ESCAPE TO CALIFORNIA & MAKE IT RAMADA!

California is a lot more than miles of beautiful, sun-kissed beaches and sparkling water. Pet the dolphins at Sea World,® shake hands with Mickey Mouse,® ride the Malibu waves, stroll along Hollywood Boulevard's Walk of Fame, taste the seafood at Fisherman's Wharf, visit a local museum and then watch the sunset behind the Golden Gate Bridge.

After all that fun, unwind and relax at a Ramada location where the friendliest faces ensure all the comforts of home. Be sure to ask about our **AAA rates** at Ramada locations throughout the state. Whatever Ramada you choose, you'll have all the comforts and friendly service to make your sunny days in California even brighter!

PARTICIPATING LOCATIONS

Northern California
Antioch
  Ramada Inn
Carmel
  Ramada Ltd.
Eureka
  Ramada Ltd.
Half Moon Bay
  Ramada Ltd.
Monterey
  Ramada Ltd.
Mountain View
  Ramada Ltd.
SAN FRANCISCO
Airport/Burlingame
  Ramada Inn
Airport/South
  Ramada Inn
Civic Center
  Ramada Plaza
Downtown
  Ramada Ltd.
Fisherman's Wharf
  Ramada Plaza Hotel
Vallejo
  Ramada Inn
Santa Cruz
  Ramada Ltd.
Sunnyvale
  Ramada Inn
Central California
Fresno
  Ramada Inn

Merced
  Ramada Inn
Oakdale
  Ramada Inn
Southern California
Corona
  Ramada Ltd.
Huntington Beach
  Ramada Ltd.
L.A. DISNEY PARK AREA
Anaheim
  Ramada Ltd.
Anaheim
  Ramada Inn/
  Conestoga
Anaheim
  Ramada Inn
LOS ANGELES
Commerce
  Ramada Inn
Chatsworth
  Ramada Inn
Culver City
  Ramada Plaza
Hollywood
  Ramada Inn
Inglewood
  Ramada Ltd.
Marina Del Rey
  Ramada Ltd.
Torrance
  Ramada Inn

Torrance
  Ramada Ltd.
West Hollywood
  Ramada Plaza
Palm Springs
  Ramada Inn
SAN DIEGO
Hotel Circle
  Ramada Plaza
Old Town
  Ramada Ltd.

South Bay
  Ramada Ltd.
San Marcos
  Ramada Ltd.
Santa Barbara
  Ramada Ltd.
Temecula
  Ramada Inn

For Reservations Call
1•800•2•RAMADA
and ask for the **AAA Rate**.

RAMADA®
LIMITEDS • INNS • PLAZA HOTELS
www.ramada.com

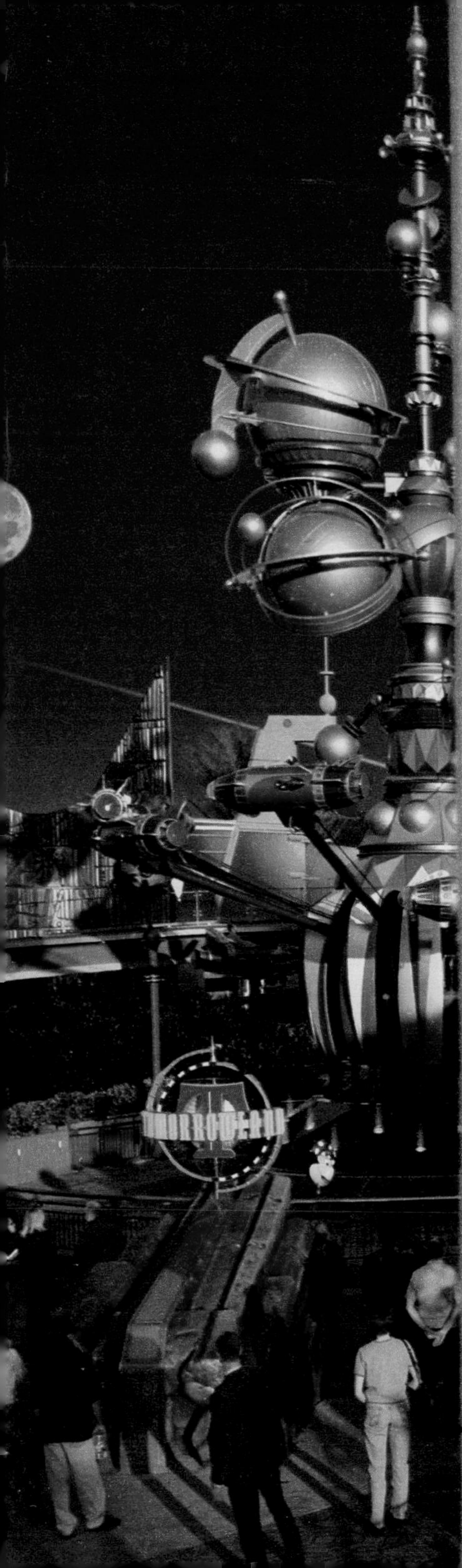

California Nevada

Valid through January 2000

Published by:
AAA Publishing
1000 AAA Drive
Heathrow, FL 32746-5063
Copyright AAA 1998.

Send Written Comments to:
AAA Member Comments
Box 61, 1000 AAA Drive
Heathrow, FL 32746-5063

Advertising Rate and Circulation Information
Call: (407) 444-8280

Printed in the USA by Quebecor Printing, Buffalo, NY

California
Nevada

TourBook
Navigator

Follow our simple guide to
make the most of this member benefit ... 7-23

Comprehensive
City Index

Alphabetical list for the entire book 1160

■ *California*

Featured Information

■ *Nevada*

4

Congratulations. You made it.

It's a place where you can kick off your shoes and take it easy.

Where you can take a load off your mind as well as your feet.

Where you can relax, because you know we don't.

Call 1-800-HAMPTON® or visit us at hampton-inn.com.

We make it easy to take it easy.℠

When it comes to personal trip planning, nobody beats trained AAA travel counselors.

Our highly trained counselors can assist you with all facets of planning your trip, from designing the route to making reservations. In addition, only AAA travel counselors can provide our exclusive collection of travel materials selected especially for you.

TourBook® guides are comprehensive travel guides listing AAA-approved attractions, lodgings and restaurants. In addition to the coveted diamond ratings, you'll find descriptions of towns and cities and information on discounts available only to AAA members. TourBooks are updated annually and cover every state and province in the United States and Canada.

TripTik® routings trace your route mile-by-mile and are clearly marked with the vital information you need while on the road, such as highway exits and rest stops. These handy spiral-bound maps are custom-configured by your AAA travel counselor and can highlight the quickest, shortest or most scenic routes, as well as highway construction projects along the way.

Sheet maps are updated annually and cover every state and province, plus regional areas throughout North America. An extensive network of road reporters and club staff work with AAA cartographers to ensure that AAA maps are the most detailed and accurate maps available.

CampBook® guides list AAA-approved camping and RV facilities, both public and private, throughout the United States and Canada.

So the next time you're planning a trip, remember to visit your local AAA travel counselor, and *Travel With Someone You Trust.*®

Only AAA offers an integrated travel information system that is tailored to your individual needs.

6

SUDDENLY, YOU'VE GOT COMPANY.

JUST WHEN YOUR EYES ARE AT THEIR WEARIEST, THE KIDS ARE AT THEIR CRANKIEST AND MOTHER NATURE AT HER STORMIEST, YOU SEE **THE KNIGHT**— LIKE AN ESCAPE TO THE COAST AFTER HITTING THE JACKPOT— COMING TO YOUR RESCUE WITH A **GREAT NIGHT'S REST** AT TRUE **BUDGET RATES.** WITH OVER 250 LOCATIONS COAST-TO-COAST, KNIGHTS INN IS WITH YOU WHEREVER YOU TRAVEL— **CONVENIENT, COMFORTABLE, AFFORDABLE... JUST RIGHT.**

Knights Inn®

EVERY KNIGHT. JUST RIGHT.℠

CALL 800-THE KNIGHTS

800-843-5644 • WWW.KNIGHTSINN.COM

TRUST the AAA TourBook for objective travel information. Follow the pages of TourBook Navigator to thoroughly understand this unique member benefit.

Each attraction, lodging and restaurant is listed on the basis of merit alone after careful evaluation, approval and rating by one of our full-time inspectors or, in rare cases, a designated representative.

Annual lodging inspections are unannounced and conducted on site by random room sample. Learn how to use the diamonds on pages 14-15.

An establishment's decision to advertise in TourBooks has no bearing on its inspection, evaluation or rating. Advertising for services or products does not imply AAA endorsement.

Casino gambling establishments not contained within hotels, as well as recreational activities of a participatory nature (requiring physical exertion or special skills), are not inspected but are presented in a bulleted format for informational purposes.

All information in this TourBook was reviewed for accuracy before publication. However, since changes inevitably occur between annual editions, we suggest you contact establishments directly to confirm prices and schedules.

How the TourBook is Organized

Geographic listing is used for accuracy and consistency. This means attractions, lodgings and restaurants are listed under the city or town in which they physically are located—or in some cases under the nearest recognized city or town. See the comprehensive City Index on page xx for an A-to-Z list of towns in this TourBook.

Most listings are alphabetically organized by state or province, city, and establishment name. Reflecting contemporary travel patterns, TourBooks cluster information in two additional ways that illustrate geographic relationships among major travel targets:

- **Destination cities** are metro areas we define with local expertise supplementing government models. Our defined metro areas comprise core cities along with vicinity communities.

- **Destination areas** are regions with broad tourist appeal beyond the local. Several cities will comprise the area.

Note: If a city is grouped in a destination vicinity section, the city name will still appear at its alphabetical location in the book—and a handy cross reference will give the exact page on which listings for that city begin.

Map illustrations at the beginning of their sections orient you to these major destinations. A color bar across the top of the page indicates you are in a destination section.

Additional color tabs on the sides of pages are coded to a state or province. Match the color tabs to easily switch from attractions to lodgings and restaurants.

Sample Lodging Listing

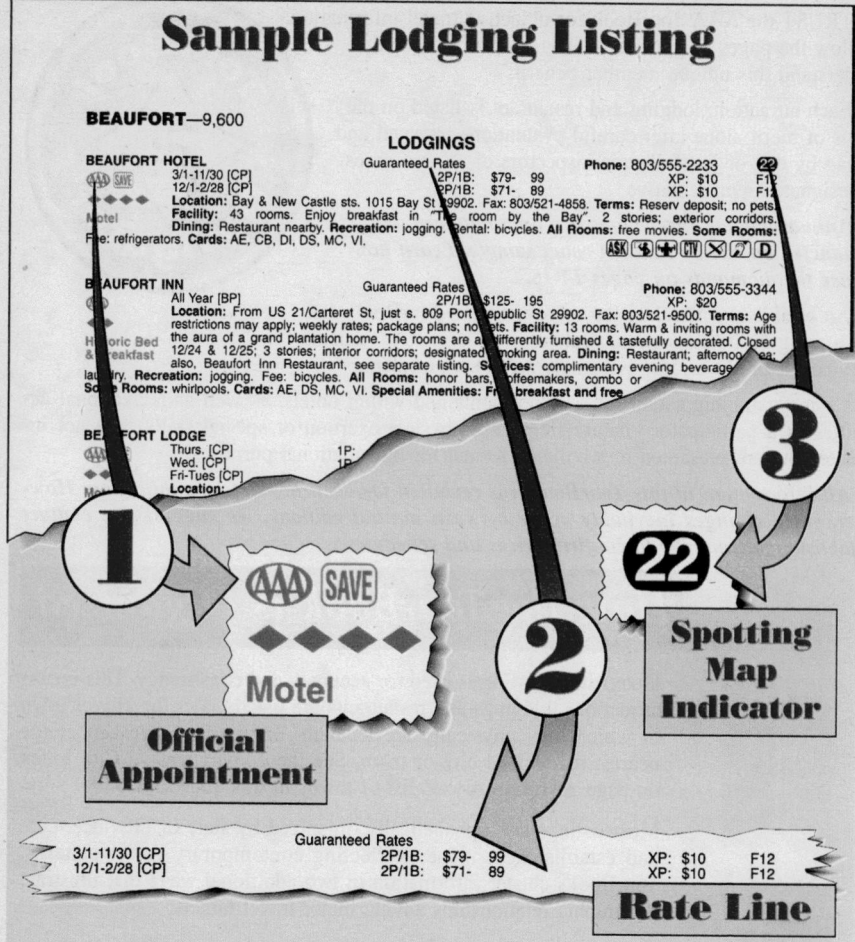

BEAUFORT—9,600

LODGINGS

BEAUFORT HOTEL
Guaranteed Rates Phone: 803/555-2233
3/1-11/30 [CP] 2P/1B: $79- 99 XP: $10 F12
12/1-2/28 [CP] 2P/1B: $71- 89 XP: $10 F12
Location: Bay & New Castle sts. 1015 Bay St 29902. Fax: 803/521-4858. **Terms:** Reserv deposit; no pets. **Facility:** 43 rooms. Enjoy breakfast in "The room by the Bay". 2 stories; exterior corridors. **Dining:** Restaurant nearby. **Recreation:** jogging. Rental: bicycles. **All Rooms:** free movies. **Some Rooms:** Fee: refrigerators. **Cards:** AE, CB, DI, DS, MC, VI.

BEAUFORT INN
Guaranteed Rates Phone: 803/555-3344
All Year [BP] 2P/1B: $125- 195 XP: $20
Location: From US 21/Carteret St, just s. 809 Port Republic St 29902. Fax: 803/521-9500. **Terms:** Age restrictions may apply; weekly rates; package plans; no pets. **Facility:** 13 rooms. Warm & inviting rooms with the aura of a grand plantation home. The rooms are differently furnished & tastefully decorated. Closed 12/24 & 12/25; 3 stories; interior corridors; designated smoking area. **Dining:** Restaurant; afternoon tea; also, Beaufort Inn Restaurant, see separate listing. **Services:** complimentary evening beverage; laundry. **Recreation:** jogging. Fee: bicycles. **All Rooms:** honor bars, coffeemakers, combo or Some **Rooms:** whirlpools. **Cards:** AE, DS, MC, VI. **Special Amenities:** Free breakfast and free

BEAUFORT LODGE
Thurs. [CP] 1P:
Wed. [CP] 1P:
Fri-Tues [CP]
Location:

Official Appointment

Spotting Map Indicator

Rate Line

3/1-11/30 [CP] Guaranteed Rates 2P/1B: $79- 99 XP: $10 F12
12/1-2/28 [CP] 2P/1B: $71- 89 XP: $10 F12

① ◆◆◆ or ◆◆◆ The number of diamonds—not the color—informs you of the overall level of quality in a lodging's amenities and service. More diamond details on pages 14-15.

Motel or Motel Diamond ratings are applied in the context of lodging type, or classification. See pages 16-17 for our Lodging Classifications.

🆔 or 🆔 indicates our Official Appointment (OA) lodgings. The OA Program permits properties to display and advertise the 🆔 or 🆔 emblem. **We highlight these properties with red diamonds and classification.** OAs have a special interest in serving members like you. Some OA listings include special amenities such as free breakfast; early check-in/late check-out; free room upgrade or preferred room, such as ocean view or poolside (subject to availability); free local phone calls; and free daily newspaper. This does not imply that only these properties offer these amenities. The 🆔 or 🆔 sign helps traveling members find accommodations that want member business.

Discounts

[SAVE] is used to highlight Official Appointment properties that guarantee members a minimum 10% discount off the published TourBook rates.

[SAVE] appears in "icon row" below the listing and indicates that the following Show Your Card & Save® chain partners provide special values to our members: Choice Hotels, Days Inn, Hilton, Hyatt and La Quinta. Individual properties in these chains appearing in the TourBook have been inspected and approved by AAA. Be sure to read "How to Get the Best Room Rates," page 12.

[S$] identifies establishments offering a senior discount with either the Guaranteed Rates or Rates Subject to Change options (see below). Where [S$] appears in "icon row," a minimum discount of 10% off the prevailing or guaranteed rates is available to members who are 60 or older.

[ASK] in "icon row" below the listing points out the many TourBook properties that offer discounts to members even though the lodgings do not participate in a formal discount program. The [ASK] is another reminder to *ask* about available discounts when making your reservations or at check-in.

NOTE: Discounts normally offered at some lodgings may not apply during special events or holiday periods. Special rates and discounts may not appply to all room types.

Rate Lines and Rate Options

Rate Lines

Shown from left to right: dates the rates are effective, any meal plan included, the number of Persons/Beds allowed/provided, the rates charged, the extra person (XP) charge and any applicable family plan indicator. (See next page for meal and family plan codes.) Rates are for typical or standard rooms, not special units.

Rate Options

If a lodging chooses not to offer a discount to our members, then it must select one of the following rate options:

   Guaranteed Rates—The establishment guarantees our members will not be charged more than the maximum rates printed in the TourBook.

   Rates Subject to Change—Rates may vary for the life of the TourBook but are guaranteed not to exceed a 15% increase on the printed rates.

Printed rates are based on rack rates and last room availability and are rounded to the nearest dollar. Rates do not include taxes and discounts. U.S. rates are in U.S. dollars; rates for Canadian lodgings are in Canadian dollars. Lodgings may temporarily increase room rates or modify policies during a special event or holiday.

Always Verify Rates and Discounts

To obtain published rates or discounts, you must identify yourself as a AAA or CAA member and request them when making reservations. The SAVE or senior discounts may not be used in conjunction with other discounts. Show your card at registration and verify the room rate.

[22] are numerals used to locate, or "spot," lodgings on maps we provide for larger cities. We spot restaurants with black numerals on white background ovals [22] .

What the Icons Mean

Member Services

Ⓨ Cocktail Lounge
🍴 Restaurant on Premises
🍴 Restaurant off Premises (walking distance)
🛎 24 Hour Room Service
🌃 Nightclub
🎭 Entertainment
✈ Transportation to Airport
🐾 Pets Allowed

Special Features

🧒 Child Care
💼 Business Services
👕 Laundry Service
♿ Fully Accessible
🛗 Semi-Accessible
🚿 Roll-in Showers
👂 Hearing Impaired
🅿 Valet Parking

Room Amenities

☕ Coffee Maker in Room
🍸 Honor Bar
💻 Data Port/Modem Line
📺 No Cable TV
🎬 Movies
📼 VCR
📻 Radio
🚭 Non-Smoking Rooms
🔲 Microwaves
🧊 Refrigerator
❄ No Air Conditioning
☎ No Telephones

Sports/Recreation

🏊 Pool
🏋 Fitness Center
🎱 Recreation Facilities

Safety Features

Ⓢ Sprinklers
Ⓓ Smoke Detectors
Ⓢ Safe

Fees may be charged for some of the services represented by the icons listed above; please inquire when making reservations. Check-in times are shown in the listing only if they are after 3 p.m.; check-out times are shown only if they are before 10 a.m. Parking is on the premises and free unless otherwise noted. If a pet icon is not present, assume that the property does not accept pets; although deposits and fees are stated in the listing, check policies and restrictions when making reservations.

Meal Plan Indicators

CP = Continental Plan of pastry, juice and another beverage or may offer expanded breakfast items
BP = Breakfast Plan of full hot breakfast
AP = American Plan of three meals daily
MAP = Modified American Plan of two meals daily
EP = European Plan, where rate includes only room

Family Plan Indicators

The establishment may limit the number of children to whom the family plan applies.
F17 = children 17 and under stay free (age displayed will reflect property's policy)
D17 = discount for children 17 and under
F = children stay free
D = discounts for children

Access for Disabled Travelers

Qualified properties listed in this book have symbols indicating they are either *Fully Accessible or Semi-Accessible*. This two-tiered standard was developed to meet members' varying degrees of accessibility needs.

Fully Accessible properties meet the needs of those who are significantly disabled and primarily confined to a wheelchair. A fully accessible lodging will provide at least one guest room meeting the designated criteria. A traveler with these disabilities will be able to park and access public areas, including restrooms, check-in facilities and at least one food and beverage outlet. A *Fully Accessible* restaurant indicates that parking, dining rooms and restrooms are accessible.

Semi-Accessible properties meet the needs of those who are disabled but have some mobility and are not confined to a wheelchair. Such travelers would include people using a cane or walker, or a disabled individual with good mobility but a limited arm or hand range of motion. A *Semi-Accessible* lodging will provide at least one guest room meeting the designated criteria. A traveler with these disabilities will be able to park and access public areas, including restrooms, check-in facilities and at least one food and beverage outlet. A *Semi-Accessible* restaurant indicates that parking, dining rooms and restrooms are accessible.

This symbol indicates a property with the following equipment available for *Hearing Impaired* travelers: TDD at front desk or switchboard; visual notification of fire alarm, incoming telephone calls, door knock or bell; closed caption decoder available; text telephone or TDD available for guest room use; telephone amplification device available, with shelf and electric outlet next to guest room telephone.

AAA/CAA urges members with disabilities to always phone ahead to fully understand the accommodation's offerings. Some properties do not fully comply with AAA/CAA's exacting accessibility standards but may offer some property design standards that meet the needs of some guests with disabilities.

AAA/CAA does not evaluate recreational facilities, banquet rooms or convention and meeting facilities for accessibility. Call a property directly to inquire about your needs for these areas.

The criteria used by AAA/CAA do not represent the full scope of the Americans With Disabilities Act of 1990 Accessibility Guidelines (ADAAG); they are, however, consistent with the ADAAG. Members can obtain from their local AAA/CAA club the AAA brochure "Accessibility Criteria for Travelers With Disabilities," which describes the specific criteria pertaining to the *Fully Accessible* and *Semi-Accessible* standards.

The Americans With Disabilities Act (ADA) prohibits businesses that serve the public from discriminating against persons with disabilities who are aided by service animals. Some businesses have mistakenly denied access to their properties to persons with disabilities who use service animals. ADA has priority over all state and local laws, as well as a business owner's standard of business, that might bar animals from the premises. Businesses must permit guests and their service animal entry, as well as allow service animals to accompany guests to all public areas of a property. A property is permitted to ask whether the animal is a service animal or a pet, or whether a guest has a disability. The property may not, however, ask questions about the nature of a disability or require proof of one.

How to Get the Best Room Rates

You'll find the best room rate if you book your reservation in advance with the help of a travel counselor or agent at your local AAA/CAA office.

If you're not yet ready to make firm vacation plans or if you prefer a more spontaneous trip, take advantage of the partnerships that preferred hotel chains have arranged with AAA. Call the toll-free numbers on the opposite page that have been set up exclusively for the purpose of reserving with these *Show Your Card & Save®* chain partners.

Even if you were unable to make a reservation, be sure to show your membership card at the desk and ask if you're being offered the lowest rate available for that time. Many lodgings offer reduced rates to members.

Making Reservations

Give Proper Identification

When making reservations, you must identify yourself as a AAA/CAA member. Give all pertinent information about your planned stay. Request written confirmation to guarantee: type of room, rate, dates of stay, and cancellation and refund policies. **Note:** Age restrictions may apply.

Confirm Deposit, Refund and Cancellation Policies

Most establishments give full deposit refunds if they have been notified at least 48 hours before the normal check-in time. However, when making reservations, confirm the property's deposit, cancellation and refund policies. Some properties may charge a cancellation or handling fee. When this applies, "handling fee imposed" will appear in the listing. If you cancel too late, you have little recourse if a refund is denied. When an establishment requires a full or partial payment in advance, and your trip is cut short, a refund may not be given.

When canceling reservations, call the lodging immediately. Make a note of the date and time you called, the cancellation number if there is one, and the name of the person who handled the cancellation. If your AAA/CAA club made your reservation, allow them to make the cancellation for you as well so you will have proof of cancellation.

Review Charges for Appropriate Rates

When you are charged more than the rate listed in the TourBook, under the option **Guaranteed Rates,** or you qualify for the **Senior Discount** and did not receive it, question the additional charge. If management refuses to adhere to the published rate, pay for the room and submit your receipt and membership number to AAA/CAA *within 30 days.* Include all pertinent information: dates of stay, rate paid, itemized paid receipts, number of persons in your party, the room number you occupied, and list any extra room equipment used. A refund of the amount paid in excess of the stated maximum will be made if our investigation indicates that unjustified charging has occurred.

Get the Room You Reserved

When you find your room is not as specified, and you have written confirmation of reservations for a certain type of accommodation, you should be given the option of choosing a different room or finding one elsewhere. Should you choose to go elsewhere and a refund is refused or resisted, submit the matter to AAA/CAA *within 30 days* along with complete documentation, including your reasons for refusing the room and copies of your written confirmation and any receipts or canceled checks associated with this problem.

Preferred Lodging Partners

Call the member-only toll-free numbers or your club to get these member benefits.

Choice Hotel brands
◄ *(800) 228-1222*

SAVE Save 10% at Sleep, Comfort, Quality and Econo Lodge
SAVE Save 20% at Clarion Hotels and Clarion Carriage House Inns
SAVE Guaranteed stay - If you're not satisfied with your stay, it's free

Days Inn
◄ *(800) 432-9755*

SAVE Guaranteed lowest rates available for dates of stay when booked in advance

Hilton Worldwide
◄ *(800) 916-2221*

SAVE Guaranteed lowest rates available for dates of stay when booked in advance

Hyatt Hotels
◄ *(800) 532-1496*

SAVE Guaranteed lowest rates available for dates of stay when booked in advance
SAVE Receive second dinner entree at half-price in Hyatt dining room when staying at the hotel

La Quinta Inns
◄ *(800) 221-4731*

SAVE Guaranteed lowest public rate for dates of stay for standard room
SAVE Children under 18 and spouse sharing room stay free
SAVE Guaranteed stay - If you're not satisfied with your stay, it's free

Red Roof Inns
◄ *(877) 222-7663*

SAVE Save 10% at all Red Roof Inns
SAVE Guaranteed stay - If you're not happy with your night's stay and the problem can't be corrected, it's free

Special rates and discounts may not apply to all room types. Not available to groups and cannot be combined with other discounts. Restrictions apply to stay guarantees. Valid AAA/CAA membership card must be presented at check-in. Offers good at time of publication; chains and offers may change without notice.

Show Your Card & Save

The Lodging Diamonds

AAA-RATED® lodgings are evaluated annually during unannounced visits by full-time inspectors. Properties must satisfy a set of minimum requirements that reflect the basic lodging needs members have identified. An increased number of diamonds reflects higher levels of quality in service and amenities.

The few lodgings with ⟦FYI⟧ in place of diamonds are included as an "informational only" service for members. It indicates that a property has not been rated for one or more of the following reasons: too new to rate; under construction; under major renovation; not inspected; or may not meet all AAA requirements.

Properties meet all Listing Requirements. They are clean and well-maintained.

Properties maintain the attributes offered at the one diamond level while showing noticeable enhancements in room decor and quality of furnishings.

Properties show a marked upgrade in physical attributes, services and comfort. Additional amenities, services and facilities may be offered.

Properties reflect an exceptional degree of hospitality, service and attention to detail, while offering upscale facilities and a variety of amenities.

Property facilities and operations exemplify an impeccable standard of excellence while exceeding guest expectations in hospitality and service. These renowned properties are both striking and luxurious, offering many extra amenities.

The Restaurant Diamonds

Diamond ratings are assigned based on conditions noted at the time of the evaluation. Food quality is the most critical to the overall rating, but other factors also are considered, such as service and atmosphere. Restaurants are classified by cuisine type. Some listings include additional information, such as the availability of a senior citizen menu, children's menu or "early bird specials," if offered at least 5 days a week. The dinner price range is approximate and includes a salad or appetizer, an entree, a vegetable and a non-alcoholic beverage for one person. Taxes and tip are not included. *Note: Major restaurant chains are not listed due to their widespread recognition.*

Provides a simple, family or specialty meal in clean, pleasant surroundings. Food is basic and wholesome. Service is casual, limited or self-serve. Decor is informal.

More extensive menus for family or adult dining. Food is prepared with standard ingredients. Service is attentive but may be informal, casual, limited or self-serve. The decor presents a unified theme that is comfortable but also may be trendy, casual or upbeat.

An upscale or special family dining experience. Food is cooked to order and creatively prepared with quality ingredients. A wine list is available. A skilled, often uniformed staff provides service. The usually professional and inviting decor projects a trendy, upbeat, casual or formal atmosphere.

A high degree of sophistication, thus creating an adult dining experience. Complex food is creatively presented. An extensive wine list is offered. The service staff, often formally attired, is professionally trained. The decor is distinctive, stylish and elegant; some establishments are casual while still offering refinement or formality.

A memorable occasion—the ultimate in adult dining. Food shows the highest culinary skills, evident in all areas of preparation and presentation. An extensive wine list is available. A professional staff—often in formal attire—provides flawless and pampering service. The decor has classic details, often formal, and reflects comfort and luxury.

Lodging Classifications

AAA inspectors evaluate lodgings based on classification, since all lodging types by definition do not provide the same level of service and facilities. Thus, hotels are rated in comparison to other hotels–and so on. A lodging's classification appears beneath its diamond rating in the listing.

Motel
(limited service)

Low-rise or multistory establishment offering limited public and recreational facilities.

Hotel
(full service)

Usually high-rise establishments, offering a full range of on-premises food and beverage service, cocktail lounge, entertainment, conference facilities, business services, shops and recreational activities. Wide range of services provided by uniformed staff on duty 24 hours. Parking arrangements vary.

Motor Inn
(moderate service)

Single or multistory establishment offering on-premises food and beverage service. Meeting and banquet facilities and some recreational activities. Usually complimentary on-site parking.

Bed and Breakfast
(limited service)

Usually smaller establishments emphasizing a more personal relationship between operators and guests, leading to an "at home" feeling. Guest units tend to be individually decorated. Rooms may not include some modern amenities such as televisions and telephones, and may have a shared bathroom. Usually owner-operated, with a common room or parlor, separate from the innkeeper's living quarters, where guests and operators can interact during evening and breakfast hours. Evening office closures are normal. A continental or full, hot breakfast is served and is included in the room rate.

Country Inn
(moderate service)

Although similar in definition to a bed and breakfast, country inns are usually larger in size, provide more spacious public areas and offer a dining facility that serves at least breakfast and dinner. May be located in a rural setting or downtown area.

Apartment
(limited service)

Establishments that primarily offer transient guest accommodations with one or more bedrooms, a living room, a full kitchen and an eating area. Studio-type apartments may combine the sleeping and living areas into one room.

Condominium
(limited service)

Establishments that primarily offer guest accommodations that are privately owned by individuals and available for rent. These can include apartment-style units or homes. A variety of room styles and decor treatments as well as limited housekeeping service is typical. May have off-site registration.

Lodging Classifications

Complex
(service varies depending on type of lodgings)

A combination of two or more types of lodging classifications.

Cottage
(limited service)

Establishments that primarily provide individual housing units that may offer one or more separate sleeping rooms, a living room and cooking facilities. Usually incorporate rustic decor treatments and are geared to vacationers.

Lodge
(moderate service)

Typically two or more stories with all facilities in one building, rustic decor. Located in vacation, ski, fishing areas, etc. Usually has food and beverage service.

Ranch
(moderate service)

Often offers rustic decor treatments and food and beverage facilities. Entertainment and recreational activities are geared to a Western-style adventure vacation. May provide some meeting facilities.

Resort
(full service)

Geared to vacation travelers. It is a destination offering varied food and beverage outlets, specialty shops, meeting or conference facilities, entertainment, and extensive recreational facilities for special interests such as golf, tennis, skiing, fishing and water sports. Assorted social and recreational programs are typically offered in season, and a variety of package plans are usually available, including meal plans incorporated into the rates. Larger resorts may offer a variety of guest accommodations.

Subclassifications

The following are subclassifications that may appear along with the classifications listed above to provide a more specific description of the lodging:

Suite

One or more bedrooms and a living room/sitting area, which is closed off by a full wall. *Note:* May not have a partition bedroom door.

Extended Stay

Properties catering to longer-term guest stays. Will have kitchens or efficiencies. May have a separate living room area, evening office closure and limited housekeeping services.

Historic

Accommodations in restored structures built prior to 1920, reflecting the ambiance of yesteryear and the surrounding area. Antique furnishings complement the overall decor of the property. Rooms may lack some modern amenities and may have shared bathrooms.

Precautions Can Save A Vacation!

Travelers are faced with the task of protecting themselves while in a strange environment. Although there is no way to guarantee absolute protection from crime, the experts—law enforcement officials—advise travelers to take a pro-active approach to securing their property and ensuring their safety.

1 Make sure the hotel desk clerk does not announce your room number; if so, quietly request a new room assignment.

2 Ask front desk personnel which areas of town to avoid and what, if any, special precautions should be taken when driving a rental car (some criminals target tourists driving rental cars).

3 Never open the door to a stranger; use the peephole and request identification. If you are still unsure, call the front desk to verify the identity of the person and the purpose of his/her visit.

4 Carry money separately from credit cards or use a "fanny pack." Carry your purse close to your body and your wallet in an inside coat or front trouser pocket. Never leave luggage unattended, and use your business address, if possible, on luggage tags.

5 Beware of distractions staged by would-be scam artists, especially groups of children that surround you or a stranger who accidentally spills something on you. They may be lifting your wallet.

6 If using an automatic teller machine (ATM), choose one in a well-lit area with plenty of foot traffic, such as one at a grocery store. Law enforcement officials suggest that machines inside establishments are generally safer to use.

7 Use room safes or safety deposit boxes provided by the hotel. Store all valuables out of sight, even when you are in the room.

8 Law enforcement agencies consider card-key (electronic) door locks the most secure.

Guest Safety

In order to be approved for listing in AAA/CAA TourBook® guides for the United States and Canada, all lodgings must comply with AAA's guest room security requirements.

In response to AAA/CAA members' concern about their safety at properties, AAA RATED® accommodations must have deadbolt locks on all guest room entry doors and connecting room doors.

If the area outside the guest room door is not visible from inside the room through a window or door panel, viewports must be installed on all guest room entry doors. Bed and breakfast properties and country inns are not required to have viewports. Ground floor and easily accessible sliding doors must be equipped with some other type of secondary security locks.

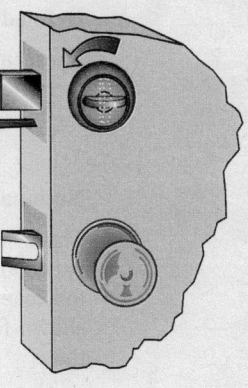

Field inspectors view a percentage of rooms at each property. It is not feasible for the inspectors to evaluate every room in every lodging establishment, So, AAA cannot guarantee that there are working locks on all doors and windows in all guest rooms.

Because of the highly specialized skills needed to conduct professional fire safety inspections, AAA/CAA inspectors cannot assess fire safety. However, guest rooms in U.S. lodging properties must be equipped with an operational, single-station smoke detector, and all public areas must have operational smoke detectors or an automatic sprinkler system. **Note:** Some Canadian lodgings are an exception to this requirement. There may be some Canadian properties that were approved prior to 1988 that use heat sensors in place of smoke detectors and/or automatic sprinkler systems.

Since all U.S. lodgings must be equipped as described above, no special notation is made in the U.S. listings. Canadian listings reflect with icons (shown on page 8) the type of fire safety equipment provided. A AAA/CAA inspector has evaluated a sampling of the rooms to verify this equipment is in place. For additional fire safety information read the page posted on the back of your guest room door, or write:

National Fire Protection Association,
1 Batterymarch Park, P.O. Box 9101,
Quincy, MA 02269-9101.

TourBook Maps

Attractions Section

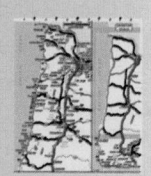

Orientation maps

These maps near the start of each Attractions section show only those places we call points of interest. Stars accent towns with "must see" attractions. And the black ovals with white numerals locate items listed in the nearby Recreation Areas chart.

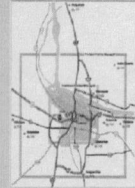

Defined metro and destination area maps

These maps illustrate key travel areas defined by local travel experts. Communities shown have listings for AAA approved attractions.

National park maps

These maps represent the area in and around the park. Some campground sites and lodges spotted on the maps do not meet AAA/CAA criteria, but are shown for members who nevertheless wish to stay there.

City maps

These maps show areas where numerous points of interest are concentrated and indicate their location in relation to major roads, parks, airports and other landmarks.

Walking or self-guiding tour maps

These maps correspond to specific routes described in TourBook text.

Driving Distance Maps

Driving distance maps

These maps located in the Featured Information section of the book are intended to be used only for trip-distance and driving-time planning.

TourBook Maps

Lodgings & Restaurants Section

State or province orientation maps
These maps appear before the property listings in the Lodgings & Restaurants section of selected TourBooks. These maps show the relative positions of major metropolitan areas and the vicinity towns in those areas.

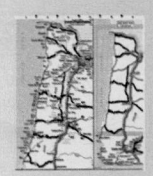

Area maps
These maps denote large geographical areas in which there are many towns containing lodgings and/or restaurants. Due to these maps' small scale, lodgings and restaurants are not shown; towns with lodgings and/or restaurants are printed in magenta type.

Defined metro and destination area maps
These maps illustrate key travel areas defined by local travel experts. Communities shown have listings for AAA RATED® lodgings and/or restaurants.

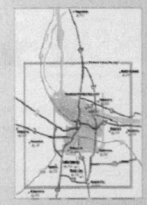

Spotting maps
These maps show the location of lodgings and restaurants. Lodgings are spotted with a black-background numeral (🀆, for example); restaurants are spotted with a white-background numeral (⑳ for example). Spotting map indexes have been placed after the main city heading to provide the user with a convenient method to identify what an area has to offer at a glance. The index references the map page number where the property is spotted, indicates if a property is an Official Appointment and contains an advertising reference if applicable. It also lists the property's diamond rating, high season rate range and listing page number.

Downtown/city spotting maps
These maps are provided when spotted facilities are very concentrated. Starred points of interest also appear on these maps.

Vicinity spotting maps
These maps spot those properties that are outside the downtown or city area. Major roads, landmarks, airports and starred points of interest are shown on vicinity spotting maps as well. The names of suburban communities that have AAA RATED® accommodations are shown in magenta type.

Sample Attraction Listing

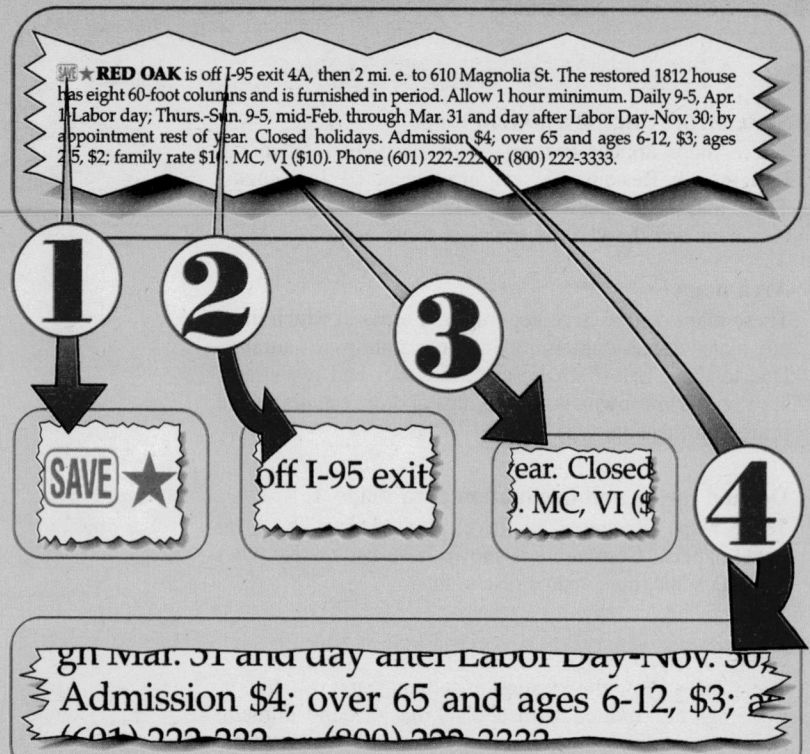

★ RED OAK is off I-95 exit 4A, then 2 mi. e. to 610 Magnolia St. The restored 1812 house has eight 60-foot columns and is furnished in period. Allow 1 hour minimum. Daily 9-5, Apr. 1-Labor day; Thurs.-Sun. 9-5, mid-Feb. through Mar. 31 and day after Labor Day-Nov. 30; by appointment rest of year. Closed holidays. Admission $4; over 65 and ages 6-12, $3; ages 2-5, $2; family rate $10. MC, VI ($10). Phone (601) 222-222 or (800) 222-3333.

off I-95 exit

ear. Closed
). MC, VI ($

gh Mar. 31 and day after Labor Day-Nov. 30;
Admission $4; over 65 and ages 6-12, $3; a
(601) 222-222 or (800) 222-3333

① ⬛ participants offer AAA/CAA cardholders and up to six family members at least 10% off admission for the validity period of the TourBook. Present your card at the admissions desk. A list of participating attractions appears in the Indexes section of the book. The SAVE discount may not be used in conjunction with other discounts. Discounts may not apply during special events or particular days or seasons.

★—Attraction is of exceptional interest and quality.

② Unless otherwise specified, directions are given from the center of town, using the following highway designations: I (interstate highway), US (federal highway), Hwy. (Canadian highway), SR (state route), CR (county road), FM (farm to market road), FR (forest road), MM (mile marker).

③
AE=American Express	DS=Discover	MC=MasterCard
CB=Carte Blanche	JC=Japanese Credit Bureau	VI=VISA
DI=Diners Club		

Minimum amounts that may be charged appear in parentheses when applicable.

④ Admission prices are quoted *without* sales tax. Children under the lowest age specified are admitted free when accompanied by an adult. Days, months and age groups written with a hyphen are *inclusive*. Prices pertaining to attractions in the United States are quoted in U.S. dollars; Canadian province and territory attraction prices are quoted in Canadian dollars.

Confirm Prices and Schedules

All information was reviewed for accuracy before publication. However, since changes often occur between annual editions, please use the phone numbers in the listings to confirm prices and schedules.

Attraction Partners

These Show Your Card & Save® attraction partners provide the listed member benefits. Admission tickets that offer greater discounts may be available for purchase at the local AAA club.

Universal Studios (Florida and Hollywood)

SAVE Save $3 on admission at the gate

SAVE Save 10% on selected souvenirs and dining

SeaWorld/Busch Gardens

Save at SeaWorld, Busch Gardens, Sesame Place, Water Country U.S.A. and Adventure Island

SAVE Save 10% on general admission

SAVE Save 10% at a selected restaurant and retail shops inside the park

Offers at the attractions listed above are good at the time of publication and are subject to change without notice.

Golden Passports

Citizens or permanent residents of the United States who are 62 and older can obtain Golden Age Passports for a one-time $10 fee. Golden Access Passports are free to citizens or permanent residents of the United States (regardless of age) who are medically blind or permanently disabled. Both cover entrance fees for the holder and accompanying private party to all national parks and historic sites, monuments and battlefields within the U.S. national park system, plus half off camping and other fees. Apply in person at most federally operated areas.

Rack Up The Miles.
Reap The Rewards.

TRAVELODGE MILES℠
The Guest Rewards Program

Hit the road to exceptional value! At Travelodge® locations our great value starts with a comfortable room at a very affordable rate. Then we add lots of special extras* like free fresh-brewed in-room coffee, a free weekday lobby newspaper, free cable TV including movies, news and sports, and no long distance access charges. **Plus there's the added value of Travelodge Miles,** our Guest Rewards program. Start racking up Travelodge Miles℠ and you can earn a Free Night's Stay,† frequent flyer airline miles, or your choice of dozens of other great new Guest Rewards — everything from cameras to cookware — fast and easy. So call us now for reservations, and get ready for a very rewarding travel experience!

For Reservations Call:
1-800-367-2250
www.travelodge.com

Also available at participating Thriftlodge locations.

California

Majestic Redwoods

These magnificent trees tower over the emerald green rain forests of the north-western coast

Oases in the Desert

Lush islands in a sun-scorched sea of rock and sand, oases such as Palm Springs dot the southeast

Alpine Lakes and Valleys

Lake Tahoe and the Yosemite Valley nestle among the lofty crags of the Sierra Nevada

Picturesque Spanish Missions

Symbols of Spanish Colonial times, historic missions bask in the golden light of the coast

Sheer Cliffs and Scenic Vistas

Wave-swept beaches and breathtaking, cliff-spanning bridges highlight the Big Sur

the promised land

The allure of the Golden State must be powerful: More than 30 million people can't be wrong. Abundant resources, some of the nation's most agreeable weather and a stunningly varied landscape go a long way toward explaining the attraction.

Most Americans who have never set foot west of the Rockies have heard of the Yosemite Valley, Lake Tahoe, Big Sur, Death Valley, the Golden Gate Bridge, the San Diego Zoo and L.A.'s Getty Center. Thanks to Hollywood movies and TV shows, California and all its associations—surfing, sun, starlets lounging by pools, environmentalists chaining themselves to condemned trees, urban sprawl, pollution, earthquakes— have all entered the popular imagination.

When a fad sweeps the country, odds are good that it started in California. The sense of style here is often imitated, the native cuisine savored around the world.

Besides physical appeal, perhaps nothing epitomizes the "Left Coast" more than the people and their almost mythical lifestyle. Populated by entrepreneurs, visionaries, counterculture radicals, trendsetters, go-getters and—truth be told—a few eccentrics as well, the state has long been fertile ground for innovative ideas, technological breakthroughs and entirely new ways of living. No wonder Americans looking toward the future often face west.

Fade in: A snow-clad mountainside. A man and woman dressed in ski gear swoosh down an alpine slope. Cut to: A sun-washed beach hours later. The same couple stroll along the shore, waves rolling in, water lapping at their feet. Next scene: A swank urban bistro an hour later. The twosome sit across from each other savoring a sumptuous dinner as they discuss which of the many local nightclubs they should visit. Fade out.

Although unusually energetic, the happy duo described above is realistic enough. It's the setting that seems unreal, dreamed up. Skiing in the mountains within hours of a walk on a picture-postcard beach? Both within reach of a major city? A place that could only exist in movies, right?

Well, no. Though the beautiful scenery is nearly unbelievable, the place is real, and it is where movies are *made*. As you've probably guessed, this far-fetched locale could only be California.

Appropriately named after a fictional island rich with gold from a Spanish romance novel, the state attracted early movie-making pioneers with its plentiful sunshine, mild climate and tremendously varied terrain. What better background for drama?

And drama has long been a hallmark of the state. From that first emotion-filled cry of "Eureka!" at Sutter's Mill to the chaotic human tidal wave of the ensuing gold rush and the tragedy of the San Francisco earthquake decades later, drama has been one of the state's most notable characteristics.

Better Than Fiction

Those first filmmakers arriving in the early 1900s must have realized they couldn't dream up a better setting for their celluloid fantasies; the California landscape itself is dramatic. Breathtaking only begins to describe the rocky, sea-splashed cliffs of Big Sur, the snow-capped cone of volcanic Mount Shasta or the jagged, glacier-sculpted peaks of the Sierra Nevada.

And vistas that are impossible to truly capture on film abound in the Yosemite Valley and the surrounding national park. Even frequent visitors find it difficult to comprehend the size of the park's colossal escarpments and the height of its waterfalls. And what camera could do justice to the super-saturated blues of frigid Lake Tahoe or the emerald greens of Muir Woods?

There's also drama in the diversity of landscapes: the nation's second tallest

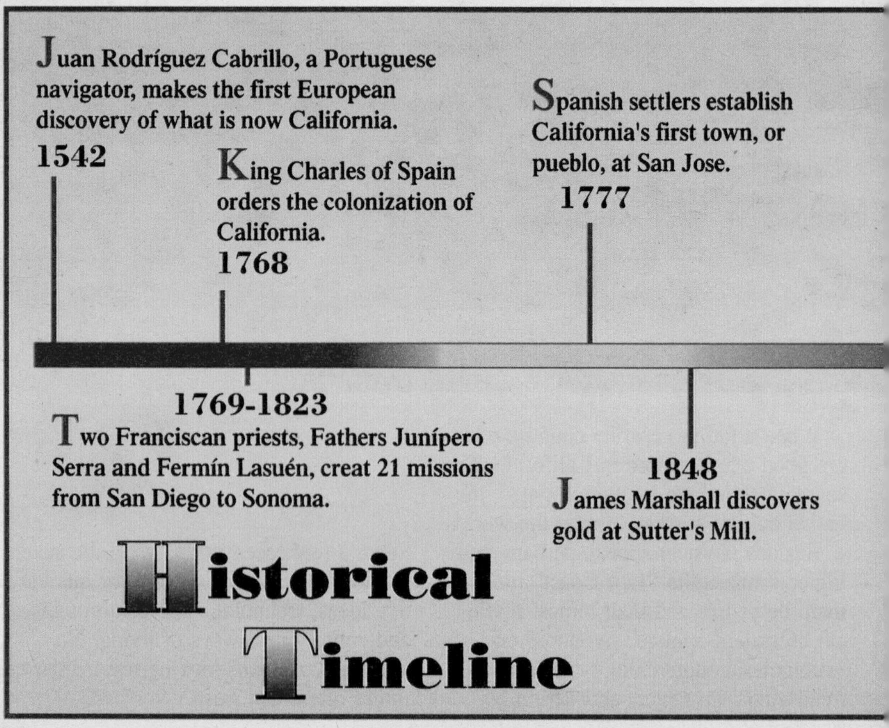

Juan Rodríguez Cabrillo, a Portuguese navigator, makes the first European discovery of what is now California.

1542

King Charles of Spain orders the colonization of California.

1768

Spanish settlers establish California's first town, or pueblo, at San Jose.

1777

1769-1823
Two Franciscan priests, Fathers Junípero Serra and Fermín Lasuén, creat 21 missions from San Diego to Sonoma.

1848
James Marshall discovers gold at Sutter's Mill.

Historical Timeline

mountain, Mount Whitney, stands within 90 miles of Death Valley, the Western Hemisphere's lowest point. Even the lighting varies enough to please the fussiest cinematographer, ranging from the soft, mist-dimmed glow of the northwest coast to the harsh, unfiltered glare of the southeast deserts. And speaking of lighting, who can count the number of movies that have ended with a lingering view of heroes and heroines riding off into trademark, technicolor California sunset?

And like a movie star from Hollywood's golden age, the state's ready for its close-up. Zoom in on the mountains, valleys, deserts and shore areas and you'll find a fascinating array of plants and animals. Off the coast, migrating gray and humpback whales are the stars while sea lions, elephant seals and playful sea otters make their appearances closer to shore. California's signature flora includes chaparral scrub, desert-loving joshua trees, giant sequoias and ancient bristlecone pines.

Following the Sun

But what motion picture would be complete without actors? Even before the flood of fortune hunters following the sun from the East arrived, the lands west of the Sierra Nevada were home to a cast of characters that included Franciscan missionaries, Spanish ranchers and the American Indians who had lived in the region for thousands of years. Then the gold rush created cities and towns almost overnight, and people have never stopped being drawn to the spectacle of the place. Since the '60s more people have called the Golden State home than any other in the union.

The results of their labors take myriad forms: centuries-old Spanish missions that dot the coast; the futuristic glass-and-steel skyscrapers of Los Angeles and San Francisco; the lovely beach resorts of Carmel and Santa Cruz; the unlikely desert oasis of Palm Springs; and the quaint gold rush towns sprinkled along the western slopes of the Sierra Nevada. And what more fitting testament to surreal beauty than the magnificent Hearst Castle or the celebration of imagination that is Disneyland?

Of course, no better symbol of California's blend of the fantastic and the real exists than Hollywood: the capital of an industry which has for nearly a century drawn inspiration from a location that seems like make-believe but somehow isn't.

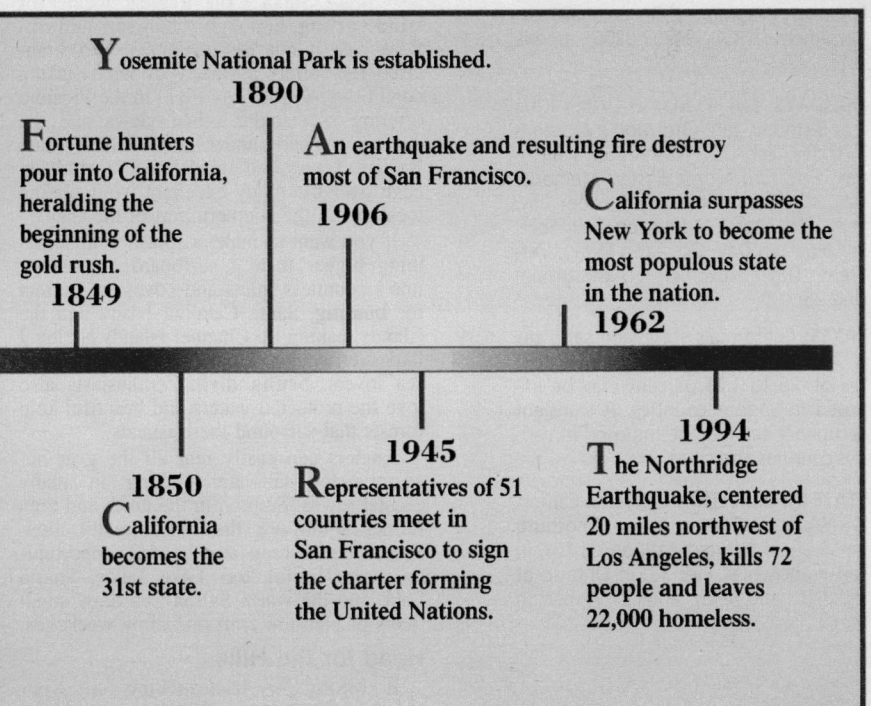

Yosemite National Park is established.
1890

Fortune hunters pour into California, heralding the beginning of the gold rush.
1849

An earthquake and resulting fire destroy most of San Francisco.
1906

California surpasses New York to become the most populous state in the nation.
1962

1850
California becomes the 31st state.

1945
Representatives of 51 countries meet in San Francisco to sign the charter forming the United Nations.

1994
The Northridge Earthquake, centered 20 miles northwest of Los Angeles, kills 72 people and leaves 22,000 homeless.

FAST FACTS

POPULATION: 32,268,300.

AREA: 158,693 square miles; ranks 3rd.

CAPITAL: Sacramento.

HIGHEST POINT: 14,494 ft., Mount Whitney

LOWEST POINT: -282 ft., Death Valley

TIME ZONE: Pacific. DST.

MINIMUM AGE FOR DRIVERS: 16 with drivers' training, 18 without.

SEAT BELT/CHILD RESTRAINT LAWS: Safety belts required for driver and all passengers; child restraints required for children under age 5 (regardless of weight) or under 40 pounds (regardless of age).

HELMETS FOR MOTORCYCLISTS: Required.

RADAR DETECTORS: Permitted.

FIREARMS LAWS: Vary by state and/or county. Contact Department of Justice, Firearms Program, P.O. Box 820200, Sacramento, CA 94203-0200; phone (916) 227-3703.

HOLIDAYS: Jan. 1; Martin Luther King Jr.'s Birthday, Jan. (3rd Mon.); Lincoln's Birthday, Feb. 12; Washington's Birthday, Feb. (3rd Mon.); Easter; Memorial Day, May (last Mon.); July 4; Labor Day, Sept. (1st Mon.); Admission Day, Sept. 9; Columbus Day, Oct. (2nd Mon.); Veterans Day, Nov. 11; Thanksgiving; Dec. 25.

TAXES: California's statewide sales tax is 7.25 percent; an additional district tax of .25 to 1.25 percent may be imposed in various counties. A transient occupancy tax may be imposed in various counties and cities.

STATE INFORMATION CENTERS: California Welcome Centers are in Kingsburg on SR 99, in Rohnert Park on US 101, in San Francisco at Pier 39, in Ontario at jct. I-10 and I-15, and in Anderson on I-5.

Recreation

Enjoying life out-of-doors in California is easy; choosing from the many options is where things get difficult. The great outdoors truly is great here, and the amazing variety of landscapes and activities attracts nature lovers from far and wide.

Splish Splash

California's scenic coastline isn't just for taking snapshots. Water sports enthusiasts have it made in the Golden State, and of course the **surfing** here is legendary. The beaches around Los Angeles are one of the most popular (and famous) areas to hang ten. Hermosa City Beach, Manhattan State Beach, Redondo Beach and Venice Beach offer some of the best waves.

South of L.A. you can ride exceptional waves at Huntington Beach, a center of surfing culture, and also north of the city at Rincon Beach near Santa Barbara. Some of the best surfing on the West Coast is at La Jolla, near San Diego: Tourmaline Surfing Park and Windansea Beach are standouts here. In northern California wet-suited surfers flock to the chilly waters of Monterey Bay, especially around Santa Cruz's renowned Steamer Lane.

Consistent winds March through October also make Santa Cruz a great locale for **wind surfing**, although rough surf and riptides rule it out for beginners. San Francisco Bay offers a variety of wind surfing conditions, with Crissy Field in the Presidio offering spectacular urban views and the chance to sail under the Golden Gate Bridge. Year-round winds give Ventura an edge over the many excellent wind surfing locations in the southern part of the state.

If you want to make a splash with something bigger than a surfboard, the coastline's countless inlets and coves are perfect for **boating**. Santa Catalina Island and the islands making up Channel Islands National Park are popular destinations for sailors and sea lovers. **Scuba diving** enthusiasts also love the protected waters and beautiful kelp forests that surround these islands.

Anglers can easily rent all the gear necessary for saltwater **fishing** in many coastal towns. Salmon in the north and tuna farther south are the most sought after. Freshwater fishing and boating opportunities are plentiful, too. Lake Tahoe, Shasta Lake and the warm Salton Sea draw small fleets of pleasure craft on balmy weekends.

Head for the Hills

If **hiking** or **backpacking** are your sports, lace up your boots, strap on your pack and head for any section of the 600-mile-long California Coastal Trail or the Pacific Crest Trail, which stretches from Mexico to Canada. And you won't have to travel far from California's big cities to enjoy tromping through the outdoors. Check out Topanga State Park in Los Angeles; Torrey Pines State Reserve near San Diego; or Mount Tamalpais State Park, Mount Diablo State Park and the Golden Gate National Recreation Area near San Francisco. By the way, Marin County, on the north end of the Golden Gate Bridge, offers several great trails for **mountain biking** in case your feet get tired.

No self-respecting hiker visiting Lake Tahoe should miss the incredible views from the Tahoe Rim Trail. And then there's Yosemite, which fully deserves its reputation for amazing scenery. But don't limit yourself to the valley floor; the park's high country, accessible during the summer months, offers spectacular panoramas.

If the strange, otherworldly landscapes of the desert interest you, try backpacking or off-road biking through Anza-Borrego Desert State Park or Joshua Tree and Death Valley national parks. Just remember to bring water and plenty of sunscreen. Want to just sit still a bit? Many of these parks and recreation areas are great for **camping**, too.

When temperatures drop, Californians head outdoors for great **skiing** and **snowboarding**. The Lake Tahoe area alone is sprinkled with more than a dozen different ski areas, including Squaw Valley, site of the 1960 Winter Olympics. Add to this the San Bernardino Mountains in the south; Bear Valley, Yosemite Valley and Mammoth Lakes in the Sierra Nevada; and Mount Shasta in the north, and you could basically ski from one end of the state to the other.

Recreational Activities

Throughout the TourBook, you may notice a Recreational Activities heading with bulleted listings of recreation-oriented establishments listed underneath. Since normal AAA inspection criteria cannot be applied, these establishments are presented for information only. Age, height and weight restrictions may apply. Reservations are often recommended and sometimes required. Visitors should phone or write the attraction for additional information, and the address and phone number are provided for this purpose.

FOR YOUR INFORMATION

SPECIAL REGULATIONS: The State Department of Food and Agriculture inspects all produce, plant materials and wild animals at the borders to see if they are admissible under current quarantine regulations. For California regulations concerning plants phone (916) 654-0312; for regulations concerning animals phone (916) 654-1447. Dogs older than 4 months must be accompanied by a current rabies vaccination certificate.

ROAD CONDITIONS: CalTrans provides current information about road conditions; phone (800) 427-7623.

FURTHER INFORMATION FOR VISITORS:
California Division of Tourism
P.O. Box 1499
Sacramento, CA 95812-1499
(800) 862-2543

RECREATION INFORMATION:
State Parks:
California State Park System
Department of Parks and Recreation
P.O. Box 942896
Sacramento, CA 94296-0001
(916) 653-6995
(800) 444-7275 (reservations)
National Forests:
Pacific-Southwest Region,
U.S. Forest Service
630 Sansome St., Room 807
San Francisco, CA 94111
(415) 705-2874
(800) 365-2267 (information and reservations)
National Parks:
National Park Service
Fort Mason, Bldg. 201
Bay and Franklin sts.
San Francisco, CA 94123
(415) 556-0560
(800) 365-2267 (reservations)

FISHING AND HUNTING REGULATIONS:
Department of Fish and Game
1416 9th St.
Sacramento, CA 95814
(916) 653-7664

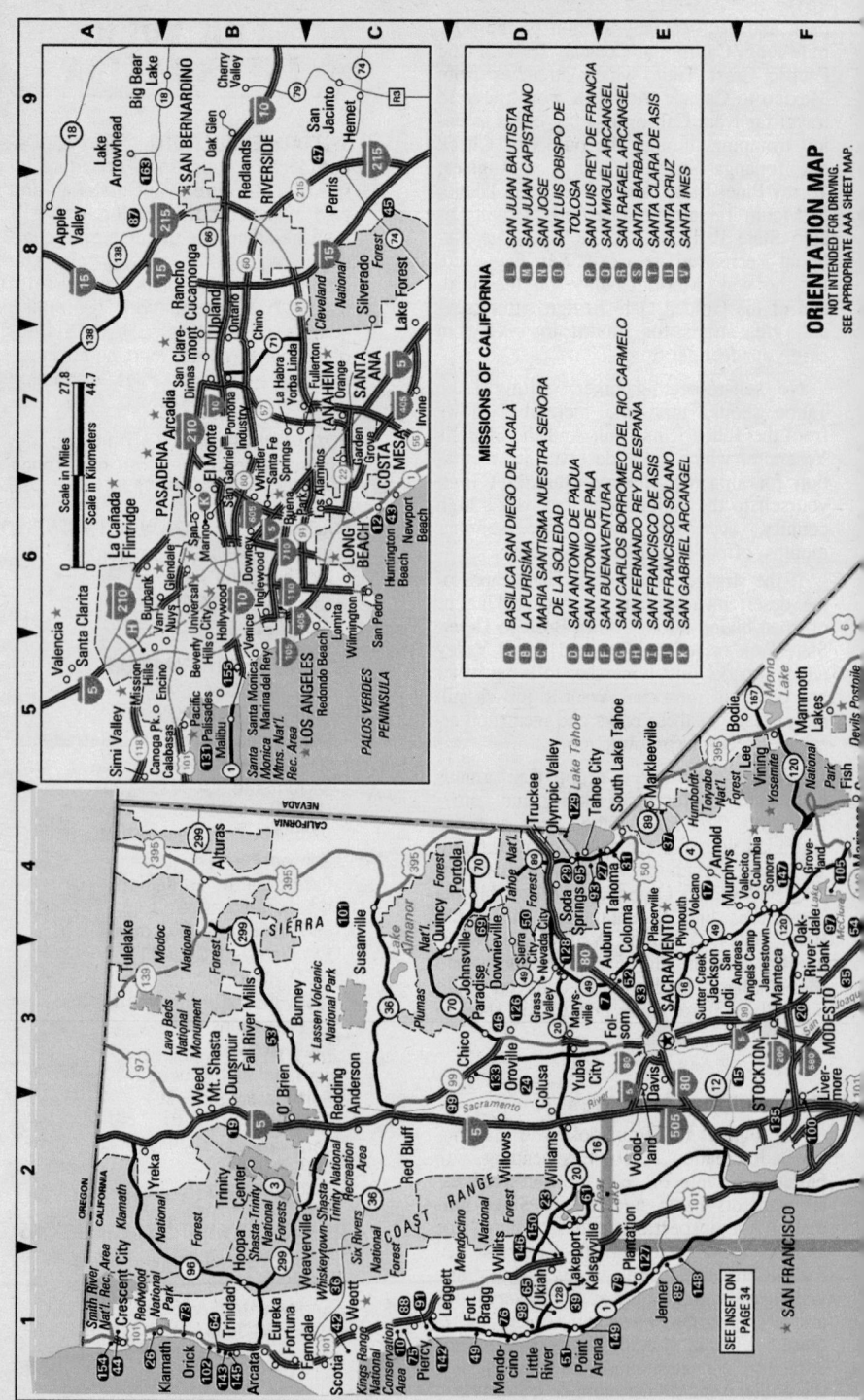

SEE INSET ON PAGE 34

Scale in Miles

0   27.8

Scale in Kilometers

0   44.7

MISSIONS OF CALIFORNIA

- A BASILICA SAN DIEGO DE ALCALÁ
- B LA PURÍSIMA
- C MARÍA SANTÍSIMA NUESTRA SEÑORA DE LA SOLEDAD
- D SAN ANTONIO DE PADUA
- E SAN ANTONIO DE PALA
- F SAN BUENAVENTURA
- G SAN CARLOS BORROMEO DEL RÍO CARMELO
- H SAN FERNANDO REY DE ESPAÑA
- I SAN FRANCISCO SOLANO
- X SAN GABRIEL ARCÁNGEL

- J SAN JUAN BAUTISTA
- K SAN JUAN CAPISTRANO
- L SAN JOSE
- M SAN LUIS OBISPO DE TOLOSA
- N SAN LUIS REY DE FRANCIA
- O SAN MIGUEL ARCÁNGEL
- P SAN RAFAEL ARCÁNGEL
- Q SANTA BARBARA
- S SANTA CLARA DE ASÍS
- T SANTA CRUZ
- V SANTA INES

ORIENTATION MAP

NOT INTENDED FOR DRIVING.
SEE APPROPRIATE AAA SHEET MAP.

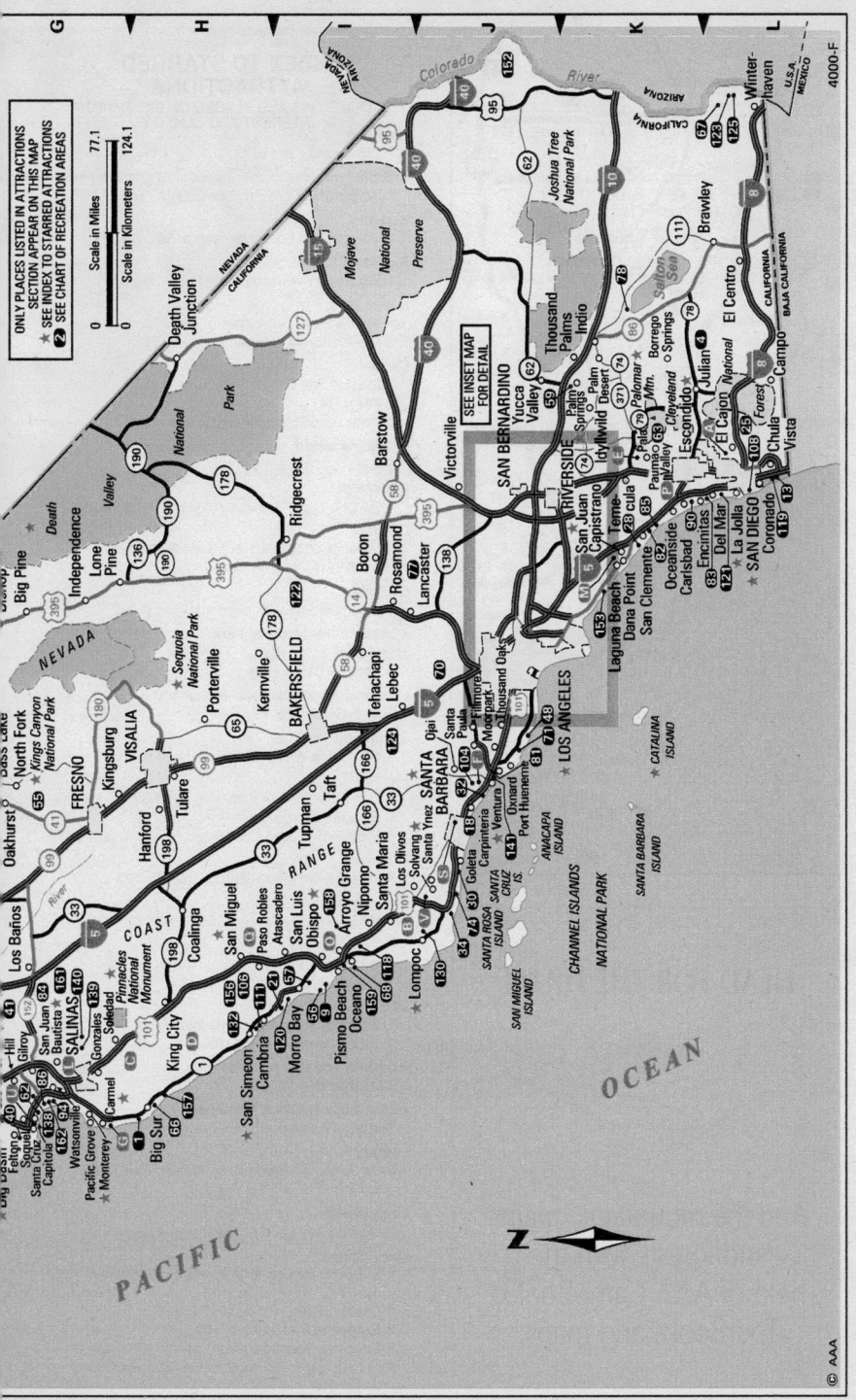

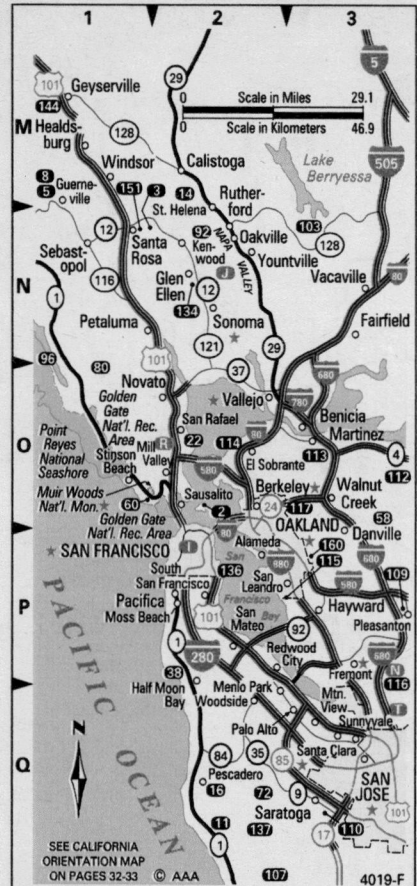

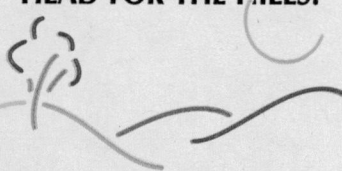

HEAD FOR THE HILLS!

And the mountains, plains
and forests with the
help of AAA CampBooks,
TourBooks and maps.

INDEX TO STARRED ATTRACTIONS

ATTRACTIONS AND PLACES OF EXCEPTIONAL INTEREST AND QUALITY

Anaheim
★ Disneyland - see p. 47

Arcadia
★ Arboretum of Los Angeles County - see p. 118

Berkeley
★ University of California - see p. 58

Big Basin
★ Big Basin Redwoods State Park - see p. 59

Buena Park
★ Knott's Berry Farm - see p. 61
★ Movieland Wax Museum - see p. 61

Carmel
★ Mission San Carlos Borromeo del Rio Carmelo - see p. 141
★ Point Lobos State Reserve - see p. 141

★ **Catalina Island**
See place listing p. 63

Claremont
★ Rancho Santa Ana Botanic Garden - see p. 120

Coloma
★ Marshall Gold Discovery State Historic Park - see p. 67

Columbia
★ Columbia State Historic Park - see p. 67

★ **Death Valley National Park**
See place listing p. 70
★ Scotty's Castle - see p. 71

★ **Devils Postpile National Monument**
See place listing p. 71

Escondido
★ San Diego Wild Animal Park - see p. 73

Fremont
★ Don Edwards San Francisco Bay National Wildlife Refuge - see p. 77
★ Mission San Jose Chapel and Museum - see p. 77

Glendale
★ Forest Lawn Memorial-Park - see p. 121

Hollywood
★ Hollywood Bowl - see p. 122
★ Mann's Chinese Theatre - see p. 122

La Cañada Flintridge
★ Descanso Gardens - see p. 123

La Jolla
★ Birch Aquarium At Scripps Institute of Oceanography - see p. 188

★ **Lassen Volcanic National Park**
See place listing p. 93

★ **Lava Beds National Monument**
See place listing p. 95

Lompoc
★ La Purísima Mission State Historic Park - see p. 96

Long Beach
★ Queen Mary - see p. 124

Los Angeles
★ El Pueblo de Los Angeles Historic Monument - see p. 107
★ Olvera Street - see p. 107
★ Exposition Park - see p. 107
★ California Science Center - see p. 107
★ Natural History Museum of Los Angeles County - see p. 108

INDEX TO STARRED ATTRACTIONS
CONTINUED

Sunburn can ruin a vacation.
Be careful when you're
on the beach or
in the water.

RECREATION AREAS

	MAP LOCATION	CAMPING	PICNICKING	HIKING TRAILS	BOATING	BOAT RAMP	BOAT RENTAL	FISHING	SWIMMING	PETS ON LEASH	BICYCLE TRAILS	NATURE PROGS.	VISITOR CENTER	LODGE/CABINS	FOOD SERVICE
NATIONAL PARKS *(See place listings)*															
Channel Islands 249,515 acres.															
Anacapa (J-4) Skin diving.		•	•	•	•			•	•				•	•	
San Miguel (J-3) Skin diving.		•	•	•	•			•	•				•	•	
Santa Barbara (K-4) Skin diving.		•	•	•	•			•	•				•	•	
Santa Cruz (J-4) Skin diving.					•			•	•						•
Santa Rosa (J-3) Skin diving.		•	•	•	•			•	•				•		
Death Valley (H-7) 3,367,628 acres. Wildflower viewing.		•	•	•				•	•			•	•	•	•
Joshua Tree (K-8) 793,000 acres.		•	•	•						•			•		
Lassen Volcanic (C-3) 106,000 acres.		•	•	•	•			•	•	•		•	•	•	•
Redwood (A-1) 110,246 acres. Kayaking; horse rental.		•	•	•				•	•	•	•	•	•	•	•
Sequoia and Kings Canyon (H-5 & G-5) 1,351 square miles. Horse rental.		•	•	•				•		•		•	•	•	•
Yosemite (F-5) 1,189 square miles. Horse rental. Motorized vessels prohibited.		•	•	•	•			•	•	•	•	•	•	•	•
NATIONAL RECREATION AREAS *(See place listings)*															
Golden Gate (O-1) 74,000 acres. Bird-watching, golfing, sailing; horse rental.		•	•	•		•		•	•	•	•	•	•	•	•
Santa Monica Mountains (B-5) 150,000 acres. Horse rental.		•	•	•				•	•	•	•		•		
Smith River (A-1) 305,337 acres. Historic. Gold panning, scuba diving; horse trails, scenic byway. *(See Six Rivers National Forest p. 226)*		•	•	•	•	•		•	•	•	•	•	•		•
Whiskeytown-Shasta-Trinity (C-2) 42,500 acres. Horse rental.		•	•	•	•	•	•	•	•	•	•	•	•	•	•
NATIONAL FORESTS *(See place listings)*															
Angeles 651,874 acres. Southern California.		•	•	•	•	•		•	•	•	•	•	•		•
Cleveland 420,630 acres. Southwestern California.		•	•	•				•		•		•	•		•
Eldorado 676,780 acres. Central California. Bird-watching, rock climbing; motorcycle trails.		•	•	•	•	•		•	•	•	•	•	•	•	•
Inyo 1,944,040 acres. Central California. Horse rental.		•	•	•	•	•	•	•	•	•	•	•	•	•	•
Klamath 1,726,000 acres. Northern California. Bird-watching, cross-country skiing, horseback riding.		•	•	•	•	•		•	•	•	•	•	•		•
Lassen 1,375,000 acres. Northern California.		•	•	•	•	•		•	•	•	•	•	•	•	•
Los Padres 1,752,539 acres. Southern California. Horse rental.		•	•	•				•	•	•	•	•	•		•
Mendocino 886,048 acres. Northwestern California.		•	•	•	•	•		•	•	•	•	•	•		•
Modoc 1,654,392 acres. Northeastern California.		•	•	•	•	•		•	•	•	•	•	•		•
Plumas 1,162,863 acres. Northern California. Horse rental, motorcycle trails.		•	•	•	•	•		•	•	•	•	•	•	•	•
San Bernardino 657,360 acres. Southern California. Horse rental.		•	•	•	•	•		•	•	•	•	•	•	•	•
Sequoia 1,139,519 acres. South-central California. Horse rental.		•	•	•	•	•		•	•	•	•	•	•	•	•
Shasta-Trinity 2,129,524 acres. Northern California. Horse rental.		•	•	•	•	•		•	•	•	•	•	•	•	•
Sierra 1,304,476 acres. Central California. Horse rental.		•	•	•	•	•		•	•	•	•	•	•	•	•
Six Rivers 958,543 acres. Northwestern California. Kayaking.		•	•	•	•	•		•	•	•		•	•		•
Stanislaus 898,602 acres. Central California. Horse rental.		•	•	•	•	•		•	•	•	•	•	•	•	•
Tahoe 797,205 acres. North-central California. Horse rental.		•	•	•	•	•		•	•	•	•	•	•	•	•
NATIONAL CONSERVATION AREA															
King Range (C-1) 60,000 acres w. of Garberville. Horseback riding, wildlife viewing.		•	•	•	•			•	•	•	•		•	•	•
NATIONAL PRESERVE *(See place listing)*															
Mojave (I-8) 1,400,000 acres.		•	•	•						•			•	•	•

RECREATION AREAS

	MAP LOCATION	CAMPING	PICNICKING	HIKING TRAILS	BOATING	BOAT RAMP	BOAT RENTAL	FISHING	SWIMMING	PETS ON LEASH	BICYCLE TRAILS	NATURE PROGS.	VISITOR CENTER	LODGE/CABINS	FOOD SERVICE
NATIONAL SEASHORE *(See place listing)*															
Point Reyes (O-1) 65,300 acres. Wildlife viewing; horse rental.		•	•	•				•		•	•	•	•		•
ARMY CORPS OF ENGINEERS															
Lake Mendocino (D-2) 5,000 acres 5 mi. n.w. of Ukiah on SR 20. Nature trails.	150	•	•	•	•	•	•	•	•	•	•	•	•		•
Lake Sonoma (M-1) 17,600 acres 26 mi. n.w. of Santa Rosa on Dry Creek Rd. Horseback riding; fish hatchery, interpretive trails.	144	•	•	•	•	•	•	•	•	•	•	•	•		•
STATE															
Anderson Marsh (D-2) 871 acres .75 mi. n. of Lower Lake on SR 53. Bird-watching; nature trail.	61		•	•	•			•				•	•		
Andrew Molera (H-2) 4,800 acres 21 mi. s. of Carmel on SR 1. Bird-watching, beachcombing; horse rental.	1	•	•	•				•		•		•			
Angel Island (O-2) 758 acres in San Francisco Bay; ferry from San Francisco or Tiburon. Historic. Beachcombing, kayaking; bicycle rentals, interpretive services, museum, nature trails, tours.	2	•	•	•	•	•		•		•	•	•	•		
Annadel (M-2) 4,913 acres s.e. of Santa Rosa on Channel Dr. Horse rental.	3							•		•	•	•			
Anza-Borrego Desert (K-7) 600,000 acres. Horse rental, nature and off-road-vehicle trails. *(See Borrego Springs p. 60)*	4	•	•	•						•	•	•	•		
Armstrong Redwoods (M-1) 752 acres 2 mi. n. of Guerneville on Armstrong Woods Rd. Horse rental, nature trails.	5		•	•						•		•	•		
Auburn (E-3) 30,000 acres 1 mi. s. of Auburn on SR 49. Historic. Gold panning, hunting, rafting, water skiing; farm, marina, pond.	7	•	•	•	•	•	•		•	•	•				
Austin Creek (M-1) 4,236 acres 2 mi. n. of Guerneville on Armstrong Woods Rd. Horse rental.	8	•	•	•				•							
Benbow Lake (C-1) 786 acres 3 mi. s. of Garberville on US 101. Motorboats not permitted. Golfing.	10	•	•	•	•		•	•	•	•		•			
Bethany Reservoir (F-2) 600 acres 7 mi. n. of I-580 via Altamont Pass, Mountain House and Christensen rds. Windsurfing.	135	•			•	•		•		•		•			
Bidwell/Sacramento River (D-3) 180 acres 5 mi. w. of Chico on River Rd. Canoeing, kayaking, rafting, tubing.	133	•	•	•	•			•	•						
Big Basin Redwoods (Q-2) 18,000 acres. Horse rental, nature trails. *(See Big Basin p. 59)*	11	•								•	•	•	•	•	•
Bolsa Chica Beach (C-6) 164 acres 3 mi. n. of Huntington Beach on SR 1.	12		•						•	•		•			
Border Field (L-7) 680 acres 15 mi. s. of San Diego on Monument Rd. Horse rental, nature trails.	13		•	•				•		•		•	•		
Bothe-Napa Valley (M-2) 1,916 acres 4 mi. n. of St. Helena on SR 29. Bird-watching, wildlife viewing; horse rental.	14	•	•	•					•	•		•			
Brannan Island (F-3) 336 acres 3.25 mi. s. of Rio Vista. Water skiing, windsurfing; nature trails, wildlife habitat.	15	•	•	•	•	•	•	•	•	•		•			•
Butano (Q-2) 3,200 acres 7 mi. s. of Pescadero on Cloverdale Rd. Wildlife viewing.	16	•	•	•				•				•			
Calaveras Big Trees (E-4) 6,073 acres. Cross-country skiing; nature trails; wildlife site. *(See Arnold p. 53)*	17	•							•	•		•			
Candlestick Point (P-2) 37 acres e. of US 101 via Candlestick exit. Windsurfing; cultural programs, guided nature walks.	136		•	•				•				•	•		
Carpinteria Beach (J-4) 84 acres at Carpinteria off SR 224.	18	•	•					•	•						
Castaic Lake (J-5) 8,000 acres .5 mi. e. of Castaic on Ridge Route Rd.	70	•	•		•	•	•	•	•	•		•			•
Castle Crags (B-2) 6,218 acres. Nature trails. *(See Dunsmuir p. 71)*	19	•	•	•	•			•		•	•		•		

RECREATION AREAS

	MAP LOCATION	CAMPING	PICNICKING	HIKING TRAILS	BOATING	BOAT RAMP	BOAT RENTAL	FISHING	SWIMMING	PETS ON LEASH	BICYCLE TRAILS	NATURE PROGS.	VISITOR CENTER	LODGE/CABINS	FOOD SERVICE
Castle Rock (Q-3) 3,600 acres 2 mi. s. of SRs 9 and 35 on Skyline Blvd. Wildlife viewing; horse trails, nature trails.	137	•		•								•	•		
Caswell Memorial (F-3) 258 acres 6 mi. s.w. of Ripon on Austin Rd. Wildlife habitat.	20	•	•	•	•			•	•	•	•	•			
China Camp (O-2) 1,640 acres n. of San Rafael via US 101 and N. San Pedro Rd. Windsurfing; wildlife site.	22	•	•	•	•			•		•	•		•	•	•
Clear Lake (D-2) 565 acres 3.5 mi. n. of Kelseyville on Soda Bay Rd. Water skiing, wildflower viewing; nature trails. *(See Kelseyville p. 85)*	23	•	•	•	•	•	•	•	•	•	•	•	•	•	•
Colusa-Sacramento River (D-3) 67 acres near downtown Colusa on SR 20. Nature trails.	24	•	•		•	•		•	•	•					
Crystal Cove (K-6) 2,791 acres n. of Dana Point on SR 1.	153	•		•				•	•		•				
Cuyamaca Rancho (L-7) 24,677 acres 6 mi. n. of Descanso on SR 79. Horse rental, nature trails.	25	•	•	•				•		•		•	•		
Del Norte Coast Redwoods (A-1) 6,400 acres 7 mi. s. of Crescent City on US 101. Nature trails.	26	•	•	•				•		•		•	•		
D.L. Bliss (E-4) 1,237 acres 17 mi. s. of Tahoe City on SR 89. Nature trails. *(See South Lake Tahoe in Lake Tahoe Area p. 91)*	27	•	•	•				•	•	•		•			
Doheny State Beach (K-6) 62 acres 1 mi. s. of Dana Point on Del Obispo St.	28	•	•					•	•	•		•	•		•
Donner Memorial (D-4) 353 acres. Cross-country skiing; nature trails. *(See Truckee in Lake Tahoe Area p. 92)*	29	•	•	•	•	•		•	•	•		•	•		
El Capitan State Beach (J-4) 133 acres 20 mi. w. of Santa Barbara off US 101. Nature trails.	30	•	•	•				•	•	•		•	•		•
Emerald Bay (E-4) 593 acres on the s.w. shore of Lake Tahoe.	31	•	•	•	•			•	•	•		•			
Emma Wood State Beach (J-4) 116 acres 4 mi. n. of Ventura on US 101.	32	•	•					•	•	•					
Empire Mine (D-3) 788 acres. Horse rental. *(See Grass Valley p. 79)*	128			•						•		•	•		
Folsom Lake (E-3) 17,718 acres 2 mi. n.w. of Folsom off US 50. Water skiing, windsurfing; horse rental, nature trails.	33	•	•	•	•	•	•	•	•	•	•	•	•		•
Forest of Nisene Marks (G-2) 9,960 acres 4 mi. n. of Aptos on Aptos Creek Rd.	138	•	•	•						•	•				
Fort Ross (E-1) 3,386 acres. *(See Jenner p. 83)*	127	•	•	•				•				•	•		
Fremont Peak (G-3) 244 acres 11 mi. s. of San Juan Bautista on San Juan Canyon Rd. Nature trails.	139	•	•	•						•		•			
Gaviota (J-4) 2,776 acres at Gaviota, 30 mi. w. of Santa Barbara on US 101. Horse rental.	34	•	•	•	•	•		•		•		•			•
George J. Hatfield (F-3) 47 acres 28 mi. w. of Merced on Kelly Rd.	35	•	•			•	•		•		•				
Grizzly Creek Redwoods (C-1) 390 acres 15 mi. e. of Fortuna on SR 36. Nature trails.	36	•	•	•				•	•			•			
Grover Hot Springs (E-4) 539 acres 4 mi. w. of Markleeville on Hot Springs Rd. Nature trails.	37	•	•	•					•	•	•	•	•		
Half Moon Bay Beach (P-2) 170 acres .5 mi. w. of US 1 on Kelly Ave. Horse rental.	38	•	•	•				•		•	•				
Hendy Woods (D-1) 693 acres 3 mi. w. of Philo off SR 128. Nature trails.	39	•	•	•					•	•		•			
Henry Cowell Redwoods (G-2) 4,082 acres 3 mi. e. of Felton on Graham Hill Rd. Nature trails.	40	•	•	•					•	•		•	•		
Henry W. Coe (G-3) 80,000 acres 14 mi. e. of Morgan Hill on E. Dunne Ave. Nature trails.	41	•	•	•				•		•			•		
Hollister Hills (G-3) 3,322 acres 8 mi. s. of Hollister via Cienega Rd. Nature trails, motorcycle trails, trails for four-wheel-drive vehicles.	140	•	•	•						•	•	•			•
Humboldt Lagoons (B-1) 1,886 acres 4 mi. s. of Orick on US 101. *(See Orick p. 153)*	102	•	•	•	•	•		•	•	•		•	•		

RECREATION AREAS

	MAP LOCATION	CAMPING	PICNICKING	HIKING TRAILS	BOATING	BOAT RAMP	BOAT RENTAL	FISHING	SWIMMING	PETS ON LEASH	BICYCLE TRAILS	NATURE PROGS.	VISITOR CENTER	LODGE/CABINS	FOOD SERVICE
Humboldt Redwoods (C-1) 51,000 acres. Horse rental, nature trails. *(See Weott p. 236)*	42	•	•	•	•			•	•		•		•		
Huntington Beach (C-6) 78 acres at the s. edge of Huntington Beach on SR 1 opposite Magnolia Ave.	43		•					•	•	•		•			•
Jack London (N-2) 800 acres. Horse rental. *(See Glen Ellen p. 79)*	134		•	•						•		•	•	•	•
Jedediah Smith Redwoods (A-1) 9,560 acres 9 mi. n.e. of Crescent City on US 199. Horse rentals, nature trails.	44	•	•	•	•			•	•	•		•	•		
Julia Pfeiffer Burns (H-2) 3,583 acres 37 mi. s. of Carmel on SR 1.	157	•	•	•					•						
Kings Beach (D-4) 8 acres 12 mi. n.e. of Tahoe City on SR 28.	129		•		•	•	•	•	•						
Lake Elsinore (C-8) 2,954 acres 1 mi. w. of Elsinore on SR 74. Water skiing, windsurfing.	45	•	•		•	•	•	•	•	•					•
Lake Oroville (D-3) 31,600 acres 6 mi. n.e. of Oroville off SR 70. Water skiing, windsurfing; horse rental, nature trails.	46	•	•	•	•	•	•	•	•	•		•	•		
Lake Perris (C-9) 8,000 acres 4 mi. n.e. of Perris on the Ramona Expwy. Rock climbing, water skiing; horse rental.	47	•	•	•	•	•	•	•	•	•		•	•		•
Lakes Earl and Talawa (A-1) 5,000 acres n. of Crescent City off US 101. Horse rental.	154	•	•	•	•	•	•	•			•	•			
La Purísima Mission (J-3) 967 acres. Horse rental. *(See Lompoc p. 96)*	130		•	•									•	•	
Leo Carrillo Beach (J-5) 2,000 acres 22 mi. n. of Santa Monica on SR 1. Windsurfing.	48	•	•	•				•	•						
Los Baños Creek Reservoir (G-3) 10 mi. s.w. of Los Baños via SR 165, Pioneer and Canyon rds. Horseback riding trails.	161	•	•	•	•			•	•	•					
MacKerricher (D-1) 2,030 acres 3 mi. n. of Fort Bragg on SR 1. Horse rental.	49	•	•	•	•	•		•		•	•	•			
Malakoff Diggins (D-3) 3,000 acres n.e. of Nevada City on N. Bloomfield Rd. Historic. Nature trails.	50	•	•	•				•	•	•		•	•	•	
Malibu Creek (B-5) 6,600 acres 4 mi. s. of US 101 on Las Virgenes/Malibu Canyon Rd. in Calabasas. Horse rental.	131	•	•	•				•	•	•	•				
Malibu Lagoon Beach (B-5) 76 acres at US 101 and Malibu Creek. Nature trails.	155		•	•				•	•			•			
Manchester Beach (D-1) 1,419 acres 7 mi. n of Point Arena on SR 1.	51	•	•					•		•		•			
Manresa Beach (G-2) 83 acrea 5 mi. w. of Watsonville.	162	•	•					•	•	•					
Marshall Gold Discovery (E-3) 280 acres 8 mi. n. of Placerville on SR 49. Historic. Nature trails.	52		•	•	•	•		•		•		•	•		•
McArthur-Burney Falls Memorial (B-3) 910 acres. Scenic. Water skiing, nature trails. *(See Burney p. 61)*	53	•	•	•	•			•	•			•	•		•
McConnell (F-4) 74 acres 5 mi. e. of Delhi on Merced River.	54	•	•		•			•	•			•			
McGrath Beach (J-4) 295 acres s. of Ventura on Harbor Blvd. Nature trails.	141	•		•				•	•			•			
Millerton Lake (G-4) 6,553 acres 21 mi. n.e. of Fresno via SR 41. Historic. Water skiing, windsurfing.	55	•	•	•	•	•	•	•	•	•	•	•	•		
Montaña de Oro (I-3) 8,066 acres 7 mi. s. of Los Osos on Pecho Rd. Horse rental, nature trails.	56	•	•	•				•				•	•		•
Morro Bay (I-3) 2,435 acres 3 mi. s. of Morro Bay. Birdwatching, golf.	57	•	•	•	•	•	•	•		•		•	•		•
Morro Strand Beach (I-3) 117 acres 1 mi. n. of Morro Bay on SR 1. Surfing.	120	•	•					•	•	•					
Mount Diablo (O-3) 18,000 acres. Horse rental. *(See Walnut Creek p. 236)*	58	•	•	•							•	•	•		•
Mount San Jacinto (J-7) 13,522 acres. Horse rental. *(See San Bernardino National Forest p. 171)*	59	•	•	•						•		•	•		
Mount Tamalpais (O-1) 6,233 acres. Horse rental, nature trails. *(See Mill Valley p. 209)*	60	•	•	•						•	•	•	•	•	•

RECREATION AREAS

	MAP LOCATION	CAMPING	PICNICKING	HIKING TRAILS	BOATING	BOAT RAMP	BOAT RENTAL	FISHING	SWIMMING	PETS ON LEASH	BICYCLE TRAILS	NATURE PROGS.	VISITOR CENTER	LODGE/CABINS	FOOD SERVICE
Navarro River Redwoods (D-1) 12 acres 6 mi. w. of Navarro on SR 128.	65	•	•	•				•	•	•					
New Brighton Beach (G-2) 94 acres 4 mi. s. of Santa Cruz.	62	•	•	•				•	•				•		
Oceano Dunes (I-3) 2,500 acres 3 mi. s. of city of Pismo Beach on SR 1. Off-road vehicles permitted. Surfing; horse rental.	118	•	•	•				•	•				•		
Palomar Mountain (K-7) 1,897 acres 4 mi. n. of jct. CR S6 and CR 57 via park road. Nature trails.	63	•	•	•				•		•					
Patrick's Point (B-1) 632 acres. Nature trails. *(See Trinidad p. 232)*	64	•	•	•				•		•		•	•	•	•
Pfeiffer Big Sur (H-2) 821 acres. Nature trails. *(See Big Sur p. 60)*	66								•		•	•	•	•	•
Picacho (L-9) 4,880 acres 23 mi. n. of Winterhaven. Water skiing.	67	•	•	•	•	•	•	•	•			•			
Pismo Beach (I-3) 1,051 acres 3 mi. s. of city of Pismo Beach on SR 1. Surfing; nature trails.	68	•	•	•				•	•		•	•			•
Plumas-Eureka (D-4) 6,749 acres 5 mi. w. of Graeagle on CR A14. Horse rental, nature trails.	69	•	•	•				•		•		•	•	•	
Point Mugu (J-5) 13,360 acres 15 mi. s. of Oxnard on SR 1. Horse rental.	71	•	•	•				•	•	•		•			
Portola (Q-2) 2,010 acres 20 mi. s.w. of Palo Alto off SR 35. Nature trails.	72	•	•	•				•		•		•	•		
Prairie Creek Redwoods (B-1) 40,000 acres. *(See Orick p. 153)*	73	•	•	•				•		•		•	•		
Pyramid Lake (I-5) 1,297 acres 12 mi. n. of Frazier Park off I-5.	124	•	•		•	•	•	•	•	•	•				•
Red Rock Canyon (I-6) 4,000 acres. Scenic. Nature trails. *(See place listing p. 164)*	122	•	•	•								•			
Refugio Beach (J-4) 155 acres 22 mi. n.w. of Santa Barbara off US 101.	74	•	•	•				•	•	•					
Richardson Grove (C-1) 1,000 acres 8 mi. s. of Garberville on US 101. Nature trails.	75	•	•	•				•	•	•		•	•		•
Russian Gulch (D-1) 1,300 acres 2 mi. n. of Mendocino on US 101. Skin diving.	76	•	•	•				•	•	•		•			
Saddleback Butte (I-6) 2,875 acres 17 mi. e. of Lancaster at E. Ave. J and 170th St. Nature trails.	77	•	•	•						•					
Salton Sea (K-8) 17,900 acres 11 mi. s.e. of Mecca via SR 111. Water skiing; nature trails.	78	•	•	•	•	•		•	•			•			
Salt Point (E-1) 5,676 acres 24 mi. n. of Jenner on SR 1. Skin diving.	79	•	•	•	•	•		•		•		•	•		
Samuel P. Taylor (O-1) 2,708 acres 15 mi. w. of San Rafael on Sir Francis Drake Blvd. Nature trails.	80	•	•	•			•			•	•	•	•		
San Buenaventura Beach (J-5) 114 acres in Ventura.	81		•						•	•		•			•
San Clemente Beach (K-5) 110 acres at the s. edge of San Clemente via the Avenida Calafia exit off I-5.	82	•	•	•					•	•		•			
San Elijo Beach (L-6) 39 acres 1 mi. s. of Encinitas.	83	•							•	•			•		
San Luis Reservoir (G-3) 26,026 acres 12 mi. w. of Los Banos on SR 152. Water skiing, windsurfing; motor-bike area.	84	•	•		•	•		•	•	•					
San Onofre Beach (K-6) 3,036 acres 1.5 mi. s. of San Clemente off I-5.	85	•		•					•	•					
San Simeon Beach (H-3) 541 acres 5 mi. s. of San Simeon on SR 1.	111	•	•	•				•	•						
Seacliff Beach (G-2) 85 acres 5.5 mi. s. of Santa Cruz on SR 1.	86	•	•					•	•			•	•		
Silver Strand Beach (L-6) 428 acres 4.5 mi. s. of Coronado on SR 75.	119		•						•	•					
Silverwood Lake (A-8) 2,200 acres, e. of Cajon Junction on SR 138. Water skiing; nature trails.	87	•	•	•	•	•	•	•	•	•		•	•		•
Sinkyone Wilderness (C-1) 7,000 acres 30 mi. w. of Redway on CR 435 (Briceland Rd.).	142	•	•	•											

RECREATION AREAS

	MAP LOCATION	CAMPING	PICNICKING	HIKING TRAILS	BOATING	BOAT RAMP	BOAT RENTAL	FISHING	SWIMMING	PETS ON LEASH	BICYCLE TRAILS	NATURE PROGS.	VISITOR CENTER	LODGE/CABINS	FOOD SERVICE
Smithe Redwoods (C-1) 622 acres 4 mi. n. of Leggett on US 101.	88		•					•	•	•		•			
Sonoma Coast Beach (E-1) 5,333 acres n. of Bodega Bay on SR 1. Horse rental.	89	•	•	•	•	•	•		•	•	•	•		•	
South Carlsbad Beach (K-6) 135 acres 4 mi. n. of Encinitas.	90	•						•	•						
South Yuba River Project (D-3) 2,000 acres 8 mi. n.w. of Nevada City on SR 49. Nature trail.	126	•	•	•				•	•	•		•	•		
Standish-Hickey (C-1) 1,020 acres 2 mi. n. of Leggett on US 101. Nature trail.	91	•	•	•				•	•	•		•			
Sugarloaf Ridge (N-2) 2,700 acres 7 mi. e. of Santa Rosa on SR 12. Horse rental, nature trails.	92	•	•	•				•	•	•	•	•			
Sugar Pine Point (D-4) 2,011 acres 10 mi. s. of Tahoe City on SR 89. Historic. Nature trails, cross-country ski trails.	93	•	•	•	•			•	•	•		•	•		
Sunset Beach (G-3) 324 acres 4 mi. w. of Watsonville.	94	•	•					•	•	•					
Tahoe (E-4) 57 acres on Lake Tahoe .25 mi. s. of Tahoe City.	95	•	•		•			•	•	•	•				
Tomales Bay (N-1) 1,857 acres 4 mi. n. of Inverness on Pierce Pt. Rd. Nature trails.	96	•	•	•				•	•	•		•	•		
Torrey Pines Beach (L-6) 41 acres 1 mi. s. of Del Mar on N. Torrey Pines Rd.	121		•					•	•						
Trinidad Beach (B-1) 159 acres 19 mi. n. of Eureka on US 101.	143	•	•	•	•	•	•	•	•		•				
Turlock Lake (F-4) 408 acres 23 mi. e. of Modesto off SR 132. Water skiing.	97	•	•	•	•	•		•	•			•			
Van Damme (D-1) 2,163 acres 3 mi. s. of Mendocino on SR 1. Nature trails.	98	•	•	•				•		•		•	•		
William Randolph Hearst Memorial Beach (H-3) 8 acres in San Simeon on SR 1.	132		•		•			•	•			•			•
Woodson Bridge (D-2) 428 acres 6 mi. e. of Corning and I-5. Nature trails.	99	•	•	•	•	•		•		•		•			
OTHER															
Anthony Chabot Regional Park and Lake Chabot Marina (P-3) 5,242 acres e. of Oakland. Horse rental, horse trails.	160	•	•	•	•		•	•		•	•	•			•
Avila Beach (I-3) 10 acres in Avila. Surfing.	9		•					•	•						•
Big Lagoon (B-1) 50 acres 7 mi. n. of Trinidad on US 101.	145	•	•	•		•		•	•	•					
Cayucos Beach (I-3) 16 acres s.w. of Cayucos on SR 1. Surfing.	21		•	•				•	•	•					
Contra Loma (O-3) 776 acres 1 mi. s. of Antioch. Wind-surfing, sailboarding.	112		•	•	•	•	•	•	•	•	•				•
Cow Mountain (D-2) 50,000 acres e. of Ukiah on Talmage Rd.	146	•	•					•		•			•		
Del Valle (F-2) 4,500 acres 10 mi. s. of Livermore.	100	•	•	•	•	•	•	•	•	•	•				•
Don Pedro Lake (F-4) 12,960 acres n.e. of La Grange on Bond's Flat Rd.	147	•	•	•	•	•	•	•	•	•				•	•
Doran (E-1) 120 acres on Doran Park Rd., Bodega Bay.	148	•	•	•	•	•	•	•	•	•					
Eagle Lake (C-4) 22,000 acres 20 mi. n.w. of Susanville.	101	•	•	•	•	•	•	•	•	•		•		•	•
Empire Landing (J-9) 10 acres 7 mi. s.w. of Parker Dam (Calif. side of Colorado River).	152	•	•	•	•			•	•						
Gualala Point (E-1) 300 acres off SR 1 s. of Gualala.	149	•	•	•	•			•		•			•		
Lake Berryessa (N-3) 13,000 acres 20 mi. n.w. of Napa on SR 121.	103	•	•	•	•	•	•	•	•	•				•	•
Lake Casitas (J-5) 6,000 acres 5 mi. s.w. of Ojai off SR 150.	104	•	•	•	•	•	•	•		•					•
Lake Gregory (A-8) 150 acres in Crestline.	163		•					•	•					•	•
Lake McClure (F-4) 7,100 acres 4 mi. w. of Coulterville on SR 132.	105	•	•		•	•	•	•	•	•			•	•	•
Lake Nacimiento (H-3) 5,370 acres 17 mi. w. of Paso Robles off US 101.	106	•	•		•	•	•	•	•	•	•	•	•	•	•

RECREATION AREAS

	MAP LOCATION	CAMPING	PICNICKING	HIKING TRAILS	BOATING	BOAT RAMP	BOAT RENTAL	FISHING	SWIMMING	PETS ON LEASH	BICYCLE TRAILS	NATURE PROGS.	VISITOR CENTER	LODGE/CABINS	FOOD SERVICE
Lake San Antonio (H-3) 5,000 acres 40 mi. s. of King City off US 101. Birdwatching; horse rental.	156	•	•	•	•	•	•	•	•	•		•		•	•
Loch Lomond (Q-2) 2,100 acres n. of Ben Lomond.	107	•	•	•	•	•	•	•		•		•			•
Lopez Lake (I-4) 4,376 acres 11 mi. n.e. of Arroyo Grande on Lopez Dr.	158	•	•	•	•	•	•	•	•	•					
Martinez Shoreline (O-3) 343 acres in Martinez. Birdwatching; nature trails.	113	•	•	•	•	•	•	•		•	•	•	•		
Martin Luther King Jr. Shoreline (P-3) 1,220 acres in Oakland. Birdwatching; fishing pier.	115	•	•	•	•	•		•		•	•	•			•
Mission Bay (L-7) 4,600 acres. *(See San Diego p. 178)*	108	•	•		•	•	•	•	•	•	•		•	•	•
Oceano Memorial (I-3) 11.8 acres on Dewey Rd. in Oceano.	159	•	•					•	•						
Point Pinole Shoreline (O-2) 2,147 acres n.w. of San Pablo. Fishing pier.	114	•	•					•		•	•	•	•		
Senator Wash Reservoir (L-9) 6 acres 20 mi. n. of Winterhaven on Senator Wash Rd. Skin diving.	123	•	•		•	•		•	•						
Shadow Cliffs East Bay Regional Recreation Area (P-3) 249 acres at Pleasanton. Waterslide. *(See Pleasanton p. 160)*	109	•	•	•	•	•	•	•	•	•	•	•			•
Spring Lake (M-1) 320 acres e. of Santa Rosa at Newanga Ave.	151	•	•	•	•	•	•	•	•	•	•	•			•
Squaw Lake (L-9) 18 acres 20 mi. n. of Winterhaven at end of Senator Wash Rd.	125	•	•	•	•	•		•	•	•					
Sunol Wilderness (Q-3) 6,858 acres 6 mi. s. of Sunol. Birdwatching; nature trails.	116	•	•	•						•	•	•	•		
Temescal (O-3) 48 acres in Oakland.	117	•	•					•	•	•		•			•
Vasona Park and Reservoir (Q-3) 151 acres near Los Gatos. Motorboats not permitted.	110	•	•	•	•		•	•	•	•		•	•		•

CALIFORNIA'S SESQUICENTENNIAL

California continues its 3-year celebration of its sesquicentennial with the observance of the 150th anniversary of the gold rush that brought a tidal wave of fortune seekers and dreamers to the state. The celebration will culminate in the commemoration of the 150th anniversary of statehood in 2000.

Towns, festivals and attractions across the state will gear their annual events toward the celebration of the state's heritage. In addition, many other one-time-only events and festivals are being planned specifically for the sesquicentennial.

For information about what's happening during California's sesquicentennial, contact California Gold Discovery to Statehood Sesquicentennial, 900 N St., Suite 500, Sacramento, CA 95814; phone (916) 653-9599.

BLAST OFF FOR

Disneyland®
PARK

©Disney

TOMORROWLAND
IS HERE TODAY.

Let your imagination soar in the new Tomorrowland at Disneyland Park. It's the land redone for total fun! Ride the futuristic fast track of Rocket Rods. Pilot your own soaring starship on Astro Orbitor. Experience the 3-D sensory sensation of "Honey, I Shrunk The Audience." To Tomorrowland and beyond!

"Honey, I Shrunk The Audience"

Shrink with delight and rock with laughter in 3-D.

3 FLEXIBLE WAYS TO SAVE WITH AAA

Save up to $60 with **AAA Disney Magic Moments** on a AAA Vacations® Disneyland package when staying at participating hotels.*

If you're driving, check out **AAA Disney Driveaway Vacations** featuring special discounts on en route accommodations plus a Travel Activity Kit.

Or choose the flexibility of either the new 3-Day or 5-Day **Disneyland Flex Passport** to fit your travel itinerary. Enjoy 1 FREE Early Admission into the Park 1½ hours before it opens** and FREE Disneyland parking. For even more Flex fun, purchase the 5-Day Disneyland Flex Passport and receive 1 breakfast inside Disneyland plus Early Admission every day your Disneyland Flex Passport is valid.** Disneyland Flex Passports are available at participating AAA Travel Offices.

To plan your Disneyland Vacation, call or visit your nearest AAA Travel Office, today!

Disneyland
Park
IN SOUTHERN CALIFORNIA

*Subject to limited availability. **Does not operate daily. Some restrictions apply. Attraction and entertainment schedules may vary. ©Disney

STARRED ATTRACTIONS

Arboretum of Los Angeles County—Stroll through acres and acres of lush gardens filled with exotic trees and shrubs surrounding ponds and a spring-fed lake. See Arcadia p. 118.

Avenue of the Giants—Some of California's most beautiful redwood groves line this 33-mile section of highway in Humboldt Redwoods State Park. See Weott p. 237.

Balboa Park—The 200-foot California Tower soars above the many museums, gardens and recreation areas that make up this impressive park at the edge of the city's business district. See San Diego p. 174.

Big Basin Redwoods State Park—California's first state park features the giant redwoods, some as tall as 330 feet, that California is famous for. See Big Basin p. 59.

Birch Aquarium at Scripps Institute of Oceanography—Perched on a hillside above the Scripps Institution of Oceanography, the aquarium is home to marine life from both the cold and warm waters of the Pacific. See La Jolla p. 188.

Cabrillo National Monument—Take in terrific views of the Pacific from where this monument stands on Point Loma. See San Diego p. 180.

California Academy of Sciences—This Golden Gate Park institution features a natural history museum, an aquarium and a planetarium. See San Francisco p. 199.

California Science Center—Hands-on exhibits dealing with mathematics, space, the environment, health and earthquakes take center stage at this museum in Exposition Park. See Los Angeles p. 107.

California State Railroad Museum—Several restored locomotives along with exhibits describing railroad history are housed in this museum's striking brick and glass building. See Sacramento p. 168.

Continued on p. 48.

Points of Interest

ALAMEDA (P-2) pop. 76,500, elev. 30′

Fall and winter in Alameda are the best times to observe such sea birds as loons, grebes and ducks at Robert W. Crown Memorial Beach. Crab Cove has been designated a marine reserve. Crab Cove Visitor Center, on McKay near Central, features free exhibits about shoreline and undersea life and a saltwater aquarium with live bay creatures; phone (510) 521-6887.

Daily ferry service through Harbor Bay Ferry is available between the Ferry Building, at the foot of Market Street across from the Embarcadero in San Francisco, and Bay Farm Island, in Alameda at 2990 Main St.; seasonal service to Candlestick Point for sporting events also is offered. Phone (510) 769-5500 or (415) 247-1600, for departure times and rates. Alameda/Oakland Ferry, with service from Alameda, Jack London Square in Oakland and San Francisco, connects with Blue and Gold Fleet, which takes passengers to Alcatraz; phone (510) 522-3300 for schedule.

Alameda Chamber of Commerce: 2447 Santa Clara Ave., Suite 302, Alameda, CA 94501; phone (510) 522-0414 or 521-8677.

ALAMEDA HISTORICAL MUSEUM AND CULTURAL CENTER, 2324 Alameda Ave., contains city memorabilia. Displayed are vintage clothing, photographs, art, toys, household furnishings and a bicycle built for six. A gallery features changing exhibits of contemporary arts and crafts created by local artists. Allow 30 minutes minimum. Wed.-Sun. 1:30-4 (also Sat. 11-1:30), Jan.-Nov.; closed holidays. Free. Phone (510) 521-1233.

ALTURAS (B-4) pop. 3,200, elev. 4,366′

Until 1874 Alturas was called Dorris Bridge after the Dorris family, the town's first European settlers. The Dorrises built a simple wooden bridge across the Pit River at the south end of town and later erected a house that served as a stopover for travelers. The county seat, Alturas is a marketing center for ranchers who raise livestock, potatoes and alfalfa.

Alturas Chamber of Commerce: 522 S. Main St., Alturas, CA 96101; phone (530) 233-4434.

MODOC COUNTY HISTORICAL MUSEUM, 600 S. Main St., documents area development via displays of American Indian artifacts and firearms, including pieces dating from the 15th century to World War II. A steam engine once used locally is outside. Tues.-Sat. 10-4, May-Oct. Donations. Phone (530) 233-6328 or 233-2944.

ANAHEIM (C-7) pop. 266,400, elev. 160'

Its name taken from the Santa Ana River and the German word for home, Anaheim was settled by German emigrants in 1857. They brought cuttings from their Rhineland vineyards and developed Anaheim into California's wine capital. In the late 1800s a blight destroyed the vineyards, and the grape growers began growing oranges, thus beginning a new industry.

No longer a small town surrounded by orange groves, Anaheim is now a bustling suburb of Los Angeles. Exhibitions, concerts and sports events take place at Anaheim Convention Center on Harbor Boulevard. Home games of baseball's Anaheim Angels are held in Edison International Field of Anaheim; for Angels ticket information phone (714) 634-2000. The Mighty Ducks professional ice hockey team plays at Arrowhead Pond; phone (714) 704-2700 for ticket information.

Anaheim/Orange County Visitor & Convention Bureau: 800 W. Katella Ave., Anaheim, CA 92803; phone (714) 765-8888.

★ **DISNEYLAND** is at 1313 Harbor Blvd. via I-5. The park encompasses more than 60 major rides, 50 shops and 30 restaurants divided among eight themed lands. Entering Disneyland through a 19th-century railroad station, guests can board one of four trains of the Disneyland Railroad and circle the park, passing the 1890s Main Street, U.S.A., and seven other theme areas: Tomorrowland, Frontierland, Fantasyland, Adventureland, Critter Country, Mickey's Toontown and New Orleans Square. Town Square faces the station; old-fashioned streetcars rumble past an ice cream parlor, bank and other enterprises—all open for business.

"The Mulan Parade" is a colorful new nighttime parade inspired by Walt Disney Pictures' newest animated feature. The parade celebrates the adventures of Mulan, the heroine of the story, and employs a wide range of entertainment techniques and special effects. Additional highlights include choreography inspired by Asian martial arts; monumental floats and rolling stages; and elaborate, colorful Chinese costuming. Among the performers is a troupe of Chinese acrobats.

During the day, Disneyland presents the "Hercules Victory Parade." The "Fantasmic!" special effects show starring Mickey Mouse is presented nightly each summer and on weekends along the Rivers of America in Frontierland.

Main Street, U.S.A., is a composite of the nation's small towns as they appeared at the turn of the 20th century. The thoroughfare leads to all Disneyland attractions and is flanked by a theater featuring "Great Moments with Mr. Lincoln" and "The Walt Disney Story," a tribute to the park's founder. It also is lined with specialty shops, a penny arcade, a silent cinema, Candy Palace and City Hall.

Adventureland reproduces the exotic surroundings of Asia, the Middle East and the South

STARRED ATTRACTIONS

Catalina Island—Just 21 miles off the California coast, this resort island offers all sorts of opportunities for outdoor fun including sport fishing, boating and hiking. See place listing p. 63.

Chinatown—Enjoy a taste of the Far East in this bustling "city within a city" where Chinese shops and restaurants abound. See San Francisco p. 106.

Columbia State Historic Park—Once a Mother Lode mining town, Columbia boasts a restored business district that evokes the town's heady gold rush days. See Columbia p. 67.

County Courthouse—Balconies, turrets, and ornately carved doors and archways reveal a Spanish-Moorish flair that makes this 1929 public building a memorable sight. See Santa Barbara p. 217.

Death Valley National Park—The Western Hemisphere's lowest point, Death Valley is blazingly hot and prone to flash floods, yet is home to rare foliage and geological phenomena. See place listing p. 70.

Descanso Gardens—Camellias, roses, lilacs, irises, daylilies: no matter what time of year something is blooming at this woodland botanic garden. See La Cañada Flintridge p. 123.

Devils Postpile National Monument—A sheer wall of 60-foot high basaltic columns distinguishes this monument in the eastern Sierra Nevada range. See place listing p. 71.

Disneyland—This classic theme park features a revamped Tomorrowland, new parades and several new attractions. See Anaheim p. 47.

Don Edwards San Francisco Bay National Wildlife Refuge—A 20,000-acre habitat for migratory birds and local endangered species, this refuge also features an interpretive center. See Fremont p. 77.

Seas. Here, in a vine-covered Polynesian hut called the Enchanted Tiki Room, 225 audio-animatronic birds, flowers and tiki gods serenade visitors. The Jungle Cruise takes passengers through a simulated tropical rain forest that includes elephants, hippopotamuses, a bengal tiger and a waterfall. Nearby is the Swiss Family Treehouse, the arboreal abode of the shipwrecked family whose adventures were portrayed in the Disney film, "The Swiss Family Robinson."

Visitors to Adventureland can continue their journeys to far-off locales at the Indiana Jones™ Adventure, based upon the Indiana Jones film trilogy. Aboard four-wheel-drive vehicles, passengers encounter ancient temple ruins, clouds of smoke and fire, bubbling lava pits and a menacing temple deity.

New Orleans Square recaptures the city of a century ago with iron-trellised balconies; narrow, winding streets; sidewalk cafes; and wandering Dixieland jazz minstrels. Guests can board boats and follow a band of audio-animatronic buccaneers as they burn and plunder a town in Pirates of the Caribbean. Above the attraction's entrance is the Disney Gallery, an art gallery showcasing the pre-opening conceptual artwork of Disneyland's lands and attractions. The nearby Haunted Mansion is the domain of 999 ghosts, ghouls and goblins who cavort through dark, cobwebbed halls.

Critter Country is home to Splash Mountain, a hollowed-out log ride through the world of Brer Rabbit, Brer Bear and Brer Fox which climaxes with a plunge down a five-story waterfall. The Country Bear Vacation Hoedown musical revue stars 18 audio-animatronic bears.

Frontierland re-creates the American West of the 19th century. At Big Thunder Mountain Railroad guests depart from an 1890s mining camp aboard open-air ore cars and encounter a swarm of bats, a raging waterfall and an underground earthquake. Nearby, the Golden Horseshoe Revue presents Western-themed entertainment.

Plying the Rivers of America are other sights from yesteryear. The *Mark Twain* riverboat paddles past plantation docks while the square-masted schooner *Columbia* unleashes a cannonade at Fort Wilderness. Visitors to Tom Sawyer's Island can walk across a shifting barrel bridge, explore Injun Joe's Cave and climb Tom Sawyer's treehouse.

Symbol of Disneyland, Sleeping Beauty Castle is the gateway to Fantasyland. Rides based upon the adventures of such storybook characters as Snow White, Peter Pan, Mr. Toad, Dumbo the Flying Elephant and Alice from "Alice in Wonderland" can be found here. It's a Small World offers a cruise around the globe during which nearly 600 audio-animatronic children wearing bright native costumes sing and dance. The Matterhorn roller coaster simulates a bobsled run through the Alps.

The Jolly Trolley travels through Mickey's Toontown, which features Disney characters in fanciful community settings. Within Toontown are Gadget's Go-Coaster, a miniature roller coaster made of oversized toys, and Roger Rabbit's Car Toon Spin, where passenger's board cartoon cabs for an unpredictable automobile chase.

Tomorrowland has been extensively updated and, in addition to park favorites such as Space Mountain and Star Tours, offers several new rides and attractions. Guests can experience the recently opened 3-D adventure, "Honey, I Shrunk The Audience." At the entrance to the land guests will find the striking new Astro Orbitor attraction where they can pilot their own "spaceships." A new attraction called "Rocket Rods," is the longest and fastest thrill ride in Disneyland history. "Innoventions," located in the former Carousel Theater, takes guests on a journey through new technologies and explores how these achievements will affect lives today and in the future.

Visitors should be prepared for lengthy lines at many rides with wait times frequently lasting an hour or more. It is best to take advantage of newer rides where the lines will be longest during the early morning and late evening hours or during parades and major shows.

Immediately west of Disneyland and connected to the park by the Monorail System is the Disneyland Resort Hotels complex made up of the Disneyland Hotel and the Disneyland Pacific Hotel. The resort complex features a twice-nightly Fantasy Waters Show, remote-control tugboats and dune buggies, video arcades, two hotels, restaurants, lounges and shops. For information phone (714) 778-6600.

Disneyland is open Mon.-Fri. 10-6, Sat.-Sun. 9 a.m.-midnight, with extended hours during summer and on some holidays.

The Unlimited Passport covers admission to the park plus all rides and attractions, except the arcades: One-day Passport $38; over 60, $36; ages 3-11, $28. Two-day Passport $68; ages 3-11, $51. Three-day Passport $95; ages 3-11, $75. Parking $7. AE, DS, MC, VI. Those holding A through E coupons from past visits may apply them toward the purchase of an Unlimited Passport.

Disneyland's parking lot can be entered from Harbor Boulevard or West Street. The Disneyland Resort is undergoing a major expansion and when completed in 2001 will include a second theme park, a third hotel and a retail, dining and entertainment district. Due to construction some routes into parking lots may periodically change. Visitors are advised to look for directional signs. Pets can be left in the kennel at the main gate for a fee. Phone (714) 781-4565. *See color ads starting on p. 43.*

HOBBY CITY AND ADVENTURE CITY, 1238 S. Beach Blvd., comprises hobby shops and a toy and doll museum housed in a half-scale model of the White House. The museum includes more than 4,000 dolls and toys, including foreign dolls, composition dolls, antique French and Ger-

STARRED ATTRACTIONS

El Pueblo de Los Angeles Historic Monument—See the site where the city of angels got its start at this 44-acre historic district in the heart of the metropolis. See Los Angeles p. 107.

Exploratorium—With more than 600 interactive exhibits, this science museum inside the Palace of Fine Arts teaches visitors about a wide variety of topics. See San Francisco p. 201.

Exposition Park—Three museums and the L.A. Memorial Coliseum occupy this city park along with a 7-acre rose garden. See Los Angeles p. 107.

Farmers Market—Shop among the more than 100 vendors or sip a cappuccino at a sidewalk cafe at this large outdoor market. See Los Angeles p. 117.

Forest Lawn Memorial-Park—Wander around the marble statuary of this 300-acre park or behold the impressive stained glass windows, paintings and gem and coin collections within the Forest Lawn Museum and other park buildings. See Glendale p. 121.

Getty Center—The centerpiece of this complex in the foothills of the Santa Monica Mountains is the J. Paul Getty Museum and its world-renowned art collection. See Los Angeles p. 108.

Golden Gate Park—This magnificent city park has it all: museums, gardens, recreation facilities, ponds, streams, lakes—even a buffalo enclosure and a Dutch-style windmill. See San Francisco p. 201.

Griffith Park—Boasting museums, a zoo and a planetarium/observatory complex, this huge municipal park also features hiking trails, a bird sanctuary and several family-oriented attractions. See Los Angeles p. 108.

Hearst Castle—Overlooking the Pacific Ocean, this palatial Mediterranean Revival-style mansion pays homage to the wealth and vision of its late owner, newspaper tycoon William Randolph Hearst. See San Simeon p. 216.

STARRED ATTRACTIONS

Hollywood Bowl—Occupying a natural amphitheater, the bowl plays host to concerts by the Los Angeles Philharmonic and the Hollywood Bowl Orchestra. See Hollywood p. 122.

Huntington Library, Art Collections and Botanical Gardens—Housing one of the world's great collections of rare books, this library also features galleries exhibiting an impressive art collection and is surrounded by a 150-acre botanical garden. See San Marino p. 129.

Knott's Berry Farm—A theme park that re-creates the Old West, this popular attraction is divided into six main areas: Ghost Town, Indian Trails, Fiesta Village, the Boardwalk, Wild Water Wilderness and Camp Snoopy. See Buena Park p. 61.

La Purísima Mission State Historic Park—With nearly a dozen 19th-century buildings, this is one of California's most extensively restored missions. See Lompoc p. 96.

Lassen Volcanic National Park—Four types of volcanoes as well as lava flows, boiling springs and lakes, fumaroles and mudpots are among the uncommon sights in this national park. See place listing p. 93.

Lava Beds National Monument—Exploring the national monument's rugged terrain will lead to lava tube caves and volcanic formations used as fortifications by the Modoc Indians. See place listing p. 95.

Lick Observatory—Dedicated in 1888, this facility on the summit of 4,209-foot Mount Hamilton now serves as an observation station overlooking the Santa Clara Valley. See San Jose p. 213.

Little Tokyo—Cultural pride is readily evident in the heart of Southern California's Japanese community; here you'll find the Japanese American Cultural and Community Center, a museum, shops and restaurants. See Los Angeles p. 110.

man dolls, teddy bears and antique toy soldiers. Adventure City, an outdoor theme park for children under 13, includes rides, face-painting, hands-on exhibits, a petting zoo and play areas.

Hobby City open daily 10-6. Adventure City open Mon.-Fri. 10-5 (also Fri. 5-8), Sat.-Sun. 11-8, (also Sat. 8-9 p.m.) mid-June through mid-Sept.; otherwise varies. Hobby City free. Adventure City $4.95, unlimited ride pass $10.95. Phone (714) 236-9300 for Adventure City or (714) 527-2323 for Hobby City.

ANDERSON (C-3) pop. 8,300, elev. 430'

The railroad arrived in the area near Anderson in 1872. The town was named for Elias Anderson, the owner of the largest land grant in the area at that time. Today part of that grant is Anderson River Park which offers free summer concerts.

Anderson Chamber of Commerce: P.O. Box 1144, Anderson, CA 96007; phone (530) 365-8095.

COLEMAN NATIONAL FISH HATCHERY is 11 mi. s.e. via Balls Ferry Rd. to Ashcreek and Gover rds., then onto Coleman Fish Hatchery Rd. The hatchery raises fingerlings in the rearing ponds year-round. Salmon and steelhead migrate up the ladders to the hatchery early October to early February. Picnicking is permitted. Self-guiding tours are available. Daily 8-4. Free. Phone (530) 365-8622.

ANGELES NATIONAL FOREST

Forest elevations range from 1,234 ft. in the San Gabriel Canyons to 10,064 ft. at the top of Mount San Antonio (Old Baldy). Refer to AAA maps for additional elevation information.

John Muir described the San Gabriel Mountains as "one vast bee pasture, a rolling wilderness of honey-bloom." Covering more than 690,000 acres of these rugged mountains on the northern rim of the Los Angeles Basin, Angeles National Forest encompasses terrain ranging from arid desert to heavily timbered high mountain ridges and meadows.

Year-round recreation is available in the generally warm and dry climate. The forest, which includes the San Gabriel Wilderness and Sheep Mountain Wilderness, has more than 80 campgrounds as well as picnic areas and hiking trails for all levels of experience. During the summer three major areas—Chilao, Big Pines and Crystal Lake—offer films, nature walks and other interpretive programs. Visitor centers are available at all three areas.

A particularly scenic route is the 64-mile Angeles Crest Highway (SR 2), which runs from La Cañada Flintridge to Wrightwood. It continues along Hwy. 138 to connect with Rim of the World Drive *(see San Bernardino p. 171)*.

Six major areas offer skiing and other snow sports in winter. Although forest highways are generally open all year, heavy snows sometimes close the roads. Check with forest headquarters for information about weather conditions and wildland fire danger. For more information contact the Supervisor's Office, Angeles National Forest, 701 N. Santa Anita Ave., Arcadia, CA 91006; phone (626) 574-5200. *See Recreation Chart and the AAA California/Nevada CampBook.*

ANGELS CAMP (F-3) pop. 2,400, elev. 1,379′

Named after shopkeeper Henry Angel who started a trading post at this site in 1848, Angels Camp was a popular spot for gold miners. Early diggers uncovered riches, and within one year approximately 4,000 miners populated the town to try their luck. Angels Camp sits atop numerous tunnels, which proved to be successful mines.

Angels Camp inspired Mark Twain to write his famous short story "The Celebrated Jumping Frog of Calaveras County"—his first published success.

Calaveras County Visitor Center: 1211 S. Main St., P.O. Box 637, Angels Camp, CA 95222; phone (209) 736-0049 or (800) 225-3764.

Self-guiding tours: A packet that includes a walking-tour map and information about the historic district is available for 25c from the visitor center.

ANGELS CAMP MUSEUM, 753 S. Main St., features early mining equipment, wagons, a blacksmith shop, minerals and artifacts from the Gold Rush era and a carriage house with horse-drawn vehicles from the gold-rush days. Allow 1 hour minimum. Daily 10-3, Mar.-Nov.; Sat.-Sun. 10-3, Jan.-Feb. Closed holidays. Admission $2; ages 6-12, 50c. Phone (209) 736-2963.

 RECREATIONAL ACTIVITIES
White-water Rafting
• SAVE **O.A.R.S. River Trips,** 1.7 mi. s. on SR 49, P.O. Box 67, Angels Camp, CA 95222. Daily Apr.-Oct. Phone (209) 736-4677 or (800) 346-6277.

APPLE VALLEY (A-8) pop. 46,100

Once home to Hollywood's cowboy king and queen Roy Rogers and Dale Evans, Apple Valley provides opportunities for fishing, horseback riding and rodeo competition.

STARRED ATTRACTIONS

Los Angeles County Museum of Art—It takes five buildings to hold the museum's extensive collections of paintings, sculptures, costumes, textiles, decorative art, photography, prints and drawings from around the world. See Los Angeles p. 110.

Los Angeles Zoo—More than 1,200 animals from around the world live in this Griffith Park landmark. See Los Angeles p. 109.

Mann's Chinese Theatre—By accidentally stepping in wet cement, silent screen star Norma Talmadge started the tradition of immortalizing celebrity hand- and footprints in the theater's forecourt. See Hollywood p. 122.

The Marine World Theme Park—Denizens of the deep are not the only attractions at this wildlife park; elephants, Bengal tigers, exotic birds, shows and interactive exhibits also are part of the entertainment. See Vallejo p. 234.

Maritime Museum of San Diego—Nautical exhibits featured aboard three historic ships—a windjammer, a ferry and a yacht—are the stars of this museum. See San Diego p. 181.

Marshall Gold Discovery State Historic Park—This is where the great California gold rush of 1849 began; James Marshall discovered the precious metal here near Capt. John Sutter's mill, and the rest is history. See Coloma p. 67.

Mission Basilica San Diego de Alcalà—The white stucco 1769 basilica, California's first mission, has massive walls and is fully restored. Noteworthy features are religious artifacts and gardens. See San Diego p. 181.

Mission San Carlos Borromeo del Rio Carmelo—Called Carmel Mission, this church was founded in 1770. Relics of the mission's early days as well as books and documents are displayed. A moorish bell tower and courtyard gardens are of interest. See Carmel p. 141.

STARRED ATTRACTIONS

Mission San Fernando Rey de España— Restored structures include the church, monastery, majordomo's house, workrooms and living quarters. A 35-bell carillon rings hourly 9-5. See Mission Hills p. 126.

Mission San Francisco de Asis— One of the oldest buildings in San Francisco, the mission's redwood roof timbers still are lashed together with rawhide. A small museum displays relics and old manuscripts. See San Francisco p. 202.

Mission San Jose Chapel and Museum— An unusually elegant interior features crystal chandeliers, murals, religious paintings and an ornate altar. A museum displays photographs, paintings and artifacts. See Fremont p. 77.

Mission San Juan Bautista— Still an active Roman Catholic Church, the 1797 mission features a three-aisle entrance to the altar. Displays include relics and period furnishings. See San Juan Bautista p. 214.

Mission San Juan Capistrano— Known for the swallows that arrive in mid-March and leave in mid-October, the mission also contains a museum devoted to the American Indian, Spanish and Mexican periods of its history. See San Juan Capistrano p. 214.

Mission San Luis Obispo de Tolosa— In order to repel flaming arrow attacks by unfriendly natives, the mission was built with a tile roof rather than the usual ignitable thatch roof. A museum contains Chumash Indian artifacts and memorabilia from early settlers. See San Luis Obispo p. 215.

Mission San Miguel Arcangel— Many original decorations, frescoes and paintings adorn the 1797 mission. The vaulted corridor is known for its arches. See San Miguel p. 215.

Mission Santa Barbara— One of the best preserved of the missions, its original living quarters are now museum rooms that feature period artifacts. The church also contains 18th- and 19th-century Mexican art. See Santa Barbara p. 217.

Apple Valley Chamber of Commerce: 17874 Hwy. 18, P.O. Box 1073, Apple Valley, CA 92307; phone (760) 242-2753.

VICTOR VALLEY MUSEUM AND ART GALLERY, 1 blk. s. of Bear Valley Rd. at 11873 Apple Valley Rd., features exhibits about the nature and history of the Victor Valley and Mojave Desert regions. Displays include American Indian woven baskets and other artifacts as well as displays of barbed wire and early 20th-century household appliances and furniture. The museum also features a hands-on area for children. Wed.-Sat. 10-4, Sun. noon-4; closed Jan. 1, Easter, Thanksgiving and Dec. 25. Admission $3, over 55 and students with ID $2, under 12 free with an adult. Phone (760) 240-2111.

ARCADIA—
see Los Angeles p. 118.

ARCATA (B-1) pop. 15,200, elev. 33′

Founded in 1858 as a mining supply center, Arcata also was where author Bret Harte once worked as a journalist and miner; he used Arcata as the setting for some of his stories of mining camp life. Humboldt State University is in Arcata.

Southwest on Humboldt Bay is the 175-acre Arcata Marsh and Wildlife Sanctuary, a recently transformed industrial area and county landfill that now is host to more than 200 species of birds. About 4.5 miles of foot trails wind past seven wetland habitats.

Arcata Chamber of Commerce: 1062 G St., Arcata, CA 95521-5816; phone (707) 822-3619.

Self-guiding tours: Maps detailing a walking tour of Greek Revival structures and Victorian houses, as well as maps of the city-owned Redwood Park within Arcata Community Forest can be obtained at the chamber of commerce.

AZALEA STATE RESERVE is 5 mi. n. off US 101 McKinleyville exit, then 2 mi. e. on North Blank Rd. The reserve is loveliest when the flowers bloom from May through June. Parking is limited; the reserve is not recommended for trailers. Allow 30 minutes minimum. Daily dawn-dusk. Free. Phone (707) 488-2041.

HUMBOLDT STATE UNIVERSITY NATURAL HISTORY MUSEUM, 1315 G St., exhibits almost 2,000 animal and plant specimens from around the world. Fossil displays date from 500 million years ago. Highlights include a 60-gallon tidepool tank, live local salamanders, toads, turtles, snakes and freshwater fish, a fossil of a dire wolf jaw, the intricate skeleton of a 50 million-year-old fish, a saber-toothed cat skeleton, butterflies and Pacific seashells. Exhibits change periodically. Tues.-Sat. 10-4; closed Jan. 1, Thanksgiving and Dec. 25. Donations. Phone (707) 826-4479.

ARNOLD (E-4) pop. 2,400, elev. 4,000'

The logging industry sustained Arnold until Blagen Mill closed in 1962. The city provides a full slate of winter recreation, from snowmobiling to skiing, as well as summer activities in area parks, lakes and rivers.

CALAVERAS BIG TREES STATE PARK, 6,073 acres 4 mi. e. on SR 4, contains some of the finest specimens of Sierra redwoods. Horseback tours are offered May through October. Interpretive programs are available in summer; snowshoeing and cross-country skiing are available in winter. Daily 24 hours. Day use fee $5 per private vehicle; over 62, $4. Phone (209) 795-2334. *See Recreation Chart and the AAA California/ Nevada CampBook.*

ARROYO GRANDE (I-3)
pop. 14,400, elev. 114'

Although Spanish explorers discovered the creek flowing from the Santa Lucia Mountain Range to the ocean, Arroyo Grande was not founded until 1862; it was another 5 years before the first two structures—a smithy and a schoolhouse—were built.

To bridge the gap between the town's two sections, which grew on opposite banks of the river, a rope bridge was constructed during the 1880s. A local landmark, the Swinging Bridge still is used by pedestrians. Arroyo Grande Village, .2 miles east of US 101 along E. Branch Street, reflects an 1890s atmosphere.

Arroyo Grande Chamber of Commerce: 800A W. Branch St., Arroyo Grande, CA 93420-1999; phone (805) 489-1488.

Self-guiding tours: A walking-tour brochure outlining historic structures is available from the chamber.

ATASCADERO (I-4)
pop. 23,100, elev. 834'

Atascadero City Administration Building, Palma Avenue at West Mall, was built in the Italian Renaissance style. Completed in 1918, it houses the city hall and Atascadero Historical Society Museum, which has photographs and household items pertaining to Atascadero's early days. About 2 miles west off SR 41, Atascadero Lake Park offers fishing, picnicking and Charles Paddock Zoo.

Atascadero Chamber of Commerce: 6550 El Camino Real, Atascadero, CA 93422; phone (805) 466-2044.

ATWATER (F-3) pop. 22,300, elev. 151'

The 1991 announcement that Castle Air Force Base would close—as well as its closure four years later—thrust Atwater into a temporary eco-

STARRED ATTRACTIONS

Mission Santa Clara de Asis—Relics displayed include three bells given to the mission by the king of Spain. Gardens and artifacts also are noteworthy. See Santa Clara p. 218.

Monterey Bay Aquarium—More than 500 species of marine life are exhibited. Touch pools, life-size models, a shorebird aviary, a theater and historical displays also are featured. See Monterey p. 144.

Monterey State Historic Park—A 7-acre site preserves the historical and architectural heritage of old Monterey. Guided walking tours are available. See Monterey p. 144.

Movieland Wax Museum—Figures of more than 300 movie and television stars are displayed in realistic settings. Sets from major film and television productions also are shown. See Buena Park p. 61.

Muir Woods National Monument—Named for noted conservationist John Muir, Muir Woods is one of the most beautiful and accessible of the noted redwood groves. Some coast redwoods reach a height of 250 feet with diameters of more than 12 feet. Trails for hiking and exploring are available. See place listing p. 209.

The Music Center—Tour some of Los Angeles' landmark theaters including the Dorothy Chandler Pavilion, which hosts the Oscar ceremony each year. See Los Angeles p. 111.

Natural History Museum of Los Angeles County—Follow the evolution of such diverse creatures as beetles, sharks and dinosaurs. See Los Angeles p. 108.

Norton Simon Museum—More than 2,000 years of Western and Asian art are represented at this museum known for its Renaissance, baroque and rococo masterpieces. See Pasadena p. 127.

Oakland Museum of California—The state's natural and cultural history can be traced through artwork and exhibits. See Oakland p. 151.

STARRED ATTRACTIONS

Old Mission Santa Ines—Built in 1804, this mission displays artifacts dating back more than 100 years, reflecting the artistry and traditions of 19th-century life. See Solvang p. 227.

Olvera Street—Mexican-American vendors sell traditional wares and preserve their heritage in this colorful marketplace. See Los Angeles p. 107.

Palm Springs Aerial Tramway—Travel above terrain ranging from desert palms to an alpine forest. See Palm Springs p. 156.

Palomar Observatory—Learn about asteroids, comets and stars that span the Milky Way. See Palomar Mountain p. 157.

Paramount's Great America—Five themed areas offer thrilling rides, dazzling shows and magical children's attractions. See Santa Clara p. 218.

Pinnacles National Monument—Jagged crags and stark spires that serve as remnants of an ancient volcano rise above a countryside rich with flora and fauna. See place listing p. 159.

Point Lobos State Reserve—Rocky bluffs along the sea are home to rare plants, archeological sites and unusual geological formations. See Carmel p. 141.

Queen Mary—Come aboard one of the world's largest luxury liners and explore its rich history. See Long Beach p. 124.

Rancho Santa Ana Botanic Garden—Plantings native to California's deserts, coastal dunes and channel islands are spread along the outwash plain of the San Gabriel Mountains. See Claremont p. 120.

Rim of the World Drive—This 107-mile scenic byway stretches across the San Bernardino Mountains. See San Bernardino p. 171.

nomic crisis that waned as local markets flourished and interest rates remained steady.

Atwater Chamber of Commerce: 1181 Third St., CA 95301; phone (209) 358-4251.

CASTLE AIR MUSEUM, .5 mi. e. of SR 99 on Buhach Rd., then n. on Santa Fe Dr., is housed in a remodeled barracks. The museum is named for Brig. Gen. Frederick W. Castle, who earned a posthumous Medal of Honor for his role in a bombing mission over Europe in World War II. Historical photographs, weapons, uniforms and 44 vintage aircraft, including the SR-71 Blackbird, depict the development of the U.S. Air Force. Guided tours and food are available.

Allow 1 hour minimum. Daily 9-5, Memorial Day-Sept. 30; Sun. 10-4, rest of year. Closed Jan. 1, Easter, Thanksgiving and Dec. 25. Admission $5; over 59, $3; ages 12-18, $2. Phone (209) 723-2178.

AUBURN (E-3) pop. 10,600, elev. 1,255'

Historic Old Auburn, the central section of the city, has many restored mid-1800s buildings, including a firehouse and the oldest continuously used post office in California.

Auburn Visitor Center: 13464 Lincoln Way, Auburn, CA 95603; phone (530) 887-2111 or (800) 427-6463 in Calif.

GOLD COUNTRY MUSEUM, 1273 High St. on the fairgrounds, depicts the early days of Placer County through old mining equipment and exhibits pertaining to early transportation and mining methods. Also featured are a stamp mill and period saloon. Visitors may try gold-panning at a small stream. Bernhard Museum has a restored Victorian house and outbuildings with coopering, blacksmithing and winemaking displays. Guided tours are available.

Allow 1 hour. Gold Country Museum open Tues.-Fri. 10-3:30, Sat.-Sun. 11-4. Bernhard Museum open Tues.-Fri. 10:30-3, Sat.-Sun. noon-4. Both closed holidays. Both museums $1; over 65 and ages 6-16, 50c. Phone (530) 889-6500.

PLACER COUNTY MUSEUM & COURTHOUSE, 101 Maple St., features an American Indian habitat complete with a light and sound show and a ten-minute videotape presentation about the history of the transcontinental highway that runs through the county. Also inside the 1898-courthouse is a restored sheriff's office circa 1915 and the Pate Native American Collection, which contains more than 400 American Indian artifacts from around the country. Allow 1 hour minimum. Tues.-Sun. 10-4. Free. Phone (530) 889-6500.

AVALON—
see Catalina Island p. 63.

BAKERSFIELD (I-5)
pop. 175,000, elev. 408′

Bakersfield, near the southern end of the San Joaquin Valley, is an important shipping and marketing center for oil, natural gas and farm products. It also is known as California's country music capital. Mesa Marin Raceway is host to NASCAR stock car races in March and mid-October.

Greater Bakersfield Chamber of Commerce: 1725 Eye St., P.O. Box 1947, Bakersfield, CA 93301; phone (805) 327-4421.

Shopping areas: The Valley Plaza Shopping Center, SR 99 at Ming Avenue, has a Gottschalks, JCPenney, Macy's, Robinsons-May and Sears. East Hills Mall, at Mall View Road and Oswell Street off SR 178, offers Gottschalks, Harris' and Mervyn's.

SAVE **CALIFORNIA LIVING MUSEUM,** 3.5 mi. n.w. off SR 178 at 14000 Alfred Harrell Hwy., contains a cross-section of California wildlife and native plants, some of which are rare or endangered. Included are the mountain lion, desert tortoise, kit fox and bald eagle. Exhibits include a reptile building and indoor fossil and geologic displays. Picnic facilities are available. Tues.-Sun. 9-5; closed Thanksgiving and Dec. 25. Admission $3.50; over 60, $2.50; students with ID and ages 3-12, $2. Phone (805) 872-2256.

SAVE **KERN COUNTY MUSEUM,** 3801 Chester Ave., contains exhibits that represent the human and natural history of the area. The 16-acre, 56-building museum depicts life in the late 19th and early 20th centuries. Lori Brock Children's Discovery Center features hands-on exhibits. Mon.-Fri. 8-5, Sat. and some holidays 10-5, Sun. noon-5. Last admission is 2 hours before closing. Closed Jan. 1, Thanksgiving and Dec. 24-25. Admission $5; over 60, $4; ages 3-12, $3. Phone (805) 861-2132.

BARSTOW (I-7) pop. 21,500, elev. 2,106′

A thriving mining center in the late 19th century, Barstow is at the junction of three major highways—I-15, I-40 and SR 58—that provide access to the Mojave Desert. Several local military installations anchor the city's economy.

Barstow Area Chamber of Commerce: 222 E. Main St., Suite 216, Mercado Mall, P.O. Box 698, Barstow, CA 92311; phone (760) 256-8617.

Shopping areas: Approximately 95 outlet stores draw bargain hunters to Factory Merchants Outlet Plaza, 4 miles south near the SR 15 Lenwood Road exit, and Tanger Outlet Center, across the street.

STARRED ATTRACTIONS

Rosicrucian Egyptian Museum and Planetarium—In the beautiful gardens of Rosicrucian Park, this museum showcases one of the country's largest collections of Egyptian, Babylonian and Assyrian antiquities. See San Jose p. 213.

San Buenaventura Mission—Since its completion in 1809, the present church has withstood earthquakes, a tidal wave, pirates, secularization and modernization. See Ventura p. 235.

San Diego Wild Animal Park—They are not just monkeying around at this breeding facility for rare and endangered species—just ask the shoebill stork. See Escondido p. 73.

San Diego Zoo—Party the night away with 4,238 specimens from 816 species and subspecies during a summer Safari Sleep-over. See San Diego p. 177.

San Juan Bautista State Historic Park—In the early 1800s, the town which sprang up around the mission was the largest in central California. See place listing p. 214.

Santa Barbara Museum of Art—You can bet your Monet the works in this former post office will create a good Impression. See Santa Barbara p. 217.

Santa Barbara Zoological Gardens—In 1963 this zoo opened with a llama, two sheep, a goat, a turkey and a pair of spider monkeys; today its 40 acres is home to more than 600 animals. See Santa Barbara p. 218.

Scotty's Castle—Walter E. Scott had been a prospector, a mule team driver and a member of Buffalo Bill's Wild West Show before he began this nine-building, Moorish-Mexican-Spanish-style home for Chicago businessman Albert Johnson. See Death Valley National Park p. 71.

SeaWorld—See the dwellers of the deep and the Antarctic antics of flightless birds. See San Diego p. 179.

Continued on p. 57.

CALICO EARLY MAN ARCHAEOLOGICAL SITE, 15 mi. n.e. via I-15 and Minneola Rd., is an excavation begun by Dr. Louis Leakey in 1964. More than 12,000 stone tools dating back possibly 200,000 years have been unearthed, making this one of the oldest prehistoric tool sites yet discovered in the Western Hemisphere. Examples of early tools can be seen in the walls and floors of the excavated pits, in the visitor center and in the county museum. Guided tours are available. Thurs.-Sun. 9-4:30, Wed. noon-4:30; closed holidays. Donations. Phone (760) 256-5102.

SAVE **CALICO GHOST TOWN REGIONAL PARK** is 11 mi. n.e. via I-15. Named for the varicolored surrounding mountains, Calico was a booming silver-mining town 1881-96. Its mines produced more than $13 million in ore. In 1895 the price of silver dropped, the mines quit producing and the town fell into ruin. Attractions include a mine tour, mystery shack, shooting gallery and train ride. Gunfights and historic tours are offered. Camping is permitted. Food is available.

Daily 9-5; closed Dec. 25. Town admission $6; ages 6-15, $3. Train ride and mystery shack each $2; ages 6-15, $1. Mine tour $1. Shooting gallery $1 per round of ammunition. Phone (760) 254-2122 or (800) 862-2542. *See ad.*

RAINBOW BASIN NATIONAL NATURAL LAND-MARK is 8 mi. n. via SR 58 to Irwin Rd., then n. to Fossil Bed Rd. (last 3 mi. unpaved). The sediment of the desert basin was formed by millions of years of the shifting and upheaval of the Earth's crust. The rock walls, in shades of red, brown, green and white, hold fossils and an abundance of minerals.

The 4-mile loop from Fossil Bed Road offers good views of the colorful rock formations. Only vehicles less than 25 feet in length are permitted on the loop; motorhomes, buses and towed vehicles are prohibited. Hiking and camping are permitted at Owl Canyon Campground; a fee is required for camping. Phone (760) 252-6060.

BASS LAKE (G-5)

BASS LAKE YOSEMITE TOURS & TRANSPORTATION picks up passengers at area hotels for narrated tours of Yosemite National Park. Visitors can see Yosemite Valley, the Mariposa Grove of giant sequoias and Glacier Point. Daily 8-5. Fare $38; senior citizens $33; under 12, $16. Reservations are required. Phone (209) 658-8687.

BENICIA (O-3) pop. 24,400, elev. 33'

Named after the wife of Mariano Guadalupe Vallejo, one of its founders, Benicia boasts California's oldest standing capitol building. The city supported an Army arsenal and barracks as well as the Pacific Mail Steamship Co. before becoming the state's third capital in 1853. Several well-preserved houses date back to those early years of statehood.

Benicia also boasts the oldest Masonic temple in the state and Saint Paul's Episcopal Church, the first Episcopal cathedral in northern California. Scandinavian shipwrights who worked on the church created a ceiling that resembles an inverted ship's hull, a design similar to those of Norwegian stave churches. Other historic structures include the four sandstone buildings of Benicia Camel Barn Museum built 1853-57. The museum contains exhibits recounting the histories of Benicia and the U.S. Army Arsenal.

Benicia Chamber of Commerce: 601 First St., Benicia, CA 94510; phone (707) 745-2120 or (800) 559-7377.

Self-guiding tours: The chamber distributes a visitors guide that includes information about driving and walking tours of historic Benicia.

BENICIA CAPITOL STATE HISTORIC PARK, First and West G sts., preserves the Greek Revival building that served as the third state capitol Feb. 4, 1853-Feb. 25, 1854. The structure is restored and furnished in period. Fischer-Hanlon House, next to the park, is a renovated gold rush hotel furnished in period. Allow 30 minutes minimum. Park open daily 10-5; closed Jan. 1,

Thanksgiving and Dec. 25. Fischer-Hanlon House open most Sats. noon-4. Admission, includes Fischer-Hanlon House, $2; ages 6-12, $1. Phone (707) 745-3385.

BERKELEY (O-2)
pop. 102,700, elev. 152'

Lively, inquiring and experimental, Berkeley exudes an atmosphere befitting its position as one of the country's leading educational centers. The University of California is often the vanguard of any campus movement, be it political, artistic or philosophical.

At the foot of University Avenue lies the center for one of the city's favorite activities—sport fishing. Berkeley Marina, base for a large charter boat fleet, also has a free fishing pier; phone (510) 644-6376. No license is required. Water sports and model yacht racing are popular on the milelong saltwater lake in Aquatic Park at the foot of Bancroft Avenue. Golden Gate Fields in nearby Albany offers seasonal horse racing; phone (510) 559-7300.

Note: Policies concerning admittance of children to pari-mutuel betting facilities vary. Phone for information.

Phone (510) 549-8710 for 24-hour recorded information about attractions, events, the arts and city facilities.

Berkeley Convention & Visitors Bureau: 2015 Center St., Berkeley, CA 94704; phone (510) 549-7040 or (800) 847-4823.

Self-guiding tour: A brochure of a walking tour that outlines the architectural flavor downtown is available from the bureau.

BERKELEY MUNICIPAL ROSE GARDEN, Euclid Ave. at Bayview Pl., contains more than 4,000 varieties of roses and is best viewed in late spring and early summer. A terraced amphitheater and arbor overlook the bay and Golden Gate Bridge. Daily dawn-dusk. The garden may be closed during special occasions; phone ahead. Free. Phone (510) 644-6530.

CHARLES LEE TILDEN REGIONAL PARK, adjoining the city on the n.e. edge, features a botanic garden, golf course, picnic grounds, camping facilities, nature area and hiking, biking and horse trails. Environmental Education Center near Jewel Lake has a miniature farm with livestock, farm implements and an exhibit hall. Swimming and fishing in Lake Anza, a merry-go-round, and pony and miniature train rides also are available. Hours and prices vary with the season; phone (510) 848-3385.

Park open daily 8 a.m.-10 p.m. Environmental center open Tues.-Sun. 10-5; closed Jan. 1, Thanksgiving and Dec. 25. Park admission free. Swimming fee $2.50; under 16 and over 61, $1.50. Pony rides $2.50. Train rides $1.50. Merry-go-round $1. Phone (510) 562-7275 or

STARRED ATTRACTIONS

Sequoia and Kings Canyon National Parks—For variety you can't beat this second-oldest national park: rivers, waterfalls, meadows, caves, played-out gold mines, trees 200 feet high and marmots that eat radiator hoses. See place listing p. 222.

Shasta State Historic Park—In 1849, Shasta—the "Queen City"—was the supply point for the gold mines in the northern Klamath Range. See Redding p. 163.

Six Flags Magic Mountain—Thrill rides, a man-made, white-water river, animal shows, action shows, a petting zoo—there is something here to amuse almost everyone. See Valencia p. 131.

Solvang—This Danish town has everything you would expect, except the Northern Lights. See place listing p. 227.

Sonoma State Historic Park—Sonoma, completed in 1823, is the last of California's 21 missions; the surrounding buildings were constructed 1823-55. See Sonoma p. 227.

State Capitol—The 40 acres of gardens surrounding the restored 1869 capitol include the Vietnam Veterans' Memorial. See Sacramento p. 169.

Sutter's Fort State Historic Park—The site, once part of a 48,000-acre ranch named New Helvetia (New Switzerland), has been restored to the way it was 2 years before gold was discovered here in 1849. See Sacramento p. 169.

Universal Studios Hollywood—Go behind the scenes to see how TV shows and movies are made and when you're done you can experience one of the many movie-themed rides. See Universal City p. 131.

University of California—This college campus encompasses more than a thousand scenic acres that include archives, art and science museums, a botanical garden and a 307-foot-tall bell tower. See Berkeley p. 58.

STARRED ATTRACTIONS

University of California, Los Angeles (UCLA)—Set in the foothills of the Santa Monica Mountains, this university features a cultural history museum, a botanical garden and a sculpture garden. See Los Angeles p. 112.

Will Rogers State Historic Park—The former home of cowboy humorist Will Rogers is open to visitors along with several hiking trails and picnic facilities. See Pacific Palisades p. 126.

Winchester Mystery House—Told by a psychic she was being tormented by vengeful spirits, rifle heiress Sarah Winchester fled her home in Connecticut and built this elaborate and unusual West Coast mansion in which to hide. See San Jose p. 213.

Yosemite National Park—One of the jewels of the national park system, Yosemite includes the spectacular valley for which it was named along with more than 1,100 square miles of nearly pristine land in the Sierra Nevada. See place listing p. 238.

AREA CODE CHANGE FOR BAKERSFIELD AREA

In February 1999 an area code split will occur in Kern County and the northern portion of Los Angeles County. The western portion of the area will retain the 805 area code. The new 661 area code will be assumed by the eastern portion of the area. The affected area includes the following communities: Bakersfield, California Hot Springs, Cuyama, Earlimart, Tehachapi, Taft, Mojave, Frazier Park, Gorman, Lancaster, Palmdale, Newhall and McKittrick.

Permissive dialing begins Feb. 13, 1999. Mandatory use of the 661 area code begins Aug. 14, 1999.

635-0135 for park, 525-2233 for environmental center, 548-6100 for train, 527-0421 for pony rides, or 524-6773 for merry-go-round.

GRIZZLY PEAK BOULEVARD, which can be reached from the head of Spruce Street or from other points along the city's northeastern edge, winds along the crest of the hills behind the city at elevations up to 1,600 feet. The scenic drive provides access to attractions within Charles Lee Tilden Regional Park as well as a view of San Francisco Bay.

JUDAH L. MAGNES MUSEUM (Jewish Museum of the West), 2911 Russell St., displays ceremonial art and changing exhibits of Jewish art and history, a Judaica library and Western history archives. Tours are offered Sunday and Wednesday. Allow 1 hour minimum. Sun.-Thurs. 10-4; closed Jewish and federal holidays. Donations. Phone (510) 549-6950.

PACIFIC SCHOOL OF RELIGION, LeConte and Scenic aves., is an interdenominational seminary. A museum displays Palestinian artifacts dating from 3200 B.C. Allow 30 minutes minimum. Mon.-Fri. 9-4; closed major holidays. Free. Phone (510) 848-0528.

TAKARA SAKE USA INC., 708 Addison St., presents on request a slide show pertaining to the production of Japanese rice and plum wines. A tasting room also is available. Mon.-Fri. 1-5, Sat.-Sun. noon-6; closed Jan. 1, Easter, July 4, Thanksgiving and Dec. 25. Free. Phone (510) 540-8250.

★**UNIVERSITY OF CALIFORNIA** occupies a beautiful 1,232-acre campus e. of Oxford St., between Hearst St. and Bancroft Way. Guided 90-minute campus walking tours depart from the visitor center in the lobby of University Hall at Oxford Street and University Avenue Mon.-Fri. at 10, and from the clock tower Sat. at 10 and Sun. at 1. Phone (510) 642-5215.

Botanical Garden, 34 acres in Strawberry Canyon off Centennial Dr., contains 12,000 species of plants arranged according to their native regions. The complex includes a Chinese herb garden and a large collection of cactuses and other succulents. Greenhouse exhibits and a visitor center also are available. Allow 1 hour minimum. Daily 9-7, Memorial Day-Labor Day; 9-4:45, rest of year. Tours Thurs. and Sat.-Sun. at 1:30. Closed Dec. 25. Admission $3; over 65, $2; ages 3-18, $1; free to all Thurs. Phone (510) 642-3343.

Campanile, at the center of the campus, is 307 feet tall and contains a 61-bell carillon which chimes on the hour and plays music at 7:50, noon and 6. An elevator to the viewing platform operates Mon.-Fri. 10-4, Sat. 10-5, Sun. 10-1:30 and 3-5; closed university holidays. Recitals lasting 45 minutes are performed Sat. at noon and 6, Sun. at 2 and 2:45. Admission $1. Phone (510) 642-3666.

Ernest Orlando Lawrence Berkeley National Laboratory, above campus on Cyclotron Rd., is a Department of Energy laboratory that performs scientific research and operates national scientific user facilities in the energy, life and physical sciences. Tours are offered Mon.-Fri. Reservations are required 2 weeks in advance. Comfortable clothing and walking shoes are recommended. Phone (510) 486-4387.

Lawrence Hall of Science, Centennial Dr. on the e. side of the campus, is a public science center with hands-on exhibits involving computers, telescopes, laboratory equipment and animals. Allow 2 hours minimum. Science hall open daily 10-5; closed Thanksgiving and Dec. 25. Holt Planetarium presents shows daily at 1, 2:15 and 3:30, June-Aug.; Sat.-Sun. and holidays at 1, 2:15 and 3:30, rest of year. Admission $6; over 61 and ages 7-18, $4; ages 3-6, $2. Planetarium shows an additional $2. Phone (510) 642-5132.

Pacific Film Archive, at the University Art Museum, 2625 Durant Ave., houses a large collection of films and videotapes from around the world. Showings are held nightly. Admission $6; over 65 and under 12, $3.50; second feature $1.50 extra. Phone (510) 642-1412.

Phoebe Apperson Hearst Museum of Anthropology, in Kroeber Hall on Bancroft Way, has exhibits about ethnology, archeology and anthropology. Wed.-Sun. 10-4:30 (also Thurs. 4:30-9, Sept.-May); closed major holidays. Admission $2; over 59, $1; under 16, 50c; free to all Thurs. Phone (510) 643-7648.

UC Berkeley Art Museum, 2626 Bancroft Way between College Ave. and Bowditch St., features contemporary and Asian art as well as 18th- and 19th-century works and touring exhibits. Allow 1 hour, 30 minutes minimum. Wed.-Sun. 11-5 (also Thurs. 5-9). Admission $6; over 64 and ages 12-17, $4; under 12 free; free to all Thurs. 11-noon and 5-9. Phone (510) 642-0808.

BEVERLY HILLS—
see Los Angeles p. 118.

BIG BASIN (G-2) pop. 100, elev. 1,000′

★**BIG BASIN REDWOODS STATE PARK** is on SR 236; the headquarters is 9 mi. n.w. of Boulder Creek. Covering more than 18,000 acres surrounding Big Basin, the park was established in 1902 as California's first state park. Some trees have attained a diameter of 18 feet and a height of 330 feet. A natural history museum is on the grounds. Camping supplies and naturalist services are available June through October.

Allow 2 hours minimum. Park and museum open daily 8-dusk. Day use fee $6 per private vehicle; over 61, $5 per private vehicle. Phone (831) 338-8860. *See Recreation Chart.*

BIG BEAR LAKE (A-9)
pop. 5,400, elev. 6,754′

One of California's largest year-round recreation areas, Big Bear Lake and Valley lie about 30 miles northeast of San Bernardino in the eastern San Bernardino Mountains. Camping, picnicking and horseback riding are popular in summer; with seven resorts in the area, skiing and sledding are popular winter pastimes. Hunting and fishing are permitted in season. Swimming is permitted only in designated areas, including Meadow Park Swim Beach. Boat rentals and scenic boat tours are available.

Big Bear Chamber of Commerce: 630 Bartlett Rd., P.O. Box 2860, Big Bear Lake, CA 92315; phone (909) 866-4608.

Self-guiding tours: The Gold Fever Trail Guide, a 3-hour auto tour map, covers several sites of the 1860-75 gold rush that occurred in Holcomb Valley just north of the lake. The free guide is available at Big Bear Ranger Station, 3 miles east of Fawnskin on SR 38; phone (909) 866-3437.

⟨SAVE⟩ **BIG BEAR JEEP TOURS,** off SR 18 on Village Dr., offers narrated 2- to 4-hour tours to off-road areas of Big Bear Valley and the surrounding mountains. Information is provided about area history, flora, fauna and geology; colorful tales of the gold and silver mining days are recounted. Daily 9-5, May-Oct. Fare $37.95-$89.95. AE, DS, MC, VI. Phone (909) 878-5337.

BIG BEAR LAKE SCENIC BOAT TOUR, Pine Knot Landing at the foot of Pine Knot Ave., takes up to 40 passengers in a tri-hull excursion boat on an 80-minute narrated tour of Big Bear Lake, with views of China Island, the solar observatory and San Gorgonio Mountain. Tours depart daily every 2 hours 10-6, Apr.-Nov. (weather permitting); otherwise varies. Fare $8.50; over 52, $6.50; ages 4-12, $5. The 10 a.m. tour is half-price. Phone (909) 866-2628.

BIG PINE (G-6) pop. 1,500, elev. 3,985′

ANCIENT BRISTLECONE PINE FOREST, 28,000 acres in Inyo National Forest *(see place listing p. 82),* preserves these gnarled trees, some more than 4,000 years old—a millennium older than the oldest redwoods. Two self-guiding trails are available. Naturalist services sometimes are available at Schulman Visitor Center in the White Mountain District, open daily mid-June through Labor Day.

The bristlecone area is reached from Big Pine by the Westgard Pass road (SR 168) and White Mountain Road to Schulman Grove (elev. 10,000 ft.). Dress warmly, bring adequate water and have a full tank of gas; there are no telephones, gas or water in the area. Daily early June-late Oct. (weather permitting). Admission $2 ($5 maximum per private vehicle), under 18 free. Phone (760) 873-2500.

BIG SUR (H-2) pop. 1,000, elev. 155'

Point Sur State Historic Park, facing SR 1, encompasses Point Sur Lighthouse and its seven light-station buildings as well as an interpretive center. Because access is through private land, the park is open only by guided tour. Phone (831) 625-4419 for 24-hour information. Camping facilities are found at Limekiln State Park, south on SR 1 near Lucia.

PFEIFFER BIG SUR STATE PARK, s. on SR 1, covers 821 acres of coastal redwood and chaparral on the Big Sur River. Visitors can see groves of redwood trees while traversing the hiking trails within the park. Rangers conduct naturalist and campfire programs Memorial Day through Labor Day. Year-round overnight camping is permitted. Park open daily 9-dusk. Day use fee $6 per private vehicle; camping fee $20-$23. Phone (831) 667-2315 or 667-2316. *See Recreation Chart.*

BISHOP (G-6) pop. 3,500, elev. 4,147'

Near the northern end of the Owens River Valley, between the state's two highest mountain ranges, Bishop is the center of a vast recreation and resort area and an outfitting point for pack trips. Bishop Creek Canyon is west on Bishop Creek Highway (SR 168) within Inyo National Forest *(see place listing p. 82).*

Bishop Chamber of Commerce: 690 N. Main St., Bishop, CA 93514; phone (760) 873-8405.

LAWS RAILROAD MUSEUM AND HISTORICAL SITE, 5 mi. n.e. on US 6, features the original narrow-gauge railroad depot that served the once-active railroad community of Laws. On site are exhibit buildings such as an old time doctor's office, an agent's house and a carriage house, all with Owens Valley artifacts. Also shown is Locomotive No. 9, with its string of cars. Daily 10-4 (weather permitting); closed Jan. 1, Thanksgiving and Dec. 25. Donations. Phone (760) 873-5950.

OWENS VALLEY PAIUTE-SHOSHONE INDIAN CULTURAL CENTER, 2300 W. Line St. on Bishop Paiute Reservation, features exhibits of historic American Indian food sources, clothing, shelter, tools and basketry. Mon.-Fri. 9-5, Sat.-Sun. 10-4; closed Jan. 1, Easter, Thanksgiving and Dec. 25. Donations. Phone (760) 873-4478.

BODIE (E-5) elev. 8,375'

Once a bustling mining town with an estimated population of 10,000, Bodie was notorious for its saloons, brothels, gambling halls and opium dens. Devastated in the early 1900s by fire and earthquake, the town now is said to house only an assortment of colorful spirits.

BODIE STATE HISTORIC PARK, more than 1,000 acres embracing the ghost town of Bodie, is reached via SR 270 (last 3 mi. unpaved). It is often inaccessible in winter. The former community of 10,000 reportedly deserved and sustained its reputation as one of the toughest and most lawless gold-mining camps in the West. The local diggings yielded almost $100 million in ore. The 170 buildings that remain are preserved in a state of arrested decay; they will not be restored, but are prevented from decaying further. There also is a museum in the park.

Park open daily 8-7, Memorial Day weekend-Sept. 30; 8-6, May 1-day before Memorial Day weekend, Oct. 1 to mid-Oct. and Nov.-Feb.; 8-5, rest of year. Museum open daily 9:30-5, Memorial Day weekend to mid-Oct. Admission $2. A $1 fee is charged for pets; leashes are required. Phone (760) 647-6445.

BORON (I-6) pop. 2,000, elev. 2,460'

TWENTY MULE TEAM MUSEUM, at 26962 Twenty Mule Team Rd., is a renovated and enlarged house that once stood near a borax mine campsite. The museum has an F-4 jet fighter as well as exhibits about area history, Edwards Air Force Base and NASA, minerals, and local flora and fauna. Video presentations explore borax mining, alternative power generation and the air force base. On the grounds are a turn-of-the-20th-century railroad depot and mining equipment. Daily 10-4; closed Jan. 1, Thanksgiving and Dec. 25. Donations. Phone (760) 762-5810.

BORREGO SPRINGS (K-7)
pop. 2,200, elev. 590'

Although Juan Bautiste De Anza passed the town in 1774 while en route from Sonora, Mexico, to Monterey, Borrego Springs failed to lure many inhabitants until nearly 100 years later.

ANZA-BORREGO DESERT STATE PARK, surrounding the town, encompasses 600,000 acres of the Colorado Desert. The desert blooms with a colorful display of annuals in spring. Points of interest include Butterfield Overland Stagecoach Road; the fossil-laden Carrizo Badlands; Font's Point; Split Mountain; Seventeen Palms Oasis and several canyons. Visitor center displays explain geology, history, desert plants and wildlife. A slide or video presentation is shown every 20 minutes. Check with the visitor center for road conditions before leaving the pavement.

Daily 9-5, Oct.-May; Sat.-Sun. and holidays 9-5, rest of year. Day use fee $5 per private vehicle. All but three campgrounds are on a first-come, first-served basis; phone Parknet at (800) 444-7275 for reservations. Phone (760) 767-5311 for park information, or 767-4684 for recorded wildflower information. *See Recreation Chart and the AAA California/Nevada CampBook.*

BRAWLEY (L-8) pop. 18,900, elev. -113'

While the Imperial Valley around Brawley produces cantaloupes, lettuce and alfalfa, the town is best known as a cattle-raising center.

Brawley Chamber of Commerce: 204 S. Imperial Ave., P.O. Box 218, Brawley, CA 92227; phone (760) 344-3160.

ALGODONES DUNES is 19.5 mi. e. off SR 78. Formed of sand from an ancient lake, wind-sculpted crests and ripples extend more than 40 miles; some sand crests reach heights of more than 300 feet. Next to SR 78 in the middle of the sand dunes is Hugh Osborne Scenic Overlook, a high point that provides panoramas of the dunes. Algodones Dunes consists of two areas—Algodones Dunes Off-Highway Vehicle Area and the Imperial Sand Hills National Natural Landmark. No water is available. Daily 24 hours. Free. Phone (760) 337-4400.

BUENA PARK (B-6) pop. 68,800, elev. 74'

Although its agriculture once was dominated by avocados, oranges and lima beans, Buena Park became known for the boysenberry, which Walter Knott and his neighbor Rudolph Boysen created by grafting the blackberry, the red raspberry and the loganberry. A humble roadside stand that once sold boysenberry preserves burgeoned into one of the nation's most well-known amusement parks, Knott's Berry Farm.

Buena Park Convention & Visitors Office: 6280 Manchester Blvd., Suite 103, Buena Park, CA 90621; phone (714) 562-3560 and (800) 541-3953.

Shopping areas: Buena Park Mall, at La Palma and Stanton avenues, houses JCPenney, Fedco and Sears.

[SAVE] ★**KNOTT'S BERRY FARM,** 8039 Beach Blvd., re-creates the atmosphere of the Old West and encompasses six theme areas: Ghost Town, an 1880s Western boom town with cowboys, gun fights, stagecoaches and panning for gold; Indian Trails with the Native American Interpretive Center; Fiesta Village; The Boardwalk, a coastal amusement park of the 1920s; Wild Water Wilderness; and Camp Snoopy, especially for the younger crowd.

In addition to rides there are shops, a full-size reproduction of Independence Hall and the Good Time Theatre, where major entertainers perform. Mystery Lodge is a theatrical production which combines actors and special effects to dramatize the history of North American Indians. Food is available.

Sun.-Thurs. 9 a.m.-11 p.m., Fri.-Sat. 9 a.m.-1 a.m., June 1-Labor Day; Mon.-Fri. 10-6, Sat. 10-10, Sun. 10-7, rest of year. Closed Dec. 25. Hours may vary; extended hours during most holiday periods. Unlimited-use ticket $36; over 59 and ages 3-11, $26. Admission after 4 p.m. $17.50; over 59 and ages 3-11, $12.50. AE, DI, DS, MC, VI. Phone (714) 220-5200.

[SAVE] **MEDIEVAL TIMES,** 7662 Beach Blvd., offers 11th-century entertainment—tournament feats of skill and combat performed by costumed knights on horseback—in a castle setting, while guests feast on a four-course dinner. Performances nightly; phone for exact times. Admission $34.95; over 65, $31.95; under 12, $22.95. Reservations are required. AE, DS, MC, VI. Phone (714) 521-4740 or (800) 899-6600.

[SAVE] ★**MOVIELAND WAX MUSEUM,** 7711 Beach Blvd., displays more than 300 figures of movie and television stars in realistic settings. Ed Asner, Barbra Streisand, John Wayne, Julie Andrews, Sylvester Stallone and Michael Jackson are among the stars featured. Sets from productions such as "Wizard of Oz," "African Queen," "Dr. Zhivago," "Star Trek" and "Bonanza" are shown. Mon.-Fri. 10-6, Sat.-Sun. 9-7. Admission $12.95; over 54, $10.55; ages 4-11, $6.95. MC, VI. Phone (714) 522-1155.

[SAVE] **RIPLEY'S BELIEVE IT OR NOT! MUSEUM,** 7850 Beach Blvd., exhibits interesting, humorous and bizarre items collected from around the world. Mon.-Fri. 11-5, Sat.-Sun. 10-6. Admission $8.95; over 55, $6.95; ages 4-11, $5.25. MC, VI. Phone (714) 522-7045.

WILD BILL'S WILD WEST DINNER EXTRAVAGANZA, 7600 Beach Blvd., presents old-fashioned Western-style entertainment that includes lariat twirling, live music and cancan dancing; audience participation is encouraged. A family-style meal is served. Shows nightly; phone for times. Admission $35.95; ages 3-11, $22.95. Reservations are required. Phone (714) 522-6414 or (800) 883-1546.

BURBANK—
see Los Angeles p. 118.

BURNEY (B-3) pop. 3,200, elev. 3,173'

Named for an early English settler killed in an American Indian raid in 1857, Burney is a marketing center for lumber, produce and livestock. Its location between Lassen National Forest and Mount Shasta makes it popular with campers and anglers; see place listings p. 93 and 146.

Burney Chamber of Commerce: 37088 N. Main St., P.O. Box 36, Burney, CA 96013; phone (530) 335-2111.

McARTHUR-BURNEY FALLS MEMORIAL STATE PARK, 6 mi. n. on SR 89, features a 129-foot waterfall that flows down several levels over moss-covered lava rock in a lush forest setting. Daily dawn-dusk. Admission $5 per private vehicle; over 62, $4 per private vehicle. A $1 fee is charged for each dog. Phone (530) 335-2777. See Recreation Chart.

The AAA Promise:
Ready to help
no matter where you are!

★ **CABRILLO NATIONAL
MONUMENT—**
see San Diego p. 180.

CALABASAS—
see Los Angeles p. 120.

CALICO GHOST TOWN—
see Barstow p. 56.

CALISTOGA (M-2) pop. 4,500, elev. 362'

At the head of Napa Valley, Calistoga is a health resort with natural hot-water geysers, mineral springs and mineralized mud baths. Some of California's finest vineyards cover the surrounding region. An extinct volcano lies north of town.

Calistoga is the southern terminus of a scenic 94-mile stretch of SR 128 that heads northwest to the coastal city of Albion. Scenic SR 29 runs 28 miles south to Napa through the valley.

Calistoga Chamber of Commerce: 1458 Lincoln #9, Calistoga, CA 94515; phone (707) 942-6333.

HOT AIR BALLOON RIDES over Napa Valley vineyards are available through Calistoga Balloon Adventures, (707) 942-6546 or (800) 333-4359. One-hour sunrise flights depart daily. Fare $165. Flights include a champagne breakfast and transportation to and from the launch site. Under 5 are not permitted. Reservations are required. AE, MC, VI.

Note: The mention of the preceding hot air balloon rides is for information only and does **not** imply endorsement by AAA.

SAVE **OLD FAITHFUL GEYSER OF CALIFORNIA,** 1 mi. n. on Tubbs Ln. between SRs 29 and 128, is one of the few regularly erupting geysers in the world. Fed by an underground river, the water heats to 350 degrees Fahrenheit and erupts about every 30 minutes for 1 to 2 minutes on average, spewing 60 feet into the air. Earthquake activity might disrupt normal eruption patterns. Self-guiding geothermal tours are available. Picnicking is permitted. Daily 9-6, May-Sept.; 9-5, rest of year. Admission $6; over 60, $5; ages 6-12, $2. Phone (707) 942-6463.

PETRIFIED FOREST, 5 mi. w. on Petrified Forest Rd., preserves the texture and fiber of giant petrified redwoods. The grounds also contain a museum and picnic facilities. Allow 30 minutes minimum. Daily 10-6; closed Dec. 25. Admission $4; over 55 and ages 12-17, $3; ages 4-11, $1. Phone (707) 942-6667.

SHARPSTEEN MUSEUM, 1311 Washington St., displays artifacts, photographs and dioramas depicting 19th-century Calistoga; a scale model of Calistoga Hot Springs Resort is included. Next to the museum is one of the resort's 1860s cottages. Exhibits change every 3 months and include an interactive geothermal display. Docents conduct tours on request. Daily 10-4, Apr.-Oct.; noon-4, rest of year. Closed Thanksgiving and Dec. 25. Donations. Phone (707) 942-5911.

 WINERIES

• **Sterling Vineyards,** between SR 29 and Silverado Trail at 1111 Dunaweal Ln. Daily 10:30-4:30; closed Jan. 1, Thanksgiving and Dec. 25. Phone (707) 942-3344 or (800) 726-6136.

CAMBRIA (H-3) pop. 3,100, elev. 60'

Cambria, with its stately pines and panoramic ocean views, lies about 33 miles northwest of San Luis Obispo off SR 1. Originally developed in 1866, the town became a center for shipping, lumbering, whaling and mining. Today specialty shops, art galleries and restaurants line Main Street.

Two coastal parks, Shamel County Park and Leffingwell Landing, a state day-use park, offer picnic areas, beachcombing, tidepools and vantage points for viewing sea otters, sea lions and the winter migration of California gray whales. Cambria lies on a scenic stretch of SR 1 that extends from San Francisco to San Luis Obispo.

Cambria Chamber of Commerce: 767 Main St., Cambria, CA 93428; phone (805) 927-3624.

CAMPO (L-7) pop. 1,100, elev. 2,638'

SAN DIEGO RAILROAD MUSEUM, off SR 94 at the old Campo depot on Forest Gate Rd., has a large collection of vintage locomotives in addition to freight and passenger cars. Tours of the equipment shops and restoration areas are offered. A 16-mile round trip on a train pulled by a restored vintage steam or diesel locomotive is available. One or two Saturdays a month a round-trip excursion to rural Tecate, Mexico, lets passengers stay south of the border for 3 hours. Picnic areas and food are available.

Sat.-Sun. and some holidays 9-5. Train rides depart at 11 and 2:30. Museum free. Train ride $10; over 62 and military with ID $8; ages 6-12, $3. Tecate trip $35; ages 6-12, $20. Phone (619) 595-3030, or (619) 478-9937 Sat.-Sun.

CANOGA PARK—
see Los Angeles p. 120.

CAPITOLA (G-2) pop. 10,200, elev. 50'

Capitola is a resort community on the north shore of Monterey Bay facing New Brighton

Beach State Park *(see Recreation Chart)*. Capitola's begonia gardens bloom July through September. Capitola lies on a scenic stretch of SR 1 that extends from San Francisco to San Luis Obispo.

Capitola Chamber of Commerce: 716-G Capitola Ave., Capitola, CA 95010; phone (831) 475-6522 or (800) 474-6522.

CARLSBAD (K-6) pop. 63,100, elev. 42′

Named for the popular 19th-century Karlsbad spa in Europe, Carlsbad today is known as a major commercial flower growing center, beach resort and antique mecca. Its European background can be seen in the Old World architecture of some of the town's buildings. Just off I-5 is Batiquitos Lagoon, a wetlands area surrounding a freshwater lake that opens into the ocean. Guided hikes along a nature trail are available. Not far away, Legoland California *(see color ad p. 186)*, a theme park designed around the popular toy, is scheduled to open in spring 1999.

Carlsbad Convention & Visitors Bureau: 400 Carlsbad Village Dr., P.O. Box 1246, Carlsbad, CA 92018-1246; phone (760) 434-6093.

SAVE **CARLSBAD CHILDREN'S MUSEUM,** in Carlsbad Village Faire Shopping Centre at 300 Carlsbad Village Dr., #103, provides hands-on activities geared to children. Exhibits include a marketplace, fishing boat and a solar-energy-powered toy train. Daily 10-5, July 1-early Sept.; Tues., Thurs. and Sun. noon-5, Fri.-Sat. 10-5, rest of year. Admission $3.50, under 2 free. Phone (760) 720-0737.

THE FLOWER FIELDS AT CARLSBAD RANCH are e. of I-5 at Palomar Airport Rd. and Paseo del Norte. On a gently sloping hillside which affords an ocean view are 50 acres that turn vibrant each spring with the gold, pink, red, orange, salmon, yellow and white of the thousands of ranunculus. Visitors walking along the wide paths between the fields can view these members of the buttercup family; comfortable shoes are recommended. Daily 9-dusk, Feb. 28-May 30. Hours may vary; phone ahead. Admission $2, under 3 free; prices may vary. Phone (760) 431-0352.

CARMEL—
see Monterey Peninsula p. 140.

CARPINTERIA (J-4)
pop. 13,700, elev. 14′

Carpinteria is a popular resort community and a commercial flower- and avocado-growing center 12 miles southeast of Santa Barbara. It is noted for its sandy beach and for its natural reef breakwater which prevents riptides. Nearby Carpinteria State Beach, which has one of California's largest public beach camping facilities, provides recreational opportunities *(see Recreation Chart)*. Carpinteria lies on a scenic stretch of US 101 that extends from San Luis Obispo to Los Angeles.

Carpinteria Valley Chamber of Commerce: 5320 Carpinteria Ave., Suite J, P.O. Box 956, Carpinteria, CA 93013-0956; phone (805) 684-5479.

CARPINTERIA VALLEY MUSEUM OF HISTORY, 956 Maple Ave., uses antique household objects and specialized tools to depict the area's multicultural history. Among the displays are the Chumash Room, highlighting the centuries-old lifestyle of the valley's American Indians, and exhibits that depict turn-of-the-20th-century asphalt mining, farming and schooling. Tues.-Sat. 1-4 (also Sat. 11-1); closed holidays. Donations. Phone (805) 684-3112.

★CATALINA ISLAND (K-5)

Twenty-two miles from the mainland, Catalina Island is 21 miles long and 8 miles wide, with Avalon the principal town. The settlement of Two Harbors at Catalina's isthmus is about two-thirds of the way toward the island's northwest end. Although Gabrielino Indians settled the island circa 500 B.C., it was not discovered by Europeans until 1542, when Juan Rodríguez Cabrillo found it during his search for the mythical passage between the Atlantic and Pacific oceans. During its Spanish-Mexican period, Catalina was used as a smuggling and piracy base.

Santa Catalina Island Co., originally owned by the Banning family and later by chewing-gum magnate William Wrigley Jr., was responsible for all phases of the island's development as a resort and sport fisherman's paradise. In 1972 the Santa Catalina Island Conservancy was established as a non-profit organization dedicated to the preservation of the island's native flora and fauna and geographical features. The conservancy now owns 86 percent of the island and will maintain much of it in its present state.

The island can be reached by sea and air. Channel crossing time by sea ranges from 1 to 4 hours, depending upon the point of departure; service is provided by the following companies:

Catalina Express, (310) 519-1212 or (800) 360-1212 (see ad p. 63), departing Long Beach and San Pedro; Catalina Cruises, (800) 228-2546, departing Long Beach; and Catalina Passenger Service, (949) 673-5245, departing Newport Bay. See color ad below & p. 123.

Catalina-Vegas Airlines, (619) 292-7311, has a 40-minute flight from San Diego. Helicopter flight time averages 15 to 20 minutes via Island Express, (310) 510-2525; helicopters depart from Long Beach and San Pedro. It is necessary to make reservations well in advance, particularly during summer.

One of the leading resorts in the Los Angeles area, the island has fine beaches, tennis courts,

horseback riding, hiking, camping, a golf course and deep-sea and pier fishing. It is, however, a fragile environment. Thus you may not bring cars to the island; bicycles and small gasoline-powered carts can be rented for use around Avalon. Permits must be obtained from the Santa Catalina Island Conservancy, (310) 510-2595, for bicycling in the interior. Only pedestrians and tour buses are permitted outside the Avalon area.

Catalina Island Visitors Bureau and Chamber of Commerce: #1 Green Pier, P.O. Box 217, Avalon, CA 90704; phone (310) 510-1520. See color ad p. 64.

CATALINA ISLAND MUSEUM, in the former casino at the w. end of Avalon Bay, contains artifacts and mementos of the island's past. Daily 10:30-4. Admission $1.50; over 55, $1; ages 5-11, 50c. Phone (310) 510-2414.

TOURS of the island and surrounding waters are available from several companies; phone the Santa Catalina Island Company's Discovery Tours Center, (310) 510-2500 or (800) 428-2566, or Catalina Adventure Tours, (310) 510-2888. Except where noted, regular fares usually begin at about $8.50; over 54, $7.50; and ages 2-11, $4.25.

Avalon Scenic Tour consists of a 50-minute tram tour along the bay and into the hills above Avalon. Frequent departures daily.

Casino Tour is a guided tour of the Casino, an island landmark. Of interest are the ballroom, theater and circular balcony. Admittance to Catalina Island Museum is included. Departures daily.

Catalina Adventure Tours offers glass-bottom boat trips to Lover's Cove Undersea Gardens, where passengers can spot colorful fish. The 2-hour Inside Adventure Tour, a narrated trip through the island's scenic backcountry, also is available. Frequent departures daily (weather permitting) for daylight and evening trips; evening trips are offered only during summer. Fare $16.50; over 54, $14; ages 2-11, $12.50.

Catalina Interior Safari offers 2.5 hour guided motor tours departing from Two Harbors. The tours explore the island's natural history and include stops at various points of interest in the interior. Fare $18.

Flying Fish Boat Trip provides views of nocturnal flying fish by the use of searchlights during 1-hour night tours Memorial Day-Labor Day.

Glass-Bottom Boat Trip in waters just outside the harbor offers 40-minute tours with views of marine life. Frequent departures daily for daylight trips. Evening tours offered daily, June-Sept.; Wed. and Fri.-Sat., rest of year.

Inland Motor Tour is a 3.75-hour trip through the island's mountainous interior and along Skyline Drive overlooking the coast. Refreshments are included. Departs daily at 9. Fare $29.50; over 55, $26; ages 2-11, $14.75. Reservations are recommended.

Seal Rocks Cruise travels along Catalina's coastline to its eastern tip, where a large seal colony often resides. Frequent departures daily May-Sept.

Skyline Drive affords views of Avalon and the island interior. The 2-hour tour includes a stop at Catalina Airport. Frequent daily tours Memorial Day-Labor Day. Fare $17; over 55, $15; ages 2-11, $8.50.

Sundown Isthmus Cruise is a 4.5-hour cruise along 14 miles of scenic coastline to Two Harbors, where a guided tour across the isthmus is provided. The flying fish tour is included on the return trip. Twice weekly departures mid-June through Sept. 30. Fare $26.50; over 55, $23.50; ages 2-11, $13.25.

Twilight Safari is a 2.5-hour motor trip running through Catalina's interior from Two Harbors to Little Harbor. Late afternoon departures. Fare $18.

Undersea Tour is 40-minute day or evening trip aboard boats with underwater windows. Daily; phone for schedule. Fare $21; over 55, $18; ages 2-11, $13.

WRIGLEY MEMORIAL AND BOTANICAL GARDEN is 2 mi. s. of Avalon via Avalon Canyon Rd. The memorial honors William Wrigley Jr., the person responsible for developing the island into a resort. The adjoining garden features plants native to the island. Daily 8-5. Admission $1, under 12 free. Phone (310) 510-2288.

CHANNEL ISLANDS NATIONAL PARK (K-4)

Elevations in the park range from sea level to 2,450 ft. on Santa Cruz Island. Refer to AAA maps for additional elevation information.

Of the eight islands in Southern California's Channel Islands chain, Anacapa, San Miguel, Santa Barbara, Santa Cruz and Santa Rosa constitute Channel Islands National Park. The water around these five islands is protected as Channel Islands National Marine Sanctuary. Access to the islands can be arranged at locations in and around Ventura and from Santa Barbara.

The plants and animals in these isolated havens display traits that let them thrive amid the constant wind and surging tides of the island environment. Among native species are cormorants, seals, sea lions and sea birds, most notably the endangered California brown pelican. Giant kelp forests shelter more than 1,000 species of ocean life. Fossils and evidence of volcanism and faulting also are found in the park.

General Information and Activities

Visitors are expected to remain on the trails; all objects, including plants, animals and archeological remains, should be left undisturbed. Sections of the islands may be closed to protect the wildlife. Primitive camping is permitted on Anacapa, San Miguel, Santa Cruz, Santa Rosa and Santa Barbara; reservations are required.

Because provisions are not available on the islands, visitors must bring food and water. Clothing should be appropriate for both hot and cold weather. There is no shade on some islands; those with sensitive skin should prepare accordingly.

Rangers conduct walks on San Miguel and Santa Rosa islands; make arrangements in advance through park headquarters in the visitor center; phone (805) 658-5711 for permit applications. The Nature Conservancy owns most of Santa Cruz Island; phone (805) 964-7839 for permission to visit.

Several businesses offer transportation to the islands. Island Packers Co., next to the park headquarters in Ventura, offers trips to Santa Barbara, Santa Cruz, Santa Rosa and San Miguel islands. Boats to Anacapa Island depart from both Ventura Harbor and Channel Islands Harbor in Oxnard daily; phone for schedule. Half-day, non-landing excursions to Anacapa also are available.

Round-trip fare to Anacapa Island $32-$37; under 12, $20. Fares to Santa Barbara, San Miguel, Santa Rosa and Santa Cruz vary. Channel Islands Aviation in Camarillo offers flights to the park for $85 to $139; phone (805) 987-1301. Overnight camping is allowed at all islands. Make reservations 2 or more weeks in advance through Island Packers Co., 1867 Spinnaker Dr., Ventura, CA 93001; phone (805) 642-1393. *See Recreation Chart.*

VISITOR CENTER, 1901 Spinnaker Dr. in Ventura Harbor, contains the park headquarters and features exhibits, slide programs and a film about the islands. Weekend programs are offered. Mon.-Fri. 8:30-4:30, Sat.-Sun. 8-5. Closed Thanksgiving and Dec. 25. Free. Phone (805) 658-5730.

ADMISSION to the visitor center is free. Camping and landing permits are free.

PETS are not permitted on the islands or at the visitor center.

ADDRESS inquiries to the Superintendent, Channel Islands National Park, 1901 Spinnaker Dr., Ventura, CA 93001. Phone (805) 658-5730.

 **Your signal to turn in.**

CHERRY VALLEY (B-9)
pop. 5,000, elev. 2,783′

Cherry Valley Chamber of Commerce: P.O. Box 790, Cherry Valley, CA 92223; phone (909) 845-8466.

EDWARD-DEAN MUSEUM OF DECORATIVE ARTS, 9401 Oak Glen Rd., exhibits furniture and 17th-, 18th- and 19th-century European and Asian decorative art. Changing displays present international art in various media. Tues.-Fri. 1-4:30, Sat.-Sun. 10-4:30, Sept.-July; closed holidays. Admission $3, over 60 and students with ID $2, under 12 free. Phone (909) 845-2626.

CHICO (D-3) pop. 40,100, elev. 200′

Bidwell Park, a 2,250-acre city park spanning an area from downtown to the foothills of the Sierra Nevada, offers hiking and bicycling trails, a playground and various sports facilities.

Chico Chamber of Commerce & Visitor Bureau: 300 Salem St., Chico, CA 95928; phone (530) 891-5556 or (800) 852-8570.

BIDWELL MANSION STATE HISTORIC PARK, 525 The Esplanade, preserves a 26-room Victorian residence built 1865-68 for city founder Gen. John Bidwell. Allow 1 hour minimum. Mon.-Fri. noon-5, Sat.-Sun. 10-5; closed Jan. 1, Thanksgiving and Dec. 25. Tours are given daily on the hour. Last tour begins 1 hour before closing. Admission $3; ages 6-12, $1.50. Phone (530) 895-6144.

CHICO MUSEUM, 2nd and Salem sts., offers permanent and changing exhibits of regional history and art as well as a late-1800s Chinese Taoist temple that was used in Chico 1860-1939. Guided tours are available. Wed.-Sun. noon-4. Donations. Phone (530) 891-4336.

CHINO (B-7) pop. 59,700, elev. 735′

Richard Gird, a wealthy silver miner, moved to the area from Arizona in 1881 and purchased the 48,000-acre Rancho Santa Ana del Chino. There he raised cattle and grew sugar beets and at one time owned the nation's largest sugar refinery. In 1887 Gird began selling parcels of his land to create the town of Chino.

Chino Valley Chamber of Commerce: 13134 Central Ave., Chino, CA 91710; phone (909) 627-6177.

SAVE **PLANES OF FAME AIR MUSEUM,** 4.5 mi. s. of SR 60 off Euclid Ave. at Chino Airport, displays restored American, British, German and Japanese military aircraft. A collection of early aircraft includes an 1896 glider. The Jet Fighter Museum houses jet fighters that range from the early P-59 to the F-104; most jets reflect the Korean War era. Daily 9-5; closed Thanksgiving and Dec. 25. Admission $8.95; ages 5-11, $1.95. Phone (909) 597-3722.

CHULA VISTA—
see San Diego p. 187.

CLAREMONT—
see Los Angeles p. 120.

CLEVELAND NATIONAL FOREST

Elevations in the forest range from 460 ft. in the San Mateo Wilderness to 6,271 ft. at Monument Peak. Refer to AAA maps for additional elevation information.

Divided among three separate areas in Southern California, Cleveland National Forest covers more than 420,000 acres of land in San Diego, Orange and Riverside counties. These areas include chaparral and conifer woodlands and offer many recreational opportunities, the most popular of which are camping and hiking.

Information about all forest activities is available at the following offices: Descanso Ranger District, 3348 Alpine Blvd., Alpine, CA 91901, phone (619) 445-6235; Palomar Ranger District, 1634 Black Canyon Rd., Ramona, CA 92065, phone (760) 788-0250; and Trabuco Ranger District, 1147 E. Sixth St., Corona, CA 91719, phone (909) 736-1811.

Forest information also can be obtained from the Laguna Mountain Visitor Information Office on Sunrise Highway, phone (619) 473-8547.

The Forest Supervisor's Office is at 10845 Rancho Bernardo Rd., Suite 200, San Diego, CA 92127-2107; phone (619) 674-2901. It is open Mon.-Fri. 8-4:30. *See Recreation Chart and the AAA California/Nevada CampBook.*

COALINGA (H-3) pop. 8,200, elev. 671'

Coalinga began as a loading point for the Southern Pacific Railroad Co., which transported coal from area mines. Eventually "Coaling Station A" grew into a permanent oil-boomer settlement and its name was abbreviated. Nine miles north is a group of oil pumps decorated as animals, clowns and imaginary creatures.

Coalinga Area Chamber of Commerce: 380 Coalinga Plaza, Coalinga, CA 93210; phone (559) 935-2948 or (800) 854-3885.

R.C. BAKER MEMORIAL MUSEUM, 297 W. Elm St., displays fossils, American Indian artifacts, Western ranch hand equipment, early 20th-century household items, a 1924 American La France fire engine and a large collection of oil-field equipment. Allow 1 hour minimum. Mon.-Fri. 10-noon and 1-5, Sat. 11-5, Sun. and holidays 1-5; closed Jan. 1, Easter, Thanksgiving and Dec. 24-25. Donations. Phone (559) 935-1914.

COLOMA (E-4) pop. 1,100, elev. 750'

In January 1848, near Capt. John Sutter's sawmill on the American River, James Marshall discovered the first yellow flecks of metal that launched the great California gold rush. By the summer more than 2,000 miners were sifting for gold along the river near Sutter's mill, and Coloma, the first of the gold rush towns, was born. Finds grew scarce within a few years, and the once thriving city of 10,000 dwindled to the quiet village it is today.

★MARSHALL GOLD DISCOVERY STATE HISTORIC PARK, 276 acres on SR 49, includes the 1860 cabin in which James Marshall lived. A statue of Marshall points toward the site of his discovery, a half-mile away. A replica of Sutter's mill stands nearby. Picnic facilities, a visitor center and a museum are available; fishing is permitted in season.

Allow 1 hour minimum. Park open daily 8-dusk. Museum open daily 10-5, Apr.-Oct.; 10-4:30, rest of year. Closed Jan. 1, Thanksgiving and Dec. 25. Day use fee $5 per private vehicle; over 62, $4 per private vehicle. Phone (530) 622-3470 for the park, or 622-1116 for the museum.

☀❄ RECREATIONAL ACTIVITIES
White-water Rafting

• **Whitewater Connection** departs from Point Pleasant Beach campground, .2 mi. n. of Sutter's Mill on SR 49. Write P.O. Box 270, Coloma, CA 95613-0270. Daily Apr.-Sept. Phone (530) 622-6446 or (800) 336-7238.

COLUMBIA (F-4) pop. 400, elev. 2,143'

In the foothills of the Sierra Nevada, Columbia was one of the largest and most important mining towns along the Mother Lode. Local placer mines yielded $87 million in gold 1850-70.

★COLUMBIA STATE HISTORIC PARK, covering 12 square blocks in the old business district, has been partially restored to its appearance in gold-rush days. Among the buildings are a schoolhouse, bank, newspaper building, barbershop, saloons, the Wells Fargo Express Co. building, Fallon Hotel and the City Hotel, which still houses guests. The Masonic Temple has been reconstructed on its original site.

A museum presents slide shows about Columbia history. The Firemen's Muster is held the first weekend in May. Plays are presented in the

THE SEA OTTER

That pointy-nosed, long-whiskered creature floating on its back in central and northern California's waters isn't one of California's typical sunbathers—it's the sea otter.

The sea otter is a thickset, sturdy, fur-bearing marine mammal with small ears and short limbs. Its large hind feet are webbed and flipper-like; its front feet are comparatively small but agile enough to use rocks as tools to break open shellfish. The average adult weighs up to 80 pounds and can be 5 feet long including its tail, making it the largest otter.

The sea otter differs from most marine animals in that it doesn't have a layer of blubber under its skin to keep it warm. Instead, air trapped in its fur serves as a waterproof blanket, insulating the animal and helping it stay afloat.

Weaving through the water at speeds up to 10 miles per hour and diving as deep as 100 feet, sea otters swim with the ease of fish, but they're not fast enough to escape their natural enemies, killer whales and sharks. Vast populations of sea otters once lived in kelp beds along the northern Pacific coast until man proved to be their worst enemy.

Like many species, the friendly sea otter learned to fear man when hunters virtually exterminated the species for its lustrous, brown-black fur. One pelt could bring as much as $2,500. By 1910 the U.S. government prohibited the hunting of sea otters in the Aleutian Islands; in 1911 Russia, Japan, Great Britain and the United States signed an international treaty protecting them.

The sea otter has reoccupied about one-fifth of its original range, re-establishing colonies in California, western Alaska and near the Commander and Kurile islands. Slowly, but in steadily increasing numbers, the bewhiskered sea otter is reclaiming its place in the Pacific ecosystem.

restored Fallon House Theater. Stagecoach rides, horseback tours, gold panning and gold-mine tours also are available.

Park open daily 24 hours. The museum and most stores are open 10-5. Plays are presented Thurs.-Sat. at 8 p.m., Sun. at 2 (also Sat. at 2 if the production is a musical), except during breaks between one closing and another opening. Stagecoach and horseback rides daily 10-6, Memorial Day-Labor Day; Sat.-Sun. and holidays 10-6, rest of year (weather permitting).

Park admission free. Play admission $16; over 62, $15; students with ID $8. Stagecoach fare $4.50; ages 5-12, $4 (shotgun prices $1 additional). Beginner horseback tours $5-$35. Experienced horseback tours $20-$75. Gold mine tour $8; ages 5-12, $7. Gold panning $3-$10. Phone (209) 532-0150 for park office, (209) 532-4644 for play information, (209) 532-0663 for stagecoach or horseback rides, or (209) 532-9693 for gold panning and gold-mine tours.

COURTNEY AVIATION offers scenic tours departing from Columbia Airport at 10723 Airport Rd. Passengers can choose from various tours that fly over such scenic areas as the Yosemite Valley, Mt. Lyell Glacier, Mammoth Lakes, John Muir Wilderness, Kings Canyon and Sequoia National Parks, Mt. Whitney and Mono Lake. Flights depart daily. Fares range from $59-$229. Reservations are required. AE, DS, MC, VI. Phone (209) 532-2345.

Note: The mention of the preceding airplane tour is for information only and does **not** imply endorsement by AAA.

COLUSA (D-3) pop. 4,900, elev. 61'

More than 4,000 acres of seasonal marsh, permanent ponds, watergrass and uplands west of Colusa shelter large flocks of ducks and geese during fall and winter; the best viewing is during November and December. The Colusa National Wildlife Refuge's 3-mile self-guiding auto tour route and 1-mile walking trail lead through part of the area; phone (530) 934-2801.

CORONADO—
see San Diego p. 187.

COSTA MESA (C-7) pop. 96,400, elev. 100'

A budding cultural center, Costa Mesa is the home of South Coast Repertory Theater. Huntington State Beach is nearby. *See Recreation Chart.*

Costa Mesa Tourism & Promotion Council: P.O. Box 5071, Costa Mesa, CA 92628-5071; phone (800) 399-5499.

Shopping areas: South Coast Plaza, at I-405 and Bristol Street, has Macy's, Nordstrom, Robinsons-May, Saks Fifth Avenue and Sears.

ORANGE COUNTY MUSEUM OF ART SOUTH COAST PLAZA GALLERY, 3333 Bristol St., is a satellite facility of Orange County Museum of Art in Newport Beach *(see attraction listing p. 149).* Mon.-Fri. 10-9, Sat. 10-7, Sun. 11-6:30. Free. Phone (714) 662-3366.

ORANGE COUNTY PERFORMING ARTS CENTER, 600 Town Center Dr. in South Coast Plaza Town Center, features the 3,000-seat Segerstrom Hall, where major symphony concerts, operas, ballets and Broadway musicals are presented. Near the center is a 1.6-acre sculpture garden featuring works by Isamu Noguchi. Guided 45-minute tours of the backstage areas, dressing and rehearsal rooms and lobbies are offered Mon., Wed. and Sat. at 10:30. Tours free. Phone (714) 556-2787 for ticket and tour information.

CRESCENT CITY (A-1)
pop. 4,400, elev. 44'

Founded in 1853 as a gold mining supply center, Crescent City edges a harbor defined by a crescent-shaped beach. Point St. George, just above the harbor, protects the city from strong north winds; it was on Point St. George Reef that the sidewheeler *Brother Jonathan* wrecked on July 30, 1865; Brother Jonathan Cemetery, 9th Street and Pebble Beach Drive, contains the graves of many victims.

Lake Earl Wildlife Area, 5 miles north at the junction of Northcrest Drive and Old Mill Road, is 5,000 acres of wildlife habitat open for nature study, boating, hiking, waterfowl hunting and fishing.

Crescent City is the southern terminus of a scenic 42-mile stretch of US 199 that heads northeast to the Oregon border through Smith River National Recreation Area.

Crescent City-Del Norte County Chamber of Commerce: 1001 Front St., Crescent City, CA 95531; phone (707) 464-3174 or (800) 343-8300.

BATTERY POINT LIGHTHOUSE, on Battery Point Island at the end of A St., is a working 1856 lighthouse that houses a museum, nautical artifacts, antique clocks, and photographs of shipwrecks and American and foreign lighthouses. Guided tours are available, tide permitting. Allow 30 minutes minimum. Wed.-Sun. 10-4, Apr.-Sept. Admission $2; under 12, 50c. To confirm hours phone (707) 464-3089.

DEL NORTE COAST REDWOODS STATE PARK, 6,400 acres 7 mi. s. on US 101, contains 15 memorial redwood groves. The growths extend down steep slopes almost to the ocean shore.

Wildlife can be seen. Daily 24 hours. Day use fee $5 per private vehicle; over 65, $4 per private vehicle. Camping $16 May 1-Sept. 15, $14 rest of year. Phone (707) 464-6101, ext. 5101.For camping information phone Parknet at (800) 444-7275. *See Recreation Chart.*

OCEAN WORLD, 304 US 101S, features a half-million-gallon tank with a sandy bottom and reef exhibit. Other highlights include a touch tide-pool, river otter exhibit, shark petting tank and performances by trained sea lions. Guided aquarium tours are available. Daily 8 a.m.-9 p.m., May-Sept.; 9-6, rest of year. Closed Thanksgiving and Dec. 25. Admission $5.95; ages 3-10, $3.95. AE, DS, MC, VI. Phone (707) 464-3522.

DANA POINT (K-6) pop. 31,900, elev. 10'

At the turn of the 19th century Dana Point was the only major port between Santa Barbara and San Diego. Now the natural cove boasts a modern marina from which whale-watching cruises depart late November through March.

Dana Point Chamber of Commerce: 24681 La Plaza # 115, P.O. Box 12, Dana Point, CA 92629; phone (949) 496-1555.

Shopping areas: Dana Point Harbor, Golden Lantern at Harbor Drive, consists of two dockside villages that offer shopping with a view.

ORANGE COUNTY MARINE INSTITUTE, 24200 Dana Point Harbor Dr., contains sea-life exhibits. Next to the institute is a full-size replica of Richard Henry Dana's ship *Pilgrim,* which he described in the seafaring novel, "Two Years Before the Mast." In July and August nautical-themed musicals and dramas are performed on the ship's deck. Marine biologists conduct wildlife cruises aboard a research vessel on weekends; dolphins, sea lions and whales may be seen in season. Harbor cruises also are available.

Daily 10-4:30; closed holidays. Ship tours are given Sun. 10-2:30. Institute admission is by donation. Production $20; under 13, $15. Wildlife cruise $20; under 13, $14. Harbor cruise $11; under 13, $8. Reservations are required for productions and cruises. Phone (949) 496-2274.

DANVILLE (P-3) pop. 31,300, elev. 368'

Early buildings and narrow downtown roads connect Danville to its Old West past. In addition to its eight parks, which offer varied recreational activities, the city offers Iron Horse Trail, a popular biking and walking route. Mount Diablo State Park *(see attraction listing in Walnut Creek p. 236)* is east on Diablo Road. Eugene O'Neill National Historic Site, a park for the performing arts, can be toured Wed.-Sun. at 10 and 12:30; phone (925) 838-0249 for reservations.

Danville Area Chamber of Commerce: 117-E Town and Country Dr., Danville, CA 94526; phone (925) 837-4400.

BLACKHAWK AUTOMOTIVE MUSEUM, 3700 Blackhawk Plaza Cir., at the intersection of Crow Canyon Rd., Camino Tassajara and Blackhawk Rd., features rotating exhibits of about 120 distinctive automobiles from 1897 to the 1980s. The Automotive Art Collection is in the museum. Wed.-Sun. 10-5; closed Jan. 1, Thanksgiving and Dec. 25. Guided tours are given Sat.-Sun. at 2. Admission $8, over 65 and students with ID $5, under 6 free with adult. Phone (925) 736-2277.

DAVIS (E-3) pop. 46,200, elev. 50'

As a result of its foresight and commitment to conservation, Davis has received several energy conservation awards. The University of California, Davis ranks among the top 25 research universities in the United States. Tours of the campus, available Sat.-Sun. at 11:30 and 1:30 and weekdays by appointment, depart from Buehler Alumni and Visitors Center; phone (530) 752-0539.

Davis Chamber of Commerce: 130 G St., Davis, CA 95616; phone (530) 756-5160.

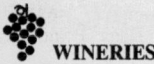

WINERIES

• **Satiety Winery,** 8 mi. n. of I-80 at SR 113 and CR 25-A. Mon.-Fri. 6 a.m.-7 p.m., Sat. 8-7, Sun. 11-7. Phone (530) 661-0680.

DEATH VALLEY JUNCTION (H-8) pop. 100, elev. 2,042'

MARTA BECKET'S AMARGOSA OPERA HOUSE, near jct. SRs 127 and 190, is the backdrop for dance-mime performances created and presented by Marta Becket. Murals painted by Becket adorn the walls and ceiling of the opera house. Performances Mon. and Sat. at 8:15 p.m., Feb.-Apr.; Sat. at 8:15 in Jan., first two Sat. in May, and in Oct. and Dec. Admission $10; ages 2-12, $8. Phone (760) 852-4441.

★DEATH VALLEY NATIONAL PARK (H-7)

Elevations in the park range from -282 ft. near Badwater to 11,049 ft. at Telescope Peak. Refer to AAA maps for additional elevation information.

Death Valley's formation began about 3 million years ago when forces within the Earth broke the crust into blocks. Some of these blocks tilted and rotated, creating the alternating mountain and valley pattern. During the ice ages large lakes intermittently occupied the basin; their evaporation left alternating layers of mud and large salt deposits that still are visible.

Several American Indian cultures have occupied the area during the past 9,000 years, but the valley gained its forbidding name and reputation relatively recently. In the winter of 1849 a band of gold seekers started across the valley, believing that it was a shortcut to the gold fields. After running low on food and water, the band splintered into several frantic groups, each trying to escape the area on its own. Some of the pioneers died.

Although miners later found precious metal in the area, the discovery of another mineral—borax—initiated the exploitation of the valley. The first borax prospectors built the roads over which the famous 20-mule teams drew wagon loads weighing as much as 40 tons.

A place of unexpected contrasts, Death Valley encompasses 3,336,000 acres, and ranges from less than 10 miles to about 61 miles in width and is about 146 miles long. Elevations range from 282 feet below sea level near Badwater (the lowest point in the Western Hemisphere) to 11,049 feet above sea level at Telescope Peak. One of the hottest regions in the world, the valley can experience daytime temperatures as high as 134 F. Although summer thunderstorms often send flash floods tearing down narrow canyons, the average yearly rainfall on the valley floor is less than 2 inches.

Of the more than 900 species of plants and trees found, 21 are unique to the valley, including the Panamint daisy, the Death Valley sage and the Death Valley sandpaper plant.

The area also contains a wealth of geological phenomena: large sand dune formations, sculpted rocks, isolated valleys and volcanic craters. The canyon and mountain walls change color with the shifting sunlight.

Mankind's marks on the desert are limited. The park boundaries encompass the route of the Jayhawkers Trail taken from Utah's Great Salt Lake in 1849; the route taken by the Darwin-French party in 1860; the first mine worked in the region; several beehive charcoal kilns; and the ghost town site of Skidoo.

General Information and Activities

Death Valley attracts many visitors between early November and late April. Washington's Birthday, Easter Week, Thanksgiving, Christmas and Death Valley Encampment in early November are particularly popular times.

Artists Drive is a scenic 9-mile route among the foothills of the Black Mountains. Golden Canyon, about 5 miles north of the entrance to Artists Drive, is cut by an easy 2-mile trail that winds through carved rock formations; parking and trail guides are available at the trail entrance. East of Furnace Creek, SR 190 leads to Zabriskie Point and views of an area of eroded, contoured hills.

Furnace Creek Visitor Center, on SR 190, has exhibits, literature and an 18-minute film about the park. It is open daily 8-6; phone (760) 786-2331. Evening programs and naturalist walks are conducted Nov.-Apr. Horses can be rented at Furnace Creek Ranch.

Note: Travelers are cautioned that the valley is subject to intense heat during the summer. Those affected by extreme temperatures should plan to travel in the cooler evening or nighttime hours. Carry extra water and boil or purify any water taken from valley springs before drinking it.

ADMISSION fee $10 per private vehicle, $5 per person arriving by other means, free to holders of Golden Age or Golden Access passports. *See Recreation Chart and the AAA California/Nevada CampBook.*

PETS on leash are allowed in the valley but not in public facilities or on the trails.

ADDRESS inquiries to the Superintendent, Death Valley National Park, P.O. Box 579, Death Valley, CA 92328. Phone (760) 786-2331.

Points of Interest

★**SCOTTY'S CASTLE**, at the valley's north boundary, is an amazing sight in this isolated region. Built in the 1920s as a vacation retreat by a wealthy Chicagoan, it contains beautiful furnishings and art. Allow 1 hour minimum. Rangers conduct tours on the hour daily 9-5. Admission $8; over 62 and ages 6-11, $4. Phone (760) 786-2392.

DEL MAR—
see San Diego p. 187.

★DEVILS POSTPILE NATIONAL MONUMENT (F-5)

Near Mammoth Lakes and surrounded by Inyo National Forest *(see place listing p. 82),* Devils Postpile National Monument lies at an elevation of 7,600 feet in the eastern Sierra Nevada. The highlight of this 800-acre monument is a sheer wall of symmetrical basaltic columns more than 60 feet high. The formation is a remnant of a basalt flow worn smooth on top by glacial action. A trail leads to the top where the surface resembles a tile inlay.

The Middle Fork of the San Joaquin River drops more than 100 feet at Rainbow Falls, 2 miles by trail from the Postpile. Fishing is permitted; anyone over 16 must have a California license. Hunting is prohibited.

The monument is reached via SR 203, which leads west from US 395 and Mammoth Visitor Center to the Mammoth Mountain Ski Area parking lot, then by shuttle bus to the Postpile ranger station; phone (760) 934-0686 or *see Inyo National Forest p. 82 for shuttle bus information.* A half-mile trail leads to the Postpile. Except for

vehicles with camping permits, private vehicles are not allowed beyond Minaret Summit (just beyond the ski area parking lot) during the day, mid-June through Labor Day.

Rangers conduct interpretive walks and campfire programs early July through Labor Day, weather permitting. Leashed pets are permitted. Monument open mid-June through Oct. 31. Ranger station open daily 8-5, July 1-Labor Day. Shuttle bus (round trip) $9; ages 13-18, $7; ages 5-12, $4. Phone (760) 934-2289 mid-June through Oct. 31, or (760) 872-4881 the rest of the year.

★DISNEYLAND—
see Anaheim p. 47.

DOWNEY—
see Los Angeles p. 120.

DOWNIEVILLE (D-4)
pop. 400, elev. 2,899'

Once the center of enormously rich gold diggings, Downieville retains much of its earlier atmosphere. Old brick and stone buildings with picturesque iron doors and shutters flank narrow, tree-lined Main Street. Some sections of sidewalk still are made of planks. Gold panning is available downtown in the Yuba River.

DOWNIEVILLE MUSEUM, Main St., was built in 1852 and features artifacts donated by a former town sheriff and a collection of horse snowshoes. The stone structure once was a Chinese store and gambling house. Tours are available by reservation daily 10-5, Memorial Day weekend-second weekend in Oct. Donations. Phone (530) 289-3423.

DUNSMUIR (B-3) pop. 2,100, elev. 2,289'

Dunsmuir is an old railroad town just south of Mount Shasta. The Sacramento River, which runs through town, offers fishing. Other recreational opportunities in the area include camping, hiking and skiing. Dunsmuir Museum, 4101 Pine St., has displays about railroad history.

Dunsmuir Chamber of Commerce: P.O. Box 17, Dunsmuir, CA 96025; phone (530) 235-2177.

CASTLE CRAGS STATE PARK lies 6 mi. s. off I-5. The granite crags tower more than 4,000 feet over the nearby Sacramento River. Camping is available. Park open daily 7:30 a.m.-10 p.m. Day use fee $5 per private vehicle; over 62, $4 per private vehicle; physically impaired $2.50. Pets $1 additional; must be leashed. Camping fee $16; over 65, $15; physically impaired $8. Phone (530) 235-2684, or Parknet at (800) 444-7275 for camping reservations. *See Recreation Chart.*

EL CAJON—
see San Diego p. 187.

EL CENTRO (L-8) pop. 31,400, elev. -45'

El Centro is the market center for the Imperial Valley, one of the richest farming areas in the world. Irrigation has transformed a barren desert—much of it below sea level—into a verdant patchwork of productive fields and pastures. Tomatoes, cotton, sugar beets, melons and lettuce are raised. The Navy's Blue Angels flying team does its winter training at the nearby Naval Air Facility.

El Centro Chamber of Commerce & Visitors Bureau: 1095 S. 4th St., P.O. Box 3006, El Centro, CA 92244-3006; phone (760) 352-3681.

ELDORADO NATIONAL FOREST

Elevations in the forest range from 3,382 ft. in the foothills to 9,983 ft. at Pyramid Peak. Refer to AAA maps for additional elevation information.

Bounded on the west by the Mother Lode Country and on the east by Lake Tahoe, Eldorado National Forest encompasses 676,780 acres in the rugged, lake-strewn Sierra Nevada. US 50 and SR 88 provide access to most of the forest's recreational facilities. Carson Pass Highway (SR 88) is a 58-mile scenic route through the forest.

Although the forest is most popular in spring and summer, three downhill ski areas and trails for cross-country skiing and snowmobiling attract winter visitors as well. Segments of the Pacific Crest National Scenic Trail pass through the forest; snow renders some sections impassable until mid-June or July. Hikers wishing to camp on the trail should obtain campfire permits. Permits also are required for day use and overnight stays in the Desolation Wilderness and Mokelumne Wilderness.

Designated routes for off-road vehicles are outlined on a Vehicle Travel Plan Map. For information contact Eldorado National Forest Visitor Center, 3070 Camino Heights Dr., Camino, CA 95709; phone (530) 644-6048. *See Recreation Chart and the AAA California/Nevada CampBook.*

Serving the
American traveler since 1902.

EL MONTE—
see Los Angeles p. 120.

EL SOBRANTE (O-2) pop. 9,900

 RECREATIONAL ACTIVITIES

White-water Rafting

- **Whitewater Voyages,** 5225 San Pablo Dam Rd., P.O. Box 20400, El Sobrante, CA 94820. Daily 9-5. Phone (510) 222-5994 or (800) 488-7238.

ENCINITAS (K-6) pop. 55,400, elev. 92'

QUAIL BOTANICAL GARDENS, 230 Quail Gardens Dr., encompasses 30 acres of rare plants, a waterfall and self-guiding trails. Exotic tropical plants, palms, ferns, bamboos and unusual plant collections thrive in the gardens' deep canyons and sunny hillsides. A chaparral area serves as a natural bird refuge. Daily 9-5; closed Jan. 1, Thanksgiving and Dec. 25. Tours are given Sat. at 10. Admission $5; over 64, $4; ages 5-12, $2; free to all first Tues. of the month. Phone (760) 436-3036.

ENCINO—
see Los Angeles p. 121.

ESCONDIDO (K-7)
pop. 108,600, elev. 684'

The Heritage Walk and Museum, in Grape Day Park on Broadway, features Escondido's first library (now the museum office), a furnished 1890 Victorian house and other 19th-century buildings, including a restored 1888 Santa Fe train depot. The California Center for the Arts, 340 N. Escondido Blvd., consists of a concert hall, theater, museum and conference center.

Escondido Chamber of Commerce: 720 N. Broadway, Escondido, CA 92025; phone (760) 745-2125.

Shopping areas: North County Fair, I-15 and Via Rancho Parkway, contains Macy's, Robinsons-May and Sears.

DEER PARK, 29013 Champagne Blvd., combines a car museum and a winery. The museum occupies three buildings and displays about 130 automobiles—all convertibles—dating from 1903 to the 1970s. Included are two 18-foot-long 1959 Cadillacs and a small post-World War II Messerschmidt. Museum open daily 10-4; winery open daily 10-5. Closed Thanksgiving and Dec. 25. Admission (includes museum and winery tour) $6; over 54, $4; under 12 free. Phone (760) 749-1666.

SAVE ★**SAN DIEGO WILD ANIMAL PARK** embraces 2,100 acres about 5 mi. e. of I-15 via Rancho Pkwy. exit, following signs. Begun as a breeding facility for the San Diego Zoo's large animals, San Diego Wild Animal Park today is home to more than 3,000 animals, including elephants, tigers, rhinoceroses, zebras and giraffes. These creatures roam over expanses of land that simulate Africa, Asia and Australia. The park also contains more than 3,000 species of exotic plants.

Visitors can view the preserve during a 50-minute monorail ride or from lookout points along a 1.75-mile walking trail. Animal and bird shows are presented daily in the African atmosphere of Nairobi Village, which also has small mammal exhibits and aviaries.

Park open daily at 9; closing times vary. All-inclusive admission $21.95; over 60, $19.75; ages 3-11, $14.95. Parking $3. Pets are not permitted. DS, MC, VI. Phone (619) 234-6541.

SAN PASQUAL BATTLEFIELD STATE HISTORIC PARK, 8 mi. e. on SR 78, covers 50 acres and commemorates an important battle in the conquest of California. In 1846 Gen. Stephen Watts Kearny and his American troops from Fort Leavenworth clashed with Californians under Gen. Andrés Pico. A pamphlet outlining a self-guiding .5-mile loop nature trail is available at the visitor center. The trail affords an introduction to native plants and a view of the San Pasqual Valley. On the first Sunday of each month, guides in period attire demonstrate 19th-century crafts and domestic skills. Sat.-Sun. and holidays 10-5; closed Jan. 1, Thanksgiving and Dec. 25. Free. Phone (619) 220-5430 or (760) 489-0076.

WELK RESORT THEATRE, 7 mi. n. off I-15 at 8860 Lawrence Welk Dr. in Welk Resort Center/San Diego, is a 330-seat dinner theater that offers musical comedy and variety productions. A museum contains memorabilia of bandleader Lawrence Welk's life and musical career. Museum open daily at 10; closing time varies. Museum free. Phone (760) 749-3448.

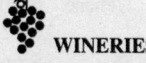

WINERIES

• **Bernardo Winery,** off Pomerado Rd. at 13330 Paseo del Verano Norte. Daily 9-5. Phone (619) 487-1866.

• **Ferrara Winery,** 1120 W. 15th Ave. Daily 10-5; closed holidays. Phone (760) 745-7632.

EUREKA (B-1) pop. 27,000, elev. 44'

The chief port between San Francisco Bay and the Columbia River, Eureka is a lumbering, industrial and commercial city on Humboldt Bay. Such ornate Victorian dwellings as Carson Mansion at 2nd and M streets reflect the days of the lumber barons. Fort Humboldt, the 1853 head-

quarters of Gen. Ulysses S. Grant, houses exhibits about past methods of logging.

The renovated 19th-century Old Town consists of specialty shops, restaurants, art galleries and studios. Three- and 6-hour tours of the city's commercial and Victorian residential districts depart daily all year; phone (707) 445-2117 or (800) 400-1849.

Humboldt Bay also is an important fishing port, boasting generous catches of crab, salmon, shrimp, albacore and bottom fish. Fishing fleets dock just across the Samoa bridge at Woodley Island Marina, where a copper statue of a fisherman commemorates fishermen lost at sea. Humboldt Bay Maritime Museum, 1410 2nd St., displays marine artifacts and early photographs of the area.

Eureka/Humboldt County Convention and Visitors Bureau: 1034 Second St., Eureka, CA 95501; phone (707) 443-5097 or (800) 346-3482.

Self-guiding tours: A map of a driving tour that passes 100 vintage residences is available from the Greater Eureka Chamber of Commerce, 2112 Broadway, Eureka, CA 95501-2189; phone (707) 442-3738 or (800) 356-6381.

BLUE OX MILLWORKS, at the foot of X St., 4 blks. n. of US 101, is a Victorian mill-work shop that includes a sawmill building, molding building, smithy and a re-creation of a logging "Skid Camp." Vintage equipment dating 1852-1940 is used in production. Visitors may watch the artisans at work via a self-guiding tour; casual dress and low-heeled shoes are advised. Mon.-Sat. 9-5. Admission $5; over 64 and ages 12-18, $4; ages 8-11, $2.50. Phone (707) 444-3437 or (800) 248-4259.

CLARKE MEMORIAL MUSEUM, 240 E St., displays American Indian artifacts, antique weapons and exhibits about regional and natural history. The museum also has a significant collection of northwestern California Indian basketry, including examples of Yurok, Karuk and Hupa ceremonial regalia as well as Wiyot basketry and stone artifacts. Allow 1 hour minimum. Tues.-Sat. noon-4; closed Jan. 1, Thanksgiving and Dec. 25. Donations. Phone (707) 443-1947.

SAVE **HUMBOLDT BAY HARBOUR CRUISE** leaves from the foot of C St. The MV *Madaket,* an original 1910 ferry, takes visitors on a 75-minute narrated history cruise around Humboldt Bay. Bring a sweater or jacket. Harbor cruise departs Mon.-Sat. at 1, 2:30 and 4, Sun. at 1 and 2:30, May-Oct. Holiday brunch cruises are available. Harbor cruise $9.50; over 60 and ages 12-17, $8.50; ages 5-11, $6.50. Phone (707) 445-1910.

SAMOA COOKHOUSE MUSEUM off US 101 across the Samoa Bridge at 79 Cookhouse Ln., was established in the late 1800s as a large lumber camp chowhouse. The museum and dining rooms contain equipment, utensils and memorabilia from the lumber and logging industry. Food is available. Daily 6-3:30 and 5-10, Memorial Day weekend-Labor Day; 6-3 and 5-9 (Thanksgiving noon-8 and Dec. 24 6 a.m.-3 p.m.), rest of year. Closed Dec. 25. Free. Phone (707) 442-1659.

SEQUOIA PARK, Glatt and W sts., contains a 52-acre grove of virgin redwoods, a formal flower garden, duck pond, zoo, bear grotto and deer and African nyala and llama paddocks. A playground and picnic facilities are available. Park open daily 10-dusk. Zoo open Tues.-Sun. 10-7, May-Sept; 10-5, rest of year. Petting zoo open Tues.-Sun. 11:30-3:30, mid-June through Labor Day. Free. Phone (707) 442-6552.

FAIRFIELD (N-3) pop. 77,200, elev. 15'

Founded in 1903, Fairfield sits southeast of the Vaca Mountains. Major industries sustaining Fairfield include agriculture, manufacturing and the military.

Fairfield-Suisun Chamber of Commerce: 1111 Webster St., Fairfield, CA 94533; phone (707) 425-4625.

Shopping areas: Solano Mall, off I-80 at jct. Travis Boulevard and Pennsylvania Avenue, houses Macy's, JCPenney, Emporium, Mervyn's and Sears.

NORTH SAN DIEGO'S

GREAT GOLF GETAWAY

In the peaceful hills of North San Diego • Just minutes from the wineries of Temecula • Par 72 championship golf course • Lighted tennis courts • Fitness Center • Heated pool & spa • Friendly and attentive hospitality.

GOLF PACKAGES AVAILABLE YEAR ROUND

AAA MEMBERS RECEIVE
15% OFF PUBLISHED RATES

PALA MESA
R E S O R T

800-722-4700 or 760-728-5881

2001 Old Hwy 395 • Fallbrook, CA • www.palamesa.com

ANHEUSER-BUSCH FAIRFIELD BREWERY TOUR, 3101 Busch Dr., details the brewing process via a 1-hour guided tour of the brewery. A film also is shown. Tours are given on the hour Mon.-Sat. 9-4, June-Aug.; Tues.-Sat. 9-4, rest of year. Free. Under 5 are not allowed on the production floor. Phone (707) 429-7595.

JELLY BELLY FACTORY TOUR is offered at the Herman Goelitz Candy Co. at 2400 N. Watney Way. The company offers tours of its jelly-bean-making facilities. Visitors can see the entire process which includes pouring and curing the jelly centers, coating the centers with a candy shell and polishing and seasoning the jelly beans before they are packaged. Allow 30 minutes minimum. Daily 9-3, early July-late June; closed Easter, Thanksgiving and Dec. 25. Free. Phone (707) 428-2838 or (800) 522-3267.

🅢🅐🅥🅔 **SCANDIA FAMILY FUN CENTER,** I-80 and Suisun Valley Rd., includes two 18-hole miniature golf courses, a large arcade, waterbug bumper boats, little Indy race cars and a 10-minute train ride on the Copenhagen Express. A children's club house also is part of the center. Food is available.

Allow 2 hours minimum. Indoor activities daily 10-10. Outdoor activities Sun.-Thurs. 10-8:30; Fri.-Sat. 10-10. Admission, including 10 game tokens, golf, Indy cars, junior track, boats and train, $14.95; individual prices for other rides $2.95-$5.95. Golf $5.50; over 55 and ages 6-10, $4; under 5 free. Phone (707) 864-8558.

TRAVIS AIR FORCE MUSEUM is on Travis Air Force Base in Bldg. 80 on Burgan Blvd.; enter the base at the main gate. Photographs, uniforms and memorabilia detail base history. The aircraft outside, mostly transport, relate the growth of airlift aviation. Allow 1 hour minimum. Mon.-Fri. 9-4, Sat. 9-5, Sun. hours vary, closed federal holidays. Free. Visitor passes and self-guiding tour brochures are available at the main gate. Visitors must obtain a vehicle pass by showing a valid drivers license, vehicle registration and proof of vehicle insurance. Phone (707) 424-5605.

WESTERN RAILWAY MUSEUM, 12 mi. e. on SR 12, operates vintage streetcars, including Key System trains, California's last 5-cent street car and other equipment on 5-mile trips. Diesel 15-mile train rides from Rio Vista Junction to Dozier are available Mar.-May for wildflower viewing; other trips are offered in early Dec. Picnicking is permitted.

Wed.-Sun. 11-5, July 4-Labor Day; Sat.-Sun. 11-5, rest of year. Closed Jan. 1, Thanksgiving and Dec. 25. Admission $6; over 65, $5; ages 4-12, $3; family rate $18. Train ride $12; ages 4-12, $8. Reservations are required for train ride. AE, DS, MC, VI. Phone (707) 374-2978, or (800) 900-7245 only for train reservations.

FALL RIVER MILLS (B-3) elev. 3,291'

FORT CROOK MUSEUM, Fort Crook Ave., displays American Indian artifacts, photographs and memorabilia from the 1800s, an authentic dugout canoe and a 360-degree view of Fall River Mills. Next to the museum is a turn-of-the-20th-century schoolhouse, a barn that houses a 1911 Wichita Flat-Bed Motorstage, an 1860 log cabin, a jailhouse and the James Showcase building. Genealogical records are available. Allow 30 minutes minimum. Tues.-Sun. noon-4, May-Oct. Donations. Phone (530) 336-5110.

FELTON (G-2) pop. 4,600, elev. 286'

One of the tallest covered bridges in the United States—and the only one made of redwood—can be found in Felton. Felton lies on a scenic stretch of SR 9 that extends from Los Gatos to Santa Cruz.

San Lorenzo Valley Chamber of Commerce: P.O. Box 67, Felton, CA 95018-0067; phone (831) 335-2764.

ROARING CAMP & BIG TREES NARROW GAUGE RAILROAD, 1 mi. s.e. on Graham Hill Rd., runs s. from Roaring Camp Station through the redwoods of Santa Cruz County. An 1880 steam train makes a 6-mile, 75-minute round trip as the conductor recounts the history of the Santa Cruz Mountains. Picnicking is permitted at Roaring Camp; a barbecue lunch is offered Saturday and Sunday noon-3, May through October. Departures several times daily; phone for schedule. Closed Dec. 25. Fare $13.50; ages 3-12, $9.50. AE, DS, MC, VI. Phone (831) 335-4400. *See color ad p. 925-926.*

Santa Cruz Big Trees and Pacific Railway departs Roaring Camp Station for a 3-hour round-trip excursion to the beach boardwalk at Santa Cruz. The 1920s-style passenger coaches travel through Henry Cowell Redwoods State Park and along the San Lorenzo River Canyon. Conductors comment on the central coast's "golden age" of railroading 1910-25. Departures several times daily, mid-May through Nov. 30; otherwise varies. Fare $15; ages 3-12, $11. AE, DS, MC, VI. Phone (831) 335-4400.

FERNDALE (C-1) pop. 1,300, elev. 30'

Ferndale was settled in 1852 by Vermonters Seth and Stephen Shaw, but it was Danish pioneers who established the town's dairying industry in the 1850s, producing the butter that Ferndale has been identified with ever since. The houses that the Danish and Portuguese dairymen built, known as "butterfat palaces," reflect the town's past and present. Fern Cottage, 3 mi. w. on Ocean Ave., features 19th-century items. The village is a state historical landmark; it plays host to a December Christmas gala.

Ferndale Repertory Theatre offers eight productions each year, including contemporary American,

musical and classic plays; phone (707) 725-2378 for schedule and ticket information.

Ferndale Chamber of Commerce: P.O. Box 325, Ferndale, CA 95536-0325; phone (707) 786-4477.

Self-guiding tours: A souvenir newspaper detailing walking and driving tours can be obtained at various shops on Main Street.

FERNDALE MUSEUM, Third and Shaw sts., features period rooms, a smithy, a seismograph, farm and logging equipment, and microfilmed newspapers dating from 1878. Tues.-Sat. 11-4, Sun. 1-4, June-Sept.; Wed.-Sat. 11-4, Sun. 1-4, Feb.-May and Oct.-Dec. Admission $1; ages 6-16, 50c. Phone (707) 786-4466.

FILLMORE (J-5) pop. 12,000, elev. 469'

FILLMORE & WESTERN RAILWAY, departing from Central Park Plaza, offers 1-hour scenic rides to Santa Paula aboard vintage train cars including a 1920s-style Pullman and restored dining, sleeper and commuter cars. Train workers dress in vintage costumes. Themed dinner train tours also are available. Allow 2 hours minimum. Sightseeing tours depart Sat. at 2, Sun. at 11 and 2; closed Jan. 1, July 4 and Dec. 25. Fare $15; senior citizens $12; ages 3-11, $8. Phone (805) 524-2546.

FISH CAMP (F-5) pop. 100, elev. 4,990'

[SAVE] **YOSEMITE MOUNTAIN-SUGAR PINE RAILROAD** is 2 mi. s. on SR 41. The scenic narrow-gauge railroad offers 4-mile excursions through Sierra National Forest aboard authentic steam-powered trains or gas-powered railcars. A Moonlight Special journey with barbecue dinner and entertainment also is available.

The scenic narrow-gauge train runs daily mid-Mar. through Oct. 31 and some fall and winter holidays. Departure times for the Logger steam train vary, May.-Oct.; phone for schedule. Jenny Rail cars operate daily every half-hour 9-4, mid-Mar. through Oct. 31, except when the steam train is running; phone for limited winter schedule. Moonlight Special runs Sat. evenings, early June-early Oct.; reservations are recommended. Steam train $10.50; over 62, $9.45; ages 3-12, $5.75. Rail cars $6.75; ages 3-12, $3.75. Moonlite Special $32; over 62, $29.25; ages 3-12, $18. MC, VI. Phone (559) 683-7273.

FOLSOM (E-3) pop. 29,800, elev. 218'

A gold-mining town dating from the 1860s, Folsom retains much of its historic character. Many restored houses and buildings of that era line Sutter Street; they include the Wells Fargo Office—the terminus of the Pony Express.

The old Southern Pacific Depot, 200 Wool St., now houses the chamber of commerce. A Southern Pacific railcar, boxcar and caboose are displayed. Alongside the cars is the 1868 Ashland

Freight Depot, said to be the oldest standing station west of the Mississippi River.

Folsom City Park and Zoo, behind the city hall complex on Natoma Street, has picnic facilities, a children's play area, a railway and a small zoo. Two miles north of town is the massive granite Folsom State Prison. A museum contains displays of photographs and other items that describe the prison's history. An arts and gift shop at the main gate has items crafted by inmates; sales contribute to trust funds for the creators upon their release.

Folsom Chamber of Commerce: 200 Wool St., Folsom, CA 95630; phone (916) 985-2698 or (800) 377-1414.

Shopping areas: Folsom Station Factory Outlet, 13000 Folsom Blvd., has more than 50 factory-direct and specialty stores.

HISTORIC FOLSOM POWERHOUSE, on the American River at the foot of Riley St., performed the first long-distance transmission of hydroelectric power to Sacramento in 1895. Now a state historic park and national landmark, it is part of Folsom Lake State Recreation Area *(see Recreation Chart)*. Wed.-Sun. noon-4; closed major holidays. Tours of powerhouse and dam free. Parking $2. Phone (916) 985-4843 or 988-0205 to arrange powerhouse tours, (916) 989-7275 for dam tours, or (916) 988-1707 for additional information.

FORT BRAGG (D-1) pop. 6,100, elev. 80′

Fort Bragg was established in 1857 to oversee the Mendocino Indian Reservation. When the reservation was moved, the fort was abandoned and subsequently became a lumber and port town. Noyo Harbor, at the south end of town, is a small commercial fishing port; fishing and whale-watching cruises are available. Fort Bragg lies on a scenic stretch of SR 1 that extends from Leggett to Sausalito.

Fort Bragg-Mendocino Coast Chamber of Commerce: 332 N. Main St., P.O. Box 1141, Fort Bragg, CA 95437; phone (707) 961-6300 or (800) 726-2780.

SAVE **MENDOCINO COAST BOTANICAL GARDENS,** 2 mi. s. on SR 1, encompasses 47 acres of lush woods, meadows and gardens. Paths lead from a nursery through the gardens, "Fern Canyon" and native forest to scenic ocean bluffs. The 1-mile loop trail to the Pacific is a leisurely 30-minute walk. Other paths pass rhododendrons and fuchsias. Free electric carts are available. Food is available. Allow 1 hour minimum. Daily 9-5, Mar.-Oct.; 9-4, rest of year. Closed Thanksgiving and Dec. 25. Admission $6; over 60, $5; ages 13-17, $3; ages 6-12, $1. Phone (707) 964-4352.

SAVE **SKUNK TRAIN,** departing from Skunk Depot on Laurel St. w. off SR 1, travels from coastal

Fort Bragg to Willits through Northspur, at an elevation of 1,750 feet. The 40-mile trip passes through redwood groves, two tunnels and crosses and recrosses the Noyo River. The train's unusual name derives from the gas engines used to power the passenger rail cars that went into use in 1925. The Skunk Line operates different trains, including vintage 1925 and 1935 motorcars as well as engines powered by diesel and steam. For reservations write Skunk Train, P.O. Box 907, Fort Bragg, CA 95437.

One-way, full- and half-day trips daily from Fort Bragg or Willits, June-Sept.; one-way trips daily from Fort Bragg and Willits, and full- and half-day trips daily only from Fort Bragg, rest of year. Closed Jan. 1, Thanksgiving and Dec. 25. Super Skunk, with open observation cars, also makes the run in summer. Full-day round-trip fare $35; ages 3-11, $18. Half-day fare $25; ages 3-11, $13. Round-trip to Northspur (3.5 hours) $25; ages 3-11, $13. MC, VI. Phone (707) 964-6371 or (800) 777-5865. *See ad p. 448.*

FORTUNA (B-1) pop. 8,800, elev. 51′

Established in 1875 as Springville, after the numerous springs in the surrounding hills, Fortuna was renamed Slide and finally, Fortuna by its "fortunate" citizens. The Redwood Empire surrounds the town.

Fortuna Chamber of Commerce: 735 14th St., P.O. Box 797, Fortuna, CA 95540; phone (707) 725-3959.

CHAPMAN'S GEM AND MINERAL SHOP AND MUSEUM, 4 mi. s. off US 101, has displays of fossils, gems, minerals, petrified wood and American Indian artifacts. Allow 30 minutes minimum. Mon.-Sat. 10-5, Sun. 1-5, May-Sept.; Mon. and Wed.-Sat. 10-5, Sun. 1-5, rest of year. Closed Easter, Thanksgiving and Dec. 25. Donations. Phone (707) 725-4732.

THE FORTUNA DEPOT MUSEUM, e. of US 101 in Rohner Park, presents local history exhibits in a restored 1893 Northwestern-Pacific depot. Included are displays about fishing, logging, railroading and barbed wire. Allow 30 minutes minimum. Daily 10-4:30, June 1-Labor Day; Wed.-Sun. noon-4:30, rest of year. Free. Phone (707) 725-7645.

FREMONT (P-3) pop. 173,300, elev. 53′

Fremont was created in 1956 by the incorporation of five southeastern San Francisco Bay communities and their adjacent agricultural lands.

Spanish priests and native Ohlones founded a mission in this area in 1797. Reputedly, pioneer John Fremont, for whom the city is named, was so taken with the mission that he offered to buy the adjacent property for his house. The gold rush transformed the mission-based trade and agricultural center into a boisterous supply stop for miners. The use of salt in extracting silver from the Comstock Lode stimulated salt production along San Francisco Bay.

By the 1800s artesian springs had turned Fremont into a resort area. It was a motion picture location as well; Essanay Studio began a 4-year production stint in 1912, and Charlie Chaplin filmed "The Tramp" in 1915. Traces of the past provide a backdrop for the futuristic city hall that overlooks Lake Elizabeth and Central Park.

Fremont Chamber of Commerce: 39488 Stevenson Pl., Ste. 100, Fremont, CA 94539; phone (510) 795-2244.

ARDENWOOD HISTORIC FARM, on Ardenwood/ Newark Blvd., .2 mi. n. of SR 84, is a living-history project depicting farm life from the 1870s to the 1920s. The complex contains the Patterson house, a farmyard, gardens, period shops, a picnic area and farm animals. Haywagon and horse-drawn rail car rides as well as guided house tours are available. The farm is open for Christmas tours in early December.

Tues.-Sun. 10-4. Admission Thurs.-Sun. $5; over 62 and ages 13-17, $4; ages 4-12, $3.50. Admission Tues.-Wed. $1; ages 4-17, 50c. Additional admission is charged during events. Phone (510) 796-0663, or 791-4196 for information about house tours, or 797-5621 for picnic reservations.

COYOTE HILLS REGIONAL PARK is at 8000 Patterson Ranch Rd. The park is a 966-acre wildlife sanctuary containing 2,400-year-old Indian shell mounds and a reconstructed Indian village. The park also has more than 40 miles of hiking, bicycling and jogging trails; a museum; a visitor center; a boardwalk through a freshwater marsh; picnic facilities; and weekend nature programs.

Park open daily 8-dusk. Visitor center and museum open Tues.-Sun. 9:30-5; closed Thanksgiving and Dec. 25. Day-use fee $3.50 per private vehicle. Leashed dogs are permitted; fee $1. Phone (510) 795-9385.

★ **DON EDWARDS SAN FRANCISCO BAY NATIONAL WILDLIFE REFUGE,** on Marshlands Rd., protects 20,000 acres for migratory birds using the Pacific flyway and for the endangered species of San Francisco Bay. An interpretive center overlooking Dumbarton Bridge has dioramas depicting area wildlife as well as a changing film series and weekend interpretive walks. The road to a fishing pier, 2.5 miles from the center, is closed to automobile traffic April through August. Wildlife viewing is best October through April. Trails open 7 a.m.-dusk. Center open Tues.-Sun 10-5. Free. Phone (510) 792-0222.

FREMONT CENTRAL PARK, 40000 Paseo Padre Pkwy., includes a waterfowl refuge, lake, bicycling and jogging trails, and sailboat, kayak, canoe and paddleboat rentals. Picnicking is permitted. A golf driving range and tennis courts are available. Daily dawn-10 p.m. Free. Nonmotorized boat launch fee $3. Swimming fee $2.50, in summer. Phone (510) 791-4340.

★ **MISSION SAN JOSE CHAPEL AND MUSEUM,** 43300 Mission Blvd., was founded in 1797. The reconstructed church has an unusually elegant interior, containing crystal chandeliers, murals, religious paintings and a gold leaf altar. The mission contains a small museum, which displays old paintings, photographs, mission period artifacts and exhibits about the Ohlone Indians and the mission restoration. Daily 10-5; closed Jan. 1, Easter, Thanksgiving and Dec. 25. Donations. Phone (510) 657-1797.

FRESNO (G-4) pop. 354,200, elev. 294′

More than a million acres in the San Joaquin Valley are irrigated; on this land grow the grapes, oranges and cotton that make Fresno County one of the nation's agricultural leaders. More turkeys are raised in this area than anywhere else in the country.

Blossom Trail is a scenic 63-mile self-guiding tour encompassing vineyards, orchards and historical points of interest. The trail is a profusion of almond, apricot, peach, plum and nectarine blossoms from late February through March. A map of the trail is available from the convention & visitors bureau.

Guided tours of Kearney Mansion Museum, 7160 W. Kearney Blvd. in Kearney Park, feature many original furnishings and wallcoverings; phone (559) 441-0862 Also of historical interest is the 1889 Meux Home Museum, 1007 R St. at Tulare. Guided tours are offered weekends; phone (559) 233-8007.

Fresno Convention & Visitors Bureau: 808 M St., Fresno, CA 93721; phone (559) 233-0836 or (800) 788-0836.

FRESNO ART MUSEUM, 2233 N. First St. in Radio Park, offers changing exhibits of national and international artists in eight galleries. Bonner Auditorium features a Fresno Public Theater and concert series. Allow 1 hour minimum. Tues.-Fri. 10-5, Sat.-Sun. noon-5; closed holidays and 1 full week in Aug. Admission $2, over 62 and students with ID $1, under 15 free; free to all Tues. Phone (559) 441-4221.

FRESNO METROPOLITAN MUSEUM OF ART, HISTORY AND SCIENCE, 1555 Van Ness Ave., features an Asian art collection and the Salzer collection of European and American still-life paintings displayed alternately with regional history, hands-on and temporary exhibits. Allow 1 hour minimum. Tues.-Sun. 11-5; closed Jan. 1, Easter, Thanksgiving and Dec. 25. Admission $4; over 64, students with ID and ages 4-12, $3; $1 to all first Wed. of the month. Phone (559) 441-1444.

ROEDING PARK, US 99 via the Olive Ave. or Belmont Ave. exits, features recreational facilities; Rotary Playland, which has a carrousel, rides and a miniature railway; historic Fort Miller Blockhouse; and the Japanese-American

War Memorial. Allow 1 hour, 30 minutes minimum. Daily 7 a.m.-10 p.m.. Park fee $1 per private vehicle. Phone (559) 498-4239.

Chaffee Zoological Gardens, on Olive Ave., houses mammals, birds and reptiles amid dense vegetation and winding pathways. The computerized Reptile House modifies temperature, humidity and light cycles to mimic the environment from which each species comes. South American plants and animals share the rain forest habitat. Food is available. Daily 9-5, Mar.-Oct.; 10-4, rest of year. Admission $4.95; over 62, $3.50; ages 2-11, $2.50. Phone (559) 498-2671.

Storyland, 890 W. Belmont Ave., is a children's attraction with a fairytale theme featuring a castle. Mon.-Fri. 10-3, Sat.-Sun. 10-5, May 1-Labor Day; Sat.-Sun. and school holidays 10-5, day after Labor Day-Oct. 31 and President's Day weekend-Apr. 30; Sat.-Sun. 10-4 in Nov. Admission $2.75; over 62, $2.25; ages 3-12, $1.75. Phone (559) 264-2235.

WILD WATER ADVENTURES, 11413 E. Shaw Ave., 7 mi. e. of Clovis Ave., offers more than 20 water rides and amusements, including water slides and flumes; Gold Rush Mountain, a water tube ride; Vortex, an enclosed inner tube with special effects; a large wave pool; large swimming pool; a small fishing lake; and Adventure Bay, a children's play area. Picnic facilities, baseball fields, volleyball courts, horseshoe pits and food are available. Glass items and containers are not permitted.

Open mid-May through Sept. 30. Hours may vary; phone ahead. Admission $19.99; age 3 to under 48 inches tall $15.99; over age 62, $6.99; under age 2 free. DS, MC, VI. Phone (559) 299-9453, or (800) 564-9453 in the Central Valley area.

FULLERTON (C-7)
pop. 114,100, elev. 157'

Established in 1887, Fullerton was typical of western towns of the era. The chaos of the years of railroad construction gave way to the influx of stable families. Citrus crops and oil fields were instrumental to building the city's economic base.

Fullerton Chamber of Commerce: 219 E. Commonwealth Ave., Fullerton, CA 92832-0529; phone (714) 871-3100.

FULLERTON ARBORETUM, 1900 Associated Rd. at Yorba Linda Blvd., is a 26-acre botanical garden. Paths meander through the cultivated grounds passing lakes, streams and a waterfall. The 1894 Victorian Heritage House, on the premises, is open for tours Sun. 2-4, weekdays by appointment. Arboretum open daily 8-4:45; closed Jan. 1, Thanksgiving and Dec. 25. Donations. Phone (714) 278-3579.

MUCKENTHALER CULTURAL CENTER, 1201 W. Malvern Ave., was built in 1924 in the Italian Renaissance style. The first floor houses changing art exhibits. Dinner theater performances are held in the summer. Tues.-Sat. 10-4, Sun. noon-5; closed holidays. Admission $2, over 59 and students with ID $1. Phone (714) 738-6595.

GARDEN GROVE (C-7)
pop. 143,100, elev. 85'

The arrival of the railroad in 1905 drastically changed the face of this once-quiet farming community. Garden Grove's spirit twice was tested in the early 20th century: A 1916 flood left the town center under four feet of water, and an earthquake damaged the old town sector in 1933. The city persevered, however, and is now a dynamic presence.

Garden Grove Chamber of Commerce: 11277 Garden Grove Blvd., Suite A, Garden Grove, CA 92843; phone (714) 638-7950.

CRYSTAL CATHEDRAL OF THE REFORMED CHURCH IN AMERICA, 12141 Lewis St. at Chapman Ave., is an all-glass sanctuary enclosed by 10,000 mirrored windows; it was designed by Philip Johnson. Crean Tower contains Arvella Schuller Carillon and Mary Hood Prayer Chapel. Tours are given Mon.-Sat. 9-3:30 (church functions affect tour times); closed holidays. Donations. Phone (714) 971-4013.

GEYSERVILLE (M-1) elev. 209'

LAKE SONOMA VISITOR CENTER, 3333 Skaggs Springs Rd., displays local flora and fauna and provides information about recreational activities in the Lake Sonoma/Warm Springs Dam area. King salmon, silver salmon and steelhead are raised at Don Clausen Fish Hatchery. A swim area is available at Yorty Creek. Allow 2 hours minimum. Daily 9:30-7, Memorial Day-Labor Day; Thurs.-Mon. 9:30-4, rest of year. Free. Phone (707) 433-9483.

GILROY (G-3) pop. 31,500, elev. 194'

When Scotsman John Cameron jumped a British ship in Monterey Bay and traveled to Ortega Ranch, he adopted his mother's maiden name, Gilroy, and married the ranch owner's daughter. A small town developed around his property; orchards were planted and cattle introduced, and the railroad found its way to the settlement. By 1870 Gilroy had lost the ranch to gambling debts, but the town was incorporated and continued to thrive.

Gilroy Historical Museum, in the Carnegie Library Building on the corner of Fifth and Church streets, displays historical photographs and artifacts of the area; phone (408) 848-0470.

Gilroy Visitors Bureau: 7780 Monterey St., Gilroy, CA 95020; phone (408) 842-6436.

Self-guiding tours: The visitors bureau and Gilroy Historical Museum offer a walking-tour booklet for 60c.

GLENDALE—
see Los Angeles p. 121.

GLEN ELLEN (N-2) pop. 1,000, elev. 230'

JACK LONDON STATE HISTORIC PARK, 800 acres 1 mi. w. on London Ranch Rd., encompasses the author's ranch, home and grave. The two-story house contains his papers, personal belongings and mementos of his travels, including South Pacific art objects. The burnt ruins of Wolf House, the 26-room mansion he built but never lived in, are nearby. The original cottage which London purchased is open weekends. No off-road vehicles are allowed.

Allow 1 hour, 30 minutes minimum. Park open daily 9:30-7, Apr.-Oct.; 9:30-5, rest of year. Museum open daily 10-5; closed Jan. 1, Thanksgiving and Dec. 25. Fee $6 per private vehicle; over 62, $5 per private vehicle. Leashed dogs are permitted except on back trails; fee $1. Phone (707) 938-5216. *See Recreation Chart.*

GOLDEN GATE NATIONAL RECREATION AREA—
see San Francisco p. 208.

GOLETA (J-4) pop. 30,000, elev. 33'

Once a vast orchard, Goleta now is known for its recreational offerings. Its proximity to both forests and beaches attracts outdoor enthusiasts.

Goleta Valley Chamber of Commerce: 5730 Hollister Ave., Suite 1, Goleta, CA 93117; phone (805) 967-4618.

SOUTH COAST RAILROAD MUSEUM, 300 N. Los Carneros Rd., is centered on the wooden Goleta Depot that was built in 1901 and used until 1973. Antique railroad artifacts, photographs and hands-on exhibits are in the agency office and passenger waiting room. A 300-square-foot HO-scale model railroad is displayed, and an old Southern Pacific caboose is open for inspection. Allow 30 minutes minimum. Wed.-Sun. 1-4. Miniature train rides Wed. and Fri. 2-3:30, Sat.-Sun. 1:15-3:45. Donations. Phone (805) 964-3540.

UNIVERSITY OF CALIFORNIA, SANTA BARBARA, 2 mi. s. of US 101 via Ward Memorial Blvd. (SR 217), occupies 989 acres near the ocean. A major landmark is the 175-foot-high Storke Tower, which houses a 61-bell carillon heard twice each hour. Campus tours are given regularly Mon.-Fri. at 11 and 2. Admission Mon.-Fri. is by a $5 pass (includes campus map and parking fee) which can be purchased at the entrance gate. Phone (805) 893-8175.

GONZALES (G-3) pop. 4,700, elev. 131'

In the heart of the Salinas Valley, Gonzales is sustained by agriculture; products include lettuce, broccoli, strawberries and grapes. Among recreational offerings are boating, water skiing, swimming and hiking.

Gonzales Chamber of Commerce: Box 216, Gonzales, CA 93926; phone (831) 675-9019.

GRASS VALLEY (D-3) pop. 9,000, elev. 2,420'

In 1850 George Knight stubbed his toe on a piece of quartz laced with gold and put Grass Valley on the map. Aided by advanced mining techniques that first were developed and used in this region, Grass Valley ultimately became the richest gold-mining town in California. Unlike most gold-rush towns, Grass Valley achieved prosperity that outlasted its mining industry. Agriculture, high-tech manufacturing and tourism now anchor the economy.

Grass Valley & Nevada County Chamber of Commerce: 248 Mill St., Grass Valley, CA 95945-6783; phone (530) 273-4667 or (800) 655-4667.

EMPIRE MINE STATE HISTORIC PARK, 1 mi. e. of SR 49 at 10791 E. Empire St., produced nearly 6 million ounces of gold during its operation. The park has 10 miles of hiking trails and a mine with 367 miles of passageways; restored buildings include the owner's cottage, clubhouse, a smithy, a hoist house and a machine shop. Films are shown daily at the visitor center. Tours and lectures are offered daily.

Allow 2 hours minimum. Daily 10-5, Sept.-Apr.; 9-5, in May; 9-6, rest of year. Admission $3; ages 6-12, $1. Fee for dogs $1. Phone (530) 273-8522. *See Recreation Chart.*

NORTH STAR MINING MUSEUM, on Allison Ranch Rd. at the s. end of Mill St., houses the three-story Pelton wheel, a type of water wheel used for hydroelectric power; an assay room; a smithy; a stamp mill; and a dynamite-packing machine. The museum features one of the few operable Cornish pumps in the country. A collection of gold samples also is shown. Picnicking is permitted. Daily 10-5, May-Oct. Donations. Phone (530) 273-4255.

GROVELAND (F-4) elev. 2,846'

In its formative years, the gold-boom town went through a pair of unpleasant names—Savage's Diggings and Garrotte—before its citizens agreed on a more placid one, Groveland.

RECREATIONAL ACTIVITIES
White-water Rafting

- [SAVE] **ARTA River Trips** has departure points on several rivers. Write 24000 Casa Loma Rd.,

Groveland, CA 95321. Daily Apr.-Oct. Phone (209) 962-7873 or (800) 323-2782.

GUERNEVILLE (M-1)
pop. 2,000, elev. 56'

Lumber mills flourished during Guerneville's early years. Railroads were built to ship wood from the town, and agricultural endeavors were undertaken on the cleared land.

The Russian River Chamber of Commerce: 16200 First St., P.O. Box 331, Guerneville, CA 95446; phone (707) 869-9000.

WINERIES

• **Korbel Champagne Cellars**, 13250 River Rd. Daily 9-5, May-Sept.; 9-4, rest of year. Phone (707) 887-2294.

HALF MOON BAY—
see San Francisco p. 209.

HANFORD (H-4) pop. 30,900, elev. 248'

Founded in 1882 in the San Joaquin Valley, Hanford was named for a Southern Pacific Railroad paymaster who became a power in the community. He paid millions of dollars of workers' wages in gold. Hanford once claimed one of the largest Chinese communities in California. In China Alley, a remnant of that community, are Taoist Temple and a landmark restaurant operated by the descendants of the family who started the business in 1883.

Courthouse Square, the center of historic Hanford, includes a renovated carrousel and many specialty shops.

Hanford Visitor Agency: 200 Santa Fe Ave., Suite D, Hanford, CA 93230; phone (559) 582-5024.

Self-guiding tours: Maps for tours of historic Hanford are available from the visitor agency.

HANFORD CARNEGIE MUSEUM, 109 E. Eighth St., is in a Romanesque-style library built in 1906. Among items depicting Hanford and Kings County history are clothes, including a dress that belonged to Amelia Earhart, furniture and photographs. Guided tours are available by appointment. Allow 30 minutes minimum. Tues.-Fri. noon-3, Sat. noon-4. Admission $1, students 50c. Phone (559) 584-1367.

HAYWARD (P-3) pop. 111,300, elev. 111'

HAYWARD AREA HISTORICAL SOCIETY MUSEUM, 22701 Main St., is a former post office that houses memorabilia of early Hayward and southern Alameda County. Photographs, maps, tools and a vintage fire truck are displayed.

Changing exhibits also are presented. Allow 1 hour minimum. Mon.-Fri. 11-4, Sat. noon-4, Sun. 1-4; closed holidays. Admission $1; ages 6-12, 50c. Phone (510) 581-0223.

JAPANESE GARDENS, 22373 N. Third St. off Crescent Ave., encompasses 3.3 acres of Japanese and native California trees, rocks and plants arranged in the traditional Japanese style. The area includes a small pond containing koi and goldfish, and a teahouse. Daily 8:30-4. Free. Phone (510) 881-6700.

THE McCONAGHY HOME & CARRIAGE HOUSE, 18701 Hesperian Blvd. next to Kennedy Park, is a spacious 1886 house, restored and furnished in period. A carriage house is next to the house. Between the two buildings is a tank house that once pumped water for the estate. Allow 1 hour minimum. Guided tours Thurs.-Sun. 1-3:30, Feb.-Dec. Last tour at closing. Closed holidays and Thanksgiving week. Admission $3; over 64, $2; ages 6-12, 50c. Special rates apply during Victorian Christmas. Phone (510) 276-3010.

HEALDSBURG (M-1)
pop. 9,500, elev. 106'

Healdsburg, founded in 1867, was once a part of the 48,800-acre Sotoyome Rancho owned by widow Josefa Fitch and her 11 children. While the family sought refuge at Sutter's Fort during American Indian uprisings and the Mexican War, Harmon Heald and many other failed gold miners illegally squatted on her land. Fitch won ownership of the original title to the rancho, but Heald donated some of the rancho he had bought for a park, school, cemetery and church and then named this new town after himself.

Healdsburg Chamber of Commerce: 217 Healdsburg Ave., Healdsburg, CA 95448; phone (707) 433-6935, or (800) 648-9922 in Calif.

Self-guiding tours: Maps for tours of historic buildings as well as a winery map are available at the chamber of commerce for $1.

THE HEALDSBURG MUSEUM is 2 blks. e. of the downtown plaza at 221 Matheson St. Housed in the refurbished 1910 Healdsburg Carnegie Library, the museum preserves and exhibits a range of relics and documents pertaining to northern Sonoma County history. Items displayed include 19th-century weapons, tools, textiles and crafts along with Pomo Indian basketry and other artifacts. Allow 30 minutes minimum. Tues.-Sun. 11-4; closed major holidays. Free. Phone (707) 431-3325.

WINERIES

• **Johnson's Alexander Valley Wines**, 7 mi. n.e. at 8333 SR 128. Daily 10-5; closed Jan. 1, Thanksgiving and Dec. 25. Phone (707) 433-2319.

- **Simi Winery**, US 101 to Dry Creek Rd., e. to Healdsburg Ave., then 1 mi. n. Daily 10-4:30; closed holidays. Phone (707) 433-6981.

★ HEARST CASTLE—
see San Simeon p. 216.

HEMET (C-9) pop. 36,100, elev. 1,597′

Hemet Visitor & Tourism Council: 395 E. Latham Ave., Hemet, CA 92543; phone (909) 658-3211 or (800) 334-9344.

RAMONA PAGEANT, presented in the Ramona Bowl, 2 mi. s.e., is a dramatization of Helen Hunt Jackson's 1884 novel. This historical drama is a love story depicting American Indian life 1870-80 and features a cast of more than 400. Send a request for a ticket application form with a stamped reply envelope to: Ramona Pageant Assoc., 27400 Ramona Bowl Rd., Hemet, CA 92544. Sat.-Sun. afternoons, late Apr.-early May. Admission $16-$25. Phone (909) 658-3111 or (800) 645-4465.

HOLLYWOOD—
see Los Angeles p. 121.

HOOPA (B-1) pop. 1,000, elev. 300′

HOOPA TRIBAL MUSEUM, on SR 96 in Hoopa Shopping Mall, displays baskets, jewelry, tools, a redwood canoe, hats and ceremonial clothing still used in Hoopa tribal events. Tours to the ceremonial grounds and villages may be arranged by appointment. Displayed are collections of new and restored baskets. Allow 1 hour minimum. Mon.-Fri. 8-5, Sat. 10-4. Donations. Phone (530) 625-4110.

HUMBOLDT-TOIYABE NATIONAL FOREST—
see Nevada p. 260.

HUNTINGTON BEACH (C-6) pop. 181,500, elev. 28′

Named after Henry E. Huntington, who brought the Redline-Pacific Electric Railway to what was then a small seaside village, Huntington Beach was incorporated in 1909. In 1920 an oil boom increased the population from 1,500 to 5,000 in less than a month, and in the following years agriculture and oil provided a base for continued growth. One of Orange County's largest cities, Huntington Beach boasts numerous parks and 8.5 miles of uninterrupted beach, all connected by a paved path in the sand.

Along the Pacific Coast Highway between Goldenwest and Brookhurst streets, Bolsa Chica and Huntington state beaches and Huntington City Beach provide areas for swimming, picnicking and surfing *(see Recreation Chart)*. Parking fees are charged. Huntington Beach International Surfing Museum, 411 Olive Ave., displays surfboards, photographs and other memorabilia commemorating this ocean sport.

The largest city park is Central Park, on Golden West Street between Slater and Ellis avenues. The park is home to hundreds of bird species, with walking and bicycling trails that wind past ponds, waterways and groves. Park Bench Cafe caters to a canine clientele. The park also has equestrian and nature centers.

Huntington Beach Central Library and Cultural Center, 7777 Talbert Ave., has a large children's library and one of the state's largest genealogy departments. Its 320-seat -Huntington Beach Playhouse has performances year-round. Fishing from the 1,583-foot-long concrete municipal pier is a favorite pastime.

Huntington Beach Conference and Visitors Bureau: 417 Main St., Huntington Beach, CA 92648-5131; phone (714) 969-3492 or (800) 729-6232.

Shopping areas: Huntington Beach Mall, at Beach Boulevard and Center Avenue near I-405, has a three-story Barnes & Noble Booksellers, major chain stores and specialty shops. Old World Village, on Center Avenue across from the H.B. Mall, maintains a Bavarian atmosphere with cobblestone streets winding among specialty shops and restaurants.

BOLSA CHICA INTERPRETIVE CENTER, off the Pacific Coast Hwy. at 3842 Warner Ave., features displays describing the surrounding Bolsa Chica Ecological Reserve, which contains 185 acres of restored wetlands. The reserve supports such rare waterfowl as avocets, egrets, plovers and least terns. A 1.5-mile walkway with explanatory signs leads through the reserve. Center open Tues.-Fri. 10-4. Trail open daily dawn-dusk. Closed Jan. 1, Easter, July 4, Thanksgiving and Dec. 25. Free. Phone (714) 846-1114.

IDYLLWILD (K-7) elev. 5,500′

Idyllwild is a resort community in the San Jacinto Mountains. Founded as a logging community in the late 1800s, the area today is known for hiking trails and rock-climbing opportunities. Phone the chamber of commerce for 24-hour recorded information about road conditions, accommodations and events.

Idyllwild Chamber of Commerce: 54295 Village Center Dr., P.O. Box 304, Idyllwild, CA 92549; phone (909) 659-3259.

INDEPENDENCE (G-6) elev. 3,925′

EASTERN CALIFORNIA MUSEUM, 3 blks. w. of the courthouse at 155 Grant St., illustrates area history, anthropology, botany and geology. Highlights include antique farm and mining equipment. Little Pine Village features restored and re-created structures from the 1880s, including a smithy and assay office. Of interest is the exhibit dealing with the Manzanar World War II Relocation Camp for Japanese-Americans; the camp, a national historic site, is 5 miles from Independence. Wed.-Mon. 10-4; closed Jan. 1, Easter, Thanksgiving and Dec. 25. Donations. Phone (760) 878-0364 or 878-0258.

INDIO (K-8) pop. 36,800, elev. -22'

Often called the date capital of the nation, Indio is a distribution point for the dates, grapefruit, grapes and melons produced in the Coachella Valley.

Indio Chamber of Commerce: 82-503 Hwy. 111, P.O. Box TTT, Indio, CA 92202; phone (760) 347-0676.

COACHELLA VALLEY MUSEUM AND CULTURAL CENTER, 82616 Miles Ave., is in a former house and medical office built in 1926. The museum displays American Indian artifacts, old farm and household equipment, changing art exhibits and a smithy. A sawmill is on the grounds. A large relief map shows the development of the desert's water system, and dioramas explain the date-growing industry. Wed.-Sat. 10-4, Sun. 1-4, Oct.-May; Fri.-Sun. 1-4 in June and Sept. Closed holidays. Admission $2; over 54 and under 12, $1. Phone (760) 342-6651.

GENERAL PATTON MEMORIAL MUSEUM, 30 mi. e. off I-10 at Chiriaco Summit, is built on the site of the Gen. George S. Patton Desert Training Center. The museum contains memorabilia from World War II and other eras of American military history and includes displays of tanks and artillery. A 26-minute video highlights the general's life and career. The development of Southern California's water system and 11 desert training camp sites are indicated on a relief map. Daily 9:30-4:30; closed Thanksgiving and Dec. 25. Admission $4; over 62, $3.50; under 12 free with adult. Phone (760) 227-3483.

A Starred Attraction

When you see a ★ before an attraction, it's a **must** see!

INDUSTRY—
see Los Angeles p. 122.

INGLEWOOD—
see Los Angeles p. 122.

INYO NATIONAL FOREST

Elevations in the forest range from 3,700 ft. in Owens Valley to 14,494 ft. at the summit of Mount Whitney. Refer to AAA maps for additional elevation information.

Inyo National Forest parallels US 6 and US 395 for 165 miles between the eastern California towns of Inyokern and Lee Vining. Mount Whitney, at 14,494 feet, is the highest point in the contiguous United States. The forest also contains portions of the Pacific Crest Trail and the John Muir Trail. The eastern escarpment of the Sierra Nevada and the Ancient Bristlecone Pine Forest in the White Mountains rise to 14,246 feet between US 6 and the Nevada border. Almost all of the Sierra's highest peaks are within 10 to 15 miles of US 395.

Vehicle travel is restricted in Devils Postpile National Monument *(see place listing p. 71)* and the Reds Meadow area of the forest: Only vehicles with camping permits are allowed beyond the Minaret Vista turnoff between 7:30 a.m. and 5:30 p.m., June 1-Labor Day.

All others are required to use a shuttle bus that operates during the restricted times. The 2-hour round trip makes 10 stops, including the Devils Postpile ranger station, where trails lead to recreation areas. Tickets and schedule and fare information are available at Mammoth Mountain Inn. Parking is free.

Mammoth and June mountains have ski areas that are popular in winter, while mountain biking, hiking, camping, fishing and backpacking are the main summertime diversions. Chairlift rides to the top of Mammoth Mountain provide outstanding views and access to hiking trails. Chairlift rides are available daily 9:30-5:30, mid-June to mid-Sept. (weather and wind permitting). Fare $10; ages 7-12, $5. Phone (760) 934-2571.

Minaret Vista, at 9,175 feet, offers a sweeping view of Ritter Range. A store and cafe, as well as saddle and pack horses, are available at Reds Meadow. Permits are required for all overnight trips in wilderness areas. Contact the Inyo National Forest Wilderness Reservation Service, P.O. Box 430, Big Pine, CA 93513; phone (888) 374-3773.

Roads throughout the remainder of the forest provide scenic drives. An interagency visitor center is south of Lone Pine at the junction of US 395 and SR 136. Center open daily 8-4:50; hours are extended in summer. Closed Jan. 1, Thanksgiving and Dec. 24-25. Phone (760) 876-4252. For additional information the forest supervisor's office is at 873 N. Main St., Bishop, CA 93514; phone (760) 873-2400. *See Recreation Chart and the AAA California/Nevada CampBook.*

BISHOP CREEK CANYON is 9 mi. w. of Bishop on SR 168. Lined by 1,000-foot granite cliffs, the canyon is a popular fishing area late April through October. Developed campgrounds, hiking trails and food are available.

JUNE LAKE LOOP RECREATION AREA off SR 158, covers approximately 60,000 acres and contains portions of the Pacific Crest and John Muir trails, Mono Basin National Forest Scenic Area *(see place listing p. 139)* and June Mountain Winter Sports Area. Mono Craters, Lee Vining Canyon and Tioga Pass are nearby. Free. Phone (760) 647-3044.

IRVINE (C-7) pop. 110,300, elev. 208'

Irvine is a planned community built on Irvine Ranch, a former Spanish land grant. Old Town Irvine on Sand Canyon Rd. incorporates historic buildings that once were part of Irvine Ranch. A lima bean warehouse built in 1895 houses shops and a restaurant; former grain silos have become one wing of a major hotel. Among smaller buildings built in the early 1900s, one is now a post office. The Irvine campus of the University of California overlooks Upper Newport Bay.

Irvine Museum exhibits American impressionist landscapes (1890-1930) which depict well-known and lesser-known areas of the state. The museum is on the 12th floor of the Tower 17 Corporate Offices Building at 18881 Von Karman Ave.; phone (949) 476-2565.

Irvine Meadows Amphitheatre, 8808 Irvine Center Dr., presents outdoor concerts May through September. Amphitheater and lawn seating are available; phone (949) 855-2863.

Irvine Chamber of Commerce: 17755 Sky Park E., #101, Irvine, CA 92614; phone (949) 660-9112.

WILD RIVERS WATERPARK, 8770 Irvine Center Dr., encompasses 20 acres devoted to more than 40 water rides and attractions. The park includes inner tube rides, waterslides, two wave pools, activity pools, lounging areas, children's play areas and picnic facilities. Open mid-May through late Sept.; phone for days and hours. Admission (includes most rides) $20.95; spectators $20.95 with a $7 refund; ages 3-9, $16.95; over 54, $9.95. After 4 p.m. $9.95. Parking $4. MC, VI. Phone (949) 768-9453.

JACKSON (E-3) pop. 3,500, elev. 1,200'

Many buildings along Jackson's narrow streets were destroyed by fire in 1862 and subsequently were rebuilt. North of town are several mine headframes; one shaft is approximately 6,000 feet deep. Kennedy Gold Mine Tours offers visitors tours of the buildings and other structures that made up a mining site closed in 1942; phone (209) 223-9542.

Amador County Chamber of Commerce: 125 Peek St., Suite B, P.O. Box 596, Jackson, CA 95642; phone (209) 223-0350 or (800) 649-4988.

AMADOR COUNTY MUSEUM is at 225 Church St. The museum features a working scale model of Kennedy Mine. Allow 30 minutes minimum. Wed.-Sun. 10-4. Mine model tours are offered Sat.-Sun. on the hour 11-3. Donations. Mine model tours $1. Phone (209) 223-6386.

JAMESTOWN (F-3) pop. 2,200, elev. 1,405'

The first gold discovery in Tuolumne County was made near Jamestown in 1848. "Jimtown," as it once was called, has served as a backdrop for such movies as "High Noon" and "Butch Cassidy and the Sundance Kid." Several buildings in town date to the 1870s.

JIMTOWN 1849 GOLD MINING CAMP, 18170 Main St., is a living-history re-creation. Among the camp's buildings is a cabin said to be once inhabited by Mark Twain. Gold panning is available. Allow 1 hour minimum. Daily 9-5. Admission free. Gold panning $10-$70. MC, VI. Phone (209) 984-4653.

RAILTOWN 1897 STATE HISTORIC PARK, on 5th Ave., comprises 26 acres which include an interpretive center, a roundhouse, station, trains and yard facilities. Sierra Railway Co. began operating from Jamestown in 1897, carrying passengers and freight throughout the gold-mining area. Visitors can observe the maintenance and restoration of the railroad equipment.

Guided tours include a videotape presentation. Tours of the roundhouse and shop are given daily 9:30-4:30. Train rides are given Sat.-Sun. on the hour 11-3, early Apr.-Oct. 31. Tours $2; ages 6-12, $1. Train $6; ages 6-12, $3. Phone (209) 984-3953 or 984-1600.

JENNER (E-1) elev. 12'

FORT ROSS STATE HISTORIC PARK, 12 mi. n. on SR 1, was the site of a trading post and fort established by Russians in 1812 to protect their claim against the Spanish. Restored or reconstructed buildings within the stockade include the chapel, officers' barracks, commandant's house and blockhouses. The visitor center includes a museum. Living History Day is held the last Saturday in July. Russian Orthodox services are held Memorial Day and July 4.

Allow 1 hour minimum. Grounds daily dawn-dusk. Visitor center daily 10-4:30. Closed Jan. 1, Thanksgiving and Dec. 25. Fee $6 per private vehicle; over 62, $5 per private vehicle. Living History Day admission $10. Phone (707) 847-3286. *See Recreation Chart.*

JOHNSVILLE (D-3)

Johnsville was established in 1872 on the flat at the base of Eureka Peak. Two fires destroyed many of the town's original structures. Ski racing, which originated nearby, is among the popular recreational pursuits.

PLUMAS-EUREKA STATE PARK AND MUSEUM, 4 mi. w. on CR A14 at 310 Johnsville Rd., has a collection of photographs, tools and memorabilia of mining days. A partially restored stamp mill is featured. Allow 30 minutes minimum. Park open daily 24 hours, early May to mid-Oct. Museum open daily 8-4:30, early June to mid-Oct.; schedule may vary according to staff availability, rest of year. Closed Jan. 1, Thanksgiving and Dec. 25. Park admission free. Museum $2; ages 6-12, $1. Camping $16 May 15-Labor Day; $14 rest of year. Phone (530) 836-2380. *See Recreation Chart.*

Elevations in the park range from about 1,800 ft. at Pinto Basin to 5,813 ft. at Quail Mountain. Refer to AAA maps for additional elevation information.

Joshua Tree National Park covers more than 1,238 square miles north of I-10 and east of Desert Hot Springs. This California desert country contains striking granite formations and mountain ranges rising from flat valleys about 1,800 feet above sea level to elevations of more than 5,000 feet. The many spectacular desert plants include Joshua trees, cactuses, ocotillos, smoke trees, palo verdes, piñon pines, Mojave yuccas and an array of spring wildflowers.

The desert supports a wide variety of wildlife, including many resident and migratory birds. The park's largest animal is the desert bighorn sheep.

Wood, gas and supplies must be carried into all of the park's nine primitive campgrounds, and water must be carried into all but Cottonwood and Black Rock. There are entrance stations at Cottonwood Spring, Twentynine Palms and Joshua Tree. The Cottonwood station is open daily 8-4:30. Oasis Visitor Center at Twentynine Palms has displays providing an introduction to the flora, fauna and history of the desert park. The center is open daily 8-5. Park admission $10 per vehicle.

Direct inquiries to the Superintendent, Joshua Tree National Park, 74485 National Park Dr., Twentynine Palms, CA 92277-3597; phone (760) 367-5500. Phone Biospherics Incorporated at (800) 365-2267 for reservations at Black Rock Canyon. *See Recreation Chart and the AAA California/Nevada CampBook.*

JULIAN (L-7) pop. 1,300, elev. 4,220'

Julian is a late 1800s mining town known for its spring wildflowers and autumn apple harvest. Orchards cover the surrounding land, and fall festivals celebrate the harvests.

Julian Chamber of Commerce: 2129 Main St., P.O. Box 1866, Julian, CA 92036; phone (760) 765-1857.

EAGLE MINING CO., n. end of C St., offers a guided tour through a gold mine. Dug through a mountain, the mine brought gold seekers into the area more than 100 years ago. A 1-hour tour details mine history and gold excavation. Daily 10-3 (weather permitting). Admission $7; ages 5-15, $3; under 5, $1. Phone (760) 765-0036.

JULIAN PIONEER MUSEUM, 2811 Washington St., housed in a late 1800s structure, contains

19th-century clothing, household furnishings, photographs of early Julian and tools. There also are American Indian artifacts and mounted animals indigenous to the area. Tues.-Sun. 10-4, Apr.-Nov.; Sat.-Sun. and legal holidays 10-4, rest of year. Closed Jan. 1, Thanksgiving and Dec. 25. Admission $1. Phone (760) 765-0227.

KELSEYVILLE (D-1) pop. 2,900, elev. 1,386'

Called the "Bartlett Pear Capital of the World," Kelseyville is the agricultural center of Lake County. Pear and walnut orchards share the surrounding valley with vineyards.

CLEAR LAKE STATE PARK VISITORS CENTER, 3 mi. n.e. at 5300 Soda Bay Rd., has wildlife dioramas and exhibits depicting the lake environment both on land and in water. A theater presents videos, films and demonstrations. Allow 1 hour minimum. Fri.-Sun. 10-4, May-Sept. Park admission $5 per private vehicle; over 62, $4 per private vehicle. Fee for dogs on leash $1. Phone (707) 279-4293. *See Recreation Chart.*

KENWOOD (N-2) pop. 1,000, elev. 415'

WINERIES

- **Chateau St. Jean Winery,** 8555 Sonoma Hwy. Daily 10-4:30. Phone (707) 833-4134.

KERNVILLE (H-5) pop. 1,700, elev. 2,251'

 RECREATIONAL ACTIVITIES

White-water Rafting

- **Chuck Richards' Whitewater Inc.,** 11316 Kernville Rd., Box W.W. Whitewater, Lake Isabella, CA 93240. Daily May-Sept. Phone (760) 379-4444 or (800) 624-5950.

KING CITY (H-3) pop. 7,600, elev. 330'

King City takes its name from pioneer Charles H. King who bought 13,000 acres of land in 1884 and founded King Ranch. The town was incorporated in 1911. Agriculture sustains King City; products range from broccoli and beets to barley and beans.

King City & Southern Monterey County Chamber of Commerce & Agriculture: 203 Broadway, King City, CA 93930; phone (831) 385-3814.

MISSION SAN ANTONIO DE PADUA is 29 mi. s.w. in Fort Hunter Liggett via Jolon Rd. Founded by Father Junípero Serra on July 14, 1771, it is one of the largest restored and rebuilt missions. Original remains include the well, gristmill, tannery and parts of the aqueduct system. A museum exhibits American Indian artifacts. The mission's annual fiesta is held the second weekend in June. Mon.-Sat. 10-4:30, Sun. 11-5. Donations. Phone (831) 385-4478.

MONTEREY COUNTY AGRICULTURAL AND RURAL LIFE MUSEUM, in San Lorenzo County Park at 1160 Broadway, features a barn with more than 20 exhibits tracing the evolution of agriculture in Monterey County. Other buildings include a restored Spreckels farmhouse, a smithy, a turn-of-the-century schoolhouse of the late 1800s, and an 1887 train depot. Picnicking is permitted. Guided tours are available by appointment.

Allow 30 minutes minimum. Museum open daily 10-4; school, farmhouse and smithy open Sat.-Sun. (also July 4) 11-2, or by appointment. Closed Jan. 1, Thanksgiving and Dec. 25. Donations. Parking Mon.-Thurs. $3, Fri.-Sun. $5. Phone (408) 385-8020.

KINGSBURG (G-5) pop. 7,200, elev. 297'

Kingsburg was established in 1875 by the Southern Pacific Railroad. Swedish emigrants influenced the town's customs and architecture. Today Kingsburg is known as a Swedish village, with many restored buildings dating back to the early 1900s and featuring steep wood-shingled roofs, dormer windows and half-timbers.

California Welcome Center-Kingsburg District Chamber of Commerce: 1776 6th Avenue Dr., Kingsburg, CA 93631; phone (559) 897-2925.

★KINGS CANYON NATIONAL PARK—
see Sequoia and Kings Canyon National Parks p. 222.

KLAMATH (B-1) pop. 200, elev. 29'

Above the Klamath River on aptly named Bear Bridge, two golden bears welcome visitors to the city. Originally gray, the bears were painted in the late '50s or early '60s by a group of residents who set out to give the town a facelift. State government officials repeatedly painted the bears gray to expunge what they had believed was the work of vandals. Upon realizing that the citizens were behind the golden bears, the government relented.

TREES OF MYSTERY PARK, 4 mi. n. on US 101, is a forest of redwoods containing a number of oddly formed trees. Along the Trail of Tall Tales are chainsaw-carved redwood sculptures that depict the legend of Paul Bunyan and other loggers' stories. The End of the Trail Indian Museum contains displays of artifacts and crafts from Plains and Western Indian tribes. Daily dawn-dusk; closed Thanksgiving and Dec. 25. Admission $6.50; over 60, $5; ages 6-12, $4; family rates available. AE, DI, DS, MC, VI. Phone (707) 482-2251 or (800) 848-2982. *See ad p. 485.*

KLAMATH NATIONAL FOREST

Elevations in the forest range from 523 ft. at Somes Bar to 8,563 ft. at Caribou Mountain. Refer to AAA maps for additional elevation information.

Characterized by rugged forested ridges, rushing rivers and high mountain lakes and streams, Klamath National Forest covers about 1,726,000 acres. A small segment of the forest extends into Oregon. Much of this scenic area is included in the Marble Mountain Wilderness and Trinity Alps Wilderness, which are accessible only by trail. Vehicular traffic is prohibited in wilderness areas. Hunting, fishing and white-water rafting opportunities are available.

Good fishing spots abound, and the forest is a prime location for anglers in search of steelhead and salmon. Trout fishing is popular in creeks and high mountain lakes. Outdoor enthusiasts also can camp, hike, horseback ride, ski and snowmobile.

Klamath River Highway and forest roads and trails provide access to the region. For information contact the Forest Supervisor, Klamath National Forest, 1312 Fairlane Rd., Yreka, CA 96097; phone (530) 842-6131. *See Recreation Chart and the AAA California/Nevada CampBook.*

KLAMATH NATIONAL FOREST INTERPRETIVE MUSEUM, 1312 Fairlane Rd. in Yreka, has exhibits about national forests and how they are managed. Displays include dioramas about timber and wildlife preservation, geology, soils, mining and fire prevention. Another exhibit honors Hallie Daggett, the first female forest-fire lookout in the country. Mon.-Fri. 8-4:30; closed holidays. Free. Phone (530) 842-6131 or 841-4484.

RECREATIONAL ACTIVITIES
White-water Rafting

- 〔SAVE〕 **Marble Mountain Ranch/Access to Adventure Whitewater Rafting** departs from various points. Write 92520 Hwy. 96, Somes Bar, CA 95568. Daily Apr.-Oct. Phone (530) 469-3322 or (800) 552-6284.

LA CAÑADA FLINTRIDGE—
see Los Angeles p. 123.

LAGUNA BEACH (K-5)
pop. 23,200, elev. 25'

Laguna Beach, a picturesque resort community with steep hills rising from the coast, has long been a popular artists' colony. Park and beach areas line the oceanfront between Hawthorne Drive and Forest Avenue. The professional, resident company of Laguna Playhouse stages six adult-fare plays and four productions for youths during its September through June season; phone (949) 497-2787.

Laguna Beach Visitor Information Center: 252 Broadway, P.O. Box 221, Laguna Beach, CA 92651; phone (949) 497-9229, ext. 0, or (800) 877-1115.

〔SAVE〕 **FESTIVAL OF ARTS AND PAGEANT OF THE MASTERS** in Irvine Bowl Park, 650 Laguna Canyon Rd., highlights the original works of more than 160 artists. The pageant re-creates classical and contemporary works of art posed as living tableaux by citizens from area communities. To obtain a pageant ticket order form, send a self-addressed stamped envelope to Festival of Arts, P.O. Box 1659, Laguna Beach, CA 92652. The pageant is presented nightly at 8:30, early July-late Aug.

Art festival admission $5; over 55 and students with ID, $3; under 13 free with an adult. Pageant tickets $10-$50. Pageant reservations, which can be made several months in advance, are recommended. Phone (949) 494-1145 for general information, or (800) 487-3378 for tickets.

LA HABRA (B-7) pop. 51,300, elev. 298'

CHILDREN'S MUSEUM AT LA HABRA, 301 S. Euclid St., offers a creative, hands-on environment for children, including activities geared to toddlers as well as school-aged children. Highlights include a carrousel, model trains, nature walk, mini-market, science gallery, train caboose, dino-dig, theater and a bee observatory. There also are changing exhibits. Mon.-Sat. 10-5, Sun. 1-5; closed holidays. Admission $4, under 2 free. Phone (562) 905-9793 or 905-9693.

LA JOLLA—
see San Diego p. 187.

LAKE ARROWHEAD (A-9)
pop. 6,300, elev. 5,191'

Strict zoning laws have protected the appearance of Lake Arrowhead, a popular mountain resort town and a highlight of the scenic Rim of the World Drive from San Bernardino *(see place listing p. 170)*. Fishing, hiking and winter sports are popular in this area, and nearby San Bernardino National Forest *(see place listing p. 171)* provides winter recreation facilities.

Lake Arrowhead Communities Chamber of Commerce and Visitor Center: 28200 Hwy. 189, Bldg. F, P.O. Box 219, Lake Arrowhead, CA 92352; phone (909) 337-3705.

THE *ARROWHEAD QUEEN,* which departs Lake Arrowhead Village waterfront, gives a 50-minute narrated tour of Lake Arrowhead. Trips depart daily 11-5 (weather permitting); closed Dec. 25. Fare $10; over 60, $9; ages 2-12, $6.50. Tickets are available at LeRoy's Sports in Lake Arrowhead Village. Phone (909) 336-6992.

LAKE FOREST (C-8)
pop. 56,100, elev. 394'

HERITAGE HILL HISTORICAL PARK, 25151 Serrano Rd., has four preserved and restored structures that reflect part of Orange County's history: the 1863 Serrano Adobe, St. George's Episcopal Mission, the 1890 El Toro Grammar School and the 1908 Bennett Ranch House. Wed.-Sun. 9-5. Tours are given Wed.-Fri. at 2, Sat.-Sun. at 11 and 2; closed holidays. Donations. Phone (949) 855-2028.

LAKEPORT (D-1) pop. 4,400, elev. 1,343'

On the western shore of Clear Lake *(see Recreation Chart)*, one of California's largest, Lakeport is known for its excellent fishing (especially bass) and water recreation.

Lake County Visitor Information & Economic Development: 875 Lakeport Blvd., Lakeport, CA 95453-5405; phone (707) 263-9564 or (800) 525-3743.

LAKE COUNTY HISTORICAL MUSEUM, 255 N. Main St., contains displays of items depicting Pomo Indian culture, period rooms of the late 1800s and early 1900s, and a gem and mineral collection that includes Lake County diamonds. Changing exhibits also are featured. Allow 1 hour minimum. Wed.-Sat. 11-4, Memorial Day-Labor Day. Donations. Phone (707) 263-4555.

Time–not coffee–will sober you up.

Lake Tahoe Area

Lake Tahoe, which holds enough water to cover the entire state of California to a depth of 14 inches, was named "big water" by the Washoe Indians. Their legend says Lake Tahoe was created when an Evil Spirit was in pursuit of an innocent Indian. Attempting to aid the Indian, the Great Spirit gave him a branch of leaves; each leaf dropped would produce a body of water that the Evil Spirit would have to circumvent. But during the chase, the Indian dropped the whole branch in fright—creating Lake Tahoe.

It is said that the water in Lake Tahoe is 97 percent pure, nearly the same as distilled water. Remarkably clear and deep blue, the lake is 22 miles long and 12 miles wide; about one-third lies in Nevada. Its average depth is 989 feet; the deepest point is 1,645 feet, making Tahoe the third deepest lake in North America. The first 12 feet below the surface can warm to 68 F in summer, while depths below 700 feet remain a constant 39 F.

The "lake in the sky," at an elevation of 6,229 feet, lies in a valley between the main Sierra Nevada and an eastern offshoot, the Carson Range. The mountains rise more than 4,000 feet above the resort-lined shore. Most of the surrounding area is within the Eldorado, Humboldt-Toiyabe and Tahoe national forests *(see place listings p. 72, 260 and 230).*

Immigrants and miners were lured to the rugged Sierra by tales of fortunes made during the California gold rush. The discovery of the Comstock Lode increased traffic and depleted the Tahoe Basin's natural resources to a dangerously low level. Between 1860 and 1890 lumber was needed for fuel and to support the web of mines constructed beneath Virginia City. The decline of the Comstock Lode was likely the saving grace for Tahoe's forests.

By the early 1900s the lake had become a retreat for the rich. Elaborate hotels began dotting the shores. Roads were paved during the 1920s and '30s, and Lake Tahoe no longer was available only to the wealthy. As development continued in the 1950s, roads were plowed during the winter, enabling year-round residence. In 1968 the Tahoe Regional Planning Agency was established, ensuring environmentally responsible development for years to come.

Snow skiing enthusiasts flock to Lake Tahoe each year to enjoy their favorite winter sport. Well-known Tahoe ski areas include Heavenly, Alpine Meadows and Squaw Valley.

The headquarters of the U.S. Forest Service-Lake Tahoe Basin Management Unit provides year-round information about forest activities, including camping and hiking in summer and cross-country skiing in winter. The headquarters is open Mon.-Fri. 8-4:30, weather permitting. For information contact Lake Tahoe Basin Management Unit, 870 Emerald Bay Rd., South Lake Tahoe, CA 96150; phone (530) 573-2600, or TDD (530) 541-4036.

The U.S. Forest Visitor Center on SR 89 between Camp Richardson and Emerald Bay offers free orientation programs; a Stream Profile Chamber, an underground viewing chamber allowing an underwater cross-section view of Taylor Creek; and a quarter-mile walking trail. Open daily 8-5, mid-June through Sept. 30; Sat.-Sun. 8-5, Memorial Day to mid-June (weather permitting). Phone (530) 573-2674.

The lake has two distinct approaches: the North Shore via I-80 and the South Shore via US 50. The North Shore has a more rural atmosphere with small lakeside towns, while the South Shore places such as South Lake Tahoe and Stateline, Nev., are more metropolitan and have casinos, more shopping areas and restaurants.

Both roads that surround the lake are two-lane highways providing excellent views and interesting drives. SR 89 on the west side around Emerald Bay occasionally is closed in times of heavy snow. Road information is available from CalTrans; phone (800) 427-7623 in California. Rotary phone users and those outside California should phone (916) 445-1534.

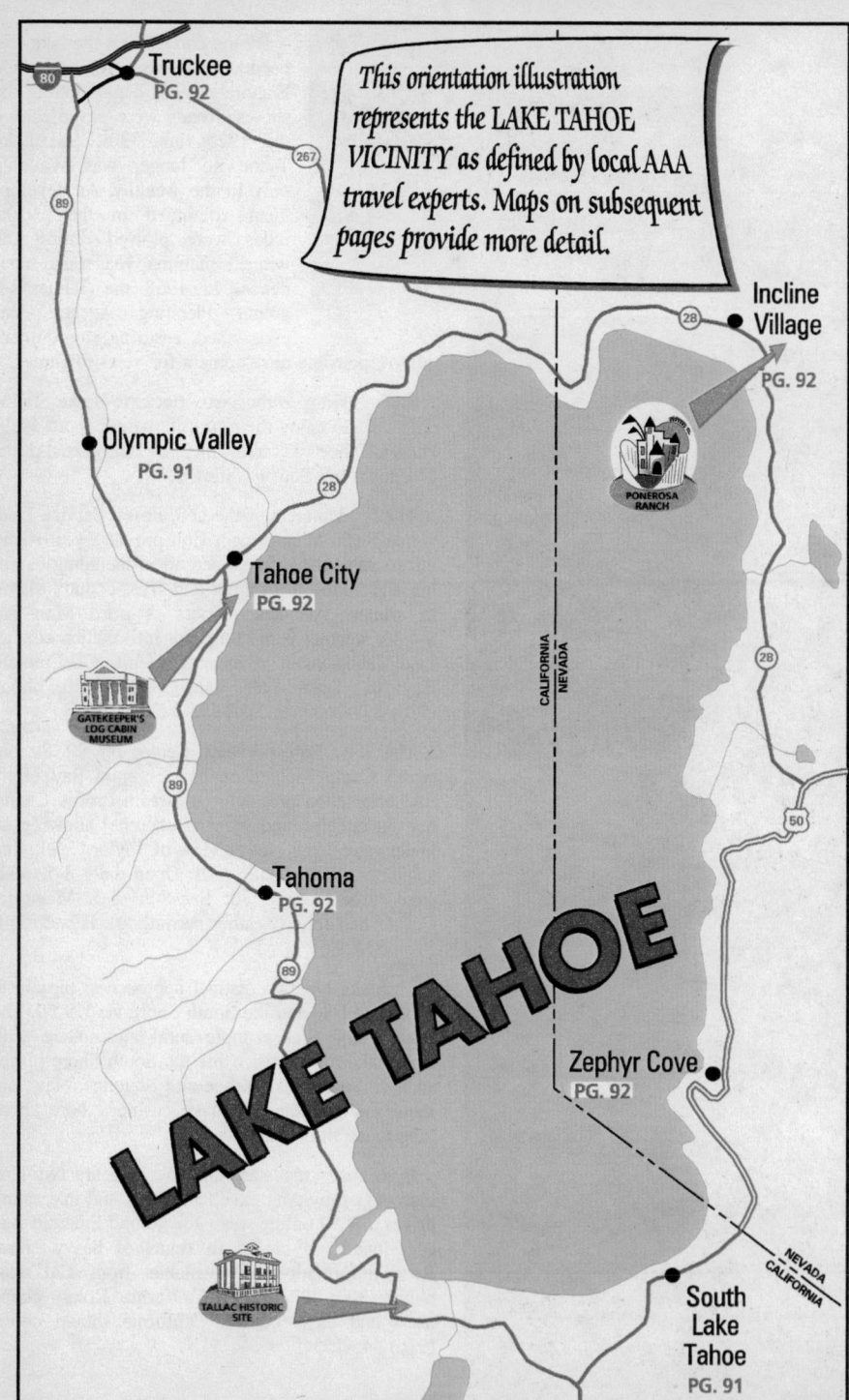

This orientation illustration represents the LAKE TAHOE VICINITY as defined by local AAA travel experts. Maps on subsequent pages provide more detail.

OLYMPIC VALLEY (D-4)

SQUAW VALLEY CABLE CAR, 1960 Squaw Valley Rd., provides a full aerial view of Lake Tahoe and Squaw Valley, site of the 1960 Winter Olympics and a year-round recreation area. Passengers are taken to the trailhead of the Pacific Crest Trail, where activities such as ice skating and swimming are offered. Activities packages are available. Daily 9-9, Nov.-Sept. (weather permitting). Closed 3 weeks for repairs; phone ahead. Fare $14; ages 3-12, $5. Fee charged for activities. AE, DS, MC, VI. Phone (530) 583-6985.

SOUTH LAKE TAHOE (E-4)
pop. 21,600, elev. 6,254'

Lake Tahoe Visitors Authority: 1156 Ski Run Blvd., South Lake Tahoe, CA 96150; phone (530) 544-5050 or (800) 288-2463.

D.L. BLISS STATE PARK, on the w. shore of Lake Tahoe between Meeks and Emerald bays, occupies 1,237 acres of forested mountain terrain. A sandy beach is at Rubicon Point, 2 miles north of Emerald Bay. Naturalist programs are available in the summer. Allow 3 hours minimum. Daily 8 a.m.-dusk, mid-June to mid-Sept. Day use fee $5 per private vehicle; over 62, $4 per private vehicle. Phone (530) 525-7277. *See Recreation Chart.*

HEAVENLY TRAM, top of Ski Run Blvd., offers a 7-minute tram ride 2,000 feet above lake level. A panorama of the lake is possible from the summit. Hiking trails are available. Trips depart every 15 minutes daily 10-9, Memorial Day weekend-late Sept.; Mon.-Fri. 9-4, Sat.-Sun. 8:30-4, Thanksgiving weekend-March 31. Summer fare $12; under 13, $7.50. Winter fare $13; under 13, $6.50. AE, DS, MC, VI. Phone (702) 586-7000.

TALLAC HISTORIC SITE is on SR 89 n. of Camp Richardson. This historic site is where elaborate summer estates were built by California's newly rich during the late 19th and early 20th centuries. Three estates on the shore of Lake Tahoe are open to visitors. Some buildings are being restored. Highlights include a visitor center and an art gallery where visitors may watch artists at work. Picnicking is permitted. Guided tours are available.

Site open daily dawn-dusk, Memorial Day weekend-Labor Day. Artists in Action program Mon.-Sat. 11-3, late June-early Sept. Visitor center open daily 8-5, mid-June through Labor Day; Sat.-Sun. 8-5, Memorial Day to mid-June. Free. Phone (530) 573-2600 year-round to verify

schedule, (530) 573-2674 for visitor center, or 542-4166 for Artists in Action.

VIKINGSHOLM, at the s.w. end of Emerald Bay, is a 38-room reproduction of a ninth-century Norse fortress. It is accessible by boat or by a steep 1-mile hiking trail; park in the Harvey West parking lot by SR 89 at Emerald Bay. Allow 1 hour minimum. Guided tours every half-hour daily 10-4, mid-June through Labor Day; Sat.-Sun. 10-4, Memorial Day weekend to mid-June. Admission $3; ages 6-12, $2. Phone (530) 525-7277 or 541-3030 for the campground.

TAHOE CITY (D-4) elev. 6,302'

North Lake Tahoe Resort Association: 245 North Lake Blvd. and 950 N. Lake Tahoe Blvd., #3, P.O. Box 884, Tahoe City, CA 96145; phone (530) 581-6900.

GATEKEEPER'S LOG CABIN MUSEUM is 1 blk. s. on SR 89. The museum is a reconstruction of the original gatekeeper's cabin, which served as the residence for the dam attendant. Included are displays about pioneer, Lake Tahoe and natural history; American Indian baskets and artifacts; and photographs. Picnicking is permitted. Allow 30 minutes minimum. Daily 11-5, June 15-Labor Day; Wed.-Sun. 11-5, May 1-June 14 and day after Labor Day-Oct. 1. Donations. Phone (530) 583-1762.

TAHOMA (E-4) pop. 500

EHRMAN MANSION is 1 mi. s. on SR 89 in Sugar Pine Point State Park. The two-story Queen Anne-style house was built in 1902 and is a fine example of a Tahoe summer house. Exhibits pertaining to the Hellman-Ehrman family can be seen on the second floor. On the grounds are an 1870 cabin, a nature center and nature trails. Rangers conduct guided tours of the mansion daily on the hour 11-4, July 1-Labor Day. Park entrance fee $5 per private vehicle; over 61, $4 per private vehicle. Tour $2; ages 6-12, $1. Phone (530) 525-7982.

TRUCKEE (D-4) pop. 2,400, elev. 5,820'

Truckee, named for Washoe Indian Chief Trokay, was once a lawless lumber and railroad town, and much of its Old West charm remains; 19th-century false-front buildings and a train that runs through the middle of town can be seen.

Truckee-Donner Chamber of Commerce: 10065 Donner Pass Rd., Truckee, CA 96161; phone (530) 587-2757.

Self-guiding tours: Free maps outlining a self-guiding walking tour of the historic downtown district are available from the chamber of commerce.

DONNER MEMORIAL STATE PARK, 2 mi. w. on Donner Pass Rd., covers 353 acres near the site where the Donner party was stranded without food as they tried to cross the Sierra Nevada Mountains during the severe winter of 1846-47. As members of the 89-person party died, some of those remaining resorted to cannibalism. Only 47 were rescued. A 25-minute slide show is presented at 10:15 and on the hour 11-3. Emigrant Trail Museum features exhibits of railroad history, logging, natural history and immigrants.

Park open daily 8-dusk, Memorial Day weekend to mid-Oct. Museum open daily 9-4; closed Jan. 1, Thanksgiving and Dec. 25. Day use fee $5 per private vehicle. Museum admission $2; ages 6-12, $1. Phone (530) 582-7892. *See Recreation Chart.*

Nearby Nevada

INCLINE VILLAGE pop. 7,100

Incline Village & Crystal Bay Chamber of Commerce: 969 Tahoe Blvd., Incline Bay, NV 89451; phone (702) 831-4440.

PONDEROSA RANCH, 100 Ponderosa Ranch Rd. off SR 28, is a Western-style theme park featuring the original Cartwright ranch house from the television show "Bonanza." Park highlights include a saloon, museum, kiddyland, playground, petting farm and mystery mine. Allow 2 hours minimum. Daily 9:30-5, mid-Apr. through Oct. 31. Breakfast hay rides 8-9:30, Memorial Day-Labor Day. Admission $9.50; ages 5-11, $5.50.

Breakfast (includes ranch admission) $11.50; ages 5-11, $7.50; ages 2-4, $2. AE, DS, MC, VI. Phone (702) 831-0691.

ZEPHYR COVE pop. 6,100

SAVE THE MS *DIXIE II* offers 2-hour sightseeing cruises daily at 11 and 2, mid-June-Labor Day; at 11, 12 and 2, day after Labor Day-Oct. 15; at noon, rest of year. Breakfast, brunch and dinner dance cruises also are available. Fare $16; over 60, $14; ages 3-11, $5. Reservations are recommended. AE, DS, MC, VI. Phone (702) 588-3508 or 882-0786.

LANCASTER (J-6)
pop. 97,300, elev. 2,355'

The high desert city of Lancaster in the Antelope Valley was established in 1884 along the Southern Pacific Railroad line. The community grew through farming and mining activities. Edwards Air Force Base's predecessor, Muroc Bombing and Gunnery Range, was established in 1933 and became an important part of Lancaster's economy. The city's population expanded beginning in the 1980s as Lancaster became a bedroom community for Los Angeles and other Southern California locations.

The Antelope Valley is well-known for its abundant springtime display of poppies at California Poppy Reserve. The reserve and an interpretive center, on Lancaster Road between 130th and 170th streets west, are open mid-March through April 30; phone (805) 724-1180 or 942-0662.

Lancaster Performing Arts Center, 750 W. Lancaster Blvd., presents musical, dance, drama and children's events September through May. Also along Lancaster Boulevard, the Aerospace Walk of Honor pays tribute to distinguished test pilots who have flown out of Edwards Air Force Base.

Lancaster Chamber of Commerce: 554 W. Lancaster Blvd., Lancaster, CA 93534-2534; phone (805) 948-4518.

HOT AIR BALLOON RIDES over the Antelope Valley, during which passengers may sometimes assist with lift-off and pack-up operations, are available (weather permitting) through the following companies: Boondoc Balloon Team, (310) 545-7725; Don's Early Light Hot Air Balloon Flights, (800) 943-7616; and Dreams Unlimited, (805) 251-0553 or (800) 246-8247. Rides last 30 minutes-1 hour. Fares range $90-$125. Beverages and snacks are included. Reservations are required. Rides are not advisable for children under age 8. All pilots are FAA certified.

Note: The mention of the preceding hot air balloon rides is for information only and does **not** imply endorsement by AAA.

LANCASTER MUSEUM/ART GALLERY, 44801 N. Sierra Hwy., presents changing exhibitions of art from various media as well as exhibits of historical interest. Tues.-Sat. 11-4, Sun. 1-4; closed holidays and between exhibits. Donations. Phone (805) 723-6250.

★ means attractions
of unusual interest
and exceptionally
high quality.

LASSEN NATIONAL FOREST

Elevations in the forest range
from 800 ft. near Butte Meadows
to 8,172 ft. at West Prospect Peak.
Refer to AAA maps for additional
elevation information.

Lassen National Forest covers approximately 1,375,000 acres surrounding Lassen Volcanic National Park *(see place listing p. 93)*. Within the region are numerous lakes formed by ancient volcanic action.

Several highways, forest roads and trails afford access to the region. The Caribou, Thousand Lakes and Ishi wilderness areas allow backpacking. Campfire permits are required, except in campgrounds with developed facilities. Obtain permits in person at any Forest Service, Bureau of Land Management or California Department of Forestry Office. Hunting, fishing, cross-country skiing and snowmobiling are permitted.

Lake Almanor, one of the largest man-made bodies of water in California, and Eagle Lake, the second largest natural lake in California, offer fishing, sailing, water skiing and swimming. Eagle Lake and Hat Creek offer trout fishing. Recreation sites usually are open mid-May to mid-October (weather permitting); the season is shorter at higher elevations. For more information contact the Supervisor's Office, Lassen National Forest, 55 S. Sacramento St., Susanville, CA 96130; phone (530) 257-2151. *See Recreation Chart and the AAA California/Nevada CampBook.*

SUBWAY CAVE is off SR 89 about .1 mi. n. of SR 44. This lava tube winds 1,300 feet through a lava flow that covered the Hat Creek Valley nearly 2,000 years ago. Carry a jacket and a reliable lantern or flashlight while exploring this self-guiding interpretive trail through this cave. Free. Phone (530) 336-5521.

★ LASSEN VOLCANIC NATIONAL PARK (C-3)

Elevations in the park range
from 6,000 ft. at Manzanita Lake
to 10,457 ft. at Lassen Peak. Refer
to AAA maps for additional
elevation information.

Lassen Volcanic National Park covers 106,000 acres in northeastern California where the Cascades join the Sierra Nevada. The park is accessible via SR 36, 9 miles east of Mineral. In addition to Lassen Peak (10,457 ft.) and Cinder Cone (6,907 ft.), the park boasts Prospect Peak (8,338 ft.) and Mount Harkness (8,045 ft.), two shield volcanoes topped by cinder cones with trails leading to their summits. Other features include smaller volcanoes and lava flows, fumaroles, boiling springs, boiling lakes and mudpots.

For a period of several thousand years Lassen Peak was quiescent; then in the spring of 1914 a series of relatively small eruptions began. After reaching its peak in 1915, the activity continued until about 1921.

A plug dome volcano, Lassen Peak once protruded from the north flank of ancestral Mount Tehama. This great stratovolcano was destroyed by glaciers, hydrothermal activity and erosion by Mill Creek and other water. Lassen Park Road winds around Lassen Peak, affording views of the volcano and evidence of its destructive might.

In the southern half of the park gurgling mudpots and roaring fumaroles contribute to the bizarre atmosphere. The eastern sector encompasses a splendid chain of lakes, extending from Juniper Lake at the northern base of Mount Harkness to Butte Lake near the eastern base of Prospect Peak.

General Information and Activities

Although the park is open all year, heavy snows render most sections inaccessible from late October to early June. Winter roads are maintained from the northern gate to the district ranger's office (about 1 mile) and from the southern gate to the winter sports area at Lassen Chalet, the hub of winter sports activity. Cross-country skiing is usually possible from early December to late spring. Mountain bikes are not permitted on trails in the park.

Some of the park's many lakes and streams contain trout. A state fishing license is required, and catch limits are posted. Wilderness permits issued by the park are required for back-country camping. Permits are available by mail; phone the park headquarters 2 weeks in advance. Gates are open 24 hours daily, but the hours they are attended vary. Motorists entering the park in summer when the station is unattended must obtain a permit before leaving.

Park headquarters is 1 mile west of Mineral on SR 36. Maps, information and bulletins can be obtained at the headquarters and Loomis Museum. Interpretive and evening programs, guided nature walks and self-guiding trails are available. Daily 9-5, mid-June to late Sept.; Sat.-Sun. 9-5, late May-early June (weather permitting). *See Recreation Chart.*

Note: Stay on established trails at all times in boiling springs or steaming areas; small children should be kept under strict control. Ground crusts that appear safe can be dangerously thin.

ADMISSION to the park is $10 per private vehicle, $4 per person over age 16 by other means. Entrance fees are good for 7 days, with a receipt.

PETS are permitted in the park only if they are on a leash, crated or otherwise physically restrained at all times. Pets are not allowed on trails or in buildings.

ADDRESS inquiries to the Superintendent, Lassen Volcanic National Park, Box 100, Mineral, CA 96063-0100. Phone (530) 595-4444.

Points of Interest

BUMPASS HELL TRAIL, about .5 mi. beyond Emerald Lake, leads 1.5 mi. off the Lassen Park Rd. to Bumpass Hell, a large area of spectacular boiling springs, mudpots, boiling pools and other types of hydrothermal activity.

BUTTE LAKE is 6 mi. off SR 44 in the n.e. corner of the park. A marked nature trail leads to the Cinder Cone summit; interpretive leaflets are available at the trailhead.

CINDER CONE, accessible from a trail beginning at Butte Lake, is known for Fantastic Lava Beds and multicolored volcanic ejecta. It is possible that some lava flows occurred as recently as the mid-1700s.

LASSEN PARK ROAD is a 30-mile drive between the s. entrance and Manzanita Lake in the n.w. region. A road guide to points of interest along the route is available for a fee at the park's headquarters and at Loomis Museum. Most of the road is impassable late Oct.-early June due to heavy snowfall.

Chaos Crags and Chaos Jumbles are 2 mi. s. from the n.w. boundary. The Chaos Crags are lava plugs believed to have been pushed up more than 1,000 years ago; subsequent rockfalls formed the Chaos Jumbles. The small coniferous trees in the Chaos Jumbles—some more than 300 years old—constitute the Dwarf Forest.

Devastated Area begins about 2.5 mi. n. of Summit Lake. It was stripped of all vegetation by hot blasts, avalanches and mudflows from the May 1915 eruptions of Lassen Peak. Natural reforestation is taking place. Another eruption remnant is Hot Rock, a large black lava rock near the north end of the area.

Diamond Peak is reached by Lassen Park Rd., which, from 2 mi. n. of the Sulphur Works, winds up the remains of old Mount Tehama. The road, which encompasses Diamond Peak, offers a glimpse of steam vents across the canyon in Little Hot Springs Valley.

Kings Creek Meadows (7,400 ft.) are 4.5 mi. n. from the summit. A trail leads 1.3 miles to beautiful Kings Creek Falls. Both the cascades and falls are visible from the left side of the creek downstream.

Loomis Museum, .5 mi. beyond the n.w. entrance station, has a visitor contact station where park information, exhibits, books, wilderness maps and assistance are available.

Sulphur Works Thermal Area, about 1 mi. n. of the s.w. entrance station, has steam vents and mudpots. Stay on the trails in these areas at all times. Ground that appears safe might be dangerously thin.

Summit Lake, 5 mi. n.e. of Kings Creek Meadows, has two lakeside campgrounds with trailer spaces. They are convenient to hiking, fishing and points of interest. Campfire programs several nights a week are available in summer.

LASSEN PEAK TRAIL leaves Lassen Park Rd. less than 1 mi. beyond Lake Helen and travels 2.5 miles to the top of the volcano. Round trip requires 4 to 5 hours.

WARNER VALLEY, in the s. part of the park, is reached by road from Chester or by trail from Summit Lake to Drakesbad. Marked trails lead to Boiling Springs Lake and Devils Kitchen, a large area of boiling pools and other volcanic features.

★ LAVA BEDS NATIONAL MONUMENT (B-3)

Centuries ago molten lava spewing from Medicine Lake volcano cooled to form the rugged terrain of Lava Beds National Monument. The 46,500-acre area is characterized by cinder cones, deep chasms and more than 300 lava tube caves of various sizes. Some of the caves contain permanent ice. Free-use flashlights for cave exploration are available at the visitor center. The Modoc Indians used the volcanic formations as fortifications 1872-73 during the only major Indian war fought in California.

Camping is allowed, but no lodgings, supplies, gas or oil are available. Pets on leash are permitted in certain areas of the park. The monument is open all year, and although there are no specified visiting hours, those planning to camp should arrive before 5 p.m. The geology and history of the area is interpreted at a visitor center. Daily 8-6, June 15-Labor Day; 8-5, rest of year. Admission $4 per private vehicle; $2 per motorcycle, bi-

cycle or on foot. For more information contact the Supervisor's Office, P.O. Box 867, Tulelake, CA 96134; phone (530) 667-2282. *See the AAA California/Nevada CampBook.*

LEBEC (I-5) elev. 3,570'

In Grapevine Canyon, Lebec was named after Peter le Beck. Little is known about the man except for his epitaph, carved deeply into the wood of an oak tree: "Peter le Beck, killed by a bear, Oct. 17, 1873."

FORT TEJON STATE HISTORIC PARK, 3.5 mi. n. on I-5, is a restored U.S. Army Dragoon post in use 1854-64. Patrols from the post guarded the supply route from Los Angeles to Fort Mojave; protected travelers; and watched over southern California. Fort Tejon also was the site of the experimental U.S. Camel Corps, a group of 34 camels that hauled supplies from San Antonio and surveyed the California-Nevada border. The park also contains a small museum, officers' quarters and barracks.

Daily 10-4:30; closed Jan. 1, Thanksgiving and Dec. 25. Civil War re-enactments are staged the third Sun. of the month at 10, noon and 2, Apr.-Oct. Daily fee $2; ages 6-12, $1. Events $5; ages 6-12, $3. Phone (805) 248-6692, or (805) 398-9199 for the Fort Tejon Historical Society.

LEE VINING (F-5) pop. 300, elev. 6,781'

Lee Vining is a center for recreational and scenic attractions around Mono Lake. Mono Lake County Park, 5 miles north off US 395, has a shady streamside picnic area and a boardwalk trail that winds through meadows to the lakeshore. Contact the information center for details on naturalist tours and canoe trips.

Mono Lake Committee Information Center and Bookstore: US 395, P.O. Box 29, Lee Vining, CA 93541; phone (760) 647-6595.

What's your MPG? Find out in four easy steps:

Step 1: Fill your tank completely and write down your odometer reading.

Step 2: When it's time to refuel, again fill your tank completely and write down your odometer reading. Also write down how many gallons of fuel your tank took.

Step 3: Subtract your first odometer reading from your second odometer reading.

Step 4: Divide the result of Step 3 by how many gallons your tank took during your second refueling. This result is your MPG – miles per gallon.

MONO LAKE TUFA STATE RESERVE, at S. Tufa Area off SR 120, 5 mi. e. of US 395, preserves tufa, a calcium-carbonate rock created by the interaction of freshwater springs under the lake with the alkaline lake waters. The lowering of the lake level due to stream diversion has exposed unusual tower formations. Daily 24 hours. Guided tours are given daily in summer. Free. Phone (760) 647-6331.

LEGGETT (C-1) pop. 200

Leggett is at the crossroads of the Redwood Highway (US 101) and scenic SR 1. The town is near the ocean, wine country and redwood forests. The area also contains several historic sites.

CHANDELIER TREE, in Drive-Thru Tree Park on US 101, towers 315 feet into the air and is 21 feet in diameter. Visitors can drive a full-size automobile through the hand-hewn opening at the base of the tree. Picnicking is permitted. Daily 9-dusk. Admission $3 per private vehicle. Phone (707) 925-6464.

LITTLE RIVER (D-1) elev. 90′

Founded as a lumber and shipbuilding town in the mid-19th century, Little River boasts architecture to reflect its settlers' New England heritage. The town is a popular spot for divers. Little River lies on a scenic stretch of SR 1 on the north coast that runs from Leggett southward to Sausalito and the San Francisco Bay.

PYGMY FOREST, s. edge on SR 1 and 3 mi. e. on Little River Airport Rd., is thought to be the result of acidic soil. Even though they are decades old, some of the rare pygmy pine and pygmy cypress trees are only 2 feet high.

LIVERMORE (F-3) pop. 56,700, elev. 486′

Livermore is the principal community in Livermore Valley, a scenic area with vineyards and cattle lands. Sycamore trees—some more than 2 centuries old—grow along the banks of the Arroyo del Valle.

Livermore Chamber of Commerce: 2157 First St., Livermore, CA 94550-4543; phone (925) 447-1606.

LAWRENCE LIVERMORE NATIONAL LABORATORY VISITORS CENTER, off Greenville Rd. about 2.2 mi. s. of I-580, presents a broad-based display of the scientific technology developed at the laboratory and highlights the laboratory's research about new energy sources through photographs and a short video wall overview.
   Allow 30 minutes minimum. Mon.-Fri. 1:30-4; holiday hours vary. Tours lasting 90 minutes are given Thurs. at 1:30; reservations are required at least 2 weeks in advance. Free. Under 18 not permitted. Non-U.S. citizens must make reservations 45 days in advance. Phone (925) 422-4599, or 422-6408 for reservations.

 WINERIES

- **Livermore Valley Cellars,** 1 mi. s. off SR 84 at 1508 Wetmore Rd. Daily 11:30-5. Phone (925) 447-1751.

- **Wente Vineyards,** off I-580, 3 mi. s. on Vasco Rd., then w. to 5565 Tesla Rd. Daily 11-4:30. Phone (925) 456-2305.

LODI (E-3) pop. 51,900, elev. 52′

With more than a dozen wineries nearby, Lodi is an important wine-producing center. Nearby Lake Lodi Park offers water skiing, boating, picnicking and swimming. Hill House Museum is one of the few Victorian houses in Lodi.

Lodi Chamber of Commerce: 35 S. School St., Lodi, CA 95241; phone (209) 367-7840.

MICKE GROVE REGIONAL PARK, 11793 N. Micke Grove Rd., has picnic facilities, amusement rides, a Japanese garden, historical museum and zoo. Park open daily 8-dusk. Zoo open daily 10-5. Park admission per private vehicle Mon.-Fri. $2, Sat.-Sun. $4, holidays $5. Zoo admission $1.50; ages 6-17, $1. Phone (209) 331-7400.

San Joaquin County Historical Museum contains permanent and changing exhibits about local history, agriculture, transportation and American Indian culture. Of interest is the Sunshine Trail, which re-creates a trip across California from west to east. An enclosed garden contains native California plants and a waterfall. Weber Gallery contains personal belongings and a model of the first home site of Capt. Charles Weber, the founder of the city of Stockton. Allow 2 hours minimum. Wed.-Sun. 1-4:45. Admission $2; over 59 and ages 6-12, $1. Phone (209) 331-2055.

LOMITA—
see Los Angeles p. 123.

LOMPOC (I-3) pop. 37,600, elev. 104′

Many of the nation's flower seeds are grown in Lompoc; local flower fields bloom May through September. Civic Center Plaza between C and E streets has a display garden where new varieties of plants are identified.

Lompoc Valley Chamber of Commerce and Visitor Center: 111 S. I St., P.O. Box 626, Lompoc, CA 93438-0626; phone (805) 736-4567.

★**LA PURÍSIMA MISSION STATE HISTORIC PARK** is at 2295 Purisima Rd. The original mission, founded in 1787, was demolished by an earthquake in 1812. Chumash Indians, directed by Franciscan priests, rebuilt it 1813-22 a few miles from the original site. One of the most complete mission restorations, the park includes

10 buildings and a water system consisting of an historic aqueduct. The grounds comprise more than 1,900 acres and have 25 miles of hiking and riding trails. Rooms are furnished as they would have been in the 1820s; mission crafts are demonstrated periodically during the summer.

Daily 9-5; closed Jan. 1, Thanksgiving and Dec. 25. Admission $5 per private vehicle; over 61, $4 per private vehicle. Phone (805) 733-3713. *See Recreation Chart.*

LOMPOC MUSEUM, 200 S. H St., contains a large collection of American Indian artifacts representing the Chumash and other tribes. Exhibits trace Lompoc Valley history from the founding of La Purísima Mission to the present. Tues.-Fri. 1-5, Sat.-Sun. 1-4; closed holidays. Admission $1; under 12, 25c. Phone (805) 736-3888.

LONE PINE (G-6) pop. 1,700, elev. 3,733'

Many Western movies have been filmed among the Alabama Hills, a mass of weatherbeaten rock bordering US 395 west and northwest of Lone Pine.

Eastern Sierra Interagency Visitor Center, at US 395 and SR 136, has information and exhibits about Inyo National Forest, Sequoia and Kings Canyon National Parks, Yosemite National Park, Death Valley National Park and Inyo and Mono counties recreation areas; phone (760) 876-6222.

Vestiges of Manzanar are about 9 miles north off SR 395. This internment camp, the first of several established to hold Japanese-Americans during World War II, ultimately had 10,000 inhabitants. Today little remains but stone entrance gates, some concrete foundations, a cemetery and roads in varying stages of disrepair.

Lone Pine Chamber of Commerce: 126 S. Main St., P.O. Box 749, Lone Pine, CA 93545; phone (760) 876-4444.

MOUNT WHITNEY, west of Lone Pine, rises to 14,494 feet, making it the highest mountain in the contiguous United States. The summit is 11 miles by a strenuous trail from the end of Whitney Portal Road (8,367 ft.). Wilderness permits are required year-round, and overnight-use quotas are in effect late May to mid-October; for details or permit reservations write Inyo National Forest Wilderness Reservation Service, P.O. Box 430, Big Pine, CA 93513, or phone (888) 374-3773. Mount Whitney Ranger Station in Lone Pine is open daily 8-4:30, late May to mid-Oct.; Mon.-Fri. 8-4:30, rest of year. Phone (760) 876-6200 for general information.

LONG BEACH—
see Los Angeles p. 123.

LOS ALAMITOS (C-6) pop. 11,700, elev. 25'

Los Alamitos Race Course, 4961 E. Katella Ave., conducts Thoroughbred, quarter horse and harness racing. For schedule information phone (714) 995-1234.

Note: Policies concerning admittance of children to pari-mutuel betting facilities vary. Phone for information.

Los Alamitos Area Chamber of Commerce: 3231 Katella Ave., P.O. Box 111, Los Alamitos, CA 90720; phone (562) 598-6659.

Los Angeles

Los Angeles is California's largest city, both in population and in territory (469.3 sq. mi.). The city ranks second in city and metropolitan area population in the United States.

Los Angeles is hardly a city in the traditional sense of the word; it has no concentrated urban center with relatively distinct limits. Rather, it is a collection of intermingling communities, each with its own identity and character. For example, Hollywood lies entirely within the Los Angeles city limits. It is possible to travel 25 miles from city hall and still remain in the city; on the other hand, you can travel less than 3 miles in another direction and be in another town.

Early in this century towns that wanted to take advantage of water piped to Los Angeles from the Owens River had to become part of the city. Communities that refused to subscribe to the project under this stipulation remained separate from Los Angeles but in some cases found themselves entirely surrounded by it. Officially, the name Los Angeles applies to both city and county. The name often is used to designate the downtown nucleus, but it also can refer to the entire metropolitan area.

A Spanish expedition in search of the port of Monterey first visited the area in 1769. In 1781 Governor Felipe de Neve and 11 families founded El Pueblo de Nuestra Señora la Reina de Los Angeles (the Village of Our Lady the Queen of the Angels). Following Mexican independence from Spain in the early 19th century, Los Angeles sporadically served as capital of the Mexican province of Alta California. It was the last place to surrender to the United States in the Mexican War in 1847.

The original pueblo slowly branched into thriving cattle ranches and varied agricultural pursuits and trade. The climate, so conducive to the good life, undoubtedly contributed to an increasingly secular philosophy and the decline of the once-influential missions. By the 1800s many of the mission friars were complaining that the Angelenos were paying "more attention to gambling and playing the guitar than to tilling their lands and educating their children."

More recently the city's growth has been due to the development of a variety of industries. More than three-fourths of all motion pictures made in the United States are produced in the Los Angeles metropolitan area. This enormous amount of film production, combined with the major radio and television broadcasting companies, has made Los Angeles the entertainment center of the West.

The city also thrives on tourism, world trade and highly diversified industries—predominantly oil, electronics, finance, entertainment, real estate, aircraft and aerospace. But the city has not forgotten its past; it has preserved many early 19th-century houses.

The Museum Village at Heritage Square in the Highland Park district is a haven for the ornate Victorian structures that reflect the lifestyle of the city 1865-1914. A short distance from downtown, the Victorian-style suburb of Angelino Heights boasts stately 19th-century houses that have been restored to their original grandeur.

The city's educational institutions include the University of California at Los Angeles (UCLA), a campus of the state's oldest and most renowned university. Among the city's private institutions are the University of Southern California (USC), Loyola-Marymount University and Occidental College.

Behind all the broad boulevards, palm-planted parks, gleaming new buildings and other physical features of the city is that intangible quality which is the essence of Los Angeles: the hopeful dreams of its citizens. Here flock the aspiring star, the artist, the laborer, the imaginative businessperson and the student, each in search of his or her own El Dorado.

Some make it big; most do not. But many stay, and their collective aspirations produce the zest and variety that characterize their city. Smog and congestion, though undeniable, fail to smother the irrepressible enthusiasm that is Los Angeles.

Approaches

By Car

The major north-south route, I-5, is a heavily traveled freeway that bisects both Los Angeles proper and the entire metropolitan area. From the north this inland route approaches through the San Joaquin Valley, crosses the Tehachapi Mountains and enters the city as the Golden State Freeway; from the south at San Diego it follows the coast to Capistrano Beach, turns inland, then, as the Santa Ana Freeway, passes through Anaheim and sweeps into central Los Angeles.

I-405 (San Diego Freeway) joins I-5 at San Fernando and south of Irvine; a good alternate route, it avoids the busy downtown area, although it is typically as heavily traveled as the central route.

From the north, two other controlled-access routes, SR 99 and US 101, roughly parallel I-5 on the east and the west, respectively. SR 99 crosses the San Joaquin Valley and merges with I-5 a few miles south of Bakersfield. US 101 is a 204-mile scenic stretch from San Luis Obispo.

THE INFORMED TRAVELER

City Population: 3,485,400

Elevation: 267 ft.

Sales Tax: State and county sales taxes total 8.25% in Los Angeles. A lodging tax called a transient occupancy tax of 14% also is levied along with an 8.25% rental car tax.

WHOM TO CALL

Emergency: 911

Police (non-emergency): (213) 625-3311

Time: 853-1212 (all area codes)

Weather: (213) 554-1212

Hospitals: Cedars-Sinai Medical Center, (310) 855-5000; San Pedro Peninsula, (310) 832-3311; UCLA Medical Center, (310) 825-9111.

WHERE TO LOOK

Newspapers

The major daily newspapers in Los Angeles are the *Los Angeles Times* and the *Daily News*. Many surrounding communities publish daily newspapers as well; foreign-language and special-interest papers also are plentiful.

Radio and TV

Los Angeles radio station KFWB (980 AM) is an all-news/weather station; KCRW (89.9 FM) is a member of National Public Radio; KKTR (1650 AM) offers continuous traffic reports 24 hours a day. Several stations in the Los Angeles area broadcast in Spanish, such as KLAX (97.9 FM), and other languages as well as in English. The major TV channels are 2 (CBS), 4 (NBC), 7 (ABC), 11 (FOX), 28 (PBS) and 34 (MEX). For a complete list of radio and television programs, consult the daily newspapers.

Almost continuously in sight of the coast ranges, US 101 follows the Salinas River Valley, runs along the coastline through Santa Barbara and terminates at I-5 in the center of Los Angeles. SR 1, which traverses the rugged coast, is slower and more dangerous when fog sets in or rain increases the possibility of slides. Outstanding coastal views make it the most scenic north-south route.

I-15 links Las Vegas and San Diego. Passing east of Los Angeles, it provides access to the area via freeway connections at San Bernardino, Ontario and Riverside.

Direct access from the east is via I-10, which enters Los Angeles as the San Bernardino Freeway and ends at Santa Monica. Indirect access from points east is provided by I-40, a fast route across the desert that ends at I-15 in Barstow.

Getting Around

Street System

In sprawling Los Angeles the most popular way of getting around is by car. The result is a routine traffic volume seldom encountered elsewhere; in Los Angeles alone there is one car for every 1.8 residents.

City driving is usually least complicated on the major boulevards, such as Wilshire or Olympic. One big help is oversized street signs, easily legible from far enough away to permit decisions before reaching important intersections. In some outlying communities signs carry not only the name of the street but the name of the town as well.

The speed limit on most streets is 35 mph or as posted; residential areas have a limit of 25 mph. Freeway speed is generally 65 mph. Motorists might be ticketed for driving at speeds considered dangerously slow as well as dangerously fast. Right turns on red are permitted unless otherwise posted. U-turns at intersections also are permitted unless otherwise posted.

Pedestrians crossing the street in a marked crosswalk or at an intersection in an unmarked crosswalk **always** have the right-of-way.

The Freeways

Los Angeles has an extensive freeway system. Its involved interchanges, myriad access ramps and potentially confusing exit signs can bewilder a motorist unfamiliar with the territory. Without the freeways, getting around the metropolitan area would be nearly impossible. Although traffic flow on the city's surface streets is good, the freeways generally provide faster and safer transportation for the greater distances that area residents are accustomed to traveling daily.

The San Diego Freeway (I-405), the Foothill Freeway (I-210) and the Ventura Freeway (US 101, SR 134) are the completed freeway bypasses of downtown Los Angeles. Others, usually named for their ultimate destination, radiate from a loop around the central city. For example, the southbound Harbor Freeway (I-110) leads to San Pedro and the harbor district; it is one of the most heavily traveled highways in the country.

The cardinal rule for driving the Los Angeles freeways is PLAN AHEAD. Before you start, study your map carefully and know the exact route that you intend to take. You might find it helpful to jot down highway numbers and directions, major interchanges and the names of a few main cross streets that precede the exit ramp you want to take.

It is especially important for a newcomer to avoid the rush hours, 6:30-9:30 a.m. and about 3:30-6:30 p.m. If you must drive during these times, have an alternate route in mind in case of exceptionally heavy congestion. Keep your radio on to catch Sigalert bulletins, which warn of freeway tie-ups.

Parking

Although downtown on-street parking is prohibited in most areas during the day, Los Angeles has hundreds of convenient lots and garages. Prices vary according to location. They are highest in the central city: about $2-$5 per half-hour and $12-$25 per day. Some hotels and stores provide free parking with validation.

Public Transportation

The public transportation system in Los Angeles is becoming as diversified as in many other large cities. Bus lines provide comprehensive coverage of the entire metropolitan region. Information and maps are available at the MTA Customer Centers on Level C of ARCO Plaza, 515 S. Flower St., Mon.-Fri. 7:30-3:30; Union Station/Gateway Center, East Portal, Mon.-Fri. 6 a.m.-6:30 p.m.; East Los Angeles, 4501 "B" Whittier Blvd. (on Ford north of Whittier), Tues.-Sat. 10-6; Hollywood, 6249 Hollywood Blvd., Mon.-Fri. 10-6; Baldwin Hills/Crenshaw Plaza, 3650 Martin Luther King Blvd., Suite 101B, Tues.-Sat. 10-6; San Fernando Valley, 14435 Sherman Way, Suite 107 (Van Nuys), Mon.-Fri. 10-6; Wilshire District, 5301 Wilshire Blvd., Mon.-Fri. 9-5.

The Metro Rail system has three lines in daily operation. The Blue Line runs 22 miles from Los Angeles to downtown Long Beach. The Metro Red Line subway runs from Union Station/Gateway Center (downtown Los Angeles at Cesar E. Chavez Avenue and Alameda Street) to Wilshire Boulevard and Western Avenue in the Wilshire district. The 20-mile Green Line serves an east-west corridor across southern Los Angeles County and provides access to Los Angeles International Airport via shuttle buses from the Aviation Station. The basic fare is $1.35; discount tokens are available for 90c. Trains operate daily.

Metrolink, a regional commuter rail system, operates lines serving 44 stations from Union Station/Gateway Center, connecting downtown Los Angeles with Lancaster, Oxnard, San Ber-

THE INFORMED TRAVELER

Visitor Information

The following groups distribute visitor information: Los Angeles Convention and Visitors Bureau, 685 S. Figueroa St., Los Angeles, CA 90017 and 6541 Hollywood Blvd., Hollywood, CA 90028, (213) 689-8822; the chamber of commerce, (213) 580-7500, 350 S. Bixel St., Los Angeles, CA 90017; and Los Angeles City Recreation and Parks Department, (213) 485-5555, City Hall East, 200 N. Main St., Los Angeles, CA 90012.

WHAT TO WEAR

Many people might consider the climate of Los Angeles perfect. The average annual rainfall is just 14 inches, most occurring November through March. Winters are mild; days average 60 to 75 degrees Fahrenheit and nights about 20 degrees cooler. However, temperature fluctuations can be quick and unpredictable; the Christmas season can vary from 28 to 95 degrees.

Late spring is cool and often overcast. Summer days might dawn cloudy, but the skies usually clear before noon. Summer weather is comfortable, ranging from the low 80s in the daytime to the low 60s at night. The warmest months are August through November, when the hot, dry Santa Ana desert winds periodically blow in from the east or northeast.

DID YOU KNOW?

The full name of Los Angeles is El Pueblo de Nuestra Señora de Reina de Los Angeles.

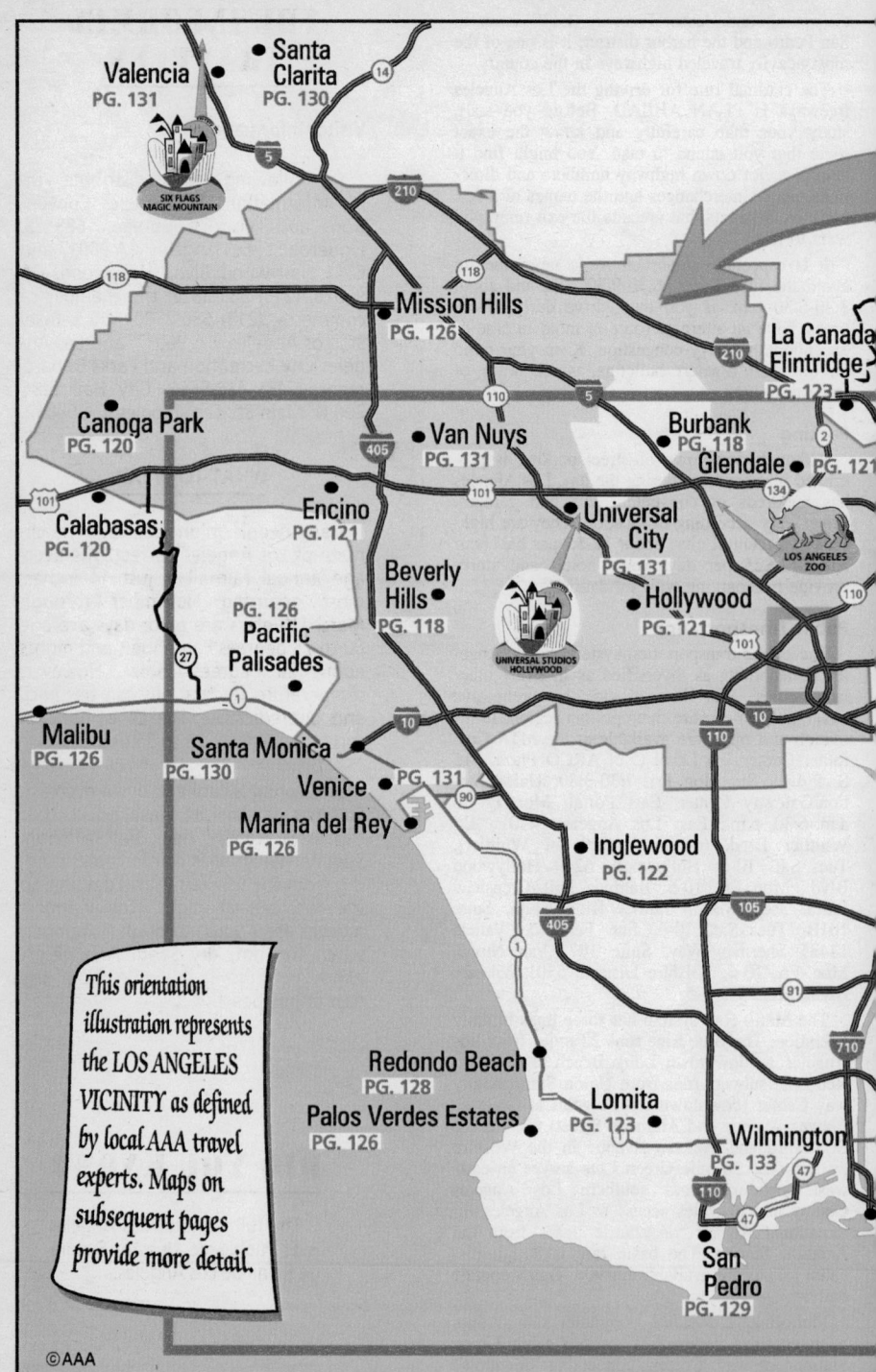

Valencia PG. 131

Santa Clarita PG. 130

SIX FLAGS MAGIC MOUNTAIN

Mission Hills PG. 126

La Canada Flintridge PG. 123

Canoga Park PG. 120

Van Nuys PG. 131

Burbank PG. 118

Glendale PG. 121

LOS ANGELES ZOO

Calabasas PG. 120

Encino PG. 121

Universal City PG. 131

Hollywood PG. 121

UNIVERSAL STUDIOS HOLLYWOOD

Beverly Hills PG. 118

Pacific Palisades PG. 126

Malibu PG. 126

Santa Monica PG. 130

Venice PG. 131

Marina del Rey PG. 126

Inglewood PG. 122

This orientation illustration represents the LOS ANGELES VICINITY as defined by local AAA travel experts. Maps on subsequent pages provide more detail.

Redondo Beach PG. 128

Palos Verdes Estates PG. 126

Lomita PG. 123

Wilmington PG. 133

San Pedro PG. 129

©AAA

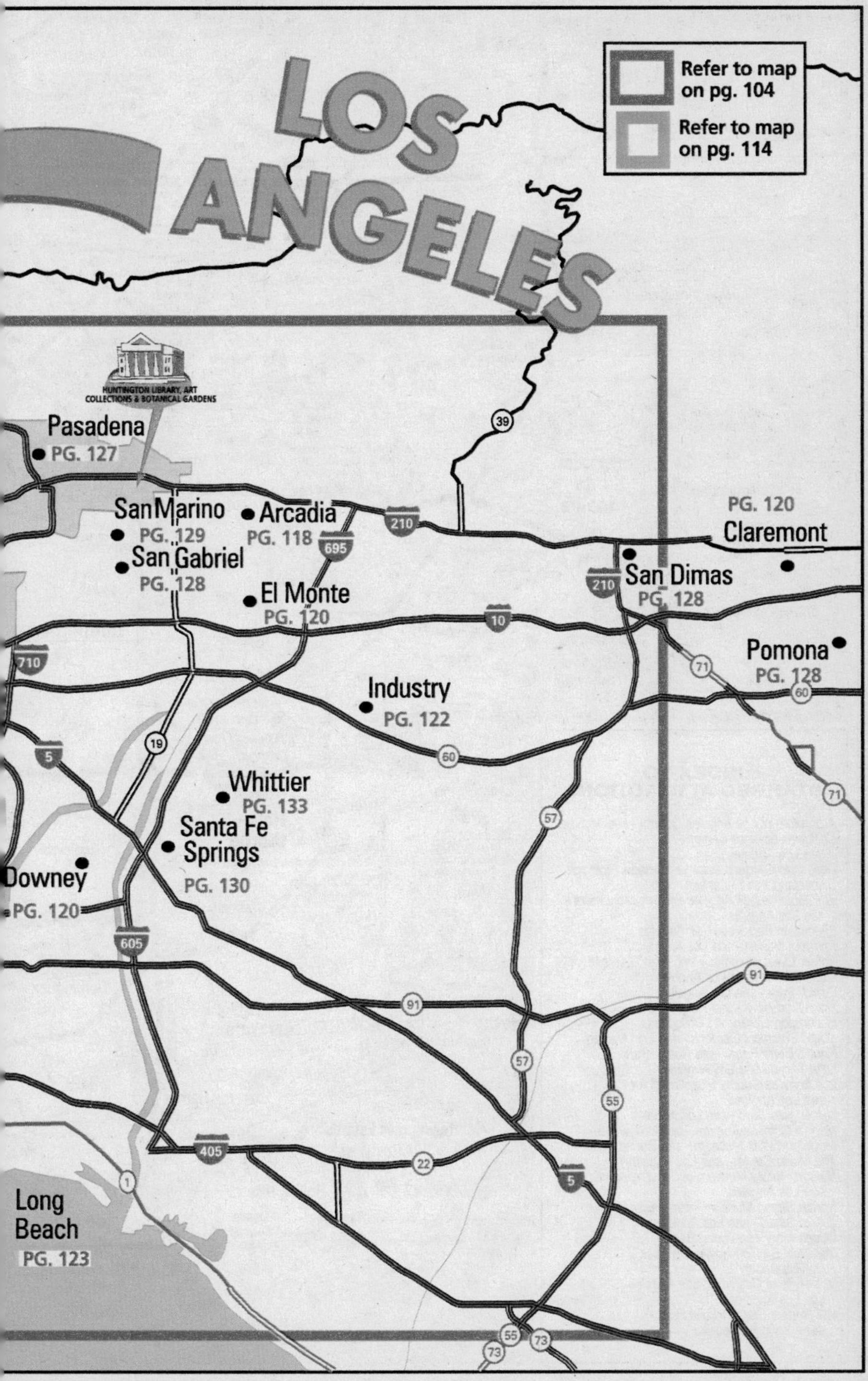

LOS ANGELES

Refer to map on pg. 104

Refer to map on pg. 114

HUNTINGTON LIBRARY, ART COLLECTIONS & BOTANICAL GARDENS

Pasadena
PG. 127

39

PG. 120

Claremont

San Marino
PG. 129

Arcadia
PG. 118

210

695

San Gabriel
PG. 128

San Dimas
PG. 128

210

El Monte
PG. 120

10

Pomona
PG. 128

710

71

60

Industry
PG. 122

19

60

5

Whittier
PG. 133

57

Santa Fe Springs
PG. 130

71

Downey
PG. 120

91

605

91

57

55

405

91

1

22

5

Long Beach
PG. 123

55

73

73

INDEX TO STARRED ATTRACTIONS

2049-F

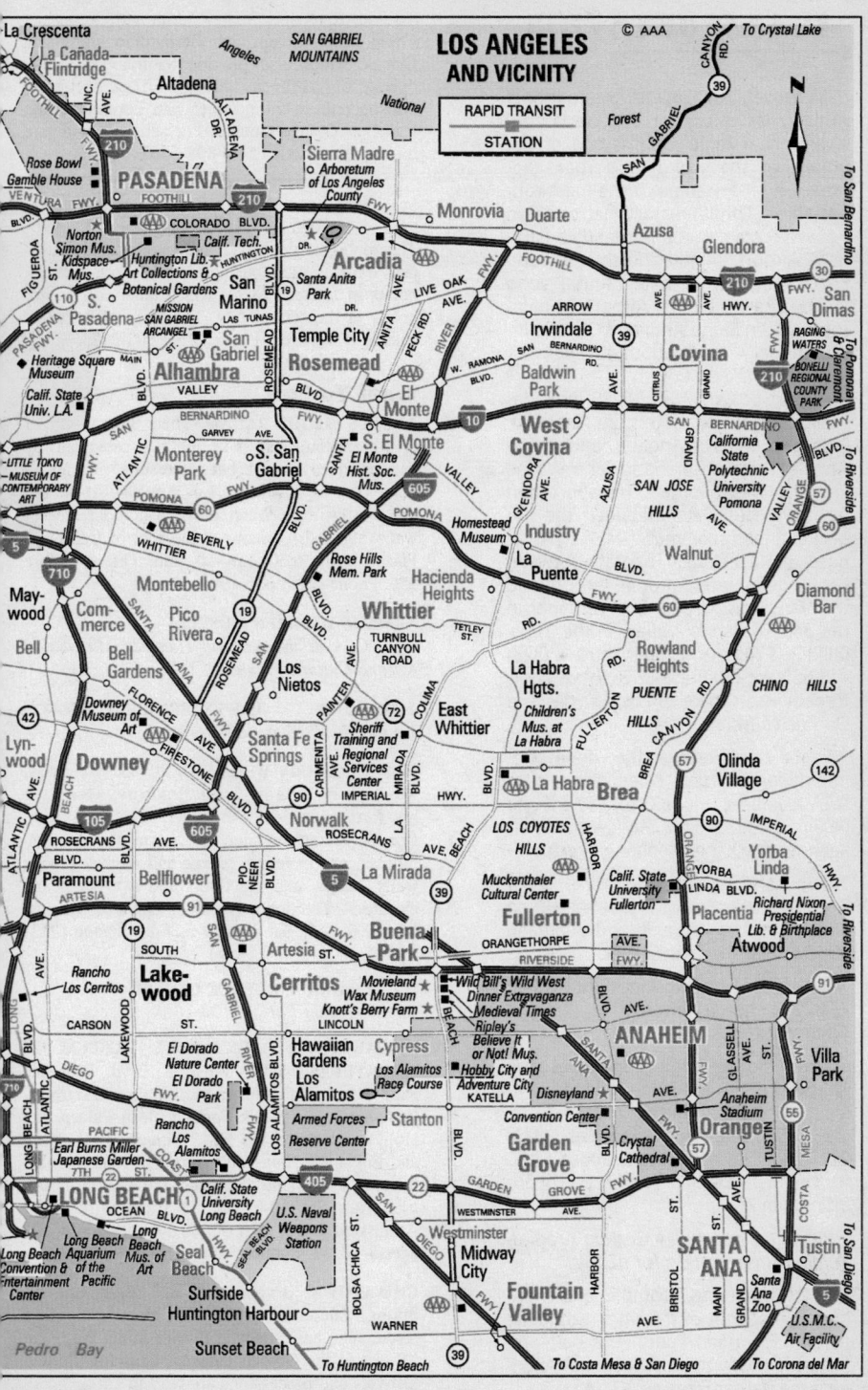

LOS ANGELES
AND VICINITY

© AAA

RAPID TRANSIT
STATION

To Crystal Lake

La Crescenta
La Cañada-Flintridge
Altadena
SAN GABRIEL MOUNTAINS
Angeles
National
Forest
CANYON RD.
To San Bernardino

Rose Bowl
Gamble House
PASADENA
FOOTHILL
Sierra Madre
Arboretum of Los Angeles County
Monrovia
Duarte
Azusa
Glendora

Norton Simon Mus.
Kidspace Mus.
Huntington Lib. Art Collections & Botanical Gardens
Calif. Tech.
San Marino
Santa Anita Park
Arcadia
LIVE OAK AVE.
FOOTHILL
ARROW
San Dimas
Raging Waters
Bonelli Regional County Park

Heritage Square Museum
Calif. State Univ. L.A.
MISSION SAN GABRIEL ARCANGEL
San Gabriel
Alhambra
Temple City
Rosemead
El Monte
Irwindale
Baldwin Park
Covina
California State Polytechnic University Pomona

LITTLE TOKYO MUSEUM OF CONTEMPORARY ART
Monterey Park
S. San Gabriel
El Monte Hist. Soc. Mus.
S. El Monte
West Covina
SAN JOSE HILLS
Walnut
Diamond Bar

Maywood
Commerce
Montebello
Pico Rivera
Bell Gardens
Bell
Homestead Museum
Industry
La Puente
Hacienda Heights
Whittier
Rose Hills Mem. Park
TURNBULL CANYON ROAD
Los Nietos
East Whittier
La Habra Hgts.
Children's Mus. at La Habra
Rowland Heights
PUENTE HILLS
CHINO HILLS

Lynwood
Downey Museum of Art
Downey
Santa Fe Springs
Sheriff Training and Regional Services Center
La Habra
Brea
Olinda Village

Paramount
Bellflower
Norwalk
La Mirada
LOS COYOTES HILLS
Muckenthaler Cultural Center
Fullerton
Calif. State University Fullerton
Yorba Linda
Richard Nixon Presidential Lib. & Birthplace
Atwood
Placentia

Rancho Los Cerritos
Lakewood
Cerritos
Buena Park
Movieland Wax Museum
Knott's Berry Farm
Wild Bill's Wild West Dinner Extravaganza
Medieval Times
ORANGETHORPE
ANAHEIM
Villa Park

El Dorado Nature Center
El Dorado Park
Hawaiian Gardens
Los Alamitos
Cypress
Los Alamitos Race Course
Ripley's Believe It or Not! Mus.
Hobby City and Adventure City
KATELLA
Disneyland
Orange
Anaheim Stadium

Earl Burns Miller Japanese Garden
Rancho Los Alamitos
Armed Forces Reserve Center
Stanton
Convention Center
Garden Grove
Crystal Cathedral

LONG BEACH
Calif. State University Long Beach
Long Beach Mus. of Art
Seal Beach
U.S. Naval Weapons Station
Westminster
Midway City
SANTA ANA
Santa Ana Zoo
Tustin

Long Beach Aquarium of the Pacific
Long Beach Convention & Entertainment Center
Surfside
Huntington Harbour
Sunset Beach
Fountain Valley
WARNER
U.S.M.C. Air Facility

Pedro Bay
To Huntington Beach
To Costa Mesa & San Diego
To Corona del Mar

TRANSPORTATION

Air travel: Los Angeles International Airport, at Century and Sepulveda boulevards near Inglewood, is one of the busiest in the world, and roads approaching it are some of the most congested. Other major metropolitan airports are Burbank-Glendale-Pasadena Airport, 14 miles northwest; Long Beach Airport, 22 miles south; John Wayne Orange County Airport, 30 miles southeast in Santa Ana; and Ontario International Airport, about 40 miles east in San Bernardino County.

Airport Bus, (800) 772-5299, provides service to major hotels in Anaheim, Pasadena and Los Angeles, and to Los Angeles International and John Wayne airports. Metropolitan Transportation Authority buses run between the airport and many communities. FlyAway buses, (818) 994-5554, operate between Los Angeles International Airport and the Van Nuys Airport Bus Terminal in the San Fernando Valley. Prime Time, (800) 262-7433, and Super Shuttle, (323) 775-6600 or (800) 258-3826, have door-to-door van service in Los Angeles and Orange counties.

Rental cars: Hertz, at the Los Angeles International Airport, offers discounts to AAA members; phone (310) 568-3400 or (800) 654-3080. For listings of other agencies check the telephone directory.

Rail service: Amtrak trains, (800) 872-7245, use the Art Deco-style Union Station at Los Angeles and Alameda streets, near the Civic Center.

Buses: Greyhound Lines Inc., (800) 231-2222, has a terminal at 7th and Alameda streets.

Taxis: Some large companies are Checker, (213) 482-3456; Independent, (213) 385-8294; United Independent, (323) 653-5050; and Yellow Cab, (323) 222-1234. The base rate is about $3.50 for the first mile and $1.80 for each additional mile.

Public transport: See Getting Around, Public Transportation for details.

Boats: Numerous steamship and cruise lines operate out of the city's man-made harbor. From San Pedro, the best and fastest highway to downtown Los Angeles is the Harbor Freeway (I-110).

nardino, Riverside, Santa Clarita and Oceanside. These lines—except San Bernardino and Santa Clarita, which also provide Saturday service—operate only Monday through Friday. Metrolink also operates a line between San Bernardino and Irvine in Orange County. For schedule and fare information phone (213) 808-5465.

DASH (Downtown Area Short Hop), a minibus shuttle system, operates throughout downtown Los Angeles with frequent service daily. The routes of the silver and magenta minibuses pass close to most business centers, retail stores, points of interest, Metro Rail stations and major hotels in the central city. The fare is 25c; exact change is required. Phone (213) 808-2273.

What To See

ANGELS FLIGHT RAILWAY, near the n.w. corner of 4th and Hill sts., is an inclined cable railway that provides a brief but interesting ride and a good view of downtown Los Angeles. At the top one can visit the Watercourt, an outdoor area of walkways and fountains at the foot of California Plaza. Daily 6:30 a.m.-10 p.m. One-way fare 25c. Phone (213) 626-1901.

ARMAND HAMMER MUSEUM—
see UCLA at the Armand Hammer Museum of Art and Cultural Center p. 112.

AUTRY MUSEUM OF WESTERN HERITAGE—
see Griffith Park p. 109.

THE BRADBURY BUILDING, 304 S. Broadway, was built in 1893 by Louis Bradbury, who made his fortune in Mexican silver mining. A five-story skylit atrium includes ornate wrought-iron railings, oak paneling, glazed and unglazed brick walls, marble and tile floors and two open-cage elevators. The lobby level is open to visitors. Mon.-Fri. 9-6, Sat.-Sun. 9-5. Free. Phone (213) 626-1893.

★ **CALIFORNIA SCIENCE CENTER—**
see Exposition Park p. 107.

SAVE **CAROLE & BARRY KAYE MUSEUM OF MINIATURES,** 5900 Wilshire Blvd., features handcrafted miniatures in more than 190 settings. Included are France's Fontainebleau Palace, the Hollywood Bowl, the HMS Titanic, the Vatican and England's Hampton Court. The museum also features a diorama depicting the O.J. Simpson trial. Tues.-Sat. 10-5, Sun. 11-5; closed holidays. Admission $7.50; over 60, $6.50; ages 12-18, $5; ages 3-11, $3. Phone (323) 937-6464.

CHINATOWN is bordered by Cesar Chavez, Spring, Yale and Bernard sts. Chinese shops and restaurants line streets off Gin Ling Way, the "Street of the Golden Palace." Colorful Chinese festivals and processions are held in this area. The Chinese Chamber of Commerce sponsors a 1-hour walking tour of the district departing from 960 N. Broadway; phone (213) 617-0396.

CIVIC CENTER, roughly bounded by Cesar E. Chavez and Grand aves. and 2nd and San Pedro sts., houses city, county, state and federal offices. The Arthur Will Memorial Fountain is on Grand Avenue. The Department of Water and Power Building across from the Music Center is surrounded by reflecting pools.

★ DISNEYLAND—see Anaheim p. 47.

DODGER STADIUM, 1000 Elysian Park Ave., n. of the Civic Center, is visible from Academy Rd. The cantilevered structure, which seats 56,000, is open only for baseball games and events. The Dodgers baseball season usually runs early April to early October. Phone (323) 224-1400 for schedule and ticket information.

★ EL PUEBLO DE LOS ANGELES HISTORIC MONUMENT consists of 44 acres bounded by Alameda, Arcadia and Spring sts. and Chavez Ave. Near the site of the pueblo where Los Angeles was established in 1781, this oldest section of the city reflects the ethnic background and heritage of the diverse groups who settled here and contributed to the city's development. Some historic landmarks have been restored. For more information contact the visitor information center in Sepulveda House.

Free guided walking tours are given Tues.-Sat. on the hour 10-1, except Thanksgiving and Dec. 25. Phone (213) 628-1274.

Avila Adobe, 10 E. Olvera St., was built in 1818 by rancher Don Francisco Avila. This adobe has been restored to exemplify the California lifestyle of the 1840s. Daily 9-5, Apr.-Sept.; 9-4, rest of year. Closed Thanksgiving and Dec. 25. Free.

Masonic Hall, 416-418 N. Main St., was built in 1858. It has been restored with many furnishings and fixtures that were brought around Cape Horn by sailing ships. Tues.-Fri. 10-3; closed holidays. Free.

Old Plaza, N. Main St., was the center of activity in the old pueblo of Los Angeles. It contains an ornate kiosk; century-old Moreton Bay fig trees; a statue of Felipe de Neve, leader of the group that founded the city in 1781; and a statue of King Carlos III, ruler of Spain at that time.

Old Plaza Church (Nuestra Señora la Reina de Los Angeles), on N. Main St. at the Plaza, is the oldest church in the city. Completed in 1822, it still serves an active parish.

Old Plaza Firehouse, 134 Paseo de la Plaza, was built in 1884. It houses an original chemical wagon, antique firefighting equipment and historic photographs. Tues.-Sun. 10-3; closed holidays. Free.

★ Olvera Street is n. of the Plaza between N. Main and Alameda sts. Named after Agustin Olvera, Los Angeles' first judge, the blocklong street is one of the oldest streets in the city; it was revitalized in 1930 as a Mexican marketplace. Sidewalk shops and stalls sell Mexican handicrafts; restaurants serve Mexican dishes. Las Posadas, the Mexican Christmas festival, is celebrated in December. Daily 10-7; some shops close at 8 p.m. Apr.-Sept. Free.

Pico House, 424-436 N. Main St., once was an elegant hotel built in 1870 by Pio Pico, the last governor of California under the Mexican flag. The building is partially restored but is not open to the public.

Sepulveda House, 622 N. Main. St., is a two-story Eastlake Victorian building built in 1887. The original owner, Eloisa Martínez de Sepulveda, used the structure as a boarding house with shops and as her own residence. The partially restored house includes a visitor center. An 18-minute film about the history of Los Angeles is shown on request. Mon.-Sat. 10-3; closed holidays. Free. Phone (213) 628-1274.

★ EXPOSITION PARK, bounded by Figueroa St., Exposition Blvd., Menlo Ave. and Martin Luther King Jr. Blvd., is a civic, cultural and recreational center. Within the park is a 7-acre sunken rose garden, where 16,000 specimens of 190 varieties are cultivated. Los Angeles Memorial Sports Arena holds sporting events and varied entertainment (see Sports and Recreation p. 116). Free.

California African-American Museum is at 600 State Dr. The museum has a permanent fine arts and history collection relating to African-American life. There also are changing exhibits of paintings, photographs, films and artifacts. Tues.-Sun. 10-5; closed Jan. 1, Thanksgiving and Dec. 25. Free. Phone (213) 744-7432.

[SAVE] ★ California Science Center, 700 State Dr., has hands-on exhibits relating to physics, space, the environment and health. World of Life features BodyWorks in which a 50-foot human figure explains how organs work. Creative World features Digital Jam Session where visitors can create music with drums, keyboards and guitars and then alter their creations using computers. The Space Docking Simulator is a virtual reality ride simulating a zero-gravity environment. Visitors can ride the High-Wire Bicycle across a one-inch cable 43 feet above the ground.

The IMAX® Theater uses a five-story screen and surround sound to take audiences on a simulated 2-D and 3-D journey across continents, over oceans and into space. The Weingart Gallery contains special exhibits. Food is available.

Museum open daily 10-5; closed Jan. 1, Thanksgiving and Dec. 25. IMAX theater open daily 10-9; closed Thanksgiving and Dec. 25. Museum free. IMAX admission $6.25; students with ID $4.75; over 60, $4.25; ages 4-12, $3.75. IMAX 3-D admission $7.25; students with ID $5.75; over 60, $5.25; ages 4-12, $4.75. Parking $5. MC, VI. Phone (213) 724-3623, or 744-7400 for museum and 744-2014 for theater.

⭐ Natural History Museum of Los Angeles County is at 900 Exposition Blvd. The museum contains detailed habitats of African, North American and exotic mammals. Exhibits include birds, insects and marine life; displays of dinosaurs and prehistoric fossils; a mineral collection; a cut gemstone collection; Megamouth, said to be the world's rarest shark; and the Times Mirror Hall of Native American Cultures. Skeletons of a tyrannosaurus rex and a triceratops face off in the main foyer.

History galleries depict life in California and the Southwest 1540-1940, U.S. history from the Colonial period through 1914 and pre-Columbian archeology. The Discovery Center has hands-on exhibits for children and an insect zoo. Permanent and rotating exhibits are displayed.

Mon.-Fri. 9:30-5, Sat.-Sun. 10-5; closed major holidays. Admission $8; over 62 and ages 13-18, $5.50; ages 5-12, $2; free to all first Tues. of the month. Phone (213) 763-3466.

⭐ FARMERS MARKET—*see Shopping p. 116.*

FIRST BAPTIST CHURCH is at 760 S. Westmoreland Ave. The rose windows are patterned after those in the cathedral at Chartres, France, and the goldleaf embossed ceiling replicates that of an Italian palace. Mon.-Fri. 9-4:30, Sun. 9-1; closed holidays. Donations. Phone (213) 384-2151.

FOREST LAWN MEMORIAL-PARK—HOLLYWOOD HILLS, 6300 Forest Lawn Dr., w. of Griffith Park, is a 340-acre cemetery featuring Carrara marble and bronze statuary. The Court of Liberty contains Thomas Ball's bronze and marble Washington Memorial, a replica of the Liberty Bell and a mosaic, "The Birth of Liberty." The Hall of Liberty presents the film "The Birth of Liberty" daily 11-4. Also in the hall is the Museum of Mexican History; an outdoor plaza contains reproductions of pre-Columbian Mexican sculpture.

The park also contains a replica of Boston's Old North Church which is closed during private services. Daily 8-5. Free. Phone (818) 241-4151 or (800) 204-3131.

GEORGE C. PAGE MUSEUM OF LA BREA DISCOVERIES, 5801 Wilshire Blvd., exhibits reconstructed fossils of ice-age animals such as mammoths, dire wolves, birds of prey and sabertoothed cats. A 14-minute film, "The La Brea Story," provides an introduction to the museum and depicts prehistoric life in Southern California. Visitors can watch fossils being cleaned, identified and catalogued in the paleontological laboratory. Tues.-Sun. 10-5; closed Jan. 1, July 4, Labor Day, Thanksgiving and Dec. 25. Admission, includes tar pits tour, $6; over 65 and students with ID $3.50; ages 5-10, $2; free to all first Tues. of the month. While a $7.50 fee is charged for parking in the lot behind the museum, the museum validates for $2.50; there is metered on-street parking. Phone (323) 934-7243.

Rancho La Brea Tar Pits, Wilshire Blvd. and Curson Ave., are among the richest sources of ice-age fossils. These sticky asphalt beds trapped and preserved prehistoric plant and animal life. More than 3 million fossils have been recovered from the tar pits. The viewing station and observation pit show how specimens appeared when they were discovered. Findings are displayed in Page Museum. Visitors can view paleontologists excavating the site in July and August.

Guided tours of the grounds start at the observation pit Thurs.-Sun. at 1. Observation pit open Sat.-Sun. 10-3; no tours Jan. 1, July 4, Labor Day, Thanksgiving and Dec. 25. Free.

⭐ GETTY CENTER, off I-405 at 1200 Getty Center Dr., unites the J. Paul Getty Trust's museum, institutes and grant program in the foothills of the Santa Monica Mountains. The centerpiece of the 110-acre complex is the museum and its collections of pre-20th-century European paintings, drawings, illuminated manuscripts, sculpture, decorative arts and photographs.

The site of the former J. Paul Getty Museum in Malibu is under renovation. The replica of an ancient Roman villa is scheduled to reopen in 2001 as a center for comparative archeology and ancient art.

Tues.-Wed. 11-7, Thurs.-Fri. 11-9, Sat.-Sun. 10-6. Free. Parking reservations must be made in advance; no parking in the neighborhood. **Note:** Visitors without parking reservations (including those arriving on foot, by taxi or by public transportation) will experience long lines and may not be allowed inside if the center's capacity is reached. Phone (310) 440-7300 for information and parking reservations.

⭐ GRIFFITH PARK, 4,107 acres at the e. end of the Santa Monica Mountains, just w. of the Golden State Frwy. (I-5), roughly between Los Feliz Blvd. on the s. and the Ventura Frwy. (SR 134) on the n., is said to be the largest urban municipal park in the United States. Originally a part of the Rancho Los Feliz Spanish land grant, the park was named for its 1896 donor, Griffith J. Griffith, a Welsh emigrant who made a fortune in gold mining.

The park contains attractions and recreational facilities, including educational and cultural institutions, wilderness areas and hiking trails. A bird sanctuary on Vermont Canyon Road provides glimpses of many species in their natural habitat. The visitor center and park ranger headquarters at 4730 Crystal Springs Dr., provides park information.

Greek Theatre is a natural amphtitheater at 2700 N. Vermont Ave. Ticket prices for summer concerts range from $15 to $65 and do not include parking. Phone (323) 665-1927.

Griffith Park Merry-Go-Round, in Park Center between Los Angeles Zoo and the Los Feliz park entrance, has 68 elaborately detailed and decorated horses. An automated band organ plays selections of marches and waltz music as an accompaniment. For information phone (323) 665-3051. Interpretive hikes conducted by the Sierra Club leave the upper or middle merry-go-round parking lots; for information about these and other hikes contact ranger headquarters.

Pony rides and a train that runs a 1.5-mile route through the park are near the Los Feliz Boulevard entrance. Near the train station is the SR2 Simulator, which uses film, sound effects and hydraulic motion to make participants feel as if they are driving a racing car, riding a roller coaster and flying in acrobatic airplanes. For pony ride information, phone (323) 664-3266.

The park is open and a ranger is on duty daily 6 a.m.-10 p.m. The 54 miles of bridle trails and hiking paths close at dusk. Carrousel runs daily 11-5 in summer; Sat.-Sun. and holidays 11-5, rest of year. Park admission free. Carrousel $1. Phone (323) 913-4688.

[SAVE] **Autry Museum of Western Heritage,** 4700 Western Heritage Way, uses art, artifacts and audiovisual materials to present the history of America's westward movement and its depiction on the big and small screens. Permanent and changing exhibits feature clothing, tools and a Colt gun collection. The display devoted to film and television cowboy heroes includes their silver saddles, hats and clothing. Also on-site are a theater that shows Westerns and a children's gallery. Food is available. Tues.-Sun. 10-5; closed Thanksgiving and Dec. 25. Admission $7.50; over 60 and ages 13-18, $5; ages 2-12, $3. Phone (323) 667-2000.

Griffith Observatory and Planetarium, on the s. slopes of Mount Hollywood at 2800 E. Obser-vatory Rd., is popular for viewing both city lights and stars. A bronze bust of James Dean is along the walkway of the observatory, where two scenes of "Rebel Without A Cause" were filmed. The planetarium reproduces the night sky; special effects replicate celestial phenomena visible to the naked eye. A twin refracting telescope is available on clear evenings. The Science Center has exhibits about our relationship with the universe. Laserium laser-light shows are coordinated with music.

Planetarium open daily 12:30-10, mid-June through Labor Day; Tues.-Fri. 2-10 and Sat.-Sun. 12:30-10, rest of year. Closed Thanksgiving and Dec. 24-25. Telescope available Tues.-Sun. dusk-9:45. Planetarium shows are presented daily at 3 and 7:30 (also Sat.-Sun. at 1:30 and 4:30). Laserium shows are presented Tues.-Sun.; phone for times. Box office opens 30 minutes before each show; there are no reserved seats.

Planetarium $4; over 64, $3; ages 5-12, $2. Laserium shows $7-$8; over 64 and ages 5-12, $6-$7. Under 5 admitted only to 1:30 planetarium show, with adult; under 5 not admitted to laserium shows. Phone (323) 664-1191 or 663-8171, or (818) 901-9405 for recorded laserium information.

[SAVE] ★**Los Angeles Zoo,** near the jct. of the Golden State and Ventura frwys., covers 113 acres of landscaped hills. The zoo is home to more than 1,200 mammals, birds and reptiles, including many rare and endangered species. Highlights include great ape families, a reptile house and an aviary. Animals native to the Southwest are showcased in their natural habitats on Adventure Island. Wildlife shows are offered. Picnicking is permitted. Daily 10-5. Last admission 1 hour before closing. Closed Dec. 25. Admission $8.25; over 64, $5.25; ages 2-12, $3.25. Phone (323) 644-4200.

Travel Town, n. side of Griffith Park on N. Zoo Dr., is an outdoor transportation museum with steam locomotives and other early railroad equipment. An indoor area features wagons, period automobiles and Los Angeles firefighting equipment used 1869-1940. A miniature train circles the area. Docent tours or free rides on a full-scale caboose are offered the first Sunday of the month.

Mon.-Fri. 10-5, Sat.-Sun. and holidays 10-6, Apr.-Oct.; Mon.-Fri. 10-4, Sat.-Sun. and holidays 10-5, rest of year. Closed Dec. 25. Donations. Train rides $1.75; ages 18 months-13 years, $1.25; over 64, $1. Phone (323) 662-5874.

[SAVE] **HERITAGE SQUARE MUSEUM,** 3800 Homer St., is an open-air museum featuring relocated and restored historically and architecturally significant buildings that reflect everyday life in Los Angeles 1865-1914. The museum's collections, exhibits and programs are displayed in villagelike settings. Guided tours are available. Grounds open Fri. 10-3; grounds and buildings open Sat.-Sun. 11:30-4:30, with guided tours on the hour noon-3. Admission $5; over 64 and ages 13-17, $4; ages 7-12, $2; under 7 free with adult; free to all Fri. Phone (626) 449-0193.

HOLLYHOCK HOUSE, 4800 Hollywood Blvd. in Barnsdall Park, is considered one of Frank Lloyd Wright's finest works. Tours are given on the hour Wed.-Sun. noon-4. Admission $2; over 61, $1; under 13 free with adult. Phone (323) 913-4157.

★ **KNOTT'S BERRY FARM—** *see Buena Park p. 61.*

LA BREA TAR PITS—*see George C. Page Museum of La Brea Discoveries p. 108.*

★ **LITTLE TOKYO,** roughly bounded by 1st, Alameda, 3rd and Los Angeles sts., is the social, cultural and economic center of Southern California's Japanese community. The 21-story New Otani Hotel, the Japanese American Cultural and Community Center and the Japanese American National Museum attest to the area's vitality. Four shopping centers—Japanese Village Plaza, Weller Court, Yaohan Plaza and Honda Plaza—contain restaurants and shops.

[SAVE] **Japanese American National Museum,** 1st and Central sts., occupies a remodeled Buddhist temple with displays of photographs, personal objects, art and artifacts reflecting the history of Japanese immigration to and assimilation into America. Other highlights include an area where visitors may experiment with origami, examine Japanese family photo albums, learn about World War II internment camps and view the 15-minute film, "Moving Memories."

Tues.-Wed. and Fri.-Sun. 10-5, Thurs. 10-8; closed Jan. 1, Thanksgiving and Dec. 25. Admission $4; over 61, college students with ID and ages 6-17, $3. Phone (213) 625-0414.

LOS ANGELES CHILDREN'S MUSEUM, downtown at 310 N. Main St., offers a hands-on environment for ages 2-10, designed to demystify everyday experiences. Interactive exhibits include a video studio and a recording studio; Club ECO; H2O, the Story of Water; and Art Workshops. Mon.-Fri. 11:30-5, Sat.-Sun. 10-5, late June to mid-Sept.; Sat.-Sun. 10-5, rest of year. Closed holidays. Admission $5, under 2 free. Phone (213) 687-8800.

★ **LOS ANGELES COUNTY MUSEUM OF ART,** 5905 Wilshire Blvd., is a five-building complex housing paintings, sculpture, costumes, textiles and decorative art from around the world. The collections comprise more than 150,000 works and span the history of art from ancient times to the present. In addition to presenting more than 30 exhibitions each year, the museum also sponsors concerts, film programs and lectures that complement its collections.

The museum's West Building, in the former May Co. Building at the corner of Wilshire Blvd. and Fairfax St., features the Southwestern Art Museum, the Experimental Gallery and special exhibits. Guided tours are offered daily. Food is available. Thurs.-Tues. noon-8 (also Fri. 8-9 p.m.); closed Thanksgiving and Dec. 25. Admission $6; over 61 and students with ID $4; ages 6-17, $1; free to all second Tues. of the month. Parking $5. Phone (323) 857-6000.

LOS ANGELES MUNICIPAL ART GALLERY, 4800 Hollywood Blvd. in Barnsdall Art Park, presents changing exhibits of contemporary art from Southern California. Wed.-Sun. 12:30-5 (also Fri. 5-8:30); closed holidays and between exhibits. Admission $1.50, under 12 free with adult. Phone (213) 485-4581.

LOS ANGELES PUBLIC LIBRARY'S CENTRAL LIBRARY, 630 W. 5th St. between Grand Ave. and Flower St., is a landmark structure designed by noted architect Bertram Goodhue. The library's extensive collection includes more than 2.1 million books and 500,000 historical photographs. Damaged by fire in 1986, the 1926 building has been restored and expanded; the grounds offer gardens and a 250-seat auditorium. Mon. and Thurs.-Sat. 10-5:30, Sun. 1-5, Tues.-Wed. noon-8. Guided tours Mon.-Fri. at 12:30, Sat. at 11 and 2, Sun. at 2. Free. Phone (213) 228-7000.

LOS ANGELES TIMES, 202 W. 1st St. (entrance at 145 S. Spring St.), offers 35-minute tours of its editorial operations Mon.-Fri. at 11:15; closed holidays. Free. Under 10 are not permitted. Phone (213) 237-5757.

★ **LOS ANGELES ZOO—** *see Griffith Park p. 109.*

★ **MOVIELAND WAX MUSEUM—** *see Buena Park p. 61.*

THE MUSEUM OF CONTEMPORARY ART, 250 S. Grand Ave. at California Plaza, houses international works, including paintings, sculptures and environmental pieces, from the 1940s to the present. Mixed media and performing arts programs also are presented. The building, designed by Arata Isozaki in 1982, is itself considered a work of art. The Geffen Contemporary at MOCA, the museum's other building, is near Little Tokyo at 152 N. Central Ave.

Tues.-Sun. 11-5 (also Thurs. 5-8); closed Jan. 1, Thanksgiving and Dec. 25. Combined admission $6, over 64 and students with ID $4, under 12 free; free to all Thurs. 5-8. Phone (213) 626-6222.

MUSEUM OF MINIATURES—see *Carole & Barry Kaye Museum of Miniatures p. 106.*

SAVE **MUSEUM OF NEON ART,** 501 W. Olympic Blvd., contains "modern sculpture in neon." Displays are colorful, frenetic, and imaginative. The collection includes fine art, old signs, kinetic art and information about the history and technology of neon signage. Wed.-Sat. 11-5 (also second Thurs. of the month 5-8), Sun. noon-5. Admission $5; over 64 and ages 13-22, $3.50; under 12 free with an adult. Parking in Renaissance Tower free with validation; entrance is on Grand Avenue north of Olympic. Phone (213) 489-9918.

SAVE **MUSEUM OF TOLERANCE,** 9786 W. Pico Blvd., has interactive exhibits about racism and prejudice in America. Using films, reconstructions, photographs and artifacts, a major installation depicts the history of the Holocaust. The Point of View Diner is an interactive exhibit dealing with personal responsibility as it relates to drunk driving, and hate speech versus First Amendment rights issues. A learning center allows additional research. Food is available. Comfortable walking shoes and a sweater or jacket are advised.

Two-and-a-half-hour museum tours depart every 12 minutes Mon.-Thurs. 10-4, Fri. 10-1 (also Fri. 1-3, Apr.-Oct.), Sun. 11-5; closed Jewish holidays. Admission $8; over 61, $6; students with ID $5; ages 3-10, $3. Free underground parking is available. Phone (310) 553-8403. *See color ad.*

★**THE MUSIC CENTER,** 135 Grand Ave. at 1st St., is a three-theater complex at the crown of the Civic Center. One-hour guided tours include Dorothy Chandler Pavilion (the center's largest building), Ahmanson Theatre and Mark Taper Forum. Tours are given Mon.-Sat. 10-noon. Hours may vary; phone ahead. Tours free. Phone (213) 972-7483, or (213) 972-7211 for show information.

★**NATURAL HISTORY MUSEUM OF LOS ANGELES COUNTY—** see *Exposition Park p. 108.*

★**OLVERA STREET—**see *El Pueblo de Los Angeles Historic Monument p. 107.*

SAVE **PETERSEN AUTOMOTIVE MUSEUM,** 6060 Wilshire Blvd., contains exhibits dedicated to the history of the automobile and includes a full-scale reproduction of scenes and buildings that marked important milestones in the development of the motor car and Los Angeles. Five galleries house changing exhibitions of various types of vehicles, while other galleries display automotive memorabilia and changing exhibits. Tues.-Sun. and Mon. holidays 10-6. Admission $7; over 62 and students with ID $5; ages 5-12, $3. Parking $4. Phone (323) 930-2277.

ST. JOHN'S CHURCH (Episcopal), 514 W. Adams Blvd. just e. of Figueroa St., replicates an 11th-century church in Toscanella, Italy. The Martin Luther King Jr. window, dedicated in 1977, is on the west side of the clerestory. Mon. and Wed.-Fri. 9-3:30, Sat.-Sun. 9-noon, June-Sept.; Mon. and Thurs. 9-5, Wed. 9-7, Fri. 9-3, Sat.-Sun. 9-noon, rest of year. Closed holidays. Free. Phone (213) 747-6285.

ST. SOPHIA CATHEDRAL (Greek Orthodox) is at 1324 S. Normandie Ave. Stained-glass windows, large-scale murals, gilded woodwork and crystal chandeliers highlight the domed interior. Photography is not permitted. Fri.-Wed. 10-2; closed holidays. Free. Phone (323) 737-2424.

ST. VINCENT DE PAUL CHURCH (Catholic), 621 W. Adams Blvd. at Figueroa St., is an elaborate Spanish Colonial-style church with mosaic tile from Mexico. Daily 7-4:30. Free. Phone (213) 749-8950.

SIX FLAGS MAGIC MOUNTAIN—
see Valencia p. 131.

SKIRBALL CULTURAL CENTER AND MUSEUM
is at 2701 N. Sepulveda Blvd. near I-405 at the
top of Sepulveda Pass in the Santa Monica
Mountains, and was designed by Moshe Safde.
The center seeks to interpret the Jewish experience through a range of cultural programs including exhibitions of religious objects, statuary,
pottery, mosaics, clothing and photographs.
Films, concerts, lectures and symposia offer the
visitor exposure to the customs and traditions of
the world's Jews. The Children's Discovery Center explores the world of archeology through
hands-on sand exhibits. Food is available. Tues.-
Sat. noon-5, Sun. 11-5. Admission $8, over 64
and students with ID $6, under 12 free. Phone
(310) 440-4500.

SAVE SOUTHWEST MUSEUM, 234 Museum Dr.,
offers art exhibits and artifacts representing the
diversity of Native American cultures from prehistoric times to the present, and from Alaska to
South America. Collections include basketry, pottery, paintings, textiles and decorative arts.
Changing exhibits explore various cultural aspects of different regions. Lectures, demonstrations and other programs are scheduled
periodically. Tues.-Sun. 10-5; closed holidays.
Admission $5; over 54 and students with ID $3;
ages 7-18, $2. Phone (323) 221-2164.

**UCLA AT THE ARMAND HAMMER MUSEUM
OF ART AND CULTURAL CENTER,** 10899
Wilshire Blvd. in Westwood Village, is a meeting
place and showcase for the arts. In addition to
offering a diverse schedule of historical and contemporary art exhibitions, the museum also presents music, dance, poetry, gallery talks,
symposia and docent-led tours.

Tues.-Sat. 11-7 (also Thurs. 7-9 p.m.), Sun.
11-5; closed Jan. 1, July 4, Thanksgiving and
Dec. 25. Admission $4.50, over 64 and college
students with ID $3, under 18 free; free to all
Thurs. 6-9 p.m. Parking is $2.75 for the first 3
hours, and $1.75 for each 20 minutes thereafter;
maximum daily fee is $12. Phone (310)
443-7000.

**★ UNIVERSITY OF CALIFORNIA, LOS ANGE-
LES (UCLA),** 405 Hilgard Ave., occupies 419
acres in the foothills of the Santa Monica Mountains. Relocated here in 1929, the university encompasses several major complexes, including a
large medical center, and enrolls approximately
34,000 students each year.

The UCLA School of the Arts and Architecture offers events, including concerts, recitals,
festivals, lectures, exhibitions, dance showcases
and forums October to mid-June in Schoenberg
Hall and other campus venues; most are free.
Roger Hall, scheduled to reopen in spring 1998,
is host to other performances. For 24-hour event
information, phone (310) 825-2278.

Visitors can pick up a map at information
booths around campus. Guided walking tours are

offered Mon.-Fri. at 10:15 and 2:15; reservations
are required. Tours free; parking $5. Phone (310)
825-8764.

Edwin W. Pauley Pavilion, on the w. side of
campus off Westwood Blvd., is a 13,000-seat
arena that accommodates UCLA basketball, volleyball and gymnastic events. For tickets phone
(310) 825-2101.

Franklin D. Murphy Sculpture Garden, on the
n. portion of the campus in front of Dickson Art
Center, is an outdoor museum featuring more
than 70 works by 19th- and 20th-century masters
such as Joan Miro, Henry Moore and Auguste
Rodin. It is reputed to have one of the most distinguished collections in the country. Daily 24
hours. Free.

Mildred E. Mathias Botanical Garden, Hilgard
and Le Conte aves., consists of 8 acres of native,
subtropical and exotic plants. Walking paths
through the garden are open Mon.-Fri. 8-5, Sat.-
Sun. 8-4; closed university holidays. Free. Phone
(310) 825-3620.

UCLA Fowler Museum of Cultural History,
on the n. side of campus w. of Royce Hall, has
four galleries presenting six to eight changing
exhibits a year representing the art and culture of
past and present peoples from around the world.
Wed.-Sun. noon-5 (also Thurs. 5-8). Admission
$5, over 64 and students with ID $3, under 18
free; free to all Thurs. and Sun. Phone (310)
825-4361.

**UNIVERSITY OF SOUTHERN CALIFORNIA
(USC),** with its University Park campus at Exposition Blvd. and S. Figueroa St., was founded in
1880. Widney Alumni House, USC's first building, is the said to be the oldest university building in California. A bronze Trojan warrior stands
near the entrance to Bovard Administration
Building. A 400-pound boulder quarried more
than 3,000 years ago from near the ancient city
of Troy is displayed in Founders Park. The
School of Cinema-Television, established in 1929
and the first of its kind, can be toured Friday afternoons by appointment; phone (213) 740-2892.

The School of Theatre presents drama in Bing
Theater; phone (213) 740-7111 for schedule.
Hancock Memorial Museum, in Hancock Foundation Building, offers tours by appointment
through four rooms of the 1907-09 Hancock
Mansion; phone (213) 740-5144. Many campus
buildings feature Romanesque architecture and
have been backdrops for films, including "For-
rest Gump." One-hour walking tours are available by appointment Mon.-Fri. 10-3. Tours free;
parking $6. Phone (213) 740-6605.

Fisher Gallery, 823 Exposition Blvd., displays
rotating exhibits, including works of European
old masters and contemporary artworks. Tues.-
Fri. noon-5, Sat. 11-3, early Sept.-Apr. 30; closed
between exhibitions. Free. Phone (213)
740-4561.

WATTS TOWERS OF SIMON RODIA STATE HISTORIC PARK, 1765 E. 107th St., feature the Towers of Simon (Sabato) Rodia, eight weblike towers of concrete-coated steel rods encrusted with shells, tile, pottery and glass. A tilesetter, Simon Rodia spent 33 years creating these remarkable works of folk art. Watts Towers Art Center, next to the towers, sponsors exhibits, classes and cultural events. The upper portions of the towers are readily visible from the center.

Tours are suspended while the towers are closed for restoration. However, visitors to the park can see the towers from the outside. Park open daily 24 hours. Free. Phone (213) 847-4646.

WELLS FARGO HISTORY MUSEUM is in Wells Fargo Center, 333 S. Grand Ave. Exhibits and a video presentation depict the history and development of the West and Wells Fargo Bank since its 1852 founding. Highlights include a 19th-century stagecoach, a 2-pound gold nugget, prospecting and assaying equipment, bank notes, photographs and lithographs from the 1800s. Visitors can board the stagecoach and listen to a firsthand description of a 3-week journey from St. Louis to San Francisco taken in 1859. Mon.-Fri. 10-5; closed bank holidays. Free. Phone (213) 253-7166.

WILSHIRE BOULEVARD TEMPLE, 3663 Wilshire Blvd. at Hobart Blvd., is dominated by a 135-foot dome inlaid with mosaics. The interior walls have murals with Biblical and post-Biblical themes. A gallery contains exhibits explaining the history and customs of various Jewish celebrations. Mon.-Fri. 8:30-5; closed Jewish holidays. Free. Phone (213) 388-2401.

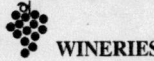 **WINERIES**

• **San Antonio Winery**, 737 Lamar St. Daily 11-3. Phone (323) 223-1401.

What To Do

Sightseeing

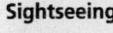 **Boat Tours**

Boat tours of the Los Angeles harbor depart Ports O' Call Village *(see San Pedro p. 130)*. Ships also leave San Pedro for Catalina Island.

 **Bus and Limousine Tours**

One way to get a comprehensive picture of Los Angeles is by taking an organized bus or limousine tour. Prices vary according to the itinerary and length of tour.

Free bus tours of downtown Los Angeles depart on the first and third Wednesday mornings of the month from the Docent Center adjoining Old Plaza Firehouse in El Pueblo de Los Angeles Historic Monument *(see attraction listing p.*

107). Sponsored by Las Angelitas del Pueblo, the 2-hour tours visit Little Tokyo, Bunker Hill, California Plaza, Chinatown and Carroll Avenue. Reservations are required; phone (213) 628-1274.

 Plane Tours

Scenic air tours over Los Angeles County's inland and coastal areas in an open-cockpit biplane are available through Bird's Nest, (818) 753-0070 Security Aviation, (310) 676-2206 also offers tours. Rides last from 15 to 60 minutes and reservations are recommended. All pilots are FAA certified.

Note: The mention of the preceding airplane rides is for information only and does **not** imply endorsement by AAA.

Studio Tours

NBC STUDIO TOURS—*see Burbank p. 118.*

TELEVISION STUDIOS of the major broadcasting companies offer many studio audience shows. Ticket requests should be made well in advance; some shows have waiting lists several months long. Audiences Unlimited Ticket Line can provide further information; phone (818) 506-0067.

★**UNIVERSAL STUDIOS HOLLYWOOD**—*see Universal City p. 131.*

THE WARNER BROS. STUDIOS V.I.P. TOUR—*see Burbank p. 120.*

 Walking Tours

The Los Angeles Conservancy offers 12 guided, 1- and 2-hour walking tours of historic downtown Los Angeles. The Pershing Square Landmarks, Broadway Theaters and Art Deco tours are among offerings. A tour of Little Tokyo is given on the first Saturday of the month. One-hour tours are given of Regal Biltmore Hotel, City Hall and Union Station. All tours cost $5; reservations are required. Phone (213) 623-2489.

Walking tours of El Pueblo de Los Angeles Historic Monument *(see attraction listing p. 107)* depart Tuesday through Saturday on the hour 10-1 from the Docent Center adjoining Old Plaza Firehouse. The free tours last approximately 1 hour. Guided walking tours of Chinatown *(see attraction listing p. 106)* are sponsored by the Chinese Chamber of Commerce.

 Self-guiding Tour

The best way to see downtown Los Angeles is on foot. The walking tour outlined here *(see map following)* is approximately 3 miles long and will take at least 4 hours, allowing time for lunch and browsing. The names of sites listed in detail in the Attractions section are printed in bold type. Even if you do not tour a listed site, reading the listing when you reach that point will make the tour more interesting.

The tour is designed to return you to the starting point via the convenient DASH minibus, which operates daily together with the Red Line subway to facilitate getting around in the downtown area.

The tour starts in front of the imposing and inviting **Los Angeles Central Library** on 5th St. between Flower St. and Grand Ave. Rising from the north side of 5th are the Bunker Hill Steps, a series of gradually ascending steps bordered by small waterfalls and edged by skyscrapers. On either side of the steps climbing Bunker Hill are eating establishments. Follow the steps to the top and continue north on Hope St. to 4th St. At this corner, the top of the ARCO garage, next to Ket-

cham YMCA, can be reached by the garage elevator or from the bridge linking it with the futuristic Westin Bonaventure. The impressive buildings of the financial district are visible on all sides. Each building is distinct in color and shape, yet all blend harmoniously and are spaced to allow plenty of sunlight to reach the plazas and streets below.

Extensive landscaping and artwork also play an important role in this district. The Bank of America water garden (1 block north), Wells Fargo Center (diagonally across at 4th and Hope) and the forecourt and tiered plazas of Citibank Center are particularly attractive.

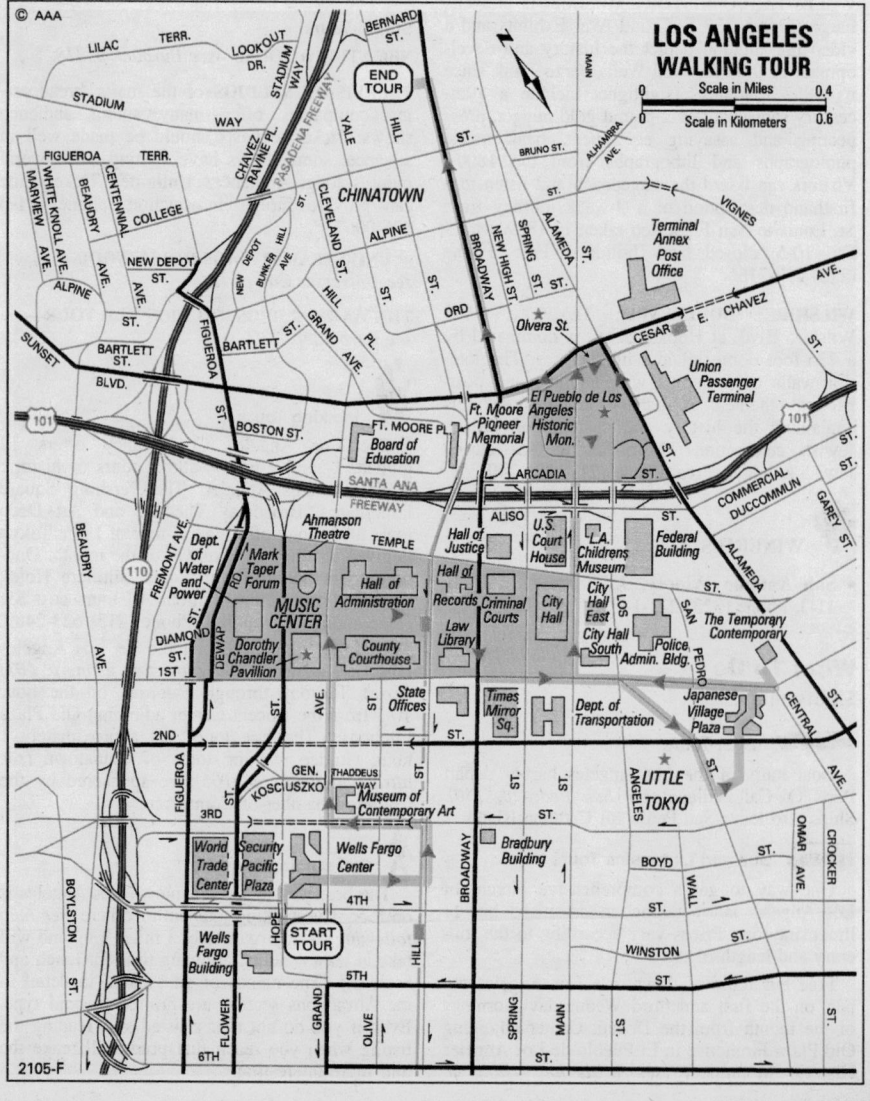

Library Tower, with its dramatic crownlike top, is America's tallest building west of Chicago. Next to the 1,017-foot tower is a beautiful Spanish-style stairway that leads in a series of cascades down to 5th Street.

While still atop the ARCO garage, walk to the edge opposite the Westin Bonaventure. The landscaped parks covering the roofs of the buildings below also were a design requirement, as was the pedestrian skyway system that links the complexes.

Leave the rooftop at 4th and Hope and walk through Wells Fargo Center to Grand Ave. (The Court is the glass-enclosed garden pavilion between the huge granite towers housing Wells Fargo Bank and IBM.) Across Grand is California Plaza and the **Museum of Contemporary Art.**

Detour across the Watercourt, a plaza enhanced by fountains and eating establishments set among towering skyscrapers. On the east side of the Watercourt, across Grand Ave. from Wells Fargo Center, is **Angels Flight Railway**, a restored funicular ride known as the world's shortest railway. For 25 cents you can take a one-minute ride that drops down to Hill St. Across the street stands Grand Central Market, containing blocklong rows of food stalls. There are fruit and vegetable stands, lunch counters, bakeries and ethnic foods.

Although some construction remains to be done, the massive Bunker Hill project includes three towering office buildings, nearly a thousand apartments, a major hotel, shops and restaurants, and an impressive series of waterfalls and fountains.

Going back to Grand via Angels Flight, and continuing north, you will notice that the roadway is elevated. Below is lower Grand Ave., which provides access to underground garages, thereby keeping the sidewalks on upper Grand free of automobile entranceways. Two blocks north is the **Music Center**, home of major musical and theatrical companies.

The huge building just west of the Music Center is the headquarters of the Los Angeles Department of Water and Power, the nation's largest public utility. The reflecting pool surrounding it is lined by a promenade from which you can see much of central Los Angeles.

Moving east, cross Grand Ave. to the plaza that leads toward **City Hall** (closed temporarily for renovation), which is the tall, pyramid-topped building straight ahead. You will pass the impressive Arthur Will Memorial Fountain and see a great variety of subtropical foliage. The brilliant orange blooms of the bird-of-paradise plant—the city's official flower—can be found throughout the **Civic Center** from fall through spring.

Many Civic Center buildings surround the mall. Together they constitute one of the largest government complexes in the entire country outside of those in Washington, D.C.

At the "Court of Flags" is an entrance to Los Angeles' subway. Take the escalator down to view the cavernous station. Proceed east through the "Court of Flags" to Broadway, then turn south a half block to 1st St. and continue east past the mammoth headquarters of the *Los Angeles Times.*

Two blocks farther east on 1st and next to New Otani Hotel is Weller Court. An attractive development in the **Little Tokyo** district, the court contains many restaurants and shops. An excellent place to take a break is the Japanese Garden atop the south wing of New Otani Hotel. The bustling city below and the skyscrapers on the horizon provide an intriguing contrast to the tumbling waterfalls, placid streams and serene landscaping of the garden.

An equally lovely garden is found at the Japanese American Cultural and Community Center, a half block south of 2nd St. on San Pedro St. It lies just beyond the spacious JACCC Plaza, whose main focus is a striking work by the sculptor Isamu Noguchi. Fronting the plaza are the community center building and the Japan America Theatre, which offers performances from both Eastern and Western cultures.

Leading north from JACCC Plaza, a pedestrian lane crosses 2nd St. and enters Japanese Village Plaza, a pleasant collection of small restaurants and stores. Cross the plaza to 1st St. At 1st and Central is the **Japanese American National Museum,** providing insight into Japanese family life in the United States. Also on Central is the Geffen Contemporary at MOCA, the second building of The Museum of Contemporary Art.

Redeveloped artists' galleries and lofts now occupy the once-drab area east and south of Little Tokyo. The Calendar section of Sunday's *Los Angeles Times* lists galleries and museums in the area and throughout the city.

Turning back on 1st St. to Main St., you will re-enter the Civic Center. Go north on Main past City Hall, Los Angeles Mall, a sunken shopping plaza containing the **Los Angeles Children's Museum,** to **El Pueblo de Los Angeles Historic Monument,** the birthplace of Los Angeles. Historic **Pico House** and the **Old Plaza Firehouse** face the plaza. A visitor information center has brochures and information about the park.

Proceed northeast through **Olvera Street** to Alameda St. Across the street is the impressive 1939 Union Station, now the focus of a 460-mile commuter rail transit system as well as the focus of transcontinental Amtrak service. Return to Olvera St. and turn west to Main St. and the city's oldest religious structure—**Old Plaza Church.** Follow Main north to Chavez Ave., then take Chavez west to Broadway.

A 3.5-block walk north on Broadway brings you to **Chinatown**, with its distinctive architecture, shops, restaurants and dragons. To return to the starting point, catch a DASH bus southbound on Broadway and get off at Westin Bonaventure

Hotel at 5th and Flower sts. For a pleasant end to the tour, stop off at the revolving lounge atop the hotel for a panorama of the city; casual dress is acceptable.

Sports and Recreation

Sloping south from the San Gabriel Mountains over the Hollywood Hills to the Pacific Ocean, the Los Angeles Basin and surrounding valleys are blessed with a climate permitting outdoor activities throughout the year. It is possible to hit the ski slopes in the morning and have lunch at the beach on the same day.

Golf courses and tennis courts, many open for public use, are numerous. Nearly all beaches are open to the public; many offer swimming, surfing, scuba diving, surf fishing and snorkeling. Check locally for restrictions. Some coastal areas offer pier or deep-sea fishing and have marinas and facilities for boating and water skiing. Numerous concessions sell bait and rent fishing gear as well as surfboards and boats. As in many places, parking fees are charged at or near beaches.

Spectator sports are many and varied. Santa Anita Park, (626) 574-7223, is among the country's most famous Thoroughbred horse racing tracks; more than a score of $100,000 racing stakes are run here. Hollywood Park in Inglewood, known as the "track of lakes and flowers," also plays host to Thoroughbred racing; phone (310) 419-1500. Los Alamitos Race Course has both quarter horse and harness racing; phone (714) 995-1234.

Note: Policies concerning admittance of children to pari-mutuel betting facilities vary. Phone ahead for information.

Polo is frequently played at Will Rogers State Historic Park in Pacific Palisades, usually on Saturday and Sunday (weather permitting).

The college football event of the year is the Rose Bowl Game, played in Pasadena on New Year's Day. The home games of USC are played at Los Angeles Memorial Coliseum in Exposition Park. UCLA plays its home football games at the Rose Bowl.

The home of the Los Angeles Lakers basketball and Kings ice hockey teams, as well as the Sparks women's basketball team, is Great Western Forum in Inglewood; phone (310) 673-1300 for ticket information. Both the Lakers and the Kings play from late October to mid-March. The Mighty Ducks ice hockey team plays at Arrowhead Pond in Anaheim. Los Angeles Clippers basketball games, as well as circuses, athletic meets and other events, are held in Exposition Park at Los Angeles Memorial Sports Arena; phone (213) 748-8000.

Professional baseball is played in Dodger Stadium, (323) 224-1400, near the Civic Center and at Edison Field in Anaheim, home field of the Anaheim Angels; phone (714) 634-2000.

For information about sports and recreation in other nearby areas see place listings for Angeles National Forest p. 50, Big Bear Lake p. 59, Catalina Island p. 63, Lake Arrowhead p. 86, San Bernardino National Forest p. 171 and Santa Monica Mountains National Recreation Area p. 220.

Shopping

The decentralization of Los Angeles has given rise to a number of shopping centers scattered throughout the city and the metropolitan area. Major downtown shopping areas include Macy's Plaza, bounded by 7th, Hope, 8th and Flower streets, and Seventh Market Place, bounded by 7th, Figueroa and 8th streets and the Harbor Freeway. Other shopping areas include Beverly Hills, Century City and Westwood Village near UCLA.

Major suburban areas have regional shopping centers, many of which have distinctive architecture. These include Beverly Center in Los Angeles, Del Amo Fashion Center in Torrance, Fashion Island in Newport Beach, Fox Hills Mall in Culver City, Glendale Galleria, Santa Anita Fashion Park in Arcadia, Santa Monica Place, South Coast Plaza in Costa Mesa, Topanga Plaza in Woodland Hills, Ventura Boulevard in the San Fernando Valley and Westside Pavilion in West Los Angeles.

The major stores dotting the metropolitan landscape include Macy's, Neiman-Marcus,

Nordstrom, Robinsons-May and Saks Fifth Avenue. Most have many branches and prices that range from moderate to expensive.

You can find gifts and unusual souvenirs from the Orient in the Chinatown and Little Tokyo districts. Mexican handicraft shops are abundant on Olvera Street. Many art galleries grace La Cienega Boulevard from Santa Monica to Beverly boulevards, and others are scattered throughout the area, particularly on the west side of Los Angeles.

Also downtown is the garment district, where numerous wholesalers offer discount prices to the public, and the expanding jewelry district along Hill Street offers good value. At 7th and Wall streets is the Flower Mart, a huge wholesale flower center. Also popular is Grand Central Public Market, a bustling grocery and meat market at 3rd and Hill streets, which rivals Farmers Market for color and variety.

The massive ARCO and Macy's plazas and the Westin Bonaventure combine modern shopping complexes and dramatic architecture. Fisherman's Village in Marina del Rey and Shoreline Village in Long Beach feature many art, craft and specialty shops.

★ **FARMERS MARKET**, 6333 W. 3rd St. at Fairfax Ave., consists of more than 100 merchants selling food, clothing and gift items. The market's outdoor cafes also are popular. Mon.-Sat. 9-7, Sun. 10-6, June-Sept.; Mon.-Sat. 9-6:30, Sun. 10-5, rest of year. Closed holidays. Free. Phone (323) 933-9211.

Theater and Concerts

Thanks in part to The Music Center and the enormous talent pool created by the film and television industries, Los Angeles has become the nation's second major theatrical city.

Again, the best source of information is the Calendar section of the Sunday *Los Angeles Times*; it lists current and coming movie and stage features as well as lectures, classical and pop music concerts, nightlife, museum exhibits and art shows. Universities and community colleges present student productions and touring professional shows. Tickets for most theaters can be obtained at the box office or through ticket agencies.

Presentations range from comedic theater in various media, such as that found at the Improv in Santa Monica, to more serious works at such

places as the Ahmanson, Mark Taper and UCLA James A. Doolittle theaters. Many small theaters present dramas that range from classical to contemporary.

The Music Center in downtown Los Angeles is host to opera, musical comedy, a celebrity series, symphony concerts and productions of the Center Theatre Group, the Los Angeles Opera, Los Angeles Master Chorale and the Los Angeles Philharmonic; phone (213) 972-7211. Wiltern Theatre, noted for its elaborate art deco design, presents stage events.

Shubert Theatre in Century City stages plays and musicals. Universal Amphitheatre in Universal City is an enclosed year-round entertainment complex. Pantages Theatre in Hollywood presents musical comedies and stage plays with top-name entertainers. Henry Fonda Theatre in Hollywood and Wilshire Theatre in Beverly Hills present dramatic fare with professional actors. Outdoor theaters offering summer productions include the Greek Theatre in Griffith Park and the Hollywood Bowl.

Cerritos Center for the Performing Arts in Cerritos presents an international spectrum of entertainment; pop, jazz, classical and virtuoso musical offerings complement performances of opera, ballet and theater.

Special Events

Oshogatsui, the Japanese New Year, is celebrated in early January, while the Sunkist Invitational Indoor Track Meet is held mid-month. The Chinese New Year is celebrated in early February. The UCLA Gymnastics Invitational, held in Westwood, and the Nissan Los Angeles Open Golf Tournament occur later in the month. The Los Angeles Marathon is held in early March.

The Hispanic L.A. Fiesta fills the Broadway shopping district downtown with 500,000 people in late April. Cinco de Mayo celebrations in early May are scattered throughout the city at various locations. The Volvo Tennis Tournament at UCLA is held in early August, and Japanese Americans celebrate Nisei Week during the second week of August. The Los Angeles Senior PGA Golf Tournament is held in late October.

For further information about Los Angeles events contact the district offices of the Automobile Club of Southern California or the Los Angeles Convention and Visitors Bureau.

Words to the Wise.

No matter how far you travel, you never will escape totally the need to guard against theft and personal crime. In a new locale, use the same prudence that you would at home. Be aware of your surroundings, and don't invite petty thievery by careless actions. Leave valuables in your hotel safe; use travelers checks instead of cash. Always lock your car, even when you are in it. And do your on-foot sightseeing in daylight hours, preferably with two or more companions.

The Los Angeles Vicinity

ARCADIA (B-7) pop. 48,300, elev. 485'

Part of an enormous land grant given to the San Gabriel Mission by a Spanish king in the mid-1800s, Arcadia experienced a population explosion after World War II. The city is known primarily as a bedroom community.

Arcadia Chamber of Commerce: 388 W. Huntington Dr., Arcadia, CA 91007-3402; phone (626) 447-2159 or 445-1400.

Shopping areas: Santa Anita Fashion Park, Huntington Drive and Baldwin Avenue, includes JCPenney, Macy's, Nordstrom and Robinsons-May.

★**ARBORETUM OF LOS ANGELES COUNTY,** just s. of I-210 at 301 N. Baldwin Ave., encompasses 127 acres of trees and shrubs arranged by continent of origin. The horticultural research center also has tropical and begonia greenhouses, a reference library and a bird sanctuary. Of interest are the historic Queen Anne Cottage and coach barn, the Hugo Reid Adobe and the Santa Anita railroad depot.

Within the boundaries of the arboretum is Lake Baldwin, a small natural lake fed by underground springs. The Tropical Forest includes plants and trees from rain forest areas of Central and South America and the Northwestern United States as well as an inviting system of ponds that support aquatic plants. Picnic areas and food are available.

Guides conduct walking tours Wed. at 11. Arboretum open Mon.-Fri. 9-6:30, Sat.-Sun. 9-4:30, June 1-Sept. 3; daily 9-5, rest of year. Begonia and tropical greenhouses open daily 9-4. Tram tours Mon.-Fri. 12:15-3, Sat.-Sun. 10:30-3. Closed Dec. 25. Last admission is 30 minutes before closing. Admission $5; over 62, students with ID and ages 13-17, $3; ages 5-12, $1. Tram $1.50. Phone (626) 821-3222.

SANTA ANITA PARK, 285 W. Huntington Dr., is one of the most famous Thoroughbred horse racing tracks in the country. Since its 1934 inception, Santa Anita has introduced and developed the magnetically-controlled starting gate, the photo finish, electrical timing and the totalisator. Racing Wed.-Sun., early Oct.-early Nov. and late Dec.-late Apr.; post time 12:30 or 1, depending on season. Morning workouts daily 7:30-9:30 during the racing seasons. Minimum betting age is 18. Admission $4-$10, under 17 free with adult. Morning workouts free. Parking $3-$8. Phone (626) 574-7223.

Note: Policies concerning admittance of children to pari-mutuel betting facilities vary. Phone for information.

BEVERLY HILLS (B-5)
pop. 32,000, elev. 225'

One of the most elegant residential communities in Southern California, Beverly Hills is completely surrounded by Los Angeles. Many well-known personalities of stage, screen and television live here.

Beverly Hills Visitors Bureau: 239 S. Beverly Dr., Beverly Hills, CA 90212; phone (310) 248-1015 or (800) 345-2210.

Self-guiding tours: A visitor's guide, which provides historical commentary and walking-tour information, is available free from the visitors bureau.

Shopping areas: Rodeo Drive is famous for its many art galleries and upscale clothing and jewelry shops.

THE MUSEUM OF TELEVISION AND RADIO IN CALIFORNIA is at 465 N. Beverly Dr. The museum offers a collection of more than 95,000 historical and contemporary television and radio programs and advertisements. Visitors can view or listen to selected programming at an individual console or attend special screenings in one of the museum's two theaters. Parking is available in the museum lot off South Santa Monica Boulevard.

Wed.-Sun. noon-5 (also Thurs. 5-9); closed Jan. 1, July 4, Thanksgiving and Dec. 25. Admission $6; over 63 and students with ID $4; under 13, $3. Two hours of parking free with validation. Phone (310) 786-1030.

BURBANK (A-6) pop. 93,600, elev. 598'

Among the largest cities in the San Fernando Valley, Burbank is best known for its film and television studios.

Burbank Chamber of Commerce: 200 W. Magnolia Blvd., Burbank, CA 91502-1724; phone (818) 846-3111.

Shopping areas: Media City Center, 201 E. Magnolia Blvd., includes a restored 1895 Loof carrousel along with Ikea, Macy's, Mervyn's, Sears and more than 100 other stores.

NBC STUDIO TOURS, 3000 W. Alameda Ave., offers a 75-minute tour of the broadcasting complex. Featured are special-effects demonstrations, wardrobe and make-up departments, sound-effects room and—when available—Studio 3, where "The Tonight Show" originates. Comfortable walking shoes are recommended. Tours are given on a first-come, first-served basis on the hour Mon.-Fri. 9-3. Admission $7; over 59, $6.25; ages 5-12, $3.75. No cameras or tape recorders are permitted. Phone (818) 840-3537.

Your key to **savings** is actually a card.

Hilton offers special room rates to all AAA members.

Wherever you travel in the United States, there's a Hilton hotel or resort waiting to serve you. And now, AAA members can receive members-only room rates when you *Show Your Card & Save*® at Hiltons. Advance reservations are required. **Just call your AAA travel office or Hilton's private AAA number, 1-800-916-2221.**

It happens at the Hilton.™

CALIFORNIA:
Anaheim & Towers
Anaheim/Orange-Suites
Beverly Hills
Concord
Huntington Beach-
  Waterfront Resort
Irvine/Orange County Airport
Los Angeles Airport
Burbank Airport
Los Angeles/Carson
Los Angeles/Long Beach
Los Angeles/Pasadena
Los Angeles/San Pedro
Los Angeles/Torrance
Los Angeles/Universal City
  & Towers

Los Angeles/ Valencia
  Six Flags®-Garden Inn
Los Angeles/Whittier
Los Angeles/Woodland Hills
  & Towers
Monterey
Oakland Airport
Ontario Airport
Palm Springs Resort
Roseville-Garden Inn
Sacramento
San Bernardino
San Diego/Del Mar
San Diego Resort
San Diego Mission Valley
San Francisco & Towers
San Francisco/Pleasanton
San Jose & Towers

San Jose/Cupertino-
  Garden Inn
San Jose/Milpitas-
  Garden Inn
San Jose/Newark/Fremont
San Jose/Sunnyvale
Santa Maria
Sonoma County/Santa Rosa

NEVADA:
Las Vegas
Las Vegas-Bally's
Las Vegas-Flamingo
Las Vegas-Hilton Grand
  Vacations Club Flamingo
  Hilton
Laughlin-Flamingo
Reno
Reno-Flamingo

THE WARNER BROS. STUDIOS V.I.P. TOUR, Hollywood Way and Olive Ave. and entered via Gate 4, showcases the many facets of a movie and television studio, including recording stages, prop shops and live filming when possible. Included in the tour is a stop in Warner Bros. Museum to view historic film memorabilia.

Tours are given on the half-hour Mon.-Fri. 9-4, Memorial Day-Labor Day; on the hour Mon.-Fri. 9-3, rest of year. Closed holidays. Admission $30. Reservations are required. Under 10 are not permitted. Limited still photography is permitted. No video cameras or tape recorders are allowed. Comfortable walking shoes are recommended. Phone (818) 954-1669.

CALABASAS (B-5)
pop. 16,600, elev. 928'

The origin of Calabasas' name is debated. Some believe the Indian word for "where the wild geese fly" is at its root; others say it is derived from the Spanish *calabaza*, or "pumpkin."

Calabasas Chamber of Commerce: 23564 Calabasas Rd., Suite 101, Calabasas, CA 91302; phone (818) 222-5680.

THE LEONIS ADOBE, 23537 Calabasas Rd., is a restored two-story ranch house built about 1844. Once the home of Miguel Leonis, a colorful figure prominent in early Los Angeles history, it is one of the best preserved Monterey-style adobes in the area. Plummer House, the first house built in Hollywood, has been relocated here. Completely renovated, it serves as an entrance and visitor center and contains dioramas and period costumes. Also on the grounds are outbuildings and farm animals. Wed.-Sun. 1-4; closed Thanksgiving and Dec. 25. Donations. Phone (818) 222-6511.

CANOGA PARK (A-5)
pop. 89,300, elev. 795'

A Spanish possession 1796-1922, Canoga Park then became a Mexican prize and finally was awarded to the United States as reparation after the Mexican War of 1845.

Canoga Park Chamber of Commerce: 7248 Owensmouth Ave., Canoga Park, CA 91303; phone (818) 884-4222.

Shopping areas: In Topanga Plaza, Topanga Canyon Boulevard and Vanowen Street, more than 150 specialty stores share space with department stores, including Sears, Nordstrom and Robinsons-May.

ORCUTT RANCH HORTICULTURE CENTER, 23600 Roscoe Blvd., embraces a Spanish-style ranch house surrounded by huge oak trees, gardens and 16 acres of citrus trees. Grounds open daily 8-5; closed holidays. House tours are given by appointment. Free. Phone (818) 346-7449.

CLAREMONT (B-7)
pop. 32,500, elev. 1,165'

Claremont is best known as a college community that comprises six schools known collectively as the Claremont Colleges: Pomona College, The Claremont Graduate School, Scripps College, Claremont McKenna College, Harvey Mudd College and Pitzer College. The city also is home to the School of Theology at Claremont. Claremont Heritage offers 90-minute guided walking tours the first Saturday of each month at 10 for $5; phone (909) 621-0848.

Claremont Chamber of Commerce: 205 Yale Ave., Claremont, CA 91711; phone (909) 624-1681.

Shopping areas: More than 75 shops, art galleries and eateries are found in The Village, which is bounded by 1st and 4th streets and Yale and Harvard avenues.

★**RANCHO SANTA ANA BOTANIC GARDEN,** 1500 N. College Ave., contains 85 acres dedicated to the cultivation and display of native California plants and flowers. The garden is divided into three distinct areas.

Indian Hill Mesa is a flat-topped hill featuring plant strains originated under cultivation, as well as wild species of plants native to California. The East Alluvial Gardens include plantings native to California deserts, coastal dunes and channel islands, while the Plant Communities display native specimens in naturalistic settings. The gardens are most colorful February through June.

Daily 8-5; closed Jan. 1, July 4, Thanksgiving and Dec. 25. Donations. Phone (909) 625-8767.

DOWNEY (B-6) pop. 91,400, elev. 118'

The first Southern Pacific Railroad train reached Downey a year after its 1873 founding. With fertile soil, abundant water and a temperate climate, the city became a center for agriculture and animal husbandry.

Downey Chamber of Commerce: 11131 Brookshire Ave., Downey, CA 90241; phone (562) 923-2191.

DOWNEY MUSEUM OF ART, in Furman Park at 10419 S. Rives Ave., displays changing contemporary exhibits of professional art works that include paintings, sketches, ceramics, sculpture and other media. Wed.-Fri. noon-5, Sun. 1-4; closed holidays and between exhibits. Donations. Phone (562) 861-0419.

EL MONTE (B-7) pop. 106,200, elev. 283'

El Monte was known as the end of the Santa Fe Trail for westbound travelers. The water sources they found in the woodland in the 1850s now nourish the area's diminishing orange and walnut groves.

El Monte/South El Monte Chamber of Commerce: 10501 Valley Blvd., P.O. Box 5866, El Monte, CA 91734-1866; phone (626) 443-0180.

EL MONTE HISTORICAL SOCIETY MUSEUM, 3150 N. Tyler Ave., occupies the town's former library. Period furniture, clothing, household items and photographs are among the displays, many dating back to the late 19th century. An early 1900s schoolroom and Victorian-era parlor are replicated. Tues.-Fri. 10-4, Sun. 1-3; closed holidays and the first 2 weeks of Aug. Donations. Phone (626) 580-2232 or 444-3813.

ENCINO (A-5) pop. 62,000, elev. 750'

A community within the San Fernando Valley portion of Los Angeles, Encino includes both urban and wildnerness areas. The Sepulveda Basin Recreation Area offers miles of walking and bicycling paths, a Japanese Garden, Lake Balboa, a wildlife refuge and an undeveloped stretch of the Los Angeles River. Encino also includes a portion of the Santa Monica Mountains.

Encino Chamber of Commerce: 4933 Balboa Blvd., Encino, CA 91316; phone (818) 789-4711.

LOS ENCINOS STATE HISTORIC PARK, 16756 Moorpark St., contains a spring-fed lake, a smithy and other American period buildings. The site is all that remains of Rancho El Encino, a 4,500-acre cattle and sheep ranch and stagecoach stop 1845-1915. Picnicking is permitted; reservations are required Sat.-Sun. Grounds open Wed.-Sun. 10-5. House tours Wed.-Sun. 1-4. Closed Jan. 1, Thanksgiving and Dec. 25. Grounds free. Tours $2; ages 6-17, $1. Phone (818) 784-4849.

GLENDALE (B-6) pop. 180,000, elev. 563'

At the east entrance to the San Fernando Valley, Glendale occupies the first land grant in California, given in 1784 by King Charles IV of Spain.

Glendale Chamber of Commerce: 200 S. Louise St., P.O. Box 112, Glendale, CA 91205; phone (818) 240-7870.

Shopping areas: Glendale Galleria, a 250-store mall featuring JCPenney, Macy's, Mervyn's and Nordstrom, is bounded by Broadway, Central Avenue, Colorado Street and Columbus Avenue.

BRAND LIBRARY AND ART GALLERIES, 1601 W. Mountain St. in Brand Park, is a 1904 Moorish-style mansion with an art and music library and gallery, and studio and performance facilities. Tues.-Thurs. 1-6 (also Tues. and Thurs. 6-9 p.m.), Fri.-Sat. 1-5; closed holidays. Free. Phone (818) 548-2051.

★**FOREST LAWN MEMORIAL-PARK,** 1712 S. Glendale Ave., comprises 300 landscaped acres and contains a collection of large Carrara marble statuary and stained-glass windows. The Memorial Terrace houses a stained-glass re-creation of Leonardo da Vinci's "Last Supper." In the Hall of the Crucifixion-Resurrection is one of the world's largest religious oil paintings, Jan Styka's 45- by 195-foot "Crucifixion." Its companion, "Resurrection," is 51 by 70 feet.

The Forest Lawn Museum displays all types of coins mentioned in the Bible, a gem collection, American bronze statuary, 11th- to 15th-century cathedral stained glass, a Michelangelo exhibit and photographic illustrations of the history of Forest Lawn. Park open daily 8-5. Museum open daily 10-5. "Last Supper" shown daily on the half-hour 9:30-4. "Crucifixion" and "Resurrection" shown daily on the hour 10-4. Free. Artworks shown by donations. Phone (323) 254-3131 or (800) 204-3131.

HOLLYWOOD (B-6) pop. 165,800, elev. 300'

Hollywood began as a religion-oriented agricultural community in 1903 and became part of Los Angeles in 1910. A year later the first motion picture studio was established, and the fabulous legends of Hollywood began.

In keeping with the legends, the "Walk of Fame" extends for about a mile along Hollywood Boulevard between Gower Street and La Brea Avenue, and along a portion of Vine Street south of Hollywood Boulevard. Large metal stars

embedded in the sidewalk honor past and present stars of the entertainment industry.

Today several major studios produce motion pictures, while some 60 independent companies are largely engaged in television productions. Entering the studios usually requires a personal contact, but some lots do have tours *(see Burbank and Universal City p. 118 and 131).* ABC, CBS, FOX and NBC television studios offer audience participation shows *(see Studio Tours p. 113).*

Hollywood Chamber of Commerce: 7018 Hollywood Blvd., Hollywood, CA 90028; phone (323) 469-8311.

GUINNESS WORLD OF RECORDS MUSEUM, 6764 Hollywood Blvd., has video and hands-on displays illustrating historical and statistical information ranging from the comical to the scientific. Sun.-Thurs. 10 a.m.-midnight, Fri.-Sat. 10 a.m.-2 a.m. Admission $9.95; over 65, $8.50; ages 6-12, $6.95. Combination ticket with Hollywood Wax Museum $14.95; over 65, $12.95; ages 6-12, $8.95. Phone (323) 463-6433.

★**HOLLYWOOD BOWL** occupies a natural amphitheater in the foothills off Highland Ave. just w. of Cahuenga Blvd. Seating 18,000, the bowl plays host to concerts by the Los Angeles Philharmonic and the Hollywood Bowl Orchestra.

Grounds open daily 9-5. Concerts are presented Tues.-Sat. at 8:30 p.m., six Sunday Sunset Concerts at 7:30 p.m., and jazz concerts on five Wednesdays at 7:30 p.m., late June to mid-Sept. The Open House performances take place Mon.-Fri. at 10 and 11:15, early July to mid-Aug. Ticket prices vary. AE, MC, VI. Phone (323) 850-2000; for tickets phone (213) 480-3232.

The Edmund D. Edelman Hollywood Bowl Museum, near the pedestrian and vehicle entrance to the bowl grounds, features a multimedia look at the illustrious history of the Hollywood Bowl from its 1922 beginnings. Tues.-Sat. 10-4 (also 4-8:30 on concert nights) Free. Phone (323) 850-2058.

HOLLYWOOD WAX MUSEUM, 6767 Hollywood Blvd., presents life-size figures of people and sets, including displays about television, motion pictures, politics and religion. Low-heeled shoes are advised. Sun.-Thurs. 10 a.m.-midnight, Fri.-Sat. 10 a.m.-1 a.m.; closed holidays. Admission $9.95; over 65, $8.50; ages 6-12, $6.95. Combination ticket with Guinness World of Records $14.95; over 65, $12.95; ages 6-12, $8.95. Phone (323) 462-8860.

★**MANN'S CHINESE THEATRE** is at 6925 Hollywood Blvd. When visiting the newly constructed Chinese Theatre in May 1927, silent film star Norma Talmadge stepped into a sidewalk of wet cement, thus beginning the tradition of immortalizing the prints of legendary Hollywood stars in the concrete of the theater's forecourt.

The footprints of Mary Pickford and Douglas Fairbanks Sr. were added to celebrate the theater's opening, and over the years nearly 200 stars—including Marilyn Monroe, Whoopi Goldberg, Tom Cruise and the original cast members of "Star Trek"—have been immortalized. While some legends left only hand and/or footprints, others have imprinted their trademarks—Betty Grable's leg, Jimmy Durante's nose, John Barrymore's profile and John Wayne's fist. Others have left personal messages such as "You made my day" from Clint Eastwood.

RIPLEY'S BELIEVE IT OR NOT! ODDITORIUM, 6780 Hollywood Blvd., displays nearly 300 unusual and amazing items collected from around the world. Sun.-Thurs. 10-10, Fri.-Sat. 10 a.m.-11 p.m. Admission $8.95; over 55, $7.95; ages 5-11, $5.95. Phone (323) 466-6335.

SIGHTSEEING TOURS are a good way to see Hollywood landmarks and to catch glimpses of celebrities' homes. Tour lengths and prices vary according to destination. Reservations should be made 24 hours in advance during the peak summer season. Casablanca Sightseeing Tours, (213) 461-0156, and Starline Tours of Hollywood, (213) 463-3333, *(see ad p. 121)* offer a variety of tours from which to choose. Area accommodations can provide literature about other available tours. Consult the telephone directory for additional listings.

INDUSTRY (B-7) pop. 600, elev. 329′

Devoted to the business community, City of Industry is a center for commerce. Because of restrictions on residential growth, approximately 100 times as many people work in the city than live in it.

Industry Chamber of Commerce: 255 N. Hacienda Blvd., Suite 100, City of Industry, CA 91744-2841; phone (626) 968-3737.

Shopping areas: Sears and Robinsons-May anchor Puente Hills Mall.

WORKMAN AND TEMPLE FAMILY HOMESTEAD MUSEUM is at 15415 E. Don Julian Rd. The Workman House is a Victorian home constructed around an 1840s adobe. A 1920s Spanish Colonial Revival home, La Casa Nueva, features stained glass, Mexican and American tile and a courtyard with a fountain. A mausoleum in El Campo Santo contains the remains of Gov. Pio Pico of Mexican California. Exotic gardens beautify the grounds. Tours are given on the hour Wed.-Sun. 1-4; closed holidays and the fourth weekend of each month. Free. Phone (626) 968-8492.

INGLEWOOD (B-6) pop. 109,600, elev. 118′

Inglewood is home to Great Western Forum, which is host to the NBA's Lakers, the WNBA's

Sparks and the Kings hockey team. *See Sports and Recreation p. 116.*

HOLLYWOOD PARK, 1050 S. Prairie Ave. at Century Blvd., includes one of the West Coast's largest racetracks. Free morning workouts are at 8. Racing post time Wed.-Sun. is at 1, mid-Apr. to late July and mid-Nov. to late Dec. (also Fri. night racing Apr.-July; phone for schedule). Admission $6-$25, under 18 free. Program and parking free. Phone (310) 419-1500.

Note: Policies concerning admittance of children to pari-mutuel betting facilities vary. Phone for information.

LA CAÑADA FLINTRIDGE (A-6)
pop. 19,400, elev. 1,318'

In the foothills of the San Gabriel Mountains, La Cañada Flintridge is the gateway to an array of winter and summer recreational activities.

La Cañada Flintridge Chamber of Commerce: 4529 Angeles Crest Hwy., Suite 102, La Cañada Flintridge, CA 91011; phone (818) 790-4289.

★**DESCANSO GARDENS,** s. of Foothill Blvd. at 1418 Descanso Dr., is a woodland garden in the midst of California chaparral. The 165-acre botanic garden contains almost 100,000 camellia shrubs growing in a 25-acre California live oak forest. The camellias bloom October through March. The 5-acre International Rosarium showcases 4,000 antique and modern roses informally planted with shrubs, annuals and perennials, with peak bloom Aprilthrough December. The 250 lilac shrubs bloom March to April. Iris gardens, daylily beds, water gardens and outdoor orchids bloom in spring and summer.

Georgie Van de Kamp Hall and Rose Pavilion accommodate horticultural events, lectures, classes, demonstrations and flower shows throughout the year. A teahouse in the Japanese Garden and guided tram tours also are available. Food is available.

Gardens open daily 9-4:30; closed Dec. 25. Tram tours Tues.-Fri. 1-3, Sat.-Sun. and holidays 11-3. Admission $5; over 61 and students with ID $3; ages 5-12, $1. Tram tours $1.50. Pets, bicycles and radios are not permitted. Under 18 must be with an adult. Phone (818) 952-4401.

JET PROPULSION LABORATORY—
see Pasadena p. 127.

LOMITA (C-6) pop. 19,400, elev. 98'

LOMITA RAILROAD MUSEUM, 250th St. and Woodward Ave., is a Victorian-style passenger depot containing scale models, photographs and paintings of locomotives, and assorted railroad memorabilia. A 1902 Mogul locomotive and an all-wood 1910 Union Pacific caboose are outside. The museum annex has a 1913 box car and a 1923 oil tanker; picnicking is permitted. Wed.-Sun. 10-5; closed Thanksgiving and Dec. 25. Admission $1; under 12, 50c. Children must be with an adult. Phone (310) 326-6255.

LONG BEACH (C-6)
pop. 429,400, elev. 32'

California's fifth largest city, Long Beach became popular in the late 19th century as a seaside resort. Long Beach Harbor, next to the Port of Los Angeles, is one of the busiest shipping centers on the Pacific Coast, and four airlines serve the city's airport. The area is rich in petroleum resources, both on land and offshore.

Long Beach Convention and Entertainment Center at Ocean and Long Beach boulevards includes the Long Beach Arena, Terrace Theater and Center Theater; concerts, plays, trade shows and sporting events are held here. Boat cruises to Catalina Island *(see place listing p. 63)* leave from the foot of Golden Shore Boulevard and from near the *Queen Mary.* The roar of Grand Prix race cars echoes through the city streets in mid-April during the Toyota Grand Prix of Long Beach.

Long Beach Area Convention & Visitors Bureau: One World Trade Center, Suite 300, Long Beach, CA 90831-0300; phone (562) 436-3645 or (800) 452-7829.

Shopping areas: Specialty shops abound along the waterfront. The Queen's Marketplace, near

CALIFORNIA MISSIONS

To secure its northern territorial claims in the New World, Spain ordered the creation of a series of Franciscan missions in California. Begun under the leadership of Father Junípero Serra, who died in 1784, 21 missions and one asistencia were established 1769-1823, spaced about a day's journey apart along the northern extension of El Camino Real, the Royal Road.

Each mission had its own herd of cattle, fields and vegetable gardens, which were tended by native converts. For furniture, clothing, tools and other implements, the missions traded their surplus of meal, wine, oil, hemp, hides and tallow. Their attempts to "civilize" the indigenous population yielded mixed results: For the thousands of Indians brought under the wing of the church, thousands of others died at the hands of the Spanish or from their diseases. But the missions succeeded in other regards: Around them and their accompanying presidios, or military posts, grew the first permanent settlements in California.

After winning its independence from Spain and during the secularization, Mexico removed control of the missions from the Franciscans and subdivided much of their land among the Mexican soldiers and settlers. During the ensuing years, neglect and earthquakes took their toll; many of the missions were severely damaged or destroyed. Subsequent restoration and reconstruction have revitalized these historic structures, and today US 101 roughly traces the route of the old El Camino Real.

Pier J, is an open-air mall designed to resemble an old English village. Shoreline Village, on Shoreline Village Drive at the foot of Pine Street, is a harborside shopping center with specialty stores, restaurants, a restored Looff carrousel and occasional live boardwalk entertainment.

EARL BURNS MILLER JAPANESE GARDEN is at 1250 Bellflower Blvd. on the campus of California State University, Long Beach. This traditional Japanese Garden features a koi-filled lake and a path that winds among Japanese black pines, Chinese willows, golden bamboo, irises and camellias, among other foliage. The path also meanders past waterfalls, Buddhist statues, stone lanterns and a pagoda. A tea house and Zen dry garden complete this tranquil, Asian-themed setting. Tues.-Fri. 8-3:30, Sun. noon-4. Free. Phone (310) 985-8885.

EL DORADO NATURE CENTER, 7550 E. Spring St., is an 102-acre wildlife sanctuary with native plant areas, nature trails, programs and classes, and a museum containing ecology displays, hands-on exhibits for children, photographs and artwork. Museum open Tues.-Fri. 10-4, Sat.-Sun. 8:30-4. Trails open Tues.-Sun. 8-5. Museum free. Parking Mon.-Fri. $3, Sat.-Sun and holidays $5. Phone (562) 570-1745.

LONG BEACH AQUARIUM OF THE PACIFIC, off of Shoreline Dr. at 100 Aquarium Way, features 17 major habitats and 30 smaller exhibits representing three regions of the Pacific Ocean: Southern California/Baja, Tropical Pacific and Northern Pacific. Sharks, giant groupers, harbor seals, sea lions, Pacific octopus, sea stars and giant Japanese spider crabs are just a few of the 550 species that can be seen. Daily 10-6. Admission $13.95; over 59, $11.95; ages 3-11, $6.95. Phone (562) 590-3100. *See color ad.*

LONG BEACH MUSEUM OF ART, 2300 E. Ocean Blvd., is housed in a 1912 mansion overlooking the Pacific Ocean and features permanent and changing exhibitions of modern and contemporary paintings, sculpture, video art and photographs. A garden contains sculptures and a fountain. Food is available. Wed.-Sun. 10-5 (also Fri. 5-8); closed holidays and occasionally to change exhibits. Admission $2, over 54 and students with ID $1, under 12 free. Phone (562) 439-2119.

★*QUEEN MARY* is at 1126 Queens Hwy. and can be reached via Queen's Way Bridge or I-710. The *Queen Mary,* one of the largest passenger liners ever built, is permanently moored in Long Beach Harbor. A self-guiding tour includes the bridge, officers' quarters, engine rooms and upper decks. A guided tour takes visitors behind the scenes, to areas usually inaccessible to the public. A fireworks display is presented Saturday evenings in the summer. Queen Mary Seaport, adjoining the ship's berth, includes shops and restaurants.

Daily 9-9, late June-Labor Day; 10-6, rest of year. Last admission is 90 minutes before closing Sun.-Thurs. and 30 minutes before closing on Sat. Admission $13; over 54 and military with ID $11; ages 4-11, $8. Guided tours $7; ages 4-11, $4. While the first 30 minutes of parking is free, hourly rates are charged thereafter; the maximum parking fee is $7 per day. Phone (562) 435-3511. *See color ad.*

***Scorpion* Submarine,** at the bow of the *Queen Mary*, is a Cold War-era Soviet submarine. A tour of the torpedo room, crew's quarters, galley and formerly top-secret communications center is available. Comfortable clothing and low-heeled shoes are recommended. Daily 9-9, late June-Labor Day; 10-6, rest of year. Last admission is 90 minutes before closing Sun.-Thurs. and 30 minutes before closing on Sat. Guided tours $10; over 54, military with ID and ages 4-11, $9. Phone (562) 435-3511.

RANCHO LOS ALAMITOS, 6400 E. Bixby Hill Rd., is a 7-acre historic ranch. An adobe ranch house dates from 1800. Also featured are a smithy, six early 20th-century barns and lush garden areas. Guided tours are offered Wed.-Sun. 1-5; closed holidays. Last tour begins 1 hour before closing. Free. Phone (562) 431-3541.

RANCHO LOS CERRITOS, 4600 Virginia Rd., is one of the few remaining early Monterey-style adobes in Southern California. The 1844 house originally served as headquarters for a 27,000-acre cattle ranch. Remodeled in 1930 in the Monterey Colonial style, the house is now furnished in 1870s decor to reflect the rancho's days as one of the few sheep ranches in the region.

More than four acres of gardens still surround the house, which also features a visitor center. Picnicking is permitted. Events are offered throughout the year. Wed.-Sun. 1-5. Tours on the hour Sat.-Sun. 1-4. Closed holidays. Free. Phone (562) 570-1755.

MALIBU (B-5) pop. 11,700, elev. 5'

Stretching 27 miles along SR 1, Malibu is wedged between the Santa Monica Mountains and the Pacific Ocean. Many artists, writers and well-known entertainers are among its residents.

Malibu Chamber of Commerce: 23805 Stuart Ranch Rd., #100, Malibu, CA 90265; phone (310) 456-9025.

★**J. PAUL GETTY MUSEUM—**
see Getty Center in Los Angeles p. 108.

MALIBU LAGOON MUSEUM AND HISTORIC ADAMSON HOUSE, 23200 Pacific Coast Hwy., is a Moorish-Spanish Colonial-style residence built in the 1920s. Colorful tile, handcrafted woodwork and ironwork and other decorative features are found throughout the house. The adjoining museum depicts Malibu history. Guided tours are given Wed.-Sat. 11-3; closed holidays. Last tour begins 1 hour before closing. Tour $2; ages 7-17, $1. Parking $6. Phone (310) 456-8432.

MARINA DEL REY (B-5)
pop. 7,400, elev. 5'

FISHERMAN'S VILLAGE, 13755 Fiji Way, overlooks the Marina del Rey harbor. The colorful New England-style buildings house specialty shops and restaurants. Sailboats, electric boats, ocean wave riders and kayaks are available for rent from Marina Boat Rentals, (310) 574-2822. Marina del Rey Sportfishing, (310) 822-3625, offers deep-sea sportfishing and whale-watching trips. Phone for schedules, fares and reservations.

Shops and restaurants are open daily; most will validate for 2 hours of free parking. Free Sunday afternoon concerts are given. Phone (310) 823-5411 for village information.

HORNBLOWER DINING YACHTS, 13755 Fiji Way, offers 45-minute harbor sightseeing tours. Dinner/dance and champagne brunch cruises also are available. Harbor tour departs daily on the hour noon-5, June-Aug.; Sat.-Sun. on the hour noon-5, rest of year. Harbor tour $8; over 59 and under 12, $4. AE, DI, DS, MC, VI. Phone (310) 301-6000.

MISSION HILLS (A-5)
pop. 32,000, elev. 914'

★**MISSION SAN FERNANDO REY DE ESPAÑA,** midway between I-5 and I-405 at 15151 San Fernando Mission Blvd., was founded Sept. 8, 1797. Restored structures include the church, monastery, majordomo's house, workrooms and living quarters around the quadrangle. The old gardens, now Brand Park, have flowers and shrubs from the other 20 missions. A 35-bell carillon rings hourly 9-5. An Archival Center preserves and interprets historic documents and records of California's Catholic heritage.

A museum theater offers three films illustrating the history of the mission, the Archdiocese of Los Angeles and the life of Father Junípero Serra. An American Indian craft room is featured. Mission and museum open daily 9-4:30. Last admission 45 minutes before closing. Archival Center open Mon. and Thurs. 1-3; closed Thanksgiving and Dec. 25. Admission $4; ages 7-15, $3. Phone (818) 361-0186.

PACIFIC PALISADES (B-5)
pop. 23,100, elev. 260'

Many elaborate houses are perched precariously on Pacific Palisades' steep bluffs, overlooking the beaches below.

Pacific Palisades Chamber of Commerce: 15330 Antioch St., Pacific Palisades, CA 90272; phone (310) 459-7963.

SELF-REALIZATION FELLOWSHIP LAKE SHRINE, 17190 Sunset Blvd., is a 10-acre site that includes a picturesque lake and a "wall-less temple" housing Gandhi World Peace Memorial. A pathway encircling the lake affords views of a bird refuge, a sunken garden and various structures representing the five major religions of the world. There also is a small museum. Tues.-Sat. 9-4:30, Sun. 12:30-4:30; closed holidays and some Sat. Free. Phone (310) 454-4114.

★**WILL ROGERS STATE HISTORIC PARK,** 186 acres at 1501 Will Rogers State Park Rd., includes the humorist's home as well as hiking trails and picnic facilities. Polo games are played Sat. at 2 and Sun. at 10 (weather permitting). Park open daily 8-dusk. House tours depart daily on the half-hour 10:30-4:30; closed Jan. 1, Thanksgiving and Dec. 25. Admission $6 per private vehicle; over 62, $5 per private vehicle. Phone (310) 454-8212.

PALOS VERDES PENINSULA (C-5)
elev. 800'

Palos Verdes Peninsula is contoured by three coves. The widest and most easily reached is Malaga Cove, next to Torrance City Beach on Paseo de la Playa. Follow Paseo del Mar west to a turnout for Bluff Cove; a trail winds down to the rocky inlet. A short, steep hike off the roadside turnoff on Paseo del Mar reaches Lunada Bay, a sand and pebble cove. Collecting plants or animals is prohibited in all coves. Just north of the peninsula are Redondo, Hermosa and Manhattan beaches.

Palos Verdes Peninsula Chamber of Commerce: 550 Deep Valley Dr., Suite 253, Rolling Hills Estates, CA 90274; phone (310) 377-8111.

PALOS VERDES ART CENTER, 5504 W. Crestridge Rd., features exhibitions of Southern Californian as well as nationally known artists. Tours are available. Mon.-Fri. 9-5, Sat. 10-4, Sun. 1-4. Free. Phone (310) 541-2479.

POINT VICENTE INTERPRETIVE CENTER, next to Point Vicente Lighthouse off Palos Verdes Dr. W., has exhibits about the Pacific gray whale and the human, geologic and natural history of Palos Verdes Peninsula. An inside observation area on the second floor offers a panorama of the coast. The best season for whale-watching is December through April. Daily 10-7, Memorial Day-Labor Day; 10-5, rest of year. Closed Jan. 1, Thanksgiving and Dec. 24-25. Admission $2; over 54 and ages 4-14, $1. Phone (310) 377-5370.

SOUTH COAST BOTANIC GARDEN, 26300 Crenshaw Blvd., represents more than 150,000 plant species. Featured are semi-drought tolerable plants suitable to the Southern California landscape. A children's garden is developed around fairy tale themes. Daily 9-5. Tram tours depart at 11, 1 and 3. Admission $5; over 62, students with ID and ages 13-17, $3; ages 5-12, $1. Tram fare $1.50. Phone (310) 544-6815.

WAYFARERS CHAPEL, 5755 Palos Verdes Dr. S., was designed by Lloyd Wright, son of Frank Lloyd Wright. Built almost entirely of glass and stone, the "Glass Church" is a memorial to Emanuel Swedenborg, an 18th-century mystic and theologian. The church is surrounded by redwoods and 3.5 acres of gardens on a bluff overlooking the Pacific. Self-guiding tour brochures are available. Daily 9-5. Free. Phone (310) 377-1650.

PASADENA (A-6)
pop. 131,600, elev. 865'

Pasadena, a residential community with stately houses and the prestigious California Institute of Technology, is the site of the famed Tournament of Roses Parade, held Jan. 1 or 2, and the attendant Rose Bowl football game. Tickets for grandstand seats for the parade must be obtained months in advance. Football game tickets can be purchased from participating schools.

The Pasadena Center, a major auditorium and convention facility, plays host to cultural events. Pasadena Playhouse presents stage productions; phone (626) 356-7529. Nearby is the historic Old Town section of the city, featuring numerous shops and restaurants in an area bounded by Union and Green streets and Raymond and Pasadena avenues.

Pasadena Chamber of Commerce and Civic Association: 117 E. Colorado Blvd. #100, Pasadena, CA 91105-1993; phone (626) 795-3355.

Shopping areas: Plaza Pasadena, bounded by Colorado Boulevard, Los Robles Avenue, and Green and Marengo streets, is an enclosed mall with a JCPenney and Macy's.

CALIFORNIA INSTITUTE OF TECHNOLOGY, 1200 E. California Blvd., is noted for its extensive research and instruction in science and engineering. Campus tours begin at the public relations office, 315 S. Hill Ave., Mon.-Fri. at 2. Architectural tours are given at 11 on the fourth Thursday of the month, Jan.-June and Sept.-Oct., and on the third Thursday in Nov. No tours on holidays, rainy days or during winter break. Both tours are free. Reservations are required for architectural tour. Phone (626) 395-6327.

Jet Propulsion Laboratory (JPL), NASA's center for robotic space exploration and home of the *Mars Pathfinder*, is at the north end of Oak Grove Drive in La Cañada Flintridge. Two-hour tours are given occasionally only by reservation. Phone (818) 354-9314.

THE GAMBLE HOUSE, 4 Westmoreland Pl., parallel to the 300 blk. of N. Orange Grove Blvd., just n. jct. Walnut, is a program of the University of Southern California School of Architecture. Designed by renowned architects Charles and Henry Greene, this 1908 bungalow-style house features sculptured woodwork, hand-shaped beams, distinctive stained glass and original furnishings. One-hour tours are given Thurs.-Sun. noon-3; closed holidays. Admission $5; over 65, $4; full-time students with ID $3; under 12 free. Phone (626) 793-3334.

KIDSPACE MUSEUM, 390 S. El Molino Ave., is a participatory museum for ages 2-10. Children are encouraged to explore hands-on exhibits that include a TV studio, fire station and beach exhibit. The museum also has programs and workshops. Sun.-Thurs. 1-5, Fri.-Sat. 10-5, early June-early Sept.; Wed.-Thurs. and Sun. 1-5, Sat. 10-5, Tues. 1:30-5, rest of year. Admission $5; over 65, $3.50; ages 1-2, $2.50. Phone (626) 449-9143.

★**NORTON SIMON MUSEUM,** 411 W. Colorado Blvd. at Orange Grove Blvd., exhibits art from the early Renaissance through the mid-20th century, including paintings by Edgar Degas, Claude Monet, Rembrandt, Pierre Auguste Renoir and Vincent Van Gogh, and southeast Asian and American Indian sculpture. Thurs.-Sun. noon-6; closed Jan. 1 and Dec. 25. Admission $4, over 62 and students with ID $2, under 12 free. Phone (626) 449-6840.

PACIFIC ASIA MUSEUM, 46 N. Los Robles Ave., houses historical, cultural and art exhibits of Asia and the Pacific Islands. The building, designed like a Chinese treasure house, surrounds a Chinese Imperial Palace garden and koi pond. Major exhibits change biannually. The museum also has a students' gallery. Wed.-Sun. 10-5; closed holidays. Admission $5, over 61 and students with ID $3, under 12 free; free to all third Sat. of the month. Phone (626) 449-2742.

(SAVE) **PASADENA HISTORICAL MUSEUM,** 470 W. Walnut St., features Fenyes Mansion, a Beaux Art-style house built in 1905. Rooms contain original furnishings including period pieces, artwork and antiques. Also on the grounds is Finnish Folk Art Museum, with exhibits that include handmade furniture, utensils and decorative pieces.

Tours of Fenyes Mansion are offered Thurs.-Sun. 1-4. Last mansion tour begins 1 hour before closing. Closed Jan. 1, Thanksgiving and Dec. 25. Admission $4, over 55 and students with ID $3, under 13 free. Phone (626) 577-1660.

ROSE BOWL, in Brookside Park, is the site of the celebrated football game played Jan. 1 or 2. The bowl is home to the Los Angeles Galaxy soccer team, UCLA home football games and other sporting events throughout the year. A huge swap meet is held on the grounds the second Sunday of each month; admission $5, parking $2. The Rose Bowl is open to the public for viewing Mon.-Fri. 9-4; closed alternate Fridays, holidays and during events. Admission $2. Phone (626) 577-3100.

POMONA (B-7) pop. 131,700, elev. 850'

Pomona is the home of California State Polytechnic University, Pomona. Its beautifully landscaped campus reflects a full curriculum that includes agriculture and environmental design. Foals, piglets, lambs, calves and ducklings are seasonal residents. Self-guiding and guided campus tours are available; phone (909) 869-3529.

Pomona Chamber of Commerce: 485 N. Garey, P.O. Box 1457, Pomona, CA 91769-1457; phone (909) 622-1256.

W.K. KELLOGG ARABIAN HORSE CENTER, off Kellogg Dr. on the campus of California State Polytechnic University, was part of the ranch that W.K. Kellogg donated to the university to perpetuate the breeding of Arabian horses. Daily 9-4. Horse shows are held the first Sun. of the month at 2, Oct.-June. Grounds free. Horse show $3; over 59 and ages 6-17, $2. Phone (909) 869-2224.

REDONDO BEACH (C-5)
pop. 60,200, elev. 59'

A drive along SR 1 leads south to Palos Verdes Boulevard, affording views of the coastline and, on a clear day, Catalina Island.

Redondo Beach Pier, at the foot of Torrance Boulevard, offers souvenir shops and seafood restaurants. King Harbor, along Harbor Drive between Herondo and Beryl streets, has restaurants, hotels and facilities for such activities as boating, sport fishing, bicycling and racquetball. A wide pathway leads bicyclists and pedestrians to International Boardwalk, which has souvenir shops, an amusement center and fresh fish markets.

Redondo Beach Visitors Bureau: 200 N. Pacific Coast Hwy., Redondo Beach, CA 90277; phone (310) 374-2171 or (800) 282-0333.

Shopping areas: The Galleria at South Bay, at Hawthorne and Artesia boulevards, has Mervyn's, Nordstrom and Robinsons-May. The Pier at Redondo Beach, Horseshoe and Monstad piers at the foot of Torrance Boulevard, is a waterfront marketplace.

SAN DIMAS (B-7) pop. 32,400, elev. 940'

RAGING WATERS, 111 Raging Waters Dr., is a 50-acre aquatic recreation park featuring waterslides and speed slides, rides, chutes, lagoons, children's activity pools and beaches for sunbathing. Open daily at 10, early June-early Sept.; open Sat.-Sun. at 10, Apr. 1 to early June and early Sept.-Sept. 30. Closing times vary. Over 48 inches tall $23.99, over age 54 and 42-48 inches tall $14.99, under age 2 free. Parking $6. Phone (909) 802-2200. *See color ad p. 129.*

SAN GABRIEL (B-7)
pop. 37,100, elev. 430'

In 1771 Mission San Gabriel Arcángel was established at the crossing of three heavily traveled trails, two from Mexico to Upper California and one that later brought settlers from the East to California. The community that took shape around the mission initially was devoted to agriculture and later to light industry. Incorporated as a city in 1913, San Gabriel today takes pride in its mission and its history.

Self-guiding tours: A free brochure of a walking tour of the Mission District is available from Mission San Gabriel Arcangel and from the City of San Gabriel offices, 532 W. Mission Dr.; phone (626) 308-2800.

(SAVE) **MISSION SAN GABRIEL ARCANGEL,** 428 S. Mission Dr. at Junipero Serra Dr., was founded Sept. 8, 1771. The mission bell tower was damaged by an earthquake in 1812 and moved to its present position. Daily 9-5; closed Easter, Thanksgiving and Dec. 25. Admission $4; over 64, $3; ages 6-12, $1. Phone (626) 457-3035.

Freeway driving requires special caution: Drive carefully.

SAN MARINO (B-6)
pop. 13,000, elev. 566'

EL MOLINO VIEJO (The Old Mill), 1120 Old Mill Rd. off Oak Knoll Ave., is a former gristmill built by American Indians under supervision of the padres around 1816 for Mission San Gabriel. A working model of the mill, photographs and changing exhibits of California are displayed. Tues.-Sun. 1-4; closed holidays. Free. Phone (626) 449-5458.

★HUNTINGTON LIBRARY, ART COLLECTIONS AND BOTANICAL GARDENS, 1151 Oxford Rd. (second entrance at Orlando Rd. and Allen Ave.), houses one of the world's great collections of rare books and manuscripts, including a Gutenberg Bible, the Ellesmere Chaucer, and early editions of works by William Shakespeare. Huntington Art Gallery contains 18th-century British and European paintings, rare tapestries, porcelains, miniatures, sculpture and period furniture.

Virginia Steele Scott Gallery of American Art displays paintings from the 1730s to the 1930s as well as period furnishings. The botanical gardens cover 150 acres of the 207-acre estate and embrace 15,000 varieties of plants, shrubs and trees. Garden tours depart Tues.-Sun. at 1; self-guiding tour brochures are available. Tues.-Sun. 10:30-4:30, Memorial Day-Labor Day; Tues.-Fri. noon-4:30, Sat.-Sun. 10:30-4:30, rest of year. Closed holidays. Admission $8.50; over 65, $7; students with ID $4; under 13 free; free to all first Thurs. of the month. Phone (626) 405-2141.

SAN PEDRO (C-6) pop. 70,900, elev. 100'

With Wilmington and Terminal Island, San Pedro forms the Port of Los Angeles, one of the largest deep-water ports in the nation. Fort MacArthur, now an inactive base but once a formidable coastal defense, overlooks the harbor; Cabrillo Beach lies south. Cruises to Catalina Island *(see place listing p. 63)* leave the Catalina terminal near the Vincent Thomas Bridge. Harbor cruises are available as well.

The Marine Mammal Care Center at Fort MacArthur is a rehabilitation facility where ill or injured seals and sea lions are nursed back to health for return to their natural environment. Visitors can view the animals from a fenced area surrounding the center. Phone (310) 548-5677.

San Pedro Peninsula Chamber of Commerce: 390 W. Seventh St., San Pedro, CA 90731; phone (310) 832-7272.

CABRILLO MARINE AQUARIUM, 3720 Stephen M. White Dr., specializes in the marine life of Southern California. Displays include a touch tank and 35 seawater aquariums with sea life native to Southern California. Daily multimedia shows, seasonal events, grunion programs and whale-watching tours are offered. Tues.-Fri. noon-5, Sat.-Sun. 10-5; closed Thanksgiving and Dec. 25. Free. Parking $6.50. Phone (310) 548-7562.

LOS ANGELES MARITIME MUSEUM, berth 84 at the foot of 6th St., contains local nautical memorabilia, including historical photographs of Los Angeles Harbor, ship models and assorted maritime equipment from the USS *Los Angeles.* The museum also houses a 21-foot scale model of the *Queen Mary* and an 18-foot model of the *Titanic.* Allow 30 minutes minimum. Tues.-Sun. 10-5; closed Jan. 1, Thanksgiving and Dec. 25. Donations. Phone (310) 548-7618.

PORTS O' CALL VILLAGE, on the main channel of Los Angeles Harbor at the s. end of Harbor Frwy., is a picturesque waterfront area featuring restaurants, shops and entertainment. Mon.-Fri. 11-7, Sat.-Sun. 11-8; closed Thanksgiving and Dec. 25. Free. Phone (310) 831-0287.

Los Angeles Harbor Cruises, departing from the Village Boat House, Berth 78, offers 1-hour cruises of the inner and outer harbor past supertankers, cruise ships, a Coast Guard station, Terminal Island, Federal Prison and Angels Gate Lighthouse. Seasonal whale-watching cruises and 2-hour coastline cruises along Palos Verdes Peninsula also are available.

Harbor cruises depart Mon.-Fri. noon-4, Sat.-Sun. and holidays noon-5. Coastline cruises depart Sat.-Sun. at 11:30, 1:30 and 3:30. Closed Thanksgiving and Dec. 25. Harbor cruise $8; ages 2-12, $4. Coastline cruise $12; ages 2-12, $5. Phone (310) 831-0996.

SAVE Spirit Cruises, departing from Ports O' Call Village, offers trips aboard a 90-foot motor yacht, an 85-foot schooner or a 65-foot cruise boat. Cruises lasting 45 minutes and 1.5-hours are offered daily, June-Sept.; Sat.-Sun., rest of year. Whale-watching cruises lasting 2.5 hours are offered Jan.-Mar. Dinner cruises also are available. Cruise lasting 45 minutes $6; ages 2-12, $3. Ninety-minute cruise $12; ages 2-12, $6. Whale-watching cruise $15; ages 2-12, $8. Reservations are suggested. Phone (310) 548-8080.

SS *LANE VICTORY*, Berth 94 off Harbor Blvd., is a museum and memorial to Merchant Marines buried at sea. Built in 1945, this Merchant Marine ship saw service in three wars and was decommissioned in 1971. Visitors can tour most areas of this operational ship. Daily 9-4; closed occasional summer weekends for cruises. Admission $3; ages 5-15, $1. Phone (310) 519-9545.

SANTA CLARITA (A-5)
pop. 110,700, elev. 1,270'

WILLIAM S. HART COUNTY PARK AND MUSEUM, 1.7 mi. n.w. of SR 14 via San Fernando Rd., embraces the home and 265-acre park of the Western movie star. Hart's home, which sits on a hill at the end of a winding nature trail, contains original furnishings and Western art, American Indian artifacts and historical objects. The park also offers a large picnic area, a barnyard animal display, numerous trails and a herd of buffalo.

Park open daily 7-dusk; closed Jan. 1, Thanksgiving and Dec. 25. Home open Wed.-Sun. 11-3:30, mid-June to mid-Sept.; Wed.-Fri. 10-12:30, Sat.-Sun. 11-3:30, rest of year. Tours are conducted about every half-hour. Free. Phone (805) 254-4584 or 259-0855.

SANTA FE SPRINGS (B-7)
pop. 15,500, elev. 158'

HERITAGE PARK 12100 Mora Dr., was developed on the site of an 1880s citrus ranch. Highlights include the reconstructed carriage barn, now used as a museum to exhibit items reflecting a turn-of-the-20th-century lifestyle, an operating windmill, remains of the ranch house, a Victorian-style formal garden, an aviary and a plant conservatory. A railroad exhibit features the A.T. & S.F. No. 870, a turn-of-the-20th-century steam locomotive.

Picnicking is permitted. Food is available Mon.-Fri. Park open daily 7 a.m.-10 p.m. Museum open Tues.-Sun. noon-4. Free. Phone (562) 946-6476.

SANTA MONICA (B-5)
pop. 86,900, elev. 101'

Bounded by Los Angeles on three sides and by the Pacific on the fourth, Santa Monica is a popular ocean resort. Shops, restaurants and boutiques line sections of Main Street, Montana Avenue and Third Street. Santa Monica Municipal Pier at the foot of Colorado Avenue also has shops and restaurants as well as a fishing pier, carnival games, an amusement park and a restored antique carrousel with hand-carved wooden horses.

Palisades Park lies along the cliff tops overlooking Santa Monica's broad beachfront and affords scenic spots for picnicking.

Santa Monica Visitor Center: 1400 Ocean Ave., Santa Monica, CA 90401; phone (310) 393-7593.

Shopping areas: Santa Monica Place, bounded by Broadway and 4th, Colorado and 2nd streets, is anchored by Macy's and Robinsons-May. A holiday atmosphere prevails at Farmers Market on Arizona Avenue between 2nd and 4th sts., where shoppers can buy produce and plants Wednesday 9-2 and Saturday 9-1.

ANGELS ATTIC, 516 Colorado Ave., is a restored Victorian house containing antique dollhouses, miniatures, dolls and toys. Thurs.-Sun. 12:30-4:30; closed holidays and the first week in Sept. Admission $6.50; over 64, $4; under 13, $3.50. Phone (310) 394-8331.

BERGAMOT STATION, 2525 Michigan Ave., is an art gallery complex and cultural center on nearly six acres. Twenty-two galleries in renovated warehouses display sketches, contemporary paintings, photographs, sculpture and functional art. Food is available. Most galleries open Tues.-Fri. 10-5, Sat. 11-5. Free. Phone (310) 453-7535.

SAVE CALIFORNIA HERITAGE MUSEUM, 2612 Main St., contains restored period rooms dating from the 1890s through the 1930s. The museum also has changing exhibits and displays depicting

California's history and culture. Tours are available. Wed.-Sat. 11-4, Sun. 10-4; closed holidays. Admission $3, senior citizens and students with ID $2, under 13 free. Phone (310) 392-8537.

(SAVE) **MUSEUM OF FLYING,** 2772 Donald Douglas Loop N. near the s. end of 28th St., is on the site where Donald Douglas built the first DC 3. The museum houses more than 30 vintage aircraft, many in flight-ready condition. Among the three stories of displays is Airventure, an interactive flight area. Wed.-Sun. 10-5; closed Jan. 1 and Dec. 25. Admission $7; over 64, $5; ages 3-17, $3. AE, DS, MC, VI. Phone (310) 392-8822.

UNIVERSAL CITY (B-6) elev. 609′

UNIVERSAL CITYWALK, a three-block entertainment and shopping promenade, provides a pedestrian link between Universal Studios Hollywood, Universal Amphitheatre and a movie theater complex. CityWalk incorporates elements of architecturally diverse streets and is enlivened with live performers and more than 20 vintage neon signs. Retail outlets include apparel stores, juice and coffee bars, jewelry shops, toy and gift emporiums and a play area for children. Sun.-Thurs. 11-9, Fri.-Sat. 11-11. Free. Parking $6. Phone (818) 622-4455.

(SAVE) ★ **UNIVERSAL STUDIOS HOLLYWOOD,** Hollywood Frwy. (US 101) at Lankershim Blvd., takes visitors behind the scenes of a major film and TV studio. A narrated tram tour shows where and how movies are made; visitors see props, sound stages, demonstrations of special effects, and sets from such films as "The Lost World: Jurassic Park."

Other highlights include a bike ride with E.T. the extraterrestrial, while "Jurassic Park—The Ride" brings visitors face-to-face with dinosaurs in a tropical habitat. "Back to the Future—the Ride" and "Backdraft" offer, respectively, a sense of high-speed time travel and being trapped in a fiery inferno. "Waterworld," a sea war-themed stunt show featuring pyrotechnics, is based on the Kevin Costner movie of the same name. The Entertainment Center takes visitors where live shows—"Wild, Wild, Wild West Stunt Show," "Animal Actors Stage" and "Totally Nickelodeon"—are performed. Tours are offered continuously.

Daily 8 a.m.-10 p.m. in the summer; 9-7, rest of year. Box office closes at 5 in the summer, at 4 the rest of the year. Tours in Spanish are available Sat.-Sun. Closed Thanksgiving and Dec. 25. Admission $36; over 59, $29; ages 3-11, $26. Parking $6, $7 for RVs. AE, CB, DI, MC, VI. Phone (818) 622-3801. *See color ad p. 132.*

VALENCIA (A-5)

(SAVE) ★ **SIX FLAGS MAGIC MOUNTAIN,** just w. of I-5 Magic Mountain Pkwy. exit at 26101 Magic Mountain Pkwy., is a 260-acre entertainment complex with more than 100 rides, shows and attractions. Highlights include Tidal Wave, which plunges over a 50-foot waterfall; Ninja, a coaster suspended from an overhead track; Freefall, which gives the sensation of leaping from a 10-story building; Viper, a coaster with an initial drop of 188 feet, then vertical loops, a corkscrew and a boomerang turn; Psyclone, a classic wooden roller coaster; the 384-foot Sky Tower and the Riddler's Revenge, a stand-up roller coaster.

The 6-acre Gotham City Backlot features the dark, Gothic-style architecture that is the urban setting for the adventures of comic book and movie crime fighter, Batman. The centerpiece of this themed land is Batman The Ride, a roller coaster with high-speed suspended vehicles that travel through loops, corkscrews and a zero-gravity heartline spin. The "Batman and Robin Live Action Show" takes place at Batman Action Theatre. High Sierra Territory features a river raft ride, rock maze and echo cave. An animal farm and Bugs Bunny World were designed especially for children. Food is available.

Complex open daily at 10, early Apr.-late Oct.; Sat.-Sun. and most school holidays, rest of year. Closing hours vary. Closed Dec. 25. Admission $35; over age 54, $20; under 48 inches tall $17; under age 3 free. Parking $7. Combination with Hurricane Harbor $50. AE, MC, VI. Phone (805) 255-4111 or (818) 367-5965.

(SAVE) **Six Flags Hurricane Harbor** features 22 slides, including the 75-foot speed slides of Black Snake Summit, the racing slides on Bamboo Racer and open flumes at Reptile Ridge; a recreational pool; volleyball courts; and other water-play areas. Admission $18; over age 54, and under 48 inches tall $11; under age 3 free. Parking $7. Combination with Magic Mountain $50. AE, MC, VI.

VAN NUYS (B-6) elev. 708′

Van Nuys Chamber of Commerce: 14540 Victory Blvd., Suite 100, Van Nuys, CA 91411; phone (818) 989-0300.

THE JAPANESE GARDEN AT THE TILLMAN WATER RECLAMATION PLANT, 6100 Woodley Ave., is a water-treatment facility highlighted by a 6.5-acre Japanese garden. Paths wind by small lakes and among lawns, bonsai trees and decorative stones. The garden features a tea house, zigzag bridge and stone lanterns.

Tours of the garden and treatment plant depart Mon.-Thurs. on the half-hour 9:30-10:30, Sat. on the half-hour 9:30-10:30. Self-guiding tours Mon.-Thurs. noon-4. Evening tours are given in summer; phone for schedule. Admission $3; over 61, students with ID and under 11, $2. Reservations are required. Phone (818) 756-8166.

VENICE (B-5) pop. 37,700

Founded in 1905, Venice originally boasted many miles of interconnected canals; today only

Speed down an 8-story drop, and narrowly escape the clutches of a man-eating T-Rex on Jurassic Park®–The Ride. Fly through the decades on Back To The Future...The Ride, feel the heat from Backdraft and bike to the moon on the E.T. Adventure. You can even go Totally Nickelodeon, where kids rule, live every day. Experience the one-of-a-kind world of Universal Studios today.

UNIVERSAL STUDIOS HOLLYWOOD®
THEME PARK

six canals form a network of waterways lined by contemporary and historic homes. Venice is probably most known for its Ocean Front Walk, alive every day with bicyclists, weightlifters, bikini-clad in-line-skaters, and tourists who come to look at the many artisan booths, body-piercing studios and risqué street performers.

Venice has served as the backdrop for a number of movie and television productions, including "Baywatch."

Venice Area Chamber of Commerce and Visitors Bureau: 583 Venice Blvd., Venice, CA 90291; phone (310) 396-7016.

Self-guiding tours: A pamphlet of a 3-mile walking tour, which features murals and sculptures, is available from the visitors bureau.

WHITTIER (B-7) pop. 77,700, elev. 365'

Whittier Area Chamber of Commerce: 8158 Painter Ave., Whittier, CA 90602; phone (562) 698-9554.

Shopping areas: Whittwood Mall, Whittier and Santa Gertrudes boulevards, contains JCPenney, Sears and Mervyn's.

PIO PICO STATE HISTORIC PARK, 6003 Pioneer Blvd., contains the home of Pio Pico, the last governor of California under the Mexican flag. A portion of the 1850s adobe mansion can be seen. Picnicking is permitted. Park open Wed.-Sun. 10-5; closed Jan. 1, Thanksgiving and Dec. 25. Guided tours of the house are available by appointment. Free. Phone (562) 695-1217.

ROSE HILLS MEMORIAL PARK, 3888 S. Workman Mill Rd., is one of the world's largest memorial parks. The east park features the 3.5-acre Pageant of Roses Garden with more than 7,000 bushes and 600 varieties. The west park has a Japanese garden with a meditation house; lakes and arched bridges further enhance the park. Daily 8-7. Free. Phone (562) 699-0921.

SHERIFFS TRAINING AND REGIONAL SERVICES (STARS) CENTER, 11515 S. Colima Rd., near the n.w. corner of S. Colima and Telegraph rds., includes a museum depicting the history and current activities of the Los Angeles County Sheriffs Department. Highlights are a Hughes 300 helicopter, a replica of a 19th-century sheriff's office and jail and videotapes of famous cases that involved the department. Mon.-Fri. 9-4. Free. Guided tours of the museum and a portion of the campus are available by reservation. Phone (562) 946-7081 Wed.-Fri.

WILMINGTON (C-6) pop. 40,000, elev. 22'

BANNING RESIDENCE MUSEUM, 401 E. M St., is the restored 18-room 1864 Greek Revival home of Gen. Phineas Banning, who founded Wilmington in 1858. The museum is a major center for the interpretation of 19th-century Los Angeles history. Guided tours are given on the half-hour Tues.-Thurs. 12:30-2:30, Sat.-Sun. 12:30-3:30; closed holidays. Donations. Phone (310) 548-7777.

DRUM BARRACKS CIVIL WAR MUSEUM, 1052 Banning Blvd., once was the "Accompanied Officers Quarters" and is the only remaining structure of the more than 20 that composed Camp Drum 1862-73. The camp, quartering up to 7,000 men, was established as a Civil War Garrison and depot and also served as a base of operations in the Indian Wars.

The rooms now display items from that period, including a rare 1872 model naval Gatling gun, furniture, photographs, documents and a scale model of the original 60-acre camp. Tours depart Tues.-Thurs. on the hour 10-1, Sat.-Sun. on the half-hour 11:30-2:30. Donations. Phone (310) 548-7509.

**This ends listings for the Los Angeles Vicinity.
The following page resumes the alphabetical listings of cities in California.**

LOS BAÑOS (G-3) pop. 14,500, elev. 120'

The town is named for Los Baños Creek, once a popular bathing spot for missionaries. Cotton, rice and alfalfa crops were introduced to the town's hardy soil in the mid- to late 1800s. Agriculture remains the key industry.

Los Baños Chamber of Commerce: 503 J St., Los Baños, CA 93635; phone (209) 826-2495 or (800) 336-6354.

SAN LUIS DAM COMPLEX, 12 mi. w. on SR 152, is an important link in the Central Valley Project and the California Water Project. Swimming, windsurfing, boating, camping and picnicking are permitted at San Luis Reservoir, San Luis Creek, Los Baños Detention Dam and O'Neill Forebay state recreation areas. Romero Visitors Center has movies, slide programs, telescopes and information about the projects.

Park open daily 24 hours. Visitor center open daily 9-5; closed Jan. 1, Thanksgiving and Dec. 25. Day use pass $5. Visitor center free. Boat pass $10. Phone (209) 826-1196 for dam complex information, or (209) 826-0718, ext. 253, for visitor center.

LOS GATOS (G-2) pop. 27,400, elev. 385'

Los Gatos is guarded by two mountain ridges, El Sombroso (the shadowing one) and El Sereno (the night watchman). The town was founded about 1868 on a portion of an 1840 Spanish land grant. The original grant was known as *La Rinconada de los Gatos* (corner of the cats), a name derived from the many mountain lions and wildcats that inhabited the nearby hills.

By the early 1900s, Los Gatos was a rural community supporting mostly orchards. The town was thrust into urbanization with the onset of World War II. Forbes Mill Museum at 75 Church St. has exhibits about local and regional history. Los Gatos is the northern terminus of a scenic 38-mile stretch of SR 9 to Santa Cruz.

Los Gatos Chamber of Commerce: 333 N. Santa Cruz Ave., P.O. Box 1355, Los Gatos, CA 95031; phone (408) 354-9300.

Shopping areas: Oldtown, 50 University Ave., with its many restored buildings of Spanish and Victorian architecture, topiary trees and gardens, encompasses shops, restaurants and an outdoor amphitheater.

LOS GATOS ARTS & NATURAL HISTORY MUSEUM, at W. Main St. and Tait Ave., has art, science and nature displays. Wed.-Sun. noon-4; closed holidays. Donations. Phone (408) 354-2646.

OAK MEADOW PARK/VASONA PARK are at University Ave. and Blossom Hill Rd. Vasona Park has a playground and fishing and boating facilities; boat rentals are available. Daily 8 a.m.-dusk. Free. Parking fee of $5 charged daily, mid-June to mid-Sept. and Sat.-Sun., Mar. 1 to mid-June; free other days. Phone (408) 354-6809 for Oak Meadow Park, or 358-3751 for Vasona Park, or 399-5781 for the Parks and Recreation Dept.

Billy Jones Wildcat Railroad, in Oak Meadow Park, is a restored 1905 steam train, although a diesel train occasionally is featured. A 1910 English carrousel also is available. Train departs daily 10:30-4:30, mid-June through Labor Day; Sat.-Sun. 11-3, Nov. 1 to mid-Mar. (weather permitting). Fare $1 per ride, physically impaired and under age 2 with paying adult free. Phone (408) 395-7433.

LOS OLIVOS (I-4) elev. 825'

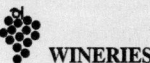

WINERIES

- **The Firestone Vineyard**, 2 mi. n. of jct. US 101 and SR 154 on Zaca Station Rd. Daily 10-5. Phone (805) 688-3940.

- **Zaca Mesa Winery**, approximately 9 mi. n.w. on Foxen Canyon Rd. Daily 10-4. Phone (805) 688-3310.

LOS PADRES NATIONAL FOREST

Elevations in the forest range from sea level at Big Sur to 8,831 ft. at the summit of Mount Pinos. Refer to AAA maps for additional elevation information.

With more than 1,750,000 acres in Southern California, Los Padres National Forest covers terrain ranging from coastal areas through semi-desert to pine-timbered elevations of almost 9,000 feet. Within this region are the Ventana, Machesna, San Rafael, Santa Lucia and Dick Smith wilderness areas as well as condor sanctuaries. Due to this diverse terrain and climate, the forest encompasses a wide variety of flora and fauna. Recreational opportunities also are varied, with camping, swimming, cross-country skiing, hiking, backpacking and horseback riding among the possibilities.

For additional information contact the Forest Supervisor, Los Padres National Forest, 6144 Calle Real, Goleta, CA 93117; phone (805) 683-6711, or TTY/TDD (805) 967-4487. *See Recreation Chart and the AAA California/Nevada CampBook.*

MALIBU—
see Los Angeles p. 126.

MAMMOTH LAKES (F-5)
pop. 4,800, elev. 7,860'

One of California's most popular four-season resorts, Mammoth Lakes provides access to the recreational facilities and points of interest in Inyo National Forest *(see place listing p. 82).*

Mammoth Lakes Visitors Bureau: P.O. Box 48, Mammoth Lakes, CA 93546; phone (888) 466-2666. *See ad p. 656.*

MAMMOTH LAKES RECREATION AREA, 200,000 acres, contains portions of Pacific Crest Trail, John Muir Trail, Devils Postpile National Monument *(see place listing p. 71),* Mammoth Mountain Ski Area, Rainbow Falls, Mammoth City Historical Site, Mammoth Lakes Basin and geothermal springs. Self-guiding trails tour alpine lakes, mountain vistas, lodgepole and Jeffrey pine forests and unusual geologic formations. The area has facilities for fishing, boating, snowmobiling, cross-country and downhill skiing and hiking. Naturalists conduct interpretive programs.

The visitor center-ranger station, on SR 203 at the entrance to town, is open daily 8-6 (also Fri. 6-8 p.m.), July 1-Labor Day; 8-5, rest of year. Closed Jan. 1, Thanksgiving and Dec. 25 Visitor center free. Phone (760) 924-5500 for visitor center, or (800) 427-7623 for weather and road information.

MANTECA (F-3) pop. 40,800, elev. 38'

[SAVE] **OAKWOOD LAKE WATER THEME PARK** is between I-5 and SR 99 at 874 E. Woodward. The park features more than 30 water rides and a wading pool. A 75-acre lake adjoins a campground and picnic sites. Daily 10-7, mid-June through Labor Day; Sat.-Sun. 10-5, May 1 to mid-June and day after Labor Day-Sept. 30. All-inclusive pass $19, 42-48 inches tall $11, under 42 inches tall free. Only children's area and wading pool $10. DS, MC, VI. Phone (209) 239-9566 or 239-2500.

MARINA DEL REY—
see Los Angeles p. 126.

MARIPOSA (F-4) pop. 1,200, elev. 1,953'

Originally called Logtown, Mariposa was renamed after the Spanish word for butterfly. Gold mining has been supplanted by the scenic riches of nearby Yosemite Valley, which draw thousands of visitors each year.

Mariposa County Chamber of Commerce: 5158 Hwy. 140, P.O. Box 425, Mariposa, CA 95338; phone (209) 966-2456 or (800) 208-2434. *See color ad p. 241.*

CALIFORNIA STATE MINING AND MINERAL MUSEUM, 1.8 mi. s. on SR 49 at the county fairgrounds, contains a collection of minerals, gold, diamonds and other gems that reflect the wealth found in Mariposa mines. Benitoite, the California state gemstone, is displayed. Other exhibits include models of an assay office and stamp mill and a full-scale replica of a mine. The museum also features temporary exhibits of gem and mineral specimens from other institutions and private collections.

Allow 1 hour minimum. Wed.-Mon. 10-9, May-Sept.; Wed.-Sun. 10-4, rest of year. Hours may vary; phone ahead. Closed Memorial Day weekend, Thanksgiving and Dec. 25. Admission $3.50; over 59, students with ID and ages 14-18, $2.50. Phone (209) 742-7625.

COURTHOUSE, 5088 Bullion St., was built in 1854 and is the oldest courthouse in the state still in use. Wooden pegs were used in the construction of the two-story white pine building; the second floor contains original furnishings. The old clock in the square clock tower was brought by way of Cape Horn, at the southern tip of South America. Daily 8-5, Memorial Day weekend-Labor Day; Mon.-Fri. 8-5, rest of year. Guided tours Fri. 5-9, Sat. 10-8, Sun. and holidays noon-5, June-Sept. Free. Phone (209) 966-7081.

MARIPOSA MUSEUM AND HISTORY CENTER INC., SR 140 at 12th and Jessie sts., contains a re-created 1850s street, including a five-stamp mill, horse-drawn vehicles and mining and printing equipment. Featured are replicas of a schoolroom, an American Indian village, a miner's cabin, a print shop, a sheriff's office, a saloon and an apothecary as well as the restored house of the 1860s county treasurer. Allow 1 hour minimum. Daily 10-4:30, Mar.-Oct.; Sat.-Sun. 10-4 in Feb. and Nov.-Dec. Donations. Phone (209) 966-2924.

MARKLEEVILLE (E-5)
pop. 100, elev. 5,525'

ALPINE COUNTY HISTORICAL COMPLEX, .2 mi. w. of SR 89 at School and Montgomery sts., includes an 1882 schoolhouse and a jail that have been restored and furnished in period. A museum contains exhibits about the history and culture of the Washoe Indians and the history of the Vaquero Camp. Wed.-Mon. noon-5, Memorial Day weekend-Oct. 31. Donations. Phone (530) 694-2317.

MARTINEZ (O-3) pop. 31,300, elev. 23'

JOHN MUIR NATIONAL HISTORIC SITE, 4202 Alhambra Ave., was the residence of the conservationist and founder of the Sierra Club. His crusade for wilderness preservation aided in the establishment of national parks and forests. The 1882 house contains original furnishings. Visitors may tour the 17-room mansion and the surrounding orchards. A film about Muir's life is shown at 10, 11, noon, 1:30, 2:30 and 3:30. The two-story Martinez Adobe, built in 1848, is the former home of Muir's daughter.

Allow 1 hour, 30 minutes minimum. Wed.-Sun. 10-4:30; closed Jan. 1, Thanksgiving and Dec. 25. Admission $2, under 16 free. Phone (925) 228-8860.

MARYSVILLE (D-3)
pop. 12,300, elev. 63'

Central to Marysville is Ellis Lake, named for W.T. Ellis, a prosperous town merchant in the early 1900s. The boulevard along the shore testifies to the merchant's efforts to beautify the lake; a jogging/exercise course also circles the lake. Paddleboats are available seasonally.

Mary Aaron Museum, 704 D St., is a restored Victorian house built in 1856. The museum features changing exhibits of various items of Victorian life; phone (530) 743-1004.

Riverfront Park is beneath the 5th and 10th street bridges, which link Marysville and Yuba City. Recreational facilities include a boat-launching dock, picnic area, playgrounds, soccer fields, baseball fields and motorbike trails. The park also has a concert bowl with grassy slopes for seating.

Yuba-Sutter Chamber of Commerce: 429 10th St., P.O. Box 1429, Marysville, CA 95901; phone (530) 743-6501.

MENDOCINO (D-1) pop. 1,000, elev. 90'

A picturesque community off scenic SR 1 on the rugged northern California coast, Mendocino has many well-preserved 19th-century buildings and houses. The architecture reflects the New England roots of early settlers, who were drawn by the rich timber resources of the surrounding countryside. The stark beauty of the region attracts many artists to the town. Mendocino Art Center, 45200 Little Lake Rd., offers exhibits and festivals.

KELLEY HOUSE HISTORICAL MUSEUM, 45007 Albion St., contains photographs, watercolors and brief histories of many private buildings and houses in the area. The 1861 house has been restored. Daily 1-4, June-Sept.; Fri.-Mon. 1-4, rest of year. Admission $2. Phone (707) 937-5791.

 RECREATIONAL ACTIVITIES

Canoeing

- **Catch a Canoe & Bicycles, Too!**, SR 1 and Comptche-Ukiah Rd. Write P.O. Box 487, Mendocino, CA 95460. Daily 9-5:30. Phone (707) 937-0273 or (800) 320-2453.

MENDOCINO NATIONAL FOREST

Elevations in the forest range from 1,000 ft. at Elk Creek to 8,110 ft. at the summit of Mount Linn. Refer to AAA maps for additional elevation information.

Encompassing nearly 886,048 acres, Mendocino National Forest lies in the North Coast Mountain Range north of San Francisco. Hang gliding and motorcycling areas are available. Roads and trails afford access to scenic points. Many roads within the forest are unsurfaced; driving can be hazardous, especially in the dusty, dry months.

Yolla Bolly-Middle Eel Wilderness at the north end of the forest and Snow Mountain Wilderness in the south provide peaceful settings for horseback riding and hiking. Wilderness entry permits are not required, but users should sign the registry at trailheads.

Campfire permits are required in some areas; check with the Forest Supervisor, 420 E. Laurel St., Willows, CA 95988, or a district ranger. For recorded information phone (530) 934-2350, 934-3316, or TDD (530) 934-7724. *See Recreation Chart and the AAA California/Nevada CampBook.*

MENLO PARK (Q-2)
pop. 28,000, elev. 70'

ALLIED ARTS GUILD, off SR 82 at the end of Cambridge Ave. on Arbor Rd., stands on 3.5 acres of land granted by the King of Spain to the Commandant of the Presidio de San Francisco in the early 19th century. Spanish-style buildings, courtyards, gardens, fountains, murals and frescoes create an Old World atmosphere where artisans practice their crafts. Mon.-Sat. 10-5 (also Sun. noon-5 in Dec.). Free. Phone (650) 325-3259.

SUNSET PUBLISHING CORP., 80 Willow Rd. at Middlefield Rd., the publisher of *Sunset* magazine, offers self-guiding walking tours of the gardens. Divided into zones that represent the West, the gardens contain more than 300 varieties of trees, shrubs, vines, ground cover, annuals and perennials. Allow 1 hour minimum. Mon.-Fri. 9-4:30; closed holidays. Free. Phone (650) 321-3600.

MERCED (G-4) pop. 56,200, elev. 167'

Merced, in the agricultural San Joaquin Valley, is the principal western gateway to Yosemite National Park for travelers from the north.

The 1875 Old County Courthouse at 21st and N streets in Courthouse Park is built in the Italianate Renaissance style and resembles the state

Capitol building. Merced County Museum in the courthouse contains exhibits about local history. Merced National Wildlife Refuge is 16 miles southwest. Water sports are offered 7 miles northeast at Lake Yosemite. Applegate Park and Zoo on 25th and R streets features wild animals, birds and children's rides.

Merced Conference and Visitors Bureau: 690 W. 16th St., Merced, CA 95340; phone (209) 384-3333 or (800) 446-5353. *See ad p. 668.*

Self-guiding tours: The visitors bureau distributes a guide to historic Merced as well as a blossom guide.

MILL VALLEY—
see San Francisco p. 209.

MISSION HILLS—
see Los Angeles p. 126.

MODESTO (F-3) pop. 164,700, elev. 88'

In the northern San Joaquin Valley on the Tuolumne River, Modesto is near the geographic center of the state. When the Central Pacific Railroad brought about the city's founding in 1870, its proponents wanted to name it after a San Francisco banker. When the banker rejected the idea, his modesty was commemorated in the chosen name. Modesto provides access to Sonora Pass in Stanislaus National Forest, the Mother Lode Country and the Big Oak Flat route to Yosemite.

Miller's California Ranch, 10 miles east on SR 132 at 9425 Yosemite Blvd., has a small collection of motor vehicles and wagons and an old-fashioned store featuring antique and unusual bicycles; phone (209) 522-1781. Great Valley Museum of Natural History, 1100 Stoddard Ave., features exhibits about Central Valley ecosystems; phone (209) 575-6190. St. Stan's Brewery at 9th and L streets offers tours and tastings; phone (209) 524-4782.

Modesto Convention and Visitors Bureau: 1114 J St., P.O. Box 844, Modesto, CA 95353; phone (209) 571-6480 or (800) 266-4282.

BLUE DIAMOND ALMOND, 4800 Sisk Rd., offers a videotape presentation about the growing and harvesting of almonds. A tasting room is available. Mon.-Fri. 10-5, Sat. 10-4; closed holidays. Last videotape presentation is shown at 4:30. Free. Phone (209) 545-3222.

McHENRY MANSION, 15th and I sts., is a restored 19th-century Victorian house furnished with period artwork and antiques. Tours are given Thurs. and Sun. 1-4, Fri. noon-3. Donations. Phone (209) 577-5341.

McHENRY MUSEUM, 1402 I St., includes a schoolroom, smithy, dentist's and doctor's offices, kitchen, country store, historical photographs and documents, and changing exhibits. Tues.-Sun. noon-4; closed holidays. Donations. Phone (209) 577-5366.

MODOC NATIONAL FOREST

Elevations in the forest range from 4,500 ft. at Devils Gardens to 9,892 ft. at Eagle Peak. Refer to AAA maps for additional elevation information.

Modoc National Forest's 1,654,392 acres encompass much of the state's remote northeastern corner, which was covered millions of years ago by an immense lava flow. Although geologically the area is known as the Modoc Plateau, it doesn't look like a plateau. The region is distinguished by basins, mountains, lakes and meadows. And despite the relatively dry climate, the plateau supports some of the country's most significant wetlands.

The forest is home to more than 300 species of wildlife, including Rocky Mountain mule deer, pronghorn antelopes, bald and golden eagles and wild horses. The Pacific Flyway for migratory birds crosses directly over the forest.

Volcanism has left many marks on the forest's terrain, and some of the most dramatic examples are in the Medicine Lake highlands. There are such unusual features as Glass Mountain, a huge flow of obsidian, and the Burnt Lava Flow, which is a jumble of black lava interspersed with islands of timber. Medicine Lake itself fills an old volcanic crater and is popular for boating and swimming.

On the forest's eastern boundary, the Warner Mountains are a rolling upland that drops steeply on its eastern edge. Most of the range is above 5,000 feet, and some of the peaks reach an altitude over 9,000 feet in the 70,385-acre South Warner Wilderness, which includes Modoc's highest mountain, Eagle Peak. The forest has 118 miles of trails, accessible by eight trailheads, suited for hikers and horseback riders. Carrying a topography map is advised. Fishing is prime in many reservoirs. Cross-country skiing is a popular wintertime diversion.

Maps, brochures and information about recreational opportunities are available at the district ranger stations and the forest headquarters in Alturas. For more information write the Forest Supervisor, Modoc National Forest, 800 W. 12th St., Alturas, CA 96101; phone (530) 233-5811. *See the Recreation Chart and AAA California/ Nevada CampBook.*

MOJAVE NATIONAL PRESERVE (I-8)

Designated a national preserve in 1994, Mojave National Preserve comprises 1.6 million acres between I-15 and I-40 in southeastern California. It was established to protect the prehistoric, historic and natural resources found at this convergence of ecosystems.

The preserve ranges in elevation from less than 1,000 feet to almost 8,000 feet. The diverse landscape encompasses mountains, mesas, red volcanic spires, cinder cones and sand dunes. Since summer daytime temperatures typically exceed 100 F at lower elevations, the best months for visiting are October through May. Although yearly rainfall averages between 5 and 10 inches, summer storms sometimes cause flash floods, and occasional winter storms bring rain and even snow to the higher mountains.

Though not always visible, wildlife is abundant. Some of the nearly 300 species of animals living in this area include bighorn sheep, mule deer, porcupines and mountain lions in the mountains; coyotes, kit foxes, desert tortoises and antelope ground squirrels inhabit lower elevations.

To survive the desert climate, many plants have small leaves to minimize moisture loss. Cactuses store water in their tissues, and mesquites send roots as deep as 100 feet. Common plants include yucca, sage, rabbitbrush and the spindly Joshua tree. Wildflower displays are colorful in April and May.

Mojave National Preserve is rich in archeological and historical features that are protected by law. The many examples of Indian rock art include petroglyphs more than 10,000 years old. More recent are the abandoned mines and desert camps, evidence of the mining that once flourished and continues to a limited extent today. Cattle ranching, also important during the 1800s, is still practiced.

Developed campgrounds are open all year at Mid Hills and Hole-in-the-Wall; the fee at both is $10 per night. Primitive camping is permitted at other designated sites. Hiking, backpacking and horseback riding are permitted, but horses are not allowed at developed campsites. Camping or parking within .25 mile of a watering spot is not allowed. Birdwatching, photography and star tracking also are popular.

Several paved roads and hundreds of miles of gravel and dirt roads lace the area. Vehicles must stay on designated roads; there are no off-road vehicle areas. Because gasoline availability is unpredictable, you should fill your tank at Needles, Ludlow or Baker before entering the region and check ahead for weather and road conditions.

For further information contact the Mojave National Preserve, 222 E. Main St., Barstow, CA 92311; phone (760) 733-4040. The preserve office is open Mon.-Fri. 8-5. Information can be obtained daily 9-5 from the California Desert Information Center, 831 Barstow Rd., Barstow, CA 92311; phone (760) 255-8760. *See Recreation Chart.*

CEDAR CANYON ROAD runs east and west between the Kelso-Cima and Lanfair roads, passing remnants of old ranches and homesteads—stark reminders of life in the preserve during the late 1800s. Part of this road follows Mojave Road, or Old Government Road, one of the first routes developed through this region for wagon use in the 1850s and '60s. Most of Mojave Road is accessible only by four-wheel-drive vehicles. Guidebooks for the 130-mile route are available on loan from the Bureau of Land Management offices in Barstow, Needles and Riverside.

CIMA ROAD heads south from I-15 at Valley Wells; it passes east of the rounded and weathered granite of Cima Dome, which has one of the densest Joshua tree forests in California.

IVANPAH-LANFAIR ROAD begins 6.5 mi. w. of Nipton near I-15 and extends s. to Goffs near I-40. The first stretch through Ivanpah Valley is one of the best places in California to spot the desert tortoise in spring. The road continues over the New York Mountains, where the presence of water accounts for the existence of 288 species of plants and a variety of wildlife. Both abandoned and working mines are scattered throughout the area.

KELBAKER ROAD provides north-south access between I-15 at Baker and I-40. Heading south from Baker, the road passes the historic town of Kelso, the site of a classic Neo-Spanish railroad depot along the Union Pacific Railroad. Kelso Dunes southwest of town is one of the few dune fields in the continental United States where the sand cascading down the steep slopes emits a booming sound. Farther south the road passes between two of the area's highest ranges, the Providence Mountains on the east and the Granite Mountains on the west.

PROVIDENCE MOUNTAINS STATE RECREATION AREA is 17 mi. n. of I-40 on Essex Rd. The nearby countryside consists of high desert framed by red volcanic peaks. A self-guiding nature trail begins near the visitor center. Essex-Black Canyon Road continues north to the Hole-in-the-Wall country, the setting for the area's two developed campgrounds. Hills and mesas scattered with pinyon and juniper surround the broad sagebrush-covered valleys. Volcanic in origin, the mesas and buttes around Hole-in-the-Wall are pocked with holes that produce eerie sounds when the wind blows.

Mitchell Caverns, approximately 15 miles north of I-40 off Essex Rd., is known for its limestone caves. Old mines dot the area, making it a favorite with rockhounds. For information or reservations write P.O. Box 1, Essex, CA 92332. Guided tours of the caverns are offered Mon.-Fri. at 1:30, Sat.-Sun. and holidays at 10, 1:30 and 3, Sept.-May (weather permitting); Sat.-Sun. at

1:30, rest of year. Tours $6; ages 6-17, $3. There is a $2 per person reservation fee. Parking $5. Phone (760) 928-2586.

MONO BASIN NATIONAL FOREST SCENIC AREA

Accessible via SRs 120 and 167, the scenic area is within Inyo National Forest *(see place listing p. 82)* near Lee Vining. The area covers 116,000 acres surrounding Mono Lake and includes volcanic hills on its borders. The Bodie Hills to the north and the Anchorite Hills to the east are about 11 million years old, while the Mono Craters to the south are the youngest mountain range in North America. One of the craters erupted about 600 years ago. The islands in Mono Lake also are volcanic, as evidenced by hot springs and steam vents.

The lake itself is more than 700,000 years old. Over time the salts and minerals in the water have become too concentrated for most species, but brine shrimp and flies attract millions of migratory birds and waterfowl. Most tourists come to see the tufa, spires and knobs formed of calcium carbonate that have been exposed as the lake's water level has dropped. Tufa, pumice and obsidian are protected by state and federal laws and may not be collected or damaged.

Many basin roads are unsuitable for conventional vehicles; off-road driving is not permitted. Self-guiding nature trails and interpretive exhibits are at the South Tufa and Panum Crater dayuse areas. The scenic area is open daily 24 hours. A visitor center 1 mile north of Lee Vining is open daily 9-5, Apr. 1-Labor Day; otherwise varies. Free. For more information contact Lee Vining Ranger District, P.O. Box 429, Lee Vining, CA 93541; phone (760) 647-3044.

Monterey Peninsula

Although Spanish explorer Juan Rodriguez Cabrillo, the first European to reach Monterey Bay, came within visual contact of the bay's beaches and pine forests in 1542, he was unable to land due to high seas. It would be 60 years before Sebastián Vizcaíno explored the bay and named it for the Count of Monte Rey, viceroy of Mexico. Vizcaíno also was responsible for naming a nearby valley after his patron saint, Our Lady of Carmel.

Although officially claimed for Spain, the area was not settled until Franciscan priest Junípero Serra and Spanish governor Gaspar de Portolá arrived in 1770 to build a mission and establish a seat of government, respectively.

The fishing industry was the original anchor of the area's economy, with whaling the mainstay. By the 1880s tourism took economic precedence over whaling. But it was only natural that the ocean should beckon once again, and sardine harvesting led to the birth of Monterey's Cannery Row during the 1920s.

The peninsula's natural beauty restored tourism to the economic forefront after the collapse of the sardine industry. In addition to the obvious attractions offered by the dramatic coastline, beaches and the surf, the Monterey Peninsula also consists of gently rolling hills, streams and forests, and the area has become a mecca for golf aficionados.

For those seeking more active pursuits, the Monterey Peninsula Recreational Trail is a walking and biking path that parallels the coastline from Seaside, through Monterey to Pacific Grove.

CARMEL (G-2) pop. 4,200, elev. 20′

Carmel was established in 1904 by a group of artists and writers as a bucolic retreat. As the settlement grew, its founders fought the encroachment of paved streets, gas, electricity and other modern amenities, and stringent zoning ordinances have preserved Carmel's village flavor and individuality. Carmel is an architectural conglomerate of international styles, reflecting the whims of the residents.

Each summer the Outdoor Forest Theatre delivers live performances and the audience is encouraged to picnic.

Downtown parking time limits are strictly enforced. A city lot on Third at Torres offers free, unlimited parking; enter from Third.

Carmel lies on a scenic stretch of SR 1 that extends from San Francisco to San Luis Obispo. North of

Carmel's white sand beach is an entrance to Seventeen-Mile Drive, a scenic route from Pacific Grove to Carmel *(see Monterey p. 145)*.

Carmel Business Association: San Carlos between 5th and 6th streets, P.O. Box 4444, Carmel, CA 93921; phone (831) 624-2522.

Shopping areas: The compact business center contains unusual shops and galleries that display the work of local artists. The Barnyard, SR 1 and Carmel Valley Road with access from Carmel Rancho Boulevard, is as popular for its garden setting and country atmosphere as for its galleries and specialty shops. The Crossroads, east of SR 1 and Father Serra's Carmel Mission, offers nearly 100 boutiques and specialty shops.

★**MISSION SAN CARLOS BORROMEO DEL RIO CARMELO,** called Carmel Mission, is at 3080 Rio Rd. Established by Father Junípero Serra at Monterey in 1770 and moved to its present site the following year, the mission was Father Serra's residence and headquarters until his death in 1784. He is buried beneath the church floor in front of the altar. Relics of the mission's early days and some of Father Serra's books and documents are displayed. The courtyard gardens and Moorish bell tower are of interest. A fiesta usually is held the last Sunday in September.

Allow 1 hour minimum. Mon.-Sat. 9:30-4:30, Sun. 10:30-4:30. Closed Thanksgiving and Dec. 25. Admission $2; ages 5-17, $1. Phone (831) 624-3600.

★**POINT LOBOS STATE RESERVE,** 3 mi. s. on SR 1, covers 1,225 acres of land and water along the rugged seacoast. There are many well-marked trails along the cliffs. Maps of the 10 miles of trails are available at the entrance station. Plants specially adapted to the coastal climate abound in and among the rocks, particularly the Monterey cypress, Monterey pine, seaside daisy and bluff lettuce. The reserve also has varied wildlife, including deer, squirrels and rabbits.

About half the reserve is designated as an underwater reserve. Harbor seals, gray whales and the California sea lion frequent the area, and the California sea otter also can be seen. Numerous sea birds, including cormorants and pelicans, nest along the coast. Diving is permitted only by permit; phone (831) 624-8413 for reservations. Nature walks are offered; phone for schedule. Pets are not permitted.

Allow 2 hours minimum. Daily 9-6:30, Memorial Day-Labor Day; 9-5, rest of year. Admission $7 per private vehicle; over 62, $6 per private vehicle. Phone (831) 624-4909.

MONTEREY (G-2) pop. 32,000, elev. 25'

The capital of Alta California under the Spanish, Mexican and American flags, Monterey lies on the Monterey Peninsula and ranges in altitude from sea level to 360 feet. The peninsula is a popular year-round playground boasting several golf courses. South of Monterey SR 1 winds through redwood forests and along the cliffs of the spectacular Big Sur coast.

This orientation illustration represents the MONTEREY VICINITY as defined by local AAA travel experts.

MONTEREY BAY AQUARIUM

Pacific Grove
PG. 145

MONTEREY

Carmel-By-The-Sea
PG. 140

MISSION SAN CARLOS BORROMEO DEL RIO CARMELO

68

1

MONTEREY PENINSULA

©AAA

On Cannery Row, the colorful locale of John Steinbeck's novels "Cannery Row" and "Sweet Thursday," galleries, shops and restaurants have replaced the sardine canneries. Along Fisherman's Wharf an art gallery, handicraft shops and Wharf Theater have superseded the commercial fishing activities of the early 20th century.

Every Tuesday afternoon bargain hunters flock to Monterey Farmers Market to meander among the produce, food, and arts and crafts booths.

The Monterey Presidio, 1 block from the theater on Pacific Street, was founded in 1770 by Capt. Gaspar de Portolá, assisted by fathers Junípero Serra and Juan Crespi. It is now the Defense Language Institute Presidio of Monterey.

Monterey Peninsula Visitors and Convention Bureau: 380 Alvarado St., Monterey, CA 93940; phone (831) 649-1770.

Self-guiding tours: Maps for a 2-mile Monterey Path of History walking tour, detailing gardens, adobes and historic sites, are available from the chamber of commerce and from the visitor center at 201 El Estero.

DENNIS THE MENACE PLAYGROUND is in the park on Lake El Estero. Hank Ketcham, creator of "Dennis the Menace," aided in its development. It contains climbing structures, slides, a balancing bridge, a maze, a railroad switch engine and a lion-shaped drinking fountain. Daily

10-dusk, June-Aug.; Tues.-Sun. 10-dusk, rest of year. Free. Phone (831) 646-3866.

MARITIME MUSEUM, 5 Custom House Plaza, contains the collections of Allen Knight, a seaman who built a stone ship next to his home to store his collected artifacts. The Fresnel lens of Point Sur Lighthouse, weighing nearly 10,000 pounds, illuminates the museum's exhibits, including navigational instruments, ship models, chronicles, photos and charts. A 14-minute film of regional history is presented every 20 minutes.

Allow 1 hour minimum. Daily 10-5; closed Thanksgiving and Dec. 25. Last film is shown at 4:30. Admission $5; over 64 and military $4; ages 13-18, $3; ages 6-12, $2. Phone (831) 373-2469.

★**MONTEREY BAY AQUARIUM,** 886 Cannery Row, houses more than 500 species of marine life in more than 100 galleries and exhibits. The "Outer Bay" galleries present the mysteries of the open ocean. Included is a million-gallon tank whose denizens, including sunfish, barracudas, tuna, sharks and green sea turtles, are visible through an acrylic panel 54 feet long, 15 feet high and 13 inches thick. Other exhibits include an elliptical, overhead 15,000-gallon anchovy tank and a remarkable display of jellyfish species.

The aquarium also has a touch pool, life-size models of whales and other marine animals, a shorebird aviary, a theater and historical displays. Feeding demonstrations take place daily at the sea otter and kelp forest exhibits.

"Mysteries of the Deep" features deep-sea animals from Monterey Bay. The exhibit includes live broadcasts from a research submarine in the bay, working at depths to 6,000 feet. New exhibits open each March. Food is available.

Allow 3 hours minimum. Daily 9:30-6, Memorial Day-Labor Day and on holidays; 10-6, rest of year. Closed Dec. 25. Admission $15.95; over 65 and students with ID $11.95; physically impaired and ages 3-12, $6.95. AE, MC, VI. Phone (831) 648-4888 for information, or (800) 756-3737 in Calif. for advance tickets. *See color ad p. 143.*

MONTEREY PENINSULA MUSEUM OF ART, 559 Pacific St., presents permanent and changing displays of regional, Oriental and folk art as well as photography. Allow 1 hour minimum. Wed.-Sat. 11-5 (also third Thurs. of the month 5-7), Sun. 1-4; closed Jan. 1, Thanksgiving and Dec. 25. Admission $3, students with ID $1.50. Phone (831) 372-7591.

★**MONTEREY STATE HISTORIC PARK,** 20 Custom House Plaza, is a 7-acre site that preserves the historical and architectural heritage of old Monterey. Nearby is the original 1602 landing site of Sebastián Vizcaíno and—more than 150 years later—Father Junípero Serra. Guided walking tours are available from the visitors center at 5 Custom House Plaza; the center also offers brochures and free showings of a film about Monterey history.

Daily 10-5, Memorial Day weekend-Labor Day; 10-4, rest of year. Gardens are open daily 10-4. Closed Jan. 1, Thanksgiving and Dec. 25. Tours $5; ages 13-17, $3; physically impaired $2.50; ages 6-12, $2. Phone (831) 649-7118 to verify schedule.

Casa Soberanes and Garden, 336 Pacific St., was built in 1842 and occupied by members of the Soberanes family until 1922. The well-preserved house contains period antiques. Guided tours are available at noon and 2.

Colton Hall, in the civic center on Pacific St. facing Friendly Plaza, is where the first Constitution of California was written in 1849. It now contains a museum dedicated to city history. Adjoining Colton Hall, completed in 1849, is the old jail, built in 1854. Allow 30 minutes minimum. Daily 10-noon and 1-5, Mar.-Oct.; 10-noon and 1-4, rest of year. Closed Jan. 1, Thanksgiving and Dec. 25. Donations. Phone (831) 646-5640.

Cooper-Molera Adobe and Garden, at 525 Polk St., is the restored Victorian home of the Yankee sea captain, rancher and adventurer who married the sister of Gen. Mariano Vallejo. The grounds also have four other structures and a period garden that are open to the public. Visitor center open daily 10-4. Guided tours available Tues. and Thurs.-Sun. at 10, 11 and noon, July-Aug.; at 10 and 11, rest of year.

Custom House and Garden, on Custom House Plaza at Fisherman's Wharf, is the oldest government building in California, its north section having been constructed about 1827. When Commodore John Drake Sloat raised the American flag over the building in 1846, approximately 600,000 square miles became part of the United States. The house displays trade goods from the 1840s. Daily 10-5, June-Aug.; 10-4, rest of year.

First Theater and Garden, Pacific and Scott sts., once was a lodging house for sailors as well as the first building in Monterey to charge admission for a theatrical performance. The 1846 building contains relics of early California. Dramatic productions still are staged. Daily 10-5. Fees for theatrical productions vary; phone (831) 375-4916 for information and reservations, 649-7118 for garden tours.

Larkin House and Garden is at Calle Principal and Jefferson St. Its combination of Mexican Colonial and New England architectural features reflects the New England origins of the builder. The 1835 house served as the American consulate 1843-46. Its rooms hold antiques from many parts of the world. Guided tours are available.

Stevenson House and Garden, 530 Houston St., is the old French Hotel where Robert Louis Stevenson spent the fall of 1879. Here he wrote "Vendetta of the West" and an essay about Thoreau, and blocked out the "Amateur Emigrant" and "Prince Otto." Restored and furnished in period, the house can be seen only via a 30-minute guided tour.

SAN CARLOS CATHEDRAL, also known as Royal Presidio Chapel, is at 550 Church St. Founded in 1770 to be the mission church of the port, San Carlos Cathedral became the church for the Spanish colonists and soldiers instead, as the mission was moved to Carmel the following year. The present church has been in continuous use since 1795. Daily 8-6. Donations. Phone (831) 373-2628.

SEVENTEEN-MILE DRIVE is the scenic route from Pacific Grove to Carmel and a highlight of any visit to this coastal region. Points of interest along the way include Seal Rock, Cypress Point and Lone Cypress. Among the six golf courses on the route are the Pebble Beach, Cypress Point, Spy Glass Hill and Monterey Peninsula, scene of the AT&T Pro-Am Golf Tournament at the end of January and the beginning of February.

Allow at least 1 hour to complete the drive. Bicycles are permitted during daylight hours when no major sporting event is scheduled; no motorcycles or motorbikes are permitted on the drive. Bicyclists must enter through the Pacific Grove gate on weekends, holidays and when events are scheduled, and must sign a release before using the drive. The toll includes a map listing 21 points of interest along the road. The toll for cars is $7.50. For hours of operation and toll information phone the security office at (831) 625-8426 or 624-6669.

STEINBECK SPIRIT OF MONTEREY WAX MUSEUM, 700 Cannery Row in the Monterey Cannery Building, displays wax figures from Monterey's turbulent history. Allow 30 minutes minimum. Daily 9 a.m.-10 p.m. Admission $6.95; over 55, military with ID and students with ID $5; ages 13-18, $3.95; ages 6-12, $2.95. Phone (831) 375-3770. *See color ad p. 143.*

TRIPS ON TAPE, for the Monterey Peninsula and Big Sur, is a self-guiding audio tape tour that describes the history, landmarks, events and attractions of Monterey, Pacific Grove, Carmel, Carmel Valley, Point Lobos and the Big Sur Coast. Maps are included. Tapes are available for $12.95 from Bay Area bookstores, or by mail from The Rider's

Guide, 484 Lake Park Ave., Suite 255, Oakland, CA 94610. Add $2.50 for postage; Calif. residents add sales tax. Phone (510) 653-2553.

 RECREATIONAL ACTIVITIES

Kayaking

• **Monterey Bay Kayaks,** 693 Del Monte Ave., Monterey, CA 93940. Daily 9-6; closed Jan. 1, Thanksgiving and Dec. 25. Phone (831) 373-5357 or (800) 649-5357.

PACIFIC GROVE (G-2)
pop. 16,100, elev. 55'

Adjoining Monterey, Pacific Grove is the starting point for the popular Seventeen-Mile Drive *(see Monterey p. 145).* Point Piños Lighthouse, in operation since 1855, is on Asilomar Boulevard, off Lighthouse Avenue. The lighthouse's levels, connected by a spiral staircase, depict a typical lightkeeper's quarters in the 1800s and early 1900s; phone (831) 648-3116. Downtown residential neighborhoods contain numbers of well-preserved Victorian houses.

For years thousands of monarch butterflies visited an area of pine trees on Ridge Road off Lighthouse Avenue from early October through March; sadly, their number is greatly diminished.

Pacific Grove Chamber of Commerce: First and Central aves., P.O. Box 167, Pacific Grove, CA 93950; phone (831) 373-3304.

Shopping areas: American Tin Cannery, 125 Ocean View Blvd., has more than 45 factory-direct and specialty stores.

MUSEUM OF NATURAL HISTORY, 165 Forest Ave., emphasizes the natural history of Monterey County through an extensive collection of rocks and minerals, 400 mounted birds and a monarch butterfly display. Changing exhibits focus on American Indians. Allow 1 hour minimum. Tues.-Sun. and holidays 10-5; closed Jan. 1, Thanksgiving and Dec. 24-25. Free. Phone (831) 648-3116.

This ends listings for the Los Angeles Vicinity.
The following page resumes the alphabetical listings of cities in California.

MORGAN HILL (G-3)
pop. 23,900, elev. 345'

Before the arrival of Spanish soldiers and priests in 1776, the area was home to the peaceful Costanoan Indians. The first English-speaking community sprang up around a prosperous estate known as Morgan Hill's Ranch in 1845 and was incorporated in 1906. Morgan Hill is at the southern end of the agriculturally rich Santa Clara Valley, where the French prune was developed.

Morgan Hill Chamber of Commerce: 25 W. First St., P.O. Box 786, Morgan Hill, CA 95038-0786; phone (408) 779-9444.

MORRO BAY (I-3) pop. 9,700, elev. 80'

Both the town of Morro Bay and the bay that fronts it are named for Morro Rock, the great conical rock that juts 578 feet out of the Pacific Ocean. In the 1870s Morro Bay was a port for the region's cattle ranching and dairy industries. Later commercial fishing and oyster farming became prominent. Morro Bay still maintains a large commercial fishing fleet.

Boat tours and boat rentals are available at Marina Square on the Embarcadero. A few miles south of SR 1 is Morro Bay State Park *(see Recreation Chart and the AAA California CampBook).*

Morro Bay Chamber of Commerce: 880 Main St., P.O. Box 876, Morro Bay, CA 93442; phone (805) 772-4467.

MORRO BAY STATE PARK MUSEUM OF NATURAL HISTORY, in Morro Bay State Park, includes interpretive displays and dioramas about animals and marine life native to the central coast, the area's geology and the lives of the Chumash who once made their home around the bay. Audiovisual presentations, nature walks and lectures are featured. Trails from the museum lead to scenic viewpoints. Daily 10-5; closed Jan. 1, Thanksgiving and Dec. 25. Admission $3; ages 7-12, $1. Phone (805) 772-2694.

SUB-SEA TOURS, which departs from Marina Sq. at the Embarcadero at Pacific St., lets visitors view sea life—including eels, fish and diving birds—from both above and below the water. Kayak and canoe rentals as well as ocean sailing tours also are available. Allow 1 hour minimum. Daily 9-5. Fare $12.50; under 13, $5.50. MC, VI. Phone (805) 772-9463 for office or (310) 379-8826 for marina.

TIGER'S FOLLY II **HARBOR CRUISES** depart from 1205 Embarcadero. One-hour narrated trips on the stern-wheeler cruise past Morro Rock, the harbor entrance and the Embarcadero. Sunday brunch and weekend dinner cruises also are available. One-hour trips offered daily, June-Sept.; Sat.-Sun. and holidays, rest of year. Fare $8; under 12, $4. AE, DS, MC, VI. Phone (805) 772-2257.

MOSS BEACH—
see San Francisco p. 209.

MOUNTAIN VIEW (Q-3)
pop. 67,500, elev. 97'

Mountain View is a busy industrial city in the Santa Clara Valley. To the east is Moffett Field, a combined-services military field.

Mountain View Chamber of Commerce: 580 Castro St., Mountain View, CA 94041; phone (650) 968-8378.

AMES RESEARCH CENTER, off US 101, Moffett Field exit, is a NASA research center that includes what is thought to be the world's largest wind tunnels, and experimental research hangars. Guided tours of the facility are offered. The 2-hour tours involve a 2-mile walk.

A visitor center features a moon rock, space shuttle model, artwork and actual prototypes and models of vehicles designed by Ames. Occasional rotating exhibits highlight past and current projects. Visitor center open Mon.-Fri. 8-4:30; closed federal holidays. Tours offered Mon.-Fri. by reservation made 6 months in advance; under 9 are not permitted. Free. Phone (650) 604-6497 for tours or 604-6274 for the visitor center.

MOUNT SHASTA (B-3)
pop. 3,500, elev. 3,554'

A small city named for a tall mountain, Mount Shasta is the northern gateway via scenic SR 89 to Whiskeytown-Shasta-Trinity National Recreation Area, Shasta-Trinity National Forests and nearby Lake Siskiyou.

Mount Shasta Visitors Bureau: 300 Pine St., Mount Shasta, CA 96067; phone (530) 926-4865 or (800) 926-4865.

MOUNT SHASTA STATE FISH HATCHERY AND SISSON HATCHERY MUSEUM, .5 mi. w. of I-5 via central Mount Shasta exit at Three, Old Stage Rd., produces 3 to 5 million trout annually to stock the streams and lakes of northern California. The museum has exhibits pertaining to the geological and human history of the region. Allow 1 hour minimum. Museum open Mon.-Sat. 10-4, Sun. 1-4, early May-Sept. 30; daily 1-4, Mar. 1-early May and Oct.-Dec. Hatchery open daily 7-5. Free. Phone (530) 926-2215, or 926-5508 for the museum.

MUIR WOODS NATIONAL MONUMENT—
see San Francisco p. 209.

MURPHYS (E-4) pop. 1,500, elev. 2,171'

MERCER CAVERNS, 1.5 mi. n. via Sheep Ranch Rd., has been open since 1885. Guided tours lasting 45 to 50 minutes visit 10 rooms with various crystalline formations. Mon.-Fri. 9-6, Sat.-Sun. 9-8, Memorial Day weekend-Labor Day; daily 10-4:30, rest of year. Closed Dec. 25. Admission $7; ages 5-11, $3.50. Phone (209) 728-2101.

WINERIES

• **Stevenot Winery**, 2 mi. n. on Sheep Ranch Rd., then left .2 mi. on San Domingo Rd. Daily 10-5; closed Dec. 25. Phone (209) 728-3436.

NAPA VALLEY (N-2)

Napa Valley, one of California's most famous wine producing regions, began in the 1850s as a gold-rush center. The original grapevine cuttings were supplied by priests from the missions at Sonoma and San Rafael. Today Napa Valley is a leader in the American table wine industry. Popular tours of wineries and vineyards in Napa Valley are listed under Calistoga, Oakville, Rutherford, St. Helena and Yountville. Napa is the southern terminus of a scenic 28-mile stretch of SR 29 that heads northwest through the valley to Calistoga.

Napa Valley Conference and Visitors Bureau: 1310 Napa Town Center, Napa, CA 94559; phone (707) 226-7459.

Self-guiding tours: Winery maps are available from the conference and visitors bureau.

HOT AIR BALLOON RIDES over Napa Valley are available (weather permitting) through several companies, including Above The West Ballooning, (707) 944-8638 or (800) 627-2759; Adventures Aloft, (707) 944-4408 or (800) 944-4408; Balloon Aviation, (707) 944-4400 or (800) 367-6272; 〔SAVE〕 Balloons Above the Valley, (707) 253-2222 or (800) 464-6824; Bonaventura Balloon, (707) 944-2822, (800) 359-6272, or (800) 243-6743 in Calif.; Calistoga Balloon Adventures, (707) 942-2282 or (800) 333-4359; or

Napa Valley Balloons, (707) 944-0228 or (800) 253-2224.

Flights last about an hour and often include champagne afterward. Fares range $165-$185. All pilots are FAA certified. Professional Balloon Pilots Association of Napa Valley Inc. answers general questions about planning a flight; phone (707) 944-8793.

Note: The mention of the preceding hot air balloon rides is for information only and does **not** imply endorsement by AAA.

NAPA VALLEY WINE TRAIN, 1275 McKinstry St., is 36-mile journey that winds through the heart of Napa Valley wine country. Pullman dining cars offer brunch, lunch and dinner, while hors d'oeuvres and wine tasting are offered in lounge cars. Allow 3 hours minimum. Departures daily, times vary. Lunch train $33, brunch train $30, dinner train $25; meal and beverages not included. Reservations and deposit are required. AE, CB, DI, DS, JCB, MC, VI. Phone (707) 253-2111 or (800) 427-4124. *See color ad.*

TRIPS ON TAPE is a self-guiding audio tape tour that describes the history, events, wineries and local attractions in the Napa Valley. Maps are included. Tapes are available for $12.95 by mail from The Rider's Guide, 484 Lake Park Ave., Suite 255, Oakland, CA 94610. Add $2.50 for postage; Calif. residents add sales tax. Phone (510) 653-2553.

NEVADA CITY (D-3)
pop. 2,900, elev. 2,525'

In the foothills of the High Sierras, Nevada City has been a gold-mining center for more than a century. It also is the seat of Nevada County, whose lode and placer mines have yielded more than one-half of California's total production of gold. Among the buildings dating from gold rush days is Old Nevada Theater, said to be the oldest theater in California. It opened in July 1865.

Nevada City Chamber of Commerce: 132 Main St., Nevada City, CA 95959; phone (530) 265-2692 or (800) 655-6569.

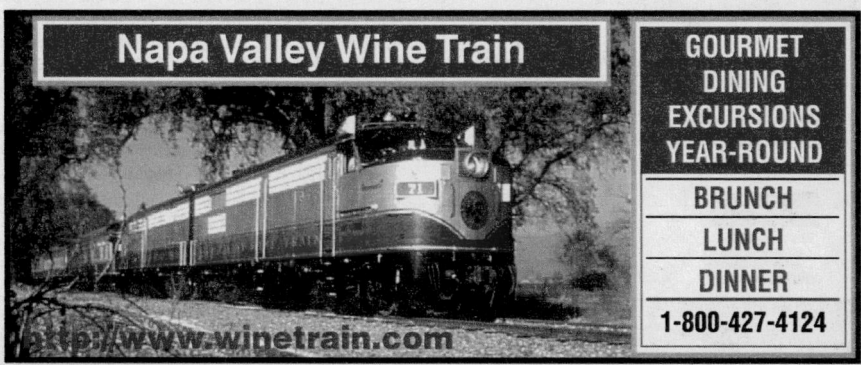

FIREHOUSE MUSEUM, at 214 Main St. in Firehouse No. 1, displays pioneer relics, American Indian artifacts, a Chinese altar and Donner Party artifacts. Allow 30 minutes minimum. Daily 11-4, Apr.-Oct. (weather permitting). Donations. Phone (530) 265-5468.

MALAKOFF DIGGINS STATE HISTORIC PARK, 27 mi. n.e. of SR 49 off Tyler Foote Crossing Rd., was the world's largest hydraulic gold mine before it ceased operation in 1884. The park museum has exhibits and a 20-minute film explaining hydraulic mining methods and describing the miners' way of life. Highlights include a restored church, 1860s general store, drugstore, barber shop, livery stable and house. The homecoming celebration is held in mid-June.

Camping and picnicking facilities are available; reservations are required and are available through Parknet at (800) 444-7275. Allow 1 hour minimum. Daily 10-5, June-Labor Day; Sat.-Sun. 10-4, rest of year. Admission $5 per vehicle; over 61, $4 per vehicle. Additional fee of $1 per dog. Dogs must be leashed and are not permitted in buildings or on trails. Phone (530) 265-2740 for information and cabin reservations.

MINERS FOUNDRY CULTURAL CENTER, 325 Spring St., was built in 1856 for industrial metal working and metal casting. The complex is now a cultural center with performing arts facilities. A

hall built of stones native to the area also is featured. A free self-guiding tour of the historic site is available; guided tours are available by appointment. Programs are scheduled October through December and in March. Mon.-Fri. 9-5. Free. Phone (530) 265-5040 for information about programs.

NEWPORT BEACH (C-6)
pop. 66,600, elev. 10'

The city of Newport Beach comprises Balboa, Balboa Island, Bay Shores, Corona del Mar, Harbor Island, Lido Isle, Linda Isle and Newport Heights. A 6-mile beach lies along the peninsula between the bay and the ocean. Newport Harbor is a leading Pacific Coast yacht rendezvous; it has one of the largest concentrations of pleasure craft in the nation with nearly 9,000 boats docked at the harbor.

SAVE Balboa Fun Zone, at the Newport Bay end of Main Street on the Balboa peninsula, is an amusement area with a carrousel, Ferris wheel, shops and restaurants. In the same area is Balboa Pavilion. Built in 1905 as an electric railway terminus, it now houses various businesses. Catalina Passenger Service has regularly scheduled trips to Catalina Island *(see place listing p. 63).* Small ferry boats ply the channel between the peninsula and Balboa Island, and boat tours of the bay are offered. Davy's Locker Sport Fishing and Whale Watching operates 2.5-hour spotting cruises in the winter; phone (949) 673-1434.

Newport Harbor Area Chamber of Commerce: 1470 Jamboree Rd., Newport Beach, CA 92660; phone (949) 729-4400.

Shopping areas: Macy's, Neiman-Marcus, Bloomingdale's and Robinsons-May all are at Fashion Island, an open-air Mediterranean-style village on Newport Center Drive.

SAVE **NEWPORT HARBOR CRUISE, BALBOA PAVILION,** which departs from Balboa Pavilion, offers 45- and 90-minute narrated cruises aboard the double-deck riverboats *Pavilion Queen* or *Pavilion Paddy.* Departures daily 11-7, mid-June to Labor Day; 11-3, rest of year. Closed Dec. 24-25. Fare for the 45-minute cruise $6; over 55, $4; ages 5-12, $1. Fare for the 90-minute cruise $8; over 55, $4; ages 5-12, $1. Phone (949) 673-5245.

NEWPORT HARBOR NAUTICAL MUSEUM is housed aboard the riverboat *Pride of Newport* docked at 151 E. Pacific Coast Hwy. Boats, ships models, ships in bottles, navigational and nautical equipment, fishing trophies and nautical art are displayed. The museum also houses exhibits that tell the history of the harbor through memorabilia and photographs. Food is available. Tues.-Sun. 10-5; closed Thanksgiving and Dec. 25. Admission $4, under 12 free. Phone (949) 675-8915.

NEWPORT HARBOR SHOWBOAT CRUISES leave from 600 E. Edgewater Place. A 45-minute cruise departs daily on the hour 11-7, Memorial Day-Labor Day; 11-4, rest of year. A 90-minute cruise leaves daily on the hour 11-6, Memorial Day-Labor Day; 11-3, rest of year. Closed Dec. 24-25. Fare for the 45-minute cruise $6; ages 5-11, $2. Fare for the 90-minute cruise $9; ages 5-11, $2. Phone (949) 673-0240.

ORANGE COUNTY MUSEUM OF ART, 850 San Clemente Dr., offers exhibitions and programs focusing on California's artistic heritage and its provocative contemporary art. The permanent collection comprises more than 6,000 works dating from the turn of the 20th century to the present. Tues.-Sun. 11-5; closed holidays. Tours are given Tues.-Sun. at 1. Admission $5, senior citizens and students with ID $4, under 16 free. Phone (949) 759-1122.

SHERMAN LIBRARY AND GARDENS, 2647 E. Coast Hwy., is a cultural center with a research library and botanical gardens displaying tropical and subtropical flora. The complex also has a touch and smell garden and a tea garden. Gardens open daily 10:30-4; library open Mon.-Fri. 9-4:30. Closed Jan. 1, Thanksgiving and Dec. 25. Admission $3; ages 12-16, $1. Phone (949) 673-2261.

NIPOMO (I-4) pop. 10,000, elev. 330′

Originally a private 38,000-acre ranch, Nipomo grew into a stopover on El Camino Real between missions San Luis Obispo and Santa Barbara. Citrus orchards, vegetable farms and commercial nurseries thrive in the rich soil that washes down from the Nipomo Foothills. Thousands of blue gum eucalyptus trees, unsuccessfully planted to yield hardwood, populate the mesa area of Nipomo. The Dana Adobe, built in 1839 with the help of mission Indians, still stands. Nipomo is on a scenic stretch of US 101.

Nipomo Chamber of Commerce: 267 W. Taft, P.O. Box 386, Nipomo, CA 93444; phone (805) 929-1583.

WINERIES

• **Ross-Keller Winery,** 985 Orchard Ave. Daily noon-5. Phone (805) 929-3627.

NORTH FORK (G-5)
pop. 600, elev. 2,629′

SIERRA MONO INDIAN MUSEUM, jct. of CRs 225, 228 and 274, displays artifacts and items unique to the Mono Indians. Central to the museum's exhibits, as well as to the Mono culture, is an extensive collection of baskets. Other highlights include wildlife exhibits and tools, jewelry and baskets from other North American Indian tribes.

Mon.-Sat. 9-4; closed Jan. 1, Thanksgiving and Dec. 25. Admission $2, over 60 and physically impaired $1.50, high school students $1, elementary school students 75c. Phone (559) 877-2115.

NOVATO (O-1) pop. 47,600, elev. 18′

North of San Francisco on US 101, Novato was named for a chief of the Coast Miwok Indians. Although a national leader in the production of CD-ROMs, the area still retains an outlying dairy region. Novato History Museum, 815 DeLong Ave., is in the circa 1856 house of the town's first postmaster. Exhibits include photographs and relics depicting life in Novato from its earliest days.

Novato Chamber of Commerce: 807 DeLong Ave., Novato, CA 94945; phone (415) 897-1164 or (800) 897-1164.

MARIN MUSEUM OF THE AMERICAN INDIAN, 2200 Novato Blvd. in Miwok Park, displays American Indian art and culture as well as exhibits of the prehistoric period in Marin County. The museum also has a native plant garden. Changing exhibits highlight various other American Indian cultures. Allow 30 minutes minimum. Tues.-Fri. 10-3, Sat.-Sun. noon-4. Donations. Phone (415) 897-4064.

OLOMPALI STATE HISTORIC PARK, 2.5 mi. n. on US 101, is a 700-acre park featuring several historic buildings including the ruins of the 1913 Burdell Mansion, which consists of three older structures built 1830-66. A traditional Victorian garden surrounds the ruins and an 1870s frame house stands nearby. A reconstruction of a Coast Miwok village from which the state park takes its name also is featured. Allow 30 minutes minimum. Daily 8:30-5. Admission $5 per private vehicle. Phone (415) 892-3383.

OAKDALE (F-3) pop. 12,000, elev. 155′

HERSHEY CHOCOLATE U.S.A., a division of Hershey Foods, is at 1400 S. Yosemite Ave. The visitor center is at S. Sierra Ave. and G St. Thirty-minute tours are given Mon.-Fri. 8:30-3. Visitor center open Mon.-Fri. 8:30-5. Closed Good Friday and holidays. Free. Phone (209) 848-8126.

OAK GLEN (B-9) elev. 4,840′

Oak Glen is one of the largest apple-growing communities in Southern California. Most orchards, including ranches where people may pick their own fruit, are open September through December. Oak Tree Village near the summit of Oak Glen Road has a live-animal park, a small fishing pond and Mountaintown, where mounted animals from around the world are displayed.

OAKHURST (G-4)
pop. 2,000, elev. 2,289'

FRESNO FLATS HISTORICAL PARK, n.e. via SR 41 and CR 426 on School Rd., has a museum and a collection of historic buildings typical of those found in a local late 19th-century community. Highlights include Taylor Log House; Laramore House with its collection of antiques; a smithy; a logging exhibit; a late 1800s agricultural barn; a schoolhouse; and a collection of wagons and stagecoaches. A research library is available. Picnicking is permitted. Park open daily 24 hours. Research library open Mon.-Fri. 10-4. Tours of the buildings Wed.-Sat. 1-3, Sun. 1-4, and by appointment, Mar.-Dec. Closed Dec. 25. Donations. Phone (559) 683-6570.

OAKLAND (O-3) pop. 372,200, elev. 42'.

Oakland is a major West Coast port and manufacturing center that stretches along the mainland side of San Francisco Bay and varies in elevation from sea level to 1,500 feet. The San Francisco-Oakland Bay Bridge links the city with San Francisco; a westbound toll of $2 is charged.

The city's rich cultural heritage is demonstrated through ethnic festivals and varied events. Rolling hills and forested areas offer hiking and riding trails, and lakes and parks dot the countryside.

Nine regional parks adjoin Oakland: Anthony Chabot *(see Recreation Chart),* Charles Lee Tilden *(see Berkeley p. 57),* Claremont Canyon Regional Preserve, Huckleberry Botanic Regional Preserve, Lake Temescal *(see Recreation Chart),* Martin Luther King Jr. Shoreline *(see Recreation Chart),* Miller/Knox, Redwood, and Robert Sibley Volcanic Regional Preserve. Opportunities for hiking, picnicking, fishing and swimming are available. Facilities vary from park to park.

Bret Harte Boardwalk on 5th Street between Jefferson and Clay streets adjoins the site of the author's boyhood home. A block of renovated Victorian houses and barns has been converted to shops and restaurants. Visitor centers are at 14th Street and Broadway and at Jack London Square, Broadway and Embarcadero.

Oakland-Alameda County Coliseum Complex, off Nimitz Freeway (I-880) at the 66th Avenue exit, includes a stadium, indoor arena and exhibit hall. The complex is the home of Oakland's professional sports teams—the A's (baseball), Raiders (football) and Warriors (basketball)—as well

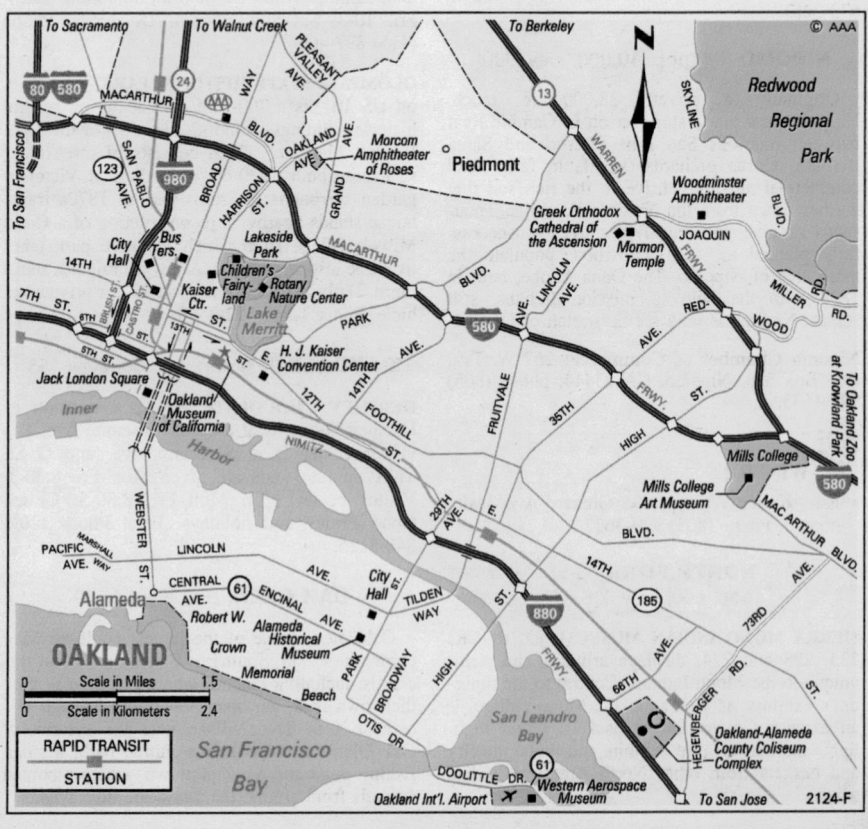

as concerts, wrestling and the circus; phone (510) 569-2121.

Oakland Convention & Visitors Authority: 550 10th St., Suite 214, Oakland, CA 94607; phone (510) 839-9000 or (800) 262-5526.

GREEK ORTHODOX CATHEDRAL OF THE ASCENSION, 4700 Lincoln Ave., overlooks Oakland and the bay. Designed in the Byzantine style, the copper-domed church houses colorful mosaics and icons of Christ and the disciples. It is crowned with a 12-foot cross set with light-catching Baccarat crystals. A 3-day Greek festival is held in mid-May. Allow 1 hour minimum. Mon.-Fri. 9-4; closed holidays. Free. Phone (510) 531-3400.

JACK LONDON SQUARE, bounded by Clay St., Alice St., the Embarcadero and the Oakland estuary, is a colorful waterfront area. Heinolds' First and Last Chance Saloon, a favorite haunt of the author, is at the foot of Webster Street. The area also contains an Amtrak station and several museums. A concert series is presented in summer; phone (510) 208-4646. Jack London Village is an early 19th-century-style shopping and restaurant complex; phone (510) 814-6000.

Round-trip ferry service via Alameda-Oakland Ferry to Pier 1 and Pier 39 in San Francisco, as well as to Angel Island in the summer, is available daily; phone (510) 522-3300. Most stores open Mon.-Fri. 10:30-6, Sat.-Sun. noon-6. Phone (510) 893-7956.

KAISER CENTER ART GALLERY, 300 Lakeside Dr. on the second floor of Kaiser Center, houses changing exhibits. A roof garden is on the third floor. Allow 30 minutes minimum. Gallery open Mon.-Fri. 8-5. Roof garden open Mon.-Sat. 7-6:30. Closed holidays. Free. Phone (510) 271-6157.

LAKESIDE PARK embraces the n. shore of Lake Merritt, a saltwater tidal lake in the center of the city. Boat rentals, wind-surfing and sailing lessons and bowling greens are available. Picnicking is permitted. A tour boat plies the lake Sat.-Sun. noon-5. Park admission free; parking $2, Sat.-Sun. and holidays. Boat fare $1.50; over 54 and under 12, 75c. Phone (510) 444-3807.

Children's Fairyland, corner of Grand Ave. and Bellevue Ave., is a child-size attraction depicting fairy tales and nursery rhymes. Children's rides are available. Allow 2 hours minimum. Mon.-Fri. 10-4:30, Sat.-Sun. 10-5:30, mid-June through Labor Day; Wed.-Sun. 10-4:30, Apr. 1 to mid-June and day after Labor Day-Oct. 31; Sat.-Sun. 10-4:30, rest of year. Closed Jan. 1, Thanksgiving and Dec. 25. Puppet shows are presented at 11, 2 and 4. Admission $3.25; ages 1-12, $2.75. Parking $2 Sat.-Sun. and holidays. Phone (510) 238-6876 or 452-2259.

Lakeside Park Garden Center, 666 Bellevue Ave., is surrounded by Japanese, Polynesian, cactus, dahlia, palm, fuchsia, firescape and chrysanthemum gardens, and also has an herb and fragrance garden. The center presents flower shows in season. Allow 2 hours minimum. Mon.-Fri. 10-3, Sat.-Sun. and holidays 10-5, May-Nov.; Mon.-Fri. 10-3, Sat.-Sun. 10-4, rest of year. Closed Jan. 1, Thanksgiving and Dec. 25. Parking $2 Sat.-Sun. and holidays. Phone (510) 238-3208.

Rotary Nature Center, Bellevue Ave. and Perkins St., has seasonal displays of birds, mammals and reptiles. In winter hundreds of wild geese, herons, egrets and ducks take sanctuary at the wildlife refuge outside the museum. The nature center also contains a native plant garden. Allow 30 minutes minimum. Daily 10-5. Free. Phone (510) 238-3739.

MILLS COLLEGE ART MUSEUM, on campus, offers changing exhibits by contemporary artists and senior art students. Allow 1 hour, 30 minutes minimum. Tues.-Sat. 11-4, Sun. noon-4, early Sept.-late May; closed holidays. Free. Phone (510) 430-2164.

MORCOM AMPHITHEATER OF ROSES, 1 blk. w. of Grand Ave. at 700 Jean St., has 8 acres of gardens, reflecting pools and trees. Various species are in bloom May through November; the peak season is May through September. Garden information is available. Additional street parking is available on Olive Avenue. Daily dawn-dusk. Free. Phone (510) 238-3187.

MORMON TEMPLE, 4770 Lincoln Ave., is a magnificent example of religious architecture and offers a scenic vista of Oakland and San Francisco. Guided tours of the gardens and worship houses include a 12-minute slide show about the temple. The interior of the temple is closed to non-Mormons. Allow 1 hour minimum. Grounds open 6 a.m.-10 p.m. Visitor Center open 9-9. Last tour departs 30 minutes before closing. Free. Phone (510) 531-3200, or 531-1475 for the visitor center.

★**OAKLAND MUSEUM OF CALIFORNIA,** 10th and Oak sts., is a complex of terraced gardens and three main galleries reflecting the ecology, history and art of California.

The Gallery of Natural Sciences depicts the ecology of California through a walk across the state's biotic zones from ocean to mountains and desert, while Cowell Hall of California History preserves the history of the state from its pre-Spanish Native American period to current times. The Gallery of California Art presents a chronological survey of the state's art from early 19th century to the present. The museum also displays traveling exhibits throughout the year.

Allow 1 hour minimum. Wed.-Sat. 10-5 (also Fri. 5-9), Sun. noon-5; closed Jan. 1, July 4, Thanksgiving and Dec. 25. Admission $6; over 65, students with ID and ages 6-17, $4; free to all Fri. 5-9. Phone (510) 238-2200.

OAKLAND ZOO AT KNOWLAND PARK, 9777
Golf Links Rd. off I-580, offers picnic facilities,
playgrounds, amusement rides, a children's zoo
and more than 300 exotic and native animals in
naturalistic habitats. An aerial tram affords a
bird's-eye view of the area. Allow 1 hour minimum. Zoo open daily 10-4. Park open daily 9-5.
Closed Thanksgiving and Dec. 25. Zoo admission $5.50; over 54 and ages 2-14, $3. Park admission $3 per private vehicle; pedestrians free.
Parking free first Mon. of each month, except
holidays. Phone (510) 632-9525.

SKYLINE BOULEVARD follows the rim of Oakland's low hills through a section of parks and
private estates. On clear days the entire East Bay
area is visible.

WESTERN AEROSPACE MUSEUM, is off
I-880, 1 mi. w. on Hegenberger Rd., .7 mi. n. on
Earhart Rd., then e. past Hangar 6 (Alaska Airlines) to 8260 Boeing St., Building 621, on Oakland Airport's North Field. This museum, housed
in a 1940 hangar, presents a collection of unusual aircraft as well as exhibits about the history of aviation and aviators. Wed.-Sun. 10-4;
closed Jan. 1, Thanksgiving and Dec. 25. Admission $4; ages 6-12, $2. Phone (510) 638-7100.

WOODMINSTER AMPHITHEATER is 1 mi.
above Mormon Temple off SR 13 at 3300
Joaquin Miller Rd. in Joaquin Miller Park. Mon.-
Fri. 10-2. Presentations are scheduled at 8 p.m.,
mid-July to mid-Sept. Tickets $14-$23; under 16
free with adult. AE, MC, VI. Phone (510)
687-4225.

OAKVILLE (N-2) elev. 155'

WINERIES

- **Robert Mondavi Winery,** .5 mi. n. on SR 29.
  Daily 9-5, May-Oct.; 10-4:30, rest of year.
  Closed holidays. Phone (707) 259-9463.

O'BRIEN (B-3)

LAKE SHASTA CAVERNS is reached from Shasta
Caverns Rd., 1.5 mi. e. of I-5. The 2-hour tour
includes more than 600 steps. Round-trip boat
and bus transportation are provided. Food is
available. Allow 3 hours minimum. Tours depart
every half-hour daily 9-4, Memorial Day
weekend-Labor Day; every hour 9-3, Apr. 1-day
before Memorial Day weekend and day after Labor Day-Sept. 30; at 10, noon and 2, rest of year
(weather permitting). Closed Thanksgiving and
Dec. 25. Admission $14; ages 4-12, $7. MC, VI.
Phone (530) 238-2341 or (800) 795-2283.

OCEANO (I-3) pop. 5,000, elev. 25'

**THE GREAT AMERICAN MELODRAMA AND
VAUDEVILLE,** 1863 Pacific Blvd. (SR 1), presents 19th-century vaudeville shows, melodra-
mas, comedies and thrillers. Food is available.
Shows are staged Wed.-Thurs. at 7 p.m., Fri. at 8
p.m., Sat. at 4:30 and 8:30 p.m., Sun. at 6 p.m.;
closed holidays. Box office open Mon.-Sat. 10-6,
Sun. 11-5. Tickets $10-$14; over 61 and under
13, $6-$16. Reservations are recommended.
Phone (805) 489-2499.

OCEANSIDE (K-6) pop. 128,400, elev. 47'

At the mouth of the San Luis Rey Valley,
Oceanside's 3.5 miles of beaches offer year-
round opportunities for ocean recreation. The
harbor has facilities for boating and sport fishing;
whale-watching takes place during winter.

Oceanside Chamber of Commerce: 928 N.
Coast Hwy., Oceanside, CA 92054; phone (760)
722-1534.

CAMP PENDLETON, a Marine Corps base covering approximately 125,000 acres, is one of the
world's leading amphibious training camps; it
also serves as a historical and ecological preserve. Self-guiding tours include the Amphibious
Vehicle Museum, where amphibious vehicles
used in combat are displayed.

Visitor passes and self-guiding tour brochures
are available at the main gate on Vandegrift
Boulevard. Visitors must present a driver's license, vehicle registration and verification of
auto insurance to enter. Mon.-Fri. dawn-dusk;
closed holidays. Guided tours are given the third
Tues. of the month 9:30-3. Reservations are required. Free. Phone (760) 725-5569.

MISSION SAN LUIS REY DE FRANCIA, 4 mi.
e. on SR 76 at 4050 Mission Ave., was 18th in
the chain of missions and one of the largest established in Alta (Upper) California. Founded in
1798 by Father Fermín de Lasuén, it was named
for Louis IX, King of France. The splendid sanctuary interior has a wooden double-dome construction and lofty beamed ceilings; the colorful,
original decorations were done by American Indians. A museum includes artifacts from 18th-
and 19th-century mission life. Picnicking facilities are available.

Mon.-Sat. and holidays 10-4:30, Sun. 11:30-
4:30; closed Jan. 1, Thanksgiving and Dec. 25.
Admission $3; ages 7-12, $1. Phone (760)
757-3651.

OJAI (J-5) pop. 7,600, elev. 746'

In a valley surrounded by high mountains,
Ojai (O-hi) is a popular artists' colony and re-
treat. Attractions include Ojai Valley Historical
Museum, (805) 640-1390, in the old historic St.
Thomas chapel. An introduction to the Ojai Val-
ley and its surrounding mountains is provided by
Pink Moment Jeep Tours; phone (805) 646-2903.

Ojai Center for the Arts presents community
theater productions and works of California artists; phone (805) 646-0117.

Ojai Valley Chamber of Commerce and Visitors Center: 150 W. Ojai Ave., P.O. Box 1134, Ojai, CA 93024; phone (805) 646-8126.

OLYMPIC VALLEY—
see Lake Tahoe Area p. 91.

ONTARIO (B-8) pop. 133,200, elev. 988'

Once an agricultural center, Ontario is now a largely residential community and the location of the Los Angeles area's second international airport.

Ontario Convention Center Corporation: 2151 Convention Center Way, Suite 203A, Ontario, CA 91764; phone (909) 937-3000.

Shopping areas: Ontario Mills Mall, jct. I-10 and I-15 at Haven Ave. exit, counts Off 5th—Saks Fifth Avenue Outlet, Off Rodeo Drive Beverly Hills, Ann Taylor Loft and JCPenney Outlet among its more than 200 shops.

GRABER OLIVE HOUSE, 315 E. Fourth St., was established in 1894. Tours are conducted daily. During the fall harvest season visitors can watch the grading, curing and canning of olives. Picnicking is permitted. Mon.-Sat. 9-5:30, Sun. 9:30-6; closed holidays. Free. Phone (909) 983-1761 or (800) 996-5483.

MUSEUM OF HISTORY AND ART, ONTARIO, 225 S. Euclid Ave., is housed in Spanish-Mediterranean-style former city hall completed in 1937. The history section interprets the region's agricultural past of orchards, citrus groves and vineyards; its industrial heritage derived from hydroelectric development; and local aviation history. Changing exhibits are featured in the history section as well as the Art Wing. Wed.-Sun. noon-4; closed holidays. Free. Phone (909) 983-3198.

ORANGE (C-7) pop. 110,700, elev. 187'

In 1869 two lawyers planned the city of Orange from 1,300 acres they had received as payment from a client. The town was built around the circular central plaza at Chapman Avenue and Glassell Street. Chapman University is 2 blocks north of the plaza.

Orange Chamber of Commerce: 531 E. Chapman Ave., Suite A, Orange, CA 92866; phone (714) 538-3581.

Self-guiding tours: Information about walking tours of restored Victorian-style neighborhoods is available from the chamber of commerce.

Shopping areas: Antique and specialty shops line Glassell Street just north of the plaza. Orange Circle Antique Mall, with 50 shops under one roof, is at 118 S. Glassell St. JCPenney and Sears have branches at the Mall of Orange, Tustin and Meats avenues. Stadium Promenade at 1523 W. Katella Ave. features several stores and restaurants.

ORICK (B-1) pop. 700, elev. 34'

HUMBOLDT LAGOONS STATE PARK, 1,886 acres 4 mi. s. on US 101, has a sandy marshland with more than 200 bird species, a lagoon and rocky headlands. Wild azaleas and lilacs bloom in June. Park open daily 24 hours. Visitor center open daily 10-3, June-Sept. Free. Phone (707) 488-2041. *See Recreation Chart.*

PRAIRIE CREEK REDWOODS STATE PARK, 40,000 acres, is 6 mi. n. on US 101. A coastal redwood park, it protects one of the last herds of native Roosevelt elks. Daily 24 hours. Beach access, guided nature hikes and campfire programs are available June 1-Labor Day. Day use fee $5 per private vehicle; over 61, $4 per private vehicle, $1 per dog (must be leashed). Phone (707) 464-6101, ext. 5301. *See Recreation Chart.*

OROVILLE (D-3) pop. 12,000, elev. 174'

Cherokee Indians migrated to Oroville from Georgia in the 1850s to work in gold mines north of town. In 1870 alone, hydraulic mining operations at the site yielded $5 million in gold. Later diamonds were discovered; Cherokee Diamond Mine opened in 1873 and produced some 300 diamonds of industrial quality.

The reserves soon were depleted however, and the town of Cherokee, like so many other mining towns in California, was forgotten. Ruins of brick stores and foundations identified by markers are all that remain in this ghost town on Cherokee Road, 10 miles north via SR 70, the Feather River Scenic Byway.

Oroville Area Chamber of Commerce: 1789 Montgomery St., Oroville, CA 95965; phone (530) 538-2542 or (800) 655-4653.

[SAVE] **CHINESE TEMPLE** is at 1500 Broderick St. The 1863 temple contains furnishings donated by the Emperor of China. A self-guiding tour includes three temples—Confucianism, Taoism and Buddhism, a courtyard garden and collections of puppets, costumes and tapestries. Allow 1 hour minimum. Thurs.-Mon. 11-4:30, Tues.-Wed. 1-4, Feb. 1-Dec. 14. Admission $2, under 12 free. Phone (530) 538-2496.

FEATHER RIVER HATCHERY, 5 Table Mountain Blvd., releases more than 10 million salmon and steelhead yearlings into Feather River each year. The best time to visit the hatchery is during the spawning season, October 1 to mid-November. Allow 30 minutes minimum. Daily 8-dusk. Guided tours are available by appointment. Free. Phone (530) 538-2222, or 534-2306 for guided tours.

LAKE OROVILLE VISITOR CENTER is 7 mi. n.e. of SR 162 to Kelly Ridge, then 1.5 mi. n.

The center, overlooking Lake Oroville and Oroville Dam, displays exhibits depicting the gold-rush era, state water projects, wildlife, the Beckwourth Trail and the Maidu Indians. Films are shown on request. Allow 1 hour minimum. Daily 9-5; closed Jan. 1, Thanksgiving and Dec. 25. Guided tours of the power plant are offered by appointment. Free. Phone (530) 538-2219, or 534-2306 for power plant tour.

LOTT HOME MUSEUM is between 3rd and 4th aves. at 1067 Montgomery St. The 1856 house is furnished in period. Picnic facilities are available. House open Sun.-Mon. and Fri. noon-4, and by appointment, Feb. 1-Dec. 14. Park open daily 9-8. House $2, under 12 free. Park free. Phone (530) 538-2497.

OXNARD (J-4) pop. 142,200, elev. 52'

With a busy harbor and 7 miles of beaches, Oxnard offers opportunities for boating, sport fishing, swimming and bicycling.

Greater Oxnard and Harbors Tourism Bureau: 200 W. Seventh St., Oxnard, CA 93030; phone (805) 385-7545 or (800) 269-6273.

Shopping areas: The Esplanade, Vineyard Avenue and Esplanade Drive, has a Robinsons-May and a Sears. Fisherman's Wharf is at the corner of Victoria Avenue and Channel Islands Boulevard. Styled after an Early-American seacoast village, the complex houses specialty shops.

Waterfront shops are the attraction at Harbor Landing at Harbor and Channel Islands boulevards. Off Gonzales Road near Rice Avenue, the Oxnard Factory Outlet reflects the citrus-growing and packing-shed history of the town.

CARNEGIE ART MUSEUM, 424 S. C St., is in a 1906 neoclassical building in historic downtown. The permanent collection focuses on contemporary California painters. Exhibits feature fine and decorative arts, photography and works by Ventura County artists. Thurs.-Sat. 10-5, Sun. 1-5; closed Jan. 1, Thanksgiving, Dec. 25 and periodically between exhibits. Admission $3; over 54 and students with ID $2; ages 6-16, $1. Phone (805) 385-8157.

VENTURA COUNTY GULL WINGS CHILDREN'S MUSEUM, 418 W. 4th St., has more than 12 hands-on exhibits and activities that include a puppet theater, an optical illusions room, a career costumes area with a stage and videotape camera, a make-believe campground with a tent and "fishing pond," a medical room with cutaway anatomical models and medical equipment, a farmers market, computers and a room with rocks and fossils. Tues.-Sun. 10-5; events Sat. at 2. Admission $3.50. Phone (805) 483-3005.

VENTURA COUNTY MARITIME MUSEUM, 2731 S. Victoria Ave., just past Channel Islands Blvd., harbors ship models and artwork that reflects maritime history from ancient times to the present. Changing guest artist exhibits detail maritime commerce, the Channel Islands, shipwrecks, whaling and the California coast. Daily 11-5, Memorial Day-Labor Day; Thurs.-Mon. 11-5, rest of year. Closed Jan. 1, Thanksgiving and Dec. 25. Donations. Phone (805) 984-6260.

PACIFICA—
see San Francisco p. 209.

PACIFIC GROVE—
see Monterey Peninsula p. 145.

PACIFIC PALISADES—
see Los Angeles p. 126.

PALA (K-7) pop. 500, elev. 410'

MISSION SAN ANTONIO DE PALA, n. of SR 76 on Pala Mission Rd., was originally a branch of Mission San Luis Rey de Francia. The first building, the granary, was built in 1810; the mission itself was built in 1816. Planned as part of a second chain of inland missions, it fell into disrepair during the period of secularization. The mission since has been restored and includes a museum, mineral room, gardens and chapel. Tues.-Sun. 10-4, Apr.-Oct.; 10-3, rest of year. Closed Thanksgiving and Dec. 25. Mission free. Museum $2; under 12, $1. Phone (760) 742-1600.

PALM DESERT (K-7)
pop. 23,300, elev. 243'

At the base of the Santa Rosa Mountains, Palm Desert is one of the satellite cities of Palm Springs. Bob Hope Cultural Center presents live musical entertainment.

Palm Desert Chamber of Commerce: 72-990 Hwy. 111, Palm Desert, CA 92260; phone (760) 346-6111.

Shopping areas: Palm Desert Town Center Mall, SR 111 and Monterey Avenue, has Macy's, JCPenney and Robinsons-May.

HOT AIR BALLOON RIDES over the Coachella Valley offer an unusual perspective of the desert landscape. Contact Desert Balloons, (760) 346-8575 or 398-8575; Dream Flights Hot Air Balloon Adventures, (760) 321-5154 or (800) 933-5628; or Fantasy Balloon Flights, (760) 398-6322 or (800) 462-2683. Flights usually last an hour and depart daily (weather permitting), mid-September through May. Fares range $95-$150; beverages and snacks usually are included. Rides are not advisable for children under age 8. Reservations are required. All pilots are FAA certified.

Note: The mention of the preceding hot air balloon rides is for information only and does **not** imply endorsement by AAA.

THE LIVING DESERT, 1.5 mi. s. off SR 111 at 47-900 Portola Ave., is a 1,200-acre wildlife and botanical park featuring rare plant and animal species from the world's deserts. Among the animals are bighorn sheep, zebras, mountain lions, Mexican wolves and birds of prey. Live animal shows, picnic areas, tram tours, hiking trails and food are available. Daily 9-4:30, Sept. 1 to mid-June; otherwise varies, mid-June through July 31. Admission $7.50; over 61, $6.50; ages 3-12, $3.50. Phone (760) 346-5694.

PALM SPRINGS (K-7)
pop. 40,200, elev. 466′

The fashionable resort city of Palm Springs lies in the upper Colorado Desert at the foot of 10,804-foot San Jacinto Peak. The mineral springs have attracted visitors for years, and the idyllic setting has been the location of many Hollywood productions. Nationally known golf tournaments are held on courses in Palm Springs and in neighboring communities.

Palm Springs Desert Resorts Convention and Visitors Bureau: 69-930 Hwy. 111, Suite 201, Rancho Mirage, CA 92270; phone (760) 770-9000. A visitor center is at 2781 N. Palm Canyon Dr.; phone (800) 967-3767. *See color ad.*

Shopping areas: Desert Fashion Plaza, at Palm Canyon Drive and Tahquitz Way, specializes in haute couture from the likes of Gucci and Saks.

AGUA CALIENTE INDIAN RESERVATION, 5 mi. s., is a vast scenic area that includes hiking trails and picnic areas set aside for visitors by the Tribal Council. Daily 8-6, Apr.-Aug.; 8-5, rest of year. Reservation entrance fee (includes Andreas, Murray and Palm canyons) $5; military and students with ID $3.50; over 62, $2.50; ages 6-12, $1. Phone (760) 325-5673.

Andreas Canyon offers many unusual rock formations, a hiking trail that follows a stream and

picnic facilities. There also are grinding stones and caves once used by Agua Caliente Indians.

Murray Canyon is less accessible than Andreas and Palm canyons, but contains spectacular rock formations, mortar holes and caves.

Palm Canyon is lined for 15 miles with 1,500- to 2,000-year-old Washingtonian palms that can be viewed by taking a steep walk down into the valley.

MOORTEN BOTANICAL GARDEN, 1701 S. Palm Canyon Dr., displays 3,000 varieties of desert plants from around the world and also serves as a bird sanctuary. Mon.-Sat. 9-4:30, Sun. 10-4. Admission $2; ages 5-15, 75c. Phone (760) 327-6555.

OASIS WATERPARK, 1500 Gene Autry Tr., has a wave pool, 13 waterslides, 5 toddler waterslides, a river, a spa and an outdoor pavilion. Daily 11-6, early June-Labor Day.; daily 11-5, mid-Mar. to early June; Sat.-Sun. 11-5, day after Labor Day-Oct. 31. Admission $18.95; 36-60 inches tall, $11.50; over age 55, $10.95; under 36 inches tall free; reduced rates at 3 and 3:30. Parking $3. Phone (760) 327-0499.

SAVE ★ **PALM SPRINGS AERIAL TRAMWAY,** on Tramway Rd., 3 mi. s.w. of SR 111, transports passengers 2.5 mi. from Valley Station (2,643 ft.) in Chino Canyon to and from Mountain Station

(8,516 ft.) at the e. edge of Long Valley. The tram affords spectacular views and access to the rugged San Jacinto Mountains. Both stations have observation decks and picnic areas; food is available.

Fifty miles of trails in San Jacinto Wilderness Park make the area popular with hikers and cross-country skiers. Pets are not permitted on the tramway; there are no restrictions or extra fees for hiking or backpacking gear.

Tram rides are offered Mon.-Fri. beginning at 10 a.m., Sat.-Sun. and holidays beginning at 8 a.m. Last trip up departs at 9 p.m. and returns at 10:45 p.m., during DST; last trip up departs at 8 p.m. and returns at 9:45 p.m., rest of year. **Note:** The tramway will be closed June 28-Sept. 13, 1999, for the installation of new tram cars. Fare $17.65; over 55, $14.65; ages 5-12, $11.65. AE, DS, MC, VI. Phone (760) 325-1391. *See ad p. 156.*

[SAVE] **PALM SPRINGS DESERT MUSEUM,** 101 Museum Dr., encompasses more than 100,000 square-feet dedicated to art, natural science and the performing arts. Exhibitions focus on Western and contemporary art and the human and natural history of the Coachella Valley. Performances of music, drama and dance take place in Annenberg Theater. Tues.-Sat. 10-5, Sun. noon-5; closed holidays. Admission $7.50; over 62, $6.50; military and students with ID and ages 6-17, $3.50; free to all first Fri. of the month, except during selected exhibitions. Phone (760) 325-0189.

[icon] **RECREATIONAL ACTIVITIES**

Rock Climbing

- **Uprising Rock Climbing Center,** 1500 S. Gene Autry Tr., Palm Springs, CA 92264. Mon.-Fri. 10-8, Sat.-Sun. 9-6, mid-Dec. through May 31; Mon.-Fri. noon-8, Sat.-Sun. 10-6, rest of year. Phone (760) 320-6630.

PALO ALTO (Q-2) pop. 55,900, elev. 23'

Palo Alto (Spanish for tall tree) was named for a double-trunked redwood tree, a landmark used by travelers and explorers as early as 1769. A likeness of the tree appears on the seal of Stanford University. The opening of the university in 1891 provided the impetus for Palo Alto's growth, and the livelihoods of the two remain closely intertwined. Palo Alto is the southeastern terminus of a scenic 31-mile stretch of I-280 that heads northwest to San Francisco.

Palo Alto Chamber of Commerce: 325 Forest Ave., Palo Alto, CA 94301; phone (650) 324-3121.

STANFORD UNIVERSITY stands on what is known as the "Stanford Farm," an estate of 8,200 acres. The main buildings are about 1 mile from the city. Frederick Law Olmstead created the general concept for the grounds and the unifying architectural theme: Romanesque sandstone buildings with arched arcades and red-tiled roofs. One-hour campus tours depart Memorial Hall, across from Hoover Tower on Serra Street, daily at 11 and 3:15. Phone (650) 723-2560.

Hoover Tower, next to Main Quad., houses the Hoover Institution on War, Revolution and Peace, devoted to the study of world conflict. The building and observation platform are open daily 10-4:30; closed holidays, examination weeks and during school breaks. Allow 30 minutes minimum. Admission $2; over 64 and under 14, $1.

Stanford Linear Accelerator Center (SLAC) is a research facility with a 2-mile-long linear accelerator that generates high-energy electron beams. Stanford University operates the 426-acre basic research laboratory for the U.S. Department of Energy. An orientation precedes the guided bus tour. Allow 2 hours minimum. Visitor center open Mon.-Fri. 8-5. Tour schedule varies; phone ahead. Free. Phone (650) 926-2204 for schedule and reservations.

PALOMAR MOUNTAIN (K-7)
pop. 200, elev. 5,202'

★**PALOMAR OBSERVATORY,** 4.5 mi. n. on CR S6, consists of four domes; the largest houses the 200-inch Hale telescope, which is used to study distant celestial bodies. Also included are 48-inch Oschin and 18-inch Schmidt telescopes and a 60-inch reflecting telescope. These telescopes are used for astronomical research by measuring the physical properties of planets, stars and galaxies. Greenway Museum contains a photographic display of some observatory sightings.

Museum and visitors' gallery at the 200-inch telescope open daily 9-4; closed Dec. 24-25. Free. Phone (760) 742-2119.

PALOS VERDES PENINSULA—
see Los Angeles p. 126.

PARADISE (D-3) pop. 25,400, elev. 1,708'

GOLD NUGGET MUSEUM, 502 Pearson Rd., exhibits a miner's cabin, smithy, general store and a replica of a gold mine. Also displayed are exhibits depicting the history of Paradise and Magalia Ridge, and a doll collection. A research library is available. Allow 1 hour minimum. Wed.-Sun. noon-4. Donations. Phone (530) 872-8722.

PASADENA—
see Los Angeles p. 127.

PASO ROBLES (H-4)
pop. 18,600, elev. 721′

Twenty-five miles east on SR 46 is Cholame, the small town where motion-picture legend James Dean died in an automobile accident; a stainless steel monument is beside the road.

Paso Robles Chamber of Commerce: 1225 Park St., Paso Robles, CA 93446-2234; phone (805) 238-0506.

EL PASO DE ROBLES AREA PIONEER MUSEUM, 2010 Riverside Ave., is dedicated to preserving the history of the Paso Robles area. Objects displayed include American Indian artifacts, vintage farm and ranching equipment, early 20th-century trucks, household items, furniture, clothing and business machinery. Thurs.-Sun. 1-4. Guided tours available by appointment. Free. Phone (805) 239-4556.

HELEN MOE ANTIQUE DOLL MUSEUM, US 101 at Wellsona Rd., houses about 800 antique dolls. The oldest doll exhibited dates from 1540 and belonged to Edward VI, son of England's King Henry VIII. Some room settings depict the early 1900s. Mon.-Sat. 10-5; closed holidays. Admission $3; under 13, $1. Phone (805) 238-2740.

 WINERIES

- **Arciero Winery,** 6 mi. e. on SR 46. Daily 10-5 (also Sat.-Sun. 5-6, June-Aug.). Phone (805) 239-2562.

- **Eberle Winery,** 4 mi. e. on SR 46. Daily 10-6, mid-May through Sept. 30; 10-5, rest of year. Closed Thanksgiving and Dec. 25. Phone (805) 238-9607.

PAUMA VALLEY (K-7)
pop. 900, elev. 840′

[SAVE] **SENGME OAKS WATER PARK,** on La Jolla Indian Reservation, 10.5 mi. s.e. on SR 76, has waterslides and a children's pool in a wooded setting. Picnic facilities, a volleyball court, showers and lockers are available. Daily 10-6, mid-June through Labor Day; Sat.-Sun. 10-6, late May to mid-June and day after Labor Day-Sept. 30. Admission $11.95; ages 4-11, $7.95. Phone (760) 742-1921.

PERRIS (C-8) pop. 21,500, elev. 1,457′

HOT AIR BALLOON RIDES over Perris Valley are available (weather permitting) through Adventure Flights Inc., (909) 678-4334; Boondoc Balloon Team, (310) 545-7725; or Full of Hot Air Balloon Co. (714) 530-0110. Rides last from 15 minutes to 1 hour. Fares range $39-$140. Beverages and snacks often are included. Rides are not advisable for children under 6. Reservations are required. All pilots are FAA certified.

Note: The mention of the preceding hot air balloon rides is for information only and does **not** imply endorsement by AAA.

ORANGE EMPIRE RAILWAY MUSEUM, 2201 S. A St., exhibits a collection of more than 200 steam, diesel and electric locomotives as well as passenger and freight cars, streetcars, and other railway equipment on a 64-acre site. Rail transportation in the West from the late 1870s through the 1960s is depicted. On weekends, exhibit buildings are open and rides on restored cars and locomotives are available. Picnicking is permitted.

Museum open daily 9-5; closed Thanksgiving and Dec. 25. Exhibit buildings open and train rides offered Sat.-Sun. 11-5. Donations; admission charged during events. All-day ride pass $7; ages 4-11, $4. MC, VI. Phone (909) 657-2605.

PESCADERO (Q-2) elev. 30′

AÑO NUEVO STATE RESERVE is 13 mi. s on SR 1. The reserve is best known for its colony of northern elephant seals, which come ashore to give birth, breed and molt. Guided 3-mile walks, which last 2.5 hours, are scheduled during the best viewing months, December through March. All walks operate regardless of weather; no refunds are issued. Tickets must be bought in advance by phone through Parknet; phone (800) 444-4445. Pets are not allowed. Hiking permits for the wildlife protection area, required Apr.-Nov., can be obtained on a first-come, first-served basis daily 8:30-3:30 at the entrance station or visitor center.

Park open daily 8-dusk, year-round; wildlife protection has some seasonal restrictions. Guided walks every quarter-hour daily 8:45-2:30, mid-Dec. through Mar. 31; closed Jan. 24 and Dec. 25. Donations. Guided walk tickets $4 per person. Parking $5 per private vehicle. Layered clothing and sturdy shoes are recommended. Phone (650) 879-0227 or 879-2025.

PETALUMA (N-1) pop. 43,200, elev. 12′

Petaluma began as a hunter's camp on the Petaluma River and grew quickly as discouraged gold miners returned from the fields to take up hunting and farming. Today poultry and dairy industries comprise much of the local economy.

The *Petaluma Queen,* an authentic 350-passenger paddlewheeler, offers dining and entertainment cruises departing from 255 Weller St. in the Port of Petaluma; phone (707) 762-2100 or (800) 750-7501.

Petaluma Visitor Program: 799 Baywood Dr., Suite 1, Petaluma, CA 94954; phone (707) 769-0429 or 769-5640. *See ad p. 792.*

Self-guiding tours: Brochures detailing a walking tour of 19th-century iron-front buildings and Victorian houses, survivors of the 1906 earthquake, and a Petaluma River walk can be obtained from the Petaluma Visitor Program.

MARIN FRENCH CHEESE FACTORY, 12 mi. s.w. at 7500 Red Hill Rd. (Petaluma-Point Reyes Rd.), offers tours of its cheesemaking operation. Picnicking is permitted. Allow 30 minutes minimum. Tours are given daily on the hour 10-4. Closed Jan. 1, Thanksgiving and Dec. 25. Free. Phone (707) 762-6001, 938-1519 or (800) 292-6001.

PETALUMA ADOBE STATE HISTORIC PARK, .7 mi. e. on Adobe Rd., preserves a large adobe ranch headquarters built about 1836. Exhibits include candles, leather goods, clothing and tools, all made in this period. Allow 1 hour minimum. Daily 10-5; closed Jan. 1, Thanksgiving and Dec. 25. Admission, including house, $2; ages 6-12, $1. Phone (707) 762-4871.

PETALUMA HISTORICAL MUSEUM/LIBRARY, 20 4th St., houses permanent and rotating exhibits reflecting life in early 19th-century Petaluma. Philanthropist Andrew Carnegie awarded the town $12,500 toward the building's construction in 1903. Exhibits include photographs, reference materials about the poultry industry and a collection of iron-front building facades popular in the last century. Allow 30 minutes minimum. Mon. and Thurs.-Sat. 10-4, Sun. 1-4. Costumed docents offer 1-hour guided tours Sat. at 10:30. Donations. Phone (707) 778-4398.

PIERCY (C-1) pop. 200, elev. 622′

CONFUSION HILL, on US 101, is an experience in contradictory optical and physical sensations in an apparently confused gravitational field. An optional 1.25-mile, 17-minute miniature train ride meanders (weather permitting) through a redwood forest and a tree tunnel to the top of the hill, where a logging museum contains exhibits dating back to 1800. Allow 1 hour minimum. Daily 8-7, late May-Labor Day; 11-4, rest of year. Train operates and museum open daily 10-7, late May-Labor Day. Admission $3; under 13, $2. Train ride $3; under 13, $2.50. Phone (707) 925-6456.

WORLD FAMOUS TREE HOUSE, 5 mi. s. on US 101, is in a 4,000-year-old living tree—250 feet high, 33 feet in diameter and 101.5 feet in circumference. The room is built in a 50-foot-high cavity in the tree. Allow 30 minutes minimum. Daily 9-8, June-Sept.; 9-5, rest of year. Closed Thanksgiving and Dec. 25. Free. Phone (707) 925-6406.

★ PINNACLES NATIONAL MONUMENT (G-3)

Pinnacles National Monument is entered from the east, 35 miles south of Hollister and 35 miles north of King City via SR 25 or CR G13 to SR 146, or from the west via SR 146, off US 101 in Soledad. It embraces about 16,000 acres of precipitous bluffs, spires and crags of colorful volcanic rock. In addition to volcanic action, the forces of heat, cold, water and wind also have worn the contours of the rock formations.

Bear Gulch Visitor Center is accessible by car from the east entrance. The west entrance has a ranger station; the entrance road is winding and narrow. Trailers and motorhomes are advised to use the east entrance. No roads connect the east and west districts. The visitor center is open daily 9-5; closed Dec. 25.

Pinnacles is strictly a hiking park, although some major formations can be seen from the roadway into the monument. The best viewing by car is from the west side. Hiking trails range from easy 1-mile treks to strenuous hikes of more than 7 miles.

The monument is bisected from north to south by a 1,000-foot-high ridge. Most of the spirelike formations, some more than 600 feet high, are found on or alongside the ridge. This central backbone has been cut in two places by streams; huge fragments of rock have fallen into the resulting deep clefts, creating caves. Bear Gulch Caves and Balconies Caves require visitors to carry flashlights. The caves have been closed but are scheduled to reopen in May 1999.

In addition to geological and scenic interest, the monument has an abundant bird population as well as deer and wildflowers. The plants and animals within the national monument are examples of a chaparral ecosystem. An example of Coast Range chaparral thrives here. Picnic facilities are available. Pets must be kept under physical control and are not permitted on trails. Admission is $5 per private vehicle; parking areas fill up early during spring, the monument's busiest season. Phone (831) 389-4485. *See the AAA California/Nevada CampBook.*

PISMO BEACH (I-3) pop. 7,700, elev. 70′

Pismo Beach is perhaps best known for its namesake mollusk, the Pismo clam. At one time the clams were so plentiful that 45,000 could be harvested commercially in a day. Decades of unrestricted clamming and the appetites of sea otters have depleted the supply, resulting in strict limits. Clamming for no more than 10 of the legal-size mollusks is permitted with a California state license.

These days butterflies outrank clams as a local attraction. From late October through February thousands of migrating monarchs alight on Pismo Beach's Butterfly Trees, a grove of Monterey pine and eucalyptus. Some come from as far as Canada to pass the winter in this mild climate.

The region offers opportunities for fishing, scuba diving, bicycling and other activity. Pismo State Beach *(see Recreation Chart)* has camping and a dune area where off-highway vehicles are allowed. Vehicles are prohibited in Pismo Dunes Preserve, which contains extensive coastal dunes. Pismo Beach lies on a scenic stretch of US 101 that extends from San Luis Obispo to Los Angeles.

Pismo Beach Chamber of Commerce: 581 Dolliver St., Pismo Beach, CA 93449; phone (805) 773-4382. *See color ad p. 794.*

PLACERVILLE (E-4)
pop. 8,400, elev. 1,860'

Placerville, originally known as Old Dry Diggin's, became so prosperous and lawless that lawbreakers were hanged first singly, then in pairs. As a result, the settlement was named Hangtown. By working as a wheelwright in a smithy, John Studebaker accumulated enough capital to establish the factory where the first Studebaker automobile was produced.

El Dorado County Chamber of Commerce: 542 Main St., Placerville, CA 95667; phone (530) 621-5885 or (800) 457-6279.

EL DORADO COUNTY HISTORICAL MUSEUM is 2 mi. w. at 104 Placerville Dr. in the El Dorado County Fairgrounds. Exhibits—which include ranching, logging, mining equipment, farming, housing, a country store, a stagecoach, a Shay locomotive and other railroad rolling stock—reflect local history and the gold-rush days. Changing exhibits also are offered. Allow 1 hour minimum. Wed.-Sat. 10-4 (also Sun. noon-4, Mar.-Oct.) or by appointment; closed Jan. 1, Easter, Thanksgiving and Dec. 25. Donations. Phone (530) 621-5865.

GOLD BUG MINE is off US 50 exit N. Bedford Ave., then 1 mi. to entrance of Gold Bug Park; the mine is just inside the park. The nation's only municipally owned mine, Gold Bug Mine lies on the eastern side of the Mother Lode vein. A replica of a stamp mill, which crushed gold-bearing quartz, can be seen. Picnicking is permitted. Guided and self-guiding tours as well as audiotapes with recorders are available.

Allow 30 minutes minimum. Self-guiding tours daily 10-4, mid-Apr. through Oct.; Sat.-Sun. noon-4, Mar. to mid-Apr. and in Nov. Guided tours by appointment. Admission $3; ages 8-16, $1. Audiotape and recorder rental $1. Children must be with an adult. Phone (530) 642-5232 to confirm schedule, or (530) 642-5238 for guided tours and reservations.

PLANTATION (E-2) pop. 200, elev. 741'

KRUSE RHODODENDRON STATE RESERVE, 317 acres, is .5 mi. e. off SR 1 on Kruse Ranch Rd. The rhododendrons, some growing to 14 feet tall, usually reach full bloom in April to early June. A variety of mosses, ferns, sorrel and other forest undergrowth bloom even earlier. Four miles of hiking trails wind through the reserve.

Allow 1 hour minimum. Daily dawn-dusk. Free. The reserve is not suitable for vehicles larger than a van or pickup truck; trailers are not permitted. Phone (707) 865-2391.

PLEASANTON (P-3)
pop. 50,600, elev. 352'

Many well-maintained old buildings and houses lend Pleasanton an early 19th-century atmosphere. Amador-Livermore Valley Historical Society Museum at 603 Main St. depicts regional history; phone (925) 462-2766.

The Alameda County Fairgrounds has one of the oldest racetracks in America; it was built in 1858 by the sons of a Spanish don, Augustin Bernal. The presence of limestone in the soil is credited with making this an exceptionally fine track.

Shadow Cliffs East Bay Regional Recreation Area on the outskirts of town was developed from an abandoned gravel quarry. A lake in the park offers swimming, boating and fishing. *See Recreation Chart.*

Pleasanton Chamber of Commerce: 777 Peters Ave., Pleasanton, CA 94566; phone (925) 846-5858.

RAPIDS WATERSLIDE AT SHADOW CLIFFS EAST BAY REGIONAL PARK, 2 mi. e. at 2500 Stanley Blvd., has four flumes in a rustic corner of the site. Under 42 inches tall are not permitted on the slides. Daily 10:30-5:30, June 1-Labor Day; Sat.-Sun. 10:30-5:30, Apr.-May and day after Labor Day-Sept. 30 (weather permitting). All-day pass $12.50; half-day pass (Mon.-Fri. 10:30-2 or 2-5:30) $8; regular admission $5 per hour. Parking $4-$5. Phone (925) 846-4900, or 829-6230 for reservations.

PLUMAS NATIONAL FOREST

Elevations in the forest range from 1,000 ft. at Feather River Canyon to 8,372 ft. at the summit of Mount Ingalls. Refer to AAA maps for additional elevation information.

The 1,162,863 acres of Plumas National Forest straddle the transition zone between two of the West's great mountain ranges, the Sierra Nevada and the Cascades. Although the Sierra block disappears under the younger volcanic rock of the Cascades on the forest's northern boundary near Lake Almanor, it is difficult to tell where one range ends and the other begins.

The mountains of the northern Sierra Nevada, which make up most of the forest lands, are neither as high nor as spectacular as those south of

Lake Tahoe. Yet within these mountains are a history of hidden treasure and a wealth of scenery.

The forest's principal gem is the Feather River watershed. The Feather River has carved numerous canyons and ravines full of cascades and white water. Portions of the Middle Fork of the river and three of its tributaries have been designated Feather Falls Scenic Area. The centerpiece of this 15,000-acre scenic area is 640-foot Feather Falls, which is just above Lake Oroville and is the highest of the numerous waterfalls on the 93-mile-long Middle Fork of the Feather River—a designated wild and scenic river. Water from this forest creates the headwaters for the California state water system.

Because of the rugged terrain and dangerous rapids, canoeing and tubing are recommended only in the recreation zone. Hiking trails and campgrounds are available along the river. Near the headwaters of the South Fork is Little Grass Valley Lake Recreation Area, which offers swimming, fishing and camping.

An extensive network of roads criss-crosses the national forest. Many routes, such as the Feather River National Scenic Byway, which crosses the lowest pass in the Sierra Nevadas, are a legacy of the gold era when such towns as Rich Bar, Pulga and La Porte were flourishing mining camps. Anglers and hikers have replaced the miners and frequent such popular areas as Bucks Lake, Lake Davis, Frenchman Lake and Antelope Lake. Seventy-one miles of the Pacific Crest Trail run through the national forest.

Information about campgrounds and recreational opportunities is available at the District Ranger stations and the Forest Headquarters in Quincy. Maps and guides to the Pacific Crest Trail and the Feather Falls Scenic Area also are available at the headquarters. For more information contact Plumas National Forest, 159 Lawrence St., P.O. Box 11500, Quincy, CA 95971; phone (530) 283-2050. *See the Recreation Chart and AAA California/Nevada CampBook.*

PLYMOUTH (E-4) pop. 800, elev. 1,086'

WINERIES

• **Sobon Estate**, 7.5 mi. n.e. of SR 49 at 14430 Shenandoah Rd. Daily 10-5; closed Jan. 1, Easter and Dec. 25. Phone (209) 245-6554.

POINT ARENA (D-1) pop. 400, elev. 220'

POINT ARENA LIGHTHOUSE AND MUSEUM are 1 mi. n.w. of SR 1 on Lighthouse Rd. The steel-reinforced concrete lighthouse opened in 1908 to replace an earlier structure that was destroyed by the 1906 earthquake; guided tours are available. The lighthouse also is a popular spot for whale

WINE COUNTRY

The Automobile Club of Southern California publishes *Central and Southern California Wineries* and *Northern California Wineries* which feature maps and information about the process of winemaking and its history in the state. The publications are available at offices of the Automobile Club of Southern California and the California State Automobile Association and are free to AAA/CAA members.

Spotlight's Wine Country Guide, a 100-page brochure providing maps and detailed information about towns, events, wineries, attractions, accommodations and retail establishments in Lake, Lower Mendocino, Napa and Sonoma counties is available free at the concierge desk of most Bay Area hotels, at most retail establishments in Wine Country and at northern California AAA offices. The brochure's four-month calendar of events is updated monthly.

The brochure is available from the publisher for $3 to cover postage and handling. Write *Spotlight's Wine Country Guide*, 5 Kenilworth Ct., Novato, CA 94945; phone (415) 898-7908, or fax 898-7751.

DID YOU KNOW?

According to estimates, 70 percent of California's gold remains to be discovered.

Between 1860 and 1960 California's population doubled on average once every 20 years.

People speaking nearly 100 languages comprise the ethnically diverse population of Los Angeles.

watching. Historical items are displayed in the adjacent maritime museum. Mon.-Fri. 11-3:30, Sat.-Sun. 10-3:30, May-Sept.; daily 11-2:30, Sept.-Dec. and Mar.-May; Sat.-Sun. 10-3:30, rest of year. Closed Thanksgiving and Dec. 25. Admission $3; under 12, $1. Phone (707) 882-2777.

POINT REYES NATIONAL SEASHORE—
see San Francisco p. 210.

POMONA—
see Los Angeles p. 128.

PORTERVILLE (H-5)
pop. 29,600, elev. 455'

PORTERVILLE HISTORICAL MUSEUM, 257 N. D St., is housed in a 1913 Southern Pacific passenger station. The museum's exhibits include vignettes of a dentist's office, drug store and attorney's office. China, glassware, furniture and American Indian artifacts, including baskets created by Yokuts, are displayed. Thurs.-Sat. 10-4; closed Jan. 1, during Porterville Fair Week in May, Thanksgiving and Dec. 25. Admission $1, students with ID 50c. Phone (559) 784-2053.

ZALUD HOUSE, 393 Hockett St. at Morton Ave., was built about 1891 for an established Porterville family. The rococo-style house with a mansard roof contains most of its original furnishings. The flower garden, originally planted in the 1930s, retains its original design. Guided tours are given Wed.-Sat. 10-4, Sun. 2-4, Feb.-Dec.; closed holidays. Admission $2; under 18, 50c. Phone (559) 782-7548.

PORT HUENEME (J-4)
pop. 20,300, elev. 13'

CEC/SEABEE MUSEUM, U.S. Naval Construction Battalion at Ventura Rd. and Sunkist Ave., presents models of equipment and battle scenes, weapons, uniforms, and arts and crafts by and about the U.S. Navy Civil Engineer Corps and the Navy Seabees. Obtain a visitor pass at the Ventura Road Gate. Mon.-Fri. 8-4:30, Sat. 9:30-4:30, Sun. 12:30-4:30; closed Easter and federal holidays. Phone to confirm hours. Free. Visitors must obtain a vehicle pass from the Sunkist Avenue gate by showing a valid drivers license, vehicle registration and proof of vehicle insurance. Under 16 must be with an adult. Phone (805) 982-5163.

PORTOLA (D-4) pop. 2,200, elev. 4,850'

PORTOLA RAILROAD MUSEUM, 1 mi. s. of SR 70 on CR A15, contains more than 100 historical Western railroad locomotives and railcars, including a 1950 streamline diesel and a Union Pacific Centennial, billed as the world's largest diesel locomotive. Housed in a former diesel shop, the museum also displays railroad relics. By reservation and for a fee, instruction in the operation of a locomotive is available. Picnic facilities are available.

Allow 1 hour minimum. Daily 10-5. Caboose train rides every half-hour, Sat.-Sun. 11-4, Memorial Day weekend-Labor Day. Museum admission by donations. Admission charged during events. All-day train ride pass $2, family pass $5. Phone (530) 832-4131, or 832-4532 for engineer instruction.

QUINCY (C-4) elev. 3,432'

PLUMAS COUNTY MUSEUM, 500 Jackson St., displays historical documents and photographs; permanent and rotating exhibits; cultural and natural history displays that illustrate area history since the 1850s; mining, logging and railroad exhibits; and woven baskets and artifacts from the native Maidu Indians. The restored 1878 Victorian house next to the museum is furnished with museum-quality pieces. Allow 30 minutes minimum. Mon.-Fri. 8-5 (also Sat.-Sun. and holidays 10-4, May-Sept.). Admission $1; ages 12-17, 50c. Phone (530) 283-6320.

RANCHO CUCAMONGA (B-8)
pop. 101,400, elev. 1,200'

The Serrano and Gabrielino Indians called this area *Kukamonga*, sandy place. The first Europeans arrived in 1774 and shortly thereafter established a mission. In 1839 the Mexican governor of California granted to Tabrucio Tapia 13,000 acres and Cucamonga Rancho began. In the early 1960s the area began changing from an agricultural economy to one of industry and commerce.

RED BLUFF (C-2) pop. 12,400, elev. 304'

Named for the colored sand and gravel cliffs characteristic of the surrounding area, Red Bluff is a gateway to Lassen Volcanic National Park *(see place listing p. 93).*

Red Bluff-Tehama County Chamber of Commerce: 100 Main St., P.O. Box 850, Red Bluff, CA 96080; phone (530) 527-6220 or (800) 655-6225.

SALMON VIEWING PLAZA, .1 mi. e. of I-5 on SR 36, then 2 mi. s. on Sale Ln., is at Diversion Dam on the Sacramento River. Underwater television cameras monitor the fish ladders. There is no viewing mid-September through mid-May. The plaza has exhibits about salmon as well as camping, picnicking and boat-launching facilities. Nearby is Sacramento River Discovery Center; phone (530) 527-1196. Daily 6 a.m.-8 p.m. River ramp closed in Aug. Free. Phone (530) 824-5196 for camping information or 527-3043 in the off-season.

WILLIAM B. IDE ADOBE STATE HISTORIC PARK, 2 mi. n. on Adobe Rd., is an 1850 adobe that serves as a memorial to the founder and president of the short-lived California Republic. In 1846 rumors that Mexican authorities were planning to expel American settlers compelled Ide to join a band of settlers in the Bear Flag Revolt. Subsequently, California became an independent country with Ide as its president for 24 days until the outbreak of the Mexican-American War and the occupation of the area by U.S. troops. Picnicking is permitted. Daily 8-dusk. Free. Parking $3. Phone (530) 529-8599 or 538-2200.

REDDING (C-2) pop. 66,500, elev. 560'

Redding provides scenic access via I-5 to the surrounding Shasta-Trinity National Forests and Whiskeytown-Shasta-Trinity National Recreation Area *(see place listings p. 225 and 237).*

Greater Redding Chamber of Commerce: 747 Auditorium Dr., Redding, CA 96001; phone (530) 225-4433.

CARTER HOUSE NATURAL SCIENCE MUSEUM, 48 Quartz Hill Rd. in Caldwell Park, has displays about the natural history of northern California, featuring native animals. Changing exhibits also are presented. Tues.-Sun. 10-5. Admission $2; ages 2-16, $1. Phone (530) 243-5457.

REDDING MUSEUM OF ART AND HISTORY, 56 Quartz Hill Rd., in Caldwell Park, has changing contemporary art exhibits, items depicting Shasta County history and displays of ethnic art, including American Indian works. An arts and crafts fair is held in September. Tues.-Sun. 10-5; closed holidays. Admission $2. Phone (530) 243-8801.

SHASTA DAM is 10 mi. n.w. off I-5 Shasta Dam Blvd. exit, following signs. Shasta Dam is reputedly the world's highest center-overflow spillway. A 30-minute film depicting water usage in California is shown at the visitor center on request. A 1-hour tour of the dam departs daily on the hour 9-4, Memorial Day weekend-Oct. 31; at 10, noon and 2, rest of year. Visitor center open Mon.-Fri. 8:30-4, Sat.-Sun. 8:30-5, Memorial Day weekend-Labor Day; otherwise varies. Closed federal holidays. Free. Phone (530) 275-4463.

★**SHASTA STATE HISTORIC PARK** is 6 mi. w. on SR 299. Formerly a robust mining town with a population of 2,500, Shasta was the gateway to a large area of riches and a rendezvous for gamblers; it is now an interesting gold-rush relic. The old courthouse has been converted to a museum; a restored barn and stagecoach also can be seen. Also displayed in the park is the Boggs Collection—100 Years of California Art. Picnic facilities are available. Wed.-Sun. 10-5; closed Jan. 1, Thanksgiving and Dec. 25. Admission $2; ages 6-12, $1. Phone (530) 243-8194 or 225-2065.

WATERWORKS PARK, .2 mi. e. of SR 299 at 151 N. Boulder Dr., has three flumes, the Flash Flood, an inner tube ride, an activity pool, a children's pool with slides and a fountain, and facilities for beach volleyball, basketball and video games. Lockers, dressing rooms, picnic tables and food are available. Daily 10-8, Memorial Day weekend-Labor Day. Admission $13.50; ages 3-11, $11.50; over 65 free. Reduced admission after 5. DS, MC, VI. Phone (530) 246-9550.

REDLANDS (B-9)
pop. 60,400, elev. 1,356'

Named for the color of the local soil, Redlands once was an important packing and distribution point for citrus fruit. Today the University of Redlands plays an important role in the life of the area; its campus occupies approximately 130 acres northeast of the city center. Redlands also is known for its carefully restored Victorian houses.

Redlands Bowl, in Smiley Park at Grant and Eureka streets, presents music and dance programs late June through late August; phone (909) 793-7316.

Redlands Chamber of Commerce: 1 E. Redlands Blvd., Redlands, CA 93273; phone (909) 793-2546.

KIMBERLY CREST HOUSE AND GARDENS, 1325 Prospect Dr., comprises a three-story, 1897 house built in the French chateau style along with formal Mediterranean gardens. The house, which sits on a hill, contains furnishings dating from the late 19th and early 20th centuries. Thurs.-Sun. 1-4, Sept.-July; closed holidays. Admission $, senior citizens $4, under 13 free. Phone (909) 792-2111.

LINCOLN MEMORIAL SHRINE, at 125 W. Vine St. on the grounds of the Smiley Public Library, is dedicated to Abraham Lincoln and contains memorabilia along with books about the president and the Civil War. Busts of Lincoln, Confederate general Robert E. Lee and Union general Ulysses S. Grant line the shrine's walls. Tues.-Sat. 1-5. Free. Phone (909) 798-7636.

PHAROAH'S LOST KINGDOM, off I-10 at 1101 California St., is an Egyptian-themed amusement park offering a variety of midway rides and attractions. The park includes a carrousel, a train, a long-boat swing, bumper boats, miniature golf and a children's play area. A waterpark is open during the summer. Sun.-Thurs. 10-10, Fri.-Sat. 10 a.m.-midnight. Single ride tickets $1-$5. Waterpark $14.95; ages 2-10, $10.95. Gold Passport (includes unlimited rides, attractions and admission to waterpark) $29.95; ages 2-10, $19.95. Parking $3. DS, MC, VI. Phone (909) 335-7275.

SAN BERNARDINO ASISTENCIA is 1.5 mi. w. at 26930 Barton Rd. Built about 1830, this was a branch of the San Gabriel Mission and part of the second chain of missions. During the 1840s its buildings became part of the Lugo ranch. Today these restored structures include a museum, a historic dining room, a wedding chapel and a gatehouse. Wed.-Sat. 10-5, Sun. 1-5; closed Jan. 1, Thanksgiving and Dec. 25. Admission $1; under 13, 50c. Phone (909) 793-5402.

SAN BERNARDINO COUNTY MUSEUM, n. of I-10 at 2024 Orange Tree Ln. at California St., has regional anthropology, history and geology exhibits, an extensive collection of mammals, birds and bird eggs as well as fine arts and special exhibits. Tues.-Sun. 9-5; closed Jan. 1, Thanksgiving and Dec. 25. Admission $4; over 61 and students with ID $3; ages 5-12, $2. Additional charge for special exhibits may apply. Phone (909) 307-2669.

REDONDO BEACH—
see Los Angeles p. 128.

RED ROCK CANYON STATE PARK

Red Rock Canyon State Park is 23 miles northeast of Mojave via SR 14. Red, brown and gray sandstone cliffs have eroded into spectacular shapes. The colorful formations served as landmarks for freight wagons that stopped for refreshment at the canyon's springs. Included in this desert community are Joshua trees, cholla cactus, golden eagles, desert tortoises and coyotes. A visitor center provides information about geology and history, and a pamphlet for a self-guiding half-mile nature trail is available.

Approximately 3 miles north of the park off I-14, Opal Canyon Road (a rough, dirt road) leads to a fire opal mine open to the public for prospecting on weekends; a nominal fee is charged.

The park is open daily 24 hours. The visitor center is open Sat.-Sun. 8-4, mid-Sept. through Memorial Day. Park admission $5 per private vehicle; over 64, $4. An additional fee is charged for camping. Phone (805) 942-0662. *See Recreation Chart and AAA California/Nevada CampBook.*

REDWOOD CITY (P-3)
pop. 66,100, elev. 15'

LATHROP HOUSE is off Marshall St. at 627 Hamilton St. The restored 1863 house, built by Benjamin Lathrop, is an example of early Gothic Revival architecture and is furnished in period. Its two floors feature period clothing and changing exhibits. The house was moved to its present site in 1905 and survived the earthquake of 1906. Tues.-Thurs. 11-3, Sept.-July; closed holidays and the last 2 weeks in Dec. Donations. Phone (650) 365-5564.

REDWOOD NATIONAL PARK (A-1)

Elevations in the park range from sea level at Crescent City to 3,262 ft. at an unnamed peak. Refer to AAA maps for additional elevation information.

Encompassing 105,516 acres, Redwood National Park lies along the northern California coast between Crescent City and Orick, 330 miles north of San Francisco on US 101. Within its boundaries are the 34,780 combined acres of Del Norte Coast, Jedediah Smith and Prairie Creek Redwoods state parks *(see Recreation Chart).* In addition to dense forests of coast redwoods, the park embraces marshland, beaches, rugged coastline, rivers, streams, prairies and oak woodlands.

General Information and Activities

The beaches are open all year, but visitors should use caution when swimming or surfing. The coastline in northern California is a dangerous combination of steeply descending beaches, heavy undertows, very cold water and jagged rocky shoals. Visitors to the beach should be aware of the tides.

Coastal Drive, reached from the US 101 Klamath Beach Road exit, affords 8 miles of spectacular coastal scenery. Gold Bluffs Beach, off US 101 on Davison Road about 2 miles north of Orick, was the site of gold-mining operations in the 1850s. Howland Hill Road east of Crescent City is a 6-mile drive through old-growth redwoods along an unimproved stage route. Coastal Drive, Gold Bluffs and Howland Road are not suitable for RV or trailer travel.

Some public roads also serve adjoining private forest lands; logging truck traffic and other private activities take place along some of the routes.

Trails traverse the 33 miles of wild and untouched coastline along rock promontories that protrude into the sea, affording vistas of sea lion colonies and migrating whales. Birds inhabit bluffs, lagoons and offshore rocks; birdwatching is particularly rewarding during the waterfowl migrations. More than 150 miles of trails provide access to the magnificent redwood groves.

The park staff provides free guided walks, evening programs and other activities from mid-June through Labor Day. Information stations are in Crescent City, Hiouchi and Orick.

Developed campgrounds are within the state parks and along US 101 nearby. There also are five primitive walk-in campsites in the national park although space is limited. Freshwater and surf fishing are permitted; a California fishing license is required. *See Recreation Chart.*

ADMISSION to the national park is free. The state parks charge day use and overnight fees of $5 for developed picnicking and camping areas.

PETS must be kept under physical restraint while in the park and are prohibited on most trails. Campers are required to have proof of rabies shots for pets.

ADDRESS inquiries to the Superintendents, Redwood National and State Parks, 1111 2nd St., Crescent City, CA 95531. Phone (707) 464-6101.

RIDGECREST (I-6)
pop. 27,700, elev. 2,289'

MATURANGO MUSEUM, E. Las Flores Ave. at China Lake Blvd., has exhibits pertaining to the natural and cultural history of the upper Mojave Desert. Highlights include ancient American Indian petroglyphs and a gallery of changing artworks. A children's section offers hands-on displays. Daily 10-5; closed holidays. Admission $2; over 54, military with ID and ages 6-18, $1. Phone (760) 375-6900.

RIVERBANK (F-3) pop. 8,500, elev. 135'

RECREATIONAL ACTIVITIES
White-water Rafting
- **Beyond Limits Adventure,** P.O. Box 215, Riverbank, CA 95367. Daily Mar.-Oct. Phone (209) 869-6060 or (800) 234-7238. *See color ad p. 91.*

RIVERSIDE (B-8) pop. 226,500, elev. 852'

Since rich soil and mild climate made it the ideal location for growing navel oranges, Riverside grew rapidly. By 1895 Riverside, then the metropolitan center of Southern California, was the wealthiest city per capita in the nation. The 1873 Parent Navel Orange Tree is at the corner of Magnolia and Arlington avenues.

The citrus industry remains vital to the economy and is under constant scrutiny by the strong agricultural curriculum at the University of California at Riverside, on the east edge of town.

The Italian Renaissance-style old City Hall is a 1912 Classic Revival municipal museum. Several elaborate Victorian houses and many fine examples of mission architecture and adobe houses reflect the city's early wealth and prestige. The Queen Anne-style Heritage House at 8193 Magnolia Ave. is open for tours; phone (909) 689-1333.

Chino Hills State Park, which includes 13,000 acres of rolling hills dotted with oaks and sycamores, offers 65 miles of trails for hiking, biking and horseback riding; phone (909) 780-6222.

Visitors and Convention Bureau: 3443 Orange St., Riverside, CA 92501; phone (909) 787-7950.

Shopping areas: Galleria at Tyler, at the Tyler Street intersection of Riverside Freeway (SR 91), contains a JCPenney, Macy's, Nordstrom and Robinsons-May as well as 145 specialty shops.

CALIFORNIA CITRUS STATE HISTORIC PARK, Van Buren Blvd. at Dufferin Ave., pays tribute to the citrus industry for which Riverside was famous between the 1880s and 1940s. The park features hundreds of navel orange trees as well as a varietal grove with about 80 types of citrus. The visitor center is a replica of a middle-class home typical of those occupied by growers during the early 1900s. Walking trails and a picnic area also are available. Daily 8-5. Free. Phone (909) 780-6222.

CASTLE AMUSEMENT PARK, 3500 Polk St., offers four 18-hole miniature golf courses, a three-story arcade and more than 35 rides, including Go-Karts. Food is available. The miniature golf courses and arcade open daily at 10; closing times vary. Ride park schedule varies. Admission to grounds free. Prices for rides and games vary. Phone (909) 785-4141.

JURUPA MOUNTAINS CULTURAL CENTER, 7621 Granite Hill Dr., houses displays of minerals, dinosaur fossils and American Indian relics. The 104-acre grounds include a natural spring and several American Indian trails but can only be toured with one of the center's guides. Tues. and Thurs. noon-4, Sat. 7:30-4; closed Jan. 1, July 4 and Dec. 25. Free. Phone (909) 685-5818.

MARCH FIELD MUSEUM, s. on I-215 to Van Buren Blvd. at March Air Reserve Base, emphasizes the evolution of military air power. Displays feature military aviation artifacts, engines and trainers from 1918 to the present. Flight line aircraft include bombers, fighters, helicopters, the SR-71 and the F-14 "Tomcat." Mon.-Fri. 10-4, Sat.-Sun. 10-5, Memorial Day-Labor Day; daily 10-4, rest of year. Closed Jan. 1, Easter, Thanksgiving and Dec. 25. Admission $5; ages 5-12, $2; family rate $10. Phone (909) 697-6600.

MISSION INN, 3696 Main St., features towers and campanarios that reflect California missions. Buildings and courtyards brim with antique bells, stained glass, statues, paintings and gardens. The first wing was built in 1902. St. Francis Chapel contains a massive gold-leaf Mexican altar and seven Tiffany mosaic and stained-glass windows. A small museum uses photographs and artifacts to reflect the history of the inn and the city.

Guided tours last 1.25 hours and are offered Mon.-Fri. at 10, 10:30, 1:30 and 2, Sat.-Sun. every half-hour 10-3. Museum open daily 9:30-4; closed Easter, Mother's Day, Thanksgiving and Dec. 25. Tour $8. Museum $1. Reservations are suggested for the tour. Phone (909) 781-8241 Mon.-Fri. for the tour, (909) 784-0300, ext. 5035, Sat.-Sun. for the tour or (909) 788-9556 for the museum.

MOUNT RUBIDOUX, at 1,337 feet, rises above the Santa Ana River at the city's w. edge. On the summit are Father Serra Cross and the World Peace Tower. At the western foot of the mountain is St. Francis Fountain. The summit road, which begins at 9th Street and Mount Rubidoux Drive, is a walking trail which leads to the top.

RIVERSIDE MUNICIPAL MUSEUM, 3720 Orange St., houses exhibits depicting Riverside's human and natural history, including displays about American Indian cultures. Tues.-Fri. 9-5, Sat. 10-5, Sun. 11-5, Mon. 9-1; closed holidays. Free. Phone (909) 782-5273.

UCR BOTANIC GARDENS, on the e. side of the University of California Riverside campus off N. Campus Circle Dr. near parking lot 13, occupies 39 hilly acres. Emphasis is on dry-climate plants; many of the 3,500 species bloom in the winter and spring, usually January through May. Allow 30 minutes minimum. Daily 8-5; closed Jan. 1, July 4, Thanksgiving and Dec. 25. Free. Under 16 must be with an adult. Phone (909) 787-4650.

SAVE **UCR/CALIFORNIA MUSEUM OF PHOTOG-RAPHY,** 3824 Main St., presents changing exhibits of contemporary photography and related new media. The permanent collection features historic photographs, cameras and equipment. Photographs range from early daguerreotypes to contemporary prints. Some of the many cameras displayed date back to the invention of photography. Also available are a children's Interactive Gallery and an Internet Gallery.

Wed.-Sat. 11-5, Sun. noon-5; closed Jan. 1, Easter, Thanksgiving and Dec. 25. Admission $2, over 64 and students with ID $1, under 12 free with adult; free to all Wed. Phone (909) 784-3686.

ROSAMOND (I-6) pop. 7,400, elev. 2,330'

EXOTIC FELINE BREEDING COMPOUND, 3.5 mi. w. of SR 14 on Rosamond Blvd., is a breeding, research and educational facility with more than 50 rare and exotic cats in outdoor enclosures. Fourteen species, including leopards, tigers, cougars and ocelots, are represented. Tour guides provide detailed information about these endangered felines. Thurs.-Tues. 10-4. Last tour departs 30 minutes before closing. Closed Dec. 25. Free. No pets are allowed. Phone (805) 256-3332.

NASA DRYDEN FLIGHT RESEARCH CENTER, 15 mi. e. on Rosamond Blvd. to Edwards Air Reserve Base, develops and tests new forms of aircraft design and flight operation techniques. Guided tours, which last 90 minutes, begin with a film describing the history of the test programs, then continue with a walk through a hangar and a look at experimental aircraft. Tours are given Mon.-Fri. at 10:15 and 1:15; closed holidays and space shuttle landing days. Free. Reservations are required. Phone (805) 258-3460.

RUTHERFORD (M-2) elev. 170'

WINERIES

• **Beaulieu Vineyard,** off SR 29 at 1960 St. Helena Hwy. Daily 10-5. Closed holidays. Phone (707) 963-2411 or 967-5231.

• **Rutherford Hill Winery,** e. off Silverado Tr. at the end of Rutherford Hill Rd. Daily 11:30-3:30. Phone (707) 963-7194 or 963-1871.

SACRAMENTO (E-3) pop. 369,400, elev. 30'.

Capt. John Sutter, a Swiss emigrant, settled at the confluence of the American and Sacramento rivers in 1839 on a 50,000-acre land grant from the Mexican government. The town of Sacramento was laid out on Sutter's property in 1848—the same year that James Marshall discovered gold near the South Fork of the American River to start the great California gold rush.

Sacramento quickly grew into a major supply center for the northern Mother Lode country. It was devastated 1849-1853 by two floods and two fires that leveled two-thirds of the town. Nonetheless, it was chosen as the state capital in 1854 and fought off subsequent challenges by Berkeley, San Jose and Monterey.

In 1856 the first railroad in California connected Sacramento with Folsom and became the western terminus of the Pony Express line from St. Joseph, Mo. The transcontinental railroad was completed in 1869. Agriculture took hold in the fertile Sacramento Valley, and the city's continued prosperity was assured.

Today Sacramento is an important highway, rail and river hub; the state capital; and the marketing center for a rich agricultural region. Nearby military installations and the space and aviation industries also contribute to Sacramento's economy. A deepwater channel to San Francisco Bay was completed in 1963, making the city a major inland port.

Wells Fargo History Museum, in Wells Fargo Center at 400 Capitol Mall, has exhibits illustrating the commercial development of Wells Fargo Bank and its role during the gold rush, including historical items such as a fully restored Concord stagecoach, photographs and lithographs; phone (916) 440-4161.

Arco Arena, at 1 Sports Pkwy. near the intersection of I-5 and I-80, is the home of the Sacramento Kings professional basketball team. The arena also is the scene of many other events and performances; phone (916) 928-8499 for ticket information. Gray Line offers daily sightseeing tours of the area; phone (916) 648-0181 or (800) 356-9838.

Sacramento is the northern terminus of a scenic 33-mile stretch of SR 160 that heads south to Isleton along the Sacramento River.

Sacramento Convention and Visitors Bureau: 1421 K St., Sacramento, CA 95814; phone (916) 264-7777 or (800) 392-2334.

Self-guiding tours: Maps and brochures for walking tours of Old Sacramento are available at the Old Sacramento Visitor Center at 1102 2nd St.; phone (916) 442-7644.

BLUE DIAMOND GROWERS, 1701 C St., presents a 20-minute videotape about almond growing and processing and offers tastings. Allow 1 hour minimum. Mon.-Fri. 10-5, Sat. 10-4. Free. Phone (916) 446-8439.

CALIFORNIA VIETNAM VETERANS MEMORIAL is at 15th and L sts., at the e. end of State Capitol Park. The 22 shiny black granite panels, built entirely with donations, are engraved with the 5,822 names of California's dead and missing. Full-relief bronze figures depict daily life during the war.

SAVE **CROCKER ART MUSEUM,** 216 O St., exhibits paintings, drawings, sculpture and decorative arts, featuring both European and northern California artists. Traveling exhibits are displayed in the main room. Guided tours are available on request. Tues.-Sun. 10-5 (also Thurs. 5-9); closed Jan. 1, July 4, Thanksgiving and Dec. 25. Admission $4.50; ages 7-17, $2. Phone (916) 264-5423.

GOVERNOR'S MANSION STATE HISTORIC PARK, 16th and H sts., features the 19th-century governor's mansion. Furnishings and personal items of former governors are displayed. Included are a 1902 Steinway piano, Persian carpets acquired by Mrs. Earl Warren in 1943 and many reminders of the Victorian era. The mansion grounds contain flowers, shrubs and trees, some dating to 1877. Tours daily on the hour 10-4; closed Jan. 1, Thanksgiving and Dec. 25. Admission $3; ages 6-12, $1.50. Phone (916) 323-3047.

THE HISTORIC PADDLEWHEELER *SPIRIT OF SACRAMENTO,* departing from the L St. Landing in Old Sacramento, is a 110-foot paddlewheel riverboat that conducts 1-hour sightseeing cruises

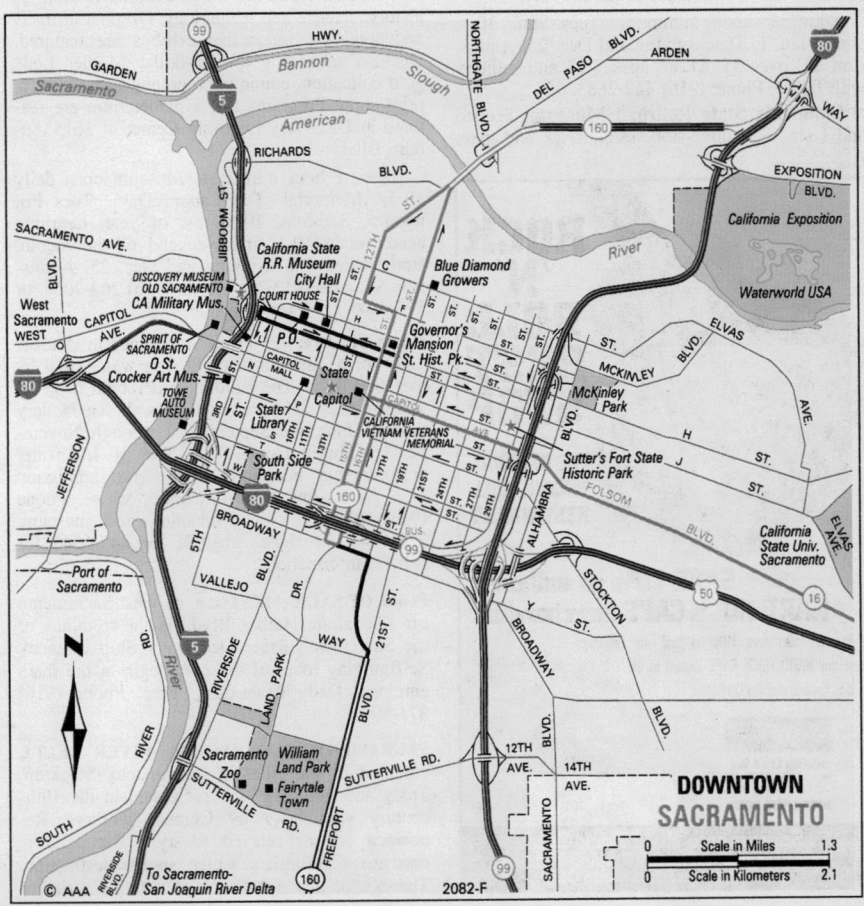

DOWNTOWN SACRAMENTO

on the Sacramento River. Dinner, brunch, happy hour and murder mystery excursions also are available. Sightseeing cruises depart Wed.-Sun. at 1:30 and 3, June-Aug.; otherwise varies. Sunday sunset cruises are offered year-round. Sightseeing fare $10; under 12, $5. Reservations are recommended. MC, VI. Phone (916) 552-2933 or (800) 433-0263.

OLD SACRAMENTO, a four-block section delineated by Capitol Mall, I and Second sts., and the Sacramento River, was the commercial district during the gold rush. The area has been redeveloped with museums, restaurants and shops that preserve its historical character.

The California Military Museum, 1119 Second St., honors Californians who have served and protected their state and country in times of war, peace and disaster. Artifacts exhibited include weapons, uniforms, battle flags, photographs, medals and documents dating from the time of the Spanish explorers through the Civil War, World Wars I and II, Korea, Vietnam, Desert Storm and California earthquakes. A research center covers all branches of the military.

Allow 1 hour minimum. Tues.-Sun. 10-4; closed Jan. 1, Thanksgiving and Dec. 25. Admission $3; over 55, $1.50; ages 7-17 and military with ID $1. Phone (916) 442-2883.

★ **California State Railroad Museum,** Second and I sts., is a three-story steel, brick and glass

structure housing 21 restored locomotives and train cars. More than 40 interpretive exhibits, dioramas, pictures, murals and film presentations document the history of American railroading 1860-1960. A film is presented in the museum's theaters. The building's striking design and gleaming exhibits are impressive.

Allow 2 hours minimum. Daily 10-5; closed Jan. 1, Thanksgiving and Dec. 25. Admission $6; ages 6-12, $3. Tickets are good for a same-day visit to the Central Pacific Passenger Station. Phone (916) 323-9280 for the lobby and ticket office, 324-0539 for recorded information, or 445-6645 for 24-hour events and information.

Central Pacific Passenger Station, Front and J sts. across from the railroad museum, was the first California terminal for the transcontinental railroad. The self-guiding tour of the reconstructed building recalls the 1870s. Allow 30 minutes minimum. Daily 10-5. Admission $6; ages 6-12, $3. Tickets are good for same-day visit to the California State Railroad Museum.

[SAVE] **Discovery Museum,** 101 I St., comprises five themed areas that offer exhibits relating to history, science and technology. Original artifacts and hands-on, interactive exhibits are featured. Displays include a million-dollar Mother Lode gold collection, ethnic photographs and a historic print shop. Programs and a planetarium are featured at Discovery Learning Center at 3615 Auburn Blvd.

Allow 1 hour minimum. Museum open daily 10-5, Memorial Day-Labor Day; Tues.-Fri. noon-5, Sat.-Sun. 10-5, rest of year. Learning center open 10-5 first weekend of the month. Both closed Thanksgiving and Dec. 25. Admission $4; ages 6-12, $2. Phone (916) 264-7057, or 575-3941 for learning center.

Eagle Theatre, 925 Front St., opened in October 1849 for a 3-month run and then was closed by the 1850 flood. The building was rebuilt in 1974. A 13-minute slide presentation is shown January through June and September 1 through November 15. Museum open Tues.-Sun. 10-4. Theater performances occasionally. Museum admission free. Admission to performances varies. Phone (916) 207-1226 for production and museum, 323-6343 for show schedule, or 445-6645 for general information.

PORT OF SACRAMENTO, s. of West Sacramento off I-80 along Harbor Blvd., is the terminus of the Sacramento River Deepwater Ship Channel. Self-guiding tours of the port begin at the main entrance. Daily dawn-dusk. Free. Phone (916) 371-8000.

SACRAMENTO-SAN JOAQUIN RIVER DELTA, bounded by the cities of Sacramento, Stockton, Tracy and Pittsburg, was reclaimed in the 19th-century with labor by Chinese workers. Renowned for its relaxed lifestyle, the delta is northern California's water sports destination. Throughout this rich farmland winds a series of waterways punctuated by hundreds of islands, historical towns, marinas and resorts. Houseboating is a favorite means of exploring the delta. Fishing, camping and picnicking also are popular. Phone (916) 777-5007.

★STATE CAPITOL, bounded by 10th, 15th, L and N sts., was built 1860-74 and is noted for its lofty glass dome, which rises 210 feet above the street. The main building contains historical and art exhibits, murals and statuary. Free guided tours cover the restored main building and chambers. A 10-minute film about the capitol's history and construction is presented in the basement. The surrounding park has trees, shrubs and other plants from around the world. Children must be with an adult.

Allow 1 hour minimum. Daily 9-5; closed Jan. 1, Thanksgiving and Dec. 25. A Capitol Tour is offered daily on the hour 9-4. Additional tours are offered, and tickets are available 30 minutes before tours; phone for schedule and location. Free. Phone (916) 324-0333.

STATE LIBRARY, 914 Capitol Mall, is a handsome granite structure with a 100-foot mural by Maynard Dixon. The files of early state newspapers are especially interesting. A second building at 900 N. Street houses the state history section. Mon.-Fri. 9:30-4. Free. Phone (916) 654-0261.

★SUTTER'S FORT STATE HISTORIC PARK, 27th and L sts., was the first European outpost in the California interior. The restored 1839 adobe fort has relics of pioneer and gold rush days; a diorama depicts life in the fort in the 1800s. Allow 1 hour minimum. Daily 10-5; 10-4 during events. Last tour departs 45 minutes before closing. Closed Jan. 1, Thanksgiving and Dec. 25. Admission mid-May to mid-Sept. and during events $5; ages 6-12, $3. Admission rest of year $3; ages 6-12, $1.50. Phone (916) 445-4422 or 324-0539.

State Indian Museum, 2618 K St., on the grounds of Sutter's Fort, depicts aspects of California's American Indian cultures with displays of feather baskets, jewelry, clothing and art. Daily 10-5; closed Jan. 1, Thanksgiving and Dec. 25. Admission $3; ages 6-12, $1.50. Phone (916) 324-0971 or 324-0539.

SAVE TOWE AUTO MUSEUM, Front St. at V St., displays more than 180 vintage automobiles. The development of the automobile is depicted via representations of varied models, including Model A's, Model T's and early Ford V-8s. Antique fire trucks, mail vehicles and early commercial Ford vehicles are also displayed. Allow 30 minutes minimum. Daily 10-6; closed Jan. 1, Thanksgiving and Dec. 25. Admission $5; over 64, $4.50; ages 14-18, $2.50; ages 5-13, $1. Phone (916) 442-6802.

WATERWORLD USA, 1600 Exposition Blvd., has a wading pool, wave pool, waterslides, a river tube ride, an in-line water luge and a children's play area featuring a five-story interactive playhouse. Daily 10:30-6, Memorial Day weekend-Labor Day. Admission, including all rides, $16.95; under 48 inches tall $11; under age 3 free. Additional charges for parking, lockers, inner tubes and observers. AE, MC, VI. Phone (916) 924-0556 or 924-3747.

WILLIAM LAND PARK, bounded by Freeport and Riverside blvds., 13th Ave. and Sutterville Rd., encompasses 600 acres, including picnic facilities, a public golf course and a grove of cherry trees. Phone (916) 455-5014 for golf information.

Fairytale Town, 39091 Land Park Dr. across from Sacramento Zoo, is a 2.5-acre park with sets based on themes from popular children's nursery rhymes and fairy tales. Puppet shows and other activities take place daily. Daily 10-5, Mar.-Dec.; Sat.-Sun. 10-5, rest of year. Closed Dec. 25. Last admission 1 hour before closing. Admission Mon.-Fri. $3.25; ages 3-12, $2.75. Admission Sat.-Sun. and holidays $3.50; ages 3-12, $3. Phone (916) 264-7060, or 264-5233 for schedule and price information.

SAVE Sacramento Zoo, at the corner of Sutterville Rd. and W. Land Park Dr., exhibits more than 350 animals, including Asian lions, Siberian tigers, Grevy zebras, African cheetahs and chimpanzees. A reptile house maintains 53 species in 60 exhibits. Daily 10-4; closed Thanksgiving and Dec. 25. Admission Mon.-Fri. $4.50; ages 3-12, $3. Admission Sat.-Sun. and holidays $5; ages 3-12, $3.50. Phone (916) 264-5885.

ST. HELENA (N-2) pop. 5,000, elev. 255'

In addition to its many wineries, St. Helena in Napa Valley has other industries, such as the production of handcrafted candles by Hurd Beeswax Candle Factory, 2.5 miles north on SR 29 in the Freemark Abbey complex,. St. Helena lies on a scenic stretch of SR 29 from Calistoga to Napa.

St. Helena Chamber of Commerce: 1010-A Main St., P.O. Box 124, St. Helena, CA 94574; phone (707) 963-4456 or (800) 799-6456.

BALE GRIST MILL STATE HISTORIC PARK is 3 mi. n.w. on SR 29. The 1847 mill has a 36-foot-diameter wheel that was once used to grind flour for local farmers. It has been restored and once again grinds flour and cornmeal. Hiking trails lead from the access road to the mill pond as well as to Bothe-Napa Valley State Park (see Recreation Chart). Daily 10-5; closed Jan. 1, Thanksgiving and Dec. 25. Admission $5 per private vehicle; physically impaired with pass $4; ages 5-10, $2.50. Phone (707) 942-4575.

SILVERADO MUSEUM, 1490 Library Ln., off E. Adams St., contains more than 8,000 items related to Robert Louis Stevenson. Tues.-Sun. noon-4; closed holidays. Donations. Phone (707) 963-3757.

WINERIES

- **Beringer Winery**, 2000 Main St. Daily 9:30-6, May-Oct.; 9:30-5, rest of year. Closed holidays. Phone (707) 963-7115.

- **Charles Krug Winery**, 2800 Main St. (SR 29). Daily 10:30-5:30; closed holidays. Phone (707) 963-2761 or 967-2200.

- **Louis M. Martini Winery**, 254 St. Helena Hwy. S. Daily 10-4:30. Closed holidays. Phone (707) 963-2736 or (800) 321-9463.

SALINAS (G-3) pop. 108,800, elev. 55'

Salinas is best known as the birthplace of John Steinbeck and the setting for many of his novels. Winner of the Nobel and Pulitzer prizes, Steinbeck continues to be a source of pride in Salinas. First editions, letters, photographs and memorabilia are displayed in a room of John Steinbeck Public Library, 350 Lincoln Ave.; phone (831) 758-7311. The vast quantities and varieties of vegetables and fruits grown in the area have earned the Salinas Valley the nickname "Salad Bowl of the Nation."

Salinas Area Chamber of Commerce: 119 E. Alisal St., P.O. Box 1170, Salinas, CA 93902; phone (831) 424-7611.

JOSE EUSEBIO BORONDA ADOBE, 333 Boronda Rd., was built 1844-48 and is the town's oldest structure. The wood shingles used on the restored adobe are a departure from the traditional red-clay tiles. The 1897 Old Lagunita School House also is at the site. Allow 30 minutes minimum. Tours are given Mon.-Fri. 10-2, Sun. 1-4. Donations. Phone (831) 757-8085.

SALINAS COMMUNITY CENTER, 940 N. Main St., displays varied artwork and stages musical and theatrical performances throughout the year. Allow 30 minutes minimum. Mon.-Fri. 8-5. Free. Phone (831) 758-7351.

"Hat In Three Stages of Landing" is on the lawn of Salinas Community Center. It is a giant sculpture by Claes Oldenberg. The three hats, at various elevations, are painted a vivid yellow and weigh 3,500 pounds each. The sculpture is a tribute to farmers and ranchers and represents a Western hat tossed in the air from the nearby rodeo stands.

SALTON SEA (K-8)

The 35- by 15-mile Salton Sea, 20 miles south of Indio, is one of the world's largest inland bodies of saltwater. Created by flood waters from the Colorado River in 1905, the sea is shallow, having an average depth of less than 20 feet. The climate of the desert terrain surrounding the sea is typically hot and dry; summer temperatures regularly exceed 100 F. The area is most inviting to visitors between October and May, when temperatures fall to the 70s and 80s.

Camping, hiking, swimming, boating, fishing and water skiing are among the recreational opportunities in the area. Limited supplies are sold in the surrounding small towns. Parking fee $5. For information contact the Salton Sea State Recreation Headquarters, 100-225 State Park Rd., North Shore, CA 92254; phone (760) 393-3052.

SAN ANDREAS (E-3)
pop. 2,100, elev. 1,008'

Just 16 miles west of San Andreas via SR 12, Paloma Road, Watertown Road and Campo Seco-Chile Camp Road are the remains of Campo Seco, a once thriving gold and copper town. Dubbed Campo Seco (dry camp) by prospectors, the site produced some gold, but the real treasure was copper. In the early 1860s Penn Copper Co. supplied the Union Army with the metal during the Civil War. Though considered a ghost town, Campo Seco has a post office and claims the largest cork oak tree in California.

Calaveras County Visitor Center: 1211 S. Main St., P.O. Box 637, Angels Camp, CA 95222-0637; phone (209) 736-0049 or (800) 225-3764.

CALAVERAS COUNTY MUSEUM, 30 N. Main St., served as the county jail and the county courthouse 1867-1962. Featured are a garden of native California plants and trees, Miwok Indian artifacts, mining relics and 1850-1900 period exhibits. Allow 30 minutes minimum. Daily 10-4; closed holidays. Admission $1, students with ID 50c, under 6 free. Phone (209) 754-6579.

CALIFORNIA CAVERNS AT CAVE CITY is 8 mi. e. on Mountain Ranch Rd., then about 2.5 mi. s.e. on Michel and Cave City Rd. Chambers and passageways contain glittering formations ranging from fragile soda straws on the ceiling to colossal stalagmites rising from the floor. The cavern was discovered in 1849, and many signatures dating back to the 1850s are visible on the walls. John Muir was reportedly among the signers, but his name has yet to be found.

A 4-hour Wild Downstream Circuit (spelunking) trip and an introductory spelunking trip lasting 2 to 3 hours are available by reservation. An 80-minute guided tour leaves (weather permitting) daily on the hour 10-5, May-Sept.; 10-4, Oct.-Nov. Phone ahead to verify schedule. Tour fee $8; over 60, $7.50; ages 6-12, $4.50. MC, VI. Phone (209) 736-2708.

SAN BERNARDINO (B-9)
pop. 164,700, elev. 1,040'

Settled by Mormons in the 1850s, San Bernardino lies in San Bernardino County, the largest county in the United States. The city is the gateway to the resort areas of the San Bernardino

Mountains, including Big Bear Lake and Lake Arrowhead *(see place listings p. 59 and 86).*

San Bernardino Convention and Visitors Bureau: 201 N. E St., Suite 103, San Bernardino, CA 92401; phone (909) 889-3980.

Shopping areas: Carousel Mall, bounded by 4th, E, 2nd and G streets, has Harris, JCPenney and Montgomery Wards. Macy's, Gottschalks and Sears have stores at Inland Center, I-215 and Inland Center Drive.

★ **RIM OF THE WORLD DRIVE,** SR 18, leads to Lake Arrowhead, Big Bear Lake and other resort areas. This winding 40-mile road, at elevations of 5,000 to 7,200 feet, offers many panoramic views. One spectacular vista is from 7,203-foot Lakeview Point, which overlooks Big Bear Lake and the road ahead as it twists among the cliffs around the head of Bear Canyon. Visitors can take either SR 38 or SR 18 around Big Bear Lake and continue past Baldwin Lake and over the Johnson and Cushenbury grades to Lucerne Valley, Apple Valley and Victorville.

SAN BERNARDINO NATIONAL FOREST

Elevations in the forest range from 1,000 ft. at the forest boundaries to 11,502 ft. at the summit of Mount San Gorgonio. Refer to AAA maps for additional elevation information.

Wide variations in climate, vegetation, scenery, natural resources and outdoor recreation can be found within the nearly 660,000 acres of San Bernardino National Forest. The forest encompasses the highest mountains in Southern California, including 11,502-foot Mount San Gorgonio. Some 114,000 acres are set aside as the Cucamonga, San Gorgonio, Santa Rosa and San Jacinto wilderness areas.

In addition to the resort centers of Lake Arrowhead, Big Bear Lake and Idyllwild, there are campgrounds, picnic areas and six winter sports areas. Other recreational opportunities include hiking, skiing, horseback riding, fishing and hunting. Information about walking, driving and self-guiding tours of the historic mining area in Holcomb Valley is available at any of the five ranger stations.

The 107-mile-long Rim of the World National Scenic Byway begins in Cajon Pass, travels through the San Bernardino Mountains and ends near the Mill Creek ranger station, near Redlands. Tour brochures are available for 50c at forest ranger stations.

For more information contact the Forest Supervisor, San Bernardino National Forest, 1824 S. Commercenter Cir., San Bernardino, CA 92408-3430; phone (909) 383-5588. *See Recreation Chart and the AAA California/Nevada CampBook.*

MOUNT SAN JACINTO STATE PARK, encompassing the state park and a wilderness area, embraces 13,522 acres at the e. edge of the forest, w. of Palm Springs and n. of Idyllwild. Crowned by 10,804-foot Mount San Jacinto, it is a popular area for backpacking. Other park activities include hiking, camping, picnicking, cross-country skiing and bird watching. Free day-use permits are available at any ranger station. Phone (909) 659-2607. *See Recreation Chart.*

SAN CLEMENTE (K-6)
pop. 41,100, elev. 208′

Built on hillsides overlooking the Pacific Ocean, San Clemente is known for its palm-fringed beach. The municipal pier is popular among fishermen and sightseers. The city beach offers swimming, surfing and picnic facilities. Camping is available at San Clemente State Beach *(see Recreation Chart).*

San Clemente Chamber of Commerce: 1100 N. El Camino Real, San Clemente, CA 92672-4653; phone (949) 492-1131.

San Diego

Second largest city in California, San Diego is both a modern metropolis and a popular year-round resort. Spreading from the coast to the desert, encompassing cliffs, hills, mesas, canyons and valleys, San Diego possesses one of California's largest natural harbors; peninsulas shelter San Diego Bay from the ocean and provide miles of shoreline for both business and pleasure. This ideal location has been a dominant factor in determining the city's history, economy and development.

Considered the birthplace of California, San Diego was first discovered by Europeans in 1542 when Juan Rodríguez Cabrillo, landed at Point Loma and claimed what is now California for the Spanish Crown. The first settlement came more than 2 centuries later in 1769, when Gaspar de Portolá and a group of Spanish settlers founded a military outpost on what is now Presidio Hill.

Accompanying Portolá was Franciscan friar Junípero Serra, who founded Mission Basilica San Diego de Alcalá, the first of a chain of 21 missions established in California. In 1774 Serra moved the mission a few miles up the San Diego River to better soil and a more abundant water supply. The sites of the original mission and the fort still can be seen in Old Town San Diego.

After California achieved statehood in 1850, San Diego grew slowly, deferring to the northern coastal cities, Los Angeles and San Francisco. It maintained a fairly insular existence until the late 1800s when San Francisco merchant Alonzo E. Horton decided to move the nucleus of the town closer to its valuable harbor. Horton bought 960 acres of waterfront land and developed it into New Town, which is now part of downtown San Diego.

During the early 1900s San Diego made a concerted effort to attract people, industry, and shipping and railroad commerce, but Los Angeles remained the leader. World War II had a major impact on the city: The United States, forced to move its Pacific naval headquarters from Pearl Harbor, chose San Diego as the new command center. This relocation produced an increase in industry and brought thousands of military personnel, many of whom stayed after the war.

San Diego is the home of the largest naval air station on the West Coast and is headquarters for many Pacific Fleet operations of the U.S. Navy. The federal government and the aerospace equipment industry rank high in economic importance, closely followed by tourism and agriculture.

San Diego has spread more than 20 miles north, south and east. It sprawls over the natural contours of the land, rather than following the traditional grid concept, and encompasses several distinct communities.

Mission Bay, once a shallow wasteland, is a 4,600-acre aquatic park. Southeast of Mission Bay, Old Town preserves the town's rich Spanish-Mexican heritage, while downtown supports the business community, a convention center, theaters and naval and commercial shipping operations.

Balboa Park, an oasis in the midst of the city, provides numerous tourist attractions and recreational opportunities. Point Loma boasts two man-made resorts—Shelter Island and Harbor Island—and contains Cabrillo National Monument, where California began. A spectacular 2.3-mile bridge over San Diego Bay links the Coronado peninsula with downtown.

San Diego's institutions of higher education include San Diego State University, the University of California, San Diego and the University of San Diego. Within the city lies the community of La Jolla, home to Scripps Institute of Oceanography, a world-renowned marine studies center, and the Salk Institute, an outstanding biological research facility.

Business and pleasure coexist in unusual harmony. San Diego's climate, attractive setting and recreational facilities promote a casual lifestyle that has enticed many visitors to become permanent residents.

Approaches
By Car

Two major north-south routes, both originating at the Canadian border, converge on San Diego. I-5 comes down through Los Angeles, then heads for the coast; nearing San Diego it bisects the University of California San Diego campus at La Jolla, skirts Mission Bay Park and passes Old Town before entering the city center.

I-15 comes inland through Las Vegas and the Mojave Desert but changes to SR 15 as it avoids downtown San Diego and terminates at I-5 just south of the city proper. SR 163 (Cabrillo Freeway) leaves I-15 at the Miramar Marine Corps Air Station, swings southwestward through Balboa Park, interchanges with I-5 and finally becomes Market Street in the heart of San Diego.

From the south the main route is I-5, which begins at the Mexican border, passes along the east side of San Diego Bay, then heads for the downtown area.

I-805 is the north-south bypass. It leaves I-5 north of La Jolla and rejoins I-5 just north of the Mexican border customs stations.

From points east, I-8 funnels traffic across the Colorado River at Yuma, Ariz., and roughly parallels the Mexican border to the town of Boulevard, from which it arcs northwestward through Alpine, interchanges with the major north-south routes just north of downtown San Diego and ends near the mouth of the San Diego River.

From I-8 at Boulevard, two-lane SR 94 continues to the border town of Tecate, then heads for San Diego via Spring Valley and La Mesa, where it becomes a multilane divided highway; this route ends at the I-5 interchange in downtown San Diego.

THE INFORMED TRAVELER

City Population: 1,110,500

Elevation: 13 ft.

Sales Tax: State and county sales taxes total 7.75% in San Diego. A lodging tax called a transient occupancy tax of 10.5% also is levied along with an 7.75% rental car tax.

WHOM TO CALL

Emergency: 911

Police (non-emergency): (619) 531-2000

Time: (619) 853-1212

Temperature: (619) 289-1212

Hospitals: Kaiser Foundation, (619) 528-5000; Columbia Mission Bay, (619) 274-7721.

WHERE TO LOOK

Newspapers

The major daily in San Diego is the morning *San Diego Union-Tribune*. Other foreign-language and community papers also are published.

Radio and TV

San Diego radio station KSDO (1130 AM) is a news/talk station; KPBS (89.5 FM) is a member of National Public Radio.

Major TV channels are 6 (FOX), 8 (CBS), 10 (ABC), 15 (PBS) and 39 (NBC). For a complete list of radio and television programs, consult the daily newspapers.

Visitor Information

The San Diego International Visitors Information Center, (619) 236-1212, is at 11 Horton Plaza, San Diego, CA 92101. On the corner of First and F sts., the center offers brochures and city maps. Guides of Old Town San Diego can be purchased for $2 at the State Park Visitor Center, (619) 220-5422, in Old Town. Another visitor information center, (619) 276-8200, is at 2688 E. Mission Bay Dr., San Diego, CA 92109.

WHAT TO WEAR

With an average daily temperature of 70, San Diego has an almost perfect climate. The average annual rainfall of 9.5 inches falls mainly during December, January and February. Winters are mild, with daytime temperatures in the mid-60s.

Getting Around

Street System

Generally the most convenient way to get around San Diego is by car. Most major attractions and shopping areas are within easy freeway access. Traffic delays are infrequent except downtown during rush hours. Main thoroughfares, which include Pacific Highway, Harbor and Mission Bay drives, Nimitz and El Cajon boulevards, University Avenue, Friars Road and Market Street, also are easy travel routes.

Speed limits are usually 35 mph on streets and 65 mph on freeways. It is important to maintain freeway speed limits; drivers moving at dangerously slow speeds will be ticketed. Right turns on red and U-turns at intersections are both legal unless otherwise posted. Pedestrians crossing the street at intersections or in crosswalks **always** have the right-of-way.

Parking

San Diego has metered on-street parking downtown in addition to many lots and garages. Charges vary, but most average from $3 per half-hour to $10 per day. Some downtown hotels and stores provide free parking. Parking in other parts of the city is rarely a problem.

What To See

Balboa Park

★ **BALBOA PARK** is a 1,200-acre recreation and cultural center at the n.e. edge of the business district. The park's most prominent feature, the 200-foot California Tower, contains a 100-bell carillon that chimes every 15 minutes. The park was the site of the Panama-California International Exposition in 1915-16, and many Moorish and Spanish Renaissance-style exhibit halls, such as the California Building and the ornate Casa del Prado, still remain along El Prado (The Promenade).

A $21, 1-week passport allows admission to up to 12 Balboa Park museums, one ticket per museum. Passports are available at participating museums and at Balboa Park Visitors Center in the Plaza de Panama parking lot at the House of Hospitality Building. Phone (619) 239-0512.

Botanical Building, at the n. end of the lily pond, is a reassembled Santa Fe Railroad station in which tropical and subtropical plants are displayed. Fri.-Wed. 10-4; closed Jan. 1, Thanksgiving and Dec. 25. Free. Phone (619) 235-1100.

Japanese Friendship Garden, just n.e. of Spreckels Organ Pavilion, includes a small entry garden, the Exhibit House, a traditional sand and stone garden and a picnic area overlooking a wooded canyon. Tues. and Fri.-Sun. 10-4. Admission $2, over 64, military and students with ID $1, family rate $5; free to all third Tues. of the month. Phone (619) 232-2780.

Mingei International Museum, 1439 El Prado, features folk art from around the world. Permanent and rotating exhibits occupy the museum's

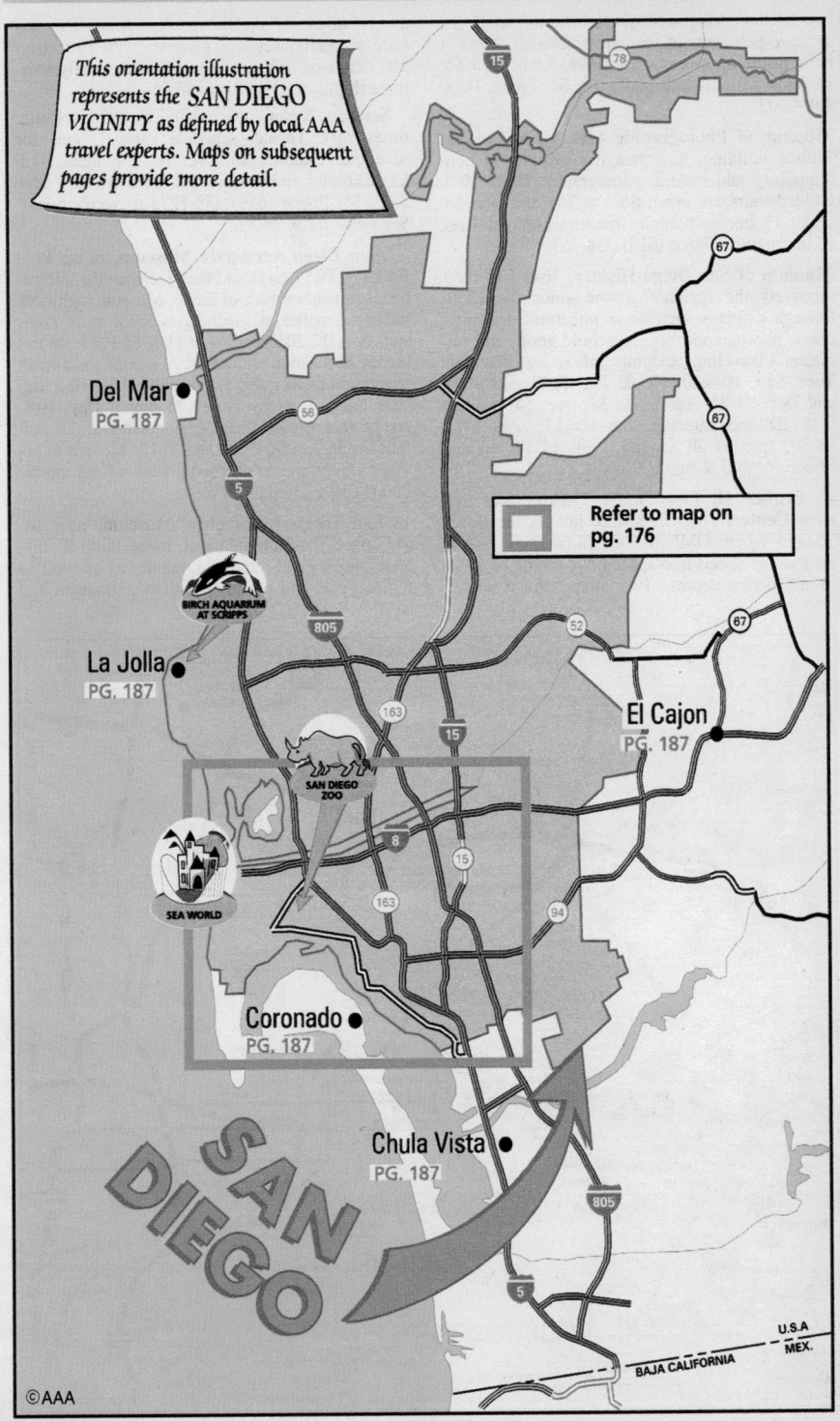

This orientation illustration represents the *SAN DIEGO VICINITY* as defined by local AAA travel experts. Maps on subsequent pages provide more detail.

Del Mar
PG. 187

BIRCH AQUARIUM AT SCRIPPS

La Jolla
PG. 187

Refer to map on pg. 176

El Cajon
PG. 187

SAN DIEGO ZOO

SEA WORLD

Coronado
PG. 187

SAN DIEGO

Chula Vista
PG. 187

U.S.A
MEX.

BAJA CALIFORNIA

©AAA

two floors. Videotape presentations detail the creative processes of the native cultures. Allow 1 hour minimum. Tues.-Sun. 10-4. Admission $5; students with ID and under 18, $2. Phone (619) 239-0003.

Museum of Photographic Arts, in the Casa de Balboa building, has changing exhibits of contemporary and historic photography. Daily 10-5. Guided tours are given Sun. at 2. Admission $4, under 12 free with adult; free to all second Tues. of the month. Phone (619) 238-7559.

Museum of San Diego History, 1649 El Prado, interprets the region's growth since the 1850s through displays such as architectural drawings, maps, photographs, art, household goods and furniture. Traveling exhibits also are featured. Tues.-Sun. 10-4:30; closed Jan. 1, Thanksgiving and Dec. 24-25. Admission $4; over 54, military with ID and students with ID $3; ages 5-12, $1.50; free to all second Tues. of the month. Phone (619) 232-6203.

SAVE **Reuben H. Fleet Space Theater and Science Center,** 1875 El Prado, houses the Space Theater where OMNIMAX® films allow one to vicariously speed into space on a shuttle or swim in the ocean depths. Two afternoon screenings

are subtitled for the hearing impaired. The science center houses five galleries with more than 100 hands-on exhibits, as well as nationally touring exhibitions. Food is available.

Science center open daily at 9:30; closing times vary. Theater schedule varies; phone for schedule. Exhibits $5; over 64, $4; ages 3-12, $3. Exhibits and theater $8; over 64, $7; ages 3-12, $5. Phone (619) 238-1233 to verify prices. *See color ad p. 180.*

SAVE **San Diego Aerospace Museum,** in the Ford Building, Pan American Plaza, includes the International Aerospace Hall of Fame. Museum highlights include a replica of Lindbergh's *Spirit of St. Louis* and an A-12 Blackbird. The Hall of Fame honors heroes of aviation and space. A tour of the aircraft restoration facility also is available. Daily 10-5, day after Labor Day-day before Memorial Day; 10-4, rest of year. Closed Thanksgiving and Dec. 25. Admission $6; over 64, $5; ages 6-17, $2; free to active military and to all fourth Tues. of the month. Phone (619) 234-8291.

SAVE **San Diego Automotive Museum,** near the aerospace museum, features more than 60 historic and special-interest automobiles as well as motorcycles and prototypes in its permanent and

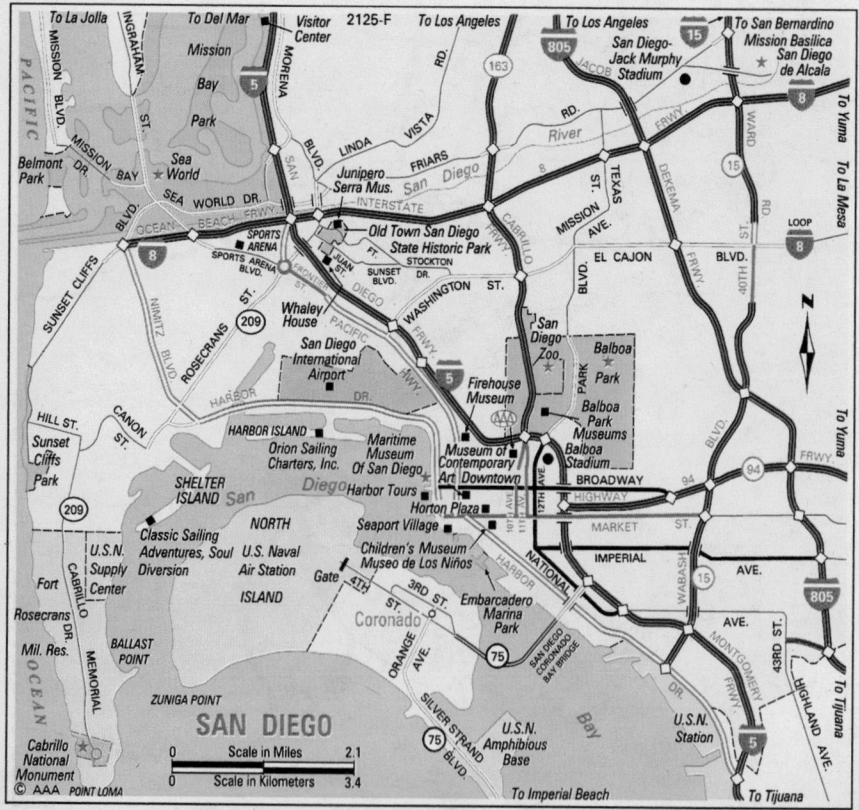

rotating collections. A collection of reference works and memorabilia also is on site. Daily 10-5:30 in summer; 10-4:30, rest of year. Last admission 30 minutes before closing. Closed Jan. 1, Thanksgiving and Dec. 25. Admission $6; over 64 and military with ID $5; ages 6-15, $2. Phone (619) 231-2886.

San Diego Model Railroad Museum in the Casa de Balboa building, has five scale-model railroad layouts that detail the geography and historical development of railroading in Southern California. A hands-on model railroad for children also is offered. Allow 30 minutes minimum. Tues.-Fri. and some holidays 11-4; Sat.-Sun. 11-5. Admission $3, over 55 and students and military with ID $2.50; free to all first Tues. of the month. Phone (619) 696-0199.

San Diego Museum of Art, in the center of the park, has a permanent collection of Italian Renaissance works; Spanish baroque old masters; American, Asian and American Indian art and sculpture; contemporary California art; and special exhibitions. Tues.-Sun. 10-4:30; closed Jan. 1, Thanksgiving and Dec. 25. Tours are given Tues.-Thurs. at 10, 11, 12:30 and 1:30; Fri. at 12:30 and 1:30; Sat. on the hour 10-2; Sun. at 1 and 2. Admission $8; over 64 and college students with ID $6; military with ID $5; ages 6-17, $3. Phone (619) 232-7931.

SAVE **San Diego Museum of Man** comprises a group of buildings around the California Quadrangle. Exhibits explore the nature and origins of humankind and feature the cultures of American Indians, Ancient Egypt, Mexico and Latin America. Exhibits also highlight human reproduction, folk art, textiles and early man. Daily 10-4:30; closed Jan. 1, Thanksgiving and Dec. 25. Admission $5; over 64, $4.50; ages 6-17, $3; free to uniformed military and to all third Tues. of the month. Phone (619) 239-2001.

San Diego Natural History Museum, e. end of Balboa Park, houses permanent and changing exhibits about plants, animals and the geology of San Diego County and Baja, California. Daily 9:30-5:30 (also Thurs. 5:30-6:30), Memorial Day weekend-Labor Day; 9:30-4:30 (also Thurs. 4:30-6:30), rest of year. Hours may be extended during special exhibits. Closed Jan. 1, Thanksgiving and Dec. 25. Admission $6; over 59 and military with ID $5; ages 6-17, $2; free to all first Tues. of the month, except during special exhibits. Prices may increase during special exhibits. Phone (619) 232-3821.

★ **SAN DIEGO WILD ANIMAL PARK**— *see Escondido p. 73.*

SAVE ★ **San Diego Zoo,** from I-5 take Pershing Dr. exit, then follow signs, one of the largest zoos in the world, exhibits some of the rarest specimens in captivity. More than 4,000 animals live in enclosures closely simulating their natural environments. Highlights include walk-through aviaries, koalas, an impressive assemblage of primates and a large reptile collection. Habitats also in-

TRANSPORTATION

Air travel: San Diego International Airport (Lindbergh Field) off Harbor Drive is served by major domestic and foreign carriers. Taxi service to downtown averages $6 to $8. San Diego Transit Corporation's buses provide frequent service to downtown for $2; phone (619) 233-3004 or 231-2100.

Rental cars: Hertz, at the airport, offers discounts to AAA members; phone (619)220-5222 or (800) 654-3080. For listings of other agencies check the telephone directory.

Rail service: Amtrak, (800) 872-7245, has daily service to Los Angeles. The Amtrak (Santa Fe) depot is at Broadway and Kettner Boulevard. Coaster is a commuter rail service from Oceanside to downtown San Diego; phone (800) 262-7837.

Buses: Greyhound Lines Inc., (800) 231-2222, has a depot at 1st Avenue and Broadway. Greyhound and Five Star Tours, (619) 232-5049, offer daily service between to downtown Tijuana, Mexico.

Taxis: Cab companies include San Diego, (619) 232-6566; Red Cab, (619) 428-1107; USA, (619) 231-1144; and Yellow, (619) 234-6161. Base fare is $3.20, with rate of $1.80 for each additional mile.

Public transport: San Diego Metropolitan Transit System (MTS) serves the area from Oceanside to the Mexican border. One-way bus fare ranges from $1.50 to $3. Some transfers may require an upgrade fee.
The San Diego Trolley provides daily service on two lines that operate from 5 a.m. to 1 a.m. The Blue Line connects Mission San Diego in Mission Valley with the international border at San Ysidro via Old Town and downtown. The Orange Line runs from downtown to Santee. Trolley fares are $1 to $2.25.
The Transit Store, downtown on Broadway at 1st Avenue, sells money-saving passes and multi-ride tickets for buses and trolleys and provides maps, schedules and brochures. For information phone (619) 233-3004; phone for recorded trolley information (619) 231-8549; phone TDD (619) 234-5005.

clude Gorilla Tropics, Tiger River and the Sun Bear Forest.

Hippo Beach, a hippopotamus habitat resembling an African marsh, lets visitors view these enormous creatures through an underwater observation window. Polar Bear Plunge is a recreation of a summer tundra habitat, complete with a pool with an underwater viewing area. The Giant Panda Research Station exhibits two pandas on a 12-year loan from China. The pandas occasionally are off-exhibit for conservation research; phone (888) 697-2632 for viewing hours.

The zoo is landscaped with more than 6,500 plant species, including tropical and subtropical vegetation. Moving sidewalks stretch from the deep canyons to upper levels. An aerial tramway runs from the main entrance to the Horn and Hoof Mesa, .3 mile away. The Children's Zoo lets children pet the more gentle creatures and see newborn animals. Live animal shows are presented at Wegeforth Bowl and Hunte Amphitheatre. Narrated bus tours and picnic facilities also are available. Pets are not permitted.

October is a special month at the zoo. The first Monday of the month is Founder's Day, and general admission for all is free. If a sponsor was found, all children under age 12 are provided free general admission all month.

Zoo opens at 9; closing time varies. General admission $16; ages 3-11, $7. Deluxe ticket package (including admission, bus tour, aerial tram and children's zoo) $22; over 59, $19.80; ages 3-11, $12. Phone (619) 234-3153.

Spanish Village Art Center contains more than 40 studios where artisans create, display and sell their wares. Studios open daily 11-4; closed Jan. 1, Thanksgiving and Dec. 25. Free. Phone (619) 233-9050.

Spreckels Organ Pavilion contains an outdoor pipe organ said to be the largest in the world. Free concerts Sun. at 2 and Mon. at 8 p.m., mid-June to Aug. 31. Phone (619) 235-1100.

Timken Museum of Art houses a collection of works by European Old Masters from the 14th through 19th centuries as well as 18th- and 19th-century American paintings and Russian icons. Tues.-Sat. 10-4:30, Sun. 1:30-4:30, Oct.-Aug.; closed holidays. Guided tours are given Tues.-Thurs. 10-noon. Free. Phone (619) 239-5548.

Mission Bay

Northwest of downtown, Mission Bay has two islands and many coves and inlets. Mission Bay Park has facilities for boating, boat rental, camping and fishing as well as miles of shoreline for picnicking and swimming.

SAVE **BELMONT PARK**, W. Mission Bay Dr. and W. Mission Blvd., is an oceanside amusement park featuring a renovated 1925 wooden roller coaster; a carrousel; a 175-foot-long indoor swimming pool; and an indoor family playland.

Other amusements also are offered. Sun.-Thurs. 11-10, Fri.-Sat. 11-11, Memorial Day-Labor Day; Sun.-Thurs. 11-7, Fri.-Sat. 11-9, rest of year. Phone to verify schedule. Park admission free. Prices for rides vary. Phone (619) 491-2988.

[SAVE] ★ SEAWORLD, on Mission Bay's south shore, is a 150-acre marine zoological park with shows, aquariums, marine-life attractions and rides. Star performers include the "killer whales" Shamu and Baby Shamu, along with dolphins, sea lions, otters and walruses.

Other highlights include "Wild Arctic," a simulated ride into the Arctic's frozen landscape; the Rocky Point Preserve, a habitat for dolphins; Penguin Encounter, an exhibit containing more than 300 penguins; Shark Encounter; and Forbidden Reef, where guests can feed bat rays. Shamu's Happy Harbor is a 2.2-acre interactive play area. Guided tours are offered. Pets are not permitted. Evening entertainment is offered in summer.

Park open daily at 9, mid-June through Labor Day; at 10, rest of year. Closing times vary. Admission $34.95; over 55, $26.20; ages 3-11, $26.95. Extra fee for some rides. Parking fee $5, RVs $7. DS, MC, VI. Phone (619) 226-3901 or (760) 939-6212.

Old Town San Diego

JUNÍPERO SERRA MUSEUM, 2727 Presidio Dr. in Presidio Park, interprets San Diego's historical American Indian, Spanish and Mexican periods. Exhibits include artifacts from archeological excavations at the Presidio site. The museum stands above the sites of the 18th-century presidio and Father Junípero Serra's first mission in Alta California. Tues.-Sat. 10-4, Sun. noon-4; closed Jan. 1, Thanksgiving and Dec. 24-25. Admission $3, under 13 free. Phone (619) 297-3258.

OLD TOWN SAN DIEGO STATE HISTORIC PARK, a six-block area bounded by Wallace, Juan, Twiggs and Congress sts., commemorates the founding of the first permanent settlement in California. It contains many of San Diego's original buildings. Nearby Presidio Park is the site of California's first mission and military fortress, established in 1769.

Daily 10-5. Free guided walking tours depart the Seeley Stables Visitor Information Center daily at 10:30 and 2. All buildings are closed Thanksgiving and Dec. 25. Brochures for self-guiding tours of Old Town are available at Seeley Stables and Cascade Estudillo for $2. Phone (619) 220-5422.

Black Hawk Smithy & Stable, Mason and Juan sts. behind Casa de Bandini, was opened in the 1860s. Vintage blacksmithing techniques are demonstrated Wed. and most Sat. 10-2.

Colorado House/Wells Fargo Museum, on San Diego Ave. facing the plaza, occupies the 1851

Colorado House Hotel. The museum features historical documents and artifacts as well as an 1868 Concord stagecoach. Daily 10-5. Free. Phone (619) 238-3929.

The Courthouse, 2731 San Diego Ave., on the plaza next to Colorado House, was built by the Mormon Battalion in 1847 and is said to have been the town's first fired-brick building. Originally used as a town hall, the structure served as the first courthouse and civic center 1850-72. The present building has been reconstructed. Daily 10-5. Free.

La Casa de Estudillo is at 4001 Mason St. The restored 1827 adobe features Spanish and Early American relics, period furnishings and a garden. The house was built by the former commander of the San Diego Presidio. Daily 10-5. Free.

Machado-Stewart Adobe is next to Mason Street School. The restored adobe, built in the 1830s, depicts the everyday lifestyle during the Mexican period of early San Diego. Daily 10-5. Living history demonstrations of crafts, candle making, and cooking are presented Wed. 10-noon. Free.

Mason Street School, Mason and Congress sts., is a one-room frame building erected in 1865. After being moved to another location and used for other purposes, the building was returned to its original site and restored. Daily 10-4. Free.

Old Town Dental Museum is on San Diego Ave. A replica of a late 19th-century dentist's office, the museum displays period furnishings and dental equipment. Daily 10-5. Free.

Old Town Plaza, bounded by San Diego Ave. and Wallace, Calhoun and Mason sts., was the center of community life after the formation of the pueblo of San Diego in 1821.

Robinson-Rose Building, 4002 Wallace St., is a two-story adobe built in 1853 by a successful attorney. Today it houses the park's headquarters and has photo murals and a carefully crafted scale model of Old Town as it appeared until 1872. Daily 10-5. Free.

San Diego Union Museum, 2602 San Diego Ave., is in a restored pre-fabricated wooden building erected in 1851. The newspaper was founded here in 1868. The museum is furnished to reflect the 1860s. Daily 10-5. Free.

Seeley Stables Visitor Information Center, 2648 Calhoun St., is a reconstructed 1869 stable. Now a museum, the building houses a collection of horse-drawn vehicles, including covered wagons and stagecoaches; Western memorabilia; and American Indian artifacts. Slide shows are presented on the hour. Daily 10-5. Guided walking tours depart daily at 10:30 and 2. Free.

WHALEY HOUSE, 2482 San Diego Ave., dates from 1857 and is thought to be the first two-story brick house built in Southern California. The building has served as a residence, store, courthouse and theater; it now showcases restored period furnishings. Also displayed is an 1860 life mask of Abraham Lincoln. Daily 10-4:30; closed holidays. Admission $4; over 64, $3; ages 5-17, $2. Phone (619) 298-2482.

Point Loma

★**CABRILLO NATIONAL MONUMENT,** overlooking the city and harbor, is at the s. end of Cabrillo Memorial Dr. (SR 209) on Point Loma; it is approached through the gates of the Naval Ocean Systems Center. The monument commemorates Juan Rodríguez Cabrillo's exploration of the West Coast of the United States in 1542. The lighthouse, which beaconed ships to San Diego Harbor 1855-91, has been refurbished.

An overlook provides a good vantage for observing the migration of Pacific gray whales from December through February. Tidepools offer a chance to explore coastal marine life. Recorded information is provided at the lighthouse and whale overlook.

A coast artillery system that defended San Diego Harbor during World Wars I and II is visible from Bayside Trail. The trail follows an old military road and allows glimpses of the plants and animals that comprise a coastal sage scrub community.

The visitor center presents films, has exhibits about Cabrillo's voyage and provides information about park activities. Daily 9-5:15; possible extended hours in summer. Admission $5 per private vehicle or $2 per person arriving by other means; permanent U.S. residents with Golden Age Passport and under 17 free. For more information contact Cabrillo National Monument, 1800 Cabrillo Memorial Dr., San Diego, CA 92106-0670; phone (619) 557-5450.

SUNSET CLIFFS along Sunset Cliffs Blvd. between Hill St. and Point Loma Ave., affords seascape views from rocky cliffs that have been carved into unusual shapes by the surf.

San Diego Bay
The U.S. Coast Guard Base, U.S. Marine Training Center and the U.S. Marine Corps Air Station flank the bay.

[SAVE] ★ **MARITIME MUSEUM OF SAN DIEGO**, on the Embarcadero at 1306 N. Harbor Dr., encompasses three historic vessels: the 1863 tall ship *Star of India*, the 289-foot 1898 ferry *Berkeley*, and the 1904 steam yacht *Medea*. Nautical and oceanographic exhibits are featured. Allow 1 hour minimum. Daily 9-8. Admission $5; over 61 and ages 13-17, $4; ages 6-12, $2. DS, MC, VI. Phone (619) 234-9153.

SEAPORT VILLAGE, at Kettner Blvd. and West Harbor Dr., is a 14-acre landscaped dining, shopping and entertainment complex in a harborside setting. Within the village is a restored Looff carrousel and an 8-acre park. Daily 10-10, June-Aug.; 10-9, rest of year. Free. Parking free for 2

hours with validation, $1 per half-hour thereafter. Phone (619) 235-4014.

Other Points of Interest
CHILDREN'S MUSEUM/MUSEO DE LOS NIÑOS, downtown at 200 W. Island Ave. at the corner of Front St., introduces children to various cultures via hands-on activities such as Curious Canvas, a 1952 Dodge truck that kids can paint. The Improv Theatre offers costumes and a stage for make believe, while creative talents can paint and shape clay. Educational displays change monthly. Tues.-Sun. 10-5. Admission $5; over 65, $3; under 2 free. Phone (619) 233-5437.

[SAVE] **FIREHOUSE MUSEUM,** downtown at 1572 Columbia St., contains antique fire equipment, an old steamer, helmets and other items from around the world. Thurs.-Fri. 10-2, Sat.-Sun. 10-4; closed holidays. Admission $2; over 64, ages 13-17 and military in uniform $1; firefighters free; free to all first Thurs. of the month. Phone (619) 232-3473.

★ **MISSION BASILICA SAN DIEGO DE ALCALÀ**, 10818 San Diego Mission Rd. in Mission Valley, is reached via Mission Gorge Rd. (off I-8) and Twain Ave. The first of California's missions, it was founded July 16, 1769, by Father Junípero Serra at Presidio Hill, moved to its present site in 1774, destroyed by earthquakes in 1803 and 1812 and subsequently rebuilt. Taped tours are

available at the visitor center. Daily 9-5; closed Thanksgiving and Dec. 25. Admission $2; over 54 and students $1; under 12, 50c. Phone (619) 281-8449.

MISSION TRAILS REGIONAL PARK VISITOR & INTERPRETIVE CENTER, 8 mi. n.e. at 1 Junipero Serra Tr., is an imaginatively designed and spacious structure housing displays and hands-on equipment interpreting the natural history, plants and wildlife of the park's nearly 5,200 acres. Free hiking trail maps and videotape presentations about various aspects of the park are available. Picnicking is permitted. Pets must be kept on a leash. Park open daily dawn-dusk. Visitor center open daily 9-5; closed Jan. 1, Thanksgiving and Dec. 25. Free. Phone (619) 668-3275.

[SAVE] **MUSEUM OF CONTEMPORARY ART DOWNTOWN,** downtown at 1001 Kettner Blvd. at Broadway, is the auxiliary facility of the main museum in La Jolla. Four galleries on two levels have permanent and changing exhibits of contemporary paintings, sculptures, prints, drawings and videotapes. Tues.-Sat. 10-5, Sun. noon-5; closed Jan. 1, Thanksgiving and Dec. 25. Admission $2, under 13 free; free to all first Tues. of the month. Phone (619) 234-1001.

★ **SAN DIEGO WILD ANIMAL PARK—** *see Escondido p. 73.*

What To Do
Sightseeing

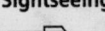
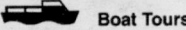 **Boat Tours**

Since much of San Diego's activity centers on its harbor, a cruise provides an excellent perspective of the city.

CLASSIC SEA ADVENTURES, *SOUL DIVERSION,* Best Western Island Palms Hotel on Shelter Island, is a 35-foot sailing craft that offers afternoon and evening cruises on the ocean or in San Diego Bay. Passengers may take the helm and participate in the sailing. Daily 1-5 and 5:30-7:30, mid-Mar. to mid-Dec.; 8:30-12:30 and 1-5, rest of year. Fare $50. There is a limit of six passengers per cruise. Reservations are required. DS, MC, VI. Phone (619) 224-0800 or (800) 659-0141.

HORNBLOWER DINING YACHTS, 1066 N. Harbor Dr., next to the cruise ship terminal, offers 1- and 2-hour narrated tours of San Diego Bay. The 1-hour trip offers views of the San Diego skyline, historic ships, shipyards and Navy vessels. Nightly dinner/dance, Sunday champagne brunch and winter whale watching cruises also are available; reservations are required.

One-hour trip departs daily at 10, 11:15, 12:45 and 4:15 (also at 2:30, Memorial Day-Labor Day). The 2-hour cruise departs at 2 (also at 9:45 and 12:15, Memorial Day-Labor Day). One-hour tour $12; over 55 and military with ID $10; un-der 12, $6. Two-hour tour $17; over 55 and military with ID $15; ages 3-12, $8.50. AE, DI, DS, MC, VI. Phone (619) 234-8687.

[SAVE] **ORION SAILING CHARTERS** is at 3842 Liggett Dr. behind the Sheraton San Diego Hotel and Marina. This company offers guided sailing tours and whale-watching excursions. Sightseeing tours depart daily at 9, 1 and 5:30. Whale-watching tours are available Dec.-Mar. Fare $45. Phone (619) 574-7504.

SAN DIEGO-CORONADO FERRY runs between the dock at Broadway and Harbor Dr. in San Diego and the Ferry Landing Marketplace at B Ave. and 1st St. in Coronado. The ferry leaves San Diego on the hour and Coronado on the half-hour; crossings take approximately 15 minutes. Sun.-Thurs. 9-9, Fri.-Sat. 9 a.m.-10 p.m. One-way fare $2; 50c additional for bicycles. Phone (619) 234-4111.

SAN DIEGO HARBOR EXCURSION departs from 1050 N. Harbor Dr. near the foot of Broadway. Sights include the largest Navy fleet in the continental United States and the San Diego-Coronado Bay Bridge. Dinner cruises also are offered. The 1-hour trip departs daily 10-5:30, mid-June through Sept. 30; 10-4:15, rest of year. The 2-hour cruise departs daily at 9:45, 12:30 and 2, mid-June through Sept. 30; Mon.-Fri. at 2:45 and 5:30, Sat.-Sun. and holidays at 9:45, 12:30 and 2, rest of year.

One-hour fare $12; over 55 and military with ID $10; ages 4-12, $6. Two-hour fare $17; over 55 and military with ID $15; ages 4-12, $8.50. AE, DI, DS, MC, VI. Phone (619) 234-4111 or (800) 442-7847.

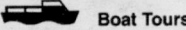 **Bus, Limousine and Trolley Tours**

A good way to become acquainted with the city is to take a bus or limousine tour. Bus tour destinations range from Los Angeles to Ensenada, Mexico. Gray Line San Diego Tours, (619) 491-0011, at 1775 Hancock St., Suite 130, offers more than 15 trips varying in price and itinerary. Tours pick up from most major hotels and depart from the terminal at 1775 Hancock St.

San Diego Mini-Tours, (619) 477-8687, offers narrated bus tours of San Diego as well as trips to Tijuana, Ensenada and Rosarito. Other touring companies are listed in the telephone directory. Reservations should be made a day in advance.

OLD TOWN TROLLEY TOURS, with departure points at various locations, hotels and attractions throughout town, offers 2-hour trolley-bus excursions that visit Balboa Park, Horton Plaza, the Gaslamp Quarter, Seaport Village, the Embarcadero, Old Town and Coronado. Passengers have boarding and reboarding privileges at each stop. Daily 9-5, early June-early Oct.; 9-4, rest of year. Closed Jan. 1, Thanksgiving and Dec. 25. Fare $20; ages 4-12, $8. Phone (619) 298-8687.

SAVE SAN DIEGO SCENIC TOURS picks up passengers from most local hotels. Narrated half- and full-day tours are offered aboard air-conditioned minibuses. The San Diego tour counts Balboa Park, Embarcadero, Gaslamp Quarter and La Jolla Cove among its numerous highlights. Also offered are hour-long San Diego Bay harbor tours, which are available only in conjunction with other tours; tours of Tijuana; and combination tours.

Tours depart daily at 8:30 and 2, depending on the tour. Fares $24-$48; over 59, $22-$46; ages 3-11, $9-$19. Some tours offer family rates. Reservations are required. MC, VI. Phone (619) 273-8687.

 **Driving Tours**

A 59-mile scenic drive is marked at frequent intervals by blue and gold signs with a white sea gull. The drive begins at Broadway Pier, although it can be joined at any point. It takes in the Embarcadero, Shelter and Harbor islands, Point Loma, Mission Bay, La Jolla, Old Town and Balboa Park. The loop can be driven in about 3 hours, but time should be allowed for sightseeing. Avoid driving during rush hours.

 Hot Air Balloon Tours

HOT AIR BALLOON RIDES provide panoramic views of San Diego County areas. Sunset Balloon Flights, (800) 558-5828, offer tours year-round (weather permitting). Flights last approximately 1 hour. Fares range $125-$150. Beverages and snacks usually are included. Reservations are required. Rides are not advisable for children under age 8. All pilots are FAA certified.

Note: The mention of the preceding hot air balloon rides is for information only and does **not** imply endorsement by AAA.

 Plane Tours

BIPLANE & AIR COMBAT ADVENTURES departs from McClellan-Palomar Airport, 3 mi. e. of I-5 on Palomar Airport Rd. in Carlsbad. Scenic tours over San Diego County as well as mock combat flights are offered in vintage aircraft. Flights last 20 minutes to an hour. Daily 10-dusk. Fares range $49-$149 for biplane trips; $179-$249 for air combat trips. Reservations are required. MC, VI. Phone (760) 438-7680 or (800) 759-5667.

Note: The mention of the preceding airplane ride is for information only and does **not** imply endorsement by AAA.

 Walking Tours

Pedestrians can take a self-guiding tour of Old Town San Diego State Historic Park, which is closed to vehicular traffic. Guide booklets giving a brief history of Old Town are available for $2 at the park headquarters in Robinson-Rose Building, 4002 Wallace St.

Within the following description of the tour, the names of sites listed in detail in the Attractions section are printed in bold type. Even if you do not tour a listed site, reading the listing when you reach that point should make the tour more interesting.

Go south from the visitor center and turn east on San Diego Ave.; you will pass a number of historic one-story buildings, including the 1840s Machado-Silvas Adobe. At the reconstructed first San Diego **Courthouse** and the **Colorado House/Wells Fargo Museum,** turn south on the walkway to **Machado-Stewart Adobe,** once the home of a shipmate of author Richard Henry Dana. A visit to the adobe was described in Dana's classic "Two Years Before the Mast."

Diagonally north of Machado-Stewart Adobe on Mason St. is **Mason Street School,** a one-room frame building erected in 1865. This building served as the city's first publicly owned schoolhouse. Walk north on Mason St. to San Diego Ave. and the **Old Town Dental Museum** and continue east to Dodson's Corner, a group of small false-front shops where merchants sometimes dress in period costumes. Across San Diego Ave. is the **San Diego Union Museum,** birthplace of Southern California's oldest continuously published newspaper.

Walk northward on Twiggs St.; around the corner at 2648 Calhoun St. are the **Seeley Stables.** Head north along the west side of the stables, then slightly east, to **Black Hawk Smithy & Stable.** Adjacent stands Casa de Bandini, an L-shaped structure built in 1827 for Juan Bandini. A second floor was added in 1869 and the building became a hotel; today it is a Mexican restaurant.

Walk west on Calhoun St. to **Johnson House** and the neighboring Alvarado House. Retrace your steps and head south on Mason St., stopping for a visit at historic **La Casa de Estudillo.** Directly across the street on Mason is **Old Town Plaza,** a good place to end the tour.

A stroll around downtown's Gaslamp Quarter, bounded by Broadway, 4th Ave., 6th Ave. and Harbor Dr., provides an overview of the city's architectural and commercial history. Many buildings in this 16.5-block, 38-acre area have been restored to their original beauty. Surrounded by gaslamps and brick sidewalks, the Victorian craftsmanship evident in the historic district blends with an abundance of restaurants, antique shops and galleries.

Adjoining the district, particularly along the 600 and 800 blocks of G St., are arts and crafts shops and coffee houses well worth exploring. For more information about the area, phone the Gaslamp Quarter Association at (619) 233-5227 of 233-4691.

The Gaslamp Quarter Historical Foundation maintains an office in the 1850 William Heath Davis House at 4th and Island aves. Guided walking tours of The Gaslamp area depart from this museum Sat. at 11; audiocassette tours also are available. The museum is open Mon.-Fri. 10-2, Sat. 10-4, and Sun. noon-4. Admission to the museum is free. The guided tour costs $5 for over age 11; the audiocassette tour fee is $5. Phone (619) 233-4692.

Nature lovers will enjoy monthly bird-watching walks at Point Loma. Led by knowledgeable volunteers, the tours leave from the Cabrillo National Monument visitor center. For information phone (619) 557-5450.

Sports and Recreation

Because of its mild climate, San Diego is a haven for year-round recreation. Outdoor sports draw nearly as many visitors to the city as the sightseeing attractions.

Miles of shoreline and two large, protected bays provide ideal settings for all types of water sports. **Swimming** opportunities include the ocean, Mission Bay and public pools. Ocean swimming is best June through November. The more popular beaches have lifeguards on duty daily.

Surfing is an all-year activity, but wet suits are advised in winter. Among the popular surfing beaches are La Jolla Shores Beach, Pacific Beach Park, Mission Beach, Tourmaline Surfing Park, Windansea Park and Imperial Beach.

Water skiing conditions are excellent on the calm waters of the bays. San Diego Bay has restricted areas due to naval and commercial traffic, but water skiing is permitted within Glorietta Bay. Skiing is permitted in certain sections of Mission Bay from dawn to dusk.

Boating is a favorite pastime; hundreds of pleasure boats dot the ocean and bays daily. The major boating centers are Shelter and Harbor islands, Glorietta Bay and Mission Bay marinas. Rental and launching facilities for paddle and fishing boats, sailboats and powerboats are available at these areas.

Fishing enthusiasts can enjoy many varieties of the sport: deep-sea, surf, pier, bay, shell and freshwater. Bottom-feeding fish are attracted by offshore kelp beds, and nearby Mexican waters contain barracuda, bass, bonito and yellowtail. Public piers are at Shelter Island, Ocean Beach and Imperial Beach. Fishing charters depart from Point Loma and Quivira Basin at Mission Bay Park.

Golf courses in San Diego County number more than 80, ranging from seaside to desert locations. Mission Bay Golf Center is lighted for evening play.

Tennis courts for public play are scattered throughout the area. The best are in La Jolla, Coronado and Mission Bay. Most resort areas also have tennis facilities.

Bicycling is a good way to tour this sunshine city. There are several marked bike routes and numerous rental shops.

Horseback riding clubs offer horse rentals and riding facilities, and there are several horse rental agencies throughout the area. Bright Valley Farm, in Spring Valley, has hundreds of acres of riding trails.

Spectator sports are many and varied. Qualcomm Stadium is the home of two major league teams: the Padres, **baseball**, and the Chargers, **football**. San Diego Sports Arena plays host to special sports events. Local college and university teams provide added entertainment.

Horse racing takes place at Del Mar Racetrack, 20 miles north. Across the border in Tijuana, Agua Caliente Racetrack has **dog racing**. Another prominent spectator sport in Mexico is **bullfighting**.

Note: Policies concerning admittance of children to pari-mutuel betting facilities vary. Phone ahead for information.

For more information about sports and recreation contact the Automobile Club of Southern California, 815 Date St., P.O. Box 1031, San Diego, CA 92112-1031; phone (619) 233-1000. Information about recreational opportunities can be obtained from the Community Park and Recreation Division, (619) 685-1300.

Shopping

Mission Valley is the premier shopping area in the city. Its emergence can be attributed to its easy freeway access and its two large shopping centers—Fashion Valley and Mission Valley. The two centers are within a few minutes of each other and have a combined total of more than 175 stores and restaurants. Fashion Valley, at SR 163 and Friars Road, is anchored by JCPenney, Macy's and Neiman-Marcus, while Mission Valley, at I-8 and Mission Center Road offers Macy's and Robinsons-May.

Other regional shopping centers include Grossmont Center in La Mesa, near the intersection of the I-8 and SR 125 freeways, and La Jolla Village Square, west of I-5, and University Towne Centre, east of I-5, in La Jolla. These contain a variety of department stores, including Macy's, JCPenney, Robinsons-May and Saks Fifth Avenue.

Seaport Village at Kettner Boulevard and Harbor Drive has specialty shops (see San Diego Bay p. 181). The Olde Cracker Factory, 448 W. Market St., is an antique buff's delight. Within the three-story building more than 40 dealers display antiques and collectibles.

Among historic sites in Old Town are numerous attractive shops, including those at Old San Diego Galleria. International items can be found at Bazaar del Mundo, and Dodson's Corner recreates a 19th-century shopping atmosphere. At

Rosecrans, Taylor and San Diego avenues is Pottery Village, where small exhibits about 19th-century California life are interspersed with departments of gift items.

Along the Embarcadero are boutiques featuring clothing, jewelry and sea-related items. Downtown at 7th and L streets fresh fruits and vegetables, homemade foods and hand-crafted gifts attract shoppers to the Farmers Bazaar. Art, craft and specialty shops are featured in the downtown Gaslamp Quarter.

Shoppers in San Diego also will be lured to the Mexican border city of Tijuana. Because of its free port status, Tijuana offers tempting bargains on imported goods. Prices of Mexican products also are reasonable. Major shopping areas include Mercado de Artesanías (Mexican Arts and Crafts), Plaza Río Tijuana Shopping Center and Avenida Revolución, the city's oldest tourist shopping area.

HORTON PLAZA is between Broadway, G St. and 1st and 4th aves. downtown. Distinguished by its multicolored architecture and outdoor entertainment, the five-level plaza houses three major department stores, more than 140 specialty shops, a 14-screen cinema, a theater and restaurants. Stores open Mon.-Sat. 10-9, Sun. 11-7, July-Aug.; Mon.-Fri. 10-9, Sat. 10-6, Sun. 11-7 (with extended holiday hours), rest of year. Restaurants, theaters and some shops have extended hours. Parking is available in an adjacent garage; 3 hours are free with validation. Phone (800) 214-7467.

Theater and Concerts

San Diego has become a major city in terms of its varied cultural offerings. The San Diego Concourse on 1st Avenue between A and C streets contains the City Administration Building, exhibit halls, the 3,000-seat Civic Theatre and the 4,000-seat Golden Hall. The theater and hall are venues for ballets, operas, plays, musicals and concerts. Copley Symphony Hall, a converted 1929 movie house at 7th and B streets, is the cornerstone of Symphony Towers, which also contains a hotel and shopping arcade.

San Diego Convention Center, 111 W. Harbor Dr., is done in a modern architectural style, with a portion of its roof line suggesting huge sails. The center has exhibit rooms, an open-air covered pavilion and an amphitheater.

The Civic Theatre is home to the San Diego Opera Company; free backstage-tours of the building are offered early Friday evening before performances. For opera information phone (619) 232-7636.

Balboa Park's Simon Edison Centre for the Performing Arts encompasses Lowell Davies Festival Theatre; Old Globe Theatre; and Cassius Carter Centre Stage. Contemporary and classic works are presented throughout the year; Shakespeare is emphasized in the summer.

The Coronado Playhouse on the Silver Strand stages cabaret-style musicals, while Welk Resort Theatre in Escondido entertains guests with Broadway hits. Theater in Old Town offers classic and experimental plays. Mystery Café offers interactive theater.

Mandell-Weiss Center on the University of California San Diego campus in La Jolla presents plays and musicals by professional touring groups in La Jolla Playhouse. San Diego Sports Arena often books top-name shows.

TIMES ARTS TIX, a public service of the San Diego Performing Arts League, sells half-price performance-day tickets for many attractions. The box office is downtown at Broadway and Broadway Circle in Horton Plaza Park. Phone (619) 497-5000 Tues.-Thurs. 11-6, Fri.-Sat. 10-6.

Special Events

San Diego celebrates St. Patrick's Day with a parade in mid-March. April activities include the San Diego Crew Classic at Mission Bay, while May brings the Cinco de Mayo celebration.

Miramar's Naval Air Show takes place in late July or early August. In mid-September the Budweiser APA Thunderboat Gold Cup Races are held in Mission Bay. The Dixieland Jazz Festival, held Thanksgiving weekend, is a popular event, as is the Holiday Bowl football game in late December.

AREA CODE CHANGE FOR SOUTHERN CALIFORNIA

In June 1999 an area code split will occur in Southern California. The southern portion of the area will retain the 619 area code. The new 858 area code will be assumed by the northern portion of the area, which includes the following communities: Del Mar, La Jolla, Poway and Rancho Bernardo.

Permissive dialing begins June 12, 1999. Mandatory use of the 858 area code begins Dec. 11, 1999.

The San Diego Vicinity

CHULA VISTA (L-7)
pop. 135,200, elev. 75'

ARCO OLYMPIC TRAINING CENTER OF THE UNITED STATES OLYMPIC COMMITTEE is 8 mi. e. of I-805 on Telegraph Canyon Rd., then 2 mi. s. on Wueste Rd. Eucalyptus trees line the paths that traverse the grounds of this training 152-acre facility for top-notch athletes. Guided 1- to 1.5-hour tours begin in Copley Visitor Center, where a 30-minute videotape presentation about the Olympics is shown. Mon.-Sat. 9-5, Sun. noon-5. Free. Phone (619) 482-6222. *See color ad p. 181.*

SAVE CHULA VISTA NATURE CENTER is at 1000 Gunpowder Point Dr.; access is by shuttle bus, departing every 20 minutes from a parking lot just w. of I-5 at E St. The center offers a 1.5-mile walking trail as well as hands-on exhibits interpreting the surrounding marshland habitat. Observation decks allow views of indigenous flora and fauna and migratory birds. Tues.-Sun. (also Mon., Memorial Day-Labor Day); closed holidays. Last shuttle departs 1 hour before closing. Admission $3.50; over 64, $2.50; ages 6-17, $1; free to all first Tues. of the month. Phone (619) 422-2473.

CORONADO (L-6) pop. 26,500, elev. 27'

On a peninsula between San Diego Bay and the Pacific Ocean, Coronado is a beach resort, convention center and attractive residential town. The San Diego-Coronado Bay Bridge connects Coronado to San Diego. The 1888 Hotel del Coronado, commonly called "the Del," is a well-known landmark and resort with Victorian turrets and cupolas. During the holiday season white lights adorn the hotel's exterior and establishments along Orange Avenue leading to it also are decorated.

Boat rentals and sightseeing charters are available at the dock next to the boathouse on Glorietta Bay. A ferry service runs from Ferry Landing Marketplace at B Avenue and 1st Street to San Diego *(see Boat Tours p. 182).* Gondola di Venezia offers cruises through Coronado Cays aboard traditional, handcrafted Venetian gondolas; phone (619) 221-2999.

Local businesses offer bicycle rentals. Silver Strand State Beach, 4.5 miles south of town, allows picnicking, surfing and swimming *(see Recreation Chart).*

Hotel de Coronado and SAVE Coronado Touring both offer guided walking tours that detail Coronado's history. The hotel tours depart Wednesday throughThursday at 10 and 11 and cost $15 per person. Coronado Touring trips depart from Glorietta Bay Inn, 1630 Glorietta Blvd., on Tuesday, Thursday and Saturday at 11 and cost $6; phone (619) 435-5892 or 435-5993.

Coronado Visitor Information Center: 1047 B Ave., Coronado, CA 92118; (619) 437-8788.

DEL MAR (L-6) pop. 4,900, elev. 122'

Del Mar's fairgrounds complex is home to Thoroughbred racing from late July to mid-September.

Greater Del Mar Chamber of Commerce: 1104 Camino Del Mar #214, Del Mar, CA 92014; phone (619) 755-4844.

HOT AIR BALLOON RIDES over Del Mar provide views of the coastline, rolling hills and reservoir-dotted valleys. Pre- or post-flight beverages and snacks usually are included. The following two companies fly year-round (weather permitting): A Skysurfer Balloon Co., (619) 481-6800 or (800) 660-6809, and California Dreamin' Balloon Tours, (760) 438-9550 or (800) 373-3359.

Flights are about 1 hour and depart just after dawn or just before dusk. Reservations are required. Fares range $135-$160. Rides are not advisable for children under age 8. All pilots are FAA certified.

Note: The mention of the preceding hot air balloon rides is for information only and does not imply endorsement by AAA.

TORREY PINES STATE RESERVE, 1,750 acres on N. Torrey Pines Rd., is the natural habitat of the Torrey pine, which Pacific winds often twist into unusual shapes. Self-guiding tours, nature walks and a museum are available; camping, pets and picnicking are not permitted. Reserve open daily 9-dusk. Museum daily 11-5. Nature walks conducted Sat.-Sun. at 11:30 and 1:30. Fee $4 per private vehicle; over 61, $3 per private vehicle. Pedestrians and bicyclists free. Phone (619) 755-2063.

EL CAJON (L-7) pop. 88,700, elev. 435'

SAVE HERITAGE OF THE AMERICAS MUSEUM is at 12110 Cuyamaca College Dr. W. Set atop a hill commanding a sweeping view of the campus and surrounding area, the museum is a cultural and educational center reflecting the natural and human history of the Americas. Exhibits include minerals and meteorites, fossils, seashells, tribal tools, effigies, ornaments, baskets and jewelry as well as a small art gallery. Tues.-Fri. 10-4, Sat. 1-5. Admission $3; over 55, $2; students with ID $1; under 13 free. Phone (619) 670-5194.

LA JOLLA (L-6) pop. 28,800, elev. 110'

Within the city limits of San Diego, La Jolla (Lah HOY-yah) is a popular resort graced with a rocky coast and fine beaches. Carved out of sandstone cliffs by centuries of wave action, Sunny Jim Cave is accessible via a staircase in a souvenir shop at 1325 Coast Blvd. La Jolla Cove affords excellent swimming, beachcombing, and scuba and skin diving.

[SAVE] La Jolla Tours offers 90-minute to 2-hour guided walking tours of historic buildings, scenic areas of the downtown coast, and Sunny Jim Cave. Trips depart from Colonial Inn at 910 Prospect St. Reservations are required; phone (619) 453-8219.

La Jolla Town Council: 7734 Herschel, Suite E, La Jolla, CA 92037; phone (619) 454-1444.

[SAVE] ★ **BIRCH AQUARIUM AT SCRIPPS INSTITUTE OF OCEANOGRAPHY,** 2300 Expedition Way, is on a hillside above Scripps Institution of Oceanography at the University of California, San Diego. The aquarium features marine life from both the cold northern waters and the warm tropical seas of the Pacific Ocean. Interactive exhibits and changing displays explore the latest developments in oceanography. During January and February exhibits about the migrating California gray whales are presented. The aquarium also offers whale-watching boat rides. Daily 9-5; closed Thanksgiving and Dec. 25. Admission

$7.50; over 60, $6.50; ages 13-17, $4.50; ages 3-12, $3.50. Parking $3. Phone (619) 534-3474.

[SAVE] **MUSEUM OF CONTEMPORARY ART SAN DIEGO,** 700 Prospect St., features gallery viewing on two levels as well as a sculpture garden. Rotating exhibitions of paintings, sculpture, prints, drawings and other works are presented throughout the year. The permanent collection includes examples of minimalist, conceptual and California art. Tues.-Sat. 10-5 (also Wed. 5-8), Sun. noon-5. Admission $4, senior citizens, military and students with ID $2, under 12 free; free to all first Tues. and Sun. of the month. Phone (619) 454-3541.

THE SALK INSTITUTE FOR BIOLOGICAL STUDIES, 10010 N. Torrey Pines Rd., is one of the world's foremost centers conducting biomedical research. Areas of focus include molecular biology, genetics, and the neurosciences. The 26-acre campus overlooks the Pacific Ocean; its laboratories are housed in buildings designed by modernist architect Louis I. Kahn for the institute's founding director Jonas Salk. Guided architectural tours are given Mon.-Fri. by appointment; closed holidays. Free. Phone (619) 453-4100, ext. 1200.

This ends listings for the San Diego Vicinity.
The following page resumes the alphabetical listings of
cities in California.

Now You Can Count on AAA for Financial Services Too!

*N*ow, your AAA membership offers even more. Choose from a full range of financial products and services with special AAA member-only rates and features.

AAA Member Select℠ Prime Access℠ Credit Card

AAA Member Select℠ Rewards Credit Card

AAA Member Select℠ Platinum VISA® Credit Card

Auto Loans & Leasing

Home Equity Loans[1]

Personal Loans

Market Rate Checking

Money Market Accounts

Certificates of Deposit[2]

Financial Services

MAKE THE MOST OF YOUR MEMBERSHIP.℠

1-800-680-AAA4

24 HOURS A DAY. 7 DAYS A WEEK.

Available only through participating AAA clubs.

Equal Housing Lender

San Francisco

Civic devotion is the most noticeable characteristic of San Francisco residents; indeed, it is one of the few matters upon which they unanimously agree. The city is comparatively young, yet seldom is there found a greater passion for preservation of the past with all its colorful legends and architecture. This spirit is evident in the preservation of historic buildings as well as the famous cable cars.

Combined with this love of the city is the great determination and courage that rebuilt the city not once but seven times after devastating fires. Six of them came within a period of two boomtown years; the last one, which destroyed four-fifths of the town (28,000 buildings), blazed for days after the 1906 earthquake broke the water mains and rendered the firefighting equipment useless.

Possibly it is the beauty of San Francisco's setting that commands such loyalty. Varying in altitude from sea level to 929 feet, the city rests on 40 hills at the tip of a narrow peninsula, bounded on one side by the Pacific Ocean and on the other by San Francisco Bay, one of the largest land-locked harbors in the world.

It was the city's bayside location that attracted its earliest colonizers. A permanent European settlement was established in 1776, when the presidio, or Spanish military post, was begun at the end of the peninsula. During that same year the Franciscan fathers founded the Mission San Francisco de Asis.

A trail from the presidio to the mission was established, and about halfway between the two there sprang up a halting place known as El Paraje de Yerba Buena, the place of the good herb, around what is now Portsmouth Square. It was not until 1835 that the town of Yerba Buena—later to be called San Francisco—was founded.

For more than 13 years the village had fewer than 100 inhabitants, but with the discovery of gold in the American River in 1848 the population rapidly increased to well over 10,000. Through San Francisco poured thousands of hopefuls from all over the world, and back to it came most of the '49ers, both the successful and the disappointed, when it was all over.

San Francisco's population comprises citizens of Chinese, Japanese, Hispanic, Italian, Russian and other ancestry. This diversity contributes to a spirit of broadminded sophistication and tolerance. Cultural, cosmopolitan San Francisco has given birth to interesting

offspring as well, from the United Nations to the topless dancer.

The best example of San Francisco's good-humored tolerance took place during the years jokingly called the Reign of Emperor Norton. A British businessman driven insane by financial failure, Joshua Norton in 1859 declared himself Emperor of these United States and Protector of Mexico.

For 21 years he "ruled" San Francisco, the residents of which gladly indulged his grandiose whims. Even some of his edicts were followed, for beneath his grand and flowery language flowed a strong, sane sense of humanitarian reform and practical public interest. When Emperor Norton I died in 1880, more than 30,000 San Franciscans attended his funeral.

Today's San Francisco, still fun-loving, also is an important industrial, tourist and financial center. Its financial district at the lower end of Montgomery Street is often called "Wall Street West." Furthermore, the city port handles huge amounts of cargo annually and ranks among the top 10 ports in the world for passenger traffic. George R. Moscone Convention Center occupies a city block between Third and Fourth streets and Howard and Folsom streets and is built almost entirely underground. Across the street is the Center for the Arts at the Yerba Buena Gardens, a visual and performing arts complex.

A fine example of San Francisco's Victorian architecture is the 1886 Queen Anne Haas-Lilienthal House, a mansion at 2007 Franklin Street.

San Francisco provides scenic access via I-280 to San Jose and SR 1 to San Luis Obispo along the coast.

The crests of many city hills, particularly Twin Peaks, afford matchless views of downtown and the East Bay. At night when the bridges are lighted, the view is even more impressive. Standing on a hilltop, watching the fog swirl in through the Golden Gate and looking at the city's skyline, it is easy to understand Rudyard Kipling's lament: "San Francisco has only one drawback—'tis hard to leave."

Approaches

By Car

Scenic north-south routes passing directly through San Francisco are US 101 and SR 1. They enter the city separately from the south, merge on the San Francisco approach to the Golden Gate Bridge and continue as one through a few miles of southern Marin County. Because SR 1, the coastal route, is subject to dense fog and the likelihood of landslides, you should check weather and road conditions before driving it.

The fast north-south route, I-5, lies east of San Francisco; connections to the San Francisco-Oakland Bay Bridge are via I-580 and I-880 from the north and I-580 and I-880 (with a detour on I-980) from the south. Another route, SR 99, closely parallels I-5 and also has connections into the city.

THE INFORMED TRAVELER

City Population: 724,000

Elevation: 63 ft.

Sales Tax: State and county sales taxes total 8.6% in San Francisco. A lodging tax called a transient occupancy tax of 12% also is levied.

WHOM TO CALL

Emergency: 911

Police (non-emergency): (415) 553-0123

Time: (415) 767-1111

Hospitals: University of California San Francisco, (415) 476-1000; Davies Medical Center, (415) 565-6000; St. Francis Memorial, (415) 353-6000; St. Mary's Medical Center, (415) 668-1000.

WHERE TO LOOK

Newspapers

San Francisco has a number of papers in Chinese, Japanese and other foreign languages, but the major daily newspapers are the morning *Chronicle* and the evening *Examiner*. The two combine to produce a Sunday paper.

Radio and TV

San Francisco radio station KCBS (740 AM) is an all-news/weather station; KQED (88.5 FM) is a member of National Public Radio.

Major TV channels are 2 (FOX), 4 (NBC), 5 (CBS), 7 (ABC) and 9 (PBS). Several stations have programs in Spanish and other languages. For a complete list of radio and television programs, consult the daily newspapers.

Visitor Information

The San Francisco Visitor Information Center, (415) 391-2000, is in Hallidie Plaza at 900 Market St., San Francisco, CA 94102. The center is open Mon.-Fri. 9-5:30, Sat. 9-3, Sun. 10-2; closed Jan. 1, Thanksgiving and Dec. 25.

Information about northern California is available at the Redwood Empire Association Visitor Information Center, (415) 543-8334 or (800) 200-8334, 2801 Leavenworth, 2nd Floor, San Francisco, CA 94133. The center is open daily 10-6, July-Sept.; Tues.-Sat. 10-6, rest of year.

Continued on p. 198.

Most traffic from the east approaches via I-80 across the Sierra. I-80 is closely paralleled by US 50 to Sacramento, from where the Interstate heads west, leading into the city over the San Francisco-Oakland Bay Bridge.

Getting Around

Street System

Market Street, the main thoroughfare, runs diagonally through the city. Major east-west arteries are Bush and Pine, one-way streets with synchronized traffic signals; Bush goes into the city, Pine out. The numbered streets are in the eastern section; the numbered avenues are in the western section. The many one-way streets make a street map helpful.

San Francisco intersections are subject to strict enforcement of the Anti-Gridlock Act, which prohibits pulling into an intersection when traffic makes it questionable that you'll get through before the light turns red. Motorists convicted of violating the act are subject to a fine of $103.

"The Boot" (also known as "The Denver Boot") is a metal clamp which immobilizes a car when attached to the wheel. This device is applied when 5 or more parking tickets have accumulated or if registration is not current; it is removed only when all outstanding fines and/or registration fees and a $50 de-booting fee have been paid. If the fines are not paid, the car may be towed within 72 hours.

The downtown speed limit, unless otherwise posted, is 25 mph—15 mph at blind intersections. Right turns on red are legal unless otherwise posted. Pedestrians using designated crosswalks **always** have the right-of-way. Rush hours are generally 7-9 a.m. and 4-6 p.m.

Parking

Parking can present a problem, but downtown has some large garages and many convenient smaller garages and lots. On-street meter parking is permitted in some areas. Garage fees downtown range from $1.20 per 20 minutes to $6 per hour and from $13 to $29 per day. The only public parking available for recreational vehicles in San Francisco is at 3Com Park.

On-street parking in hilly San Francisco is strictly regulated. In addition to posted tow-away zones, the color of the curb also governs parking. Red means no stopping, standing or parking whatsoever; yellow curbs indicate limited stops for loading and unloading passengers or freight (7 a.m.-6 p.m.). Passenger cars left unattended in downtown yellow or loading zones are subject to heavy fines and towing. Visitors must obtain a release from the nearest district police department before picking up the car at the towing company.

White curbs, usually found at entrances to public buildings, allow short stops to take on or discharge passengers during the hours that the building is in use. Green curbs indicate 10-minute parking 9 a.m.-6 p.m. Blue marks spaces for use by the disabled; the fine for illegal parking in designated spaces for the disabled or bus

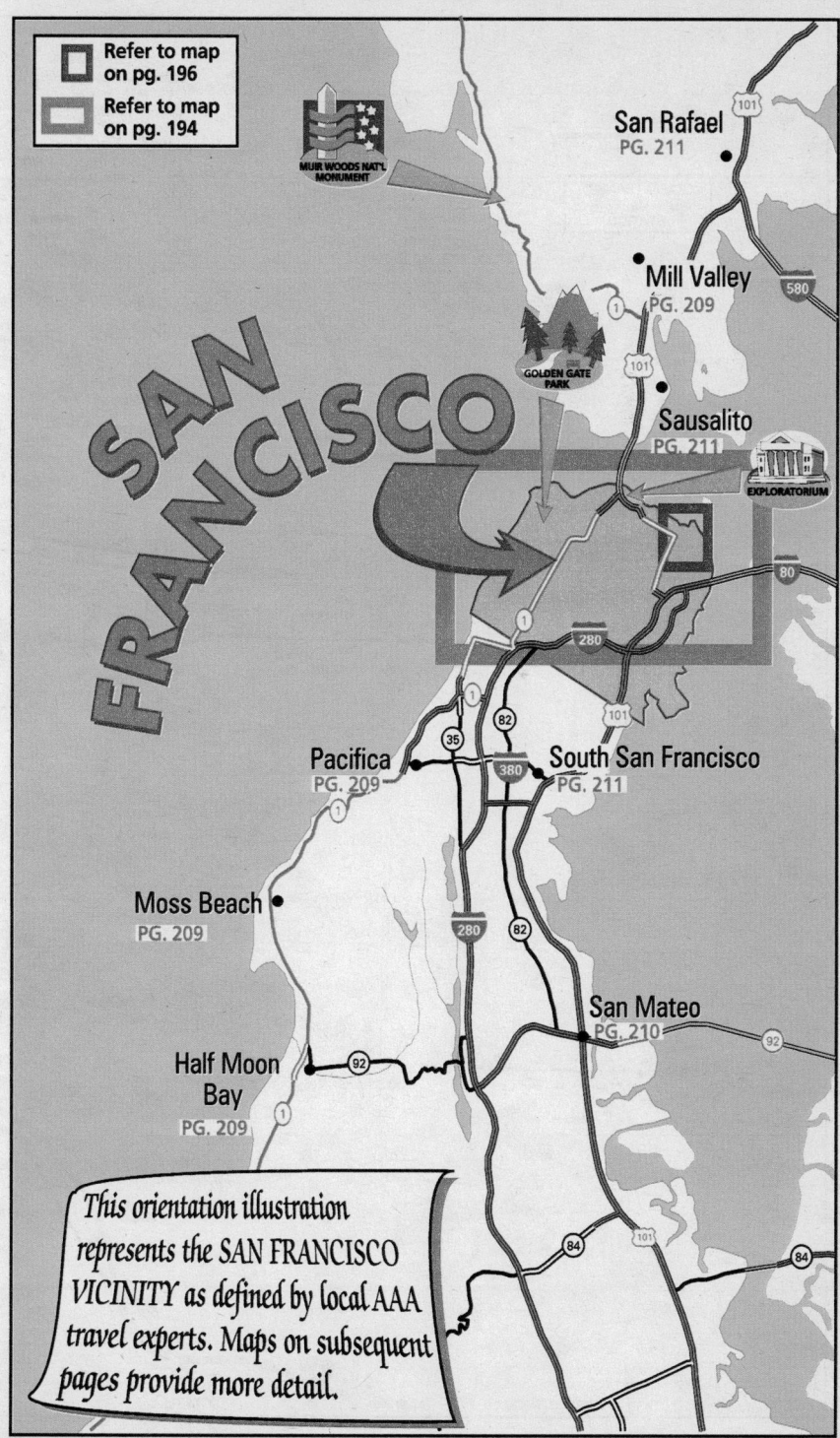

Refer to map on pg. 196

Refer to map on pg. 194

MUIR WOODS NAT'L. MONUMENT

San Rafael
PG. 211

Mill Valley
PG. 209

GOLDEN GATE PARK

Sausalito
PG. 211

EXPLORATORIUM

SAN FRANCISCO

Pacifica
PG. 209

South San Francisco
PG. 211

Moss Beach
PG. 209

San Mateo
PG. 210

Half Moon Bay
PG. 209

This orientation illustration represents the SAN FRANCISCO VICINITY as defined by local AAA travel experts. Maps on subsequent pages provide more detail.

SAN FRANCISCO

Scale in Miles   0 — .95
Scale in Kilometers 0 — 1.5

RAPID TRANSIT
■ STATION

GOLDEN GATE BRIDGE
(TOLL SOUTH BOUND)

To Marin County & Redwood Empire
Fort Point National Historic Site

U.S. Coast Guard Station
Golden Gate National Recreation Area
★ Exploratorium

Marina Small Craft Harbor
MARINA BLVD.
CERVANTES BLVD.
Palace of Fine Arts
LOMBARD

Recreation Area
Baker Beach
National Beach
South Bay

LANDS END
Golden Gate China Beach
DEL MAR

Presidio

Letterman Army Medical Center
Presidio Museum
JACKSON
CALIFORNIA

Lincoln Park
California Palace of the Legion of Honor
EL CAMINO DEL MAR
LEGION OF HONOR DR.
Veterans Hospital

Cliff House
POINT LOBOS AVE.
GEARY BLVD.

S.F. Fire Dept. Museum
University of San Francisco
TURK
GOLDEN GATE

De Young Memorial Museum
FULTON ST.
Spreckles Lake
KENNEDY DR.
Chain of Lakes
J.F.
Golden Gate Park
MARTIN LUTHER KING JR. DR.
Stow Lake
Japanese Tea Garden
Asian Art Museum
California Academy of Sciences
University of California San Francisco Medical Center

Beach Chalet
GREAT

LINCOLN
Strybing Arboretum
7TH AVE.
CLARENDON AVE.

FELL
OAK ST.
HAIGHT ST.
Randall Museum
STANYAN ST.
CLAYTON ST.

PACIFIC

SUNSET BLVD.
19TH AVE.
1
TWIN PEAKS
EL 904 FT.
EL 910 FT.
TWIN PEAKS
MARKET ST.

LAGUNA HONDA BLVD.
WOODSIDE AVE.
DEWEY BLVD.

Golden
Gate
National
Recreation
Area

TARAVAL ST.

O'SHAUGHNESSY BLVD.
Glen Canyon Park

PORTOLA DR.
Mt. Davidson Park
EL 927 FT.
ST. FRANCIS BLVD.
BOSWORTH ST.

MONTEREY BLVD.

SLOAT BLVD.
35

San Francisco Zoo

OCEAN

LAKE MERCED BLVD.
WINSTON DR.
Lake Merced

Harding Park

San Francisco State University

JUNIPERO SERRA BLVD.
OCEAN AVE.

City College of San Francisco
Balboa Park
GENEVA

Harding Park Golf Course
Lake Merced

Fort Funston
35

JUNIPERO SERRA BLVD.
1
SOUTHERN
280
82
SAN
To San Jose
MISSION

To Santa Cruz

To San Jose

2107-F

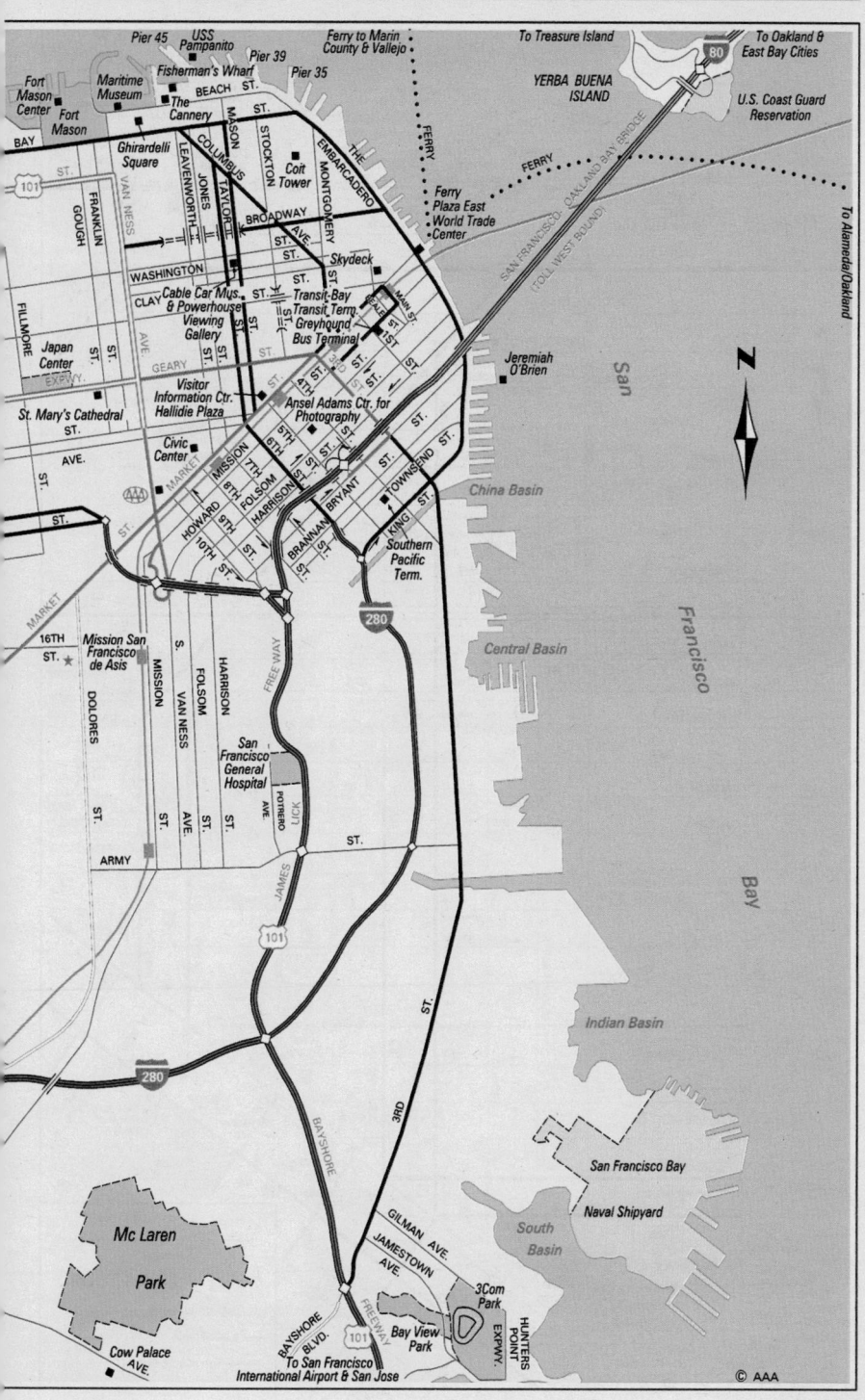

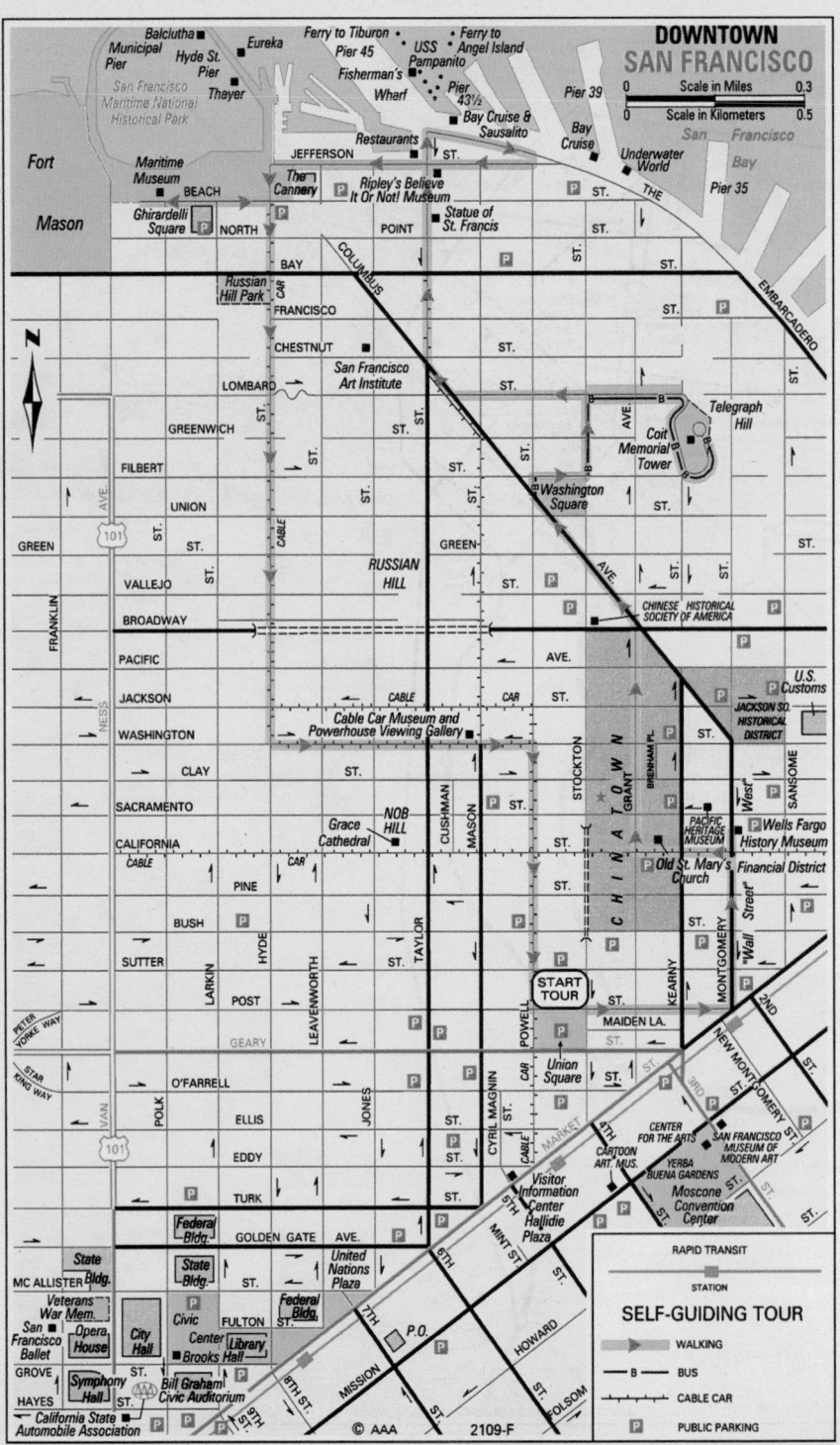

zone spaces is $250. In several areas of the city local residents have priority parking rights; be sure to check all posted regulations wherever you park.

It is illegal to park a vehicle on any grade exceeding 3 percent without effectively setting the brakes and blocking the wheels by turning them against the curb or by other means. The minimum penalty for this violation is $23.

When parking uphill, the front wheels must be "heeled," or turned out, so that a tire is resting securely against the curb. They must be "toed," or turned in, when parking downhill. If there is no curb you must use a block. The emergency brake must always be firmly set, and it is strongly recommended that you have your brakes thoroughly checked before driving or parking in hilly San Francisco. For additional parking information phone the City of San Francisco Parking and Traffic Department, (415) 553-1200.

Public Transportation

San Francisco Municipal Railway (Muni) provides public transportation, which consists of buses, streetcars and cable cars. The fare is $1; over 64, the physically impaired and ages 5-17, 35c. Fare includes a free transfer good for use on any two other vehicles within a 90-minute period; ask for a transfer when paying your fare. The Muni-F Market Line of colorful streetcars operates on Market Street between Castro and the Transbay Terminal at First and Mission streets, for easy access to attractions. E-Embarcadero Line is a light-rail service running from Embarcadero Station on Market Street to Fourth and King streets.

Service on some lines is available 24 hours a day. The Muni Passport, valid on all Muni buses and cable cars, offers unlimited usage each day and is $6 for a daily pass, $10 for a 3-day pass, and $15 for a 7- day pass. The $35 fast pass is valid for one month; over 64 and ages 5-17, $8. Drivers do not carry change. For schedules, routing and other information phone (415) 673-6864. AC Transit is a bus service that runs from the Transbay Terminal to various destinations in East Bay Area and Alameda and Contra Costa counties.

BART (Bay Area Rapid Transit) connects San Francisco with East Bay cities, terminating at Richmond (north), Pittsburg/Bay Point (east), Pleasanton (southeast) and Fremont (south). On the West Bay side the terminus is Colma, approximately 17 minutes south of the Civic Center area. BART operates Mon.-Fri. 4 a.m.-midnight, Sat. 6 a.m.-midnight and Sun. 8 a.m.-midnight. Tickets must be purchased from dispensing machines. Information is posted near the machines; phone (650) 992-2278.

In addition, passenger ferries link San Francisco with the north Bay Area. The Blue and

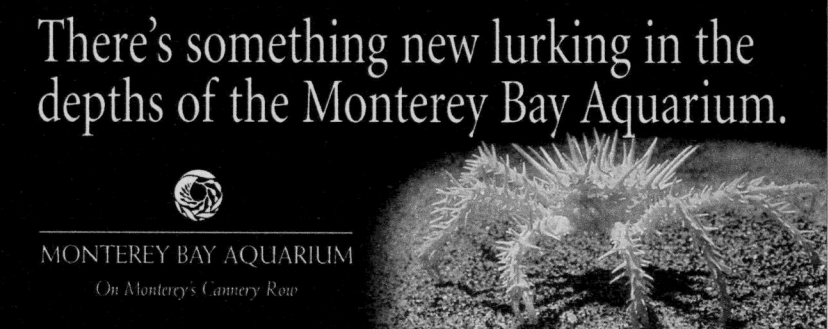

THE INFORMED TRAVELER

WHAT TO WEAR

San Francisco's weather is noted not for its extremes but for its consistency. Temperatures usually do not rise above 80 or fall below 40. August and September are generally the warmest months; January is the coldest. Most of the average yearly rainfall of just over 20 inches falls in the winter, but the summer fog also dampens the air in mornings and evenings, making a raincoat useful throughout the year.

CITYPASS

CityPass offers savings to those who plan visits to many San Francisco attractions. The pass covers the price of admission to seven sites—Blue & Gold Fleet's San Francisco Bay Cruise, California Academy of Sciences and Steinhart Aquarium, California Palace of the Legion of Honor, Exploratorium, De Young Memorial Museum and San Francisco Museum of Modern Art.

A pass, valid for 9 days once the first attraction is visited, is $27.75; over 64, $19.75; ages 12-17, $17.25. CityPass is available from visitor information centers, participating attractions and most major hotels.

Gold Fleet, (415) 773-1188, operates daily commuter service to Tiburon and Sausalito.

Golden Gate Transit, (415) 332-6600, operates ferries to Larkspur and Sausalito; no service is available Jan. 1, Thanksgiving or Dec. 25. Larkspur ferry one-way rates Mon.-Fri. are $2.75; ages 6-12, $2.05; over 65 and the physically impaired $1.35. Sat.-Sun. and holidays $4.70; ages 6-12, $3.55; over 65 and the physically impaired $2.35. Sausalito ferry one-way rates daily are $4.70; ages 6-12, $3.55; over 65 and the physically impaired $2.35. Bus service linking San Francisco to Marin County and the cities of Sausalito, Mill Valley, Tiburon and Santa Rosa in Sonoma County via the Golden Gate Bridge is available; phone (415) 923-2000.

Harbor Bay Maritime, (510) 769-5500, operates ferries from Alameda to the San Francisco Ferry Building. Fares are $4; over 61 and military $3; ages 6-12, $2. The Alameda/Oakland Ferry, (510) 522-3300, provides service to Alameda, Angel Island, Oakland and San Francisco. The Alameda/Oakland/San Francisco one-way fare is $4.50; over 64, military and the physically impaired $2.75; ages 5-12, $1.75. The round-trip Angel Island fares are $13, $9 and $6.

Golden Gate and Harbor Bay Maritime ferries depart from the Ferry Building at the foot of Market Street and north of the San Francisco-Oakland Bay Bridge. Red and White ferries depart Pier 41, Fisherman's Wharf. For schedules phone the respective companies at the above numbers.

What To See

ACRES OF ORCHIDS—
see South San Francisco p. 211.

ALCATRAZ ISLAND—*see Golden Gate National Recreation Area p. 208.*

ANSEL ADAMS CENTER FOR PHOTOGRAPHY (The Friends of Photography), 250 Fourth St., features five galleries with ongoing displays of work by Ansel Adams and changing exhibits of contemporary and historical photography. Allow 1 hour minimum. Tues.-Sun. 11-5 (also 5-8 the first Thurs. of the month). Admission $5; students with ID $3; over 61 and ages 13-17, $2. Phone (415) 495-7000.

ASIAN ART MUSEUM, in Golden Gate Park, houses a collection of 12,000 pieces spanning 6,000 years. Jades, bronzes, textiles, porcelain, ceramics, paintings and other objects illustrate the major periods and stylistic development of Asian art. Wed.-Sun. 9:30-4:45 (also first Wed. of the month 4:45-8:45). Admission $7; over 64, $5; ages 12-17, $4; free to all first Wed. of the month. Phone (415) 379-8800.

CABLE CAR MUSEUM AND POWERHOUSE VIEWING GALLERY, 1201 Mason St. at Washington St., contains models, photographs and relics of San Francisco's early transit system, including the first cable car, built in 1873. A videotape about cable cars describes how they work, and an underground viewing room enables visitors to observe the huge sheaves that guide the vehicles from under the street. Allow 1 hour minimum. Daily 10-6, Apr.-Sept.; 10-5, rest of year. Closed Jan. 1, Thanksgiving and Dec. 25. Donations. Phone (415) 474-1887.

★ CALIFORNIA ACADEMY OF SCIENCES, in Golden Gate Park, includes Morrison Planetarium, the Natural History Museum and Steinhart Aquarium. Daily 10-5, Memorial Day weekend-Labor Day; 9-6, rest of year. Admission $8.50; over 65 and students with ID $5.50; ages 4-11, $2.50; free to all first Wed. of the month. Admission includes the museum and aquarium; planetarium extra. Phone (415) 750-7145.

Morrison Planetarium houses a 5,000-pound star projector—an instrument built specially for the planetarium—under a 65-foot dome. Star shows are given Sat.-Sun. and holidays on the hour noon-4, Mon.-Fri. at 2, mid-June through Labor Day; daily at 2, rest of year. Additional shows are given Sat.-Sun. and holidays at 11; closed during program changeovers. Planetarium shows change every 2-3 months; phone for times and program titles.

Admission (in addition to academy admission) $2.50; over 64 and under 18, $1.25. Phone (415) 750-7141 or (415) 750-7138 for Laserium.

Natural History Museum encompasses Wild California Hall, Simson African Hall, Hall of Gems and Minerals, The Far Side of Science Gallery and Earth and Space Hall, where a shake table lets visitors safely experience a simulated California earthquake. Another exhibit hall, Life Through Time—The Age of the Dinosaurs, demonstrates evolution based on scientific evidence. There also is a Discovery Room with hands-on exhibits for children; open Tues.-Fri. noon-4, Sat.-Sun. 10-4.

Steinhart Aquarium houses some 14,000 aquatic animals, including octopuses, alligators, turtles, reptiles, sharks, anemones and sea horses, presented in 189 displays. Highlights include the Fish Roundabout and Sharks of the Tropics, featuring several species of sharks in a re-created tropical reef habitat. Sharks are fed daily every 2 hours 10:30-4:30; penguins are fed at 11:30 and 4.

CALIFORNIA PALACE OF THE LEGION OF HONOR is in Lincoln Park near 34th Ave. and Clement St. overlooking the Golden Gate Bridge. Founded to honor Californians who died during World War I, the building is a replica of the Palais de la Légion d'Honneur in Paris. The collection includes decorative arts, sculpture, tapestries and more than 87,000 paintings spanning 4,000 years. Ancient and medieval art is featured as are works by El Greco, Rembrandt, Claude Monet, Pablo Picasso and Pierre Auguste Renoir.

Food is available. Allow 3 hours minimum. Tues.-Sun. 9:30-5; closed holidays. Admission

TRANSPORTATION

Air travel: San Francisco International Airport is about 12 miles south near San Bruno. Airporter Coaches, (415) 495-8404, travels to major downtown hotels every 15 minutes, 6 a.m.-midnight. One-way fare is $10; ages 2-16, $5.

Minivans make frequent pickups from the red-and-white-striped zones on pedestrian islands on the airport upper level. One-way fare is $10-$20 per person. Airport shuttle buses pick up passengers on the lower level pedestrian islands near the blue columns. Taxi fares to downtown average $28-$30; limousine service costs $35-$60.

Rental cars: Hertz, at the airport, offers discounts to AAA members; phone (415) 771-2200 or (800) 654-3080. For listings of other agencies check the telephone directory.

Rail service: Most rail service terminates in Oakland at Jack London Square, Alice and Embarcadero, and passengers are transported by bus to the Ferry Building and Caltrain Depot on Townsend Street. Phone Amtrak at (800) 872-7245.

Buses: Greyhound Lines Inc., (800) 231-2222, depart from the Trans-Bay Terminal at First and Mission streets.

Taxis: Taxi companies are listed in the local telephone directory. The base fare for most rides is $2 for the first mile, $1.80 for each additional mile.

Public transport: Preserved as national historic landmarks and purportedly the only such on wheels, San Francisco's famous cable cars are painted in their original 1873 colors—maroon with cream and blue trim. They operate 6 a.m.-1 a.m. along the following routes: Powell and Market to Fisherman's Wharf; Powell and Market to Victorian Park at Beach and Hyde; and on California from Market to Van Ness. The fare is $2; no transfers are available.

See Getting Around, Public Transportation for details about other public transportation.

Boats: Oceangoing steamship lines and cruise lines arrive and depart at the piers that radiate from the Embarcadero and southern waterfront.

$7; over 65, $5; ages 12-17, $4; free to all second Wed. of the month. An additional fee is charged for special exhibitions. Phone (415) 863-3330.

CARTOON ART MUSEUM is at 814 Mission St. in the Yerba Buena Gardens district. Founded in 1984, the museum contains original art from comic books, animated movies, magazines, advertisements and newspapers as well as sculpture and videotapes. Works date from the 1730s to the present. Exhibits change every 4 months. Wed.-Fri. 11-5, Sat. 10-5, Sun. 1-5. Admission $5; over 61 and students with ID $3; ages 6-12, $2. Phone (415) 227-8666.

★ **CHINATOWN** covers about 16 square blks. and is bounded by Broadway, Bush, Kearny and Stockton sts. More Chinese live in this "city within a city" than in any other place in the world outside of China.

Grant Avenue, the main thoroughfare, is lined with tearooms, shops, temples, Christian missions, Chinese schools, theaters and grocery stores. The Bank of Canton, 743 Washington St., has an unusual exterior.

Chinese Culture Center, 3rd floor of the Holiday Inn at 750 Kearny St., is a source for information about Chinatown and displays Chinese art. The center also offers walking tours of Chinatown Saturday and Sunday at 2 or by reservation. Phone (415) 986-1822. The center is open Tues.-Sat. 10-4, Sun. noon-4; closed holidays. Center free. Heritage Tour $15; under 18, $5. Culinary Tour $30; under 12, $15.

All About Chinatown! Walking Tours features the history, culture and traditions of the area. Two-hour tours are given daily at 10. Fee $25. Tours require six or more participants. Phone (415) 982-8839. The Wok Wiz Chinatown Tours offers one of five culinary and historical walking tours of Chinatown daily. Fee $25-$75. Phone (650) 355-9657.

CHINESE HISTORICAL SOCIETY OF AMERICA, 644 Broadway, Suite 401, recalls the important role of the Chinese in the settlement of the city and the West through a variety of exhibits. Tues.-Fri. 10-4, Sat. hours vary; closed Jan. 1, Thanksgiving and Dec. 25. Donations. Phone (415) 391-1188.

CIVIC CENTER, bordered by Market, Hayes and Franklin sts. and Golden Gate Ave., covers eight blocks and groups federal, state and city structures and parklands. Crowned by a dome taller than the U.S. Capitol, City Hall commands a view of the plaza, which is surrounded by the State Building, Main Public Library, Federal Building, Auditorium and the Health Center, all of French and Neo-Renaissance style. The United Nations Conference on International Organization, which culminated in the signing of the Charter of the United Nations, was held at the Civic Center in 1945.

Performing Arts Center is across Van Ness Ave. opposite City Hall. The center comprises San Francisco Performing Arts Library, Herbst Theater in the Veterans Memorial Building, War Memorial Opera House, Davies Symphony Hall and San Francisco Ballet Association. San Francisco Symphony's electro-pneumatic Ruffatti organ comprises more than 10,000 pipes, five manuals and 163 ranks. Four-hour center tours are given Mon. at 10, except on holidays. Tours of Davies Symphony Hall Wed. and Sat. are available by request. Tours $5, over 65 and students with ID $3. Phone (415) 552-8338 for reservations, or (415) 255-4800 for library information.

CLIFF HOUSE—see *Golden Gate National Recreation Area p. 208.*

DE YOUNG MEMORIAL MUSEUM, 75 Teagarden Dr. in Golden Gate Park, features American art from the Colonial period through the 20th century. Included are paintings, sculpture, furniture and decorative arts by such artists as Winslow Homer, Albert Bierstadt, James McNeill Whistler, John Singer Sargent and Paul Revere. Also included are pieces from Egypt, Greece, Rome and Africa and costumes and textiles. Rotating exhibits also are presented; an additional fee may be charged. Guided tours are offered.

Allow 2 hours minimum. Wed.-Sun. 9:30-5 (also first Wed. of the month 5-8:45); closed Thanksgiving and Dec. 25. Admission $7; over 65, $5; ages 12-17, $3; free to all the first Wed. of the month, except during special exhibitions. Phone (415) 863-3330.

★**EXPLORATORIUM**, 3601 Lyon St. inside the Palace of Fine Arts, contains more than 600 interactive exhibits that invite visitors to see, touch, hear, feel and explore the fields of science, mathematics, technology, animal behavior and human perception. Subjects covered include color, electricity, language, motion, touch and weather. Food is available.

Allow 2 hours minimum. Daily 10-6 (also Wed. 6-9:30 p.m.), Memorial Day-Labor Day; Tues.-Sun. 10-5 (also Wed. 5-9:30), rest of year. Admission $9; over 64 and students with ID $7; physically impaired and ages 6-17, $5; ages 3-5, $2.50; free to all first Wed. of the month. Phone (415) 561-0360.

FORT MASON CENTER, Buchanan St. and Marina Blvd., is a World War II embarkation point that has been transformed into a regional cultural center. Among the art galleries converted from former warehouses are The Mexican Museum; Museo Italo-Americano; and San Francisco Craft & Folk Art Museum. Six theaters also are here. Events are presented weekly. Daily 8 a.m.-midnight. Tours are given second Sat. of the month (also fourth Sat. of the month, Nov.-Dec.). Free; charges for some events and galleries. Reservations are recommended for tours. Phone (415) 979-3010.

FORT POINT NATIONAL HISTORIC SITE—*see Golden Gate National Recreation Area p. 208.*

GOLDEN GATE BRIDGE, over the bay, connects San Francisco with Marin County and the Redwood Hwy. (US 101). With a length of 8,981 feet and main span length of 4,200 feet, it is one of the longest single-span suspension bridges ever built. Its two massive towers are the world's highest bridge towers, at 746 feet above the water. A clearance of 220 feet allows passage of the largest oceangoing vessels. A crew of painters constantly maintains the bridge's distinctive coat of international orange. Toll of $3 is charged southbound; northbound free.

GOLDEN GATE NATIONAL RECREATION AREA—*see place listing p. 208.*

★**GOLDEN GATE PARK** is bordered by the Great Hwy. on the west, Lincoln Way on the south, Stanyan St. on the east and Fulton St. on the north. John McLaren, a Scottish landscape gardener and park superintendent 1887-1943, transformed a barren wasteland lapped by shifting dunes into this lush oasis with a dozen artificial lakes and a collection of trees and other plants of worldwide scope. Miles of roads, bridle paths and foot trails weave through the 1,017-

acre park, which extends 3 miles from Fell and Stanyan streets to the ocean.

Among its many attractions are a bison paddock, a restored Dutch-style windmill, an equestrian center, trotting track, tennis courts, archery field, golf course, the polo field stadium and an outdoor music concourse, which offers concerts all year. Portals of the Past, a remnant of the 1906 earthquake, is on Kennedy Drive across from Speedway Meadows. Severely damaged in December 1995, Conservatory of Flowers is not yet open to the public; phone (415) 666-7017. The visitor center, housed in the Beach Chalet on Great Highway, features murals with scenes of the city during the Great Depression, mosaics and wood carvings. Daily 10-dusk.

In the southeast corner of the park on Bowling Green is the playground with a restored 1912 Herschel Spillman carrousel. Boats can be rented at Stowe Lake, a moat ringing the steep slopes of Strawberry Hill, whose summit of over 400 feet is the highest point in the park. Certain roads are closed to automobile traffic Sunday. Picnic facilities are available. Guided tours of various parts of the park are offered Sat. at 11 and Sun. at 11 and 2, May-Oct.; most tours last 1 to 2 hours, but duration varies greatly, and tours are not restricted to the hours listed. For tour information phone (415) 263-0991. Park open daily 24 hours. Phone (415) 831-2700.

Japanese Tea Garden, 8th Ave. and Kennedy Dr., is landscaped with bridges, walks, ponds, miniature waterfalls, statuary and pagodas. The garden is spectacular in spring when the cherry trees bloom. Daily 9-6:30, Mar.-Sept.; 9-5, rest of year. Admission $2.50; over 64 and ages 6-12, $1. Phone (415) 752-1171.

Strybing Arboretum, 9th Ave. and Lincoln Way, has more than 7,000 species of plants from around the world. Within its 70 acres are demonstration gardens, a Mediterranean collection, a New World Cloud Forest collection, the Garden of Fragrance for the visually impaired and the Moonviewing Pavilion and adjacent waterfall. Guided tours are available. Mon.-Fri. 8:30-4:30, Sat.-Sun. and holidays 10-5. Tours are given daily at 1:30 (also Sat.-Sun. at 10:30). Closed holidays. Donations. Phone (415) 661-1316.

JAPAN CENTER (Nihonmachi), bounded by Post, Geary, Laguna and Fillmore sts., is a 5-acre complex with diverse cultural and commercial points of interest. Miyako Hotel adjoins the offices of the Japanese consulate. The Peace Pagoda, gift of the people of Japan, stands in the central plaza. Music, dance, tea ceremonies and martial arts presentations are given many weekends in summer. The area has restaurants, art galleries, movie theaters, gardens, Japanese baths and shops *(see Shopping p. 206).* Underground parking is available. Phone (415) 922-6776.

JAPANESE TEA GARDEN—
see Golden Gate Park p. 202.

THE *JEREMIAH O'BRIEN*, berthed at Pier 32 at the end of Brannan St., is the only unaltered World War II liberty ship in operating condition. During "steaming" weekends, usually the third weekend of the month, the ship's engine is in operation, the coal stove galley is open and the ship's store is set up. Mon.-Fri. 9-3, Sat.-Sun. 9-4; closed Jan. 1, Easter, Thanksgiving and Dec. 24-25 and 31. Cruises are offered in May and Oct. Admission $5; over 64, $3; ages 10-18, $2; ages 1-9, $1. Phone (415) 441-3101.

LANDS END, overlooking the Pacific Ocean and the Golden Gate Bridge, is part of Golden Gate National Recreation Area *(see place listing p. 208).* It has a memorial to the men who died on the USS *San Francisco* during the Battle of Guadalcanal, Nov. 12-13, 1942. The memorial is a part of the ship's bridge.

LINCOLN PARK, 193 acres at 34th Ave. and Clement St., contains American artist George Segal's memorial to the victims of the World War II Holocaust. The park is noted for its encompassing views of the Golden Gate area and includes California Palace of the Legion of Honor *(see attraction listing p. 199).*

LOMBARD STREET, between Hyde and Leavenworth sts., is often referred to as "the crookedest street in the world." In a series of S-curves, this one-block portion descends a 40-degree slope. Stairs are available. Campers and trailers are prohibited on this block of Lombard St.

★ **MISSION SAN FRANCISCO DE ASIS** (Mission Dolores) is at 3321 16th St. at Dolores St. One of the oldest buildings in San Francisco, it was founded June 29 and opened Oct. 9, 1776, by Father Junípero Serra. The rough-hewn redwood roof timbers still are lashed together with rawhide. The altar was one of the most ornate among the missions; the original books and decorations were brought from Spain and Mexico. California's first book—Palou's "Life of Junípero Serra"—was written here. A small museum displays old manuscripts and mission relics.

The basilica next door, with its combination of Moorish, Mission and Corinthian styles, is a striking contrast to the mission's appearance. Daily 9-4; closed Thanksgiving and Dec. 25. Admission $2; over 64 and under 12, $1. Limited street parking is available. Phone (415) 621-8203.

MORRISON PLANETARIUM—
see California Academy of Sciences p. 199.

NATURAL HISTORY MUSEUM—
see California Academy of Sciences p. 199.

NOB HILL, in the vicinity of California, Sacramento, Jones and Taylor sts., was the center of luxurious living in the last half of the 19th century, when men who had made fortunes in railroading and gold mining built their houses in this territory. Elegant apartment buildings and hotels now occupy the hilltop. Grace Cathedral (Episcopal), one of the nation's oldest cathedrals, contains replicas of the bronze doors of the Baptistry in Florence by Lorenzo Ghiberti. Tours Mon.-Fri. 1-3, Sat. 11:30-1:30, Sun. 12:30-2. Special choral performances Thurs. at 4:45. Donations. Phone (415) 749-6300.

NORTH BEACH, spread around Telegraph Hill and down to the waterfront, is noted for its art galleries, bookshops, international restaurants and informal approach to life. The area once was on the water, but landfill efforts have moved it farther inland.

OLD ST. MARY'S CHURCH is in Chinatown at Grant Ave. and California St. The 1854 church's interior was patterned after the Spanish church of California's first bishop, Joseph Sadoc Alemany. Sun.-Fri. 7-3:30, Sat. 11-6. Donations. Phone (415) 986-4388.

PACIFIC HERITAGE MUSEUM, 608 Commercial St., displays changing exhibits chronicling the history and culture of emigrants from both sides of the Pacific Basin. Housed in the restored U.S. Subtreasury building, the museum features an exhibit depicting the building's history. Allow 30 minutes minimum. Tues.-Sat. 10-4; closed holidays. Free. Phone (415) 399-1124 or 362-4100.

PALACE OF FINE ARTS, s.e. approach to the Golden Gate Bridge at Bay and Lyon Sts., is the last remaining structure of the 1915 Panama-Pacific Exposition. The temporary structure survived until 1962 when the Beaux Arts rotunda and colonnade were re-created in concrete from castings of the original ornamentation. The palace is now in a park with a lagoon where swans and ducks swim. Also in the park is a 1,000-seat theater. Daily dawn-dusk. Free. Phone (415) 567-6642 for theater information.

PRESIDIO—*see Golden Gate National Recreation Area p. 209.*

RANDALL MUSEUM, off Roosevelt Way at 199 Museum Way, has animals, arts and crafts and exhibits about sciences and model trains. Tues.-Sat. 10-5. Donations. Phone (415) 554-9600.

RIPLEY'S BELIEVE IT OR NOT! MUSEUM, 175 Jefferson St. at Fisherman's Wharf, displays the bizarre and unusual. Sun.-Thurs. 9 a.m.-11 p.m., Fri.-Sat. 9 a.m.-midnight, July 4-Labor Day; Sun.-Thurs. 10-10, Fri.-Sat. 10 a.m.-midnight, rest of year. Admission $8.50; over 59, $7; ages 5-12, $5.50. AE, MC, VI. Phone (415) 771-6188.

ST. MARY'S CATHEDRAL, 1111 Gough St. on Cathedral Hill, is a modern structure of Italian marble. A baldachino, or canopy, of aluminum and gold; a large mosaic; and a Ruffati organ highlight the interior of the cathedral. Mon.-Fri. 6:30-4:30, Sat. 6:30 a.m.-7 p.m., Sun. 7:30-4:30, except during Masses. Donations. Phone (415) 567-2020.

SAN FRANCISCO ART INSTITUTE, 800 Chestnut St. at Jones St., presents artworks in two galleries, one of which contains a mural by Diego Rivera. The architecture effectively combines the traditional Spanish style of the original structure with the contemporary look of the addition. Tues.-Sat. 10-5 (also Thurs. 5-8), Sun. noon-5; closed holidays. The mural can be viewed daily 9-9. Free. Phone (415) 771-7020.

SAN FRANCISCO MARITIME NATIONAL HISTORICAL PARK, at the west end of Fisherman's Wharf, includes Aquatic Park, a bayside park and recreation area with a quarter-mile stretch of beach and a lagoon.

Hyde Street Pier, at the foot of Hyde St., displays ships dating from the late 19th century. Visitors can board three ships: *Balclutha,* a three-masted square-rigged sailing vessel which contains ship relics, marine paintings and photographs; *C.A. Thayer,* a coastal lumber schooner; and *Eureka,* the largest ferry operating on San Francisco Bay in her time. The tugboats *Eppleton Hall* and *Hercules* also are anchored nearby. Programs and demonstrations are offered.

Daily 10-6, May 15-Sept. 15; 9:30-5, rest of year. Closed Jan. 1, Thanksgiving and Dec. 25.

Admission $4; ages 12-17, $2; over 61 free; free to all first Tues. of the month. Phone (415) 556-3002.

Maritime Museum displays the history of water transportation from the 1800s to the present. Model ships, maritime artifacts, fine arts and photographs are displayed. Daily 10-5; closed Jan. 1, Thanksgiving and Dec. 25. Free. Phone (415) 556-3002.

San Francisco Maritime Library is at Fort Mason, Building E, and houses more than 250,000 historic photographs, documents and maritime literature. Wed.-Fri. 1-5, Sat. 10-5, Tues. 5-8. Free. Phone (415) 556-9870.

SAN FRANCISCO MUSEUM OF MODERN ART, 151 Third St., is in a modernistic, five-story building designed by Swiss architect Mario Botta in 1994. A brick, granite and glass exterior contains spaceous galleries illuminated by a skylight. The museum houses a comprehensive collection of contemporary art, including traditional paintings and sculpture, multimedia installations and photography. Rotating exhibits are featured. Food is available.

Fri.-Tues. 10:30-6:30, Thurs. 10:30-9; closed Jan. 1, July 4, Thanksgiving and Dec. 25. Admission $8; over 62, $5; students with ID $3.50; under 12 free; free to all first Tues. of the month. Admission Thurs. 6-9 p.m., $4; over 62, $2.50; students with ID $2; under 12 free. Under 12 must be with an adult. Phone (415) 357-4000, 357-4095, 357-4096 for guided tours or TDD 357-4154.

SAN FRANCISCO-OAKLAND BAY BRIDGE spans San Francisco Bay and links San Francisco with the East Bay cities. Including approaches, it is 8.4 miles long, 4.5 miles of it over navigable water. The east and west spans are connected by a double-deck tunnel through Yerba Buena Island. A $2 toll is charged westbound only. Phone (510) 286-1148.

SAN FRANCISCO ZOO, on Sloat Blvd. with an entrance near 45th Ave., has approximately 1,000 mammals and birds. Of interest are the Primate Discovery Center, Gorilla World, Koala Crossing which features an Australian Walk-About, a feline conservation center, a warthog exhibit, broad-snouted caymans and an antique carrousel. Big cats are fed Tues.-Sun. at 2. Daily 10-5. Admission $9; over 64 and ages 12-17, $6; ages 3-11, $3; free to all first Wed. of month. Carrousel ride $2. Phone (415) 753-7080.

Children's Zoo includes nature trails, a barnyard, an insect zoo and animals that may be petted and fed. Daily 10:30-4:30 in summer; 11-4, rest of year. Admission $1, under 3 free.

SKYDECK, on the 41st floor of 1 Embarcadero Center, affords views of the city. On a clear day, the view may encompass 35 miles, displaying Alcatraz, numerous islands and 96 high-rise buildings. Wed.-Fri. 5-10, Sat.-Sun. and holidays 10-10; closed Jan. 1, Thanksgiving and Dec. 25. Admission $4; over 61 and students with ID $3.50; ages 5-12, $3. Phone (888) 737-5933.

STEINHART AQUARIUM—
see California Academy of Sciences p. 199.

STRYBING ARBORETUM—
see Golden Gate Park p. 202.

TELEGRAPH HILL, topped by a park, rises near the e. end of Lombard St. and provides a panorama. Coit Memorial Tower, built roughly in the shape of a fire hose nozzle, memorializes volunteer firefighters. The observation deck is 542 feet above the bay. Tower open daily 10-6. Tower admission $3; over 64, $2; ages 6-12, $1. Phone (415) 362-0808.

UNDERWATER WORLD, Pier 39 at the Embarcadero and Beach St., is a "diver's eye" view aquarium. Clear acrylic tunnels give visitors a subsea perspective on such marine life as sharks, rays, jellyfish and eels. Guided tours through the tanks last an hour. Daily 9-9. Admission $12.95; over 64, $9.95; ages 3-11, $6.50. Public transit riders receive $2 discount. Parking $5 per hour. MC, VI. Phone (415) 623-5300.

USS *PAMPANITO*, at the end of Taylor St. at Pier 45, is a World War II submarine that saw action in the Pacific theater. Self-guiding audio tours require stooping through low bulkheads. Daily 9-8, mid-May to mid-Oct.; Fri.-Sat. 9-8, Sun.-Thurs. 9-6, rest of year. Admission $7; over 62 and ages 6-12, $4; family rate (two adults and up to four family members) $20. Phone (415) 775-1943.

WELLS FARGO HISTORY MUSEUM is in Wells Fargo Bank Building at 420 Montgomery St. The museum contains a stagecoach, relics of the gold rush, nuggets, Western franks and stamps and other articles from 1848 to the present. Mon.-Fri. 9-5; closed bank holidays. Free. Phone (415) 396-2619.

YERBA BUENA GARDENS, bordered by Mission, Howard and Third sts., comprises three galleries, an esplanade, an outdoor stage, a theater, a waterfall, a sculpture court and a garden. The complex emphasizes a range of art forms, from painting and electronic music to ballet and video. Lectures and workshops are offered. Food is available. Galleries open Tues.-Sun 11-6 (also first Thurs. of the month 6-8 p.m.). Admission to galleries $5; senior citizens, students with ID and under 16, $3; free to senior citizens and students with ID Thurs. 11-3 and to all first Thurs. of the month 6-8 p.m. Phone (415) 978-2787.

What To Do

Sightseeing

Sightseeing tours are available by land, sea and air; if your time is limited, the bus tours that touch briefly on city highlights are recommended. A list of events and sightseeing tips is recorded daily by the San Francisco Convention & Visitors Bureau; phone (415) 391-2000. *See color ad p. 200.*

 Boat Tours

Tours of the harbor operate from Fisherman's Wharf. The Red and White Fleet, (415) 447-0597 or (800) 229-2784, schedules hourlong daytime cruises that depart from Pier 43½. Tours to Sonoma and the Napa wine country as well as tours of the city and Yosemite National Park depart from Pier 43½ or from area hotels with advance notice. *See color ad p. 925-926.*

Cruises to Marine World Africa USA in Vallejo and to Angel Island are scheduled by Vallejo Ferry and depart from the Ferry Building; phone (707) 643-3779.

The Angel Island-Tiburon Ferry, (415) 435-2131, runs daily; times vary with the season. Angel Island State Park offers picnic facilities, beaches and hiking trails. The park includes the Angel Island Immigration Station, which received thousands of Chinese emigrants 1910-40 *(see Recreation Chart).*

Blue and Gold Fleet Bay Cruises and Motor Coach Tours, (415) 705-5555, has 60-minute bay cruises leaving Pier 39 at frequent intervals daily. The company also offers daily San Francisco, Napa and Sonoma wine country, Muir Woods,

Monterey, Carmel and Yosemite trips; phone (415) 773-1188.

Hornblower Dining Yachts, (415) 788-8866, Pier 33 on the Embarcadero, offers daily dinner and lunch cruises, and weekend brunch cruises aboard the motor yacht *California Hornblower.* Live music is provided with dinner and brunch, and there are dance floors on two decks. Reservations are required and credit cards are accepted.

 Bus and Limousine Tours

Many companies offer limousine tours of San Francisco, the Bay Area and Wine Country. See the telephone directory for information.

GRAY LINE offers full- and half-day excursions of San Francisco and the Bay Area. Day tours depart from Trans-Bay Terminal at First and Mission streets, and night tours depart from Union Square at Powell and Geary streets. The 3.5-hour Deluxe City tour departs daily at 9, 10, 11, 1:30 and 2:30 (also at 3:30, June-Aug.). Deluxe City fare $28; ages 5-11, $14. Reservations are required. AE, MC, VI. Phone (415) 558-9400.

 Driving Tours

Skyline Boulevard (SR 35) follows the scenic peninsula divide south of the city into the Santa Cruz Mountains, affording simultaneous views of the bay and ocean.

Upon presentation of your AAA membership card, the California State Automobile Association can furnish a map with a suggested tour covering much of San Francisco. This 49-Mile Scenic Drive map also is available from the San Francisco Convention & Visitors Bureau Visitor Information Center on the lower level of Hallidie Plaza at Market and Powell streets, where the cable cars turn around.

TRIPS ON TAPE, available at selected bookstores, is a self-guiding audiotape tour of San Francisco. It features 10 excursions of major attractions by foot, ferry, car and cable car. Tapes cost $12.95 and also are available by mail from The Rider's Guide, 484 Lake Park Ave., Suite 255, Oakland, CA 94610. Add $2.50 for postage; California residents should add sales tax. Phone (510) 653-2553.

 Walking Tours

Perhaps the best way to get the feeling that instills such deep civic devotion in San Franciscans is to take a walking tour. The tour can be followed using this book's map of downtown San Francisco. The names of sites listed in detail in the What To See and Shopping sections are printed in bold type. Even if you do not tour a listed site, reading the listing when you reach that point should make the tour more interesting.

Union Square is a good starting point. Stroll east on Post to Montgomery St. and make a

sharp left. Here between Market and Sacramento sts. is "Wall Street West." Continue north on Montgomery to the Wells Fargo Bank Building, which houses **Wells Fargo History Museum.**

Return a quarter block to California St., turn right and continue up the hill on California to Grant Ave., passing **Old St. Mary's Church.** You now enter **Chinatown;** turn right on Grant Ave., which is lined with many Chinese shops and restaurants.

At Columbus Ave. bear left to Union St., and, for the sake of your feet, take a number 39 bus ($1 fare) to the top of **Telegraph Hill** and a breathtaking view from Coit Memorial Tower. Be sure to look west to view the section of **Lombard Street** known as "the crookedest street in the world." Descend via Lombard and return to Columbus Ave. for a block.

From Columbus make a right onto Taylor St.; 3 blocks farther is a fine statue of St. Francis by Bufano. At the end of Taylor St. is **Fisherman's Wharf;** of interest are **Ripley's Believe It Or Not! Museum,** the The Wax Museum and the wharf itself, which boasts many fine seafood restaurants.

Walk a few blocks east to Pier 39 or a few blocks west to **The Cannery;** both have interesting shops, boutiques and restaurants. **Hyde Street Pier,** a floating museum of ships, is at the foot of Hyde St.

Proceed south on Hyde St. and turn right onto Beach St. Continuing west on Beach, you will

find the **Maritime Museum** on your right and **Ghirardelli Square** on your left. Do an about-face and return to the corner of Beach and Hyde sts., then take a cable car up one of the city's steepest hills and return to Union Square.

City Guides Walking Tours, a part of the San Francisco Friends of the Library, provides free 1.5- to 2-hour tours of historic Market Street, the Civic Center, North Beach, Chinatown, Golden Gate Bridge, the mission murals, the Palace of Fine Arts, Victorian San Francisco, Pacific Heights mansions and other parts of the city; phone (415) 557-4266 for schedules and information. Heritage Walks offers tours of the Pacific Heights Victorians, of Haas-Lilienthal House and of Yerba Buena. Tours last 2 hours and cost $5; over 65 and under 12, $3; phone (415) 441-3004 or 441-3000.

The highlights of Haig Partigian StatueWalks tours, beginning at City Hall facing Polk Street, include statues, artwork, plaques and a rose garden. Fee $20; phone (510) 834-3617 for reservations.

The murals along Balmy Alley in the Mission District can be viewed via walking tours. Tours depart Sat. at 1:30 from Precita Eyes Mural Arts Center at 348 Precita Ave. Fee $5; over 64, $4; students with ID and under 18, $1. Monthly bicycle and Mexican bus tours also are available. Phone (415) 285-2287.

Another interesting opportunity to take in the magnificent vistas and experience some neighborhood history is via the city's stairways, more than 300 of which are scattered throughout the city. Some stairways, such as those on Telegraph Hill and Russian Hill, provide links to well-known scenic vantage points, while others offer short-cuts from one street to another. Many are lined with well-kept private gardens, and most offer great exercise—though visitors are cautioned not to rush the climb.

Alamo Square, at Hayes and Steiner streets, is an historic area of Victorian row houses backdropped by downtown skyscrapers. The grassy square itself is a good spot for a mid-day break. The area contains several bed and breakfast inns.

Sports and Recreation

The recreational center of San Francisco is wooded Golden Gate Park, which offers facilities for all sorts of sports, including **hiking, bicycling,** boating, **horseback riding,** golf and tennis. The local telephone directory contains listings of bicycle rental agencies and riding academies.

The San Francisco Recreation and Park Department, (415) 831-7107, maintains 151 public **tennis** courts, eight indoor **swimming** pools and an outdoor pool open June through September.

Boating and **fishing** are popular on Lake Merced. Rental boats with fishing gear are available; phone (415) 753-1101.

Municipal **golf** courses include Golden Gate Park Golf Course (nine holes) at 47th Avenue and John F. Kennedy Drive; Harding Park Golf Course on Lake Merced, Harding Road off Skyline Boulevard; Jack Fleming Golf Course (nine holes), Harding Road off Skyline Boulevard; Lincoln Park Municipal Golf Course, at 34th Avenue and Clement Street, overlooking the Golden Gate Bridge; and the Presidio Golf Course on Finley at Arguello.

There also are private golf and country clubs that extend privileges to visitors who are members of recognized clubs in their hometowns; check with your own club.

3Com Park on Candlestick Point in southeastern San Francisco is the home of the San Francisco Giants **baseball** team and the 49ers **football** team. The Oakland-Alameda County Coliseum Complex is home to the "Hail Mary pass" inventors, the Oakland Raiders, baseball's Oakland A's and the bay area's **basketball** team, the Golden State Warriors. One-hour south, San Jose Arena's National **Hockey** League Sharks circle their prey.

Cow Palace, 2600 Geneva Ave. at Santos St., is host to rodeos, ice shows and other events; phone (415) 469-6000.

Shopping

Many San Francisco shopping areas would be attractions on their own without the shops they offer. In general, the hours for downtown department stores are Mon.-Sat. 9:30-5:30; some stores are open evenings and Sun. noon-5.

Embarcadero Center is bounded by Sacramento, California, Clay, Battery and Drumm streets. The four-tower complex houses Hyatt Regency Hotel, shops, restaurants, offices and galleries; sculptures and tapestries are displayed throughout.

Chinatown, bounded by Broadway, Bush, Kearny and Stockton streets, has a variety of imports, including fine ivory and jade items.

Japan Center is bordered by Post, Geary, Laguna and Fillmore streets. Three buildings (Kintetsu, East and Kinokuniya) contain malls that are lined with art galleries, antique stores, restaurants and many shops selling Japanese goods.

Union Square, with its flower stands, is the heart of the city's downtown shopping district; it is bounded by Powell, Geary, Post and Stockton streets. Around the square itself and extending a few blocks down each street are Neiman-Marcus and Saks Fifth Avenue, both elegant stores devoted mainly to apparel; Alfred Dunhill of London Inc., Brooks Brothers, Bullock and Jones, Gucci and Hermes, where designer fashions may be found; and Macy's department store.

Also there is Gump's, famous for its selection of fine gifts, china and glass as well as its jade collection; fine jewelers like Shreve and Co. and Tiffany and Co.; FAO Schwarz Fifth Avenue, the toy store for children of all ages; and bookstores and art galleries.

Near Union Square and bordered by Post, Kearney, Sutter and Montgomery streets, Crocker Galleria offers more than 50 shops, restaurants and services under a glass dome modeled after Galleria Vittorio Emmanuelle in Milan, Italy. The three-level pavilion features a rooftop garden and one-of-a-kind collectibles by American and European designers.

At Fifth and Market streets, more than 100 establishments call San Francisco Shopping Centre home. The mall offers nine stories of vertical shopping, including a five-story Nordstrom complete with six spiral escalators. The 150-foot-high atrium is covered by a retractable skylight.

A section of Union Street between Van Ness Avenue and Steiner Street features boutiques, antique stores and gift shops. This is the "main street" of historic Cow Hollow, serving residents of Marina and Pacific Heights as well as visitors.

THE CANNERY is on the e. side of the block bordered by Jefferson, Leavenworth, Beach and Hyde sts. Formerly a Del Monte fruit cannery, it houses specialty shops, art galleries and restaurants, all linked by arcades, bridges and balconies. Phone (415) 771-3112.

FISHERMAN'S WHARF, with its picturesque sights and pungent smells, attracts millions of visitors annually. Along the waterfront are many restaurants, markets, import houses and souvenir shops. Fresh seafood and sourdough bread are favorite buys. Parking is available in public lots along Beach, North Point, Bay and Francisco streets.

GHIRARDELLI SQUARE, between Beach, Polk, North Point and Larkin sts., is within walking distance of Fisherman's Wharf and the Cannery. The 2.5-acre site comprises a complex of crenellated, white-trimmed brick buildings of the old Ghirardelli chocolate company, a woolen mill, apartments and other buildings that have been refurbished to house specialty shops, bakeries and international restaurants. Many "human statues" and mimes perform next to the square. Phone (415) 775-5500.

PIER 39, at the foot of Stockton St. on the Embarcadero, is a waterfront shopping and dining complex. Three stage areas present live entertainment, and the Palace of Fun Arts provides an amusement section for children. An information center is at the pier's entrance. Phone (415) 705-5500.

Theater and Concerts

The San Francisco Opera presents a full season of productions in the Opera House from mid-September into December. The San Francisco Symphony performs in Louise M. Davies Symphony Hall from September through May; it also presents a Beethoven Festival in June and gives pops concerts in July.

Free Sunday orchestral and band concerts take place in Sigmund Stern Memorial Grove at Sloat Boulevard and 19th Avenue in summer and in Golden Gate Park all year. During the academic year the San Francisco Conservatory of Music holds concerts by students and graduates at Hellman Hall; phone (415) 759-3477 for 24-hour

schedule and price information, or for tickets phone 759-3475 Mon.-Fri. 10-3.

The San Francisco Ballet's repertory season is between late January and early May. The company also presents the Nutcracker Suite in December. All performances are at War Memorial Opera House. Other principal theaters are the Curran, 445 Geary St.; the Orpheum, 1192 Market St.; Exit Theatre, 156 Eddy St.; Cowell Theatre, at Fort Mason, Marina Boulevard at Buchanan; and the Golden Gate, at the intersection of Market and Taylor streets and Golden Gate Avenue. These feature Broadway hits or occasional pre-Broadway tryouts.

The American Conservatory Theater, a repertory group, presents plays in the restored, Edwardian-style, 1910 Geary Theatre; phone (415) 749-2228 for information. A uniquely San Francisco theater experience is "Beach Blanket Babylon" at Club Fugazi, 678 Green St.; phone (415) 421-4222 for reservations. Community theater also flourishes in San Francisco.

Special Events

San Francisco's calendar is packed with events ranging from gigantic exhibits of boats, cars, vacation equipment, furniture and antiques to small one-man sidewalk art shows.

The year begins with the East-West Shrine Game, held in January at Stanford University in Palo Alto. The Sports and Boat Show is a huge exhibition held in January at either Moscone Center or the Cow Palace. Following is one of the most colorful of all celebrations—Chinese New Year. Featuring a parade, complete with dragon, it is held in February or early March in Chinatown. March's main event, the St. Patrick's Day Parade, is held the Sunday nearest the 17th; it starts at the Civic Center and ends in the financial district.

Spring blossoms with The Union Street Easter Parade and Celebration. Mid-April brings the Japanese Cherry Blossom Festival. The San Francisco International Film Festival, held nearly every spring since 1956, is presented in various locations.

In May Armed Forces Day is observed; the festivities include a parade, entertainment, arts and crafts and an open house at several nearby military installations. Also in May is the Bay to Breakers Footrace, involving as many as 100,000 runners. In late May or early June, Carnaval takes place in the Mission District; a parade is followed by a masquerade ball. A parade from the Civic Center to the Embarcadero is the highlight of the Lesbian-Gay Freedom Day Parade and Celebration in late June.

The California Shakespeare Festival is held in Orinda from July through September. The Chinatown Autumn Moon Festival is observed in September as well. Mid-October presents the Italian Heritage Day Parade and Fleet Week, and in late October the Cow Palace is the scene of the Grand National Rodeo, Horse and Stock Show. The San Francisco International Auto Show revs up in late November at Moscone Center.

The San Francisco Vicinity

GOLDEN GATE NATIONAL RECREATION AREA (O-1)

Golden Gate National Recreation Area encompasses both the rolling coastal hill country north of the Golden Gate Bridge and the diverse urban parklands strung around San Francisco's northern and western edges.

The Marin Headlands across the Golden Gate Bridge contrast dramatically with the cityscape to the south. Smooth grassy ridges slope down through valleys to a craggy shoreline scalloped with sandy coves. Abandoned gun emplacements stud the hillsides above the Golden Gate and provide good vantage points for viewing the bridge and the city.

Northward from the Marin Headlands are Mount Tamalpais State Park (see Mill Valley p. 209) and Muir Woods National Monument (see place listing p. 209). Beyond the state park, the Olema Valley section of the recreation area abuts Point Reyes National Seashore (see place listing p. 210).

About 100 miles of hiking and riding trails traverse the pastoral countryside between Point Reyes and the Golden Gate. Hikers should stay on the trails, as the hillsides are often laced with poison oak. Because of the cool ocean winds and frequent fog, visitors should be prepared for changeable weather by dressing in layers. Swimming is permitted at Stinson Beach, China Beach, Muir Beach and Aquatic Park. Backcountry campsites are available and require reservations. Fishing spots and picnic facilities are scattered throughout the parklands.

California Marine Mammal Center, 4 miles west of US 101 in the Marin Headlands, is an animal hospital that rescues and rehabilitates sick, injured or distressed marine animals from the California coast. Self-guiding tours are available.

The southern extreme of the recreation area is Fort Funston, where hang gliders commonly fly along the cliffs. The long windswept strand of Ocean Beach links Fort Funston with Cliff House, the Victorian gardens of Sutro Heights and Lands End at the northwestern shoulder of the city. The Coastal Trail threads through Lands End to China and Baker beaches and the abandoned coastal batteries just south of the Golden Gate Bridge.

The Golden Gate Promenade extends 3.5 miles along San Francisco Bay and connects Fort Point below the Golden Gate Bridge with Crissy Field and Fort Mason. Alcatraz Island in the bay also is part of the recreation area.

For further information write the Information Center, Golden Gate National Recreation Area, Building 201, Fort Mason, San Francisco, CA 94123; phone (415) 556-0560. The center is open Mon.-Fri. 9:30-4:30. See Recreation Chart.

ALCATRAZ ISLAND, in San Francisco Bay, can be reached via ferries that leave Pier 41 at Fisherman's Wharf. Alcatraz was a maximum security federal penitentiary that once incarcerated such notorious criminals as Al Capone, Machine Gun Kelly and Robert Stroud, the "Birdman of Alcatraz." A self-guiding trail, cellblock tour, slide show and ranger programs are available.

Ferries depart daily at 9:30 and 10:15, then every half-hour 10:45-4:15, mid-May through Aug. 31; at 9:30 and 10:15, then every half-hour 10:45-2:15, rest of year. Round-trip fare with admission (includes audiotape tour) $11; over 61, $9.25; ages 5-11, $5.75. Wear comfortable shoes and warm clothing. Visitors are strongly advised to buy tickets 2 to 4 weeks in advance, May-Sept.; 2 days in advance, rest of year. Orders can be completed by phone for a $2 fee. AE, MC, VI. Phone (415) 705-5555.

BAY AREA DISCOVERY MUSEUM is off US 101 at 557 McReynolds Rd. in Golden Gate National Recreation Area at the n. end of Golden Gate Bridge. The hands-on children's museum features both indoor exhibitions and outdoor activities. Crawling through an underwater sea tunnel, decorating a doll house and fishing off a boat or pier are some of the activities offered. Tot Spot is a storybook environment for ages 1-3. All children must be with an adult. Food is available.

Tues.-Sun. 10-5, June 15-Sept. 15; Tues.-Thurs. 10-5, Fri.-Sun. 10-5, rest of year. Closed Jan. 1, Easter, July 4, Thanksgiving and Dec. 24-25. Admission $7; ages 1-18, $6. MC, VI. Phone (415) 487-4398.

CLIFF HOUSE, Great Hwy. and Point Lobos Ave., overlooks the ocean and nearby Seal Rocks, habitat of sea lions September through June. A visitor center under the aegis of Golden Gate National Recreation Area is at the viewing platform. Mechanical Museum (Musee Mecanique) displays coin-operated, automatic musical instruments. Mon.-Fri. 11-7, Sat.-Sun. 10-8. Free. Phone (415) 386-1170.

FORT POINT NATIONAL HISTORIC SITE, reached by turning off Lincoln Blvd. at Long Ave. to the fort, is part of Golden Gate National Recreation Area. Built by the U.S. Army 1853-1861, Fort Point is similar in design to Fort Sumter, S.C. Although it once was the principal defense bastion on the West Coast, no battle ever occurred at Fort Point. Videotape presentations about the history of the fort and the building of the Golden Gate Bridge are provided. Tours and cannon-loading demonstrations are offered. An audio tape narrating a tour can be rented.

Wed.-Sun. 10-5. Cannon-loading demonstrations are given at noon. Closed Jan. 1, Thanksgiving and Dec. 25. Donations. Phone (415) 556-1693.

PRESIDIO, in the n.w. corner of the city, served as an active military garrison almost continuously for 218 years. The Presidio was closed as an Army post in 1994, and its 1,480 acres transferred to the National Park Service. Within its boundaries are Fort Point, San Francisco National Cemetery, Fort Winfield Scott, Letterman Hospital and Crissy Field. The higher hills offer spectacular bay and ocean vistas. Visitors can join guided tours or participate in recreational activities.

A visitor center in Building 102 on Montgomery Street at Lincoln Boulevard contains displays, maps and brochures. Visitor center is open daily 9-5; closed Jan. 1, Thanksgiving and Dec. 25. Park admission free. Phone (415) 561-4323, or TTY (415) 561-4314.

Presidio Museum, Funston Ave. at Lincoln Blvd., depicts more than 200 years of Presidio history. Two cottages behind the museum were among thousands built to house refugees following the city's 1906 earthquake and fire. A guided tour is offered Saturday. Wed.-Sun. noon-4; closed Jan. 1, Thanksgiving and Dec. 25. Free. Phone (415) 561-4331.

HALF MOON BAY (Q-2)
pop. 8,900, elev. 69'

Half Moon Bay has a rugged coastline with many sandy beaches for walking and exploring. The bay is a popular launching spot for sightseeing, fishing and whale-watching cruises; contact Huck Finn Sport Fishing at (650) 726-7133. The town also is known for its flower market, held every third Saturday of the month at Kelly and Main streets. Half Moon Bay lies on a scenic stretch of SR 1 that extends from San Francisco to San Luis Obispo.

Half Moon Bay Coastside Chamber of Commerce: 520 Kelly Ave., Half Moon Bay, CA 94019; phone (650) 726-5202.

MILL VALLEY (O-2)
pop. 13,000, elev. 70'

Mill Valley is a residential community at the base of Mount Tamalpais. The heavy redwood frame of the sawmill for which the town was named still stands in Old Mill Park on Throckmorton Avenue. Hikers can follow a nearby trail up the mountain.

Mill Valley Chamber of Commerce: 85 Throckmorton Ave., P.O. Box 5123, Mill Valley, CA 94942; phone (415) 388-9700.

MOUNT TAMALPAIS STATE PARK, 6 mi. w., covers 6,233 acres of picturesque coastal hill country dominated by triple-peaked Mount Tamalpais, whose profile from the south is said to resemble a sleeping American Indian girl. Hiking and bicycling trails and a winding road lead to the summit, which offers spectacular vistas. A visitor center is at the summit. Plays are presented May through June in Mountain Theater; phone (415) 383-1100. Park open daily dawn-dusk. Visitor center open Sat.-Sun 10-5. Parking $5 per private vehicle. Phone (415) 388-2070. *See Recreation Chart.*

MOSS BEACH (P-1) pop. 1,900, elev. 80'

JAMES V. FITZGERALD MARINE RESERVE, w. off SR 1 via California Ave., preserves marine life in one of the state's most diverse intertidal regions. Marine life typically visible includes crabs, abalone, mussels, starfish, sea slugs and isopods. Low tide is the best time to explore; consult a local tide chart or phone the reserve for information. Collecting shells, rocks and plants is strictly prohibited. Daily dawn-dusk. Free. Phone (650) 728-3584.

★ MUIR WOODS NATIONAL MONUMENT (O-1)

The 560-acre Muir Woods National Monument, 17 miles northwest of San Francisco on the southwestern slope of Mount Tamalpais, is reached via the Golden Gate Bridge and SR 1. Named for noted conservationist John Muir, Muir Woods is one of the most beautiful and accessible of the famous redwood groves which 140 million years ago blanketed much of the Northern Hemisphere. The Sequoia sempervirens, tallest of all tree life—though not as large in girth as the Sequoia gigantea—is well represented. Some coast redwoods reach a height of 250 feet with diameters of more than 12 feet.

Although coast redwood trees are most common in the forest, Douglas fir, maple, oak and bay laurel also thrive. Due to a lack of food caused by the shady forest conditions, animal life is sparse. Trails for hiking and exploring range from a half-mile to 2 miles long. Some trails combine with others in Mount Tamalpais State Park *(see Mill Valley p. 209)*.

Neither picnicking nor camping is permitted at the monument, and pets are not allowed. Since roads leading to the park are steep and winding, vehicles longer than 35 feet are not permitted. Food is available. Monument open daily 8-dusk. A visitor center is open daily 9-6, Memorial Day-Labor Day; 9-5, rest of year. Free. For additional information contact the Site Supervisor, Muir Woods National Monument, Mill Valley, CA 94941; phone (415) 388-2595, or TDD (916) 556-2766.

PACIFICA (P-2) pop. 37,700, elev. 60'

One of California's newest towns, Pacifica was formed in 1957. Its history, however, goes back to 1769, when Gaspar de Portolá first sighted San Francisco Bay from Discovery Point in the mountains behind present-day Pacifica. Francisco Sanchez, an alcalde of San Francisco under the Spanish government, later was awarded the land in return for his service to Mexico. His adobe was built 1842-46. The two-story house, a half-mile east of SR 1 at 1000

Linda Mar Blvd., is preserved as Sanchez Adobe Historic Site and is decorated with period furniture, objects, implements and clothing.

Pacifica Chamber of Commerce and Visitors Center: 225 Rockaway Beach Ave., Suite 1, Pacifica, CA 94044; phone (650) 355-4122.

POINT REYES NATIONAL SEASHORE (O-1)

Blunt headlands jut into the sea, and grass-tufted dunes lie along miles of secluded beaches on Point Reyes, north of San Francisco. Inland are rolling hills, freshwater lakes and Inverness Ridge, where the Douglas fir, typical of the northern California coastal ranges, and the Bishop pine of the southern forest areas merge. More than 350 species of birds and 72 species of mammals inhabit Point Reyes National Seashore's 65,300 acres. In addition fragile tidepool life can be observed at several locations.

Park headquarters is at Bear Valley, .2 miles west of Olema on Bear Valley Road. The headquarters is adjacent to Bear Valley Visitor Center, which provides information about facilities, nature trails and exhibits; it is open daily. Point Reyes Lighthouse and Visitor Center is open Thurs.-Mon. 10-5 (weather permitting). Kenneth C. Patrick Visitor Center at Drakes Beach is open Sat.-Sun. and holidays 10-5 (weather permitting). Admission, backpack camping and use of facilities are free; reservations are suggested for camping.

Point Reyes Morgan Horse Ranch; Kule Loklo, a replica of a Miwok Indian village; the Pierce Ranch, a former dairy ranch with self-guiding trail exhibits; and the Earthquake Trail are near park headquarters. At the end of Mesa Road is Point Reyes Bird Observatory. Bird-banding demonstrations are held Saturday and Sunday mornings. Popular activities within the seashore include hiking, bird-watching, beachcombing, picnicking and swimming. Panoramic views are available at many observation spots and overlooks; from some locations it is possible to spot harbor seals, sea lions and migrating gray whales.

The park has four hike-in campgrounds; the required free permits can be obtained at Bear Valley Visitor Center; phone (415) 663-8054 daily 9-2 for camping reservations. More than 140 miles of foot and horse trails fan out from the Bear Valley trailhead. Some 35 miles of trails are open to bicyclists; trail maps are available at the visitor centers. Hikers and campers should carry a canteen, since the stream water is not potable. Pets are barred from all trails and campgrounds, but may be taken to North and South beaches and a portion of Limantour Beach if leashed.

Point Reyes National Seashore lies on a scenic stretch of SR 1 that extends from Leggett to Sausalito.

Varied programs are conducted; for additional information contact the Superintendent, Point Reyes National Seashore, Point Reyes, CA 94956; phone (415) 663-1092. *See Recreation Chart and the AAA California/Nevada CampBook.*

SAN MATEO (P-2) pop. 85,500, elev. 29′

San Mateo is a residential suburb of San Francisco. Central Park contains a lovely Japanese garden. San Mateo-Hayward Bridge, constructed with five steel spans, is one of the longest highway bridges in the country. Bay Meadows Race Track features horse racing; phone (650) 574-7223.

Note: Policies concerning admittance of children to pari-mutuel betting facilities vary. Phone for information.

San Mateo Chamber of Commerce: 1021 S. El Camino, 2nd floor, San Mateo, CA 94402; phone (650) 341-5679.

SAVE **COYOTE POINT MUSEUM FOR ENVIRONMENTAL EDUCATION** is on Coyote Point Dr. in Coyote Point Park. Environmental Hall exhibits are on four descending levels of ramps to symbolize the eastward flow of water from the Santa Cruz Mountains to San Francisco Bay and its westward flow to the Pacific. Displays include environmental dioramas, a working beehive and other insect colonies. Interactive demonstration stations stress man's impact on nature. The wildlife habitats feature reptiles, birds and mammals. Picnicking is permitted.

Tues.-Sat. 10-5, Sun. noon-5; closed Jan. 1, Thanksgiving and Dec. 25. Admission (includes museum and wildlife habitats) $3; over 61 and ages 13-17, $2; ages 4-12, $1; free to all first Wed. of the month. Park admission $4 per private vehicle. Phone (650) 342-7755.

JAPANESE GARDEN AT CENTRAL PARK, El Camino at 5th Ave., was designed by Nagao Sakurai, the chief landscape architect at Imperial Palace in Tokyo. The garden has labeled plants, evergreens, waterfalls and koi ponds. Parking lots are under the tennis courts. Daily 8 a.m.-10 p.m. Free. Phone (650) 377-4640.

SAN RAFAEL (O-2)
pop. 48,400, elev. 34'

San Rafael began as a village that developed in the early 19th century around Mission San Rafael. It is now a residential area.

San Rafael Chamber of Commerce: 817 Mission Ave., San Rafael, CA 94901; phone (415) 454-4163 or (800) 454-4163.

MARIN COUNTY CIVIC CENTER, just n. off US 101, was the last major project of Frank Lloyd Wright. The 140 landscaped acres include fairgrounds, theaters, a lake and water conservation garden with drought-resistant plants. The building itself is divided into the administrative offices and the Hall of Justice; both parts of the building are included on a tour, which can be arranged by appointment. Allow 1 hour minimum. Mon.-Fri. 9-6; guided tours by appointment. Closed holidays. Free. Phone (415) 499-7407.

MISSION SAN RAFAEL ARCANGEL, 1104 5th Ave. at A St., is a replica built in 1949 on the approximate site of the original mission. Relics and old pictures are displayed. A self-guiding audio tape tour is available. Allow 30 minutes minimum. Mon.-Sat. 11-4, Sun. 10-4. Free. Phone (415) 454-8141.

WILDCARE—TERWILLIGER NATURE EDUCATION AND WILDLIFE REHABILITATION is at 76 Albert Park Ln. off B St. The hospital treats and shelters injured animals until they are able to return to their natural habitats. An exhibit hall offers photographic and California wildlife displays in addition to hands-on exhibits for children. Allow 30 minutes minimum. Daily 9-5. Donations. Phone (415) 456-7283.

SAUSALITO (O-2) pop. 7,200, elev. 14'

A focal point for artists, Sausalito (originally *Saucelito,* meaning "little willow") is a pleasant blending of bohemian and marine influences. Its setting on hilly terrain plunging into the bay contributes to its popularity.

Ferry service links Sausalito with San Francisco; the entire bay area is visible from Sausalito and from Vista Point at the north end of the Golden Gate Bridge. Sausalito is the southern terminus of a scenic 212-mile stretch of SR 1 that heads north along the ocean to Leggett.

Sausalito Chamber of Commerce: 333 Caledonia St., P.O. Box 566, Sausalito, CA 94965; phone (415) 332-0505.

BAY MODEL VISITOR CENTER, 2100 Bridgeway at the foot of Spring St. from Marinship Way access rd., reproduces the tidal action, flow and current as well as the mixing of salt and freshwater in a 2-acre scale model of the San Francisco Bay and Delta region. The model operates only when an experiment is in progress. Audio tours, videotapes and interactive exhibits are available. For guided tour information phone (415) 332-3871. Tues.-Fri. 9-4, Sat. and holidays 10-6, Memorial Day-Labor Day; Tues.-Sat. 9-4, rest of year. Summer hours may vary; phone ahead. Free. Phone (415) 332-3870.

SOUTH SAN FRANCISCO (P-2)
pop. 54,300, elev. 19'

ACRES OF ORCHIDS (Rod McLellan Co.) is e. of I-280 on Hickey Blvd., then s. to 1450 El Camino Real (SR 82). It displays a large variety of orchids and floral crops. Daily 9-6; closed holidays. Free. Phone (650) 871-5655.

This ends listings for the San Francisco Vicinity. The following page resumes the alphabetical listings of cities in California.

SAN GABRIEL—
see Los Angeles p. 128.

SAN JACINTO (C-9)
pop. 16,200, elev. 1,564'

San Jacinto was incorporated in 1888 on land that once was part of Rancho San Jacinto Viejo, a Mexican land grant given to Jose Antonia Estudillo in 1842. The town's heritage includes American Indian, Spanish and Mexican influences along with more recently introduced cultural traditions.

San Jacinto Chamber of Commerce: 188 E. Main St., San Jacinto, CA 92583-4228; phone (909) 654-9246.

SAN JACINTO MUNICIPAL MUSEUM, 181 E. Main St., contains items pertaining to the geologic and human history of Hemet and the San Jacinto Valley. Allow 30 minutes minimum. Tues.-Sat. noon-4; closed Jan. 1, Thanksgiving and Dec. 25. Free. Phone (909) 654-4952.

SAN JOSE (Q-3) pop. 782,200, elev. 94'

San Jose lies in the Santa Clara Valley between the Mount Hamilton and Santa Cruz ranges. Founded as Pueblo de San Jose de Guadalupe in November 1777, the settlement was established to raise crops and cattle for the nearby presidios of San Francisco and Monterey. In 1849 San Jose became the state's first capital—until 1851. The town claims as its oldest structure SAVE Peralta Adobe at 184 W. St. John St. San Jose now is known as the "Capital of Silicon Valley" for the technological innovations that have been forthcoming.

The San Jose area has more than 50 wineries ranging from family-run establishments to large corporations. Throughout the year there are festivals, concerts and other events celebrating viticulture.

San Jose is host to community events as well; Mexican, Japanese, Italian, Spanish, German, Portuguese and Vietnamese festivals take place throughout the year. San Jose's FYI Events Line is answered daily 24 hours at (408) 295-2265, with a touch-tone phone. Santa Clara Valley Transit Authority offers transportation to the various wineries.

San Jose Arena at W. Santa Clara and Autumn streets is home to the San Jose Sharks hockey team. College and professional sporting events, in addition to musical and entertainment events, are held at the arena.

San Jose Convention/Visitors Bureau: 333 W. San Carlos St., Suite 1000, San Jose, CA 95110-2720; phone (408) 295-9600 or 977-0900.

Self-guiding tours: Driving-tour maps are available from the convention/visitors bureau. The

San Jose Visitor Information and Business Center is in the lobby of San Jose McEnery Convention Center, 150 W. San Carlos St.

Shopping areas: Oakridge Mall, Blossom Hill Road and Santa Teresa Boulevard, features Macy's. The anchor sites of Eastridge Mall, e. of US 101 on Tully Road, are occupied by JCPenney, Macy's and Sears. Great Mall of the Bay Area, off I-880 in nearby Milpitas, features more than 180 outlet stores, including Off 5th—Saks Fifth Avenue Outlet, Donna Karan and The Sharper Image. The San Jose Flea Market, 12000 Berryessa Rd., which features thousands of booths and 25 restaurants, draws an average of 80,000 people on a sunny weekend.

ALUM ROCK PARK, 730 acres in the foothills, is e. of US 101 on Alum Rock Ave. The park contains picnic facilities, mineral springs, marked trails and Youth Science Institute. Allow 30 minutes minimum. Park open daily 8 a.m. until 30 minutes after dusk. Institute open Tues.-Sat. noon-4:30. Because of brush-fire danger, the park may be closed at times June-Oct.; phone ahead.

Park free. Institute admission 50c. Parking $3 per private vehicle, Memorial Day weekend-Labor Day and Sat.-Sun. and holidays, rest of year; free other times. Dogs are not permitted. Phone (408) 259-5477, or 258-4322 for the Institute.

CHILDREN'S DISCOVERY MUSEUM OF SAN JOSE, intersection of Woz Way and Auzerais St., offers changing interactive exhibits and programs that lead children to discoveries about themselves and the world around them. Guadalupe Park surrounds the museum. Tues.-Sat. 10-5, Sun. and some Mon. holidays noon-5. Admission $6; over 64, $5; ages 2-18, $4. Under 13 must be with an adult. Phone (408) 298-5437.

KELLEY PARK is at Senter and Story rds. Daily 8 a.m. until 30 minutes after dusk. Parking fee $3 per private vehicle. Phone (408) 277-5738.

Happy Hollow, 1300 Senter Rd., is a family park with a playground, riverboat replica, treehouse, rides and a zoo. Allow 1 hour minimum. Daily 10-5. Closed Dec. 25. Combination ticket for playground, rides and zoo $4.50; ages 65-74, $4. Phone (408) 295-8383.

SAVE **History Museum at Kelley Park,** 1650 Senter Rd. at Phelan Ave., comprises 28 structures that highlight the history and culture of San Jose and the Santa Clara Valley. Visitors can experience a Chinese temple and a Portuguese imperio, observe letterpress printing and hop aboard a historic trolley. The Peralta Adobe is the last remaining structure from El Pueblo de San José de Guadalupe. It is furnished and features a "horno," or outside oven. The Fallon House is a Victorian mansion showcasing 15 period rooms.

Allow 2 hours minimum. Tues.-Fri. 9-5, Sat.-Sun. noon-5; closed Jan. 1, Thanksgiving and Dec. 25. Admission $6; over 64, $5; ages 6-17, $4. Rates vary for events. Phone (408) 287-2290.

Japanese Friendship Garden, 1500 Senter Rd., features landscaping and lanterns representing Japanese culture. Free guided tours are available by reservation. Daily 10-4. Free. Phone (408) 277-4192, or 277-5254 for guided tours.

★**LICK OBSERVATORY,** on the 4,209-foot summit of Mount Hamilton, is e. via Alum Rock Rd. and 19-mile long, narrow, winding Mount Hamilton Rd. Mount Hamilton Rd. is closed when there is snow at the observatory. The observatory, now an observation station overlooking the Santa Clara Valley, was dedicated in 1888. The observatory is a division of the University of California, Santa Cruz. **Note:** Food and automotive services are not available nearby.

Allow 2 hours minimum. Free tours are available for the visitor center in the main building every half-hour Mon.-Fri. 1-4:30, Sat.-Sun. 10:30-4:30. The main building is open 30 minutes before and 30 minutes after the tours begin. A visitor gallery at the 120-inch telescope is open daily 10-5; closed Thanksgiving and Dec. 24-25. Phone to verify schedule. Free. Phone (408) 274-5061 for information and detailed directions.

MUNICIPAL ROSE GARDENS is on Naglee Ave. between Dana Ave. and Garden Dr. The gardens contain more than 5,000 plants and 186 varieties of roses. The peak of color is in May and June, but blooms continue throughout the summer. Allow 30 minutes minimum. Daily dawn-30 minutes after dusk. Free. Phone (408) 277-5422.

OVERFELT GARDENS, Educational Park Dr. and McKee Rd., has a self-guiding arboreal trail, wildflower path, fragrance garden and three small lakes. The 5-acre Chinese Cultural Garden contains statues, memorials and displays devoted to ancient Chinese architecture and culture. Allow 1 hour, 30 minutes minimum. Daily 10-dusk; closed Jan. 1, Thanksgiving and Dec. 25. Free. Phone (408) 251-3323.

RAGING WATERS, off Capitol Expwy. at Tully Rd. in Lake Cunningham Regional Park, is a 16-acre water park with more than 10 waterslides and a wave pool set in a tropical atmosphere. Allow 4 hours minimum. Open daily at 10 (closing time varies), mid-June through Labor Day; Sat.-Sun. 10-7, mid-May to mid-June and day after Labor Day to mid-Sept. (weather permitting). Admission $20.99; under 42 inches tall $16.99; over age 59, $10; under age 3 free. After 3 p.m. $14.99. Parking $3. AE, MC, VI. Phone (408) 654-5450.

⟦SAVE⟧ ★ **ROSICRUCIAN EGYPTIAN MUSEUM AND PLANETARIUM,** on Park Ave. between Naglee and Randol, has a collection of Egyptian artifacts, including mummies, sculptures, jewelry and objects from daily life; a replica of an Egyptian rock tomb; and Babylonian, Sumerian and Assyrian artifacts. Open only for group shows, the planetarium is undergoing renovations; phone for schedule.

Allow 2 hours minimum. Daily 10-5. Last admission 30 minutes before closing. Closed Jan. 1, Thanksgiving and Dec. 25. Museum admission $7; over 64 and students with ID $5; ages 7-15, $3.50. Planetarium admission $4; over 64 and students with ID $3.50; ages 6-15, $3. Under 5 are not admitted to planetarium show. AE, DS, MC, VI. Phone (408) 947-3636.

SAN JOSE MUSEUM OF ART, 110 S. Market St., was built in 1892 by local architect Willoughby Edbrooke. The museum contains changing exhibits of contemporary art. Text panels are available in several languages. Allow 2 hours minimum. Daily 10-5 (also Thurs. 5-8); closed holidays. Tours are given Tues.-Sun. at 12:30 and 2:30. Admission $6; over 62, students with ID and ages 6-17, $3; half-price to all Thurs. 5-8; free to all first Thurs. of the month; free to over 62 first Tues. of the month. AE, MC, VI. Phone (408) 294-2787.

TECH MUSEUM OF INNOVATION, jct. Park Ave. and Market St., contains nearly 300 permanent exhibits and interactive displays designed to show how technology affects everyday life. The museum comprises four themed galleries that focus on high-technology, communication, the human body and exploration. Films are shown in the Hackworth IMAX® Dome Theater.

Daily 10-6 (also Thurs. 6-8 p.m.), Memorial Day-Labor Day; Tues.-Sun. 10-5 (also 5-8 third Thurs. of the month), rest of year. Closed Jan. 1, Easter, Thanksgiving and Dec. 25. Exhibits *or* IMAX film $8; over 64, $7; ages 6-18, $6. Exhibits *and* IMAX film $12; over 64, $11; ages 6-18, $10. AE, DS, MC, VI. Phone (408) 279-7150.

★**WINCHESTER MYSTERY HOUSE,** 525 S. Winchester Blvd. between I-280 and Stevens Creek Blvd., is a Victorian mansion designed to baffle the evil spirits that haunted Sarah Winchester, eccentric heiress to the Winchester Arms fortune, and mistress of the house. With 160 rooms, 2,000 doors, 13 bathrooms, 10,000 windows, 47 fireplaces, blind closets, secret passageways and 40 staircases, the house is so complex that even the owner and servants needed maps to find their way.

One tour includes a 65-minute guided tour of the mansion interior and a self-guiding tour of the gardens. The behind-the-scenes tour lets visitors see how the estate operated when Winchester lived in it.

Allow 2 hours minimum. Daily 9-8, mid-June through Labor Day; Sun.-Thurs. 9-5, Fri.-Sat. 9-8, Apr. 1 to mid-June; daily 9-5 in Mar. and day after Labor Day-Oct. 31; daily 9:30-4, rest of year. Closed Dec. 25. Tour of the mansion, gardens and museums $13.95; over 64, $10.95; ages 6-12, $7.95. AE, MC, VI. Phone (408) 247-2101. *See color ad p. 925-926.*

MISSION ARCHITECTURE

The architecture of the 21 Spanish missions built along El Camino Real 1769-1823 reflects both the simple tastes of their Franciscan founders and the limited resources of material and skilled labor available in the California wilderness. The missions were constructed of stone and adobe, finished inside and out with whitewashed mud plaster and topped with pitched roofs of hewn timber covered with red tile. They were modestly adorned, compared to much of the Spanish architecture in the New World at that time.

The mission usually centered on a courtyard, which was enclosed by the church and a variety of other buildings. These minor structures included quarters for friars, native workers, servants and soldiers; guest rooms; workshops; a convent; a kitchen; and a dining hall. Cloisters—arched covered passageways—fronted the courtyard and often the surrounding outer plaza as well.

The mission church followed one of three general designs. The first, typified by Mission San Miguel Arcangel in San Miguel, consisted of a simple nave, or central hall. A more elaborate design, such as San Buenaventura Mission in Ventura, included a single bell tower. Two belfry towers adorned churches of the third design, exemplified by the graceful Mission Santa Barbara.

After the secularization of the missions in 1833, earthquakes and neglect took their toll; many of the missions were severely damaged or destroyed. Subsequent restoration and reconstruction have revitalized these historic structures, which remain the oldest and perhaps the most elegant architecture in California.

 WINERIES

- **Mirassou Vineyards**, 3000 Aborn Rd. Mon.-Sat. noon-5, Sun. noon-4; closed holidays. Phone (408) 274-4000.

SAN JUAN BAUTISTA (G-3)
pop. 1,600, elev. 200′

★ **MISSION SAN JUAN BAUTISTA** is at 2nd and Mariposa St. Founded June 24, 1797, it was the largest of the mission churches. In recognition of its importance, a set of nine bells once graced the chapel area; only three remain. It is the only mission with a three-aisle entrance to the altar. The mission has period furnishings, and the convent wing contains relics. It is still an active Catholic church. Mon.-Sat. 9:30-5, Sun. 10-5; closed Jan. 1, Thanksgiving and Dec. 25. Donations. Phone (831) 623-4528, or 623-2127 for the office.

★ **SAN JUAN BAUTISTA STATE HISTORIC PARK,** on the plaza, includes the old Plaza Hotel, built in 1858 on the site of the old Spanish soldiers' barracks, and the 1840 Castro House, headquarters of the Mexican government and later home of the Patrick Breen family, survivors of the ill-fated Donner party. Other attractions are the 1868 Zanetta House, gardens, a Spanish orchard, a livery stable with old wagons and a slide show about the history of San Juan Bautista. Allow 30 minutes minimum. Daily 10-4:30; closed Jan. 1, Thanksgiving and Dec. 25. Admission $2; ages 6-12, $1. Phone (831) 623-4881.

SAN JUAN CAPISTRANO (K-6)
pop. 26,200, elev. 130′

San Juan Capistrano is set in rolling hills between the Santa Ana Mountains and the sea. It has several historic adobe buildings, and its restored 1895 Santa Fe Railroad station is now an Amtrak terminal and restaurant.

A guided walking tour departs from the station every Saturday at 10. The tour covers the old mission, the library, the city's oldest residential neighborhood and a few historic adobes; phone (949) 489-0736. Across the tracks from the station is the Jones Family Mini Farm which features a petting zoo and pony rides; phone (949) 831-6550.

San Juan Capistrano Chamber of Commerce: 31871 Camino Capistrano, Suite 306, San Juan Capistrano, CA 92675; phone (949) 493-4700.

★ **MISSION SAN JUAN CAPISTRANO,** 2 blks. w. of the SR 74/I-5 jct., was founded Nov. 1, 1776, by Father Junípero Serra. The mission had three churches: the Great Stone Church, of which only ruins remain; its likeness, the new seven-domed parish church containing a 104-foot belltower; and Padre Serra's Church, dedicated in 1778 and used daily. The cruciform stone church, built

1797-1806, was one of the most ambitious and elaborately adorned of the mission churches. The earthquake of 1812 razed the tower and heavy roof.

Today the mission is famous for the swallows that arrive in mid-March and leave in mid-October. These remarkably constant birds fly approximately 6,000 miles from Goya, Argentina, to nest and rear their young in San Juan Capistrano. By 1777, when a record of their return first was noted in the mission archives, ceremonies welcoming the swallows were already a village tradition.

The 10-acre site contains museum rooms devoted to the Native American, Spanish and Mexican periods of the mission's history. A self-guiding tour features artifacts, work buildings, the padres' living quarters, the soldiers' barracks, an American Indian cemetery and a kitchen. Gardens, arches and Moorish fountains grace the grounds. Daily 8:30-5; closed Good Friday afternoon, Thanksgiving and Dec. 25. Admission $5; over 54 and ages 3-12, $4. Phone (949) 248-2048 or 248-2049.

SAN LEANDRO (P-2)
pop. 68,200, elev. 59'

San Leandro Chamber of Commerce: 262 Davis St., P.O. Box 607, San Leandro, CA 94577; phone (510) 351-1481.

CASA PERALTA is at 384 W. Estudillo. This 1901 casa has been restored to its 1920s appearance. Spanish tiles inside the fence relate the story of Don Quixote. Allow 30 minutes minimum. Fri.-Sun. noon-4; closed holidays. Donations. Phone (510) 577-3474 or 577-3491.

SAN LUIS OBISPO (I-4)
pop. 42,000, elev. 230'

Founded as a mission in 1772, San Luis Obispo grew into a full-fledged town only after completion of the Southern Pacific Railroad in 1894. Today the city is accessible via US 101 and is known as the home of California Polytechnic State University; for information about free guided tours phone (805) 756-5734. The university's Christopher Cohan Center for Performing Arts holds cultural events; phone (805) 756-2787 for ticket information.

A Farmers Market takes place on the 600-900 blocks of Higuera Street each Thursday evening from 6:30 to 9. There are stalls of fresh produce as well as barbecue stands serving cooked food. Many retail stores remain open, and free street entertainment includes bands, jugglers and puppet shows.

Mission Plaza, a developed wooded creek and urban oasis, offers events all year. San Luis Obispo is part of a scenic 252-mile stretch of SR 1 to San Francisco. Continuing southward, San Luis Obispo provides access to an interesting 204-mile drive on US 101 to Los Angeles.

San Luis Obispo Chamber of Commerce: 1039 Chorro St., San Luis Obispo, CA 93401-3278; phone (805) 781-2777.

APPLE FARM, 2015 Monterey St., features a working reproduction of a 19th-century millhouse on San Luis Creek. Visitors can watch a 14-foot water wheel that, through a series of pulleys and gears, powers a gristmill, ice cream maker and cider press. Food is available. Tours are available. Daily 9-6. Free. Phone (805) 544-2040.

★**MISSION SAN LUIS OBISPO DE TOLOSA**, Chorro and Monterey sts., is often called "The Prince of Missions." Named for a 13th-century French saint, the Bishop of Toulouse, the 1772 mission is now a parish church. In order to repel flaming arrow attacks by unfriendly natives, the mission was built with a tile roof instead of the usual ignitable thatch roof. A museum contains Chumash Indian artifacts and memorabilia from early settlers. There also are gardens. Daily 9-5, Memorial Day-Dec. 31; 9-4, rest of year. Closed Jan. 1, Easter, Thanksgiving and Dec. 25. Donations. Phone (805) 543-6850.

SAN LUIS OBISPO CHILDREN'S MUSEUM, 1010 Nipomo St., lets children learn through play and exploration in more than 25 interactive exhibits. Budding thespians can perform at the Kids' Theater; future firefighters can learn to extinguish fires. Mon.-Tues. and Thurs.-Sat. 10-5, Sun. 1-5, mid-June through Aug. 31; Thurs.-Fri. and Sun. 1-5, Mon. and Sat. 10-5, rest of year. Closed holidays. Admission $4, under 2 free. Phone (805) 544-6212.

SAN LUIS OBISPO COUNTY HISTORICAL MUSEUM, 696 Monterey St. in the historic Carnegie Library building, contains exhibits covering local history from the Chumash and Salinan Indian periods to the present. Wed.-Sun. 10-4; closed holidays. Donations. Phone (805) 543-0638.

SAN MARINO—
see Los Angeles p. 129.

SAN MATEO—
see San Francisco p. 210.

SAN MIGUEL (H-4) pop. 1,100, elev. 620'

★**MISSION SAN MIGUEL ARCANGEL**, 775 Mission St. on the s. edge of US 101, is still a parish church. In good repair, the 1797 mission has many original decorations, frescoes and paintings. The vaulted corridor is noted for its arches. The mission holds a fiesta the third Sunday in September. Daily 9:30-4:30; closed Jan. 1, Easter, Thanksgiving and Dec. 25. Donations. Phone (805) 467-3256.

RIOS-CALEDONIA ADOBE is at 700 S. Mission St. The adobe served as an inn and stage stop

1868-90; it is restored and furnished in period. Daily 10-4; closed Thanksgiving and Dec. 25. Donations. Phone (805) 467-3357.

SAN PEDRO—
see Los Angeles p. 129.

SAN RAFAEL—
see San Francisco p. 211.

SAN SIMEON (H-3) elev. 20'

San Simeon lies on a scenic stretch of SR 1 that extends from San Francisco to San Luis Obispo.

San Simeon Chamber of Commerce: 9255 Hearst Dr., P.O. Box 1, San Simeon, CA 93452; phone (805) 927-3500 or (800) 342-5613.

★ **HEARST CASTLE** has visitor parking in a lot off SR 1; buses provide transportation to the castle. The Castle consists of 165 rooms which include the main house of 115 rooms and three guesthouses, as well as and 127 acres of what was once the estate of newspaper publisher William Randolph Hearst. The grounds and dwellings are on a 1,600-foot mountain (named La Cuesta Encantada—"The Enchanted Hill") overlooking San Simeon and the Pacific Ocean. The castle is decorated during December.

The main residence is a huge Mediterranean Revival-style building called Casa Grande, where Hearst's art collection and antiques are displayed. Pools, fountains and statuary grace the landscaped gardens. Construction began in 1919 and continued until 1947, when ill health forced Hearst to abandon the project. He still had not completed Casa Grande at his death in 1951.

The estate is open only by tour. Four distinct 1.75-hour daytime tours and one 2-hour evening tour are available.

Tour 1 conducts visitors through the gardens, one guesthouse, both pools and the ground floor of the main building, where a Hearst home movie is shown in the theater. *Tour 2* visits the upper floors of the main building, including Hearst's private quarters, study, guest library, guestrooms, kitchen and both pools.

Tour 3 includes the north wing of the main building, one guesthouse, gardens, both pools and a videotape about the castle's construction. *Tour 4* covers mostly the gardens and includes the wine cellar, Neptune pool dressing rooms, two levels of the largest and most elaborate guesthouse and both pools. Evening tours cover highlights of the estate and feature a living-history program. Tour 1 is suggested for first-time visitors.

Comfortable shoes are recommended; there are many stairways. A sweater or jacket is advised; part of each tour is outdoors. Photography without the use of supports or flash attachments is permitted. A visitor center at the foot of the hill has exhibits highlighting the lives of Hearst and the estate's architect, Julia Morgan. Visitors also can watch conservators doing restoration.

Estate tours daily 8:20-3:20. Hours vary depending upon the season. Tour 4 offered Apr.-Oct. Evening tours available Fri.-Sat., Mar.-May and Sept.-Dec. Closed Jan. 1, Thanksgiving and Dec. 25. Day tours $14; ages 6-12, $8. Evening tours $25; ages 6-12, $13. Reservations are recommended and can be made by phone up to 8 weeks in advance. Wheelchair-accessible tours are available with at least 10 days advance notice. DS, MC, VI. To charge by telephone, phone (800) 444-4445. Phone (805) 927-2020.

SANTA ANA (C-7)
pop. 293,700, elev. 110'

Santa Ana Chamber of Commerce: P.O. Box 205, Santa Ana, CA 92702; phone (714) 541-5353.

Shopping areas: South Coast Plaza Village, a European-style marketplace, is at Bear Street and Sunflower Avenue. MainPlace/Santa Ana is on Main St.

SAVE **BOWERS MUSEUM OF CULTURAL ART,** 2002 N. Main St., occupies a landmark mission-style building with bell tower and open courtyard. Extensive permanent and changing exhibits reflect the cultural arts of the Americas, Pacific Rim and Africa. The adjacent Kidseum offers interactive experiences geared to children. Food is available. Tues.-Sun. 10-4 (also Thurs. 4-9); closed holidays. Admission $6; over 61 and students with ID $4; ages 5-12, $2. Phone (714) 567-3600.

SAVE **SANTA ANA ZOO AT PRENTICE PARK,** 1801 E. Chestnut Ave., features a variety of animals, including exotic birds, monkeys, a mountain lion and barnyard animals. There also is a playground. Food is available. Daily 10-5, Memorial Day weekend-Labor Day; 10-4, rest of year. Closed Jan. 1 and Dec. 25. Admission $3.50; over 59 and ages 3-12, $1.50; physically impaired free. Phone (714) 835-7484.

SANTA BARBARA (J-5)
pop. 85,600, elev. 33'

Resting on a narrow shelf between the Santa Ynez Mountains and the Pacific coast, Santa Barbara is one of Southern California's foremost vacation areas. A scenic approach is by way of US 101.

Santa Barbara traces its history back to the earliest days of Spanish settlement in Upper California. In 1602 Spanish conquistador Sebastián Vizcaíno sailed into Santa Barbara Bay and named it for the saint who had that birthdate. A military fortress was established in 1782; the mission was founded 4 years later by Father Fermín Francisco de Lasuén.

Santa Barbara's heritage is evident in its many whitewashed, tile-roofed buildings and Spanish street names. The Santa Barbara Historical Society administers the 1862 Fernald Mansion, a traditional upper-class Victorian home with many original period furnishings, and the 1854 Trussell-Winchester Adobe, which represents the intermingling of New England and adobe architecture at 414 W. Montecito St. Phone (805) 966-1601.

Sea Landing offers jet ski rentals, fishing and diving charters, dinner excursions and whale-watching cruises; phone (805) 568-0460.

Santa Barbara Conference & Visitors Bureau Visitor Center: 1 Santa Barbara St., Santa Barbara, CA 93103; phone (800) 676-1266.

Self-guiding tours: Maps of the Red Tile Tour, which covers a section of downtown roughly bordered by Victoria, Santa Barbara, de la Guerra and State streets, are available from the information center near Stearns Wharf.

Shopping areas: Two major stores, Robinsons-May and Sears, are in La Cumbre Plaza at State Street and La Cumbre Road. Paseo Nuevo, anchored by a Macy's and Nordstrom, is on State Street between Cañon Perdido and Ortega streets.

ALAMEDA PLAZA, bounded by Micheltorena, Sola, Anacapa and Garden sts., has picnic areas, playgrounds and more than 70 species of trees. Daily 24 hours. Free.

ALICE KECK PARK MEMORIAL GARDEN, bounded by Arrelaga, Garden, Santa Barbara and Micheltorena sts., contains a pond and a 4.5-acre botanical garden landscaped with native ground covers, trees, shrubs and flowers. Daily 24 hours. Free.

★**COUNTY COURTHOUSE,** 1100 Anacapa St., was built in 1929 and is a fine example of Spanish-Moorish-style architecture. Architectural highlights include specially-designed windows, staircases, balconies, turrets, ornately carved doors and archways. Murals and Tunisian tile decorate the interior, while the tower offers fine views of the city and coast. Mon.-Fri. 8-5, Sat.-Sun. 10-5; closed Dec. 25. Guided tours are given Mon.-Tues. and Fri. at 10:30 and 2, Wed.-Thurs. and Sat. at 10:30. Free. Phone (805) 962-6464.

EL PRESIDIO DE SANTA BARBARA STATE HISTORIC PARK, 100 and 200 blocks of E. Canon Perdido St., is the site of the 1782 Spanish outpost that first brought settlers to the area. Historic buildings within the park include the 1788 El Cuartel, the second-oldest surviving structure in California; the restored Cañedo Adobe; the reconstructed Padre's Quarters; the Chapel; the Commandant's office; and the Northeast Corner. A slide show and guided tours are available upon request. Daily 10:30-4:30; closed Jan. 1, Easter, Thanksgiving and Dec. 25. Free. Phone (805) 965-0093.

HISTORIC ADOBES, downtown, are colorful reminders of the city's past. The 1828 Casa de la Guerra, 15 E. de la Guerra St., is part of El Paseo, a restoration. The 1817 Casa Covarrubias, 715 Santa Barbara St., is believed to have been used briefly as headquarters by the last Mexican governor of California, Pío Pico. The 1836 Historic Adobe, next to the Covarrubias, serves as the office of the Rancheros Visitadores. The 1826 Hill-Carrillo Adobe is at 11-15 E. Carrillo St. The 1854 Trussell-Winchester Adobe, 414 W. Montecito St., is a "Yankee Adobe" typical of the hybrid architecture between Santa Barbara's Mexican and American periods.

The structures are closed to the public, but may be seen on a self-guiding walking tour. Maps are available from the Santa Barbara Visitor Information Center.

KARPELES MANUSCRIPT LIBRARY MUSEUM, 21 W. Anapamu St., displays an extensive collection of original and facsimile manuscripts that includes books, treaties, letters, maps, illustrations and music scores. Many items date back several centuries. Daily 10-4; closed Dec. 25. Free. Phone (805) 962-5322.

★**MISSION SANTA BARBARA** is at E. Los Olivos and Laguna sts. Called "Queen of the Missions," Mission Santa Barbara was founded on Dec. 4, 1786, the Feast of St. Barbara. Completed in 1820, it is one of the best preserved of the missions. The original living quarters for missionaries and guests are now museum rooms which feature collections of period artifacts.

The mission church contains examples of 18th- and 19th-century Mexican art, and a Moorish fountain, built in 1808, graces the front of the mission. Daily 9-5; closed Easter, Thanksgiving and Dec. 25. Admission $3, under 12 free. Phone (805) 682-4149 or 682-4713.

SAVE **SANTA BARBARA BOTANIC GARDEN,** 1212 Mission Canyon Rd., consists of 65 acres devoted to native California trees, flowers, shrubs and cactuses; 5.5 miles of trails wind through native plant habitats ranging from redwoods to desert. Mon.-Fri. 9-5, Sat.-Sun. 9-6, Mar.-Oct.; Mon.-Fri. 9-4, Sat.-Sun. 9-5, rest of year. Guided tours daily at 2 (also Thurs. and Sat.-Sun at 10:30). Admission $3; over 59 and full-time students with ID $2; ages 5-12, $1. Phone (805) 682-4726.

SANTA BARBARA HISTORICAL MUSEUM, 136 E. de la Guerra, has local historical exhibits. Allow 30 minutes minimum. Tues.-Sat. 10-5, Sun. noon-5; closed Jan. 1, Thanksgiving and Dec. 25. Guided tours Wed. and Sat.-Sun. at 1:30. Donations. Phone (805) 966-1601.

★**SANTA BARBARA MUSEUM OF ART,** 1130 State St., displays American, Asian and 19th-century European art; contemporary works; Greek and Roman antiquities; a major photographic collection; and changing exhibitions throughout the year. The collections include works by Claude Monet and other impressionists. Tues.-Thurs. and Sat. 11-5, Fri. 11-1, Sun. noon-5. Tours are given Tues.-Thurs. and Sat.-Sun. at 1. Closed Jan. 1, Thanksgiving and Dec. 25. Admission $5; over 62, $3; ages 6-17 and students with ID $2; free to all Thurs. and first Sun. of the month. Phone (805) 963-4364.

SANTA BARBARA MUSEUM OF NATURAL HISTORY, 2559 Puesta del Sol Rd., houses exhibits about American Indian tribes as well as animals, birds, insects, plants, minerals, marine science and geology. A large skeleton of a baby blue whale is displayed at the entrance. The museum also contains a planetarium. Mon.-Sat. 9-5, Sun. and holidays 10-5; closed Jan. 1, Thanksgiving and Dec. 25. Admission $5; over 64 and ages 13-17, $4; under 13, $3; free to all first Sun. of the month. Phone (805) 682-4711, or 682-3224 for planetarium information.

SAVE ★ **SANTA BARBARA ZOOLOGICAL GARDENS,** a 40-acre park at 500 Niños Dr., has 80 exhibits displaying more than 600 animals in naturalistic habitats. Picnic areas, a playground and a miniature train also are featured. The landscaped grounds also include a fine botanical collection. Food is available. Daily 10-5; closed Thanksgiving and Dec. 25. Last admission 1 hour before closing. Admission $6; over 60 and ages 2-12, $4. Train rides $1; ages 2-12, 50c. Phone (805) 962-5339.

STEARNS WHARF is at the foot of State St. on the east end of the harbor. A landmark in Santa Barbara, it was built in 1872 to serve cargo and passenger ships. In the 1930s, it was the departure point for people trying to get aboard floating casinos, while during World War II the wharf served as a naval installation. Today it is the site of specialty shops, restaurants and a small museum. It also affords excellent views of the harbor and the mountains behind Santa Barbara. Parking $2 per hour; 2 hours free with validation. Phone (805) 564-5518.

Sea Center, at the wharf, features a life-size model of a California gray whale and her calf. Through models, aquariums, photographs and a touch tank, this small museum gives a comprehensive introduction to the marine and bird life of the Santa Barbara Channel and the Channel Islands National Marine Sanctuary. Museum open daily 10-5; closed Jan. 1, Thanksgiving and Dec. 25. Touch tank open daily noon-4. Admission $3; over 62 and ages 13-17, $2; ages 3-12, $1.50. Phone (805) 962-0885.

UNIVERSITY OF CALIFORNIA, SANTA BARBARA—see Goleta p. 79.

★ **SANTA CATALINA ISLAND—**
see Catalina Island p. 63.

SANTA CLARA (Q-3)
pop. 93,600, elev. 88'

Once an agricultural community renowned for its orchards, Santa Clara is now world-famous as the core of the Silicon Valley. The seeds and fruit of the information revolution can be examined at Intel Museum, 2200 Mission College Blvd., whose various exhibits focus on the manufacture and use of computer chips; phone (408) 765-0503.

Shopping areas: Valley Fair, off I-880 at Stevens Creek Boulevard, features Macy's, Nordstrom and 165 specialty stores.

DE SAISSET MUSEUM, on the Santa Clara University campus, displays paintings, decorative arts, an early California history collection relating to Mission Santa Clara and changing exhibits. Allow 1 hour minimum. Tues.-Sun. 11-4; closed holidays. Donations. Phone (408) 554-4528.

★ **MISSION SANTA CLARA DE ASIS,** on the Santa Clara University campus, off US 101 De La Cruz exit to 500 El Camino Real, was founded in 1777. The present building is a replica of the third mission, which was built in 1825. Relics include three bells given to the mission by the king of Spain. The original garden still can be seen; it is in full bloom April through May. Allow 30 minutes minimum. Mission church open daily 8-6; office open Mon.-Fri. 1-5. Free. Phone (408) 554-4023.

SAVE ★ **PARAMOUNT'S GREAT AMERICA,** on Great America Pkwy. between US 101 and SR 237, is a 100-acre family entertainment center. Through architecture and landscaping, boutiques, restaurants, craft shops and entertainment, it evokes North America's past in five major theme areas: Hometown Square, Yukon Territory, Yankee Harbor, County Fair and Orleans Place.

Among the 35 amusement rides are a double-decker carrousel; a three-armed Ferris wheel that stands 110 feet tall; Drop Zone Stunt Tower, a 22-story free-fall ride; a pendulum-like swinging ship; and seven roller coasters—Invertigo, Vortex, the Demon, Top-Gun, Skyhawk, Tidal Wave and the Grizzly wooden coaster.

Other highlights include Rip Roaring Rapids, a 1,600-foot white-water raft ride and the Days of Thunder motion simulator which re-creates a high-speed stock car race through the use of special effects, digital sound, movie footage shown on a giant screen and seats that move. There also are children's rides, an aerial gondola, a narrow-gauge railway, water flume rides, an antique auto turnpike ride and roaming "Star Trek" characters.

Nickelodeon Splat City, an area for kids, features Mega Mess-a-Mania, a participatory game show held in the outdoor Green Slime Bowl arena, and the Green Slime Zone, an interactive maze of pipework.

Theaters present stage shows and films, and concerts are held in an outdoor amphitheater. Sidewalk entertainment, an ice show and game arcades also are featured. Open daily at 10 (closing time varies) during Easter season and late May-Labor Day; Sat.-Sun. 10-7, late Mar. through mid-May (except during Easter season) and day after Labor Day to mid-Oct. Hours and dates may vary. Closed Easter. Admission $31.99; over 60, $20.99; ages 3-6, $18.50. Parking $6. AE, DS, MC, VI. Phone (408) 988-1776. *See color p. 925-926.*

SANTA CLARITA—
see Los Angeles p. 130.

SANTA CRUZ (G-2)
pop. 49,000, elev. 20'

Santa Cruz, on the coast off scenic SR 1, is the site of one of Father Junípero Serra's 21 missions. A half-scale replica of the mission is on the grounds of Holy Cross Church facing the plaza. All that remains of the original mission, built in 1791 and destroyed by the 1857 earthquake, are the ruins of the soldiers' barracks and part of the stone foundation. The chapel is open to visitors.

Also of interest are McPherson Center for Art and History at Santa Cruz County Art Museum, 705 Front St., which has family programs featuring exhibitions, films and lectures; and Santa Cruz County Historical Trust Museum at McPherson Center, with exhibits and programs relating to local history. The Surfing Museum, on the ground level of Mark Abbott Memorial Lighthouse on West Cliff Drive, displays a collection of surfboards and surfing photographs from the 1930s to the present; phone (831) 425-7278.

Santa Cruz County Conference and Visitors Council: 701 Front St., Santa Cruz, CA 95060; phone (831) 425-1234 or (800) 833-3494.

SAVE CHARDONNAY SAILING CHARTERS departs from Santa Cruz Yacht Harbor. Two-hour ecology and 3-hour whale-watching cruises through Monterey Bay National Marine Sanctuary are available aboard a 70-foot sailing yacht. Other cruise adventures are available. Ecology cruises depart Sun. at 1, Apr.-Oct. Whale-watch cruises depart Fri.-Sun. at 10, Jan.-Mar.; Fri.-Sat. at 10, July-Aug. Each cruise $39.50. Reservations are required. AE, MC, VI. Phone (831) 423-1213 to verify schedule.

JOSEPH M. LONG MARINE LABORATORY, at the end of Delaware Ave. near Natural Bridges State Park, is a marine research and educational facility of the University of California. Examples of ongoing research, an aquarium, touch tank,

marine mammal research pools, interactive exhibits and a museum are featured. Allow 1 hour minimum. Guided tours Tues.-Sun. 1-4; closed holidays. Admission $2, over 64 and students with ID $1, under 17 free; free to all first Tues. of the month. Phone (831) 459-4308.

MYSTERY SPOT, 2.5 mi. n. on Market St., which becomes Branciforte Dr., is a section of redwood forest where the law of gravity seemingly does not apply. Allow 30 minutes minimum. Tours are given daily 9-7. Admission $4; ages 5-11, $2. Phone (831) 423-8897.

NATURAL BRIDGES STATE BEACH, 65 acres on West Cliff Dr., has many tide pools for exploring. The migration of monarch butterflies can be observed from about mid-October through February; a boardwalk leads to the grove. A visitor center offers exhibits about area ecology and wildlife. Allow 2 hours minimum. Beach open daily 8-dusk. Visitor center open Fri.-Sun 10-4. Day use fee $6 per private vehicle; over 61, $5 per private vehicle. Phone (831) 423-4609. *See Recreation Chart.*

SANTA CRUZ ART LEAGUE GALLERIES, 526 Broadway, presents changing art exhibits in all forms of media as well as performance space for theater, dance and music. Allow 30 minutes minimum. Wed.-Sat. 11-5, Sun. noon-4; closed Jan. 1, Thanksgiving and Dec. 25. Donations. Phone (831) 426-5787.

SAVE SANTA CRUZ BEACH BOARDWALK, off SR 1 following signs to beach area, was established in 1904. A magnificent casino built in 1907 has been renovated to house an entertainment facility. The carrousel dates from 1911; the Giant Dipper roller coaster, built in 1924, ranks among the nation's most thrilling.

The boardwalk features Neptune's Kingdom Adventure Center, which includes miniature golf, games and historical displays. Allow 1 hour minimum. Opens daily at 11, closing times vary, Memorial Day-Labor Day; Sat.-Sun. and holidays 11-7, Jan. 1-day before Memorial Day and day after Labor Day-Nov. 30. Boardwalk free. Individual rides $1.50-$3; unlimited rides $18.95. DS, MC, VI. Phone (831) 426-7433 or 423-5590. *See color ad p. 1027.*

SANTA CRUZ CITY MUSEUM OF NATURAL HISTORY, 1305 E. Cliff Dr., contains displays of American Indian artifacts, rocks, fossils, a touch tide pool exhibit and specimens of local flora and fauna. The museum sponsors programs, field trips and special events. Allow 1 hour minimum. Tues.-Sun. 10-5; closed holidays. Donations. Phone (831) 429-3773.

UNIVERSITY OF CALIFORNIA AT SANTA CRUZ (UCSC), corner of Bay and High sts., was founded in 1965 on a 2,000-acre portion of the Cowell Ranch overlooking Monterey Bay and Santa Cruz. Roads and walkways situated amid redwoods and meadows connect eight residential colleges. Barn Theater, just inside the main entrance, is a converted horse barn that now functions as a 158-seat theater used by campus and community groups.

Self-guiding tour maps are available at the main entrance information booth. Student-led tours are given Mon.-Fri. and some Sat. at 10:30 and 1:30; Mon.-Fri. hours may vary. Reservations are required at least 2 to 3 weeks in advance. Parking permits $4; limited metered spaces. Phone (831) 459-4008.

Arboretum, on High St., .5 mi. w. of the main entrance, maintains rare plant collections. Many specimens are not otherwise available for study in American botanical gardens. Hummingbirds and butterflies frequently can be seen. Arboretum open daily 9-5; docents are on duty Tues.-Sat. 10-4, Sun 1-4. Free. Phone (831) 427-2998.

Center for Agroecology & Sustainable Food Program, reached by footpath from Coolidge Dr., is a 25-acre teaching and research facility. The organic farm supports vegetable crops, flowers, herbs and fruit trees. Self-guiding tours are available daily dawn-dusk. Docents are available Thurs. at noon and Sun. at 2. Free. Phone (831) 459-3248.

Cook House, now the college's admissions office, is the former Cowell Ranch cookhouse. The well-preserved building also has served as the chancellor's office and headquarters for the campus police.

Performing Arts Center, Meyer Dr., is an open-air complex that contains a 530-seat indoor theater as well as dance, drama and sound recording studios; a 231-seat second stage; an outdoor Shakespeare Santa Cruz Festival glen seating 700; a 390-seat music and recital hall; and specialized visual arts facilities. Phone (831) 459-2121.

SANTA FE SPRINGS—
see Los Angeles p. 130.

SANTA MARIA (I-4)
pop. 61,300, elev. 217′

Santa Maria's scenic location can best be viewed by a drive along US 101.

Santa Maria Valley Chamber of Commerce: 614 S. Broadway, Santa Maria, CA 93454; phone (805) 925-2403 or (800) 331-3779.

Shopping areas: Santa Maria Town Center, at Broadway and Main Street, has Gottschalks, Robinsons-May Co. and Sears.

SANTA MARIA MUSEUM OF FLIGHT, 3015 Airpark Dr., displays within two hangars such airplanes as the Fleet Model 2 and the Stinson V77-Reliant. An extensive collection of model planes depicts aviation history from the Wright brothers'

pioneering effort to the "flying wing" Stealth bomber. Also on view is the once-secret Norden bombsight and its accessories. Picnicking is permitted. Fri.-Sun. 9-5, Apr.-Nov.; 10-4, rest of year. Closed Jan. 1 and Dec. 25. Donations. Phone (805) 922-8758.

SANTA MARIA VALLEY HISTORICAL MUSEUM, 616 S. Broadway, depicts early area history. Changing displays include artifacts from the Chumash Indian, Spanish rancho and American pioneer eras. The museum also has a replica of a portion of a turn-of-the-20th-century schoolroom. Tues.-Sat. noon-5; closed holidays. Free. Phone (805) 922-3130.

WINERIES

• **Byron Vineyard & Winery,** 12 mi. s.e. at 5230 Tepusquet Rd. Daily 10-4; closed holidays. Phone (805) 937-7288.

SANTA MONICA—
see Los Angeles p. 130.

SANTA MONICA MOUNTAINS NATIONAL RECREATION AREA (B-5)

Santa Monica Mountains National Recreation Area, stretching west from Griffith Park in Los Angeles to the Ventura County line, embraces 150,000 acres of rugged mountains, steep canyons, rolling woodlands and 50 miles of beach. Within its boundaries are 70,000 acres of city, county, state and federal parklands. Major state parks include Leo Carrillo, Malibu Creek, Point Mugu, Topanga Canyon and Will Rogers; in addition there are state and county beaches and parks from Point Mugu to Santa Monica.

Among the many scenic crest line and canyon roads within the recreation area are Decker, Encinal Canyon, Potrero and Yerba Buena roads. Tuna Canyon and Saddle Peak roads provide coastal views, while Corral Canyon Road offers a view of the interior canyons and rugged crests.

Paralleling the Pacific Coast Highway (SR 1) and the Ventura Freeway (US 101), the Mulholland Highway traverses the Santa Monica Mountains from the Hollywood Freeway (US 101) on the east to the Pacific Ocean at Leo Carrillo State Beach on the west.

Note: A 10-mile section of Mulholland Highway from the San Diego Freeway (I-405) west to Topanga Canyon Boulevard is a graded dirt road that can be hazardous in rainy weather.

Recreation includes hiking, picnicking, birdwatching, camping, swimming, snorkeling, fishing, surfing, bicycling and horseback riding. Rangers conduct nature hikes and educational programs; check with the park service for schedules. Reservations are required on some hikes.

For information contact the Santa Monica Mountains National Recreation Area, 401 Hillcrest Dr., Thousand Oaks, CA 91360; phone (818) 597-9192, or (805) 370-2300 in Calif. Phone to confirm all schedules *See Recreation Chart and the AAA California/Nevada CampBook.*

CHEESEBORO CANYON, off Cheeseboro Rd. in Agoura, has more than 2,000 acres of rolling oak woodland that is suitable for hiking, horseback riding and picnicking. Daily 8-dusk. Free.

CIRCLE X RANCH, 5 mi. off Pacific Coast Hwy. on Yerba Buena Rd., has 1,665 acres of trails. Camping, picnicking, hiking and horseback riding are available. Daily 8-dusk. Ranch free; fee for camping.

FRANKLIN CANYON RANCH, on Lake Dr. off Franklin Canyon Dr. n. of Beverly Hills, is a wilderness area amid a highly developed suburban neighborhood. Mountaintop trails provide both mountain and city vistas; streamside walks and grassy picnic areas also are available. Nature walks and educational programs are offered periodically. Food is not available. Daily 8-dusk. Free.

Note: Part of Franklin Canyon Drive is unpaved and can be hazardous in rainy weather.

PARAMOUNT RANCH, on Cornell Rd. off Kanan Rd. in Agoura, was owned by Paramount Studios and used as a Western movie set. Picnicking, hiking and equestrian trails are available; rangers lead hikes and conduct naturalist programs. Daily 8-dusk. Free.

PETER STRAUSS RANCH (Lake Enchanto), 30000 Mulholland Hwy., has a 250-seat outdoor amphitheater, loop nature trails, ranger-conducted hikes and picnic tables. Concerts are held periodically at 2 on Sundays. Daily 8-dusk. Free.

RANCHO SIERRA VISTA/SATWIWA, on Potrero Rd. off Wendy Dr. s. of Newbury Park, is an area of chaparral-covered hillsides and large grassy fields ideal for picnicking, hiking and horseback riding. Rancho Sierra Vista also provides access to the extensive trail system of Point Mugu State Park. Rangers periodically conduct hikes, nature tours and naturalist programs. Satwiwa Native American Culture Center presents exhibits and craft demonstrations every Sunday. Ranch open daily 8-dusk. Center open Sat.-Sun. 10-5. Free.

ROCKY OAKS, Kanan Rd. and Mulholland Hwy. in Agoura, is a park consisting of shady oak groves and a small pond. Popular pursuits include picnicking, hiking, bird-watching and horseback riding. Daily 8-dusk. Free.

SANTA PAULA (J-5)
pop. 25,100, elev. 274'

SANTA PAULA UNION OIL MUSEUM, 1001 E. Main St., depicts the art and science of oil exploration in California through relics, photographs, computer games, videos and a working model of a drilling rig. Housed in an 1890 Queen Anne-Italianate-style building constructed by the founders of Union Oil Co., the museum also displays period offices and a 1930s apartment. Guided tours are offered Fri.-Sun. Open Wed.-Sun. 10-4; closed holidays. Donations. Phone (805) 933-0076.

SANTA ROSA (N-1)
pop. 113,300, elev. 164'

LUTHER BURBANK HOME AND GARDENS is at the corner of Santa Rosa and Sonoma aves. The 30-minute guided tours describe the life and work of the horticulturist who introduced 800 varieties of fruits, vegetables, nuts, grains and ornamental flowers. Examples of roses, fruit trees and other plants developed by Burbank are featured on the grounds. The home, greenhouse and carriage house museum contain original furnishings and changing exhibits.

Gardens open daily 8-7, Apr.-Oct.; 8-5, rest of year. Home tours available Wed.-Sun. 10-3:30, Apr.-Oct. only. Gardens free. Home tours $3, under 12 free. Phone (707) 524-5445.

SONOMA COUNTY MUSEUM, in the restored post office building at 425 7th St., exhibits photographs, paintings and other items pertaining to regional history and culture. Programs and lectures are offered periodically. Allow 30 minutes minimum. Wed.-Sun. 11-4. Admission $2; over 64 and ages 12-18, $1. Phone (707) 579-1500.

SANTA YNEZ (J-4) pop. 3,300, elev. 600'

SANTA YNEZ VALLEY HISTORICAL SOCIETY MUSEUM AND PARKS-JANEWAY CARRIAGE HOUSE is at 3596 Sagunto St. The museum has exhibits about the Chumash Indian culture and 19th- and early 20th-century life in the Santa Ynez Valley. A large collection of North American Indian baskets, pottery, beadwork, porcupine quillwork and weaving also is displayed. The carriage house holds many horse-drawn vehicles including surreys, stagecoaches, phaetons, a shooting brake and a military supply wagon. Many fine examples of Western saddles and tack, including silver-mounted saddles, also are displayed.

A complete blacksmith shop and an old pioneer jailhouse can be seen as well. Museum open Fri.-Sun. 1-4. Carriage house open Tues.-Sat. 10-4, Sun. 1-4. Closed major holidays. Donations. Phone (805) 688-7889.

WINDHAVEN GLIDER RIDES, at Santa Ynez Airport off SR 246, offers glider rides of varying duration over the hills, towns and vineyards of the Santa Ynez Valley. Picnic tables are available. Daily 10-5 (weather permitting); closed Dec. 25. Fare for 15-20 min. Scenic Flight (at 2,500 ft.) $65; 25-30 min. Mountain Adventure

Flight (at 4,000 ft.) $110; 35-40 min. Mile-High Flight (at 5,280 ft.) $135. Reservations are suggested. Phone (805) 688-2517.

WINERIES

- **The Gainey Vineyard,** 1 mi. e. on SR 246. Tours depart at 11, 1, 2 and 3; closed Jan. 1, Thanksgiving and Dec. 25. Phone (805) 688-0558.

- **LinCourt Vineyards at Santa Ynez Winery,** s. of SR 246 at 343 N. Refugio Rd. Daily 10-5; closed Jan. 1, Thanksgiving and Dec. 25. Phone (805) 688-8381.

SARATOGA (Q-2) pop. 28,000, elev. 480'

Saratoga is the northern terminus of a scenic 38-mile stretch of SR 9.

Saratoga Chamber of Commerce: 20460 Saratoga-Los Gatos Rd., Saratoga, CA 95070; phone (408) 867-0753.

HAKONE GARDENS, 21000 Big Basin Way, is a 15-acre park containing four gardens—Hill and Pond Garden; Tea Garden; Zen Garden; and Kizuna En, a bamboo garden. A tea ceremony is performed the first Thursday of the month. Allow 1 hour minimum. Mon.-Fri. 10-5, Sat.-Sun. and holidays 11-5; closed Jan. 1 and Dec. 25. Donations. Parking $5 per private vehicle Phone (408) 741-4994.

VILLA MONTALVO CENTER FOR THE ARTS AND ARBORETUM is .5 mi. s.e. on SR 9, then 1 mi. s.w. on Montalvo Rd.; from SR 17 at Los Gatos take SR 9 n.w. 3.5 mi. Formerly the summer home of U.S. senator and San Francisco mayor James D. Phelan, the estate now serves as a center for fine arts. The 1912 Mediterranean-style structure has a formal garden and trails to lookout points on the surrounding hills. The villa regularly sponsors art exhibits, theater events and concerts. The arboretum has approximately 400 species of plants and 85 species of birds.

Allow 1 hour minimum. Arboretum open Mon.-Fri. 8-5, Sat.-Sun. and holidays 9-5, Oct.-Apr.; otherwise varies, rest of year. Gallery open Thurs.-Fri. 1-4, Sat.-Sun. 11-4. The garden occasionally closes for events. Hours may vary; phone ahead. Center and arboretum free. Phone (408) 961-5800 for recorded information.

SAUSALITO—
see San Francisco p. 211.

SCOTIA (C-1) elev. 164'

PACIFIC LUMBER CO., Main St., offers self-guiding tours of their redwood-processing plant. A logging museum features samples of former and current products, logging equipment, Scotia coins (produced for and used by employees), and photographs. Allow 1 hour minimum. Plant tours Mon.-Fri. 7:30-10:30 and 11:30-2. Museum open Mon.-Fri. 8-4:30, day after Memorial Day-Labor Day; closed holidays. Free. Phone (707) 764-2222.

SEBASTOPOL (N-1) pop. 7,000, elev. 78'

Named after Sevastopol, the Russian seaport on the Crimean peninsula, Sebastopol became a center of canned applesauce production in the late 19th century. The industry is still important to the town today.

Sebastopol Chamber of Commerce and Visitors Center: 265 S. Main St., Sebastopol, CA 95472; phone (707) 823-3032.

HOT AIR BALLOON RIDES, over the Sonoma Valley, are available (weather permitting) through Above the Wine Country Balloons & Tours, (707) 829-3695 or (800) 759-5638. Flights depart daily at dawn. Fare $175. Rides are not advisable for children under age 5. Reservations are required.

Note: The mention of the preceding hot air balloon ride is for information only and does **not** imply endorsement by AAA.

★SEQUOIA AND KINGS CANYON NATIONAL PARKS (H-5) & (G-5)

Elevations in the parks range from 1,300 ft. near the headquarters at Ash Mountain to 14,494 ft. at the summit of Mount Whitney. Refer to AAA maps for additional elevation information.

One way to turn back the clock 3,000 years is to take a trip through Sequoia and Kings Canyon National Parks. The landscape is studded with the largest of trees, the giant sequoia trees (Sequoiadendron giganteum). Many of the trees are more than 200 feet high and some have trunks more than 30 feet in diameter. The parks, which abut, extend from the foothills of the San Joaquin Valley to the crest of the High Sierra. Mount Whitney, at 14,494 feet the highest point in the contiguous United States, is on the eastern edge of Sequoia National Park.

Although the sequoias sparked the formation of these parks, magnificent forests of sugar and ponderosa pine, white and red fir and incense-cedar also exist here. Sugar pines have been known to grow to a base diameter of 11 feet.

Its variable climate has endowed this region with a significant variety of plants. About 1,200 trees, shrubs, plants and flowers have been identified.

Mule deer, marmots, chipmunks and squirrels are common. American black bears frequently are seen in campgrounds; proper food storage is strictly enforced. Raccoons, gray foxes and bob-cats can be seen occasionally at night. Rarely seen, however, are Sierra bighorns, mountain li-ons, pine martens, wolverines and fishers. About 150 species of birds, including the golden eagle, have been spotted, and the streams along with some high-country lakes support rainbow, brook, brown and golden trout.

Only trails penetrate the alpine wilderness of both parks; therefore, the beauties of the High Sierra or back country are available only to hik-ers and horseback riders. *See Recreation Chart and the AAA California/Nevada CampBook.*

General Information and Activities

Sequoia and Kings Canyon National Parks are open all year, although the more remote areas are inaccessible in winter. High mountain passes are seldom open to travel before July 1. The roads to Giant Forest, Lodgepole and the Big Stump en-trance are open all year; however, the Generals Highway between Lodgepole in Sequoia Na-tional Park and Grant Grove in Kings Canyon is closed by heavy snow for periods during winter. Tire chains may be necessary at any time.

Vehicles longer than 22 feet are not recom-mended on the Generals Highway in Sequoia National Park between Potwisha Campground and the Giant Forest Village. It is recommended they use SR 180 via Kings Canyon National Park to access the area.

Bus tours within the parks are available daily in summer. Accommodations and campgrounds usually operate from late May to late September. Some facilities are open throughout the year. A shuttle bus operates hourly in summer between Lodgepole Campground and Crescent Meadow, with stops at the General Sherman Tree, Giant Forest Village and Moro Rock.

Lodgepole and Grant Grove visitor centers, in Sequoia and Kings Canyon National Parks, re-spectively, are headquarters for activities. Natu-ralists give illustrated talks or campfire programs several nights a week in summer at Cedar Grove, Dorst, Grant Grove, Lodgepole, and Mineral King amphitheaters. Schedules of programs and daily guided walks are posted on bulletin boards and in prominent public places. The parks' free newspaper, the *Sequoia Bark*, contains informa-tion. It is available at park entrance stations and visitor centers.

A state fishing license is required for all persons 16 years and over; fee for residents $24.95, non-residents $65.90. A 1-day resident or non-resident license costs $8.95. Hunting is prohibited.

Horseback trips over the hundreds of miles of backpacking trails are popular. Current informa-tion is available at the park visitor centers. Guided trail rides and pack trips or rental saddle stock are available from Grant Grove, Cedar Grove, Wolverton near Giant Forest, and Mineral

King at the southern section of Sequoia. Pack trips also can be arranged from the Owens Valley area on the east side of the Sierra. Cross-country ski rentals and lessons are available at Grant Grove and Wolverton.

Headquarters for both parks, which are admin-istered jointly, is at Ash Mountain, on the Gener-als Hwy. 7 mi. above Three Rivers via SR 198. The center includes a photographic exhibit de-picting life in the foothills.

ADMISSION to the parks is $10 per private ve-hicle, good for 7 days, or $5 per person by other means.

PETS are permitted only if they are on a leash, crated or otherwise restricted at all times. They are prohibited on all trails and in buildings.

ADDRESS inquiries to the Superintendent, Se-quoia and Kings Canyon National Parks, Three Rivers, CA 93271; phone (559) 565-3341.

Points of Interest

Connecting the two national parks is the Gen-erals Highway, a 46-mile-long scenic road that extends from SR 198 at Ash Mountain through Giant Forest to SR 180 at Grant Grove in Kings Canyon National Park. The highway reaches 7,643 feet at Big Baldy Saddle. From Ash Moun-tain to Giant Forest, the road is particularly diffi-cult for motor homes and large trailers. Vehicles longer than 22 feet are not recommended. Ve-hicle combinations over 50 feet are prohibited between Hospital Rock and Giant Forest.

ALTA PEAK (Sequoia), 11,204 feet high, is about 7 mi. from the Wolverton parking area; it can be reached on foot by strenuous hike.

CEDAR GROVE (Kings Canyon) is within the canyon of the South Fork of the Kings River. Peaks rise nearly a mile above the stream, and spectacular views are available from road and trail. The level valley floor is especially well suited to leisurely bicycling. Cedar Grove also is a popular base point for trail trips into the high country. The area is inaccessible during winter.

CRYSTAL CAVE is the only one of more than 200 caves within the national parks open to the public. It is 14 mi. from Lodgepole Visitor Cen-ter and is reached by a narrow, winding road that descends 2,000 feet to Marble Fork Kaweah River Bridge, and then from the parking area down a steep .5-mi. trail to the cave entrance. Vehicles longer than 20 feet are prohibited on the road. Stalagmites and stalactites are highlights of the Organ Room, the Dome Room and the Marble Hall. The temperature inside the cave is a constant 48 F; visitors should bring warm clothing.

Tickets must be bought at least 1.5 hours in advance at Lodgepole Visitor Center or 2 hours in advance at Foothills Visitor Center. Tours last-ing 50 minutes are offered daily every 30 min-utes 11-4, mid-June through Labor Day; Fri.-Mon. on the hour 11-4, mid-May to mid-June and day after Labor Day-Sept. 30. Admission $5; ages 6-12, $2.50. Phone (559) 565-3759.

GENERAL GRANT AND REDWOOD MOUNTAIN GROVES are in Kings Canyon. In Grant Grove is General Grant Tree, third largest of known sequoias. It is 267 feet high with a circumference of 107.6 feet. Robert E. Lee is the second largest sequoia in Grant Grove. Centennial Stump was cut in 1875 as an exhibit for the Philadelphia World's Fair, and Big Stump Basin, the result of early lumbering pursuits, is nearby. Hart Tree, another large sequoia, is in Redwood Mountain Grove.

Grant Grove Visitor Center is 3 mi. e. of Big Stump entrance station on SR 180. The center contains exhibits about the logging history of the sequoias and the wildlife and early native inhabitants. Daily 8-6, June-Sept.; 8-5, rest of year. Free.

GIANT FOREST (Sequoia), 16 mi. from park entrance station via the steep and winding Generals Hwy., was named in 1875 by conservationist John Muir. It is one of the largest sequoia groves. General Sherman Tree is approximately 275 feet high and 103 feet in circumference, with a maximum diameter of 36.5 feet at the base. The volume of its trunk alone is 52,500 cubic feet; it is the largest known sequoia.

HEATHER LAKE (Sequoia), 4 mi. by trail from Wolverton, is the most easily accessible of the parks' alpine lakes. Two miles beyond is Pear Lake, in a barren granite basin.

THE HIGH COUNTRY extends from Coyote Peaks at the s. border of Sequoia to the n. boundary of Kings Canyon at Pavilion Dome. Trail trips are the only way to become acquainted with this rugged country. Mount Whitney is 72 miles from Giant Forest along the High Sierra Trail.

HOSPITAL ROCK (Sequoia) is 5 mi. beyond Ash Mountain entrance station on the road to Giant Forest. American Indian pictographs on the boulder mark an old village site once occupied by the Potwisha tribe of the Western Mono Indians. Also at the site are 71 mortar holes used by the Indian women to grind acorns into flour. Exhibits are on the site of an ancient village.

LODGEPOLE VISITOR CENTER (Sequoia) is 4 mi. n.e. of Giant Forest on the Generals Hwy. The center has displays about the sequoias, geologic history and plant life. Daily 8-6, mid-June to Labor Day; 9-5, rest of year. Free. For camping reservations (in summer only) phone Biospherics Incorporated at (800) 365-2267. Phone (559) 565-3782.

MINERAL KING is 29 mi. e. of Three Rivers via Mineral King Rd. and a steep, narrow, winding and partially paved road. Once a silver-mining area, it is now a peaceful valley retreat lying at

an altitude of 7,500 feet beneath the towering peaks of the Great Western Divide. Rangers lead walks and campfire programs in summer. The area is unsuitable for RVs (trailers are not permitted) and is inaccessible in winter.

MORO ROCK (Sequoia), 2 mi. by narrow road or trail from Giant Forest, is 6,725 feet above sea level and more than 6,000 feet above the San Joaquin Valley floor. Scenic views of the Great Western Divide, especially at sunset, are the rewards of reaching the top. A steep stairway, inaccessible in winter, leads to the summit.

PANORAMIC POINT (Kings Canyon), at the e. boundary of General Grant Grove, offers views of the High Sierra to the east and the San Joaquin Valley and Coast Range to the west. Within walking distance is another observation point at Park Ridge. The roads are narrow and winding; motor homes are prohibited.

THARP'S LOG (Sequoia) is at the end of Log Meadow, a mile by trail from Crescent Meadow; or by Circle Meadow and Congress trails. An old pioneer cabin was built within a hollow sequoia log.

SEQUOIA NATIONAL FOREST

Elevations in the forest range from 1,000 ft. at the Kings and Kern rivers along the forest's western edge to 12,432 ft. at Florence Peak in the Golden Trout Wilderness. Refer to AAA maps for additional elevation information.

Sequoia National Forest, in central California at the southern end of the Sierra Nevada, extends from Kings River southward to the Kern River and Piute Mountains and westward from the Sierra Nevada summit to the brush-covered foothills of the San Joaquin Valley.

Giant sequoias, the Kern Plateau and the Golden Trout, Monarch, Jennie Lakes, South Sierra, Dome Land and Kiavah wildernesses are among the most popular attractions of this approximately 1,139,500-acre forest. South Fork Kings Wild and Scenic River, Kings River Special Management Area, North Fork Kern Wild and Scenic River, and South Fork Kern Wild and Scenic River also are among the attractions.

More than 50 campgrounds and picnic areas provide bases for fishing, swimming, boating, hiking, horseback riding, rock climbing and hunting. White-water rafting is popular on the Kern and Kings rivers. Swimming along the shoreline is permitted on 87-acre Hume Lake. Fall color is particularly spectacular at Quaking Aspen, Indian Basin and Kern Plateau. Winter activities include cross-country and downhill skiing and snowmobiling.

For information contact the Information Receptionist, Sequoia National Forest, 900 W. Grand Ave., Porterville, CA 93257-2035; phone (559) 784-1500. *See Recreation Chart and the AAA California/Nevada CampBook.*

BALCH PARK is a 160-acre county park within Mountain Home State Forest and the general boundary of the Sequoia National Forest, 32 mi. n.e. of Porterville. At an elevation of 6,325 feet stands a beautiful sequoia grove. Two small stocked ponds are in the park. Free.

[SAVE] **BOYDEN CAVERNS** is 22 mi. n.e. of Grant Grove on SR 180 within Sequoia National Forest. Guided tours wind through a variety of underground formations. The temperature inside is a cool 55 F; a sweater or jacket is advised. Allow 1 hour minimum. Forty-five minute tours are offered daily 10-5, June-Sept.; 11-4 in May and Oct. Tour $6; over 62, $5.50; ages 6-12, $3. MC, VI. Phone (209) 736-2708.

LAKE ISABELLA, off SR 178, is one of Southern California's largest reservoirs, with more than 11,000 surface acres. With fishing, boating, camping and picnicking, the lake offers freshwater recreation well within a half-day's drive of either Los Angeles or Bakersfield. Phone (760) 379-5646.

SHASTA-TRINITY NATIONAL FORESTS

Elevations in the forests range from 620 ft. at Lake Shasta to 14,162 ft. at Mount Shasta. Refer to AAA maps for additional elevation information.

Shasta-Trinity National Forests in northern California cover more than 2,100,000 acres, including portions of Yolla Bolly-Middle Eel Wilderness Area and Trinity Alps Wilderness. Mount Shasta, a dormant volcano with five living glaciers, towers to 14,162 feet.

Three impounded lakes—Whiskeytown, Shasta and Clair Engle—are within Whiskeytown-Shasta-Trinity National Recreation Area *(see place listing p. 237)*. Some 1,269 miles of trails lace the area, including 154 miles of the Pacific Crest Trail. The forest offers opportunities for lake and stream fishing as well as hunting for waterfowls, upland birds, deer, bears and small game. For forest reservations phone the U.S. National Forest Service Reservation Center at (800) 280-2267, TDD (800) 879-4496.

For more information contact the Forest Supervisor, Shasta-Trinity National Forests, 2400 Washington Ave., Redding, CA 96001; phone (530) 246-5222. *See Recreation Chart and the AAA California/Nevada CampBook.*

SIERRA CITY (D-4)
pop. 100, elev. 4,187′

KENTUCKY MINE PARK AND MUSEUM, 1 mi. n.e. via SR 49 in Sierra County Historical Park, is on the site of a hard-rock gold mine. Guided walking tours go from the mine portal through an operable tin stamp mill. Tools, photographs, documents and mineral samples displayed in the museum depict mining-camp life during California's gold rush era. Other exhibits include Native American and Chinese artifacts. Picnic facilities are available. Concerts take place Friday evenings July 4 weekend through Labor Day in the outdoor amphitheater; phone for concert information.

Wed.-Sun. 10-5, Memorial Day weekend-Sept. 30; Sat.-Sun. 10-5, in Oct. (weather permitting). Tours, including museum admission, $5; ages 7-17, $2.50. Museum $1. Phone (530) 862-1310.

SIERRA NATIONAL FOREST

Elevations in the forest range from 990 ft. at the Merced River to 13,157 ft. at the summit of Mount Ritter. Refer to AAA maps for additional elevation information.

Sierra National Forest is a gem set between two of California's crown jewels, Kings Canyon and Yosemite national parks *(see place listings p. 222 and 238)*. The forest's 1,300,000 acres embrace almost all the land between these national parks—from the gently rolling foothills bordering the San Joaquin Valley to the jagged Sierra crest. Within the forest's boundaries is much of John Muir's famed "Range of Light." More commonly called the High Sierra, this is a landscape of craggy peaks, giant glacial stairways, and mountainside amphitheaters filled with lakes and open meadows.

How this rugged landscape came to be was a major issue among many 19th-century scientists. Yet it was Muir's remark that "tender snowflowers noiselessly falling through unnumbered centuries" came closest to the truth. Glacial ice gave these peaks their distinctive shape, a profile further refined by the swift streams and rivers fed by the yearly snowpack. Such major rivers as the San Joaquin, the Merced, the Kings and their tributaries carved deep canyons and gorges within the forest.

Hidden deep within these watersheds are clusters of sequoias. One stand of these majestic trees is the Nelder Grove south of Yosemite National Park near Bass Lake; another is farther south near Dinkey Creek in the McKinley Grove.

Two major highways that penetrate the forest are SRs 41 and 168; the most accessible recreation areas lie along or just off these routes. Shaver and Bass lakes are two popular destinations, offering camping and water sports. Other recreation areas, such as Florence Lake, Edison Lake, Redinger Lake and Pine Flat Reservoir, are accessible from forest roads branching off SR 168.

The John Muir and Ansel Adams wilderness areas straddle the forest's eastern border and the Sierra crest. The former, with its snowcapped peaks, dense forests and numerous lakes, is one of California's largest wilderness areas. Highlights of this wild area include John Muir Trail—a segment of Pacific Crest Trail—and Humphreys Basin, with its countless lakes and views of Mount Humphreys, a favorite for world-class climbers.

Within Ansel Adams Wilderness Area are the jagged peaks of Ritter Range, one of the most dramatic mountain ranges in the national forest. Smaller areas include the Monarch, Dinkey Lakes and Kaiser wilderness areas. The John Muir, Kaiser and portions of the Ansel Adams wilderness areas are so popular that a quota system for visitors is in effect; reservations at least 3 weeks in advance are recommended. Other recreation highlights include 1,100 miles of hiking trails, 411 lakes and five wilderness areas.

Wildlife native to the forest include deer, bears, quails, bobcats, foxes, beavers and coyotes. Anglers can expect to find an abundance of rainbow, golden, brown and eastern brook trout as well as large and small mouth bass, crappie and bluegill.

Although the forest has no visitor center, information about campgrounds and recreational opportunities is available at the district ranger stations and the forest headquarters in Clovis. Campground reservations, usually required for June, July and August at Shaver Lake, Huntington Lake, Dinkey Creek and Bass Lake, can be made through the U.S. National Forest Service Reservation Center, (800) 280-2267. Downhill skiing is available nearby.

For more information contact the Forest Headquarters, Sierra National Forest, 1600 Tollhouse Rd., Clovis, CA 93611; phone (559) 297-0706. *See Recreation Chart and the AAA California/Nevada CampBook.*

SILVERADO (C-8) pop. 800, elev. 1,800'

TUCKER WILDLIFE SANCTUARY, 7 mi. s. off Santiago Canyon Rd. at 29322 Modjeska Canyon Rd., is notable for its hummingbirds and native plants. An observation porch affords views of the area, and plaques aid in identification. A nature center displays several small native animals, live as well as stuffed and mounted. Nature trails wind

through the 12-acre site. Daily 9-4; closed Dec. 25. Admission $1.50. Phone (714) 649-2760.

SIMI VALLEY (A-5)
pop. 100,200, elev. 820'

SAVE **RONALD REAGAN PRESIDENTIAL LIBRARY,** 40 Presidential Dr., is a Spanish Mission-style structure built around a courtyard and set on a hilltop that affords a view of the surrounding countryside. Within the library's museum are photographs and memorabilia of President Reagan's life, gifts of state received during his administration, a full-scale replica of the Oval Office and a large section of the Berlin Wall. Daily 10-5; closed Jan. 1, Thanksgiving and Dec. 25. Admission $4; over 61, $2; under 16 free. Phone (805) 522-8444.

SIX RIVERS NATIONAL FOREST

Elevations in the forest range from 350 ft. at Adams Station to 6,957 ft. at the summit of Salmon Mountain. Refer to AAA maps for additional elevation information.

Covering almost 990,000 acres, Six Rivers National Forest extends 135 miles south from the Oregon border along the west slope of the Coast Range; it is named for the Smith, Klamath, Trinity, Mad, Van Duzen and Eel rivers.

Many routes, including SR 96 along the Trinity and Klamath rivers northward from Willow Creek through the Hoopa Valley Indian Reservation, penetrate the forest. Much of the region is accessible only on foot or by horseback.

As the forest's name implies, many recreational opportunities center around the rivers. Rafting and kayaking are especially popular on the Klamath, Trinity and Smith rivers. Trout, steelhead and salmon fishing and deer hunting also are popular pastimes.

Within the national forest is Smith River National Recreation Area, which offers numerous leisure activities. More than 65 miles of trails accommodate horseback riders, mountain bikers or hikers, and animals lovers will find rare and endangered species such as the bald eagle and peregrine falcon. For information contact the Forest Supervisor, Six Rivers National Forest, 1330 Bayshore Way, Eureka, CA 95501; phone (707) 441-3523. *See Recreation Chart and the AAA California/Nevada CampBook.*

SODA SPRINGS (D-4)
pop. 300, elev. 6,768'

WESTERN SKISPORT MUSEUM, s. of I-80 at the Boreal Ski Area, has displays depicting the development of snow skiing as a sport. Exhibits date from 1850 to the present. Films are shown by request. Allow 30 minutes minimum. Wed.-Sun. 10-4, June 15 through mid-Apr. Free. Phone (530) 426-3313.

SOLEDAD (G-3) pop. 7,200, elev. 190'

MISSION MARIA SANTISIMA NUESTRA SEÑORA DOLORISISIMA DE LA SOLEDAD, 1.3 mi. w. off US 101 at 36641 Fort Romie Rd., was founded in 1791. It consists of adobe ruins, a museum and a restored chapel. Allow 30 minutes minimum. Wed.-Mon. 10-4; closed Jan. 1, Easter, July 4, Thanksgiving and Dec. 25. Donations. Phone (831) 678-2586.

★ SOLVANG (I-4) pop. 4,700, elev. 480'

Danish in heritage, customs and atmosphere, Solvang is about 45 miles northwest of Santa Barbara in the Santa Ynez Valley. The town was established in 1911 by a group of Danish educators from the Midwest who were looking for a site on which to build a Danish folk school. Visitors delight in the traditional Danish architecture, windmills, gaslights and cobblestone walks. A Danish streetcar, drawn by blonde Belgian horses, tours the town. Perched on many roofs are artificial nesting storks, considered good luck charms by the Danes.

Solvang Business Association & Chamber of Commerce: 1693 Mission Dr., P.O. Box 465, Solvang, CA 93464; phone (805) 688-0701 or (800) 468-6765.

Shopping areas: A Danish flavor pervades roughly 300 stores, which sell everything from hand-crafted furniture to freshly baked bread.

ELVERHJ MUSEUM, 1624 Elverhoy Way, is devoted to the presentation of Solvang's history and Danish heritage. Displays in this reconstruction of an 18th-century Danish farmhouse include pre-industrial Danish artifacts and memorabilia, as well as artworks. Wed.-Sun. 1-4. Free. Phone (805) 686-1211.

NOJOQUI FALLS COUNTY PARK, 6.5 mi. s.w. on Alisal Rd., was named for a 164-foot-high falls that, after a sufficient rainy season, cascades over a mossy cliff. The park offers picnic facilities, a ball field, volleyball courts, playgrounds and a trail to the falls. Phone (805) 934-6211.

★ OLD MISSION SANTA INES, 1760 Mission Dr., contrasts with the town's Scandinavian motif. The mission, named for St. Agnes, was founded in 1804; at the peak of its prosperity in 1820, it owned 12,000 head of stock. The mission now contains a museum which exhibits collections of vestments, church records and religious texts. Daily 9-7, June 1 through mid-Sept.; 9-5:30, rest of year. Closed Jan. 1, Easter, Thanksgiving and Dec. 25. Admission $3, under 16 free with adult. Phone (805) 688-4815.

SONOMA (N-2) pop. 8,100, elev. 84'

To proclaim California a republic, the Bear Flag was raised on June 14, 1846, in Sonoma Plaza; on July 9 it was replaced by the Stars and Stripes. Depot Museum in the original town depot preserves the history of the California Republic through displays of 19th-century clothing and furniture; phone (707) 938-1762.

Sonoma Valley Visitors Bureau: 453 1st St. E., Sonoma, CA 95476; phone (707) 996-1090.

★ SONOMA STATE HISTORIC PARK, 20 E. Spain St. on Sonoma Plaza, includes Toscano Hotel and Sonoma Barracks on the Plaza, Mission San Francisco Solano and the home of Sonoma's founder, Gen. Mariano Guadalupe Vallejo. The mission houses the Jorgensen watercolors of Missions of California. The Vallejo house has gardens and furnishings from the family estate.

Self-guiding tours of the mission are available; depending upon the availability of docents, guided tours of the Vallejo house are offered Mon.-Fri. and some weekends. Allow 1 hour minimum. Daily 10-5; closed Jan. 1, Thanksgiving and Dec. 25. Park free. Mission, barracks and house $2; ages 6-12, $1. Phone (707) 938-1519.

TRAIN TOWN, 1 mi. s. on SR 12, offers a 20-minute miniature steam train ride through a forested railroad park past scaled-down

THE MOTHER LODE

Mexican miners called it "La Veta Madre"—the Mother Lode—a rich vein of gold lacing the western slopes of the Sierra Nevada for 120 miles. The name eventually came to denote the entire band of territory extending roughly from Mariposa to Sierra City, where the gleaming metal was mined during the frenetic years of the California gold rush.

The discovery of gold near Coloma in 1848 lured thousands of prospectors to the Mother Lode. Tales of nuggets littering the hillsides were not entirely unfounded during the early years of the gold rush, and the possibility of unearthing a mammoth find, like the 195-pound nugget found near Carson Hill, stoked the get-rich-quick dreams of many a '49er.

Nearly 550 mining towns proliferated in the Mother Lode; fewer than half remain today. Like the fortunes of many of the miners, the towns rose and fell precipitately and often were simply abandoned when the miners moved on to more profitable stakes. A few, such as Sonora, Placerville, Auburn and Grass Valley, weathered the diminishing reserves to become prosperous small cities. Others survive as little more than intriguing names on a map.

Aptly numbered SR 49 traverses the length of the Mother Lode country. The facades of the surviving buildings, the historical parks along the route and the ghost towns and empty mines scattered throughout the hills still retain a sense of the atmosphere from this colorful period.

DID YOU KNOW?

Thanks to the gold rush of the '40s and '50s, California's population exploded from 26,000 to almost 380,000 12 years.

reproductions of buildings and waterfalls. A diesel engine is featured Monday through Friday, while a steam engine is used Saturday, Sunday and holidays. A petting zoo, Ferris wheel, merry-go-round and other rides are on the grounds. Allow 30 minutes minimum. Trips daily 10-5, June-Sept.; Fri.-Sun. and some holidays 10-5, rest of year. Closed Thanksgiving and Dec. 25. Admission $3.75; over 54 and ages 16 months-16 years, $2.75. Merry-go-round $1.25. Phone (707) 938-3912.

TRIPS ON TAPE, for the Sonoma Valley, is a self-guiding audio tape tour featuring the valley's wineries and tasting rooms, historic Sonoma Plaza, Jack London State Historic Park, community events and Sonoma Valley landmarks. Maps are included. The $12.95 tapes are available by mail from The Rider's Guide, 484 Lake Park Ave., Suite 255, Oakland, CA 94610. Add $2.50 for postage; California residents should add sales tax. Phone (510) 653-2553.

 WINERIES

- **Buena Vista Winery** is 2 mi. n.e. at 18000 Old Winery Rd. Daily 10:30-5; closed Jan. 1, Thanksgiving and Dec. 25. Phone (707) 938-1266 or (800) 926-1266.

- **Sebastiani Vineyards,** 389 4th St. E. Daily 10-5; closed holidays. Phone (707) 938-5532 or (800) 888-5532.

SONORA (F-4) pop. 4,200, elev. 1,796'

Sonora was first settled by miners from Sonora, Mexico, and became one of the largest and wealthiest towns in the Mother Lode country. Still a bustling community, Sonora now relies on tourism, lumbering and agriculture. It also is the seat of Tuolumne County and a market center for the surrounding region. Sonora's past is proudly reflected in its fine collection of Victorian houses.

Tuolumne County Visitors Bureau: 55 Stockton St., Sonora, CA 95370; phone (209) 533-4420 or (800) 446-1333.

BRADFORD STREET PARK, Bradford St. at SR 49, has exhibits of mining equipment used in Sonora during the gold rush era. An arrastra, stamp mill and pelton wheel are included. Picnic areas are available. Daily 24 hours. Free.

TUOLUMNE COUNTY MUSEUM, 158 W. Bradford Ave., is housed in the 1857 county jail. Displays depicting the gold-rush era include photographs, guns, antiques, artifacts and gold exhibits. A Pioneer Trails exhibit is available. Picnicking is permitted. Tues.-Fri. 10-4, Sat. 10-3:30, Sun.-Mon. 9-4; closed Jan. 1 and Dec. 24-25 and 31. Donations. Phone (209) 532-1317.

SOQUEL (G-2) pop. 6,200, elev. 40'

WINERIES

- **Bargetto's Santa Cruz Winery**, 3535 N. Main St. Mon.-Sat. 9-5, Sun. 11-5; closed holidays. Tours are given Mon.-Fri. at 11 and 2; reservations are required. Phone (831) 475-2258.

SOUTH LAKE TAHOE—
see Lake Tahoe Area p. 91.

SOUTH SAN FRANCISCO—
see San Francisco p. 211.

STANISLAUS NATIONAL FOREST

Elevations in the forest range from 1,200 ft. in the Lumsden area to 11,462 ft. at Sonora Peak. Refer to AAA maps for additional elevation information.

Covering nearly 900,000 acres on the western slope of the Sierra Nevada Range, Stanislaus National Forest outlines the northwestern boundary of Yosemite National Park *(see place listing p. 238)*. The Merced, Mokelumne, Clavey, Stanislaus and Tuolumne rivers cut deep canyons through this region.

Popular summer activities include swimming, camping, picnicking, boating, rafting, canoeing and hunting. More than 800 miles of rivers and streams offer myriad opportunities for fishing. The forest offers an abundance of trails suitable for hiking, horseback riding, backpacking, off-roading and mountain biking. Snow skiing is available at Dodge Ridge off SR 108 and at Mount Reba off SR 4. Snowmobiling and cross-country skiing also are popular during the winter.

Reservations for Pinecrest campground can be made through the U.S. National Forest Service Reservation Center, (800) 280-2267 in summer.

Visitor tours and programs are offered June through August in Pinecrest. The Emigrant and Carson-Iceberg wildernesses are on the eastern side of the forest. Permits may be obtained at any Stanislaus National Forest office. For general forest information contact the Supervisor's Office, Stanislaus National Forest, 19777 Greenley Rd., Sonora, CA 95370; phone (209) 532-3671. *See Recreation Chart and the AAA California/ Nevada CampBook.*

STINSON BEACH (O-1)
pop. 800, elev. 18'

AUDUBON CANYON RANCH, 3.5 mi. n. on SR 1, is a former dairy ranch that is now a wildlife sanctuary and educational center. The ranch contains a major heronry frequented by great blue herons and great egrets. Allow 2 hours minimum. Sat.-Sun. and holidays 10-4, during the mid-Mar. to mid-July nesting period. Donations. Phone (415) 868-9244.

STOCKTON (F-3) pop. 210,900, elev. 14'

The first of California's two inland seaports, Stockton is connected with San Francisco Bay by a channel 60 miles long and 37 feet deep. The San Joaquin waterways, 1,000 miles of navigable inland waters, offer boating and fishing. The city also is the home of the University of the Pacific, the first chartered university in California.

Greater Stockton Chamber of Commerce: 445 W. Weber Ave., Suite 220, Stockton, CA 95203; phone (209) 547-2770.

THE HAGGIN MUSEUM, Rose St. and Pershing Ave. in Victory Park, houses European and American paintings and local historical artifacts. Tours are available by appointment. Tues.-Sun. 1:30-5; closed Jan. 1, Thanksgiving and Dec. 25. Donations. Phone (209) 462-4116.

PIXIE WOODS WONDERLAND, jct. Occidental Ave. and Monte Diablo Blvd. in Louis Park, is a children's playland featuring sets from popular children's stories and legends. Theater programs are held during the afternoon. The park also offers amusement rides. Wed.-Fri. and holidays 11-5, Sat.-Sun. 11-6, early June-early Sept.; Sat.-Sun. and holidays noon-5, late Feb.-early June and mid-Sept. to late Oct. Admission $1.75; under 13, $1.25. Rides 60c each. Phone (209) 937-8220 or 937-7366.

SUNNYVALE (Q-3)
pop. 117,200, elev. 105'

Although Silicon Valley doesn't appear on any map, people the world over know that the nickname refers to the area around Sunnyvale. The city is the headquarters of more than 650 computer-related manufacturers whose products, whether software or hardware, are based on silicon chip technology.

Local manufacturers make good use of The Sunnyvale Center for Innovation, Invention and Ideas (SCI3) at 465 S. Mathilda Ave., Suite 300. The center, which has facilities for patent and trademark research, also has on-line access to the full patent database used by the Patent and Trademark Office in Washington, D.C. A research library features patents from 1790 to the present as well as trademark/logo information. Phone (408) 730-7290.

Sunnyvale Chamber of Commerce: 499 S. Murphy Ave., Sunnyvale, CA 94086; phone (408) 736-4971.

SUSANVILLE (C-4)
pop. 7,300, elev. 4,258'

Founded by pioneer Isaac Roop in 1854 and named for his daughter, the town of Susanville lies at the head of the Honey Lake Valley and is flanked by the cliffs of the Susan River Canyon. In the 19th century Susanville served as a stopping point on the Nobles Emigrant Trail, a popular alternate route to the Donner Pass Overland Trail.

The Bizz Johnson Trail follows an old branch line of the Southern Pacific Railroad for approximately 26 miles between Susanville and Westwood. Administered by the Bureau of Land Management and Lassen National Forest, the trail is popular with hikers, railroad history buffs and cross-country skiers. The Susanville Depot & Museum at the beginning of the trail houses historic photographs and railroad memorabilia in a restored 1920s train station.

Lassen County Chamber of Commerce: 84 N. Lassen St., P.O. Box 338, Susanville, CA 96130; phone (530) 257-4323.

EAGLE LAKE, 16 mi. n.w. on Eagle Lake Rd., is the second largest natural lake in California. In summer campfire programs are held Wednesday evenings, and slide presentations are shown Saturday evenings. Daily dawn-dusk, mid-May to mid-Oct. Free. Phone (530) 257-4188. *See Recreation Chart.*

SUTTER CREEK (E-3)
pop. 1,800, elev. 1,198'

In the Sierra foothills, Sutter Creek is popular with outdoor enthusiasts due to its mild climate. On SR 49, wayfarers are often waylaid by the 1850s charm of this small town's antiques shops and bed and breakfasts.

Sutter Creek Visitor Information: 40 Main St., P.O. Box 600, Sutter Creek, CA 95685; phone (800) 400-0305.

Self-guiding tours: A brochure of a walking tour is available from the visitor information.

TAFT (I-4) pop. 5,900, elev. 984'

WEST KERN OIL MUSEUM, w. of SR 33 at 1168 Wood St., preserves artifacts and equipment from the early oil fields on an 8-acre property. Exhibits include American Indian artifacts, gas engines, handwrought cable tools, photographs and a wooden derrick constructed in 1917. Tues.-Sat. 10-4, Sun. 1-4; closed Jan. 1, Thanksgiving and Dec. 25. Donations. Phone (805) 765-6664.

TAHOE CITY—
see Lake Tahoe Area p. 92.

TAHOE NATIONAL FOREST

Elevations in the forest range from 1,300 ft. on the Middle Fork of the American River to 9,143 ft. at the summit of Mount Lola. Refer to AAA maps for additional elevation information.

Despite its name, Tahoe National Forest has little to do with the lake. All of its 797,205 acres are north and west of Lake Tahoe, while the lake and its immediate environs are part of the Lake Tahoe Basin Management Unit. Much of the national forest lies in the Yuba River drainage. Here miners used the placer pan, pick and hydraulic cannon, which used tons of pressurized water to tear away the hillsides, in their frantic pursuit of gold.

Today, where pack trains and stagecoaches once traveled, automobiles now follow SR 49 past the remnants of mining camps since reclaimed by forest. Along the twisting course of the North Yuba River are steep-walled canyons and the dramatic Sierra Buttes, which are riddled with old quartz mines.

Miners weren't the only ones to leave their mark on the landscape. Touring the region as an entertainer in 1853, famed *femme-fatale* Lola Montez christened Independence Lake during a Fourth of July picnic. Just north of the site of her picnic, Mount Lola honors the adventuress.

Independence Lake is but one of many lakes within the forest boundaries. Some of the most popular areas are the French Meadows Reservoir, cradled in the upper reaches of the American River watershed; a cluster of glacial lakes north of Sierra City; and Bullards Bar Reservoir, on the edge of the Sacramento Valley.

Recreational opportunities abound in the forest. Alpine and Nordic skiing and snowmobiling are popular winter diversions, while hiking, camping, boating, horseback riding and fishing are available the rest of the year. Hikers enjoy the 400 miles of trails, and those who prefer water sports are attracted to the sailing, waterskiing, swimming, rafting, kayaking and canoeing available within the forest. Reservations for Logger Campground can be made through the U.S. National Forest Service Reservation Center; phone (800) 280-2267.

Publications about recreational opportunities and maps are available at most forest service stations and the forest headquarters in Nevada City. For more information contact the Forest Supervisor, Tahoe National Forest, 631 Coyote St., P.O.

Box 6003, Nevada City, CA 95959; phone (530) 265-4531. *See Recreation Chart and the AAA California/Nevada CampBook.*

TAHOMA—
see Lake Tahoe Area p. 92.

TEHACHAPI (I-5) pop. 5,800, elev. 3,973'

This old railroad town in the Tehachapi Mountains is in an area known as the Tehachapi-Mojave Wind Resource Area, site of more than 4,900 wind turbines. These turbines collectively generate 1.3 billion kilowatt-hours of electricity per year, enough to meet the annual residential needs of almost 500,000 people. The best time to see the turbines spinning is late afternoon when hot winds blow from the nearby Mojave Desert. For guided tours or a brochure outlining a self-guiding tour contact the Kern Wind Energy Association at (805) 822-7956.

Mourning Cloak Ranch and Botanical Gardens has more than 2,200 species of plants on 20 acres of hillside. Open by appointment only, the ranch and gardens also feature a horse-drawn carriage collection; phone (805) 822-1661 or 822-5062.

Greater Tehachapi Chamber of Commerce: 209 E. Tehachapi Blvd., Tehachapi, CA 93581; phone (805) 822-4180.

Self-guiding tours: Brochures outlining walking tours of the downtown historic district and the surrounding area are available from the chamber of commerce.

TEHACHAPI LOOP, 8.5 mi. n.w. on the railroad, was conceived by a railroad engineer in 1876 to surmount a steep grade. The loop enables the last car of an 85-car train to pass above the engine in the tunnel below. For more information phone the chamber of commerce at (805) 822-4180.

TEHACHAPI MUSEUM, 310 S. Green St., displays items of local historical significance including ranching, farming and mining equipment, along with exhibits describing the importance of the lumber, cement, railroad and wind-power industries to the area. Sat.-Sun. noon-4, Tues. and Thurs. 9-noon. Free. Phone (805) 822-8152 or 822-3937.

TEMECULA (K-6)
pop. 27,100, elev. 1,006'

Having served as an important stop for the Butterfield Stagecoach Route and later as a station on the railroad between San Bernardino and San Diego, Temecula was founded in 1882 and today is a fast-growing bedroom community for Riverside and San Diego counties. "Old Town Temecula," on Front Street between Moreno Road and 3rd Street, preserves historic buildings and is an antique shopper's delight. The country-

side, known as Temecula Wine Country, supports extensive horse ranches, vineyards and wineries.

Temecula Valley Chamber of Commerce: 27450 Ynez Rd. #104, Temecula, CA 92591; phone (909) 676-5090.

HOT AIR BALLOON RIDES provide panoramic views of the Temecula wine country, often including scenic portions of northern San Diego County. Pre- or post-flight beverages and snacks usually are provided. Rides last approximately 1 hour. Companies include Balloon Adventures by California Dreamin'; phone (760) 438-9550 or (800) 373-3359. Trips depart Sat.-Sun. year-round (weather permitting). Fare $125-$135. Reservations are required. Rides are not advisable for children under age 5. All pilots are FAA certified.

Note: The mention of the preceding hot air balloon ride is for information only and does **not** imply endorsement by AAA.

TEMECULA MUSEUM, in Sam Hicks Park at Mercedes St. and Moreno Rd., houses a collection of household items, tools, historic documents and photographs that describe the history of the area. American Indian artifacts found locally can be seen as well. A diorama depicts the town as it looked around 1914. A collection of Earle Stanley Gardner memorabila also is displayed. Gardner, author of the Perry Mason mystery novels, lived in Temecula for more than 30 years until his death in 1970. Wed.-Sun. 11-4; closed Jan. 1, Thanksgiving and Dec. 25. Free. Phone (909) 676-0021.

TEMECULA SHUTTLE WINE COUNTRY TOURS, 28464 Front St., provides 4-hour personalized, narrated van tours to Temecula Valley wineries. Departures require a minimum of six passengers. Daily 12:30-4:30. Fare (includes light lunch, champagne and wine tastings) $52.50. Reservations are required. Phone (909) 694-0292.

 WINERIES

• **Callaway Vineyard and Winery,** 32720 Rancho California Rd. Daily 10:30-5. Tours Mon.-Fri. at 11, 1 and 3, on the hour Sat.-Sun. 11-4. Closed holidays. Phone (909) 676-4001.

• **Cilurzo Vineyard and Winery,** off Rancho California Rd. at 41220 Calle Contento. Daily 10-5; closed Thanksgiving and Dec. 25. Phone (909) 676-5250.

• **Mount Palomar Winery,** 33820 Rancho California Rd. Daily 10-5. Phone (909) 676-5047.

• **Thornton Winery,** 32575 Rancho California Rd. Daily 10-9. Tours are given on the hour Sat.-Sun. 11-4. Phone (909) 699-0099.

THOUSAND OAKS (J-5)
pop. 104,400, elev. 800'

OAKBROOK REGIONAL PARKS CHUMASH INTERPRETIVE CENTER, 3290 Lang Ranch Pkwy., offers exhibits of Chumash artifacts and narrative pictorials that portray Chumash lifesytles. Native docents demonstrate various aspects of Chumash culture in a re-created village. The Rock Art Exhibit describes the painted pictographs from various areas of the Chumash realm. The center also features changing exhibits. Tues.-Sat. 10-5; closed Jan. 1, July 4, Thanksgiving and Dec. 25. Admission $5; over 55 and ages 5-12, $3. Phone (805) 492-8076.

STAGECOACH INN MUSEUM, 51 S. Ventu Park Rd., first opened in 1876 as a stopping place for travelers journeying between Los Angeles and Santa Barbara. The reconstructed Monterey-style building houses Victorian furnishings, displays of Chumash artifacts and changing exhibits. The complex also includes a carriage house, pioneer house, one-room schoolhouse, an adobe and a Chumash hut. Wed.-Sun. 1-4; closed holidays. Admission $3; over 62 and ages 5-12, $1. Phone (805) 498-9441.

THOUSAND PALMS (K-7)
pop. 4,100, elev. 226'

Thousand Palms Chamber of Commerce: P.O. Box 365, Thousand Palms, CA 92276; phone (619) 343-1988.

COVERED WAGON TOURS is 6 mi. e. of I-10 on Ramon Rd. Mule-drawn wagons traverse the

Coachella Valley Preserve. A naturalist describes area history and flora. Jackrabbits and quail are among animals commonly seen. Daily (weather permitting) 8 a.m.-10 p.m., Oct.-May. Fare, including barbecue dinner, $55; ages 7-16, $27.50. Fare, without dinner, $40. Reservations are required. Phone (760) 347-2161 or (800) 367-2161.

TOIYABE NATIONAL FOREST—
see Humboldt-Toiyabe National Forest in Nevada p. 260.

TRINIDAD (B-1) pop. 400, elev. 175'

PATRICK'S POINT STATE PARK, 632 acres 5 mi. n. via US 101, is noted for its agate beach, numerous tide pools, American Indian village and spring wildflowers. A naturalist service is available in summer. Dogs are restricted from the beach and trails. Camping is permitted; phone Parknet at (800) 444-7275. Daily dawn-dusk. Day use fee $5 per private vehicle; over 61, $4 per private vehicle. Fee for dogs $1. Phone (707) 677-3570. *See Recreation Chart.*

TRINITY CENTER (B-2) elev. 2,311'

SCOTT MUSEUM OF TRINITY CENTER is .2 mi. e. off SR 3 on Airport Rd. Among the exhibits are horse-drawn vehicles, a barbed-wire collection, American Indian artifacts and old utensils. Free guide service is available. Tues.-Sat. 1-5, May 15-Sept. 15. Donations. Phone (530) 266-3242 or 266-3378.

TRINITY NATIONAL FOREST—
see Shasta-Trinity National Forests p. 225.

TRUCKEE—
see Lake Tahoe Area p. 92.

TULARE (H-4) pop. 33,200, elev. 288'

Tulare, in the heart of one of the country's largest milk and dairy producing areas, has become known as a dairy processing center. Agriculture also plays an important part in the area's economy.

Greater Tulare Chamber of Commerce: 260 N. L St., P.O. Box 1435, Tulare, CA 93275-1435; phone (559) 686-1547.

Shopping areas: Dozens of factory outlet stores are adjacent to the Prosperity Avenue exit from SR 99.

TULARE HISTORICAL MUSEUM, 444 W. Tulare Ave., displays dioramas, relics, photographs and replicas of rooms and small businesses which reveal the colorful history of the town, from

Yokuts Indian villages to the arrival of the railroad in 1872 to modern-day Tulare. The museum also house memorabilia of Olympians Bob Mathias and Sim Iness. Thurs.-Sat. 10-4, Sun. 12:30-4; closed holidays. Admission $1.50, students with ID $1, under 5 free. Phone (559) 686-2074.

TULELAKE (A-3) pop. 1,000, elev. 4,035′

KLAMATH BASIN NATIONAL WILDLIFE REFUGES, near Tulelake, include the Lower Klamath and Tule Lake refuges. They offer some 30 miles of self-guiding auto tour routes for observing wildlife. An estimated 60 to 70 percent of Pacific flyway waterfowl stop here in the fall; the peak migration period is from late October to mid-November. Hunting is allowed during state seasons.

The Klamath Basin regularly attracts as many as 500 bald eagles during January and February; many can be seen from the auto tour routes. A self-guiding canoe trail at Tule Lake Refuge is open July through September. The visitor center is open Mon.-Fri. 8-4:30, Sat.-Sun. and holidays 10-4; closed Jan. 1 and Dec. 25. Day-use fee $3 per private vehicle. For more information contact the Refuge Manager, Klamath Basin Refuges, Rte. 1, Box 74, Tulelake, CA 96134; phone (530) 667-2231.

TUPMAN (I-4) pop. 400

TULE ELK STATE RESERVE, 3 mi. w. of I-5 on Stockdale Hwy., protects 956 acres and a herd of Tule elk, sometimes called dwarf elk. The elk can be observed best in the viewing area near park headquarters. A visitor center offers natural history displays and information about the Tule elk. Picnicking is permitted. Reserve open daily 8-dusk. Visitor center open Tues.-Thurs. and Sat.-Sun. 10-4, mid-Mar. to mid-Nov. Day use fee $3 per private vehicle. Phone (805) 764-6881.

UKIAH (D-1) pop. 14,600, elev. 635′

Ukiah, center of a flourishing wine region, gets its name from a Pomo Indian word meaning "deep valley." It is home to the Redwood Empire Fairgrounds.

Greater Ukiah Chamber of Commerce: 200 S. School St., Ukiah, CA 95482; phone (707) 462-4705.

GRACE HUDSON MUSEUM AND SUN HOUSE, 431 S. Main St., is a complex that includes a historic house, a park and a museum of art, history and anthropology. The museum displays works by noted painter Grace Carpenter Hudson, who often chose American Indians as her subjects; a small collection of Pomo Indian basketry; family artifacts; and historical photographs. Sun House was the home of the artist, who lived there for 25 years before her death in 1937. The museum mounts three or four exhibitions annually.

Allow 1 hour minimum. Museum open Wed.-Sat. 10-4:30, Sun. noon-4:30; closed major holidays. Guided tours of Sun House are available on the hour Wed.-Sun. noon-3. Donations. Phone (707) 467-2836.

LAKE MENDOCINO VISITOR CENTER is .2 mi. s. of SR 20 at Marina Dr. The center offers information that features the lake, Pomo Indian culture and the Coyote Valley. Highlights include the Interpretive Cultural Center, featuring exhibits of Pomo Indian crafts and decorative arts. Picnicking is permitted. Guided tours are available by appointment. Wed.-Sun. 9-5, mid-Apr. through Sept. 30; Sat.-Sun. 1-5, Oct. 1 to mid-Nov. Donations. Phone (707) 485-8285 or 462-7581.

WINERIES

• **Parducci Wine Estates**, 501 Parducci Rd. Daily 9-5; closed holidays. Tours are given daily at 11 and 2. Phone (707) 463-5357.

UNIVERSAL CITY—
see Los Angeles p. 131.

VACAVILLE (N-3) pop. 71,500, elev. 179′

VACAVILLE MUSEUM, 213 Buck Ave., displays photographs, documents and memorabilia pertaining to the history of Solano County. The museum also contains changing exhibits and an interpretive garden of native plants. Guided walking tours of old downtown are offered periodically; phone for schedule. Allow 30 minutes minimum. Wed.-Sun. 1-4:30. Donations. Phone (707) 447-4513.

VALENCIA—
see Los Angeles p. 131.

VALLECITO (F-4) pop. 300, elev. 1,745′

SAVE **MOANING CAVERN**, 2 mi. s.w. on Parrots Ferry Rd., was explored in 1851 by miners, who discovered not the precious metal they sought but prehistoric human remains. Guided 45-minute tours descend 165 feet, 100 feet of which are by means of a steel spiral staircase into a room big enough to hold the Statue of Liberty.

Visitors also can descend into the cavern on a 165-foot rappel (no experience necessary) or take the 3-hour Adventure Tour to the farthest depths of the cavern. Daily 9-6 in summer; 10-5, rest of year. Admission $7.75; over 62, $7.25; ages 3-13, $4. MC, VI. Reservations are required for the Adventure Tour. Phone (209) 736-2708 or (800) 225-3764, ext. 211.

VALLEJO (O-2) pop. 109,200, elev. 40'

In 1851 Gen. Mariano Guadalupe Vallejo (val-LEH-hoh) founded the town that bears his name at the junction of the Carquinez Straits and the Napa River. The general was a citizen of California under both Mexican and U.S. rule. The town served as state capital on two occasions 1851-53. Today Vallejo is the home of California Maritime Academy and the Sperry Division of General Mills.

Service by Vallejo Ferry is offered from Pier 39 and the Ferry Building in San Francisco to Vallejo, where shuttle buses can transport visitors to The Marine World Theme Park, as well as to Napa Valley.

Vallejo Convention and Visitors Bureau: 495 Mare Island Way, Vallejo, CA 94590; phone (707) 642-3653.

SAVE ★ THE MARINE WORLD THEME PARK, Marine World Pkwy. (SR 37) exit off I-80, is a 160-acre wildlife and theme park that combines rides, shows, play areas and educational encounters with wildlife. Killer whales, sea lions, tigers and elephants perform in shows.

Interactive attractions include Butterfly World, a tropical area filled with free-flying butterflies; Elephant Encounter, where the pachyderms are featured in shows, demonstrations and rides; Lorikeet Aviary; Shark Experience, where the predators can be viewed through a clear underwater tunnel; Popeye's Spinach Factory; and Tiger Island Splash Attack. Walrus Experience depicts the sea creature's rocky beach habitat, and the Australian Walk-about highlights the country's native marsupials and birds. A water ski show operates April through October.

Other features include a 3-D motion simulator ride, an animal nursery, a veterinary clinic and Dolphin Harbor, a 2,800-seat stadium where bottlenose dolphins perform.

Children will enjoy the playground, petting zoo, life-size blue whale play area and elephant rides. Food is available. Allow a full day. Daily 10-10, Memorial Day weekend-Labor Day; daily 10-8 during spring break; Fri.-Sun. 10-8, Apr.-day before Memorial Day weekend (except spring break) and day after Labor Day-Oct. 31. Admission $28.99; over 59, $23.99; ages 4-12, $19.99. After 5 p.m. $13.99; ages 4-12, $9.99. Elephant ride $5. Parking $6. AE, CB, DI, MC, VI. Phone (707) 643-6722. *See color ad p. 925-926.*

VALLEJO NAVAL AND HISTORICAL MUSEUM, in the old Vallejo City Hall building at 734 Marin St., offers exhibits about naval history, including relics and papers from Mare Island Naval Shipyard. Ships models, murals and an operating periscope are displayed. The museum also offers changing exhibits and exhibits of local and regional history. Guided tours are available by reservation. Tues.-Sat. 10-4:30; closed holidays. Admission $1.50; over 59 and ages 12-17, 75c. There is an additional fee for guided tours. Phone (707) 643-0077.

VAN NUYS—
see Los Angeles p. 131.

VENICE—
see Los Angeles p. 131.

VENTURA (J-4) pop. 92,600, elev. 35'

Although Gaspar de Portolá reached what is now Ventura County in 1769, it was 13 years before a mission was founded. Father Junípero Serra established Mission San Buenaventura, his last mission, in 1782. After the secularization of the mission's lands in 1834, adobe houses were built near the mission site by Spanish and Mexican settlers. By the 1860s American and Europeans began arriving, and by the time the railroad arrived in 1887, San Buenaventura—by now shortened to just Ventura—was a prosperous community of houses, stores, industry, a school and churches.

Ventura today is a center of agriculture and oil production, yet it retains its link to the ocean with beaches, a public pier and marinas. It also serves as the gateway to Channel Islands National Park *(see place listing p. 65)*. Ventura lies on a scenic stretch of US 101.

Ventura Visitors and Convention Bureau: 89 S. California St., Ventura, CA 93001; phone (805) 648-2075.

Shopping areas: Buenaventura Plaza, at Mills Road and Main Street, contains JCPenney and Macy's. Ventura Harbor Village, on Spinnaker Drive about 1 mile west of Harbor Boulevard, offers specialty shops, a carrousel and live drama.

ALBINGER ARCHAEOLOGICAL MUSEUM, 113 E. Main St., displays artifacts spanning 3,500 years; all were excavated from a single site next to San Buenaventura Mission. Evidence of an early Indian culture dating from 1600 B.C. and the later Chumash Indians dating from A.D. 1500 is exhibited, along with objects dating from the mission's founding to the early 1900s. The original mission foundation and an earth oven lie outside in the dig area. An audiovisual program is presented on request.

Allow 30 minutes minimum. Wed.-Sun. 10-4, Memorial Day weekend-Labor Day; Wed.-Fri. 10-2, Sat.-Sun. 10-4, rest of year. Closed Jan. 1, Easter, Thanksgiving and Dec. 25. Free. Phone (805) 648-5823.

OLIVAS ADOBE HISTORICAL PARK is at 4200 Olivas Park Dr. The two-story adobe house was built in 1847 in the Monterey style by Raymundo Olivas and has displays of period furnishings and handicrafts reminiscent of the early California rancho period. An adjacent building contains artifacts from the adobe and rancho eras in Ventura County; an audiovisual program is presented upon request. The grounds include a small adobe and an adobe pit as well as rose and herb gardens.

Grounds open daily 10-4. House open Sat.-Sun. 10-4. Guided tours Sat.-Sun. at 11, 1 and 2. Closed holidays. Free. Phone (805) 644-4346.

PADRE SERRA CROSS is on Mission Hill in Grant Park, which offers an impressive view. The first cross was erected on this spot by Father Junípero Serra on March 31, 1782.

★ **SAN BUENAVENTURA MISSION** is at 225 E. Main St.; entrance is through a gift shop just east of the mission. Founded in 1782 and completed in 1809, the present mission includes a restored church, Holy Cross School (not open to visitors) and a small museum. The museum contains Chumash Indian artifacts as well as vestments, books and other items from the early days of the mission. Constructed in a rectangular design, the mission opens into gardens. The restored church is still used by an active congregation. Mon.-Sat. 10-5, Sun. 10-4; closed holidays. Donations. Phone (805) 648-4496.

[SAVE] **VENTURA COUNTY MUSEUM OF HISTORY & ART**, 100 E. Main St., reflects Native American, Hispanic and pioneer influences in the area. The museum includes displays of horse-drawn agricultural equipment and changing art and history exhibits. George Stuart Historical Figures®, created by the Ventura County artist, portray the famous and infamous of world history. Tues.-Sun. 10-5; closed Jan. 1, Thanksgiving and Dec. 25. Admission $3, under 16 free with adult. Phone (805) 653-0323.

VICTORVILLE (J-7)
pop. 40,700, elev. 2,714′

Victorville Chamber of Commerce: 14174 Greentree Blvd., P.O. Box 997, Victorville, CA 92392-4323; phone (760) 245-6506.

Shopping areas: The Mall of Victor Valley, I-15 and Bear Valley Road, houses Harris, JCPenney, Mervyn's and Sears.

[SAVE] **THE ROY ROGERS-DALE EVANS MUSEUM** is at 15650 Seneca Rd. From I-15 take Roy Rogers Dr. exit; turn s. Amargosa Rd., e on Seneca Rd. to museum entrance; from Palmdale Rd. (SR 18) go n. on Amargosa Rd., e. on Seneca Rd. to entrance. The museum exhibits personal and professional memorabilia of these famous Western stars. Daily 9-5; closed Easter, Thanksgiving and Dec. 25. Admission $7; over 65 and ages 13-16, $6; ages 6-12, $5. Phone (760) 243-4547.

VISALIA (G-5) pop. 75,600, elev. 331′

Founded in 1852, Visalia is the oldest city between Stockton and Los Angeles. By the early 20th century its countryside was rich with ranches and farms, and the city's prosperity was reflected in its many lavish houses.

Visalia Convention and Visitors Bureau: 301 E. Acequia St., Visalia, CA 93291; phone (559) 738-3435 or (800) 524-0303.

Self-guiding tours: Free brochures outlining walking tours of the historic district are available through the convention and visitors bureau.

MOONEY GROVE PARK, 5 mi. s., embraces 155 grassy acres covered with valley oaks and date palms, picnic areas, a lake and recreational facilities. Daily 8 a.m.-9 p.m., Memorial Day-Labor Day; Mon. and Thurs.-Fri. 8-7, Sat.-Sun. 8 a.m.-9 p.m., Mar. 1-day before Memorial Day and day after Labor Day-Sept. 30; Thurs.-Mon. 8-5, rest of year. Closed Jan. 1, Dec. 24-31 and county holidays. Admission $4 per private vehicle, over 54 free. Phone (559) 733-6612.

Tulare County Museum, in the park, displays American Indian artifacts and Tulare County pioneer memorabilia of the late 1800s. Guided tours are available by appointment. Allow 30 minutes minimum. Mon. and Wed.-Fri. 10-4, Sat.-Sun. 12:30-6:30, Memorial Day-Labor Day; Thurs.-Mon. 10-4, Mar. 1-day before Memorial Day and day after Labor Day-Oct. 31; Mon. and Thurs.-Fri. 10-4, Sat.-Sun. 1-4, rest of year. Closed holidays. Admission $2; over 54 and ages 6-12, $1. Under age 12 must be with an adult. Phone (559) 733-6616.

VOLCANO (E-4) pop. 100, elev. 2,053′

Volcano, in a deep depression resembling a crater, was aptly named. During the gold rush the city was famous for its dance halls and saloons. Daffodil Hill, 3 miles north, is covered with daffodils originally planted during the 1850s. Blooming season is late March to mid-April.

INDIAN GRINDING ROCK STATE HISTORIC PARK, .5 mi. off SR 88 at 14881 Pine Grove-Volcano Rd., is a 135-acre park where Miwok Indians chiseled in the main bedrock more than a thousand mortar cups in which they pulverized acorns and other seeds for food. A ceremonial roundhouse and re-created village are featured. Chaw Se' Regional Indian Museum includes artifacts, presentations, exhibits and audiovisual programs representing 10 Sierra Nevada Indian tribes. Camping and picnicking are permitted.

Park open daily dawn-dusk. Museum open Mon.-Fri. 11-3, Sat.-Sun. 10-4; closed Jan. 1, Thanksgiving and Dec. 25. Admission $5 per private vehicle; over 61, $4 per private vehicle. Phone (209) 296-7488.

WALNUT CREEK (O-3)
pop. 60,600, elev. 135′

THE GARDENS AT HEATHER FARM is at 1540 Marchbanks Dr. Walkways wind among the center's 5.4-acre educational garden site, which features 20 landscaped gardens and learning sites. Included are rose, English meadow, water conservation, sensory, butterfly, native plant and rock gardens. A gazebo overlooks a lagoon where ducks and birds gather. Daily dawn-dusk. Gardens free. Guided tours $2; reservations are required. Phone (925) 947-1678, or 947-6712.

⬛ **LINDSAY MUSEUM,** 1931 First Ave., houses native animals that are unfit for release into the wild. Wildlife Rehabilitation Hospital, closed to the public, tends to animals, which can be observed from the exhibit hall. Other displays include natural history items, aquariums, insects and a children's room featuring hands-on exhibits. A 35-ft. replica of Balancing Rock, cast from the real formation atop Mount Diablo, supports more than 100 plant and animal specimens native to the mountain.

Wed.-Sun. 10-5, mid-June through Labor Day; Wed.-Fri. noon-5, Sat.-Sun. 10-5, rest of year. Holiday hours vary. Admission $4.50; over 64, $3.50; ages 3-17, $2.50. Phone (925) 935-1978.

MOUNT DIABLO STATE PARK is 17 mi. s.e. on Diablo Rd. A paved road leads to the 3,849-foot summit of Mount Diablo, from which as much as 600 miles of the Sierra Nevada Range and portions of 35 counties are visible on clear days. An interpretive center is on the summit. Dogs are permitted except on trails. Park open daily 8-dusk. Interpretive center open Wed.-Sun. 11-5, Mar.-Oct.; Thurs.-Sun. 11-4, rest of year. Day use fee $5 per private vehicle; over 61, $4 per private vehicle. Per-dog fee $1. Phone (925) 837-2525. *See Recreation Chart.*

☀❄ **RECREATIONAL ACTIVITIES**

White-water Rafting

* ⬛ **All-Outdoors Whitewater Rafting Trips** depart from points along 12 rivers. Write 1250 Pine St., Suite 103, Walnut Creek, CA 94596. Daily Apr.-Oct. Phone (925) 932-8993 or (800) 247-2387.

WATSONVILLE (G-2)
pop. 31,100, elev. 23′

Watsonville's economy relies heavily on the growing of apples, strawberries and flowers. The main harvest time is celebrated in late September and early October.

Pajaro Valley Chamber of Commerce: 444 Main St., P.O. Box 1748, Watsonville, CA 95077-1748; phone (831) 724-3900.

Self-guiding tours: Maps for walking and driving tours of Watsonville and the Pajaro Valley are available from the chamber of commerce.

ELKHORN SLOUGH NATIONAL ESTUARINE RESEARCH RESERVE is e. of SR 1 off Dolan Rd. exit at 1700 Elkhorn Rd. The 1,400-acre coastal area protects the habitat of hundreds of species of birds, fish and invertebrates. It also is

an important feeding and resting ground for many waterfowl and migratory shorebirds. Walking trails wend through live oak and eucalyptus groves and along fingers of salt marsh.

Picnicking is permitted near the visitor center; smoking is prohibited on the trails. Wed.-Sun. 9-5. Guided nature walks originate at the visitor center near the Elkhorn Road entrance and are offered Sat.-Sun. at 10 and 1. Admission $2.50, under 16 free. Phone (831) 728-2822.

WEAVERVILLE (B-2)
pop. 2,800, elev. 2,045′

A mining town in the days of '49, Weaverville retains the flavor and colorful atmosphere depicted by author Bret Harte. The town is a starting point for trips into Shasta-Trinity National Forests and Whiskeytown-Shasta-Trinity National Recreation Area *(see place listings p. 225 and 237).*

Trinity County Chamber of Commerce: 210 N. Main St., P.O. Box 517, Weaverville, CA 96093; phone (530) 623-6101 or (800) 487-4648.

J.J. "JAKE" JACKSON MEMORIAL MUSEUM, 508 Main St., displays American Indian relics, Chinese weapons, fossils, a bottle collection and old jail cells with an emphasis on the early pioneer era. Picnic facilities are available. Daily 10-5, May-Oct.; daily noon-4, in Apr. and Nov.; Tues. and Sat. noon-4, rest of year. Donations. Phone (530) 623-5211.

JOSS HOUSE STATE HISTORIC PARK, at the corner of Main and Oregon sts., contains the oldest Chinese temple still in use in California. Exhibits depict Chinese life, early history and contributions to the state's development. Daily 10-5, June-Aug.; Wed.-Sun. 10-5, Apr.-May and Sept.-Nov.; Sat. 10-5, rest of year. Closed Jan. 1, Thanksgiving and Dec. 25. Tours are given every hour 10-4. Admission $2; ages 6-12, $1. Phone (530) 623-5284.

WEED (B-3) pop. 3,100, elev. 3,466′

LIVING MEMORIAL SCULPTURE GARDEN is 13 mi. e. on US 97 near jct. CR A12. This 32-acre memorial features metal sculptures grouped into nine themed areas. In addition to American veterans in general, those specifically memorialized include refugees, army nurses, prisoners of war, Korean War veterans and helicopter pilots from the Vietnam War. Daily dawn-dusk. Free. Phone (530) 938-2218.

WEOTT (C-1) pop. 400, elev. 338′

HUMBOLDT REDWOODS STATE PARK covers more than 50,000 acres along the Redwood Hwy. between Miranda and Redcrest. The park is famous for the 362-foot Dyerville Giant Tree, considered the world's tallest until it was felled by a lightning strike in 1991; the 356-foot Rockefeller Tree; and more than 100 memorial redwood groves. Naturalist service is offered in the summer. A visitor center contains redwood and wildlife exhibits.

Park open daily 24 hours. Visitor center open daily 9-5, Mar.-Oct.; Thurs.-Sun. 10-4, rest of year. Day use fee $5 per private vehicle; over 61, $4 per private vehicle. Visitor center free. Phone (707) 946-2409 for the park, or (707) 946-2263 for the visitor center. *See Recreation Chart.*

★ **Avenue of the Giants,** a 33-mile section of highway paralleling US 101 between Phillipsville and Pepperwood, winds along the course of Eel River. While the surrounding hills support oak, maple, madrone and pepperwood trees, the magnificent redwoods along this route overshadow all. The two-lane road has numerous parking areas, picnic sites and nature trails that afford a closer look at some of California's most beautiful redwood groves.

WHISKEYTOWN-SHASTA-TRINITY NATIONAL RECREATION AREA (C-2)

The 42,500-acre Whiskeytown-Shasta-Trinity National Recreation Area is at the head of the Sacramento Valley and Upper Trinity River country, north and west of Redding. Its three components embrace four major dam-created lakes: Whiskeytown, about 8 miles west of Redding via SR 299; Clair Engle and Lewiston, northeast of Weaverville; and Shasta, north of Redding.

Recreational gold panning using a metal or plastic gold pan is permitted in the Whiskeytown unit only; annual permits are required and are available at the park for $1. Other recreational activities include hiking, swimming, personal watercraft riding, boating and sailing. Area open daily dawn-dusk. Visitor center open daily 9-5 in summer; otherwise varies. Day-use fee $5 per private vehicle; a fee is charged for camping. Phone (530) 241-6584 for park information, or Parknet at (800) 444-7275 for camping reservations. *See Recreation Chart and the AAA California/Nevada CampBook.*

WHITTIER—
see Los Angeles p. 133.

WILLIAMS (D-2) pop. 2,300, elev. 80'

SACRAMENTO VALLEY MUSEUM, 1 mi. w. of I-5 at 1491 E St. in the two-story Williams High School building, includes 27 rooms that depict life in the Sacramento Valley area from the mid-1800s to the 1930s. Among them are an apothecary, a kitchen, a children's room with dolls in 1500-1920s apparel, a millinery and dress shop, an old-fashioned general store and a documents room with deeds signed by United States presidents. Thurs.-Sat. 10-4, Apr.-Oct.; Fri.-Sat. 10-4,

rest of year. Closed major holidays. Tours are available by appointment Wed.-Sat. 10-3. Admission $1. Additional charge for events. Phone (530) 473-2978.

WILLITS (D-1) pop. 5,000, elev. 1,364'

Willits is the terminus for the California Western Railroad trip aboard "The Skunk" from Fort Bragg *(see place listing p. 76).*

Willits Chamber of Commerce: 239 S. Main St., Willits, CA 95490-3591; phone (707) 459-7910.

MENDOCINO COUNTY MUSEUM, 400 E. Commercial St., displays collections of Pomo and Yuki Indian baskets, artifacts of Mendocino County, steam-powered equipment and locomotives, and contemporary and traditional art. Allow 30 minutes minimum. Wed.-Sun. 10-4:30; closed holidays except July 4. Donations. Phone (707) 459-2736.

WILLOWS (D-2) pop. 6,000, elev. 135'

SACRAMENTO NATIONAL WILDLIFE REFUGE, 7 mi. s. on SR 99W, affords a 10,783-acre wintering area for migratory birds, especially ducks and geese. The best season to view waterfowl is November through January. Among the more than 265 bird species frequenting the area are hawks, egrets and herons. A 6-mile auto route and 2-mile self-guiding walking trail meanders through part of the refuge. Visitors should contact the visitor center for information. Other refuges that constitute the Sacramento Valley National Wildlife Refuge Complex are Colusa *(see place listing p. 68),* Delevan, Sacramento River and Sutter.

Refuge open daily dawn-dusk. Visitor center open daily 7:30-4, Oct.-Mar.; Mon.-Fri. 8-4:30, rest of year. Admission $3 per private vehicle. Phone (530) 934-2801, or 934-7774 for recorded information.

WILMINGTON—
see Los Angeles p. 133.

WINDSOR (M-1) pop. 13,400, elev. 118'

WINDSOR WATERWORKS AND SLIDES, 8225 Conde Ln., has a children's slide, a speed slide, an inner-tube ride, an aqua tube, a splash fountain and a heated pool. Height requirements are imposed on certain rides and all slides. Picnic facilities and food are available.

Allow 4 hours minimum. Daily 11-7, mid-June to early Sept.; Sat.-Sun. 11-7, May 1 to mid-June. Afternoon splash daily 4-7, mid-June to early July. All-day pass Sat.-Sun. $13.25. After 4 p.m. (mid-June to early July) $9.75. AE, MC, VI. Phone (707) 838-7760.

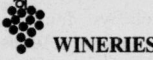

WINERIES

- **Rodney Strong Vineyards,** 11455 Old Redwood Hwy. Daily 10-5. Tours are given daily at 11 and 3. Closed Jan. 1, Thanksgiving and Dec. 25. Phone (707) 431-1533.

WINTERHAVEN (L-9)
pop. 1,100, elev. 1,100'

FORT YUMA QUECHAN MUSEUM, Fort Yuma Indian Hill, has displays about Native American culture, the early military era and Spanish expeditions. Nearby are the old Methodist Indian Mission and St. Thomas Mission buildings. Sun.-Fri. 8-5, Sat. 10-4. Closed major holidays. Admission $1, under 12 free. Phone (760) 572-0661.

WOODLAND (E-3) pop. 39,800, elev. 65'

First known as Yolo City, Woodland was a gold rush town established in 1861. Agriculture and industrial plants feed the economy.

Woodland Chamber of Commerce: 520 Main St., Woodland, CA 95695; phone (530) 662-7327.

SAVE **HAYS ANTIQUE TRUCK MUSEUM,** 1962 Hays Ln., houses a collection of antique trucks and chronicles the history of the trucking industry. Trucks dating from 1903 through the '50s represent many manufacturers. Also displayed are vehicles powered by steam, gas, diesel and electricity. A section of the Old Plank Road, which crossed the sand dunes from Yuma, Ariz., to El Centro, is on display. Guided tours are available. Open Mon.-Fri. 10-5, Sat.-Sun. 10-6, Easter-Labor Day; Wed.-Fri. 10-5, Sat.-Sun. 10-6, rest of year. Closed holidays. Admission $6; over 62 and ages 6-14, $4. Phone (530) 666-1044.

WOODSIDE (Q-2) pop. 5,000, elev. 382'

Woodside came into being in 1849 when the gold-rush drastically increased the size and population of San Francisco. The wood needed for wharves, houses and commercial buildings was harvested from virgin redwood forests in this section of San Mateo County. At one time there were 14 lumber mills here. Reminders of those rough-and-tumble days appear in the 1854 Woodside Store, now a museum; phone (650) 851-7615.

FILOLI, off I-280 via Edgewood Rd. to Cañada Rd., is a 654-acre estate built 1916-19 for Mr. and Mrs. William B. Bourn II, wealthy San Franciscans. The estate includes a 43-room mansion and 16 acres of themed formal gardens. The focal points of the garden are the Italian Renaissance tea house and the nearby carriage house, which is dominated by a bell tower.

Estate may be seen via guided tour Tues.-Thurs. at 9:30, 11:30 and 1:30, Apr.-June; at 10 and 1, mid-Feb. through Mar. 31 and July 1-Nov. 1. Estate is open for self-guiding tours Thurs.-Sat. 10-2, mid-Feb. through Oct. 31. Admission $10; ages 2-12, $1. Reservations are required for guided tours. Phone (650) 364-8300, ext. 507.

YORBA LINDA (B-7)
pop. 52,400, elev. 397'

RICHARD NIXON PRESIDENTIAL LIBRARY AND BIRTHPLACE, 18001 Yorba Linda Blvd., includes a museum gallery, theaters, gardens and the small house in which Nixon was born. Within the museum are films, interactive video displays, exhibits and personal memorabilia that reflect the president's life. The museum also features a re-creation of the White House's Lincoln Sitting Room and Nixon's post-presidency study. Nixon and his wife, Pat, are buried on the grounds.

Mon.-Sat. 10-5, Sun. 11-5; closed Thanksgiving and Dec. 25. Admission $5.95; military $4.95; over 62, $3.95; ages 8-11, $2. Phone (714) 993-5075.

★ YOSEMITE NATIONAL PARK (F-5)

See map page 240.

Elevations in the park range from 2,000 ft. at the park boundary at El Portal on SR 140 to 13,014 ft. at the summit of Mount Lyell. Refer to AAA maps for additional elevation information.

Glaciers transformed the rolling hills and meandering streams of pre-Pleistocene Yosemite into the colossal landscape of the present. To preserve it for posterity, Abraham Lincoln set aside the Mariposa grove of giant sequoias in the Yosemite Valley as the nation's first state park on June 30, 1864. Twenty-six years later Yosemite became a national park.

A region of unusual beauty, Yosemite National Park lies in central California on the western slope of the Sierra Nevada. The park is much greater both in area and beauty than most people generally realize; Yosemite Valley actually comprises only 7 of the 1,169 square miles of park land. The territory above the rim of the valley is less celebrated principally because it is less well-known. However, 196 miles of primary roads and more than 800 miles of trails now make much of this mountain region easily accessible to both motorist and hiker.

The crest of the Sierra Nevada is the park's eastern boundary, and the two rivers that flow through the park—the Merced and Tuolumne—originate among the snowy peaks. The Merced River flows through Yosemite Valley, and the Tuolumne River carves a magnificent gorge through the northern half of the park. Though spectacular through most of the year, many of the park's famous waterfalls are often dry during the late summer months.

The park can be reached by SR 140 (El Portal Rd.) from Merced; SR 41 (Wawona Rd.) from Fresno; and SR 120 (Big Oak Flat Rd.) from Stockton. With the exception of the Tioga Pass Road portion of SR 120, the Glacier Point Road and the Mariposa Grove Road, all of which are closed late fall through early summer, all roads are open year round; chains may be needed in winter.

The road to Mirror Lake and Happy Isles, at the eastern end of Yosemite Valley, is closed to most cars but is served by a free shuttle bus. Southside Drive is one-way eastbound from Bridalveil Fall to Curry Village; Northside Drive is one-way westbound from Yosemite Lodge; and the road between Curry Village and Yosemite Village also is one-way westbound.

General Information and Activities

Yosemite National Park is open daily all year. Maps and information are available at the Yosemite Valley Visitor Center, and schedules of events are provided at park entrances and posted throughout the valley. A free shuttle bus operates in the east end of the valley daily 7:30 a.m.-10 p.m., mid-May to mid-Sept.; 9 a.m.-10 p.m., rest of year. In the winter a shuttle runs from Yosemite Lodge to the Badger Pass Ski Area.

Wilderness permits, required of all overnight backpackers, are free at the Yosemite Valley Wilderness Center or $3 if obtained by phone or mail; phone (209) 372-0740. To make reservations by mail write Wilderness Reservations, P.O. Box 545, Yosemite, CA 95389. For information about wilderness permits phone (209) 372-0200.

A California fishing license is required for all park waters; an annual permit costs $25.70 for residents and $69.55 for non-residents. A 1-day resident or non-resident license costs $9.20. Information about bicycle rentals is available at Curry Village and Yosemite Lodge; tour bus information also is given at these spots and at Yosemite Village and Ahwahnee Hotel.

Ranger-naturalists conduct year-round nature walks that last from a half-hour to 2 hours; snowshoe walks are available in the winter. Evening programs are presented all year at the Yosemite Lodge, and in summer at Curry Village, Lower Pines, Glacier Point, Tuolumne Meadows, Crane Flat, Wawona and White Wolf campgrounds.

An open-air tram offers frequent 2-hour tours of the valley during summer and occasional trips after Labor Day; reservations can be made at the Ahwahnee Hotel, Curry Village and Yosemite Lodge. Other tours depart daily in summer to Glacier Point and Mariposa Grove. Guided horseback tours of Wawona, Tuolumne Meadows and the valley also are available. A hiker shuttle goes to Glacier Point and Tuolumne Meadows.

Four- and 6-day saddle trips and a 7-day guided hiking trip are available; contact Yosemite Concession Services Corp., Yosemite National Park, CA 95389.

Skiing and skating can be enjoyed in winter. Curry Village has an outdoor skating rink; Badger Pass Ski Area has downhill and cross-country skiing. Cross-country ski trails lead from the Badger Pass and Crane Flat areas. Snowshoe tours are offered.

Child care is available in winter for a fee at Ski Tots Playhouse at Badger Pass. During the summer the Junior Ranger Program of nature walks and classes welcomes students in grades 3 through 6; phone (209) 372-0200.

For recorded information about camping, roads, weather conditions and recreation, phone (209) 372-0200. Campground reservations are available through the National Park Reservation System, (800) 436-7275, 9450 Carroll Park Dr., San Diego, CA 92121. *See Recreation Chart and the AAA California/Nevada CampBook.*

The visitor center in Yosemite Valley has exhibits and audiovisual programs and is open all year. The adjacent Indian Cultural Museum depicts the history of the Miwok and Paiute. The visitor centers at Big Oak Flat and Tuolumne Meadows usually are open June through September.

The Wilderness Center, in Yosemite Valley, provides detailed information about the park's back country and wilderness areas. The center, open daily 8-5 with extended hours during the summer, contains a variety of displays for hikers and climbers as well as trip planning information, including guide books and maps; phone 372-0200 for additional information, or 372-0740 for back country reservations.

ADMISSION to the park is by $20 private vehicle fee, good for 7 days. **Note:** Chains might be required at any time during winter months.

PETS are not allowed on the trails or in public buildings and accommodations and must be leashed at all times. Cats and dogs are permitted in Upper Pines in Yosemite Valley, the west end of the campground at Tuolumne Meadows, and at White Wolf (Section C), Bridalveil (Section A), Crane Flat (Section A), Wawona, Hodgdon Meadows and Yosemite Creek campgrounds. Dogs can be boarded in Yosemite Valley from late May to mid-October.

ADDRESS inquiries concerning the park to the Superintendent, P.O. Box 577, Yosemite National Park, CA 95389. Phone (209) 372-0200.

Points of Interest

GLACIER POINT, 30 mi. from Yosemite Valley via Wawona Rd. to Chinquapin, then Glacier

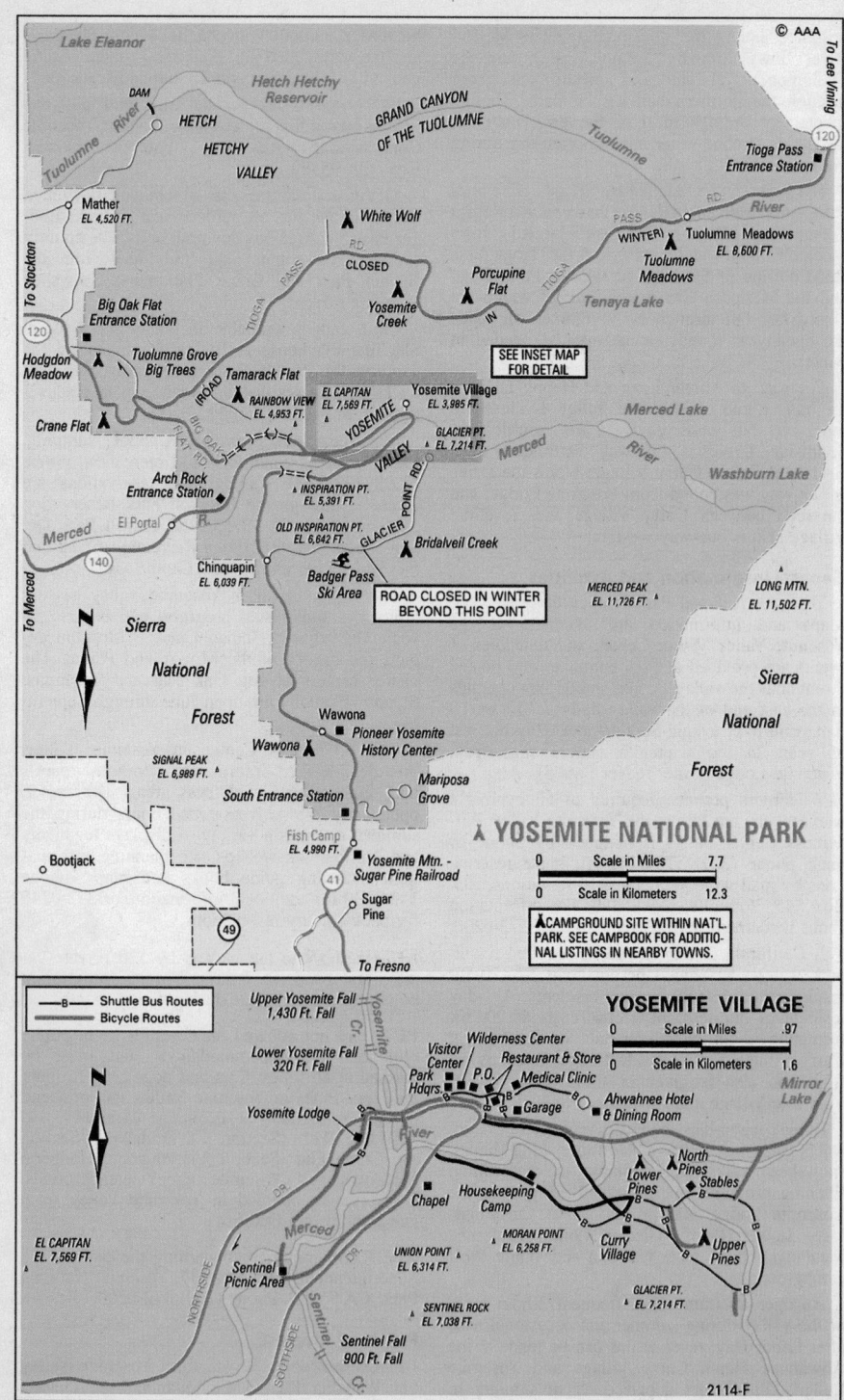

© AAA

To Lee Vining

Lake Eleanor

Hetch Hetchy
Reservoir

GRAND CANYON
OF THE TUOLUMNE

Tuolumne

120

DAM

HETCH

HETCHY

VALLEY

Tioga Pass
Entrance Station

To Stockton

Mather
EL 4,520 FT.

PASS

WINTER

Tuolumne Meadows
EL 8,600 FT.

Tuolumne
Meadows

River

RD.

CLOSED

White Wolf

Porcupine
Flat

TIOGA

Big Oak Flat
Entrance Station

120

Hodgdon
Meadow

Tuolumne Grove
Big Trees

ROAD

Yosemite
Creek

Tenaya Lake

SEE INSET MAP
FOR DETAIL

Merced Lake

Crane Flat

FLAT

Tamarack Flat

RAINBOW VIEW
EL 4,953 FT.

EL CAPITAN
EL 7,569 FT.

Yosemite Village
EL 3,985 FT.

OAK

YOSEMITE

GLACIER PT.
EL 7,214 FT.

Merced

River

Washburn Lake

BIG

Arch Rock
Entrance Station

INSPIRATION PT.
EL 5,391 FT.

VALLEY

To Merced

Merced

R.

El Portal

140

OLD INSPIRATION PT.
EL 6,642 FT.

POINT

GLACIER

RD.

Bridalveil Creek

Chinquapin
EL 6,039 FT.

Badger Pass
Ski Area

ROAD CLOSED IN WINTER
BEYOND THIS POINT

MERCED PEAK
EL 11,726 FT.

LONG MTN.
EL 11,502 FT.

Sierra

N

National

Forest

Wawona

Pioneer Yosemite
History Center

Sierra

National

Wawona

Forest

SIGNAL PEAK
EL 6,989 FT.

South Entrance Station

Mariposa
Grove

YOSEMITE NATIONAL PARK

Bootjack

Fish Camp
EL 4,990 FT.

41

Yosemite Mtn. -
Sugar Pine Railroad

0   Scale in Miles   7.7

0   Scale in Kilometers   12.3

49

Sugar
Pine

CAMPGROUND SITE WITHIN NAT'L.
PARK. SEE CAMPBOOK FOR ADDITIO-
NAL LISTINGS IN NEARBY TOWNS.

To Fresno

B Shuttle Bus Routes
Bicycle Routes

Upper Yosemite Fall
1,430 Ft. Fall

Yosemite
Cr.

YOSEMITE VILLAGE

0   Scale in Miles   .97

Lower Yosemite Fall
320 Ft. Fall

Wilderness Center

Visitor
Center

Restaurant & Store

P.O.

Medical Clinic

0   Scale in Kilometers   1.6

Mirror
Lake

N

Park
Hdqrs.

Garage

Ahwahnee Hotel
& Dining Room

Yosemite Lodge

River

North
Pines

Stables

Upper
Pines

EL CAPITAN
EL 7,569 FT.

Merced

Chapel

Housekeeping
Camp

MORAN POINT
EL 6,258 FT.

Lower
Pines

Curry
Village

Sentinel
Picnic Area

UNION POINT
EL 6,314 FT.

GLACIER PT.
EL 7,214 FT.

Sentinel

SENTINEL ROCK
EL 7,038 FT.

NORTHSIDE

SOUTHSIDE

Sentinel Fall
900 Ft. Fall

2114-F

Point Rd., offers a panorama of area domes, pinnacles, waterfalls and—dominating all—Half Dome. On the valley floor 3,214 feet below, automobiles appear as moving specks, and the Merced River resembles a silver thread. From the stone lookout you can study the detail of the High Sierra and its flanking ranges, miles away.

The paved road to the point winds through forests of pine and fir. During summer, bus tours and hiker shuttles to Glacier Point are available and ranger-naturalists are on duty. A 1.5-mile walk from the parking area leads to Sentinel Dome at 8,122 feet. The road to Glacier Point normally is open late May through October.

THE GRAND CANYON of the Tuolumne can be traversed only on foot. Waterwheel Falls is accessible by a trail 6 miles from Tioga Road along the Tuolumne River Gorge to Glen Aulin High Sierra Camp, then 3 miles down the river. At the falls, the river rushing down the canyon hits shelves of projecting rock with terrific force, throwing enormous arcs of water into the air. This spectacle is best viewed mid-June to mid-July.

Below the waterfalls the river descends abruptly, plunging through a mile-deep gorge. Trails penetrate to the heart of the region and lead to Pate Valley, where only ancient mortar holes remain as a reminder of the American Indians who once lived in this region.

North of the Tuolumne River is a vast area of lakes and valleys. Though it is threaded with numerous trails, it remains lightly visited and offers a true wilderness experience. Hikers should inquire in advance about trail conditions.

HETCH HETCHY RESERVOIR is reached from Yosemite Valley via Big Oak Flat Rd. (You should carry tire chains in the fall, winter and spring.) The 38-mile drive from the valley through fine stands of sugar pine and white fir can be covered easily in 2 hours. A paved road leads 7 miles from Mather to the 312-foot dam, which impounds San Francisco's water supply. Before the dam was built in the 1920s, the Hetch Hetchy Valley rivaled Yosemite Valley in beauty. The Hetch Hetchy Valley floor is now under 300 feet of water.

MARIPOSA GROVE, in the extreme southern end of the park, is reached via Wawona Road (SR 41). The easy 36-mile paved drive from Yosemite Valley is closed during winter and spring. The giant sequoia grove is one of the finest in the Sierra.

Grizzly Giant, the oldest tree in Mariposa Grove, has a maximum base diameter of 30.7 feet, a girth of 96.5 feet and a height of 210 feet. Two tunnel trees are in the park: the 232-foot California Tree in Mariposa Grove and the 40-foot stump Dead Giant in Tuolumne Grove. The Wawona Tunnel Tree fell during the 1968-69 winter storms.

HIGH-ALTITUDE HEALTH

Temples throbbing, gasping for breath and nauseated, you barely notice the sparkling snow, the scudding clouds or the spectacular view below.

You might be suffering from Acute Mountain Sickness (AMS). Usually striking at around 8,000 feet (2,500 m) in altitude, AMS is your body's way of coping with the reduced oxygen and humidity of high altitudes. Among the symptoms are headaches, shortness of breath, loss of appetite, insomnia and lethargy. Some people complain of temporary weight gain or swelling in the face, hands and feet.

If your AMS is severe, you should stop ascending; you will recover in a few days. On the other hand, a quick descent will end the suffering immediately.

You can reduce the impact of high altitude by being in top condition. If you smoke or suffer from heart or lung ailments, consult your physician. Alcohol and certain drugs will intensify the symptoms.

A gradual ascent with a couple days of acclimatization is the best bet if you have time. On the way up, eat light, nutritious meals and drink water copiously. A spicy, high-carbohydrate diet might mitigate the effects of low oxygen and encourage you to drink more. But beware of those crystal-clear mountain streams where parasites might lurk. Boil such water at least 10 minutes.

Other high-altitude health problems include sunburn and hypothermia. Dress in layers to protect yourself from the intense sun and wide fluctuations in temperature.

Finally, after you unwind in the sauna or whirlpool bath at your lodgings, remember to stand up carefully, for the heat has relaxed your blood vessels and lowered your blood pressure.

Mariposa Grove Museum contains exhibits about giant sequoias. During the summer a naturalist gives talks about the park. Nearby is the fallen Massachusetts Tree, 280 feet long and 28 feet in diameter; several broken sections provide opportunities to study the wood.

Guided bus tours run from the valley to the grove, with a stop in Wawona. Along the way an overlook at the east portal of the 4,233-foot Wawona tunnel offers a view of the entire valley; farther south is the Merced South Fork Basin. Cars are not permitted in the upper grove. For those who want to explore on foot, a 2.5-mile trail leads to the upper grove. Every 15-20 minutes 1-hour tram tours leave from the parking area. Tram tours and museum daily 9-6, early May-Oct. 31. Museum free. Tram fare $8; over 61, $7.25; ages 5-12, $4.

TIOGA PASS ROAD (SR 120) traverses the park and provides the only entrance from the east; it begins at the junction of SR 120 with US 395 just south of Lee Vining.

The first 12 miles of the two-lane paved road ascend nearly a mile and overlook a vast canyon. The road traverses Tuolumne Meadows and descends to Tenaya Lake. From the rocky area surrounding the lake it continues west to a junction with Big Oak Flat Road. This route offers a very pleasant and scenic trip with frequent overlooks.

Although portions of the drive are more demanding than relaxing, the magnificent scenery attracts many motorists. The road is usually open late May-October 31 (weather permitting). Motorists should carry tire chains, since weather and road conditions can change quickly. For road conditions phone (209) 372-0200.

TUOLUMNE GROVE, on old Big Oak Flat Rd., 17 mi. from Yosemite Valley, contains 20 giant sequoia trees, including the Dead Giant stump. Automobiles are no longer permitted on the section of Big Oak Flat Rd. adjacent to the grove. Visitors may park their cars near the Crane Flat Junction at a lot off of Tioga Rd. and walk to Tuolumne Grove; however, the mile-long route descends approximately 700 feet and the return ascent to the parking lot is a moderately strenuous climb.

TUOLUMNE MEADOWS is in the High Sierra, about 56 miles from Yosemite Valley over the Big Oak Flat and Tioga roads. At 8,600 feet in elevation and surrounded by lofty peaks, this area is an ideal camping place and an excellent starting point for fishing, hiking and mountain-climbing trips. It is accessible by car from about early June through October.

Trips can be taken on foot or horseback to Waterwheel Falls, Mount Lyell and Lyell Glacier, Lembert Dome, Glen Aulin, Muir Gorge, Soda Springs, Tenaya Lake and other points.

Daily bus service is available early June through Labor Day (weather permitting) from Yosemite Valley to Tuolumne Meadows. Nature walks, hikes and evening campfire programs are conducted early June through Labor Day (weather permitting); saddle horses and gas station, store and post office services also are available, along with a mountaineering school and guide service.

WASHBURN AND MERCED LAKES, accessible by trail only from Yosemite Valley, are typical of the many lakes bordering the western slopes of the Sierra. One of six High Sierra camps is at the head of Merced Lake and can be reached by trail from Yosemite Valley, Tenaya Lake or Tuolumne Meadows.

WAWONA BASIN provides a recreation area of several square miles that includes camping, riding, golf, swimming and tennis facilities. Wawona, in a beautiful meadow on Wawona Road, is 27 miles south of the Yosemite Valley near Mariposa Grove. Saddle and pack animals are available in summer.

YOSEMITE PIONEER HISTORY CENTER, at Wawona, has historic cabins and exhibits about stagecoach days in Yosemite. Living-history demonstrations are offered.

YOSEMITE VALLEY, 27 mi. n. on SR 41 or also accessible from SRs 120 and 140, is open all year. The valley extends for 7 miles and averages .75 miles in width; its walls rise to 3,200 feet. Immense precipices on either side of the valley and lofty waterfalls are impressive natural features.

Upper Yosemite Fall drops 1,430 feet in one fall, a height equal to nine Niagaras. Lower Yosemite Fall, immediately below, has a comparatively modest drop of 320 feet. Counting the cascades in between, the total drop from the crest of Yosemite Falls to the valley floor is 2,425 feet—nearly half a mile. Vernal Fall drops 317 feet; Illilouette Fall, 370 feet; Nevada Fall, 594 feet; Bridalveil Fall, 620 feet; and Ribbon Fall, 1,612 feet.

The falls are at their fullest in May and June while winter snows are melting. Fairly abundant up to mid-July, many of the falls practically disappear for the balance of the summer, then reappear with the first storm of autumn and run lightly during winter.

The great domes and pinnacles of Yosemite Valley—Three Brothers, El Capitan, Cathedral Spires, North Dome and Half Dome—are as celebrated as the falls.

YOUNTVILLE (N-2)
pop. 3,300, elev. 100'

Yountville lies on a scenic stretch of SR 29 that extends from Calistoga to Napa.

Yountville Chamber of Commerce: 6516 Yount St., P.O. Box 2064, Yountville, CA 94599; phone (707) 944-0904.

Shopping areas: Vintage 1870 offers shopping and dining in a restored 19th-century winery.

HOT AIR BALLOON RIDES over Napa Valley vineyards are available (weather permitting) through the following companies: Adventures Aloft, (707) 255-8688; Balloon Aviation, (707) 252-7067; and Napa Valley Balloons, (707) 944-0228, or (800) 253-2224 in Calif. Flights usually last 1 hour and depart in the early morning. Fares range $100-$195. Reservations are required. Rides are not advisable for children under age 8; under age 5 are not permitted. All pilots are FAA certified.

Note: The mention of the preceding hot air balloon rides is for information only and does **not** imply endorsement by AAA.

WINERIES

• **Domaine Chandon,** 1 California Dr. Daily 11-5, May-Oct.; Wed.-Sun. 11-5, rest of year. Closed holidays. Phone (707) 944-2280.

YREKA (A-2) pop. 6,900, elev. 2,625'

Yreka was incorporated in 1857, 6 years after Abraham Thompson's mules pulled gold flecks up on the roots of the grass they were eating. Miners soon swarmed into this lush valley, which had long been a home to the Modoc and Shasta Indians. I-5 provides a scenic route.

Yreka Chamber of Commerce: 117 W. Miner St., Yreka, CA 96097; phone (530) 842-1649.

BLUE-GOOSE STEAM TRAIN departs the depot at the Center exit. The 3-hour tour provides views of Mount Shasta, Shasta Valley and cattle ranch country as well as a visit to the old railroad town of Montague. Steam train departs Wed.-Sun. at 10, mid-June through Labor Day; Sat.-Sun. at 10, late May to mid-June and Sept.-Oct. Fare $9; ages 3-12, $4.50. DS, MC, VI. Phone (530) 842-4146.

GREENHORN PARK, s. off Greenhorn Rd. at Greenhorn Reservoir, features a restored miner's cabin and mining equipment. A nature trail, playground and picnic facilities are available. Fishing is permitted. Daily 7 a.m.-10 p.m., May-Sept.; 7-6, rest of year. Free. Phone (530) 841-2386.

SISKIYOU COUNTY COURTHOUSE, 311 Fourth St., exhibits various forms of gold. Mon.-Fri. 8-5; closed holidays. Free. Phone (530) 842-8084 or (888) 854-2000.

SISKIYOU COUNTY MUSEUM, 910 S. Main St., contains exhibits of the region dating from prehistoric times to the 20th century. Featured are displays about American Indians, fur trappers and the military. The outdoor museum displays equipment and restored buildings in an 1800s village setting. A candlelight tour takes place in early March. Allow 2 hours minimum. Tues.-Sat. 9-5; closed holidays. Admission $1; ages 7-12, 75c. Phone (530) 842-3836.

 RECREATIONAL ACTIVITIES

White-water Rafting

- **Orange Torpedo Trips** travels the Klamath River. Write P.O. Box 1111, Grants Pass, OR 97526-0294. Daily Apr.-Oct. Phone (541) 479-5061.

YUBA CITY (D-3) pop. 27,400, elev. 60'

Yuba City was founded in 1849 as a gold rush development; it is now a marketing center for the surrounding agricultural area.

COMMUNITY MEMORIAL MUSEUM, 1333 Butte House Rd., contains American Indian and pioneer artifacts, furniture, clothing, agricultural equipment, photographs and historical documents from Sutter County. Tues.-Fri. 9-5, Sat.-Sun. noon-4. Donations. Phone (530) 822-7141.

GRAY LODGE WILDLIFE REFUGE, 15 mi. n.w. off SR 99, comprises 8,400 acres. The refuge is an important Pacific flyway stopover for waterfowls, in addition to being a nesting ground for doves, pheasants, coots and hawks. In all, more than 200 species of birds use the refuge. An auto route traverses the area; fishing and hunting are permitted in season.

Daily dawn-dusk, except during waterfowl season, when hours coincide with the operational hunting regulations. Admission $2.50; free to holders of current California fishing and hunting licenses or California Wildlife Pass. For more information contact the area headquarters office at

3207 Rutherford Rd., Gridley, CA 95948; phone (530) 846-3315. For information about interpretive programs phone (530) 846-5176.

SUTTER BUTTES, 10 mi. w. on Butte House Rd., are sometimes referred to as the world's smallest mountain range. This brooding cluster of dark rocks rises some 2,000 feet above the surrounding plain and covers about 75 square miles. The buttes are a volcanic upthrust formation—something of a geologic anomaly for this area—and are popular with nature lovers, who enjoy the abundant bird life and wildflowers.

Although much of the region is private property, visitors can join nature study groups and guided hikes. For more information contact Yuba College Community Education, 2088 N. Beale Rd., Marysville, CA 95901; phone (530) 741-6825.

YUCCA VALLEY (J-7)
pop. 16,500, elev. 3,279'

Yucca Valley Chamber of Commerce: 55569 29 Palms Hwy., Yucca Valley, CA 92284; phone (760) 365-6323.

HI-DESERT NATURE MUSEUM, 1 blk. n. of 29 Palms Hwy./SR 62 on Dumosa Ave., offers permanent and changing exhibitions relating the Hi-Desert's natural and historical elements. Included are displays of American Indian artifacts, a rock and mineral collection and a mini-zoo featuring small desert animals. At South Park, one nature trail offers views of Joshua Tree National Park (*see place listing p. 84*). Tues.-Sun. 10-5; closed major holidays. Donations. Phone (760) 369-7212.

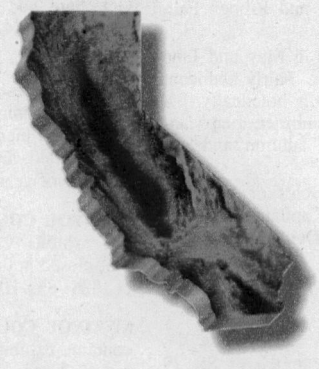

Nevada

"The City that Never Sleeps"

Non-stop gambling, neon signs, flashy shows— this is Las Vegas

The Extraterrestrial Highway

Bring your binoculars and watch for UFOs along this lonely stretch of road

Sandy Lows and Icy Highs

Nevada's terrain ranges from parched deserts to snowcapped peaks

Pioneer Routes

Many Nevada highways retrace the routes blazed by intrepid pioneers

Ghost Towns Still Live

Old mining towns such as Virginia City, Rhyolite and Eureka are open for business

take a closer look

Y ou could drive completely
across Nevada and see nothing
but lonely, deserted highway, or
you could drive across Nevada and see
everything. It's all in your expectations
and attitude.

You can see it as it is now, some of
the most arid territory in the entire country. Or you could imagine what this land
must have been like millions of years
ago when it was a vast inland sea.

You might glance at your surroundings and think: hot, sandy, dry. Or you
could look a little further and see snow-
capped peaks and green valleys with
fertile farms.

You might think that nothing could
live in such a desolate place. But closer

inspection might reveal wild horses, tortoises and any number of raptors.

You could look toward the horizon and see only sage, juniper and yucca palms. Or you could venture off the beaten path and find pines, firs, roses and wild strawberries.

You might conclude that all the people you see are tourists or visiting weekend gamblers.

Yet a little investigation will show that the state is one of the fastest growing in the country and that Clark County has more than tripled its citizenry over the past 25 years.

So take a second look at Nevada. Don't be fooled by what you think you see.

OK, you were lured to Nevada by the temptation of turning a quarter into a million dollars. Hitting the jackpot. Early retirement. A life of ease. Then reality sets in. As it turns out, you don't have the Midas touch after all. But here you are in Nevada, the Silver State, with no silver to show for your troubles. What should you do?

Your dreams of monetary riches may have faded, but there are other riches to be had here: wide open spaces, endless blue skies, deserts, mountains and the culture of the American Indians who lived here long before neon invaded the Las Vegas Valley.

Las Vegas is man's excuse for excess. In the beginning there were slot machines, which begat all-you-can-eat buffets, which begat elaborate star-studded shows, which begat themed megaresorts. But leave the glitz and glamor of Vegas and you will find the Nevada of the ancient Anasazi, of the early pioneers who braved the harsh extremes of barren deserts and inhospitable mountains, of the dashing pony express riders and the ghost towns left behind by grizzled miners.

For there's another side to this state, one where Mother Nature, history and geography are intertwined. Take a gamble on what

you will find here. You might discover that you struck it rich after all.

Of Deserts and Mountains

Some of Nevada's earliest inhabitants left their calling cards at Grimes Point near Fallon. Follow a trail past 150 boulders inscribed with rock art etched by these ancient peoples. But don't become too engrossed in deciphering their symbolism. You might be rudely returned to the present by the roar of jet aircraft engines—the Navy Fighter Weapons School, commonly known as "Top Gun," is nearby.

When you consider Nevada's setting in the Great Basin—an area characterized by dry deserts, mountain ranges, and valleys often interrupted by mesas and buttes—it's easy to understand why permanent settlement did not occur until the 1850s. It was greed and the potential of hitting pay dirt in the burgeoning mining districts that finally brought rudimentary civilization to this part of the nation.

It takes hardy species such as yucca, cacti and sagebrush to survive the arid climate, where annual rainfall in some areas is no more than 4 inches. While geckos and rattlesnakes handle the desert heat, bighorn sheep and pronghorn antelopes have adapted to the

Francisco Garcés, a Spanish Franciscan priest, is the first person of European descent to visit the area.

1775

A year after Hudson's Bay Co. trapper Peter Skene Ogden crosses the Humboldt River, explorer Jedediah Smith leads a party into the Las Vegas Valley.

1826

Following the Mexican War, the Treaty of Guadalupe Hidalgo grants the U. S. possession of former Mexican lands, including present-day Nevada.

1848

1843-45

Capt. John C. Frémont explores the area for the purpose of expanding the United States.

1851

Mormons establish the first permanent settlement, Mormon Station, now called Genoa.

Historical Timeline

higher elevations, where some peaks are snow-covered most of the year.

E.T. Meets the Old West

If this reminds you of the Old West, you have an accurate picture of much of Nevada. The occupation of cowboy still thrives in this part of the country, where old Pony Express stations line US 50, now known as "The Loneliest Road in America." But more futuristic means of travel are sought out along SR 375, designated the Extraterrestrial Highway for its many UFO sightings and proximity to the Air Force's top-secret Area 51.

Head away from the population hubs of Las Vegas and Reno and you will find highways leading to historic outposts. Old mining towns such as Virginia City retain their 19th-century boomtown appearance from the days when the Comstock Lode's vast deposits generated prosperity and a surge in population, as well as saloons and brothels. The assay office is open again in the ghost town of Berlin, east of Gabbs on SR 844, but this time strictly for the edification of visitors to the state park encompassing the site.

Present-day reminders of Nevada's heritage include rodeos, powwows and exhibits about the American Indians who lived here before Capt. John C. Frémont explored this land. For a look at one tribe's legacy, visit the Lost City Museum in Overton, which is on the site of a prehistoric Anasazi village. On the cowboy side of the ledger, get a ticket for June's Helldorado Days rodeo in Las Vegas for bull riding and bucking bronco action.

Wealth from Different Sources

As spectacular as the man-made scenery is in Las Vegas and Reno, it pales in comparison with that created by Mother Nature. Seemingly crafted with a heavy hand, Nevada's landscape is studded with jagged peaks, vividly hued rock formations and alkali flats—sometimes surreal, always majestic. The high desert setting of Red Rock Canyon, a short drive west of Las Vegas; the eroded sandstone formations at Valley of Fire, near Overton; and the spires and pillars of Cathedral Gorge, outside Caliente, attest to nature's prowess.

Nevada appeals to the gambler in each of us, from pioneers seeking fortune and wealth to today's casino cowboys, who pursue instant riches—not from the sweat of their brows, but with poker chips or a lucky roll of the dice.

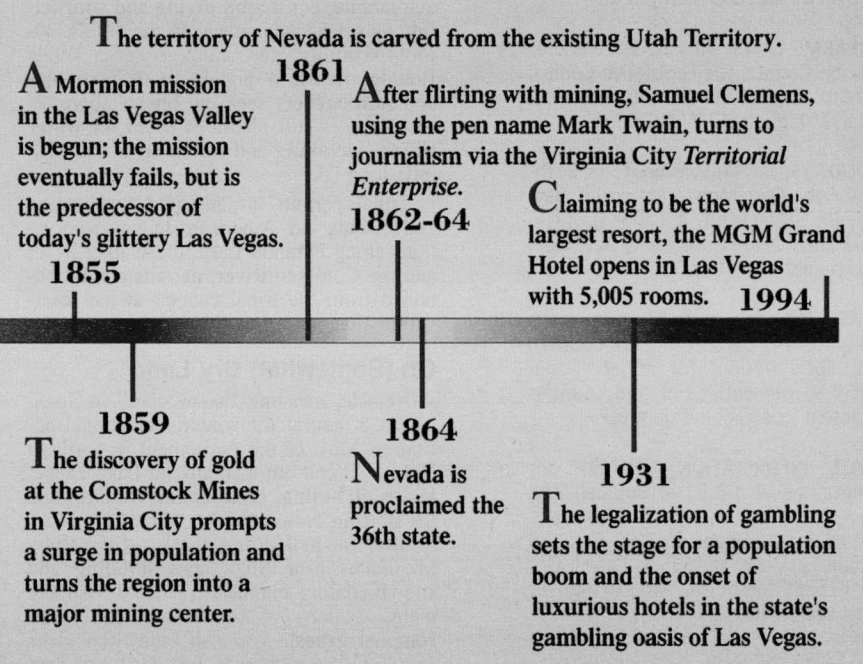

The territory of Nevada is carved from the existing Utah Territory.

1861

A Mormon mission in the Las Vegas Valley is begun; the mission eventually fails, but is the predecessor of today's glittery Las Vegas.

1855

After flirting with mining, Samuel Clemens, using the pen name Mark Twain, turns to journalism via the Virginia City *Territorial Enterprise.*

1862-64

Claiming to be the world's largest resort, the MGM Grand Hotel opens in Las Vegas with 5,005 rooms. **1994**

1859

The discovery of gold at the Comstock Mines in Virginia City prompts a surge in population and turns the region into a major mining center.

1864

Nevada is proclaimed the 36th state.

1931

The legalization of gambling sets the stage for a population boom and the onset of luxurious hotels in the state's gambling oasis of Las Vegas.

FAST FACTS

POPULATION: 1,676,800.

AREA: 110,540 square miles; ranks 7th.

CAPITAL: Carson City.

HIGHEST POINT: 13,143 ft., Boundary Peak, White Mountains.

LOWEST POINT: 470 ft., on the Colorado River.

TIME ZONE: Pacific. DST.

MINIMUM AGE FOR DRIVERS: 16.

MINIMUM AGE FOR GAMBLING: 21.

SEAT BELT/CHILD RESTRAINT LAWS: Seat belts required for driver and all passengers; restraints required for children under 5 and under 40 pounds.

HELMETS FOR MOTORCYCLISTS: Required.

RADAR DETECTORS: Permitted.

FIREARMS LAWS: Vary by state and/or county. Contact the Legislative Council Bureau, Capitol Complex, Carson City, NV 89710; phone (775) 687-6800.

HOLIDAYS: Jan. 1; Washington's Birthday, Feb. (3rd Mon.); Memorial Day, May (last Mon.); July 4; Labor Day; Nevada Day, Oct. 31; Veterans Day, Nov. 11; Thanksgiving; Dec. 25.

TAXES: Nevada's statewide sales tax is 6.5 percent (7 percent in Clark County), with local options for an additional 0.25-0.50 percent. Cities and counties impose a 1 percent lodgings tax.

STATE INFORMATION CENTERS are maintained on US 93 at Boulder City; on I-15 at Jean; at 195 US 50 at Lake Tahoe; in Las Vegas at 3150 Paradise Rd.; in Laughlin at 1555 S. Casino Dr.; on I-15 at Mesquite; and on I-80 at West Wendover.

Recreation

Conventional wisdom holds that recreational opportunities would be clustered near a state's largest cities. And you *can* enjoy **swimming, golf, tennis** and **racquetball** at any number of places in Las Vegas and Reno. However, the rest of the state holds its own as far as outdoor pursuits are concerned.

In or On the Water

If **fishing** is on the agenda, Nevada is the right place to be. Grab your pole and head to lakes Mead or Mohave in Lake Mead National Recreation Area for some of the nation's premier sport fishing spots. Lake Mead, created when Hoover Dam was built in 1936, is known for striped bass, while rainbow trout prefer the waters of Lake Mohave. Other prime fishing holes can be found at Cave Lake State Park near Ely. where German brown trout are prevalent, and at Wild Horse State Recreation Area, off SR 225 between Mountain City and North Fork, where several varieties of trout populate the reservoir. State fishing licenses and/or special use stamps may be required.

Lake Mead is where to go for just about any water-based activity. **Boating** enthusiasts enjoy hidden coves not reachable by automobile, and **scuba diving** and **snorkeling** fans take advantage of the lake's 30-foot visibility and calm waters. While Boulder Beach is popular with swimmers and **sailboarders** seek out breezy shore areas, there is still plenty of room for **water skiing, kayaking** and **canoeing** at this 110-mile-long lake.

Tribal permits are required for boating and fishing on American Indian reservations along Pyramid Lake, the Walker River and the Colorado River; permits can be obtained from the tribal council at the reservation site.

On (Somewhat) Dry Land

Nevada, meaning "snow clad" in Spanish, is a natural for winter recreational activities. Most of the excitement in northern Nevada is concentrated around Lake Tahoe. **Downhill skiing, cross-country skiing** and **ice skating** draw crowds to the area's many resorts. For **heli-skiing** check out the Ruby Mountains near Elko; **snowmobiling** and **snowboarding** enthusiasts should visit the many sections of the Humboldt-Toiyabe National Forest. You can enjoy the same sports farther south at Lee Canyon, near Mount Charleston northwest of Las Vegas.

Lace up your **hiking** boots and explore Nevada. Miles of trails within most state parks await the adventurous. Just west of Las Vegas, Red Rock Canyon has more than 30 miles of hiking trails, including Pine Creek Canyon Trail, where eagle eyes might spot wild burros. Trekking cross-country through Lake Mead National Recreation Area can lead you to colorful sandstone formations, centuries-old petroglyphs and panoramic views. Brochures describing various trails as well as safety hints are available from the USDA Forest Service, Las Vegas Ranger Division, 2881 Valley View Blvd., Suite 16, Las Vegas, NV 89102; phone (702) 873-8800.

Among the miles of **backpacking** and hiking trails in Humboldt-Toiyabe National Forest are those in the Ruby Mountains outside Elko where mountain goats and bighorn sheep can be seen among the high mountain lakes. But don't forget your long johns, as evening temperatures can drop below freezing even during the summer. There also are many miles of trails suitable for **horseback riding.**

Duck hunters should head to the national wildlife refuges of Pahranagat, south of Alamo; Ruby Lake, in the Ruby Valley; and Stillwater, in the Fallon area. Other huntable wildlife include rabbits, quails and pheasants. Controlled **hunting** for deer, elk and antelopes takes place at the Desert National Wildlife Range northwest of Las Vegas.

Most state parks are open all year, although severe winter weather may limit their accessibility. The majority charge user fees for **camping**, day use and boat launching. For information about camping *see the AAA California/Nevada Campbook.*

And for those more attuned to spectator sports, Las Vegas has more to offer than casinos and nightclubs. The Las Vegas Motor Speedway complex, northeast off I-15 exit 54, offers all forms of **automobile racing.**

Recreational Activities

Throughout the TourBook, you may notice a Recreational Activities heading with bulleted listings of recreation-oriented establishments listed underneath. Since normal AAA inspection criteria cannot be applied, these establishments are presented for information only. Age, height and weight restrictions may apply. Reservations are often recommended and sometimes required. Visitors should phone or write the attraction for additional information, and the address and phone number are provided for this purpose.

FOR YOUR INFORMATION

FURTHER INFORMATION FOR VISITORS:

Commission on Tourism
Capitol Complex
Carson City, NV 89710
(775) 687-4322
(800) 638-2328

RECREATION INFORMATION:

Nevada Division of State Parks
1300 S. Curry St.
Carson City, NV 89703
(775) 687-4384

FISHING AND HUNTING REGULATIONS:

Nevada Division of Wildlife
State Headquarters
1100 Valley Rd.
Reno, NV 89512
(775) 688-1500

NATIONAL FOREST INFORMATION:

Intermountain Region
2501 Wall Ave.
Ogden, UT 84401
(801) 625-5306
(800) 280-2267 (reservations only)

DID YOU KNOW?

Nevada has the lowest rainfall of any state; Las Vegas, Reno and Winnemucca are among the 10 driest cities in the country.

Lake Mead, formed by Hoover Dam, is one of the world's largest artificially created lakes.

More than 85 percent of the land in Nevada is owned by the federal government.

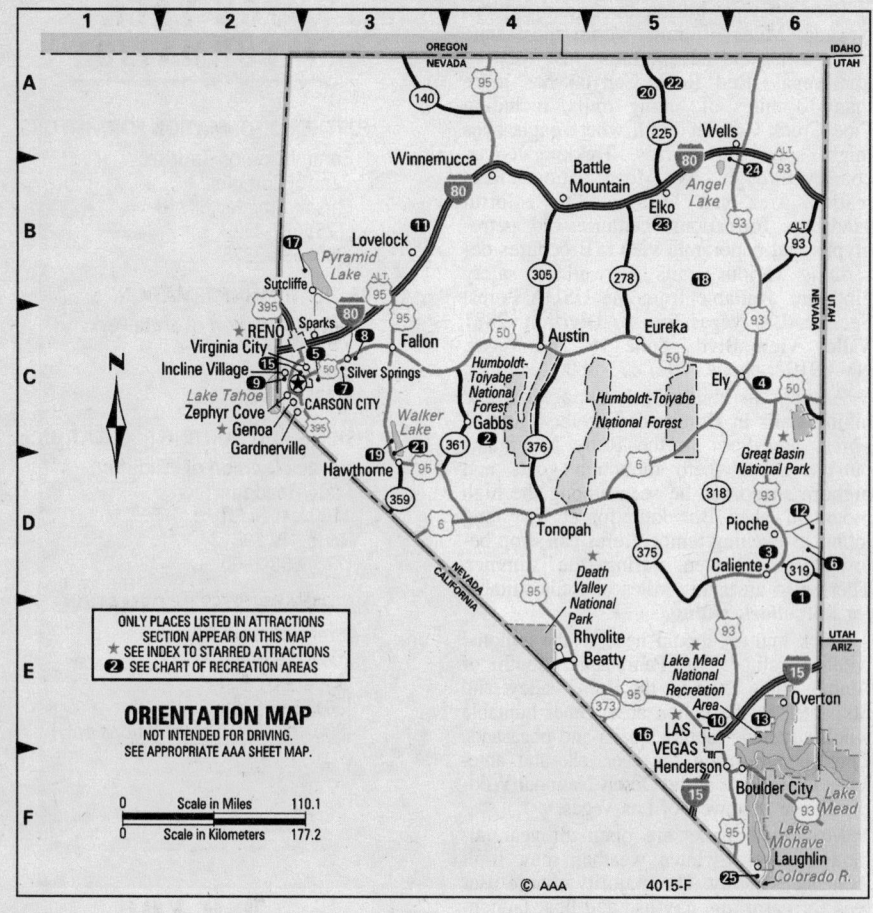

ONLY PLACES LISTED IN ATTRACTIONS
SECTION APPEAR ON THIS MAP
★ SEE INDEX TO STARRED ATTRACTIONS
❷ SEE CHART OF RECREATION AREAS

ORIENTATION MAP
NOT INTENDED FOR DRIVING.
SEE APPROPRIATE AAA SHEET MAP.

| 0 | Scale in Miles | 110.1 |
| 0 | Scale in Kilometers | 177.2 |

© AAA   4015-F

INDEX TO STARRED ATTRACTIONS
ATTRACTIONS AND PLACES OF EXCEPTIONAL INTEREST AND QUALITY

★**Death Valley National Park**
See place listing in California p. 70

Genoa
 ★ Mormon Station State Historic Park - see p. 258

★**Great Basin National Park**
See place listing p. 259
 ★ Lehman Caves - see p. 259

★**Lake Mead National Recreation Area**
See place listing p. 260
 ★ Hoover Dam - see p. 260

Las Vegas
 ★ The Liberace Museum - see p. 267
 ★ Siegfried & Roy - see p. 269

Reno
 ★ Fleischmann Planetarium - see p. 275
 ★ National Automobile Museum - see p. 275

A STARRED ATTRACTION
When you see a ★ before an attraction, it's a **must** see!

RECREATION AREAS

RECREATION AREAS	MAP LOCATION	CAMPING	PICNICKING	HIKING TRAILS	BOATING	BOAT RAMP	BOAT RENTAL	FISHING	SWIMMING	PETS ON LEASH	BICYCLE TRAILS	WINTER SPORTS	VISITOR CENTER	LODGE/CABINS	FOOD SERVICE
NATIONAL PARK *(See place listing)*															
Great Basin 77,100 acres 5 mi. w. of Baker near the Nevada-Utah border.		•	•	•				•		•			•		•
NATIONAL FORESTS *(See place listing)*															
Humboldt-Toiyabe 6,343,735 acres. Central, western, southern and northern Nevada and eastern California. Horse rental, interpretive trails.		•	•	•	•		•	•		•		•	•		•
NATIONAL RECREATION AREA *(See place listing)*															
Lake Mead (E-5) Southeastern Nevada. Scuba diving.		•	•	•	•	•	•	•	•	•			•	•	•
STATE															
Beaver Dam (D-6) 2,393 acres 3.5 mi. n.e. of Caliente on US 93, then 28 mi. e. on a gravel road. Interpretive trails.	❶	•	•	•	•	•			•	•					
Berlin-Ichthyosaur (C-4) 1,127 acres 23 mi. e. of Gabbs via SR 844. Historic. Horse trails, interpretive trails. *(See Gabbs p. 258)*	❷	•	•							•		•	•		
Big Bend of the Colorado (F-6) 2,500 acres 5 mi. s. of Laughlin on the Needles Hwy. Scenic.	㉕		•		•	•		•	•						
Cathedral Gorge (D-6) 1,633 acres 2 mi. n. of Panaca off US 93. Scenic. Horse trails, interpretive trails.	❸	•	•	•						•			•		
Cave Lake (C-6) 1,240 acres 8 mi. s. of Ely off US 93, then 7 mi. e. on Success Summit Rd. Cross-country skiing, snowmobiling.	❹	•	•	•	•	•		•		•		•			
Dayton (C-3) 152 acres in Dayton on US 50. Historic. Nature trail.	❺	•	•	•				•		•					
Echo Canyon (D-6) 1,080 acres 12 mi. e. of Pioche via SRs 322 and 323. Interpretive trail.	❻	•	•		•	•		•		•					
Floyd Lamb (E-5) 2,040 acres 15 mi. n.w. of Las Vegas on US 95.	❿		•					•		•					
Fort Churchill (C-3) 4,461 acres 7 mi. s. on US 95, then 1 mi. w. on Old Fort Churchill Rd. Historic. Interpretive trail. *(See Silver Springs p. 276)*	❼	•	•	•						•			•		
Lahontan (C-3) 30,522 acres 18 mi. w. of Fallon off US 50. Water sports. Scenic drives.	❽	•	•	•	•	•	•	•	•	•					
Lake Tahoe Nevada (C-2) 14,242 acres 4 mi. s. of Incline Village on SR 28. Water skiing, cross-country skiing.	❾	•	•	•	•	•		•	•	•	•	•			
Rye Patch (B-3) 20,241 acres 22 mi. n.e. of Lovelock off I-80.	⓫	•	•		•	•		•	•	•					
South Fork (B-5) 3,924 acres 16 mi. s.w. of Elko via SR 228 to Lower South Fork Rd. Water skiing.	㉓	•	•	•	•	•		•	•	•			•		
Spring Valley (D-6) 1,281 acres 20 mi. e. of Pioche via SR 322.	⓬	•	•	•	•	•		•		•		•			
Valley of Fire (E-6) 34,830 acres 14 mi. s.w. of Overton via SR 169. Historic sites. Birdwatching; horse trails. *(See Overton p. 274)*	⓭	•	•	•						•			•		
Walker Lake (C-3) 280 acres 11 mi. n.w. of Hawthorne on US 95. Water skiing.	㉑	•	•	•	•	•	•	•	•	•					
Washoe Lake (C-2) 8,038 acres between Reno and Carson City e. of US 395.	⓯	•	•	•	•	•		•	•	•					
Wild Horse (A-5) 120 acres 65 mi. n. of Elko via SR 225. Birdwatching, cross-country skiing, snowmobiling.	⓴	•	•		•	•		•		•		•			
OTHER															
Angel Lake (B-5) 13 mi. s.w. of Wells via SR 582.	㉔	•	•		•	•		•	•	•			•		
Mount Charleston (E-5) 30 mi. n.w. of Las Vegas via US 95 and SR 157.	⓰	•	•	•					•	•	•	•	•	•	•
Pyramid Lake (B-2) off SR 445. *(See Sutcliffe p. 276)*	⓱	•	•		•	•	•	•	•	•			•	•	•
Ruby Lake (B-5) 60 mi. s.e. of Elko.	⓲	•	•		•	•		•		•			•		•
Walker Lake (D-3) 4 mi. n. of Hawthorne. Water skiing.	⓳	•	•		•	•		•	•	•					
Wild Horse Reservoir (A-5) 65 mi. n. of Elko on SR 225.	㉒	•	•	•	•	•		•	•	•		•		•	•

STARRED ATTRACTIONS

Death Valley National Park—The Western Hemisphere's lowest point, Death Valley is blazingly hot and prone to flash floods, yet is home to rare foliage and geological phenomena. See place listing in California p. 70.

Fleischmann Planetarium—Realistic images projected on the planetarium's domed screen transport visitors to the stars and beyond. See Reno p. 275.

Great Basin National Park—Flora and fauna in this mountainous park range from that typically found in arid climates to examples that survive in frigid tundra conditions. See place listing p. 259.

Hoover Dam—As an alternative to the standard guided tours of the dam and power plant, "hard hat" tours allow a close-up look at what makes the turbines operate. See Lake Mead National Recreation Area p. 260.

Lake Mead National Recreation Area—A year-round recreation mecca, Lake Mead beckons boaters, fishermen, hikers and water skiers as well as those simply in search of scenic drives. See place listing p. 261.

Lehman Caves—Marble and limestone passageways are the focus of this cave at the base of Wheeler Peak. See Great Basin National Park p. 259.

The Liberace Museum—The glittering costumes and jewelry and the elaborate pianos and automobiles collected by the legendary pianist and entertainer are the highlights of this museum. See Las Vegas p. 267.

Mormon Station State Historic Park—The log trading post at Mormon Station has been rebuilt to portray its place in history as a way station on the grueling overland trek to California. See Genoa p. 258.

Points of Interest

AUSTIN (C-4) pop. 400, elev. 6,527'

Popular legend says that Austin sprang up in 1862 just west of the present townsite after a Pony Express horse kicked over a rock that capped the mouth of a silver-laden cavern. Within 2 years Austin boasted a population of 10,000, as bullion poured from 11 ore-reduction mills. By 1867 some 6,000 mining claims had been filed.

A reminder of Austin's former affluence is Stoke's Castle, built in 1897 for Anson Phelps Stokes, an eastern financier who had considerable mining interests in the area. Built of hand-hewn granite slabs, the deserted three-story replica of a Roman tower can be seen for miles in the desert. Also of interest is Lander County Courthouse, the second-story balcony of which was used by vigilantes as a gallows.

Near Austin are a number of historical sites. Hickson Petroglyph Recreation Site, 24 miles east on US 50 near the old Pony Express Trail, and the Toquima Caves, 6 miles farther east, feature stones etched with American Indian drawings dating from 1000 B.C. to A.D. 1500. About 65 miles west of Austin off SR 50 are the remains of the Cold Springs Pony Express Station. A sign near the highway explains the history of the site and marks the beginning of an interpretive 1.5-mile trail to the Pony Express station site.

Mountain biking and hiking as well as trout fishing and waterfowl hunting are available in the Humboldt-Toiyabe National Forest *(see place listing p. 260)*.

Greater Austin Chamber of Commerce: Austin Courthouse, P.O. Box 212, Austin, NV 89310; phone (775) 964-2200 or 964-2418.

BATTLE MOUNTAIN (B-5) pop. 3,500, elev. 4,507'

Battle Mountain is named for a nearby mountain range that commemorates an American Indian raid against pioneers in 1857. The discovery of minerals in Copper Canyon in 1870 brought permanent settlers, and Battle Mountain became the point of transfer for mining supplies between stage lines and railroads.

Ranching and transportation have largely replaced mining. There are two barite mines near Battle Mountain and a gold and silver mine at Copper Canyon. Battle Mountain straddles I-80, which follows the old Bidwell, Donner and Fremont pioneer trails. To the south along SR 305 is the scenic Reese River Valley, part of the Arc Dome Wilderness in the Humboldt-Toiyabe National Forest.

Battle Mountain Chamber of Commerce: 625 S. Broad, P.O. Box 333, Battle Mountain, NV 89820; phone (775) 635-8245.

BEATTY (E-5) pop. 1,600, elev. 3,308'

A picturesque desert town in the Amargosa River Valley, Beatty is the Nevada approach to Death Valley National Monument *(see place listing in California p. 70)*. Chloride Cliff, reached via a rough 5-mile dirt road off SR 374, offers an excellent view of Death Valley. Also en route to the national monument are the ghost towns of Rhyolite *(see place listing p. 276)* and Bullfrog. Six miles north of Beatty on US 95 is Bailey's Hot Springs. With a water temperature of about 104 degrees Fahrenheit, the springs are open year-round.

Beatty Chamber of Commerce: 119 E. Main, P.O. Box 956, Beatty, NV 89003; phone (775) 553-2424.

BOULDER CITY—
see Las Vegas p. 273.

CALIENTE (D-6) pop. 1,100, elev. 4,403'

Caliente, named for the hot springs originally found in the area, is near several state parks, including Beaver Dam, Cathedral Gorge, Echo Canyon and Spring Valley *(see Recreation Chart)*. Also nearby is the ghost town Delamar, marked by a few stone buildings, mill ruins and a cemetery; check locally for road conditions.

A mural displaying points of interest in Lincoln and Clark counties is in the lobby of the Amtrak station, a Spanish-style railroad depot built in 1923. Guided tours of the Lincoln County Art Room, also in the lobby of the station, and other area attractions can be arranged through the chamber of commerce.

Caliente Chamber of Commerce: Depot Building, P.O. Box 553, Caliente, NV 89008; phone (775) 726-3129.

CARSON CITY (C-3)
pop. 40,400, elev. 4,660'

Carson City, founded in 1858 and named for Kit Carson, was designated as the state capital in 1864. The original silver-domed Capitol, with additions and restorations, still is in use. The old Assembly and Senate chambers, including a museum display about the Capitol, can be visited. Self-guiding tour brochures are available at the Capitol; at the Nevada State Library and Archives at 100 S. Stewart St., phone (775) 687-5160; or from the State Historic Preservation Office, phone (775) 687-1311. The Legislative Building, south of the Capitol, also is open to the public; phone (775) 687-6800.

As the social center for nearby mining settlements in the mid-1800s, Carson City prospered.

STARRED ATTRACTIONS

National Automobile Museum—Drive on over and check out the more than 200 classic automobiles on display in period street scenes and galleries. See Reno p. 275.

Siegfried & Roy—White tigers and elephants appear and disappear in illusions performed by Siegfried and Roy in an appropriate setting—the Mirage Hotel. See Las Vegas p. 269.

DID YOU KNOW?

Nevada has the lowest rainfall of any state; Las Vegas, Reno and Winnemucca are among the 10 driest cities in the country.

Mark Twain worked as a reporter for the state's first newspaper 1862-64.

Nevada was part of Mormon leader Brigham Young's proposed State of Deseret.

A sucker fish called cui-ui lives only in Nevada's Pyramid Lake.

During Virginia City's heydey the city had 100 saloons and a population of 2,200.

The federal government established a mint for coining the copious silver output of the Comstock Lode, 15 miles northeast near Virginia City *(see place listing p. 277)*. Gold found its way here also, as evidenced by the rare gold display at the Carson City Nugget, across from the Capitol.

Antique firefighting equipment, old photographs and a series of Currier & Ives prints dealing with firefighters are displayed at Warren Engine Company No. 1 Fire Museum at 777 S. Stewart St.; phone (775) 887-2210.

The Sierra Seminary, one of the first coeducational schools in the West, was established in Carson City in 1860 by Hannah Clapp. An outspoken advocate of women's rights, Clapp operated the school for about 25 years before moving to Reno. There she and the university president temporarily served as the entire staff of the infant University of Nevada.

Carson City lies along US 50, which has been called "the loneliest road in America." Once part of the Pony Express Trail across central Nevada, the route has long stretches without roadside services and passes through such historic mining towns as Austin *(see place listing p. 254)*, Ely *(see place listing p. 257)* and Eureka *(see place listing p. 257)*.

The portion of US 50 heading west to Lake Tahoe and the California border is especially scenic. From its junction with US 395 downtown, US 50 cuts through the Humboldt-Toiyabe National Forest *(see place listing p. 260)* and then follows the lake's southeastern shoreline. Beginning at its junction with US 50 at Spooner Summit, SR 28, another scenic route, follows the lake's northeastern shoreline into California.

Carson City Convention and Visitors Bureau: 1900 S. Carson St., Ste. 200, Carson City, NV 89701; phone (775) 687-7410 or (800) 638-2321.

Self-guiding tours: A walking-tour map containing illustrations and descriptions of the town's historic sites is available from the convention and visitors bureau.

BOWERS MANSION PARK, 10 mi. n. on old US 395, overlooks Washoe Lake. The restored mansion, built by a Comstock Lode millionaire at a cost of $200,000 in 1864, contains some of the original furnishings. The surrounding park has picnic facilities, a playground and a swimming pool.

Park open daily 8 a.m.-9 p.m., Memorial Day-Labor Day; 8-7, first weekend in Apr.-day before Memorial Day and day after Labor Day-Oct. 31; 8-5, rest of year. Closed Thanksgiving and Dec. 25. Guided mansion tours are given daily every 30 minutes 11-4:30, June 1-Labor Day; Sat.-Sun. 11-4:30, in May and day after Labor Day-Oct. 31. Park free. Mansion tours $4; over 63 and under 12, $2. Pool $2.50; ages 13-17, $2; over 63 and under 13, $1.50. Phone the mansion at (775) 849-0201 or the ranger station at 849-1825.

NEVADA STATE RAILROAD MUSEUM, 2180 S. Carson St. (US 395), consists of more than 60 pieces of rolling stock, most from the Virginia and Truckee Railroad line, including seven restored steam engines. Established in 1869, the celebrated line carried ore from the Comstock Lode to the Carson River for 69 of its 81 years. In retirement, the line was discovered by Hollywood, which used V & T passenger cars, freight cars and vintage engines in movies from the late 1930s through the 1950s. Rides on the historic trains are available.

Allow 30 minutes minimum for museum, 1 hour for museum and train ride. Museum open daily 8:30-4:30; closed Jan. 1, Thanksgiving and Dec. 25. Train rides depart Fri.-Sun. 10-4, Memorial Day-Labor Day. Schedule may vary; phone ahead. Museum admission $2, under 18 free. Train ride $2.50; ages 6-11, $1. Motorcar ride $1; ages 6-11, 50c. Phone (775) 687-6953.

STATE MUSEUM, 600 N. Carson St., is in the former United States Branch Mint Building where Carson City silver dollars were stamped 1870-93. Exhibits include historical relics, a ghost town replica, a gun collection, one of the largest mammoths ever found in North America, a mint-mark coin collection, minerals and ores. The basement features a walk-through reproduction of an underground mine. In addition, an American Indian room displays willow baskets woven by Dot-So-La-Lee of the Washoe tribe.

Allow 1 hour, 30 minutes minimum. Daily 9-5:30, Memorial Day-October 31; 8:30-4:30, rest of year. Closed Jan. 1, Thanksgiving and Dec. 25. Admission $3, senior citizens $2.50, under 18 free. Phone (775) 687-4810.

STEWART INDIAN MUSEUM, 5366 Snyder Ave., has displays of American Indian artifacts, basketry, pottery, arrowheads and E.S. Curtis photogravures. Changing exhibits highlight American Indian history and culture. Allow 1 hour minimum. Mon.-Sat. 9-5:30, Sun. 9-4. Donations. Phone (775) 882-1808.

★ DEATH VALLEY NATIONAL PARK—
see place listing in California p. 70.

ELKO (B-5) pop. 14,700, elev. 5,060'

The center of Nevada's cattle country, Elko served as a way station for wagon trains during the western migration. Tourism accounts for a large portion of the town's revenue. The Cowboy Poetry Gathering, the nation's first such festival, is held from late January to early February. The event helps preserve the culture of the cowboy through music, stories, tall tales, dance, exhibits of cowboy gear and poetry.

South of Elko lie the Ruby Mountains, where miles of trails lead to back-country lakes and marshes offering hunting, fishing and boating. Lamoille Canyon *(see Humboldt-Toiyabe National Forest p. 260)* in the Ruby Mountains is known for its 12-mile-long steep glacial walls, free-flowing streams and scenic vistas.

Elko Chamber of Commerce: 1601 Idaho St., Elko, NV 89801; phone (775) 738-7135 or (800) 428-7143.

NORTHEASTERN NEVADA MUSEUM, 1515 Idaho St., chronicles natural history with exhibits pertaining to the area's American Indian heritage, mining, ranching and railroad tradition. Frontier displays include a pioneer kitchen, a schoolroom and a printing plant. Also included are wildlife displays, a photograph library and an antique gun collection.

An 1860 Pony Express cabin and a "mudwagon" stagecoach are on the grounds as well as a 1918 Dodge touring car and a 1925 Seagraves fire engine. Allow 1 hour minimum. Mon.-Sat. 9-5, Sun. 1-5; closed Jan. 1, Thanksgiving and Dec. 25. Donations. Phone (775) 738-3418.

ELY (C-5) pop. 4,800, elev. 6,421'

Founded in 1868 as a silver-mining camp, Ely bloomed with the arrival of the Nevada Northern Railway, which chugged into town in 1906 bedecked with flags, bunting and sagebrush wreaths. When Ely converted to large-scale copper mining, the town grew from 500 to 3,000 residents in a year.

Kennecott Copper Corp.'s renowned Liberty Pit produced more than $550 million in copper, gold and silver deposits. Kennecott also operated the giant Ruth pit, which produced from about 1905 to the late 1970s. Ely continues to be a center for mining as well as ranching and recreation.

The surrounding mountain ranges provide fine hunting and trout fishing. High-country hikers are fond of nearby Wheeler Peak Scenic Area, which includes 13,063-foot Wheeler Peak, Baker and Snake creeks, Big Wash Canyon and the upper parts of Lehman Creek. The garnet-studded rhyolite outcropping at the peak of Garnet Hill, 5 miles west off US 50, is popular with rockhounds. Swimming and fishing are available at Cave Lake State Recreation Area *(see Recreation Chart and the AAA California/Nevada CampBook).*

Several old mining camps and ghost towns still can be found in the Ely vicinity; these include Cherry Creek, Fort Schellbourne, Hamilton, Lane City, Osceola, Taylor and Ward. Ely also is the western terminus of a scenic route consisting of US 93, US 50/6 and SR 487. Crossing the Schell Creek and Snake ranges, the route leads to the Utah border and Great Basin National Park *(see place listing p. 259).*

Bristlecone Convention Center & Visitor's Authority: 150 6th St., P.O. Box 958, Ely, NV 89301; phone (775) 289-3720 or (800) 496-9350.

NEVADA NORTHERN RAILWAY MUSEUM, at 1100 Ave. A in East Ely, includes a restored depot, a dispatcher's office, a roundhouse and a machine shop in addition to cars and locomotives from various eras. On weekends from Memorial Day through Labor Day, the Ghost Train of Old Ely makes a 1.5-hour trip from the museum around downtown Ely, the Lane City ghost town, Robinson Canyon and the Keystone mining district.

The train consists of preserved Nevada Northern Railway cars, including a Pullman coach, a baggage car, a flat car, a 1910 Baldwin steam engine and a 1909 American locomotive. Riders in flat cars should wear protective eye and headgear. Museum open Tues.-Sun. 9-5, Memorial Day-Labor Day. Guided tours are given at 11 and 2. Museum admission $2.50, under 10 free. Train departures and prices vary; phone ahead. Phone (775) 289-2085.

WARD CHARCOAL OVENS STATE HISTORIC PARK is 5 mi. s.e. on US 6/50/93, then 11 mi. s. on Cave Valley Rd. The six 30-foot-high stone "beehive" kilns, constructed during the 1870s mining boom, burned wood to produce charcoal for use in area smelters. The monument is open all year, but may not be accessible during winter months. Phone (775) 728-4467.

WHITE PINE COUNTY MUSEUM, 2000 Aultman St., displays gems and minerals, mining equipment, Pony Express memorabilia, American Indian relics, furniture, clothes and guns. In addition, the museum has a collection of 700 dolls, 200 of which are displayed at a time on a rotating basis. An outdoor train exhibit includes a 1905 coach and 1909 and 1917 steam locomotives. Mon.-Wed. 8:30-1, Thurs. 8:30-1:30, Fri. 8:30-12:30, Sat.-Sun. 10-4; closed major holidays. Donations. Phone (775) 289-4710.

EUREKA (C-5) pop. 800, elev. 6,837'

Eureka lies along US 50 at the southern end of scenic SR 278. During the town's heyday in the 1870s, its lead-based economy and the attendant smelters led the town to be called the "Pittsburgh of the West." The population, which at one point reached nearly 11,000, supported 100 saloons, several newspapers, hotels, an opera house, five fire companies and a brass band.

The renovated Eureka Opera House, 31 S. Main St., which dates from 1880, presents a variety of cultural shows and serves as a convention, visitor and cultural arts center. A videotape describing Eureka's history also is featured. For further information phone (775) 237-6006.

Eureka Sentinel Museum, at Bateman and Monroe roads, houses the original printing equipment of the newspaper, which began operations in 1870, and displays reprints, posters and placards printed by the *Sentinel* in the 1870s and '80s. Phone (775) 237-5010.

Eureka County Chamber of Commerce: Monroe and Bateman Rds., P.O. Box 14, Eureka, NV 89316; phone (775) 237-5484.

FALLON (C-3) pop. 6,400, elev. 3,963'

Completion of Lahontan Dam in 1914 and subsequent reclamation and irrigation changed the area from barren desert to one of the state's largest farming districts. Major farm products include livestock, alfalfa and "Hearts o' Gold" cantaloupes. Besides supplying water for irrigation, the impounded lake is popular for recreation as part of the 30,522-acre Lahontan State Recreation Area *(see Recreation Chart and the AAA California/Nevada Campbook).*

East of Fallon US 50 parallels the old route of the Pony Express for a number of miles. About 20 miles east of town is a 1-mile-long road that leads to Sand Mountain and Sand Springs Pony Express Station. One of the few "singing mountains" in the country, Sand Mountain is composed of grains of sand that sometimes create a low moan as they shift. A more contemporary means of getting across the desert now exists, however, as Fallon is the headquarters for the U.S. Navy Fighter Weapons School; the flight school is more commonly known as "Top Gun."

The Bureau of Land Management offers free expeditions on the second and fourth Saturday of each month to Hidden Cave, an archeological zone 12 miles east of Fallon on US 50; phone (702) 885-6000. Tours depart from Churchill County Museum and Archives *(see attraction listing)* at 9:30. Visitors also can explore nearby Grimes Point, which contains petroglyphs.

Fallon Convention & Tourism Authority: 100 Campus Way, Fallon, NV 89406; phone (775) 423-4556 or (800) 874-0903.

CHURCHILL COUNTY MUSEUM AND ARCHIVES, 1050 S. Maine St., features an extensive collection of Western Americana focusing on the history of Churchill County and the Lahontan Valley. Displays of memorabilia pertain to the Emigrant Trail, Pony Express and the transcontinental telegraph, while notable collections include rocks, minerals and gemstones, artifacts of Nevada Indian tribes and an early 1900s novelty store.

Allow 1 hour minimum. Mon.-Sat. 10-5, Sun. noon-5, Apr.-Dec.; Mon.-Wed. and Fri.-Sat. 10-4, Sun. noon-4, rest of year. Donations. Phone (775) 423-3677.

GABBS (C-4) pop. 700, elev. 4,597'

BERLIN-ICHTHYOSAUR STATE PARK is 23 mi. e. via SR 844. This 1,127-acre park has fossils of gigantic fish dinosaurs known as ichthyosaurs that once swam the ocean covering Nevada 225 million years ago. The Ichthyosaur Fossil Shelter is a fossil bed protected by a large shed. The park also contains the late 19th-century ghost town of Berlin. Interpretive signs outline self-guiding tours among the town's 13 preserved buildings. Camping is available.

Park open daily 24 hours (weather permitting). Guided tours of the townsite are given Sat.-Sun. at 11, Memorial Day-Labor Day. Guided tours of the Ichthyosaur Fossil Shelter are given Fri.-Mon. at 10, 2 and 4, Memorial Day-Labor Day; Sat.-Sun. at 10 and 2, Mar. 1-day before Memorial Day and day after Labor Day-Nov. 30. Park free. Guided tours $1; ages 6-12, 50c. Phone (775) 964-2440. *See Recreation Chart and the AAA California/Nevada CampBook.*

GARDNERVILLE (C-2) pop. 2,200, elev. 4,746'

The Lahontan National Fish Hatchery, 4 miles south on US 395, raises the threatened Lahontan cutthroat trout for stocking in western Nevada waters. Self-guiding tour maps are available. Picnicking is permitted. The hatchery is open daily 8-3; phone (775) 265-2425.

Carson Valley Chamber of Commerce and Visitors Authority: 1512 US 395, Suite 1, Gardnerville, NV 89410; phone (775) 782-8144 or (800) 727-7677.

GENOA (C-2) elev. 4,800'

Founded by one of the traders sent out by Brigham Young in 1849, Genoa became the first permanent settlement in Nevada. In 1859 Nevada's first territorial legislature met in Genoa for a 9-day session that drafted a declaration of cause for separation from Utah Territory. Recognizing the value of the famed Comstock Lode in financing the Union's efforts in the Civil War, Congress established the Territory of Nevada in 1861.

GENOA COURTHOUSE MUSEUM is on Main St. The restored courthouse, built in 1865, contains a Virginia and Truckee Railroad display, replicas of an old schoolroom, a courtroom, a jail and a kitchen as well as American Indian basketry, needlework and artifacts. The museum also features an exhibit about the original Ferris wheel. A display about Snowshoe Thompson, a man who carried mail between Genoa and Sacramento, Calif., for many years, also is presented. Allow 1 hour minimum. Daily 10-4:30, mid-May to mid-Oct. Donations. Phone (775) 782-4325.

★ **MORMON STATION STATE HISTORIC PARK,** off US 395 then w. on Genoa Ln. to jct. SR 206 (Foothill Rd.), is a restored log stockade and trading post built in 1851 in the Carson Valley, where pioneers often rested before continuing over the Sierra Nevada to California. There also is a museum on the grounds with state history exhibits. Picnicking is permitted. Daily 9-5, May 15 to mid-Oct. (weather permitting). Donations. Phone (702) 782-2590 or 687-4379.

★ GREAT BASIN NATIONAL PARK (D-6)

Elevations in the park range from 6,200 ft. at Snake Creek to 13,063 ft. at Wheeler Peak. Refer to AAA maps for additional elevation information.

Great Basin National Park is 5 miles west of Baker on SR 488 near the Nevada-Utah border. Established in 1986, the 77,100-acre park contains many of the features common to the Great Basin, including impressive mountain peaks, lush meadows, sparkling streams, alpine lakes and a small glacier.

Rising abruptly 7,700 feet from the desert floor, the park exhibits a wide variety of plant and animal habitats that range from the Upper Sonoran life zone with its jack rabbits, sagebrush and cacti to the frigid Arctic-Alpine Tundra life zone at the highest elevations.

In spring and summer many kinds of wildflowers bloom on the mountain slopes. Pine, spruce, fir and mountain mahogany make up the forests, and wildlife includes mule deer, mountain lions, coyotes, porcupines and golden eagles. Rocky Mountain bighorn sheep, once locally extinct, were reintroduced to this area in 1971.

General Information and Activities

A highlight of the park is Lehman Caves, a limestone-solution cave. The park's visitor center is open daily 8-5 Memorial Day-Labor Day; 8:30-4:30, rest of year. Phone (775) 234-7331, ext. 212. Sixty- and 90-minute cave walks, exhibits films, maps and park information are offered. Food is available April through October.

Wheeler Peak Scenic Drive extends 12 miles to the 10,000-foot elevation on the flank of Wheeler Peak. Hiking trails lead past several alpine lakes to the 13,063-foot summit or to a rare ancient bristlecone pine forest. Park interpreters conduct various campfire programs in the summer. It is recommended that motor homes and trailers longer than 24 feet not attempt Wheeler Peak Scenic Drive.

Camping is permitted at three campgrounds along Wheeler Peak Scenic Drive and at Baker Creek Campground on Baker Creek Road. Fishing for rainbow trout is popular in the park's many clear creeks. Anglers over age 11 need a Nevada fishing license and a trout stamp; both are available in Ely and Baker. There are no developed cross-country ski trails, but winter brings ample opportunity for back-country skiing.

A few warnings should be kept in mind when visiting the park. The area is dry, so carry plenty of drinking water when hiking and treat any surface water before use. Rattlesnakes are found at all elevations during warm weather, and extreme weather conditions are likely throughout the year. *See Recreation Chart and the AAA California/ Nevada CampBook.*

ADMISSION to the park is free. There is a fee for cave walks and camping.

PETS must be on a leash at all times. They are not allowed in buildings, in the cave or on trails.

ADDRESS inquiries to the Superintendent, Great Basin National Park, Baker, NV 89311-9700; phone (775) 234-7331.

Points of Interest

BRISTLECONE PINE FOREST consists of 150 acres of trees considered to be among the oldest living things on Earth. One stand includes pines approaching 4,000 years old. An interpretive trail through the forest branches off the scenic area's main loop trail. Another spur off the main loop climbs to the summit of Wheeler Peak, the second highest peak in Nevada. Park interpreters lead walks through the bristlecone pine forest daily in summer (weather permitting).

★ **LEHMAN CAVES**, 5 mi. w. of Baker at the foot of Wheeler Peak, consists of illuminated marble and limestone passages that have many colorful formations and curious shield or palette shapes.

Although the first written mention of the cave was found in an 1885 newspaper, it is possible the cave was discovered earlier by homesteaders or miners. Absalom S. Lehman probably was the first to realize the significance of the underground galleries. After conducting his own exploration, he guided parties through the cave until his death in 1891.

The tour covers about a half-mile and includes six stairways. Flash cameras are allowed, but tripods and backpacks are not. The cave temperature is 50 degrees Fahrenheit, so a sweater or light jacket is recommended.

Guided 1- and 1.5-hour cave tours are given daily year-round. Tour times vary; phone ahead. Closed Jan. 1, Thanksgiving and Dec. 25. Tickets may be purchased up to 30 days in advance. Fee $4, ages 6-15 (with an adult) $3, bearers of Golden Age Passports $2. MC, VI. Phone (775) 234-7331, ext. 242 Mon.-Fri. 7:30-4:30.

HAWTHORNE (D-3)
pop. 4,200, elev. 4,375'

MINERAL COUNTY MUSEUM, 10th and D sts., features old mining, firefighting and railroad equipment, clothing, housewares and archeological specimens from the area's early days. Tues.-Sat. 11-5, Apr.-Oct.; noon-4, rest of year. Donations. Phone (775) 945-5142.

HENDERSON—
see Las Vegas p. 273.

HUMBOLDT-TOIYABE NATIONAL FOREST (C-5)

Elevations in the forest range
from 100 ft. below sea level at
Death Valley in Calif. to 12,374 ft.
at Castle Peak. Refer to AAA maps
for additional elevation
information.

The 6,343,735 acres of Humboldt-Toiyabe National Forest are scattered among divisions in central, northern, western and southern Nevada and in eastern California, making it the second largest national forest in the country. Ranges in north-central Nevada include the Independence, Santa Rosa, Ruby, White Pine, Jarbidge, Schell Creek and Quinn Canyon. Part of the forest lies along the rugged Monitor, Toquima, Toiyabe, Shoshone and Paradise ranges of central Nevada and along the eastern slopes of the Sierra Nevada and the Spring Mountains near Las Vegas.

Jarbidge Wilderness is north of Elko; no motorized vehicles are allowed, but six trails suitable for hiking and horseback riding traverse the area. The Ruby Mountains Wilderness, southeast of Elko, offers backpacking and other recreational opportunities within 90,000 acres of alpine lakes, glaciated canyons and rugged mountains. Other wilderness areas include East Humboldt, Mount Moriah, Currant Mountain, Quinn Canyon, Grant Range and Santa Rosa-Paradise Peak.

Three national hiking trails are within the forest. The Pacific Crest National Scenic Trail traverses 74 miles of forest land; the Toiyabe Crest National Recreation Trail runs 67 miles along the Toiyabe Range; and the Mount Charleston National Recreation Trail ascends the 11,918-foot summit of Charleston Peak. Due to unpredictable weather conditions, hiking on these trails should be limited to June through October; high elevations can receive snow during any month of the year.

Recreational activities within the forest include backpacking and hiking on nearly 900 miles of trails, fishing, hunting, camping and picnicking. Several mountain biking trails have been developed near Austin in central Nevada. Winter sports areas are at Lee Canyon, Heavenly Valley and Mount Rose. Winter sports such as heli-skiing, snowmobiling and cross-country skiing are becoming increasingly popular. Other areas noted for visual and recreational appeal are Lake Tahoe, the Sierra Nevada near Bridgeport, Calif., and Mount Rose.

For further information contact the Forest Supervisor, Humboldt-Toiyabe National Forest, 1200 Franklin Way, Sparks, NV 89431; phone (775) 331-6444. *See Recreation Chart and the AAA California/Nevada CampBook.*

LAMOILLE CANYON SCENIC AREA is in Humboldt-Toiyabe National Forest, 20 mi. s.e. of Elko via SR 227. A paved, two-lane scenic drive, overshadowed by towering cliffs, winds 12 miles along the canyon. Several overlooks with posted information enable visitors to observe the effects of glacial activity. Picnicking, rest areas and limited campgrounds are available.

INCLINE VILLAGE—
see Lake Tahoe Area in California p. 92.

★ LAKE MEAD NATIONAL RECREATION AREA (E-5)

Extending about 140 miles along the Colorado River from Grand Canyon National Park, Ariz., to Bullhead City, Ariz., Lake Mead National Recreation Area embraces 1.5 million acres in western Arizona and southern Nevada. Included are Lake Mohave and Lake Mead as well as an isolated pocket of land north of the lower portion of Grand Canyon National Park.

Three of America's four desert ecosystems— the Mojave, the Great Basin and the Sonoran deserts—meet in Lake Mead National Recreation Area, and the area is home to bighorn sheep, mule deer, coyotes, foxes and bobcats as well as lizards and snakes. Such threatened and endangered species as the desert tortoise and peregrine falcon also live here.

Fishing is popular in both lakes all year; licenses are required. Largemouth bass, striped bass and catfish are the chief catches in Lake Mead, while rainbow trout and bass are plentiful in Lake Mohave. The recreation area can be enjoyed year-round and is a prime destination for swimming, boating and skiing as well as fishing.

Area open daily 24 hours. Free. For further information contact the Superintendent, Lake Mead National Recreation Area, 601 Nevada Hwy., Boulder City, NV 89005; phone (702) 293-8906. *See Recreation Chart and the AAA California/Nevada CampBook.*

★ **HOOVER DAM**, on SR 93, stands 726 feet high and is one of the highest concrete dams ever constructed. Completed in 1936 for flood control and water storage, it impounds Lake Mead, one of the largest man-made lakes in the United States by volume of water. Originally intended to be built in Boulder Canyon, the more structurally sound Black Canyon was used when construction began in 1931.

A 25-minute film is presented at the Hoover Dam Visitor Center; phone (702) 294-3523. An overlook atop the center provides views of the dam, Lake Mead and Black Canyon. Thirty-five-minute guided tours of the dam and power plant are featured. Elevators descend 520 feet through the rock wall of Black Canyon to the bottom of the dam, where visitors can view several hydroelectric generators. The Exhibit Building at the west end of the dam houses a model of the river basin; a recorded lecture can be played.

A 1-hour Hard Hat tour goes behind the scenes where visitors can see the inner workings of the dam. Visitor center daily 8:30-5:30, Memorial Day-Labor Day; 8:30-4:30, rest of year. Closed Dec. 25. Admission $8; over 61, $7; ages 6-16, $2. Hard Hat tour $25. AE, MC, VI. Phone (702) 294-8321.

LAKE MEAD is 110 miles long and averages 200 feet in depth (500 ft. at its deepest point). The 550-mile shoreline encircles 157,900 acres of water *(see Lake Mead National Recreation Area for fishing information).* There are six major recreational centers with marinas and launch facilities on the lake. Temple Bar in Arizona is about 80 miles north of Kingman. In Nevada are Boulder Beach, 6 miles northeast of Boulder City; Las Vegas Wash, 13 miles northeast of Boulder City; Callville Bay, 22 miles east of North Las Vegas; and the Overton Beach and Echo Bay areas, both south of Overton.

Films and exhibits about natural and cultural history are offered at the Alan Bible Visitor Center, 4 miles east of Boulder City at US 93 and Lakeshore Road, overlooking Lake Mead. A botanical garden has desert flora. Information also is available at district ranger stations and the headquarters office, 601 Nevada Hwy., Boulder City, NV 89005; phone (702) 293-8907.

Visitor center daily 8:30-5:30, Memorial Day-Labor Day; 8:30-4:30, rest of year. Closed Dec. 25. Free. Phone (702) 293-8990. *See Recreation Chart and the AAA California/Nevada CampBook.*

Desert Princess departs from the Lake Mead Ferry Terminal on Lakeshore Rd. (SR 166). Excursion cruises on a paddlewheeler include a narration about area history and the construction of Hoover Dam. Breakfast, dinner and dance cruises also are available. Two-hour round-trip excursion cruises depart daily 10-5. Fare $16; ages 2-12, $6. Reservations are recommended. AE, DS, MC, VI. Phone (702) 293-6180.

LAKE MOHAVE extends 67 mi. s. from Hoover Dam to Davis Dam. Recreational developments offering launching ramps, trailer sites, refreshment concessions, boat rentals and overnight accommodations are available at Katherine Landing, about 35 miles west of Kingman, Ariz., and at Cottonwood Cove, 14 miles east of Searchlight. Other accommodations are available a short distance away in Needles, Calif., and Bullhead City, Ariz.

Willow Beach, 28 miles east of Boulder City on US 93, offers a launch ramp and concession facilities. Information regarding recreational facilities is available at all three sites (*see Lake Mead National Recreation Area for fishing information*). Davis Dam is open daily 7:30-3:30 (Mountain Standard Time) for self-guiding tours.

LAKE TAHOE—

see Lake Tahoe Area in California.

Las Vegas

A neon tribute to tinseled affluence, Las Vegas booms 24 hours a day with a heady "get rich quick" atmosphere. The lure of easy money, the whirling wheels and gaming tables and the numerous plush hotels provide ready entertainment.

Las Vegas, once an oasis on the route to California, began as a Mormon settlement and briefly boomed during the silver rush. But unlike towns that went bust and stayed busted, the townsite revived with ranching in the late 1800s and the coming of the railroad in 1905. The Union Pacific successfully auctioned off 1,200 lots in one day, upon which saloons, gambling houses and other businesses quickly sprang up.

During the Great Depression a stampede of unemployed men streamed into the Las Vegas-Boulder City area to find work constructing Hoover Dam on the Colorado River. The hydroelectric wonder they created helped to light the neon signs now synonymous with the city.

In 1931, the same year construction began on Hoover Dam, the desert town received its greatest windfall: legalized gambling. The ever-practical state legislators, cognizant of widespread gambling, decided to capitalize on it and eliminate the attendant bribery and corruption. Casinos sprang up downtown almost overnight; gamblers flooded the city and Las Vegas began to grow.

After World War II came the big resort hotels, and with them big entertainment. The purpose was simply to lure people in to sample the thrill of slot machines and blackjack. As more hotels moved onto the Strip, each vied with the others for the most opulent casino and the showroom with the most glamorous stars.

The siren song was simple: Visit Las Vegas and see the world's largest and best collection of singers, comedians, dancers and musicians. People heeded the call in increasing numbers. Hotels and casinos, enriched by the increased revenue, offered more and more—shows grew bigger, the Strip flashier, the casinos slicker. Las Vegas became a city that thrived on illusion and fantasy.

Glitz and escapist fun are supplied in quantity by colossal hotel/casino complexes. The Excalibur is a castlelike structure with four stone turrets and 14 red, blue and gold spires. Visitors must cross a moat, complete with a drawbridge guarded by a fire-breathing dragon, to gain access. Once inside, they can witness a jousting tournament. At the Luxor Hotel a 10-story sphinx serves as a front door. A replica of King Tut's tomb and a seven-story motion simulator are among the many adventures found within the hotel.

For those who like money, visit Binions Horseshoe; it features 100 U.S. bank notes bound between sheets

of bulletproof glass. Worth $10,000 each, the bills display the visage of Salmon P. Chase, chief justice of the U.S. Supreme Court 1864-73.

Fremont Street Experience boasts a canopy of more than 2 million lights arching across a four-block expanse of downtown Las Vegas. This pedestrian gambling mall features nightly animated sound and light shows—for 6-minute periods each hour the glittering casino lights are turned off and visitors are treated to themed productions of computer-generated graphics and music.

The New York-New York Hotel and Casino contains a re-creation of the Manhattan skyline—a western version of the Big Apple. The property includes a replica of the Statue of Liberty, a 300-foot-long Brooklyn Bridge, 12 skyscrapers and a roller coaster modeled after those found at Coney Island.

Circus Circus is a tent-shaped hotel casino featuring trapeze stars, high-wire artists, clowns, unicyclists and aerial dancers, all performing high above the floor to a brass band. Bordering the floor at performer level is an observation gallery lined with food, games and carnival concessions.

With more than 5,000 rooms, the MGM Grand Hotel, Casino and Theme Park is one of the largest hotels on Earth. A bronze lion serves as the entrance into this land of fantasy. Discoveries within the complex include man-made rivers, giant-size videotape displays and a 33-acre indoor amusement park.

The Mirage offers gardens, a tropical rain forest, waterfalls and a man-made volcano, which erupts 100 feet above the water every 15 minutes from dusk to midnight. A 20,000-gallon aquarium next to the front lobby is stocked with sharks, stingrays and angelfish. A 1.5-million-gallon tank houses eight bottlenose dolphins, and an elaborate habitat exists for the white tigers used in the Siegfried & Roy show.

The "Battle at Buccaneer Bay" is re-enacted every 90 minutes from 1:30 to 10:30 in front of Treasure Island Hotel. The staged battle takes place in a 65-foot-deep lagoon equipped with a full-scale British pirate ship, major explosions and more than 20 dueling actors.

And the building frenzy goes on. In addition to new construction and the ongoing expansion and modernization of existing properties, older hotels are being razed and replaced by newer, glitzier megaresorts. With more than 100,000 hotel rooms, the abundant excess that is Las Vegas seems primed for the next century.

Approaches
By Car

The major route into Las Vegas is I-15, which passes through the city from southern California to Arizona and Utah. Other routes are US 95 from the northwest, which becomes the Las Vegas Expressway in the downtown area, and US 93/95 from the southeast.

Travelers from California should be prepared for desert driving, regardless of their departure point. Basic precautions include making certain that the car's

THE INFORMED TRAVELER

City Population: 258,300

Elevation: 2,174 ft.

Sales Tax: Nevada's statewide sales tax is 6.5 percent; local option increases the sales tax in Clark County to 7 percent. There is an additional lodging tax of between 9 and 11 percent and a tax of 6 percent on automobile rentals. An entertainment tax of 10 percent is charged for hotel shows.

WHOM TO CALL

Emergency: 911

Police (non-emergency): (702) 795-3111 or TDD (702) 795-4703

Fire: (702) 383-2888

Weather: (702) 736-3854

Time: (775) 782-3456

Hospitals: Columbia Sunrise Hospital, (702) 731-8000; Valley Hospital Medical Center, (702) 388-4000.

WHERE TO LOOK

Newspapers
Las Vegas has two daily newspapers, the morning *Review-Journal* and the evening *Sun*. Check the daily events section for current entertainment offerings.

Radio and TV
Las Vegas radio station KNUU (970 AM) is an all-news/weather station; KNPR (89.5 FM) is a member of National Public Radio.

The major TV channels are 3 (NBC), 5 (FOX), 8 (CBS), 10 (PBS) and 13 (ABC).

Continued on p. 267.

engine and cooling system are working well, that tires are inflated properly, and that the gas tank is filled adequately. It always is prudent to carry extra coolant or water in case of overheating.

Getting Around
Street System
Las Vegas Boulevard, known as the Strip, and Main Street are the primary north-south thoroughfares. The primary east-west thoroughfares are Charleston Boulevard and Sahara Avenue. Four east-west streets that intersect both the Strip and I-15 are Sahara Avenue, Spring Mountain Road, Dunes-Flamingo Road and Tropicana Avenue. There also is an interchange for the Strip on I-15.

Downtown is bordered roughly by Charleston Boulevard on the south, Bonanza Road on the north, Maryland Parkway on the east and Main Street on the west. Since Las Vegas is laid out in the traditional grid system, most streets in the city travel north to south or east to west.

Parking
Parking seldom is a problem since most hotels, casinos and businesses provide guest, valet and customer parking. Should neither free nor on-street parking be available, rates at lots and garages average from $1-$2 per hour. If you leave your car in a commercial lot, check the hours of the lot's operation, since many commercial lots close at 6 p.m. However, several downtown hotels and the city of Las Vegas operate 24-hour garages.

What To See
GRAND SLAM CANYON is in Circus Circus Hotel at 2880 Las Vegas Blvd. Encased in a pink glass dome, the 5-acre indoor theme park showcases the Canyon Blaster, a double-loop, double-corkscrew roller coaster that whips past life-size animated dinosaurs and cascading waterfalls. A white-water raft ride, a tubular slide, virtual-reality games and an arcade also are included. Food is available.

Allow 2 hours minimum. Sun.-Thurs. 10-6, Fri.-Sat. 10 a.m.-midnight. Fees for rides and games vary. All-day ride pass $15.95, under 48 inches tall $11.95. AE, CB, DS, MC, VI. Phone (702) 794-3745 or 794-3939.

SAVE **GUINNESS WORLD OF RECORDS MUSEUM,** 2780 Las Vegas Blvd. S., features exhibits, videotape presentations, computerized data banks and interactive computers containing world records, feats and facts from the "Guinness Book of Records." A display highlights the history of Las Vegas. Daily 9-8, June-Aug.; 9-6, rest of year. Admission $4.95; over 62, military with ID and ages 13-18, $3.95; ages 5-12, $2.95. AE, DS, MC, VI. Phone (702) 792-3766.

IMPERIAL PALACE ANTIQUE AND CLASSIC AUTO COLLECTION, on the parking terrace of the Imperial Palace Hotel, includes more than

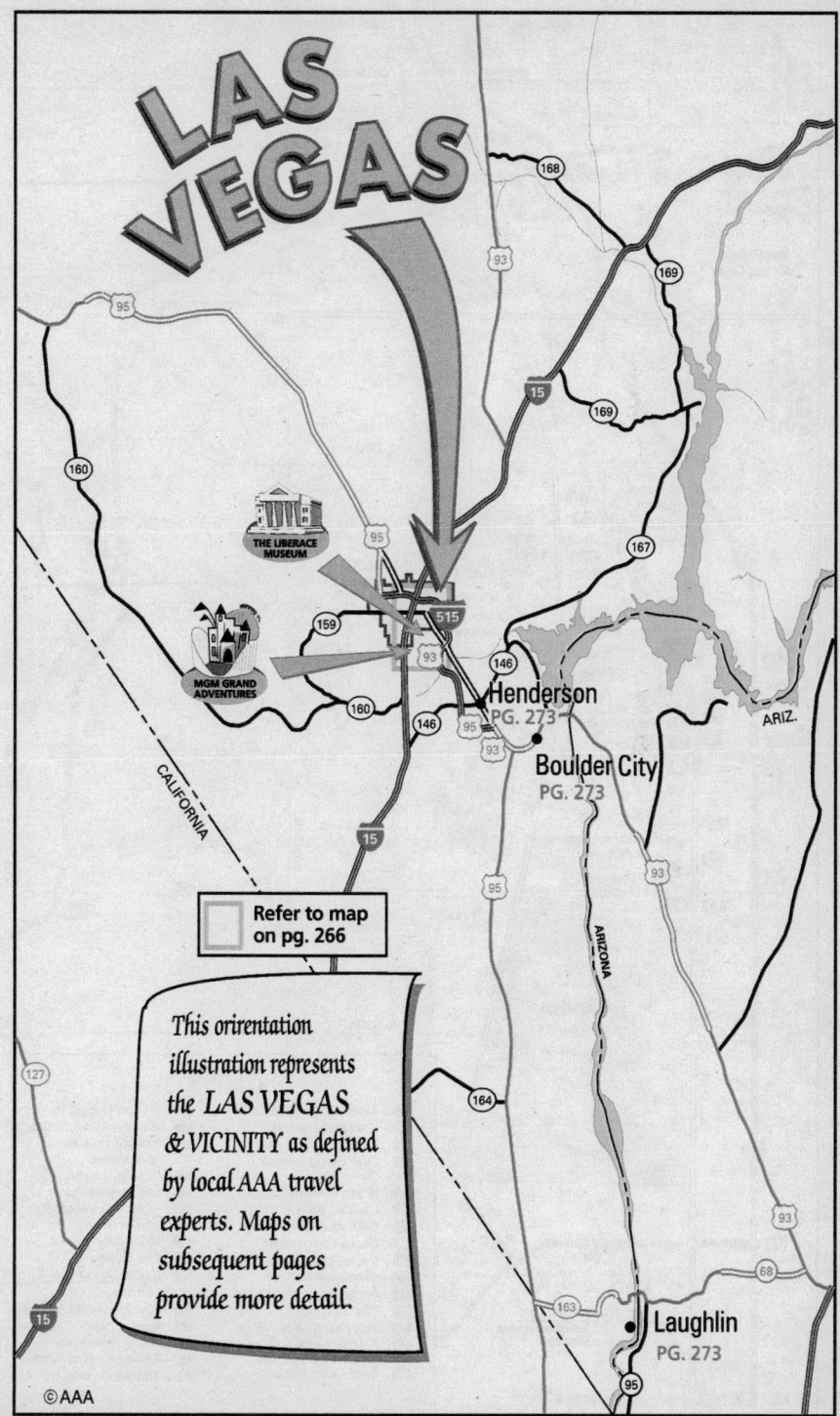

Refer to map
on pg. 266

This orirentation
illustration represents
the *LAS VEGAS*
& VICINITY as defined
by local AAA travel
experts. Maps on
subsequent pages
provide more detail.

THE LIBERACE
MUSEUM

MGM GRAND
ADVENTURES

Henderson
PG. 273

Boulder City
PG. 273

Laughlin
PG. 273

CALIFORNIA

ARIZONA

ARIZ.

© AAA

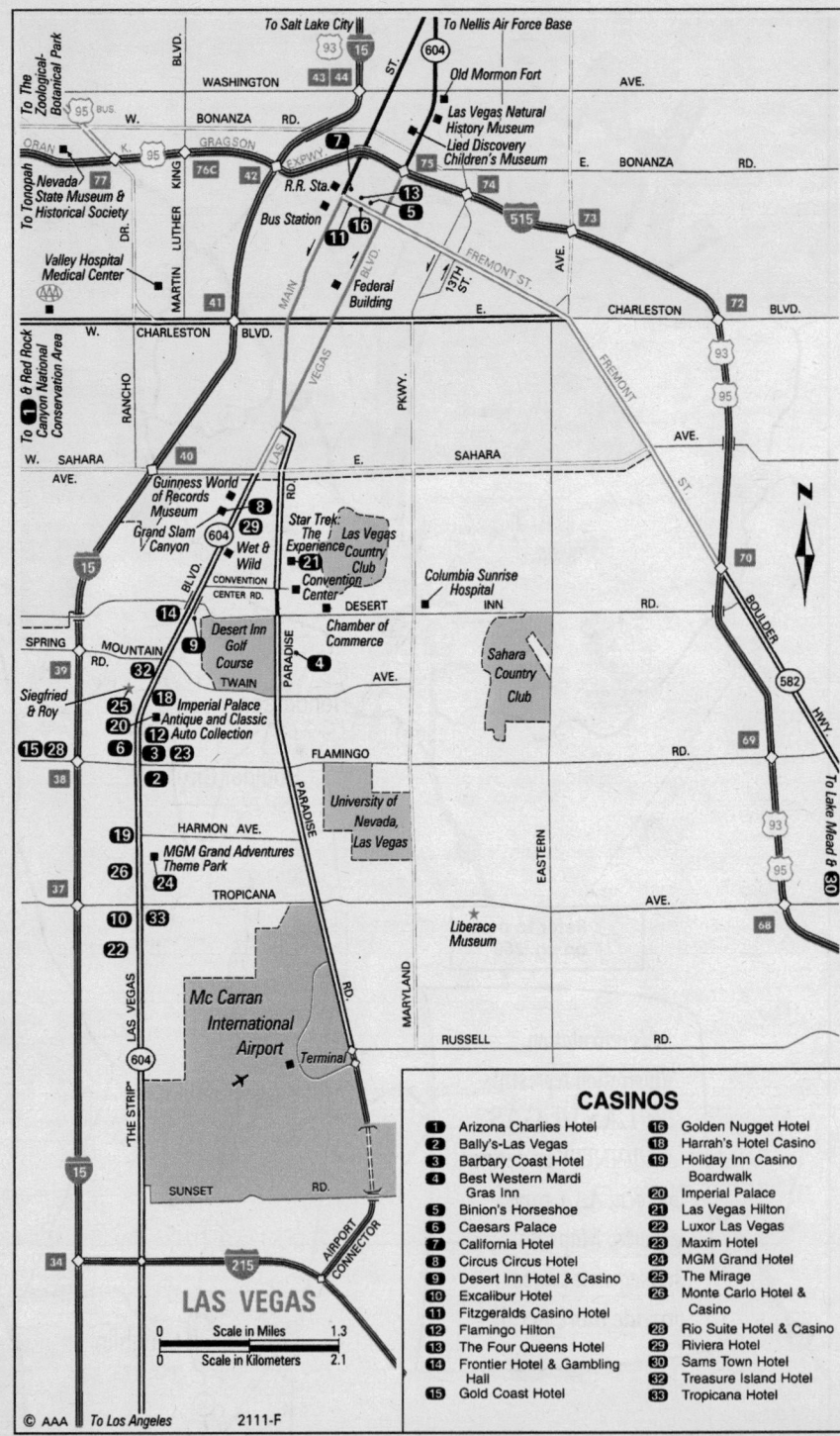

WASHINGTON   AVE.

To The
Zoological-
Botanical Park

BONANZA   RD.

Las Vegas Natural
History Museum
Lied Discovery
Children's Museum

E.   BONANZA   RD.

To Tonopah

Nevada
State Museum &
Historical Society

R.R. Sta.

Bus Station

Valley Hospital
Medical Center

Federal
Building

CHARLESTON   BLVD.

To ① & Red Rock
Canyon National
Conservation Area

W.   CHARLESTON   BLVD.

W.   SAHARA
AVE.

E.   SAHARA   AVE.

Guinness World
of Records
Museum

Grand Slam
Canyon

Star Trek:
The Las Vegas
Experience

Wet &
Wild

Las Vegas
Country
Club

Columbia Sunrise
Hospital

CONVENTION
CENTER RD.

Convention
Center

DESERT   INN   RD.

Desert Inn
Golf
Course

Chamber of
Commerce

Sahara
Country
Club

SPRING

MOUNTAIN   RD.

TWAIN

AVE.

Siegfried
& Roy

Imperial Palace
Antique and Classic
Auto Collection

FLAMINGO   RD.

HARMON   AVE.

University
of
Nevada,
Las Vegas

MGM Grand Adventures
Theme Park

TROPICANA   AVE.

Liberace
Museum

RUSSELL   RD.

Mc Carran
International
Airport

Terminal

SUNSET   RD.

To Los Angeles

2111-F

CASINOS

❶	Arizona Charlies Hotel	⓰	Golden Nugget Hotel
❷	Bally's-Las Vegas	⓲	Harrah's Hotel Casino
❸	Barbary Coast Hotel	⓳	Holiday Inn Casino
❹	Best Western Mardi		Boardwalk
	Gras Inn	⓴	Imperial Palace
❺	Binion's Horseshoe	㉑	Las Vegas Hilton
❻	Caesars Palace	㉒	Luxor Las Vegas
❼	California Hotel	㉓	Maxim Hotel
❽	Circus Circus Hotel	㉔	MGM Grand Hotel
❾	Desert Inn Hotel & Casino	㉕	The Mirage
❿	Excalibur Hotel	㉖	Monte Carlo Hotel &
⓫	Fitzgeralds Casino Hotel		Casino
⓬	Flamingo Hilton	㉘	Rio Suite Hotel & Casino
⓭	The Four Queens Hotel	㉙	Riviera Hotel
⓮	Frontier Hotel & Gambling	㉚	Sams Town Hotel
	Hall	㉜	Treasure Island Hotel
⓯	Gold Coast Hotel	㉝	Tropicana Hotel

LAS VEGAS

Scale in Miles   0 — 1.3

Scale in Kilometers   0 — 2.1

© AAA

250 antique, classic and special-interest automobiles displayed in a gallery setting. The collection, which includes more than 800 vehicles, is shown on a rotating basis.

The automobiles date back to an 1897 Haynes-Apperson and include the King of Siam's 1928 Delage limousine, a 1947 Tucker, President Eisenhower's parade car, President Kennedy's 1962 Lincoln Continental "bubble top," Elvis Presley's 1976 Cadillac El Dorado and one of the largest collections of Model J Duesenbergs.

Allow 1 hour minimum. Daily 9:30 a.m.-11:30 p.m. Admission $6.95; senior citizens, military with ID and ages 5-11, $3. AE, DS, JC, MC, VI. Phone (702) 731-3311.

LAS VEGAS NATURAL HISTORY MUSEUM, 900 Las Vegas Blvd. N., features walk-through dioramas representing animals in their natural habitats. The museum displays marine life and species from around the world. A prehistoric room contains animated dinosaurs. Also highlighted are 21 mounted sharks, a 3,000-gallon shark tank, a videotape presentation about sharks, an exhibit of plants and animals indigenous to Nevada and hands-on exhibits.

Allow 30 minutes minimum. Daily 9-4; closed Thanksgiving and Dec. 25. Admission $5; senior citizens, military and students with ID $4; ages 4-12, $2.50. AE, DS, MC, VI. Phone (702) 384-3466.

★ **THE LIBERACE MUSEUM,** 1775 E. Tropicana Ave., houses a rare piano collection, antiques, jewelry, customized automobiles and elaborate costumes from the entertainer's million-dollar wardrobe. Of particular interest are a Louis XV desk owned by Czar Nicholas II of Russia, an authentic uniform that belonged to Czar Nicholas, a piano played by Frédéric François Chopin and a concert grand owned by George Gershwin.

Allow 1 hour, 30 minutes minimum. Mon.-Sat. 10-5, Sun. 1-5; closed Jan. 1, Thanksgiving and Dec. 25. Last admission 45 minutes before closing. Admission $6.95; over 60, $4.50; students with ID $3.50; ages 6-12, $2. AE, DS, MC, VI. Phone (702) 798-5595.

[SAVE] **LIED DISCOVERY CHILDREN'S MUSEUM,** 833 Las Vegas Blvd. N., consists of 100 hands-on exhibits about science, arts and humanities that teach as well as entertain. An everyday-living section, where children pretend to pick a job, earn a paycheck, deposit savings in a bank and buy groceries, offers an opportunity to sample adult life. Another section lets children simulate what it is like to be physically impaired. A science tower with fiber optics and a weather station also are featured.

Allow 2 hours minimum. Tues.-Sat. 10-5 (also Mon. during school holidays), Sun. noon-5. Admission $5; over 59, military and students with ID $4; ages 3-11, $3. AE, DS, MC, VI. Phone (702) 382-3445.

MGM GRAND ADVENTURES THEME PARK is in the MGM Grand Hotel/Casino at 3799 Las

THE INFORMED TRAVELER

Visitor Information

The Las Vegas Convention and Visitors Authority, 3150 S. Paradise Rd., Las Vegas, NV 89109, and the Las Vegas Chamber of Commerce, 711 E. Desert Inn Rd., Las Vegas, NV 89104, provide entertainment, transportation, recreation, city tour and visitor information. The authority is open Mon.-Fri. 8-6, Sat.-Sun. 8-5; phone (702) 892-7575. The chamber is open Mon.-Fri. 8-5; phone (702) 735-1616.

WHAT TO WEAR

Las Vegas receives roughly 4 inches of rain and an estimated 250 days of sunshine annually. Though days can be furnace-hot from May to October, low humidity and air conditioning dispel discomfort.

Temperatures range between 25 and 70 degrees Fahrenheit from November through February, climb to warmer levels in March and reach well over 100 degrees Fahrenheit from June through August.

MORE TIPS

Before you pack, study this book's "Temperature Chart" from the U.S. National Weather Service.

Pack fresh fruits, whole-wheat crackers or popcorn rather than sugary sweets for on-the-road snacking.

TRANSPORTATION

Air travel: McCarran International Airport is 5 miles south of the business district via Paradise Road and the Strip. Limousine, taxi and bus service are available. Citizens Area Transit (CAT) buses pick up passengers every 10 minutes, 5:30 a.m.-1:30 a.m.

Rental cars: Hertz offers discounts to AAA members; phone (702) 736-4900 for the airport, 735-4597 for the Strip or (800) 654-3080. For listings of other agencies check the telephone directory.

Buses: Greyhound Lines Inc., 1 Main St., serves Las Vegas; phone (702) 384-8009 or (800) 231-2222.

Taxis: Cab companies include ABC Union, (702) 736-8444; Ace, (702) 736-8383; Checker, (702) 873-2227; and Yellow Cab, (702) 873-2227. Base fare is $2.20 for the first mile, $1.50 for each additional mile; airport trips incur a $1.50 surcharge. The tip is usually 15 to 20 percent of the meter reading.

Public transport: Citizens Area Transit (CAT) provides bus service to most of the city. Buses serving the Strip, or Las Vegas Boulevard, run every 15-20 minutes until 1 a.m., then every 30 minutes until 4:15 a.m., then every hour until 7 a.m. The fare is $1.50; senior citizens, physically impaired and ages 5-17, 50c. Transfers are free, exact change is required.

A monthly unlimited ride pass costs $20; senior citizens and ages 5-17, $10. Buses serve other Las Vegas routes from 5:30 a.m.-1:30 a.m. The fare is $1; senior citizens, physically impaired and ages 5-17, 50c. For schedule and route information phone (702) 228-7433.

Trolleys run along the Strip every 20 minutes from the Stratosphere Hotel to the Luxor Hotel for a fare of $1.30; exact change is required. Phone (702) 382-1404 for information. Downtown trolleys run every 20 minutes from the South Plaza of the Downtown Transportation Center to the Stratosphere Hotel for 50c; exact change is required. The Meadows Mall Shopping Express trolley departs from the Downtown Transportation Center Mon.-Sat. 10:30-5; the fare is $1.10.

Vegas Blvd. The 33-acre outdoor entertainment complex features a variety of adventure rides and shows. Highlights include Grand Canyon Rapids, a white-water rafting ride that travels through an exploding tunnel; Over the Edge, a log flume ride consisting of a 42-foot drop; Skyscreamer, a combination of skydiving and hang gliding from 250 feet above ground; Lightning Bolt, a twisting, turning roller coaster; and the Parisian Taxis bumper cars.

Asian Village, New Orleans Square, Gold Rush Junction and Salem Village also are featured. Shows include the Dueling Pirates Stunt Spectacular, the Magic Screen Theatre and the Gold Rush Theatre. Food is available. Thurs.-Mon. 10-6, June-Aug.; 11-7, rest of year. Hours may vary; phone ahead. Admission for rides and shows $13, hotel guests $10, under 42 inches tall free. Skyscreamer $23. Some rides may enforce a minimum height requirement. AE, DI, DS, JC, MC, VI. Phone (702) 891-7979.

NEVADA STATE MUSEUM AND HISTORICAL SOCIETY, 700 Twin Lakes Dr. in Lorenzi Park, portrays the history, cultures, geography and wildlife of southern Nevada from the Ice Age to the present. The rambling Spanish Colonial-style museum also houses the Nevada Historical Society's research library. Daily 9-5. Admission $2, under 18 free. Phone (702) 486-5205.

OLD LAS VEGAS MORMON FORT STATE HISTORIC PARK, at Washington Ave. and Las Vegas Blvd., is the site where a 150-foot-square adobe fort was built by Mormons in 1855 to give refuge to travelers bound for California. After the departure of the Mormons in 1858, the site was developed as a ranch that supplied blacksmith services and supplies to westward bound pioneers; it later become a railroad stop, prompting land speculation that transformed the town into what would become Las Vegas. Antiques and relics help re-create a late 19th-century Mormon living room.

Guided tours are available; there also is a self-guiding exhibit. Allow 30 minutes minimum. Daily 8:30-3:30; closed Dec. 25-Jan. 1. Donations. Phone (702) 486-3511 or 486-5126.

RED ROCK CANYON NATIONAL CONSERVATION AREA, 20 mi. w. off Charleston Blvd. (SR 159), is a 67,500-acre preserve containing such outstanding geological formations as the Keystone Thrust Fault, which reveals the contrast between layers of gray limestone and red sandstone. A 13-mile scenic loop road passes a visitor center that winds through unusual high desert terrain, which includes the 3,000-foot-high Red Rock Escarpment.

Self-guiding hiking trails lead to a spring, a waterfall, water catchment areas, small canyons and the ruins of an old homestead. Because of the danger of flash floods, avoid low-lying areas. Picnicking at Willow Spring on the scenic loop road and primitive camping at Oak Creek Canyon are permitted. Scenic loop road open daily 7 a.m.-dusk. Visitor center daily 8:30-4:30; closed Thanksgiving and Dec. 25. Admission $5 per private vehicle. Phone (702) 363-1921.

★ **SIEGFRIED & ROY,** in the Mirage Hotel at 3400 Las Vegas Blvd., perform illusions with disappearing animals and rare royal white tigers in a $25 million theater designed especially for their show. Food is available at the 7:30 show only. Allow 2 hours minimum. Performances Fri.-Tues. at 7:30 and 11, Wed.-Thurs. at 7:30. Admission (includes 2 drinks) $89.95. AE, DI, DS, MC, VI. Phone (702) 792-7777 or (800) 374-9000.

STAR TREK: THE EXPERIENCE, in the Las Vegas Hilton Hotel at 3000 Paradise Rd., features an interactive 24th-century space adventure aboard the USS *Enterprise*. A highlight is the simulated voyage on a shuttlecraft that emulates warp speed and battles Klingons. Costumes, props and memorabilia from "Star Trek" films are displayed in the museum. Food is available. Daily 11-11. Hours may vary; phone ahead. Admission $14.95. Under 42 inches tall not allowed on motion simulator voyage. AE, CB, DI, DS, JC, MC, VI. Phone (888) 462-6535.

UNIVERSITY OF NEVADA, LAS VEGAS is 1.5 mi. e. of the Strip at 4505 Maryland Pkwy. UNLV, one of the nation's fastest-growing universities, offers 1-hour tours of its 335-acre campus Mon.-Fri. at 9 a.m. Phone (702) 895-3443. *Also see What To Do, Theater and Concerts.*

Donna Beam Fine Art Gallery, in the Alta Ham Fine Arts Building on campus, displays works of modern art by professional touring artists, faculty and students. Guided tours are available. Allow 30 minutes minimum. Mon.-Fri. 9-5, Sat. 10-2; closed holidays and Oct. 31. Free. Phone (702) 895-3893.

Flashlight is in the small plaza next to the Judy Bayley Theatre on Maryland Ave. on campus. The university commissioned Claes Oldenburg to create a work symbolizing the school. The resulting sculpture is a 38-foot black steel flashlight that is mounted lens down.

Marjorie Barrick Museum of Natural History, at the corner of Swenson and Harmon sts. on campus, focuses on the natural history of southern Nevada and the Mojave Desert. Traveling exhibits also are featured. An outdoor garden features drought-resistant plants from deserts around the world. Allow 1 hour minimum. Mon.-Fri. 8-4:45, Sat. 10-2; closed holidays and Oct. 31. Free. Phone (702) 895-3381.

VALLEY OF FIRE STATE PARK—
see Overton p. 274.

SAVE **WET 'N WILD,** 2601 Las Vegas Blvd., is a 26-acre water park. Attractions include a wave pool, water flumes, water roller coaster, a hydra-hurricane ride that carries riders on inner tubes around a pool at 15 miles per hour, and a capsule

ENTERTAINMENT TIPS

Las Vegas entertainment falls into two categories: big room and lounge. Big rooms, seating 600-1,500, offer different types of shows, the best known of which is a star performer backed by an orchestra and supported by a lesser-known singer or comic. Extravagant production shows are another option; most feature some combination of elaborately costumed singers and dancers, comics, illusionists, impressionists, celebrity hosts, female impersonators and special effects.

Big room shows run about 90 minutes. One or two performances per night are the norm. Check in advance for show times, prices and reservation policies. Guests for cocktail shows should arrive about 45 minutes early; for dinner shows, 2 hours in advance. Children are not admitted to shows with nude performers.

There is no cover charge for big room shows, but depending on the entertainer, admission can range from $25 to close to $90 per person. Production shows are $10-$25 per person. Big rooms usually require reservations; for popular performances, make reservations 24-48 hours in advance and give the name of your hotel. Chances of getting into a show are better when staying at a hotel where an entertainer is performing. Ticket agencies often have reservations for tables; refer to the phone directory. A reservation, however, usually only admits a guest to the room—tipping the maitre d' $5-$10 per couple and double that for a larger party helps get a good seat. Dinner show waiters also expect a tip; rules for tipping in restaurants apply here. But remember that the bill includes entertainment costs as well as food.

Lounges seat 200-400 in more intimate surroundings and can provide visitors on a budget moderate- to big-name performers with supporting acts. Lounge shows vary from those offering 24-hour entertainment to those featuring two or three acts a night, usually from 7 p.m. to 4 a.m. Here, too, a tip will spur the captain to seat you quickly and at a good table. To ensure the act you want to see is performing (Mon.-Tues. are commonly dark nights), and to find out times and prices, check in advance. Both big room and lounge shows normally include two drinks per person.

that drops riders feet-first into the water. Allow 3 hours minimum. Park open daily at 10, last weekend in Apr.-last weekend in Sept. Closing times vary; phone ahead. Admission $23.95; ages 3-9, $17.95; over 55, $12. AE, MC, VI. Phone (702) 737-3819.

THE ZOOLOGICAL-BOTANICAL PARK, 1.5 mi. n. of US 95N at 1775 N. Rancho Dr., is a 4-acre zoo featuring African, Asian and Western American animals along with more than 50 varieties of plants. Of interest is the children's petting zoo. Allow 30 minutes minimum. Daily 9-5; closed Jan. 1, Thanksgiving and Dec. 25. Admission $5.95; over 62 and ages 2-12, $3.95. AE, MC, VI. Phone (702) 648-5955.

What To Do

Gambling

The rattle of the "bones," then a sigh of disappointment or a cry of exultation—such are the sounds of Las Vegas, where gambling is by no means limited to the craps table. Slot machines, "21" or blackjack, keno, bingo, poker, baccarat and roulette all await the hopeful.

Gambling is easier than buying toothpaste, since casinos never close and most drugstores do. Many hotels strategically place their casinos near the registration desk; visitors are immediately greeted with the lure of fortune. Rows of slot machines stand like sentries in most establishments—restaurants, drugstores, supermarkets, even laundromats.

Visitors who resist the temptation to gamble are rare. If you decide to take a chance, obtain a book about gambling and bone up. Generally speaking, beginners never should approach any gaming table without some knowledge about the game to be played. Many casinos provide literature and some even give classes for novice patrons. Although the state regulates casinos and gambling, the odds ultimately favor the house.

In terms of betting and playing strategies, poker in all its varieties can be termed the most complex. Baccarat requires a high stake to be successful, though "mini-baccarat," in which the dealer keeps the bank, provides cheaper play.

The many ways of playing number combinations, the difficulty in understanding the payoffs and general unfamiliarity with the game have made craps the most challenging game of all. It also is a difficult game for dealers to learn. While not a game for the novice, craps is mesmerizing to watch.

Casinos and separate betting parlors also have sports books that allow patrons to wager on almost any horse race, boxing match or professional or collegiate game.

Remember that if you are a first-time visitor to Las Vegas, credit at the gaming tables will be tight or nonexistent. With further visits, once credit has been established, gamblers will be able to obtain $1,000 as easily as $1.

Sightseeing

There are other ways to spend time and money in Las Vegas than inside a casino. A day-long sightseeing tour of the city and nearby attractions can be a relaxing intermission from the hectic agenda of casino hopping and shows.

 Boat Tours

A combination tour of Hoover Dam and a cruise on Lake Mead is offered by Lake Mead Cruises; phone (702) 293-6180.

 Bus Tours

Guided bus tours of downtown and surrounding points of interest, including the Grand Canyon, Hoover Dam, Red Rock Canyon, Bryce Canyon, Death Valley, Lake Mead and Valley of Fire State Park, are offered by Gray Line; phone (702) 384-1234 or (800) 634-6579.

 Driving Tours

A 13-mile scenic road in nearby Red Rock Canyon winds through unusual high-desert terrain. In the vicinity is Spring Mountain Ranch, a working ranch which served as a luxurious retreat for Vera Krupp, the wife of a wealthy German munitions industrialist.

The ranch, now a state park, has a visitor center that is open to the public. Guided tours of the park leave from the center on weekends and Nevada state holidays; self-guiding tours of the ranch house are permitted daily. Both the park and visitor center are open daily. Phone (702) 875-4141 for the park or (702) 363-1921 for the visitor center.

Plane or Helicopter Tours

Air tours of the Grand Canyon or Lake Mead area are available from Las Vegas or Boulder City; companies include Biplane Rides of Las Vegas, (702) 375-0048; Eagle Canyon Airlines, (702) 736-4247 or (800) 446-4584; A Grand Canyon Tour, (702) 361-7628; Lake Mead Air, (702) 293-1848 *(see ad p. 271);* Maverick Helicopters, (702) 261-0007; SAVE Scenic Airlines, (702) 638-3300 or (800) 634-6801; and Sundance Helicopters, (702) 597-5525 or (800) 653-1881.

Sports and Recreation

Las Vegas has a royal flush of recreational pursuits that include **golf, tennis, racquetball** and **swimming**. Lake Mead *(see place listing p. 261),* 24 miles south, is ideal for water sports. Less than an hour's drive northwest is Humboldt-Toiyabe National Forest *(see place listing p. 260).* Mount Charleston, within the forest, offers **hunting, mountain climbing** and **winter sports** and includes the Lee Canyon Ski Area *(see Recreation Chart).*

Golf enthusiasts enjoy the excellent playing conditions of Las Vegas' desert climate. Numerous championship and less demanding golf courses are open to the public.

Area courses include Angel Park Golf Club (18 holes), 8 miles west via Summerlin Parkway to 100 S. Rampart Blvd.; Badlands Golf Club (18), 8 miles west via Summerlin Parkway at 9115 Alta Dr. at Rampart Boulevard; Craig Ranch (18), 2.5 miles north off I-15 at 628 W. Craig Rd. (North Las Vegas); Desert Inn Golf Club (18), .7 miles east of I-15 off Flamingo Road at 3145 Las Vegas Blvd.; Desert Pines (18), 2 miles east of I-15 at 3415 E. Bonanza Rd.; Desert Rose Golf Course (18), 6 miles east of I-15 off Sahara Avenue at 5483 Clubhouse Dr.; and Las Vegas Golf Club (18), 5 miles west of US 95 on Washington Avenue.

Others include the two 18-hole courses at Las Vegas Paiute Golf Resort, 23 miles northwest via US 95 at 10325 Nu-Wav Kaiv Blvd., Snow Mountain (Nu-Wav Kai) and Sun Mountain (Tav-Ai Kaiv); Los Prados Golf Course (18), 2.5 miles west of US 95 via Lone Mountain Road and Los Prados Boulevard at 5150 Los Prados Cir.; North Las Vegas Community Golf Course (nine), .5 miles west of I-15 off Cheyenne Avenue at 324 E. Brooks Ave.; Painted Desert Golf Course (18), 8.5 miles northwest off US 95 and Ann Road at 5555 Painted Mirage Rd.; and Sun City Las Vegas' Palm Valley Golf Club (18), 10 miles northwest of US 95 and Lake Mead Boulevard at 9101 Del Webb Blvd.

All courses include a clubhouse, golf shop, equipment rental and some food service. None are lighted for night play. Early starts are recommended during the summer months.

Tennis players seldom have difficulty finding an empty court, since there are many public courts scattered throughout the city. Those that follow have at least two lighted courts: East Las Vegas Park and Recreation Center, Missouri Avenue and Boulder Highway; Paradise Park Recreation Center, 4770 S. Harrison Dr.; Sunrise Recreation Center, 2240 Linn Ln.; Sunset Park, Sunset Drive and Eastern Avenue; Winchester Recreation Center, 3130 S. McLeod; and Winterwood Park, Sahara Avenue and Winterwood Boulevard.

Many resort hotels and private clubs have tennis courts that visitors are allowed to use, but it is always a good idea to confirm the hotel's current visitor policy by phone.

Many swimming pools are open daily Memorial Day through Labor Day. Contact the Las Vegas Parks and Recreation Department for information about pools with different schedules; phone (702) 229-6309.

The Las Vegas Thunder, part of the International **Hockey** League, make their home at the Thomas & Mack Center at the University of Nevada, Las Vegas. Their season runs from October through April; phone (702) 895-3900 for schedule and ticket information.

Bowling is available at several locations. The Showboat Hotel, 2800 E. Fremont St., has 106

lanes and an attended room where children can be watched for a fee; phone (702) 385-9153. Other bowling centers can be found at Gold Coast Hotel, 4000 W. Flamingo Rd.; The Orleans, 4500 W. Tropicana Ave.; and Sam's Town Hotel, 5111 Boulder Hwy. The Santa Fe Hotel, 4949 N. Rancho Dr., has bowling and **ice skating** facilities.

Fans of **baseball** will find the Las Vegas Stars, the AAA farm club of the San Diego Padres, playing at Cashman Field, 850 Las Vegas Blvd. N., April through the first week in September. Phone (702) 386-7200 for ticket and schedule information.

Fans of **automobile racing** will find plenty of company at the Las Vegas Motor Speedway, 7000 Las Vegas Blvd. N., 17 miles northeast of Las Vegas off I-15 Speedway Boulevard exit. The facility, set on 1,500 acres, has 24 race tracks, seating for 107,000, plus 75,000 square feet of meeting and exhibit space. The complex hosts NASCAR events as well as American Motorcycle Association races; phone (702) 644-4444 for information.

Shopping

Las Vegas offers a wide range of boutiques, menswear shops and specialty stores. The Boulevard and Meadows malls generally are open Mon.-Fri. 10-9, Sat. 10-6 and Sun. noon-5.

The Fashion Show Mall, at Las Vegas Boulevard and Spring Mountain Road, contains such major department stores as Bullock's, Dillard's, May-Robinson's, Neiman-Marcus and Saks Fifth Avenue. The Forum Shops at Caesars Palace on the Strip is an upscale complex with 70 specialty shops and restaurants in a setting designed to recall a winding street in Italy. To reach the 31 stores at The Tower Shops, at the Stratosphere Hotel and Casino, 2000 Las Vegas Blvd. S., requires passing through themed street scenes of Hong Kong, Paris and New York.

Outlet shopping is another shopping option in Las Vegas. Belz Factory Outlet World, 7400 Las Vegas Blvd. S., has Off 5th-Saks Fifth Avenue Outlet as its anchor store, plus more than 140 other outlets, including Esprit, Lenox and Nike; Factory Stores of America, 9155 Las Vegas Blvd. S., contains more than 50 factory-direct shops such as Geoffrey Beene, London Fog and Mikasa in its Spanish-themed setting.

Theater and Concerts

Concerts and plays are presented periodically at Reed Whipple Cultural Center on Las Vegas Boulevard and at Charleston Heights Arts Center, on Brust Street west of Decatur Boulevard north of Charleston Boulevard.

The award-winning Theatre Arts Department of the University of Nevada stages both contemporary plays and the classics throughout the year in the 600-seat Judy Bayley Theater on Maryland Parkway. The popular Nevada Dance Theater also performs on a regular basis; phone (702) 895-3801.

Artemus W. Ham Concert Hall, also on the University of Nevada campus and a few miles from the Strip, presents symphony, ballet, opera, jazz and popular music performances, often under the direction of internationally renowned musicians. Phone (702) 895-3801 for schedule information.

For a different form of theater, Caesars Palace's futuristic Omnimax® Theater offers a different film every few months on a huge screen with a "sensaround" sound system designed to allow the audience to experience the action. Housed in a geodesic dome, the theater is accessible via a moving sidewalk or the Olympic Tower escalator. Shows are presented on the hour Fri.-Sat. noon-11, Sun.-Thurs. 2-10; phone (702) 731-7900.

Red Rock Theaters, 5201 W. Charleston Blvd., consists of 11 movie theaters in an enclosed mall decorated with antiques; phone (702) 870-1423.

Information regarding performances and exhibits is available from the newspapers or from the Allied Arts Council, 401 S. 4th St., #110, Mon.-Fri. 9-5; phone (702) 386-4804.

Special Events

Events in Las Vegas are as varied as entertainment on the Strip. The Desert Inn LPGA Golf Tournament tees off in March, and the All Indian Pow Wow is held in April. In May the Old West is relived during Helldorado Days, which features Western costumes, parades and a championship rodeo.

The Fairshow, held in North Las Vegas in late October, includes national championship hot air balloon races, a chili cook-off, a bicycle relay and softball tournaments.

Computer enthusiasts should be sure to include the American Mega Shows in their itinerary. The computer expos are held six times per year at Cashman Field, 850 Las Vegas Blvd. N.; phone (702) 368-6266 for more information.

Las Vegas' sports events are of both the indoor and outdoor variety. They include the Showboat Invitational Bowling Tournament in January; the Nissan/400 Off-Road Race, the Las Vegas Invitational Golf Tournament and the World Series of Poker, all held in the spring; and the National Rodeo Finals in December.

The world's largest motoring club

The Las Vegas Vicinity

BOULDER CITY (F-6)
pop. 12,600, elev. 2,501'

An access point to the Lake Mead National Recreation Area *(see place listing p. 261),* Boulder City was built by the federal government as a residential community for employees of the Bureau of Reclamation, Park Service and Bureau of Mines branches in the area. Because gambling was prohibited in Boulder City under the original land agreement, the town remains the only community in Nevada without legalized gambling.

Boulder City Chamber of Commerce: 1305 Arizona St., Boulder City, NV 89005; phone (702) 293-2034.

DESERT PRINCESS—
see Lake Mead National Recreation Area p. 261.

★ **HOOVER DAM—**
see Lake Mead National Recreation Area p. 260.

HENDERSON (F-5)
pop. 64,900, elev. 1,881'

Henderson was settled during World War II as a housing area for employees of a magnesium plant. The town since has expanded into Nevada's main industrial center, with many plants concerned principally with chemical and metal production. Henderson is the southwest terminus of scenic SR 147, which follows the spectacular Lake Mead shoreline from Hoover Dam to Overton Beach.

Henderson Chamber of Commerce: 590 S. Boulder Hwy., Henderson, NV 89015; phone (702) 565-8951.

CLARK COUNTY HERITAGE MUSEUM, 1830 S. Boulder Hwy., offers three exhibit areas: a chronological history of southern Nevada from dinosaurs to the first white settlements; a group of historic residential and commercial structures called Heritage Street; and a re-created ghost town with a number of original structures and old railroad cars. Allow 1 hour minimum. Daily 9-4:30; closed Jan. 1 and Dec. 25. Admission $1.50; over 55 and ages 3-15, $1. Phone (702) 455-7955.

ETHEL M. CHOCOLATE FACTORY AND CACTUS GARDEN is in the Green Valley Business Park at 2 Cactus Garden Dr. The factory makes gourmet chocolates. Adjacent is the Cactus Garden, a 2.5-acre collection of more than 350 species of desert plants from the Southwest and other arid areas. Guided tours of the Cactus Garden are available by appointment; phone (702) 435-2641. Self-guiding tours of the chocolate factory are available daily 8:30-7; closed Dec. 25. Free. Phone (702) 433-2500, 458-8864, or (888) 627-0990.

LAUGHLIN (F-6) pop. 3,000

Laughlin, near the California border and across the Colorado River from Arizona, was little more than a nameless bait shack on the Colorado River in 1970. It is now a gambling mecca in the middle of the desert, a destination which attracted 4.8 million visitors in 1992. Buses and ferries provide transportation between the glittery casinos in Laughlin and parking areas in nearby Bullhead, Ariz.

Laughlin Chamber of Commerce: 1725 Casino Dr., P.O. Box 2280, Laughlin, NV 89029; phone (702) 298-2214 or (800) 227-5245.

This ends listings for the Las Vegas Vicinity.
The following page resumes the alphabetical listings of
cities in Nevada.

LAUGHLIN—
see Las Vegas p. 273.

LOVELOCK (B-3) pop. 2,100, elev. 3,900'

Lovelock is an agricultural town founded by immigrant pioneers as a stopping point before beginning a 40-mile desert crossing. It is said to have the only round courthouse in use in the country and offers such recreational diversions as gaming casinos, stock car races and rodeos. Hunting and fishing are profitable in the surrounding area. Small Tufa Park, 5 miles west of town, features geological deposits created by ancient Lake Lahontan, which covered the area thousands of years ago.

About 22 miles northeast is the 20,241-acre Rye Patch State Recreation Area, with facilities for camping, fishing, swimming, boating and picnicking. *See Recreation Chart and the AAA California/Nevada CampBook.*

Lovelock/Pershing County Chamber of Commerce: Marzen Lane, P.O. Box 821, Lovelock, NV 89419; phone (775) 273-7213.

MARZEN HOUSE, at the s.w. end of Cornell Ave., houses the Pershing County Museum. Displays of antiques, mineral ores, pioneer memorabilia and Paiute Indian artifacts are exhibited in the 1874 two-story frame house. A cave exhibit, an old fire engine and an ambulance also are featured. Tues.-Fri. 9-4, Sat.-Sun. 1:30-4, May-Oct.; otherwise varies. Closed Jan. 1, Thanksgiving and Dec. 25. Donations. Phone (775) 273-2115.

OVERTON (E-6) pop. 1,800, elev. 1,250'

Founded by Mormon pioneers, Overton lies just north of the site of a prehistoric Anasazi Indian Pueblo, Pueblo Grande de Nevada, known as the Lost City, which extended 30 miles on both sides of the Muddy River. The Puebloans who lived in Lost City were farmers who built above-ground dwellings with several rooms that were used to store crops.

Overton also lies at the northern end of a scenic route that follows the northwestern shore of Lake Mead. The route is made up of SR 169 to Overton Beach and SR 147 from Overton Beach to US 95/93 and Hoover Dam.

Moapa Valley Chamber of Commerce: P.O. Box 361, Overton, NV 89040; phone (702) 397-2160 or 397-2193.

LOST CITY MUSEUM OF ARCHEOLOGY, 721 S. Moapa Valley Blvd., preserves and interprets the prehistory of the Moapa Valley, focusing on the prehistoric Anasazi settlement. The museum contains artifacts of the Anasazi Indians, who settled the Moapa Valley during the first century.

An actual archeological site is interpreted within the museum. In addition, changing art and traveling exhibits are featured. Several Pueblo-type houses of wattle and daub are reconstructed on their original foundations. Allow 30 minutes minimum. Daily 8:30-4:30; closed Jan. 1, Thanksgiving and Dec. 25. Admission $2, under 18 free. Phone (702) 397-2193.

VALLEY OF FIRE STATE PARK, 14 mi. s.w. on SR 169, occupies a basin about 6 miles long and 3 to 4 miles wide. The rough floor and jagged walls contain formations of eroded red sandstone, said to date back 150 million years, that often appear to be on fire when reflecting the sun's rays.

Some cliffs and rocks, mainly in the area of Atlatl Rock, are covered with prehistoric petroglyphs probably carved from 300 B.C. to A.D. 1150 by the Basket Maker people and the Anasazi Pueblo farmers. An *atlatl* (Aztec for spear thrower) was a device used, before the invention of the bow and arrow, to increase the speed and distance a spear could be thrown. Atlatl Rock contains a petroglyph depiction of this tool.

Mouse Tank, a natural basin that collects scarce rainwater, was named for a reclusive Paiute Indian who lived in this area in the early 1900s. A quarter-mile trail to the tank offers views of prehistoric petroglyphs.

Exhibits about the park's history, geology and ecology are housed in the visitor center on SR 169, about 7 miles east of the park boundary. Park open daily dawn-dusk. Visitor center daily 8:30-4:30. Closed Jan. 1 and Dec. 25. Entry $5 per private vehicle. Phone (702) 397-2088. *See Recreation Chart and the AAA California/Nevada CampBook.*

PIOCHE (D-6) pop. 800, elev. 6,018'

Pioche was one of the roughest mining camps in the West during the 1870s. The town's Boot Hill boasted 75 graves before its first interment due to natural causes. Residents balanced their lack of creativity in solving disagreements with such epitaphs as "Fanny Peterson, July 12, 1872. They loved til death did them part. He killed her."

Pioche is known for its Million Dollar Courthouse, a $30,000 building that cost the county almost $1 million by the time it was completed in the late 1800s. Condemned in 1933, the building and the four lots on which it stands were sold 25 years later for $150. The courthouse has been restored and is open for guided tours.

Pioche Chamber of Commerce: Main St., P.O. Box 127, Pioche, NV 89043; phone (775) 962-5544 or 962-5245.

LINCOLN COUNTY HISTORICAL MUSEUM, on Main St. next to the library, houses local historical items that include mining tools, furniture, musical instruments, photographs, documents and early 20th-century clothing. Daily 10-1 and 2-4; closed Thanksgiving and Dec. 25. Donations. Phone (775) 962-5207.

RENO (C-2) pop. 133,900, elev. 4,490'

Full of stage shows and gambling establishments that operate 24 hours a day, Reno is a city of diverse extremes, calling itself "The Biggest Little City in the World." Its neon lights supply the same excitement as Las Vegas, but Reno also is an important distribution and merchandising center, has extensive residential areas and is the home of the University of Nevada, Reno.

Reno's sunny, dry climate attracts summer and winter sports enthusiasts. Skiers flock to the Sierra Nevada in California for downhill and cross-country skiing. Facilities for boating, biking, snowmobiling, hiking and white-water rafting are available in the Reno area.

A more sedate side of Reno can be found along the banks of the Truckee River. The brass and marble Truckee River Walk features several fountains and is the location for various family events throughout the year.

The Silver Legacy Resort Casino, 407 N. Virginia St., features a 120-foot-tall mining rig that mints coins before your eyes, while free circus acts are offered at Circus Circus Hotel/Casino, 500 N. Sierra St. Exhibitions of works by international, regional and local artists are held by Nevada Museum of Art at 160 W. Liberty St.

Reno is at the southwestern end of a scenic route consisting of SRs 445, 446 and 447. These highways run through Pyramid Lake Indian Reservation and follow the southern shoreline of Pyramid Lake *(see attraction listing).*

Reno/Sparks Convention and Visitor Authority: 4590 S. Virginia St., P.O. Box 837, Reno, NV 89504; phone (775) 827-7366 or (800) 367-7366.

CHURCH FINE ARTS BUILDING, at the University of Nevada, Reno, presents changing exhibits, principally of contemporary art, in Sheppard Fine Arts Gallery. Theatrical productions are staged by the university in the Church Fine Arts Theatre, and concerts are held in Nightingale Music Hall. Allow 30 minutes minimum. Building open Mon.-Fri. 9-5 (also Wed. 5-7); closed major holidays and during school breaks. Building free.

Phone (775) 784-6658 for theater and music hall prices, 784-6839 or 784-6145 for the music hall.

SAVE ★ **FLEISCHMANN PLANETARIUM,** at the n. edge of the University of Nevada, Reno campus on N. Virginia St., presents programs about the night sky. Periodically changing Star Shows depict astronomical events of the past, present and future. Films shown on the Skydome screen surround the audience with realistic images. Each performance includes both planetarium and Skydome shows. Astronomy and earth science exhibits also are featured. Hours and programs vary.

Allow 1 hour, 30 minutes minimum. Mon.-Fri. 8 a.m.-10 p.m., Sat.-Sun. 11-10; closed Jan. 1, Thanksgiving, Dec. 24-25 and 31. Star Show schedule varies after 5 p.m.; phone ahead. Planetarium building free. Star Show and Skydome movie $6; over 59 and under 13, $4. Under 6 are admitted to daytime shows only. DS, MC, VI. Phone (775) 784-4811 for recorded show information, 784-4812 for reservations or 784-1759 for recorded Skyline information.

SAVE ★ **NATIONAL AUTOMOBILE MUSEUM,** 10 Lake St. S., displays more than 200 antique, vintage, classic and special-interest automobiles. Four street scenes with period automobiles and artifacts depict different eras of the 20th century. The facility also offers interactive exhibits, a multimedia theater presentation, antique clothing and an automotive research library. Many of the cars on display have been featured in movies. Food is available in the summer.

Allow 1 hour, 30 minutes minimum. Mon.-Sat. 9:30-5:30, Sun. 10-4; closed Thanksgiving and Dec. 25. Admission $7.50; over 62, $6.50; ages 6-18, $2.50. AE, DS, MC, VI. Phone (775) 333-9300. *See ad.*

NEVADA HISTORICAL SOCIETY MUSEUM is at 1650 N. Virginia St. Founded in 1904, it is the state's oldest museum. Displays include American Indian artifacts, pioneer relics, antique furniture, guns and rocks. A research library contains records dating from 1859. Museum Mon.-Sat. 10-5. Library Tues.-Sat. noon-4. Closed Jan. 1,

July 4, Oct. 31, Thanksgiving and Dec. 25. Admission $2, under 18 free. Phone (775) 688-1190.

PYRAMID LAKE—*see Sutcliffe p. 276.*

WILBUR D. MAY CENTER is in Rancho San Rafael Park at 1502 Washington St. and includes the ⛶ Wilbur D. May Museum, Arboretum and Botanical Garden and Great Basin Adventure. Containing objects collected by adventurer Wilbur D. May during his world travels, the museum is a replica of his Double Diamond Ranch. Highlights of the collection include souvenirs of his African safaris, rare Tang Dynasty horse sculptures and 18th-century sterling silver. One wing of the museum features changing exhibits.

The adjacent arboretum consists of 12 gardens representing plant habitats at different elevations in the eastern Sierra Nevada. Great Basin Adventure, a nearby children's park, includes a log flume ride, a petting zoo, a stamp mill, exhibits about mining and dinosaurs of the Great Basin and pony rides. A discovery room offers plenty to see and touch, from x-rays to rocks. Picnicking is permitted.

Allow 1 hour minimum. Museum Mon.-Sat. 10-5, Sun. noon-5. Arboretum daily 8 a.m.-dusk. Great Basin Adventure Mon.-Sat. 10-5, Sun. noon-5, Memorial Day weekend-Labor Day. Museum $2.50; over 54 and ages 3-12, $1.50. Arboretum free. Great Basin Adventure $3; ages 3-12, $2. Pony and flume rides $1. Phone (775) 785-5961 for the museum, 785-4153 for the arboretum or 785-4844 for Great Basin Adventure.

RHYOLITE (E-5)

On a dirt road 2.5 miles west of Beatty, Rhyolite was a city of 12,000 inhabitants in 1907. Mine failure caused its desertion, and only stone foundations and brick fronts remain. The town once boasted telephone service, water companies, saloons, hundreds of houses, an opera house, electric street lights and even a red-light district.

An elaborate railroad depot and a house constructed almost entirely of bottles are two of the few surviving structures in Rhyolite; neither is open to the public. Visitors are cautioned to be careful if climbing the old remains; trembling caused by mining in nearby areas could make it dangerous.

Beatty Chamber of Commerce: P.O. Box 956, Beatty, NV 89003; phone (775) 553-2424.

SILVER SPRINGS (C-3)
pop. 2,300, elev. 4,209′

FORT CHURCHILL STATE HISTORIC PARK is 7 mi. s. on US 95, then 1 mi. w. on Old Fort Churchill Rd. Built in 1860 as protection against American Indian attacks, this U.S. Army outpost also guarded the Pony Express and other mail routes. Although the fort is now in ruins, the site

is a 4,461-acre park with an interpretive trail. A visitor center reconstructs the fort's colorful history with exhibits.

Park open daily 24 hours. Visitor center daily 8-4, Memorial Day-Labor Day; otherwise varies. Admission $3 per private vehicle. Camping $7. Phone (775) 577-2345. *See Recreation Chart.*

SPARKS (C-3) pop. 53,400, elev. 4,407′

Sparks was established in 1904 when railroad buildings were moved by the Southern Pacific Railroad to Reno's eastern border. It was named after the state's governor, John Sparks.

An outdoor railroad exhibit, the chamber of commerce and a number of casinos are on Victorian Avenue. Victorian Square, a pedestrian mall off I-80 via Rock Boulevard or Pyramid Way, holds events year-round at the mall and in the 400-seat Victorian Amphitheater. It also is the site of casinos, hotels and Sparks Heritage Museum.

Sparks Community Chamber of Commerce: 831 Victorian Ave., Sparks, NV 89431-5088; phone (775) 358-1976.

⛶ **WILD ISLAND,** I-80E and Sparks Blvd. at 250 Wild Island Ct., has 10 outdoor water rides, a wave pool, a volleyball court, a children's play area, a game arcade, picnic facilities, miniature golf and miniature race tracks. Food is available. Daily 11-7, mid-June through Labor Day; 11-5, mid-May to mid-June. Admission $16.95; under 48 inches tall $11.95; over 63, $4.95. Golf $4.25. Indy racers $3.50. Sprint racers $2.50. DS, MC, VI. Phone (775) 359-2927.

SUTCLIFFE (B-2) elev. 3,900′

PYRAMID LAKE is off SR 445. Though smaller in size than prehistoric Lake Lahontan, which once covered 8,400 square miles of western Nevada and northeastern California, Pyramid Lake is still Nevada's largest natural lake. About 30 miles long and 7 to 9 miles wide, it is surrounded by red and brown sandstone mountains and is punctuated by porous rock islands.

Long before it became a 475,000-acre Paiute Indian reservation in 1874, the lake area served as the tribe's homeland. The lake's north end, surrounded by huge rock monoliths, is sacred to the Paiutes and off-limits to visitors. Fragmentary remains of an elephant, bison and camel found at the nearby Astor Pass railroad excavations offer clues to the area's prehistoric inhabitants.

Pyramid Lake is considered one of the state's best recreation areas. Unique to the lake are the cui-cui fish—an endangered lake sucker fish—and trout weighing up to 40 pounds. Warrior Point, a park 9 miles north of Sutcliffe, offers various shoreline facilities. Applications for fishing and boating permits can be obtained at the ranger station or from Pyramid Lake Indian

Paiute Tribe, P.O. Box 256, Nixon, NV 89424. Phone (775) 574-1000. *See Recreation Chart.*

TOIYABE NATIONAL FOREST—
see Humboldt-Toiyabe National Forest p. 260.

TONOPAH (D-4) pop. 3,600, elev. 6,030'

Tonopah had its beginning in 1900 when prospector Jim Butler idly chipped away at a ledge that sheltered him during a thunderstorm and noticed that the rock looked like silver ore. By the time the boom he started reached its peak 13 years later, production in the area had netted $9.5 million. The town shared the area's mineral wealth with nearby Goldfield.

Tonopah Chamber of Commerce: 301 Brougher Ave., P.O. Box 869, Tonopah, NV 89049; phone (775) 482-3859.

CENTRAL NEVADA MUSEUM, on Logan Field Rd. s. of Nye General Hospital, depicts the history of the area through displays dealing with American Indians, settlements, boomtowns, railroads and mining. A research library also is available. The grounds contain heavy industrial and mining equipment. Allow 30 minutes minimum. Daily 9-5, Apr.-Sept.; Mon.-Sat. 11-5, rest of year. Closed Jan. 1, Thanksgiving and Dec. 25. Donations. Phone (775) 482-9676.

VIRGINIA CITY (C-2) pop. 1,500, elev. 6,220'

With 35,000 residents, banks, churches, theaters, 110 saloons and the only elevator between Chicago and San Francisco, the Virginia City of the 1870s was the West's mining metropolis. The Comstock Lode had given the town unequaled prosperity. The ore extracted from the Consolidated Virginia Mine has been estimated to have a gross value of at least $234 million, some of which was used to build San Francisco and finance the Union Army during the Civil War.

Notable residents included Mark Twain and Bret Harte, who worked as reporters on the *Territorial Enterprise*, Nevada's first newspaper and one known for occasionally making up the news. The International Championship Camel Races, held on the first weekend in September, began as a fictitious story in 1959 and has since become one of the state's major events.

Much has been done to restore Virginia City to its 1870 boomtown appearance. Many small museums along C Street preserve the town's illustrious past. They include The Way It Was Museum and Ponderosa Mine, which offers underground mine tours every 20 minutes.

Mark Twain Bookstore, on C and Taylor streets, contains a collection of historic memorabilia and rare books; phone (775) 847-0454.

Saint Mary's in the Mountains is a brick church built on the site of a church destroyed by fire in 1875. The building has been restored and can be visited daily in summer and on weekends all year.

Virginia City lies along a scenic route consisting of SR 341 northwest to the junction of US 395. From that point the route follows SR 431 through Toiyabe National Forest to the northern shore of Lake Tahoe.

Virginia City Chamber of Commerce: 131 S. C St., P.O. Box 464, Virginia City, NV 89440; phone (775) 847-0311.

THE CASTLE, 70 S. B St., is an 1868 structure that reflects the prosperity of mining towns through original antique furnishings, 200-year-old Czechoslovakian crystal chandeliers, Italian marble fireplaces and silver doorknobs. Allow 30 minutes minimum. Guided tours are given daily 11-5, Memorial Day weekend-last Sun. in Oct. Fee $3.50; ages 6-12, 50c. Phone (775) 847-0275.

CHOLLAR MINE, S. F St., is an 1861 Comstock gold and silver mine with original square-set timbering. Allow 30 minutes minimum. Daily noon-5, June-Sept.; Sat.-Thurs. 1-4, in May and Oct. (weather permitting). Admission $5; ages 4-14, $1. Phone (775) 847-0155.

COMSTOCK FIREMEN'S MUSEUM, 125 S. C St., displays antique fire wagons dating from 1859 as well as firefighters' uniforms, leather helmets, photographs and firefighting accessories. The collection spans the early volunteer fire department period in the Virginia City-Gold Hill area 1861-77 and includes relics from later periods. Daily 10-5, May-Oct. Donations. Phone (775) 847-0717.

SAVE **MACKAY MANSION,** 129 S. D St., is a 10-room, 1860 building that served as the original headquarters of the Gould and Curry Mine Co. Later it was the residence of silver king John Mackay, owner of the Consolidated Virginia Mine and an early leader of Virginia City who donated millions to Nevada education.

Pieces of Mrs. Mackay's Tiffany silver collection, original furnishings, an old Chinese laundry and a woodshed with original implements have been retained. Daily 10-6, May-Oct.; 11-4, rest of year (weather permitting). Admission $3, under 14 free. Phone (775) 847-0173.

PIPER'S OPERA HOUSE, B and Union sts., witnessed the coming of age of many traveling players following its construction in the 1880s. Such greats as Maude Adams, Wilson Barrett, David Belasco, Edwin Booth, Lotta Crabtree and Adah Isaacs Menken performed for the bonanza kings of Comstock silver wealth.

Features include original 19th-century scenery, an auditorium floor built on ore car springs, a raked stage and a suspended balcony as well as a museum of playbills, posters, photographs and other theater memorabilia. **Note:** The opera house is closed for renovation; reopening is planned for spring 1999. Daily 11-4:30, mid-May to late Oct. Admission $2, under 10 free with paying adult. Phone (775) 847-0433.

SAVE **VIRGINIA AND TRUCKEE RAILROAD,** departing from the Washington and F St. station, is a partially restored standard gauge railroad. It operates a 35-minute round trip steam train run, narrated by a conductor, between Virginia City and Gold Hill. Daily 10:30-5:45, Memorial Day weekend-last weekend in Oct. (weather permitting). All-day pass $9.50. Round-trip fare $4.75; ages 5-12, $2.50. Phone (775) 847-0380.

WELLS (A-5) pop. 1,300, elev. 5,625'

Wells took its name from a number of calm springs. This area, where I-80 and US 93 intersect, was an important stop for late 19th-century pioneers following the Humboldt Trail. The ruts left by the iron-rimmed wheels of their wagons still can be seen in nearby rocks.

For a panorama of the area, summer visitors can hike on trails leading from nearby Angel Lake *(see Recreation Chart and the AAA California/Nevada CampBook)* to the 11,000-foot "Hole-in-the-Mountain Peak." Angel Lake is accessible from Wells from mid-June through September via SR 582, a precipitous two-lane road.

Wells Chamber of Commerce: 279 Clover Ave., P.O. Box 615, Wells, NV 89835; phone (775) 752-3540.

WINNEMUCCA (B-3) pop. 6,100, elev. 4,324'

Thousands of pioneers passed through Winnemucca on their way to California and Oregon. In 1845 children in a wagon train bound for California played a game of tossing pebbles into blue buckets hanging from the wagons. The "pebbles" were later identified as gold nuggets, and although many have searched, the "Blue Bucket Mine" never has been found.

The infamous Butch Cassidy and the Sundance Kid were said to have left their mark on Winnemucca. In 1900 they purportedly celebrated their robbery of the First National Bank by sending the bank president a studio portrait of themselves.

Humboldt County Museum, at Maple Avenue and Jungo Road, chronicles the region's history with antiques and memorabilia; phone (775) 623-2912. Minerals found in the area include gold, silver, tungsten, barite and mercury, in addition to opals and turquoise.

Humboldt Convention and Visitor Bureau: 50 Winnemucca Blvd. W., Winnemucca, NV 89445; phone (775) 623-5071 or (800) 962-2638.

ZEPHYR COVE—
see Lake Tahoe Area in California p. 92.

Capture the moment...

Tips for successful photographs

Know your camera, and be sure it's in good working order. Before going on a trip, shoot a roll of film so you won't have any surprises when it really counts.Use film best suited to your purpose; camera shop personnel can help you choose the right kind. Then, follow the instructions that come with it.

● Compose your picture. Try framing it with a foreground feature (a fence or tree), making sure that parts of the subject are not being cut off. Get close enough so that your subject won't be dwarfed in an expanse of background.

● When taking close-ups of people, have them stand against a simple backdrop, and be sure they do something other than stare stiffly at the camera.

● Mid-morning and mid-afternoon, when the sun's angle creates definite but not overpowering shadows, are the best times for general photography. Pictures taken during the shadowless high noon hours tend to be flat.

● If the weather turns bad, take pictures anyway. Rain and fog can add a special magic to your efforts.

We help you master the art of family travel. Remarkably, everything and everyone is taken care of. So you all feel free to have your own brand of fun. Here we do more than take care of you — we empower you — with an attentive staff, a comfortable room and all the best services, which include in-room communications from AT&T. You can rely on AT&T to stay better connected to friends, family and work, anywhere, anytime. So it's never been easier to pick up the phone and express your happiness. For your next trip, choose a hotel that lets you be you.

express yourself

Laurel Inn Motel
801 W. Laurel Drive
Salinas, CA 93906
408-449-2474

49er Motel
718 Main; P.O. 1608
Weaverville, CA 96093
530-623-49er (4937)

Pine Inn
Ocean Avenue and
Monte Verde Street
Carmel, CA 93921
800-228-3851

It's all within your reach.  **AT&T**

California

California Orientation Map to Destinations

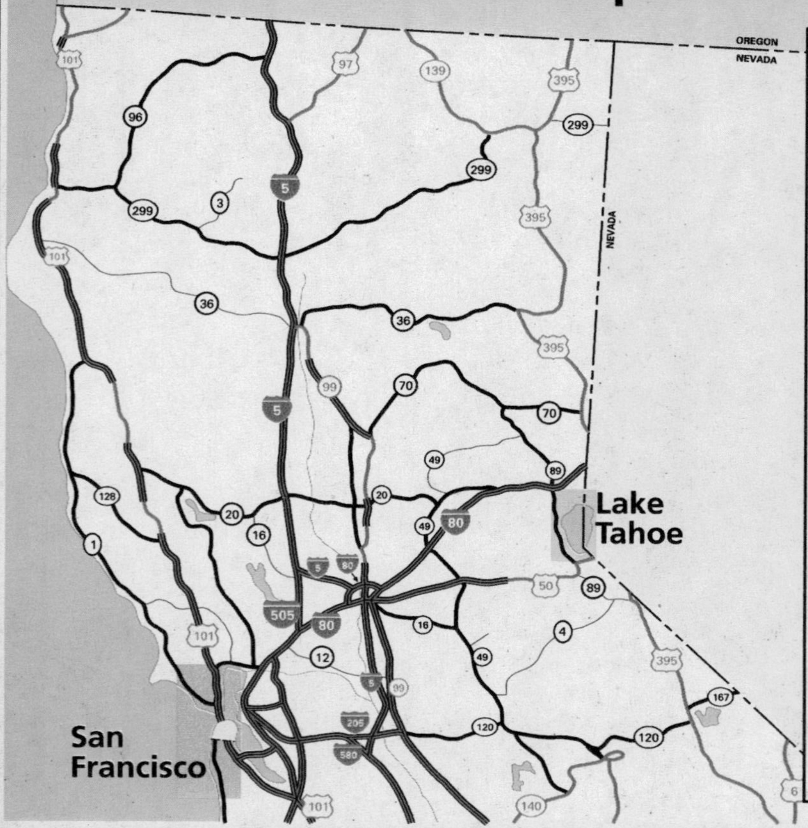

OREGON
IDAHO

OREGON
NEVADA

NEVADA

Lake
Tahoe

San
Francisco

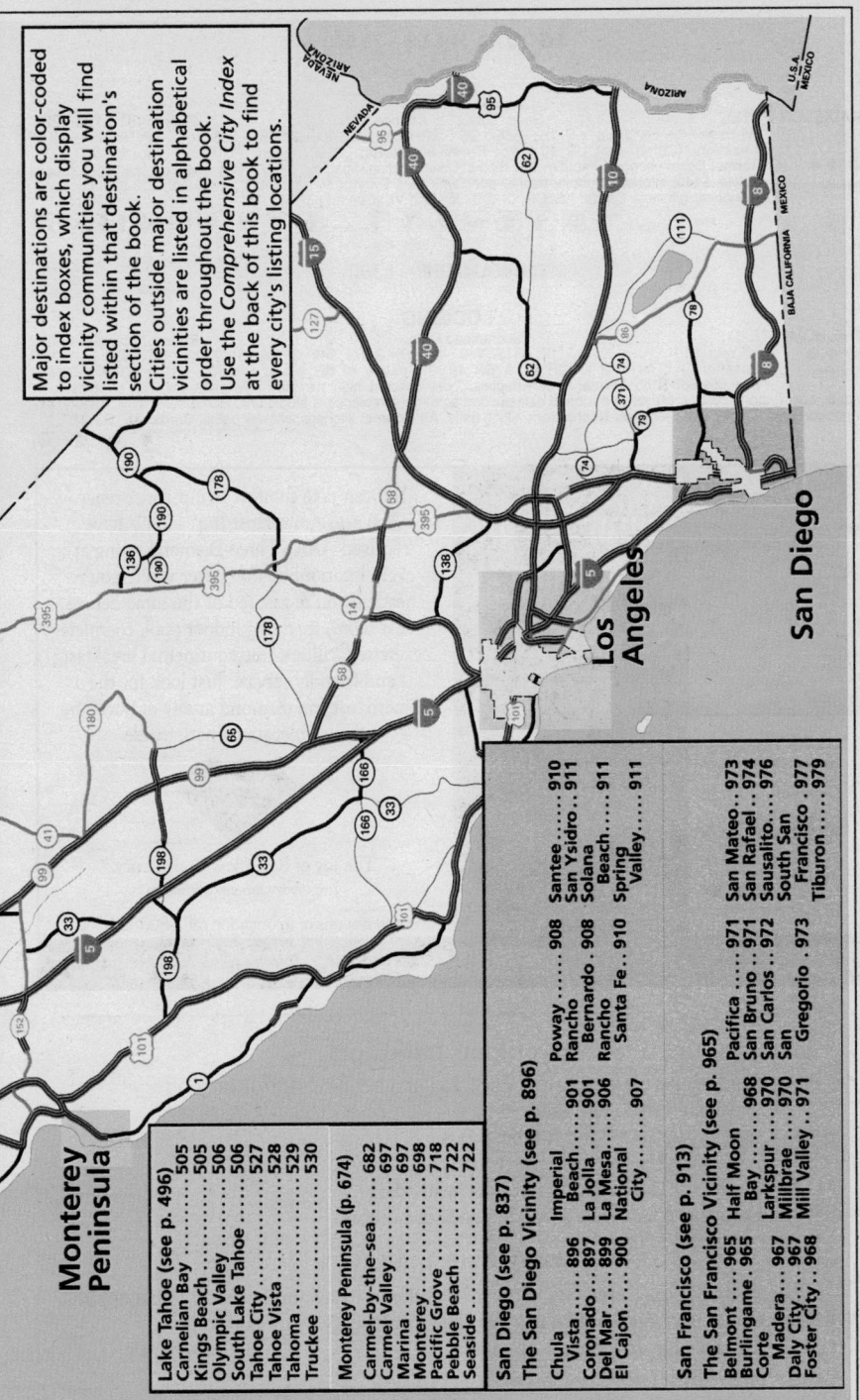

Major destinations are color-coded to index boxes, which display vicinity communities you will find listed within that destination's section of the book. Cities outside major destination vicinities are listed in alphabetical order throughout the book. Use the *Comprehensive City Index* at the back of this book to find every city's listing locations.

Los Angeles

San Diego

AGOURA HILLS—20,400

LODGING

RADISSON HOTEL
Rates Subject to Change
Phone: (818)707-1220
All Year   1P: $85- 95   2P/1B: $95- 105 2P/2B: $95- 105   XP: $10   F17
Location: 0.3 mi s of US 101, exit Reyes Abode Rd. 30100 Agoura Rd 91301. Fax: 818/707-6298.
Terms: Reserv deposit. **Facility:** 281 rooms. Quiet location. Spacious lobby. Many balconies. 14 one-bedroom
suites, $140; interior corridors; heated pool, whirlpool. **Dining:** Restaurant; 7 am-10 pm; $12-$25; cocktails.
Services: giftshop. **Cards:** AE, CB, DI, DS, JC, MC, VI. *(See ad p 615)*

Hotel

AHWAHNEE—1,300

LODGING

THE HOMESTEAD
Guaranteed Rates
Phone: (559)683-0495
All Year [CP]   1P: $115- 149   2P/1B: $115- 149 2P/2B: $149- 205   XP: $50
Location: 4.5 mi n of jct SR 41 & SR 49, 2.5 mi sw of SR 49 on CR 600. 41110 Rd 600 93601.
Fax: 559/683-8165. **Terms:** Reserv deposit, 7 day notice; 2 night min stay, weekends. **Facility:** 5 rooms. Indi-
vidual, adobe-stone-cedar cottages in secluded oak-studded acreage. Fireplaces. 1 studio unit. Horse-stalls avail. 1 story; ex-
terior corridors; smoke free premises. **Recreation:** hiking trails. **All Rooms:** kitchens, shower baths. **Cards:** AE, DS, MC, VI.

Cottage

Meal Plan Indicators

CP = Continental Plan of pastry, juice and another beverage or may offer
expanded breakfast items
BP = Breakfast Plan of full hot breakfast
AP = American Plan of three meals daily
MAP = Modified American Plan of two meals daily
EP = European Plan, where rate includes only room

Family Plan Indicators

The establishment may limit the number of children to whom the family plan applies.
F17 = children 17 and under stay free (age displayed will reflect property's policy)
D17 = discount for children 17 and under
F = children stay free
D = discounts for children

ALAMEDA—76,500   (See map p. 752; index p. 751)

LODGINGS

CORAL REEF MOTEL & SUITES   **Phone:** (510)521-2330   59
(AAA) [SAVE]   All Year [CP]   1P: $81   2P/1B: $88   2P/2B: $88   XP: $7
◆◆◆   **Location:** Exit I-880 at 23rd Ave, 1 mi se. 400 Park St 94501. Fax: 510/521-4707. **Terms:** Weekly/monthly
Motel   rates. **Facility:** 93 rooms. Most rooms have balcony or patio; overlooking lagoon. 1 blk to South Shore Beach.
Landscaped grounds. 2 stories; exterior corridors. **Dining:** Restaurant nearby. **All Rooms:** kitchens.
Cards: AE, CB, DI, DS, MC, VI. **Special Amenities: Free breakfast.** *(See color ad below)*

MARINA VILLAGE INN   **Phone:** (510)523-9450   60
(AAA) [SAVE]   All Year [CP]   1P: $80- 99   2P/1B: $89- 105   2P/2B: $95- 115   XP: $8   F16
◆◆◆   **Location:** From Webster St Tube: E Atlantic; 0.5 mi to n on Triumph to end. 1151 Pacific Marina 94501.
Motel   Fax: 510/523-6315. **Facility:** 51 rooms. Some rooms with harbor views, most rooms with private deck or bal-
cony. 2 stories; interior/exterior corridors; heated pool; marina. **Dining:** Restaurant nearby.
Recreation: complimentary guest berthing. **All Rooms:** combo or shower baths. **Cards:** AE, CB, DI, DS,
MC, VI. **Special Amenities: Free breakfast and free local telephone calls.** *(See color ad p 755)*

ALBION—400

LODGING

ALBION RIVER INN   Rates Subject to Change   **Phone:** 707/937-1919
◆◆◆   All Year [BP]   1P: $170- 260   2P/1B: $170- 260   2P/2B: $170- 260   XP: $20   D9
Cottage   **Location:** On SR 1, 6 mi s of Mendocino; nw end of bridge. 3790 Hwy #1 N 95410 (PO Box 100).
Fax: 707/937-2604. **Terms:** Reserv deposit, 7 day notice; handling fee imposed; 2 night min stay, with Sat.
Facility: 20 rooms. On a bluff; fireplace & ocean view; most with deck. 2 stories; exterior corridors. **All Rooms:** combo or
shower baths. **Cards:** AE, MC, VI.

RESTAURANT

ALBION RIVER INN RESTAURANT   **Dinner:** $15-$25   **Phone:** 707/937-4044
◆◆◆   **Location:** SR 1, 6 mi s of Mendocino; nw end of bridge; at Albion River Inn. 3790 N Hwy 1 95410.
American   **Hours:** 5:30 pm-9:30 pm. **Reservations:** required. **Features:** No A/C; casual dress; cocktails; a la carte.
Fresh seafood. On cliff overlooking river & ocean. Smoke free premises. **Cards:** AE, MC, VI.

ALPINE—5,400

LODGING

COUNTRY SIDE INN   Rates Subject to Change   **Phone:** (619)445-5800
◆◆◆   All Year [CP]   1P: $60- 70   2P/1B: $60- 70   2P/2B: $70- 80   XP: $10   F12
Motel   **Location:** Adjacent to I-8, exit Tavern Rd. 1251 Tavern Rd 91901. Fax: 619/445-6730. **Facility:** 99 rooms. Next
to a shopping center. Nicely landscaped grounds. Barbecue & picnic area. Dep req during major holidays; 2
stories; exterior corridors; heated pool. **Cards:** AE, CB, DI, DS, MC, VI.

RESTAURANTS

DONATO'S   **Lunch:** $6-$9   **Dinner:** $8-$14   **Phone:** 619/445-4006
◆   **Location:** 0.5 mi e. 2654 Alpine Blvd 91901. **Hours:** 11 am-10 pm. Closed major holidays.
Italian   **Reservations:** suggested; Fri & Sat. **Features:** casual dress; children's menu; carryout; cocktails & lounge.
Nice selection of pasta, pizza, seafood & veal. Smoke free premises. **Cards:** DS, MC, VI.

MEDITERRANEO BISTRO & GRILL   **Lunch:** $7-$11   **Dinner:** $8-$14   **Phone:** 619/445-9902
◆◆   **Location:** 0.3 mi s of I-8, exit Tavern Rd. In Alpine Creek Shopping Center. 1347 Tavern Rd 91901.
Italian   **Hours:** 11 am-9:30 pm, Fri & Sat-10:30 pm. Closed: 1/1, 11/25, 12/25 & Easter. **Features:** beer & wine only;
a la carte. A small restaurant with indoor & patio dining. Imaginative selection of pasta, seafood, chicken, &
veal entrees. Gourmet pizza also avail. **Cards:** AE, MC, VI.

ALTURAS—3,200—See also CEDARVILLE.

LODGINGS

BEST WESTERN TRAILSIDE INN
◆◆   5/1-10/31   Guaranteed Rates   **Phone:** (530)233-4111
Motel   5/1-10/31   1P: $52-   59   2P/1B: $56-   64   2P/2B: $66   XP: $5
        2/1-4/30 & 11/1-1/31   1P: $50-   55   2P/1B: $52-   60   2P/2B: $58   XP: $5
Location: On US 395. 343 N Main St 96101. Fax: 530/233-3180. **Facility:** 38 rooms. 2 stories; exterior corridors. **Cards:** AE, CB, DI, DS, MC, VI.

SUPER 8 MOTEL
🅰🅰🅰   All Year   Rates Subject to Change   **Phone:** (530)233-3545
◆◆   1P: $52-   65   2P/1B: $54-   65   2P/2B: $59-   65   XP: $5   F12
Motel   **Location:** On US 395. 511 N Main St 96101. Fax: 530/233-3305. **Facility:** 48 rooms. 2 stories; exterior corridors. **Dining:** Coffee shop nearby. **Cards:** AE, CB, DI, DS, MC, VI.

AMADOR CITY—200

RESTAURANT

IMPERIAL HOTEL RESTAURANT   **Dinner:** $14-$22   **Phone:** 209/267-9172
◆◆   **Location:** Center. 14202 Hwy 49 95601. **Hours:** 5 pm-9 pm; Sun 10 am-2 & 5-9 pm. Closed: 12/24.
Continental   **Reservations:** suggested. **Features:** casual dress; Sunday brunch; cocktails; a la carte. Smoke free premises. **Cards:** AE, CB, DI, DS, MC, VI.

HEADING FOR THE BIG CITY?

It might pay to investigate AAA lodgings in the smaller nearby towns. A AAA map and the appropriate TourBook, with its many cross-references, can help.

ANAHEIM

pop. 266,400

This index helps you "spot" where approved accommodations are located on the detailed maps that follow. Rate ranges are for comparison only and show the property's high season. Turn to the listing page for more detailed rate information and consult display ads for special promotions. Restaurant rate range is for dinner unless only lunch (L) is served.

ANAHEIM

Spotter/Map Pg.Number	OA	ANAHEIM - Lodgings	Rating	Rate	Listing Page
1 / p. 294		Embassy Suites-Disneyland Park Area - see ad p 338	◆◆◆	$129-199	338
2 / p. 294	⊕	Park Inn International - see color ad p 344	◆◆◆	$119-219 ⟨SAVE⟩	345
3 / p. 294		Hawthorn Suites, Ltd - see color ad p 310	◆◆◆	$109-209	340
4 / p. 294	⊕	Super 8 Motel - see color ad p 353	◆◆	$65 ⟨SAVE⟩	351
5 / p. 294	⊕	Ramada near Disneyland Park	◆◆	$79-89 ⟨SAVE⟩	348
7 / p. 294	⊕	Castle Inn & Suites - see color ad starting on p 322 , p 341, p 324	◆◆◆	$72-92 ⟨SAVE⟩	327
8 / p. 294	⊕	Super 8 Motel Disneyland Park	◆◆	$69	351
9 / p. 294	⊕	Anaheim Desert Palm Inn & Suites - see color ad starting on p 300	◆◆◆	$64-89	312
10 / p. 294		Radisson Hotel Maingate-Anaheim	◆◆◆	$95-105	346
11 / p. 294	⊕	Best Western Raffles Inn & Suites - see color ad p 326	◆◆◆	$79-99 ⟨SAVE⟩	325
12 / p. 294	⊕	Travelodge International Inn - see color ad p 353	◆◆	$79-98 ⟨SAVE⟩	351
13 / p. 294	⊕	Anaheim Comfort Inn Maingate - see color ad p 286	◆◆	$59-109 ⟨SAVE⟩	311
14 / p. 294	⊕	Red Roof Inn - see color ad p 350	◆◆	$76 ⟨SAVE⟩	350
15 / p. 294	⊕	Hyatt Regency Alicante - see color ad p 565 , p 304	◆◆◆	$164-180 ⟨SAVE⟩	341
16 / p. 294	⊕	Anaheim Stadium Travelodge - see color ad p 324	◆◆	$67 ⟨SAVE⟩	318
17 / p. 294	⊕	Comfort Suites at the Park - see color ad p 332	◆◆◆	$89-119 ⟨SAVE⟩	328
18 / p. 294	⊕	Anaheim Heritage Inn & Suites - see color ad p 315		$99-120 ⟨SAVE⟩	312
19 / p. 294	⊕	Anaheim Carriage Inn - see color ad p 303	◆◆◆	$59-89 ⟨SAVE⟩	309
20 / p. 294	⊕	Quality Hotel Maingate - see color ad p 308	◆◆◆	$105-150 ⟨SAVE⟩	345
21 / p. 294	⊕	Anaheim Marriott Hotel	◆◆◆	$189 ⟨SAVE⟩	316
22 / p. 294	⊕	Anaheim Hilton and Towers - see ad p 119, p 319	◆◆◆	$119-370	316
24 / p. 294	⊕	Westcoast Anaheim Hotel	◆◆◆	$99-109 ⟨SAVE⟩	353
25 / p. 294	⊕	Jolly Roger Inn Hotel - see color ad p 306	◆◆◆	$79-139 ⟨SAVE⟩	342
26 / p. 294	⊕	Dolphin's Cove Resort	◆◆◆	$150-200 ⟨SAVE⟩	336
27 / p. 294		Magic Inn & Suites	◆	$55-59	342
28 / p. 294	⊕	Alpine Motel - see color ad p 308	◆	$54-59	308
29 / p. 294	⊕	Anaheim Angel Inn - see ad p 309	◆	$59-64 ⟨SAVE⟩	309
33 / p. 294	⊕	Ramada Maingate Saga Inn - see color ad p 311 , p 349	◆◆◆	$79-99 ⟨SAVE⟩	348
34 / p. 294	⊕	Best Western Anaheim Inn - see color ad p 327	◆◆◆	$65-125 ⟨SAVE⟩	318
35 / p. 294	⊕	Anaheim Days Inn Maingate - see color ad p 297	◆◆	$69-129	312
36 / p. 294	⊕	Anaheim Desert Inn & Suites - see color ad starting on p 298	◆◆◆	$69-89	312
37 / p. 294	⊕	Best Western Park Place Inn - see color ad p 327	◆◆◆	$119-129 ⟨SAVE⟩	325
38 / p. 294	⊕	Anaheim Penny Sleeper Inn - see color ad p 318	◆◆	$69-89	317
39 / p. 294	⊕	Howard Johnson Plaza Hotel - see color ad p 342, opposite inside back cover	◆◆	$84-94 ⟨SAVE⟩	341
40 / p. 294	⊕	Holiday Inn Anaheim at the Park - see color ad p 340	◆◆◆	$109-139 ⟨SAVE⟩	340

Spotter/Map Pg.Number	OA	ANAHEIM - Lodgings (contd.)	Rating	Rate	Listing Page
41 / p. 294	🏠	Anaheim Courtesy Lodge - see color ad p 309	◆	$39-48	311
42 / p. 294	🏠	Anaheim Fairfield Inn - see color ad p 312	◆ ◆ ◆	$114 🈯	312
43 / p. 294		Residence Inn By Marriott - see color ad p 351	◆ ◆ ◆	$194-224	350
44 / p. 294	🏠	Peacock Suite Resort	◆ ◆ ◆	$99-119 🈯	345
46 / p. 294	🏠	Sheraton-Anaheim Hotel	◆ ◆ ◆	$90 🈯	351
47 / p. 294	🏠	Best Western Anaheim Stardust - see color ad p 324	◆ ◆	$54-89 🈯	324
48 / p. 294	🏠	Days Inn Anaheim West - see color ad p 334	◆	$42-69 🈯	334
49 / p. 294	🏠	Park Vue Inn - see color ad p 345	◆	$69-79 🈯	345
50 / p. 294	🏠	Days Inn Suites - see color ad p 335	◆ ◆	$59-145 🈯	336
51 / p. 294	🏠	Best Western Courtesy Inn - see color ad p 325	◆ ◆	$69-99 🈯	325
52 / p. 294	🏠	Ramada Inn Conestoga at Disneyland Park - see color ad opposite title page, p 345	◆ ◆ ◆	$119 🈯	346
53 / p. 294	🏠	Candy Cane Inn - see color ad p 328	◆ ◆ ◆	$74-129 🈯	326
56 / p. 294	🏠	The Disneyland Pacific Hotel - see color ad p 337	◆ ◆ ◆	$190-225	336
57 / p. 294	🏠	Abby's Anaheimer Inn - see color ad p 308	◆	$39-69 🈯	308
58 / p. 294	🏠	Best Western Stovall's Inn - see color ad p 327	◆ ◆	$98-116 🈯	326
59 / p. 294	🏠	Best Western Pavilions - see color ad p 327	◆ ◆ ◆	$59-129 🈯	325
60 / p. 294	🏠	Disneyland Hotel - see color ad p 337	◆ ◆ ◆	$190-225	336
61 / p. 294	🏠	Crystal Inn - see color ad p 334	◆	$36-44	328
62 / p. 294	🏠	Anaheim Days Inn Park South - see color ad p 313	◆ ◆	$69-129	312
63 / p. 294	🏠	Anaheim Islander Inn & Suites - see color ad p 316	◆	$46-69	316
64 / p. 294	🏠	Anaheim Maingate Inn - see color ad p 317	◆ ◆	$69 🈯	316
66 / p. 294	🏠	Carousel Inn & Suites	◆ ◆ ◆	$89-99 🈯	327
67 / p. 294	🏠	Tropicana Inn - see color ad p 344	◆ ◆	$99-189 🈯	351
75 / p. 294	🏠	Comfort Inn & Suites - see color ad p 330	◆ ◆ ◆	$89-99 🈯	328
77 / p. 294	🏠	Econo Lodge/Maingate - see color ad p 339	◆	$55-90 🈯	338
78 / p. 294	🏠	Ramada Limited Maingate North - see color ad p 305	◆ ◆	$69-79 🈯	347
79 / p. 294	🏠	Holiday Inn Express - see color ad p 341	◆ ◆ ◆	$95-99 🈯	340
82 / p. 294	🏠	Anaheim Coachman Inn - see color ad p 286 , p 302	◆ ◆	$49-69 🈯	309
83 / p. 294	🏠	Anaheim Plaza Hotel & Suites - see color ad starting on p 320	◆ ◆	$99 🈯	317
84 / p. 294	🏠	Comfort Inn & Suites/Anaheim West - see color ad p 331	◆ ◆ ◆	$79-99 🈯	328
85 / p. 294	🏠	Ramada Limited Disneyland Area - see color ad p 347	◆	$95 🈯	347
		ANAHEIM - Restaurants			
2 / p. 294		Thee White House Restaurant	◆ ◆ ◆	$16-26	354
3 / p. 294	🏠	Mr Stox Restaurant	◆ ◆ ◆	$14-26	354
6 / p. 294		The Catch	◆ ◆	$20-31	353
7 / p. 294	🏠	Hansa House Smorgasbord	◆ ◆	$10	354
13 / p. 294		Cattleman's Wharf	◆ ◆ ◆	$18-37	354
14 / p. 294		Overland Stage Restaurant	◆ ◆	$14-21	354
15 / p. 294		Garden Court Bistro	◆ ◆	$9-18	354
16 / p. 294		Plantation Restaurant	◆	$6-8	354

Nearby Accommodations

Spotter/Map Pg.Number	OA	NEWPORT BEACH - Lodgings	Rating	Rate	Listing Page
1 / p. 296	🏠	Sheraton Newport Beach Hotel	◆ ◆ ◆	$99-119 🈯	746
2 / p. 296	🏠	The Sutton Place Hotel	◆ ◆ ◆ ◆	$220-875 🈯	746
3 / p. 296		Newport Beach Marriott Suites	◆ ◆ ◆	$149	745

Spotter/Map Pg.Number	OA	NEWPORT BEACH - Lodgings (contd.)	Rating	Rate	Listing Page
4 / p. 296	⊕	Newport Channel Inn - see color ad p 745	◆◆	$79-119 SAVE	745
5 / p. 296	⊕	Holiday Inn Express - see color ad p 743		$79-139	744
6 / p. 296	⊕	Newport Classic Inn	◆◆	$76-86 SAVE	745
10 / p. 296	⊕	Portofino Beach Hotel	◆◆◆	$159-399 SAVE	745
12 / p. 296		Doryman's Oceanfront Inn	◆◆◆	$135-275	743
15 / p. 296	⊕	Best Western Bay Shores Inn - see color ad p 743	◆◆◆	$169-369 SAVE	742
16 / p. 296	⊕	Hyatt Newporter - see color ad p 565	◆◆◆	$184-270 SAVE	744
18 / p. 296	⊕	Four Seasons Hotel	◆◆◆◆◆	$250-305 SAVE	743
20 / p. 296		Newport Beach Marriott Hotel & Tennis Club	◆◆◆	$149	744
		NEWPORT BEACH - Restaurants			
1 / p. 296		Pascal	◆◆◆	$20-29	747
2 / p. 296		Kitayama	◆◆	$21-29	746
4 / p. 296		Bistro 201	◆◆◆	$10-23	746
7 / p. 296		Josh Slocum's Restaurant	◆◆	$15-32	746
8 / p. 296		Ristorante Mamma Gina	◆◆◆	$16-26	747
9 / p. 296		Oysters Restaurant	◆◆◆	$11-27	746
10 / p. 296		The Cannery Restaurant	◆◆	$17-21	746
12 / p. 296		21 Ocean Front	◆◆◆	$18-32	747
15 / p. 296		Yankee Tavern	◆◆	$12-20	747
18 / p. 296		The Pavilion	◆◆◆◆	$18-28	747
20 / p. 296		Daily Grill	◆◆	$9-19	746
21 / p. 296		P F Chang's China Bistro	◆◆	$8-15	747
22 / p. 296		The Ritz	◆◆◆◆	$18-29	747
24 / p. 296		Five Crowns	◆◆◆◆	$16-26	746
		LAKE FOREST - Lodgings			
24 / p. 296	⊕	Best Western Laguna/El Toro Inn - see color ad p 352	◆◆◆	$79-89 SAVE	495
25 / p. 296	⊕	Irvine Suites Hotel	◆◆◆	$89-149	495
26 / p. 296		Hampton Inn South Orange County - see color ad p 338	◆◆◆	$119	495
		LAGUNA HILLS - Lodgings			
28 / p. 296	⊕	Comfort Inn Laguna Hills/Irvine - see color ad p 478, p 490	◆◆	$59-69 SAVE	493
29 / p. 296		Courtyard By Marriott - see color ad p 311	◆◆◆	$94-129	493
30 / p. 296		Laguna Hills Lodge	◆◆	$70	493
32 / p. 296		Holiday Inn - see color ad p 493	◆◆◆	$85-119	493
		LAGUNA HILLS - Restaurant			
30 / p. 296		Claim Jumper Restaurant	◆◆	$9-15	493
		MISSION VIEJO - Lodgings			
34 / p. 296	⊕	Fairfield Inn by Marriott	◆◆	$66 SAVE	670
		MISSION VIEJO - Restaurant			
32 / p. 296		Trabuco Oaks SteakHouse	◆◆	$9-19	671
		LAGUNA BEACH - Lodgings			
37 / p. 296	⊕	Bayview Laguna Inn	◆◆	$85-140 SAVE	487
38 / p. 296	⊕	By-The-Sea Inn - see color ad p 487	◆◆	$99-189 SAVE	487
40 / p. 296	⊕	Inn at Laguna Beach - see color ad p 491	◆◆◆	$169-489 SAVE	492
41 / p. 296	⊕	Hotel Laguna		$105-200 SAVE	489
42 / p. 296	⊕	Holiday Inn Laguna Beach - see ad p 491	◆◆◆	$99-159 SAVE	489
44 / p. 296	⊕	Laguna Riviera Beach Resort & Spa - see color ad p 491	◆◆	$75-179	492
45 / p. 296		The Carriage House-Bed & Breakfast	◆◆◆	$125-150	487
46 / p. 296	⊕	Capri Laguna	◆◆	$150-235 SAVE	487
48 / p. 296	⊕	Best Western Laguna Brisas Spa Hotel - see color ad p 488	◆◆◆	$139-329 SAVE	487
50 / p. 296	⊕	Surf & Sand Hotel - see ad p 489	◆◆◆◆	$295-425 SAVE	492
52 / p. 296	⊕	Casa Laguna Inn - see ad p 489	◆◆	$105-220 SAVE	489
53 / p. 296	⊕	Best Western Laguna Reef Inn	◆◆◆	$120-165 SAVE	487

Spotter/Map Pg.Number	OA	**LAGUNA BEACH** - Lodgings (contd.)	Rating	Rate	Listing Page
55 / p. 296	AAA	Aliso Creek Inn - see ad p 486	◆◆◆	$154-326 SAVE	486
		LAGUNA BEACH - Restaurants			
34 / p. 296		Las Brisas	◆◆◆	$10-25	492
35 / p. 296		Cedar Creek Inn	◆◆	$6-23	492
36 / p. 296		Claes Seafood Etc	◆◆	$18-30	492
37 / p. 296		Ristorante Rumari	◆◆	$11-20	492
38 / p. 296	AAA	The Beach House	◆◆	$10-22	492
		DANA POINT - Lodgings			
57 / p. 296	AAA	Quality Inn & Suites - see color ad p 490	◆◆	$75 SAVE	430
58 / p. 296	AAA	The Ritz-Carlton, Laguna Niguel	◆◆◆◆◆	$365-560	430
59 / p. 296	AAA	Dana Point Harbor Inn	◆◆	$69-79 SAVE	430
60 / p. 296		Blue Lantern Inn	◆◆◆◆	$140-500	429
61 / p. 296	AAA	Best Western Marina Inn - see color ad p 429	◆◆◆	$89-99 SAVE	429
62 / p. 296		Marriott's Laguna Cliffs Resort/Dana Point	◆◆◆	$120-215	430
63 / p. 296	AAA	Doubletree Guest Suites Dana Point - see color ad p 423	◆◆◆	$129-250 SAVE	430
64 / p. 296	AAA	Capistrano Surfside Inn - see ad p 429	◆◆◆	$140-175 SAVE	430
66 / p. 296	AAA	Holiday Inn Express Dana Point Edgewater - see color ad p 986	◆◆◆	$89-169 SAVE	430
		DANA POINT - Restaurants			
44 / p. 296		The Dining Room	◆◆◆◆	$35-53	430
45 / p. 296		The Club Grill & Bar	◆◆◆◆	$35-48	430
48 / p. 296		Delaney's	◆◆	$12-29	430
		SAN JUAN CAPISTRANO - Lodgings			
70 / p. 296	AAA	Best Western Capistrano Inn - see color ad p 327	◆◆◆	$89-99 SAVE	986
71 / p. 296	AAA	Laguna Inn & Suites	◆◆◆	$55-80	986
		SAN JUAN CAPISTRANO - Restaurants			
51 / p. 296		Cedar Creek Inn	◆◆◆	$13-23	987
52 / p. 296		El Adobe de Capistrano	◆◆	$9-17	987
53 / p. 296		Cafe Mozart	◆◆	$8-20	987
		SAN CLEMENTE - Lodgings			
73 / p. 296		Country Side Inn - see ad p 834	◆◆◆	$79-84	835
74 / p. 296	AAA	Best Western Casablanca Inn	◆◆◆	$74-109 SAVE	834
76 / p. 296		Holiday Inn-San Clemente Resort	◆◆◆	$119-149	835
77 / p. 296	AAA	Motel San Clemente	◆◆	$40-85 SAVE	835
78 / p. 296	AAA	Casa Tropicana Bed & Breakfast Inn	◆◆◆	$120-350	834
80 / p. 296	AAA	San Clemente Beach Travelodge - see color ad p 834	◆◆	$49-109 SAVE	835
81 / p. 296	AAA	Quality Suites Hotel - see color ad p 835	◆◆◆	$89-135 SAVE	835
82 / p. 296	AAA	Comfort Suites	◆◆◆	$89-109 SAVE	834
		SAN CLEMENTE - Restaurants			
56 / p. 296		Swiss Chalet	◆◆	$11-18	835
57 / p. 296		The Vintage Restaurant	◆◆	$9-18	835
		BUENA PARK - Lodgings			
92 / p. 294		Fairfield Inn by Marriott - see color ad p 338	◆◆	$53-56	388
93 / p. 294	AAA	Hanford Hotel - see color ad p 336, p 389	◆◆◆	$79-99	388
94 / p. 294	AAA	Red Roof Inn	◆	$50-73 SAVE	390
95 / p. 294	AAA	Super 8 Motel - see color ad p 390	◆◆	$50-58 SAVE	391
96 / p. 294	AAA	Travelodge/Buena Park - see color ad p 391	◆◆	$58-60 SAVE	391
98 / p. 294	AAA	Best Western Buena Park Inn - see color ad p 388	◆◆	$42-62 SAVE	388
99 / p. 294		Embassy Suites Hotel-Buena Park	◆◆◆	$134	388
100 / p. 294		Courtyard by Marriott - see color ad p 311	◆◆◆	$76	388
101 / p. 294	AAA	Innsuites Hotels Buena Park Suite Hotel - see color ad p 390	◆◆	$89	390

Spotter/Map Pg.Number	OA	BUENA PARK - Lodgings (contd.)	Rating	Rate	Listing Page
102 / p. 294	⚜	Holiday Inn Buena Park - see color ad p 389	◆◆◆	$89 🆂	390
		BUENA PARK - Restaurant			
23 / p. 294		Knott's Berry Farm Chicken Dinner Restaurant	◆	$10-12	391
		ANAHEIM HILLS - Lodgings			
106 / p. 294	⚜	**Best Western Anaheim Hills**	◆◆◆	$84-114 🆂	354
107 / p. 294	⚜	Hanford Hotel Anaheim Hills - see color ad p 336	◆◆◆	$79-89	354
		ANAHEIM HILLS - Restaurants			
25 / p. 294		Foscari Italian Restaurant	◆◆	$8-24	354
26 / p. 294		Foxfire Restaurant	◆◆◆	$16-29	354
27 / p. 294		Mandarin Taste Restaurant	◆◆	$7-19	354
		LA PALMA - Lodgings			
108 / p. 294	⚜	**La Quinta Inn**	◆◆◆	$69-82 🆂	535
		LA PALMA - Restaurant			
30 / p. 294		A'Roma Trattoria-Ristorante	◆◆	$9-24	535
		SANTA ANA - Lodgings			
112 / p. 294	⚜	**Comfort Suites - Orange County Airport**	◆◆◆	$79	1000
113 / p. 294		**Courtyard by Marriott - see color ad p 311**	◆◆◆	$80	1000
114 / p. 294		Embassy Suites/Orange County Airport North	◆◆◆	$154	1000
115 / p. 294	⚜	Doubletree Club Hotel-Orange County Airport - see ad p 1000	◆◆◆	$170	1000
116 / p. 294		Holiday Inn Express	◆◆	$75-95	1000
117 / p. 294	⚜	Best Western Orange County Airport North - see color ad p 329	◆◆◆	$62	1000
118 / p. 294	⚜	Red Roof Inn - see color ad p 350	◆◆	$78 🆂	1001
119 / p. 294	⚜	**Tustin Suites**	◆	$54-94 🆂	1001
120 / p. 294		Quality Suites - Orange County Airport - see color ad p 1001	◆◆◆	$119	1001
121 / p. 294	⚜	Radisson Suite Hotel-Santa Ana - see color ad p 346, p 1001	◆◆◆	$115-170 🆂	1001
122 / p. 294	⚜	Holiday Inn-Orange County Airport/Central Business District - see color ad p 478, p 343	◆◆◆	$99-129 🆂	1001
123 / p. 294	⚜	**Woolley's Petite Suites Hotel**	◆◆◆	$95 🆂	1002
		SANTA ANA - Restaurants			
32 / p. 294		Topaz Cafe	◆◆◆	$10-17	1002
33 / p. 294		Crazy Horse Steakhouse	◆◆	$8-23	1002
34 / p. 294		Gustaf Anders	◆◆◆	$16-30	1002
35 / p. 294		Antonello Ristorante	◆◆◆◆	$16-35	1002
		PLACENTIA - Lodgings			
130 / p. 294		Fairfield Inn By Marriott - see color ad p 338	◆◆	$58-61	800
131 / p. 294		Holiday Inn Placentia - see color ad p 342	◆◆◆	$70-80	800
		ORANGE - Lodgings			
138 / p. 294		Country Side Inn	◆◆◆	$95-105	762
139 / p. 294	⚜	**Howard Johnson Express Inn**	◆	$65-90 🆂	762
140 / p. 294	⚜	Anaheim/Orange County Doubletree Hotel - see ad p 347	◆◆◆	$109 🆂	762
142 / p. 294	⚜	Anaheim/Orange Hilton Suites - see ad p 119	◆◆◆	$169 🆂	762
143 / p. 294	⚜	**Orange Travelodge**	◆◆	$65-70 🆂	763
145 / p. 294		Residence Inn by Marriott - see color ad p 351	◆◆◆	$114	763
146 / p. 294	⚜	**Hawthorn Suites**	◆◆◆	$130 🆂	762
		ORANGE - Restaurants			
39 / p. 294		Cafe Francais	◆◆◆	$14-20	763
40 / p. 294		Gaetano's Ristorante	◆◆	$8-16	763
41 / p. 294		Rockwell's Cafe' & Bakery	◆◆	$9-17	763
42 / p. 294		The Hobbit	◆◆◆	$50	763
43 / p. 294		Moreno's Restaurant	◆	$5-14	763

Spotter/Map Pg.Number	OA	COSTA MESA - Lodgings	Rating	Rate	Listing Page
170 / p. 294	∰	Best Western Newport Mesa Inn - see color ad p 422	◆◆	$59-79	422
171 / p. 294	∰	Comfort Inn	◆◆	$69-120	422
172 / p. 294		Costa Mesa Marriott Suites	◆◆◆	$129	423
173 / p. 294	∰	Country Side Inn & Suites - see color ad p 744	◆◆◆	$109-119	423
174 / p. 294	∰	Days Inn	◆	$84-94	423
175 / p. 294		Holiday Inn-Costa Mesa/Orange County Airport	◆◆◆	$95-115	423
176 / p. 294	∰	Inn at Costa Mesa	◆◆	$42-46	424
177 / p. 294	∰	La Quinta Inn	◆◆◆	$59-69	424
178 / p. 294	∰	Costa Mesa Holiday Inn Express - see color ad p 422, p 744, p 340	◆◆◆	$69-109	423
180 / p. 294	∰	Ramada Limited - see color ad p 745, p 424, opposite title page	◆◆	$69-89	424
181 / p. 294	∰	Doubletree Hotel/Orange County Airport - see color ad p 423	◆◆◆	$119	423
182 / p. 294		Residence Inn by Marriott	◆◆◆	$119	424
183 / p. 294	∰	Super 8 Motel, Costa Mesa - see color ad p 424	◆◆	$56-66	425
184 / p. 294	∰	Cozy Inn	◆◆	$42-46	423
185 / p. 294	∰	Vagabond Inn	◆◆	$99	425
186 / p. 294	∰	The Westin South Coast Plaza Hotel	◆◆◆◆	$199-239	425
187 / p. 294	∰	Wyndham Garden Hotel - see color ad p 425	◆◆◆	$116	425
188 / p. 294	∰	TraveLodge-Hacienda Inn - see ad p 746	◆◆	$65-85	425
189 / p. 294	∰	Sandpiper Motel	◆	$54-60	424
		COSTA MESA - Restaurants			
68 / p. 294		Diva	◆◆◆	$12-20	425
69 / p. 294		Birraporetti's	◆◆	$8-13	425
70 / p. 294		The Golden Truffle	◆◆	$12-18	425
71 / p. 294		Mimi's Cafe	◆	$8-13	426
72 / p. 294		Troquet	◆◆◆	$28-34	426
73 / p. 294		Scott's Seafood Grill & Bar	◆◆◆	$20-38	426
74 / p. 294		Kaplan's Deli	◆	$7-12	426
		WESTMINSTER - Lodgings			
192 / p. 294	∰	Best Western Westminster Inn	◆◆◆	$62-108	1081
194 / p. 294		Travelodge Westminster/Huntington Beach - see color ad p 1082	◆◆	$55-65	1081
195 / p. 294	∰	Westminster Gateway Travelodge	◆	$55	1082
196 / p. 294	∰	Westminster Super 8	◆	$55-60	1082
		STANTON - Lodgings			
201 / p. 294		Holiday Inn Express-Stanton/Disneyland Park Area - see color ad p 352	◆◆	$65-85	1055
		CYPRESS - Lodgings			
206 / p. 294		Woodfin Suite Hotel-Cypress - see color ad p 333	◆◆◆	$99-199	597
207 / p. 294		Cypress Courtyard By Marriott - see color ad p 311	◆◆◆	$69-89	597
		FOUNTAIN VALLEY - Lodgings			
211 / p. 294	∰	Ramada Limited-Huntington Beach/Fountain Valley - see color ad opposite title page	◆◆	$74-79	454
212 / p. 294		Courtyard by Marriott - see color ad p 311	◆◆◆	$86	454
213 / p. 294		Residence Inn by Marriott	◆◆◆	$124	454
		FOUNTAIN VALLEY - Restaurant			
81 / p. 294		Mimi's Cafe	◆◆	$7-13	454
		FULLERTON - Lodgings			
218 / p. 294	∰	Fullerton Inn	◆◆	$45-55	460
220 / p. 294	∰	Heritage Inn	◆◆	$50	460
221 / p. 294	∰	Radisson Hotel Fullerton	◆◆◆	$88	460

Spotter/Map Pg.Number	OA	**FULLERTON** - Lodgings (contd.)	Rating	Rate	Listing Page
222 / p. 294		Chase Suite Hotel - see color ad p 333	◆◆◆	$109-169	460
223 / p. 294	⊕	**Four Points Hotel by Sheraton - see color ad p 335**	◆◆◆	$99-159 SAVE	460
		FULLERTON - Restaurants			
83 / p. 294		The Cellar	◆◆◆◆	$22-33	461
84 / p. 294		Summit House	◆◆◆	$20-30	461
		GARDEN GROVE - Lodgings			
228 / p. 294	⊕	**Best Western Plaza International Inn**	◆◆	$49-69 SAVE	462
229 / p. 294	⊕	**Ramada Plaza Hotel-Disneyland South**	◆◆◆	$79 SAVE	462
		GARDEN GROVE - Restaurant			
89 / p. 294		Mimi's Cafe	◆◆	$7-13	462
		HUNTINGTON BEACH - Lodgings			
232 / p. 294		Ramada Ocean Front - see color ad p 473, p 348	◆◆	$99-129	474
234 / p. 294	⊕	**Harbour Inn - see ad p 473**	◆◆◆	$79-109 SAVE	473
235 / p. 294	⊕	**Comfort Suites**	◆	$69-99 SAVE	473
236 / p. 294	⊕	**Beach Inn Motel**	◆	$65-110	472
237 / p. 294		Holiday Inn-Huntington Beach	◆◆	$88	473
238 / p. 294		Ritz Inn	◆◆	$75-85	474
239 / p. 294		Best Western Regency Inn	◆◆	$75-95 SAVE	473
240 / p. 294	⊕	Quality Inn	◆◆	$130-140 SAVE	473
241 / p. 294	⊕	Sun'n Sands Motel	◆	$99-140	474
242 / p. 294	⊕	**Waterfront Hilton Beach Resort - see ad p 119 , p 474**	◆◆◆◆	$179-299	474
		HUNTINGTON BEACH - Restaurants			
92 / p. 294		Market Broiler	◆◆	$8-18	474
93 / p. 294		Palm Court	◆◆◆	$12-31	474
		IRVINE - Lodgings			
250 / p. 294	⊕	Atrium Hotel at Orange County Airport	◆◆◆	$105 SAVE	477
251 / p. 294		Courtyard By Marriott Irvine/Orange County Airport - see color ad p 311	◆◆◆	$79-129	477
252 / p. 294	⊕	**Embassy Suites Hotel-Orange County Airport**	◆◆◆	$144 SAVE	478
253 / p. 294		Crowne Plaza-Irvine/Orange County Airport	◆◆◆	$154-179	477
254 / p. 294	⊕	**Hyatt Regency Irvine - see color ad p 565**	◆◆◆◆	$200-239 SAVE	478
255 / p. 294		Irvine Marriott Hotel	◆◆◆	$89-169	479
256 / p. 294		La Quinta Inn	◆◆◆	$75-95	479
257 / p. 294	⊕	Orange County Airport Hilton - see color ad p 350 & ad p 119	◆◆◆	$109	479
258 / p. 294		Residence Inn by Marriott-Irvine Spectrum	◆◆◆	$104-119	479
259 / p. 294		Homestead Village	◆◆◆	$89-99	478
		IRVINE - Restaurants			
99 / p. 294		Bistango	◆◆◆	$15-24	479
100 / p. 294		Chanteclair	◆◆◆◆	$20-28	479
101 / p. 294		McCormick & Schmick's	◆◆◆	$10-20	479
102 / p. 294		Mimi's Cafe	◆◆	$8-12	479
103 / p. 294		Prego Ristorante	◆◆◆	$10-20	479
104 / p. 294		Ciao Mein	◆◆◆	$11-18	479
106 / p. 294		Il Fornaio Cucina Italiana	◆◆◆	$10-22	479
		TUSTIN - Restaurants			
110 / p. 294		The Barn Restaurant & Saloon	◆	$9-21	1068
111 / p. 294		Mimi's Cafe	◆◆	$7-13	1068
112 / p. 294		Nieuport 17 Restaurant	◆◆◆	$18-24	1068
113 / p. 294		The Black Sheep Bistro	◆◆	$14-26	1068

"Rates Subject To Change." The printed rates are the establishment's estimated charges for the periods noted.

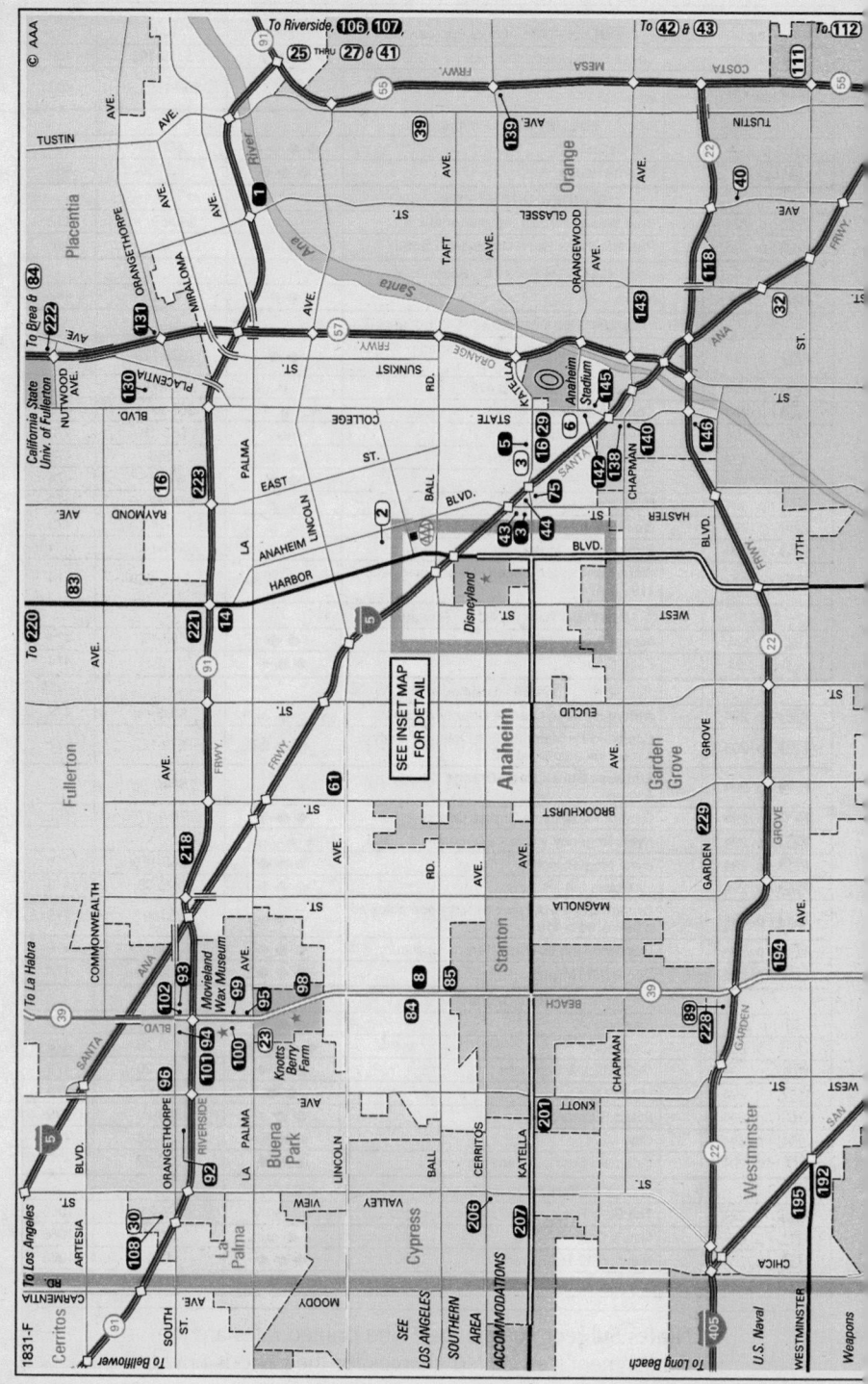

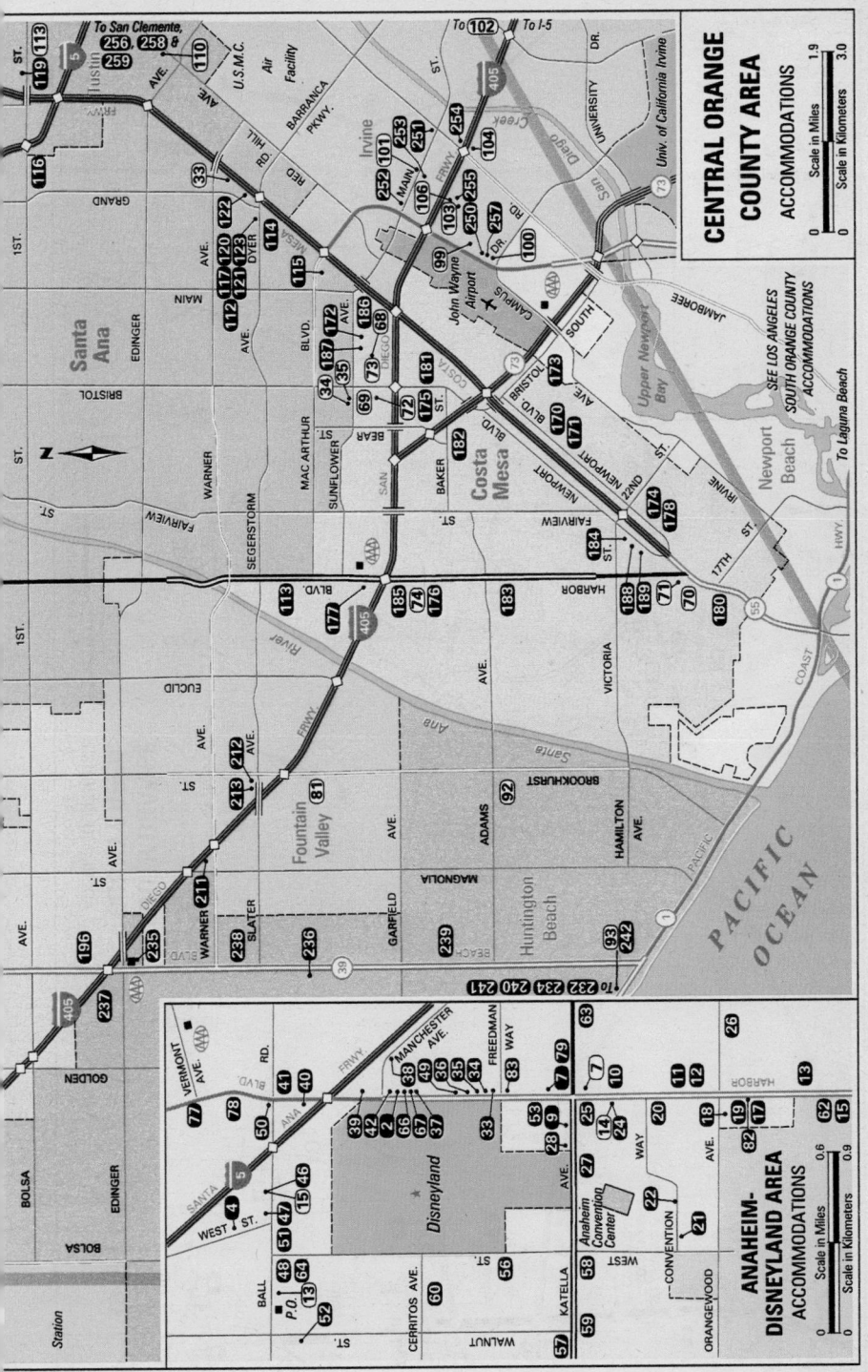

CENTRAL ORANGE COUNTY AREA
ACCOMMODATIONS

Scale in Miles   1.9
Scale in Kilometers   3.0

ANAHEIM-DISNEYLAND AREA
ACCOMMODATIONS

Scale in Miles   0.6
Scale in Kilometers   0.9

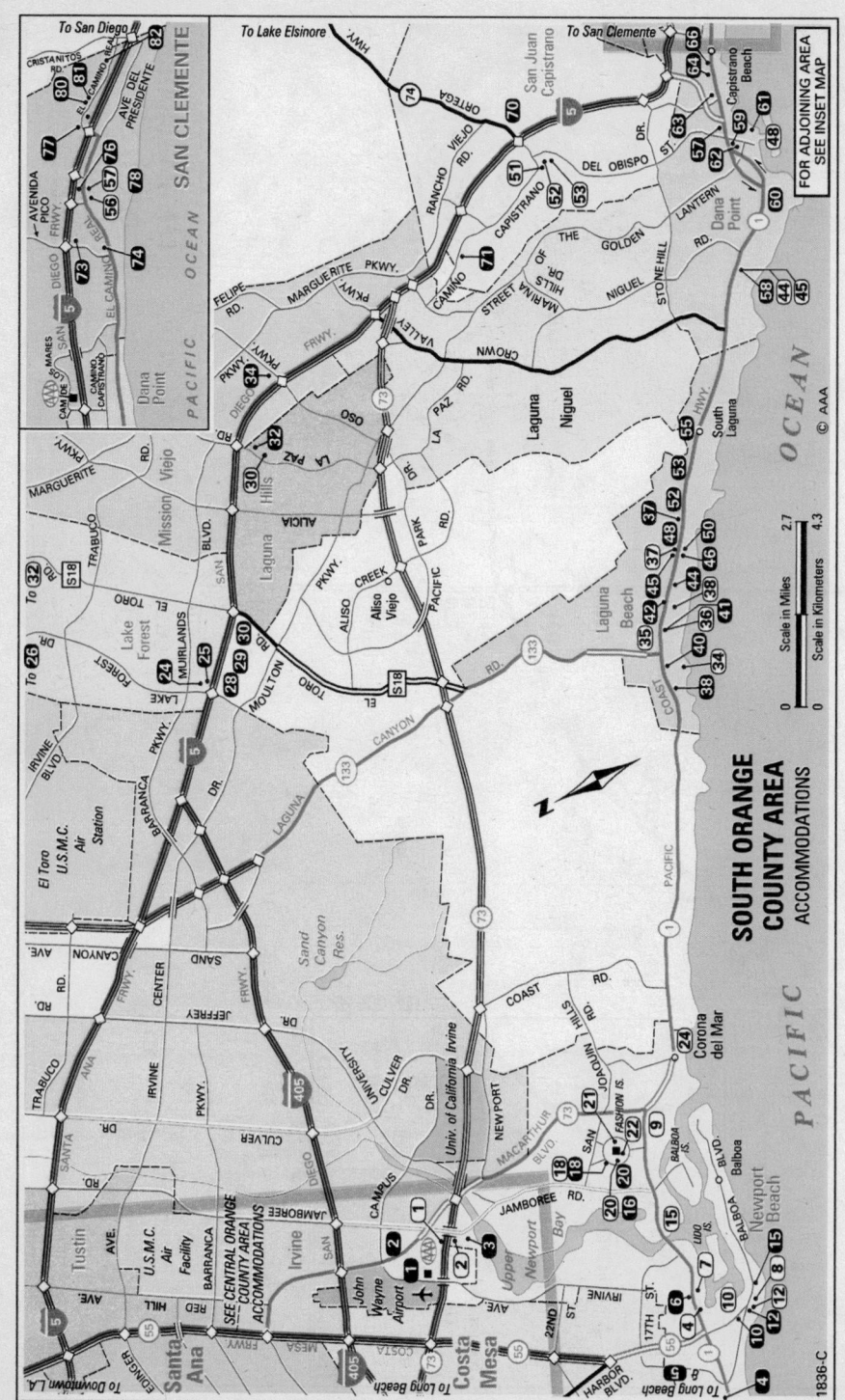

SOUTH ORANGE
COUNTY AREA
ACCOMMODATIONS

1836-C

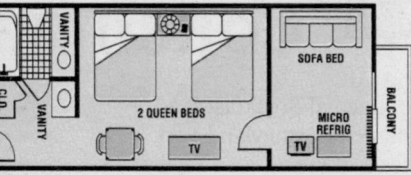
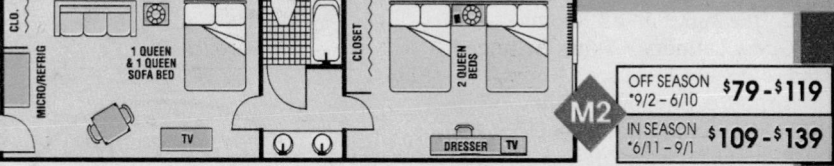
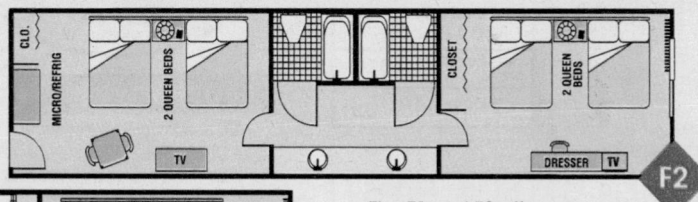
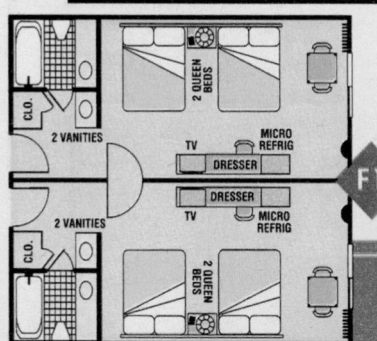
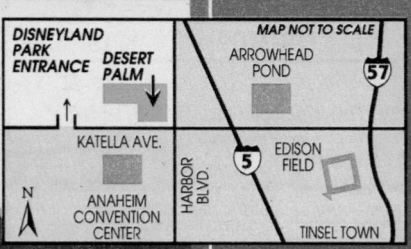

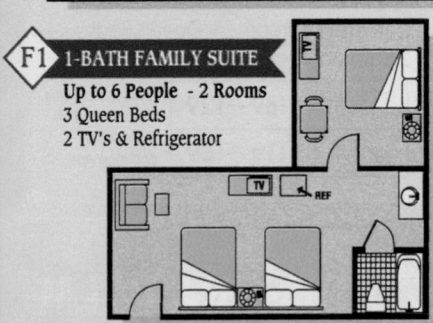
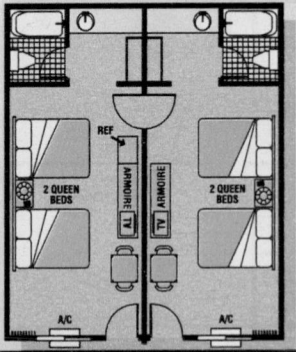

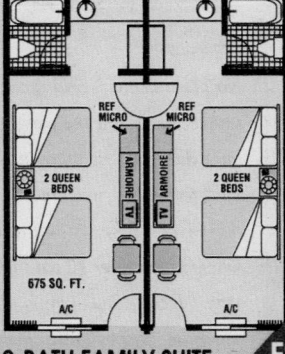
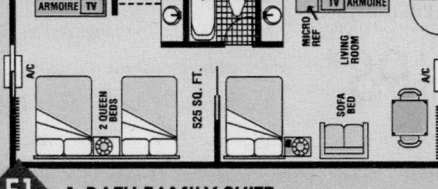

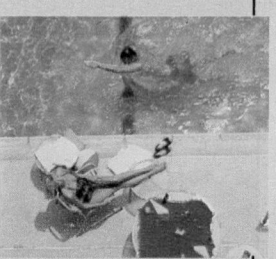
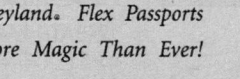

"Suite Dreams" at Disneyland ® Park

Great rooms, 2 1/2 blocks from Disneyland, AND a choice of hot breakfasts every day of your stay.

© Disney

1-4 Persons

$ **59** *

Including
HOT Breakfast!

- Group Rates available
- Disney Flex Packages
- Free Disneyland hourly shuttle
- Deluxe Continental Breakfast
- Ask about hot breakfast upgrade
- Comfortable, spacious guest room
- Deluxe King or Queen sized beds
- In-room refrigerator, coffee maker, hair dryer and safe
- Heated outdoor pool
- Microwave ovens available
- Guest laundry facility
- 25" Remote televisions
- Carrow's restaurant on property

1-4 Persons

$ **49** *

ROOM ONLY

SUITE B
Has 2 rooms with 3 Queen Beds, 1 sofa bed, 2 baths, 2 televisions.
High season $95-$150
Low season $85-$135

1-8 Persons

$ **95** *

Including
HOT Breakfast!

SUITE C

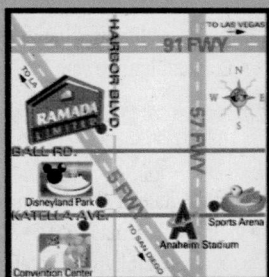

Approved

Award Winning
Gold Key Ramada

Reservations Only
(800) 235-3399

The Name You Can Trust
Local: (714) 999-0684 • Fax: (714) 956-8839
921 S. Harbor Blvd., Anaheim, CA 92805

Rates are subject to change without notice and are based upon availability. 72-Hr Cancellation Notice is required for a full refund. Rates are higher during Summer, Holiday & Special Events.

to Disneyland® Park

$59*⁹⁵

UP TO 4 PERSONS

November thru February........$59⁹⁵*

March, April, May, September
and October from $64⁹⁵*

June, July & August from $74⁹⁵*

*Higher rates apply during holiday periods,
conventions and some weekends.
Rate reflects 10% AAA member discount.

© THE WALT DISNEY COMPANY

Disneyland Park Packages

5 DAYS FOR THE PRICE OF 2!
DISNEYLAND FLEX PASSPORT

Includes: Deluxe Room
- Shuttle to Disneyland Park
- All taxes included
- No charge for kids under 3

PRICE PER PACKAGE **NOT** PER PERSON

Package A: 2 nights accommodations and
1 day admission to Disneyland Park

2 PERSONS	3 PERSONS	4 PERSONS	5 PERSONS
$255	$296	$337	$401

Package B: 2 nights accommodations and
5 days admission to Disneyland Park

2 PERSONS	3 PERSONS	4 PERSONS	5 PERSONS
$309	$377	$445	$536

Package C: 3 nights accommodations and
5 days admission to Disneyland Park

2 PERSONS	3 PERSONS	4 PERSONS	5 PERSONS
$395	$463	$531	$634

June-August Add $25 for Package A & B
Add $35 for Package C

Extra nights available from $59⁹⁵

THE Jolly Roger HOTEL

ANAHEIM—266,400   (See map p. 294; index p. 287)

LODGINGS

ABBY'S ANAHEIMER INN   Phone: (714)774-0211   **57**

3/16-4/30 & 6/1-8/31	1P: $39- 59	2P/1B: $39- 59	2P/2B: $39- 69	XP: $10	F16
2/1-3/15 & 1/1-1/31	1P: $29- 49	2P/1B: $29- 49	2P/2B: $39- 59	XP: $10	F16
5/1-5/31 & 9/1-12/31	1P: $29- 49	2P/1B: $29- 49	2P/2B: $35- 55	XP: $10	F16

Motel   **Location:** At Walnut. 1201 W Katella Ave 92802. Fax: 714/774-0211. **Facility:** 28 rooms. 2 stories; exterior corridors; small heated pool, whirlpool. **Cards:** AE, CB, DI, DS, JC, MC, VI. **Special Amenities:** Early check-in/late check-out and free breakfast. *(See color ad below)*

ALPINE MOTEL   Rates Subject to Change   Phone: 714/535-2186   **28**

6/1-9/5 [CP]	1P: $50- 59	2P/1B: $52- 59	2P/2B: $54- 59	XP: $4
2/1-5/31 & 9/6-1/31 [CP]	1P: $39- 49	2P/1B: $39- 49	2P/2B: $39- 49	XP: $4

Motel   **Location:** 715 W Katella Ave 92802. Fax: 714/535-3714. **Terms:** Reserv deposit. **Facility:** 41 rooms. 7 two-bedroom units. 2 stories; exterior corridors; heated pool. **Dining:** Restaurant nearby. **All Rooms:** combo or shower baths. **Cards:** AE, DI, DS, MC, VI. *(See color ad below)*

(See map p. 294)

ANAHEIM ANGEL INN **Phone:** (714)634-9121
(AAA) (SAVE)
| | 6/15-8/31 | | 1P: | $49- | 54 | 2P/1B: | $54- | 59 | 2P/2B: | $59- | 64 |
| | 2/1-6/14 & 9/1-1/31 | | 1P: | $36- | 39 | 2P/1B: | $39- | 42 | 2P/2B: | $45- | 49 |

◆ **Location:** 1 mi e of I-5, exit Katella Ave. 1800 E Katella Ave at State Clge Blvd 92805. Fax: 714/978-1608.
Motel **Terms:** Reserv deposit; weekly rates. **Facility:** 61 rooms. 2 stories; exterior corridors; heated pool. **Dining:** Restaurant nearby. **Cards:** AE, DS, MC, VI. **Special Amenities: Free room upgrade and preferred room (each subject to availability with advanced reservations).** *(See ad below)*

ANAHEIM CARRIAGE INN **Phone:** (714)740-1440 19
(AAA) (SAVE)
| | 3/12-4/18, 6/11-9/6 & | | | | | | | | | | |
| | 12/17-1/31 [CP] | | 1P: | $59- | 89 | 2P/1B: | $59- | 89 | 2P/2B: | $59- | 89 |
◆◆◆ | 2/1-3/11, 4/19-6/10 & | | | | | | | | | | |
Motel | 9/7-12/16 [CP] | | 1P: | $49- | 79 | 2P/1B: | $49- | 79 | 2P/2B: | $49- | 79 |

Location: Just s of Orangewood Ave. 2125 S Harbor Blvd 92802. Fax: 714/971-5330. **Terms:** Reserv deposit; handling fee imposed. **Facility:** 66 rooms. Limited parking. 3 stories; exterior corridors; heated pool, whirlpool. **Dining:** Coffee shop nearby. **Services:** area transportation, Disneyland Park. **Some Rooms:** 5 efficiencies. **Cards:** AE, CB, DI, DS, JC, MC, VI. **Special Amenities: Free breakfast.** *(See color ad p 303)*

ANAHEIM COACHMAN INN **Phone:** (714)971-5556 82
(AAA) (SAVE)
| | 6/12-9/1 [CP] | | 1P: | $49- | 69 | 2P/1B: | $49- | 69 | 2P/2B: | $49- | 69 |
| | 2/1-6/11 & 9/2-1/31 [CP] | | 1P: | $39- | 59 | 2P/1B: | $39- | 59 | 2P/2B: | $39- | 59 |
◆◆ **Location:** Just s of Orangewood Ave. 2145 S Harbor Blvd 92802. Fax: 714/971-5580. **Facility:** 60 rooms. 5
Motel two-bedroom units. 2 stories; exterior corridors; heated pool, whirlpool. **Cards:** AE, CB, DI, DS, MC, VI. **Special Amenities: Early check-in/late check-out and free breakfast.** IMA.
(See color ad p 286 & p 302)

(See map p. 294)

ANAHEIM COMFORT INN MAINGATE
Phone: (714)750-5211 **13**

			1P:	$59-	99	2P/1B:	$59-	99	2P/2B:	$59-	109	XP:	$5	F18
	6/1-9/3 [CP]													
	2/1-5/31 & 9/4-1/31 [CP]		1P:	$49-	79	2P/1B:	$49-	79	2P/2B:	$49-	89	XP:	$5	F18

Location: 0.8 mi s of Katella Ave. 2200 S Harbor Blvd 92802. **Fax:** 714/750-2226. **Terms:** Reserv deposit.
Motel **Facility:** 66 rooms. 2 stories; exterior corridors; small heated pool, whirlpool. **Cards:** AE, DI, DS, MC, VI.
(See color ad p 286)

ANAHEIM COURTESY LODGE
Rates Subject to Change
Phone: 714/533-2570 **41**

			1P:	$39-	48	2P/1B:	$39-	48	2P/2B:	$39-	48	XP:	$4
	6/6-9/5 [CP]												
	2/1-6/5 & 9/6-1/31 [CP]		1P:	$33-	39	2P/1B:	$33-	39	2P/2B:	$33-	39	XP:	$4

Location: 0.3 mi e of I-5; just e of Harbor Blvd. 414 W Ball Rd 92805. **Terms:** Reserv deposit, 3 day notice.
Motel **Facility:** 26 rooms. 1 two-bedroom unit. 1 kitchen, $5-$7 extra; no utensils; 2 stories; exterior corridors.
Cards: AE, DS, MC, VI. *(See color ad p 309)*

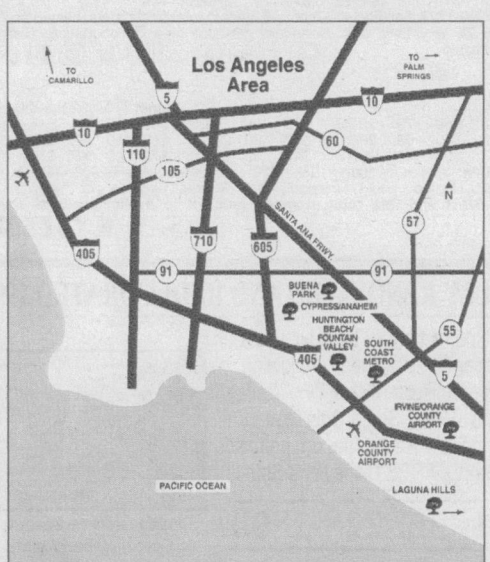

(See map p. 294)

ANAHEIM DAYS INN MAINGATE — Rates Subject to Change — Phone: (714)635-3630 🔢35

4/1-4/15, 6/1-9/4 & 12/20-1/3
[CP] — 1P: $59- 109 — 2P/1B: $59- 109 — 2P/2B: $69- 129 — XP: $10
2/1-3/31, 4/16-5/31,
9/5-12/19 & 1/4-1/31 [CP] — 1P: $49- 89 — 2P/1B: $49- 89 — 2P/2B: $49- 109 — XP: $10
Location: 1604 S Harbor Blvd 92802. Fax: 714/520-3290. **Terms:** Reserv deposit, 3 day notice. **Facility:** 58 rooms. Limited parking. 1 two-bedroom unit. 2 stories; exterior corridors; heated pool, whirlpool. **Dining:** Coffee shop nearby. **Cards:** AE, DI, DS, MC, VI. *(See color ad p 297)*

ANAHEIM DAYS INN PARK SOUTH — Rates Subject to Change — Phone: (714)703-1220 🔢62

6/1-9/4 & 12/20-1/31 [CP] — 1P: $59- 109 — 2P/1B: $59- 109 — 2P/2B: $69- 129 — XP: $10
2/1-5/31 & 9/5-12/19 [CP] — 1P: $49- 89 — 2P/1B: $49- 89 — 2P/2B: $49- 109 — XP: $10
Location: Just s of Orangewood Ave. 2171 S Harbor Blvd 92802. Fax: 714/703-1401. **Terms:** Reserv deposit, 3 day notice. **Facility:** 128 rooms. 2 stories; exterior corridors; heated pool, whirlpool. **Dining:** Coffee shop nearby. **Cards:** AE, DI, DS, MC, VI. *(See color ad p 313)*

ANAHEIM DESERT INN & SUITES — Guaranteed Rates — Phone: (714)772-5050 🔢36

3/12-4/12, 6/11-9/1 &
12/17-1/31 [CP] — 1P: $59- 79 — 2P/1B: $59- 79 — 2P/2B: $69- 89
2/1-3/11, 4/13-6/10 &
9/2-12/16 [CP] — 1P: $44- 69 — 2P/1B: $44- 69 — 2P/2B: $49- 79
Location: 1600 S Harbor Blvd 92802. Fax: 714/778-2754. **Terms:** Reserv deposit; handling fee imposed. **Facility:** 143 rooms. Contemporary exterior with some underground parking. 2 & 3-room suites for 5-10 persons, $64-$169. 12 whirlpool rms, $69-$119 for 2-6 persons; 5 stories; exterior corridors; heated indoor pool, whirlpool. **Dining:** Coffee shop nearby. **Services:** giftshop; area transportation, Disneyland, Conv. Ctr. **Recreation:** Video game room. **Cards:** AE, CB, DI, DS, JC, MC, VI. *(See color ad starting on p 298)*

ANAHEIM DESERT PALM INN & SUITES — Guaranteed Rates — Phone: (714)535-1133 🔢9

3/12-4/12, 6/11-9/1 &
12/17-1/31 [CP] — 1P: $59- 79 — 2P/1B: $59- 79 — 2P/2B: $64- 89
2/1-3/11, 4/13-6/10 &
9/2-12/16 [CP] — 1P: $46- 69 — 2P/1B: $46- 69 — 2P/2B: $49- 79
Location: 631 W Katella Ave 92802. Fax: 714/491-7409. **Terms:** Reserv deposit; handling fee imposed. **Facility:** 105 rooms. Limited parking. 35 two-bedroom units. 35 two-bedroom units for up to 8 persons, $89-$169; 4 stories; interior corridors; heated pool, sauna, whirlpool. **Dining:** Restaurant nearby. **Some Rooms:** whirlpools. **Cards:** AE, CB, DI, DS, JC, MC, VI. *(See color ad starting on p 300)*

ANAHEIM FAIRFIELD INN — Phone: (714)772-6777 🔢42

12/17-1/3 — 1P: $104 — 2P/1B: $104 — 2P/2B: $114
3/26-4/10 — 1P: $94 — 2P/1B: $94 — 2P/2B: $94
5/27-8/28 — 1P: $89 — 2P/1B: $89 — 2P/2B: $94
2/1-3/25, 4/11-5/26,
8/29-12/16 & 1/4-1/31 — 1P: $79 — 2P/1B: $79 — 2P/2B: $84
Location: 1460 S Harbor Blvd 92802. Fax: 714/999-1727. **Facility:** 467 rooms. 9 stories; exterior corridors; heated pool. **Dining:** Restaurant; 6 am-midnight; $6-$9; wine/beer only. **Services:** giftshop; area transportation, Disneyland. **Cards:** AE, CB, DI, DS, MC, VI. *(See color ad below)*

ANAHEIM HERITAGE INN & SUITES — Phone: (714)971-9000 🔢18

6/1-8/31 — 1P: $69- 79 — 2P/1B: $79- 99 — 2P/2B: $99- 120 — XP: $10
9/1-1/2 — 1P: $59- 69 — 2P/1B: $69- 89 — 2P/2B: $89- 110 — XP: $10
2/1-5/31 & 1/3-1/31 — 1P: $39- 49 — 2P/1B: $49- 59 — 2P/2B: $79- 99 — XP: $10
Under major renovation. **Location:** Just w of Harbor Blvd. 620 Orangewood Ave 92802. **Terms:** Reserv deposit. **Facility:** 63 rooms. Heated pool, whirlpool. **All Rooms:** combo or shower baths. **Special Amenities:** Free breakfast and free room upgrade (subject to availability with advanced reservations). *(See color ad p 315)*

DAYS INN

At Disneyland® Park

Located two short blocks from Disneyland® Park

$*49⁰⁰

Double Occupancy

Reservations
(800) 547-8270

- 1-1/2 Blocks from the Anaheim Convention Center.
- Complimentary shuttle service to/from Disneyland® Park & Continental breakfast daily.
- Heated pool and spa
- Refrigerator, hair dryer, and Tea & Coffee makers in all guest rooms. Restaurants within walking distance.
- Non-smoking rooms available.
- Choice of king or 2 queen beds.
- Family units with 4 queen size beds, accommodates up to 8.

	*Rates	
	Off-Season	In-Season
1-King	$49-69	$59-89
2-Queen	$49-69	$59-89

In Season Rates apply during summer, Holidays and Special Events. Limited Availability. Double Occupancy.

2171 South Harbor Blvd. • Anaheim, CA   92802
(714) 703-1220 • Fax (714) 703-1401

*Off season rate; In-season rates apply during Summer, Holidays & Special Events. Subject to Limited Availability.

Use Your AAA Membership Card to SAVE BIG!

Whenever you see the Show Your Card & Save* symbol at thousands of participating businesses, show your AAA membership card for exclusive discounts. Save big on hotel rooms, theme park tickets, car rentals, and more — just for being a AAA member! For more information, call your local AAA office. Have your membership card handy when calling.

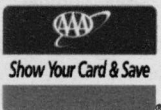

The Show Your Card & Save program is the official discount program of AAA and CAA.
Valid AAA membership card required. Various restrictions apply. Not valid with other discounts.
Good at participating locations only. Offers subject to change without notice. Offers expire 12/31/99.

(See map p. 294)

ANAHEIM HILTON AND TOWERS — Rates Subject to Change — Phone: (714)750-4321 — 22
All Year — 1P: $89- 300 — 2P/1B: $119- 370 — 2P/2B: $119- 370 — XP:$30-60 — F18
Location: Just s of Katella Ave. 777 Convention Way 92802. Fax: 714/740-4460. **Terms:** Reserv deposit, 7 day notice; small pets only. **Facility:** 1576 rooms. Next to Anaheim Convention Center. Large convention resort hotel with many recreational facilities & specialty shops. 96 1- & 2-bedroom suites avail; 14 stories; interior corridors; heated pool, whirlpools. Fee: parking; indoor pool. **Dining:** 2 restaurants, coffee shop, deli; 6 am-midnight; $8-$30; cocktails; sushi bar. **Services:** giftshop. Fee: massage. **Recreation:** children's program, 5/31 & 9/1; golf practice driving net. **Cards:** AE, CB, DI, DS, JC, MC, VI. *(See ad p 119 & p 319)*
Hotel

ANAHEIM ISLANDER INN & SUITES — Guaranteed Rates — Phone: (714)778-6565 — 63
3/12-4/12, 6/11-9/1 &
12/17-1/31 [CP] — 1P: $42- 56 — 2P/1B: $42- 56 — 2P/2B: $46- 69
2/1-3/11, 4/13-6/10 &
9/2-12/16 [CP] — 1P: $36- 46 — 2P/1B: $36- 46 — 2P/2B: $38- 52
Location: 1 blk e of Harbor Blvd. 424 W Katella Ave 92802. Fax: 714/535-6567. **Terms:** Reserv deposit. **Facility:** 34 rooms. 12 two-bedroom units. 2-room units, some with full kitchen, no utensils $65-$89; 2 stories; exterior corridors. **Cards:** AE, CB, DI, DS, JC, MC, VI. *(See color ad below)*
Motel

ANAHEIM MAINGATE INN — Phone: (714)533-2500 — 64
6/1-8/31 [CP] — 1P: $69 — 2P/1B: $69 — 2P/2B: $69
2/1-5/31 & 9/1-1/31 [CP] — 1P: $59 — 2P/1B: $59 — 2P/2B: $59
Location: Just w of I-5 at Ball Rd. 1211 S West St 92802. Fax: 714/520-0578. **Terms:** Reserv deposit. **Facility:** 33 rooms. 2 stories; exterior corridors; whirlpool. **Cards:** AE, DS, MC, VI. **Special Amenities:** Early check-in/late check-out and free breakfast. *(See color ad p 317)*
Motel

ANAHEIM MARRIOTT HOTEL — Phone: 714/750-8000 — 21
All Year — 1P: $169 — 2P/1B: $189 — 2P/2B: $189
Location: Just w of Harbor Blvd. 700 W Convention Way 92802. Fax: 714/750-9100. **Terms:** Check-in 4 pm; reserv deposit; small pets only. **Facility:** 1033 rooms. Adjacent to Anaheim Convention Center. 19 stories; interior corridors; heated indoor/outdoor pool, saunas, whirlpools. Fee: parking. **Dining:** 3 restaurants; 6:30 am-11 pm; $8-$30; cocktails. **Services:** giftshop. **All Rooms:** combo or shower baths. **Cards:** AE, CB, DI, DS, JC, MC, VI.
Hotel

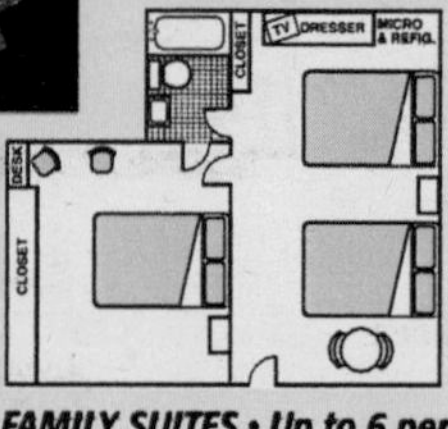

(See map p. 294)

ANAHEIM PENNY SLEEPER INN   Rates Subject to Change   Phone: (714)991-8100   38
ⒶⒶⒶ   3/12-4/12, 6/11-9/7 &
◆◆   12/17-1/3   1P: $59- 79 2P/1B: $59- 79 2P/2B: $69- 89
Motel   2/1-3/11, 4/13-6/10, 9/8-12/16
           & 1/4-1/31   1P: $49- 69 2P/1B: $49- 69 2P/2B: $59- 79
           Location: Adjacent to I-5; northbound Harbor Blvd exit, southbound Katella Ave exit; just e of Harbor Blvd.
1441 S Manchester Ave 92802. Fax: 714/533-6430. **Terms:** Reserv deposit. **Facility:** 189 rooms. 2 stories; exterior corridors;
heated pool. **Services:** giftshop. **Cards:** AE, DS, MC, VI. *(See color ad p 318)*

ASK 🛅 �

ANAHEIM PLAZA HOTEL & SUITES   Phone: (714)772-5900   83
ⒶⒶⒶ SAVE   6/1-9/1 [CP]   1P: $99   2P/1B: $99   2P/2B: $99
◆◆   2/1-5/31 & 9/2-1/31 [CP]   1P: $79   2P/1B: $79   2P/2B: $79
Motor Inn **Location:** 1700 S Harbor Blvd 92802. Fax: 714/772-8386. **Terms:** Package plans. **Facility:** 299 rooms. Large
           fenced swimming pool area. Two rm family suites, $89-$129; 2 stories; exterior corridors; heated pool, whirl-
           pool. **Dining:** Dining room; 6:30 am-11 & 5-10 pm; $8-$15; cocktails. **Services:** giftshop. **Cards:** AE, CB, DI,
DS, MC, VI. **Special Amenities: Free breakfast and preferred room (subject to availability with advanced
reservations).** *(See color ad starting on p 320)*

(See map p. 294)

ANAHEIM STADIUM TRAVELODGE

Phone: (714)634-1920 ⓰

| 6/10-9/10 [CP] | 1P: $54 | 2P/1B: $57 | 2P/2B: $67 |
| 2/1-6/9 & 9/11-1/31 [CP] | 1P: $44 | 2P/1B: $47 | 2P/2B: $57 |

Location: Just w of State College Blvd & Anaheim Stadium. 1700 E Katella Ave 92805. Fax: 714/634-0366. **Terms:** Reserv deposit. **Facility:** 72 rooms. 2 stories; exterior corridors; heated pool, whirlpool. **Cards:** AE, CB, DI, DS, JC, MC, VI. **Special Amenities:** Free breakfast and free newspaper. *(See color ad p 324)*

Motel

BEST WESTERN ANAHEIM INN

Phone: (714)774-1050 ㉞

All Year   1P: $65- 125   2P/1B: $65- 125   2P/2B: $65- 125
Location: 1630 S Harbor Blvd 92802. Fax: 714/776-6305. **Terms:** Reserv deposit. **Facility:** 88 rooms. Limited parking. 5 two-bedroom units. 3 stories; exterior corridors; small heated pool, saunas, whirlpool. **Dining:** Restaurant nearby. **Some Rooms:** kitchen. **Cards:** AE, DI, DS, JC, MC, VI. *(See color ad p 327)*

Motel

777 Convention Way
Anaheim, CA 92802
714-750-4321

AAA members can receive members–only room rates when you
Show Your Card & Save® at the Hilton Anaheim & Towers. We've
recently redecorated and feature on-site Disneyland® Park passports
and free shuttle; a 25,000 square foot fitness center,
shopping and video game arcade; plus seven
restaurants and lounges. **Just call your AAA travel
office or Hilton's private AAA number, 1-800-916-2221.**

from
$**144**-
$**195**
per room
per night

Your key to **savings** is actually a card.

It happens at the Hilton.™

Directly Opposite the Main

ANAHEIM PLAZA
~ HOTEL & SUITES ~

Olympic Size Pool

Unique Resort Hotel

❖ The Parkside Grill offers an excellent menu for breakfast or dinner.

	Harbor Blvd.	Freedman Way
✳ DISNEYLAND PARK®	✳ ANAHEIM PLAZA HOTEL & SUITES	
❖ Convention Center	Katella Ave.	

❖ Seven two story buildings on nine acres surrounded by majestic trees, landscaped walks and flowerbeds.

Entrance to Disneyland Park

Newly Renovated Rooms

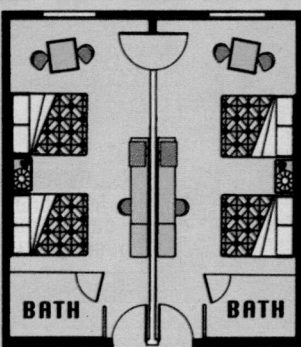

BATH   BATH

DELUXE ROOMS $49-$69*
1-4 PERSONS

6/15 thru 8/31 Add $10
1 King or 2 Queen beds.
TV with SHOWTIME,
and Coffee maker.

FAMILY SUITES $89-$139*
2-8 PERSONS

Two connecting rooms with 2
Double or 2 Queen beds, 2 full
baths, 2 TVs with SHOWTIME,
2 Coffee makers and Refrigerator.

AAA Members Guaranteed Special Amenities
Complimentary Continental Breakfast and Deluxe Rooms

FEATURES: Guest coin laundry • Free Parking • Tour/Bell Desk
In-room Coffee & Tea Maker • Complimentary shuttle to Disneyland Park
Gift Shops • Game Room • Rooms with Balconies and Patios Available

 *Disneyland Park Bargain Fun Packages*

PACKAGE FEATURES: • Accommodations in a spacious room • Continental
Breakfast Daily • Shuttle to Disneyland Park • Disneyland Park Pass
• T-shirt for children age 3 to 11 • All Taxes • Children under 3 Free

PRICE IS PER PACKAGE, NOT PER PERSON

Applicable Dates	1/1-6/14 & 9/1-12/31*			6/15 - 8/31*		
No. Persons	2	3	4	2	3	4
2 Nights, 1 Day Pass	$240	$295	$350	$273	$317	$383
3 Nights, 5 Day Pass	$339	$438	$537	$383	$493	$581
4 Nights, 5 Day Pass	$383	$493	$603	$438	$537	$658
5 Nights, 5 Day Pass	$449	$559	$680	$515	$625	$746

RESERVATIONS 1-800-522-6415

ANAHEIM PLAZA HOTEL & SUITES 1700 S. Harbor Blvd.
Anaheim, CA 92802 714-772-5900 FAX 714-772-8386

** Higher rates apply during Holiday Periods, Special Events and Conventions.
Two day cancellation notice required. Subject to availability. Check-in after 3:00PM*

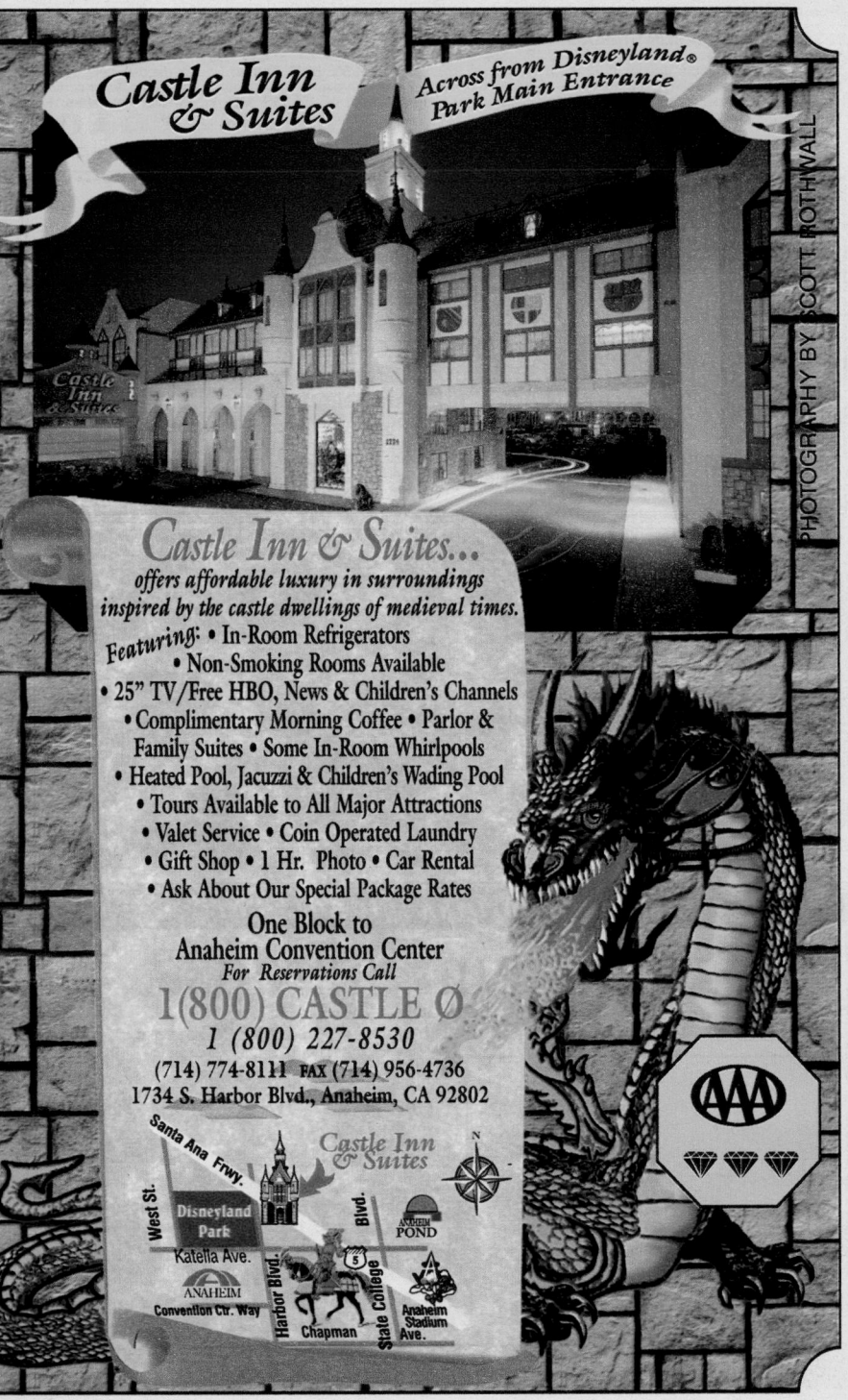

(See map p. 294)

BEST WESTERN ANAHEIM STARDUST   **Phone:** (714)774-7600

AAA   SAVE   All Year [CP]   1P: $54- 89   2P/1B: $54- 89   2P/2B: $54- 89

◆◆   **Location:** Just w of I-5. 1057 W Ball Rd 92802. Fax: 714/535-6953. **Terms:** Reserv deposit; pets, $50 dep
Motel   req. **Facility:** 103 rooms. 14 rooms with balcony. 7 rms with oversized bathtub; 2-3 stories; exterior corridors;
heated pool, whirlpool. **Dining:** Restaurant nearby. **Cards:** AE, DI, DS, MC, VI. **Special Amenities:** Free
breakfast. *(See color ad below)*

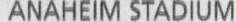

 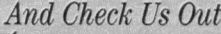

(See map p. 294)

BEST WESTERN COURTESY INN   Phone: (714)772-2470   🗹51

		1P:		2P/1B:		2P/2B:		XP:		
🆎 SAVE	6/12-9/5 & 12/23-12/31 [CP]	1P:	$69- 99	2P/1B:	$69- 99	2P/2B:	$69- 99	XP:	$4	F12
	3/15-6/11 [CP]	1P:	$59- 89	2P/1B:	$59- 89	2P/2B:	$59- 89	XP:	$4	F12
◆ ◆	2/1-3/14, 9/6-12/22 &									
Motel	1/1-1/31 [CP]	1P:	$49- 79	2P/1B:	$55- 79	2P/2B:	$55- 79	XP:	$4	F12

Location: Just w of I-5. 1200 S West St at Ball Rd 92802. Fax: 714/774-3425. **Terms:** Reserv deposit; 3 day notice; weekly rates. **Facility:** 37 rooms. 3 stories; exterior corridors; small pool, whirlpool. **Cards:** AE, CB, DI, DS, JC, MC, VI. **Special Amenities:** Free breakfast. *(See color ad below)*   🖥️ 🏊 🎇 💻 🖨️ 🔌 ⊠

BEST WESTERN PARK PLACE INN   Phone: (714)776-4800   🗹37

		1P:		2P/1B:		2P/2B:	
🆎 SAVE	12/17-1/2 [CP]	1P:	$109- 119	2P/1B:	$109- 119	2P/2B:	$119- 129
	2/1-3/14, 4/11-5/27 &						
◆ ◆ ◆	9/6-12/16 [CP]	1P:	$99- 119	2P/1B:	$99- 119	2P/2B:	$119- 129
Motor Inn	1/3-1/31 [CP]	1P:	$89- 99	2P/1B:	$89- 99	2P/2B:	$109- 119
	3/15-4/10 & 5/28-9/5 [CP]	1P:	$79- 99	2P/1B:	$79- 99	2P/2B:	$99- 109

Location: 1544 S Harbor Blvd 92802. Fax: 714/758-1396. **Terms:** Reserv deposit. **Facility:** 199 rooms. Limited parking, 3 stories; exterior corridors; heated pool, sauna, whirlpool. **Dining:** Restaurant; 7 am-11 pm; $6-$12; cocktails. **Services:** giftshop. **Cards:** AE, CB, DI, DS, JC, MC, VI. **Special Amenities:** Free breakfast. *(See color ad p 327)*   🖥️ 🏨 🎇 🏊 🍴 ⛱️ 🎇 💻 🖨️ 🔌 ⊠

BEST WESTERN PAVILIONS   Phone: (714)776-0140   🗹59

		1P:		2P/1B:		2P/2B:	
🆎 SAVE	All Year	1P:	$59- 129	2P/1B:	$59- 129	2P/2B:	$59- 129

Location: 1 mi w of I-5. 1176 W Katella Ave 92802. Fax: 714/776-5801. **Terms:** Reserv deposit; handling fee imposed. **Facility:** 100 rooms. 1 two-bedroom unit. 2 stories; exterior corridors; heated pool, sauna, whirlpool. **Dining:** Restaurant nearby. **Cards:** AE, CB, DI, DS, MC, VI. **Special Amenities:** Free newspaper. *(See color ad p 327)*   🖥️ 🏊 📺 🎇 VCR 💻 🖨️ 🔌 ⊠

BEST WESTERN RAFFLES INN & SUITES   Phone: (714)750-6100   🗹11

		1P:		2P/1B:		2P/2B:		XP:		
🆎 SAVE	3/26-4/10, 5/28-8/28 &									
	12/17-1/1 [CP]	1P:	$79- 99	2P/1B:	$79- 99	2P/2B:	$79- 99	XP:	$10	F17
◆ ◆ ◆	2/1-3/25, 4/11-5/27,									
Motel	8/29-12/16 & 1/2-1/31 [CP]	1P:	$59- 85	2P/1B:	$59- 85	2P/2B:	$59- 85	XP:	$10	F17

Location: 0.3 mi s of Katella Ave. 2040 S Harbor Blvd 92802. Fax: 714/740-0639. **Terms:** Pets, $10 extra charge. **Facility:** 122 rooms. Limited parking. 8 two-bedroom units. Units for up to 4 persons, $59-$79; 3 stories; exterior corridors; heated pool, whirlpool. **Services:** giftshop. **All Rooms:** extended cable TV. **Some Rooms:** whirlpools. **Cards:** AE, CB, DI, DS, MC, VI. **Special Amenities:** Early check-in/late check-out and free breakfast. *(See color ad p 326)*   🖥️ 🐕 🎇 🏊 ⛱️ 🎇 💻 🖨️ 🔌 ⊠

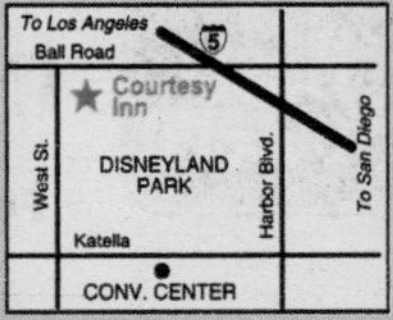

(See map p. 294)

BEST WESTERN STOVALL'S INN   Phone: (714)778-1880   58

	3/19-4/10, 5/28-9/5 &				
AAA SAVE	12/17-12/31	1P: $90- 110	2P/1B: $96- 114	2P/2B: $98- 116	XP: $6-10 F17
◆◆	2/1-3/18, 4/11-5/27, 9/6-12/16				
Motel	& 1/1-1/31	1P: $70- 88	2P/1B: $76- 90	2P/2B: $76- 94	XP: $6-10 F17

Location: Katella Ave at S West St. 1110 W Katella Ave 92802. Fax: 714/778-3805. **Terms:** Reserv deposit.
Facility: 290 rooms. Landscaped in topiary trees & bushes. 3 stories; exterior corridors; heated pool, wading pool, whirlpools.
Dining: Coffee shop nearby. **Services:** giftshop. **Cards:** AE, CB, DI, DS, JC, MC, VI. **Special Amenities:** Early check-in/late check-out and free room upgrade (subject to availability with advanced reservations).
(See color ad p 327)

CANDY CANE INN   Phone: (714)774-5284   53

	All Year [CP]	1P: $74- 129	2P/1B: $74- 129	2P/2B: $74- 129

AAA SAVE
◆◆◆
Motel

Location: Just n of Katella Ave. 1747 S Harbor Blvd 92802. Fax: 714/772-5462. **Terms:** Reserv deposit.
Facility: 172 rooms. Beautifully landscaped grounds. 2 stories; exterior corridors; heated pool, wading pool, whirlpool. **Dining:** Restaurant nearby. **Services:** giftshop; area transportation, Disneyland hotel & park. **Cards:** AE, DI, DS, MC, VI. *(See color ad p 328)*

(See map p. 294)

CAROUSEL INN & SUITES
Phone: (714)758-0444 [66]
All Year [CP]   1P: $59- 69 2P/1B: $69- 79 2P/2B: $89- 99 XP: $12   F17
Location: 1530 S Harbor Blvd 92802. Fax: 714/772-9960. **Terms:** Reserv deposit. **Facility:** 131 rooms. 2-5 stories; exterior corridors; rooftop heated pool. **Dining:** Restaurant nearby. **Cards:** AE, DS, MC, VI.
Motel

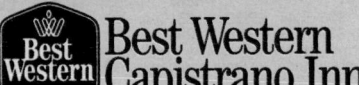

CASTLE INN & SUITES
Phone: (714)774-8111 [7]
All Year   1P: $72- 82 2P/1B: $72- 82 2P/2B: $72- 92
Location: Just n of Katella Ave. 1734 S Harbor Blvd 92802. Fax: 714/956-4736. **Terms:** Reserv deposit. **Facility:** 198 rooms. 2 room suites with microwave & refrigerator, $92-$122; 4 stories; exterior corridors; heated pool, wading pool, whirlpool. **Dining:** Restaurant nearby. **Services:** giftshop; area transportation; Disneyland Park. **Some Rooms:** whirlpools. **Cards:** AE, DI, DS, MC, VI.
Motel
(See color ad starting on p 322, p 341 & p 324 & p 333)

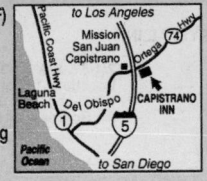

For <u>guaranteed</u> rates, you MUST show your membership card.

(See map p. 294)

COMFORT INN & SUITES   **Phone:** (714)772-8713   **75**

All Year [CP]   1P: $69- 79 2P/1B: $79- 89 2P/2B: $89- 99 XP: $5
Location: Just w of I-5, Katella Ave exit. 300 E Katella Way 92802. Fax: 714/778-1235. **Terms:** Reserv deposit, 3 day notice. **Facility:** 136 rooms. 5 stories; interior corridors; heated pool, whirlpool. **Services:** area transportation, Disneyland Park. **Cards:** AE, DI, DS, JC, MC, VI. **Special Amenities: Free breakfast and free newspaper.** *(See color ad p 330)*

Motel

COMFORT INN & SUITES/ANAHEIM WEST   **Phone:** (714)220-0100   **84**

6/1-9/4 [CP]   1P: $79- 99 2P/1B: $79- 99 2P/2B: $79- 99
2/1-5/31 & 9/5-1/31 [CP] 1P: $69- 99 2P/1B: $69- 99 2P/2B: $69- 99
Location: On SR 39; just n of Ball Rd. 727 S Beach Blvd 92804. **Terms:** Reserv deposit. **Facility:** 101 rooms. 3 stories; interior/exterior corridors; heated pool, whirlpool. **Cards:** AE, CB, DI, DS, MC, VI. **Special Amenities: Free breakfast and free room upgrade (subject to availability with advanced reservations).** *(See color ad p 331)*

Motel

COMFORT SUITES AT THE PARK   **Phone:** (714)971-3553   **17**

6/1-8/31 [CP]   1P: $79- 99 2P/1B: $79- 99 2P/2B: $89- 119 XP: $10   F17
2/1-5/31 & 9/1-1/31 [CP] 1P: $69- 89 2P/1B: $69- 89 2P/2B: $79- 109 XP: $10   F17
Location: 2141 S Harbor Blvd 92802. Fax: 714/971-4609. **Facility:** 94 rooms. Limited parking. 4 stories; exterior corridors; small heated pool, whirlpool. **Some Rooms:** whirlpools. **Cards:** AE, CB, DI, DS, JC, MC, VI. *(See color ad p 332)*

Motel

CRYSTAL INN   Rates Subject to Change   **Phone:** 714/535-8446   **61**

6/6-9/5   1P: $36- 44 2P/1B: $36- 44 2P/2B: $36- 44 XP: $4-5
2/1-6/5 & 9/6-1/31   1P: $29- 39 2P/1B: $29- 39 2P/2B: $29- 39 XP: $4-5
Location: 1.5 mi w of I-5. 2123 W Lincoln Ave 92801. **Terms:** Reserv deposit, 3 day notice. **Facility:** 23 rooms. 1 two-bedroom unit. 3 efficiencies, $5-$7 extra, no utensils; 1 story; exterior corridors; small pool, whirlpool. **All Rooms:** combo or shower baths. **Cards:** AE, DS, MC, VI. *(See color ad p 334)*

Motel

◆ Diamonds are a guest's best friend. ◆

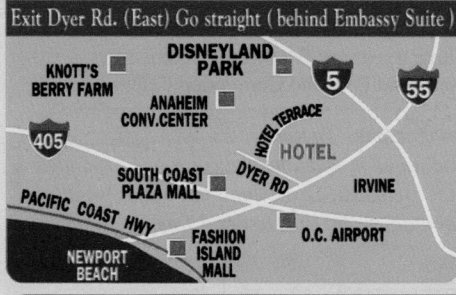

2 Blocks to Disneyland® Park
2 Blocks to Convention Center

Recently Built
AAA ◆◆◆ Rating

$**69**

**1-4 Persons
June thru Aug.
Add $10**

ACCOMMODATIONS

Rooms with 2 double beds,
2 queen or 1 King. Executive
rooms w/King bed & Sleeper
sofa. All rooms have data ports,
fridges, micros, hair dryers, iron/board. NS & HC .

FEATURES & SERVICES   Remote cable TV

& pay per view movies • Heated Pool & Spa • Spacious lobby lounge with 24
hour coffee • Free ice, safe deposit boxes, and parking • Car rental, valet,
laundry, FAX and copying services • Meeting room • Tours arranged
with front door pick up and front door airport service

COMPLIMENTARY   Deluxe Expanded Breakfast • Shuttle to
Disneyland Park and Convention Center

*Disneyland® Park
Bargain Packages*

Package Features Include:
*Accommodations in spacious deluxe room, expanded
continental breakfast, Disneyland Park pass, shuttle
to park, and all taxes. Kids under 3 free.*

**PRICE IS PER
PACKAGE
NOT PER
PERSON**

PERSONS	2	3	4	2	3	4
2 NIGHTS 1 DAY PASS	$214	$252	$290	$234	$272	$310
2 NIGHTS 5 DAY PASS	$274	$342	$410	$294	$362	$430
3 NIGHTS 5 DAY PASS	$343	$411	$479	$373	$441	$509
4 NIGHTS 5 DAY PASS	$412	$480	$548	$452	$520	$588
5 NIGHTS 5 DAY PASS	$481	$549	$617	$531	$599	$667

JAN.-MAY/SEPT.-DEC.   JUNE - AUG.

Comfort
Inn & Suites

300 E. Katella Way
Anaheim, CA 92802
714-772-8713
Fax 714-778-1235

Reservations
1-800-982-8239
email: merco816@msn.com

*Subject to Availability. Higher Rates Holiday Periods Conventions & Special Events. 72 Hr. Cancellation Policy

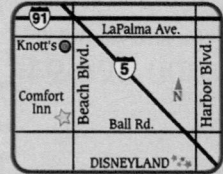

(See map p. 294)

DAYS INN ANAHEIM WEST　　　　　　　　　　　　　　　　　**Phone:** (714)520-0101　48

| | 3/3-1/3 | 1P: | $69 | 2P/1B: | $69 | 2P/2B: | $79 | XP: | $8 | F17 |
| | 2/1-3/2 & 1/4-1/31 | 1P: | $42 | 2P/1B: | $42- | 49 2P/2B: | $49 | XP: | $8 | F17 |

Location: 1030 W Ball Rd 92802. Fax: 714/758-9406. **Terms:** Reserv deposit. **Facility:** 45 rooms. 2 two-bedroom units. 2 stories; exterior corridors; heated pool, whirlpool. **Services:** area transportation, Disneyland. **Some Rooms:** whirlpools. **Cards:** AE, CB, DI, DS, JC, MC, VI. **Special Amenities:** Free breakfast and free newspaper. *(See color ad below)*

Motel

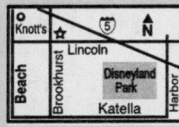

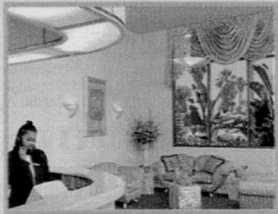

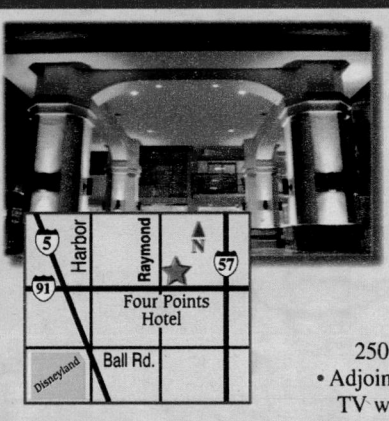

(See map p. 294)

DAYS INN SUITES

Phone: (714)533-8830   [50]

(AAA) [SAVE]

3/26-4/17, 6/1-9/1 &
12/17-1/2 [CP]   2P/2B: $59- 145
2/1-3/25, 4/18-5/31,

◆◆

Motel

9/2-12/16 & 1/3-1/31 [CP]   2P/2B: $49- 130
Location: Just n of Ball Rd. 1111 S Harbor Blvd 92805. Fax: 714/758-0573. **Terms:** Reserv deposit.
Facility: 81 rooms. 2 stories; exterior corridors; heated pool, whirlpool. **Dining:** Coffee shop nearby. **All Rooms:** extended cable TV. **Cards:** AE, CB, DS, MC, VI. **Special Amenities:** Free breakfast and free room upgrade (subject to availability with advanced reservations). *(See color ad p 335)*   [symbols]

DISNEYLAND HOTEL

Rates Subject to Change   Phone: (714)778-6600   [60]

(AAA)

All Year   1P: $190- 225   2P/1B: $190- 225 2P/2B: $190- 225   XP: $15   F17

◆◆◆

Resort
Complex

Location: 1150 W Cerritos Ave 92802. Fax: 714/956-6597. **Terms:** Reserv deposit, 3 day notice.
Facility: 1036 rooms. Rooms in towers & 2-story buildings on several acres of nicely landscaped grounds. Many recreational & shopping facilities. 1, 2 & 3 bedroom suites $325-$675; 2-14 stories; interior/exterior corridors; heated pool, whirlpool; playground. Fee: parking. **Dining:** 3 restaurants; 6 am-1 am; $6-$42; cocktails. **Services:** giftshop. **Recreation:** waterslide; Disneyland Monorail Station, Man made sand beach. **Cards:** AE, CB, DI, DS, JC, MC, VI. *(See color ad p 335)*   [symbols]

THE DISNEYLAND PACIFIC HOTEL

Rates Subject to Change   Phone: (714)999-0990   [56]

(AAA)

All Year   1P: $190- 225   2P/1B: $190- 225 2P/2B: $190- 225   XP: $15   F17

◆◆◆

Hotel

Location: Just n of Katella Ave. 1717 S West St 92802. Fax: 714/776-5763. **Terms:** Reserv deposit, 3 day notice. **Facility:** 502 rooms. All recreational & entertainment facilities at adjacent Disneyland Hotel avail to hotel guests. 15 stories; interior corridors; heated pool, whirlpool. Fee: parking. **Dining:** Dining room, restaurant; 6:30 am-11 pm; $7-$24; cocktails. **Services:** giftshop. **Recreation:** video game room, ping pong, shuffleboard court. **Cards:** AE, CB, DI, DS, JC, MC, VI. *(See color ad p 337)*   [symbols]

DOLPHIN'S COVE RESORT

Phone: (714)980-0830   [26]

(AAA) [SAVE]

All Year   1P: $150- 200   2P/1B: $150- 200 2P/2B: $150- 200

◆◆◆

Condo
Complex

Location: Just e of Harbor Blvd. 465 W Orangewood Ave 90802. Fax: 714/750-1647. **Terms:** Check-in 4 pm; reserv deposit; handling fee imposed. **Facility:** 136 rooms. Beautifully landscaped grounds. 1-, 2- & 3-bedroom units with 1 or 2 bathrooms. Full kitchen. 16 three-bedroom units. 2 stories; exterior corridors; heated pool, wading pool, whirlpool. **Dining:** Pool snack bar, limited hrs. **Recreation:** pool equipment, ping pong table, pool table. **All Rooms:** kitchens, extended cable TV. **Cards:** DS, MC, VI.   [symbols]

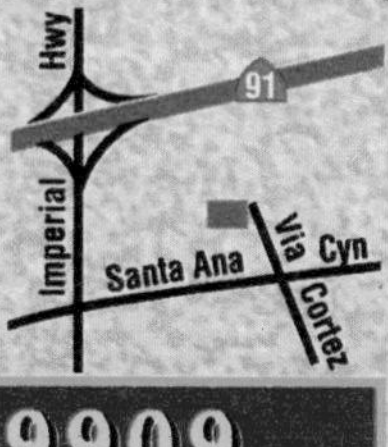

There's only **one** Disneyland, but there are **two** Disneyland® Resort Hotels.

Now serving breakfast with a sprinkling of magic.

Rise and shine with Disney Character wake up calls.

Stay at an official Disneyland Resort Hotel. Enjoy award-winning dining, swimming pools, tropical beach and fitness centers. Plus Early Admission to select attractions 1½ hours before Disneyland Park opens.* For a AAA Disneyland vacation, visit a AAA Travel Office and ask about the AAA member benefit or call **(714) 956-MICKEY.**

PACIFIC HOTEL
Disneyland.

Disneyland.
Hotel

*Available with valid Disneyland Passport, does not operate daily. AAA members must present membership card upon check-in. Rooms subject to availability. Advance reservations required. Complimentary Disneyland Resort Hotels parking. ©Disney

(See map p. 294)

ECONO LODGE/MAINGATE   Phone: (714)535-7878

		1P:	$50-	70	2P/1B:	$55-	75	2P/2B:	$55-	90	XP: $5-10	F1
6/1-8/31 [CP]												
3/1-5/31 [CP]		1P:	$45-	60	2P/1B:	$50-	65	2P/2B:	$50-	65	XP: $5-10	F1
2/1-2/28 & 9/1-1/31 [CP]		1P:	$40-	55	2P/1B:	$45-	60	2P/2B:	$45-	60	XP: $5-10	F1

Motel   **Location:** Just n of Ball Rd. 871 S Harbor Blvd 92805. **Fax:** 714/535-8186. **Terms:** Reserv deposit.
Facility: 51 rooms. 3 stories; exterior corridors; heated pool, whirlpool. **Some Rooms:** whirlpools.
Cards: AE, DI, DS, MC, VI. **Special Amenities:** Early check-in/late check-out and free breakfast. *(See color ad p 339)*

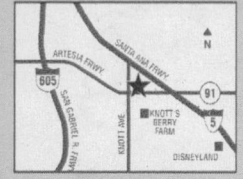

EMBASSY SUITES-DISNEYLAND PARK AREA   Rates Subject to Change   Phone: (714)632-1221

All Year   1P: $129- 199   2P/1B: $129- 199   2P/2B: $129- 199   XP: $10-20   F1
Suite Motor Inn **Location:** Adjacent to SR 91, Glassell St exit. 3100 E Frontera St 92806. Fax: 714/632-9963. **Facility:** 22
rooms. Attractively decorated & landscaped atrium area. 7 stories; interior corridors; heated indoor pool.
Services: giftshop; area transportation. **Cards:** AE, CB, DI, DS, JC, MC, VI. *(See ad below)*

(See map p. 294)

FOUR POINTS HOTEL ANAHEIM BY SHERATON Phone: (714)774-8899
AAA SAVE All Year 1P: $99 2P/1B: $99 2P/2B: $100 XP: $10 F10
Too new to rate. **Location:** Just e of Harbor Blvd. 515 W Katella Ave 92802. Fax: 714/774-7722.
FYI **Terms:** Reserv deposit. **Facility:** 105 rooms. 4 stories; interior corridors; heated pool, sauna, whirlpool.
Dining: Restaurant; 6:30 am-midnight; $8-$16; cocktails. **Services:** area transportation, local attractions.
Motor Inn **Cards:** AE, DI, DS, MC, VI. *(See color ad p 339)*

HAWTHORN SUITES, LTD Rates Subject to Change Phone: (714)535-7773 [3]
◆◆◆ 6/15-9/8 & 12/15-12/31 [BP] 1P: $109- 209 2P/1B: $109- 209 2P/2B: $109- 209 XP: $10 F17
Suite Motel 3/2-4/15 [BP] 1P: $89- 189 2P/1B: $89- 189 2P/2B: $89- 189 XP: $10 F17
2/1-3/1 & 1/1-1/31 [BP] 1P: $79- 159 2P/1B: $79- 159 2P/2B: $79- 159 XP: $10 F17
4/16-6/14 & 9/9-12/14 [BP] 1P: $99- 109 2P/1B: $99- 109 2P/2B: $99- 109 XP: $10 F17
Location: Just n of Katella Ave. 1752 S Clementine St 92802. Fax: 714/776-9073. **Facility:** 130 rooms. 7 two-bedroom 2-bath suites, $139-$189 for up to 8 persons; 4 stories; interior corridors; heated pool. **Services:** giftshop. **Cards:** AE, CB, DI, DS, JC, MC, VI. *(See color ad p 310)*

HOLIDAY INN ANAHEIM AT THE PARK Phone: (714)758-0900 [40]
AAA SAVE 3/26-4/10, 5/28-8/28 &
12/17-1/31 1P: $109- 139 2P/1B: $109- 139 2P/2B: $109- 139
◆◆◆ 2/1-3/25, 4/11-5/27 &
Motor Inn 8/29-12/16 1P: $89- 129 2P/1B: $89- 129 2P/2B: $89- 129
Location: Adjacent to I-5, southbound exit Ball Rd, northbound Harbor Blvd. 1221 S Harbor Blvd at Ball Rd 92805. Fax: 714/533-1804. **Terms:** Reserv deposit. **Facility:** 254 rooms. Attractively landscaped pool area. 5 stories; exterior corridors; heated pool, whirlpool. **Dining:** Restaurant; 6:30 am-10 pm; $10-$15; cocktails. **Services:** giftshop; area transportation, major attractions & malls. **Recreation:** video game room. **Cards:** AE, CB, DI, DS, JC, MC, VI.
(See color ad below)

HOLIDAY INN EXPRESS Phone: (714)772-7755 [79]
AAA SAVE 6/3-9/3 [CP] 1P: $95- 99 2P/1B: $95- 99 2P/2B: $95- 99 XP: $10
2/1-6/2 & 9/4-1/31 [CP] 1P: $89- 95 2P/1B: $89- 95 2P/2B: $89- 95 XP: $10
◆◆◆ **Location:** Just e of Harbor Blvd. 435 W Katella Ave 92802. Fax: 714/772-2727. **Facility:** 104 rooms. Underground parking. 5 whirlpool rms, extra charge; 4 stories; interior/exterior corridors; heated pool, sauna, whirlpool. **Dining:** Restaurant nearby. **Cards:** AE, DI, MC, VI. **Special Amenities:** Free breakfast.
Motel
(See color ad p 341)

(See map p. 294)

HOWARD JOHNSON PLAZA HOTEL
Phone: (714)776-6120 **39**

(AAA) (SAVE)

Motor Inn

3/26-4/10, 5/28-8/28 & 12/17-12/31		1P: $74		2P/1B: $74		2P/2B: $84- 94
2/1-3/25, 4/11-5/27,						
8/29-12/16 & 1/1-1/31		1P: $69		2P/1B: $69		2P/2B: $74- 84

Location: Adjacent west side I-5, exit Harbor Blvd. 1380 S Harbor Blvd 92802. Fax: 714/533-3578. **Terms:** Reserv deposit. **Facility:** 284 rooms. 7 stories; interior/exterior corridors; heated pool, wading pool, whirlpool. **Dining:** Restaurant; 6 am-midnight; $6-$12; wine/beer only. **Services:** giftshop. **Recreation:** video game room. **Cards:** AE, CB, DI, DS, JC, MC, VI. **Special Amenities:** Free room upgrade and preferred room (each subject to availability with advanced reservations).** (See color ad p 342 & opposite inside back cover)

HYATT REGENCY ALICANTE
Phone: (714)750-1234 **15**

(AAA) (SAVE)

Hotel

All Year   1P: $139- 155   2P/1B: $164- 180   2P/2B: $164- 180   XP: $25   F18
Location: Chapman Ave at Harbor Blvd. 100 Plaza Alicante 92840 (PO Box 4669). Fax: 714/740-0465. **Facility:** 396 rooms. Contemporary decor. 17-story atrium area. 13 two-room suites with wet bar & refrigerator, $225; 17 stories; interior corridors; heated pool, whirlpool; 2 tennis courts. Fee: parking. **Dining:** Dining room, restaurant; 6:30 am-midnight; $7-$22; cocktails. **Services:** giftshop; area transportation, Disneyland & Conv Center. **Recreation:** video game room, fee for driving range & putting green. **Some Rooms:** whirlpools. **Cards:** AE, CB, DI, DS, JC, MC, VI. (See color ad p 565 & p 304)

(See map p. 294)

JOLLY ROGER INN HOTEL　　　　　　　　　　　　　　　　　　　Phone: (714)772-7621　25
All Year　　　　　1P: $79- 139　2P/1B:　$79- 139　2P/2B:　$79- 139　XP: $10　F12

Location: 640 W Katella Ave at Harbor Blvd 92802. Fax: 714/772-2308. **Facility:** 238 rooms. 10 two-bedroom units. 1 unit with private pool, $200; 2-5 stories; interior/exterior corridors; heated pool, wading pool, whirlpool. Motor Inn　**Dining:** Dining room, coffee shop; 6:30 am-12:30 am; $10-$18; cocktails. **Services:** giftshop. **All Rooms:** combo or shower baths. **Cards:** AE, CB, DI, DS, JC, MC, VI. **Special Amenities:** Preferred room (subject to availability with advanced reservations). *(See color ad p 306)*

MAGIC INN & SUITES　　　　　　　Rates Subject to Change　　　　　　　Phone: (714)772-7242　27
◆　　　　　6/1-12/31　　　1P: $49- 52　2P/1B:　$49- 52　2P/2B:　$55- 59　XP: $5　F17
Motel　　　2/1-5/31 & 1/1-1/31　1P: $45- 49　2P/1B:　$45- 49　2P/2B:　$49- 54
Location: 1 mi w of I-5, adjacent to Anaheim Convention Center. 1030 W Katella Ave 92802. Fax: 714/772-5461. **Terms:** Reserv deposit. **Facility:** 217 rooms. Limited parking. 37 two-bedroom units. 3 stories; exterior corridors; heated pool. **All Rooms:** combo or shower baths. **Cards:** AE, DS, MC, VI.

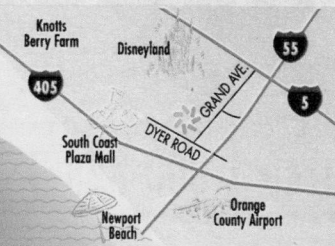

(See map p. 294)

PARK INN INTERNATIONAL Phone: (714)635-7275 **2**
(AAA) [SAVE] All Year [CP] 1P: $119- 219 2P/1B: $119- 219 2P/2B: $119- 219
◆◆◆ **Location:** 1520 S Harbor Blvd 92802. Fax: 714/635-7276. **Terms:** Reserv deposit. **Facility:** 121 rooms.
Motel Across from Disneyland Park. 4th floor sundeck & pool area with good view of surrounding area. 39 two-
bedroom units. 39 suites with wetbar, microwave & refrigerator; 5 stories; exterior corridors; heated pool, whirl-
pool. **Dining:** Restaurant nearby. **Services:** giftshop; area transportation, Disneyland Park.
Some Rooms: whirlpools. **Cards:** AE, DI, DS, MC, VI. *(See color ad p 344)*

[icons]

PARK VUE INN Phone: (714)772-3691 **49**
(AAA) [SAVE] 9/16-1/31 [CP] 1P: $49- 59 2P/1B: $59- 69 2P/2B: $69- 79 XP: $10 F14
◆ 6/15-9/15 [CP] 1P: $59 2P/1B: $69 2P/2B: $79 XP: $10 F14
Motel 2/1-6/14 [CP] 1P: $49 2P/1B: $49 2P/2B: $49 XP: $10 F14
Location: 1570 S Harbor Blvd 92802. Fax: 714/635-5305. **Terms:** Reserv deposit, 7 day notice; package
plans. **Facility:** 88 rooms. 6 two-bedroom units. 2 stories; exterior corridors; heated pool, wading pool.
Dining: Restaurant nearby. **Services:** giftshop. **Cards:** AE, DS, MC, VI. *(See color ad below)*

[icons]

PEACOCK SUITE RESORT Phone: (714)535-8255 **44**
(AAA) [SAVE] 6/1-8/31 [CP] 1P: $89- 109 2P/1B: $89- 109 2P/2B: $99- 119
◆◆◆ 2/1-5/31 & 9/1-1/31 [CP] 1P: $79- 89 2P/1B: $79- 89 2P/2B: $89- 109
Suite Motel **Location:** Just n of Katella Ave. 1745 S Anaheim Blvd 92802. Fax: 714/535-8914. **Terms:** Check-in 4 pm;
reserv deposit. **Facility:** 140 rooms. Sun deck on 4th floor. 12 two-bedroom 2-bath suites, $129-$159 for up to
8 persons; 4 stories; interior corridors; heated indoor/outdoor pool, whirlpools. **Services:** giftshop; area
transportation, Disneyland Park. **Recreation:** video game room. **Some Rooms:** whirlpools. **Cards:** AE, CB, DI, DS, MC, VI.
Special Amenities: Free breakfast and preferred room (subject to availability with advanced reservations).

[icons]

QUALITY HOTEL MAINGATE Phone: (714)750-3131 **20**
(AAA) [SAVE] All Year 1P: $99- 139 2P/1B: $105- 150 2P/2B: $105- 150 XP: $10 F17
◆◆◆ **Location:** Just s of Katella Ave. 616 Convention Way at Harbor Blvd 92802. Fax: 714/750-9027.
Motor Inn **Terms:** Check-in 4 pm; reserv deposit; small pets only. **Facility:** 284 rooms. 96 rooms with microwave & refrigerator, $20 extra; 9 stories; interior corridors; heated pool. Fee: parking. **Dining:** Dining room, coffee
shop; 6 am-10 pm; $7-$18; cocktails. **Services:** giftshop. **Recreation:** recreation room with pool table &
video games. **Cards:** AE, CB, DI, DS, JC, MC, VI. **Special Amenities:** Early check-in/late check-out and free room
upgrade (subject to availability with advanced reservations). *(See color ad p 308)*

[icons]

(See map p. 294)

RADISSON HOTEL MAINGATE-ANAHEIM   Rates Subject to Change   **Phone:** (714)750-2801   🔟
◆◆◆   All Year   1P: $95- 105   2P/1B: $95- 105   2P/2B: $95- 105   XP: $10   F18
Motor Inn   **Location:** 1850 S Harbor Blvd 92802. Fax: 714/971-4754. **Facility:** 314 rooms. 5-8 stories; interior corridors; heated pool. **Services:** giftshop; area transportation. **Cards:** AE, DI, DS, JC, MC, VI.

(ASK) 🛏️ 🐕 📶 🏊 🍴 🛎️ 🛗 🎾 🖥️ 📇 📠 🚫 ⏲️

RAMADA INN CONESTOGA AT DISNEYLAND PARK   **Phone:** (714)535-0300   52
🅰🅰🅰 (SAVE)   6/1-9/5   1P: $99   2P/1B: $99   2P/2B: $119   XP: $10   F17
            2/1-5/31 & 9/6-1/31   1P: $94   2P/1B: $94   2P/2B: $109   XP: $10   F17
◆◆◆   **Location:** 0.5 mi w of I-5; just s of Ball Rd. 1240 S Walnut St 92802. Fax: 714/491-8953. **Terms:** Check-in 4
Hotel   pm; reserv deposit. **Facility:** 252 rooms. 2-6 stories; interior corridors; heated pool, whirlpool.
Dining: Restaurant, coffee shop; 6:30 am-1 & 5:30-9:30 pm; $8-$15; cocktails; also, Cattleman's Wharf, see
separate listing. **Services:** giftshop; area transportation, to Disneyland Park. **Recreation:** video game room. **Cards:** AE, DI,
DS, JC, MC, VI. *(See color ad opposite title page & p 345)*   🛏️ 🐕 📶 🏊 🍴 🛎️ 🛗 🎾 🖥️ 🔲 📠 🚫

(See map p. 294)

RAMADA LIMITED DISNEYLAND AREA Phone: (714)995-5700 85 F18

Motel

6/1-9/30 [CP]	1P:	$85	2P/1B:	$90	2P/2B:	$95	XP:	$10
2/1-5/31 & 10/1-1/31 [CP]	1P:	$55	2P/1B:	$60	2P/2B:	$65		

Location: ON SR 39, 0.5 mi n of Ball Rd. 800 S Beach Blvd 92804. Fax: 714/826-6021. **Terms:** Check-in 4 pm; handling fee imposed. **Facility:** 78 rooms. 3 stories; exterior corridors; heated pool, whirlpool. **All Rooms:** combo or shower baths. **Cards:** AE, CB, DI, DS, MC, VI. **Special Amenities:** Free breakfast and free room upgrade (subject to availability with advanced reservations). (See color ad below)

RAMADA LIMITED MAINGATE NORTH Phone: (714)999-0684 78

Motel

6/1-9/7 [CP]	1P:	$59- 69	2P/1B:	$59- 69	2P/2B:	$69- 79
2/1-5/31 & 9/8-1/31 [CP]	1P:	$39- 49	2P/1B:	$39- 49	2P/2B:	$49- 59

Location: Just n of Ball Rd. 921 S Harbor Blvd 92805. Fax: 714/956-8839. **Terms:** Reserv deposit, 3 day notice. **Facility:** 93 rooms. 1 two-bedroom unit. 2 stories; exterior corridors; heated pool. **Dining:** Restaurant nearby. **Cards:** AE, CB, DI, DS, JC, MC, VI. (See color ad p 305)

(See map p. 294)

RAMADA MAINGATE SAGA INN   Phone: (714)772-0440   [33]

| | 3/16-9/30 [CP] | 1P: $79- 89 | 2P/1B: $79- 99 | 2P/2B: $79- 99 | XP: $10 | F18 |
| | 2/1-3/15 & 10/1-1/31 [CP] | 1P: $69- 78 | 2P/1B: $79- 89 | 2P/2B: $79- 89 | XP: $10 | F18 |

(AAA) (SAVE)   ♦♦♦   Motel   **Location:** 1650 S Harbor Blvd 92802. Fax: 714/991-8219. **Terms:** Reserv deposit, 3 day notice. **Facility:** 185 rooms. 7 whirlpool rms, extra charge. 8 two-room suites, $90-$120; 3 stories; exterior corridors; heated pool, whirlpool. **Dining:** Restaurant nearby. **Services:** giftshop; area transportation, Disneyland Park. **Cards:** AE, CB, DI, DS, JC, MC, VI. **Special Amenities:** Free breakfast and preferred room (subject to availability with advanced reservations). *(See color ad p 311 & p 349)*

🆂♦ 🏊 ⑪ 🛆 📶 ⌨ 🎥 Ⓥⓒⓡ 🖨 🛅 ✕

RAMADA NEAR DISNEYLAND PARK   Phone: (714)978-8088   [5]

| | 3/15-9/15 | 1P: $69- 79 | 2P/1B: $79- 89 | 2P/2B: $79- 89 | XP: $10 | F17 |
| | 2/1-3/14 & 9/16-1/31 | 1P: $59- 69 | 2P/1B: $69- 79 | 2P/2B: $69- 79 | XP: $10 | F17 |

(AAA) (SAVE)   ♦♦   Motor Inn   **Location:** 0.8 mi e of I-5, Katella Ave exit. 1331 E Katella Ave 92805. Fax: 714/937-5622. **Facility:** 232 rooms. 2 stories; exterior corridors; heated pool, saunas, whirlpool. **Dining:** Restaurant; 6 am-10 pm; $5-$10; cocktails. **Services:** giftshop; area transportation. **Cards:** AE, CB, DI, DS, MC, VI. **Special Amenities:** Free newspaper and free room upgrade (subject to availability with advanced reservations).

🆂♦ 🛗 🐾 🏊 ⑪ 🛆 🕯 🎥 🍽 🖥 🖨 🛅 ⑪ ✕

(See map p. 294)

RED ROOF INN   Phone: (714)635-6461

	6/1-9/30	1P: $62	2P/1B: $69	2P/2B: $76	XP: $7	F18
	5/1-5/31	1P: $55	2P/1B: $62	2P/2B: $69	XP: $7	F18
	2/1-4/30 & 10/1-1/31	1P: $51	2P/1B: $58	2P/2B: $65	XP: $7	F18

Motel **Location:** Just s of SR 91. 1251 N Harbor Blvd 92801. Fax: 714/502-9014. **Terms:** Pets. **Facility:** 117 rooms. 3 stories; exterior corridors; heated pool, whirlpool. **Cards:** AE, CB, DI, DS, JC, MC, VI. **Special Amenities:** Free local telephone calls. *(See color ad below)*

RESIDENCE INN BY MARRIOTT   Rates Subject to Change   Phone: 714/533-3555
◆◆◆   All Year [CP]   1P: $178- 224   2P/1B: $178- 224 2P/2B: $194- 224
Apartment **Location:** Just sw of I-5, exit Katella Ave. 1700 S Clementine St at Freedman Way 92802.
Motel Fax: 714/535-7626. **Terms:** Check-in 4 pm. **Facility:** 200 rooms. Nicely landscaped grounds. Many rooms with fireplace. Complimentary barbecue Thurs evening in summer. 57 two-bedroom units. 4 rooms with private patio & outdoor whirlpool, $259; 2 stories; exterior corridors; heated pool. **Services:** giftshop; area transportation. **Recreation:** sports court. **All Rooms:** kitchens. **Cards:** AE, CB, DI, DS, MC, VI. *(See color ad p 351)*

(See map p. 294)

SHERATON-ANAHEIM HOTEL

AAA SAVE — ◆◆◆ — Hotel

All Year   1P: $90   2P/1B: $90   2P/2B: $90   XP: $20   **46** F17
Location: Adjacent to I-5. 1015 W Ball Rd 92802. Fax: 714/535-3889. **Facility:** 490 rooms. Medieval castle exterior. Nicely landscaped grounds. 21 two-rm suites; 4 stories; interior corridors; heated pool, whirlpool. **Dining:** Restaurant; 6 am-11 pm; $8-$16; cocktails; also, Garden Court Bistro, see separate listing. **Services:** giftshop; area transportation, Disneyland. **Recreation:** game room with pool tables, video games, air hockey & miscellaneous electronic games. **Cards:** AE, CB, DI, DS, JC, MC, VI. **Special Amenities:** Free newspaper.

SUPER 8 MOTEL

AAA SAVE — ◆◆ — Motel

6/10-9/6 & 12/15-1/4 [CP]   1P: $55   2P/1B: $55   2P/2B: $65   XP: $10   **4** F18
2/1-6/9, 9/7-12/14 & 1/5-1/31 [CP]
[CP]   1P: $45   2P/1B: $45   2P/2B: $55   XP: $10   F18
Location: Just n of Ball Rd. 915 S West St 92802. Fax: 714/778-3878. **Facility:** 111 rooms. 3 stories; exterior corridors; heated pool, whirlpool. **Dining:** Restaurant nearby. **All Rooms:** combo or shower baths. **Cards:** AE, CB, DI, DS, MC, VI. **Special Amenities:** Free breakfast and free local telephone calls. (See color ad p 353)

SUPER 8 MOTEL DISNEYLAND PARK

AAA — ◆◆ — Motel

All Year   Rates Subject to Change   Phone: 714/778-6900   **8**
   1P: $69   2P/1B: $69   2P/2B: $69
Location: Just e of Harbor Blvd. 415 W Katella Ave 92802. Fax: 714/535-5659. **Terms:** Reserv deposit, 14 day notice. **Facility:** 173 rooms. 2 stories; exterior corridors; heated pool, whirlpool. **Dining:** Restaurant nearby. **Services:** giftshop. **Cards:** AE, DI, DS, JC, MC, VI.

TRAVELODGE INTERNATIONAL INN

AAA SAVE — ◆◆ — Motel

6/1-9/5 [CP]   1P: $69-79   2P/1B: $79-98   2P/2B: $79-98   XP: $8   **12** F17
3/22-5/31 & 9/6-1/31 [CP]   1P: $69   2P/1B: $69-79   2P/2B: $69-79   XP: $8   F17
2/1-3/21 [CP]   1P: $59   2P/1B: $69   2P/2B: $69   XP: $8   F17
Location: Just n of Orangewood Ave. 2060 S Harbor Blvd 92802. Fax: 714/971-2706. **Terms:** Reserv deposit, 3 day notice. **Facility:** 119 rooms. Tudor style exterior. Limited parking. 3 two-bedroom units. 3 stories; exterior corridors; heated pool, whirlpool. **Dining:** Coffee shop nearby. **All Rooms:** combo or shower baths. **Some Rooms:** 6 efficiencies, no utensils. **Cards:** AE, CB, DI, DS, MC, VI. **Special Amenities:** Free breakfast and free newspaper. (See color ad p 353)

TROPICANA INN

AAA SAVE — ◆◆ — Motel

All Year [CP]   1P: $99-189   2P/1B: $99-189   2P/2B: $99-189   **67**
Location: 1540 S Harbor Blvd 92802. Fax: 714/635-1535. **Terms:** Reserv deposit. **Facility:** 195 rooms. Limited parking. Across from Disneyland Park. 6 two-bedroom units. 14 efficiencies, $15 extra charge. 4 suites with whirlpool, $110-$190; 3 stories; interior/exterior corridors; heated pool, whirlpool. **Dining:** Restaurant nearby. **Services:** giftshop; area transportation, to Disneyland & Conv Ctr. **All Rooms:** combo or shower baths. **Cards:** AE, DI, DS, MC, VI. (See color ad p 344)

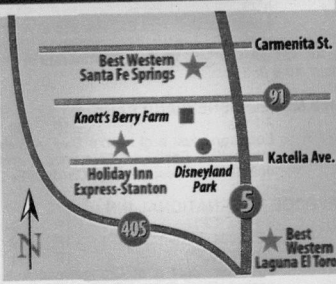

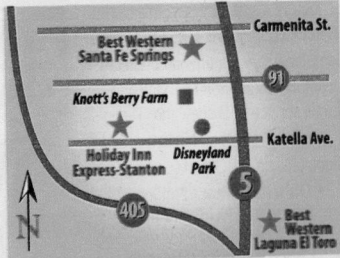

(See map p. 294)

WESTCOAST ANAHEIM HOTEL   **Phone:** (714)750-1811   24

All Year   1P: $99- 109   2P/1B: $99- 109 2P/2B: $99- 109 XP: $15   F18

(AAA) (SAVE) **Location:** Just s of Katella Ave. 1855 S Harbor Blvd 92802. Fax: 714/971-3626. **Terms:** Reserv deposit, 3

◆◆◆   day notice. **Facility:** 500 rooms. Many rooms with patio & balcony. 14 stories; interior corridors; heated pool,

Hotel   whirlpool. Fee: parking. **Dining:** Restaurant, coffee shop; 6 am-11 pm; $7-$18; cocktails; also, Overland

        Stage Restaurant, see separate listing. **Services:** giftshop; area transportation, Disneyland. **Cards:** AE, CB,

DI, DS, JC, MC, VI. **Special Amenities: Free room upgrade (subject to availability with advanced reservations).**

RESTAURANTS

THE CATCH   **Lunch:** $10-$14   **Dinner:** $20-$31   **Phone:** 714/634-1829   6

◆◆   **Location:** 0.3 mi s of Katella Ave, opposite Anaheim Stadium. 1929 S State College Blvd 92806.

Steak and   **Hours:** 11:30 am-2:30 & 5-9:30 pm, Fri-10 pm, Sat 5 pm-10 pm, Sun 5 pm-9 pm. Closed major holidays.

Seafood   **Reservations:** suggested. **Features:** children's menu; carryout; cocktails & lounge; valet parking; a la carte.

        Attractive 1920's decor. **Cards:** AE, CB, DI, DS, MC, VI.

(See map p. 294)

CATTLEMAN'S WHARF **Dinner:** $18-$37 **Phone:** 714/535-1622 ⑬
◆◆◆   **Location:** 1160 W Ball Rd 92802. **Hours:** 5 pm-10 pm, Sun 10 am-2 & 5-10 pm. **Reservations:** suggested.
American   **Features:** casual dress; Sunday brunch; children's menu; cocktails & lounge; entertainment; fee for valet parking; a la carte. Attractive restaurant with 5 theme dining rooms. Nice selection of beef, steaks, prime rib, seafood & poultry. Smoke free premises. **Cards:** AE, MC, VI.   ✕

GARDEN COURT BISTRO **Lunch:** $7-$11 **Dinner:** $9-$18 **Phone:** 714/778-1700 ⑮
◆◆   **Location:** In the Sheraton-Anaheim Hotel. 1015 W Ball Rd 92802. **Hours:** 6 am-2 & 5-11 pm.
American   **Features:** casual dress; children's menu; health conscious menu; cocktails & lounge; a la carte. Salad, sandwiches, chicken, steak, seafood & prime rib. A few Japanese & Italian entrees. Patio dining in season.
Smoke free premises. **Cards:** AE, CB, DI, DS, JC, MC, VI.   ✕

HANSA HOUSE SMORGASBORD **Lunch:** $6 **Dinner:** $10 **Phone:** 714/750-2411 ⑦
Ⓐ   **Location:** Just s of Katella Ave. 1840 S Harbor Blvd 92802. **Hours:** 7 am-11 & noon-9 pm.
◆◆   **Features:** Sunday brunch; children's menu; salad bar; cocktails. Scandinavian decor. Large selection of salads & entrees served buffet style. Smoke free premises. **Cards:** AE, DS, MC, VI.
Ethnic   ✕

MR STOX RESTAURANT **Lunch:** $10-$16 **Dinner:** $14-$26 **Phone:** 714/634-2994 ③
Ⓐ   **Location:** 0.3 mi e of I-5. 1105 E Katella Ave 92805. **Hours:** 11:30 am-10 pm, Sat from 5:30 pm, Sun 5:30-9
◆◆◆   pm. Closed major holidays, 1/1 & 12/25. **Reservations:** suggested. **Features:** semi-formal attire; children's
American   menu; cocktails & lounge; entertainment; fee for valet parking; a la carte. Pleasant dining featuring California contemporary cuisine. Limited menu 2:30 pm-5:30 pm. **Cards:** AE, CB, DI, DS, MC, VI.   ✕

OVERLAND STAGE RESTAURANT **Dinner:** $14-$21 **Phone:** 714/750-1811 ⑭
◆◆   **Location:** Just s of Katella Ave; in Westcoast Anaheim Hotel. 1855 S Harbor Blvd 92802. **Hours:** 5 pm-10
American   pm. **Reservations:** suggested. **Features:** casual dress; children's menu; carryout; salad bar; cocktails & lounge. Attractive Western decor. Features grilled steaks, seafood, poultry & pasta. Smoke free premises.
Cards: AE, CB, DI, DS, JC, MC, VI.   ✕

PLANTATION RESTAURANT **Lunch:** $4 **Dinner:** $6-$8 **Phone:** 714/870-1020 ⑯
◆   **Location:** 0.3 mi w of Raymond Ave. 601 E Orangethorpe Ave 92801. **Hours:** 11 am-8 pm. Closed: 12/25 &
American   Mon. **Features:** casual dress; children's menu; early bird specials; carryout; beer & wine only; cafeteria.
Attractive decor. Smoke free premises. **Cards:** DS, MC, VI.   ✕

THEE WHITE HOUSE RESTAURANT **Lunch:** $9-$16 **Dinner:** $16-$26 **Phone:** 714/772-1381 ②
◆◆◆   **Location:** Just n of Ball Rd. 887 S Anaheim Blvd 92805. **Hours:** 11:30 am-2 & 5:30-10 pm, Sat & Sun from
Northern   5 pm. Closed: 12/25. **Reservations:** suggested. **Features:** cocktails; fee for valet parking; a la carte. Fine
Italian   dining in a restored home with colonial theme. Outdoor seating, weather permitting. Smoke free premises.
Cards: AE, MC, VI.   ✕

ANAHEIM HILLS   (See map p. 294; index p. 291)

LODGINGS

BEST WESTERN ANAHEIM HILLS **Phone:** (714)779-0252 🔲106
Ⓐ ⓢⒶⓥⒺ   All Year [CP] 1P: $74- 104 2P/1B: $79- 104 2P/2B: $84- 114 XP: $7 F12
◆◆◆   **Location:** 0.3 mi n of SR 91; exit Imperial Hwy. 5710 E La Palma Ave 92807. **Fax:** 714/693-1073.
Motel   **Terms:** Reserv deposit; weekly rates; pets, $5. **Facility:** 120 rooms. Landscaped courtyard. 3 miles south of
Richard Nixon Library. Attractively decorated rooms. 1 room with pet run. 16 two-room suites with refrigerator & microwave; 2 stories; interior/exterior corridors; heated pool, sauna, steamroom, indoor whirlpool.
Dining: Restaurant nearby. **Services:** area transportation, to major attractions. **Cards:** AE, CB, DI, DS, JC, MC, VI.
Special Amenities: Free breakfast and free local telephone calls.

🆂🅾 🐕 🔧 🎛 ➦ 🛗 ✈ 🛥 💪 🍴 📼 ▣ ▢ 🔒 ✕

HANFORD HOTEL ANAHEIM HILLS Guaranteed Rates **Phone:** (714)921-1100 🔲107
Ⓐ   6/15-8/31 [CP] 1P: $79- 89 2P/1B: $79- 89 2P/2B: $79- 89 XP: $5 F17
◆◆◆   2/1-6/14 & 9/1-1/31 [CP] 1P: $69- 79 2P/1B: $69- 79 2P/2B: $69- 79 XP: $5 F17
Motel   **Location:** Adjacent to SR 91, exit Imperial Ave, just s to Santa Ana Canyon Rd, just e to Via Cortez. 201 N
Via Cortez St 92807. **Fax:** 714/637-8790. **Facility:** 163 rooms. Located adjacent to Canyon Plaza Shopping
Center. Nicely decorated rooms. 25 whirlpool rms, extra charge; 4 stories; exterior corridors; heated pool,
sauna, whirlpool. **Dining:** Restaurant nearby. **Cards:** AE, DI, DS, MC, VI. *(See color ad p 336)*

🆂🅾 🔧 ➦ 🛗 🛥 💪 🍴 ▣ 🔒 🔒 Ⓘ ✕

RESTAURANTS

FOSCARI ITALIAN RESTAURANT **Lunch:** $8-$15 **Dinner:** $8-$24 **Phone:** 714/779-1777 ㉕
◆◆   **Location:** Located in Imperial Promenade, corner of La Palma Ave & Imperial Hwy. 5645 E La Palma Av
Italian   Hwy 92807. **Hours:** 11:30 am-2 & 5-10 pm, Sat & Sun 5 pm-10 pm. Closed: 11/25 & 12/25.
Reservations: suggested. **Features:** casual dress; children's menu; carryout; cocktails. Bistro style
restaurant. Selection of pasta, meat & fish entrees excellently prepared. Delivery within 5 mi; $3.50. Popular restaurant -
reservations a must on weekends. Smoke free premises. **Cards:** AE, DI, DS, MC, VI.   ✕

FOXFIRE RESTAURANT **Lunch:** $9-$15 **Dinner:** $16-$29 **Phone:** 714/974-5400 ㉖
◆◆◆   **Location:** Adjacent to SR 91, Imperial Hwy exit; in Canyon Plaza Shopping Center. 5717 E Santa Ana
American   Canyon Rd 92807. **Hours:** 11:30 am-2:30 & 5-9 pm, Fri-Sat from 5 pm, Sun 10 am-2 & 5-9 pm. Closed
major holidays. **Reservations:** suggested. **Features:** casual dress; Sunday brunch; children's menu;
cocktails & lounge; entertainment. Dining in casual elegance. Patio seating avail. **Cards:** AE, CB, DI, MC, VI.   ✕

MANDARIN TASTE RESTAURANT **Lunch:** $5-$10 **Dinner:** $7-$19 **Phone:** 714/974-8889 ㉗
◆◆   **Location:** 0.4 mi w of Imperial Hwy. 5555 E Santa Ana Canyon Rd 92807. **Hours:** 11 am-10 pm. Closed:
Chinese   11/25. **Features:** casual dress; Sunday brunch; children's menu; early bird specials; health conscious menu;
carryout; cocktails; a la carte. Hunan & Szechuan cuisine served in an attractive setting. Smoke free
premises. **Cards:** AE, MC, VI.   ✕

ANDERSON—8,300

LODGINGS

AMERIHOST INN-ANDERSON
Phone: (530)365-6100
(AAA) (SAVE) All Year [CP]   1P: $60- 75   2P/1B: $65- 80   2P/2B: $69- 79   XP: $10   F17
◆◆◆ **Location:** Northbound exit off I-5 hwy 273, e Deschutes; southbound exit Deschutes Rd w. 2040 Deschutes
Motel Rd 96007. Fax: 530/365-3231. **Terms:** Small pets only. **Facility:** 61 rooms. 5 whirlpool rooms, extra charge;
interior corridors; heated indoor pool, sauna, whirlpool. **Dining:** Coffee shop nearby. **All Rooms:** combo or
shower baths. **Cards:** AE, CB, DI, DS, JC, MC, VI. **Special Amenities: Free breakfast and free**
newspaper. *(See color ad p 284)*   🖧 📶 🎙️ 🍳 ⊃ 🍽️ ✈️ 🎥 💻 🖵 🛏️ 🔋 🔟 ❄️ ⊠

ANDERSON VALLEY INN   Rates Subject to Change   Phone: (530)365-2566
(AAA) All Year [CP]   1P: $45   2P/1B: $55   2P/2B: $55   XP: $5   D12
◆◆ **Location:** E of & adjacent to I-5, exit Central Anderson. 2861 Mc Murry Dr 96007. Fax: 530/378-2810.
Motel **Terms:** Handling fee imposed; pets. **Facility:** 62 rooms. 2 stories; exterior corridors; small pool.
Dining: Coffee shop nearby. **Cards:** AE, CB, DI, DS, MC, VI.   🐾 ⊃ 🍽️ 🎥 ⊠

BEST WESTERN KNIGHTS INN   Guaranteed Rates   Phone: (530)365-2753
◆◆ All Year   1P: $47- 52   2P/1B: $51- 56   2P/2B: $53- 58   XP: $4   F12
Motel **Location:** Exit I-5 at the Central Anderson, Lassen Park exit. 2688 Gateway Dr 96007. Fax: 530/365-6083.
Terms: Reserv deposit. **Facility:** 40 rooms. 2 stories; exterior corridors. **Cards:** AE, CB, DI, DS, MC, VI.
(ASK) 🖧 🐾 🎙️ ⊃ 🍽️ 🎥 💻 🖵 🛏️ ⊠

RESTAURANT

AMIGO'S ON THE RIVER   **Lunch:** $6-$12   **Dinner:** $8-$12   Phone: 530/365-6142
◆ **Location:** E of I-5, exit Riverside, 1 mi to Sacramento River. 1542 Claude Ln 96049. **Hours:** 11 am-9 pm,
Mexican Fri & Sat-10 pm. Closed: 12/25 & Easter. **Features:** casual dress; children's menu; cocktails; a la carte. All
year enclosed patio, opened for outside dining in summer; steak, seafood, vegetarian & salads featured. On
the Sacramento River. Smoke free premises. **Cards:** AE, MC, VI.   ⊠

ANGELS CAMP—2,400

LODGINGS

ANGELS INN MOTEL
Phone: (209)736-4242
(AAA) (SAVE) 5/1-9/30   1P: $65   2P/1B: $65- 150 2P/2B: $65- 150 XP: $5   F12
◆◆◆ 2/1-4/30 & 10/1-1/31   1P: $65- 120 2P/1B: $65- 120 2P/2B: $65- 120 XP: $5   F12
Motel **Location:** SR 49, n end of town. 600 N Main 95221 (PO Box 1121). Fax: 209/736-6758. **Terms:** Reserv
deposit; pets, $40 dep req. **Facility:** 57 rooms. Large comfortable rooms. 2 stories; exterior corridors.
Dining: Coffee shop nearby. **Recreation:** seasonal pool. **Some Rooms:** efficiency. **Cards:** AE, DS, MC, VI.
(See color ad below)   🖧 🐾 🎙️ ⊃ 🍽️ 🏊 📺 🎥 VCR 💻 🖵 🛏️ ⊠

GOLD COUNTRY INN
Phone: (209)736-4611
(AAA) (SAVE) All Year   1P: $49   2P/1B: $54   2P/2B: $59   XP: $5   F10
◆◆ **Location:** 1 mi s of jct SR 49 & SR 4. 720 S Main St 95222 (PO Box 188). Fax: 209/736-4832.
Motel **Terms:** Reserv deposit. **Facility:** 40 rooms. Comfortable rooms. 2 stories; exterior corridors. **Dining:** Coffee
shop nearby. **Cards:** AE, DS, MC, VI. **Special Amenities: Free local telephone calls.**
🍽️ 🎥 💻 🖵 ⊠

ANTIOCH—62,200

LODGINGS

BEST WESTERN HERITAGE INN
Phone: (925)778-2000
(AAA) (SAVE) All Year [CP]   1P: $60- 75   2P/2B: $65- 80   XP: $5   F12
◆◆◆ **Location:** Exit SR 4 at Somersville Rd. 3210 Delta Fair Blvd 94509. Fax: 925/778-2000. **Facility:** 73 rooms.
Motel 26 whirlpool rms, extra charge; 3 stories; exterior corridors; whirlpool. **Dining:** Coffee shop nearby.
Cards: AE, CB, DI, DS, JC, MC, VI. **Special Amenities: Free breakfast and free local telephone calls.**
🖧 🎙️ 🎙️ ⊃ 🍽️ 🎥 💻 🖵 🛏️ ⊠

RAMADA INN
◆◆ Motel
All Year [CP]   Rates Subject to Change   **Phone:** 925/754-6600
1P: $69- 99 2P/1B: $69- 99 2P/2B: $79   XP: $10   F12
Location: At Hwy 4 & Somersville Rd. 2436 Mahogany Way 94509. Fax: 925/754-6828. **Terms:** Reserv deposit. **Facility:** 116 rooms. Complimentary evening social Wed. 3 stories; exterior corridors.
Services: area transportation. **All Rooms:** combo or shower baths. **Cards:** AE, CB, DI, DS, JC, MC, VI.
(See color ad opposite title page)

RESTAURANT

RIVERVIEW LODGE RESTAURANT   **Lunch:** $5-$20   **Dinner:** $7-$20   **Phone:** 925/757-2272
◆ Seafood
Location: 0.5 mi n off SR 4 on river, at foot of I St. 94509. **Hours:** 11 am-11:30 pm. Closed: 12/25.
Reservations: suggested. **Features:** children's menu; cocktails & lounge; a la carte. Rustic decor. Varied menu; steak specialties. **Cards:** AE, CB, DI, DS, MC, VI.

APTOS—7,000—*See also CAPITOLA, FELTON, SANTA CRUZ & SCOTTS VALLEY.*

LODGINGS

BAYVIEW HOTEL
◆◆ Historic Bed & Breakfast
All Year [CP]   Rates Subject to Change   **Phone:** (831)688-8654
2P/2B: $90- 160 XP: $20
Location: 1 mi ne of SR 1, Seacliff exit; in Aptos Village. 8041 Soquel Dr 95003. Fax: 831/688-5128. **Terms:** Reserv deposit, 7 day notice. **Facility:** 11 rooms. 1878 Victorian, convenient to Nisene Marks S P. 2 rms with fireplace & oversize soaking tub; 3 stories, no elevator; interior corridors; smoke free premises.
All Rooms: combo or shower baths. **Some Rooms:** color TV. **Cards:** AE, MC, VI.

BEST WESTERN SEACLIFF INN
◆◆◆ Motor Inn
Fri & Sat 4/2-10/30 [EP]   1P: $129   2P/1B: $149   2P/2B: $139   XP: $10   F16
Sun-Thurs 4/2-10/30 [CP]   1P: $119   2P/1B: $139   2P/2B: $129   XP: $10   F16
10/31-1/31 [EP]   1P: $99   2P/1B: $119   2P/2B: $109   XP: $10   F16
2/1-4/1 [EP]   1P: $89   2P/1B: $109   2P/2B: $99   XP: $10   F16
Phone: (831)688-7300
Location: Just n of SR 1, Seacliff exit. 7500 Old Dominion Ct 95003. Fax: 831/685-3603. **Terms:** Package plans; 2 night min stay, in summer. **Facility:** 140 rooms. 6 buildings clustered around ample, nicely landscaped grounds with koi pond water fall by dining room deck. 10 units with parlor, wet bar, 2 baths & whirlpool tub $139-$229 for up to 2 persons; 2 stories; interior/exterior corridors; whirlpool. **Dining:** Dining room; 6:30 am-2 & 5-9 pm; $12-$26; cocktails. **Cards:** AE, CB, DI, DS, MC, VI. **Special Amenities:** Free local telephone calls and free newspaper.

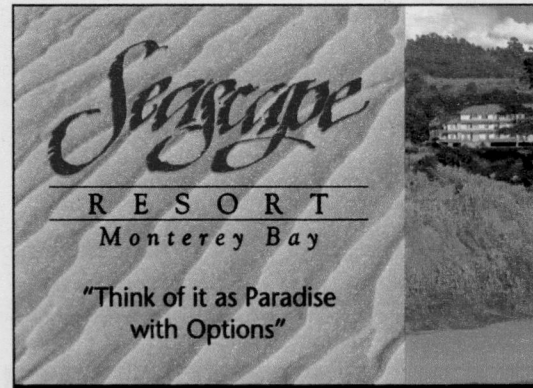

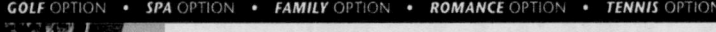

RIO SANDS MOTEL Rates Subject to Change **Phone:** (831)688-3207

7/1-9/5 [CP] 2P/1B: $119- 139 2P/2B: $119- 139 XP: $10 F6
5/28-6/30 & 9/6-10/31 [CP] 2P/1B: $79- 119 2P/2B: $79- 119 XP: $10 F6
2/1-5/27 & 11/1-1/31 [CP] 2P/1B: $69- 99 2P/2B: $69- 99 XP: $10 F6

Apartment Motel

Location: 1.2 mi w of SR 1, Rio Del Mar Blvd exit. 116 Aptos Beach Dr 95003. Fax: 831/688-6107. **Terms:** Reserv deposit; weekly rates; 2 night min stay, weekends. **Facility:** 50 rooms. 24 kitchens, $79-$159 for 2 persons; 2 stories; interior/exterior corridors; whirlpool. **All Rooms:** combo or shower baths. **Cards:** DS, MC, VI. *(See color ad p 1030)*

SEASCAPE RESORT **Phone:** (831)688-6800

All Year 1P: $220- 325 2P/1B: $220- 325 2P/2B: $340- 429

Condo Hotel

Location: 1 mi w of SR 1; San Andreas Rd exit, n on Seascape Blvd. One Seascape Resort Dr 95003. Fax: 831/685-0615. **Terms:** Check-in 4 pm; reserv deposit, 3 day notice; handling fee imposed; weekly rates; package plans; 2 night min stay, 5/22-9/30 weekends. **Facility:** 285 rooms. Gas fireplace, patio or deck. Studio, 1- & 2-bedroom condos. On bluff above the beach. 201 two-bedroom units. Rates for up to 6 persons; 3 stories; exterior corridors; smoke free premises; beach, whirlpools. **Dining:** Restaurant; 7 am-11 pm; $14-$25; cocktails. **Services:** area transportation. Fee: massage. **Recreation:** swimming. Fee: privileges with 1/3 starting times at Seascape Golf courts, tennis court, volleyball & badminton, kids camp in summer. Rental: bicycles. **All Rooms:** combo or shower baths. **Some Rooms:** 84 efficiencies, 201 kitchens. **Cards:** AE, DI, DS, MC, VI. *(See color ad p 356)*

RESTAURANTS

CAFE RIO **Dinner:** $12-$23 **Phone:** 831/688-8917

Steak and Seafood

Location: 1.2 mi w of SR 1, Rio Del Mar Blvd exit. 131 Esplanade 95003. **Hours:** 5 pm-9:30 pm, Sun from 4 pm. Closed: 11/25 & 12/25. **Reservations:** suggested. **Features:** No A/C; casual dress; children's menu; cocktails & lounge; a la carte. Casual atmosphere; at the beach. Smoke free premises. **Cards:** AE, MC, VI.

PALAPAS **Lunch:** $8-$16 **Dinner:** $11-$20 **Phone:** 831/662-9000

Mexican

Location: 1 mi w of SR 1; San Andreas Rd exit, n on Seascape Blvd. 21 Seascape Village 95003. **Hours:** 11:30 am-2:30 & 5-10 pm, Sun 11:30 am-2:30 & 4:30-9:30 pm. Closed: 11/25 & 12/25. **Reservations:** suggested. **Features:** casual dress; children's menu; cocktails & lounge; a la carte. Emphasis on fresh ingredients & own sauces, also seafoods Smoking in lounge only. Smoke free premises. **Cards:** AE, CB, DI, MC, VI.

ARCADIA—*See Los Angeles p. 586.*

ARCATA—15,200

LODGINGS

ARCATA SUPER 8 Rates Subject to Change **Phone:** (707)822-8888

All Year 1P: $49- 55 2P/1B: $54- 59 2P/2B: $57- 62 XP: $6 F12

Motel

Location: 2 mi n, e of US 101, exit Guintoli Ln E. 4887 Valley West Blvd 95521. Fax: 707/822-2513. **Facility:** 62 rooms. 2 stories; interior corridors. **Cards:** AE, CB, DI, DS, MC, VI.

BEST WESTERN ARCATA INN **Phone:** (707)826-0313

5/15-9/15 [CP] 1P: $79 2P/1B: $83 2P/2B: $83 XP: $5
2/1-5/14 & 9/16-1/31 [CP] 1P: $56 2P/1B: $66 2P/2B: $66 XP: $5

Motel

Location: 2 mi n, e of US 101, exit Guintoli Rd. 4827 Valley West Blvd 95521. Fax: 707/826-0365. **Terms:** Pets, $5 extra charge. **Facility:** 62 rooms. 4 whirlpool rms, extra charge; 2 stories; exterior corridors; heated indoor/outdoor pool, indoor whirlpool. **Dining:** Restaurants nearby. **All Rooms:** combo or shower baths. **Cards:** AE, CB, DI, DS, MC, VI. **Special Amenities:** Free breakfast and free local telephone calls.

COMFORT INN **Phone:** (707)826-2827

6/1-9/15 [CP] 1P: $72- 99 2P/1B: $78- 120 2P/2B: $79- 130 XP: $6 F18
2/1-2/28 & 9/16-1/31 [CP] 1P: $51- 85 2P/1B: $57- 98 2P/2B: $58- 110 XP: $6 F18
3/1-5/31 [CP] 1P: $55- 85 2P/1B: $59- 98 2P/2B: $60- 110 XP: $6 F18

Motel

Location: 2 mi n, e of US 101, exit Guintoli Ln. 4701 Valley West Blvd 95521. Fax: 707/826-9344. **Terms:** Reserv deposit; pets, manager's discretion. **Facility:** 55 rooms. 1 two-bedroom unit. 2 whirlpool rms, $98-$150 for up to 2 persons; 8 mini suites $75-$130 for up to 2 persons; 2 stories; exterior corridors; heated indoor pool, indoor whirlpool. **Dining:** Restaurant nearby. **All Rooms:** combo or shower baths. **Cards:** AE, CB, DI, DS, JC, MC, VI. **Special Amenities:** Early check-in/late check-out and free newspaper.

FAIRWINDS MOTEL **Phone:** (707)822-4824

All Year 1P: $45- 85 2P/1B: $50- 85 2P/2B: $60- 85 XP: $5-10 F18

Motel

Location: Northbound exit. US 101 14th St, w to G St, 0.3 mi n; southbound exit Sunset, e on 16th St, n on G St. 1674 G St 95521. **Terms:** Weekly rates. **Facility:** 27 rooms. Modern comfortable rooms. 1 two-bedroom unit. 2 stories; exterior corridors. **All Rooms:** shower baths. **Cards:** AE, DS, MC, VI. **Special Amenities:** Early check-in/late check-out and free local telephone calls.

HOTEL ARCATA **Phone:** (707)826-0217

All Year [CP] 1P: $60- 65 2P/1B: $65- 70 2P/2B: $70- 75

Historic Hotel

Location: At Central Plaza. 708 9th St 95521. Fax: 707/826-1737. **Terms:** Pets, $50 dep req. **Facility:** 32 rooms. Refurbished 1915 hotel. 3 stories; interior corridors; street parking only. **Dining:** Restaurant; 11 am-2:30 & 5-9 pm, Fri-Sun-midnight; $12-$20. **Services:** giftshop. **Cards:** AE, CB, DI, DS, MC, VI. **Special Amenities:** Early check-in/late check-out and free breakfast.

HOWARD JOHNSON EXPRESS INN

Rates Subject to Change   Phone: 707/826-9660

7/1-9/15 [CP]	1P:	$60-	70	2P/1B:	$56-	90	2P/2B: $70- 150	XP: $8
3/16-6/30 & 9/16-10/31 [CP]	1P:	$50-	70	2P/1B:	$56-	76	2P/2B: $66- 130	XP: $8
2/1-3/15 & 11/1-1/31 [CP]	1P:	$44-	64	2P/1B:	$50-	70	2P/2B: $60- 100	XP: $8

Motel   Too new to rate. **Location:** US 101, exit Guintola LA, just e. 4700 Valley West Blvd 95521. Fax: 707/826-9319. **Facility:** 48 rooms. 2 stories; interior corridors; indoor pool, whirlpool. **Dining:** Restaurant nearby. **Cards:** AE, DI, DS, MC, VI.

NORTH COAST INN

Guaranteed Rates   Phone: 707/822-4861

5/1-8/31	1P:	$95	2P/1B:	$110	2P/2B:	$115	XP: $5
2/1-4/30 & 9/1-1/31	1P:	$65	2P/1B:	$70	2P/2B:	$79	XP: $5

Motel   **Location:** 2 mi n of exit US 101 Guintoli Ln e. 4975 Valley West Blvd 95521. Fax: 707/822-2036. **Facility:** 78 rooms. 2 stories; interior corridors; heated indoor pool. **Cards:** AE, DI, DS, JC, MC, VI.

QUALITY INN-MAD RIVER

Phone: (707)822-0409

6/1-9/30 [CP]	1P:	$79-	110	2P/1B:	$86-	115	2P/2B:	$86- 115	XP: $5 F18
3/1-5/31 [CP]	1P:	$55-	83	2P/1B:	$59-	88	2P/2B:	$59- 88	XP: $5 F18
2/1-2/28 & 10/1-1/31 [CP]	1P:	$52-	78	2P/1B:	$57-	83	2P/2B:	$57- 83	XP: $5 F18

Motor Inn   **Location:** W of US-101, exit Guintoli Rd 0.3 mi. 3535 Janes Rd 95521. Fax: 707/822-1074. **Terms:** Pets, 5 extra charge. **Facility:** 64 rooms. 2 whirlpool rms, extra charge; 2 stories; interior corridors; whirlpool; 1 tennis court; playground. **Dining:** Restaurant; 11 am-9 pm; $9-$18; cocktails. **Recreation:** sports court, video game room. **Cards:** AE, DI, DS, MC, VI. **Special Amenities:** Free breakfast and free local telephone calls. *(See color ad p 443)*

RESTAURANTS

ABRUZZI

Dinner: $10-$20   Phone: 707/826-2345

Italian   **Location:** On ground level of Jacoby's Storehouse. 791 8th St 95521. **Hours:** 5:30-9 pm. Closed: 11/25. **Reservations:** suggested. **Features:** No A/C; casual dress; early bird specials; cocktails. Housemade sauces, pasta & desserts. Quiet, comfortable atmosphere. Smoke free premises. **Cards:** AE, DI, DS, MC, VI.

PLAZA GRILL

Dinner: $6-$13   Phone: 707/826-0860

American   **Location:** 3rd floor of Jacoby's Storehouse. 791 8th St 95521. **Hours:** 5 pm-10 pm, Fri & Sat-11 pm. Closed: 12/25. **Reservations:** suggested. **Features:** No A/C; casual dress; cocktails. Popular, very lively atmosphere. Fresh grilled fish, steaks & chicken. Smoke free premises. **Cards:** AE, DI, DS, MC, VI.

ARROYO GRANDE—14,400

LODGINGS

BEST WESTERN CASA GRANDE RESORT & SUITES

Phone: (805)481-7398

5/15-9/15 [CP]	1P:	$80-	95	2P/1B:	$85-	110	2P/2B:	$80- 120	XP: $10 F12
2/1-5/14 & 9/16-1/31 [CP]	1P:	$65-	75	2P/1B:	$75-	85	2P/2B:	$75- 95	XP: $10 F12

Motor Inn   **Location:** Just e of US 101, Oak Park exit; 1 mi s of Pismo Beach. 850 Oak Park Rd 93420. Fax: 805/481-4859. **Facility:** 113 rooms. Suites with private balcony. 2 room suites, $100-$150; 3 stories; interior/exterior corridors; heated pool, saunas, whirlpool. **Dining:** Restaurant; 11:30 am-10:30 pm; complimentary tea & cookies in afternoon; $8-$18; cocktails. **All Rooms:** combo or shower baths. **Cards:** AE, CB, DI, DS, JC, MC, VI. **Special Amenities:** Free breakfast and free local telephone calls. *(See color ad p 798)*

CRYSTAL ROSE INN

Rates Subject to Change   Phone: 805/481-1854

All Year [MAP]	1P:	$85- 185	2P/1B:	$95- 185	2P/2B:	$165	XP: $35

Historic Country Inn   **Location:** W of US 101. Southbound exit Fair Oak to Valley Rd, 1.5 mi s. Northbound exit Los Berros Rd, 4.5 mi nw. 789 Valley Rd 93420. Fax: 805/481-9541. **Terms:** Reserv deposit, 7 day notice. **Facility:** 8 rooms. 1890 Victorian house on 1 1/2 acres of landscaped gardens. Rooms individually decorated in period furnishings. Smoking permited in garden areas only. 2 stories; interior/exterior corridors. **Services:** giftshop. **Recreation:** bicycles. **All Rooms:** combo or shower baths. **Cards:** AE, DS, MC.

ECONO LODGE

Phone: (805)489-9300

Fri & Sat [CP]	1P:	$69-	110	2P/1B:	$69-	110	2P/2B: $79- 125	XP: $5-10 F17
Sun-Thurs [CP]	1P:	$45-	55	2P/1B:	$45-	55	2P/2B: $60- 75	XP: $5-10 F17

Motel   **Location:** Adjacent to US 101, northbound exit Brisco, southbound exit Halcyon Rd. 611 El Camino Real 93420. Fax: 805/473-8318. **Terms:** Reserv deposit, 3 day notice. **Facility:** 40 rooms. 2 stories; exterior corridors; pool heated in season. **Dining:** Restaurant nearby. **All Rooms:** combo or shower baths. **Cards:** AE, CB, DI, DS, MC, VI. **Special Amenities:** Free breakfast and free local telephone calls.

GRAND AVE MOTEL

Phone: (805)489-5633

All Year	1P:	$35-	45	2P/1B:	$40-	50	2P/2B: $45- 65 XP: $5 D12

Motel   **Location:** 0.5 mi w of US 101, Grand Ave exit. 617 Grand Ave 93420. Fax: 805/489-3471. **Terms:** Reserv deposit, 7 day notice; handling fee imposed; 2 night min stay. **Facility:** 15 rooms. 2 stories; exterior corridors. **Dining:** Coffee shop nearby. **Cards:** DS, MC, VI.

RESTAURANT

THE HUNT CLUB

Lunch: $7-$12   Dinner: $13-$24   Phone: 805/481-0610

American   **Location:** W of US 101. Southbound exit Fair Oak to Valley Rd, 1.5 mi s. Northbound exit Los Berros Rd, 4.5 mi nw in Crystal Rose Inn. 789 Valley Rd 93420. **Hours:** 11:30 am-2 pm & 5:30-9 pm, Sun 5:30-9 pm. Closed: Mon. **Reservations:** suggested. **Features:** No A/C; casual dress; cocktails & lounge. Small restaurant located in a restored Victorian home. Entrees include beef, lamb, chicken & fowl. Smoke free premises. **Cards:** AE, DS, MC, VI.

ARTESIA—See Los Angeles p. 586.

ATASCADERO—23,100

LODGINGS

BEST WESTERN COLONY INN Phone: (805)466-4449
AAA SAVE | 4/1-10/18 [CP] | 1P: $49- 125 | 2P/1B: $49- 125 | 2P/2B: $58- 129 | XP: $8 | F12
| 2/1-3/31 & 10/19-1/31 [CP] | 1P: $49- 99 | 2P/1B: $49- 99 | 2P/2B: $49- 109 | XP: $8 | F12
◆◆◆ **Location:** East side of US 101; exit San Anselmo Rd, then 0.5 mi n. 3600 El Camino Real 93422.
Motor Inn **Fax:** 805/466-2119. **Terms:** Reserv deposit. **Facility:** 75 rooms. 2-3 stories; interior corridors; heated pool, saunas, whirlpool, pool heated in season. **Dining:** Restaurant; 4:30 am-10 pm; $9-$16; cocktails.
Some Rooms: whirlpools. **Cards:** AE, DI, DS, MC, VI. **Special Amenities:** Free breakfast and free local telephone calls.
(See ad p 993) ⬛⬛⬛⬛⬛⬛⬛⬛⬛⬛⬛⬛

RANCHO TEE MOTEL Phone: (805)466-2231
AAA SAVE | Fri & Sat | 1P: $85- 95 | 2P/1B: $95- 110 | 2P/2B: $110- 120 | XP: $10
| Sun-Thurs | 1P: $46- 55 | 2P/1B: $50- 65 | 2P/2B: $55- 75 | XP: $5
◆ **Location:** Just ne of jct US 101, exit SR 41 (Morro Rd). 6895 El Camino Real 93422. Fax: 805/466-0214.
Motel **Terms:** Reserv deposit, 3 day notice; weekly rates. **Facility:** 27 rooms. 2 stories; exterior corridors; pool heated in season. **Dining:** Restaurant nearby. **Some Rooms:** 2 kitchens. **Cards:** AE, DS, MC, VI.
⬛⬛⬛⬛⬛

SUPER 8 MOTEL Phone: (805)466-0794
AAA SAVE | Sun-Thurs | 1P: $45- 95 | 2P/1B: $49- 99 | 2P/2B: $55- 120 | XP: $10-30
| Fri & Sat | 1P: $55- 110 | 2P/1B: $59- 110 | 2P/2B: $59- 110 | XP: $10-30
◆ **Location:** On SR 41, just w of jct US 101. 6505 Morro Rd 93422. Fax: 805/461-9500. **Terms:** Reserv
Motel deposit, 4 day notice; weekly rates; small pets only, $10 extra charge, $100 dep req. **Facility:** 30 rooms. 2 stories; exterior corridors. **Cards:** AE, CB, DI, DS, MC, VI. **Special Amenities:** Free breakfast and free local telephone calls. ⬛⬛⬛⬛⬛⬛⬛⬛

RESTAURANTS

GENIE'S STEAK HOUSE **Lunch:** $5-$8 **Dinner:** $11-$20 Phone: 805/466-6515
◆◆ **Location:** Just e of US 101, exit SR 41 (Morro Rd). 7030 El Camino Real 93422. **Hours:** 11 am-9 pm, Fri &
Steakhouse Sat-10 pm, Sat & Sun from 10 am. **Reservations:** suggested. **Features:** Sunday brunch; children's menu; cocktails & lounge. Aged choice beef, pasta & seafood. Live piano music Thurs-Sat evenings. Smoke free
premises. **Cards:** AE, CB, DI, DS, MC, VI. ⬛

SALSITAS **Lunch:** $3-$10 **Dinner:** $5-$10 Phone: 805/461-5500
◆ **Location:** 0.5 mi e & n of US 101, exit Santa Rosa, in Atascadero Oaks Shopping Center. 8783 El Camino
Mexican Real 93422. **Hours:** 11 am-8 pm, Fri-8:30 pm, Sat noon-8:30 pm, Sun noon-8 pm. **Features:** children's menu; health conscious menu; carryout; beer & wine only. An informal restaurant with indoor & outdoor patio dining. Menu features tacos, tostadas, burritos & an imaginative selection of beef, chicken and seafood specialties. Smoke
free premises. **Cards:** AE, MC, VI. ⬛

VILLAGE CAFFE' **Lunch:** $6-$9 **Dinner:** $8-$16 Phone: 805/462-1900
◆◆ **Location:** On El Camino Real, just s of jct US 101 & SR 41; in Adobe Plaza shopping center. 7377 El
Italian Camino Real 93422. **Hours:** 11:30 am-9 pm, Sat 5:30 pm-9 pm, Sun 5:30 pm-8 pm. Closed major holidays. **Reservations:** suggested; weekends. **Features:** casual dress; children's menu; early bird specials; beer & wine only; a la carte. Nice selection of pasta, chicken, veal & seafood. Smoke free premises. **Cards:** MC, VI. ⬛

ATWATER—22,300

LODGING

SUPER 8 Phone: 209/357-0202
AAA SAVE | All Year | 1P: $45 | 2P/1B: $50 | 2P/2B: $50- 55 | XP: $5 | F
◆◆◆ **Location:** Just ne of SR 99, Applegate Rd exit. 1501 Sycamore Ave 95301. Fax: 209/357-0798.
Motel **Terms:** Reserv deposit; handling fee imposed. **Facility:** 80 rooms. Some units near railroad tracks. 2 stories; exterior corridors. **Dining:** Coffee shop nearby. **Cards:** AE, CB, DI, DS, JC, MC, VI.
⬛⬛⬛⬛⬛⬛

AUBURN—10,600

LODGINGS

AUBURN INN Rates Subject to Change Phone: (530)885-1800
◆◆◆ | All Year [CP] | 1P: $54- 64 | 2P/1B: $62- 70 | 2P/2B: $66- 72 | XP: $6 | F12
Motel **Location:** 1.3 mi e; exit I-80N via Foresthill & Auburn Ravine rds. 1875 Auburn Ravine Rd 95603.
Fax: 530/888-6424. **Terms:** Check-in 4 pm. **Facility:** 81 rooms. 2 stories; interior corridors; heated pool.
All Rooms: combo or shower baths. **Cards:** AE, CB, DI, DS, MC, VI. ⬛⬛⬛⬛⬛⬛⬛⬛⬛⬛

BEST WESTERN GOLDEN KEY MOTEL Phone: (530)885-8611
AAA SAVE | All Year [CP] | 1P: $56- 76 | 2P/1B: $56- 76 | 2P/2B: $66- 86 | XP: $6 | F17
◆◆◆ **Location:** Off & adjacent to I-80; via Foresthill Rd. 13450 Lincoln Way 95603. Fax: 530/888-0319.
Motel **Terms:** Reserv deposit, 14 day notice; handling fee imposed; pets, $10 extra charge. **Facility:** 68 rooms. Spacious lawn area with many seasonal flowers. 2 stories; exterior corridors; heated pool. **Dining:** Restaurant nearby. **All Rooms:** combo or shower baths. **Cards:** AE, CB, DI, DS, JC, MC, VI. **Special Amenities:** Free breakfast and free local telephone calls. ⬛⬛⬛⬛⬛⬛⬛⬛

HOLIDAY INN-AUBURN Rates Subject to Change Phone: (530)887-8787
◆◆◆ | 5/1-8/31 | 1P: $78- 98 | 2P/1B: $78- 98 | 2P/2B: $82- 102 | XP: $10 | F18
Motor Inn | 9/1-1/31 | 1P: $76- 96 | 2P/1B: $76- 96 | 2P/2B: $80- 100 | XP: $10 | F18
| 2/1-4/30 | 1P: $74- 94 | 2P/1B: $74- 94 | 2P/2B: $78- 98 | XP: $10 | F18
Location: Jct I-80 & SR 49. 120 Grass Valley Hwy 95603. Fax: 530/887-9824. **Facility:** 96 rooms. Suites $90-$140 for up to 2 persons; 2-3 stories; interior corridors. **Cards:** AE, CB, DI, DS, MC, VI. *(See color ad p 360)* ⬛⬛⬛⬛⬛⬛⬛⬛⬛⬛

SLEEP INN·

(AAA) (SAVE)

◆◆
Motel

All Year [CP]   1P: $49- 56 2P/1B: $52- 62 2P/2B: $60- 70 XP: $5   F12
Location: Exit I-80 Auburn Ravine/Foothill Rd. 1819 Auburn Ravine Rd 95603. Fax: 530/888-6200.
Facility: 57 rooms. 3 stories, no elevator; interior corridors; heated pool, whirlpool. **All Rooms:** combo or shower baths. **Cards:** AE, CB, DI, DS, JC, MC, VI. **Special Amenities: Free breakfast and free newspaper.** *(See color ad below)*

Phone: (530)888-7829

SUPER 8 MOTEL

(AAA) (SAVE)

◆◆
Motel

All Year   1P: $49- 56 2P/1B: $52- 60 2P/2B: $60- 70 XP: $5   F16
Location: 1.3 mi e; exit I-80 n via Foresthill & Auburn Ravine rds. 140 E Hillcrest Dr 95603.
Fax: 530/885-3588. **Terms:** Reserv deposit. **Facility:** 51 rooms. 6 whirlpool rms, $75 for 2 persons; 2 stories; exterior corridors; heated pool, whirlpool. **Cards:** AE, CB, DI, DS, JC, MC, VI. **Special Amenities: Free breakfast.** *(See color ad below)*

Phone: (530)888-8808

RESTAURANTS

THE HEADQUARTER HOUSE AT RASPBERRY HILL **Lunch:** $7-$19 **Dinner:** $13-$34 **Phone:** 530/878-1906
◆◆
American
Location: 1.5 mi e; s off I-80 via Bell Rd. 14500 Musso Rd 95603. **Hours:** 11:30 am-9 pm, Sat-10 pm, Sun 10 am-9:30 pm. Closed: 12/25. **Reservations:** suggested. **Features:** casual dress; Sunday brunch; children's menu; cocktails & lounge; entertainment; a la carte. On the Dunipace Angus Ranch, in the pines. Beef, seafood & chicken. Smoke free premises. **Cards:** AE, CB, DS, MC, VI. ⊠

LATITUDES **Lunch:** $5-$10 **Dinner:** $10-$19 **Phone:** 530/885-9535
Ethnic
Location: Exit I-80 at Hwy 49, Placerville exit, 0.3 mi s to Lincoln Way, 0.3 mi w to Maple St opposite the County Court House. 130 Maple St #200 95603. **Hours:** 11:30 am-3 & 5-9 pm, Sat & Sun-10 pm, Sunday brunch 10 am-3 pm. Closed: Mon, Tues for dinner & 12/25. **Reservations:** suggested. **Features:** casual dress; Sunday brunch; children's menu; beer & wine only; a la carte. Dishes from different cultural regions, natural ingredients. Smoke free premises. **Cards:** AE, MC, VI. ⊠

AZUSA—See Los Angeles p. 587.

BADGER—200—See also SEQUOIA AND KINGS CANYON NATIONAL PARKS.

LODGING

BADGER INN MOTEL Rates Subject to Change **Phone:** 559/337-0022
◆◆
Motel
2/1-4/30 & 10/1-1/31	1P: $65	2P/1B: $65- 170	2P/2B: $65- 170	XP: $5
5/1-9/30	1P: $75	2P/1B: $75- 170	2P/2B: $75- 170	XP: $5

Location: On SR 245, 12 mi s of entrance to Kings Canyon National Park. 49496 Hwy 245 (PO Box 43, 93603). **Facility:** 9 rooms. Located in a quiet country setting. Cozy rooms. One 2-level suite; 1 story; exterior corridors. **Recreation:** hiking trails. **All Rooms:** shower baths. **Cards:** AE, CB, DI, DS, MC, VI. 🛏 ➔ 🍴 ⊠ 📺 📼 ✂ 🐾 ⊠

BAKER—600

LODGING

BUN BOY MOTEL **Phone:** (760)733-4363
AAA SAVE
◆
Motor Inn
Fri & Sat	1P: $40	2P/1B: $49	2P/2B: $53	XP: $10	D12
Sun-Thurs	1P: $30	2P/1B: $39	2P/2B: $43	XP: $10	D12

Location: At jct I-15 & SR 127. 72155 Baker Blvd 92309 (PO Box 130). Fax: 760/733-4595. **Terms:** Small pets only, credit card dep req. **Facility:** 20 rooms. 1 story; exterior corridors. **Dining:** Restaurant; 24 hours; $6-$12; cocktails. **All Rooms:** shower baths, extended cable TV. **Cards:** AE, DS, MC, VI.
Special Amenities: Preferred room (subject to availability with advanced reservations). 🛏 🍴 🐾 ⊠

BAKERSFIELD—175,000

LODGINGS

BEST WESTERN HERITAGE INN **Phone:** (805)764-6268
AAA SAVE
◆◆◆
Motel
All Year [CP] 1P: $49- 52 2P/1B: $52- 60 2P/2B: $60- 65 XP: $5 F12
Location: 15 mi w of Bakersfield, at jct I-5 & Stockdale Hwy. 253 Trask St 93312. Fax: 805/764-5181. **Terms:** Reserv deposit; small pets only. **Facility:** 47 rooms. 1 whirlpool rm, extra charge; 2 stories; exterior corridors. **Dining:** Restaurant nearby. **Cards:** AE, CB, DI, DS, JC, MC, VI. **Special Amenities:** Free local telephone calls and free newspaper. 🛏 🛏 ➔ 🍴 🐾 ⊠

BEST WESTERN HILL HOUSE **Phone:** (805)327-4064
AAA SAVE
◆◆◆
Motor Inn
All Year [CP] 1P: $48- 50 2P/1B: $50- 54 2P/2B: $50- 60 XP: $5
Location: 2 mi e of SR 99, California Ave exit to Chester Ave, n to Truxtun Ave. 700 Truxtun Ave St 93301. Fax: 805/327-1247. **Terms:** Reserv deposit, 7 day notice; pets, $3 per pet extra charge. **Facility:** 99 rooms. Just east of downtown, near convention center & government offices. 2 stories; interior corridors. **Dining:** Dining room, coffee shop; 6:30 am-9 pm, Sat & Sun 7 am-2 pm; $7-$12; cocktails. **Cards:** AE, CB, DI, DS, MC, VI. **Special Amenities:** Early check-in/late check-out and free local telephone calls. 🛏 🐾 ➔ 🍴 🐾 ✂ 📷 📠 ⊠

BEST WESTERN INN
Phone: (805)327-9651
(AAA) (SAVE)　All Year [BP]　　　1P: $48- 78　2P/1B:　$54- 78　2P/2B:　$54- 78　XP: $10　　F18
◆◆　**Location:** E side of SR 99, Northbound exit Buck Owens Blvd, southbound exit Rosedale Hwy. 2620 Buck
Motor Inn　Owens Blvd 93308. Fax: 805/334-1820. **Terms:** Weekly/monthly rates; pets, $10 per pet. **Facility:** 198 rooms.
Large nicely landscaped courtyard & pool area. 2 stories; interior corridors; whirlpool. **Dining:** Restaurant,
coffee shop; 6 am-10 pm; $8-$14; cocktails. **Cards:** AE, CB, DI, DS, JC, MC, VI. **Special Amenities:** Free
local telephone calls and free room upgrade (subject to availability with advanced reservations).
(See color ad p 361)

BEST WESTERN OAK INN
Phone: (805)324-9686
(AAA) (SAVE)　All Year　　　　1P: $40- 44　2P/1B:　$44- 52　2P/2B:　$48- 52　XP: $5
◆◆　**Location:** E side of SR 99, exit California Ave, s on Oak St. 889 Oak St 93304. Fax: 805/325-4427.
Motel　**Terms:** Small pets only, $5. **Facility:** 42 rooms. 2 stories; exterior corridors. **All Rooms:** combo or shower
baths, extended cable TV. **Cards:** AE, CB, DI, DS, JC, MC, VI. **Special Amenities:** Free breakfast and free
local telephone calls.

CALIFORNIA INN
Phone: (805)328-1100
(AAA) (SAVE)　All Year　　　　1P: $39- 49　2P/1B:　$41- 49　2P/2B:　$43- 49　XP: $4
◆◆　**Location:** Just w of SR 99 & s of California Ave on Real Rd. From SR 99, exit California Ave. 3400 Chester
Motel　Ln 93309. Fax: 805/328-0433. **Facility:** 74 rooms. 3 whirlpool rms, extra charge; 3 stories; interior corridors;
small pool, sauna, whirlpool. **Dining:** Restaurant nearby. **All Rooms:** extended cable TV. **Cards:** AE, CB, DI,
DS, MC, VI. **Special Amenities:** Free breakfast and free local telephone calls.

CALIFORNIA INN WIBLE
Phone: (805)834-3377
(AAA) (SAVE)　All Year [CP]　　1P: $36- 38　2P/1B:　$38- 40　2P/2B:　$39- 42　XP: $4
◆◆　**Location:** E side of SR 99, exit Ming Ave; 0.4 mi n on Wible Rd. 830 Wible Rd 93304. Fax: 805/834-4439.
Motel　**Terms:** Weekly/monthly rates. **Facility:** 61 rooms. 1/2 mi n of Valley Plaza Mall. 2 stories; exterior corridors;
small pool, sauna, whirlpool. **All Rooms:** extended cable TV. **Cards:** AE, CB, DI, DS, MC, VI.
Special Amenities: Free breakfast and free local telephone calls.

COMFORT INN-CENTRAL
Phone: (805)831-1922
(AAA) (SAVE)　All Year [CP]　　1P: $38- 40　2P/1B:　$40- 45　2P/2B:　$45- 50　XP: $5　　F17
◆　**Location:** Adjacent to SR 99; 0.8 mi ne of Ming Ave exit. 1030 Wible Rd 93304. Fax: 805/831-1879.
Motel　**Terms:** Reserv deposit; weekly rates; pets, $5 extra charge. **Facility:** 53 rooms. 2 stories; exterior corridors;
small pool, whirlpool. **All Rooms:** combo or shower baths. **Some Rooms:** 10 efficiencies, no utensils.
Cards: AE, CB, DI, DS, JC, MC, VI. **Special Amenities:** Early check-in/late check-out and free
breakfast.

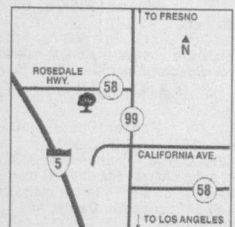

COURTYARD BY MARRIOTT
◆◆◆
Motor Inn
Rates Subject to Change
Phone: 805/324-6660
All Year — 1P: $82 — 2P/1B: $82 — 2P/2B: $82
Location: Just w of SR 99, exit SR 58 Rosedale Hwy; just s on Camino Del Rio. 3601 Marriott Dr 93308. Fax: 805/324-1185. **Facility:** 146 rooms. Nicely landscaped courtyard area. 12 suites, $105/2 persons; 3 stories; interior corridors; heated pool. **Cards:** AE, CB, DI, DS, MC, VI. *(See color ad p 362)*

DAYS INN
Ⓐ Ⓐ Ⓐ SAVE
◆◆◆
Motor Inn
Phone: (805)326-1111
All Year [CP] — 1P: $65- 90 — 2P/1B: $70- 95 — 2P/2B: $70- 95 — XP: $5-10 — F18
Location: SR 58, just w of jct SR 99; Rosedale Hwy exit. 3540 Rosedale Hwy 93308. Fax: 805/326-1513. **Facility:** 122 rooms. 5 stories; interior corridors; heated pool, whirlpool. **Dining:** Coffee shop; 6 am-11 am. **All Rooms:** extended cable TV. **Cards:** AE, CB, DI, DS, MC, VI. **Special Amenities:** Free local telephone calls and free newspaper. *(See color ad p 362)*

DOUBLETREE HOTEL
Ⓐ Ⓐ SAVE
◆◆◆
Hotel
Phone: (805)323-7111
Mon-Thurs — 1P: $89 — 2P/1B: $89 — 2P/2B: $89 — XP: $15 — F18
Fri-Sun — 1P: $79 — 2P/1B: $79 — 2P/2B: $79 — XP: $15 — F18
Location: On SR 58, just w of jct SR 99, Rosedale Hwy exit. 3100 Camino Del Rio Ct 93308. Fax: 805/323-0331. **Terms:** Pets. **Facility:** 262 rooms. Spacious rooms. Attractive courtyard. 7 two-bedroom units. 3 stories; interior corridors; heated pool, whirlpool. **Dining:** Restaurant; 6 am-10 pm; $7-$17; cocktails; also, California Grill, see separate listing. **Services:** giftshop. **Cards:** AE, CB, DI, DS, JC, MC, VI. **Special Amenities:** Early check-in/late check-out and free newspaper.

FOUR POINTS HOTEL BY SHERATON
Ⓐ Ⓐ SAVE
◆◆◆
Motor Inn
Phone: (805)325-9700
All Year — 1P: $135 — 2P/1B: $135- 145 — 2P/2B: $135- 145
Location: 1.3 mi sw of SR 99, exit California Ave. 5101 California Ave 93309. Fax: 805/323-3508. **Facility:** 197 rooms. Located in a Business Park area on nicely landscaped, tree-shaded grounds with ponds & creeks. 2 stories; interior corridors; heated pool, whirlpool. **Dining:** The Bistro, see separate listing. **All Rooms:** extended cable TV. **Cards:** AE, CB, DI, DS, MC, VI. **Special Amenities:** Early check-in/late check-out and preferred room (subject to availability with advanced reservations). *(See color ad below)*

GARDEN SUITES INN
Ⓐ Ⓐ Ⓐ SAVE
◆◆
Suite Motel
Phone: (805)833-6066
All Year [CP] — 1P: $39- 54 — 2P/1B: $44- 60 — 2P/2B: $44- 64 — XP: $5 — F18
Location: E side of SR 99, Ming Ave exit; just s on Wible Rd. 2310 Wible Rd 93304. Fax: 805/397-5464. **Terms:** Reserv deposit; weekly rates. **Facility:** 64 rooms. 1 block s of Valley Plaza Mall. 1-bedroom suites & a few hotel rooms. 8 whirlpool rms, extra charge; 3 stories; interior corridors; small pool, whirlpool. **All Rooms:** extended cable TV. **Cards:** AE, CB, DI, DS, MC, VI. **Special Amenities:** Free breakfast and free local telephone calls.

GOOD NITE INN
◆◆
Motor Inn
Rates Subject to Change
Phone: (805)327-0681
All Year — 1P: $45- 55 — 2P/1B: $45- 55 — 2P/2B: $45- 55 — XP: $6
Location: West side of SR 99, exit SR 58 Rosedale Hwy, just s on Camino Del Real Ct. 3535 Rosedale Hwy 93308. Fax: 805/324-1648. **Facility:** 185 rooms. Many rooms with balcony or patio overlooking central courtyard. 2 stories; interior/exterior corridors. **Cards:** AE, CB, DI, DS, MC, VI.

HAMPTON INN
◆◆◆
Motel
Rates Subject to Change
Phone: 805/633-0333
All Year [CP] — 1P: $64- 69 — 2P/1B: $72- 75 — 2P/2B: $70
Location: E side of SR 99, California Ave exit. 1017 Oak St 93304. Fax: 805/633-0669. **Facility:** 95 rooms. 4 stories; interior corridors; small heated pool. **Cards:** AE, CB, DI, DS, JC, MC, VI.

HOLIDAY INN EXPRESS
Ⓐ Ⓐ Ⓐ SAVE
◆◆◆
Motel
Phone: (805)833-3000
All Year [CP] — 1P: $56- 99 — 2P/1B: $56- 99 — 2P/2B: $56- 89 — XP: $5 — F18
Location: From SR 99, exit White Ln, 0.3 mi e, just s on Hughes Ln. 4400 Hughes Ln 93304. Fax: 805/833-3736. **Facility:** 108 rooms. 4 stories; interior corridors; whirlpool. **All Rooms:** extended cable TV. **Some Rooms:** whirlpools. **Cards:** AE, DI, DS, MC, VI. **Special Amenities:** Free breakfast and free local telephone calls. *(See color ad p 364)*

HOLIDAY INN SELECT
◆◆◆ All Year
Hotel
Rates Subject to Change
1P: $100   2P/1B: $100   2P/2B: $100   XP: $10   F18
Phone: (805)323-1900
Location: 1.8 mi e of SR 99, California Ave exit to Chester Ave, n to Truxtun. 801 Truxtun Ave 93301. Fax: 805/323-2844. **Facility:** 258 rooms. A contemporary downtown hotel, adjacent to Bakersfield Convention Center. Large, nicely furnished rooms. 9 stories; interior corridors. **Services:** giftshop. **Cards:** AE, CB, DI, MC, VI.

LA QUINTA INN
(AAA) (SAVE)
◆◆◆
Motel
All Year [CP]
1P: $62- 75   2P/1B: $62- 75   2P/2B: $62- 75
Phone: (805)325-7400
Location: E side of SR 99, southbound exit Rosedale Hwy, northbound exit Buck Owens Blvd, just n of Rosedale Hwy. 3232 Riverside Dr 93308. Fax: 805/324-6032. **Terms:** Small pets only, $8 per pet. **Facility:** 129 rooms. 3 stories; exterior corridors; heated pool. **Dining:** Restaurant nearby. **Cards:** AE, CB, DI, DS, JC, MC, VI. **Special Amenities:** Free breakfast and free local telephone calls.

LONE OAK INN
◆
Motel
Rates Subject to Change
1P: $39   2P/1B: $43   2P/2B: $49   XP: $5
Phone: 805/589-6600
Location: On SR 58, 4.5 mi w of jct SR 99. 10614 Rosedale Hwy 93312. Fax: 805/588-2026. **Facility:** 19 rooms. 2 stories; exterior corridors. **All Rooms:** efficiencies. **Cards:** AE, DS, MC, VI.

OXFORD INN & SUITES
(AAA) (SAVE)
◆◆
Motel
All Year [CP]
1P: $48- 58   2P/1B: $48- 58   2P/2B: $53- 63   XP: $5   F12
Phone: (805)324-5555
Location: Just e of SR 99, 1 mi n of Rosedale Hwy. From SR 99, southbound exit Rosedale Hwy, northbound Duck Owens Blvd. 4500 Buck Owens Blvd 93308. Fax: 805/325-0106. **Terms:** Pets, $6 extra charge. **Facility:** 203 rooms. Attractive tree shaded pool area. 24 mini-suites with efficiency & patio; 3 stories; exterior corridors; 9-hole 3-par golf; whirlpool. **Dining:** Coffee shop nearby. **All Rooms:** extended cable TV. **Cards:** AE, CB, DI, DS, JC, MC, VI. **Special Amenities:** Free local telephone calls and preferred room (subject to availability with advanced reservations).

QUALITY INN
(AAA) (SAVE)
◆◆◆
Motel
All Year [CP]
1P: $46- 56   2P/1B: $50- 65   2P/2B: $55- 65   XP: $5   F16
Phone: (805)325-0772
Location: E side of SR 99, exit California Ave, just s. 1011 Oak St 93304. Fax: 805/325-4646. **Terms:** Pets. **Facility:** 89 rooms. Some rooms with patio or balcony. 2 stories; interior/exterior corridors; heated pool, sauna, indoor whirlpool. **Dining:** Coffee shop nearby. **Cards:** AE, CB, DI, DS, JC, MC, VI. **Special Amenities:** Early check-in/late check-out and free breakfast. *(See color ad p 365)*

RADISSON SUITES
(AAA) (SAVE)
◆◆◆
Motel
All Year [CP]
1P: $69- 89   2P/1B: $79- 99   2P/2B: $79- 99   XP: $10   F18
Phone: (805)322-9988
Location: W side of SR 99, exit California Ave; just s on Real Rd. 828 Real Rd 93309. Fax: 805/322-3668. **Terms:** Reserv deposit; weekly rates. **Facility:** 80 rooms. One 1-bedroom apartment. 4 whirlpool rms, extra charge; 4 stories; interior corridors; sauna, whirlpool. **Dining:** Restaurant nearby. **All Rooms:** extended cable TV. **Cards:** AE, CB, DI, DS, JC, MC, VI. **Special Amenities:** Free breakfast and free local telephone calls.

RESIDENCE INN BY MARRIOTT
◆◆◆
Apartment
Motel
All Year [CP]
Rates Subject to Change
1P: $115- 135   2P/1B: $115- 135   2P/2B: $115- 135
Phone: 805/321-9800
Location: Just w of SR 99, exit California Ave, just n on Chester Ln. 4241 Chester Ln 93309. Fax: 805/321-0721. **Facility:** 114 rooms. Studios, 1- & 2-bedroom suites with kitchen, some with fireplace. Central courtyard with attractive grounds. 28 two-bedroom units. 2 stories; exterior corridors; putting green; heated pool. **Recreation:** sports court. **Cards:** AE, DI, DS, JC, MC, VI.

O BRAVO RESORT   Phone: (805)872-5000

	Fri & Sat 3/1-6/30 & 9/1-11/15	1P: $98	2P/1B: $108	2P/2B: $108
esort Motor	Sun-Thurs 3/1-6/30 & 9/1-11/15	1P: $75	2P/1B: $75	2P/2B: $75
n	7/1-8/31	1P: $70	2P/1B: $70	2P/2B: $70
	2/1-2/28 & 11/16-1/31	1P: $60	2P/1B: $60	2P/2B: $60

cation: 12 mi e on SR 178, 2.5 mi n on Alfred Harrell Hwy. 11200 Lake Ming Rd 93306. Fax: 805/872-6546.
rms: Package plans; pets, $50 dep req. **Facility:** 100 rooms. On spacious grounds near Lake Ming. Large rooms with patio balcony. 5 one-bedroom suites; 2 stories; interior corridors; heated pool, whirlpools; 18 lighted tennis courts.
ning: Dining room, restaurant; 7 am-11 pm, Fri & Sat-midnight; $11-$16; cocktails. **Services:** Fee: massage.
creation: hiking trails, arrangements thru resort for golf courses & water sports nearby. **Cards:** AE, CB, DI, DS, MC, VI.
ecial Amenities: Free local telephone calls and free room upgrade (subject to availability with advanced servations).

RAVELODGE HOTEL & ENTERTAINMENT CENTER   Rates Subject to Change   Phone: (805)324-6666

| | All Year | 1P: $45- 57 | 2P/1B: $51- 63 | 2P/2B: $51- 63 | XP: $10 | F18 |

tor Inn   **Location:** W side of SR 99, exit White Ln, then s. 818 Real Rd 93309. Fax: 805/324-6670. **Facility:** 181 rooms. Suites, $79-$89; 2 stories; interior/exterior corridors; heated pool. **Services:** area transportation.
ards: AE, CB, DI, DS, MC, VI.

RAVELODGE SOUTH   Phone: (805)833-1000

| | All Year [CP] | 1P: $50 | 2P/1B: $55 | 2P/2B: $60 | XP: $5 | F12 |

Location: W side of SR 99, exit White Ln, just n on Wible Rd. 3620 Wible Rd 93309. Fax: 805/832-3212.
otel   **Facility:** 60 rooms. Whirlpool rms $75-$85; 2 stories; exterior corridors; whirlpool. **Dining:** Coffee shop nearby. **All Rooms:** extended cable TV. **Cards:** AE, DI, DS, MC, VI. **Special Amenities:** Early check-in/late check-out and free breakfast.

RESTAURANTS

ENJIS FRENCH BASQUE RESTAURANT   **Lunch:** $7-$13   **Dinner:** $13-$19   Phone: 805/328-0400
Location: On SR 58, 0.3 mi w of jct SR 99, exit Rosedale Hwy. 4001 Rosedale Hwy 93308. **Hours:** 11:30
asque   am-2 pm & 5:30-9:30 pm. Closed major holidays & Tues. **Features:** casual dress; children's menu; cocktails.
Complete Basque meals served in traditional style with soup, salad, condiments & entree; featuring lamb,
icken, beef & fish. Smoke free premises. **Cards:** AE, MC, VI.

HE BISTRO   **Lunch:** $8-$18   **Dinner:** $14-$22   Phone: 805/323-3905
Location: 1.3 mi sw of SR 99, exit California Ave; at Four Points Hotel By Sheraton. 5101 California Ave
ontinental   93309. **Hours:** 6:30-10 am, 11-2 & 6-10 pm, Sat 7:30-10 am, 11-2 & 6-10 pm, Sun 7:30 am-2 & 6-10 pm.
Reservations: suggested. **Features:** Sunday brunch; children's menu; cocktails & lounge. Menu features a
ariety of French & California cuisine. Smoke free premises. **Cards:** AE, DI, DS, MC, VI. *(See color ad p 363)*

CALIFORNIA GRILL   Lunch: $7-$12   Dinner: $12-$21   Phone: 805/323-711
◆◆◆ **Location:** On SR 58, just w of jct SR 99, Rosedale Hwy exit; in Doubletree Hotel. 3100 Camino Del Rio C
American 93308. **Hours:** 11:30 am-1:30 & 5:30-10 pm, Fri-11 pm, Sat 5:30 pm-11 pm, Sun 9 am-2 & 5:30-10 pm
Reservations: suggested. **Features:** casual dress; Sunday brunch; children's menu; cocktails & lounge.
large, attractive dining room featuring a nice selection of steak & seafood. Smoke free premises. **Cards:** AE, CB, DI, DS
JC, MC, VI.

CHALET BASQUE   Lunch: $7-$12   Dinner: $14-$20   Phone: 805/327-2915
◆ **Location:** E side of SR 99, just n of Brundage Ln, exit Stockdale Hwy/Brundage Ln. 200 Oak St 93304
Basque **Hours:** 11:30 am-2 & 5:30-9:30 pm, Sat 5-9:30 pm. Closed major holidays, Sun & Mor
Reservations: accepted. **Features:** casual dress; children's menu; cocktails & lounge. Complete Basque
meals served in traditional style with soup, salad, condiments & entree; featuring lamb, chicken, beef & fish. Smoke free
premises. **Cards:** AE, MC, VI.

MAMA TOSCA'S RISTORANTE ITALIANO   Lunch: $9-$12   Dinner: $13-$28   Phone: 805/831-1242
◆◆◆ **Location:** 2 mi w of SR 99, exit Ming Ave; in Laurelglen Plaza. 6631 Ming Ave 93309. **Hours:** 11:30 am-2 &
Italian 5:30-10 pm, Sat from 5:30 pm. Closed major holidays & Sun. **Reservations:** suggested
Features: children's menu; cocktails & lounge. Fine dining in an attractive setting. Selections of pasta
chicken, veal, fish, steak & lamb. Dessert made on premises. Smoke free premises. **Cards:** AE, CB, DI, DS, MC, VI.

TAVERN BY THE GREEN   Lunch: $8-$15   Dinner: $13-$25   Phone: 805/831-5225
◆◆◆ **Location:** 0.4 mi w of New Stine Rd at Sundale Country Club. 6218 Sundale Ave 93309. **Hours:** 11:30 am-2
Continental & 5:30-9:30 pm, Sat 5:30 pm-10 pm, Sun 10 am-2 & 5:30-9:30 pm. Closed: 1/1, 12/25 & Mor
Reservations: suggested. **Features:** Sunday brunch; cocktails & lounge. Attractive dining room on 2nd floor
overlooking the golf driving range. Smoke free premises. **Cards:** AE, DS, MC, VI.

URICCHIO'S TRATTORIA   Lunch: $7-$16   Dinner: $10-$18   Phone: 805/326-8870
◆◆◆ **Location:** Downtown; just e of Chester Ave. 1400 17th St 93301. **Hours:** 11 am-2 & 5-9 pm, Fri & Sat-10
Italian pm. Closed: 11/25, 12/25 & Sun. **Features:** cocktails & lounge; street parking. Casual, contemporary dining
in a restored downtown building. Smoke free premises. **Cards:** AE, CB, DI, DS, MC, VI.

BALDWIN PARK—See Los Angeles p. 587.

ALLARD

LODGING

THE BALLARD INN   Rates Subject to Change   Phone: (805)688-7770
◆◆◆◆ All Year [BP]   1P: $170- 250   2P/1B: $170- 250   XP: $50
Country Inn **Location:** 3.5 mi ne of Solvang, via Alamo Pintado Rd. 2436 Baseline 93463. Fax: 805/688-9560
Terms: Reserv deposit, 7 day notice; handling fee imposed; 10% service charge; 2 night min stay
weekends. **Facility:** 15 rooms. A charming inn with individually decorated rooms, 7 with fireplace. Afternoon wine tasting & hors
d'oeuvres. Phone jacks & cable TV hookups in all rooms. TV & phone avail upon request. Closed 12/25. 2 stories;
interior/exterior corridors; smoke free premises. **All Rooms:** combo or shower baths. **Cards:** AE, MC, VI.

RESTAURANTS

THE BALLARD STORE RESTAURANT   Dinner: $15-$21   Phone: 805/688-5319
◆◆◆ **Location:** 3.5 mi ne of Solvang, via Alamo Pintado Rd. 2449 Baseline Ave 93463. **Hours:** 5:30 pm-9:30 pm,
Continental Sat 6 pm-9:30 pm, Sun 10:30 am-2 & 5-8:30 pm. Closed: Mon, Tues, 12/24 & 12/25.
Reservations: suggested. **Features:** casual dress; Sunday brunch; children's menu; cocktails. Fine dining in
a French country atmosphere. International cuisine. Extensive selection of California wine. Also prixe fixe menu $19.95.
Gourmet picnic boxes avail with advance arrangements 26 years in business. Smoke free premises. **Cards:** AE, DI, DS,
MC, VI.

CAFE CHARDONNAY   Dinner: $15-$26   Phone: 805/688-7770
◆◆◆ **Location:** In The Ballard Inn; 3.5 mi ne of Solvang, via Alamo Pintado Rd. 2436 Baseline 93463. **Hours:** 6
American pm-9 pm. Closed: Mon, Tues & 12/25. **Reservations:** suggested. **Features:** casual dress; beer & wine only;
a la carte. Small, intimate restaurant. Nicely prepared selection of fish, poultry & meat dishes compatible with
large selection of local wines. Smoke free premises. **Cards:** AE, MC, VI.

BANNING—20,600

LODGINGS

BANNING TRAVELODGE   Rates Subject to Change   Phone: (909)849-1000
Ⓐ All Year [CP]   1P: $47- 57   2P/1B: $53- 63   2P/2B: $57- 67   XP:$5-15   F8
◆◆ **Location:** Adjacent to I-10, exit 22nd St, 0.5 mi e. 1700 W Ramsey St 92220. Fax: 909/849-4071.
Motel **Terms:** Reserv deposit; weekly rates; pets, $3 extra charge. **Facility:** 41 rooms. 4 whirlpool rms, $78; 2 sto-
ries; exterior corridors; small pool. **All Rooms:** extended cable TV. **Some Rooms:** whirlpools. **Cards:** AE,
CB, DI, DS, JC, MC, VI. *(See color ad p 367)*

SUPER 8 MOTEL

Phone: 909/849-6887

[AAA] [SAVE]
◆◆
Motel

All Year [CP]   1P: $48- 58   2P/1B: $54- 59   2P/2B: $59- 69   XP: $5-10
Location: Adjacent to I-10, 22nd St exit, 0.5 mi e. 1690 W Ramsey St 92220. Fax: 909/922-9157.
Terms: Reserv deposit; weekly rates; small pets only, $3 extra charge. **Facility:** 51 rooms. 2 stories; interior corridors. **All Rooms:** extended cable TV. **Cards:** AE, DI, DS, MC, VI.

BARSTOW—21,500

LODGINGS

BARSTOW-SUPER 8 MOTEL

Phone: 760/256-8443

[AAA] [SAVE]
◆◆
Motel

1P: $50   2P/1B: $50   2P/2B: $50   XP: $5   F13
Location: I-15 exit Main St; 0.3 mi w, then s on Coolwater Ln. 170 Coolwater Ln 92311. Fax: 760/256-0997.
Terms: Pets, $3 extra charge. **Facility:** 51 rooms. Exterior corridors. **Dining:** Restaurant nearby. **Cards:** AE, CB, DI, DS, JC, MC, VI.

BEST MOTEL

Phone: (760)256-6836

[AAA] [SAVE]
◆
Motel

All Year [CP]   1P: $30   2P/1B: $34   2P/2B: $38   XP: $5
Location: 0.5 mi w of I-15; from I-15 & Westbound I-40, E Main St exit. 1281 E Main St 92311.
Fax: 760/255-1029. **Terms:** Small pets only. **Facility:** 29 rooms. 2 stories; exterior corridors.
Dining: Restaurant nearby. **All Rooms:** extended cable TV. **Cards:** AE, DS, MC, VI. **Special Amenities:** Early check-in/late check-out and free local telephone calls. *(See ad below)*

BEST WESTERN DESERT VILLA INN

Phone: (760)256-1781

[AAA] [SAVE]
◆◆◆
Motel

All Year [CP]   1P: $66- 80   2P/1B: $68- 82   2P/2B: $71- 84   XP: $5   F16
Location: Adjacent to I-40, westbound exit Main St, eastbound exit Montara; 0.5 mi e of I-15. 1984 E Main St 92311. Fax: 760/256-9265. **Facility:** 95 rooms. 2 stories; exterior corridors; whirlpool. **Dining:** Dining room; 5 pm-8:30 pm; $7-$13; cocktails. **Services:** giftshop. **All Rooms:** extended cable TV. **Some Rooms:** whirlpools. **Cards:** AE, CB, DI, DS, JC, MC, VI. **Special Amenities:** Free breakfast and free local telephone calls.

COMFORT INN

Phone: (760)256-0661

[AAA] [SAVE]
◆◆
Motel

All Year [CP]   1P: $35- 55   2P/1B: $40- 60   2P/2B: $45- 75   XP: $7   F12
Location: 0.4 mi w of I-15; from I-15 & westbound I-40, exit E Main St. 1431 E Main St 92311.
Fax: 760/256-8392. **Terms:** Small pets only, $10 extra charge. **Facility:** 64 rooms. 2 stories; interior corridors; wading pool. **Dining:** Restaurant nearby. **Cards:** AE, CB, DI, DS, MC, VI. **Special Amenities:** Free breakfast and free local telephone calls. *(See color ad p 368)*

DAYS INN

AAA SAVE
◆
Motel

Phone: (760)256-1737
All Year [CP]　　　　　　1P: $26- 46　2P/1B: $26- 46　2P/2B: $36- 59　XP: $5　　F12
Location: Just w of I-15, E Main St exit; then s on Roberta St. 1590 Coolwater Ln 92311.
Fax: 760/256-7771. **Terms:** Pets, $10 extra charge. **Facility:** 113 rooms. 2 stories; exterior corridors.
Some Rooms: color TV. **Cards:** AE, CB, DI, DS, MC, VI. **Special Amenities:** Free breakfast and free local telephone calls.

ECONOLODGE

AAA SAVE
◆
Motel

Phone: (760)256-2133
6/15-9/15 [CP]　　　　1P: $28- 43　2P/1B: $33- 53　2P/2B: $35- 55　XP: $5　　F12
2/1-6/14 & 9/16-1/31 [CP]　1P: $25- 35　2P/1B: $29- 49　2P/2B: $29- 49　XP: $5　　F12
Location: 0.8 mi w of I-15; from I-15 & westbound I-40, E Main St exits. 1230 E Main St 92311.
Terms: Reserv deposit, 5 day notice; weekly rates; pets, $5 extra charge. **Facility:** 51 rooms. 2 stories; exterior corridors; heated pool. **All Rooms:** combo or shower baths. **Some Rooms:** 4 kitchens, no utensils.
Cards: AE, CB, DI, DS, MC, VI. **Special Amenities:** Free local telephone calls. *(See color ad below)*

EXECUTIVE INN

AAA SAVE
◆
Motel

Phone: (760)256-7581
All Year　　　　　　　1P: $25- 45　2P/1B: $30- 45　2P/2B: $35- 50　XP: $5
Location: 0.8 mi w of I-15; from I-15 & westbound I-40, E Main St exits. 1261 E Main St 92311.
Fax: 760/256-0155. **Terms:** Reserv deposit; weekly rates; small pets only. **Facility:** 33 rooms. 10 kitchens, no extra, no utensils; 2 stories; exterior corridors; small pool. **All Rooms:** extended cable TV. **Cards:** AE, CB, DI, DS, JC, MC, VI. **Special Amenities:** Free local telephone calls and preferred room (subject to availability with advanced reservations).

GATEWAY MOTEL

AAA SAVE
◆
Motel

Phone: (760)256-8931
All Year　　　　　　　1P: $25- 45　2P/1B: $30- 55　2P/2B: $33- 60　XP: $3-5　　D
Location: Just e of I-15; from I-15 & westbound I-40, E Main St exits. 1630 E Main St 92311.
Terms: Reserv deposit; weekly rates; small pets only, in smoking rooms. **Facility:** 33 rooms. Modest rooms. 2 stories; exterior corridors. **Dining:** Coffee shop nearby. **All Rooms:** extended cable TV. **Cards:** AE, CB, DI, DS, JC, MC, VI. **Special Amenities:** Free local telephone calls and preferred room (subject to availability with advanced reservations).

GOOD NITE INN

AAA SAVE
◆
Motel

Phone: (760)253-2121
All Year　　　　　　　1P: $40　　2P/1B: $46　　2P/2B: $52　　XP: $6　　F18
Location: 8 mi s on I-15. 2551 Commerce Pkwy 92311. Fax: 760/253-2086. **Terms:** Small pets only.
Facility: 110 rooms. Across freeway from factory outlet shopping mall. 3 stories; exterior corridors; whirlpool.
Dining: Restaurant nearby. **Cards:** AE, CB, DI, DS, JC, MC, VI. **Special Amenities:** Free local telephone calls.

HOLIDAY INN

◆◆◆
Motor Inn

Rates Subject to Change　　　　　　　　Phone: 760/256-5673
All Year　　　　　　　1P: $75- 125　2P/1B: $85- 140　2P/2B: $90- 145　XP: $5　　F12
Location: 0.3 mi w of I-15; from I-15 & westbound I-40, E Main St exits. 1511 E Main St 92311.
Fax: 760/256-5917. **Facility:** 148 rooms. 3 stories; interior corridors; heated pool. **Cards:** AE, DI, MC, VI.

HOLIDAY INN EXPRESS

◆◆◆
Motel

VI.

Rates Subject to Change　　　　　　　　Phone: (760)256-1300
All Year　　　　　　　1P: $59- 85　2P/1B: $59- 85　2P/2B: $59- 85
Location: 0.8 mi ne of I-15, exit W Main St. 1861 W Main St 92311. Fax: 760/256-6807. **Facility:** 65 rooms. 3 stories; interior corridors; small pool. **All Rooms:** combo or shower baths. **Cards:** AE, CB, DI, DS, JC, MC,

QUALITY INN

◆◆
Motor Inn

Rates Subject to Change　　　　　　　　Phone: (760)256-6891
All Year　　　　　　　1P: $49- 64　2P/1B: $58- 64　2P/2B: $58- 64　XP: $6　　F18
Location: 0.3 mi w of I-15; from I-15 & I-40 westbound, E Main St exit. 1520 E Main St 92311.
Fax: 760/256-3850. **Terms:** Reserv deposit, 7 day notice. **Facility:** 100 rooms. Large lawn area. 2 stories; exterior corridors; heated pool. **Cards:** AE, CB, DI, DS, MC, VI.

STARDUST INN

AAA SAVE
◆
Motel

Phone: (760)256-7116
All Year　　　　　　　1P: $30- 35　2P/1B: $35- 45　2P/2B: $40- 50　XP: $5　　F10
Location: I-15, Barstow Rd exit; 0.8 mi n, then 0.4 mi e. 901 E Main St 92311. Fax: 760/256-1408.
Terms: Reserv deposit; weekly rates; small pets only, $3 fee. **Facility:** 24 rooms. 2 stories; exterior corridors; small pool. **All Rooms:** extended cable TV. **Some Rooms:** 6 kitchens, no utensils. **Cards:** AE, CB, DI, DS, MC, VI. **Special Amenities:** Early check-in/late check-out and free local telephone calls.

RESTAURANT

LE SPURS STEAK HOUSE **Lunch:** $7-$11 **Dinner:** $12-$19 **Phone:** 760/256-8888
Location: 1.7 mi n of downtown via First Ave. 690 Old Hwy 58 92311. **Hours:** 11 am-9 pm, Fri-9:30 pm, Sat
4 pm-9:30 pm, Sun 4 pm-9 pm. Closed: 1/1, 11/25 & 12/25. **Features:** casual dress; cocktails & lounge.
Attractive western decor. Features prime rib, steak & seafood. **Cards:** AE, DS, MC, VI.

teakhouse

BASS LAKE—200

LODGINGS

INES RESORT CHALETS Rates Subject to Change **Phone:** 559/642-3121

4/1-8/31	1P: $199- 249	2P/1B: $199- 249	2P/2B: $199- 249	XP: $10 F16
9/1-12/31	1P: $129- 159	2P/1B: $129- 159	2P/2B: $129- 159	XP: $10 F16
2/1-3/31 & 1/1-1/31	1P: $59- 109	2P/1B: $59- 109	2P/2B: $59- 109	XP: $10 F16

ocation: 6 mi e of SR 41; CR 222 exit, e on CR 274 & s on SR 434; in Pine Village. 54432 Road 432 93604 (PO Box
09). Fax: 559/642-3902. **Terms:** Check-in 4 pm; reserv deposit, 7 day notice; 3 night min stay, weekends in summer.
acility: 84 rooms. 1-bedroom bilevel duplexes with deck. Some with view of lake; most with fireplace. Midweek discounts; 2
tories; exterior corridors; 2 tennis courts. Fee: boat ramp, marina. **Services:** giftshop. **Recreation:** fishing. Fee: boating,
aterskiing; snowmobiling. **Cards:** AE, CB, DI, DS, JC, MC, VI. *(See color ad p 1089)*

INES RESORT SUITES Rates Subject to Change **Phone:** 559/642-3131

4/1-8/31 [CP]	1P: $249- 369	2P/1B: $249- 369		XP: $15
9/1-12/31 [CP]	1P: $159- 259	2P/1B: $159- 259		XP: $15
2/1-3/31 & 1/1-1/31 [CP]	1P: $69- 129	2P/1B: $69- 129		XP: $15

esort Lodge
ocation: 6 mi e of SR 41 CR 222 exit, e on CR 274 & s on CR 434; in Pines Village. 54432 Road 432 93604 (PO Box
09). Fax: 559/642-3902. **Terms:** Reserv deposit, 7 day notice; 3 night min stay, weekends, in season. **Facility:** 20 rooms.
ireplaces, wet bars, decks & step-down parlor. 2 stories; interior corridors; 2 tennis courts. Fee: boat ramp, marina.
ecreation: fishing. Fee: boating, waterskiing; snowmobiling. **Cards:** CB, DI, DS, JC, MC, VI.

BEAUMONT—9,700

LODGINGS

EST WESTERN EL RANCHO MOTEL Rates Subject to Change **Phone:** (909)845-2176
All Year 1P: $49- 73 2P/1B: $54- 73 2P/2B: $57- 70 XP: $5 F12
Motel **Location:** Just n of I-10, exit Beaumont Ave. 480 E Fifth St 92223. Fax: 909/845-7559. **Facility:** 52 rooms. 4
two-bedroom units. 2 stories; exterior corridors. **All Rooms:** combo or shower baths. **Cards:** AE, CB, DI, DS,
MC, VI.

BUDGET HOST INN **Phone:** (909)845-2185
All Year 1P: $36- 40 2P/1B: $40- 46 2P/2B: $45- 50 XP: $3-5
Motel **Location:** Adjacent to I-10, exit Beaumont Ave; just e. 625 E 5th St 92223. **Terms:** Weekly rates; pets, $2
extra charge. **Facility:** 24 rooms. 2 two-bedroom units. 2 stories; exterior corridors. **All Rooms:** shower
baths. **Cards:** AE, CB, DI, DS, MC, VI. **Special Amenities:** Free local telephone calls and preferred
room (subject to availability with advanced reservations). *(See color ad below)*

WINDSOR MOTEL **Phone:** 909/845-1436
All Year [CP] 1P: $32- 34 2P/1B: $32- 36 2P/2B: $37- 41 XP: $3-5
Motel **Location:** From I-10, westbound exit Pennsylvania Ave, 1 blk n, then e; eastbound take first Beaumont exit,
2 mi e. 1265 E 6th St 92223. Fax: 909/845-1436. **Terms:** Reserv deposit; handling fee imposed; weekly
rates; pets, $3 extra charge. **Facility:** 16 rooms. Whirlpool rm, $75-$99; 1 story; exterior corridors.
All Rooms: combo or shower baths. **Some Rooms:** 2 efficiencies, whirlpools. **Cards:** AE, DS, MC, VI.

BELL—*See Los Angeles p. 587.*

BELLFLOWER—*See Los Angeles p. 587.*

BELL GARDENS—See Los Angeles p. 588.

BELMONT—See San Francisco p. 965.

BENICIA—24,400

LODGING

BEST WESTERN HERITAGE INN
Phone: (707)746-0401

AAA SAVE ◆◆◆ Motel

All Year [CP]
    1P: $60- 85 2P/1B: $60- 85 2P/2B: $60- 85 XP: $5 F12
Location: E off I-780, exit Central Benicia/E 2nd St. 1955 E 2nd St 94510. Fax: 707/745-0842.
Terms: Small pets only, $25 dep req. **Facility:** 99 rooms. Spacious rooms. 30 whirlpool rms, extra charge; 3 stories; interior corridors; whirlpool. **Some Rooms:** 5 efficiencies. **Cards:** AE, CB, DI, DS, MC, VI.

RESTAURANT

UNION HOTEL & GARDENS
  Lunch: $7-$11   **Dinner:** $12-$18   Phone: 707/746-0100
◆◆ American

Location: 401 1st St 94510. **Hours:** 11:30 am-2:30 & 6-10 pm, Sat 9:30 am-2:30 & 6-10 pm, Sun 9:30 am-11 & 5:30-9 pm. **Reservations:** suggested. **Features:** semi-formal attire; Sunday brunch; children's menu; cocktails & lounge; entertainment; street parking; a la carte. Historic 1882 hotel, emphasis on fresh local ingredients & creative preparation. Smoking in cocktail lounge only. Smoke free premises. **Cards:** AE, CB, DI, DS, MC, VI.

BEN LOMOND—7,200

LODGINGS

ECONO LODGE
Phone: (831)336-2292

AAA SAVE ◆◆ Motel

Fri & Sat 5/1-9/30 [CP]	1P: $69- 165	2P/1B: $69- 165	2P/2B: $79- 175	XP: $10	F12
Sun-Thurs 5/1-9/30 [CP]	1P: $59- 145	2P/1B: $59- 145	2P/2B: $69- 165	XP: $10	F12
2/1-4/30 & 10/1-1/31 [CP]	1P: $48- 115	2P/1B: $48- 115	2P/2B: $58- 135	XP: $10	F12

Location: 0.3 mi n on SR 9; on San Lorenzo River. 9733 Hwy 9 95005. Fax: 831/336-0554. **Terms:** Reserv deposit, 3 day notice. **Facility:** 21 rooms. In the redwoods. 1 housekeeping cottage & whirlpool rooms $100-$185 for 2 persons; 2 stories; exterior corridors. **Recreation:** fishing. **All Rooms:** combo or shower baths. **Cards:** AE, DI, DS, MC, VI. **Special Amenities:** Free breakfast and preferred room (subject to availability with advanced reservations).

JAYE'S TIMBERLANE RESORT
  Rates Subject to Change   Phone: 831/336-5479
AAA
    All Year 1P: $70- 110 2P/1B: $70- 110 XP: $10
◆◆ Cottage

Location: 0.5 mi s on SR 9. 8705 Hwy 9 95005. **Terms:** Reserv deposit, 7 day notice; weekly rates; 2 night min stay, weekends & in summer. **Facility:** 10 rooms. In Redwoods hillside. 2 units with fireplace. Private deck or porch. 1 two-bedroom unit. Lower rates, in winter; 1 story; exterior corridors. **All Rooms:** efficiencies, shower baths. **Cards:** MC, VI.

BERKELEY—102,700   (See map p. 752; index p. 750)

LODGINGS

BERKELEY MARINA RADISSON
Phone: (510)548-7920

AAA SAVE ◆◆◆ Motor Inn

All Year   1P: $99- 149 2P/1B: $99- 149 2P/2B: $99- 149
Location: On Berkeley Marina, exit I-80 University Ave w 0.5 mi. 200 Marina Blvd 94710. Fax: 510/548-7944. **Facility:** 375 rooms. Some rooms with view of Marina & San Francisco Bay. 1 whirlpool rm, extra charge; interior corridors; indoor pool, sauna, 2 indoor whirlpools; boat dock. **Dining:** Restaurant; 6:30 am-2:30 & 4:30-10 pm, Sat 7 am-2:30 & 4:30-11 pm; $11-$20; cocktails. **Services:** giftshop; area transportation, to Bart. **Recreation:** jogging, pier. **Cards:** AE, CB, DI, DS, JC, MC, VI. **Special Amenities:** Free newspaper.

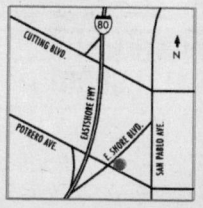

(see map p. 752)

GOLDEN BEAR MOTEL   Rates Subject to Change   **Phone:** 510/525-6770   29
All Year   1P: $60- 65   2P/1B: $60- 65   2P/2B: $70- 75   XP: $5
Location: Exit I-80 Gilman St e, 0.8 mi s. 1620 San Pablo Ave 94702. Fax: 510/525-6999. **Terms:** Small
pets only, $5 extra charge. **Facility:** 43 rooms. 8 two-bedroom units. 4 two-bedroom cottages with kitchen,
$99-$125 for up to 4 persons; 2 stories; exterior corridors. **Dining:** Restaurant nearby. **All Rooms:** combo or
shower baths. **Cards:** AE, CB, DI, DS, JC, MC, VI.

HOTEL DURANT   Rates Subject to Change   **Phone:** (510)845-8981   31
All Year [CP]   1P: $95   2P/1B: $105   2P/2B: $105   XP: $15   F12
Location: E off I-80 on Ashby to Telegraph n to Durant; westbound from SR 13 & 24 exit Berkeley, w on
Ashby to Telegraph, then n to Durant at Bowditch. 2600 Durant Ave 94704. Fax: 510/486-8336.
Terms: Handling fee imposed. **Facility:** 140 rooms. 1 block from university. A refurbished 1928 hotel. 6 stories;
interior corridors. Fee: parking. **Dining:** Restaurant; 7 am-10 & 11-10 pm; $12-$20; cocktails.
All Rooms: combo or shower baths. **Cards:** AE, CB, DI, DS, JC, MC, VI.

RESTAURANTS

CHEZ PANISSE   **Lunch:** $25   **Dinner:** $45-$65   **Phone:** 510/548-5525   16
Location: At Cedar St. 1517 Shattuck Ave 94709. **Hours:** 6 pm & 9 pm seatings, Cafe Panisse 11:30 am-3
& 5-10:30 pm, Fri & Sat-11:30 pm. Closed major holidays. **Reservations:** required; 1 mth advance.
Features: casual dress; beer & wine only; street parking; prix fixe. California, French & strong Mediterranean
influence. At same location "Cafe Panisse" is open for lunch, serves a full menu, upstairs dining, less
restrictive in reservation policy. Smoke free premises. **Cards:** AE, MC, VI.

JORDAN'S AT THE CLAREMONT   **Lunch:** $12-$18   **Dinner:** $27-$40   **Phone:** 510/843-3000   15
Location: In Oakland/Berkeley Hills; on SR 13, 1 mi n of jct SR 24, exit SR 24 via Claremont Ave. 41
Tunnel Rd 94705. **Hours:** 6:30 am-10 pm. **Reservations:** suggested. **Features:** casual dress; Sunday
brunch; health conscious menu; cocktails & lounge; fee for valet parking; a la carte. Extraordinary views of
San Francisco Bay & sunset. Inovative nutritionally balanced items with emphasis on fresh local seasonal
ingredients. Herbs from the Claremont's own gardens. Warm, luxurious atmosphere. Smoke free premises. **Cards:** AE, CB,
DS, JC, MC, VI.

SKATES ON THE BAY   **Lunch:** $10-$15   **Dinner:** $11-$19   **Phone:** 510/549-1900   17
Location: On Berkeley Marina, exit I-80 University Ave, w 0.3 mi. 100 Seawall Dr 94710. **Hours:** 11:30 am-3
& 5-10 pm, Sat 11:30 am-3 & 4-10:30 pm, Sun 10:30 am-10 pm. Closed: 12/25. **Reservations:** suggested.
Features: casual dress; Sunday brunch; children's menu; cocktails & lounge; a la carte. Varied menu,
mesquite grilled fish, duck & pasta. Casual atmosphere with view of bay. Smoke free premises. **Cards:** AE, DI, DS, MC, VI.

BERRY CREEK

LODGING

LAKE OROVILLE BED & BREAKFAST   Guaranteed Rates   **Phone:** 530/589-0700
All Year [BP]   1P: $75- 135   2P/1B: $75- 135   2P/2B: $75- 135   XP: $10
Location: Exit SR 70 at SR 162, 15 mi e on SR 162 to Bell Ranch Rd, 0.5 mi w to Sunday Dr. 240 Sunday
Dr 95916. Fax: 530/589-5313. **Facility:** 6 rooms. Picturesque setting overlooking Lake Oroville. 2 stories; inte-
rior corridors. **Cards:** AE, DS, MC, VI.

BEVERLY HILLS—See Los Angeles p. 588.

BIG BEAR CITY—11,200

LODGINGS

CATHY'S COUNTRY COTTAGES   **Phone:** 909/866-7444
Fri-Sun [CP]   2P/1B: $79- 199
Mon-Thurs [CP]   1P: $39   2P/1B: $40- 99
Location: On SR 18; 0.7 mi e of Division St across from airport entrance. 600 W Big Bear Blvd 92315 (PO
Box 3706, BIG BEAR LAKE). Fax: 909/866-1822. **Terms:** Reserv deposit, 14 day notice; handling fee
imposed; weekly rates; 2 night min stay, weekends. **Facility:** 6 rooms. Charming country motif. All rooms with
fireplace & whirlpool tub. 1 small unit on 2nd floor. Wedding chapel. 1 story; exterior corridors. **All Rooms:** combo or shower
baths. **Cards:** AE, CB, DI, DS, JC, MC, VI. (See color ad p 376)

GOLD MOUNTAIN MANOR BED & BREAKFAST   Rates Subject to Change   **Phone:** (909)585-6997
All Year [BP]   1P: $125- 190   2P/1B: $125- 190   XP: $25
Location: Just w of Greenway Dr, just n of North Shore Dr (SR 38). 1117 Anita 92314 (PO Box 2027).
Fax: 909/585-0327. **Terms:** Reserv deposit, 7 day notice; handling fee imposed; 2 night min stay, weekends.
Facility: 6 rooms. Log mansion built in 1928. Located on 1 acre of pine trees & grassy areas. 6 rooms with
woodburning fireplace, one suite with spa. 2 stories; interior corridors; smoke free premises. **Recreation:** hiking trails.
All Rooms: combo or shower baths. **Cards:** AE, DS, MC, VI.

RESTAURANT

MADLON'S RESTAURANT   **Lunch:** $6-$10   **Dinner:** $14-$21   **Phone:** 909/585-3762
Location: On SR 18. 829 W Big Bear Blvd 92314. **Hours:** 11 am-2 & 5-8 pm, Sat & Sun 8 am-2:30 & 5-9
pm. Closed: 1/1, 11/25 & Mon. **Reservations:** suggested. **Features:** casual dress; beer & wine only. Fine
dining in a charming, cozy restaurant. Large selection of seafood, poultry, beef & pasta. Smoke free
premises. **Cards:** DI, DS, MC, VI.

BIG BEAR LAKE—5,400

LODGINGS

ALPENHORN BED & BREAKFAST
Phone: 909/866-570

(AAA) [SAVE]   Fri & Sat [BP]   2P/1B: $155- 185
              Sun-Thurs [BP]   2P/1B: $135- 165
[FYI]   Too new to rate. **Location:** 601 Knight Ave 92315 (PO Box 2912). Fax: 909/866-8221. **Terms:** Check-in
Bed &   pm; reserv deposit; 2 night min stay, weekends. **Facility:** 7 rooms. Mountain modern pine inn. Rooms with ga
Breakfast   fireplace & whirlpool, most with balcony. 2 stories; interior corridors; designated smoking area; whirlpool
              Services: complimentary evening beverages. **Cards:** MC, VI.   [VCR] [X] [X]

ALPINE VILLAGE SUITES
Phone: 909/866-546

(AAA) [SAVE]   Fri & Sat 2/1-4/15 &
              11/22-1/31   1P: $129- 149   2P/1B: $129- 149   2P/2B: $129- 149
◆ ◆   Sun-Thurs 2/1-4/15, Fri & Sat
Suite Motel   4/16-11/21 & Sun-Thurs
              11/22-1/31   1P: $98- 128   2P/1B: $98- 128   2P/2B: $98- 128
              Sun-Thurs 4/16-11/21   1P: $79- 109   2P/1B: $79- 109   2P/2B: $79- 109
Location: In the Village area; on SR 18 Business Rt. 546 Pine Knot Ave 92315 (PO Box 1713). Fax: 909/866-0031
Terms: Reserv deposit; small pets only, dep req. **Facility:** 6 rooms. Spacious 1-bedroom suites with gas fireplace. 2 stories
interior/exterior corridors. **Dining:** Restaurant nearby. **All Rooms:** kitchens, extended cable TV. **Some Rooms:** whirlpools
Cards: AE, DS, MC, VI.   [X] [X] [X] [VCR] [X] [X] [X]

BEAR MANOR CABINS
Phone: 909/866-680

(AAA) [SAVE]   12/17-1/3   1P: $119- 169   2P/1B: $119- 169   2P/2B: $149- 169
              Fri-Sun 2/1-12/16 & 1/4-1/31 1P: $109- 149 2P/1B: $109- 149 2P/2B: $129- 149
◆ ◆   Mon-Thurs 2/1-4/1 & 1/4-1/31 1P: $59- 109 2P/1B: $59- 109 2P/2B: $79- 119
Cottage   Mon-Thurs 4/2-12/16   1P: $49- 89   2P/1B: $49- 89   2P/2B: $59- 99
              Location: 0.8 mi w on SR 18. 40375 Big Bear Blvd 92315 (PO Box 3874). Fax: 909/866-8644. **Facility:** 1
rooms. Tree-shaded grounds. Attractive cabins with knotty pine walls & rock fireplaces, most with whirlpool. Registration at the
adjacent Accommodation by Reservation office. 1 two-bedroom unit. 1 story; exterior corridors. **Cards:** AE, DS, MC, VI.
                                                                [X] [X] [X] [X]

BIG BEAR CABINS
Phone: (909)866-272

(AAA) [SAVE]   2/1-3/14 & 11/16-1/31 1P: $59- 99   2P/1B: $59- 109   2P/2B: $89- 139   XP: $10   F1
◆   3/15-11/15   1P: $59- 89   2P/1B: $59- 99   2P/2B: $79- 129   XP: $10   F1
              Location: 1.3 mi w on SR 18. 39774 Big Bear Blvd 92315 (PO Box 1533). **Terms:** Reserv deposit, 3 da
Cottage   notice; handling fee imposed; weekly rates; pets, $10 extra charge, designated rooms. **Facility:** 14 rooms
              Spacious grounds. Small, rustic to spacious cabins with fireplace. 2 two-bedroom units. 1 story; exterior corri
dors; heated pool, whirlpool. **All Rooms:** combo or shower baths, extended cable TV. **Some Rooms:** 5 efficiencies, (
kitchens. **Cards:** MC, VI. *(See color ad below)*   [X] [X] [X] [X] [X] [X]

BIG BEAR LAKE INN CIENEGA
Phone: (909)866-347

(AAA) [SAVE]   Fri & Sat [CP]   2P/1B: $75- 81   2P/2B: $89- 96   XP: $5
◆   Sun-Thurs [CP]   1P: $51   2P/1B: $53- 57   2P/2B: $60- 64   XP: $5
Motel   **Location:** 2.3 mi w on SR 18. 39471 Big Bear Blvd 92315 (PO Box 1665). Fax: 909/878-9187
              Terms: Reserv deposit, 3 day notice. **Facility:** 52 rooms. Large rooms, all with king beds. 9 efficiencies, $10
              extra, no utensils; 2 stories; exterior corridors; heated pool, whirlpool. **Cards:** AE, DS, MC, VI
Special Amenities: Free breakfast and free local telephone calls.   [X] [X] [X] [X]

COZY HOLLOW LODGE
Phone: 909/866-8888

◆ ◆   Fri-Sun [CP]   1P: $49- 95   2P/1B: $69- 95   2P/2B: $79- 159   XP: $10
Cottage   Mon-Thurs [CP]   1P: $49- 86   2P/1B: $49- 86   2P/2B: $69- 159   XP: $10
              Location: 0.8 mi w on SR 18. 40409 Big Bear Blvd 92315 (PO Box 1288). Fax: 909/866-2692
Terms: Reserv deposit, 10 day notice; 2 night min stay, weekends. **Facility:** 13 rooms. Tree-shaded grounds. Comfortable
nicely furnished cabins with fireplace. 2 two-bedroom units. 3 units with whirlpool, $99-$169; 1 story; exterior corridors; playground. **Some Rooms:** 5 efficiencies, 2 kitchens. **Cards:** AE, CB, DI, DS, MC, VI.   [X] [X] [X] [X] [X] [X]

EAGLE'S NEST BED & BREAKFAST
Phone: (909)866-646

◆ ◆   All Year [BP]   1P: $85- 170   2P/1B: $85- 170   2P/2B: $85- 170
Bed &   **Location:** 1 mi e on SR 18. 41675 Big Bear Blvd 92315 (PO Box 1003). **Terms:** Reserv deposit, 5 day
Breakfast   notice; 2 night min stay, weekends. **Facility:** 10 rooms. Charming bed & breakfast inn in a log cabin building
              with country antiques. Also 5 cottage units with fireplace, TV, microwave, refrigerator & coffee maker. Break-
fast avail for guests in cottage units, extra charge. 1-2 stories; interior/exterior corridors. **Recreation:** bicycles.
All Rooms: combo or shower baths. **Some Rooms:** kitchen. **Cards:** AE, DS, MC, VI.   [X] [X] [X] [X] [X] [X]

GEWATER INN
Phone: (909)866-4161
SAVE   All Year   1P: $49- 105   2P/1B: $49- 125   2P/2B: $49- 125   XP: $20-30   F16
otel   **Location:** Just n of SR 18. 40570 Simonds Dr 92315 (PO Box 4294). **Terms:** Reserv deposit; handling fee
        imposed; pets, $10 extra charge. **Facility:** 9 rooms. Lakefront, next to Big Bear Marina. 2 stories; exterior cor-
        ridors. **All Rooms:** kitchens, extended cable TV. **Cards:** AE, DS, MC, VI. **Special Amenities:** Early
        check-in/late check-out and free local telephone calls.

RESIDE LODGE
Phone: (909)866-2253
        2/1-3/31 & 11/1-1/31 [CP]   1P: $90- 100   2P/1B: $90- 100
◆ ◆   4/1-10/31 [CP]   1P: $70- 80   2P/1B: $70- 80
otel   **Location:** SR 18, just w of Pine Knot Ave. 40660 Lakeview Dr 92315 (PO Box 635). Fax: 909/866-8113.
        Terms: Reserv deposit, 14 day notice; handling fee imposed; 2 night min stay, weekends. **Facility:** 32 rooms.
        A variety of attractively decorated rooms, studios, suites & spa units. Some gas or woodburning fireplaces.
me with lake view. 3 two-bedroom units. Suites & spa units, $120-$190; 1-2 stories; exterior corridors; heated pool.
Rooms: extended cable TV. **Some Rooms:** 20 efficiencies. **Cards:** AE, DS, MC, VI. **Special Amenities:** Free breakfast
d free local telephone calls.

REST SHORES INN
Rates Subject to Change   Phone: 909/866-6551
        Fri & Sat 2/1-4/14 & All Year 1P: $105- 135   2P/1B: $105- 135   2P/2B: $185- 250
◆ ◆   **Location:** On SR 18, just w of Pine Knot Ave. 40670 Lakeview Dr 92315 (PO Box 946). Fax: 909/866-6406.
ando Motel **Terms:** Weekly rates; 2 night min stay, weekends. **Facility:** 23 rooms. Lakefront. Studio units with efficiency &
        1- to 3-bedroom apartments with gas fireplace. Barbecue on patio or balcony, overlooking the lake. 3 stories;
        exterior corridors; heated pool, sauna, whirlpool; boat dock. **Recreation:** fishing, waterskiing.
Rooms: extended cable TV. **Cards:** AE, CB, DI, DS, MC, VI. *(See color ad below)*

RONTIER LODGE & MOTEL
Phone: (909)866-5888
        All Year [CP]   1P: $79- 115   2P/1B: $84- 195   2P/2B: $80- 195   XP: $10
◆ ◆   **Location:** 0.5 mi w on SR 18. 40472 Big Bear Blvd 92315 (PO Box 1966). Fax: 909/866-4372.
ottage **Terms:** Reserv deposit, 14 day notice; 2 night min stay, weekends; pets, $10 extra charge, $75 dep req, ltd
        rms. **Facility:** 44 rooms. Studio units & 1- to 3-bedroom housekeeping cabins with fireplace, 6 with spa tubs.
        Lakefront motel units. Cabins with whirlpool, $150-$250. 2-bedroom Lakefront cottage with whirlpool tub, $289-
10; 1-2 stories; exterior corridors; pool heated in summer only; boat dock; playground. **All Rooms:** comb, shower or tub
ths. **Some Rooms:** 12 efficiencies, 16 kitchens. **Cards:** AE, CB, DI, DS, MC. **Special Amenities:** Free breakfast.

OLDEN BEAR COTTAGES
Guaranteed Rates   Phone: (909)866-2010
        All Year   1P: $59- 89   2P/1B: $69- 119   XP: $10   F12
◆ ◆   **Location:** 2 mi w on SR 18. 39367 Big Bear Blvd 92315 (PO Box 1731). Fax: 909/866-9547. **Terms:** Reserv
ottage deposit, 14 day notice; pets, $10 extra charge. **Facility:** 23 rooms. Rustic cabins & motel rooms with fireplace,
        most with kitchen & outdoor barbecue. 1 three-bedroom unit, 12 two-bedroom units. 1 four-bedroom cabin with
        fireplace, kitchen & dining room for up to 14 persons $229-$299; 2 stories; exterior corridors; heated pool,
hirlpool; playground. **Services:** winter plug-ins. **Recreation:** barbecue area, basketball, shuffleboard & volleyball.
Rooms: combo or shower baths, extended cable TV. **Some Rooms:** 4 efficiencies, 17 kitchens. **Cards:** AE, DS, MC, VI.

OLDMINE LODGE
Phone: (909)866-5118
SAVE   All Year [CP]   1P: $35- 75   2P/1B: $45- 105   2P/2B: $75- 105   XP: $10
◆ ◆ ◆   **Location:** 1.5 mi e on SR 18; 0.3 mi s on Moonridge Rd. 42268 Moonridge Rd 92315 (PO Box 198).
otel   Fax: 909/806-5041. **Terms:** Reserv deposit, 3 day notice; handling fee imposed; 2 night min stay, weekends.
        Facility: 11 rooms. On attractive pine-shaded grounds with barbecue area & playground. 6 suites with living
        room, bedroom, kitchen & woodburning fireplace; 2 stories; exterior corridors; whirlpool. **All Rooms:** combo
shower baths, extended cable TV. **Cards:** AE, DS, MC, VI.

REY SQUIRREL RESORT
Phone: (909)866-4335
SAVE   All Year   1P: $75- 115   2P/1B: $75- 115   2P/2B: $75- 132   XP: $10-25
◆ ◆ ◆   **Location:** 2.5 mi e of dam on SR 18. 39372 Big Bear Blvd 92315 (PO Box 1711). Fax: 909/866-6271.
ottage **Terms:** Reserv deposit, 14 day notice; 2 night min stay, weekends; pets, $10 extra charge, $100 dep req.
        Facility: 18 rooms. Spacious grounds in a park like setting. Charming 1- to 3-bedroom cottages & 2 motel units
        with fireplace & outdoor barbecue. Fish cleaning area. 3 two-bedroom cabins for up to 6 persons. 3 three-
edroom cabins for up to 8 persons. 1 cabin for up to 20 people $325-$350; 1 story; exterior corridors; heated pool, whirlpool.
Rooms: combo or shower baths, extended cable TV. **Some Rooms:** 16 kitchens. **Cards:** AE, DS, MC, VI.
pecial Amenities: Early check-in/late check-out and free local telephone calls.

HILLCREST LODGE

Phone: (909)866-733█

(AAA) [SAVE]
◆◆◆
Motel

		1P:	2P/1B:		2P/2B:
Fri & Sat 2/1-4/15 & 12/15-1/31		$64- 149	$64- 149		$115- 139
Fri & Sat 4/16-12/14		$49- 139	$49- 139		$79- 118
Sun-Thurs 2/1-4/15 & 12/15-1/31		$39- 99	$39- 99		$74- 84
Sun-Thurs 4/16-12/14		$35- 84	$35- 84		$57- 75

Location: 0.8 mi w on SR 18. 40241 Big Bear Blvd 92315 (PO Box 3945). Fax: 909/866-1171. **Terms:** Reserv deposit, day notice. **Facility:** 12 rooms. Nicely decorated rooms & suites in cabins & 2-story building. 10 rooms with fireplace, 2 wi█ whirlpool. 1 two-bedroom unit. 1-2 stories; exterior corridors; whirlpool. **All Rooms:** combo or shower baths, extended cabl█ TV. **Some Rooms:** 10 kitchens. **Cards:** AE, CB, DI, DS, MC, VI. **Special Amenities:** Early check-in/late check-out an█ free local telephone calls.

HOLIDAY INN-BIG BEAR CHATEAU

Phone: (909)866-666█

(AAA) [SAVE]
◆◆◆
Hotel

	1P:	2P/1B:		2P/2B:
2/1-5/30 & 11/1-1/31	$189- 299	$209- 399		$209- 399
5/31-10/31	$69- 99	$89- 109		$89- 109

Location: 1.5 mi e on SR 18, just s on Moonridge Rd. 42200 Moonridge Rd 92315 (PO Box 1814█ Fax: 909/866-8988. **Facility:** 80 rooms. Elegant, European chateau decor. 2 stories; interior corridors; heate█ pool, whirlpool. **Dining:** Dining room; 7 am-11, noon-2 & 5-9 pm; $12-$29; cocktails. **All Rooms:** extende█ cable TV. **Some Rooms:** whirlpools. **Cards:** AE, CB, DI, DS, MC, VI. *(See ad below)*

HONEY BEAR LODGE

Phone: (909)866-782█

(AAA) [SAVE]
◆◆
Motel

		2P/1B:	2P/2B:	XP:
Fri-Sun		$89- 169	$89- 169	$8
Mon-Thurs		$39- 89	$39- 89	$8

Location: Just e of SR 18 Business Rt (Pine Knot Ave). 40994 Pennsylvania Ave 92315 (Box 2879█ Fax: 909/866-1958. **Terms:** Check-in 4 pm; reserv deposit, 7 day notice; pets, $5 extra charge, $200 de█ req. **Facility:** 20 rooms. Rooms with woodburning fireplace, some with lake view. Close to the village shoppin█ area. 6 rooms with loft; 1-2 stories; exterior corridors. **Some Rooms:** 5 efficiencies, 2 kitchens, whirlpools. **Cards:** AE, DS█ MC, VI. **Special Amenities:** Free local telephone calls and free room upgrade (subject to availability with advance█ reservations).

THE INN AT FAWNSKIN BED & BREAKFAST

Guaranteed Rates   Phone: 909/866-320█

◆◆
Bed & Breakfast

	1P:	2P/1B:	2P/2B:	XP:	
Fri & Sat [BP]	$72- 165	$85- 175		$5-10	D█
Sun-Thurs [BP]	$62- 138	$72- 148		$5-10	D█

Location: SR 38, 0.8 mi e of Fawnskin. 880 Canyon Rd 92333 (PO Box 378, FAWNSKIN). **Terms:** Reser█ deposit, 7 day notice; handling fee imposed; 2 night min stay, weekends. **Facility:** 4 rooms. 2-story log hom█ surrounded by pine trees. Features a knotty pine interior with country decor. 2 stories; interior corridors; designated smokin█ area. **Some Rooms:** color TV. **Cards:** AE, MC, VI.

MARINA RIVIERA RESORT

Phone: 909/866-754█

(AAA) [SAVE]
◆◆◆
Motel

	1P:	2P/1B:	2P/2B:	XP:	
Fri & Sat [CP]	$120- 210	$120- 210	$132- 231	$8-10	F18
Sun-Thurs [CP]	$99- 165	$99- 165	$99- 165	$8	F18

Location: SR 18, 1 blk w of Pine Knot Blvd. 40770 Lakeview Dr 92315 (Box 2824). Fax: 909/866-6705█ **Terms:** Reserv deposit. **Facility:** 42 rooms. On spacious, Lakefront grounds. All rooms with lake view, many with balcony & 4 with gas fireplace. Picnic & barbecue area. 1 suite with whirlpool & kitchen; 3 stories; exterio█ corridors; putting green, golf driving net; beach, heated pool, whirlpool. Fee: boat dock. **Dining:** Restaurant nearby **All Rooms:** extended cable TV. **Some Rooms:** 3 efficiencies, whirlpools. **Cards:** AE, DS, MC, VI. *(See color ad p 375)*

NORTHWOODS RESORT HOTEL

Phone: (909)866-312█

(AAA) [SAVE]
◆◆◆
Motor Inn

	1P:	2P/1B:	2P/2B:	XP:	
12/17-1/31	$154- 194	$154- 194	$154- 194	$10	F18
2/1-4/10 & 6/18-12/16	$144- 184	$144- 184	$144- 184	$10	F18
4/11-6/17	$139- 174	$139- 174	$139- 174	$10	F18

Location: Just e of SR 18, in The Village. 40650 Village Dr 92315 (PO Box 2943). Fax: 909/878-2122█ **Terms:** Check-in 4 pm; reserv deposit, 3 day notice; handling fee imposed; 2 night min stay, winte█ weekends. **Facility:** 141 rooms. Uniquely furnished rooms & suites, many with gas fireplace, some suites with VCP, coffee█ maker, microwave, refrigerator and spa tubs. 4 stories; interior corridors; heated pool, sauna, whirlpool. **Dining:** Restaurant 7 am-10 pm; $12-$24; cocktails. **Services:** giftshop. **All Rooms:** extended cable TV. **Cards:** AE, DI, DS, MC, VI **Special Amenities:** Free room upgrade (subject to availability with advanced reservations). *(See color ad p 375)*

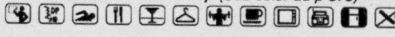

E KNOT GUEST RANCH

Phone: 909/866-6500

| | Fri & Sat | 1P: $119- 149 | 2P/1B: $119- 149 | 2P/2B: $119- 149 | XP: $10 | F12 |
| | Sun-Thurs | 1P: $89 | 2P/1B: $99 | | XP: $10 | F12 |

Location: Just s of SR 18 Business Rt & Downtown area. 908 Pine Knot Ave 92315 (PO Box 3446). **Terms:** Reserv deposit, 7 day notice; weekly rates; 2 night min stay, weekends. **Facility:** 8 rooms. Spacious grounds. 2-room cabins decorated in light colors with fireplace, whirlpool tub & skylight. Also 2-story, edroom family cabin. 1 story; exterior corridors; designated smoking area; playground. **Recreation:** bicycles. **Rooms:** shower baths, extended cable TV. **Some Rooms:** kitchen. **Cards:** AE, DI, DS, MC, VI.

AIL COVE LAKESIDE CABINS

Rates Subject to Change   Phone: (909)866-5957

| All Year | | 2P/1B: $99- 109 | 2P/2B: $99- 109 | XP: $10 | D10 |
| | 1P: $99 | | | | |

Location: Just sw of Fawnskin on SR 38. 39117 N Shore Dr 92333 (PO Box 117, FAWNSKIN). **Fax:** 909/866-5135. **Terms:** Reserv deposit, 10 day notice; handling fee imposed. **Facility:** 6 rooms. Near the e. One-bedroom cabins with kitchen & fireplace. 1 two-bedroom unit. 2 bedroom a-frame cabin, $139-$169; 1-2 stories; ex- or corridors. **All Rooms:** kitchens, combo or shower baths. **Cards:** AE, MC, VI.

ROBINHOOD INN

(AAA)

◆◆

Motor Inn

Rates Subject to Change

Phone: (909)866-46◻

2/1-3/31, 7/1-9/5 & 11/1-1/31 1P: $69- 169 2P/1B: $69- 169 2P/2B: $99- 269
4/1-6/30 & 9/6-10/31   1P: $59- 159 2P/1B: $64- 169 2P/2B: $84- 249

Location: SR 18, Lakeview Dr at Pine Knot Ave. 40797 Lakeview Dr 92315 (PO Box 188◻ Fax: 909/866-4645. **Terms:** Reserv deposit, 4 day notice; weekly/monthly rates; 2 night min stay, weeken◻ pets, $10 extra charge, in designated rooms. **Facility:** 21 rooms. Village area, just s of the lake. 11 rooms w◻ fireplace. 4 suites with whirlpool & fireplace; 2 stories; exterior corridors; whirlpool. **Dining:** Restaurant; 11 am-10 p◻ continental breakfast weekends and major holidays; $8-$12; cocktails. **All Rooms:** extended cable ◻ **Some Rooms:** kitchen. **Cards:** AE, MC, VI.

SHORE ACRES LODGE

(AAA) [SAVE]

◆◆

Cottage

Fri & Sat   1P: $95- 195 2P/1B: $95- 195 2P/2B: $95- 195 XP: $10
2/1-3/31 & Sun-Thurs 1P: $75- 155 2P/1B: $75- 155 2P/2B: $75- 155 XP: $10

Phone: (909)866-82◻

Location: 0.8 mi w of village. 40090 Lakeview Dr 92315 (Box 110410). Fax: 909/866-3248. **Terms:** Rese◻ deposit, 14 day notice; handling fee imposed; weekly rates; package plans, mid-week; 2 night min sta◻ weekends; pets, $5 extra charge. **Facility:** 11 rooms. Pine shaded lakefront grounds. 1 & 2-bedroom cottag◻ with patio, barbecue & fireplace. 4 two-bedroom units. 1 story; exterior corridors; beach, whirlpool, heated pool open 5/28-10◻ boat dock. **Recreation:** fishing. **All Rooms:** kitchens, combo or shower baths, extended cable TV. **Cards:** AE, MC, VI. *(See color ad below)*

SLEEPY FOREST COTTAGES

(AAA) [SAVE]

◆◆◆

Cottage

Fri-Sun [CP]   2P/1B: $119- 199 2P/2B: $149- 199 XP: $10   F
Mon-Thurs [CP]   1P: $59   2P/1B: $59- 99 2P/2B: $74- 99 XP: $10   ◻

Phone: 909/866-74◻

Terms: Reserv deposit, 14 day notice; handling fee imposed; weekly/monthly rates; 2 night min sta◻ weekends. **Facility:** 16 rooms. Cozy country cottages on pine-shaded grounds. Gas or woodburning fireplac◻ 2 two-bedroom units. 3-story unit with loft bedroom; 1 story; exterior corridors. **All Rooms:** combo or shower bath◻ **Some Rooms:** 8 kitchens, whirlpools. **Cards:** AE, CB, DI, DS, JC, MC, VI. *(See color ad below)*

Location: 1 mi e on SR 18, just n on Eureka Dr. 426 Eureka Dr 92315 (PO Box 3706). Fax: 909/866-182◻

STAGE COACH LODGE

(AAA) [SAVE]

◆

Cottage

All Year [CP]   1P: $79- 120 2P/1B: $79- 120 2P/2B: $90- 150 XP: $10

Phone: (909)878-30◻

Location: 0.5 mi e on SR 18, just s. 652 Jeffries 92315 (PO Box 687). Fax: 909/878-2634. **Terms:** Rese◻ deposit, 14 day notice; weekly rates; pets, $100 dep req; in designated units, $10 extra charge. **Facility:** ◻ rooms. Spacious 1- & 2-bedroom, 2-story cottages and 1-2 bedroom rustic cabins, many with fireplace. Als◻ one 4-bedroom cottage. 8 two-bedroom units. 1-2 stories; exterior corridors; playgroun◻ **Recreation:** barbecue. **All Rooms:** combo or shower baths. **Some Rooms:** 13 kitchens, whirlpools. **Cards:** AE, DS, M◻ VI. **Special Amenities:** Free breakfast and free room upgrade (subject to availability with advanced reservations). *(See color ad p 377)*

Cathy's Country Cottages
photo by Marcus Dietz

WITZERLAND HAUS BED & BREAKFAST INN   Rates Subject to Change   **Phone:** (909)866-3729
◆◆◆
ed &
eakfast
2/1-4/15 & 11/15-1/31 [BP]   2P/1B: $125- 175   2P/2B: $125- 175   XP: $20
4/16-11/14 [EP]   1P: $50- 68   2P/1B: $68- 115   2P/2B: $165
Location: Located by Snow Summit ski area, 0.5 mi s of SR 18 via Summit Blvd. 41829 Switzerland Dr 92315 (PO Box 177). **Terms:** Reserv deposit, 7 day notice. **Facility:** 5 rooms. Swiss-style house. Nicely deco-
ated rooms. Garden area with view of Snow Summit ski area. 1 suite with fireplace; 2 stories; interior corridors.
ervices: area transportation. **All Rooms:** combo or shower baths. **Cards:** AE, DS, MC, VI.

HUNDERCLOUD RESORT   Rates Subject to Change   **Phone:** (909)866-7594
ⓐ
◆◆
Motel
Fri & Sat [CP]   1P: $74- 99   2P/1B: $74- 99   2P/2B: $84- 99   XP: $10   F15
Sun-Thurs [CP]   1P: $64- 84   2P/1B: $64- 84   2P/2B: $74- 84   XP: $10   F15
Location: On SR 18, 0.3 mi w of Pine Knot Ave. 40598 Lakeview Dr 92315 (PO Box 1773).
Fax: 909/866-4543. **Terms:** Handling fee imposed. **Facility:** 64 rooms. Located on pine shaded grounds, with
picnic and BBQ area. Family units for up to 6 persons. Some rooms with fireplace. 1 two-bedroom unit. 2 sto-
es; interior/exterior corridors; heated indoor pool, saunas, indoor whirlpool. **All Rooms:** shower baths. **Some Rooms:** 16
itchens. **Cards:** AE, CB, DI, DS, MC, VI. *(See ad below)*

TIMBER HAVEN LODGE
(AAA) (SAVE)

◆◆
Cottage

							Phone: (909)866-3568
Mon-Thurs [CP]	1P:	$49	2P/1B:	$79- 139		XP: $10	F18
Fri-Sun [CP]			2P/1B:	$109- 159		XP: $10	F18

Location: 1.8 mi w on SR 18, 0.3 mi s. 877 Tulip Ln 92315 (PO Box 430). Fax: 909/866-4577
Terms: Reserv deposit, 14 day notice; pets, $10 extra charge, $30-$50 dep req. **Facility:** 9 rooms. Nicely landscaped, pine-shaded grounds in a quiet area. All units with fireplace. 1 two-bedroom unit. 1 large cabin, up to 6 persons; one 2-bedroom, 2-story cottage; 1 story; exterior corridors; whirlpool. **All Rooms:** combo or shower baths. **Some Rooms:** efficiency, 8 kitchens, whirlpools. **Cards:** AE, DS, MC, VI. **Special Amenities:** Free breakfast and free local telephone calls. *(See color ad p 377)*

TIMBERLINE LODGE
(AAA) (SAVE)

◆◆◆
Cottage

MC, VI.

							Phone: 909/866-4141
All Year	1P:	$71- 106	2P/1B:	$71- 126	2P/2B: $89- 200	XP: $10	F3

Location: 1.5 mi w on SR 18. 39921 Big Bear Blvd 92315 (PO Box 1955). Fax: 909/866-0707.
Terms: Reserv deposit, 10 day notice; pets, $10 extra charge. **Facility:** 13 rooms. Studios & 1-to 3-bedroom housekeeping units, many with fireplace. 6 two-bedroom units. 1-2 stories; exterior corridors; heated pool; playground. **All Rooms:** combo or shower baths, extended cable TV. **Some Rooms:** 8 kitchens. **Cards:** AE, DS,

TRUFFLES BED & BREAKFAST
◆◆◆
Bed &
Breakfast

Rates Subject to Change
Phone: 909/585-2772

All Year [BP]	1P: $115- 150	2P/1B: $115- 150		

Location: SR 18, Moonridge Rd 1.7 mi s to Sand Canyon, 0.1 mi to Bow Canyon Dr, then 0.7 mi. 43591 Bow Canyon Dr 92315 (PO Box 130649). **Terms:** Reserv deposit, 7 day notice. **Facility:** 5 rooms. Ranch style building located in a quiet residential area. Beautifully furnished & decorated rooms. 1 room with gas fireplace. 2 stories; interior corridors; smoke free premises. **All Rooms:** comb, shower or tub baths. **Cards:** AE, DS, MC, VI.

WILDWOOD RESORT
(AAA) (SAVE)

◆◆
Cottage

All Year	1P: $55- 108	2P/1B: $55- 108	2P/2B: $55- 155	XP: $10	Phone: (909)878-2178

Location: 0.8 mi w of village on SR 18. 40210 Big Bear Blvd 92315 (PO Box 2885). Fax: 909/878-3036.
Terms: Reserv deposit, 14 day notice; weekly rates; 2 night min stay, weekends; pets, $10 extra charge, $100 dep req. **Facility:** 19 rooms. 1- & 2-bedroom housekeeping cottages & 4 lodge units; most with fireplace. 5 two-bedroom units. 1-2 stories; interior/exterior corridors; heated pool, whirlpool; playground. **Dining:** Restaurant nearby. **Recreation:** barbecue. **All Rooms:** combo or shower baths. **Some Rooms:** 13 kitchens. **Cards:** AE, DS, MC, VI. **Special Amenities:** Free local telephone calls and preferred room (subject to availability with advanced reservations).

WISHING WELL MOTEL
(AAA) (SAVE)

◆◆
Motel

							Phone: 909/866-3505
Fri & Sat [CP]	1P:	$59- 69	2P/1B:	$69- 79	2P/2B: $79- 89	XP: $10	
Sun-Thurs [CP]	1P:	$49- 59	2P/1B:	$59- 69	2P/2B: $69- 79	XP: $10	

Location: SR 18 Business Rt. 540 Pine Knot Blvd 92315 (PO Box 577). Fax: 909/866-6821. **Terms:** Reserv deposit, 3 day notice; pets, $50 dep req. **Facility:** 15 rooms. Pine-shaded grounds in downtown area. 2 stories; exterior corridors. **Dining:** Restaurant nearby. **All Rooms:** shower baths. **Cards:** AE, CB, DI, MC, VI.

RESTAURANTS

CHE' FACCIA RISTORANTE
◆◆
Italian

Lunch: $6-$8   Dinner: $11-$20   Phone: 909/878-3222
Location: In the Village area. 607 Pine Knot Ave 92315. **Hours:** 11:30 am-9 pm, Fri & Sat-10 pm, Mon-Wed 5 pm-9 pm. **Closed:** 12/25. **Reservations:** suggested; weekends. **Features:** casual dress; children's menu; beer & wine only; street parking. Light, contemporary decor. Very nice selection of pasta, chicken, veal & seafood. Smoke free premises. **Cards:** AE, MC, VI.

THE IRON SQUIRREL RESTAURANT
◆◆
Continental

Lunch: $7-$12   Dinner: $15-$22   Phone: 909/866-9121
Location: In the Village area. 646 Pine Knot Blvd 92315. **Hours:** 5 pm-9 pm, Sun 10 am-2 & 5 pm-9 pm, also Wed-Fri 11:30 am-2 pm. **Closed:** 12/25. **Reservations:** suggested. **Features:** casual dress; cocktails & lounge. Charming, early American decor. Nice selection of veal, poultry, seafood & beef. Smoke free premises. **Cards:** AE, MC, VI.

MOZART'S BISTRO
◆◆
American

Lunch: $7-$10   Dinner: $15-$25   Phone: 909/866-9497
Location: In the Village area, just w of Pine Knot Blvd. 40701 Village Dr 92315. **Hours:** 11:30 am-2 & 4:30-9 pm, Fri & Sat-10 pm. **Closed:** 12/25 & Mon. **Features:** casual dress; children's menu; cocktails & lounge; a la carte. Attractive chalet style building. Menu features a variety of American & German cuisine & specialties including elk, quail & rack of pork. Smoke free premises. **Cards:** AE, CB, DI, DS, MC, VI.

BIG PINE—1,500

LODGINGS

BIG PINE MOTEL
(AAA)

◆◆
Motel

All Year	1P: $30- 42	2P/1B: $38- 42	2P/2B: $42- 60	XP: $4-6	Guaranteed Rates

Phone: 760/938-2282
Location: On US 395. 370 S Main 93513 (PO Box 759). **Terms:** Reserv deposit; pets, $4 extra charge. **Facility:** 14 rooms. Tree-shaded lawn area with picnic tables & barbecues. 2 units with kitchen, $5 extra; 1 story; exterior corridors. **All Rooms:** combo or shower baths. **Cards:** AE, CB, DI, DS, JC, MC, VI.

BRISTLECONE MOTEL
(AAA) (SAVE)

◆
Motel

All Year	1P: $34	2P/1B: $40	2P/2B: $48	XP: $4	Phone: (760)938-2067

D12
Location: On US 395. 101 N Main 93513 (PO Box 849). Fax: 760/938-3107. **Terms:** Pets. **Facility:** 17 rooms. 4 efficiencies, $6 extra charge; 1 story; exterior corridors. **Dining:** Restaurant nearby. **Some Rooms:** 4 kitchens. **Cards:** AE, DI, DS, JC, MC, VI. **Special Amenities:** Early check-in/late check-out and free local telephone calls.

STARLIGHT MOTEL
(AAA)

◆◆
Motel

All Year [CP]	1P: $32- 38	2P/1B: $35- 42	2P/2B: $38- 46	XP: $5	Rates Subject to Change

Phone: 760/938-2011
Location: On US 395. 511 S Main St 93513 (PO Box 575). **Terms:** Reserv deposit, 3 day notice. **Facility:** 8 rooms. 1 story; exterior corridors. **Recreation:** fish cleaning & freezing facilities. **All Rooms:** shower baths. **Cards:** AE, CB, DI, DS, JC, MC, VI.

RESTAURANT

ROSSI'S STEAK & SPAGHETTI
AAA
◆◆
American

Dinner: $10-$17
Location: On US 395. 100 N Main St 93513. **Hours:** 5:30 pm-10 pm, in winter from 5 pm. Closed major
holidays. **Reservations:** suggested; weekends. **Features:** cocktails & lounge. Casual dining in pleasant
surroundings. Interesting collection of family & regional memorabilia. Wine cellar & wine lounge room.
Banquet facilities. Smoke free premises. **Cards:** MC, VI.
Phone: 760/938-2254
⊠

BIG SUR—1,000

LODGINGS

BIG SUR LODGE
AAA
◆◆
Cottage

Rates Subject to Change
Phone: (831)667-3100

	2P/1B:	2P/2B:	XP:
6/1-9/15	$139	$199	$20
4/1-5/31 & 9/16-11/30	$109	$139	$20
2/1-3/31 & 12/1-1/31	$89	$119	$20

Location: 26 mi s of Carmel on SR 1; in Pfeiffer Big Sur State Park. (PO Box 190, 93920).
Fax: 831/667-3110. **Terms:** Check-in 4 pm; package plans; 2 night min stay, weekends. **Facility:** 61 rooms.
Spacious wooded surroundings. Deck or balcony. 40 two-bedroom units. Few units with fireplace or kitchen, $20 extra charge;
1 story; exterior corridors. **Dining:** Restaurant; 7:30 am-9 pm; $20-$30; wine/beer only. **Services:** giftshop.
Recreation: hiking trails, jogging. **All Rooms:** combo or shower baths. **Cards:** AE, MC, VI. *(See color ad below)*
🔲 🔄 🍴 ⊠ 🎦 🚗 🐾 🛏 ⊠

VENTANA INN
◆◆◆
Complex

Rates Subject to Change
Phone: (831)667-2331
All Year [CP]   1P: $260- 725   2P/1B: $260- 725   2P/2B: $260- 725   XP: $50
Location: 28 mi s of Carmel; 0.5 mi e of SR 1. SR 1 93920. Fax: 831/667-2419. **Terms:** Check-in 4:30 pm;
reserv deposit, 7 day notice; 2 night min stay, weekends. **Facility:** 63 rooms. Wooded hilltop location; some
ocean views; unfinished-cedar interior. Many with woodburning fireplace. Townhouses. 2 stories; exterior corridors.
Services: giftshop. Fee: massage. **Recreation:** hiking trails, jogging. **All Rooms:** combo or shower baths. **Cards:** AE, CB,
DI, DS, MC, VI.
🔲 🎦 🔄 🍴 ⊠ 🔥 🎾 📼 🍸 🛏 🔲 🏊 🛁 📶 🗝 ⊠ 🔓

RESTAURANTS

TRAIL'S HEAD CAFE
◆◆
American

Lunch: $10-$20   **Dinner:** $20-$30   **Phone:** 831/667-3111
Location: At Big Sur Lodge, just e of SR 1. 93920. **Hours:** 8 am-10:30, 11-2:30 & 5-9 pm. **Features:** No
A/C; casual dress; children's menu; beer & wine only; a la carte. Fresh seafood & local produce, California
style. Smoke free premises. **Cards:** AE, MC, VI.
♿ ⊠

VENTANA
◆◆◆
American

Lunch: $10-$17   **Dinner:** $20-$30   **Phone:** 831/667-2331
Location: 0.3 mi e of SR 1. Hwy 1 93920. **Hours:** noon-3 & 6-9 pm, Sat & Sun 11 am-9:30 pm. Closed:
12/1-12/12. **Reservations:** accepted; dinner only. **Features:** casual dress; health conscious menu items;
cocktails & lounge; a la carte. California Mediteranean cuisine, also few prix fixe, oakwood broiler. Casual
atmosphere on wooded hilltop. Smoke free premises. **Cards:** AE, CB, DI, DS, MC, VI.
♿ ⊠

BISHOP—3,500

LODGINGS

BEST WESTERN BISHOP HOLIDAY SPA LODGE
AAA SAVE
◆◆◆
Motel

Phone: (760)873-3543
All Year [CP]   1P: $60- 72   2P/1B: $68- 84   2P/2B: $78- 90   XP: $5   F12
Location: 0.8 mi n on US 395. 1025 N Main St 93514. Fax: 760/872-4777. **Terms:** Small pets only.
Facility: 89 rooms. 2 stories; exterior corridors; indoor whirlpool. **Dining:** Restaurant nearby.
Recreation: fish cleaning & freezing facilities. Guest barbecue. **Cards:** AE, CB, DI, DS, JC, MC, VI.
Special Amenities: Free breakfast and free local telephone calls. *(See color ad p 380)*
🆘 🐾 🎦 🔄 🍴 🛁 🎾 📼 🍸 🛏 🔲 🏊 🍸 ⊠

BEST WESTERN CREEKSIDE INN
AAA SAVE
◆◆◆
Motel

Phone: (760)872-3044

	1P:	2P/1B:	2P/2B:	XP:	
5/16-10/31 [CP]	$99- 139	$99- 139	$99- 139	$12	F12
2/1-5/15 & 11/1-1/31 [CP]	$89- 109	$89- 109	$89- 109	$12	F12

Location: Just n of downtown on US 395. 725 N Main St 93514. Fax: 760/872-1300. **Terms:** Pets, $10 extra
charge. **Facility:** 89 rooms. Nicely landscaped grounds with a running creek. Large, very nicely furnished
rooms, many with balcony or patio. 2 stories; interior corridors; heated pool; whirlpool. **Dining:** Restaurant
nearby. **Recreation:** fish cleaning & freezing facilities. **All Rooms:** extended cable TV. **Some Rooms:** 12 kitchens.
Cards: AE, CB, DI, DS, MC, VI. **Special Amenities:** Free breakfast and free local telephone calls.
(See color ad p 380)
🛏 🎦 🔄 🍴 🛁 🎾 🔲 ⊠

BISHOP DAYS INN   **Phone:** (760)872-1095

All Year [CP]   1P: $54- 60 2P/1B: $59- 74 2P/2B: $69- 79 XP: $5-10
Location: On SR 168, 0.4 mi w of US 395. 724 W Line St 93514. Fax: 760/872-1097. **Facility:** 34 rooms. 1
suite with whirlpool tub $75-$95; 2 stories; exterior corridors; indoor whirlpool. **Dining:** Restaurant nearby.
Motel   **Cards:** AE, CB, DI, DS, MC, VI. **Special Amenities:** Free breakfast and free local telephone calls.

CHALFANT HOUSE BED & BREAKFAST   Guaranteed Rates   **Phone:** 760/872-1790
◆◆◆   All Year [BP]   1P: $50- 80   2P/1B: $60- 100 2P/2B: $65- 100 XP: $15
Historic Bed   **Location:** Downtown area, just w of US 395. 213 Academy St 93514. **Facility:** 7 rooms. Charming Victorian
& Breakfast   decor in a restored 1898 house. Antique shop on premises. 1 one-bedroom apartment for 2-4 persons $90-
$120; 2 stories; interior/exterior corridors; smoke free premises. **All Rooms:** combo or shower baths.
Some Rooms: color TV. **Cards:** AE, DS, MC, VI.

Checkout time is noted in the listing if the
required time is before 10 a.m.

COMFORT INN
Phone: (760)873-4284
(AAA) (SAVE) All Year [CP]   1P: $59- 69   2P/1B: $69- 79   2P/2B: $79- 89   XP: $5   F18
◆◆◆ Location: 0.5 mi n on US 395. 805 N Main St 93514. Fax: 760/873-8563. Terms: Pets. Facility: 52 rooms. 1
Motel two-bedroom unit. 2 stories; exterior corridors; whirlpool. Dining: Restaurant nearby. Recreation: fish
cleaning & freezing facilities. Cards: AE, CB, DI, DS, MC, VI. Special Amenities: Free local telephone
calls and preferred room (subject to availability with advanced reservations). (See color ad below)
⬛❄️ 🐕 ⊅ 🏋️ 🛆 💥 💷 ▢ 🎁 ✕

ELMS MOTEL
Phone: (760)873-8118
(AAA) (SAVE) 5/15-10/31   1P: $37- 43   2P/1B: $40- 45   2P/2B: $45- 55   XP: $5
◆ 2/1-5/14 & 11/1-1/31   1P: $34- 40   2P/1B: $37- 42   2P/2B: $42- 45   XP: $5
Motel Location: Just e of US 395. 233 E Elm St 93514. Fax: 760/873-6254. Facility: 19 rooms. Quiet location ad-
jacent to public park. Cozy rooms. 1 story; exterior corridors. Dining: Restaurant nearby. Recreation: fish
cleaning & freezing facilities; barbecues. All Rooms: shower baths, extended cable TV. Cards: DS, MC, VI.
Special Amenities: Preferred room (subject to availability with advanced reservations). 🏋️ 💷 🎁 ✕

EL RANCHO MOTEL
Phone: (760)872-9251
(AAA) (SAVE) All Year   1P: $32- 47   2P/1B: $34- 47   2P/2B: $38- 54   XP: $4   F10
◆◆ Location: Just w of US 395. 274 Lagoon St 93514. Facility: 16 rooms. 3 kitchens, $8 extra; 1 story; exterior
Motel corridors. Recreation: fish cleaning & freezing facilities. All Rooms: combo or shower baths, extended cable
TV. Cards: MC, VI. Special Amenities: Free room upgrade and preferred room (each subject to
availability with advanced reservations). ⬛❄️ 💷 🎁 🎁 ✕

THE MATLICK HOUSE BED & BREAKFAST   Rates Subject to Change   Phone: (760)873-3133
All Year [BP]   1P: $75- 85   2P/1B: $75- 85   2P/2B: $75- 85   XP: $19   F13
Bed & Location: 2 mi nw on US 375. 1313 Rowan Ln 93515. Terms: Reserv deposit, 7 day notice; handling fee
Breakfast imposed. Facility: 5 rooms. Charming home built in 1906. 2 stories; interior corridors; designated smoking
area. All Rooms: combo or shower baths. Some Rooms: color TV. Cards: AE, DS, MC, VI.
(ASK) ⬛❄️ 🎁 ✕

MOTEL 6 - 4094   Rates Subject to Change   Phone: 760/873-8426
(AAA) All Year   1P: $40- 50   2P/1B: $50- 60   2P/2B: $50- 60   XP: $5   F17
◆◆ Location: 0.8 mi n on US 395. 1005 N Main St 93514. Fax: 760/873-8060. Terms: Small pets only.
Motel Facility: 52 rooms. 2 stories; exterior corridors; small pool, indoor whirlpool. Dining: Restaurant nearby.
Recreation: fish cleaning & freezing facilities. All Rooms: extended cable TV. Some Rooms: 2 efficiencies.
Cards: AE, CB, DI, DS, JC, MC, VI. 🐕 🦺 ⊅ 🏋️ 🛆 💥 🎁 ✕

MOUNTAIN VIEW MOTEL
Phone: (760)873-4242
(AAA) (SAVE) All Year [CP]   1P: $45- 55   2P/1B: $57- 67   2P/2B: $59- 69   XP: $6   F12
◆◆◆ Location: SR 168, 0.4 mi w of US 395. 730 W Line St 93514. Fax: 760/873-3409. Terms: Reserv deposit.
Motel Facility: 35 rooms. Nicely landscaped grounds. 3 efficiency units, $69-$79; 2 kitchen suites, $95-$105; 2 sto-
ries; exterior corridors; heated pool. Recreation: fish cleaning & freezing facilities. All Rooms: combo or
shower baths, extended cable TV. Cards: AE, CB, DI, DS, MC, VI. Special Amenities: Free breakfast and
free local telephone calls. ⬛❄️ ⊅ ✕

RODEWAY INN
Phone: (760)873-3564
(AAA) (SAVE) 5/1-10/31   1P: $53- 58   2P/1B: $58- 63   2P/2B: $60- 70   XP: $5
◆◆ 2/1-4/30 & 11/1-1/31   1P: $47- 53   2P/1B: $53- 63   2P/2B: $55- 65   XP: $5
Motel Location: just n of Downtown, & e of US 395. 150 E Elm St 93514. Fax: 760/873-6936. Terms: Small pets
only. Facility: 55 rooms. 1 two-bedroom unit. 2 stories; interior/exterior corridors. Dining: Restaurant nearby.
Recreation: fish cleaning & freezing facilities. All Rooms: combo or shower baths. Cards: AE, CB, DI, DS,
JC, MC, VI. Special Amenities: Free local telephone calls and free newspaper.
🐕 ⊅ 🏋️ 💥 💷 ▢ 🛎️ 🎁 ✕

SUPER 8 MOTEL
Phone: (760)872-1386
(AAA) (SAVE) All Year   1P: $58   2P/1B: $65   2P/2B: $70   XP: $5
◆◆ Location: 0.3 mi s on US 395. 535 S Main St 93514. Fax: 760/873-3262. Terms: Pets. Facility: 43 rooms. 2
Motel stories; exterior corridors; sauna, indoor whirlpool. Recreation: fish cleaning & freezing facilities.
All Rooms: extended cable TV. Cards: AE, DS, MC, VI. 🐕 ⊅ 💥 💷 ✕

THUNDERBIRD MOTEL
Phone: 760/873-4215
(AAA) (SAVE) All Year   1P: $40- 65   2P/1B: $45- 75   2P/2B: $50- 80   XP: $5
◆ Location: Downtown, just w of US 395. 190 W Pine St 93514. Fax: 760/873-6870. Terms: Reserv deposit,
Motel 10 day notice; small pets only, $4 extra charge. Facility: 23 rooms. 2 stories; exterior corridors.
Recreation: fish freezing facilities. All Rooms: extended cable TV. Cards: AE, CB, DI, DS, MC, VI.
⬛❄️ 🐕 💷 ▢ 🎁 ✕

VAGABOND INN

AAA SAVE
◆◆
Motel

3/16-10/15 [CP]   1P: $70   2P/1B: $76   2P/2B: $82   XP: $5 F18
2/1-3/15 & 10/16-1/31 [CP] 1P: $66 2P/1B: $71- 72 2P/2B: $76 XP: $5 F18

Phone: (760)873-6351

Location: 0.8 mi n on US 395. 1030 N Main St 93514. Fax: 760/873-3067. **Terms:** Pets, $5 extra charge. **Facility:** 80 rooms. 4 two-room units with king bed & 4 bunk beds; 2 stories; exterior corridors; sauna. **Dining:** Restaurants nearby. **Recreation:** fish cleaning & freezing facilities; barbecue area with picnic table.
All Rooms: extended cable TV. **Cards:** AE, CB, DI, DS, MC, VI. **Special Amenities:** Free breakfast and free local telephone calls.

RESTAURANTS

FIREHOUSE GRILL
◆◆
American

Location: 1.8 mi n on US 395. 2206 N Sierra Hwy 93514. **Hours:** 4:30 pm-10 pm. **Features:** casual dress; children's menu; early bird specials; carryout; cocktails. Country decor. Nice selection of steaks, seafood, chicken & pasta. **Cards:** AE, DI, DS, MC, VI.

Dinner: $15-$22   Phone: 760/873-4888

WHISKEY CREEK AT BISHOP
AAA
◆◆
American

Lunch: $6-$19   Dinner: $10-$22   Phone: 760/873-7174

Location: On US 395, just n of downtown. 524 N Main St 93514. **Hours:** 7 am-9 pm, weekends & summer-10 pm. Closed: 12/25. **Reservations:** suggested. **Features:** casual dress; early bird specials; carryout; cocktails & lounge. Country decor. Menu features a nice variety of sandwiches, steaks, seafood, BBQ & pasta. Patio dining weather permitting. Bakery & gift shop. Smoke free premises. **Cards:** AE, CB, DI, DS, MC, VI.

BLYTHE—8,400

LODGINGS

BEST WESTERN SAHARA MOTEL

AAA SAVE
◆◆
Motel

2/1-2/13 & 1/16-1/31 [CP] 1P: $75- 110 2P/1B: $75- 110 2P/2B: $75- 110 XP: $5 F12
2/14-1/15 [CP] 1P: $49- 70 2P/1B: $59- 70 2P/2B: $59- 70 XP: $5 F12

Phone: (760)922-7105

Location: Just n of I-10, Lovekin Blvd exit. 825 W Hobsonway 92225. Fax: 760/922-5836. **Terms:** Small pets only. **Facility:** 46 rooms. Palm-shaded grounds. 1 story; exterior corridors; whirlpool. **Dining:** Coffee shop nearby. **Cards:** AE, CB, DI, DS, MC, VI. **Special Amenities:** Free breakfast and free newspaper.

(See ad below)

BEST WESTERN TROPICS MOTOR INN

AAA SAVE
◆◆
Motel

2/1-2/11 & 1/20-1/31 1P: $55- 75 2P/1B: $60- 85 2P/2B: $64- 94 XP: $10 F17
2/12-1/19 1P: $39- 44 2P/1B: $44- 49 2P/2B: $44- 58 XP: $5 F17

Phone: (760)922-5101

Location: From I-10, exit Intake Blvd, 1 blk n, then 0.3 mi w. 1721 E Hobsonway 92225. Fax: 760/921-2610. **Terms:** Reserv deposit; weekly rates; small pets only, $20 extra charge. **Facility:** 56 rooms. 2 stories; exterior corridors; whirlpool. **Dining:** Coffee shop nearby. **All Rooms:** combo or shower baths. **Cards:** AE, CB, DI, DS, JC, MC, VI. **Special Amenities:** Early check-in/late check-out and free local telephone calls.

BLYTHE TRAVELODGE

AAA SAVE
◆◆
Motel

2/1-2/10 & 1/21-1/31 [CP] 1P: $65- 75 2P/1B: $65- 79 2P/2B: $80- 99 XP: $5-10 F17
2/11-1/20 [CP] 1P: $44- 49 2P/1B: $49- 54 2P/2B: $50- 55 XP: $3-5 F17

Phone: (760)922-5145

Location: Just nw of I-10, exit Lovekin Blvd. 850 W Hobsonway 92225. Fax: 760/922-8422. **Terms:** Weekly rates. **Facility:** 50 rooms. 1-2 stories; exterior corridors. **Dining:** Restaurant nearby. **All Rooms:** combo or shower baths. **Cards:** AE, CB, DI, DS, MC, VI. **Special Amenities:** Free breakfast and free newspaper.

COMFORT INN

AAA SAVE
◆◆
Motel

2/1-2/11 & 8/31-1/31 [CP] 1P: $75- 80 2P/1B: $85- 90 2P/2B: $85- 95 XP: $5 F16
2/12-8/30 [CP] 1P: $45- 55 2P/1B: $52- 56 2P/2B: $58- 62 XP: $5 F16

Phone: (760)922-4146

Location: Just n of I-10, exit Lovekin Blvd. 903 W Hobsonway 92225. Fax: 760/922-8481. **Terms:** Reserv deposit; small pets only, in smoking rooms only. **Facility:** 48 rooms. 1-2 stories; exterior corridors; whirlpool. **Dining:** Restaurants nearby. **Cards:** AE, DI, DS, MC, VI. **Special Amenities:** Free breakfast and free newspaper.

COMFORT SUITES   Phone: (760)922-9209

(AAA) (SAVE)	2/1-2/15 & 1/14-1/31 [CP]	1P:	$79	2P/1B:	$89	2P/2B:	$109	XP: $10	F12
	2/16-1/13 [CP]	1P:	$59- 69	2P/1B:	$69- 79	2P/2B:	$79- 89	XP: $8	F12

Location: 0.3 mi nw of I-10; exit 7th St. 545 E Hobsonway 92225. Fax: 760/922-0427. **Terms:** Reserv
Motel   deposit. **Facility:** 67 rooms. 2 stories; exterior corridors; whirlpool. **Cards:** AE, CB, DI, DS, JC, MC, VI.

ECONOMY INN   Rates Subject to Change   Phone: (760)922-3334

(AAA)	2/1-2/15 & 1/15-1/31	1P:	$60- 70	2P/1B:	$60- 70	2P/2B:	$70- 80	XP: $5	F12
	2/16-1/14	1P:	$40- 45	2P/1B:	$40- 45	2P/2B:	$45- 50	XP: $5	F12

Location: From I-10, exit Intake Blvd, just n, then just w. 1781 E Hobson Way 92225. **Facility:** 36 rooms. 1
Motel   story; exterior corridors. **Cards:** AE, DS, MC, VI.

HAMPTON INN   Phone: (760)922-9000

(AAA) (SAVE)	2/1-2/15 [CP]	1P:	$78- 85	2P/1B:	$85- 94	2P/2B:	$85- 94		
	2/16-4/30 & 1/1-1/31 [CP]	1P:	$60- 70	2P/1B:	$65- 75	2P/2B:	$65- 75		
	5/1-12/31 [CP]	1P:	$56- 64	2P/1B:	$62- 68	2P/2B:	$62- 68		

Location: Just nw of I-10; exit Lovekin Blvd. 900 W Hobsonway 92225. Fax: 760/922-9011. **Terms:** Pets, in
Motel   smoking rooms only. **Facility:** 59 rooms. 4 suites; 2 stories; exterior corridors; whirlpool. **Dining:** Restaurant
nearby. **Cards:** AE, CB, DI, DS, JC, MC, VI.

HOLIDAY INN EXPRESS   Phone: (760)921-2300

(AAA) (SAVE)	2/1-2/15 & 1/15-1/31 [CP]	1P:	$79- 89	2P/1B:	$79- 99	2P/2B:	$89-109	XP: $10	F17
	2/16-1/14 [CP]	1P:	$55- 65	2P/1B:	$60- 70	2P/2B:	$65- 75	XP: $8	F17

Location: Adjacent to s side of I-10, Lovekin Blvd exit. 600 W Donlon St 92225. Fax: 760/921-2307.
Motel   **Terms:** Reserv deposit; weekly/monthly rates; pets, $10 dep req. **Facility:** 66 rooms. 2 stories; exterior corri-
DI, DS, JC, MC, VI. **Special Amenities:** Free breakfast and free local telephone calls.   dors; heated indoor pool, whirlpool. **Dining:** Restaurant nearby. **Some Rooms:** whirlpools. **Cards:** AE, CB,

---

BODEGA BAY—300

LODGINGS

BODEGA BAY LODGE   Phone: (707)875-3525

(AAA) (SAVE)	Fri & Sat	1P: $195- 375	2P/1B:	$195- 375	2P/2B:	$195- 375	XP: $10	F18
	Sun-Thurs	1P: $170- 375	2P/1B:	$170- 295	2P/2B:	$170- 295	XP: $10	F18

Location: 0.5 mi s off SR 1 via Doran Beach Rd. 103 SR 1 94923. Fax: 707/875-2428. **Terms:** Reserv
Motel   deposit; handling fee imposed. **Facility:** 84 rooms. Balconies or patios with view of bay & ocean. Many fire-
places. 4 two-bedroom units. 8 whirlpool rms, extra charge; 2 stories; exterior corridors; sauna, whirlpool.
Dining: Restaurant; 8 am-10 & 6-9 pm; $15-$30. **Services:** complimentary evening beverages. Rental: bicycles. **Cards:** AE,
DI, DS, MC, VI. **Special Amenities:** Free local telephone calls and free newspaper. *(See color ad inside back
cover & below)*

BODEGA COAST INN

(AAA)
◆◆◆
Motel

Rates Subject to Change

				Phone: (707)875-2217
Fri & Sat 4/1-11/30 Fri & Sat 2/1-3/31 & 12/1-1/31	1P: $129- 190	2P/1B: $129- 190	2P/2B: $129- 210	XP: $10 F12
Sun-Thurs 4/1-11/30	1P: $119- 179	2P/1B: $119- 179	2P/2B: $129- 189	XP: $10 F12
Sun-Thurs 2/1-3/31 & 12/1-1/31	1P: $99- 149	2P/1B: $99- 149	2P/2B: $119- 160	XP: $10 F12
	1P: $79- 109	2P/1B: $79- 119	2P/2B: $89- 139	XP: $10 F12

Location: 2 blks s on SR 1. 521 SR 1 N 94923 (PO Box 55). **Fax:** 707/875-2964. **Terms:** Reserv deposit; pets, $10 extra charge. **Facility:** 45 rooms. Many rooms with view of bay; some with patio or balcony. Few rooms with woodburning fireplace and/or whirlpool. 3 stories; exterior corridors; whirlpool. **Dining:** Restaurant nearby. **Some Rooms:** whirlpools. **Cards:** AE, DI, DS, MC, VI. *(See color ad p 383)*

🐕 🛅 🍴 📺 📼 💻 🎿 🖨 🛢 ✕

INN AT THE TIDES

(AAA) [SAVE]
◆◆◆
Motel

			Phone: (707)875-2751
All Year [CP]	1P: $124- 249	2P/1B: $124- 249	2P/2B: $124- 189 XP: $20 F12

Location: Center; on SR 1. 800 SR 1 94923 (PO Box 640). **Fax:** 707/875-2669. **Terms:** Reserv deposit. **Facility:** 86 rooms. Many with woodburning fireplace & view of bay. 2 stories; exterior corridors; sauna, whirlpool. **Dining:** Dining room; Wed-Sun 6 pm-10 pm; $16-$24; cocktails. **Cards:** AE, DS, JC, MC, VI. **Special Amenities: Free newspaper and preferred room (subject to availability with advanced reservations).** *(See color ad below)*

🛅 🚐 🍴 🛋 🎿 📼 💻 🎿 🖨 🛢

RESTAURANT

LUCAS WHARF RESTAURANT

(AAA)
◆◆
Seafood

Lunch: $8-$17	**Dinner:** $8-$17	**Phone:** 707/875-3522

Location: Center. 595 SR 1 94923. **Hours:** 11 am-9:30 pm, Fri & Sat-10 pm. Closed: 11/28 & 12/25. **Features:** No A/C; casual dress; children's menu; cocktails & lounge; a la carte. Also, steak & pasta. On the bay. Smoke free premises. **Cards:** DS, MC, VI.

♿ ✕

BONSALL—1,900

RESTAURANT

RIO RICO RESTAURANT
◆◆
Mexican

Lunch: $6-$10	**Dinner:** $8-$14	**Phone:** 760/945-1250

Location: 1 mi e on SR 76, in River Village Shopping Center. 5256 S Mission Rd 92003. **Hours:** 11 am-9 pm, Fri & Sat-10 pm. Closed: 11/25 & 12/25. **Features:** casual dress; children's menu; carryout; cocktails & lounge. Colorfully decorated dining room & outdoor second floor deck. Nice selection of seafood & traditional Mexican cuisine. **Cards:** AE, DI, DS, MC, VI.

✕

BORREGO SPRINGS—2,200

LODGINGS

BORREGO SPRINGS RESORT HOTEL
◆◆◆
Resort Motor Inn

Rates Subject to Change

				Phone: (760)767-5700
Fri & Sat 2/1-5/31 & 11/1-1/31	1P: $120	2P/1B: $120	2P/2B: $120	XP: $15 F10
Sun-Thurs 2/1-5/31 & 11/1-1/31	1P: $105	2P/1B: $105	2P/2B: $105	XP: $15 F10
Fri & Sat 6/1-10/31	1P: $94	2P/1B: $94	2P/2B: $94	XP: $15 F10
Sun-Thurs 6/1-10/31	1P: $79	2P/1B: $79	2P/2B: $79	XP: $15 F10

Location: 1112 Tilting T Dr 92004 (PO Box 981). **Fax:** 760/767-5710. **Terms:** Reserv deposit. **Facility:** 100 rooms. 2 stories; interior/exterior corridors; putting green; heated pool. **Fee:** 18 holes golf; 6 lighted tennis courts. **All Rooms:** efficiencies. **Cards:** AE, DI, DS, MC, VI.

[ASK] 🛅 🚐 🍴 🍸 🛋 ✕ 📶 🖨 🛢 ✕

GOING UP? Expect elevators in establishments of three or more stories. We tell you in the listings if there are none.

LA CASA DEL ZORRO RESORT HOTEL Phone: (760)767-5323

AAA SAVE

♦♦♦♦
Resort
Complex

		1P:	2P/1B:	2P/2B:	XP:	
2/1-4/30		1P: $100- 815	2P/1B: $100- 815	2P/2B: $100- 815	XP: $10	F18
5/1-5/31 & 10/1-1/31		1P: $90- 550	2P/1B: $90- 550	2P/2B: $90- 550	XP: $10	F18
6/1-9/30		1P: $80- 445	2P/1B: $80- 445	2P/2B: $80- 445	XP: $10	F18

Location: 5.5 mi se on CR S-3 at jct Yaqui Pass Rd & Borrego Springs Rd. 3845 Yaqui Pass Rd 92004. **Fax:** 760/767-5963. **Terms:** Check-in 4 pm; reserv deposit, 3 day notice; weekly rates; 2 night min stay, weekends. **Facility:** 104 rooms. Long-established resort on several acres of attractive, tree-shaded & open grounds. Beautifully appointed rooms, suites, villas & 2- to 4-bedroom casitas; many with woodburning fireplace. 1-2 stories; exterior corridors; putting green; heated pool, whirlpools. Fee: 6 lighted tennis courts. **Dining:** Restaurant, see separate listing. **Services:** giftshop. Fee: massage. Rental: bicycles. **All Rooms:** combo or shower baths. **Cards:** AE, CB, DI, DS, MC, VI. **Special Amenities:** Free local telephone calls and free newspaper. *(See color ad p 178)*

PALM CANYON RESORT Guaranteed Rates Phone: (760)767-5341

AAA

♦♦♦
Motor Inn

		1P:	2P/1B:	2P/2B:	XP:	
Sun-Thurs 2/1-5/31 & 11/1-1/31		1P: $75- 115	2P/1B: $75- 115	2P/2B: $75- 115	XP: $10	F12
Fri & Sat 2/1-5/31 & 11/1-1/31		1P: $90- 150	2P/1B: $90- 150	2P/2B: $90- 110	XP: $10	F12
Fri & Sat 6/1-10/31		1P: $70- 95	2P/1B: $70- 95	2P/2B: $70- 95	XP: $10	F12
Sun-Thurs 6/1-10/31		1P: $55- 75	2P/1B: $55- 75	2P/2B: $55- 75	XP: $10	F12

Location: 1.5 mi w on CR S-22. 221 Palm Canyon Dr (PO Box 956). **Facility:** 60 rooms. Spacious grounds; western atmosphere. 1 two-bedroom unit. 2 stories; exterior corridors; heated pool, whirlpool. **Dining:** Restaurant; 7 am-10 pm; 5/1-12/31 11 am-5 pm; $6-$12; cocktails. **Services:** giftshop. **Cards:** AE, CB, DI, DS, MC, VI. *(See color ad below)*

RESTAURANTS

CROSS WINDS RESTAURANT **Lunch:** $5-$12 **Dinner:** $5-$15 Phone: 760/767-4646

♦
American

Location: On CR S-22 4 mi e of Traffic Circle, at airport. 1816 Palm Canyon Dr 92004. **Hours:** 11 am-9 pm. **Reservations:** required. **Features:** casual dress; carryout; cocktails & lounge; a la carte. Local restaurant, with view of airplanes landing & taking off, serving steak, seafood & Buffalo dishes. Smoke free premises. **Cards:** AE, MC, VI.

LA CASA DEL ZORRO RESORT HOTEL DINING ROOM **Lunch:** $7-$11 **Dinner:** $15-$29 Phone: 760/767-5323

♦♦♦
American

Location: 3845 Yaqui Pass Rd 92004. **Hours:** 7 am-2 & 5-10 pm. **Reservations:** suggested. **Features:** semi-formal attire; children's menu; early bird specials; cocktails & lounge; entertainment. Attractive dining in an early California atmosphere. Patio seating avail. **Cards:** AE, CB, DI, DS, MC, VI.

BOULDER CREEK—5,700

LODGING

MERRYBROOK LODGE Rates Subject to Change Phone: 831/338-6813

AAA

♦♦
Cottage

		1P:	2P/1B:	XP:	
2/1-4/30 & 10/1-1/31		1P: $74- 90	2P/1B: $84- 100	XP: $10	
5/1-9/30		1P: $74- 90	2P/1B: $94- 120	XP: $10	

Location: Just n on Big Basin Hwy, SR 236. 13420 Big Basin Way 95006 (PO Box 845). **Terms:** Reserv deposit, 7 day notice; weekly rates; 2 night min stay, weekends. **Facility:** 9 rooms. Rustic setting in redwood grove; few units overlooking creek. 6 housekeeping cottages with wood stoves & 3 motel units; 1 story; exterior corridors. **All Rooms:** shower baths. **Cards:** MC, VI.

BRAWLEY—18,900

LODGINGS

BRAWLEY INN
AAA SAVE
◆ ◆ ◆
Motel

Phone: (760)344-1199

2/1-5/31 & 9/2-1/31 [CP]	1P: $65	2P/1B: $69	2P/2B: $65- 69	XP: $5
6/1-9/1 [CP]	1P: $59	2P/1B: $64	2P/2B: $64- 69	XP: $5

Location: On SR 86. 575 W Main St 92227. Fax: 760/344-2251. **Terms:** Reserv deposit. **Facility:** 87 rooms. 8 mini suites $80-$100; Presidential suite $150-$200; 2 stories; interior/exterior corridors; heated pool, whirlpool. **Dining:** Restaurant nearby. **Cards:** AE, CB, DI, DS, MC, VI. **Special Amenities:** Early check-in/late check-out and free breakfast.

TOWN HOUSE LODGE
AAA SAVE
◆ ◆
Motel

Phone: (760)344-5120

All Year   1P: $49- 75   2P/1B: $53- 75   2P/2B: $55- 80   XP: $3   F12
Location: At jct SR 78 & 86. 135 Main St 92227. Fax: 760/344-5120. **Terms:** Reserv deposit; weekly/monthly rates; small pets only. **Facility:** 39 rooms. Comfortable, compact rooms. 2 stories; exterior corridors; small pool. **Cards:** AE, CB, DI, DS, MC, VI. **Special Amenities:** Free local telephone calls and free newspaper.

BREA—32,900

LODGINGS

EMBASSY SUITES HOTEL
AAA SAVE
◆ ◆ ◆
Suite Hotel

Phone: (714)990-6000

Sun-Thurs [BP]	1P: $159	2P/1B: $159	2P/2B: $159	XP: $10	F12
Fri & Sat [BP]	1P: $129	2P/1B: $129	2P/2B: $129	XP: $10	F12

Location: 0.5 mi w of SR 57, exit Imperial Hwy, opposite Brea Mall & adjacent to Brea Civic Center. 900 E Birch St 92821. Fax: 714/990-1653. **Terms:** Reserv deposit. **Facility:** 229 rooms. 2 room suites with wet bar. Guestrooms located around landscaped atrium area. Public areas attractively decorated in Egyptian theme. 7 stories; interior corridors; heated pool, sauna, whirlpool. **Dining:** Restaurant; 11 am-2:30 & 5-10 pm, Fri & Sat-11 pm; $10-$18. **Services:** giftshop; complimentary evening beverages. **Cards:** AE, CB, DI, DS, JC, MC, VI. **Special Amenities:** Free breakfast and free newspaper.

HOMESTEAD VILLAGE
◆ ◆ ◆
Extended Stay Motel

Rates Subject to Change   **Phone:** (714)528-2500

All Year   1P: $62- 72   2P/1B: $82- 92   2P/2B: $82- 92   XP: $20   F15
Location: 1 mi e of SR 57 at Saturn St. 3050 E Imperial Blvd 92821. Fax: 714/528-4900. **Terms:** Check-in 4 pm; reserv deposit; handling fee imposed. **Facility:** 133 rooms. 3 stories; exterior corridors. **All Rooms:** kitchens, combo or shower baths. **Cards:** AE, DS, MC, VI.

HYLAND MOTEL
AAA SAVE
◆
Motel

Phone: (714)990-6867

All Year   1P: $40   2P/1B: $42   2P/2B: $45   XP: $5
Location: 0.8 mi ne of Bastanchury Rd. 727 S Brea Blvd 92821. Fax: 714/990-2697. **Terms:** Reserv deposit, 3 day notice; handling fee imposed; weekly rates; pets. **Facility:** 26 rooms. Clean, modestly furnished rooms. 1 story; exterior corridors. **Cards:** AE, DS, MC, VI. **Special Amenities:** Early check-in/late check-out and free room upgrade (subject to availability with advanced reservations).

WOODFIN SUITE HOTEL-BREA
◆ ◆ ◆
Suite Motel

Guaranteed Rates   **Phone:** (714)579-3200

All Year [BP]   1P: $79- 199   2P/1B: $79- 199   2P/2B: $79- 199   XP: $10   F12
Location: 1.8 mi e of SR 57, exit Imperial Hwy. 3100 E Imperial Hwy 92821. Fax: 714/996-5984. **Terms:** Check-in 4 pm. **Facility:** 88 rooms. In suburban commercial area, 2 mi e of Brea Mall. Some suites with woodburning fireplace. 11 two-bedroom suites with kitchen. 2 stories; exterior corridors; heated pool. **Services:** area transportation. **Some Rooms:** 20 efficiencies, 68 kitchens. **Cards:** AE, CB, DI, DS, JC, MC, VI. *(See color ad p 333)*

RESTAURANT

LA VIE EN ROSE
◆ ◆ ◆
French

Lunch: $7-$15   **Dinner:** $25-$38   **Phone:** 714/529-8333

Location: Adjacent to SR 57, Imperial Hwy exit. 240 S State College Blvd 92821. **Hours:** 11:30 am-2:30 & 5:30-9:30 pm, Sat from 5:30 pm. Closed major holidays & Sun. **Reservations:** suggested. **Features:** cocktails & lounge; a la carte. Cozy atmosphere reminiscent of French chateau. Located across from Brea Mall. Smoke free premises. **Cards:** AE, MC, VI.

BRIDGEPORT—500

LODGINGS

BEST WESTERN RUBY INN
AAA SAVE
◆ ◆ ◆
Motel

Phone: (760)932-7241

4/1-10/31	1P: $75- 165	2P/1B: $80- 165	2P/2B: $85- 165	XP: $5-10	F12
2/1-3/31 & 11/1-1/31	1P: $65- 100	2P/1B: $70- 110	2P/2B: $75- 110	XP: $5-10	F12

Location: Center on US 395, across from the courthouse. 333 Main St 93517 (PO Box 475). Fax: 760/932-7531. **Terms:** Small pets only. **Facility:** 30 rooms. 1 two-bedroom unit. 1-2 stories; exterior corridors; whirlpool. **Recreation:** fish cleaning & freezing facilities. **All Rooms:** extended cable TV. **Cards:** AE, CB, DI, DS, MC, VI. **Special Amenities:** Early check-in/late check-out and free local telephone calls.

THE CAIN HOUSE
AAA
◆ ◆ ◆
Historic Bed & Breakfast

Rates Subject to Change   **Phone:** (760)932-7040

4/25-10/25 [BP]   1P: $90- 140   2P/1B: $90- 140
Location: Center; on US 395. 340 Main St 93517 (PO Box 428). Fax: 760/932-7419. **Terms:** Open 4/25-10/25; reserv deposit. **Facility:** 7 rooms. Historical western home restored with a comfortable elegance. 2 stories; interior corridors; smoke free premises. **Dining:** Restaurant nearby. **Services:** complimentary evening beverages. **All Rooms:** extended cable TV. **Cards:** AE, DS, MC, VI.

REDWOOD MOTEL
Rates Subject to Change
Phone: (760)932-7060

(AAA)
6/15-12/31   1P: $60- 70   2P/1B: $65- 75   2P/2B: $80- 95   XP: $10
4/1-6/14   1P: $50- 60   2P/1B: $55- 65   2P/2B: $70- 85   XP: $5

◆
Motel
Location: N side of town, on US 395. 425 Main St 93517 (PO Box 674). **Terms:** Open 4/1-12/31; reserv deposit; small pets only. **Facility:** 19 rooms. 1 story; exterior corridors. **Recreation:** fish cleaning & freezing facilities. **All Rooms:** combo or shower baths, extended cable TV. **Cards:** AE, MC, VI.

SILVER MAPLE INN
Rates Subject to Change
Phone: 760/932-7383

(AAA)
4/25-10/25   1P: $60- 80   2P/1B: $70- 90   2P/2B: $70- 95   XP: $10

◆
Motel
Location: Center; on US 395, next to the courthouse. 310 Main St 93517 (PO Box 327). **Terms:** Open 4/25-10/25; pets. **Facility:** 20 rooms. Tree-shaded lawn area. 1 story; exterior corridors. **Dining:** Restaurant nearby. **Recreation:** fish cleaning & freezing facilities. **All Rooms:** combo or shower baths. **Cards:** AE, DS, MC, VI.

WALKER RIVER LODGE
Rates Subject to Change
Phone: 760/932-7021

(AAA)
11/1-1/31   1P: $60- 115   2P/1B: $70- 125   2P/2B: $90- 125   XP: $10-15
2/1-10/31   1P: $70- 120   2P/1B: $80- 125   2P/2B: $105- 125   XP: $10-15

◆◆◆
Motel
Location: South end of town, on US 395. **Terms:** Reserv deposit, 3 day notice; pets. **Facility:** 36 rooms. Rooms on the East Walker River. Large lawn area with barbecues & picnic tables. 4 two-bedroom units. 2 two-bedroom suites with kitchen; 1-2 stories; exterior corridors; heated pool, whirlpool. **Services:** giftshop. **Recreation:** fishing, fish cleaning & freezing facilities. **All Rooms:** extended cable TV. **Cards:** AE, CB, DI, DS, MC, VI. *(See color ad below)*

BUELLTON—2,400

LODGINGS

BEST WESTERN PEA SOUP ANDERSEN'S INN
Phone: (805)688-3216

(AAA) [SAVE]
5/1-9/30 [CP]   1P: $69- 89   2P/1B: $69- 89   2P/2B: $69- 89   XP: $10   F12
2/1-4/30 & 10/1-1/31 [CP]   1P: $59- 79   2P/1B: $59- 79   2P/2B: $59- 79   XP: $10   F12

◆◆◆
Motel
Location: On SR 246; just w of jct US 101. 51 E Hwy 246 93427 (PO Box 197). Fax: 805/688-9767. **Terms:** Monthly rates; package plans, golf. **Facility:** 97 rooms. 2 stories; exterior corridors; putting green; heated pool, whirlpool. **Dining:** Restaurant nearby. **All Rooms:** extended cable TV. **Cards:** AE, CB, DI, DS, MC, VI. **Special Amenities:** Free breakfast.

ECONO LODGE
Rates Subject to Change
Phone: 805/688-0022

◆◆
Motel
2/1-3/31   1P: $40- 75   2P/1B: $50- 75   2P/2B: $56- 85   XP: $8   F18
4/1-1/31   1P: $40- 60   2P/1B: $50- 65   2P/2B: $56- 70   XP: $8   F18
Location: Adjacent to US 101; southbound first Buellton exit; northbound Frontage Rd exit, just w over the frwy. 630 Ave of Flags 93427. Fax: 805/688-7448. **Facility:** 60 rooms. 16 efficiencies, $39-$89 for 2 persons; 2-3 stories; interior/exterior corridors. **Cards:** AE, DS, MC, VI.

RANCHO SANTA BARBARA MARRIOTT
Phone: (805)688-1000

(AAA) [SAVE]
Sun-Thurs   1P: $79- 200   2P/1B: $89- 200   2P/2B: $89- 200   XP: $10   F17
Fri & Sat   1P: $89- 200   2P/1B: $99- 200   2P/2B: $99- 200   XP: $10   F17

◆◆◆
Motor Inn
Location: Adjacent to US 101, exit SR 246, 0.3 mi n. 555 McMurray Rd 93427. Fax: 805/688-0380. **Facility:** 149 rooms. 7 suites with whirlpool tub; 4 stories; interior corridors; heated pool, steamroom, whirlpool; racquetball court, 1 tennis court. **Dining:** Restaurant; 6:30 am-10 pm; $7-$15. **Services:** area transportation. Fee: massage. **Recreation:** sports court, video game room. **Cards:** AE, CB, DI, DS, JC, MC, VI. **Special Amenities:** Early check-in/late check-out and free newspaper.

WINDMILL MOTOR INN
Phone: 805/688-8448

(AAA) [SAVE]
Fri & Sat   1R: $76- 86   2P/1B: $86- 92   2P/2B: $86- 92   XP: $8   F12
Sun-Thurs   1P: $56- 69   2P/1B: $69- 76   2P/2B: $69- 76   XP: $8   F12

◆◆◆
Motel
Location: Adjacent to US 101, at jct SR 246. 114 E Hwy 246 93427. Fax: 805/686-1338. **Terms:** Reserv deposit, 7 day notice; weekly/monthly rates. **Facility:** 108 rooms. 2 stories; exterior corridors; heated pool, whirlpool. **Some Rooms:** 9 efficiencies. **Cards:** AE, CB, DI, DS, JC, MC, VI.

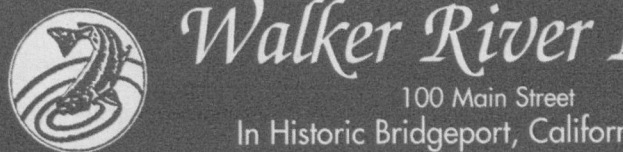

RESTAURANTS

A J SPURS
AAA
◆◆
American

Dinner: $14-$28

Phone: 805/686-165●

Location: On SR 246, 0.3 mi e of US 101. 350 E Hwy 246 93427. **Hours:** 4 pm-9:30 pm. Closed: 1/1 11/25, 12/24 & 12/25. **Reservations:** suggested; except Sat. **Features:** casual dress; children's menu; early bird specials; cocktails & lounge. Casual, western-style family dining featuring steak, ribs, barbecue chicken & seafood. Large portions. Extra plate fee $6.95. Smoke free premises. **Cards:** AE, MC, VI.
✕

FEDERICO'S
◆◆
Mexican

Lunch: $5-$12

Dinner: $7-$16

Phone: 805/688-060●

Location: Adjacent to US 101, exit SR 246, 0.3 mi n. 585 McMurray Rd 93427. **Hours:** 11:30-3 & 5-9, Fri & Sat-10:30 pm; Sun 10:30-9:30 pm. Closed major holidays. **Features:** casual dress; Sunday brunch children's menu; senior's menu; carryout; cocktails & lounge. Large, attractively decorated. Small gift shop Sun brunch 10:30 am-3 pm $10.95. **Cards:** AE, CB, DI, DS, MC, VI.
✕

THE HITCHING POST II
◆◆
Steakhouse

Dinner: $12-$32

Phone: 805/688-067●

Location: On SR 246, 0.5 mi e of jct US 101. 406 E Hwy 246 93427. **Hours:** 5 pm-9:30 pm. Closed major holidays. **Reservations:** suggested. **Features:** casual dress; children's menu; carryout; cocktails & lounge Well-known for steak & barbecue specialties. Restaurant also makes own wine. Smoke free premises **Cards:** AE, MC, VI.
✕

BUENA PARK—68,800   (See map p. 294; index p. 290)

LODGINGS

BEST WESTERN BUENA PARK INN
AAA SAVE
◆◆
Motel

All Year

2P/1B: $39- 49 2P/2B: $42- 62

Phone: (714)828-5211   98

Location: Just e of SR 39, just s of Crescent Ave. 8580 Stanton Ave 90620. Fax: 714/826-3716. **Facility:** 62 rooms. 2 two-bedroom units. 2 stories; exterior corridors; heated pool. **Dining:** Restaurant nearby. **Cards:** AE, CB, DI, DS, MC, VI. **Special Amenities:** Free breakfast and preferred room (subject to availability with advanced reservations). (See color ad below)

COURTYARD BY MARRIOTT
◆◆◆
Motor Inn

Rates Subject to Change
All Year

1P: $76   2P/1B: $76   2P/2B: $76

Phone: (714)670-6600   100

Location: SR 39, 0.3 mi s of jct SR 91. 7621 Beach Blvd 90620. Fax: 714/670-0360. **Facility:** 145 rooms. Patio or balcony. 2 stories; interior corridors; heated pool. **Cards:** AE, DI, DS, MC, VI. (See color ad p 311)

EMBASSY SUITES HOTEL-BUENA PARK
◆◆◆
Suite Motor Inn

Rates Subject to Change
6/1-8/31 [BP]   1P: $124   2P/1B: $134   2P/2B: $134   XP: $15   F19
2/1-5/31 & 9/1-1/31 [BP] 1P: $109   2P/1B: $124   2P/2B: $124   XP: $15   F19

Phone: 714/739-5600   99

Location: SR 39, 0.5 mi s of jct SR 91. 7762 Beach Blvd 90620. Fax: 714/521-9650. **Terms:** Check-in 4 pm; reserv deposit. **Facility:** 202 rooms. Landscaped courtyard. 1-bedroom suites with refrigerator & microwave; 4 stories; exterior corridors; heated pool. **Services:** giftshop; area transportation. **Cards:** AE, CB, DI, DS, JC, MC, VI.

FAIRFIELD INN BY MARRIOTT
◆◆
Motel

Rates Subject to Change
All Year [CP]   1P: $48- 50   2P/2B: $53- 56

Phone: 714/523-1488   92

Location: Just n of SR 91, exit Knott Ave. 7032 Orangethorpe Ave 90621. Fax: 714/523-1488. **Facility:** 135 rooms. 3 stories; interior/exterior corridors; heated pool. **Cards:** AE, CB, DI, DS, MC, VI. (See color ad p 338)

HANFORD HOTEL
AAA
◆◆◆
Motel

Guaranteed Rates
6/1-8/15 [CP]   1P: $79- 99 2P/1B: $79- 99 2P/2B: $79- 99 XP: $5 F17
2/1-5/31 & 8/16-1/31 [CP] 1P: $69- 89 2P/1B: $69- 89 2P/2B: $69- 89 XP: $5 F17

Phone: (714)670-7200   93

Location: 1 blk n of SR 91, exit Beach Blvd. 7828 Orangethorpe Ave 90621. Fax: 714/522-3319. **Terms:** Monthly rates. **Facility:** 173 rooms. 7 stories; interior corridors; heated pool, whirlpool. **Dining:** Restaurant nearby. **Services:** area transportation, within 5 mi. **Cards:** AE, DI, DS, MC, VI. (See color ad p 336 & p 389)

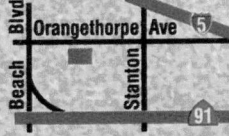

(See map p. 294)

HOLIDAY INN BUENA PARK
Phone: (714)522-7000
All Year   1P: $89   2P/1B: $89   2P/2B: $89   XP: $10
Location: On SR 39, at jct SR 91. 7000 Beach Blvd 90620. Fax: 714/522-3230. Terms: Reserv deposit, day notice. Facility: 246 rooms. 4-5 stories; interior corridors; heated pool, wading pool, whirlpo
Motor Inn   Dining: Dining room; 6:30 am-3 & 5-10 pm; $9-$15; cocktails. Services: giftshop. Cards: AE, CB, DI, D MC, VI. *(See color ad p 389)*

INNSUITES HOTELS BUENA PARK SUITE HOTEL   Rates Subject to Change   Phone: (714)522-7360
6/1-9/15 & 12/15-1/31 [CP]   1P: $69   2P/1B: $79   2P/2B: $89
2/1-5/31 & 9/16-12/14 [CP]   1P: $49   2P/1B: $59   2P/2B: $69
Location: Just s of SR 91. 7555 Beach Blvd 90620. .Fax: 714/523-2883. Terms: Reserv deposit, 7 d
Motel   notice; pets, $25 refundable dep req. Facility: 185 rooms. 2 stories; exterior corridors; heated pool, saur whirlpool. Services: complimentary evening beverages; area transportation, area attraction
Recreation: billiard room, video arcade. Some Rooms: whirlpools. Cards: AE, CB, DI, DS, MC, VI. *(See color ad below)*

RED ROOF INN
Phone: (714)670-9000
5/15-1/31   1P: $43- 66   2P/1B: $50- 73   2P/2B: $50- 73   XP: $4
2/1-5/14   1P: $42- 66   2P/1B: $50- 73   2P/2B: $50- 73   XP: $4
Location: Adjacent to SR 91 at jct SR 39. 7121 Beach Blvd 90620. Fax: 714/522-7280. Terms: Rese
Motel   deposit. Facility: 128 rooms. 4 stories; exterior corridors; heated pool, whirlpool. Dining: Restaurant nearb Cards: AE, CB, DI, DS, MC, VI. Special Amenities: Free local telephone calls and free newspaper.

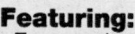

The best reservation is a *confirmed* reservation.

(See map p. 294)

SUPER 8 MOTEL   Phone: (714)522-2422 [95]
AAA SAVE   6/1-9/6 [CP]   1P: $38- 48   2P/1B: $38- 48   2P/2B: $50- 58   XP: $4   F11
          2/1-5/31 & 9/7-1/31 [CP] 1P: $38- 42   2P/1B: $38- 42   2P/2B: $42- 48   XP: $4   F11
◆◆   **Location:** SR 39, 0.5 mi s of jct SR 91. 7930 Beach Blvd 90620. Fax: 714/994-3874. **Terms:** Weekly rates.
Motel   **Facility:** 78 rooms. Many balconies. 4 two-bedroom units. 2 stories; interior corridors; heated pool, whirlpool.
          Dining: Coffee shop nearby. **Some Rooms:** 40 efficiencies. **Cards:** AE, CB, DI, DS, JC, MC, VI.
Special Amenities: Free breakfast and free newspaper. *(See color ad p 390)* [icons]

TRAVELODGE/BUENA PARK   Phone: (714)521-9220 [96]
AAA SAVE   6/1-8/31 [CP]   1P: $44- 46   2P/1B: $44- 46   2P/2B: $58- 60   XP: $4   F17
          2/1-5/31 & 9/1-1/31 [CP] 1P: $42- 44   2P/1B: $42- 44   2P/2B: $50- 54   XP: $4   F17
◆◆   **Location:** Just e of Knott Ave. 7039 Orangethorpe Ave 90621. Fax: 714/521-6706. **Terms:** Weekly rates.
Motel   **Facility:** 100 rooms. 2 stories; interior/exterior corridors; heated pool. **Dining:** Restaurant
          nearby. **Some Rooms:** 63 efficiencies. **Cards:** AE, CB, DI, DS, MC, VI. *(See color ad below)* [icons]

RESTAURANT

KNOTT'S BERRY FARM CHICKEN
DINNER RESTAURANT   **Lunch:** $6-$7   **Dinner:** $10-$12   **Phone:** 714/220-5080 [23]
◆   **Location:** 8039 Beach Blvd 90620. **Hours:** 7 am-8:30 pm, Fri & Sun-9 pm, Sat-10 pm. Closed: 12/25.
American **Features:** children's menu; beer & wine only. Very popular, well-known restaurant specializing in complete
          chicken dinners. Also sandwiches & salads at lunch. Smoke free premises. **Cards:** AE, DI, DS, JC, MC, VI.
          [icon]

BURBANK—*See Los Angeles p. 590.*

BURLINGAME—*See San Francisco p. 965.*

BURNEY—3,200

LODGINGS

BURNEY MOTEL   Rates Subject to Change   Phone: 530/335-4500
AAA   All Year   1P: $42- 52   2P/1B: $47- 57   2P/2B: $52- 62   XP: $6
◆   **Location:** 0.8 mi e on SR 299. 37448 Main St 96013. **Facility:** 10 rooms. 5 two-bedroom units. 2 efficiency
Motel   units, $10 extra charge; 1 story; exterior corridors; putting green. **Dining:** Coffee shop nearby.
          Recreation: horseshoe pit & picnic area. **All Rooms:** combo or shower baths. **Cards:** AE, DS, MC, VI.
          [icons]

CHARM MOTEL   Phone: (530)335-2254
AAA SAVE   4/21-9/9   1P: $45   2P/1B: $51   2P/2B: $57   XP: $6   F5
          2/1-4/20 & 9/10-1/31 1P: $35   2P/1B: $41   2P/2B: $47   XP: $6   F5
◆   **Location:** 0.8 mi e on SR 299. 37363 Main St 96013. Fax: 530/335-4147. **Terms:** Pets, $5 per pet per night
Motel   manager discretion extra charge. **Facility:** 42 rooms. Some small units. 1 two-bedroom unit. 2 stories; exterior
          corridors. **Recreation:** barbecue & picnic area. **All Rooms:** combo or shower baths. **Some Rooms:** 5
kitchens. **Cards:** AE, DI, DS, MC, VI.   [icons]

GREEN GABLES MOTEL　　　　　　　　　　　　　　　　　　　　　　　　　　　**Phone:** (530)335-2264
(AAA) [SAVE]　All Year　　　　1P: $46- 54　2P/1B: $53- 58　2P/2B: $54- 60　XP: $7　　F3
◆　　**Location:** 0.8 mi e on SR 299. 37385 Main St 96013. Fax: 530/335-5037. **Terms:** Reserv deposit; small
Motel　pets only, $6 extra charge. **Facility:** 26 rooms. 2 two-bedroom units. 2-bedroom 1-bath apt, $99 for up to 4
　　persons; 1 story; exterior corridors. **Dining:** Restaurant nearby. **All Rooms:** combo or shower baths.
　　Some Rooms: 6 kitchens. **Cards:** AE, CB, DI, MC, VI.

SHASTA PINES MOTEL　　　　　　　Rates Subject to Change　　　　　　**Phone:** (530)335-2201
(AAA)　All Year [CP]　　　1P: $35- 67　2P/1B: $39- 69　2P/2B: $49- 69　XP: $7
◆ ◆　**Location:** 0.8 mi e on SR 299. 37386 Main St 96013. Fax: 530/335-2202. **Terms:** Reserv deposit, 4 day
Motel　notice; pets, $5 extra charge. **Facility:** 30 rooms. Lawns, barbecue & picnic area. 1-2 stories; exterior corri-
　　dors; sauna, whirlpool, seasonal heated pool. **Dining:** Restaurant nearby. **All Rooms:** combo or shower
　　baths. **Some Rooms:** 2 efficiencies. **Cards:** AE, DI, DS, MC, VI.

BUTTONWILLOW—1,400

LODGINGS

GOOD NITE INN　　　　　　　　　　　　　　　　　　　　　　　　　　　**Phone:** (805)764-5121
(AAA) [SAVE]　All Year　　　　1P: $35　　2P/1B: $41　　2P/2B: $47　　XP: $5
◆　　**Location:** Adjacent to I-5 at jct SR 58. 20645 Tracy Road 93206 (PO Box 877). Fax: 805/764-5891
Motel　**Terms:** Weekly rates; small pets only, one pet only. **Facility:** 82 rooms. 2 stories; exterior corridors; heated
　　pool, whirlpool. **Dining:** Restaurant nearby. **Cards:** AE, CB, DI, DS, JC, MC, VI. **Special Amenities:** Free
　　breakfast and free local telephone calls.

SUPER 8 MOTEL　　　　　　　　　　　　　　　　　　　　　　　　　　　**Phone:** (805)764-5117
(AAA) [SAVE]　4/1-9/30　　　　　1P: $36　　2P/1B: $41　　2P/2B: $46　　XP: $4　　F12
　　10/1-1/31　　　　1P: $35　　2P/1B: $40　　2P/2B: $45　　XP: $4　　F12
◆ ◆　2/1-3/31　　　　1P: $34　　2P/1B: $39　　2P/2B: $44　　XP: $4　　F12
Motel　**Location:** Adjacent to I-5, exit SR 58. 20681 Tracy Ave 93206 (PO Box 921). Fax: 805/764-6676.
Terms: Pets. **Facility:** 86 rooms. 2 stories; exterior corridors; whirlpool. **Dining:** Restaurant nearby.
All Rooms: combo or shower baths. **Cards:** AE, CB, DI, DS, MC, VI. **Special Amenities:** Early check-in/late check-out
and free local telephone calls.

CALABASAS—See Los Angeles p. 591.

CALEXICO—18,600

LODGINGS

BEST WESTERN JOHN JAY INN　　　　　　　　　　　　　　　　　　　**Phone:** (760)768-0442
(AAA) [SAVE]　All Year [CP]　　1P: $50- 95　2P/1B: $55- 95　2P/2B: $55- 95　XP: $5　　F12
◆ ◆ ◆　**Location:** C/Cole Rd, 2.5 mi n of Mexico border. 2421 Scaroni Rd 92231. Fax: 760/768-1733. **Facility:** 58
Motel　rooms. Interior corridors; heated pool, sauna, whirlpool. **Cards:** AE, CB, DI, DS, JC, MC, VI.
　　Special Amenities: Free breakfast and free local telephone calls.

QUALITY INN　　　　　　　　　　　　　　　　　　　　　　　　　　　　**Phone:** (760)357-3271
(AAA) [SAVE]　All Year　　　1P: $58- 65　2P/1B: $58- 65　2P/2B: $62- 68　XP: $6　　F18
◆　　**Location:** SR 111, 0.5 mi n of Mexico Border. 801 Imperial Ave 92231. Fax: 760/357-7975. **Terms:** Reserv
Motor Inn　deposit, 3 day notice; weekly/monthly rates. **Facility:** 57 rooms. 2 stories; interior corridors. **Dining:** Dining
　　room, restaurant; 6 am-10 pm, Sun to 3 pm; $10-$14; cocktails. **All Rooms:** extended cable TV.
　　Some Rooms: 8 efficiencies. **Cards:** AE, CB, DI, DS, MC, VI. **Special Amenities:** Early check-in/late
check-out and free local telephone calls.

CALIMESA—6,700

LODGING

CALIMESA INN MOTEL　　　　　　　　　　　　　　　　　　　　　　　　**Phone:** (909)795-2536
(AAA) [SAVE]　All Year　　　　1P: $45　　2P/1B: $48　　2P/2B: $55　　XP: $5
◆ ◆　**Location:** Just n of I-10, exit Calimesa Blvd. 1205 Calimesa Blvd 92320. Fax: 909/795-8468. **Terms:** Reserv
Motel　deposit; weekly rates; small pets only, $6 extra charge. **Facility:** 36 rooms. 2 stories; exterior corridors; whirl-
　　pool. **Dining:** Restaurant nearby. **Cards:** AE, CB, DI, DS, JC, MC, VI.

CALIPATRIA—2,700

LODGING

CALIPATRIA INN　　　　　　　　　　　　　　　　　　　　　　　　　　**Phone:** (760)348-7348
(AAA) [SAVE]　All Year [CP]　　1P: $59- 130　2P/1B: $59- 130　2P/2B: $64- 70　XP: $5-10　F12
◆ ◆ ◆　**Location:** 0.5 mi n on SR 111. 700 N Sorenson 92233 (PO Box 30). Fax: 760/348-7348. **Terms:** Reserv
Motel　deposit; monthly rates; small pets only, $10 dep req. **Facility:** 40 rooms. 1 two-bedroom unit. 1 bedroom suites
　　with efficiency, $88; large whirlpool rm, $79-$100; 1-2 stories; exterior corridors; heated pool, whirlpool.
　　Recreation: bird cleaning area, barbecues. **Cards:** AE, DS, MC, VI. **Special Amenities:** Free breakfast
and free local telephone calls.

CALISTOGA—4,500

LODGINGS

CALISTOGA VILLAGE INN AND SPA

Guaranteed Rates   **Phone:** (707)942-0991

Fri & Sat	1P: $79- 175	2P/1B: $79- 175	2P/2B: $99- 119	XP: $10	F16
Sun-Thurs 5/4-11/15	1P: $65- 125	2P/1B: $65- 125	2P/2B: $80	XP: $10	F16
Sun-Thurs 2/1-5/3 & 11/16-1/31	1P: $50- 125	2P/1B: $50- 125	2P/2B: $65	XP: $10	F16

Resort Motel **Location:** 0.8 mi n on SR 29. 1880 Lincoln Ave 94515. Fax: 707/942-5306. **Terms:** Reserv deposit; package plans. **Facility:** 41 rooms. 10 two-bedroom units. 1 cottage $135-$300 for 2 persons; 1 story; exterior corridors; wading pool, whirlpool, geothermal mineral water pool & tubs. Fee: mudbaths. **Dining:** Restaurant nearby. **All Rooms:** combo or shower baths. **Some Rooms:** whirlpools. **Cards:** AE, CB, DI, DS, JC, MC, VI. *(See ad below)*

[icons]

CARLIN COUNTRY COTTAGES

Rates Subject to Change   **Phone:** 707/942-9102

Mon-Thurs	1P: $89- 150	2P/1B: $89- 150	XP: $15	F12
Fri-Sun	1P: $115- 175	2P/1B: $115- 175	XP: $15	F12

Cottage **Location:** 0.5 mi w of SR 29. 1623 Lake St 94515. Fax: 707/942-2295. **Facility:** 15 rooms. 1 two-bedroom unit. 1 story; exterior corridors. **Some Rooms:** 8 kitchens. **Cards:** AE, MC, VI.

[icons]

COMFORT INN NAPA VALLEY NORTH

    Phone: (707)942-9400

Fri & Sat [CP]	1P: $75- 125	2P/1B: $80- 135	2P/2B: $90- 150	XP: $7	F19
Sun-Thurs 4/1-10/31 [CP]	1P: $75	2P/1B: $80	2P/2B: $90	XP: $7	F19
Sun-Thurs 2/1-3/31 & 11/1-1/31 [CP]	1P: $55	2P/1B: $60	2P/2B: $80	XP: $7	F19

Motel **Location:** 0.5 mi n on SR 29. 1865 Lincoln Ave 94515. Fax: 707/942-5262. **Terms:** Package plans. **Facility:** 54 rooms. Many units with view of gardens or hills. 2 stories; exterior corridors; sauna, small geothermal pool & whirlpool. **Dining:** Restaurant nearby. **Cards:** AE, CB, DI, DS, JC, MC, VI. **Special Amenities:** Free breakfast and free newspaper.

[icons]

COTTAGE GROVE INN

Rates Subject to Change   **Phone:** 707/942-8400

Sun-Thurs [CP]	1P: $195	2P/1B: $195	XP: $25
Fri & Sat [CP]	1P: $215	2P/1B: $215	XP: $25

Cottage **Location:** On SR 29, at Wapoo St. 1711 Lincoln Ave 94515. Fax: 707/942-2653. **Terms:** Reserv deposit, 7 day notice; handling fee imposed. **Facility:** 16 rooms. Cozy individually decorated cottages with fireplace, wet bar & stereo system. 1 story; exterior corridors; smoke free premises. **Cards:** AE, DI, DS, MC, VI.

[icons]

ROMAN SPA

Resort Motel

Rates Subject to Change

Phone: 707/942-444

Fri & Sat & Sun-Thurs
6/11-9/5 — 2P/1B: $96- 160 2P/2B: $104- 135 XP: $10-15

Sun-Thurs 3/12-6/10 &
9/6-11/14 — 2P/1B: $80- 140 2P/2B: $89- 115 XP: $10-15

Sun-Thurs 2/1-3/11 &
11/15-1/31 — 2P/1B: $70- 125 2P/2B: $82- 105 XP: $10-15

Location: Center; just n of Lincoln Ave, SR 29. 1300 Washington St 94515. **Terms:** Reserv deposit, 3 day notice, Check money order deposit req; weekly rates; 2 night min stay, weekends. **Facility:** 60 rooms. Cluster of buildings with several land scaped patios, one with BBQ facilities; arbor & pond. 2 two-bedroom units. 2-bedroom unit, $125-$210 for up to 4 persons; stories; exterior corridors; saunas, 3 hot mineral pools, 2 with jets, 1 indoors. **Dining:** Restaurant nearby. **Recreation** Fee: facials, geothermal tubs, jet tubs, mudbaths, spa services. **All Rooms:** combo or shower baths. **Some Rooms:** 2 kitchens, whirlpools. **Cards:** AE, MC, VI. *(See ad p 393)*

STEVENSON MANOR INN

Motel

Rates Subject to Change

Phone: (707)942-111

Fri & Sat & Sun-Thurs
4/1-10/31 — 1P: $69- 159 2P/1B: $69- 159 2P/2B: $89- 159

Sun-Thurs 2/1-3/31 &
11/1-1/31 — 1P: $59- 139 2P/1B: $59- 139 2P/2B: $79- 139

Location: 0.5 mi n on SR 29. 1830 Lincoln Ave 94515. Fax: 707/942-0318. **Facility:** 34 rooms. 2 stories; e terior corridors; sauna, steamroom, whirlpool. **Some Rooms:** whirlpools. **Cards:** AE, CB, DI, DS, JC, MC, VI. *(See ad p 393)*

CAMARILLO—52,300

LODGINGS

BEST WESTERN CAMARILLO INN

Motel

Rates Subject to Change

Phone: (805)987-499

All Year [CP] — 1P: $62 2P/1B: $67 2P/2B: $72 XP: $5 F1

Location: Adjacent to US 101; 0.3 mi ne, Los Posas Rd exit. 295 E Daily Dr 93010. Fax: 805/388-367 **Facility:** 58 rooms. 2 stories; exterior corridors; small pool, whirlpool. **Dining:** Restaurant nearb **Some Rooms:** whirlpools. **Cards:** AE, CB, DI, DS, JC, MC, VI.

COMFORT INN

Motel

Phone: (805)987-418

All Year — 1P: $54- 86 2P/1B: $59- 89 2P/2B: $65- 99 XP: $6 F1

Location: Adjacent to US 101, 0.5 mi se; Central Ave exit. 984 Ventura Blvd 93010. Fax: 805/987-345 **Terms:** Weekly/monthly rates. **Facility:** 72 rooms. 11 suites, $65-$69; 3 stories; exterior corridors; small heate pool, whirlpool. **Cards:** AE, CB, DI, DS, MC, VI. **Special Amenities:** Free breakfast and free newspaper. *(See color ad below)*

COUNTRY INN AT CAMARILLO
◆◆◆
Motel
MC, VI. *(See color ad p 394)*

Guaranteed Rates
All Year [BP]   1P: $94   2P/1B: $94   2P/2B: $94   XP: $10   F12
Location: Adjacent to US 101, n side, 0.5 mi w; Central Ave exit. 1405 Del Norte Rd 93010.
Fax: 805/983-1838. **Facility:** 100 rooms. 3 stories; interior corridors; heated pool. **Cards:** AE, CB, DI, DS,

Phone: (805)983-7171

COURTYARD BY MARRIOTT
◆◆◆
Motor Inn
Cards: AE, DI, DS, MC, VI. *(See color ad below)*

Rates Subject to Change
Mon-Thurs   1P: $97   2P/1B: $97   2P/2B: $97
Fri-Sun   1P: $76   2P/1B: $76   2P/2B: $82
Location: Adjacent n side of US 101; Pleasant Valley Rd/Santa Rosa Rd exit. 4994 Verdugo Way 93012.
Fax: 805/987-6274. **Facility:** 130 rooms. Many units with patio & balcony. 10 suites; 2 stories; interior corridors; heated pool.

Phone: (805)388-1020

DAYS INN
🆁🅰🅰 SAVE
◆◆
Motel

All Year [CP]   1P: $57   2P/1B: $62   2P/2B: $67   XP: $7   F12
Location: Adjacent to US 101; Los Posas Rd exit. 165 Daily Dr 93010. Fax: 805/388-3679. **Facility:** 82 rooms.
Adjacent to shopping plaza. 2 stories; exterior corridors. **Dining:** Restaurant nearby. **All Rooms:** combo or
shower baths. **Some Rooms:** whirlpools. **Cards:** AE, CB, DI, DS, MC, VI. **Special Amenities:** Free
breakfast and free local telephone calls.

Phone: (805)482-0761

GOOD NITE INN
(AAA) (SAVE)
◆ ◆
Motel

All Year   1P: $43   2P/1B: $49   2P/2B: $55   XP: $6   F
Phone: (805)388-56
Location: Adj to US 101, exit Carmen Dr. 1100 Ventura Blvd 93010. Fax: 805/987-7062. **Terms:** Pets, 2 d stay only. **Facility:** 129 rooms. 1 suite with kitchenette, $64; 2 stories; exterior corridors; whirlpo **Some Rooms:** efficiency. **Cards:** AE, CB, DI, DS, JC, MC, VI. **Special Amenities:** Free local telepho calls.

HOLIDAY INN EXPRESS
(AAA)
◆ ◆ ◆
Motel

Rates Subject to Change   **Phone: (805)485-39**
6/15-9/4 [CP]   1P: $69- 99   2P/1B: $69- 99   2P/2B: $75- 105   XP: $6
2/1-6/14 & 9/5-1/31 [CP]   1P: $59- 79   2P/1B: $59- 79   2P/2B: $69- 89   XP: $6
Location: Adjacent to US 101, n side; Central Ave exit. 4444 E Central Ave 93010. Fax: 805/485-182 **Facility:** 110 rooms. Patio or balcony. 3 stories; interior corridors; small heated pool, whirlpo **Dining:** Restaurant nearby. **Some Rooms:** 24 efficiencies. **Cards:** AE, CB, DI, DS, MC, VI.
(See color ad p 395)

RESTAURANT

OTTAVIO'S
◆ ◆
Italian

Lunch: $6-$12   **Dinner:** $8-$20   **Phone:** 805/482-38
Location: Just se of US 101; Carmen Dr exit. 1620 Ventura Blvd 93010. **Hours:** 11 am-9 p Closed major holidays. **Reservations:** suggested. **Features:** children's menu; early bird specials; senio menu; carryout; cocktails & lounge. Informal atmosphere. Selection of seafood, steak & pasta. Buffet lun Mon-Fri 11:30 am-1:30 pm. Smoke free premises. **Cards:** AE, DS, MC, VI.

CAMBRIA—3,100

LODGINGS

BEST WESTERN FIRESIDE INN BY THE SEA
(AAA) (SAVE)
◆ ◆ ◆
Motel

Phone: (805)927-86
5/22-9/24 [CP]   1P: $99- 169   2P/1B: $99- 169   2P/2B: $99- 169   XP: $10   F
2/1-5/21 & 9/25-1/31 [CP]   1P: $79- 149   2P/1B: $79- 149   2P/2B: $79- 149   XP: $10   F
Location: 2.3 mi n, adjacent to SR 1. 6700 Moonstone Beach Dr 93428. Fax: 805/927-8584. **Facility:** rooms. Across from beach. Spacious rooms, many with gas fireplace. 1 story; interior/exterior corridors; heat pool, whirlpool. **Some Rooms:** whirlpools. **Cards:** AE, CB, DI, DS, MC, VI. *(See color ad below)*

.UEBIRD MOTEL

Rates Subject to Change

Phone: 805/927-4634

Fri & Sat 6/15-9/15	1P: $64- 150	2P/1B: $66- 150	2P/2B: $78- 150 XP: $6
Fri & Sat 2/1-6/14, Sun-Thurs 6/15-9/15 & Fri & Sat 9/16-1/31	1P: $54- 120	2P/1B: $60- 120	2P/2B: $60- 130 XP: $6
Sun-Thurs 2/1-6/14 & 9/16-1/31	1P: $48- 120	2P/1B: $48- 120	2P/2B: $58- 120 XP: $6

cation: In East Village area, just w of Burton Dr. 1880 Main St 93428. Fax: 805/927-5215. **Terms:** Reserv deposit. **cility:** 37 rooms. Attractive Creekside garden area, 11 creekside rooms & suites with refrigerator, fireplce & VCP. 1 two-droom unit. 1-2 stories; exterior corridors. **Dining:** Restaurant nearby. **All Rooms:** combo or shower baths. **Cards:** AE, , DI, DS, JC, MC, VI. *(See ad p 396)*

Blue Dolphin Inn

Come experience the quiet contentment of this charming, elegant seaside haven OVERLOOKING THE OCEAN

♦ Each of the eighteen rooms is individually decorated with English Country style fabrics, wall-coverings and luxurious custom made furniture.

Four Diamond Award
AAA

♦ In each room there is a fireplace, a mini-refrigerator, a hair dryer and a TV with a VCP.

♦ Many rooms offer a separate dressing area, canopy bed, whirl-pool tub, garden patio and SPECTACULAR OCEAN VIEWS.

♦ Spend your leisure time in the lovely main sitting room. Each day enjoy a complimentary morning newspaper, Continental Breakfast and Afternoon tea with refreshments in the delightful Tea Room.

RESERVATIONS 805-927-3300

6470 Moonstone Beach Dr. Cambria, CA 93428

FIGHT NOISE POLLUTION!
If there's too much bump in the night at your lodging, phone the 24-hour attendant.

BLUE DOLPHIN INN Rates Subject to Change Phone: (805)927-3:

Fri & Sat 2/1-3/31, 4/1-10/31
& Fri & Sat 11/1-1/31 [CP] 1P: $95- 220 2P/1B: $95- 220 2P/2B: $95- 220 XP: $10
Sun-Thurs 2/1-3/31 &
11/1-1/31 [CP] 1P: $75- 195 2P/1B: $75- 195 2P/2B: $75- 195 XP: $10

Motel **Location:** 2.5 mi n; adjacent to SR 1. 6470 Moonstone Beach Dr 93428. Fax: 805/927-7311. **Terms:** Res
deposit, 3 day notice. **Facility:** 18 rooms. Many ocean view rooms. Attractively decorated rooms in French country decor
gas fireplace. 5 whirlpool tub rms, $125-$210; 2 stories; interior corridors. **All Rooms:** extended cable TV. **Cards:** AE,
VI. *(See color ad p 397)*

BLUE WHALE INN BED & BREAKFAST Rates Subject to Change Phone: 805/927-4:

Fri & Sat [BP] 1P: $170- 190 2P/1B: $170- 190 XP: $30
Sun-Thurs [BP] 1P: $160- 190 2P/1B: $160- 190 XP: $30

Bed & **Location:** 2.3 mi n, adjacent to SR 1. 6736 Moonstone Beach Dr 93428. Fax: 805/927-4647. **Terms:** Res
Breakfast deposit, 10 day notice; handling fee imposed; 2 night min stay, weekends. **Facility:** 6 rooms. Across from
ocean. Beautifully furnished rooms in European country decor with canopy beds & gas fireplaces. Complim
tary afternoon refreshments. 1 story; exterior corridors; smoke free premises. **All Rooms:** extended ca
TV. **Cards:** MC, VI. *(See color ad below)*

The Blue Whale Inn

Four Diamond Award

BED & BREAKFAST
Six romantic, ocean view
mini-suites with canopy beds
and fireplaces. Full breakfast.
Afternoon tea.

805/927-4647
MOONSTONE BEACH
CAMBRIA, CA
www.bluewhaleinn.com

Burton Drive
(Sylvia's) **INN**

Beautiful Spacious Suites

Walk to shops &
restaurants.

Just minutes from the
beach &
Hearst Castle.

In the heart of
Cambria's
picturesque village.

www. burtondriveinn.com

Resv: (800) 572-7442 • 4022 Burton Dr. • Cambria • CA 93428

URTON DRIVE INN SYLVIA'S　　　　Guaranteed Rates　　　　Phone: 805/927-5125
All Year [CP]　　1P: $79- 145　2P/1B: $85- 155　2P/2B: $85- 155　XP: $10　　D12
Location: East Village, just s of Main St. 4022 Burton Dr 93428. Fax: 805/927-9637. **Terms:** Reserv deposit, 3 day notice. **Facility:** 10 rooms. A charming inn in the center of Old Cambria. Very spacious, beautifully furnished rooms & 1-bedroom suites. 2 stories; interior corridors; smoke free premises. **All Rooms:** extended cable TV. **Cards:** AE, DI, DS, MC, VI. *(See color ad p 398)*

uite Motel

AMBRIA LANDING ON MOONSTONE BEACH　　Rates Subject to Change　　Phone: (805)927-1619
All Year　　1P: $95- 225　2P/1B: $95- 225　2P/2B: $95- 225　XP: $25
Location: 2.3 mi n, adjacent to SR 1. 6530 Moonstone Beach Dr 93428. **Terms:** Reserv deposit, 7 day notice. **Facility:** 26 rooms. Across from beach. All rooms with gas fireplace, some with balcony & ocean view. 6 cottage units with whirlpool & a/c; 1-2 stories; interior/exterior corridors; 2 indoor whirlpools. **Dining:** Restaurant nearby. **Cards:** MC, VI. *(See color ad p 997)*

otel

CAMBRIA SHORES INN
Phone: 805/927-8644
AAA
Motel

Rates Subject to Change

Fri & Sat [CP]	1P:	$75- 100	2P/1B:	$85- 110	2P/2B:	$85- 120	XP: $5
Sun-Thurs 6/1-9/30 [CP]	1P:	$85	2P/1B:	$95	2P/2B:	$110	XP: $5
Sun-Thurs 4/1-5/31 & 10/1-12/1 [CP]	1P:	$75	2P/1B:	$85	2P/2B:	$95	XP: $5
Sun-Thurs 2/1-3/31 & 12/2-1/31 [CP]	1P:	$45	2P/1B:	$55	2P/2B:	$65	XP: $5

Location: 2 mi n, adjacent to SR 1. 6276 Moonstone Beach Dr 93428. Fax: 805/927-4070. **Terms:** Reserv deposit, 3 day notice; handling fee imposed; pets, $5 extra charge. **Facility:** 24 rooms. Across from beach. Nice lawn area overlooking the ocean. Exterior corridors. **All Rooms:** combo or shower baths, extended cable TV. **Cards:** AE, DS, MC, VI.
(See color ad p 399)

CAMBRIA'S PELICAN SUITES
Phone: (805)927-1500
AAA [FYI]
Motel

Rates Subject to Change

All Year [CP]   1P: $100- 250   2P/1B: $100- 250   2P/2B: $100- 250   XP: $10
Too new to rate. **Location:** 2 mi n; adjacent to SR 1. 6316 Moonstone Beach Dr 93428. Fax: 805/927-3249.
Terms: Reserv deposit, 3 day notice. **Facility:** 24 rooms. Overlooking the beach. All rooms with gas fireplace. Scheduled to open August 1998; 2 stories; heated pool. **All Rooms:** extended cable TV.
Some Rooms: whirlpools. **Cards:** AE, MC, VI. *(See color ad p 399)*

CAPTAIN'S COVE INN
Phone: (805)927-8581
AAA
Motel

Rates Subject to Change

All Year [CP]   1P: $85- 185   2P/1B: $85- 185   2P/2B: $85- 125   XP: $5
Location: 2.5 mi n, adjacent to SR 1. 6454 Moonstone Beach Dr 93428. Fax: 805/927-8581. **Facility:** 5 rooms. Across from beach. Charming units nicely decorated in a country motif. Gas fireplace in all rooms. 1 oceanview rm with gas fireplace & whirlpool $145-$185; 1 story; exterior corridors; designated smoking area.
All Rooms: extended cable TV. **Cards:** DS, JC, MC, VI. *(See ad below)*

CASTLE INN BY THE SEA
Phone: 805/927-8605
AAA
Motel

Rates Subject to Change

Sun-Thurs 6/1-9/30	1P:	$85- 125	2P/1B:	$95- 125	2P/2B:	$110- 125	XP: $110-125
Fri & Sat	1P:	$85- 115	2P/1B:	$95- 125	2P/2B:	$95- 125	XP: $5
Sun-Thurs 4/1-5/31 & 10/1-12/1	1P:	$65- 115	2P/1B:	$75- 120	2P/2B:	$85- 125	XP: $5
Sun-Thurs 2/1-3/31 & 12/2-1/31	1P:	$50- 85	2P/1B:	$55- 95	2P/2B:	$65- 110	XP: $5

Location: 2.3 mi n, adjacent to SR 1. 6620 Moonstone Beach Dr 93428. Fax: 805/927-3179. **Terms:** Reserv deposit, 3 day notice. **Facility:** 30 rooms. Across from beach. Many oceanview rooms. 2 stories; exterior corridors; heated pool, whirlpool.
Dining: Restaurant nearby. **All Rooms:** combo or shower baths. **Cards:** AE, DS, MC, VI. *(See color ad below)*

CREEKSIDE INN   Rates Subject to Change   **Phone:** 805/927-4021
◆◆   All Year & Fri & Sat 2/1-5/21 1P: $55- 80   2P/1B: $55- 80 2P/2B: $55- 80 XP: $5   F3
Motel   **Location:** 0.3 mi e of the East Village business area. 2618 Main St 93428. **Facility:** 23 rooms. 14 creekside rooms with balcony. 2 suites, $120; 2 stories; exterior corridors. **All Rooms:** combo or shower baths.
Cards: AE, CB, DI, DS, MC, VI. *(See color ad below)*

CYPRESS COVE INN   **Phone:** 805/927-2600
AAA SAVE   Fri & Sat 2/1-5/27, 5/28-9/5 &
     Fri & Sat 9/6-1/31 [CP]   1P: $105- 160   2P/1B: $105- 160 2P/2B: $105- 160 XP: $5
◆◆◆   Sun-Thurs 2/1-5/27 &
Motel   9/6-1/31 [CP]   1P: $90- 145   2P/1B: $90- 145 2P/2B: $90- 145 XP: $5
     Location: 2.5 mi n; adjacent to SR 1. 6348 Moonstone Beach Dr 93428. Fax: 827/927-0204. **Facility:** 22 rooms. All rooms with gas fireplace. 1 two-bedroom unit. Two rm suite with balcony & ocean view, $175; 2 stories; interior corridors; designated smoking area; whirlpool. **Some Rooms:** whirlpools. **Cards:** AE, CB, DI, DS, MC, VI.
(See color ad below)

FOG CATCHER INN   Phone: 805/927-1400

AAA SAVE   ◆◆◆   Motel

7/1-9/5 [BP]	1P: $115- 170	2P/1B: $115- 170	2P/2B: $115- 170	XP: $5
Fri & Sat 2/1-6/30 & 9/6-1/31 [BP]	1P: $105- 160	2P/1B: $105- 160	2P/2B: $105- 160	XP: $5
Sun-Thurs 2/1-6/30 & 9/6-1/31 [BP]	1P: $90- 145	2P/1B: $90- 145	2P/2B: $90- 145	XP: $5

Location: 2.5 mi n; adjacent to SR 1. 6400 Moonstone Beach Dr 93428. Fax: 805/927-0204. **Facility:** 60 rooms. Across from beach. Charming English village motif. Attractively landscaped grounds. Country decor, all rooms with gas fireplace. 1 two-bedroom unit. 1 large unit with private balcony & ocean view, $220; 1-2 stories; exterior corridors; heated pool, whirlpool. **Cards:** AE, CB, DI, DS, MC, VI. *(See color ad p 401)*

THE J PATRICK HOUSE BED AND BREAKFAST INN   Rates Subject to Change   Phone: 805/927-3812

◆◆◆   Bed & Breakfast

Fri & Sat 2/1-7/31, 8/1-8/31 & Fri & Sat 9/1-1/31 [BP]	1P: $135- 180	2P/1B: $135- 180	XP: $20
Sun-Thurs 2/1-7/31 & 9/1-1/31 [BP]	1P: $115- 180	2P/1B: $115- 180	XP: $20

Location: SR 1, take Burton Dr, 0.5 mi n. 2990 Burton Dr 93428. Fax: 805/927-6759. **Terms:** Reserv deposit, 7 day notice; handling fee imposed. **Facility:** 8 rooms. Rustic log home & guest house on nicely landscaped, tree-shaded grounds. Country decor. 6 rooms with fireplace, 1 with wood-burning stove. 2 stories; interior corridors; smoke free premises. **All Rooms:** combo or shower baths. **Cards:** AE, DS, MC, VI.

MARINERS INN Rates Subject to Change **Phone:** 805/927-4624

Fri & Sat 6/1-9/15 [CP] 1P: $98- 210 2P/1B: $98- 210 2P/2B: $139- 210 XP: $10
Fri & Sat 2/1-5/31 &
9/16-1/31 [CP] 1P: $69- 185 2P/1B: $69- 185 2P/2B: $89- 149 XP: $10
Sun-Thurs 6/1-9/15 [CP] 1P: $55- 165 2P/1B: $55- 165 2P/2B: $89- 139 XP: $10
Sun-Thurs 2/1-5/31 &
9/16-1/31 [CP] 1P: $45- 149 2P/1B: $45- 149 2P/2B: $65- 139 XP: $10

Location: 1.8 mi n; adjacent to SR 1. 6180 Moonstone Beach Dr 93428. Fax: 805/927-3425. **Terms:** Reserv deposit. **Facility:** 26 rooms. Across from beach. Sun deck overlooking ocean. Many rooms with gas fireplace. 1 story; exterior corridors; designated smoking area; whirlpool. **All Rooms:** extended cable TV. **Some Rooms:** whirlpools. **Cards:** AE, DS, MC, VI.

MOONSTONE INN MOTEL Rates Subject to Change **Phone:** 805/927-4815
4/2-10/31 [CP] 1P: $110- 150 2P/1B: $110- 150 2P/2B: $110- 150 XP: $10
2/1-4/1 & 11/1-1/31 [CP] 1P: $75- 150 2P/1B: $75- 150 2P/2B: $75- 150 XP: $10

Location: 1.8 mi n; adjacent to SR 1. 5860 Moonstone Beach Dr 93428. Fax: 805/927-3944. **Terms:** Reserv deposit, 7 day notice; 2 night min stay, weekends. **Facility:** 10 rooms. A small, charming motel with the friendly atmosphere of a country inn. Across from beach. Many ocean view rooms. Beautifully appointed rooms; most with gas fireplace. 1-2 stories; exterior corridors; designated smoking area; whirlpool. **Dining:** Complimentary afternoon refreshments. **All Rooms:** combo or shower baths. **Some Rooms:** whirlpools. **Cards:** AE, CB, DI, DS, MC, VI.
(See color ad below)

OLALLIEBERRY INN   Guaranteed Rates   **Phone:** (805)927-3222

Fri & Sat & Sun-Thurs
7/1-9/6 [BP]   1P: $100- 185   2P/1B: $100- 185   XP: $20
Sun-Thurs 2/1-6/30 &
9/7-1/31 [BP]   1P: $90- 175   2P/1B: $90- 175   XP: $20
Location: Just e of Burton Dr, in East Village area. 2476 Main St 93428. **Fax:** 805/927-0202. **Terms:** Reserv deposit, 7 day notice. **Facility:** 9 rooms. Restored 1873 Greek Revival house & cottage with turn-of-the-century antiques. Cozy, comfortable rooms, some with gas log fireplace. 2 stories; interior/exterior corridors; smoke free premises. **Services:** complimentary evening beverages. **All Rooms:** comb, shower or tub baths. **Cards:** AE, MC, VI.

Historic Bed & Breakfast

SAND PEBBLES INN   Rates Subject to Change   **Phone:** (805)927-5600

Fri & Sat 2/1-3/31, 4/1-10/31
& Fri & Sat 11/1-1/31 [CP]   1P: $95- 220   2P/1B: $95- 220 2P/2B: $95- 220 XP: $10
Sun-Thurs 2/1-3/31 &
11/1-1/31 [CP]   1P: $75- 195   2P/1B: $75- 195 2P/2B: $75- 195 XP: $10
Location: 2 mi n; adjacent to SR 1. 6252 Moonstone Beach Dr 93428. **Fax:** 805/927-0393. **Terms:** Reserv deposit, 3 day notice. **Facility:** 23 rooms. Overlooking the beach. Attractively decorated rooms in French country decor with gas fireplace. 6 whirlpool rms, $125-$210; 2 stories; interior corridors. **All Rooms:** extended cable TV. **Cards:** AE, MC, VI. *(See color ad p 402)*

Motel

SAN SIMEON PINES SEASIDE RESORT   Rates Subject to Change   **Phone:** 805/927-4648

All Year [CP]   1P: $78- 110   2P/2B: $78- 110
Location: 3 mi n, adjacent to SR 1. 7200 Moonstone Beach Dr 93436 (PO Box 117, SAN SIMEON). **Terms:** Reserv deposit, 3 day notice. **Facility:** 60 rooms. On several acres of tree shaded & nicely landscaped grounds. Private access to beach. 22 rooms with fireplace. 1-2 stories; exterior corridors; 9 hole par 3 golf course; heated pool; playground. **Recreation:** Croquet, shuffleboard. **All Rooms:** combo or shower baths. **Cards:** AE, MC, VI. *(See ad p 998 & p 403)*

Motel

SEA OTTER INN   **Phone:** 805/927-5888

Fri & Sat 2/1-5/27, 5/28-9/5 &
Fri & Sat 9/6-1/31   1P: $100- 130   2P/1B: $100- 130 2P/2B: $100- 130 XP: $5
Sun-Thurs 2/1-5/27 &
9/6-1/31   1P: $70- 100   2P/1B: $70- 100 2P/2B: $70- 100 XP: $5
Location: 2.3 mi n; adjacent to SR 1. 6656 Moonstone Beach Dr 93428. **Fax:** 805/927-0204. **Facility:** 25 rooms. Across from beach. Attractive grounds. Gas fireplace in all rooms. Exterior corridors; heated pool, whirlpool. **All Rooms:** extended cable TV. **Some Rooms:** whirlpools. **Cards:** AE, CB, DI, DS, MC, VI. *(See color ad p 401)*

Motel

THE SQUIBB HOUSE BED & BREAKFAST   Rates Subject to Change   **Phone:** (805)927-9600

All Year [CP]   1P: $95- 140   2P/1B: $95- 140
Location: In East Village, just off Main St. 4063 Burton Dr 93428. **Fax:** 805/962-9606. **Terms:** Reserv deposit, 7 day notice; handling fee imposed. **Facility:** 5 rooms. 1877 well preserved historical house with period furnishings made for each room. Nicely landscaped grounds. Each room with gas fireplace. No check-in after 9 pm; 2 stories; interior corridors; smoke free premises. **All Rooms:** combo or shower baths. **Cards:** MC, VI.

Historic Bed & Breakfast

WHITE WATER INN   **Phone:** 805/927-1066

All Year [CP]   1P: $70- 150   2P/1B: $80- 150 2P/2B: $80- 150 XP:$5-10
Location: 2.5 mi n, adjacent to SR 1, near Leffingwell Landing. 6790 Moonstone Beach Dr 93428. **Fax:** 805/927-0921. **Facility:** 17 rooms. Across from beach. Many ocean view rooms, all with gas fireplace. 2 mini-suites with private patio & whirlpool, $160-$200; exterior corridors; smoke free premises. **All Rooms:** extended cable TV. **Some Rooms:** whirlpools. **Cards:** DS, MC, VI. *(See color ad p 403)*

Motel

RESTAURANTS

THE BRAMBLES DINNER HOUSE   **Dinner:** $11-$25   **Phone:** 805/927-4716

Location: East Village area, 2 blks s of Main St. 4005 Burton Dr 93428. **Hours:** 4 pm-9:30 pm, Sat-10 pm, Sun 9:30 am-2 & 4-9:30 pm. **Reservations:** suggested. **Features:** No A/C; casual dress; Sunday brunch; children's menu; early bird specials; cocktails & lounge. Several dining areas in a charming English cottage. Selection of steak, prime rib, chicken, seafood & pasta. Extensive selection of California wines. **Cards:** AE, CB, DI, DS, MC, VI.

American

IAN'S   **Dinner:** $9-$27   **Phone:** 805/927-8649

Location: East Village area, just w of Burton Dr. 2150 Center St 93428. **Hours:** 5 pm-9 pm, Fri & Sat-10 pm. **Reservations:** suggested. **Features:** casual dress; early bird specials; cocktails & lounge; a la carte. Contemporary decor in a turn-of-the-century bungalow. Nice selection of beef, lamb, seafood, pasta & pizza. Smoke free premises. **Cards:** AE, MC, VI.

American

LINN'S   **Lunch:** $7-$11   **Dinner:** $9-$13   **Phone:** 805/927-0371

Location: In East Village, just e of Burton Dr. 2277 Main St 93428. **Hours:** 8 am-10 pm; weekdays in winter-9:30 pm. **Closed:** 12/25. **Features:** No A/C; casual dress; Sunday brunch; children's menu; carryout; beer & wine only. Nice selection of soups, salads, sandwiches & entrees. Chicken & beef pot pies a specialty. Own baked pies & pastries. Gift shop. Smoke free premises. **Cards:** AE, DS, MC, VI.

American

MOONSTONE BEACH BAR & GRILL   **Lunch:** $7-$12   **Dinner:** $15-$19   **Phone:** 805/927-3859

Location: 2.3 mi n; adjacent to SR 1. 6550 Moonstone Beach Dr 93428. **Hours:** 8 am-9 pm, Sun 10 am-9 pm. **Reservations:** suggested. **Features:** No A/C; casual dress; Sunday brunch; children's menu; carryout; cocktails; a la carte. Attractive setting with ocean view. Indoor & outdoor patio dining; smoking allowed on patio. **Cards:** MC, VI.

American

MUSTACHE PETE'S ITALIAN EATERY   **Lunch:** $5-$10   **Dinner:** $11-$21   **Phone:** 805/927-8589

Location: In East Village area, just s of Main St. 4090 Burton Dr 93428. **Hours:** 11 am-9 pm, Fri & Sat-10 pm, Sun 10 am-9 pm. **Closed:** 12/25. **Features:** No A/C; casual dress; Sunday brunch; children's menu; early bird specials; carryout; cocktails & lounge. Casual family dining. Selection of seafood, chicken, beef & pasta. Large variety of pizza & calzones. **Cards:** AE, CB, DI, DS, MC, VI.

Italian

ROBIN'S
Lunch: $7-$11   **Dinner:** $10-$18   **Phone:** 805/927-5007
Location: In East Village, just s of Main St. 4095 Burton Dr 93428. **Hours:** 11 am-9 pm. Closed: 11/25 &
12/25. **Reservations:** suggested; weekends. **Features:** No A/C; casual dress; children's menu; carryout;
beer & wine only; a la carte. Charming dining room & outdoor semi-enclosed patio. A variety of ethnic
Ethnic   cuisines, including Mexican, Italian, Indian, Thai & Chinese. Smoke free premises. **Cards:** MC, VI.   ☒

SEA CHEST RESTAURANT & OYSTER BAR   **Dinner:** $14-$20   **Phone:** 805/927-4514
Location: 6216 Moonstone Beach Dr 93428. **Hours:** 5:30 pm-10 pm, Sun-9 pm. Closed: 11/25-12/26.
Seafood   **Features:** No A/C; casual dress; beer & wine only. California coast atmosphere. Features a nice selection of
fresh seafood. Reservations not accepted. Smoke free premises.   ☒

THE SOW'S EAR CAFE   **Dinner:** $14-$20   **Phone:** 805/927-4865
Location: East Village area, just e of Burton Dr. 2248 Main St 93428. **Hours:** 5-9 pm, Fri & Sat-9:30 pm.
American   Closed: 12/24 & 12/25. **Reservations:** suggested. **Features:** No A/C; casual dress; children's menu; early
bird specials; beer & wine only; street parking. A cozy, comfortable restaurant with nice selection of fresh
seafood, baby back ribs & chicken. Breads & desserts made on premises. Smoke free premises. **Cards:** DS, MC, VI.   ☒

CAMERON PARK—5,600

LODGINGS

BEST WESTERN CAMERON PARK INN   **Phone:** (530)677-2203
All Year [CP]   1P: $60- 70   2P/1B: $65- 75   2P/2B: $65- 75   XP: $6
Location: 12 mi w of Placerville on US 50, exit Cameron Park Dr. 3361 Coach Ln 95682.
Fax: 530/676-1422. **Terms:** Small pets only. **Facility:** 63 rooms. Large attractive rooms. 9 kitchens, $10 extra;
Motel   2 stories; exterior corridors. **Dining:** Coffee shop nearby. **Some Rooms:** 10 kitchens. **Cards:** AE, DI, DS,
JC, MC, VI. **Special Amenities:** Free breakfast and free local telephone calls. *(See ad below)*

SUPER 8 MOTEL   Rates Subject to Change   **Phone:** 530/677-7177
All Year [CP]   1P: $55- 60   2P/1B: $55- 60   2P/2B: $60- 65   XP: $5-7   F10
Motel   **Location:** 12 mi w of Placerville on US 50, exit Cameron Park Dr. 3444 Coach Ln 95682.
Fax: 530/672-1980. **Facility:** 60 rooms. 3 extra large rooms, $48.50-$58.50 for up to 2 persons; 2 stories; in-
terior corridors; small pool. **Cards:** AE, CB, DI, DS, JC, MC, VI.

CAMPBELL—36,000

LODGINGS

CAMPBELL INN   **Phone:** (408)374-4300
All Year [BP]   1P: $135- 185   2P/1B: $155- 225   2P/2B: $165- 225   XP: $10   F12
Location: Exit SR 17 Hamilton Ave E; 0.3 mi to Bascom Ave, 0.3 mi s; 0.3 mi w. 675 E Campbell Ave
95008. Fax: 408/379-0695. **Facility:** 95 rooms. Tastefully appointed. Some with fireplace. 2 stories; exterior
Motel   corridors; heated pool, whirlpool; 1 lighted tennis court. **Dining:** Restaurant nearby. **Recreation:** bicycles,
jogging. **Some Rooms:** whirlpools. **Cards:** AE, DI, DS, MC, VI. **Special Amenities:** Free breakfast and
free room upgrade (subject to availability with advanced reservations).

EXECUTIVE INN SUITES   **Phone:** (408)559-3600
All Year [CP]   1P: $130   2P/1B: $140   2P/2B: $140   XP: $10   F12
Location: Exit SR 17 at Camden Ave E. 1300 Camden Ave 95008. Fax: 408/371-5721.
Terms: Weekly/monthly rates. **Facility:** 38 rooms. Attractively appointed rooms. 3 stories; interior corridors.
Motel   **Dining:** Coffee shop nearby. **All Rooms:** efficiencies, no utensils, combo or shower baths.
Some Rooms: whirlpools. **Cards:** AE, CB, DI, DS, MC, VI. **Special Amenities:** Free breakfast and free
room upgrade (subject to availability with advanced reservations).

THE PRUNEYARD INN   Rates Subject to Change   **Phone:** (408)559-4300
Sun-Thurs [EP]   1P: $165   2P/1B: $165   2P/2B: $165   XP: $10-20   F18
Fri & Sat [BP]   1P: $109   2P/1B: $109   2P/2B: $109   XP: $10-20   F18
Motel   **Location:** Exit SR 17 Hamilton Ave, 0.3 mi e, s on Bascom Ave, at nw corner of Pruneyard Shopping
Center. 1995 S Bascom Ave 95008. Fax: 408/559-9919. **Facility:** 172 rooms. Attractive decor. Some rooms with fireplace; 3
stories; interior corridors; heated pool. **Services:** area transportation. **Recreation:** bicycles. **All Rooms:** combo or shower
baths. **Some Rooms:** 11 efficiencies. **Cards:** AE, CB, DI, DS, JC, MC, VI.

RESIDENCE INN BY MARRIOTT-SAN JOSE
◆◆◆   Sun-Thurs   1P: $109   2P/1B: $109   2P/2B: $135
Suite Motel   Fri & Sat   1P: $79   2P/1B: $79   2P/2B: $109
      Location: Exit SR 17 via Camden Ave E; then n. 2761 S Bascom Ave 95008. Fax: 408/371-9808.
Facility: 80 rooms. 1-& 2-bedroom suites with living room, dining area & kitchen; some with fireplace. 2 stories; exterior corridors; heated pool. **Recreation:** bicycles. **Cards:** AE, DI, DS, MC, VI.

Rates Subject to Change   **Phone:** 408/559-1551

CANOGA PARK—See Los Angeles p. 591.

CAPITOLA—10,200—See also APTOS, FELTON, SANTA CRUZ & SCOTTS VALLEY.

LODGINGS

CAPITOLA INN   **Phone:** (831)462-3004
(AAA) (SAVE)   Fri & Sat 5/1-9/30   1P: $85- 145   2P/1B: $85- 145   2P/2B: $95- 165   XP: $10
         Sun-Thurs 5/1-9/30   1P: $65- 110   2P/1B: $65- 110   2P/2B: $75- 120   XP: $10
◆◆◆   Fri & Sat 2/1-4/30 &
Motel   10/1-1/31   1P: $75- 100   2P/1B: $75- 100   2P/2B: $85- 110   XP: $10
         Sun-Thurs 2/1-4/30 &
         10/1-1/31   1P: $65- 80   2P/1B: $65- 80   2P/2B: $75- 90   XP: $10
Location: Just w of SR 1, Bay Ave exit. 822 Bay Ave 95010. Fax: 831/462-3004. **Terms:** 2 night min stay, weekends in summer; small pets only, $20 extra charge, by reservation only. **Facility:** 56 rooms. All units have small deck or patio. 7 efficiencies, $15 extra charge. 3 units with gas fireplace & whirlpool, $125-$195 for up to 4 persons; 2 stories; interior/exterior corridors. **Cards:** AE, CB, DI, DS, MC, VI.

THE INN AT DEPOT HILL   **Phone:** (831)462-3376
(AAA) (SAVE)   All Year [BP]   1P: $190- 275   2P/1B: $190- 275   2P/2B: $190- 275   XP: $25
         Location: 1 mi w of SR 1, Park Ave exit. 250 Monterey Ave 95010. Fax: 831/462-3697. **Terms:** Reserv
◆◆◆   deposit, 10 day notice; 2 night min stay, with Sat. **Facility:** 12 rooms. Individually decorated rooms & common
Bed &   areas in converted former railroad station & annex; fireplaces. 2 stories; interior corridors; smoke free prem-
Breakfast   ises. **Dining:** Complimentary wine, hors d'oeuvres & dessert. **All Rooms:** combo or shower baths.
Some Rooms: whirlpools. **Cards:** AE, DI, DS, MC, VI. **Special Amenities: Free breakfast and free local telephone calls.**

RESTAURANTS

OSTRICH GRILL   **Lunch:** $8-$10   **Dinner:** $13-$23   **Phone:** 831/477-9181
◆◆   **Location:** At Crossroads Ctr, on 2nd floor. 820 Bay Ave 95010. **Hours:** 11:30 am-2 & 5:30-9 pm, Fri &
American   Sat-10 pm. Closed: 11/25 & 12/25. **Reservations:** accepted. **Features:** No A/C; casual dress; children's
         menu; cocktails. Wood-grilled meat, including ostrich for dinner. Smoke free premises. **Cards:** AE, CB,
DS, MC, VI.

SHADOWBROOK   **Dinner:** $15-$29   **Phone:** 831/475-1511
◆◆◆   **Location:** 0.5 mi s of SR 1, 41st Ave exit, then 0.5 mi e on Capitola Rd. 1750 Wharf Rd 95010. **Hours:** 5:30
Regional   pm-9:30 pm, Sat 4 pm-10:30 pm, Sun 10 am-2:30 & 4-9 pm. **Reservations:** suggested. **Features:** No A/C;
American   casual dress; Sunday brunch; children's menu; cocktails & lounge; a la carte. Unique rustic setting
         overlooking creek. Lush landscaping. Funicular railway down to dining rooms. Prime rib. Variety of fresh,
ocean caught fish & seasonal California specialties. Entertainment weekends. Smoke free premises. **Cards:** AE, CB, DI, DS,
MC, VI.

CARDIFF-BY-THE-SEA—10,100

LODGING

COUNTRY SIDE INN   Rates Subject to Change   **Phone:** (760)944-0427
◆◆◆   5/22-9/12 [BP]   1P: $119   2P/1B: $125   2P/2B: $125   XP: $8   F12
Motel   2/1-5/21 & 9/13-1/31 [BP]   1P: $88   2P/1B: $94   2P/2B: $94   XP: $8   F12
      Location: Adjacent to I-5, Birmingham Dr exit. 1661 Villa Cardiff Dr 92007. Fax: 760/944-7708.
Terms: Reserv deposit. **Facility:** 102 rooms. Attractive, country decor. 2 stories; interior corridors; small heated pool.
Cards: AE, CB, DI, DS, MC, VI. *(See ad below)*

RESTAURANT

THE BEACH HOUSE   **Lunch:** $7-$13   **Dinner:** $15-$22   **Phone:** 760/753-1321
◆◆
American   **Location:** 0.5 mi s of Chesterfield. 2530 S Coast Hwy 101 92007. **Hours:** 11 am-2:30 & 4:30-10 pm, Sun 10
am-2:30 & 4:30-10 pm. Closed: 11/25 & 12/25. **Reservations:** suggested. **Features:** casual dress; Sunday
brunch; children's menu; early bird specials; health conscious menu; cocktails & lounge; entertainment; valet
parking; a la carte. Seafood. Overlooking ocean. Patio seating also. Sat & Sun champagne brunch $9.95. **Cards:** AE, MC,
VI.

CARLSBAD—63,100

LODGINGS

BEST WESTERN BEACH TERRACE INN   Rates Subject to Change   **Phone:** (760)729-5951
   6/1-9/30 [CP]   1P: $119- 199   2P/1B: $129- 209   2P/2B: $129- 209   XP: $10   F12
   2/1-5/31 & 10/1-1/31 [CP]   1P: $109- 159   2P/1B: $119- 169   2P/2B: $129- 179   XP: $10   F12
   Location: From I-5, exit Carlsbad Village Dr, 1 mi w, just n. 2775 Ocean St 92008. Fax: 760/729-1078.
Motel   **Facility:** 49 rooms. Directly on beach. Many rooms with balcony & ocean view. Most rooms with gas fireplace.
3-4 stories; exterior corridors; heated pool, sauna, whirlpool. **Some Rooms:** 6 efficiencies, 34 kitchens.
Cards: AE, CB, DI, DS, JC, MC, VI. *(See color ad below)*

BEST WESTERN BEACH VIEW LODGE

Motel

Rates Subject to Change · Phone: (760)729-1151

	1P	2P/1B	2P/2B	XP	
6/1-9/30 [CP]	\$109- 149	\$119- 169	\$129- 189	\$10	F12
2/1-5/31 [CP]	\$99- 139	\$109- 149	\$119- 159	\$10	F12
10/1-1/31 [CP]	\$99- 139	\$109- 149	\$119- 159	\$10	F12

Location: I-5, exit Carlsbad Village Dr, 0.8 mi w, just s. 3180 Carlsbad Blvd 92008. Fax: 760/434-5405. **Terms:** Monthly rates, Oct-Apr. **Facility:** 41 rooms. Across from Carlsbad State Beach. Few ocean view rooms. Some with gas fireplace & balcony. 6 one-bedroom apartments, \$110-\$135 for 2 persons; 3 stories; exterior corridors; heated pool, whirlpool. **All Rooms:** extended cable TV. **Some Rooms:** 12 efficiencies. **Cards:** AE, CB, DI, DS, JC, MC, VI. *(See color ad p 407)*

CARLSBAD INN BEACH RESORT

Motor Inn

Rates Subject to Change · Phone: (760)434-7020

	1P	2P/1B	2P/2B	XP	
All Year	\$169- 238	\$169- 238	\$169- 238	\$15	F12

Location: 0.8 mi w of I-5, exit Carlsbad Village Dr. 3075 Carlsbad Blvd 92008. Fax: 760/729-4853. **Terms:** Check-in 4 pm; reserv deposit. **Facility:** 62 rooms. Across the street from stairway to beach. Old World decor. 3 stories; interior corridors; heated pool, sauna, whirlpool; playground. **Dining:** Restaurants nearby. **Recreation:** bicycles, volleyball. **All Rooms:** combo or shower baths. **Some Rooms:** 29 efficiencies, whirlpools. **Cards:** AE, DI, DS, MC, VI.

CARLSBAD SUPER 8

Motel

Rates Subject to Change · Phone: (760)720-0808

	1P	2P/1B	2P/2B	XP
Fri & Sat 6/15-9/11	\$64- 79	\$64- 99	\$74- 109	\$10-20
Fri & Sat 2/1-6/14 & 9/12-1/31	\$59- 79	\$59- 79	\$69- 99	\$10-20
Sun-Thurs 6/15-9/11	\$54- 69	\$54- 89	\$64- 99	\$10-20
Sun-Thurs 2/1-6/14 & 9/12-1/31	\$49- 69	\$49- 69	\$59- 89	\$10-20

Location: E side of I-5, exit Tamarack Ave; just n. 3700 Pio Pico Dr 92008. Fax: 760/720-0380. **Terms:** Reserv deposit. **Facility:** 47 rooms. 3 two-bedroom units. Exterior corridors; small pool. **Cards:** AE, CB, DI, DS, MC, VI.

FOUR SEASONS RESORT AVIARA

Resort Complex

Rates Subject to Change · Phone: (760)603-6800

	1P	2P/1B	2P/2B	XP	
All Year	\$345- 600	\$345- 600	\$345- 600	\$30	F18

Location: 2 mi se of I-5 on Batiquitos Lagoon, exit Poinsettia Ln/Aviara Pkwy. 7100 Four Seasons Point 92009. Fax: 760/603-6828. **Terms:** Reserv deposit, 3 day notice; handling fee imposed. **Facility:** 331 rooms. Hilltop location overlooking the lagoon & golf course with views of the ocean. 1 three-bedroom unit, 3 two-bedroom units. Suites, \$750-\$4000; 5 stories; putting green; heated pool. Fee: 18 holes golf; 6 lighted tennis courts. **Services:** giftshop. Fee: massage. **Recreation:** hiking trails, jogging. Fee: bicycles. **Cards:** AE, DI, DS, JC, MC, VI.

HOLIDAY INN CARLSBAD BY THE SEA

Motor Inn

Rates Subject to Change · Phone: (760)438-7880

	1P	2P/1B	2P/2B	XP	
4/1-9/15	\$119- 129	\$139- 149	\$139- 149	\$10	F17
2/1-3/31 & 9/16-1/31	\$99- 109	\$109- 119	\$109- 119	\$10	F17

Location: Adjacent to I-5; exit Palomar Airport Rd. 850 Palomar Airport Rd 92008. Fax: 760/438-1015. **Terms:** Reserv deposit, 3 day notice. **Facility:** 148 rooms. Spacious, nicely landscaped grounds. 2 stories; exterior corridors; heated pool, whirlpool. **Dining:** Pea Soup Andersen's Restaurant, see separate listing. **Services:** giftshop. **Cards:** AE, CB, DI, DS, MC, VI. **Special Amenities:** Free room upgrade (subject to availability with advanced reservations). *(See color ad below)*

INNS OF AMERICA

Motor Inn

Phone: (760)931-1185

	1P	2P/1B	2P/2B	XP
6/27-9/7 [CP]	\$58	\$61	\$61	\$5
9/8-1/31 [CP]	\$47	\$52	\$57	\$5
2/1-6/26 [CP]	\$51	\$56	\$57	\$5

Location: Adjacent to I-5, Poinsettia Ln exit; just w to Ave Encinas, just n. 751 Raintree Dr 92009. Fax: 760/431-9212. **Terms:** Pets. **Facility:** 126 rooms. 3 stories; exterior corridors; heated pool. **Dining:** Restaurant; 11:30 am-11 pm, Sun 9:30 am-11 pm; \$10-\$17; cocktails. **Cards:** AE, MC, VI. **Special Amenities:** Free breakfast and free local telephone calls.

\ COSTA RESORT AND SPA   Phone: (760)438-9111
(SAVE)   All Year   1P: $300- 485 2P/1B: $300- 485 2P/2B: $300- 485 XP: $35   F17
◆◆◆   **Location:** I-5, exit La Costa Ave 2 mi e, 0.3 mi n on El Camino Real. Costa Del Mar Rd 92009.
─sort   Fax: 760/438-3758. **Terms:** Check-in 4 pm; reserv deposit; package plans. **Facility:** 480 rooms. Acres of nicely
mplex   landscaped grounds. Extensive recreational facilities & shops. Full service spa. 2-3 stories; interior/exterior corridors; heated pool; playground. Fee: 36 holes golf; 21 tennis courts (7 lighted). **Dining:** 4 restaurants; 6
am-11 pm; $15-$35; cocktails. **Services:** giftshop. **Recreation:** jogging. Fee: bicycles. **Cards:** AE, CB, DI,
, JC, MC, VI. **Special Amenities: Free newspaper and free room upgrade (subject to availability with advanced
servations).**

DTEL 6 - 1021   Rates Subject to Change   Phone: 760/434-7135
          6/17-1/31   1P: $45- 55 2P/1B: $51- 57 2P/2B: $51- 57 XP: $3-6   F17
          2/1-6/16   1P: $38- 43 2P/1B: $44- 49 2P/2B: $44- 49 XP: $3-6   F17
          Location: Just w of I-5. 1006 Carlsbad Village Dr 92008. Fax: 760/730-0159. **Terms:** Small pets only.
otel   **Facility:** 109 rooms. 2 stories; exterior corridors. **Dining:** Coffee shop nearby. **All Rooms:** combo or shower
baths. **Cards:** AE, CB, DI, DS, MC, VI.

CEAN PALMS BEACH RESORT   Phone: (760)729-2493
(SAVE)   7/1-9/2   1P: $84- 143 2P/1B: $103- 125 2P/2B: $159- 186
          2/1-6/30 & 9/3-1/31   1P: $69- 99 2P/1B: $79- 99 2P/2B: $109- 139
          Location: From I-5, exit Carlsbad Village Dr, 1 mi w then just n. 2950 Ocean St 92008. Fax: 760/729-0579.
artment   **Terms:** Reserv deposit, 30 day notice; weekly/monthly rates, 10/1-5/31. **Facility:** 56 rooms. Across from
otel   stairway to beach. Studio, 1- & 2-bedroom apartments with kitchen or efficiency. 2 stories; exterior corridors;
designated smoking area; heated pool, sauna, whirlpool; playground. **Services:** giftshop. **All Rooms:** combo
shower baths. **Cards:** AE, CB, DI, DS, MC, VI.

LYMPIC RESORT HOTEL & SPA   Phone: (760)438-8330
(SAVE)   All Year   1P: $78- 89 2P/1B: $98   2P/2B: $98   XP: $10   F12
          Location: I-5, exit Palomar Airport Rd, 3.5 mi e, just s. 6111 El Camino Real 92009. Fax: 760/431-0838.
◆◆   **Terms:** Reserv deposit; package plans. **Facility:** 78 rooms. Tennis resort with full service spa. All rooms with
esort Motor   patio or balcony. 2 stories; interior corridors; putting green; heated pool, saunas, steamrooms, whirlpool.
Fee: 5 lighted tennis courts. **Dining:** Restaurant; 7 am-2:30 & 5-9 pm, Sun 7 am-2:30 pm; $8-$14; cocktails.
          Services: giftshop; area transportation, within 5 mi. Fee: massage. **Recreation:** driving range.
l **Rooms:** combo or shower baths. **Cards:** AE, CB, DI, DS, JC, MC, VI. **Special Amenities: Early check-in/late
eck-out and free newspaper.**

ELICAN COVE INN   Rates Subject to Change   Phone: (760)434-5995
◆◆   All Year [BP]   1P: $90- 180 2P/1B: $90- 180 2P/2B: $90- 180 XP: $15   F8
ed &   **Location:** I-5, Carlsbad Village Dr exit; 0.8 mi w, just s on Carlsbad Blvd, 0.3 mi e. 320 Walnut Ave 92008.
eakfast   Fax: 760/434-7649. **Terms:** Reserv deposit, 7 day notice; 2 night min stay. **Facility:** 8 rooms. Beautifully decorated rooms. Gas fireplaces. Feather beds. Located in quiet residential area. Telephone jacks in all rooms.
lephones avail. 2 stories; exterior corridors; designated smoking area. **All Rooms:** combo or shower baths. **Cards:** AE,
C, VI.

JRF MOTEL   Rates Subject to Change   Phone: (760)729-7961
          4/1-4/15, 6/1-9/4 & 12/20-1/3
          [CP]   1P: $69- 119 2P/1B: $69- 119 2P/2B: $69- 119 XP: $10   F12
          2/1-3/31, 4/16-5/31,
otel   9/5-12/19 & 1/4-1/31 [CP] 1P: $49- 89 2P/1B: $49- 89 2P/2B: $59- 99 XP: $10   F12
          Location: From I-5, exit Carlsbad Village Dr, 0.8 mi/w, just s. 3136 Carlsbad Blvd 92008. Fax: 760/434-6642.
rms: Reserv deposit, 3 day notice. **Facility:** 28 rooms. 5 whirlpool rms, extra charge; 2 stories; exterior corridors; heated
ol. **All Rooms:** combo or shower baths, extended cable TV. **Some Rooms:** 5 efficiencies, 2 kitchens, utensil deposit.
ards: AE, DI, DS, MC, VI. *(See color ad p 842 & p 407)*

RESTAURANTS

DYOTE BAR & GRILL   **Lunch:** $6-$11   **Dinner:** $7-$14   Phone: 760/729-4695
          Location: 0.8 mi w of I-5, exit Carlsbad Village Dr; in Village Faire Shopping Center. 300 Carlsbad Village Dr
outhwest   92008. **Hours:** 11 am-1:30 am, Fri & Sat-2 am. **Features:** casual dress; children's menu; carryout; cocktails
merican   & lounge; entertainment; a la carte. Interesting selection of southwestern cuisine served in a casual, lively
atmosphere. Large selection of appetizers. **Cards:** AE, MC, VI.

OMINICS CUCINA ITALIANA   **Lunch:** $6-$11   **Dinner:** $9-$16   Phone: 760/720-3737
◆   **Location:** 0.8 mi w of I-5, exit Carlsbad Village Dr. 264 Carlsbad Village Dr 92008. **Hours:** 11 am-10 pm, Fri
lian   & Sat-11 pm. **Closed:** Some major holidays. **Features:** casual dress; cocktails; entertainment. Tastefully
decorated restaurant with display cooking. Patio seating, weather permitting. Smoke free premises.
ards: AE, DI, DS, MC, VI.

DEL'S NORTE   **Lunch:** $6-$10   **Dinner:** $8-$10   Phone: 760/729-0903
          Location: 1 mi w of I-5, exit Carlsbad Village Dr. 3003 Carlsbad Blvd 92008. **Hours:** 11:30 am-9:30 pm, Fri
exican   & Sat-10 pm. **Closed:** 11/25 & 12/25. **Features:** casual dress; early bird specials; cocktails & lounge; a la
carte. Colorful, informal restaurant featuring nice selection of Mexican cuisine. Indoor & patio dining.
ards: MC, VI.

EIMAN'S   **Lunch:** $6-$9   **Dinner:** $10-$20   Phone: 760/729-4131
◆◆   **Location:** 0.8 mi w of I-5, exit Carlsbad Village Dr. 2978 Carlsbad Blvd 92008. **Hours:** 11 am-1 am, Sun
merican   from 9:30 am. **Features:** casual dress; Sunday brunch; children's menu; salad bar; cocktails & lounge;
entertainment. In restored Victorian building. Very attractive restaurant featuring seafood, chicken & prime
. Smoke free premises. **Cards:** AE, CB, DS, MC, VI.

EA SOUP ANDERSEN'S RESTAURANT **Lunch:** $9-$14   **Dinner:** $9-$14   Phone: 760/438-7880
          Location: Adjacent to I-5; exit Palomar Airport Rd; in Holiday Inn Carlsbad By The Sea. 850 Palomar Airport
merican   Rd 92008. **Hours:** 6:30 am-10 pm. **Features:** casual dress; Sunday brunch; children's menu; salad bar;
cocktails & lounge. Coffeeshop & dining room featuring a nice selection of salad, sandwiches & entrees.
eakfast buffet $5.95, lunch buffet 11:30 am-2 pm $6.95. Smoke free premises. **Cards:** AE, CB, DI, DS, MC, VI.

CARMEL-BY-THE-SEA—*See Monterey Peninsula p. 682.*

CARMEL VALLEY—See Monterey Peninsula p. 697.

CARNELIAN BAY—See Lake Tahoe Area p. 505.

CARPINTERIA—13,700

LODGINGS

BEST WESTERN CARPINTERIA INN   **Phone:** (805)684-0473
(AAA) [SAVE]   5/1-10/1   1P: $105- 115   2P/1B: $115- 135   2P/2B: $115- 135   XP: $10   F18
              2/1-4/30 & 10/2-1/31   1P: $89- 99   2P/1B: $99- 109   2P/2B: $99- 109   XP: $10   F18
◆ ◆   **Location:** Adjacent to US 101; northbound exit Santa Monica Rd, southbound exit Reynolds Ave. 4558
Motor Inn   Carpinteria Ave 93013. Fax: 805/684-4015. **Terms:** Pets. **Facility:** 143 rooms. Many rooms with patio or balcony surrounding landscaped garden area. Some smaller rooms. 3 suites avail, 2 with kitchens $150-$225; 3
stories; interior corridors; small heated pool, whirlpool. **Dining:** Dining room; 7 am-10:30 & 5:30-9:30 pm, Fri & Sat 7 am-11
& 5:30-10 pm; $8-$17; cocktails. **Cards:** AE, CB, DI, DS, VI.

COMFORT SUITES   Rates Subject to Change   **Phone:** (805)566-9499
[FYI]   5/1-9/30 [CP]   1P: $89- 129   2P/1B: $89- 129   2P/2B: $89- 129   XP: $10   F12
          10/1-1/31 [CP]   1P: $79- 109   2P/1B: $79- 109   2P/2B: $79- 109   XP: $10   F12
Motel   2/1-4/30 [CP]   1P: $79- 99   2P/1B: $79- 99   2P/2B: $79- 99   XP: $10   F12
          Too new to rate. **Location:** Adjacent to US 101; northbound exit Bilard Rd, southbound exit Casitas Pass
Rd. 5606 Carpinteria Ave 93013. Fax: 805/566-9433. **Facility:** 75 rooms. 2 stories; interior corridors. **Cards:** AE, DI, DS,
MC, VI. *(See color ad p 1011)*

PRUFROCK'S GARDEN INN   Rates Subject to Change   **Phone:** 805/566-9696
◆ ◆   Fri & Sat & Sun-Thurs
Historic Bed   6/15-10/31 [BP]   1P: $99- 229   2P/1B: $99- 229   XP: $20
& Breakfast   Sun-Thurs 2/1-2/28 &
               11/1-1/31 [BP]   1P: $69- 169   2P/1B: $69- 169   XP: $20
               Sun-Thurs 3/1-6/14 [EP] 1P: $79- 199   2P/1B: $79- 199
Location: 0.5 mi s of US 101, northbound exit Casitas Pass Rd; southbound exit Linden Ave. 600 Linden Ave 93013.
Fax: 805/566-9696. **Terms:** Check-in 4 pm; reserv deposit, 7 day notice; handling fee imposed. **Facility:** 7 rooms. Restored 1904 California cottage-style house with antique furnishings & colorful gardens. 3 blks from beach.
Phone for guest use in public area. 2 suites with fireplace & whirlpool, $129-$199; 2 stories; interior corridors; designated
smoking area. **Some Rooms:** combo or shower baths, shared bathrooms, color TV. **Cards:** MC, VI.

CARSON—See Los Angeles p. 592.

CASTAIC—1,100

LODGINGS

CASTAIC INN   **Phone:** (805)257-0229
(AAA) [SAVE]   All Year [CP]   1P: $35- 69   2P/1B: $36- 79   2P/2B: $38- 79   XP: $14   F14
◆ ◆   **Location:** Adjacent to I-5; northbound exit Parker Rd, southbound exit Lake Hughes Rd, 0.8 mi se. 31411
Motel   Ridge Rt 91384. Fax: 805/257-0980. **Terms:** Reserv deposit, 7 day notice; handling fee imposed;
weekly/monthly rates, in winter. **Facility:** 50 rooms. 6 whirlpool rms, $50-$79; 2 stories; exterior corridors; small
pool, whirlpool. **Dining:** Restaurant nearby. **Cards:** AE, DS, JC, MC, VI. **Special Amenities:** Early
check-in/late check-out and free breakfast. *(See ad p 645 & below)*

COMFORT INN   **Phone:** (805)295-1100
(AAA) [SAVE]   All Year [CP]   1P: $40- 75   2P/1B: $40- 80   2P/2B: $40- 85   XP: $7
◆ ◆   **Location:** I-5, northbound exit Parker Rd, 0.3 mi ne, southbound exit Lake Hughes Rd, 0.5 mi se. 31558
Motel   Castaic Rd 91384. Fax: 805/295-0379. **Terms:** Weekly/monthly rates; small pets only, in smoking rooms.
Facility: 120 rooms. 2 stories; exterior corridors; small heated pool. **Cards:** AE, CB, DI, DS, JC, MC, VI.
Special Amenities: Free breakfast and free newspaper.

DAYS INN
Phone: 805/295-1070

4/1-9/30	1P:	$64	2P/1B:	$69	2P/2B:	$79	XP: $5
2/1-3/31 & 10/1-1/31	1P:	$45	2P/1B:	$49	2P/2B:	$54	XP: $5

Rates Subject to Change

Motel **Location:** I-5, exit Lake Hughes Rd. 31410 Castaic Rd 91384. Fax: 805/295-6758. **Facility:** 54 rooms. 2 stories; exterior corridors. **Cards:** AE, DS, MC, VI.

[SAVE] [icons]

CASTRO VALLEY—48,600   (See map p. 752; index p. 750)

LODGINGS

ECONO LODGE [SAVE]
Phone: (510)537-8833   **6**

All Year   1P: $65- 70   2P/1B: $75   2P/2B: $70   XP: $10   F12

◆◆ **Location:** N of I-580, eastbound exit Crow Canyon Rd; westbound exit Castro Valley Blvd, 0.3 mi e. 3928 E Castro Valley Blvd 94552. Fax: 510/538-9584. **Terms:** Reserv deposit, 3 day notice. **Facility:** 33 rooms. Most rooms with vista of San Francisco Bay. 14 whirlpool rms, extra charge; 2 stories; exterior corridors; whirlpool.
Motel **Cards:** AE, CB, DI, DS, JC, MC, VI.

[icons]

HOLIDAY INN EXPRESS [SAVE]
Phone: (510)538-9501   **7**

All Year [CP]   1P: $79- 137   2P/1B: $79- 137   2P/2B: $79- 137   XP: $10   F18

◆◆◆ **Location:** Exit I-580 Castro Valley Blvd, 0.3 mi n. 2532 Castro Valley Blvd 94546. Fax: 510/538-9487.
Motel **Facility:** 61 rooms. All rooms with hair dryers, iron & ironing boards. 7 whirlpool rms & 2 master suites, extra charge; 3 stories; interior corridors; small heated indoor/outdoor pool. **Dining:** Coffee shop nearby. **Cards:** AE, DI, DS, JC, MC, VI. **Special Amenities:** Free breakfast and free local telephone calls.

[icons]

CATALINA ISLAND

LODGINGS

BANNING HOUSE LODGE
Phone: (310)510-2800

6/19-9/19 [CP]	1P:	$110- 210	2P/1B:	$110- 210	2P/2B:	$110- 210	XP: $20
3/20-6/18 & 9/20-10/31 [CP]	1P:	$75- 160	2P/1B:	$75- 160	2P/2B:	$75- 160	XP: $20
2/1-3/19 & 11/1-1/31 [CP]	1P:	$60- 150	2P/1B:	$60- 150	2P/2B:	$60- 150	XP: $20

Rates Subject to Change

Motel **Location:** In two harbors. (PO Box 737, AVALON, 90704). Fax: 310/510-0244. **Terms:** Reserv deposit, 3 day notice. **Facility:** 11 rooms. Craftsman style inn. Some ocean view rooms. 2 stories; exterior corridors. **All Rooms:** shower baths. **Cards:** AE, DS, MC, VI.

[icons]

BEST WESTERN CATALINA CANYON RESORT & SPA
Phone: (310)510-0325

6/16-10/17	1P:	$159- 199	2P/1B:	$159- 199	2P/2B:	$159- 199	XP: $10	F17
4/2-6/15	1P:	$109- 149	2P/1B:	$109- 149	2P/2B:	$109- 149	XP: $10	F17
2/1-4/1 & 10/18-1/31	1P:	$89- 119	2P/1B:	$89- 119	2P/2B:	$89- 119	XP: $10	F17

Rates Subject to Change

◆◆◆ Motor Inn **Location:** In Avalon, 0.5 mi from the harbor. 888 Country Club Dr 90704 (PO Box 736, AVALON). Fax: 310/510-0900. **Terms:** 2 night min stay, weekends. **Facility:** 75 rooms. On the hillside near country club. Compact room arrangement, attractive pool area, full service spa. Suite w/full kitchen $250-$500; 3 stories; exterior corridors; heated pool. **Services:** Fee: massage. **Cards:** AE, CB, DI, DS, MC, VI. (See color ad p 64)

[icons]

CATALINA ISLAND SEACREST INN
Rates Subject to Change   Phone: 310/510-0800

Fri-Sun & Mon-Thurs			
6/1-10/1 [CP]	1P: $105- 195	2P/1B: $105- 195	
Mon-Thurs 2/1-5/31 &			
10/2-1/31 [CP]	1P: $75- 145	2P/1B: $75- 145	

◆◆ Motel **Terms:** Reserv deposit, 7 day notice; handling fee imposed; package plans; 2 night min stay, weekends. **Facility:** 8 rooms. Small well-appointed Victorian style rooms. 3rd floor sun deck with view of Avalon. 2 stories; interior corridors; smoke free premises. **All Rooms:** combo or shower baths. **Some Rooms:** whirlpools. **Cards:** DI, DS, MC, VI.

[icons]

EL TERADO TERRACE [SAVE]
Phone: (310)510-0831

5/1-10/31	1P:	$80- 130	2P/1B:	$80- 130	2P/2B:	$140- 180	XP: $10
2/1-4/30 & 11/1-1/31	1P:	$55- 80	2P/1B:	$55- 80	2P/2B:	$90- 130	XP: $10

◆◆ Motel **Location:** In Avalon. 230 Marilla Ave 90704 (PO Box 1295, AVALON). Fax: 310/510-1582. **Terms:** Reserv deposit, 5 day notice; 2 night min stay. **Facility:** 18 rooms. On hill, 1 1/2 blocks from harbor. Some rooms with ocean view. 2 & 3 room units with full kitchen $130-$220; 1-2 stories; exterior corridors; whirlpool. **All Rooms:** combo or shower baths. **Some Rooms:** 9 efficiencies. **Cards:** AE, DS, MC, VI.

[icons]

HOTEL ATWATER
Rates Subject to Change   Phone: (310)510-1788

Fri & Sat 6/18-9/25	1P:	$86- 323	2P/1B:	$86- 323	2P/2B:	$86- 323	XP: $10	F11
Sun-Thurs 6/18-9/25	1P:	$68- 264	2P/1B:	$68- 264	2P/2B:	$68- 264	XP: $10	F11
2/1-6/17 & 9/26-10/30	1P:	$55- 243	2P/1B:	$55- 243	2P/2B:	$55- 243	XP: $10	F11
10/31-1/31	1P:	$54- 178	2P/1B:	$54- 178	2P/2B:	$54- 178	XP: $10	F11

◆ Motel **Location:** 4.5 blks from Crescent Ave. 125 Sumner Ave 90704 (PO Box 737, AVALON). Fax: 310/510-2073. **Terms:** Reserv deposit, 3 day notice; 2 night min stay, weekends. **Facility:** 92 rooms. Hotel open on weekends only off season. Some smaller rooms. 2 suites w/refrigerator & microwave $138-$278; 2 stories; interior corridors. **All Rooms:** combo or shower baths. **Cards:** AE, CB, DI, DS, JC, MC, VI.

[icons]

HOTEL MAC RAE
Rates Subject to Change   Phone: (310)510-0246

Fri & Sat 4/30-10/11 [CP]	1P: $140- 190	2P/1B: $140- 190	2P/2B: $140- 160	
Sun-Thurs 4/30-10/11 [CP]	1P: $120- 170	2P/1B: $120- 170	2P/2B: $120- 140	
Fri & Sat 2/1-4/29 &				
10/12-1/31 [CP]	1P: $80- 120	2P/1B: $80- 120	2P/2B: $80- 90	
Sun-Thurs 2/1-4/29 &				
10/12-1/31 [CP]	1P: $55- 95	2P/1B: $55- 95	2P/2B: $55- 65	

◆ Motel **Location:** In Avalon. 409 Crescent Ave 90704 (PO Box 246, AVALON). Fax: 310/510-9632. **Terms:** Reserv deposit, 3 day notice. **Facility:** 24 rooms. Across from beach. Nicely decorated, cozy rooms surrounding interior patio. **All Rooms:** combo or shower baths. **Cards:** MC, VI. (See ad p 412)

[icons]

HOTEL METROPOLE
△△△ Motel
◆◆◆

	Guaranteed Rates					**Phone:** 310/510-1884	
5/1-10/31 [CP]	1P: $119- 355	2P/1B: $119- 355	2P/2B: $165- 795	XP: $10	F18
2/1-4/30 & 11/1-1/31 [CP]	1P: $89- 245	2P/1B: $80- 245	2P/2B: $115- 795	XP: $10	F18

Location: In Avalon; corner of Crescent Av & Whittley. 208 Crescent Ave 90704 (PO Box 1900, AVALON). **Fax:** 310/510-2534. **Terms:** Reserv deposit, 3 day notice. **Facility:** 48 rooms. Across from harbor at Metropole Market Place. Some ocean view rooms, many with balconies. Gas fireplace in many rooms. 1 two-bedroom apartment with whirlpool, fireplace, big screen TV, kitchen & deck $495-$695. 11 whirlpool rms, extra charge; 3 stories; interior/exterior corridors; smoke free premises; whirlpool. **Dining:** Restaurant nearby. **Cards:** AE, MC, VI.
(See color ad p 64)

HOTEL ST. LAUREN
△△△ Motel
◆◆

	Rates Subject to Change				**Phone:** (310)510-2299
5/1-11/1	1P: $90- 275	2P/1B: $90- 275	2P/2B: $150- 250	XP: $20
2/1-4/30 & 11/2-1/31	1P: $40- 250	2P/1B: $40- 250	2P/2B: $120- 225	XP: $20

Location: In Avalon. 231 Beacon St at Metropole 90704 (PO Box 2166, AVALON). **Fax:** 310/510-1369. **Terms:** Reserv deposit, 7 day notice; handling fee imposed; 2 night min stay, weekends. **Facility:** 42 rooms. Victorian style hotel. 1 block from harbor. Many ocean view rooms. 6 stories; interior corridors.
Some Rooms: whirlpools. **Cards:** AE, MC, VI. *(See color ad p 64)*

HOTEL VILLA PORTOFINO
△△△ Motor Inn
◆◆◆

	Rates Subject to Change				**Phone:** 310/510-0555
[CP]	1P: $110- 345	2P/1B: $110- 345	2P/2B: $155- 345	XP: $10-20
Sun-Thurs 6/1-9/30 [CP]	1P: $90- 345	2P/1B: $90- 345	2P/2B: $100- 345	XP: $10-20
Sun-Thurs 2/1-5/31 & 10/1-1/31 [CP]	1P: $65- 245	2P/1B: $65- 245	2P/2B: $65- 245	XP: $10-20

Location: In Avalon. 111 Crescent Ave 90704 (PO Box 127, AVALON). **Fax:** 310/510-0839. **Terms:** Reserv deposit, 7 day notice; handling fee imposed; 2 night min stay, weekends 3/1-10/26. **Facility:** 34 rooms. Across from harbor. Some ocean view rooms. Sun deck with view of the harbor. 3 two-bedroom units. 2 stories; exterior corridors. **Dining:** Ristorante Villa Portofino, see separate listing. **All Rooms:** combo or shower baths. **Cards:** AE, CB, DI, DS, MC, VI.

HOTEL VINCENTES
△△△ SAVE Motel
◆◆

					Phone: (310)510-1115
Fri-Sun 4/15-10/31 [CP]	1P: $99- 140	2P/1B: $99- 140	2P/2B: $175	XP: $20	F5
Mon-Thurs 4/15-10/31 [CP]	1P: $85- 140	2P/1B: $85- 140	2P/2B: $125- 175	XP: $20	F5
Mon-Thurs 2/1-4/14 & 11/1-1/31 [CP]	1P: $55- 125	2P/1B: $55- 125	2P/2B: $65- 125	XP: $20	F5
Fri-Sun 2/1-4/14 & 11/1-1/31 [CP]	1P: $79- 89	2P/1B: $79- 89	2P/2B: $110- 125	XP: $20	F5

Location: In Avalon; 1/4 blk from Harbor. 108 Marilla Ave 90704 (PO Box 187, AVALON). **Fax:** 310/510-1709. **Terms:** Reserv deposit, 10 day notice; 2 night min stay, weekends 4/1-10/31. **Facility:** 12 rooms. Located close to harbor & shops. Attractive interior patio area. 2 ocean view suites, with efficiency $140-$275 for up to 2 persons; $110-$195 off season. Handling fe imposed; no elevator. **Recreation:** free videos. **All Rooms:** combo or shower baths. **Cards:** AE, DS, MC, VI.

HOTEL VISTA DEL MAR
△△△ Motel
◆◆◆

	Rates Subject to Change				**Phone:** (310)510-1452
5/1-10/31 [CP]	1P: $95- 325	2P/1B: $95- 325	2P/2B: $95- 325	XP: $10-15
2/1-4/30 & 11/1-1/31 [CP]	1P: $75- 225	2P/1B: $75- 225	2P/2B: $75- 225	XP: $10-15

Location: In Avalon. 417 Crescent Ave 90704 (PO Box 1979, AVALON). **Fax:** 310/510-2917. **Terms:** Reserv deposit, 5 day notice; handling fee imposed; package plans, non-cancellable; 2 night min stay, weekends. **Facility:** 15 rooms. Across from beach. Most rooms with gas fireplace & some with whirlpool bathtub. Rooms surround an attractive atrium area with a balcony overlooking the harbor. 2 stories; interior corridors. **Dining:** Restaurant nearby. **Cards:** AE, DS, MC, VI.

THE OLD TURNER INN
△△△ Bed & Breakfast
◆◆

| | Rates Subject to Change | | **Phone:** (310)510-2236 |
| All Year [CP] | 1P: $135- 210 | | XP: $20-35 |

Location: 232 Catalina Ave 90704 (PO Box 97, AVALON). **Terms:** Reserv deposit, 10 day notice; handling fee imposed; 2 night min stay, weekends. **Facility:** 5 rooms. Located in residential area. Tastefully decorated rooms, some with fireplace. 2 stories; interior corridors; smoke free premises. **Services:** complimentary evening beverages. **All Rooms:** combo or shower baths. **Cards:** DS, MC, VI.

AVILION LODGE Rates Subject to Change Phone: (310)510-1788

Fri & Sat 6/18-9/25 [CP] 1P: $199 2P/1B: $199 2P/2B: $199 XP: $10 F11
Sun-Thurs 6/18-9/25 [CP] 1P: $149 2P/1B: $149 2P/2B: $149 XP: $10 F11
2/1-6/17 & 9/26-10/30 [CP] 1P: $99- 139 2P/1B: $99- 139 2P/2B: $99- 139 XP: $10 F11
10/31-1/31 [CP] 1P: $62- 99 2P/1B: $62- 99 2P/2B: $62- 99 XP: $10 F11

Motel **Location:** In Avalon. 513 Crescent Ave 90704 (PO Box 737, AVALON). Fax: 310/510-2073. **Terms:** Reserv deposit, 3 day notice; 2 night min stay, weekends 2/1-11/30. **Facility:** 73 rooms. Across from beach. Nicely landscaped grounds. For reservations call 800-851-0215. 2 stories; exterior corridors. **All Rooms:** combo or shower baths. **Cards:** AE, DI, DS, JC, MC, VI. *(See color ad p 64 & ad below)*

🐾 📼 💳 ☎ 🖨 📶 ✕

SEAPORT VILLAGE INN Rates Subject to Change Phone: 310/5100344

Fri & Sat 4/12-10/31 &
Sun-Thurs 6/15-9/15 1P: $99- 199 2P/1B: $99- 199 2P/2B: $99- 199 XP: $15
Fri & Sat 2/1-4/11, Sun-Thurs
4/12-6/14, 9/16-10/31 &
11/1-1/31 1P: $69- 149 2P/1B: $69- 149 2P/2B: $69- 149 XP: $15
Sun-Thurs 2/1-4/11 &
11/1-1/31 1P: $39- 109 2P/1B: $39- 109 2P/2B: $39- 109 XP: $15

Motel **Location:** Just w of Crescent Ave at end of Maiden Ln in Avalon. 119 Maiden Ln 90704 (PO Box 2411, AVALON). Fax: 310/5101156. **Terms:** Reserv deposit, 7 day notice; handling fee imposed; 2 night min stay, weekends. **Facility:** 34 rooms. Nestled against a southern hillside 0.5 block from beach, bay & town. 9 studio with kitchen some with whirlpool, $79 - $179; 5 one-bedroom suites with kitchen $79-$179 1 view suite with kitchen $275-$399; 4 stories; exterior corridors. **Services:** area transportation. **All Rooms:** combo or shower baths. **Cards:** AE, MC, VI. *(See color ad p 64)*

💱 💳 🖨 📶 ✕

SNUG HARBOR INN Rates Subject to Change Phone: (310)510-8400

2/1-10/31 [CP] 1P: $195- 325 2P/1B: $195- 325
11/1-1/31 [CP] 1P: $140- 295 2P/1B: $140- 295

Motel **Location:** In Avalon; 1/2 blk from Crescent Av. 108 Sumner 90704 (PO Box 2470, AVALON). Fax: 310/510-8418. **Terms:** Reserv deposit, 5 day notice; handling fee imposed; 2 night min stay, weekends. **Facility:** 6 rooms. Beautiful appointed rooms with nautical theme. Some rooms with bay view. 2 stories; interior corridors. **Services:** complimentary evening beverages. **Recreation:** complimentary videos. **Cards:** AE, DS, MC, VI.

📼 🖨 🔟 ✕

RESTAURANTS

THE BLUE PARROT Lunch: $5-$8 Dinner: $10-$15 Phone: 310/510-2465

American **Location:** At Metropole Center. 205 Crescent Ave 90704. **Hours:** 11 am-10 pm, Fri & Sat-11 pm. Closed: 11/25 & 12/25. **Features:** No A/C; casual dress; Sunday brunch; children's menu; early bird specials; carryout; cocktails & lounge. Casual restaurant with tropical decor. Located on upper level with good view of harbor. Smoke free premises. **Cards:** AE, DI, DS, MC, VI.

✕

CAFE PREGO Lunch: $6-$10 Dinner: $9-$26 Phone: 310/510-1218

Italian **Location:** In Avalon. 605 Crescent Ave 90704. **Hours:** 4:30 pm-9 pm, Fri & Sat-10 pm, open for lunch Fri-Mon. Closed: 11/25 & 12/20/12/25. **Reservations:** suggested; in summer. **Features:** No A/C; casual dress; children's menu; early bird specials; senior's menu; cocktails. A variety of Italian entrees. Smoke free premises. **Cards:** AE, CB, DI, DS, MC, VI.

✕

THE CHANNEL HOUSE Lunch: $6-$16 Dinner: $12-$25 Phone: 310/510-1617

Continental **Location:** At Metropole Market Place in Avalon. 205 Crescent Ave 90704. **Hours:** 11 am-2 & 5-10 pm. Closed: Mon 11/1-6/15. **Reservations:** suggested. **Features:** casual dress; children's menu; cocktails & lounge. Attractive dining room & outdoor patio seating located across street from the harbor. Excellently prepared beef, poultry, fish & pasta entrees. Smoke free premises. **Cards:** AE, DS, MC, VI.

✕

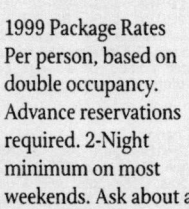

EL GALLEON **Lunch:** $7-$14 **Dinner:** $12-$25 **Phone:** 310/510-1188
🔷🔷🔷 **Location:** Across from harbor & beach; in Avalon. 411 Crescent Ave 90704. **Hours:** 11 am-4 & 5-10 pm.
◆ **Features:** No A/C; casual dress; children's menu; early bird specials; carryout; cocktails & lounge;
Steak and entertainment. Nautical decor. Selection of seafood & steak. Smoke free premises. **Cards:** AE, MC, VI. 🆇
Seafood

THE LANDING BAR & GRILLE **Lunch:** $5-$8 **Dinner:** $13-$18 **Phone:** 310/510-1474
◆ **Location:** In Avalon. 101 Marilla at Crescent Ave 90704. **Hours:** 11 am-10 pm, Fri & Sat-midnight, Sun 11
American am-10 pm. Closed: Mon off season & 12/25. **Features:** casual dress; children's menu; early bird specials;
carryout; cocktails & lounge. Indoor & outdoor patio dining overlooking harbor. Dancing weekends during
summer season. Smoke free premises. **Cards:** AE, DI, MC, VI. 🆇

RISTORANTE VILLA PORTOFINO **Dinner:** $15-$30 **Phone:** 310/510-0508
🔷🔷🔷 **Location:** At the Hotel Villa Portofino in Avalon. 111 Crescent Ave 90704. **Hours:** 5 pm-10 pm 4/1-10/31.
Italian Closed: Mon & Tues 11/1 - 3/31. **Reservations:** suggested. **Features:** No A/C; casual dress; children's
menu; early bird specials; cocktails; a la carte. Attractive dining room with a nice selection of seafood, pasta
& veal. May close some evenings during off season. Smoke free premises. **Cards:** AE, CB, DI, DS, MC, VI. 🆇

CATHEDRAL CITY—30,100 (See map p. 774; index p. 772)

LODGINGS

CATHEDRAL CITY TRAVELODGE **Phone:** (760)328-2616 🔢20
🔷🔷🔷 SAVE Fri & Sat 2/1-5/31 &
  1/15-1/31 1P: $60- 74 2P/1B: $60- 74 2P/2B: $70- 79 XP: $5 F17
◆ ◆ Fri & Sat 10/1-1/14 1P: $50- 60 2P/1B: $50- 60 2P/2B: $55- 65 XP: $5 F17
Motel Fri & Sat 6/1-9/30 1P: $36- 48 2P/1B: $36- 48 2P/2B: $44- 56 XP: $5 F17
  Sun-Thurs 1P: $34- 48 2P/1B: $38- 52 2P/2B: $44- 56 XP: $5 F17
Location: 2 mi w. 67-495 Highway 111 92234. Fax: 760/328-0577. **Facility:** 43 rooms. Across the street from Camelot Amusement Park. 2 stories; interior corridors; heated pool, whirlpool. **Dining:** Restaurant nearby. **Cards:** AE, CB, DI, DS, MC, VI.
Special Amenities: Free local telephone calls and free newspaper. Ⓢ🔊 ⌚ 🔟 🎥 🆇

DAYS INN SUITES **Phone:** (760)324-5939 🔢21
🔷🔷🔷 SAVE 2/1-5/31 & 12/31-1/31 [CP] 1P: $85 2P/1B: 2P/2B: $105- 145 XP: $10 F16
  10/1-12/30 [CP] 1P: $55 2P/1B: $65- 75 2P/2B: $75- 105 XP: $10 F16
◆ ◆ 6/1-9/30 [CP] 1P: $55 2P/1B: $59- 69 2P/2B: $69- 89 XP: $10 F16
Motel **Location:** SR 111 just e of Date Palm Rd. 69-151 E Palm Canyon Dr 92234. Fax: 760/324-3034.
Terms: Small pets only. **Facility:** 97 rooms. Studios, 1- & 2-bedroom suites with kitchen. 3 stories; exterior
corridors; heated pool, whirlpool. **Dining:** Complimentary barbecue Wed evening. **All Rooms:** extended cable TV.
Cards: AE, CB, DI, DS, MC, VI. **Special Amenities:** Free breakfast. Ⓢ🔊 🛏 ⑂ ⌚ ➕ 🛎 📺 🖨 🆇

DOUBLETREE RESORT AT DESERT PRINCESS COUNTRY CLUB **Phone:** (760)322-7000 🔢18
🔷🔷🔷 SAVE 2/1-4/30 & 1/1-1/31 1P: $149- 179 2P/1B: $149- 179 2P/2B: $149- 179 XP: $15 F18
  5/1-6/15 & 10/1-12/31 1P: $79- 99 2P/1B: $79- 99 2P/2B: $79- 99 XP: $15 F18
🔷🔷🔷 6/16-9/30 1P: $59- 79 2P/1B: $59- 79 2P/2B: $59- 79 XP: $15 F18
Resort **Location:** 1.8 mi sw of I-10, exit Date Palm Dr. 67-967 Vista Chino 92234 (PO Box 1644, PALM SPRINGS,
Complex 92263). Fax: 760/322-6853. **Terms:** Reserv deposit, 3 day notice; weekly/monthly rates; small pets only,
$125 dep req. **Facility:** 285 rooms. Spacious grounds. Nicely furnished rooms with patio or balcony. 4 stories;
interior corridors; heated pool, whirlpools. Fee: 27 holes golf; racquetball court, 10 tennis courts (5 lighted). **Dining:** Dining
room; 6:30 am-10 pm, Sat-11 pm; $10-$20; cocktails. **Services:** giftshop. Fee: massage. **Cards:** AE, CB, DI, DS, JC, MC,
VI. **Special Amenities:** Early check-in/late check-out and free local telephone calls. *(See ad p 784)*
Ⓢ🔊 🛏 ⑂ ⌚ 🏊 🍴 ➕ 🆇 🎥 📺 🖨 📦 🔟 🆇

CAYUCOS—2,300

LODGINGS

BEACHWALKER INN **Phone:** (805)995-2133
🔷🔷🔷 SAVE 2/1-5/31 & 10/1-1/31 [CP] 1P: $85- 150 2P/1B: $85- 150 2P/2B: $85- 150 XP: $10 F12
  6/1-9/30 [CP] 1P: $75- 130 2P/1B: $75- 130 2P/2B: $75- 130 XP: $10 F12
🔷🔷🔷 **Location:** SR 1 business route. 501 S Ocean Ave 93430. Fax: 805/995-3139. **Terms:** Reserv deposit, 7 day
Motel notice; weekly/monthly rates; 2 night min stay, weekends in season. **Facility:** 25 rooms. 1 block to beach.
Some ocean view rooms & 1-bedroom suites with efficiency, can be combined to 2-bedroom suites. Gas fireplace. Country decor. Two room suite with kitchen & wood burning fireplace, $150-$225; 2 stories; exterior corridors; designated smoking area. **All Rooms:** extended cable TV. **Cards:** AE, CB, DI, DS, JC, MC, VI. **Special Amenities:** Free
breakfast and free newspaper. *(See color ad p 415)* Ⓢ🔊 🔟 🎥 VCR 📺 🆇 🖨 🆇

CYPRESS TREE MOTEL **Phone:** (805)995-3917
🔷🔷🔷 SAVE 5/16-9/15 1P: $45- 70 2P/1B: $45- 70 2P/2B: $55- 80 XP: $5 F16
  2/1-5/15 & 9/16-1/31 1P: $30- 55 2P/1B: $30- 55 2P/2B: $40- 65 XP: $5 F16
◆ **Location:** On SR 1 business route. 125 S Ocean Ave 93430. **Terms:** Weekly/monthly rates; pets, $5 dep
Motel req. **Facility:** 12 rooms. 1 blk to beach. Small rooms. 3 kitchens; $10 extra charge; 1-2 stories; exterior corri-
dors. **Dining:** Restaurant nearby. **All Rooms:** combo or shower baths. **Cards:** AE, DS, MC, VI.
Special Amenities: Free local telephone calls and preferred room (subject to availability with advanced
reservations). 🛏 🔟 VCR 📺 🎥 🖨 🆇

DOLPHIN INN Rates Subject to Change **Phone:** (805)995-3810
🔷🔷🔷 All Year [CP] 1P: $45- 95 2P/1B: $45- 95 2P/2B: $65- 140 XP: $10 F16
◆ **Location:** SR 1 business route. 399 S Ocean Ave 93430. Fax: 805/995-0200. **Terms:** Reserv deposit; pets,
Motel $10 extra charge, limited rooms. **Facility:** 19 rooms. Cozy motel units & cottages. 1 blk to beach. 2 whirlpool
rms, $85; 1 story; exterior corridors. **All Rooms:** combo or shower baths. **Some Rooms:** 5 kitchens,
whirlpools. **Cards:** AE, DS, MC, VI. 🛏 🎥 VCR 📺 🔟 🆇 🖨 🆇

In the listings, the meal plan included in the rates follows the open dates.

ESTERO BAY MOTEL
Phone: (805)995-3614

6/1-9/30	1P: $65- 120	2P/1B: $65- 120	2P/2B: $65- 120	XP: $10		F14
2/1-5/31 & 10/1-1/31	1P: $38- 85	2P/1B: $38- 85	2P/2B: $42- 92	XP: $10		F14

Location: SR 1 business route. 25 S Ocean Ave 93430. **Terms:** Reserv deposit, 3 day notice; weekly/monthly rates; pets, $15 extra charge. **Facility:** 12 rooms. 1/2 blk to beach. 4 kitchens & 1 efficiency, $10 extra charge; 1 story; exterior corridors. **All Rooms:** combo or shower baths. **Cards:** AE, DS, MC, VI. **Special Amenities:** Free local telephone calls and free room upgrade (subject to availability with advanced reservations).

Motel

SHORELINE INN
Phone: (805)995-3681

Fri & Sat 5/16-9/15	1P: $105- 140	2P/1B: $105- 140	2P/2B: $105- 140
Sun-Thurs 5/16-9/15	1P: $90- 120	2P/1B: $90- 120	2P/2B: $90- 120
Fri & Sat 2/1-5/15 & 9/16-1/31	1P: $75- 120	2P/1B: $75- 120	2P/2B: $75- 120
Sun-Thurs 2/1-5/15 & 9/16-1/31	1P: $60- 110	2P/1B: $60- 110	2P/2B: $60- 110

Location: #1 N Ocean Ave 93430 (PO Box 376). Fax: 805/995-3064. **Terms:** Pets, $10 extra charge. **Facility:** 29 rooms. At the beach, rooms have full or partial ocean view. 2 rms with fireplace & refrigerator, $100-$150; 2 stories; exterior corridors. **All Rooms:** combo or shower baths, extended cable TV. **Cards:** AE, CB, DI, DS, JC, MC, VI. **Special Amenities:** Free breakfast and free newspaper.

Motel

CEDARVILLE—1,100—See also ALTURAS.

LODGING

SUNRISE MOTEL
Phone: (530)279-2161

All Year	1P: $35- 40	2P/1B: $45- 50	2P/2B: $53- 58	XP: $10

Location: 0.5 mi w on Hwy 299. 54889 Hwy 299 96104 (PO Box 345). Fax: 530/279-6261. **Terms:** Handling fee imposed; weekly/monthly rates; small pets only. **Facility:** 14 rooms. Horseshoe pits & barbecue area. RV parking avail; 1 story; exterior corridors. **All Rooms:** combo or shower baths. **Cards:** AE, CB, DI, JC, MC, VI. **Special Amenities:** Free local telephone calls and free newspaper.

Motel

CERRITOS—See Los Angeles p. 593.

CHATSWORTH—See Los Angeles p. 593.

CHESTER—2,100

LODGING

THE BIDWELL HOUSE
Guaranteed Rates
Phone: 530/258-3338

All Year [BP]	2P/1B: $60- 140	

Location: On SR 36. 1 Main St 96020 (PO Box 1790). Fax: 530/258-3338. **Terms:** Reserv deposit, 3 day notice. **Facility:** 14 rooms. 1901 renovated farmhouse at e edge of town near Lake Almanor. 3 rooms with woodburning fireplaces. Office closes noon-3 pm. 2 stories; interior corridors. **Some Rooms:** kitchen, color TV. **Cards:** MC, VI.

Bed & Breakfast

For the easiest and most accurate navigation possible, always use your AAA sheet map *in conjunction with* your TourBook.

CHICO—40,100

LODGINGS

BEST WESTERN HERITAGE INN
Phone: (530)894-8600
⊕ SAVE
All Year [CP]   1P: $64- 86 2P/1B: $71- 86 2P/2B: $71- 86 XP: $7   F12
Location: Just e of SR 99, via Cohasset Rd. 25 Heritage Ln 95926. Fax: 530/894-8600. **Facility:** 101 rooms.
◆◆◆   3 stories; interior corridors; whirlpool. **Some Rooms:** whirlpools. **Cards:** AE, CB, DI, DS, JC, MC, VI.
Motel   **Special Amenities:** Free breakfast and free local telephone calls.

DELUXE INN
Phone: (530)342-8386
⊕ SAVE
All Year [BP]   1P: $39- 49 2P/1B: $46- 56 2P/2B: $46- 56 XP: $4-6   F16
Location: 2 mi n on SR 99 business route. 2507 Esplanade 95926. **Terms:** Small pets only, $4 extra
◆   charge. **Facility:** 35 rooms. 1 story; exterior corridors. **Dining:** Restaurant nearby. **All Rooms:** combo or
Motel   shower baths. **Some Rooms:** 8 kitchens. **Cards:** AE, DI, DS, MC, VI. **Special Amenities:** Early
check-in/late check-out and free local telephone calls.

HOLIDAY INN OF CHICO
Rates Subject to Change   Phone: 530/345-2491
◆◆◆   All Year   1P: $79- 89 2P/1B: $85- 95 2P/2B: $85- 95 XP: $6   F19
Motor Inn   **Location:** Just w of SR 99, via Cohasset Rd. 685 Manzanita Ct 95926. Fax: 530/893-3040. **Terms:** Reserv
deposit. **Facility:** 172 rooms. 5 stories; interior corridors; smoke free premises. **Cards:** AE, CB, DI, DS, JC,
MC, VI. *(See color ad below)*

JOHNSON'S COUNTRY INN
Guaranteed Rates   Phone: 530/345-7829
◆◆◆   Fri & Sat [BP]   1P: $80- 125 2P/1B: $80- 125 2P/2B: $80- 125
Bed &   Sun-Thurs [BP]   1P: $70- 105 2P/1B: $70- 125 2P/2B: $70- 125
Breakfast   **Location:** 2 mi w on W 5th St. 3935 Morehead Ave 95928. **Terms:** Handling fee imposed. **Facility:** 4 rooms.
Surrounded by almond tree orchards & flowering gardens. 2 stories; interior corridors; designated smoking
area. **All Rooms:** combo or shower baths. **Cards:** MC, VI.

MUSIC EXPRESS INN
Guaranteed Rates   Phone: 530/345-8376
◆◆◆   All Year [BP]   1P: $55- 65 2P/1B: $75- 85 2P/2B: $75- 85
Bed &   **Location:** Exit SR 99 at SR 32, 1 mi e to El Monte Ave, just n. 1091 El Monte Ave 95928.
Breakfast   Fax: 530/893-8521. **Terms:** Reserv deposit. **Facility:** 9 rooms. 2 stories; interior/exterior corridors.
Cards: AE, DS, MC, VI.

OXFORD SUITES
Rates Subject to Change   Phone: (530)899-9090
◆◆   All Year [BP]   1P: $63- 129 2P/1B: $70- 136 2P/2B: $71- 78 XP: $7   F10
Motor Inn   **Location:** SR 99, exit 20th St e. 2035 Business Ln 95928. Fax: 530/899-9476. **Terms:** Reserv deposit.
Facility: 183 rooms. Conveniently located within walking distance to the Chico Mall. 4 stories; interior corridors.
Services: giftshop. **Cards:** AE, DI, DS, MC, VI.

SAFARI GARDEN MOTEL
Phone: (530)343-3201
⊕ SAVE
All Year   1P: $42- 45 2P/1B: $45- 48 2P/2B: $45- 48 XP: $5   F12
Location: 2 mi n on SR 99 business rt. 2352 Esplanade 95926. Fax: 530/343-2364. **Terms:** Small pets only,
◆ $25 dep req. **Facility:** 50 rooms. Tree-shaded grounds. 4 kitchens & 1 efficiency, $8 extra charge; 1-2 stories;
Motel   exterior corridors. **All Rooms:** combo or shower baths. **Cards:** AE, CB, DI, DS, JC, MC, VI.
Special Amenities: Free local telephone calls.

SUPER 8 MOTEL
Rates Subject to Change   Phone: (530)345-2533
◆   All Year   1P: $44- 56 2P/1B: $50- 62 2P/2B: $50- 62 XP: $6   F12
Motel   **Location:** Just w of SR 99, via Cohasset Rd. 655 Manzanita Ct 95926. Fax: 530/345-6762. **Terms:** Reserv
deposit. **Facility:** 53 rooms. 3 stories, no elevator; interior corridors. **All Rooms:** combo or shower baths.
Cards: AE, CB, DI, DS, MC, VI.

TOWN HOUSE MOTEL
Phone: 530/343-1621
⊕ SAVE
All Year [CP]   1P: $32- 44 2P/1B: $35- 48 2P/2B: $40- 50 XP: $5
Location: 1.8 mi n on SR 99 business route. 2231 Esplanade 95926. Fax: 530/894-6159. **Terms:** Small pets
◆   only, $25 dep req. **Facility:** 29 rooms. 1 story; exterior corridors. **Dining:** Coffee shop nearby.
Motel   **All Rooms:** shower baths. **Some Rooms:** 2 efficiencies, no utensils. **Cards:** AE, DS, MC, VI.

RESTAURANT

ATCH COVER
Dinner: $8-$23
Phone: 530/345-5862

◆
eak and
eafood

Location: 1.5 mi n on SR 99 business rt. 1720 Esplanade 95926. **Hours:** 5 pm-9:30 pm, Fri & Sat-10 pm. Closed: 1/1, 11/28 & 12/25. **Reservations:** suggested. **Features:** casual dress; children's menu; early bird specials; cocktails & lounge; a la carte. Varied menu. Smoke free premises. **Cards:** AE, DS, MC, VI.

CHINO—59,700

LODGINGS

EST WESTERN PINE TREE MOTEL
Phone: (909)628-6021

All Year
1P: $39- 46   2P/1B: $45- 53   2P/2B: $47- 59   XP: $4-5   F12

otel

Location: Just n of SR 60, Chino/Montclair (Central Ave) exit. 12018 Central Ave 91710. Fax: 909/465-0748. **Facility:** 43 rooms. 2 stories; exterior corridors. **All Rooms:** combo or shower baths. **Cards:** AE, CB, DI, DS, MC, VI. **Special Amenities:** Free local telephone calls.

HINO MOTEL
Rates Subject to Change
Phone: (909)591-9505

All Year
1P: $45   2P/1B: $50   2P/2B: $52   XP: $4-5

◆ ◆
otel

Location: 0.5 mi n of SR 60, Chino/Montclair (Central Ave) exit. 11885 Central Ave 91710. Fax: 909/591-9470. **Terms:** Reserv deposit, 3 day notice. **Facility:** 52 rooms. 2 stories; exterior corridors; small pool. **Cards:** AE, DI, DS, MC, VI.

CHOWCHILLA—5,900

LODGING

AYS INN
Phone: 559-665-4821

5/1-9/30
1P: $48   2P/1B: $53   2P/2B: $57

2/1-4/30 & 10/1-1/31
1P: $40   2P/1B: $40   2P/2B: $53

◆ ◆
otel

Location: SR 99 exit Robertson Blvd W. 220 E Robertson Blvd 93610. Fax: 559/665-4821. **Facility:** 30 rooms. 2 stories; exterior corridors. **Cards:** AE, DI, DS, MC, VI. **Special Amenities:** Free breakfast and free local telephone calls.

CHULA VISTA—See San Diego p. 896.

CITRUS HEIGHTS—107,400   (See map p. 821; index p. 820)

LODGING

LIVE GROVE SUITES
Phone: (916)725-0100   **57**

All Year
1P: $65- 85   2P/1B: $75- 95   2P/2B: $75- 95

otel

Location: Exit I-80 at Greenback Ln, 1 mi s to Auburn Blvd. 6143 Auburn Blvd 95621-4701. Fax: 916/726-5091. **Terms:** Pets, $50 dep req. **Facility:** 80 rooms. Spacious suites include seperate bedrooms, living rooms & full kitchens. 2 stories; exterior corridors. **Dining:** Restaurant nearby. **All Rooms:** kitchens. **Cards:** AE, DI, DS, MC, VI. **Special Amenities:** Early check-in/late check-out and ee room upgrade (subject to availability with advanced reservations).

CLAREMONT—See Los Angeles p. 594.

CLEARLAKE—11,800

LODGINGS

EST WESTERN EL GRANDE INN
Phone: (707)994-2000

4/1-10/15
1P: $64- 72   2P/1B: $71- 89   2P/2B: $71- 89   XP: $7   F12

2/1-3/31 & 10/16-1/31
1P: $66- 74   2P/1B: $66- 79   2P/2B: $71- 79   XP: $7   F12

otor Inn

Location: 0.2 mi w of SR 53, Lakeshore Dr exit. 15135 Lakeshore Dr 95422 (PO Box 4598). Fax: 707/994-2042. **Facility:** 68 rooms. 4 stories; interior corridors; whirlpool, indoor sitting pool. **Dining:** Dining room; 7 am-1:30 & 5-9:30 pm; $10-$17; cocktails. **All Rooms:** combo or shower baths. ards: AE, CB, DI, DS, MC, VI.

AYS INN
Rates Subject to Change
Phone: 707/994-8982

5/26-9/30
1P: $45- 85   2P/1B: $50- 85   2P/2B: $75   XP: $6

2/1-5/25 & 10/1-1/31
1P: $35- 45   2P/1B: $45- 55   2P/2B: $60   XP: $6

◆ ◆
otel

Location: 0.8 mi w of SR 53, Lakeshore Dr exit. 13865 Lakeshore Dr 95422. Fax: 707/994-0613. **Terms:** Reserv deposit, 3 day notice; BP avail. **Facility:** 20 rooms. On the lake; view rooms. 1 suite, $80-$125; 10/1-5/26 $55-$90, for up to 2 persons; 2 stories; exterior corridors; small pool in summer; boat dock. ecreation: swimming, fishing, waterskiing. **Cards:** AE, CB, DI, DS, MC, VI.

CLEARLAKE OAKS—2,400

LODGING

AKE POINT LODGE
Phone: (707)998-4350

All Year [CP]
1P: $49- 54   2P/1B: $56- 61   2P/2B: $62- 68   XP: $6   F12

◆ ◆
otel

Location: 3 mi nw of jct SR 53. 13440 E Hwy 20 95423 (PO Box 708). Fax: 707/998-2144. **Facility:** 40 rooms. Approximately 2 mi from lake. Rates for up to 4 persons; 2 stories; exterior corridors; whirlpool, small pool in summer. **Dining:** Restaurant nearby. **Some Rooms:** whirlpools. **Cards:** AE, DI, DS, MC, VI. **Special Amenities:** Free breakfast and free local telephone calls.

CLOVIS—50,300

LODGING

BEST WESTERN CLOVIS COLE　　　　　　　　　　　　　　　　　　　　**Phone:** (559)299-1547
(AAA) [SAVE]　All Year [CP]　　　　　1P: $60- 125　2P/1B: $65- 130　2P/2B: $65- 130　XP: $6　　　F12
◆◆　　**Location:** Center; on SR 168 at 4th St. 415 Clovis Ave 93612. **Fax:** 559/325-9128. **Facility:** 58 rooms. A John
Motel　　Jay Motel. 3 stories; interior corridors; sauna, whirlpool. **All Rooms:** combo or shower baths. **Cards:** AE,
　　　　CB, DI, DS, JC, MC, VI. **Special Amenities:** Free breakfast and free local telephone calls.

COALINGA—8,200

LODGINGS

BIG COUNTRY INN　　　　　　　　　　　　　　　　　　　　　　　**Phone:** (559)935-0866
(AAA) [SAVE]　All Year [CP]　　　　　1P: $48- 52　2P/1B: $54- 58　2P/2B: $62- 66　XP: $5-7　　　F5
◆◆　　**Location:** W of & adjacent to I-5, at SR 198, Hanford-Lemoore off-ramp. 25020 W Dorris Ave 93210.
Motel　　**Fax:** 559/935-0644. **Terms:** Small pets only, $3. **Facility:** 48 rooms. Spacious landscaped grounds. 1 story;
　　　　exterior corridors. **Dining:** Coffee shop nearby. **Cards:** AE, DS, JC, MC, VI. **Special Amenities:** Free
breakfast and free local telephone calls.

THE INN AT HARRIS RANCH　　　　　　　　　　　　　　　　　　　**Phone:** (559)935-0717
(AAA) [SAVE]　All Year　　　　　　　1P: $80- 100　2P/1B: $86- 105　2P/2B: $86- 91　XP: $8　　　F12
◆◆◆　**Location:** E side & adjacent to I-5; at SR 198, Hanford-Lemoore off-ramp. 24505 W Doris Ave 93210 (Rt 1,
Motor Inn　Box 777). **Fax:** 559/935-5061. **Terms:** Pets, $10 extra charge. **Facility:** 123 rooms. Spacious landscaped
　　　　grounds. Spanish architecture. 1-bedroom suite, $215 for up to 2 persons; 2-3 stories; interior/exterior corri-
　　　　dors; heated pool, whirlpools. **Dining:** Restaurant; 6 am-11 pm; $8-$25. **Recreation:** private airstrip.
All Rooms: combo or shower baths. **Cards:** AE, CB, DI, DS, JC, MC, VI.

RESTAURANT

HARRIS RANCH RESTAURANT　　**Lunch:** $5-$11　　　**Dinner:** $8-$23　　　**Phone:** 559/935-0717
◆◆◆　　**Location:** In The Inn at Harris Ranch. 24505 W Dorris Ave 93210. **Hours:** 6 am-11 pm. **Features:** casual
Steakhouse　dress; children's menu; cocktails & lounge; a la carte. Coffeeshop & dining room. Specializing in
　　　　Harris-raised beef & Harris-grown fruit & vegetables. Early California elegance. Smoke free premises.
Cards: AE, CB, DI, MC, VI.

COLFAX—1,300

RESTAURANT

DINGUS MCGEES　　　　**Lunch:** $6-$8　　　　**Dinner:** $9-$16　　　　**Phone:** 530/346-6368
◆◆　　**Location:** 16 mi n of Auburn; n side of I-80; westbound exit via Placer Hills Rd; eastbound exit Canyon Way.
American　2121 S Auburn St 95713. **Hours:** 3 pm-9 pm, Fri & Sat 11:30 am-2 & 3-9 pm, Sun from 10 am. **Closed:**
　　　　12/25. **Reservations:** suggested. **Features:** casual dress; Sunday brunch; children's menu; cocktails. Beef,
seafood & pasta. Smoke free premises. **Cards:** AE, MC, VI.

COLTON—40,200

RESTAURANT

JEAN'S　　　　　**Lunch:** $7-$12　　　　　**Dinner:** $10-$18　　　　**Phone:** 909/825-0905
◆◆　　**Location:** Across from Civic Center. 592 N La Cadena Dr 92324. **Hours:** 11:30 am-2 pm & 5 pm-9 pm.
French　　Closed major holidays Sun & Mon. **Features:** casual dress; beer & wine only; street parking. Small,
　　　　charming restaurant serving a nice selection of French cuisine. Smoke free premises.

COLUMBIA—400

LODGINGS

COLUMBIA CITY HOTEL　　　　　　Guaranteed Rates　　　　　　　　**Phone:** (209)532-1479
◆◆　　　All Year [BP]　　　　　1P: $90- 110　2P/1B: $95- 115　2P/2B: $95- 105　XP: $10-15　　F4
Historic Bed　**Location:** Center Columbia State Historic Park. Main St 95310 (PO Box 1870). **Fax:** 209/532-7027.
& Breakfast　**Terms:** Reserv deposit, 7 day notice. **Facility:** 10 rooms. Authentically restored 1856 Gold Rush Era hotel.
　　　　Closed 12/24 & 12/25. 2 stories; interior corridors. **Cards:** AE, DS, VI.

COLUMBIA INN MOTEL　　　　　　　　　　　　　　　　　　　　**Phone:** (209)533-0446
(AAA) [SAVE]　4/1-10/31　　　　　　1P: $42- 56　2P/1B: $46- 56　2P/2B: $56- 76　XP: $4-6　　F12
◆　　　2/1-3/31 & 11/1-1/31　　　1P: $32- 38　2P/1B: $36- 42　2P/2B: $42- 56　XP: $4　　　F12
Motel　　**Location:** Adjacent to Columbia State Historic Park. 22646 Broadway St 95310 (PO Box 298).
　　　　Fax: 209/536-9571. **Terms:** Reserv deposit. **Facility:** 24 rooms. 4 two-bedroom units. 4 suites, $76 for up to
　　　　4 persons in season; 2 stories; exterior corridors. **Cards:** AE, MC, VI. **Special Amenities:** Free local
telephone calls and preferred room (subject to availability with advanced reservations).

FALLON HOTEL　　　　　　　　　Guaranteed Rates　　　　　　　　**Phone:** (209)532-1470
◆◆　　　All Year [BP]　　　　　1P: $65- 110　2P/1B: $70- 115　2P/2B: $80- 115　XP: $10-15　　F4
Historic Bed　**Location:** Entrance to Columbia State Historic Park; adjacent Fallon Theatre. 11175 Washington St 95310
& Breakfast　(PO Box 1870). **Fax:** 209/532-7027. **Terms:** Reserv deposit, 7 day notice. **Facility:** 14 rooms. Authentically re-
　　　　stored 1857 Victorian Hotel. Closed Mon; Tues-Wed 11/1-11/30 & 1/1-5/31. 1 two-bedroom unit. 1 two-room
suite $145 for up to 4 persons; 2 stories; interior corridors. **Cards:** AE, DS, MC, VI.

RESTAURANT

TY HOTEL DINING ROOM Historical **Dinner:** $30-$39 **Phone:** 209/532-1479
◆◆ **Location:** Center Columbia State Historic Park; in Columbia City Hotel. 22768 Main St 95310. **Hours:** 5
ench pm-8:30 pm, Sat-9 pm; Sun brunch 11 am-2 pm. Closed: 1/6-1/16, 12/25 & Mon. **Reservations:** suggested.
Features: Sunday brunch; cocktails; a la carte, also prix fixe. Authentically furnished dining room & saloon of
e Gold Rush Days; fine California wine selection in restored landmark circa 1870's. Smoke free premises. **Cards:** AE, DS,
C, VI.

COMMERCE—See Los Angeles p. 594.

COMPTON—See Los Angeles p. 595.

CONCORD—111,300

LODGINGS

EST WESTERN HERITAGE INN Rates Subject to Change **Phone:** 925/686-4466
◆ All Year 1P: $51- 61 2P/1B: $51- 61 XP: $7
otel **Location:** 3 mi e at Wharton Way. 4600 Clayton Rd 94521. Fax: 925/825-0581. **Facility:** 125 rooms. Spacious
attractive rooms. 40 whirlpool rms, extra charge; 2 stories; exterior corridors. **Some Rooms:** 7 efficiencies.
ards: AE, CB, DI, DS, MC, VI.

OMFORT INN **Phone:** (925)827-8998
[AD] [SAVE] 6/1-9/30 [CP] 1P: $79- 89 2P/1B: $79- 89 2P/2B: $84- 94 XP: $5 F18
2/1-5/31 [CP] 1P: $74- 84 2P/1B: $74- 84 2P/2B: $79- 89 XP: $5 F18
◆◆ 10/1-1/31 [CP] 1P: $74- 84 2P/1B: $74- 84 2P/2B: $79- 89 XP: $5 F18
partment **Location:** 0.5 mi e of I-680, northbound exit Monument Blvd; southbound exit Gregory Ln. 1370 Monument
otel Blvd 94520. Fax: 925/798-3374. **Terms:** Reserv deposit; weekly rates. **Facility:** 41 rooms. 11 two-bedroom
units. 3 stories; interior corridors; seasonal pool. **Dining:** Restaurant nearby. **All Rooms:** efficiencies, combo
shower baths. **Cards:** AE, CB, DI, DS, MC, VI.

ONCORD HILTON Rates Subject to Change **Phone:** 925/827-2000
◆◆ All Year 1P: $125 2P/1B: $125 2P/2B: $125 XP: $10
tel **Location:** E of I-680 via Willow Pass Rd. 1970 Diamond Blvd 94520. Fax: 925/671-0984. **Facility:** 330 rooms.
Beautiful public areas, comfortable rooms. 2 whirlpool rms, extra charge; 11 stories; interior corridors.
rvices: giftshop; area transportation. **Cards:** AE, CB, DI, DS, MC, VI. *(See ad p 119)*

CONOMY INN **Phone:** (925)682-7850
[AD] [SAVE] All Year [CP] 1P: $49- 59 2P/1B: $59- 75 2P/2B: $64- 79 XP: $5 F12
◆ **Location:** 1 mi e at Babel Rd. 3606 Clayton Rd 94521. Fax: 925/676-7547. **Terms:** Reserv deposit.
otel **Facility:** 63 rooms. Some suites with wet bar & large whirlpool tub, $85-$105 for 2 persons; 2 stories; exterior
corridors. **Some Rooms:** whirlpools. **Cards:** AE, DS, MC, VI.

. MONTE MOTOR INN Rates Subject to Change **Phone:** 925/682-1601
[AD] All Year [CP] 1P: $53- 55 2P/1B: $53- 55 2P/2B: $62- 65 XP: $5 F6
◆ **Location:** 2 mi e of jct I-680 & SR 24, exit SR 242 at Clayton Rd. 3555 Clayton Rd 94519.
otel Fax: 925/827-4756. **Terms:** Weekly rates. **Facility:** 42 rooms. Spanish style, well-kept. 2 stories;
interior/exterior corridors; whirlpool. **All Rooms:** combo or shower baths. **Some Rooms:** 24 kitchens.
Cards: AE, DI, DS, MC, VI.

OLIDAY INN EXPRESS Guaranteed Rates **Phone:** (925)674-9400
[AD] All Year [BP] 1P: $85- 95 2P/1B: $85- 95 2P/2B: $85- 95 XP: $5 F12
otel **Location:** 6.5 mi e of jct I-680 & SR 24; exit SR 242 at Clayton Rd 5.5 e. 5370 Clayton Rd 94521.
Fax: 925/674-9595. **Terms:** Reserv deposit. **Facility:** 30 rooms. 2 stories; exterior corridors. **Cards:** AE, CB,
DS, JC, MC, VI.

HERATON CONCORD HOTEL Rates Subject to Change **Phone:** 925/825-7700
◆◆◆ Mon-Thurs 1P: $125 2P/1B: $125 2P/2B: $145 XP: $20 F18
tor Inn Fri-Sun 1P: $89 2P/1B: $89 2P/2B: $89 XP: $20 F18
Location: E off I-680 exit Concord Ave. 45 John Glenn Dr 94520. Fax: 925/674-9567. **Facility:** 324 rooms. 3
ries; interior corridors; putting green; small indoor pool. **Services:** giftshop. **Cards:** AE, DS, MC, VI.

COPPEROPOLIS—1,000

LODGING

KE TULLOCH RESORT Rates Subject to Change **Phone:** (209)785-8200
◆ Fri & Sat 4/16-10/16 1P: $129- 145 2P/1B: $129- 145 2P/2B: $129- 145 XP: $10 F17
tel Sun-Thurs 5/1-9/30 1P: $105- 115 2P/1B: $105- 115 2P/2B: $105- 115 XP: $10 F17
Fri & Sat 2/1-4/15 &
10/17-1/31 1P: $99- 115 2P/1B: $99- 115 2P/2B: $99- 115 XP: $10 F17
Sun-Thurs 2/1-4/30 &
10/1-1/31 1P: $89- 99 2P/1B: $89- 99 2P/2B: $89- 99 XP: $10 F17
cation: 5 mi n off SR 108/120; 7 mi s off SR 4. 7260 O'Byrnes Ferry Rd 95228. Fax: 209/785-8202. **Terms:** Reserv
osit, 3 day notice. **Facility:** 46 rooms. Lakeside setting. 1 two-bedroom unit. 2 stories; exterior corridors; heated pool; boat
ck, boat ramp, marina. **Recreation:** swimming, boating, fishing, sailboating, waterskiing. **All Rooms:** shower baths.
rds: AE, DI, DS, MC, VI. *(See ad p 1054)*

CORNING—5,900

LODGINGS

AMERIHOST INN-CORNING
Phone: (530)824-52
All Year [CP]   1P: $50- 54   2P/1B: $58   2P/2B: $54   XP: $5-10   F
Location: I-5, exit Solano St, e of & adjacent. 910 Hwy 99 W 96021. Fax: 530/824-5400. **Terms:** Small p only. **Facility:** 61 rooms. 2 stories; interior corridors; heated indoor pool, sauna, whirlpo
Motor Inn   **Dining:** Restaurant nearby. **All Rooms:** combo or shower baths. **Some Rooms:** whirlpools. **Cards:** AE, C DI, DS, JC, MC, VI. **Special Amenities:** Free breakfast and free newspaper. *(See color ad p 284)*

BEST WESTERN INN-CORNING
Phone: (530)824-24
All Year [CP]   1P: $47- 57   2P/1B: $52- 62   2P/2B: $59- 69   XP: $7
Location: Exit I-5 e via Corning exit, 1 blk e. 2165 Solano St 96021. **Facility:** 41 rooms. 2 s
Motel   ries; exterior corridors. **Dining:** Coffee shop nearby. **Cards:** AE, CB, DI, DS, JC, MC, VI.

DAYS INN
Phone: (530)824-20
All Year [CP]   1P: $32- 35   2P/1B: $38- 42   2P/2B: $45- 55   XP: $3-5   F
Location: Exit I-5 at South Ave, 0.3 mi s. 3475 Hwy 99W 96021. Fax: 530/824-2736. **Terms:** Pets, $5 ex charge, $25 dep req. **Facility:** 62 rooms. 2 stories; interior corridors. **All Rooms:** combo or shower bat
Motel   **Cards:** AE, CB, DI, DS, JC, MC, VI. **Special Amenities:** Free breakfast and free local telephone calls.

SHILO INN
Rates Subject to Change   Phone: (530)824 29
All Year [CP]   1P: $65- 95   2P/1B: $65- 95   2P/2B: $65- 95   XP: $10   F
Motel   **Location:** 1 mi s; e & adjacent to I-5, exit South Ave. 3350 Sunrise Way 96021. Fax: 530/824-291
Facility: 78 rooms. Some rooms with wet bar, microwave & refrigerator $59-$65; 4 stories; interior corrido small pool. **Cards:** AE, CB, DI, DS, JC, MC, VI.

RESTAURANT

D2 (SQUARED)   **Lunch:** $3-$9   **Dinner:** $8-$16   Phone: 530/824-41
Location: Exit Central Corning, 1 mi e. 410 Solano St 96021. **Hours:** 11 am-2 & 5-9 pm, Sat from 5 p
Continental   Closed: Sun (except Mothers Day & Easter), Mon, 1/1, 11/25 & 12/25. **Reservations:** suggest
Features: casual dress; children's menu; senior's menu; beer & wine only. Comfortable atmosphe emphasis on fresh ingredients. Creative preparation. **Cards:** CB, DI, MC, VI.

CORONA—76,100

LODGINGS

BEST WESTERN KINGS INN
Phone: (909)734-42
All Year [CP]   1P: $59- 69   2P/1B: $64- 74   2P/2B: $64- 74   XP: $5   F
Location: Just n of SR 91, Lincoln Ave exit. 1084 Pomona Rd 91720. Fax: 909/279-5371. **Facility:** 87 roor 2 stories; exterior corridors; heated pool, whirlpool. **Dining:** Restaurant nearby. **All Rooms:** combo
Motel   shower baths, extended cable TV. **Cards:** AE, CB, DI, DS, MC, VI. **Special Amenities:** Free breakfast a free local telephone calls.

CORONA TRAVELODGE
Phone: (909)735-55
All Year [CP]   1P: $45- 53   2P/1B: $49- 55   2P/2B: $55- 62   XP: $8   F
Location: S side of SR 91, eastbound exit 6th St, westbound exit Maple St. 1701 W 6th St 917
Terms: Reserv deposit. **Facility:** 46 rooms. 2 stories; exterior corridors. **Dining:** Restaurant nea
Motel   **Cards:** AE, CB, DI, DS, JC, MC, VI. **Special Amenities:** Free breakfast.

COUNTRY SIDE INN
Rates Subject to Change   Phone: (909)734-21
All Year [BP]   1P: $65- 75   2P/1B: $75- 85   2P/2B: $75- 85   XP: $10   F
Motel   **Location:** Just ne of SR 91, exit McKinley St; 1.8 mi e of jct I-15. 2260 Griffin Way 917
Fax: 909/734-4056. **Facility:** 100 rooms. Very attractive country French decor. 2 stories; interior corrido small heated pool. **Cards:** AE, DI, DS, MC, VI. *(See ad below)*

OUNTRY SUITES-CORONA   Rates Subject to Change   Phone: (909)738-9113
All Year [BP]   1P: $65- 75   2P/1B: $75- 85   2P/2B: $75- 85   XP: $10   F12
Too new to rate. **Location:** Just s of SR 91, eastbound exit 6th St; westbound exit Maple St. 1900 Frontage
Rd 91720. **Facility:** 114 rooms. Scheduled to open September, 1998; 2 stories; exterior corridors; heated pool.
Cards: AE, DI, DS, MC, VI. *(See ad p 420)*

NASTY SUITES-CORONA   Guaranteed Rates   Phone: (909)371-7185
All Year [CP]   1P: $47- 53   2P/1B: $47- 53   2P/2B: $55- 60   XP: $5-10   D12
Location: S side of SR 91, westbound exit 6th St; westbound exit Maple St. 1805 W 6th St 91720.
Fax: 909/371-0401. **Terms:** Small pets only, $10. **Facility:** 56 rooms. 1 two-bedroom unit. 1 two-bedroom unit
with kitchen. 6 whirlpool rms, extra charge; 2 stories; exterior corridors; small pool, whirlpool.
Dining: Restaurant nearby. **Cards:** AE, CB, DI, DS, JC, MC, VI. *(See color ad below)*

AMADA LIMITED   Phone: (909)272-4900
6/15-9/15 & 12/1-12/31 [CP]   1P: $58- 75   2P/1B: $63- 75   2P/2B: $63- 68   XP: $5-10   F16
2/1-6/14, 9/16-11/30 &
1/1-1/31 [CP]   1P: $53- 70   2P/1B: $58- 70   2P/2B: $58- 63   XP: $5-10   F16
Location: SR 91, exit Lincoln Ave; just s, then 0.3 mi w on 6th St. 1248 W 6th St 91720. Fax: 909/272-4127.
Terms: Small pets only. **Facility:** 54 rooms. Efficiencies, $4 extra charge; 10 one-bedroom suites. 2 whirlpool
s, extra charge; 2 stories; exterior corridors; small pool, whirlpool. **Dining:** Restaurant nearby. **Cards:** AE, MC, VI.
ecial Amenities: Free breakfast and free room upgrade (subject to availability with advanced reservations).

RESTAURANTS

AIM JUMPER RESTAURANT   Lunch: $8-$23   Dinner: $12-$23   Phone: 909/735-6567
Location: Just nw of SR 91, exit McKinley St; in Corona Hills Plaza. 380 McKinley St 91719. **Hours:** 11
herican   am-11 pm, Sun & Mon-10 pm. Closed: 7/4, 11/25 & 12/25. **Features:** casual dress; children's menu; salad
bar; cocktails & lounge. Large, popular restaurant. Mining camp decor. Nice selection of salad, sandwiches &
trees. Generous portions. Smoke free premises. **Cards:** AE, DI, DS, MC, VI.

MI'S CAFE   Lunch: $6-$12   Dinner: $8-$12   Phone: 909/734-2073
Location: Just n of SR 91, exit McKinley St; 1.8 mi e of I-15. 2230 Griffin Way 91719. **Hours:** 7 am-11 pm.
herican   Closed: 12/25. **Features:** casual dress; children's menu; carryout; beer & wine only. Attractive French cafe
atmosphere. Nice selection of salad, sandwiches & entrees. Smoke free premises. **Cards:** AE, MC, VI.

B SCOTT'S SEAFOOD LANDING   Lunch: $7-$11   Dinner: $13-$19   Phone: 909/340-3474
Location: N side of SR 91, exit Lincoln Ave. 103 N Lincoln Ave 91720. **Hours:** 11 am-10 pm, Fri-11 pm, Sat
herican   4 pm-11 pm, Sun 9 am-10 pm. **Reservations:** suggested. **Features:** casual dress; children's menu; early
bird specials; cocktails & lounge. Nice selection of mesquite grilled, blackened or sauteed seafood. Also
ultry and pasta specialties. Luncheon buffet Mon-Fri. Smoke free premises. **Cards:** AE, MC, VI.

LA AMALFI RISTORANTE   Lunch: $7-$11   Dinner: $8-$15   Phone: 909/278-3393
Location: From SR 91, just s on Lincoln Ave, then w on 6th St. 1237 W 6th St 91720. **Hours:** 11:30 am-9
ian   pm, Fri-10 pm, Sat 4:30 pm-10 pm. Closed major holidays. **Reservations:** suggested. **Features:** casual
dress; beer & wine only; a la carte. Charming restaurant featuring a nice selection of pasta, seafood, veal,
cken & pizza. Smoke free premises. **Cards:** AE, CB, DI, DS, MC, VI.

CORONADO—See San Diego p. 897.

CORTE MADERA—See San Francisco p. 967.

COSTA MESA—96,400   (See map p. 294; index p. 292)

LODGINGS

BEST WESTERN NEWPORT MESA INN   **Phone: (949)650-3020**
⟨AAA⟩ SAVE   6/1-8/31 [CP]   1P: $59- 79   2P/1B: $59- 79 2P/2B: $59- 79 XP: $10
         2/1-5/31 & 9/1-1/31 [CP]   1P: $49- 69   2P/1B: $49- 69 2P/2B: $49- 69 XP: $10
◆◆   **Location:** E side of SR 55, on frontage road, exit Fair Dr/Del Mar. 2642 Newport Blvd 926:
Motel   Fax: 949/642-1220. **Terms:** Reserv deposit. **Facility:** 96 rooms. 3 whirlpool rms, extra charge; 3 stories; ir
         rior corridors; heated pool, sauna, whirlpool, indoor whirlpool. **Cards:** AE, CB, DI, DS, JC, MC,
Special Amenities: Free breakfast and free local telephone calls. *(See color ad below)*

COMFORT INN   **Phone: (949)631-7840**
⟨AAA⟩ SAVE   All Year [CP]   1P: $38- 110 2P/1B: $69- 110 2P/2B: $69- 120 XP: $5-10
◆◆   **Location:** Adjacent to SR 55, 1.5 mi n of jct Harbor Blvd. 2430 Newport Blvd 92627. Fax: 949/548-37
Motel   **Terms:** Reserv deposit. **Facility:** 58 rooms. 2 stories; exterior corridors; whirlpool. **Cards:** AE, CB, DI, I
         JC, MC, VI.

(See map p. 294)

COSTA MESA HOLIDAY INN EXPRESS
Rates Subject to Change   Phone: (949)631-6000   **178**
otel

7/1-9/4 & 12/25-1/3 [CP]	1P: $69- 109	2P/1B: $69- 109	2P/2B: $69- 109 XP: $10
2/1-6/30, 9/5-12/24 &			
1/4-1/31 [CP]	1P: $59- 89	2P/1B: $59- 89	2P/2B: $59- 89 XP: $10

Location: Adjacent to SR 55; 0.8 mi n of jct Harbor Blvd. 2070 Newport Blvd 92627. Fax: 949/631-4952. **Terms:** Reserv deposit, 3 day notice; weekly rates. **Facility:** 62 rooms. 3 stories; interior corridors. *Recreation:* sun deck. **All Rooms:** combo or shower baths. **Cards:** AE, DI, DS, MC, VI.
(See color ad p 422, p 744 & p 340)

COSTA MESA MARRIOTT SUITES
Rates Subject to Change   Phone: 714/957-1100   **172**
Suite Hotel

Mon-Thurs	1P: $129	2P/1B: $129	2P/2B: $129
Fri-Sun	1P: $79	2P/1B: $79	2P/2B: $79

Location: From I-405, use Bristol St exit; 1 blk n, then 3 blks e. 500 Anton Blvd 92626. Fax: 714/966-8495. **Terms:** Check-in 4 pm; reserv deposit. **Facility:** 253 rooms. Attractively landscaped pool area in a park-like setting. One-bedroom suites. 11 stories; interior corridors; heated pool. **Cards:** AE, DI, DS, JC, MC, VI.

COUNTRY SIDE INN & SUITES
Phone: (714)549-0300   **173**
Motor Inn

2/1-8/31 [BP]	1P: $99- 109	2P/1B: $109- 119	2P/2B: $109- 119 XP: $10 F12
9/1-1/31 [BP]	1P: $89- 99	2P/1B: $99- 109	2P/2B: $99- 109 XP: $10 F12

Location: Adjacent to SR 73; just e of Red Hill Ave. 325 S Bristol St 92626. Fax: 714/662-0828. **Terms:** Weekly/monthly rates. **Facility:** 279 rooms. Attractive French, country atmosphere, 27 one-bedroom suites. 4 stories; interior corridors; heated pool, whirlpools. **Dining:** Dining room; 6:30 am-10 pm; $8-$20; *cocktails.* **Services:** giftshop; complimentary evening beverages. **All Rooms:** combo or shower baths. *Some Rooms:* whirlpools. **Cards:** AE, DI, DS, MC, VI. **Special Amenities:** Free breakfast and free newspaper.
(See color ad p 744)

COZY INN
Rates Subject to Change   Phone: (949)650-2055   **184**
otel

5/15-9/15	1P: $38- 40	2P/1B: $42- 46	2P/2B: $48 XP: $4 D12
2/1-5/14 & 9/16-1/31	1P: $36- 38	2P/1B: $40- 44	2P/2B: $46 XP: $4 D12

Location: SR 55, southbound exit 22nd St/Victoria St, s on frontage road (Newport Blvd); northbound take n frontage road to Bay St, just w of SR 55. 325 W Bay St 92627. Fax: 949/650-6281. **Facility:** 29 rooms. 8 efficiencies $8 extra charge, no utensils; 2 stories; exterior corridors; small heated pool. **Cards:** AE, CB, DI, DS, C, MC, VI.

DAYS INN
Phone: (949)642-2670   **174**
otel

Fri & Sat 5/15-9/15 [CP]	1P: $69- 79	2P/1B: $79- 89	2P/2B: $84- 94 XP: $5-10 F12
Sun-Thurs 5/15-9/15 [CP]	1P: $56- 69	2P/1B: $59- 69	2P/2B: $64- 79 XP: $5 F12
2/1-5/14 & 9/16-1/31 [CP]	1P: $49- 59	2P/1B: $54- 64	2P/2B: $59- 74 XP: $5-10 F12

Location: Adjacent to SR 55; 0.8 mi n of jct Harbor Blvd. 2100 Newport Blvd 92627. Fax: 949/646-7242. **Facility:** 31 rooms. 3 two-bedroom units. 2 stories; exterior corridors. **Cards:** AE, CB, DI, DS, MC, VI.

DOUBLETREE HOTEL/ORANGE COUNTY AIRPORT
Phone: (714)540-7000   **181**
otel

Sun-Thurs	1P: $119	2P/1B: $119	2P/2B: $119 XP: $10 F18
Fri & Sat	1P: $84	2P/1B: $84	2P/2B: $84 XP: $10 F18

Location: Just s of I-405, exit Bristol St. 3050 Bristol St 92626. Fax: 714/540-9176. **Terms:** Handling fee imposed; small pets only, $25 extra charge. **Facility:** 484 rooms. Large, contemporary atrium lobby. 7 stories; interior corridors; heated pool, sauna, steamroom, whirlpool. **Dining:** Dining room, restaurant; 6 am-midnight; -$25; cocktails. **Services:** giftshop; area transportation, South Coast Plaza. Fee: massage. **Some Rooms:** whirlpools. **Cards:** AE, CB, DI, DS, JC, MC, VI. **Special Amenities:** Early check-in/late check-out and preferred room (subject to availability with advanced reservations).** *(See color ad below)*

HOLIDAY INN-COSTA MESA/ORANGE COUNTY AIRPORT
Rates Subject to Change   Phone: (714)557-3000   **175**
Motor Inn

All Year	1P: $95- 115	2P/1B: $95- 115	2P/2B: $95- 115 XP: $10 F18

Location: Just s of I-405, Bristol St exit. 3131 Bristol St 92626. Fax: 714/957-8185. **Facility:** 230 rooms. Just s of South Coast Plaza. 3-5 stories; interior corridors; heated pool. **Services:** area transportation. **Cards:** AE, B, DI, DS, JC, MC, VI.

(See map p. 294)

INN AT COSTA MESA   Rates Subject to Change   **Phone:** (714)540-8571   **17**
All Year   1P: $35- 38   2P/1B: $38- 40   2P/2B: $42- 46
Location: Just s of I-405. 3151 Harbor Blvd 92626. Fax: 714/979-9647. **Terms:** Reserv deposit; handling fe imposed; weekly rates. **Facility:** 50 rooms. 1 two-bedroom unit. 2 stories; exterior corridors; heated po
Motel   **Cards:** AE, CB, DI, DS, MC, VI.

LA QUINTA INN   **Phone:** (714)957-5841   **1**
All Year [CP]   1P: $59- 69   2P/1B: $59- 69   2P/2B: $59- 69
Location: Just nw of I-405, Harbor Blvd exit. 1515 South Coast Dr 92626. Fax: 714/432-7159. **Terms:** Sm pets only. **Facility:** 160 rooms. 3 stories; exterior corridors; heated pool. **Dining:** Restaurant near
Motel   **Services:** area transportation, within 5 mi. **Recreation:** in-room video games. **Cards:** AE, CB, DI, DS, J MC, VI. **Special Amenities:** Free breakfast and free local telephone calls.

RAMADA LIMITED   **Phone:** (949)645-2221   **1**
5/30-9/5 [CP]   1P: $64- 84   2P/1B: $69- 89   2P/2B: $69- 89   XP: $5   F
2/1-5/29 & 9/6-1/31 [CP]   1P: $59- 79   2P/1B: $64- 84   2P/2B: $64- 84   XP: $5   F
Location: Just w of SR 55, Newport Blvd. 1680 Superior Ave at 17th St 92627. Fax: 949/650-912
Motel   **Terms:** Weekly/monthly rates. **Facility:** 140 rooms. Nicely decorated rooms & suites. 2 two-bedroom units. stories; exterior corridors; heated pool, whirlpool. **Services:** area transportation, Catalina Flyer, Hoag Hos
Cards: AE, CB, DI, DS, JC, MC, VI. **Special Amenities:** Free breakfast and free newspaper.
(See color ad p 745, below & opposite title page)

RESIDENCE INN BY MARRIOTT   Rates Subject to Change   **Phone:** 714/241-8800   **1**
All Year [CP]   1P: $119   2P/1B: $119   2P/2B: $119
Apartment   **Location:** Adjacent to s side of SR 73, Bear St exit; from SR 55, Baker St exit. 881 W Baker St 9262
Motel   Fax: 714/546-4308. **Facility:** 144 rooms. 1-bedroom studios & split level, 2-bedroom suites with living room kitchen. Half of units with woodburning fireplace. 2 bedroom suites with living room & kitchen, $149 for up 5 persons; 2 stories; exterior corridors; heated pool. **Services:** area transportation. **Recreation:** sports court. **Cards:** A CB, DI, DS, JC, MC, VI.

SANDPIPER MOTEL   **Phone:** (949)645-9137   **1**
2/1-5/14 & 10/1-1/31 [CP]   1P: $42- 48   2P/1B: $42- 48   2P/2B: $54- 60
5/15-9/30 [EP]   1P: $48- 51   2P/1B: $48- 51   2P/2B: $48- 51
Location: Adjacent to SR 55, exit Victoria. 1967 Newport Blvd 92627. Fax: 949/650-1702. **Terms:** Week
Motel   rates. **Facility:** 43 rooms. 2 stories; exterior corridors. **All Rooms:** combo or shower bat **Some Rooms:** 14 efficiencies. **Cards:** AE, DS, MC, VI. **Special Amenities:** Free breakfast.

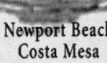
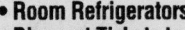

See map p. 294)

SUPER 8 MOTEL, COSTA MESA **Phone:** (714)545-9471 **183**
All Year [CP] 1P: $48- 58 2P/1B: $53- 63 2P/2B: $56- 66 XP: $5 F12
Location: 1 mi s of I-405, exit Harbor Blvd. 2645 Harbor Blvd 92626. Fax: 714/432-8129. **Facility:** 71 rooms.
Kitchens, $7; 4 suites with whirlpool, wetbar, refrigerator & microwave; 2 stories; exterior corridors; heated pool,
sauna, whirlpool. **Services:** complimentary evening beverages. **Some Rooms:** whirlpools. **Cards:** AE, CB,
DI, DS, JC, MC, VI. **Special Amenities:** Free local telephone calls and free newspaper.
See color ad p 424)

TRAVELODGE-HACIENDA INN **Phone:** (949)650-2999 **188**
5/21-9/7 [CP] 1P: $62- 79 2P/1B: $62- 79 2P/2B: $65- 85 XP: $5 F18
2/1-5/20 & 9/8-1/31 [CP] 1P: $52- 69 2P/1B: $52- 69 2P/2B: $57- 74 XP: $5 F18
Location: At end of SR 55 Frwy; southbound exit Victoria, s on frontage road, northbound take frontage rd
to Bay St, s on frontage rd. 1951 Newport Blvd 92627. Fax: 949/650-2699. **Facility:** 56 rooms. 2 rm suite with
full kitchen, extra charge; 2 stories; exterior corridors; whirlpool. **Cards:** AE, CB, DI, DS, JC, MC, VI.
Special Amenities: Free breakfast and preferred room (subject to availability with advanced reservations).
See ad p 746)

VAGABOND INN **Phone:** (714)557-8360 **185**
2/1-2/28 [CP] 1P: $88 2P/1B: $75 2P/2B: $99 XP: $7 F18
3/1-1/31 [CP] 1P: $66 2P/1B: $73 2P/2B: $77 XP: $7 F18
Location: Just s of I-405, Harbor Blvd exit (entrance from Gisler, just w of Harbor). 3205 Harbor Blvd 92626.
Fax: 714/662-7596. **Terms:** Weekly rates; small pets only, $5. **Facility:** 127 rooms. 3 two-bedroom units. 2
stories; exterior corridors; heated pool, whirlpool. **Dining:** Restaurant nearby. **Cards:** AE, CB, DI, DS, MC,
VI. **Special Amenities:** Free breakfast and free local telephone calls.

THE WESTIN SOUTH COAST PLAZA HOTEL **Phone:** (714)540-2500 **186**
1/1-1/31 1P: $199- 239 2P/1B: $199- 239 2P/2B: $199- 239 XP: $20 F18
2/1-12/31 1P: $189- 229 2P/1B: $189- 229 2P/2B: $189- 229 XP: $20 F18
Location: Just n of I-405, Bristol St exit. 686 Anton Blvd 92626. Fax: 714/662-6695. **Terms:** Small pets only.
Facility: 390 rooms. Across from South Coast Plaza & 1/2 block from Orange County Performing Arts Center.
16 stories; interior corridors; heated pool; 2 lighted tennis courts. Fee: parking. **Dining:** Restaurant; 6:30
am-10 pm; $13-$25; cocktails. **Services:** giftshop. Fee: massage. **Cards:** AE, CB, DI, DS, JC, MC, VI.

WYNDHAM GARDEN HOTEL **Phone:** (714)751-5100 **187**
Mon-Thurs [EP] 1P: $116 2P/1B: $116 2P/2B: $116 XP: $10-20 F18
Fri-Sun [BP] 1P: $89 2P/1B: $89 2P/2B: $89 XP: $10-20 F18
Location: I-405, exit Bristol St; n to Anton Blvd, 2 blks e, 1 blk n on Ave of the Arts. 3350 Ave of the Arts
92626. Fax: 714/751-0129. **Terms:** Monthly rates; small pets only, $25 extra charge. **Facility:** 238 rooms. Just
e of Orange County Performing Arts Center. 24 one-bedroom suites with refrigerator; 6 stories; interior corridors; heated pool, whirlpool. **Dining:** Restaurant; 6 am-10 pm, Sun from 7:30 am; $8-$20; cocktails. **Cards:** AE, CB, DI, DS,
JC, MC, VI. **Special Amenities:** Early check-in/late check-out and preferred room (subject to availability with
advanced reservations). *(See color ad below)*

RESTAURANTS

SIRRAPORETTI'S **Lunch:** $8-$13 **Dinner:** $8-$13 **Phone:** 714/850-9090 **69**
Location: 0.3 mi n of I-405, in South Coast Plaza, adjacent to Sears. 3333 Bristol St 92626. **Hours:** 11
Italian am-11 pm, Fri & Sat-11:30 pm. Closed: 11/25 & 12/25. **Reservations:** accepted. **Features:** casual dress;
cocktails & lounge. A large, popular restaurant featuring a nice selection of pasta, chicken, veal, seafood &
Pizza. **Cards:** AE, DI, DS, MC, VI.

DIVA **Lunch:** $7-$12 **Dinner:** $12-$20 **Phone:** 714/754-0600 **68**
Location: Just s of Orange County Performing Arts Center. 600 Anton Blvd 92626. **Hours:** 11:30 am-3 &
American 5-10 pm, Fri-midnight, Sun 4:30-9 pm. Closed major holidays. **Reservations:** suggested.
Features: semi-formal attire; cocktails & lounge; valet parking; a la carte. Contemporary restaurant featuring
an imaginative selection of California cuisine. Live Jazz Fri-Sat night. **Cards:** AE, DI, MC, VI.

THE GOLDEN TRUFFLE **Lunch:** $7-$15 **Dinner:** $12-$18 **Phone:** 949/645-9858 **70**
Location: SR 55, just s of jct Harbor Blvd. 1767 Newport Blvd 92627. **Hours:** 11:30 am-2:30 & 5:30-10 pm.
French Closed: Sun, Mon & 12/25. **Reservations:** suggested. **Features:** casual dress; beer & wine only; street
parking; a la carte. Interesting selection of French-Caribbean cuisine. **Cards:** AE, CB, MC, VI.

(See map p. 294)

KAPLAN'S DELI
◆
Ethnic
DS, MC, VI.

Lunch: $6-$9   **Dinner:** $7-$12   **Phone:** 714/557-6611   ⑦
Location: Just s of I-405, exit Harbor Blvd. 3211 Harbor Blvd 92626. **Hours:** 6 am-10 pm, Fri-Sun to 11 pr
Features: casual dress; early bird specials; carryout; cocktails. Selection of pastrami, beef, chicken & d
specialties. Bakery on premises. Patio dining weather permitting. Smoke free premises. **Cards:** AE, CB, [
ᐳ

MIMI'S CAFE
◆
American

Lunch: $7-$13   **Dinner:** $8-$13   **Phone:** 949/722-6722   ⑦
Location: On SR 55. 1835 Newport Blvd at Harbor Blvd 92627. **Hours:** 7 am-11 pm. Closed: 12/2
Features: casual dress; children's menu; beer & wine only. Colorful French cafe atmosphere. Nice selectio
of salads, sandwiches & entrees. Patio dining, smoking allowed on patio. **Cards:** AE, MC, VI.
ᐳ

SCOTT'S SEAFOOD GRILL & BAR
◆◆◆
Steak and
Seafood
Cards: AE, CB, DI, MC, VI.

Lunch: $8-$18   **Dinner:** $20-$38   **Phone:** 714/979-2400   ⑦
Location: Just n of I-405, exit Bristol St; Across from South Coast Plaza. 3300 Bristol St 92626. **Hours:**
am-10 pm, Fri & Sat-11 pm, Sun from 10 am. Closed: 1/1, 11/25 & 12/25. **Reservations:** suggeste
Features: casual dress; Sunday brunch; cocktails & lounge; valet parking; a la carte. A popular attracti
restaurant featuring fresh seafood & steak. Outdoor seating, weather permitting. Smoke free premise

TROQUET
◆◆◆
French
of French nouvelle cuisine. Patio dining avail. Smoke free premises. **Cards:** AE, CB, DI, DS, MC, VI.

Lunch: $21-$27   **Dinner:** $28-$34   **Phone:** 714/708-6865   ⑦
Location: Just n of I-405, in South Coast Plaza shopping center, near Nordstrom (third level). 3333 S Bris
St 92626. **Hours:** 11:30 am-4 & 6-9:30 pm, Fri & Sat-10 pm. Closed: 12/25 & Sun. **Reservations:** require
Features: cocktails; fee for valet parking; a la carte. Bistro ambiance with open kitchen area. Nice selectio
ᐳ

COULTERVILLE—100

LODGING

HOTEL JEFFERY
ⓐⓐⓐ
◆
Historic Hotel

All Year   Rates Subject to Change   **Phone:** (209)878-347
                           2P/1B: $59- 74 2P/2B: $59- 99 XP: $10
Location: At jct SR 49 & SR 132. 1 Main St 95311 (PO Box 440). Fax: 209/878-3473. **Terms:** Rese
deposit. **Facility:** 21 rooms. Built in 1851. Adjacent to city recreational park. 1 two-bedroom unit. 3 stories, I
elevator; interior corridors. **Dining:** Restaurant nearby. **Cards:** AE, DS, MC, VI. *(See ad p 1088)*
🅢ⓜ ⑪ ⓟⓥ ⓩ ⓧ ᐳ

COVINA—*See Los Angeles p. 595.*

CRESCENT CITY—4,400

LODGINGS

ANCHOR BEACH INN
ⓕⓨⓘ

Under construction. **Location:** US 101 at Anchor Way. 880 Hwy US 101 S 95531. **Facility:** 52 rooms. Whi
pool rms, extra charge. Scheduled to open February, 1999;   **Phone:** 707/464-26(

BAY VIEW INN
◆◆
Motel
$89-$95; 3 stories, no elevator; interior/exterior corridors. **All Rooms:** combo or shower baths. **Cards:** AE, DI, DS, MC, VI.

                    Rates Subject to Change   **Phone:** 707/465-205
6/15-10/14   1P: $59- 69 2P/1B: $59- 69 2P/2B: $59- 69
2/1-6/14 & 10/15-1/31   1P: $45- 55 2P/1B: $45- 55 2P/2B: $45- 55
Location: W of US 101 S. 310 Highway 101 S 95531. Fax: 707/465-3690. **Facility:** 66 rooms. Whirlpool rm
⑪ ⓐ ⓧ ⓟ ⎕ ⓐ ⓗ ⓕ ᐳ

BEST WESTERN NORTHWOODS INN

Phone: (707)464-9771

7/1-9/4 [BP]	1P:	$69-	79	2P/1B:	$69-	79	2P/2B:	$89-	99	XP: $6-8	F14
5/29-6/30 & 9/5-10/16 [BP]	1P:	$59-	69	2P/1B:	$59-	69	2P/2B:	$65-	79	XP: $6	F14
4/1-5/28 [BP]	1P:	$55-	65	2P/1B:	$55-	65	2P/2B:	$59-	69	XP: $5	F14
2/1-3/31 & 10/17-1/31 [BP]	1P:	$49-	59	2P/1B:	$49-	59	2P/2B:	$55-	65	XP: $5	F14

Location: On US 101. 655 Hwy 101S 95531. Fax: 707/464-9461. **Facility:** 89 rooms. Comfortable modern rooms. 1 whirlpool rm, extra charge; 2 stories; interior/exterior corridors. **Dining:** Restaurant; cocktails. **Cards:** AE, CB, DI, DS, JC, MC, VI. **Special Amenities:** Free breakfast and free local telephone calls. *(See ad p 426)*

CRESCENT CITY TRAVELODGE

Phone: (707)464-6124

7/1-9/4 [CP]	1P:	$55-	65	2P/1B:	$55-	65	2P/2B:	$65-	69	XP: $8	F14
5/28-6/30 & 9/5-10/31 [CP]	1P:	$49-	55	2P/1B:	$49-	55	2P/2B:	$55-	59	XP: $6	F14
4/1-5/27 [CP]	1P:	$39-	49	2P/1B:	$39-	49	2P/2B:	$49-	55	XP: $6	F14
2/1-3/31 & 11/1-1/31 [CP]	1P:	$35-	39	2P/1B:	$35-	39	2P/2B:	$45-	55	XP: $5	F14

Location: Between US 101 northbound & southbound at 4th St. 353 L St 95531. Fax: 707/464-4781. **Facility:** 27 rooms. Comfortable rooms. 2 stories; exterior corridors; sauna. **Dining:** Coffee shop nearby. **All Rooms:** combo or shower baths. **Cards:** AE, CB, DI, DS, MC, VI. **Special Amenities:** Early check-in/late check-out and free breakfast. *(See ad p 426)*

CURLY REDWOOD LODGE

Rates Subject to Change   Phone: 707/464-2137

7/1-8/31	1P:	$60	2P/1B:	$60	2P/2B:	$65	XP: $5
6/1-6/30 & 9/1-9/30	1P:	$52	2P/1B:	$52	2P/2B:	$56	XP: $5
2/1-5/31 & 10/1-1/31	1P:	$37	2P/1B:	$37	2P/2B:	$39	XP: $5

Location: S on US 101. 701 Redwood Hwy S 95531. Fax: 707/464-1655. **Facility:** 36 rooms. Many large rooms. Entirely built from one curly redwood tree. 3 two-bedroom units, $68-$86; 1-2 stories; interior/exterior corridors. **All Rooms:** combo or shower baths. **Cards:** AE, CB, DI, MC, VI. *(See ad below)*

ECONO LODGE

Phone: (707)464-2181

7/1-9/15 [CP]	1P:	$45-	50	2P/1B:	$50-	55	2P/2B:	$55-	70	XP: $5	F18
5/1-6/30 & 9/16-10/15 [CP]	1P:	$35-	40	2P/1B:	$40-	45	2P/2B:	$45-	50	XP: $5	F18
2/1-4/30 & 10/16-1/31 [CP]	1P:	$30-	35	2P/1B:	$35-	40	2P/2B:	$35-	45	XP: $5	F18

Location: US 101 southbound at Front St. 119 L St 95531. Fax: 707/464-7329. **Terms:** Pets, $5 extra charge. **Facility:** 48 rooms. Modern rooms. 2 stories; exterior corridors. **All Rooms:** shower baths. **Cards:** AE, CB, DI, DS, JC, MC, VI. **Special Amenities:** Free breakfast and free local telephone calls.

HIOUCHI MOTEL

Rates Subject to Change   Phone: 707/458-3041

All Year	1P:	$30	2P/1B:	$48	2P/2B:	$55

Location: US 101, US 199 exit; 5 mi e. 2097 Hwy 199 95531. **Facility:** 17 rooms. 2 stories; exterior corridors. **All Rooms:** combo or shower baths. **Cards:** DS, MC, VI.

HOLIDAY INN EXPRESS

Phone: (707)464-3885

5/25-10/1 [CP]	1P:	$68- 90	2P/1B:	$68- 90	2P/2B:	$68- 90	XP:	$5	F12
2/1-5/24 & 10/2-1/31 [CP]	1P:	$56- 65	2P/1B:	$56- 65	2P/2B:	$56- 65	XP:	$5	F12

Location: W of Citizen Dock & US 101S. 100 Walton St 95531. Fax: 707/464-5311. **Facility:** 46 rooms. Some rooms view harbor. 6 rooms with kitchen & whirlpool tub, $110 for 2 persons; 2 stories; exterior corridors. **All Rooms:** combo or shower baths. **Cards:** AE, CB, DI, DS, JC, MC, VI. **Special Amenities:** Free breakfast and free local telephone calls.

AAA SAVE ◆◆◆ Motel

PACIFIC MOTOR HOTEL

Rates Subject to Change   **Phone: 707/464-4141**

5/1-10/15	1P: $52	2P/1B:	$62	2P/2B:	$65	XP:	$5
2/1-4/30 & 10/16-1/31	1P: $39	2P/1B:	$52	2P/2B:	$57	XP:	$5

Location: On US 101. 440 Hwy 101N 95531 (PO Box 595). Fax: 707/465-3274. **Terms:** Pets, $5 extra charge, small dogs only. **Facility:** 62 rooms. Family Owned. 3 two-bedroom units. 2 stories; exterior corridors; sauna, indoor whirlpool. **Dining:** Restaurant nearby. **All Rooms:** combo or shower baths. **Cards:** AE, CB, DI, DS, MC, VI.

AAA ◆◆ Motel

QUALITY INN

Phone: (707)464-6100

6/16-9/15 [CP]	1P:	$62	2P/1B:	$67	2P/2B:	$73	XP:	$3	F12
2/1-6/15 & 9/16-1/31 [CP]	1P:	$45	2P/1B:	$49	2P/2B:	$55	XP:	$3	F12

Location: On US 101 N. 725 Hwy 101N 95531. Fax: 707/464-8210. **Facility:** 52 rooms. North of county fair grounds. 1 story; exterior corridors; sauna, whirlpool. **Cards:** AE, CB, DI, DS, JC, MC, VI. **Special Amenities:** Free breakfast and free local telephone calls.

AAA SAVE ◆◆ Motel

SUPER 8

Phone: (707)464-4111

6/25-9/5 [CP]	1P:	$65- 75	2P/1B:	$69- 79	2P/2B:	$74- 84	XP:	$5	F12
5/28-6/24 & 9/6-10/9 [CP]	1P:	$56- 66	2P/1B:	$60- 70	2P/2B:	$65- 75	XP:	$5	F12
4/1-5/27 & 10/10-1/31 [CP]	1P:	$46- 56	2P/1B:	$50- 60	2P/2B:	$55- 65	XP:	$5	F12
2/1-3/31 [CP]	1P:	$42- 52	2P/1B:	$44- 54	2P/2B:	$50- 60	XP:	$5	F12

Location: 0.3 mi s on US 101; opposite harbor. 685 Hwy 101 S 95531. Fax: 707/465-8916. **Terms:** Small pets only, $5 extra charge, dogs only. **Facility:** 49 rooms. Large modern rooms, few with harbor view. 2 stories; exterior corridors. **Dining:** Restaurant nearby. **All Rooms:** combo or shower baths. **Cards:** AE, DS, MC, VI. **Special Amenities:** Early check-in/late check-out and free local telephone calls.

AAA SAVE ◆◆ Motel

RESTAURANTS

DA LUCIANNA RISTORANTE
Lunch: $5-$8   **Dinner: $20-$30**   **Phone: 707/465-6566**

Location: 575 Hwy 101 S 95531. **Hours:** 11 am-2 & 5-10 pm, Sat 5 pm-10 pm, Sun & holidays 4 pm-10 pm. Closed: 1/1 & 12/25. **Reservations:** suggested. **Features:** casual dress; cocktails. Smoking permitted in lounge. Opposite harbor. **Cards:** AE, MC, VI.

◆◆◆ Steak and Seafood

HARBOR VIEW GROTTO
Lunch: $5-$8   **Dinner: $7-$29**   **Phone: 707/464-3815**

Location: At dock. 150 Starfish Way 95531. **Hours:** 11:30 am-10 pm, in winter-9 pm. Closed: 1/1, 11/25, 12/24 & 12/25. **Reservations:** suggested. **Features:** casual dress; children's menu; senior's menu; cocktails & lounge; a la carte. Informal dining. Smoke free premises. **Cards:** MC, VI.

AAA ◆◆ Steak and Seafood

NORTHWOOD'S RESTAURANT
Lunch: $4-$9   **Dinner: $7-$16**   **Phone: 707/465-5656**

Location: At BW Northwoods Inn. 675 Hwy 101S 95531. **Hours:** 7 am-9 pm, in summer 6:30 am-10 pm. Closed: 12/25. **Features:** No A/C; children's menu; cocktails & lounge; a la carte. Fresh seafood specials in casual atmosphere. Booth seating. Smoke free premises. **Cards:** AE, DS, MC, VI.

AAA ◆◆ American

CROMBERG

LODGING

LONG VALLEY RESORT
Rates Subject to Change   **Phone: 530/836-0750**

All Year	1P: $50- 60	2P/1B:	$50- 60	2P/2B:	$50- 60	XP: $6

Location: 59532 Hwy 70 96103. **Terms:** Weekly rates. **Facility:** 9 rooms. Motel rooms & cottages in forest setting. 4 two-bedroom units. 1 story; exterior corridors. **Recreation:** badminton, horseshoes, volleyball. **All Rooms:** combo or shower baths. **Some Rooms:** 5 kitchens. **Cards:** MC, VI.

AAA ◆ Complex

CULVER CITY—See Los Angeles p. 596.

CUPERTINO—40,300

LODGINGS

COURTYARD BY MARRIOTT
Rates Subject to Change   **Phone: (408)252-9100**

Sun-Thurs	1P: $174- 194	2P/1B: $174- 194	2P/2B: $174- 194
Fri & Sat	1P: $89- 139	2P/1B: $89- 139	2P/2B: $89- 139

Location: N of & adjacent to I-280; exit Wolfe Rd N, w on Pruneridge Rd. 10605 N Wolfe Rd 95014. Fax: 408/252-0632. **Terms:** Reserv deposit; handling fee imposed. **Facility:** 149 rooms. Attractive courtyard gardens. 3 stories; interior corridors; heated pool. **Cards:** AE, CB, DI, DS, MC, VI.

◆◆◆ Motor Inn

CUPERTINO INN
Rates Subject to Change   **Phone: (408)996-7700**

All Year [BP]	1P: $99- 199	2P/1B: $99- 214	2P/2B: $99- 214	XP: $15 F14

Location: N of & adjacent to I-280; exit Sunnyvale-Saratoga Rd. 10889 N De Anza Blvd 95014. Fax: 408/257-0578. **Terms:** Check-in 4 pm; reserv deposit. **Facility:** 125 rooms. Attractive central courtyard & public areas, nicely appointed rooms, some with fireplace. 4 stories; interior corridors; heated pool. **Cards:** AE, DI, DS, JC, MC, VI.

◆◆◆ Motel

RESTAURANT

FONTANA'S ITALIAN RESTAURANT **Lunch:** $7-$15 **Dinner:** $16-$26 **Phone:** 408/725-0188
◆◆◆ **Location:** Exit I-280 at Saratoga-Sunnyvale W; 0.3 mi w. 20840 Stevens Creek Blvd 95014. **Hours:** 11:30
Italian am-4 pm & 4:30-9:30 pm, Fri & Sat-10 pm, Sun 4:30 pm-9:30 pm. Closed: 11/28 & 12/25 for lunch on major
holidays. **Reservations:** suggested. **Features:** casual dress; early bird specials; health conscious menu
items; beer & wine only; a la carte. Cozy fireplace, display kitchen. Variety of fresh fish, housemade pastas & desserts.
Cards: AE, CB, DI, MC, VI.   ☒

CYPRESS—*See Los Angeles p. 597.*

DALY CITY—*See San Francisco p. 967.*

DANA POINT—31,900 (See map p. 296; index p. 290)

LODGINGS

BEST WESTERN MARINA INN **Phone:** (949)496-1203 61
AAA SAVE 5/16-9/10 1P: $75- 85 2P/1B: $80- 90 2P/2B: $89- 99 XP: $6 F12
2/1-5/15 & 9/11-1/31 1P: $70- 80 2P/1B: $75- 85 2P/2B: $86- 96 XP: $6 F12
◆◆◆ **Location:** 0.5 mi w of SR 1, Pacific Coast Hwy. At Dana Point Harbor. 24800 Dana Point Harbor Dr 92629.
Motel Fax: 949/248-0360. **Terms:** Weekly rates. **Facility:** 136 rooms. Suites. $120-$150; 3 stories; interior corridors;
heated pool. **Dining:** Restaurant nearby. **Some Rooms:** 44 efficiencies. **Cards:** AE, CB, DI, DS, JC, MC, VI.
Special Amenities: Free breakfast and free newspaper. *(See color ad below)*
🅂🄵 🄵 ≈ ⑪⁺ 🄰 ✚ 🄺 🖥 🖵 🅟 🔒 ☒

BLUE LANTERN INN Rates Subject to Change **Phone:** (949)661-1304 60
◆◆◆◆ All Year [BP] 1P: $140- 500 2P/1B: $140- 500 2P/2B: $140- 500 XP: $15
Bed & **Location:** Just w of Pacific Coast Hwy. 34343 Street of Blue Lantern 92629. Fax: 949/496-1483.
Breakfast **Terms:** Reserv deposit. **Facility:** 29 rooms. Beautifully decorated rooms & public areas. On bluff overlooking
Dana Point Harbor. Many rooms with ocean view. All rooms with fireplace & whirlpool bathtub; tower suite with
panoramic view deck, $350; 3 stories; interior corridors. **Recreation:** bicycles. **Cards:** AE, DI, MC, VI.
🄵 🄿⁺ ⑪⁺ 🄰 ☒ 🖥 🖶 🖵 🅟 🔒 ☒

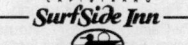

(See map p. 296)

CAPISTRANO SURFSIDE INN
Phone: (949)240-7681

(AAA) SAVE

6/15-9/15	1P: $140- 175	2P/1B: $140- 175	2P/2B: $140- 175
4/1-6/14 & 9/16-10/31	1P: $125- 155	2P/1B: $125- 155	2P/2B: $125- 155
2/1-3/31 & 11/1-1/31	1P: $105- 130	2P/1B: $105- 130	2P/2B: $105- 130

Suite Motel **Location:** 34680 Pacific Coast Hwy 92624. Fax: 949/493-5793. **Terms:** Check-in 4 pm; reserv deposit, day notice; weekly/monthly rates. **Facility:** 37 rooms. Balconies with gas barbecue. Some ocean views. two-bedroom units. 3 stories; interior corridors; heated pool, whirlpool, beach equipment avail. **Recreation:** bicycle recreation room with large screen TV & pool table, tanning bed. **All Rooms:** kitchens. **Cards:** AE, DI, DS, MC, V **Special Amenities:** Free newspaper. (See ad p 429)

DANA POINT HARBOR INN
Phone: (949)493-5001

(AAA) SAVE

All Year [CP]	1P: $59- 69	2P/1B: $59- 69	2P/2B: $69- 79 XP: $5

Motel **Location:** 25325 Dana Point Harbor Dr 92629. Fax: 949/661-6895. **Terms:** Reserv deposit, 3 day notic **Facility:** 46 rooms. 2 stories; exterior corridors; pool heated in summer. **Cards:** AE, CB, DI, DS, MC, V **Special Amenities:** Early check-in/late check-out and free breakfast.

DOUBLETREE GUEST SUITES DANA POINT
Phone: (949)661-1100

(AAA) SAVE

Sun-Thurs	1P: $109- 250	2P/1B: $109- 250	2P/2B: $109- 250 XP: $15
Fri & Sat	1P: $129- 250	2P/1B: $129- 250	2P/2B: $129- 250 XP: $15

Suite Hotel **Location:** Exit I-5 northbound Beach Cities Dr, southbound Pacific Coast highway, make a u-turn at Dohne Park Plaza Dr, 8 mi s. 34402 Pacific Coast Hwy 92629. Fax: 949/489-0628. **Terms:** Check-in 4 pm; rese deposit, 3 day notice. **Facility:** 196 rooms. Comfortable contemporary decor. 13 suites with ocean view, pati whirlpool tub & fireplace; 4 stories; interior corridors; heated pool, sauna, whirlpool. Fee: parking. **Dining:** Restaurant; 6:3 am-2 & 5-11 pm; $8-$15; cocktails. **Services:** giftshop. Fee: massage. **Recreation:** video game room. Rental: bicycle **Cards:** AE, CB, DI, DS, JC, MC, VI. **Special Amenities:** Early check-in/late check-out and free room upgrade (subje to availability with advanced reservations). (See color ad p 423)

HOLIDAY INN EXPRESS DANA POINT EDGEWATER
Phone: (949)240-0150

(AAA) SAVE

All Year	1P: $89- 169	2P/1B: $89- 169	2P/2B: $89- 169

Motel **Location:** I-5, southbound exit Beach Cities, northbound exit Beach Cities; then exit Coast Hwy s fro Transition Rd, 0.8 mi. 34744 Pacific Coast Hwy 92624. Fax: 949/240-4862. **Terms:** Reserv deposit; week rates; 2 night min stay, weekends. **Facility:** 30 rooms. Across from beach & near harbor. Most rooms wi ocean view & private balcony. 1 room with gas fireplace. 28 rooms with efficiency. 2-3 stories; exterior cor dors; sauna, glass enclosed whirlpool with panoramic ocean view. **Some Rooms:** whirlpools. **Cards:** AE, DI, DS, MC, V **Special Amenities:** Free breakfast and free local telephone calls. (See color ad p 986)

MARRIOTT'S LAGUNA CLIFFS RESORT/DANA POINT
Rates Subject to Change   Phone: 949/661-5000

(AAA)

All Year	1P: $120- 215	2P/1B: $120- 215	2P/2B: $120- 215

Hotel **Location:** Just w of SR 1, Pacific Coast Hwy. 25135 Park Lantern 92629. Fax: 949/661-3688. **Facility:** 34 rooms. On a bluff above Dana Point Harbor. Many rooms with ocean view & view of Yacht Harbor. Some wi patio or balcony. 11 two-room suites, most with balcony, $350; 3 stories; interior corridors; heated pool. Fee: 2 lighted tenn courts. **Services:** giftshop. Fee: massage. **Cards:** AE, DI, DS, MC, VI.

QUALITY INN & SUITES
Phone: (949)248-1000

(AAA) SAVE

4/2-9/1 [CP]	1P: $75	2P/1B: $75	2P/2B: $75 XP: $10
2/1-4/1 & 9/2-1/31 [CP]	1P: $65	2P/1B: $65	2P/2B: $65 XP: $10

Motel **Location:** 34280 Coast Hwy 92629. Fax: 949/661-3136. **Facility:** 86 rooms. 3 stories; interior/exterior cor dors; heated pool, sauna. **All Rooms:** combo or shower baths. **Cards:** AE, CB, DI, DS, MC, V **Special Amenities:** Free breakfast and free room upgrade (subject to availability with advance reservations). (See color ad p 490)

THE RITZ-CARLTON, LAGUNA NIGUEL
Rates Subject to Change   Phone: (949)240-2000

(AAA)

7/2-9/6	1P: $365- 560	2P/1B: $365- 560	2P/2B: $365- 560 XP: $50
2/1-7/1 & 9/7-1/31	1P: $335- 445	2P/1B: $335- 445	2P/2B: $335- 445 XP: $50

Resort Hotel **Location:** Just w of SR 1. One Ritz-Carlton Dr 92629. Fax: 949/240-1061. **Terms:** Check-in 4 pm; rese deposit, 7 day notice; $15 service charge. **Facility:** 393 rooms. An elegant hotel on a bluff overlooking th ocean. Beautiful public facilities, pool area & guest rooms. 4 stories; interior corridors; beach, heated poo saunas, whirlpools. Fee: 18 holes golf; 4 tennis courts. **Dining:** 2 dining rooms, restaurant; 6:30 am-10:30 pm; $12-$4 cocktails; afternoon tea; also, The Dining Room, The Club Grill & Bar, see separate listing. **Services:** giftsho, Fee: massage, area transportation. **Recreation:** in-room video games. **Cards:** AE, CB, DI, DS, MC, VI.

RESTAURANTS

THE CLUB GRILL & BAR
Dinner: $35-$48   Phone: 949/240-2000

◆◆◆◆ **Location:** Just w of SR 1; in The Ritz-Carlton, Laguna Niguel. One Ritz Carlton Dr 92627. **Hours:** 7-10 pr Fri & Sat-10:30 pm. Closed: Tues & Wed. **Reservations:** suggested. **Features:** semi-formal attire; cocktail American entertainment; fee for valet parking; a la carte. Supper club ambiance. Variety of fish & meat entree excellently prepared. Smoke free premises. **Cards:** AE, CB, DI, DS, JC, MC, VI.

DELANEY'S
Lunch: $9-$15   Dinner: $12-$29   Phone: 949/496-6195

◆◆ **Location:** On Dana Island. 25001 Dana Dr 92629. **Hours:** 11:30 am-9 pm, Fri & Sat-10 pm. Closed: 12/2 Seafood **Reservations:** suggested; weekends. **Features:** casual dress; Sunday brunch; children's menu; carryou cocktails & lounge. Overlooking marina. **Cards:** AE, DS, MC, VI.

THE DINING ROOM
Dinner: $35-$53   Phone: 949/240-2000

◆◆◆◆ **Location:** Just w of SR 1; in The Ritz-Carlton, Laguna Niguel. One Ritz-Carlton Dr 92627. **Hours:** 6:3 pm-10 pm, Fri & Sat-10:30 pm. Closed: Sun & Mon. **Reservations:** suggested. **Features:** semi-formal attir French health conscious menu; cocktails; fee for valet parking; a la carte. Formal, beautifully decorated dining roo Vegetarian Menu avail. Smoke free premises. **Cards:** AE, CB, DI, DS, JC, MC, VI.

DANVILLE—31,300 (See map p. 752; index p. 751)

LODGING

DANVILLE INN   Guaranteed Rates   **Phone:** (925)838-8080   **51**
All Year   1P: $60- 65 2P/1B: $65- 70 2P/2B: $70- 75 XP: $5   F12
Location: E of & adjacent to I-680; exit via Sycamore Valley Rd. 803 Camino Ramon 94526.
Fax: 925/838-5902. **Terms:** Small pets only. **Facility:** 60 rooms. Convenient Location. 2 stories;
Motel   interior/exterior corridors. **Dining:** Coffee shop nearby. **Cards:** AE, CB, DI, MC, VI.

RESTAURANT

BLACKHAWK GRILLE   **Lunch:** $10-$16   **Dinner:** $13-$27   **Phone:** 925/736-4295   **35**
Location: Intersection of Sycamore Valley, Crow Canyon Rd & Camino Tassajara in the Blackhawk Plaza.
Regional   3540 Blackhawk Plaza Cir 94506. **Hours:** 11:30 am-2:30 & 5:30-10 pm, Sat-11 pm, Sun 11 am-2:30 &
American   5-9:30 pm. **Reservations:** suggested. **Features:** casual dress; Sunday brunch; children's menu; health
conscious menu; cocktails & lounge; entertainment; a la carte. Patio seating avail, weather permitting.
Smoke free premises. **Cards:** AE, CB, DI, DS, MC, VI.

DAVIS—46,200

LODGINGS

AGGIE INN   **Phone:** (530)756-0352
All Year [CP]   1P: $85- 119 2P/1B: $85- 119 2P/2B: $99-109 XP: $5
Location: 0.5 mi n of I-80; Davis exit, w on First St, then 2 blks. 245 First St 95616. Fax: 530/753-5738.
Facility: 31 rooms. 1 block from University of California campus. 2 stories; interior/exterior corridors; sauna,
Motel   whirlpool. **Cards:** AE, DI, DS, MC, VI.

BEST WESTERN PALM COURT HOTEL   **Phone:** (530)753-7100
All Year [CP]   1P: $145- 230 2P/1B: $155- 240 2P/2B: $155- 240 XP: $10   F12
Location: Exit I-80 at Centra/Davis exit. Downtown. 234 D St 95616. Fax: 530/753-8761. **Facility:** 26 rooms.
Elegantly furnished rooms. Centrally located in downtown area. 3 stories; interior corridors.
Motel   **Some Rooms:** whirlpools. **Cards:** AE, DI, DS, MC, VI.

BEST WESTERN UNIVERSITY LODGE   **Phone:** (530)756-7890
All Year   1P: $69- 79 2P/1B: $69- 79 2P/2B: $75- 85 XP: $5   F14
Location: Just e of U of C campus. 123 B St 95616. Fax: 530/756-0245. **Terms:** Reserv deposit; small pets
only, $5. **Facility:** 53 rooms. Some large rooms. 2 stories; exterior corridors; whirlpool. **Dining:** Restaurants
Motel   nearby. **Recreation:** bicycles. **All Rooms:** combo or shower baths. **Some Rooms:** efficiency, 2 kitchens, no
utensils. **Cards:** AE, CB, DI, MC, VI. **Special Amenities:** Free local telephone calls and free room
upgrade (subject to availability with advanced reservations).

HALLMARK INN   **Phone:** (530)753-3600
All Year   1P: $59 2P/1B: $75 2P/2B: $65   XP: $6
Location: I-80 westbound exit Davis, eastbound exit Central Davis. 110 F St 95616. Fax: 530/758-8623.
Terms: Reserv deposit. **Facility:** 135 rooms. Center of town. Walking distance to University of California
Motor Inn   campus. 2-3 stories; interior corridors; heated pool. **Dining:** Coffee shop nearby. **Cards:** AE, DI, DS, MC, VI.

HOLIDAY INN EXPRESS HOTEL & SUITES   **Phone:** (530)758-2600
All Year [CP]   1P: $85- 135 2P/1B: $90- 145 2P/2B: $90- 145 XP: $10
Location: Exit I-80 at Richards Blvd, e. 1771 Research Park Dr 95616. Fax: 530/758-1771.
Facility: 50 rooms. 3 stories; interior corridors; whirlpool. **Cards:** AE, CB, DI, DS, JC, MC, VI.
Motel   **Special Amenities:** Free breakfast and free local telephone calls. *(See color ad below)*

UNIVERSITY PARK INN   Rates Subject to Change   **Phone:** 530/756-0910
All Year   1P: $70- 130 2P/1B: $70- 130 2P/2B: $70- 130
Too new to rate. **Location:** I-80, exit Richards Blvd, just n. 1111 Richards Blvd 95616. **Terms:** Reserv
Motel   deposit, 14 day notice. **Facility:** 54 rooms. Scheduled to open December, 1998; 2 stories; exterior corridors.
Cards: AE, CB, DI, DS, MC, VI.

DEATH VALLEY NATIONAL PARK

LODGINGS

FURNACE CREEK INN
Rates Subject to Change
Phone: (760)786-234■
(AAA)
2/12-4/17 & 10/11-1/3   1P: $245- 340   2P/1B: $245- 340   2P/2B: $245- 340   XP: $15   F1
2/1-2/11, 4/18-5/10 &
♦♦♦♦
1/4-1/31   1P: $230- 325   2P/1B: $230- 325   2P/2B: $230- 325   XP: $15   F1
Resort Hotel
5/11-10/10   1P: $150- 205   2P/1B: $150- 205   2P/2B: $150- 205   XP: $15   F1
Location: On SR 190; 1 mi s of visitor center. SR 190 92328 (PO Box 1). Fax: 760/786-251■
Terms: Check-in 4 pm; reserv deposit. **Facility:** 66 rooms. Historic hotel. Opened 1927. Picturesque location overlookin■
Death Valley. Palm-shaded terrace grounds. A variety of rooms from small & cozy to large, nicely decorated. 3-4 storie■
interior/exterior corridors; heated pool, saunas; 4 lighted tennis courts. Fee: 18 holes golf. **Dining:** Dining room; cocktail■
afternoon tea; also, The Inn Dining Room, see separate listing. **Services:** giftshop. **Recreation:** Fee: horseback ridin■
All Rooms: combo or shower baths. **Cards:** AE, CB, DI, DS, MC, VI.

FURNACE CREEK RANCH
Rates Subject to Change
Phone: 760/786-234■
♦♦
All Year   1P: $94- 134   2P/1B: $94- 134   2P/2B: $94- 134   XP: $15   F1
Resort
Location: On SR 190, adjacent to Visitor Center. 92328 (PO Box 1). Fax: 760/786-9945. **Terms:** Check-in ■
Complex
pm; reserv deposit. **Facility:** 224 rooms. 2 stories; interior/exterior corridors; heated pool; 2 lighted tenn■
courts; playground. Fee: 18 holes golf. **Recreation:** Fee: horseback riding. **All Rooms:** combo or show■
baths. **Some Rooms:** color TV. **Cards:** AE, CB, DI, DS, MC, VI.

STOVEPIPE WELLS VILLAGE
Rates Subject to Change
Phone: 760/786-238■
(FYI)
All Year   1P: $58- 80   2P/2B: $58- 80   XP: $10   F1
Doesn't meet listing requirements. **Location:** On SR 190, 24 mi nw of Visitor Center. SR 190 9232■
Motor Inn
Fax: 760/786-2389. **Terms:** Check-in 4 pm; reserv deposit. **Facility:** 83 rooms. Located just west of the San■
Dunes. Water in some rooms unsuitable for drinking. Modest to large, nicely furnished rooms. Meets AAA fir■
safety requirements. 1 story; exterior corridors; heated pool. **Services:** giftshop. **All Rooms:** combo or shower bath■
Some Rooms: color TV. **Cards:** AE, DS, MC, VI.

RESTAURANT

THE INN DINING ROOM   **Lunch:** $8-$14   **Dinner:** $19-$26   Phone: 760/786-234■
♦♦♦
Location: On SR 190; 1 mi s of visitor center; in Furnace Creek Inn. 92328. **Hours:** 7 am-2:30 & 5:30-9:3■
American
pm; closed for lunch in summer. **Reservations:** suggested. **Features:** semi-formal attire; Sunday brunc■
cocktails & lounge; a la carte. Elegant dining. Formal service. Smoke free premises. **Cards:** AE, DI, DS, M■
VI.

DELANO—22,800

LODGINGS

COMFORT INN
Phone: (805)725-102■
(AAA) (SAVE)
All Year [CP]   1P: $45- 49   2P/1B: $49- 52   2P/2B: $57- 60   XP: $5   F1
Location: Just e of SR 99; County Line exit. 2211 Girard St 93215. Fax: 805/725-1104. **Terms:** Reser■
♦
deposit, 3 day notice; small pets only. **Facility:** 45 rooms. 2 whirlpool rms, extra charge; 2 stories; exterior co■
Motel
ridors; small pool. **Dining:** Restaurant nearby. **Cards:** AE, CB, DI, DS, JC, MC, VI. **Special Amenities:** Fre■
local telephone calls and free newspaper.

SHILO INN
Rates Subject to Change
Phone: (805)725-755■
♦♦
All Year [CP]   1P: $49- 75   2P/1B: $49- 75   2P/2B: $49- 75   XP: $9   F1
Motel
Location: Just e of SR 99; County Line exit. 2231 Girard St 93215. Fax: 805/725-7524. **Facility:** 48 rooms.
stories; interior corridors; heated pool. **Cards:** AE, CB, DI, DS, JC, MC, VI.

DEL MAR—See San Diego p. 899.

DESERT HOT SPRINGS—11,700   (See map p. 774; index p. 772)

LODGINGS

AGUA CALIENTE HOTEL & MINERAL WATER SPA   Phone: (760)329-4481   ■
(AAA) (SAVE)
2/1-5/31 & 12/24-1/31   1P: $59- 74   2P/1B: $59- 74   2P/2B: $74- 84   XP: $6   F1
9/3-12/23   1P: $54- 69   2P/1B: $54- 69   2P/2B: $69- 79   XP: $6   F1
♦♦
6/1-9/2   1P: $44- 59   2P/1B: $44- 59   2P/2B: $59- 69   XP: $6   F1
Motor Inn
Location: 1.5 mi s. 14500 Palm Dr 92240. Fax: 760/329-1409. **Terms:** Reserv deposit; weekly/month■
rates. **Facility:** 115 rooms. 1 two-bedroom unit. 10 rooms with small private pool, refrigerator $99-$129; ■
kitchens $64-$94; 2 stories; exterior corridors; sauna, heated mineral pool, 2 hot mineral whirlpools, 1 enclose■
Dining: Coffee shop; 6:30 am-9 pm; $6-$12; wine/beer only. **Services:** Fee: massage. **Recreation:** fitness clu■
All Rooms: extended cable TV. **Cards:** AE, CB, DI, DS, MC, VI. *(See ad p 433)*

DESERT HOT SPRINGS SPA HOTEL   Phone: (760)329-6000   ■
(AAA) (SAVE)
2/1-5/31   1P: $59- 119   2P/1B: $59- 119 2P/2B: $59- 119 XP: $10   F■
10/1-1/31   1P: $49- 89   2P/1B: $49- 89   2P/2B: $49- 89   XP: $10   F■
♦♦♦
6/1-9/30   1P: $39- 79   2P/1B: $39- 79   2P/2B: $39- 79   XP: $10   F■
Motor Inn
Location: 1 mi n. 10805 Palm Dr 92240. Fax: 760/329-6915. **Terms:** Package plans; 2 night min sta■
weekends 12/24-5/31. **Facility:** 50 rooms. Popular spa facility. 2 stories; exterior corridors; wading pool, sau■
4 hot natural mineral water pools, 4 mineral water whirlpools. **Dining:** Dining room; 7 am-11 pm; $7-$13; cocktai■
Services: giftshop. Fee: massage. **Cards:** AE, DI, DS, MC, VI. **Special Amenities:** Early check-in/late check-out.
(See color ad p 433, inside front cover, p 773 & p 155)

(See map p. 774)

MIRACLE SPRINGS HOTEL & SPA
Phone: (760)251-6000 [1]

	2/1-5/31	1P:	$69- 189	2P/1B:	$69- 189	2P/2B:	$69- 189	XP: $10	F11
	10/1-1/31	1P:	$59- 179	2P/1B:	$59- 179	2P/2B:	$59- 179	XP: $10	F11
	6/1-9/30	1P:	$49- 169	2P/1B:	$49- 169	2P/2B:	$49- 169	XP: $10	F11

Motor Inn **Location:** 1 mi n. 10625 Palm Dr 92240. Fax: 760/251-0460. **Terms:** Reserv deposit, 3 day notice. **Facility:** 110 rooms. Large, nicely landscaped pool area. 2 stories; interior corridors; hot natural mineral water pool 7 natural mineral water whirlpools. **Dining:** Dining room; 7 am-9 pm; $10-$18; cocktails. **Services:** giftshop. Fee: massage. **All Rooms:** extended cable TV. **Cards:** AE, DI, DS, MC, VI. **Special Amenities: Early check-in/late check-out.** *(See color ad below, p 773, p 155 & inside front cover)*

SAM'S FAMILY SPA MOTEL
Rates Subject to Change   Phone: 760/329-6457 [9]

| | All Year | 1P: | $55- 92 | 2P/1B: | $55- 72 | 2P/2B: | $72- 92 | XP: $7 |

Motel **Location:** 4.3 mi e of Palm Dr. 70-875 Dillon Rd 92241. Fax: 760/329-8267. **Terms:** Reserv deposit; 2 night min stay, weekends. **Facility:** 13 rooms. Extensive grounds including park area with large lake where guests may observe & feed ducks, birds & other fowl. Park area has picnic tables & barbecues avail to public. 1 two-bedroom unit. 2 stories; interior corridors; heated pool; playground. **All Rooms:** combo or shower baths. **Some Rooms:** 5 kitchens.

STARDUST MOTEL
Phone: (760)329-5443 [4]

	2/1-5/15 & 12/1-1/31	1P:	$46- 48	2P/1B:	$46- 48	2P/2B:	$50- 52	XP: $7
	5/16-6/30 & 10/1-11/30	1P:	$43- 45	2P/1B:	$43- 45	2P/2B:	$48- 50	XP: $7
	7/1-9/30	1P:	$40- 42	2P/1B:	$40- 42	2P/2B:	$43- 45	XP: $7

Motel **Location:** 0.5 mi n, just e of Palm Dr. 66634 5th St 92240. Fax: 760/329-1912. **Terms:** Reserv deposit; weekly/monthly rates; pets. **Facility:** 16 rooms. Located in quiet, residential area. 9 kitchens, $9-$14 extra charge; 2 stories; exterior corridors; heated pool. **Recreation:** hot mineral water whirlpool. **All Rooms:** combo or shower baths, extended cable TV. **Cards:** MC, VI.

(See map p. 774)

TRAVELLERS REPOSE BED & BREAKFAST   Guaranteed Rates   **Phone:** 760/329-9584
◆◆   2/1-6/30 & 9/1-1/31 [CP]   1P: $58- 76   2P/1B: $65- 85
Bed &   **Location:** 0.4 mi e of town center. 66920 First St 92240 (PO Box 655). **Terms:** Open 2/1-6/30 & 9/1-1/31
Breakfast   reserv deposit, 7 day notice. **Facility:** 3 rooms. Victorian style house in quiet residential area. Some rooms with
antique or country style furnishings. Views of San Gorgonio & Mt. San Jacinto. 2 stories; interior corridors
smoke free premises. **All Rooms:** combo or shower baths.

DIAMOND BAR—*See Los Angeles p. 597.*

DINUBA—12,700

LODGINGS

BEST WESTERN AMERICANA INN   **Phone:** (559)595-840
All Year [CP]   1P: $45- 80   2P/1B: $50- 85   2P/2B: $50- 85   XP: $5   F
Location: 0.6 mi sw of downtown. 1450 S Alta Ave 93618. Fax: 559/595-9450. **Facility:** 38 rooms. Decorate
◆◆◆   in a New England provincial motif. 4 one-bedroom suites; 2 stories; interior corridors; whirlpoo
Motel   **All Rooms:** combo or shower baths. **Cards:** AE, CB, DI, DS, JC, MC, VI. **Special Amenities:** Fre
breakfast and free local telephone calls.

REEDLEY COUNTRY INN   Rates Subject to Change   **Phone:** (559)638-258
◆◆◆   All Year [BP]   1P: $85- 105   2P/1B: $85- 105   XP: $15   F1
Historic Bed   **Location:** 1 mi s of Reedley via Reed St. (43137 Road 52, REEDLEY, 93654). Fax: 559/638-809
& Breakfast   **Terms:** Reserv deposit, 3 day notice; handling fee imposed. **Facility:** 5 rooms. 2 restored country farm house
set in a plum & peach orchard with lush gardens & roses. 1 two-bedroom unit. Telephones avail on reques
1-2 stories; interior/exterior corridors; designated smoking area. **All Rooms:** combo or shower baths. **Cards:** AE, MC, VI.

DIXON—10,400

LODGING

BEST WESTERN INN   **Phone:** (916)678-140
◆◆◆   5/1-9/30 [CP]   1P: $60- 73   2P/1B: $60- 73   2P/2B: $73- 85   XP: $5   F
2/1-4/30 & 10/1-1/31 [CP]   1P: $57- 70   2P/1B: $57- 70   2P/2B: $63- 73   XP: $5   F
Motel   **Location:** Adjacent to I-80, exit Pitt School Road, 8 mi west of U.C. Davis Campus. 1345 Commercial Wa
95620. Fax: 916/678-0754. **Terms:** Reserv deposit; small pets only, $50 dep req. **Facility:** 55 rooms. 2 storie
exterior corridors; heated pool, sauna, whirlpool. **Some Rooms:** whirlpools. **Cards:** AE, CB, DI, DS, MC, V
Special Amenities: Free breakfast and free local telephone calls. *(See color ad below)*

DOWNEY—*See Los Angeles p. 598.*

DUARTE—*See Los Angeles p. 598.*

Look for the ⦿ in our listings!

DUBLIN—23,200

LODGING

BEST WESTERN MONARCH HOTEL Phone: (925)828-7750
AAA SAVE
Sun-Thurs 1P: $119 2P/1B: $129 XP: $10
Fri & Sat 1P: $79 2P/1B: $89 XP: $10
◆◆◆ **Location:** Exit I-580 San Ramon Rd exit, at nw quadrant of I-580 & I-680. 6680 Regional St 94568.
Motor Inn Fax: 925/828-3650. **Facility:** 239 rooms. 3 stories; interior corridors; indoor pool, sauna, whirlpool.
Dining: Restaurant; 6 am-10:30 & 4:30-10 pm; $9-$15. **Some Rooms:** 3 kitchens. **Cards:** AE, DI, DS, MC,
VI. **Special Amenities:** Free breakfast and free local telephone calls. (See ad p 803)

DUNNIGAN—300

LODGINGS

BEST WESTERN COUNTRY Phone: (530)724-3471
AAA SAVE
5/28-9/30 [CP] 1P: $52- 59 2P/1B: $65- 69 2P/2B: $69- 79 XP: $5 F17
2/1-5/27 & 10/1-1/31 [CP] 1P: $52- 59 2P/1B: $62- 66 2P/2B: $65- 69 XP: $5 F17
◆◆◆ **Location:** I-5, Dunnigan exit. 3930 Road 89 95937 (PO Box 740). Fax: 530/724-4233. **Terms:** Small pets
Motel only. **Facility:** 55 rooms. Large comfortable rooms. Attractive landscapd grounds. 6 kitchens, $69-$85; no uten-
sils. 8 suites, $75-$85; 1 story; exterior corridors; whirlpool. **Dining:** Coffee shop nearby. **Cards:** AE, CB, DI,
DS, MC, VI. (See color ad below)

IMA VALUE LODGE Phone: (530)724-3333
AAA SAVE
5/28-9/30 [CP] 1P: $46 2P/1B: $55 2P/2B: $58 XP: $4 F17
2/1-5/27 & 10/1-1/31 [CP] 1P: $41 2P/1B: $50 2P/2B: $52 XP: $4 F17
◆◆ **Location:** I-5, Dunnigan exit. 3930 Road 89 95937 (PO Box 740). Fax: 530/724-4233. **Terms:** Small pets
Motel only. **Facility:** 40 rooms. Comfortable rooms. 2 stories; interior corridors. **Dining:** Coffee shop nearby.
Cards: AE, MC, VI. **Special Amenities:** Free breakfast and preferred room (subject to availability with
advanced reservations). IMA. (See color ad p 286)

DUNSMUIR—2,100

LODGINGS

CABOOSE MOTEL-RAILROAD PARK RESORT Rates Subject to Change Phone: (530)235-4440
AAA
5/16-10/14 1P: $60- 70 2P/1B: $65- 85 2P/2B: $68 XP: $8
2/1-5/15 & 10/15-1/31 1P: $55- 65 2P/1B: $60- 70 2P/2B: $63 XP: $8
◆◆◆ **Location:** 1 mi s exit I-5, Railroad Park Rd. 100 Railroad Park Rd 96025. Fax: 530/235-4470.
Motel **Terms:** Reserv deposit; small pets only, $8 extra charge with prior approval. **Facility:** 27 rooms. Restored &
nicely furnished caboose cars; 4 motel rooms. Attractively landscaped with views of Castle Crags Peaks. 1
two-bedroom unit. Whirlpool. **Dining:** Railroad Park Resort Restaurant, see separate listing. **Services:** giftshop.
All Rooms: combo or shower baths. **Some Rooms:** 3 kitchens. **Cards:** AE, DS, MC, VI.

CEDAR LODGE MOTEL Phone: 530/235-4331
AAA SAVE
5/1-1/31 1P: $35- 39 2P/1B: $42- 48 2P/2B: $44- 50 XP: $5
2/1-4/30 1P: $33- 36 2P/1B: $40- 44 2P/2B: $40- 46 XP: $4
◆◆ **Location:** Exit I-5 at Dunsmuir/Siskiyou; w 0.5 mi. 4201 Dunsmuir Ave 96025. Fax: 530/235-4000.
Motel **Terms:** Reserv deposit; small pets only, $5 extra charge. **Facility:** 16 rooms. Quiet tree-shaded grounds. 3
two-bedroom units. 4 family units for 2-8 person $65-$125, with woodburning fireplace or stove, 1 or 2 bedrooms, living rooms, kitchens. 2 kitchenettes, $10 extra; 1 story; exterior corridors; whirlpool. **Cards:** AE, DS, MC, VI.

DUNSMUIR TRAVELODGE Phone: (530)235-4395
AAA SAVE
5/25-9/4 1P: $45 2P/1B: $55 2P/2B: $60 XP: $5 F15
2/1-5/24 & 9/5-1/31 1P: $40 2P/1B: $45 2P/2B: $50 XP: $5 F15
◆◆ **Location:** Exit I-5 Central Dunsmuir. 5400 Dunsmuir Ave 96025. Fax: 530/235-0229. **Terms:** Reserv deposit.
Motel **Facility:** 18 rooms. Attractive comfortable modern rooms. 3 two-bedroom units, $75-$85 for 4-6 persons; 2
stories; exterior corridors. **Cards:** AE, DS, MC, VI. **Special Amenities:** Free local telephone calls and free
newspaper.

RESTAURANT

RAILROAD PARK RESORT RESTAURANT   **Dinner:** $10-$28   **Phone:** 530/235-461
◆◆   **Location:** 1 mi s exit I-5, Railroad Park Rd; in Caboose Motel-Railroad Park Resort. 100 Railroad Park R
American   96025. **Hours:** 5 pm-9 pm; in summmer to 10 pm; winter hours vary (from 9/15-5/15). Closed: 1/1, 11/2
     12/25, Mon & Tues. **Reservations:** suggested. **Features:** children's menu; cocktails & lounge. Attractive
restored 100 year old railroad cars; varied menu. Smoke free premises. **Cards:** AE, DS, MC, VI.   [X]

EL CAJON—*See San Diego p. 900.*

EL CENTRO—31,400

LODGINGS

BARBARA WORTH GOLF RESORT & CONVENTION CENTER   **Phone:** (760)356-280
(AAA) (SAVE)   All Year   1P: $63   2P/1B: $70   2P/2B: $70   XP: $6   F1
     Location: 9 mi e of El Centro; 2.3 mi w of Holtville; from I-8, take Bowker Rd 2 mi n, then 3 mi e c
◆◆◆   CRS-80. 2050 Country Club Dr 92250. Fax: 760/356-4653. **Terms:** Handling fee imposed; weekly/month
Resort Motor   rates; small pets only, with prior approval. **Facility:** 104 rooms. Quiet, restful setting. Large, nicely furnishe
Inn   rooms, most overlooking the golf course. 4 suites with kitchen; 4 whirlpool rms, extra charge; 2 storie
     interior/exterior corridors; putting green; heated pool, whirlpool. Fee: 18 holes golf. **Dining:** Dining roor
restaurant, see separate listing. **Cards:** AE, CB, DI, DS, JC, MC, VI.

[icons]

BEST WESTERN JOHN JAY INN   **Phone:** (760)337-867
(AAA) (SAVE)   All Year [CP]   1P: $55- 95   2P/1B: $60- 95 2P/2B: $60- 95 XP: $6   F1
     Location: Adjacent to I-8, exit Fourth St. 2352 S Fourth St 92243. Fax: 760/337-8693. **Facility:** 58 rooms.
◆◆◆   stories; interior corridors; sauna, whirlpool. **Cards:** AE, CB, DI, DS, JC, MC, VI. **Special Amenities:** Fre
Motel   breakfast and free local telephone calls.

[icons]

BRUNNER'S   **Phone:** (760)352-643
(AAA) (SAVE)   All Year   1P: $46- 53   2P/1B: $49- 55 2P/2B: $52- 55 XP: $3   F1
     Location: 1 mi n of I-8, exit Imperial Ave. 215 N Imperial Ave 92243. Fax: 760/352-643
◆◆   **Terms:** Weekly/monthly rates; pets. **Facility:** 88 rooms. Wide variety of nicely decorated rooms. 20 one
Motor Inn   bedroom apartments, $70-$80 for 2 persons; 1-2 stories; exterior corridors; whirlpool. **Dining:** Restaurar
     coffee shop; 5 am-9 pm; $5-$23; cocktails. **Cards:** AE, CB, DI, DS, MC, VI. **Special Amenities:** Free loc
telephone calls and free newspaper.

[icons]

LAGUNA INN   Phone: (760)353-7750
(AAA) (SAVE)   All Year   1P: $40- 48   2P/1B: $40- 48   2P/2B: $44- 52
◆   Location: Just nw of I-8, exit Imperial Ave. 2030 Cottonwood Cir 92243. Fax: 760/353-7755. Facility: 27
Motel   rooms. 4 one-bedroom suites with efficiency, $58; 2 stories; exterior corridors; whirlpool, lap pool.
Dining: Restaurant nearby. Cards: AE, CB, DS, MC, VI.

RAMADA INN   Phone: (760)352-5152
(AAA) (SAVE)   All Year   1P: $51- 57   2P/1B: $57- 63   2P/2B: $57- 63   XP: $6   F18
◆◆◆   Location: Adjacent to I-8, exit Imperial Ave. 1455 Ocotillo Dr 92243. Fax: 760/337-1567. Terms: Monthly
Motor Inn   rates; small pets only. Facility: 147 rooms. 2 stories; interior/exterior corridors; heated pool, wading pool, whirl-
pool. Dining: Restaurant; 24 hours; $6-$9; cocktails. Cards: AE, CB, DI, DS, MC, VI. Special Amenities:
Free local telephone calls and preferred room (subject to availability with advanced reservations).
(See color ad p 436)

VACATION INN   Phone: (760)352-9523
(AAA) (SAVE)   All Year [CP]   1P: $44- 49   2P/1B: $44- 49   2P/2B: $49- 54
◆◆   Location: Adjacent to I-8, exit Imperial Ave. 2015 Cottonwood Cir 92243. Fax: 760/353-7620.
Motor Inn   Terms: Weekly/monthly rates; pets. Facility: 186 rooms. 2 stories; exterior corridors; heated pool, whirl-
pools. Dining: Restaurant; 5:30 am-10 pm, Sun from 7 am; $10-$16; cocktails. Some Rooms: 18
efficiencies. Cards: AE, CB, DI, DS, MC, VI. *(See ad p 436)*

RESTAURANTS

BARBARA WORTH GOLF RESORT RESTAURANT   Lunch: $5-$9   Dinner: $10-$18   Phone: 760-356-2806
◆◆◆   Location: At Barbara Worth Golf Resort. 2050 Country Club Dr 92250. Hours: 6 am-10 pm. Closed: 12/25.
American   Reservations: accepted. Features: casual dress; Sunday brunch; children's menu; carryout; cocktails &
lounge. Attractive restaurant with view of golf course. Friday seafood buffet, 5 pm-9 pm & Saturday prime rib
buffet, 5 pm-10 pm. Smoke free premises. Cards: AE, CB, DI, DS, JC, MC, VI.

GRASSO'S ITALIAN RESTAURANT   Dinner: $8-$18   Phone: 760/352-4635
◆   Location: 0.5 mi w of Imperial Ave. 1902 W Main 92243. Hours: 5:30 pm-10 pm. Closed major holidays,
Italian   Mon & Tues. Features: children's menu; beer & wine only; a la carte. A small, unpretentious restaurant
serving a selection of pasta, pizza, veal & a few steak & chicken entrees. Very casual atmosphere. Smoke
free premises. Cards: AE, MC, VI.

EL CERRITO—22,900

LODGING

TRAVELODGE-EL CERRITO   Phone: (510)232-0900
(AAA) (SAVE)   All Year   1P: $60- 80   2P/1B: $70- 90   2P/2B: $80- 100   XP: $8-15   D12
◆   Location: Eastbound exit I-80 Potrero Ave; westbound exit El Cerrito/San Rafael Bridge; E Cutting; S San
Motel   Pablo; S Eastshore Blvd. 6009 Potrero Ave 94530. Fax: 510/231-0209. Terms: Reserv deposit, 7 day notice.
Facility: 48 rooms. 2 whirlpool rms, extra charge; 3 stories; interior corridors. Dining: Restaurant nearby.
All Rooms: combo or shower baths. Cards: AE, CB, DI, DS, MC, VI. *(See color ad p 370)*

ELK—300

LODGING

ELK COVE INN   Rates Subject to Change   Phone: (707)877-3321
◆◆   Fri & Sat & Sun-Thurs
Cottage   7/1-10/31 [BP]   2P/1B: $108- 278   2P/2B: $108- 278   XP: $30
Sun-Thurs 2/1-6/30 &
11/1-1/31 [BP]   2P/1B: $98- 248   2P/2B: $98- 248   XP: $30
Location: 6.5 s of jct SR 128. 6300 S Hwy 1 95432 (PO Box 367). Fax: 707/877-1808. Terms: Reserv deposit, 14 day
notice; handling fee imposed. Facility: 14 rooms. Many fireplaces, ocean garden views. 2 stories; interior/exterior corridors.
All Rooms: combo or shower baths. Cards: AE, MC, VI.

EL MONTE—See Los Angeles p. 599.

EL PORTAL—500

LODGINGS

CEDAR LODGE   Rates Subject to Change   Phone: (209)379-2612
(AAA)   All Year   1P: $85- 129   2P/1B: $85- 129   2P/2B: $99- 129
◆◆   Location: 6 mi w of YNP Westgate. 9966 Hwy 140 95318 (PO Box C). Fax: 209/379-2712. Terms: Reserv
Motel   deposit, 7 day notice; handling fee imposed. Facility: 206 rooms. Few small rooms. 2 three-bedroom apartments with kitchen, $279; 1 with private swimming pool, $399 for up to 8 persons; 2 stories; exterior corridors;
heated indoor pool, whirlpool. Dining: Cocktails; restaurant nearby. Services: giftshop. All Rooms: combo
or shower baths. Some Rooms: 12 efficiencies, whirlpools. Cards: AE, MC, VI. *(See color ad p 1087)*

YOSEMITE VIEW LODGE   Rates Subject to Change   Phone: 209/379-2681
(AAA)   All Year   1P: $129- 169   2P/1B: $129- 169   2P/2B: $99- 139
◆◆◆   Location: Just w of Y N P West Gate. 11136 Hwy 140 95318 (PO Box D). Fax: 209/379-2704.
Motel   Terms: Reserv deposit, 7 day notice; handling fee imposed; pets, $5 extra charge. Facility: 278 rooms. Many
balconies on the Merced River. Many gas fireplaces. Few with loft. 14 two-bedroom units. 1-3 stories; exterior
corridors; indoor pool, whirlpools. Dining: Cocktails; restaurant nearby. Services: giftshop.
Recreation: fishing. All Rooms: efficiencies, combo or shower baths. Some Rooms: whirlpools. Cards: MC, VI.
(See color ad p 1087)

EL SEGUNDO—See Los Angeles p. 599.

EMERYVILLE—5,700   (See map p. 752; index p. 750)

LODGINGS

**FOUR POINTS BY SHERATON-
SAN FRANCISCO BAY BRIDGE**   Rates Subject to Change   **Phone:** (510)547-7888   🏨34
All Year [CP]   1P: $109- 129   2P/1B: $119- 139   2P/2B: $119- 139   XP: $10   F14
Location: Off I-80 via Powell St exit, 1 mi n of Oakland-San Francisco Bay Bridge. 1603 Powell St 94608.
Motel   Fax: 510/652-4426. **Facility:** 153 rooms. Some rooms with bay view. 7 stories; interior corridors; whirlpool.
Dining: Coffee shop nearby. **Cards:** AE, DI, DS, MC, VI.

HOLIDAY INN-BAY BRIDGE   Rates Subject to Change   **Phone:** (510)658-9300   🏨33
All Year   1P: $130- 145   2P/1B: $145- 165   2P/2B: $145- 165   XP: $10   F17
Motor Inn   **Location:** Off I-80 via Powell-Emeryville exit; 1 mi n of Oakland-San Francisco Bay Bridge. 1800 Powell St
94608. Fax: 510/547-8166. **Facility:** 279 rooms. Some rooms with view of San Francisco Bay. 3 bay view
suites, $300 for 2 persons; 12 stories; interior corridors. **Services:** giftshop. **All Rooms:** combo or shower baths. **Cards:** AE,
DI, DS, JC, MC, VI.

ENCINITAS—55,400

LODGINGS

ENCINITAS INN & SUITES   **Phone:** (760)942-7455
All Year [CP]   1P: $95- 115   2P/1B: $95- 115   2P/2B: $95- 115   XP: $10   F12
Location: Just w of I-5, exit Encinitas Blvd. 85 Encinitas Blvd 92024. Fax: 760/632-9481. **Terms:** Reserv
Motel   deposit. **Facility:** 90 rooms. Hillside location. Spacious rooms with balcony, some with ocean view. 3 stories;
exterior corridors; heated pool, whirlpool. **All Rooms:** combo or shower baths. **Some Rooms:** 30
efficiencies, whirlpools. **Cards:** AE, CB, DI, DS, MC, VI. **Special Amenities:** Free breakfast and free
newspaper.

HOLIDAY INN EXPRESS   **Phone:** (760)944-3800
7/1-9/30 [CP]   1P: $99- 109   2P/1B: $99- 109   2P/2B: $99- 109   XP: $5   F18
5/1-6/30 & 10/1-1/31 [CP]   1P: $89- 99   2P/1B: $89- 99   2P/2B: $89- 99   XP: $5   F18
2/1-4/30 [CP]   1P: $79- 89   2P/1B: $79- 89   2P/2B: $79- 89   XP: $5   F18
Motel   **Location:** E side of I-5, Leucadia Blve exit. 607 Leucadia Blvd 92024. Fax: 760/944-6217. **Terms:** Weekly
rates. **Facility:** 100 rooms. 3 stories; exterior corridors; small heated pool, whirlpool. **Cards:** AE, CB, DI, DS,
JC, MC, VI. **Special Amenities:** Free breakfast and free local telephone calls.

LEUCADIA INN-BY-THE-SEA   Rates Subject to Change   **Phone:** (760)942-1668
6/1-10/1 [BP]   2P/1B: $89- 109
Motel   2/1-5/31 & 10/2-1/31 [EP]   2P/1B: $79- 99
Location: 0.5 mi w of I-5, exit Encinitas Blvd. 960 N Coast Hwy 101 92024. Fax: 760/942-1065.
Terms: Reserv deposit, 7 day notice. **Facility:** 7 rooms. Individually decorated theme rooms. One block to the beach. 2 sto-
ries; exterior corridors; designated smoking area. **All Rooms:** shower baths. **Cards:** DS, MC, VI.

OCEAN INN   **Phone:** (760)436-1988
5/21-12/31 [CP]   1P: $89- 99   2P/1B: $99- 109   2P/2B: $99- 109   XP: $10   F12
2/1-5/20 & 1/1-1/31 [CP]   1P: $69- 79   2P/1B: $79- 89   2P/2B: $79- 89   XP: $10   F12
Location: I-5, exit Leucadia Blvd 1 mi w, 1 mi n on Hwy 101. 1444 N Coast Hwy 101 92024.
Motel   Fax: 760/436-3921. **Facility:** 48 rooms. 2 stories; exterior corridors; beach access. **All Rooms:** efficiencies,
no utensils. **Some Rooms:** whirlpools. **Cards:** AE, DS, MC, VI. **Special Amenities:** Early check-in/late
check-out and free breakfast.

SEABREEZE BED & BREAKFAST INN   Rates Subject to Change   **Phone:** (760)944-0318
All Year [CP]   1P: $60- 150   2P/1B: $75- 150   XP: $10-20   F13
Bed &   **Location:** I-5, Encinitas Blvd exit; 0.3 mi w. 121 N Vulcan Ave 92024. **Terms:** Reserv deposit, 7 day notice;
Breakfast   handling fee imposed; 2 night min stay, weekends. **Facility:** 5 rooms. One room with refrigerator, whirlpool
bathtub & private hot tub. One apartment with fireplace, kitchen, living room & separate bedroom. 2 stories;
interior/exterior corridors; designated smoking area. **Services:** area transportation. **All Rooms:** combo or shower baths.
Cards: DS, MC, VI.

RESTAURANT

WHEN IN ROME   **Dinner:** $12-$20   **Phone:** 760/944-1771
Location: 0.8 mi s of Encinitas Blvd at Ave J. 1108 S Coast Hwy 101 92024. **Hours:** 5:30-10 pm, Sun
Italian   5-9:30 pm. Closed major holidays. **Reservations:** suggested. **Features:** No A/C; casual dress; carryout;
cocktails; a la carte. Fine dining in a very attractive atmosphere. Patio seating available. Smoking allowed on
patio. **Cards:** AE, MC, VI.

ENCINO—See Los Angeles p. 600.

ESCONDIDO—108,600

LODGINGS

BEST WESTERN ESCONDIDO
Phone: (760)740-1700
All Year [CP]   1P: $69- 89 2P/1B: $69- 89 2P/2B: $69- 89 XP: $6   F12
Location: Just e of I-15; exit El Norte Pkwy. 1700 Seven Oaks Rd 92026. Fax: 760/740-9832. **Facility:** 100 rooms. 19 suites, $112 for up to 2 persons; 4 stories; interior corridors; heated pool, whirlpool. **Cards:** AE, CB, DI, DS, MC, VI. **Special Amenities:** Early check-in/late check-out and free breakfast.
(See color ad below)

COMFORT INN ESCONDIDO-SAN DIEGO
Phone: (760)489-1010
6/1-9/10 [CP]   1P: $59- 89 2P/1B: $59- 89 2P/2B: $59- 99 XP: $10   F17
2/1-5/31 & 9/11-1/31 [CP] 1P: $49- 69 2P/1B: $49- 69 2P/2B: $49- 79 XP: $10   F17
Location: Just w of I-15, exit Valley Pkwy. 1290 W Valley Pkwy 92029. Fax: 760/489-7847. **Facility:** 93 rooms. Interior corridors; whirlpool. **Dining:** Restaurant nearby. **Cards:** AE, DI, DS, JC, MC, VI. **Special Amenities:** Early check-in/late check-out and free breakfast.

HOLIDAY INN EXPRESS/WILD ANIMAL PARK
Phone: (760)741-7117
6/2-9/15 [CP]   1P: $59- 99 2P/1B: $59- 99 2P/2B: $69- 109 XP: $10
2/1-6/1 & 9/16-1/31 [CP] 1P: $49- 89 2P/1B: $49- 89 2P/2B: $49- 99 XP: $10
Location: Just w of I-15, exit Valley Pkwy. 1250 W Valley Pkwy 92029. Fax: 760/747-0443. **Terms:** Weekly/monthly rates. **Facility:** 84 rooms. 24 two-rm suites with microwave & refrigerator, $119-$139; 3 stories; interior corridors; heated pool, whirlpool. **Dining:** Restaurant nearby. **Some Rooms:** 25 efficiencies. **Cards:** AE, DI, DS, MC, VI.

PALMS INN
Phone: (760)743-9733
Rates Subject to Change
All Year [CP]   1P: $38- 44 2P/1B: $42- 48 2P/2B: $46- 52 XP: $6   F14
Location: 0.5 mi e of I-15, northbound exit Centre City Pkwy, southbound exit Felicita Rd, then e on Citracado. 2650 S Escondido Blvd 92025. Fax: 760/743-0866. **Terms:** Reserv deposit; weekly rates. **Facility:** 44 rooms. 2 stories; exterior corridors; whirlpool. **Dining:** Restaurant nearby. **Cards:** AE, DS, MC, VI.

RODEWAY INN
Phone: (760)746-0441
5/1-9/30   1P: $42- 67 2P/1B: $42- 60 2P/2B: $42- 67
2/1-4/30   1P: $35- 53 2P/1B: $35- 53 2P/2B: $39- 53
10/1-1/31   1P: $35- 53 2P/1B: $35- 53 2P/2B: $39- 53
Location: 1 mi e of I-15, exit El Norte to Centre City Pkwy. 250 W El Norte 92026. Fax: 760/746-0537. **Terms:** Reserv deposit. **Facility:** 23 rooms. 2 stories; exterior corridors. **Dining:** Restaurant nearby. **All Rooms:** combo or shower baths. **Some Rooms:** 4 efficiencies. **Cards:** AE, CB, DI, DS, MC, VI. **Special Amenities:** Free breakfast and free local telephone calls.

THE SHERIDAN INN
Phone: (760)743-8338
All Year [CP]   1P: $49- 65 2P/1B: $56- 69 2P/2B: $59- 75
Location: 1 mi e of I-15; Exit El Norte, just e of Centre City Pkwy. 1341 N Escondido Blvd 92026. Fax: 760/743-0840. **Facility:** 54 rooms. 2 stories; exterior corridors; heated pool, whirlpool. **Cards:** AE, DI, DS, JC, MC, VI. **Special Amenities:** Early check-in/late check-out and free breakfast.

SUPER 8 MOTEL-ESCONDIDO
Phone: 760/747-3711
All Year [CP]   1P: $40- 50 2P/1B: $45- 55 2P/2B: $50- 60 XP: $5-10   F12
Location: Center, just sw of I-15 business loop (Centre City Pkwy); from SR 78E exit Centre City Parkway S. 528 W Washington Ave 92025. Fax: 760/747-8385. **Terms:** Reserv deposit, 7 day notice; small pets only, $10 dep req. **Facility:** 52 rooms. 3 stories; exterior corridors; whirlpool. **Cards:** AE, CB, DI, DS, MC, VI.

WELK RESORT CENTER

(AAA) [SAVE]

◆◆◆
Resort Motor
Inn

Phone: (760)749-3000

All Year   1P: $160- 190   2P/1B: $160- 190   2P/2B: $160- 190   XP: $10   F12
Location: 9 mi n on I-15, between Deer Springs & Old Castle Rd exits. 8860 Lawrence Welk Dr 92026.
Fax: 760/749-6182. **Terms:** Weekly rates; package plans; pets, $50 dep req. **Facility:** 137 rooms. Extensive recreational facilities & shopping plaza located in a valley surrounded by rugged hills. Large rooms with balcony or patio. 4 two-bedroom units. Two 2-bedroom suites with full kitchen & bathtub, $250-$500; two 2-bedroom suites with refrigerator, $225-$450; 2-3 stories; exterior corridors; putting green, 18 hole executive course, 18 hole par 3 course,; heated pool, whirlpools; 3 lighted tennis courts. **Dining:** Deli; 7 am-9 pm; cocktails; also, Welk Resort Center Restaurant, see separate listing. **Services:** giftshop. Fee: massage. **Recreation:** Welk Resort Theatre & Museum. **Cards:** AE, CB, DI, DS, MC, VI. **Special Amenities:** Free local telephone calls and preferred room (subject to availability with advanced reservations). *(See color ad p 879)*

ZOSA GARDENS BED & BREAKFAST

(AAA) [SAVE]

◆◆◆
Bed &
Breakfast

Phone: (760)723-9093

Mon-Thurs [BP]   1P: $122- 177   2P/1B: $122- 177   XP: $20-25   F10
Fri-Sun [BP]   1P: $135- 195   2P/1B: $135- 195   XP: $20-25   F10
Location: 12 mi n of Escondido; 1.4 mi e of I-15 & Old Highway 395. 9381 W Lilac Rd 92026.
Fax: 760/723-3460. **Terms:** Reserv deposit, 3 day notice; handling fee imposed. **Facility:** 9 rooms. A hacienda-style home on 22 acres of beautifully landscaped grounds in a country setting with orchards & flowering plants. 2 stories; interior corridors; designated smoking area; whirlpool; 1 tennis court. **Services:** Fee: massage. **Recreation:** volleyball court, croquet lawn. **Some Rooms:** combo or shower baths, shared bathrooms, color TV. **Cards:** AE, CB, DI, DS, MC, VI. **Special Amenities:** Free breakfast and preferred room (subject to availability with advanced reservations).

RESTAURANTS

THE BRIGANTINE

◆◆
Seafood

Lunch: $8-$12   **Dinner:** $11-$25   **Phone:** 760/743-4718
Location: 1.5 mi s on I-15 business loop, (Centre City Pkwy). 421 W Felicita Pkwy 92025. **Hours:** 11:30 am-2:30 & 5-9:30 pm, Fri-10:30 pm, Sat 5 pm-10:30 pm, Sun 4:30 pm-9:30 pm. **Closed:** 11/25 & 12/25.
Features: casual dress; children's menu; early bird specials; cocktails & lounge. Nautical decor. Nice selection of seafood, steak & pasta. Smoke free premises. **Cards:** AE, CB, DI, MC, VI.

FIRESIDE RESTAURANT

◆◆
American

Lunch: $5-$12   **Dinner:** $13-$19   **Phone:** 760/745-1931
Location: On I-15 business loop (Centre City Pkwy). 439 W Washington Ave 92025. **Hours:** 11:30 am-2:30 & 5-9 pm, Fri & Sat-10 pm, Sun 10 am-3 & 4:30-9 pm. **Features:** casual dress; Sunday brunch; children's menu; early bird specials; carryout; cocktails & lounge. Nice selection of steak, prime rib, seafood & pasta. Smoke free premises. **Cards:** AE, CB, DI, DS, MC, VI.

LA TAPATIA

◆
Mexican

Lunch: $7-$15   **Dinner:** $8-$15   **Phone:** 760/747-8282
Location: Downtown area, just e of Centre City Pkwy. 340 W Grand Ave 92025. **Hours:** Mon-Thurs 11 am-10 pm, Fri-Sun 7 am-10 pm. **Features:** casual dress; children's menu; early bird specials; carryout; cocktails & lounge. A popular, long established restaurant. Smoking allowed on patio. Sunday breakfast buffet, $9.95. **Cards:** AE, DS, MC, VI.

150 GRAND CAFE

◆◆◆
American

Lunch: $7-$11   **Dinner:** $14-$23   **Phone:** 760/738-6868
Location: Downtown. 150 W Grand Ave 92025. **Hours:** 11:30 am-3 & 5-9 pm, Sat 5 pm-9:30 pm. **Closed:** 11/25, 12/25 & Sun. **Reservations:** suggested. **Features:** casual dress; cocktails & lounge. Contemporary dining. Interesting selection of California cuisine Smoking allowed on patio. **Cards:** AE, CB, DI, MC, VI.

SIRINO'S RESTAURANT

◆◆◆
Continental

Lunch: $8-$11   **Dinner:** $14-$22   **Phone:** 760/745-3835
Location: Downtown. 113 W Grand Ave 92025. **Hours:** 11:30 am-2 & 4:30-9:30 pm. **Closed:** 12/25, Sun & Mon. **Reservations:** suggested. **Features:** casual dress; early bird specials; cocktails; street parking. A small, charming restaurant. Limited patio seating. **Cards:** AE, CB, DI, DS, MC, VI.

WELK RESORT CENTER RESTAURANT

◆◆
American

Lunch: $5-$10   **Dinner:** $9-$18   **Phone:** 760/749-3000
Location: 9 mi n on I-15, between Deer Springs & Old Castle Rd exits. 8860 Lawrence Welk Dr 92026.
Hours: 7 am-9 pm. **Features:** casual dress; children's menu; early bird specials; salad bar; cocktails & lounge. Large dining room overlooking the golf course. Varied selection of beef, fish & chicken. Chicken & dumplings a specialty. Buffet lunch or dinner avail prior to performances at Welk Resort Theatre. Smoke free premises. **Cards:** AE, CB, DI, DS, MC, VI.

ETNA—800

LODGING

MOTEL ETNA

[FYI]

Motel

Rates Subject to Change   **Phone:** 530/467-5330
6/1-9/30   1P: $33   2P/1B: $38   2P/2B: $38   XP: $5
2/1-5/31 & 10/1-1/31   1P: $30   2P/1B: $35   2P/2B: $35   XP: $5
Has not been inspected. **Location:** 317 Collier Way 96027 (PO Box 754). **Facility:** 6 rooms. Best available in area. Meets AAA fire safety requirements. 1 story; exterior corridors. **All Rooms:** shower baths. **Cards:** AE, CB, DI, DS, MC, VI.

EUREKA—27,000

LODGINGS

AN ELEGANT VICTORIAN MANSION BED & BREAKFAST INN

(AAA) [SAVE]

◆◆◆
Historic Bed
& Breakfast

Phone: (707)444-3144

5/1-10/31 [BP]   1P: $98- 195   2P/1B: $135- 225   2P/2B: $235   XP: $50
2/1-4/30 & 11/1-1/4 [BP]   1P: $88- 185   2P/1B: $125- 215   2P/2B: $225   XP: $50
Location: US 101, C St exit; 0.5 mi e. 1406 C St 95501. **Fax:** 707/442-5594. **Terms:** Open 2/1-1/4; reserv deposit, 14 day notice; handling fee imposed. **Facility:** 4 rooms. Authentically restored 1888 national historic landmark. Victorian flower garden. Exceptional personal service from host-historian. Antique car collection, gramaphone & film collection. Located in quiet residential neighborhood. 1 two-bedroom unit. 2 stories; interior corridors; smoke free premises; sauna. **Dining:** Breakfast includes Lilys Belgian pastry & egg dish, quiches, fruit cobblers, variety of fruits & juices. House-blend coffee. **Recreation:** bicycles, croquet field. **Some Rooms:** color TV. **Cards:** MC, VI. **Special Amenities:** Free local telephone calls and preferred room (subject to availability with advanced reservations).

BEST WESTERN BAYSHORE INN

Phone: (707)268-8005

	5/1-9/30	1P:	$90- 140	2P/1B:	$95- 145	2P/2B:	$95- 145	XP:	$5	F12
(AAA) (SAVE)	2/1-4/30	1P:	$70- 120	2P/1B:	$75- 125	2P/2B:	$75- 125	XP:	$5	F12
◆◆◆	10/1-1/31	1P:	$70- 120	2P/1B:	$75- 125	2P/2B:	$75- 125	XP:	$5	F12

Motel   **Location:** On US 101, s of Bayshore Mall. 3500 Broadway 95503. Fax: 707/268-8002. **Terms:** Pets, $50 dep req. **Facility:** 82 rooms. Some rooms have view or bay & some with fireplaces. 8 two-bedroom units. 11 whirlpool rms, extra charge; 3 stories; exterior corridors; heated indoor/outdoor pool, sauna, whirlpool. **Dining:** Restaurant; 7:30 am-10 pm, Fri & Sat to 11 pm; $10-$20; cocktails. **Services:** giftshop. **Recreation:** video game room. **Some Rooms:** 2 kitchens. **Cards:** AE, CB, DI, DS, JC, MC, VI. **Special Amenities:** Early check-in/late check-out and free local telephone calls.

BEST WESTERN THUNDERBIRD INN

Phone: (707)443-2234

	7/1-9/30	1P:	$85- 99	2P/1B:	$89- 105	2P/2B:	$89- 105	XP:	$5	F18
(AAA) (SAVE)	5/15-6/30	1P:	$75- 89	2P/1B:	$79- 95	2P/2B:	$79- 95	XP:	$5	F18
◆◆◆	2/1-5/14 & 10/1-1/31	1P:	$69- 85	2P/1B:	$72- 87	2P/2B:	$72- 87	XP:	$5	F18

Motel   **Location:** On US 101, at Broadway. 232 W 5th St 95501. Fax: 707/443-3489. **Facility:** 115 rooms. Enclosed patio with barbeque area. 3 two-bedroom units. 2 stories; exterior corridors; heated pool, whirlpool. **Dining:** Restaurant; 6 am-10 pm; $10-$20. **Recreation:** Fee: Super Nintendo. **All Rooms:** combo or shower baths. **Some Rooms:** Fee: whirlpools. **Cards:** AE, CB, DI, DS, JC, MC, VI. **Special Amenities:** Early check-in/late check-out and free local telephone calls. *(See color ad below)*

COMFORT INN

Phone: (707)444-0401

	5/1-10/31 [CP]	1P:	$50- 95	2P/1B:	$55- 100	2P/2B:	$60- 100	XP:	$5	F16
(AAA) (SAVE)	2/1-4/30 & 11/1-1/31 [CP]	1P:	$45- 90	2P/1B:	$45- 90	2P/2B:	$48- 90	XP:	$5	F16

◆◆◆   **Location:** US 101 southbound, corner 4th & V sts. 2014 4th St 95501. Fax: 707/442-8145. **Facility:** 30 rooms. Motel   Modern, attractive decor. 1 two-bedroom unit, $90-$160 for 4-6 persons; 2 stories; exterior corridors. **All Rooms:** combo or shower baths. **Cards:** AE, CB, DI, DS, JC, MC, VI. **Special Amenities:** Free breakfast and free newspaper.

THE DALY INN-BED & BREAKFAST

Phone: (707)445-3638

	5/1-10/31 [BP]	1P:	$80- 140	2P/1B:	$125- 150	2P/2B:	$85- 150	XP:	$20
(AAA) (SAVE)	2/1-4/30 & 11/1-1/31 [BP]	1P:	$75- 110	2P/1B:	$100- 120	2P/2B:	$80- 120	XP:	$20

◆◆◆   **Location:** E of US 101. 1125 H St 95501. Fax: 707/444-3636. **Terms:** Check-in 4 pm; reserv deposit, 7 day Bed & notice. **Facility:** 5 rooms. 1905 Colonial revival house in residential area, antique furnishings, porch with wicker Breakfast   rockers overlooks garden. Closed 1 week for major holidays. 2 stories; interior corridors; smoke free premises. **Dining:** Breakfast specialities include grandmother's sticky buns & noodle kugle. **Services:** complimentary evening beverages. **Some Rooms:** shared bathrooms, color TV. **Cards:** AE, DS, MC, VI. **Special Amenities:** Free local telephone calls and free room upgrade (subject to availability with advanced reservations).

DAYS INN EUREKA

Phone: (707)444-2019

	6/1-9/15 [CP]	1P:	$60- 80	2P/1B:	$65- 85	2P/2B:	$70- 90	XP:	$8	F12
(AAA) (SAVE)	2/1-5/31 & 9/16-1/31 [CP]	1P:	$48- 52	2P/1B:	$54- 64	2P/2B:	$59- 68	XP:	$8	F12

◆◆◆   **Location:** US 101, s end of town. 4260 Broadway 95503. **Terms:** Reserv deposit; handling fee imposed. Motel   **Facility:** 48 rooms. 4 whirlpool rms, extra charge; 2 stories; interior corridors; heated indoor pool, indoor whirlpool. **Dining:** Restaurant nearby. **Cards:** AE, CB, DI, DS, JC, MC, VI. **Special Amenities:** Early check-in/late check-out and free local telephone calls. *(See color ad p 442)*

DOUBLETREE HOTEL

Rates Subject to Change   **Phone: (707)445-0844**

	7/1-9/30	1P:	$84- 94	2P/1B:	$84- 94	2P/2B:	$84- 94	XP:	$15	F18
◆◆◆	2/1-6/30 & 10/1-1/31	1P:	$74- 84	2P/1B:	$74- 84	2P/2B:	$74- 84	XP:	$15	F18

Motor Inn   **Location:** US 101 southbound between T & V sts. 1929 4th St 95501. Fax: 707/445-2752. **Facility:** 178 rooms. Attractively decorated rooms. 8 two-bedroom units. 8 two-bedroom family suites, $104-$114 for up to 2 persons; 3 stories; interior corridors; small pool. **All Rooms:** combo or shower baths. **Cards:** AE, CB, DI, DS, JC, MC, VI. *(See color ad p 442)*

DOWNTOWNER MOTEL
Rates Subject to Change
Phone: 707/443-5061
All Year [CP]   1P: $59   2P/1B: $59   2P/2B: $59   XP: $10   F16
Location: E of US 101, exit E St. 424 8th St 95501. Fax: 707/442-0637. **Terms:** Check-in 4 pm. **Facility:** 77 rooms. 1 two-bedroom unit. 2 stories; interior/exterior corridors. **Dining:** Restaurant. **Some Rooms:** kitchen.
Cards: AE, DI, DS, MC, VI.
Motel

EUREKA INN
Phone: (707)442-6441
All Year   1P: $115- 260   2P/1B: $115- 260   2P/2B: $115- 260   XP: $10   F16
Location: E of US 101 N. 518 7th St 95501. Fax: 707/442-0637. **Terms:** Check-in 4 pm; small pets only, 1st floor rooms only. **Facility:** 105 rooms. Charming English Tudor design. Excellent facilities. 2 two-bedroom units. 1 whirlpool rm, extra charge; 4 stories; interior corridors; seasonal pool. **Dining:** Dining room, restaurant;
Historic Hotel
6:30 am-2 &5-10 pm; $5-$17; cocktails; also, The Rib Room, see separate listing. **All Rooms:** combo or shower baths. **Cards:** AE, DI, DS, MC, VI. **Special Amenities:** Free local telephone calls and free newspaper.
(See color ad below)

Respect Property—Public and Private.

EUREKA RAMADA LIMITED
Phone: (707)443-2206

(AAA) (SAVE)

◆◆
Motel

			1P:	$59-	79	2P/1B:	$69-	89	2P/2B:	$69-	89	XP:	$8	F16
6/1-9/30 [CP]														
2/1-5/31 & 10/1-1/31 [CP]			1P:	$49-	69	2P/1B:	$59-	79	2P/2B:	$59-	79	XP:	$8	F16

Location: On US 101 northbound. 270 5th St 95501. Fax: 707/443-2029. **Terms:** Small pets only, $6 extra charge. **Facility:** 40 rooms. Very attractive & comfortable rooms. 2 two-bedroom units. 1 efficiency, $6 extra. 1 kitchen apartment, $92-$110 for 2 persons; 3 stories; interior corridors; sauna, indoor whirlpool. **Cards:** AE, CB, DI, DS, JC, MC, VI. **Special Amenities:** Free breakfast and free local telephone calls.
(See color ad below & opposite title page)

(icons)

EUREKA SUPER 8 MOTEL
Phone: (707)443-3193

(AAA) (SAVE)

◆◆◆
Motel

| 6/1-9/15 [CP] | | | 1P: | $60- | 67 | 2P/1B: | $62- | 75 | 2P/2B: | $64- | 79 | XP: | $6 | D |
| 2/1-5/31 & 9/16-1/31 [CP] | | | 1P: | $40- | 45 | 2P/1B: | $43- | 49 | 2P/2B: | $45- | 50 | XP: | $6 | D |

Location: US 101 S, at N St. 1304 4th St 95501. **Terms:** Reserv deposit; handling fee imposed. **Facility:** 50 rooms. 1 two-bedroom unit. 2 room apartment, $110-$185 for up to 6 persons; 2 stories; interior/exterior corridors; small indoor pool, sauna, indoor whirlpool. **Dining:** Coffee shop nearby. **All Rooms:** combo or shower baths. **Some Rooms:** 2 efficiencies, no utensils. **Cards:** AE, CB, DI, DS, MC, VI. **Special Amenities:** Early check-in/late check-out and free local telephone calls. *(See color ad below)*

(icons)

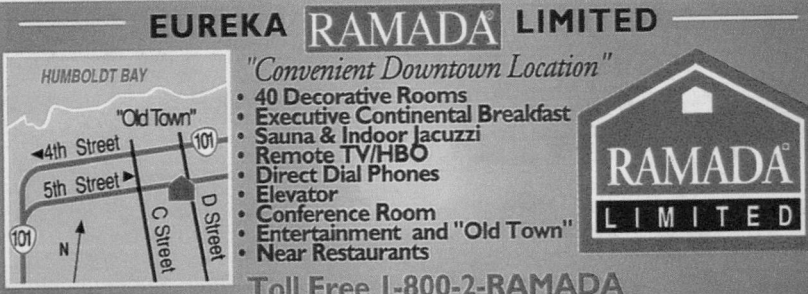

EUREKA TOWN HOUSE MOTEL

Phone: 707/443-4536

(AAA) [SAVE]

7/1-9/5	1P:	$42-	45	2P/1B:	$48-	50	2P/2B:	$50- 58	XP: $6	F12
5/14-6/30 & 9/6-9/30	1P:	$36-	42	2P/1B:	$39-	48	2P/2B:	$45- 54	XP: $6	F12
2/1-5/13 & 10/1-1/31	1P:	$32-	36	2P/1B:	$36-	38	2P/2B:	$39- 44	XP: $5	F12

◆ Motel
Location: US 101 southbound, corner 4th & K sts. 933 4th St 95501. Fax: 707/444-2099. **Terms:** Reserv deposit; weekly rates; small pets only, $5 extra charge. **Facility:** 20 rooms. Unusual design. Very well-kept. 1 three-bedroom unit, 3 two-bedroom units. 6 whirlpool rms, extra charge; 2 stories; exterior corridors. **All Rooms:** combo or shower baths. **Cards:** AE, CB, DI, DS, MC, VI. *(See ad p 444)*

HOLIDAY INN EXPRESS

Phone: (707)442-3261

(AAA) [SAVE]

5/14-9/2 [CP]	1P:	$65-	75	2P/1B:	$68-	85	2P/2B:	$68- 85	XP: $5
2/14-5/13 & 9/3-1/31 [CP]	1P:	$50-	65	2P/1B:	$55-	70	2P/2B:	$55- 70	XP: $5

◆◆◆ Motel
Location: Northbound exit US 101 w on V St, n on 3rd, southbound exit US 101 at X St. 2223 4th St 95501. Fax: 707/442-2317. **Facility:** 45 rooms. 7 whirlpool rms, extra charge; 2 stories; exterior corridors; heated indoor pool. **Dining:** Restaurant nearby. **All Rooms:** combo or shower baths. **Some Rooms:** 5 kitchens. **Cards:** AE, CB, DI, DS, MC, VI. **Special Amenities:** Free breakfast and free local telephone calls.

HOTEL CARTER

Phone: (707)444-8062

(AAA) [SAVE]

All Year [BP]	1P: $125- 500	2P/1B: $152- 500	2P/2B: $168- 285	XP: $25

◆◆◆ Bed & Breakfast
Location: Just w of US 101S. 301 L St 95501. Fax: 707/444-8067. **Terms:** Reserv deposit, 3 day notice; handling fee imposed; AP, EP avail. **Facility:** 23 rooms. 5 additional units available at Carter House, 3 at Bell Cottage & 1 at Honeymoon Cottage across street from hotel. 4 rooms with fireplace & whirlpool bath, $185- $275 for 2 persons; 3 stories; interior corridors; smoke free premises. **Dining:** Dining room; 6 pm-9 pm; $14-$26; cocktails; also, Carter House (Rest 301), see separate listing. **Services:** complimentary evening beverages. **Some Rooms:** whirlpools. **Cards:** AE, CB, DI, DS, JC, MC, VI. **Special Amenities:** Early check-in/late check-out and free room upgrade (subject to availability with advanced reservations). *(See color ad p 444)*

QUALITY INN

Phone: (707)443-1601

(AAA) [SAVE]

5/10-9/15	1P:	$75-	95	2P/1B:	$85-	125	2P/2B:	$95- 150	XP: $15	F13
2/1-5/9 & 9/16-1/31	1P:	$65-	85	2P/1B:	$75-	98	2P/2B:	$85- 115	XP: $15	F13

◆◆◆ Motel
Location: On US 101 southbound, between M & N sts; 1 blk from the Carson Mansion. 1209 4th St 95501. Fax: 707/444-8365. **Terms:** Reserv deposit; pets. **Facility:** 60 rooms. Spacious rooms. 4 two-bedroom units. 3 rooms in a 1911 American arts & crafts style house, $95-$150 for up to 2 persons; entire house with kitchen $250-$400 for 3-6 persons; 2 stories; exterior corridors; wading pool, indoor whirlpool & sauna. **Dining:** Coffee shop nearby. **Some Rooms:** Fee: whirlpools. **Cards:** AE, CB, DI, DS, JC, MC, VI. **Special Amenities:** Free breakfast and free local telephone calls. *(See color ad p 444)*

SUNRISE INN & SUITES

Phone: (707)443-9751

(AAA) [SAVE]

5/1-10/31	1P:	$49-	54	2P/1B:	$58-	63	2P/2B:	$64- 72	XP: $6	F6
2/1-4/30 & 11/1-1/31	1P:	$43-	48	2P/1B:	$51-	56	2P/2B:	$57- 63	XP: $6	F6

◆◆ Motel
Location: US 101 southbound at C St, northbound exit C St West. 129 4th St 95501. Fax: 707/443-9751. **Terms:** Reserv deposit; small pets only, $4 extra charge. **Facility:** 25 rooms. 5 two-bedroom units. 5 two-bedroom whirlpool units, $80-$120 for up to 4 persons; 2 stories; exterior corridors. **All Rooms:** combo or shower baths. **Some Rooms:** whirlpools. **Cards:** AE, CB, DI, DS, JC, MC, VI. **Special Amenities:** Early check-in/late check-out and free local telephone calls. *(See ad p 444)*

RESTAURANTS

CAFE MARINA
Lunch: $4-$10   **Dinner:** $10-$20   **Phone:** 707/443-2233
◆◆ American
Location: Exit US 101 at SR 255W, exit to Marina on Woodley Island. 601 Startare Dr 95501. **Hours:** 7 am-10 pm. Closed: 11/25 & 12/25. **Features:** casual dress; children's menu; early bird specials; senior's menu; cocktails & lounge. Specializing in fresh local seafood; casual atmosphere overlooking marina. Outside dining, weather permitting. **Cards:** AE, CB, DI, DS, MC, VI.

CARTER HOUSE (REST 301)

Dinner: $14-$38

Phone: 707/446-1390

△△△
◆ ◆
American

Location: Just w of US 101S; in Hotel Carter. 301 L St 95501. **Hours:** 6 pm-10 pm. **Reservations:** suggested. **Features:** No A/C; casual dress; cocktails; street parking. Weekly seasonal specials, fresh ingredients, unique & creative preparation. Smoke free premises. **Cards:** AE, CB, DI, MC, VI.

⊠

THE RIB ROOM

Dinner: $20-$35

Phone: 707/442-6441

◆ ◆ ◆
Continental

Location: In Eureka Inn. 518 Seventh St 95501. **Hours:** 5 pm-10 pm, Sat & Sun-11 pm. **Reservations:** suggested. **Features:** casual dress; cocktails & lounge; entertainment. English Tudor decor. Prime rib & fresh seafood in season. **Cards:** AE, CB, DI, MC, VI.

🔥 ⊠

SAMOA COOKHOUSE

Lunch: $8

Dinner: $12

Phone: 707/442-1659

△△△
◆
American

Location: US 101, SR 255 exit, w via Samoa Bridge. Samoa Rd 95501. **Hours:** 6 am-3:30 & 5-9 pm; to 10 pm, in summer. Closed: 12/25. **Features:** No A/C; casual dress. The west's last surviving lumber-camp cookhouse, built in 1885. Family-style dining. Display room has relics of bygone days. **Cards:** AE, CB, DI, DS, MC, VI.

THE SEA GRILL

Lunch: $5-$11

Dinner: $12-$20

Phone: 707/443-7187

◆ ◆
Seafood

Location: W off US 101. 316 E St 95501. **Hours:** 11 am-2 & 5-9:15 pm, Sat & Mon from 5 pm. Closed major holidaysSun & 11/1-11/14. **Reservations:** suggested. **Features:** No A/C; casual dress; children's menu; salad bar; cocktails & lounge; street parking. Varied menu, emphasis on seafood but steaks, prime rib featured. Comfortable attractive dining. Smoke free premises. **Cards:** DI, DS, MC, VI.

⊠

EXETER—7,300

LODGINGS

BEST WESTERN EXETER INN & SUITES

Phone: (559)592-8118

△△△ SAVE
[FYI]
Motel

All Year [CP]   1P: $49- 149   2P/1B: $49- 149   2P/2B: $49- 149
Too new to rate. **Location:** 0.5 mi s on SR 65. 805 S Kaweah Ave 93221. Fax: 559/592-5226. **Terms:** Check-in 4 pm. **Facility:** 32 rooms. Scheduled to open January, 1999; 2 stories; exterior corridors; whirlpool. **Some Rooms:** whirlpools. **Cards:** AE, CB, DI, DS, MC, VI. **Special Amenities:** Free breakfast and preferred room (subject to availability with advanced reservations).

KAWEAH MOTEL

Phone: (559)592-2961

△△△ SAVE
◆
Motel

All Year   1P: $39- 55   2P/1B: $42- 55   2P/2B: $48- 65 XP: $5
Location: SR 65, just se of downtown. 319 S Kaweah Ave 93221. Fax: 559/592-4393. **Terms:** Reserv deposit, 3 day notice. **Facility:** 19 rooms. 1 story; exterior corridors. **All Rooms:** shower baths. **Cards:** AE, DS, MC, VI.

FAIRFIELD—77,200

LODGINGS

BEST WESTERN CORDELIA INN

Rates Subject to Change

Phone: (707)864-2029

△△△
◆ ◆
Motel

All Year [CP]   1P: $60- 66   2P/1B: $66- 72   2P/2B: $74- 80 XP: $6   F18
Location: 3.5 mi w; exit I-80 Suisun Valley Rd, 1 blk s to Central Pl at Cordelia Village. 4373 Central Pl 94585. Fax: 707/864-5834. **Facility:** 60 rooms. Quiet location. 2 stories; exterior corridors; whirlpool. **Dining:** Coffee shop nearby. **Cards:** AE, CB, DI, DS, JC, MC, VI. *(See color ad below)*

HAMPTON INN

Phone: (707)864-1446

△△△ SAVE
◆ ◆ ◆
Motel

4/25-1/31 [CP]   1P: $69- 76   2P/1B: $79- 86   2P/2B: $79- 86
2/1-4/24 [CP]   1P: $65- 72   2P/1B: $75- 82   2P/2B: $75- 82
Location: Exit I-80 at Suisun Valley Rd; S. 4441 Central Pl 94585. Fax: 707/864-4288. **Facility:** 57 rooms. Modern design, attractive breakfast room. 3 whirlpool rms, extra charge; 3 stories; interior/exterior corridors; heated pool. **Dining:** Coffee shop nearby. **Cards:** AE, CB, DI, DS, MC, VI. **Special Amenities:** Free breakfast and free local telephone calls. *(See color ad p 447)*

HOLIDAY INN SELECT
◆◆◆
Motor Inn

Rates Subject to Change   **Phone:** 707/422-4111
1P: $70- 88 2P/1B: $78- 98 2P/2B: $78- 88 XP: $10
Location: I-80, Travis Blvd W exit, 0.3 mi s. 1350 Holiday Ln 94533. Fax: 707/428-3452. **Facility:** 142 rooms. 1 whirlpool rm, extra charge; 4 stories; interior corridors; heated pool. **Cards:** AE, DI, DS, JC, MC, VI.

FALLBROOK—22,100

LODGINGS

BEST WESTERN FRANCISCAN INN
(AAA) SAVE
◆◆
Motel

Phone: (760)728-6174
All Year [CP]   1P: $62- 72 2P/1B: $62- 72 2P/2B: $65- 75 XP: $5   F11
Location: 1 mi s on CR S-13. 1635 S Mission Rd 92028. Fax: 760/731-6404. **Terms:** Reserv deposit; small pets only, $5. **Facility:** 51 rooms. Some rooms with patio or balcony. 2 stories; exterior corridors; heated pool, whirlpool. **Dining:** Restaurant nearby. **Some Rooms:** 14 efficiencies. **Cards:** AE, DI, DS, MC, VI.

FALLBROOK COUNTRY INN
◆◆
Motel

Rates Subject to Change   **Phone:** (760)728-1114
All Year [CP]   1P: $70   2P/1B: $70- 80 2P/2B: $80   XP: $5
Location: 0.5 mi s on CR 5-13. 1425 S Mission Rd 92028. Fax: 760/731-6754. **Terms:** Reserv deposit. **Facility:** 28 rooms. Nicely landscaped grounds. Rooms decorated in a colorful country theme. 1 story; exterior corridors. **All Rooms:** combo or shower baths. **Cards:** AE, CB, DI, DS, MC, VI.

LA ESTANCIA INN
◆◆◆
Motel

Rates Subject to Change   **Phone:** 760/723-2888
All Year   1P: $49- 79 2P/1B: $49- 79 2P/2B: $49- 79 XP: $10   F12
Location: Adjacent to I-15, exit Pala Rd & SR 76, 0.3 mi n. 3135 S Old Hwy 395 92028. Fax: 760/723-2888. **Terms:** Reserv deposit. **Facility:** 40 rooms. Rooms decorated in a Southwest motif. 2 stories; interior/exterior corridors. **Some Rooms:** 6 efficiencies. **Cards:** AE, CB, DI, MC, VI.

PALA MESA RESORT
◆◆◆
Resort
Complex

Guaranteed Rates   **Phone:** 760/728-5881
All Year   1P: $110- 160 2P/1B: $110- 160 2P/2B: $110- 160
Location: Adjacent to I-15; 1.3 mi n of jct SR 76. 2001 Old Hwy 395 92028. Fax: 760/723-8292. **Terms:** Check-in 4 pm; reserv deposit. **Facility:** 133 rooms. Attractively landscaped grounds. Country Club atmosphere. Spacious rooms. Some with patio or balcony. 2 stories; exterior corridors; heated pool. Fee: 18 holes golf; 4 lighted tennis courts. **Recreation:** sports court. **All Rooms:** combo or shower baths. **Cards:** AE, DI, MC, VI.
(See color ad p 74)

RESTAURANTS

ALEXANDER'S
◆◆◆
American

Lunch: $8-$15   Dinner: $12-$25   **Phone:** 760/728-5881
Location: Adjacent to I-15; 1.3 mi n of jct SR 76, at Pala Mesa Resort. 2001 Old Hwy 395 92028. **Hours:** 6 am-2 & 5:30-10 pm. **Reservations:** suggested. **Features:** casual dress; Sunday brunch; children's menu; early bird specials; cocktails & lounge; a la carte. Attractive, formal, early California decor. Golf course view. Smoke free premises. **Cards:** AE, DI, MC, VI.

LE BISTRO RESTAURANT
◆
American

Lunch: $7-$12   Dinner: $11-$24   **Phone:** 760/723-3559
Location: Downtown. 119 N Main 92028. **Hours:** 11:30 am-2:30 & 5-9 pm; Sun 5-9 pm. Closed: 11/25, 12/25, 1/1 & Mon. **Features:** No A/C; casual dress; early bird specials; beer & wine only; street parking. Casual dining in a charming outdoor patio area & indoor dining rooms. More formal dining in upper level dining rooms. Features California & Continental cuisine. **Cards:** AE, DI, DS, MC, VI.

FALL RIVER MILLS—1,500

LODGINGS

HI-MONT MOTEL
(AAA) SAVE
◆
Motel

Phone: (530)336-5541
All Year   1P: $47- 62 2P/1B: $54- 69 2P/2B: $54- 70 XP: $8   F3
Location: 1 mi w on Hwy 299. 43021 Hwy 299 96028 (PO Box 353). Fax: 530/336-7051. **Terms:** Reserv deposit; pets; $10 extra charge. **Facility:** 21 rooms. Barbecue area with picnic tables. 3 RV sites, full hookups, $15; 2 stories; exterior corridors. **All Rooms:** combo or shower baths. **Some Rooms:** 2 kitchens. **Cards:** AE, CB, DI, DS, MC, VI.

LAVA CREEK LODGE
◆ All Year
Resort
Complex

Rates Subject to Change
1P: $95- 135   2P/1B: $95- 135   2P/2B: $95- 135   XP: $20
Phone: 530/336-6288

Location: 12 mi n of SR 299 via Glenburn Rd, e on Brown Rd & n on CR A19, bear right on Island Rd to gravel driveway. One Island Rd 96028. Fax: 530/336-1087. **Terms:** Reserv deposit, 21 day notice. **Facility:** 17 rooms. Secluded, rustic cabins & lodge rooms on wooded lakeside setting adjacent to Ahjumawi Lava Springs State Park. 2 three-bedroom units. Lower rates Mon-Thurs; 1 story; exterior corridors; boat dock, boat ramp. **Recreation:** fishing; hiking trails. Fee: boating, canoeing. **All Rooms:** shower baths. **Cards:** MC, VI.

🛏️ 🍴 ⊠ 📺 ⃠ 🅇 ⊠

FELTON—4,600—See also APTOS, CAPITOLA, SANTA CRUZ & SCOTTS VALLEY.

LODGING

FERN RIVER RESORT
〓 5/1-9/30
2/1-4/30 & 10/1-1/31
◆◆
Cottage

Rates Subject to Change
1P: $65- 97   2P/1B: $67- 99   XP: $7-9
1P: $48- 68   2P/1B: $50- 75   XP: $7-9
Phone: (831)335-4412

Location: 1 mi s on SR 9; across river from Henry Cowell State Park. 5250 Hwy 9 95018. Fax: 831/335-2418. **Terms:** Reserv deposit, 30 day notice; handling fee imposed; 10% service charge; weekly/monthly rates. **Facility:** 13 rooms. Rustic setting along San Lorenzo River. Single & duplex housekeeping cottages. Few fireplaces. 2 two-bedroom units. 1 story; exterior corridors; designated smoking area; playground. **Recreation:** swimming, fishing; volleyball, pingpong. **All Rooms:** shower baths. **Some Rooms:** 2 efficiencies, 10 kitchens, no utensils. **Cards:** AE, MC, VI.

⊠ ⃠ 🅇 🔒 ⊠

FERNDALE—1,300

LODGINGS

GINGERBREAD MANSION
〓 All Year [BP]
Historic Bed
& Breakfast

Guaranteed Rates
1P: $120- 330   2P/1B: $140- 350   2P/2B: $160   XP: $40
Phone: (707)786-4000

Location: Just e of Main St. 400 Berding St 95536. Fax: 707/786-4381. **Terms:** Reserv deposit, 7 day notice; handling fee imposed. **Facility:** 11 rooms. 1899 Victorian mansion in Queen Anne & Eastlake style. Formal English garden with sitting areas. Generous elegant rooms, Victorian bathing areas, some with fireplace, stain glass windows and clawfoot tubs. Empire suite, 2 fireplaces, 8 shower heads, wet bar refrigerator. Renaisance revival style 2 person $350; 3 stories, no elevator; interior corridors; smoke free premises. **Dining:** Full breakfast in formal dining room. Stuffed french toast, baked eggs Benedict are house specialty. Mansion's own coffee. High tea, variety of pastry. **All Rooms:** combo or shower baths. **Some Rooms:** B/W TV. **Cards:** AE, MC, VI.

🍴 📺 🅇 🔒 🔒

SHAW HOUSE BED & BREAKFAST INN
〓 All Year [BP]
◆◆◆
Historic Bed
& Breakfast

Guaranteed Rates
1P: $70- 140   2P/1B: $75- 145
Phone: (707)786-9958

Location: 703 Main St 95536 (PO Box 1125). Fax: 707/786-9958. **Terms:** Check-in 4 pm; reserv deposit, 7 day notice; handling fee imposed. **Facility:** 7 rooms. 1854 Carpenter Gothic; home of city founder. 1 acre of beautifully landscaped grounds. 2 stories; interior corridors; smoke free premises. **Dining:** Breakfast features dutch babies (puff pancake), quiche, filled croissants, homemade jams, jellies, & sauces. **Services:** giftshop. **All Rooms:** comb, shower or tub baths. **Cards:** AE, MC, VI.

📺 🅇

FILLMORE—12,000

LODGING

BEST WESTERN LA POSADA MOTEL
〓 All Year
◆◆
Motel

Rates Subject to Change
1P: $48- 58   2P/1B: $54- 64   2P/2B: $56- 70   XP: $6
Phone: (805)524-0440

Location: 0.5 mi w on SR 126. 827 Ventura St 93015. Fax: 805/524-1463. **Facility:** 49 rooms. 2 stories; exterior corridors; sauna, whirlpool. **Dining:** Restaurant nearby. **All Rooms:** combo or shower baths, extended cable TV. **Some Rooms:** 3 efficiencies. **Cards:** AE, DI, DS, MC, VI.

🔌 🛁⁺ 🏊 🆅🅲🆁 🖥️ 🔒 ⊠

FISH CAMP—100—See also YOSEMITE NATIONAL PARK.

LODGINGS

APPLE TREE INN
〓 SAVE   5/28-9/5 [BP]
9/6-12/31 [BP]
◆◆◆   3/1-5/27 [BP]
Cottage   2/1-2/28 & 1/1-1/31 [BP]

1P: $80- 180   2P/1B: $80- 180   2P/2B: $80- 180   XP: $5
1P: $70- 160   2P/1B: $70- 160   2P/2B: $70- 160   XP: $5
1P: $60- 140   2P/1B: $60- 140   2P/2B: $60- 140   XP: $5
1P: $50- 120   2P/1B: $50- 120   2P/2B: $50- 120   XP: $5
Phone: (559)683-5111

Location: 2 mi from South Gate to YNP. 1110 Hwy 41 93623 (PO Box 41). Fax: 559/642-6280. **Terms:** 2 night min stay, weekends, in summer. **Facility:** 54 rooms. 17 duplex & triplex, 1- & 2-story bldgs in forest setting. Most with fireplace, deck or porch. 16 two-bedroom units. 2 stories; exterior corridors; heated indoor pool, whirlpool; racquetball court, 1 indoor tennis court. **Dining:** Dining room; 7:30 am-10 & 5-9 pm; $9-$11. **Services:** giftshop. **Recreation:** cross country skiing; hiking trails. Fee: horseback riding. **All Rooms:** combo or shower baths. **Some Rooms:** efficiency, kitchen. **Cards:** AE, CB, DI, DS, MC, VI. (See ad p 1091)

🔒 🦽 🔌 🍴 ⛄ ⊠ 📺 🆅🅲🆁 🖥️ 🖥️ 🅇 🖨️ 🔒 🏋️ ⊠ 🏓

THE NARROW GAUGE INN
◆◆   4/1-10/31
Motor Inn

Rates Subject to Change
1P: $70- 195   2P/1B: $70- 195   2P/2B: $85- 95   XP: $5   F3
Phone: (559)683-7720

Location: 4 mi from South Gate to YNP. 48571 Hwy 41 93623. Fax: 559/683-2139. **Terms:** Open 4/1-10/31; reserv deposit, 4 day notice. **Facility:** 25 rooms. Picturesque mountain setting. All units with balcony or deck & forest view. 2 stories; exterior corridors; small pool. **Recreation:** hiking trails. **All Rooms:** combo or shower baths. **Cards:** AE, DS, MC, VI. (See color ad p 1088)

⛄ 🔌 🍴 ⊠ 📺 🆅🅲🆁 🖥️ ⊠

OWL'S NEST CABINS
〓 4/1-11/1
◆
Cottage

Rates Subject to Change
1P: $70- 95   2P/1B: $70- 95   2P/2B: $95   XP: $15
Phone: (559)683-3484

Location: 2 mi from Southgate to YNP. 1237 Hwy 41 93623. Fax: 559/683-3486. **Terms:** Open 4/1-11/1. **Facility:** 4 rooms. 3 two-level cottages & 1 room in owner's home. 2 stories; exterior corridors. **Dining:** Restaurant nearby. **Some Rooms:** 2 kitchens. **Cards:** MC, VI.

🛁⁺ 🆅🅲🆁 🖥️ 🖥️ ⃠ 🅇 🔒 ⊠

TENAYA LODGE AT YOSEMITE   Rates Subject to Change   **Phone:** (559)683-6555

6/21-9/6, 11/25-11/28 & 12/23-1/2 [BP]	1P: $229- 259	2P/1B: $229- 259	2P/2B: $229- 259	XP: $15-25 F17
3/28-6/20 & 9/7-11/24 [BP]	1P: $149- 219	2P/1B: $149- 219	2P/2B: $149- 219	XP: $15-25 F17
2/1-3/27, 11/29-12/22 & 1/3-1/31 [BP]	1P: $109- 169	2P/1B: $109- 169	2P/2B: $109- 169	XP: $15-25 F17

Resort Hotel

Location: 2 mi from south gate to YNP. 1122 Hwy 41 93623 (PO Box 159). Fax: 559/683-8684. **Terms:** Reserv deposit, 10 day notice; pets, $50 extra charge. **Facility:** 242 rooms. Landscaped grounds, surrounded by national forest. 3-4 stories; interior corridors; smoke free premises; heated indoor pool, saunas, steamrooms, whirlpools. **Dining:** Dining room, restaurant, coffee shop, deli; 7 am-11 pm; $14-$30; cocktails. **Services:** giftshop. Fee: massage. **Recreation:** cross country skiing; hiking trails. Fee: downhill skiing; bicycles, horseback riding. **Some Rooms:** whirlpools. **Cards:** AE, DI, DS, JC, MC, VI. *(See color ad p 1090)*

FOLSOM—29,800

LODGINGS

HILTON GARDEN INN   **Phone:** 916/353-1717

Under construction. **Location:** Exit US 50 at Folsom Blvd, 0.5 mi n to Iron Point Rd, 0.3 mi e. 221 Iron Point Rd 95630. **Facility:** 100 rooms. Scheduled to open spring, 1999; *(See ad p 119)*

LAKE NATOMA INN   Rates Subject to Change   **Phone:** (916)351-1500

Sun-Thurs [CP]	1P: $99	2P/1B: $99	2P/2B: $99	XP: $10 F18
Fri & Sat [CP]	1P: $89	2P/1B: $89	2P/2B: $89	XP: $10 F18

Hotel

Location: US 50 exit Folsom Blvd 3 mi n, behind The Lakes Specialty Shopping Center. 702 Gold Lake Dr 95630. Fax: 916/351-1511. **Facility:** 132 rooms. Rural setting. 4 stories; interior corridors; putting green; heated pool. **Services:** giftshop. Fee: massage. **Recreation:** Fee: bicycles. **Cards:** AE, CB, DI, DS, JC, MC, VI.

LARKSPUR LANDING   **Phone:** 916/355-1616

Under construction. **Location:** Exit US 50 at Folsom Blvd, 0.5 mi n to Iron Point Rd, 0.3 mi e. 121 Iron Point Rd 95630. **Facility:** 84 rooms. Scheduled to open spring, 1999;

FONTANA—87,500

LODGINGS

COMFORT INN   **Phone:** (909)822-3350

All Year [CP]   1P: $50- 55 2P/1B: $55- 60 2P/2B: $58- 65 XP: $4   F16

Location: Just nw of I-10, exit Sierra Ave. 16780 Valley Blvd 92335. Fax: 909/822-0337. **Terms:** Reserv deposit. **Facility:** 50 rooms. Across from shopping center. Comfortable, attractive rooms. 2 stories; exterior corridors. **Dining:** Restaurant nearby. **All Rooms:** combo or shower baths. **Cards:** AE, CB, DI, DS, MC, VI.

Motel

Special Amenities: Free breakfast and free newspaper.

ECONO LODGE   **Phone:** (909)822-5411

All Year   1P: $40- 45 2P/1B: $40- 45 2P/2B: $45- 50 XP: $4

Location: 0.4 mi ne of I-10, exit Sierra Ave. 17133 Valley Blvd 92335. Fax: 909/822-9174. **Facility:** 60 rooms. Across from Kaiser Medical Center. 2 stories; interior corridors; whirlpool. **Dining:** Restaurant nearby.

Motel

Cards: AE, CB, DI, DS, MC, VI.

FORT BRAGG—6,100

LODGINGS

BEACHCOMBER MOTEL   Rates Subject to Change   **Phone:** 707/964-2402

5/1-9/30	1P: $59	2P/1B: $59	2P/2B: $175	XP: $10 F12
2/1-4/30 & 10/1-1/31	1P: $45	2P/1B: $45	2P/2B: $95	XP: $10 F12

Motel

Location: 1 mi n on SR 1. 1111 N Main St 95437. Fax: 707/964-8925. **Terms:** Reserv deposit, 3 day notice; pets, $10. **Facility:** 27 rooms. Many rooms with oceanview. 3 two-bedroom units. 3 whirlpool rms, $195-$250; exterior corridors. **All Rooms:** combo or shower baths. **Some Rooms:** 5 kitchens.

BEACH HOUSE INN
[FYI]
Motel

5/16-11/15	1P: $79- 150	2P/1B: $79- 150	2P/2B: $125- 150	XP: $5-10	F12
2/1-5/15 & 11/16-1/31	1P: $59- 79	2P/1B: $59- 79	2P/2B: $79- 125	XP: $5-10	F12

Rates Subject to Change   **Phone:** (707)961-1700
Too new to rate. **Location:** 0.7 mi n on SR-1. 100 Pudding Creek Rd 95437. **Fax:** 707/961-1627. **Facility:** 30 rooms. Many units with private balconies. Spa & fireplace suites, $110-$175; 2 stories; interior corridors.
Cards: AE, CB, DI, DS, JC, MC, VI. *(See color ad p 449)*

BEST WESTERN VISTA MANOR LODGE
(AAA) [SAVE]
◆◆
Motel

5/1-10/31 [CP]	1P: $67- 95	2P/1B: $79- 110	2P/2B: $79- 110	XP: $5
2/1-4/30 & 11/1-1/31 [CP]	1P: $46- 80	2P/1B: $53- 90	2P/2B: $53- 90	XP: $5

Phone: (707)964-4776
Location: 1 mi n on SR 1. 1100 N Main St 95437. **Fax:** 707/964-4779. **Terms:** Reserv deposit, 3 day notice. **Facility:** 55 rooms. Many rooms with ocean view. 2 two-bedroom cottages, $110-$200 for up to 6 persons; 2 stories; exterior corridors; heated indoor pool. **All Rooms:** combo or shower baths. **Some Rooms:** 2 kitchens. **Cards:** AE, DI, DS, MC, VI. **Special Amenities:** Free breakfast.

CLEONE LODGE INN
◆◆
Cottage

All Year	1P: $78- 150	2P/1B: $78- 150	2P/2B: $86- 160	XP: $10-12

Rates Subject to Change   **Phone:** 707/964-2788
Location: 3 mi n on SR 1. 24600 N Hwy One 95437. **Terms:** Reserv deposit, 3 day notice; handling fee imposed. **Facility:** 12 rooms. Large picnic area with barbecue, easy access to beach. 4 two-bedroom units. 1 story; exterior corridors. **All Rooms:** combo or shower baths. **Some Rooms:** 4 kitchens. **Cards:** AE, DS, MC, VI.

THE GREY WHALE INN
(AAA) [SAVE]
◆◆◆
Bed & Breakfast

All Year [BP]	1P: $80- 160	2P/1B: $100- 180	2P/2B: $100- 180	XP: $25

Phone: (707)964-0640
Location: 0.5 mi n on SR 1. 615 N Main St 95437. **Fax:** 707/964-4408. **Terms:** Reserv deposit, 7 day notice; handling fee imposed; 2 night min stay, weekends. **Facility:** 14 rooms. Lounge with fireplace. TV room with VCP, game room with pool table, parlor with teas. Some rooms with private deck, fireplace & ocean view. 3 stories, no elevator; interior corridors; smoke free premises. **Dining:** Restaurant nearby. **All Rooms:** combo or shower baths. **Some Rooms:** 3 kitchens, whirlpools. **Cards:** AE, DS, JC, MC, VI. **Special Amenities:** Free room upgrade and preferred room (each subject to availability with advanced reservations). *(See ad p 664)*

[SAVE]   Take advantage of member discounts.
When you see this icon, you'll save money!

HARBOR LITE LODGE

AAA
◆◆
Motel

Phone: 707/964-0221

Rates Subject to Change

	1P:		2P/1B:		2P/2B:		XP:		
6/11-9/18	1P:	$64- 86	2P/1B:	$64- 86	2P/2B:	$68- 78	XP:	$6	F3
4/30-6/10 & 9/19-10/30	1P:	$61- 79	2P/1B:	$61- 79	2P/2B:	$65- 72	XP:	$6	F3
Fri & Sat 2/1-4/29 & 10/31-1/31	1P:	$61- 79	2P/1B:	$61- 79	2P/2B:	$65- 72	XP:	$6	F3
Sun-Thurs 2/1-4/29 & 10/31-1/31	1P:	$45- 70	2P/1B:	$45- 70	2P/2B:	$45- 55	XP:	$6	F3

Location: 0.5 mi s at n end of Noyo Bridge, off SR 1. 120 N Harbor Dr 95437. **Terms:** Reserv deposit. **Facility:** 79 rooms. Many balconies with view of Noyo Harbor & fishing fleet. 1 two-bedroom unit. 6 units with woodburning fireplace, $96-$106 for up to 2 persons; 2 stories; exterior corridors; sauna. **Cards:** AE, CB, DI, DS, MC, VI. *(See color ad p 450)*

THE LODGE AT NOYO RIVER

AAA SAVE
◆◆◆
Bed &
Breakfast

Phone: (707)964-8045

	2P/1B:	$105- 160	2P/2B:	$105- 149	XP:	$15	F6
All Year [BP]							

Location: 3 blks e of SR 1 via Harbor Dr. 500 Casa del Noyo Dr 95437. Fax: 707/964-9366. **Terms:** Reserv deposit, 3 day notice; 2 night min stay, weekends. **Facility:** 16 rooms. Some units overlooking river & fishing fleet. Some fireplaces & balconies. 2 stories; interior/exterior corridors. **All Rooms:** combo or shower baths. **Some Rooms:** color TV. **Cards:** AE, MC, VI. **Special Amenities:** Free breakfast and free local telephone calls.

NORTH CLIFF HOTEL

FYI
Motor Inn

Phone: 707/962-2500

Rates Subject to Change

	1P:		2P/1B:		2P/2B:	
Fri & Sat	1P:	$175- 225	2P/1B:	$175- 225	2P/2B:	$175- 225
Sun-Thurs	1P:	$135- 175	2P/1B:	$135- 175	2P/2B:	$135- 175

Too new to rate. **Location:** N end of Noyo River Bridge. 1005 S Main St 95437. Fax: 707/962-2572. **Terms:** Reserv deposit. **Facility:** 39 rooms. Many units with harbor & ocean view. 3 stories; exterior corridors. **Cards:** AE, CB, DI, DS, MC, VI.

OCEAN BREEZE LODGE

AAA
◆◆
Motel

Phone: 707/961-1177

Guaranteed Rates

	1P:		2P/1B:		2P/2B:		XP:	
6/1-9/15	1P:	$79	2P/1B:	$79	2P/2B:	$85	XP:	$10
2/1-5/31 & 9/16-1/31	1P:	$59	2P/1B:	$59	2P/2B:	$85	XP:	$10

Location: Center. 212 S Main St 95437. **Terms:** Reserv deposit, 3 day notice. **Facility:** 10 rooms. 2 stories; interior/exterior corridors. **Dining:** Restaurant nearby. **All Rooms:** combo or shower baths. **Some Rooms:** 2 kitchens. **Cards:** MC, VI.

OLD STEWART HOUSE INN

◆◆
Bed &
Breakfast

Phone: (707)961-0775

Guaranteed Rates

	1P:		2P/1B:		2P/2B:		XP:	
All Year [BP]	1P:	$75- 100	2P/1B:	$85- 110	2P/2B:	$85- 110	XP:	$15	F12

Location: Just w of SR-1 via Pine St. 511 Stewart St 95437. Fax: 707/962-0559. **Terms:** Reserv deposit, 3 day notice; handling fee imposed. **Facility:** 5 rooms. 2 stories; interior/exterior corridors. **All Rooms:** combo or shower baths. **Cards:** MC, VI.

PINE BEACH INN & SUITES

AAA SAVE
◆◆
Motor Inn

Phone: (707)964-5603

	1P:		2P/1B:		2P/2B:	
5/28-9/30	1P:	$85- 125	2P/1B:	$85- 125	2P/2B:	$85- 125
3/26-5/27 & 10/1-10/31	1P:	$75- 105	2P/1B:	$75- 105	2P/2B:	$75- 105
2/1-3/25 & 11/1-1/31	1P:	$65- 95	2P/1B:	$65- 95	2P/2B:	$65- 95

Location: 4 mi s on SR 1. 16801 N Hwy #1 95437 (PO Box 1173). Fax: 707/964-4237. **Facility:** 50 rooms. Spacious grounds. Some units with ocean view. 9 suites, $100-$160 for up to 6 persons; 1-2 stories; exterior corridors; beach; 2 tennis courts. **Dining:** Restaurant; 7 am-10:30 & 5:30-9 pm, Sun 8 am-1 pm, 4/1-10/28; $11-$18; cocktails. **Recreation:** fishing. **All Rooms:** combo or shower baths. **Cards:** AE, MC, VI. **Special Amenities:** Free local telephone calls and preferred room (subject to availability with advanced reservations). IMA. *(See color ad below)*

SEABIRD LODGE

AAA SAVE
◆◆
Motel

Phone: (707)964-4731

	1P:		2P/1B:		2P/2B:		XP:		
5/28-9/30	1P:	$75- 90	2P/1B:	$88- 98	2P/2B:	$92- 98	XP:	$6	F12
3/26-5/27 & 10/1-10/31	1P:	$70- 80	2P/1B:	$75- 88	2P/2B:	$78- 88	XP:	$6	F12
2/1-3/25 & 11/1-1/31	1P:	$60- 70	2P/1B:	$65- 78	2P/2B:	$68- 78	XP:	$6	F12

Location: 0.8 mi n of Noyo Bridge; 1 blk e off SR 1. 191 South St 95437. Fax: 707/961-1779. **Facility:** 65 rooms. 3 kitchens, $15 extra charge; 2 stories; exterior corridors; heated indoor pool, whirlpool. **Dining:** Restaurant nearby. **Cards:** AE, MC, VI. **Special Amenities:** Free local telephone calls and preferred room (subject to availability with advanced reservations). IMA. *(See color ad p 452 & p 286)*

SURF MOTEL
Phone: (707)964-5361

Rates Subject to Change

		1P:		2P/1B:			2P/2B:		XP:		
5/21-10/24		$62-	82		$66-	84		$73-	90	$6	F6
2/1-4/1 & 11/29-1/31		$42-	70		$47-	70		$51-	75	$6	F6
4/2-5/20 & 10/25-11/28		$48-	66		$56-	70		$63-	74	$6	F6

Location: 1 mi s on SR 1; s of Noyo River Bridge; 0.3 mi n of jct SR 20. 1220 S Main St 95437 (PO Box 488). Fax: 707/964-3187. **Facility:** 54 rooms. Spacious landscaped grounds. 2 apartment units $125 for up to 6 persons; 1 story; exterior corridors. **Recreation:** fish cleaning facilities; barbecue & picnic area. **All Rooms:** combo or shower baths. **Cards:** AE, CB, DI, DS, MC, VI.

Motel

SURF 'N SAND LODGE
Phone: (707)964-9383

Rates Subject to Change

		1P:		2P/1B:		2P/2B:		XP:	
All Year		$69-	125		$98- 175		$98- 150		$10

Location: 1 mi n on SR 1. 1131 N Main St 95437. Fax: 707/964-0314. **Terms:** Reserv deposit, 3 day notice. **Facility:** 30 rooms. Many rooms with balconies overlooking the ocean. Junior suite, $98-$150 for up to 2 persons. Spa & fireplace suite, $125-$150 for up to 2 persons; 2 stories; interior corridors. **Some Rooms:** whirlpools. **Cards:** AE, CB, DI, DS, JC, MC, VI. *(See color ad p 452)*

Motel

SURREY INN
Phone: 707/964-4003

Rates Subject to Change

		1P:		2P/1B:			2P/2B:		XP:		
5/1-10/31		$52-	57		$59-	64		$64-	69	$5	F5
2/1-4/30 & 11/1-1/31		$35-	40		$38-	43		$43-	48	$5	F5

Location: 0.5 mi s; n end of Noyo Bridge on SR 1. 888 S Main St 95437. Fax: 707/964-4076. **Terms:** Reserv deposit. **Facility:** 53 rooms. Some rooms with ocean view. 2 stories; exterior corridors. **Dining:** Coffee shop nearby. **Cards:** AE, DS, MC, VI.

Motel

TRADEWINDS LODGE
Phone: (707)964-4761

		1P:		2P/1B:			2P/2B:		XP:		
5/1-9/30		$65-	75		$69-	79		$79-	89	$8-10	F12
2/1-4/30 & 10/1-10/31		$54-	64		$59-	69		$69-	79	$8-10	F12
11/1-1/31		$45-	55		$49-	59		$59-	69	$8-10	F12

Location: 6 blks s on SR 1. 400 S Main St 95437. Fax: 707/964-0372. **Facility:** 92 rooms. Many large rooms. 9 two-bedroom units. 7 units, $85-$120 for up to 6 persons; 2 stories; exterior corridors; heated indoor pool, whirlpool. **Dining:** Restaurant; 4:30 am-midnight; $7-$15; cocktails. **Services:** area transportation, Ft Bragg Skunk Depot. **All Rooms:** combo or shower baths. **Cards:** AE, CB, DI, DS, MC, VI. **Special Amenities:** Early check-in/late check-out and free local telephone calls. *(See color ad p 452)*

Motor Inn

RESTAURANTS

CLIFF HOUSE
Dinner: $11-$19
Phone: 707/961-0255

Location: 8 blks s on SR 1; at s end of Noyo Bridge. 1011 S Main St 95437. **Hours:** 4 pm-9 pm, Sat til 10 pm. Closed: 12/24 & 12/25. **Reservations:** suggested. **Features:** casual dress; children's menu; early bird specials; cocktails & lounge. Overlooking ocean & Noyo River entrance from four dining levels. **Cards:** AE, DS, MC, VI.

American

OLD COAST HOTEL
Lunch: $5-$10
Dinner: $8-$19
Phone: 707/961-4488

Location: 1.5 mi n of jct Hwy 1 & SR 20; just e on Oak. 101 N Franklin 95437. **Hours:** 11:30 am-10 pm. **Reservations:** required. **Features:** No A/C; casual dress; Sunday brunch; children's menu; cocktails; a la carte. Innovative menus. Smoke free premises. **Cards:** AE, MC, VI.

American

THE RESTAURANT
Lunch: $7-$9
Dinner: $11-$19
Phone: 707/964-9800

Location: 2 blks n on SR 1. 418 N Main St 95437. **Hours:** 5 pm-9 pm, Thurs & Fri 11:30 am-2 & 5-9 pm, Sun 9 am-1 & 5-9 pm. Closed: Wed, 11/28, 12/25. **Reservations:** suggested. **Features:** No A/C; casual dress; Sunday brunch; children's menu; beer & wine only; a la carte. California cuisine. Family owned & operated since 1973. Smoke free premises. **Cards:** MC, VI.

Continental

FORTUNA—8,800

LODGINGS

BEST WESTERN COUNTRY INN
Phone: (707)725-6822

		1P:		2P/1B:			2P/2B:			XP:		
5/1-9/30 [CP]		$73-	93		$78-	98		$78-	98	$5	F12
2/1-4/30 [CP]		$53-	73		$58-	78		$58-	78	$5	F12
10/1-1/31 [EP]		$53-	73		$58-	78		$58-	78	$5	F12

Location: W of US 101, exit Kenmar Rd. 2025 Riverwalk Dr 95540. Fax: 707/725-5270. **Terms:** Small pets only. **Facility:** 66 rooms. Attractive, comfortable rooms. 2 two-bedroom units. Family units, $30 extra charge. 8 whirlpool rms, extra charge; 2 stories; exterior corridors; heated indoor/outdoor pool, indoor whirlpool. **Dining:** Restaurants nearby. **All Rooms:** combo or shower baths. **Cards:** AE, CB, DI, DS, JC, MC, VI. **Special Amenities:** Free breakfast and free local telephone calls.

Motel

FORTUNA SUPER 8
Phone: 707/725-2888

		1P:		2P/1B:			2P/2B:		XP:	
7/1-9/6 [CP]		$49-	55		$58-	70		$60-	75	$6
5/1-6/30 & 9/7-9/30 [CP]		$45-	50		$49-	65		$55-	65	$6
2/1-4/30 & 10/1-1/31 [CP]		$42-	45		$45-	50		$48-	55	$6

Location: w of US 101 exit Kenmar Rd. 1805 Alamar Way 95540. Fax: 707/725-2888. **Terms:** Pets, $5 extra charge, $20 dep req. **Facility:** 47 rooms. Nicely decorated, comfortable rooms. 4 whirlpool rms, extra charge; 2 stories; exterior corridors. **Dining:** Restaurant nearby. **All Rooms:** combo or shower baths. **Cards:** AE, CB, DI, DS, MC, VI.

Motel

HOLIDAY INN EXPRESS
Phone: (707)725-5500

		1P:		2P/1B:			2P/2B:		XP:		
6/15-9/14 [CP]		$65-	85		$65-	85		$65-	85	$10	F18
5/1-6/14 & 9/15-9/30 [CP]		$45-	69		$45-	69		$49-	69	$10	F18
2/1-4/30 & 10/1-1/31 [CP]		$45-	59		$45-	59		$45-	59	$10	F18

Location: W of US 101, exit Kenmar Rd. 1859 Alamar Way 95540. Fax: 707/725-2379. **Terms:** Pets, $25 dep req. **Facility:** 46 rooms. Off hwy. Nicely decorated rooms. 2 whirlpool rms, extra charge; 2 stories; exterior corridors; heated indoor pool. **Dining:** Restaurant nearby. **Cards:** AE, CB, DI, DS, MC, VI.

Motel

FOSTER CITY—See San Francisco p. 968.

FOUNTAIN VALLEY—53,700   (See map p. 294; index p. 292)

LODGINGS

COURTYARD BY MARRIOTT   Rates Subject to Change   **Phone:** 714/968-5775   [212]
◆◆◆   All Year   1P: $86   2P/1B: $86   2P/2B: $86
Motor Inn   **Location:** Just n of I-405, exit Brookhurst St. 9950 Slater Ave 92708. Fax: 714/968-0112. **Facility:** 150 rooms.
3 stories; interior corridors; heated pool. **Cards:** AE, CB, DI, DS, MC, VI. *(See color ad p 311)*

RAMADA LIMITED-HUNTINGTON BEACH/FOUNTAIN VALLEY   **Phone:** (714)847-3388   [211]
(AAA) [SAVE]   6/15-9/15 [EP]   1P: $74- 79   2P/1B: $79   2P/2B: $79   XP: $5   F17
◆◆   2/1-6/14 & 9/16-1/31 [CP]   1P: $59   2P/1B: $59   2P/2B: $64   XP: $10   F17
Motel   **Location:** Adj to I-405; northbound exit Warner Ave W, southbound exit Magnolia just e. 9125 Recreation Cir
92708. Fax: 714/842-4192. **Terms:** Small pets only, $25 dep req, $10 extra charge. **Facility:** 68 rooms. Located adjacent to Family Fun Center. 3 two-bedroom units. Rooms with whirlpool $69-$99. Efficiency units $59-
$69; 3 stories; exterior corridors; whirlpool. **Some Rooms:** 10 efficiencies, whirlpools. **Cards:** AE, CB, DI, DS, JC, MC, VI.
(See color ad opposite title page)

RESIDENCE INN BY MARRIOTT   Rates Subject to Change   **Phone:** 714/965-8000   [213]
◆◆◆   Mon-Thurs 5/25-9/27   1P: $124   2P/1B: $124   2P/2B: $124
Apartment   Mon-Thurs 2/1-5/24, Fri-Sun
Motel   5/25-9/27 & Mon-Thurs
9/28-1/31   1P: $114   2P/1B: $114   2P/2B: $114
Fri-Sun 9/28-1/31   1P: $89   2P/1B: $89   2P/2B: $89
Fri-Sun 2/1-5/24   1P: $79   2P/1B: $79   2P/2B: $79   XP: $10
Location: Just n of I-405, exit Brookhurst St. 9930 Slater Ave 92708. Fax: 714/962-3439. **Facility:** 122 rooms. Studio, 1- &
2-bedroom apartments. Some with fireplace. 2 stories; exterior corridors; heated pool. **Recreation:** sports court. **Cards:** AE,
CB, DI, DS, JC, MC, VI.

RESTAURANT

MIMI'S CAFE   **Lunch:** $7-$13   **Dinner:** $7-$13   **Phone:** 714/964-2533   [81]
◆◆   **Location:** Corner of Ellis. 18461 Brookhurst St 92708. **Hours:** 7 am-11 pm. Closed: 12/25. **Features:** casual
American   dress; children's menu; carryout; beer & wine only. French country decor. Varied selection of fish, beef,
chicken, sandwiches & salads. Patio dining avail. **Cards:** AE, MC, VI.

FREMONT—173,300

LODGINGS

BEST WESTERN GARDEN COURT INN   **Phone:** (510)792-4300
(AAA) [SAVE]   All Year [CP]   1P: $85- 129   2P/1B: $85- 129   2P/2B: $85- 129   XP: $10   F12
◆◆◆   **Location:** Exit I-880 Mowry Ave E. 5400 Mowry Ave 94538. Fax: 510/792-2643. **Terms:** Pets, $50, $25
Motel   non-refundable dep req. **Facility:** 125 rooms. Spacious, landscaped grounds. 2 stories; interior corridors;
sauna, whirlpool. **Dining:** Restaurant nearby. **Cards:** AE, DI, DS, MC, VI. **Special Amenities:** Free
breakfast and free local telephone calls.

COURTYARD BY MARRIOTT   Rates Subject to Change   **Phone:** 510/656-1800
◆◆◆   Mon-Thurs   1P: $169   2P/1B: $169   2P/2B: $169
Motor Inn   Fri-Sun   1P: $74   2P/1B: $74   2P/2B: $74
Location: W of & adjacent to I-880; northbound exit Gateway Blvd, southbound exit Warren Ave. 47000
Lakeview Blvd 94538. Fax: 510/656-2441. **Facility:** 146 rooms. Attractive courtyard setting. In-room coffee. 3 stories; interior
corridors; indoor pool. **Recreation:** jogging. **Cards:** AE, DI, DS, MC, VI.

FREMONT ECONO LODGE   Rates Subject to Change   **Phone:** 510/656-2800
◆◆   All Year   1P: $75   2P/1B: $85   2P/2B: $95   XP: $20
Motel   **Location:** I-680 exit e at Warren Ave - Mission Blvd, 0.5 mi n. 46101 Warm Springs Blvd 94539.
Fax: 510/659-0352. **Facility:** 49 rooms. 3 stories; interior corridors. **All Rooms:** combo or shower baths.
Cards: AE, DI, DS, MC, VI.

RESIDENCE INN BY MARRIOTT   Rates Subject to Change   **Phone:** 510/794-5900
◆◆◆   All Year [CP]   1P: $159   2P/1B: $159   2P/2B: $179
Suite Motel   **Location:** E of I-880, exit Mowry Ave. 5400 Farwell Pl 94536. Fax: 510/793-6587. **Facility:** 80 rooms. Attrac-
tively appointed rooms, some with fireplace. 20 two-bedroom units. 2 stories; exterior corridors.
Services: area transportation. **Recreation:** sports court. **All Rooms:** kitchens. **Cards:** AE, CB, DI, DS, JC, MC, VI.

RESTAURANT

FREMONT MARKET BROILER   **Lunch:** $5-$12   **Dinner:** $8-$25   **Phone:** 510/791-8675
◆   **Location:** Exit I-990 Mowry E, 0.3 mi s. 39195 Farwell Dr 94538. **Hours:** 11 am-10 pm, Fri & Sat-11 pm.
Steak and   Closed: 11/25 & 12/25. **Features:** casual dress; children's menu; carryout; cocktails. Mesquite grilled
Seafood   seafood, fresh pasta & steak. Take-out fish market. Smoke free premises. **Cards:** AE, DS, MC, VI.

FRESNO—354,200

LODGINGS

BEST WESTERN GARDEN COURT INN   Phone: (559)237-1881
All Year [BP]   1P: $52- 58   2P/1B: $56- 64   2P/2B: $58- 68   XP: $5   F12
Location: Just w of SR 99, Clinton Ave exit. 2141 N Parkway Dr 93705. Fax: 559/237-9719.
Terms: Handling fee imposed; pets, $5 extra charge. **Facility:** 106 rooms. Spacious landscaped courtyard.
Garden view rooms. 2 stories; exterior corridors; whirlpool. **Dining:** Restaurant; 6:30 am-10 & 5-9 pm;
$10-$18; cocktails. **All Rooms:** combo or shower baths. **Cards:** AE, CB, DI, DS, JC, MC, VI.
Special Amenities: Free breakfast and free local telephone calls. *(See color ad p 456)*

BEST WESTERN PARKSIDE INN   Rates Subject to Change   Phone: 559-237-2086
All Year   1P: $50- 54   2P/1B: $54- 60   2P/2B: $56- 62   XP: $4   F12
Location: Just e of SR 99, Olive Ave exit. 1415 W Olive Ave 93728. Fax: 559/264-9304. **Facility:** 48 rooms.
3 whirlpool rms, extra charge; 2 stories; exterior corridors. **Cards:** AE, DI, DS, JC, MC, VI. *(See ad p 456)*

BEST WESTERN VILLAGE INN   Phone: 559/226-2110
All Year [CP]   1P: $50- 56   2P/1B: $56- 62   2P/2B: $58- 64   XP: $4   F12
Location: 0.3 mi w of SR 41, Shields Ave exit. 3110 N Blackstone Ave 93703. Fax: 559/226-0539.
Facility: 153 rooms. Some small rooms. 2 stories; interior corridors; whirlpool. **Dining:** Coffee shop nearby.
Cards: AE, CB, DI, DS, MC, VI. **Special Amenities:** Free breakfast and free local telephone calls.

BEST WESTERN WATER TREE INN   Phone: 559/222-4445
All Year [CP]   1P: $59- 69   2P/1B: $59- 69   2P/2B: $59- 69   XP: $4   F12
Location: 0.3 mi w of SR 41, Ashlan Ave exit. 4141 N Blackstone Ave 93726. Fax: 559/226-4589.
Facility: 136 rooms. 2 stories; interior corridors. **Dining:** Restaurant nearby. **Recreation:** discount at
adjacent gym. **Cards:** AE, CB, DI, DS, JC, MC, VI. **Special Amenities:** Free breakfast and free local
telephone calls.

CHATEAU INN BY PICCADILLY INN HOTELS   Rates Subject to Change   Phone: 559/456-1418
All Year   1P: $58- 71   2P/1B: $64- 77   2P/2B: $64- 77   XP: $6-12   F17
Location: 4 mi e of SR 41, McKinley Ave exit. 5113 E McKinley 93727. Fax: 559/456-4643. **Facility:** 78 rooms.
2 stories; interior corridors. **Dining:** Coffee shop nearby. **All Rooms:** combo or shower baths. **Cards:** AE,
CB, DI, DS, JC, MC, VI.

COMFORT SUITES   Phone: (559)435-5650
All Year [CP]   1P: $59- 109   2P/1B: $59- 109   2P/2B: $79- 119   XP: $7   F18
Location: W of SR 41; Herndon exit. 102 E Herndon Ave 93720. Fax: 559/435-0175. **Facility:** 70 rooms.
3 stories; interior corridors; heated indoor pool, whirlpool. **All Rooms:** combo or shower baths.
Some Rooms: whirlpools. **Cards:** AE, CB, DI, DS, JC, MC, VI. **Special Amenities:** Free breakfast and
free local telephone calls.

COURTYARD BY MARRIOTT-AIRPORT
◆◆◆   Sun-Thurs   1P: $79   2P/1B: $89   2P/2B: $89   Phone: 559/251-5200
Motel   Fri & Sat   1P: $69   2P/1B: $69   2P/2B: $69   XP: $10   F12

Rates Subject to Change   XP: $10   F12

Location: 4 mi e of SR 41, McKinley Ave exit. 1551 N Peach Ave 93727. Fax: 559/454-0552. **Facility:** 116 rooms. 4 stories; interior corridors. **Cards:** AE, DI, DS, MC, VI.

COURTYARD BY MARRIOTT-SHAW
◆◆◆   Sun-Thurs   1P: $89   2P/1B: $89   2P/2B: $89   Phone: 559/221-6000
Motor Inn   Fri & Sat   1P: $74   2P/1B: $74   2P/2B: $79

Guaranteed Rates

Location: Just w of SR 41, Shaw Ave exit. 140 E Shaw Ave 93710. Fax: 559/221-0368. **Terms:** Check-in 4 pm. **Facility:** 146 rooms. Nicely landscaped grounds. Maximum rates for up to 4 persons; 3 stories; interior corridors. **Cards:** AE, DI, DS, MC, VI.

DAYS INN-BLACKSTONE
Ⓐ   6/1-8/31 [CP]   1P: $45- 47   2P/1B: $51- 53   2P/2B: $51- 53   XP: $6   F16
   2/1-5/31 & 9/1-1/31 [CP]   1P: $45   2P/1B: $45   2P/2B: $47   XP: $6   F16
◆◆   **Location:** 0.5 mi w of SR 41, Ashland Ave exit. 4061 N Blackstone Ave 93726. Fax: 559/225-0144.
Motel   **Facility:** 111 rooms. 2 stories; interior/exterior corridors; whirlpool. **Dining:** Coffee shop nearby. **Cards:** AE, DS, MC, VI.

Rates Subject to Change   Phone: 559/222-5641

DAYS INN-PARKWAY
Ⓐ SAVE   5/15-9/15   1P: $36- 64   2P/1B: $36- 64   2P/2B: $48- 64   XP: $5
   2/1-5/14 & 9/16-1/31   1P: $36   2P/1B: $36   2P/2B: $42   XP: $5
◆◆   **Location:** W of SR 99, Olive St exit. 1101 N Parkway Dr 93728. Fax: 559/268-6211. **Terms:** CP avail; pets,
Motel $5 extra charge. **Facility:** 98 rooms. Spacious grounds. 2 two-bedroom units. 2 stories; exterior corridors; playground. **Dining:** Coffee shop nearby. **All Rooms:** combo or shower baths. **Cards:** AE, CB, DI, DS, MC, VI.
Special Amenities: Free breakfast and free local telephone calls.

Phone: (559)268-6211

DOUBLETREE HOTEL
◆◆◆
Hotel
Rates Subject to Change
All Year   1P: $79- 119   2P/1B: $79- 119   2P/2B: $79- 119   XP: $10   F18
Phone: 559/485-9000
Location: 0.5 mi e of SR 99; Ventura St exit. 1055 Van Ness Ave 93721. Fax: 559/485-3210. **Facility:** 193 rooms. 9 stories; interior corridors. **Cards:** AE, CB, DI, DS, MC, VI.

FAIRFIELD INN BY MARRIOTT
◆◆
Motel
Rates Subject to Change
All Year [CP]   1P: $65- 99   2P/1B: $65- 99   2P/2B: $65- 99
Phone: (559)435-5838
Location: Just e of SR 41, Bullard Ave exit. 6065 N Thesta Ave 93710. Fax: 559/435-6439. **Facility:** 62 rooms. Rates for up to 4 persons; 3 stories; interior/exterior corridors; indoor pool. **All Rooms:** combo or shower baths. **Cards:** AE, CB, DI, DS, JC, MC, VI. *(See color ad below)*

FOUR POINTS HOTEL BY ITT SHERATON
(AAA) (SAVE)
◆◆◆◆
Motor Inn
Sun-Thurs   1P: $72- 107   2P/1B: $72- 112   2P/2B: $72- 112   XP: $5   F18
Fri & Sat   1P: $69- 107   2P/1B: $69- 112   2P/2B: $69- 112   XP: $5   F18
Phone: (559)226-2200
Location: 0.3 mi w of SR 41, Shields Ave exit. 3737 N Blackstone Ave 93726. Fax: 559/222-7147. **Terms:** Package plans. **Facility:** 204 rooms. Nicely landscaped grounds. Some patios. 2 stories; interior corridors; whirlpool. **Dining:** Restaurant; 6:30-10:30 am, 11-3 & 5-10 pm, Sun-9 pm; $10-$18; cocktails. **Cards:** AE, CB, DI, DS, JC, MC, VI. **Special Amenities:** Early check-in/late check-out and free newspaper.
(See color ad below)

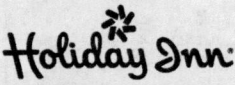

HOLIDAY INN-AIRPORT
◆◆◆
Motor Inn

		Rates Subject to Change					Phone: (559)252-3611
Mon-Thurs	1P: $72	2P/1B: $82	2P/2B: $82	XP: $10	F19
Fri-Sun	1P: $67	2P/1B: $67	2P/2B: $67	XP: $10	F19

Location: 4 mi e of SR 41, McKinley Ave exit. 5090 E Clinton Ave 93727. Fax: 559/456-8243. **Facility:** 210 rooms. Some rooms facing Holidome recreation area. 2 stories; interior corridors; heated indoor pool. **All Rooms:** combo or shower baths. **Cards:** AE, CB, DI, DS, JC, MC, VI. (See ad p 457)

🔲🔲🔲🔲🔲🔲🔲🔲🔲🔲🔲🔲🔲🔲🔲

HOLIDAY INN CENTRE PLAZA
◆◆◆
Hotel

| | | Rates Subject to Change | | | | Phone: (559)268-1000 |
| All Year | 1P: $99- 120 | 2P/1B: $109- 130 | 2P/2B: $109- 130 | XP: $10 | F17 |

Location: E of SR 99, Ventura St exit; adjacent to Convention Center. 2233 Ventura St 93709. Fax: 559/486-6625. **Terms:** Reserv deposit. **Facility:** 320 rooms. All units open to atrium. 9 stories; interior corridors; indoor/outdoor pool. **Services:** giftshop. **Cards:** AE, CB, DI, DS, JC, MC, VI.

🔲🔲🔲🔲🔲🔲🔲🔲🔲🔲🔲🔲🔲🔲🔲🔲

HOLIDAY INN EXPRESS-BARCUS
◆◆
Motel

| | | Rates Subject to Change | | | Phone: (559)277-5700 |
| All Year [CP] | 1P: $79- 159 | 2P/1B: $79- 159 | 2P/2B: $79- 159 | XP: $5-25 |

Location: Just e of SR 99, Shaw Ave exit. 5046 N Barcus 93722. Fax: 559/277-2244. **Terms:** Check-in 4 pm. **Facility:** 50 rooms. 3 stories; interior corridors; indoor/outdoor pool. **Some Rooms:** 3 kitchens. **Cards:** AE, CB, DI, DS, JC, MC, VI.

🔲🔲🔲🔲🔲🔲🔲🔲🔲🔲🔲

HOLIDAY INN EXPRESS-THESTA
◆◆
Motel

| | | Rates Subject to Change | | | Phone: (559)435-6593 |
| All Year [CP] | 1P: $68- 85 | 2P/1B: $68- 85 | 2P/2B: $68- 85 | XP: $10 | F17 |

Location: Just e of SR 41, Bullard Ave exit. 6051 N Thesta Ave 93710. Fax: 559/435-8694. **Facility:** 56 rooms. 2 whirlpool rms, extra charge; 2 stories; exterior corridors. **All Rooms:** combo or shower baths. **Cards:** AE, CB, DI, DS, JC, MC, VI. (See color ad below)

🔲🔲🔲🔲🔲🔲🔲🔲🔲🔲🔲🔲🔲

KNIGHTS INN
🅰🅰🅰 SAVE
FYI
Motel

| | | | | | Phone: (559)275-7766 |
| All Year | 1P: $49 | 2P/1B: $54 | 2P/2B: $59 | XP: $5 |

Too new to rate. **Location:** Just w of SR 99, Shields Ave exit. 3093 N Parkway 93722. Fax: 559/271-7966. **Terms:** Reserv deposit, 7 day notice; pets, $5 per pet per day extra charge. **Facility:** 85 rooms. Shares lobby with Travelodge. Scheduled to open Summer, 1998; 2 stories; exterior corridors; heated pool. **All Rooms:** combo or shower baths. **Cards:** AE, DI, MC, VI. **Special Amenities:** Free breakfast and free room upgrade (subject to availability with advanced reservations).

🔲🔲🔲🔲🔲🔲🔲🔲

LA QUINTA INN
🅰🅰🅰 SAVE
◆◆◆
Motel

| | | | | Phone: (559)442-1110 |
| All Year [CP] | 1P: $59- 69 | 2P/1B: $59- 69 | 2P/2B: $59- 69 |

Location: Just w of SR 41, Tulare St exit. 2926 Tulare St 93721. Fax: 559/237-0415. **Terms:** Pets. **Facility:** 130 rooms. 3 stories; exterior corridors. **Dining:** Restaurant nearby. **Cards:** AE, DI, DS, JC, MC, VI. **Special Amenities:** Free breakfast and free local telephone calls.

🔲🔲🔲🔲🔲🔲🔲🔲🔲🔲🔲🔲

NATIONAL 9 INN
🅰🅰🅰
◆
Motel

		Rates Subject to Change				
Mon-Sat 4/1-9/30 [CP]	1P: $29- 39	2P/1B: $34- 44	2P/2B: $39- 49	XP: $5-10	F12	Phone: (559)442-1082
Mon-Sat 2/1-3/31 & 10/1-1/31 [CP]	1P: $29- 39	2P/1B: $32- 40	2P/2B: $35- 45	XP: $5-10	F12	
Sun [CP]	1P: $26- 35	2P/1B: $32- 38	2P/2B: $35- 40	XP: $5-10	F12	

Location: 0.2 mi w of SR 99, Olive Ave exit. 1804 W Olive Ave 93728. Fax: 559/497-9545. **Terms:** Pets. **Facility:** 54 rooms. 2 stories; exterior corridors. **Dining:** Restaurant nearby. **Cards:** AE, CB, DI, DS, MC, VI.

🔲🔲🔲🔲🔲🔲🔲🔲🔲

PICCADILLY INN AIRPORT
🅰🅰🅰
◆◆◆◆
Motor Inn

		Rates Subject to Change				Phone: (559)251-6000
Mon-Thurs [CP]	1P: $79- 85	2P/1B: $79- 85	2P/2B: $79- 85	XP: $10	F17
Fri-Sun [CP]	1P: $74	2P/1B: $74	2P/2B: $74	XP: $10	F17

Location: 4 mi e of SR 41, McKinley Ave exit. 5115 E McKinley 93727. Fax: 559/251-6956. **Facility:** 185 rooms. Nicely landscaped courtyard. Balconies or patios. 4 Evergreen rms; 2 stories; interior corridors; whirlpool. **Dining:** Restaurant, coffee shop; 6 am-10 pm; $12-$20; cocktails. **Services:** giftshop. **Cards:** AE, CB, DI, DS, JC, MC, VI.

🔲🔲🔲🔲🔲🔲🔲🔲🔲🔲🔲🔲🔲🔲

PICCADILLY INN-SHAW
AAA
◆◆◆ Motor Inn
C, MC, VI.

Rates Subject to Change | Phone: (559)226-3850
Mon-Thurs [CP] 1P: $79- 85 2P/1B: $79- 85 2P/2B: $79- 85 XP: $10 F17
Fri-Sun [CP] 1P: $74 2P/1B: $74 2P/2B: $74 XP: $10 F17
Location: 3 mi e of SR 99, Shaw Ave exit. 2305 W Shaw Ave 93711. Fax: 559/226-2448. **Terms:** Package plans. **Facility:** 194 rooms. Quiet location. Spacious grounds. 6 "Evergreen rooms". 2 stories; interior/exterior corridors; whirlpool. **Dining:** Food service in lounge 4 pm-9 pm; $8-$20; cocktails. **Cards:** AE, CB, DI, DS,

PICCADILLY INN-UNIVERSITY
AAA
◆◆◆ Motel

Rates Subject to Change | Phone: (559)224-4200
Mon-Thurs [CP] 1P: $79- 85 2P/1B: $79- 85 2P/2B: $79- 85 XP: $10 F17
Fri-Sun [CP] 1P: $74 2P/1B: $74 2P/2B: $74 XP: $10 F17
Location: 1.5 mi ne; e of SR 41, Shaw Ave exit. 4961 N Cedar Ave 93726. Fax: 559/227-2382. **Facility:** 190 rooms. Large rooms. 6 evergreen rooms; 3 stories; interior corridors; whirlpool. **Dining:** Restaurant nearby. **Some Rooms:** whirlpools. **Cards:** AE, CB, DI, DS, JC, MC, VI.

QUALITY INN & SUITES
◆◆◆ Motel

Rates Subject to Change | Phone: (559)229-5811
All Year [CP] 1P: $79- 99 2P/1B: $79- 99 2P/2B: $89-109 XP: $10 F18
Location: Just e of SR 41, Shaw Ave exit. 480 E Shaw Ave 93710. Fax: 559/229-5911. **Facility:** 53 rooms. 3 stories; interior corridors; smoke free premises; heated pool, small pool. **Cards:** AE, CB, DI, DS, MC, VI.
(See color ad p 455 & p 1089)

RAMADA INN-SHAW
AAA SAVE
◆◆◆ Motor Inn

Phone: (559)224-4040
All Year 1P: $72 2P/1B: $78 2P/2B: $78 XP: $10 F18
Location: Just e of SR 41, Shaw Ave exit. 324 E Shaw Ave 93710. Fax: 559/222-4017. **Terms:** Package plans. **Facility:** 168 rooms. Lower rates, in winter; 2 stories; interior/exterior corridors; whirlpool. **Dining:** Dining room, coffee shop; 6:30 am-10 pm, Sat & Sun 7 am-9 pm; $11-$15; cocktails. **Services:** Fee: massage. **Cards:** AE, CB, DI, DS, JC, MC, VI. **Special Amenities:** Free local telephone calls and free newspaper. *(See color ad below & opposite title page)*

RESIDENCE INN BY MARRIOTT
◆◆◆ Suite Motel

Rates Subject to Change | Phone: (559)222-8900
All Year [CP] 1P: $79- 125 2P/1B: $79- 125 2P/2B: $99- 159
Location: 0.3 mi w of SR 41, Shaw Ave exit, n on Blackstone & e on Barstow. 5322 N Diana Ave 93710. Fax: 559/222-9089. **Facility:** 120 rooms. Few fireplaces; barbecue. 18 two-bedroom units. Rates for up to 5 persons; 3 stories; interior corridors. **All Rooms:** combo or shower baths. **Some Rooms:** 102 efficiencies, 18 kitchens. **Cards:** AE, CB, DI, DS, JC, MC, VI.

RODEWAY INN
AAA
◆ Motel

Rates Subject to Change | Phone: 559/268-0363
All Year 1P: $32 2P/1B: $34 2P/2B: $36 XP: $5
Location: SR 99 exit Olive Ave; w to Parkway Dr. 949 N Parkway Dr 93728. Fax: 559/268-0363. **Terms:** Pets, $5 fee, $10 dep req. **Facility:** 45 rooms. 2 stories; exterior corridors; small pool. **All Rooms:** shower baths. **Cards:** AE, DI, DS, MC, VI.

THE SAN JOAQUIN
AAA SAVE
◆◆◆ Suite Motel

Phone: (559)225-1309
All Year [CP] 1P: $82- 125 2P/1B: $82- 125 2P/2B: $99- 165
Location: 3.5 mi e of SR 99, Shaw Ave exit. 1309 W Shaw Ave 93711. Fax: 559/225-6021. **Terms:** Weekly/monthly rates. **Facility:** 68 rooms. Attractive landscaped grounds. 8 two-bedroom units, 2 three-bedroom units. Max rates for up to 6 persons; 2 stories; exterior corridors; whirlpool. **All Rooms:** combo or shower baths. **Some Rooms:** 18 kitchens. **Cards:** AE, CB, DI, DS, MC, VI. **Special Amenities:** Free breakfast and free local telephone calls.

SUPER 8-DOWNTOWN
AAA SAVE
◆ Motel

Phone: (559)268-0621
All Year [CP] 1P: $45- 50 2P/1B: $45- 50 2P/2B: $55- 65 XP: $5-10 F12
Location: 0.5 mi e of SR 99, Ventura St exit. 2127 Inyo St 93721. Fax: 559/233-9300. **Terms:** Reserv deposit, 7 day notice; pets, $5 extra charge. **Facility:** 50 rooms. Near convention center. 2 stories; exterior corridors. **Cards:** AE, DS, MC, VI. **Special Amenities:** Free breakfast and preferred room (subject to availability with advanced reservations).

SUPER 8 - PARKWAY

Phone: (559)268-074

(AAA) (SAVE)
◆ ◆
Motel

Mon-Sat 4/1-9/30 [CP]	1P:	$39- 49	2P/1B:	$44- 54	2P/2B:	$49- 59	XP: $5-10	F1
Sun [CP]	1P:	$28- 35	2P/1B:	$32- 40	2P/2B:	$38- 55	XP: $5-10	F1
Mon-Sat 2/1-3/31 &							
10/1-1/31 [CP]	1P:	$34- 45	2P/1B:	$36- 50	2P/2B:	$40- 50	XP: $5-10	F1

Location: Just w of SR 99; Olive Ave. exit. 1087 N Parkway Dr 93728. Fax: 559/237-2293. **Terms:** Week rates; pets, $5 extra charge. **Facility:** 48 rooms. 2 stories; exterior corridors; sitting pool. **Dining:** Coffee shop nearb **Services:** area transportation. **Cards:** AE, DS, MC, VI. **Special Amenities: Free breakfast and free local telephone calls**

TRAVELODGE

Phone: (559)276-774

(AAA) (SAVE)
[FYI]
Motel

All Year   1P: $59   2P/1B: $65   2P/2B: $69   XP: $5
Too new to rate. **Location:** Just w of SR 99, Sheilds Ave exit. 3093 N Parkway 93722. Fax: 559/271-796 **Terms:** Reserv deposit, 7 day notice; pets, $5 extra charge. **Facility:** 115 rooms. Shares lobby with Knight Inn. 3 whirlpool rms, $79-$89. Scheduled to open summer, 1998; 2 stories; exterior corridors; heated poo sauna. **All Rooms:** combo or shower baths. **Cards:** AE, DI, MC, VI. **Special Amenities: Free breakfa and free local telephone calls.** *(See color ad below)*

FULLERTON—114,100   (See map p. 294; index p. 292)

LODGINGS

CHASE SUITE HOTEL
◆ ◆ ◆
Motel

Rates Subject to Change   **Phone: (714)579-7400**   22
All Year [CP]   1P: $99- 169   2P/1B: $99- 169   2P/2B: $109- 169   XP: $10   F1
Location: Adjacent to e side of SR 57; exit Nutwood Ave. 2932 E Nutwood Ave 92831. Fax: 714/528-794 **Terms:** Reserv deposit. **Facility:** 97 rooms. 5 stories; interior corridors; small heated pool. **Some Rooms:** kitchens. **Cards:** AE, CB, DI, DS, JC, MC, VI. *(See color ad p 333)*

FOUR POINTS HOTEL BY SHERATON
(AAA) (SAVE)
◆ ◆ ◆
Motor Inn

Phone: (714)635-9000   22
All Year [CP]   1P: $99- 129   2P/1B: $99- 139   2P/2B: $99- 159   XP: $10-15   F1
Location: Adjacent to SR 91, exit Raymond Ave. 1500 S Raymond Ave 92831. Fax: 714/520-462 **Facility:** 250 rooms. 3-6 stories; interior/exterior corridors; heated pool. **Dining:** Restaurant; 6:30 am-10 pr $8-$14; cocktails. **Cards:** AE, CB, DI, DS, JC, MC, VI. **Special Amenities: Free breakfast and fre newspaper.** *(See color ad p 335)*

FULLERTON INN
(AAA) (SAVE)
◆ ◆
Motel

Phone: (714)773-4900   21
All Year   1P: $36- 43   2P/1B: $36- 43   2P/2B: $45- 55
Location: 0.3 mi ne of SR 91, Riverside Frwy, exit Magnolia Ave. 2601 W Orangethorpe Ave 9283 Fax: 714/773-9386. **Terms:** Reserv deposit; weekly rates; small pets only. **Facility:** 43 rooms. 2 stories; e terior corridors; small heated pool, whirlpool. **Cards:** AE, CB, DI, DS, JC, MC, VI.

HERITAGE INN
(AAA) (SAVE)
◆ ◆
Motel

Phone: (714)447-9200   22
All Year [CP]   1P: $50   2P/1B: $50   2P/2B: $50   XP: $5   F1
Location: On SR 90, just e of Harbor Blvd. 333 E Imperial Hwy 92835. Fax: 714/773-0685. **Facility:** 12 rooms. Located in suburban commercial area. Large lobby area. 3 suites & 10 large rooms with refrigerator microwave, $80-$95 for up to 2 persons; 4 stories; interior corridors; heated pool, whirlpoo **Recreation:** video game room. **Cards:** AE, CB, DI, DS, JC, MC, VI.

RADISSON HOTEL FULLERTON
(AAA) (SAVE)
◆ ◆ ◆
Motor Inn

Phone: (714)992-1700   22
All Year   1P: $78   2P/1B: $88   2P/2B: $88   XP: $10   F1
Location: Adjacent to SR 91, exit Harbor Blvd, Fullerton. 222 W Houston Ave 92832. Fax: 714/992-484 **Facility:** 289 rooms. Located adjacent to large shopping mall. 4-7 stories; interior corridors; heated poo wading pool. **Dining:** Dining room; 6 am-2 & 4-10 pm; 6/1-9/1 to 11:30 pm; $8-$15; cocktail **Services:** giftshop; area transportation, within 5 mi. **Recreation:** video game room. **Cards:** AE, CB, DI, DS JC, MC, VI. **Special Amenities: Free newspaper and free room upgrade (subject to availability with advance reservations).**

(See map p. 294)

RESTAURANTS

THE CELLAR   **Dinner: $22-$33**   **Phone: 714/525-5682**   (83)
◆◆◆   **Location:** 1.3 mi n of SR 91, exit Harbor Blvd; in Villa Del Sol Shopping Plaza. 305 N Harbor Blvd 92832.
French   **Hours:** 5:30 pm-10 pm, Fri & Sat-11 pm. Closed major holidays, Sun & Mon. **Reservations:** suggested.
  Features: casual dress; early bird specials; cocktails & lounge; valet parking; a la carte. Refined
atmosphere. Expertly prepared cuisine. Smoke free premises. **Cards:** AE, DI, DS, MC, VI.   ⊗

SUMMIT HOUSE   **Lunch: $9-$13**   **Dinner: $20-$30**   **Phone: 714/671-4111** (84)
◆◆◆   **Location:** At State College Blvd. 2000 E Bastanchury Rd 92835. **Hours:** 11:30 am-2:30 & 5 pm-10 pm, Sun 5
American   pm-10 pm, Sun 5 pm-9:30 pm. Closed: 1/1 & 12/25. **Reservations:** suggested. **Features:** semi-formal attire;
  children's menu; cocktails & lounge; valet parking; a la carte. Located on a bluff with a spectacular city view.
Nicely prepared meat, poultry & fish entrees. Smoke free premises. **Cards:** AE, DI, DS, MC, VI.   ⊗

GALT—8,900

LODGING

HOLIDAY INN EXPRESS-GALT   Guaranteed Rates   **Phone: (209)745-9500**
  All Year [CP]   1P: $69- 99   1P: $69- 99   2P/2B: $69- 99   XP: $10   F18
Motel   **Location:** Northbound SR-99, exit Simmerhorn Rd; southbound SR-99, exit Pringle Ave. 620 N Lincoln Way
  95632. Fax: 209/745-9300. **Facility:** 44 rooms. 2 stories; interior corridors. **Cards:** AE, CB, DI, DS, MC, VI.

ASK 🅂ⅅ 🔁 🖨 ⊗

GARBERVILLE—1,000

LODGINGS

BENBOW INN   **Phone: (707)923-2124**
AAA SAVE   4/30-11/27 & 12/23-1/2   1P: $115- 189   2P/1B: $115- 189   2P/2B: $115- 189   XP: $20
   4/2-4/29 & 11/28-12/22   1P: $89- 170   2P/1B: $89- 170   2P/2B: $89- 170   XP: $20
◆◆◆   **Location:** 2 mi s on US 101, Benbow exit. 445 Lake Benbow Dr 95542. Fax: 707/923-2897. **Terms:** Open
Historic   4/2-1/2; handling fee imposed. **Facility:** 55 rooms. Tudor English Inn design. Afternoon tea & scones. Desig-
Country Inn   nated as a national historic landmark. Cassette players & complimentary sherry in all rooms. 3 units with fireplace, $215-$295. Large garden unit with fireplace, for 2 persons $295. Whirlpool rms, extra charge; 3 stories,
  no elevator; interior/exterior corridors; smoke free premises; seasonal swimming, nearby pool available. **Dining:** Restaurant,
see separate listing. **Services:** giftshop. **Recreation:** bicycles. **All Rooms:** combo or shower baths. **Some Rooms:** color
TV. **Cards:** AE, DI, DS, MC, VI. **Special Amenities:** Free room upgrade **(subject to availability with advanced
reservations).**

🔗 🔁 ⑪ 🍸 ⊗ VCR 💻 🖨 🎞

BEST WESTERN HUMBOLDT HOUSE INN   **Phone: (707)923-2771**
AAA SAVE   5/10-10/31 [CP]   1P: $69- 85   2P/1B: $69- 85   2P/2B: $69- 85   XP: $5   D
   2/1-5/9 & 11/1-1/31 [CP]   1P: $52- 62   2P/1B: $57- 67   2P/2B: $60- 70   XP: $5   D
◆◆◆   **Location:** US 101 1st exit. 701 Redwood Dr 95542. Fax: 707/923-4259. **Terms:** Small pets only. **Facility:** 76
Motel   rooms. Many rooms with balcony or patio. 6 two-bedroom units. 2 stories; exterior corridors; whirlpool.
  Dining: Restaurant nearby. **All Rooms:** combo or shower baths. **Some Rooms:** 3 kitchens. **Cards:** AE, CB,
DI, DS, MC, VI. **Special Amenities:** Free breakfast and free local telephone calls. *(See ad below)*

🐾 🔗 🔁 ⑪ 🛆 🐾 ▢ 🎞 ♿ ⊗

HUMBOLDT REDWOODS INN   **Phone:** 707/923-245
Motel   (AAA) (SAVE)
| | 5/22-9/30 | 1P: | $50- | 82 | 2P/1B: | $50- | 82 | 2P/2B: | $50- | 82 | XP: | $6 |
| | 2/1-5/21 & 10/1-1/31 | 1P: | $42- | 52 | 2P/1B: | $45- | 55 | 2P/2B: | $45- | 55 | XP: | $5 |

Location: On US 101 business rt. 987 Redwood Dr 95542. Fax: 707/923-2451. **Terms:** Reserv depos
Facility: 22 rooms. 2 two-bedroom units. 1 story; exterior corridors; pool seasonal. **All Rooms:** combo
shower baths. **Cards:** AE, CB, DI, DS, JC, MC, VI.

MOTEL GARBERVILLE   **Phone:** (707)923-242
Motel   (AAA) (SAVE)
| | 5/1-9/30 | 1P: | $39- | 49 | 2P/1B: | $48- | 58 | 2P/2B: | $55- | 65 | XP: | $5 | F1 |
| | 2/1-4/30 & 10/1-1/31 | 1P: | $35- | 45 | 2P/1B: | $39- | 49 | 2P/2B: | $55- | 55 | XP: | $5 | F1 |

Location: On US 101 business rt. 948 Redwood Dr 95542. Fax: 707/923-2427. **Terms:** Reserv depos
pets. **Facility:** 30 rooms. 1 two-bedroom unit. 1 story; exterior corridors. **Dining:** Restaurant nearb
All Rooms: combo or shower baths. **Cards:** AE, CB, DI, DS, MC, VI. **Special Amenities: Free loc.**
telephone calls and free room upgrade (subject to availability with advanced reservations).

SHERWOOD FOREST MOTEL   Guaranteed Rates   **Phone:** 707/923-272
Motel   (AAA)
| | 5/1-10/31 | 1P: | $56 | 2P/1B: | $60 | 2P/2B: | $62 | XP: | $5 |
| | 2/1-4/30 & 11/1-1/31 | 1P: | $50 | 2P/1B: | $54 | 2P/2B: | $58 | XP: | $5 |

Location: North & southbound US 101 1st exit. 814 Redwood Dr 95542. Fax: 707/923-3677. **Terms:** Sma
pets only, limited to few rooms. **Facility:** 32 rooms. 1 two-bedroom unit. 2 kitchens, $15 extra charge; 1 stor
exterior corridors; whirlpool. **Dining:** Coffee shop nearby. **All Rooms:** combo or shower baths. **Cards:** A
DS, MC, VI.

RESTAURANT

BENBOW INN RESTAURANT Historical   **Lunch:** $6-$12   **Dinner:** $19-$30   **Phone:** 707/923-212
American   ◆◆◆
Location: In Benbow Inn. 445 Lake Benbow Dr 95542. **Hours:** Open 4/2-1/2; 8 am-11 & 6-9 pm; Sun
am-1:30 & 6-9 pm; noon-1:30 pm 6/1-10/31 & 12/1-12/31. Closed: 1/3-4/1 & lunch 11/1-5/3
Reservations: required. **Features:** No A/C; casual dress; Sunday brunch; children's menu; cocktails
lounge; a la carte. Pleasant dining. Patio service weather permitting. Varied menu, fresh local ingredients. Listed as
National Historic landmark. Extensive wine list. Smoke free premises. **Cards:** AE, DS, MC, VI.

GARDENA—See Los Angeles p. 600.

GARDEN GROVE—143,100   (See map p. 294; index p. 293)

LODGINGS

BEST WESTERN PLAZA INTERNATIONAL INN   **Phone:** (714)894-7568
Motel   (AAA) (SAVE)
| | All Year [CP] | 1P: | $39- | 49 | 2P/1B: | $44- | 55 | 2P/2B: | $49- | 69 | XP: | $3-5 | F1 |

Location: Adjacent to SR 22, n of jct SR 39 Beach Blvd. 7912 Garden Grove 9284
Fax: 714/894-6308. **Terms:** Reserv deposit, 3 day notice; weekly/monthly rates. **Facility:** 99 rooms. 2 storie
exterior corridors; heated pool, saunas. **Dining:** Restaurant nearby. **Cards:** AE, CB, DI, DS, JC, MC, V
Special Amenities: Early check-in/late check-out and free breakfast.

RAMADA PLAZA HOTEL-DISNEYLAND SOUTH   **Phone:** (714)534-1818
Motor Inn   (AAA) (SAVE)
| | All Year | 1P: | $69 | 2P/1B: | $79 | 2P/2B: | $79 | XP: | $10 | F1 |

Location: Just w of Brookhurst. 10022 Garden Grove Blvd 92844. Fax: 714/539-9930. **Facility:** 116 room
Some larger rooms with refrigerator, $99-$139; 4 stories; interior corridors; heated pool, whirlpoc
Dining: Restaurant; 7 am-11 pm; $9-$14; cocktails. **Services:** giftshop; area transportation, Disneyland Par
Cards: AE, CB, DI, DS, MC, VI. **Special Amenities: Free breakfast and free room upgrade (subject**
availability with advanced reservations).

RESTAURANT

MIMI'S CAFE   **Lunch:** $7-$13   **Dinner:** $7-$13   **Phone:** 714/898-5042
American   ◆◆
Location: SR 39, just n of SR 22. 7955 Garden Grove Blvd 92841. **Hours:** 7 am-11 pm. Closed: 12/2
Features: casual dress; children's menu; carryout; beer & wine only. Delightful restaurant with decor of
French cafe, patio dining avail. Nice selection of salads, sandwiches & entrees. **Cards:** AE, MC, VI.

GEYSERVILLE—1,300

LODGINGS

EYSERVILLE INN   Phone: (707)857-4343
All Year [CP]   1P: $99- 129 2P/1B: $99- 129 2P/2B: $139   XP: $10   F18
Location: Just se of US 101, Canyon Rd exit. 21714 Geyserville Ave 95441. Fax: 707/857-4411. **Facility:** 38
rooms. Few units with gas fireplace or balcony. Few with vineyard view. Carport parking. 2 stories; interior corridors; smoke free premises; whirlpool. **Dining:** Deli nearby. **Cards:** AE, DS, MC, VI. **Special Amenities:**
Free breakfast. *(See color ad p 1041)*

OPE-MERRILL HOUSE   Rates Subject to Change   Phone: (707)857-3356
All Year [BP]   1P: $95- 140   2P/1B: $111- 179   XP: $20   D
Location: 0.5 mi E of US 101, Geyserville exit. 21253 Geyserville Ave 95441. Fax: 707/857-4673.
Terms: Check-in 4 pm; reserv deposit, 8 day notice; handling fee imposed; 2 night min stay, weekends.
Facility: 12 rooms. Late 1800's Victorian; 4 units at the Hope-Bosworth House, acros street. 2 stories; interior
corridors; smoke free premises; pool 5/1-10/31. **All Rooms:** comb, shower or tub baths.
Some Rooms: color TV, whirlpools. **Cards:** AE, MC, VI.

GILROY—31,500

LODGINGS

EST WESTERN INN   Phone: (408)848-1467
5/1-9/30   1P: $54   2P/1B: $57   2P/2B: $64   XP: $10   F12
2/1-4/30 & 10/1-1/31 1P: $50   2P/1B: $53   2P/2B: $58   XP: $10   F12
Location: Just w of US 101, Leavesley Rd exit. 360 Leavesley Rd 95020. Fax: 408/848-1424. **Terms:** CP
avail. **Facility:** 42 rooms. Near convenience foods store. 1 two-bedroom unit. 2 stories; exterior corridors; whirlpool. **Dining:** Coffee shop nearby. **Cards:** AE, CB, DI, DS, MC, VI. **Special Amenities: Free breakfast and
ee local telephone calls.**

OMFORT INN   Rates Subject to Change   Phone: 408/848-3500
All Year [CP]   1P: $49- 79 2P/1B: $59- 89 2P/2B: $69- 89 XP: $10   F17
Location: Just w of US 101, Leavesley Rd exit. 8292 Murray Ave 95020. Fax: 408/848-1569. **Facility:** 65
rooms. Convenient to gas station, trucks. 2 whirlpool rms, extra charge; 2 stories; exterior corridors.
ards: AE, CB, DI, DS, JC, MC, VI.

OREST PARK INN   Phone: (408)848-5144
All Year   1P: $50   2P/1B: $60   2P/2B: $62   XP: $5
Location: Just w of US 101, Leavesley Rd exit. 375 Leavesley Rd 95020. Fax: 408/848-1138. **Facility:** 123
rooms. Private balconies. 4 two-bedroom units. 21 rms with gas fireplace, $10-$20 extra charge; 3 stories; interior corridors; sauna, whirlpool; 1 tennis court. **Dining:** Coffee shop nearby. **Some Rooms:** whirlpools.
Cards: AE, CB, DI, DS, MC, VI. **Special Amenities: Free local telephone calls.**

EAVESLEY INN   Phone: (408)847-5500
All Year [CP]   1P: $45   2P/1B: $50   2P/2B: $60   XP: $5   F12
Location: Just w of US 101; Leavesley Rd exit. 8430 Murray Ave 95020. Fax: 408/847-2241. **Terms:** Pets,
$10 extra charge. **Facility:** 48 rooms. Some units have sitting area with sofabed. 2 stories; exterior corridors;
whirlpool. **Dining:** Restaurant nearby. **Cards:** AE, CB, DI, DS, MC, VI. **Special Amenities: Free breakfast
and free local telephone calls.**

ODEWAY INN   Phone: (408)847-0688
6/1-8/31 [CP]   1P: $48- 58 2P/1B: $58- 68 2P/2B: $68- 79 XP: $10   F16
2/1-5/31 [CP]   1P: $50- 55 2P/1B: $55- 58 2P/2B: $58- 62 XP: $5   F16
9/1-1/31 [CP]   1P: $48- 52 2P/1B: $55- 58 2P/2B: $58- 62 XP: $10   F16
Location: Just e of US 101, Leavesley Rd exit. 611 Leavesley Rd 95020. Fax: 408/847-4400. **Terms:** CP
avail; small pets only, $25 dep req. **Facility:** 43 rooms. Near outlet shopping center. 2 stories; exterior corridors; small pool. **Dining:** Coffee shop nearby. **All Rooms:** combo or shower baths. **Cards:** AE, CB, DI, DS, JC, MC, VI.
pecial Amenities: Free breakfast and free local telephone calls.

UPER 8 MOTEL   Phone: (408)848-4108
6/1-9/30   1P: $55- 65 2P/1B: $60- 69 2P/2B: $63- 73 XP: $5   F12
2/1-5/31 & 10/1-1/31 1P: $49   2P/1B: $53   2P/2B: $57   XP: $5   F12
Location: Just e of to US 101, Leavesley Rd exit. 8435 Leavesley Rd 95020. Fax: 408/848-2651.
Terms: Reserv deposit; weekly/monthly rates. **Facility:** 53 rooms. Few larger rooms with sitting area, recliners.
Near outlet stores shopping center. 3 stories; interior corridors. **Dining:** Coffee shop nearby. **Cards:** AE, DI,
S, MC, VI. Special Amenities: Free breakfast and free local telephone calls.

GLENDALE—*See Los Angeles p. 600.*

GLENDORA—*See Los Angeles p. 602.*

GRAEAGLE—300—See also PORTOLA & QUINCY.

LODGING

GRAEAGLE MEADOWS
◆◆◆
Resort
Complex
Rates Subject to Change
5/24-9/24   2P/2B: $110
2/1-5/23 & 9/25-1/31   2P/2B: $93
Phone: 530/836-11
Location: 0.3 mi s on SR 89; 1.5 mi s of jct SR 70, Feather River Hwy. 96103 (PO Box 76
Fax: 530/836-1629. **Terms:** Reserv deposit, 14 day notice; 2 night min stay. **Facility:** 64 rooms. 2-
3-bedroom, 2-bath, duplex homes with fireplace, patio & laundry. 12 three-bedroom units. Damage deposit $200. Two ni
rate $290-360 for 2 persons; 2 stories; exterior corridors. Fee: 18 holes golf; 4 tennis courts. **Recreation:** hiking trai
Fee: horseback riding. **All Rooms:** kitchens.

GRASS VALLEY—9,000

LODGINGS

ALTA SIERRA VILLAGE INN
◆◆
Motel
Rates Subject to Change
All Year   1P: $49- 100   2P/1B: $49- 100   2P/2B: $59- 150   XP: $10
Phone: (530)273-91
Location: 6 mi s; e 1.1 mi on Alta Sierra Dr; s 0.8 mi on Norlene; e 0.5 mi on Tammy; follow signs to A
Sierra Country Club. 11858 Tammy Way 95949. Fax: 530/273-8031. **Terms:** Reserv deposit, 14 day notic
handling fee imposed. **Facility:** 14 rooms. Decks overlooking small lake. Rustic decor. 2-bedroom unit $145, M
Thurs $115 for up to 4 persons; 1 story; exterior corridors. **All Rooms:** combo or shower baths. **Some Rooms:** kitche
Cards: DS, MC, VI.

BEST WESTERN GOLD COUNTRY INN
ⒶⒶⒶ SAVE
◆◆
Motel
Phone: (530)273-13
3/16-9/30 [CP]   1P: $65- 90   2P/1B: $75- 90   2P/2B: $78- 90   XP: $8-10
2/1-3/15 & 1/1-1/31 [CP] 1P: $52- 75   2P/1B: $56- 75   2P/2B: $63- 85   XP: $5-8
Location: 1 mi e; off & adjacent to SR 20 & 49; midway between Grass Valley & Nevada City; e
Brunswick Rd 11972 Sutton Way 95945. Fax: 530/273-4229. **Terms:** 2 night min stay, weekends 4/1-10/3
pets, $10 extra charge. **Facility:** 84 rooms. 3 two-bedroom units. 1-2 stories; exterior corridors; whirlpo
Some Rooms: 4 efficiencies, 10 kitchens. **Cards:** AE, CB, DI, DS, JC, MC, VI. **Special Amenities: Free breakfast an
free local telephone calls.**

COACH N' FOUR MOTEL
ⒶⒶⒶ
◆
Motel
Rates Subject to Change
All Year [CP]   1P: $42- 65   2P/1B: $42- 65   2P/2B: $50- 65   XP: $10
Phone: 530/273-80
Location: SR 49, exit W Empire St, 0.3 mi n. 628 S Auburn St 95945. Fax: 530/272-2696. **Terms:** Rese
deposit; pets, $50 dep req. **Facility:** 16 rooms. 2-bedroom family suite, $85-$100 for up to 6 persons; 2 st
ries; exterior corridors. **All Rooms:** combo or shower baths. **Cards:** AE, MC, VI.

ELAM BIGGS BED AND BREAKFAST
◆◆◆
Bed &
Breakfast
Guaranteed Rates
All Year [BP]   1P: $70- 105   2P/1B: $75- 110   2P/2B: $75   XP: $20
Phone: (530)477-09
Location: Just e of jct of SR 49 & Hwy 174 (Colfax Hwy). 220 Colfax Ave 95945. **Terms:** Reserv depos
Facility: 4 rooms. 1892 Queen Anne Victorian. 2 stories; interior corridors. **Cards:** MC, VI.

GOLDEN CHAIN RESORT MOTEL
ⒶⒶⒶ
◆◆
Motel
Phone: 530/273-72
Fri & Sat 5/1-10/15 [CP]   1P: $58- 68   2P/1B: $62- 72   2P/2B: $62- 82   XP: $6-10
Sun-Thurs 5/1-10/15 [CP]   1P: $48- 58   2P/1B: $52- 62   2P/2B: $52- 72   XP: $6-10
Fri & Sat 2/1-4/30 &
10/16-1/31 [EP]   1P: $44- 54   2P/1B: $48- 58   2P/2B: $48- 68   XP: $6-10
Sun-Thurs 2/1-4/30 &
10/16-1/31 [CP]   1P: $42- 48   2P/1B: $44- 52   2P/2B: $44- 54   XP: $6-10
Location: 2.5 mi s on SR 49. 13363 SR 49 95949. Fax: 530/274-1888. **Terms:** Reserv deposit, 3 day notice; pets, $6 ext
charge, limited rooms. **Facility:** 21 rooms. Spacious tree-shaded grounds. 1 story; exterior corridors; putting green; heat
pool. **All Rooms:** combo or shower baths. **Cards:** AE, JC, MC, VI.

HOLBROOKE HOTEL
ⒶⒶⒶ SAVE
◆◆
Historic Hotel
Phone: (530)273-135
4/1-12/31 [CP]   2P/1B: $71- 150   XP: $15
2/1-3/31 & 1/1-1/31 [CP]   2P/1B: $55- 120   XP: $15
Location: SR 49 exit Central Grass Valley. 212 W Main St 95945. Fax: 530/273-0434. **Terms:** Handling f
imposed. **Facility:** 28 rooms. 1851 restored hotel. 10 rooms located in restored 1870 Victorian annex. A Ca
fornia historical landmark. 2 stories; interior corridors. **Dining:** Dining room; 11:30 am-2 & 5:30-9 pm, S
brunch 10 am-2 pm; $10-$21; cocktails. **All Rooms:** combo or shower baths. **Cards:** AE, CB, DI, DS, JC, MC, V
Special Amenities: Free breakfast.

HOLIDAY LODGE
ⒶⒶⒶ SAVE
◆
Motel
Phone: (530)273-44
4/1-9/30   1P: $48- 50   2P/1B: $55- 60   2P/2B: $60- 65   XP: $5
2/1-3/31, 10/1-1/31 &
10/16-1/31   1P: $40- 45   2P/1B: $45- 50   2P/2B: $55- 60   XP: $5
Location: 1.3 mi e; 0.8 mi e on Old Hwy 20 & 49; exit SR 49 Frwy via Idaho-Maryland Rd exits. 1221
Main St 95945. Fax: 530/477-2878. **Terms:** Reserv deposit; small pets only, 1 dog only, $20 dep re
Facility: 36 rooms. Some gold rush theme rooms, $65-$75 for 2 persons; 2 stories; exterior corridors. **All Rooms:** combo
shower baths. **Cards:** AE, CB, DI, DS, MC, VI. **Special Amenities: Free breakfast and free local telephone calls.**

STAGECOACH MOTEL
◆
Motel
Guaranteed Rates
All Year [CP]   1P: $50   2P/1B: $50   2P/2B: $50   XP: $10
Phone: 530/272-37
Location: Exit SR 49 at Colfax Ave, 0.4 mi s. 405 S Auburn St 95945. **Terms:** Reserv deposit. **Facility:**
rooms. 2 stories; exterior corridors. **Cards:** AE, DS, MC, VI.

RESTAURANTS

PAULETTE'S COUNTRY KITCHEN
◆◆
American
Lunch: $4-$7   Dinner: $6-$9   **Phone: 530/273-40**
Location: Exit SR 49 & 20 at Brunswick Rd, just n. 11875 Sutton Way 95945. **Hours:** 6 am-8 pm, Fri-3 p
Sat & Sun 7 am-3 pm. Closed: 1/1, 11/25 & 12/25. **Reservations:** suggested. **Features:** casual dres
children's menu; early bird specials; beer & wine only; a la carte. Family restaurant located in shoppi
center. Smoke free premises. **Cards:** AE, DS, MC, VI.

CHEIDEL'S OLD EUROPEAN RESTAURANT   **Dinner:** $13-$22   **Phone:** 530/273-5553
◆◆
erman   **Location:** 6 mi s on SR 49, at entrance to Alta Sierra Dr. 10100 Alta Sierra Dr 95945. **Hours:** 5:30 pm-9:30 pm, Sat-10 pm, Sun 4 pm-9:30 pm. Closed: Mon, Tues, 5/27, 9/2 & 2 wks in Jan. **Reservations:** suggested. **Features:** casual dress; children's menu; cocktails & lounge; minimum charge-$9. Charming Bavarian
'mosphere. European & continental specialties. **Cards:** MC, VI.   ☒

GRIDLEY—4,600

LODGING

ACIFIC MOTEL   Guaranteed Rates   **Phone:** 530/846-4580
ⒶⒶ   All Year   1P: $37- 47   2P/1B: $42- 52   2P/2B: $48- 58   XP: $5   F6
   Location: 1 mi s on SR 99. 1308 Hwy 99 95948. **Terms:** Pets, $3 extra charge. **Facility:** 15 rooms. Attrac-
◆◆   tively landscaped center courtyard including shaded picnic area. 1 story; exterior corridors.
lotel   **All Rooms:** combo or shower baths. **Cards:** AE, MC, VI.   🛏🖘💻☐🔒☒

GROVELAND—1,500

LODGINGS

ROVELAND HOTEL   **Phone:** (209)962-4000
ⒶⒶ (SAVE)   All Year [CP]   1P: $115- 195   2P/1B: $115- 195   2P/2B: $115- 195   XP: $15-25
   Location: Center. 18767 Main St 95321 (PO Box 481). Fax: 209/962-6674. **Terms:** Reserv deposit; handling
◆◆   fee imposed; pets, $25 dep req. **Facility:** 17 rooms. Restored 1849 adobe & 1914 Queen Anne hotel. Modeled
istoric   after the Larkin house, the first American mansion. 3 whirlpool, rms, extra charge. 3 suites with sitting room
ountry Inn $175; 2 stories. **Dining:** Dining room; 6 pm-10 pm; $14-$22; wine/beer only. **Recreation:** Guests have
   access to Pine Mountain Lake Golf. **All Rooms:** combo or shower baths. **Some Rooms:** color TV.
ards: AE, CB, DI, DS, JC, MC, VI. **Special Amenities:** Free breakfast and free local telephone calls.
🛏🕭🍽🍸(VCR)💻🖨☒

OSEMITE WESTGATE MOTEL   **Phone:** 209/962-5281
ⒶⒶ (SAVE)   5/1-10/31   1P: $89- 139   2P/1B: $89- 139   2P/2B: $89- 139   XP: $8   F12
   2/1-4/30 & 11/1-1/31   1P: $59- 125   2P/1B: $59- 125   2P/2B: $59- 125   XP: $5   F12
◆◆   **Location:** 12 mi e on SR 120. 7633 Hwy 120 95321. Fax: 209/962-5285. **Terms:** Reserv deposit; pets, $10
lotel   extra charge. **Facility:** 44 rooms. Close to Yosemite National Park. 2 stories; exterior corridors.
   All Rooms: combo or shower baths. **Cards:** AE, DI, DS, MC, VI. IMA. *(See color ad p 286 & below)*
🅂🛏🖘🏊🐾☐🖨🔒☒

GROVER BEACH—11,700

LODGING

OLIDAY INN EXPRESS GROVER BEACH   **Phone:** (805)481-4448
ⒶⒶ (SAVE)   5/15-10/1 [CP]   1P: $59- 95   2P/1B: $59- 95   2P/2B: $59- 95   XP: $10
   2/1-5/14 & 10/2-1/31 [CP]   1P: $49- 65   2P/1B: $49- 75   2P/2B: $55- 79   XP: $10
◆◆◆   **Location:** Just w of US 101, exit Oak Park Blvd. 775 Oak Park Blvd 93433. Fax: 805/473-3609.
lotor Inn   **Terms:** Reserv deposit. **Facility:** 78 rooms. Attractive hillside location. 2 rooms with whirlpool & gas fireplace,
   $79-$99; 11 rooms with fireplace; 3 stories; interior corridors; heated pool, whirlpool. **Dining:** Wm Cody's
teakhouse & Saloon, see separate listing. **Cards:** AE, CB, DI, DS, JC, MC, VI. **Special Amenities:** Free breakfast and
ee local telephone calls. *(See color ad p 799)*   🕭🔔🖘🍽🍸☐🖨🔒☒

RESTAURANT

WM CODY'S STEAKHOUSE & SALOON   **Lunch:** $6-$10   **Dinner:** $15-$23   **Phone:** 805/489-77...
◆   **Location:** Just w of US 101, exit Oak Park Blvd; at Holiday Inn Express Grover Beach. 777 Oak Park B...
American   93433. **Hours:** 11:30 am-2 & 4-9 pm, Fri & Sat-10 pm, Sun from 9 am. **Reservations:** suggeste...
          Features: casual dress; Sunday brunch; children's menu; early bird specials; cocktails & loung...
entertainment. Old west atmosphere. Large selection of steaks, BBQ, chicken & seafood. Live band & dancing Fri & S...
Cards: AE, DI, DS, JC, MC, VI.   ▷

GUALALA—600—See also POINT ARENA.

LODGINGS

BREAKERS INN   Rates Subject to Change   **Phone:** 707/884-32...
◆◆◆   Fri & Sat [CP]   1P: $125- 235   2P/1B: $125- 235   XP: $20
Motel   Sun-Thurs [CP]   1P: $88- 185   2P/1B: $88- 185   XP: $20
          Location: Center. 39300 S Highway 1 95445 (PO Box 389, 95445-0389). Fax: 707/884-34...
Terms: Reserv deposit, 5 day notice; handling fee imposed. **Facility:** 27 rooms. All rooms with deck, ocean view, fireplace...
wet bar. 3 stories. **All Rooms:** shower baths. **Cards:** AE, DS, MC, VI. *(See ad below)*

GUALALA COUNTRY INN   Guaranteed Rates   **Phone:** (707)884-43...
Ⓐ   All Year [CP]   1P: $79- 149   2P/1B: $79- 149 2P/2B: $95- 105
◆◆   **Location:** E side of SR 1. 47955 Center St 95445 (PO Box 697). Fax: 707/884-1018. **Terms:** Pets, $...
Motel   extra charge. **Facility:** 20 rooms. Few woodburning fireplace & ocean view. 2 stories; interior/exterior corrido...
          Some Rooms: whirlpools. **Cards:** AE, CB, DI, DS, MC, VI. *(See color ad below)*

URF MOTEL   Guaranteed Rates   **Phone:** (707)884-3571
AD   All Year   1P: $79- 145   2P/1B: $79- 145 2P/2B: $99
◆   **Location:** W side of Hwy SR 1. 39170 Hwy 1 95445 (PO Box 695). Fax: 707/884-3009. **Terms:** Pets, $10
Motel   extra charge. **Facility:** 20 rooms. Few units with oceanview. Maximum rates for up to 4 persons; 1 story; ex-
         terior corridors. **Dining:** Restaurant nearby. **All Rooms:** combo or shower baths. **Some Rooms:** 5 kitchens.
         Cards: AE, CB, DI, DS, MC, VI. *(See color ad p 466)*

RESTAURANT

T ORRES   **Dinner:** $30   **Phone:** 707/884-3335
◆◆◆   **Location:** 2 mi n on SR 1. 36601 S Hwy 1 95445. **Hours:** 6 pm-9:15 pm, Sat 5:15 pm-9:45 pm. Closed:
merican Tues & Wed 1/1-4/30, Wed-May,Oct,Nov & first 2 wks in Dec. **Reservations:** required. **Features:** No A/C;
         casual dress; beer & wine only; prix fixe, a la carte. Unique Russian architecture. 3-story domed dining room.
-course dinner with several choices of entrees. Also choice of daily specials, including wild game. Fresh appetizers &
esserts extra charge. Smoke free premises.   ☒

GUERNEVILLE—2,000—*See also MONTE RIO.*

LODGING

ROOKSIDE LODGE   **Phone:** 707/869-2874
AD [SAVE]   All Year   1P: $82- 150   2P/1B: $92- 168 2P/2B: $102- 150 XP: $12
◆◆   **Location:** Just n of SR 16. 14100 Brookside Ln 95446 (PO Box 382). Fax: 707/869-0714. **Terms:** Reserv
omplex   deposit, 14 day notice; handling fee imposed; 2 night min stay, weekends. **Facility:** 36 rooms. Cottages &
         motel rooms. Few fireplaces. 2 two-bedroom units. 20 units with kitchen $15 extra charge, no utensils. Per-
         sonal checks not accepted; 1-2 stories; exterior corridors; sauna, whirlpool, pool 4/15-10/31. **Recreation:**
ee: towels. **Some Rooms:** whirlpools. **Cards:** AE, MC, VI. *(See color ad below)*

HACIENDA HEIGHTS—*See Los Angeles p. 603.*

HALF MOON BAY—*See San Francisco p. 968.*

HANFORD—30,900

LODGINGS

EST WESTERN HANFORD INN   Rates Subject to Change   **Phone:** (559)583-7300
AD   All Year   1P: $42- 45   2P/1B: $46- 47 2P/2B: $48   XP: $6
◆◆   **Location:** S of & adj to SR 198, eastbound exit 11th Ave; westbound exit Redington St. 755 Cadillac Ln
Motel   93230. Fax: 559/582-8455. **Facility:** 40 rooms. Easy highway access. 2 stories; exterior corridors.
         Dining: Coffee shop nearby. **Cards:** AE, CB, DI, DS, MC, VI.

RWIN STREET INN   **Phone:** (559)583-8000
AD [SAVE]   Fri & Sat [CP]   1P: $79   2P/1B: $79   2P/2B: $90   XP: $5
         Sun-Thurs [CP]   1P: $69   2P/1B: $69   2P/2B: $80   XP: $5
◆◆◆   **Location:** Downtown Hanford Historic District. 522 N Irwin St 93230. Fax: 559/583-8793. **Terms:** Reserv
ed &   deposit, 3 day notice. **Facility:** 30 rooms. Suites, $99-$125; 2 stories; exterior corridors; heated pool.
reakfast **Dining:** Restaurant; 7 am-2 & 5-9 pm, Sun-2 pm; $9-$18. **Cards:** AE, CB, DI, DS, MC, VI.
         Special Amenities: Free breakfast and free local telephone calls.

EQUOIA INN   **Phone:** (559)582-0338
AD [SAVE]   All Year [CP]   1P: $63- 69   2P/1B: $66- 69 2P/2B: $70- 76 XP: $6-12
◆◆◆   **Location:** Exit SR 198 at 12th Ave, n to Mall Dr. 1655 Mall Dr 93230. Fax: 559/582-1392. **Terms:** Small pets
Motel   only, $10 extra charge at manager's discretion. **Facility:** 58 rooms. 3 stories; interior corridors; whirlpool.
         Dining: Restaurant nearby. **All Rooms:** combo or shower baths. **Cards:** AE, CB, DI, DS, JC, MC, VI.
         Special Amenities: Free breakfast and free local telephone calls.

HAPPY CAMP—1,100

RESTAURANT

INDIAN CREEK CAFE
🔷🔷🔷
◆
American

        Lunch: $4-$9   **Dinner:** $11-$25   **Phone:** 530/493-51∎
Location: S off SR 96, 0.3 mi e. 106 Indian Creek Rd 96039. **Hours:** 8 am-8 pm. Closed: 4/12, 11/26 &
weeks at Christmas. **Reservations:** suggested. **Features:** casual dress; children's menu; early bird specia
beer & wine only; a la carte. Homemade bread, soups & desserts. Steaks, chops & seafood, Mexican,
vegetarian specialities. Smoke free premises. **Cards:** AE, DI, MC, VI.

HAYWARD—111,300

LODGINGS

BEST WESTERN INN OF HAYWARD
🔷🔷🔷 [SAVE]
◆◆◆
Motel

                                                        Phone: (510)785-87∎
All Year [CP]   1P: $65- 85   2P/1B: $69- 99 2P/2B: $75- 90 XP: $7
Location: E of I-880. 360 West A St 94541. Fax: 510/782-0850. **Facility:** 91 rooms. 4 kitchens, $8 ext
charge. 2 units with hot tub $140. 16 whirlpool rms, extra charge; 3 stories; interior/exterior corridors; saun
whirlpool. **Dining:** Restaurant nearby. **All Rooms:** combo or shower baths. **Some Rooms:** color T
Cards: AE, CB, DI, DS, MC, VI. **Special Amenities: Free breakfast and free room upgrade (subject
availability with advanced reservations).**

COMFORT INN
🔷🔷🔷 [SAVE]
◆◆
Motel

                                                        Phone: (510)538-44∎
All Year [CP]   1P: $75- 125 2P/1B: $75- 125 2P/2B: $90- 150 XP: $5-20   F
Location: 1.8 mi e of I-880; exit Jackson Blvd/SR92, s 0.5 mi on SR 238 (Mission Blvd). 24997 Mission Bl
94541. Fax: 510/581-8029. **Terms:** Reserv deposit. **Facility:** 62 rooms. Attractive decor. Exceptionally we
maintained. 2 stories; exterior corridors; sauna. **Dining:** Restaurant nearby. **Some Rooms:** 18 efficiencie
no utensils. Fee: whirlpools. **Cards:** AE, CB, DI, DS, JC, MC, VI. **Special Amenities: Free breakfast ar
free local telephone calls.** *(See color ad p 937)*

DAYS INN AIRPORT
🔷🔷🔷 [SAVE]
◆◆◆
Motel

                                                        Phone: (510)670-055∎
All Year [CP]   1P: $65- 85   2P/1B: $70- 90 2P/2B: $80- 95 XP: $5   F
Location: Exit I-880 A St W. 450 W A St 94541. Fax: 510/670-0440. **Facility:** 32 rooms. 3 stories; exterior co
ridors. **Some Rooms:** whirlpools. **Cards:** AE, CB, DI, DS, JC, MC, VI. **Special Amenities: Free breakfa
and free local telephone calls.** *(See color ad below)*

DISCOVERY INN
🔷🔷🔷 [SAVE]
◆◆
Motel

                                                        Phone: (510)886-711
All Year [CP]   1P: $55- 67   2P/1B: $55- 75 2P/2B: $64- 80 XP: $5
Location: 1 mi e of I-880 on SR 92 (Jackson St). 333 Jackson St 94544. Fax: 510/727-141
Terms: Package plans. **Facility:** 21 rooms. 2 rms with whirlpool $95 for 2 persons; 2 stories; exterior corrido
Some Rooms: Fee: whirlpools. **Cards:** AE, CB, DI, DS, JC, MC, VI. **Special Amenities: Free breakfa
and free local telephone calls.**

EXECUTIVE INN-A HANFORD HOTEL
🔷🔷🔷
◆◆◆
Motel

                     Guaranteed Rates   **Phone:** (510)732-630
Mon-Thurs [CP]   1P: $85- 99   2P/1B: $85- 99 2P/2B: $85- 99 XP: $10   F1
Fri-Sun [CP]   1P: $79   2P/1B: $79   2P/2B: $79   XP: $10   F1
Location: Exit I-880; A St, 0.5 mi w. 20777 Hesperian Blvd 94541. Fax: 510/783-2265. **Facility:** 146 room
Modern attractive decor, spacious rooms. 3 stories; interior corridors; heated pool, whirlpoo
Dining: Restaurant nearby. **Recreation:** Nintendo. **All Rooms:** combo or shower baths. **Cards:** AE, CB, D
DS, JC, MC, VI.

PHOENIX LODGE
🔷🔷🔷 [SAVE]
◆
Motel

                                                        Phone: 510/786-041
All Year   1P: $40- 50   2P/1B: $45- 55 2P/2B: $45- 55 XP: $5   F1
Location: W of I-880, A St exit. 500 West A St 94541. Fax: 510/783-4531. **Terms:** Small pets only, $10 ext
charge. **Facility:** 70 rooms. 3 stories, no elevator; interior corridors. **All Rooms:** combo or shower bath
Cards: AE, CB, DI, DS, JC, MC, VI.

RAMADA LIMITED
◆
Motel

                     Guaranteed Rates   **Phone:** 510/538-438
All Year [CP]   1P: $59   2P/1B: $59   2P/2B: $59   XP: $10
Location: Se of I-580 & I-238 interchange. 21598 Foothill Blvd 94541. Fax: 510/889-0728. **Facility:** 70 room
2 stories; exterior corridors. **Cards:** AE, CB, DI, DS, MC, VI. *(See color ad p 953)*

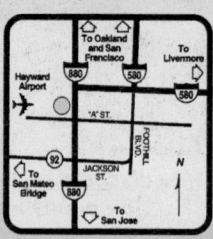

RESTAURANT

E DE MAIN RESTAURANT FRANCAIS   **Lunch:** $10-$15   **Dinner:** $15-$34   **Phone:** 510/537-0812
◆◆   **Location:** Exit 880 at A St, e 1.5 mi; s on Main St between B & C sts. 22622 Main St 94541. **Hours:** 11:30
nch   am-2:15 & 5:30-9:30 pm, Fri & Sat 5:30 pm-10:30 pm. Closed major holidays, Sun & Mon.
Reservations: suggested. **Features:** casual dress; children's menu; beer & wine only; a la carte. Creative
paration & presentation, unique Paris street-cafe decor. Pleasant, quiet atmosphere. **Cards:** AE, CB, DI, MC, VI.

HEALDSBURG—9,500

LODGINGS

ST WESTERN DRY CREEK INN		Rates Subject to Change				**Phone:** (707)433-0300	
7/1-10/31 & 12/17-1/1 [CP]	1P:	$79- 149	2P/1B:	$79- 149	2P/2B:	$79- 149	XP: $15	F16
4/11-6/30 & 11/1-11/30 [CP]	1P:	$69- 129	2P/1B:	$69- 129	2P/2B:	$69- 129	XP: $15	F16
2/1-4/10, 12/1-12/16 &							
1/2-1/31 [CP]	1P:	$55- 99	2P/1B:	$55- 99	2P/2B:	$55- 99	XP: $15	F16

Location: just e of US 101, Dry Creek Rd exit. 198 Dry Creek Rd 95448. Fax: 707/433-1129.
rms: Package plans, all year; pets, $10 extra charge. **Facility:** 102 rooms. Spanish-style building. 3 stories; exterior corri-
s; small pool, covered whirlpool. **Dining:** Coffee shop nearby. **Cards:** AE, CB, DI, DS, MC, VI. *(See color ad below)*

RVIEW MOTEL		Rates Subject to Change				**Phone:** (707)433-5548	
Fri & Sat 4/1-11/30 [CP]	1P:	$60- 70	2P/1B:	$60- 70	2P/2B:	$70- 80	XP: $10	F10
Fri & Sat 2/1-3/31 &							
12/1-1/31 [CP]	1P:	$50- 60	2P/1B:	$50- 60	2P/2B:	$60- 70	XP: $10	F10
Sun-Thurs [CP]	1P:	$46- 56	2P/1B:	$46- 56	2P/2B:	$46- 60	XP: $10	F10

Location: Just e of US 101; central Healdsburg exit. 74 Healdsburg Ave 95448. Fax: 707/433-4512.
rms: Reserv deposit, 3 day notice; handling fee imposed; 2 night min stay, summer weekends; small pets only, $10 dep
. **Facility:** 18 rooms. Older, well kept motel. No checks accepted; 1 story; exterior corridors; whirlpool; playground.
Rooms: combo or shower baths. **Cards:** AE, DS, MC, VI.

E HONOR MANSION		Rates Subject to Change				**Phone:** 707/433-4277	
All Year [BP]	1P:	$130- 250	2P/1B:	$130- 250	2P/2B:	$160	XP: $25

Location: Just e of US 101, Dry Creek Rd exit; just s. 14891 Grove St 95448. Fax: 707/431-7173.
◆◆◆   **Terms:** Check-in 4 pm; reserv deposit, 15 day notice; handling fee imposed; 2 night min stay, weekends.
storic Bed   **Facility:** 6 rooms. 1883 Italianate Victorian & a studio-cottage. Few fireplaces; decks, koi pond. 2 stories;
Breakfast   interior/exterior corridors; smoke free premises. **Dining:** 24 hr cappuccino machine, tea, bottled water &
cookies. **Services:** complimentary evening beverages. **All Rooms:** combo or shower baths.
me Rooms: color TV. **Cards:** DS, MC, VI.

AVELODGE		Rates Subject to Change				**Phone:** 707/433-0101	
4/1-11/30 [CP]	1P:	$65- 99	2P/1B:	$65- 99	2P/2B:	$65- 99	XP: $10-20
Fri & Sat 2/1-3/31 &							
12/1-1/31 [CP]	1P:	$45- 89	2P/1B:	$45- 89	2P/2B:	$45- 89	XP: $10-20
Sun-Thurs 2/1-3/31 &							
12/1-1/31 [EP]	1P:	$45	2P/1B:	$45	2P/2B:	$55	XP: $25

cation: Just e of US 101; Dry Creek Rd exit. 178 Dry Creek Rd 95448. Fax: 707/433-1466. **Terms:** Reserv deposit, 3
y notice; handling fee imposed. **Facility:** 23 rooms. Contemporary-style building. 1 unit with refrigerator, microwave & whirl-
ol, $90-$150 for up to 2 persons; 3 stories, no elevator; interior corridors; sauna, indoor whirlpool. **Dining:** Coffee shop
arby. **Cards:** AE, CB, DI, DS, JC, MC, VI.

HEMET—36,100

LODGINGS

ST WESTERN HEMET MOTOR INN						**Phone:** (909)925-6605	
2/1-5/31 [CP]	1P:	$52- 126	2P/1B:	$52- 126	2P/2B:	$52- 136	XP: $6	F18
6/1-1/31 [CP]	1P:	$46- 96	2P/1B:	$46- 96	2P/2B:	$46- 96	XP: $6	F18

Location: 1.3 mi w on SR 74 & 79. 2625 W Florida Ave 92545. Fax: 909/925-7095. **Terms:** Handling fee
imposed; weekly/monthly rates; pets, $10. **Facility:** 68 rooms. 2 two-bedroom units. 29 efficiencies, $6 extra
tel   charge; 2 stories; exterior corridors; heated pool, whirlpool. **Dining:** Coffee shop nearby.
creation: shuffleboard courts. **All Rooms:** extended cable TV. **Cards:** AE, DI, DS, MC, VI. **Special Amenities:** Free
eakfast and free local telephone calls. *(See ad p 470)*

COACH LIGHT MOTEL   Phone: (909)658-3
🔵 SAVE   All Year   1P: $31- 35 2P/1B: $35- 43 2P/2B: $38- 46 XP: $4
◆   Location: 1 mi w on SR 74 & SR 79. 1640 W Florida Ave 92543. Terms: Weekly/monthly rates; pets
Motel   extra charge. Facility: 32 rooms. 1 story; exterior corridors. All Rooms: combo or shower baths. Cards:
                 CB, DI, DS, JC, MC, VI. Special Amenities: Free room upgrade and preferred room (each subje
                 availability with advanced reservations).   [icons]

HEMET INN   Phone: (909)929-6
🔵 SAVE   All Year [CP]   1P: $35- 38 2P/1B: $38- 42 2P/2B: $38- 42 XP: $4-5
◆◆   Location: 0.7 mi w on SR 74 & 79. 800 W Florida Ave 92543. Fax: 909/925-3016. Terms: Weekly/mo
Motel   rates; pets, $10 extra charge. Facility: 65 rooms. 2 stories; exterior corridors; heated pool, whirlp
                 Dining: Restaurant nearby. All Rooms: combo or shower baths, extended cable TV. Some Rooms
                 efficiencies, utensil deposit. Cards: AE, DI, DS, MC, VI. Special Amenities: Free breakfast and prefe
room (subject to availability with advanced reservations).   [icons]

HEMET TRAVELODGE   Phone: (909)766-1
🔵 SAVE   All Year   1P: $38   2P/1B: $43   2P/2B: $43   XP: $5
◆◆   Location: 0.8 mi w on SR 74 & 79. 1201 W Florida Ave 92543. Fax: 909/766-7739. Terms: Reserv dep
Motel   small pets only, $5. Facility: 46 rooms. 5 whirlpool rooms, extra charge; 2 stories; exterior corridors; he
                 pool, whirlpool. All Rooms: extended cable TV. Cards: AE, CB, DI, DS, JC, MC, VI.   [icons]

RAMADA INN   Phone: (909)929-8
🔵 SAVE   All Year & 2/1-3/31 [CP] 1P: $44- 48 2P/1B: $50- 56 2P/2B: $56- 66 XP: $8
◆◆   Location: 2 mi w on SR 74 & 79. 3885 W Florida Ave 92545. Fax: 909/925-3716. Terms: Weekly/mo
Motel   rates; pets, $8 extra charge. Facility: 99 rooms. 2 stories; exterior corridors; heated pool, whirl
                 Dining: Restaurant nearby. Some Rooms: 14 efficiencies, whirlpools. Cards: AE, DI, DS, MC,
                 Special Amenities: Free breakfast and free room upgrade (subject to availability with advan
reservations).   [icons]

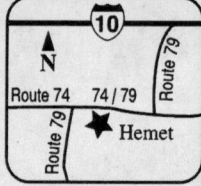

PER 8 MOTEL   **Phone:** (909)658-2281
) [SAVE]   All Year [CP]   1P: $34- 38   2P/1B: $38- 42 2P/2B: $42- 46 XP: $6   F12
         Location: 2 mi w on SR 74 & 79. 3510 W Florida Ave 92545. Fax: 909/925-6492. **Terms:** Reserv deposit;
tel   weekly/monthly rates. **Facility:** 68 rooms. 3 stories; interior corridors; small heated pool, whirlpool.
         Cards: AE, CB, DI, DS, MC, VI. **Special Amenities: Free breakfast and preferred room (subject to**
         availability with advanced reservations). (See ad p 470)

RESTAURANT

:JANDRO'S   **Lunch:** $4-$10   **Dinner:** $6-$13   **Phone:** 909/766-1192
         Location: 2.3 mi w on SR 74 & 79. 3909 W Florida Ave 92545. **Hours:** 11 am-10 pm, Fri & Sat-11 pm, Sun
xican   9 am-9 pm. Closed: 11/25 & 12/25. **Features:** casual dress; Sunday brunch; cocktails & lounge. Colorfully
         decorated. **Cards:** MC, VI.

HERMOSA BEACH—See Los Angeles p. 603.

HESPERIA—50,400

LODGINGS

'S INN SUITES   **Phone:** (760)948-0600
) [SAVE]   All Year [CP]   1P: $45- 78   2P/1B: $45- 78 2P/2B: $45- 78 XP: $5   F18
         Location: Just e of I-15, exit Bear Valley Rd; 0.5 mi e of Victor Valley Mall. 14865 Bear Valley Rd 92345.
el   Fax: 760/956-8645. **Terms:** Reserv deposit; pets, $10 dep req. **Facility:** 24 rooms. 3 two-bedroom units. 2
         stories; exterior corridors; indoor whirlpool. **Dining:** Restaurant nearby. **Some Rooms:** whirlpools.
         Cards: AE, CB, DI, DS, JC, MC, VI. **Special Amenities: Free local telephone calls and preferred room**
bject to availability with advanced reservations).

DNO LODGE   **Phone:** (760)949-1515
) [SAVE]   All Year   1P: $42   2P/1B: $46   2P/2B: $48   XP: $4   F17
         Location: E side of I-15, exit Bear Valley Rd, just s. 11976 Mariposa Rd 92345. **Terms:** Small pets only.
tel   **Facility:** 53 rooms. 2 stories; exterior corridors. **Cards:** AE, MC, VI.

PER 8 MOTEL   **Phone:** (760)949-3231
) [SAVE]   All Year   1P: $40- 50   2P/1B: $50- 65 2P/2B: $50- 65 XP: $4   F10
         Location: Just se of I-15, exit Bear Valley Rd. 12033 Oakwood Ave 92345. Fax: 760/949-0237. **Facility:** 72
◆   rooms. Across freeway from Victor Valley Mall. 2 stories; exterior corridors; whirlpool. **Recreation:** small
tel   pool. **Some Rooms:** whirlpools. **Cards:** AE, DI, DS, MC, VI. **Special Amenities: Early check-in/late**
         check-out and free breakfast.

RESTAURANT

GANO'S RESTAURANT   **Lunch:** $8-$11   **Dinner:** $14-$18   **Phone:** 760/948-4880
)   **Location:** Just e of I-15, Bear Valley Rd exit. 14747 Bear Valley Rd 92345. **Hours:** 11:30 am-2 & 5-10 pm,
◆   Sat & Sun 5 pm-10 pm. Closed: 11/25, 12/25, Mon & Tues. **Reservations:** suggested. **Features:** casual
ian   dress; beer & wine only. Charming restaurant featuring a nice selection of well-prepared Italian cuisine.
         Smoke free premises. **Cards:** AE, DS, MC, VI.

HIGHLAND—34,400

LODGING

PER 8 MOTEL   **Phone:** (909)864-0100
) [SAVE]   All Year [CP]   1P: $44   2P/1B: $44   2P/2B: $48   XP: $4   F12
         Location: 0.5 mi e of jct SR 30. 26667 E Highland Ave 92346. Fax: 909/425-0612. **Facility:** 39 rooms. Across
◆   from Patton State Hospital. 2 stories; exterior corridors. **Dining:** Restaurant nearby. **Cards:** AE, CB, DI, DS,
tel   MC, VI. **Special Amenities: Free local telephone calls and free room upgrade (subject to availability**
         with advanced reservations).

HOLLISTER—19,200

LODGINGS

ST WESTERN SAN BENITO INN   Rates Subject to Change   **Phone:** 831/637-9248
)   5/1-9/30 [CP]   1P: $55   2P/1B: $65   2P/2B: $75   XP: $5   F12
         2/1-4/30 & 10/1-1/31 [CP]   1P: $50   2P/1B: $55   2P/2B: $65   XP: $5   F12
         Location: 1.5 mi n on SR 25 & 156. 660 San Felipe Rd 95023. Fax: 831/637-4584. **Facility:** 42 rooms. 4 larger
el   units with wet bar $70-$100 for up to 2 persons; 2 stories; exterior corridors. **Cards:** CB, DI, DS, MC, VI.

SA DE FRUTA GARDEN MOTEL   Rates Subject to Change   **Phone:** 408/842-9316
◆   Fri & Sat   1P: $56- 60   2P/1B: $61- 65 2P/2B: $65   XP: $5
el   Sun-Thurs   1P: $45- 47   2P/1B: $50- 52 2P/2B: $52   XP: $5
         Location: Just s of SR 152. 10031 Pacheco Pass Hwy 95023. Fax: 831/637-1293. **Facility:** 14 rooms. Con-
ient to gas station & store. 1 story; exterior corridors; playground. **Services:** giftshop. **Cards:** MC, VI.

HOLLISTER INN Phone: (831)637-1

(AAA) [SAVE]

◆ ◆
Motel

		1P:		2P/1B:		2P/2B:		XP:
Fri & Sat 5/1-10/31		$65- 72		$72- 79		$89- 99		$10
Fri & Sat 2/1-4/30 & 11/1-1/31		$62- 65		$62- 69		$69- 76		$10
Sun-Thurs 5/1-10/31		$52- 58		$59- 65		$65- 72		$6
Sun-Thurs 2/1-4/30 & 11/1-1/31		$50- 56		$56- 62		$62- 69		$6

Location: Just n on SR 25 & 156. 152 San Felipe Rd 95023. Fax: 831/637-8423. **Facility:** 31 rooms. Across from small s
ping mall. 2 stories; exterior corridors. **Dining:** Coffee shop nearby. **Cards:** AE, CB, DI, DS, MC, VI. **Special Ameni**
Free local telephone calls and free room upgrade (subject to availability with advanced reservations).

[TI+] [🎬] [VCR] [▣] [◻] [🖨] [🗝]

RIDGEMARK GUEST COTTAGES Rates Subject to Change Phone: (831)637-8

◆ ◆ ◆
Resort Motor
Inn

		1P:		2P/1B:		2P/2B:		XP:
Fri & Sat		$85- 120		$85- 110		$105- 125		$10-14
Sun-Thurs		$90- 105		$100- 105		$100- 105		$5

Location: 2.5 mi se on SR 25; at Ridgemark Golf & Country Club. 3800 Airline Hwy 95
Fax: 831/636-3168. **Terms:** Reserv deposit, 3 day notice; handling fee imposed. **Facility:** 32 rooms. M
rooms overlooking golf course. 22 whirlpool rms, extra charge; 1 story; exterior corridors; 6 lighted tennis courts. Fee
holes golf. **Cards:** AE, DI, DS, MC, VI.

[ASK] [3P] [TI] [⚦] [✕] [🎬] [▣] [🖨] [🗝]

HOLLYWOOD—See Los Angeles p. 604.

HOMELAND—3,300

LODGING

PIERSON'S COUNTRY PLACE Rates Subject to Change Phone: (909)926-4

◆ ◆ ◆
Bed &
Breakfast

		1P:		2P/1B:	
Fri & Sat [BP]		$125		$125	
Sun-Thurs [BP]		$85- 100		$85- 100	

Location: 4 mi e of I-215; 7 mi w of Hemet; SR 74, 0.8 mi e on Sultanas Rd, 0.3 mi e on Alicante Dr. 25
Pierson Rd 92548. Fax: 909/926-1456. **Terms:** Reserv deposit, 5 day notice; handling fee impo
Facility: 5 rooms. New Mediterranean style home in the country with a view of the valley. Designated smoking a
All Rooms: combo or shower baths. **Some Rooms:** color TV. **Cards:** MC, VI.

[ASK] [So] [CTV] [✆]

HOOPA—1,000

LODGING

TSEWENALDIN INN Phone: (530)625-4

(AAA) [SAVE]

◆ ◆ ◆
Motel

		1P:		2P/1B:		2P/2B:		XP:
All Year		$60		$65		$80		$10

Location: On Hoopa Indian reservation at Hoopa Shopping Center. Hwy 96 95546 (PO Box 2
Fax: 530/625-4351. **Facility:** 21 rooms. Very attractive decor. All rooms have view of Trinity River. 2 sto
exterior corridors; whirlpool. **Dining:** Restaurant nearby. **Cards:** AE, CB, DI, DS, MC, VI. **Special Ameni**
Free breakfast and free local telephone calls.

[🎬] [3P] [⊃] [TI+] [CTV] [🎬] [▣] [◻] [🖨] [🗝]

HOPE VALLEY

LODGING

SORENSEN'S Rates Subject to Change Phone: 530/694-2

(AAA)

◆ ◆
Resort
Cottage

		1P:		2P/1B:		2P/2B:		XP:
2/1-4/15 & 11/15-1/31		$70- 110		$105- 180		$160- 250		$15
4/16-11/14		$60- 95		$90- 150		$125- 195		$15

Location: On Hwy 88, 1 mi e of Jct 89. 14255 Hwy 88 96120. **Terms:** Check-in 4 pm; reserv deposit
day notice; 2 night min stay, weekends. **Facility:** 29 rooms. All seasons resort in the Sierra Nevada; incl
cross-country skiing, backpacking & bicycling. 6 two-bedroom units. 1 story; exterior corric
Dining: Restaurant; 7:30 am-4 & 5:30-8:30 pm; $11-$17. **Recreation:** cross country skiing; hiking t
All Rooms: combo or shower baths. **Some Rooms:** 24 kitchens. **Cards:** DS, MC, VI.

[TI] [✕] [CTV] [✆] [🐾]

HOPLAND—1,200

LODGING

THATCHER INN Phone: (707)744-1

(AAA) [SAVE]

◆ ◆
Historic
Country Inn

		1P:		2P/1B:		2P/2B:		XP:
All Year [BP]		$100- 110		$105- 110		$105- 110		$25

Location: Center. 13401 S Hwy 101 95449 (PO Box 660). Fax: 707/744-1219. **Terms:** Reserv depos
day notice. **Facility:** 20 rooms. Restored 1890's Victorian hotel with interesting library. 3 stories, no elev
interior corridors; smoke free premises; small pool open 6/1-10/31. **Dining:** Dining room; 7:30 am-10
11:30 am-2 pm & 5:30 pm-9:30 pm; $11-$20; cocktails. **All Rooms:** comb, shower or tub baths. **Cards:**
MC, VI. **Special Amenities: Free breakfast.**

[🎬] [3P] [⊃] [TI] [CTV] [🖨]

HUNTINGTON BEACH—181,500   (See map p. 294; index p. 293)

LODGINGS

BEACH INN MOTEL Rates Subject to Change Phone: (714)841-6606

(AAA)

◆
Motel

		1P:		2P/1B:		2P/2B:		XP:
5/15-9/30		$50- 65		$55- 70		$65- 110		$10-15
2/1-5/14 & 10/1-1/31		$45- 60		$50- 65		$55- 70		$10-15

Location: 2.8 mi s of I-405. 18112 Beach Blvd 92648. Fax: 714/848-9288. **Terms:** Reserv dep
Facility: 38 rooms. 8 efficiencies, $7-$10 extra charge; 2 stories; exterior corridors; small heated pool, w
pool. **Some Rooms:** whirlpools. **Cards:** AE, DS, JC, MC, VI.

[⊃] [🎬] [🗝]

e map p. 294)

ST WESTERN REGENCY INN   Phone: (714)962-4244   239

[SAVE]
All Year [CP]   1P: $65- 85   2P/1B: $65- 85 2P/2B: $75- 95 XP: $10   F12
el
Location: 2 mi n on SR 39, 4 mi s of I-405. 19360 Beach Blvd 92648. Fax: 714/963-4724. **Terms:** Reserv
deposit, 3 day notice; weekly rates. **Facility:** 63 rooms. 11 efficiencies $79-$89, no utensils. 14 whirlpool rms,
$79-$99; 3 stories; exterior corridors; whirlpool. **Cards:** AE, CB, DI, DS, JC, MC, VI. **Special Amenities:**
Free breakfast and free local telephone calls.

MFORT SUITES   Phone: (714)841-1812   235

[SAVE]
5/1-9/30 [CP]   1P: $64- 89   2P/1B: $69- 99 2P/2B: $69- 99 XP: $5-10   F18
10/1-1/31 [CP]   1P: $59- 69   2P/1B: $64- 89 2P/2B: $69- 99 XP: $5-10   F18
el
2/1-4/30 [CP]   1P: $59- 89   2P/1B: $64- 99 2P/2B: $69- 99 XP: $5-10   F18
Location: SR 39, 0.4 mi s of I-405. 16301 Beach Blvd 92647. Fax: 714/841-0214. **Facility:** 102 rooms. 3 whirlpool rms, extra charge; 3 stories; exterior corridors; heated pool, whirlpool. **Dining:** Restaurant nearby.
ds: AE, CB, DI, DS, JC, MC, VI. **Special Amenities: Free breakfast and free newspaper.**

RBOUR INN   Phone: (562)592-4770   234

[SAVE]
All Year [CP]   1P: $69- 109 2P/1B: $69- 109 2P/2B: $79- 109 XP: $10   F9
◆
Location: SR 1, at Sunset Beach. 16912 Pacific Coast Hwy 90742 (PO Box 1439, SUNSET BEACH).
el
Fax: 562/592-3547. **Terms:** Reserv deposit; weekly rates. **Facility:** 25 rooms. Spacious rooms.
Some rooms with view of Huntington Harbor. 2 two-room suites; 3 stories; interior corridors. **Cards:** AE, CB,
DI, DS, MC, VI. *(See ad below)*

LIDAY INN-HUNTINGTON BEACH   Rates Subject to Change   Phone: (714)891-0123   237

◆
al
All Year   1P: $88   2P/1B: $88   2P/2B: $88
Location: I-405, Beach Blvd exit; 0.5 mi w on Center Dr across from Huntington Center Shopping Plaza.
7667 Center Ave 92647. Fax: 714/895-4591. **Facility:** 224 rooms. 8 stories; interior corridors; heated indoor
l. **Services:** giftshop. **Cards:** AE, CB, DI, DS, MC, VI.

ALITY INN   Phone: (714)536-7500   240

[SAVE]
Sun-Thurs 5/1-9/15 [CP]   1P: $89- 199 2P/1B: $89- 199 2P/2B: $130- 140 XP: $10   F18
Fri & Sat 5/1-9/15 [CP]   1P: $99- 210 2P/1B: $99- 210 2P/2B: $140   XP: $10   F18
◆
el
Sun-Thurs 2/1-4/30 &
9/16-1/31 [CP]   1P: $79- 189 2P/1B: $79- 189 2P/2B: $99- 110 XP: $10   F18
Fri & Sat 2/1-4/30 &
9/16-1/31 [CP]   1P: $89- 199 2P/1B: $89- 199 2P/2B: $110   XP: $10   F18
ation: SR 1, 3 blks nw of Huntington Beach Pier. 800 Pacific Coast Hwy 92648. Fax: 714/536-6846. **Terms:** Reserv
osit. **Facility:** 50 rooms. Many rooms with balcony & ocean view. 6 rms with whirlpool tub, extra charge; 3 stories; interior
dors; whirlpool. **Cards:** AE, CB, DI, DS, JC, MC, VI. **Special Amenities: Free breakfast and free newspaper.**

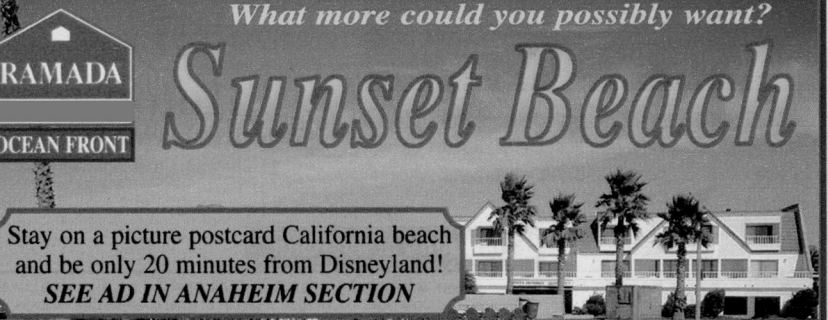

(See map p. 294)

RAMADA OCEAN FRONT
◆◆
Motel

All Year [CP]	1P: $89- 109	2P/1B: $99- 109	2P/2B: $99- 129	XP: $5-10

Rates Subject to Change Phone: 714/840-2431
Location: On SR 1; in Sunset Beach. 17205 Pacific Coast Hwy 90742 (PO Box 1188, SUNSET BEA
Fax: 562/592-4093. **Terms:** Reserv deposit. **Facility:** 50 rooms. Most rooms with patio or balcony, some
ocean view. Located adjacent to Bolsa Chica State Beach. 2 stories; interior corridors. **Cards:** AE, CB, DI, DS, MC, VI.
(See color ad p 473 & p 348)

RITZ INN
◆◆
Motel

Rates Subject to Change Phone: 714/375-0250

6/1-1/31 [CP]	1P: $55- 75	2P/1B: $69- 75	2P/2B: $75- 85	
2/1-3/31 [CP]	1P: $53- 65	2P/1B: $60- 65	2P/2B: $65- 75	
4/1-5/31 [CP]	1P: $53- 64	2P/1B: $59- 64	2P/2B: $70- 75	

Location: SR 39, 1.5 mi s of jct I-405. 17251 Beach Blvd 92647. Fax: 714/375-0251. **Facility:** 65 rooms. 20 one-bedr
suites. 4 suites with whirlpool tub; 3 stories; exterior corridors. **Cards:** AE, CB, DI, DS, JC, MC, VI.

SUN'N SANDS MOTEL
ⓐⓐ
◆
Motel

Rates Subject to Change Phone: 714/536-2543

5/16-9/15	1P: $79- 89	2P/1B: $89- 110	2P/2B: $99- 140	XP: $10-20
2/1-5/15 & 9/16-1/31	1P: $59- 69	2P/1B: $69- 79	2P/2B: $79- 89	XP: $5-10

Location: On SR1, 5 blks NW of Huntington Beach Pier. 1102 Pacific Coast Hwy 92648. Fax: 714/960-5
Terms: Reserv deposit, 3 day notice; handling fee imposed; weekly/monthly rates. **Facility:** 17 rooms. Ac
highway from beach. 2 stories; exterior corridors; heated pool. **All Rooms:** combo or shower ba
Cards: AE, CB, DI, DS, JC, MC, VI.

WATERFRONT HILTON BEACH RESORT
ⓐⓐ
◆◆◆◆
Hotel

Rates Subject to Change Phone: (714)960-7873

6/12-9/5	1P: $179- 299	2P/1B: $179- 299	2P/2B: $179- 299	XP: $15
2/1-6/11 & 9/6-1/31	1P: $179- 259	2P/1B: $179- 259	2P/2B: $179- 259	XP: $15

Location: 0.3 mi se on SR 1. 21100 Pacific Coast Hwy 92648. Fax: 714/960-2642. **Terms:** Check-in 4
Facility: 290 rooms. Across from beach. Most rooms have ocean view. 12 stories; interior corridors; he
pool, whirlpool; 2 lighted tennis courts. **Dining:** Deli; also, Palm Court, see separate lis
Services: giftshop. **Recreation:** Fee: bicycles. **Some Rooms:** whirlpools. **Cards:** AE, CB, DI, DS, JC, MC, VI.
(See ad p 119 & below)

RESTAURANTS

MARKET BROILER
◆◆
Seafood

Lunch: $6-$10 **Dinner:** $8-$18 Phone: 714/963-7796
Location: 2 mi s of I-405, exit Brookhurst St. 20111 Brookhurst St 92646. **Hours:** 11 am-10 pm, Fri & Sa
pm. Closed: 11/25 & 12/25. **Features:** casual dress; carryout; cocktails. A popular restaurant featuri
large variety of mesquite broiled seafood. A selection of chicken, steak & pasta also avail. Smoke
premises. **Cards:** AE, DS, MC, VI.

PALM COURT
◆◆◆
Continental

Lunch: $6-$18 **Dinner:** $12-$31 Phone: 714/960-7873
Location: 0.3 mi se on SR 1; in Waterfront Hilton Beach Resort. 21100 Pacific Coast Hwy 92
Hours: 6:30 am-3 & 5-10 pm, Fri & Sat-11 pm. **Reservations:** suggested. **Features:** children's m
cocktails & lounge; entertainment; valet parking; a la carte. Overlooking ocean. Casual day dining; fo
dining during evening meal. Patio dining avail. **Cards:** AE, CB, DI, DS, JC, MC, VI.

IDYLLWILD—3,000

LODGINGS

CEDAR STREET INN
◆◆
Cottage

All Year	1P: $75- 105	2P/1B: $75- 105	2P/2B: $115- 145	XP: $20

Rates Subject to Change Phone: 909/659-4
Location: 0.3 mi e of SR 243 via North Circle Dr. 25880 Cedar St 92549 (Box 627). **Terms:** Reserv dep
10 day notice; handling fee imposed; 2 night min stay, weekends. **Facility:** 9 rooms. In a quiet, forest se
with decks & patios. Themed rooms in cottages & 2-story building. Separate cabin with fireplace, kitchen & 2 bedrooms, $
$145 for up to 4 people; 1-2 stories; exterior corridors; smoke free premises. **All Rooms:** combo or shower ba
Cards: AE, DS, MC, VI.

EEKSTONE INN BED & BREAKFAST   Rates Subject to Change   **Phone:** (909)659-3342
◆◆   Fri-Sun [BP]   2P/1B: $95- 145
&   Mon-Thurs [BP]   2P/1B: $75- 125
akfast   **Location:** 0.8 mi e of village center. 54950 Pine Crest Ave 92549 (PO Box 1897). Fax: 909/659-2499.
Terms: Reserv deposit, 14 day notice; 2 night min stay, weekends. **Facility:** 9 rooms. Rooms decorated in
ntry decor & antiques. 7 rooms with fireplace. 3 whirlpool rms, extra charge; 2 stories; interior corridors; designated
king area. **Cards:** DS, MC, VI.

ESIDE INN   Guaranteed Rates   **Phone:** 909/659-2966
    All Year   1P: $55- 100   2P/1B: $65- 100   2P/2B: $55-   85   XP: $10
    Location: 0.3 mi ne of SR 243 & Village Center. 54540 N Circle Dr 92549 (PO Box 313).
◆   Fax: 909/659-4286. **Terms:** Reserv deposit, 10 day notice; handling fee imposed; 2 night min stay,
tage   weekends; small pets only. **Facility:** 8 rooms. Duplex cottages tree-shaded grounds. 1 two-
bedroom unit. Historic cabin with loft, $100; 1 story; exterior corridors; designated smoking area.
Rooms: combo or shower baths, extended cable TV. **Some Rooms:** efficiency, 7 kitchens. **Cards:** AE, CB, DI, DS, JC,
VI.

E HIGH COUNTRY INN   Rates Subject to Change   **Phone:** 909/659-2931
    Fri & Sat [CP]   1P: $65- 110   2P/1B: $65- 110   2P/2B: $110   XP: $10   D12
    Sun-Thurs [CP]   1P: $50-   75   2P/1B: $60-   75   2P/2B: $85   XP: $10   D12
    Location: 0.4 mi e of SR 243. 54635 N Circle Dr 92549 (PO Box 1685). Fax: 909/659-4926. **Terms:** Reserv
el   deposit, 10 day notice; weekly rates; 2 night min stay, weekends. **Facility:** 8 rooms.
Cozy, compact units. Closed 3/1-3/15 & 12/1-12/15. 1 two-bedroom unit. Woodburning fireplaces. One cabin
whirlpool; 1 story; exterior corridors; designated smoking area. **All Rooms:** combo or shower baths, extended cable TV.
ne **Rooms:** 3 efficiencies. **Cards:** AE, CB, DI, DS, MC, VI.

ET CREEK INN   Guaranteed Rates   **Phone:** 909/659-6110
    All Year   1P: $73- 89   2P/1B: $73- 89   2P/2B: $89
    Location: 0.8 mi s on SR 243, 0.4 mi w on Toll Gate Rd, just n. 26345 Delano Dr 92549 (PO Box 240).
    Terms: Reserv deposit, 10 day notice. **Facility:** 10 rooms. Duplex cottages on spacious pine shaded grounds.
tage   5 suites with living room & efficiency. Woodburning fireplaces. All units have private decks overlooking Strawberry Creek. 5 studio units. 1 story; exterior corridors. **All Rooms:** shower baths, extended cable TV.
ds: AE, JC, MC, VI.

RAWBERRY CREEK INN   Rates Subject to Change   **Phone:** 909/659-3202
    All Year [BP]   1P: $85- 105   2P/1B: $85- 105
    Location: 0.3 mi s on SR 243. 26370 SR 243 92549 (PO Box 1818). **Terms:** Reserv deposit, 14 day notice;
    2 night min stay, weekends. **Facility:** 10 rooms. Two story bed & breakfast inn; surrounded by oaks & pines;
◆   4 adjacent courtyard rooms with fireplace & skylight. 1-bedroom cottage with living room & kitchen, $150; Mon-
&   Thurs, $110; breakfast not included; extra person $20; 1-2 stories; interior/exterior corridors; smoke free prem-
akfast   ises. **All Rooms:** combo or shower baths. **Some Rooms:** color TV, whirlpools. **Cards:** DS, MC, VI.

ODLAND PARK MANOR   Guaranteed Rates   **Phone:** 909/659-2657
    All Year   2P/1B: $75- 95   2P/2B: $95- 150
age   **Location:** 1 mi e of SR 243. 55350 S Circle Dr 92549 (PO Box 86). **Terms:** Reserv deposit, 10 day notice;
    2 night min stay, weekends. **Facility:** 11 rooms. Duplex cottages & one separate cottage, all with woodburning
lace. Large, wooded area with picnic tables. 1 story; exterior corridors; designated smoking area; heated pool.
Rooms: combo or shower baths. **Some Rooms:** 5 efficiencies, 6 kitchens. **Cards:** MC, VI.

RESTAURANTS

TONELLI'S SEAFOOD RISTORANTE   **Dinner:** $12-$19   **Phone:** 909/659-5500
    Location: On SR 243, 0.3 mi s of Village Center. 26345 Hwy 243 92549. **Hours:** 5 pm-9 pm. Closed: Mon &
    Tues. **Reservations:** suggested; on weekends. **Features:** No A/C; children's menu; carryout; beer & wine
◆   only. Well prepared pasta & seafood entrees. Patio dining in summer. **Cards:** AE, DI, DS, MC, VI.
an

STROGNOME RESTAURANT   **Lunch:** $8-$12   **Dinner:** $12-$22   **Phone:** 909/659-5055
    Location: Just e of SR 243, in Village Center. 54381 Ridgeview Dr 92549. **Hours:** 11:30 am-2:30 & 5-9 pm,
    Fri & Sat-10 pm. **Reservations:** suggested; weekends. **Features:** No A/C; casual dress; Sunday brunch;
erican   children's menu; carryout; cocktails; a la carte. Attractive restaurant featuring steak, seafood & Continental
ees. Smoke free premises. **Cards:** CB, DI, DS, MC, VI.

LLWILD CAFE   **Lunch:** $5-$7   **Phone:** 909/659-2210
    Location: 0.5 mi s; on SR 243. 26600 Hwy 243 92549. **Hours:** 7 am-2 pm. **Features:** No A/C; casual dress.
erican   Large selection of omelettes, pancakes, sandwiches & hamburgers. Smoke free premises. **Cards:** DS, MC,
VI.

ER ROCK CAFE   **Dinner:** $16-$26   **Phone:** 909/659-5047
◆   **Location:** 0.3 mi s of Village Center. 26290 Hwy 243 92549. **Hours:** 5 pm-9 pm, Fri & Sat-10 pm. Closed:
erican   12/25, Mon, Tues & Wed. **Features:** casual dress; children's menu; carryout; beer & wine only. Attractive
restaurant featuring beef, chicken, seafood & pasta. Smoke free premises. **Cards:** DS, MC, VI.

IMPERIAL—4,100

LODGING

ST WESTERN IMPERIAL VALLEY INN   **Phone:** (760)355-4500
SAVE   2/1-6/30 & 9/1-1/31 [CP]   1P: $44- 77   2P/1B: $50- 77   2P/2B: $54- 79   XP: $6
    7/1-8/31 [CP]   1P: $42- 75   2P/1B: $48- 75   2P/2B: $51- 79   XP: $6
◆   **Location:** On SR 86, 2.5 mi n of El Centro. 1093 Airport Blvd 92251. Fax: 760/355-8645. **Terms:** Small pets
or Inn   only. **Facility:** 90 rooms. Next to Imperial County Airport. 10 suites, $77; 2 stories; exterior corridors; heated
pool, sauna, whirlpool. **Dining:** Restaurant; 5:30 am-10 pm; $7-$12; cocktails. **Cards:** AE, CB, DI, DS, JC,
VI. **Special Amenities: Free breakfast and free local telephone calls.**

IMPERIAL BEACH—*See San Diego p. 901.*

INDEPENDENCE—800

LODGING

RAY'S DEN MOTEL   Phone: (760)878-1

(AAA) [SAVE] 5/1-10/31   1P: $42- 56   2P/1B: $42- 56   2P/2B: $42- 56
◆   2/1-4/30 & 11/1-1/31 1P: $38- 51   2P/1B: $38- 51   2P/2B: $38- 51
Motel   **Location:** On US 395. 405 N Edwards 93526 (PO Box 68). **Terms:** Pets, $5.50 extra charge. **Facili**
            rooms. 1 story; exterior corridors. **All Rooms:** shower baths. **Cards:** AE, CB, DI, DS, JC, MC
            Special Amenities: Free local telephone calls.

INDIAN WELLS—2,600   (See map p. 774; index p. 772)

LODGINGS

HYATT GRAND CHAMPIONS RESORT   Phone: (760)341-1000

(AAA) [SAVE] 2/1-4/30 & 1/1-1/31   1P: $290- 375   2P/1B: $290- 375   2P/2B: $290- 375   XP: $25
            5/1-6/30 & 10/1-12/31 1P: $230- 300   2P/1B: $230- 300   2P/2B: $230- 300   XP: $25
◆◆◆◆   7/1-9/30   1P: $140- 205   2P/1B: $140- 205   2P/2B: $140- 205   XP: $25
Resort Hotel **Location:** On SR 111. 44-600 Indian Wells Ln 92210. Fax: 760/568-2236. **Terms:** Check-in 4 pm; re
            deposit, 7 day notice; pets. **Facility:** 338 rooms. Spacious, beautifully landscaped grounds. Large, attrac
decorated rooms with step down parlor area & patio or balcony. 19 one & two-bedroom villas with fireplace whirlpool & I
service $350-$950; 5 stories; interior/exterior corridors; heated pool, wading pool, saunas, steamrooms, waterslide, whirlp
playground. Fee: 36 holes golf; 12 tennis courts, 8 lighted including 2 clay courts & 2 grass courts. **Dining:** Dining I
restaurant, deli; 6:30 am-10 pm; $14-$25; cocktails. **Services:** giftshop. **Recreation:** volleyball court. **All Rooms:** exte
cable TV. **Cards:** AE, CB, DI, DS, JC, MC, VI. *(See color ad p 565)*

INDIAN WELLS RESORT HOTEL   Phone: (760)345-6466

(AAA) [SAVE] 2/1-4/25 & 1/7-1/31 [BP]   1P: $169- 249   2P/1B: $169- 249   2P/2B: $169- 249
◆◆◆   4/26-5/30 & 9/17-1/6 [BP]   1P: $119- 189   2P/1B: $119- 189   2P/2B: $119- 189
Hotel   5/31-7/4 [CP]   1P: $89- 139   2P/1B: $89- 139   2P/2B: $89- 139
            7/5-9/16 [CP]   1P: $59- 119   2P/1B: $59- 119   2P/2B: $59- 119
            Location: On SR 111. 76-661 Hwy 111 92210. Fax: 760/772-5083. **Terms:** Monthly rates. **Facility:** 151 rc
Adjoining Indian Wells Country Club. Many rooms with view of golf course. 3 stories; interior corridors; heated pool, whir
2 tennis courts. Fee: 36 holes golf. **Dining:** Dining room; 6:30 am-2 & 5-10 pm, Fri & Sat-10:30 pm; $12-$20; cock
Services: giftshop. **All Rooms:** extended cable TV. **Cards:** AE, CB, DI, DS, JC, MC, VI. **Special Amenities:**
breakfast and preferred room (subject to availability with advanced reservations).

MIRAMONTE RESORT   Rates Subject to Change   Phone: (760)341-2200

(AAA)   2/1-5/23   1P: $249- 279   2P/1B: $249- 279   2P/2B: $249- 279   XP: $25
            11/1-1/31   1P: $219- 239   2P/1B: $219- 239   2P/2B: $219- 239   XP: $25
◆◆◆◆   5/24-7/5   1P: $179- 199   2P/1B: $179- 199   2P/2B: $179- 199   XP: $25
Hotel   7/6-10/31   1P: $109- 119   2P/1B: $109- 119   2P/2B: $109- 119   XP: $25
            Location: SR 111. 76-477 Hwy 111 92210. Fax: 760/568-0541. **Terms:** 2 night min stay; small pets
Facility: 226 rooms. Attractively landscaped grounds. Elegant Mediterranean atmosphere. 2 stories; interior/exterior corr
heated pool, saunas, whirlpools. **Dining:** Restaurant; 5:30 am-2:30 & 5-10 pm, Fri & Sat-11 pm; $15-$26; cock
Services: giftshop; area transportation. **Cards:** AE, CB, DI, DS, MC, VI.

RENAISSANCE ESMERALDA RESORT   Rates Subject to Change   Phone: 760/773-4444

◆◆◆◆   All Year   1P: $240- 288   2P/1B: $240- 288   2P/2B: $240- 288   XP: $25
Resort Hotel **Location:** On SR 111. 44-400 Indian Wells Ln 92210. **Facility:** 560 rooms. Unique
staircase leads down to restaurants & pool area. 7 stories; interior corridors; heated pool; 4 tennis cou
lighted). Fee: 36 holes golf. **Services:** giftshop. Fee: massage. Rental: bicycles. **Cards:** AE, CB, DI, DS, JC, MC, VI.

RESTAURANTS

DON DIEGO'S   Lunch: $7-$11   Dinner: $11-$17   Phone: 760/340-5588
◆◆   **Location:** At Cook St; in the Village Shopping Center. 74-969 Hwy 111 92210. **Hours:** 11 am-9 pm,
Mexican   Sat-10 pm, Sun 10 am-9 pm. Closed: 11/25 & 12/25. **Reservations:** suggested. **Features:** casual d
Cards: AE, CB, DI, DS, MC, VI.   Sunday brunch; children's menu; cocktails. Colorfully decorated restaurant. Smoke free prem

LE ST GERMAIN   Lunch: $12-$15   Dinner: $20-$32   Phone: 760/773-6511
◆◆◆   **Location:** SR 111 at Cook St. 74-985 Hwy 111 92210. **Hours:** 11:30 am-2:30 & 5-10 pm. Closed: close
French   lunch in summer. **Reservations:** suggested. **Features:** semi-formal attire; cocktails & lounge; valet pa
            a la carte. An elegant restaurant featuring French Mediterranean cuisine. Smoke free premises. **Cards**
CB, DI, DS, MC, VI.

SIROCCO   Lunch: $9-$15   Dinner: $16-$27   Phone: 760/773-4444
◆◆◆   **Location:** On SR 111; in Renaissance Esmeralda Resort. 44-400 Indian Wells Ln 92210. **Hours:**
Continental am-2:30 & 6-10 pm, Sat & Sun 6 pm-10 pm. Closed: 7/1-9/15. **Reservations:** suggested. **Features:** ca
            dress; cocktails & lounge; valet parking; a la carte. Mediterranean cuisine served in an elegant, but rel
atmosphere. Smoke free premises. **Cards:** AE, CB, DI, DS, JC, MC, VI.

INDIO—36,800   (See map p. 774; index p. 773)

LODGINGS

⸱T WESTERN DATE TREE HOTEL   Phone: (760)347-3421   [65]
[SAVE]

		1P:		2P/1B:		2P/2B:		XP:	
2/1-4/25 & 10/2-1/31 [CP]	1P:	$49- 129	2P/1B:	$59- 129	2P/2B:	$59- 129	XP:	$10	F18
4/26-10/1 [CP]	1P:	$49- 69	2P/1B:	$49- 89	2P/2B:	$59- 89	XP:	$6	F18

◆◆ **Location:** 0.5 mi s of I-10; westbound Monroe St exit, eastbound Indio Blvd exit. 81-909 Indio Blvd 92201.
⸱el   Fax: 760/347-3421. **Terms:** Weekly/monthly rates; pets, $50 dep req. **Facility:** 119 rooms. Large pool area. Grounds landscaped with palms, fruit trees & cactus. 3 two-bedroom units. Heated pool, whirlpool; playground.
⸱ng: Restaurant nearby. **All Rooms:** combo or shower baths, extended cable TV. **Some Rooms:** 5 efficiencies,
⸱lpools. **Cards:** AE, CB, DI, DS, JC, MC, VI. **Special Amenities: Free breakfast and free room upgrade (subject to ⸱ilability with advanced reservations).**

⸱MFORT INN   Phone: (760)347-4044   [66]
) [SAVE]

	1P:		2P/1B:		2P/2B:		XP:	
2/1-4/14 [CP]	1P:	$49- 99	2P/1B:	$59- 109	2P/2B:	$59- 119	XP:	$6	F18
1/1-1/31 [CP]	1P:	$59- 99	2P/1B:	$59- 99	2P/2B:	$59- 109	XP:	$6	F18
4/15-12/31 [CP]	1P:	$49- 69	2P/1B:	$49- 69	2P/2B:	$49- 79	XP:	$6	F18

⸱el   **Location:** 0.5 mi s of I-10. 80-761 Hwy 111 92201. Fax: 760/347-1287. **Terms:** Reserv deposit; pets. **Facility:** 63 rooms. 4 whirlpool rms, extra charge; 2 stories; interior corridors; heated pool, whirl-
⸱. **All Rooms:** extended cable TV. **Cards:** AE, CB, DI, DS, JC, MC, VI. **Special Amenities: Free local telephone calls ⸱ free newspaper.**

⸱LM SHADOW INN   Phone: (760)347-3476   [68]
⸱ [SAVE]

	1P:		2P/1B:		2P/2B:		XP:	
2/1-4/30	1P:	$79- 129	2P/1B:	$79- 129	2P/2B:	$97- 129	XP:	$10-15	F6
11/1-1/31	1P:	$59- 97	2P/1B:	$59- 97	2P/2B:	$69- 97	XP:	$10-15	F6
5/1-10/31	1P:	$44- 79	2P/1B:	$44- 79	2P/2B:	$59- 79	XP:	$10-15	F6

⸱el   **Location:** SR 111, 0.8 mi e of Jefferson Ave. 80-761 Hwy 111 92201. Fax: 760/342-8333. **Terms:** Reserv deposit, 7 day notice; weekly/monthly rates; pets, $5 extra charge. **Facility:** 18 rooms. Nicely furnished rooms.
⸱e pool & lawn area. $10-$15 extra charge for efficiency. In-room fax machine & office supplies avail at extra charge; 1
⸱y; exterior corridors; heated pool, whirlpool. **Dining:** Restaurant nearby. **Recreation:** croquet, horseshoe pit, barbecue.
⸱Rooms:** combo or shower baths, extended cable TV. **Cards:** AE, DI, DS, MC, VI. **Special Amenities: Free local ⸱phone calls and free room upgrade (subject to availability with advanced reservations).**

⸱YAL PLAZA INN   Phone: (760)347-0911   [70]
) [SAVE]

	1P:		2P/1B:		2P/2B:	
2/1-3/31 & 1/1-1/31	1P:	$64- 95	2P/1B:	$68- 95	2P/2B:	$68- 89
4/1-6/30 & 10/1-12/31	1P:	$52- 89	2P/1B:	$59- 89	2P/2B:	$59- 89
7/1-9/30	1P:	$44- 49	2P/1B:	$48- 54	2P/2B:	$48- 54

⸱or Inn   **Location:** SR 111, 0.4 mi e.of Monroe St. 82-347 Hwy 111 92201. Fax: 760/347-8644. **Terms:** Weekly rates; pets. **Facility:** 99 rooms. Just w of Riverside County Government complex, Desert Expo Centre & Larson Jus-
Center. 2 stories; interior corridors; heated pool, whirlpool. **Dining:** Restaurant; 5 am-10 pm, Fri & Sat-11 pm; $9-$20;
⸱ktails. **Recreation:** shuffleboard courts. **All Rooms:** extended cable TV. **Cards:** AE, CB, DI, DS, MC, VI.

INDUSTRY—See Los Angeles p. 608.

INGLEWOOD—See Los Angeles p. 609.

IRVINE—110,300   (See map p. 294; index p. 293)

LODGINGS

⸱RIUM HOTEL AT ORANGE COUNTY AIRPORT   Phone: (949)833-2770   [250]
) [SAVE]

	1P:	2P/1B:	2P/2B:	XP:	
Mon-Thurs	1P: $105	2P/1B: $105	2P/2B: $105	XP: $10	F18
Fri-Sun	1P: $84	2P/1B: $84	2P/2B: $84	XP: $10	F18

◆◆ **Location:** 0.5 mi s of I-405. 18700 MacArthur Blvd 92612. Fax: 949/757-1228. **Terms:** Reserv deposit; pets,
⸱el $50 extra charge. **Facility:** 214 rooms. Opposite John Wayne/Orange County Airport. Nicely landscaped court-
yard area. 1 room with private whirlpool. 3 stories; interior corridors; heated pool. **Dining:** Coffee shop; 6
-10 pm; $6-$27; cocktails. **Services:** giftshop; area transportation, within 5 mi. **Recreation:** Billiard room.
⸱Rooms:** combo or shower baths. **Cards:** AE, CB, DI, DS, JC, MC, VI. **Special Amenities: Early check-in/late ⸱ck-out and free newspaper.**

⸱URTYARD BY MARRIOTT IRVINE/ORANGE
⸱UNTY AIRPORT   Rates Subject to Change   Phone: 949/757-1200   [251]
◆◆ All Year   1P: $79- 129   2P/1B: $79- 129   2P/2B: $79- 129
⸱or Inn   **Location:** 0.5 mi n of I-405, exit Jamboree Rd. 2701 Main St 92614. Fax: 949/757-1596. **Facility:** 153 rooms.
4 stories; interior corridors; heated pool. **Cards:** AE, CB, DI, DS, MC, VI. *(See color ad p 311)*

⸱OWNE PLAZA-IRVINE/ORANGE
⸱UNTY AIRPORT   Rates Subject to Change   Phone: (949)863-1999   [253]

	1P:	2P/1B:	2P/2B:	XP:	
Sun-Thurs	1P: $139- 154	2P/1B: $154- 179	2P/2B: $154- 179	XP: $15	F18
Fri & Sat	1P: $79- 94	2P/1B: $94- 109	2P/2B: $94- 109		

⸱el   **Location:** Adjacent to I-405, Jamboree Rd exit; n to Main, w to Von Karman Ave. 17941 Von Karman Ave.
14. Fax: 949/474-7236. **Facility:** 335 rooms. Located in an attractive office park area. 13 stories; interior corridors; heated
⸱or pool. **Services:** giftshop; area transportation. **Cards:** AE, CB, DI, DS, JC, MC, VI.

(See map p. 294)

EMBASSY SUITES HOTEL-ORANGE COUNTY AIRPORT
Phone: (949)553-8332

AAA SAVE
◆◆◆
Suite Hotel

| | Sun-Thurs [BP] | 1P: $134 | 2P/1B: $144 | 2P/2B: $144 | XP: $10 |
| | Fri & Sat [BP] | 1P: $99 | 2P/1B: $99 | 2P/2B: $99 | XP: $10 |

Fax: 949/261-5301. **Location:** I-405, exit MacArthur Blvd; exit n to Main St, then 0.5 mi e. 2120 Main St 92 **Facility:** 293 rooms. Attractive atrium area. 1-bedroom suites. A few smaller non rooms. 2 two-bedroom units. 10 stories; interior corridors; heated indoor pool, sauna, whirl **Dining:** Restaurant; 11 am-2 & 5-10 pm; $8-$18; cocktails. **Services:** giftshop; complimentary evening beverages; transportation, within 5 mi. **Recreation:** video game room. **Cards:** AE, DI, DS, JC, MC, VI. **Special Amenities:** breakfast and free newspaper.

HOMESTEAD VILLAGE
◆◆◆
Extended Stay Motel

| All Year [CP] | Rates Subject to Change | | Phone: 949/727-4228 |
| | 1P: $69- 79 | 2P/1B: $89- 99 | 2P/2B: $89- 99 | XP: $20 |

Location: E side of I-5, exit Alton Pkwy. 30 Technology Dr 92618. Fax: 949/727-3917. **Terms:** Check pm. **Facility:** 149 rooms. 2 stories; exterior corridors. **All Rooms:** kitchens, combo or shower ba **Cards:** AE, CB, DI, DS, JC, MC, VI.

HYATT REGENCY IRVINE
Phone: (949)975-1234

AAA SAVE
◆◆◆◆
Hotel

| All Year | 1P: $175- 214 | 2P/1B: $200- 239 | 2P/2B: $200- 239 | XP: $25 |

Location: Adjacent to I-405, exit Jamboree Rd. 17900 Jamboree Rd 92614. Fax: 949/863-0 **Terms:** Monthly rates. **Facility:** 536 rooms. In a suburban business park location. Business plan rms, $15 charge; Regency Club Rooms, $25 extra charge; 14 stories; interior corridors; heated pool, whirlpool; 3 lig tennis courts. Fee: parking. **Dining:** Restaurant, coffee shop; 6 am-11 pm; also, Ciao Mein, see sepa listing. **Services:** giftshop; area transportation, within 5 mi. Fee: massage. **Recreation:** bicycles. **Some Rooms:** whirlp **Cards:** AE, CB, DI, DS, JC, MC, VI. *(See color ad p 565)*

(See map p. 294)

IRVINE MARRIOTT HOTEL Rates Subject to Change Phone: (949)553-0100 ⟨255⟩
◆◆◆ All Year [BP] 1P: $89- 169 2P/1B: $89- 169 2P/2B: $89- 169
Hotel **Location:** Adjacent to I-405, exit Jamboree Rd; s to Michelson Dr, w to Von Karman Ave. 18000 Von
Karman Ave 92612. Fax: 949/261-7059. **Terms:** Check-in 4 pm. **Facility:** 485 rooms. Contemporary Hi-Rise
hotel in a corporate area. 16 stories; interior corridors; heated indoor/outdoor pool; 3 lighted tennis courts. Fee: parking.
Services: giftshop; area transportation. Fee: massage. **Cards:** AE, DI, DS, JC, MC, VI.

(ASK) (S⌂) ⟨▤⟩ ⟨✦⟩ ⟨30P⟩ ⟨⇌⟩ ⟨†1⟩ ⟨⊕⟩ ⟨⌂⟩ ⟨△⟩ ⟨✕⟩ ⟨♦⟩ ⟨♦⟩ ⟨▢⟩ ⟨▦⟩ ⟨∎⟩ ⟨✕⟩

LA QUINTA INN Rates Subject to Change Phone: (949)551-0909 ⟨256⟩
◆◆◆ All Year [CP] 1P: $75- 95 2P/1B: $75- 95 2P/2B: $75- 95
Motel **Location:** Just w of I-5, exit Sand Canyon Ave. 14972 Sand Canyon Ave 92618. Fax: 949/551-2945.
Facility: 145 rooms. Units vary from modern, contemporary style to unique rooms situated in historic hex-
agonal grain silos; each decorated in turn-of-century replica furnishings. 3-4 stories; interior/exterior corridors; heated pool.
Cards: AE, CB, DI, DS, JC, MC, VI.

(SAVE) ⟨✦⟩ ⟨30P⟩ ⟨⇌⟩ ⟨†1⟩ ⟨⊕⟩ ⟨△⟩ ⟨♦⟩ ⟨♦⟩ ⟨▢⟩ ⟨▦⟩ ⟨∎⟩ ⟨✕⟩

ORANGE COUNTY AIRPORT HILTON Guaranteed Rates Phone: (949)833-9999 ⟨257⟩
ⓐ Mon-Thurs 1P: $109 2P/1B: $109 2P/2B: $109 XP: $15 F
Fri-Sun 1P: $79 2P/1B: $79 2P/2B: $79 XP: $15 F
Hotel **Location:** 0.5 mi s of I-405. 18800 MacArthur Blvd 92612. Fax: 949/833-3317. **Terms:** Small pets only, $50
dep req. **Facility:** 289 rooms. Located in a busy corporate center area across from John Wayne Airport. 10
stories; interior corridors; heated pool, whirlpool; 1 lighted tennis court. **Dining:** Dining room; 6 am-11 pm;
$10-$22; cocktails. **Services:** giftshop; area transportation, within 5 mi. **Cards:** AE, DS, MC, VI.
See color ad p 350 & ad p 119)

(SAVE) ⟨▤⟩ ⟨✦⟩ ⟨30P⟩ ⟨⇌⟩ ⟨†1⟩ ⟨⊕⟩ ⟨△⟩ ⟨✕⟩ ⟨♦⟩ ⟨♦⟩ ⟨▢⟩ ⟨▦⟩ ⟨∎⟩ ⟨✕⟩

RESIDENCE INN BY MARRIOTT-IRVINE SPECTRUM Guaranteed Rates Phone: 949/380-3000 ⟨258⟩
◆◆◆ 6/12-9/6 [CP] 1P: $104- 119 2P/1B: $104- 119 2P/2B: $104- 119
Apartment 2/1-6/11 & 9/7-1/31 [CP] 1P: $94- 109 2P/1B: $94- 109 2P/2B: $94- 109 **Facility:** 112
Motel rooms. Located in a corporate business park area. Studios & 1-bedroom split-level apartments, some with fire-
place. 2 stories; exterior corridors; heated pool. **Services:** area transportation. **Recreation:** sports court.
All Rooms: kitchens. **Cards:** AE, CB, DI, DS, JC, MC, VI. **Location:** 2 mi e of I-5, exit Alton Pkwy. 10 Morgan at Alton Pkwy 92618. Fax: 949/588-7743.

⟨▤⟩ ⟨✦⟩ ⟨30P⟩ ⟨⇌⟩ ⟨⊕⟩ ⟨△⟩ ⟨✕⟩ ⟨♦⟩ ⟨VCR⟩ ⟨▦⟩ ⟨✕⟩

RESTAURANTS

BISTANGO Lunch: $7-$15 Dinner: $15-$24 Phone: 949/752-5222 ⟨99⟩
◆◆◆ **Location:** 0.3 mi s of Michelson Dr; In the Atrium Bldg. 19100 Von Karman Ave 92612. **Hours:** 11:30 am-3
American & 5:30-11 pm, Sat & Sun from 5:30 pm. Closed: 1/1, 11/25 & 12/25. **Reservations:** suggested.
Features: casual dress; cocktails & lounge; entertainment; valet parking; a la carte. Attractive decor with
contemporary art displays. Menu selection includes pasta, pizza, steak & seafood. **Cards:** AE, CB, DI, DS, MC, VI. ⟨✕⟩

CHANTECLAIR Lunch: $10-$15 Dinner: $20-$28 Phone: 949/752-8001 ⟨100⟩
◆◆◆◆ **Location:** 0.7 mi s of I-405. 18912 MacArthur Blvd 92612. **Hours:** 11:30 am-2:30 & 6-10 pm, Sat 6-10 pm,
French Sun 10 am-9 pm. Closed major holidays. **Reservations:** suggested. **Features:** semi-formal attire; cocktails &
lounge; valet parking; a la carte. An elegant restaurant with the atmosphere of a French country inn. Cigar
lounge. **Cards:** AE, DI, DS, MC, VI. ⟨✕⟩

CIAO MEIN Lunch: $8-$16 Dinner: $11-$18 Phone: 949/756-2426 ⟨104⟩
◆◆◆ **Location:** In Hyatt Regency Irvine; Adjacent to I-405, exit Jamboree Rd. 17900 Jamboree Rd 92614.
Ethnic **Hours:** 11:30 am-2 & 3-11 pm, Sat & Sun 3 pm-11 pm. **Reservations:** suggested. **Features:** semi-formal
attire; children's menu; carryout; cocktails & lounge; fee for valet parking; a la carte. Contemporary dining
room with an innovative selection of Chinese & Italian cuisines. American fare. Smoke free premises. **Cards:** AE, CB, DI,
DS, JC, MC, VI. ⟨✕⟩

IL FORNAIO CUCINA ITALIANA Lunch: $10-$22 Dinner: $10-$22 Phone: 949/261-1444 ⟨106⟩
◆◆◆ **Location:** 18051 Von Karman Ave 92612. **Hours:** 11 am-11 pm, Fri & Sat-midnight, Sun 5-10 pm.
Italian **Reservations:** suggested. **Features:** casual dress; cocktails & lounge; valet parking; a la carte. A large,
popular restaurant serving pasta, pizza, steaks, veal & chicken. Some patio seating avail. **Cards:** AE, DI,
DS, MC, VI. ⟨✕⟩

MCCORMICK & SCHMICK'S Lunch: $6-$20 Dinner: $10-$20 Phone: 949/756-0505 ⟨101⟩
◆◆◆ **Location:** Just w of Von Karman Ave. 2000 Main St 92614. **Hours:** 11 am-11 pm, Sat from 5 pm, Sun 5
Seafood pm-10 pm. Closed: 12/25, 1/1. **Reservations:** suggested. **Features:** casual dress; cocktails & lounge; valet
parking; a la carte. Large selection of fresh seafood. Beef, poultry & pasta entrees also available. **Cards:** AE,
CB, DI, DS, MC, VI. ⟨✕⟩

MIMI'S CAFE Lunch: $6-$12 Dinner: $8-$12 Phone: 949/559-8840 ⟨102⟩
◆◆ **Location:** Just e of Culver Dr. 4030 Barranca Pkwy 92614. **Hours:** 7 am-11 pm. Closed: 12/25.
American **Features:** casual dress; children's menu; beer & wine only. Colorful French cafe atmosphere. Nice selection
of salads, sandwiches & entrees. Patio dining avail. **Cards:** AE, MC, VI. ⟨✕⟩

PREGO RISTORANTE Lunch: $10-$20 Dinner: $10-$20 Phone: 949/553-1333 ⟨103⟩
◆◆◆ **Location:** Michelson at Von Karman; in Koll Center Irvine. 18420 Von Karman Ave 92612. **Hours:** 11:30
Italian am-11 pm, Sat 5 pm-11 pm, Sun 5 pm-10 pm. Closed major holidays. **Reservations:** suggested.
Features: casual dress; cocktails & lounge; valet parking; a la carte. Attractive, popular restaurant serving a
nice selection of regional Italian cuisine. **Cards:** AE, DI, MC, VI. ⟨✕⟩

JACKSON—3,500

LODGINGS

AMADOR MOTEL
Motel
Guaranteed Rates
Phone: 209/223-0970

		1P:	2P/1B:		2P/2B:		XP:
Fri & Sat 2/1-10/31 & Sun-Thurs 2/1-10/31 &		$40	$52		$45- 57		$5
11/1-1/31		$33	$45		$45- 55		$5

Location: 1.5 mi n at jct SR 49 & 88 on Frontage Rd. 12408 Kennedy Flat Rd 95642. **Terms:** Reserv deposit; pets. **Facility:** 10 rooms. Large back patio with unique flower & herb garden. Some small, all comfortable rooms. Exterior corridors. **Recreation:** outdoor BBQ & picnic facilities. **All Rooms:** shower baths. **Cards:** AE, DS, MC, VI.

BEST WESTERN AMADOR INN
Motor Inn
Phone: (209)223-0211

		1P:	2P/1B:		2P/2B:		XP:	
Fri & Sat		$63	$82		$82		$12	F12
Sun-Thurs		$59	$72		$72		$12	F12

Location: On SR 49. 200 s Hwy 49 95642 (PO Box 758). Fax: 209/223-4836. **Facility:** 118 rooms. Comfortable rooms. Walking distance to downtown shops. 4 shops. **Dining:** Coffee shop nearby. **Cards:** AE, CB, DI, DS, JC, MC, VI. **Special Amenities:** Free local telephone calls.

EL CAMPO CASA RESORT MOTEL
Motel
Phone: (209)223-0100

		1P:		2P/1B:		2P/2B:		XP:
5/1-9/30		$41- 57		$46- 57		$51- 77		$6
2/1-4/30 & 10/1-12/31		$37- 51		$41- 51		$45- 67		$6

Location: 1.5 mi w in Martell, at jct SR 49 & 88 on Frontage Rd; approach off SR 88. 12548 Kennedy Flat Rd 95642. **Terms:** Open 2/1-12/31; reserv deposit; pets, one room available. **Facility:** 15 rooms. Attractively landscaped backyard & garden area. 2 stories; exterior corridors; playground. **Recreation:** barbeque & picnic facilities. **All Rooms:** shower baths. **Cards:** AE, MC, VI.

GATE HOUSE INN
Historic Bed & Breakfast
Rates Subject to Change
Phone: (209)223-3500

		1P:	2P/1B:		XP:
All Year [BP]		$100- 150	$105- 160		$20

Location: 2 mi n on SR 49; then 1.5 mi e on Jackson Gate Rd. 1330 Jackson Gate Rd 95642. Fax: 209/223-1299. **Terms:** Reserv deposit, 7 day notice. **Facility:** 5 rooms. A turn-of-the-century rural Victorian. 1 two-bedroom unit. 2 stories; interior corridors. **All Rooms:** combo or shower baths. **Cards:** AE, CB, DS, MC, VI.

JACKSON GOLD LODGE
Motel
Phone: (209)223-0486

		1P:		2P/1B:		2P/2B:		XP:	
5/1-9/30 [CP]		$55- 85		$57- 85		$59- 85		$6	F16
2/1-4/30 & 10/1-1/31 [CP]		$50- 72		$50- 72		$57- 75		$6	F16

Location: 0.5 mi w on SR 49 & 88. 850 N SR 49 95642 (PO Box 1147). Fax: 209/223-2905. **Terms:** Pets, $10 extra charge. **Facility:** 36 rooms. Comfortable rooms & cottages. 8 duplex housekeeping cottages, $75-$90 for up to 2 persons; 1-2 stories; exterior corridors. **All Rooms:** combo or shower baths. **Cards:** AE, CB, DI, DS, MC, VI. **Special Amenities:** Free breakfast and free local telephone calls. *(See ad below)*

THE WEDGEWOOD INN
Bed & Breakfast
Guaranteed Rates
Phone: (209)296-4300

		1P:	2P/1B:		2P/2B:		XP:	
All Year [BP]		$90- 165	$100- 165		$100- 165		$25	D5

Location: 6.5 mi e of jct SR 49 & SR 88, exit SR 88 Irishtown-Clinton rds, r on Clinton Rd 0.6 mi s to Narcissus Rd, 0.4 mi e to Wedgewood Dr (don't exit W Clinton). 11941 Narcissus Rd 95642. Fax: 209/296-4301. **Terms:** Reserv deposit, 7 day notice; handling fee imposed. **Facility:** 6 rooms. Beautiful Queen Ann Victorian replica furnished in European & American antiques & memorabilia. English country style grounds. 1 two-bedroom suite with whirlpool tub, $165; rates up to 2 persons; 3 stories; interior corridors; smoke free premises. **Some Rooms:** color TV. **Cards:** AE, DS, MC, VI.

RESTAURANT

UPSTAIRS RESTAURANT & STREETSIDE BISTRO
West American
Lunch: $3-$10   **Dinner:** $13-$22   **Phone:** 209/223-3342

Location: Center. 164 Main St 95642. **Hours:** 11:30 am-2:30 & 5:30-9 pm, Sat & Sun 11:30 am-3:30 & 5:30 pm-9 pm. Closed: Mon & 12/25. **Reservations:** suggested. **Features:** casual dress; children's menu; beer & wine only; street parking. Smoke free premises. **Cards:** DI, DS, MC, VI.

JAMESTOWN—2,200

LODGING

PALM HOTEL BED & BREAKFAST
◆◆◆
Historic Bed
& Breakfast
Rates Subject to Change   **Phone:** 209/984-3429
All Year [BP]   1P: $85- 145   2P/1B: $85- 145   2P/2B: $85- 145   XP: $15
Location: Center. 10382 Willow St 95327. Fax: 209/984-4929. **Terms:** Reserv deposit, 5 day notice; handling fee imposed; 2 night min stay, with saturday. **Facility:** 8 rooms. 2 stories; interior corridors. **All Rooms:** shower or tub baths. **Cards:** AE, MC, VI.
⊞ ☎ 🔒 ✕

RESTAURANT

NATIONAL HOTEL RESTAURANT   Lunch: $6-$10   Dinner: $9-$17   **Phone:** 209/984-3446
American
Location: Center, Main St. 77 Main St 95327. **Hours:** 11:30 am-4:30 & 5-9 pm, Sun 10 am-3:30 & 4-9 pm, Sat-10 pm. **Reservations:** suggested. **Features:** casual dress; Sunday brunch; children's menu; cocktails & lounge; minimum charge-$5; street parking. Casual elegance. Restored landmark established in 1859. Smoke free premises. **Cards:** AE, CB, DI, DS, MC, VI.
✕

JENNER—200

LODGING

JENNER INN & COTTAGES
◆◆
Cottage
Rates Subject to Change   **Phone:** (707)865-2377
All Year [CP]   1P: $95- 225   2P/1B: $95- 225   2P/2B: $150- 225   XP: $15   F4
Location: 10400 Hwy 1 95450. Fax: 707/865-0829. **Terms:** Reserv deposit; handling fee imposed. **Facility:** 18 rooms. Cottages at various locations, three along bluff n of main bldg, overlooking river. Few rooms with fireplace. 2 stories; exterior corridors. **All Rooms:** combo or shower baths. **Some Rooms:** 5 kitchens. **Cards:** AE, MC, VI.
⊞ 🐂 ▭ ☎ 🐕 🔒 ✕

JULIAN—1,300

LODGINGS

APPLE TREE INN   **Phone:** (760)765-0222
AAA SAVE
◆◆
Motel
All Year   1P: $77- 87   2P/1B: $77- 87   2P/2B: $87   XP: $7   F12
Location: 3 mi w on SR 78 & 79. 4360 Hwy 78 92070 (4360 Highway 78, SANTA YSABEL). **Terms:** Reserv deposit; weekly rates; pets, $50, $10 extra charge dep req. **Facility:** 16 rooms. 1 story; exterior corridors. **Dining:** Restaurant nearby. **Cards:** AE, CB, DI, DS, JC, MC, VI. **Special Amenities:** Early check-in/late check-out and preferred room (subject to availability with advanced reservations).
$↓ 🛏 ⇆ ⊞ 🐕 ☎ ✕

BUTTERFIELD BED & BREAKFAST   **Phone:** (760)765-2179
AAA SAVE
◆◆◆
Bed &
Breakfast
Fri & Sat [BP]   1P: $110- 145   2P/1B: $110- 145
Sun-Thurs [BP]   1P: $99- 129   2P/1B: $99- 129
Location: 1.5 mi e on SR 78 to Sunset Dr & Whispering Pines. 2284 Sunset Dr 92036 (PO Box 1115). Fax: 760/765-1229. **Terms:** Reserv deposit, 7 day notice; package plans. **Facility:** 5 rooms. A charming inn on a tree-shaded, hillside location. Cozy, comfortable rooms, 2 with fireplace. 2 stories; interior/exterior corridors; designated smoking area. **All Rooms:** combo or shower baths, extended cable TV. **Some Rooms:** color TV. **Cards:** AE, DS, MC, VI. **Special Amenities:** Free breakfast and free room upgrade (subject to availability with advanced reservations).
$↓ 🖥 ☎ 🐕 🖨 ✕

HOMESTEAD BED & BREAKFAST   Rates Subject to Change   **Phone:** (760)765-1536
AAA
◆◆◆
Bed &
Breakfast
All Year [BP]   1P: $99- 140   2P/1B: $99- 140   2P/2B: $99- 140
Location: 4.5 mi s on SR 79. 4924 Hwy 79 92036 (PO Box 1208). **Terms:** Reserv deposit, 7 day notice; 2 night min stay, weekends. **Facility:** 4 rooms. An attractive mountain home in a quiet, forest location with antiques & a stone fireplace. 2 stories; interior corridors; designated smoking area. **All Rooms:** combo or shower baths. **Cards:** MC, VI.
🐕 ☎ ✕

JULIAN GOLD RUSH HOTEL BED & BREAKFAST   **Phone:** (760)765-0201
AAA SAVE
◆◆
Historic Bed
& Breakfast
Fri & Sat 2/1-5/31 & 9/1-1/31
[BP]   1P: $110- 155   2P/1B: $110- 115   2P/2B: $135
Fri & Sat 6/1-8/31 [BP]   1P: $96- 140   2P/1B: $96- 140   2P/2B: $115
Sun-Thurs 2/1-5/31 &
9/1-1/31 [BP]   1P: $55- 125   2P/1B: $86- 125   2P/2B: $98
Sun-Thurs 6/1-8/31 [BP]   1P: $55- 115   2P/1B: $76- 115   2P/2B: $86
Location: Center of town, on SR 78 & 79. 2032 Main St 92036 (PO Box 1856). Fax: 760/765-0327. **Terms:** Reserv deposit, 3 day notice; 2 night min stay, weekends. **Facility:** 14 rooms. Historic hotel built in 1897. Victorian decor. Small rooms. One bedroom suite with wood burning fireplace $160 weekends, $125 weekdays; 2 stories; interior/exterior corridors; designated smoking area. **Dining:** Afternoon refreshments; afternoon tea. **All Rooms:** combo or shower baths. **Cards:** AE, MC, VI. **Special Amenities:** Free breakfast and free local telephone calls.
$↓ 🐕 ☎ 🐕 🖨 ✕

JULIAN LODGE   **Phone:** (760)765-1420
AAA SAVE
◆◆
Lodge
All Year [CP]   1P: $72- 92   2P/1B: $72- 92   2P/2B: $82   XP: $10
Location: In town, just S of Main St (SR 78 & 79). 2720 C St 92036 (PO Box 1930). **Terms:** Reserv deposit. **Facility:** 23 rooms. Attractive country atmosphere. 2 stories; interior/exterior corridors. **Cards:** AE, DS, MC, VI.
🖥 ☎ 🔒 ✕

THE JULIAN WHITE HOUSE BED & BREAKFAST INN   **Phone:** (760)765-1764
AAA SAVE
◆◆
Bed &
Breakfast
All Year [BP]   1P: $95- 145   2P/1B: $95- 145   XP: $25
Location: 0.8 mi w on SR 78 & 79, 2 mi s on Pine Hills Rd; 0.5 mi w on Blue Jay Dr. 3014 Blue Jay Dr 92036 (PO Box 824). **Terms:** Check-in 4 pm; reserv deposit, 7 day notice; handling fee imposed; 2 night min stay, weekends. **Facility:** 4 rooms. Petite southern colonial mansion in a wooded area. Each guest room is individually decorated with antiques & Victorian decor, some with fireplace. 2 stories; interior corridors; designated smoking area; whirlpool. **Dining:** Evening refreshments. **All Rooms:** combo or shower baths. **Cards:** MC, VI. **Special Amenities:** Free breakfast and free local telephone calls.
🐕 ☎ ✕

ORCHARD HILL COUNTRY INN   Rates Subject to Change   Phone: (760)765-1700
AAA   All Year [BP]   1P: $155- 225   2P/1B: $155- 225   2P/2B: $155- 255   XP: $25
◆◆◆◆   **Location:** Just n of Main St (SR 78 & 79). 2502 Washington St 92036 (PO Box 425). Fax: 760/765-0290.
Country Inn   **Terms:** Reserv deposit, 7 day notice; 2 night min stay, weekends. **Facility:** 22 rooms. California craftsman lodge rooms & spacious cottages with American country decor; 11 rooms with fireplace, 8 with whirlpool. On a hillside above town on several acres landscaped with native plants & picnic areas. 8 whirlpool rms, extra charge; 1-2 stories; interior/exterior corridors; designated smoking area; whirlpools. **Dining:** Dining room; 6:30 pm-8 pm, open Wed & Sat for guests only, other days on a seasonal basis, reservations advised; afternoon refreshments; wine/beer only. **Services:** Fee: massage. **Recreation:** hiking trails. **All Rooms:** combo or shower baths. **Cards:** AE, MC, VI.
(See color ad p 84)   [ASK] [🛁] [🍽] [⊗] [VCR] [▭] [🖨] [🔒] [✕]

RESTAURANTS

JULIAN GRILLE   **Lunch:** $8-$10   **Dinner:** $14-$21   Phone: 760/765-0173
◆   **Location:** Just w of SR 78 & 79. 2224 Main St. **Hours:** 11 am-3 & 5-9 pm; Sun 9:30 am-3 & 5-9 pm. Closed: 11/25 & 12/25. **Features:** casual dress; Sunday brunch; children's menu;
American   cocktails; street parking. Dining in a restored home & outdoor patio. **Cards:** AE, MC, VI.   [✕]

ROMANO'S RESTAURANT   **Lunch:** $6-$15   **Dinner:** $10-$17   Phone: 760/765-1003
◆   **Location:** In town, just s of Main St (SR 78 & 79). 2718 B St 92036. **Hours:** 11 am-8 pm. Closed holidaysTues. **Reservations:** suggested. **Features:** No A/C; casual dress; cocktails & lounge; street parking;
Italian   a la carte. Rustic, country decor. Features a nice selection of pasta, pizza & Italian specialties. Credit cards not accepted. Limited outdoor seating. Smoke free premises.   [✕]

JUNE LAKE—600

LODGINGS

DOUBLE EAGLE RESORT/SPA   Phone: 760/648-7004
AAA [SAVE]   Fri & Sat   1P: $130- 142   2P/2B: $130- 142   XP: $10
   Sun-Thurs   1P: $116- 128   2P/2B: $116- 128   XP: $10
[FYI]   Too new to rate. **Location:** On SR 158, 3 mi w of Village Center. 5587 Hwy 158 93529 (Rt 3, Box 14-C). Fax: 760/648-7017. **Terms:** Pets. **Facility:** 7 rooms. On several acres of open & tree-shaded grounds.
Cottage   2-bedroom cabins with kitchen, 2 fireplace. Rates for up to 4-6 persons; 1 story; exterior corridors.
   All Rooms: kitchens, combo or shower baths.   [🛏] [🍴] [✕]

GULL LAKE LODGE   Rates Subject to Change   Phone: (760)648-7516
◆   Fri & Sat 2/1-4/30 & 11/1-1/31   1P: $55- 84   2P/1B: $55- 84   2P/2B: $55- 84   XP: $5-9   F5
Apartment   5/1-10/31   1P: $60- 84   2P/1B: $60- 84   2P/2B: $60- 84   XP: $5-9   F5
Motel   Sun-Thurs 2/1-4/30 & 11/1-1/31   1P: $40- 60   2P/1B: $40- 60   2P/2B: $40- 60   XP: $5-9   F5
Location: In the village area just N of SR 158, via Knoll & Bruce sts. 132 Leonard Ave 93529 (PO Box 25). **Terms:** Reserv deposit, 21 day notice; handling fee imposed. **Facility:** 14 rooms. Within walking distance of June & Gull lakes. 13 one-bedroom suites with kitchen and one 2-bedroom housekeeping cottage. 2 stories; exterior corridors. **All Rooms:** combo or shower baths. **Cards:** AE, DS, MC, VI.   [ASK] [🛏] [⛱] [🎣] [▭] [▢] [Ⓩ] [✕] [🖨] [✕]

JUNE LAKE MOTEL & CABINS   Rates Subject to Change   Phone: 760/648-7547
AAA   Fri & Sat 2/1-4/30 & 11/1-1/31   2P/1B: $56   2P/2B: $58- 87   XP: $8
◆◆   5/1-11/31   2P/1B: $52   2P/2B: $54- 85   XP: $8
Motel   Sun-Thurs 2/1-4/30 & 11/1-1/31   2P/1B: $50   2P/2B: $52- 70   XP: $8
Location: SR 158, in center of village. 2716 Boulder Dr 93529 (PO Box 98). Fax: 760/648-7147. **Terms:** Reserv deposit, 14 day notice; handling fee imposed; weekly rates, in summer; pets, $5 extra charge. **Facility:** 30 rooms. Motel units, some with kitchen; also one & two-bedroom housekeeping cabins with fireplace. 8 two-bedroom units. 1-2 stories; exterior corridors; sauna, indoor whirlpool. **Recreation:** fish cleaning & freezing facilities. **All Rooms:** combo or shower baths. **Cards:** AE, DS, MC, VI.   [🛏] [🛏] [↔] [🎣] [▭] [▢] [✕] [🔒] [✕]

JUNE LAKE VILLAGER   Rates Subject to Change   Phone: 760/648-7712
AAA   Fri & Sat 2/1-4/8 & 11/27-1/31   1P: $45- 60   2P/1B: $50- 65   2P/2B: $50- 65   XP: $8
◆◆   Sun-Thurs 2/1-4/8 & 11/27-1/31   1P: $40- 55   2P/1B: $45- 60   2P/2B: $45- 60   XP: $8
Motel   4/9-11/26   1P: $35- 55   2P/1B: $40- 55   2P/2B: $40- 60   XP: $8
Location: Center of village, on SR 158. 85 Boulder Dr 93529 (PO Box 127). Fax: 760/648-7003. **Terms:** Check-in 4 pm; reserv deposit, 14 day notice; small pets only. **Facility:** 23 rooms. A variety of motel & housekeeping units. 8 with fireplace. 1 two-bedroom unit, 3 three-bedroom units. 1-2 stories; exterior corridors; indoor whirlpool. **Dining:** Restaurant nearby. **All Rooms:** combo or shower baths. **Some Rooms:** 3 efficiencies, 9 kitchens, color TV. **Cards:** AE, DS, MC, VI.   [🛏] [↔] [🍴] [⛱] [🎣] [▭] [▢] [✕] [✕]

WHISPERING PINES CHALETS & MOTEL   Phone: (760)648-7762
AAA [SAVE]   Fri & Sat 2/1-4/30 & 11/1-1/31 [CP]   2P/1B: $65- 70   2P/2B: $65- 155   XP: $10   D12
◆◆   5/1-7/31 & 9/7-10/31 [CP]   2P/1B: $55- 69   2P/2B: $55- 145   XP: $10   D12
Motel   8/1-9/6 [CP]   2P/1B: $69- 90   2P/2B: $69- 145   XP: $10   D12
   Sun-Thurs 2/1-4/30 & 11/1-1/31 [CP]   1P: $28- 70   2P/1B: $38- 70   2P/2B: $48- 70   XP: $10   D12
Location: On SR 158, 3 mi W of village center. 93529 (Rt 3, Box 14B). Fax: 760/648-7589. **Terms:** Reserv deposit, 14 day notice. **Facility:** 24 rooms. Motel units with kitchens, housekeeping cabins & hillside A-frame chalets; spectacular mountain view. 6 two-bedroom units. Exterior corridors; indoor whirlpool. **Recreation:** fish cleaning & freezing facilities. **All Rooms:** kitchens, combo or shower baths. **Cards:** AE, DS, MC, VI. **Special Amenities:** Free breakfast and preferred room (subject to availability with advanced reservations).   [🛏] [🛏] [↔] [🎣] [VCR] [▢] [✕] [🖨] [✕]

RESTAURANT

CARSON PEAK INN   **Dinner:** $11-$20   Phone: 760/648-7575
◆◆   **Location:** 2 mi w on SR 158. 93529. **Hours:** 5 pm-10 pm. **Reservations:** suggested. **Features:** No A/C;
American   casual dress; children's menu; carryout; beer & wine only. Beautiful country setting at foot of Carson Peak. Menu features a variety of steak, seafood, barbeque back ribs & combination plates. Smoke free premises.
Cards: MC, VI.   [✕]

KELSEYVILLE—2,900

LODGINGS

BELL HAVEN RESORT
◆
Cottage
All Year — Rates Subject to Change — 2P/1B: $85 — 2P/2B: $85 — XP: $5 — Phone: (707)279-4329
Location: 6 mi e of SR 29, just no of Soda Bay Rd. 3415 White Oak Way 95451. Fax: 707/279-9049. **Terms:** Reserv deposit, 14 day notice, in summer; 2 night min stay. **Facility:** 10 rooms. Nice wooded area on southwest shore of Clear Lake. 1 three-bedroom unit, 7 two-bedroom units. 1 two-bedroom & 1 three-bedroom house, $105-$275 for up to 8 persons; 1 story; exterior corridors; boat dock. **Recreation:** swimming, boating, fishing, paddleboats, sailboating. **All Rooms:** shower baths. **Some Rooms:** 9 kitchens, color TV. **Cards:** DS, MC, VI.

KONOCTI HARBOR RESORT & SPA
◆◆◆
Resort Complex
All Year — Rates Subject to Change — 1P: $49- 100 — 2P/1B: $49- 100 — 2P/2B: $49- 100 — XP: $10 — Phone: 707/279-4281
Location: 5 mi ne of SR 29 via SR 281. 8727 Soda Bay Rd 95451. Fax: 707/279-9205. **Terms:** Check-in 4 pm. **Facility:** 250 rooms. Beautifully landscaped, terraced hillside location. Excellent recreational facilities. Few modest motel rooms. Cottages & apartments, some with gas fireplace, balcony; most with lake view. 100 kitchen apartments $135-$225 for up to 2 persons. Midweek rates may vary; 2 stories; exterior corridors; lake view; indoor pool; 8 lighted tennis courts; boat ramp; playground. Fee: miniature golf; marina. **Services:** giftshop. Fee: massage. **Recreation:** fishing, waterskiing. Rental: boats. **All Rooms:** combo or shower baths. **Cards:** AE, CB, DI, DS, MC, VI.

KERNVILLE—1,700

LODGINGS

BAREWOOD MOTEL
◆◆
Motel
All Year — Rates Subject to Change — 2P/1B: $65 — 2P/2B: $65 — XP: $10 — Phone: 760-376-1910
Location: 4 mi s in Wofford Heights. 7013 Wofford Blvd 93285 (PO Box 3791, WOFFORD HEIGHTS). Fax: 760/376-1931. **Facility:** 10 rooms. Hillside location with view of Lake Isabella. Large whirlpool rm, $85; 1 story; exterior corridors; playground. **Cards:** AE, DS, MC, VI.

HI-HO LODGE
AAA
◆
Motel
All Year — Rates Subject to Change — 1P: $65 — 2P/1B: $65 — 2P/2B: $85 — XP: $10 — Phone: 760/376-2671
Location: 1.2 mi s on Sierra Way. 11901 Sierra Hwy 93238 (Rt 1, Box 21). **Terms:** Reserv deposit, 5 day notice; weekly/monthly rates; small pets only, $10. **Facility:** 7 rooms. 1- & 2-bedroom units with kitchen. 4 two-bedroom units. 1 story; exterior corridors; whirlpool; playground. **Recreation:** fish cleaning facilities. **All Rooms:** kitchens, extended cable TV. **Cards:** AE, DS, MC, VI.

THE KERN LODGE
◆◆
Motel
All Year — Rates Subject to Change — 1P: $60- 100 — 2P/1B: $60- 100 — 2P/2B: $70- 100 — XP: $5-10 — F18 — Phone: 760/376-2223
Location: Sierra Way, Just n of Jct Kernville Rd. 67 Valley View 93238. Fax: 760/376-2225. **Terms:** Reserv deposit, 3 day notice; handling fee imposed. **Facility:** 15 rooms. Barbecue & picnic area. 2 two-bedroom units for up to 5 persons; 1 story; exterior corridors. **All Rooms:** shower baths. **Some Rooms:** 6 kitchens. **Cards:** DS, MC, VI.

KERN RIVER INN BED & BREAKFAST
AAA
◆◆◆
Bed & Breakfast
4/1-10/31 [BP] — 1P: $79- 89 — 2P/1B: $89- 99 — XP: $15 — Guaranteed Rates — Phone: (760)376-6750
2/1-3/31 & 11/1-1/31 [BP] — 1P: $69- 79 — 2P/1B: $79- 89 — XP: $15
Location: In town just s of Kernville Rd. 119 Kern River Dr 93238 (PO Box 1725). Fax: 760/376-6643. **Terms:** Reserv deposit, 7 day notice. **Facility:** 6 rooms. Across from Riverside Park & Kern River. Afternoon refreshments. Very comfortable individually decorated rooms with river view, 3 with woodburning fireplace, 2 with whirlpool tub. 2 stories; interior corridors; smoke free premises. **Cards:** AE, MC, VI.

KERNVILLE INN
AAA [SAVE]
◆◆
Motel
All Year — 1P: $49- 74 — 2P/1B: $49- 74 — 2P/2B: $54- 59 — XP: $10 — Phone: (760)376-2206
Location: Center of town, across from Circle Park. 11042 Kernville Rd 93238 (Rt 1, Box 41). Fax: 760/376-3735. **Facility:** 26 rooms. A variety of rooms, some with river view. Suites with kitchen, $99; 1 story; exterior corridors. **Dining:** Restaurant nearby. **All Rooms:** combo or shower baths, extended cable TV. **Some Rooms:** 8 efficiencies. **Cards:** AE, DS, MC, VI. **Special Amenities:** Early check-in/late check-out and preferred room (subject to availability with advanced reservations).

RIVER VIEW LODGE
AAA [SAVE]
◆
Motel
All Year [CP] — 1P: $55- 90 — 2P/1B: $55- 90 — 2P/2B: $75- 95 — Phone: (760)376-6019
Location: In center of town, on Kernville Rd, at the bridge. 2 Sirretta St 93238 (PO Box 745). Fax: 760/376-4147. **Terms:** Pets, $5 extra charge. **Facility:** 10 rooms. Rustic buildings, tree-shaded lawn area. Rooms decorated in a country decor. 1 story; exterior corridors. **Dining:** Restaurant nearby. **Services:** area transportation. **Recreation:** fishing; hiking trails. **All Rooms:** shower baths, extended cable TV. **Cards:** AE, CB, DI, JC, MC, VI. **Special Amenities:** Free breakfast and free local telephone calls.

WHISPERING PINES LODGE BED & BREAKFAST
AAA [SAVE]
◆◆◆
Lodge
All Year [BP] — 1P: $99- 159 — 2P/1B: $99- 159 — 2P/2B: $99- 159 — XP: $15 — Phone: (760)376-3733
Location: 0.3 mi n. 13745 Sierra Way 93238 (Rt 1, Box 41). Fax: 760/376-3735. **Facility:** 17 rooms. Lodge and cottage type units on spacious grounds with access to river. Several rooms with gas fireplace. 1 suite with kitchen, fireplace & large porch overlooking the river; 1-2 stories; exterior corridors; designated smoking area; whirlpools. **Recreation:** video rentals. **Some Rooms:** 4 efficiencies, kitchen, whirlpools. **Cards:** AE, DS, MC, VI. **Special Amenities:** Free breakfast and preferred room (subject to availability with advanced reservations).

RESTAURANTS

EWING'S ON THE KERN
◆◆
American
VI.
Dinner: $11-$22 — Phone: 760/376-2411
Location: Just e across the bridge, then n. 125 Buena Vista Dr 93238. **Hours:** 4 pm-9 pm, Fri & Sat-10 pm, Sun 9 am-2 & 4-9 pm. Closed: 12/25. **Features:** casual dress; Sunday brunch; early bird specials; cocktails & lounge. Hillside restaurant overlooking the Kern River. Smoke free premises. **Cards:** AE, CB, DI, DS, MC,

JOHNNY MCNALLY'S FAIRVIEW LODGE
◆
Steakhouse
Dinner: $9-$27   **Phone:** 760/376-2430
Location: 15 mi ne on Sierra Way. 93238. **Hours:** 5pm-10 pm, Sun 4 pm-9 pm. Closed: Dec & Jan. Open weekends Nov, Feb, Mar; Daily 4/1-10/31. **Reservations:** suggested. **Features:** No A/C; casual dress; children's menu; cocktails & lounge. Old West decor. Features oversize steaks including 40 oz Porterhouse, also fish & poultry. Located on Kern River. **Cards:** DS, MC, VI.

PEACOCK INN
◆
Chinese
Lunch: $5-$7   **Dinner:** $9-$13   **Phone:** 760/376-3937
Location: Just e of bridge & n of Kernville Rd. 21 Sierra Dr 93238. **Hours:** 11 am-9 pm. Closed: 11/25 , 12/25 & Tues. **Reservations:** suggested. **Features:** No A/C; carryout; beer & wine only; a la carte. Casual atmosphere. Features Mandarin & Szechuan cuisine. Smoke free premises. **Cards:** MC, VI. ☒

THAT'S ITALIAN RESTAURANT
◆◆
Italian
Lunch: $6-$8   **Dinner:** $9-$14   **Phone:** 760/376-6020
Location: Center of town at Circle Park. 9 Big Blue Rd 93238. **Hours:** 11 am-9 pm, 9/15-5/15 4 pm-9 pm. Closed: Mon & Tues. **Features:** casual dress; beer & wine only. Nice variety of pasta, chicken & seafood entrees. Smoke free premises. ☒

KETTLEMAN CITY—600

LODGINGS

BEST WESTERN INN
AAA SAVE
◆◆
Motel
All Year [CP]   1P: $55- 65   2P/1B: $60- 70   2P/2B: $65- 75   XP: $5-8   F12
Phone: (559)386-0804
Location: East of & adjacent to I-5, exit SR 41 n, 0.3 mi to Bernard, n 0.3 mi. 33410 Powers DR 93239. Fax: 559/386-4526. **Terms:** Small pets only, $2 extra charge, $20 dep req. **Facility:** 56 rooms. 2 whirlpool rms, $75-$95. Deluxe mini suites, $60-$80; 2 stories; exterior corridors; whirlpool. **Dining:** Restaurant nearby. **Cards:** AE, CB, DI, DS, MC, VI. **Special Amenities:** Free breakfast and free local telephone calls.
🆔 🐾 ➡ 🍽 ⚬ 🏊 🐕 🍴 ▤ 🖨 🎱 ☒

SUPER 8
AAA SAVE
◆◆
Motel
All Year   1P: $49- 69   2P/1B: $49- 69   2P/2B: $49- 69   XP: $3-5
Phone: 559/386-9530
Location: 2 mi sw; 0.5 blk e off I-5, jct SR 41; exit Kettleman City-Paso Robles. 33415 Powers Dr 93239. Fax: 559/386-9530. **Terms:** Pets, $50 dep req, $10 fee. **Facility:** 60 rooms. 2 stories; exterior corridors. **Dining:** Coffee shop nearby. **Cards:** AE, DI, DS, MC, VI.
🆔 🐾 ➡ 🍽 🐕 🍴 ☒

KING CITY—7,600

LODGINGS

BEST WESTERN KING CITY INN
AAA SAVE
◆◆
Motel
4/1-10/31 [CP]   1P: $49- 85   2P/1B: $59- 95   2P/2B: $61- 68   XP: $8   F12
2/1-3/31 [CP]   1P: $42- 75   2P/1B: $52- 85   2P/2B: $54- 61   XP: $8   F12
11/1-1/31 [CP]   1P: $42- 75   2P/1B: $52- 85   2P/2B: $54- 61   XP: $8   F12
Phone: (831)385-6733
Location: Just e of US 101, Broadway exit. 1190 Broadway 93930. Fax: 831/385-0714. **Terms:** Reserv deposit. **Facility:** 47 rooms. 6 whirlpool rms, extra charge; 2 stories; exterior corridors; small pool, whirlpool. **Cards:** AE, CB, DI, DS, JC, MC, VI. **Special Amenities:** Free breakfast and free local telephone calls. *(See ad below)*
➡ 🍴 ▢ 🖨 🎱 ☒

COURTESY INN
Phone: (831)385-4646

△△△ SAVE

All Year [CP]   1P: $39- 89   2P/1B: $44- 139   2P/2B: $44- 139   XP: $6   F14
Location: Just w of US 101; Broadway exit. 4 Broadway Cir 93930. Fax: 831/385-6024. **Terms:** Pets, $10 extra charge. **Facility:** 63 rooms. Few units have sitting area with sofabed. 2 stories; exterior corridors; small heated pool, whirlpool. **Dining:** Coffee shop nearby. **Cards:** AE, CB, DI, DS, MC, VI. **Special Amenities:** Early check-in/late check-out and free breakfast. *(See color ad p 484)*

◆◆◆
Motel

KEEFER'S INN
Phone: 831/385-4843

△△△ SAVE

All Year [CP]   1P: $43- 60   2P/1B: $48- 70   2P/2B: $48- 70   XP: $5   F12
Location: Just w of US 101, Canal St exit. 615 Canal St 93930. Fax: 831/385-1254. **Terms:** Reserv deposit. **Facility:** 47 rooms. Near shopping mall & fairgrounds. 2 stories; interior/exterior corridors; small pool, whirlpool. **Dining:** Coffee shop nearby. **Cards:** AE, DI, DS, JC, MC, VI.

◆◆
Motor Inn

RESTAURANT

KEEFER'S RESTAURANT   Lunch: $6-$12   Dinner: $12-$21   Phone: 831/385-3543

△△△

Location: Just w of US 101, Canal St exit. 611 Canal St 93930. **Hours:** 7 am-9:30 pm. Closed: 12/25. **Reservations:** suggested. **Features:** casual dress; children's menu; early bird specials; salad bar; cocktails; a la carte. Family restaurant. Gift shop. Smoke free premises. **Cards:** AE, MC, VI.

◆◆
American

KINGS BEACH—*See Lake Tahoe Area p. 505.*

KINGSBURG—7,200

LODGING

SWEDISH INN   Guaranteed Rates   Phone: 559/897-1022

△△△

All Year   1P: $44- 48   2P/1B: $48- 54   2P/2B: $48- 54   XP: $5
Location: Just w of SR 99; Conejo exit. 401 Conejo St 93631. Fax: 559/897-0134. **Terms:** MAP avail; pets. **Facility:** 47 rooms. Scandinavian decorations. 3 units with sitting area, $52-$89 for up to 2 persons; 2 stories; exterior corridors; whirlpool. **Dining:** Restaurant nearby. **Some Rooms:** kitchen. **Cards:** AE, DS, MC.

◆◆
Motel

KIT CARSON—300

LODGING

KIT CARSON LODGE   Rates Subject to Change   Phone: 209/258-8500

◆◆

6/4-10/11   1P: $115- 190   2P/1B: $115- 190   2P/2B: $115- 190
Location: 0.3 mi off SR 88, on Silver Lake. 32000 Kit Carson Rd 95644. Fax: 209/258-8315. **Terms:** Open 6/4-10/11; check-in 4 pm; reserv deposit, 30 day notice; handling fee imposed. **Facility:** 27 rooms. Wooded mountainside location at 7200 ft elevation. Many units with fireplace. 8 two-bedroom units. 8 motel units for up to 3 persons; 19 efficiency cottages for up to 6 persons; 1 story; exterior corridors; boat dock. **Recreation:** swimming, boating, fishing. Rental: canoes. **All Rooms:** shower baths. **Cards:** MC, VI.

Resort
Cottage

KLAMATH—200

LODGING

MOTEL TREES
Phone: 707/482-3152

△△△ SAVE

All Year   1P: $40   2P/1B: $44   2P/2B: $48   XP: $4
Location: 4 mi n on US 101. 15495 Hwy 101 N 95548 (PO Box 309). **Facility:** 23 rooms. Opposite Trees of Mystery. 4 two-bedroom units, $65 for up to 4 persons; 1 story; exterior corridors; 1 tennis court. **Dining:** Coffee shop nearby. **Services:** giftshop. **All Rooms:** combo or shower baths. **Cards:** AE, DS, MC, VI. *(See ad below)*

◆◆
Motel

LA CANADA FLINTRIDGE—*See Los Angeles p. 610.*

LAFAYETTE—23,500   (See map p. 752; index p. 751)

LODGING

LAFAYETTE PARK HOTEL   Phone: (925)283-3700   [36]
All Year   1P: $170- 190   2P/1B: $180- 200 2P/2B: $180- 200 XP: $10   F18
Location: Exit SR 24 at Pleasant Hill Rd, 1 blk s. 3287 Mt Diablo Blvd 94549. Fax: 925/284-1621.
Hotel
Terms: Monthly rates. **Facility:** 139 rooms. Norman French architecture. Spacious elegant rooms, some with fireplace. 3 stories; interior corridors; sauna, whirlpool. Fee: parking. **Dining:** Restaurant; 6:30 am-9:30 pm, Fri & Sat-10 pm; $13-$25; cocktails. **Cards:** AE, CB, DI, DS, MC, VI. **Special Amenities:** Early check-in/late check-out and free newspaper. *(See color ad inside back cover)*

RESTAURANTS

CAPE COD HOUSE   **Lunch:** $6-$10   **Dinner:** $9-$15   **Phone:** 925/283-8288   [26]
Location: Exit SR 24 Central, 1 mi e. 3666 Mt Diablo Blvd 94549. **Hours:** 11:30 am-9:30 pm, Sun-9 pm.
Seafood
Reservations: suggested. **Features:** casual dress; children's menu; early bird specials; cocktails & lounge; a la carte. Quiet comfortable atmosphere, nice selection of meats & poultry. Smoke free premises. **Cards:** AE, DI, MC, VI.

THE DUCK CLUB RESTAURANT   **Lunch:** $8-$13   **Dinner:** $22-$40   **Phone:** 925/283-7108   [25]
Location: In the Lafayette Park Hotel. 3287 Mt Diablo Blvd 94549. **Hours:** 6:30-10:30 am, 11:30-2, & 6-9:30
American
pm, Sun champagne brunch 10:30 am-2:30 pm $22.95; 6 pm-9 pm. Closed: 1/1. **Reservations:** suggested. **Features:** casual dress; cocktails & lounge; valet parking; a la carte. Artistic, light fare with continental flair; comfortable, attractive, warm surroundings. Smoke free premises. **Cards:** AE, CB, DI, DS, MC, VI.
(See color ad inside back cover & p 383)

LAGUNA BEACH—23,200   (See map p. 296; index p. 289)

LODGINGS

ALISO CREEK INN   Phone: (949)499-2271   [55]
6/23-9/6   1P: $154- 326   2P/1B: $154- 326 2P/2B: $154- 326 XP: $10   F12
Sun-Thurs 2/1-6/22 &
9/7-1/31   1P: $112- 294   2P/1B: $112- 294 2P/2B: $112- 294 XP: $10   F12
Resort   Fri & Sat 2/1-6/22 & 9/7-1/31 1P: $124- 294 2P/1B: $124- 294 2P/2B: $124- 294 XP: $10   F12
Complex   **Location:** 2 mi se on SR 1; 0.3 mi e of Aliso Beach Park. 31106 S Coast Hwy 92677. Fax: 949/499-4601.
Terms: Reserv deposit; monthly rates. **Facility:** 62 rooms. Picturesque canyon setting adjoining golf course. Studio & 1 to 2-bedroom, 1 & 2 story suites with full kitchen. All units have patio or deck. 4 two-story suites with living room, kitchen, 2 bedrooms, fireplace and whirlpool; $225-275 for up to 4 persons; 1-2 stories; exterior corridors; putting green; heated pool, wading pool, whirlpool. Fee: 9 holes golf. **Dining:** Restaurant; 8 am-10 pm, Fri & Sat-10:30 pm, Sun 8 am-3 & 5-9 pm, Entertainment Fri & Sat; $11-$17; cocktails. **Cards:** AE, DS, MC, VI. *(See ad below)*

KNOW THE ZERO HOUR. Confirm the checkout time with the front desk employee before planning your departure time.

(See map p. 296)

AYVIEW LAGUNA INN   Phone: (949)494-5450   **37**

| | 6/15-9/16 | 1P: $80- 140 | 2P/1B: $80- 140 | 2P/2B: $85- 140 | XP: $10 |
| | 2/1-6/14 & 9/17-1/31 | 1P: $65- 120 | 2P/1B: $65- 120 | 2P/2B: $65- 120 | XP: $10 |

Location: 1 mi se on SR 1. 2020 S Coast Hwy 92651. Fax: 949/494-0597. **Terms:** Reserv deposit, 3 day notice. **Facility:** 22 rooms. Half block to Woods Cove Beach. 2 stories; exterior corridors; small pool. **All Rooms:** combo or shower baths. **Cards:** AE, DS, MC, VI. **Special Amenities:** Free breakfast and referred room (subject to availability with advanced reservations).

EST WESTERN LAGUNA BRISAS SPA HOTEL   Phone: (949)497-7272   **48**

	7/1-8/31 [CP]	1P: $139- 329	2P/1B: $139- 329	2P/2B: $139- 329	XP: $10-20	F12
	3/1-6/30 [CP]	1P: $119- 289	2P/1B: $119- 289	2P/2B: $119- 289	XP: $10-20	F12
	2/1-2/28 & 9/1-1/31 [CP]	1P: $99- 259	2P/1B: $99- 259	2P/2B: $99- 259	XP: $10-20	F12

Location: 1 mi se on SR 1. 1600 S Coast Hwy 92651. Fax: 949/497-8306. **Facility:** 64 rooms. Tastefully furnished rooms, some with ocean view or partial ocean view. 4 stories; interior corridors; small heated pool, whirlpool, sundeck with ocean view. **Cards:** AE, CB, DI, DS, JC, MC, VI. **Special Amenities:** Free breakfast and free newspaper. *(See color ad p 488)*

EST WESTERN LAGUNA REEF INN   Phone: (949)499-2227   **53**

	7/1-9/7 [CP]	1P: $120- 165	2P/1B: $120- 165	2P/2B: $120- 165	XP: $10	F12
	2/1-6/30 [CP]	1P: $92- 130	2P/1B: $92- 130	2P/2B: $92- 130	XP: $10	F12
	9/8-1/31 [CP]	1P: $73- 115	2P/1B: $73- 115	2P/2B: $73- 115	XP: $10	F12

Location: 1.8 mi n on SR 1. 30806 S Coast Hwy 92651. Fax: 949/499-5575. **Terms:** Reserv deposit; weekly rates. **Facility:** 43 rooms. Tastefully decorated rooms surrounding colorful botanical gardens with many peciman plants. Some rooms with ocean view, $15 extra charge; 2 stories; exterior corridors; heated pool, sauna, whirlpool. **Recreation:** free videos. **All Rooms:** combo or shower baths. **Some Rooms:** 3 efficiencies. **Cards:** AE, CB, DI, DS, MC, VI. **Special Amenities:** Free breakfast.

Y-THE-SEA INN   Phone: 949/497-6645   **38**

| | 6/11-9/11 [CP] | 1P: $89- 189 | 2P/1B: $89- 189 | 2P/2B: $99- 189 | XP: $10-20 | F12 |
| | 2/1-6/10 & 9/12-1/31 [CP] | 1P: $69- 159 | 2P/1B: $69- 159 | 2P/2B: $89- 159 | XP: $10-20 | F12 |

Location: 0.5 mi n on SR 1. 475 N Coast Hwy 92651. Fax: 949/497-6962. **Terms:** Reserv deposit, 3 day notice. **Facility:** 36 rooms. 1 blk to oceanfront. Some rooms with patio& oceanview. 3 stories; exterior corridors; small heated pool, sauna, steamroom, whirlpool. **Recreation:** video movie rental. **Some Rooms:** whirlpools. **Cards:** AE, DI, DS, MC, VI. *(See color ad below)*

APRI LAGUNA   Phone: (949)494-6533   **46**

	6/1-9/30 [CP]	1P: $150- 235	2P/1B: $150- 235	2P/2B: $150- 235	XP: $10	F14
	2/1-5/31 & 10/1-10/31 [CP]	1P: $110- 175	2P/1B: $110- 175	2P/2B: $110- 175	XP: $10	F14
	11/1-1/31 [CP]	1P: $99- 160	2P/1B: $99- 160	2P/2B: $99- 160	XP: $10	F14

Location: 1 mi se on SR 1. 1441 S Coast Hwy 92651. Fax: 949/497-6962. **Terms:** Weekly rates; 2 night min stay, 6/4-9/13 weekends. **Facility:** 35 rooms. Some rooms with ocean view & patios. Limited on premises parking. 5 stories; exterior corridors; designated smoking area; beach, heated pool, sauna. **Some Rooms:** 28 efficiencies, 3 tchens. **Cards:** AE, CB, DI, DS, MC, VI. **Special Amenities:** Early check-in/late check-out and free breakfast.

HE CARRIAGE HOUSE-BED & BREAKFAST   Rates Subject to Change   Phone: 949/494-8945   **45**

| | All Year [CP] | 1P: $95- 150 | 2P/1B: $95- 150 | 2P/2B: $125- 150 | XP: $10-20 | F6 |

Location: 1 mi s; just e of SR 1, via Cress St. 1322 Catalina St 92651. Fax: 949/494-8945. **Terms:** Reserv deposit, 7 day notice; 2 night min stay, weekends. **Facility:** 6 rooms. A charming bed & breakfast inn with 1- & 2-bedroom suites. 2 stories; exterior corridors; designated smoking area. **All Rooms:** combo or tub baths. **Some Rooms:** 5 kitchens. **Cards:** AE, MC, VI.

IN AAA LISTINGS, "WEEKENDS" MEANS FRIDAY AND SATURDAY NIGHTS.

Laguna Beach's Best Kept Secret

...with Spectacular Ocean View Terrace

All Rooms Include Breakfast & In Room Spa for Two

Location

Pacific Coast Highway is all that separates you from the beach. Amid many boutiques. restaurants, art galleries & shops. You will enjoy the serenity of the City & the sights & sounds of the beckoning blue Pacific. A great place for a romantic getaway.

Features

65 unique rooms. each with an in room spa for 2 · Ocean view rooms available · Complimentary continental breakfast · Heated pool. hot spa, sun terrace with ocean view · Free parking · Cable TV & HBO · Guest laundry · In-room coffeemakers & irons/boards

1600 So. Coast Hwy.
Laguna Beach. 92651
(949) 497-7272
www.lagunabrisas.com

Rates Up to 4 persons	Weekdays FROM	Weekends FROM
Sept.- Feb.	79⁹⁵*	99⁹⁵*
March-June	89⁹⁵*	119⁹⁵*
July-August	109⁹⁵*	159⁹⁵*

*Subject to limited availability.
Holidays and special events higher.
Rate reflects 10% AAA discount.

800-682-9723

Laguna Brisas
SPA HOTEL

(See map p. 296)

ASA LAGUNA INN
Phone: (949)494-2996 52

Historic Bed Breakfast

Fri & Sat 7/1-8/31 & 12/24-1/31 [CP]	1P:	$105- 220	2P/1B:	$105- 220	2P/2B:	$105- 220	XP: $20	D12
Sun-Thurs 2/1-6/30 & 9/1-12/23 [CP]	1P:	$79- 199	2P/1B:	$79- 199	2P/2B:	$79- 199	XP: $20	D12
Fri & Sat 2/1-6/30 & 9/1-12/23 [CP]	1P:	$99- 199	2P/1B:	$99- 199	2P/2B:	$99- 199	XP: $20	D12
Sun-Thurs 7/1-8/31 & 12/24-1/31 [CP]	1P:	$89- 199	2P/1B:	$89- 199	2P/2B:	$89- 199	XP: $20	D12

Location: 1.3 mi se on SR 1. 2510 S Coast Hwy 92651. Fax: 949/494-5009. **Terms:** Weekly/monthly rates; small pets only, extra charge, by reservation only. **Facility:** 20 rooms. Landscaped, terraced grounds overlooking the ocean. Smaller, nicely furnished rooms to spacious suites. Entry to parking lot off Upland. 2 two-bedroom units. 2 night minimum stay weekends, 7/1-31; 1 cottage $169-205; 2 stories; exterior corridors; heated pool. **Dining:** Afternoon tea. **All Rooms:** shower baths. **Some Rooms:** 6 kitchens. **Cards:** AE, DS, MC, VI. **Special Amenities:** Free breakfast. (See ad below)

HOLIDAY INN LAGUNA BEACH
Phone: (949)494-1001 42

Motor Inn

6/13-9/14	1P: $159		2P/1B: $159		2P/2B: $159		XP: $10	F17
2/1-6/12 & 9/15-1/31	1P: $99- 129		2P/1B: $99- 129		2P/2B: $99- 129		XP: $10	F17

Location: SR 1, 0.5 mi s of SR 33. Entrance to parking lot on Cleo. 696 S Coast Hwy 92651. Fax: 949/497-7107. **Terms:** Reserv deposit; weekly/monthly rates. **Facility:** 54 rooms. Rooms surround attractive pool & garden area. Rooms decorated in French Country theme. 4 whirlpool rms, extra charge; 2-3 stories; exterior corridors; heated pool. **Dining:** Restaurant; 7:30 am-10 pm; $7-$17; cocktails. **All Rooms:** combo or shower baths. **Cards:** AE, CB, DI, DS, JC, MC, VI. (See ad p 491)

HOTEL LAGUNA
Phone: (949)494-1151 41

Historic Hotel

Sun-Thurs 2/1-5/27 & 9/8-1/31 [CP]	1P:	$80- 165	2P/1B:	$80- 165	2P/2B:	$80- 165
5/28-9/7 [CP]	1P:	$105- 200	2P/1B:	$105- 200	2P/2B:	$105- 145
Fri & Sat 2/1-5/27 & 9/8-1/31 [CP]	1P:	$90- 200	2P/1B:	$90- 200	2P/2B:	$90- 125

Location: On SR 1, 0.5 mi s of SR 33. 425 S Coast Hwy 92651. Fax: 949/497-2163. **Terms:** Reserv deposit, 4 day notice; monthly rates. **Facility:** 65 rooms. Oceanfront hotel built in 1930. Many ocean or mountain view rooms. Private beach club with food & beverage service on the beach. 3 stories; interior corridors; beach. **Dining:** Dining room, 2 restaurants; 7 am-11 pm; $15-$25; also, Claes Seafood Etc, see separate listing. **Services:** giftshop; complimentary evening beverages, Mon-Fri. **All Rooms:** combo or shower baths. **Cards:** AE, CB, DI, DS, MC, VI. **Special Amenities:** Free breakfast and free newspaper.

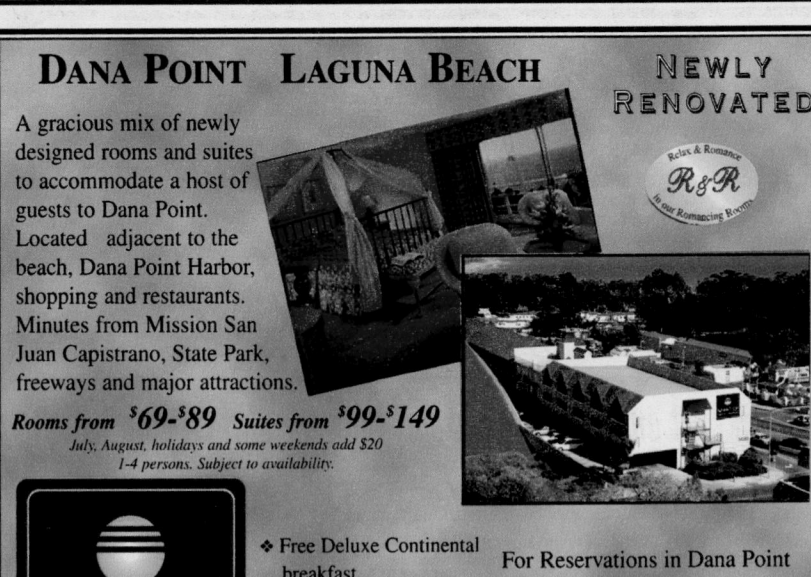

(See map p. 296)

INN AT LAGUNA BEACH   Phone: (949)497-9722   40
⬧⬧⬧ [SAVE]   5/28-9/5 [CP]   1P: $169- 489 2P/1B: $169- 489 2P/2B: $169- 489 XP: $20   F16
            2/1-5/27 & 9/6-1/31 [CP]   1P: $139- 489 2P/1B: $139- 489 2P/2B: $169- 489 XP: $20   F16
◆◆◆   **Location:** 211 N Coast Hwy 92651. Fax: 949/497-9972. **Terms:** Check-in 4 pm. **Facility:** 70 rooms. Located
Motel   on bluff above the ocean. Many rooms with ocean view & patio. 3 stories; interior/exterior corridors; beach
           heated pool, whirlpool. **Services:** Fee: massage. **All Rooms:** combo or shower baths. **Cards:** AE, CB, DI
DS, MC, VI. **Special Amenities: Free breakfast and free newspaper.** *(See color ad p 491)*

LAGUNA RIVIERA BEACH RESORT & SPA   Rates Subject to Change   Phone: 949/494-1196   44
⬧⬧⬧   5/29-9/12 [CP]   1P: $75- 179 2P/1B: $75- 179 2P/2B: $75- 179 XP: $10   F5
            2/1-5/28 & 9/13-1/31 [CP] 1P: $62- 155 2P/1B: $62- 155 2P/2B: $62- 155 XP: $10   F5
◆◆   **Location:** 0.5 mi se on SR 1. 825 S Coast Hwy 92651. Fax: 949/494-8421. **Terms:** Reserv deposit
Motel   weekly/monthly rates; 2 night min stay, weekends 6/15-9/15. **Facility:** 41 rooms. 5 terrace levels on oceanfront
           Large variety of rooms, some with ocean view & enclosed lanai. 5 two-bedroom units. 2 stories; exterior corri
dors; beach, heated indoor pool, sauna, whirlpool. **All Rooms:** combo or shower baths. **Some Rooms:** 16 efficiencies, 10
kitchens, whirlpools. **Cards:** AE, CB, DI, DS, JC, MC, VI. *(See color ad p 491)*

SURF & SAND HOTEL   Phone: (949)497-4477   50
⬧⬧⬧ [SAVE]   5/28-10/15 & 1/1-1/31   1P: $295- 425 2P/1B: $295- 425 2P/2B: $295- 425 XP: $15   F
            3/26-5/27   1P: $255- 335 2P/1B: $255- 335 2P/2B: $255- 335 XP: $15   F
◆◆◆◆   2/1-3/25 & 10/16-12/31   1P: $250- 300 2P/1B: $250- 300 2P/2B: $250- 300 XP: $15   F
Hotel   **Location:** 1 mi se on SR 1. 1555 S Coast Hwy 92651. Fax: 949/494-7653. **Terms:** Reserv deposit, 3 day
           notice. **Facility:** 164 rooms. Oceanfront. Most rooms with ocean view & balcony. A few rooms with fireplace
2 two-bedroom units. 2-night minimum stay 7/1-7/31; also weekends 1/30-5/31 & 9/1-12/31; 3-day minimum stay 8/1-8/31. 1
& 2-bedroom suites, $400-$1000; 9 stories; beach, heated pool. Fee: parking. **Dining:** Dining room; 7 am-11 pm; $11-$25
cocktails. **Services:** giftshop; area transportation, charge for large groups. **Some Rooms:** whirlpools. **Cards:** AE, CB, DI
DS, MC, VI. *(See ad p 489)*

RESTAURANTS

THE BEACH HOUSE   **Lunch:** $6-$13   **Dinner:** $10-$22   **Phone:** 949/494-9707   38
⬧⬧   **Location:** 0.5 mi se on SR 1; just w. 619 Sleepy Hollow Ln 92651. **Hours:** 8 am-11:15, 11:30-3:30 &
◆◆   4:30-10 pm, Sat 8 am-11:45, noon-3:30 & 4:30-11 pm, Sun 8 am-3:30 & 4:30-10 pm. Closed: 11/26 & 12/25
Seafood   **Reservations:** suggested. **Features:** No A/C; casual dress; Sunday brunch; children's menu; early bird
           specials; cocktails & lounge; fee for valet parking; a la carte. Charming restaurant located on the beach
           Cards: AE, MC, VI.   ☒

CEDAR CREEK INN   **Lunch:** $6-$11   **Dinner:** $6-$23   **Phone:** 949/497-8696   35
◆◆   **Location:** Downtown, 2 blks e of SR 1. 384 Forest Ave 92651. **Hours:** 11 am-10 pm. Closed major holidays
American   **Reservations:** suggested. **Features:** casual dress; Sunday brunch; children's menu; cocktails & lounge
           entertainment. Very attractive restaurant featuring a large selection of homemade dessert, fresh fish, beef
chicken, veal & sandwiches. Oyster bar 4 pm-midnight. Patio seating avail. **Cards:** AE, DI, MC, VI.   ☒

CLAES SEAFOOD ETC   **Lunch:** $10-$15   **Dinner:** $18-$30   **Phone:** 949/376-9283   36
◆◆   **Location:** In Hotel Laguna. 425 S Coast Hwy 92651. **Hours:** 7 am-2:30 & 5:30-10 pm, Mon 7 am-2:30 pm
Seafood   **Features:** No A/C; casual dress; Sunday brunch; children's menu; cocktails & lounge; entertainment; fee fo
           valet parking; a la carte. Seafood restaurant with full ocean views, also outdoor dining. Mon-Sat breakfas
buffet $6.95. Smoke free premises. **Cards:** AE, DI, DS, MC, VI.   ☒

LAS BRISAS   **Lunch:** $7-$11   **Dinner:** $10-$25   **Phone:** 949/497-5434   34
◆◆◆   **Location:** 0.3 mi nw on SR 1. 361 Cliff Dr 92652. **Hours:** 8 am-10:30 am 11-3:30 & 5-10 pm, Fri & Sat 5-11
Mexican   pm, Sun 9 am-3 & 4-10 pm. Closed: 12/25. **Reservations:** suggested. **Features:** casual dress; Sunday
           brunch; children's menu; cocktails & lounge; minimum charge-$7-lunch, $9-dinner; fee for valet parking; a la
carte. Beautiful ocean view. Features cuisine of the west coast of Mexico. Sun brunch 9 am-3 pm $18. All you can eat buffe
Mon-Sat 8 am-11am $7. Mariachi music Wed night, 4-10 pm during summer. **Cards:** AE, CB, DI, DS, MC, VI. ☒

RISTORANTE RUMARI   **Dinner:** $11-$20   **Phone:** 949/494-0400   37
◆◆   **Location:** 1 mi se on SR 1. 1826 S Coast Hwy 92651. **Hours:** 5 pm-9:30 pm, Fri & Sat-10:30 pm. Closed
Italian   11/25, 12/25, 1/1. **Reservations:** suggested. **Features:** No A/C; casual dress; beer & wine only; a la carte
           Intimate atmosphere. A nice selection of pasta, seafood, chicken & beef. Smoke free premises. **Cards:** AE
CB, DS, MC, VI.   ☒

LAGUNA HILLS—33,600 (See map p. 296; index p. 289)

LODGINGS

COMFORT INN LAGUNA HILLS/IRVINE Phone: (949)859-0166 [28]
All Year 1P: $59- 69 2P/1B: $59- 69 2P/2B: $59- 69
Motel **Location:** 0.3 mi sw of I-5, exit Lake Forest Dr. 23061 Avenida De La Carlota 92653. Fax: 949/859-2468. **Terms:** Reserv deposit. **Facility:** 76 rooms. Located in a commercial area. 3 stories; exterior corridors; heated pool, whirlpool. **Dining:** Restaurant nearby. **Cards:** AE, CB, DS, MC, VI. **Special Amenities: Free breakfast and free local telephone calls.** *(See color ad p 478 & p 490)*

COURTYARD BY MARRIOTT Rates Subject to Change Phone: 949/859-5500 [29]
Sun-Thurs 1P: $94- 129 2P/1B: $94- 129 2P/2B: $94- 129
Motor Inn Fri & Sat 1P: $84- 119 2P/1B: $84- 119 2P/2B: $84- 119
Location: I-5, Lake Forest Dr exit; 0.7 mi sw. 23175 Avenida De La Carlota 92653. Fax: 949/454-2158.
Facility: 136 rooms. Nicely landscaped grounds. 5 stories; interior corridors; heated pool. **Cards:** AE, CB, DI, DS, MC, VI.
(See color ad p 311)

HOLIDAY INN Guaranteed Rates Phone: (949)586-5000 [32]
All Year 1P: $75- 109 2P/1B: $85- 119 2P/2B: $85- 119 XP: $10 F19
Motor Inn **Location:** Just w of I-5, La Paz Rd exit. 25205 La Paz Rd 92653. Fax: 949/581-7410. **Facility:** 147 rooms. Tree shaded pool area. Large rooms. 4 stories; interior corridors; heated pool. **Cards:** AE, CB, DI, DS, MC, VI. *(See color ad below)*

LAGUNA HILLS LODGE Rates Subject to Change Phone: (949)830-2550 [30]
All Year 1P: $50 2P/1B: $60 2P/2B: $70 XP: $5-10
Motel **Location:** Just w of I-5, El Toro Rd exit. 23932 Paseo De Valencia 92653. Fax: 949/581-0819. **Terms:** Reserv deposit. **Facility:** 121 rooms. 2 two-bedroom units. 2-3 stories; interior/exterior corridors; heated pool. **All Rooms:** combo or shower baths. **Cards:** AE, CB, DI, DS, JC, MC, VI.

RESTAURANT

CLAIM JUMPER RESTAURANT **Lunch:** $7-$12 **Dinner:** $9-$15 Phone: 949/768-0662 [30]
Traditional American **Location:** 0.3 mi sw exit La Paz Rd from I-5; in La Paz Center. 25332 McIntyre St 92653. **Hours:** 11 am-10 pm, Tues-Thurs to 11 pm, Fri & Sat to midnight. **Closed:** 7/4, 11/25 & 12/25. **Features:** casual dress; children's menu; carryout; salad bar; cocktails & lounge. Generous portions of entrees & sandwiches. Western theme. Smoke free premises. **Cards:** AE, DI, DS, MC, VI.

LA HABRA—51,300

RESTAURANTS

CAFE EL CHOLO **Lunch:** $8-$15 **Dinner:** $8-$15 Phone: 562/691-4618
Mexican **Location:** 1.5 mi e of Hwy 39 (Beach Blvd). 840 E Whittier Blvd 90631. **Hours:** 11 am-9 pm, Fri & Sat-10 pm. **Closed:** 7/4, 11/25 & 12/25. **Features:** casual dress; Sunday brunch; children's menu; carryout; cocktails & lounge; a la carte. Burro Alley Tortilla Factory specializing in foods from Baja CA, Mexico also located on premises. **Cards:** AE, CB, DI, MC, VI.

THE CAT & THE CUSTARD CUP **Lunch:** $8-$16 **Dinner:** $17-$26 Phone: 562/694-3812
American **Location:** 1.5 mi e of Hwy 39 (Beach Blvd). 800 E Whittier Blvd 90631. **Hours:** 11:30 am-2:30 & 5:30-9 pm, Fri 10 pm, Sat 5:30-10 pm, Sun 5-9pm. **Closed:** 7/4 & 12/25. **Reservations:** suggested. **Features:** cocktails & lounge; entertainment; a la carte. English inn & pub atmosphere. Pastries made on premises. Smoke free premises. **Cards:** AE, DI, MC, VI.

LA JOLLA—*See San Diego p. 901.*

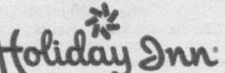

LAKE ARROWHEAD—6,300

LODGINGS

ARROWHEAD SADDLEBACK INN
Rates Subject to Change   **Phone:** (909)336-3571
All Year   1P: $85- 160 2P/1B: $85- 160 2P/2B: $85- 160
Location: SR 173, at jct SR 189, across from entrance to Lake Arrowhead Village. 92352 (PO Box 1890).
Historic
Country Inn
Fax: 909/337-4277. **Terms:** Reserv deposit, 7 day notice; 2 night min stay, weekends 7/1-8/31; pets, in designated rooms. **Facility:** 34 rooms. Attractive country motif. Cozy rooms & 1- to 3-bedroom suites in main lodge & individual chalets. Many gas fireplaces. 1 two-bedroom unit, 2 three-bedroom units. 1-2 stories; interior/exterior corridors; beach privileges. **Dining:** Dining room; 11 am-3 & 5-9 pm; Fri & Sat-10 pm;
$14-$22; cocktails. **All Rooms:** combo or shower baths. **Some Rooms:** whirlpools. **Cards:** AE, CB, DI, DS, JC, MC, VI.

ARROWHEAD TREE TOP LODGE
Phone: (909)337-2311
6/15-1/2   2P/1B: $68- 108 2P/2B: $79- 128
2/1-6/14 & 1/3-1/31   2P/1B: $59- 94 2P/2B: $74- 125
Motel
Location: SR 173, 0.3 mi s of Lake Arrowhead Village. 27992 Rainbow Dr 92352 (PO Box 186).
Terms: Reserv deposit, 7 day notice; handling fee imposed; weekly/monthly rates; 2 night min stay, 7/1-8/31 weekends; pets, in designated rooms, $8 extra charge. **Facility:** 19 rooms. Picturesque forest setting. Some fireplaces. Outdoor barbecue area & nature trail. 6 efficiency apartments, $85-$157 for up to 6 persons; 1-2 stories; exterior corridors; heated pool. **Recreation:** video rentals. **All Rooms:** shower baths. **Cards:** AE, DI, MC, VI. **Special Amenities:** Free local telephone calls and free room upgrade (subject to availability with advanced reservations).

BRACKEN FERN MANOR
Rates Subject to Change   **Phone:** (909)337-8557
All Year [BP] 1P: $65- 185 2P/1B: $80- 185 2P/2B: $115- 150 XP: $20 D14
Location: 0.5 mi n of SR 18. 815 Arrowhead Villas Rd 92352 (PO Box 1006). Fax: 909/337-3323.
Historic Bed
& Breakfast
Terms: Check-in 3:30 pm; reserv deposit, 7 day notice; handling fee imposed; weekly rates. **Facility:** 10 rooms. Restored English Tudor style building built in 1929. 3 stories; interior corridors; sauna, whirlpool. **Services:** complimentary evening beverages. **Some Rooms:** whirlpools. **Cards:** MC, VI.

CHATEAU DU LAC BED & BREAKFAST INN
Rates Subject to Change   **Phone:** 909/337-6488
All Year [BP]   2P/1B: $125- 225
Location: 911 Hospital Rd 92352 (PO Box 1098). Fax: 909/337-6746. **Terms:** Reserv deposit, 3 day notice;
Bed &
Breakfast
2 night min stay, weekends in summer. **Facility:** 5 rooms. Victorian house with Country French decor overlooking the lake. 3 stories; interior corridors; smoke free premises. **All Rooms:** combo or shower baths.
Cards: AE, DI, DS, MC, VI.

LAKE ARROWHEAD RESORT
Phone: (909)336-1511
7/1-9/30 1P: $169- 229 2P/1B: $169- 229 2P/2B: $169- 229 XP: $20 F18
2/1-6/30 & 10/1-1/31 1P: $139- 199 2P/1B: $139- 199 2P/2B: $139- 199 XP: $20 F18
Resort
Complex
Location: In Lake Arrowhead Village. 27984 Hwy 189 92352 (PO Box 1699). Fax: 909/336-1378.
Terms: Check-in 4 pm. **Facility:** 177 rooms. On several acres of lakefront grounds. 1- & 2-bedroom suites, $259-$399; 3 stories; interior corridors; beach, heated pool, whirlpools. Fee: racquetball courts, 2 tennis courts (1 lighted). **Dining:** Dining room, restaurant; 7 am-11 pm; $8-$25; cocktails. **Services:** giftshop.
Fee: massage. **Recreation:** children's program, wknds & summer. Fee: fishing. **Cards:** AE, CB, DI, DS, MC, VI.

ROMANTIQUE LAKEVIEW LODGE
Guaranteed Rates   **Phone:** 909/337-6633
Fri & Sat 7/1-1/2 [CP] 1P: $95- 215 2P/1B: $95- 215 2P/2B: $175- 225
Lodge
Fri & Sat 2/1-6/30 & 1/3-1/31
[CP] 1P: $75- 175 2P/1B: $75- 175 2P/2B: $145- 175
Sun-Thurs 6/30-1/2 [CP] 1P: $75- 125 2P/1B: $75- 125 2P/2B: $95- 125
Sun-Thurs 2/1-6/29 &
1/3-1/31 [CP] 1P: $65- 120 2P/1B: $65- 120 2P/2B: $95- 120
Location: SR 189, just w of jct SR 173. 28051 Hwy 189 92352 (PO Box 128). Fax: 909/337-5966. **Terms:** Reserv deposit, 7 day notice; 2 night min stay, wknds 7/1-12/31. **Facility:** 9 rooms. Charming rooms with Victorian decor; many with gas fireplace. 2 stories; interior/exterior corridors; designated smoking area. **All Rooms:** combo or shower baths. **Cards:** AE, DS, MC, VI.

RESTAURANTS

CASUAL ELEGANCE
Dinner: $17-$25   **Phone:** 909/337-8932
Location: SR 189, in Aqua Fria, 0.7 mi w of Blue Jay. 26848 Hwy 189 92317. **Hours:** From 5 pm, closing
American
hrs vary, 10 am-1:30 pm Sun brunch. Closed: 12/25, 1/1, Mon & Tues. **Reservations:** suggested.
Features: casual dress; beer & wine only. Fine dining in a cozy, country cottage. Menu features selections of beef, seafood, poultry & pasta. Menu changed weekly. Smoke free premises. **Cards:** AE, DI, DS, MC, VI.

THE CHEF'S INN & TAVERN
Lunch: $6-$13   **Dinner:** $12-$20   **Phone:** 909/336-4488
Location: In Cedar Glen, 1.5 mi ne of Lake Arrowhead Village. 29020 Oak Terrace 92321. **Hours:** 11:30
American
am-2 & 5-9 pm, Sat-10 pm, Sun from 10 am. Closed: Mon for lunch. **Reservations:** suggested.
Features: No A/C; casual dress; Sunday brunch; cocktails & lounge. Located in a historic building. Victorian decor. European & American cuisine. Smoke free premises. **Cards:** AE, DS, MC, VI.

THE ROYAL OAK RESTAURANT
Lunch: $8-$13   **Dinner:** $14-$25   **Phone:** 909/337-6018
Location: In Blue Jay; 1.5 mi sw of Lake Arrowhead Village. 27187 Hwy 189 92317. **Hours:** 11:30 am-3 &
American
5-9 pm, Fri & Sat-10 pm, Sun & Mon 5 pm-9 pm. Closed: 4/4, 11/24, 12/25 & Easter.
Reservations: suggested. **Features:** casual dress; children's menu; early bird specials; carryout; cocktails & lounge. Large selection of seafood, beef, pasta & continental entrees. Olde English Tudor atmosphere. Smoke free premises. **Cards:** AE, DS, MC, VI.

LAKE ELSINORE—18,300

LODGING

LAKEVIEW INN
AAA SAVE
◆◆
Motel

Phone: (909)674-9694

All Year [CP]   1P: $48- 57   2P/1B: $48   2P/2B: $57   XP: $5   F11
Location: W side of I-15, exit Diamond Dr, 0.5 mi s on Casino Dr. 31808 Casino Dr 92530.
Fax: 909/245-9249. **Facility:** 55 rooms. Hillside location looking towards the lake. 4 whirlpool rms, extra charge; 2 stories; exterior corridors; heated pool, whirlpool. **Cards:** AE, CB, DI, DS, MC, VI.

LAKE FOREST—300   (See map p. 296; index p. 289)

LODGINGS

BEST WESTERN LAGUNA/EL TORO INN
AAA SAVE
◆◆◆
Motor Inn

Phone: (949)458-1900   24

5/15-9/10 [CP]   1P: $69- 79   2P/1B: $75- 85   2P/2B: $79- 89   XP: $8-10   F12
2/1-5/14 & 9/11-1/31 [CP]   1P: $69- 75   2P/1B: $75- 81   2P/2B: $79- 85   XP: $8-10   F12
Location: I-5, exit Lake Forest Dr; 0.3 mi e. 23702 Rockfield Blvd 92630. Fax: 949/830-3325.
Terms: Reserv deposit. **Facility:** 113 rooms. 3 stories; interior corridors; sauna, whirlpool.
Dining: Restaurant; 11:30 am-2:30 & 4:30-9:30 pm; closed Sun; $6-$11; cocktails. **Services:** complimentary evening beverages, Mon-Fri. **Some Rooms:** whirlpools. **Cards:** AE, DI, DS, MC, VI. **Special Amenities: Early check-in/late check-out and free breakfast.** (See color ad p 352)

HAMPTON INN SOUTH ORANGE COUNTY   Rates Subject to Change   Phone: (949)597-8700   26
◆◆◆
Motel

6/15-9/6 [CP]   1P: $99   2P/1B: $119   2P/2B: $119
2/1-6/14 & 9/7-1/31 [CP]   1P: $89   2P/1B: $99   2P/2B: $99
Location: 5 mi e of I-5 via Lake Forest Dr. (27102 Towne Center Dr, BRIDGEPORT, 92610).
Fax: 949/597-8777. **Terms:** Check-in 4 pm. **Facility:** 84 rooms. 3 stories; interior corridors; heated pool. **Cards:** AE, CB, DI, DS, MC, VI. (See color ad p 338)

IRVINE SUITES HOTEL   Rates Subject to Change   Phone: (949)380-9888   25
AAA
◆◆◆
Suite Motor
Inn

All Year [BP]   1P: $79- 139   2P/1B: $89- 149   2P/2B: $89- 149   XP: $10-15
Location: 0.5 mi se of I-5, via Lake Forest Dr exit; Rockfield Blvd & Boeing. 23192 Lake Center Dr 92630.
Fax: 949/380-8307. **Terms:** Weekly/monthly rates. **Facility:** 90 rooms. 1-bedroom suites with living room. 10 suites with whirlpool, 2 with loft. 9 whirlpool rms, extra charge; 4 stories; exterior corridors; heated pool, whirlpool. **Dining:** Coffee shop. **Services:** giftshop; complimentary evening beverages, Mon-Fri; area transportation, within 5 mi. **Cards:** AE, CB, DI, DS, JC, MC, VI.

LAKE ISABELLA—3,300—See KERNVILLE.

LAKEPORT—4,400

LODGINGS

ANCHORAGE INN   Rates Subject to Change   Phone: 707/263-5417
AAA
◆
Motel

5/15-10/15   1P: $54   2P/1B: $54   2P/2B: $65   XP: $10
2/1-5/14 & 10/16-1/31   1P: $40   2P/1B: $40   2P/2B: $47   XP: $10
Location: 1 mi e of SR 29, 11th St exit. 950 N Main St 95453. Fax: 707/263-5453. **Terms:** Reserv deposit, 5 day notice; weekly/monthly rates, in winter. **Facility:** 34 rooms. A few units with decks facing lake. 8 two-bedroom units. Housekeeping/family units $80-$135 for up to 6 persons; $69-$99 in winter; 2 stories; exterior corridors; sauna, whirlpool, small pool 5/10-10/15. Fee: boat dock. **Recreation:** boating, fishing, waterskiing. **All Rooms:** combo or shower baths. **Some Rooms:** 20 kitchens. **Cards:** AE, DI, DS, MC, VI.

CLEAR LAKE INN   Phone: (707)263-3551
AAA SAVE
◆
Motel

3/15-10/15   1P: $49- 59   2P/1B: $59- 69   2P/2B: $69- 79   XP: $5-15   F4
2/1-3/14 & 10/16-1/31   1P: $42- 45   2P/1B: $45- 49   2P/2B: $55- 69   XP: $5   F4
Location: 1 mi e of SR 29, 11th St exit. 1010 N Main St 95453. Fax: 707/263-4762. **Terms:** Reserv deposit, 7 day notice. **Facility:** 40 rooms. 2 units facing lake. 2 stories; exterior corridors; small pool in summer; boat dock. **Recreation:** boating, fishing, waterskiing. **Cards:** AE, DI, DS, MC, VI. **Special Amenities: Free local telephone calls and preferred room (subject to availability with advanced reservations).**

SKYLARK SHORES MOTEL RESORT   Rates Subject to Change   Phone: (707)263-6151
◆◆
Complex

5/23-9/21   1P: $66- 118   2P/1B: $68- 118   2P/2B: $76- 118   XP: $6
4/4-5/22 & 9/22-11/2   1P: $53- 95   2P/1B: $53- 95   2P/2B: $63- 95   XP: $6
2/1-4/3 & 11/3-1/31   1P: $42- 82   2P/1B: $42- 82   2P/2B: $52- 82   XP: $6
Location: 1 mi e of SR 29, 11th St exit. 1120 N Main St 95453. Fax: 707/263-7733. **Terms:** Reserv deposit, 3 day notice. **Facility:** 45 rooms. On spacious grounds. 16 lakefront units with patio or balcony. Motel rooms & cottages. 10 two-bedroom units. 9 efficiencies, $15 extra. 5 one- & 2-bedroom cottages, with kitchen, $560-$800 weekly for 2-8 persons; 1-2 stories; exterior corridors; small pool; boat dock; playground. **Dining:** Coffee shop nearby. **Recreation:** swimming, boating, fishing, waterskiing. **All Rooms:** combo or shower baths. **Cards:** AE, CB, DI, DS, JC, MC, VI.

RESTAURANT

ANTHONY'S   Dinner: $9-$18   Phone: 707/263-4905
AAA
◆
Italian

Location: 0.8 mi n on SR 29 business route. 2509 Lakeshore Blvd 95453. **Hours:** 5 pm-10 pm. Closed: 11/25, 12/25, Tues, Weds, Oct & Easter. **Reservations:** suggested. **Features:** casual dress; children's menu; carryout; cocktails & lounge; minimum charge-$10; a la carte. Also American cuisine. Smoke free premises. **Cards:** AE, DS, MC, VI.

**AAA CampBooks—valuable additions for
members who enjoy outdoor vacations.**

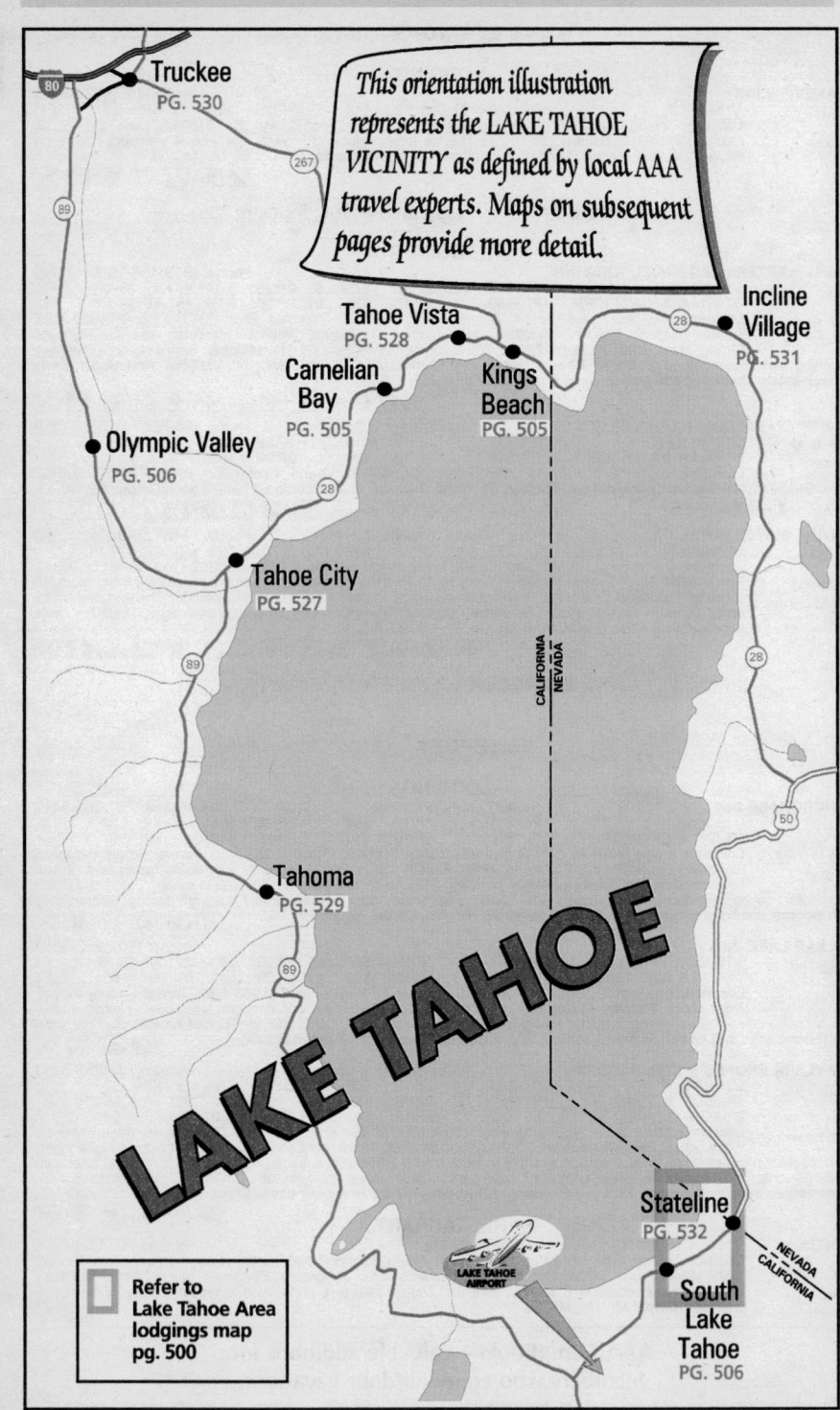

Lake Tahoe Area

his index helps you "spot" where approved accommodations are located on the detailed maps that follow. Rate ranges are for comparison only and show the property's high season. Turn to the listing page for more detailed rate information and consult display ads for special promotions. Restaurant rate range is for dinner unless only lunch (L) is served.

Lake Tahoe Area Vicinity

Spotter/Map Pg.Number	OA	INCLINE VILLAGE - Lodgings	Rating	Rate	Listing Page
1 / p. 500		Hyatt Regency Lake Tahoe Resort & Casino - see color ad p 531	◆◆◆◆	$225-380	531
2 / p. 500		Club Tahoe	◆◆◆	$180	531
3 / p. 500	ⓐ	The Inn at Incline	◆◆	$99-135 SAVE	531
		INCLINE VILLAGE - Restaurants			
① / p. 500		Azzara's Italian Restaurant	◆◆	$10-17	531
② / p. 500		Cafe 333	◆◆	$11-22	532
		OLYMPIC VALLEY - Lodgings			
5 / p. 500	ⓐ	**Resort at Squaw Creek**	◆◆◆◆	$325-415 SAVE	506
6 / p. 500	ⓐ	**Squaw Valley Lodge - see ad p 504**	◆◆◆◆	$375-625 SAVE	506
8 / p. 500		Squaw Tahoe Resort	◆◆	$210-300	506
		OLYMPIC VALLEY - Restaurant			
⑤ / p. 500		Glissandi	◆◆◆◆	$27-45	506
		TAHOE VISTA - Lodgings			
10 / p. 500	ⓐ	The Shore House at Lake Tahoe	◆◆◆	$150-225	529
11 / p. 500	ⓐ	Cedar Glen Lodge - see color ad p 502, p 286	◆◆	$79-95 SAVE	528
12 / p. 500	ⓐ	Charmey Chalet Resort - see color ad p 502	◆◆	$70-90 SAVE	528
13 / p. 500	ⓐ	Franciscan Lakeside Lodge - see color ad p 502	◆◆	$95-160	529
14 / p. 500	ⓐ	Woodvista Lodge	◆	$65-110 SAVE	529
15 / p. 500	ⓐ	Vista Shores Resort - see ad p 499	◆◆	$95-190	529
16 / p. 500	ⓐ	Firelite Lodge	◆	$56-79	528
		TAHOE VISTA - Restaurants			
⑪ / p. 500		Le Petit Pier	◆◆◆	$31-45	529
⑫ / p. 500		Sunsets on the Lake	◆◆◆	$14-24	529
		TAHOE CITY - Lodgings			
19 / p. 500	ⓐ	Lake of the Sky Motor Inn - see ad p 504	◆◆	$55-105 SAVE	527
20 / p. 500		The Cottage Inn at Lake Tahoe	◆◆◆	$140-210	527
21 / p. 500		Granlibakken Resort & Conference Center	◆◆◆	$156	527
22 / p. 500		River Ranch Lodge	◆◆	$135	528
24 / p. 500	ⓐ	Tahoe City Travelodge - see ad p 501	◆◆	$82-131 SAVE	528
25 / p. 500		Sunnyside Resort	◆◆◆	$160-200	528
26 / p. 500	ⓐ	Pepper Tree Inn	◆◆	$70-95 SAVE	527
		TAHOE CITY - Restaurants			
⑭ / p. 500		Christy Hill Restaurant	◆◆◆	$30-40	528
⑮ / p. 500		Tahoe House	◆◆◆	$8-18	528
		TRUCKEE - Lodgings			
30 / p. 500	ⓐ	Best Western Truckee Tahoe Inn - see color ad p 503	◆◆◆	$92-135 SAVE	530
31 / p. 500	ⓐ	Donner Lake Village Resort - see color ad p 503	◆◆◆	$100-225 SAVE	530
32 / p. 500	ⓐ	Northstar at Tahoe	◆◆◆	$139-448	531
		STATELINE - Lodgings			
37 / p. 500		Horizon Casino Resort	◆◆◆	$129	532
38 / p. 500		Caesars Tahoe	◆◆◆◆	$89-185	532
39 / p. 500	ⓐ	Harrah's Hotel & Casino	◆◆◆◆	$149-249 SAVE	532

Spotter/Map Pg.Number	OA	**STATELINE** - Lodgings (contd.)	Rating	Rate	Listing Page
④⓪ / p. 500	🚗	Harvey's Resort Hotel - see color ad p 515	◆◆◆◆	$120-235 🆂	532
④① / p. 500	🚗	Lakeside Inn - see color ad p 519	◆◆◆	$69-89 🆂	532
④② / p. 500	🚗	The Ridge Tahoe - see ad p 521	◆◆◆◆	$270-395 🆂	533
		STATELINE - Restaurants			
㉑ / p. 500	🚗	Llewellyn's	◆◆◆◆	$17-27	533
㉒ / p. 500	🚗	The Summit Room	◆◆◆◆	$26-32	533
㉓ / p. 500		Sage Room Steak House	◆◆◆	$18-24	533
㉔ / p. 500		The Eagles' Nest	◆◆◆	$9-19	533
		KINGS BEACH - Lodgings			
⑤⑤ / p. 500		Stevenson's Holliday Inn	◆	$60-99 🆂	505
⑤⑥ / p. 500		Falcon Motor Lodge - see color ad p 502	◆	$69-129	505
⑤⑦ / p. 500	🚗	Goldcrest Resort Motel - see color ad p 501	◆	$85-195 🆂	505
⑤⑧ / p. 500	🚗	Crown Motel - see color ad p 505	◆	$85-130 🆂	505
⑤⑨ / p. 500	🚗	Sun N' Sand Lodge - see ad p 504	◆	$84-100 🆂	506
		SOUTH LAKE TAHOE - Lodgings			
⑥③ / p. 500	🚗	Bavarian Village	◆◆	$150 🆂	506
⑥④ / p. 500		Dream Inn	◆	$75-89	513
⑥⑤ / p. 500	🚗	Alder Inn	◆◆	$66-96 🆂	506
⑥⑥ / p. 500		Tahoe Hacienda Motel	◆	$75-85	523
⑥⑦ / p. 500	🚗	Viking Motor Lodge	◆◆	$69-99 🆂	527
⑥⑧ / p. 500	🚗	Trade Winds Resort & Suites - see color ad p 526	◆	$95-105 🆂	525
⑥⑨ / p. 500	🚗	Tahoe Chalet Inn - see ad p 523	◆◆	$72-128 🆂	522
⑦⓪ / p. 500	🚗	South Tahoe Travelodge - see color ad p 511	◆◆◆	$91-111 🆂	521
⑦① / p. 500		Stardust Lodge	◆◆	$126-162	522
⑦② / p. 500		Pacifica Lodge	◆◆	$70-75	519
⑦③ / p. 500	🚗	Best Western Station House Inn - see color ad p 509	◆◆◆	$200-250 🆂	508
⑦④ / p. 500	🚗	Best Tahoe West Inn - see color ad p 507, inside front cover, p 501	◆◆	$60-99 🆂	507
⑦⑤ / p. 500	🚗	Holiday Lodge - see color ad p 517	◆	$85 🆂	515
⑦⑥ / p. 500	🚗	La Baer Inn - see ad p 517	◆◆	$67-109 🆂	517
⑦⑦ / p. 500	🚗	Lakepark Lodge	◆◆	$50-80 🆂	517
⑦⑧ / p. 500	🚗	Beachside Inn & Suites - see color ad p 526	◆	$95-105 🆂	507
⑦⑨ / p. 500	🚗	Blue Jay Lodge - see color ad p 510	◆◆	$69-149 🆂	510
⑧⓪ / p. 500	🚗	Alpenrose Inn	◆◆	$60-80 🆂	506
⑧② / p. 500		Days Inn Lake Tahoe - see color ad p 512	◆◆	$89-130	512
⑧③ / p. 500	🚗	Cedar Inn & Suites	◆	$89-99	510
⑧④ / p. 500	🚗	Elizabeth Lodge	◆	$65-89 🆂	513
⑧⑤ / p. 500		Quality Inn & Suites - see color ad p 504	◆◆	$89-130	520
⑧⑥ / p. 500	🚗	Rodeway Inn	◆	$39-95 🆂	520
⑧⑦ / p. 500	🚗	Tahoe Keys Resort - see color ad p 524	◆◆◆	$180-440 🆂	523
⑧⑧ / p. 500	🚗	Royal Valhalla Motor Lodge	◆◆◆	$92-112	520
⑨⓪ / p. 500	🚗	7 Seas Motel - see color ad p 521	◆	$69-79 🆂	521
⑨① / p. 500	🚗	Embassy Suites Resort	◆◆◆◆	$249-349 🆂	513
⑨② / p. 500	🚗	Pioneer Inn Motel	◆	$55-155	520
⑨③ / p. 500	🚗	Green Lantern Motel	◆	$50-95 🆂	513
⑨④ / p. 500		South Shore Inn	◆◆	$48-148 🆂	521
⑨⑤ / p. 500	🚗	Tahoe Marina Inn	◆◆	$99-150	523
⑨⑥ / p. 500	🚗	Cedar Lodge	◆◆	$64-94 🆂	511
⑨⑦ / p. 500	🚗	Lakeland Village - see color ad p 519	◆◆◆	$175-280 🆂	517
⑨⑧ / p. 500	🚗	Econo Lodge - see color ad p 503	◆	$89-125 🆂	513
⑨⑨ / p. 500	🚗	Lampliter Motel	◆◆	$80-100 🆂	519
⑩⓪ / p. 500	🚗	Tahoe Sunset Lodge	◆	$45-90	523
⑩① / p. 500		Stateline Lodge	◆	$65	522
⑩② / p. 500	🚗	Thunderchief Motel	◆	$95-125 🆂	525

Spotter/Map Pg.Number	OA	SOUTH LAKE TAHOE - Lodgings (contd.)	Rating	Rate	Listing Page
103 / p. 500	AAA	Casino Area Travelodge - see color ad p 511	◆◆	$91-111 [SAVE]	510
104 / p. 500	AAA	Ridgewood Inn	◆	$70-75	520
105 / p. 500	AAA	Best Western Lake Tahoe Inn	◆◆	$135-165 [SAVE]	507
106 / p. 500	AAA	Best Western Timber Cove Lodge - see color ad p 508	◆◆◆	$135-185 [SAVE]	510
107 / p. 500	AAA	High Country Lodge	◆◆	$70 [SAVE]	514
108 / p. 500	AAA	Inn By The Lake - see ad p 518	◆◆◆	$200-250 [SAVE]	515
109 / p. 500	AAA	Stateline Travelodge	◆◆	$91-111 [SAVE]	522
110 / p. 500	AAA	Emerald Bay Inn	◆	$55-85 [SAVE]	513
111 / p. 500	AAA	Tahoe Valley Lodge - see ad p 525	◆◆	$175 [SAVE]	524
112 / p. 500	AAA	Forest Inn Suites - see color ad p 514	◆◆◆	$210-460 [SAVE]	513
113 / p. 500	AAA	Parkwood Lodge - see color ad p 520	◆◆	$68-88 [SAVE]	520
114 / p. 500	AAA	Holiday Inn Express - see color ad p 516	◆◆◆	$139-149 [SAVE]	515
115 / p. 500	AAA	Days Inn-Casino Area/South Lake Tahoe - see color ad p 512	◆◆	$78-98 [SAVE]	512
116 / p. 500	AAA	Paradice Motel	◆	$58-68	519
117 / p. 500	AAA	Mark Twain Motel	◆	$58-78	519
118 / p. 500	AAA	Torchlite Inn & Suites - see color ad p 525	◆◆	$78-98 [SAVE]	525
119 / p. 500	AAA	Super 8 - see color ad p 522	◆◆	$50-108 [SAVE]	522
120 / p. 500	AAA	The Tahoe Seasons Resort	◆◆◆	$170-240 [SAVE]	523
122 / p. 500	AAA	Tahoe Sundowner Motel	◆	$65-85	523
		SOUTH LAKE TAHOE - Restaurants			
30 / p. 500		Evans American Gourmet Cafe	◆◆◆	$25-40	527
31 / p. 500	AAA	Heidi's Restaurant	◆	$5-9(L)	527
33 / p. 500	AAA	Tep's Villa Roma	◆	$7-17	527
35 / p. 500	AAA	The Swiss Chalet	◆◆	$13-21	527
36 / p. 500		Zackary's	◆◆◆	$14-22	527
37 / p. 500	AAA	LewMarNel's	◆◆◆	$14-25	527
		TAHOMA - Lodgings			
125 / p. 500	AAA	Norfolk Woods Inn & Restaurant	◆◆	$90-155	529
126 / p. 500		Tahoe Cedars Lodge	◆	$55	530
		CARNELIAN BAY - Restaurant			
44 / p. 500	AAA	Gar Woods Grill & Pier	◆◆◆	$12-18	505

Fire Safety Conscious?

All AAA lodgings must have a smoke detector in each sleeping room.

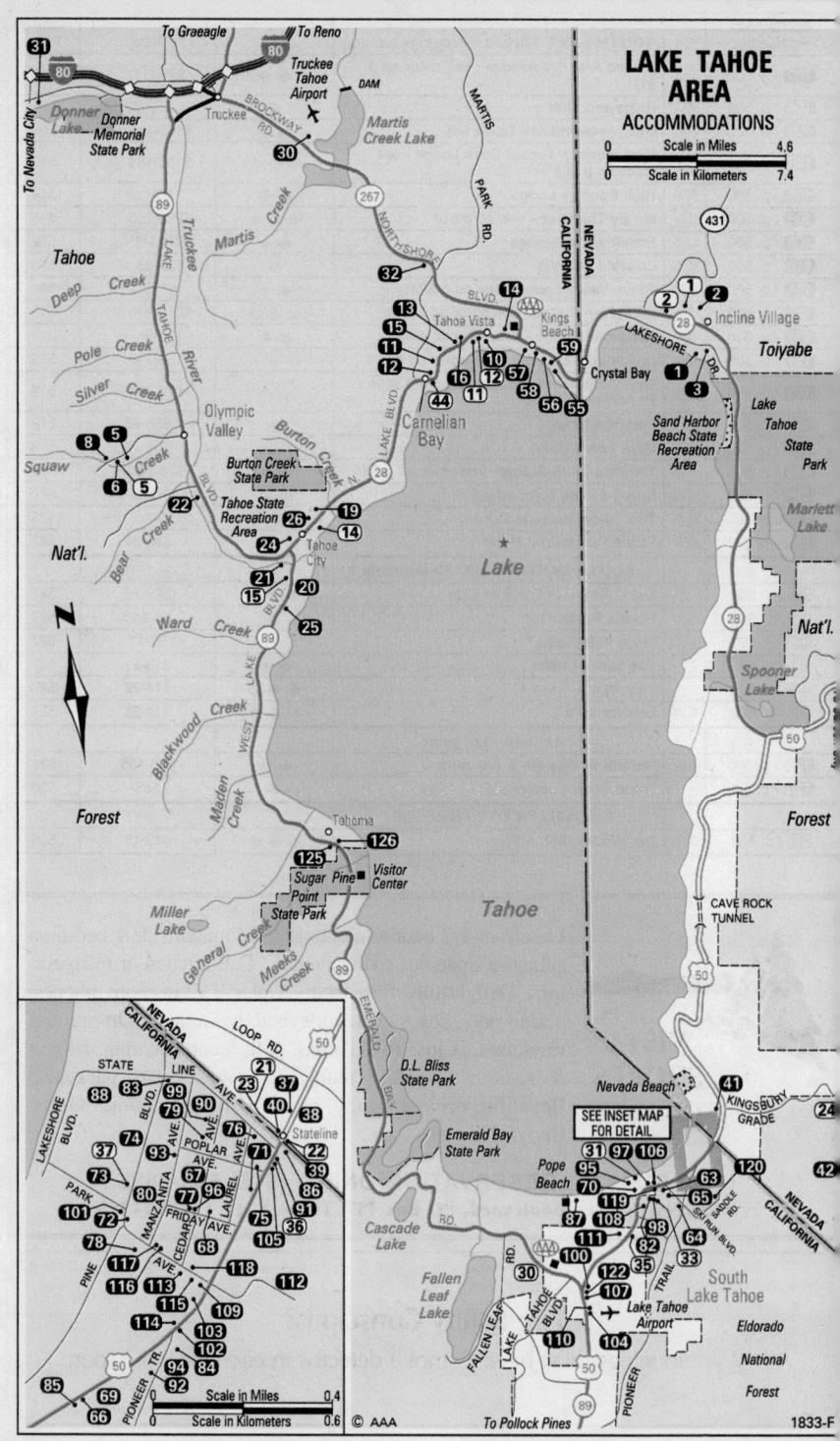

LAKE TAHOE AREA
ACCOMMODATIONS

Scale in Miles　　0　　4.6
Scale in Kilometers　0　　7.4

© AAA

1833-F

When making reservations, state:

1. Your AAA/CAA membership.
2. Number of persons in your party.
3. Ages of any children.
4. Type of accommodations desired.
5. Rate preferred.
6. Date and estimated arrival time.
7. Length of stay.

CARNELIAN BAY—1,400 (See map p. 500; index p. 499)

RESTAURANT

GAR WOODS GRILL & PIER   **Lunch:** $7-$11   **Dinner:** $12-$18   **Phone:** 530/546-3366   44
Location: On SR 28, 6 mi e of SR 89. 5000 N Lake Blvd 96140. **Hours:** 10:30 am-10 pm.
Reservations: suggested. **Features:** No A/C; casual dress; cocktail lounge; a la carte. Lakefront view on
Tahoe's north shore. **Cards:** AE, MC, VI.   ♿ ☒

Traditional
Continental

KINGS BEACH—2,800 (See map p. 500; index p. 498)

LODGINGS

CROWN MOTEL   **Phone:** (530)546-3388   58

Fri & Sat 2/1-3/31 & 6/18-9/18	1P:	$65- 120	2P/1B:	$85- 130	2P/2B:	$85- 130	XP: $5-10	F10
12/16-1/2 & Fri & Sat 1/3-1/31	1P:	$65- 120	2P/1B:	$85- 130	2P/2B:	$85- 130	XP: $5-10	F10
Sun-Thurs 2/1-3/31, 4/1-6/17 & 9/19-12/15	1P:	$45- 85	2P/1B:	$45- 90	2P/2B:	$50- 95	XP: $5-10	F10
Sun-Thurs 1/3-1/31	1P:	$45- 85	2P/1B:	$45- 90	2P/2B:	$50- 95	XP: $5-10	F10

Location: SR 28, 0.3 mi e of SR 267. 8200 N Lake Blvd 96143 (PO Box 845). **Terms:** Reserv deposit, 7 day notice; handling fee imposed. **Facility:** 37 rooms. 12 attractively decorated units with gas fireplace & lakeviews. Some smaller units. 8 two-bedroom units. 2 stories; exterior corridors; lakefront; beach, whirlpool. **Recreation:** swimming. **All Rooms:** combo or shower baths. **Cards:** AE, DS, MC, VI. **Special Amenities:** Early check-in/late check-out and free local telephone calls. *(See color ad below)*   🛥 ☒ 🖵 ☐ 🔋 ☒

FALCON MOTOR LODGE   Rates Subject to Change   **Phone:** 530/546-2583   56

Fri & Sat 2/1-6/14, 6/15-9/15 & Fri & Sat 9/16-1/31	1P:	$59- 129	2P/1B:	$69- 129	2P/2B:	$69- 129	XP: $5	F12
Sun-Thurs 2/1-6/14 & 9/16-1/31	1P:	$39- 89	2P/1B:	$49- 89	2P/2B:	$49- 89	XP: $5	F12

Location: 2 blks e of SR 267, on SR 28. 8258 N Lake Blvd 96143 (PO Box 249). Fax: 530/546-8680. **Terms:** Reserv deposit, 3 day notice. **Facility:** 31 rooms. Some rooms with lake view; few small rooms. 1 three-bedroom unit, 4 two-bedroom units. 2 stories; exterior corridors; heated pool. **Recreation:** swimming. **All Rooms:** combo or shower baths. **Some Rooms:** 2 kitchens. **Cards:** AE, DI, DS, MC, VI. *(See color ad p 502)*   🐾 🛥 ⛰ ☒ 🖵 ☐ 🎿 🔋 ☒

GOLDCREST RESORT MOTEL   **Phone:** (530)546-3301   57

6/10-9/15 & 12/20-1/3 [CP]	1P:	$60- 135	2P/1B:	$60- 135	2P/2B:	$85- 195	XP: $5
2/1-6/9, 9/16-12/19 & 1/4-1/31 [CP]	1P:	$45- 125	2P/1B:	$45- 125	2P/2B:	$65- 175	XP: $5

Location: SR 28, 0.3 mi e of SR 267. 8194 North Lake Blvd 96143 (PO Box 579). Fax: 530/546-4395.
Terms: Reserv deposit, 30 day notice; handling fee imposed. **Facility:** 25 rooms. 4 two-bedroom units. 4 kitchens, $15 extra charge; 1-2 stories; exterior corridors; beach, heated pool, whirlpool. **Dining:** Coffee shop nearby. **Recreation:** swimming. Fee: waterskiing. **All Rooms:** combo or shower baths. **Cards:** AE, CB, DI, DS, MC, VI. **Special Amenities:** Free breakfast and free local telephone calls. *(See color ad p 501)*   🛥 🍴 ☒ 🎿 🔋 ☒

STEVENSON'S HOLLIDAY INN   **Phone:** (530)546-2269   55

6/16-9/20	1P:	$55- 85	2P/1B:	$55- 85	2P/2B:	$60- 99	XP: $5
2/1-6/15 & 9/21-1/31	1P:	$38- 75	2P/1B:	$38- 75	2P/2B:	$48- 79	XP: $5

Location: SR 28, 1 mi e of SR 267. 8742 N Lake Blvd 96143 (PO Box 235). **Terms:** Reserv deposit, 5 day notice; small pets only, $25 dep req. **Facility:** 22 rooms. Recreation room with video games & ping-pong. 4 two-bedroom units. 1 story; exterior corridors; heated pool, whirlpool. **Dining:** Coffee shop nearby. **All Rooms:** combo or shower baths. **Some Rooms:** 3 kitchens. **Cards:** AE, DI, DS, MC, VI. **Special Amenities:** Early check-in/late check-out and free local telephone calls.   🐾 🛥 🍴 ☐ 🎿 🔋 ☒

(See map p. 500)

SUN N' SAND LODGE
Phone: (530)546-2515
6/30-9/3   1P: $63- 115   2P/1B: $63- 115   2P/2B: $84- 100   XP: $10
2/1-6/29 & 9/4-1/31   1P: $45- 115   2P/1B: $45- 115   2P/2B: $53- 96   XP: $10
Motel
Location: SR 28, 0.3 mi e of SR 267. 8308 N Lake Blvd 96143. **Fax:** 530/546-0112. **Terms:** Reserv deposi
Facility: 26 rooms. 2 stories; exterior corridors. **Dining:** Coffee shop nearby. **All Rooms:** shower baths
Cards: AE, DI, DS, MC, VI. *(See ad p 504)*

OLYMPIC VALLEY—1,000   (See map p. 500; index p. 497)

LODGINGS

RESORT AT SQUAW CREEK
Phone: (530)583-6300
12/19-1/4   2P/2B: $325- 415   XP: $35
2/1-3/29 & 1/5-1/31   2P/2B: $275- 390   XP: $35
6/15-8/30   2P/2B: $255- 370   XP: $35
Resort   3/30-6/14 & 8/31-12/18   2P/2B: $225- 350   XP: $35
Complex
Location: 0.3 mi from entrance to Squaw Valley. 400 Squaw Creek Rd 96146 (P O Box 3333)
Fax: 530/581-5407. **Terms:** Check-in 4 pm; reserv deposit, 30 day notice. **Facility:** 405 rooms. All season re
sort, exceptional facilities. Choice of mountain or valley view. 18 two-bedroom units. 18 bi-level suites, $525-$855; 9 stories
interior corridors; heated pool, wading pool, saunas, whirlpools, waterslide pool open 7/1-9/7; indoor whirlpool. Fee: 18 hole
golf; 2 tennis courts. **Dining:** Dining room, 2 restaurants; 6:30 am-10 pm; $15-$55; cocktails; also, Glissandi, see separate
listing. **Recreation:** ice skating. Fee: downhill skiing; horseback riding. Rental: bicycles. **Some Rooms:** 14 kitchens
Cards: AE, DI, DS, MC, VI.

SQUAW TAHOE RESORT   Rates Subject to Change   Phone: 530/583-7226
12/19-1/3   1P: $210   2P/1B: $260   2P/2B: $300
Motel   2/1-4/11, 11/20-12/18 &
1/4-1/31   1P: $130- 180   2P/1B: $160- 240   2P/2B: $210- 270
4/12-11/19   1P: $70- 80   2P/1B: $120- 130   2P/2B: $120- 130
Location: Located at Squaw Valley Ski Area. 2000 Squaw Loop Road 96146. **Fax:** 530/583-8808. **Terms:** Reserv deposit,
day notice. **Facility:** 26 rooms. 8 two-bedroom units. 3 stories; interior corridors. **All Rooms:** kitchens, combo or showe
baths. **Cards:** AE, MC, VI.

SQUAW VALLEY LODGE
Phone: (530)583-5500
12/17-1/1   1P: $275   2P/1B: $305- 325   2P/2B: $375- 625
2/1-4/10 & 1/2-1/31 1P: $160- 210   2P/1B: $210- 260   2P/2B: $260- 310
4/11-12/16   1P: $120- 150   2P/1B: $160- 190   2P/2B: $180- 210
Condo Lodge **Location:** In Olympic Valley at Squaw Valley Ski area. 201 Squaw Peak Rd 96146 (PO Box 3730)
Fax: 530/583-0326. **Terms:** Check-in 4 pm; reserv deposit, 30 day notice. **Facility:** 154 rooms. Located at foc
of slopes, 150 feet from cable car. Most rooms with view of slopes or valley. 3 stories; interior corridors; heated pool, sauna
whirlpool, 3 indoor whirlpools; 2 tennis courts. **Recreation:** Fee: downhill skiing. **All Rooms:** kitchens. **Cards:** AE, DI, MC
VI. *(See ad p 504)*

RESTAURANT

GLISSANDI   **Dinner:** $27-$45   Phone: 530/581-6621
French
Location: In Olympic Valley at Resort, Squaw Creek. 1000 Squaw Creek Rd 96146. **Hours:** WK: 6 pm-1
pm. Closed: Sun. **Reservations:** required. **Features:** No A/C; semi-formal attire; cocktails & lounge; vale
parking; a la carte. **Cards:** AE, CB, DI, MC, VI.

SOUTH LAKE TAHOE—21,600   (See map p. 500; index p. 498)

LODGINGS

ALDER INN
Phone: (530)544-4485
Fri & Sat [CP]   1P: $66- 96   2P/1B: $66- 96   2P/2B: $66- 96
Sun-Thurs [CP]   1P: $43- 66   2P/1B: $43- 66   2P/2B: $43- 66
Motel   **Location:** 2 1/2 blks s off US 50 on Ski Run Blvd; 0.8 mi below Heavenly Valley ski lift terminal. 1072 Sk
Run Blvd 96150. **Fax:** 530/541-4816. **Terms:** Reserv deposit, 3 day notice; handling fee imposed; pets, $1
extra charge. **Facility:** 24 rooms. Quiet location. 2 stories; exterior corridors; heated pool, whirlpool, enclose
whirlpool. **Cards:** AE, DS, MC, VI. **Special Amenities:** Early check-in/late check-out and free breakfast.

ALPENROSE INN
Phone: (530)544-2985
Fri & Sat 6/11-9/11 [CP]   1P: $55- 80   2P/1B: $55- 85   2P/2B: $60- 80   XP: $5
Fri & Sat 2/1-6/10 &
9/12-1/31 [CP]   1P: $50- 70   2P/1B: $50- 70   2P/2B: $50- 70   XP: $5
Motel   Sun-Thurs 6/11-9/11 [CP]
Sun-Thurs 2/1-6/10 &   1P: $45- 60   2P/1B: $45- 60   2P/2B: $45- 65   XP: $5
9/12-1/31 [CP]   1P: $33- 60   2P/1B: $35- 60   2P/2B: $40- 65   XP: $5
Location: 0.3 mi n of US 50 via Park Ave. 4074 Pine Blvd 96150. **Fax:** 530/543-0299. **Terms:** Reserv deposit, 3 day notice
small pets only, $10 extra charge, $50 dep req. **Facility:** 19 rooms. Few rooms with fireplace. 2 stories; exterior corridors
whirlpool. **Dining:** Restaurant nearby. **All Rooms:** combo or shower baths. **Some Rooms:** 4 kitchens. **Cards:** AE, DS, MC
VI. **Special Amenities:** Free breakfast and free local telephone calls.

BAVARIAN VILLAGE
Phone: 530/541-8191
2/1-4/10, 6/15-9/15 &
11/21-1/31   1P: $95   2P/1B: $130   2P/2B: $150
Condo   4/11-6/14 & 9/16-11/20   1P: $70   2P/1B: $90   2P/2B: $110
Complex   **Location:** Just w of Ski Run Blvd, 0.3 mi s of US 50. 1140-B Herbert Ave 96150 (PO Box 709, 96156)
Fax: 530/544-3082. **Terms:** Reserv deposit. **Facility:** 55 rooms. 2 & 3-bedroom units; 2 stories; exterior corr
dors; heated pool, whirlpool; playground. **All Rooms:** kitchens. **Cards:** AE, DS, MC, VI.

(See map p. 500)

BEACHSIDE INN & SUITES　　　　　　　　　　　　　　Phone: (530)544-2400　**78**

AAA SAVE

◆

Motel

		1P:	$75- 85	2P/1B:	$85- 95	2P/2B:	$95- 105	XP: $10	F12
Fri & Sat 2/1-3/31, 6/16-10/15 & 12/23-1/31									
Fri & Sat 4/1-6/15 & 10/16-12/22		1P:	$45- 55	2P/1B:	$55- 65	2P/2B:	$65- 75	XP: $10	F12
Sun-Thurs 6/15-9/15		1P:	$40- 50	2P/1B:	$40- 50	2P/2B:	$50- 60	XP: $5	F12
Sun-Thurs 2/1-6/14 & 9/16-12/22		1P:	$35- 45	2P/1B:	$35- 45	2P/2B:	$45- 55	XP: $5	F12

Location: 3 blks from casino center. 930 Park Av 96150. Fax: 530/544-0600. **Terms:** Reserv deposit, 10 day notice; handling fee imposed; 2 night min stay, weekends; pets, $5 extra charge, $50 dep req. **Facility:** 17 rooms. 2 stories; exterior corridors; whirlpool. **Dining:** Restaurant nearby. **All Rooms:** combo or shower baths. **Some Rooms:** whirlpools. **Cards:** AE, DS, MC, VI. **Special Amenities:** Free breakfast and free local telephone calls. *(See color ad p 526)*

🛏️ 🍴 🐾 ▢ ▢ ⚙️ 🖥️

BEST TAHOE WEST INN　　　　　　　　　　　　　　Phone: (530)544-6455　**74**

AAA SAVE

◆ ◆

Motel

		1P:	$55- 89	2P/1B:	$55- 89	2P/2B:	$60- 99	XP: $10	F11
Fri & Sat 6/11-9/11									
Fri & Sat 2/1-6/10, Sun-Thurs 6/11-9/9 & Fri & Sat 9/12-1/31		1P:	$44- 79	2P/1B:	$44- 79	2P/2B:	$55- 89	XP: $10	F11
Sun-Thurs 2/1-6/10 & 9/10-1/31		1P:	$33- 69	2P/1B:	$33- 69	2P/2B:	$44- 79	XP: $10	F11

Location: N off US 50, via Park Ave; on Pine Blvd, between Stateline & Park aves. 4107 Pine Blvd 96150. Fax: 530/544-0508. **Terms:** Reserv deposit, 3 day notice. **Facility:** 61 rooms. On both sides of Pine Blvd. 11 efficiencies, $7 extra charge; 2-3 stories, no elevator; exterior corridors; small heated pool, sauna, whirlpool. **All Rooms:** combo or shower baths. **Cards:** AE, DI, DS, MC, VI. **Special Amenities:** Early check-in/late check-out and free local telephone calls. *(See color ad below, inside front cover & p 501)*

🅂🄳 🏊 ⚙️ ✕

BEST WESTERN LAKE TAHOE INN　　　　　　　　　Phone: (530)541-2010　**105**

AAA SAVE

◆ ◆

Motor Inn

		1P:	$125- 155	2P/1B:	$125- 155	2P/2B:	$135- 165	XP: $10	F16
12/25-1/2 [BP]									
2/1-12/24 & 1/3-1/31 [BP]		1P:	$49- 94	2P/1B:	$49- 94	2P/2B:	$59- 104	XP: $10	F16

Location: US 50, adjacent to casinos. 4110 Lake Tahoe Blvd 96150. Fax: 530/542-1428. **Terms:** Reserv deposit, 3 day notice. **Facility:** 400 rooms. Spacious grounds. 8 two-bedroom units. 2 stories; exterior corridors; heated pool, whirlpool. **Dining:** Coffee shop; 6:30 am-1 pm; cocktails. **All Rooms:** combo or shower baths. **Cards:** AE, CB, DI, DS, JC, MC, VI. **Special Amenities:** Free breakfast and free room upgrade (subject to availability with advanced reservations).

🏊 🍴 🐾 🖥️ 📠 ✕

(See map p. 500)

BEST WESTERN STATION HOUSE INN　　　　　　　　　　　　　　　　**Phone:** (530)542-1101　　🆖

ⒶⒶⒶ ⓈⒶⓋⒺ	12/23-1/6 [BP]	1P: $200- 250	2P/1B: $200- 250	2P/2B: $200- 250 XP: $25-50

F12

◆◆◆　　2/1-3/31, 6/15-10/21 &

Motor Inn

1/7-1/31 [BP]	1P: $98- 118	2P/1B: $98- 118	2P/2B: $118- 128 XP: $10
4/1-6/14 & 10/22-12/22 [BP]	1P: $88- 108	2P/1B: $88- 108	2P/2B: $108- 118 XP: $10

F12
F12

Location: 3 1/2 blks from casino center; 2 blks n off US 50 via Lake Park Ave. 901 Park Ave 96150. Fax: 530/542-1714. **Terms:** Reserv deposit, 3 day notice. **Facility:** 102 rooms. Attractive rooms. 1 three-bedroom unit. 1 two-bedroom cabin & 1 three-bedroom cabin, $150-$200 for up to 6 persons; 2 whirlpool suites, $125-$150; 2 stories; exterior corridors; heated pool, whirlpool. **Dining:** Restaurant; also, LewMarNel's, see separate listing. **All Rooms:** combo or shower baths. **Cards:** AE, CB, DI, DS, MC, VI. **Special Amenities:** Free breakfast and free room upgrade (subject to availability with advanced reservations). *(See color ad p 509)*

Relax over good food: Follow the recommendations
in the Lodgings & Restaurants listings.

(See map p. 500)

BEST WESTERN TIMBER COVE LODGE   Phone: (530)541-6722 ⑩

AAA SAVE

		1P:		2P/1B:		2P/2B:		XP:	
	12/25-1/2	1P:	$125- 175	2P/1B:	$125- 175	2P/2B:	$135- 185	XP:	$10	F1
	6/19-9/6	1P:	$100- 150	2P/1B:	$100- 150	2P/2B:	$100- 160	XP:	$10	F1
	9/7-9/26	1P:	$65- 150	2P/1B:	$65- 150	2P/2B:	$75- 160	XP:	$10	F1
Motor Inn	2/1-6/18, 9/27-12/24 &									
	1/3-1/31	1P:	$65- 130	2P/1B:	$65- 130	2P/2B:	$75- 140	XP:	$10	F1

Location: On lake 1.5 mi w of casino center, 0.5 mi w of Ski Run Blvd. 3411 Lake Tahoe Blvd 96150. Fax: 530/541-7795. **Terms:** Reserv deposit. **Facility:** 262 rooms. Spacious grounds; some rooms with lake view. 3 stories; exterior corridor; beach, heated pool, whirlpool; marina. **Dining:** Restaurant; 7 am-10 pm; to 9 pm, in winter; $9-$20; cocktail. **Recreation:** swimming, fishing, waterskiing. Rental: boats. **All Rooms:** combo or shower baths. **Cards:** AE, CB, DI, DS, MC, VI. **Special Amenities:** Free breakfast and free local telephone calls. (See color ad p 508)

BLUE JAY LODGE   Phone: (530)544-5232 ⑦

AAA SAVE

		1P:		2P/1B:		2P/2B:		XP:	
	2/1-3/31, 6/13-9/15 &									
	12/23-1/3	1P:	$59- 139	2P/1B:	$59- 139	2P/2B:	$69- 149	XP:	$6	F1
	4/1-6/12, 9/16-12/22 &									
Motel	1/4-1/31	1P:	$49- 119	2P/1B:	$49- 119	2P/2B:	$59- 129	XP:	$6	F1

Location: 2 blks from casino center. 4133 Cedar Ave 96150. Fax: 530/544-0453. **Terms:** Reserv deposit; pets, $10 extra charge, $100 dep req. **Facility:** 65 rooms. Some rooms with fireplaces. Honeymoon suite with spa $98-$16; 2 stories; exterior corridors; heated pool, whirlpool. **Dining:** Restaurant nearby. **All Rooms:** combo or shower bath. **Some Rooms:** 11 kitchens. **Cards:** AE, DI, DS, MC, VI. **Special Amenities:** Free local telephone calls and free room upgrade (subject to availability with advanced reservations). (See color ad below)

CASINO AREA TRAVELODGE   Phone: (530)541-5000 ⑩

AAA SAVE

		1P:		2P/1B:		2P/2B:		XP:	
	7/1-8/31	1P:	$81- 101	2P/1B:	$86- 106	2P/2B:	$91- 111	XP:	$5	F1
	5/1-6/30 & 9/1-10/31	1P:	$71- 91	2P/1B:	$76- 96	2P/2B:	$81- 101	XP:	$5	F1
	1/1-1/31	1P:	$62- 82	2P/1B:	$67- 87	2P/2B:	$72- 92	XP:	$5	F1
Motel	2/1-4/30 & 11/1-12/31	1P:	$59- 79	2P/1B:	$64- 84	2P/2B:	$69- 89	XP:	$5	F1

Location: 2 blks w of casino center, on US 50. 4003 Lake Tahoe Blvd 96150. Fax: 530/544-6918. **Terms:** Reserv deposit. **Facility:** 66 rooms. Nicely decorated rooms. 2 stories; exterior corridors; heated pool, whirlpool. **All Rooms:** shower baths. **Cards:** AE, CB, DI, DS, JC, MC, VI. **Special Amenities:** Free local telephone calls and free newspaper. (See color ad p 511)

CEDAR INN & SUITES   Guaranteed Rates   Phone: 530/543-0159 ⑧

AAA

		1P:		2P/1B:		2P/2B:		XP:	
	Fri & Sat	1P:	$75- 99	2P/1B:	$75- 99	2P/2B:	$89- 99	XP:	$8	F1
	Sun-Thurs 6/15-9/15	1P:	$52- 77	2P/1B:	$52- 77	2P/2B:	$65- 77	XP:	$8	F1
	Sun-Thurs 2/1-6/14 &									
Motel	9/16-1/31	1P:	$45- 70	2P/1B:	$45- 70	2P/2B:	$60- 70	XP:	$8	F1

Location: 2 blks n of US 50, at Stateline & Manzanita. 890 Stateline Ave 96150. Fax: 530/543-0300. **Facility:** 39 rooms. 2 stories; exterior corridors; heated pool, whirlpool. **Dining:** Restaurant nearby. **All Rooms:** combo or shower baths. **Some Rooms:** 4 kitchens. **Cards:** AE, DI, DS, MC, VI.

Choose an establishment with the AAA next to its listing!

See map p. 500)

CEDAR LODGE

	6/15-9/15 [CP]		2P/1B:	$56-	86	2P/2B:	$64- 94	XP: $10
	2/1-3/31 & 12/23-1/31 [CP]		2P/1B:	$39-	69	2P/2B:	$49- 79	XP: $8
	4/1-6/14 [CP]		2P/1B:	$39-	56	2P/2B:	$46- 66	XP: $8
	9/16-12/22 [CP]		2P/1B:	$36-	56	2P/2B:	$46- 66	XP: $8

Phone: (530)544-6453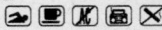

Location: N off US 50, toward the lake; at Cedar & Friday aves; 3 blks from the casino center. 4069 Cedar ve 96150. Fax: 530/542-1290. **Terms:** Reserv deposit, 3 day notice; package plans. **Facility:** 34 rooms. Very well maintained rooms. 2 two-bedroom units. 2 stories; exterior corridors; heated pool, whirlpool, whirlpool open 10/1-5/15. ll **Rooms:** combo or shower baths. **Cards:** MC, VI. **Special Amenities:** Free local telephone calls.

(See map p. 500)

DAYS INN-CASINO AREA/SOUTH LAKE TAHOE   **Phone:** (530)541-4800
6/15-9/15 [CP]   1P: $66- 80   2P/1B: $70- 84 2P/2B: $78- 98 XP: $6
2/1-6/14 & 9/16-1/31 [CP] 1P: $59- 69   2P/1B: $59- 74 2P/2B: $70- 88 XP: $6
Location: 3 blks w of casino center; 1 blk n off US 50 toward lake at Park & Cedar aves. 968 Park
Motel   96157 (PO Box 6499). Fax: 530/544-4643. **Terms:** Reserv deposit, 3 day notice; pets, $5 extra charge, $
dep req. **Facility:** 59 rooms. Weekend rates same as high season. 3 two-bedroom units for up to 4 perso
$100; 3 stories; interior corridors; small pool, sauna, whirlpool. **Cards:** AE, DI, DS, MC, VI. **Special Amenities:** Fr
breakfast and free newspaper. *(See color ad below)*

DAYS INN LAKE TAHOE   Rates Subject to Change   **Phone:** (530)544-3445
◆◆   Fri & Sat 6/18-9/25 &
Motel   12/24-1/3 [CP]   1P: $79- 99   2P/1B: $79- 110 2P/2B: $89- 130 XP: $10-15
         Fri & Sat 2/1-6/17,
         9/26-12/23 & 1/4-1/31 [CP] 1P: $59- 79   2P/1B: $69- 89 2P/2B: $79- 99 XP: $10
         Sun-Thurs 6/18-9/25 [CP]   1P: $49- 69   2P/1B: $59- 79 2P/2B: $69- 89 XP: $10
         Sun-Thurs 2/1-6/17,
         9/26-12/23 & 1/4-1/31 [CP] 1P: $39- 69   2P/1B: $49- 79 2P/2B: $59- 89 XP: $10
Location: US 50, 1.5 mi w of casino center. 3530 Lake Tahoe Blvd 96150. Fax: 530/544-3466. **Terms:** Reserv deposi
day notice; handling fee imposed. **Facility:** 42 rooms. 1 story; exterior corridors; heated pool. **All Rooms:** combo or show
baths. **Cards:** AE, CB, DI, DS, JC, MC, VI. *(See color ad below)*

Going to the Caribbean?
Ask for the AAA Caribbean TravelBook, Including Bermuda.

(See map p. 500)

DREAM INN Rates Subject to Change Phone: 530/544-6228 [64]

Motel

Fri & Sat 7/1-9/15 & 12/25-1/1	1P: $65- 79	2P/1B: $65- 79	2P/2B: $75- 89	XP: $10
Fri & Sat 2/1-3/31 & 1/2-1/31	1P: $55- 65	2P/1B: $55- 65	2P/2B: $65- 75	XP: $10
Fri & Sat 4/1-6/30 & 9/16-12/24	1P: $40- 55	2P/1B: $40- 55	2P/2B: $49- 65	XP: $5
Sun-Thurs 2/1-3/31, 4/1-6/30, 7/1-9/15, 9/16-12/24 & 12/25-1/31	1P: $24- 34	2P/1B: $24- 34	2P/2B: $30- 39	XP: $5

Location: 0.5 mi s of US 50. 1200 Ski Run Blvd 96150. Fax: 530/544-2560. **Terms:** Reserv deposit, 3 day notice. **Facility:** 23 rooms. 2 stories; exterior corridors. **All Rooms:** combo or shower baths. **Cards:** AE, DI, DS, MC, VI.

ECONO LODGE Rates Subject to Change Phone: (530)544-2036 [98]

Motel

Fri & Sat 6/18-9/25	1P: $79- 99	2P/1B: $79- 99	2P/2B: $89- 125	XP: $10	F14
Fri & Sat 2/1-6/17 & 9/26-1/31	1P: $59- 79	2P/1B: $59- 79	2P/2B: $79- 99	XP: $10	F14
Sun-Thurs 6/18-9/25	1P: $45- 69	2P/1B: $49- 69	2P/2B: $69- 89	XP: $10	F14
Sun-Thurs 2/1-6/17 & 9/26-1/31	1P: $39- 69	2P/1B: $39- 69	2P/2B: $49- 89	XP: $10	F14

Location: US 50, 1.5 mi w of Casino Center. 3536 Lake Tahoe Blvd 96150. Fax: 530/544-3466. **Terms:** Reserv deposit, 3 day notice; handling fee imposed; small pets only, $5 extra charge. **Facility:** 36 rooms. Exterior corridors; whirlpool. **Dining:** Restaurant nearby. **All Rooms:** combo or shower baths. **Cards:** AE, CB, DI, DS, JC, MC, VI.
See color ad p 503)

ELIZABETH LODGE Phone: (530)544-2417 [84]

Motel

Sat	1P: $55- 68	2P/1B: $55- 68	2P/2B: $65- 89	XP: $6
Fri	1P: $30- 45	2P/1B: $30- 45	2P/2B: $40- 55	XP: $6
Sun-Thurs	1P: $22- 28	2P/1B: $22- 28	2P/2B: $25- 38	XP: $6

Location: 4 blks w of casino center. 3918 Pioneer Tr 96150. Fax: 530/543-1746. **Terms:** Reserv deposit; handling fee imposed. **Facility:** 20 rooms. 1 story; exterior corridors. **All Rooms:** combo or shower baths. **Cards:** AE, DS, MC, VI. **Special Amenities:** Free breakfast and free local telephone calls.

EMBASSY SUITES RESORT Phone: (530)544-5400 [91]

Suite Hotel

2/1-3/31, 6/18-9/6 & 12/17-1/4 [BP]	1P: $199- 299	2P/1B: $219- 319	2P/2B: $249- 349	XP: $30-60	F12
10/24-12/16 [BP]	1P: $159- 199	2P/1B: $179- 219	2P/2B: $189- 249	XP: $30-60	F12
4/1-6/17, 9/7-10/23 & 1/5-1/31 [BP]	1P: $169- 209	2P/1B: $189- 229	2P/2B: $189- 239	XP: $30-60	F12

Location: At Casino Center. 4130 Lake Tahoe Blvd 96150. Fax: 530/544-7643. **Terms:** Reserv deposit, 3 day notice; 2 night min stay, weekends. **Facility:** 400 rooms. 9 stories; interior corridors; heated indoor pool, sauna, whirlpool. **Dining:** Restaurant; cocktails; also, Zackary's, see separate listing. **Services:** complimentary evening beverages. **All Rooms:** efficiencies, no utensils. **Cards:** AE, CB, DI, DS, JC, MC, VI. **Special Amenities:** Free breakfast and free newspaper.

EMBASSY VACATION RESORT-LAKE TAHOE Rates Subject to Change Phone: 530/541-6122

Motel

12/18-1/2 [CP]	1P: $169- 389	2P/1B: $169- 389	2P/2B: $169- 389	XP: $20	F12
2/1-3/29, 7/1-9/19 & 1/3-1/31 [CP]	1P: $139- 389	2P/1B: $139- 389	2P/2B: $139- 389	XP: $20	F12
3/30-6/30 & 9/20-12/17 [CP]	1P: $99- 379	2P/1B: $99- 379	2P/2B: $99- 379	XP: $20	F12

Too new to rate. **Location:** Jct of US 50 & Ski Run Blvd, 1 mi w of Casino center. 916 Ski Run Blvd 96150. Fax: 530/541-2028. **Terms:** Reserv deposit; 2 night min stay, wknds. **Facility:** 124 rooms. 1 and 2 bedroom condos with kitchen, fireplace & private patio. Adjacent to Ski Rkun Marina which offers a variety of lake activities & excursions. 62 two-bedroom units. 5 stories; interior corridors. **Services:** giftshop. **Some Rooms:** 62 efficiencies, 62 kitchens. **Cards:** AE, DI, DS, MC, VI.

EMERALD BAY INN Phone: (530)541-2333 [110]

Motel

All Year [CP]	1P: $48- 74	2P/1B: $48- 74	2P/2B: $55- 85	XP: $10	F16

Location: On US 50, 0.5 mi n of airport. 1313 Emerald Bay Rd 96150. Fax: 530/541-0331. **Terms:** Reserv deposit, 7 day notice; handling fee imposed. **Facility:** 12 rooms. 1 story; exterior corridors. **All Rooms:** shower baths. **Cards:** AE, DI, MC, VI. **Special Amenities:** Early check-in/late check-out and preferred room (subject to availability with advanced reservations).

FOREST INN SUITES Phone: (530)541-6655 [112]

Apartment Motel

12/23-1/3 [CP]	1P: $170- 360	2P/1B: $175- 365	2P/2B: $210- 460	XP: $10	F17
2/1-4/5, 6/14-9/19 & 1/4-1/31 [CP]	1P: $100- 170	2P/1B: $105- 175	2P/2B: $130- 205	XP: $10	F17
4/6-6/13 & 9/20-12/22 [CP]	1P: $90- 150	2P/1B: $95- 155	2P/2B: $115- 180	XP: $10	F17

Location: Just se off US 50, adjacent to casinos. One Lake Pkwy 96150. Fax: 530/544-3135. **Terms:** Reserv deposit, 4 day notice. **Facility:** 116 rooms. Shaded, landscaped grounds. Some motel units. 1-bedroom suites for up to 4 persons, $115-$185; 100 kitchens; 2 stories; interior/exterior corridors; heated pool, sauna, steam-room, whirlpools. **Cards:** AE, DI, DS, MC, VI. **Special Amenities:** Free breakfast and free newspaper.
See color ad p 514)

GREEN LANTERN MOTEL Phone: (530)544-6336 [93]

Motel

Fri & Sat, Sun-Thurs 7/1-9/7 & 12/21-1/31	1P: $46- 80	2P/1B: $46- 80	2P/2B: $50- 95	XP: $5
Sun-Thurs 5/22-6/30 & 9/8-10/17	1P: $40- 60	2P/1B: $40- 60	2P/2B: $46- 70	XP: $5
Sun-Thurs 2/1-5/21 & 10/18-12/20	1P: $36- 55	2P/1B: $36- 55	2P/2B: $46- 60	XP: $5

Location: 3 blks toward the lake from casino area, on Manzanita Ave at Poplar St. 4097 Manzanita 96157 (PO Box SV). Fax: 530/544-0276. **Terms:** Reserv deposit, 5 day notice. **Facility:** 37 rooms. Well cared for, comfortable rooms. 2 stories; exterior corridors; whirlpools. **All Rooms:** shower baths. **Cards:** AE, CB, DI, DS, MC, VI. **Special Amenities:** Free breakfast and free local telephone calls.

(See map p. 500)

HIGH COUNTRY LODGE   Phone: (530)541-0508

Fri & Sat 6/30-9/30	1P:	$60	2P/1B:	$60	2P/2B:	$70	XP:	$5

Fri & Sat 2/1-6/29 &

10/1-1/31	1P:	$50	2P/1B:	$55	2P/2B:	$60	XP:	$5
Sun-Thurs	1P:	$25	2P/1B:	$28	2P/2B:	$35	XP:	$5

Motel

Location: 0.5 mi n of airport; on US 50. 1227 Emerald Bay Rd 96150. Fax: 530/544-7518. **Terms:** Rese deposit, 7 day notice; handling fee imposed; pets, $5 extra charge; $50 dep req. **Facility:** 15 rooms. Tree shaded grounds story; exterior corridors; whirlpool. **All Rooms:** shower baths. **Cards:** AE, DS, MC, VI. **Special Amenities: Free loc telephone calls and preferred room (subject to availability with advanced reservations).**

Don't forget your AAA membership card.
More than 3,700 accommodations and 1,500 attractions
offer discounts to AAA members.

(See map p. 500)

HOLIDAY INN EXPRESS
Phone: (530)544-5900   114

(AAA) SAVE
◆◆◆
Motel

Fri & Sat 6/18-9/18 & 12/24-1/2 [CP]	1P: $139- 149	2P/1B: $139- 149	2P/2B: $139- 149
Fri & Sat 2/1-6/17, Sun-Thurs 6/27-8/28, Fri & Sat 9/19-12/23 & 1/3-1/31 [CP]	1P: $109- 119	2P/1B: $109- 119	2P/2B: $109- 119
Sun-Thurs 6/6-6/26 & 8/29-9/30 [CP]	1P: $89- 99	2P/1B: $89- 99	2P/2B: $89- 99
Sun-Thurs 2/1-6/5, 10/1-12/23 & 1/3-1/31 [CP]	1P: $69- 79	2P/1B: $69- 79	2P/2B: $69- 79

Location: 0.3 mi w of casino center, on US 50; at Pioneer Tr. 3961 Lake Tahoe Blvd 96150. Fax: 530/544-5333. **Terms:** Reserv deposit. **Facility:** 89 rooms. Very attractive decor. 8 suites, $139-$209; exterior corridors; heated pool, sauna, whirlpool, indoor & outdoor whirlpool. **Dining:** Coffee shop nearby. **All Rooms:** combo or shower baths. **Cards:** AE, CB, DI, DS, JC, MC, VI. **Special Amenities:** Free breakfast and free local telephone calls. (See color ad p 516)

HOLIDAY LODGE
Phone: (530)544-4101   75

(AAA) SAVE
◆
Motel

Fri & Sat 6/16-9/21	1P: $75	2P/1B: $85	2P/2B: $85	XP: $5
Sun-Thurs 6/16-9/21	1P: $65	2P/1B: $80	2P/2B: $80	XP: $5
2/1-6/15 & 9/22-1/31	1P: $65	2P/1B: $70	2P/2B: $70	XP: $5

Location: 1 blk w of casinos & US 50. 4095 Laurel Ave 96157 (PO Box 4007). Fax: 530/542-4932. **Terms:** Reserv deposit. **Facility:** 165 rooms. 2 stories; exterior corridors; indoor pool, sauna, whirlpool. **Dining:** Restaurant nearby. **All Rooms:** combo or shower baths. **Some Rooms:** 6 efficiencies. **Cards:** AE, CB, MC, VI. **Special Amenities:** Free local telephone calls and free room upgrade (subject to availability with advanced reservations). (See color ad p 517)

INN BY THE LAKE
Phone: (530)542-0330   108

(AAA) SAVE
◆◆◆
Motel

12/17-1/2 [CP]	1P: $150- 250	2P/1B: $150- 250	2P/2B: $200- 250
6/25-9/5 [CP]	1P: $98- 165	2P/1B: $98- 165	2P/2B: $148- 165
2/1-6/24, 9/6-12/16 & 1/3-1/31 [CP]	1P: $98- 138	2P/1B: $98- 138	2P/2B: $128- 138

Location: 2 mi s of casino center on US 50. 3300 Lake Tahoe Blvd 96150. Fax: 530/541-6596. **Terms:** Reserv deposit; handling fee imposed; 2 night min stay, weekends. **Facility:** 99 rooms. Attractive landscaped grounds. 2 two-bedroom units. Rates for up to 4 persons; 3 stories; interior corridors; designated smoking area; lake view; heated pool, sauna, whirlpool. **Dining:** Coffee shop nearby. **Recreation:** Fee: bicycles. **All Rooms:** combo or shower baths. **Some Rooms:** 6 kitchens, whirlpools. **Cards:** AE, CB, DI, DS, MC, VI. **Special Amenities:** Free breakfast. (See ad p 518)

(See map p. 500)

LA BAER INN   Phone: (530)544-2139   76
AAA SAVE 7/1-8/31   1P: $59- 99   2P/1B: $59- 99   2P/2B: $67-109   XP: $5   F16
          5/1-6/30 & 9/1-10/31 1P: $49- 99   2P/1B: $49- 99   2P/2B: $49- 99   XP: $5   F16
◆ ◆   2/1-4/30 & 11/1-1/31 1P: $39- 99   2P/1B: $39- 99   2P/2B: $39- 99   XP: $5   F16
Motel   **Location:** On US 50, 1 blk w of Casino Center. 4133 Lake Tahoe Blvd 96150. **Fax:** 530/542-4825.
          Terms: Small pets only, $10 dep req. **Facility:** 32 rooms. 2 stories; exterior corridors. **Dining:** Restaurant
nearby. **All Rooms:** combo or shower baths. **Cards:** AE, DS, MC, VI. *(See ad below)*   ⊠ 🖭 🚪 📶 🐾 ⊠

LAKELAND VILLAGE   Phone: (530)544-1685   97
AAA SAVE 7/2-7/5 & 12/18-1/2   1P: $110- 175   2P/1B: $110- 175   2P/2B: $175- 280
          2/1-3/28, 6/19-7/1, 7/6-9/6 &
◆ ◆ ◆   1/3-1/31   1P: $89- 170   2P/1B: $89- 170   2P/2B: $139- 225
Apartment 3/29-6/18 & 9/7-12/17 1P: $80- 145   2P/1B: $80- 145   2P/2B: $130- 195
Motel   **Location:** 1.3 mi w of casino center, on US 50. 3535 Lake Tahoe Blvd 96150. **Fax:** 530/541-6278.
          Terms: Reserv deposit, 30 day notice. **Facility:** 210 rooms. Spacious grounds. Some units on lakefront. 1- to
4-bedroom housekeeping townhouse units with fireplace, $140-$460 for up to 10 persons; 1-3 stories; interior/exterior corri-
dors; beach, heated pool, wading pool, saunas, whirlpool; boat dock. **Fee:** 2 tennis courts. **Dining:** Restaurant nearby.
Recreation: swimming. **Rental:** boats. **Cards:** AE, MC, VI. *(See color ad p 519)*   🏊 📶 ⊠ 🐾 🗲 🖥

LAKEPARK LODGE   Phone: (530)541-5004   77
AAA SAVE All Year [CP]   1P: $40- 75   2P/1B: $45- 80   2P/2B: $50- 80   XP: $5   F12
◆ ◆   **Location:** Just off Hwy 50, near Stateline Casinos. 4081 Cedar Ave 96150. **Fax:** 530/541-3539.
Motel   **Terms:** Reserv deposit, 3 day notice; small pets only, $10 extra charge, $50 dep req, no cats. **Facility:** 22
          rooms. 2 stories; exterior corridors; whirlpool. **Dining:** Restaurant nearby. **All Rooms:** shower baths.
          Cards: AE, MC, VI. **Special Amenities:** Early check-in/late check-out and free local telephone calls.
                                                                              🚪 📶 ⊟ 🛜 ⊠

(See map p. 500)

LAMPLITER MOTEL Phone: (530)544-2936 [99]

AAA SAVE Fri & Sat 6/1-9/30 [CP] 1P: $70- 80 2P/1B: $75- 95 2P/2B: $80- 100 XP: $8
◆◆ Fri & Sat 2/1-5/31 &
Motel 10/1-1/31 [CP] 1P: $60- 80 2P/1B: $60- 80 2P/2B: $70- 90 XP: $8
  Sun-Thurs 6/1-9/30 [CP] 1P: $50- 70 2P/1B: $50- 70 2P/2B: $60- 80 XP: $8
  Sun-Thurs 2/1-5/31 &
  10/1-1/31 [CP] 1P: $40- 60 2P/1B: $40- 60 2P/2B: $45- 65 XP: $8

Location: 2 blks n of US 50, adjacent to Casino Center. 4143 Cedar Ave 96150. Fax: 530/544-5249. **Terms:** Reserv deposit, 3 day notice; pets, $8 extra charge, $100 dep req. **Facility:** 28 rooms. 2 stories; exterior corridors; whirlpool. **Dining:** Restaurant nearby. **All Rooms:** combo or shower baths. **Cards:** AE, DI, DS, MC, VI. **Special Amenities: Free breakfast and free local telephone calls.**

MARK TWAIN MOTEL Rates Subject to Change Phone: (530)544-5733 [117]

AAA Fri & Sat 6/15-9/15 1P: $48- 68 2P/1B: $48- 68 2P/2B: $58- 78 XP: $5 D12
◆ Fri & Sat 2/1-6/14 &
Motel 9/16-1/31 1P: $38- 58 2P/1B: $38- 58 2P/2B: $48- 68 XP: $5 D12
  Sun-Thurs 2/1-4/30 &
  6/1-1/31 1P: $28- 48 2P/1B: $28- 48 2P/2B: $38- 58 XP: $5 D12
  Sun-Thurs 5/1-5/31 1P: $20 2P/1B: $20 2P/2B: $30 XP: $5 D12

Location: 1 blk n of US 50, toward lake. 947 Park Ave 96150. Fax: 530/544-2482. **Facility:** 22 rooms. 2 stories; exterior corridors; whirlpool. **All Rooms:** shower baths. **Cards:** AE, DI, MC, VI.

PACIFICA LODGE Rates Subject to Change Phone: 530/544-4131 [72]
◆◆ 6/15-9/14 & 12/22-1/1 1P: $70- 75 2P/1B: $70- 75 2P/2B: $70- 75 XP: $6 F12
Motel 2/1-6/14, 9/15-12/21 &
  1/2-1/31 1P: $55- 65 2P/1B: $55- 65 2P/2B: $55- 65 XP: $6 F12

Location: 6 blks w of casino center; 2 blks n off US 50 toward lake at Park & Manzanita Ave. 931 Park Ave 96150. **Facility:** 44 rooms. Some woodburning fireplace units. 2 stories; exterior corridors; heated pool. **Cards:** AE, CB, DI, DS, MC, VI.

PARADICE MOTEL Rates Subject to Change Phone: (530)544-6800 [116]

AAA Fri & Sat 6/15-9/15 1P: $48- 58 2P/1B: $48- 58 2P/2B: $58- 68 XP: $5 F12
◆ Fri & Sat 2/1-6/14 &
Motel 9/16-1/31 1P: $38- 48 2P/1B: $38- 48 2P/2B: $48- 58 XP: $5 F12
  Sun-Thurs 2/1-4/30 &
  6/1-1/31 1P: $25- 28 2P/1B: $25- 28 2P/2B: $35- 45 XP: $5 F12
  Sun-Thurs 5/1-5/31 1P: $20 2P/1B: $20 2P/2B: $25 XP: $5 F12

Location: Just n of US 50, toward the lake. 953 Park Ave 96150. Fax: 530/544-9145. **Terms:** Handling fee imposed. **Facility:** 14 rooms. 2 stories; exterior corridors; whirlpool. **All Rooms:** combo or shower baths. **Cards:** AE, DS, MC, VI.

(See map p. 500)

PARKWOOD LODGE

Phone: (530)544-4114   **113**

AAA SAVE — ◆ ◆ — Motel

		1P:		2P/1B:			2P/2B:		XP:
Fri & Sat 6/15-9/15		1P:	$48- 78	2P/1B:	$48- 78	2P/2B:	$68- 88	XP:	$10
Fri & Sat 2/1-6/14, Sun-Thurs 6/15-9/15 & Fri & Sat									
9/16-1/31		1P:	$38- 68	2P/1B:	$38- 68	2P/2B:	$58- 88	XP:	$10
Sun-Thurs 2/1-6/14 & 9/16-1/31		1P:	$28- 48	2P/1B:	$28- 48	2P/2B:	$38- 68	XP:	$10

Location: 1 blk n off US 50 toward lake, at Park & Cedar aves; 3 blks w of casino center. 954 Park Ave 96150. Fax: 530/541-7519. **Terms:** Reserv deposit, 3 day notice. **Facility:** 16 rooms. Very well kept. 2 stories; interior/exterior corridors; whirlpool. **Cards:** AE, DS, MC, VI. **Special Amenities:** Free local telephone calls and preferred room (subject to availability with advanced reservations). *(See color ad below)*

PIONEER INN MOTEL

Rates Subject to Change   Phone: 530/544-5728   **92**

AAA — ◆ — Motel

	1P:		2P/1B:			2P/2B:		XP:	
Sat	1P:	$55- 125	2P/1B:	$55- 130	2P/2B:	$55- 155	XP:	$6
Fri	1P:	$30- 38	2P/1B:	$30- 65	2P/2B:	$40- 75	XP:	$6
Sun-Thurs	1P:	$22- 28	2P/1B:	$26- 36	2P/2B:	$28- 38	XP:	$6

Location: 0.6 mi w of Casino Center. 3863 Pioneer Trail 96150. Fax: 530/541-4810. **Facility:** 20 rooms. 2 stories; exterior corridors. **All Rooms:** shower baths. **Cards:** AE, DS, MC, VI.

QUALITY INN & SUITES

Rates Subject to Change   Phone: (530)541-5400   **85**

◆ ◆ — Motel

	1P:		2P/1B:		2P/2B:		XP:	
Fri & Sat 6/18-9/25 & 12/24-1/3 [CP]	1P: $79- 99	2P/1B: $79- 110	2P/2B: $89- 130	XP: $10-15	F14
Fri & Sat 2/1-6/17, 9/26-12/23 & 1/4-1/31 [CP]	1P: $59- 79	2P/1B: $69- 89	2P/2B: $79- 99	XP: $10	F14
Sun-Thurs 6/18-9/25 [CP]	1P: $49- 69	2P/1B: $59- 79	2P/2B: $69- 89	XP: $10	F14
Sun-Thurs 2/1-6/17, 9/26-12/23 & 1/4-1/31 [CP]	1P: $39- 49	2P/1B: $49- 79	2P/2B: $59- 89	XP: $10	F14

Location: US 50, 0.7 mi w of Casino Center. 3838 Lake Tahoe Blvd 96150. Fax: 530/541-7170. **Terms:** Reserv deposit, 3 day notice; handling fee imposed. **Facility:** 120 rooms. 20 two-bedroom units. 2 stories; exterior corridors. **Some Rooms:** 20 kitchens. **Cards:** AE, CB, DI, DS, JC, MC, VI. *(See color ad p 504)*

RIDGEWOOD INN

Rates Subject to Change   Phone: 530/541-8589   **104**

AAA — ◆ — Motel

	1P:		2P/1B:		2P/2B:		XP:	
6/15-9/7 & 12/23-1/3	1P: $60- 65	2P/1B: $65- 70	2P/2B: $70- 75	XP: $5	F12
2/1-6/14, 9/8-12/22 & 1/4-1/31	1P: $40- 45	2P/1B: $45- 50	2P/2B: $50- 55	XP: $5	F12

Location: US 50, 0.5 mi n of airport. 1341 Emerald Bay Rd 96150. Fax: 530/541-8712. **Terms:** Reserv deposit, 3 day notice; handling fee imposed; pets, $20 dep req. **Facility:** 12 rooms. 1 story; exterior corridors; whirlpool. **All Rooms:** combo or shower baths. **Some Rooms:** 2 kitchens. **Cards:** AE, MC, VI.

RODEWAY INN

Phone: (530)541-7900   **86**

AAA SAVE — ◆ — Motel

	1P:		2P/1B:		2P/2B:	
Fri & Sat [CP]	1P: $39- 95	2P/1B: $39- 95	2P/2B: $39- 95
Sun-Thurs [CP]	1P: $29- 55	2P/1B: $29- 55	2P/2B: $29- 55

Location: US 50, 1 blk w of casino center. 4082 Lake Tahoe Blvd 96150. Fax: 530/544-1336. **Terms:** Reserv deposit; pets, $15 extra charge. **Facility:** 100 rooms. 2 stories; exterior corridors; heated pool, whirlpool. **Dining:** Restaurant nearby. **All Rooms:** shower baths. **Cards:** AE, DI, DS, MC, VI.

ROYAL VALHALLA MOTOR LODGE

Rates Subject to Change   Phone: (530)544-2233   **88**

AAA — ◆ ◆ ◆ — Motel

5/15-9/30 [CP]	2P/1B: $82- 102	2P/2B: $92- 112	XP: $5
2/1-5/14 & 10/1-1/31 [CP]	2P/1B: $59- 79	2P/2B: $69- 89	XP: $5

Location: N off Hwy 50; at Lakeshore & Stateline Ave. 4104 Lakeshore Blvd 96157 (PO Box GG). Fax: 530/544-1436. **Terms:** Reserv deposit. **Facility:** 80 rooms. Beach opposite. Some rooms with balcony. 2- & 3-bedroom bi-level suites; some with covered parking. Attractive rooms. 26 two-bedroom units. 29 kitchens, $5 extra charge; 2 stories; interior corridors; lake view; heated pool, whirlpool. **All Rooms:** combo or shower baths. **Cards:** AE, CB, DI, MC, VI.

(See map p. 500)

7 SEAS MOTEL   Phone: (530)544-7031   **90**

AAA SAVE ◆ Motel

Fri & Sat 6/25-9/23 [CP]	1P:	$59- 74	2P/1B:	$59- 79	2P/2B:	$69- 79	XP: $5-10	F12
Fri & Sat 5/21-6/24 & 9/24-10/21 [CP]	1P:	$49- 64	2P/1B:	$49- 69	2P/2B:	$59- 69	XP: $5-7	F12
Fri & Sat 2/1-5/20, Sun-Thurs 6/18-9/23 & Fri & Sat 10/22-1/31 [CP]	1P:	$39- 49	2P/1B:	$39- 59	2P/2B:	$49- 65	XP: $5	F12
Sun-Thurs 2/1-6/17 & 9/24-1/31 [CP]	1P:	$29- 39	2P/1B:	$29- 49	2P/2B:	$39- 59	XP: $5	F12

Location: 2 blks from casino center; 2 blks n off US 50 towards lake on Manzanita Ave. 4145 Manzanita Ave 96150. **Fax:** 530/544-1208. **Terms:** Reserv deposit, 3 day notice. **Facility:** 17 rooms. Some small rooms. 2 stories; exterior corridors; whirlpool. **All Rooms:** combo or shower baths. **Cards:** AE, DS, JC, MC, VI. **Special Amenities:** Free local telephone calls and free room upgrade (subject to availability with advanced reservations). *(See color ad below)*

SOUTH SHORE INN   Phone: (530)544-1000   **94**

AAA SAVE ◆◆ Motel

6/15-9/30 & 12/15-1/2	1P:	$36- 128	2P/1B:	$40- 128	2P/2B:	$48- 148	XP: $10	F4
Fri & Sat 2/1-6/14, 10/1-12/14 & 1/3-1/31	1P:	$32- 58	2P/1B:	$36- 58	2P/2B:	$48- 68	XP: $10	F4
Sun-Thurs 2/1-6/14, 10/1-12/14 & 1/3-1/31	1P:	$28	2P/1B:	$32	2P/2B:	$38	XP: $5	F4

Location: 4 blks w of casino area. 3900 Pioneer Tr 96157 (PO Box 6470). **Terms:** Reserv deposit, 3 day notice; handling fee imposed. **Facility:** 22 rooms. Quiet location. Some covered parking. 2 two-bedroom units. 2 stories; exterior corridors. **Cards:** MC, VI. **Special Amenities:** Free local telephone calls.

SOUTH TAHOE TRAVELODGE   Phone: (530)544-5266   **70**

AAA SAVE ◆◆◆ Motel

7/1-8/31	1P:	$81- 101	2P/1B:	$86- 106	2P/2B:	$91- 111	XP: $5	F18
5/1-6/30 & 9/1-10/31	1P:	$71- 91	2P/1B:	$76- 96	2P/2B:	$81- 101	XP: $5	F18
1/1-1/31	1P:	$62- 82	2P/1B:	$67- 87	2P/2B:	$72- 92	XP: $5	F18
2/1-4/30 & 11/1-12/31	1P:	$59- 79	2P/1B:	$64- 84	2P/2B:	$69- 89	XP: $5	F18

Location: 1.5 mi w of casino center. 3489 Lake Tahoe Blvd 96150. **Fax:** 530/544-6985. **Terms:** Reserv deposit. **Facility:** 59 rooms. Nicely decorated rooms. 2 stories; exterior corridors; whirlpool. **Dining:** Restaurant nearby. **All Rooms:** combo or shower baths. **Cards:** AE, CB, DI, DS, JC, MC, VI. **Special Amenities:** Free local telephone calls and free newspaper. *(See color ad p 511)*

See the Sample Lodging Listing.

(See map p. 500)

STARDUST LODGE

◆◆ Motel

	Rates Subject to Change			
Fri & Sat 5/22-9/30 [CP]	1P: $126- 162	2P/1B: $126- 162	2P/2B: $126- 162	
Sun-Thurs 5/22-9/30 [CP]	1P: $110- 145	2P/1B: $110- 145	2P/2B: $110- 145	
Fri & Sat 2/1-5/21 & 10/1-1/31 [CP]	1P: $95- 135	2P/1B: $95- 135	2P/2B: $95- 135	
Sun-Thurs 2/1-5/21 & 10/1-1/31 [CP]	1P: $85- 125	2P/1B: $85- 125	2P/2B: $85- 125	

Phone: 530/544-5211   **71**

Location: US 50, just w of Casino Center. 4061 Lake Tahoe Blvd 96150. Fax: 530/544-3617. **Terms:** Reserv deposit. **Facility:** 86 rooms. 2 stories; exterior corridors. **All Rooms:** combo or shower baths. **Some Rooms:** 72 efficiencies, 14 kitchens. **Cards:** AE, DS, MC, VI.

STATELINE LODGE

◆ Motel

	Rates Subject to Change			
Fri & Sat	1P: $50	2P/1B: $50	2P/2B: $65	
Sun-Thurs	1P: $30	2P/1B: $30	2P/2B: $45	

Phone: (530)544-3340   **101**

Location: 0.4 mi from casino center. 910 Park Ave 96150. Fax: 530/544-1817. **Terms:** Handling fee imposed. **Facility:** 15 rooms. 1 story; exterior corridors. **All Rooms:** combo or shower baths. **Cards:** AE, DI, JC, MC, VI.

STATELINE TRAVELODGE

(AAA) [SAVE] ◆◆ Motel

Phone: (530)544-6000   **109**

						XP:	
7/1-8/31	1P: $81- 101	2P/1B: $86- 106	2P/2B: $91- 111	XP: $5	F18
5/1-6/30 & 9/1-10/31	1P: $71- 91	2P/1B: $76- 96	2P/2B: $81- 101	XP: $5	F18
1/1-1/31	1P: $62- 82	2P/1B: $67- 87	2P/2B: $72- 92	XP: $5	F18
2/1-4/30 & 11/1-12/31	1P: $59- 79	2P/1B: $64- 84	2P/2B: $69- 89	XP: $5	F18

Location: 2 blks w of Casino Center, on US 50. 4011 Lake Tahoe Blvd 96150. Fax: 530/544-6869. **Terms:** Reserv deposit. **Facility:** 50 rooms. Some small rooms. 2 stories; exterior corridors; whirlpool. **All Rooms:** shower baths. **Cards:** AE, CB, DI, DS, JC, MC, VI. **Special Amenities:** Free local telephone calls and free newspaper.

SUPER 8

(AAA) [SAVE] ◆◆ Motel

Phone: (530)544-3476   **119**

				XP:	
Fri & Sat 6/19-9/27	1P: $88	2P/1B: $98	2P/2B: $108	XP: $6
Fri & Sat 2/1-6/18 & 9/28-1/31	1P: $50	2P/1B: $50	2P/2B: $60	XP: $6
Sun-Thurs	1P: $42- 50	2P/1B: $42- 50	2P/2B: $50- 60	XP: $6

Location: US 50, just w of Ski Run Blvd. 3600 Lake Tahoe Blvd 96150. Fax: 530/542-4011. **Terms:** Pets, $10 extra charge. **Facility:** 110 rooms. Attractively landscaped grounds. 1 two-bedroom unit. 1 large suite with fireplace, $85-$110 for 2 persons; 2 stories; exterior corridors; heated pool, whirlpool; playground. **Dining:** Coffee shop; 6 am-2 pm. **All Rooms:** combo or shower baths. **Some Rooms:** efficiency, kitchen. **Cards:** AE, CB, DI, DS, MC, VI. **Special Amenities:** Free local telephone calls. *(See color ad below)*

TAHOE CHALET INN

(AAA) [SAVE] ◆◆ Motel

Phone: (530)544-3311   **69**

2/1-4/15, 6/16-9/30 & 12/16-1/31 [CP]	1P: $58- 82	2P/1B: $58- 82	2P/2B: $72- 128	
4/16-6/15 & 10/1-12/15 [CP]	1P: $42- 70	2P/1B: $42- 70	2P/2B: $52- 108	

Location: 0.5 mi s of Casino Center. 3860 Lake Tahoe Blvd 96150. Fax: 530/544-4069. **Terms:** Reserv deposit, 7 day notice. **Facility:** 66 rooms. 2 stories; exterior corridors; sauna, whirlpool. **All Rooms:** combo or shower baths. **Some Rooms:** 14 kitchens, whirlpools. **Cards:** AE, CB, DI, DS, MC, VI. **Special Amenities:** Free breakfast and free local telephone calls. *(See ad p 523)*

(See map p. 500)

TAHOE HACIENDA MOTEL
◆
Motel

Rates Subject to Change				Phone: (530)541-3805		66
Fri & Sat 6/15-9/15	1P: $65- 70	2P/1B:	$70- 75	2P/2B: $75- 85	XP: $5	F
Fri & Sat 2/1-6/14, Sun-Thurs 6/15-9/15 & Fri & Sat 9/16-1/31	1P: $55- 65	2P/1B:	$55- 65	2P/2B: $65- 70	XP: $5	F
Sun-Thurs 2/1-6/14 & 9/16-1/31	1P: $30- 35	2P/1B:	$30- 35	2P/2B: $40- 42	XP: $5	F

Location: On US 50, 0.7 mi w of Casino Center. 3820 Lake Tahoe Blvd 96150. Fax: 530/541-7763. **Terms:** Reserv deposit, 3 day notice. **Facility:** 33 rooms. 1 story; exterior corridors; heated pool. **Some Rooms:** 2 kitchens. **Cards:** AE, DS, MC, VI.

TAHOE KEYS RESORT
AAA SAVE
◆◆◆
Resort
Complex

				Phone: (530)544-5397	87
All Year	1P: $108- 220	2P/1B: $140- 275	2P/2B: $180- 440		

Location: Exit SR 50 at Tahoe Keys Blvd, 1 mi w. 599 Tahoe Keys Blvd 96150. Fax: 530/544-2741. **Terms:** Reserv deposit; handling fee imposed; pets, $25 extra charge, $100 dep req. **Facility:** 80 rooms. Waterfront condos, homes & villas. 30 two-bedroom units, 15 three-bedroom units. Some larger homes & villas $500-$1750; 2 stories; exterior corridors; heated indoor pool, whirlpool; 6 lighted tennis courts; marina. **Dining:** Restaurant nearby. **Recreation:** swimming, boating, fishing; bicycles. **All Rooms:** kitchens. **Cards:** AE, DS, MC, VI. **Special Amenities:** Early check-in/late check-out and free local telephone calls.
(See color ad p 524)

TAHOE MARINA INN
AAA
◆◆
Apartment
Motel

Rates Subject to Change				Phone: (530)541-2180		95
6/1-9/30	1P: $89- 99	2P/1B:	$89- 99	2P/2B: $99- 150	XP: $5-10	F6
Sun-Thurs 2/1-5/31 & 10/1-1/31		2P/1B:	$79- 99	2P/2B: $89- 130	XP: $5	F6
Fri & Sat 2/1-5/31 & 10/1-1/31	1P: $69- 89	2P/1B:	$69- 89	2P/2B: $79- 99	XP: $5-10	F6

Location: On lake, 1.5 mi w of casino center; off US 50. 930 Bal BiJou Rd 96150. **Terms:** Reserv deposit, 7 day notice; small pets only. **Facility:** 77 rooms. Some spacious rooms. 29 condominiums with kitchen & fireplace, $99-$190; 3 stories; interior/exterior corridors; lake view; beach, heated pool. **Dining:** Restaurant nearby. **Recreation:** swimming. **All Rooms:** combo or shower baths. **Some Rooms:** 43 kitchens. **Cards:** MC, VI.

THE TAHOE SEASONS RESORT
AAA SAVE
◆◆◆
Hotel

				Phone: (530)541-6700	120
12/18-1/2	1P: $170- 240	2P/1B: $170- 240	2P/2B: $170- 240		
2/1-3/31 & 1/3-1/31	1P: $160- 225	2P/1B: $160- 225	2P/2B: $160- 225		
6/16-9/15	1P: $150- 215	2P/1B: $150- 215	2P/2B: $150- 215		
4/1-6/15 & 9/16-12/17	1P: $110- 180	2P/1B: $110- 180	2P/2B: $110- 180		

Location: 1.3 mi se off US 50; 0.5 mi ne on Saddle Rd; across from Heavenly Valley ski area. Saddle Rd at Keller Rd 96157 (PO Box 5656). Fax: 530/541-0653. **Terms:** Check-in 4 pm; package plans. **Facility:** 160 rooms. In the pines. 12 two-bedroom units. Max rates for up to 4 persons; 8 stories; interior corridors; heated pool, whirlpool; 2 tennis courts. **Dining:** Restaurant; 7 am-noon; open for lunch & dinner in ski season; $8-$15; cocktails. **Recreation:** paddleball-1 court. **All Rooms:** combo or shower baths. **Some Rooms:** whirlpools. **Cards:** AE, DI, MC, VI.

TAHOE SUNDOWNER MOTEL
AAA
◆
Motel

Rates Subject to Change				Phone: 530/541-2282		122
Fri & Sat 6/30-9/30	1P: $55- 75	2P/1B:	$55- 75	2P/2B: $65- 85	XP: $5	F10
Fri & Sat 2/1-6/29 & 10/1-1/31	1P: $45- 65	2P/1B:	$45- 65	2P/2B: $55- 75	XP: $5	F10
Sun-Thurs	1P: $30- 40	2P/1B:	$30- 40	2P/2B: $35- 55	XP: $5	F10

Location: On US 50, 0.5 mi n of airport. 1211 Emerald Bay Rd 96150. Fax: 530/541-6388. **Terms:** Reserv deposit, 3 day notice; handling fee imposed; pets, $5 extra charge, $50 dep req. **Facility:** 16 rooms. 1 story; exterior corridors; whirlpool. **Dining:** Coffee shop nearby. **All Rooms:** shower baths. **Cards:** AE, DI, MC, VI.

TAHOE SUNSET LODGE
AAA
◆
Motel

Guaranteed Rates				Phone: (530)541-2940		100
Fri & Sat	1P: $35- 70	2P/1B:	$40- 80	2P/2B: $45- 90	XP: $5	D
Sun-Thurs	1P: $25	2P/1B:	$30	2P/2B: $35	XP: $5	D

Location: US 50, 0.5 mi n of airport. 1171 Emerald Bay Rd 96150. Fax: 530/544-1750. **Terms:** Reserv deposit, 7 day notice; handling fee imposed; pets, $5 extra charge. **Facility:** 15 rooms. 2 stories; exterior corridors; whirlpool. **Dining:** Coffee shop nearby. **All Rooms:** shower baths. **Cards:** AE, DI, MC, VI.

(See map p. 500)

TAHOE VALLEY LODGE   Phone: (530)541-0353   111

| | 2/12-2/14, 9/3-9/5 &
12/24-1/1 [CP] | 1P: $125 | 2P/1B: $125 | 2P/2B: $175 | XP: $30 |
| Motel | 2/1-2/11, 2/15-9/2, 9/6-12/23
& 1/2-1/31 [CP] | 1P: $95 | 2P/1B: $95 | 2P/2B: $125 | XP: $30 |

Location: 0.5 mi e of jct US 50 & SR 89, at Tahoe Keys Blvd. 2241 Lake Tahoe Blvd 96150. **Terms:** Reserv deposit, 7 day notice; handling fee imposed; 2 night min stay; weekends; small pets only, $10 extra charge. **Facility:** 21 rooms. All rooms with gas fireplace. 2 stories; exterior corridors; whirlpool. **All Rooms:** combo or shower baths. **Some Rooms:** whirlpools. **Cards:** AE, CB, DI, DS, MC, VI. **Special Amenities:** Free breakfast and free local telephone calls. *(See ad p 525)*

(See map p. 500)

THUNDERCHIEF MOTEL　　　　　　　　　　　　　　　　　　　　Phone: (530)541-6231　[102]

	12/23-1/2	1P:	$85- 110	2P/1B:	$85- 110	2P/2B:	$95- 125	XP:	$10	F10
	Fri & Sat 2/1-3/31 &									
	6/16-9/15	1P:	$49- 59	2P/1B:	$49- 69	2P/2B:	$59- 79	XP:	$6	F10
	Fri & Sat 4/1-6/15,									
	9/16-12/22 & 1/3-1/31	1P:	$29- 49	2P/1B:	$29- 49	2P/2B:	$39- 59	XP:	$6	F10
	Sun-Thurs 2/1-12/22 &									
	1/3-1/31	1P:	$22- 30	2P/1B:	$22- 30	2P/2B:	$24- 38	XP:	$6	F10

(AAA) (SAVE)
◆
Motel

Location: Corner of Echo Rd & Pioneer Trail. 1008 Echo Rd 96150. Fax: 530/541-1544. **Terms:** Reserv deposit; handling fee imposed. **Facility:** 15 rooms. 2 stories; exterior corridors. **All Rooms:** combo or shower baths. **Cards:** AE, DS, MC, VI. **Special Amenities: Free local telephone calls and preferred room (subject to availability with advanced reservations).**　　　　　　　　　　　　　　　　　　　　　　　　　　(K) (🖨) (🛡) (X)

TORCHLITE INN & SUITES　　　　　　　　　　　　　　　　　　Phone: (530)541-2363　[118]

	Fri & Sat 6/15-9/15 [CP]	1P:	$58- 78	2P/1B:	$68- 88	2P/2B:	$78- 98	XP:	$10	F18
	Fri & Sat 2/1-6/14 &									
	9/16-1/31 [CP]	1P:	$58	2P/1B:	$68	2P/2B:	$68	XP:	$5	F18
	Sun-Thurs 6/15-9/15 [CP]	1P:	$48	2P/1B:	$58	2P/2B:	$68	XP:	$5	F18
	Sun-Thurs 2/1-6/14 &									
	9/16-1/31 [CP]	1P:	$38	2P/1B:	$48	2P/2B:	$58	XP:	$5	F18

(AAA) (SAVE)
◆◆
Motel

Location: 1 1/2 blks from casino center; 1 blk n off US 50 via Park-Loop Rd. 965 Park Ave 96150. Fax: 530/541-1988. **Terms:** Reserv deposit, 7 day notice. **Facility:** 33 rooms. Convenient location. 2 stories; interior/exterior corridors; whirlpool. **Cards:** AE, DS, MC, VI. **Special Amenities: Free breakfast and free local telephone calls.** *(See color ad below)*

　　　　　　　　　　　　　　　　　　　　　　　　　　　　　　　　　(🖥) (K) (X)

TRADE WINDS RESORT & SUITES　　　　　　　　　　　　　　Phone: (530)544-6459　[68]

	Fri & Sat 2/1-3/31,									
	6/16-10/15 & 12/23-1/31	1P:	$75- 85	2P/1B:	$85- 95	2P/2B:	$95- 105	XP:	$10	F12
	Fri & Sat 4/1-6/15 &									
	10/16-12/22	1P:	$45- 55	2P/1B:	$55- 65	2P/2B:	$65- 75	XP:	$10	F12
	Sun-Thurs 6/15-9/15	1P:	$40- 50	2P/1B:	$40- 50	2P/2B:	$50- 60	XP:	$5	F12
	Sun-Thurs 2/1-6/14 &									
	9/16-12/22	1P:	$35- 45	2P/1B:	$35- 45	2P/2B:	$45- 55	XP:	$5	F12

(AAA) (SAVE)
◆
Motel

Location: 0.2 mi s of casino center, at Friday & Cedar aves. 944 Friday Ave 96150. Fax: 530/544-1272. **Terms:** Reserv deposit, 10 day notice; handling fee imposed; 2 night min stay, weekends; small pets only, $5 extra charge, $50 dep req. **Facility:** 68 rooms. 2 stories; exterior corridors; heated pool, whirlpool. **Dining:** Restaurant nearby. **Some Rooms:** whirlpools. **Cards:** AE, DS, MC, VI. **Special Amenities: Free breakfast and free local telephone calls.** *(See color ad p 526)*

　　　　(🐕) (➰) (🍴) (⛷) (🎿) (🖥) (🗄) (K) (🖨) (🛡) (X)

VIKING MOTOR LODGE   Phone: (530)541-5155   67

	6/12-9/5 [CP]	1P:	$59-	89	2P/1B:	$59-	89	2P/2B:	$69-	99	XP: $5	F12
	2/1-6/11 & 9/6-1/31 [CP]	1P:	$46-	66	2P/1B:	$46-	66	2P/2B:	$49-	69	XP: $5	F12

Location: Just off Hwy 50, via Friday Ave, toward lake on Cedar Ave; near casino Center. 4083 Cedar Ave 96150. **Fax:** 530/541-5643. **Terms:** Reserv deposit, 3 day notice. **Facility:** 74 rooms. Some compact rooms. 14 efficiencies, $5 extra charge; 2 stories; exterior corridors; whirlpool. **All Rooms:** utensils extra charge, combo or shower baths. **Cards:** AE, CB, DI, DS, JC, MC, VI. **Special Amenities:** Free local telephone calls and free room upgrade (subject to availability with advanced reservations).

RESTAURANTS

EVANS AMERICAN GOURMET CAFE   **Dinner:** $25-$40   Phone: 530/542-1990   30

♦♦♦ American

Location: On SR 89; 1 mi n of US 50. 536 Emerald Bay Rd 96150. **Hours:** 6 pm-10 pm. Closed: Sun, 4/7, 11/28, 12/25 & first 3 weeks of Nov. **Reservations:** suggested. **Features:** semi-formal attire; beer & wine only; minimum charge-$8; a la carte. Quiet cozy atmosphere; creative California cuisine with emphasis on fresh ingredients. Smoke free premises. **Cards:** MC, VI.

HEIDI'S RESTAURANT   **Lunch:** $5-$9   Phone: 530/544-8113   31

♦ American

Location: 1.5 mi w of Stateline on US 50. 3485 Lake Tahoe Blvd 96150. **Hours:** 7 am-2 pm. **Features:** casual dress; children's menu. Family restaurant. Breakfast & lunch, American & European dishes. **Cards:** MC, VI.

LEWMARNEL'S   **Lunch:** $4-$7   **Dinner:** $14-$25   Phone: 530/542-1072   37

♦♦♦ Continental

Location: 3 1/2 blks from casino center; 2 blks n off US 50 via Lake Park Ave; in Best Western Station House Inn. 901 Park Ave 96157. **Hours:** 7:30 am-10, 11-4 & 5:30-10 pm, Sat & Sun 7 am-4 & 5:30-10:30 pm. Closed: Wed & 12/1-17. **Reservations:** suggested. **Features:** casual dress; cocktails & lounge. Rustic, Western atmosphere. Varied menu featuring steak & seafood. **Cards:** AE, CB, DI, MC, VI.

THE SWISS CHALET   **Dinner:** $13-$21   Phone: 530/544-3304   35

♦♦ Continental

Location: 4 mi w of Stateline; on US 50 at Sierra Blvd. 2544 Lake Tahoe Blvd 96158. **Hours:** 5 pm-10 pm. Closed: Mon, 11/15-12/3, 12/25 & 4/7. **Reservations:** suggested. **Features:** casual dress; children's menu; cocktails & lounge; minimum charge-$7; a la carte. Chalet decor & atmosphere, casual dining. European, German & Swiss cuisine, also steaks & seafood. **Cards:** AE, MC, VI.

TEP'S VILLA ROMA   **Dinner:** $7-$17   Phone: 530/541-8227   33

♦ Italian

Location: 1.5 mi w of Stateline. 3450 Lake Tahoe Blvd 96150. **Hours:** 5-10 pm, Sat-10:30 pm. Closed: 11/28. **Features:** casual dress; children's menu; cocktails & lounge. Casual atmosphere, large varied salad bar & fresh seafood specialties. Smoke free premises. **Cards:** AE, MC, VI.

ZACKARY'S   **Lunch:** $4-$9   **Dinner:** $14-$22   Phone: 530/544-5400   36

♦♦♦ Continental

Location: In Embassy Suites. 4130 Lake Tahoe Blvd 96150. **Hours:** 11 am-2 & 5-9 pm, Sat-10 pm. **Reservations:** suggested. **Features:** casual dress; children's menu; cocktails & lounge; valet parking; a la carte. Casual atmosphere, varied menu featuring fresh local ingredients & fresh seafood specialties. Lunch on Deck Weather permitting. **Cards:** AE, CB, DI, DS, MC, VI.

TAHOE CITY—1,100   (See map p. 500; index p. 497)

LODGINGS

THE COTTAGE INN AT LAKE TAHOE   Guaranteed Rates   Phone: 530/581-4073   20

♦♦♦ Bed & Breakfast

All Year [BP]	1P: $140- 210	2P/1B: $140- 210	2P/2B: $140- 210	XP: $15	

Location: SR 89, 2 mi s. 1690 W Lake Blvd 96145 (PO Box 66). **Fax:** 530/581-0226. **Terms:** Reserv deposit, 3 day notice. **Facility:** 15 rooms. 2 stories; exterior corridors. **All Rooms:** combo or shower baths. **Some Rooms:** 2 kitchens. **Cards:** MC, VI.

GRANLIBAKKEN RESORT & CONFERENCE CENTER   Rates Subject to Change   Phone: (530)583-4242   21

♦♦♦ Resort Complex

12/18-1/3 [BP]	1P: $100	2P/1B: $124	2P/2B: $156	XP: $25	F3
Fri & Sat 2/1-12/17 & 1/4-1/31 [BP]	1P: $90	2P/1B: $114	2P/2B: $136	XP: $22	F3
Sun-Thurs 2/1-12/17 & 1/4-1/31 [BP]	1P: $85	2P/1B: $104	2P/2B: $121	XP: $20	F3

Location: 0.8 mi s of jct SR 89 & SR 28, 0.6 mi w. Granlibakken Rd 96145 (PO Box 6329). **Fax:** 530/583-7641. **Terms:** Reserv deposit, 30 day notice; handling fee imposed. **Facility:** 110 rooms. 74 picturesque wooded acres within walking distance of Lake Tahoe. Few smaller units in main lodge building. 20 two-bedroom units, 10 three-bedroom units. Larger condo units, $300-$900; 3 stories; interior corridors; heated pool, whirlpool, 6 tennis courts. **Dining:** Restaurant; 7 am-9 pm; $11-$19. **Recreation:** hiking trails, jogging. **Some Rooms:** 30 kitchens. **Cards:** AE, DI, DS, JC, MC, VI.

LAKE OF THE SKY MOTOR INN   Phone: (530)583-3305   19

♦♦ Motel

All Year	1P: $50- 100	2P/1B: $50- 100	2P/2B: $55- 105	XP: $5	F12

Location: 1 mi e of jct SR 89. 955 North Lake Blvd 96145 (PO Box 227). **Terms:** Reserv deposit, 7 day notice. **Facility:** 23 rooms. Some rooms have lake view. 1 story; exterior corridors; lake view. **All Rooms:** shower baths. **Cards:** AE, DI, DS, MC, VI. *(See ad p 504)*

PEPPER TREE INN   Phone: 530/583-3711   26

♦♦ Motel

2/1-4/17, 6/18-9/18 & 12/17-1/31	1P: $60- 85	2P/1B: $65- 90	2P/2B: $70- 95	XP: $5	F12
4/18-6/17 & 9/19-12/16	1P: $40- 60	2P/1B: $45- 60	2P/2B: $45- 55	XP: $5	F12

Location: SR 28, 0.5 mi e of SR 89. 645 N Lake Blvd 96145 (PO Box 29). **Fax:** 530/583-6938. **Terms:** Reserv deposit, 3 day notice. **Facility:** 51 rooms. 2-7 stories; exterior corridors; heated pool, whirlpool. **Dining:** Restaurant nearby. **All Rooms:** shower baths. **Cards:** AE, CB, DI, DS, JC, MC, VI.

(See map p. 500)

RIVER RANCH LODGE ◆◆

	Rates Subject to Change			Phone: 530/583-4264	22
12/15-1/1 [CP]	1P: $135	2P/1B: $135	2P/2B: $135	XP: $15	F6
Lodge 2/1-4/20 & 1/2-1/31 [CP]	1P: $95	2P/1B: $125	2P/2B: $125	XP: $15	F6
6/14-9/21 [CP]	1P: $85	2P/1B: $110	2P/2B: $110	XP: $15	F6
4/21-6/13 & 9/22-12/14 [CP]	1P: $59	2P/1B: $85	2P/2B: $85	XP: $15	F6

Location: Exit I-80 at SR 89, 11 mi s on SR 89. SR 89 & Alpine Meadows Rd 96145 (PO Box 197). Fax: 530/583-7237. **Terms:** Reserv deposit, 3 day notice; handling fee imposed. **Facility:** 19 rooms. Located adjacent to Alpine Meadows Ski Resort. 2 stories; interior/exterior corridors. **Recreation:** hiking trails, jogging. **All Rooms:** combo or shower baths. **Cards:** AE, MC, VI.

SUNNYSIDE RESORT ◆◆◆

	Rates Subject to Change			Phone: (530)583-7200	25
5/21-10/9 [CP]	1P: $160- 200	2P/1B: $160- 200	2P/2B: $160- 200	XP: $15	F4
Lodge 2/1-4/3 & 12/10-1/31 [CP]	1P: $110- 175	2P/1B: $110- 175	2P/2B: $110- 175	XP: $15	F4
4/4-5/20 & 10/10-12/9 [CP]	1P: $90- 155	2P/1B: $90- 155	2P/2B: $90- 155	XP: $15	F4

Location: SR 89, 2 mi s. 1850 W Lake Blvd 96145 (PO Box 5969). Fax: 530/583-2551. **Terms:** 2 night min stay, weekends. **Facility:** 23 rooms. Completely refurbished 1908 residence, most rooms face lake. Comfortably furnished units, some with fireplace. 2 stories; interior/exterior corridors. Fee: boat dock. **Recreation:** swimming, fishing. Fee: sailboating, waterskiing. Rental: boats, canoes. **Cards:** AE, MC, VI.

TAHOE CITY TRAVELODGE (AAA) (SAVE) ◆◆
Motel

				Phone: (530)583-3766	24
2/1-4/10, 6/25-9/5 & 12/17-1/31	1P: $71- 115	2P/1B: $76- 120	2P/2B: $82- 131	XP: $5-10	F17
4/11-6/24 & 9/6-10/16	1P: $60- 98	2P/1B: $65- 103	2P/2B: $70- 109	XP: $5	F17
10/17-12/16	1P: $49- 79	2P/1B: $52- 82	2P/2B: $56- 91	XP: $5	F17

Location: SR 28, 0.3 mi e of jct SR 89. 455 North Lake Blvd 96145 (PO Box 84). Fax: 530/583-8045. **Facility:** 47 rooms. Lake opposite & golfing adjacent; attractive comfortable rooms. Well-maintained. 2 stories; interior/exterior corridors; heated pool, sauna, whirlpool. **Dining:** Restaurant nearby. **All Rooms:** combo or shower baths. **Cards:** AE, CB, DI, DS, MC, VI. **Special Amenities:** Free newspaper and preferred room (subject to availability with advanced reservations).** *(See ad p 501)*

RESTAURANTS

CHRISTY HILL RESTAURANT ◆◆◆
American

Dinner: $30-$40   **Phone:** 530/583-8551   14
Location: E off SR 28 toward lake. 115 Grove St, Tahoe City 96145. **Hours:** 5:30 pm-9:30 pm. Closed: 11/26, 12/25, Mon & first 2 weeks in December. **Reservations:** suggested. **Features:** No A/C; casual dress; beer & wine only; a la carte. Varied menu with emphasis on California & French style; fresh local ingredients & pacific seafood. Attractive decor, view of lake. Smoke free premises. **Cards:** AE, MC, VI.

TAHOE HOUSE ◆◆◆
Ethnic

Dinner: $8-$18   **Phone:** 530/583-1377   15
Location: 0.8 mi s of Tahoe City on SR 89. 625 W Lake Blvd 96145. **Hours:** 5 pm-10 pm. **Reservations:** suggested. **Features:** children's menu; cocktails & lounge; a la carte. Swiss, also California cuisine. Fresh baked breads. Homemade desserts; European atmosphere. Smoke free premises. **Cards:** AE, CB, DI, MC, VI.

TAHOE VISTA—1,100   (See map p. 500; index p. 497)

LODGINGS

CEDAR GLEN LODGE (AAA) (SAVE) ◆◆
Motel

				Phone: (530)546-4281	11
Fri & Sat 2/1-4/18, 6/18-9/25 & 12/18-1/31 [CP]	1P: $55- 60	2P/1B: $55- 65	2P/2B: $79- 95	XP: $10	
Sun-Thurs 2/1-4/18, 4/19-6/17 & 9/26-12/17 [CP]	1P: $45- 75	2P/1B: $45- 75	2P/2B: $55- 85	XP: $10	

Location: SR 28, 1.5 mi w of SR 267; 3 mi w of casino center. 6589 North Lake Blvd 96148 (PO Box 188). Fax: 530/546-2250. **Terms:** Reserv deposit, 7 day notice; handling fee imposed; 3 night min stay, in housekeeping unit. **Facility:** 31 rooms. Motel & cottages. 2 two-bedroom units. 2 two-bedroom kitchen units, $95-$120 for up to 6 persons; 1-2 stories; exterior corridors; sauna, whirlpool; playground. **All Rooms:** combo or shower baths. **Some Rooms:** 10 efficiencies. **Cards:** AE, DS, MC, VI. IMA. *(See color ad p 502 & p 286)*

CHARMEY CHALET RESORT (AAA) (SAVE) ◆◆
Motel

				Phone: 530/546-2529	12
Fri & Sat 6/19-9/17	1P: $65- 85	2P/1B: $65- 85	2P/2B: $70- 90	XP: $7	
Sun-Thurs 6/26-9/8	1P: $55- 75	2P/1B: $55- 75	2P/2B: $60- 80	XP: $7	
Fri & Sat 2/1-6/18 & 9/18-1/31	1P: $55- 65	2P/1B: $55- 65	2P/2B: $60- 70	XP: $7	
Sun-Thurs 2/1-6/25 & 9/9-1/31	1P: $45- 55	2P/1B: $45- 55	2P/2B: $50- 60	XP: $7	

Location: SR 28, 1.5 mi w of SR 267. 6549 North Lake Blvd 96148 (PO Box 316). Fax: 530/546-0308. **Terms:** Reserv deposit, 3 day notice. **Facility:** 29 rooms. In the pines. Garden patios & few rooms with lake view. 2 two-bedroom efficiencies with fireplace, $140-$160 for up to 6 persons; $90-$120 for 2 persons. 1 whirlpool unit, $75-$95 for 2 persons; 1 story; exterior corridors; heated pool, whirlpool, beach opposite. **All Rooms:** combo or shower baths. **Some Rooms:** 10 efficiencies. **Cards:** AE, DS, MC, VI. *(See color ad p 502)*

FIRELITE LODGE (AAA) ◆
Motel

	Guaranteed Rates			Phone: 530/546-7222	16
2/1-4/30, 6/19-9/13 & 11/26-1/31	1P: $46- 69	2P/1B: $46- 69	2P/2B: $56- 79	XP: $5	
5/1-6/18 & 9/14-11/25	1P: $39- 48	2P/1B: $39- 48	2P/2B: $44- 56	XP: $5	

Location: On SR 28, 1 mi w of SR 267. 7035 N Lake Blvd 96148 (PO Box 135). Fax: 530/546-7770. **Facility:** 25 rooms. 2 stories; exterior corridors; whirlpool. **Dining:** Restaurant nearby. **Cards:** AE, MC, VI.

(See map p. 500)

FRANCISCAN LAKESIDE LODGE Rates Subject to Change Phone: 530/546-6300 **13**
2/1-4/15, 5/20-9/5 &
11/15-1/31 1P: $75- 160 2P/1B: $75- 160 2P/2B: $95- 160 XP: $10
4/16-5/19 & 9/6-11/14 1P: $56- 120 2P/1B: $56- 120 2P/2B: $71- 120 XP: $10
Location: SR 28, 1 mi w of SR 267. 6944 N Lake Blvd 96148 (PO Box 280). Fax: 530/546-0348.
Cottage **Terms:** Reserv deposit, 14 day notice, in high season. **Facility:** 63 rooms. Some motel rooms in pines, few
cottages on lake. 6 two-bedroom units, $130-$155 for up to 7 persons; 1-2 stories; exterior corridors; beach, heated pool open
5/30-10/1; playground. **Recreation:** swimming, fishing. **All Rooms:** kitchens, combo or shower baths. **Cards:** AE, DS, MC,
VI. (See color ad p 502)

THE SHORE HOUSE AT LAKE TAHOE Rates Subject to Change Phone: (530)546-7270 **10**
All Year [BP] 1P: $150- 225 2P/1B: $150- 225 2P/2B: $150- 225 XP: $20-25 F18
Location: SR 28, 1 mi w of jct SR 28 & SR 267. 7170 North Lake Blvd 96148 (PO Box 343).
Fax: 530/546-7130. **Terms:** Reserv deposit, 14 day notice; handling fee imposed. **Facility:** 9 rooms. Lake ac-
Bed & cess with private dock. 2 stories; exterior corridors; lakefront. **Dining:** Restaurant nearby. **All Rooms:** combo
Breakfast or shower baths. **Some Rooms:** 2 kitchens, whirlpools. **Cards:** DS, MC, VI.

VISTA SHORES RESORT Rates Subject to Change Phone: 530/546-3635 **15**
6/15-9/15 1P: $65- 90 2P/1B: $65- 125 2P/2B: $95- 190 XP: $10
2/1-6/14 & 9/16-1/31 1P: $60- 85 2P/1B: $60- 95 2P/2B: $75- 150 XP: $10
Location: SR 28, 1 mi w of SR 267. 6731 North Lake Blvd 96148 (PO Box 487). Fax: 530/546-7145.
Motel **Terms:** Reserv deposit, 31 day notice. **Facility:** 27 rooms. Some cottages on the beach.
1 three-bedroom unit, 4 two-bedroom units. 1 three-bedroom cottage, $75-$180 for 2-4 persons; 1 story; exterior corridors; beach, sauna, whirlpool. **Dining:** Restaurant nearby. **All Rooms:** combo or shower baths. **Some Rooms:** 2
efficiencies, 14 kitchens. **Cards:** DS, MC, VI. (See ad p 499)

WOODVISTA LODGE Phone: (530)546-3839 **14**
All Year 1P: $55- 75 2P/1B: $55- 75 2P/2B: $65- 110 XP: $5-10 F
Location: North Lake Tahoe Area, on SR 28, 0.2 mi W of SR 267. 7699 N Lake Blvd 96148 (PO Box 439).
Fax: 530/546-2747. **Terms:** Reserv deposit, 3 day notice. **Facility:** 16 rooms. Tree-shaded grounds. Spacious
Motel lawn. 1 story; exterior corridors; whirlpool; playground. **Dining:** Restaurant nearby. **All Rooms:** shower
baths. **Cards:** AE, DI, DS, JC, MC, VI. **Special Amenities:** Free local telephone calls and preferred room
(subject to availability with advanced reservations).

RESTAURANTS

LE PETIT PIER Dinner: $31-$45 Phone: 530/546-4464 **11**
Location: On SR 28; 0.5 mi w of SR 267. 7238 N Lake Blvd 96148. **Hours:** 6 pm-10 pm. Closed: Tues.
French **Reservations:** suggested. **Features:** cocktails & lounge; a la carte. View of lake & mountains; quiet
atmosphere. **Cards:** AE, DI, MC, VI.

SUNSETS ON THE LAKE Lunch: $7-$13 Dinner: $14-$24 Phone: 530/546-3640 **12**
Location: 0.7 mi w of SR 267. 7320 North Lake Blvd 96148. **Hours:** 11:30 am-2:30 & 5-9 pm. Closed major
Continental holidays. **Reservations:** suggested. **Features:** No A/C; casual dress; children's menu; cocktails & lounge.
California Northern Italian; lakefront. Smoke free premises. **Cards:** AE, CB, DI, MC, VI.

TAHOMA—500 (See map p. 500; index p. 499)

LODGINGS

NORFOLK WOODS INN & RESTAURANT Rates Subject to Change Phone: (530)525-5000 **125**
2/1-4/7, 6/16-10/12 &
12/16-1/31 1P: $80- 155 2P/1B: $80- 155 2P/2B: $90- 155 XP: $12 F12
4/8-6/15 & 10/13-12/15 1P: $75- 140 2P/1B: $75- 140 2P/2B: $80- 140 XP: $12 F12
Location: On SR 89, 9 mi s of Tahoe City. 6941 West Lake Blvd 96142 (PO Box 262). Fax: 530/525-5266.
Country Inn **Terms:** Reserv deposit, 14 day notice; handling fee imposed; pets, $10 extra charge. **Facility:** 13 rooms. 6
two-bedroom units. 4 cabins with kitchen, $120-$155, breakfast not included. 2 two-bedroom suites, $115-$135, breakfast included; 2 stories; interior/exterior corridors; smoke free premises; heated pool, whirlpool, pool open 5/24-10/1.
Dining: Restaurant; 8 am-2 & 5:30-9:30 pm; $14-$25; cocktails. **Some Rooms:** 5 kitchens, color TV. **Cards:** AE, MC, VI.

Meal Plan Indicators

CP = Continental Plan of pastry, juice and another beverage or may offer
expanded breakfast items

BP = Breakfast Plan of full hot breakfast

AP = American Plan of three meals daily

MAP = Modified American Plan of two meals daily

EP = European Plan, where rate includes only room

Family Plan Indicators

The establishment may limit the number of children to whom the family plan applies.

F17 = children 17 and under stay free (age displayed will reflect property's policy)

D17 = discount for children 17 and under

F = children stay free

D = discounts for children

(See map p. 500)

TAHOE CEDARS LODGE — Guaranteed Rates — Phone: 530/525-7515 [126]

◆ 5/1-10/1 — 1P: $52 — 2P/1B: $52 — 2P/2B: $55 — XP: $6

Cottage — **Location:** 9 mi s of Tahoe City, on SR 89. 6980 W Lake Blvd 96142 (PO Box 269). **Terms:** Open 5/1-10/1; reserv deposit, 5 day notice. **Facility:** 19 rooms. Spacious lakefront grounds. Rustic cottages. 3 two-bedroom units. 9 kitchens, $67-$70 for 2 persons. 4 duplex units for up to 5 persons, $117-$127 also 2 two-story units, $127-$137 for up to 6 persons; 1 story; exterior corridors; boat dock. **Recreation:** swimming. **All Rooms:** shower baths.

TRUCKEE—2,400 (See map p. 500; index p. 497)

LODGINGS

BEST WESTERN TRUCKEE TAHOE INN — Phone: (530)587-4525 [30]

AAA SAVE

Fri & Sat [CP] — 1P: $82- 135 — 2P/1B: $92- 135 — 2P/2B: $88- 135 — XP: $7 — F13
Sun-Thurs [CP] — 1P: $71- 125 — 2P/1B: $80- 125 — 2P/2B: $78- 125 — XP: $7 — F13

◆◆◆ Motel — **Location:** 1.5 mi se of I-80, via SR 267 exit. 11331 SR 267 96161. Fax: 530/587-8173. **Terms:** Reserv deposit. **Facility:** 100 rooms. Attractive courtyard garden, pool & spa area. 2 stories; interior corridors; heated pool, sauna, whirlpool. **Dining:** Cafeteria. **Cards:** AE, DI, DS, MC, VI. **Special Amenities:** Early check-in/late check-out and free breakfast. *(See color ad p 503)*

DONNER LAKE VILLAGE RESORT — Phone: (530)587-6081 [31]

AAA SAVE

6/21-9/5 & 12/15-1/2 — 1P: $100- 225 — 2P/1B: $100- 225 — 2P/2B: $100- 225 — XP: $10 — F12
2/1-3/31, 9/6-9/30 & 1/3-1/31 — 1P: $80- 175 — 2P/1B: $80- 175 — 2P/2B: $80- 175 — XP: $10 — F12
4/1-6/20 & 10/1-12/14 — 1P: $70- 145 — 2P/1B: $70- 145 — 2P/2B: $70- 145 — XP: $10 — F12

◆◆◆ Resort Motel — Fax: 530/587-8782. **Terms:** Reserv deposit, 5 day notice. **Facility:** 64 rooms. Studio, 1- & 2-bedroom units. **Location:** 4 mi w; I-80 exit Donner Lake, on Old Hwy 40 at w end of lake. 15695 Donner Pass Rd 96161. Some lakefront units. 2 stories; interior/exterior corridors; beach, saunas; marina. **Recreation:** swimming, fishing, waterskiing; hiking trails. Fee: jet ski. Rental: boats, canoes, paddleboats. **Cards:** AE, DI, DS, MC, VI. **Special Amenities:** Early check-in/late check-out and preferred room (subject to availability with advanced reservations). *(See color ad p 503)*

HOLIDAY INN EXPRESS — Phone: 530/582-9999

[FYI] Under construction. **Location:** Exit I-80 at Donner Pass Rd, adjacent to Donner Memorial State Park. 10527 Cold Stream Rd 96161. **Facility:** 65 rooms. Scheduled to open winter, 1998; *(See color ad below)*

(See map p. 500)

NORTHSTAR AT TAHOE   Rates Subject to Change   Phone: (530)562-1010   🔲32
ⒶⒶⒶ
◆◆◆   11/22-1/31   2P/2B: $139- 448
Complex   6/6-10/26   2P/2B: $99- 303
Location: Exit I-80 at SR 267, 7 mi se; exit SR 28 at Kings Beach SR 267 n 6 mi. SR 267 & Northstar Dr 96160 (PO Box 129). Fax: 530/562-2215. **Terms:** Open 6/6-10/26 & 11/22-1/31; check-in 5 pm; reserv deposit, 7 day notice, written refund notice; handling fee imposed; 2 night min stay. **Facility:** 254 rooms. Spacious grounds, mountain setting. Varied accommodations in 1- to 4-bedroom housekeeping units, most with fireplace. 2-night minimum stay 6/26-9/13 & 11/16-4/30; 2-3 stories, no elevator; interior/exterior corridors; heated pool, saunas, whirlpools; 10 tennis courts. Fee: 18 holes golf. **Dining:** Restaurant, coffee shop; 8 am-9 pm; $11-$18; cocktails. **Recreation:** Fee: downhill & cross country skiing, ski equipment; horseback riding. Rental: bicycles. **Cards:** AE, DS, MC, VI.

🏊 🍴 ⛄ ✕ 💻 🎿 🖨 ✕

Nearby Nevada

INCLINE VILLAGE—7,500   (See map p. 500; index p. 497)

LODGINGS

CLUB TAHOE   Rates Subject to Change   Phone: 775/831-5750   🔲2
◆◆◆   12/17-1/5   1P: $180   2P/1B: $180   2P/2B: $180
Apartment   6/18-9/16   1P: $160   2P/1B: $160   2P/2B: $160
Complex   11/19-12/16 & 1/6-1/31   1P: $140   2P/1B: $140   2P/2B: $140
2/1-6/17 & 9/17-11/18   1P: $125   2P/1B: $125   2P/2B: $125
Location: North Lake Tahoe Area, Exit SR28 at Village Blvd N, 0.3 mi e. 914 Northwood Blvd 89452 (PO Box 7440). Fax: 775/832-9400. **Terms:** Check-in 4 pm; reserv deposit, 14 day notice; 7 night min stay, in season. **Facility:** 92 rooms. Attractive landscaped grounds with creek & tall pine trees. 2-bedroom units, with fireplace, deck, loft & laundry facilities. Rates for up to 6 persons. 2-night minimum stay off season; 2 stories; exterior corridors; heated pool; racquetball courts, 2 lighted tennis courts. **All Rooms:** kitchens. **Cards:** DS, MC, VI.

🏊 🍴 🍸 ✕ 🎿 🖨

HYATT REGENCY LAKE TAHOE RESORT & CASINO   Rates Subject to Change   Phone: (775)832-1234   🔲1
◆◆◆◆   Fri & Sat 7/1-9/30 &
Resort Hotel   12/24-1/31   1P: $225- 355   2P/1B: $225- 380   2P/2B: $225- 380   XP: $25   F18
Sun-Thurs 7/1-9/30   1P: $205- 330   2P/1B: $205- 355   2P/2B: $205- 355   XP: $25   F18
Fri & Sat 2/1-6/30 &
10/1-12/23   1P: $195- 250   2P/1B: $195- 275   2P/2B: $195- 275   XP: $25   F18
Sun-Thurs 2/1-6/30 &
10/1-12/23   1P: $155- 215   2P/1B: $155- 240   2P/2B: $155- 240   XP: $25   F18
Location: 0.5 mi w of SR 28, toward lake via Country Club Dr; 2 mi s of Mt Rose Hwy. Lakeshore at Country Club Dr 89450 (PO Box 3239). Fax: 775/831-7508. **Terms:** Reserv deposit, 21 day notice. **Facility:** 458 rooms. Exceptional facilities; nestled in the pines on beautifully landscaped grounds. 24 one & 2-bedroom lakeside cottages, suites & regency level rooms, $210-705 for 2 to 4 persons; 12 stories; interior corridors; heated pool; 2 tennis courts. **Recreation:** swimming. Fee: sailboating. Rental: bicycles. **Cards:** AE, CB, DI, DS, JC, MC, VI. *(See color ad below)*

SAVE 🅥 🏊 🍴 🛗 🖨 ✕ 🐕 🖨 ✕

THE INN AT INCLINE   Phone: (775)831-1052   🔲3
ⒶⒶⒶ SAVE   6/18-9/18 [CP]   1P: $89- 135   2P/1B: $89- 135   2P/2B: $99- 135   XP: $10   F12
◆◆   2/1-6/17 & 9/19-1/31 [CP]   1P: $69- 109   2P/1B: $69- 109   2P/2B: $79- 109   XP: $10   F12
Motel   **Location:** North Lake Tahoe Area, on SR28 n of Country Club Dr. 1003 Tahoe Blvd 89451. Fax: 775/831-3016. **Terms:** Reserv deposit, 7 day notice. **Facility:** 38 rooms. Convenient to village & activities. 2 stories; interior/exterior corridors; heated indoor pool, sauna, whirlpool. **Cards:** AE, DS, MC, VI.
Special Amenities: Free breakfast and free local telephone calls.

🆂 🏊 🐕 🎿 🖨

RESTAURANTS

AZZARA'S ITALIAN RESTAURANT   Dinner: $10-$17   Phone: 775/831-0346   🔲1
◆◆   **Location:** 930 Tahoe Blvd 89450. **Hours:** 5 pm-9:30 pm. Closed: Mon, 4/7, 11/28, 12/24 & 12/25.
Italian   **Features:** casual dress; cocktails & lounge; minimum charge-$5; a la carte. Charming European decor, varied menu with seafood specialties, very popular. Smoke free premises. **Cards:** AE, MC, VI.

✕

(See map p. 500)

CAFE 333
◆◆
Traditional
American

Lunch: $5-$11   **Dinner:** $11-$22   **Phone:** 775/832-7333   ②
Location: 0.3 mi n of SR-28. 333 Village Blvd 89451. **Hours:** 7 am-3 pm & 5:30 pm-9:30 pm. Closed major holidays. **Reservations:** suggested. **Features:** No A/C; casual dress; children's menu; early bird specials; cocktails. French country decor. Beautiful garden dining overlooking a waterfall. Smoke free premises. **Cards:** MC, VI.

STATELINE—1,400   (See map p. 500; index p. 497)

LODGINGS

CAESARS TAHOE
◆◆◆◆
Hotel

	Rates Subject to Change			**Phone:** (775)588-3515	㊳
All Year	1P: $89- 185	2P/1B: $89- 185	2P/2B: $89- 185	XP: $10	F

Location: At casino center. (PO Box 5800, 89449). Fax: 775/586-2068. **Facility:** 440 rooms. Many rooms with view of Lake Tahoe. 14 stories; interior corridors; heated indoor pool. Fee: 4 lighted tennis courts.
All Rooms: combo or shower baths. **Cards:** AE, DI, DS, MC, VI.

HARRAH'S HOTEL & CASINO
(AAA) [SAVE]
◆◆◆◆
Hotel

				Phone: (775)588-6611	㊴
6/18-9/4	1P: $149- 249	2P/1B: $249	2P/2B: $149- 249	XP: $20-60	F
2/1-6/17 & 9/5-1/31	1P: $119- 209	2P/1B: $119- 209	2P/2B: $119- 209	XP: $20-60	F

Location: In casino area. In Casino area 89449 (PO Box 8). Fax: 775/586-6607. **Terms:** Check-in 4 pm; reserv deposit, 3 day notice; handling fee imposed; pets, in kennel. **Facility:** 534 rooms. Many with views of mountains or lake. 18 stories; interior corridors; heated indoor pool, whirlpools, 2 indoor whirlpools. **Dining:** 5 restaurants, coffee shop; 24 hours; $8-$60; cocktails; also, The Summit Room, see separate listing. **Services:** Fee: massage. **Cards:** AE, CB, DI, DS, JC, MC, VI. **Special Amenities: Early check-in/late check-out and preferred room (subject to availability with advanced reservations).**

HARVEY'S RESORT HOTEL
(AAA) [SAVE]
◆◆◆◆
Hotel

				Phone: (775)588-2411	㊵
6/26-9/6 & 12/18-1/2 [CP]	1P: $120- 235	2P/1B: $120- 235	2P/2B: $120- 235	XP: $20	F12
2/1-6/25, 9/7-12/17 & 1/3-1/31 [CP]	1P: $99- 225	2P/1B: $99- 225	2P/2B: $99- 225	XP: $20	F12

Location: On US 50, casino center. In casino center 89449 (PO Box 128). Fax: 775/588-6643. **Terms:** Reserv deposit; package plans. **Facility:** 740 rooms. Beautifully decorated rooms, exceptional facilities. Whirlpool suites; most with balcony, $300; 19 stories; interior corridors; lake view; heated pool, whirlpool. **Dining:** 4 restaurants, coffee shop; 24 hours; $10-$31; cocktails; also, Sage Room Steak House, see separate listing. **Services:** giftshop. Fee: massage. **Recreation:** large video game room, complimentary board games. Fee: bicycles. **All Rooms:** combo or shower baths. **Cards:** AE, CB, DI, DS, JC, MC, VI. **Special Amenities: Free breakfast and free room upgrade (subject to availability with advanced reservations).** *(See color ad p 515)*

HORIZON CASINO RESORT
◆◆◆
Hotel

	Rates Subject to Change			**Phone:** 775/588-6211	㊲
Fri & Sat 6/12-9/12	1P: $129	2P/1B: $129	2P/2B: $129	XP: $10	F11
Fri & Sat 2/1-6/11, Sun-Thurs 6/12-9/12 & Fri & Sat 9/13-1/31	1P: $119	2P/1B: $119	2P/2B: $119	XP: $10	F11
Sun-Thurs 3/1-6/11 & 9/13-10/24	1P: $99	2P/1B: $99	2P/2B: $99	XP: $10	F11
Sun-Thurs 2/1-2/28 & 10/25-1/31	1P: $89	2P/1B: $89	2P/2B: $89	XP: $10	F11

Location: On US 50 in the casino area. 50 Hwy 50 89449 (PO Box C). Fax: 775/588-1344. **Terms:** Reserv deposit. **Facility:** 539 rooms. Lake view rms, $10 extra charge; 9-15 stories; interior corridors; heated pool. **Cards:** AE, DI, DS, MC, VI.

LAKESIDE INN
(AAA) [SAVE]
◆◆◆
Motor Inn

				Phone: 775/588-7777	㊶
6/12-10/22	1P: $69- 89	2P/1B: $69- 89	2P/2B: $69- 89	XP: $10	F16
2/1-6/11 & 10/23-1/31	1P: $59- 79	2P/1B: $59- 79	2P/2B: $59- 79	XP: $10	F16

Location: On US 50; 1 mi e of state line at Kingsbury Grade. US 50 89449 (PO Box 5640). Fax: 775/588-4092. **Terms:** Check-in 3:30 pm; reserv deposit. **Facility:** 124 rooms. Some units open onto pool deck, some spacious rooms. 1 two-bedroom unit. 1 & 2-bedroom suites with wet bar & whirlpool tub, $210 for up to 4 persons; 2 stories; interior/exterior corridors; heated pool, Heated pool open 6/1-9/30. **Dining:** Restaurant; 24 hrs; $8-$18; cocktails. **Cards:** AE, CB, DI, DS, MC, VI. *(See color ad p 519)*

(See map p. 500)

THE RIDGE TAHOE **Phone:** (775)588-3553 **42**

(AAA) [SAVE]
     2/1-4/18, 6/7-9/12 &
     12/6-1/31   1P: $160- 260   2P/1B: $160- 260   2P/2B: $270- 395
◆◆◆◆ 4/19-6/6 & 9/13-12/5   1P: $105- 180   2P/1B: $105- 180   2P/2B: $270- 300

Resort
Complex

Location: 3 mi e of US 50 via Kingsbury Grade, 0.8 mi s via Tramway Dr, then 1.3 mi e on Quaking Aspen Ln. 400 Ridge Club Dr 89449 (PO Box 5790). Fax: 775/588-7099. **Terms:** Check-in 4 pm; reserv deposit, 15 day notice, in high season. **Facility:** 447 rooms. A resort at 7600 ft elevation, gondola to ski lift. 1- & 2-bedroom units with fully equipped kitchen & gas fireplace; some hotel units, some with view of Carson Valley. 254 two-bedroom units. Maximum rates for up to 6 persons; 4-11 stories; interior/exterior corridors; putting green; heated indoor/outdoor pool, saunas, indoor & outdoor whirlpools; racquetball courts, 4 tennis courts (1 indoor, 2 lighted); playground. **Dining:** Dining room, coffee shop; 9 am-10 pm, dining room closed Mon & Tues; Sun brunch 10 am-1:30 pm, for resort guests only. Outside dining; $10-$30; cocktails. **Services:** area transportation, to casinos. **Recreation:** game room, children's sled area. Fee: downhill skiing. **Some Rooms:** 389 kitchens. **Cards:** AE, CB, DI, DS, MC, VI. **Special Amenities:** Free newspaper.
(See ad p 521)

🏊 🍴 ⬇ ❌ 🎾 VCR 🅰 📠 🔒 ❌

RESTAURANTS

THE EAGLES' NEST   **Dinner:** $9-$19   **Phone:** 775/588-3245 **24**

◆◆◆
American

Location: 3 mi e of US 50 on Kingsbury Grade. 472 Needle Peak Rd 89449. **Hours:** 5 pm-9 pm, Fri & Sat-10 pm. **Reservations:** suggested. **Features:** casual dress; cocktail lounge; beer & wine only. Sunset views over Lake Tahoe. **Cards:** AE, MC, VI. ❌

LLEWELLYN'S   **Lunch:** $6-$17   **Dinner:** $17-$27   **Phone:** 775/588-2411 **21**

(AAA)

◆◆◆◆
Continental

Location: Atop Harvey's Resort Hotel. US 50 89449. **Hours:** 11:30 am-2:30 & 6-9:30 pm, Sat-10 pm, Sun 10 am-2 pm & 6-9:30 pm. Closed: for lunch Mon & Tues. **Reservations:** suggested; in season. **Features:** semi-formal attire; cocktails & lounge; entertainment; minimum charge-$12; valet parking; a la carte, a la carte. Elegant surroundings, spectacular view of Lake Tahoe & mountains. Inovative preparation. **Cards:** AE, CB, DI, MC, VI. ♿ ❌

SAGE ROOM STEAK HOUSE   **Dinner:** $18-$24   **Phone:** 775/588-2411 **23**

◆◆◆
Steakhouse

Location: In Harvey's Hotel. 89449. **Hours:** 6 pm-10 pm, Sat & Sun from 5:30 pm. **Reservations:** suggested. **Features:** semi-formal attire; cocktails & lounge; minimum charge-$12; valet parking. Rustic quiet atmosphere, extensive selection of beef. **Cards:** AE, CB, DI, MC, VI. ♿ ❌

THE SUMMIT ROOM   **Dinner:** $26-$32   **Phone:** 775/588-6611 **22**

(AAA)

◆◆◆◆
Continental

Location: On 16th floor of Harrah's Tahoe Hotel. US 50 89449. **Hours:** 5:30 pm-10 pm, Sat & holidays-11 pm. Closed: Tues. **Reservations:** suggested. **Features:** semi-formal attire; cocktails & lounge; entertainment; valet parking; a la carte, a la carte. Excellently prepared dishes. An intimate, elegant environment that was previously the "Star Suite". **Cards:** AE, CB, DI, MC, VI. ❌

This ends listings for the Lake Tahoe Area.
The following page resumes the alphabetical listings of
cities in California.

LA MESA—See San Diego p. 906.

LA MIRADA—See Los Angeles p. 610.

LANCASTER—97,300

LODGINGS

BEST WESTERN ANTELOPE VALLEY INN　　　　　　　　　　　　　　Phone: (805)948-4651
(AAA) [SAVE]　All Year　　　　　　　1P: $56- 62　2P/1B:　$62- 68　2P/2B:　$68- 73　XP: $6　　F16
　◆◆　　Location: 2.3 mi e of SR 14 & 138, Ave K exit. 44055 N Sierra Hwy 93534. Fax: 805/948-4651.
Motor Inn　Terms: Monthly rates; pets, $25 extra charge. Facility: 148 rooms. Large landscaped courtyard. 3 stories;
　　　　　interior/exterior corridors; heated pool, whirlpool. Dining: Coffee shop; 5 am-9 pm, Sat & Sun 6 am-9 pm;
$10-$20; also, Desert Rose, see separate listing. All Rooms: combo or shower baths. Cards: AE, CB, DI,
DS, JC, MC, VI. Special Amenities: Early check-in/late check-out and free local telephone calls.

DESERT INN HOTEL　　　　　　　　　　　　　　　　　　　　　　Phone: 805/942-8401
(AAA) [SAVE]　All Year [CP]　　　　　1P: $70- 100　2P/1B:　$75- 105　2P/2B:　$75- 105　XP: $5　　F10
　◆◆　　Location: 2 mi e of SR 14 & 138; Ave J exit. 44219 N Sierra Hwy 93534. Fax: 805/942-8950.
Motor Inn　Terms: Weekly rates. Facility: 144 rooms. Nicely landscaped grounds. 2 two-bedroom units. 1-2 stories; ex-
　　　　　terior corridors; wading pool, sauna, whirlpool; racquetball courts. Dining: Coffee shop; 5:30 am-10 pm;
$7-$15; cocktails; also, Granada Room, see separate listing. Services: Fee: massage. All Rooms: combo
or shower baths, extended cable TV. Some Rooms: 25 kitchens. Cards: AE, CB, DI, DS, MC, VI. (See color ad below)

INN OF LANCASTER　　　　　　　　　　Guaranteed Rates　　　　　　　　Phone: 805/945-8771
　◆◆◆　　All Year [CP]　　　　　　1P: $55- 65　2P/1B:　$55- 65　2P/2B:　$61- 71
Motel　　Location: 2 mi e of SR 14 & 138, exit Ave J. 44131 Sierra Hwy 93534. Fax: 805/948-3355. Facility: 103
rooms. Tuesday night complimentary barbecue. 2 stories; exterior corridors; heated pool. Cards: AE, CB, DI,
DS, MC, VI.

RIO MIRADA INN　　　　　　　　　　　Guaranteed Rates　　　　　　　　Phone: (805)949-3423
　◆◆　　All Year　　　　　　　　1P: $55- 65　2P/1B:　$60- 70　2P/2B:　$65- 69　XP: $5　　F5
Motel　　Location: Adjacent to SR 14, exit Ave K, then just w. 1651 West Avenue K 93534. Fax: 805/949-0896.
　　　　Terms: Reserv deposit, 3 day notice. Facility: 171 rooms. 68 suites with kitchenettes $65-$70; 4 stories; in-
terior corridors; heated pool. Some Rooms: 68 efficiencies. Cards: AE, DI, DS, MC, VI.

RESTAURANTS

DESERT ROSE　　　　　　　　　Dinner: $10-$20　　　　　　　　　　Phone: 805/948-4651
　◆◆　　Location: 2.3 mi e of SR 14 & 138, Ave K exit; in Best Western Antelope Valley Inn. 44055 N Sierra Hwy
Steakhouse　93534. Hours: 5-9 pm. Closed: Sun. Features: casual dress; children's menu; carryout; salad bar; cocktails
　　　　& lounge; entertainment. Chicken, lamb, salad, seafood, steak & prime rib. Smoke free premises. Cards: AE,
CB, DI, DS, JC, MC, VI.

DOWNTOWN BISTRO & CAFE　　　Lunch: $5-$11　　　　Dinner: $7-$14　　　　Phone: 805/948-2253
　◆◆　　Location: Just e of 10th St W. 858 W Lancaster Blvd 93534. Hours: 7:30 am-2:30 & 5-8:30 pm, Fri-9:30
American　pm, Sat 8:30 am-2:30 & 5-9:30 pm, Sun 8:30 am-2:30 & 5-8:30 pm. Closed major holidaysMon-also closed
　　　　one week in summer. Reservations: suggested. Features: casual dress; Sunday brunch; children's menu;
health conscious menu; carryout; cocktails. Sandwiches, salads, chicken, lamb, duck, pasta, steak & fresh seafood. Fresh
breads prepared & baked on premises. Smoke free premises. Cards: AE, DS, MC, VI.

GRANADA ROOM　　　　　　　Lunch: $7-$10　　　　　Dinner: $12-$25　　　　Phone: 805/942-8401
　◆◆　　Location: 2 mi e of SR 14 & 138; Ave J exit; in Desert Inn Hotel. 44219 N Sierra Hwy 93534. Hours: 11
American　am-2 & 5-10 pm, Sat 5 pm-10 pm, Sun 10 am-2 & 5 pm-10 pm. Closed: 12/25. Features: Sunday brunch;
　　　　cocktails & lounge; entertainment; a la carte. Attractive dining room with a nice selection of entrees.
Semi-formal atmosphere. Cards: AE, CB, DI, MC, VI.

LA PALMA—15,400   (See map p. 294; index p. 291)

LODGING

LA QUINTA INN   **Phone:** (714)670-1400   108
All Year [CP]   1P: $69- 82 2P/1B: $69- 82 2P/2B: $69- 82
Location: 0.3 mi nw of SR 91, Orangethorpe Ave/Valley View St exit; located in Centerpointe La Palma
Business Park. 3 Centerpointe Dr 90623. Fax: 714/522-4698. **Facility:** 158 rooms. Many balconies. Transpor-
tation to Disneyland & Knotts Berry Farm. 7 stories; interior corridors; heated pool, whirlpool.
Dining: Restaurant nearby. **Cards:** AE, CB, DI, DS, JC, MC, VI. **Special Amenities:** Free breakfast and
free local telephone calls.

RESTAURANT

A'ROMA TRATTORIA-RISTORANTE   **Lunch:** $6-$15   **Dinner:** $9-$24   **Phone:** 714/523-3729   30
Location: Located in Center Pointe Plaza, adjacent to Orangethorpe Ave, just w of Valley View Ave. 30
Italian   Center Pointe Dr; Ste 1 90623. **Hours:** 11 am-10 pm, Sat 4 pm-10 pm. Closed major holidays & Sun.
Features: children's menu; carryout; cocktails. Attractive, contemporary decor. Good food, nicely presented.
Smoking permitted on heated patio. **Cards:** AE, DI, MC, VI.

LA QUINTA—11,200   (See map p. 774; index p. 773)

LODGING

TWO ANGELS INN   Rates Subject to Change   **Phone:** (760)564-7332   60
2/1-5/31 & 10/1-1/31 [BP]   1P: $175- 340 2P/1B: $185- 350
Bed &   6/1-6/30 [BP]   1P: $148- 280 2P/1B: $148- 280
Breakfast   7/1-9/30 [BP]   1P: $148- 263 2P/1B: $139- 263
Location: 0.5 mi s of SR 111 on Washington St, just e between Ave 47 & Ave 48. 78-120 Caleo Bay 92253.
Fax: 760/564-6356. **Terms:** Reserv deposit, 14 day notice. **Facility:** 11 rooms. French chateau style building. Individually deco-
rated rooms with fireplace & patio or balcony overlooking the lake. 2 stories; interior corridors; smoke free premises; heated
pool. **All Rooms:** combo or shower baths. **Cards:** AE, DS, MC, VI.

RESTAURANTS

LA QUINTA CLIFFHOUSE   **Lunch:** $8-$12   **Dinner:** $13-$20   **Phone:** 760/360-5991   38
Location: Just W of Washington. 78-250 Highway 111 92253. **Hours:** 5 pm-9:30 pm, Fri & Sat-10 pm;
American   1/1-5/31 11:30 am-2 & 5-9:30 pm. Closed: 12/25. **Features:** casual dress; children's menu; early bird
specials; cocktails & lounge; valet parking; a la carte. Located on hillside with a mountain view. Beautifully
landscaped terraces with plants & a waterfall. Sun brunch 10 am-2 pm 1/1-5/31. Smoke free premises. **Cards:** AE, DI, DS,
MC, VI.

THE LA QUINTA GRILL   **Dinner:** $20-$35   **Phone:** 760/564-4443   40
Location: SR 111, 2.8 mi s on Washington St, 0.5 mi w on 52nd Ave, just n. 78-045 Calle Cadiz 92253.
Continental   **Hours:** Open 2/1-6/1 & 10/15-1/31; 6 pm-10 pm. Closed: 1/1 & 12/25. **Reservations:** suggested.
Features: semi-formal attire; cocktails & lounge; a la carte. Fine dining in an elegant 1930's ranch house.
Several dining areas. Smoke free premises. **Cards:** AE, CB, DI, MC, VI.

LARKSPUR—*See San Francisco p. 970.*

LASSEN VOLCANIC NATIONAL PARK—*See also RED BLUFF & REDDING.*

LODGING

DRAKESBAD GUEST RANCH   Guaranteed Rates
FYI   7/11-10/10 [AP]   1P: $130- 150 2P/1B: $220- 250 2P/2B: $220- 250 XP: $90-98   D12
Has not been inspected. **Location:** 47 mi se of Park Hdqtrs; 17 mi nw of Chester on CR Chester-Warner
Resort   Valley; last 3 mi rocky-gravel/dirt road. CR Chester-Warner Valley 96020. **Terms:** Open 7/11-10/10; reserv
Complex   deposit, 30 day notice. **Facility:** 19 rooms. Beautiful primitive wilderness setting overlooking meadows; Sus-
anville operator (530), Drakesbad No. 2, through your long-distance operator; in winter (530) 529-9820. Meets
AAA fire safety requirements. 1 two-bedroom unit. 4 cabins & 6 lodge rooms with half-bath for up to 4 persons, $125-$448. No
electricity. $10 N.P. admission fee; 2 stories; interior/exterior corridors. **Recreation:** fishing; hiking trails. Fee: horseback
riding. **Cards:** DS, MC, VI.

LATHROP—6,800

LODGINGS

DAYS INN   **Phone:** (209)982-1959
All Year [CP]   1P: $60- 85 2P/1B: $60- 85 2P/2B: $70- 85 XP: $5-10   F12
Location: Exit I-5 at Lathrop Rd. 14750 S Harlan Rd 95330. Fax: 209/982-4978. **Terms:** Reserv deposit, 3
day notice; pets, $10 extra charge. **Facility:** 40 rooms. 2 two-bedroom units. Interior corridors; sauna.
Motel   **Cards:** AE, MC, VI. **Special Amenities:** Free breakfast and free local telephone calls.

HOLIDAY INN EXPRESS   **Phone:** (209)858-1234
All Year [CP]   1P: $65- 85 2P/1B: $65- 85 2P/2B: $75- 95 XP: $10   F18
Location: Exit I-5 at Louise Rd. 16855 S Harlan Rd 95330. Fax: 209/858-1800. **Facility:** 65 rooms. 2 stories;
exterior corridors; sauna, whirlpool. **Dining:** Restaurant nearby. **Cards:** AE, CB, DI, DS, JC, MC, VI.
Motel   **Special Amenities:** Free breakfast and free newspaper. *(See color ad p 1056)*

LAWNDALE—*See Los Angeles p. 611.*

LEBEC—1,200

LODGINGS

BEST REST INN
◆◆
Motor Inn
All Year — Rates Subject to Change — 1P: $50- 60 2P/1B: $55- 65 2P/2B: $55- 65 XP: $7 — Phone: 805/248-2700
Location: Just w of I-5; exit Frazier Park. 42810 Frazier Mtn Park Rd 93243. Fax: 805/248-2720. **Facility:** 80 rooms. Convenience store, service station, truck garage & barber shop on property. 2 stories; interior corridors; heated pool. **Services:** giftshop. **Cards:** AE, DS, MC, VI.

COUNTRY SIDE INN-GRAPEVINE
◆◆◆
Motel
All Year [CP] — Rates Subject to Change — 1P: $45 2P/1B: $52 2P/2B: $55 XP: $7 F10 — Phone: 805/248-1530
Location: Adj to I-5, exit Grapevine; 5 mi s of jct I-5 & SR 99; 28 mi s of Bakersfield. 9000 Country Side Ct 93243. Fax: 805/248-3149. **Facility:** 74 rooms. Located in a country setting at the foot of the mountains. Attractive southwestern ranch decor. 3 one-bedroom suites with microwave & refrigerator $90; 2 stories; exterior corridors; heated pool. **All Rooms:** combo or shower baths. **Cards:** AE, CB, DI, DS, MC, VI.

LEE VINING—300

LODGINGS

BEST WESTERN LAKE VIEW LODGE
AAA
◆◆◆
Motel
Rates Subject to Change — Phone: (760)647-6543

6/21-9/8	1P:	$78- 108	2P/1B:	$78- 108	2P/2B:	$78- 108	XP: $4
4/21-6/20 & 9/9-1/31	1P:	$48- 108	2P/1B:	$48- 108	2P/2B:	$48- 108	XP: $4
2/1-4/20	1P:	$42- 82	2P/1B:	$42- 82	2P/2B:	$42- 82	XP: $4

Location: On US 395. 30 Main St 93541 (PO Box 345). **Terms:** Check-in 4 pm. **Facility:** 46 rooms. Tree-shaded lawn areas. Some rooms with view of Mono Lake. 3 two-bedroom units. 3-night minimum stay in 3 kitchens, $8 extra charge; 2 stories; exterior corridors. **Dining:** Restaurant nearby. **Cards:** AE, CB, DI, DS, JC, MC, VI.

MURPHEY'S MOTEL
AAA
◆◆
Motel
Rates Subject to Change — Phone: 760/647-6316

6/16-9/30	1P:	$63- 73	2P/1B:	$68- 88	2P/2B:	$78- 98	XP: $5
5/24-6/15 & 10/1-11/15	1P:	$48- 68	2P/1B:	$48- 88	2P/2B:	$48- 98	XP: $5
2/1-5/23 & 11/16-1/31	1P:	$38- 68	2P/1B:	$38- 78	2P/2B:	$38- 78	XP: $5

Location: On US 395. 93541 (PO Box 57). **Terms:** Handling fee imposed; small pets only, $5 extra charge. **Facility:** 43 rooms. Rustic exterior & contemporary rooms. 2 stories; exterior corridors; sauna, whirlpool open 5/1-11/1. **Dining:** Restaurant nearby. **Recreation:** fish cleaning & freezing facilities. **All Rooms:** combo or shower baths. **Some Rooms:** 2 kitchens. **Cards:** AE, DS, MC, VI.

RESTAURANT

THE MONO INN RESTAURANT & ANSEL ADAMS GALLERY
◆◆◆
American
Dinner: $14-$21 — **Phone:** 760/647-6581
Location: 4 mi n. 55620 Hwy 395 93541. **Hours:** 5 pm-10 pm. Closed: Tues in summer, Mon-Wed in winter. **Reservations:** suggested. **Features:** casual dress; Sunday brunch; beer & wine only. Fine dining with a spectacular view of Mono Lake. Smoke free premises. **Cards:** AE, MC, VI.

LEGGETT—200

LODGINGS

REDWOODS RIVER RESORT
AAA SAVE
◆
Cottage
Phone: (707)925-6249

5/1-9/30	1P:	$55- 65	2P/1B:	$55- 65	2P/2B:	$55- 65	XP: $5
2/1-4/30 & 10/1-1/31	1P:	$50	2P/1B:	$50- 55	2P/2B:	$50- 55	XP: $5

Location: 7 mi n on US 101. 75000 Highway 101 95585. Fax: 707/925-6413. **Facility:** 16 rooms. Small grocery on premises. Lodge rooms & cottages. 2 stories; exterior corridors; smoke free premises. **Recreation:** fishing. Rental: canoes. **All Rooms:** kitchens. **Cards:** AE, DS, MC, VI.

STONEGATE VILLA'S
◆
Motel
All Year — Rates Subject to Change — 1P: $36 2P/1B: $42 2P/2B: $52 XP: $10 — Phone: 707/925-6226
Location: Exit US 101 at South Leggett, Drive Thru Tree Rd e, 0.7 mi. 65260 Drive Thru Tree Rd 95585 (PO Box 239). **Facility:** 7 rooms. 2 two-bedroom units. Efficiencies $62 for up to 2 persons; 1 story; exterior corridors; designated smoking area. **All Rooms:** shower baths. **Some Rooms:** 3 efficiencies. **Cards:** AE, MC, VI.

LEMOORE—13,600

LODGINGS

BEST WESTERN VINEYARD INN
AAA SAVE
◆◆
Motor Inn
All Year [CP] — 1P: $50 2P/1B: $55 2P/2B: $55 XP: $5 F12 — Phone: (559)924-1261
Location: 0.8 mi nw of SR 198; Houston St exit eastbound; D St exit westbound. 877 East D St 93245. Fax: 559/924-4270. **Terms:** Reserv deposit; handling fee imposed; pets, limited rooms. **Facility:** 67 rooms. Back-to-back units. 2 stories; exterior corridors. **Dining:** Restaurant nearby. **Recreation:** barbecue facilities. **Cards:** AE, CB, DI, DS, MC, VI. **Special Amenities:** Free breakfast and free local telephone calls.

HOLIDAY INN EXPRESS
◆◆◆
Motel
All Year [CP] — Rates Subject to Change — 1P: $69 2P/1B: $74 2P/2B: $65 XP: $5 — Phone: 559/924-3200
Location: 0.8 mi nw of SR 198; Houston St exit eastbound; D St westbound. 820 E Bush St 93245. Fax: 559/924-0198. **Facility:** 61 rooms. 4 whirlpool rms, extra charge; 2 stories; exterior corridors. **Some Rooms:** kitchen. **Cards:** AE, DI, DS, MC, VI.

LINDSAY—8,300

LODGING

OLIVE TREE INN
Rates Subject to Change
Phone: (559)562-5188
All Year [CP]   1P: $47   2P/1B: $52   2P/2B: $57   XP: $5   F12
Location: On SR 65. 390 N Hwy 65 93247. Fax: 559/562-2113. **Terms:** Reserv deposit; pets, $10 extra charge. **Facility:** 51 rooms. 6 efficiencies, $5 extra charge; 2 stories; exterior corridors; whirlpool.
Motel
Dining: Restaurant nearby. **All Rooms:** extended cable TV. **Cards:** AE, DI, DS, JC, MC, VI.

LITTLE RIVER—800

LODGINGS

GLENDEVEN
Rates Subject to Change
Phone: 707/937-0083
Fri-Sun 2/1-7/31, 8/1-8/31 &
Fri-Sun 9/1-1/31 [BP]   1P: $98- 200   2P/1B: $118- 200   2P/2B: $155- 200   XP: $20-30
Bed & Breakfast
Mon-Thurs 2/1-7/31 &
9/1-1/31 [BP]   1P: $78- 185   2P/1B: $98- 185   2P/2B: $135- 185   XP: $20-30
Location: 2 mi s of Mendocino, e of SR 1. 8221 N Hwy 1 95456. Fax: 707/937-6108. **Terms:** Reserv deposit, 7 day notice; handling fee imposed; 2 night min stay, weekends. **Facility:** 10 rooms. 1867 New England-style farmhouse, converted barn & annex; in landscaped wooded setting; most with fireplace. 1 two-bedroom unit. 2-3 stories, no elevator; interior/exterior corridors; smoke free premises. **Some Rooms:** kitchen. **Cards:** AE, MC, VI.

THE INN AT SCHOOLHOUSE CREEK
Rates Subject to Change
Phone: (707)937-5525
Fri-Sun & Mon-Thurs
5/16-10/31   1P: $100- 185   2P/1B: $100- 185   2P/2B: $115- 200   XP: $10-15   F2
Mon-Thurs 2/1-5/15 &
Complex
11/1-1/31   1P: $85- 170   2P/1B: $85- 170   2P/2B: $100- 185   XP: $15   F2
Location: 3 mi s of Mendocino; e of Coast Hwy. 7051 N Hwy 1 95456 (PO Box 1637, MENDOCINO, 95460). Fax: 708/937-2012. **Terms:** Reserv deposit, 14 day notice; handling fee imposed; 2 night min stay, weekends; pets extra charge. **Facility:** 13 rooms. On 8.5 landscaped acres; small single & duplex units & 6 cottages. Office & guest lounge in former home, circa 1862. Many with ocean view & fireplaces. 1 story; exterior corridors. **Services:** complimentary evening beverages. **All Rooms:** combo or shower baths. **Some Rooms:** efficiency, 4 kitchens, color TV, whirlpools. **Cards:** AE, DS, MC, VI. *(See ad p 663)*

RACHEL'S INN
Rates Subject to Change
Phone: (707)937-0088
Fri-Sun 2/1-6/30, 7/1-10/31 &
Fri-Sun 11/1-1/31 [BP]   1P: $115- 215   2P/1B: $115- 215   2P/2B: $115- 215   XP: $18
Mon-Thurs 2/1-6/30 &
Bed & Breakfast
11/1-1/31 [BP]   1P: $96- 190   2P/1B: $96- 190   2P/2B: $96- 190   XP: $18
Location: 2 mi s of Mendocino, w of SR 1. 8200 N Hwy 1 95456. Fax: 707/937-3620. **Terms:** Reserv deposit, 7 day notice; handling fee imposed; 2 night min stay, weekends. **Facility:** 9 rooms. 1860's farmhouse & converted barn. Many units with fireplace & balcony. Unit with piano & ocean view. 2 stories; interior corridors. **Recreation:** hiking trails. **All Rooms:** comb, shower or tub baths. **Cards:** MC, VI. *(See color ad p 663)*

STEVENSWOOD LODGE
Guaranteed Rates
Phone: (707)937-2810
All Year   1P: $150- 250   2P/1B: $150- 250   2P/2B: $175- 250   XP: $25   D12
Location: 2 mi s of Mendocino; e of SR 1. 8211 N Hwy 1 95456. Fax: 707/937-1237. **Terms:** Reserv deposit, 7 day notice; handling fee imposed; 2 night min stay, weekends. **Facility:** 10 rooms. Quiet forest setting. Forest or oceanview. Many rooms with fireplace. 2 stories; interior corridors; smoke free premises; whirlpools. **Dining:** Restaurant; 8 am-11 & 5:30-10 pm; prix fixe dinners; $45-$50; wine/beer only.
Country Inn
Recreation: hiking trails. **All Rooms:** combo or shower baths. **Some Rooms:** whirlpools. **Cards:** AE, DI, DS, MC, VI.
(See color ad p 664)

RESTAURANT

LITTLE RIVER INN RESTAURANT Country Inn
Dinner: $13-$21
Phone: 707/937-5942
Location: E side of SR 1, on a knoll. 7751 N Hwy 1 95456. **Hours:** 7:30 am-10:30 & 6-9 pm, Sat 7:30 am-11 & 6-10 pm, Sun 7:30 am-1 & 6-9 pm. **Reservations:** suggested. **Features:** No A/C; casual dress;
American
children's menu; cocktails & lounge. Prime rib Sat. Charming Victorian circa 1853. Garden view. Smoke free premises. **Cards:** MC, VI.

LIVERMORE—56,700

LODGINGS

COMFORT INN
Phone: (925)606-6200
All Year [CP]   1P: $88- 98   2P/1B: $98- 108   2P/2B: $108- 118   XP: $10   F14
Location: Exit I-580 Airway/Collier Canyon Rd N. 475 Collier Canyon Rd 94550. Fax: 925/606-6014.
Terms: Reserv deposit. **Facility:** 60 rooms. Attractive design. 2 rooms with whirlpool, $128 for 2 persons; 2
Motel
stories; exterior corridors; heated pool, whirlpool. **Some Rooms:** 2 kitchens. **Cards:** AE, CB, DI, DS, JC.
Special Amenities: Free breakfast and free newspaper.

HAMPTON INN
Guaranteed Rates
Phone: (925)606-6400
Sun-Thurs [CP]   1P: $83- 89   2P/1B: $92- 98   2P/2B: $98   XP: $10   F18
Fri & Sat [CP]   1P: $69- 79   2P/1B: $69- 79   2P/2B: $69- 79   XP: $10   F18
Motel
Location: Exit I-580 Airway/Collier Canyon Rd N. 2850 Constitution Dr 94550. Fax: 925/606-6410.
Facility: 80 rooms. 2 stories; interior corridors. **All Rooms:** combo or shower baths. **Cards:** AE, CB, DI, DS, MC, VI.

HOLIDAY INN-LIVERMORE
◆◆ Motor Inn
All Year — Rates Subject to Change — Phone: (925)443-4950
1P: $89- 99 2P/1B: $97- 105 2P/2B: $97- 105 XP: $8 F19
Location: N of & adjacent to I-580, exit Springtown Blvd. 720 Las Flores Rd 94550. Fax: 925/449-9059. **Facility:** 125 rooms. 4 stories; interior corridors. **Cards:** AE, CB, DI, DS, JC, MC, VI.

RESIDENCE INN BY MARRIOTT
◆◆◆ Suite Motel
All Year [CP] — Rates Subject to Change — Phone: 925/373-1800
1P: $99- 139 2P/2B: $109- 149
Location: Exit I-580 Airway/Collier Canyon Rd N. 1000 Airway Blvd 94550. Fax: 925/373-7252. **Facility:** 96 rooms. Some rooms with 2 double beds, some units have loft bedrooms. 36 two-bedroom units. 2 stories; exterior corridors. **Recreation:** sports court. **All Rooms:** kitchens. **Cards:** AE, CB, DI, DS, MC, VI.

RESTAURANT

WENTE VINEYARDS RESTAURANT
◆◆◆ American
Lunch: $6-$15 — Dinner: $6-$26 — Phone: 925/447-3696
Location: Exit I-580 n Livermore Ave; 1.2 mi s to 1st St, 0.8 mi w to s L St; 4.5 mi s via : L St & Arroyo Rd. 5050 Arroyo Rd 94550. **Hours:** 11:30 am-2:30 & 5:30-9:30 pm, Sun 10:30 am-2:30 & 5-9:30 pm. Closed major holidays. **Reservations:** suggested. **Features:** wine only; a la carte. Serving New American fare; attractive vineyard surroundings. Smoke free premises. **Cards:** AE, MC, VI.

LODI—51,900

LODGINGS

BEST WESTERN ROYAL HOST INN
AAA SAVE
◆◆ Motel
All Year [CP] — Phone: (209)369-8484
1P: $45- 50 2P/1B: $49- 55 2P/2B: $52- 65 XP: $8 F12
Location: 0.8 mi s on SR 99 business route. 710 S Cherokee Ln 95240. Fax: 209/369-0654. **Terms:** Small pets only. **Facility:** 48 rooms. Large rooms. 4 two-bedroom units. 2 stories; exterior corridors. **Dining:** Restaurant nearby. **All Rooms:** combo or shower baths. **Cards:** AE, CB, DI, DS, MC, VI. **Special Amenities:** Free breakfast and free newspaper.

COMFORT INN
AAA SAVE
◆◆ Motel
All Year [CP] — Phone: (209)367-4848
1P: $65 2P/1B: $69 XP: $5 F18
Location: 0.3 mi n on business Rt SR 99. 118 N Cherokee Ln 95240. Fax: 209/367-4898. **Terms:** Pets, $5 extra charge. **Facility:** 53 rooms. 2 stories; exterior corridors; whirlpool. **Dining:** Restaurant nearby. **Cards:** AE, CB, DI, DS, JC, MC, VI. **Special Amenities:** Early check-in/late check-out and free breakfast.

HOLIDAY INN EXPRESS-LODI
AAA SAVE
◆◆ Motel
All Year [CP] — Phone: (209)334-6422
1P: $76 2P/1B: $76 2P/2B: $76 XP: $6 F18
Location: 1 blk w of jct SR 99 & 12; exit SR 99, Kettlemen. Ln. 1140 S Cherokee Ln 95240. Fax: 209/368-7967. **Facility:** 95 rooms. Large comfortable rooms. 2 stories; exterior corridors; sauna, whirlpool. **Dining:** Coffee shop nearby. **Cards:** AE, CB, DI, DS, MC, VI. **Special Amenities:** Free breakfast and free local telephone calls.

WINE AND ROSES COUNTRY INN
AAA SAVE
◆◆◆ Bed & Breakfast
All Year [BP] — Phone: (209)334-6988
1P: $81- 115 2P/1B: $99- 125 2P/2B: $125- 140 XP: $15 D
Location: I-5 exit Turner Rd, e 5 mi; SR 99 exit Turner Rd, w 2 mi. 2505 W Turner Rd 95242. Fax: 209/334-6570. **Terms:** Reserv deposit, 7 day notice; handling fee imposed; AP avail. **Facility:** 10 rooms. 1902 historical estate located on 5 acres of landscaped grounds. 2 stories; interior corridors. **Dining:** Dining room; Lunch Tues-Fri 11:30-1:30 pm; dinner Wed-Sat 6 pm-9 pm, Sun brunch 10:30 am-2 pm; $13-$24. **All Rooms:** combo or shower baths. **Cards:** AE, CB, DI, DS, MC, VI. **Special Amenities:** Free breakfast and free local telephone calls.

LOMPOC—37,600

LODGINGS

BEST WESTERN VANDENBERG INN
AAA SAVE
◆◆◆ Motel
All Year [CP] — Phone: (805)735-7731
1P: $40- 90 2P/1B: $45- 95 2P/2B: $45- 95 XP: $5 F12
Location: 1 mi e on SR 1 & 246. 940 E Ocean Ave 93436. Fax: 805/737-0012. **Terms:** Small pets only, $20 extra charge. **Facility:** 83 rooms. 11 one-bedroom suites with efficiency, $100-$105; 2 stories; exterior corridors; heated pool, sauna, whirlpool. **Cards:** AE, CB, DI, DS, JC, MC, VI. **Special Amenities:** Free breakfast and free local telephone calls.

EMBASSY SUITES HOTEL
◆◆◆ Suite Motor Inn
7/1-12/31 [BP] — Rates Subject to Change — Phone: 805/735-8311
1P: $109 2P/1B: $109 XP: $10 F18
2/1-6/30 & 1/1-1/31 [BP]
1P: $99 2P/1B: $109 XP: $10 F18
Location: 1.3 mi n on SR 1. 1117 North H St 93436. Fax: 805/735-8459. **Terms:** Reserv deposit. **Facility:** 155 rooms. 2 room suites surrounding outdoor pool & garden area. 3 stories; exterior corridors; heated pool. **All Rooms:** combo or shower baths. **Cards:** AE, CB, DI, DS, JC, MC, VI.

HOLIDAY INN EXPRESS
AAA SAVE
◆◆◆ Motel
Phone: (805)736-2391
Fri & Sat 2/1-12/31 & 1/1-1/31 [CP]
1P: $109 2P/1B: $119 2P/2B: $119 XP: $6 F18
Sun-Thurs 2/1-12/31 [CP]
1P: $89 2P/1B: $99 2P/2B: $99 XP: $6 F18
Sun-Thurs 1/1-1/31 [CP]
1P: $99 2P/1B: $109 2P/2B: $99 XP: $6 F18
Location: 1417 N H St 93436. Fax: 805/736-6410. **Facility:** 90 rooms. 2 stories; interior corridors; heated pool, whirlpool. **All Rooms:** extended cable TV. **Cards:** AE, CB, DI, DS, MC, VI. **Special Amenities:** Free breakfast and free local telephone calls.

INN OF LOMPOC
AAA (SAVE)

◆◆◆
Motel

| | All Year [CP] | 1P: $69 | 2P/1B: $69 | 2P/2B: $79 | XP: $10 | F12 |

Phone: (805)735-7744

Location: 1.2 mi n on SR 1. 1122 North H St 93436. Fax: 805/736-0421. **Terms:** Reserv deposit; weekly/monthly rates; package plans; pets, $15 dep req. **Facility:** 90 rooms. Nicely furnished rooms. Attractive landscaping. 2 stories; interior/exterior corridors; heated indoor pool, whirlpool. **Services:** complimentary evening beverages. **All Rooms:** combo or shower baths. **Cards:** AE, CB, DI, DS, MC, VI. **Special Amenities: Early check-in/late check-out and free breakfast.**

(amenity icons)

QUALITY INN & EXECUTIVE SUITES
AAA (SAVE)

◆◆◆
Motel

| | 5/1-9/30 | 1P: $79- 109 | 2P/1B: $79- 109 | 2P/2B: $79- 109 | XP: $10 | F18 |
| | 2/1-4/30 & 10/1-1/31 | 1P: $69- 99 | 2P/1B: $69- 99 | 2P/2B: $69- 99 | XP: $10 | F18 |

Phone: (805)735-8555

Location: 1.8 mi n on SR 1. 1621 North H St 93436. Fax: 805/735-8566. **Terms:** Reserv deposit; package plans; pets, $25. **Facility:** 218 rooms. Standard rooms & larger rooms with efficiency. 92 executive suites with efficiency $75-$80; 4 stories; interior corridors; heated pool, whirlpool. **Dining:** Restaurant nearby. **Services:** Fee: massage. **Recreation:** in-room video games. **All Rooms:** extended cable TV. **Some Rooms:** 92 efficiencies. **Cards:** AE, CB, DI, DS, JC, MC, VI. **Special Amenities: Early check-in/late check-out and free local telephone calls.** *(See color ad below)*

(amenity icons)

SPACEPORT INN
◆◆
Motel

| | All Year [CP] | Rates Subject to Change | 1P: $73 | 2P/1B: $73 | 2P/2B: $73 | XP: $10 |

Phone: 805/733-5000

Location: 3.5 mi nw, adjacent to SR 1, exit Constellation Blvd. 3955 Apollo Way 93436. Fax: 805/733-0633. **Facility:** 63 rooms. 4 suites w/wet bars, $70-$84; 2 stories; interior/exterior corridors; heated pool. **Cards:** AE, DS, MC, VI.

(amenity icons)

TALLY HO MOTOR INN
AAA (SAVE)

◆◆
Motel

	Fri & Sat 7/1-9/14	1P: $49- 54	2P/1B: $49- 54	2P/2B: $54- 59	XP: $5
	Fri & Sat 2/1-6/30 & 9/15-12/31	1P: $40- 45	2P/1B: $45- 50	2P/2B: $50- 55	XP: $5
	Sun-Thurs 7/1-9/14	1P: $39- 44	2P/1B: $44- 49	2P/2B: $49- 54	XP: $5
	Sun-Thurs 2/1-6/30, 9/15-12/31 & 1/1-1/31	1P: $35- 40	2P/1B: $40- 45	2P/2B: $45- 50	XP: $5

Phone: (805)735-6444

Location: 1 mi e on SR 1 & 246. 1020 E Ocean Ave 93436. Fax: 805/735-5558. **Terms:** Monthly rates; pets, $10 extra charge. **Facility:** 53 rooms. Few smaller economy rooms. 4 two-room units with efficiency, $55; 2 stories; exterior corridors; sauna, indoor whirlpool. **Cards:** AE, CB, DI, DS, MC, VI. **Special Amenities: Free breakfast and free local telephone calls.**

(amenity icons)

RESTAURANT

THE JETTY
◆
Seafood

Lunch: $6-$11   **Dinner:** $9-$21   **Phone:** 805/735-2400

Location: 0.3 mi w on Ocean Ave. 304 W Ocean Ave 93436. **Hours:** 11:30 am-9 pm, Fri & Sat-10 pm. Closed major holidays. **Features:** casual dress; children's menu; health conscious menu; carryout; beer & wine only. All you can eat fish night-Tues. All you can eat crab night-Thurs. Nice selection of fresh seafood entrees. Smoke free premises. **Cards:** MC, VI.

(icon)

LONE PINE—1,700

LODGINGS

ALABAMA HILLS INN
Phone: 760/876-8700

AAA [SAVE]
◆◆◆
Motel

All Year [CP]　　　　　　　1P: $53- 68　2P/1B: $53- 58　2P/2B: $63- 68　XP: $5
Location: 1.5 mi s on US 395. 1920 S Main St 93545 (PO Box C). Fax: 760/876-8704. **Terms:** Pets, $5 extra charge. **Facility:** 58 rooms. Many units with balcony or patio. 2 stories; interior corridors; heated pool.
Cards: AE, DI, DS, MC, VI.

BEST WESTERN FRONTIER MOTEL
Phone: (760)876-5571

AAA [SAVE]
◆◆◆
Motel

4/1-10/15 [CP]　　　　　　1P: $47- 84　2P/1B: $52- 89　2P/2B: $52- 89　XP: $5　F12
2/1-3/31 & 10/16-1/31 [CP]　1P: $37- 64　2P/1B: $42- 69　2P/2B: $42- 69　XP: $5　F12
Location: 0.5 mi s on US 395. 1008 S Main St 93545. Fax: 760/876-5357. **Terms:** Pets. **Facility:** 73 rooms. A variety of rooms from cozy, nicely furnished original units to spacious newer units. 2 whirlpool rms, one extra charge; exterior corridors; heated pool. **All Rooms:** combo or shower baths. **Cards:** AE, CB, DI, DS, MC, VI.
Special Amenities: Free breakfast and free local telephone calls. *(See color ad below)*

DOW VILLA MOTEL
Phone: (760)876-5521

AAA [SAVE]
◆◆◆
Motel

4/1-10/31　　　　　　　　　1P: $75- 90　2P/1B: $75- 90　2P/2B: $85- 100
2/1-3/31 & 11/1-1/31　　　　1P: $58- 70　2P/1B: $58- 70　2P/2B: $64- 70
Location: US 395. 310 S Main St 93545 (PO Box 205). Fax: 760/876-5643. **Terms:** Pets, in smoking rms only. **Facility:** 42 rooms. 1-2 stories; exterior corridors; heated pool, whirlpool. **Dining:** Restaurant nearby. **All Rooms:** extended cable TV. **Cards:** AE, CB, DI, DS, MC, VI. **Special Amenities:** Free local telephone calls and preferred room (subject to availability with advanced reservations). *(See ad below)*

MT. WHITNEY MOTEL
Rates Subject to Change
Phone: (760)876-4207

AAA
◆
Motel

5/1-10/31　　　　　　　　　1P: $49- 70　2P/1B: $49- 70　2P/2B: $49- 79
2/1-4/30 & 11/1-1/31　　　　1P: $36- 49　2P/1B: $36- 49　2P/2B: $38- 55
Location: US 395. 305 N Main St 93545 (PO Box 722). Fax: 760/876-8818. **Terms:** Reserv deposit, 3 day notice. **Facility:** 29 rooms. Small rooms in original section to large, nicely furnished newer units. 2 stories; exterior corridors; small pool. **Dining:** Restaurant nearby. **All Rooms:** combo or shower baths, extended cable TV. **Some Rooms:** whirlpools. **Cards:** AE, DI, DS, MC, VI.

NATIONAL 9 TRAILS MOTEL
Rates Subject to Change
Phone: (760)876-5555

AAA
◆
Motel

3/1-10/31　　　　　　　　　1P: $45- 70　2P/1B: $49- 70　2P/2B: $49- 80　XP: $5
2/1-2/28 & 11/1-1/31　　　　1P: $36- 49　2P/1B: $36- 49　2P/2B: $39- 49　XP: $5
Location: 0.3 mi s on US 395. 633 S Main St 93545 (P.O. Box 65). Fax: 760/876-4650. **Terms:** Pets, $5 in smoking rooms only extra charge. **Facility:** 17 rooms. 1 story; exterior corridors; small pool. **Recreation:** fish freezing facilities. **All Rooms:** combo or shower baths. **Cards:** AE, CB, DI, DS, MC, VI.

THE PORTAL MOTEL

Rates Subject to Change

Phone: (760)876-5930

5/1-10/31	1P:	$49- 70	2P/1B:	$49- 70	2P/2B:	$49- 79	XP:	$4
2/1-4/30 & 11/1-1/31	1P:	$36- 49	2P/1B:	$36- 49	2P/2B:	$38- 55	XP:	$4

Ⓐ
◆
Motel

Location: US 395. 425 S Main St 93545 (PO Box 97). **Terms:** Reserv deposit, 3 day notice. **Facility:** 17 rooms. 1 story; exterior corridors. **Dining:** Coffee shop nearby. **All Rooms:** combo or shower baths. **Cards:** AE, DS, MC, VI.

RESTAURANTS

MERRY GO ROUND DINNER HOUSE Dinner: $10-$19 Phone: 760/876-4115

Ⓐ
◆
American

Location: On US 395 in center of town. 212 S Main St 93545. **Hours:** 5 pm-9 pm; 5/15-10/15 to 10 pm. Closed: 11/25 & 12/25. **Reservations:** suggested. **Features:** casual dress; carryout; beer & wine only; street parking. Small restaurant features charbroiled steak, lamb chops, chicken & seafood. Smoke free premises. **Cards:** CB, DI, DS, MC, VI.

SEASONS RESTAURANT Dinner: $15-$19 Phone: 760/876-8927

Ⓐ
◆◆
Continental

Location: Center, On US 395. 206 S Main St 93545. **Hours:** 5-9 pm, summer to 10 pm. Closed: 12/25 & Tue, Wed 11/1-4/1. **Reservations:** suggested. **Features:** casual dress; children's menu; health conscious menu; cocktails & lounge. Popular restaurant features chicken, seafood, lamb, veal, steak & pasta. Smoke free premises. **Cards:** DS, MC, VI.

LONG BEACH—*See Los Angeles p. 611.*

LOS ALTOS—26,300

RESTAURANT

PICCOLO MONDO RISTORANTE ITALIANO Lunch: $8-$14 Dinner: $20-$30 Phone: 650/968-5450

◆◆◆
Northern
Italian

Location: Between San Antonio & Rengstorff. 4926 El Camino Real 94022. **Hours:** 11:30 am-2:30 & 5:30-10:30 pm, Sat from 5:30. Closed major holidays & Sun. **Reservations:** suggested. **Features:** casual dress; cocktails & lounge; minimum charge-$8. Housemade pasta, good selection of traditional Italian dishes. Comfortable attractive atmosphere. **Cards:** AE, CB, DI, MC, VI.

What the Icons Mean

Member Services

- 🍸 Cocktail Lounge
- 🍴 Restaurant on Premises
- 🍴→ Restaurant off Premises *(walking distance)*
- 🛎 24 Hour Room Service
- 🎦 Nightclub
- 🎭 Entertainment
- ✈ Transportation to Airport
- 🐾 Pets Allowed

Special Features

- 🧒 Child Care
- 💼 Business Services
- 🧺 Laundry Service
- ♿ Fully Accessible
- 🚹 Semi-Accessible
- 🚿 Roll-in Showers
- 👂 Hearing Impaired
- 🅿 Valet Parking

Room Amenities

- ☕ Coffee Maker in Room
- 🍸 Honor Bar
- 💻 Data Port/Modem Line
- 📺 No Cable TV
- 🎬 Movies
- 📼 VCR
- 📻 Radio
- ⊠ Non-Smoking Rooms
- ▭ Microwaves
- 🔌 Refrigerator
- 🅰 No Air Conditioning
- ☎ No Telephones

Sports/Recreation

- 🏊 Pool
- 🏋 Fitness Center
- ⊠ Recreation Facilities

Safety Features

- Ⓢ Sprinklers
- Ⓓ Smoke Detectors
- 🔒 Safe

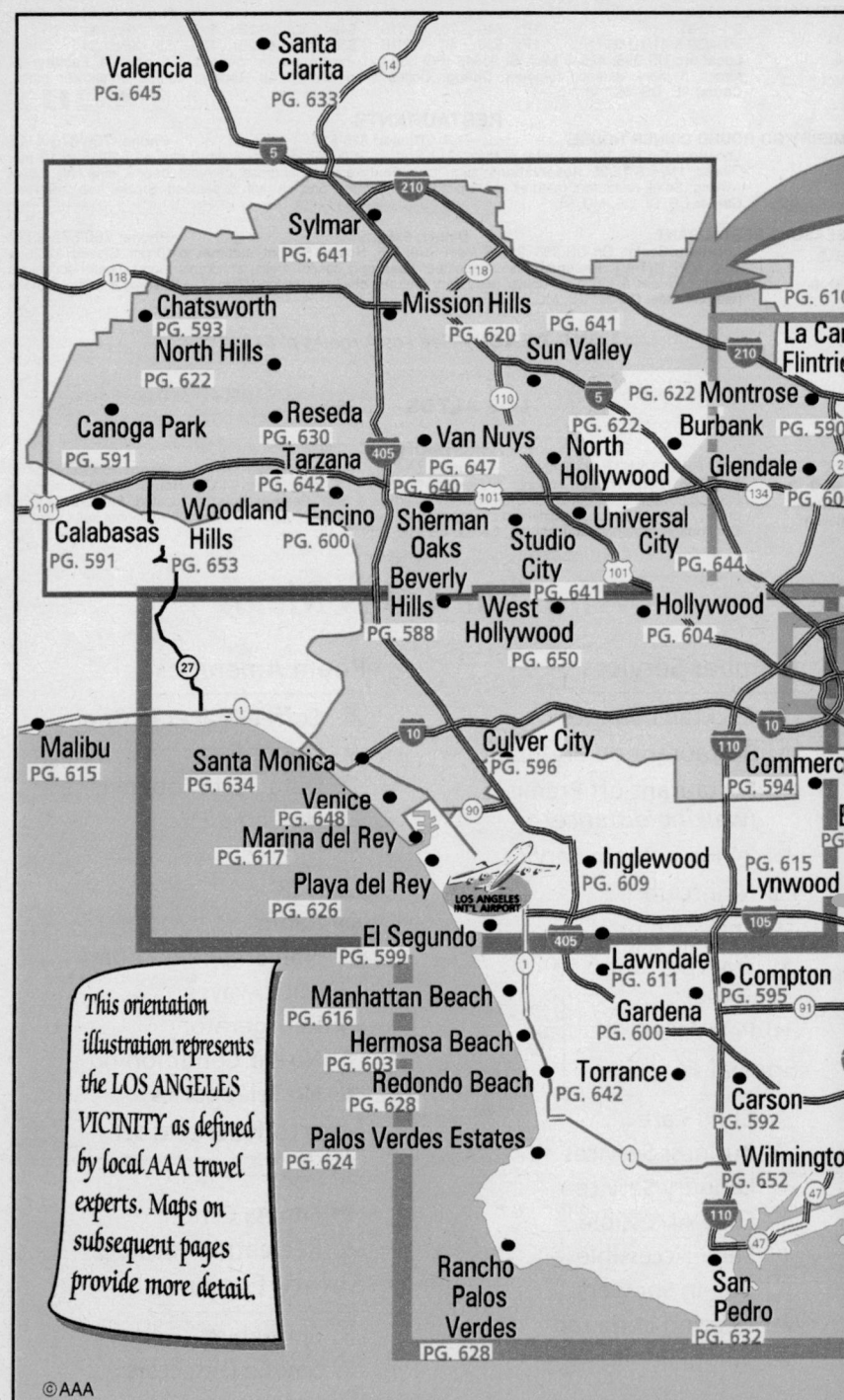

Valencia
PG. 645

Santa
Clarita
PG. 633

14

Sylmar
PG. 641

210

118

118

Chatsworth
PG. 593

North Hills
PG. 622

Mission Hills
PG. 620

PG. 641

Sun Valley

PG. 610

La Ca
Flintri

210

Canoga Park
PG. 591

Reseda
PG. 630

Tarzana
PG. 642

Van Nuys
PG. 647

5

110

PG. 622

PG. 622

North
Hollywood

Montrose
PG. 590

Burbank

Glendale
PG. 60

Woodland
Hills
PG. 653

Encino
PG. 600

405

Sherman
Oaks
PG. 640

Studio
City

Universal
City

PG. 644

134

101

2

Calabasas
PG. 591

101

Beverly
Hills
PG. 588

West
Hollywood
PG. 650

Studio
City
PG. 641

Hollywood
PG. 604

101

27

Malibu
PG. 615

1

Santa Monica
PG. 634

10

Culver City
PG. 596

10

110

Commerc
PG. 594

Venice
PG. 648

Marina del Rey
PG. 617

90

PG

Playa del Rey
PG. 626

LOS ANGELES
INT'L AIRPORT

Inglewood
PG. 609

PG. 615

Lynwood

El Segundo
PG. 599

405

105

This orientation
illustration represents
the LOS ANGELES
VICINITY as defined
by local AAA travel
experts. Maps on
subsequent pages
provide more detail.

Manhattan Beach
PG. 616

Hermosa Beach
PG. 603

Redondo Beach
PG. 628

Palos Verdes Estates
PG. 624

Lawndale
PG. 611

Gardena
PG. 600

Compton
PG. 595

91

Torrance
PG. 642

Carson
PG. 592

Wilmingto
PG. 652

1

47

Rancho
Palos
Verdes
PG. 628

110

47

San
Pedro
PG. 632

© AAA

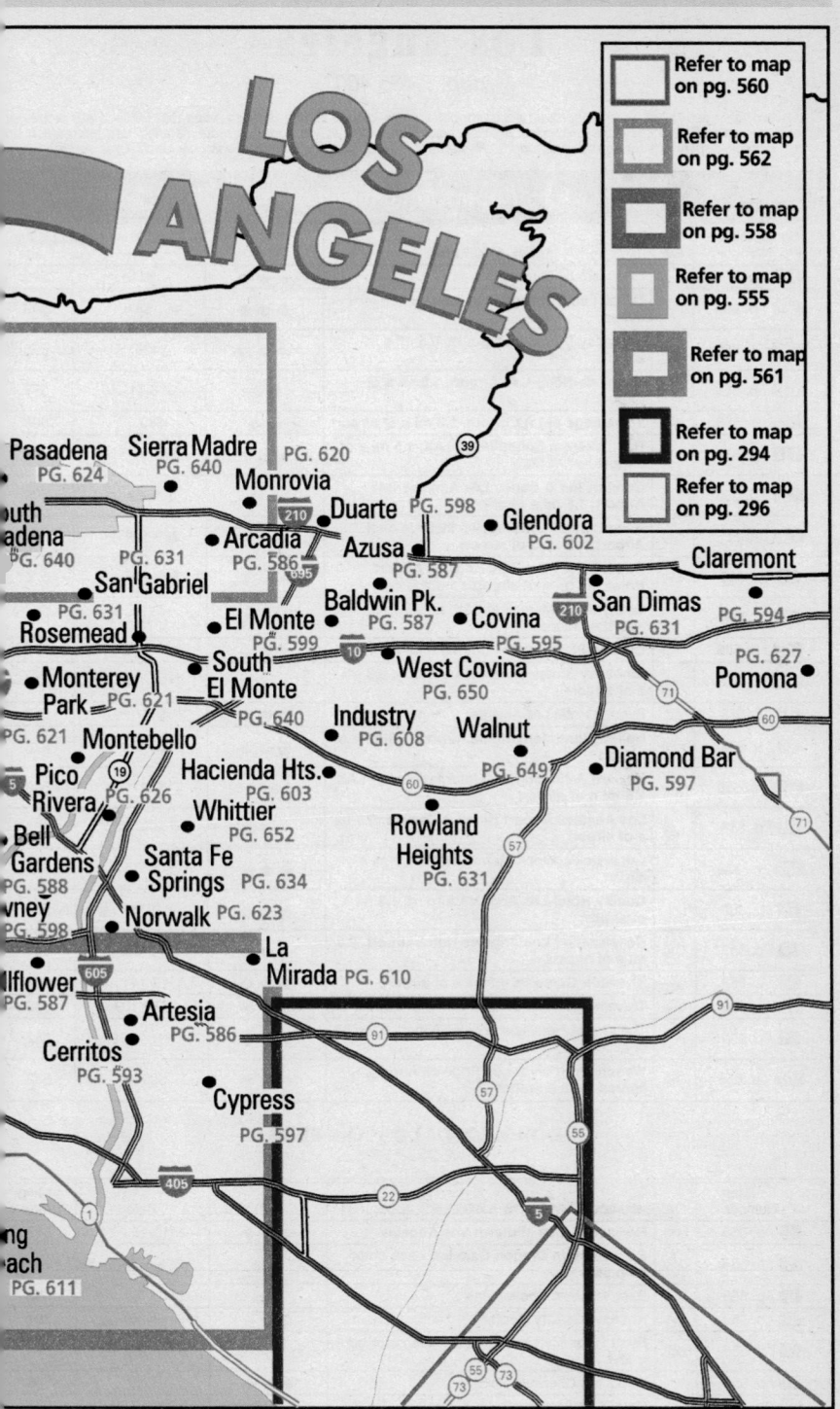

Refer to map on pg. 560
Refer to map on pg. 562
Refer to map on pg. 558
Refer to map on pg. 555
Refer to map on pg. 561
Refer to map on pg. 294
Refer to map on pg. 296

Pasadena PG. 624
Sierra Madre PG. 640
South Pasadena PG. 640
Monrovia
Duarte PG. 598
Glendora PG. 602
Claremont
Arcadia PG. 586
Azusa PG. 587
San Gabriel PG. 631
Baldwin Pk. PG. 587
Covina
San Dimas PG. 631
PG. 594
Rosemead PG. 631
El Monte PG. 599
West Covina PG. 650
PG. 595
Pomona PG. 627
Monterey Park PG. 621
South El Monte PG. 640
Industry PG. 608
Walnut PG. 649
Diamond Bar PG. 597
PG. 621
Montebello PG. 626
Hacienda Hts. PG. 603
Pico Rivera
Whittier PG. 652
Rowland Heights PG. 631
Bell Gardens PG. 588
Santa Fe Springs PG. 634
wney PG. 598
Norwalk PG. 623
La Mirada PG. 610
Ilflower PG. 587
Artesia PG. 586
Cerritos PG. 593
Cypress PG. 597
ng ach PG. 611

Los Angeles
pop. 3,485,400

This index helps you "spot" where approved accommodations are located on the detailed maps that follow. Rate ranges are for comparison only and show the property's high season. Turn to the listing page for more detailed rate information and consult display ads for special promotions. Restaurant rate range is for dinner unless only lunch (L) is served.

✈ Airport Accommodations

Spotter/Map Pg. Number	OA	LOS ANGELES	Rating	Rate	Listing Page
163 / p. 558		Courtyard by Marriott, 1.8 mi s of airport	◆◆◆	$119	599
165 / p. 558		Doubletree Club Hotel Los Angeles, 1.8 mi s of airport	◆◆◆	$87	599
164 / p. 558	⊕	Embassy Suites-LAX South, 0.5 mi s of airport	◆◆◆	$139 SAVE	599
160 / p. 558	⊕	Hacienda Hotel-L.A. Airport, 1.5 mi s of airport	◆◆	$58-71 SAVE	599
162 / p. 558	⊕	Travelodge at LAX South, 1.3 mi s of airport	◆◆	$69 SAVE	600
117 / p. 558	⊕	Best Western Suites Hotel-LAX, 1.5 mi e of airport	◆◆◆	$99-119 SAVE	609
126 / p. 558	⊕	Comfort Inn & Suites Los Angeles Int'l Airport, 1.5 mi e of airport	◆◆	$69-89 SAVE	609
115 / p. 558	⊕	Hampton Inn-Los Angeles International Airport, 1.5 mi e of airport	◆◆◆	$89-129 SAVE	609
95 / p. 558		Continental Plaza Los Angeles Airport Hotel, 0.5 mi e of airport	◆◆◆	$95-145 SAVE	570
66 / p. 558		Courtyard by Marriott at LAX, across from airport entrance	◆◆◆	$109-119	572
105 / p. 558	⊕	Crowne Plaza LA Airport, 0.3 mi e of airport	◆◆◆	$129 SAVE	573
103 / p. 558	⊕	Embassy Suites Hotel-LAX/Century, 0.5 mi e of airport	◆◆◆	$119-139 SAVE	575
84 / p. 558		Furama Hotel Los Angeles, 2 mi nw of airport	◆◆◆	$99-129	577
86 / p. 558	⊕	Holiday Inn-International Airport, 1.3 mi e of airport	◆◆◆	$129-159 SAVE	578
112 / p. 558	⊕	Howard Johnson Hotel International at LAX, 1.5 mi n of airport	◆◆	$79 SAVE	580
69 / p. 558	⊕	Los Angeles Airport Hilton & Towers, 0.8 mi e of airport	◆◆◆	$99 SAVE	580
104 / p. 558		Los Angeles Airport Marriott Hotel, 0.5 mi e of airport	◆◆◆	$145	580
76 / p. 558	⊕	Quality Hotel-Los Angeles Airport, 1.3 mi e of airport	◆◆◆	$110-150 SAVE	580
77 / p. 558	⊕	Renaissance Los Angeles Hotel-Airport, 0.5 mi e of airport	◆◆◆	$129	581
83 / p. 558		Sheraton Gateway, 0.3 mi e of airport	◆◆◆	$119-144 SAVE	582
92 / p. 558		Travelodge Hotel at Lax, 1 mi e of airport	◆◆◆	$79-109	582
71 / p. 558		The Westin Hotel-Los Angeles Airport, 1.3 mi e of airport	◆◆◆	$169-179	582
107 / p. 558	⊕	Wyndham Hotel at Los Angeles Airport, across from entrance	◆◆◆	$99 SAVE	582

DOWNTOWN LOS ANGELES

Spotter/Map Pg.Number	OA	DOWNTOWN LOS ANGELES - Lodgings	Rating	Rate	Listing Page
1 / p. 555	⊕	Radisson Hotel Midtown Los Angeles	◆◆◆	$110-150 SAVE	567
3 / p. 555	⊕	Best Western Dragon Gate Inn - see color ad p 563	◆◆	$69-109 SAVE	563
4 / p. 555		Best Western The Mayfair	◆◆	$113-133 SAVE	563
6 / p. 555		Holiday Inn City Center	◆◆◆	$119-149 SAVE	564
9 / p. 555	⊕	Hyatt Regency Los Angeles - see color ad p 565	◆◆◆◆	$190-225 SAVE	566
11 / p. 555		Wyndham Checkers Hotel	◆◆◆	$161	568
12 / p. 555	⊕	Omni Los Angeles Hotel & Centre	◆◆◆◆	$109-129	567

Spotter/Map Pg.Number	OA	DOWNTOWN LOS ANGELES - Lodgings (contd.)	Rating	Rate	Listing Page
13 / p. 555	⬡	The Regal Biltmore Hotel	◆◆◆◆	$235-315 ⬛	567
14 / p. 555	⬡	The Westin Bonaventure	◆◆◆	$95-199 ⬛	568
15 / p. 555	⬡	Los Angeles Downtown Marriott Hotel - see color ad p 566	◆◆◆	$145 ⬛	566
17 / p. 555		The New Otani Hotel	◆◆◆	$99	567
18 / p. 555		Kawada Hotel	◆◆	$99-109	566
19 / p. 555	⬡	Metro Plaza Hotel - see color ad p 567	◆◆	$75 ⬛	566
21 / p. 555		Hotel Inter-Continental Los Angeles at California Plaza	◆◆◆	$270	566
22 / p. 555		Wilshire Royale Howard Johnson Plaza	◆◆	$159-179	568
23 / p. 555	⬡	Ramada Inn-L.A. Downtown	◆◆◆	$75-118 ⬛	567
24 / p. 555	⬡	Holiday Inn-Downtown	◆◆◆	$89-99 ⬛	564
25 / p. 555		The Inn at 657	◆◆	$180	566
26 / p. 555		InTown Hotel	◆	$70-80	566
27 / p. 555		Miyako Inn	◆◆	$113-126	567
28 / p. 555	⬡	Vagabond Inn Figueroa	◆	$85 ⬛	567
29 / p. 555		Comfort Inn	◆	$69-96	564
		DOWNTOWN LOS ANGELES - Restaurants			
1 / p. 555	⬡	The Tower	◆◆◆	$35-45	569
3 / p. 555		Bernard's	◆◆◆◆	$25-34	568
5 / p. 555		A Thousand Cranes Restaurant	◆◆◆	$40-60	568
6 / p. 555		Little Joe's	◆	$8-22	568
7 / p. 555		Golden Dragon Restaurant	◆	$6-25	568
8 / p. 555		Engine Company No 28	◆◆	$10-20	568
11 / p. 555		Top of Five	◆◆◆	$20-30	568
12 / p. 555		McCormick & Schmick's	◆◆	$9-20	568
13 / p. 555		Orchid Gardens Restaurant	◆◆	$9-28	568
18 / p. 555		Water Grill	◆◆◆	$14-30	569
19 / p. 555		Brandy's Restaurant & Lounge	◆◆	$12-19	568
20 / p. 555		Checkers Restaurant	◆◆◆	$16-32	568

LOS ANGELES CENTRAL & WEST

Spotter/Map Pg.Number	OA	LOS ANGELES CENTRAL & WEST - Lodgings	Rating	Rate	Listing Page
63 / p. 558	⬡	Days Inn-Los Angeles	◆	$79 ⬛	574
64 / p. 558	⬡	Radisson Wilshire Plaza Hotel - see ad p 581	◆◆◆	$149-199 ⬛	581
65 / p. 558	⬡	Comfort Inn Towne - see ad p 573	◆	$72 ⬛	570
66 / p. 558		Courtyard by Marriott at LAX	◆◆◆	$109-119	572
67 / p. 558	⬡	Renaissance Beverly Hills	◆◆◆	$205-250 ⬛	581
68 / p. 558	⬡	Beverly Laurel Motor Hotel - see ad p 571	◆	$69-79 ⬛	570
69 / p. 558	⬡	Los Angeles Airport Hilton & Towers - see ad p 119	◆◆◆	$99 ⬛	580
70 / p. 558	⬡	Four Seasons Hotel	◆◆◆◆	$355-400 ⬛	576
71 / p. 558		The Westin Hotel-Los Angeles Airport	◆◆◆	$169-179	582
72 / p. 558	⬡	Best Western Mid-Wilshire Plaza Hotel	◆◆	$64-74 ⬛	569
73 / p. 558	⬡	Farmer's Daughter Motel	◆	$65-69 ⬛	575
75 / p. 558	⬡	Doubletree Hotel-Los Angeles/Westwood, Beverly Hills Area - see color ad p 574	◆◆◆	$140-175 ⬛	575
76 / p. 558	⬡	Quality Hotel-Los Angeles Airport - see color ad p 570	◆◆◆	$110-150 ⬛	580
77 / p. 558	⬡	Renaissance Los Angeles Hotel-Airport	◆◆◆	$129	581
79 / p. 558	⬡	Dunes Motor Hotel-Wilshire - see ad p 575	◆◆	$73	575
80 / p. 558	⬡	Beverly Plaza Hotel	◆◆◆	$165 ⬛	570
82 / p. 558		Holiday Inn Select	◆◆◆	$129	578
83 / p. 558	⬡	Sheraton Gateway	◆◆◆	$119-144 ⬛	582

Spotter/Map Pg.Number	OA	LOS ANGELES CENTRAL & WEST - Lodgings (contd.)	Rating	Rate	Listing Page
84 / p. 558		Furama Hotel Los Angeles - see color ad p 577	◆◆◆	$99-129	577
85 / p. 558	ⓐ	Econo Lodge Mid-Wilshire - see color ad p 575	◆	$59-69 SAVE	575
86 / p. 558	ⓐ	Holiday Inn-International Airport - see color ad p 578	◆◆◆	$129-159 SAVE	578
87 / p. 558	ⓐ	Century Plaza Hotel & Tower	◆◆◆◆	$330-435 SAVE	570
88 / p. 558	ⓐ	Courtyard by Marriott Century City/Beverly Hills - see color ad p 573	◆◆◆	$126 SAVE	572
89 / p. 558	ⓐ	Holiday Inn Express- Century City	◆◆◆	$109 SAVE	578
90 / p. 558		Oxford Palace Hotel	◆◆◆	$90-105	580
91 / p. 558	ⓐ	Best Western Westwood Pacific Hotel	◆◆◆	$105 SAVE	569
92 / p. 558	ⓐ	Travelodge Hotel at Lax - see color ad p 569	◆◆◆	$79-109	582
93 / p. 558		Hotel Bel-Air	◆◆◆◆	$410-2500	578
94 / p. 558		Hotel Del Capri	◆◆◆	$105-150 SAVE	580
95 / p. 558	ⓐ	Continental Plaza Los Angeles Airport Hotel	◆◆◆	$95-145 SAVE	570
96 / p. 558	ⓐ	Hilgard House Hotel - see ad p 578	◆◆◆	$124 SAVE	578
97 / p. 558		Ramada Limited/West Los Angeles/UCLA	◆◆	$95-120	581
98 / p. 558		Westwood Marquis Hotel and Gardens	◆◆◆◆	$260-650	582
99 / p. 558	ⓐ	Best Western Royal Palace Inn & Suites	◆◆◆	$69-110 SAVE	569
100 / p. 558	ⓐ	Travelodge-Los Angeles West	◆	$85-95 SAVE	582
101 / p. 558	ⓐ	Summit Hotel, Bel-Air	◆◆◆	$130	582
102 / p. 558	ⓐ	Park Hyatt Los Angeles at Century City - see color ad p 565	◆◆◆◆	$294-424 SAVE	580
103 / p. 558	ⓐ	Embassy Suites Hotel-LAX/Century	◆◆◆	$119-139 SAVE	575
104 / p. 558		Los Angeles Airport Marriott Hotel	◆◆◆	$145	580
105 / p. 558	ⓐ	Crowne Plaza LA Airport - see ad p 573	◆◆◆	$129 SAVE	573
107 / p. 558	ⓐ	Wyndham Hotel at Los Angeles Airport - see color ad p 581	◆◆◆	$99 SAVE	582
108 / p. 558		Hotel Sofitel	◆◆◆◆	$340-400	580
109 / p. 558	ⓐ	Carlyle Inn - see color ad p 571	◆◆◆	$109-129 SAVE	570
111 / p. 558	ⓐ	Hotel Nikko at Beverly Hills	◆◆◆◆	$335-720 SAVE	580
112 / p. 558	ⓐ	Howard Johnson Hotel International at LAX - see color ad opposite inside back cover	◆◆	$79 SAVE	580
113 / p. 558	ⓐ	La Mirage Inn	◆	$60 SAVE	580
114 / p. 558		Brentwood Motor Hotel	◆	$94	570
		LOS ANGELES CENTRAL & WEST - Restaurants			
42 / p. 558		The Restaurant	◆◆◆◆	$35-55	584
43 / p. 558		Dynasty Room	◆◆◆◆	$50-75	583
44 / p. 558		Daily Grill	◆◆	$9-19	583
45 / p. 558		Sisley Italian Kitchen	◆◆	$8-22	584
46 / p. 558		Gardens	◆◆◆◆	$28-38	583
47 / p. 558		Campanile	◆◆◆	$22-50	582
49 / p. 558		Panda Inn	◆◆	$9-13	583
50 / p. 558		La Cachette Restaurant	◆◆◆	$18-30	583
51 / p. 558		The Chez	◆◆◆	$12-23	582
52 / p. 558		Sonora Cafe	◆◆	$15-25	584
53 / p. 558		Chaya Brasserie	◆◆◆	$25-40	582
54 / p. 558		El Cholo	◆◆	$6-12	583
55 / p. 558	ⓐ	Junior's Restaurant	◆	$7-10	583
61 / p. 558		Primi	◆◆◆	$12-25	584
62 / p. 558		Le Chardonnay	◆◆◆◆	$19-28	583
63 / p. 558		Patina	◆◆◆◆	$25-35	584
64 / p. 558		Citrus	◆◆◆	$24-30	582
66 / p. 558		La Bruschetta	◆◆	$12-22	583
68 / p. 558		Four Oaks	◆◆◆	$20-30	583
69 / p. 558		Lunaria	◆◆◆	$15-35	583
70 / p. 558		L'Orangerie	◆◆◆◆◆	$35-50	583

Los Angeles Vicinity

Spotter/Map Pg.Number	OA	LAWNDALE - Lodgings	Rating	Rate	Listing Page
1 / p. 561	⊕	Best Western South Bay Hotel	◆◆	$59-125 SAVE	611
2 / p. 561	⊕	Days Inn Airport South Bay - see color ad p 576	◆◆	$58-74 SAVE	611
		ARCADIA - Lodgings			
1 / p. 562		Embassy Suites	◆◆◆	$149-169	586
2 / p. 562		Hampton Inn	◆◆◆	$89-109	586
4 / p. 562		Residence Inn by Marriott	◆◆◆	$101-139	586
		ARCADIA - Restaurants			
① / p. 562		Chez Sateau	◆◆	$10-21	586
② / p. 562		Sesame Grill	◆◆	$9-17	586
③ / p. 562		The Derby Restaurant	◆◆	$11-26	586
		COMPTON - Lodgings			
3 / p. 561		Radisson The New Crystal Park Hotel & Casino	◆◆◆	$79	595
		MONROVIA - Lodgings			
6 / p. 562		Homestead Village	◆◆◆	$329-434	621
7 / p. 562		Holiday Inn - see ad p 620	◆◆◆	$89-159	620
8 / p. 562		Wyndham Garden Hotel - see color ad p 621	◆◆◆	$99	621
9 / p. 562	⊕	Oak Tree Inn - see ad p 620	◆	$49-60	621
10 / p. 562		Comfort Inn Monrovia/Duarte	◆◆	$60-70	620
		MONROVIA - Restaurants			
④ / p. 562		Claim Jumper Restaurant	◆◆	$10-25	621
⑤ / p. 562		La Parisienne	◆◆	$15-23	621
⑥ / p. 562		Restaurant Devon	◆◆◆	$11-27	621
		HERMOSA BEACH - Lodgings			
9 / p. 561		Beach House Inn At Hermosa Beach - see color ad p 603	◆◆◆	$179-299	603
10 / p. 561	⊕	Hotel Hermosa	◆◆◆	$79-165 SAVE	603
11 / p. 561	⊕	Quality Inn & Suites - see color ad p 603	◆◆◆	$84-104 SAVE	604
		PASADENA - Lodgings			
14 / p. 562	⊕	Comfort Inn	◆◆◆	$67-80 SAVE	624
15 / p. 562	⊕	Best Western Colorado Inn	◆◆	$70 SAVE	624
16 / p. 562	⊕	Saga Motor Hotel - see color ad p 625	◆◆	$69-74 SAVE	625
17 / p. 562		The Ritz Carlton, Huntington Hotel	◆◆◆◆	$215-325	625
18 / p. 562		Pasadena Hilton - see ad p 119	◆◆◆	$109	624
19 / p. 562		Holiday Inn-Convention Center	◆◆◆	$144-154	624
20 / p. 562	⊕	Doubletree Hotel-Pasadena	◆◆◆◆	$165-319 SAVE	624
21 / p. 562	⊕	Westway Inn	◆◆	$65-72 SAVE	625
22 / p. 562	⊕	Best Western Pasadena Royale - see ad p 624	◆◆◆	$70-96 SAVE	624
23 / p. 562	⊕	Best Western Pasadena Inn - see ad p 624	◆◆	$67-85 SAVE	624
24 / p. 562	⊕	Quality Inn Pasadena	◆◆◆	$69-75 SAVE	625
25 / p. 562	⊕	Super 8	◆	$56	625
27 / p. 562	⊕	Travelodge-Pasadena Central	◆	$60-65 SAVE	625
29 / p. 562	⊕	Vagabond Inn	◆◆	$73 SAVE	625
		PASADENA - Restaurants			
⑦ / p. 562		Patakan	◆	$8-12	626
⑧ / p. 562		Parkway Grill	◆◆◆	$12-24	626
⑨ / p. 562		Saladang	◆◆	$9-15	626
⑩ / p. 562		McCormick & Schmicks	◆◆	$7-22	626
⑪ / p. 562		Bistro 45	◆◆◆	$20-30	625
⑫ / p. 562		The Raymond Restaurant	◆◆◆	$26-45	626
⑬ / p. 562		Yujean Kang's	◆◆	$9-18	626
⑭ / p. 562		The Grill	◆◆◆	$24-50	626
⑮ / p. 562		Mi Piace	◆◆	$7-13	626

Spotter/Map Pg.Number	OA	PASADENA - Restaurants (contd.)	Rating	Rate	Listing Page
⑯ / p. 562		Kathleen's	◆◆	$12-18	626
⑰ / p. 562		Arroyo Chop House	◆◆◆	$30-60	625
⑲ / p. 562		Spencers	◆◆◆	$10-24	626
		REDONDO BEACH - Lodgings			
⑮ / p. 561	⊕	**Best Western Galleria Inn - see color ad p 571 , p 628**	◆◆◆	$64-84 ⛊	628
⑯ / p. 561	⊕	**Crowne Plaza Redondo Beach & Marina Hotel**	◆◆◆	$119	629
⑱ / p. 561	⊕	**Best Western Sunrise at Redondo Beach - see color ad p 629**	◆◆◆	$109-119 ⛊	629
⑲ / p. 561	⊕	**Portofino Hotel & Yacht Club**	◆◆◆	$150-194	629
⑳ / p. 561	⊕	**Travelodge-Redondo Beach Pier**	◆	$77 ⛊	630
㉒ / p. 561	⊕	**Palos Verdes Inn - see ad p 629**	◆◆◆	$120-140 ⛊	629
㉓ / p. 561	⊕	**Vagabond Inn**	◆	$90 ⛊	630
㉔ / p. 561	⊕	**Best Western Redondo Beach Inn - see ad p 628**	◆◆◆	$79-94 ⛊	628
		REDONDO BEACH - Restaurants			
⑧ / p. 561		The Blue Moon Saloon	◆	$17-27	630
⑩ / p. 561		Splash	◆◆◆	$10-28	630
⑪ / p. 561		Le Beaujolais	◆◆	$16-27	630
⑭ / p. 561		Chez Melange	◆◆◆	$12-22	630
		NORTH HOLLYWOOD - Lodgings			
㉕ / p. 560	⊕	**Colony Inn - see color ad p 622**	◆◆	$71-79 ⛊	623
㉖ / p. 560	⊕	**Beverly Garland's Holiday Inn - see color ad p 623**	◆◆◆	$99-134	622
㉗ / p. 560	⊕	**Mikado Best Western Motor Hotel**	◆◆	$99-109 ⛊	623
		NORTH HOLLYWOOD - Restaurants			
⑲ / p. 560	⊕	**Mikado Restaurant**	◆◆	$16-20	623
⑳ / p. 560		Paradise Restaurant	◆	$8-16	623
		TORRANCE - Lodgings			
㉘ / p. 561		Summerfield Suites Hotel	◆◆◆	$135	643
㉙ / p. 561	⊕	Del Amo Inn	◆	$60-65 ⛊	642
㉚ / p. 561		Residence Inn by Marriott	◆◆◆	$109-168	643
㉛ / p. 561		Ramada Limited	◆◆	$65	643
㉜ / p. 561		Torrance Hilton at South Bay - see ad p 119	◆◆◆	$144-179	643
㉞ / p. 561		Torrance Marriott	◆◆◆	$84-174	643
㉟ / p. 561		Courtyard by Marriott/Torrance South Bay - see color ad p 618, p 563	◆◆◆	$99	642
㊱ / p. 561	⊕	**Holiday Inn Torrance**	◆◆◆	$160-170 ⛊	643
㊳ / p. 561		Courtyard by Marriott/Torrance Del Amo - see color ad p 563	◆◆◆	$69-99	642
㊴ / p. 561	⊕	**Travelodge**	◆◆	$65 ⛊	643
㊵ / p. 561	⊕	**Ramada Inn - see ad p 643**	◆◆	$65-75 ⛊	643
		TORRANCE - Restaurants			
⑱ / p. 561		Jasmines	◆◆◆	$15-35	644
⑳ / p. 561		The Ginger Cafe	◆◆	$8-18	644
㉑ / p. 561		South Bay Grill	◆◆	$7-15	644
		SHERMAN OAKS - Lodgings			
㉘ / p. 560	⊕	**Radisson Valley Center - see color ad p 584**	◆◆◆	$129	640
㉙ / p. 560	⊕	**Carriage Inn**	◆◆	$85 ⛊	640
		SHERMAN OAKS - Restaurant			
㉑ / p. 560		Valley Inn	◆◆	$14-27	640
		UNIVERSAL CITY - Lodgings			
㉛ / p. 560	⊕	**Sheraton Universal Hotel, at Universal Studios**	◆◆◆	$178 ⛊	644
㉜ / p. 560	⊕	**Universal City Hilton & Towers, at Universal Studios - see ad p 119, p 645**	◆◆◆	$150-190 ⛊	645

Spotter/Map Pg.Number	OA	GLENDALE - Lodgings	Rating	Rate	Listing Page
32 / p. 562	AAA	Best Western Eagle Rock Inn - see ad p 600	◆◆	$85-110 SAVE	600
33 / p. 562	AAA	Comfort Inn-Eagle Rock	◆◆	$59-110 SAVE	601
34 / p. 562	AAA	Econo Lodge - see ad p 601	◆	$60-70 SAVE	602
35 / p. 562	AAA	Best Western Golden Key Motor Hotel - see color ad p 601	◆◆◆	$119-149 SAVE	600
36 / p. 562	AAA	Red Lion Hotel/Glendale	◆◆◆	$149-169 SAVE	602
38 / p. 562	AAA	Chariot Inn Motel - see color ad p 601	◆	$60-70 SAVE	601
39 / p. 562	AAA	Vagabond Inn	◆	$85-95 SAVE	602
		GLENDALE - Restaurants			
20 / p. 562		Rusty Pelican	◆◆	$13-26	602
21 / p. 562		La Fontana Italian Kitchen	◆◆◆	$9-16	602
22 / p. 562		Panda Inn	◆◆	$10-16	602
24 / p. 562		Far Niente	◆◆	$9-20	602
25 / p. 562		Fresco Ristorante	◆◆◆	$16-25	602
26 / p. 562		Tam O'Shanter Inn	◆◆	$10-20	602
27 / p. 562		Fortune Inn	◆◆	$6-12	602
28 / p. 562		Jax Bar & Grill	◆◆	$10-20	602
		VAN NUYS - Lodgings			
33 / p. 560	AAA	Travelodge Van Nuys-Sepulveda - see color ad p 648	◆	$55 SAVE	648
34 / p. 560	AAA	Airtel Plaza Hotel - see ad p 648	◆◆◆	$94	647
		VAN NUYS - Restaurant			
22 / p. 560		Matterhorn Chef Restaurant	◆◆	$8-20	648
		SUN VALLEY - Lodgings			
37 / p. 560	AAA	Emerson Inn	◆	$43-45	641
		STUDIO CITY - Lodgings			
39 / p. 560	AAA	Sportsmen's Lodge Hotel - see color ad p 585	◆◆◆	$120-135 SAVE	641
40 / p. 560	AAA	Days Inn	◆	$79 SAVE	641
41 / p. 560		Universal City Inn	◆◆	$70	641
		STUDIO CITY - Restaurant			
24 / p. 560		Marrakesh Restaurant	◆◆	$17-22	641
		CANOGA PARK - Lodgings			
42 / p. 560	AAA	Best Western Canoga Park Motor Inn - see ad p 592	◆	$59-69 SAVE	591
43 / p. 560		Clarion Suites Warner Center - see color ad p 592	◆◆◆	$114-154	592
44 / p. 560		Days Inn	◆	$70-95	592
		SOUTH PASADENA - Lodgings			
45 / p. 562		Artist's Inn	◆◆◆	$115-165	640
46 / p. 562		The Bissell House Bed & Breakfast	◆◆◆	$115-160	640
		SOUTH PASADENA - Restaurants			
30 / p. 562		Oak Tree Inn	◆◆	$7-15	641
31 / p. 562		Shiro	◆◆◆	$14-20	641
		CHATSWORTH - Lodgings			
46 / p. 560		The Chatsworth Hotel	◆◆◆	$140-200	593
47 / p. 560		Ramada Inn - see color ad p 593	◆	$69-79	593
48 / p. 560	AAA	7-Star Suites Hotel - see color ad p 593	◆◆◆	$49-119 SAVE	594
49 / p. 560		Summerfield Suites Hotel	◆◆◆	$164	594
		WILMINGTON - Lodgings			
46 / p. 561	AAA	Best Western Los Angeles Worldport - see color ad p 652	◆◆◆	$64-135 SAVE	652
		SAN PEDRO - Lodgings			
48 / p. 561	AAA	Holiday Inn San Pedro-LA Harbor - see color ad p 632	◆◆◆	$99-149 SAVE	632
49 / p. 561	AAA	Vagabond Inn	◆	$85 SAVE	633

Spotter/Map Pg.Number	OA	SAN PEDRO - Lodgings (contd.)	Rating	Rate	Listing Page
50 / p. 561	⊕	**Best Western Sunrise Hotel - see color ad p 632**	◆◆	$80-95 ⛨	632
51 / p. 561		Sheraton-Los Angeles Harbor Hotel	◆◆◆	$118-158	633
52 / p. 561		San Pedro Hilton at Cabrillo Marina - see color ad p 633 & ad p 119	◆◆◆	$189-199	633
		SAN PEDRO - Restaurants			
31 / p. 561		Simon's Restaurant	◆◆	$18-30	633
32 / p. 561		Madeo Ristorante	◆◆◆	$11-21	633
		WOODLAND HILLS - Lodgings			
51 / p. 560	⊕	**Holiday Inn-Woodland Hills**	◆◆◆	$109-119 ⛨	653
52 / p. 560	⊕	**Vagabond Inn**	◆◆	$80 ⛨	653
53 / p. 560		Woodland Hills Hilton & Towers - see ad p 119	◆◆◆	$169	653
54 / p. 560	⊕	**Warner Center Marriott Hotel**	◆◆◆	$155 ⛨	653
		WOODLAND HILLS - Restaurants			
28 / p. 560		Piacere	◆◆	$9-20	653
29 / p. 560		Plum Tree Inn	◆◆	$10-16	653
31 / p. 560		Bob Burns Restaurant	◆◆	$15-30	653
32 / p. 560		Adagio Ristorante	◆◆	$15-25	653
		SAN GABRIEL - Lodgings			
51 / p. 562	⊕	**Quality Inn**	◆◆	$60-66 ⛨	631
		SAN GABRIEL - Restaurant			
45 / p. 562		Tung Lai Shun Restaurant	◆	$6-19	631
		TARZANA - Lodgings			
56 / p. 560	⊕	**Days Inn - see color ad p 642**	◆◆	$79-89 ⛨	642
		CARSON - Lodgings			
57 / p. 561		Hampton Inn	◆◆◆	$62-70	592
59 / p. 561		Carson Hilton at The Civic Plaza Conference Center - see ad p 119	◆◆◆	$89	592
60 / p. 561	⊕	**Comfort Inn**	◆◆	$65-85 ⛨	592
		ENCINO - Lodgings			
58 / p. 560	⊕	**Tokyo Princess Inn**	◆◆◆	$99-129	600
		CALABASAS - Lodgings			
59 / p. 560		Country Inn at Calabasas - see color ad p 591	◆◆◆	$99	591
		CALABASAS - Restaurants			
38 / p. 560		Gaetano's Ristorante	◆◆◆	$13-26	591
39 / p. 560		Saddle Peak Lodge	◆◆◆◆	$25-50	591
40 / p. 560	⊕	**Cosmos Grill & Rotisserie**	◆◆	$5-13	591
		BURBANK - Lodgings			
60 / p. 560	⊕	**Burbank Airport Hilton & Convention Center - see ad p 119, p 644**	◆◆◆	$155-205 ⛨	590
61 / p. 560		Holiday Inn-Burbank	◆◆◆	$119-145	590
62 / p. 560	⊕	**The Anabelle - see color ad p 590**	◆	$160-210 ⛨	590
63 / p. 560	⊕	**Safari Inn - see color ad p 590**	◆◆	$94-124 ⛨	590
64 / p. 560	⊕	**Burbank Inn & Suites**	◆◆◆	$77-87	590
		BURBANK - Restaurants			
41 / p. 560		Bobby McGee's Comglomeration	◆	$7-20	591
42 / p. 560		Dalt's Classic American Grill	◆◆	$6-13	591
		ARTESIA - Lodgings			
63 / p. 561		Best Western Pioneer Inn - see color ad p 586	◆◆	$69-99	586
		CERRITOS - Lodgings			
66 / p. 561		Sheraton Cerritos Hotel at Towne Center	◆◆◆	$97	593
		CERRITOS - Restaurant			
35 / p. 561		Arte Cafe	◆◆◆	$11-19	593

Spotter/Map Pg.Number	OA	**LONG BEACH** - Lodgings	Rating	Rate	Listing Page
68 / p. 561	⊕	**Best Western of Long Beach** - see color ad p 611	◆ ◆	$64 〔SAVE〕	611
69 / p. 561	⊕	**Comfort Inn Downtown**	◆ ◆	$79-89 〔SAVE〕	612
70 / p. 561	⊕	**Long Beach Hilton** - see ad p 119	◆ ◆ ◆ ◆	$119-189 〔SAVE〕	613
71 / p. 561	⊕	**Super 8 Motel-Long Beach Traffic Circle** - see color ad p 613	◆ ◆	$59-69 〔SAVE〕	614
72 / p. 561		**Renaissance Long Beach Hotel**	◆ ◆ ◆ ◆	$129-149	614
73 / p. 561	⊕	**Hyatt Regency Long Beach** - see color ad p 565	◆ ◆ ◆	$195-235 〔SAVE〕	613
74 / p. 561		The Westin Long Beach	◆ ◆ ◆	$218-236	614
75 / p. 561		Courtyard by Marriott - Downtown - see color ad p 612	◆ ◆ ◆	$92	612
76 / p. 561	⊕	**Travelodge Convention Center**	◆	$49-99 〔SAVE〕	614
77 / p. 561	⊕	**Inn of Long Beach**	◆	$55-89	613
78 / p. 561	⊕	**GuestHouse Hotel** - see color ad p 612	◆ ◆ ◆	$73 〔SAVE〕	613
80 / p. 561	⊕	**Best Western Golden Sails Hotel** - see ad p 611	◆ ◆	$128-148 〔SAVE〕	611
81 / p. 561		Long Beach Marriott	◆ ◆ ◆	$170	614
82 / p. 561	⊕	**Holiday Inn-Long Beach Airport** - see color ad p 612	◆ ◆	$75-85 〔SAVE〕	613
83 / p. 561		West Coast Long Beach Hotel - see color ad p 613	◆ ◆ ◆	$89	614
		LONG BEACH - Restaurants			
43 / p. 561		Parkers' Lighthouse	◆ ◆	$13-29	614
44 / p. 561		Johnny Reb's	◆	$9-13	614
46 / p. 561		L'Opera Ristorante	◆ ◆ ◆	$14-27	614
47 / p. 561		Colonial Buffet	◆ ◆	$8	614
48 / p. 561		Gazzella	◆ ◆	$8-17	614
50 / p. 561		Simon & Seafort's Steak, Chop & Oyster House	◆ ◆	$16-25	615
52 / p. 561		555 East	◆ ◆ ◆	$16-28	614
54 / p. 561		Fish Tale	◆ ◆	$12-26	614
56 / p. 561		Shenandoah Cafe	◆ ◆ ◆	$12-22	615
		MISSION HILLS - Lodgings			
69 / p. 560	⊕	**Best Western Mission Hills Inn** - see color ad p 585	◆ ◆	$72-78 〔SAVE〕	620
		RESEDA - Lodgings			
77 / p. 560	⊕	**Howard Johnson Lodge** - see color ad opposite inside back cover, p 630	◆ ◆	$55 〔SAVE〕	630
		SYLMAR - Lodgings			
80 / p. 560	⊕	**Rodeway Inn**	◆ ◆	$62 〔SAVE〕	641
81 / p. 560	⊕	**Good Nite Inn**	◆	$56 〔SAVE〕	641
		SEAL BEACH - Lodgings			
84 / p. 561		Radisson Inn of Seal Beach	◆ ◆ ◆	$118	1043
		SEAL BEACH - Restaurant			
60 / p. 561		Spaghettini	◆ ◆ ◆	$14-19	1043
		NORTH HILLS - Lodgings			
85 / p. 560	⊕	**Howard Johnson Inn** - see color ad opposite inside back cover	◆	$49-69 〔SAVE〕	622
		INGLEWOOD - Lodgings			
115 / p. 558	⊕	**Hampton Inn-Los Angeles International Airport** - see color ad p 599, p 564	◆ ◆ ◆	$89-129 〔SAVE〕	609
116 / p. 558	⊕	**Econo Lodge LAX**	◆	$50 〔SAVE〕	609
117 / p. 558	⊕	**Best Western Suites Hotel-LAX** - see color ad p 572	◆ ◆ ◆	$99-119 〔SAVE〕	609
118 / p. 558	⊕	**Touristlodge Inglewood-LAX**	◆ ◆	$45 〔SAVE〕	609
119 / p. 558	⊕	**Best Western Airport Plaza Inn** - see color ad p 576	◆ ◆	$68-86 〔SAVE〕	609
120 / p. 558	⊕	**Ramada Limited LAX**	◆ ◆	$78-88 〔SAVE〕	609
122 / p. 558	⊕	**Rodeway Inn**	◆ ◆	$55-70 〔SAVE〕	609

Spotter/Map Pg.Number	OA	INGLEWOOD - Lodgings (contd.)	Rating	Rate	Listing Page
123 / p. 558	⊕	Super 8 Motel-Airport	◆◆	$49-59 SAVE	609
124 / p. 558	⊕	Days Inn Airport Maingate - see color ad p 576	◆	$64-74 SAVE	609
125 / p. 558	⊕	Best Western Airpark Hotel - see color ad p 572	◆◆◆	$74-88 SAVE	609
126 / p. 558	⊕	Comfort Inn & Suites Los Angeles Int'l Airport - see color ad p 574	◆◆	$69-89 SAVE	609
		CULVER CITY - Lodgings			
127 / p. 558	⊕	Sunburst Motel	◆	$69-99 SAVE	597
128 / p. 558	⊕	Holiday Inn Express - see color ad p 596	◆◆	$89-99 SAVE	596
129 / p. 558		Culver City Travelodge - see ad p 596	◆◆	$63-70	596
130 / p. 558		Wyndham Garden Hotel - see color ad p 595	◆◆◆	$89	597
131 / p. 558	⊕	Ramada Plaza Hotel-Lax International Airport North - see color ad p 597	◆◆	$99	597
132 / p. 558	⊕	Radisson Hotel-Los Angeles Airport	◆◆◆	$210 SAVE	596
		WEST HOLLYWOOD - Lodgings			
133 / p. 558	⊕	Ramada Plaza Hotel	◆◆◆	$149-249 SAVE	651
134 / p. 558		Wyndham Bel Age Hotel	◆◆◆	$214	651
135 / p. 558	⊕	Park Sunset Hotel	◆◆	$79 SAVE	651
137 / p. 558	⊕	Hyatt West Hollywood - see color ad p 565	◆◆◆	$199-274 SAVE	651
138 / p. 558	⊕	Best Western Sunset Plaza Hotel - see ad p 579	◆◆◆	$85-115 SAVE	650
139 / p. 558	⊕	Le Reve Hotel	◆◆◆	$129-205 SAVE	651
140 / p. 558		Le Parc Hotel	◆◆◆	$225-275	651
141 / p. 558		Sunset Marquis Hotel & Villas	◆◆◆◆	$275-1500	651
142 / p. 558		Le Montrose Suite Hotel De Gran Luxe	◆◆◆	$270-440	651
143 / p. 558		Summerfield Suites Hotel	◆◆◆	$169-199	651
144 / p. 558		The Argyle	◆◆◆	$219	650
		WEST HOLLYWOOD - Restaurants			
72 / p. 558		Le Dome	◆◆◆	$18-26	652
73 / p. 558		Diaghilev	◆◆◆◆	$50-75	651
75 / p. 558		Palm Restaurant	◆◆	$35-50	652
76 / p. 558		Fenix at the Argyle	◆◆◆	$12-27	651
		HOLLYWOOD - Lodgings			
145 / p. 558	⊕	Hollywood Orchid Suites	◆◆	$85-119 SAVE	606
146 / p. 558	⊕	Club Hotel by Doubletree - see color ad p 605	◆◆◆	$149-159 SAVE	605
147 / p. 558	⊕	Best Western Hollywood Plaza Inn - see color ad p 604	◆◆◆	$89-119 SAVE	604
148 / p. 558	⊕	Best Western Hollywood Hills - see ad p 571	◆◆◆	$79-129 SAVE	604
149 / p. 558	⊕	Dunes Motel-Sunset - see ad p 575	◆	$73	606
150 / p. 558	⊕	Days Inn-Hollywood - see color ad p 605	◆◆	$65-199 SAVE	605
151 / p. 558	⊕	Travelodge-Sunset/La Brea	◆	$65-75 SAVE	608
152 / p. 558	⊕	Ramada Limited - see ad p 607	◆◆◆	$69-99 SAVE	608
153 / p. 558	⊕	Hollywood Hills Magic Hotel	◆◆	$89-149 SAVE	606
154 / p. 558		Budget Inn	◆◆	$80	604
156 / p. 558	⊕	Econo Lodge-Hollywood - see color ad p 606	◆	$63 SAVE	606
157 / p. 558	⊕	Hollywood Roosevelt Hotel (A Clarion Hotel)	◆◆◆	$159 SAVE	608
158 / p. 558	⊕	Hollywood Metropolitan Hotel - see color ad p 606	◆◆	$89-149 SAVE	606
		HOLLYWOOD - Restaurants			
80 / p. 558		Dar Maghreb	◆◆◆	$30	608
81 / p. 558		Musso & Frank Grill	◆	$8-28	608
		EL SEGUNDO - Lodgings			
159 / p. 558		Summerfield Suites Hotel-El Segundo/LAX	◆◆◆	$150-160	600
160 / p. 558	⊕	Hacienda Hotel-L.A. Airport - see color ad p 571	◆◆	$58-71 SAVE	599

Spotter/Map Pg.Number	OA	EL SEGUNDO - Lodgings (contd.)	Rating	Rate	Listing Page
161 / p. 558		Homestead Village	◆◆◆	$399	600
162 / p. 558	⊕	Travelodge at LAX South - see color ad p 577	◆◆	$69 SAVE	600
163 / p. 558		Courtyard by Marriott - see color ad p 563	◆◆◆	$119	599
164 / p. 558	⊕	Embassy Suites-LAX South	◆◆◆	$139 SAVE	599
165 / p. 558		Doubletree Club Hotel Los Angeles	◆◆◆	$87	599
		SANTA MONICA - Lodgings			
169 / p. 558	⊕	Travelodge-Santa Monica Beach	◆	$115-220 SAVE	639
170 / p. 558	⊕	The Georgian	◆◆◆	$210-340 SAVE	636
171 / p. 558	⊕	Comfort Inn - see ad p 635	◆◆	$79-150 SAVE	635
172 / p. 558	⊕	Hotel Oceana	◆◆◆	$300-600	563
173 / p. 558	⊕	Best Western Gateway Hotel Santa Monica - see color ad p 635	◆◆◆	$109-159 SAVE	634
174 / p. 558	⊕	Radisson Huntley Hotel - see color ad p 637	◆◆◆	$164 SAVE	637
175 / p. 558		Miramar Sheraton Hotel	◆◆◆	$295-345	637
176 / p. 558	⊕	Pacific Shore Hotel - see color ad p 637	◆◆	$120 SAVE	637
177 / p. 558	⊕	Four Points by Sheraton, Santa Monica	◆◆◆	$149	636
178 / p. 558	⊕	Shangri-La Hotel - see ad p 638	◆◆◆	$185 SAVE	638
179 / p. 558	⊕	Loews Santa Monica Beach Hotel	◆◆◆◆	$310-495	637
180 / p. 558		Channel Road Inn Bed & Breakfast	◆◆◆	$215-275	634
181 / p. 558	⊕	Doubletree Guest Suites - see color ad p 636	◆◆◆	$159-179	636
182 / p. 558	⊕	Holiday Inn-Santa Monica Beach - see color ad p 636	◆◆◆	$169 SAVE	636
183 / p. 558	⊕	Best Western Ocean View Hotel - see color ad p 635	◆◆	$129-249 SAVE	634
184 / p. 558	⊕	Days Inn Santa Monica	◆◆	$89-119	635
185 / p. 558		Shutters on the Beach	◆◆◆◆	$355-555	639
186 / p. 558	⊕	Travelodge-Santa Monica/Pico Blvd - see color ad p 638	◆◆	$89 SAVE	639
		SANTA MONICA - Restaurants			
86 / p. 558		Ocean Avenue Seafood	◆◆◆	$15-25	639
87 / p. 558		Valentino Restaurant	◆◆◆◆	$20-40	640
88 / p. 558		Knoll's Black Forest Inn	◆◆◆	$13-25	639
91 / p. 558		Bistro of Santa Monica	◆◆	$10-13	639
92 / p. 558		Bob Burns Restaurant	◆	$11-25	639
93 / p. 558		DC 3	◆◆	$15-25	639
94 / p. 558		Michael's	◆◆	$20-30	639
95 / p. 558		Locanda Del Lago	◆◆◆	$11-22	639
96 / p. 558		Rockenwagner	◆◆◆	$18-22	640
97 / p. 558		Chinois on Main	◆◆◆	$50-55	639
98 / p. 558		Izzy's Deli	◆	$8-12	639
99 / p. 558		The Fish Company	◆◆	$10-18	639
		BEVERLY HILLS - Lodgings			
188 / p. 558		Avalon Hotel		$150-235	588
189 / p. 558		Regent Beverly Wilshire	◆◆◆◆	$365-600	589
190 / p. 558	⊕	Beverly Hilton - see ad p 119, p 588	◆◆◆◆	$330-355 SAVE	588
191 / p. 558		The Beverly Hills Hotel	◆◆◆◆	$335-390	588
192 / p. 558	⊕	The Peninsula Beverly Hills	◆◆◆◆◆	$350 SAVE	589
193 / p. 558	⊕	Summit Hotel Rodeo Drive	◆◆	$150	589
194 / p. 558		Beverly Hills Inn	◆◆◆	$150	588
		BEVERLY HILLS - Restaurants			
100 / p. 558		The Belvedere	◆◆◆◆◆	$16-30	589
101 / p. 558		Lawry's The Prime Rib	◆◆◆	$19-26	589
102 / p. 558		La Scala Boutique	◆◆	$10-25	589
103 / p. 558		Cafe Rodeo	◆◆	$13-18	589
105 / p. 558		Trader Vic's	◆◆◆	$20-30	589
109 / p. 558		Prego	◆◆◆	$16-19	589

Spotter/Map Pg.Number	OA	BEVERLY HILLS - Restaurants (contd.)	Rating	Rate	Listing Page
⑩ / p. 558		Matsuhisa	◆◆◆	$30-40	589
⑪ / p. 558		Crustacean	◆◆◆	$18-38	589
⑬ / p. 558		The Dining Room	◆◆◆◆	$25-60	589
⑮ / p. 558		Spago	◆◆◆	$18-27	589
		MARINA DEL REY - Lodgings			
197 / p. 558		Marina Beach Marriott Hotel	◆◆◆	$169-250	618
198 / p. 558	⏣	**Best Western-Jamaica Bay Inn - see color ad p 618**	◆◆◆	$109-139 📖	617
199 / p. 558	⏣	**Courtyard by Marriott - see color ad p 618**	◆◆◆	$125 📖	617
200 / p. 558	⏣	Marina Del Rey Hotel - see color ad p 619	◆◆◆	$180-260	618
202 / p. 558		Marina International Hotel	◆◆	$130-180	618
203 / p. 558	⏣	**The Ritz-Carlton, Marina del Rey**	◆◆◆◆◆	$240	619
205 / p. 558	⏣	**Foghorn Beachfront Hotel**	◆◆	$119-149	618
		MARINA DEL REY - Restaurants			
⑫ / p. 558		The Dining Room	◆◆◆◆	$21-40	620
⑬ / p. 558		Cafe Del Rey	◆◆◆	$12-25	620
		VENICE - Lodgings			
211 / p. 558	⏣	**Holiday Inn Express-Marina Del Rey/Venice - see color ad p 619**	◆◆◆	$89-99 📖	648
212 / p. 558	⏣	**Inn at Venice Beach - see color ad p 649**	◆◆◆	$99-129 📖	649
213 / p. 558	⏣	**Lincoln Inn**	◆◆	$95-99 📖	649
216 / p. 558		Marina Pacific Hotel & Suites	◆◆	$140-200	649
217 / p. 558		**The Venice Beach House**	◆◆◆	$95-165 📖	649
219 / p. 558	⏣	**Ramada Limited - see color ad p 619**	◆◆◆	$89-99 📖	649
		VENICE - Restaurant			
⑫ / p. 558		72 Market St	◆◆	$13-26	649
		LYNWOOD - Lodgings			
225 / p. 558		Lynwood Century Freeway Travelodge	◆◆	$65	615
		PLAYA DEL REY - Lodgings			
230 / p. 558		Inn at Playa Del Rey	◆◆◆	$125-275	626
		MANHATTAN BEACH - Lodgings			
235 / p. 558	⏣	**Sea View Inn at the Beach**	◆◆	$90-155	617
236 / p. 558		Barnabey's Hotel - see color ad p 616	◆◆◆	$135-144	616
238 / p. 558	⏣	**Manhattan Beach Marriott**	◆◆◆	$150-195	617
239 / p. 558		Residence Inn by Marriott	◆◆◆	$160-250	617
240 / p. 558	⏣	**Holiday Inn Express - see color ad p 617**	◆◆◆	$110-120 📖	617
241 / p. 558	⏣	**Comfort Inn - see color ad p 616**	◆◆◆	$85-90 📖	617
		NORTHRIDGE - Restaurant			
㊺ / p. 560		Pagoda Inn	◆◆	$8-20	747
		SIERRA MADRE - Restaurant			
㊿ / p. 562		Restaurant Lozano	◆◆	$12-19	640
		LA CANADA FLINTRIDGE - Restaurants			
㊕ / p. 562		Flintridge Inn	◆◆◆	$16-24	610
㊟ / p. 562		The Barkley Restaurant & Bar	◆	$6-16	610
		MONTROSE - Restaurants			
⑥⓪ / p. 562		Star Cafe	◆◆	$6-16	622
⑥① / p. 562		Divina Cucina	◆◆	$8-13	622
⑥② / p. 562		El Charro Mexican Restaurant	◆	$8-14	622
⑥③ / p. 562		Oceanview Bar & Grill	◆◆	$9-20	622
		GARDENA - Restaurant			
⑥② / p. 561		Paradise Restaurant	◆◆	$9-16	600
		PALOS VERDES ESTATES - Restaurant			
⑥⑤ / p. 561		La Rive Gauche	◆◆◆	$16-27	624
		RANCHO PALOS VERDES - Restaurant			
⑦⓪ / p. 561	⏣	**Admiral Risty Restaurant**	◆◆	$17-30	628

Spotter/Map Pg.Number	OA	BELLFLOWER - Restaurants	Rating	Rate	Listing Page
⑦⑤ / p. 561		Johnny Rebs'	◆	$10-13	588
⑦⑥ / p. 561		Cafe Camellia	◆◆	$12-20	587

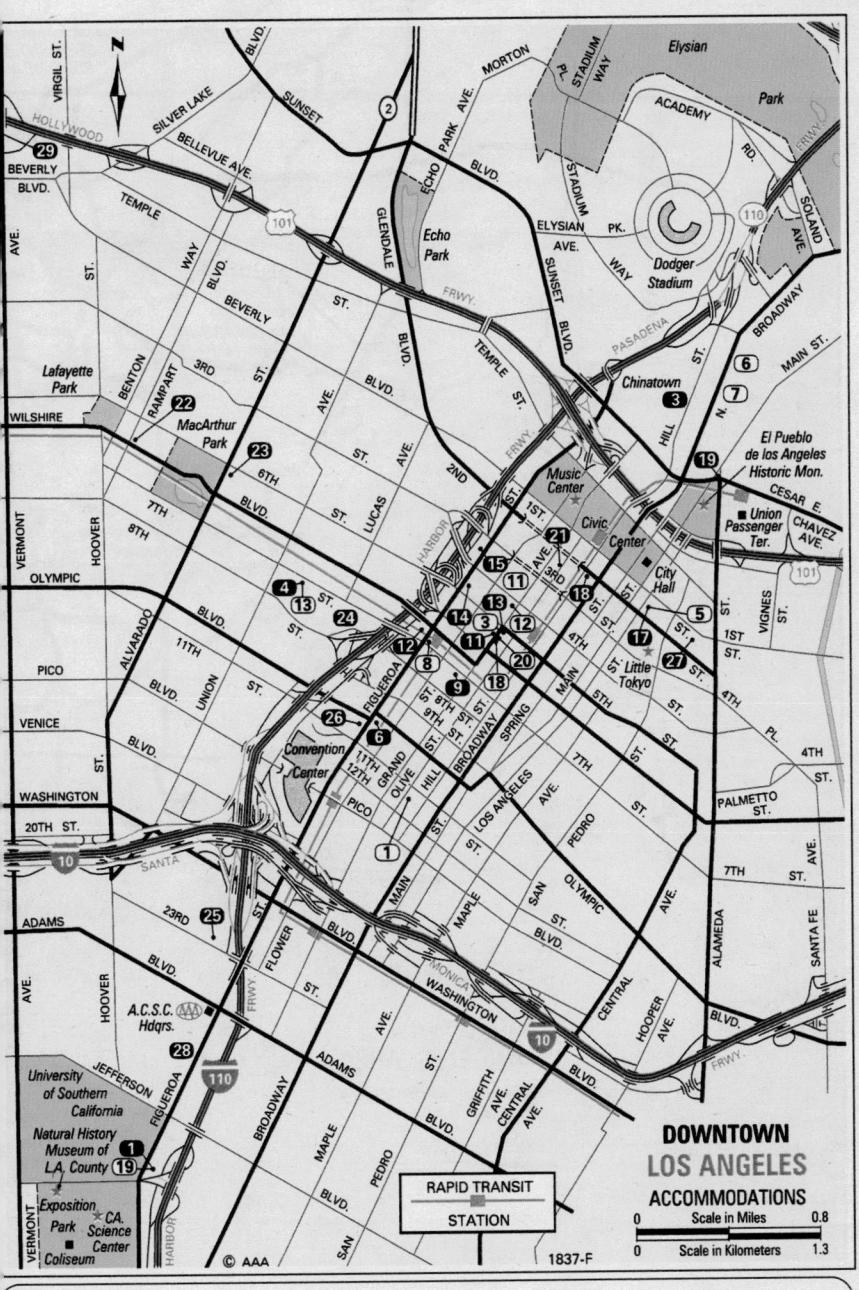

DOWNTOWN
LOS ANGELES
ACCOMMODATIONS

RAPID TRANSIT

STATION

© AAA

1837-F

ACCOMMODATIONS IN THE
LOS ANGELES AREA
See appropriate map/index
for each region

0	Scale in Miles	6.7
0	Scale in Kilometers	10.7

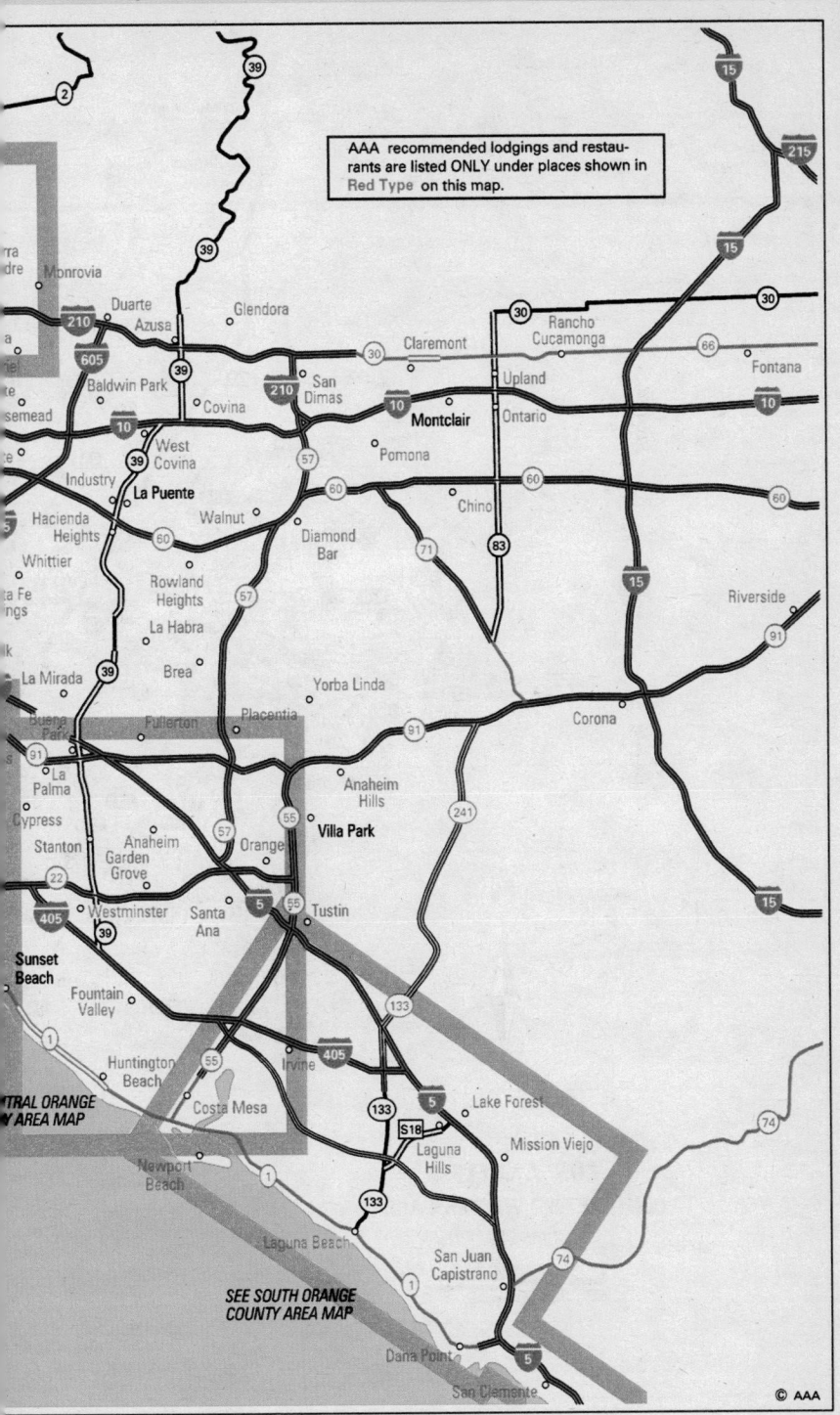

AAA recommended lodgings and restaurants are listed ONLY under places shown in Red Type on this map.

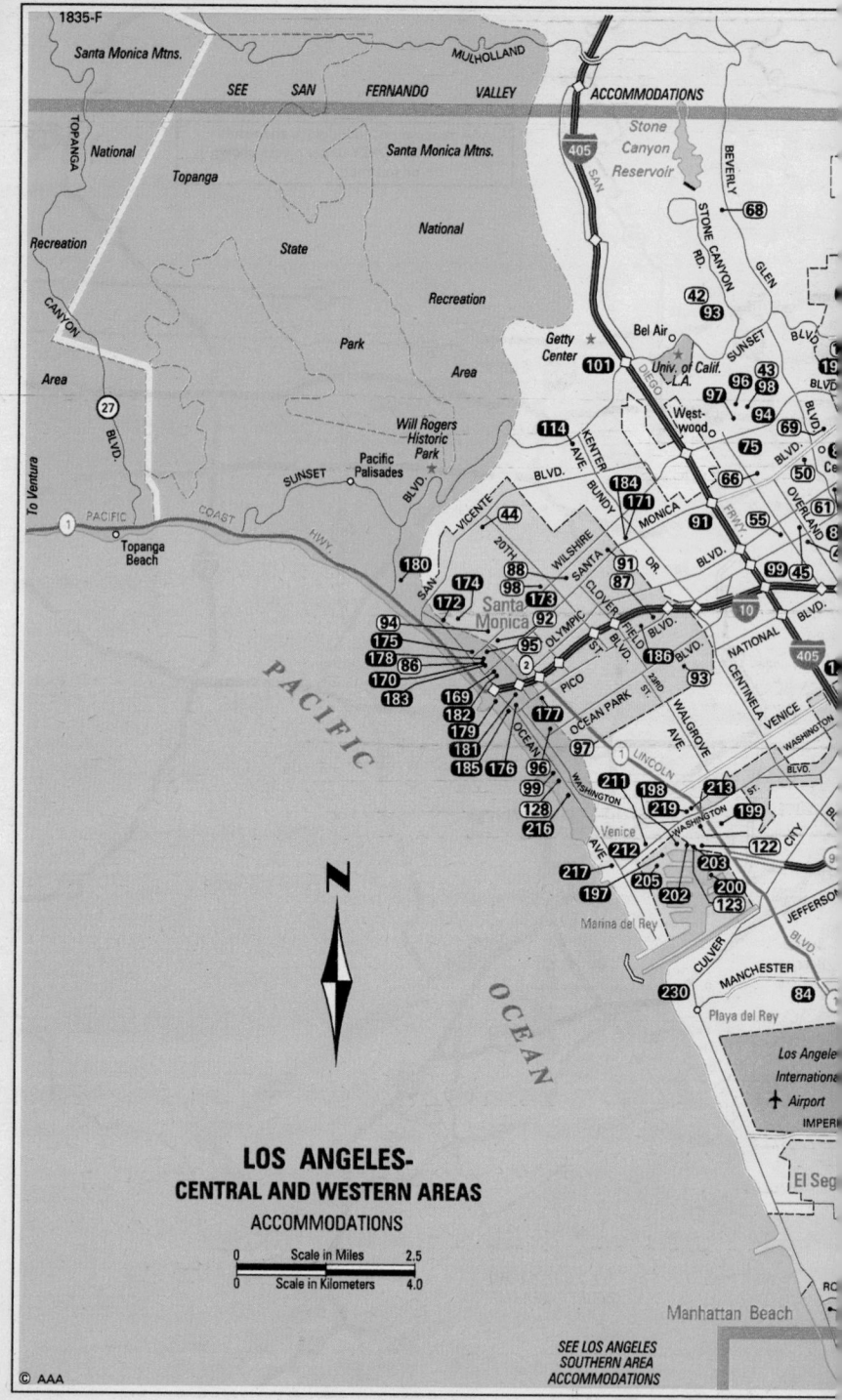

LOS ANGELES-
CENTRAL AND WESTERN AREAS
ACCOMMODATIONS

© AAA

SEE LOS ANGELES
SOUTHERN AREA
ACCOMMODATIONS

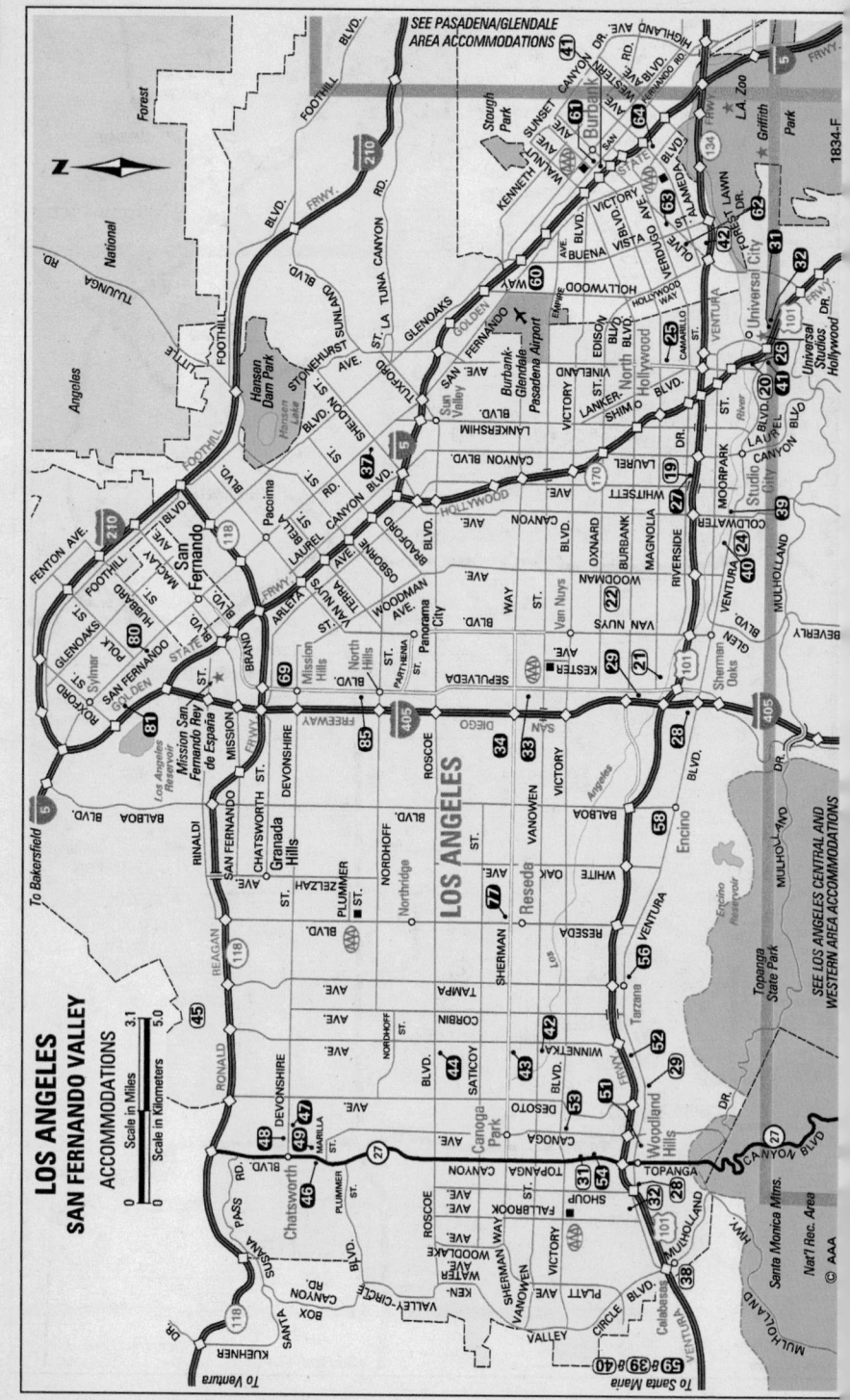

LOS ANGELES
SAN FERNANDO VALLEY
ACCOMMODATIONS

SEE PASADENA/GLENDALE
AREA ACCOMMODATIONS

SEE LOS ANGELES CENTRAL AND
WESTERN AREA ACCOMMODATIONS

© AAA

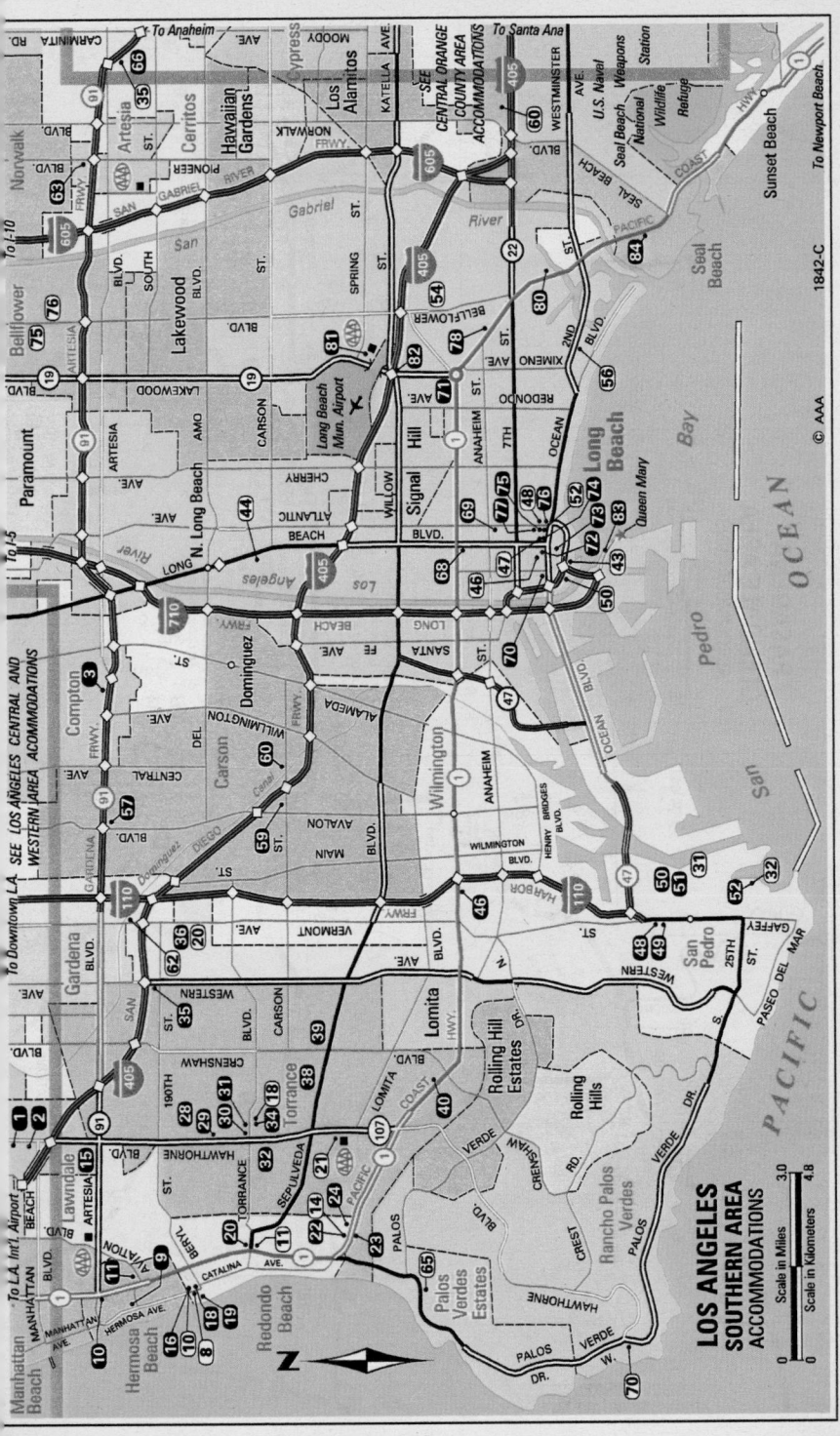

LOS ANGELES
SOUTHERN AREA
ACCOMMODATIONS

Scale in Miles
0   3.0

Scale in Kilometers
0   4.8

© AAA

1842-C

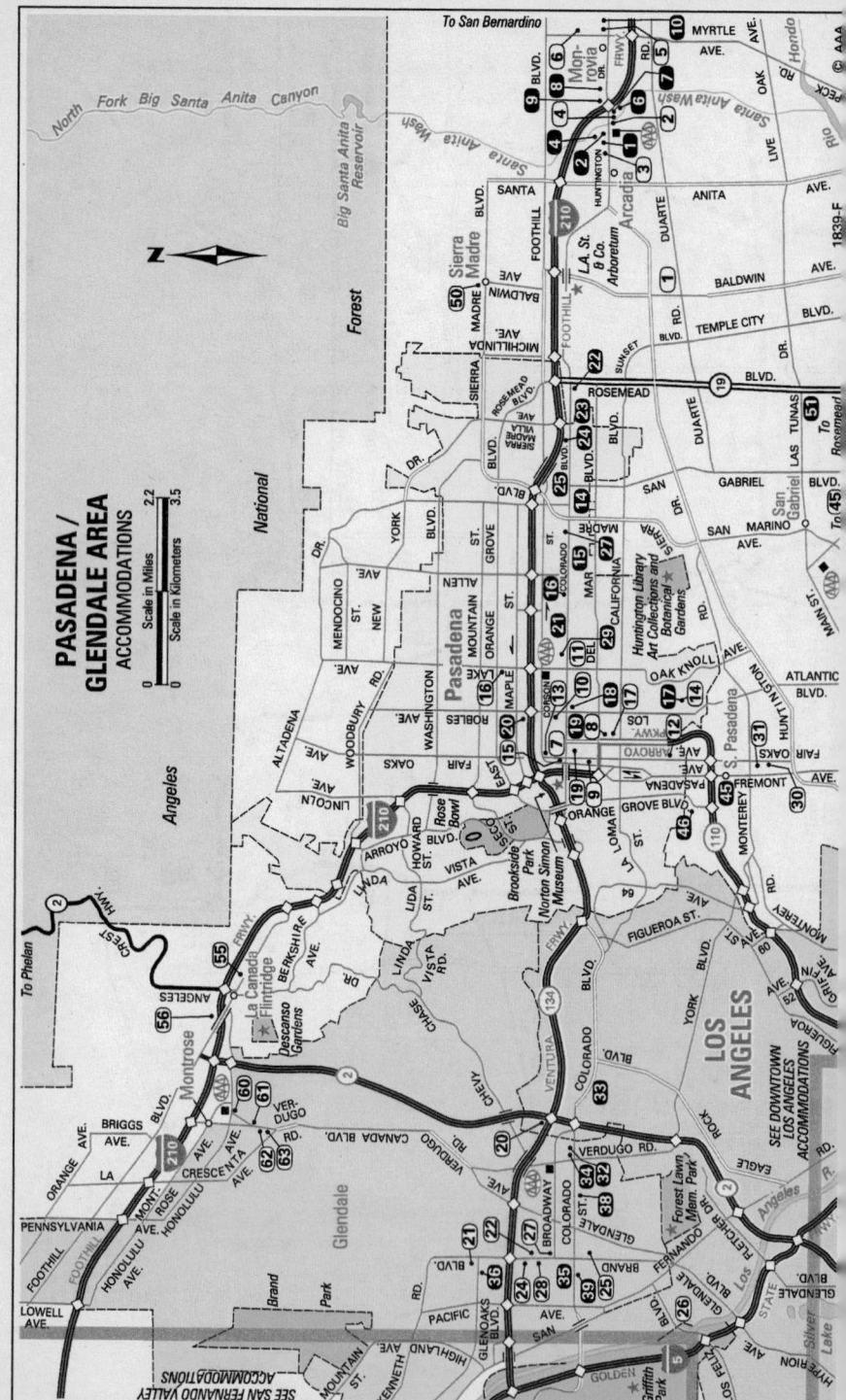

PASADENA / GLENDALE AREA ACCOMMODATIONS

DOWNTOWN LOS ANGELES   (See map p. 555; index p. 544)

LODGINGS

EST WESTERN DRAGON GATE INN   Phone: (213)617-3077   **3**
 **[SAVE]**   All Year [CP]   1P: $69- 109   2P/1B: $69- 109   2P/2B: $69- 109   XP: $10   F18
Location: 2 blks n of US 101 in Chinatown. 818 N Hill St 90012. Fax: 213/680-3753. **Facility:** 50 rooms.
◆◆   Downtown location in Chinatown. Shops & Restaurants in courtyard. 3 stories; exterior corridors.
Motor Inn   Fee: parking. **Dining:** Restaurant nearby. **Services:** giftshop. **Recreation:** Fee: car wash avail.
All Rooms: combo or shower baths. **Cards:** AE, DI, DS, MC, VI. **Special Amenities: Free breakfast and**
free room upgrade (subject to availability with advanced reservations). *(See color ad below)*

EST WESTERN THE MAYFAIR   Phone: (213)484-9789   **4**
 **[SAVE]**   All Year   1P: $93- 103   2P/1B: $103- 113   2P/2B: $113- 133   XP: $15   F12
Location: 5 blks w of Figueroa St. 1256 W 7th St 90017. Fax: 213/484-2769. **Terms:** Reserv deposit, 14
◆◆   day notice; handling fee imposed. **Facility:** 295 rooms. Located downtown, large lobby. 15 stories; interior cor-
Hotel   ridors. **Dining:** Orchid Gardens Restaurant, see separate listing. **Recreation:** Fee: in room video games.
All Rooms: combo or shower baths. **Cards:** AE, CB, DI, DS, JC, MC, VI. **Special Amenities: Free room**
upgrade and preferred room (each subject to availability with advanced reservations).

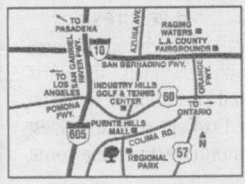
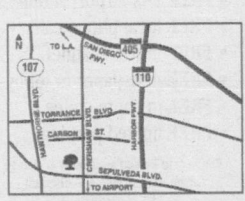
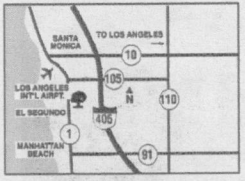

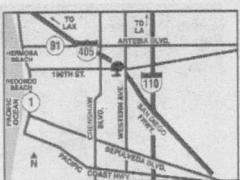

(See map p. 555)

COMFORT INN ◆ Motel
Rates Subject to Change
Phone: (323)665-0344
All Year [CP]   1P: $69- 96   2P/1B: $69- 96 2P/2B: $69- 96 XP: $10
Location: Just s of US 101, exit Vermont Ave. 321 N Vermont Ave 90004. Fax: 323/665-1152. **Facility:** 70 rooms. 15 whirlpool rms, extra charge; 3 stories; interior corridors. **Cards:** AE,DI,DS,JC,MC,VI.

HOLIDAY INN CITY CENTER (AAA) (SAVE) ◆◆◆ Hotel
Phone: (213)748-1291
All Year   1P: $109- 139   2P/1B: $119- 149 2P/2B: $119- 149 XP: $10
Location: 1020 S Figueroa St at Olympic Blvd 90015. Fax: 213/748-6028. **Terms:** Small pets only. **Facility:** 19 rooms. Across from Convention Center. 9 stories; interior corridors; small heated pool, sauna. Fee: parking. **Dining:** Dining room; 6 am-10 pm; $9-$20; cocktails. **Services:** giftshop. **All Rooms:** extended cable TV. **Cards:** AE, CB, DI, DS, JC, MC, VI. **Special Amenities:** Early check-in/late check-out and free room upgrade (subject to availability with advanced reservations).

HOLIDAY INN-DOWNTOWN (AAA) (SAVE) ◆◆◆ Hotel
Phone: (213)628-9900
All Year   1P: $79- 89   2P/1B: $89- 99 2P/2B: $89- 99 XP: $10
Location: Just w of SR 110 at 8th St. 750 Garland Ave 90017. Fax: 213/628-1201. **Terms:** Small pets only, $15. **Facility:** 204 rooms. Downtown location with garage parking. 6 stories; interior corridors; whirlpool. **Dining:** Dining room; 6 am-2 & 5-10 pm; $8-$15; cocktails. **Services:** giftshop. **All Rooms:** extended cable TV. **Cards:** AE, CB, DI, DS, JC, MC, VI. **Special Amenities:** Early check-in/late check-out and free room upgrade (subject to availability with advanced reservations).

The Hyatt touch is applied 365 days a year.

So are these special AAA Member Services offers:

Preferred nightly rates. . .half price dinner entree!

Now through December 29, 1999, a superb dining offer is yours to enjoy at your choice of fifteen spectacular Hyatt destinations in sunny Southern California. Purchase one dinner entree and receive a second entree of equal or lesser value at half price. Simply show your AAA card at check-in and ask for your "Dining  *Discount" coupon. You'll also sleep better at Hyatt, knowing you will receive the lowest room rate available. For reservations call your travel planner or Hyatt at 1-800 532-1496.*

Hyatt Westlake Plaza (Thousand Oaks)
Park Hyatt Los Angeles (Century City)
Hyatt Regency Los Angeles
Hyatt West Hollywood
Hyatt Regency Long Beach
Hyatt Regency Alicante (Anaheim)
Hyatt Irvine (Orange County)
Hyatt Islandia (San Diego)
Hyatt Regency La Jolla (San Diego)
Hyatt Regency San Diego
Hyatt Newporter (Newport Beach)
Hyatt Regency Suites Palm Springs
Hyatt Grand Champions Resort
(Near Palm Springs)
Hyatt Rickeys (Palo Alto)
Hyatt Valencia (Six Flags/Santa Clarita)

Feel the Hyatt Touch®

(See map p. 555)

HOTEL INTER-CONTINENTAL LOS ANGELES
AT CALIFORNIA PLAZA
◆◆◆   All Year
Hotel
Services: giftshop; area transportation. Fee: massage. **Cards:** AE, CB, DI, DS, JC, MC, VI.

Rates Subject to Change   **Phone:** 213/617-3300
1P: $250   2P/1B: $270   2P/2B: $270   XP: $30
Location: Just n of 4th St. 251 S Olive St 90012. Fax: 213/617-3399. **Facility:** 434 rooms. Adjacent to the seum of Contemporary Art, at California Plaza. 4 two-bedroom units. 17 stories; interior corridors; heated p

HYATT REGENCY LOS ANGELES   **Phone:** (213)683-1234
(AAA) (SAVE)   All Year   1P: $165- 200   2P/1B: $190- 225   2P/2B: $190- 225   XP: $25
◆◆◆◆   **Location:** Just e of SR 110; at Broadway Plaza. 711 S Hope St at 7th St 90017. Fax: 213/629-32
Hotel   **Facility:** 485 rooms. Lobby adjoins shopping plaza. 24 stories; interior corridors; whirlpool. Fee: park
Dining: 2 restaurants; 6 am-midnight; $10-$30; cocktails. **Services:** giftshop. **Cards:** AE, CB, DI, DS,
VI. *(See color ad p 565)*

THE INN AT 657   Rates Subject to Change   **Phone:** 213/741-2200
◆◆   All Year [BP]   1P: $125   2P/1B: $145   2P/2B: $180   XP: $25
Bed &   **Location:** Just w of Figueroa. 657 W 23rd St 90007. **Terms:** Reserv deposit, 5 day notice. **Facility:** 5 roo
Breakfast   House built in 1948, in an older residential neighborhood. One room & 4 apartments; each apartment ha
kitchen, 2 are 2-bedroom. 2 stories; interior/exterior corridors.

INTOWN HOTEL   Rates Subject to Change   **Phone:** (213)628-2222
◆   All Year   1P: $60   2P/1B: $70   2P/2B: $70- 80   XP: $10-12
Motel   **Location:** SR 110 exit 9th St E, just s of 9th St. 913 S Figueroa St 90015. Fax: 213/687-05
Terms: Reserv deposit. **Facility:** 170 rooms. 2 suites with refrigerator $120-$140; 3 stories; interior/exte
corridors. **Cards:** AE, CB, DI, DS, JC, MC, VI.

KAWADA HOTEL   Rates Subject to Change   **Phone:** (213)621-4455
◆◆   Mon-Thurs   1P: $89- 99   2P/1B: $99- 109   2P/2B: $99- 109   XP: $15
Hotel   Fri-Sun   1P: $75   2P/1B: $75   2P/2B: $75   XP: $15
Location: S on SR 110, exit Hill St, then 1.5 mi s; n on SR 110, exit 9th St, just e to Figueroa St, then
mi n to 2nd St, just e, corner of Hill & 2nd St. 200 S Hill St 90012. Fax: 213/687-4455. **Terms:** Reserv deposit. **Facility:**
rooms. Small nicely furnished rooms. In downtown business district. 4 stories; interior corridors. **Services:** a
transportation. **All Rooms:** combo or shower baths. **Some Rooms:** 85 efficiencies. **Cards:** AE, CB, DI, DS, JC, MC, VI.

LOS ANGELES DOWNTOWN MARRIOTT HOTEL   **Phone:** (213)617-1133
(AAA) (SAVE)   Mon-Thurs   1P: $145   2P/1B: $145   2P/2B: $145   XP: $25
Fri-Sun   1P: $99   2P/1B: $99   2P/2B: $99   XP: $25
◆◆◆   **Location:** Adjacent to SR 110. 333 S Figueroa St 90071. Fax: 213/613-0291. **Facility:** 469 rooms. Busin
Hotel   services, extra charge; 14 stories; interior corridors; heated pool. Fee: parking. **Dining:** Dining room
restaurants; 6:30 am-11 pm; $12-$25; cocktails. **Services:** giftshop. **Cards:** AE, CB, DI, DS, JC, MC, VI.
(See color ad below)

METRO PLAZA HOTEL   **Phone:** (213)680-0200
(AAA) (SAVE)   All Year   1P: $59   2P/1B: $69   2P/2B: $75   XP: $10-20
◆◆   **Location:** Corner of Main & Cesar Chavez. 711 N Main St 90012. Fax: 213/620-0200. **Terms:** Res
Motel   deposit; handling fee imposed. **Facility:** 80 rooms. Across from Olvera St & Chinatown; 1/2 blk from Amtra
Metro Rail station. 2 rooms with whirlpool, $109; 1 loft unit, $139; 4 stories; interior corrid
All Rooms: extended cable TV. **Cards:** AE, DI, DS, JC, MC, VI. **Special Amenities:** Early check-in/
check-out and free room upgrade (subject to availability with advanced reservations). *(See color ad p 567)*

(see map p. 555)

YAKO INN ◆
All Year — Rates Subject to Change — Phone: 213/617-2000 — ⊠27 F12
1P: $103- 116   2P/1B: $113- 126   2P/2B: $113- 126   XP: $15
Location: In Little Tokyo area. 328 E First St 90012. Fax: 213/617-2700. **Terms:** Reserv deposit. **Facility:** 174 rooms. Downtown location with garage parking. 11 stories; interior corridors. Services: giftshop. Fee: massage. **Cards:** AE, CB, DI, DS, JC, MC, VI.

THE NEW OTANI HOTEL ◆◆
All Year — Rates Subject to Change — Phone: (213)629-1200 — ⊠17 F12
1P: $99   2P/1B: $99   2P/2B: $99   XP: $25
Location: In Civic Center-Little Tokyo area. 120 S Los Angeles St 90012. Fax: 213/622-0980. **Facility:** 434 rooms. Extensive public facilities & shopping areas. Second floor Japanese garden. 21 stories; interior corridors. Fee: parking. **Services:** giftshop. Fee: massage. **Cards:** AE, CB, DI, DS, JC, MC, VI.

OMNI LOS ANGELES HOTEL & CENTRE ◆◆◆
Mon-Thurs — Rates Subject to Change — Phone: (213)688-7777 — ⊠12 F18
1P: $109- 129   2P/1B: $129   2P/2B: $129   XP: $25
Fri-Sun   1P: $109   2P/1B: $109   2P/2B: $109   XP: $25   F18
Location: Adjacent to SR 110. 930 Wilshire Blvd at Figueroa St 90017. Fax: 213/612-3989. **Facility:** 900 rooms. Extensive public facilities & shopping areas. 1- & 2-bedroom suites $275-475. Deluxe rooms $139-$189; 16 stories; interior corridors; heated pool, whirlpool. Fee: parking. **Dining:** 3 restaurants, coffee shop; 10 am-1 am; $10-$30; cocktails. **Services:** giftshop. Fee: massage. **Cards:** AE, CB, DI, DS, JC, MC, VI.

RADISSON HOTEL MIDTOWN LOS ANGELES ◆◆
All Year — Phone: (213)748-4141 — ⊠1 F18
1P: $95- 135   2P/1B: $110- 150   2P/2B: $110- 150   XP: $15
Location: 1 blk w of SR 110, Harbor Frwy, exit Exposition Blvd. 3540 S Figueroa St 90007. Fax: 213/746-3255. **Terms:** Reserv deposit, 3 day notice. **Facility:** 240 rooms. Downtown location, near University of Southern California. 11 stories; interior corridors; heated pool, whirlpool. Fee: parking. **Dining:** Dining room, coffee shop; 6:30 am-10 pm; $7-$15; cocktails. **Services:** giftshop; area transportation, 1/4 mi radius. **Recreation:** video games. **All Rooms:** extended cable TV. **Cards:** AE, CB, DI, DS, JC, MC, VI.

RAMADA INN-L.A. DOWNTOWN ◆◆
All Year [CP] — Phone: (213)483-6363 — ⊠23 F18
1P: $68- 118   2P/1B: $68- 118   2P/2B: $75- 118   XP: $8
Location: Just s of 6th St, near Alvarado St. 611 S Westlake Ave 90057. Fax: 213/483-0088. **Facility:** 67 rooms. 5 stories; interior corridors; sauna. **Some Rooms:** whirlpools. **Cards:** AE, DI, DS, MC, VI. **Special Amenities:** Early check-in/late check-out and free breakfast.

THE REGAL BILTMORE HOTEL ◆◆◆
Sun-Thurs 8/1-11/7 — Phone: (213)624-1011 — ⊠13 F18
1P: $235- 315   2P/1B: $235- 315   2P/2B: $235- 315   XP: $30
Sun-Thurs 2/1-6/15 & 12/29-1/31
1P: $175- 255   2P/1B: $175- 255   2P/2B: $175- 255   XP: $30   F18
Fri & Sat & Sun-Thurs 11/8-12/28
1P: $155- 235   2P/1B: $155- 235   2P/2B: $155- 235   XP: $30   F18
Sun-Thurs 6/16-7/31   1P: $125- 205   2P/1B: $125- 205   2P/2B: $125- 205   XP: $30   F18
Location: 506 S Grand Ave at 5th St 90071. Fax: 213/612-1628. **Facility:** 683 rooms. A long established hotel. Beautifully decorated lobby & public facilities. 25 one-bedroom suites, $450-$500; 11 stories; interior corridors; heated indoor pool, sauna, whirlpool. **Dining:** 3 restaurants, coffee shop; 6:30 am-11 pm; $10-$34; cocktails; also, Bernard's, see separate listing. **Services:** giftshop; area transportation, Central Business District. Fee: massage. **Cards:** AE, CB, DI, DS, JC, MC, VI.

VAGABOND INN FIGUEROA ◆
All Year [CP] — Phone: (213)746-1531 — ⊠28 F18
1P: $75   2P/1B: $80   2P/2B: $85   XP: $5
Location: 0.5 mi sw of SR 110, Adams Blvd exit. 3101 S Figueroa St 90007. Fax: 213/746-9106. **Terms:** Pets, $5. **Facility:** 72 rooms. Coffee & tea in lobby. 6 two-bedroom units. 2 stories; exterior corridors; heated pool. **Dining:** Coffee shop; 6 am-midnight; $5-$8. **All Rooms:** extended cable TV. **Cards:** AE, CB, DI, DS, MC, VI. **Special Amenities:** Free breakfast and free local telephone calls.

(See map p. 555)

THE WESTIN BONAVENTURE   Phone: (213)624-1000
AAA SAVE   All Year   1P: $95- 179   2P/1B: $95- 199   2P/2B: $199   XP: $25
◆◆◆   **Location:** 404 S Figueroa St 90071. **Fax:** 213/612-4800. **Terms:** Check-in 4 pm; reserv depo
Hotel   **Facility:** 1354 rooms. Dramatically designed lobby area. Extensive public facilities & shopping areas.
          suites, $195-$2500; 35 stories; interior corridors; heated pool. Fee: parking. **Dining:** Dining room
          restaurants, coffee shop; microbrewery & food court; 5:30 am-11 pm; $7-$30; cocktails; also, Top of F
see separate listing. **Services:** giftshop. Fee: massage. **Recreation:** full service Japanese style spa. **Cards:** AE, CB,
DS, JC, MC, VI.

🛏️🏊🏋️🅿️🍴🍽️🚭🔒🛎️🧺♿🎾 📼 💻 📶 🖥️ 🖨️ 🎧 📠 🔋 🐕 🖐️ ❌

WILSHIRE ROYALE HOWARD JOHNSON PLAZA   Rates Subject to Change   Phone: 213/387-5311
◆◆   4/1-9/30   1P: $109- 129   2P/1B: $139- 149   2P/2B: $159- 179   XP: $10-20
Hotel   2/1-3/31 & 10/1-1/31 1P: $89- 109 2P/1B: $119- 129   2P/2B: $139- 159   XP: $10-20
          Location: 1.5 mi w of SR 110, corner of Wilshire Blvd & Rampart Blvd. 2619 Wilshire Blvd 900
Fax: 213/380-8174. **Facility:** 198 rooms. 65 1-bedroom suites, $125-$160; 12 stories; interior corridors; small heated p
Services: giftshop. **All Rooms:** combo or shower baths. **Some Rooms:** 40 efficiencies. **Cards:** AE, CB, DI, DS, JC,
VI.

ASK 🏋️🅿️🍴🍽️🚭🔒🧺💻 📶 🖥️ 📠 🔋

WYNDHAM CHECKERS HOTEL   Rates Subject to Change   Phone: (213)624-0000
◆◆◆   Sun-Thurs [EP]   1P: $161   2P/1B: $161   2P/2B: $161   XP: $10-20
Hotel   Fri & Sat [BP]   1P: $109   2P/1B: $109   2P/2B: $109   XP: $10-20
          Location: 535 S Grand Ave 90071. **Fax:** 213/626-9906. **Facility:** 188 rooms. Downtown location, w
appointed lobby & guest rooms. 15 stories; interior corridors. **Services:** area transportation. **Cards:** AE, CB, DI, DS, JC,
VI. Wyndham.

🏋️🅿️🍴🍽️🚭🔒🧺♿🎾 📼 💻 📶 🖥️ 📠 🔋

RESTAURANTS

A THOUSAND CRANES RESTAURANT   Lunch: $12-$20   Dinner: $40-$60   Phone: 213/253-9255
◆◆◆   **Location:** In The New Otani Hotel. 120 S Los Angeles St 90012. **Hours:** 7-10 am, 11:30-2 & 6-9:30
Ethnic   Sun brunch 11 am-2 pm. **Reservations:** suggested. **Features:** semi-formal attire; cocktails; entertainme
           valet parking; a la carte. Japanese restaurant with 3- to 6-person & 1- to 25-person tatami rooms. Tempura
sushi bar. Garden view from most areas. Smoke free premises. **Cards:** AE, CB, DI, DS, JC, MC, VI.

BERNARD'S   Dinner: $25-$34   Phone: 213/612-1580
◆◆◆◆   **Location:** In the Regal Biltmore Hotel. 506 S Grand Ave 90071. **Hours:** 5:30 pm-9:30 pm, Fri & Sat-10
Continental Closed major holidays, Sun & Mon. **Reservations:** suggested. **Features:** semi-formal attire; cocktails; v
           parking; a la carte. An elegant dining room featuring expertly prepared cuisine. Smoke free premis
Cards: AE, CB, DI, DS, JC, MC, VI.

BRANDY'S RESTAURANT & LOUNGE   Lunch: $10-$16   Dinner: $12-$19   Phone: 213/748-4141
◆◆   **Location:** At the Crowne Plaza-Los Angeles Downtown. 3540 S Figueroa St 90007. **Hours:** 11 am-10
American   **Features:** casual dress; cocktails; entertainment. Chicken, pasta, salads, steak & seafood. **Cards:** AE,
           DI, DS, JC, MC, VI.

CHECKERS RESTAURANT   Lunch: $13-$20   Dinner: $16-$32   Phone: 213/891-0519
◆◆◆   **Location:** In Wyndham Checkers Hotel. 535 S Grand Ave 90071. **Hours:** 7 am-10:30 pm, Sun brunch
Continental am-2:30 pm. **Reservations:** suggested. **Features:** semi-formal attire; Sunday brunch; cocktails & lounge;
           for valet parking; a la carte. Excellent selection of seafood, steak, lamb, chicken & pasta dishes. Smoke f
premises. **Cards:** AE, CB, DI, DS, JC, MC, VI.

ENGINE COMPANY NO 28   Lunch: $10-$20   Dinner: $10-$20   Phone: 213/624-6996
◆◆   **Location:** Just n of 7th St. 644 S Figueroa St 90017. **Hours:** 11:15 am-9 pm, Sat & Sun 5 pm-9 pm. Clos
American   major holidays. **Reservations:** suggested. **Features:** semi-formal attire; cocktails & lounge; fee for parking
           la carte. Pasta, beef & fresh seafood entrees. Popular downtown location in a historic converted firehou
Valet parking after 5 pm. Complementary shuttle to Music Center Tues-Sat. Validated parking in Home Savings Tower
Lebanon St. **Cards:** AE, DI, MC, VI.

GOLDEN DRAGON RESTAURANT   Lunch: $6-$25   Dinner: $6-$25   Phone: 213/626-2039
◆   **Location:** In Chinatown. 960 N Broadway 90012. **Hours:** 9 am-9:30 pm. **Features:** casual dress; Sund
Chinese   brunch; carryout; cocktails & lounge; fee for parking; a la carte. Good selection of dim sum & Chine
           entrees. Magic show brunch Sat & Sun. Smoke free premises. **Cards:** MC, VI.

LITTLE JOE'S   Lunch: $8-$13   Dinner: $8-$22   Phone: 213/489-4900
◆   **Location:** 1.3 mi n of US 101, in Chinatown area, ne corner of College & Broadway. 900 N Broadw
Italian   90012. **Hours:** 11 am-9 pm, Sat 3 pm-9 pm. Closed major holidays & Sun. **Features:** casual dre
           children's menu; carryout; cocktails & lounge; minimum charge-$4; fee for parking; valet parking; a la ca
Extensive selection of entrees. Informal atmosphere. **Cards:** AE, CB, DI, DS, MC, VI.

MCCORMICK & SCHMICK'S   Lunch: $9-$20   Dinner: $9-$20   Phone: 213/629-1929
◆◆   **Location:** Just s of 4th St via Hope St, on the 4th floor of the First Interstate World Center Bldg. 633 W
Seafood   St 90071. **Hours:** 11:30 am-10 pm, Fri-11 pm, Sat 4:30-11 pm, Sun 4:30-10 pm. Closed major holida
           Reservations: suggested. **Features:** semi-formal attire; cocktails & lounge; area transportation; a la carte
Fresh seafood flown in daily. Fee for parking, complimentary self parking after 4 pm. **Cards:** AE, CB, DI, DS, MC, VI.

ORCHID GARDENS RESTAURANT   Lunch: $8-$20   Dinner: $9-$28   Phone: 213/484-9789
◆◆   **Location:** 5 blks w of Figueroa St; in Best Western The Mayfair. 1256 W 7th St 90017. **Hours:** 6:30-9
Continental am, 11:30-2 & 6-10 pm, Sat & Sun 6:30 am-9:30 & 6-10 pm. **Reservations:** required. **Features:** cas
           dress; salad bar; cocktails. Sandwiches, salads, chicken, pasta, lamb, seafood & steak. Smoke f
premises. **Cards:** AE, CB, DI, DS, JC, MC, VI.

TOP OF FIVE   Dinner: $20-$30   Phone: 213/612-4743
◆◆◆   **Location:** On the 35th floor of the Westin Bonaventure. 404 S Figueroa St 90071. **Hours:** 11 am-2:30
Continental 5-10 pm, Fri & Sat 5 pm-11 pm. **Reservations:** suggested. **Features:** casual dress; Sunday brun
           children's menu; senior's menu; cocktails & lounge; entertainment; fee for valet parking; a la carte
Panoramic view. Mesquite broiled seafood, black angus steak, lamb, chicken, veal & pasta. Hot rock cooking by guest
tableside. Smoke free premises. **Cards:** AE, CB, DI, DS, JC, MC, VI.

ee map p. 555)

E TOWER   Lunch: $30-$35   Dinner: $35-$45   Phone: 213/746-1554   ①
Location: 1150 S Olive St 90015. **Hours:** 11:30 am-2 & 5:30-10 pm, Sat from 5:30 pm-11 pm. Closed major holidays & Sun. **Reservations:** suggested. **Features:** semi-formal attire; cocktails & lounge; valet parking; a la carte. On 32nd floor of Transamerica Center Building with panoramic view of city. Smoke free premises.
ntinental **Cards:** AE, CB, DI, MC, VI.   Ⓧ

ATER GRILL   Lunch: $8-$28   Dinner: $14-$30   Phone: 213/891-0900   ⑱
Location: Between 5th & 6th sts. 544 S Grand Ave 90071. **Hours:** 11:30 am-9 pm, Wed-Fri to 10 pm, Sat 5
afood   pm-10 pm, Sun 4:30 pm-9 pm. Closed: 11/25 & 12/25. **Reservations:** suggested. **Features:** semi-formal attire; cocktails & lounge; fee for valet parking; a la carte. Richly decorated setting in the Pacific Center building.
aturing fresh seafood & oyster bar. Menu changes daily. Smoke free premises. **Cards:** AE, CB, DI, DS, MC, VI.   Ⓧ

LOS ANGELES CENTRAL & WEST (See map p. 558; index p. 545)

LODGINGS

ST WESTERN MID-WILSHIRE PLAZA HOTEL   Phone: (213)385-4444   ⑫
SAVE   5/28-9/5 [CP]   1P: $64- 74 2P/1B: $64- 74 2P/2B: $74   XP: $5   F12
       2/1-5/27 & 9/6-1/31 [CP] 1P: $59- 69 2P/1B: $59- 69 2P/2B: $69   XP: $5   F12
tel **Location:** Just n of Wilshire Blvd. 603 S New Hampshire Ave 90005. Fax: 213/380-5413. **Terms:** Reserv deposit. **Facility:** 89 rooms. Limited parking. 5 stories; interior corridors; indoor pool, sauna, whirlpool.
Cards: AE, CB, DI, DS, MC, VI. **Special Amenities: Free breakfast and free newspaper.**
⑤ⓓ ⊇ △ ⊞ ⊕ ⊟ Ⓧ

ST WESTERN ROYAL PALACE INN & SUITES   Phone: (310)477-9066   ⑨⑨
SAVE   6/15-9/15 [CP]   1P: $65- 99 2P/1B: $65- 99 2P/2B: $69- 110 XP: $6-8   F12
       2/1-6/14 & 9/16-1/31 [CP] 1P: $59- 99 2P/1B: $59- 90 2P/2B: $66- 105 XP: $6-8   F12
tel **Location:** 0.3 mi s of Pico Blvd. 2528 S Sepulveda Blvd 90064. Fax: 310/478-4133. **Terms:** Reserv deposit; weekly rates. **Facility:** 55 rooms. 2 stories; interior corridors; small heated pool, sauna, whirlpool. **Recreation:** billard room. **All Rooms:** comb, shower or tub baths. **Cards:** AE, CB, DI, DS, JC, MC, VI.
ecial Amenities: Free breakfast and free room upgrade (subject to availability with advanced reservations).
⑤ⓓ ⑳⊓ ⊇ △ ⊞ ⊕ VCR ⊟ ⊡ ⊟ Ⓧ

ST WESTERN WESTWOOD PACIFIC HOTEL   Phone: (310)478-1400   ⑨①
SAVE   6/1-9/15 [CP]   1P: $99   2P/1B: $105   2P/2B: $105   XP: $10   F12
       9/16-1/31 [CP]   1P: $94   2P/1B: $99   2P/2B: $103   XP: $10   F12
tel   2/1-5/31 [CP]   1P: $84   2P/1B: $89   2P/2B: $89   XP: $10   F12
Location: 1 blk w of I-405 at Sawtelle. 11250 Santa Monica Blvd 90025. Fax: 310/478-1401. **Facility:** 76 rooms. 4 stories; exterior corridors; whirlpool. **Recreation:** in-room video games. **Cards:** AE, CB, DI, DS, JC,
:, VI. **Special Amenities: Free breakfast and free newspaper.**
⑤ⓓ △ ⊞ ⊕ ⊡ ⊟ ⊟ Ⓧ

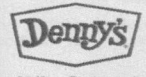
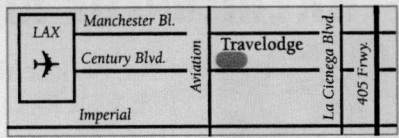

(See map p. 558)

BEVERLY LAUREL MOTOR HOTEL　　　　　　　　Phone: (323)651-2441
All Year　　　　　1P: $65- 75　2P/1B:　$69- 79　2P/2B:　$69- 79　XP:　$5
Motor Inn　　**Location:** Just w of Fairfax Ave. 8018 Beverly Blvd 90048. Fax: 323/651-5225. **Terms:** Weekly rates; pe $5 extra charge. **Facility:** 52 rooms. Underground garage parking. 3 stories; exterior corrido **Dining:** Coffee shop; 6:30 am-4 am; $6-$11. **All Rooms:** combo or shower baths. **Some Rooms:** kitchens. **Cards:** AE, DI, MC, VI. *(See ad p 571)*

BEVERLY PLAZA HOTEL　　　　　　　　　　　Phone: (323)658-6600
All Year　　　　　1P: $165　　　2P/1B:　$165　　　2P/2B: $165　　　XP: $10
Hotel　　**Location:** Just e of La Cienega Blvd. 8384 W 3rd St 90048. Fax: 323/653-3464. **Facility:** 98 rooms. Tastefu furnished rooms. 5 stories; interior corridors; street parking only; heated pool, saunas. **Dining:** Restaura supper club with dining & dancing; 6 pm-midnight; $12-$18; cocktails. **Services:** area transportation, withir mi. Fee: massage. **Cards:** AE, DI, MC, VI. **Special Amenities:** Free newspaper and free room upgra (subject to availability with advanced reservations).

BRENTWOOD MOTOR HOTEL　　　Guaranteed Rates　　　Phone: (310)476-9981
Motel　　5/1-9/30　　　　　1P: $84　　　2P/1B:　$89　　　2P/2B:　$94　　　XP: $5
2/1-4/30 & 10/1-1/31　　1P: $79　　　2P/1B:　$84　　　2P/2B:　$89　　　XP: $5
　　　Location: In Brentwood; 1 mi w of I-405. 12200 W Sunset Blvd 90049. Fax: 310/471-0768. **Terms:** Res deposit. **Facility:** 20 rooms. 1-2 stories; exterior corridors. **All Rooms:** shower baths. **Cards:** DI, DS, MC, VI.

CARLYLE INN [BP]　　　　　　　　　　　　Phone: (310)275-4445
6/1-9/15 [BP]　　　　　1P: $109- 129　2P/1B:　$109- 129　2P/2B: $109- 129　XP: $10
2/1-5/31 & 9/16-1/31 [BP]　1P: $95- 115　2P/1B:　$99- 119　2P/2B:　$99- 119　XP: $10
Motor Inn　　**Location:** Just s of Olympic Blvd. 1119 S Robertson Blvd 90035. Fax: 310/859-0496. **Facility:** 32 room Charming rooms & suites overlooking courtyard area. Executive suites, $190 for up to 3 persons; 4 stories; terior corridors; whirlpool. Fee: parking. **Dining:** 4 pm-6 pm, Mon-Fri; complimentary wine & chee **Services:** area transportation, within 5 mi, 7 am-6 pm. **Recreation:** sun deck. **Cards:** AE, CB, DI, DS, JC, MC, VI. *(See color ad p 571)*

CENTURY PLAZA HOTEL & TOWER　　　　　　Phone: (310)277-2000
All Year　　　　　1P: $300- 410　2P/1B:　$330- 435　2P/2B: $330- 435　XP: $25-50
Hotel　　**Location:** Century City. 2025 Avenue of the Stars 90067. Fax: 310/551-3355. **Terms:** Reserv deposit, 3 d notice; small pets only. **Facility:** 1072 rooms. An impressive hotel with many public facilities & shops. Acro from ABC Entertainment Center. 30 stories; interior corridors; heated pool, whirlpool. Fee: parkir **Dining:** Dining room, restaurant; 6:30 am-11 pm; $11-$26; cocktails. **Services:** giftshop; area transportatic to local shopping. Fee: massage. **All Rooms:** combo or shower baths. **Some Rooms:** whirlpools. **Cards:** AE, CB, DI, C JC, MC, VI. **Special Amenities:** Free newspaper. Westin Hotels.

COMFORT INN TOWNE　　　　　　　　　　　Phone: (323)294-5200
All Year [CP]　　　　1P: $62　　　2P/1B:　$72　　　2P/2B:　$67　　　XP: $10
Motel　　**Location:** Just s of Martin Luther King Blvd. 4122 S Western Ave 90062. Fax: 323/294-9343. **Facility:** rooms. Urban motel, 4 rooms with fireplace. 1 two-bedroom unit. 3 stories; exterior corridors; indoor whirlp **All Rooms:** shower or tub baths. **Cards:** AE, CB, DI, DS, JC, MC, VI. **Special Amenities:** Free breakfa and free newspaper. *(See ad p 573)*

CONTINENTAL PLAZA LOS ANGELES AIRPORT HOTEL　　Phone: (310)645-4600
4/1-9/30　　　　　1P: $95- 145　2P/1B:　$95- 145　2P/2B:　$95- 145　XP: $10
2/1-3/31 & 10/1-1/31　　1P: $85- 145　2P/1B:　$85- 145　2P/2B:　$85- 145　XP: $10
Hotel　　**Location:** 0.5 mi e of airport; 1 blk n of Century Blvd. 9750 Airport Blvd 90045. Fax: 310/216-702 **Terms:** Pets, $20 dep req. **Facility:** 562 rooms. 20 suites with refrigerators, $125; 9 stories; interior/exter corridors; heated pool. Fee: parking. **Dining:** Restaurant; 6 am-10:30 pm; $8-$20; cockta **Services:** giftshop; area transportation, Fox Hill Malls. **Cards:** AE, DI, DS, JC, MC, VI. **Special Amenities:** Ea check-in/late check-out and free room upgrade (subject to availability with advanced reservations).

(See map p. 558)

COURTYARD BY MARRIOTT AT LAX   Rates Subject to Change   **Phone:** (310)649-1400   66
♦♦♦   All Year   1P: $109- 119   2P/1B: $109- 119 2P/2B: $109- 119
Hotel   **Location:** 6161 W Century Blvd 90045. Fax: 310/649-0964. **Terms:** Reserv deposit. **Facility:** 178 rooms. 7
stories; interior corridors. **Services:** giftshop. **Cards:** AE, CB, DI, DS, JC, MC, VI.

COURTYARD BY MARRIOTT CENTURY CITY/BEVERLY HILLS   **Phone:** (310)556-2777   88
(AAA) (SAVE)   Mon-Thurs   1P: $126   2P/1B: $126   2P/2B: $126
♦♦♦   Fri-Sun   1P: $113   2P/1B: $113   2P/2B: $113
Motor Inn   **Location:** Just e of Beverly Glen. 10320 W Olympic Blvd 90064. Fax: 310/203-0563. **Facility:** 134 rooms.
Contemporary decor. 4 stories; interior corridors; whirlpool. **Dining:** Cafeteria; 6:30 am-10 am, breakfast
buffet avail. **Services:** area transportation, 7 am-10 pm, within 3 mi. **Recreation:** video games system in
rooms. **Cards:** AE, DI, DS, MC, VI. **Special Amenities:** Early check-in/late check-out and preferred room (subject to
availability with advanced reservations). *(See color ad p 573)*

(See map p. 558)

CROWNE PLAZA LA AIRPORT
Phone: (310)642-7500 **105**

Sun-Thurs	1P: $129	2P/1B: $129	2P/2B: $129	XP: $15	F12
Fri & Sat	1P: $99	2P/1B: $99	2P/2B: $99	XP: $15	F12

Location: 0.3 mi e of airport. 5985 W Century Blvd 90045. **Fax:** 310/417-3608. **Facility:** 615 rooms. Refrigerators available on request. Some rooms with FAX machine. 16 stories; interior corridors; heated pool, sauna, steamroom, whirlpool. **Fee:** parking. **Dining:** Dining room, restaurant; 6 am-midnight; $8-$27; cocktails. **Services:** giftshop; area transportation. **Recreation:** in-room video game. **Cards:** AE, CB, DI, DS, JC, MC, VI.
(See ad below)

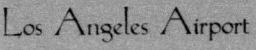

(See map p. 558)

DAYS INN-LOS ANGELES Phone: (213)380-6910 [63]

	Fri & Sat 2/1-4/30 & Sun-Thurs 5/1-8/31	1P: $69	2P/1B: $75	2P/2B: $79	XP: $6	F13
	Sun-Thurs 2/1-4/30, Fri & Sat 5/1-8/31 & Sun-Thurs 12/1-1/31	1P: $65	2P/1B: $70	2P/2B: $75	XP: $6	F13
	9/1-11/30 & Fri & Sat 12/1-1/31	1P: $60	2P/1B: $65	2P/2B: $70	XP: $6	F13

Motel

Location: Just n of Wilshire Blvd. 457 S Mariposa Ave 90020. Fax: 213/382-3888. **Facility:** 47 rooms. 3 whirlpool rms, extra charge; 4 stories; interior/exterior corridors; sauna, whirlpool. **All Rooms:** extended cable TV. **Cards:** AE, CB, DI, DS, JC, MC, VI. **Special Amenities:** Free breakfast and free newspaper.

Do you need a room AND an 18-hole golf course? Let the **Resorts Index lead you** to accommodations with on-site recreational facilities.

(See map p. 558)

DOUBLETREE HOTEL-LOS ANGELES/WESTWOOD, BEVERLY HILLS AREA Phone: (310)475-8711 **75**
  All Year 1P: $140- 175 2P/1B: $140- 175 2P/2B: $140- 175 XP: $10 F18
  Location: 10740 Wilshire Blvd 90024. Fax: 310/475-5220. **Terms:** Reserv deposit. **Facility:** 295 rooms. 19 stories; interior corridors; heated pool, sauna, whirlpool. Fee: parking. **Dining:** Dining room; 6:30 am-2 pm & 5 pm-10 pm; $7-$16; cocktails. **Services:** giftshop; area transportation, J Paul Getty Museum. **Recreation:** video game room. **Cards:** AE, CB, DI, DS, MC, VI. **Special Amenities:** Free newspaper and free room upgrade (subject to availability with advanced reservations). *(See color ad p 574)*
Hotel

DUNES MOTOR HOTEL-WILSHIRE Rates Subject to Change Phone: 323/938-3616 **79**
  6/10-9/15 1P: $65 2P/1B: $65 2P/2B: $73 XP: $4 F12
  2/1-6/9 & 9/16-1/31 1P: $58 2P/1B: $58 2P/2B: $65 XP: $5 F12
  Location: 2 blks w of Crenshaw Blvd. 4300 Wilshire Blvd 90010. Fax: 323/938-8661. **Terms:** Reserv deposit. **Facility:** 63 rooms. 6 efficiencies, $10 extra charge; 3 stories; interior/exterior corridors; heated pool. **Cards:** AE, CB, DI, DS, MC, VI. *(See ad below)*
Motel

ECONO LODGE MID-WILSHIRE Phone: (213)385-0061 **85**
  6/16-9/10 [CP] 1P: $54- 59 2P/1B: $59- 64 2P/2B: $59- 69 XP: $5-8 F18
  2/1-6/15 & 9/11-1/31 [CP] 1P: $49- 55 2P/1B: $54- 59 2P/2B: $54- 59 XP: $5-8 F18
  Location: Just e of Vermont Ave. 3400 W 3rd St 90020. Fax: 213/385-8517. **Facility:** 100 rooms. 4 kitchen units, $5 extra charge; 2 stories; interior/exterior corridors. **All Rooms:** combo or shower baths. **Cards:** AE, CB, DI, DS, JC, MC, VI. *(See color ad below)*
Motel

EMBASSY SUITES HOTEL-LAX/CENTURY Phone: (310)215-1000 **103**
  Mon-Thurs [BP] 1P: $139 2P/1B: $139 2P/2B: $139 XP: $15 F17
  Fri-Sun [BP] 1P: $119- 129 2P/1B: $119- 129 2P/2B: $119- 129 XP: $15 F17
  Location: Just n of Century Blvd; 0.5 mi e of airport. 9801 Airport Blvd 90045. Fax: 310/215-1952. **Terms:** Reserv deposit, 3 day notice; monthly rates. **Facility:** 215 rooms. Atrium lavishly decorated with greenery. 8 stories; interior corridors; heated indoor pool, sauna, whirlpool. Fee: parking. **Dining:** Restaurant; 11 am-11 pm; $12-$17. **Services:** giftshop; complimentary evening beverages. **Cards:** AE, CB, DI, DS, JC, MC, VI. **Special Amenities:** Free breakfast and free newspaper.
Suite Hotel

FARMER'S DAUGHTER MOTEL Phone: (323)937-3930 **73**
  6/20-8/31 1P: $63- 67 2P/1B: $65- 69 2P/2B: $65- 69 XP: $5
  2/1-6/19 & 9/1-1/31 1P: $58- 63 2P/1B: $63- 67 2P/2B: $63- 67 XP: $5
  Location: Opposite Farmers Market & CBS Studio. 115 S Fairfax Ave 90036. Fax: 323/932-1608. **Terms:** Reserv deposit. **Facility:** 66 rooms. 3 stories; exterior corridors; small heated pool. **Cards:** AE, MC, VI. **Special Amenities:** Free local telephone calls and preferred room (subject to availability with advanced reservations).
Motel

(See map p. 558)

FOUR SEASONS HOTEL   Phone: (310)273-2222 **70**
 All Year   1P: $325- 400   2P/1B: $355- 400 2P/2B: $355- 400 XP: $30   F18
◆◆◆◆   **Location:** Corner of Burton Way. 300 S Doheny Dr 90048. **Fax:** 310/859-3824. **Terms:** Weekly/monthly
Hotel   rates; pets. **Facility:** 285 rooms. Impressive hotel. In-room fax machines. 16 stories; interior corridors; heated
              pool, whirlpool. **Dining:** Dining room, restaurant; 6:30 am-11:30 pm; $15-$33; cocktails; afternoon tea; also,
              Gardens, see separate listing. **Services:** giftshop; area transportation, to local shopping. Fee: massage.
Cards: AE, CB, DI, DS, JC, MC, VI.

ee map p. 558)

RAMA HOTEL LOS ANGELES — Rates Subject to Change — Phone: (310)670-8111 **84**
◆◆ All Year — 1P: $99- 129 2P/1B: $99- 129 2P/2B: $99- 129 XP: $10 — **F17**
tel **Location:** On SR 1. 8601 Lincoln at Manchester Blvd 90045. Fax: 310/337-1883. **Facility:** 763 rooms. 3-12 stories; interior corridors; heated pool. **Services:** giftshop; area transportation. **All Rooms:** combo or shower hs. **Cards:** AE, CB, DI, DS, JC, MC, VI. *(See color ad below)*

(See map p. 558)

HILGARD HOUSE HOTEL
Phone: (310)208-3945
(AAA) (SAVE)   All Year [CP]   1P: $114   2P/1B: $124   2P/2B: $124   XP: $10
◆◆◆   **Location:** 3 blks n of Wilshire Blvd in Westwood. 927 Hilgard Ave 90024. Fax: 310/208-1972. **Facility:**
Motel   rooms. Residential area. Tastefully furnished guest rooms. 3 stories; interior corridors. **Dining:** Restaura
nearby. **Some Rooms:** whirlpools. **Cards:** AE, CB, DI, DS, JC, MC, VI. **Special Amenities: Free breakfas**
(See ad below)

HOLIDAY INN EXPRESS- CENTURY CITY
Phone: (310)553-1000
(AAA) (SAVE)   All Year [CP]   1P: $109   2P/1B: $109   2P/2B: $109   XP: $10
◆◆◆   **Location:** Just e of Beverly Glen. 10330 W Olympic Blvd 90064. Fax: 310/277-1633. **Terms:** Rese
Motel   deposit. **Facility:** 47 rooms. Some rooms have lofts. Suites, $159; 4 stories; interior corrido
All Rooms: combo or shower baths. **Some Rooms:** whirlpools. **Cards:** AE, CB, DI, DS, JC, MC,
Special Amenities: Early check-in/late check-out and free room upgrade (subject to availability w
advanced reservations).

HOLIDAY INN-INTERNATIONAL AIRPORT
Phone: (310)649-5151
(AAA) (SAVE)   All Year   1P: $129- 149   2P/1B: $129- 159   2P/2B: $129- 159   XP: $10
◆◆◆   **Location:** Just n of Century Blvd. 9901 S La Cienega Blvd 90045. Fax: 310/670-3619. **Facility:** 401 roon
Hotel   Some rooms with fax machine. 12 stories; interior corridors; heated pool. Fee: parking. **Dining:** Dining roo
6 am-11 pm; $7-$13; cocktails. **Services:** giftshop. **Recreation:** video games. **Cards:** AE, CB, DI, DS, J
MC, VI. (See color ad below)

HOLIDAY INN SELECT
Rates Subject to Change   Phone: 310/553-6561
◆◆◆   Fri-Sun   1P: $129   2P/1B: $129   2P/2B: $129   XP: $10
Hotel   Mon-Thurs   1P: $119   2P/1B: $119   2P/2B: $119   XP: $10
Location: Just n of Pico Blvd. 1150 S Beverly Dr 90035. Fax: 310/277-4469. **Facility:** 260 rooms. 12 storie
interior corridors; heated pool. **Services:** giftshop; area transportation. **Cards:** AE, CB, DI, DS, JC, MC, VI.

HOTEL BEL-AIR
Rates Subject to Change   Phone: (310)472-1211
◆◆◆◆   All Year   1P: $350-2500   2P/1B: $350-2500   2P/2B: $410-2500   XP: $30
Hotel   **Location:** 0.5 mi n of Sunset Blvd. 701 Stone Canyon Rd 90077. Fax: 310/476-5890. **Facility:** 92 roon
Quiet, secluded location on extensive, beautifully landscaped grounds. Suites & apartments. 5 two-bedroo
units. 1 story; exterior corridors; heated pool. **Services:** Fee: massage. **Some Rooms:** 5 kitchens. **Cards:** AE, DI, JC, M
VI. A Preferred Hotel.

(See map p. 558)

HOTEL DEL CAPRI
Phone: (310)474-3511
All Year [CP]   1P: $95- 150   2P/1B: $105- 150   2P/2B: $105- 150   XP: $10
Location: Just e of Westwood Blvd. 10587 Wilshire Blvd 90024. Fax: 310/470-9999. **Terms:** Monthly rate
pets, $70-$140 non-refundable fee req. **Facility:** 79 rooms. Attractively landscaped. 12 deluxe suites, $14
Suite Motel $275 for 2-8 persons; 4 stories; interior/exterior baths. **Services:** area transportation, with
3 mi. **All Rooms:** combo or shower baths. **Some Rooms:** 46 efficiencies, whirlpools. **Cards:** AE, CB, D
MC, VI. **Special Amenities:** Free breakfast.

HOTEL NIKKO AT BEVERLY HILLS
Phone: (310)247-0400
All Year   1P: $310- 720   2P/1B: $335- 720   2P/2B: $335- 720   XP: $25
Location: La Cienega Blvd at San Vicente. 465 S La Cienega Blvd 90048. Fax: 310/247-031
Terms: Reserv deposit; package plans; pets, $25 extra charge, $100 dep req. **Facility:** 297 rooms. Spaciou
Hotel   rooms decorated in a contemporary oriental motif. CD, stereo system & fax machine in each room. 1 tw
bedroom unit. 9 suites, with living room, business amenities & some with wet bar, $600-$950, also, Preside
tial suite avail $1800-$2070 for up to 4 persons; 7 stories; exterior corridors; heated pool, saunas. **Dining:** Dining roon
restaurant; 6:30 am-2:30 & 6 pm-10:30 pm; $30-$50; cocktails. **Services:** giftshop. Fee: massage, area transportation
Cards: AE, CB, DI, DS, JC, MC, VI. **Special Amenities:** Free newspaper and preferred room (subject to availabilit
with advanced reservations).

HOTEL SOFITEL
Rates Subject to Change   Phone: (310)278-5444
Sun-Thurs   1P: $340- 400   2P/1B: $400   2P/2B: $340- 400   XP: $25
Hotel   Fri & Sat   1P: $300- 340   2P/1B: $400   2P/2B: $300- 340   XP: $25
Location: 2.5 mi n of I-10, exit La Cienega Blvd; across from Beverly Center. 8555 Beverly Blvd 9004
Fax: 310/657-2816. **Facility:** 311 rooms. Spacious, attractive lobby, well-appointed rooms. 10 stories; interior corridors; heate
pool. **Services:** giftshop. Fee: massage. **Cards:** AE, CB, DI, MC, VI.

HOWARD JOHNSON HOTEL INTERNATIONAL AT LAX
Phone: (310)645-7700
All Year   1P: $59   2P/1B: $69   2P/2B: $79   XP: $10
Location: Just s of Manchester Ave. 8620 Airport Blvd 90045. Fax: 310/645-2958. **Facility:** 160 rooms. Mi
suites $89. 10 whirlpool rms, extra charge; 6 stories; interior corridors; heated pool, whirlpoo
Motor Inn   **Dining:** Restaurant; 6:30 am-9:30 pm; $7-$25; Sushi Bar 6 pm-11 pm. **Services:** giftshop; area
transportation, within 5 miles. **Cards:** AE, CB, DI, DS, JC, MC, VI. **Special Amenities:** Early check-in/lat
check-out and free room upgrade (subject to availability with advanced reservations).
(See color ad opposite inside back cover)

LA MIRAGE INN
Phone: (323)418-0888
All Year   1P: $45   2P/1B: $45   2P/2B: $60
Location: Just s of Imperial Hwy. 11711 S Western Ave 90047. Fax: 323/777-6091. **Terms:** Reserv depos
5 day notice. **Facility:** 34 rooms. 4 whirlpool rms, extra charge; 2 stories; exterior corridors. **Cards:** AE, DS
Motel   MC, VI.

LOS ANGELES AIRPORT HILTON & TOWERS
Phone: (310)410-4000
All Year   1P: $99   2P/1B: $99   2P/2B: $99   XP: $20
Location: 0.8 mi e of airport. 5711 W Century Blvd 90045. Fax: 310/410-6250. **Terms:** Pets, $15 extr
charge. **Facility:** 1234 rooms. Contemporary decor. 17 stories; interior corridors; heated pool, saunas, whir
Hotel   pools. Fee: parking. **Dining:** Dining room, restaurant; 6 am-10 pm; $7-$25; cocktails; deli, 24 hr
Services: giftshop. **Cards:** AE, CB, DI, DS, JC, MC, VI. **Special Amenities:** Free newspaper and fre
room upgrade (subject to availability with advanced reservations). *(See ad p 119)*

LOS ANGELES AIRPORT MARRIOTT HOTEL
Rates Subject to Change   Phone: 310/641-5700
All Year   1P: $145   2P/1B: $145   2P/2B: $145
Hotel   **Location:** 0.5 mi e of airport. 5855 W Century Blvd 90045. Fax: 310/337-5358. **Terms:** Reserv deposi
Facility: 1010 rooms. Some rooms with fax machine; internet access through TV in rooms. 18 stories; interio
corridors; heated pool. Fee: parking. **Services:** giftshop. **Cards:** AE, CB, DI, DS, JC, MC, VI.

OXFORD PALACE HOTEL
Rates Subject to Change   Phone: (213)389-8000
All Year   1P: $84- 98   2P/1B: $90- 105   2P/2B: $149   XP: $20
Hotel   **Location:** In Koreatown, just e of Western Ave, between 7th & 8th sts. 845 S Oxford Ave 9000
Fax: 213/389-8500. **Facility:** 86 rooms. Nine 1-bedroom suites, $110-$370; 4 stories; interio
corridors. **Services:** giftshop. Fee: area transportation. **Cards:** AE, CB, DI, DS, MC, VI.

PARK HYATT LOS ANGELES AT CENTURY CITY
Phone: (310)277-2777
All Year   1P: $269- 399   2P/1B: $294- 424   2P/2B: $294- 424   XP: $25
Location: 0.5 mi s of Santa Monica Blvd. 2151 Avenue of the Stars 90067. Fax: 310/785-9240. **Facility:** 36
Hotel   rooms. Nicely decorated rooms, many with balcony or patio. In-room fax machines. 17 stories; interior cor
dors; heated indoor pool, saunas, steamrooms, whirlpool. Fee: parking. **Dining:** Dining room; 6:30 am-10:3
pm, Sat & Sun from 7 am; $18-$30; afternoon tea. **Services:** giftshop; area transportation, Century City
Rodeo Dr. Fee: massage. **Recreation:** in-room fax machines. **Cards:** AE, CB, DI, DS, JC, MC, VI. *(See color ad p 565)*

QUALITY HOTEL-LOS ANGELES AIRPORT
Phone: (310)645-2200
8/22-1/31   1P: $100- 130   2P/1B: $110- 140   2P/2B: $110- 150   XP: $15
6/1-8/21   1P: $90- 115   2P/1B: $100- 130   2P/2B: $100- 140   XP: $15
2/1-5/31   1P: $80- 105   2P/1B: $90- 116   2P/2B: $90- 126   XP: $15
Hotel   **Location:** 1.5 blks w of I-405. 5249 W Century Blvd 90045. Fax: 310/641-8214. **Terms:** Pets, $50 fee fr
dogs over 20 lbs. **Facility:** 278 rooms. 10 stories; interior corridors; heated pool. Fee: parking. **Dining:** De
6 am-10 pm, summer-11 pm; Avenue Food Court; $5-$9; cocktails. **Services:** giftshop; area transportation, twice dail
Recreation: video games in all rooms, separate game room. **All Rooms:** extended cable TV. **Cards:** AE, CB, DI, DS, JC
MC, VI. **Special Amenities:** Early check-in/late check-out and free room upgrade (subject to availability wit
advanced reservations). *(See color ad p 570)*

(See map p. 558)

RADISSON WILSHIRE PLAZA HOTEL   **Phone:** (213)381-7411   [G4]
All Year   1P: $149- 199   2P/1B: $149- 199   2P/2B: $149- 199   XP: $10   F18
Location: On Wilshire Blvd at Normandie Ave. 3515 Wilshire Blvd 90010. Fax: 213/386-7379.
Terms: Monthly rates. **Facility:** 383 rooms. 12 stories; interior corridors; heated pool. Fee: parking.
Dining: Dining room, restaurant; 6 am-11 pm; $10-$21; cocktails. **Services:** giftshop. **Cards:** AE, CB, DI, DS, JC, MC, VI. **Special Amenities: Preferred room (subject to availability with advanced reservations).** *(See ad below)*

RAMADA LIMITED/WEST LOS ANGELES/UCLA   Rates Subject to Change   **Phone:** 310/208-6677   [97]
6/16-9/15 [CP]   1P: $75- 120   2P/1B: $86- 120   2P/2B: $95- 120   XP: $6-8   F12
2/1-6/15 & 9/16-1/31 [CP]   1P: $66- 120   2P/1B: $79- 120   2P/2B: $86- 120   XP: $6-8   F12
Location: Just n of Wilshire Blvd in Westwood. 1052 Tiverton Ave 90024. Fax: 310/824-3732.
Terms: Reserv deposit. **Facility:** 36 rooms. Studio & 1-bedroom apartments; 6 small units. 3 stories; interior corridors. **All Rooms:** combo or shower baths. **Some Rooms:** 29 kitchens. **Cards:** AE, CB, DI, DS, JC, MC, VI.

RENAISSANCE BEVERLY HILLS   **Phone:** (310)277-2800   [67]
All Year   1P: $205- 250   2P/1B: $205- 250   2P/2B: $205- 250   XP: $25
Location: At Rodeo Dr & Pico Blvd. 1224 S Beverwil Dr 90035. Fax: 310/203-9537. **Terms:** Reserv deposit.
Facility: 139 rooms. 2 two-bedroom units. 6 executive jacuzzi suites $700-$900 for 2 people; 12 stories; interior corridors; heated pool. **Dining:** 7 am-10 pm; $10-$25; health conscious menu items; cocktails; also, The Chez, see separate listing. **Services:** complimentary evening beverages; area transportation, within 5 mi. **Recreation:** CD players in all rooms. **Some Rooms:** whirlpools. **Cards:** AE, CB, DI, DS, JC, MC, VI. **Special Amenities: early check-in/late check-out and free newspaper.**

RENAISSANCE LOS ANGELES HOTEL-AIRPORT   Rates Subject to Change   **Phone:** (310)337-2800   [77]
Sun-Thurs   1P: $129   2P/1B: $129   2P/2B: $129
Fri & Sat   1P: $116   2P/1B: $116   2P/2B: $116
Location: 1 blk n of Century Blvd. 9620 Airport Blvd 90045. Fax: 310/216-6681. **Facility:** 499 rooms. Elegantly decorated rooms, lobby & dining areas. 11 stories; interior corridors; heated pool, saunas, whirlpool. Fee: parking. **Dining:** 2 restaurants; 5:30 am-11 pm; $13-$23; cocktails. **Services:** giftshop; area transportation, within 5 mi. **Recreation:** in-room video games. **Cards:** AE, CB, DI, DS, JC, MC, VI.

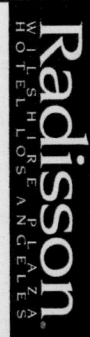

(See map p. 558)

SHERATON GATEWAY
Phone: (310)642-1111 ⑧
Ⓐ Ⓢ Ⓐ Ⓥ Ⓔ All Year 1P: $119- 144 2P/1B: $119- 144 2P/2B: $119- 144 XP: $25 F1
◆◆◆ **Location:** 6101 W Century Blvd 90045. Fax: 310/410-1267. **Terms:** Reserv deposit. **Facility:** 659 rooms. Co
Hotel temporary decor. 15 stories; interior corridors; heated pool, whirlpool. Fee: parking. **Dining:** Dining roor
restaurant; 6 am-11 pm; $13-$22; cocktails. **Services:** giftshop. **Recreation:** in room video gam
Cards: AE, CB, DI, DS, JC, MC, VI. **Special Amenities:** Free newspaper.

SUMMIT HOTEL, BEL-AIR
Rates Subject to Change Phone: 310/476-6571 ⑩
Ⓐ Ⓐ Ⓐ All Year 1P: $130 2P/1B: $130 2P/2B: $130 XP: $20 F1
◆◆◆ **Location:** In Brentwood area; just w of I-405. 11461 Sunset Blvd 90049. Fax: 310/471-6310. **Terms:** Rese
Motor Inn deposit. **Facility:** 161 rooms. Attractive grounds. Spacious, nicely decorated rooms, many with balcony
patio. 2 stories; interior corridors; heated pool; 1 tennis court. **Dining:** Dining room; 6:30 am-10:30 pr
$11-$21; cocktails. **Services:** giftshop. **Cards:** AE, CB, DI, DS, JC, MC, VI.

TRAVELODGE HOTEL AT LAX
Guaranteed Rates Phone: (310)649-4000 ⑨
Ⓐ Ⓐ Ⓐ All Year 1P: $74- 99 2P/1B: $74- 99 2P/2B: $79- 109 XP: $6-10 F1
◆◆◆ **Location:** 1 mi e of airport at Aviation Blvd. 5547 W Century Blvd 90045. Fax: 310/649-0311. **Terms:** Pet
Motor Inn $8 extra charge. **Facility:** 147 rooms. Plants in rooms, corridors & walkways create inviting tropical atmo
phere. 2 stories; interior/exterior corridors; heated pool. **Dining:** Coffee shop; 24 hrs; $5-$9; cocktail
Services: area transportation, within airport area. **Recreation:** video games. **All Rooms:** combo or showe
baths. **Cards:** AE, CB, DI, DS, JC, MC, VI. (See color ad p 569)

TRAVELODGE-LOS ANGELES WEST
Phone: (310)474-4576 ⑩
Ⓐ Ⓐ Ⓐ Ⓢ Ⓐ Ⓥ Ⓔ 6/16-9/15 [CP] 1P: $65- 89 2P/1B: $65- 95 2P/2B: $85- 95 XP: $5-8
◆ 2/1-6/15 & 9/16-1/31 [CP] 1P: $59- 89 2P/1B: $59- 90 2P/2B: $75- 90 XP: $5-8
Motel **Location:** 2 mi e from I-405, Santa Monica Blvd exit. 10740 Santa Monica Blvd 90025. Fax: 310/470-311
Terms: Reserv deposit; weekly rates. **Facility:** 55 rooms. 2 stories; exterior corridors. **All Rooms:** combo
shower baths. **Cards:** AE, CB, DI, DS, JC, MC, VI. **Special Amenities:** Free breakfast and fre
newspaper.

THE WESTIN HOTEL-LOS ANGELES AIRPORT
Rates Subject to Change Phone: (310)216-5858 ⑦
◆◆◆ All Year 1P: $169- 179 2P/1B: $169- 179 2P/2B: $169- 179 XP: $15 F1
Hotel **Location:** 5400 W Century Blvd 90045. Fax: 310/670-1948. **Terms:** Reserv deposit. **Facility:** 723 rooms. Co
temporary decor rooms. Some rooms with private outside whirlpools. 12 stories; interior corridors; heated poo
Fee: parking. **Services:** giftshop; area transportation. **Cards:** AE, CB, DI, DS, JC, MC, VI.

WESTWOOD MARQUIS HOTEL AND GARDENS
Rates Subject to Change Phone: 310/208-8765 ⑨
◆◆◆◆ All Year 1P: $225- 650 2P/1B: $225- 650 2P/2B: $260- 650
Suite Hotel **Location:** Westwood Village, just n of Wilshire Blvd. 930 Hilgard Ave 90024. Fax: 310/824-035
Facility: 257 rooms. Elegant hotel; 1- to 3-bedroom units with living room. 15 stories; interior corridors; heate
pool. **Services:** giftshop. Fee: massage. **Cards:** AE, CB, DI, DS, JC, MC, VI. A Preferred Hotel.

WYNDHAM HOTEL AT LOS ANGELES AIRPORT
Phone: (310)670-9000 ⑩
Ⓐ Ⓐ Ⓐ Ⓢ Ⓐ Ⓥ Ⓔ Sun-Thurs [EP] 1P: $99 2P/1B: $99 2P/2B: $99 XP: $10-20 F1
◆◆◆ Fri & Sat [BP] 1P: $89 2P/1B: $89 2P/2B: $89 XP: $10-20 F1
Hotel **Location:** On SR 1. 6225 W Century Blvd at Sepulveda Blvd 90045. Fax: 310/670-8110. **Facility:** 591 room
Contemporary room decor, some with fax machine. 12 stories; interior corridors; heated pool, sauna, whirlpoo
Fee: parking. **Dining:** Dining room, restaurant; 6 am-11 pm; $8-$25; cocktails. **Services:** giftsho
Cards: AE, CB, DI, DS, JC, MC, VI. (See color ad p 581)

RESTAURANTS

CAMPANILE
Lunch: $8-$16 Dinner: $22-$50 Phone: 323/938-1447 ④
◆◆◆ **Location:** Just n of Wilshire Blvd. 624 S La Brea Ave 90036. **Hours:** 11:30 am-2:30 & 6-10 pm, Fri 5:3
Italian pm-11 pm, Sat 8 am-1:30 & 5:30-11 pm, Sun 8 am-1:30 pm. Closed major holiday
Reservations: suggested. **Features:** semi-formal attire; Sunday brunch; cocktails & lounge; street parking
fee for valet parking; a la carte. Italian/Mediterranean food with a California influence served in a converted office buildir
built by Charlie Chaplin. Creative desserts & breads prepared in their adjacent bakery. Smoke free premises. **Cards:** A
CB, DI, DS, MC, VI.

CHAYA BRASSERIE
Lunch: $11-$20 Dinner: $25-$40 Phone: 310/859-8833 ⑤
◆◆◆ **Location:** Near Cedars-Sinai Medical Center. 8741 Alden Dr 90048. **Hours:** 11:30 am-2:30 & 6-10:30 pr
Ethnic Fri-11 pm, Sat 6 pm-11 pm, Sun 6 pm-10 pm. Closed: 1/1, 11/25 & 12/25. **Reservations:** require
Features: casual dress; cocktails & lounge; fee for valet parking; a la carte. Dine in a twenty-first centur
Quonset hut. French, Japanese & Italian entrees. Smoke free premises. **Cards:** AE, DI, MC, VI.

THE CHEZ
Lunch: $8-$15 Dinner: $12-$23 Phone: 310/277-2800 ⑤
◆◆◆ **Location:** At Rodeo Dr & Pico Blvd; in Renaissance Beverly Hills. 1224 S Beverwil Dr 90035. **Hours:**
Continental am-10 pm, Fri & Sat to 11 pm, Sun 8 am-9 pm. **Reservations:** suggested. **Features:** cocktails & lounge; fe
for valet parking; a la carte. California continental cuisine with a Mediterranean influence. Sat & Sun brunc
Cards: AE, CB, DI, MC, VI.

CITRUS
Lunch: $12-$18 Dinner: $24-$30 Phone: 323/857-0034 ⑥
◆◆◆ **Location:** 1 blk w of Highland Ave. 6703 Melrose Ave 90038. **Hours:** noon-2:30 & 6:30-10 pm, Fri 6:3
French pm-11 pm, Sat 6 pm-11 pm. Closed major holidays & Sun. **Reservations:** suggested. **Features:** casu
dress; cocktails; fee for valet parking; a la carte. Contemporary decor. Interesting selection of French
California cuisine. Smoke free premises. **Cards:** AE, DI, JC, MC, VI.

**Look For The Lodging Signs
Backed By A 100%
Satisfaction Guarantee**

HOW TO RUN A HOTEL.℠

Free local calls and in-room coffee makes Quality the perfect place for today's traveler. For over 50 years, Quality has been making everything just right.

It's more than a room. It's Comfort.℠

You always enjoy extra amenities when you stay at Comfort Inn & Comfort Suites. Like our Free Breakfast to help you start the day off right.

Upgrade your room, not your rate.℠

At Clarion, you'll find everything you expect at an upscale hotel. Well, everything except the high rates. And AAA members save 20% at most Clarions.

In a class by itself.℠

With low rates and state-of-the-art rooms, it's no wonder Sleep Inn is rated among the best hotels for satisfaction, service and value.

Stay longer for less.℠

The reasonably-priced option for travelers who are looking for a comfortable extended-stay hotel. A great place for visits that last a night, a week, or more.

For Reservations Call
1-800-228-1AAA
Or Contact Your Local AAA Club.

HOW TO RUN A HOTEL.℠

It's more than a room. It's Comfort.℠

Upgrade your room, not your rate.℠

In a class by itself.℠

Stay longer for less.℠

For Reservations Call
1-800-228-1AAA
Or Contact Your Local AAA Club.

(king of the road)

Don't hit the road without enrolling in the **AT&T One Rate® Calling Card Plan.** Unlike some other calling card plans that have a hidden service charge for every call, this plan has just a flat $1 monthly fee. Plus a low per minute rate for domestic AT&T Calling Card calls. Just call **1 800 378-8562 x62549** for this outstanding travel value.

It's all within your reach.

(See map p. 558)

DAILY GRILL — **Lunch:** $7-$12 — **Dinner:** $9-$19 — **Phone:** 310/442-0044 ㊹
◆◆
American — **Location:** In Brentwood Gardens. 11677 San Vicente Blvd 90049. **Hours:** 11:30 am-11 pm, Sun 10 am-10 pm. Closed: 11/25 & 12/25. **Features:** casual dress; carryout; cocktails; fee for valet parking. Casual atmosphere. Large selection salad, sandwiches & entrees. Smoke free premises. **Cards:** AE, DI, MC, VI.
⊠

DYNASTY ROOM — **Dinner:** $50-$75 — **Phone:** 310/208-8765 ㊸
◆◆◆◆
Continental — **Location:** Westwood Village, just n of Wilshire Blvd; in Westwood Marquis Hotel and Gardens. 930 Hilgard Ave 90024. **Hours:** 5:30 pm-11 pm. **Reservations:** suggested. **Features:** casual dress; children's menu; cocktails; entertainment; valet parking; a la carte. Elegant dining room with attentive service & creative dishes artfully presented. Smoke free premises. **Cards:** AE, CB, DI, JC, MC, VI.
⊠

EL CHOLO — **Lunch:** $6-$12 — **Dinner:** $6-$12 — **Phone:** 323/734-2773 ㊴
◆◆
Mexican — **Location:** 2 blks s of Olympic Blvd. 1121 S Western Ave 90006. **Hours:** 11 am-10 pm, Fri & Sat-11 pm, Sun-9 pm. Closed: 7/4, 11/25 & 12/25. **Reservations:** suggested. **Features:** casual dress; children's menu; carryout; cocktails & lounge; fee for valet parking; a la carte. A charming, long established, family owned & operated restaurant. Smoke free premises. **Cards:** AE, MC, VI.
⊠

FOUR OAKS — **Lunch:** $12-$20 — **Dinner:** $20-$30 — **Phone:** 310/470-2265 ㊲
◆◆◆
French — **Location:** In Bel Air, 0.5 mi n of Sunset Blvd. 2181 N Beverly Glen 90077. **Hours:** 11:30 am-2 & 6-10 pm, Mon 6 pm-10 pm, Sun 10:30 am-2 & 6-10 pm. **Reservations:** suggested. **Features:** semi-formal attire; Sunday brunch; cocktails & lounge; valet parking; a la carte. Charming century-old house. California-French cuisine. Smoke free premises. **Cards:** AE, MC, VI.
⊠

GARDENS — **Lunch:** $17-$22 — **Dinner:** $28-$38 — **Phone:** 310/273-2222 ㊻
◆◆◆◆
American — **Location:** Corner of Burton Way; in Four Seasons Hotel. 300 S Doheny Dr 90048. **Hours:** 7 am-10 pm. **Reservations:** suggested. **Features:** semi-formal attire; Sunday brunch; health conscious menu; cocktails; valet parking; a la carte. Comfortable dining room with soft elegant air. Creative American cuisine using fresh ingredients. Also garden dining area. **Cards:** AE, CB, DI, JC, MC, VI.
⊠

JUNIOR'S RESTAURANT — **Lunch:** $5-$8 — **Dinner:** $7-$10 — **Phone:** 310/475-5771 ㊺
ⒶⒶⒶ
Ethnic — **Location:** In Rancho Park area, just n of Pico Blvd. 2379 Westwood Blvd 90064. **Hours:** 6:30 am-11 pm, Fri-midnight, Sat 7 am-midnight, Sun 7 am-11 pm. **Features:** casual dress; children's menu; senior's menu; health conscious menu; carryout; beer & wine only; a la carte. Very popular Jewish restaurant & delicatessen. Large selection of salads, sandwiches, entrees, kosher style foods & bakery. Smoke free premises. **Cards:** AE, DS, MC, VI.
⊠

LA BRUSCHETTA — **Lunch:** $12-$18 — **Dinner:** $12-$22 — **Phone:** 310/477-1052 ㊻
◆◆
Italian — **Location:** 0.5 mi ne of I-405; Santa Monica Blvd. 1621 Westwood Blvd 90024. **Hours:** noon-2 & 6-10:30 pm, Fri & Sat 6 pm-10:30 pm. Closed major holidaysSun. **Reservations:** required. **Features:** casual dress; beer & wine only; fee for valet parking; a la carte. Smoke free premises. **Cards:** AE, DI, DS, MC, VI.
⊠

LA CACHETTE RESTAURANT — **Lunch:** $12-$22 — **Dinner:** $18-$30 — **Phone:** 310/470-4992 ㊿
◆◆
French — **Location:** 2.3 mi e of I-405; Santa Monica Blvd exit. 10506 Santa Monica Blvd 90025. **Hours:** 11:30 am-2:30 & 6-10 pm, Sat & Sun 5:30 pm-10:30 pm. **Reservations:** required. **Features:** No A/C; casual dress; beer & wine only; street parking & valet parking; a la carte. Featuring interesting selection of French cuisine. Entrance only through rear alley. Smoke free premises. **Cards:** AE, DI, MC, VI.
⊠

LE CHARDONNAY — **Dinner:** $19-$28 — **Phone:** 323/655-8880 ㊼
◆◆◆
French — **Location:** 5 blks e of La Cienega Blvd. 8284 Melrose Ave 90046. **Hours:** 6 pm-10 pm, Fri & Sat 5:30 pm-10 pm, Sun 5:30 pm-9 pm. Closed major holidays& Mon. **Reservations:** suggested. **Features:** casual dress; cocktails; fee for valet parking; a la carte. French bistro decor. Excellent food & service. Smoke free premises. **Cards:** AE, DI, MC, VI.
⊠

L'ORANGERIE — **Dinner:** $35-$50 — **Phone:** 310/652-9770 ⑰
◆◆◆◆
French — **Location:** 903 N La Cienega Blvd 90069. **Hours:** 6 pm-11 pm. Closed: 1/1, 7/4 & 12/25 & Mon. **Reservations:** suggested. **Features:** semi-formal attire; cocktails & lounge; fee for valet parking; a la carte. Formal dining in a classic French atmosphere. Smoke free premises. **Cards:** AE, CB, DI, MC, VI.
⊠

LUNARIA — **Lunch:** $10-$20 — **Dinner:** $15-$35 — **Phone:** 310/282-8870 ㊽
◆◆◆
Provincial French — **Location:** 2.3 mi e of I-405; Santa Monica Blvd exit. 10351 Santa Monica Blvd 90025. **Hours:** 11:30 am-2:30 & 6-10 pm, Mon 6-10 pm, Fri & Sat 6-11 pm. Closed major holidays & Sun. **Reservations:** required. **Features:** casual dress; cocktails & lounge; entertainment; valet parking; a la carte. Featuring an interesting selection of French cuisine. Extensive collection of Impressionist paintings. Jazz music. Smoke free premises. **Cards:** AE, CB, DI, DS, MC, VI.
⊠

PANDA INN — **Lunch:** $6-$10 — **Dinner:** $9-$13 — **Phone:** 310/470-7790 ㊾
◆◆
Chinese — **Location:** On ground level of Westside Pavilion. 10800 W Pico Blvd 90064. **Hours:** 11:30 am-10:30 pm, Fri & Sat-11 pm. Closed: 11/26. **Reservations:** suggested. **Features:** casual dress; carryout; cocktails; fee for valet parking; a la carte. Selection of Mandarin & Szechuan cuisine. Smoke free premises. **Cards:** AE, DI, MC, VI.
⊠

(See map p. 558)

PATINA **Lunch:** $15-$22 **Dinner:** $25-$35 **Phone:** 323/467-1108 ⑥
◆◆◆◆ **Location:** 1 blk w of Cahuenga Blvd. 5955 Melrose Ave 90038. **Hours:** 6 pm-10 pm, Tues noon-2 & 6-1
French pm, Sat 5:30 pm-10 pm, Sun 6 pm-10 pm. Closed: 1/1 & 12/25. **Reservations:** suggested. **Features:** casu
dress; cocktails & lounge; street parking & fee for valet parking; a la carte. Superbly prepared French
California cuisine. Smoke free premises. **Cards:** AE, DI, DS, MC, VI. ⊠

PRIMI **Lunch:** $10-$20 **Dinner:** $12-$25 **Phone:** 310/475-9235 ⑥
◆◆◆ **Location:** 2.3 mi ne of I-10, Overland Ave exit. 10543 W Pico Blvd 90064. **Hours:** 11:30 am-2:30 pm & 5:3
Northern pm-10:30 pm. Closed major holidaysSat for lunch & Sun. **Reservations:** suggested. **Features:** casual dres
Italian cocktails; valet parking; a la carte. Spacious open kitchen dominates dining area. Nice selection of entree
Pasta, bread & desserts made on premises. Patio dining. Smoke free premises. **Cards:** AE, DI, MC, VI. ⊠

THE RESTAURANT **Lunch:** $22-$40 **Dinner:** $35-$55 **Phone:** 310/472-1211 ④
◆◆◆◆ **Location:** 0.5 mi n of Sunset Blvd; in Hotel Bel-Air. 701 Stone Canyon Rd 90077. **Hours:** 7 am-1
Specialty noon-2:30 & 6:30-10 pm. **Reservations:** required. **Features:** semi-formal attire; Sunday brunch; cocktails
lounge; fee for valet parking; a la carte. Beautifully decorated dining room. French-California cuisine
Cards: AE, DI, JC, MC, VI. ⊠

SISLEY ITALIAN KITCHEN **Lunch:** $8-$15 **Dinner:** $8-$22 **Phone:** 310/446-3030 ④
◆◆ **Location:** 2.3 mi nw of I-10, Overland Ave exit, in Westside Pavilion Shopping Center. 10800 W Pico Blv
Italian 90064. **Hours:** 11:30 am-10 pm, Fri & Sat-10:30 pm, Sun 11:30-9 pm. Closed: 12/2!
Reservations: suggested. **Features:** casual dress; Sunday brunch; carryout; cocktails; valet parking; a l
carte. A nice selection of Northern & Southern Italian cuisine. Smoke free premises. **Cards:** AE, DI, MC, VI. ⊠

SONORA CAFE **Lunch:** $11-$17 **Dinner:** $15-$25 **Phone:** 323/857-1800 ⑤
◆◆ **Location:** 180 S La Brea Blvd 90036. **Hours:** 11:30 am-10 pm, Fri-11 pm, Sat from 5:30-11 pm, Sun 5 pm-
Southwest pm. Closed major holidays. **Reservations:** suggested. **Features:** casual dress; cocktails & lounge; stree
American parking & fee for valet parking; a la carte. An attractive restaurant serving a nice selection of Southwester
cuisine. Patio dining. Smoke free premises. **Cards:** AE, CB, DI, MC, VI. ⊠

LOS ANGELES (SAN FERNANDO VALLEY)

The Los Angeles Vicinity

ARCADIA—48,300   (See map p. 562; index p. 547)

LODGINGS

EMBASSY SUITES
◆◆◆   Sun-Thurs [BP]
Suite Motor Inn Fri & Sat [BP]
Rates Subject to Change
1P: $149- 159   2P/1B: $149- 169   2P/2B: $149- 169   XP: $10-20
1P: $129- 139   2P/1B: $129- 139   2P/2B: $129- 139   XP: $10-20
Phone: (626)445-8525
Location: 0.3 mi w of I-210; exit Huntington Dr. 211 E Huntington Dr 91006. Fax: 626/445-854
Facility: 194 rooms. Beautifully landscaped atrium area. 7 stories; interior corridors; heated indoor pool. **Services:** giftsho
Cards: AE, CB, DI, DS, JC, MC, VI.

HAMPTON INN
◆◆◆   All Year [CP]
Motel
Rates Subject to Change
1P: $79- 99   2P/1B: $89- 109   2P/2B: $89- 109
Phone: (626)574-5600
Location: 0.5 mi w of I-210, exit Huntington Dr. 311 E Huntington Dr 91006. Fax: 626/446-2748
Facility: 131 rooms. 4 stories; interior corridors; heated pool. **Cards:** AE, CB, DI, DS, JC, MC, VI.

RESIDENCE INN BY MARRIOTT
◆◆◆   All Year [CP]
Apartment
Motel
Guaranteed Rates
1P: $101- 139   2P/1B: $101- 139   2P/2B: $139
Phone: 626/446-6500
Location: 0.5 mi w of I-210, exit Huntington Dr. 321 E Huntington Dr 91006. Fax: 626/446-582
Facility: 120 rooms. Studios & split level 2-bedroom units, many with fireplace. 30 two-bedroom units. 2 sto
ries; exterior corridors; heated pool. **Services:** area transportation. **Recreation:** sports cou
All Rooms: kitchens. **Cards:** AE, CB, DI, DS, JC, MC, VI.

RESTAURANTS

CHEZ SATEAU
◆◆
French
Lunch: $7-$14   **Dinner:** $10-$21   Phone: 626/446-8806
Location: Just s of Huntington Dr. 850 S Baldwin Ave 91007. **Hours:** 11:30 am-2:30 & 5:30-9 pm, Sat 5:3
pm-10 pm, Sun 10:30 am-2:30 & 5:30-9 pm. Closed: Mon. **Reservations:** suggested. **Features:** early bi
specials; carryout; cocktails & lounge; valet parking; a la carte. Fine dining in attractively decorated dinin
room. Smoke free premises. **Cards:** AE, CB, DI, JC, MC, VI.

THE DERBY RESTAURANT
◆◆
American
Lunch: $7-$16   **Dinner:** $11-$26   Phone: 626/447-2430
Location: 0.5 mi w of I-210, exit Huntington Dr. 233 Huntington Dr 91006. **Hours:** 11 am-11 pm, Fri
Sat-midnight. Closed: 12/25. **Features:** casual dress; cocktails & lounge; valet parking. A cozy, comfortab
restaurant with several small dining areas. Features a large collection of horse racing memorabilia. Smo
free premises. **Cards:** AE, CB, DI, DS, MC, VI.

SESAME GRILL
◆◆
American
Lunch: $8-$10   **Dinner:** $9-$17   Phone: 626/821-0880
Location: 0.5 mi w of I-210, exit Huntington Dr. 308 E Huntington Dr 91006. **Hours:** 11:30 am-2:30 & 5-9:3
pm. Closed: 11/25, 12/25 & Sun. **Reservations:** suggested. **Features:** casual dress; beer & wine only; a
carte. A small shopping center restaurant serving a creative selection of European & Pacific Rim cuisin
Smoke free premises. **Cards:** AE, MC, VI.

ARTESIA—15,500   (See map p. 561; index p. 550)

LODGING

BEST WESTERN PIONEER INN
◆◆
Motel
(See color ad below)
Rates Subject to Change
1P: $59- 99   2P/1B: $59- 99   2P/2B: $69- 99   XP: $5
Phone: (562)402-2202
Location: Adjacent to SR 91, exit Pioneer Blvd. 16905 S Pioneer Blvd 90701. Fax: 562/924-3623
Facility: 162 rooms. 3 stories; interior/exterior corridors; heated pool. **Cards:** AE, CB, DI, DS, JC, MC, VI.

AZUSA—41,300

LODGING

SUPER 8 MOTEL   **Phone:** (626)969-8871
AAA SAVE   All Year [CP]   1P: $45   2P/1B: $45   2P/2B: $50   XP: $5   F12
◆◆   **Location:** SR 39, just n of I-210; exit Azusa Ave. 117 N Azusa Ave 91702. Fax: 626/633-9153.
Motel   **Terms:** Reserv deposit; weekly rates. **Facility:** 44 rooms. 14 efficiencies, $5 extra; no utensils; 2 stories; exterior corridors; whirlpool. **Cards:** AE, MC, VI. **Special Amenities:** Free breakfast and free local telephone calls.

RESTAURANT

EL ENCANTO INN   **Lunch:** $6-$10   **Dinner:** $13-$25   **Phone:** 626/969-8877
◆◆   **Location:** 3 mi n on SR 39, in San Gabriel Canyon. 100 N Old San Gabriel Canyon Rd 91702.
American   **Hours:** 11:30 am-2:30 & 4:30-10 pm, Fri-11 pm, Sat 4:30 pm-11 pm, Sun 4 pm-9 pm. Closed: 1/1, 12/25 & Mon. **Features:** children's menu; senior's menu; carryout; cocktails & lounge. Country setting. Selections of chicken, lamb, pork, steak, seafood & prime rib. Smoke free premises. **Cards:** AE, DI, MC, VI.

BALDWIN PARK—69,300

LODGINGS

HOWARD JOHNSON LODGE   Rates Subject to Change   **Phone:** 626/962-8761
◆   All Year   1P: $49- 58   2P/1B: $49- 67 2P/2B: $49- 71 XP: $8
Motel   **Location:** S side of I-10, exit Puente Ave. 14624 Dalewood St 91706. Fax: 626/338-7989. **Facility:** 69 rooms. 4 stories; interior corridors. **Cards:** AE, CB, DI, DS, JC, MC, VI.

RADISSON HOTEL-SAN GABRIEL VALLEY   Rates Subject to Change   **Phone:** (626)962-6000
◆◆◆   All Year   1P: $109- 139 2P/1B: $109- 139 2P/2B: $109- 139 XP: $10-15   F18
Hotel   **Location:** N side of I-10, exit Puente Ave. 14635 Baldwin Park Towne Center 91706. Fax: 626/960-6214. **Facility:** 195 rooms. 10 stories; interior corridors; heated pool. **Services:** area transportation. **Cards:** AE, CB, DI, DS, MC, VI.

RESTAURANT

ROSA RISTORANTE ITALIANO   **Lunch:** $10-$12   **Dinner:** $10-$19   **Phone:** 626/960-2788
◆◆◆   **Location:** Just n of I-10, exit Baldwin Park Blvd. 3077 Baldwin Park Blvd 91706. **Hours:** 11:30 am-2 & 5-9
Italian   pm, Mon 11:30 am-2 pm, Sat 5 pm-9 pm. Closed major holidays & Sun. **Reservations:** suggested. **Features:** casual dress; carryout; cocktails; a la carte. A small, charming restaurant featuring a nice selection of pasta, seafood & veal. Smoke free premises. **Cards:** AE, CB, DI, DS, MC, VI.

BELL—34,400

RESTAURANT

MIAMI RESTAURANT   **Lunch:** $5-$10   **Dinner:** $6-$12   **Phone:** 323/560-0672
◆◆   **Location:** 1.5 mi w of I-710, exit Florence Ave. 4021 E Florence Ave 90201. **Hours:** 10 am-10:30 pm.
Specialty   **Features:** beer & wine only. A small, charming restaurant, specializing in Cuban cuisine. Smoke free premises. **Cards:** AE, DI, DS, MC, VI.

BELLFLOWER—61,800   (See map p. 561; index p. 555)

RESTAURANTS

CAFE CAMELLIA   **Lunch:** $6-$15   **Dinner:** $12-$20   **Phone:** 562/866-2824 **76**
◆◆   **Location:** 0.3 mi n of SR 91, Bellflower Blvd exit. 16916 Bellflower Blvd 90706. **Hours:** 11 am-2:30 & 5-9
French   pm, Fri & Sat-9:30 pm. Closed: 1/1, 7/4, 12/25 & Sun. **Reservations:** suggested. **Features:** casual dress; carryout; cocktails. Very nice selection of French & Continental entrees. Smoke free premises. **Cards:** AE, DI, DS, MC, VI.

Meal Plan Indicators

CP = Continental Plan of pastry, juice and another beverage or may offer expanded breakfast items

BP = Breakfast Plan of full hot breakfast

AP = American Plan of three meals daily

MAP = Modified American Plan of two meals daily

EP = European Plan, where rate includes only room

Family Plan Indicators

The establishment may limit the number of children to whom the family plan applies.

F17 = children 17 and under stay free (age displayed will reflect property's policy)

D17 = discount for children 17 and under

F = children stay free

D = discounts for children

(See map p. 561)

JOHNNY REBS' Lunch: $6-$9 Dinner: $10-$13 Phone: 562/866-6455 ⑦⑤
◆ **Location:** 0.4 mi n of SR 91. 16639 Bellflower Blvd 90706. **Hours:** 7 am-9 pm, Fri & Sat-10 pm. Closed
American 11/25 & 12/25. **Features:** casual dress; senior's menu; carryout; beer & wine only. Southern Roadhouse
style diner serving barbecue meat, catfish & Southern cuisine. Smoke free premises. **Cards:** MC, VI. ☒

BELL GARDENS—42,400

LODGING

BEST WESTERN HOTEL BY THE CASINO Phone: (562)928-345
ⒶⒶⒶ ⓢⒶⓥⒺ 5/24-9/7 1P: $70- 129 2P/1B: $70- 129 2P/2B: $80- 129
2/1-5/23 & 9/8-1/31 1P: $62- 115 2P/1B: $62- 115 2P/2B: $73- 115
◆◆ **Location:** Just e of I-710, exit Florence Ave, just s. 7330 Eastern Ave 90201. Fax: 562/928-9851
Motel **Terms:** Reserv deposit. **Facility:** 117 rooms. 31 suites & 6 whirlpool rms; 3 stories; interior/exterior corridors
whirlpool. **Dining:** Restaurant nearby. **Cards:** AE, CB, DI, DS, MC, VI.

🛏🍴🛗🏊❄☕🖥🔒☒

BEVERLY HILLS—32,000   (See map p. 558; index p. 553)

LODGINGS

AVALON HOTEL Rates Subject to Change Phone: 310/277-5221 ⑱⑧
ⒻⓎ All Year [CP] 2P/1B: $150- 235 2P/2B: $150- 235
Under major renovation. **Location:** Just east of Beverly Dr. 9400 W Olympic Blvd 90212. Fax: 310/277-4928
Motel **Facility:** 88 rooms. 3-4 stories; interior/exterior corridors; heated pool. Fee: parking. **All Rooms:** combo c
shower baths. **Cards:** DI, DS, MC, VI.

🏊❄🖥☕📺🖥🛗☒

THE BEVERLY HILLS HOTEL Rates Subject to Change Phone: 310/276-2251 ⑲
◆◆◆◆ All Year 1P: $310- 365 2P/1B: $335- 390 2P/2B: $335- 390 XP: $25 F1
Historic Hotel **Location:** At Rodeo Dr. 9641 Sunset Blvd 90210. Fax: 310/887-2887. **Facility:** 203 rooms. Beautifully deco
rated historic hotel. Lush landscaping & grounds. 14 two-bedroom units, 7 three-bedroom units. Bungalows &
bungalow suites $685-$2750; suites $685-$4700. Bungalow with one private pool, $3595; 3-4 stories; interior corridors; heated
pool; 2 lighted tennis courts. Fee: parking. **Services:** giftshop; area transportation. **Some Rooms:** 27 kitchens. **Cards:** AE
CB, DI, JC, MC, VI. 🛏🍴🏊🖥🏊❄☕🖥🔒☒

BEVERLY HILLS INN Rates Subject to Change Phone: 310/278-0303 ⑲④
◆◆◆ All Year [BP] 1P: $145 2P/1B: $145 2P/2B: $150
Hotel **Location:** 125 S Spalding Dr 90212. Fax: 310/278-1728. **Terms:** Handling fee imposed. **Facility:** 46 rooms.
two-bedroom unit. 2-bedroom suite with living room, balcony & pool view, $275 for up to 6 persons; 4 stories
interior/exterior corridors; small heated pool. **Cards:** AE, DI, JC, MC, VI.

🏊🖥🛗☕🖥🔒☒

BEVERLY HILTON Phone: (310)274-7777 ⑲⓪
ⒶⒶⒶ ⓢⒶⓥⒺ All Year 1P: $330- 355 2P/1B: $330- 355 XP: $25 F1
Location: 9876 Wilshire at Santa Monica Blvd 90210. Fax: 310/285-1313. **Terms:** Reserv deposit; BP avai
◆◆◆◆ pets. **Facility:** 581 rooms. Very popular, elegant hotel. Two deluxe suites with full kitchen, balcony with cit
Hotel lights view & up to 4 bedrooms, $1100-$1700 for up to 8 people; 4-8 stories; interior corridors; heated pool
wading pool. Fee: parking. **Dining:** 2 restaurants, coffee shop; 6:30 am-11 pm; $8-$30; also, Trader Vic's
see separate listing. **Services:** giftshop; area transportation, within 3 mi. Fee: massage. **Cards:** AE, CB, DI, DS, JC, MC, VI
Special Amenities: Free newspaper. *(See ad p 119 & below)*

🛏🐾🍴🏊🖥🏊❄☕✈🖥🏊❄🖥📺🖥🛗☕🔒☒

L'ERMITAGE BEVERLY HILLS Rates Subject to Change Phone: (310)278-334
ⒻⓎ All Year 1P: $380 2P/1B: $380
Too new to rate. **Location:** 9291 Burton Way 90210. Fax: 310/278-8247. **Terms:** Reserv deposit
Hotel **Facility:** 124 rooms. 11 suites, $780-$880; 8 stories; exterior corridors; heated pool. Fee: parking. **Services:**
Fee: massage. **Cards:** AE, CB, DI, DS, JC, MC, VI.

🏊🖥🏊🖥🍴🛗☕🖥🔒☒

(See map p. 558)

THE PENINSULA BEVERLY HILLS
Phone: (310)551-2888 `192`
All Year 1P: $350 2P/1B: $350 2P/2B: $350 XP: $35 F16
Location: 9882 Little Santa Monica Blvd 90212. Fax: 310/788-2319. **Terms:** Reserv deposit. **Facility:** 196 rooms. An elegant boutique hotel with luxurious public areas & guest rooms, specializing in personalized service. 32 suites in main building & 16 suites in 5 2-story villas; some with private terrace & fireplace, $340-$625; 5 stories; interior corridors; heated pool, saunas, steamrooms, whirlpool. **Dining:** Dining room, restaurant; 6:30 am-5 pm; $16-$25; cocktails; afternoon tea; also, The Belvedere, see separate listing. **Services:** giftshop. Fee: massage. **Some Rooms:** 6 efficiencies, whirlpools. **Cards:** AE, CB, DI, DS, JC, MC, VI. **Special Amenities:** Early check-in/late check-out and free newspaper. A Preferred Hotel.

REGENT BEVERLY WILSHIRE
Rates Subject to Change **Phone:** (310)275-5200 `189`
All Year 1P: $325- 560 2P/1B: $365- 600 2P/2B: $365- 600 XP: $40 F16
Location: 9500 Wilshire Blvd at Rodeo Dr 90212. Fax: 310/274-2851. **Facility:** 394 rooms. Elegant, formal lobby & public areas. Comfortable, beautifully decorated rooms. 8-12 stories; interior corridors; heated pool. **Services:** giftshop. Fee: massage. **Cards:** AE, CB, DI, JC, MC, VI.

SUMMIT HOTEL RODEO DRIVE
Rates Subject to Change **Phone:** 310/273-0300 `193`
All Year 1P: $150 2P/1B: $150 2P/2B: $150 XP: $30 F12
Location: Just n of Wilshire Blvd. 360 N Rodeo Dr 90210. Fax: 310/859-8731. **Terms:** Reserv deposit; weekly/monthly rates. **Facility:** 86 rooms. 2 two-bedroom units. 4 stories; interior corridors. **Dining:** Restaurant; 7 am-10:30 pm; also, Cafe Rodeo, see separate listing. **Recreation:** transportation to off-site pool & tennis courts. **Cards:** AE, CB, DI, DS, JC, MC, VI.

RESTAURANTS

THE BELVEDERE
Lunch: $11-$20 **Dinner:** $16-$30 **Phone:** 310/788-2306 `100`
American **Location:** In the Peninsula Beverly Hills. 9882 Little Santa Monica Blvd 90212. **Hours:** 6:30-11 am, 11:30-2:30 & 6-10:30 pm. **Reservations:** suggested. **Features:** semi-formal attire; cocktails & lounge; entertainment; fee for valet parking; a la carte. Beautifully decorated dining room with creative Southern California cuisine. Wide variety of traditional & seasonal specialties. Terrace dining avail. Sophisticated dessert menu created on premises. Excellent wine list. Smoke free premises. **Cards:** AE, CB, DI, DS, JC, MC, VI.

CAFE RODEO
Lunch: $6-$14 **Dinner:** $13-$18 **Phone:** 310/273-0300 `103`
American **Location:** Just n of Wilshire Blvd; in Summit Hotel Rodeo Drive. 300 N Rodeo Dr 90210. **Hours:** 7:30 am-10:30 pm. **Reservations:** accepted. **Features:** casual dress; cocktails & lounge; fee for valet parking; a la carte. **Cards:** AE, CB, DI, DS, JC, MC, VI.

CRUSTACEAN
Lunch: $12-$22 **Dinner:** $18-$38 **Phone:** 310/205-8990 `111`
Specialty **Location:** 9646 S Santa Monica Blvd 90212. **Hours:** 11:30 am-2:30 & 5:30-10:30 pm, Fri & Sat-11:30 pm. Closed major holidays& Sun. **Reservations:** suggested. **Features:** semi-formal attire; cocktails & lounge; fee for parking & valet parking; a la carte. Euro-Asian seafood specialties Plexiglass covered koi stream. Smoke free premises. **Cards:** AE, CB, DI, MC, VI.

THE DINING ROOM
Lunch: $14-$25 **Dinner:** $25-$60 **Phone:** 310/275-5200 `113`
Continental **Location:** In the Regent Beverly Wilshire Hotel. 9500 Wilshire Blvd 90212. **Hours:** 7-10:30 am, 11:30-3 & 6-11 pm, Sat from 8 am, Sun 6 pm-10 pm. **Reservations:** suggested. **Features:** semi-formal attire; cocktails & lounge; fee for valet parking; a la carte. An elegant dining room decorated in the grand European tradition with formal service, Fri & Sat dancing to live 4 piece band. Smoke free premises. **Cards:** AE, CB, DI, DS, JC, MC, VI.

LA SCALA BOUTIQUE
Lunch: $8-$15 **Dinner:** $10-$25 **Phone:** 310/275-0579 `102`
Italian **Location:** 410 N Canon Dr 90210. **Hours:** 11:30 am-10:30 pm. Closed major holidays & Sun. **Reservations:** required. **Features:** semi-formal attire; cocktails; street parking & fee for valet parking; a la carte. Italian-oriented Continental menu. Smoke free premises. **Cards:** AE, CB, DI, DS, MC, VI.

LAWRY'S THE PRIME RIB
Dinner: $19-$26 **Phone:** 310/652-2827 `101`
American **Location:** Just n of Wilshire Blvd. 100 N La Cienega Blvd 90211. **Hours:** 5 pm-10 pm, Fri-11 pm, Sat 4:30 pm-11 pm, Sun 4 pm-10 pm. Closed: 12/25. **Reservations:** suggested. **Features:** casual dress; children's menu; cocktails & lounge; fee for valet parking; a la carte. Famous for prime rib, fresh fish also avail. **Cards:** AE, CB, DI, DS, JC, MC, VI.

MATSUHISA
Lunch: $15-$30 **Dinner:** $30-$40 **Phone:** 310/659-9639 `110`
Specialty **Location:** 129 N La Cienega Blvd 90211. **Hours:** 11:45 am-2:15 & 5:45-10:15 pm. Closed major holidays & for lunch Sat & Sun. **Reservations:** required. **Features:** casual dress; beer & wine only; fee for valet parking; a la carte. Extensive Japanese entrees featuring sushi & seafood. Smoke free premises. **Cards:** AE, DI, MC, VI.

PREGO
Lunch: $12-$19 **Dinner:** $16-$19 **Phone:** 310/277-7346 `109`
Italian **Location:** Just n of Wilshire Blvd. 362 N Camden Dr 90210. **Hours:** 11:30 am-midnight, Sun 5 pm-11 pm. Closed: 11/25 & 12/25. **Reservations:** suggested. **Features:** casual dress; cocktails & lounge; street parking & valet parking; a la carte. Northern Italian cuisine featuring homemade pasta & grilled seafood entrees. **Cards:** AE, DI, MC, VI.

SPAGO
Dinner: $18-$27 **Phone:** 310/385-0880 `115`
American **Location:** 176 N Canon 90212. **Hours:** 6 pm-11 pm. Closed major holidays. **Reservations:** required. **Features:** semi-formal attire; cocktails & lounge; fee for valet parking; a la carte. A very busy restaurant popular with celebrities. Creative California cuisine featuring a variety of pizza & pasta dishes. Smoke free premises. **Cards:** DI, DS, MC, VI.

TRADER VIC'S
Dinner: $20-$30 **Phone:** 310/276-6345 `105`
Specialty **Location:** In the Beverly Hilton. 9876 Wilshire at Santa Monica Blvd 90210. **Hours:** 5 pm-midnight, Fri & Sat-1 am. Closed: 11/25 & 12/25. **Reservations:** suggested; weekends. **Features:** casual dress; children's menu; cocktails & lounge; valet parking; a la carte. Large selection of Cantonese & Polynesian cuisine. Smoke free premises. **Cards:** AE, CB, DI, DS, JC, MC, VI.

BURBANK—93,600   (See map p. 560; index p. 550)

LODGINGS

THE ANABELLE   Phone: (818)845-7800

		1P	2P/1B	2P/2B	XP
	Sun-Thurs	$160- 210	$160- 210	$160- 210	$15
	Fri & Sat	$119- 180	$119- 180	$119- 180	$15

Location: 1.3 mi sw of I-5, exit Olive Ave. 2011 W Olive Ave 91506. Fax: 818/845-0054. **Terms:** Check-in
Motor Inn   pm. **Facility:** 47 rooms. 3 stories; interior corridors; whirlpool. **Services:** area transportation, within 5 m
All Rooms: combo or shower baths. **Some Rooms:** 7 kitchens. **Cards:** AE, CB, DI, DS, MC, VI.
(See color ad below)

BURBANK AIRPORT HILTON & CONVENTION CENTER   Phone: (818)843-6000

		1P	2P/1B	2P/2B	XP	
	1/1-1/31	$135- 185	$155- 205	$155- 205	$25	F1
	2/1-12/31	$121- 180	$141- 191	$141- 191	$20	F1

Location: 1 mi s of I-5, exit Hollywood Way. 2500 Hollywood Way 91505. Fax: 818/842-9720
Hotel   **Terms:** Monthly rates; pets, requires signed waiver. **Facility:** 486 rooms. Spacious lobby. Rooms in 2 towe
buildings. 8-9 stories; interior corridors; heated pool, saunas, whirlpool. Fee: parking. **Dining:** Dining room
coffee shop; 6 am-11 pm; $8-$14; cocktails. **Services:** gift/shop; area transportation. Fee: massage. **Cards:** AE, CB, DI, DS,
JC, MC, VI. **Special Amenities:** Free newspaper. *(See ad p 119 & p 644)*

BURBANK INN & SUITES   Rates Subject to Change   Phone: (818)842-1114

		1P	2P/1B	2P/2B	XP
	All Year	$67- 77	$67- 77	$77- 87	$10

Location: Adjacent to w side of I-5; exit Alameda Ave, w. 180 W Alameda Ave 91502. Fax: 818/842-1114
Motel   **Terms:** Reserv deposit. **Facility:** 34 rooms. 17 mini suites; 2 stories; exterior corridors; small heated poo
Dining: Coffee shop nearby. **Cards:** AE, CB, DI, DS, JC, MC, VI.

HOLIDAY INN-BURBANK   Rates Subject to Change   Phone: 818/841-4770

		1P	2P/1B	2P/2B	XP
	All Year	$109- 135	$119- 145	$119- 145	$10

Location: Just e of I-5; northbound exit Olive Ave, southbound exit Verdugo Ave. 150 E Angeleno 91502
Hotel   Fax: 818/566-7886. **Facility:** 490 rooms. 19-20 stories; interior corridors; heated pool. **Services:** gift/shop
Some Rooms: 102 efficiencies. **Cards:** AE, CB, DI, DS, JC, MC, VI.

SAFARI INN   Phone: (818)845-8586

		1P	2P/1B	2P/2B	XP
	All Year	$94- 124	$94- 124	$94- 124	$15

Location: 1.3 mi sw of I-5, Olive Ave exit. 1911 W Olive Ave 91506. Fax: 818/845-0054. **Terms:** Check-in
Motor Inn   pm; weekly/monthly rates. **Facility:** 55 rooms. 2-3 stories; interior/exterior corridors; heated pool, whirlpo
Dining: Restaurant nearby. **Services:** area transportation, within 5 mi. **All Rooms:** combo or shower baths
Some Rooms: 10 kitchens. **Cards:** AE, CB, DI, DS, MC, VI. *(See color ad below)*

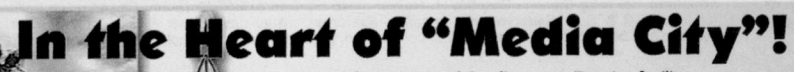

(See map p. 560)

RESTAURANTS

BOBBY MCGEE'S COMGLOMERATION **Dinner:** $7-$20 **Phone:** 818/841-1935 🔳
◆ **Location:** Adjacent to n side of I-5; northbound exit Olive Ave, southbound exit Verdugo Ave. 107 S 1st St
American 91502. **Hours:** 5-10 pm, Fri-11 pm, Sat 6 pm-11 pm, Sun 4 pm-10 pm. Closed: 12/25.
Reservations: suggested. **Features:** casual dress; children's menu; early bird specials; cocktails & lounge;
entertainment; fee for valet parking. Uniquely decorated restaurant. Informal, casual service by costumed staff. Features
steaks, prime rib & seafood, chicken & pasta. **Cards:** AE, DI, MC, VI. 🔳

DALT'S CLASSIC AMERICAN GRILL **Lunch:** $6-$13 **Dinner:** $6-$13 **Phone:** 818/953-7750 🔳
◆◆ **Location:** 0.5 w of SR 134 exit Hollywood Way across from Media Center. 3500 W Olive Ave 91505.
American **Hours:** 11 am-midnight, Fri & Sat 11 am-1 am, Sun 9am-midnight. Closed: 11/25 & 12/25. **Features:** No
A/C; casual dress; Sunday brunch; children's menu; carryout; cocktails & lounge. Nice selections of
sandwiches, burgers, pasta & entrees. Upscale 1950's decor. Validated parking in garage. Wide selection of premium beers.
Smoke free premises. **Cards:** AE, DI, DS, MC, VI. 🔳

CALABASAS—16,600 (See map p. 560; index p. 550)

LODGING

COUNTRY INN AT CALABASAS Guaranteed Rates **Phone:** (818)222-5300 🔳
◆◆◆ All Year [BP] 1P: $99 2P/1B: $99 2P/2B: $99 XP: $99 F12
Motel **Location:** Adjacent to US 101, Mulholland Dr exit; left over to Calabasas Rd, then 0.6 mi n. 23627
Calabasas Rd 91302. Fax: 818/591-0870. **Facility:** 122 rooms. 10 units with gas fireplace. 2 two-bedroom
units. 4 stories; interior corridors; heated pool. **Cards:** AE, CB, DI, DS, MC, VI. *(See color ad below)*

(ASK) 🔳 🔳 🔳 🔳 🔳 🔳 🔳 🔳 🔳 🔳

RESTAURANTS

COSMOS GRILL & ROTISSERIE **Lunch:** $5-$13 **Dinner:** $5-$13 **Phone:** 818/591-2211 🔳
◆◆◆ **Location:** Just s of US 101, Mulholland Dr exit. 23631 Calabasas Rd 91302. **Hours:** 11:30 am-10 pm, Fri &
Sat-11 pm, Sun 4:30-10 pm. **Features:** casual dress; children's menu; carryout; beer & wine only; a la carte.
◆◆ Selections of chicken, duck, steak, fish & pasta expertly prepared. Patio dining also avail. Smoke free
American premises. **Cards:** AE, DI, MC, VI. 🔳

GAETANO'S RISTORANTE **Lunch:** $8-$15 **Dinner:** $13-$26 **Phone:** 818/223-9600 🔳
◆◆◆ **Location:** US 101, exit Valley Circle/Mulholland Dr, 2 mi w, then 0.3 mi n. 20536 Calabasas Rd 91302.
Italian **Hours:** 11:30 am-2:30 & 5-10 pm, Fri & Sat-10:30 pm, Sun 5 pm-10 pm. Closed major holidays & Mon.
Reservations: suggested. **Features:** semi-formal attire; cocktails; fee for valet parking; a la carte. Excellent
selection of Northern Italain cuisine. Intimate & charming atmosphere. Extensive selection of California & imported wines.
Smoke free premises. **Cards:** AE, MC, VI. 🔳

SADDLE PEAK LODGE **Dinner:** $25-$50 **Phone:** 818/222-3888 🔳
◆◆◆◆ **Location:** US 101 exit Las Virgenes/Malibu Canyon Rd; w 5 mi to Piuma Rd; s on Piuma Rd; 1 mi to Cold
American Canyon Rd. 419 Cold Canyon Rd 91302. **Hours:** 6 pm-9:30 pm, Sat 5:30 pm-9:30 pm, Sun 11 am-2 &
5-9:30 pm. Closed: 12/25, Mon & Tues. **Reservations:** required. **Features:** semi-formal attire; Sunday
brunch; cocktails & lounge; fee for valet parking; a la carte. Beautiful 3 level hunting lodge with attractive landscaping &
sportsmen's theme & decor. Game trophies on walls. Furniture crafted from tree limbs & branches. Outdoor dining avail.
Featuring fresh & exotic game dishes. **Cards:** AE, MC, VI. 🔳

CANOGA PARK (See map p. 560; index p. 549)

LODGINGS

BEST WESTERN CANOGA PARK MOTOR INN **Phone:** (818)883-1200 🔳
All Year [CP] 1P: $59- 69 2P/1B: $59- 69 2P/2B: $59- 69 XP: $5
Location: 1.5 mi n of US 101. 20122 Vanowen St at Winnetka Ave 91306. Fax: 818/883-1202.
◆ **Terms:** Weekly rates; small pets only, $25 non-refundable extra charge. **Facility:** 46 rooms. Central courtyard.
Motor Inn Bowling alley adjacent. 8 efficiencies with microwave, $10 extra charge; 2 stories; interior corridors; heated
pool, sauna, whirlpool. **Dining:** Coffee shop; 7 am-11 pm; $5-$9; cocktails. **Cards:** AE, CB, DI, DS, MC, VI. **Special Amenities:** Early check-in/late check-out and free
breakfast. *(See ad p 592)* 🔳 🔳 🔳 🔳 🔳 🔳 🔳 🔳 🔳

(See map p. 560)

CLARION SUITES WARNER CENTER   Rates Subject to Change   **Phone:** (818)883-8250   **43**
◆◆◆   All Year [CP]   1P: $104- 139   2P/1B: $114- 144   2P/2B: $114- 154   XP: $10   F18
Suite Motel   **Location:** Just w of Winnetka Ave. 20200 Sherman Way 91306. Fax: 818/883-8268. **Facility:** 99 rooms. Most
rooms are 1-bedroom suites with living room, some with patio or balcony. 3 stories; interior/exterior corridors;
1 lighted tennis court. **Recreation:** sports court. **Cards:** AE, CB, DI, DS, JC, MC, VI. *(See color ad below)*

SAVE ⬛⬛⬛⬛⬛⬛⬛⬛⬛⬛⬛⬛⬛ ✕

DAYS INN   Rates Subject to Change   **Phone:** 818/341-7200   **44**
◆   4/1-9/30   1P: $50- 65   2P/1B: $55- 80   2P/2B: $70- 95   XP: $5   F12
Motel   2/1-3/31 & 10/1-1/31   1P: $45   2P/1B: $50   2P/2B: $50   XP: $5   F12
   Location: 1 blk w of Winnetka Ave. 20128 Roscoe Blvd 91306. Fax: 818/341-5741. **Facility:** 57 rooms. 2 one-
bedroom suites with kitchen, $70-$95; 3 stories; exterior corridors; heated indoor pool. **Cards:** AE, DI, DS, MC, VI.

SAVE ⬛⬛⬛⬛⬛⬛ ✕

CARSON—84,000   (See map p. 561; index p. 550)

LODGINGS

CARSON HILTON AT
THE CIVIC PLAZA CONFERENCE CENTER   Rates Subject to Change   **Phone:** (310)830-9200   **59**
◆◆◆   Mon-Thurs   1P: $89   2P/1B: $89   2P/2B: $89
Hotel   Fri-Sun   1P: $69   2P/1B: $69   2P/2B: $69
   Location: Adjacent to I-405, exit Carson St. 2 Civic Plaza 90745. Fax: 310/518-2969. **Facility:** 220 rooms. 8
stories; interior corridors; heated pool. **Cards:** AE, CB, DI, DS, JC, MC, VI. *(See ad p 119)*

SAVE ⬛⬛⬛⬛⬛⬛⬛⬛⬛⬛⬛⬛ ✕

COMFORT INN   **Phone:** (310)830-8044   **60**
AAA SAVE   All Year [CP]   1P: $49- 65   2P/1B: $50- 75   2P/2B: $65- 85   XP: $8-9   F
   Location: Just e of I-405, Carson St exit. 1325 E Carson St 90745. Fax: 310/518-5575. **Facility:** 31 rooms. 2
◆◆   stories; exterior corridors; small pool. **Cards:** AE, CB, DI, DS, JC, MC, VI. **Special Amenities:** Free room
Motel   upgrade and preferred room (each subject to availability with advanced reservations).

⬛⬛⬛⬛⬛⬛ ✕

HAMPTON INN   Rates Subject to Change   **Phone:** (310)768-8833   **57**
◆◆◆   All Year [CP]   1P: $60- 68   2P/1B: $62- 70   2P/2B: $62
Motel   **Location:** Adjacent to s side of SR 91; exit Avalon Blvd. 767 Albertoni St 90746. Fax: 310/768-2022.
   Terms: Reserv deposit. **Facility:** 134 rooms. 5 stories; interior corridors. **Cards:** AE, DI, DS, MC, VI.

⬛⬛⬛⬛⬛⬛ ✕

CERRITOS—53,200 (See map p. 561; index p. 550)

LODGING

SHERATON CERRITOS HOTEL AT TOWNE CENTER — Rates Subject to Change — **Phone: 562/809-1500** [66]

◆◆◆ Sun-Thurs 1P: $97 2P/1B: $97 2P/2B: $97 XP: $15

Hotel Fri & Sat 1P: $85 2P/1B: $85 2P/2B: $85 XP: $15

Location: Just s of SR 91; westbound exit Artesia/Bloomfield, eastbound exit Shoemaker Rd. 12725 Center Court Dr 90703. Fax: 562/403-2080. **Facility:** 203 rooms. Attractive contemporary decor. Adjacent to Cerritos Center for Performing Arts. 56 club level rms with printer, copier, fax & scanner, $195; 8 stories; interior corridors; heated pool. **Services:** giftshop. **Cards:** AE, CB, DI, DS, JC, MC, VI.

RESTAURANT

ARTE CAFE — **Lunch:** $7-$12 — **Dinner:** $11-$19 — **Phone:** 562/403-1080 [35]

◆◆◆ **Location:** Just s of SR 91 & e of Bloomfield Dr. 12741 Towne Center Dr 90701. **Hours:** 11 am-10 pm, Fri &

American Sat 11 am-11 pm. Closed: 1/1 & 12/25. **Reservations:** suggested. **Features:** casual dress; Sunday brunch; children's menu; cocktails. In Cerritos Towne Center, adjacent to Barnes & Noble Bookstore. A contemporary restaurant with indoor & heated outdoor dining. Selection of French & Pacific Rim cuisine. Smoking allowed on patio. **Cards:** AE, DI, DS, MC, VI.

CHATSWORTH (See map p. 560; index p. 549)

LODGINGS

THE CHATSWORTH HOTEL — Rates Subject to Change — **Phone: (818)709-7054** [46]

◆◆◆ All Year [BP] 1P: $140- 200 2P/1B: $140- 200 2P/2B: $140 XP: $10 F17

Motor Inn **Location:** 2 mi s of SR 118, Topanga Canyon Rd exit. 9777 Topanga Canyon Rd 91311. Fax: 818/998-3573.

Terms: Handling fee imposed. **Facility:** 147 rooms. Large lobby with lounge area. 6 suites, $130-$165. 2 suites with living room, bedroom & kitchen, $210; 4 stories; interior/exterior corridors; heated pool. **Cards:** AE, CB, DI, DS, MC, VI.

RAMADA INN — Rates Subject to Change — **Phone: 818/998-5289** [47]

◆ Fri & Sat [CP] 1P: $69- 79 2P/1B: $69- 79 2P/2B: $69- 79 XP: $5

Motel Sun-Thurs [CP] 1P: $65- 75 2P/1B: $65- 75 2P/2B: $65- 75 XP: $5

Location: SR 118, De Soto Ave exit; 1.5 mi e, then 0.5 mi n. 21340 Devonshire St 91311. Fax: 818/998-0257. **Terms:** Reserv deposit. **Facility:** 72 rooms. Rates for up to 2 persons. 14 one-bedroom suites with wet bar & microwave, $65-$79; 3 stories; interior corridors. **Cards:** AE, CB, DI, DS, JC, MC, VI. *(See color ad below)*

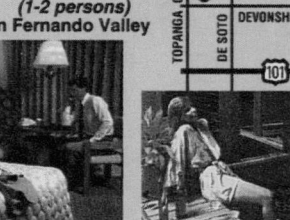

(See map p. 560)

7-STAR SUITES HOTEL
Phone: (818)998-8888
All Year [CP]   1P: $49- 119   2P/1B: $49- 119   2P/2B: $49- 119   XP: $7
Location: Just e of Topanga Canyon Blvd. 21603 Devonshire St 91311. Fax: 818/718-6666. Terms: Reser
deposit; weekly rates. Facility: 73 rooms. 1 unit with living room, bedroom, sauna, whirlpool & suntan boot
$119; 3 stories; exterior corridors; small heated pool, whirlpool. Some Rooms: whirlpools. Cards: AE, CB
DI, DS, MC, VI. Special Amenities: Free breakfast. *(See color ad p 593)*

SUMMERFIELD SUITES HOTEL
Rates Subject to Change
Phone: 818/773-0707
All Year [BP]   1P: $124   2P/1B: $124   2P/2B: $164   XP: $10
Suite Motel
Location: Just e of Topanga Canyon Blvd. 21902 Lassen St 91311. Fax: 818/773-0351. Facility: 114 rooms
1- & 2-bedroom suites with living room & kitchen. Many fireplaces. 27 two-bedroom units. 2-3 stories, no e
evator; exterior corridors; heated pool. Recreation: sports court. Cards: AE, DI, DS, JC, MC, VI.

CLAREMONT—32,500

LODGING

THE CLAREMONT INN
Phone: (909)626-241
All Year   1P: $69- 89   2P/1B: $69- 89   2P/2B: $69- 89   XP: $6
Location: 1.8 mi n of I-10; just w of Indian Hill Blvd. 555 W Foothill Blvd 91711. Fax: 909/624-0756
Motor Inn
Facility: 264 rooms. Nicely landscaped grounds. 2-3 stories; interior/exterior corridors; heated pool, whirlpoo
Dining: Candlelight Pavilion dinner theater adjacent. Services: giftshop; area transportation. Cards: AE, CE
DI, DS, MC, VI. *(See color ad below)*

RESTAURANTS

ARUFFO'S
Lunch: $8-$14   Dinner: $13-$20   Phone: 909/624-962
Italian
Location: In Claremont Village, just e of Indian Hill Blvd. 126 Yale Ave 91711. Hours: 11 am-8:30 pm, Fri
Sat-9:30 pm, Sun from 5 pm. Closed: 12/25. Reservations: suggested. Features: casual dress; children
menu; cocktails; street parking. Charming restaurant serving a nice variety of pasta, veal, seafood & hous
specialties. Large selection of wines & cappuccino. Smoke free premises. Cards: AE, CB, DI, DS, MC, VI.

TUTTI MANGIA ITALIAN GRILL
Lunch: $6-$10   Dinner: $8-$18   Phone: 909/625-466
Italian
Location: In Claremont Village, at 1st & Harvard, just e of Indian Hill Blvd. 102 Harvard Ave 91711
Hours: 11 am-9 pm, Fri & Sat-10 pm, Sun 4 pm-9 pm. Closed major holidays. Reservations: suggested
Features: early bird specials; carryout; cocktails & lounge; street parking; a la carte. Casual, contemporal
dining. Smoke free premises. Cards: AE, CB, DI, DS, MC, VI.

WALTER'S RESTAURANT
Lunch: $7-$12   Dinner: $11-$15   Phone: 909/624-277
Afghan
Location: In Claremont Village, just e of Indian Hill Blvd. 308 N Yale Ave 91711. Hours: 7 am-9 pm, Su
from 8 am. Closed: 11/25 & 12/25. Reservations: suggested. Features: casual dress; Sunday brunch; bee
& wine only. Indoor & a large covered patio dining area. A wide variety of entrees with an emphasis o
Afghan cuisine. Cards: MC, VI.

COMMERCE—12,100

LODGINGS

COMMERCE PLAZA HOTEL
Rates Subject to Change
Phone: (323)888-887
All Year   1P: $59- 69   2P/1B: $59- 69   2P/2B: $59- 69   XP: $10
Hotel
Location: Adjacent to I-5, Washington Blvd exit. 6300 E Telegraph Rd 90040. Fax: 323/888-8871
Facility: 267 rooms. 6 stories; interior corridors; heated pool. All Rooms: combo or shower baths
Cards: AE, CB, DI, DS, MC, VI.

RAMADA INN
Guaranteed Rates
Phone: 562/806-477
All Year   1P: $59- 80   2P/1B: $59- 80   2P/2B: $59- 80   XP: $10
Motel
Location: Just sw of I-5, exit Slauson Ave. 7272 Gage Ave 90040. Fax: 562/928-2907. Facility: 156 rooms.
stories; interior corridors; heated pool. Services: area transportation. Cards: AE, CB, DI, DS, JC, MC, VI.

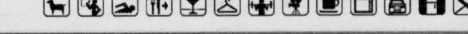

UPER 8 MOTEL — Rates Subject to Change — Phone: (562)806-3791
◆◆ lotel — All Year [CP] — 1P: $45 — 2P/1B: $49 — 2P/2B: $49 — XP: $5 — F11
Location: Just se of I-5; exit Slauson Ave. 7810 E Telegraph Rd 90040. Fax: 562/806-4741. **Terms:** Reserv deposit; handling fee imposed. **Facility:** 120 rooms. 3 stories; exterior corridors. **Services:** area ansportation. **Cards:** AE, DI, DS, MC, VI.

YNDHAM GARDEN HOTEL — Rates Subject to Change — Phone: 323/887-8100
◆◆◆ lotel — Sun-Thurs [EP] — 1P: $116 — 2P/1B: $116 — 2P/2B: $116 — XP: $10-20 — F18
Fri & Sat [BP] — 1P: $69 — 2P/1B: $69 — 2P/2B: $69 — XP: $10-20 — F18
Location: Adjacent e side of I-5, between Washington Blvd & Atlantic Ave off ramps. 5757 Telegraph Rd 0040. Fax: 323/887-4343. **Facility:** 201 rooms. South end of The Citadel. 14 suites with living room & bedroom, $129-$139; stories; interior corridors; heated pool. **Cards:** AE, CB, DI, DS, JC, MC, VI. *(See color ad below)*

RESTAURANTS

TEVENS STEAK HOUSE — Lunch: $6-$15 — Dinner: $8-$25 — Phone: 323/723-9856
◆◆ merican — **Location:** Just w of I-5, exit Atlantic Ave. 5332 Stevens Pl 90040. **Hours:** 11 am-Midnight, Fri & Sat-1 am, Sun 3 pm-10 pm. **Closed:** 12/25 & 1/1. **Reservations:** suggested. **Features:** No A/C; casual dress; cocktails & lounge; entertainment; valet parking. Large, attractive restaurant featuring a nice variety of steaks, prime , seafood & pasta. Smoke free premises. **Cards:** AE, MC, VI.

AMAYO RESTAURANT — Lunch: $7-$17 — Dinner: $7-$17 — Phone: 323/260-4700
◆◆ lexican — **Location:** From I-5, exit Atlantic Ave, 0.5 mi n, just e. 5300 E Olympic Blvd 90022. **Hours:** 7 am-10 pm, Fri-11 pm, Sat 5 pm-11 pm. **Closed:** 11/25, 12/25 & Sun. **Reservations:** suggested. **Features:** casual dress; cocktails & lounge; valet parking. Large restaurant in a restored Spanish style building. Contemporary lexican cuisine featuring spit-roasted meat, chicken & seafood. Smoke free premises. **Cards:** AE, CB, DI, MC, VI.

COMPTON—90,500 (See map p. 561; index p. 547)

LODGING

ADISSON THE NEW CRYSTAL PARK HOTEL & CASINO — Rates Subject to Change — Phone: (310)631-3838
◆◆◆ lotel — All Year — 1P: $79 — 2P/1B: $79 — 2P/2B: $79 — XP: $10 — F16
Location: Adjacent to SR 91, westbound exit Sante Fe, eastbound Acacia. 123 E Artesia Blvd 90221. Fax: 310/631-0809. **Facility:** 282 rooms. 9 stories; interior corridors. **Services:** Fee: massage. **Cards:** AE, I, DS, MC, VI.

COVINA—43,200

LODGING

MBASSY SUITES HOTEL — Guaranteed Rates — Phone: (626)915-3441
Sun-Thurs Wkly [BP] — 1P: $99 — 2P/1B: $109 — 2P/2B: $109 — XP: $12 — F18
Fri & Sat Wkly [BP] — 1P: $89 — 2P/1B: $99 — 2P/2B: $99 — XP: $12 — F18
◆◆◆ uite Motor an — **Location:** Adjacent to I-10, Holt Ave exit. 1211 E Garvey St 91724. Fax: 626/331-0773. **Terms:** Reserv deposit. **Facility:** 260 rooms. Nicely landscaped, tree-shaded grounds. 3 stories; exterior corridors; heated pool, whirlpool. **Dining:** Restaurant; 11 am-3 & 5-10 pm; $14-$22; cocktails. **Services:** giftshop; complimentary evening beverages; area transportation, within 10 mi. **Cards:** AE, DI, DS, MC, VI.

CULVER CITY—38,800   (See map p. 558; index p. 552)

LODGINGS

CULVER CITY TRAVELODGE   Rates Subject to Change   **Phone:** 310/839-1111   [12]
◆◆   5/1-9/30   1P: $63- 70   2P/1B: $63- 70   2P/2B: $63- 70   XP: $5   F
Motel   2/1-4/30 & 10/1-1/31   1P: $54- 60   2P/1B: $54- 60   2P/2B: $54- 60   XP: $5   F
            Location: Just e of Sepulveda Blvd. 11180 Washington Pl 90232. Fax: 310/839-1111. **Terms:** Rese
deposit. **Facility:** 36 rooms. 3 stories; exterior corridors. **All Rooms:** combo or shower baths. **Cards:** AE, CB, DI, DS, J
MC, VI. *(See ad below)*

HOLIDAY INN EXPRESS   **Phone:** (310)390-2189   [12]
(AAA) [SAVE]   6/1-8/31 [CP]   1P: $79- 99   2P/1B: $79- 99   2P/2B: $89- 99   XP: $5   F
            2/1-5/31 & 9/1-1/31 [CP]   1P: $69- 79   2P/1B: $69- 79   2P/2B: $79- 89   XP: $5   F
◆◆   **Location:** Just n of Washington Blvd. 3930 Sepulveda Blvd 90230. Fax: 310/391-4529. **Terms:** Week
Motel   rates. **Facility:** 49 rooms. 8 rooms with whirlpool, $89-$110; 3 stories; exterior corridors. **Cards:** AE, CB, D
            DS, JC, MC, VI. **Special Amenities: Free breakfast and free room upgrade (subject to availability w**
advanced reservations). *(See color ad below)*

RADISSON HOTEL-LOS ANGELES AIRPORT   **Phone:** (310)649-1776   [13]
(AAA) [SAVE]   10/1-1/31   1P: $210   2P/1B: $210   2P/2B: $210
            5/1-9/30   1P: $200   2P/1B: $200   2P/2B: $200
◆◆◆   3/1-4/30   1P: $160   2P/1B: $160   2P/2B: $160
Hotel   2/1-2/28   1P: $150   2P/1B: $150   2P/2B: $150
            Location: Adjacent to I-405, Jefferson Blvd exit. 6161 Centinela Ave 90230 (PO Box 3200
Fax: 310/649-4411. **Terms:** Small pets only, $50 dep req. **Facility:** 371 rooms. 12 stories; interior corridors; heated pool, whi
pool. **Dining:** Dining room, coffee shop; 6 am-11 pm; $7-$17; cocktails. **Services:** giftshop; area transportation, to Fox Hil
mall. **Cards:** AE, CB, DI, DS, JC, MC, VI. **Special Amenities: Early check-in/late check-out and free newspaper.**

(see map p. 558)

**RAMADA PLAZA HOTEL-LAX
INTERNATIONAL AIRPORT NORTH** Rates Subject to Change Phone: (310)670-3200 131
  5/1-10/31 1P: $99 2P/1B: $99 2P/2B: $99
  2/1-4/30 & 11/1-1/31 1P: $89 2P/1B: $89 2P/2B: $89
Location: Adjacent to I-405, Sepulveda Blvd exit, just n of Centinela Ave. 6333 Bristol Pkwy 90230. Fax: 310/670-9026. **Terms:** Reserv deposit. **Facility:** 259 rooms. 8 suites avail $150-$275; 12 stories; interior corridors; heated pool, whirlpool. **Dining:** Dining room; 6 am-11 pm; $10-$18; cocktails. **Services:** giftshop; area transportation, within 5 mi. **Recreation:** in-room video games. **Cards:** AE, CB, DI, DS, JC, MC, VI.
(See color ad below)

SUNBURST MOTEL Phone: (310)398-7523 127
  All Year [CP] 1P: $59- 99 2P/1B: $59- 99 2P/2B: $69- 99 XP: $10 F11
Location: just n of Washington Blvd. 3900 Sepulveda Blvd 90230. Fax: 310/398-0344. **Terms:** Reserv deposit. **Facility:** 35 rooms. 2 stories; exterior corridors; whirlpool. **Some Rooms:** Fee: whirlpools. **Cards:** AE, CB, DI, DS, JC, MC, VI. **Special Amenities:** Early check-in/late check-out and free breakfast.

WYNDHAM GARDEN HOTEL Rates Subject to Change Phone: 310/641-7740 130
  Sun-Thurs 1P: $89 2P/1B: $89 2P/2B: $89 XP: $10 F18
  Fri & Sat 1P: $79 2P/1B: $79 2P/2B: $79 XP: $10 F18
Location: Just e of I-405, Sepulveda Blvd exit. 5990 Green Valley Cir 90230. Fax: 310/645-7045. **Facility:** 199 rooms. Just south of Fox Hills Mall. 8 stories; interior corridors; heated pool. **Services:** giftshop; area transportation. **Cards:** AE, CB, DI, DS, JC, MC, VI. (See color ad p 595)

CYPRESS—42,700 (See map p. 294; index p. 292)

LODGINGS

CYPRESS COURTYARD BY MARRIOTT Rates Subject to Change Phone: (714)827-1010 207
  All Year 1P: $69- 89 2P/1B: $69- 89 2P/2B: $69- 89
Location: just w of Valley View. 5865 Katella Ave 90630. Fax: 714/220-0543. **Facility:** 180 rooms. 7 stories; interior corridors; heated pool. **Services:** giftshop; area transportation. **Cards:** AE, DI, DS, MC, VI.
(See color ad p 311)

WOODFIN SUITE HOTEL-CYPRESS Guaranteed Rates Phone: (714)828-4000 206
  All Year [BP] 1P: $99- 199 2P/1B: $99- 199 2P/2B: $99- 199 XP: $10 F12
Location: Just s of Cerritos Ave & just w of Valley View. 5905 Corporate Ave 90630. Fax: 714/229-0566. **Facility:** 142 rooms. 2-bedroom suites with living room & full kitchen or wet bar, $50 extra charge; 3 stories; exterior corridors; heated pool. **Services:** giftshop; area transportation. **Cards:** AE, CB, DI, DS, JC, MC, VI.
(See color ad p 333)

DIAMOND BAR—53,700

LODGINGS

BEST WESTERN DIAMOND BAR Phone: (909)860-3700
  All Year [CP] 1P: $59- 89 2P/1B: $79- 99 2P/2B: $79- 99 XP: $5 F12
Location: Adj to jct SR 60 & 57; just w of Diamond Bar Blvd. 259 Gentle Springs Ln 91765. Fax: 909/860-2110. **Terms:** Weekly rates. **Facility:** 94 rooms. Spacious rooms. 2 stories; exterior corridors; whirlpool. **All Rooms:** extended cable TV. **Cards:** AE, DI, DS, MC, VI. **Special Amenities:** Free breakfast and free newspaper.

COUNTRY SUITES BY AYRES Rates Subject to Change Phone: (909)860-6290
  All Year [BP] 1P: $70- 100 2P/1B: $80- 110 2P/2B: $80- 110 XP: $10 F12
Location: Adjacent to SR 57/60, Grand Ave exit, then 0.5 mi w. 21951 Golden Springs Dr 91765. Fax: 909/860-5469. **Facility:** 101 rooms. Charming European country decor. 3 stories; interior corridors; heated pool. **Cards:** AE, CB, DI, DS, JC, MC, VI.

HOLIDAY INN SELECT
Phone: (909)860-5‹
(AAA) (SAVE)   All Year   1P: $89- 145   2P/1B: $89- 145   2P/2B: $89- 145   XP: $10
◆◆   **Location:** Adjacent to SR 57 & 60, exit Grand Ave, 0.8 mi w on Golden Springs Dr; in Gateway Corpo
Hotel   Center. 21725 E Gateway Center Dr 91765. Fax: 909/860-8224. **Facility:** 175 rooms. 6 stories; interior c‹
dors; heated pool, whirlpool. **Dining:** Restaurant; 6 am-10 pm; $8-$11; cocktails. **Cards:** AE, CB, DI,
MC, VI. **Special Amenities: Free local telephone calls and free newspaper.**

DOWNEY—91,400

LODGINGS

COMFORT INN
Phone: (562)803-35
(AAA) (SAVE)   All Year [CP]   1P: $44   2P/1B: $49   2P/2B: $54   XP: $5
◆◆   **Location:** 1 mi w of I-605, Firestone Blvd exit. 9438 Firestone Blvd 90241. Fax: 562/803-08
Motel   **Terms:** Reserv deposit; handling fee imposed. **Facility:** 33 rooms. 3 stories; exterior corridors; whirlp
Cards: AE, CB, DI, DS, JC, MC, VI. **Special Amenities: Free breakfast.**

DAYS INN-STONEWOOD   Rates Subject to Change   Phone: (562)861-09
(AAA)   All Year [CP]   1P: $70- 100   2P/1B: $70- 120   2P/2B: $75- 120   XP: $5
◆◆   **Location:** On SR 19, just n of Firestone Blvd; 1.5 mi w of I-605 exit Firestone Blvd. 11102 Lakewood E
Motel   90241. Fax: 562/862-5206. **Facility:** 33 rooms. Next to Stonewood Shopping Center. 2 rooms with whirlp
$100; 2 stories; exterior corridors. **Cards:** AE, CB, DI, DS, JC, MC, VI.

DOWNEY INN
Phone: (562)862-50
(AAA) (SAVE)   All Year   1P: $49- 89   2P/1B: $49- 89   2P/2B: $54   XP: $6
◆◆   **Location:** On SR 19, just s of Firestone Blvd. 11510 Lakewood Blvd 90241. Fax: 562/923-4240. **Facility:**
Motel   rooms. 5 one-bedroom suites with whirlpool, $69-89; 3 stories; exterior corridors; sau
Some Rooms: whirlpools. **Cards:** AE, DI, DS, MC, VI. **Special Amenities:** Early check-in/late check-
and free breakfast. *(See ad below)*

EMBASSY SUITES HOTEL
Phone: (562)861-19
(AAA) (SAVE)   Sun-Thurs [BP]   1P: $139- 154   2P/1B: $164- 169   2P/2B: $154- 159   XP: $15-20
◆◆◆   Fri & Sat [BP]   1P: $125- 135   2P/1B: $140   2P/2B: $150   XP: $15-20
Suite Hotel   **Location:** 2 mi w of I-605, exit Firestone Blvd. 8425 Firestone Blvd 90241. Fax: 562/923-58
Terms: Monthly rates; pets, $15 extra charge. **Facility:** 219 rooms. Next to Downey Theatre & Civic Cer
Large, attractive lobby & atrium area. 8 stories; interior corridors; heated indoor pool, sauna, steamroom, w
pool. **Dining:** Restaurant; 11 am-3 & 5-10 pm; $11-$18; cocktails. **Services:** giftshop; complimentary evening beverac
area transportation, within 10 mi. **Cards:** AE, CB, DI, DS, JC, MC, VI. **Special Amenities: Free breakfast and f
newspaper.**

RESTAURANT

MIMI'S CAFE   **Lunch:** $6-$13   **Dinner:** $9-$13   Phone: 562/862-28
◆◆   **Location:** 0.5 mi w of Lakewood Blvd, adjacent to Downey Theatre. 8455 Firestone Blvd. **Hours**
American   am-11 pm. Closed: 12/25. **Features:** casual dress; children's menu; beer & wine only. Colorful French c
atmosphere. Nice selection of salads, sandwiches & entrees. Smoke free premises. **Cards:** AE, MC, VI.

DUARTE—20,700

LODGING

DAYS INN-DUARTE
Phone: (626)303-45
(AAA) (SAVE)   All Year [CP]   1P: $50- 55   2P/1B: $60- 65   2P/2B: $65   XP: $10
◆◆   **Location:** 0.5 mi ne of I-210, use Buena Vista St exit. 1533 E Huntington Dr 91010. Fax: 626/303-64
Motel   **Terms:** Weekly/monthly rates. **Facility:** 50 rooms. 2 stories; exterior corridors; whirlp
Some Rooms: whirlpools. **Cards:** AE, CB, DI, DS, JC, MC, VI. **Special Amenities: Free breakfast a
free newspaper.**

RESTAURANT

ANARA'S ITALIAN RESTAURANT   **Lunch:** $7-$11   **Dinner:** $8-$16   **Phone:** 626/358-0128
Location: 1 mi ne of I-210, Buena Vista exit. 1845 E Huntington Dr 91010. **Hours:** 11 am-9 pm, Sat 4:30
Italian   pm-10 pm, Sun 4:30 pm-9 pm. Closed: 11/25 & 12/25. **Features:** casual dress; children's menu; carryout;
cocktails. A nice selection of pasta, veal, chicken & seafood. Patio dining weather permitting. Smoke free
premises. **Cards:** AE, DS, MC, VI.

EL MONTE—106,200

LODGING

SUPER 8 MOTEL   **Phone:** (626)442-8354

6/1-9/30 [CP]	1P:	$49	2P/1B:	$49	2P/2B:	$57	XP: $5	D12
2/1-5/31 & 10/1-1/31 [CP]	1P:	$46	2P/1B:	$46	2P/2B:	$51	XP: $5	D12

Location: From I-10 westbound exit Garvey Ave, just w; eastbound exit Valley Blvd, 0.8 mi e. 12047 Valley
Motel   BL 91732 (12040 Garvey Ave). Fax: 626/442-8357. **Terms:** Pets, 1 per room. **Facility:** 50 rooms. 3 stories; exterior corridors; whirlpool. **Cards:** AE, CB, DI, DS, MC, VI. **Special Amenities:** Free breakfast and free
newspaper.

RESTAURANT

OWARD'S   **Lunch:** $8-$19   **Dinner:** $10-$19   **Phone:** 626/442-2400
Location: South side of I-10, exit Rosemead Blvd, just s to Flair Dr, then 0.8 mi e. 9600 Flair Dr 91731.
American   **Hours:** 11:15 am-10:15 pm, Sat 3 pm-11 pm, Sun 1 pm-9 pm. Closed: 7/4, 11/25, 12/25.
Features: children's menu; health conscious menu; cocktails & lounge. Informal dining. Western/Victorian
atmosphere. Smoke free premises. **Cards:** AE, DI, DS, MC, VI.

EL SEGUNDO—15,200   (See map p. 558; index p. 552)

LODGINGS

COURTYARD BY MARRIOTT   Rates Subject to Change   **Phone:** 310/322-0700   `163`
All Year   1P: $119   2P/1B: $119   2P/2B: $119   XP: $10   F18
Motor Inn   **Location:** Just e of SR 1, Sepulveda Blvd. 2000 E Mariposa Ave 90245. Fax: 310/322-4401. **Facility:** 146
rooms. Many rooms with balcony overlooking courtyard. 3 stories; interior corridors; heated pool. **Cards:** AE,
DS, MC, VI. *(See color ad p 563)*

DOUBLETREE CLUB HOTEL LOS ANGELES   Rates Subject to Change   **Phone:** (310)322-0999   `165`
Sun-Thurs   1P: $87   2P/1B: $87   2P/2B: $87   XP: $10   F12
Motor Inn   Fri & Sat   1P: $65   2P/1B: $65   2P/2B: $65   XP: $10   F12
Location: Just e of SR 1, Sepulveda Blvd. 1985 E Grand Ave 90245. Fax: 310/322-4758. **Facility:** 215 rooms.
Located in business park. 7 stories; interior corridors; heated pool. **Services:** giftshop; area transportation. **Cards:** AE, CB,
DS, JC, MC, VI.

EMBASSY SUITES-LAX SOUTH   **Phone:** (310)640-3600   `164`
Mon-Thurs [BP]   1P: $139   2P/1B: $139   2P/2B: $139   XP: $10   F18
Fri-Sun [BP]   1P: $109   2P/1B: $119   2P/2B: $119   XP: $10   F18
Suite Motor   **Location:** 1 blk w of Sepulveda Blvd. 1440 E Imperial Ave 90245. Fax: 310/322-0954. **Terms:** Small pets
Inn   only, $10 extra charge. **Facility:** 350 rooms. Beautifully decorated & landscaped interior courtyard. 5 stories;
interior corridors; heated pool, indoor whirlpool. **Dining:** Restaurant; 11 am-11 pm; $8-$20; cocktails.
Services: giftshop; complimentary evening beverages; area transportation. Local shopping & beaches.
Cards: AE, CB, DI, DS, JC, MC, VI. **Special Amenities:** Free breakfast and free newspaper.

HACIENDA HOTEL-L.A. AIRPORT   **Phone:** (310)615-0015   `160`
All Year   1P: $52- 65   2P/1B: $58- 71   2P/2B: $58- 71   XP: $6   F18
Location: On SR 1, Sepulveda Blvd. 525 Sepulveda Blvd 90245. Fax: 310/615-0217. **Terms:** Reserv
deposit. **Facility:** 630 rooms. Commercial area. Some rooms overlook Spanish style courtyard. 5-9 stories; in-
Motel   terior corridors; heated pool, whirlpool. **Dining:** Coffee shop; 24 hrs; $7-$17; cocktails. **Services:** giftshop;
area transportation, within 5 mi radius. **All Rooms:** combo or shower baths. **Cards:** AE, CB, DI, DS, JC,
MC, VI. **Special Amenities:** Early check-in/late check-out and preferred room (subject to availability with advanced
reservations). *(See color ad p 571)*

(See map p. 558)

HOMESTEAD VILLAGE
◆◆◆   All Year Wkly
Extended Stay   **Location:** Just e of SR 1 (Sepulveda Blvd). 1910 E Mariposa Ave 90245. Fax: 310/607-46
Motel   **Terms:** Check-in 4 pm; reserv deposit. **Facility:** 150 rooms. 2 stories; exterior corrido
All Rooms: kitchens, combo or shower baths. **Cards:** AE, CB, DI, DS, MC, VI.

Rates Subject to Change   **Phone:** 310/607-4000
1P: $299   2P/1B: $319   2P/2B: $399   XP: $20

SUMMERFIELD SUITES HOTEL-EL SEGUNDO/LAX   Rates Subject to Change   **Phone:** 310/725-0100
◆◆◆   All Year [CP]   1P: $135- 145   2P/1B: $135- 145   2P/2B: $150- 160   XP: $10
Suite Hotel   **Location:** Just w of Aviation Blvd at Rosecrans. 810 S Douglas Ave 90245. Fax: 310/725-09
Terms: Reserv deposit. **Facility:** 122 rooms. All rooms are 1- or 2-bedroom suites. 60 two-bedroom units
stories, no elevator; interior/exterior corridors; heated pool. **Recreation:** sports court. **All Rooms:** kitchens. **Cards:** AE, C
DI, DS, JC, MC, VI.

TRAVELODGE AT LAX SOUTH   **Phone:** (310)615-1073
◆◆   6/1-9/10 [CP]   1P: $64   2P/1B: $64   2P/2B: $69   XP: $5
2/1-5/31 & 9/11-1/31 [CP]   1P: $49   2P/1B: $52   2P/2B: $55   XP: $4
Motel   **Location:** On SR 1. 1804 E Sycamore at Sepulveda Blvd 90245. Fax: 310/322-4475. **Terms:** Res
deposit, 15 day notice; weekly rates; small pets only, $25 dep req. **Facility:** 94 rooms. A variety of nicely
nished units. 2 stories; interior/exterior corridors; heated pool. **All Rooms:** combo or shower bat
Some Rooms: 44 kitchens, utensils extra charge. **Cards:** AE, CB, DI, DS, MC, VI. **Special Amenities:** Free breakfast a
free newspaper. *(See color ad p 577)*

ENCINO   (See map p. 560; index p. 550)

LODGING

TOKYO PRINCESS INN   Guaranteed Rates   **Phone:** (818)788-3820
◆◆   All Year [CP]   1P: $79- 109   2P/1B: $89- 119   2P/2B: $99- 129   XP: $20
Location: SR 101, Balboa Blvd exit, 0.3 mi s, then 0.4 mi w. 17448 Ventura Blvd 91316. Fax: 818/788-38
◆◆◆   **Terms:** Reserv deposit; handling fee imposed. **Facility:** 26 rooms. Nicely decorated rooms in oriental deco
Motel   stories; exterior corridors; whirlpool. **Dining:** Restaurant nearby. **All Rooms:** combo or shower bat
extended cable TV. **Cards:** AE, MC, VI.

GARDENA—49,800   (See map p. 561; index p. 554)

RESTAURANT

PARADISE RESTAURANT   **Lunch:** $7-$13   **Dinner:** $9-$16   **Phone:** 310/324-4800
◆◆   **Location:** At Vermont Ave. 889 W 190th St 90248. **Hours:** 11 am-2:30 & 5-9 pm, Fri & Sat 4:30 pm-10 p
American   Sun 4 pm-8 pm. Closed major holidays. **Features:** casual dress; children's menu; health conscious me
cocktails & lounge; a la carte. Popular restaurant, decorated in oasis theme. **Cards:** AE, CB, DI, DS, MC,

GLENDALE—180,000   (See map p. 562; index p. 549)

LODGINGS

BEST WESTERN EAGLE ROCK INN   **Phone:** (323)256-7711
◆◆   All Year [CP]   1P: $75- 100   2P/1B: $75- 100   2P/2B: $85- 110   XP: $5
Location: Just e of Verdugo Rd. (2911 Colorado St, LOS ANGELES, 90041). Fax: 323/255-67
◆◆   **Facility:** 50 rooms. 3 stories; exterior corridors; small pool, whirlpool. **All Rooms:** extended cable
Motel   Some Rooms: whirlpools. **Cards:** AE, CB, DI, DS, MC, VI. **Special Amenities:** Free breakfast and fr
newspaper. *(See ad below)*

BEST WESTERN GOLDEN KEY MOTOR HOTEL   **Phone:** (818)247-0111
◆◆   All Year [CP]   1P: $109- 149   2P/1B: $109- 149   2P/2B: $119- 149   XP: $5
Location: 1 mi s of SR 134, Brand Blvd exit. 123 W Colorado St 91204. Fax: 818/545-9393. **Facility:**
◆◆◆   rooms. 3 stories; exterior corridors; heated pool, whirlpool. **Dining:** Coffee shop nearby. **Cards:** AE, CB,
Motel   DS, MC, VI. **Special Amenities:** Free breakfast and free local telephone calls. *(See color ad p 601)*

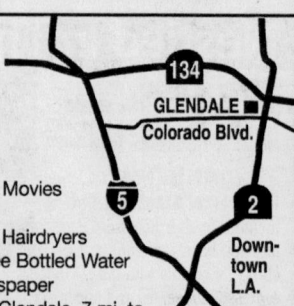

ee map p. 562)

ARIOT INN MOTEL   **Phone:** (818)507-9600   38
[SAVE]   All Year   1P: $50- 65   2P/1B: $50- 65   2P/2B: $60- 70   XP: $5
    Location: 1.5 mi se of SR 134, exit Glendale Ave. 1118 E Colorado Blvd 91205. Fax: 818/507-9774.
tel   **Terms:** Reserv deposit. **Facility:** 30 rooms. 2 stories; exterior corridors; whirlpool. **Dining:** Coffee shop
nearby. **Some Rooms:** whirlpools. **Cards:** AE, CB, DI, DS, MC, VI. **Special Amenities: Free breakfast and**
preferred room (subject to availability with advanced reservations). *(See color ad below)*

OMFORT INN-EAGLE ROCK   **Phone:** (323)256-1199   33
[SAVE]   All Year [CP]   1P: $50- 90   2P/1B: $50- 90   2P/2B: $59- 110   XP: $5-10   F18
    Location: From SR 134, exit Harvey Dr, just s, then just e on Broadway & 0.3 mi e on Colorado Blvd. (2300
tel   Colorado Blvd, LOS ANGELES, 90051). Fax: 323/255-7768. **Terms:** Reserv deposit. **Facility:** 56 rooms. 2 stories; exterior corridors; heated pool, whirlpool. **All Rooms:** extended cable TV. **Cards:** AE, CB, DI, DS, JC,
MC, VI. **Special Amenities: Free breakfast and free newspaper.**

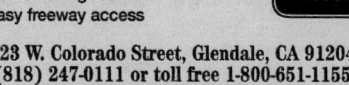

(See map p. 562)

ECONO LODGE Phone: (818)246-8367
AAA SAVE   All Year   1P: $50- 65   2P/1B: $50- 65   2P/2B: $60- 70   XP: $5
◆   **Location:** Just e of Verdugo Rd. 1437 E Colorado St 91205. Fax: 818/246-8374. **Terms:** Reserv depo
Motel   **Facility:** 30 rooms. 4 efficiencies, $5 extra; 2 stories; exterior corridors; small pool, whirlpool. **Cards:**
CB, DI, DS, JC, MC, VI. *(See ad p 601)*

RED LION HOTEL/GLENDALE Phone: (818)956-5466
AAA SAVE   Sun-Thurs   1P: $149- 169   2P/1B: $149- 169   2P/2B: $149- 169   XP: $10
◆◆◆   Fri & Sat   1P: $99- 139   2P/1B: $99- 139   2P/2B: $99- 139   XP: $10
Hotel   **Location:** Just n of SR 134; between Central Ave & Brand Blvd. 100 W Glenoaks Blvd 912
Fax: 818/956-5490. **Facility:** 348 rooms. 19 stories; interior corridors; heated pool, sauna, whirlp
Fee: parking. **Dining:** 2 restaurants; 6 am-11 pm; $8-$18; cocktails. **Services:** giftshop. **Cards:** AE, DI,
JC, MC, VI. **Special Amenities:** Early check-in/late check-out and free newspaper.

VAGABOND INN Phone: (818)240-1700
AAA SAVE   All Year [CP]   1P: $76   2P/1B: $81   2P/2B: $85- 95   XP: $5
◆   **Location:** 1 mi s of SR 134, Brand Blvd exit. 120 W Colorado St 91204. Fax: 818/548-8428. **Terms:** P
Motel $5 extra charge. **Facility:** 52 rooms. 3 stories; exterior corridors; heated pool. **Dining:** Coffee shop nea
Cards: AE, CB, DI, DS, MC, VI. **Special Amenities:** Free breakfast and free local telephone calls.

RESTAURANTS

FAR NIENTE   Lunch: $7-$20   Dinner: $9-$20   Phone: 818/242-3835
◆◆   **Location:** SR 134, exit Brand Blvd; then 0.8 mi s. 204 1/2 N Brand Blvd 91203. **Hours:** 11:30 am-10:30
Italian   Fri 11:30 am-11 pm, Sat 5:30 pm-11 pm, Sun 5 pm-9:30 pm. Closed major holidays. **Features:** casual dre
children's menu; carryout; cocktails & lounge; street parking. Traditional pasta selections as well as m
game & seafood entrees. Metered parking in rear lot. Smoke free premises. **Cards:** AE, CB, DI, DS, MC, VI.

FORTUNE INN   Lunch: $5-$7   Dinner: $6-$12   Phone: 818/547-2832
◆◆   **Location:** near The Exchange, 0.2 mi e of Brand Blvd, corner of Maryland Ave. 117 E Broadway St 912
Chinese   **Hours:** 11 am-10 pm. Closed: 11/26. **Features:** casual dress; carryout; cocktails. Excellent selectio
Mandarin cuisine. Validated parking in garage on Maryland Ave. Smoke free premises. **Cards:** AE, CB,
MC, VI.

FRESCO RISTORANTE   Lunch: $7-$14   Dinner: $16-$25   Phone: 818/247-5541
◆◆◆   **Location:** Just s of Colorado Blvd. 514 S Brand Blvd 91204. **Hours:** 11:30 am-2:30 & 5:30-10 pm, F
Italian   Sat-10:30 pm. Closed major holidays & Sun. **Reservations:** suggested. **Features:** semi-formal at
cocktails & lounge; street parking & fee for valet parking; a la carte. Selections of salads, pasta, seafo
chicken, beef & veal. **Cards:** AE, MC, VI.

JAX BAR & GRILL   Lunch: $6-$12   Dinner: $10-$20   Phone: 818/500-1604
◆◆   **Location:** 0.5 mi s of SR 134, exit Brand Blvd. 339 N Brand Blvd 91203. **Hours:** 11 am-1 am, Sat fro
American   pm, Sun from 4 pm. Closed: 11/25 & 12/25. **Reservations:** suggested. **Features:** casual dress; early
specials; cocktails & lounge; street parking. Excellent selection of steaks & pasta. Live jazz & bl
entertainment nightly. Metered parking lot in rear. Smoke free premises. **Cards:** AE, CB, DI, DS, MC, VI.

LA FONTANA ITALIAN KITCHEN   Lunch: $8-$14   Dinner: $9-$16   Phone: 818/247-6256
◆◆◆   **Location:** Just n of SR 134, corner of Brand & Glenoaks blvds. 933 N Brand Blvd 91202. **Hours:** 11 am
Northern   pm, Fri-11 pm, Sat noon-11 pm, Sun noon-10 pm. Closed: 1/1, 11/25 & 12/25. **Reservations:** sugges
Italian   **Features:** casual dress; children's menu; health conscious menu; carryout; cocktails; entertainment; a
carte. Salad, sandwiches, pasta, pizza, chicken, veal & seafood. Breads & pastries prepared & baked
premises. Patio dining weather permitting. Smoke free premises. **Cards:** AE, CB, DI, DS, MC, VI.

PANDA INN   Lunch: $5-$9   Dinner: $10-$16   Phone: 818/502-1234
◆◆   **Location:** Just e of Brand Blvd. 111 E Wilson Ave 91206. **Hours:** 11:30 am-10:30 pm. Closed: 11.
Chinese   **Reservations:** suggested. **Features:** casual dress; carryout; cocktails & lounge; a la carte. Selectio
Mandarin & Szechuan cuisine. Metered parking until 8 pm. Validated parking in Exchange parking struc
on Maryland Ave. **Cards:** AE, DI, DS, MC, VI.

RUSTY PELICAN   Lunch: $7-$11   Dinner: $13-$26   Phone: 818/242-9191
◆◆   **Location:** At SR 134 & Glendale Frwy. 300 Harvey Dr 91206. **Hours:** 11:30 am-10 pm, Fri & Sat-11:30
Seafood   Sun 10 am-2:30 & 3-10 pm. **Reservations:** suggested. **Features:** casual dress; Sunday brunch; childr
menu; early bird specials; carryout; cocktails & lounge; entertainment; valet parking. Informal atmosph
Chicken, lamb, salad, prime rib & seafood. **Cards:** AE, CB, DI, DS, MC, VI.

TAM O'SHANTER INN   Lunch: $7-$12   Dinner: $10-$20   Phone: 323/664-0228
◆◆   **Location:** 0.5 mi e of I-5. 2980 Los Feliz Blvd 90039. **Hours:** 11 am-3 & 5-10 pm, Fri & Sat-11 pm,
American   10:30 am-2:30 & 4-10 pm. Closed: 7/4 & 12/25. **Reservations:** suggested. **Features:** casual dress; Sur
brunch; children's menu; health conscious menu; carryout; cocktails & lounge; valet parking; a la carte
popular, long-established restaurant. Attractive, early Scottish decor. Ale & sandwich bar 11 am-10 pm, Fri & Sat-11 pm,
1 pm-10 pm. Patio dining, weather permitting. **Cards:** AE, CB, DI, DS, MC, VI.

GLENDORA—47,800

LODGING

COMFORT INN Phone: (626)963-9;
AAA SAVE   All Year [CP]   1P: $59- 79   2P/1B: $69- 89   2P/2B: $69- 89   XP: $6
◆◆   **Location:** 0.8 mi n of I-210, exit Grand Ave, just w. 606 W Alosta 91740. Fax: 626/914-2037. **Facility:**
Motel   rooms. 2 stories; exterior corridors; indoor whirlpool. **Some Rooms:** 30 efficiencies. **Cards:** AE, CB, DI,
JC, MC, VI. **Special Amenities:** Free room upgrade and preferred room (each subject to availab
with advanced reservations).

RESTAURANT

DERBY EAST　　**Lunch:** $7-$15　　**Dinner:** $11-$20　　**Phone:** 626/914-2977
◆◆
American　**Location:** 0.5 mi n of I-210, exit Grand Ave. 545 W Alosta Ave 91740. **Hours:** 11 am-10 pm, Sat 4 pm-11 pm, Sun 10 am-2 & 4-9 pm. Closed: 12/25. **Features:** casual dress; Sunday brunch; early bird specials; cocktails & lounge. Comfortable western atmosphere. Menu selections include steaks, seafood, rack of lamb & pasta. Smoke free premises. **Cards:** AE, CB, DI, DS, MC, VI.

HACIENDA HEIGHTS—52,400

LODGING

COURTYARD BY MARRIOTT　　Rates Subject to Change　　**Phone:** 626/965-1700
◆◆◆　All Year　　1P: $69- 84　2P/1B: $69- 84　2P/2B: $69- 84
Motor Inn　**Location:** 0.5 mi s of SR 60, exit Azusa Ave. 1905 S Azusa Ave 91745. Fax: 626/965-1367. **Facility:** 150 rooms. Just S of Puente Hills Mall. Large landscaped courtyard. 2-3 stories; interior corridors; heated pool. **Cards:** AE, DI, DS, MC, VI. (See color ad p 563)

HERMOSA BEACH—18,200　　(See map p. 561; index p. 547)

LODGINGS

BEACH HOUSE INN AT HERMOSA BEACH　　Rates Subject to Change　　**Phone:** (310)374-3001　**9**
◆◆◆　Sun-Thurs [CP]　1P: $169- 259　2P/1B: $169- 259　　XP: $25　F18
Suite Motel　Fri & Sat [CP]　1P: $179- 299　2P/1B: $179- 299　　XP: $25　F18
Location: Just w of Pacific Coast Hwy (#1) & Aviation Blvd. 1300 The Strand 90254. Fax: 310/372-2115. **Terms:** Check-in 4 pm. **Facility:** 56 rooms. All rooms with patio or deck & fireplace. 3 stories; interior corridors; designated smoking area; beachfront. **Services:** Fee: massage. **Recreation:** Fee: bicycles. **All Rooms:** efficiencies. **Cards:** AE, CB, DI, DS, MC, VI. (See color ad below)

HOTEL HERMOSA　　**Phone:** (310)318-6000　**10**
AAA SAVE　All Year [CP]　1P: $69- 165　2P/1B: $69- 165　2P/2B: $79- 165　XP: $10　F15
◆◆◆　**Location:** Corner of Artesia Blvd & Pacific Coast Hwy. 2515 Pacific Coast Hwy 90254. Fax: 310/318-6936.
Motel　**Facility:** 80 rooms. Many rooms with ocean view & balcony. 8 loft units, $119-$139. 8 whirlpool rms, $109-$119; 3 stories; interior corridors; small heated pool, whirlpool. **Some Rooms:** 14 efficiencies, no utensils. **Cards:** AE, DI, DS, JC, MC, VI.

(See map p. 561)

QUALITY INN & SUITES　　　　　　　　　　　　　　　　　Phone: (310)374-2666　**1**
AAA SAVE　6/1-9/15 [CP]　　　1P: $84- 104　2P/1B:　$84- 104　2P/2B:　$84- 104　XP: $10
　　　　　2/1-5/31 & 9/16-1/31 [CP]　1P: $74- 94　2P/1B:　$74- 94　2P/2B:　$74- 94　XP: $10
◆◆◆　**Location:** Just e of SR 1, Pacific Coast Hwy. 901 Aviation Blvd 90254. Fax: 310/379-3797. **Terms:** Reser
Motel　deposit. **Facility:** 68 rooms. Covered parking, some rooms with patios. 1 two-bedroom unit. 3 family suite
　　　　$89-109; 4 stories; interior/exterior corridors; whirlpool. **Some Rooms:** Fee: whirlpools. **Cards:** AE, CB, D
DS, JC, MC, VI. **Special Amenities:** Free breakfast. *(See color ad p 603)*

HOLLYWOOD　(See map p. 558; index p. 552)

LODGINGS

BEST WESTERN HOLLYWOOD HILLS　　　　　　　　　　　Phone: (323)464-5181　**14**
AAA SAVE　6/1-10/31　　　1P: $79- 129　2P/1B:　$79- 129　2P/2B:　$79- 129　XP: $10　F1
　　　　　2/1-5/31 & 11/1-1/31　1P: $69- 109　2P/1B:　$79- 109　2P/2B:　$79- 109　XP: $10　F1
◆◆◆　**Location:** Just e of Vine St. 6141 Franklin Ave 90028. Fax: 323/962-0536. **Terms:** Reserv deposit; sma
Motor Inn　pets only, $25 extra charge. **Facility:** 86 rooms. 50 efficiencies, $10 extra charge; 3-4 stories; interior/exterie
　　　　corridors; heated pool. **Dining:** Coffee shop; 7 am-10 pm; $8-$12. **Some Rooms:** 50 efficiencie
Cards: AE, CB, DI, DS, MC, VI. **Special Amenities:** Early check-in/late check-out and free room upgrade (subject
availability with advanced reservations). *(See ad p 571)*

BEST WESTERN HOLLYWOOD PLAZA INN　　　　　　　　Phone: (323)851-1800　**14**
AAA SAVE　6/15-9/30　　　1P: $79- 95　2P/1B:　$89- 109　2P/2B:　$89- 119　XP: $10　F1
　　　　　2/1-6/14 & 10/1-1/31　1P: $69- 79　2P/1B:　$75- 89　2P/2B:　$75- 89　XP: $10　F1
◆◆◆　**Location:** 0.5 mi n of Hollywood Blvd. 2011 N Highland Ave 90068. Fax: 323/851-1836. **Terms:** Reser
Motor Inn　deposit; weekly rates. **Facility:** 82 rooms. Some covered parking. 3 stories; exterior corridor
　　　　Dining: Coffee shop; 6:30 am-1 & 5:30-8 pm; $5-$8. **Some Rooms:** whirlpools. **Cards:** AE, CB, DI, DS, JC
MC, VI. *(See color ad below)*

BUDGET INN　　　　　Rates Subject to Change　　　　　Phone: 323/465-7186　**15**
◆◆　6/1-9/30　　　1P: $60　　2P/1B:　$70　　2P/2B:　$80　　XP: $10　F1
Motel　2/1-5/31 & 10/1-1/31　1P: $50　　2P/1B:　$55　　2P/2B:　$70　　XP: $10　F1
　　　Location: Just w of Highland Ave. 6826 Sunset Blvd 90028. Fax: 323/962-7663. **Facility:** 30 rooms. 2 storie
exterior corridors. **Cards:** AE, CB, DI, DS, JC, MC, VI.

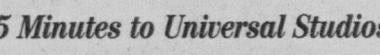
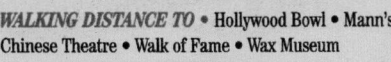
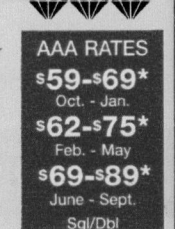

(See map p. 558)

CLUB HOTEL BY DOUBLETREE   **Phone: (323)850-5811**   **146**

[AAA] [SAVE]   6/11-10/30   1P: $149- 159   2P/1B: $149- 159   2P/2B: $149- 159   XP: $10   F17

         2/1-6/10 & 10/31-1/31   1P: $129- 139   2P/1B: $129- 139   2P/2B: $129- 139   XP: $10   F17

♦♦♦   **Location:** 0.5 mi n of Hollywood Blvd. 2005 N Highland Ave 90068. Fax: 323/876-3272. **Facility:** 160 rooms.

Motor Inn   Business friendly. Private workstation avail. 7 stories; interior corridors; heated pool, whirlpool. **Dining:** Deli;

         6 am-11 pm; $4-$7. **All Rooms:** extended cable TV. **Cards:** AE, CB, DI, DS, JC, MC, VI.

Special Amenities: Early check-in/late check-out and free newspaper. *(See color ad below)*

[icons]

DAYS INN-HOLLYWOOD   **Phone: (323)464-8344**   **150**

[AAA] [SAVE]   All Year [CP]   1P: $65- 199   2P/1B: $65- 199   2P/2B: $65- 199

♦♦   **Location:** Just e of La Brea Ave. 7023 Sunset Blvd 90028. Fax: 323/962-9748. **Terms:** Handling fee

Motel   imposed. **Facility:** 72 rooms. Few smaller rooms. 2 stories; exterior corridors; heated pool.

         All Rooms: combo or shower baths. **Some Rooms:** whirlpools. **Cards:** AE, DI, DS, JC, MC, VI.

         Special Amenities: Early check-in/late check-out and free breakfast. *(See color ad below)*

[icons]

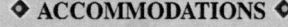

(See map p. 558)

DUNES MOTEL-SUNSET　　　　　　　Rates Subject to Change　　　　　　　**Phone:** 323/467-5171
🔶🔶🔶　　6/10-9/15　　　　　　　1P:　$65　　2P/1B:　$65　　2P/2B:　$73　　XP:　$5
◆　　　　2/1-6/9 & 9/16-1/31　　1P:　$58　　2P/1B:　$58　　2P/2B:　$65　　XP:　$5
Motor Inn　**Location:** 1 blk e of US 101, exit Sunset Blvd. 5625 Sunset Blvd 90028. Fax: 323/469-1962. **Terms:** Rese
deposit. **Facility:** 57 rooms. 2 stories; exterior corridors. **Dining:** Restaurant; 7 am-9 pm, Sat 8 am-3 p
closed Sun; $5-$8; cocktails. **Cards:** AE, CB, DI, DS, MC, VI. *(See ad p 575)*

ECONO LODGE-HOLLYWOOD　　　　　　　　　　　　　　　　　**Phone:** (323)463-5671
🔶🔶🔶 [SAVE]　All Year [CP]　　　　　1P:　$49　　2P/1B:　$55　　2P/2B:　$63　　XP:　$5
◆　　　　**Location:** Just n of Melrose Ave. 777 N Vine St 90038. Fax: 323/463-5675. **Facility:** 43 rooms. 2 stories; e
Motel　　terior corridors. **Dining:** Restaurant nearby. **Cards:** AE, CB, DI, DS, JC, MC, VI. **Special Amenities:** Ea
check-in/late check-out and free breakfast. *(See color ad below)*

HOLLYWOOD HILLS MAGIC HOTEL　　　　　　　　　　　　　**Phone:** (323)851-0800
🔶🔶🔶 [SAVE]　6/11-9/20　　　　　1P:　$69- 89　2P/1B:　$69- 99　2P/2B:　$89- 149　XP:　$10
◆◆　　　2/1-6/10 & 9/21-1/31　1P:　$59- 79　2P/1B:　$59- 79　2P/2B:　$75- 119　XP:　$10
Motel　　**Location:** 0.3 mi n of Hollywood Blvd. 7025 Franklin Ave 90028. Fax: 323/874-5246. **Terms:** Weekly rate
Facility: 40 rooms. Most units are 1-bedroom apartments with full kitchen. Also executive suites with kitche
ette & 7 studio apartments. 2 bedroom suite with kitchen, $119-$139 for up to 6 persons; 2-3 stories; exter
corridors; heated pool. **All Rooms:** extended cable TV. **Cards:** AE, CB, DI, DS, JC, MC, VI.

HOLLYWOOD METROPOLITAN HOTEL　　　　　　　　　　　**Phone:** (323)962-5800
🔶🔶🔶 [SAVE]　All Year　　　　　　1P:　$89- 149　2P/1B:　$89- 149　2P/2B:　$95　　XP:　$10
◆◆　　　**Location:** Just w of US 101, exit Sunset Blvd. 5825 Sunset Blvd 90028. Fax: 323/466-0646. **Facility:**
Hotel　　rooms. Interior corridors. **Dining:** Restaurant; 7-11 am. **Cards:** AE, CB, DI, DS, MC, VI.
(See color ad below)

HOLLYWOOD ORCHID SUITES　　　　　　　　　　　　　　**Phone:** (323)874-9678
🔶🔶🔶 [SAVE]　6/11-9/20　　　　　1P:　$80- 109　2P/1B:　$85- 109　2P/2B:　$85- 119　XP:　$10
◆◆　　　2/1-6/10 & 9/21-1/31　1P:　$65- 89　2P/1B:　$75- 89　2P/2B:　$65- 99　XP:　$10
Apartment　**Location:** Just n of Hollywood Blvd. 1753 N Orchid Ave 90028. Fax: 323/874-5246. **Terms:** Weekly rate
Motel　　**Facility:** 39 rooms. Located near Hollywood Blvd & the celebrated Manns Chinese Theatre. 1-bedroom suit
with kitchen, $75-$109 for up to 4 persons; 3 stories; interior/exterior corridors; heated po
Dining: Restaurant nearby. **Some Rooms:** 4 efficiencies, 35 kitchens. **Cards:** AE, CB, DI, DS, JC, MC, VI.

(See map p. 558)

HOLLYWOOD ROOSEVELT HOTEL (A CLARION HOTEL)　　Phone: (323)466-7000

AAA SAVE	5/1-10/31	1P: $139	2P/1B: $159	2P/2B: $159	XP: $20	F
	11/1-1/31	1P: $129	2P/1B: $149	2P/2B: $149	XP: $20	F
◆◆◆	2/1-4/30	1P: $119	2P/1B: $139	2P/2B: $139	XP: $20	F

Historic Hotel　**Location:** 7000 Hollywood Blvd 90028. **Fax:** 323/462-8056. **Terms:** Reserv deposit, 4 day notic
Facility: 331 rooms. Hollywood memorabilia on display throughout the legendary hotel. On the Hollywood Wa
of Fame & directly across from the Mann's Chinese Theatre. A variety of room sizes. 12 stories; interior corridors; heated
whirlpool. Fee: parking. **Dining:** Dining room; 6 am-11 pm; coffee house; $12-$18; cocktails. **Services:** giftsho
Fee: massage. **Cards:** AE, CB, DI, DS, JC, MC, VI.

RAMADA LIMITED　　Phone: (323)660-1788

AAA SAVE　All Year [CP]　1P: $59- 89　2P/1B: $69- 99　2P/2B: $69- 99　XP: $10
Location: 0.5 mi n of US 101. 1160 N Vermont Ave 90029. **Fax:** 323/660-8069. **Terms:** Reserv depos
◆◆◆　weekly/monthly rates. **Facility:** 128 rooms. Seasonal central heating and air conditioning. Suites with refr
Motel　erator, microwave & coffeemaker, $79-$129; 4 stories; interior corridors; heated pool, saunas, steamroon
Fee: parking. **Recreation:** Fee: video games & video game room. **All Rooms:** combo or shower bath
Cards: AE, CB, DI, DS, JC, MC, VI. **Special Amenities: Free breakfast and free room upgrade (subject to availabil
with advanced reservations).** (See ad p 607)

TRAVELODGE-SUNSET/LA BREA　　Phone: (323)462-0905

AAA SAVE　Fri & Sat　1P: $55- 65　2P/1B: $60- 70　2P/2B: $65- 75　XP: $5
◆　Sun-Thurs　1P: $50- 60　2P/1B: $55- 65　2P/2B: $60- 70　XP: $5
Location: 7051 Sunset Blvd 90028. **Fax:** 323/465-6088. **Terms:** Reserv deposit. **Facility:** 43 rooms. 3 storie
Motel　exterior corridors. **All Rooms:** combo or shower baths. **Cards:** AE, CB, DI, DS, JC, MC,
Special Amenities: Free breakfast and free newspaper.

RESTAURANTS

DAR MAGHREB　　Dinner: $30　　Phone: 323/876-7651
◆◆◆　**Location:** 7651 Sunset Blvd 90046. **Hours:** 6 pm-11 pm, Sat 5:30 pm-11 pm, Sun 5:30 pm-10:30 p
Ethnic　Closed: 11/25 & 12/25. **Reservations:** suggested. **Features:** casual dress; cocktails; fee for valet parking
la carte. Traditional Moroccan cuisine in a recreated palace. Seating on couches & pillows, food eaten w
hands. Belly dancing. Price fixe 7-course menu, $29.95, vegetarian, $26. Smoke free premises. **Cards:** CB, DI, MC, VI.

MUSSO & FRANK GRILL　Historical　**Lunch:** $8-$28　**Dinner:** $8-$28　Phone: 323/467-5123
◆　**Location:** 3 blks w of Cahuenga Blvd. 6667 Hollywood Blvd 90028. **Hours:** 11 am-11 pm. Closed ma
American　holidays, Sun & Mon. **Reservations:** accepted. **Features:** casual dress; children's menu; carryout; cockta
& lounge; fee for parking; a la carte. A Hollywood tradition since 1919 serving breakfast, sandwiches
American entrees throughout the day. Original decor with seating at tables, counter & booths. Smoke free premis
Cards: AE, CB, DI, MC, VI.

INDUSTRY—600

LODGING

INDUSTRY HILLS SHERATON RESORT & CONFERENCE CENTER

Rates Subject to Change　　Phone: (626)810-44
AAA　All Year　1P: $150- 175　2P/1B: $165- 190　2P/2B: $165- 190　XP: $15　F
Location: 1.8 mi n of SR 60, Azusa Ave exit. One Industry Hills Pkwy 91744. **Fax:** 626/964-95
◆◆◆　**Terms:** Reserv deposit, 14 day notice. **Facility:** 294 rooms. Hilltop location on spacious grounds. 14 stori
Resort Hotel　interior corridors; golf library; heated pool, saunas, whirlpools. Fee: 36 holes golf; 17 lighted tennis cou
Dining: Coffee shop; 6 am-11:30 pm; $8-$16; also, The Brae, see separate listing. **Services:** giftsh
Recreation: competition swim complex. **All Rooms:** combo or shower baths. **Cards:** AE, CB, DI, DS, JC, MC, VI.

RESTAURANTS

THE BRAE　**Lunch:** $8-$14　**Dinner:** $17-$30　Phone: 626/854-23
◆◆◆　**Location:** 1.8 mi n of SR 60, Exit Azusa Ave, in the Industry Hills Sheraton Resort & Conference Cent
American　One Industry Hills Pkwy 91744. **Hours:** 11:30 am-3 & 6-10:30 pm, Sat 5:30 pm-10:30 pm, Sun 9:30 am-2
& 6-10 pm. **Reservations:** suggested. **Features:** semi-formal attire; Sunday brunch; cocktails & loun
entertainment; fee for valet parking; a la carte. Formal dining overlooking the golf course. Unique selection of entre
including specialties such as Bison, Antelope & Venison. Smoke free premises. **Cards:** AE, CB, DI, DS, MC, VI.

CLAIM JUMPER RESTAURANT　**Lunch:** $8-$23　**Dinner:** $12-$23　Phone: 626/964-11
◆◆　**Location:** N side of SR 60 between Azusa Ave & Fullerton Rd exits. 18061 Gale Ave 91745. **Hours:** Sur
American　Mon 11 am-10 pm, Tues-Thurs to 11 pm, Fri & Sat-midnight. Closed: 7/4, 11/25 & 12/25. **Features:** cas
dress; children's menu; carryout; salad bar; cocktails & lounge. Generous portions of entrees, sala
sandwiches & desserts. Smoke free premises. **Cards:** AE, DI, DS, MC, VI.

MIMI'S CAFE　**Lunch:** $6-$11　**Dinner:** $7-$11　Phone: 626/912-33
◆◆　**Location:** Northside of SR 60, between Azusa Ave & Fullerton Ave exits. 17919 E Gale 91748. **Hours**
American　am-11 pm. Closed: 12/25. **Features:** children's menu; beer & wine only. Casual dining in a French c
atmosphere. Nice selection of salads, sandwiches & entrees. Smoke free premises. **Cards:** AE, MC, VI.

INGLEWOOD—109,600 (See map p. 558; index p. 551)

LODGINGS

EST WESTERN AIRPARK HOTEL   Phone: (310)677-7378   125
) SAVE
6/1-8/31 [CP]   1P: $68- 78   2P/1B: $68- 88   2P/2B: $74- 88   XP: $6-10   F12
2/1-5/31 & 9/1-1/31 [CP]   1P: $62- 79   2P/1B: $66- 86   2P/2B: $66- 86   XP: $6-10   F12
◆◆   **Location:** Adjacent to I-405, Manchester Blvd E exit. 640 W Manchester Blvd 90301. Fax: 310/674-1137.
otel   **Terms:** Reserv deposit, 3 day notice. **Facility:** 70 rooms. 5 whirlpool rms, extra charge; 4 stories; exterior corridors; sauna, steamroom, whirlpools, 1 indoor whirlpool. **Dining:** Restaurant nearby. **Cards:** AE, CB, DI, DS, MC, VI. **Special Amenities:** Free breakfast and free newspaper. *(See color ad p 572)*

EST WESTERN AIRPORT PLAZA INN   Phone: (310)568-0071   119
) SAVE
2/1-6/30 & 9/1-1/31 [CP]   1P: $62- 79   2P/1B: $66- 86   2P/2B: $66- 86   XP: $6-10   F12
7/1-8/31 [CP]   1P: $68- 78   2P/1B: $68- 78   XP: $6-10   F12
◆   **Location:** Just e of I-405, exit La Tijera Blvd to Centinela. 1730 Centinela Ave 90302. Fax: 310/337-1919.
otel   **Terms:** Reserv deposit. **Facility:** 54 rooms. 3 whirlpool rms, extra charge; 3 stories; exterior corridors; whirlpool. **Services:** area transportation. **Cards:** AE, CB, DI, DS, MC, VI. **Special Amenities:** Early
eck-in/late check-out and free breakfast. *(See color ad p 576)*

EST WESTERN SUITES HOTEL-LAX   Phone: (310)677-7733   117
) SAVE
6/1-8/31 [CP]   1P: $89- 119   2P/1B: $89- 119   2P/2B: $99- 119   XP: $10   F12
2/1-5/31 & 9/1-1/31 [CP]   1P: $79- 109   2P/1B: $89- 109   2P/2B: $89- 109   XP: $10   F12
◆◆   **Location:** 1 blk E of I-405, Century Blvd E exit, 1.5 mi e of airport. 5005 W Century Blvd 90304.
Fax: 310/671-7722. **Terms:** Reserv deposit, 3 day notice. **Facility:** 80 rooms. Park & fly rates avail; 4 stories; interior corridors; heated pool, whirlpool. **Services:** area transportation. **Some Rooms:** Fee: whirlpools.
rds: AE, CB, DI, DS, JC, MC, VI. **Special Amenities:** Early check-in/late check-out and free breakfast.
ee color ad p 572)

OMFORT INN & SUITES LOS ANGELES INT'L AIRPORT   Phone: (310)671-7213   126
) SAVE
6/1-8/31 [CP]   1P: $64- 79   2P/1B: $69- 89   2P/2B: $69- 89   XP: $5   F12
2/1-5/31 & 9/1-1/31 [CP]   1P: $64- 74   2P/1B: $69- 84   2P/2B: $69- 84   XP: $5   F12
◆   **Location:** Just e of I-405; exit Century Blvd. 4922 W Century Blvd 90304. Fax: 310/671-1804.
tel   **Terms:** Reserv deposit, 3 day notice. **Facility:** 105 rooms. 33 1-bedroom whirlpool suites with coffeemaker $79-$109; 4 stories; interior/exterior corridors; heated pool. **Cards:** AE, CB, DI, DS, JC, MC, VI.
ecial Amenities: Free local telephone calls and free newspaper. *(See color ad p 574)*

YS INN AIRPORT MAINGATE   Phone: (310)649-0800   124
) SAVE
6/1-8/31   1P: $59- 69   2P/1B: $54- 74   2P/2B: $64- 74   XP: $5   F12
2/1-5/31 & 9/1-1/31   1P: $54- 64   2P/1B: $59- 69   2P/2B: $59- 69   XP: $5   F12
◆   **Location:** Just w of I-405, Manchester Blvd exit. 901 W Manchester Blvd 90301. Fax: 310/649-3837.
tor Inn   **Terms:** Reserv deposit, 3 day notice; weekly rates. **Facility:** 47 rooms. 11 two-bedroom units, $60-$79; 2 stories; exterior corridors. **Dining:** Coffee shop; 6 am-2 pm; wine/beer only. **Cards:** AE, CB, DI, DS, JC, MC, VI.
ee color ad p 576)

ONO LODGE LAX   Phone: (310)672-7285   116
) SAVE
5/1-8/31   1P: $38   2P/1B: $45   2P/2B: $50   XP: $5
2/1-4/30   1P: $35   2P/1B: $42   2P/2B: $50   XP: $5
9/1-1/31   1P: $38   2P/1B: $40   2P/2B: $45   XP: $5
tel   **Location:** 1.8 mi e I-405. 4123 W Century Blvd 90304. Fax: 310/672-1046. **Terms:** Reserv deposit.
Facility: 41 rooms. 3 stories; exterior corridors. **Cards:** AE, DS, MC, VI.

MPTON INN-LOS ANGELES INTERNATIONAL AIRPORT   Phone: (310)337-1000   115
) SAVE
Mon-Thurs [CP]   1P: $89- 129   2P/1B: $89- 129   2P/2B: $89- 129
Fri-Sun [CP]   1P: $79- 109   2P/1B: $79- 109   2P/2B: $79- 109
◆◆   **Location:** Just w of I-405, exit Century Blvd, 1.5 mi e of LAX. 10300 La Cienega Blvd 90304.
tel   Fax: 310/645-6925. **Terms:** Pets. **Facility:** 148 rooms. 7 stories; interior corridors. **Cards:** AE, CB, DI, DS, JC, MC, VI. **Special Amenities:** Free breakfast. *(See color ad p 599 & p 564)*

MADA LIMITED LAX   Phone: (310)419-1011   120
) SAVE
6/15-9/15   1P: $58- 68   2P/1B: $63- 73   2P/2B: $78- 88   XP: $10   F17
2/1-6/14 & 9/16-1/31   1P: $58- 63   2P/1B: $58- 63   2P/2B: $78- 83   XP: $10   F17
◆   **Location:** 1.3 mi e of I-405. 4300 W Century Blvd 90304. Fax: 310/412-1294. **Facility:** 46 rooms. 4 mini suites
tel   with whirlpool tubs, $100; 3 stories; exterior corridors; whirlpool. **Cards:** AE, CB, DI, DS, JC, MC, VI.

DEWAY INN   Phone: (310)672-4570   122
) SAVE
All Year [CP]   1P: $45- 55   2P/1B: $45- 55   2P/2B: $55- 70   XP: $5-15   F17
◆   **Location:** Just e of Prairie Ave, across from Hollywood Park Racetrack & Casino. 3940 W Century Blvd
90303. Fax: 310/671-7410. **Facility:** 36 rooms. 6 one-bedroom suites $65-$80; 2 stories; exterior corridors.
tel   **Some Rooms:** whirlpools. **Cards:** AE, DS, MC, VI. **Special Amenities:** Free breakfast and free newspaper.

PER 8 MOTEL-AIRPORT   Phone: (310)672-0740   123
) SAVE
All Year [CP]   1P: $39- 49   2P/1B: $43- 53   2P/2B: $49- 59   XP: $3-5   F12
◆   **Location:** 4238 W Century Blvd 90303. Fax: 310/672-1904. **Terms:** Reserv deposit. **Facility:** 39 rooms. 4
tel   whirlpool rms, extra charge; 3 stories; exterior corridors. **Cards:** AE, CB, DI, DS, JC, MC, VI.

URISTLODGE INGLEWOOD-LAX   Phone: (310)677-0112   118
) SAVE
All Year   1P: $35   2P/1B: $38   2P/2B: $45   XP: $3-5   D15
◆   **Location:** 1 mi e of Hawthorne Blvd. 3649 W Imperial Hwy 90303. Fax: 310/674-2325. **Terms:** Reserv
deposit. **Facility:** 39 rooms. 5 whirlpool rms, extra charge; 2 stories; exterior corridors. **Cards:** AE, CB, DI,
tel   DS, MC, VI. **Special Amenities:** Free local telephone calls.

LA CANADA FLINTRIDGE—19,400   (See map p. 562; index p. 554)

RESTAURANTS

THE BARKLEY RESTAURANT & BAR   **Lunch:** $5-$9   **Dinner:** $6-$16   **Phone:** 818/790-2348   5◆
◆   **Location:** SR 210, Angeles Crest Hwy exit s, to Foothill Blvd; then 1 mi w. 1438 Foothill Blvd 9101
American   **Hours:** 7 am-10 pm. **Closed:** 12/25. **Reservations:** suggested. **Features:** casual dress; children's menu
carryout; cocktails. Friendly family restaurant with good selection of pasta, sandwiches & entrees. Smoke
free premises. **Cards:** AE, CB, DI, DS, MC, VI.   ⊠

FLINTRIDGE INN   **Lunch:** $6-$10   **Dinner:** $16-$24   **Phone:** 818/790-5355   5◆
◆◆◆   **Location:** SR 210, exit Angeles Crest Hwy s; e on Foothill Blvd, 0.5 mi n of Glendale. 734 Foothill Blv
Continental   91011. **Hours:** 11 am-3 & 5-9 pm, Fri-10 pm, Sat 5 pm-10 pm, Sun 5 pm-9 pm. **Closed:** 12/2
Reservations: accepted. **Features:** casual dress; children's menu; early bird specials; cocktails & loung
Nicely decorated in unusual interior design. Excellent selection of meat, chicken, seafood & pasta dishes. Smoke fre
premises. **Cards:** AE, CB, DI, MC, VI.   ⊠

LA MIRADA—40,500

LODGINGS

HOLIDAY INN SELECT   Rates Subject to Change   **Phone:** (714)739-850
◆◆◆   All Year   1P: $89   2P/2B: $99
Hotel   **Location:** Just ne of I-5, Valley View exit. 14299 Firestone Blvd 90638. Fax: 714/739-4272. **Facility:** 28
rooms. 8 stories; interior corridors; heated pool. **Services:** giftshop; area transportation. **Cards:** AE, CB, D
JC, MC, VI. *(See color ad below)*

RESIDENCE INN BY MARRIOTT   Rates Subject to Change   **Phone:** 714/523-280
◆◆◆   All Year [BP]   1P: $84- 99   2P/1B: $84- 99 2P/2B: $127- 149
Suite Motel   **Location:** E side of I-5, exit Valley View, 0.5 mi se on Firestone Blvd. 14419 Firestone Blvd 9063
Fax: 714/522-5884. **Facility:** 146 rooms. Studio & 2-bedroom suites with living room & kitchen; many with fire
place. 2 stories; exterior corridors; heated pool. **Services:** area transportation. **Recreation:** sports court. **Cards:** AE, DI, DS
JC, MC, VI.

LAWNDALE—27,300   (See map p. 561; index p. 547)

LODGINGS

BEST WESTERN SOUTH BAY HOTEL   Phone: (310)973-0998   **1**
All Year [CP]   1P: $55- 105   2P/1B: $59- 125 2P/2B: $59- 125 XP: $5-10   F12
Location: SR 107, 0.8 mi n of jct I-405, San Diego Frwy. 15000 Hawthorne Blvd 90260. Fax: 310/978-0022.
Terms: Reserv deposit, 3 day notice; weekly rates. **Facility:** 100 rooms. 2 whirlpool rms, extra charge; 3 stories; interior corridors; sauna, whirlpool. **Dining:** Dining room; 11 am-2:30 & 5-9 pm; $6-$10; cocktails.
Cards: AE, CB, DI, DS, MC, VI. **Special Amenities: Free breakfast and free newspaper.**

Motor Inn

DAYS INN AIRPORT SOUTH BAY   Phone: (310)676-7378   **2**
6/15-8/31 [CP]   1P: $54- 68   2P/1B: $58- 72 2P/2B: $58- 74 XP: $6   F12
2/1-6/14 & 9/1-1/31 [CP]   1P: $50- 65   2P/1B: $54- 64 2P/2B: $54- 68 XP: $5   F12
Location: SR 107, 0.5 mi n of jct I-405, San Diego Frwy. 15636 Hawthorne Blvd 90260. Fax: 310/676-3138.
Terms: Reserv deposit, 3 day notice. **Facility:** 43 rooms. 2 whirlpool rms, $85-$100; 4 stories; exterior corridors; whirlpool. **Dining:** Restaurant nearby. **Cards:** AE, CB, DI, DS, JC, MC, VI. *(See color ad p 576)*

Motel

LONG BEACH—429,400   (See map p. 561; index p. 551)

LODGINGS

BEST WESTERN GOLDEN SAILS HOTEL   Phone: (562)596-1631   **80**
All Year   1P: $118- 138   2P/1B: $128- 148 2P/2B: $128- 148 XP: $10   F12
Location: On SR 1, just ne of Marina Pacific Plaza & Naples area. 6285 E Pacific Coast Hwy 90803.
Fax: 562/594-0623. **Terms:** Reserv deposit, 3 day notice. **Facility:** 172 rooms. 2-4 stories; interior/exterior corridors; heated pool, whirlpool. **Dining:** Restaurant; 6 am-2 & 5-9:30 pm, Sun 9:30 am-2 & 5-9 pm; $9-$16; cocktails. **All Rooms:** combo or shower baths. **Some Rooms:** 28 efficiencies, whirlpools. **Cards:** AE, CB, DI, JC, MC, VI. **Special Amenities: Free newspaper and free room upgrade (subject to availability with advanced reservations).** *(See ad below)*

Motor Inn

BEST WESTERN OF LONG BEACH   Phone: (562)599-5555   **68**
All Year [CP]   1P: $58   2P/1B: $64   2P/2B: $64   XP: $6   F18
Location: Just s of SR 1 (Pacific Coast Hwy). 1725 Long Beach Blvd 90813. Fax: 562/599-1212.
Terms: Reserv deposit; small pets only. **Facility:** 102 rooms. 3 two-bedroom units. 4 stories; interior corridors; heated pool. **Cards:** AE, DI, DS, MC, VI. **Special Amenities: Free breakfast and free newspaper.**
(See color ad below)

Motel

(See map p. 561)

COMFORT INN DOWNTOWN
Phone: (562)590-8858 **69**
All Year   1P: $59- 89   2P/1B: $69- 89 2P/2B: $79- 89 XP: $10   F17
Location: 1 mi n of Ocean Blvd. 1133 Atlantic Ave 90813. Fax: 562/983-1607. **Facility:** 134 rooms. 4 stories; interior corridors; small heated pool, whirlpool. **Dining:** Restaurant; 6:30 am-2 & 6-10 pm; $6-$12; wine/beer only. **Cards:** AE, CB, DI, DS, JC, MC, VI.
Motor Inn

COURTYARD BY MARRIOTT - DOWNTOWN   Rates Subject to Change   Phone: 562/435-8511 **75**
All Year   1P: $92   2P/1B: $92   2P/2B: $92
Location: Just n of Ocean Blvd at Atlantic. 500 E 1st 90802. Fax: 562/435-1370. **Terms:** Check-in 4 pm; reserv deposit, 3 day notice. **Facility:** 216 rooms. 9 stories; interior corridors; heated pool. **Cards:** AE, DI, DS, MC, VI. *(See color ad below)*
Motor Inn

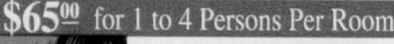

MAIL YOUR RESERVATION DEPOSIT EARLY!

(See map p. 561)

GUESTHOUSE HOTEL
Phone: (562)597-1341   **78**
AAA SAVE   All Year   1P: $73   2P/1B: $73   2P/2B: $73   XP: $10   F18
Location: On SR 1. 5325 E Pacific Coast Hwy 90804. Fax: 562/597-1664. **Terms:** Pets, $50 dep req.
◆◆◆ **Facility:** 143 rooms. 0.75 mi w of California State University Long Beach. 4 two-bedroom units. 2 stories; ex-
Motor Inn   terior corridors; heated pool. **Dining:** Restaurant; 8 am-10 pm, Sun-9 pm; $9-$15; cocktails.
Some Rooms: whirlpools. **Cards:** AE, CB, DI, DS, JC, MC, VI. *(See color ad p 612)*

HOLIDAY INN-LONG BEACH AIRPORT
Phone: (562)597-4401   **82**
AAA SAVE   All Year   1P: $75- 85   2P/1B: $75- 85   2P/2B: $75- 85   XP: $10-20   F19
Location: On SR 19, just s of I-405. 2640 Lakewood Blvd 90815. Fax: 562/597-0601. **Terms:** Monthly rates.
◆◆ **Facility:** 230 rooms. Dining room & lounge on top floor with view of airport & surrounding area. 13 stories; in-
Motor Inn   terior corridors; heated pool. **Dining:** Dining room; 6 am-2 & 5:30-10 pm, Sat & Sun from 6:30 am; $10-$15;
cocktails. **Cards:** AE, DI, DS, JC, MC, VI. *(See color ad p 612)*

HYATT REGENCY LONG BEACH
Phone: (562)491-1234   **73**
AAA SAVE   All Year   1P: $170- 210   2P/1B: $195- 235   2P/2B: $195- 235   XP: $25   F18
Location: Downtown. 200 S Pine Ave at Shoreline Dr 90802. Fax: 562/432-1972. **Facility:** 521 rooms. Adja-
◆◆◆ cent to Long Beach Convention & Entertainment Center. 16 stories; interior corridors; heated pool, whirlpool.
Hotel   **Fee:** parking. **Dining:** Restaurant; 6 am-midnight; coffee bar avail; $7-$25. **Services:** giftshop. **Cards:** AE,
CB, DI, DS, JC, MC, VI. *(See color ad p 565)*

INN OF LONG BEACH
Rates Subject to Change   **Phone:** (562)435-3791   **77**
AAA   5/27-10/9 [CP]   1P: $48- 69   2P/1B: $48- 69   2P/2B: $55- 89   XP: $5-10   D14
2/1-5/26 [CP]   1P: $48- 63   2P/1B: $48- 63   2P/2B: $55- 79   XP: $5-10   D14
◆ 10/10-1/31 [CP]   1P: $48- 59   2P/1B: $48- 59   2P/2B: $52- 79   XP: $5-10   D14
Motel   **Location:** Just n of Ocean Blvd. 185 Atlantic Ave 90802. Fax: 562/436-7510. **Terms:** Reserv deposit, 3 day
notice. **Facility:** 46 rooms. 2 stories; exterior corridors; heated pool, whirlpool. **Cards:** AE, DI, DS, MC, VI.

LONG BEACH HILTON
Phone: (562)983-3400   **70**
AAA SAVE   All Year   1P: $119- 189   2P/1B: $119- 189   2P/2B: $119- 189
Location: Downtown area, just e of I-710, exit Broadway. Two World Trade Center 90831.
◆◆◆◆ Fax: 562/983-1200. **Terms:** Small pets only, $25. **Facility:** 393 rooms. At The World Trade Center. Public areas
Hotel   decorated in an oriental theme. 1 three-bedroom unit, 2 two-bedroom units. 15 stories; interior corridors;
heated pool, whirlpool. **Fee:** parking. **Dining:** Restaurant; 6 am-11 pm; $8-$17; cocktails. **Services:** giftshop.
Fee: massage. **Cards:** AE, CB, DI, DS, JC, MC, VI. *(See ad p 119)*

(See map p. 561)

LONG BEACH MARRIOTT
◆◆◆   Mon-Thurs [EP]
Hotel   Fri-Sun [BP]
Rates Subject to Change   Phone: 562/425-5210   **81**
1P: $170   2P/1B: $170   2P/2B: $170   XP: $15   F18
1P: $99   2P/1B: $99   2P/2B: $99   XP: $15   F18
Location: 1 mi n of I-405, exit Lakewood Blvd; 0.5 mi s of Long Beach Airport. 4700 Airport Plaza Dr & Spring St 90815. Fax: 562/421-1075. **Facility:** 311 rooms. 8 stories; interior corridors; heated indoor pool. **Services:** giftshop. **Cards:** AE, CB, DI, DS, JC, MC, VI.

RENAISSANCE LONG BEACH HOTEL
(AAA)   All Year
◆◆◆◆
Hotel
Rates Subject to Change   Phone: (562)437-5900   **72**
1P: $129- 149   2P/1B: $129- 149   2P/2B: $129- 149
Location: Downtown. 111 E Ocean Blvd at Pine Ave 90802. Fax: 562/499-2509. **Facility:** 374 rooms. Across from Long Beach Convention Center. Many rooms with ocean view. 12 stories; interior corridors; heated pool, saunas, whirlpool. **Dining:** Dining room, restaurant; 6 am-11 pm; $12-$25; cocktails. **Services:** giftshop. Fee: massage. **Cards:** AE, CB, DI, DS, JC, MC, VI.

SUPER 8 MOTEL-LONG BEACH TRAFFIC CIRCLE
(AAA) (SAVE)   All Year [CP]
◆◆
Motel
Phone: (562)597-7701   **71**
1P: $50- 60   2P/1B: $56- 66   2P/2B: $59- 69   XP: $5   F12
Location: On SR 1; 1 mi s of I-405, exit Lakewood Blvd. 4201 E Pacific Coast Hwy 90804. Fax: 562/494-7373. **Terms:** Weekly rates. **Facility:** 49 rooms. Opposite Long Beach Community Hospital. 10 kitchen units, $7 extra charge; 2 stories; exterior corridors; heated pool, wading pool, sauna, whirlpool. **Services:** complimentary evening beverages. **Some Rooms:** whirlpools. **Cards:** AE, CB, DI, DS, JC, MC, VI. **Special Amenities:** Free local telephone calls and free newspaper. *(See color ad p 613)*

TRAVELODGE CONVENTION CENTER
(AAA) (SAVE)   All Year
◆
Motor Inn
Phone: (562)435-2471   **76**
1P: $49- 99   2P/1B: $49- 99   2P/2B: $49- 99   XP: $5   F17
Location: Downtown area, just n of Ocean Blvd. 80 Atlantic Ave 90802. Fax: 562/437-1995. **Facility:** 63 rooms. 3 stories; exterior corridors. **Dining:** Restaurant; 6 am-10 pm; $6-$8; wine/beer only. **All Rooms:** combo or shower baths. **Cards:** AE, CB, DI, DS, JC, MC, VI.

WEST COAST LONG BEACH HOTEL
◆◆◆   All Year
Motor Inn
Rates Subject to Change   Phone: 562/435-7676   **83**
1P: $79   2P/1B: $79   2P/2B: $89   XP: $10
Location: Southern terminus of I-710, just n of The Queen Mary. 700 Queensway Dr 90802. Fax: 562/437-0866. **Facility:** 196 rooms. Most rooms with balcony or patio & view of harbor. 5 stories; exterior corridors; heated pool; 2 lighted tennis courts. **Services:** giftshop. **Cards:** AE, CB, DI, DS, MC, VI. *(See color ad p 613)*

THE WESTIN LONG BEACH
◆◆◆   All Year
Hotel
Rates Subject to Change   Phone: 562/436-3000   **74**
1P: $218- 236   2P/1B: $218- 236   XP: $20   F18
Location: Downtown. 333 E Ocean Blvd 90802. Fax: 562/436-9176. **Facility:** 460 rooms. Across from Long Beach Convention & Entertainment Center. 15 stories; heated pool. Fee: parking. **Services:** giftshop. **Cards:** AE, DI, DS, MC, VI.

RESTAURANTS

COLONIAL BUFFET
◆◆
American
Lunch: $6   **Dinner:** $8   **Phone:** 562/590-0220   **47**
Location: Downtown. 355 E First St 90802. **Hours:** 11 am-8 pm. **Features:** casual dress; Sunday brunch; children's menu; beer & wine only; buffet. Attractive early American decor. Smoke free premises. **Cards:** MC, VI.

FISH TALE
◆◆
Seafood
Lunch: $8-$15   **Dinner:** $12-$26   **Phone:** 562/594-8771   **54**
Location: 0.8 mi s of I-405, in Los Altos Market Center. 5506 Britton Dr 90815. **Hours:** 11 am-10 pm, Fri & Sat-11 pm, Sun 10 am. Closed: 11/25 & 12/25. **Features:** casual dress; children's menu; cocktails & lounge. Rustic, nautical decor. Large selection of seafood. Heated outdoor patio. Smoke free premises. **Cards:** AE, CB, DI, DS, MC, VI.

555 EAST
◆◆◆
American
Lunch: $10-$17   **Dinner:** $16-$28   **Phone:** 562/437-0626   **52**
Location: Downtown at Linden Ave. 555 E Ocean Blvd 90802. **Hours:** 11:30 am-3 & 5:30-10 pm, Fri-11 pm, Sat 5:30 pm-11 pm, Sun 5:30 pm-9 pm. Closed: 1/1, 7/4 & 12/25. **Reservations:** suggested. **Features:** casual dress; cocktails & lounge; valet parking; a la carte. Menu features prime beef. Also a selection of chicken, pasta & seafood. Smoke free premises. **Cards:** AE, DI, DS, MC, VI.

GAZZELLA
◆◆
Italian
Lunch: $7-$11   **Dinner:** $8-$17   **Phone:** 562/495-7252   **48**
Location: downtown area just n of Ocean Blvd, corner of Atlantic & Broadway. 525 E Broadway 90802. **Hours:** 11 am-2 & 5-10 pm, Sat & Sun 5-10 pm. Closed: 11/25 & 12/25. **Reservations:** suggested. **Features:** cocktails & lounge; valet parking. Dining in an atmosphere of an Italian Villa. Selections of veal, chicken, seafood, lamb & pasta. Smoke free premises. **Cards:** AE, DI, MC, VI.

JOHNNY REB'S
◆
American
Lunch: $5-$13   **Dinner:** $9-$13   **Phone:** 562/423-7327   **44**
Location: 2 mi n of I-405, exit Long Beach Blvd. 4663 Long Beach Blvd 90805. **Hours:** 7 am-9 pm, Fri & Sat-10 pm. Closed: 11/25 & 12/25. **Features:** casual dress; senior's menu; carryout; beer & wine only. Modest appearing Alabama "Roadhouse" atmosphere serving barbeque meats, catfish & southern cuisine. Smoke free premises. **Cards:** MC, VI.

L'OPERA RISTORANTE
◆◆◆
Italian
Lunch: $9-$20   **Dinner:** $14-$27   **Phone:** 562/491-0066   **46**
Location: Downtown, just n of Ocean Blvd. 101 Pine Ave 90802. **Hours:** 11:30 am-11 pm, Fri-midnight, Sat 5 pm-midnight, Sun 5 pm-10 pm. Closed major holidays. **Reservations:** suggested. **Features:** cocktails; valet parking; a la carte. Fine dining in a restored bank building. Classic & modern Italian dishes. Smoke free premises. **Cards:** AE, DI, DS, MC, VI.

PARKERS' LIGHTHOUSE
◆◆
Seafood
Lunch: $6-$14   **Dinner:** $13-$29   **Phone:** 526/432-6500   **43**
Location: Just s of downtown; in Shoreline Village. 43 Shoreline Dr 90802. **Hours:** 11 am-3 & 5-10 pm, Fri-11 pm, Sat 11 am-11 pm, Sun 10 am-11 & 3-9:30 pm. Closed: 12/25. **Reservations:** suggested. **Features:** casual dress; Sunday brunch; children's menu; cocktails & lounge; a la carte. Waterfront restaurant with view of harbor & the Queen Mary. Nice selection of seafood & a limited selection of beef, poultry & pasta. **Cards:** AE, CB, DI, DS, MC, VI.

(See map p. 561)

SHENANDOAH CAFE   **Lunch:** $7-$10   **Dinner:** $12-$22   **Phone:** 562/434-3469 [56]
◆◆◆   **Location:** In Belmont Shore area. 4722 E 2nd St 90803. **Hours:** 11:30 am-2:30 & 5-10 pm, Sat 4:30-11 pm,
American   Sun 4:30-10 pm. Closed major holidays. **Reservations:** suggested. **Features:** children's menu; beer & wine
    only; street parking. Features a nice selection of Regional American cuisine with a Southern emphasis.
Smoke free premises. **Cards:** AE, DI, MC, VI.   ⊠

SIMON & SEAFORT'S STEAK, CHOP &
OYSTER HOUSE   **Lunch:** $9-$15   **Dinner:** $16-$25   **Phone:** 562/435-2333 [50]
◆◆   **Location:** 2 blks s of Ocean Ave, at Catalina Landing. 340 Golden Shore 90802. **Hours:** 11 am-2:15 & 5-10
American   pm, Sat 5 pm-10 pm, Sun 4:30 pm-9 pm. Closed: 7/4, 11/25 & 12/25. **Reservations:** suggested.
    Features: casual dress; children's menu; cocktails & lounge. Nice selection of fresh seafood; also steaks,
chops & roasts . Smoke free premises. **Cards:** AE, DI, MC, VI.   ⊠

LYNWOOD—61,900   (See map p. 558; index p. 554)

LODGING

LYNWOOD CENTURY FREEWAY TRAVELODGE   Rates Subject to Change   **Phone:** 310/763-4029 [225]
◆◆   All Year   1P: $54   2P/1B: $54   2P/2B: $65   XP: $5
Motel   **Location:** Just n of I-105, exit Long Beach Blvd. Motel reached by driving through adjacent shopping center.
    11401 Long Beach Blvd 90262. Fax: 310/763-0548. **Facility:** 49 rooms. 7 whirlpool rms, extra charge; 2 sto-
ries; exterior corridors. **Cards:** AE, MC, VI.

MALIBU—11,700

LODGINGS

MALIBU BEACH INN   Guaranteed Rates   **Phone:** 310/456-6444
◆◆◆   5/29-10/31 [CP]   1P: $159- 229   2P/1B: $159- 229   2P/2B: $159- 229   XP: $15   F12
Motor Inn   11/1-1/31 [CP]   1P: $164- 219   2P/1B: $164- 219   2P/2B: $164- 219   XP: $15   F12
    Fri & Sat 2/1-5/28 [CP]   1P: $160- 209   2P/1B: $160- 209   2P/2B: $160- 209   XP: $15   F12
    Sun-Thurs 2/1-5/28 [CP]   1P: $149- 209   2P/1B: $149- 209   2P/2B: $149- 209   XP: $15   F12
Location: Adjacent to Malibu Pier. 22878 Pacific Coast Hwy 90265. Fax: 310/456-1499. **Terms:** Reserv deposit, 3 day
notice; 2 night min stay, weekends 5/1-10/31. **Facility:** 47 rooms. Balconies with ocean view, 42 fireplaces. 3 stories; exterior
corridors. **Services:** giftshop. **Recreation:** swimming, fishing. **Cards:** AE, CB, DI, JC, MC, VI. *(See color ad below)*

MALIBU COUNTRY INN   Phone: (310)457-9622

(AAA) SAVE   5/22-9/30 [CP]   1P: $165- 225   2P/1B: $165- 225   2P/2B: $165- 225   XP: $10   F12
             2/1-5/21 & 10/1-1/31 [CP] 1P: $125- 225   2P/1B: $125- 225   2P/2B: $125- 225   XP: $10   F12
◆ ◆   **Location:** 7 mi n, corner of Westward Beach Rd & SR 1 (Pacific Coast Hwy). 6506 Westward Beach Rd
Motor Inn   90265. Fax: 310/457-1349. **Terms:** Reserv deposit, 3 day notice; handling fee imposed; weekly rates.
             Facility: 15 rooms. Some rooms with fireplace. 1-2 stories; exterior corridors; heated pool, small heated pool.
Dining: Restaurant; 8 am-11 pm. **All Rooms:** combo or shower baths. **Cards:** AE, CB, DI, MC, VI. **Special Amenities:**
Free breakfast.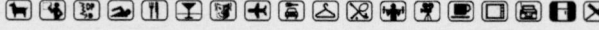

RESTAURANTS

BEAU RIVAGE   **Dinner:** $15-$35   Phone: 310/456-5733
◆ ◆   **Location:** 2 mi n of Malibu Canyon Rd. 26025 Pacific Coast Hwy 90265. **Hours:** 5 pm-11 pm, Sun 11 am-10
Ethnic   pm. Closed major holidays. **Reservations:** required. **Features:** casual dress; Sunday brunch; cocktails;
             entertainment; a la carte. Mediterranean cuisine with emphasis on French & Italian entrees. Smoke free
premises. **Cards:** AE, DI, DS, MC, VI.   ⊠

GEOFFREY'S/MALIBU   **Lunch:** $10-$20   **Dinner:** $14-$34   Phone: 310/457-1519
◆ ◆   **Location:** Hwy 1, 4 mi n of Pepperdine University. 27400 Pacific Coast Hwy 90265. **Hours:** noon-10 pm,
Continental Sat from 10:30 pm, Sun from 11 am. **Reservations:** suggested. **Features:** No A/C; casual dress; Sunday
             brunch; cocktails & lounge; fee for valet parking; a la carte. California/Continental menu with an Italian
influence. Pleasant patio setting overlooking the ocean.   ⊠

GRANITA   **Lunch:** $12-$18   **Dinner:** $40-$45   Phone: 310/456-0488
◆ ◆ ◆   **Location:** 5.5 mi n, in Malibu Colony Plaza. 23725 W Malibu Rd 90265. **Hours:** 6 pm-10:30 pm, Sat & Sun
Specialty   11 am-2 & 5:30-10:30 pm. Closed: 1/1, 11/25 & 12/25. **Reservations:** suggested. **Features:** casual dress;
             Sunday brunch; cocktails & lounge; a la carte. Featuring Mediterranean cuisine. Outdoor dining weather
permitting. Smoke free premises. **Cards:** DI, DS, MC, VI.   ⊠

MANHATTAN BEACH—32,100   (See map p. 558; index p. 554)

LODGINGS

BARNABEY'S HOTEL   Rates Subject to Change   Phone: 310/545-8466   [236]
◆ ◆ ◆   All Year   1P: $119- 129   2P/1B: $135- 144 2P/2B: $135- 144   XP: $15   F12
Hotel   **Location:** On SR 1, just s of Rosecrans Ave. 3501 N Sepulveda Blvd 90266. Fax: 310/545-8621.
             Facility: 123 rooms. Charming Old English atmosphere. 3 stories; interior corridors; heated pool.
Services: giftshop; area transportation. **Recreation:** Fee: bicycles. **Cards:** AE, CB, DI, DS, MC, VI. *(See color ad below)*

Welcome to the garden spot of Los Angeles.

Barnabey's Hotel, in Manhattan Beach, features gracious accommodations, superb service and fine dining. A little bit of Eden in Southern California, Barnabey's seems like Paradise.

For reservations call 310-545-8466 or 800-552-5285 or see your travel professional. For reservations at any Grand Heritage Hotel call 800-HERITAGE.

Barnabey's Hotel
Manhattan Beach, CA

(See map p. 558)

COMFORT INN
Phone: (310)318-1020 — 241
AAA SAVE All Year [CP] 1P: $85- 90 2P/1B: $85- 90 2P/2B: $85- 90 XP: $8 F12
◆◆◆ **Location:** On SR 1. 850 N Sepulveda Blvd 90266. Fax: 310/376-3545. **Terms:** Reserv deposit, 3 day notice.
Motel **Facility:** 45 rooms. 2-room units & spa room, $105-135. 8 whirlpool rms, extra charge; 2 stories; exterior corridors; heated pool, sauna, whirlpool. **Cards:** AE, CB, DI, DS, MC, VI. **Special Amenities:** Free breakfast and free newspaper. *(See color ad p 616)*

HOLIDAY INN EXPRESS
Phone: (310)318-6132 — 240
AAA SAVE All Year [CP] 1P: $99- 105 2P/1B: $105- 110 2P/2B: $110- 120 XP: $8 F12
◆◆◆ **Location:** On SR 1. 900 N Sepulveda Blvd 90266. Fax: 310/372-9134. **Terms:** Reserv deposit, 3 day notice.
Motel **Facility:** 44 rooms. 9 whirlpool rms, $139-$147; 2 suites with fireplace & whirlpool, $179-$187; 4 two-bedroom units, $145-$165; 3 stories; exterior corridors; heated pool, sauna, whirlpool. **Some Rooms:** whirlpools. **Cards:** AE, CB, DI, MC, VI. **Special Amenities:** Free breakfast and free local telephone calls.
(See color ad below)

MANHATTAN BEACH MARRIOTT
Rates Subject to Change Phone: 310/546-7511 — 238
AAA Sun-Thurs 1P: $150- 195 2P/1B: $150- 195 2P/2B: $150- 195 XP: $15 F16
Fri & Sat 1P: $89- 195 2P/1B: $89- 195 2P/2B: $89- 195 XP: $15 F16
◆◆◆ **Location:** 0.5 mi e of SR 1 via Rosecrans Ave. 1400 Parkview Ave 90266. Fax: 310/546-7520. **Facility:** 380 Hotel rooms. Spacious lobby, many rooms overlook golf course. 7 stories; interior corridors; heated pool, saunas, whirlpool. Fee: parking; 9 hole golf course. **Dining:** Dining room, restaurant; 6 am-10 pm; $7-$30; cocktails.
Services: giftshop; area transportation, to Manhattan Beach Pier. **Cards:** AE, CB, DI, DS, MC, VI.

RESIDENCE INN BY MARRIOTT
Rates Subject to Change Phone: 310/546-7627 — 239
◆◆◆ All Year [BP] 1P: $125- 198 2P/1B: $125- 198 2P/2B: $160- 250 XP: $10
Apartment **Location:** On SR 1, 1 mi s of Rosecrans Ave. 1700 N Sepulveda Blvd 90266. Fax: 310/545-1327.
Motel **Facility:** 176 rooms. 1-bedroom studios & split level, 2-bedroom units with living room & kitchen. Many fireplaces. 2 stories; exterior corridors; heated pool. **Services:** area transportation. **Recreation:** sports court.
Cards: AE, CB, DI, DS, MC, VI.

SEA VIEW INN AT THE BEACH
Rates Subject to Change Phone: 310/545-1504 — 235
AAA 5/1-9/30 1P: $90- 155 2P/1B: $90- 155 2P/2B: $90- 155
2/1-4/30 & 10/1-1/31 1P: $80- 130 2P/1B: $80- 130 2P/2B: $80- 130
◆◆ **Location:** Just s of Rosecrans Ave. 3400 Highland Ave 90266. Fax: 310/545-4052. **Terms:** Reserv deposit; Motel weekly rates. **Facility:** 13 rooms. Partial ocean view, located 2 blks from beach. Some smaller rooms. 2 stories; exterior corridors; heated pool. **Recreation:** bicycles. **All Rooms:** combo or shower baths. **Cards:** AE, MC, VI.

MARINA DEL REY—7,400 (See map p. 558; index p. 554)

LODGINGS

BEST WESTERN-JAMAICA BAY INN
Phone: (310)823-5333 — 198
AAA SAVE 6/1-9/15 1P: $109- 139 2P/1B: $109- 139 2P/2B: $109- 139 XP: $10 F12
2/1-5/31 & 9/16-1/31 1P: $99- 129 2P/1B: $99- 129 2P/2B: $99- 129 XP: $10 F12
◆◆◆ **Location:** 0.8 mi w of SR 1 (Lincoln Blvd). 4175 Admiralty Way 90292. Fax: 310/823-1325. **Facility:** 42 rooms.
Motor Inn At Marina del Rey Beach. Spacious rooms, some with marina view. 2 stories; interior corridors; heated pool, whirlpool. **Dining:** Restaurant, coffee shop; 6 am-8 pm; $6-$10; cocktails. Rental: bicycles. **Cards:** AE, CB, DI, DS, JC, MC, VI. *(See color ad p 618)*

COURTYARD BY MARRIOTT
Phone: (310)822-8555 — 199
AAA SAVE Sun-Thurs 1P: $125 2P/1B: $125 2P/2B: $125 XP: $10 F
Fri & Sat 1P: $116 2P/1B: $116 2P/2B: $116 XP: $10 F
◆◆◆ **Location:** Just e of SR 1 (Lincoln Blvd), just n of jct SR 90. 13480 Maxella Ave 90292. Fax: 310/823-2996.
Motor Inn **Terms:** Handling fee imposed; BP avail. **Facility:** 276 rooms. Next to shopping center. 6 suites at $169 includes microwave & refrigerator; 5 stories; interior corridors; heated pool, whirlpool. **Dining:** Dining room; 6:30 am-11 pm; $7-$12; cocktails. **Recreation:** in-line skate rentals. Fee: bicycles. **Cards:** AE, CB, DI, DS, MC, VI. **Special Amenities:** Early check-in/late check-out and preferred room (subject to availability with advanced reservations). *(See color ad p 618)*

(See map p. 558)

FOGHORN BEACHFRONT HOTEL
Rates Subject to Change
Phone: (310)823-4626 205

5/14-9/5 [CP] 1P: $119- 149 2P/1B: $119- 149 2P/2B: $119- 149 XP: $10 F14
3/2-5/13 & 9/6-11/30 [CP] 1P: $109- 139 2P/1B: $109- 139 2P/2B: $109- 139 XP: $10 F14
2/1-3/1 & 12/1-1/31 [CP] 1P: $99- 129 2P/1B: $99- 129 2P/2B: $99- 129 XP: $10 F14
Motel **Location:** Just s of Washington St. 4140 Via Marina 90292. Fax: 310/578-1964. **Terms:** Reserv deposit. **Facility:** 23 rooms. At Marina Del Rey Beach. Cozy rooms with patio. 2 stories; interior corridors. **Dining:** Restaurant nearby. **All Rooms:** combo or shower baths. **Cards:** AE, CB, DI, DS, MC, VI.

MARINA BEACH MARRIOTT HOTEL
Rates Subject to Change
Phone: (310)301-3000 197

All Year 1P: $169- 250 2P/1B: $169- 250 2P/2B: $169- 250 XP: $20 F12
Hotel **Location:** 0.8 mi w of SR 1 (Lincoln Blvd). 4100 Admiralty Way 90292. Fax: 310/448-4870. **Terms:** Reserv deposit. **Facility:** 371 rooms. Many rooms with view of marina or coastline. 10 stories; interior corridors; heated pool. Fee: parking. **Services:** giftshop. **All Rooms:** combo or shower baths. **Cards:** AE, CB, DI, DS, JC, MC, VI.

MARINA DEL REY HOTEL
Rates Subject to Change
Phone: 310/301-1000 200

All Year 1P: $160- 240 2P/1B: $180- 260 2P/2B: $180- 260 XP: $20-40 F12
Motor Inn **Location:** 0.5 mi w of SR 1 (Lincoln Blvd). 13534 Bali Way 90292. Fax: 310/301-8167. **Facility:** 159 rooms. Many rooms with marina view. 3 stories; interior corridors; heated pool. **Services:** giftshop; area transportation. **Cards:** AE, CB, DI, DS, MC, VI. *(See color ad p 619)*

MARINA INTERNATIONAL HOTEL
Rates Subject to Change
Phone: (310)301-2000 202

All Year 1P: $130- 180 2P/1B: $130- 180 2P/2B: $130- 180 XP: $15-25 F12
Motor Inn **Location:** 0.8 mi w of SR 1 (Lincoln Blvd). 4200 Admiralty Way 90292. Fax: 310/301-6687. **Terms:** Reserv deposit. **Facility:** 134 rooms. Large rooms. 25 individually decorated courtyard rooms. 3 stories; interior/exterior corridors; heated pool. **Services:** giftshop. **All Rooms:** combo or shower baths. **Cards:** AE, CB, DI, JC, MC, VI.

(See map p. 558)

THE RITZ-CARLTON, MARINA DEL REY		Rates Subject to Change		Phone: (310)823-1700		203
2/1-3/31	1P: $240	2P/1B: $240	2P/2B: $240	XP: $20		F18
4/1-6/15 & 9/8-1/31	1P: $219	2P/1B: $219	2P/2B: $219	XP: $20		F18
6/16-9/7	1P: $209	2P/1B: $209	2P/2B: $209	XP: $20		F18

Hotel **Location:** 4375 Admiralty Way 90292. Fax: 310/823-2403. **Facility:** 306 rooms. An elegant hotel overlooking the marina. 12 stories; interior corridors; charter yachts; heated pool, saunas, whirlpool; 12 tennis courts (2 lighted). **Dining:** Dining room, restaurant; 6:30 am-10:30 pm; $15-$40; also, The Dining Room, see separate listing. **Services:** giftshop. Fee: massage, area transportation. **Recreation:** basketball. Rental: bicycles. **Cards:** AE, CB, DI, DS, JC, MC, VI.

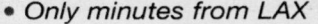

(See map p. 558)

RESTAURANTS

CAFE DEL REY   **Lunch:** $8-$14   **Dinner:** $12-$25   **Phone:** 310/823-6395   123
◆◆◆   **Location:** 4451 Admiralty Way 90292. **Hours:** 11:30 am-2:30 & 5:30-10:30 pm, Fri & Sat-10:30 pm, Sun
American   10:30 am-2:30 & 5-9:30 pm. **Closed:** 12/25. **Reservations:** suggested. **Features:** casual dress; Sunday
brunch; carryout; cocktails & lounge; valet parking; a la carte. Contemporary decor. Overlooks yacht harbor.
Imaginative selection of California & Pacific Rim cuisine. Extensive selection of California wines. Smoke free premises.
Cards: AE, CB, DI, DS, MC, VI.   ⊠

THE DINING ROOM   **Dinner:** $21-$40   **Phone:** 310/823-1700   122
◆◆◆◆   **Location:** In The Ritz-Carlton, Marina del Rey. 4375 Admiralty Way 90045. **Hours:** 6:30 pm-10 pm. **Closed:**
Continental   Sun & Mon. **Reservations:** suggested. **Features:** semi-formal attire; cocktails & lounge; valet parking; a la
carte. A beautiful, elegant dining room with marina view. Features Mediterranean cuisine. Smoke free
premises. **Cards:** AE, CB, DI, DS, JC, MC, VI.   ⊠

MISSION HILLS—32,000   (See map p. 560; index p. 551)

LODGING

BEST WESTERN MISSION HILLS INN   **Phone:** (818)891-1771   69
ⒶⒶⒶ ⓈⒶⓥⒺ   5/16-9/15 [CP]   1P: $64- 72   2P/1B: $68- 76   2P/2B: $72- 78   XP: $10   F12
    2/1-5/15 & 9/16-1/31 [CP]   1P: $61- 68   2P/1B: $64- 71   2P/2B: $68- 74   XP: $10   F12
◆◆   **Location:** Just s of SR 118, 0.3 mi e of I-405. 10621 Sepulveda Blvd 91345. **Fax:** 818/891-6921.
Motel   **Terms:** Weekly rates; pets, $50 dep req. **Facility:** 113 rooms. Patios or balconies. 2 stories; exterior corridors.
Dining: Coffee shop nearby. **Cards:** AE, CB, DI, DS, MC, VI. **Special Amenities:** Free breakfast and free
newspaper. *(See color ad p 585)*   🖧 📶 🎛 ⛱ 🛅 🅟 📟 🖥 📠 🛗 ⊠ 🅿

MONROVIA—35,800   (See map p. 562; index p. 547)

LODGINGS

COMFORT INN MONROVIA/DUARTE   Rates Subject to Change   **Phone:** (626)358-0430   10
◆◆   All Year [CP]   1P: $45- 50   2P/1B: $54- 59   2P/2B: $60- 70   XP: $5-9   F18
Motel   **Location:** 0.5 mi nw of I-210; exit Buena Vista. 1125 E Huntington Dr 91016. **Fax:** 626/359-9458. **Facility:** 39
rooms. 4 rooms with whirlpool $99-$159 for up to 2 persons; 2 stories; exterior corridors; small pool.
Cards: AE, DS, JC, MC, VI.   ⓈⒶⓥⒺ 🅢🄶 📶 🎛 🅟 🛗 📟 📠 🛗 ⊠

HOLIDAY INN   Rates Subject to Change   **Phone:** (626)357-1900   7
◆◆◆   All Year [CP]   1P: $89- 159   2P/1B: $89- 159   2P/2B: $89- 159
Motor Inn   **Location:** Adjacent to I-210, exit Huntington Dr. 924 W Huntington Dr 91016. **Fax:** 626/359-1386.
Facility: 174 rooms. 10 stories; interior corridors; heated pool. **Cards:** AE, CB, DI, DS, JC, MC, VI.
(See ad below)   🄰🅂🄺 🅢🄶 🕭 📶 🎛 🛅 🅟 🍽 🛅 🅟 📟 📠 🛗 ⊠

(See map p. 562)

HOMESTEAD VILLAGE ◆◆◆   Rates Subject to Change   **Phone: 626/256-6999**   **6**
All Year Wkly [CP]   1P: $308- 413   2P/1B: $329- 434
Extended Stay   **Location:** S side of I-210, exit Huntington Dr. 930 S Fifth Ave 91016. **Fax:** 626/256-6969. **Facility:** 122 rooms.
Motel   3 stories; interior corridors. **All Rooms:** efficiencies. **Cards:** AE, CB, DI, DS, MC, VI.

OAK TREE INN   Rates Subject to Change   **Phone: (626)358-8981**   **9**
(AAA)   All Year   1P: $47- 60   2P/1B: $49- 60   2P/2B: $49- 60   XP:$5-10
◆   **Location:** Adjacent to I-210, exit Huntington Dr. 788 W Huntington Dr 91016. **Fax:** 626/301-0657.
Motel   **Terms:** Weekly/monthly rates. **Facility:** 56 rooms. 3 stories; exterior corridors; whirlpool. **Cards:** AE, DI, DS, MC, VI. *(See ad p 620)*

WYNDHAM GARDEN HOTEL ◆◆◆   Rates Subject to Change   **Phone: 626/357-5211**   **8**
All Year   1P: $89   2P/1B: $99   2P/2B: $99   XP: $10-20   F18
Motor Inn   **Location:** Adjacent to I-210,exit Huntington Dr. 700 W Huntington Dr 91016. **Fax:** 626/357-2786.
  Facility: 150 rooms. 9 stories; interior corridors; heated pool. **Cards:** AE, CB, DI, DS, MC, VI.
(See color ad below)

RESTAURANTS

CLAIM JUMPER RESTAURANT ◆◆   **Lunch:** $8-$25   **Dinner:** $10-$25   **Phone:** 626/359-0463   **4**
American   **Location:** Adjacent to I-210, exit Huntington Dr. 820 W Huntington Dr 91016. **Hours:** 11 am-10 pm,
Tues-Thur to 11 pm, Fri & Sat-midnight. Closed: 7/4 & 12/25. **Features:** casual dress; carryout; salad bar;
cocktails. Generous portions of beef, chicken, ribs & sandwiches. Old west theme. Smoke free premises.
Cards: AE, DI, DS, MC, VI.

LA PARISIENNE ◆◆   **Lunch:** $9-$18   **Dinner:** $15-$23   **Phone:** 626/357-3359   **5**
French   **Location:** 0.6 mi nw of I-210, Buena Vista exit. 1101 E Huntington Dr 91016. **Hours:** 11 am-2 & 5-10 pm,
Sat 5 pm-10 pm. Closed: 1/1, 12/25 & Sun. **Reservations:** suggested. **Features:** cocktails & lounge. Cozy,
comfortable European decor. Smoke free premises. **Cards:** AE, DI, MC, VI.

RESTAURANT DEVON ◆◆◆   **Lunch:** $5-$12   **Dinner:** $11-$27   **Phone:** 626/305-0013   **6**
French   **Location:** Downtown, just e of Myrtle Ave. 109 E Lemon Ave 91016. **Hours:** 11:30 am-2 & 6-9 pm, Fri-10
pm, Sat 6 pm-10 pm, Sun 5 pm-8:30 pm. Closed major holidays & Mon. **Reservations:** suggested.
Features: cocktails; street parking; a la carte. A small store-front restaurant serving a nice variety of
California-French cuisine. Smoke free premises. **Cards:** AE, MC, VI.

MONTEBELLO—59,600

LODGING

HOWARD JOHNSON-MONTEBELLO/LOS ANGELES   Guaranteed Rates   **Phone:** (323)724-1400
◆◆◆   All Year   1P: $49   2P/1B: $49   2P/2B: $49   XP: $10   F18
Motor Inn   **Location:** Just ne of I-5, exit Slauson Ave. 7709 Telegraph Rd 90640. **Fax:** 323/721-4410. **Terms:** Reserv
deposit. **Facility:** 150 rooms. 5 stories; interior corridors; heated pool. **Services:** area transportation.
Cards: AE, CB, DI, DS, JC, MC, VI. *(See color ad opposite inside back cover)*

MONTEREY PARK—60,700

LODGING

BEST WESTERN MONTEREY PARK INN   **Phone:** (626)289-5090
(AAA) [SAVE]   All Year [CP]   1P: $54- 90   2P/1B: $54- 90   2P/2B: $64-120   XP: $5
◆   **Location:** Just s of I-10, exit Atlantic Blvd. 420 N Atlantic Blvd 91754. **Fax:** 626/281-6499. **Facility:** 55 rooms.
Motel   2 stories; exterior corridors; whirlpool. **Cards:** AE, MC, VI. **Special Amenities:** Free breakfast and
preferred room (subject to availability with advanced reservations).

RESTAURANT

HARBOR VILLAGE RESTAURANT **Lunch:** $5-$12 **Dinner:** $10-$18 **Phone:** 626/300-8833
◆◆ **Location:** On 3rd level of Atlantic Place Shopping Center. 111 N Atlantic Blvd 91754. **Hours:** 11 am-2:30 &
Chinese 5:30-10 pm, Sat & Sun from 10 am. **Reservations:** suggested. **Features:** casual dress; cocktails; a la carte.
Hong Kong style Cantonese restaurant. Well known for large selection of Dim Sum served during lunch.
Smoke free premises. **Cards:** AE, DI, DS, JC, MC, VI. ⊠

MONTROSE—4,100 (See map p. 562; index p. 554)

RESTAURANTS

DIVINA CUCINA **Lunch:** $7-$9 **Dinner:** $8-$13 **Phone:** 818/248-3077 [61]
◆◆ **Location:** Just n of Glendale; SR 2, exit Verdugo Blvd, then 0.5 mi w at corner of Verdugo Rd. 3730 N
Italian Verdugo Rd 91021. **Hours:** 11:30 am-3 & 5-10:30 pm; Sat & Sun 5 pm-10:30 pm. Closed: Easter & Labor
Day. **Features:** casual dress; children's menu; health conscious menu; carryout; beer & wine only. Excellent
selection of pasta, pizza & italian entrees. Outdoor dining available. Smoke free premises. **Cards:** AE, CB, DI, DS, MC, VI.
⊠

EL CHARRO MEXICAN RESTAURANT **Lunch:** $5 **Dinner:** $8-$14 **Phone:** 818/249-2405 [62]
◆ **Location:** SR 2, Verdugo Blvd exit; then 0.5 mi w corner of Honolulu Ave & Verdugo Rd. 3741 N Verdugo
Mexican Rd 91020. **Hours:** 11 am-9:30 pm. Closed major holidays& Sun. **Features:** No A/C; casual dress; Sunday
brunch; carryout; cocktails. Long established restaurant popular with locals. Good selection of traditional
Mexican dishes. Smoke free premises. **Cards:** MC, VI. ⊠

OCEANVIEW BAR & GRILL **Lunch:** $7-$10 **Dinner:** $9-$20 **Phone:** 818/248-2722 [63]
◆◆ **Location:** SR 210, Oceanview Blvd exit; then 0.4 mi s. 3826 Oceanview Blvd 91020. **Hours:** 11:30 am-2:30
American & 5-10 pm, Sat 5 pm-10 pm. Closed major holidays & Sun. **Reservations:** suggested. **Features:** casual
dress; children's menu; cocktails. Intimate grill serving good selection of appetizers, seafood, meat & pasta
dishes. Outdoor dining avail. Smoke free premises. **Cards:** AE, CB, DI, DS, MC, VI. ⊠

STAR CAFE **Lunch:** $6-$9 **Dinner:** $6-$16 **Phone:** 818/957-7827 [60]
◆◆ **Location:** Just s of SR210, exit Oceanview; just s, then just e on Honolulu Ave. 2217 Honolulu Ave 91020.
American **Hours:** 11 am-10:30 pm, Sat 10 am-11 pm, Sun 10 am-10 pm. Closed: 11/25 & 12/25.
Reservations: accepted; for 6 or more. **Features:** casual dress; Sunday brunch; children's menu; health
conscious menu; carryout; beer & wine only; a la carte. Nice selection of American & Italian entrees. Busy restaurant, lively
atmosphere. Outdoor patio dining avail, weather permitting. Smoke free premises. **Cards:** AE, DS, MC, VI. ⊠

NORTH HILLS (See map p. 560; index p. 551)

LODGING

HOWARD JOHNSON INN **Phone:** (818)892-0751 [85]
(AAA) [SAVE] 5/25-9/3 [CP] 1P: $44- 59 2P/1B: $49- 69 2P/2B: $49- 69 XP: $5
2/1-5/24 & 9/4-1/31 [CP] 1P: $39- 54 2P/1B: $44- 64 2P/2B: $44- 64 XP: $5
◆ **Location:** 0.8 mi ne of I-405, exit Nordhoff St. 9401 Sepulveda Blvd 91343. Fax: 818/893-3150.
Motel **Terms:** Reserv deposit; weekly/monthly rates. **Facility:** 62 rooms. 2 stories; interior/exterior corridors.
Dining: Coffee shop; 8 am-9 pm; Tues 8-11 am. **All Rooms:** combo or shower baths. **Some Rooms:** 12
efficiencies. **Cards:** AE, CB, DI, DS, MC, VI. **Special Amenities:** Early check-in/late check-out and preferred room
(subject to availability with advanced reservations). *(See color ad opposite inside back cover)*
🛇 🖾 🍴 🍷 🖵 ▢ 🗄 ⊠

NORTH HOLLYWOOD (See map p. 560; index p. 548)

LODGINGS

BEVERLY GARLAND'S HOLIDAY INN Guaranteed Rates **Phone:** (818)980-8000 [26]
(AAA) All Year 1P: $99- 134 2P/1B: $99- 134 XP: $15 F12
◆◆◆ **Location:** Adjacent to US 101. 4222 Vineland Ave 91602. Fax: 818/766-5230. **Facility:** 255 rooms. All rooms
Hotel with patio or balcony. 2 suites with microwave & refrigerator, $204-$295; 6-7 stories; interior corridors; heated
pool, wading pool, sauna; 2 lighted tennis courts. **Dining:** $8-$15; cocktails; also, Paradise Restaurant, see
separate listing. **Services:** giftshop; area transportation, to Universal Studios. **Cards:** AE, JC, MC, VI.
(See color ad p 623) 🛇 🖾 🍴 🍷 🖾 🗄 ⊠

(See map p. 560)

COLONY INN   Phone: (818)763-2787   25
△△△ SAVE   All Year [CP]   1P: $61- 69   2P/1B: $61- 69   2P/2B: $71- 79   XP: $10   F13
   Location: 1 mi n of US 101, exit Vineland Ave. 4917 Vineland Ave 91601. Fax: 818/763-0909.
◆ ◆   Terms: Reserv deposit, 3 day notice. Facility: 27 rooms. 4 suites, $125; 3 stories; exterior corridors.
Motel   Cards: AE, CB, DI, DS, JC, MC, VI. Special Amenities: Free breakfast and preferred room (subject to availability with advanced reservations). (See color ad p 622)

MIKADO BEST WESTERN MOTOR HOTEL   Phone: (818)763-9141   27
△△△ SAVE   All Year [BP]   1P: $99- 109   2P/1B: $99- 109   2P/2B: $99- 109   XP: $10   F12
   Location: Adjacent to US 101, between Coldwater Canyon & Laurel Canyon Ave exits. 12600 Riverside Dr
◆ ◆   91607. Fax: 818/752-1045. Facility: 58 rooms. Landscaped courtyard with blue tile pool. 1 bedroom apart-
Motor Inn   ment, $100-$150; 2 stories; exterior corridors; whirlpool. Dining: Restaurant, see separate listing.
   Cards: AE, CB, DI, DS, JC, MC, VI. Special Amenities: Free breakfast and free room upgrade (subject
to availability with advanced reservations).

RESTAURANTS

MIKADO RESTAURANT   Lunch: $9-$12   Dinner: $16-$20   Phone: 818/763-1963   19
△△△   Location: At Mikado Best Western Motor Hotel. 12600 Riverside Dr 91607. Hours: 11:30 am-2 & 5:30-10
   pm, Sat from 5:30 pm, Sun 5 pm-9:30 pm. Closed: 11/25 & lunch major holidays. Features: casual dress;
◆ ◆   cocktails & lounge; a la carte. Features Japanese food & sushi bar. Casual atmosphere. Smoke free
Ethnic   premises. Cards: AE, CB, DI, DS, JC, MC, VI.

PARADISE RESTAURANT   Lunch: $7-$10   Dinner: $8-$16   Phone: 818/985-6567   20
◆   Location: Adjacent to US 101; in Beverly Garland's Holiday Inn. 4222 Vineland Ave 91602. Hours: 6 am-11
American   pm. Features: casual dress; carryout; cocktails & lounge. Nice selection of sandwiches, pastas, meat &
   seafood entrees. Cards: AE, CB, DI, DS, MC, VI.

NORWALK—94,300

LODGINGS

BEST WESTERN NORWALK INN   Phone: (562)929-8831
△△△ SAVE   All Year [CP]   1P: $40- 49   2P/1B: $45- 55   2P/2B: $45- 65   XP: $5-10   F18
   Location: Just e of I-605. 10902 Firestone Blvd 90650. Fax: 562/929-4027. Terms: Weekly rates.
◆ ◆   Facility: 88 rooms. Coffeemaker avail upon request. 3 stories; interior/exterior corridors; sauna, whirlpool.
Motel   Cards: AE, CB, DI, DS, JC, MC, VI. Special Amenities: Free breakfast and free newspaper.

COMFORT INN-NORWALK   Phone: (562)868-3453
△△△ SAVE   All Year [CP]   1P: $49- 69   2P/1B: $49- 69   2P/2B: $59- 79   XP: $5   F15
   Location: Adjacent to I-5, southbound exit Pioneer; northbound exit Imperial Ave, then w. 12512 Pioneer
◆ ◆   Blvd 90650. Fax: 562/868-5385. Facility: 79 rooms. 3 stories; exterior corridors; whirlpool. Cards: AE, CB,
Motel   DI, DS, JC, MC, VI. Special Amenities: Free breakfast and free newspaper.

NORWALK MARRIOTT HOTEL   Phone: (562)863-5555
△△△ SAVE   All Year   1P: $99   2P/1B: $99   2P/2B: $99   XP: $15   F18
   Location: Adjacent to I-5, exit Norwalk Blvd. 13111 Sycamore Dr 90650. Fax: 562/868-4486.
◆ ◆ ◆   Terms: Weekly/monthly rates. Facility: 173 rooms. Attractive, modern hotel located next to a 20 screen movie
Hotel   theatre. Large rooms. 26 mini-suites avail; 8 stories; interior corridors; heated pool, whirlpool.
   Dining: Restaurant; 6 am-10:30 pm, Sat & Sun from 7 am; $9-$25; cocktails. Services: giftshop; area
transportation, Disneyland. Cards: AE, CB, DI, DS, JC, MC, VI.

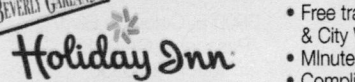

PALOS VERDES ESTATES—13,500   (See map p. 561; index p. 554)

RESTAURANT

LA RIVE GAUCHE   **Lunch:** $7-$13   **Dinner:** $16-$27   **Phone:** 310/378-0267   65
◆◆◆   **Location:** 1 blk w of Malaga Cove Plaza. 320 Tejon Pl 90274. **Hours:** 5:30 pm-10 pm, also Tues-Sat 11:30
French   am-3 pm, Sun brunch 10 am-3 pm. **Reservations:** suggested. **Features:** semi-formal attire; Sunday brunch;
cocktails; entertainment. French provincial decor. Features fresh fish, rack of lamb & duck. Summer garden
patio. Smoke free premises. **Cards:** AE, CB, DI, DS, MC, VI.   ☒

PASADENA—131,600   (See map p. 562; index p. 547)

LODGINGS

BEST WESTERN COLORADO INN   **Phone:** (626)793-9339   15
(AAA) SAVE   All Year [CP]   1P: $54   2P/1B: $62   2P/2B: $70   XP: $8   F12
◆◆   **Location:** 0.8 mi sw of I-210, exit Sierra Madre Blvd. 2156 E Colorado Blvd 91107. Fax: 626/568-2731.
Motel   **Terms:** Reserv deposit; weekly/monthly rates. **Facility:** 77 rooms. 3 stories; exterior corridors; small heated
pool, whirlpool. **Cards:** AE, CB, DI, DS, JC, MC, VI. **Special Amenities:** Free breakfast and free local
telephone calls.   ⬛⬛⬛⬛⬛⬛⬛☒

BEST WESTERN PASADENA INN   **Phone:** (626)796-9100   23
(AAA) SAVE   All Year [CP]   1P: $53- 70   2P/1B: $62- 80   2P/2B: $67- 85   XP: $8-15   F12
◆◆   **Location:** I-210, exit Rosemead Blvd S; just w of Rosemead Blvd. 3570 E Colorado Blvd 91107.
Motel   Fax: 626/405-9948. **Terms:** Reserv deposit, 30 day notice; weekly rates. **Facility:** 63 rooms. 2 stories; exterior
corridors; sauna, whirlpool. **Cards:** AE, CB, DI, DS, JC, MC, VI. **Special Amenities:** Free breakfast and
free local telephone calls. *(See ad below)*   ⬛⬛⬛⬛⬛⬛

BEST WESTERN PASADENA ROYALE   **Phone:** (626)793-0950   22
(AAA) SAVE   All Year [CP]   1P: $56- 87   2P/1B: $65- 96   2P/2B: $70- 96   XP: $8-15   F12
◆◆◆   **Location:** I-210, exit Rosemead Blvd S; just w of Rosemead Blvd. 3600 E Colorado Blvd 91107.
Motel   Fax: 626/568-2827. **Terms:** Reserv deposit, 30 day notice; weekly rates, 21 one-bedroom suites. **Facility:** 63
rooms. 3 stories; exterior corridors; sauna, whirlpool. **Cards:** AE, CB, DI, DS, JC, MC, VI.
Special Amenities: Free breakfast and free local telephone calls. *(See ad below)*   ⬛⬛⬛⬛⬛⬛

COMFORT INN   **Phone:** (626)405-0811   14
(AAA) SAVE   All Year   1P: $64- 80   2P/1B: $67- 80   2P/2B: $67- 80   XP: $6   F17
◆◆◆   **Location:** 0.5 mi se of I-210; exit Sierra Madre Blvd. 2462 E Colorado Blvd 91107. Fax: 626/796-0966.
Motel   **Terms:** Reserv deposit. **Facility:** 53 rooms. 3 stories; exterior corridors; small pool, sauna, whirlpool.
Cards: AE, CB, DI, DS, JC, MC, VI. **Special Amenities:** Free local telephone calls and free newspaper.
⬛⬛⬛⬛⬛⬛⬛⬛☒

DOUBLETREE HOTEL-PASADENA   **Phone:** (626)792-2727   20
(AAA) SAVE   Mon-Thurs   1P: $165- 319   2P/1B: $165- 319   2P/2B: $165- 319   XP: $15
Fri-Sun   1P: $109- 219   2P/1B: $109- 219   2P/2B: $109- 219   XP: $15
◆◆◆◆   **Location:** Just n of Colorado Blvd. 191 N Los Robles Ave at Walnut 91101. Fax: 626/795-7669.
Hotel   **Terms:** Reserv deposit. **Facility:** 350 rooms. Spacious lobby & picturesque plaza area. 12 stories; interior cor-
ridors; heated pool, saunas, whirlpool. Fee: parking. **Dining:** Dining room; 6 am-11 pm; $10-$20; cocktails.
Services: giftshop; area transportation, within Pasadena area. **All Rooms:** extended cable TV. **Cards:** AE, CB, DI, DS, JC,
MC, VI.   ⬛⬛⬛⬛⬛⬛⬛⬛⬛⬛⬛⬛⬛⬛☒

HOLIDAY INN-CONVENTION CENTER   Rates Subject to Change   **Phone:** 626/449-4000   19
◆◆◆   All Year   1P: $129- 139   2P/1B: $129- 139   2P/2B: $144- 154   XP: $15   F19
Motor Inn   **Location:** Just s of Colorado Blvd via Marengo Ave. 303 E Cordova St 91101. Fax: 626/584-1390.
Terms: Check-in 4 pm. **Facility:** 320 rooms. 5 stories; interior corridors; heated pool; 2 lighted tennis courts.
Fee: parking. **Services:** giftshop. **Cards:** AE, CB, DI, DS, MC, VI.   ⬛⬛⬛⬛⬛⬛⬛⬛⬛⬛☒

PASADENA HILTON   Rates Subject to Change   **Phone:** 626/577-1000   18
◆◆◆   All Year   1P: $109   2P/1B: $109   2P/2B: $109   XP: $15
Hotel   **Location:** Just s of Colorado Blvd. 150 S Los Robles Ave 91101. Fax: 626/584-3148. **Facility:** 291 rooms. 13
stories; interior corridors; heated pool. Fee: parking. **Services:** giftshop; area transportation. **Cards:** AE, CB,
DI, DS, JC, MC, VI. *(See ad p 119)*   ⬛⬛⬛⬛⬛⬛⬛⬛⬛⬛☒

(See map p. 562)

QUALITY INN PASADENA
Phone: (626)796-9291 **24**
All Year [CP] 1P: $59- 65 2P/1B: $62- 68 2P/2B: $69- 75 XP: $6
Location: Just SW of I-210, exit Madre St. 3321 E Colorado Blvd 91107. Fax: 626/796-9780. **Facility:** 70 rooms. 2 suites with whirlpool tub, $120; 3 stories; exterior corridors; small pool, sauna, whirlpool. **Dining:** Restaurant nearby. **Cards:** AE, CB, DI, DS, MC, VI. **Special Amenities:** Free breakfast and free local telephone calls.

THE RITZ CARLTON, HUNTINGTON HOTEL Rates Subject to Change Phone: 626/568-3900 **17**
All Year 1P: $215- 325 2P/1B: $215- 325 2P/2B: $215- 325 XP: $25 F18
Location: 2 mi s of I-210 via Lake Ave & Oak Knoll Ave. 1401 S Oak Knoll Ave 91106. Fax: 626/568-3700. **Terms:** Reserv deposit; handling fee imposed. **Facility:** 387 rooms. An elegant hotel in a quiet residential area. Main building, garden units & cottages on 23 acres of nicely landscaped grounds. 1-8 stories; interior/exterior corridors; heated pool. Fee: parking; 3 lighted tennis courts. **Services:** giftshop. Fee: massage. **Recreation:** Fee: bicycles. **Cards:** AE, CB, DI, DS, JC, MC, VI.

SAGA MOTOR HOTEL
Phone: (626)795-0431 **16**
All Year [CP] 1P: $63- 69 2P/1B: $66- 74 2P/2B: $69- 74 XP: $5 F16
Location: 0.8 mi s of I-210; westbound Allen Ave exit, eastbound Hill Ave exit, across from Pasadena City College. 1633 E Colorado Blvd 91106. Fax: 626/792-0559. **Facility:** 70 rooms. 3 stories; interior/exterior corridors; heated pool. **Dining:** Restaurant nearby. **Cards:** AE, CB, DI, DS, MC, VI. **Special Amenities:** Free breakfast and free newspaper. *(See color ad below)*

SUPER 8
Rates Subject to Change Phone: 626/449-3020 **25**
7/1-8/31 1P: $40 2P/1B: $48 2P/2B: $56 XP: $5
2/1-6/30 & 9/1-1/31 1P: $36 2P/1B: $40 2P/2B: $50 XP: $5
Location: SR 210, San Gabriel Blvd exit, 0.4 mi s, then 0.2 mi e. 2863 E Colorado Blvd 91107. Fax: 626/578-9791. **Terms:** Pets, $5 extra charge. **Facility:** 71 rooms. 3 stories; exterior corridors. **Dining:** Restaurant nearby. **Cards:** AE, DS, MC, VI.

TRAVELODGE-PASADENA CENTRAL
Phone: (626)796-3121 **27**
5/2-9/1 [CP] 1P: $45- 50 2P/1B: $50- 55 2P/2B: $60- 65 XP:$5-10 F16
2/1-5/1 & 9/2-1/31 [CP] 1P: $39- 45 2P/1B: $45- 50 2P/2B: $55- 60 XP:$5-10 F16
Location: Just w of Sierra Madre Blvd. 2131 E Colorado Blvd 91107. Fax: 626/793-4713. **Terms:** Reserv deposit. **Facility:** 53 rooms. 3 stories; exterior corridors; whirlpool. **Cards:** AE, DI, DS, MC, VI. **Special Amenities:** Free breakfast and free newspaper.

VAGABOND INN
Phone: (626)449-3170 **29**
All Year [CP] 1P: $61 2P/1B: $66 2P/2B: $73 XP: $5 F18
Location: 0.3 mi s of I-210, exit Hill St. 1203 E Colorado Blvd 91106. Fax: 626/577-8873. **Terms:** Pets, $5 extra charge. **Facility:** 54 rooms. 3 stories; interior/exterior corridors; heated pool. **Some Rooms:** 3 kitchens. **Cards:** AE, CB, DI, DS, MC, VI. **Special Amenities:** Free local telephone calls.

WESTWAY INN
Phone: (626)304-9678 **21**
All Year 1P: $55- 62 2P/1B: $61- 68 2P/2B: $65- 72 XP: $5 F12
Location: 0.8 mi s of I-210, westbound Allen Ave exit, eastbound Hill Ave exit, across from Pasadena City College. 1599 E Colorado Blvd 91106. Fax: 626/449-3493. **Terms:** Reserv deposit; pets, $5 extra charge. **Facility:** 61 rooms. 23 one bedroom suites, $55-$62. 4 whirlpool rms, extra charge; 4 stories; exterior corridors; small pool, sauna, whirlpool. **Cards:** AE, CB, DI, DS, MC, VI. **Special Amenities:** Free breakfast and free newspaper.

RESTAURANTS

ARROYO CHOP HOUSE Dinner: $30-$60 Phone: 626/577-7463 **17**
Location: 536 S Arroyo Pkwy 91105. **Hours:** 5 pm-10 pm. Closed: 7/4, 11/25 & 12/25. **Reservations:** suggested. **Features:** semi-formal attire; cocktails; valet parking; a la carte. Excellent selection of steak, chops & prime rib. Smoke free premises. **Cards:** AE, DI, MC, VI.
Steakhouse

BISTRO 45 Lunch: $8-$15 Dinner: $20-$30 Phone: 626/795-2478 **11**
Location: Just s of Colorado Blvd. 45 S Mentor Ave 91106. **Hours:** 11:30 am-2:30 & 6-10 pm, Fri & Sat 5:30-11 pm, Sun 5-9 pm. Closed major holidays1/1, 11/25, 12/25 & Mon. **Reservations:** suggested. **Features:** semi-formal attire; cocktails & lounge; fee for valet parking; a la carte. Seasonal selection of French & California cuisine. Smoke free premises. **Cards:** AE, CB, DI, MC, VI.
French

(See map p. 562)

THE GRILL　　　**Dinner:** $24-$50　　　**Phone:** 626/568-3900　⑭
◆◆◆　**Location:** 2 mi s of I-210, via Lake Ave & Oak Knoll Ave; in The Ritz Carlton, Huntington Hotel. 1401 S Oak
Continental　Knoll Ave 91106. **Hours:** 6 pm-9 pm. **Reservations:** accepted. **Features:** semi-formal attire; health
conscious menu; cocktails & lounge; fee for valet parking; a la carte. Dining in an elegant club atmosphere.
Menu features a nice variety of steak, seafood & specialties, including rack of lamb, chateaubriand, roasted venison. Smoke
free premises. **Cards:** AE, CB, DI, DS, JC, MC, VI.
🗙

KATHLEEN'S　　　**Lunch:** $5-$10　　　**Dinner:** $12-$18　　　**Phone:** 626/578-0722　⑯
◆◆　**Location:** SR 210, Lake Ave exit; then 0.3 mi n. 595 N Lake Ave 91101. **Hours:** 11 am-9 pm, Sat 8 am-9
American　pm, Sun 8 am-2 pm. Closed major holidays& Mon. **Features:** No A/C; casual dress; children's menu; health
conscious menu; carryout; beer & wine only. Popular long established family restaurant. A favorite with the
locals. Separate full dinner menu features good selection of California cuisine. Smoke free premises. **Cards:** AE, DS, MC,
VI.
🗙

MCCORMICK & SCHMICKS　　**Lunch:** $8-$20　　**Dinner:** $7-$22　　**Phone:** 626/405-0064　⑩
◆◆　**Location:** Just n of Colorado Blvd. 111 N Los Robles 91101. **Hours:** 11:30 am-11 pm, Sun 10:30 am-10 pm.
Seafood　**Reservations:** suggested. **Features:** casual dress; Sunday brunch; early bird specials; carryout; cocktails;
fee for parking; a la carte. A comfortable club-like atmosphere. Features a large selection of fresh seafood.
Also a limited selection of pasta, meat & poultry. **Cards:** AE, DI, DS, MC, VI.
🗙

MI PIACE　　　**Lunch:** $7-$13　　　**Dinner:** $7-$13　　　**Phone:** 626/795-3131　⑮
◆◆　**Location:** In Old Town area. 25 E Colorado Blvd 91105. **Hours:** 11:30 am-11:30 pm; Fri & Sat-1 am. Closed:
Italian　11/25 & 12/25. **Reservations:** suggested. **Features:** casual dress; cocktails; fee for valet parking; a la carte.
A popular, contemporary restaurant serving a wide selection of Italian cuisine. Desserts made on premises.
Smoke free premises. **Cards:** AE, CB, DI, MC, VI.
🗙

PARKWAY GRILL　　**Lunch:** $8-$16　　　**Dinner:** $12-$24　　　**Phone:** 626/795-1001　⑧
◆◆◆　**Location:** 510 S Arroyo Pkwy 91105. **Hours:** 11:30 am-2:30 & 5:30-10 pm, Fri-midnight, Sat 5 pm-11 pm,
American　Sun 11 am-2:30 & 5-10 pm. Closed: 11/25 & 12/25. **Reservations:** suggested. **Features:** casual dress;
Sunday brunch; cocktails & lounge; valet parking; a la carte. Popular restaurant serving an interesting
selection of creative dishes artfully presented. Organic garden tours avail. Smoke free premises. **Cards:** AE, CB, DI, MC, VI.
🗙

PATAKAN　　　**Lunch:** $7-$8　　　**Dinner:** $8-$12　　　**Phone:** 626/449-4418　⑦
◆　**Location:** In Old Town area between Raymond & Fair Oaks Ave, just n of Colorado Blvd. 43 E Union St
Ethnic　91103. **Hours:** 11:30 am-3 & 5-10 pm, Fri & Sat-10:30 pm. Closed major holidays& Sun.
Reservations: suggested. **Features:** casual dress; carryout; beer & wine only; street parking; a la carte.
Thai & Southeast Asian cuisine. Smoke free premises. **Cards:** AE, CB, DI, DS, MC, VI.
🗙

THE RAYMOND RESTAURANT　　**Lunch:** $9-$18　　**Dinner:** $26-$45　　**Phone:** 626/441-3136　⑫
◆◆◆　**Location:** SR 210 exit Fairoaks Ave, 3 mi s at Columbia St. 1250 S Fairoaks Ave 91105. **Hours:** 11:30
Continental　am-2:30 & 6-10 pm; Fri 11:30am-2:30 & 5:45-10 pm; Sat 11 am-2:30 & 5:45-10 pm; Sun 10 am-2:30 &
4:30-8 pm. Closed: 1/1, 12/25 & Mon. **Reservations:** suggested. **Features:** semi-formal attire; Sunday
brunch; cocktails; a la carte, also prix fixe. Beautifully restored & decorated 1901 craftsman cottage. Delightful, varied menu
changes frequently & offers excellen selection of continental & american dishes. Smoke free premises. **Cards:** AE, DI, DS,
MC, VI.
🗙

SALADANG　　　**Lunch:** $7-$13　　　**Dinner:** $9-$15　　　**Phone:** 626/793-8123　⑨
◆◆　**Location:** just s of Del Mar Ave. 363 S Fair Oaks 91105. **Hours:** 10 am-10 pm. Closed major holidays.
Ethnic　**Features:** casual dress; carryout; beer & wine only; a la carte. Thai cuisine with an extensive selection of
creative dishes. Smoke free premises. **Cards:** AE, CB, DI, MC, VI.
🗙

SPENCERS　　　**Lunch:** $7-$13　　　**Dinner:** $10-$24　　　**Phone:** 626/583-8275　⑲
◆◆◆　**Location:** In Old Town, Raymond at Green St. 70 S Raymond Ave 91106. **Hours:** 11:30 am-2:30 & 5-10 pm,
American　Fri-midnight　&　Sat 5 pm-midnight. Closed: 12/24, 1/1 & Sun. **Reservations:** suggested.
Features: semi-formal attire; children's menu; carryout; cocktails; fee for valet parking; a la carte. Attractive
contemporary dining room & garden patio. Continental & California cuisine. Smoke free premises. **Cards:** AE, CB, DI, DS,
MC, VI.
🗙

YUJEAN KANG'S　　**Lunch:** $7-$9　　　**Dinner:** $9-$18　　　**Phone:** 626/585-0855　⑬
◆◆　**Location:** In Old Town area, just n of Colorado Blvd. 67 N Raymond Ave 91103. **Hours:** 11:30 am-2:30 &
Chinese　5-9:30 pm; Fri & Sat-10 pm. Closed: lunch 11/25 & 12/25. **Reservations:** suggested. **Features:** beer & wine
only; street parking & fee for valet parking; a la carte. Creative and fascinating California-influenced Chinese
dishes. Desserts creatively presented. Smoke free premises. **Cards:** AE, CB, DI, DS, MC, VI.
🗙

PICO RIVERA—59,200

LODGING

PICO RIVERA TRAVELODGE　　　　　　　　　　　**Phone:** (562)949-6648
🆎 SAVE　All Year [CP]　　　1P: $42- 45　2P/1B: $48- 52　2P/2B: $55　XP: $5　F16
Location: On SR 19; 1.6 mi n of I-5. 7222 Rosemead Blvd 90660. Fax: 562/942-7807. **Terms:** Small pets
◆◆　only. **Facility:** 47 rooms. 2 stories; exterior corridors. **Some Rooms:** whirlpools. **Cards:** AE, CB, DI, DS, MC,
Motel　VI. **Special Amenities:** Early check-in/late check-out and free breakfast.
🔊 🛏 🛋 📺 🐾 🖨 🔒 🗙

PLAYA DEL REY   (See map p. 558; index p. 554)

LODGING

INN AT PLAYA DEL REY　　　Rates Subject to Change　　　**Phone:** (310)574-1920　230
◆◆◆　All Year [BP]　　　1P: $125- 275　1P/2P: $125- 275　2P/2B: $125- 275　XP: $15　F21
Bed &　**Location:** 1 mi w of SR 1, via Culver Blvd or Jefferson. 435 Culver Blvd 90293. Fax: 310/574-9920.
Breakfast　**Terms:** Reserv deposit. **Facility:** 22 rooms. Spacious, beautifully decorated rooms, many looking towards Ma-
rina Del Rey & the Ballona Wetlands Bird Sanctuary. 3 stories; interior corridors; designated smoking area.
Recreation: bicycles. **Cards:** AE, MC, VI.
📺 🗙 📼 🖨 🔒 🗙

POMONA—131,700

LODGINGS

SHERATON SUITES FAIRPLEX
Phone: (909)622-2220
(AAA) [SAVE]
All Year   1P: $165   2P/1B: $165   2P/2B: $165   XP: $10   F17
♦♦♦ **Location:** N of I-10; eastbound exit White Ave, westbound exit Fairplex Dr. 601 W McKinley Ave 91768.
Suite Hotel   **Fax:** 909/622-3577. **Terms:** Reserv deposit; pets, $10 extra charge, $75 dep req. **Facility:** 247 rooms. At Los Angeles County Fairgrounds. One bedroom suites. 8 stories; interior corridors; heated pool, sauna, whirlpool. **Dining:** Restaurant; 6 am-10 pm; $10-$15; cocktails. **Cards:** AE, CB, DI, DS, JC, MC, VI.
Special Amenities: Free newspaper. *(See color ad p 129)*

[icon row]

SHILO HILLTOP SUITES-POMONA
Rates Subject to Change
Phone: (909)598-7666
♦♦♦ All Year [BP]   1P: $95- 175   2P/1B: $95- 175   2P/2B: $95- 175   XP: $12   F12
Motor Inn   **Location:** Adjacent to SR 57, Temple Ave exit. 3101 Temple Ave 91768. Fax: 909/598-5654.
Terms: Check-in 4 pm. **Facility:** 129 rooms. Hilltop location. Large, contemporary rooms. 3 stories; interior corridors; heated pool. **Cards:** AE, CB, DI, DS, JC, MC, VI. *(See ad below, p 1091, p 658 & below)*

[icon row]

SHILO HOTEL-POMONA
Rates Subject to Change
Phone: (909)598-0073
♦♦♦ All Year [BP]   1P: $69- 155   2P/1B: $69- 155   2P/2B: $69- 155   XP: $12   F12
Motor Inn   **Location:** Adjacent to SR 57, Temple Ave exit. 3200 Temple Ave 91768. Fax: 909/594-5862. **Facility:** 160 rooms. 4 stories; interior corridors; heated pool. **Cards:** AE, CB, DI, DS, JC, MC, VI.
(See ad below, p 1091 & p 658)

[icon row]

RESTAURANT

RILLO'S RESTAURANT
Lunch: $8-$13   Dinner: $10-$20
Phone: 909-621-4954
♦♦ **Location:** 0.3 mi w of Towne Ave. 510 E Foothill Blvd 91767. **Hours:** 11:30 am-2:30 & 4:30-10 pm, Sat &
Italian   Sun from 4:30 pm. Closed major holidays 7/1-7/15. **Features:** early bird specials; cocktails & lounge. Large selection of pasta, veal, chicken & seafood. Smoke free premises. **Cards:** AE, MC, VI.

AAA Plus® provides you extended services, such as up to 100 miles of free towing.

RANCHO PALOS VERDES—41,700   (See map p. 561; index p. 554)

RESTAURANT

ADMIRAL RISTY RESTAURANT   **Dinner:** $17-$30   **Phone:** 310/377-0050   70
(AAA)   **Location:** Just s of Hawthorne Blvd. 31250 Palos Verdes Dr W 90274. **Hours:** 5 pm-10 pm, Fri & Sat-11
pm, Sun 10 am-3 & 5-10 pm. Closed: 11/25 & 12/25. **Reservations:** suggested; Fri & Sat. **Features:** casual
◆ ◆   dress; Sunday brunch; children's menu; cocktails & lounge; entertainment. Seafood, steak, chicken, salad &
Seafood   pasta. 4 styles of seafood preparation. Ocean view. Smoke free premises. **Cards:** AE, CB, DI, DS, MC, VI.

REDONDO BEACH—60,200   (See map p. 561; index p. 548)

LODGINGS

BEST WESTERN GALLERIA INN   **Phone:** (310)370-4353   15
(AAA) [SAVE]   All Year [CP]   1P: $54- 74 2P/1B: $64- 84 2P/2B: $64- 84 XP: $6   F12
◆ ◆ ◆   **Location:** 1 mi w of I-405. 2740 Artesia Blvd 90278. **Fax:** 310/793-7135. **Terms:** Reserv deposit, 3 day
Motel   notice. **Facility:** 51 rooms. 6 whirlpool rms, extra charge; 3 stories; exterior corridors; sauna, whirlpool.
Cards: AE, CB, DI, DS, MC, VI. **Special Amenities: Free breakfast.** *(See color ad p 571 & below)*

BEST WESTERN REDONDO BEACH INN   **Phone:** (310)540-3700   24
(AAA) [SAVE]   6/1-8/31   1P: $79- 94 2P/1B: $79- 94 2P/2B: $79- 94 XP: $5   F18
  2/1-5/31 & 9/1-1/31 1P: $74- 89 2P/1B: $74- 89 2P/2B: $74- 89 XP: $5   F18
◆ ◆ ◆   **Location:** 1.8 mi se on SR 1. 1850 S Pacific Coast Hwy 90277. **Fax:** 310/540-3675. **Terms:** Weekly/monthly
Motor Inn   rates. **Facility:** 108 rooms. Some rooms with patio. 1 suite with whirlpool, $160; 3 stories; interior/exterior cor-
ridors; heated pool, sauna, indoor whirlpool. **Dining:** Coffee shop; 6 am-1 pm. **Recreation:** bicycles.
Cards: AE, CB, DI, DS, JC, MC, VI. *(See ad below)*

(See map p. 561)

BEST WESTERN SUNRISE AT REDONDO BEACH Phone: (310)376-0746 **18**
SAVE 6/1-9/15 1P: $109- 119 2P/1B: $109- 119 2P/2B: $109- 119 XP: $10 F16
2/1-5/31 & 9/16-1/31 1P: $99- 109 2P/1B: $99- 109 2P/2B: $99- 109 XP: $10 F16
Motor Inn **Location:** 0.5 mi w of SR 1 (Pacific Coast Hwy). 400 N Harbor Dr 90277. Fax: 310/376-7384. **Facility:** 111 rooms. Some rooms with ocean view. 3 stories; interior corridors; heated pool, whirlpool. **Dining:** Dining room, restaurant; 6 am-10 pm, Sat & Sun from 7 am; $7-$14; cocktails. **Recreation:** Fee: bicycles.
Cards: AE, CB, DI, DS, JC, MC, VI. *(See color ad below)* [icons]

CROWNE PLAZA REDONDO BEACH & MARINA HOTEL Rates Subject to Change Phone: (310)318-8888 **16**
All Year 1P: $119 2P/1B: $119 2P/2B: $119 XP: $10-25 F19
Hotel **Location:** 0.5 mi w of SR 1 (Pacific Coast Hwy) at King Harbor. 300 N Harbor Dr 90277. Fax: 310/376-1930. **Terms:** Reserv deposit. **Facility:** 340 rooms. Many rooms with harbor view & balcony. Nearby gym/athletic club free to guests. 5 stories; interior corridors; heated pool, saunas, whirlpool; 1 lighted tennis court. Fee: parking. **Dining:** Cafeteria; 6:30 am-10:30 & 11:30-2:30 pm; $13-$24; cocktails; also, Splash, see separate listing. **Services:** giftshop; area transportation, shuttle to shopping mall. Fee: massage. **Recreation:** deli, salon & cigar room. Rental: bicycles. **Cards:** AE, CB, DI, DS, JC, MC, VI. [icons]

PALOS VERDES INN Phone: (310)316-4211 **22**
SAVE All Year 1P: $110- 120 2P/1B: $120- 140 2P/2B: $120- 140 XP: $10-20 F12
Motor Inn **Location:** 1.5 mi se on SR 1. 1700 S Pacific Coast Hwy 90277. Fax: 310/316-4863. **Terms:** Reserv deposit. **Facility:** 110 rooms. Many rooms with balcony. 4 stories; interior corridors; heated pool, whirlpool. **Dining:** Dining room, restaurant; 7 am-11 pm; $12-$22; cocktails; also, Chez Melange, see separate listing. **Recreation:** bicycles. **Cards:** AE, CB, DI, DS, JC, MC, VI. **Special Amenities:** Early check-in/late check-out and free newspaper. *(See ad below)* [icons]

PORTOFINO HOTEL & YACHT CLUB Rates Subject to Change Phone: (310)379-8481 **19**
All Year 1P: $140- 184 2P/1B: $150- 194 2P/2B: $150- 194 XP: $10 F15
Motor Inn **Location:** At the marina at King Harbor, 0.8 mi w of SR 1 (Pacific Coast Hwy); 0.3 mi w of Harbor Dr. 260 Portofino Way 90277. Fax: 310/372-7329. **Terms:** Weekly/monthly rates. **Facility:** 163 rooms. Patio or balcony. Most rooms have a harbor or ocean view. 8 whirlpool rms, extra charge; 3 stories; interior corridors; small heated pool, whirlpool. **Dining:** Restaurant, coffee shop; 6 am-10 pm; $15-$25; cocktails. **Recreation:** bicycles, Video games in all rooms. Fee: boating, canoeing. **Cards:** AE, CB, DI, DS, JC, MC, VI. [icons]

(See map p. 561)

TRAVELODGE-REDONDO BEACH PIER   Phone: (310)318-1811   [20]
⬥ SAVE   6/1-9/7 [CP]   1P: $65   2P/1B: $69   2P/2B: $77   XP: $6   F17
            2/1-5/31 & 9/8-1/31 [CP] 1P: $59   2P/1B: $63   2P/2B: $65
◆   **Location:** Just n of Torrance Blvd. 206 S Pacific Coast Hwy 90277. Fax: 310/379-0190. **Terms:** Reserv
Motel   deposit; weekly rates. **Facility:** 37 rooms. 1 whirlpool rm, extra charge; 3 stories; exterior corridors; small
            heated pool, whirlpool. **Cards:** AE, CB, DI, DS, JC, MC, VI. **Special Amenities:** Early check-in/late
check-out and free newspaper.

🔲🆕🛏️🎯🖨️📠❌

VAGABOND INN   Phone: (310)378-8555   [23]
⬥ SAVE   All Year [CP]   1P: $80   2P/1B: $80   2P/2B: $90   XP: $5   F18
◆   **Location:** 1.5 mi se on SR 1. 6226 Pacific Coast Hwy 90277. Fax: 310/791-7034. **Terms:** Small pets only,
Motel $5 extra charge. **Facility:** 40 rooms. 1 two-bedroom unit. Heated pool. **Dining:** Restaurant nearby.
            Cards: AE, CB, DI, DS, MC, VI. **Special Amenities:** Free breakfast and free local telephone calls.

🔲🐾🆕🍴🎯🖨️📠❌

RESTAURANTS

THE BLUE MOON SALOON   **Lunch:** $7-$15   **Dinner:** $17-$27   **Phone:** 310/374-3411   [8]
◆   **Location:** On the waterfront in Redondo Beach Marina. 207 N Harbor Dr 90277. **Hours:** 5 pm-11 pm, Fri &
Seafood   Sat 11 am-11 pm, Sun 11 am-10 pm. Closed: 11/25 & 12/24. **Reservations:** suggested; weekends.
            Features: casual dress; Sunday brunch; early bird specials; cocktails & lounge; fee for parking. Casual
atmosphere & harbor view. Seafood, steaks, chicken, pasta & salads. Patio dining available weather permitting. Smoke free
premises. **Cards:** AE, MC, VI.

❌

CHEZ MELANGE   **Lunch:** $10-$13   **Dinner:** $12-$22   **Phone:** 310/540-1222   [14]
◆◆◆   **Location:** In Palos Verdes Inn. 1700 S Pacific Coast Hwy 90277. **Hours:** 7 am-2:30 & 5-10 pm, Sun 8
Continental am-2:30 & 5-10 pm. **Reservations:** suggested. **Features:** casual dress; Sunday brunch; cocktails & lounge;
            a la carte. Selection of chicken, steak, duck, lamb, salads & pastas prepared in the southwestern, Italian, or
oriental flair. Oyster, caviar & champagne bar. Smoke free premises. **Cards:** AE, DI, MC, VI.

❌

LE BEAUJOLAIS   **Lunch:** $9-$15   **Dinner:** $16-$27   **Phone:** 310/543-5100   [11]
◆◆   **Location:** Just n of Francica Ave. 522 S Pacific Coast Hwy 90277. **Hours:** 11:30 am-3 & 5-10 pm, Fri &
French   Sat-11 pm. **Reservations:** suggested. **Features:** semi-formal attire; Sunday brunch; cocktails. Fresh
            seafood, chicken, duck, quiche, pasta & salads. Sat & Sun brunch, 10 am-3 pm. Smoke free premises.
Cards: AE, DI, DS, MC, VI.

❌

SPLASH   **Lunch:** $8-$13   **Dinner:** $10-$28   **Phone:** 310/798-5348   [10]
◆◆◆   **Location:** 0.5 mi w of SR 1 (Pacific Coast Hwy) at King Harbor; in Crowne Plaza Redondo Beach & Marina
Specialty   Hotel. 300 N Harbor Dr 90277. **Hours:** 11:30 am-2:30 pm & 6 pm-10 pm; Fri & Sat to 11 pm.
            Reservations: suggested. **Features:** casual dress; Sunday brunch; children's menu; health conscious menu;
cocktails & lounge; fee for parking & valet parking; a la carte. Upscale restaurant serving excellent selection of
Euro-Cal-Asian cuisine. Outdoor dining avail, cigar room off lounge area. Smoke free premises. **Cards:** AE, DI, DS, JC, MC,
VI.

❌

RESEDA—79,800   (See map p. 560; index p. 551)

LODGING

HOWARD JOHNSON LODGE   Phone: (818)344-0324   [77]
⬥ SAVE   All Year [CP]   1P: $55   2P/1B: $55   2P/2B: $55   XP: $5
◆◆   **Location:** 2 blks n of Sherman Way. 7432 Reseda Blvd 91335. Fax: 818/344-7188. **Facility:** 72 rooms. 3
Motel   rooms with whirlpool, $99; 2 stories; exterior corridors; whirlpool. **All Rooms:** extended cable TV. **Cards:** AE,
            CB, DI, DS, JC, MC, VI. *(See color ad opposite inside back cover & below)*

💲🆕🛏️🎯🖥️🖨️📠❌

ROSEMEAD—51,600

LODGINGS

HOLIDAY INN EXPRESS
♦♦♦ Motel
Rates Subject to Change
Phone: (323)726-1111
All Year [CP] 1P: $69 2P/1B: $69 2P/2B: $69 XP: $5 F19
Location: S side of SR 60, exit San Gabriel Blvd. 705 N San Gabriel Blvd 91770. Fax: 323/887-9236. **Terms:** Reserv deposit. **Facility:** 69 rooms. 3 one-bedroom suites, $190; 3 stories; interior corridors.
Cards: AE, CB, DI, DS, MC, VI.

SHERATON ROSEMEAD HOTEL
Guaranteed Rates
Phone: (323)722-8800
Mon-Thurs 1P: $98 2P/1B: $98 2P/2B: $98 XP: $10 F17
Fri-Sun 1P: $85 2P/1B: $85 2P/2B: $85 XP: $10 F17
♦♦♦ Hotel
Location: S side of SR 60, exit San Gabriel Blvd. 888 Montebello Blvd 91770. Fax: 323/721-8028. **Facility:** 146 rooms. Next to Montebello Towne Center. 4-5 stories; interior corridors; heated pool, sauna, whirlpool. **Dining:** Dining room; 6:30 am-10:30 pm; $8-$17; cocktails. **Some Rooms:** whirlpools. **Cards:** AE, CB, DI, DS, JC, MC, VI.

RESTAURANT

CHAMELI RESTAURANT
Lunch: $5-$10 **Dinner:** $10-$12 **Phone:** 626/280-1947
♦♦ Indian
Location: 0.3 mi w of Rosemead Blvd. 8752 Valley Blvd 91770. **Hours:** 11 am-10 pm. Closed: Tues. **Reservations:** suggested. **Features:** casual dress; beer & wine only; a la carte. Northern Indian vegetarian dishes. Daily lunch buffet. Smoke free premises. **Cards:** AE, DS, MC, VI.

ROWLAND HEIGHTS—42,600

LODGING

BEST WESTERN EXECUTIVE INN
Guaranteed Rates
Phone: (626)810-1818
♦♦♦ Motel
All Year [CP] 1P: $65- 99 2P/1B: $65- 99 2P/2B: $65- 99 XP: $6 D17
Location: North side of SR 60, exit Nogales St, then 0.3 mi w. 18880 E Gale Ave 91748. Fax: 626/810-3222. **Facility:** 134 rooms. 3 stories; interior/exterior corridors. **Cards:** AE, CB, DI, DS, MC, VI.

SAN DIMAS—32,400

LODGINGS

COMFORT SUITES
Phone: (909)592-0500
SAVE
All Year [BP] 1P: $85 2P/1B: $95 2P/2B: $95 XP: $10 F18
♦♦♦ Motel
Location: 0.3 mi e of I-210, exit Arrow Hwy. 501 W Bonita 91773. Fax: 909/394-4912. **Terms:** Reserv deposit; weekly/monthly rates. **Facility:** 60 rooms. Nicely landscaped courtyard. 2 stories; exterior corridors; heated pool, whirlpool. **Dining:** Restaurant nearby. **Services:** complimentary evening beverages. **All Rooms:** efficiencies, no utensils. **Cards:** AE, CB, DI, DS, MC, VI. **Special Amenities:** Free breakfast and free newspaper.

RED ROOF INN
Phone: (909)599-2362
SAVE
All Year 1P: $40 2P/1B: $55 2P/2B: $50 XP: $5 F18
♦♦ Motel
Location: E side of I-210, exit Arrow Hwy. 204 N Village Ct 91773. Fax: 909/592-7903. **Terms:** Small pets only. **Facility:** 134 rooms. Nicely landscaped courtyard. 2 stories; exterior corridors; heated pool, whirlpool. **Dining:** Restaurant nearby. **All Rooms:** combo or shower baths. **Cards:** AE, CB, DI, DS, JC, MC, VI. **Special Amenities:** Free local telephone calls. *(See ad p 761)*

RESTAURANT

CASK N CLEAVER
Lunch: $5-$8 **Dinner:** $9-$20 **Phone:** 909/592-1646
♦ American
Location: E side of I-210, exit Arrow Hwy. 125 N Village Ct 91773. **Hours:** 11:30 am-2 & 5-9 pm, Fri-10 pm, Sat 5 pm-10 pm, Sun 4:30 pm-9 pm. Closed major holidays. **Features:** casual dress; children's menu; carryout; salad bar; cocktails & lounge. Casual dining. Nice selection of steak, seafood & chicken. Smoke free premises. **Cards:** AE, DS, MC, VI.

SAN GABRIEL—37,100 (See map p. 562; index p. 550)

LODGING

QUALITY INN
Phone: (626)285-0921
SAVE
All Year [CP] 1P: $50- 58 2P/1B: $58- 60 2P/2B: $60- 66 XP: $15 F16
♦♦ Motel
Location: 2 mi n of I-10, San Gabriel Blvd exit; n to Las Tunas, then 0.5 mi e. 1114 E Las Tunas Dr 91776. Fax: 626/285-8391. **Terms:** Reserv deposit, 3 day notice. **Facility:** 42 rooms. 2 stories; exterior corridors; small pool, whirlpool. **Cards:** AE, MC, VI. **Special Amenities:** Free breakfast and free local telephone calls.

RESTAURANT

TUNG LAI SHUN RESTAURANT
Lunch: $6-$19 **Dinner:** $6-$19 **Phone:** 626/288-6588
♦ Chinese
Location: 0.5 mi n of I-10 exit Del Mar Ave; in San Gabriel Square, just w of Del Mar Ave ground level, north end. 140 W Valley Blvd #118c 91776. **Hours:** 11 am-10:30 pm. **Features:** casual dress; a la carte. Extensive selection of Islamic & Chinese cuisine. Smoke free premises. **Cards:** MC, VI.

SAN PEDRO—70,900   (See map p. 561; index p. 549)

LODGINGS

BEST WESTERN SUNRISE HOTEL   **Phone:** (310)548-1080   [50]
 [SAVE]   All Year   1P: $70- 99 2P/1B: $70- 99 2P/2B: $80- 95 XP: $5-10   F16
Location: 0.5 mi s of I-110, Harbor Blvd exit. 525 S Harbor Blvd 90731. Fax: 310/519-0380. **Terms:** Reserv
◆◆ deposit. **Facility:** 110 rooms. Across from Los Angeles Maritime Museum. 3 stories; interior corridors; heated
Motel pool, whirlpool. **Dining:** Coffee shop nearby. **Services:** area transportation, to cruise ships. **Cards:** AE, CB,
DI, DS, JC, MC, VI. **Special Amenities: Early check-in/late check-out and free breakfast.**
(See color ad below)   [icons]

HOLIDAY INN SAN PEDRO-LA HARBOR   **Phone:** (310)514-1414   [48]
[AAA] [SAVE]   All Year   1P: $99- 149 2P/1B: $99- 149 2P/2B: $99- 149 XP: $10   F17
Location: Just s of I-110, Gaffey St exit. 111 S Gaffey St 90731. Fax: 310/831-8262. **Facility:** 60 rooms. Old
◆◆◆ World, European ambiance. 4 efficiencies, $10 extra charge. 4 suites with gas fireplace; 2-4 stories; interior
Hotel corridors; whirlpool. **Dining:** Dining room; 6 am-9:30 & 5:30-9:30 pm, Sun 6:30 am-2 pm & 5-9 pm; $11-$18;
telephone calls. *(See color ad below)* cocktails. **Cards:** AE, CB, DI, DS, JC, MC, VI. **Special Amenities: Free breakfast and free local**
[icons]

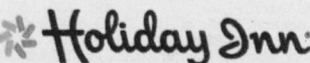

(See map p. 561)

SAN PEDRO HILTON AT CABRILLO MARINA   Rates Subject to Change   **Phone:** 310/514-3344   52
◆◆◆   All Year   1P: $179- 189   2P/1B: $179- 189   2P/2B: $189- 199   XP: $10   F18
Hotel   **Location:** 0.3 mi w of 22nd St, at Cabrillo Marina. 2800 Via Cabrillo Marina 90731. Fax: 310/514-8945.
Facility: 226 rooms. Many rooms overlooking marina. 3 stories; interior corridors; heated pool; 2 lighted tennis
courts. **Services:** giftshop. **Cards:** AE, DI, DS, JC, MC, VI. *(See color ad below & ad p 119)*

SHERATON-LOS ANGELES HARBOR HOTEL   Rates Subject to Change   **Phone:** 310/519-8200   51
◆◆◆   All Year   1P: $118- 158   2P/1B: $118- 158   2P/2B: $118- 158   XP: $20   F17
Hotel   **Location:** Downtown area. 601 S Palos Verdes St at 6th 90731. Fax: 310/519-8421. **Terms:** Reserv deposit.
Facility: 244 rooms. Some rooms with harbor view. 10 stories; interior corridors; heated pool.
Services: giftshop; area transportation. **Cards:** AE, CB, DI, DS, MC, VI.

VAGABOND INN   **Phone:** (310)831-8911   49
AAA SAVE   All Year [CP]   1P: $75   2P/1B: $80   2P/2B: $85   XP: $5   F18
◆   **Location:** Just s of I-110. 215 S Gaffey 90731. Fax: 310/831-2649. **Terms:** Pets, $5 extra charge.
Motel   **Facility:** 72 rooms. 4 stories; exterior corridors; heated pool. **Dining:** Restaurant nearby. **Cards:** AE, CB, DI,
DS, MC, VI. **Special Amenities:** Free breakfast and free local telephone calls.

RESTAURANTS

MADEO RISTORANTE   Lunch: $8-$12   Dinner: $11-$21   **Phone:** 310/521-5333   32
◆◆◆   **Location:** 0.3 mi w of 22nd St, at Cabrillo Marina; in San Pedro Hilton at Cabrillo Marina. 2800 Via Cabrillo
Italian   Marina 90731. **Hours:** 11:30 am-2:30 & 5-10:30 pm, Fri-11:30 pm, Sat 5 pm-11:30 pm, Sun 5 pm-10:30 pm.
Closed: 1/1 & 12/25. **Reservations:** suggested; weekends. **Features:** cocktails & lounge; a la carte. Bright,
colorful dining room with a nice selection of pasta, seafood & steaks. Smoke free premises. **Cards:** AE, DI, DS, MC, VI.

SIMON'S RESTAURANT   Lunch: $9-$15   Dinner: $18-$30   **Phone:** 310/514-1050   31
◆◆   **Location:** Entrance to Ports O'Call Village. 1050 Nagoya Way 90731. **Hours:** 11:30 am-2 & 5-9:30 pm; Fri &
American   Sat-10 pm; Sun 4:30 pm-9 pm. **Reservations:** suggested. **Features:** casual dress; cocktails & lounge.
Beautiful view of Los Angeles Harbor. Nice selection of fresh seafood; also steak, poultry & pasta. Smoke
free premises. **Cards:** AE, DI, MC, VI.

SANTA CLARITA—110,700

LODGINGS

BEST WESTERN RANCH HOUSE INN   Guaranteed Rates   **Phone:** 805/255-0555
◆◆   4/1-9/30   1P: $80- 100   2P/1B: $90- 110   2P/2B: $90- 110   XP: $10   F17
Motor Inn   2/1-3/31 & 10/1-1/31   1P: $70- 90   2P/1B: $80- 100   2P/2B: $80- 100   XP: $10   F17
Location: Adjacent to I-5, Magic Mountain Pkwy exit. 27413 Tourney Rd 91355. Fax: 805/255-2216.
Facility: 183 rooms. 2 suites avail at $175; 2 stories; interior/exterior corridors; heated pool. **Cards:** AE, CB, DI, DS, MC, VI.
(See color ad starting on p 646)

COMFORT SUITES   Rates Subject to Change   **Phone:** (805)254-7700
◆◆◆   All Year [CP]   1P: $89- 119   2P/1B: $89- 119   2P/2B: $89- 119   XP: $10   F18
Motel   **Location:** Just w of I-5, exit Lyons Ave. 25380 The Old Road 91381. Fax: 805/254-7736. **Facility:** 101 rooms.
11 whirlpool rms, extra charge; 3 stories; interior corridors; heated pool. **Cards:** AE, CB, DI, DS, JC, MC, VI.
(See color ad starting on p 646)

FAIRFIELD INN BY MARRIOTT
Phone: (805)290-2828

(AAA) (SAVE)
◆◆◆
Motel

All Year [CP]   1P: $83   2P/1B: $83   2P/2B: $83
Location: Adjacent to I-5, w side; exit Lyons Ave. 25340 The Old Rd 91381. Fax: 805/209-2835.
Terms: Check-in 4 pm. **Facility:** 66 rooms. 3 stories; interior/exterior corridors; heated pool, whirlpool.
Dining: Restaurant nearby. **Cards:** AE, CB, DI, DS, JC, MC, VI. **Special Amenities:** Free local telephone calls and free newspaper. *(See color ad starting on p 646)*

HAMPTON INN
Phone: (805)253-2400

◆◆◆
Motel

Rates Subject to Change
5/1-9/30 [CP]   1P: $99   2P/1B: $119   2P/2B: $119   XP: $10
2/1-4/30 & 10/1-1/31 [CP] 1P: $89   2P/1B: $99   2P/2B: $99   XP: $10
Location: Adjacent to I-5 w side; exit Lyons Ave. 25259 The Old Rd 91381. Fax: 805/253-1683. **Facility:** 130 rooms. 4 stories; interior corridors; heated pool. **Cards:** AE, CB, DI, DS, JC, MC, VI. *(See color ad starting on p 646)*

RESIDENCE INN BY MARRIOTT
Phone: (805)290-2800

(AAA) (SAVE)
◆◆◆
Suite Motel

6/1-8/31 [CP]   1P: $90- 115   2P/1B: $90- 115 2P/2B: $109- 169
2/1-5/31 & 10/1-1/31 [CP] 1P: $85- 109 2P/1B: $85- 109 2P/2B: $104- 165
Location: Adjacent to I-5 w side; exit Lyons Ave. 25320 The Old Rd 91381. Fax: 805/290-2802.
Terms: Check-in 4 pm; weekly/monthly rates. **Facility:** 90 rooms. Studio & 1 & 2-bedroom suites with living room & kitchen; many with fireplace. 3 stories; interior corridors; heated pool, whirlpool. **Dining:** Restaurant nearby. **Services:** complimentary evening beverages, Mon-Thur. **Recreation:** sports court. **Cards:** AE, CB, DI, DS, JC, MC, VI. **Special Amenities:** Free breakfast and free newspaper.

SANTA CLARITA TRAVELODGE
Phone: (805)252-1716

(AAA) (SAVE)
◆◆
Motel

6/1-9/30   1P: $65   2P/1B: $65   2P/2B: $70   XP: $1-5 F17
5/31 & 10/1-1/31   1P: $55   2P/1B: $55   2P/2B: $60   XP: $1-5 F17
Location: 1.5 mi nw of SR 14; northbound exit Sierra Hwy, southbound exit Sand Canyon Rd just n to Soledad Canyon Rd, then e 1.5 mi to Sierra Way, then just n 1 mi. 17843 Sierra Hwy 91351. Fax: 805/252-5286. **Terms:** Reserv deposit. **Facility:** 54 rooms. 2 stories; interior corridors; small heated pool, whirlpool. **Dining:** Restaurant nearby. **Cards:** AE, CB, DI, DS, JC, MC, VI. **Special Amenities:** Free breakfast and free newspaper. *(See color ad starting on p 646)*

SUPER 8 MOTEL
Phone: (805)252-1722

(AAA) (SAVE)
◆◆
Motel

5/23-9/6 [CP]   1P: $60   2P/1B: $60   2P/2B: $70   XP: $8 F12
2/1-5/22 & 9/7-1/31 [CP] 1P: $55   2P/1B: $55   2P/2B: $65   XP: $8 F12
Location: SR 14 exit Via Princessa, just w, then 1.5 mi n. 17901 Sierra Hwy 91351. Fax: 805/252-3234.
Terms: Reserv deposit; pets. **Facility:** 50 rooms. Nicely decorated. 5 rooms with fireplace. 2 stories; interior corridors; whirlpool. **All Rooms:** extended cable TV. **Cards:** AE, DS, MC, VI. **Special Amenities:** Free breakfast and free newspaper.

SANTA FE SPRINGS—15,500

LODGINGS

BEST WESTERN-SANTA FE SPRINGS
Phone: 562/404-4114

◆
Motel

Rates Subject to Change
All Year [CP]   1P: $39   2P/1B: $45   2P/2B: $49   XP: $5
Location: W side of I-5, Carmenita Ave exit. 13420 E Firestone Blvd 90670. Fax: 562/404-4114. **Facility:** 102 rooms. 1 two-bedroom unit. 6 whirlpool rms, extra charge; 2 stories; exterior corridors; heated pool.
Cards: AE, DS, MC, VI. *(See color ad p 352)*

DYNASTY SUITES-SANTA FE SPRINGS
Phone: 562/921-8571

(AAA)
◆◆
Motel

Guaranteed Rates
All Year [BP]   1P: $47- 53 2P/1B: $47- 53 2P/2B: $55- 60 XP: $5-10 D12
Location: W side of I-5, exit Carmenita Rd. 13530 E Firestone Blvd 90670. Fax: 562/921-2451. **Facility:** 49 rooms. 2 stories; exterior corridors. **Some Rooms:** whirlpools. **Cards:** AE, CB, DI, DS, MC, VI.
(See color ad p 610)

SANTA MONICA—86,900   (See map p. 558; index p. 553)

LODGINGS

BEST WESTERN GATEWAY HOTEL SANTA MONICA
Phone: (310)829-9100 **173**

(AAA) (SAVE)
◆◆◆
Motor Inn

2/1-5/31 & 10/1-1/31 1P: $79- 159 2P/1B: $79- 159 2P/2B: $79- 159 XP: $5 F18
6/1-6/30 & 9/1-9/30   1P: $89- 159 2P/1B: $89- 159 2P/2B: $89- 159 XP: $5 F18
7/1-8/31   1P: $109- 159 2P/1B: $109- 159 2P/2B: $109- 159 XP: $5 F18
Location: N of I-10, exit Cloverfield Rd. 1920 Santa Monica Blvd 90404. Fax: 310/829-9211. **Facility:** 125 rooms. 4 stories; interior corridors. **Dining:** Restaurant; 6:30 am-10 pm; $4-$10; wine/beer only.
Services: area transportation, to the beach. **Recreation:** in-room video games. **Cards:** AE, CB, DI, DS, JC, MC, VI. **Special Amenities:** Free newspaper. *(See color ad p 635)*

BEST WESTERN OCEAN VIEW HOTEL
Phone: (310)458-4888 **183**

(AAA) (SAVE)
◆◆
Motel

6/15-9/14   1P: $129- 249 2P/1B: $129- 249 2P/2B: $129- 249 XP: $10 D12
2/1-6/14 & 9/15-11/14 1P: $99- 189 2P/1B: $99- 189 2P/2B: $99- 189 XP: $10 D12
11/15-1/31   1P: $89- 189 2P/1B: $89- 189 2P/2B: $89- 189 XP: $10 D12
Location: At Broadway. 1447 Ocean Ave 90401. Fax: 310/458-0848. **Facility:** 65 rooms. Many rooms with ocean view. 4 stories; interior corridors. Fee: parking. **Dining:** Restaurant nearby. **Cards:** AE, CB, DI, DS, JC, MC, VI. **Special Amenities:** Early check-in/late check-out. *(See color ad p 635)*

CHANNEL ROAD INN BED & BREAKFAST
Phone: (310)459-1920 **180**

◆◆◆
Historic Bed
& Breakfast

Rates Subject to Change
All Year [BP]   1P: $125- 275 2P/1B: $125- 275 2P/2B: $215- 275 XP: $15
Location: Just e of Pacific Coast Hwy. 219 W Channel Rd 90402. Fax: 310/454-9920. **Terms:** Reserv deposit, 3 day notice; handling fee imposed. **Facility:** 14 rooms. 1910 Colonial Revival house furnished with period antiques. 1 blk from beach, some rooms with ocean view. 2 rms include fireplace with either sitting rm or patio & ocean view; 3 stories; interior/exterior corridors; smoke free premises. **Recreation:** bicycles. **All Rooms:** combo or shower baths. **Cards:** AE, MC, VI.

(See map p. 558)

COMFORT INN

Phone: (310)828-5517   **171**

5/1-9/30 [CP]   1P: $69- 99   2P/1B: $79- 109   2P/2B: $79- 150   XP: $10   F18
2/1-4/30 & 10/1-1/31 [CP]   1P: $59- 89   2P/1B: $69- 99   2P/2B: $69- 139   XP: $10   F18

Motel   **Location:** 1.5 mi e of SR 1 (Lincoln Blvd). 2815 Santa Monica Blvd 90404. Fax: 310/829-6084. **Terms:** Reserv deposit. **Facility:** 108 rooms. 2 stories; exterior corridors; heated pool. **All Rooms:** combo or shower baths. **Cards:** AE, CB, DI, DS, MC, VI. **Special Amenities: Free breakfast and free newspaper.**

(See ad below)

DAYS INN SANTA MONICA   Rates Subject to Change   Phone: (310)829-6333   **184**

All Year [CP]   1P: $79- 109   2P/1B: $79- 109   2P/2B: $89- 119   XP: $10   F6

Motel   **Location:** 3007 Santa Monica Blvd 90404. Fax: 310/829-1983. **Terms:** Reserv deposit; handling fee imposed. **Facility:** 68 rooms. 4 stories; interior corridors; sauna, whirlpool. **All Rooms:** combo or tub baths. **Some Rooms:** whirlpools. **Cards:** AE, CB, DI, DS, MC, VI.

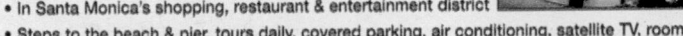

(See map p. 558)

DOUBLETREE GUEST SUITES
AAA
♦♦♦
Suite Hotel

Rates Subject to Change

Phone: (310)395-3332   [181]

All Year   1P: $149- 169   2P/1B: $149- 169   2P/2B: $159- 179   XP: $10-20   F18
Location: Adjacent to I-10, exit 4th St; just s. 1707 Fourth St 90401. Fax: 310/452-7399. **Terms:** Handling fee imposed; monthly rates. **Facility:** 253 rooms. 1-bedroom suites with living room & balcony overlooking atrium. 8 stories; interior corridors; heated pool, sauna, whirlpool. Fee: parking. **Dining:** Restaurant; 6 am-11 pm; $8-$20; cocktails. **Services:** giftshop. **Cards:** AE, DI, DS, MC, VI. *(See color ad below)*

FOUR POINTS BY SHERATON, SANTA MONICA
AAA
♦♦♦
Hotel

Guaranteed Rates

Phone: (310)399-9344   [177]

4/1-10/31   1P: $149   2P/1B: $149   2P/2B: $149   XP: $10   F17
2/1-3/31 & 11/1-1/31   1P: $129   2P/1B: $129   2P/2B: $129   XP: $10   F17
Location: Just w of Lincoln Ave. 530 Pico Blvd 90405. Fax: 310/399-2504. **Terms:** Check-in 4 pm; reserv deposit, 3 day notice; handling fee imposed; BP avail. **Facility:** 311 rooms. Large lobby; tastefully furnished guest rooms. 4 suites with whirlpool tub on balcony; 9 stories; interior corridors; heated pool, whirlpools.
Dining: Dining room; 6:30 am-11 pm; $15-$25; cocktails. **Services:** giftshop. **Cards:** AE, DI, DS, JC, MC, VI.

THE GEORGIAN
AAA [SAVE]
♦♦♦
Historic Hotel

Phone: (310)395-9945   [170]

7/1-8/31   1P: $200- 240   2P/1B: $200- 240   2P/2B: $200- 340   XP: $25   F16
2/1-6/30 & 9/1-1/31   1P: $185- 225   2P/1B: $185- 225   2P/2B: $210- 325   XP: $25   F16
Location: 1415 Ocean Ave 90401. Fax: 310/451-3374. **Terms:** Weekly rates; small pets only, $250 dep req; $100 extra charge. **Facility:** 84 rooms. Many rooms with ocean view. 28 one-bedroom suites, $285-$315; 8 stories; interior corridors. **Dining:** Restaurant; 6:30 am-10:30 pm, lunch & dinner served on patio; manager's reception Wed 5 pm-6 pm; afternoon tea. **Recreation:** in-room video games. **Cards:** AE, DI, JC, MC, VI.
Special Amenities: Free newspaper.

HOLIDAY INN-SANTA MONICA BEACH
AAA [SAVE]
♦♦♦
Hotel

Phone: (310)451-0676   [182]

6/1-10/31   1P: $169   2P/1B: $169   2P/2B: $169   XP: $15   F17
2/1-5/31   1P: $149   2P/1B: $149   2P/2B: $149   XP: $15   F17
11/1-1/31   1P: $139   2P/1B: $139   2P/2B: $139   F17
Location: 120 Colorado Blvd 90401. Fax: 310/393-7145. **Terms:** Reserv deposit, 3 day notice; weekly/monthly rates; BP avail; small pets only, $200 extra charge. **Facility:** 132 rooms. 7 stories; interior corridors; heated pool. Fee: parking. **Dining:** Restaurant; 6:30-10:30 am & 6:30-10:30 pm; $9-$16. **Services:** giftshop. **Recreation:** video game system in all rooms. Fee: bicycles. **Cards:** AE, CB, DI, DS, JC, MC, VI. *(See color ad below)*

(See map p. 558)

HOTEL OCEANA
Ⓐ
♦♦♦
Suite Motel

Rates Subject to Change **Phone:** (310)393-0486 **172**
All Year [CP] 1P: $300- 600 2P/1B: $300- 600 2P/2B: $300- 600 XP: $20-40 **F12**
Location: 3 blks n of Wilshire Blvd. 849 Ocean Ave 90403. Fax: 310/458-1182. **Facility:** 63 rooms. 50 one-bedroom & 9 two-bedroom kitchen suites; also 4 studio units. Balconies or patios, some with ocean view. 3 stories; exterior corridors; heated pool. **Recreation:** in-room video games. **Cards:** AE, CB, DI, DS, JC, MC, VI.

🔲 🔁 📶 🛄 ➕ 🍽 VCR 💻 ▢ ✕

LOEWS SANTA MONICA BEACH HOTEL
Ⓐ
♦♦♦♦
Hotel

Rates Subject to Change **Phone:** (310)458-6700 **179**
7/1-8/31 1P: $310- 495 2P/1B: $310- 495 2P/2B: $310- 495 XP: $20-40
3/1-6/30 & 9/1-11/15 1P: $300- 490 2P/1B: $300- 490 2P/2B: $300- 490 XP: $20-40
2/1-2/28 & 11/16-1/31 1P: $280- 470 2P/1B: $280- 470 2P/2B: $280- 470 XP: $20-40
Location: 1700 Ocean Ave 90401. Fax: 310/458-0020. **Terms:** Reserv deposit; pets, $50 dep req. **Facility:** 343 rooms. Many ocean view rooms; some with ocean view. 8 stories; interior corridors; heated indoor/outdoor pool, saunas, steamrooms, whirlpool; playground. **Dining:** Restaurant, coffee shop; 6:30 am-11 pm; $15-$27; cocktails; Sun brunch 10:30 am-2:30 pm. **Services:** giftshop. Fee: massage. Rental: bicycles. **Cards:** AE, CB, DI, DS, JC, MC, VI.

🐾 ♿ 📶 🔁 🍴 🍽 📶 🔌 🚰 📶 🛄 ✕ ➕ 🍽 VCR 🛗 🔲 🍽 ✕

MIRAMAR SHERATON HOTEL
♦♦♦
Hotel

Rates Subject to Change **Phone:** (310)576-7777 **175**
All Year 1P: $295- 345 2P/1B: $295- 345 2P/2B: $295- 345 XP: $20 **F17**
Location: 101 Wilshire Blvd at Ocean Ave 90401. Fax: 310/458-7912. **Facility:** 300 rooms. Many rooms with balcony overlooking ocean. 31 beautifully appointed bungalows. Special suites $275-$1000; 1-10 stories; interior/exterior corridors; heated pool. Fee: parking. **Services:** giftshop. **Cards:** AE, CB, DI, DS, JC, MC, VI.

S🔲 ♿ 📶 🔁 🍴 🍽 📶 🔌 ➕ 🛄 ➕ 🍽 💻 🛗 🍽 🔌 ✕

PACIFIC SHORE HOTEL
Ⓐ SAVE
♦♦
Hotel

Phone: (310)451-8711 **176**
6/1-9/30 1P: $120 2P/1B: $120 2P/2B: $120
2/1-5/31 & 10/1-1/31 1P: $94 2P/1B: $94 2P/2B: $94
Location: 1819 Ocean Ave & Pico Blvd 90401. Fax: 310/394-6657. **Terms:** Reserv deposit, 3 day notice. **Facility:** 168 rooms. Some rooms with ocean view. $1 per day security insurance charge; 8 stories; interior corridors; heated pool, whirlpool. **Dining:** Restaurant; 6 am-10 pm; $7-$12. **Recreation:** in-room video game. **Cards:** AE, CB, DI, DS, JC, MC, VI. **Special Amenities:** Free room upgrade (subject to availability with advanced reservations).** *(See color ad below)*

S🔲 ♿ 📶 🔁 🍴 🍽 🛄 ➕ 🍽 🍽 🔌 🔌 ✕

RADISSON HUNTLEY HOTEL
Ⓐ SAVE
♦♦♦
Hotel

Phone: (310)394-5454 **174**
7/15-10/31 1P: $164 2P/1B: $164 2P/2B: $164 XP: $20 **F17**
2/1-7/14 & 11/1-1/31 1P: $145 2P/1B: $145 2P/2B: $145 XP: $20 **F17**
Location: Just n of Wilshire Blvd. 1111 Second St 90403. Fax: 310/458-9776. **Terms:** Weekly/monthly rates. **Facility:** 213 rooms. Large lobby; attractively furnished guest rooms. 18 stories; interior corridors. Fee: parking. **Dining:** Restaurant; 6 am-11 pm; $8-$20; cocktails. **Services:** giftshop. **Recreation:** in-room video games. **Cards:** AE, CB, DI, DS, JC, MC, VI. *(See color ad below)*

S🔲 ♿ 📶 🍴 🍽 🛄 ➕ 🍽 VCR 🛗 🔲 🍽 🔌 ✕

(See map p. 558)

SHANGRI-LA HOTEL

All Year [CP]

Phone: (310)394-2791   **178**

1P: $130   2P/1B: $170   2P/2B: $185   XP: $15

Location: Just s of Wilshire Blvd. 1301 Ocean Ave 90401. Fax: 310/451-3351. **Terms:** Reserv deposit; handling fee imposed. **Facility:** 55 rooms. Built in 1939. Designed in art deco style. 2-bedroom suite $250, penthouses $365-$450; 7 stories; exterior corridors. **Dining:** Afternoon tea. **Some Rooms:** 47 kitchens. **Cards:** AE, CB, DI, DS, JC, MC, VI. **Special Amenities:** Free breakfast and free newspaper.

Motel

(See ad below)

(See map p. 558)

SHUTTERS ON THE BEACH Rates Subject to Change **Phone:** (310)458-0030 185
◆◆◆◆
Hotel

	1/1-1/31	1P: $355- 555	2P/1B: $355- 555	2P/2B: $355- 555
	6/1-12/31	1P: $345- 545	2P/1B: $345- 545	2P/2B: $345- 545
	2/1-5/31	1P: $335- 535	2P/1B: $335- 535	2P/2B: $335- 535

Location: One Pico Blvd 90405. Fax: 310/458-4589. **Terms:** Reserv deposit. **Facility:** 198 rooms. Many rooms with ocean view. 3-7 stories; interior corridors; heated pool. **Services:** giftshop. **Fee:** massage. **Recreation:** swimming; jogging. **Fee:** bicycles. **Cards:** AE, CB, DI, JC, MC, VI.

TRAVELODGE-SANTA MONICA BEACH **Phone:** (310)451-0761 169
🔺🔺 SAVE
◆
Motel

	6/1-9/30	1P: $110- 200	2P/1B: $110- 200	2P/2B: $115- 220	XP: $10	F12
	2/1-5/31	1P: $80- 130	2P/1B: $80- 130	2P/2B: $85- 140	XP: $10	F12
	10/1-12/20	1P: $80- 125	2P/1B: $80- 125	2P/2B: $85- 125	XP: $10	F12
	12/21-1/31	1P: $80- 110	2P/1B: $80- 110	2P/2B: $80- 115	XP: $5	F12

Location: 1525 Ocean Ave 90401. Fax: 310/393-5311. **Facility:** 29 rooms. 6 two-bedroom units. 2 stories; exterior corridors; heated pool. **All Rooms:** combo or shower baths. **Cards:** AE, DI, DS, MC, VI. **Special Amenities:** Free newspaper.

TRAVELODGE-SANTA MONICA/PICO BLVD **Phone:** (310)450-5766 186
🔺🔺 SAVE
◆◆
Motel

| | 5/16-9/30 [CP] | 1P: $79 | 2P/1B: $79 | 2P/2B: $89 | XP: $6 | F17 |
| | 2/1-5/15 & 10/1-1/31 [CP] | 1P: $59 | 2P/1B: $59 | 2P/2B: $69 | XP: $6 | F17 |

Location: I-10, Centinela Ave exit; 3 blks w. 3102 W Pico Blvd 90405. Fax: 310/450-8843. **Terms:** Weekly rates. **Facility:** 84 rooms. A few small rooms. 2-4 stories; exterior corridors. **Dining:** Restaurant nearby. **All Rooms:** combo or shower baths. **Some Rooms:** 47 kitchens. **Cards:** AE, CB, DI, DS, JC, MC, VI. **Special Amenities:** Free breakfast and free newspaper. *(See color ad p 638)*

RESTAURANTS

BISTRO OF SANTA MONICA **Lunch:** $7-$12 **Dinner:** $10-$13 **Phone:** 310/453-5442 91
◆◆
Italian
Location: At 23rd St. 2301 Santa Monica Blvd 90404. **Hours:** 11 am-10:30 pm. **Closed:** Sun. **Features:** carryout; cocktails; entertainment; a la carte. A Northern Italian menu featuring seafood & pasta dishes in a pleasant Bistro setting. **Cards:** AE, DS, MC, VI.

BOB BURNS RESTAURANT **Lunch:** $9-$14 **Dinner:** $11-$25 **Phone:** 310/393-6777 92
◆
American
Location: 202 Wilshire Blvd 90401. **Hours:** 11:30 am-11 pm, Fri & Sat-midnight, Sun 11 am-10:30 pm. **Closed:** 12/25. **Reservations:** suggested; weekends. **Features:** casual dress; cocktails & lounge; fee for valet parking. Nice selection of seafood and other entrees. **Cards:** AE, CB, DI, DS, MC, VI.

CHINOIS ON MAIN **Lunch:** $20-$28 **Dinner:** $50-$55 **Phone:** 310/392-9025 97
◆◆◆
Specialty
Location: 0.5 mi w of SR 1 (Lincoln Blvd). 2709 Main St 90405. **Hours:** 11:30 am-2 & 6-10:30 pm, Sat from 6 pm, Sun 5:30 pm-10 pm. **Closed:** for lunch Mon & Tues. **Reservations:** required. **Features:** casual dress; cocktails & lounge; fee for parking; valet parking; a la carte. California-Chinese cuisine. Smoke free premises. **Cards:** AE, CB, DI, DS, MC, VI.

DC 3 **Lunch:** $8-$16 **Dinner:** $15-$25 **Phone:** 310/399-2323 93
◆◆
American
Location: 2 blks s of Ocean Park on 28th. 2800 Donald Douglas Loop N 90405. **Hours:** 11:30 am-2 & 6-10 pm, Fri & Sat-10 pm. **Closed:** 1/1, 12/24, 12/25 & Mon for dinner & Sun. **Reservations:** suggested. **Features:** casual dress; cocktails & lounge; fee for valet parking. Entrees are Californian grill prepared. **Cards:** AE, CB, DI, MC, VI.

THE FISH COMPANY **Lunch:** $7-$10 **Dinner:** $10-$18 **Phone:** 310/392-8366 99
◆◆
Seafood
Location: 0.5 mi w of SR 1(Lincoln Blvd). 174 Kinney St 90405. **Hours:** 11:30 am-10 pm, Fri & Sat-11 pm, Sun-10 pm. **Closed:** 11/25 & 12/25. **Reservations:** suggested. **Features:** casual dress; children's menu; carryout; cocktails; fee for parking. Nautical decor. Large selection of mesquite broiled seafood. Patio dining also avail. **Cards:** AE, MC, VI.

IZZY'S DELI **Lunch:** $6-$10 **Dinner:** $8-$12 **Phone:** 310/394-1131 98
◆
Specialty
Location: At 15th St. 1433 Wilshire Blvd 90403. **Hours:** 24 hours. **Features:** casual dress; children's menu; early bird specials; carryout; beer & wine only; street parking & valet parking. Excellent selection of pastrami, beef, chicken & deli specialties. Smoke free premises. **Cards:** AE, CB, DI, DS, MC, VI.

KNOLL'S BLACK FOREST INN **Lunch:** $9-$17 **Dinner:** $13-$25 **Phone:** 310/395-2212 88
◆◆◆
German
Location: 2454 Wilshire Blvd 90403. **Hours:** 11:30 am-2:30 & 5-10:30 pm, Sat & Sun 5 pm-10:30 pm. **Closed:** 12/25 & Mon. **Reservations:** suggested. **Features:** casual dress; cocktails & lounge; valet parking. Charming restaurant. **Cards:** AE, CB, DI, DS, MC, VI.

LOCANDA DEL LAGO **Lunch:** $9-$18 **Dinner:** $11-$22 **Phone:** 310/451-3525 95
◆◆◆
Northern Italian
Location: At Third St Promenade. 231 Arizona Ave 90401. **Hours:** 11:30 am-10:30 pm, Sat & Sun brunch 11:30 am-4 pm. **Reservations:** suggested. **Features:** casual dress; cocktails; valet parking; a la carte. Featuring pasta, seafood, meat & poultry from the Bellagio region. Patio dining overlooking Third St Promenade weather permitting. **Cards:** AE, CB, DI, DS, MC, VI.

MICHAEL'S **Lunch:** $11-$20 **Dinner:** $20-$30 **Phone:** 310/451-0843 94
◆◆
American
Location: Just n of Wilshire Blvd. 1147 3rd St 90403. **Hours:** 11:30 am-2 & 5:30-10 pm, Sat 5:30 am-10 pm. **Closed** major holidays, Sun & Mon. **Reservations:** suggested. **Features:** semi-formal attire; cocktails; fee for valet parking; a la carte. Patio dining in attractive garden, weather permitting. Sat & Sun brunch, 10:30 am-2 pm. 15% service charge. **Cards:** AE, DI, DS, MC, VI.

OCEAN AVENUE SEAFOOD **Lunch:** $10-$23 **Dinner:** $15-$25 **Phone:** 310/394-5669 86
◆◆◆
Seafood
Location: 1401 Ocean Ave 90401. **Hours:** 11:30 am-11 pm, Sun 11:30 am-9:30 pm. **Closed:** 11/25 & 12/25. **Reservations:** suggested. **Features:** casual dress; Sunday brunch; children's menu; cocktails & lounge; fee for valet parking; a la carte. Menus change daily to reflect current availability of quality seafood. Excellent selection of seafood & pasta dishes. Lovely ocean view. Oyster bar. **Cards:** AE, CB, DI, DS, MC, VI.

(See map p. 558)

ROCKENWAGNER Lunch: $7-$14 Dinner: $18-$22 Phone: 310/399-6504 [96]
◆◆◆ Location: 1 mi s of I-10 via Lincoln Blvd and Pico Blvd. 2435 Main St 90405. Hours: 11:30 am-2:30 & 6-10
French pm, Mon 6 pm-10 pm, Sat & Sun 9 am-2:30 & 5:30-10 pm. Closed major holidays.
Reservations: suggested. Features: semi-formal attire; Sunday brunch; children's menu; cocktails; fee for
parking & valet parking; a la carte. Creative French/California food served in a modern casual setting with professional,
friendly staff. Smoke free premises. Cards: AE, DI, MC, VI. ⊠

VALENTINO RESTAURANT Dinner: $20-$40 Phone: 310/829-4313 [87]
◆◆◆◆ Location: 0.3 mi w of Centinela Ave. 3115 Pico Blvd 90405. Hours: 5:30 pm-10:30 pm, Fri 11:30 am-2:30 &
Italian 5:30-11:30 pm, Sat 5:30 pm-11:30 pm. Closed major holidays & Sun. Reservations: suggested.
Features: semi-formal attire; cocktails; fee for valet parking; a la carte. Patio dining avail, extensive wine list.
Smoke free premises. Cards: AE, CB, DI, MC, VI. ⊠

SHERMAN OAKS (See map p. 560; index p. 548)

LODGINGS

CARRIAGE INN Phone: (818)787-2300 [29]
AAA SAVE 7/1-9/9 1P: $85 2P/1B: $85 2P/2B: $85 XP: $10 F18
2/1-6/30 & 9/10-1/31 1P: $75 2P/1B: $75 2P/2B: $75 XP: $10 F18
◆◆ Location: Adjacent to I-405, Burbank Blvd exit. 5525 Sepulveda Blvd 91411. Fax: 818/782-9373.
Motor Inn Terms: Reserv deposit; handling fee imposed; weekly/monthly rates. Facility: 184 rooms. 2-3 stories;
interior/exterior corridors; heated pool, whirlpool. Dining: Dining room, coffee shop; 6 am-10 pm; $9-$16;
cocktails. Cards: AE, DI, DS, MC, VI.

RADISSON VALLEY CENTER Rates Subject to Change Phone: (818)981-5400 [28]
AAA Fri & Sat 1P: $99 2P/1B: $99 2P/2B: $99 XP: $10 F17
Sun-Thurs 1P: $129 2P/1B: $129 2P/2B: $29 XP: $10 F17
◆◆◆ Location: At jct of I-405 & US 101, just w of Sepulveda Blvd. 15433 Ventura Blvd 91403.
Hotel Fax: 818/981-3175. Terms: Monthly rates. Facility: 201 rooms. 2 blks from Galleria Shopping Center. 12 sto-
ries; interior corridors; heated pool, whirlpool. Fee: parking. Dining: Dining room; 6:30 am-10 pm, Fri &
Sat-midnight; $7-$18; cocktails. Services: giftshop. Cards: AE, CB, DI, DS, JC, MC, VI. (See color ad p 584)

RESTAURANT

VALLEY INN Lunch: $6-$13 Dinner: $14-$27 Phone: 818/784-1163 [21]
◆◆ Location: Just s of Ventura Blvd, just w of Sepulveda near SR 405 & US 101. 4557 Sherman Oaks Ave
American 91403. Hours: 11 am-11 pm, Sat 5-11 pm, Sun 5-10 pm. Closed: 12/25. Features: casual dress; children's
menu; carryout; cocktails & lounge; minimum charge-$4 lunch, $8 dinner; street parking. Nice selection of
steak, chops, chicken & seafood. Smoke free premises. Cards: AE, CB, DI, DS, MC, VI. ⊠

SIERRA MADRE—10,800 (See map p. 562; index p. 554)

RESTAURANT

RESTAURANT LOZANO Lunch: $7-$10 Dinner: $12-$19 Phone: 626/355-5945 [50]
◆◆ Location: 1 mi n of I-210, downtown. 44 N Baldwin Ave 91024. Hours: 11 am-2 pm & 5-9 pm; Fri & Sat-10
American pm. Closed: 7/4, 11/25 & 12/25. Reservations: suggested. Features: Sunday brunch; children's menu;
carryout; beer & wine only; entertainment; street parking. Interesting selection of southwestern, Italian &
Caribbean cuisine. Smoke free premises. Cards: AE, CB, DI, MC, VI. ⊠

SOUTH EL MONTE—20,900

LODGING

RAMADA INN & SUITES Rates Subject to Change Phone: 626/350-9588
◆◆ All Year 1P: $79- 99 2P/1B: $87- 107 2P/2B: $87- 107 XP: $8 F18
Suite Motor Inn Location: Just n of SR 60, Santa Anita Ave exit. 1089 Santa Anita Ave 91733. Fax: 626/350-3849.
Facility: 105 rooms. 1-bedroom suites with microwave, refrigerator & VCR. 6 suites with whirlpool & gas fire-
place $210; 4 stories; exterior corridors; heated pool. Cards: AE, CB, DI, DS, JC, MC, VI.

SOUTH PASADENA—23,900 (See map p. 562; index p. 549)

LODGINGS

ARTIST'S INN Rates Subject to Change Phone: (626)799-5668 [45]
◆◆◆ All Year [BP] 1P: $115- 165 2P/1B: $115- 165 2P/2B: $115- 165 XP: $20
Historic Bed Location: Just w of Fair Oaks and n of Mission St. 1038 Magnolia St 91030. Fax: 626/799-3678.
& Breakfast Terms: Reserv deposit, 7 day notice; handling fee imposed. Facility: 5 rooms. 1895 Victorian farmhouse with
spacious porch & gardens with rose bushes. Rooms decorated in artist's theme with period antiques. 2 stories;
interior corridors; designated smoking area. All Rooms: combo or shower baths. Cards: AE, MC, VI.

THE BISSELL HOUSE BED & BREAKFAST Rates Subject to Change Phone: 626/441-3535 [46]
◆◆◆ All Year [BP] 1P: $115- 160 2P/1B: $115- 160
Bed & Location: Just n of SR 110 (Pasadena Fwy), at sw corner of Orange Grove & Columbia. 201 Orange Grove
Breakfast Ave 91030. Fax: 626/441-3671. Facility: 5 rooms. 1887 restored Victorian house with leaded glass windows
& furnished with antiques. Landscaped grounds surrounded by 40 foot hedge for privacy. Full breakfast on
weekends; expanded continental breakfast on weekdays. Evening refreshments; 3 stories; interior corridors; designated
smoking area. All Rooms: combo or shower baths. Cards: AE, MC, VI.

(See map p. 562)

RESTAURANTS

OAK TREE INN   **Lunch:** $5-$15   **Dinner:** $7-$15   **Phone:** 323/682-2882   30
◆◆
Chinese   **Location:** 0.3 mi n of Huntington Dr. 1315 Fair Oaks Ave 91030. **Hours:** 11 am-10 pm. **Reservations:** accepted. **Features:** casual dress; carryout; cocktails; a la carte. Attractive dining room with a variety of Cantonese & Mandarin dishes. Popular local trade. Smoke free premises. **Cards:** AE, CB, DI, DS, MC, VI.   ⊠

SHIRO   **Dinner:** $14-$20   **Phone:** 626/799-4774   31
◆◆◆
French   **Location:** Just w of Fair Oaks Ave. 626 Mission St 91030. **Hours:** 6-9 pm, Fri & Sat-10 pm, Sun 5:30 pm-9 pm. Closed major holidays & Mon. **Reservations:** suggested. **Features:** semi-formal attire; cocktails; street parking; a la carte. Small contemporary restaurant. Creative dishes specializing in seafood with a Japanese influence. Smoke free premises. **Cards:** AE, DI, DS, MC, VI.   ⊠

STUDIO CITY   (See map p. 560; index p. 549)

LODGINGS

DAYS INN   **Phone:** (818)789-6900   40
(AAA) SAVE   6/1-9/30   1P: $69   2P/1B: $69   2P/2B: $79
◆   2/1-5/31 & 10/1-1/31   1P: $59   2P/1B: $59   2P/2B: $69
Motel   **Location:** US 101, exit Coldwater Canyon Blvd, just mi w, then just n on Ventura Blvd. 12933 Ventura Blvd 91604. **Fax:** 818/789-6980. **Terms:** Reserv deposit. **Facility:** 65 rooms. 2 stories; exterior corridors. **All Rooms:** combo or shower baths. **Cards:** AE, CB, DI, DS, MC, VI. **Special Amenities: Early check-in/late check-out and free breakfast.**

SPORTSMEN'S LODGE HOTEL   **Phone:** (818)769-4700   39
(AAA) SAVE   Mon-Thurs   1P: $120- 135   2P/1B: $135   2P/2B: $120- 135   XP: $10   F17
      Fri-Sun   1P: $115- 129   2P/1B: $129   2P/2B: $115- 129   XP: $10   F17
◆◆◆   **Location:** 1 mi s of US 101, Coldwater Canyon Ave exit. 12825 Ventura Blvd 91604. **Fax:** 323/877-3896.
Hotel   **Terms:** Weekly/monthly rates. **Facility:** 191 rooms. Many balconies. All rooms have fax machines. Rates for up to four persons; 1-5 stories; interior/exterior corridors; heated pool, whirlpool. **Dining:** Restaurant; 6:30 am-10 pm; $10-$18; cocktails. **Services:** giftshop; area transportation, to Universal Studios. **Cards:** AE, CB, DI, DS, JC, MC, VI. *(See color ad p 585)*

UNIVERSAL CITY INN   Rates Subject to Change   **Phone:** 818/760-8737   41
◆◆   All Year   1P: $60   2P/1B: $65   2P/2B: $70
Motel   **Location:** 0.4 mi sw of US 101, Lankershim Blvd exit. 10730 Ventura Blvd 91604. **Fax:** 818/762-5159. **Terms:** Reserv deposit. **Facility:** 39 rooms. 2 stories; exterior corridors. **Cards:** AE, CB, DI, DS, JC, MC, VI.

RESTAURANT

MARRAKESH RESTAURANT   **Dinner:** $17-$22   **Phone:** 818/788-6354   24
◆◆   **Location:** 0.5 mi w of Coldwater Cyn Ave. 13003 Ventura Blvd 91604. **Hours:** 5 pm-10 pm, Fri & Sat-11 pm.
Ethnic   **Reservations:** suggested; Fri & Sat. **Features:** casual dress; children's menu; early bird specials; carryout; cocktails & lounge; entertainment; fee for valet parking; a la carte. Authentic Moroccan cuisine, service, dress & furnishings. Smoke free premises. **Cards:** AE, CB, DI, DS, MC, VI.   ⊠

SUN VALLEY   (See map p. 560; index p. 549)

LODGING

EMERSON INN   Rates Subject to Change   **Phone:** (818)768-6600   37
(AAA)   All Year   1P: $43- 45   2P/1B: $43- 45   2P/2B: $48   XP: $3-5
◆   **Location:** 0.8 mi ne of I-5 exit Sheldon. 9417 San Fernando Rd 91352. **Terms:** Reserv deposit, 3 day
Motel   notice. **Facility:** 31 rooms. Whirlpool rms, $55; 3 stories, no elevator; exterior corridors. **Some Rooms:** whirlpools. **Cards:** AE, DS, MC, VI.

SYLMAR   (See map p. 560; index p. 551)

LODGINGS

GOOD NITE INN   **Phone:** (818)362-8899   81
(AAA) SAVE   All Year   1P: $44   2P/1B: $50   2P/2B: $56   XP: $6   F18
◆   **Location:** I-5 exit Roxford St, just e to Encinitas Ave, then just s. 12835 Encinitas Ave 91342.
Motel   **Fax:** 818/362-0627. **Terms:** Small pets only, 2 day max. **Facility:** 90 rooms. 3 stories; whirlpool. **Dining:** Restaurant nearby. **Some Rooms:** color TV. **Cards:** AE, CB, DI, DS, JC, MC, VI. **Special Amenities: Free local telephone calls.**

RODEWAY INN   **Phone:** (818)367-1223   80
(AAA) SAVE   5/28-9/6   1P: $45   2P/1B: $45   2P/2B: $62   XP: $6   F16
◆◆   2/1-5/27 & 9/7-1/31   1P: $40   2P/1B: $42   2P/2B: $52   XP: $6   F16
Motel   **Location:** I-5, Roxford St exit; 0.5 mi e, then 0.7 mi s. 12783 San Fernando Rd 91342. **Fax:** 818/367-3136. **Terms:** Reserv deposit. **Facility:** 32 rooms. 2 whirlpool rms, $80. **All Rooms:** combo or shower baths, extended cable TV. **Cards:** AE, CB, DI, DS, JC, MC, VI.

TARZANA   (See map p. 560; index p. 550)

LODGING

DAYS INN   Phone: (818)345-9410   56
AAA SAVE   All Year [CP]   1P: $60- 69 2P/1B: $60- 69 2P/2B: $79- 89 XP: $5   F12
◆◆   **Location:** 0.3 mi se of US 101; exit Tampa. 19170 Ventura Blvd 91356. Fax: 818/705-4524. **Facility:** 47
Motel   rooms. 2 stories; exterior corridors; heated pool, whirlpool. **Dining:** Coffee shop nearby. **All Rooms:** combo
or shower baths. **Cards:** AE, DI, DS, JC, MC, VI. **Special Amenities:** Early check-in/late check-out and
free breakfast. *(See color ad below)*

TORRANCE—133,100   (See map p. 561; index p. 548)

LODGINGS

COURTYARD BY MARRIOTT/TORRANCE SOUTH BAY   Rates Subject to Change   **Phone:** 310/532-1722   35
◆◆◆   Sun-Thurs 2/1-4/1   1P: $99   2P/1B: $99   2P/2B: $99
Motor Inn   Sun-Thurs 4/2-1/31   1P: $94   2P/1B: $94   2P/2B: $94
Fri & Sat   1P: $59   2P/1B: $59   2P/2B: $59
Location: Adjacent to I-405; exit Western Ave. 1925 W 190th St 90504. Fax: 310/532-9161. **Facility:** 150 rooms. Large land-
scaped courtyard. Attractively furnished guest rooms. 4 stories; interior corridors; heated pool. **Cards:** AE, CB, DI, DS, MC,
VI. *(See color ad p 618 & p 563)*

COURTYARD BY MARRIOTT/TORRENCE DEL AMO   Rates Subject to Change   **Phone:** 310/533-8000   38
◆◆◆   All Year   1P: $69- 99 2P/1B: $69- 99 2P/2B: $69- 99
Motor Inn   **Location:** Just w of Crenshaw Blvd. 2633 W Sepulveda Blvd 90505. Fax: 310/533-0564. **Facility:** 149 rooms.
Large landscaped courtyard. 3 stories; interior corridors; heated pool. **Cards:** AE, CB, DI, DS, MC, VI.
(See color ad p 563)

DEL AMO INN   Phone: (310)542-9417   29
AAA SAVE   All Year   1P: $50- 55 2P/1B: $55- 60 2P/2B: $60- 65
◆   **Location:** 0.5 mi n of Torrance Blvd. 20534 Hawthorne Blvd 90503. Fax: 310/370-6653. **Terms:** Weekly
Motel   rates. **Facility:** 31 rooms. 2 stories; exterior corridors. **Dining:** Coffee shop nearby. **Cards:** AE, DI, DS, MC,
VI. **Special Amenities:** Free room upgrade and preferred room (each subject to availability with
advanced reservations).

(See map p. 561)

HOLIDAY INN TORRANCE

Phone: (310)781-9100 **36**

🔺🔺🔺 [SAVE]
Hotel

All Year   1P: $150- 160   2P/1B: $160- 170   2P/2B: $160- 170   XP: $10   F18
Location: S of jct I-110 & I-405, 0.5 mi s of 190th St. 19800 S Vermont Ave 90502. Fax: 310/324-1695. **Facility:** 327 rooms. 12 stories; interior corridors; heated pool, sauna, whirlpool. **Dining:** Restaurant; $6-$12; also, The Ginger Cafe, see separate listing. **Services:** giftshop; area transportation, within 7 mi. **Some Rooms:** whirlpools. **Cards:** AE, CB, DI, DS, JC, MC, VI. **Special Amenities: Early check-in/late check-out and free room upgrade (subject to availability with advanced reservations).**

RAMADA INN

Phone: (310)325-0660 **40**

🔺🔺 [SAVE]
Motor Inn

All Year   1P: $59- 62   2P/1B: $62- 65   2P/2B: $65- 75
Location: Between Hawthorne Blvd & Crenshaw Blvd. 2880 Pacific Coast Hwy 90505. Fax: 310/325-6661. **Facility:** 88 rooms. 4 suites $60-$70; 2 stories; exterior corridors; whirlpool. **Dining:** Coffee shop; 6 am-10 pm; $7-$10. **Cards:** AE, CB, DI, DS, JC, MC, VI. **Special Amenities: Free newspaper and free room upgrade (subject to availability with advanced reservations).** *(See ad below)*

RAMADA LIMITED

Phone: 310/316-5570 **31**

🔺🔺
Motel

All Year [CP]   1P: $60   2P/1B: $65   2P/2B: $65   XP: $5
Location: Just e of Hawthorne Blvd. 3673 Torrance Blvd 90503. Fax: 310/316-9349. **Terms:** Reserv deposit. **Facility:** 51 rooms. 1 kitchen unit, $125 for up to 4 persons; 3 stories; exterior corridors. **Cards:** AE, CB, DI, DS, JC, MC, VI.

RESIDENCE INN BY MARRIOTT

Phone: 310/543-4566 **30**

🔺🔺🔺
Apartment
Motel

Guaranteed Rates
All Year [CP]   1P: $99- 158   2P/1B: $99- 158   2P/2B: $109- 168   XP: $10   F19
Location: Just e of Hawthorne Blvd. 3701 Torrance Blvd 90503. Fax: 310/543-3026. **Facility:** 247 rooms. 1 & 2-bedroom suites with living room, many with fireplace. Fully equipped kitchen in every unit. 61 two-bedroom units. 2 stories; exterior corridors; heated pool. **Recreation:** sports court. **Cards:** AE, CB, DI, DS, JC, MC, VI.

SUMMERFIELD SUITES HOTEL

Phone: 310/371-8525 **28**

🔺🔺🔺
Suite Motel

Rates Subject to Change
All Year [CP]   1P: $115   2P/1B: $115   2P/2B: $135   XP: $10   F10
Location: Between 190th St & Del Amo Blvd. 19901 Prairie Ave 90503. Fax: 310/542-9628. **Facility:** 144 rooms. 1- & 2-bedroom suites with living room, some with fireplace. 49 two-bedroom units. 2-3 stories; no elevator; interior/exterior corridors; heated pool. **Services:** area transportation. **Recreation:** sports court. **All Rooms:** kitchens. **Cards:** AE, CB, DI, DS, JC, MC, VI.

TORRANCE HILTON AT SOUTH BAY

Phone: 310/540-0500 **32**

🔺🔺🔺
Hotel

Rates Subject to Change
All Year   1P: $134- 169   2P/1B: $144- 179   2P/2B: $144- 179   XP: $10   F16
Location: Just s of Torrance Blvd. 21333 Hawthorne Blvd 90503. Fax: 310/540-2065. **Facility:** 371 rooms. 12 stories; interior/exterior corridors; heated pool. **Services:** giftshop; area transportation. **Rental:** bicycles. **Cards:** AE, CB, DI, DS, JC, MC, VI. *(See ad p 119)*

TORRANCE MARRIOTT

Phone: (310)316-3636 **34**

🔺🔺🔺
Hotel

Rates Subject to Change
All Year   1P: $84- 174   2P/1B: $84- 174   2P/2B: $84- 174
Location: Just s of Torrance Blvd; off Hawthorne Blvd. 3635 Fashion Way 90503. Fax: 310/543-6076. **Facility:** 487 rooms. Across from Del Amo Fashion Shopping Center. 17 stories; interior corridors; heated indoor/outdoor pool. **Services:** giftshop. **Cards:** AE, CB, DI, DS, JC, MC, VI.

TRAVELODGE

Phone: (310)539-9888 **39**

🔺🔺🔺 [SAVE]
🔺🔺
Motel

All Year   1P: $58   2P/1B: $58   2P/2B: $65   XP: $6   F17
Location: Just e of Crenshaw Blvd. 2448 Sepulveda Blvd 90501. Fax: 310/539-6420. **Facility:** 53 rooms. 1 two-bedroom unit. 2 stories; exterior corridors; small pool. **Cards:** AE, CB, DI, DS, JC, MC, VI. **Special Amenities: Free newspaper and preferred room (subject to availability with advanced reservations).**

(See map p. 561)

RESTAURANTS

THE GINGER CAFE   **Lunch:** $8-$15   **Dinner:** $8-$18   **Phone:** 310/515-0600   ⓴
◆◆   **Location:** In the Holiday Inn Torrance. 19800 S Vermont Ave 90502. **Hours:** 6 am-2 pm & 5:30 pm-10 pm.
Continental   **Features:** casual dress; children's menu; cocktails & lounge. Selections of steak, seafood, chicken, veal
          chops, salad, pizza, calzone & pasta. Traditional & Japanese dishes. Smoke free premises. **Cards:** AE, CB,
DI, DS, JC, MC, VI.   ⊠

JASMINES   **Dinner:** $15-$35   **Phone:** 310/316-3636   ⓲
◆◆◆   **Location:** Just s of Torrance Blvd; off Hawthorne Blvd; in Torrance Marriott. 3635 Fashion Way 90503-4897.
American   **Hours:** 6 pm-10 pm, Fri & Sat-11 pm. Closed: Sun & Mon. **Features:** semi-formal attire; valet parking; a la
          carte. Informal atmosphere. Featuring seafood, steaks, duck & pasta. Japanese breakfast, 6-9 am. Smoke
free premises. **Cards:** AE, CB, DI, DS, JC, MC, VI.   ⊠

SOUTH BAY GRILL   **Lunch:** $5-$9   **Dinner:** $7-$15   **Phone:** 310/378-0344   ㉑
◆◆   **Location:** On Hawthorne Blvd, just n of Lomita Blvd. 23805 Hawthorne Blvd 90505. **Hours:** 11 am-9 pm; Fri
Seafood   & Sat-10 pm, Sun noon-9 pm. Closed: 1/1, 11/26 & 12/25. **Features:** casual dress; children's menu; early
          bird specials; senior's menu; health conscious menu; carryout; cocktails & lounge. Excellent selection of
seafood as well as meat & pastas. Also fresh trout. Nautical decor with fresh fish market. **Cards:** AE, DI, DS, MC, VI. ⊠

UNIVERSAL CITY   (See map p. 560; index p. 548)

LODGINGS

SHERATON UNIVERSAL HOTEL, AT UNIVERSAL STUDIOS   **Phone:** (818)980-1212   ㉛
Ⓐ Ⓐ Ⓐ Ⓢ Ⓐ Ⓥ Ⓔ   All Year   1P: $162   2P/1B: $178   2P/2B: $178   XP: $25   F17
◆◆◆   **Location:** Adjacent to US 101, exit Lankershim Blvd, at Universal Studios. 333 Universal Terrace Pkwy
Hotel   91608. Fax: 818/985-4980. **Terms:** Reserv deposit. **Facility:** 442 rooms. 21 stories; interior corridors; heated
          pool, whirlpool. Fee: parking. **Dining:** Restaurant; 6 am-10:30 pm; $11-$20; cocktails. **Services:** giftshop;
          area transportation, to Universal Studios. **Recreation:** video games in all rooms. **All Rooms:** extended cable
TV. **Cards:** AE, CB, DI, DS, JC, MC, VI. **Special Amenities:** Early check-in/late check-out and free newspaper.

Ⓢ Ⓥ Ⓒ ⒓ ⚓ 🍴 ⒜ Ⓐ ⬗ ⬧ ✈ Ⓡ ⓋⒸⓇ 💻 ⒤⒤ 🖥 Ⓘ Ⓞ ⊠

(See map p. 560)

UNIVERSAL CITY HILTON & TOWERS, AT UNIVERSAL STUDIOS   **Phone:** (818)506-2500   🔲 32

All Year   1P: $150- 190   2P/1B: $150- 190   2P/2B: $150- 190   XP: $35   F18
Location: Adjacent to US 101, exit Lankershim Blvd. 555 Universal Terrace Pkwy 91608.
Fax: 818/509-2058. **Terms:** Package plans. **Facility:** 484 rooms. 24 stories; interior corridors; heated pool.
Fee: parking. **Dining:** Dining room; 6:30 am-11 pm; $20-$30; cocktails. **Services:** giftshop. **Cards:** AE, CB,
DI, DS, JC, MC, VI. **Special Amenities: Free newspaper and preferred room (subject to availability with
advanced reservations).** *(See ad p 119 & below)*

Hotel

VALENCIA

LODGINGS

HYATT VALENCIA   **Phone:** (805)799-1234

Sun-Thurs   1P: $169- 240   2P/1B: $169- 265   2P/2B: $169- 265   XP: $25   F18
Fri & Sat   1P: $129- 155   2P/1B: $129- 180   2P/2B: $129- 180   XP: $25   F18
Too new to rate. **Location:** 24500 Town Center Dr 91355. Fax: 805/799-1233. **Terms:** Check-in 4 pm.
Facility: 244 rooms. 6 stories; interior corridors; heated pool, whirlpool. **Dining:** Restaurant; 6 am-midnight;
cocktails. **Services:** giftshop. **Cards:** AE, CB, DI, DS, JC, MC, VI.
(See color ad starting on p 646 & p 565)

Hotel

LA QUINTA INN & SUITES-VALENCIA

Under construction. **Location:** The Old Rd & Lyons Ave. **Facility:** 143 rooms. Scheduled to open August,
1999.

DIAMOND Accommodations. What does it mean to you?

To earn even a single diamond, an accommodation must attend
to your needs in pleasant and attractive surroundings—
and offer you much more in services and facilities as well.

VALENCIA HILTON GARDEN INN-AT SIX FLAGS   **Phone:** (805)254-8800

All Year   1P: $139- 209   2P/1B: $139- 234   2P/2B: $139- 234   XP: $10

Location: Adjacent to I-5, 0.3 mi nw, exit Magic Mountain Pkwy. 27710 The Old Rd 91355. Fax: 805/254-9399. **Facility:** 152 rooms. Landscaped courtyard. Some rooms with balcony. Two 1-bedroom suites, $240-$249; 2 stories; interior corridors; heated pool, whirlpool. **Dining:** Restaurant; 6:30-10:30 am, 11:30-1:30 & 5:30-10 pm, Sat & Sun 7 am-1 & 5:30-10 pm; $8-$13; cocktails; Room service 5:30 pm-10 pm.

Motor Inn

Cards: AE, CB, DI, DS, JC, MC, VI. **Special Amenities: Free newspaper.** *(See color ad starting on p 646 & ad p 119)*

VAN NUYS (See map p. 560; index p. 549)

LODGINGS

AIRTEL PLAZA HOTEL   Rates Subject to Change   **Phone:** (818)997-7676   **34**

Mon-Thurs   1P: $94   2P/1B: $94   2P/2B: $94   XP: $10   F18

Fri-Sun   1P: $69   2P/1B: $69   2P/2B: $69   XP: $10   F18

Hotel

Location: 0.8 mi w of I-405; exit Sherman Way. 7277 Valjean Ave at Sherman Way 91406. Fax: 818/785-8864. **Terms:** Weekly/monthly rates. **Facility:** 268 rooms. Adjacent to Van Nuys Airport. Spacious rooms. 3-5 stories; interior corridors; heated pool, whirlpools. **Dining:** Dining room, coffee shop; 6 am-10 pm; $10-$18; cocktails; DJ Fri & Sat night. **Services:** giftshop; area transportation, within 5 mi. **Recreation:** parking spaces for private planes. **Some Rooms:** whirlpools. **Cards:** AE, CB, DI, DS, MC, VI. *(See ad p 648)*

As a AAA member, take advantage of **discounts on admissions** to more than 1,200 attractions throughout North America, **plus discounts at restaurants, hotels, ski resorts, seasonal attractions and more**.

(See map p. 560)

TRAVELODGE VAN NUYS-SEPULVEDA   **Phone:** (818)787-5400   33
Ⓐ Ⓢ   All Year [CP]   1P: $49   2P/1B: $55   2P/2B: $55   XP: $6   F17
◆   **Location:** 0.8 mi se of I-405, Sherman Way exit. 6909 Sepulveda Blvd 91405. Fax: 818/782-0239.
Motel   **Terms:** Weekly rates. **Facility:** 74 rooms. 3 stories; interior corridors; small pool. **Cards:** AE, CB, DI, DS, JC,
         MC, VI. **Special Amenities:** Free breakfast and free local telephone calls. *(See color ad below)*

🄢 🄫 ➤ 🍴 🖃 🖨 🔒 ⊠

RESTAURANT

MATTERHORN CHEF RESTAURANT   **Lunch:** $8-$14   **Dinner:** $8-$20   **Phone:** 818/781-4330   22
◆◆   **Location:** Just w of Woodman Ave. 13726 Oxnard St 91401. **Hours:** 11 am-10 pm, Fri & Sat-11 pm, Sun 4
German   pm-9 pm. **Closed:** 12/25, 1/1 & Mon. **Reservations:** accepted. **Features:** casual dress; children's menu;
         carryout; cocktails & lounge; valet parking; a la carte. Old World atmosphere, nice selection of German,
Swiss & Continental dishes. **Cards:** AE, CB, DI, DS, MC, VI.

⊠

VENICE (See map p. 558; index p. 554)

LODGINGS

HOLIDAY INN EXPRESS-MARINA DEL REY/VENICE   **Phone:** (310)821-4455   211
Ⓐ Ⓢ   6/1-9/15 [CP]   1P: $89- 99   2P/1B: $89- 99 2P/2B: $89- 99 XP: $10   F12
◆◆◆   2/1-5/31 & 9/16-1/31 [CP] 1P: $79- 89 2P/1B: $79- 89 2P/2B: $79- 89 XP: $10   F12
Motel   **Location:** 0.5 mi w of Lincoln Ave. 737 Washington Blvd 90292. Fax: 310/821-8098. **Terms:** Weekly rates.
         Facility: 68 rooms. Nicely decorated suites & hotel rooms. 3 stories; interior/exterior corridors; small heated
         pool, whirlpool. **Cards:** AE, CB, DI, DS, JC, MC, VI. **Special Amenities:** Free breakfast.
(See color ad p 619)

🄢 🕐 ➤ 🛌 🍴 🖃 🖨 🔒 ⊠

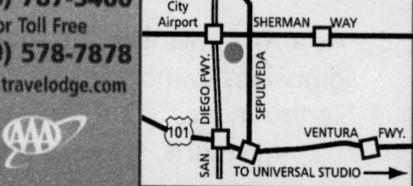

(See map p. 558)

INN AT VENICE BEACH   **Phone:** (310)821-2557 212

(AAA) SAVE   6/1-9/15 [CP]   1P: $99- 129   2P/1B: $99- 129 2P/2B: $99- 129 XP: $10   F12

           2/1-5/31 & 9/16-1/31 [CP] 1P: $89- 109   2P/1B: $89- 109 2P/2B: $99- 119 XP: $10   F12

◆◆◆   **Location:** 327 Washington Blvd 90291. Fax: 310/827-0289. **Terms:** Reserv deposit. **Facility:** 43 rooms. 2 blks

Motel   to beach. Charming, European ambiance. 5 suites with loft bedroom; 3 stories; interior/exterior corridors.

         Recreation: in-room video games. **Cards:** AE, CB, DI, DS, JC, MC, VI. *(See color ad below)*

LINCOLN INN   **Phone:** (310)822-0686 213

(AAA) SAVE   All Year [CP]   1P: $75- 79   2P/1B: $85- 89 2P/2B: $95- 99 XP: $10   F12

◆◆   **Location:** On SR 1, just n of Washington Blvd. 2447 Lincoln Blvd 90291. Fax: 310/822-3136. **Terms:** Reserv

Motel   deposit; weekly/monthly rates, in winter. **Facility:** 30 rooms. 2 stories; interior corridors. **Some Rooms:** color

         TV, whirlpools. **Cards:** AE, CB, DI, DS, MC, VI. **Special Amenities:** Free breakfast.

MARINA PACIFIC HOTEL & SUITES   Rates Subject to Change   **Phone:** (310)452-1111 216

◆◆   5/15-9/15   1P: $130- 190   2P/1B: $140- 200 2P/2B: $140- 200 XP: $10   F10

Motor Inn   2/1-5/14 & 9/16-1/31   1P: $110- 150   2P/1B: $120- 160 2P/2B: $120- 160 XP: $10   F10

         Location: 1697 Pacific Ave 90291. Fax: 310/452-5479. **Terms:** Reserv deposit. **Facility:** 92 rooms. At a busy,

beach location. Some rooms with ocean view. 35 suites with kitchen & gas fireplace, $150-$250; 3 stories; interior corridors.

All Rooms: combo or shower baths. **Cards:** AE, CB, DI, DS, MC, VI.

RAMADA LIMITED   **Phone:** (310)821-5086 219

(AAA) SAVE   All Year [CP]   1P: $79- 89   2P/1B: $79- 89 2P/2B: $89- 99 XP: $10   F14

◆◆◆   **Location:** Just w of Lincoln Blvd (SR1). 3130 Washington Blvd 90292. Fax: 310/821-6167. **Terms:** Reserv

Motel   deposit, 3 day notice. **Facility:** 33 rooms. 1 kitchenette unit with refrigerator & microwave $99; 2 stories; ex-

         terior corridors; whirlpool. **Some Rooms:** efficiency. **Cards:** AE, CB, DI, DS, JC, MC, VI. **Special Amenities:**

         Free breakfast and free newspaper. *(See color ad p 619)*

THE VENICE BEACH HOUSE   **Phone:** 310/823-1966 217

(AAA) SAVE   Fri-Sun [CP]   1P: $95- 165   2P/1B: $95- 165 2P/2B: $95   XP: $20

◆◆◆   Mon-Thurs [CP]   1P: $95- 145   2P/1B: $95- 145 2P/2B: $95   XP: $20

Historic Bed   **Location:** Just n of Washington Blvd, just w of Pacific Blvd. 15 30th Ave 90291. Fax: 310/823-1842.

& Breakfast   **Terms:** Reserv deposit, 5 day notice; handling fee imposed; weekly rates. **Facility:** 9 rooms. 1/4 block to

         beach. 1911 California Craftsman home. Parking in rear on 29th Pl. 2 stories; interior corridors; designated

         smoking area. **Cards:** AE, JC, VI.

RESTAURANT

72 MARKET ST   **Lunch:** $8-$12   **Dinner:** $13-$26   **Phone:** 310/392-8720 128

◆◆   **Location:** Just w of Pacific Ave. 72 Market St 90291. **Hours:** 11:30 am-2:30 & 6-10 pm, Fri-11 pm, Sat 6

American   pm-11 pm, Sun 5:30 pm-9:30 pm. Closed: 12/25 for lunch. **Reservations:** suggested. **Features:** casual

dress; health conscious menu; cocktails & lounge; fee for valet parking; a la carte. A popular restaurant

featuring classic American cuisine. Well-known for meatloaf & chili. **Cards:** AE, DI, MC, VI.

WALNUT—29,100

LODGING

HOLIDAY INN EXPRESS   Guaranteed Rates   **Phone:** (909)594-9999

◆◆◆   5/1-8/31 [CP]   1P: $79- 109   2P/1B: $84- 114 2P/2B: $89- 129 XP: $5-10   F17

Motel   2/1-4/30 & 9/1-1/31 [CP] 1P: $69- 99   2P/1B: $74- 104 2P/2B: $79- 119 XP: $5-10   F17

         Location: 0.3 mi s of SR 60, exit Fairway Dr. 1170 Fairway Dr 91789. Fax: 909/594-9343. **Facility:** 92 rooms.

2 stories; interior corridors; heated pool. **Services:** area transportation. **Cards:** AE, DI, DS, JC, MC, VI.

WEST COVINA—96,100

LODGINGS

BEST WESTERN WEST COVINA INN   Phone: (626)915-1611
(AAA) SAVE   All Year [CP]   1P: $56- 66 2P/1B: $59- 69 2P/2B: $69- 79 XP: $6   F12
♦♦♦   **Location:** Adjacent to I-10, exit Grand Ave. 3275 E Garvey Ave N 91791. Fax: 626/332-6977.
Motel   **Terms:** Weekly/monthly rates. **Facility:** 126 rooms. 8 whirlpool rms, extra charge; 4 stories; interior corridors;
                 whirlpool. **Dining:** Restaurant nearby. **All Rooms:** combo or shower baths. **Cards:** AE, CB, DI, DS, MC, VI.
                 Special Amenities: Free breakfast and free local telephone calls.

COMFORT INN   Phone: (626)915-6077
(AAA) SAVE   All Year [CP]   1P: $55- 75 2P/1B: $55- 75 2P/2B: $65- 99 XP: $5   F16
♦♦   **Location:** S side of I-10 between Barranca & Citrus Ave exits. 2804 E Garvey Ave S 91791.
Motel   Fax: 626/339-4587. **Terms:** Pets, designated rooms. **Facility:** 58 rooms. Whirlpool rms $129; 3 stories;
                 interior/exterior corridors; small heated pool, whirlpool. **Some Rooms:** whirlpools. **Cards:** AE, CB, DI, DS,
                 MC, VI. **Special Amenities:** Free breakfast and free room upgrade (subject to availability with
advanced reservations).

HAMPTON INN   Rates Subject to Change   Phone: (626)967-5800
♦♦♦   All Year [CP]   1P: $59- 64 2P/1B: $64- 69 2P/2B: $64- 69
Motel   **Location:** Adjacent to I-10, exit Barranca St. 3145 E Garvey Ave N 91791. Fax: 626/331-8819. **Facility:** 126
                 rooms. 5 stories; interior corridors; heated pool. **Cards:** AE, CB, DI, DS, MC, VI.

HOLIDAY INN-WEST COVINA   Phone: (626)966-8311
(AAA) SAVE   All Year [BP]   1P: $69   2P/1B: $69   2P/2B: $69   XP: $10
♦♦   **Location:** Adjacent to I-10, exit Barranca St. 3223 E Garvey Ave N 91791. Fax: 626/339-2850. **Terms:** Pets,
Motor Inn $20 extra charge. **Facility:** 134 rooms. 5 stories; interior corridors; heated pool. **Dining:** Dining room; 6 am-2
                 & 5-10 pm, Sat & Sun from 6:30 am; $9-$15; cocktails. **Cards:** AE, CB, DI, DS, JC, MC, VI.
                 Special Amenities: Free breakfast and free room upgrade (subject to availability with advanced
reservations). *(See color ad below)*

RESTAURANT

VILLA TEPEYAC   Lunch: $6-$13   Dinner: $8-$13   Phone: 626/339-5058
♦♦   **Location:** South side of I-10, between Azusa Ave & Citrus Ave exits. 2200 E Garvey Ave S 91790.
Mexican   **Hours:** 11 am-10 pm, Sat & Sun from 9 am. Closed: 12/25. **Features:** casual dress; children's menu;
                 cocktails & lounge. Family owned & operated restaurant with a large selection of beef, seafood &
combination plates. Smoke free premises. **Cards:** AE, MC, VI.

WEST HOLLYWOOD—36,100   (See map p. 558; index p. 552)

LODGINGS

THE ARGYLE   Rates Subject to Change   Phone: (323)654-7100   ⎯144⎯
♦♦♦   All Year   1P: $199   2P/1B: $219   2P/2B: $219   XP: $25   F16
Historic Hotel   **Location:** Just e of La Cienega Blvd. 8358 Sunset Blvd 90069. Fax: 323/654-9287. **Terms:** Reserv deposit,
                 3 day notice; handling fee imposed. **Facility:** 64 rooms. An art deco landmark. 16 stories; interior corridors;
heated pool. Fee: parking. **Cards:** AE, DI, DS, MC, VI.

BEST WESTERN SUNSET PLAZA HOTEL   Phone: (323)654-0750   ⎯138⎯
(AAA) SAVE   All Year   1P: $85- 115 2P/1B: $85- 115 2P/2B: $85- 115 XP: $10   F12
♦♦♦   **Location:** Just e of La Cienega Blvd. 8400 Sunset Blvd 90069. Fax: 323/656-4158. **Terms:** Reserv deposit;
Motel   weekly/monthly rates. **Facility:** 88 rooms. Attractively decorated rooms, very clean. 6 one-bedroom apart-
                 ments, $140-$165 for 2 persons; 3 stories; interior corridors; heated pool. **Some Rooms:** 28 kitchens.
(See ad p 579) **Cards:** AE, CB, DI, DS, JC, MC, VI. **Special Amenities:** Free breakfast and free newspaper.

(See map p. 558)

HYATT WEST HOLLYWOOD
AAA SAVE
◆◆◆
Hotel
Phone: (323)656-1234 — **137**
All Year   1P: $174- 249   2P/1B: $199- 274   2P/2B: $199- 274   XP: $25   F18
Location: Just e of La Cienega Blvd. 8401 Sunset Blvd 90069. **Fax:** 323/650-7024. **Facility:** 262 rooms. Full service hotel located close to many Los Angeles entertainment centers. 14 stories; interior corridors; rooftop pool. **Fee:** parking. **Dining:** Dining room; 6:30 am-11:30 pm, Sun-10 pm; $10-$20; cocktails. **Services:** giftshop. **Cards:** AE, CB, DI, DS, JC, MC, VI. *(See color ad p 565)*

LE MONTROSE SUITE HOTEL DE GRAN LUXE   Rates Subject to Change   Phone: (310)855-1115 — **142**
◆◆◆
Hotel
All Year   1P: $270- 440   2P/1B: $270- 440   2P/2B: $270- 440
Location: Just s of Sunset Blvd, just e of Doheny. 900 Hammond St at Cynthia 90069. **Fax:** 310/657-9192. **Terms:** Reserv deposit. **Facility:** 130 rooms. Spacious, attractively furnished rooms & suites. Located in residential area. All rooms with fireplace, video games & internet. 1 & 2 bedroom suites, $500; 6 stories; interior corridors; 1 lighted tennis court. **Fee:** parking. **Recreation:** bicycles. **Some Rooms:** 80 efficiencies. **Cards:** AE, CB, DI, MC, VI.

LE PARC HOTEL   Rates Subject to Change   Phone: 310/855-8888 — **140**
◆◆◆
Motor Inn
All Year   1P: $225- 275   2P/1B: $225- 275   2P/2B: $225- 275   XP: $25
Location: Just n of Melrose Ave & just w of La Cienega Blvd. 733 N West Knoll Dr 90069. **Fax:** 310/659-7812. **Facility:** 154 rooms. Spacious, comfortably furnished suites. Fireplace in all rooms. Residential area. 3 stories; interior corridors; heated pool; 1 lighted tennis court. **Some Rooms:** 44 efficiencies. **Cards:** AE, CB, DI, DS, MC, VI.

LE REVE HOTEL   Phone: (310)854-1114 — **139**
AAA SAVE
◆◆◆
Motel
All Year   1P: $129- 205   2P/1B: $129- 205   2P/2B: $129- 205   XP: $20   F11
Location: Just n of Santa Monica Blvd; just s of Sunset Blvd. 8822 Cynthia St at Larrabee 90069. **Fax:** 310/657-2623. **Terms:** Reserv deposit; monthly rates. **Facility:** 80 rooms. Rooms & 1-bedroom units with living room; most with gas fireplace. Located in a residential area. 4 stories; interior corridors; whirlpool, small rooftop heated pool. **Fee:** parking. **Some Rooms:** 23 efficiencies. **Cards:** AE, CB, DI, DS, JC, MC, VI.

PARK SUNSET HOTEL   Phone: 323-654-6470 — **135**
AAA SAVE
◆◆
Motor Inn
All Year   1P: $74   2P/1B: $79   2P/2B: $79   XP: $10
Location: Just e of La Cienega Blvd. 8462 Sunset Blvd 90069. **Fax:** 323/654-5918. **Facility:** 82 rooms. Pleasant rooms with traditional decor. 18 one-bedroom suites with microwave, refrigerator & coffeemaker, $139; 3 stories; interior corridors; heated pool. **Dining:** Restaurant; 7 am-11 pm; $6-$12; wine/beer only. **All Rooms:** combo or shower baths. **Some Rooms:** 18 kitchens. **Cards:** AE, CB, DI, DS, JC, MC, VI.

RAMADA PLAZA HOTEL   Phone: (310)652-6400 — **133**
AAA SAVE
◆◆◆
Motor Inn
All Year   1P: $149- 249   2P/1B: $149- 249   2P/2B: $149- 249   XP: $15   F16
Location: Just w of La Cienega Blvd. 8585 Santa Monica Blvd 90069. **Fax:** 310/652-2135. **Facility:** 175 rooms. Contemporary decor. 22 loft suites, $209-$350; 3 stories; interior corridors; heated pool. **Fee:** parking. **Dining:** Restaurant; 6:30 am-midnight; $7-$15; cocktails. **Recreation:** video games in all rooms. **All Rooms:** extended cable TV. **Cards:** AE, CB, DI, DS, JC, MC, VI. **Special Amenities:** Early check-in/late check-out and free newspaper.

SUMMERFIELD SUITES HOTEL   Rates Subject to Change   Phone: 310/657-7400 — **143**
◆◆◆
Motor Inn
All Year [BP]   1P: $169- 199   2P/1B: $169- 199   2P/2B: $169- 199
Location: 3 blks s of Sunset Blvd, just n of Santa Monica Blvd. 1000 Westmount Dr 90069. **Fax:** 310/854-6744. **Terms:** Reserv deposit. **Facility:** 109 rooms. 1-bedroom suites with living room & gas fireplace. Located in residential area. 4 stories; interior corridors; heated pool. **Fee:** parking. **Services:** giftshop. **Some Rooms:** 75 kitchens. **Cards:** AE, CB, DI, DS, JC, MC, VI.

SUNSET MARQUIS HOTEL & VILLAS   Rates Subject to Change   Phone: (310)657-1333 — **141**
◆◆◆◆
Suite Motor Inn
All Year   1P: $275-1500   2P/1B: $275-1500   2P/2B: $275-1500   XP: $35   F12
Location: Just s of Sunset Blvd. 1200 N Alta Loma Rd 90069. **Fax:** 310/657-1330. **Facility:** 114 rooms. 1-bedroom units with separate living room. Beautifully landscaped terraced grounds. Located in residential area. Recording studio on premises. Private 1- & 2-bedroom villas, $450-$1200. Fax machines in all villas; 3 stories; interior corridors; heated pool. **Services:** giftshop. **Some Rooms:** 9 kitchens. **Cards:** AE, DI, MC, VI.

WYNDHAM BEL AGE HOTEL   Rates Subject to Change   Phone: (310)854-1111 — **134**
◆◆◆
Suite Hotel
Fri & Sat [BP]   1P: $214   2P/1B: $214   2P/2B: $214   XP: $10-20   F18
Sun-Thurs [EP]   1P: $209   2P/1B: $209   2P/2B: $209   XP: $10-20   F18
Location: Just s of Sunset Blvd. 1020 N San Vicente Blvd 90069. **Fax:** 310/289-7763. **Facility:** 200 rooms. European elegance. 1-bedroom suites with living room. Large collection of sculptures & paintings throughout hotel. Beautifully landscaped. Rooftop pool & roof garden with spectacular city view. 10 stories; interior corridors; heated pool. **Fee:** parking. **Services:** giftshop. **Cards:** AE, CB, DI, DS, JC, MC, VI.

RESTAURANTS

DIAGHILEV   Dinner: $50-$75   Phone: 310/854-1111 — **73**
◆◆◆◆
Ethnic
Location: Just s of Sunset Blvd; in Wyndham Bel Age Hotel. 1020 N San Vincente Blvd 90069. **Hours:** 6:30 pm-10 pm. **Closed:** Sun & Mon. **Reservations:** suggested. **Features:** formal attire; cocktails & lounge; entertainment; valet parking; a la carte. An elegant dining room serving superbly prepared Russian cuisine. Smoke free premises. **Cards:** AE, CB, DI, DS, JC, MC, VI.

FENIX AT THE ARGYLE   Lunch: $8-$18   Dinner: $12-$27   Phone: 323/848-6677 — **76**
◆◆◆
French
Location: Just e of La Cienega Blvd; in The Argyle. 8358 Sunset Blvd 96069. **Hours:** 6 am-11 pm, Fri & Sat-midnight. **Reservations:** suggested. **Features:** semi-formal attire; Sunday brunch; cocktails & lounge; fee for valet parking; a la carte. French style menu with California influence. Pleasant dining room & patio with a full city view. Smoke free premises. **Cards:** AE, CB, DI, DS, MC, VI.

(See map p. 558)

LE DOME
◆◆◆
French

Dinner: $18-$26   Phone: 310/659-6919 ⑦②
Location: 2 blks w of La Cienega Blvd. 8720 Sunset Blvd 90069. **Hours:** noon-11:45 pm, Sat from 6:30 pm. Closed major holidays & Sun. **Reservations:** suggested. **Features:** semi-formal attire; cocktails & lounge; street parking & fee for valet parking; a la carte. Well known popular French restaurant with a bistro menu.
Cards: AE, DI, MC, VI.
                                                                                              ⊠

PALM RESTAURANT
◆◆
American
VI.

Lunch: $15-$20   Dinner: $35-$50   Phone: 310/550-8811 ⑦⑤
Location: 2 blks w of Robertson. 9001 Santa Monica Blvd 90069. **Hours:** noon-10:30 pm, Sat 5 pm-10:30 pm, Sun 5 pm-9:30 pm. Closed major holidays. **Reservations:** suggested. **Features:** casual dress; cocktails; fee for valet parking; a la carte. Lively, club-like atmosphere. Smoke free premises. **Cards:** AE, CB, DI, MC,
                                                                                              ⊠

WHITTIER—77,700

LODGINGS

DAYS INN WHITTIER
AAA SAVE
◆◆
Motel

                                                                          Phone: (562)944-4760
All Year [CP]   1P: $48- 60   2P/1B: $54- 65 2P/2B: $69- 99   XP: $10   F12
Location: On Telegraph Rd, just w of Colima Rd. 14330 Telegraph Rd 90604. Fax: 562/944-4376. **Terms:** Reserv deposit; weekly rates. **Facility:** 54 rooms. 8 whirlpool rms, extra charge; 2 stories; exterior corridors. **Cards:** AE, CB, DI, DS, JC, MC, VI. **Special Amenities:** Early check-in/late check-out and free room upgrade (subject to availability with advanced reservations).

                              ⑤ ⓓ ⑭ ⋙ ⌂ ⑭ ▣ □ 🖥 ⊠

VAGABOND INN
AAA SAVE
◆◆
Motel

                                                                          Phone: (562)698-9701
All Year [CP]   1P: $66   2P/1B: $71   2P/2B: $77   XP: $5   F18
Location: 2 mi e of I-605. 14125 E Whittier Blvd 90605. Fax: 562/698-8716. **Terms:** Pets, $5 extra charge. **Facility:** 49 rooms. 3 stories; exterior corridors; heated pool. **Cards:** AE, CB, DI, DS, MC, VI. **Special Amenities:** Free breakfast and free local telephone calls. ⑤ 🐕 ⑭ ⋙ ▣ 🖥 🖥 ⊠

WHITTIER HILTON
◆◆◆
Hotel

Guaranteed Rates   Phone: (562)945-8511
All Year   1P: $99- 135   2P/1B: $109- 145 2P/2B: $109- 145 XP: $10   F18
Location: In the Uptown Whittier Village area, 0.6 mi n of Whittier Blvd. 7320 Greenleaf Ave 90602. Fax: 562/945-6018. **Facility:** 202 rooms. 8 stories; interior corridors; heated pool. **Services:** giftshop.
Cards: AE, CB, DI, DS, JC, MC, VI. *(See ad p 119)*

                    SAVE ⑤ ⑭ 🄿 ⋙ ⑪ ⌂ 🖐 ▣ □ 🖥 🖥 ♿ ⊠

RESTAURANT

RESTAURANT BABALOO
◆◆
Ethnic

Lunch: $7-$8   Dinner: $10-$14   Phone: 562/945-4259
Location: In Uptown Whittier. 7051 Greenleaf Ave 90602. **Hours:** 11 am-9:30 pm, Fri, Sat & Sun-11 pm. Closed major holidays. **Features:** casual dress; beer & wine only; street parking; a la carte. A small restaurant featuring a selection of Cuban & Caribbean cuisine. Smoke free premises. **Cards:** AE, MC, VI.
                                                                                              ⊠

WILMINGTON—40,000   (See map p. 561; index p. 549)

LODGING

BEST WESTERN LOS ANGELES WORLDPORT
AAA SAVE
◆◆◆
Motel

                                                          Phone: (310)834-3400 ④⑥
All Year [CP]   1P: $57- 125   2P/1B: $64- 135 2P/2B: $64- 135 XP: $2-7   F12
Location: Just w of I-110; exit Pacific Coast Hwy. 1402 W Pacific Coast Hwy 90744. Fax: 310/835-2225. **Terms:** Weekly rates. **Facility:** 72 rooms. 4 stories; exterior corridors; heated pool, whirlpool. **Dining:** Restaurant nearby. **Cards:** AE, CB, DI, JC, MC, VI. **Special Amenities:** Free breakfast and free newspaper. *(See color ad below)*   ⑤ ⑭ ⋙ ⑪ ⌂ ▣ □ 🖥 🖥 ⊠

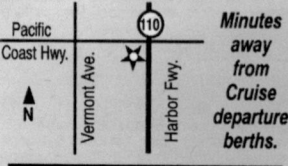

WOODLAND HILLS   (See map p. 560; index p. 550)

LODGINGS

HOLIDAY INN-WOODLAND HILLS   Phone: (818)883-6110   **51**
Sun-Thurs [BP]   1P: $99- 109   2P/1B: $109- 119   2P/2B: $109- 119   XP: $10   F18
Fri & Sat [BP]   1P: $89- 99   2P/1B: $99- 109   2P/2B: $99- 109   XP: $10   F18
Location: Adjacent to US 101, DeSoto St exit. 21101 Ventura Blvd 91364. Fax: 818/340-6550. **Terms:** Small
pets only, $100 dep req. **Facility:** 124 rooms. 6 stories; interior corridors. **Dining:** Dining room; 6:30 am-2 &
5-10 pm; $9-$12; cocktails. **Cards:** AE, CB, DI, DS, JC, MC, VI. **Special Amenities: Early check-in/late
check-out and free room upgrade (subject to availability with advanced reservations).**

VAGABOND INN   Phone: (818)347-8080   **52**
All Year [CP]   1P: $68   2P/1B: $73   2P/2B: $80   XP: $5   F18
Location: Adjacent to US 101, Winnetka Ave exit. 20157 Ventura Blvd 91364. Fax: 818/716-5333.
Terms: Small pets only, $5 extra charge. **Facility:** 96 rooms. 3 stories; exterior corridors; heated pool, whirl-
pool. **Dining:** Coffee shop; 24 hours; $5-$8; wine/beer only. **All Rooms:** extended cable TV. **Cards:** AE, CB,
DI, DS, MC, VI. **Special Amenities: Free breakfast and free local telephone calls.**

WARNER CENTER MARRIOTT HOTEL   Phone: (818)887-4800   **54**
Sun-Thurs   1P: $155   2P/1B: $155   2P/2B: $155
Fri & Sat   1P: $99   2P/1B: $99   2P/2B: $99
Location: 0.8 mi n of US 101, Topanga Canyon Blvd exit. 21850 Oxnard St 91367. Fax: 818/340-5893.
Terms: Monthly rates. **Facility:** 463 rooms. 17 stories; interior corridors; heated indoor pool, saunas, whirlpool.
Fee: parking. **Dining:** Dining room; 6:30 am-11 pm, Fri & Sat-midnight; $6-$20; cocktails. **Services:** giftshop.
Cards: AE, CB, DI, DS, JC, MC, VI.

WOODLAND HILLS HILTON & TOWERS   Rates Subject to Change   Phone: (818)595-1000   **53**
All Year   1P: $169   2P/1B: $169   2P/2B: $169   XP: $10   F18
Location: Just s of Victory Blvd. 6360 Canoga Ave 91367. Fax: 818/595-1090. **Terms:** Reserv deposit.
Facility: 322 rooms. Spacious lobby. 14 stories; interior corridors. Fee: parking. **Services:** giftshop.
Cards: AE, CB, DI, DS, JC, MC, VI. *(See ad p 119)*

RESTAURANTS

ADAGIO RISTORANTE   Dinner: $15-$25   Phone: 818/225-0533   **32**
Location: 0.5 mi w of US 101, Westbound exit Shoup, eastbound exit Topanga Canyon Blvd. 22841 Ventura
Northern Blvd 91364. **Hours:** 5:30 pm-10 pm, Thurs also 11:30 am-2 pm. Closed major holidays & Mon.
Italian **Reservations:** suggested; weekends. **Features:** casual dress; cocktails; street parking; a la carte. Selection
of pasta, veal, chicken, seafood, beef & lamb. Smoke free premises. **Cards:** AE, MC, VI.

BOB BURNS RESTAURANT   Lunch: $10-$15   Dinner: $15-$30   Phone: 818/883-2145   **31**
Location: Just e of Topanga Canyon Blvd. 21821 Oxnard St 91367. **Hours:** 11:30 am-10 pm, Fri & Sat-11
American pm, Sun 10:30 am-10 pm. Closed: 12/25. **Features:** casual dress; Sunday brunch; children's menu; cocktails
& lounge; entertainment. Attractive Scottish decor. Nice selection of seafood, steaks, prime rib, chicken, lamb
& pasta. Sandwich bar $5.25-$7.45. Smoke free premises. **Cards:** AE, CB, DI, DS, MC, VI.

PIACERE   Lunch: $8-$16   Dinner: $9-$20   Phone: 818/704-1185   **28**
Location: Just w of Topanga Canyon Blvd. 22160 Ventura Blvd 91364. **Hours:** 11:30 am-3 & 5-10 pm,
Italian Sat-11 pm, Sun from 10 am-3 & 5-10 pm. Closed: 1/1 & 12/25. **Features:** casual dress; Sunday brunch;
cocktails & lounge; fee for valet parking; a la carte. Very attractive restaurant. Outdoor patio dining weather
permitting. **Cards:** AE, DI, MC, VI.

PLUM TREE INN   Lunch: $7-$10   Dinner: $10-$16   Phone: 818/888-6001   **29**
Location: 0.6 mi nw of US 101, Winnetka Ave exit. 20461 Ventura Ave 91364. **Hours:** 11:30 am-10 pm, Fri
Chinese & Sat to 11 pm. Closed: 11/25. **Reservations:** suggested; weekends. **Features:** casual dress; carryout;
cocktails & lounge; fee for valet parking; a la carte. Excellent selection of traditional Chinese dishes. Delivery
also avail. Smoke free premises. **Cards:** AE, MC, VI.

This ends listings for the Los Angeles Vicinity.
The following page resumes the alphabetical listings of
cities in California.

LOS BANOS—14,500

LODGINGS

BEST WESTERN JOHN JAY INN
Phone: (209)827-0954
AAA SAVE
All Year [CP]   1P: $45- 80   2P/1B: $50- 85 2P/2B: $50- 90 XP: $6   F12
◆◆   **Location:** On SR 152. 301 W Pacheco Blvd 93635. Fax: 209/827-8891. **Terms:** Reserv deposit, 3 day
Motor Inn   notice; small pets only, $25 dep req. **Facility:** 57 rooms. Colonial exterior. 3 stories; interior corridors; sauna,
whirlpool. **Dining:** Coffee shop nearby. **Cards:** AE, CB, DI, DS, JC, MC, VI. **Special Amenities: Free
breakfast and free local telephone calls.**

REGENCY INN
Phone: (209)826-3871
AAA SAVE
All Year   1P: $35- 40   2P/1B: $42- 45 2P/2B: $47- 50 XP: $5   F12
◆   **Location:** On SR 152. 349 W Pacheco Blvd 93635. Fax: 209/826-2063. **Terms:** Weekly rates; small pets
Motor Inn   only, $3 extra charge, $20 dep req. **Facility:** 38 rooms. 2 stories; exterior corridors; small pool.
Dining: Coffee shop nearby. **All Rooms:** combo or shower baths. **Cards:** AE, CB, DI, DS, MC, VI.
Special Amenities: Free local telephone calls.

LOS GATOS—27,400

LODGINGS

LA HACIENDA INN   Rates Subject to Change   **Phone:** (408)354-9230
AAA
All Year [CP]   1P: $100- 150   2P/1B: $100- 150 2P/2B: $110   XP: $10   F6
◆◆◆   **Location:** 1 mi w on SR 9. 18840 Saratoga-Los Gatos Rd 95030. Fax: 408/354-7590. **Terms:** Reserv
Motor Inn   deposit. **Facility:** 20 rooms. Attractively landscaped. Some large units with fireplace, few studios. 1 story; ex-
terior corridors; whirlpool. **Dining:** Restaurant nearby. **All Rooms:** combo or shower baths. **Some Rooms:** 3
kitchens. **Cards:** AE, CB, DI, DS, JC, MC, VI.

LODGE AT VILLA FELICE
Phone: (408)395-6710
AAA SAVE
All Year [CP]   1P: $130- 240   2P/1B: $130- 240 2P/2B: $130- 240 XP: $10   F17
◆◆◆◆   **Location:** Just w of SR 17; Lark Ave or Los Gatos exits. 15350 S Winchester Blvd 95030.
Motel   Fax: 408/354-1826. **Terms:** Reserv deposit; monthly rates; package plans. **Facility:** 33 rooms. Many rooms
with view of Lake Vasona. Few fireplaces. 2 stories; interior corridors; small pool, whirlpool.
All Rooms: combo or shower baths. **Some Rooms:** kitchen, whirlpools. **Cards:** AE, CB, DI, MC, VI.

LOS GATOS LODGE
Phone: (408)354-3300
AAA SAVE
All Year   1P: $109- 150   2P/1B: $109- 150 2P/2B: $109- 150
◆◆◆   **Location:** Just e of SR 17, E Los Gatos exit. 50 Los Gatos-Saratoga Rd 95032. Fax: 408/354-5451.
Motor Inn   **Terms:** Small pets only. **Facility:** 128 rooms. Expansive landscaped grounds. Balconies & patios. 2 stories;
interior/exterior corridors; putting green; whirlpool. **Dining:** Restaurant; 7 am-9:30 pm, Fri & Sat-10 pm;
$10-$25; cocktails. **Recreation:** bocciball. **All Rooms:** combo or shower baths. **Some Rooms:** 9
efficiencies. **Cards:** AE, DI, DS, MC, VI. **Special Amenities: Free newspaper and preferred room (subject to availability
with advanced reservations).**

LOS GATOS MOTOR INN   Rates Subject to Change   **Phone:** (408)356-9191
AAA
All Year [CP]   1P: $79   2P/1B: $79   2P/2B: $84   XP: $5   F12
◆◆   **Location:** Just e of SR 17, E Los Gatos exit. 55 Los Gatos-Saratoga Rd 95032. Fax: 408/356-7502.
Motel   **Facility:** 60 rooms. Quiet location. 2 stories; exterior corridors. **Dining:** Restaurant nearby.
All Rooms: combo or shower baths. **Cards:** AE, CB, DI, MC, VI.

LOS GATOS VILLAGE INN   Rates Subject to Change   **Phone:** (408)354-8120
AAA
All Year   1P: $75- 94   2P/1B: $80- 99 2P/2B: $80- 99 XP: $5-10   F7
◆◆   **Location:** Exit SR 17 W via Saratoga-Los Gatos Rd. 235 W Main St 95030. Fax: 408/354-8121.
Motel   **Terms:** Reserv deposit. **Facility:** 23 rooms. Some rooms with balcony. Garden area with fountain. 1 family unit,
$84-$109 for up to 5 persons; 2 stories; exterior corridors. **All Rooms:** combo or shower baths. **Cards:** AE,
CB, DI, DS, JC, MC, VI.

TOLL HOUSE HOTEL   Rates Subject to Change   **Phone:** 408/395-7070
◆◆◆   All Year [CP]   1P: $144- 154   2P/1B: $154- 164 2P/2B: $154- 164 XP: $12   F
Hotel   **Location:** 0.3 mi w of I-880/SR 17; SR 9 exit. 140 S Santa Cruz Ave 95030. Fax: 408/395-3730. **Facility:** 97
rooms. Many rooms with balcony. 3 stories; interior corridors. **Cards:** AE, CB, DI, DS, MC, VI.

RESTAURANT

LA HACIENDA RESTAURANT   **Lunch:** $10-$15   **Dinner:** $16-$25   **Phone:** 408/354-6669
◆◆◆   **Location:** 1 mi w on SR 9 in; La Hacienda Inn. 18840 Saratoga-Los Gatos Rd 95030. **Hours:** 11 am-2:30 &
Continental 5-10 pm, Fri & Sat-11 pm. Closed: 9/1 & 12/25. **Reservations:** suggested. **Features:** semi-formal attire;
Sunday brunch; cocktails & lounge; entertainment; a la carte. Italian specialties & pasta. Smoke free
premises. **Cards:** AE, CB, DI, DS, MC, VI.

LOS OLIVOS—300

LODGING

FESS PARKER'S WINE COUNTRY INN   Rates Subject to Change   **Phone:** (805)688-7788
AAA
All Year   1P: $200- 350   2P/1B: $200- 350 2P/2B: $200- 350 XP: $15   F12
◆◆◆◆   **Location:** 0.5 mi s of SR 154. 2860 Grand Ave 93441 (PO Box 849). Fax: 805/688-1942. **Terms:** 2 night
Country Inn min stay, weekends. **Facility:** 21 rooms. Charming country inn atmosphere. Spacious, beautifully decorated
rooms with gas fireplaces. Located in the center of town within walking distance of shops & art galleries. 1 two-
bedroom unit. 2 stories; interior/exterior corridors; smoke free premises; heated pool, whirlpool. **Dining:** The
Vintage Room, see separate listing. **Recreation:** bicycles. **Some Rooms:** whirlpools. **Cards:** AE, MC, VI.

RESTAURANTS

MATTEI'S TAVERN Historical   **Lunch:** $7-$12   **Dinner:** $13-$23   **Phone:** 805/688-4820
◆◆   **Location:** On SR 154. 93441. **Hours:** 5:30 pm-9 pm, Sat & Sun noon-3 & 5-9 pm. **Closed:** 12/24 & 12/25.
American   **Reservations:** suggested. **Features:** casual dress; children's menu; carryout; salad bar; cocktails & lounge.
Dining in a historic stagecoach stop. Nice selection of steak, prime rib, seafood & other entrees. Smoke free
premises. **Cards:** MC, VI.   ☒

THE VINTAGE ROOM   **Lunch:** $6-$13   **Dinner:** $12-$23   **Phone:** 805/688-7788
◆◆◆   **Location:** 0.5 mi s of SR 154; in Fess Parker's Wine Country Inn. 2860 Grand Ave 93441. **Hours:** 8
Continental   am-2:30 & 5-9 pm, Fri-10 pm, Sat 8 am-3 & 5-10 pm, Sun 8 am-3 & 5-9 pm. **Features:** Sunday brunch;
cocktails. Casually elegant atmosphere. Smoke free premises. **Cards:** AE, DI, DS, MC, VI.   ☒

LOS OSOS—10,500

LODGING

BEST WESTERN SEA PINES GOLF RESORT   **Phone:** (805)528-5252

		1P:		2P/1B:		2P/2B:		XP:		
7/1-8/31		1P:	$89- 129	2P/1B:	$89- 129	2P/2B:	$89- 129	XP:	$10	F17
6/1-6/30 & 9/1-9/30		1P:	$84- 119	2P/1B:	$84- 119	2P/2B:	$84- 119	XP:	$10	F17
2/1-5/31 & 10/1-1/31		1P:	$79- 109	2P/1B:	$79- 109	2P/2B:	$79- 109	XP:	$10	F17

Motor Inn   **Location:** 1 mi w of 9th St via Los Osos Valley Rd, 0.3 mi n on Pecho Rd, just w on Skyline Dr. 1945
Solano St 93402. Fax: 805/528-8231. **Facility:** 20 rooms. Rooms with golf course or bay view. 2 one-bedroom
suites with fireplace, microwave & refrigerator, $139-$149; 2 stories; exterior corridors; putting green. Fee: 9 hole executive
golf course with driving range & pitching green. **Dining:** Restaurant; 7:30 am-9 pm; $7-$11; wine/beer only.
All Rooms: extended cable TV. **Cards:** AE, DI, DS, MC, VI. **Special Amenities:** Early check-in/late check-out and free
newspaper.

RESTAURANT

RODNEY'S   **Dinner:** $13-$20   **Phone:** 805/528-0459
◆◆   **Location:** In Baywood Park, just s of Santa Ysabel St. 1315 2nd St 93402. **Hours:** 4:30 pm-9:30 pm, Fri &
American   Sat-10 pm. **Closed:** Tues. **Reservations:** suggested. **Features:** No A/C; casual dress; children's menu; early
bird specials; beer & wine only. Small charming restaurant. Interesting selection of seafood, pasta, venison,
pheasant & other entrees. Smoke free premises. **Cards:** MC, VI.   ☒

LYNWOOD—*See Los Angeles p. 615.*

MADERA—29,300

LODGINGS

BEST WESTERN MADERA VALLEY INN   Guaranteed Rates   **Phone:** (559)673-5164
⬥⬥⬥   All Year   1P: $65- 75 2P/1B: $72- 82 2P/2B: $78- 88 XP: $4 F12
◆◆◆   **Location:** Just e of SR 99, Central Madera exit. 317 North G St 93637. Fax: 559/661-8426. **Terms:** Pets.
Motor Inn   **Facility:** 92 rooms. 5 stories; interior corridors. **Dining:** Coffee shop; 6 am-9 pm; $7-$13; cocktails.
Cards: AE, CB, DI, DS, MC, VI.

LIBERTY INN   **Phone:** (559)675-8697
⬥⬥⬥   All Year   1P: $42 2P/1B: $46 2P/2B: $49 XP: $5 F12
◆◆   **Location:** 5 min n; just w of SR 99, Ave 18 1/2 exit. 22683 Ave 18 1/2 93637. Fax: 559/662-9838.
Motel   **Terms:** Small pets only, $25 dep req. **Facility:** 40 rooms. Adjacent to truck stop. 2 stories; interior corridors;
heated indoor pool, sauna, whirlpool. **Recreation:** game room with pool table,
pin ball machine. **All Rooms:** combo or shower baths. **Cards:** AE, CB, DI, DS, MC, VI. **Special Amenities:**
Free local telephone calls and preferred room (subject to availability with advanced reservations).

RESTAURANT

LUCCA'S   **Lunch:** $7-$10   **Dinner:** $10-$22   **Phone:** 559/674-6744
◆◆◆   **Location:** Just e of SR 99, Central Madera exit. 325 N Gateway Dr 93637. **Hours:** 11:30 am-2 & 5-9 pm,
Italian   Sat 5 pm-9 pm, Sun 4 pm-8:30 pm. Closed major holidays& Mon. **Features:** casual dress; children's menu;
early bird specials; carryout; cocktails & lounge; a la carte. Homemade pasta & American dishes. Smoking in
lounge only. Smoke free premises. **Cards:** AE, CB, DI, DS, MC, VI.   ☒

MALIBU—*See Los Angeles p. 615.*

MAMMOTH LAKES—4,800

LODGINGS

ALPENHOF LODGE   Rates Subject to Change   **Phone:** (760)934-6330

		1P:		2P/1B:		2P/2B:		XP:		
11/1-1/31		1P:	$85- 103	2P/1B:	$85- 103	2P/2B:	$93- 117	XP:	$10	F12
Fri & Sat 2/1-3/31		1P:	$94- 99	2P/1B:	$94- 99	2P/2B:	$103-113	XP:	$10	F12
Sun-Thurs 2/1-3/31		1P:	$80- 85	2P/1B:	$80- 85	2P/2B:	$89- 99	XP:	$10	F12
4/1-10/31		1P:	$66- 70	2P/1B:	$66- 70	2P/2B:	$74- 81	XP:	$10	F12

Motor Inn   **Location:** On SR 203, 1.1 mi W of Old Mammoth Rd. 6080 Minaret Rd 93546 (PO Box 1157).
Fax: 760/934-7614. **Terms:** Reserv deposit, 7 day notice. **Facility:** 48 rooms. On spacious grounds. 8 rooms with fireplace.
2-3 stories, no elevator; interior/exterior corridors; sauna, whirlpool, heated pool open in summer. **Dining:** The Matterhorn
Restaurant, see separate listing. **All Rooms:** combo or shower baths. **Cards:** AE, DS, MC, VI.

AUSTRIA HOF LODGE   Phone: (760)934-2764

(AAA) [SAVE] Sun-Thurs 2/1-4/15,
◆◆   11/12-1/31 & 11/15-12/20   1P: $80- 135   2P/1B: $80- 135   2P/2B: $100- 135   XP: $10
Lodge   Fri & Sat 2/1-4/15 &
             11/12-1/31   1P: $100- 135 2P/1B: $100- 135 2P/2B: $120- 135   XP: $10
             4/16-11/11   1P: $60- 80 2P/1B: $60- 80 2P/2B: $60- 90   XP: $10
Location: Old Mammoth Rd, take SR 203 1.2 mi w, then 1 mi w on Canyon Blvd. 924 Canyon Blvd 93546 (Box 607).
Fax: 760/934-1880. **Terms:** Reserv deposit, 15 day notice, 7 days in summer; weekly rates; package plans; pets, one room
only. **Facility:** 23 rooms. Next to parking lot for Warming Hut II(Canyon Lodge). Closed late April to mid-June; interior corridors; designated smoking area; whirlpool. **Dining:** Restaurant; 7 am-10 am & 5-10 pm; 5 pm-10 pm, in summer; $12-$20;
cocktails. **Recreation:** downhill & cross country skiing, snowmobiling, walk to ski lifts. **All Rooms:** combo or shower baths,
extended cable TV. **Cards:** CB, DI, DS, JC, MC, VI.   [icons] (S

CINNAMON BEAR INN BED & BREAKFAST   Phone: (760)934-2873

(AAA) [SAVE] 2/1-4/15 & 11/15-1/31 [BP] 1P: $59- 89   2P/1B: $79- 129   2P/2B: $79- 129   XP: $10   D12
◆◆   6/15-9/15 [BP]   1P: $59- 79   2P/1B: $69- 119   2P/2B: $79- 129   XP: $10   D12
Bed &   4/16-6/14 & 9/16-11/14 [BP] 1P: $49- 69   2P/1B: $59- 99   2P/2B: $59- 99   XP: $10   D12
Breakfast   **Location:** Center St; just s of SR 203 & w of Old Mammoth Rd. 113 Center St 93546 (PO Box 3338).
Fax: 760/934-2873. **Terms:** Reserv deposit, 7 day notice; weekly rates; package plans, in season.
Facility: 14 rooms. A variety of rooms, some with four poster canopy beds. 1 two-bedroom unit. 2 stories; ex-
terior corridors; smoke free premises; whirlpool. **Dining:** Restaurant nearby. **All Rooms:** combo or shower baths, extended
cable TV. **Cards:** AE, DS, MC, VI.   [icons]

ECONOLODGE WILDWOOD INN   Phone: (760)934-6855

(AAA) [SAVE] Fri & Sat 2/1-4/30, 6/18-9/8 &
◆◆   11/1-1/31 [CP]   1P: $59- 69   2P/1B: $69- 84   2P/2B: $89- 99   XP: $10   F12
Motel   Sun-Thurs 2/1-4/30, 6/18-9/8
             & 11/1-1/31 [CP]   1P: $54- 59   2P/1B: $59- 79   2P/2B: $69- 89   XP: $10   F12
             5/1-6/17 & 9/9-10/31 [CP]   1P: $49- 54   2P/1B: $54- 69   2P/2B: $64- 79   XP: $10   F12
Location: On SR 203, 0.7 mi W of Old Mammoth Rd. 3626 Main St 93546 (PO Box 568). Fax: 760/934-3626.
Terms: Reserv deposit, 7 day notice; pets, $5 dep req. **Facility:** 32 rooms. 2 stories; exterior corridors; heated pool, whirlpool.
Dining: Restaurant nearby. **Recreation:** fish cleaning & freezing facilities. **All Rooms:** extended cable TV. **Cards:** AE, CB,
DI, DS, MC, VI. **Special Amenities:** Free breakfast and free local telephone calls.   [icons]

**The AAA Approved Auto Repair sign means
service you can depend on.**

EXECUTIVE INN

Phone: (760)934-8892

(AAA) (SAVE)
◆ ◆
Motel

Fri & Sat 2/1-4/30, 6/15-9/30 & 11/15-1/31 [CP]	1P:	$54- 79	2P/1B:	$69- 89	2P/2B:	$89- 109	XP: $10			F12
Sun-Thurs 2/1-4/30, 6/15-9/30 & 11/15-1/31 [CP]	1P:	$50- 59	2P/1B:	$59- 79	2P/2B:	$69- 89	XP: $10			F12
Fri & Sat 5/1-6/14 & 10/1-11/14 [CP]	1P:	$44- 49	2P/1B:	$49- 59	2P/2B:	$59- 79	XP: $10			F12
Sun-Thurs 5/1-6/14 & 10/1-11/14 [CP]	1P:	$40- 44	2P/1B:	$44- 49	2P/2B:	$52- 59	XP: $10			F12

Location: Just n of SR 203 (Main St); 0.6 mi w of Old Mammoth Rd. 54 Sierra Blvd 93546 (PO Box 49). Fax: 760/934-3496. **Terms:** Reserv deposit, 7 day notice; small pets only. **Facility:** 40 rooms. 2 stories; interior corridors; smoke free premises; indoor whirlpool. **All Rooms:** extended cable TV. **Cards:** AE, DS, MC, VI. **Special Amenities: Free breakfast and free local telephone calls.** 〔icons〕

HOLIDAY INN HOTEL & SUITES

(FYI) Under construction. **Location:** Just n of SR 203 & just w of Old Mammoth Rd. 3236 Main St 93546. **Facility:** 71 rooms. Scheduled to open early 1999;

INNSBRUCK LODGE

Phone: (760)934-3035

(AAA) (SAVE)
◆
Motel

Fri & Sat 2/1-4/30 & 11/1-1/31	1P:	$55- 80	2P/1B:	$55- 80	2P/2B:	$60- 90	XP: $5-10
Sun-Thurs 2/1-4/30 & 11/1-1/31	1P:	$45- 60	2P/1B:	$50- 60	2P/2B:	$55- 90	XP: $5-10
Fri & Sat 5/1-10/31	1P:	$50- 60	2P/1B:	$50- 60	2P/2B:	$55- 70	XP: $5-10
Sun-Thurs 5/1-10/31	1P:	$40- 50	2P/1B:	$40- 50	2P/2B:	$45- 60	XP: $5-10

Location: From Old Mammoth Rd, take SR 203 1.3 mi w, just e on Forest Trail. 913 Forest Trail 93546 (PO Box 758). Fax: 760/934-3530. **Terms:** Reserv deposit, 7 day notice. **Facility:** 17 rooms. Rooms located in a chalet-style lodge. 3 stories; interior corridors; designated smoking area; whirlpool. **All Rooms:** combo or shower baths, extended cable TV. **Some Rooms:** 7 kitchens. **Cards:** AE, DS, MC, VI. **Special Amenities: Early check-in/late check-out and free local telephone calls.** 〔icons〕

MAMMOTH LAKES TRAVELODGE

Phone: (760)934-8576

(AAA) (SAVE)
◆ ◆
Motel

2/1-4/25 & 11/14-1/31	1P:	$90- 150	2P/1B:	$90- 150	2P/2B:	$99- 150	
4/26-11/13	1P:	$79- 145	2P/1B:	$79- 145	2P/2B:	$89- 145	

Location: On SR 203, 1.2 mi W of Old Mammoth Rd. 6209 Minaret Rd 93546 (PO Box 353). Fax: 760/934-8007. **Terms:** Check-in 4 pm; reserv deposit, 7 day notice, 11/1-4/30; 2 night min stay, weekends 11/1-5/1. **Facility:** 126 rooms. 4 two-bedroom housekeeping cottages; 3 stories; interior corridors; heated indoor pool, saunas, 2 indoor whirlpools. Fee: whirlpools. **Dining:** Restaurants nearby. **Services:** area transportation. **All Rooms:** combo or shower baths, extended cable TV. **Cards:** AE, MC, VI. **Special Amenities: Early check-in/late check-out and free room upgrade (subject to availability with advanced reservations).** 〔icons〕

MAMMOTH MOUNTAIN INN

Phone: (760)934-2581

(AAA) (SAVE)
◆ ◆ ◆
Resort
Complex

11/15-1/31	1P:	$120- 500	2P/1B:	$120- 500	2P/2B:	$120- 500
2/1-4/25	1P:	$115- 490	2P/1B:	$115- 490	2P/2B:	$125- 490
4/26-11/14	1P:	$99- 205	2P/1B:	$99- 205	2P/2B:	$99- 205

Location: 5 mi w of town on SR 203, adjacent to Mammoth Mountain ski area. 1 Minaret Rd 93546 (PO Box 353). Fax: 760/934-0701. **Terms:** Reserv deposit, 14 day notice, in winter; handling fee imposed; weekly rates. **Facility:** 213 rooms. Alpine atmosphere at an elevation of 8900 feet. Rooms & suites located in main lodge & 2 adjacent buildings. 43 two-bedroom units, 14 three-bedroom units. 3 stories; interior corridors; whirlpools. **Dining:** Dining room, restaurant; 6:30 am-10 pm, hours vary by season; $8-$24; cocktails. **Services:** giftshop; area transportation, to village. **Recreation:** downhill & cross country skiing, snowmobiling; hiking trails, jogging. Fee: bicycles. **All Rooms:** extended cable TV. **Some Rooms:** 50 kitchens, whirlpools. **Cards:** AE, MC, VI. 〔icons〕

THE 1849 CONDOMINIUMS

Phone: (760)934-7525

(AAA) (SAVE)
◆ ◆ ◆
Condo Motel

Fri & Sat 2/1-4/22 & 11/5-1/31	2P/2B:	$200- 405
Sun-Thurs 2/1-4/22 & 11/5-1/31	2P/2B:	$165- 350
4/23-11/4	2P/2B:	$90- 250

Location: 0.8 mi n of SR 203, off Lake Mary Rd. 826 Lakeview Blvd 93546 (PO Box 835). Fax: 760/934-6501. **Terms:** Reserv deposit, 14 day notice; handling fee imposed; weekly rates; 2 night min stay. **Facility:** 46 rooms. Near Canyon Lodge (Warming Hut II), walking distance to ski lifts. A wide variety of individually furnished 1-4 bedroom apartments. Rates for 4-10 persons; 3 stories; interior/exterior corridors; heated pool, sauna, whirlpools. **Services:** area transportation. **All Rooms:** kitchens. **Cards:** AE, DS, MC, VI. 〔icons〕

QUALITY INN

Rates Subject to Change

Phone: (760)934-5114

◆ ◆ ◆
Motel

All Year [CP] 1P: $69- 120 2P/1B: $69- 120 2P/2B: $69- 120 XP: $10 F12

Location: SR 203, 0.3 mi W of Old Mammoth Rd. 3537 Main St 93546 (PO Box 3507). Fax: 760/934-5165. **Facility:** 59 rooms. 2 stories; interior corridors. **Cards:** AE, CB, DI, DS, MC, VI. 〔icons〕

ROYAL PINES RESORT

Rates Subject to Change

Phone: (760)934-2306

(AAA)
◆ ◆
Motel

Fri & Sat 2/1-4/15 & 11/15-1/31	1P:	$79	2P/1B:	$79	2P/2B:	$85- 95	XP: $10	F7
Sun-Thurs 2/1-4/15 & 11/15-1/31	1P:	$65	2P/1B:	$65	2P/2B:	$69- 76	XP: $10	F7
4/16-11/14	1P:	$54	2P/1B:	$54	2P/2B:	$59- 65	XP: $7	F7

Location: On SR 203, 0.5 mi W of Old Mammoth Rd. 3814 View Point Rd 93546 (PO Box 348). Fax: 760/934-2306. **Terms:** Pets, $5 extra charge, dogs only. **Facility:** 28 rooms. On tree-shaded grounds with mountain view. 1-2 stories; interior/exterior corridors; whirlpool. **Dining:** Restaurant nearby. **All Rooms:** combo or shower baths, extended cable TV. **Some Rooms:** 14 efficiencies, 7 kitchens. **Cards:** DS, MC, VI. 〔icons〕

SHILO INN
◆◆◆
Motel

All Year [CP]

Rates Subject to Change

1P: $109- 145   2P/1B: $109- 145   2P/2B: $109- 145   XP: $15   F12

Phone: (760)934-4500

Location: On SR 203, just e of Old Mammoth Rd. 2963 Main St 93546. Fax: 760/934-7594.
Terms: Check-in 4 pm; reserv deposit. **Facility:** 70 rooms. 4 stories; interior corridors; heated indoor pool.
Cards: AE, CB, DI, DS, JC, MC, VI. *(See ad p 627, p 1091, below & p 627)*

(ASK) (SÓ) (⌂) (🐕) (♿) (⇄) (¶✚) (⌦) (🏊) (♣) (🎤) (VCR) (🖥) (□) (▤) (🛏) (🔥) (✕)

SIERRA LODGE
(AAA) (SAVE)
◆◆◆
Motel

11/15-1/2 [CP]	1P: $130	2P/1B: $130	2P/2B: $130	XP: $10	F12
Fri & Sat 2/1-4/15 & 1/3-1/31					
[CP]	1P: $110	2P/1B: $110	2P/2B: $110	XP: $10	F12
4/16-11/14 [CP]	1P: $75	2P/1B: $75	2P/2B: $75	XP: $10	F12
Sun-Thurs 2/1-4/15 &					
1/3-1/31 [CP]	1P: $95	2P/1B: $95	2P/2B: $5	XP: $10	F12

Phone: (760)934-8881

Location: On SR 203, 0.6 mi W of Old Mammoth Rd. 3540 Main St 93546 (PO Box 918). Fax: 760/934-7231. **Facility:** 35 rooms. Attractive guest lounge with fireplace. 3 stories, no elevator; interior corridors; smoke free premises; whirlpool.
Dining: Restaurant nearby. **Cards:** MC, VI. **Special Amenities:** Free breakfast and free local telephone calls.

(¶✚) (🎤) (□) (🚗) (▤) (🛏) (✕)

SIERRA NEVADA RODEWAY INN
(AAA) (SAVE)
◆◆
Motor Inn

1/1-1/31	1P: $84- 140		2P/2B: $84- 140	XP: $10	F12
11/20-12/31	1P: $94- 129		2P/2B: $94- 129	XP: $10	F12
2/1-5/1	1P: $64- 119		2P/2B: $64- 119	XP: $10	F12
5/2-11/19	1P: $79- 119		2P/2B: $79- 119	XP: $10	F12

Phone: (760)934-2515

Location: Just s of SR 203. 164 Old Mammoth Rd 93546 (PO Box 918). **Terms:** Reserv deposit, 7 day notice; handling fee imposed; pets, in designated rooms. **Facility:** 156 rooms. Kitchen units $99-$109, family suites $149-$199; 2 stories; interior/exterior corridors; heated pool, sauna, whirlpool. **Dining:** Restaurant; 5 pm-10 pm; $14-$21; cocktails. **All Rooms:** combo or shower baths, extended cable TV. **Cards:** AE, CB, DI, DS, MC, VI.
Special Amenities: Early check-in/late check-out and free newspaper. *(See color ad below)*

(SÓ) (⌂) (🐕) (⇄) (¶) (🏊) (♣) (🎤) (🖥) (🚗) (🛏) (✕)

SNOW GOOSE INN BED & BREAKFAST
◆
Bed &
Breakfast

Rates Subject to Change

Fri & Sat 2/1-4/15 &				
11/15-1/31 [BP]	1P: $88	2P/1B: $98	2P/2B: $98	XP: $12
Sun-Thurs 2/1-4/15 &				
11/15-1/31 [BP]	1P: $68	2P/1B: $78	2P/2B: $78	XP: $12
4/16-11/14 [BP]	1P: $58	2P/1B: $68	2P/2B: $68	XP: $10

Phone: 760/934-2660

Location: Just w of Jct SR 203 & Old Mammoth Rd. 57 Forest Trail 93546 (PO Box 387). Fax: 760/934-5655.
Terms: Reserv deposit, 7 day notice; handling fee imposed. **Facility:** 19 rooms. Large gathering room with tables, couches, big screen TV, & fireplace. Cozy to large rooms. 2 efficiencies, $10 extra. 4 two-bedroom apartments with fireplace; 2 stories; interior/exterior corridors; smoke free premises. **All Rooms:** combo or shower baths. **Cards:** DS, MC, VI.

(¶✚) (🎤) (🚗) (✕)

SUMMIT ACCOMMODATIONS Phone: 760/934-7062
AAA SAVE 2/1-4/22 & 11/1-1/31 1P: $135- 285 2P/1B: $135- 285 2P/2B: $135- 285
4/23-10/31 1P: $75- 155 2P/1B: $75- 155 2P/2B: $75- 155
◆◆◆ **Location:** On Meridian Blvd, 1 mi w of Old Mammoth Rd. 3253 Meridian 93546 (PO BOx 2187).
Condo Motel Fax: 760/934-5490. **Terms:** Check-in 5 pm; reserv deposit, 21 day notice; handling fee imposed; 2 night min
stay. **Facility:** 115 rooms. Across from chairlift #15. A variety of nicely furnished, 1 to 3 bedroom apartments,
most with fireplace. 41 two-bedroom units, 5 three-bedroom units. $200 security dep; 2 stories; interior corridors; heated pool,
saunas, whirlpools; 3 tennis courts. **All Rooms:** kitchens. **Cards:** DS, MC, VI. *(See color ad below)*

🛒 ⊗ 📺 🅰 ⊗

SWISS CHALET MOTEL Rates Subject to Change Phone: 760/934-2403
◆ Fri & Sat 2/1-4/30 &
Motel 11/1-1/31 [CP] 1P: $80 2P/1B: $80 2P/2B: $85 XP: $10 F16
Sun-Thurs 2/1-4/30 &
11/1-1/31 [EP] 1P: $70 2P/1B: $70 2P/2B: $75 XP: $10 F16
5/1-10/31 [EP] 1P: $55 2P/1B: $55 2P/2B: $62 XP: $6 F16
Location: Adjacent to SR 203, 0.8 mi w of Old Mammoth Rd. 3776 Viewpoint Rd 93546 (PO Box 16). Fax: 760/934-2403.
Terms: Reserv deposit, 7 day notice; handling fee imposed. **Facility:** 21 rooms. Scenic mountain view. 2 efficiencies, $6 extra;
2 stories; exterior corridors. **All Rooms:** shower baths. **Cards:** AE, DS, MC, VI. ASK 📠 🛒 🐾 🅰 🔌 ⊗

WHITE STAG INN Rates Subject to Change Phone: 760/934-7507
AAA Fri & Sat 2/1-4/30 1P: $71 2P/1B: $71 2P/2B: $80 XP: $10
11/15-1/31 1P: $64 2P/1B: $64 2P/2B: $79 XP: $10
◆◆ Sun-Thurs 2/1-4/30 1P: $61 2P/1B: $61 2P/2B: $70 XP: $10
Motel 5/1-11/14 1P: $54 2P/1B: $54 2P/2B: $59 XP: $6
Location: SR 203, 1 mi W of Old Mammoth Rd. Main St at Minaret Rd. (PO Box 45, 93546).
Terms: Weekly rates. **Facility:** 21 rooms. 3 efficiencies, $7 extra charge; 2 stories; exterior corridors; sauna.
Dining: Restaurant nearby. **Recreation:** fish cleaning & freezing facilities. **All Rooms:** combo or shower baths, extended
cable TV. **Cards:** AE, DS, MC, VI. 📠 🍴 🐾 🅰 ⊗

RESTAURANTS

ALPENROSE RESTAURANT **Lunch:** $6-$10 **Dinner:** $11-$23 Phone: 760/934-3077
◆◆◆ **Location:** Just s of SR 203. 343 Old Mammoth Rd 93546. **Hours:** 8:30 am-9:30 pm in summer; from 5:30 in
Continental winter. **Reservations:** suggested. **Features:** casual dress; children's menu; carryout; beer & wine only. A
charming, cozy restaurant serving a nice selection of European cuisine. Closed for 2 weeks in spring & fall.
Outdoor patio dining in summer. Smoke free premises. **Cards:** AE, MC, VI. ⊗

ANGEL'S RESTAURANT **Lunch:** $6-$9 **Dinner:** $7-$15 Phone: 760/934-7427
◆ **Location:** On SR 203, 0.6 mi w of Old Mammoth Rd. 3516 Main St 93546. **Hours:** 11:30 am-10 pm; Sat
American from 4 pm, Sun from 5 pm. **Features:** children's menu; carryout; cocktails & lounge. A casual, informal
restaurant, featuring BBQ specialties, Mexican cuisine, sandwiches & salads. Smoke free premises.
Cards: AE, CB, DI, DS, MC, VI. ⊗

CERVINO'S **Dinner:** $16-$22 Phone: 760/934-4734
◆◆◆ **Location:** Adjacent to SR 203, 0.8 mi w of Old Mammoth Rd. 3752 Viewpoint Rd 93546. **Hours:** 5:30 pm-9
Northern pm, in winter-10 pm. Closed: 11/25. **Reservations:** suggested. **Features:** casual dress; beer & wine only; a
Italian la carte. Hillside location with mountain view. Imaginative selection of pasta, seafood, lamb & veal. Smoke
free premises. **Cards:** AE, CB, DI, DS, MC, VI. ⊗

THE MATTERHORN RESTAURANT **Dinner:** $13-$22 Phone: 760/934-3369
◆◆ **Location:** On SR 203, 1.1 mi w of Old Mammoth Rd, in Alpenhof Lodge. 6080 Minaret Rd 93546. **Hours:** 7
Continental am-10 & 5:30-9 pm, Sat-10 pm. Closed: 4/22-5/22 & 10/15-11/15. **Features:** No A/C; casual dress; children's
menu; beer & wine only. Cozy, Alpine decor. Menu features a nice variety of American, French & Swiss
cuisine. Smoke free premises. **Cards:** AE, DS, MC, VI. ⊗

THE MOGUL RESTAURANT **Dinner:** $12-$22 Phone: 760/934-3039
◆◆ **Location:** Just s of SR 203, just w of Old Mammoth Rd. 1528 Tavern Rd 93546. **Hours:** 5:30 pm-9:30 pm, 5
American pm-10 pm in winter. **Features:** casual dress; children's menu; salad bar; cocktails & lounge. Country decor.
Features a nice selection of steak, prime rib, chicken & seafood. Smoke free premises. **Cards:** AE, DS, MC,
VI. ⊗

NEVADOS **Dinner:** $16-$24 Phone: 760/934-4466
◆◆◆ **Location:** On SR 203, 1 mi w of Old Mammoth Rd. Minaret Rd at Main St 93546. **Hours:** 5:30 pm-10 pm.
American Closed: 2 wks in mid June. **Reservations:** suggested. **Features:** casual dress; children's menu; cocktails &
lounge; a' la carte. Contemporary dining. Menu features a selection of beef, seafood, chicken, duck & lamb.
3 course prix fixe menu avail. Smoke free premises. **Cards:** AE, DI, DS, MC, VI. ⊗

OCEAN HARVEST RESTAURANT
◆◆
Seafood
Dinner: $14-$20
Phone: 760/934-8539
Location: Just s of SR 203, at 248 Old Mammoth Rd. 242 Old Mammoth Rd 93546. **Hours:** 5:30 pm-10 pm, in summer-9:30 pm. **Closed:** 10/15-11/15. **Reservations:** suggested. **Features:** No A/C; casual dress; children's menu; carryout; cocktails & lounge. Features a nice variety of Mesquite Broiled Seafood. Also steak & chicken entrees. Smoke free premises. **Cards:** AE, CB, DI, DS, MC, VI. ⊠

THE RESTAURANT AT CONVICT LAKE
ⒶⒶ
◆◆◆◆
American
Dinner: $16-$30
Phone: 760/934-3803
Location: 9 mi se of town, 2 mi w of US 395 from Convict Lake turnoff. 93546. **Hours:** 5:30 pm-9:30 pm; also open for lunch in summer 11 am-3 pm. **Reservations:** suggested. **Features:** casual dress; children's menu; cocktails & lounge. Fine dining in a picturesque mountain setting. Smoke free premises. **Cards:** AE, CB, DI, DS, MC, VI. ⊠

SLOCUM'S ITALIAN & AMERICAN GRILL & BAR
◆◆◆
Italian
Dinner: $7-$20
Phone: 760/934-7647
Location: On SR 203, just w of Old Mammoth Rd. 3221 Main St 93546. **Hours:** 5:30 pm-10 pm. **Reservations:** suggested. **Features:** No A/C; casual dress; cocktails & lounge. Victorian decor. Menu features a variety of pasta, pizza, mesquite grilled steak, ribs, chicken & seafood entrees. Smoke free premises. **Cards:** DS, MC, VI. ⊠

WHISKEY CREEK RESTAURANT & MAMMOTH BREWING CO.
◆◆
American
Dinner: $13-$20
Phone: 760/934-2555
Location: ON SR 203, 1 mi w of Old Mammoth Rd. 24 Lake Mary Rd 93546. **Hours:** 5:30 pm-10 pm; in winter from 5 pm. **Closed:** 2 weeks in May. **Reservations:** suggested. **Features:** casual dress; children's menu; cocktails & lounge; a la carte. Popular restaurant specializing in barbecue ribs, prime rib, steak & seafood. Features a variety of handcrafted beers. Smoke free premises. **Cards:** AE, DS, MC, VI. ⊠

MANHATTAN BEACH—See Los Angeles p. 616.

MANTECA—40,800

LODGINGS

BEST WESTERN INN OF MANTECA
ⒶⒶⒶ SAVE
◆◆◆
Motel
Phone: (209)825-1415

		1P:		2P/1B:		2P/2B:		XP:	
Mon-Sat [CP]		1P: $55-	65	2P/1B: $67-	77	2P/2B: $69-	79	XP: $8	F17
Sun [CP]		1P: $47		2P/1B: $52		2P/2B: $55		XP: $8	F17

Location: At jct of SR 99 & 120, exit Yosemite Ave. 1415 E Yosemite Ave 95336. Fax: 209/825-4251. **Terms:** Weekly/monthly rates; small pets only, $20 dep req. **Facility:** 101 rooms. Some rooms with balcony. Few rooms off corridors. 28 whirlpool rms, extra charge; 3 stories; exterior corridors; sauna, whirlpool. **Dining:** Coffee shop nearby. **Cards:** AE, CB, DI, DS, JC, MC, VI. **Special Amenities:** Free breakfast and free room upgrade (subject to availability with advanced reservations).

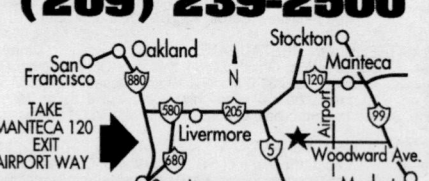

COMFORT INN OF MANTECA
◆◆◆
Motel

Guaranteed Rates
All Year [CP]　　　　　1P: $55- 65　2P/1B: $65- 75　2P/2B: $67- 77　XP: $8-10　F18
Location: SR 99, exit SR 120; 0.5 mi e. 1920 E Yosemite Ave 95336. Fax: 209/239-9011. **Facility:** 58 rooms.
2 stories; exterior corridors; heated pool. **Cards:** AE, CB, DI, DS, JC, MC, VI. *(See color ad p 660)*

Phone: (209)239-6115

MARINA—*See Monterey Peninsula p. 697.*

MARINA DEL REY—*See Los Angeles p. 617.*

MARIPOSA—1,200—*See also YOSEMITE NATIONAL PARK.*

LODGINGS

BEST WESTERN YOSEMITE WAY STATION
ⒶⒶⒶ
◆◆
Motel

Rates Subject to Change
4/1-10/31 [CP]　　　　1P: $79　　2P/1B: $79　　2P/2B: $85　　XP: $6　　F12
2/1-3/31 & 11/1-1/31 [CP]　1P: $59　　2P/1B: $59　　2P/2B: $65　　XP: $6　　F12
Location: SR 140 at SR 49S. 4999 Hwy 140 95338 (PO Box 1989). Fax: 209/966-6353. **Terms:** Reserv
deposit; small pets only, $5 extra charge. **Facility:** 78 rooms. Access to 3rd floor from 2nd level parking. 2-3
stories; exterior corridors; seasonal pool & whirlpool. **Dining:** Restaurant nearby. **All Rooms:** combo or
shower baths. **Cards:** AE, CB, DI, DS, JC, MC, VI. *(See color ad p 1087)*

Phone: (209) 966-7545

COMFORT INN-MARIPOSA
ⒶⒶⒶ
◆◆
Motel

Rates Subject to Change
4/1-10/31 [CP]　　　　1P: $75- 85　2P/1B: $75- 85　2P/2B: $85　　XP: $6　　F18
2/1-3/31 & 11/1-1/31 [CP]　1P: $65- 85　2P/1B: $65- 85　2P/2B: $75　　XP: $6　　F18
Location: Just e of jct SR 140 & SR 49 s. 4994 Bullion St 95338 (PO Box 1989). Fax: 209/966-4655.
Terms: Reserv deposit. **Facility:** 63 rooms. 2 two-bedroom units. 2-3 stories; exterior corridors; small pool,
whirlpool. **Services:** giftshop. **All Rooms:** combo or shower baths. **Some Rooms:** 2 kitchens. **Cards:** AE,
CB, DI, DS, JC, MC, VI. *(See color ad p 1087)*

Phone: (209)966-4344

E. C. YOSEMITE MOTEL
ⒶⒶⒶ
◆
Motel

Rates Subject to Change
All Year　　　　　　　1P: $55　　2P/1B: $60　　2P/2B: $60　　XP: $6　　F6
Location: Jct SR 49 & SR 140 n. 5180 Jones St 95338 (PO Box 1989). Fax: 209/742-6719. **Terms:** Reserv
deposit; small pets only, $5 extra charge. **Facility:** 28 rooms. Large rooms. 2 stories; exterior corridors; small
pool, whirlpool. **Dining:** Coffee shop nearby. **All Rooms:** combo or shower baths. **Cards:** AE, MC, VI.

Phone: (209)742-6800

HOLIDAY INN EXPRESS
◆◆
Motel

Rates Subject to Change
5/13-9/30 [CP]　　　　1P: $59- 140　2P/1B: $65- 150　2P/2B: $75- 170　XP: $10　F12
4/1-5/12 & 10/1-10/31 [CP]　1P: $49- 70　2P/1B: $55- 70　2P/2B: $60- 80　XP: $10　F12
2/1-3/31 & 11/1-1/31 [CP]　1P: $34- 44　2P/1B: $45- 55　2P/2B: $55- 65　XP: $10　F12
Location: Center. 5059 Hwy 140 95338 (PO Box 2193). Fax: 209/966-4788. **Terms:** Reserv deposit, 3 day notice.
Facility: 46 rooms. 4 stories; interior corridors; small pool. **Cards:** AE, CB, DI, DS, JC, MC, VI. *(See color ad p 1086)*

Phone: 209/966-4288

MARIPOSA HOTEL-INN
ⒶⒶⒶ
◆◆
Historic Bed
& Breakfast

Guaranteed Rates
All Year [CP]　　　　　1P: $84- 107　2P/1B: $84- 107
Location: Center. 5029 Hwy 140 95338 (PO Box 745). Fax: 209/742-5963. **Terms:** Weekly rates. **Facility:** 5
rooms. On 2nd floor of converted historic building circa 1901. Cozy individually decorated units. Smoking per-
mitted on veranda only. 2 stories; interior corridors. **Dining:** Coffee shop nearby. **Services:** giftshop.
All Rooms: combo or shower baths. **Cards:** AE, DS, MC, VI.

Phone: (209)966-4676
XP: $20

MARIPOSA LODGE
ⒶⒶⒶ
◆◆
Motel

Rates Subject to Change
4/1-10/31　　　　　　1P: $55- 85　2P/1B: $65- 85　2P/2B: $65- 85　XP: $6　　F5
2/1-3/31 & 11/1-1/31　　1P: $50　　2P/1B: $55- 65　2P/2B: $55- 65　XP: $6　　F5
Location: Center. 5052 Hwy 140 95338 (PO Box 733). Fax: 209/742-7038. **Terms:** Pets, $6 extra charge.
Facility: 44 rooms. Nicely landscaped. Many large rooms, some with balcony. 2 stories; exterior corridors;
small pool, whirlpool. **All Rooms:** combo or shower baths. **Cards:** AE, DI, DS, MC, VI. IMA.
(See color ad below, p 1091 & p 286)

Phone: (209)966-3607

MINERS INN

(AAA)

◆◆
Motel

		Rates Subject to Change				Phone: (209)742-7777
	4/1-10/31	1P: $79- 159	2P/1B: $79- 159	2P/2B: $79- 159	XP: $6	F6
	2/1-3/31 & 11/1-1/31	1P: $64- 144	2P/1B: $64- 144	2P/2B: $64- 144	XP: $6	F6

Location: SR 49, n at SR 140. 5181 Hwy 40 N 95338 (PO Box 1989). Fax: 209/966-2343. **Terms:** Reserv deposit; handling fee imposed; pets, $5 extra charge. **Facility:** 78 rooms. Some rooms with view of mountains. Few fireplaces. 2 stories; interior/exterior corridors; whirlpool. **Dining:** Coffee shop nearby. **Services:** giftshop. **All Rooms:** combo or shower baths. **Some Rooms:** 7 efficiencies, whirlpools. **Cards:** AE, CB, DI, DS, MC, VI. (See color ad p 1087)

MARTINEZ—31,800

LODGING

BEST WESTERN JOHN MUIR INN

(AAA) (SAVE)

◆◆◆
Motel

| | All Year | 1P: $62- 70 | 2P/1B: $67- 75 | 2P/2B: $72- 80 | XP: $10 | Phone: (925)229-1010 |

Location: 2.3 mi w of jct I-680 & SR 4, exit SR 4 at Pine/Center. 445 Muir Station Rd 94553. Fax: 925/228-4810. **Facility:** 113 rooms. Centrally Located. 3 stories; interior corridors; whirlpool. **Dining:** Restaurant nearby. **Services:** complimentary evening beverages, Mon-Thurs. **All Rooms:** combo or shower baths. **Some Rooms:** 8 efficiencies, 8 kitchens. **Cards:** AE, CB, DI, DS, MC, VI. **Special Amenities:** Free breakfast and free local telephone calls. (See color ad p 950)

MARYSVILLE—12,300

LODGINGS

ECONOMY INN

(AAA) (SAVE)

◆◆
Motel

| | All Year | 1P: $38- 42 | 2P/1B: $44- 46 | 2P/2B: $48- 54 | XP: $5 | Phone: (530)742-8586 |

Location: SR 20, 0.5 mi w of SR 70. 721 10th St 95901. Fax: 530/742-0132. **Terms:** Small pets only, $5 extra charge. **Facility:** 43 rooms. Centrally located. 2 stories; exterior corridors. **Dining:** Coffee shop nearby. **Cards:** AE, CB, DI, DS, MC, VI. **Special Amenities:** Free breakfast and free local telephone calls.

MARYSVILLE MOTOR LODGE

(AAA) (SAVE)

◆
Motel

| | All Year | 1P: $30- 34 | 2P/1B: $32- 36 | 2P/2B: $36- 40 | Phone: (530)743-1531 |

Location: Jct SR 70 & SR 20. 904 E Street 95901. Fax: 530/741-3119. **Terms:** Pets, $5 extra charge. **Facility:** 40 rooms. 2 stories; exterior corridors. **Dining:** Restaurant nearby. **All Rooms:** combo or shower baths. **Cards:** AE, DS, MC, VI. **Special Amenities:** Early check-in/late check-out and free local telephone calls.

SUPER 8 MOTEL

(AAA) (SAVE)

◆◆
Motel

| | All Year | 1P: $38 | 2P/1B: $40 | 2P/2B: $45 | XP: $5 | Phone: (530)742-8238 | F11 |

Location: 0.5 mi s on SR 70; exit e off N Beale Rd-Yuba College; northbound SR 70 exit Feather River Blvd. 1078 N Beale Rd 95901. Fax: 530/742-7989. **Terms:** Reserv deposit. **Facility:** 40 rooms. 2 stories; exterior corridors. **Dining:** Coffee shop nearby. **Cards:** AE, DI, DS, MC, VI. **Special Amenities:** Free breakfast and free local telephone calls.

MCCLOUD—1,600

LODGINGS

MCCLOUD HOTEL BED & BREAKFAST

(AAA) (SAVE)

◆◆◆
Historic Bed
& Breakfast

| | 4/1-9/30 [BP] | 1P: $74- 94 | 2P/1B: $74- 148 | 2P/2B: $74- 148 | XP: $15 | Phone: (530)964-2822 |
| | 2/1-3/31 & 10/1-1/31 [BP] | 1P: $67- 85 | 2P/1B: $67- 134 | 2P/2B: $67- 134 | XP: $15 | |

Location: 408 Main St 96057 (PO Box 730). Fax: 530/964-2844. **Terms:** Reserv deposit; handling fee imposed. **Facility:** 17 rooms. Restored 1916 hotel. 4 whirlpool rms, extra charge; 2 stories; interior corridors; smoke free premises. **Dining:** Restaurant nearby. **Cards:** AE, CB, DI, DS, JC, MC, VI. **Special Amenities:** Free breakfast and free local telephone calls. (See ad p 735)

MCCLOUD RIVER INN BED & BREAKFAST

◆◆◆
Historic Bed
& Breakfast

		Rates Subject to Change				Phone: 530/964-2130
	Sat 2/1-4/30 & 5/1-10/31 [BP]	1P: $85- 155	2P/1B: $85- 155	2P/2B: $85- 155	XP: $15	
	11/1-1/31 [BP]	1P: $72- 155	2P/1B: $72- 155	2P/2B: $72- 155	XP: $15	
	Sun-Fri 2/1-4/30 [BP]	1P: $72- 131	2P/1B: $72- 131	2P/2B: $72- 131	XP: $15	

Location: 325 Lawndale Ct 96057 (PO Box 1560). Fax: 530/964-2730. **Terms:** Reserv deposit, 7 day notice. **Facility:** 5 rooms. Restored 1900's office building, large lawn area with deck. 1 whirlpool rm, $135 for 2 persons; 2 stories; interior corridors; smoke free premises. **Services:** giftshop. Fee: massage. **All Rooms:** combo or shower baths. **Cards:** AE, DS, MC, VI.

PET POLICY

"Pets," "No pets" or "Kennels" is specified in the listing
when applicable; if the policy varies, pets are not mentioned.
By law, there are no restrictions on seeing-eye dogs
in the United States and Canada.

MENDOCINO—1,000

LODGINGS

AGATE COVE INN
◆◆
Bed &
Breakfast

Rates Subject to Change
All Year [BP]   1P: $109- 250   2P/1B: $109- 250   2P/2B: $109- 250   XP: $25
Location: 0.5 mi nw of SR 1, Little Lake Rd or Lansing exits. 11201 N Lansing St 95460 (PO Box 1150).
Fax: 707/937-0550. **Terms:** Reserv deposit, 7 day notice; handling fee imposed; 2 night min stay, weekends.
Facility: 10 rooms. 1860 farmhouse & guest cottages. Most with fireplace. 1 story; exterior corridors; ocean-
view. **All Rooms:** combo or shower baths. **Cards:** AE, MC, VI.
Phone: 707/937-0551

VCR Z K ⊟ X

BLACKBERRY INN
AAA
◆◆
Motel

Rates Subject to Change
All Year [CP]   1P: $90- 180   2P/1B: $95- 180   2P/2B: $100- 180   XP: $5-15   D18
Location: Just e of SR 1, Larkin Rd exit. 44951 Larkin Rd 95460. **Terms:** Reserv deposit; pets, 2 rooms
avail; $10 extra charge. **Facility:** 17 rooms. Western town facades. Attractively appointed rooms, some fire-
places or woodburning stoves; ocean view. Few with decks. 1, 2 bedroom/2 bath cottage in the woods. 1 two-
bedroom unit. 2 day min stay with Saturday 4/1-10/31 & major holidays; 1 story; exterior corridors.
Some Rooms: 2 efficiencies, kitchen, whirlpools. **Cards:** MC, VI.
Phone: 707/937-5281

🐾 ▣ K 🖥 X

THE HEADLANDS INN
◆◆
Historic Bed
& Breakfast

Rates Subject to Change
All Year [BP]   1P: $110- 195   2P/1B: $110- 195
Location: W of SR 1, Little Lake Rd exit. Albion & Howard Sts 95460 (PO Box 132). Fax: 707/937-0421.
Terms: Reserv deposit, 14 day notice; handling fee imposed; 2 night min stay, weekends. **Facility:** 6 rooms.
Remodeled 1868 Victorian; fireplaces. 1 cottage. 3 stories, no elevator; interior corridors; smoke free premises.
All Rooms: combo or shower baths. **Some Rooms:** color TV. **Cards:** AE, DS, MC, VI.
Phone: 707/937-4431

VCR Z K 🖥 X

HILL HOUSE INN
AAA
◆◆◆
Country Inn

Rates Subject to Change
All Year [CP]   1P: $125- 300   2P/1B: $125- 300   2P/2B: $125- 300   XP: $15   F18
Location: Just w of SR 1, Little Lake St exit to stop sign, right to entrance. 10701 Pallette Dr 95460 (PO
Box 625). Fax: 707/937-1123. **Terms:** Reserv deposit, 5 day notice; 2 night min stay, weekends; small pets
only. **Facility:** 44 rooms. Victorian decor; few units with ocean view. Few gas fireplaces. 2 stories;
interior/exterior corridors. **Dining:** Dining room; 11:30 am-2:30 & 6-9:30 pm; $11-$20; cocktails.
Some Rooms: whirlpools. **Cards:** AE, DI, DS, MC, VI. *(See color ad p 664)*
Phone: (707)937-0554

(ASK) SO 🐾 ▤ ▥ TI VCR ▣ K 🖥 🖥 X

JOHN DOUGHERTY HOUSE
◆◆
Historic Bed
& Breakfast

Rates Subject to Change
7/1-10/31 [BP]   1P: $105- 205   2P/1B: $105- 205
2/1-6/30 & 11/1-1/31 [BP]   1P: $95- 185   2P/1B: $95- 185
Location: Center. 571 Ukiah St 95460 (PO Box 817). **Terms:** Handling fee imposed; 2 night min stay,
weekends. **Facility:** 6 rooms. 1867 New England saltbox, cottages & water tower; English gardens11. 2 stories; interior/exterior corridors. **All Rooms:** combo or shower baths. **Cards:** AE, DI, MC, VI.
Phone: 707/937-5266
XP: $20
XP: $20

Z K 🖥 🖥 X

JOSHUA GRINDLE INN   Rates Subject to Change   **Phone:** 707/937-4143
Fri-Sun 2/1-5/31, 6/1-10/31 &
Fri-Sun 11/1-1/31 [BP]   1P: $105- 195   2P/1B: $105- 195   XP: $30
Mon-Thurs 2/1-5/31 &
Historic Bed   11/1-1/31 [BP]   1P: $100- 175   2P/1B: $100- 175   XP: $30
& Breakfast   **Location:** Just w of SR 1. 44800 Little Lake Rd 95460 (PO Box 647, 95250). **Terms:** Reserv deposit, 7 day
notice; handling fee imposed; 2 night min stay, weekends. **Facility:** 10 rooms. 1897 Victorian farmhouse, cot-
tage & "water tower". Early American antiques; some units with fireplace. 2 stories; interior/exterior corridors.
All Rooms: combo or shower baths. **Some Rooms:** color TV, whirlpools. **Cards:** MC, VI.   🅚 🖨 ⊠

MENDOCINO HOTEL & GARDEN SUITES   Rates Subject to Change   **Phone:** (707)937-0511
◆◆◆   All Year   1P: $85- 275   2P/1B: $85- 275 2P/2B: $155- 185 XP: $20   F12
Historic Hotel   **Location:** 0.2 mi w of SR 1, Little Lake Rd exit. 45080 Main St 95460 (PO Box 587). Fax: 707/937-0513.
Terms: Check-in 4 pm; reserv deposit, 3 day notice; 2 night min stay, weekends in summer. **Facility:** 51 rooms.
Restored 1878 Victorian hotel with few small rooms & large, modern garden units. 3 stories, no elevator; interior/exterior cor-
ridors. **Some Rooms:** color TV. **Cards:** AE, MC, VI. *(See color ad p 665)*   🅐🅢🅚 🆂🅾 📶 🍴 🅚 🖨 ⊠

MENOCINO SEASIDE COTTAGES ◆◆◆ Bed & Breakfast
Rates Subject to Change
Phone: 707/485-0239
All Year [CP] 1P: $101- 301 2P/1B: $101- 301
Location: 0.6 mi nw of SR 1, Little Lake Rd or Lansing St exit. 10940 Lansing St 95460. Fax: 707/485-9746.
Terms: Reserv deposit, 14 day notice. **Facility:** 4 rooms. 1997 Victorian overlooking Headlands SP fireplaces.
2 stories; interior/exterior corridors. **Recreation:** hiking trails.

REED MANOR AAA ◆◆◆◆ Bed & Breakfast
Rates Subject to Change
Phone: 707/937-5446
All Year [CP] 1P: $175- 400 2P/1B: $175- 400 XP: $50
Location: Just w of SR 1, Little Lake Rd exit, then right on Lansing & right on Palette. (PO Box 127, 95460).
Fax: 707/937-5407. **Terms:** Reserv deposit, 7 day notice; handling fee imposed; 2 night min stay, weekends.
Facility: 5 rooms. Indivdually decorated, spacious units; gas fireplaces, private decks. Few village or ocean
views. 2 stories; interior corridors; designated smoking area. **Dining:** Restaurant nearby. **Cards:** AE, MC, VI.
(See color ad below)

SEA ROCK BED & BREAKFAST INN AAA ◆◆ Complex
Rates Subject to Change
Phone: 707/937-0926
All Year [CP] 1P: $105- 250 2P/1B: $105- 250 2P/2B: $105- 250 XP: $20
Location: 0.5 mi nw of SR 1, Little Lake Rd or Lansing St exits. 11101 Lansing St 95460 (PO Box 906).
Terms: Reserv deposit, 14 day notice; handling fee imposed; 2 night min stay, weekends. **Facility:** 14 rooms.
Individual and duplex cottages & 2 Two story 4-plexes. Most with fireplace, deck, ocean or garden view. 3 two-
bedroom units. 1-2 stories; exterior corridors. **All Rooms:** combo or shower baths. **Some Rooms:** efficiency,
kitchen, whirlpools. **Cards:** AE, DI, DS, JC, MC, VI. *(See color ad below)*

Change of plans? Listings indicate when more than a 48-hour
cancellation notice is necessary for a deposit refund.

STANFORD INN BY THE SEA   Phone: (707)937-5615

AAA SAVE   All Year [BP]   1P: $215- 365   2P/1B: $215- 365   2P/2B: $215- 365   XP: $35-45
◆◆◆◆   **Location:** 0.5 mi e of SR 1, Comptche-Ukiah Rd exit. 44850 Comptche-Ukiah Rd 95460 (PO Box 487).
Complex   Fax: 707/937-0305. **Terms:** Check-in 4 pm; reserv deposit, 7 day notice; handling fee imposed; 2 night min
stay, weekends; pets, $25 extra charge. **Facility:** 35 rooms. Spacious grounds. Rustic setting. Most rooms with
ocean view. Fireplaces, VCR's, CD players/stereo & CD video library. Organic farm & Llamas. 5 two-bedroom
units. 2-3 stories; exterior corridors; heated indoor pool, sauna, whirlpool. **Dining:** Dining room; 8 am-10:30 & 6-9 pm;
vegetarian; $12-$22; wine/beer only. **Services:** complimentary evening beverages. **Recreation:** bicycles, hiking trails.
Rental: canoes. **All Rooms:** combo or shower baths. **Cards:** AE, CB, DI, DS, MC, VI. **Special Amenities: Free breakfast
and free local telephone calls.** *(See color ad below)*

🐾 🍸 📺 🏊 🍴 ⊗ 🛏 🚹 💻 🅿 📶 🖨 🛎 📠 📞 ⊠

WHITEGATE INN   Rates Subject to Change   Phone: (707)937-4892
◆◆
Historic Bed   Fri-Sun & Mon-Thurs
& Breakfast   7/1-10/31 [BP]   1P: $149- 239   2P/1B: $149- 239   2P/2B: $149- 239   XP: $30
    Mon-Thurs 2/1-6/30 &
    11/1-1/31 [BP]   1P: $129- 199   2P/1B: $129- 199   2P/2B: $129- 199   XP: $30
Location: W of SR 1, Little Lake Rd exit. 499 Howard St 95460 (PO Box 150). Fax: 707/937-1131. **Terms:** Reserv deposit,
14 day notice; handling fee imposed; 2 night min stay, weekends. **Facility:** 6 rooms. 1883 Victorian; most rooms with fireplace.
A few small units. 2 stories; exterior corridors; smoke free premises. **All Rooms:** combo or shower baths. **Cards:** AE, CB,
DI, DS, JC, MC, VI.

📶 📶 🖨 📞 ⊠

RESTAURANT

MENDOCINO HOTEL DINING ROOM   **Lunch:** $8-$12   **Dinner:** $15-$25   Phone: 707/937-0511
◆◆   **Location:** In Mendocino Hotel & Garden Suites. 45080 Main St 95460. **Hours:** 8 am-2:30 & 6-9:30 pm, Fri &
American   Sat-10 pm. **Reservations:** required. **Features:** casual dress; children's menu; cocktails & lounge; street
    parking; a la carte. Victorian decor. Lunch in glass-enclosed courtyard. California cuisine. Smoke free
premises. **Cards:** AE, MC, VI.
⊠

MENLO PARK—28,000   (See map p. 922; index p. 918)

LODGINGS

BEST WESTERN RIVIERA   Phone: (650)321-8772   [221]
AAA SAVE   All Year   1P: $125- 155   2P/1B: $135- 165   2P/2B: $145- 175   XP: $10-25   F12
◆◆◆   **Location:** On SR 82; n edge of Stanford University Campus. 15 El Camino Real 94025. Fax: 650/321-2137.
Motel   **Terms:** Reserv deposit, 7 day notice. **Facility:** 36 rooms. Kitchen units, $10 extra charge; 3 stories; exterior
corridors; sauna, whirlpool. **Cards:** AE, CB, DI, DS, JC, MC, VI. **Special Amenities: Free breakfast and
free newspaper.**

📺 🏊 🛗 🚹 🚭 💻 📶 🖨 📞 ⊠

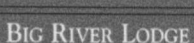

(See map p. 922)

MENLO PARK INN
Phone: (650)326-7530 **219**
AAA SAVE
All Year [CP]   1P: $95- 135 2P/1B: $95- 150 2P/2B: $95- 150 XP: $10   F16
Location: On SR 82 at Valparaiso. 1315 El Camino Real 94025. Fax: 650/328-7539. **Facility:** 30 rooms. Audio
◆◆◆   tape players. 2 stories; exterior corridors. **Dining:** Restaurant nearby. **Some Rooms:** whirlpools. **Cards:** AE,
Motel   CB, DI, DS, MC, VI. **Special Amenities: Free breakfast and free local telephone calls.**
(See color ad below)

STANFORD PARK HOTEL
Phone: (650)322-1234 **220**
AAA SAVE
All Year   1P: $250- 360 2P/1B: $265- 375 2P/2B: $265- 375 XP: $15   F13
Location: SR 82, 0.5 mi ne of Stanford University. 100 El Camino Real 94025. Fax: 650/322-0975.
◆◆◆◆ **Facility:** 163 rooms. 28 fireplaces, elegantly appointed, spacious rooms. 4 stories; interior corridors; sauna,
Hotel   whirlpool. **Dining:** Restaurant; 6:30 am-2:30 pm & 5:30-10 pm, Fri & Sat-10:30 pm; $20-$30; cocktails.
Services: complimentary evening beverages, Mon-Thurs. **Cards:** AE, CB, DI, DS, JC, MC, VI.
Special Amenities: Free newspaper and free room upgrade (subject to availability with advanced reservations).
(See color ad inside back cover)

RESTAURANTS

FONTANA'S ITALIAN RESTAURANT   **Lunch:** $7-$15   **Dinner:** $10-$20   **Phone:** 650/321-0610 **75**
◆◆◆   **Location:** 3 mi s of Woodside Rd. 1850 El Camino Real 94027. **Hours:** 11:30 am-10 pm, Fri-10 pm, Sat
Italian   5-10 pm, Sun 4:30-9:30 pm. Closed: 11/26 & 12/25. **Reservations:** suggested. **Features:** casual dress;
children's menu; cocktails & lounge; a la carte. Casual atmosphere, attractive comfortable dining rooms.
Fresh fish specials, homemade pastas & desserts. Smoke free premises. **Cards:** AE, DI, MC, VI.

GAYLORD INDIA RESTAURANT   **Lunch:** $9-$14   **Dinner:** $12-$22   **Phone:** 650/326-8761 **74**
◆◆◆   **Location:** On SR 82 at Encinal Ave. 1706 El Camino Real 94027. **Hours:** 11:30 am-2:30 & 5-10 pm.
Northern Indian Closed: 11/25 & 12/25. **Reservations:** suggested. **Features:** casual dress; cocktails; a la carte. Varied
menu, many vegetarian & seafood specialties. Attractive, comfortable surroundings. Smoke free premises.
Cards: AE, CB, DI, MC, VI.

MERCED—56,200

LODGINGS

BEST WESTERN INN
Phone: (209)723-2163
AAA SAVE
4/16-10/15 [CP]   1P: $56- 59 2P/1B: $56- 59 2P/2B: $69- 73 XP: $5   F12
2/1-4/15 [CP]   1P: $53- 56 2P/1B: $53- 56 2P/2B: $65- 69 XP: $5   F12
◆◆   10/16-1/31 [CP]   1P: $53- 56 2P/1B: $53- 56 2P/2B: $65- 69 XP: $5   F12
Motel   **Location:** Just e of SR 99, Childs Ave or SR 140 exit. 1033 Motel Dr 95340. Fax: 209/384-7272.
Terms: Reserv deposit. **Facility:** 42 rooms. 3 two-bedroom units. 5 whirlpool rms, extra charge; 2 stories; exterior corridors; small pool. **Dining:** Restaurant nearby. **Cards:** AE, CB, DI, DS, MC, VI. **Special Amenities: Free breakfast
and free local telephone calls.**

BEST WESTERN SEQUOIA INN
Phone: (209)723-3711
AAA SAVE
All Year [CP]   1P: $45- 80 2P/1B: $50- 85 2P/2B: $45- 85 XP: $8   F12
Location: Just w of SR 99, Gustine-Sonora exit. 1213 V St 95340. Fax: 209/722-8551. **Terms:** Pets, $10
◆◆◆   dep req. **Facility:** 97 rooms. 2 stories; exterior corridors. **Dining:** Restaurant nearby. **All Rooms:** combo or
Motor Inn shower baths. **Cards:** AE, CB, DI, DS, JC, MC, VI. **Special Amenities: Free breakfast and free local
telephone calls.**

DAYS INN

AAA SAVE

Motel

Phone: (209)722-2726

5/15-9/15	1P: $58- 68	2P/1B: $68	2P/2B: $78- 85	XP: $10 F17
2/1-5/14 & 9/16-1/31	1P: $58- 68	2P/1B: $58- 68	2P/2B: $68- 78	XP: $10 F17

Location: Just e of SR 99, Childs Ave or SR 140 exit. 1199 Motel Dr 95340. Fax: 209/722-7083. **Terms:** Reserv deposit; pets, $100 dep req. **Facility:** 24 rooms. Well-manicured landscaping. Exceptional units, though small. 1 story; exterior corridors. **Dining:** Restaurant nearby. **All Rooms:** combo or shower baths. **Some Rooms:** whirlpools. **Cards:** AE, CB, DI, DS, JC, MC, VI. **Special Amenities:** Early check-in/late check-out and free breakfast.

HOLIDAY INN EXPRESS
◆◆
Motel
Rates Subject to Change
All Year [CP]   1P: $69   2P/1B: $69   2P/2B: $69   XP: $6   F18
Phone: 209/383-0333
Location: Just e of SR 99; Childs Ave or SR 140 exit. 730 Motel Dr 95340. Fax: 209/383-0643. **Facility:** 65 rooms. 3 stories; exterior corridors; small pool. **Cards:** AE, CB, DI, DS, MC, VI.

MERCED-YOSEMITE TRAVELDOGE
(AAA) [SAVE]
◆
Motel
Phone: (209)722-6224
5/1-9/30 & 5/1-9/30 [CP]   1P: $55- 70   2P/1B: $55- 70   2P/2B: $65- 125   XP: $5-10   F13
2/1-4/30 & 10/1-1/31 [CP]   1P: $45- 55   2P/1B: $45- 55   2P/2B: $48- 60   XP: $5-8   F13
Location: 0.2 mi e of SR 99, Childs Ave exit. 1260 Yosemite Pkwy 95340. Fax: 209/726-3224. **Terms:** Pets, $10 extra charge, $25 dep req. **Facility:** 46 rooms. 2 stories; exterior corridors. **All Rooms:** combo or shower baths. **Some Rooms:** 4 kitchens, no utensils, whirlpools. **Cards:** AE, CB, DI, DS, JC, MC, VI.
Special Amenities: Early check-in/late check-out and free breakfast.

RAMADA INN
(AAA) [SAVE]
◆◆◆
Motor Inn
Phone: (209)723-3121
5/1-8/31 [BP]   1P: $51- 99   2P/1B: $59- 110   2P/2B: $59- 85   XP: $7   F17
2/1-4/30 & 9/1-1/31 [BP]   1P: $51- 75   2P/1B: $55- 79   2P/2B: $51- 69   XP: $7   F17
Location: Just e of SR 99, Childs Ave exit. 2000 E Childs Ave 95340. Fax: 209/723-0127. **Terms:** BP avail; package plans. **Facility:** 112 rooms. Many rooms with sitting area. 2 stories; interior/exterior corridors. **Dining:** Coffee shop; also, Eagles Nest, see separate listing. **Cards:** AE, CB, DI, DS, JC, MC, VI.
Special Amenities: Early check-in/late check-out and free local telephone calls. *(See color ad p 668)*

SUPER 8
◆◆
Motel
Rates Subject to Change
5/16-9/15   1P: $40- 55   2P/1B: $45- 60   2P/2B: $47- 60   XP: $5   F12
2/1-5/15 & 9/16-1/31   1P: $35- 45   2P/1B: $39- 47   2P/2B: $42- 50   XP: $5   F12
Phone: 209/384-1303
Location: Just e of SR 99, Childs Ave exit. 1983 E Childs Ave 95340. Fax: 209/384-1304. **Facility:** 80 rooms. 2 stories; interior corridors. **All Rooms:** combo or shower baths. **Cards:** AE, CB, DI, DS, MC, VI.

RESTAURANTS

THE BRANDING IRON
◆◆
American
Lunch: $6-$10   Dinner: $10-$21   **Phone: 209/722-1822**
Location: E of SR 99. 640 W 16th St 95340. **Hours:** 11:30 am-2 & 5:30-9:30 pm, Sat from 5:30 pm, Sun 5 pm-9 pm. Closed major holidays. **Reservations:** suggested. **Features:** casual dress; children's menu; carryout; cocktails & lounge; a la carte. Casual, Western decor; also patio dining. Smoke free premises.
Cards: AE, MC, VI.

EAGLES NEST
◆◆◆
American
Lunch: $5-$8   Dinner: $8-$17   **Phone: 209/723-1041**
Location: Just e of SR 99, Childs Ave exit; at Ramada Inn. 2000 E Childs Ave 95340. **Hours:** 6 am-10 pm. Closed: 12/25. **Reservations:** suggested. **Features:** casual dress; children's menu; health conscious menu; carryout; salad bar; cocktails & lounge. Upscale family restaurant with background music. California cuisine using fresh ingredients. Smoke free premises. **Cards:** AE, CB, DI, DS, JC, MC, VI.

SIR JAMES
◆◆
American
Dinner: $11-$42   **Phone: 209/723-5551**
Location: Just e of SR 99; Childs Ave or SR 140 exit. 1111 Motel Dr 95340. **Hours:** 5 pm-10 pm. Closed major holidays & Sun. **Reservations:** accepted. **Features:** casual dress; children's menu; early bird specials; cocktails & lounge; entertainment; a la carte. Steak, seafood & poultry. Smoke free premises. **Cards:** AE, CB, DI, MC, VI.

MILLBRAE—*See San Francisco p. 970.*

MILL VALLEY—*See San Francisco p. 971.*

MILPITAS—50,700

LODGINGS

CANDLEWOOD SUITES
[FYI]
Motel
Rates Subject to Change
Sun-Thurs   1P: $139- 159   2P/1B: $139- 159   2P/2B: $139- 159
Fri & Sat   1P: $79- 99   2P/1B: $79- 99   2P/2B: $79- 99
Phone: 408/719-1212
Too new to rate. **Location:** 40 Ranch Dr 95035. **Terms:** Reserv deposit. **Facility:** 126 rooms. Scheduled to open fall, 1998. **All Rooms:** kitchens. **Cards:** AE, CB, DI, DS, MC, VI.

EMBASSY SUITES MILPITAS/SILICON VALLEY
◆◆◆◆
Suite Hotel
Rates Subject to Change
Sun-Thurs [BP]   1P: $219- 229   2P/1B: $229- 239   2P/2B: $229- 239   XP: $10   F17
Fri & Sat [BP]   1P: $139- 149   2P/1B: $139- 149   2P/2B: $149- 159   XP: $10   F17
Phone: (408)942-0400
Location: Exit I-680 Calaveras Blvd E SR 237. 901 E Calaveras Blvd 95035. Fax: 408/262-8604. **Terms:** Reserv deposit; handling fee imposed. **Facility:** 266 rooms. Exotic atrium lobby with glass elevators, waterfall & lagoon. 8 stories; interior corridors; indoor pool. **Services:** giftshop; area transportation. **Cards:** AE, CB, DI, DS, JC, MC, VI.
(See color ad p 931)

HILTON GARDEN INN
[FYI]
Phone: 408/719-1313
Under construction. **Location:** 30 Ranch Dr 95035. **Facility:** 161 rooms. Scheduled to open winter, 1998.
(See ad p 119)

HOLIDAY INN SAN JOSE NORTH
◆◆◆
Hotel

		Rates Subject to Change		Phone: (408)321-950■
Mon-Thurs	1P: $159- 179	2P/1B: $169- 189	2P/2B: $169- 189	XP: $10	F1
Fri-Sun	1P: $75- 95	2P/1B: $85- 105	2P/2B: $85- 105	XP: $10	F1

Location: Sw quadrant of I-880 & SR 237. 777 Bellew Dr 95035. Fax: 408/321-9599. **Facility:** 305 rooms. 1 stories; interior corridors. **Services:** giftshop; area transportation. **Cards:** AE, CB, DI, DS, JC, MC, VI. *(See ad p 981)*

INNS OF AMERICA
(AAA) [SAVE]
◆◆
Motel

Phone: (408)946-888■
All Year [CP]   1P: $89- 105   2P/1B: $89- 105   2P/2B: $89- 105
Location: Exit I-880 at Calaveras Blvd; adjacent to Serra Shopping Center. 270 S Abbott Ave 95035■
Fax: 408/946-0748. **Terms:** Small pets only. **Facility:** 124 rooms. 1 bedroom unit, $125 for up to 4 persons; stories; exterior corridors; heated pool. **Cards:** AE, MC, VI. **Special Amenities: Free breakfast and free local telephone calls.**

MILPITAS TRAVELODGE
(AAA) [SAVE]
◆◆
Motel

Phone: (408)263-050■
All Year   1P: $95   2P/1B: $95   2P/2B: $105   XP: $6   F1
Location: 4 mi n of San Jose Airport, exit I-880 at Calaveras Blvd E. 378 W Calaveras Blvd 9503■
Fax: 408/263-0416. **Terms:** Reserv deposit. **Facility:** 39 rooms. Convenient Location. 2 two-bedroom units. ■ stories; exterior corridors. **Dining:** Restaurant nearby. **All Rooms:** combo or shower baths. **Cards:** AE, CB■ DI, DS, MC, VI. **Special Amenities: Free local telephone calls and free newspaper.**

RESIDENCE INN BY MARRIOTT
◆◆◆
Apartment
Hotel

	Rates Subject to Change			Phone: 408/941-922■
All Year [CP]	1P: $229- 249	2P/1B: $229- 249	2P/2B: $249- 279	

Location: I-880, exit Dixon Landing Rd E, just s. 1501 California Cr 95035. Fax: 408/941-0800. **Facility:** 12■ rooms. 24 two-bedroom units. 3 stories; interior corridors. **All Rooms:** efficiencies, combo or shower baths. **Cards:** AE, CB, DI, DS, JC, MC, VI.

SHERATON SAN JOSE AT SILICON VALLEY
(AAA) [SAVE]
◆◆◆◆
Hotel

				Phone: (408)943-060■
Mon-Thurs	1P: $209- 249	2P/1B: $219- 259	2P/2B: $219- 259	XP: $10	F1■
Fri-Sun	1P: $99- 139	2P/1B: $99- 139	2P/2B: $99- 139	XP: $10	F1■

Location: 4 mi n of San Jose Airport; 0.3 mi nw of I-880 & Montague Expwy. 1801 Barber Ln 95035■ Fax: 408/943-0484. **Terms:** Package plans, weekends. **Facility:** 229 rooms. Attractively landscaped poo■ courtyard. 24 garden suites with balcony & wet bar, $209 for up to 2 persons; 2-9 stories; interior/exterior poo■ ridors; whirlpool. **Dining:** Restaurant; 6:30 am-10 pm; $15-$25; cocktails. **Services:** giftshop; area transportation. Great Mall■ **Recreation:** jogging. **Cards:** AE, CB, DI, DS, MC, VI. **Special Amenities: Early check-in/late check-out and preferre■ room (subject to availability with advanced reservations).**

SUPER 8 MOTEL
(AAA) [SAVE]
◆◆
Motel

				Phone: (408)946-161■
3/1-10/31 [CP]	1P: $75- 90	2P/1B: $75- 90	2P/2B: $85	XP: $5	F■
2/1-2/28 & 11/1-1/31 [CP]	1P: $69- 79	2P/1B: $69- 79	2P/2B: $79	XP: $5	F■

Location: 6 mi n of San Jose Airport, exit I-880 at Montague E, then just n. 485 S Main St 95035■ Fax: 408/262-6128. **Terms:** Reserv deposit. **Facility:** 80 rooms. Modern, comfortable rooms. 2 two-bedroo■ units. 2 whirlpool rms, extra charge. 2 rm with three-beds, $85 for up to 6 persons; 2-3 stories, no elevator exterior corridors. **Dining:** Restaurant nearby. **Cards:** AE, CB, DI, DS, JC, MC, VI. **Special Amenities: Free breakfast and preferred room (subject to availability with advanced reservations).**

RESTAURANT

BRANDON'S
(AAA)
◆◆◆
Regional
American

Lunch: $8-$14   **Dinner: $13-$19**   **Phone: 408/432-631■**
Location: At Beverly Heritage Hotel. 1800 Barber Ln 95035. **Hours:** 6:30-10:30 am, 11:30-2:30 &■ 5:30-10:30 pm, Sat 7:30 am-2:30 & 5:30-10 pm, Sun 7 am-2 pm, Sun dinner in club only, 2 pm-9 pm■ Closed: 7/4 & 12/25. **Reservations:** accepted. **Features:** casual dress; Sunday brunch; cocktails & lounge■ Varied menu, attractive comfortable surroundings, fresh seafood specialties. California cuisine. Bus■ Advance reservations suggested for lunch & brunch. Smoke free premises. **Cards:** AE, CB, DI, DS, MC, VI■

MIRANDA—400

LODGING

MIRANDA GARDENS RESORT
(AAA)
◆◆
Cottage

Rates Subject to Change   **Phone: (707)943-301■**
All Year   1P: $45- 175   2P/1B: $45- 175   2P/2B: $75- 175
Location: In the village; on the Avenue of the Giants. 6766 Avenue of the Giants 95553 (PO Box 186)■ Fax: 707/943-3584. **Terms:** Pets, $10 extra charge. **Facility:** 16 rooms. Spacious, shaded grounds; quiet lo■ cation in the redwoods. Cozy single or duplex cottages. 8 two-bedroom units. 4 cabins with fireplace & 2 wit■ whirlpool tub, $115-$175; 1 story; designated smoking area; pool 5/1-10/15. **Dining:** Restaurant nearby■ **All Rooms:** combo or shower baths. **Some Rooms:** 9 efficiencies, whirlpools. **Cards:** AE, CB, DI, DS, JC, MC, VI. *(See ad p 462)*

MISSION HILLS—See Los Angeles p. 620.

MISSION VIEJO—72,800   (See map p. 296; index p. 289)

LODGING

FAIRFIELD INN BY MARRIOTT
(AAA) [SAVE]
◆◆
Motel

Phone: (949)582-7100
All Year   1P: $60   2P/1B: $64   2P/2B: $66
Location: Just e of I-5; Oso Pkwy exit. 26328 Oso Pkwy 92691. Fax: 949/582-3287. **Facility:** 147 rooms■ Nicely landscaped grounds. 5 stories; interior corridors; whirlpool. **Cards:** AE, CB, DI, DS, MC, VI■ **Special Amenities: Free breakfast and free local telephone calls.**

(See map p. 296)

RESTAURANT

TRABUCO OAKS STEAKHOUSE   Dinner: $9-$19   Phone: 949/586-0722 
◆◆   **Location:** From I-5 exit El Toro Rd, 7.3 mi ne to Cooks Corner, 4 mi se on Live Oak Canyon, just n on
Steakhouse   Trabuco Oaks Dr. 20782 Trabuco Oaks Dr 92678. **Hours:** 5 pm-9 pm, Fri & Sat-9:30 pm. Closed major
holidays & Super Bowl Sun. **Reservations:** suggested. **Features:** No A/C; casual dress; children's menu;
early bird specials; carryout; cocktails; minimum charge-$3. Located in Trabuco Canyon. Rustic, casual steakhouse. Steaks
are broiled over a mesquite charcoal fire pit. 2 lb Cowboy steak a specialty, $34. Smoke free premises. **Cards:** AE, DI, DS,
MC, VI.

MI-WUK VILLAGE—1,000

LODGINGS

CHRISTMAS TREE INN		Rates Subject to Change								Phone: (209)586-1005
⟨AAA⟩	Fri & Sat	1P: $64- 82	2P/1B: $72- 82	2P/2B: $72- 82	XP: $5
	Sun-Thurs	1P: $49- 64	2P/1B: $64- 72	2P/2B: $64- 72	XP: $5

◆◆   **Location:** 15 mi e of Sonora; on SR 108. 24685 SR 108 95346 (PO Box 700). Fax: 209/586-2247.
Motel   **Facility:** 16 rooms. Comfortable rooms. 2 stories; exterior corridors; whirlpool. **Cards:** AE, DS, MC, VI.

MI-WUK MOTOR LODGE   Phone: (209)586-3031
⟨AAA⟩ SAVE   All Year   1P: $60- 120   2P/1B: $65- 120   2P/2B: $65- 120   XP: $5
◆◆   **Location:** 15 mi e of Sonora on SR 108. 24680 SR 108 95346 (PO Box 70). Fax: 209/586-3031.
Motel   **Terms:** Reserv deposit; 2 night min stay, weekends; pets, $10 extra charge. **Facility:** 25 rooms. Wooded area.
Charming rustic decor. 4 rooms with fireplace. Kitchens, $17 extra charge. 1 housekeeping apartment, $75-$97
for 2-6 persons; 1-2 stories; exterior corridors; heated pool, whirlpool. **All Rooms:** combo or shower baths.
Some Rooms: whirlpools. **Cards:** AE, DI, MC, VI. **Special Amenities:** Free local telephone calls.

MODESTO—164,700

LODGINGS

BEST WESTERN TOWN HOUSE LODGE   Phone: (209)524-7261
⟨AAA⟩ SAVE   Mon-Sat [CP]   1P: $51- 56   2P/1B: $57- 62   2P/2B: $59- 64   XP: $8   F17
    Sun [CP]   1P: $42   2P/1B: $47   2P/2B: $49   XP: $6   F17
◆◆   **Location:** 1 mi e off Frwy 99; exit via Central Modesto at I St. 909 16th St 95354. Fax: 209/579-9546.
Motel   **Terms:** Small pets only, $20 dep req. **Facility:** 56 rooms. Comfortable rooms. 2 stories; exterior corridors;
sauna. **Dining:** Restaurant nearby. **All Rooms:** combo or shower baths. **Cards:** AE, CB, DI, DS, JC, MC, VI.
Special Amenities: Free breakfast and free local telephone calls.

CHALET MOTEL   Phone: (209)529-4370
⟨AAA⟩ SAVE   All Year [CP]   1P: $33- 38   2P/1B: $36- 40   2P/2B: $38- 42   XP: $6   F17
◆   **Location:** 0.5 mi ne on SR 108. 115 Downey Ave 95354. Fax: 209/579-9545. **Terms:** Small pets only, $20
Motel   dep req. **Facility:** 40 rooms. Walking distance to downtown. 8 whirlpool rms, extra charge; 2 stories;
interior/exterior corridors. **Dining:** Coffee shop nearby. **All Rooms:** combo or shower baths. **Cards:** AE, CB,
DI, DS, MC, VI. **Special Amenities:** Early check-in/late check-out and free breakfast.
(See color ad below)

COURTYARD BY MARRIOTT   Guaranteed Rates   Phone: (209)577-3825
⟨AAA⟩   All Year   1P: $84- 94   2P/1B: $84- 94   2P/2B: $84- 94
◆◆◆◆   **Location:** Exit SR 99 at Briggsmore Blvd, 0.3 mi n. 1720 Sisk Rd 95350. Fax: 209/577-1717. **Facility:** 126
Motel   rooms. Beautifully landscaped grounds. Attractive public areas & rooms. 2 stories; interior corridors; heated
pool, whirlpool. **Dining:** Cafeteria; 6:30 am-9:30 & 5-10 pm; $10-$15; wine/beer only. **All Rooms:** combo or
shower baths. **Some Rooms:** whirlpools. **Cards:** AE, CB, DI, DS, MC, VI.

DAYS INN

AAA SAVE

◆◆◆

Motel

(See color ad below)

All Year [CP]   1P: $60- 90   2P/1B: $65- 98 2P/2B: $65- 98   XP: $6   F1
Location: 1.8 mi n on SR 108; exit Briggsmore Ave; from SR 99, 2.3 mi e, then 0.5 mi s on McHenry Ave
1312 McHenry Ave 95350. Fax: 209/527-2033. **Facility:** 104 rooms. Large, comfortable rooms. 2 stories
interior/exterior corridors; heated pool, whirlpool. **Dining:** Restaurant nearby. **All Rooms:** combo or shower
baths. **Cards:** AE, CB, DI, JC, MC, VI. **Special Amenities:** Free breakfast and free local telephone calls.

Phone: (209)527-1010

🛎️🅿️🎱♨️📶📺🎬💻📠📞✕

DOUBLETREE

◆◆◆

Hotel

                                  Guaranteed Rates   **Phone:** 209/526-6000
6/1-8/31   1P: $105- 178   2P/1B: $120- 193 2P/2B: $120- 198   XP: $15   F1
2/1-5/31 & 9/1-1/31   1P: $89   2P/1B: $104   2P/2B: $104   XP: $15   F1
Location: SR 99 northbound exit central Modesto; southbound exit Maze Blvd; at Convention Center Plaza
1150 9th St 95354. Fax: 209/526-6096. **Facility:** 258 rooms. Tastefully appointed rooms & public areas. Suites, $225-$500 for
up to 2 persons; 15 stories; interior corridors; heated pool. **Services:** giftshop. **Cards:** AE, DI, DS, JC, MC, VI.

🛏️🅿️🎱♨️📶📺🍽️🎬🏊🅰️📞💻🖥️📠📞✕

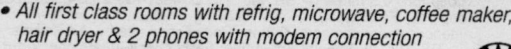
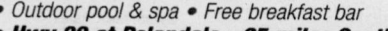

ECONO LODGE
Phone: (209)578-5400
AAA SAVE
♦
Motel
All Year [CP]   1P: $39- 44   2P/1B: $39- 44   2P/2B: $44- 55   XP: $4   F16
Location: SR 99, Kansas Ave exit. 500 Kansas Ave 95351. Fax: 209/578-5415. **Facility:** 70 rooms. Comfortable rooms. 3 stories, no elevator; interior corridors. **Dining:** Coffee shop; 5:30 am-2 pm, Thurs-Sun to 9 pm; $6-$12; wine/beer only. **All Rooms:** combo or shower baths. **Cards:** AE, CB, DI, DS, JC, MC, VI.
Special Amenities: Free breakfast and free local telephone calls.

HOLIDAY INN EXPRESS
Phone: (209)543-9000
AAA SAVE
♦♦♦
Motel
All Year [CP]   1P: $69- 79   2P/1B: $69- 79   2P/2B: $79- 89   XP: $10   F18
Location: SR 99, Pelandale Ave exit, just w. 4100 Salida Blvd 95358. Fax: 209/543-9500. **Facility:** 66 rooms. 2 stories; exterior corridors; heated pool, sauna, whirlpool. **Dining:** Restaurant nearby. **All Rooms:** combo or shower baths. **Cards:** AE, CB, DI, DS, JC, MC, VI. *(See color ad p 672)*

HOLIDAY INN OF MODESTO
Rates Subject to Change   Phone: (209)521-1612
AAA
♦♦
Hotel
All Year   1P: $95- 105   2P/1B: $95- 105   2P/2B: $95- 105   XP: $10   F18
Location: SR 99 exit Briggsmore Rd. 1612 Sisk Rd 95350. Fax: 209/527-5074. **Facility:** 186 rooms. Attractive enclosed pool & public areas. 2 stories; interior corridors; putting green; heated indoor pool, wading pool, sauna, whirlpool; 2 lighted tennis courts; playground. **Dining:** Restaurant; 6:30 am-2 & 5-10 pm; $9-$15; cocktails. **Cards:** AE, CB, DI, DS, JC, MC, VI.

HOWARD JOHNSON EXPRESS INN
Phone: (209)537-4821
AAA SAVE
♦♦
Motel
All Year [CP]   1P: $55   2P/1B: $60   2P/2B: $65- 75   XP: $5   F17
Location: Exit SR 99 Hatch Rd; s on Herndon. 1672 Herndon Rd 95307. Fax: 209/537-1040. **Terms:** Pets, $15 dep req. **Facility:** 50 rooms. 1-2 stories; exterior corridors. **Dining:** Coffee shop nearby. **All Rooms:** combo or shower baths. **Cards:** AE, CB, DI, DS, JC, MC, VI. **Special Amenities:** Free breakfast and free local telephone calls. *(See ad p 672)*

RAMADA INN
Rates Subject to Change   Phone: (209)521-9000
♦♦♦
Motel
All Year [CP]   1P: $64   2P/1B: $77   2P/2B: $77   XP: $9   F18
Location: SR 99, Briggsmore Ave exit, just s. 2001 W Orangeburg Ave 95350. Fax: 209/521-6034. **Facility:** 114 rooms. 1 whirlpool rm, extra charge; 2 stories; exterior corridors; heated pool. **Cards:** AE, CB, DI, DS, MC, VI.

SUPER 8 LODGE
Rates Subject to Change   Phone: (209)577-8008
♦
Motel
All Year   1P: $48   2P/1B: $50   2P/2B: $54   XP: $5   F13
Location: SR 99, Briggsmore Ave exit. 2025 W Orangeburg Ave 95350. Fax: 209/575-4118. **Facility:** 80 rooms. Comfortable rooms. 3 stories; interior corridors. **Cards:** AE, DI, MC, VI.

VAGABOND INN
Phone: (209)521-6340
AAA SAVE
♦
Motel
All Year   1P: $68   2P/1B: $73   2P/2B: $84   XP: $5   F18
Location: 2 mi n on SR 108; from SR 99, Briggsmore Ave exit; 2.3 mi e to McHenry Ave, then just s. 1525 McHenry Ave 95350. Fax: 209/575-2015. **Terms:** Pets, $5 extra charge. **Facility:** 99 rooms. 2 stories; exterior corridors. **Dining:** Coffee shop nearby. **Cards:** AE, CB, DI, DS, MC, VI. **Special Amenities:** Free breakfast and free local telephone calls.

MOJAVE—2,900

LODGINGS

VAGABOND INN
Phone: (805)824-2463
AAA SAVE
♦
Motel
All Year   1P: $38   2P/1B: $43   2P/2B: $53   XP: $5   F18
Location: SR 58, just e of SR 14. 2145 Hwy 58 93501. Fax: 805/824-9508. **Terms:** Pets. **Facility:** 33 rooms. 2 stories; exterior corridors. **Dining:** Restaurant nearby. **All Rooms:** extended cable TV. **Cards:** AE, CB, DI, DS, MC, VI. **Special Amenities:** Free breakfast and free local telephone calls.

WESTERN INN
Phone: (805)824-3601
AAA SAVE
♦
Motor Inn
All Year   1P: $36- 40   2P/1B: $41- 45   2P/2B: $41- 45   XP: $5
Location: On SR 14 & 58. 16200 Sierra Hwy 93501. Fax: 805/824-3605. **Terms:** Reserv deposit. **Facility:** 51 rooms. 2 stories; exterior corridors; whirlpool. **Dining:** Coffee shop; 6 am-10 pm; $6-$9; beer only. **Cards:** AE, DI, DS, MC, VI. **Special Amenities:** Free local telephone calls.

MONROVIA—See Los Angeles p. 620.

MONTEBELLO—See Los Angeles p. 621.

MONTEREY—See Monterey Peninsula p. 698.

MONTEREY PARK—See Los Angeles p. 621.

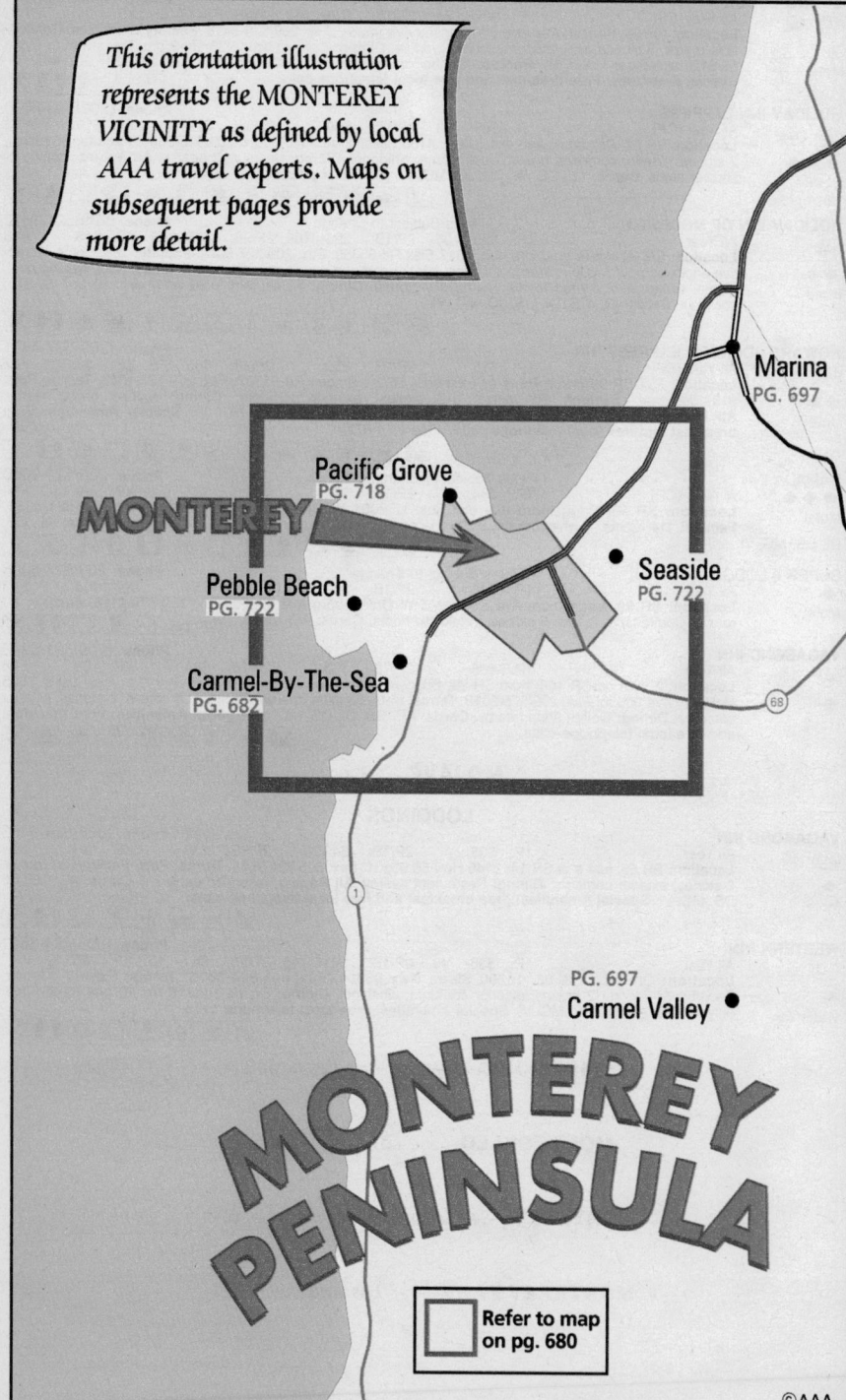

This orientation illustration represents the MONTEREY VICINITY as defined by local AAA travel experts. Maps on subsequent pages provide more detail.

Marina
PG. 697

MONTEREY

Pacific Grove
PG. 718

Pebble Beach
PG. 722

Seaside
PG. 722

Carmel-By-The-Sea
PG. 682

68

1

PG. 697
Carmel Valley

MONTEREY PENINSULA

Refer to map on pg. 680

©AAA

Monterey Peninsula

Monterey

pop. 32,000

This index helps you "spot" where approved accommodations are located on the detailed maps that follow. Rate ranges are for comparison only and show the property's high season. Turn to the listing page for more detailed rate information and consult display ads for special promotions. Restaurant rate range is for dinner unless only lunch (L) is served.

Spotter/Map Pg.Number	OA	MONTEREY - Lodgings	Rating	Rate	Listing Page
1 / p. 680	AAA	Comfort Inn-Del Monte Beach	◆◆◆	$69-179 SAVE	702
2 / p. 680	AAA	Monterey Beach Hotel-Best Western - see color ad p 710	◆◆◆	$109-219 SAVE	710
3 / p. 680	AAA	Best Western Ramona Inn	◆◆	$69-159	700
4 / p. 680	AAA	Cypress Tree Inn - see color ad p 703	◆◆	$64-99	703
5 / p. 680	AAA	Best Western De Anza Inn - see color ad p 699	◆◆◆	$85-139 SAVE	698
6 / p. 680	AAA	Econo Lodge - see color ad p 704	◆	$79-129 SAVE	705
7 / p. 680	AAA	Scottish Fairway Motel - see color ad p 713	◆	$99-119 SAVE	714
8 / p. 680	AAA	Ramada Limited-Fremont	◆◆	$95-135 SAVE	713
9 / p. 680	AAA	Super 8 Motel - see color ad p 715	◆◆	$69-109 SAVE	716
10 / p. 680	AAA	Travelodge-Monterey/Carmel	◆◆	$85 SAVE	716
11 / p. 680	AAA	Casa Verde Inn	◆	$89	701
12 / p. 680	AAA	Hilton-Monterey - see color ad p 706 & ad p 119	◆◆◆	$129 SAVE	705
13 / p. 680	AAA	Monterey Fireside Lodge	◆	$79-255 SAVE	710
14 / p. 680	AAA	I.M.A. Stage Coach Lodge - see color ad p 708 , p 286	◆◆	$95-149	708
15 / p. 680	AAA	Monterey Bay Lodge - see color ad p 709	◆◆	$89-179 SAVE	709
16 / p. 680	AAA	Doubletree Hotel	◆◆◆	$139-159 SAVE	704
17 / p. 680	AAA	Hotel Pacific - see color ad p 701	◆◆◆◆	$209-419 SAVE	706
18 / p. 680	AAA	Driftwood Motel	◆	$59-159 SAVE	704
19 / p. 680		Monterey Marriott	◆◆◆	$99-289	711
20 / p. 680	AAA	Colton Inn - see color ad p 703	◆◆◆	$110-310 SAVE	701
21 / p. 680	AAA	Monterey Downtown Travelodge - see color ad p 710	◆◆	$77-159	710
22 / p. 680	AAA	Sand Dollar Inn - see color ad p 714	◆◆	$65-125 SAVE	713
24 / p. 680	AAA	Ramada Limited-Munras	◆◆	$95-149 SAVE	713
25 / p. 680	AAA	West Wind Lodge - see color ad p 716	◆◆	$70-100 SAVE	716
26 / p. 680	AAA	El Dorado Inn - see ad p. 705	◆	$79-145	705
27 / p. 680	AAA	El Adobe Inn	◆◆	$94-134 SAVE	705
28 / p. 680	AAA	Munras Lodge - see color ad p 712	◆◆	$69-199 SAVE	712
29 / p. 680	AAA	Montero Lodge - see color ad p 712	◆	$89-115	712
30 / p. 680		Quality Inn - see color ad p 716	◆◆	$79-169	713
31 / p. 680	AAA	Best Western Park Crest Motel - see color ad p 700	◆◆◆	$85-179	699
32 / p. 680	AAA	Cypress Gardens Motel - see color ad p 685	◆◆	$104-124 SAVE	703
33 / p. 680	AAA	Surf Inn - see color ad p 715	◆	$59-159	716
34 / p. 680	AAA	Comfort Inn-Carmel Hill	◆◆	$79-119 SAVE	702
35 / p. 680	AAA	Padre Oaks	◆◆	$64-149 SAVE	713
36 / p. 680	AAA	Days Inn-Monterey - see color ad p 704	◆◆	$85-149 SAVE	703
37 / p. 680	AAA	Comfort Inn-Munras	◆◆	$79-119 SAVE	703
38 / p. 680	AAA	Best Western Steinbeck Lodge	◆◆	$89-199 SAVE	700
39 / p. 680	AAA	Carmel Hill Lodge	◆◆	$89-179 SAVE	700
40 / p. 680		Mariposa Inn - see ad p 709	◆◆	$99-139	708
41 / p. 680	AAA	Bay Park Hotel - see color ad p 698	◆◆◆	$99-160	698
42 / p. 680	AAA	Del Monte Pines Motel	◆◆	$79-169 SAVE	704
43 / p. 680	AAA	Monterey Bay Inn - see color ad p 701	◆◆◆	$199-369 SAVE	708

Spotter/Map Pg.Number	OA	MONTEREY - Lodgings (contd.)	Rating	Rate	Listing Page
44 / p. 680	◊◊◊	Monterey Plaza Hotel - see color ad inside back cover, p 711	◆◆◆◆	$195-305 ⌘	711
45 / p. 680	◊◊◊	Spindrift Inn - see color ad p 701	◆◆◆	$349-429 ⌘	714
46 / p. 680	◊◊◊	Best Western Victorian Inn - see color ad p 701	◆◆◆	$199-429 ⌘	700
47 / p. 680	◊◊◊	Holiday Inn Express-Cannery - see color ad p 706	◆◆◆	$139-249 ⌘	706
48 / p. 680	◊◊◊	Cannery Row Inn - see color ad p 701	◆◆	$79-299	700
49 / p. 680	◊◊◊	Otter Inn - see color ad p 701	◆◆	$79-299	712
50 / p. 680		Old Monterey Inn	◆◆◆◆	$200-350	712
51 / p. 680		Merritt House	◆◆	$125-190	708
52 / p. 680	◊◊◊	Way Station Inn - see color ad p 715	◆◆	$69-169 ⌘	716
53 / p. 680	◊◊◊	Lone Oak Motel - see color ad p 698	◆◆	$80-104	708
54 / p. 680		The Monterey Hotel - see color ad p 711	◆◆◆	$159-199	710
55 / p. 680	◊◊◊	San Carlos Inn - see color ad p 714	◆◆	$105-180 ⌘	713
56 / p. 680	◊◊◊	Casa Munras Garden Hotel - see color ad p 702	◆◆◆	$124-174 ⌘	701
57 / p. 680	◊◊◊	Best Western Monterey Inn - see color ad p 699	◆◆◆	$109-149	699
58 / p. 680	◊◊◊	Hyatt Regency-Monterey Resort & Conference Center - see color ad p 923	◆◆◆	$210-325 ⌘	706
		MONTEREY - Restaurants			
1 / p. 680	◊◊◊	Sandbar & Grill	◆◆	$11-19	718
3 / p. 680	◊◊◊	Domenico's on The Wharf - see ad p 717	◆◆◆	$15-36	717
6 / p. 680		The Whaler	◆◆	$10-23	718
7 / p. 680		The Duck Club - see color ad inside back cover, p 711	◆◆◆◆	$15-26	718
8 / p. 680	◊◊◊	Seafood Trattoria - see ad p 717	◆◆	$10-20	718
9 / p. 680		The Fish Hopper	◆◆	$13-24	718
10 / p. 680	◊◊◊	Whaling Station - see ad p 717	◆◆◆	$15-30	718
11 / p. 680	◊◊◊	Sardine Factory	◆◆◆◆	$16-35	718
12 / p. 680		Bradley's Harbor Front Restaurant	◆◆	$14-26	717
14 / p. 680	◊◊◊	Cafe Fina	◆◆	$13-23	717
15 / p. 680	◊◊◊	Trattoria Paradiso - see ad p 717	◆◆	$8-22	718

Monterey Peninsula Vicinity

Spotter/Map Pg.Number	OA	PACIFIC GROVE - Lodgings	Rating	Rate	Listing Page
61 / p. 680	◊◊◊	The Centrella Inn - see color ad p 685	◆◆	$144-224	719
62 / p. 680		Lovers Point Inn	◆	$79-150	720
63 / p. 680	◊◊◊	Borg's Ocean Front Motel	◆	$89-135	719
65 / p. 680		Lighthouse Lodge & Suites - see color ad p 707	◆◆	$89-268	720
66 / p. 680	◊◊◊	Best Western Monarch Resort - see color ad p 723	◆◆◆	$100-200	719
67 / p. 680		Pacific Grove Motel - see color ad p 721	◆	$69-119	720
68 / p. 680	◊◊◊	Butterfly Grove Inn		$75-149	719
69 / p. 680	◊◊◊	The Wilkies Inn	◆◆	$99-149 ⌘	721
70 / p. 680	◊◊◊	Pacific Gardens Inn	◆◆◆	$110-125	720
71 / p. 680	◊◊◊	Pacific Grove Inn - see ad p 720	◆◆◆	$142-162 ⌘	720
72 / p. 680		Asilomar - see color ad p 718	◆◆	$78-97	718
73 / p. 680	◊◊◊	Days Inn Suites - see color ad p 705, p 719	◆◆◆	$135-225 ⌘	719
74 / p. 680	◊◊◊	Rosedale Inn - see ad p 721	◆◆◆	$150-225 ⌘	720
75 / p. 680	◊◊◊	Larchwood Inn - see color ad p 719	◆◆	$69-135 ⌘	720
		PACIFIC GROVE - Restaurants			
19 / p. 680		Old Bath House	◆◆◆	$18-36	721
20 / p. 680	◊◊◊	Fandango	◆◆	$12-30	721
21 / p. 680		Crocodile Grill	◆◆	$9-17	721
22 / p. 680		Melac's	◆◆◆	$20-33	721

Spotter/Map Pg.Number	OA	PEBBLE BEACH - Lodgings	Rating	Rate	Listing Page
76 / p. 680		The Inn at Spanish Bay	◆◆◆◆	$330-2000	722
77 / p. 680		The Lodge at Pebble Beach	◆◆◆◆	$1135-1810	722
		PEBBLE BEACH - Restaurants			
25 / p. 680		Roy's	◆◆◆	$18-26	722
26 / p. 680		Club XIX	◆◆◆◆	$20-30	722
		CARMEL-BY-THE-SEA - Lodgings			
78 / p. 680	⊕	Crystal Terrace Inn Bed & Breakfast - see color ad p 691	◆◆◆	$140-275 SAVE	690
79 / p. 680	⊕	Colonial Terrace Inn - see color ad p 683	◆◆	$120-300	690
80 / p. 680	⊕	Highlands Inn	◆◆◆◆	$600-800 SAVE	692
81 / p. 680	⊕	Tickle Pink Inn - see color ad p 695	◆◆◆◆	$189-309	695
82 / p. 680	⊕	Carmel River Inn - see color ad p 683	◆◆	$100-170	687
83 / p. 680	⊕	Best Western Carmel Mission Inn - see color ad p 710	◆◆◆	$109-189 SAVE	682
84 / p. 680	⊕	Quail Lodge Resort & Golf Club - see color ad p 694	◆◆◆◆	$295-1350 SAVE	694
85 / p. 680	⊕	Hofsas House	◆◆	$80-150	692
86 / p. 680	⊕	Carmel Country Inn - see color ad p 686	◆◆◆	$105-165 SAVE	684
87 / p. 680		Carmel Tradewinds Inn	◆◆	$159-250	688
88 / p. 680	⊕	Horizon Inn & Ocean View Lodge - see color ad p 687, p 692	◆◆◆	$99-250 SAVE	692
89 / p. 680	⊕	Carmel Resort Inn - see color ad p 688	◆◆	$79-225	686
90 / p. 680	⊕	Vagabond House Inn	◆◆	$125-145 SAVE	695
91 / p. 680	⊕	Dolphin Inn - see color ad p 685	◆◆◆	$154-234 SAVE	692
92 / p. 680	⊕	Carmel Wayfarer Inn - see color ad p 689	◆◆	$142-192 SAVE	689
93 / p. 680	⊕	Carmel Garden Court - see color ad p 687	◆◆◆	$125-245	685
94 / p. 680	⊕	Carmel Fireplace Inn - see color ad p 686	◆◆◆	$155-250 SAVE	685
95 / p. 680	⊕	Briarwood Inn - see color ad p 684	◆◆◆	$125-295 SAVE	684
96 / p. 680	⊕	Candle Light Inn - see color ad p 685	◆◆◆	$154-214 SAVE	684
97 / p. 680		Carmel Oaks Inn - see color ad p 687	◆◆◆	$109-229	686
98 / p. 680	⊕	Chateau Carmel - see color ad p 691	◆◆◆	$155-245 SAVE	690
99 / p. 680	⊕	Best Western Carmel's Town House Lodge	◆◆	$100-150 SAVE	682
100 / p. 680	⊕	Carmel Sands Lodge - see color ad p 688	◆◆◆	$75-145	687
101 / p. 680	⊕	Lobos Lodge	◆◆◆	$99-185	692
102 / p. 680	⊕	Pine Inn - see color ad p 693	◆◆◆	$125-230	694
103 / p. 680	⊕	Best Western Carmel Bay View Inn - see color ad p 682	◆◆◆	$129-249	682
104 / p. 680	⊕	Sunset House	◆◆◆	$170-190 SAVE	694
105 / p. 680	⊕	Normandy Inn - see color ad p 693	◆◆◆	$98-200	693
106 / p. 680	⊕	Cypress Inn	◆◆◆	$145-285 SAVE	690
107 / p. 680	⊕	Coachman's Inn - see ad p 690	◆◆◆	$95-160 SAVE	690
108 / p. 680	⊕	Carmel Village Inn & Annex - see color ad p 689	◆◆◆	$129-200	688
109 / p. 680	⊕	Wayside Inn - see color ad p 685	◆◆◆	$154-269 SAVE	695
110 / p. 680	⊕	La Playa Hotel	◆◆◆	$155-185	692
111 / p. 680	⊕	Best Western Green Lantern Inn	◆◆	$135-250	684
112 / p. 680	⊕	Adobe Inn-Carmel - see color ad p 683	◆◆◆◆	$196-350	682
113 / p. 680	⊕	Carriage House Inn - see color ad p 685	◆◆◆◆	$234-304 SAVE	690
114 / p. 680		Cobblestone Inn	◆◆◆	$95-175	690
115 / p. 680	⊕	Svendsgaard's - see color ad p 685	◆◆◆	$124-214 SAVE	694
116 / p. 680	⊕	Carmel Valley Ranch	◆◆◆◆	$255-615 SAVE	688
		CARMEL-BY-THE-SEA - Restaurants			
28 / p. 680		From Scratch	◆	$8-25	696
29 / p. 680		Pacific's Edge	◆◆◆◆	$30-40	696
30 / p. 680	⊕	Simpson's Restaurant - see color ad p 688	◆◆◆	$14-27	696
31 / p. 680		Sans Souci	◆◆◆	$31-58	696
32 / p. 680		The Covey - see color ad p 694	◆◆◆	$19-35	696
33 / p. 680	⊕	The French Poodle Restaurant	◆◆◆◆	$15-45	696
34 / p. 680		Le Coq D'Or	◆◆◆	$18-25	696

Spotter/Map Pg.Number	OA	CARMEL-BY-THE-SEA - Restaurants (contd.)	Rating	Rate	Listing Page
㉟ / p. 680		Bully III House of Prime Rib - see color ad p 683	◆◆	$10-27	695
㊱ / p. 680	⊕⊕⊕	**Mondo's Trattoria**	◆◆◆	$10-23	696
㊲ / p. 680		Raffaello Restaurant	◆◆◆◆	$18-28	696
㊳ / p. 680	⊕⊕⊕	**The Red Lion Tavern**	◆◆◆	$11-20	696
㊴ / p. 680	⊕⊕⊕	**Anton & Michel**	◆◆◆	$17-30	695
㊵ / p. 680		Casanova	◆◆◆	$20-35	696
㊸ / p. 680		Rio Grill	◆◆◆	$20-30	696
		SEASIDE - Lodgings			
⑫⓪ / p. 680		SunBay Resort - see color ad p 723	◆◆	$89-189	724
⑫① / p. 680	⊕⊕⊕	**Bay Breeze Inn - see color ad p 722**	◆◆	$66-102 ⓜ	722
⑫② / p. 680		Seaside Inn	◆	$82-120	724
⑫③ / p. 680	⊕⊕⊕	**Sandcastle Inn**	◆◆	$110-250 ⓜ	724
⑫④ / p. 680	⊕⊕⊕	**Thunderbird Motel - see color ad p 715**	◆	$40-115	724
⑫⑤ / p. 680	⊕⊕⊕	**Howard Johnson Express Inn**	◆◆	$50-125	724
⑫⑦ / p. 680	⊕⊕⊕	**Best Western Magic Carpet Lodge - see color ad p 723**	◆◆	$79-169 ⓜ	722
⑫⑧ / p. 680	⊕⊕⊕	**Embassy Suites Hotel & Conference Center**	◆◆◆	$195-295 ⓜ	723
⑫⑨ / p. 680	⊕⊕⊕	**Pacific Best Inn**	◆	$99 ⓜ	724
⑬① / p. 680		Hampton Inn	◆◆	$89-129	724
⑬② / p. 680	⊕⊕⊕	**Economy Inn**	◆	$100 ⓜ	723
		CARMEL VALLEY - Lodgings			
⑬⑥ / p. 680	⊕⊕⊕	**Los Laureles**	◆◆◆	$110-250 ⓜ	697
⑬⑦ / p. 680	⊕⊕⊕	**Carmel Valley Lodge**	◆◆◆	$129-189 ⓜ	697
⑬⑧ / p. 680	⊕⊕⊕	**Hidden Valley Inn-Country Garden Inns - see color ad p 691**	◆◆◆	$135-168 ⓜ	697
⑬⑨ / p. 680	⊕⊕⊕	**Acacia Lodge-Country Garden Inns - see color ad p 691**	◆◆◆	$144-180 ⓜ	697
		CARMEL VALLEY - Restaurant			
㊼ / p. 680		Will's Fargo Restaurant	◆◆	$14-27	697

Meal Plan Indicators

CP = Continental Plan of pastry, juice and another beverage or may offer expanded breakfast items

BP = Breakfast Plan of full hot breakfast

AP = American Plan of three meals daily

MAP = Modified American Plan of two meals daily

EP = European Plan, where rate includes only room

Family Plan Indicators

The establishment may limit the number of children to whom the family plan applies.

F17 = children 17 and under stay free (age displayed will reflect property's policy)

D17 = discount for children 17 and under

F = children stay free

D = discounts for children

LOOK FOR THE RED

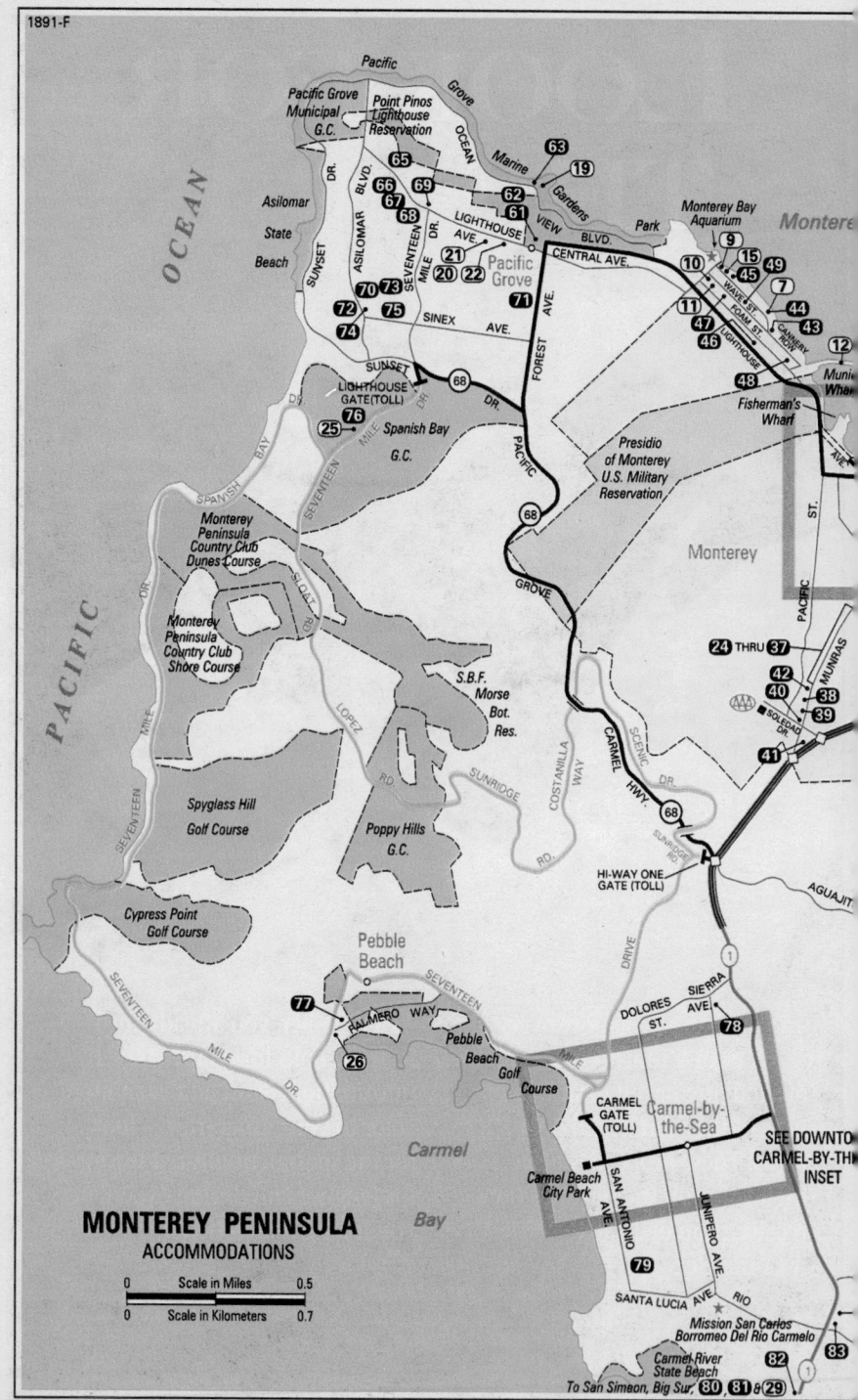

1891-F

MONTEREY PENINSULA
ACCOMMODATIONS

Scale in Miles 0 0.5
Scale in Kilometers 0 0.7

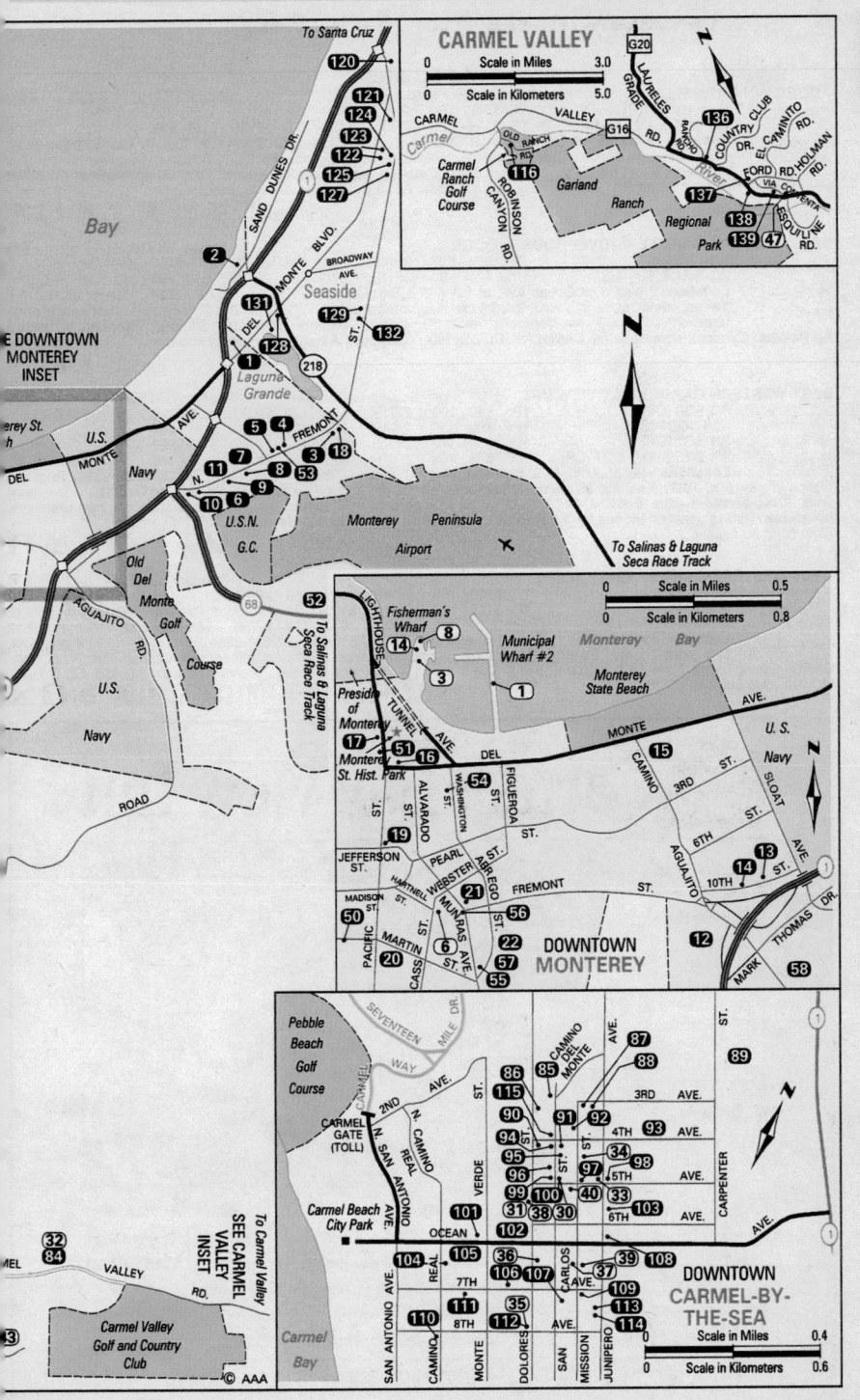

CARMEL-BY-THE-SEA—4,200 (See map p. 680; index p. 677)

LODGINGS

ADOBE INN–CARMEL   Rates Subject to Change   Phone: (831)624-3933   `112`
Ⓐ   6/15-10/31 [CP]   1P: $142- 280   2P/1B: $142- 280   2P/2B: $196- 350   XP: $20   F
        2/1-6/14 & 11/1-1/31 [CP] 1P: $126- 220   2P/1B: $126- 220   2P/2B: $156- 298   XP: $20   F
◆◆◆◆   **Location:** 2 blks s off Ocean Ave at Dolores St & 8th Ave. (PO Box 4115, 93921). Fax: 831/624-8636.
Motel   **Terms:** Reserv deposit, 3 day notice; 2 night min stay, weekends. **Facility:** 20 rooms. Gas fireplaces; many
        balconies & wet bar. 3 two-bedroom units. 2 stories; exterior corridors; small pool, sauna. **Dining:** Cocktails;
also, Bully III House of Prime Rib, see separate listing. **Cards:** AE, MC, VI. *(See color ad p 683)*

🛎 🛏 🍴 🍽 VCR 🖥 🐕 🖨 🗄 ✕

BEST WESTERN CARMEL'S TOWN HOUSE LODGE   Phone: (831)624-1261   `99`
Ⓐ SAVE   4/1-10/31   1P: $84- 97   2P/1B: $84- 97   2P/2B: $100- 150   XP: $6
          2/1-3/31 & 11/1-1/31 1P: $70- 80   2P/1B: $70- 80   2P/2B: $80- 130   XP: $6
◆◆   **Location:** 2 blks n off Ocean Ave, at 5th Ave & San Carlos St. (PO Box 3574, 93921). Fax: 831/625-6783.
Motel   **Terms:** Handling fee imposed; 2 night min stay, weekends 4/1-10/31. **Facility:** 28 rooms. In room coffee, com-
          fortable rooms. 3 two-bedroom units. 2 stories; exterior corridors. **Dining:** Restaurant nearby.
All Rooms: combo or shower baths. **Cards:** AE, DI, DS, MC, VI. **Special Amenities:** Free newspaper.

🛏 🛗 🐕 🗄 ✕

BEST WESTERN CARMEL BAY VIEW INN   Rates Subject to Change   Phone: (831)624-1831   `103`
Ⓐ   6/1-9/30 [CP]   1P: $99- 199   2P/1B: $99- 199   2P/2B: $129- 249
        10/1-10/31 [CP]   1P: $99- 189   2P/1B: $99- 189   2P/2B: $129- 239
◆◆◆   3/1-5/31 [CP]   1P: $89- 179   2P/1B: $89- 179   2P/2B: $119- 229
Motel   2/1-2/28 & 11/1-1/31 [CP] 1P: $79- 169   2P/1B: $79- 169   2P/2B: $109- 209
        Location: 1 blk n; Junipero St between 5th & 6th aves. 93921 (PO Box 3715). Fax: 831/625-2336. **Terms:** 2
night min stay, 6/15-10/31. **Facility:** 58 rooms. Hilltop units, some with balcony & most with gas burning fireplace. A few small
units. 2 two-bedroom units. 6 suites, $170-$220 for up to 4 persons; 1-5 stories; exterior corridors; smoke free premises;
oceanview. **Dining:** Restaurant nearby. **All Rooms:** combo or shower baths. **Cards:** AE, DI, DS, MC, VI.
(See color ad below)

🅢 🛏 🛗 🖥 🐕 🖨 🗄

BEST WESTERN CARMEL MISSION INN   Phone: (831)624-1841   `83`
Ⓐ SAVE   6/1-10/31   1P: $109- 189   2P/1B: $109- 189   2P/2B: $109- 189   XP: $10   F12
          4/1-5/31   1P: $109- 149   2P/1B: $109- 149   2P/2B: $109- 149   XP: $10   F12
◆◆◆   2/1-3/31 & 11/1-1/31 1P: $79- 129   2P/1B: $79- 129   2P/2B: $89- 129   XP: $10   F12
Motor Inn **Location:** 1 mi s on SR 1, at Rio Rd. 3665 Rio Rd 93923. Fax: 831/624-8684. **Terms:** Check-in 4 pm; pets,
          $25 extra charge. **Facility:** 165 rooms. Some balconies. 4 stories; interior corridors; whirlpools.
Dining: Dining room; 7 am-10 & 5-10 pm; Sat & Sun 7 am-11 & 5-10 pm; $10-$22; cocktails. **Cards:** AE, CB, DI, DS, JC,
MC, VI. *(See color ad p 710)*

🅢 🛏 🛗 🐎 🛏 🍴 🍽 ♨ 🎾 🖥 🖨 🗄 ✕

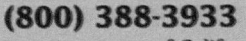

(See map p. 680)

BEST WESTERN GREEN LANTERN INN   Rates Subject to Change   **Phone:** (831)624-4392   111
6/1-9/30 [CP]   1P: $120- 175   2P/1B: $120- 175   2P/2B: $135- 250
2/1-5/31 & 10/1-1/31 [CP]   1P: $85- 145   2P/1B: $85- 145   2P/2B: $105- 225
Location: Just off Ocean Ave. 7th & Cassanova sts 93921 (PO Box 1114, CARMEL). Fax: 831/624-9591.
Terms: Reserv deposit, 3 day notice; 2 night min stay, Fri & Sat. **Facility:** 18 rooms. Attractive landscaping.
Terraced rooms. 2 stories; exterior corridors; smoke free premises. **Services:** complimentary evening
beverages. **All Rooms:** combo or shower baths. **Cards:** AE, CB, DI, DS, JC, MC, VI.

Bed & Breakfast

BRIARWOOD INN   **Phone:** (831)626-9056   95
All Year [CP]   1P: $125- 295   2P/1B: $125- 295 2P/2B: $125- 295   XP: $20
Location: 3 blks n off Ocean Ave at San Carlos St & 4th Ave. (PO Box 5245, 93921). Fax: 831/626-8900.
Terms: Reserv deposit, 7 day notice; handling fee imposed; 2 night min stay, on weekends. **Facility:** 12 rooms.
Most rooms with fireplace. 5 rooms with wet bar. 1 two-bedroom unit. 1 two-bedroom, 2 bath suite, $425 for up
to 4 person; 4 one-bedroom units, $225 for up to 4 persons; 1-2 stories; exterior corridors; smoke free prem-
ises. **Dining:** Restaurant nearby. **All Rooms:** combo or shower baths. **Cards:** AE, MC, VI. **Special Amenities: Free
breakfast and preferred room (subject to availability with advanced reservations).** *(See color ad below)*

Motel

CANDLE LIGHT INN   **Phone:** 831/624-6451   96
Fri & Sat & Sun-Thurs
7/2-10/30 [CP]   1P: $154- 214   2P/1B: $154- 214 2P/2B: $154- 214   XP: $15   F14
Sun-Thurs 2/1-7/1 &
10/31-1/31 [CP]   1P: $124- 164   2P/1B: $124- 164 2P/2B: $124- 164   XP: $15   F14
Location: 2 blks n off ocean on San Carlos St, between 4th & 5th aves. (PO Box 1900, 93921).
Fax: 831/624-6732. **Terms:** Reserv deposit, 3 day notice; 2 night min stay, weekends. **Facility:** 19 rooms. Some rooms with
fireplace. 1 two-bedroom unit. Family unit, $129-$179 for up to 4 persons. 1 whirlpool unit, $149-$199 for up to 2 persons; 2
stories; exterior corridors; small pool. **Dining:** Restaurant nearby. **All Rooms:** combo or shower baths. **Some Rooms:** 6
kitchens. **Cards:** AE, DS, MC, VI. *(See color ad p 685)*

Motel

CARMEL COUNTRY INN   **Phone:** (831)625-3263   86
All Year [CP]   1P: $105- 165   2P/1B: $105- 165 2P/2B: $105- 165   XP: $20
Location: 4 blks n of Ocean Ave; at Dolores & 3rd Ave. 93921 (PO Box 3756). Fax: 831/625-2945.
Terms: Reserv deposit, 7 day notice; handling fee imposed; 2 night min stay, weekends; small pets only, $10
extra charge, selected rooms. **Facility:** 12 rooms. Many large rooms with wet bar; most gas burning fireplaces.
5 two-bedroom units. 2 stories; exterior corridors; smoke free premises. **All Rooms:** combo or shower baths.
Cards: MC, VI. **Special Amenities: Free breakfast and preferred room (subject to availability with
advanced reservations).** *(See color ad p 686)*

Bed & Breakfast

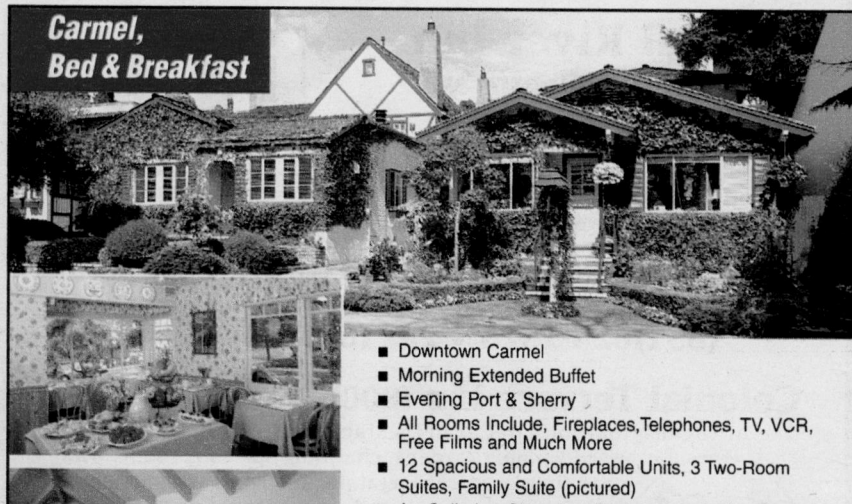
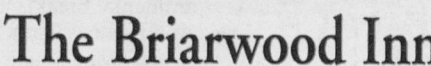

(See map p. 680)

CARMEL FIREPLACE INN

Phone: (831)624-4862 [94]

AAA SAVE All Year [CP]   1P: $85- 250   2P/1B: $85- 250   2P/2B: $155- 250   XP: $15
◆◆◆   **Location:** 3 blks n off Ocean Ave at San Carlos St & 4th Ave. (PO Box 4082, 93921). Fax: 831/626-1981.
Motel   **Terms:** Reserv deposit, 7 day notice; handling fee imposed; 2 night min stay, weekends. **Facility:** 18 rooms. Few small rooms; few large units. Many woodburning fireplaces. 1 two-bedroom unit. 2 stories; exterior corridors; smoke free premises. **Dining:** Restaurant nearby. **All Rooms:** combo or shower baths. **Cards:** AE, MC, VI. **Special Amenities:** Free breakfast and preferred room (subject to availability with advanced reservations).
(See color ad p 686)

[†+] [VCR] [▣] [K] [▨] [▤]

CARMEL GARDEN COURT

Phone: (831)624-6926 [93]

AAA SAVE All Year [CP]   1P: $125- 245   2P/1B: $125- 245   2P/2B: $125- 245   XP: $20   F10
◆◆◆   **Location:** 3 blks n at 4th Ave & Torres St. 93921 (PO Box 6226). Fax: 831/624-4935. **Terms:** Handling fee
Bed &   imposed; 2 night min stay, weekends; small pets only, $25 extra charge. **Facility:** 9 rooms. Award wining pic-
Breakfast   turesque garden area. Some flower filled private patios. Wood burning fireplaces. 1 story; exterior corridors; smoke free premises. **All Rooms:** combo or shower baths. **Some Rooms:** kitchen. **Cards:** AE, MC, VI. **Special Amenities:** Free breakfast and free newspaper. *(See color ad p 687)*

[🍽] [3⁺⁰] [VCR] [▣] [▢] [K] [▨] [▤]

(See map p. 680)

CARMEL OAKS INN — Rates Subject to Change — Phone: 831/624-5547 — 97
◆◆◆
Motel
Fri & Sat & Sun-Thurs
6/1-10/1 [CP]   1P: $89- 159   2P/1B: $89- 169 2P/2B: $109- 229   XP: $15   F16
Sun-Thurs 2/1-5/31 &
10/2-1/31 [CP]   1P: $59- 139   2P/1B: $59- 139 2P/2B: $79- 199   XP: $15   F16
Location: 2 blks n off Ocean Ave at 5th & Mission. (PO Box 3696, 93921). Fax: 831/625-5908. **Terms:** Reserv deposit, 2 day notice; 2 night min stay, weekends. **Facility:** 17 rooms. 2 stories; exterior corridors; smoke free premises. **All Rooms:** combo or shower baths. **Some Rooms:** efficiency. **Cards:** AE, MC, VI. *(See color ad p 687)*

CARMEL RESORT INN — Rates Subject to Change — Phone: (831)624-3113 — 89
ⒶⒶⒶ
◆◆
Cottage
All Year [CP]   1P: $69- 225   2P/1B: $69- 225 2P/2B: $79- 225
Location: 5 blks n at Carpenter & 2nd St. (PO Box 2266, 93921). Fax: 831/624-5456. **Terms:** Reserv deposit, 7 day notice. **Facility:** 30 rooms. Cottages located in a nicely landscaped, wooded area, 24 wood-burning fireplaces. 3 two-bedroom units. 1 story; exterior corridors; sauna, whirlpool. **Some Rooms:** efficiency. **Cards:** AE, CB, DI, DS, MC, VI. *(See color ad p 688)*

HERE'S YOUR TICKET TO FREE NIGHTS.

La Quinta® Inn

No matter where the road leads you, La Quinta® Inns and La Quinta® Inn & Suites offer more than mere comfort and convenience. You can also earn free night stays

by enrolling in our Returns® Club. There's no cost to join and by using the coupon below, we'll give you triple credits for your first stay in California or Nevada. That way you'll be well on your way to free stays and, of course, a comfy night's sleep.

La Quinta® Inn & Suites

Call 1-800-221-4731 *for reservations*
100% SATISFACTION GUARANTEE
www.laquinta.com

- -

YOU'RE ON YOUR WAY TO FREE NIGHT STAYS WITH OUR SPECIAL RETURNS CLUB® TRIPLE-CREDIT OFFER!

Present this coupon at check-in for triple credits when you stay at any CA or NV
La Quinta Inn or La Quinta Inn & Suites and join the Returns Club. Then as a regular Returns Club
member, you'll receive a free night for every 11 nights you stay, plus other great benefits.

(See map p. 680)

TICKLE PINK INN Rates Subject to Change Phone: (831)624-1244 81
(AAA) All Year [CP] 1P: $189- 309 2P/1B: $189- 309 2P/2B: $189- 309 XP: $25 F3
◆◆◆◆ **Location:** 4 mi s on SR 1 in Carmel Highlands. 155 Highland Dr 93923. Fax: 831/626-9516. **Terms:** Reserv
Motel deposit, 3 day notice; 2 night min stay, weekends. **Facility:** 35 rooms. Spectacular view. Large units with bal-
cony & some fireplace. 2-3 stories, no elevator; exterior corridors; whirlpool. **Dining:** Restaurant nearby. **All Rooms:** combo or shower baths. **Some Rooms:** kitchen,
whirlpools. **Cards:** AE, MC, VI. *(See color ad below)*

VAGABOND HOUSE INN Phone: (831)624-7738 90
(AAA) (SAVE) All Year [CP] 1P: $85- 165 2P/1B: $85- 165 2P/2B: $125- 145 XP: $20
◆◆ **Location:** N off Ocean on Dolores at 4th Ave. (PO Box 2747, 93921). Fax: 831/626-1243. **Terms:** Reserv
Bed & deposit, 3 day notice; 2 night min stay, Thurs/Fri or Sat/Sun; pets, $10 extra charge. **Facility:** 11 rooms. Cluster
Breakfast of rooms around a landscaped courtyard with fountain. 1-2 stories; exterior corridors; smoke free premises. **All Rooms:** combo or shower baths. **Some Rooms:** 8 kitchens. **Cards:** AE, MC, VI. **Special Amenities:** Free breakfast and free newspaper.

WAYSIDE INN Phone: 831/624-5336 109
(AAA) (SAVE) Fri & Sat & Sun-Thurs
7/2-10/31 [CP] 1P: $109- 269 2P/1B: $109- 269 2P/2B: $154- 269 XP: $15 F14
◆◆◆ Sun-Thurs 2/1-7/1 &
Motel 11/1-1/31 [CP] 1P: $95- 204 2P/1B: $95- 204 2P/2B: $114- 204 XP: $15 F14
Location: 1 blk s off Ocean Ave, at Mission St & 7th Ave. (PO Box 1900, 93921). Fax: 831/626-6974.
Terms: Reserv deposit, 3 day notice; handling fee imposed; 2 night min stay, weekends; small pets only. **Facility:** 22 rooms.
Most units with fireplace. 1 two-bedroom unit with kitchen, $189-$249 for up to 6 persons; 1 suite, $169-$219; 2 stories; ex-
terior corridors. **Dining:** Restaurant nearby. **All Rooms:** combo or shower baths. **Some Rooms:** 10 kitchens. **Cards:** AE,
DS, MC, VI. *(See color ad p 685)*

RESTAURANTS

ANTON & MICHEL Lunch: $5-$14 Dinner: $17-$30 Phone: 831/624-2406 39
(AAA) **Location:** Mission St at 7th St. 93921. **Hours:** 11:30 am-3 & 5:30-9:30, Sat-10 pm.
Reservations: suggested. **Features:** No A/C; dressy casual; cocktails & lounge; street parking; a la carte.
◆◆◆ Attractive courtyard view. Lamb & seafood specialties. Smoke free premises. **Cards:** AE, CB, DI, DS, MC,
Continental VI.

BULLY III HOUSE OF PRIME RIB Lunch: $5-$15 Dinner: $10-$27 Phone: 831/625-1750 35
◆◆ **Location:** 2 blks s off Ocean Ave at Dolores St & 8th Ave; in Adobe Inn-Carmel. Dolores St & 8th Ave
American 93921. **Hours:** 11:30 am-10 pm. Closed: 11/25 & 12/25. **Reservations:** suggested. **Features:** No A/C;
casual dress; children's menu; early bird specials; cocktails & lounge; street parking. Prime rib cut to order &
fresh seafood. Short order items in the pub 11:30 am-10 pm. Smoke free premises. **Cards:** AE, MC, VI.
(See color ad p 683)

(See map p. 680)

CASANOVA   Lunch: $9-$15   Dinner: $20-$35   Phone: 831/625-0501 ④⓪
◆◆◆   **Location:** On 5th Ave between San Carlos & Mission sts; 2 blks n off Ocean Ave. 93921. **Hours:** 11:30
French   am-3 & 5-10:30 pm, Sat 8 am-11, 11:30-3 & 5-10:30 pm, Sun 9am-3 & 5-10:30 pm. Closed: 12/24 at 3 pm,
12/25. **Reservations:** suggested. **Features:** No A/C; dressy casual; Sunday brunch; cocktails; street parking.
Cozy, country atmosphere. Also Italian cuisine. Smoke free premises. **Cards:** MC, VI.   (&) (X)

THE COVEY   Dinner: $19-$35   Phone: 831/624-1581 ③②
◆◆◆   **Location:** 3.5 mi e of SR 1, via Carmel Valley Rd; in Quail Lodge Resort & Golf Club. 8205 Valley Greens
Continental   Dr 93923. **Hours:** 6:30 pm-10:30 pm, Sat & Sun 6 pm-11 pm. **Reservations:** suggested. **Features:** No A/C;
semi-formal attire; health conscious menu items; cocktails & lounge; entertainment; a la carte. Overlooking
duck pond. Fresh California specialties using local produce. Smoke free premises. **Cards:** AE, CB, DI, DS, MC, VI.
(See color ad p 694)   (&) (X)

THE FRENCH POODLE RESTAURANT   Dinner: $15-$45   Phone: 831/624-8643 ③③
ⒶⒶⒶ   **Location:** 2 blks n off Ocean, at Junipero & 5th ave. 93921. **Hours:** 5:30 pm-9:30 pm. Closed: Sun & 12/25.
Reservations: required. **Features:** dressy casual; beer & wine only; street parking; a la carte. Elegant dining
◆◆◆◆   room, beautiful paintings & warm, charming atmosphere. Smoke free premises. **Cards:** AE, DI, MC, VI. (X)
French

FROM SCRATCH   Lunch: $5-$9   Dinner: $8-$25   Phone: 831/625-2448 ②⑧
◆   **Location:** 1 mi s exit SR 1 at Carmel Valley Rd, in the Barnyard Shopping Center. 3626 The Barnyard
American   93921. **Hours:** 8 am-3 Dinner: Thurs, Fri, Sat only 5:30 pm-9 pm. Closed: 11/26 & 12/25.
Reservations: suggested. **Features:** No A/C; casual dress; children's menu; beer & wine only; a la carte.
Homemade soups & quiches. Smoke free premises. **Cards:** AE, DI, DS, MC, VI.   (X)

LE COQ D'OR   Dinner: $18-$25   Phone: 831/626-9319 ③④
◆◆◆   **Location:** 3 blks n off Ocean, on Mission btwn 4th & 5th sts. **Hours:** 5 pm-9 pm. **Reservations:** suggested.
Continental   **Features:** No A/C; casual dress; beer & wine only; street parking; a la carte. European dishes,
predominately German & French. Lavish flavors. Cozy atmosphere in a homey, country-style environment,
small heated patio. Smoke free premises. **Cards:** AE, MC, VI.   (X)

MONDO'S TRATTORIA   Lunch: $6-$14   Dinner: $10-$23   Phone: 831/624-8977 ③⑤
ⒶⒶⒶ   **Location:** S off Ocean on Dolores, between Ocean & 7th Ave. **Hours:** 11:30 am-3 & 5-10 pm. Closed major
holidays. **Reservations:** suggested. **Features:** casual dress; beer & wine only; street parking; a la carte.
◆◆◆   Varied menu, traditional dishes of both northern & southern Italy, homemade dessert. Smoke free premises.
Italian   **Cards:** AE, DI, DS, MC, VI.   (X)

PACIFIC'S EDGE   Lunch: $5-$15   Dinner: $30-$40   Phone: 831/622-5445 ②⑨
◆◆◆◆   **Location:** 4 mi s on SR 1, at Carmel Highlands; in Highlands Inn. **Hours:** 11:30 am-2 & 6-10 pm, Fri &
Regional   Sat-10:30 pm, Sun brunch 10 am-2 & 6-10 pm. **Reservations:** suggested. **Features:** semi-formal attire;
American   Sunday brunch; children's menu; cocktails & lounge; valet parking; a la carte, also prix fixe. Casual but
elegant dining room with spectacular view of Pacific Ocean; emphasis on fresh local ingredients with unique
health conscious preparation, light but robust flavors. Smoke free premises. **Cards:** AE, CB, DI, DS, MC, VI.   (X)

RAFFAELLO RESTAURANT   Dinner: $18-$28   Phone: 831/624-1541 ③⑦
◆◆◆◆   **Location:** S off Ocean on Mission St between Ocean & 7th sts. 93921. **Hours:** 6 pm-10 pm.
Northern   **Reservations:** suggested. **Features:** dressy casual; beer & wine only; street parking. Traditional dishes,
Italian   prepared with a variety of wine sauces, some lighter, modern style. House made pasta, fresh ingredients,
chicken, fish & veal. Beautiful florentine dining room. Smoke free premises. **Cards:** AE, CB, DI, MC, VI. (X)

THE RED LION TAVERN   Lunch: $6-$12   Dinner: $11-$20   Phone: 831/625-6765 ③⑧
ⒶⒶⒶ   **Location:** N off Ocean, on Dolores between 5th & 6th sts. **Hours:** 11 am-10 pm, Sat-11:30 pm. Closed:
12/25. **Reservations:** suggested. **Features:** No A/C; casual dress; children's menu; cocktails & lounge;
◆◆◆   street parking; a la carte. Traditional English pub atmosphere with lively bar, separate dining room. American
American   & English dishes, varied menu featuring steak, fish, pasta & poultry. **Cards:** AE, CB, DI, DS, MC, VI. (X)

RIO GRILL   Lunch: $6-$12   Dinner: $20-$30   Phone: 831/625-5436 ④③
◆◆◆   **Location:** 1 blk e of SR 1; in the Crossroads Shopping Center. 101 Crossroads Blvd 93923. **Hours:** 11:30
American   am-10 pm, Sat-11 pm. Closed: 11/25 & 12/25, 7/4. **Reservations:** suggested. **Features:** casual dress;
Sunday brunch; cocktails & lounge; a la carte. Upbeat atmosphere, Southwestern ambiance, California
cuisine with a western flair. Interesting, creative preparation, emphasis on fresh ingredients. Smoke free premises.
Cards: AE, MC, VI.   (X)

SANS SOUCI   Dinner: $31-$58   Phone: 831/624-6220 ③①
◆◆◆   **Location:** 1 1/2 blks n of Ocean Ave, on Lincoln St between 5th & 6th aves. 93921. **Hours:** 5:30 pm-9:30
French   pm. Closed: Wed, 12/25 & 11/29-12/3. **Reservations:** suggested. **Features:** No A/C; dressy casual;
children's menu; cocktails; street parking; a la carte. Fresh seafood specialties. Cozy, warm & quiet. Smoke
free premises. **Cards:** AE, MC, VI.   (X)

SIMPSON'S RESTAURANT   Dinner: $14-$27   Phone: 831/624-5755 ③⓪
ⒶⒶⒶ   **Location:** 2 blks n off Ocean Ave; on San Carlos St & 5th ave; in Carmel Sands Lodge. Corner 5th & San
Carlos 93921. **Hours:** 5 pm-9:30 pm. Closed: Sun, Easter, 7/4; on 3 day weekends, open Sun & closed
◆◆◆   Mon, 2nd teo weeks in Jan. Reservations: suggested. **Features:** No A/C; casual dress; cocktails & lounge;
American   minimum charge-$10. Fresh seafood, prime rib, veal specialties. Smoke free premises. **Cards:** AE, MC, VI.
(See color ad p 688)   (X)

CARMEL VALLEY—4,000   (See map p. 680; index p. 678)

LODGINGS

ACACIA LODGE-COUNTRY GARDEN INNS   Phone: (831)659-2297   **139**
(AAA) (SAVE)
	7/1-9/30 [CP]	1P: $125- 158	2P/1B: $135- 168	2P/2B: $144- 180	XP: $20	D12
	2/1-6/30 & 10/1-11/30 [CP]	1P: $108- 125	2P/1B: $118- 135	2P/2B: $126- 144	XP: $20	D12
	12/1-1/31 [CP]	1P: $75- 108	2P/1B: $85- 118	2P/2B: $108- 126	XP: $20	D12

◆◆◆
Bed &
Breakfast
Location: 12.8 mi e of SR 1; in Carmel Valley Village. 20 Via Contenta 93924 (PO Box 87). Fax: 831/659-2392. **Terms:** Reserv deposit, 3 day notice; 2 night min stay, weekends. **Facility:** 18 rooms. Quiet secluded area. Nicely landscaped grounds with view of mountains. Patios. 8 kitchens, $15 extra charge; 1 story; exterior corridors; smoke free premises; heated pool, whirlpool. **Services:** complimentary evening beverages. **All Rooms:** combo or shower baths. **Cards:** AE, MC, VI. **Special Amenities:** Free breakfast and free room upgrade (subject to availability with advanced reservations). *(See color ad p 691)*

CARMEL VALLEY LODGE   Phone: (831)659-2261   **137**
(AAA) (SAVE)
	5/28-11/28 [CP]	1P: $129- 189	2P/1B: $129- 189	2P/2B: $129- 189	XP: $15
	11/29-1/31 [CP]	1P: $119- 179	2P/1B: $119- 179	2P/2B: $119- 179	XP: $15
	2/1-5/27 [CP]	1P: $109- 169	2P/1B: $109- 169	2P/2B: $109- 169	XP: $15

◆◆◆
Complex
Location: 11.5 mi e of SR 1; Carmel Valley Rd, at Ford Rd. 8 Ford Rd 93924 (PO Box 93). Fax: 831/659-4558. **Terms:** 2 night min stay, weekends; pets, $10 extra charge, dogs only. **Facility:** 31 rooms. Quiet location; landscaped grounds with garden patios. Some antiques & reproductions. Many fireplaces. 8 one-bedroom cottages, $189-$209 for 2 persons; 4 two-bedroom cottages, $269-$299 for 4 persons with kitchen & woodburning fireplace. All with micr; 2 stories; exterior corridors; sauna, whirlpool. **Some Rooms:** 8 kitchens. **Cards:** AE, MC, VI. **Special Amenities:** Free breakfast and free room upgrade (subject to availability with advanced reservations).

HIDDEN VALLEY INN-COUNTRY GARDEN INNS   Phone: (831)659-5361   **138**
(AAA) (SAVE)
	7/1-9/30 [CP]	1P: $125- 158	2P/1B: $135- 168	2P/2B: $124- 219	XP: $20	D12
	2/1-6/30 & 10/1-11/30 [CP]	1P: $108- 125	2P/1B: $118- 135	2P/2B: $109- 175	XP: $20	D12
	12/1-1/31 [CP]	1P: $75- 108	2P/1B: $85- 118	2P/2B: $85- 164	XP: $20	D12

◆◆◆
Motel
Location: 11 mi e of SR 1, Carmel Valley Rd. 102 W Carmel Valley Rd 93924 (PO Box 504). Fax: 831/659-2392. **Terms:** Reserv deposit, 3 day notice; package plans; 2 night min stay, weekends. **Facility:** 26 rooms. Quiet scenic location. Rooms with patio or deck, many overlooking pool & garden. 2 stories; exterior corridors; smoke free premises; small pool. **Services:** complimentary evening beverages. **All Rooms:** combo or shower baths. **Some Rooms:** efficiency, no utensils. **Cards:** AE, MC, VI. **Special Amenities:** Free breakfast and free room upgrade (subject to availability with advanced reservations). *(See color ad p 691)*

LOS LAURELES   Phone: (831)659-2233   **136**
(AAA) (SAVE)
| | 4/1-10/31 [EP] | 1P: $98- 250 | 2P/1B: $98- 250 | 2P/2B: $110- 250 | XP: $20 |
| | 2/1-3/31 & 11/1-1/31 [CP] | 1P: $78- 225 | 2P/1B: $78- 225 | 2P/2B: $90- 225 | XP: $20 |

◆◆◆
Motor Inn
Location: 10.5 mi e of SR 1. 313 W Carmel Valley Rd 93924 (PO Box 2310). Fax: 831/659-0481. **Terms:** Handling fee imposed; package plans. **Facility:** 30 rooms. Restored historic California ranch. Few small rooms, few with fireplace. 1 three-bedroom unit. 3-bedroom house, $450 for up to 6 persons; 1 story; exterior corridors; whirlpool; playground. **Dining:** Restaurant; 7 am-9:30 pm; 11/1-4/30 5:30 pm-9:30 pm; $15-$22; cocktails. **Services:** giftshop. **Recreation:** Fee: horseback riding. **All Rooms:** combo or shower baths. **Some Rooms:** 2 kitchens, whirlpools. **Cards:** AE, MC, VI. **Special Amenities:** Free room upgrade (subject to availability with advanced reservations).

RESTAURANT

WILL'S FARGO RESTAURANT   **Dinner:** $14-$27   Phone: 831/659-2774   **47**
◆◆
Steakhouse
Location: In the Village. 93924. **Hours:** 5:30 pm-10-pm, Sun from 5 pm-9 pm. **Reservations:** suggested. **Features:** No A/C; casual dress; children's menu; cocktails & lounge; street parking; a la carte. 1880's decor, garden setting, varied menu, steaks cut to order. Smoke free premises. **Cards:** AE, MC, VI.

MARINA—26,400

LODGINGS

COMFORT INN   Rates Subject to Change   Phone: 831/883-4000
(AAA) (FYI)
All Year [CP]   1P: $79- 215   2P/1B: $79- 215   2P/2B: $79- 215
Motel
Too new to rate. **Location:** Just e of SR 1; Reservation Rd exit. 140 Reservation Rd 93933. **Facility:** 62 rooms. Scheduled to open summer, 1998; 3 stories; interior corridors; sauna. **All Rooms:** combo or shower baths. **Cards:** AE, CB, DI, DS, MC, VI.

MONTEREY/MARINA BEACH TRAVELODGE   Phone: (831)883-0300
(AAA) (SAVE)
	7/18-10/18 [CP]	1P: $89- 104	2P/1B: $89- 104	2P/2B: $89- 104	XP: $10	F18
	5/16-7/17 [CP]	1P: $69- 89	2P/1B: $69- 89	2P/2B: $69- 89	XP: $10	F18
	2/1-5/15 & 10/19-1/31 [CP]	1P: $49- 69	2P/1B: $49- 69	2P/2B: $49- 69	XP: $10	F18

◆
Motel
Location: Just w of SR 1, Reservation Rd exit. 3290 Dunes Dr 93933. Fax: 831/384-8137. **Terms:** Weekly rates, 12/1-3/31; pets, $10 extra charge. **Facility:** 84 rooms. 2 stories; exterior corridors; whirlpool; playground. **Cards:** AE, CB, DI, DS, MC, VI. **Special Amenities:** Free breakfast and free local telephone calls.

SUPER 8   Phone: (831)384-1800
(AAA) (SAVE)
| | Fri & Sat | 1P: $84- 89 | 2P/1B: $84- 89 | 2P/2B: $94 | XP: $4 |
| | Sun-Thurs | 1P: $40- 64 | 2P/1B: $40- 64 | 2P/2B: $60- 84 | XP: $4 |

◆
Motel
Location: Just w of SR 1, Reservation Dr exit. 3290 Dunes Dr 93933. Fax: 831/384-5279. **Facility:** 114 rooms. 3 stories, no elevator; exterior corridors; whirlpool; beach access through dunes. **Cards:** AE, CB, DI, DS, MC, VI. **Special Amenities:** Free breakfast and free local telephone calls.

MONTEREY—32,000 (See map p. 680; index p. 675)

LODGINGS

BAY PARK HOTEL   Rates Subject to Change   **Phone:** (831)649-1020   **41**

	6/13-9/25	1P:	$99- 160	2P/1B:	$99- 160	2P/2B:	$99- 160	XP:	$10	F18
	4/2-6/12 & 9/26-10/31	1P:	$89- 150	2P/1B:	$89- 150	2P/2B:	$89- 150	XP:	$10	F18
	2/1-4/1 & 11/1-1/31	1P:	$79- 129	2P/1B:	$79- 129	2P/2B:	$79- 129	XP:	$10	F18

◆ ◆ ◆
Motor Inn

Location: Just w of SR 1, Munras Ave exit. 1425 Munras Ave 93940. Fax: 831/373-4258. **Terms:** Small pets only, $5 extra charge. **Facility:** 80 rooms. Across from Del Monte Center. This property recycles. 3 stories; interior corridors; whirlpool. **Dining:** Restaurant; 7 am-2 & 5:30-9 pm; $9-$16; cocktails. **Cards:** AE, CB, DI, DS, JC, MC, VI.
(See color ad below)

BEST WESTERN DE ANZA INN   **Phone:** (831)646-8300   **5**

| | 6/15-9/15 [CP] | 1P: | $70- 139 | 2P/1B: | $80- 139 | 2P/2B: | $85- 139 | XP: | $8 | F12 |
| | 2/1-6/14 & 9/16-1/31 [CP] | 1P: | $60- 129 | 2P/1B: | $65- 129 | 2P/2B: | $75- 129 | XP: | $8 | F12 |

◆ ◆ ◆
Motel

Location: 0.4 mi e of SR 1; Casa Verde or Fremont St exit. 2141 Fremont St exit. 2141 Fremont St 93940. Fax: 831/646-8130. **Terms:** 2 night min stay, weekends. **Facility:** 43 rooms. Spacious rooms. 3 stories; interior corridors; whirlpool. **Dining:** Restaurants nearby. **Cards:** AE, CB, DI, DS, JC, MC, VI. **Special Amenities:** Free breakfast and free local telephone calls. *(See color ad on p 699)*

(See map p. 680)

BEST WESTERN MONTEREY INN   Rates Subject to Change   **Phone:** (831)373-5345   57
(AAA)
6/1-10/31 [CP]	1P:	$99- 139	2P/1B:	$99- 139	2P/2B:	$109- 149	XP: $10	F12
3/1-5/31 [CP]	1P:	$79- 99	2P/1B:	$79- 99	2P/2B:	$89- 109	XP: $10	F12
2/1-2/28 & 11/1-1/31 [CP]	1P:	$69- 99	2P/1B:	$69- 99	2P/2B:	$79- 109	XP: $10	F12

Motel   **Location:** 0.7 mi w of SR 1, Munras Ave exit. 825 Abrego St 93940. **Fax:** 831/373-3246. **Terms:** Reserv deposit; 2 night min stay, weekends. **Facility:** 80 rooms. Spacious rooms, few with view. Covered parking. 9 rooms with fireplace, $99-$143 for up to 2 persons; 3 stories; interior corridors; whirlpool, small pool 4/1-10/31. **Dining:** Coffee shop nearby. **All Rooms:** combo or shower baths. **Cards:** AE, CB, DI, DS, MC, VI. *(See color ad below)*

BEST WESTERN PARK CREST MOTEL   Rates Subject to Change   **Phone:** (831)372-4576   31
(AAA)

All Year [CP]   1P: $69- 179   2P/1B: $75- 179   2P/2B: $85- 179   XP: $10   F12

Location: 0.5 mi w of SR 1, Soledad Dr or Munras Ave exits. 1100 Munras Ave 93940. **Fax:** 831/372-2317.
Motel   **Facility:** 53 rooms. Few units with view of bay. 3 two-bedroom units. Lower rates in winter; 2 stories; exterior corridors; pool open 4/15-10/31. **All Rooms:** combo or shower baths. **Some Rooms:** whirlpools. **Cards:** AE, CB, DI, DS, JC, MC, VI. *(See color ad p 700)*

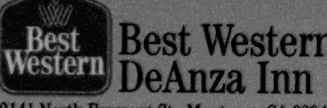

(See map p. 680)

BEST WESTERN RAMONA INN
Rates Subject to Change
Phone: (831)373-2445 **3**
All Year [CP]
1P: $59- 159   2P/1B: $59- 159   2P/2B: $69- 159   XP: $10   F12
Location: 0.7 mi e of SR 1; Del Rey Oaks (SR 218) or Fremont St exits. 2332 Fremont St 93940.
Fax: 831/373-6358. **Terms:** Reserv deposit, 7 day notice. **Facility:** 34 rooms. 2 stories; exterior corridors; whirlpool. **Dining:** Restaurant nearby. **Cards:** AE, CB, DI, DS, JC, MC, VI.
Motel

BEST WESTERN STEINBECK LODGE
Phone: (831)373-3203 **38**
7/1-8/31 [CP]   1P: $79- 179   2P/1B: $79- 179   2P/2B: $89- 199   XP: $10
4/1-6/30 & 9/1-10/31 [CP]   1P: $59- 179   2P/1B: $59- 179   2P/2B: $69- 179   XP: $10
2/1-3/31 & 11/1-1/31 [CP]   1P: $49- 179   2P/1B: $49- 179   2P/2B: $49- 179   XP: $10
Location: 0.2 mi w of SR 1, Munras Ave exit. 1300 Munras Ave 93940. Fax: 831/372-3505. **Facility:** 32 rooms.
Near Del Monte Shopping Center. 2 stories; exterior corridors. **Cards:** AE, CB, DI, DS, MC, VI.
Motel
Special Amenities: Free breakfast.

BEST WESTERN VICTORIAN INN
Phone: (831)373-8000 **46**
6/1-10/31   1P: $199- 429   2P/1B: $199- 429   2P/2B: $199- 429   XP: $10   F18
11/1-1/31   1P: $149- 399   2P/1B: $149- 399   2P/2B: $149- 399   XP: $10   F18
2/1-5/31   1P: $159- 359   2P/1B: $159- 359   2P/2B: $159- 359   XP: $10   F18
Location: 3.4 mi w of SR 1, Monterey exit. 487 Foam St 93940. Fax: 831/373-4815. **Terms:** Check-in 4 pm; reserv deposit; handling fee imposed; 2 night min stay, weekends; pets, $25 cleaning fee; $75 dep req.
Facility: 68 rooms. All units with gas burning fireplace. Near Cannery Row. Complimentary covered parking. 4 whirlpool units with featherbed; 3 stories; interior/exterior corridors; whirlpool. **Dining:** Complimentary wine & cheese 4 pm-6 pm; restaurant nearby. **All Rooms:** combo or shower baths. **Cards:** AE, CB, DI, DS, JC, MC, VI. **Special Amenities:** Free breakfast and free newspaper. (See color ad p 701)

CANNERY ROW INN
Rates Subject to Change
Phone: 831/649-8580 **48**
All Year   1P: $79- 299   2P/1B: $79- 299   2P/2B: $79- 299   XP: $10
Location: 200 Foam St 93940. Fax: 831/649-2566. **Terms:** CP avail. **Facility:** 32 rooms. Few rooms with partial bay view, most have gas fireplace. 1 two-bedroom unit. Rates for up to 4 persons; 3 stories; interior corridors; whirlpool. **Cards:** AE, DS, MC, VI. (See color ad p 701)
Motel

CARMEL HILL LODGE
Phone: (831)373-3252 **39**
Fri & Sat   1P: $89- 129   2P/1B: $89- 159   2P/2B: $89- 179   XP: $10   F18
Sun-Thurs   1P: $69- 109   2P/1B: $69- 119   2P/2B: $69- 119   XP: $10   F18
Location: Just w of SR 1, Munras Ave exit. 1374 Munras Ave 93940. Fax: 831/655-2420. **Terms:** Pets, $5 extra charge. **Facility:** 38 rooms. Near Del Monte shopping center. 2 stories; exterior corridors. **All Rooms:** combo or shower baths. **Some Rooms:** whirlpools. **Cards:** AE, DS, MC, VI.
Motel

(See map p. 680)

CASA MUNRAS GARDEN HOTEL   Phone: (831)375-2411   56
(AAA) (SAVE)
   7/1-9/30   1P: $114- 174   2P/1B: $124- 174   2P/2B: $124- 174   XP: $15   F12
◆◆◆   4/1-6/30 & 10/1-10/31   1P: $93- 153   2P/1B: $103- 153   2P/2B: $103- 153   XP: $15   F12
Motor Inn   2/1-3/31 & 11/1-1/31   1P: $83- 133   2P/1B: $93- 133   2P/2B: $93- 133   XP: $15   F12
Location: 0.8 mi w of SR 1, Munras Ave exit. 700 Munras Ave 93940 (PO Box 1351). Fax: 831/375-1365. **Facility:** 166 rooms. Some gas fireplaces & some garden view rooms. 1-2 stories; interior/exterior corridors; heated pool. **Dining:** Restaurant; 7 am-2 & 5-9 pm, Sat & Sun 7 am-noon & 5-9 pm; $9-$20; cocktails. **All Rooms:** combo or shower baths. **Cards:** AE, CB, JC, MC, VI. *(See color ad p 702)*

CASA VERDE INN   Rates Subject to Change   Phone: (831)375-5407   11
(AAA)
   4/2-10/31   1P: $60   2P/1B: $79   2P/2B: $89   XP: $8   F12
◆   2/1-4/1 & 11/1-1/31   1P: $29   2P/1B: $39   2P/2B: $49   XP: $8   F12
Motel   **Location:** Just s of SR 1, Casa Verde Way or Fremont exits. 2113 N Freemont 93940. Fax: 831/373-7261. **Terms:** Reserv deposit, 3 day notice. **Facility:** 18 rooms. Small units. 1 story; exterior corridors. **Dining:** Coffee shop nearby. **All Rooms:** combo or shower baths. **Cards:** AE, DS, MC, VI.

COLTON INN   Phone: 831/649-6500   20
(AAA) (SAVE)
   All Year [CP]   1P: $110- 310   2P/1B: $110- 310   2P/2B: $110- 310   XP: $10   F12
◆◆◆   **Location:** In Old Monterey. 707 Pacific St 93940. Fax: 831/373-6987. **Facility:** 50 rooms. Some fireplaces. 3
Motel   stories; exterior corridors; sauna. **Recreation:** sun deck. **Some Rooms:** 7 efficiencies, no utensils. whirlpools. **Cards:** AE, CB, DI, DS, MC, VI. *(See color ad p 703)*

See WHAT THE (AAA) MEANS.

(See map p. 680)

COMFORT INN-CARMEL HILL   Phone: (831)372-2908

		1P:	$69-	99	2P/1B:	$69-	109	2P/2B:	$79-	119	XP:	$5	F
	6/1-9/30 [CP]												
	4/1-5/31 [CP]	1P:	$54-	79	2P/1B:	$54-	89	2P/2B:	$59-	99	XP:	$5	F
	2/1-3/31 & 10/1-1/31 [CP]	1P:	$49-	79	2P/1B:	$49-	79	2P/2B:	$59-	89	XP:	$5	F

Motel **Location:** 0.2 mi s of SR 1, Munras Ave exit. 1252 Munras Ave 93940. Fax: 831/372-7608. **Terms:** Reserv deposit, 3 day notice; handling fee imposed. **Facility:** 30 rooms. Near Del Monte Shopping Center. 2 stories; exterior corridors. **All Rooms:** combo or shower baths. **Cards:** AE, CB, DI, DS, JC, MC, VI. **Special Amenities:** Free local telephone calls and free newspaper.

COMFORT INN-DEL MONTE BEACH   Phone: (831)373-7100   **1**

		1P:	$64-	159	2P/1B:	$64-	159	2P/2B:	$69-	179	XP:	$6
	6/29-9/30 [CP]											
	5/1-6/28 [CP]	1P:	$59-	159	2P/1B:	$59-	159	2P/2B:	$69-	169	XP:	$6
	2/1-4/30 & 10/1-1/31 [CP]	1P:	$45-	119	2P/1B:	$45-	119	2P/2B:	$50-	139	XP:	$6

Motel **Location:** Just e of SR 1; Seaside/Del Rey Oaks exit. 2401 Del Monte Ave 93940. Fax: 831/373-4813. **Terms:** Reserv deposit, 3 day notice. **Facility:** 47 rooms. Few units overlooking small lake. 3 stories; interior corridors. **Cards:** AE, DI, DS, MC, VI.

(See map p. 680)

COMFORT INN-MUNRAS
Phone: (831)372-8088 **37**

6/1-9/30 [CP]	1P: $69- 99	2P/1B: $69- 109	2P/2B: $79- 119	XP: $5 F18
4/1-5/31 [CP]	1P: $54- 79	2P/1B: $54- 89	2P/2B: $59- 99	XP: $5 F18
2/1-3/31 & 10/1-1/31 [CP]	1P: $49- 79	2P/1B: $49- 79	2P/2B: $59- 89	XP: $5 F18

Motel **Location:** Just w of SR 1, Munras Ave exit. 1262 Munras Ave 93940. Fax: 831/373-5829. **Terms:** Reserv deposit, 3 day notice; handling fee imposed. **Facility:** 36 rooms. Near Del Monte Shopping Center. 3 two-bedroom units. 2 stories; exterior corridors. **All Rooms:** combo or shower baths. **Cards:** AE, CB, DI, DS, JC, MC, VI. **Special Amenities:** Free local telephone calls and free newspaper.

CYPRESS GARDENS MOTEL
Phone: 831/373-2761 **32**

Fri & Sat & Sun-Thurs 7/2-10/30 [CP]	1P: $104- 124	2P/1B: $104- 124	2P/2B: $124	XP: $10 F14
Sun-Thurs 2/1-7/1 & 10/31-1/31 [CP]	1P: $70- 100	2P/1B: $70- 100	2P/2B: $100	XP: $10 F14

Motel **Location:** 0.5 mi w of SR 1, Munras Ave exit. 1150 Munras Ave 93940. Fax: 831/649-1329. **Terms:** Reserv deposit, 3 day notice; 2 night min stay, weekends; pets. **Facility:** 46 rooms. Nicely landscaped grounds. 1 two-bedroom unit. 1 two-bedroom suite with kitchen & fireplace, $189-$274; 2 stories; exterior corridors; whirlpool. **Cards:** AE, DS, MC, VI. (See color ad p 685)

CYPRESS TREE INN
Rates Subject to Change
Phone: (831)372-7586 **4**

All Year	1P: $48- 88	2P/1B: $58- 92	2P/2B: $64- 99	XP: $6 F12

Motel **Location:** 0.6 mi e of SR 1; Del Rey Oaks (SR 218) or Fremont St exits. 2227 N Fremont St 93940. Fax: 831/372-2940. **Terms:** Check-in 4 pm. **Facility:** 55 rooms. Few rooms with patio. 10 whirlpool rms, $90-$170 for up to 2 persons 18 RV sites adjacent, $20-$40; 2 stories; interior/exterior corridors; sauna, whirlpool. **Some Rooms:** 6 kitchens. **Cards:** MC, VI. (See color ad below)

DAYS INN-MONTEREY
Phone: (831)375-2168 **36**

5/15-9/30	1P: $65- 149	2P/1B: $75- 149	2P/2B: $85- 149	XP: $10
2/1-5/14 & 10/1-1/31	1P: $55- 118	2P/1B: $55- 118	2P/2B: $65- 118	XP: $10

Motel **Location:** 0.2 mi w of SR 1, Munras Ave exit. 1288 Munras Ave 93940. Fax: 831/375-0368. **Terms:** CP avail. **Facility:** 35 rooms. 6 units with whirlpool & fireplace, $129-$255 for up to 2 persons; 1-2 stories; exterior corridors. **All Rooms:** combo or shower baths. **Cards:** AE, CB, DI, DS, JC, MC, VI. **Special Amenities:** Free breakfast and preferred room (subject to availability with advanced reservations). (See color ad p 704)

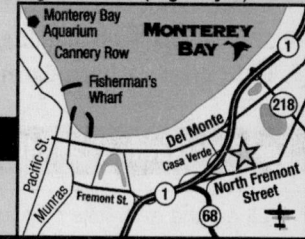

(See map p. 680)

DEL MONTE PINES MOTEL Phone: (831)375-2323 [42]

ⒶⒶⒶ ⓈⒶⓋⒺ	Fri & Sat 4/1-10/31 [CP]	1P:	$69- 149	2P/1B:	$79- 155	2P/2B:	$79- 169	XP: $10	F16
	Fri & Sat 2/1-3/31 &								
◆ ◆	11/1-1/31 [CP]	1P:	$39- 139	2P/1B:	$44- 139	2P/2B:	$44- 139	XP: $10	F16
Motel	Sun-Thurs 4/1-10/31 [CP]	1P:	$39- 99	2P/1B:	$49- 109	2P/2B:	$49- 119	XP: $10	F16
	Sun-Thurs 2/1-3/31 &								
	11/1-1/31 [CP]	1P:	$35- 89	2P/1B:	$39- 89	2P/2B:	$39- 89	XP: $10	F16

Location: Just w of SR 1, Munras Ave exit. 1298 Munras Ave 93940. Fax: 831/655-2539. **Terms:** Reserv deposit, 3 day notice; handling fee imposed; 2 night min stay, weekends in summer. **Facility:** 19 rooms. Across from Del Monte Center. 2 stories; exterior corridors; small pool. **All Rooms:** combo or shower baths. **Some Rooms:** whirlpools. **Cards:** AE, CB, DI, DS, JC, MC, VI. **Special Amenities:** Free breakfast and free local telephone calls.

ⓈⒹ 🖼 🎇 Ⓥ🅒🅡 💻 🅚 🖨 ⊠

DOUBLETREE HOTEL Phone: (831)649-4511 [16]

ⒶⒶⒶ ⓈⒶⓋⒺ	6/1-11/15	1P:	$139- 159	2P/1B:	$139- 159	XP: $20	F18
	3/1-5/31	1P:	$119- 139	2P/1B:	$119- 139	XP: $20	F18
◆ ◆ ◆	2/1-2/28 & 11/16-1/31	1P:	$99- 119	2P/1B:	$99- 119	XP: $20	F18

Hotel **Location:** 2 mi w of SR 1, Del Monte Ave or Munras Ave exits, downtown near Fisherman's Wharf. 2 Portola Plaza 93940. Fax: 831/372-0620. **Terms:** Reserv deposit; 24 day notice; package plans. **Facility:** 380 rooms. Few rooms overlooking bay & harbor. 1-7 stories; interior corridors; whirlpool. Fee: parking. **Dining:** Dining room, restaurant; 6 am-10 pm, Fri & Sat-11 pm; $15-$30; cocktails. **Services:** giftshop. Fee: massage. **All Rooms:** combo or shower baths. **Cards:** AE, CB, DI, DS, JC, MC, VI.

🅚 🎇 🖼 🍴 🖨 🅗 🕭 🎇 🖨 🅘 ⊠ 🂠

DRIFTWOOD MOTEL Phone: (831)372-5059 [18]

ⒶⒶⒶ ⓈⒶⓋⒺ	Fri & Sat 4/1-10/31 [CP]	1P:	$49- 149	2P/1B:	$49- 155	2P/2B:	$59- 159	XP: $10	F16
	Fri & Sat 2/1-3/31 &								
◆	11/1-1/31 [CP]	1P:	$33- 109	2P/1B:	$39- 119	2P/2B:	$39- 139	XP: $10	F16
Motel	Sun-Thurs 4/1-10/31 [CP]	1P:	$36- 79	2P/1B:	$39- 89	2P/2B:	$39- 99	XP: $10	F16
	Sun-Thurs 2/1-3/31 &								
	11/1-1/31 [CP]	1P:	$30- 49	2P/1B:	$33- 49	2P/2B:	$36- 59	XP: $10	F16

Location: 0.5 mi e of SR 1, Fremont St or Del Rey Oaks exits. 2362 N Fremont St 93940. Fax: 831/372-1526. **Terms:** Reserv deposit, 3 day notice; handling fee imposed; weekly rates; pets, $5 extra charge, $20 dep req. **Facility:** 15 rooms. 1 story; exterior corridors. **All Rooms:** combo or shower baths. **Cards:** AE, CB, DI, DS, JC, MC, VI.

ⓈⒹ 🅗 🅚 ⊠

Pull out the AAA state map to enhance navigation to your TourBook destination.

(See map p. 680)

ECONO LODGE  Phone: (831)372-5851 **6**
AAA SAVE Fri & Sat 6/1-9/30 [CP] 1P: $69- 99 2P/1B: $69- 119 2P/2B: $79- 129 XP: $10 F12
♦ Fri & Sat 2/1-5/31, Sun-Thurs
6/1-9/30 & Fri & Sat
Motel 10/1-1/31 [CP] 1P: $59- 79 2P/1B: $59- 89 2P/2B: $69- 99 XP: $10 F12
Sun-Thurs 2/1-5/31 &
10/1-1/31 [CP] 1P: $39- 49 2P/1B: $39- 59 2P/2B: $49- 59 XP: $10 F12
Location: Just e of SR 1, Fremont St or Casa Verde exits. 2042 Fremont St 93940. Fax: 831/372-4228. **Terms:** CP avail.
Facility: 47 rooms. Near fairgrounds. 1-2 stories; exterior corridors; whirlpool. **All Rooms:** combo or shower baths.
Some Rooms: 12 kitchens. **Cards:** AE, DI, DS, MC, VI. **Special Amenities:** Free breakfast and free local telephone
calls. *(See color ad p 704)*

EL ADOBE INN Phone: 831/372-5409 **27**
AAA SAVE Fri & Sat & Sun-Thurs
7/2-10/30 [CP] 1P: $94- 134 2P/1B: $94- 134 2P/2B: $94- 134 XP: $10 F14
♦♦ Sun-Thurs 2/1-7/1 &
Motel 10/31-1/31 [CP] 1P: $74- 100 2P/1B: $74- 100 2P/2B: $74- 100 XP: $10 F14
Location: 0.6 mi w of SR 1, Munras Ave exit. 936 Munras Ave 93940. Fax: 831/375-7236. **Terms:** Reserv
deposit, 3 day notice; pets. **Facility:** 26 rooms. 2 stories; exterior corridors; whirlpool. **All Rooms:** combo or shower baths.
Cards: AE, DS, MC, VI.

EL DORADO INN Rates Subject to Change Phone: (831)373-2921 **26**
AAA Fri & Sat 5/15-10/31 [CP] 1P: $59- 135 2P/1B: $59- 135 2P/2B: $79- 145 XP: $10 F12
Sun-Thurs 5/15-10/31 [CP] 1P: $49- 125 2P/1B: $49- 125 2P/2B: $69- 130 XP: $10 F12
♦ Fri & Sat 2/1-5/14 &
Motel 11/1-1/31 [CP] 1P: $49- 125 2P/1B: $49- 125 2P/2B: $59- 125 XP: $10 F12
Sun-Thurs 2/1-5/14 &
11/1-1/31 [CP] 1P: $39- 95 2P/1B: $39- 95 2P/2B: $49- 115 XP: $10 F12
Location: 0.6 me w of SR 1, Munras Ave exit: 900 Munras Ave 93940. **Facility:** 15 rooms. Few rooms with fireplace. 2 sto-
ries; exterior corridors. **All Rooms:** shower baths. **Cards:** CB, DI, DS, JC, MC, VI.

HILTON-MONTEREY Phone: (831)373-6141 **12**
AAA SAVE 6/14-10/31 1P: $129 2P/1B: $129 2P/2B: $129 XP: $10 F18
2/1-6/13 & 11/1-1/31 1P: $109 2P/1B: $109 2P/2B: $109 XP: $10 F18
♦♦♦ **Location:** Just w of SR 1, Aguajito Rd or Fisherman's Wharf exits. 1000 Aguajito Rd 93940.
Hotel Fax: 831/655-8608. **Terms:** Check-in 4 pm; package plans. **Facility:** 204 rooms. All rooms with balcony. 4 stories; interior corridors; putting green; sauna, whirlpool; 2 tennis courts. **Dining:** Restaurant; 6:30 am-2 & 5-10
pm; $12-$24; cocktails. **Cards:** AE, CB, DI, DS, JC, MC, VI. **Special Amenities:** Early check-in/late check-out and
preferred room (subject to availability with advanced reservations). *(See color ad p 706 & ad p 119)*

(See map p. 680)

HOLIDAY INN EXPRESS-CANNERY　　　　　　　　　　　　　　　Phone: (831)372-1800　🔢47
　　　Fri & Sat [CP]　　　　　　1P: $139- 249　2P/1B: $139- 249
　　　Sun-Thurs [CP]　　　　　1P: $99- 159　2P/1B: $99- 159
◆◆◆　**Location:** 3 mi w of SR 1, Monterey exit. 443 Wave St 93940. **Fax:** 831/372-1969. **Facility:** 43 rooms. Cozy
Motel　country inn decor. 3 stories; exterior corridors; whirlpool. **Services:** complimentary evening beverages.
　　　Cards: AE, CB, DI, DS, JC, MC, VI. **Special Amenities: Free breakfast and free local telephone calls.**
(See color ad below)　　　　　　　　　　　　　　　　　　　　🈂️ 🛏️ 📺 💻 🏧 🔌 📦 🔟 ✖️ 🏧

HOTEL PACIFIC　　　　　　　　　　　　　　　　　　　　　　Phone: (831)373-5700　🔢17
　　　7/1-10/31 [CP]　　1P: $209- 419　2P/1B: $209- 419　2P/2B: $209- 419　XP: $10　F13
　　　2/16-6/30 [CP]　　1P: $199- 349　2P/1B: $199- 349　2P/2B: $199- 349　XP: $10　F13
◆◆◆　2/1-2/15 & 11/1-1/31 [CP]　1P: $169- 299　2P/1B: $169- 299　2P/2B: $169- 299　XP: $10　F13
Suite Motel　**Location:** 2.2 mi w of SR 1, Del Monte Ave exit; near conference center. 300 Pacific St 93940.
　　　Fax: 831/373-6921. **Terms:** Check-in 4 pm; reserv deposit; handling fee imposed; package plans; 2 night
min stay, weekends. **Facility:** 105 rooms. Adobe style. All rooms have deck & gas fireplace, few with garden view. Complimentary underground parking. Two bedroom suite $319-$339 for up to 4 persons; 4 stories; interior/exterior corridors; whirlpools.
Dining: Complimentary tea & cheese 4 pm-6 pm. **Cards:** AE, CB, DI, DS, JC, MC, VI. **Special Amenities: Free breakfast
and free newspaper.** *(See color ad p 701)*　　　　🈂️ 🛏️ 📡 🏧 📼 💻 🔌 📦 🔟 ✖️ 🏧

HYATT REGENCY-MONTEREY RESORT & CONFERENCE CENTER　　　Phone: (831)372-1234　🔢58
　　　All Year　　　　　1P: $185- 300　2P/1B: $210- 325　2P/2B: $210- 325　XP: $25　F18
◆◆◆　**Location:** Just e of SR 1; Aguajito Rd or Monterey exit. 1 Old Golf Course Rd 93940. **Fax:** 831/375-3960.
Resort　**Terms:** BP avail; package plans. **Facility:** 575 rooms. Landscaped grounds. Some suites with fireplace; many
Complex　with golf course view. 2-4 stories; interior corridors; putting green; heated pool, whirlpools. Fee: 18 holes golf;
　　　6 tennis courts (2 lighted). **Dining:** Dining room; 6:30 am-11 pm; $14-$25; cocktails. **Services:** giftshop.
　　　Fee: massage. **Recreation:** jogging, croquet, basketball hoop, ping-pong, volleyball. Rental: bicycles.
All Rooms: combo or shower baths. **Cards:** AE, CB, DI, DS, JC, MC, VI. *(See color ad p 923)*
　　　　🛏️ 📡 🏊 🍴 🍽️ 📡 ✖️ 🏌️ 🎾 🔌 📦 🔟 🔟 ♿ 👤 ✖️ 🏧

(See map p. 680)

I.M.A. STAGE COACH LODGE   Rates Subject to Change   Phone: 831/373-3632   [14]

		1P:		2P/1B:		2P/2B:		XP:		
	Fri & Sat 6/1-10/31 [CP]	1P:	$85- 139	2P/1B:	$85- 139	2P/2B:	$95- 149	XP:	$10	F12
	Sun-Thurs 6/1-10/31 [CP]	1P:	$75- 129	2P/1B:	$75- 129	2P/2B:	$85- 139	XP:	$10	F12
	Fri & Sat 2/1-5/31 & 11/1-1/31 [CP]	1P:	$65- 115	2P/1B:	$65- 115	2P/2B:	$75- 125	XP:	$10	F12
	Sun-Thurs 2/1-5/31 & 11/1-1/31 [CP]	1P:	$55- 105	2P/1B:	$55- 105	2P/2B:	$65- 115	XP:	$10	F12

Motel

Location: Just w of SR 1, Aguajito Rd or Monterey exit. 1111 10th St 93940. Fax: 831/648-1734. **Terms:** Package plans. **Facility:** 25 rooms. Few rooms with view of hills. This property recycles. 2 large units with seating area, 1 with fireplace, $99-$169 for up to 2 persons; 2 stories; exterior corridors; heated pool, saunas. **Cards:** AE, CB, DI, DS, MC, VI. IMA. *(See color ad below & p 286)*

LONE OAK MOTEL   Rates Subject to Change   Phone: (831)372-4924   [53]

		1P:		2P/1B:		2P/2B:		XP:		
	Fri & Sat 6/1-8/31	1P:	$74- 102	2P/1B:	$74- 102	2P/2B:	$80- 104	XP:	$2	F12
	Fri & Sat 2/1-5/31 & 9/1-1/31	1P:	$58- 94	2P/1B:	$58- 94	2P/2B:	$64- 100	XP:	$2	F12
	Sun-Thurs 6/1-8/31	1P:	$56- 76	2P/1B:	$56- 76	2P/2B:	$62- 82	XP:	$2	F12
	Sun-Thurs 2/1-5/31 & 9/1-1/31	1P:	$44- 48	2P/1B:	$44- 48	2P/2B:	$50- 58	XP:	$2	F12

Motel

Location: 0.6 mi e of SR 1; Del Rey Oaks (SR 218) or Fremont St exit. 2221 N Fremont St 93940. Fax: 831/372-4985. **Terms:** Reserv deposit; weekly rates, 11/1-3/31. **Facility:** 46 rooms. Few duplexes & motel rooms. 3 units with whirlpool & gas fireplace $85-$140, 10 two-bedroom units $10 extra for up to 6 persons; 1 story; exterior corridors; sauna, whirlpool. **All Rooms:** combo or shower baths. **Some Rooms:** 14 kitchens. **Cards:** AE, CB, DI, DS, MC, VI. *(See color ad p 698)*

MARIPOSA INN   Rates Subject to Change   Phone: (831)649-1414   [40]

		1P:		2P/1B:		2P/2B:		XP:		
	6/11-9/25 [CP]	1P:	$89- 129	2P/1B:	$89- 129	2P/2B:	$99- 139	XP:	$10	F17
	2/1-6/10 & 9/26-1/31 [CP]	1P:	$59- 79	2P/1B:	$59- 79	2P/2B:	$69- 89	XP:	$10	F17

Motel

Location: Just w of SR 1, Soledad Dr/Munras Ave exit. 1386 Munras Ave 93940. Fax: 831/649-5308. **Terms:** Reserv deposit, 3 day notice. **Facility:** 50 rooms. Most rooms with microwaves. 3 split-level townhouses, $99-$199 for up to 4 persons, 4 whirlpool rms, extra charge; 3-4 stories; interior/exterior corridors; small pool. **Cards:** AE, CB, DI, DS, MC, VI. *(See ad p 709)*

MERRITT HOUSE   Rates Subject to Change   Phone: 831/646-9686   [51]

		1P:		2P/1B:		2P/2B:		XP:		
	6/1-11/30 [CP]	1P:	$125- 190	2P/1B:	$125- 190	2P/2B:	$140	XP:	$15	F12
	2/1-5/31 & 12/1-1/31 [CP]	1P:	$89- 135	2P/1B:	$89- 135	2P/2B:	$105	XP:	$15	F12

Complex

Location: 2 mi w of SR 1, Munras Ave exit. 386 Pacific St 93940. Fax: 831/646-5392. **Facility:** 25 rooms. Fireplaces; suites in historic adobe & motel rooms. Suite with fireplace & private patio $200; 2 stories; exterior corridors. **Cards:** AE, CB, DI, DS, MC, VI.

MONTEREY BAY INN   Phone: (831)373-6242   [43]

		1P:		2P/1B:		2P/2B:		XP:		
	6/1-10/31	1P:	$199- 369	2P/1B:	$199- 369	2P/2B:	$199- 369	XP:	$10	F18
	11/1-1/31	1P:	$179- 369	2P/1B:	$179- 369	2P/2B:	$179- 369	XP:	$10	F18
	2/1-5/31	1P:	$199- 329	2P/1B:	$199- 329	2P/2B:	$199- 329	XP:	$10	F18

Motel

Location: 3.5 mi w of SR 1, Monterey exit. 242 Cannery Row 93940. Fax: 831/373-7603. **Terms:** Check-in 4 pm; reserv deposit; handling fee imposed; package plans; 2 night min stay, weekends. **Facility:** 47 rooms. Many rooms with bay view & balcony. Rooms have sofa-sleeper, king size bed & honor snack bar. 3 units have fireplace. Complimentary covered parking. 4 stories; interior corridors; sauna, whirlpools. **Recreation:** lockers for scuba gear; exercise equipment. **Cards:** AE, DI, DS, MC, VI. **Special Amenities:** Free breakfast and free newspaper. *(See color ad p 701)*

(See map p. 680)

MONTEREY BAY LODGE　　　　　　　　　　　　　　　　　　　　　Phone: (831)372-8057　⑮

	7/1-9/30	1P:	$89- 179	2P/1B:	$89- 179	2P/2B:	$89- 159
	4/1-6/30 & 10/1-10/31	1P:	$69- 159	2P/1B:	$69- 159	2P/2B:	$89- 139
	2/1-3/31 & 11/1-1/31	1P:	$49- 139	2P/1B:	$49- 139	2P/2B:	$69- 119

Motel　**Location:** Just w of SR 1, Aguajito Rd exit. 55 Camino Aguajito 93940. Fax: 831/655-2933. **Terms:** Reserv deposit; pets, $10 extra charge, $100 dep req. **Facility:** 45 rooms. Across El Estero Lagoon & Park. 2 two-bedroom units. 2 stories; exterior corridors. **Dining:** Coffee shop nearby. **All Rooms:** combo or shower baths. **Cards:** AE, CB, DI, DS, MC, VI. **Special Amenities:** Free local telephone calls and preferred room (subject to availability with advanced reservations). *(See color ad below)*

(See map p. 680)

MONTEREY BEACH HOTEL-BEST WESTERN   Phone: (831)394-3321 [2]
 (AAA) SAVE   All Year   1P: $89- 199   2P/1B: $99- 209   2P/2B: $109- 219   XP: $10   F12
♦♦♦   **Location:** Just w of SR 1, Del Rey oaks exit. 2600 Sand Dunes Dr 93940. Fax: 831/393-1912.
Motor Inn   **Terms:** Check-in 4 pm; reserv deposit, 3 day notice; small pets only, $25 extra charge. **Facility:** 196 rooms.
              On the beach. 4 stories; exterior corridors; oceanview; beach, whirlpool. **Dining:** Restaurant; 7 am-1:30 &
              5:30-10 pm; $12-$20. **Cards:** AE, CB, DI, DS, JC, MC, VI. *(See color ad below)*

MONTEREY DOWNTOWN TRAVELODGE   Rates Subject to Change   Phone: (831)373-1876 [21]
(AAA)   All Year   1P: $73- 159   2P/1B: $73- 159   2P/2B: $77- 159   XP: $10   F18
♦♦   **Location:** 0.7 mi w of SR 1, Fremont Ave or Munras Ave exits. 675 Munras Ave 93940. Fax: 831/373-8693.
Motel   **Terms:** Reserv deposit. **Facility:** 51 rooms. Convenient to gas station. Covered & lot parking; 3 stories; ex-
              terior corridors. **Dining:** Coffee shop nearby. **All Rooms:** combo or shower baths. **Cards:** AE, CB, DI, DS,
              JC, MC, VI. *(See color ad below)*

MONTEREY FIRESIDE LODGE   Phone: (831)373-4172 [13]
(AAA) SAVE   All Year [CP]   1P: $66- 225   2P/1B: $66- 235   2P/2B: $79- 255   XP: $10   F5
♦   **Location:** Just w of SR 1, Aguajito Rd or Monterey exit. 1131 10th St 93940. Fax:831/655-5640.
Motel   **Terms:** Reserv deposit, 3 day notice; pets, $10 extra charge. **Facility:** 24 rooms. Gas fireplaces. 1-bedroom
              unit, woodburning fireplace & wet bar $169-$229 for up to 4 persons; 2 stories; exterior corridors; whirlpool.
              Some Rooms: 6 efficiencies. **Cards:** AE, DI, DS, MC, VI. **Special Amenities: Free breakfast and free**
local telephone calls.

THE MONTEREY HOTEL   Rates Subject to Change   Phone: 831/375-3184 [54]
♦♦♦   6/15-9/3 [CP]   1P: $129- 179   2P/1B: $129- 179   2P/2B: $159- 199   XP: $10   F12
Historic Hotel Fri & Sat 2/1-6/14 & 9/4-1/31
              [CP]   1P: $109- 159   2P/1B: $109- 159   2P/2B: $139- 159   XP: $10   F12
              Sun-Thurs 2/1-6/14 &
              9/4-1/31 [CP]   1P: $89- 129   2P/1B: $89- 129   2P/2B: $99- 129   XP: $10   F12
Location: Downtown. 406 Alvarado St 93940. Fax: 831/373-2899. **Terms:** 2 night min stay, weekends in summer.
Facility: 45 rooms. 1904 Victorian hotel. Some small rooms, few gas fireplaces, wet bars. 4 stories; interior corridors; smoke
free premises; off site parking only. **Cards:** AE, DI, DS, MC, VI. *(See color ad p 711)*

(See map p. 680)

MONTEREY MARRIOTT   Rates Subject to Change   **Phone:** (831)649-4234   🔟9
◆◆◆   All Year   1P: $99- 289   2P/1B: $99- 289   2P/2B: $99- 289
Hotel   **Location:** 2 mi w of SR 1, Del Monte Ave or Munras Ave exits; opposit conference center. 350 Calle Principal 93940. Fax: 831/372-2968. **Facility:** 341 rooms. Many rooms with view of bay. Rates for up to 4 persons; 10 stories; interior corridors; heated pool. Fee: parking. **Services:** giftshop. Fee: massage. **All Rooms:** combo or shower baths. **Cards:** AE, CB, DI, DS, JC, MC, VI.

🛏️ 🏃 🕴️ 🍴 🍷 📺 🏨 🛁 🐾 VCR 🖥️ 🖨️ 📠 ♿ 🦽 ✕ 🏊

MONTEREY PLAZA HOTEL   **Phone:** (831)646-1700   4️⃣4️⃣
🅰️🅰️🅰️ SAVE   All Year   1P: $195- 305   2P/1B: $195- 305   2P/2B: $195- 305   XP: $20   F17
◆◆◆◆   **Location:** 3 mi w of SR 1, Del Monte Ave or Munras Ave exits. 400 Cannery Row 93940.
Hotel   Fax: 831/646-5937. **Terms:** Check-in 4 pm; reserv deposit; package plans. **Facility:** 285 rooms. Large rooms; many on the bay with balcony. 7 two-bedroom units. 10 one- & two-bedroom suites, $325-$785 for up to 6 persons; 3-5 stories; interior corridors. Fee: parking. **Dining:** Dining room, restaurant. **Services:** giftshop. Fee: massage. **Recreation:** Fee: kayaking; bicycles. **All Rooms:** combo or shower baths. **Cards:** AE, CB, DI, DS, JC, MC, VI. *(See color ad inside back cover & below)*

🅢🅓 🏃 🕴️ 🍴 🍷 🏨 🛋️ ✕ 🐾 🖥️ 🍴 🎿 📠 ♿ 🦽 ✕ 🏊

(See map p. 680)

MONTERO LODGE   Rates Subject to Change   Phone: (831)375-6002   ㉙

Fri & Sat 6/15-9/30 [CP]	1P: $79- 99	2P/1B: $79- 109	2P/2B: $89- 115	XP: $10
Sun-Thurs 6/15-9/30 [CP]	1P: $69- 89	2P/1B: $69- 89	2P/2B: $79- 92	XP: $9

Motel

Fri & Sat 2/1-6/14 &
10/1-1/31 [CP]   1P: $55- 75   2P/1B: $59- 89   2P/2B: $59- 89   XP: $6
Sun-Thurs 2/1-6/14 &
10/1-1/31 [CP]   1P: $36- 49   2P/1B: $36- 49   2P/2B: $42- 52   XP: $6

Location: 0.5 mi w of SR 1, Soledad Dr or Munras Ave exits. 1240 Munras Ave 93940. Fax: 831/333-1603. **Facility:** 20 rooms. Near Del Monte Center. 2 stories; exterior corridors. **Dining:** Coffee shop nearby. **All Rooms:** combo or shower baths. **Cards:** AE, DI, JC, MC, VI. *(See color ad below)*

MUNRAS LODGE   Phone: (831)646-9696   ㉘

6/1-9/30 [CP]	1P: $59- 199	2P/1B: $69- 199	2P/2B: $69- 199	XP: $10-20	F13
2/1-5/31 & 10/1-1/31 [CP]	1P: $49- 169	2P/1B: $59- 169	2P/2B: $59- 169	XP: $10-20	F13

Motel

Location: 0.7 mi w of SR 1, Soledad Dr/Munras Ave exits. 1010 Munras Ave 93940. Fax: 831/647-8248. **Terms:** Weekly/monthly rates; pets, $40 dep req. **Facility:** 29 rooms. Many gas burning fireplaces. 5 suites with whirlpool & fireplace, $99-$199 for up to 2 persons; 2 stories; interior corridors; sauna, whirlpool. **Cards:** AE, DS, MC, VI. **Special Amenities:** Early check-in/late check-out and free breakfast. *(See color ad below)*

OLD MONTEREY INN   Rates Subject to Change   Phone: (831)375-8284   ㊿
◆◆◆◆   1P: $200- 350   2P/1B: $200- 350   2P/2B: $200- 350   XP: $50
Bed &   **Location:** 1 mi w of SR 1, Soledad Rd or Munras Ave exits; 1 mi s from Fishermans Wharf on Pacific St to
Breakfast   Martin St, 2 blks w. 500 Martin St 93940. Fax: 831/375-6730. **Terms:** Reserv deposit, 7 day notice; handling fee imposed; 2 night min stay, weekends. **Facility:** 10 rooms. 1929 Tudor-style garden home on wooded hillside. Individually decorated rooms, most featherbeds, some with woodburning fireplace. 1-3 stories, no elevator; interior/exterior corridors; smoke free premises. **All Rooms:** combo or shower baths. **Some Rooms:** color TV. **Cards:** MC, VI.

OTTER INN   Rates Subject to Change   Phone: 831/375-2299   ㊾
◆◆   All Year   1P: $79- 299   2P/1B: $79- 299   2P/2B: $79- 299
Motel   **Location:** 3.5 mi w of SR 1, Monterey exit; near Cannery Row. 571 Wave St 93940. Fax: 831/375-2352. **Terms:** Monthly rates. **Facility:** 31 rooms. 3 two-bedroom units for up to 6 persons, 4 rooms with fireplace & whirlpool; 4 stories; exterior corridors; whirlpool. **Cards:** AE, DS, MC, VI. *(See color ad p 701)*

(See map p. 680)

PADRE OAKS

(AAA) [SAVE]
◆◆
Motel

		1P		2P/1B		2P/2B		XP	
7/1-8/31 [CP]		1P:	$64- 139	2P/1B:	$64- 139	2P/2B:	$64- 149	XP:	$10
Fri & Sat 5/1-6/30 & 9/1-10/31 [CP]		1P:	$54- 119	2P/1B:	$54- 119	2P/2B:	$54- 129	XP:	$10
2/1-4/30 & 11/1-1/31 [CP]		1P:	$49- 99	2P/1B:	$49- 99	2P/2B:	$49- 109	XP:	$5
Sun-Thurs 5/1-6/30 & 9/1-10/31 [CP]		1P:	$54- 89	2P/1B:	$54- 89	2P/2B:	$54- 89	XP:	$10

Phone: (831)373-3741 **35**

Location: 0.3 mi w of SR 1, Soledad Dr or Munras Ave exits. 1278 Munras Ave 93940. **Facility:** 20 rooms. Landsaping includes an unusual, old oak tree. 1 two-bedroom unit. 1 story; exterior corridors. **All Rooms:** shower baths. **Cards:** AE, DS, MC, VI. **Special Amenities:** Early check-in/late check-out and free breakfast.

QUALITY INN

◆◆
Motel

	Rates Subject to Change									
Fri & Sat 6/15-10/31 [CP]		1P:	$69- 119	2P/1B:	$69- 149	2P/2B:	$79- 169	XP:	$10	F18
Fri & Sat 2/1-6/14, Sun-Thurs 6/15-10/31 & Fri & Sat 11/1-1/31 [CP]		1P:	$59- 99	2P/1B:	$59- 119	2P/2B:	$69- 129	XP:	$10	F18
Sun-Thurs 2/1-6/14 & 11/1-1/31 [CP]		1P:	$49- 79	2P/1B:	$49- 79	2P/2B:	$59- 99	XP:	$10	F18

Phone: 831/372-3381 **30** F18

Location: 0.5 mi w of SR 1; Munras Ave. exit. 1058 Munras Ave 93940. Fax: 831/372-4687. **Facility:** 55 rooms. 12 rooms with fireplace. 2 stories; exterior corridors. **Cards:** AE, DI, DS, MC, VI. *(See color ad p 716)*

RAMADA LIMITED-FREMONT

(AAA) [SAVE]
◆◆
Motel

		1P		2P/1B		2P/2B		XP		
Fri & Sat 5/2-10/31 [CP]		1P:	$80- 110	2P/1B:	$85- 125	2P/2B:	$95- 135	XP:	$10	F16
Sun-Thurs 5/2-10/31 [CP]		1P:	$55- 110	2P/1B:	$65- 110	2P/2B:	$75- 125	XP:	$10	F16
Fri & Sat 2/1-5/1 & 11/1-1/31 [CP]		1P:	$50- 70	2P/1B:	$55- 75	2P/2B:	$60- 75	XP:	$10	F16
Sun-Thurs 2/1-5/1 & 11/1-1/31 [CP]		1P:	$45- 50	2P/1B:	$48- 52	2P/2B:	$50- 55	XP:	$10	F16

Phone: (831)375-9511 **8**

Location: 0.3 mi e of SR 1; Fremont St or Casa Verde Way exits. 2058 N Fremont St 93940. Fax: 831/375-9701. **Terms:** Reserv deposit. **Facility:** 47 rooms. Some small rooms. 1-2 stories; exterior corridors; sauna, whirlpool. **All Rooms:** combo or shower baths. **Cards:** AE, CB, DI, DS, JC, MC, VI.

RAMADA LIMITED-MUNRAS

(AAA) [SAVE]
◆◆
Motel

		1P		2P/1B		2P/2B		XP		
4/1-10/31 [CP]		1P:	$65- 149	2P/1B:	$75- 149	2P/2B:	$95- 149	XP:	$10	F18
2/1-3/31 & 11/1-1/31 [CP]		1P:	$69- 79	2P/1B:	$69- 79	2P/2B:	$69- 89	XP:	$10	F18

Phone: (831)375-2679 **24**

Location: 0.5 mi of SR 1, Munras exit. 1182 Cass St 93940. Fax: 831/643-2837. **Terms:** Reserv deposit; 3 night min stay, weekends. **Facility:** 19 rooms. Few small units, few fireplaces. 1 two-bedroom unit. 2 stories; exterior corridors; smoke free premises; small pool open in summer. **Cards:** AE, CB, DI, DS, JC, MC, VI. **Special Amenities:** Free breakfast.

SAN CARLOS INN

(AAA) [SAVE]
◆◆
Motel

		1P		2P/1B		2P/2B		XP		
5/1-10/31 [CP]		1P:	$85- 105	2P/1B:	$95- 130	2P/2B:	$105- 180	XP:	$10	F13
2/1-4/30 & 11/1-1/31 [CP]		1P:	$59- 89	2P/1B:	$69- 99	2P/2B:	$79- 99	XP:	$10	F13

Phone: (831)649-6332 **55**

Location: 0.8 mi w of SR 1, Fremont St or Munras Ave exits. 850 Abrego St 93940. Fax: 831/649-6353. **Terms:** Reserv deposit, 3 day notice; package plans; 2 night min stay, weekends 5/15-10/15. **Facility:** 54 rooms. Few large rooms with view. 2-4 stories; exterior corridors; whirlpool. **All Rooms:** combo or shower baths. **Cards:** AE, CB, DI, DS, MC, VI. **Special Amenities:** Free breakfast and free local telephone calls. *(See color ad p 714)*

SAND DOLLAR INN

(AAA) [SAVE]
◆◆
Motel

		1P		2P/1B		2P/2B		XP		
All Year [CP]		1P:	$55- 115	2P/1B:	$65- 125	2P/2B:	$65- 125	XP:	$15	F12

Phone: (831)372-7551 **22**

Location: 0.8 mi w of SR 1, Fremont ST or Munras Ave exits. 755 Abrego St 93940. Fax: 831/372-0916. **Terms:** Package plans. **Facility:** 63 rooms. Some units with small deck or patio. Many with gas or woodburning fireplace. 2 two-bedroom units. 2-3 stories; interior/exterior corridors; whirlpool. **Dining:** Coffee shop nearby. **All Rooms:** combo or shower baths. **Cards:** AE, CB, DI, MC, VI. **Special Amenities:** Free breakfast and free newspaper. *(See color ad p 714)*

(See map p. 680)

SCOTTISH FAIRWAY MOTEL   Phone: (831)373-5551 **7**

Fri & Sat [CP]	1P: $79- 99	2P/1B: $89- 109	2P/2B: $99- 119	XP: $6 F10
Sun-Thurs 5/1-9/30 [CP]	1P: $49- 89	2P/1B: $49- 89	2P/2B: $69- 99	XP: $6 F10
Sun-Thurs 2/1-4/30 &				
10/1-1/31 [CP]	1P: $35- 45	2P/1B: $35- 55	2P/2B: $45- 65	XP: $6 F10

Motel

Location: 0.2 mi e of SR 1; Fremont St or Casa Verde Way exits. 2075 Fremont St 93940. Fax: 831/373-4250. **Facility:** 42 rooms. 12 two-bedroom units. 2 stories; exterior corridors. **All Rooms:** combo or shower baths. **Some Rooms:** 7 efficiencies, 6 kitchens, no utensils. **Cards:** AE, DI, DS, MC, VI. *(See color ad p 713)*

SPINDRIFT INN   Phone: (831)646-8900 **45**

6/1-1/31	1P: $219- 429	2P/1B: $219- 429	2P/2B: $349- 429
2/1-5/31	1P: $219- 369	2P/1B: $219- 369	2P/2B: $349- 369

Motel

Location: 3.7 mi w of SR 1, Monterey exit. 652 Cannery Row 93940. Fax: 831/646-5342. **Terms:** Check-in 4 pm; reserv deposit; handling fee imposed; package plans; 2 night min stay, weekends. **Facility:** 42 rooms. On the bay. All units with fireplace & elegant furnishings. 4 stories; interior corridors. Fee: parking. **Dining:** Complimentary wine & cheese 4 pm-6 pm; restaurant nearby. **Cards:** AE, DI, DS, MC, VI. **Special Amenities:** Free breakfast and free newspaper. *(See color ad p 701)*

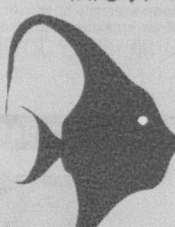

(See map p. 680)

SUPER 8 MOTEL
Phone: (831)373-3081 **9**

		1P:	2P/1B:	2P/2B:	XP:	
6/1-9/30 [CP]	79	$56-	$56- 99	$69- 109	$5	F12
4/1-5/31 [CP]	69	$44-	$44- 89	$56- 99	$5	F12
2/1-3/31 & 10/1-1/31 [CP]	64	$42-	$42- 69	$48- 79	$5	F12

Location: 0.3 mi e of SR 1; Fremont St or Casa Verde Way exits. 2050 Fremont St 93940. **Fax:** 831/372-6730. **Terms:** Reserv deposit. **Facility:** 48 rooms. Across fairgrounds. 2 stories; exterior corridors; sauna, whirlpools. **All Rooms:** combo or shower baths. **Cards:** AE, CB, DS, JC, MC, VI. **Special Amenities:** Free breakfast. *(See color ad p 715)*

SURF INN
Rates Subject to Change Phone: (831)372-5821 **33**

All Year [CP] 1P: $49- 159 2P/1B: $49- 159 2P/2B: $59- 159 XP: $10

Location: 0.5 mi w of SR 1, Soledad Dr or Munras Ave exits. 1200 Munras Ave 93940. **Terms:** Reserv deposit, 7 day notice. **Facility:** 27 rooms. 1 two-bedroom unit. 1 story; exterior corridors. **All Rooms:** combo or shower baths. **Cards:** AE, CB, DI, DS, JC, MC, VI. *(See color ad p 715)*

TRAVELODGE-MONTEREY/CARMEL
Phone: (831)373-3381 **10**

	1P:	2P/1B:	2P/2B:	XP:	
8/1-9/30	$75	$80	$85	$10	F17
6/1-7/31	$65	$70	$75	$10	F17
4/1-5/31	$60	$65	$70	$10	F17
2/1-3/31 & 10/1-1/31	$45	$50	$60	$6	F17

Location: Jct SR 1 & Fremont St at SR 68. 2030 N Fremont St 93940. **Fax:** 831/649-8741. **Facility:** 104 rooms. Accross from fairgrounds. Many large rooms. 1 two-bedroom unit. One 1-bedroom suite, $99-$175; rates for up to 6 persons; 2 stories; exterior corridors. **Dining:** Cocktails; restaurant nearby. **All Rooms:** combo or shower baths. **Cards:** AE, DI, DS, MC, VI. **Special Amenities:** Free local telephone calls and free newspaper.

WAY STATION INN
Phone: (831)372-2945 **52**

	1P:	2P/1B:	2P/2B:	XP:
7/1-10/15 [CP]	$59- 129	$59- 149	$69- 169	$10
2/1-6/30 & 10/16-1/31 [CP]	$59- 119	$59- 139	$59- 149	$10

Location: 1.5 mi e of SR 1, Airport-Salinas exit, SR 68. 1200 Olmstead Rd 93940. **Fax:** 831/375-6267. **Facility:** 46 rooms. Across from airport. 8 units with gas fireplace, $99-$149 for up to 2 persons; 2 stories; exterior corridors. **Dining:** Restaurant nearby. **Cards:** AE, CB, DI, DS, MC, VI. **Special Amenities:** Free local telephone calls and free room upgrade (subject to availability with advanced reservations). *(See color ad p 715)*

WEST WIND LODGE
Phone: (831)373-1337 **25**

	1P:	2P/1B:	2P/2B:	XP:
6/1-9/30 [CP]	$70- 100	$70- 100	$70- 100	$5
2/1-5/31 & 10/1-1/31 [CP]	$40- 90	$40- 90	$40- 90	$5

Location: 0.5 mi w of SR 1, Munras Ave exit. 1046 Munras Ave 93940. **Fax:** 831/372-2451. **Facility:** 53 rooms. Some gas fireplaces & patios. 10 two-bedroom units. 6 executive suites, $95-$175; 8 two-bedroom units, $85-$130; 2 stories; exterior corridors; heated indoor pool, sauna, whirlpool. **All Rooms:** combo or shower baths. **Some Rooms:** 6 kitchens, whirlpools. **Cards:** AE, DI, DS, MC, VI. **Special Amenities:** Free breakfast and free local telephone calls. *(See color ad below)*

(See map p. 680)

RESTAURANTS

BRADLEY'S HARBOR FRONT RESTAURANT   **Lunch:** $7-$14   **Dinner:** $14-$26   **Phone:** 831/655-6799   ⑫
◆◆   **Location:** At the Coast Guard Pier, upstairs overlooking marina. 32 Cannery Row 93940. **Hours:** 11:30
Seafood   am-2:30 & 5-9 pm. Closed: 1/1, 12/25 & Mon. **Reservations:** suggested. **Features:** casual dress; Sunday
brunch; beer & wine only; fee for parking; a la carte. Also pasta & vegetable dishes. Smoke free premises.
Cards: AE, CB, DI, DS, MC, VI.
☒

CAFE FINA   **Lunch:** $8-$18   **Dinner:** $13-$23   **Phone:** 831/372-5200   ⑭
ⒶⒶⒶ   **Location:** 47 Fisherman's Wharf 93940. **Hours:** 11:30 am-2:30 & 5-10 pm. Closed: 11/25 & 12/25.
Reservations: accepted. **Features:** No A/C; casual dress; carryout; cocktails; minimum charge-$10; fee for
◆◆   parking; a la carte. Fresh seafood, mesquite broiler, brick-oven pizza, homemade pasta. Neat & small; few
Seafood   tables & lavatories on 2nd level. Smoke free premises. **Cards:** AE, CB, DI, DS, JC, MC, VI.
☒

DOMENICO'S ON THE WHARF   **Lunch:** $7-$19   **Dinner:** $15-$36   **Phone:** 831/372-3655   ③
ⒶⒶⒶ   **Location:** 50 Fisherman's Wharf 93940. **Hours:** 11:30 am-2:30 & 4-9:30 pm, Fri & Sat-10 pm. Closed: 11/25
◆◆◆   & 12/25. **Reservations:** suggested. **Features:** No A/C; casual dress; children's menu; health conscious
Seafood   menu items; carryout; cocktails & lounge; fee for parking; a la carte. Overlooking marina. Mesquite grilled
seafood; pastas. Smoke free premises. **Cards:** AE, CB, DI, DS, MC, VI. *(See ad below)*
☒

(See map p. 680)

THE DUCK CLUB   **Dinner:** $15-$26   **Phone:** 831/646-1706   ⑦
◆◆◆◆   **Location:** 3 mi w of SR 1, Del Monte Ave or Munras Ave exits; in Monterey Plaza Hotel. 400 Cannery Row
American   93940. **Hours:** 6:30 am-11 & 5:30-10 pm. **Reservations:** accepted. **Features:** casual dress; children's
menu; health conscious menu items; cocktails & lounge; entertainment; fee for valet parking; a la carte.
Imaginative California specialties; bay views. Smoke free premises. **Cards:** AE, CB, DI, DS, JC, MC, VI.
(See color ad inside back cover & p 711)   🛆 ⊠

THE FISH HOPPER   **Lunch:** $8-$14   **Dinner:** $13-$24   **Phone:** 831/372-2406   ⑨
◆◆   **Location:** 700 Cannery Row 93940. **Hours:** 11 am-10 pm. Closed: 12/25. **Reservations:** accepted.
Seafood   **Features:** No A/C; casual dress; children's menu; early bird specials; carryout; cocktails & lounge; fee for
parking; a la carte. Over the water on the bay. Oyster bar & outdoor dining deck. Smoke free premises.
Cards: AE, MC, VI.   ⊠

SANDBAR & GRILL   **Lunch:** $7-$11   **Dinner:** $11-$19   **Phone:** 831/373-2818   ①
ⓐⓐⓐ   **Location:** #9 Wharf 2. **Hours:** 11:30 am-11 pm, Sat & Sun 10:30 am-midnight. **Features:** No A/C; casual
dress; Sunday brunch; children's menu; carryout; cocktails & lounge; entertainment; minimum charge-$5; fee
◆◆   for parking; a la carte. Overlooking marina. Also pastas, steaks & ribs. Smoke free premises. **Cards:** AE, DI,
Seafood   DS, MC, VI.   ⊠

SARDINE FACTORY   **Dinner:** $16-$35   **Phone:** 831/373-3775   ⑪
ⓐⓐⓐ   **Location:** In Cannery Row area. 701 Wave St 93940. **Hours:** 5 pm-10:30 pm, Fri & Sat-11 pm, Sun-10 pm.
Closed: week of 12/25. **Reservations:** required. **Features:** semi-formal attire; children's menu; early bird
◆◆◆◆   specials; health conscious menu items; cocktails & lounge; valet parking; a la carte. California regional.
Continental   Fresh seafood, steak & pasta. Smoke free premises. **Cards:** AE, CB, DI, DS, MC.   🛆 ⊠

SEAFOOD TRATTORIA   **Lunch:** $7-$16   **Dinner:** $10-$20   **Phone:** 831/373-1851   ⑧
ⓐⓐⓐ   **Location:** 57 Fisherman's Wharf 93940. **Hours:** 11 am-10:30 pm, Sat-11 pm. Closed: 12/25 & 1 week in
Dec. **Reservations:** accepted. **Features:** No A/C; casual dress; children's menu; carryout; cocktails &
◆◆   lounge; fee for parking; a la carte. Calamari specialties; extensive appetizer selections. Fresh seafood from
Steak and   own boat. Smoke free premises. **Cards:** AE, CB, DI, DS, JC, MC, VI. *(See ad p 717)*   ⊠
Seafood

TRATTORIA PARADISO   **Lunch:** $8-$13   **Dinner:** $8-$22   **Phone:** 831/375-4155   ⑮
ⓐⓐⓐ   **Location:** Adjacent to Spindrift Inn. 654 Cannery Row 93940. **Hours:** 11 am-10 pm, Sat & Sun from 10 am.
Closed: 11/25 & 12/25. **Reservations:** suggested. **Features:** No A/C; casual dress; Sunday brunch;
◆◆   children's menu; cocktails & lounge; minimum charge-$10; fee for parking; a la carte. Overlooking the bay.
Seafood   California & Mediterranean specialties & decor. Smoke free premises. **Cards:** AE, CB, DI, MC, VI.
(See ad p 717)   ⊠

THE WHALER   **Dinner:** $10-$23   **Phone:** 831/373-1933   ⑥
◆◆   **Location:** 635 Cass St 93940. **Hours:** 4:30 pm-9:30 pm, Sat-10 pm. **Reservations:** accepted.
Steak and   **Features:** casual dress; children's menu; early bird specials; health conscious menu; cocktails & lounge; a la
Seafood   carte. California regional specialties. Smoke free premises. **Cards:** AE, MC, VI.   ⊠

WHALING STATION   **Dinner:** $15-$30   **Phone:** 831/373-3778   ⑩
ⓐⓐⓐ   **Location:** In Cannery Row area. 763 Wave St 93940. **Hours:** 5 pm-10 pm. Closed: 1/1, 4/7, 11/25 & 12/25.
Reservations: accepted. **Features:** casual dress; children's menu; cocktails & lounge; valet parking; a la
◆◆◆   carte. Upscale Tuscan decor. Mesquite wood broiler. USDA prime beef & fresh seafood. Smoke free
Steak and   premises. **Cards:** AE, CB, DI, DS, JC, MC, VI. *(See ad p 717)*   ⊠
Seafood

PACIFIC GROVE—16,100   (See map p. 680; index p. 676)

LODGINGS

ASILOMAR   Guaranteed Rates   **Phone:** (831)372-8016   72
◆◆   All Year [BP]   1P: $74- 93   2P/1B: $78- 97   2P/2B: $78- 97   XP: $19   D12
Historic   **Location:** Just n of SR 68, on conference grounds. 800 Asilomar Blvd 93950. Fax: 831/372-7227.
Complex   **Facility:** 314 rooms. At Asilomar State Beach & Conference grounds. One 3-bedroom house, $190, for up to
2 persons; 1-2 stories; interior/exterior corridors; smoke free premises. **Services:** giftshop.
Recreation: hiking trails. **All Rooms:** combo or shower baths. **Some Rooms:** 3 kitchens, color TV. **Cards:** MC, VI.
(See color ad below)   🎇 ➰ 🍴 ⊠ 🏌 🛆 🏠 ⊠ 🖉

(See map p. 680)

BEST WESTERN MONARCH RESORT   Rates Subject to Change   **Phone:** (831)646-8885   66
All Year [CP]   1P: $80- 190   2P/1B: $90- 200   2P/2B: $100- 200   XP:$10-25   F12
Location: Just w of 17 Mile Dr. 1111 Lighthouse Ave 93950. Fax: 831/646-5976. **Terms:** Check-in 4 pm; reserv deposit, 3 day notice; handling fee imposed; 2 night min stay, weekends. **Facility:** 49 rooms. 6 two-bedroom units.
Motel   Rms with fireplace, $10 extra charge. 4 suites, $280-$400 for up to 6 persons. Lower rates, in winter; 2 stories; interior corridors; heated pool, sauna, whirlpool. **Services:** complimentary evening beverages. **Some Rooms:** 4 efficiencies. **Cards:** AE, CB, DI, DS, JC, MC, VI. *(See color ad p 723)*

BORG'S OCEAN FRONT MOTEL   Rates Subject to Change   **Phone:** 831/375-2406   63
5/28-10/31   1P: $59- 129   2P/1B: $59- 129   2P/2B: $89- 135
2/1-5/27 & 11/1-1/31   1P: $54- 99   2P/1B: $54- 99   2P/2B: $69- 109
Location: 0.5 mi n on Monterey Bay at Lovers Point. 635 Ocean View Blvd 93950. **Terms:** Reserv deposit.
Motel   **Facility:** 60 rooms. Many units with ocean view. Beach & park opposite. Near Cannery Row & Aquarium. 6 two-bedroom units. 2 stories; exterior corridors. **Dining:** Restaurant nearby. **All Rooms:** combo or shower baths. **Cards:** AE, MC, VI.

BUTTERFLY GROVE INN   Rates Subject to Change   **Phone:** (831)373-4921   68
All Year [CP]   1P: $65- 129   2P/1B: $65- 129   2P/2B: $75- 149   XP: $10   F12
Location: Just w of 17 Mile Dr. 1073 Lighthouse Ave 93950. Fax: 831/373-7596. **Facility:** 28 rooms. Few units in vintage building adjacent to pine & eucalyptus grove. Some units with fireplace. 9 two-bedroom units. Lower
Motel   rates, in winter; 2 stories; exterior corridors; whirlpool. **All Rooms:** combo or shower baths. **Some Rooms:** 4 kitchens. **Cards:** AE, DI, DS, MC, VI.

THE CENTRELLA INN   Rates Subject to Change   **Phone:** (831)372-3372   61
Fri & Sat 2/1-7/1, 7/2-10/30 &
Fri & Sat 10/31-1/31 [CP]   1P: $124- 224   2P/1B: $124- 224   2P/2B: $144- 224   XP: $15   F14
Sun-Thurs 2/1-7/1 &
10/31-1/31 [CP]   1P: $94- 174   2P/1B: $94- 174   2P/2B: $114- 174   XP: $15   F14
Historic Bed   **Location:** Center at 17th St. 612 Central Ave 93950. Fax: 831/372-2036. **Terms:** 2 night min stay,
& Breakfast   weekends. **Facility:** 24 rooms. 1890's Victorian Hotel & 5 cottages; some gas fireplaces. 3 stories, no elevator; interior/exterior corridors; smoke free premises; street parking only. **Services:** complimentary evening beverages. **All Rooms:** combo or shower baths. **Some Rooms:** color TV, whirlpools. **Cards:** AE, DS, MC, VI. *(See color ad p 685)*

DAYS INN SUITES   **Phone:** (831)373-8777   73
SAVE   Fri & Sat [CP]   1P: $135- 225   2P/1B: $135- 225   2P/2B: $135- 225   XP: $10   F17
Sun-Thurs [CP]   1P: $79- 125   2P/1B: $79- 125   2P/2B: $79- 125   XP: $10   F17
Location: Just e of SR 68 via Sinex Ave. 660 Dennett Ave 93950. Fax: 831/373-2698. **Terms:** Reserv deposit, 5 day notice. **Facility:** 30 rooms. Quiet forest setting. Some spacious rooms with balcony; some with
Motel   gas burning fireplace. 10 two-bedroom units. 2 stories; exterior corridors. **Some Rooms:** 9 efficiencies, 8 kitchens. **Cards:** AE, CB, DI, DS, MC, VI. **Special Amenities:** Early check-in/late check-out and free breakfast. *(See color ad p 705 & below)*

(See map p. 680)

LARCHWOOD INN
Phone: (831)373-1114   **75**

AAA SAVE   All Year [CP]   1P: $59- 135   2P/1B: $59- 135   2P/2B: $69- 135   XP: $10-15
◆◆   **Location:** 0.2 mi e of SR 68 via Sinex Ave. 740 Crocker Ave 93950. Fax: 831/665-5048. **Terms:** Reserv
Complex   deposit. **Facility:** 48 rooms. Most units have gas fireplace. Motel rooms & Apartments. 8 two-bedroom units.
1 & 2 bedroom suites with sauna & whirlpool access, $69-$250 for up to 2 persons; 2 stories; exterior corri-
dors. **Some Rooms:** 22 kitchens. **Cards:** AE, DS, MC, VI. **Special Amenities:** Free breakfast.
(See color ad p 719)   ⬜ 📺 📶 🖨 ✕

LIGHTHOUSE LODGE & SUITES   Rates Subject to Change   Phone: (831)655-2111   **65**
◆◆   Fri & Sat & Sun-Thurs
Motel   6/15-9/30 [CP]   1P: $89- 228   2P/1B: $89- 228   2P/2B: $89- 268   XP: $10   F12
Sun-Thurs 2/1-6/14 &
10/1-1/31 [CP]   1P: $79- 199   2P/1B: $79- 199   2P/2B: $79- 228   XP: $10   F12
Location: 0.5 mi w of 17 Mile Dr. 1150 Lighthouse Ave 93950. Fax: 831/655-4922. **Terms:** Check-in 4 pm; reserv deposit, 3
day notice; 2 night min stay, weekends in summer. **Facility:** 99 rooms. Many with balcony or patio. Few older adobe rooms;
suites across street. 1-2 stories; exterior corridors. **All Rooms:** combo or shower baths. **Some Rooms:** efficiency, 2
kitchens. **Cards:** AE, CB, DI, DS, MC, VI. *(See color ad p 707)*   🐾 🖐 🎿 🏊 📶 ⬜ 📶 🖨 📶 🔒 ✕

LOVERS POINT INN   Rates Subject to Change   Phone: 831/373-4771   **62**
◆   3/15-10/31 [CP]   1P: $79- 150   2P/1B: $79- 150   2P/2B: $79- 150   XP: $10   F12
Motel   2/1-3/14 & 11/1-1/31 [CP]   1P: $59- 99   2P/1B: $59- 99   2P/2B: $59- 99   XP: $10   F12
Location: 0.5 mi n. 625 Ocean View Blvd 93950. Fax: 831/373-4215. **Terms:** Reserv deposit, 3 day notice.
Facility: 51 rooms. 3 whirlpool rms, extra charge; 3 stories; exterior corridors. **Cards:** AE, CB, DI, DS, MC, VI.
📶➕ ⬜ 📶 🖨 🔒 ✕

PACIFIC GARDENS INN   Rates Subject to Change   Phone: (831)646-9414   **70**
AAA   3/1-10/31 [CP]   1P: $88- 110   2P/1B: $88- 115   2P/2B: $110- 125   XP: $10   F16
2/1-2/28 & 11/1-1/31 [CP]   1P: $78- 85   2P/1B: $78- 90   2P/2B: $88- 110   XP: $10   F16
◆◆◆   **Location:** Just n of SR 68; across conference grounds. 701 Asilomar Blvd 93950. Fax: 831/647-0555.
Motel   **Facility:** 28 rooms. 25 rooms with woodburning fireplace. All with popcorn makers. 2 two-bedroom units. 3
one-& two-bedroom units with parlor, $145-$175 for up to 4 persons; 2 stories; exterior corridors; whirlpools.
Services: complimentary evening beverages. **Some Rooms:** 6 kitchens. **Cards:** AE, MC, VI.
📶 🖐 🎿 📺 📶 🖨 🔒 ✕

PACIFIC GROVE INN   Phone: (831)375-2825   **71**
AAA SAVE   Fri & Sat & Sun-Thurs
7/1-10/31 [CP]   1P: $98- 122   2P/1B: $122- 142   2P/2B: $142- 162   XP: $18
◆◆◆   Sun-Thurs 3/1-6/30 [CP]   1P: $88- 112   2P/1B: $112- 122   2P/2B: $112- 132   XP: $16
Historic Bed   Sun-Thurs 2/1-2/28 &
& Breakfast   11/1-1/31 [CP]   1P: $78- 102   2P/1B: $102- 112   2P/2B: $102- 122   XP: $13
Location: 3.5 mi w of SR 1 via SR 68 & Forest Ave. 581 Pine Ave 93950. Fax: 831/625-1210. **Facility:** 16
rooms. Charming 1904 Queen Anne Victorian & annex. Most rooms with gas fireplace, some with ocean view. 3 two-bedroom
units, $225 for up to 4 persons; 2-3 stories, no elevator; interior corridors; smoke free premises. **All Rooms:** combo or
shower baths. **Cards:** AE, CB, DI, DS, MC, VI. **Special Amenities:** Free breakfast and free local telephone calls.
(See ad below)   VCR 📶 🖨 🔒 ✕

PACIFIC GROVE MOTEL   Rates Subject to Change   Phone: 831/372-3218   **67**
AAA   Fri & Sat   1P: $54- 94   2P/1B: $69- 119   2P/2B: $69- 119   XP: $10
Sun-Thurs   1P: $44- 84   2P/1B: $49- 99   2P/2B: $49- 109   XP: $10
◆   **Location:** Just w of 17 Mile Dr. Lighthouse Ave & Grove Acre 93950. **Terms:** Reserv
Motel   deposit, 3 day notice; 2 night min stay, weekends. **Facility:** 30 rooms. Few court-type units. 6 two-bedroom
units $79-$136, for up to 6 persons; 1 story; exterior corridors; smoke free premises; whirlpool; playground.
Dining: Coffee shop nearby. **All Rooms:** combo or shower baths. **Cards:** AE, DS, MC, VI. *(See color ad p 721)*
🐾 📶➕ ✕ 📺 📶 🔒 ✕

ROSEDALE INN   Phone: (831)655-1000   **74**
AAA SAVE   All Year [CP]   1P: $115- 225   2P/1B: $115- 225   2P/2B: $150- 225   XP: $10   F12
◆◆◆   **Location:** Just n of SR 68; across conference grounds. 775 Asilomar Blvd 93950. Fax: 831/655-0691.
Motel   **Terms:** Reserv deposit, 3 day notice; handling fee imposed. **Facility:** 19 rooms. 6 one-story redwood buildings
with 2 or more suites & rooms. All with fireplace & wetbar. Lower rates in winter; 1 story; exterior corridors.
Cards: AE, DI, DS, MC, VI. **Special Amenities:** Free breakfast and free newspaper. *(See ad p 721)*
🎿 📶 VCR 📺 ⬜ 📶 🖨 🔒 ✕

(See map p. 680)

THE WILKIES INN   Phone: (831)372-5960   69
(AAA) (SAVE)   6/15-9/5   1P: $89- 109   2P/1B: $99- 139   2P/2B: $99- 149   XP: $10-20   F16
♦♦   9/6-10/31   1P: $79- 99   2P/1B: $89- 129   2P/2B: $89- 139   XP: $10-20   F16
Motel   2/1-6/14 & 11/1-1/31   1P: $69- 89   2P/1B: $79- 119   2P/2B: $79- 129   XP: $10-20   F16
Location: Just w of 17 Mile Dr. 1038 Lighthouse Ave 93950. **Fax:** 831/655-1681. **Terms:** Reserv deposit, 3 day notice; 2 night min stay, weekends. **Facility:** 24 rooms. Few rooms with partial ocean view. 2 kitchens, $10 extra charge; 2 stories; exterior corridors. **All Rooms:** shower baths. **Cards:** AE, DI, DS, JC, MC, VI. **Special Amenities:** Early check-in/late check-out and preferred room (subject to availability with advanced reservations).

RESTAURANTS

CROCODILE GRILL   **Dinner:** $9-$17   Phone: 831/655-3311   21
♦♦   **Location:** Center. 701 Lighthouse Ave 93950. **Hours:** 5 pm-10 pm. Closed: 11/26, 12/25 & Tues.
Ethnic   **Reservations:** accepted. **Features:** casual dress; children's menu; carryout; beer & wine only; street parking; a la carte. Caribbean & Latin-American specialties & decor. Smoke free premises. **Cards:** AE, DI,
MC, VI.

FANDANGO   **Lunch:** $8-$16   **Dinner:** $12-$30   Phone: 831/372-3456   20
(AAA)   **Location:** Center. 223 17th St 93950. **Hours:** 11 am-3:30 & 5-9:30 pm, Sun & major holidays 10 am-2:30 & 5-9:30 pm. **Reservations:** accepted. **Features:** No A/C; casual dress; Sunday brunch; cocktails; a la carte.
♦♦   Mesquite-grilled seafood & meats. European specialties served in informal Mediterranean atmosphere.
Steak and   Smoke free premises. **Cards:** AE, CB, DI, MC, VI.
Seafood

MELAC'S   **Lunch:** $8-$15   **Dinner:** $20-$33   Phone: 831/375-1743   22
♦♦♦   **Location:** Center. 663 Lighthouse Ave 93950. **Hours:** 11:30 am-2 & 5:30-9:30 pm. Closed: Sun.
French   **Reservations:** required. **Features:** No A/C; semi-formal attire; beer & wine only; street parking; a la carte. Contemporary French cuisine with seasonal fresh ingredients & organic produce. Smoke free premises.
Cards: AE, CB, DI, DS, MC, VI.

OLD BATH HOUSE   **Dinner:** $18-$36   Phone: 831/375-5195   19
♦♦♦   **Location:** 0.5 mi n at Lovers Point. 620 Ocean View Blvd 93950. **Hours:** 5 pm-10 pm, Sat 4 pm-11 pm, Sun
Continental   4 pm-10 pm. **Reservations:** suggested. **Features:** No A/C; semi-formal attire; children's menu; early bird specials; cocktails & lounge; minimum charge-$10; street parking; a la carte. View of bay. Fresh seafood.
Mesquite grill. California specialties. Smoke free premises. **Cards:** AE, CB, DI, DS, MC, VI.

PEBBLE BEACH—4,300   (See map p. 680; index p. 677)

LODGINGS

THE INN AT SPANISH BAY
◆◆◆◆ All Year
Rates Subject to Change   1P: $330-2000 2P/1B: $330-2000 2P/2B: $330-2000   **Phone: 831/647-7500** 〔76〕
Resort Complex
Location: 3.5 mi w of SR 1; SR 68 exit. 2700 17 Mile Dr 93953. Fax: 831/644-7955. **Terms:** Check-in 4 pm; reserv deposit, 3 day notice; $17 service charge. **Facility:** 269 rooms. All rooms have bay or forest view, gas-burning fireplace; many with balcony or patio. Surrounded by Scottish-Links golf course. 3-5 stories; interior corridors; putting green. Fee: 18 holes golf; 8 tennis courts (2 lighted). **Services:** giftshop. Fee: massage. **Recreation:** scuba diving; hiking trails, jogging. Fee: horseback riding. Rental: bicycles. **All Rooms:** combo or shower baths. **Cards:** AE, DI, DS, JC, MC, VI.

THE LODGE AT PEBBLE BEACH
◆◆◆◆ All Year
Rates Subject to Change   1P: $370-1175 2P/1B: $370- 1175 2P/2B: $1135-1810 XP: $50   **Phone: 831/624-3811** 〔77〕 F
Resort Complex
Location: Off SR 1, on 17 Mile Dr. 17 Mile Dr 93953 (PO Box 1128). Fax: 831/625-8598. **Terms:** Check-in 4 pm; reserv deposit; 2 night min stay, weekends. **Facility:** 161 rooms. Beautiful panoramic view. Many units with woodburning fireplace. Smoking permitted outdoors only, by local ordinance. 2-3 stories; interior/exterior corridors; oceanfront. Fee: 18 holes golf; 12 tennis courts. **Services:** giftshop. Fee: massage. **Recreation:** jogging. Fee: horseback riding. Rental: bicycles. **Cards:** AE, CB, DI, DS, JC, MC, VI.

RESTAURANTS

CLUB XIX
◆◆◆◆
French
Lunch: $8-$20   **Dinner:** $20-$30   **Phone: 831/625-8519** 〔26〕
Location: Off SR 1, on 17 Mile Dr; in The Lodge at Pebble Beach. 17 Mile Dr 93953. **Hours:** 11:30 am-4 & 6:30-10 pm. **Reservations:** suggested. **Features:** No A/C; semi-formal attire; children's menu; cocktails & lounge; fee for valet parking; a la carte. French & California cuisine in the intimate, traditional atmosphere of the cherrywood dining room, or in the glassed in heated terrace overlooking the greens. Smoke free premises. **Cards:** AE, DI, DS, JC, MC, VI.

ROY'S
◆◆◆
Ethnic
Lunch: $10-$22   **Dinner:** $18-$26   **Phone: 831/647-7423** 〔25〕
Location: At The Inn at Spanish Bay. 2700 17 Mile Dr 93953. **Hours:** 6:30-11 am, 11:30-3 & 5:30-10 pm. **Reservations:** suggested. **Features:** casual dress; cocktails; fee for valet parking; a la carte. "Euro-Asian" cooking; relaxed, friendly atmosphere. Smoke free premises. **Cards:** AE, CB, DI, MC, VI.

SEASIDE—38,900   (See map p. 680; index p. 678)

LODGINGS

BAY BREEZE INN
(AAA) (SAVE)
◆◆
Motel
Phone: (831)899-7111 〔121〕

	1P:		2P/1B:		2P/2B:		XP:	
Fri & Sat [CP]	$46-	68	$56-	88	$66-	102	$6	F10
Sun-Thurs 5/1-9/30 [CP]	$36-	58	$39-	68	$46-	82	$6	F10
Sun-Thurs 2/1-4/30 & 10/1-1/31 [CP]	$33-	39	$35-	52	$42-	56	$6	F10

Location: Just e of SR 1, Seaside-Sand City exit. 2049 Fremont Blvd 93955. Fax: 831/899-7211. **Terms:** Pets, , small dogs only. **Facility:** 50 rooms. 1 unit with fireplace, $10 extra charge; 2 stories; interior/exterior corridors. **Cards:** AE, DI, DS, MC, VI. **Special Amenities:** Free breakfast and preferred room (subject to availability with advanced reservations). *(See color ad below)*

BEST WESTERN MAGIC CARPET LODGE
(AAA) (SAVE)
◆◆
Motel
Phone: (831)899-4221 〔127〕

	1P:		2P/1B:		2P/2B:		XP:	
5/1-10/15	$59-	129	$69-	149	$79-	169	$10	F12
2/1-4/30 & 10/16-1/31	$49-	109	$59-	129	$69-	149	$10	F12

Location: 1.5 mi e of SR 1, Seaside exit. 1875 Fremont Blvd 93955. Fax: 831/899-3377. **Terms:** Handling fee imposed; 2 night min stay, Weekends. **Facility:** 40 rooms. Few units overlooking pool. 3 stories; interior/exterior corridors. **Cards:** AE, CB, DI, DS, JC, MC, VI. **Special Amenities:** Early check-in/late check-out and free breakfast. *(See color ad p 723)*

(See map p. 680)

ECONOMY INN   Phone: (831)899-2700   [132]

(AAA) (SAVE)   Fri & Sat & Sun-Thurs
              5/1-9/30   1P: $90   2P/1B: $90   2P/2B: $100
◆   Sun-Thurs 2/1-4/30 &
Motel   10/1-1/31   1P: $35   2P/1B: $40   2P/2B: $50
              Location: 2 mi e of SR 1, Seaside exit. 1131 Fremont Blvd 93955. **Facility:** 17 rooms. Few small units. Rates
for up to 4 persons; 2 stories; exterior corridors. **Dining:** Coffee shop nearby. **Cards:** AE, CB, DI, DS, MC, VI.

EMBASSY SUITES HOTEL & CONFERENCE CENTER   Phone: (831)393-1115   [128]

(AAA) (SAVE)   7/1-10/2   1P: $175- 275   2P/1B: $195- 295   2P/2B: $195- 295   XP: $20   F18
              4/1-6/30 & 10/3-11/20 1P: $155- 255   2P/1B: $175- 275   2P/2B: $175- 275   XP: $20   F18
◆ ◆ ◆   2/1-3/31 & 11/21-1/31 1P: $135- 155   2P/1B: $155- 175   2P/2B: $155- 175   XP: $20   F18
Suite Hotel   **Location:** Just e of SR 1; Seaside/Del Rey Oaks exit. 1441 Canyon Del Rey 93955. **Fax:** 831/393-1113.
Terms: Check-in 4 pm; package plans; 2 night min stay, weekends in season. **Facility:** 225 rooms. Many
rooms with view of bay. 9 two-bedroom units. 12 stories; interior corridors; heated indoor pool, sauna, whirlpool.
Dining: Restaurant; 11 am-11 pm; $16-$25. **Services:** giftshop; complimentary evening beverages; area transportation, train
& bus terminals. Fee: massage. **All Rooms:** combo or shower baths. **Cards:** AE, DI, DS, JC, MC, VI.

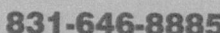

(See map p. 680)

HAMPTON INN
◆◆ Motel
Rates Subject to Change
Phone: 831/394-5335 **131**
5/1-10/31 [CP] 1P: $89- 129 2P/1B: $89- 129 2P/2B: $89- 129 XP: $10 F18
2/1-4/30 & 11/1-1/31 [CP] 1P: $59- 89 2P/1B: $59- 89 2P/2B: $59- 89 XP: $10 F18
Location: Just e of SR 1, seaside/Del Rey Oaks exit. 1400 Del Monte Blvd 93955. Fax: 831/394-7125.
Facility: 143 rooms. Some rooms overlooking lagoon. 5 stories; exterior corridors; small pool. **All Rooms:** combo or shower baths. **Cards:** AE, CB, DI, DS, MC, VI.

HOWARD JOHNSON EXPRESS INN
(AAA)
◆◆ Motel
Rates Subject to Change
Phone: (831)394-8566 **125**
7/1-9/30 [CP] 1P: $45- 95 2P/1B: $50- 105 2P/2B: $50- 125
2/1-6/30 & 10/1-1/31 [CP] 1P: $40- 60 2P/1B: $45- 95 2P/2B: $45- 95
Location: 1.2 mi e of SR 1, Seaside exit. 1893 Fremont Blvd 93955. Fax: 831/394-8568. **Facility:** 37 rooms. 6 two-bedroom units. 3 whirlpool rms, extra charge; 2 stories; exterior corridors; whirlpool. **Dining:** Coffee shop nearby. **Some Rooms:** 7 kitchens, no utensils. **Cards:** AE, DS, MC, VI.

PACIFIC BEST INN
(AAA) SAVE
◆ Motel
Phone: (831)899-1881 **129**
Fri & Sat 5/1-9/30 1P: $89 2P/1B: $89 2P/2B: $99 XP: $5 D
Fri & Sat 2/1-4/30, Sun-Thurs
5/1-9/30 & Fri & Sat
10/1-1/31 1P: $69 2P/1B: $69 2P/2B: $79 XP: $5 D
Sun-Thurs 2/1-4/30 &
10/1-1/31 1P: $39 2P/1B: $45 2P/2B: $50 XP: $5 D
Location: E of SR 1; Fremont Blvd exit. 1141 Fremont Blvd 93955. Fax: 831/392-1300. **Terms:** Reserv deposit, 3 day notice; handling fee imposed. **Facility:** 20 rooms. 2 two-bedroom units, $79-$160 for up to 4 persons; 2 stories; exterior corridors. **Dining:** Coffee shop nearby. **Cards:** AE, CB, DI, DS, JC, MC, VI. **Special Amenities:** Free local telephone calls.

SANDCASTLE INN
(AAA) SAVE
◆◆ Motel
Phone: (831)394-6556 **123**
Fri & Sat 4/1-9/30 [CP] 1P: $95- 195 2P/1B: $99- 200 2P/2B: $110- 250 XP: $20-25 F16
Fri & Sat 2/1-3/31 & 1/1-1/31
[CP] 1P: $85- 185 2P/1B: $95- 195 2P/2B: $105- 205 XP: $15-20 F16
Sun-Thurs 4/1-9/30 [CP] 1P: $50- 70 2P/1B: $55- 75 2P/2B: $60- 85 XP: $10-15 F16
Sun-Thurs 2/1-3/31,
10/1-12/31 & Sun-Thurs
1/1-1/31 [CP] 1P: $40- 60 2P/1B: $45- 65 2P/2B: $50- 75 XP: $10-15 F16
Location: Just e of SR 1; Sand City/Seaside exit. 1011 LaSalle Ave 93955. Fax: 831/394-1578. **Terms:** Reserv deposit, 5 day notice. **Facility:** 34 rooms. 2 stories; exterior corridors. **Dining:** Coffee shop nearby. **Some Rooms:** whirlpools. **Cards:** AE, DS, MC, VI. **Special Amenities:** Early check-in/late check-out and free breakfast.

SEASIDE INN
◆ Motel
Rates Subject to Change
Phone: (831)394-4041 **122**
Fri & Sat 5/1-9/30 [CP] 1P: $60- 90 2P/1B: $62- 104 2P/2B: $82- 120 XP: $10 F17
Fri & Sat 2/1-4/30 &
10/1-1/31 [CP] 1P: $54- 90 2P/1B: $58- 104 2P/2B: $74- 120 XP: $10 F17
Sun-Thurs 5/1-9/30 [CP] 1P: $45- 70 2P/1B: $50- 80 2P/2B: $56- 96 XP: $10 F17
Sun-Thurs 2/1-4/30 &
10/1-1/31 [CP] 1P: $35 2P/1B: $40- 45 2P/2B: $56 XP: $10 F17
Location: just e of SR 1, Seaside/Sand City exit. 1986 Del Monte Blvd 93955. Fax: 831/394-2806. **Terms:** Reserv deposit, 3 day notice. **Facility:** 17 rooms. Few balconies or small patios. 1-2 stories; exterior corridors. **Cards:** AE, DS, MC, VI.

SUNBAY RESORT
◆◆ Resort
Rates Subject to Change
Phone: 831/394-0136 **120**
5/1-9/30 1P: $89- 189 2P/1B: $89- 189 2P/2B: $89- 189
2/1-4/30 & 10/1-1/31 1P: $79- 169 2P/1B: $79- 169 2P/2B: $79- 169
Location: 1.2 mi e of SR 1, Sand City/Seaside or Fremont Blvd exits; immediate n on Monterey Rd & right on Coe; in Fort Ord. 5200 Coe Ave 93955. Fax: 831/394-0221. **Terms:** Check-in 4 pm; reserv deposit, 3 day notice, first night advance deposit req; 2 night min stay, weekends. **Facility:** 50 rooms. Studios, 1 & 2 bedroom/2-bath apartments. 26 two-bedroom units. Rates for up to 4 persons; 2 stories; exterior corridors; smoke free premises; racquetball courts, 2 lighted tennis courts; playground. Fee: 36 holes golf. **Recreation:** jogging. **All Rooms:** kitchens. **Cards:** AE, MC, VI.
(See color ad p 723)

THUNDERBIRD MOTEL
(AAA)
◆ Motel
Rates Subject to Change
Phone: 831/394-6797 **124**
6/1-9/15 [CP] 1P: $34- 75 2P/1B: $35- 95 2P/2B: $40- 115 XP: $5 F12
2/1-5/31 & 9/16-1/31 [CP] 1P: $29- 49 2P/1B: $30- 65 2P/2B: $34- 90 XP: $5 F12
Location: 0.3 mi n on SR 1 business rt. 1933 Fremont Blvd 93955. Fax: 831/646-0235. **Terms:** Reserv deposit, 3 day notice; handling fee imposed; weekly rates. **Facility:** 33 rooms. 2 stories; exterior corridors; small pool. **Dining:** Coffee shop nearby. **All Rooms:** combo or shower baths. **Some Rooms:** 4 efficiencies.
Cards: AE, DS, MC, VI. (See color ad p 715)

This ends listings for the Monterey Peninsula.
The following page resumes the alphabetical listings of
cities in California.

MONTE RIO —1,100—See also GUERNEVILLE.

LODGING

RIO VILLA BEACH RESORT
◆   Rates Subject to Change   Phone: 707/865-1143
        All Year   1P: $69- 179   2P/1B: $69- 179 2P/2B: $69- 189   XP: $10
Complex   **Location:** Center. 20292 Hwy 116 95462. Fax: 707/865-0115. **Terms:** Reserv deposit, 7 day notice; handling
fee imposed; 2 night min stay, weekends in summer. **Facility:** 14 rooms. Cottages, studios & motel units on
spacious, landscaped grounds & lawns by the river. 2 two-bedroom units. 1 story; exterior corridors. **Recreation:** swimming.
All Rooms: combo or shower baths. **Some Rooms:** 8 kitchens. **Cards:** AE, DS, MC, VI.

MONTROSE—See Los Angeles p. 622.

MORENO VALLEY—118,800

LODGINGS

BEST WESTERN IMAGE INN & SUITES
AAA SAVE   Phone: (909)924-4546
        All Year [CP]   1P: $49- 69   2P/1B: $49- 69 2P/2B: $49- 89   XP: $10   F17
◆◆◆   **Location:** N side of SR 60, exit Perris Blvd. 24840 Elder Ave 92557. Fax: 909/247-9337. **Facility:** 125 rooms.
Motor Inn   43 one bedroom suites; 3 stories; exterior corridors; heated pool, whirlpool. **Dining:** Coffee shop; 6-10 am,
        Sat & Sun 7-11 am. **All Rooms:** extended cable TV. **Cards:** AE, DI, DS, MC, VI. *(See ad below)*

ROADSIDE INN
AAA SAVE   Phone: (909)242-0699
        All Year   1P: $45- 49   2P/1B: $49- 59 2P/2B: $49- 59   XP: $5   F18
◆◆   **Location:** s side of SR 60, exit Pigeon Pass Rd, then 0.5 mi e on Sunnymead Blvd. 23330 Sunnymead Blvd
Motel   92553. Fax: 909/243-8635. **Terms:** Weekly rates; CP avail. **Facility:** 91 rooms. 22 one bedroom suites with
microwave & refrigerator, $59; 3 whirlpool rms, extra charge; 2-3 stories; exterior corridors; whirlpool, Small
pool. **Some Rooms:** 12 efficiencies. **Cards:** AE, DI, DS, MC, VI. **Special Amenities: Early check-in/late
check-out and free room upgrade (subject to availability with advanced reservations).**

MORGAN HILL—23,900

LODGINGS

BEST WESTERN COUNTRY INN
AAA SAVE   Phone: (408)779-0447
        All Year [CP]   1P: $70- 85   2P/1B: $75- 90 2P/2B: $90- 100   XP: $5   F12
◆◆◆   **Location:** Just e of US 101; Tennant Ave, or E Dunne Ave exit. 16525 Condit Rd 95037. Fax: 408/778-7170.
Motel   **Terms:** Small pets only. **Facility:** 84 rooms. All units with balcony; some face central courtyard. 2 stories; in-
terior corridors; whirlpool. **Dining:** Restaurant nearby. **Cards:** AE, CB, DI, DS, MC, VI. **Special Amenities:
Free breakfast and free local telephone calls.**

EXECUTIVE INN
AAA SAVE   Phone: (408)778-0404
        All Year [CP]   1P: $89- 97   2P/1B: $89- 97 2P/2B: $89- 97   XP: $10   F12
◆◆   **Location:** Just e of US 101; Dunne Ave exit. 16505 Condit Rd 95037. Fax: 408/778-2090. **Facility:** 30 rooms.
Motel   Most units with sitting area/sofa-beds. 2 stories; exterior corridors. **Some Rooms:** whirlpools. **Cards:** AE, DI,
DS, MC, VI. **Special Amenities: Free breakfast and free room upgrade (subject to availability with
advanced reservations).**

INN AT MORGAN HILL
◆◆◆   Rates Subject to Change   Phone: 408/779-7666
        All Year   1P: $130- 350   2P/1B: $130- 350 2P/2B: $130- 350   XP: $15   F12
Motel   **Location:** Just e of US 101, Tennant Ave exit. 16115 Condit Rd 95037. Fax: 408/779-8757. **Terms:** Check-in
        4 pm; reserv deposit. **Facility:** 100 rooms. 5 units with sitting room, kitchen, gas fireplace, wet bar, whirlpool
$189-$295 for 1 or 2 persons; 3 stories; interior corridors. **All Rooms:** combo or shower baths. **Cards:** AE, CB, DI, DS, MC,
VI.

MORGAN HILL INN

Phone: 408/779-1900

(AAA) (SAVE)

◆ Motel

Fri & Sat 5/1-10/31	1P:	$58- 65	2P/1B:	$65- 72	2P/2B:	$70- 78	XP: $5-10
2/1-4/30 & 11/1-1/31	1P:	$46- 52	2P/1B:	$50- 56	2P/2B:	$59- 65	XP: $5-10
Sun-Thurs 5/1-10/31 & 5/15-6/30	1P:	$50- 56	2P/1B:	$52- 58	2P/2B:	$55- 62	XP: $5-10

Location: 1 mi n on US 101 business rt. 16250 Monterey Hwy 95037. **Fax:** 408/779-1900. **Facility:** 23 rooms. 2 buildings, parking between. 1 two-bedroom unit. 2 stories; exterior corridors. **Cards:** AE, CB, DI, DS, MC, VI.

RESTAURANT

GOLDEN OAK

Lunch: $10-$20   **Dinner:** $12-$55   **Phone:** 408/779-8085

(AAA)

◆◆◆ Continental

Location: Just e of US 101; Tennant Ave, or E Dunne Ave exit. 16695 Condit Rd 95037. **Hours:** 11 am-3 & 5-9 pm; Sat 5 pm-10 pm; Sun 4 pm-9 pm. Closed major holidays. **Reservations:** accepted. **Features:** casual dress; cocktails & lounge; a la carte. Spacious, converted old winery. Also pasta & California selections. Smoke free premises. **Cards:** AE, DI, MC, VI.

MORRO BAY—9,700

LODGINGS

ASCOT INN

Phone: (805)772-4437

(AAA) (SAVE)

◆◆ Motel

5/1-10/31 [CP]	2P/1B:	$48- 95	2P/2B:	$68- 98	XP: $5	F14
2/1-4/30 & 11/1-1/31 [CP]	2P/1B:	$38- 85	2P/2B:	$58- 85	XP: $5	F14

Location: 845 Morro Ave 93442. **Fax:** 805/772-8860. **Terms:** Reserv deposit; weekly rates. **Facility:** 25 rooms. Some units with ocean view. 1 two-bedroom unit. 2 king & queen mini suites, $75-$168; 2 stories; exterior corridors. **Dining:** Restaurant nearby. **All Rooms:** combo or shower baths. **Cards:** AE, CB, DI, DS, MC, VI. **Special Amenities:** Free breakfast and free local telephone calls. (See color ad p 727)

ASCOT SUITES

Phone: (805)772-4437

(AAA) (SAVE)

(FYI) Motel

5/1-10/31 [CP]	2P/1B:	$110- 295	2P/2B:	$110- 295	XP: $10	F14
2/1-4/30 & 11/1-1/31 [CP]	2P/1B:	$85- 225	2P/2B:	$85- 225	XP: $10	F14

Too new to rate. **Location:** At Morro Ave. 260 Morro Bay Blvd 93442. **Fax:** 805/772-8860. **Terms:** Reserv deposit, 3 day notice. **Facility:** 31 rooms. English country decor. Fireplace in all rooms. Many rooms with ocean or harbor views & balcony. Most rooms have whirlpool tubs. 3 stories; interior corridors; designated smoking area; whirlpool & roof-top sun deck with panaromic view. **Dining:** Restaurant nearby. **Services:** complimentary evening beverages. **Recreation:** bicycles. **All Rooms:** extended cable TV. **Cards:** AE, CB, DI, DS, MC, VI. **Special Amenities:** Free breakfast and free local telephone calls. (See color ad p 727)

BAY VIEW LODGE

Rates Subject to Change   **Phone:** 805/772-2771

(AAA)

◆◆◆ Motel

Fri & Sat 2/1-10/31 [CP]	1P:	$65- 80	2P/1B:	$65- 80	2P/2B:	$80- 86	XP: $6
Sun-Thurs 6/11-9/30 & Fri & Sat 11/1-1/31 [CP]	1P:	$60- 74	2P/1B:	$60- 74	2P/2B:	$74- 80	XP: $6
Sun-Thurs 2/1-6/10 & 10/1-1/31 [CP]	1P:	$39- 60	2P/1B:	$50- 60	2P/2B:	$60- 72	XP: $6

Location: Just n of Morro Bay Blvd at Market Ave. 225 Harbor St 93442. **Terms:** Reserv deposit. **Facility:** 22 rooms. 1 block to Embarcadero. Some ocean view rooms, 16 with gas fireplace. 2 stories; exterior corridors; whirlpool. **All Rooms:** combo or shower baths. **Cards:** AE, MC, VI.

BEST WESTERN EL RANCHO MOTEL

Phone: (805)772-2212

(AAA) (SAVE)

◆◆ Motor Inn

5/21-9/25	1P:	$79- 89	2P/1B:	$79- 89	2P/2B:	$99	XP: $7	F12
9/26-11/27	1P:	$59- 69	2P/1B:	$59- 69	2P/2B:	$79	XP: $7	F12
2/1-5/20 & 11/28-1/31	1P:	$49- 59	2P/1B:	$49- 59	2P/2B:	$59	XP: $7	F12

Location: East side of SR 1, northbound exit SR 41, southbound exit San Jacinto St. 2460 Main St 93442. **Fax:** 805/772-2212. **Terms:** Reserv deposit; pets, $10 extra charge. **Facility:** 27 rooms. 1 story; exterior corridors; heated pool. **Dining:** Restaurant; 7 am-10 pm; $5-$10; wine/beer only. **All Rooms:** combo or shower baths, extended cable TV. **Cards:** AE, CB, DI, DS, MC, VI. **Special Amenities:** Early check-in/late check-out and free local telephone calls. (See ad below)

BEST WESTERN SAN MARCOS INN   Phone: (805)772-2248

(AAA) SAVE   6/12-8/27 [CP]   1P: $79- 149   2P/1B: $79- 149   2P/2B: $89- 159   XP: $5

           8/28-1/31 [CP]   1P: $69- 119   2P/1B: $69- 119   2P/2B: $59- 129   XP: $5

◆◆◆   2/1-6/11 [CP]   1P: $49- 99   2P/1B: $49- 99   2P/2B: $59- 109   XP: $5

Motel   **Location:** 250 Pacific St at Morro Ave 93442. Fax: 805/772-6844. **Terms:** Reserv deposit; weekly rates. **Facility:** 32 rooms. Many rooms with ocean view. Complimentary evening refreshments. 3 stories; interior corridors; whirlpool. **All Rooms:** shower baths. **Cards:** AE, CB, DI, DS, MC, VI. **Special Amenities: Free breakfast and free local telephone calls.** *(See color ad p 728)*   (icons)

BEST WESTERN TRADEWINDS MOTEL   Phone: (805)772-7376

(AAA) SAVE   All Year   1P: $49- 89   2P/1B: $49- 120   2P/2B: $49- 139   XP: $5

◆◆   **Location:** 225 Beach St & Market Ave 93442. Fax: 805/772-2090. **Terms:** Reserv deposit; small pets only, $10 extra charge. **Facility:** 24 rooms. 2 stories; exterior corridors; whirlpool. **Dining:** Coffee shop nearby.

Motel   **Cards:** AE, CB, DI, DS, JC, MC, VI. **Special Amenities: Early check-in/late check-out and free local telephone calls.** *(See ad below)*   (icons)

BLUE SAIL INN   Rates Subject to Change   Phone: 805/772-7132

(AAA)   All Year   2P/1B: $65- 95   2P/2B: $65- 95

◆◆◆   **Location:** Just n of Morro Bay Blvd. 851 Market Ave 93442. Fax: 805/772-8406. **Terms:** Reserv deposit.

Motel   **Facility:** 48 rooms. Most rooms with balcony & harbor view. 7 with gas fireplace. 2 larger rms with fireplace, wet bar, refrigerator & balcony with view of Morro Bay $110-$115; 3 stories; interior/exterior corridors; whirlpool. **Cards:** AE, CB, DI, DS, MC, VI. *(See ad below)*   (icons)

BREAKERS MOTEL   Phone: 805/772-7317

(AAA) SAVE   All Year   2P/1B: $70- 110   2P/2B: $70- 110   XP: $10   F12

◆◆◆   **Location:** Morro Bay Blvd at Market Ave. 780 Market Ave 93443 (PO Box 1447). Fax: 805/772-4771.

Motel   **Terms:** Reserv deposit. **Facility:** 25 rooms. 1 blk to the Embarcadero. Nicely decorated rooms, most with ocean view. Some with woodburning fireplace. 3 stories; exterior corridors; heated pool, whirlpool. **Dining:** Restaurant nearby. **All Rooms:** combo or shower baths. **Cards:** AE, CB, DI, DS, MC, VI.

(See color ad p 730)   (icons)

DAYS INN   Phone: (805)772-2711

⊕ SAVE | Fri & Sat 5/17-9/30 | 1P: $80- 115 | 2P/1B: $85- 140 | 2P/2B: $95- 140 | XP: $10 | F
| Fri & Sat 2/1-5/16 & |
◆◆ | 10/1-1/31 | 1P: $55 | 2P/1B: $55- 95 | 2P/2B: $65- 110 | XP: $10 | F
Motel | Sun-Thurs 5/17-9/30 | 1P: $75- 90 | 2P/1B: $75- 95 | 2P/2B: $80- 95 | XP: $10 | F
| Sun-Thurs 2/1-5/16 & |
| 10/1-1/31 | 1P: $45 | 2P/1B: $45- 60 | 2P/2B: $55- 65 | XP: $10 | F

Location: Just n of Morro Bay Blvd. 1095 Main St 93442. **Fax:** 805/772-2711. **Terms:** Reserv deposit; small pets only, $10 extra charge. **Facility:** 46 rooms. 2 stories; exterior corridors; whirlpool. **Dining:** Restaurant nearby. **All Rooms:** combo or shower baths. **Cards:** AE, CB, DI, DS, MC, VI. **Special Amenities:** Early check-in/late check-out and free breakfast.

🔊 🛏️ 📶 🖨️ 💻 📠 🔒 ✕

ECONO LODGE   Phone: (805)772-5609

⊕ SAVE | Fri & Sat 2/1-10/31 | 1P: $42- 129 | 2P/1B: $49- 139 | 2P/2B: $59- 149 | XP: $8 | F12
| 11/1-1/31 | 1P: $45- 89 | 2P/1B: $45- 95 | 2P/2B: $55- 100 | XP: $8 | F12
◆◆ | Sun-Thurs 5/1-10/31 | 1P: $52- 89 | 2P/1B: $52- 89 | 2P/2B: $65- 95 | XP: $8 | F12
Motel | Sun-Thurs 2/1-4/30 | 1P: $45- 69 | 2P/1B: $45- 74 | 2P/2B: $59- 79 | XP: $8 | F12

Location: Just n of Morro Bay Blvd. 1100 Main St 93442. **Terms:** Handling fee imposed; weekly rates. **Facility:** 18 rooms. 1 two-bedroom unit. 2 stories; exterior corridors. **Dining:** Coffee shop nearby. **Some Rooms:** 3 efficiencies, no utensils, color TV. **Cards:** AE, CB, DI, DS, MC, VI.

🔊 📶 🖨️ 🔒 ✕

EMBARCADERO INN   Guaranteed Rates   Phone: 805/772-2700

⊕ | All Year [CP] | 2P/1B: $95- 135 | 2P/2B: $95- 135 | XP: $15 | F12

◆◆◆ **Location:** S of Marina St on The Embarcadero. 456 Embarcadero 93442. Fax: 805/772-1060.
Motel **Terms:** Reserv deposit, 3 day notice. **Facility:** 32 rooms. Spacious rooms with harbor views, most with balcony, 19 with gas fireplace. 3 suites with separate living room, fireplace, wet bar, microwave & refrigerator $180; 3 stories; exterior corridors; 2 indoor whirlpools. **Cards:** AE, CB, DI, DS, JC, MC, VI.

(See color ad below)

📶 VCR 💻 🖥️ 📠 🔒 ✕

THE INN AT MORRO BAY   Rates Subject to Change   Phone: (805)772-5651

◆◆◆ | All Year | 1P: $129- 429 | 2P/1B: $129- 429 | 2P/2B: $129- 299 | XP: $15 | F18

Motor Inn **Location:** 1 mi s on Main St, at entrance to Morro Bay State Park & golf course. 60 State Park Rd 93442. Fax: 805/772-4779. **Terms:** Check-in 4 pm. **Facility:** 98 rooms. Bayfront. On nicely landscaped tree-shaded grounds. Nicely decorated rooms, some with gas fireplace, many with patio or balcony. Various size rooms from large to compact. 2 stories; exterior corridors; heated pool. **Services:** Fee: massage. **Recreation:** bicycles. **All Rooms:** combo or shower baths. **Cards:** AE, CB, DI, DS, MC, VI. *(See color ad p 731)*

A$K 🔊 📶 📶 🍴 ✕ 🖨️ 📠 🔒 ✕

KEYSTONE INN Rates Subject to Change **Phone:** 805/772-7503
◆◆ 5/15-9/30 2P/1B: $40- 85 2P/2B: $65- 95 XP: $5
Motel 2/1-5/14 & 10/1-1/31 2P/1B: $38- 65 2P/2B: $45- 75 XP: $5
Location: 0.4 mi s of Morro Bay Blvd. 540 Main St 93442. **Terms:** Reserv deposit. **Facility:** 20 rooms. Some ocean view rooms. Very clean & cozy rooms. 2 stories; exterior corridors. **Cards:** AE, DI, DS, MC, VI.

(ᔥ) (▤) (💷) (🖨) (🔒) (✕)

LA SERENA INN **Phone:** 805/772-5665
(AAA) [SAVE] All Year [CP] 1P: $79 2P/1B: $79 2P/2B: $84- 104 XP: $10 F12
Location: Just n of Morro Bay Blvd. 990 Morro Ave 93443 (PO Box 1711). Fax: 805/772-5665.
◆◆◆ **Terms:** Reserv deposit. **Facility:** 37 rooms. Spacious rooms, some with ocean view. 1 two-bedroom unit. 4
Motel king mini-suites with ocean view balcony, gas fireplace, microwave & refrigerator $125-$155. 2 room suite $160 for up to 4 persons; 3 stories; interior corridors; sauna. **Cards:** AE, CB, DI, DS, MC, VI. *(See ad below)*

(Sᴅ) (ᔥ) (▤) (💷) (🖨) (🔒) (✕)

MARINA STREET INN Guaranteed Rates **Phone:** (805)772-4016
◆◆◆ All Year [BP] 1P: $79- 130 2P/1B: $89- 140 XP: $15
Bed & **Location:** 305 Marina St 93442. **Terms:** Reserv deposit, 7 day notice; handling fee imposed. **Facility:** 4
Breakfast rooms. Evening refreshments. 2 stories; interior corridors; smoke free premises. **All Rooms:** shower baths.
Cards: AE, MC, VI.

(ASK) (🅏) (🔒) (✕)

MORRO CREST INN **Phone:** (805)772-7740
(AAA) [SAVE] Fri & Sat 5/16-9/30 1P: $45- 85 2P/1B: $50- 85 2P/2B: $55- 95 XP: $5 F12
Sun-Thurs 1P: $35- 50 2P/1B: $35- 55 2P/2B: $40- 65 XP: $5 F12
◆ Fri & Sat 2/1-5/15 &
Motel 10/1-1/31 1P: $38- 65 2P/1B: $38- 65 2P/2B: $45- 65 XP: $5 F12
Location: Just s of Morro Bay Blvd. 670 Main St 93442. **Terms:** Reserv deposit, 3 day notice; small pets only, $5 extra charge, $20 dep req. **Facility:** 17 rooms. 2 stories; exterior corridors. **Cards:** AE, DS, MC, VI.
Special Amenities: Free local telephone calls and preferred room (subject to availability with advanced reservations).

(Sᴅ) (🛏) (ᔥ) (▤) (🖨) (🔒) (✕)

SUNDOWN MOTEL Rates Subject to Change **Phone:** (805)772-7381
(AAA) Fri & Sat 6/1-9/30 1P: $45- 88 2P/1B: $50- 88 2P/2B: $55- 95 XP: $5 F10
Sat 2/1-5/31, Sun-Thurs
◆◆ 6/1-9/30 & Sat 10/1-1/31 1P: $38- 65 2P/1B: $38- 65 2P/2B: $42- 69 XP: $5 F10
Motel Sun-Fri 2/1-5/31 & 10/1-1/31 1P: $32- 45 2P/1B: $34- 48 2P/2B: $39- 50 XP: $5 F10
Location: Just s of Morro Bay Blvd. 640 Main St 93442. Fax: 805/772-7381. **Terms:** Reserv deposit; weekly/monthly rates; small pets only, $5 extra charge, 11/1-5/31. **Facility:** 17 rooms. Cozy rooms. Pets allowed in specified rooms only. 1 story; exterior corridors. **All Rooms:** shower baths. **Cards:** AE, DS, MC, VI. *(See ad p 732)*

(🛏) (ᔥ) (🔒) (✕)

SUNSET TRAVELODGE   Phone: (805)772-1259

		1P:		2P/1B:		2P/2B:		XP:
(AAA) (SAVE)	Fri & Sat 6/1-9/15	1P:	$129- 159	2P/1B:	$129- 159	2P/2B:	$149- 189	XP: $10-20
	Sat 2/1-5/31 & 9/16-1/31	1P:	$89- 125	2P/1B:	$98- 139	2P/2B:	$110- 179	XP: $10-20
◆◆	Sun-Thurs 6/1-9/15	1P:	$69- 98	2P/1B:	$69- 98	2P/2B:	$79- 110	XP: $8-12
Motel	Sun-Fri 2/1-5/31 & 9/16-1/31	1P:	$49- 89	2P/1B:	$55- 89	2P/2B:	$59- 98	XP: $5-10

Location: US 1, Morro Bay Blvd exit; right on Market. 1080 Market Ave at Beach St 93442. **Fax:** 805/772-8967. **Terms:** Reserv deposit; handling fee imposed; pets, $10 extra charge, $25 dep req. **Facility:** 31 rooms. 6 two-bedroom units. 2 stories; exterior corridors; heated pool open 4/1-10/31. **All Rooms:** combo or shower baths. **Cards:** AE, CB, DI, DS, JC, MC, VI. **Special Amenities:** Free breakfast and free local telephone calls.
(See color ad below)

THE TWIN DOLPHIN   Rates Subject to Change   **Phone:** 805/772-4483

		1P:		2P/1B:		2P/2B:		XP:	
(AAA)	All Year [CP]	1P:	$75- 130	2P/1B:	$75- 130	2P/2B:	$75- 130	XP: $10	D10

Location: Just s of Morro Bay Blvd. 590 Morro Ave 93442. **Terms:** Reserv deposit, 3 day notice. **Facility:** 31 rooms. Spacious rooms, some with ocean view. 3 stories; interior corridors; whirlpool. **All Rooms:** shower baths. **Cards:** DS, MC, VI.

VILLAGER MOTEL   **Phone:** (805)772-1235

		1P:		2P/1B:		2P/2B:		XP:
(AAA) (SAVE)	Fri & Sat 5/16-9/30	1P:	$65- 130	2P/1B:	$75- 130	2P/2B:	$85- 130	XP: $8
◆◆	Fri & Sat 2/1-5/15 & 10/1-1/31	1P:	$45- 75	2P/1B:	$55- 75	2P/2B:	$65- 80	XP: $8
Motel	Sun-Thurs	1P:	$35- 50	2P/1B:	$40- 55	2P/2B:	$45- 60	XP: $5

Location: Just n of Morro Bay Blvd. 1098 Main St 93442. **Facility:** 22 rooms. 2 stories; exterior corridors; indoor whirlpool. **Dining:** Coffee shop nearby. **All Rooms:** shower baths. **Cards:** AE, CB, DI, DS, MC, VI.

RESTAURANTS

GALLEY RESTAURANT   **Lunch:** $6-$22   **Dinner:** $14-$22   **Phone:** 805/772-2806

(AAA)   **Location:** 899 Embarcadero 93442. **Hours:** 11 am-8:30 pm, Sat, Sun & 6/1-9/15 to 9:30 pm. Closed: 12/1-12/25. **Reservations:** suggested. **Features:** casual dress; children's menu; beer & wine only; a la carte.
◆◆   Long established family operated restaurant on waterfront overlooking bay. Seafood, beef & chicken. May
Seafood   close earlier off season. Smoke free premises. **Cards:** AE, DS, MC, VI.

GREAT AMERICAN FISH COMPANY   **Lunch:** $6-$8   **Dinner:** $12-$19   **Phone:** 805/772-4407

(AAA)   **Location:** 1185 Embarcadero 93442. **Hours:** 11 am-10 pm, 11/1-4/1- to 9 pm. Closed: 11/25. **Features:** No
◆◆   A/C; casual dress; children's menu; carryout; cocktails & lounge. On waterfront, overlooking bay. Nice
Seafood   selection of mesquite broiled seafood & steaks. **Cards:** AE, DS, MC, VI.

HARADA JAPANESE RESTAURANT & SUSHI BAR   **Lunch:** $7-$9   **Dinner:** $17-$25   **Phone:** 805/772-1410
◆◆   **Location:** 630 Embarcadero 93442. **Hours:** 11:30 am-2 & 5-10 pm. **Reservations:** suggested.
Ethnic   **Features:** casual dress; beer & wine only. Attractive Japanese decor, on upper level overlooking the bay.
Smoke free premises. **Cards:** AE, MC, VI.   ☒

HARBOR HUT RESTAURANT   **Lunch:** $7-$14   **Dinner:** $12-$21   **Phone:** 805/772-2255
ⒶⒶⒶ   **Location:** 1205 Embarcadero 93442. **Hours:** 11 am-10 pm, 11/1-4/1 Sun-Thurs-9 pm; Sun brunch on
◆   sternwheeler. **Reservations:** suggested. **Features:** No A/C; casual dress; Sunday brunch; children's menu;
carryout; cocktails & lounge. On waterfront, overlooking bay. Casual, informal atmosphere. Nice selection of
Seafood   pasta, mesquite broiled steaks & seafood. Smoke free premises. **Cards:** AE, DS, MC, VI.   ☒

HOPPE'S HIP POCKET BISTRO   **Lunch:** $7-$12   **Dinner:** $7-$16   **Phone:** 805/772-5371
◆◆   **Location:** 901 Embarcadero 93442. **Hours:** 11 am-9 pm. Closed: 12/25 & some days in Jan. **Features:** No
American   A/C; casual dress; children's menu; carryout; beer & wine only; a la carte. On the Embarcadero. Bay view
dining. Specializing in fresh seafood & pasta. Some vegetarian selections avail. Children's portions avail.
Smoke free premises. **Cards:** AE, DS, MC, VI.   ☒

HOPPE'S MARINA SQUARE   **Dinner:** $14-$19   **Phone:** 805/772-5371
◆◆◆   **Location:** 699 Embarcadero 93442. **Hours:** 5 pm-9 pm, Fri & Sat-10 pm. **Reservations:** suggested.
Continental   **Features:** casual dress; cocktails & lounge; a la carte, also prix fixe. On the Embarcadero overlooking the
bay & Morro Rock; seafood, steaks prepared with French influence. **Cards:** AE, DS, MC, VI.   ☒

PARADISE RESTAURANT & LOUNGE   **Lunch:** $6-$10   **Dinner:** $11-$23   **Phone:** 805/772-2743
◆◆◆   **Location:** 1 mi s on Main St, at entrance to Morro Bay State Park & golf course; in The Inn at Morro Bay. 60
American   State Park Rd 93442. **Hours:** 7-11 am, 11:30-2 & 5-9 pm, Sun 7 am-2 & 5:30-9 pm.
Reservations: suggested; weekends. **Features:** No A/C; casual dress; Sunday brunch; children's menu;
early bird specials; cocktails & lounge; a la carte. Attractive dining room overlooking the bay. **Cards:** AE, CB, DI, DS,
VI.   ☒

MOUNTAIN VIEW—67,500

LODGINGS

BEST WESTERN MOUNTAIN VIEW INN   Rates Subject to Change   **Phone:** 650/962-9912
◆◆◆   All Year [CP]   1P: $100- 275   2P/1B: $110- 275   2P/2B: $110- 350   XP: $10   F16
Motel   **Location:** 1.3 mi s of US 101, exit Rengstorff Rd; 2 blks w on El Camino Real (SR 82). 2300 El Camino
Real W 94040. Fax: 650/962-9011. **Facility:** 72 rooms. Attractive Decor. Comfortable Rooms. 6 whirlpool rms,
extra charge; 2-3 stories, no elevator; exterior corridors; small pool. **All Rooms:** combo or shower baths. **Some Rooms:** 4
efficiencies, kitchen. **Cards:** AE, CB, DI, DS, JC, MC, VI.   🔳🔳🔳🔳🔳🔳🔳🔳🔳🔳🔳

BEST WESTERN TROPICANA LODGE   **Phone:** (650)961-0220
ⒶⒶⒶ 〔SAVE〕   All Year [CP]   1P: $85- 95   2P/1B: $85- 100   2P/2B: $85- 100   XP: $5   F12
◆◆   **Location:** Exit US 101 Shoreline S, 2 mi to SR 82, then 0.3 mi w. 1720 El Camino Real W 94040.
Fax: 650/961-1471. **Terms:** Reserv deposit; handling fee imposed; pets, at manager's discretion. **Facility:** 59
Motel   rooms. Protected pool area, comfortable rooms. 2 stories; interior/exterior corridors; sauna.
Dining: Restaurant nearby. **All Rooms:** combo or shower baths. **Cards:** AE, CB, DI, DS, JC, MC, VI.
Special Amenities: Free breakfast and free local telephone calls.   🔳🔳🔳🔳🔳🔳🔳🔳🔳

COMFORT INN   **Phone:** (650)967-7888
ⒶⒶⒶ 〔SAVE〕   All Year [CP]   1P: $95   2P/1B: $105   2P/2B: $115   XP: $10   D18
◆◆   **Location:** Exit US 101 Shoreline S, 2 mi to SR 82, just w. 1561 W El Camino Real 94040.
Fax: 650/967-3579. **Terms:** Handling fee imposed. **Facility:** 37 rooms. Covered parking. 3 whirlpool rms, $225
Motel   for up to 2 persons; Three 2-bedroom units, $120-$150; 3 stories; interior corridors; whirlpool. **Cards:** AE, DI,
DS, MC, VI. **Special Amenities: Free breakfast and free newspaper.** *(See color ad below)*
🔳🔳🔳🔳🔳🔳

COUNTY INN   **Phone:** (650)961-1131
ⒶⒶⒶ 〔SAVE〕   Mon-Thurs [CP]   1P: $109   2P/1B: $119   2P/2B: $129   XP: $10   F12
   Fri-Sun [CP]   1P: $75   2P/1B: $75   2P/2B: $85   XP: $10   F12
◆◆◆   **Location:** 1 blk s off US 101; exit via Moffett Blvd. 850 Leong Dr 94043. Fax: 650/965-9099. **Terms:** Reserv
Motel   deposit. **Facility:** 52 rooms. Attractive & comfortable rooms. 2 stories; exterior corridors. **Dining:** Restaurant
nearby. **Recreation:** some rooms have video game. **Cards:** AE, CB, DI, DS, JC, MC, VI.
Special Amenities: Free breakfast and free local telephone calls.
🔳🔳🔳🔳🔳🔳🔳🔳🔳🔳🔳

CRESTVIEW HOTEL
Phone: (650)966-8848
AAA [SAVE]
All Year [BP] 1P: $140 2P/1B: $140 2P/2B: $155 XP: $10 F12
◆◆ **Location:** SR 82, 0.5 mi e of SR 85. 901 E El Camino Real 94040. Fax: 650/966-8884. **Terms:** Reserv
Motel deposit. **Facility:** 66 rooms. Well appointed rooms. Stereo & compact disk players. 2-room suites, $175-$195
for 2 persons; 3 stories; interior corridors. **All Rooms:** efficiencies, no utensils. **Some Rooms:** whirlpools.
Cards: AE, CB, DI, DS, JC, MC, VI. **Special Amenities: Free breakfast and free newspaper.**

HOLIDAY INN EXPRESS HOTEL & SUITES
Phone: (650)967-6957
AAA [SAVE]
All Year [CP] 1P: $125- 175 2P/1B: $125- 175 2P/2B: $125- 175 XP: $10-30 F12
◆◆◆ **Location:** US 101 northbound exit SR 237 w 3 mi, just n on SR 82. US 101 southbound exit SR 85 s 0.5
Motel mi; exit Grant Rd, just n on SR 82. 93 El Camino Real W 94040. Fax: 650/967-4834. **Terms:** Reserv
deposit. **Facility:** 58 rooms. Large rooms, attractively decorated. 3 whirlpool rms, extra charge; 2 stories; ex-
terior corridors; heated pool, whirlpool. **Dining:** Restaurant nearby. **Some Rooms:** 8 efficiencies, 3 kitchens.
Cards: AE, CB, DI, DS, JC, MC, VI. **Special Amenities: Free breakfast and free local telephone calls.**
(See color ad below)

RAMADA LIMITED
Phone: (650)967-6856
AAA [SAVE]
All Year [CP] 1P: $90- 100 2P/1B: $90- 100 2P/2B: $90- 100 XP: $5 F17
◆◆ **Location:** West of and Adj to US 101, exit Ellis St, N 0.5 mi. 55 Fairchild Dr 94043. Fax: 650/964-4542.
Motel **Terms:** Reserv deposit. **Facility:** 50 rooms. Few small rooms. 7 whirlpool rms, extra charge; 2 stories; exterior
corridors; whirlpool. **Cards:** AE, CB, DI, DS, MC, VI. **Special Amenities: Free breakfast and free local
telephone calls.** (See color ad opposite title page)

RESIDENCE INN BY MARRIOTT Rates Subject to Change Phone: 650/940-1300
◆◆◆
Suite Motel
Sun-Thurs [CP] 1P: $216- 245 2P/1B: $216- 245 2P/2B: $216- 245
Fri & Sat [CP] 1P: $119- 154 2P/1B: $119- 154 2P/2B: $119- 154
Location: US 101, exit S Rengstorff; e on El Camino Real. 1854 El Camino Real 94040. Fax: 650/969-4997.
Facility: 112 rooms. 1 & 2 bedroom units, some with fireplace. 2 stories; exterior corridors. **All Rooms:** kitchens.
Cards: AE, CB, DI, DS, JC, MC, VI.

SAN ANTONIO INN Rates Subject to Change Phone: (650)948-1036
AAA
All Year [CP] 1P: $68- 95 2P/1B: $68- 98 2P/2B: $74- 99 XP: $6 F17
◆◆ **Location:** SR 82, 0.3 mi w of San Antonio Rd. 2650 El Camino Real 94040. Fax: 650/948-7214. **Facility:** 58
Motel rooms. 2 stories; exterior corridors. **Dining:** Restaurant nearby. **Cards:** AE, CB, DI, JC, MC, VI.

SUPER 8 MOTEL Rates Subject to Change Phone: 650/969-9641
AAA
All Year [CP] 1P: $75 2P/1B: $80 2P/2B: $85 XP: $5 D12
◆◆ **Location:** Exit US 101 at Shoreline, 2 mi w, n on SR 82. 1665 El Camino Real 94040. Fax: 650/938-3791.
Motel **Terms:** Reserv deposit. **Facility:** 31 rooms. 2 whirlpool rms, extra charge; 2 stories; exterior corridors.
Dining: Restaurant nearby. **Cards:** AE, DS, MC, VI.

MOUNT SHASTA—3,500

LODGINGS

BEST WESTERN TREE HOUSE MOTOR INN
Phone: (530)926-3101
AAA [SAVE]
5/28-9/25 1P: $69- 89 2P/1B: $69- 89 2P/2B: $74- 94 XP: $5 F12
2/1-5/27 & 9/26-1/31 1P: $64- 84 2P/1B: $64- 84 2P/2B: $69- 89 XP: $5 F12
◆◆◆ **Location:** E off & adjacent to I-5; exit Central Mt Shasta, 2nd exit. 111 Morgan Way 96067.
Motor Inn Fax: 530/926-3542. **Terms:** Small pets only, designated rooms. **Facility:** 95 rooms. Nicely landscaped
grounds. 7 two-bedroom units. 2-3 stories; interior/exterior corridors; heated indoor pool, whirlpool.
Dining: Restaurant; 5:30 am-2 pm, 5 pm-10 pm, Sun 5:30 am-1:30 pm & 4:30-9:30 pm; $11-$20; cocktails. **Cards:** AE, CB,
DI, DS, MC, VI. (See ad p 735)

ECONO LODGE
Phone: (530)926-3145
AAA [SAVE]
All Year 1P: $36- 45 2P/1B: $42- 49 2P/2B: $49- 59 XP: $5
◆◆ **Location:** Exit I-5 central, 0.5 mi e then 0.5 mi s. 908 S Mt Shasta Blvd 96067. Fax: 530/926-5897.
Motel **Terms:** Pets, $20 dep req. **Facility:** 20 rooms. 5 two-bedroom units. 4 kitchen units, $10 extra charge; 2 sto-
ries; exterior corridors; whirlpool. **All Rooms:** combo or shower baths. **Cards:** AE, CB, DI, DS, JC, MC, VI.
Special Amenities: Free local telephone calls and preferred room (subject to availability with
advanced reservations).

EVERGREEN LODGE   Phone: (530)926-2143
(AAA) [SAVE]   All Year   1P: $35- 45   2P/1B: $41- 49 2P/2B: $49- 59 XP: $6
              Location: Exit I-5 central, 0.5 mi e; 1 mi s. 1312 S Mount Shasta Blvd 96067. **Terms:** Reserv deposit, 3 day
◆◆   notice; handling fee imposed; pets, $5 extra charge. **Facility:** 20 rooms. 3 kitchens; $10 extra; 1 story; exterior
Motel   corridors; whirlpool. **Cards:** AE, CB, DI, DS, JC, MC, VI. **Special Amenities: Free room upgrade and
              preferred room (each subject to availability with advanced reservations).**   [icons]

MOUNTAIN AIR LODGE   Rates Subject to Change   Phone: (530)926-3411
(AAA)   5/1-8/31   1P: $39- 44   2P/1B: $42- 48 2P/2B: $51- 57 XP: $8
              2/1-4/30 & 9/1-1/31   1P: $32- 38   2P/1B: $38- 44 2P/2B: $44- 52 XP: $5
◆◆   **Location:** Exit I-5 central, 0.5 mi e, 5 mi s. 1121 S Mount Shasta Blvd 96067. **Terms:** Pets, $5 dep req.
Motel   **Facility:** 38 rooms. Shaded grounds. 13 two-bedroom units. 4 kitchens, $7 extra charge; 2 family units $130
              for up to 10 persons; 2 stories; exterior corridors; whirlpool. **Dining:** Restaurant nearby.
Recreation: recreation room. **All Rooms:** combo or shower baths. **Cards:** AE, DS, MC, VI.   [icons]

PINE NEEDLES MOTEL   Phone: (530)926-4811
(AAA) [SAVE]   All Year   1P: $35- 45   2P/1B: $42- 55 2P/2B: $45- 59 XP: $6
              Location: Exit I-5 central, 0.5 mi e then 1 mi s. 1340 S Mt Shasta Blvd 96067. Fax: 530/926-4811.
◆◆   **Terms:** Reserv deposit, 3 day notice; pets, $6 extra charge. **Facility:** 29 rooms. 2 stories; exterior corridors;
Motel   whirlpool. **All Rooms:** combo or shower baths. **Some Rooms:** 2 kitchens, no utensils. **Cards:** AE, CB, DI,
              DS, JC, MC, VI. **Special Amenities: Free local telephone calls and preferred room (subject to
availability with advanced reservations).**   [icons]

STRAWBERRY VALLEY INN   Phone: 530/926-2052
(AAA) [SAVE]   All Year [CP]   1P: $54- 57   2P/1B: $59- 79 2P/2B: $79   XP: $6   F10
              Location: Exit I-5 Central exit, 0.5 mi e, then 0.5 mi s on Mt Shasta Blvd. 1142 S Mt Shasta Blvd 96067.
◆◆◆   Fax: 530/926-0842. **Facility:** 15 rooms. Beautifully landscaped grounds. 1 story; exterior corridors; smoke free
Bed &   premises. **Services:** complimentary evening beverages. **All Rooms:** combo or shower baths. **Cards:** AE,
Breakfast   CB, DI, DS, MC, VI.   [icons]

SWISS HOLIDAY LODGE   Guaranteed Rates   Phone: (530)926-3446
(AAA)   5/1-8/31 [CP]   1P: $36- 42   2P/1B: $42- 48 2P/2B: $44- 62 XP: $5
              2/1-4/30 & 9/1-1/31 [CP]   1P: $32- 39   2P/1B: $39- 45 2P/2B: $45- 53 XP: $5
◆◆   **Location:** E of I-5 at McCloud/SR 89 exit, just n at first left. 2400 S Mt. Shasta Blvd 96067 (PO Box 335).
Motel   **Terms:** Reserv deposit, 3 day notice; small pets only. **Facility:** 21 rooms. Most rooms with view of Mt. Shasta,
              kitchen avail. 1 bedroom apartment, $98 for up to 6 persons; 2 stories; exterior corridors; small pool, whirlpool.
All Rooms: shower baths. **Cards:** AE, DI, DS, MC, VI.   [icons]

RESTAURANTS

LILY'S
◆◆
Regional
American
Lunch: $6-$9   **Dinner:** $10-$20   **Phone:** 530/926-3372
Location: E of I-5, exit Central exit, 0.5 mi e, 0.3 mi s. 1013 S Mt Shasta Blvd 96067. **Hours:** 7 am-9:30 pm. Closed: 12/25. **Reservations:** suggested. **Features:** casual dress; Sunday brunch; children's menu; senior's menu; beer & wine only. Pleasant surroundings, good selection of seafood, pasta, mexican & vegetarian specialities. Smoke free premises. **Cards:** AE, DI, MC, VI.   ⊠

MICHAEL'S RESTAURANT
◆◆
American
Lunch: $4-$9   **Dinner:** $9-$17   **Phone:** 530/926-5288
Location: Exit I-5 at Central, 0.3 mi e. 313 N Mt Shasta Blvd 96067. **Hours:** 11 am-2:30 & 5-9 pm, Sat noon-9 pm. Closed major holidays, Sun & Mon. **Reservations:** suggested. **Features:** casual dress; children's menu; beer & wine only; street parking. Casual atmosphere, varied menu. Italian specialities. Smoke free premises. **Cards:** AE, DI, DS, MC, VI.   ⊠

SERGE'S RESTAURANT
◆◆
French
Dinner: $13-$21   **Phone:** 530/926-1276
Location: Exit I-5 at Central E, 0.5 mi to Chestnut, n. 531 Chestnut St 96067. **Hours:** 5 pm-9 pm; Fri & Sat till 9:30 pm. Closed: Mon & Tues. **Reservations:** suggested. **Features:** casual dress; beer & wine only; street parking; a la carte. Classical French with low fat selections, emphasis on quality ingredients, variety. Sun deck for outside dining weather permitting. View of Mt Shasta. Smoke free premises. **Cards:** AE, MC, VI.   ⊠

MURPHYS—1,500

LODGINGS

DUNBAR HOUSE 1880
◆◆◆
Bed &
Breakfast
Rates Subject to Change   **Phone:** (209)728-2897
All Year   1P: $120- 190   2P/1B: $125- 195   XP: $20
Location: 9 mi n of jct SR 49 & SR 4; exit SR 4 Murphys, Main St. 271 Jones St 95247. Fax: 209/728-1451. **Terms:** Reserv deposit, 5 day notice; 2 night min stay, weekends. **Facility:** 4 rooms. Italianate style home built in 1880. Large porch, attractive garden landscaping. 1 two-bedroom unit. 2 stories; interior corridors; smoke free premises. **Cards:** MC, VI.   🈺 🍴 📼 🖨 🔒 ⊠

MURPHYS HISTORIC HOTEL & LODGE
AAA SAVE
◆◆
Motel
Phone: (209)728-3444
Fri & Sat [CP]   1P: $80- 85   2P/1B: $80- 85   2P/2B: $80- 85 XP: $6   F
Sun-Thurs [CP]   1P: $70- 75   2P/1B: $70- 75   2P/2B: $70- 75 XP: $6   F
Location: Center. 457 Main St 95247. Fax: 209/728-1590. **Facility:** 29 rooms. 9 rooms on the Historic Register with 19th-century atmosphere. 20 rooms located in motel section. 3 suites $75-$90 Sun-Thurs, $85-$95 Fri & Sat for up to 2 persons; 1-2 stories; interior/exterior corridors. **Dining:** Cocktails. **Some Rooms:** color TV. **Cards:** AE, DI, DS, MC, VI.   🆘 📵 ⊠

MURPHYS INN MOTEL
FYI
Phone: 209/728-1818
Under construction. **Location:** Jct SR4 & Main St. 76 Main St 95247. **Facility:** 37 rooms.

MURRIETA—1,600

RESTAURANT

THE FISH EXCHANGE
◆◆
Seafood
Lunch: $7-$10   **Dinner:** $10-$18   **Phone:** 909/677-9449
Location: From I-15, exit California Oaks Rd, 1 mi w to Washington, then 0.5 mi s. 24910 Washington Ave 92562. **Hours:** 11:30 am-3 & 5-9 pm, Sat & Sun from noon. Closed major holidays. **Reservations:** suggested. **Features:** casual dress; children's menu; beer & wine only. Casual dining. Nice selection of fresh seafood & pasta. Oyster bar. Smoke free premises. **Cards:** AE, MC, VI.   ⊠

MYERS FLAT—100

LODGING

MYERS INN
AAA SAVE
◆◆
Bed &
Breakfast
Phone: (707)943-3259
All Year [CP]   1P: $125   2P/1B: $125   2P/2B: $125   XP: $10   F12
Location: W of & adjacent to US 101, on the Avenue of the Giants. 12913 Avenue of the Giants 95554 (PO Box 173). Fax: 707/943-1800. **Terms:** Check-in 4 pm. **Facility:** 10 rooms. Most units have access to second-floor deck. Rooms furnished with white wicker. Building was a stagecoach stop, est. 1867. 2 stories; exterior corridors; smoke free premises. **Dining:** Restaurant nearby. **Cards:** AE, MC, VI. **Special Amenities:** Free breakfast and preferred room (subject to availability with advanced reservations).   🆘 🍴 ☎ 🎿 🖨

NAPA—61,800

LODGINGS

BEST WESTERN ELM HOUSE INN
AAA SAVE
◆◆◆
Motel
Phone: (707)255-1831
4/1-11/15 [BP]   1P: $119- 189   2P/1B: $119- 189   2P/2B: $119- 179 XP: $15   F12
2/1-3/31 & 11/16-1/31 [BP]   1P: $109- 149   2P/1B: $109- 149   2P/2B: $109- 149 XP: $15   F12
Location: Exit SR 29 at 1st St; 1 1/2 blks s on California Blvd. 800 California Blvd 94559. Fax: 707/255-8609. **Terms:** Reserv deposit. **Facility:** 16 rooms. Residential location. Few rooms with wood-burning fireplace, $10-$15 extra; 3 stories; interior corridors; whirlpool. **All Rooms:** combo or shower baths. **Some Rooms:** whirlpools. **Cards:** AE, CB, DI, DS, JC, MC, VI. **Special Amenities:** Free breakfast and free local telephone calls. *(See color ad p 737)*   📵 🍴 🖨 🔒 📺 📶 🖨

BEST WESTERN INN
AAA SAVE
◆◆◆
Motel
Phone: (707)257-1930
5/1-11/13   1P: $100- 180   2P/1B: $105- 180   2P/2B: $105- 180 XP: $10   F12
2/1-4/30 & 11/14-1/31   1P: $85- 165   2P/1B: $90- 165   2P/2B: $90- 165 XP: $10   F12
Location: At jct SR 121 & Soscol Ave. 100 Soscol Ave 94559. Fax: 707/255-0709. **Terms:** Reserv deposit, 3 day notice. **Facility:** 68 rooms. Large comfortable rooms. Close to Napa State Hospital. Few deluxe rooms, $120-$165 for up to 2 persons; 2-3 stories; interior/exterior corridors; heated pool, whirlpool. **Dining:** Coffee shop nearby. **Cards:** AE, CB, DI, DS, JC, MC, VI. **Special Amenities:** Free local telephone calls and free newspaper.   📵 🏊 🍴 📶 🖨 🔒 ⊠

THE CHABLIS INN

								Phone: (707)257-1944	

Rates Subject to Change   Phone: (707)257-1944

Fri & Sat 4/17-11/15	1P: $100- 120	2P/1B: $100- 125	2P/2B: $110- 130	XP: $5	F12
Fri & Sat 2/1-4/16 & 11/16-1/31	1P: $70- 95	2P/1B: $80- 100	2P/2B: $80- 105	XP: $5	F12
Sun-Thurs 5/1-11/15	1P: $75- 85	2P/1B: $80- 90	2P/2B: $80- 90	XP: $5	F12
Sun-Thurs 2/1-4/30 & 11/16-1/31	1P: $55- 70	2P/1B: $60- 80	2P/2B: $60- 80	XP: $5	F12

Motel

Location: Just w off SR 29 via Redwood Rd, just s. 3360 Solano Ave 94558. Fax: 707/226-6862. **Terms:** Reserv deposit, 3 day notice. **Facility:** 34 rooms. Comfortable rooms. 5 whirlpool rms, extra charge; 2 stories; exterior corridors; small pool, whirlpool. **Some Rooms:** 7 efficiencies. **Cards:** AE, DI, DS, MC, VI. *(See ad below)*

THE CHATEAU

Rates Subject to Change   Phone: (707)253-9300

Fri & Sat 4/1-10/31	1P: $115	2P/1B: $115	2P/2B: $120	XP: $10	F12
Sun-Thurs 4/1-10/31	1P: $105	2P/1B: $105	2P/2B: $110	XP: $10	F12
2/1-3/31 & 11/1-1/31	1P: $95	2P/1B: $95	2P/2B: $100	XP: $10	F12

Motel

Location: W of & adjacent to SR 29 at Wine Country Ave. 4195 Solano Ave 94558. Fax: 707/253-0906. **Terms:** Reserv deposit; handling fee imposed. **Facility:** 115 rooms. 5 minutes to downtown & to World Famous Wineries. 4 two-bedroom units. 2 stories; interior corridors; heated pool. **Cards:** AE, DI, DS, MC, VI. *(See color ad below)*

EMBASSY SUITES NAPA VALLEY
◆◆◆
Hotel

	Rates Subject to Change			Phone: 707/253-9540	
Fri & Sat 4/1-11/30 [BP]	1P: $189	2P/1B: $189	2P/2B: $189	XP: $15	F18
Sun-Thurs 4/1-11/30 [BP]	1P: $159	2P/1B: $159	2P/2B: $159	XP: $15	F18
Fri & Sat 2/1-3/31 & 12/1-1/31 [BP]	1P: $149	2P/1B: $149	2P/2B: $149	XP: $15	F18
Sun-Thurs 2/1-3/31 & 12/1-1/31 [BP]	1P: $139	2P/1B: $139	2P/2B: $139	XP: $15	F18

Location: Adjacent to SR 29; exit e 1st St. 1075 California Blvd 94559. **Fax:** 707/253-9202. **Terms:** Reserv deposit. **Facility:** 205 rooms. 1-bedroom suites with living room. 3 stories; interior/exterior corridors; indoor pool. Rental: bicycles. **Cards:** AE, CB, DI, DS, JC, MC, VI.

JOHN MUIR INN
ⒶⒶⒶ
◆◆◆
Motel

	Rates Subject to Change			Phone: (707)257-7220	
4/1-10/31 [CP]	1P: $105- 180	2P/1B: $105- 180	2P/2B: $105- 180	XP: $10	F14
2/1-3/31 & 11/1-1/31 [CP]	1P: $95- 160	2P/1B: $95- 160	2P/2B: $95- 160	XP: $10	F14

Location: Exit 29 at e Trower Ave. 1998 Trower Ave 94558. **Fax:** 707/258-0943. **Facility:** 59 rooms. Comfortable rooms, attractive landscaping. 3 stories; interior corridors; heated pool, whirlpool. **Dining:** Coffee shop nearby. **Some Rooms:** 18 efficiencies, whirlpools. **Cards:** AE, CB, DI, DS, MC, VI.

NAPA VALLEY BUDGET INN
ⒶⒶ
◆
Motel

	Guaranteed Rates			Phone: 707/257-6111	
Fri & Sat 5/1-10/31 [CP]	1P: $108	2P/1B: $108	2P/2B: $118	XP: $6	
Fri & Sat 2/1-4/30, Sun-Thurs 5/1-10/31 & Fri & Sat 11/1-1/31 [CP]	1P: $60	2P/1B: $64	2P/2B: $70	XP: $6	
Sun-Thurs 2/1-4/30 & 11/1-1/31 [CP]	1P: $50	2P/1B: $56	2P/2B: $60	XP: $6	

Location: Just w off SR 29 via Redwood Rd, just s. 3380 Solano Ave 94558. **Fax:** 707/252-2702. **Terms:** Reserv deposit; pets, $10 extra charge. **Facility:** 58 rooms. 2 stories; exterior corridors. **Dining:** Restaurant nearby. **All Rooms:** shower baths. **Cards:** AE, DS, MC, VI. *(See color ad p 739)*

NAPA VALLEY MARRIOTT
◆◆◆
Motor Inn

	Rates Subject to Change			Phone: 707/253-7433
Fri & Sat 4/13-11/20	1P: $149	2P/1B: $169	2P/2B: $169	
Sun-Thurs 4/13-11/20	1P: $109	2P/1B: $124	2P/2B: $124	
Fri & Sat 2/1-4/12 & 11/21-1/31	1P: $99	2P/1B: $114	2P/2B: $114	
Sun-Thurs 2/1-4/12 & 11/21-1/31	1P: $79	2P/1B: $109	2P/2B: $109	

Location: 1 blk w off SR 29 via Redwood Rd, 0.5 blk n. 3425 Solano Ave 94558. **Fax:** 707/258-1320. **Terms:** Reserv deposit. **Facility:** 191 rooms. 2 stories; interior corridors; heated pool; 2 lighted tennis courts. **Services:** giftshop. **Cards:** AE, DI, DS, MC, VI.

NAPA VALLEY TRAVELODGE
Phone: (707)226-1871

(AAA) (SAVE)

◆◆
Motel

7/1-9/30	1P: $119- 209	2P/1B: $119- 209	2P/2B: $149- 189	XP: $20	F17
5/1-6/30 & 10/1-11/30	1P: $109- 209	2P/1B: $109- 209	2P/2B: $139- 189	XP: $20	F17
2/1-4/30 & 12/1-1/31	1P: $89- 209	2P/1B: $89- 209	2P/2B: $109- 139	XP: $20	F17

Location: At 2nd & Coombs sts, across from courthouse. 853 Coombs St 94559. Fax: 707/226-1707. **Terms:** Reserv deposit, 3 day notice; handling fee imposed. **Facility:** 44 rooms. Limited parking. 3 stories; exterior corridors; small pool. **Cards:** AE, CB, DI, DS, MC, VI.

SILVERADO COUNTRY CLUB RESORT
Rates Subject to Change   Phone: 707/257-0200

◆◆◆◆
Resort
Complex

3/1-11/26	1P: $160- 500	2P/1B: $160- 500	2P/2B: $160- 500	XP: $15	F18
2/1-2/28 & 11/27-1/31	1P: $135- 375	2P/1B: $135- 375	2P/2B: $135- 375	XP: $15	F18

Location: 5.8 mi e of Napa via SR 121. 1600 Atlas Peak Rd 94558. Fax: 707/257-5400. **Terms:** Check-in 5 pm; reserv deposit, 7 day notice. **Facility:** 260 rooms. Outstanding recreational facilities. Cottages; 1- to 3-bedroom efficiency or kitchen apartments; many fireplaces. 180 two-bedroom units, 20 three-bedroom units. Some larger condominium units, $350-750; 2 stories; exterior corridors. Fee: 36 holes golf; 23 tennis courts (3 lighted). **Services:** giftshop. Rental: bicycles. **All Rooms:** combo or shower baths. **Cards:** AE, CB, DI, DS, JC, MC, VI.

RESTAURANTS

CHANTERELLE RESTAURANT
Lunch: $7-$12   Dinner: $12-$19   Phone: 707/253-7300

◆◆◆
Continental

Location: Downtown Napa. 804 1st St 94559. **Hours:** 11 am-4 pm & 5-9:30 pm, Sun 10:30-2:30 & 5-9 pm. Closed major holidays. **Reservations:** suggested. **Features:** Sunday brunch; cocktails & lounge; a la carte. Conveniently located in downtown area. Smoke free premises. **Cards:** MC, VI.

JONESY'S FAMOUS STEAK HOUSE
Lunch: $6-$16   Dinner: $8-$16   Phone: 707/255-2003

◆
Steakhouse

Location: At Napa County Airport. 2044 Airport Rd 94558. **Hours:** 11:30 am-9 pm, Fri & Sat-9 pm, 4/4-10/31 to 8 pm. Closed: Mon, 1/1, 11/25 & 12/21-12/26. **Reservations:** suggested. **Features:** casual dress; children's menu; cocktails; minimum charge-$4.50; a la carte. Also, chicken & fresh fish. **Cards:** AE, DI, DS, MC, VI.

NAPA VALLEY WINE TRAIN
Lunch: $60-$88   Dinner: $70-$97   Phone: 707/253-2111

(AAA)

◆◆◆
Continental

Location: Exit SR 29 at 1st St, e on 1st St 0.8 mi then 4 blks n on Soscal Ave. 1275 McKinstry St 94559. **Hours:** Seatings at 11:30 am & 6:30 pm, Sat & Sun seatings at 12:20 pm & 6 pm. Closed: 12/25, 1/1. **Reservations:** required. **Features:** semi-formal attire; cocktails & lounge; buffet. Restored turn-of-the-century pullman cars; 36 mi round trip excursion through scenic wine country. 3 hour fine dining experience. Prix fixe, 3 entree choices. Smoke free premises. **Cards:** AE, CB, DI, MC, VI. (See color ad p 147)

RUFFINO'S
Dinner: $11-$20   Phone: 707/255-4455

◆◆
Northern
Italian

Location: 645 First St 94559. **Hours:** 5 pm-10 pm, Sun 4 pm-9 pm. Closed major holidays & Mon. **Reservations:** suggested. **Features:** casual dress; children's menu; cocktails & lounge; a la carte. Also, steak & seafood. Smoke free premises. **Cards:** AE, DI, MC, VI.

NATIONAL CITY—See San Diego p. 907.

NEEDLES—5,200

LODGINGS

BEST WESTERN COLORADO RIVER INN
Phone: (760)326-4552

(AAA) (SAVE)

◆◆◆
Motel

5/1-8/31	1P: $55- 65	2P/1B: $60- 70	2P/2B: $60- 70	XP: $5	F12
9/1-10/31	1P: $50- 60	2P/1B: $55- 65	2P/2B: $55- 65	XP: $5	F12
2/1-4/30 & 1/1-1/31	1P: $50- 55	2P/1B: $55- 60	2P/2B: $55- 60	XP: $5	F12
11/1-12/31	1P: $45- 50	2P/1B: $50- 55	2P/2B: $50- 55	XP: $5	F12

Location: 0.3 mi e of I-40, W Broadway/River Rd exit. 2371 W Broadway 92363. Fax: 760/326-4562. **Terms:** Reserv deposit, 7 day notice; weekly/monthly rates; small pets only. **Facility:** 63 rooms. 8 mini suites $65-$150; 2 stories; exterior corridors; heated indoor pool, sauna, whirlpool. **Dining:** Restaurant nearby. **Cards:** AE, CB, DI, DS, JC, MC, VI. **Special Amenities:** Early check-in/late check-out and free local telephone calls.

BEST WESTERN ROYAL INN
Phone: (760)326-5660

(AAA) (SAVE)

◆◆◆
Motel

5/1-10/31	1P: $55- 65	2P/1B: $60- 70	2P/2B: $60- 70	XP: $5	F12
2/1-4/30	1P: $50- 55	2P/1B: $55- 60	2P/2B: $55- 60	XP: $5	F12
11/1-1/31	1P: $45- 50	2P/1B: $50- 55	2P/2B: $50- 55	XP: $5	F12

Location: Adjacent to I-40, W Broadway/River Rd exit. 1111 Pashard St 92363. Fax: 760/326-4002. **Terms:** Reserv deposit; weekly/monthly rates; small pets only. **Facility:** 60 rooms. 2 stories; exterior corridors; sauna, indoor whirlpool. **Dining:** Restaurant nearby. **Cards:** AE, CB, DI, DS, JC, MC, VI. **Special Amenities:** Early check-in/late check-out and free local telephone calls.

IMPERIAL 400 MOTOR INN
Phone: (760)326-2145

(AAA) (SAVE)

◆
Motel

All Year	1P: $22- 28	2P/1B: $25- 32	2P/2B: $29- 39	XP: $4	

Location: I-40, eastbound exit J St, westbound exit E Broadway. 644 W Broadway 92363. **Terms:** Reserv deposit; weekly/monthly rates; small pets only. **Facility:** 31 rooms. 2 stories; exterior corridors. **Dining:** Restaurant nearby. **Cards:** AE, DS, MC, VI. **Special Amenities:** Free local telephone calls and free room upgrade (subject to availability with advanced reservations).

OVERLAND INN
Rates Subject to Change   Phone: (760)326-8808

◆
Motor Inn

All Year	1P: $27- 32	2P/1B: $32- 37	2P/2B: $32- 37	XP: $5	F18

Location: On business loop I-40; exit J St eastbound; exit E Broadway westbound. 712 E Broadway 92363. Fax: 760/326-6602. **Facility:** 40 rooms. 5 two-bedroom units. 2 stories; exterior corridors. **All Rooms:** combo or shower baths. **Cards:** AE, CB, DI, DS, MC, VI.

RED ROOF INN
AAA SAVE
◆◆ Motel
Phone: (760)326-4900
Fri & Sat 5/1-9/30 1P: $43 2P/1B: $50 2P/2B: $50 XP: $4 F18
2/1-4/30, Sun-Thurs 5/1-9/30
& 10/1-1/31 1P: $33 2P/1B: $40 2P/2B: $40 XP: $4 F18
Location: Adjacent to I-40, exit J St. 1195 3rd Street Hill 92363. Fax: 760/326-4980. **Terms:** Age restrictions may apply. **Facility:** 117 rooms. 3 one-bedroom suites, $57.95 for 2 persons; 3 stories; exterior corridors. heated pool, whirlpool. **Cards:** AE, CB, DI, DS, MC, VI. **Special Amenities:** Free local telephone calls.

RIVER VALLEY MOTOR LODGE
AAA SAVE
◆ Motel
Phone: (760)326-3839
All Year 1P: $21- 27 2P/1B: $23- 29 2P/2B: $26- 35 XP: $3
Location: 1 mi nw on I-40 business loop; from I-40 westbound exit J St, eastbound exit W Broadway. 1707 W Broadway 92363. Fax: 760/326-3881. **Terms:** Reserv deposit; handling fee imposed; weekly/monthly rates; small pets only, $5 extra charge. **Facility:** 26 rooms. 1 story; exterior corridors. **Cards:** AE, CB, DI, DS, JC, MC, VI. **Special Amenities:** Early check-in/late check-out and free local telephone calls.
(See ad below)

SUPER 8 MOTEL OF NEEDLES
◆◆ Motel
Phone: 760/326-4501
All Year 1P: $37- 47 2P/1B: $45- 55 2P/2B: $45- 55 XP: $5 F12
Location: Adjacent to I-40 exit US 95, E Broadway. 1102 E Broadway 92363. Fax: 760/326-2054. **Terms:** Reserv deposit. **Facility:** 30 rooms. 2 stories; exterior corridors. **Cards:** AE, DS, MC, VI.

NEVADA CITY—2,900

LODGINGS

DEER CREEK INN
◆◆◆ Bed & Breakfast
Rates Subject to Change Phone: 530/265-0363
All Year [BP] 2P/1B: $90- 145 XP: $20
Location: In the historic district. 116 Nevada St 95959. Fax: 530/265-0980. **Terms:** Reserv deposit, 10 day notice; 2 night min stay, weekends. **Facility:** 4 rooms. Restored 1860's Queen Anne Victorian. Creek side setting. 3 stories, no elevator; interior corridors. **All Rooms:** combo or shower baths. **Cards:** MC, VI.

EMMA NEVADA HOUSE
AAA
◆◆◆ Bed & Breakfast
Guaranteed Rates Phone: (530)265-4415
All Year [BP] 1P: $100- 155 2P/1B: $100- 155 XP: $20
Location: In the historic district. 528 E Broad St 95959. Fax: 530/265-4416. **Terms:** Reserv deposit, 7 day notice; 2 night min stay, weekends 4/1-12/31. **Facility:** 6 rooms. 1856 restored pre-Victorian. Antiques. Living room with fireplace. 3 stories, no elevator; interior corridors. **All Rooms:** combo or shower baths. **Some Rooms:** whirlpools. **Cards:** AE, DI, MC, VI.

GRANDMERE'S INN
◆◆◆ Historic Bed & Breakfast
Rates Subject to Change Phone: 530/265-4660
12/1-1/2 [BP] 1P: $115- 180 2P/1B: $115- 180 XP: $20
2/1-11/30 & 1/3-1/31 [BP] 1P: $100- 165 2P/1B: $100- 165 XP: $20
Location: In the historic district. 449 Broad St 95959. Fax: 530/265-6569. **Terms:** Reserv deposit, 7 day notice; 2 night min stay, weekends 4/1-12/31. **Facility:** 7 rooms. 1856 Colonial Revival; attractive grounds; one room with private entrance. 2-3 stories, no elevator; interior corridors. **All Rooms:** combo or shower baths. **Some Rooms:** color TV. **Cards:** AE, MC, VI.

MARSH HOUSE BED & BREAKFAST INN
◆◆◆ Bed & Breakfast
Rates Subject to Change Phone: (530)265-5709
All Year [BP] 1P: $125- 165 2P/1B: $150- 175 2P/2B: $150-175 XP: $25 D12
Location: Exit SR 49 e on Broad St to Boulder, just up hill. 254 Boulder 95959. **Facility:** 6 rooms. Restored 1873 Victorian Italianate "Country Villa". 2 stories; interior corridors. **All Rooms:** combo or shower baths. **Some Rooms:** color TV. **Cards:** AE, CB, DI, DS, MC, VI.

NORTHERN QUEEN INN
AAA
◆◆ Motel
Rates Subject to Change Phone: 530/265-5824
All Year 1P: $60- 100 2P/1B: $60- 100 2P/2B: $63- 100 XP: $5
Location: 0.5 mi w, adjacent & s of SR 20 & 49, exit Sacramento Ave. 400 Railroad Ave 95959. Fax: 530/265-3720. **Facility:** 86 rooms. All cottages with woodburning stoves, all chalets overlooking creek. 8 one-story cottage units, $75-$90; 8 two-story chalets units $85-$100, for up to 2 persons; 2 stories; exterior corridors; heated pool, whirlpool. **Dining:** Dining room; 7 am-2 pm, Thurs-Sun to 9 pm; cocktails. **All Rooms:** combo or shower baths. **Cards:** AE, CB, DI, MC, VI.

RIVER VALLEY MOTOR LODGE
"One of the BEST for LESS!"
IN NEEDLES
- FREE HBO
- Refrigerators
- Microwaves
- Pool
- Non-Smoking Room
- Walking Distance to Restaurant
- King & Queen Beds
- Phones
(760) 326-3839 Reservations Call: 1-800-346-2331

PIETY HILL INN
◆
Bed & Breakfast

Rates Subject to Change
All Year [CP]   1P: $80- 130   2P/1B: $80- 130   2P/2B: $80- 130 XP: $15
Location: SR 49 & 20, exit Sacramento St. 523 Sacramento St 95959. **Facility:** 9 rooms. Single cottages & one private, 3-room cottage. Nicely landscaped grounds. Well maintained, Country American motiff. One 3-room cottage, $150; 2 persons, $150; 1 story. **All Rooms:** combo or shower baths. **Cards:** AE, MC, VI.

Phone: 530/265-2245

NEWARK—37,900

LODGINGS

HILTON HOTEL
ⒶⒶⒶ SAVE
◆◆◆
Hotel

Mon-Thurs   1P: $169   2P/1B: $169   2P/2B: $184   XP: $15   F15
Fri-Sun   1P: $89   2P/1B: $89   2P/2B: $104   XP: $15   F15
Location: I-880, Stevenson Blvd W exit. 39900 Balentine Dr 94560. Fax: 510/651-7828. **Facility:** 316 rooms. Courtyard & tower units. 3 whirlpool rms, extra charge; 2-7 stories; interior corridors; sauna, whirlpool. **Dining:** Restaurant; 6 am-10 pm; $10-$20; cocktails. **Services:** giftshop; area transportation, within 3 mi. **Cards:** AE, CB, DI, DS, JC, MC, VI. **Special Amenities:** Free newspaper. *(See ad p 119)*

Phone: (510)490-8390

PARK INN
◆◆
Motel

Rates Subject to Change
All Year [CP]   1P: $89- 129   2P/1B: $89- 129   2P/2B: $89- 129 XP: $10
Location: W of I-880, Mowry Ave ave, 0.5 mi w. 5977 Mowry Ave 94560. Fax: 510/795-0295. **Facility:** 100 rooms. 4 stories; interior corridors. **Cards:** AE, DI, DS, MC, VI. *(See ad below)*

Phone: 510/795-7995

WOODFIN SUITES
◆◆◆
Suite Motel

Rates Subject to Change
Sun-Thurs   1P: $149   2P/1B: $149   2P/2B: $149
Fri & Sat   1P: $99   2P/1B: $99   2P/2B: $99
Location: W of I-880 at Mowry Ave, 0.3 mi s on Cedar Blvd. 39150 Cedar Blvd 94560. Fax: 510/795-8874. **Terms:** Reserv deposit; handling fee imposed. **Facility:** 148 rooms. 1- & 2-bedroom suites with living room & kitchen, most with fireplace. 16 two-bedroom units. 2 stories; exterior corridors. **Services:** area transportation. **Cards:** AE, DI, DS, MC, VI.

Phone: 510/795-1200

NEWPORT BEACH—66,600   (See map p. 296; index p. 288)

LODGINGS

BEST WESTERN BAY SHORES INN
ⒶⒶⒶ SAVE
◆◆◆
Motel

7/1-9/7 [CP]   1P: $139- 229   2P/1B: $139- 229   2P/2B: $169- 369
5/1-6/30 [CP]   1P: $129- 219   2P/1B: $129- 219   2P/2B: $159- 369
2/1-4/30 & 9/8-10/31 [CP] 1P: $119- 209   2P/1B: $119- 219   2P/2B: $149- 299
11/1-1/31 [CP]   1P: $119- 209   2P/1B: $119- 209   2P/2B: $129- 249
Location: 1 mi sw of SR 1, on Balboa Peninsula. 1800 W Balboa Blvd 92663. Fax: 949/675-4977. **Terms:** 2 night min stay, wknds & 7/1-8/31. **Facility:** 26 rooms. 1 blk to beach & 1/2 blk to bay. Rooftop sun deck with partial view of ocean & bay. 1 two-bedroom suite with private balcony & efficiency $249-$350; 3 stories; exterior corridors; designated smoking area. **Dining:** Restaurant nearby. **Some Rooms:** whirlpools. **Cards:** AE, CB, DI, DS, MC, VI. **Special Amenities:** Free breakfast and free local telephone calls. *(See color ad p 743)*

Phone: (949)675-3463 ⑮

(See map p. 296)

DORYMAN'S OCEANFRONT INN
◆◆◆   All Year [CP]
Bed &
Breakfast

Rates Subject to Change
2P/1B: $135- 275

Phone: 949/675-7300   **12**
XP: $25

Location: Across from Newport Pier. 2102 W Ocean Front 92663. Fax: 949/675-7300. **Terms:** Check-in 4 pm; reserv deposit, 3 day notice. **Facility:** 10 rooms. At the beach. Elegant French & American antiques. Rooftop sun deck. 2 stories; interior corridors; designated smoking area. **Cards:** AE, MC, VI.

FOUR SEASONS HOTEL
(AAA) (SAVE)   All Year
◆◆◆◆◆
Hotel

Phone: (949)759-0808   **18**
1P: $250- 305   2P/1B: $250- 305   2P/2B: $290   XP: $30   F12

Location: In Newport Center; 1 mi e of SR 1. 690 Newport Center Dr 92660. Fax: 949/759-0568. **Terms:** Package plans; small pets only. **Facility:** 285 rooms. Across from Fashion Island. An elegant hotel in a contemporary setting. Nicely landscaped, tree-shaded pool area. 19 stories; interior corridors; heated pool, saunas, whirlpool. Fee: parking. **Dining:** Lite meals avail in The Gardens Lounge & Cafe 11 am-11 pm; cocktails; also, The Pavilion, see separate listing. **Services:** giftshop; area transportation, within 5 mi. Fee: massage. **Recreation:** bicycles. **Cards:** AE, CB, DI, DS, JC, MC, VI. **Special Amenities:** Early check-in/late check-out and free newspaper.

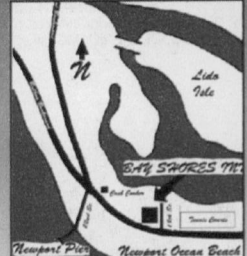

(See map p. 296)

HOLIDAY INN EXPRESS

Rates Subject to Change   Phone: (949)642-8252   **5**

(AAA) FYI   6/1-9/15 & 12/25-1/3 [CP]   1P: $79- 139   2P/1B: $79- 139   2P/2B: $79- 139   XP: $10

Motel   2/1-5/31, 9/16-12/24 &

1/4-1/31 [CP]   1P: $69- 109   2P/1B: $69- 109   2P/2B: $69- 109   XP: $10

Under major renovation. **Location:** 1 mi nw of SR 55 on SR 1. 6208 W Pacific Coast Hwy 92663. **Terms:** Reserv deposit, 3 day notice. **Facility:** 44 rooms. 4 stories; interior corridors; heated pool. **Dining:** Restaurant nearby. **Cards:** AE, DI, DS, MC, VI. *(See color ad p 743)*

HYATT NEWPORTER

Phone: (949)729-1234   **16**

(AAA) SAVE   All Year   1P: $159- 235   2P/1B: $184- 270   2P/2B: $184- 270   XP: $25   F18

◆◆◆   **Location:** 0.5 mi n of SR 1. 1107 Jamboree Rd 92660. Fax: 949/644-1552. **Terms:** Check-in 4 pm; pets,

Resort Hotel $50 non-refundable extra charge. **Facility:** 410 rooms. Colorful, California decor. Spacious, beautifully landscaped grounds. 4 three-bedroom villas with private pool; 3 stories; interior/exterior corridors; heated pool, wading pool, whirlpools. Fee: for 9 hole executive golf course; 16 lighted tennis courts. **Dining:** 2 restaurants; 6:30 am-10:30 pm; $10-$18; cocktails. **Services:** giftshop; area transportation, Fashion & Balboa Island. **Recreation:** basketball court, ping pong tables, sand volleyball court, shuffleboard court. Rental: bicycles. **Cards:** AE, CB, DI, DS, JC, MC, VI. *(See color ad p 565)*

NEWPORT BEACH MARRIOTT HOTEL & TENNIS CLUB

Rates Subject to Change   Phone: 949/640-4000   **20**

◆◆◆   All Year   1P: $149   2P/1B: $149   2P/2B: $149   XP: $20

Hotel   **Location:** 0.5 mi e of SR 1, in Newport Center. 900 Newport Center Dr 92660. Fax: 949/640-5055. **Terms:** Check-in 4 pm. **Facility:** 578 rooms. Across from Fashion Island. Some rooms with view of bay & ocean. 3-16 stories; interior/exterior corridors; heated pool. Fee: 8 lighted tennis courts. **Services:** giftshop. Fee: massage. **Cards:** AE, CB, DI, DS, JC, MC, VI.

(See map p. 296)

NEWPORT BEACH MARRIOTT SUITES

◆◆◆

Suite Hotel

		Rates Subject to Change		Phone: (949)854-4500	■ 3
Mon-Thurs 6/29-9/27	1P: $149	2P/1B: $149	2P/2B: $149		
Mon-Thurs 2/1-6/28, Fri-Sun 6/29-9/27 & Mon-Thurs					
9/28-1/31	1P: $139	2P/1B: $139	2P/2B: $139		
Fri-Sun 9/28-1/31	1P: $109	2P/1B: $109	2P/2B: $109		
Fri-Sun 2/1-6/28	1P: $99	2P/1B: $99	2P/2B: $99		

Location: At intersection of Jamboree Rd & Bayview Way. 500 Bayview Circle 92660. **Fax:** 949/854-3072. **Terms:** Check-in 4 pm. **Facility:** 250 rooms. Nicely landscaped grounds & pool area. Spacious one-bedroom suites. 9 stories; interior corridors; heated pool. **Services:** giftshop. **Cards:** AE, CB, DI, DS, JC, MC, VI.

🐕 🎿 🛗 🏊 🍽 ✈ ⛵ 🛎 🎦 ▯ 🖨 🔒 ✖

NEWPORT CHANNEL INN

Ⓐ Ⓢ🅐Ⓥ🅔

◆◆

Motel

Phone: (949)642-3030   ■ 4

	1P: $69- 109	2P/1B: $69- 109	2P/2B: $79- 119	XP: $5	F16
5/31-9/11					
2/1-5/30 & 9/12-1/31	1P: $49- 89	2P/1B: $49- 89	2P/2B: $59- 99	XP: $5	F16

Location: On SR 1, 1 mi nw of jct SR 55. 6030 W Pacific Coast Hwy 92663. **Fax:** 949/650-2666. **Terms:** Reserv deposit. **Facility:** 30 rooms. 1 blk walk to beach. Oversized rooms for up to 7 persons, $89-$145; 2 stories; exterior corridors. **Dining:** Restaurant nearby. **All Rooms:** shower baths. **Cards:** AE, CB, DI, DS, MC, VI. **Special Amenities:** Early check-in/late check-out and preferred room (subject to availability with advanced reservations).** *(See color ad below)*

🆂🅓 🛗 🍽 🎦 💻 🖨 ✖

NEWPORT CLASSIC INN

Ⓐ Ⓢ🅐Ⓥ🅔

◆◆

Motor Inn

Phone: (949)722-2999   ■ 6

All Year [CP]	1P: $65- 76	2P/1B: $65- 76	2P/2B: $76- 86

Location: On SR 1, 0.5 mi e of jct SR 55. 2300 W Coast Hwy 92663. **Fax:** 949/631-5659. **Terms:** Reserv deposit; weekly rates. **Facility:** 50 rooms. Guest rooms decorated in modern Oriental decor. 6 whirlpool rms, extra charge; 2 stories; interior corridors; heated pool, sauna, whirlpool. **Dining:** Restaurant; 11:30 am-2 & 5-10:30 pm; $12-$25; cocktails. **Cards:** AE, CB, DI, DS, JC, MC, VI. **Special Amenities:** Early check-in/late check-out and free breakfast.

🆂🅓 ⛵ 🍽 🎦 🛎 🎦 🖨 🔒 ✖

PORTOFINO BEACH HOTEL

Ⓐ Ⓢ🅐Ⓥ🅔

◆◆◆

Bed & Breakfast

Phone: (949)673-7030   ■ 10

All Year [CP]	1P: $159- 399	2P/1B: $159- 399	2P/2B: $159- 399

Location: Just n of Newport Pier. 2306 W Ocean Front 92663. **Fax:** 949/723-4370. **Terms:** Reserv deposit, 3 day notice. **Facility:** 15 rooms. At the beach. Attractive European ambiance. Some ocean view rooms. 2 stories; interior/exterior corridors; beach. **Dining:** Restaurant; 5:30 pm-10 pm; $16-$30; cocktails. **All Rooms:** combo or shower baths. **Some Rooms:** whirlpools. **Cards:** AE, CB, DI, DS, MC, VI.

🍽 🖨 ⛵ 🖨 ✖

(See map p. 296)

SHERATON NEWPORT BEACH HOTEL   Phone: (949)833-0570   **❶**

(AAA) (SAVE)

| | 6/7-8/29 | 1P: $99- 119 | 2P/1B: $99- 119 | 2P/2B: $99- 119 | XP: $10 | F16 |
| | 2/1-6/6 & 8/30-1/31 | 1P: $89- 109 | 2P/1B: $89- 109 | 2P/2B: $89- 109 | XP: $10 | F16 |

◆◆◆ Hotel   **Location:** 1 mi s of I-405, 0.5 mi s of John Wayne/Orange County Airport. 4545 MacArthur Blvd 92660. Fax: 949/833-3927. **Facility:** 337 rooms. 10 stories; interior corridors; heated pool, whirlpool; 2 lighted tennis courts. **Dining:** Restaurant; 6:30 am-10 pm; $8-$18; cocktails. **Services:** giftshop; complimentary evening beverages; area transportation, within 5 mi. **Recreation:** basketball court. **Cards:** AE, CB, DI, DS, JC, MC, VI. **Special Amenities:** Free newspaper and preferred room (subject to availability with advanced reservations).

THE SUTTON PLACE HOTEL   Phone: (949)476-2001   **❷**

(AAA) (SAVE)

| | All Year | 1P: $195- 875 | 2P/1B: $220- 875 | 2P/2B: $220- 875 | XP: $25 | F16 |

◆◆◆◆ Hotel   **Location:** 1 mi s of I-405. 4500 MacArthur Blvd 92660. Fax: 949/476-0153. **Terms:** Weekly/monthly rates; MAP avail; package plans, weekends. **Facility:** 435 rooms. Business park location. Very attractive rooms. Contemporary decor. 24 2-room suites, $290; 10 stories; interior corridors; heated pool, saunas, whirlpool; 2 lighted tennis courts. **Dining:** Dining room; 6:30 am-11 pm; $16-$26; cocktails. **Services:** giftshop; area transportation. Fee: massage. Rental: bicycles. **Cards:** AE, CB, DI, DS, JC, MC, VI. **Special Amenities:** Preferred room (subject to availability with advanced reservations).

RESTAURANTS

BISTRO 201   **Lunch:** $8-$14   **Dinner:** $10-$23   Phone: 949/631-1551   **④**

◆◆◆ American   **Location:** On Sr 1, just se of jct SR 55. 3333 Pacific Coast Hwy 92663. **Hours:** 11:30 am-10 pm, Sat 5:30-11 pm, Sun brunch 10:30 am-3 pm. **Reservations:** suggested. **Features:** casual dress; Sunday brunch; cocktails & lounge; valet parking; a la carte. Bay view dining. Contemporary decor. California cuisine. Smoke free premises. **Cards:** AE, DI, JC, MC, VI.

THE CANNERY RESTAURANT   Historical   **Lunch:** $7-$15   **Dinner:** $17-$21   Phone: 949/675-5777   **⑩**

◆◆ Steak and Seafood   **Location:** 1 mi s of SR 1; on Lido Peninsula. 3010 Lafayette Ave at 31st St 92663. **Hours:** 11:30 am-3 & 5-10 pm, Sun 10 am-2:30 & 4:30-10 pm. **Closed:** 11/25 & 12/25. **Reservations:** suggested. **Features:** casual dress; Sunday brunch; children's menu; early bird specials; carryout; cocktails & lounge; entertainment; valet parking. An interesting waterfront restaurant in the former Western Canners Co packing plant. Brunch cruises Sat & Sun, $31; lunch cruises $17.00, by prior reservation only. Patio dining weather permitting. Smoke free premises. **Cards:** AE, CB, DI, DS, JC, MC, VI.

DAILY GRILL   **Lunch:** $7-$12   **Dinner:** $9-$19   Phone: 949/644-2223   **⑳**

◆◆ American   **Location:** In Fashion Island, Newport Center. 957 Newport Center Dr 92660. **Hours:** 11:30 am-10 pm, Fri-11 pm, Sat 9 am-11 pm, Sun 9 am-10 pm. **Closed:** 11/25 & 12/25. **Features:** casual dress; children's menu; carryout; cocktails & lounge; a la carte. Casual atmosphere. Seating at booths, tables & counter. Outdoor dining also avail. Large selection of salads, sandwiches & entrees. **Cards:** AE, DI, MC, VI.

FIVE CROWNS   **Dinner:** $16-$26   Phone: 949/760-0331   **㉔**

◆◆◆◆ American   **Location:** In Corona Del Mar on SR 1. 3801 E Coast Hwy 92625. **Hours:** 5 pm-9:30 pm, Sun 10:30 am-3 & 4-10 pm. **Closed:** 12/25. **Reservations:** required. **Features:** semi-formal attire; Sunday brunch; cocktails & lounge; fee for valet parking; a la carte. Old English inn atmosphere. Nice selection of English cuisine. Specialty is prime rib. Children's portions. **Cards:** AE, DI, DS, JC, MC, VI.

JOSH SLOCUM'S RESTAURANT   **Dinner:** $15-$32   Phone: 949/642-5935   **⑦**

◆◆ Seafood   **Location:** On SR 1, 0.3 mi se of jct SR 55. 2601 W Coast Hwy 92663. **Hours:** 5 pm-10 pm, Fri & Sat-11 pm. **Closed:** 11/25 & 12/25. **Reservations:** suggested. **Features:** No A/C; casual dress; early bird specials; cocktails & lounge; valet parking; a la carte. Nautical decor, overlooking Newport Bay. Nice selection of steak & seafood. **Cards:** AE, MC, VI.

KITAYAMA   **Lunch:** $7-$15   **Dinner:** $21-$29   Phone: 949/725-0777   **②**

◆◆ Ethnic   **Location:** Bayview Pl at Bristol, just w of Jamboree. 101 Bayview Pl 92660. **Hours:** 11:30 am-2 & 6-10 pm, Sat 5:30-10 pm, Sun 5:30-9:30 pm. **Reservations:** suggested. **Features:** casual dress; cocktails & lounge. A delightful Japanese restaurant & sushi bar, in a garden setting. Smoke free premises. **Cards:** AE, DI, JC, MC, VI.

OYSTERS RESTAURANT   **Dinner:** $11-$27   Phone: 949/675-7411   **⑨**

◆◆◆ Ethnic   **Location:** In Corona del Mar, on SR 1. 2515 E Coast Hwy 92625. **Hours:** 5 pm-10 pm. **Closed:** 11/25 & 12/25. **Features:** casual dress; cocktails; entertainment; a la carte. Asian inspired selections of seafood, steak & pasta. Smoke free premises. **Cards:** AE, MC, VI.

(See map p. 296)

PASCAL   Lunch: $10-$20   Dinner: $20-$29   Phone: 949/752-0107   ①
◆◆◆   **Location:** Just w of Jamboree Rd, in Plaza Newport. 1000 Bristol St 92660. **Hours:** 11:30 am-2:30 & 6-9:30
French   pm, Fri-10 pm, Sat 6 pm-10 pm, Mon 11:30 am-2:30 pm. Closed: Sun. **Reservations:** suggested.
                   Features: casual dress; cocktails; a la carte. Charming French country decor. Excellently prepared &
presented French cuisine. Smoke free premises. **Cards:** AE, CB, DI, MC, VI.   ⊠

THE PAVILION   Lunch: $8-$15   Dinner: $18-$28   Phone: 949/759-0808   ⑱
◆◆◆◆   **Location:** In Newport Center; 1 mi e of SR 1; in Four Seasons Hotel. 690 Newport Center Dr 92660.
Continental   **Hours:** 6:30 am-2:30 & 6-10:30 pm. **Reservations:** suggested. **Features:** semi-formal attire; children's
                   menu; health conscious menu; cocktails & lounge; valet parking; a la carte. Elegant dining. Creative
presentation of seafood, veal, beef & fowl. Smoke free premises. **Cards:** AE, CB, DI, JC, MC, VI.   ⊠

P F CHANG'S CHINA BISTRO   Lunch: $6-$13   Dinner: $8-$15   Phone: 949/759-9007   ㉑
◆◆   **Location:** In Fashion Island, Newport Center. 1145 Newport Center Dr 92660. **Hours:** 11:30 am-10:30 pm,
Chinese   Fri & Sat-midnight. **Features:** casual dress; carryout; cocktails; a la carte. Menu offers a selection of cuisine
                   from the major regions of China. Smoke free premises. **Cards:** AE, CB, DI, MC, VI.   ⊠

RISTORANTE MAMMA GINA   Lunch: $8-$15   Dinner: $16-$26   Phone: 949/673-9500   ⑧
◆◆◆   **Location:** SR 1 (Pacific Coast Hwy). 251 E Coast Hwy 92660. **Hours:** 11:30 am-2:30 & 5-10 pm, Fri &
Italian   Sat-10:30 pm. Closed major holidays. **Reservations:** suggested. **Features:** casual dress; Sunday brunch;
                   early bird specials; cocktails; valet parking; a la carte. Harbor view. Tuscan Florentine Northern Italian cuisine
featuring homemade pasta, chicken & veal specialties. Smoke free premises. **Cards:** AE, CB, DI, MC, VI.   ⊠

THE RITZ   Lunch: $10-$17   Dinner: $18-$29   Phone: 949/720-1800   ㉒
◆◆◆◆   **Location:** Across from Fashion Island. 880 Newport Center Dr 92660. **Hours:** 11:30 am-3 & 6-10 pm, Fri-11
Continental   pm, Sat 5:30 pm-11 pm, Sun 5 pm-9 pm. Closed: 1/1, 7/4 & 12/25. **Reservations:** suggested.
                   Features: semi-formal attire; cocktails & lounge; valet parking; a la carte. Elegantly decorated dining rooms.
Formal service. Excellently prepared Continental cuisine. Outdoor garden dining avail weather permitting. Smoke free
premises. **Cards:** AE, DI, MC, VI.   ⊠

21 OCEAN FRONT   Dinner: $18-$32   Phone: 949/673-2100   ⑫
◆◆◆   **Location:** 2100 W Ocean Front 92663. **Hours:** 5:30 pm-10 pm, Fri & Sat-11 pm. Closed major holidays.
American   **Reservations:** suggested. **Features:** semi-formal attire; cocktails & lounge; valet parking; a la carte. At the
                   beach; across from Newport Pier. Turn-of-the-century decor. Selection of seafood, pasta, poultry & meat
entrees. Smoke free premises. **Cards:** AE, CB, DI, DS, MC, VI.   ⊠

YANKEE TAVERN   Lunch: $9-$12   Dinner: $12-$20   Phone: 949/675-5333   ⑮
◆◆   **Location:** On SR 1, (Pacific Coast Hwy). 333 Bayside Dr 92660. **Hours:** 11:30 am-4 & 5-10 pm, Fri & Sat 5
American   pm-11 pm, Sun 10:30 am-3 & 4-10 pm. Closed: 7/4 & 12/25. **Reservations:** suggested. **Features:** casual
                   dress; Sunday brunch; children's menu; cocktails; valet parking. Harbor view. Early American decor. Nice
selection of New England fare. Smoke free premises. **Cards:** AE, DI, MC, VI.   ⊠

NICE—2,100

LODGING

FEATHERBED RAILROAD CO.   Rates Subject to Change   Phone: (707)274-4434
ⓐⓐⓐ   All Year [BP]   1P: $96- 145   2P/1B: $96- 145   XP: $10   D12
◆◆   **Location:** 0.5 mi s of SR 20. 2870 Lakesshore Blvd 95464. Fax: 707/274-1415. **Terms:** Reserv deposit, 3
Bed &   day notice. **Facility:** 9 rooms. Converted nicely appointed cabooses. Few with view of lake across street.
Breakfast   Lower rates in winter; whirlpool; boat dock. **Dining:** Wine/beer only. **Recreation:** fishing; bicycles; croquet &
                   ping-pong. Fee: boating. **All Rooms:** combo or shower baths. **Some Rooms:** whirlpools. **Cards:** AE, DS,
                   MC, VI.   ➤ ⊠ 🏋 VCR ☎ 🖨 🔒 ⊠

NORCO—23,300

LODGING

HOWARD JOHNSON LODGE   Rates Subject to Change   Phone: (909)278-8886
ⓐⓐⓐ   All Year [CP]   1P: $40   2P/1B: $45   2P/2B: $45   XP: $5   F17
◆   **Location:** W side of I-15, exit Second St, just s on Hamner Ave. 1695 Hamner Ave 91760.
Motel   Fax: 909/736-5216. **Terms:** Weekly rates. **Facility:** 55 rooms. 2 stories; exterior corridors; whirlpool.
                   Cards: AE, DI, DS, MC, VI.   ➤ 🏋 ⊠

NORTH HILLS—See Los Angeles p. 622.

NORTH HOLLYWOOD—See Los Angeles p. 622.

NORTHRIDGE   (See map p. 560; index p. 554)

RESTAURANT

PAGODA INN   Lunch: $5-$7   Dinner: $8-$20   Phone: 818/368-0299   ㊺
◆◆   **Location:** SR 118, Tampa Ave exit; then 0.2 mi to Rinaldi, corner of Tampa & Rinaldi; in Porter Shopping
Chinese   Center. 19348 Rinaldi St 91326. **Hours:** 11:30 am-9 pm, Fri & Sat to 10 pm. Closed: 11/26.
                   Reservations: suggested. **Features:** No A/C; casual dress; health conscious menu; carryout; beer & wine
only. Excellent selection of mandarin & szechuan dishes. Large variety of seafood entrees. Smoke free premises.
Cards: AE, DS, MC, VI.   ⊠

NORWALK—See Los Angeles p. 623.

NOVATO—47,600

LODGINGS

BEST WESTERN NOVATO OAKS INN   Phone: (415)883-4400
(AAA) [SAVE]   All Year [CP]   1P: $79- 99 2P/1B: $84- 104 2P/2B: $84- 104 XP: $8   F17
◆◆◆   **Location:** US 101 exit w Alameda del Prado. 215 Alameda del Prado 94949. Fax: 415/883-4128.
Motor Inn   **Facility:** 105 rooms. Large rooms. Most with patio or deck. Deluxe whirlpool rms, $89-$119 for up to 2 persons; 3 stories; interior corridors; heated pool, whirlpool. **Services:** area transportation, to local restaurants. **Some Rooms:** 2 kitchens. **Cards:** AE, CB, DI, DS, JC, MC, VI. **Special Amenities:** Early check-in/late check-out and free breakfast. (See color ad p 1052)

NOVATO DAYS INN   Phone: (415)897-7111
(AAA) [SAVE]   5/1-10/31 [CP]   1P: $64- 69 2P/1B: $64- 69 2P/2B: $79   XP: $5   F12
◆◆   2/1-4/30 & 11/1-1/31 [CP] 1P: $49- 54 2P/1B: $49- 54 2P/2B: $59- 64 XP: $5   F12
Motor Inn   **Location:** US 101, exit San Marin Dr, 1 mi n. 8141 Redwood Blvd 94945. Fax: 415/897-8367. **Terms:** Reserv deposit; small pets only, $10 extra charge. **Facility:** 55 rooms. 2 suites, $110-$125; 2 stories; whirlpool. **Dining:** Restaurant; 11:30 am-2 & 4:30-9:30 pm, Sun from 4:30 pm; $9-$14; wine/beer only. **Cards:** AE, CB, DI, DS, MC, VI.

OAKDALE—12,000

LODGINGS

BEST WESTERN RAMA INN   Phone: (209)845-2500
(AAA) [SAVE]   5/1-9/30 [CP]   1P: $65- 75 2P/1B: $65- 75 2P/2B: $75- 91
◆◆◆   2/1-4/30 & 10/1-1/31 [CP] 1P: $60- 70 2P/1B: $60- 70 2P/2B: $70- 86
Motel   **Location:** 1 mi e jct SR 108/120. 1450 E F St 95361. Fax: 209/845-2523. **Terms:** Reserv deposit; handling fee imposed. **Facility:** 47 rooms. 5 whirlpool rms, extra charge; 3 stories; interior corridors; heated indoor pool, sauna, whirlpool. **Dining:** Coffee shop nearby. **Cards:** AE, CB, DI, DS, MC, VI. **Special Amenities:** Free breakfast and free room upgrade (subject to availability with advanced reservations).

HOLIDAY MOTEL   Phone: (209)847-7023
(AAA) [SAVE]   All Year [CP]   1P: $39- 51 2P/1B: $44- 56 2P/2B: $51- 63 XP: $6   F12
◆   **Location:** 1 mi e on SR 108 & 120. 950 East F St 95361. Fax: 209/847-7023. **Terms:** Reserv deposit.
Motel   **Facility:** 32 rooms. Comfortable rooms. 1 two-bedroom unit. 1 story; exterior corridors. **All Rooms:** combo or shower baths. **Cards:** AE, CB, DI, DS, JC, MC, VI.

RAMADA INN   Phone: (209)847-8181
(AAA) [SAVE]   5/1-9/30   1P: $71   2P/1B: $77   2P/2B: $77   XP: $6   F18
◆◆◆   2/1-4/30 & 10/1-1/31   1P: $65   2P/1B: $71   2P/2B: $71   XP: $6   F18
Motel   **Location:** 0.8 mi e on SR 108 & 120. 825 East F St 95361. Fax: 209/847-9546. **Facility:** 70 rooms. Short distance to Yosemite & Mother Lode. 2 stories; exterior corridors; heated pool, whirlpool. **Dining:** Coffee shop nearby. **All Rooms:** combo or shower baths. **Cards:** AE, CB, DI, DS, JC, MC, VI. **Special Amenities:** Preferred room (subject to availability with advanced reservations).

OAKHURST—2,000

LODGINGS

BEST WESTERN YOSEMITE GATEWAY INN   Phone: (559)683-2378
(AAA) [SAVE]   5/14-10/17   1P: $79- 94 2P/1B: $84- 96 2P/2B: $88- 98 XP: $6-8   F12
◆◆◆   4/1-5/13, 10/18-11/27 &
Motel   12/24-12/31   1P: $54- 60 2P/1B: $58- 65 2P/2B: $58- 65 XP: $6-8   F12
       2/1-3/31, 11/28-12/23 &
       1/1-1/31   1P: $44- 49 2P/1B: $49- 56 2P/2B: $50- 58 XP: $6   F12
Location: 0.8 mi n of jct SR 49. 40530 Hwy 41 93644. Fax: 559/683-3813. **Terms:** Reserv deposit; small pets only, limited rooms. **Facility:** 118 rooms. In nicely landscaped hillside oakgrove. 12 "evergreen" units. 15 two-bedroom units with wet bar, $124 for up to 6 persons; 2 stories; exterior corridors; heated indoor pool, sauna, whirlpools; playground. **Dining:** Restaurant nearby. **Recreation:** weight machine. **Some Rooms:** 4 efficiencies, 7 kitchens. **Cards:** AE, CB, DI, DS, MC, VI. **Special Amenities:** Early check-in/late check-out and free local telephone calls. (See color ad p 1088)

CHATEAU DU SUREAU   Rates Subject to Change   Phone: (559)683-6860
(AAA)   All Year [BP]   1P: $285- 485 2P/1B: $285- 485 2P/2B: $285- 485 XP: $65
◆◆◆◆◆   **Location:** just w of jct SR 41 & SR 49. 48688 Victoria Ln 93644 (PO Box 577). Fax: 559/683-0800.
Country Inn   **Terms:** Reserv deposit, 7 day notice; handling fee imposed; 10% service charge; 2 night min stay, weekends. **Facility:** 10 rooms. Individually, richly appointed; antiques, oils, objects D'art. Provencal ambiance. On a 7.5 acre terraced-garden estate. Closed 1/2-1/21. 2 stories; interior corridors; small pool. **Dining:** Dining room, restaurant; cocktails; also, Erna's Elderberry House, see separate listing. **Services:** complimentary evening beverages. **Recreation:** hiking trails, CD players & library in all units, outdoor granite chess court. Secluded picnic area with pond & gazebo. **Some Rooms:** color TV. **Cards:** AE, MC, VI.

COMFORT INN-OAKHURST   Rates Subject to Change   Phone: (559)683-8282
(AAA)   4/1-10/31 [CP]   1P: $80   2P/1B: $80   2P/2B: $85   XP: $6   F18
◆◆   2/1-3/31 & 11/1-1/31 [CP] 1P: $60   2P/1B: $60   2P/2B: $65   XP: $6   F18
Motel   **Location:** 0.5 mi n of jct SR 49. 40489 Hwy 41 93644. Fax: 559/658-7030. **Terms:** Reserv deposit; small pets only, $6 extra charge, $50 dep req. **Facility:** 113 rooms. 3 two-bedroom units. 3 two-bedroom family units $125 & one 2-bedroom 2-bath apartment, $225; for up to 6 persons; 2 stories; exterior corridors; whirlpool. **Dining:** Coffee shop nearby. **Services:** giftshop. **Cards:** AE, CB, DI, DS, JC, MC, VI. (See color ad p 1087)

HOLIDAY INN EXPRESS ◆◆ Motel

Rates Subject to Change

Phone: 559/642-2525

6/1-9/30 [CP]	1P:	$79- 175	2P/1B:	$79- 175	2P/2B:	$79- 175	XP:	$10	F18
4/1-5/31 & 10/1-12/31 [CP]	1P:	$59- 110	2P/1B:	$59- 110	2P/2B:	$59- 110	XP:	$10	F18
2/1-3/31 & 1/1-1/31 [CP]	1P:	$49- 89	2P/1B:	$49- 89	2P/2B:	$49- 89	XP:	$10	F18

Location: 0.8 mi n of jct SR 49. 40662 Hwy 41 93644. Fax: 559/658-8481. **Terms:** Reserv deposit, 3 day notice; handling fee imposed. **Facility:** 42 rooms. Hillside location. Most units with mountain view. Access from 1st or 4th floor parking. 1 unit whirlpool bath, $149; 4 stories, no elevator; exterior corridors. **Cards:** AE, DI, DS, JC, MC, VI. *(See color ad p 1086)*

HOUNDS TOOTH INN ◆◆◆ Bed & Breakfast

Rates Subject to Change

Phone: (559)642-6600

All Year [BP]		2P/1B:	$95- 155	XP: $20-30 F12

Location: N end of town. 42071 Hwy 41 93644. Fax: 559/658-2946. **Terms:** Reserv deposit, 3 day notice. **Facility:** 12 rooms. Few fireplaces. Smoking allowed on patios only. Few RV spaces. 2 stories; interior/exterior corridors; smoke free premises. **Cards:** AE, DS, MC, VI.

OAKHURST LODGE AAA SAVE ◆ Motel

Phone: 559/683-4417

4/1-10/31			2P/1B:	$60	2P/2B:	$65	XP: $5 F12
2/1-3/31 & 11/1-1/31	1P:	$50	2P/1B:	$50	2P/2B:	$55	XP: $5 F12

Location: Just n of jct SR 49, at CR 426. 40302 Hwy 41 93644. Fax: 559/683-4417. **Terms:** Reserv deposit. **Facility:** 60 rooms. 1-2 stories; exterior corridors; pool 4/1-10/31. **Dining:** Restaurants nearby. **All Rooms:** combo or shower baths. **Cards:** AE, CB, DI, DS, JC, MC, VI. *(See color ad p 1088)*

RAMADA LIMITED AAA SAVE ◆◆ Motel

Phone: (559)658-5500

5/16-10/31 [CP]	1P:	$89- 99	2P/1B:	$89- 119	2P/2B:	$89- 119	XP:	$5	F16
3/1-5/15 & 11/1-12/31 [CP]	1P:	$59- 79	2P/1B:	$59- 79	2P/2B:	$59- 79	XP:	$5	F16
2/1-2/28 & 1/1-1/31 [CP]	1P:	$49- 69	2P/1B:	$49- 69	2P/2B:	$49- 69	XP:	$5	F16

Location: On SR 41, just s of jct SR 49. 48800 Royal Oaks Dr 93644. Fax: 559/658-5505. **Facility:** 69 rooms. 4 rms with whirlpool/wet bar $125 for 2 persons; 2 stories; interior corridors; whirlpool. **All Rooms:** combo or shower baths. **Cards:** AE, DS, MC, VI. **Special Amenities:** Free breakfast and free local telephone calls. *(See color ad p 1086)*

SHILO INN ◆◆◆ Motel

Rates Subject to Change

Phone: 559/683-3555

All Year [CP]	1P:	$75- 119	2P/1B:	$75- 119	2P/2B:	$75- 119	XP: $10 F12

Location: 0.8 mi n of jct SR 49. 40644 Hwy 41 93644. Fax: 559/683-3386. **Terms:** Check-in 4 pm. **Facility:** 81 rooms. Large rooms. Many with mountain view. One-bedroom apartment, $150-$190 for up to 4 persons, 5/1-9/30; 4 stories; interior corridors. **Cards:** AE, CB, DI, DS, JC, MC, VI. *(See ad p 627, p 1091, p 658 & p 627)*

RESTAURANTS

ERNA'S ELDERBERRY HOUSE RESTAURANT ◆◆◆◆◆ French

Lunch: $15-$20   **Dinner:** $43-$68   **Phone:** 559/683-6800

Location: Just w of jct SR 41 & SR 49; at Chateau du Sureau. 48688 Victoria Ln 93644. **Hours:** 5:30 pm-8:30 pm, also Wed-Fri 11:30 am-1 pm. Closed: 1/2-1/23. **Reservations:** required. **Features:** semi-formal attire; Sunday brunch; cocktails & lounge; prix fixe. Elegant decor with warm Country-French ambiance & finest table settings. Inventive California cuisine with European influence. Kitchen-garden items crown a fresh seasonal menu. Cigars, smoking garden. Smoke free premises. **Cards:** AE, MC, VI.

VIEWPOINT AAA ◆◆◆ American

Dinner: $10-$23   **Phone:** 559/683-5200

Location: 0.8 mi n of jct SR 49. 40530 Hwy 41 93644. **Hours:** 7 am-10:30 & 5-9:30 pm. **Reservations:** suggested. **Features:** casual dress; Sunday brunch; children's menu; salad bar; cocktails & lounge. Smoke free premises. **Cards:** AE, CB, DI, DS, MC, VI.

OAKLAND
pop. 372,200

This index helps you "spot" where approved accommodations are located on the detailed maps that follow. Rate ranges are for comparison only and show the property's high season. Turn to the listing page for more detailed rate information and consult display ads for special promotions. Restaurant range is for dinner unless only lunch (L) is served.

✈ Airport Accommodations

Spotter/Map Pg. Number	OA	OAKLAND	Rating	Rate	Listing Page
🔢13 / p. 752		Hampton Inn-Oakland Airport, 2.5 mi e of airport	◆◆	$99	754
🔢12 / p. 752	AAA	Holiday Inn-Oakland Airport, 2.3 mi e of airport	◆◆◆	$89-129 SAVE	755
🔢11 / p. 752	AAA	Oakland Airport Hilton, 1.3 mi e of airport	◆◆◆	$109 SAVE	755
🔢18 / p. 752	AAA	Park Plaza Hotel, 1.5 mi e of airport	◆◆◆	$99-169	755
🔢1 / p. 752		San Leandro Marina Inn, 3 mi s of airport	◆◆◆	$89	987

OAKLAND

Spotter/Map Pg.Number	OA	OAKLAND - Lodgings	Rating	Rate	Listing Page
🔢10 / p. 752	AAA	Waterfront Plaza Hotel	◆◆◆	$160-325	755
🔢11 / p. 752	AAA	Oakland Airport Hilton - see ad p 119, p 941	◆◆◆	$109 SAVE	755
🔢12 / p. 752	AAA	Holiday Inn-Oakland Airport - see color ad p 754	◆◆◆	$89-129 SAVE	755
🔢13 / p. 752		Hampton Inn-Oakland Airport	◆◆	$99	754
🔢14 / p. 752		Executive Inn Embarcadero Cove - see color ad p 754	◆◆◆	$110-135	754
🔢15 / p. 752	AAA	Jack London Inn	◆	$75-125	755
🔢17 / p. 752	AAA	Best Western Inn at the Square	◆◆◆	$109-139 SAVE	754
🔢18 / p. 752	AAA	Park Plaza Hotel	◆◆◆	$99-169	755
🔢20 / p. 752		Clarion Suites Lake Merritt Hotel	◆◆	$159-229	754
		OAKLAND - Restaurants			
①1 / p. 752		Oliveto Cafe & Restaurant	◆◆◆	$20-60	756
②2 / p. 752		Le Cheval	◆◆	$10-20	756
③3 / p. 752		Bay Wolf Restaurant	◆◆◆	$30-34	755
④4 / p. 752		Il Pescatore Restaurant	◆◆◆	$10-19	756
⑥6 / p. 752	AAA	L.J. Quinn's Lighthouse	◆◆	$6-16	756
⑦7 / p. 752		Autumn Moon Cafe	◆	$15-25	755
⑧8 / p. 752		Garibaldi's on College	◆◆◆	$13-20	755

Nearby Accommodations

Spotter/Map Pg.Number	OA	SAN LEANDRO - Lodgings	Rating	Rate	Listing Page
🔢1 / p. 752		San Leandro Marina Inn	◆◆◆	$89	987
		CASTRO VALLEY - Lodgings			
🔢6 / p. 752	AAA	Econo Lodge	◆◆	$65-70 SAVE	411
🔢7 / p. 752	AAA	Holiday Inn Express	◆◆◆	$79-137 SAVE	411
		BERKELEY - Lodgings			
🔢29 / p. 752	AAA	Golden Bear Motel	◆	$70-75	371
🔢30 / p. 752	AAA	Berkeley Marina Radisson	◆◆◆	$99-149 SAVE	370
🔢31 / p. 752	AAA	Hotel Durant	◆◆	$105	371
		BERKELEY - Restaurants			
⑮15 / p. 752		Jordan's At The Claremont	◆◆◆◆	$27-40	371
⑯16 / p. 752		Chez Panisse	◆◆◆	$45-65	371
⑰17 / p. 752		Skates on the Bay	◆◆◆	$11-19	371
		EMERYVILLE - Lodgings			
🔢33 / p. 752		Holiday Inn-Bay Bridge	◆◆◆	$145-165	438

Spotter/Map Pg.Number	OA	EMERYVILLE - Lodgings (contd.)	Rating	Rate	Listing Page
34 / p. 752	⊕	Four Points by Sheraton-San Francisco Bay Bridge	◆◆◆	$119-139	438
		LAFAYETTE - Lodgings			
36 / p. 752	⊕	Lafayette Park Hotel - see color ad inside back cover	◆◆◆◆	$180-200 [SAVE]	486
		LAFAYETTE - Restaurants			
25 / p. 752		The Duck Club Restaurant - see color ad inside back cover, p 383	◆◆◆	$22-40	486
26 / p. 752		Cape Cod House	◆◆	$9-15	486
		WALNUT CREEK - Lodgings			
41 / p. 752		Marriott Hotel	◆◆◆◆	$149	1079
42 / p. 752	⊕	Walnut Creek Motor Lodge	◆◆	$70-75	1079
43 / p. 752		Holiday Inn of Walnut Creek	◆◆◆	$94	1079
44 / p. 752		Embassy Suites Hotel - see color ad p 931	◆◆◆◆	$149-169	1079
		WALNUT CREEK - Restaurants			
33 / p. 752		California Cafe Bar & Grill	◆◆◆	$10-20	1079
34 / p. 752		Massimo Ristorante	◆◆◆	$9-17	1079
		DANVILLE - Lodgings			
51 / p. 752	⊕	Danville Inn	◆◆	$70-75	431
		DANVILLE - Restaurant			
35 / p. 752		Blackhawk Grille	◆◆◆	$13-27	431
		SAN RAMON - Lodgings			
55 / p. 752		Courtyard by Marriott	◆◆◆	$69-79	996
56 / p. 752		San Ramon Marriott at Bishop Ranch	◆◆◆	$199	996
57 / p. 752		Residence Inn by Marriott	◆◆◆	$199	996
		ALAMEDA - Lodgings			
59 / p. 752	⊕	Coral Reef Motel & Suites - see color ad p 285	◆◆◆	$88 [SAVE]	285
60 / p. 752	⊕	Marina Village Inn - see color ad p 755	◆◆◆	$95-115 [SAVE]	285

Meal Plan Indicators

CP = Continental Plan of pastry, juice and another beverage or may offer expanded breakfast items

BP = Breakfast Plan of full hot breakfast

AP = American Plan of three meals daily

MAP = Modified American Plan of two meals daily

EP = European Plan, where rate includes only room

Family Plan Indicators

The establishment may limit the number of children to whom the family plan applies.

F17 = children 17 and under stay free (age displayed will reflect property's policy)

D17 = discount for children 17 and under

F = children stay free

D = discounts for children

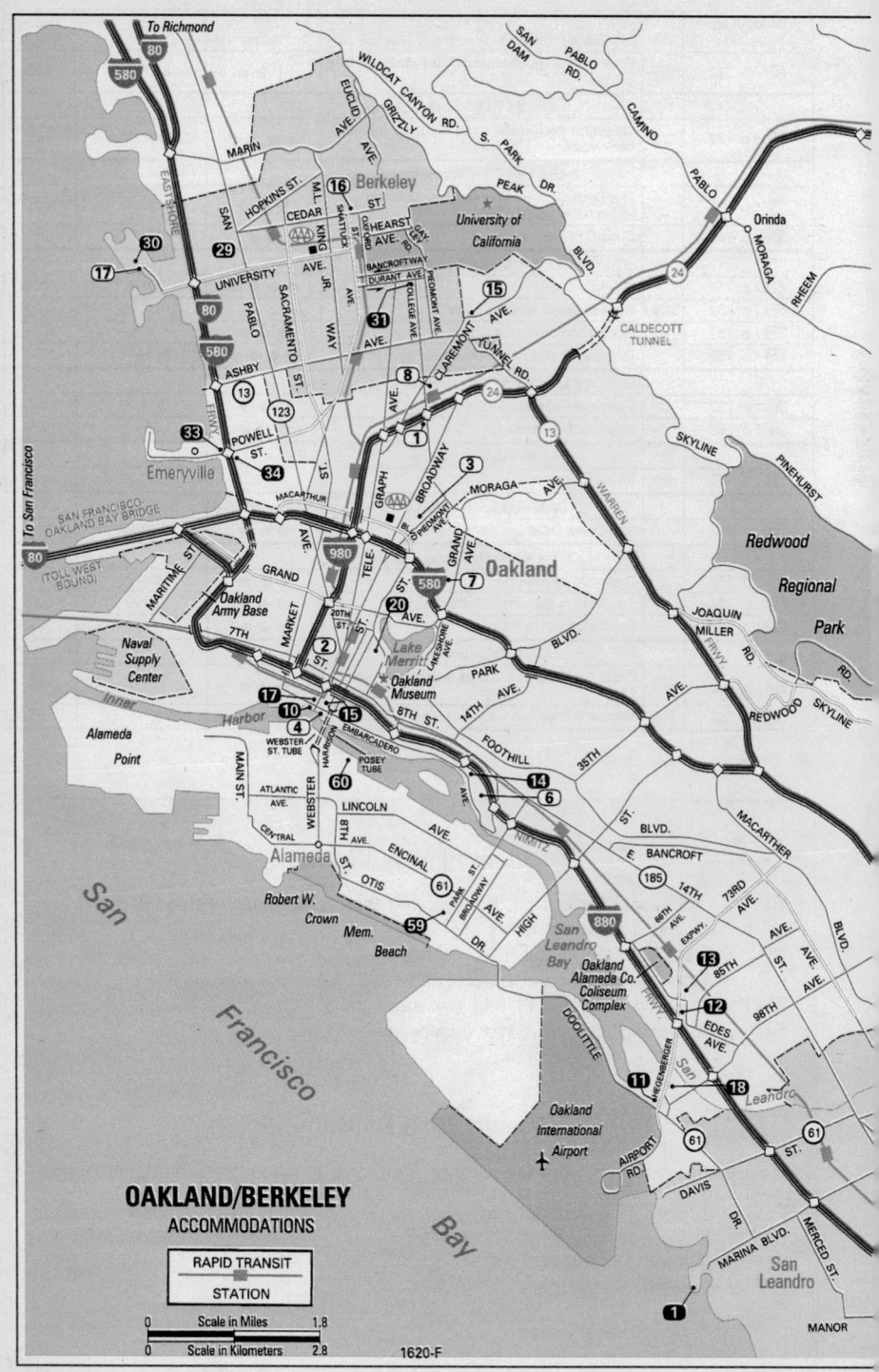

OAKLAND/BERKELEY

ACCOMMODATIONS

RAPID TRANSIT

● STATION

Scale in Miles   1.8
0

Scale in Kilometers   2.8
0

1620-F

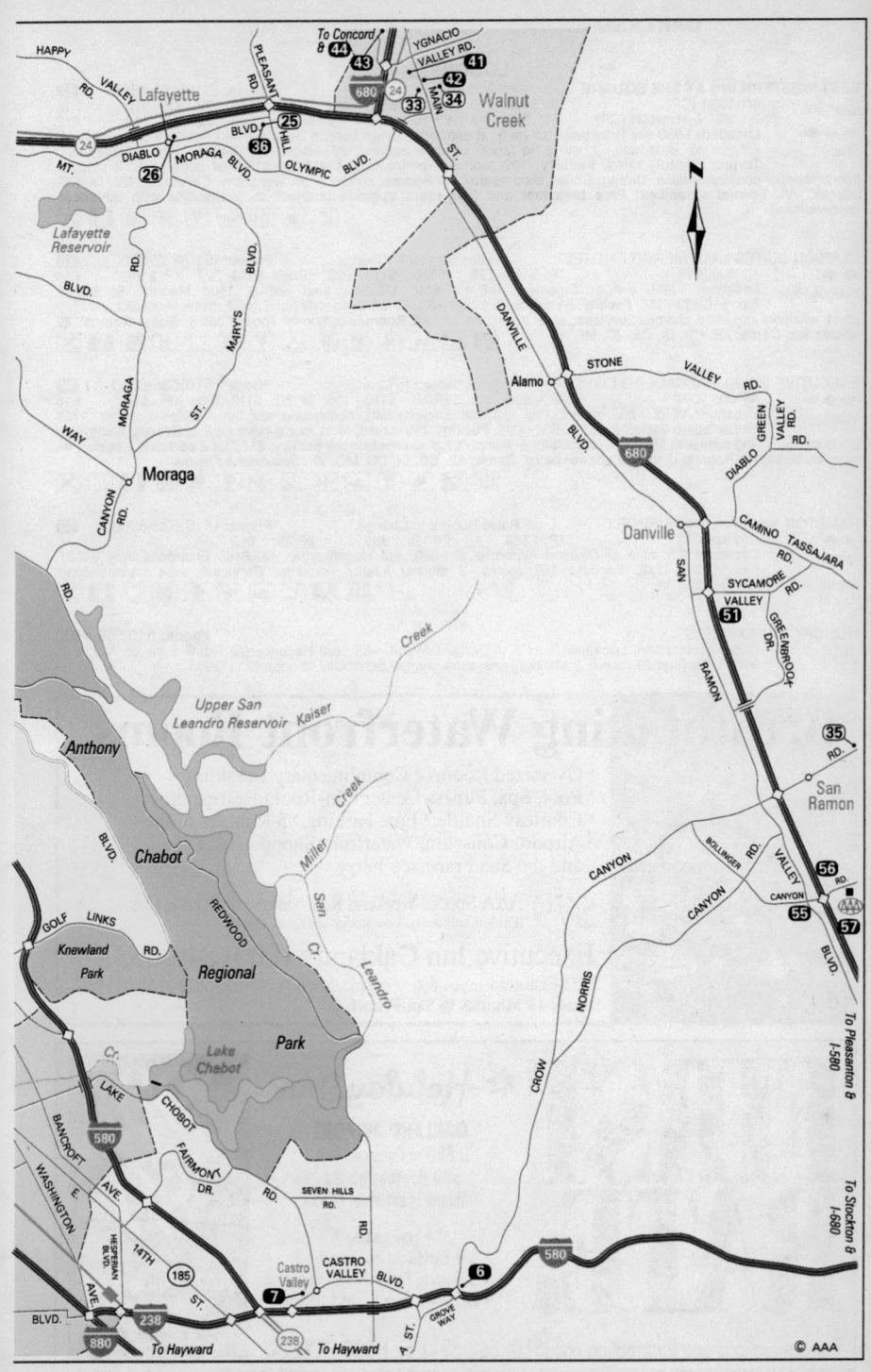

OAKLAND—372,200 (See map p. 752; index p. 750)

LODGINGS

BEST WESTERN INN AT THE SQUARE   Phone: (510)452-4565 ⑰

4/1-10/31 [CP]	1P: $109- 129	2P/1B: $109- 129	2P/2B: $109- 139	XP: $10	F12
2/1-3/31 & 11/1-1/31 [CP]	1P: $99- 119	2P/1B: $99- 119	2P/2B: $99- 129	XP: $10	F12

♦♦♦ **Location:** I-880 exit Broadway, 0.3 mi w, at entrance to Jack London Square; I-980 exit 12th E southbound,
Motel 0.7 mi to Broadway, 1 mi s to Jack London Square. 233 Broadway 94607. Fax: 510/452-4634.
Terms: Monthly rates. **Facility:** 102 rooms. 1-bedroom suites $135-$150 for 2 persons; 3 stories;
interior/exterior corridors; sauna. **Dining:** Coffee shop nearby. **All Rooms:** combo or shower baths. **Cards:** AE, CB, DI, DS,
JC, MC, VI. **Special Amenities: Free breakfast and free room upgrade (subject to availability with advanced
reservations).**

CLARION SUITES LAKE MERRITT HOTEL   Rates Subject to Change   Phone: (510)832-2300 ⑳
♦♦ All Year [CP]   1P: $119- 129   2P/1B: $119- 229   2P/2B: $159- 229   XP: $10-20   F18
Historic Hotel **Location:** I-880, exit at Broadway, 0.8 mi e to 17th St, then just s. 1800 Madison St 94612.
Fax: 510/832-7150. **Facility:** 51 rooms. Refurbished 1927 Art Deco style hotel, most rooms overlook Lake Mer-
ritt. 1 whirlpool rm, extra charge. **Services:** area transportation. **All Rooms:** combo or shower baths. **Some Rooms:** 42
efficiencies. **Cards:** AE, CB, DI, DS, JC, MC, VI.

EXECUTIVE INN EMBARCADERO COVE   Rates Subject to Change   Phone: (510)536-6633 ⑭
♦♦♦ All Year [CP]   1P: $95- 115   2P/1B: $110- 135   2P/2B: $110- 135   XP: $12   F16
Motel **Location:** W of I-880, southbound exit 16th/Embarcadero, northbound exit 5th Ave/Embarcadero. 1755
Embarcadero 94606. Fax: 510/536-6006. **Facility:** 146 rooms. Most rooms have view of Estuary, some spa-
cious rooms. 1 king suite with fireplace, refrigerator & whirlpool tub, overlooking the Estuary, $175 for 2 persons; 3 stories; in-
terior corridors. **All Rooms:** combo or shower baths. **Cards:** AE, CB, DI, DS, MC, VI. *(See color ad below)*

HAMPTON INN-OAKLAND AIRPORT   Rates Subject to Change   Phone: (510)632-8900 ⑬
♦♦ All Year   1P: $89   2P/1B: $99   2P/2B: $99
Motel **Location:** 2.5 mi e of Oakland Airport; e of I-880, exit Hegenberger Rd. 8465 Enterprise Way 94621.
Fax: 510/632-4713. **Facility:** 152 rooms. 3 stories; interior corridors. **Services:** area transportation.
Cards: AE, CB, DI, DS, MC, VI.

HOLIDAY INN EXPRESS   Phone: 510/569-4400
⟨FYI⟩ Under construction. **Location:** 1 mi e of Oakland Airport, I-880 exit Hegenberger Rd, w 1 mi. 66 Airport Dr
94621. **Facility:** 69 rooms. 3 whirlpool rms, extra charge. Scheduled to open Oct, 1998;

(See map p. 752)

HOLIDAY INN-OAKLAND AIRPORT Phone: (510)562-5311 12
AAA SAVE All Year 1P: $89- 129 2P/1B: $89- 129 2P/2B: $89- 129 XP: $10 F17
♦♦♦ **Location:** 2.3 mi e of Oakland Airport; e of I-880, exit Hegenberger Rd. 500 Hegenberger Rd 94621.
Motor Inn Fax: 510/636-1539. **Facility:** 293 rooms. 2-6 stories; interior/exterior corridors. **Dining:** Restaurant; 6:30 am-1:30 & 5-10 pm; $9-$16; cocktails. **Services:** giftshop; area transportation, within 2 mi. **Cards:** AE, CB, DI, DS, JC, MC, VI. *(See color ad p 754)*

JACK LONDON INN Rates Subject to Change Phone: 510/444-2032 15
AAA All Year 1P: $75- 125 2P/1B: $75- 125 2P/2B: $85
♦ **Location:** At Jack London Square, end of Broadway. 444 Embarcadero w 94607. Fax: 510/834-3074.
Motel **Facility:** 110 rooms. 2 blocks from Amtrak Station. 4 stories; interior corridors. **Dining:** Restaurant; $8-$14; cocktails. **All Rooms:** combo or shower baths. **Cards:** AE, CB, DI, DS, MC, VI.

OAKLAND AIRPORT HILTON Phone: (510)635-5000 11
AAA SAVE All Year 1P: $109 2P/1B: $109 2P/2B: $109 XP: $20 F17
♦♦♦ **Location:** 1.3 mi e of Oakland Airport; w of I-880, exit Hegenberger Rd 1 mi. 1 Hegenberger Rd 94614.
Motor Inn Fax: 510/729-0491. **Terms:** Small pets only, $200 dep req. **Facility:** 363 rooms. Spacious rooms. Some patio units. 3 two-bedroom units. 1 & 2-bedroom suites, $300-$500 for 2 persons; 3 stories; interior corridors. **Dining:** Restaurant, coffee shop; 6:30 am-midnight; $10-$24; cocktails. **Services:** giftshop; area transportation, to BART. **All Rooms:** combo or shower baths. **Cards:** AE, DI, DS, JC, MC, VI. **Special Amenities:** Free newspaper. *(See ad p 119 & p 941)*

PARK PLAZA HOTEL Rates Subject to Change Phone: 510/635-5300 18
AAA All Year 1P: $89- 149 2P/1B: $99- 159 2P/2B: $99- 169 XP: $20 F16
♦♦♦ **Location:** 1.5 mi e of Oakland Airport, w of I-880, exit Hegenberger Rd, 0.8 mi. 150 Hegenberger Rd 94621.
Motor Inn Fax: 510/635-9661. **Facility:** 189 rooms. 6 stories; interior corridors; sauna, indoor whirlpool. **Dining:** Restaurant; 6 am-10 pm, Sat & Sun from 7 am; $10-$20; cocktails. **Services:** area transportation, to Bart & Jack London Sq. **All Rooms:** combo or shower baths. **Cards:** AE, CB, DI, DS, JC, MC, VI.

WATERFRONT PLAZA HOTEL Rates Subject to Change Phone: 510/836-3800 10
AAA All Year 1P: $160- 325 2P/1B: $160- 325 2P/2B: $160- 325
♦♦♦ **Location:** 0.5 mi w off I-880 exit Broadway; just n of Jack London Sq. Ten Washington St 94607.
Hotel Fax: 510/832-5695. **Facility:** 144 rooms. On Estuary; many rooms with harbor view. Some balconies & fireplaces. 2 whirlpool rms, extra charge; 5 stories; interior corridors; sauna. Fee: parking; boat dock. **Dining:** Restaurant; 6:30 am-midnight; $15-$30; cocktails. **Services:** giftshop; area transportation, within 3 mi. **All Rooms:** combo or shower baths. **Cards:** AE, DI, DS, MC, VI.

RESTAURANTS

AUTUMN MOON CAFE Lunch: $6-$10 Dinner: $15-$25 Phone: 510/595-3200 7
♦ **Location:** Exit I-580 Grand Ave, n 0.5 at Sunnyside St. 3909 Grand Ave 94610. **Hours:** 7:30 am-2 &
American 5:30-9:30 pm, Sat-10 pm. Closed: 12/25, Mon, Tues lunch. **Reservations:** accepted. **Features:** No A/C; casual dress; Sunday brunch; children's menu; cocktails; street parking; a la carte. Some ethnic influences. Smoke free premises. **Cards:** MC, VI.

BAY WOLF RESTAURANT Lunch: $15-$18 Dinner: $30-$34 Phone: 510/655-6004 3
♦♦♦ **Location:** Exit I-580 at Oakland Ave, n on Mac Arthur Blvd 0.3 mi, 2 blks e on Piedmont Ave. 3853
Regional Piedmont Ave 94611. **Hours:** 11:30 am-2 & 6-9:30 pm, Sat from 5:30 pm, Sun 5:30 pm-9 pm. Closed major
American holidays. **Reservations:** suggested. **Features:** No A/C; casual dress; beer & wine only; street parking; a la carte. Attractive converted house. California cuisine with strong Mediterranean influence. Smoke free premises. **Cards:** MC, VI.

GARIBALDI'S ON COLLEGE Lunch: $8-$16 Dinner: $13-$20 Phone: 510/595-4000 8
♦♦♦ **Location:** Exit SR 24 Claremont Ave. 5356 College Ave 94618. **Hours:** 11:30 am-2:30 & 5:30-10 pm,
American Sat-10:30 pm. Closed: 12/24, 12/25, Sat & Sun for lunch. **Reservations:** suggested. **Features:** casual dress; cocktails; street parking; a la carte. California cuisine with Mediterranean influence. Smoke free premises. **Cards:** AE, MC, VI.

(See map p. 752)

IL PESCATORE RESTAURANT **Lunch:** $10-$14 **Dinner:** $10-$19 **Phone:** 510/465-2188 ④
◆◆◆ **Location:** At Jack London Sq. 57 Jack London Sq 94607. **Hours:** 11:30 am-10 pm, Sat & Sun from 11 am.
Italian Closed major holidays & Mon. **Reservations:** suggested. **Features:** casual dress; cocktails & lounge; fee for parking; a la carte. Varied menu, Tuscan cuisine, fresh seafood specialties, homemade pasta. Overlooks marina. Opera singers entertain on last Thurs of month at dinner. Smoke free premises. **Cards:** AE, CB, DI, MC, VI. 🗙

LE CHEVAL **Lunch:** $6-$8 **Dinner:** $10-$20 **Phone:** 510/763-9457 ②
◆◆ **Location:** At 11th St. 1007 Clay St 94607. **Hours:** 11 am-9:30 pm, Sat-5 pm, Sun 5 pm-10 pm. Closed:
Vietnamese 11/25 & 12/25. **Reservations:** suggested. **Features:** No A/C; casual dress; cocktails; minimum charge-$3. Southeast Asian with a French accent. Smoke free premises. **Cards:** AE, CB, DI, MC, VI. 🗙

L.J. QUINN'S LIGHTHOUSE **Lunch:** $4-$16 **Dinner:** $6-$16 **Phone:** 510/536-2050 ⑥
AAA **Location:** W of I-880, southbound exit 16th Ave, northbound exit 5th Ave. 51 Embarcadero Cove 94606.
  Hours: 11:30 am-3 & 5-9 pm, Sat-10 pm, Sun-9 pm. Closed: 1/1, 11/25 & 12/25. **Reservations:** suggested.
◆◆ **Features:** No A/C; casual dress; children's menu; early bird specials; cocktails & lounge; street parking. A
Seafood lighthouse built in 1903, overlooking marina; varied menu featuring contemporary American cooking. Pasta specialities. Casual atmosphere. **Cards:** MC, VI. 🗙

OLIVETO CAFE & RESTAURANT **Lunch:** $12-$28 **Dinner:** $20-$60 **Phone:** 510/547-5356 ①
◆◆◆ **Location:** Opposite Rockridge Bart station. 5655 College Ave 94618. **Hours:** 7 am- 10 pm, Sat 8 am-10 pm,
Italian Sun 8 am-9 pm. Closed major holidays. **Reservations:** suggested. **Features:** casual dress; beer & wine only; a la carte. Fresh seasonal ingredients prepared in the authentic Italian tradition. Smoke free premises.
Cards: AE, CB, DI, MC, VI. 🗙

OCCIDENTAL—800

LODGINGS

THE INN AT OCCIDENTAL Rates Subject to Change **Phone:** (707)874-1047
◆◆◆◆ All Year [BP] 1P: $145- 245 1P/1B: $145- 245 2P/2B: $145- 245
Bed & **Location:** Town Center. 3657 Church St 95465 (PO Box 857). Fax: 707/874-1078. **Terms:** Reserv deposit,
Breakfast 10 day notice; handling fee imposed. **Facility:** 8 rooms. 1860 restored Victorian. Covered porches with wicker furnishings. 4 rooms with fireplace. 3 stories; interior corridors. **All Rooms:** combo or shower baths.
Some Rooms: color TV. **Cards:** AE, DS, MC, VI. *(See color ad p 197)* (ASK)(📺)(🛏)(🐕)(🗙)

OCCIDENTAL LODGE Guaranteed Rates **Phone:** (707)874-3623
AAA Fri & Sat 1P: $65- 75 2P/1B: $65- 75 2P/2B: $68- 75 XP: $5-8 F12
  Sun-Thurs 1P: $44- 48 2P/1B: $48- 54 2P/2B: $54- 59 XP: $5-8 F12
◆◆ **Location:** In the village. 3610 Bohemian Hwy 95465 (PO Box 84). Fax: 707/545-5293. **Terms:** Reserv
Motel deposit; small pets only, $5. **Facility:** 24 rooms. Large comfortable rooms, some with view of surrounding hills. 2 stories; exterior corridors. **Dining:** Restaurant nearby. **Cards:** AE, DS, MC, VI. (🛏)(🛌)(🍴)(🛁)(📺)(🗙)

OCEANSIDE—128,400

LODGINGS

BEST WESTERN MARTY'S VALLEY INN **Phone:** (760)757-7700
AAA (SAVE) 5/21-9/11 [CP] 1P: $69- 75 2P/1B: $79- 85 2P/2B: $89- 95 XP: $5 F12
  2/1-5/20 [CP] 1P: $63- 68 2P/1B: $69- 75 2P/2B: $74- 80 XP: $5 F12
◆◆◆ 9/12-1/31 [CP] 1P: $63- 68 2P/1B: $69- 74 2P/2B: $74- 80 XP: $5 F12
Motel **Location:** 2 mi e on SR 76. 3240 E Mission Ave 92054. Fax: 760/439-3311. **Facility:** 111 rooms. In San Luis Rey area. 2 stories; interior/exterior corridors; heated pool. **Dining:** Restaurant nearby.
Some Rooms: efficiency, no utensils. **Cards:** AE, CB, DI, DS, MC, VI. **Special Amenities:** Free breakfast and free local telephone calls. (📶)(🛏)(📺)(🛌)(🍴)(🛁)(🐕)(🖥)(🛏)(🖥)(🗙)

BEST WESTERN OCEANSIDE INN Rates Subject to Change **Phone:** (760)722-1821
◆◆◆ All Year [CP] 1P: $79- 129 2P/1B: $79- 129 2P/2B: $79- 129 XP: $10 F17
Motel **Location:** Adjacent to I-5, exit Oceanside Blvd. 1680 Oceanside Blvd 92054. Fax: 760/967-8969. **Facility:** 80 rooms. Attractive pool & courtyard area. Large, nicely furnished rooms. 2 stories; interior/exterior corridors; heated pool. **Cards:** AE, CB, DI, DS, JC, MC, VI. (ASK)(📶)(🛌)(🛁)(🖥)(VCR)(🖥)(🛏)(🖥)(🗙)

COMFORT SUITES Rates Subject to Change **Phone:** (760)722-8880
AAA (FYI) 5/1-9/15 1P: $79- 99 2P/1B: $89- 110 2P/2B: $99- 125 XP: $5-10
  2/1-4/30 & 9/16-1/31 1P: $69- 89 2P/1B: $79- 99 2P/2B: $99- 115 XP: $5-10
Motel Too new to rate. **Location:** 888 N Coast Hwy 92054. **Terms:** Check-in 4 pm; reserv deposit. **Facility:** 64 rooms. 3 stories; interior corridors; heated pool, whirlpool. **Cards:** AE, CB, DI, MC, VI. (SAVE)(📶)(🛌)(🛁)(🖥)(🖥)(🛏)(🖥)(🗙)

DAYS INN AT THE COAST **Phone:** (760)722-7661
AAA (SAVE) 5/15-9/15 & 12/13-12/31 [CP] 1P: $65- 70 2P/1B: $70- 75 2P/2B: $80- 85 XP: $5 F12
  2/1-5/14, 9/16-12/12 &
◆ 1/1-1/31 [CP] 1P: $50- 55 2P/1B: $60- 65 2P/2B: $65- 70 XP: $5 F12
Motel **Location:** Just w of I-5, exit Oceanside Harbor Dr. 1501 Carmelo Dr 92054. Fax: 760/722-5837.
  Terms: Small pets only, $7 extra charge. **Facility:** 81 rooms. Located 0.3 mi ne of Oceanside Harbor. 2 stories; exterior corridors. **Cards:** AE, DS, MC, VI. **Special Amenities:** Free breakfast and free local telephone calls.
(See color ad p 757) (📶)(🛏)(🛌)(🖥)(🖥)(🛏)(🖥)(🗙)

DAYS INN EL CAMINO **Phone:** (760)757-2200
AAA (SAVE) 6/15-9/15 [CP] 1P: $69- 79 2P/1B: $79- 99 2P/2B: $79- 99 XP: $6 F12
  2/1-6/14 & 9/16-1/31 [CP] 1P: $59- 69 2P/1B: $69- 79 2P/2B: $69- 89 XP: $6 F12
◆◆ **Location:** N side of SR 78, 1.5 mi e of I-5; from SR 78 exit El Camino Real, just ne. 3170 Vista Way 92056.
Motel Fax: 760/757-2389. **Terms:** Reserv deposit, 3 day notice. **Facility:** 43 rooms. 2 stories; interior corridors; heated pool. **Cards:** AE, CB, DI, DS, JC, MC, VI. **Special Amenities:** Early check-in/late check-out and free breakfast. *(See color ad p 757)* (📶)(📺)(🛌)(🖥)(🖥)(🛏)(🗙)

OCEANSIDE MARINA INN — Rates Subject to Change — **Phone:** (760)722-1561
All Year [CP]   1P: $120- 135   2P/1B: $145- 165   2P/2B: $225   XP: $10   F12
AAA ◆◆◆ Suite Motel
Location: I-5, Oceanside Harbor Dr exit, just sw to Harbor Dr N, 1 mi around the harbor to the end of Harbor Dr N. 2008 Harbor Dr N 92054. Fax: 760/439-9758. **Facility:** 64 rooms. 1- & 2-bedroom suites with kitchen. Few studio units. Most rooms have fireplace & ocean or harbor view. Located on a peninsula on the north side of Oceanside Harbor. 5 two-bedroom units. 2 stories; interior/exterior corridors; designated smoking area; heated pool, sauna, whirlpool. **Recreation:** fishing; horseshoe pit, volleyball, ping pong table, shuttle boat to the beach in season, shuffleboard court. **Some Rooms:** 57 kitchens, whirlpools. **Cards:** AE, MC, VI. *(See color ad p 757)*

SOUTHERN CALIFORNIA BEACH CLUB — **Phone:** 760/722-6666
4/1-9/30   1P: $150- 170   2P/1B: $150- 170   2P/2B: $150-170   XP: $5-25   F10
2/1-3/31 & 10/1-1/31   1P: $135- 150   2P/1B: $135- 150   2P/2B: $135-150   XP: $5-25   F10
AAA SAVE ◆◆◆ Condo Complex
Location: From I-5 exit Mission Ave, 1 mi w to Pacific St just s of Mission Ave. 121 S Pacific St 92054. Fax: 760/722-8950. **Terms:** Check-in 4 pm; reserv deposit, 14 day notice; weekly rates. **Facility:** 43 rooms. 1- & 2-bedroom units with living room & kitchen. Many ocean view with deck or patio. Located adjacent to 2 city parks & near Oceanside Pier. 5 smaller studio units with efficiency or kitchen, $95-$105; fee for daily housekeeping; 4 stories; interior/exterior corridors; beach, whirlpool. **Recreation:** bicycles, game room, ping pong table. **Some Rooms:** efficiency, 42 kitchens. **Cards:** MC, VI.

RESTAURANTS

DOMINICS CUCINA ITALIANA — **Lunch:** $5-$8 — **Dinner:** $8-$16 — **Phone:** 760/630-4400
◆ Italian
Location: 2.7 mi ne of El Camino Real via Mission Ave in Mission Marketplace. 461 College Blvd 92057. **Hours:** 11 am-10 pm, Sun from 4 pm. **Features:** casual dress; beer & wine only; a la carte. Small restaurant located in strip mall. Friendly atmosphere & very good food. Italian entrees & nice selection of California style pizzas. Smoke free premises. **Cards:** AE, DI, DS, MC, VI.

ED'S COUNTRY CAFE — **Lunch:** $5-$7 — **Dinner:** $5-$8 — **Phone:** 760/721-3167
◆ American
Location: Corner of El Camino Real in Mission Center. 3768 Mission Ave 92054. **Hours:** 7 am-8 pm, Sun-2 pm. **Features:** casual dress; children's menu; early bird specials; carryout; beer & wine only. Casual, family cafe. Country decor. Large portions & friendly service. Small area of patio seating. Smoke free premises. **Cards:** AE, DI, DS, MC, VI.

OJAI—7,600

LODGINGS

BEST WESTERN CASA OJAI — **Phone:** (805)646-8175
Fri & Sat [CP]   1P: $85- 120   2P/1B: $95- 125   2P/2B: $100-135   XP: $10   F12
Sun-Thurs [CP]   1P: $56- 85   2P/1B: $66- 95   2P/2B: $69- 99   XP: $10   F12
AAA SAVE ◆◆ Motel
Location: 0.8 mi e on SR 150. 1302 E Ojai Ave 93023. Fax: 805/640-8247. **Terms:** Small pets only, $10 dep req. **Facility:** 44 rooms. 2 stories; exterior corridors; heated pool, whirlpool. **All Rooms:** extended cable TV. **Cards:** AE, CB, DI, DS, JC, MC, VI.

BLUE IGUANA INN — Rates Subject to Change — **Phone:** (805)646-5277
Fri & Sat [CP]   1P: $129- 189   2P/1B: $129- 189   2P/2B: $129-189   XP: $10   F7
Sun-Thurs [EP]   1P: $99- 149   2P/1B: $99- 149   2P/2B: $99-149   XP: $10   F7
◆◆◆ Motel
Location: 2.5 mi w on SR 33. 11794 N Ventura Ave 93023. Fax: 805/646-8078. **Terms:** 2 night min stay, weekends. **Facility:** 11 rooms. 2 two-bedroom units. 2 two-bedroom suites with kitchens, $129-$179; 1 story; exterior corridors. **All Rooms:** combo or shower baths. **Some Rooms:** 7 kitchens. **Cards:** AE, CB, DI, DS, MC, VI.

LOS PADRES INN — **Phone:** (805)646-4365
5/14-10/31 [CP]   1P: $64- 89   2P/1B: $64- 99   2P/2B: $64- 99   XP: $10   F12
2/1-5/13 & 11/1-1/31 [CP]   1P: $54- 79   2P/1B: $64- 84   2P/2B: $64- 84   XP: $10   F12
AAA SAVE ◆◆ Motel
Location: 0.8 mi e on SR 150. 1208 E Ojai Ave 93023. Fax: 805/646-0625. **Terms:** Reserv deposit; handling fee imposed; small pets only, $10 extra charge, $100 dep req. **Facility:** 31 rooms. Some rooms with patio. 1 kitchen, 1 efficiency, $10-$20 extra; 2 stories; exterior corridors; heated pool, whirlpool. **Dining:** Restaurant nearby. **All Rooms:** extended cable TV. **Cards:** AE, CB, DI, DS, MC, VI. **Special Amenities:** Free local telephone calls and free newspaper. *(See color ad below)*

OAKRIDGE INN

Phone: 805/649-4018

(AAA) (SAVE)

| | Fri & Sat [CP] | 1P: | $50- 70 | 2P/1B: | $60- 80 | 2P/2B: | $75- 95 | XP: $10 | F12 |
| | Sun-Thurs [EP] | 1P: | $45- 60 | 2P/1B: | $55- 70 | 2P/2B: | $65- 85 | XP: $10 | F12 |

◆◆
Motel

Location: In Oak View, 4 mi s on SR 33, 2 mi e of Lake Casitas. 780 N Ventura Ave 93022. Fax: 805/649-4436. **Terms:** Weekly rates; small pets only, $10 extra charge, $50 dep req. **Facility:** 33 rooms. 1 suite with kitchen & video cassette player,$245; 2 stories; exterior corridors. **All Rooms:** extended cable TV. **Some Rooms:** 4 efficiencies. **Cards:** AE, CB, DI, DS, JC, MC, VI.

🔊 🏨 🕭 🦽 🖥 📺 🍽 □ 🔒 ⊗

OJAI RANCHO MOTEL

Phone: (805)646-1434

(AAA) (SAVE)

	Fri-Sun 4/1-10/31	1P:	$95	2P/1B: $106	2P/2B: $106	XP: $25	F11
	Fri-Sun 2/1-3/31, Mon-Thurs						
	4/1-10/31 & Fri-Sun 11/1-1/31	1P:	$85	2P/1B: $95	2P/2B: $95	XP: $25	F11

◆
Motel

| | Mon-Thurs 2/1-3/31 & | | | | | | |
| | 11/1-1/31 | 1P: | $75 | 2P/1B: $85 | 2P/2B: $85 | XP: $25 | F11 |

Location: 0.5 mi on SR 150 (Ojai Ave). 615 W Ojai Ave 93023. Fax: 805/640-8455. **Terms:** Check-in 4 pm. **Facility:** 18 rooms. Cozy rooms in comfortable setting. 2 rms with fireplace, $140-$155; 1 story; exterior corridors; sauna, whirlpool. **All Rooms:** combo or shower baths, extended cable TV. **Some Rooms:** 7 efficiencies. **Cards:** AE, DS, MC, VI.

🔊 ⊇ 🖥 □ 🔒 ⊗

OJAI VALLEY INN & SPA

Rates Subject to Change

Phone: (805)646-5511

(AAA)

| | All Year | 1P: | $240- 310 | 2P/1B: | $240- 310 | 2P/2B: | $240- 310 |

◆◆◆
Resort
Complex

Location: 1 mi w on SR 150, 0.3 mi s. 905 Country Club Rd 93023. Fax: 805/646-7969. **Terms:** Check-in 4 pm; reserv deposit, 3 day notice; handling fee imposed; package plans; pets, $25 extra charge. **Facility:** 206 rooms. Charming resort on 220 acres of beautifully landscaped grounds. 15 suites with fireplaces. Full service spa. Business services, extra charge; 2 stories; interior/exterior corridors; putting green; heated pool, saunas, steamrooms, whirlpools. **Fee:** 18 holes golf; 8 tennis courts (4 lighted). **Dining:** Dining room, restaurant; 6:30 am-11 pm; $23-$55; cocktails. **Services:** giftshop. **Fee:** massage. **Recreation:** children's petting zoo; bicycles, hiking trails, jogging, video games. **Fee:** children's programs; horseback riding. **All Rooms:** extended cable TV **Some Rooms:** whirlpools. **Cards:** AE, CB, DI, DS, JC, MC, VI.

(ASK) 🔊 🏨 🦽 🖥 ⊇ 🍽 🍸 🖼 △ ⊗ 🕭 📺 □ 🏋 □ 🏨 🔒 ⊡ ⊗

RESTAURANTS

RANCH HOUSE RESTAURANT

Dinner: $18-$24

Phone: 805/646-2360

◆◆◆
Continental

Location: From jct SR 150 & 33; 0.8 mi nw on Maricopa Rd, 0.3 mi w on El Roblar, then 0.5 mi s. Corner of S Lomita & Besa Rd 93023. **Hours:** 6 pm-8:30 pm, Sun 11 am-7:30 pm. Closed: Mon & Tues. **Reservations:** suggested. **Features:** No A/C; casual dress; Sunday brunch; children's menu; health conscious menu; beer & wine only; a la carte. Colorful lush garden foliage, patio dining, homemade breads & desserts. Beef, lamb, chicken & fresh seafood. Informal atmosphere. Smoke free premises. **Cards:** AE, CB, DI, DS, MC, VI.   ⊗

SUZANNE'S CUISINE

Lunch: $7-$12

Dinner: $10-$22

Phone: 805/640-1961

◆◆
French

Location: 0.8 mi w on SR 150. 502 W Ojai Ave 93023. **Hours:** 11:30 am-3:30 & 5:30-8:30 pm. Closed: 11/25, 12/25 & Tues. **Reservations:** suggested; Fri & Sat. **Features:** casual dress; cocktails; a la carte. Sandwiches, salads, pastas, chicken, beef, lamb chops, pork & fresh seafood prepared with an Italian flair. Patio dining. Daily selections of homemade dessert. Smoke free premises. **Cards:** MC, VI.   ⊗

OLEMA—100

LODGING

POINT REYES SEASHORE LODGE

Guaranteed Rates

Phone: (415)663-9000

◆◆
Motel

	Fri & Sat [CP]	1P:	$115- 250	2P/1B: $115- 250	2P/2B: $115- 250	XP: $15
	Sun-Thurs 3/1-11/30 [CP]	1P:	$105- 225	2P/1B: $105- 225	2P/2B: $105- 225	XP: $15
	Sun-Thurs 2/1-2/28 &					
	12/1-1/31 [CP]	1P:	$85- 195	2P/1B: $85- 195	2P/2B: $85- 195	XP: $15

Location: Center, on SR 1, adjacent to Golden Gate National Recreation Area & Point Reyes National Seashore. 10021 State Rt #1 94950 (PO Box 39). Fax: 415/663-9030. **Terms:** Reserv deposit, 5 day notice. **Facility:** 22 rooms. Landscaped grounds. 9 rooms with fireplaces & decks, 4 with patios. 1 three-bedroom unit. 1 rm with 3 beds up to 6 persons-$195; 2 stories; exterior corridors. **All Rooms:** combo or shower baths. **Some Rooms:** kitchen. **Cards:** AE, DS, MC, VI.

(See color ad p 210)

📺 □ 🏨 🍴 🦽 🔒 ⊗

OLYMPIC VALLEY—See Lake Tahoe Area p. 506.

ONTARIO—133,200

✈ Airport Accommodations

OA	ONTARIO	Rating	Rate	Listing Page
(AAA)	**Best Western Ontario Airport, 1.1 mi nw of airport entrance**	◆◆ 🔊	$69 (SAVE)	760
	Country Side Suites, 1.1 mi nw of airport	◆◆◆	$92	760
	Country Suites by Ayres, 1 mi nw of airport	◆◆◆	$92	760
(AAA)	**Country Suites By Carlson, 1.2 mi nw of airport entrance**	◆◆◆	$84-114 (SAVE)	760
	Doubletree Club Hotel, 1.4 mi nw of airport	◆◆◆	$99	761
	Doubletree Hotel Ontario, 1.2 mi nw of airport entrance	◆◆◆	$99	761
(AAA)	**Good Nite Inn, 1.5 mi nw of airport entrance**	◆◆	$57 (SAVE)	761
	Ontario Airport Marriott, 0.8 mi nw of airport entrance	◆◆◆	$129	761

OA	ONTARIO (contd.)	Rating	Rate	Listing Page
🏛	Red Roof Inn-Ontario Airport, 1.2 mi w of airport entrance	◆ ◆	$50-55 ⓢ	761
	Residence Inn by Marriott, 1.1 mi nw of airport entrance	◆ ◆ ◆	$175	762
	Super 8 Lodge, 1.4 mi nw of airport entrance	◆	$79	762

LODGINGS

AMERISUITES
Phone: (909)980-2200
🏛 ⓢ All Year [CP]   1P: $80- 110   2P/1B: $80- 110   2P/2B: $80- 110   XP: $18
◆ ◆ ◆ **Location:** Jct I-10 & I-15, from I-10 take I-15 n to 4th St exit, then w, just se of Ontario Mills Mall. 4760 E
Motel Mills Circle 91764. Fax: 909/980-4433. **Facility:** 128 rooms. 6 stories; interior corridors; heated pool.
Cards: AE, DI, DS, MC, VI. **Special Amenities: Free breakfast and free local telephone calls.**

BEST ONTARIO INN
Phone: (909)391-6668
🏛 ⓢ All Year   1P: $35- 42   2P/1B: $35- 42   2P/2B: $45- 52   XP: $5   D10
◆ **Location:** 1 mi w of Euclid Ave, just e of Mountain Ave. 1045 W Mission Blvd 91762. Fax: 909/391-2815.
Motel **Terms:** Reserv deposit; weekly rates. **Facility:** 42 rooms. 1 whirlpool room, extra charge; 2 stories; exterior
corridors; small pool, whirlpool. **Cards:** AE, CB, DI, DS, JC, MC, VI.

BEST WESTERN ONTARIO AIRPORT
Phone: (909)937-6800
🏛 ⓢ All Year [CP]   1P: $60   2P/1B: $65   2P/2B: $69   XP: $5   F12
◆ ◆ **Location:** 0.4 mi s of I-10, Vineyard Ave exit. 209 N Vineyard Ave 91764. Fax: 909/937-6815. **Facility:** 150
Motel rooms. 2 stories; exterior corridors; heated pool, whirlpool. **Dining:** Restaurant nearby. **Cards:** AE, CB, DI,
DS, MC, VI. **Special Amenities: Free breakfast and free local telephone calls.**

COUNTRY SIDE SUITES   Rates Subject to Change   Phone: (909)937-9700
◆ ◆ ◆ All Year [BP]   1P: $82   2P/1B: $92   2P/2B: $92   XP: $10   F12
Motel **Location:** 0.5 mi s of I-10, Vineyard Ave exit, 1.1 mi nw of Ontario Airport entrance. 204 N Vineyard Ave
91764. Fax: 909/937-2070. **Facility:** 107 rooms. Adjacent to Ontario Convention Center. Charming country
French decor. 6 whirlpool rms, extra charge; 2 stories; interior corridors; heated pool. **Cards:** AE, DI, DS, MC, VI.

COUNTRY SUITES AT THE MILLS MALL   Rates Subject to Change   Phone: 909/481-0703
◆ ◆ ◆ All Year [BP]   1P: $87   2P/1B: $97   2P/2B: $97   XP: $10   F12
Motel **Location:** Just n of I-10, exit Milliken Ave. 4370 E Mills Cir 91764. Fax: 909/484-2601. **Facility:** 138 rooms. 3
stories; interior corridors; heated pool. **Cards:** AE, CB, DI, DS, MC, VI.

COUNTRY SUITES BY AYRES   Rates Subject to Change   Phone: (909)390-7778
◆ ◆ ◆ All Year [BP]   1P: $82   2P/1B: $92   2P/2B: $92   XP: $10   F12
Motor Inn **Location:** 0.8 mi s of I-10 exit Vineyard Ave, 1 mi nw of airport entrance. 1945 E Holt Ave 91764.
Fax: 909/937-9718. **Terms:** Reserv deposit. **Facility:** 167 rooms. Beautifully decorated rooms & public areas.
Attractively landscaped courtyard. Adjacent to Ontario Convention Center. 4 two-bedroom units. 3 stories; interior corridors;
heated pool. **Cards:** AE, DI, DS, MC, VI.

COUNTRY SUITES BY CARLSON
Phone: (909)937-6000
🏛 ⓢ All Year [CP]   1P: $74- 104   2P/1B: $84- 114   2P/2B: $84- 114   XP: $10   F18
◆ ◆ ◆ **Location:** Just s of I-10, exit Vineyard Ave. 231 N Vineyard Ave 91764. Fax: 909/937-6013. **Terms:** Pets,
Motel $50 dep req. **Facility:** 120 rooms. Studio & 1- to 2-bedroom suites with kitchen. 12 two-bedroom units. 3 sto-
ries; exterior corridors; heated pool, whirlpool. **Dining:** Restaurant nearby. **Services:** complimentary evening
beverages, Mon-Thurs. **All Rooms:** efficiencies. **Cards:** AE, DI, DS, MC, VI. **Special Amenities: Free
breakfast and free newspaper.** *(See color ad below)*

10% Off Published Rates

◆ Continental "plus" breakfast
◆ In-room coffee
◆ Weekday morning newspaper
◆ Free local phone calls and
  long distance access

COUNTRY INNS & SUITES
BY CARLSON
◆ ◆ ◆

800-456-4000
www.countryinns.com

DOUBLETREE CLUB HOTEL
◆◆◆ Sun-Thurs
Motor Inn Fri & Sat
Rates Subject to Change

| | 1P: $99 | 2P/1B: $99 | 2P/2B: $99 |
| | 1P: $79 | 2P/1B: $79 | 2P/2B: $79 |

Phone: 909/937-8000
XP: $10   F18
XP: $10   F18

Location: Just s of I-10, Vineyard Ave exit. 429 N Vineyard Ave 91764. Fax: 909/937-8028. **Facility:** 170 rooms. 6 stories; interior corridors; heated pool. **Services:** area transportation. **Cards:** AE, DI, DS, MC, VI.

DOUBLETREE HOTEL ONTARIO
◆◆◆ Mon-Thurs
Hotel Fri-Sun
Rates Subject to Change

| | 1P: $99 | 2P/1B: $99 | 2P/2B: $99 |
| | 1P: $65 | 2P/1B: $65 | 2P/2B: $65 |

Phone: 909/937-0900
XP: $15
XP: $15

Location: 0.3 mi s of I-10 Vineyard Ave exit. 222 N Vineyard Ave 91764. Fax: 909/937-0999. **Terms:** Reserv deposit. **Facility:** 339 rooms. Large, well-landscaped courtyard with ponds & streams. 4 two-bedroom units. 3-4 stories; interior corridors; heated pool. **Services:** giftshop. **Cards:** AE, CB, DI, DS, JC, MC, VI.

FAIRFIELD INN BY MARRIOTT
◆◆ All Year [CP]
Motor

Rates Subject to Change
2P/1B: $59   2P/2B: $64

Phone: (909)390-9855
XP: $5

Location: S side of I-10, exit Haven Ave; then 0.5 mi w on Guasti Rd. 3201 Centrelake Dr 91761 Fax: 909/390-9855. **Facility:** 117 rooms. 3 stories; interior/exterior corridors; heated pool. **Cards:** AE, DI, DS MC, VI.

GOOD NITE INN
All Year
◆◆
Motor Inn

Phone: (909)983-3604

| 1P: $45 | 2P/1B: $51 | 2P/2B: $57 | XP: $6   F18 |

Location: Adjacent to I-10, exit Vineyard Ave, 1 blk s, then just w. 1801 East G St 91764 Fax: 909/986-4724. **Terms:** Weekly rates; pets. **Facility:** 186 rooms. 2-3 stories; interior/exterior corridors. **Dining:** Dining room; 5 am-10 & 5-10 pm, Sat & Sun 5 am-noon; $7-$12; cocktails. **Cards:** AE, CB, DI, DS JC, MC, VI. **Special Amenities:** Free local telephone calls.

HOLIDAY INN HOTEL & SUITES
All Year [CP]
◆◆◆
Motor Inn

Phone: (909)466-9600

| 1P: $99- 125 | 2P/1B: $99- 125 | 2P/2B: $110 | XP: $10 |

Location: Adjacent to I-10, exit Haven Ave, just n, then w. 3400 Shelby St 91764. Fax: 909/941-1445 **Terms:** Weekly/monthly rates; pets, $50 dep req. **Facility:** 150 rooms. Spacious, nicely decorated rooms & suites. 42 one-bedroom suites; 3 stories; exterior corridors; heated pool, whirlpool; playground. **Dining:** Dining room; 6:30-9 am, 11:30-2 & 6-10 pm, Sat & Sun from 7:30 am; $10-$15; cocktails. **Services:** giftshop; complimentary evening beverages. **Recreation:** sports court. **Some Rooms:** whirlpools. **Cards:** AE, DI, DS, MC, VI. **Special Amenities:** Free breakfast and free local telephone calls.

LA QUINTA INN & SUITES
[FYI]
Phone: 909/476-1112

Under construction. Location: Just n of I-10, exit Haden Ave, 1.3 mi ne of airport. 3555 Inland Empire Blvd 91764. Fax: 909/476-1121. **Facility:** 144 rooms.

ONTARIO AIRPORT HILTON
◆◆◆ All Year
Hotel

Rates Subject to Change

| 1P: $115 | 2P/1B: $115 | 2P/2B: $115 | XP: $20   F18 |

Phone: 909/980-0400

Location: N side of I-10, exit Haven Ave. 700 N Haven Ave 91764. Fax: 909/948-9309. **Facility:** 309 rooms. 55 concierge level rms with fax machines; 4 whirlpool rms, extra charge; 10 stories; interior corridors; heated pool. **Services:** giftshop. **Cards:** AE, CB, DI, DS, JC, MC, VI. *(See ad p 119)*

ONTARIO AIRPORT MARRIOTT
◆◆◆ Sun-Thurs
Hotel Fri & Sat

Rates Subject to Change

| | 1P: $129 | 2P/1B: $129 | 2P/2B: $129 | |
| | 1P: $69 | 2P/1B: $69 | 2P/2B: $69 | XP: $69   F |

Phone: (909)975-5000

Location: I-10, eastbound exit Vineyard Ave, westbound Holt Blvd; on Holt Blvd, just e of Vineyard Ave. 2200 E Holt Blvd 91761. Fax: 909/975-5050. **Terms:** Reserv deposit; handling fee imposed. **Facility:** 299 rooms. Across from Ontario Convention Center. 3 stories; interior corridors; heated pool; 1 lighted tennis court. Fee: racquetball courts. **Services:** giftshop; area transportation. Fee: massage. **All Rooms:** combo or shower baths. **Cards:** AE, CB, DI, DS, JC, MC, VI.

RED ROOF INN-ONTARIO AIRPORT
All Year
◆◆
Motel

Phone: (909)988-8466

| 1P: $45- 50 | 2P/1B: $45- 50 | 2P/2B: $50- 55 | XP: $5   F18 |

Location: 1.8 mi s of I-10, Vineyard Ave exit. 1818 E Holt Blvd 91761. Fax: 909/986-5456. **Terms:** Small pets only, $25 dep req. **Facility:** 107 rooms. 3 stories; interior corridors; heated pool, sauna, whirlpool. **Cards:** AE, CB, DI, DS, JC, MC, VI. **Special Amenities:** Free local telephone calls. *(See ad below)*

RESIDENCE INN BY MARRIOTT   Rates Subject to Change   **Phone:** (909)937-6788
◆◆◆   All Year [CP]   1P: $140   2P/2B: $175
Apartment   **Location:** From I-10 exit Vineyard Ave, just s then 1 blk e. 2025 Convention Center Way 91764.
Motel   Fax: 909/937-2462. **Facility:** 200 rooms. Studio & 2-bedroom suites with living room & kitchen. Many fire-
             places. 2 stories; exterior corridors; heated pool. **Recreation:** sports court. Cards: AE, CB, DI, DS, JC, MC,
VI.

SUPER 8 LODGE   Rates Subject to Change   **Phone:** 909/937-2999
◆   All Year [CP]   1P: $62   2P/1B: $69   2P/2B: $79   XP: $8   F10
Motel   **Location:** Adjacent to I-10, Vineyard Ave exit. 514 N Vineyard Ave 91764. Fax: 909/937-2978.
             Terms: Reserv deposit, 7 day notice. **Facility:** 130 rooms. 3 stories; exterior corridors. Cards: AE, CB, DI,
DS, JC, MC, VI.

RESTAURANTS

CALLA   **Dinner:** $20-$30   **Phone:** 909/980-0400
◆◆◆   **Location:** N side of I-10, Haven Ave exit; in Ontario Airport Hilton. 700 N Haven Ave 91764. **Hours:** 6 pm-10
Continental pm. Closed: Mon. **Reservations:** suggested. **Features:** semi-formal attire; cocktails & lounge; a la carte. An
             elegant dining room. Formal service, some tableside presentation. Smoke free premises. Cards: AE, CB, DI,
DS, MC, VI.

PANDA INN   **Lunch:** $6-$8   **Dinner:** $8-$17   **Phone:** 909/390-2888
◆◆   **Location:** Adjacent to I-10; exit Haven Ave, just s then 0.5 mi w. 3223 E Centrelake Dr 91761. **Hours:** 11:30
Chinese   am-10 pm, Fri & Sat 10:30 pm. Closed: 11/25. **Reservations:** suggested. **Features:** casual dress; cocktails
             & lounge. Large, attractive restaurant serving a nice selection of Mandarin cuisine. Smoke free premises.
Cards: AE, CB, DI, MC, VI.

ROSA'S   **Lunch:** $8-$18   **Dinner:** $11-$26   **Phone:** 909/937-1220
◆◆◆   **Location:** Just s of I-10. 425 N Vineyard Ave 91764. **Hours:** 11:30 am-10 pm, Sat 5 pm-10 pm, Sun 5 pm-9
Italian   pm. Closed major holidays. **Reservations:** suggested. **Features:** semi-formal attire; cocktails & lounge; a la
             carte. Attractively decorated dining room. Formal service. Nice selection of pasta, seafood, chicken & veal.
Smoke free premises. Cards: AE, DI, MC, VI.

SAN REMO RISTORANTE ITALIANO   **Lunch:** $7-$12   **Dinner:** $12-$18   **Phone:** 909/391-2843
◆◆   **Location:** Just s of I-10, exit Mountain Ave. 1133 W 6th St 91762. **Hours:** 11:30 am-2 & 5-10 pm, Sat & Sun
Italian   5 pm-10 pm. **Reservations:** suggested. **Features:** cocktails & lounge. Features a nice variety of homemade
             pastas, veal, chicken & specialties. Smoke free premises. Cards: AE, CB, DI, DS, MC, VI.

ORANGE—110,700   (See map p. 294; index p. 291)

LODGINGS

ANAHEIM/ORANGE COUNTY DOUBLETREE HOTEL   **Phone:** (714)634-4500   **140**
AAA SAVE   Sun-Thurs   1P: $109   2P/1B: $109   2P/2B: $109   XP: $10   F18
             Fri & Sat   1P: $85   2P/1B: $85   2P/2B: $85   XP: $10   F18
◆◆◆   **Location:** Just w of I-5; southbound exit The City Dr, northbound exit Chapman Ave. 100 The City Dr at
Hotel   Chapman Ave 92868. Fax: 714/634-7115. **Terms:** Reserv deposit. **Facility:** 454 rooms. 20 stories; interior cor-
             ridors; heated pool, whirlpool; 2 lighted tennis courts. Fee: parking. **Dining:** Dining room, coffee shop; 6
am-11 pm; $9-$20; cocktails. **Services:** giftshop. Cards: AE, CB, DI, DS, JC, MC, VI. (See ad p 347)

ANAHEIM/ORANGE HILTON SUITES   **Phone:** (714)938-1111   **142**
AAA SAVE   All Year [BP]   1P: $145   2P/1B: $169   2P/2B: $169   XP: $20   F18
◆◆◆   **Location:** Just e of I-5; southbound exit State College Blvd, northbound Chapman Ave. 400 North State
Suite Hotel College Blvd 92868. Fax: 714/938-0930. **Terms:** Reserv deposit; weekly/monthly rates; small pets only.
             Facility: 230 rooms. 10 stories; interior corridors; heated indoor pool, sauna, whirlpool. **Dining:** Dining room;
11:30 am-1:30 & 5:30-10 pm; $6-$15; cocktails. **Services:** giftshop; complimentary evening beverages; area
transportation, Disneyland/Convention Ctr. Cards: AE, CB, DI, DS, JC, MC, VI. **Special Amenities: Free breakfast and
preferred room (subject to availability with advanced reservations).** (See ad p 119)

COUNTRY SIDE INN   Rates Subject to Change   **Phone:** 714/978-9168   **138**
◆◆◆   All Year [BP]   1P: $85- 95   2P/1B: $95- 105 2P/2B: $95- 105 XP: $10   F18
Motor Inn   **Location:** Just w of I-5 exit The City Dr; northbound exit Chapman Ave. 3737 W Chapman Ave
             92868. Fax: 714/385-1528. **Facility:** 129 rooms. 6 micro suites with wet bar, microwave & refrigerator; interior
corridors; heated pool. **Services:** area transportation. Cards: AE, CB, DI, DS, MC, VI.

HAWTHORN SUITES   **Phone:** (714)740-2700   **146**
AAA SAVE   6/1-8/31 [BP]   1P: $130   2P/1B: $130   2P/2B: $130
             2/1-5/31 & 9/1-1/31 [BP]   1P: $122 2P/1B: $122   2P/2B: $122
◆◆◆   **Location:** 0.3 mi s of SR 22 Garden Grove Frwy, exit the City Drive. 720 The City Drive South 92868.
Suite Motel Fax: 714/971-1692. **Terms:** Check-in 4 pm; monthly rates. **Facility:** 123 rooms. Located in business park. Cen-
             tral courtyard with fountain. 18 two-bedroom units. 2 bedroom suites, $200 for up to 6 persons; 3 stories;
interior/exterior corridors; heated pool, whirlpool. **Services:** giftshop; area transportation, Disneyland & within 5 mi.
Some Rooms: 30 kitchens, whirlpools. Cards: AE, CB, DI, MC, VI. **Special Amenities: Free breakfast and free
newspaper.**

HOWARD JOHNSON EXPRESS INN   **Phone:** (714)639-1121   **139**
AAA SAVE   5/1-9/5 & 12/22-12/31 [CP] 1P: $55- 75 2P/1B: $60- 75 2P/2B: $65- 90 XP: $5   F18
             2/1-4/30, 9/6-12/21 &
◆   1/1-1/31 [CP]   1P: $45- 60   2P/1B: $50- 65 2P/2B: $55- 70 XP: $5   F18
Motel   **Location:** Adjacent to w side of SR 55. 1930 E Katella Ave 92867. Fax: 714/639-3264. **Terms:** Reserv
             deposit; weekly rates. **Facility:** 30 rooms. Well appointed rooms. 2 stories; exterior corridors.
Dining: Restaurant nearby. Cards: AE, CB, DI, DS, JC, MC, VI. **Special Amenities: Free breakfast.**

(See map p. 294)

ORANGE TRAVELODGE   Phone: (714)633-7720   14●
(AAA) [SAVE]   5/15-9/15   1P: $55- 60   2P/1B: $55- 60   2P/2B: $65- 70   XP: $5   F1
      2/1-5/14 & 9/16-1/31   1P: $50- 55   2P/1B: $50- 55   2P/2B: $60- 65   XP: $5   F1
◆◆   **Location:** 1 mi e of I-5. 1302 W Chapman Ave 92868. Fax: 714/633-9469. **Terms:** Reserv deposit
Motel **Facility:** 32 rooms. Well appointed rooms. 8 two-bedroom units. 2 stories; exterior corridors
      All Rooms: combo or shower baths, extended cable TV. **Cards:** AE, DI, DS, MC, VI.
                                                    [S●] [3P] [≈] [♦] [▣] [🖥] [🛏] [X]

RESIDENCE INN BY MARRIOTT   Guaranteed Rates   Phone: 714/978-7700   14●
◆◆◆   6/1-8/31 [BP]   1P: $92   2P/1B: $92   2P/2B: $114   XP: $10   F1●
Apartment 2/1-5/31 & 9/1-1/31 [BP]   1P: $92   2P/1B: $92   2P/2B: $104   XP: $10   F1●
Motel **Location:** Adjacent to I-5, just n of Chapman Ave. 201 N State College Blvd 92868. Fax: 714/978-6257
      Terms: Reserv deposit, 3 day notice. **Facility:** 105 rooms. 1-bedroom studios & 26 split level 2-bedroom suites
with living room; many with fireplace. 2 stories; exterior corridors; heated pool. **Services:** area transportation
Recreation: sports court. **Cards:** AE, CB, DI, DS, MC, VI. *(See color ad p 351)*
                              [🐾] [♦] [3P] [≈] [△] [X] [♦] [VCR] [▣] [🛏] [X]

RESTAURANTS

CAFE FRANCAIS   **Dinner:** $14-$20   Phone: 714/998-6051   39●
◆◆◆   **Location:** Just e of Tustin Ave. 1736 E Meats St 92865. **Hours:** 5 pm-9:30 pm. Closed major holidays &
French Mon. **Reservations:** suggested. **Features:** casual dress; beer & wine only. Located in small strip mall. Small
      & intimate French restaurant with very good food & service. Smoke free premises. **Cards:** MC, VI.
                                                                                              [X]

GAETANO'S RISTORANTE   **Lunch:** $5-$10   **Dinner:** $8-$16   Phone: 714/637-1671   40●
◆◆   **Location:** Just s of Lincoln Ave, just e of Tustin Ave. 2658 N Santiago Blvd 92867. **Hours:** 11 am-2 & 4-1●
Italian pm, Sat & Sun from 4 pm. **Reservations:** suggested; weekends. **Features:** casual dress; carryout; beer &
      wine only. Family run Italian restaurant located in strip mall. Quaint decor. Excellent food, also pizza & Italian
sandwiches. Smoke free premises. **Cards:** AE, MC, VI.
                                                                                              [X]

THE HOBBIT   **Dinner:** $50   Phone: 714/997-1972   42●
◆◆◆   **Location:** 1 mi e of I-55. 2932 E Chapman Ave 92869. **Hours:** Closed major holidays & Mon
Continental **Reservations:** required. **Features:** semi-formal attire; cocktails; prix fixe. Located in Spanish style home buil
      in 1932. Intimate & warm atmosphere. 7 course meal, including champagne & hors d'oeuvres served in wine
cellar before dinner. One seating per evening. Smoke free premises. **Cards:** MC, VI.
                                                                                              [X]

MORENO'S RESTAURANT   **Lunch:** $5-$14   **Dinner:** $5-$14   Phone: 714/639-2181   43●
◆   **Location:** 1 mi e of SR 55. 4328 E Chapman Ave 92869. **Hours:** 11 am-9 pm, Fri & Sat-10 pm, Sun 9 am-
Mexican pm. Closed major holidays. **Features:** casual dress; Sunday brunch; children's menu; carryout; cocktails; ●
      la carte. Long established Mexican restaurant. Family owned & operated. Tortillas made on premises. Large
attractively landscaped patio. **Cards:** AE, DS, MC, VI.
                                                                                              [X]

ROCKWELL'S CAFE' & BAKERY   **Lunch:** $5-$7   **Dinner:** $9-$17   Phone: 714/921-0622   41●
◆◆   **Location:** 0.4 mi n of Katella Ave. Located in Ralph's Shopping Center in Villa Park area. 17853 Santiago
American Blvd 92867. **Hours:** 7 am-3 & 5-9 pm, Sun 7 am-1 pm, Mon & Tues 7 am-3 pm. Closed major holidays
      Features: casual dress; children's menu; early bird specials; beer & wine only. Meat, fish, chicken, & pasta
dishes. Cozy restaurant with excellent food. Bakery on premises. Smoke free premises. **Cards:** AE, MC, VI.
                                                                                              [X]

ORLAND—5,100

LODGINGS

AMBER LIGHT INN MOTEL   Rates Subject to Change   Phone: (530)865-765●
(AAA)   All Year   1P: $30- 34   2P/1B: $32- 38   2P/2B: $36- 40   XP: $2-4
◆◆   **Location:** Exit I-5 via Chico, SR 32 off-ramp, then 0.3 mi e. 828 Newville Rd 95963. Fax: 530/865-4627
Motel **Terms:** Reserv deposit; small pets only. **Facility:** 40 rooms. 2 stories; exterior corridors; whirlpool
      Dining: Coffee shop nearby. **All Rooms:** combo or shower baths. **Cards:** AE, DI, DS, MC, VI.
                                                            [🛏] [≈] [♦] [🛏] [X]

ORLAND INN   Phone: (530)865-7632
(AAA) [SAVE]   All Year   1P: $35- 40   2P/1B: $39- 44   2P/2B: $42- 44   XP: $4   F1●
◆◆   **Location:** 0.5 mi s; northbound exit I-5E via Orland-Fairgrounds, southbound exit I-5E via CR 16; adjacent
Motel to I-5 in Stony Creek Shopping Center. 1052 South St 95963. Fax: 530/865-8731. **Terms:** Weekly/monthly
      rates; pets. **Facility:** 40 rooms. 2 stories; exterior corridors. **Dining:** Coffee shop nearby. **Cards:** AE, CB, DI
      DS, JC, MC, VI. **Special Amenities:** Early check-in/late check-out and free local telephone calls.
                                                    [S●] [🛏] [≈] [♦] [🛏] [&] [X]

OROVILLE—12,000

LODGINGS

BEST WESTERN GRAND MANOR INN   Rates Subject to Change   Phone: (530)533-9673
◆◆◆   All Year [CP]   1P: $64- 67   2P/1B: $69- 74   2P/2B: $69- 79   XP: $6   F1●
Motel **Location:** SR 70 exit E Montgomery. 1470 Feather River Blvd 95965. Fax: 530/533-5862. **Facility:** 54 rooms
      Attractively appointed rooms. 3 stories; interior corridors. **Cards:** AE, CB, DI, DS, MC, VI.
                                    [ASK] [S●] [🛏] [≈] [△] [♦] [🛏] [🛏] [&] [X]

DAYS INN-OROVILLE   Guaranteed Rates   Phone: 530/533-3297
◆   All Year   1P: $47- 55   2P/1B: $47- 55   2P/2B: $57- 70   XP: $5
Motel **Location:** SR 70 exit E Montgomery St, just e to Feather River Blvd, 0.5 mi s. 1745 Feather River Blvd
      95965. Fax: 530/533-4809. **Terms:** Reserv deposit. **Facility:** 38 rooms. 2 stories; exterior corridors
All Rooms: combo or shower baths. **Cards:** AE, DS, MC, VI.
                              [SAVE] [🛏] [≈] [▣] [□] [🛏] [🛏] [X]

OROVILLE TRAVELODGE   Phone: (530)533-7070
AAA SAVE   All Year [CP]   1P: $45- 55 2P/1B: $55- 60 2P/2B: $57- 65 XP: $4   F17
◆◆   **Location:** Exit SR 70 at Oro Dam Blvd, 0.3 mi e. 580 Oro Dam Blvd 95965. Fax: 530/532-0402.
Motel   **Terms:** Pets, $5 extra charge, $20 dep req. **Facility:** 70 rooms. 1 story; exterior corridors. **Dining:** Coffee
            shop nearby. **All Rooms:** combo or shower baths. **Cards:** AE, CB, DI, DS, MC, VI. **Special Amenities:** Free
            breakfast and free local telephone calls.   🔊🕭🗺🍽🔌🛎💻🗗🔒✕

THE VILLA COURT INN   Rates Subject to Change   Phone: 530/533-3930
AAA   5/1-10/31 [CP]   1P: $46- 56 2P/1B: $52- 62 2P/2B: $56- 66 XP: $4   F12
            2/1-4/30 & 11/1-1/31 [CP] 1P: $40- 46 2P/1B: $46- 52 2P/2B: $50- 56 XP: $4   F12
◆◆   **Location:** 0.3 mi e off SR 70 exit E Montgomery; 0.5 mi n off SR 162 (Oroville Dam Blvd). 1527 Feather
Motel   River Blvd 95965. **Terms:** Reserv deposit, 3 day notice. **Facility:** 20 rooms. Comfortable rooms. 1 story; ex-
            terior corridors. **Dining:** Restaurant nearby. **All Rooms:** shower baths. **Cards:** AE, DI, MC, VI.
                                                                        🗺🍽🗗✕

RESTAURANT

THE DEPOT   **Lunch:** $5-$11   **Dinner:** $9-$21   Phone: 530/534-9101
◆◆   **Location:** 4 blks ne of courthouse. 2191 High St 95965. **Hours:** 11 am-2:30 & 4-9:30 pm, Fri-10 pm, Sat 4
Steak and   pm-10 pm, Sun 3:30 pm-9 pm. Closed: 12/25. **Features:** casual dress; children's menu; early bird specials;
Seafood   salad bar; cocktails & lounge; a la carte. Varied menu. **Cards:** AE, DS, MC, VI.   ✕

OXNARD—142,200

LODGINGS

BEST WESTERN OXNARD INN   Phone: (805)483-9581
AAA SAVE   All Year [CP]   1P: $69- 74 2P/1B: $69- 79 2P/2B: $89- 99 XP: $5   F12
◆◆◆   **Location:** 3 mi s of US 101, n/b exit Vineyard Av, then left to Oxnard Rd; s/b exit Oxnard Rd. 1156 S
Motel   Oxnard Blvd 93030. Fax: 805/483-4072. **Terms:** Reserv deposit; small pets only, $10. **Facility:** 78 rooms. 4
            suites, $125; 2 stories; exterior corridors; heated pool, whirlpool. **All Rooms:** extended cable TV.
            Some Rooms: whirlpools. **Cards:** AE, CB, DI, DS, MC, VI. **Special Amenities: Free breakfast and free**
            local telephone calls. *(See color ad below)*   🔊🕭🍴🆓🗺🔌🛎💻🗗🔒✕

CASA SIRENA HOTEL & MARINA   Guaranteed Rates   Phone: (805)985-6311
◆◆   Fri & Sat   1P: $109- 119 2P/1B: $109- 119 2P/2B: $109- 119 XP: $10   F12
Motor Inn   Sun-Thurs   1P: $89- 99   2P/1B: $89- 99   2P/2B: $89- 99 XP: $10   F12
            Location: 0.5 mi w of Victoria Blvd via Channel Islands Blvd at Channel Islands Harbor. 3605 Peninsula Rd
            93035. Fax: 805/985-4329. **Terms:** Reserv deposit. **Facility:** 272 rooms. Many rooms overlooking marina with patio or balcony.
            Spacious nicely landscaped grounds. One-bedroom suites avail, some with kitchenettes, $160; 3 stories; interior/exterior cor-
            ridors; putting green; heated pool; 1 lighted tennis court. **Services:** giftshop. Fee: massage. **Cards:** AE, CB, DI, DS, MC, VI.
            (See color ad below)   🅰🔊🕭🍴🆓🗺🍽🛗✕🕭🔌💻🗗🔒✕

CHANNEL ISLANDS INN & SUITES
Phone: (805)487-7755

All Year [BP] 1P: $69- 79 2P/1B: $69- 79 2P/2B: $69- 79 XP: $10 F16
Location: 4 mi s of US 101, exit Rose Ave. 1001 E Channel Islands Blvd 93033. Fax: 805/486-1374.
Terms: Weekly/monthly rates. Facility: 91 rooms. Spanish-style architecture. All units with dining table & utensils. Some rooms with private patio or balcony. 2 stories; exterior corridors; heated pool, whirlpool.
Motor Inn
Dining: Coffee shop nearby. Services: complimentary evening beverages. Recreation: Extensive video rental tape library. All Rooms: extended cable TV. Cards: AE, CB, DI, DS, JC, MC, VI. Special Amenities: Free breakfast and free local telephone calls.

EMBASSY SUITES MANDALAY BEACH RESORT
Phone: (805)984-2500
5/28-9/6 [BP] 1P: $189- 299 2P/1B: $189- 299 2P/2B: $189- 299 XP: $15 F18
2/1-5/27 & 9/7-1/31 [BP] 1P: $179- 269 2P/1B: $179- 269 2P/2B: $179- 269 XP: $15 F18
Suite Hotel
Location: 1 mi w of Victoria Ave via Channel Islands & Harbor blvds. 2101 Mandalay Beach Rd 93035. Fax: 805/984-8339. Terms: Check-in 4 pm; reserv deposit. Facility: 249 rooms. Many rooms with ocean view. Lovely landscaped grounds with waterfalls. 6 two-bedroom units. 6 two-bedroom suites with whirlpool, $495-$795; 2-3 stories; interior/exterior corridors; beach, heated pool, whirlpools; 2 lighted tennis courts. Fee: parking.
Dining: Restaurant; 9:30 am-10 pm, Sun brunch 10:30 am-2:30 pm; $8-$16; cocktails. Services: giftshop; complimentary evening beverages. Fee: massage. Recreation: Fee: bicycles. Cards: AE, CB, DI, DS, JC, MC, VI.

HILTON INN-OXNARD
Guaranteed Rates
Phone: 805/485-9666
All Year 1P: $99 2P/1B: $99 2P/2B: $99 XP: $10
Hotel
Location: Just s of US 101 exit Vineyard Ave. 600 Esplanade Dr 93030. Fax: 805/485-2061. Facility: 161 rooms. Nicely landscaped patio area. Many rooms with balcony. 6 stories; interior corridors; heated pool; 1 lighted tennis court. Cards: AE, CB, DI, DS, JC, MC, VI. (See color ad below)

RESIDENCE INN AT RIVER RIDGE
Rates Subject to Change
Phone: 805/278-2200
All Year [CP] 1P: $98- 134 2P/1B: $98- 134 2P/2B: $125- 134
Apartment
Motor Inn
Location: 1.8 mi sw of US 101, exit Vineyard Ave. 2101 W Vineyard Ave 93030. Fax: 805/983-4470.
Terms: Reserv deposit. Facility: 252 rooms. Nicely landscaped grounds. 60 loft units with fireplace & kitchen. 121 fireplace units; 2 stories; exterior corridors; heated pool; 5 lighted tennis courts. Fee: 18 holes golf.
Services: area transportation. Recreation: sports court. All Rooms: kitchens. Cards: AE, CB, DI, DS, JC, MC, VI.

VAGABOND INN
Phone: (805)983-0251
All Year [CP] 1P: $56 2P/1B: $61 2P/2B: $75 XP: $5 F18
Location: 1.5 mi s of US 101 on SR 1, northbound exit Vineyard, southbound exit Oxnard Bl. 1245 N Oxnard Bl 93030. Fax: 805/988-9638. Terms: Pets, $5. Facility: 69 rooms. 2 stories; exterior corridors; heated pool; playground. Dining: Restaurant nearby. All Rooms: extended cable TV. Cards: AE, CB, DI, DS, MC, VI. Special Amenities: Free breakfast and free local telephone calls.
Motor Inn

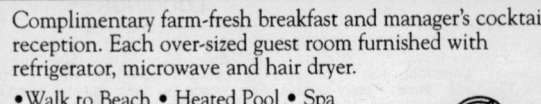

RESTAURANTS

LOBSTER TRAP RESTAURANT　　　　**Lunch:** $8-$11　　　　**Dinner:** $13-$35　　　　**Phone:** 805/985-6361
◆
Steak and
Seafood
Location: 0.5 mi w of Victoria Blvd via Channel Islands Blvd at Channel Islands Harbor; in Casa Sirena Hotel & Marina. 3605 Peninsula Rd 93035. **Hours:** 6:30 am-10 pm. **Reservations:** accepted. **Features:** casual dress; Sunday brunch; children's menu; senior's menu; cocktails & lounge; entertainment. Overlooking marina. Salads, seafood, chicken, steak & prime rib. Sun brunch 10 am-2 pm. Smoke free premises. **Cards:** AE, CB, DI, DS, MC, VI. *(See color ad p 764)*

TUGS RESTAURANT　　　　**Lunch:** $6-$10　　　　**Dinner:** $9-$25　　　　**Phone:** 805/985-8847
◆◆
Steak and
Seafood
Location: 0.5 mi se of Channel Island Blvd, via Harbor Blvd , Channel Island Harbor. 3600 S Harbor Blvd 93035. **Hours:** 8 am-9 pm. Closed: 11/25 & 12/25. **Features:** No A/C; casual dress; children's menu; carryout; cocktails. Casual atmosphere. Located on the 2nd floor of the Marine Emporium Bldg. Patio dining weather permitting. Steaks, fresh seafood, chicken, & pasta. View of harbor. Smoke free premises.
Cards: AE, DS, MC, VI.　　☒

PACIFICA—See San Francisco p. 971.

PACIFIC GROVE—See Monterey Peninsula p. 718.

PALMDALE—68,900

LODGINGS

DAYS INN PALMDALE　　　　　　　　　　　　　　　　　　　　**Phone:** (805)273-1400
(AAA) (SAVE)　　All Year　　　　　1P: $44- 49　2P/1B: $49- 54　2P/2B: $54- 59　XP: $5　　F16
◆◆
Motel
Location: Just e of SR 14, Hwy 138/Palmdale Blvd exit. 130 E Palmdale Blvd 93550. **Fax:** 805/272-9473. **Facility:** 75 rooms. 4 suites w/refrigerator, microwave & coffeemaker, $75; 2 stories; exterior corridors; whirlpool. **Dining:** Coffee shop nearby. **All Rooms:** extended cable TV. **Cards:** AE, CB, DI, DS, JC, MC, VI.

HOLIDAY INN PALMDALE-LANCASTER　　　Rates Subject to Change　　　**Phone:** 805/947-8055
◆◆◆
Motor Inn
All Year [BP]　　　1P: $89　　　2P/1B: $89　　　2P/2B: $89　　　XP: $10
Location: Palmdale Hwy & SR 14. 38630 5th St W 93551. **Fax:** 805/947-9957. **Facility:** 149 rooms. 8 suites avail $98-$135 with microwave, refrigerator & VCP; 5 stories; interior corridors; heated pool. **Recreation:** Fee: downhill skiing. **Cards:** AE, CB, DI, DS, MC, VI.

RAMADA INN　　　　　　　　　　　　　　　　　　　　　　**Phone:** (805)273-1200
(AAA) (SAVE)　　All Year [BP]　　1P: $53- 75　2P/1B: $58- 80　2P/2B: $58- 80　XP: $5-10　　F12
◆◆
Motor Inn
Location: Adjacent to SR 14. 300 W Palmdale Blvd 93551. **Fax:** 805/947-9593. **Facility:** 135 rooms. 4 stories; interior corridors; whirlpool. **Dining:** Restaurant; 7-10 am & 11-9 pm; $8-$12; cocktails. **Cards:** AE, CB, DI, DS, MC, VI. **Special Amenities:** Free breakfast and free local telephone calls.

SUPER 8 MOTEL　　　　　　　　　Rates Subject to Change　　　　　　**Phone:** 805/273-8000
◆◆
Motel
All Year [CP]　　　1P: $32- 35　2P/1B: $35- 38　2P/2B: $40- 43　XP: $3-5　　F13
Location: Adjacent to jct SR 14 & 138; exit Palmdale Blvd. 200 W Palmdale Blvd 93550. Fax: 805/266-4521. **Facility:** 91 rooms. 2 stories; interior corridors. **Cards:** AE, CB, DI, DS, MC, VI.

RESTAURANT

APPLE ANNIE'S　　　　　　**Dinner:** $6-$13　　　　　　　　　**Phone:** 805/264-2169
◆
American
Location: 19.5 mi e via Palmdale Blvd, 1.3 mi n via 170th St E; in the Lake Los Angeles area. **Hours:** 5 pm-9 pm, Fri & Sat-10 pm, Sun 4 pm-8 pm. Closed: Mon, Tues, 1/1 & 12/25. **Features:** children's menu; carryout; cocktails & lounge. Selection of beef, seafood, chicken & sandwiches. Prime rib served Fri-Sun. **Cards:** AE, DI, DS, MC, VI.　　☒

PALM DESERT—23,300　(See map p. 774; index p. 772)

LODGINGS

CASA LARREA RESORT　　　　　Rates Subject to Change　　　**Phone:** 760/568-0311　(40)
◆◆
Motel
2/1-5/31 & 10/1-1/31 [CP]　1P: $64- 104　2P/1B: $64- 104　2P/2B: $64- 104　XP: $20
6/1-9/30 [CP]　　　　　　1P: $50- 85　2P/1B: $50- 85　2P/2B: $50- 85　XP: $20
Location: Just s of SR 111, between San Luis Rey & Portola Ave. 73-771 Larrea St 92260. Fax: 760/776-1082. **Terms:** Reserv deposit, 7 day notice, 30 days, Jan-Mar; handling fee imposed. **Facility:** 11 rooms. Located in quiet, residential area. All rooms have private patios. Tastefully decorated rooms. 1 story; exterior corridors; heated pool. **All Rooms:** combo or shower baths. **Some Rooms:** 8 kitchens. **Cards:** MC, VI.

COURTYARD BY MARRIOTT　　　　　　　　　　　　　　　　**Phone:** (760)776-4150
(AAA) (SAVE)　　2/1-5/31 & 1/1-1/31　1P: $109- 119　2P/1B: $109- 119　2P/2B: $109- 129
　　　　　　　10/1-12/31　　　　1P: $65- 75　2P/1B: $65- 75　2P/2B: $65- 85
(FYI)　　　　6/1-9/30　　　　　1P: $50- 60　2P/1B: $50- 60　2P/2B: $50- 70
Motor Inn
Too new to rate. **Location:** Just s of I-10, exit Cook Rd. 74-895 Frank Sinatra Dr 92260. Fax: 760/776-1816. **Terms:** Check-in 4 pm; reserv deposit, 7 day notice; weekly rates. **Facility:** 151 rooms. 3 stories; interior corridors; heated pool, whirlpool. **Dining:** Restaurant; 6:30-10:30 am & 11:30-2:30 pm. **Cards:** AE, CB, DI, DS, MC, VI. **Special Amenities:** Free newspaper and preferred room (subject to availability with advanced reservations). *(See color ad p 768)*

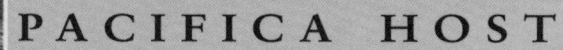

PACIFICA
HOST HOTELS

1-888-GR8-STAY

No matter where you want to stay, one call gets you connected to these great hotels that are near all the fun in San Diego! We extend this service <u>exclusively</u> to our valued <u>AAA members</u>!

Courtyard Marriott $99⁰⁰
Steps from the beach & Del Mar Race Track.

Days Inn Suites - Sea World / Airport $59⁰⁰
Free shuttle to Sea World/San Diego Zoo & complimentary full hot breakfast.

Old Town Plaza Hotel $59⁰⁰
♦♦♦ hotel in historic Old Town. Complimentary, upscale continental breakfast.

Super 8 - Mission Valley / Stadium $39⁰⁰
Free full breakfast - located near SDSU & shopping.

Holiday Inn Express - La Jolla $79⁰⁰
Near beaches & downtown La Jolla. Free deluxe continental breakfast.

Best Western Stratford Inn of Del Mar $79⁰⁰
Near beaches & Del Mar Village. Free cont'l breakfast. Kitchens avail.

Comfort Inn - Escondido $49⁰⁰
Near Performing Arts Center. Free continental breakfast.

Holiday Inn Express & Suites - Wild Animal park . . . . $ 59⁰⁰
Complimentary deluxe continental breakfast. Suites w/kitchenettes available.

Pacific Shores Inn - Pacific Beach $69⁰⁰
Steps from the beach, restaurants, shopping & nightlife.

Diamond Head Inn - Pacific Beach $79⁰⁰
Steps from beaches, restaurants and boardwalk.

Holiday Inn Express - Chula Vista $49⁰⁰
Located near International Border & Coors Amphitheater. Dlx. cont'l. brkfst.

Best Western Catalina Canyon Resort & Spa $69⁰⁰
Located on Catalina Island. Spa, restaurant and pool.

Summer, Holidays, suites & some weekends higher. Rates per night & based on availability.

www.pacificahost.com

(See map p. 774)

DESERT PATCH INN   Rates Subject to Change   **Phone:** 760/346-9161   **39**
◆◆   2/1-5/31 & 10/1-1/31 [CP]   1P: $56- 98   2P/1B: $56- 98   2P/2B: $56- 98   XP: $20
Motel   6/1-7/7 & 9/1-9/30 [CP]   1P: $47- 72   2P/1B: $47- 72   2P/2B: $47- 72   XP: $10
    Location: Just s of SR 111 between San Luis Rey & Portola Ave. 73758 Shadow Mountain Dr 92260.
Fax: 760/776-9661. **Terms:** Open 2/1-7/7 & 9/1-1/31; reserv deposit, 7 day notice; 2 night min stay, weekends. **Facility:** 14 rooms. Beautifully landscaped grounds. Located in a quiet residential area. Nicely furnished rooms & suites. 1 story; exterior corridors; putting green; heated pool. **All Rooms:** combo or shower baths. **Some Rooms:** 10 kitchens. **Cards:** AE, DS, MC, VI.

EMBASSY SUITES HOTEL   Rates Subject to Change   **Phone:** 760/340-6600   **44**
◆◆◆   2/1-4/27 & 1/1-1/31 [BP]   1P: $189- 299   2P/1B: $189- 299   2P/2B: $89- 299   XP: $15
Suite Motor Inn   4/28-6/22 & 9/21-12/31 [BP]   1P: $110- 199   2P/1B: $110- 199   2P/2B: $110- 199   XP: $15
   6/23-9/20 [BP]   1P: $89- 139   2P/1B: $89- 139   2P/2B: $89- 139   XP: $15
Location: 1.5 mi e on SR 111. 74-700 Hwy 111 92260. Fax: 760/340-9519. **Terms:** Check-in 4 pm. **Facility:** 198 rooms. Spanish-style exterior. Nicely landscaped courtyard. 3 stories; exterior corridors; putting green; heated pool; 6 lighted tennis courts. **Services:** giftshop. **Cards:** AE, DI, DS, MC, VI.

FAIRFIELD INN   **Phone:** (760)341-9100   **35**
(AAA) (SAVE)   All Year   1P: $100- 110   2P/1B: $100- 110   2P/2B: $100- 110   XP: $10   F18
◆◆◆   **Location:** On SR 111, just e of Fred Waring Dr. 72-322 Hwy 111 92260. Fax: 760/773-3515. **Facility:** 112
Motel   rooms. Centrally located in area with several shopping centers & restaurants. 3 stories; interior corridors; putting green; heated pool, whirlpool. **All Rooms:** extended cable TV. **Cards:** AE, CB, DI, DS, MC, VI.
Special Amenities: Free local telephone calls.

HOLIDAY INN EXPRESS-PALM DESERT   **Phone:** 760/340-4303   **43**
(AAA) (SAVE)   2/1-3/31 & 1/1-1/31 [CP]   1P: $99- 169   2P/1B: $99- 169   2P/2B: $99- 169   XP: $10
   4/1-6/15 [CP]   1P: $79- 119   2P/1B: $79- 119   2P/2B: $79- 119   XP: $10
◆◆◆   10/1-12/31 [CP]   1P: $69- 119   2P/1B: $69- 119   2P/2B: $69- 119
Motel   6/16-9/30 [CP]   1P: $49- 99   2P/1B: $49- 99   2P/2B: $49- 99   XP: $10
    Location: SR 111 just e of Deep Canyon Rd. 74-675 Hwy 111 92260. Fax: 760/340-3723. **Facility:** 129 rooms. 3 stories; interior corridors; heated pool, whirlpool; 1 tennis court. **Dining:** Restaurant nearby. **Recreation:** 2 lighted shuffleboard courts. **Cards:** AE, CB, DI, DS, MC, VI.

THE INN AT DEEP CANYON   **Phone:** (760)346-8061   **41**
(AAA) (SAVE)   2/1-5/31 & 12/16-1/31 [CP]   1P: $59- 99   2P/1B: $59- 99   2P/2B: $99- 129
   6/1-6/30 & 9/16-12/15 [CP]   1P: $49- 79   2P/1B: $49- 79   2P/2B: $79- 99
◆◆   7/1-9/15 [CP]   1P: $39- 69   2P/1B: $39- 69   2P/2B: $69- 89
Motel   **Location:** Just s of SR 111 via Deep Canyon Rd. 74470 Abronia Tr 92260. Fax: 760/341-9120.
   Terms: Reserv deposit, 3 day notice; weekly/monthly rates; pets. **Facility:** 32 rooms. 3 two-bedroom units. 2 stories; exterior corridors; heated pool, whirlpool. **All Rooms:** combo or shower baths, extended cable TV. **Some Rooms:** 18 efficiencies. **Cards:** AE, DS, MC, VI. **Special Amenities:** Free breakfast and preferred room (subject to availability with advanced reservations).

INTERNATIONAL LODGE   Rates Subject to Change   **Phone:** 760/346-6161   **42**
(AAA)   2/1-3/31 & 1/1-1/31   1P: $110   2P/1B: $110   2P/2B: $110   XP: $10
   4/1-5/31 & 10/1-12/31   1P: $95   2P/1B: $95   2P/2B: $95   XP: $10
◆◆◆   6/1-6/30 & 9/1-9/30   1P: $70- 80   2P/1B: $70- 80   2P/2B: $70- 80   XP: $10
Apartment   7/1-8/31   1P: $50   2P/1B: $50   2P/2B: $50   XP: $10
Motel   **Location:** Just s of SR 111 between Panorama & Deep Canyon Rd. 74-380 El Camino 92260.
   Fax: 760/568-0563. **Terms:** Weekly/monthly rates. **Facility:** 49 rooms. Spacious, individually decorated rooms. Located in quiet, residential area. 2 stories; exterior corridors; heated pool, whirlpool. **All Rooms:** kitchens, combo or shower baths. **Some Rooms:** color TV. **Cards:** AE, DS, MC, VI. *(See color ad below)*

MARRIOTT'S DESERT SPRINGS RESORT & SPA   Rates Subject to Change   **Phone:** 760/341-2211   **34**
◆◆◆◆   2/1-5/31 & 12/31-1/31   2P/1B: $369   2P/2B: $369
Resort Hotel   9/7-12/30   2P/1B: $299   2P/2B: $299
   6/1-7/5   2P/1B: $269   2P/2B: $269
   7/6-9/6   2P/1B: $189   2P/2B: $189
Location: 1.5 mi n of SR 111 via Cook St. 74-855 Country Club Dr 92260. Fax: 760/341-1872. **Terms:** Check-in 4 pm. **Facility:** 884 rooms. Tropically landscaped grounds. 8-story atrium lobby built around cascading pools & indoor & outdoor series of manmade lakes. Extensive recreational, shopping & dining facilities. 8 stories; interior/exterior corridors; mountain view; heated pool. Fee: 36 holes golf, putting green; 20 tennis courts (6 lighted). **Services:** giftshop. Fee: massage. **Cards:** AE, CB, DI, DS, JC, MC, VI.

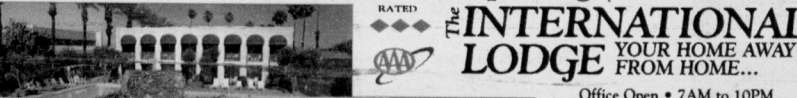

Affordable
Luxury (x 2)

Marriott, reknown for its commitment to premiere hospitality and prestigious accommodations, has created the perfect setting to present your choice of two new desert retreats providing a selection of fine amenities suited to fit your style.

The Palm Desert Residence Inn by Marriott is an all suite hotel offering all the comforts of home. Choose from spacious studios and 2-bedroom suites; perfect for short-term or long-term guests.

Featuring...

- Fully equipped kitchens
- Desk and work area
- Gas fireplaces in 2-bedroom suites
- Hot tubs in some suites
- VCP in every suite
- Daily complimentary California buffet breakfast featuring one hot item
- Daily hospitality hours featuring complimentary beer, wine, soft drinks, hot and cold hors d'ouvres and a hot entree
- Pool, spa and sports court
- Exercise facility

- Two tennis courts
- Complimentary hotel shuttle
- Laundry and dry cleaning
- Conference Center with 2000 sq. ft. of meeting/ banquet space, capacity up to 150 people

RESIDENCE INN by Marriott
38-305 Cook St.
Palm Desert, CA 92260
(760) 776-0050
(760) 776-1806 fax

The Palm Desert Courtyard by Marriott is one of the very special hotels of the desert. Work or play, you'll find our location exceptional.

COURTYARD by Marriott
74-895 Frank Sinatra Dr.
Palm Desert, CA 92260
(760) 776-4150
(760) 776-1816 fax

Enjoy these amenities...

- Relax in our spacious rooms and suites
- Enjoy our exercise facilities
- Convenient Guest Laundry
- 2 Meeting Rooms
- Luxurious Pool and 2 Spas
- Hotel Restaurant and Lounge

*Popular **Desert Willow Golf Resort**, with two championship courses, sprawls adjacent to both hotels with fabulous golf packages available.*

(See map p. 774)

RESIDENCE INN BY MARRIOTT

Phone: (760)776-0050

(AAA) (SAVE)

(FYI)

Suite Motel

2/1-5/31 & 1/1-1/31 [CP]	1P: $99- 139	2P/1B:	$99- 139	2P/2B: $159- 239	
10/1-12/31 [CP]	1P: $85- 105	2P/1B:	$85- 105	2P/2B: $135- 159	
6/1-9/30 [CP]	1P: $65- 89	2P/1B:	$65- 89	2P/2B: $119- 149	

Too new to rate. **Location:** Just s of I-10, exit Cook St. 38-305 Cook St 92260. Fax: 760/776-1806. **Terms:** Check-in 4 pm; reserv deposit, 7 day notice; weekly/monthly rates; small pets only. **Facility:** 130 rooms. Studio & 1 & 2 bedroom suites with living room & kitchen; many with fireplace. 48 two-bedroom units. 2 stories; exterior corridors; heated pool, whirlpool. **Services:** complimentary evening beverages, Mon-Thurs. **All Rooms:** kitchens. **Cards:** AE, CB, DI, DS, JC, MC, VI. **Special Amenities: Free breakfast and free newspaper.**
(See color ad p 768)

SHADOW MOUNTAIN RESORT & CLUB

Phone: (760)346-6123   **38**

(AAA) (SAVE)

♦♦♦

Resort Motor Inn

2/1-4/11 & 12/24-1/31 [CP]	1P: $160- 198	2P/1B:	$160- 198	2P/2B: $160- 198	XP: $15 F14
4/12-5/30 & 9/24-12/23 [CP]	1P: $123- 153	2P/1B:	$123- 153	2P/2B: $123- 153	XP: $15 F14
5/31-9/23 [CP]	1P: $91- 111	2P/1B:	$91- 111	2P/2B: $91- 111	XP: $15 F14

Location: 0.5 mi s of SR 111. 45-750 San Luis Rey 92260. Fax: 760/346-6518. **Terms:** Reserv deposit, 7 day notice; weekly/monthly rates; package plans. **Facility:** 100 rooms. Gated tennis resort. Studios, 1- to 3-bedroom apartments & villas. 2-bedroom units, $345-$433 in season; 2 stories; exterior corridors; designated smoking area; heated pool, saunas, whirlpools; 16 tennis courts (6 lighted), basketball, paddle tennis, volleyball courts. **Dining:** Restaurant; 7:30 am-2:30 pm weekends 9/1-12/25, closed 7/10-8/31; cocktails. **Services:** Fee: massage. Rental: bicycles. **All Rooms:** combo or shower baths, extended cable TV. **Some Rooms:** 60 efficiencies, 40 kitchens. **Cards:** AE, DI, MC, VI. *(See color ad below)*

TRES PALMAS BED & BREAKFAST

Rates Subject to Change   Phone: (760)773-9858   **36**

♦♦♦

Bed & Breakfast

2/1-6/14 & 10/16-1/31 [CP]	1P: $110- 175	2P/1B: $110- 175	XP: $20
6/15-10/15 [CP]	1P: $70- 110	2P/1B: $70- 110	XP: $20

Location: Just s of El Paseo; just e of SR 74. 73-135 Tumbleweed Ln 92260 (PO Box 2115). Fax: 760/776-9159. **Terms:** Reserv deposit, 7 day notice; 2 night min stay, weekends. **Facility:** 4 rooms. Located in residential area within walking distance of El Paseo area. Southwest decor & architecture. 1 story; interior corridors; smoke free premises; heated pool. **Cards:** AE, MC, VI.

VACATION INN

Phone: (760)340-4441   **46**

(AAA) (SAVE)

♦♦

Motel

2/1-4/14 & 12/29-1/31 [CP]	1P: $93- 108	2P/1B:	$93- 108	2P/2B: $93- 108	XP: $10 F17
4/15-5/31 & 9/15-12/28 [CP]	1P: $69- 78	2P/1B:	$69- 78	2P/2B: $69- 78	XP: $10 F17
6/1-9/14 [CP]	1P: $50- 60	2P/1B:	$50- 60	2P/2B: $50- 60	XP: $10 F17

Location: 1.5 mi e on SR 111. 74-715 Hwy 111 92260. Fax: 760/773-9413. **Facility:** 130 rooms. Balconies or patios. 3 stories; exterior corridors; heated pool, whirlpool; 2 tennis courts. **Some Rooms:** 12 efficiencies. **Cards:** AE, CB, DI, DS, JC, MC, VI. *(See color ad below)*

(See map p. 774)

RESTAURANTS

CAPTAIN COOK'S SEA GRILL   **Dinner:** $18-$27   **Phone:** 760/341-8333   ㉑
◆◆   **Location:** SR 111, just w of Fred Waring Dr. 72-191 Hwy 111 92260. **Hours:** 5 pm-9:30 pm, Fri & Sat-10
Seafood   pm. Closed: 12/25. **Reservations:** suggested. **Features:** casual dress; early bird specials; cocktails & lounge; entertainment. Attractively decorated in a nautical theme. Large outdoor deck overlooking the koi pond. Menu features seafood, beef, chicken & pasta. **Cards:** AE, DS, MC, VI.   ✖

CASUELAS CAFE   **Lunch:** $7-$13   **Dinner:** $7-$13   **Phone:** 760/568-0011   ㉖
ⓐⓐⓐ   **Location:** SR 111, between San Luis Rey & Larkspur. 73-703 Highway 111 92260. **Hours:** 10 am-10 pm,
◆   Sat 8 am-11 pm, Sun 8 am-10 pm. Closed: 11/25 & 12/25. **Features:** casual dress; cocktails & lounge.
Mexican   Popular restaurant. Indoor & patio dining. **Cards:** AE, CB, DI, DS, MC, VI.   ✖

CEDAR CREEK INN   **Lunch:** $7-$12   **Dinner:** $14-$20   **Phone:** 760/340-1236   ㉕
◆◆   **Location:** 1 blk s of SR 111, corner San Pablo & El Paseo. 73-445 El Paseo 92260. **Hours:** 11 am-10 pm.
American   Closed: 12/25. **Reservations:** suggested. **Features:** casual dress; Sunday brunch; cocktails & lounge. Attractive restaurant featuring a nice selection of salads, sandwiches, entrees & a large selection of homemade desserts. Patio dining also available. **Cards:** AE, CB, DI, MC, VI.   ✖

CLUB 74 RESTAURANT   **Lunch:** $7-$14   **Dinner:** $16-$25   **Phone:** 760/568-2782   ㉒
◆◆◆   **Location:** SR 74, just s of SR 111. 73-061 El Paseo 92260. **Hours:** 11:30 am-2:30 & 5:30-10 pm, Sun 5:30
Continental   pm-10 pm. Closed: 11/25 & 12/25. **Reservations:** suggested. **Features:** semi-formal attire; cocktails; a la carte. Located on 2nd floor. Intimate dining room & patio. **Cards:** AE, DI, DS, MC, VI.   ✖

CUISTOT   **Lunch:** $10-$15   **Phone:** 760/340-1000   ㉔
◆◆◆   **Location:** Just s of SR 111 & just e of SR 74. 73-111 El Paseo 92260. **Hours:** 11:30 am-2:30 & 6-10 pm,
French   Sun 6 pm-10 pm. Closed: Mon & 8/1-8/31. **Reservations:** suggested. **Features:** dressy casual; cocktails; a la carte. Located in the Galleria Centre. creative selection of French/California cuisine & a large selection of homemade desserts. Smoke free premises. **Cards:** AE, CB, DI, MC, VI.   ✖

DAILY GRILL   **Lunch:** $6-$14   **Dinner:** $7-$16   **Phone:** 760/779-9911   ㉓
◆◆   **Location:** Just e of SR 74. 73-061 El Paso 92260. **Hours:** 11 am-10 pm, Sun from 10 am. Closed: 11/25 &
American   12/25. **Features:** casual dress; Sunday brunch; children's menu; carryout; cocktails & lounge; a la carte. Popular restaurant featuring a wine variety of salad, sandwiches & entrees. Smoke free premises.
Cards: AE, CB, DI, DS, MC, VI.   ✖

LG'S PRIME STEAKHOUSE   **Dinner:** $18-$50   **Phone:** 760/779-9799   ㉗
◆◆◆   **Location:** At jct SR 111 & El Paseo. 74-225 Hwy 111 92260. **Hours:** 5:30 pm-10 pm, Fri & Sat-10:30 pm.
Steakhouse   Closed: 12/25. **Reservations:** suggested. **Features:** casual dress; cocktails & lounge; valet parking; a la carte. Southwestern decor. Dining in pueblo-style landmark building. Entrees include steak, chicken & seafood. Smoke free premises. **Cards:** AE, DI, DS, MC, VI.   ✖

MARIO'S RESTAURANT   **Dinner:** $18-$25   **Phone:** 760/346-0584   ㉚
◆◆◆   **Location:** Just s of SR 111. 73-399 El Paso 92260. **Hours:** Open 2/1-5/29 & 10/1-1/31; 5 pm-9:30 pm.
Italian   Closed: 11/25, 12/25 & Mon. **Reservations:** suggested. **Features:** casual dress; children's menu; cocktails & lounge; valet parking. Light opera & broadway music by strolling singers. **Cards:** AE, CB, DI, DS, MC, VI.   ✖

MAYO'S ON EL PASEO   **Dinner:** $13-$28   **Phone:** 760/346-2284   ㉙
◆◆◆   **Location:** 73-990 El Paseo 92260. **Hours:** 11:30 am-3 & 5:30-10 pm. Closed major holidays.
Continental   **Features:** casual dress; cocktails; valet parking. Contemporary intimate atmosphere. Continental cuisine with an Italian emphasis. Smoke free premises. **Cards:** AE, DI, MC, VI.   ✖

RISTORANTE MAMMA GINA   **Lunch:** $8-$15   **Dinner:** $14-$28   **Phone:** 760/568-9898   ㉘
◆◆◆   **Location:** Just s of SR 111. 73-705 El Paseo 92260. **Hours:** 11:30 am-2 pm & 5:15 pm-10:30 pm, Sun 5:15
Italian   pm-10 pm. Closed: 11/25, 12/25, Easter & closed Sun & lunch in summer. **Reservations:** suggested. **Features:** casual dress; cocktails; a la carte. Northern Italian cuisine featuring homemade pasta, chicken & veal specialties. Smoke free premises. **Cards:** AE, DI, MC, VI.   ✖

PALM SPRINGS
pop. 40,200

This index helps you "spot" where approved accommodations are located on the detailed maps that follow. Rate ranges are for comparison only and show the property's high season. Turn to the listing page for more detailed rate information and consult display ads for special promotions. Restaurant rate range is for dinner unless only lunch (L) is served.

PALM SPRINGS

Spotter/Map Pg.Number	OA	PALM SPRINGS - Lodgings	Rating	Rate	Listing Page
㊄ / p. 775		Super 8 Lodge	◆	$76-81	784
㊅ / p. 775	ⓐⓐⓐ	**Palm Court Inn - see color ad p 781**	◆	$49-79	781
㊇ / p. 775		Hampton Inn	◆◆◆	$94-104	779
㊉ / p. 775		Shilo Inn - see ad p 627, p 1091, p 658, p 627	◆◆◆	$79-139	784
㊀ / p. 775		Palm Springs Riviera Resort - see color ad p 782	◆◆◆	$129	782
㊁ / p. 775	ⓐⓐⓐ	**Ville Orleans Resort Hotel**	◆◆	$95-295	786
㊂ / p. 775	ⓐⓐⓐ	**Palm Garden Resort**	◆◆	$89-169	782

Spotter/Map Pg.Number	OA	**PALM SPRINGS** - Lodgings (contd.)	Rating	Rate	Listing Page
93 / p. 775	⊕	La Mancha Resort Village - see color ad p 777	◆◆◆	$145-695 ⓦ	780
94 / p. 775	⊕	The Willows Historic Palm Springs Inn - see color ad p 785	◆◆◆◆	$250-500 ⓦ	786
96 / p. 775	⊕	Hyatt Regency Suites Palm Springs - see color ad p 565	◆◆◆	$229-259 ⓦ	780
98 / p. 775		Spa Hotel & Casino Resort & Mineral Springs	◆◆◆	$159-199	784
99 / p. 775		Palm Springs Hilton Resort - see ad p 119	◆◆◆	$175-255	782
100 / p. 775		Wyndham Palm Springs Hotel - see color ad p 785	◆◆◆	$89-189	786
102 / p. 775		Courtyard by Marriott - see color ad p 778	◆◆◆	$119-159	778
103 / p. 775	⊕	Desert Hills Apt. Hotel	◆◆◆	$75-170 ⓦ	778
104 / p. 775		Casa Cody Country Inn	◆◆	$79-199	776
106 / p. 775	⊕	Palm Springs Conference Resort	◆◆◆	$175-245 ⓦ	782
107 / p. 775	⊕	Holiday Inn Palm Mountain Resort - see color ad p 779	◆◆◆	$115-145	779
108 / p. 775	⊕	Four Seasons Apartment Hotel	◆◆◆◆	$110-140	779
109 / p. 775		Orchid Tree Inn - see ad p 781	◆◆◆	$99-295	781
112 / p. 775	⊕	Best Western Las Brisas Hotel - see color ad p 776	◆◆◆	$99-149 ⓦ	776
113 / p. 775		Comfort Inn - see color ad p 777	◆◆◆	$129-139	776
114 / p. 775	⊕	Ingleside Inn	◆◆◆	$145-395 ⓦ	780
115 / p. 775	⊕	Estrella Inn at Palm Springs - see color ad p 778	◆◆◆	$125-325	779
116 / p. 775		Place In The Sun	◆◆◆	$69-109	782
117 / p. 775	⊕	Best Western Inn at Palm Springs	◆◆◆	$79-139 ⓦ	775
118 / p. 775		Villa Rosa Inn	◆◆	$69-125	785
119 / p. 775	⊕	Villa Royale Inn - see color ad p 785	◆◆◆	$95-295 ⓦ	785
120 / p. 775	⊕	L'Horizon Garden Hotel	◆◆	$115-255 ⓦ	781
122 / p. 775	⊕	El Rancho Lodge	◆◆	$61-80	778
123 / p. 775		Ramada Resort Inn & Conference Center - see color ad p 783	◆◆◆	$99-149	783
124 / p. 775	⊕	Vagabond Inn	◆◆◆	$80-105 ⓦ	784
125 / p. 775	⊕	Royal Sun Inn	◆◆	$99-109 ⓦ	784
126 / p. 775	⊕	Travelodge-Palm Springs	◆◆	$69-95 ⓦ	784
127 / p. 775	⊕	Hotel California	◆◆	$69-135 ⓦ	779
128 / p. 775	⊕	Quality Inn Resort - see color ad p 783	◆◆◆	$79-169 ⓦ	783
129 / p. 775		San Marino Hotel	◆◆	$125-160	784
130 / p. 775		Alpine Gardens Hotel	◆◆	$60-100	775
131 / p. 775		Palm Tee Hotel	◆◆	$70-140	782
132 / p. 775	⊕	Budget Host Inn - see color ad p 369 & ad p 776	◆◆	$59-95 ⓦ	776
133 / p. 775		Howard Johnson Inn - see color ad p 780	◆◆	$99	780
		PALM SPRINGS - Restaurants			
50 / p. 775	⊕	Billy Reed's Restaurant	◆◆	$9-18	786
53 / p. 775		Otani-A Garden Restaurant	◆◆◆	$15-29	787
54 / p. 775		Le Vallauris	◆◆◆◆	$20-30	786
55 / p. 775	⊕	Las Casuelas Terraza	◆◆	$7-14	786
56 / p. 775		Melvyn's	◆◆◆	$23-34	786
58 / p. 775	⊕	Banducci's Bit of Italy	◆◆	$8-16	786
59 / p. 775		Cedar Creek Inn	◆◆◆	$12-21	786
60 / p. 775		Lyons English Grille	◆◆	$15-25	786
61 / p. 775		LG's Prime Steakhouse	◆◆◆	$19-30	786
62 / p. 775		St James At The Vineyard	◆◆◆	$18-35	787
63 / p. 775		Purple Sage	◆◆◆	$17-22	787
64 / p. 775		Europa Restaurant	◆◆◆	$13-28	786

Nearby Accommodations

Spotter/Map Pg.Number	OA	DESERT HOT SPRINGS - Lodgings	Rating	Rate	Listing Page
1 / p. 774	⊕	Miracle Springs Hotel & Spa - see color ad p 433, p 773, p 155	◆◆◆	$69-189 SAVE	433
2 / p. 774	⊕	Desert Hot Springs Spa Hotel - see color ad p 433, inside front cover, p 773, p 155	◆◆◆	$59-119 SAVE	432
4 / p. 774	⊕	Stardust Motel	◆	$50-52 SAVE	433
6 / p. 774		Travellers Repose Bed & Breakfast	◆◆	$65-85	434
8 / p. 774	⊕	Agua Caliente Hotel & Mineral Water Spa - see ad p 433	◆◆	$74-84 SAVE	432
9 / p. 774		Sam's Family Spa Motel	◆	$72-92	433
		THOUSAND PALMS - Lodgings			
14 / p. 774	⊕	Red Roof Inn	◆◆	$56 SAVE	1064
		CATHEDRAL CITY - Lodgings			
18 / p. 774	⊕	Doubletree Resort at Desert Princess Country Club - see ad p 784	◆◆◆	$149-179 SAVE	414
20 / p. 774	⊕	Cathedral City Travelodge	◆◆	$70-79 SAVE	414
21 / p. 774	⊕	Days Inn Suites	◆◆	$105-145 SAVE	414
		RANCHO MIRAGE - Lodgings			
26 / p. 774	⊕	The Westin Mission Hills Resort	◆◆◆◆	$359-450 SAVE	807
28 / p. 774	⊕	The Ritz-Carlton, Rancho Mirage	◆◆◆◆	$375-525	806
30 / p. 774		Marriott's Rancho Las Palmas Resort	◆◆◆◆	$339	806
		RANCHO MIRAGE - Restaurants			
8 / p. 774		Kobe Japanese Steak House	◆◆	$14-30	807
10 / p. 774	⊕	Las Casuelas Nuevas	◆◆	$10-15	807
11 / p. 774		The Dining Room	◆◆◆◆	$22-36	807
14 / p. 774		Lord Fletcher Inn	◆◆	$18-23	807
15 / p. 774		Wally's Desert Turtle	◆◆◆◆	$20-35	807
18 / p. 774		Continental Cafe	◆◆	$10-19	807
		PALM DESERT - Lodgings			
34 / p. 774		Marriott's Desert Springs Resort & Spa	◆◆◆◆	$369	767
35 / p. 774	⊕	Fairfield Inn	◆◆◆	$100-110 SAVE	767
36 / p. 774		Tres Palmas Bed & Breakfast	◆◆◆	$110-175	769
38 / p. 774	⊕	Shadow Mountain Resort & Club - see color ad p 769	◆◆◆	$160-198 SAVE	769
39 / p. 774		Desert Patch Inn	◆◆	$56-98	767
40 / p. 774		Casa Larrea Resort	◆◆	$64-104	766
41 / p. 774	⊕	The Inn at Deep Canyon	◆◆	$99-129 SAVE	767
42 / p. 774	⊕	International Lodge - see color ad p 767	◆◆◆	$70-110	767
43 / p. 774	⊕	Holiday Inn Express-Palm Desert	◆◆◆	$99-169 SAVE	767
44 / p. 774		Embassy Suites Hotel	◆◆◆	$189-299	767
46 / p. 774	⊕	Vacation Inn - see color ad p 769	◆◆	$93-108 SAVE	769
		PALM DESERT - Restaurants			
21 / p. 774		Captain Cook's Sea Grill	◆◆	$18-27	770
22 / p. 774		Club 74 Restaurant	◆◆◆	$16-25	770
23 / p. 774		Daily Grill	◆◆	$7-16	770
24 / p. 774		Cuistot	◆◆◆	$18-34	770
25 / p. 774		Cedar Creek Inn	◆◆	$14-20	770
26 / p. 774	⊕	Casuelas Cafe	◆	$7-13	770
27 / p. 774		LG's Prime Steakhouse	◆◆◆	$18-50	770
28 / p. 774		Ristorante Mamma Gina	◆◆◆	$14-28	770
29 / p. 774		Mayo's on El Paseo	◆◆◆	$13-28	770
30 / p. 774		Mario's Restaurant	◆◆◆	$18-25	770
		INDIAN WELLS - Lodgings			
51 / p. 774	⊕	Hyatt Grand Champions Resort - see color ad p 565	◆◆◆◆	$290-375 SAVE	476
52 / p. 774		Renaissance Esmeralda Resort	◆◆◆◆	$240-288	476
53 / p. 774	⊕	Miramonte Resort	◆◆◆◆	$249-279	476

Spotter/Map Pg.Number	OA	**INDIAN WELLS** - Lodgings (contd.)	Rating	Rate	Listing Page
54 / p. 774	⊕	**Indian Wells Resort Hotel**	◆ ◆ ◆	$169-249 ▧	476
		INDIAN WELLS - Restaurants			
34 / p. 774		Don Diego's	◆ ◆	$11-17	476
35 / p. 774		Le St Germain	◆ ◆ ◆	$20-32	476
36 / p. 774		Sirocco	◆ ◆ ◆	$16-27	476
		LA QUINTA - Lodgings			
60 / p. 774		Two Angels Inn	◆ ◆ ◆ ◆	$185-350	535
		LA QUINTA - Restaurants			
38 / p. 774		La Quinta Cliffhouse	◆ ◆ ◆	$13-20	535
40 / p. 774		The La Quinta Grill	◆ ◆ ◆ ◆	$20-35	535
		INDIO - Lodgings			
65 / p. 774	⊕	**Best Western Date Tree Hotel**	◆ ◆ ◆	$59-129 ▧	477
66 / p. 774	⊕	**Comfort Inn**	◆	$59-119 ▧	477
68 / p. 774	⊕	**Palm Shadow Inn**	◆ ◆	$97-129 ▧	477
70 / p. 774	⊕	**Royal Plaza Inn**	◆ ◆	$68-95 ▧	477

IT'S REFUNDABLE.

A security deposit on certain personal items
may be required upon your entry into Canada.
Read Border Information.

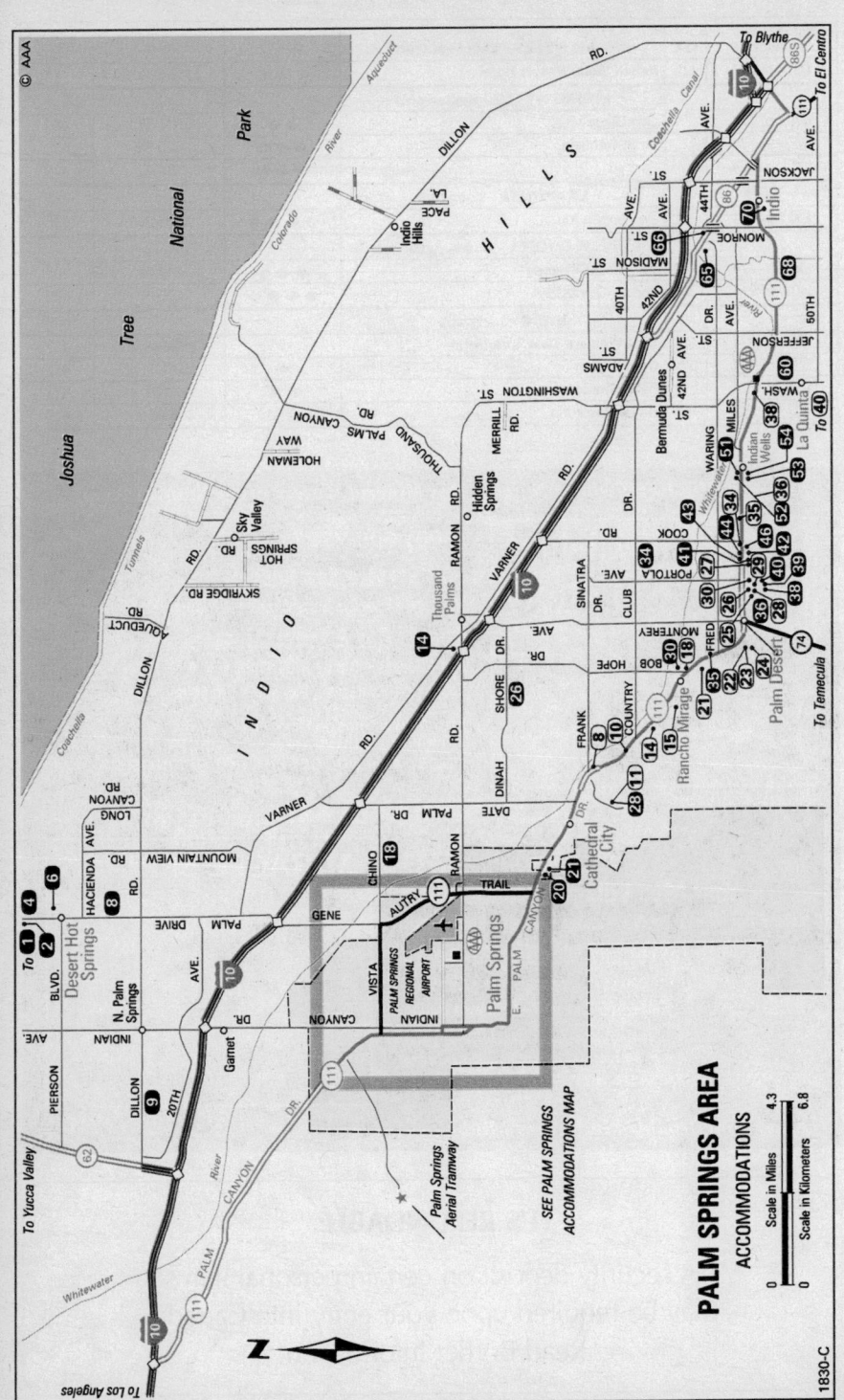

PALM SPRINGS AREA
ACCOMMODATIONS

Scale in Miles
Scale in Kilometers

1830-C

PALM SPRINGS—40,200 (See map below; index p. 770)

LODGINGS

ALPINE GARDENS HOTEL   Guaranteed Rates   **Phone: 760/323-2231** `130`
◆◆   2/1-5/31 & 9/1-1/31 [CP]   1P: $60- 100   2P/1B: $60- 100
Motel   6/1-8/31 [CP]   1P: $40- 80   2P/1B: $40- 80
Location: 2.5 mi se, just w of Sunrise Way. 1586 E Palm Canyon Dr 92264. Fax: 760/318-0155. **Facility:** 10 rooms. Cozy nicely decorated rooms. 1 two-bedroom suite; 1 story; exterior corridors; designated smoking area; heated pool. **All Rooms:** shower baths. **Some Rooms:** 5 kitchens. **Cards:** AE, DS, MC, VI.

BEST WESTERN INN AT PALM SPRINGS   **Phone: (760)325-9177** `117`
(AAA) (SAVE)   2/1-7/5 & 12/24-1/31 [CP]   1P: $79- 138   2P/1B: $79- 139   2P/2B: $79- 138   XP: $10   F12
                10/1-12/23 [CP]   1P: $49- 99   2P/1B: $49- 99   2P/2B: $49- 99   XP: $10   F12
◆◆◆   7/6-9/30 [CP]   1P: $49- 89   2P/1B: $49- 89   2P/2B: $49- 89   XP: $10   F12
Motel   **Location:** 1.5 mi s at jct E Palm Canyon Dr. 1633 S Palm Canyon Dr 92264. Fax: 760/325-9177.
Terms: Weekly/monthly rates. **Facility:** 72 rooms. Kitchen unit on 2 levels for up to 6 people $250-$300, depending on season; 2-3 stories; exterior corridors; heated pool, whirlpool. **Cards:** AE, CB, DI, DS, JC, MC, VI.
Special Amenities: Early check-in/late check-out and free breakfast.

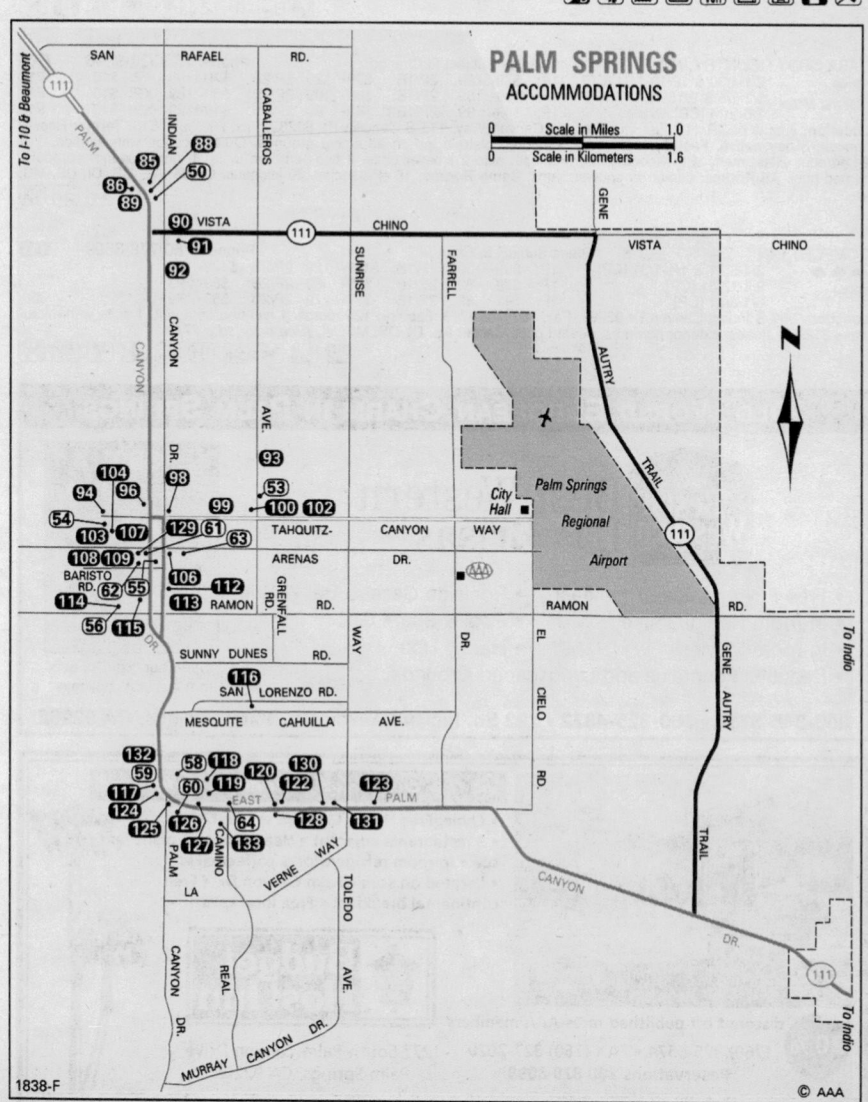

PALM SPRINGS
ACCOMMODATIONS

1838-F
© AAA

(See map p. 775)

BEST WESTERN LAS BRISAS HOTEL Phone: (760)325-4372 `112`

(AAA) (SAVE)

◆◆◆

Motel

	2/1-5/31 & 1/1-1/31 [BP]	1P: $99- 149	2P/1B: $99- 149	2P/2B: $99- 149	XP: $10
	10/1-12/31 [BP]	1P: $69- 119	2P/1B: $69- 119	2P/2B: $69- 119	XP: $10
	6/1-9/30 [BP]	1P: $49- 99	2P/1B: $49- 99	2P/2B: $49- 99	XP: $10

Location: 0.3 mi s. 222 S Indian Canyon Dr 92262. Fax: 760/320-1371. **Terms:** 2 night min stay, weekends. **Facility:** 90 rooms. Attractive garden setting. Nicely furnished rooms. 8 large rms with whirlpool tub; 3 stories; exterior corridors; heated pool, whirlpool. **Cards:** AE, CB, DI, MC, VI. **Special Amenities: Free breakfast.** *(See color ad below)*

🏊 🍸 📺 🅰 🛠 💻 🖨 📠 📶 ⊠

BUDGET HOST INN Phone: (760)325-5574 `132`

(AAA) (SAVE)

◆◆

Motel

	2/1-5/31 & 12/26-1/31 [CP]	1P: $59- 95	2P/1B: $59- 95	2P/2B: $59- 95
	9/2-12/25 [CP]	1P: $49- 69	2P/1B: $49- 69	2P/2B: $49- 69
	6/1-9/1 [CP]	1P: $39- 59	2P/1B: $39- 59	2P/2B: $39- 59

Location: 1 mi s. 1277 S Palm Canyon Dr 92264. Fax: 760/327-2020. **Facility:** 64 rooms. One suite, $79-$150; 2 stories; exterior corridors; heated pool, whirlpool. **Dining:** Restaurant nearby. **All Rooms:** combo or shower baths, extended cable TV. **Cards:** AE, DI, MC, VI. **Special Amenities: Free newspaper and preferred room (subject to availability with advanced reservations).** *(See color ad p 369 & ad below)*

⑤ 🏊 🍴 🅰 🛠 💻 🖨 📠 📶 ⊠

CASA CODY COUNTRY INN Rates Subject to Change Phone: 760/320-9346 `104`

◆◆

Historic Motel

	2/1-4/30 & 12/18-1/31 [CP]	1P: $79- 129	2P/1B: $79- 129	2P/2B: $79- 199	XP: $10	F12
	5/1-7/5 & 9/15-12/17 [CP]	1P: $69- 109	2P/1B: $69- 109	2P/2B: $69- 189	XP: $10	F12
	7/6-9/14 [CP]	1P: $49- 99	2P/1B: $49- 99	2P/2B: $49- 129	XP: $10	F12

Location: Just w of SR 111, just s of Tahquitz Canyon Way. 175 S Cahuilla Rd 92262. Fax: 760/325-8610. **Terms:** Reserv deposit, 3 day notice. **Facility:** 23 rooms. Restored historic inn on attractive grounds. Quiet location with studios, 1 & 2-bedroom villas, many with woodburning fireplace; also 2 smaller units. 1 story; exterior corridors; heated pool. **All Rooms:** combo or shower baths. **Some Rooms:** 15 efficiencies, 20 kitchens. **Cards:** AE, CB, DI, DS, MC, VI.

🐾 🛏 🚐 (VCR)

COMFORT INN Rates Subject to Change Phone: (760)778-3699 `113`

◆◆◆

Motel

	2/1-5/31 & 1/1-1/31 [CP]	1P: $99- 109	2P/1B: $119- 129	2P/2B: $129- 139
	9/1-12/31 [CP]	1P: $79- 89	2P/1B: $79- 89	2P/2B: $89- 99
	6/1-8/31 [CP]	1P: $49- 69	2P/1B: $59- 79	2P/2B: $59- 79

Location: 390 S Indian Canyon Dr 92262. Fax: 760/322-8789. **Facility:** 129 rooms. 1 two-bedroom unit. 1 suite with microwave $129; 3 stories; exterior corridors; heated pool. **Cards:** AE, DI, DS, MC, VI. *(See color ad p 777)*

(SAVE) ⑤ 🐾 🚐 🍴 🅰 🛠 🔧 💻 ⊠

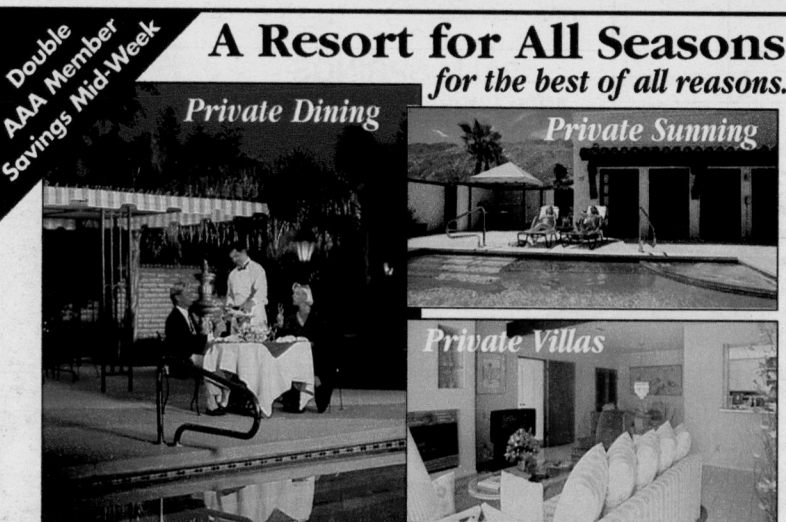

(See map p. 775)

COURTYARD BY MARRIOTT ◆◆◆   Rates Subject to Change   **Phone:** 760/322-6100   `102`

Motor Inn

2/1-5/31 & 1/1-1/31	1P: $119- 159	2P/1B: $119- 159	2P/2B: $119- 159
6/1-6/30	1P: $109- 139	2P/1B: $109- 139	2P/2B: $109- 139
9/16-12/31	1P: $69- 94	2P/1B: $69- 94	2P/2B: $69- 94
7/1-9/15	1P: $49- 59	2P/1B: $49- 59	2P/2B: $49- 59

Location: 1 mi e of Indian Canyon Dr. 1300 Tahquitz Canyon Way 92262. Fax: 760/322-6091. **Facility:** 149 rooms. Nicely landscaped interior courtyard. 3 stories; interior corridors; heated pool. **Cards:** AE, DI, DS, MC, VI. *(See color ad below)*

DESERT HILLS APT. HOTEL ⒶⒶ SAVE   **Phone:** (760)325-2777   `103`

2/1-4/26 [CP]	1P: $75- 170	2P/1B: $75- 170	2P/2B: $75- 170	XP: $10
9/14-1/31 [CP]	1P: $75- 160	2P/1B: $75- 160	2P/2B: $75- 160	XP: $10
4/27-6/14 [CP]	1P: $75- 150	2P/1B: $75- 150	2P/2B: $75- 150	XP: $10
6/15-9/13 [CP]	1P: $65- 145	2P/1B: $65- 145	2P/2B: $65- 145	XP: $10

◆◆◆
Apartment Motel

Location: 0.5 mi w of Palm Canyon Dr. 601 W Arenas Rd 92262. Fax: 760/325-6423. **Terms:** Reserv deposit, 5 day notice; monthly rates. **Facility:** 14 rooms. Spacious, attractively furnished rooms. 2 bedroom, 2-bath unit with kitchen & woodburning fireplace, $135-$160; 1 story; exterior corridors; designated smoking area; heated pool, whirlpool. **Recreation:** bicycles. **All Rooms:** combo or shower baths. **Some Rooms:** 11 kitchens. **Cards:** AE, DS, MC, VI. **Special Amenities:** Free local telephone calls and free newspaper.

EL RANCHO LODGE ⒶⒶ   Rates Subject to Change   **Phone:** (760)327-1339   `122`

2/1-5/31 & 10/1-1/31 [CP]	1P: $61- 80	2P/1B: $61- 80	2P/2B: $61- 80	XP: $20
6/1-9/30 [CP]	1P: $40- 55	2P/1B: $40- 55	2P/2B: $40- 55	XP: $20

◆◆
Motel

Location: 2 mi se on Palm Canyon Dr. 1330 E Palm Canyon Dr 92264. **Terms:** Reserv deposit; monthly rates. **Facility:** 19 rooms. 1 story; exterior corridors; heated pool, whirlpool. **All Rooms:** combo or shower baths, extended cable TV. **Some Rooms:** 6 efficiencies, 9 kitchens. **Cards:** AE, DS, MC, VI.

(See map p. 775)

ESTRELLA INN AT PALM SPRINGS
Rates Subject to Change Phone: (760)320-4117 🔲115

2/1-5/31 & 1/1-1/31 [CP]	1P: $125- 325	2P/1B: $125- 325	2P/2B: $125- 325 XP: $20 F18
10/1-12/31 [CP]	1P: $99- 250	2P/1B: $99- 250	2P/2B: $99- 250 XP: $20 F18
6/1-9/30 [CP]	1P: $75- 150	2P/1B: $75- 150	2P/2B: $75- 150 XP: $20 F18

◆◆◆ Complex **Location:** Just w of SR 111, S Palm Canyon Dr. 415 S Belardo Rd 92262. Fax: 760/323-3303. **Terms:** Reserv deposit, 3 day notice; weekly/monthly rates; pets, $20 per pet extra charge. **Facility:** 64 rooms. A wide variety of rooms, studios, suites & bungalows surround nicely landscaped courtyard areas. 8 two-bedroom units. 4 cottages with private outdoor whirlpool; 1-2 stories; interior/exterior corridors; heated pool, whirlpools. **Dining:** Restaurant; 7 am-midnight(guest only); $7-$15; cocktails. **Recreation:** shuffleboard court, volleyball court, barbecues. **All Rooms:** combo or shower baths. **Some Rooms:** 12 efficiencies, 18 kitchens. **Cards:** AE, DI, MC, VI. *(See color ad p 778)*

🔲🔲🔲🔲🔲🔲🔲🔲🔲🔲🔲🔲🔲🔲

FOUR SEASONS APARTMENT HOTEL
Rates Subject to Change Phone: (760)325-6427 🔲108

2/1-4/15 & 12/22-1/4	1P: $110- 140	2P/1B: $110- 140	2P/2B: $110- 140 XP: $10
4/16-5/31 & 1/5-1/31	1P: $105- 130	2P/1B: $105- 130	2P/2B: $105- 130 XP: $10
10/1-12/21	1P: $90- 115	2P/1B: $90- 115	2P/2B: $90- 115 XP: $10
6/1-9/30	1P: $65- 90	2P/1B: $65- 90	2P/2B: $65- 90 XP: $10

◆◆◆◆ Apartment Motel **Location:** 0.3 mi w of Palm Canyon Dr. 290 San Jacinto Dr at Baristo Dr 92262. Fax: 760/325-6427. **Terms:** Reserv deposit, 7 day notice; handling fee imposed; monthly rates. **Facility:** 11 rooms. Spacious, beautifully decorated 1-bedroom suites with kitchen, also a two-bedroom unit with gas fireplace. One smaller unit. Located in quiet residential area. 2-bedroom suite, $140-$185; exterior corridors; designated smoking area; heated pool, whirlpool. **Recreation:** bicycles. **All Rooms:** extended cable TV. **Cards:** MC, VI.

🔲🔲🔲🔲🔲🔲

HAMPTON INN
Rates Subject to Change Phone: 760/320-0555 🔲88

2/1-5/8 & 12/21-1/31 [CP]	1P: $77- 87	2P/1B: $84- 94	2P/2B: $94- 104
5/9-5/27 [CP]	1P: $67- 77	2P/1B: $74- 84	2P/2B: $84- 94
5/28-12/20 [CP]	1P: $47- 57	2P/1B: $54- 64	2P/2B: $54- 64

◆◆◆ Motel **Location:** 1.5 mi n. 2000 N Palm Canyon Dr 92262. Fax: 760/320-2261. **Facility:** 96 rooms. 2 stories; exterior corridors; heated pool. **Cards:** AE, CB, DI, DS, MC, VI.

🔲🔲🔲🔲🔲🔲🔲🔲🔲🔲

HOLIDAY INN PALM MOUNTAIN RESORT
Guaranteed Rates Phone: (760)325-1301 🔲107

2/1-5/29 & 12/24-1/31	1P: $115- 145	2P/1B: $115- 145	2P/2B: $115- 145 XP: $10 F18
10/1-12/23	1P: $99- 125	2P/1B: $99- 125	2P/2B: $99- 125 XP: $10 F18
5/30-9/30	1P: $69- 99	2P/1B: $69- 99	2P/2B: $69- 99 XP: $10 F18

◆◆◆ Motor Inn **Location:** Downtown, just w of Palm Canyon Dr. 155 S Belardo 92262. Fax: 760/323-8937. **Terms:** Reserv deposit. **Facility:** 122 rooms. 2-3 stories; exterior corridors; heated pool, whirlpool. **Dining:** Restaurant; 7 am-11 pm; $10-$20; cocktails. **All Rooms:** combo or shower baths. **Some Rooms:** whirlpools. **Cards:** AE, CB, DI, DS, JC, MC, VI. *(See color ad below)*

🔲🔲🔲🔲🔲🔲🔲🔲🔲🔲🔲🔲🔲🔲

HOTEL CALIFORNIA
Phone: (760)322-8855 🔲127

2/1-4/30 & 12/24-1/31 [CP]	1P: $69- 135	2P/1B: $69- 135	2P/2B: $69- 135 XP: $10-15
5/1-7/4 & 10/1-12/23 [CP]	1P: $59- 125	2P/1B: $59- 125	2P/2B: $59- 125 XP: $10-15
7/5-9/30 [CP]	1P: $49- 99	2P/1B: $49- 99	2P/2B: $49- 99 XP: $10-15

◆◆ Motel **Location:** 1.5 mi s. 424 E Palm Canyon Dr 92264. Fax: 760/323-0694. **Terms:** Reserv deposit, 3 day notice; weekly rates. **Facility:** 17 rooms. 2 stories; exterior corridors; heated pool. **Dining:** Restaurant nearby. **Recreation:** cabana with barbecue. **All Rooms:** combo or shower baths, extended cable TV. **Some Rooms:** 6 efficiencies, 4 kitchens. **Cards:** AE, DS, MC, VI. **Special Amenities:** Free local telephone calls and preferred room (subject to availability with advanced reservations).

🔲🔲🔲🔲🔲🔲🔲🔲🔲

(See map p. 775)

HOWARD JOHNSON INN   Rates Subject to Change   **Phone:** (760)320-2700 133
◆◆   2/1-5/31   1P: $79   2P/1B: $79   2P/2B: $99   XP: $10   F18
Motor Inn   9/1-1/31   1P: $59   2P/1B: $59   2P/2B: $79   XP: $10   F18
          6/1-8/31   1P: $49   2P/1B: $49   2P/2B: $69   XP: $10   F18
Location: 2 mi se. 701 E Palm Canyon Dr 92264. Fax: 760/322-5354. **Facility:** 205 rooms. 2 stories; exterior corridors; heated pool. **Cards:** AE, CB, DI, DS, JC, MC, VI. *(See color ad below)*   [icons]

HYATT REGENCY SUITES PALM SPRINGS   **Phone:** (760)322-9000 96
(AAA) (SAVE) 2/1-5/31 & 12/25-1/31   1P: $229- 259 2P/1B: $229- 259 2P/2B: $229- 259 XP: $25   F18
          10/1-12/24   1P: $169- 199 2P/1B: $169- 199 2P/2B: $169- 199 XP: $25   F18
◆◆◆   6/1-9/30   1P: $129- 149 2P/1B: $129- 149 2P/2B: $129- 149 XP: $25   F18
Suite Hotel **Location:** Downtown. 285 N Palm Canyon Dr 92262. Fax: 760/322-6009. **Facility:** 192 rooms. 1-bedroom units with living room & balcony. Adjacent to Desert Fashion Plaza. 5 two-bedroom units. 2 bedroom suites, $425; 6 stories; interior corridors; heated pool, whirlpool. **Dining:** 7 am-10 pm, Fri & Sat-midnight; $10-$23; cocktails. **Services:** giftshop. **Some Rooms:** whirlpools. **Cards:** AE, CB, DI, DS, JC, MC, VI. *(See color ad p 565)*   [icons]

INGLESIDE INN   **Phone:** (760)325-0046 114
(AAA) (SAVE) 2/1-5/31 & 9/1-1/31 [CP] 1P: $95- 395 2P/1B: $95- 395 2P/2B: $145- 395 XP: $20
          6/1-6/30 [CP]   1P: $95- 338 2P/1B: $86- 338 2P/2B: $145- 338 XP: $20
◆◆◆   Fri & Sat 7/1-8/31 [CP] 1P: $72- 289 2P/1B: $72- 289 2P/2B: $109- 289 XP: $20
Historic   Sun-Thurs 7/1-8/31 [CP] 1P: $48- 193 2P/1B: $48- 193 2P/2B: $72- 193 XP: $20
Country Inn **Location:** Just w of Palm Canyon Dr. 200 W Ramon Rd 92264. Fax: 760/325-0710. **Terms:** Reserv deposit; weekly/monthly rates. **Facility:** 29 rooms. Each room or villa contains beautifully restored antiques. Many rooms with woodburning fireplace, some with private patio. 2 two-bedroom units. 1-2 stories; exterior corridors; heated pool, whirlpool. **Dining:** Melvyn's, see separate listing. **Recreation:** croquet lawn. **All Rooms:** extended cable TV. **Cards:** AE, CB, DI, DS, MC, VI. **Special Amenities:** Free breakfast and free newspaper.   [icons]

LA MANCHA RESORT VILLAGE   **Phone:** (760)323-1773 93
(AAA) (SAVE) All Year   1P: $145- 695 2P/1B: $145- 695   XP: $25   F12
◆◆◆   **Location:** 0.8 mi e of Palm Canyon Dr, via Alejo Rd. 444 Avenida Caballeros 92262 (PO Box 1606).
Resort   Fax: 760/323-5928. **Terms:** Reserv deposit, 3 day notice, 7 day for weekly stays; weekly/monthly rates.
Complex   **Facility:** 67 rooms. Spacious, beautifully furnished 1 to 3-bedroom villas, some with private whirlpool; others with private pool & whirlpool. Some villas have washer & dryer. 10 two-bedroom units, 14 three-bedroom units. 2 stories; exterior corridors; putting green; heated pool, saunas, whirlpool; 2 lighted paddle courts, croquet courts. Fee: 7 tennis courts (4 lighted). **Dining:** Dining room; 7:30 am-2:30 & 5:30-9:30 pm; $15-$28; health conscious menu; cocktails; open to public by reservation only. **Services:** Fee: massage. **Recreation:** table tennis. Fee: bicycles. **All Rooms:** extended cable TV. **Some Rooms:** 52 kitchens. **Cards:** AE, DI, DS, MC, VI. **Special Amenities:** Free newspaper and preferred room (subject to availability with advanced reservations). *(See color ad p 777)*   [icons]

(See map p. 775)

L'HORIZON GARDEN HOTEL Phone: 760/323-1858 ⑫
(AAA) [SAVE] 2/1-7/8 & 12/15-1/31 [CP] 1P: $115- 255 2P/1B: $115- 255 2P/2B: $115- 255
◆◆ 10/1-12/14 [CP] 1P: $95- 210 2P/1B: $95- 210 2P/2B: $95- 210
Motel **Location:** 2.3 mi se on Palm Canyon Dr. 1050 E Palm Canyon Dr 92264. Fax: 760/327-2933. **Terms:** Open
2/1-7/8 & 10/1-1/31; reserv deposit; monthly rates. **Facility:** 22 rooms. Spacious, nicely landscaped grounds.
1 suite with fireplace; 1 story; exterior corridors; heated pool, whirlpool. **All Rooms:** combo or shower baths,
extended cable TV. **Some Rooms:** 7 kitchens. **Cards:** AE, CB, DI, DS, MC, VI. ⊇ ▣ 🖨 ✕

ORCHID TREE INN Rates Subject to Change Phone: 760/325-2791 ⑩⑨
◆◆◆ 2/1-5/31 [CP] & 10/31-1/31 [CP] 1P: $99- 295 2P/1B: $95- 295 2P/2B: $95- 295 XP: $15
Complex 6/1-7/5 & 10/3-10/30 [EP] 1P: $85- 265 2P/1B: $85- 265 2P/2B: $85- 265 XP: $15
7/6-10/2 [EP] 1P: $65- 230 2P/1B: $65- 230 2P/2B: $65- 230 XP: $15
Location: Just w of SR 111, S Palm Canyon Dr. 261 S Belardo Rd 92262. Fax: 760/325-3855. **Terms:** Reserv deposit, 7
day notice. **Facility:** 36 rooms. Nicely landscaped grounds & garden areas. 1-2 stories; exterior corridors; heated pool.
All Rooms: combo or shower baths. **Some Rooms:** 30 kitchens. **Cards:** AE, DS, MC, VI. *(See ad below)*
⊇ 🅰 [VCR] ▣ 🖨 ✕

PALM COURT INN Guaranteed Rates Phone: (760)416-2333 ⑧⑥
(AAA) 2/1-4/30 & 10/1-1/31 [CP] 1P: $39- 59 2P/1B: $45- 69 2P/2B: $49- 79 XP: $5 F17
◆ 5/1-9/30 [CP] 1P: $39- 49 2P/1B: $39- 59 2P/2B: $49- 69 XP: $5 F17
Motor Inn **Location:** 1.5 mi n of downtown on SR 111. 1983 N Palm Canyon Dr 92262. Fax: 760/416-5425. **Facility:** 80
rooms. 1-2 stories; exterior corridors; heated pool, wading pool, whirlpool. **Dining:** Restaurant nearby.
Recreation: Fee: bicycles. **All Rooms:** extended cable TV. **Cards:** AE, DS, MC, VI. *(See color ad below)*
🐕 🏊 ⊇ 🍴 🅰 ✕ 🔳 ✕

(See map p. 775)

PALM GARDEN RESORT
Phone: (760)323-1328

AAA SAVE

◆◆
Motel

	4/2-6/15	1P:	$59- 139	2P/1B:	$89- 159	2P/2B:	$89- 169	XP: $10	F16
	2/1-4/1 & 10/1-1/31	1P:	$69- 149	2P/1B:	$69- 149	2P/2B:	$79- 159	XP: $10	F16
	6/16-9/30	1P:	$40- 109	2P/1B:	$40- 109	2P/2B:	$40- 109	XP: $10	F16

Location: 1.2 mi n. 950 N Indian Canyon Dr 92262. Fax: 760/323-2971. **Terms:** Reserv deposit, 3 day notice; small pets only. **Facility:** 47 rooms. 2 stories; exterior corridors; heated pool, sauna, whirlpools. **Dining:** Restaurant nearby. **All Rooms:** combo or shower baths, extended cable TV. **Some Rooms:** 22 kitchens. **Cards:** AE, DI, DS, MC, VI. **Special Amenities:** Free breakfast and free local telephone calls.

PALM SPRINGS CONFERENCE RESORT
Phone: (760)322-2121

AAA SAVE

◆◆◆
Hotel

	1/2-1/31	1P:	$175- 245	2P/1B:	$175- 245	2P/2B:	$175- 245	XP: $20
	2/1-5/29	1P:	$169- 230	2P/1B:	$169- 230	2P/2B:	$169- 230	XP: $20
	10/1-1/1	1P:	$130- 182	2P/1B:	$130- 182	2P/2B:	$130- 182	XP: $20
	5/30-9/30	1P:	$85- 130	2P/1B:	$85- 130	2P/2B:	$85- 130	XP: $20

Location: Just s of Tahquitz Canyon Way; downtown area. 150 S Indian Canyon Dr 92262. Fax: 760/322-2180. **Terms:** Check-in 4 pm; weekly/monthly rates; package plans. **Facility:** 264 rooms. Spacious rooms, 1- & 2-bedroom suites. Patios or balconies. 3 stories; interior corridors; heated pool, wading pool, whirlpools. Fee: 2 lighted tennis courts. **Dining:** Dining room, restaurant; 7 am-10 pm; $10-$16; cocktails; also, Purple Sage, see separate listing. **Services:** giftshop. Fee: massage. **Recreation:** Kid's Camp-summer & winter weekends. **All Rooms:** extended cable TV. **Some Rooms:** 101 kitchens, utensils extra charge. **Cards:** AE, CB, DI, DS, JC, MC, VI. **Special Amenities:** Preferred room (subject to availability with advanced reservations).

PALM SPRINGS HILTON RESORT
Rates Subject to Change
Phone: (760)320-6868

◆◆◆
Hotel

	1/1-1/31	1P:	$175- 255	2P/1B:	$175- 255	2P/2B:	$175- 255	XP: $20	F18
	2/1-5/31	1P:	$165- 245	2P/1B:	$165- 245	2P/2B:	$165- 245	XP: $20	F18
	10/1-12/31	1P:	$120- 155	2P/1B:	$120- 155	2P/2B:	$120- 155	XP: $20	F18
	6/1-9/30	1P:	$70- 90	2P/1B:	$70- 90	2P/2B:	$70- 90	XP: $20	F18

Location: Just e of Indian Canyon Dr. 400 E Tahquitz Canyon Way 92262. Fax: 760/320-2126. **Terms:** Reserv deposit, 7 day notice. **Facility:** 260 rooms. Attractively landscaped courtyard & pool area. Balcony or patio. 3 stories; interior corridors; heated pool. Fee: 6 lighted tennis courts. **Services:** giftshop. Fee: massage. **Recreation:** Fee: bicycles. **Cards:** AE, CB, DI, DS, JC, MC, VI. *(See ad p 119)*

PALM SPRINGS RIVIERA RESORT
Rates Subject to Change
Phone: 760/327-8311

◆◆◆
Hotel

	2/1-5/31	1P:	$129	2P/1B:	$129	2P/2B:	$129	XP: $20
	9/1-1/31	1P:	$109	2P/1B:	$109	2P/2B:	$109	XP: $20
	6/1-8/1	1P:	$69	2P/1B:	$69	2P/2B:	$69	XP: $20

Location: 1.5 mi n. 1600 N Indian Canyon Dr 92262. Fax: 760/327-4323. **Terms:** Open 2/1-8/1 & 9/1-1/31. **Facility:** 476 rooms. 2-3 stories; interior corridors; putting green. Fee: 9 tennis courts (5 lighted). **Services:** giftshop; area transportation. **Cards:** AE, CB, DI, DS, JC, MC, VI. *(See color ad below)*

PALM TEE HOTEL
Guaranteed Rates
Phone: 760/327-1293

◆◆
Apartment
Motel

| | 2/1-5/31 & 10/1-1/31 [CP] | 1P: | $70- 140 | 2P/1B: | $70- 140 | | | XP: $10 |
| | 6/1-9/30 [CP] | 1P: | $50- 115 | 2P/1B: | $50- 115 | | | XP: $10 |

Location: 2.5 mi se; just w of Sunrise Way. 1590 E Palm Canyon Dr 92264. Fax: 760/320-4446. **Facility:** 15 rooms. Spacious rooms & one-bedroom suites. 2 stories; exterior corridors; designated smoking area; heated pool. **All Rooms:** combo or shower baths. **Some Rooms:** 9 kitchens. **Cards:** AE, CB, DS, MC, VI.

PLACE IN THE SUN
Guaranteed Rates
Phone: 760/325-0254

◆◆◆
Apartment
Motel

| | 2/1-6/1 & 12/16-1/31 | 1P: | $69- 109 | 2P/1B: | $69- 109 | 2P/2B: | $69- 109 | XP: $12 |
| | 6/2-12/15 | 1P: | $60- 90 | 2P/1B: | $60- 90 | 2P/2B: | $60- 90 | XP: $12 |

Location: Just e of Palm Canyon Dr, via Mesquite Ave & Random Rd. 754 San Lorenzo Rd 92264. Fax: 760/327-9303. **Terms:** Reserv deposit. **Facility:** 16 rooms. Attractive grounds with many fruit trees. Studio & 1-bedroom apartments. Patios. 1 story; exterior corridors; putting green; heated pool. **Some Rooms:** 2 efficiencies, 14 kitchens. **Cards:** AE, MC, VI.

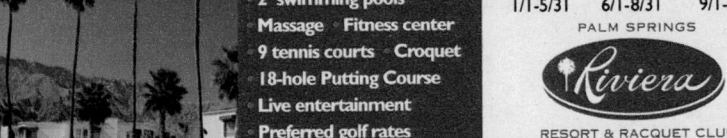

(See map p. 775)

QUALITY INN RESORT

Phone: (760)323-2775 ☒128☒

		1P:	2P/1B:	2P/2B:	XP:	
(AAA) (SAVE)	2/1-5/31 & 1/1-1/31	$69- 169	$69- 169	$79- 169	$15	F18
◆◆◆	6/1-9/30	$49- 129	$49- 129	$59- 149	$15	F18
Motel	10/1-12/31	$59- 139	$59- 139	$69- 139	$15	F18

Location: 2.3 mi se on Palm Canyon Dr. 1269 E Palm Canyon Dr 92264. Fax: 760/323-4234. **Terms:** Small pets only. **Facility:** 145 rooms. 7 one-bedroom suites, $119-$169; $79-$99 6/1-12/25. Some small room in king beds; 2 stories; exterior corridors; heated pool, wading pool, whirlpool. **Dining:** Restaurant nearby. **All Rooms:** extended cable TV. **Cards:** AE, CB, DI, DS, MC, VI. *(See color ad below)*

RAMADA RESORT INN & CONFERENCE CENTER   Rates Subject to Change   Phone: (760)323-1711 ☒123☒

		1P:	2P/1B:	2P/2B:	XP:	
◆◆◆	2/1-4/30	$99- 149	$99- 149	$89- 149	$15	F16
Motor Inn	10/1-1/31	$79- 99	$79- 99	$79- 99	$15	F16
	5/1-9/30	$69- 99	$69- 99	$69- 99	$15	F16

Location: 2.5 mi se on Palm Canyon Dr. 1800 E Palm Canyon Dr 92264. Fax: 760/327-6941. **Terms:** Reserv deposit. **Facility:** 255 rooms. 2 two-bedroom units. 3 stories; interior/exterior corridors; heated pool. **Services:** giftshop. **Cards:** AE, DI, DS, MC, VI. *(See color ad below)*

(See map p. 775)

ROYAL SUN INN
Phone: (760)327-1564 [125]

(AAA) [SAVE]

◆ ◆ Motel

	2/1-5/31 [CP]	1P:	$79- 99	2P/1B:	$79- 99	2P/2B:	$99- 109	XP: $10	F12
	10/1-1/31 [CP]	1P:	$59- 69	2P/1B:	$59- 69	2P/2B:	$69- 79	XP: $10	F12
	6/1-9/30 [CP]	1P:	$49- 59	2P/1B:	$49- 59	2P/2B:	$59- 69	XP: $10	F12

Location: 1.5 mi se on Palm Canyon Dr. 1700 S Palm Canyon Dr 92264. Fax: 760/323-9092. **Terms:** Weekly/monthly rates; small pets only, $10 extra charge. **Facility:** 66 rooms. Balconies or patios. 3 stories; exterior corridors; heated pool, sauna, whirlpool. **Dining:** Restaurant nearby. **All Rooms:** extended cable TV. **Some Rooms:** 3 efficiencies. **Cards:** AE, DS, MC, VI. **Special Amenities:** Free breakfast and preferred room (subject to availability with advanced reservations).

SAN MARINO HOTEL
Phone: (760)325-6902 [129]

◆ ◆ Motel

	Rates Subject to Change								
	2/1-5/31 & 12/16-1/31 [CP]	1P:	$85- 125	2P/1B:	$85- 125	2P/2B:	$125- 160	XP: $10	F16
	10/1-12/15 [CP]	1P:	$69- 109	2P/1B:	$69- 109	2P/2B:	$109- 140	XP: $10	F16
	6/1-9/30 [CP]	1P:	$49- 89	2P/1B:	$49- 89	2P/2B:	$89- 105		

Location: Just w of downtown area. 225 W Baristo Rd 92262. Fax: 760/325-6906. **Terms:** Handling fee imposed. **Facility:** 15 rooms. One bedroom suite, $160; 1-2 stories; exterior corridors; designated smoking area; heated pool. **All Rooms:** combo or shower baths. **Some Rooms:** 8 kitchens. **Cards:** MC, VI.

SHILO INN
Phone: (760)320-7676 [89]

◆ ◆ ◆ Motel

| | Rates Subject to Change | | | | | | | | |
| | All Year [CP] | 1P: | $79- 139 | 2P/1B: | $79- 139 | 2P/2B: | $79- 139 | XP: $12 | F12 |

Location: 1.5 mi n. 1875 N Palm Canyon Dr 92262. Fax: 760/320-9543. **Facility:** 124 rooms. Nicely landscaped grounds. Patios or balconies. 4 units with kitchen, $20 extra charge; heated pool. **Cards:** AE, CB, DI, DS, JC, MC, VI. *(See ad p 627, p 1091, p 658 & p 627)*

SPA HOTEL & CASINO RESORT & MINERAL SPRINGS
Phone: 760/325-1461 [98]

◆ ◆ ◆ Hotel

	Rates Subject to Change					
	2/1-6/15 & 12/27-1/31	2P/1B:	$159- 199	2P/2B:	$159- 199	XP: $25	F14
	9/15-12/26	2P/1B:	$129- 149	2P/2B:	$129- 149	XP: $20	F14
	6/16-9/14	2P/1B:	$69- 94	2P/2B:	$69- 94	XP: $15	F14

Location: Just e of downtown area on Tanquitz Canyon Dr. 100 N Indian Canyon Dr. Fax: 760/325-5635. **Terms:** Check-in 4 pm; reserv deposit, 3 day notice. **Facility:** 230 rooms. 5 stories; interior corridors; heated pool. **Services:** giftshop. Fee: massage. **Some Rooms:** 15 efficiencies. **Cards:** AE, CB, DI, DS, MC, VI.

SUPER 8 LODGE
Phone: (760)322-3757 [85]

◆ Motel

	Rates Subject to Change								
	2/1-5/31 & 1/1-1/31 [CP]	1P:	$66- 71	2P/1B:	$71- 76	2P/2B:	$76- 81	XP: $5	F12
	10/1-12/31 [CP]	1P:	$59- 64	2P/1B:	$64- 69	2P/2B:	$69- 74	XP: $5	F12
	6/1-9/30 [CP]	1P:	$50- 55	2P/1B:	$55- 60	2P/2B:	$60- 65	XP: $5	F12

Location: 1.5 mi n. 1900 N Palm Canyon Dr 92262. Fax: 760/323-5290. **Facility:** 62 rooms. Executive Parlor Rooms $80-$104; 2 stories; exterior corridors; heated pool. **Cards:** AE, CB, DI, DS, MC, VI.

TRAVELODGE-PALM SPRINGS
Phone: (760)327-1211 [126]

(AAA) [SAVE]

◆ ◆ Motel

	2/1-6/13 & 12/24-1/31	2P/1B:	$59- 85	2P/2B:	$69- 95	XP: $10	F18
	9/3-12/23	2P/1B:	$45- 65	2P/2B:	$55- 75	XP: $10	F18
	6/14-9/2	2P/1B:	$35- 55	2P/2B:	$43- 65	XP: $10	F18

Location: 1.5 mi s of Tahquitz Canyon. 333 E Palm Canyon Dr 92264. Fax: 760/320-4672. **Terms:** Reserv deposit; weekly rates. **Facility:** 157 rooms. 2 stories; exterior corridors; heated pool, whirlpool. **Dining:** Restaurant nearby. **Recreation:** badminton, volleyball court, shuffleboard court. **All Rooms:** combo or shower baths. **Cards:** AE, CB, DI, DS, MC, VI. **Special Amenities:** Free local telephone calls and free newspaper.

VAGABOND INN
Phone: (760)325-7211 [124]

(AAA) [SAVE]

◆ ◆ ◆ Motel

	2/1-5/16 [EP]	2P/1B:	$70- 99	2P/2B:	$80- 105	XP: $6
	10/1-1/31 [CP]	2P/1B:	$59- 69	2P/2B:	$65- 75	XP: $6
	5/17-9/30 [EP]	2P/1B:	$42- 52	2P/2B:	$46- 56	XP: $6

Location: 1.5 mi s at jct E Palm Canyon Dr. 1699 S Palm Canyon Dr 92264. Fax: 760/322-9269. **Terms:** Monthly rates. **Facility:** 120 rooms. 1 two-bedroom unit. 3 stories; exterior corridors; heated pool, saunas, whirlpool. **Dining:** Coffee shop; 7 am-3 pm. **All Rooms:** extended cable TV. **Cards:** AE, CB, DI, DS, JC, MC, VI. **Special Amenities:** Free breakfast and free local telephone calls.

(See map p. 775)

VILLA ROSA INN   Rates Subject to Change   **Phone:** (760)327-5915   118

◆◆   2/1-5/31 & 10/1-1/31 [CP]   1P: $69- 125   2P/1B: $69- 125

Motel   6/1-9/30 [CP]   1P: $49- 99   2P/1B: $49- 99

        Location: 2 mi se on Palm Canyon Dr, just n. 1577 S Indian Tr 92264. Fax: 760/416-9962. **Terms:** Reserv deposit, 3 day notice; 2 night min stay, weekends 10/1-6/1. **Facility:** 6 rooms. Tastefully decorated rooms. Quiet, garden setting. 2 one-bedroom suites with kitchen; 1 story; exterior corridors; smoke free premises; heated pool. **All Rooms:** combo or shower baths. **Cards:** AE, MC, VI.

VILLA ROYALE INN   **Phone:** (760)327-2314   119

ⒶⒶⒶ 〔SAVE〕   2/1-5/31 & 10/1-1/31 [CP]   1P: $95- 250   2P/1B: $95- 250   2P/2B: $95- 295   XP: $25

           6/1-9/30 [CP]   1P: $65- 175   2P/1B: $65- 175   2P/2B: $65- 200   XP: $25

◆◆◆   **Location:** 2 mi se on Palm Canyon Dr, just n. 1620 S Indian Tr 92264. Fax: 760/322-3794. **Terms:** Reserv

Country Inn   deposit, 10 day notice; monthly rates; 2 night min stay, weekends in season. **Facility:** 32 rooms. Old world ambiance. Nicely landscaped courtyards & individually decorated rooms & suites; some with fireplace & private outdoor whirlpools. 3 two-bedroom units. 1 story; exterior corridors; heated pool, whirlpool. **Dining:** Restaurant; also, Europa Restaurant, see separate listing. **All Rooms:** combo or shower baths, extended cable TV. **Some Rooms:** 8 efficiencies, 7 kitchens, color TV. **Cards:** AE, DI, DS, MC, VI. *(See color ad below)*

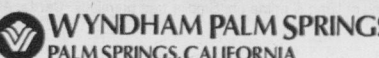

(See map p. 775)

VILLE ORLEANS RESORT HOTEL　　　　　　　　　　　　　　Phone: (760)864-6200　🏢91

(AAA) (SAVE)　2/1-5/31 & 10/1-1/31　　1P: $95- 250　2P/1B: $95- 250　2P/2B: $95- 295　XP: $25
◆◆　　6/1-9/30　　　　　　　　1P: $65- 175　2P/1B: $65- 175　2P/2B: $65- 200　XP: $25
Motel　　**Location:** 1.5 mi n of downtown; just e of Indian Canyon Dr. 269 Chuckwalla Rd 92262. Fax: 760/864-6208.
Terms: Reserv deposit; weekly/monthly rates; small pets only. **Facility:** 14 rooms. 1 two-bedroom unit.
2-bedroom 2-bath suite, $165-$225; 1-2 stories; exterior corridors; designated smoking area; heated pool,
whirlpool. **Recreation:** video library. **All Rooms:** combo or shower baths, extended cable TV. **Some Rooms:** 8 kitchens.
Cards: AE, MC, VI.

THE WILLOWS HISTORIC PALM SPRINGS INN　　　　　　Phone: (760)320-0771　🏢94

(AAA) (SAVE)　2/1-5/31 & 10/1-1/31 [BP]　1P: $250- 500　2P/1B: $250- 500
◆◆◆◆　　6/1-9/30 [BP]　　　　　　　　　　　　2P/1B: $175- 375
Historic Bed　**Location:** Just w of Palm Canyon Dr. 412 W Tahquitz Canyon Way 92262. Fax: 760/320-0780.
& Breakfast　**Terms:** Check-in 4 pm; reserv deposit, 7 day notice. **Facility:** 8 rooms. Exquisite 1927 restored historic Medi-
terranean villa. Original stone path through hillside garden; also mountain waterfall just outside dining room. 4
rooms with fireplace. 3 stories; interior corridors; smoke free premises; heated pool, whirlpool.
Services: complimentary evening beverages. **Some Rooms:** efficiency. **Cards:** AE, CB, DI, DS, MC, VI.
Special Amenities: Free local telephone calls and free newspaper. *(See color ad p 785)*

WYNDHAM PALM SPRINGS HOTEL　　　Rates Subject to Change　　Phone: (760)322-6000　🏢100
◆◆◆　　Fri & Sat [BP]　　　　　1P: $89- 189　2P/1B: $89- 189　2P/2B: $89- 189　XP:$10-20　F18
Hotel　　Sun-Thurs [EP]　　　　1P: $79- 149　2P/1B: $79- 149　2P/2B: $79- 149　XP:$10-20　F18
Location: 3 blks e of Indian Canyon Dr. 888 Tahquitz Canyon Way 92262. Fax: 760/322-5351. **Facility:** 410
rooms. 5 stories; interior corridors; heated pool. **Services:** giftshop; area transportation. Fee: massage. **Cards:** AE, CB, DI,
DS, JC, MC, VI. *(See color ad p 785)*

RESTAURANTS

BANDUCCI'S BIT OF ITALY　　　　　　　　**Dinner:** $8-$16　　　　Phone: 760/325-2537　🔲58
(AAA)　　**Location:** 1 mi s. 1260 S Palm Canyon Dr 92264. **Hours:** 5 pm-11 pm. Closed: 11/25.
Reservations: suggested; in season. **Features:** casual dress; cocktails & lounge. Popular, long established
◆◆　restaurant. Informal decor & service. Indoor & outdoor patio dining. Piano bar Wed-Sun. **Cards:** AE, DI, DS,
Italian　MC, VI.

BILLY REED'S RESTAURANT　　**Lunch:** $6-$13　　**Dinner:** $9-$18　　Phone: 760/325-1946　🔲50
(AAA)　　**Location:** 1.5 mi n. 1800 N Palm Canyon Dr 92262. **Hours:** 7 am-11 pm. **Features:** casual dress; children's
menu; early bird specials; carryout; cocktails & lounge; entertainment. Popular restaurant featuring a large
◆◆　selection of salads, sandwiches & entrees. Victorian decor. **Cards:** AE, DI, DS, MC, VI.
American

CEDAR CREEK INN　　　　**Lunch:** $8-$13　　**Dinner:** $12-$21　　Phone: 760/325-7300　🔲59
◆◆◆　　**Location:** 1 mi s. 1555 S Palm Canyon Dr 92264. **Hours:** 11 am-10 pm. Closed: 12/25. **Features:** casual
American　dress; Sunday brunch; carryout; cocktails & lounge. Colorfully decorated restaurant featuring a large
selection of salads, sandwiches, entrees & homemade desserts. **Cards:** AE, CB, DI, MC, VI.

EUROPA RESTAURANT　　　　　　　　**Dinner:** $13-$28　　　Phone: 760/327-2314　🔲64
◆◆◆　　**Location:** 2 mi se on Palm Canyon Dr, just n; in Villa Royale Inn. 1620 S Indian Tr 92264. **Hours:** 5:30-10
Continental　pm, from 6:30 pm in summer, Sat & Sun brunch 11:30 am-2 pm in season. **Reservations:** suggested.
Features: cocktails & lounge; a la carte. A cozy charming restaurant serving a nice variety of pasta, steak,
seafood, rack of lamb & veal. Smoke free premises. **Cards:** AE, CB, DI, DS, MC, VI.

LAS CASUELAS TERRAZA　　　**Lunch:** $7-$9　　**Dinner:** $7-$14　　Phone: 760/325-2794　🔲55
(AAA)　　**Location:** Downtown. 222 S Palm Canyon Dr 92262. **Hours:** 11 am-10 pm, Sun from 10 am. Closed: 11/25
& 12/25. **Reservations:** suggested; weekends. **Features:** casual dress; children's menu; carryout; cocktails
◆◆　& lounge; entertainment. Popular restaurant. Indoor & patio dining. **Cards:** AE, DI, DS, MC, VI.
Mexican

LE VALLAURIS　　　　　　**Lunch:** $13-$18　　**Dinner:** $20-$30　　Phone: 760/325-5059　🔲54
◆◆◆◆　　**Location:** Just w of Palm Canyon Dr. 385 W Tahquitz Canyon Way 92262. **Hours:** 11:30 am-2:30 & 5:30-11
French　pm. **Reservations:** suggested. **Features:** semi-formal attire; Sunday brunch; cocktails & lounge; valet
parking; a la carte. Fine dining in a beautifully decorated restaurant & tree-shaded patio. **Cards:** AE, CB, DI,
DS, MC, VI.

LG'S PRIME STEAKHOUSE　　　**Lunch:** $8-$13　　**Dinner:** $19-$30　　Phone: 760/416-1779　🔲61
◆◆◆　　**Location:** Downtown. 255 S Palm Canyon Dr 92262. **Hours:** 11:30 am-3 & 5:30-10 pm, Fri & Sat-10:30 pm.
Steakhouse　Closed: 12/25. **Reservations:** suggested. **Features:** cocktails & lounge; a la carte. Indoor & patio dining.
Features a wide variety of prime steak. Also rack of lamb & prime rib. Smoke free premises. **Cards:** AE, CB,
DI, DS, MC, VI.

LYONS ENGLISH GRILLE　　　　　　**Dinner:** $15-$25　　　Phone: 760/327-1551　🔲60
◆◆　　**Location:** 1.5 mi s. 233 E Palm Canyon Dr 92264. **Hours:** Open 2/1-6/30 & 10/2-1/31; 4:30 pm-10:30 pm.
English　**Reservations:** suggested. **Features:** casual dress; children's menu; early bird specials; carryout; cocktails;
valet parking. A long established restaurant. Old English decor. **Cards:** AE, CB, DI, MC, VI.

MELVYN'S　　　　　**Lunch:** $10-$15　　**Dinner:** $23-$34　　Phone: 760/325-2323　🔲56
◆◆◆　　**Location:** At Ingleside Inn. 200 W Ramon Rd 92264. **Hours:** 11:30-3 & 6-11:30 pm, Sat 6 pm-11:30 pm,
Continental　Sun 9 am-3 & 6-11:30 pm. **Reservations:** suggested. **Features:** casual dress; Sunday brunch; cocktails &
lounge; entertainment; valet parking. Garden setting; enclosed patio dining. Smoke free premises.
Cards: AE, CB, DI, DS, MC, VI.

(See map p. 775)

OTANI-A GARDEN RESTAURANT   **Lunch:** $7-$11   **Dinner:** $15-$29   **Phone:** 760/327-6700   ⑤③
◆◆◆   **Location:** 3 blks e of Indian Canyon Dr; across from convention center. 266 N Avenida Caballeros 92262.
Japanese   **Hours:** 11:30 am-2 & 6-9:30 pm, Sat 5 pm-9:30 pm, Sun 11 am-2 & 5:30-9:30 pm.
Reservations: suggested. **Features:** casual dress; Sunday brunch; children's menu; carryout; cocktails & lounge. Tempura, sushi, Yakatori & Teppan-yaki dining areas. Smoke free premises. **Cards:** AE, DI, DS, JC, MC, VI.   ☒

PURPLE SAGE   **Dinner:** $17-$22   **Phone:** 760/322-2121   ⑥③
◆◆◆   **Location:** Just s of Tahquitz Canyon Way; downtown area; in Palm Springs Conference Resort. 150 S
American   Indian Canyon Dr 92262. **Hours:** 5:30 pm-10 pm. Closed: Mon & Tues. **Reservations:** suggested.
Features: dressy casual; cocktails & lounge; valet parking; a la carte. Fine dining in elegant surroundings.
Smoke free premises. **Cards:** AE, CB, DI, DS, MC, VI.   ☒

ST JAMES AT THE VINEYARD   **Dinner:** $18-$35   **Phone:** 760/320-8041   ⑥②
◆◆◆   **Location:** Downtown. 265 S Palm Canyon Dr 92262. **Hours:** 5:30 pm-10:30 pm, Fri & Sat-11 pm, Sun 11
Continental   am. Closed: 1/1, 11/25 & 12/25. **Reservations:** suggested. **Features:** dressy casual; Sunday brunch;
cocktails & lounge; a la carte. Interesting selection of International cuisine. Extensive wine list. Smoke free
premises. **Cards:** AE, CB, DI, MC, VI.   ☒

PALO ALTO—55,900

LODGINGS

CABANA PALO ALTO
FYI
Hotel

	Rates Subject to Change			**Phone:** (650)857-0787
Sun-Thurs	1P: $169- 229 2P/1B: $169- 229 2P/2B: $169- 229 XP: $15			F17
Fri & Sat	1P: $109- 199 2P/1B: $109- 199 2P/2B: $109- 199 XP: $15			F17

Under major renovation. **Location:** 3.5 mi s on SR 82. 4290 El Camino Real 94306. Fax: 650/496-1939.
Facility: 200 rooms. Attractively landscaped grounds. Under renovation-scheduled completion Feb 98. 2-8 stories; interior/exterior corridors. **Cards:** AE, CB, DI, DS, JC, MC, VI.

ⒶⓈⓀ S⊘ 🛏 🐾 👤 🄿 🛗 🍽 🎥 🖥 📠 🔗 ♿ ☒ 📷

COUNTRY INN MOTEL
AAA
◆◆
Motel

	Rates Subject to Change			**Phone:** 650/948-9154
All Year	1P: $58- 68 2P/1B: $68- 72 2P/2B: $78- 84 XP: $6			F12

Location: Exit US 101 San Antonio; SR 82 n 0.3 mi. 4345 El Camino Real 94306. Fax: 650/949-4190.
Terms: Reserv deposit; weekly rates; CP avail. **Facility:** 27 rooms. Attractive, well-maintained rooms. Barbecue area. 1-2 stories; exterior corridors. **All Rooms:** combo or shower baths. **Some Rooms:** 12 kitchens.
Cards: AE, CB, DI, DS, MC, VI.

🄿 🛏 🎥 📠

CREEKSIDE INN
AAA SAVE
◆◆◆
Motor Inn

				Phone: (650)493-2411
All Year	1P: $115- 185 2P/1B: $115- 185 2P/2B: $120- 185 XP: $10			

Location: SR 82, 0.3 s of Oregon Expwy/Page Mill Rd. 3400 El Camino Real 94306. Fax: 650/493-6787.
Facility: 143 rooms. Landscaped grounds. Many spacious & beautifully decorated rooms. 6 one-bedroom suites with living room & kitchen, $155-$185 for up to 2 persons; 4 stories; interior/exterior corridors; smoke free premises. **Dining:** Restaurant, deli; 6 am-11 pm Fresco Restaurant; $15-$25; cocktails; also, Fresco Restaurant, see separate listing. **Services:** area transportation, within 5 mi. **All Rooms:** combo or shower baths.
Some Rooms: 14 efficiencies. **Cards:** AE, CB, DI, DS, JC, MC, VI. **Special Amenities:** Free local telephone calls and free newspaper. (See color ad below)

🍽 🄿 🛏 🍴 👤 🎥 VCR 🖥 📟 📠 🧳

DAYS INN
Phone: (650)493-4222
AAA SAVE
All Year [CP]   1P: $60- 145   2P/1B: $65- 165   2P/2B: $65- 185   XP: $6
Location: 2.5 mi s of Stanford University Campus, on El Camino Real. 4238 El Camino Real 94306.
Fax: 650/494-6112. **Facility:** 23 rooms. Attractive modern decor. 1-2 stories; exterior corridors.
◆ ◆
Motel
All Rooms: combo or shower baths. **Cards:** AE, CB, DI, DS, JC, MC, VI. **Special Amenities:** Free
breakfast and free newspaper.

DINAH'S GARDEN HOTEL
Rates Subject to Change   Phone: (650)493-2844
AAA
All Year   1P: $170- 220   2P/1B: $170- 220   2P/2B: $170- 220   XP: $10
Location: On SR 82, exit US 101 San Antonio W, just n on SR 82. 4261 El Camino Real 94306.
◆ ◆ ◆
Motel
Fax: 650/856-4713. **Facility:** 148 rooms. Garden units surround pool or ponds, nicely landscaped grounds. 1
two-bedroom unit. 22 suites with whirlpool or steam shower, $190-$550 for 2 persons; 1-3 stories;
interior/exterior corridors; sauna. **Dining:** 2 restaurants; 6:30 am-9:30 pm; $10-$20; cocktails.
All Rooms: combo or shower baths. **Some Rooms:** 24 efficiencies, 18 kitchens. **Cards:** AE, CB, DI, DS, JC, MC, VI.

HOWARD JOHNSON EXPRESS INN
Phone: (650)493-2760
AAA SAVE
All Year [CP]   1P: $89- 119   2P/1B: $89- 129   2P/2B: $109- 129   XP: $17
Location: US 101, exit Oregon expwy & Page Mill Rd, w 2 mi to SR 82, se on SR 82 to Ventura. 3901 El
Camino Real 94306. Fax: 650/494-7833. **Terms:** Reserv deposit; handling fee imposed. **Facility:** 53 rooms.
◆ ◆
Motel
Six 2-bedroom units, $139-$149; 1-2 stories; exterior corridors. **Cards:** AE, CB, DI, DS, MC, VI.
Special Amenities: Free breakfast and free local telephone calls.

HYATT RICKEYS
Phone: (650)493-8000
AAA SAVE
All Year   1P: $174- 244   2P/1B: $199- 269   2P/2B: $199- 269   XP: $25   F18
Location: 3.3 mi s on SR 82 in Palo Alto. 4219 El Camino Real 94306. Fax: 650/424-0836. **Facility:** 344
rooms. Attractively landscaped grounds. A few units with fireplace, balcony or patio. 1-6 stories; interior/exterior
◆ ◆ ◆
Motor Inn
corridors; putting green. **Dining:** Restaurant; 6:30 am-4 & 5-10:30 pm; $10-$19; cocktails. **Services:** area
transportation, within 5 mi. **All Rooms:** combo or shower baths. **Cards:** AE, CB, DI, DS, JC, MC, VI.
(See color ad p 565)

SHERATON PALO ALTO HOTEL
Rates Subject to Change   Phone: 650/328-2800
◆ ◆ ◆
2/1-6/10 & 6/15-1/31   1P: $189- 269   2P/1B: $189- 269   2P/2B: $189- 269   XP: $10   F
Motor Inn
6/11-6/14   1P: $209- 269   2P/1B: $209- 269   2P/2B: $209- 269
Location: Exit US 101 Embarcadero W, to SR 82, 0.5 mi n, opposite Stanford University. 625 El Camino
Real 94301. Fax: 650/327-7362. **Facility:** 342 rooms. Landscaped, tree-shaded grounds. Some units with balcony. 6 whirlpool
rms, extra charge; 4 stories; interior corridors. **Services:** giftshop; area transportation. **Some Rooms:** 14 kitchens.
Cards: AE, CB, DI, DS, JC, MC, VI.

SKY RANCH INN
Phone: (650)493-7221
AAA SAVE
All Year [CP]   1P: $60- 85   2P/1B: $65- 95   2P/2B: $75- 100   XP: $8   D16
Location: 2.5 mi s of Stanford University Campus, on El Camino Real. 4234 El Camino Real 94306.
Fax: 650/493-0858. **Terms:** Reserv deposit, 7 day notice. **Facility:** 27 rooms. 1-2 stories; exterior corridors.
◆ ◆
Motel
All Rooms: combo or shower baths. **Cards:** AE, CB, DI, DS, JC, MC, VI. **Special Amenities:** Free
breakfast and preferred room (subject to availability with advanced reservations).
(See color ad below)

STANFORD TERRACE INN
Phone: (650)857-0333
AAA SAVE
All Year [CP]   1P: $130   2P/1B: $155   2P/2B: $155   XP: $10   F12
Location: W off SR 82; s edge of Stanford University Campus. 531 Stanford Ave 94306. Fax: 650/857-0343.
Terms: Monthly rates. **Facility:** 80 rooms. Sun deck. Kitchens, $170-$195 for up to 2 persons; 2-3 stories; ex-
◆ ◆ ◆
Motel
terior corridors; small pool. **Services:** area transportation, within 5 mi. **All Rooms:** combo or shower baths.
Some Rooms: 13 kitchens. **Cards:** AE, CB, DI, DS, MC, VI.

SUPER 8
Phone: 650/493-9085
AAA SAVE
All Year [CP]   1P: $65- 75   2P/1B: $65- 75   2P/2B: $75- 85   XP: $10   F12
Location: 0.3 mi s of Oregon Expwy. 3200 El Camino Real 94306. Fax: 650/493-8405. **Terms:** Handling fee
imposed. **Facility:** 36 rooms. 4 two-bedroom units, 3 with kitchen; $85-$95 for up to 4 persons; 2 stories; ex-
◆ ◆
Motel
terior corridors. **Some Rooms:** 3 kitchens, no utensils. **Cards:** AE, CB, DI, DS, JC, MC, VI.

TOWNHOUSE INN

(AAA) (SAVE)   All Year [CP]   1P: $76- 98   2P/1B: $85- 105   2P/2B: $94- 106   XP: $8   F12

◆◆◆   Phone: (650)493-4492

Motel   **Location:** Exit US 101 Oregon Expwy; 3 mi w to SR 82 se. 4164 El Camino Real 94306. Fax: 650/493-3418. **Terms:** Reserv deposit. **Facility:** 37 rooms. 4 whirlpool rms, extra charge; 1-2 stories; exterior corridors; indoor whirlpool. **Dining:** Restaurant nearby. **Some Rooms:** 4 kitchens. **Cards:** AE, CB, DI, MC, VI. *(See color ad below)*

RESTAURANTS

CALIFORNIA CAFE BAR & GRILL   **Lunch:** $7-$17   **Dinner:** $13-$24   Phone: 650/325-2233

◆◆◆
Regional
American

Location: Exit SR 82 at Palm Dr, s to Arboroteum, w to Quarry, at Stanford Barn. 700 Welch Rd 94304. **Hours:** 11:30 am-10 pm, Sun 10:30 am-. Closed: 12/25. **Reservations:** suggested. **Features:** casual dress; Sunday brunch; children's menu; cocktails & lounge; a la carte. Contemporary California cuisine. Smoke free premises. **Cards:** AE, DI, MC, VI.

FRESCO RESTAURANT   **Lunch:** $5-$11   **Dinner:** $13-$20   Phone: 650/493-3470

◆◆
American

Location: SR 82, 0.3 s of Oregon Expwy/Page Mill Rd; in Best Western Creekside Inn. 3398 El Camino Real 94306. **Hours:** 6 am-10 pm, Fri-11 pm, Sat 7 am-11 pm, Sun 7 am-10 pm. Closed: 11/25 & 12/25. **Reservations:** suggested. **Features:** casual dress; Sunday brunch; children's menu; cocktails; a la carte. Creative California cuisine, casual atmosphere. Smoke free premises. **Cards:** AE, DI, DS, MC, VI.

MANDARIN GOURMET   **Dinner:** $8-$21   Phone: 650/328-8898

◆◆◆
Chinese

Location: Between University & Lytton. 420 Ramona St 94301. **Hours:** 11:30 am-2:30 pm, 5-10 pm, Sun 5-9:30 pm. Closed: 11/26. **Reservations:** suggested. **Features:** casual dress; cocktails & lounge; minimum charge-7.00; street parking. Modern, attractive atmosphere. Wide variety of traditional dishes. Smoke free premises. **Cards:** AE, MC, VI.

MING'S VILLA   **Lunch:** $8-$12   **Dinner:** $15-$25   Phone: 650/856-7700

◆◆
Regional
Chinese

Location: Exit US 101 Embarcadero Rd e. 1700 Embarcadero Rd 94303. **Hours:** 11 am-3 & 5-9:30 pm, Sat-10 pm, Sun 10:30 am-3 & 5-10 pm. **Reservations:** suggested. **Features:** casual dress; early bird specials; cocktails & lounge; minimum charge-$10. Specialities include dim sum on carts, fresh seafood, Chinese barbecue, Cantonese style. Comfortable seating. Smoke free premises. **Cards:** AE, DI, DS, MC, VI.

SCOTT'S SEAFOOD GRILL & BAR   **Lunch:** $16-$24   **Dinner:** $18-$38   Phone: 650/856-1046

◆◆◆
Seafood

Location: Exit US 101 at Embarcadero Rd E. 2300 E Bayshore Rd 94303. **Hours:** 6:30 am-9:30 pm, Sat & Sun 5-9:30 pm. Closed major holidays. **Reservations:** suggested. **Features:** casual dress; children's menu; early bird specials; cocktails & lounge; minimum charge-$10; a la carte. New England atmosphere; casual dining, pasta, chicken dishes & prime steak. Smoke free premises. **Cards:** AE, CB, DI, DS, MC, VI.

SUNDANCE MINE COMPANY   **Lunch:** $6-$16   **Dinner:** $11-$35   Phone: 650/321-6798

(AAA)
◆◆◆
American

Location: On SR 82 between Oregon Expressway & Embarcadero. 1921 El Camino Real 94306. **Hours:** 11:30 am-2 & 5-10 pm, Sat 5-10:30 pm, Sun 5-9 pm. Closed major holidays. **Reservations:** suggested. **Features:** casual dress; children's menu; early bird specials; cocktails & lounge; minimum charge-$20; valet parking; a la carte. Features steak, prime rib & seafood specials. Comfortable modern atmosphere. Smoke free premises. **Cards:** AE, CB, DI, DS, MC, VI.

PALOS VERDES ESTATES—*See Los Angeles p. 624.*

PARADISE—25,400

LODGINGS

BEST WESTERN TIMBERLINE LODGE   Rates Subject to Change   Phone: 530/876-0191

(FYI)   All Year   1P: $59- 82   2P/1B: $59- 88   2P/2B: $59- 88   XP: $6

Motel   Too new to rate. **Location:** On SR 191, 0.5 mi s of Pearson Rd. 5475 Clark Rd 95969. **Terms:** Reserv deposit. **Facility:** 62 rooms. Scheduled to open November, 1998; 3 stories; interior corridors. **Cards:** AE, DI, DS, MC, VI.

LANTERN MOTEL
Rates Subject to Change
Phone: (530)877-5553
⬥⬥ Motel
5/1-11/1   1P: $48   2P/1B: $48   2P/2B: $51- 56   XP: $5   F2
2/1-4/30 & 11/2-1/31   1P: $42- 44   2P/1B: $44   2P/2B: $46- 51   XP: $5   F2
Location: 1 blk w off Skyway. 5799 Wildwood Ln 95969. **Terms:** Reserv deposit. **Facility:** 16 rooms. Quiet location among pine trees. 1 story; exterior corridors. **Dining:** Coffee shop nearby. **All Rooms:** shower baths. **Cards:** AE, CB, DI, DS, JC, MC, VI.

PARADISE INN
Phone: (530)877-2127
⬥⬥ Motel
Fri & Sat 5/1-12/31   1P: $42   2P/1B: $45   2P/2B: $49   XP: $5
Sun-Thurs, Fri & Sat 2/1-4/30 & 1/1-1/31   1P: $39   2P/1B: $42   2P/2B: $45   XP: $5
Location: 1.5 mi w. 5423 Skyway 95969. Fax: 530/877-2756. **Terms:** Reserv deposit; pets, $5 extra charge. **Facility:** 17 rooms. 6 kitchens, $10 extra charge; 1-2 stories; exterior corridors. **All Rooms:** combo or shower baths. **Cards:** AE, CB, DI, DS, MC, VI. **Special Amenities:** Free breakfast and free room upgrade (subject to availability with advanced reservations).

PONDEROSA GARDENS MOTEL
Rates Subject to Change
Phone: (530)872-9094
⬥⬥⬥ Motel
All Year [CP]   1P: $55- 75   2P/1B: $55- 75   2P/2B: $60- 65   XP: $5   F3
Location: Center; 2 blks e. 7010 Skyway 95969. Fax: 530/872-2993. **Terms:** Reserv deposit; pets, $4 extra charge. **Facility:** 38 rooms. Secluded setting among pine trees. Large, comfortable rooms. 1 story; exterior corridors; whirlpool. **Some Rooms:** whirlpools. **Cards:** AE, CB, DI, MC, VI.

PASADENA—See Los Angeles p. 624.

PASO ROBLES—18,600

LODGINGS

ADELAIDE INN
Rates Subject to Change
Phone: (805)238-2770
⬥⬥⬥ Motel
4/30-10/17   1P: $45- 66   2P/1B: $47- 68   2P/2B: $62- 72   XP: $5
2/1-4/29 & 10/18-1/31   1P: $42- 58   2P/1B: $44- 60   2P/2B: $58- 68   XP: $5
Location: Just w of US 101, exit SR East 461 Fresno, Bakersfield. 1215 Ysabel Ave 93446. Fax: 805/238-3497. **Terms:** Reserv deposit. **Facility:** 67 rooms. Attractively landscaped. 1 two-bedroom unit with microwave, $85-$95; 1-2 stories; exterior corridors; 3 hole micro golf putting green; heated pool, sauna, whirlpool. **Dining:** Restaurant nearby. **All Rooms:** combo or shower baths. **Some Rooms:** whirlpools. **Cards:** AE, CB, DI, DS, JC, MC, VI.

ARBOR INN BED & BREAKFAST
Rates Subject to Change
Phone: (805)227-4673
⬥⬥⬥⬥ Bed & Breakfast
All Year [BP]   1P: $125- 235   2P/1B: $125- 235   2P/2B: $185   XP: $25
Location: 1 mi w of US 101, exit SR West 46, at Treana Winery. 2130 Arbor Rd 93447 (PO Box 3260). Fax: 805/227-1112. **Terms:** Reserv deposit. **Facility:** 9 rooms. Newly built country Victorian Inn, each room with fireplace & balcony overlooking the vineyards. 2 stories; interior/exterior corridors; designated smoking area. **Cards:** MC, VI.

BEST WESTERN BLACK OAK MOTOR LODGE
Rates Subject to Change
Phone: (805)238-4740
⬥⬥⬥ Motor Inn
4/23-10/9   1P: $58- 76   2P/1B: $58- 76   2P/2B: $66- 76   XP: $6   F12
2/1-4/22 & 10/10-1/31   1P: $54- 72   2P/1B: $54- 72   2P/2B: $62- 72   XP: $6   F12
Location: Just w of US 101, exit SR East 461 Fresno, Bakersfield. 1135 24th St 93446. Fax: 805/238-0726. **Terms:** Reserv deposit. **Facility:** 110 rooms. Attractive room decor. 2 two-bedroom units. 2 stories; exterior corridors; heated pool, wading pool, sauna, whirlpool; playground. **Dining:** Coffee shop; 6 am-9 pm; $6-$11; wine/beer only. **Recreation:** small grassy area with picnic tables & barbecue. **All Rooms:** combo or shower baths. **Some Rooms:** whirlpools. **Cards:** AE, CB, DI, DS, MC, VI.

HOLIDAY INN EXPRESS HOTEL & SUITES
[FYI]
Motel

				Rates Subject to Change				Phone: (805)237-6500
Sun-Thurs 4/1-10/16 [CP]	1P:	$59- 129	2P/1B:	$69- 149	2P/2B:	$69- 149	XP: $8-10	F12
Fri & Sat 4/1-10/16 [CP]	1P:	$79- 109	2P/1B:	$79- 129	2P/2B:	$89- 149	XP: $8-10	F12
Sun-Thurs 2/1-3/31 & 10/17-1/31 [CP]	1P:	$55- 99	2P/1B:	$59- 129	2P/2B:	$59- 129	XP: $8-10	F12
Fri & Sat 2/1-3/31 & 10/17-1/31 [CP]	1P:	$59- 99	2P/1B:	$65- 129	2P/2B:	$69- 129	XP: $8-10	F12

Too new to rate. **Location:** Just w of US 101, exit SR East 461 Fresno, Bakersfield. 2525 Riverside Ave 93446. **Terms:** Reserv deposit. **Facility:** 61 rooms. Some rms with wetbar, refrigerator & microwave; 3 stories; interior corridors; heated indoor pool. **Cards:** AE, CB, DI, DS, MC, VI.

MELODY RANCH MOTEL
(AAA)
◆
Motel

				Rates Subject to Change				Phone: 805/238-3911
5/1-10/11	1P:	$38- 44	2P/1B:	$42- 46	2P/2B:	$44- 48	XP: $2	
2/1-4/30 & 10/12-1/31	1P:	$34- 38	2P/1B:	$38- 42	2P/2B:	$40- 44	XP: $2	

Location: US 101 business route, just s of downtown. 939 Spring St 93446. **Facility:** 19 rooms. 1 story; exterior corridors; heated pool open in season. **All Rooms:** shower baths. **Cards:** AE, CB, DI, DS, MC, VI.

PASO ROBLES INN
◆◆
Historic Motor Inn

				Rates Subject to Change				Phone: 805/238-2660
3/1-10/31	1P:	$80	2P/1B:	$80	2P/2B:	$80	XP: $5	
2/1-2/28 & 11/1-1/31	1P:	$60	2P/1B:	$60	2P/2B:	$60	XP: $5	

Location: 0.5 mi w of US 101, Spring St exit. 1103 Spring St 93446. Fax: 805/238-4707. **Terms:** Reserv deposit. **Facility:** 68 rooms. Historic Inn with tree shaded landscaped grounds. 2 stories; exterior corridors. **All Rooms:** combo or shower baths. **Cards:** AE, CB, DI, DS, MC, VI. *(See ad p 790)*

TRAVELODGE PASO ROBLES
(AAA)
◆◆
Motel

				Rates Subject to Change				Phone: (805)238-0078
5/1-10/11	1P:	$44- 58	2P/1B:	$45- 62	2P/2B:	$58- 68	XP: $5	F17
2/1-4/30 & 10/12-1/31	1P:	$40- 52	2P/1B:	$42- 58	2P/2B:	$48- 65	XP: $5	F17

Location: 0.5 mi w of US 101, exit Spring St. 2701 Spring St 93446. Fax: 805/238-0822. **Terms:** Weekly/monthly rates; pets, $4 extra charge. **Facility:** 31 rooms. Tree shaded lawn area. 1-2 stories; exterior corridors. **All Rooms:** combo or shower baths. **Cards:** AE, CB, DI, DS, JC, MC, VI.

RESTAURANT

LOLO'S
(AAA)
◆
Mexican

Lunch: $4-$7 **Dinner:** $5-$8 **Phone:** 805/239-5777
Location: 0.5 mi s on US 101 business route. 305 Spring St 93446. **Hours:** 11 am-8:30 pm, Fri & Sat-9:30 pm. Closed: 11/25, 12/24, 12/25 & Easter. **Features:** casual dress; children's menu; carryout; beer & wine only; a la carte. Casual atmosphere in a restored home. Outdoor patio dining available, weather permitting. Smoke free premises. **Cards:** MC, VI.

PEBBLE BEACH—*See Monterey Peninsula p. 722.*

PERRIS—21,500

LODGING

BEST WESTERN PERRIS INN
(AAA) [SAVE]
◆◆
Motel

							Phone: (909)943-5577
All Year [CP]	1P:	$50	2P/1B:	$55	2P/2B:	$58- 63	XP: $5 F12

Location: On SR 74, just w of I-215, exit 4th St. 480 S Redlands Ave 92570. Fax: 909/943-4328. **Terms:** Reserv deposit. **Facility:** 104 rooms. 3 stories; interior corridors; whirlpool. **Dining:** Restaurant nearby. **Some Rooms:** whirlpools. **Cards:** AE, DI, MC, VI. **Special Amenities:** Early check-in/late check-out and free breakfast.

PESCADERO—900

LODGING

OLD SAW MILL LODGE
◆◆◆
Bed & Breakfast

					Phone: (650)879-0111
All Year [BP]	1P:	$105- 175	2P/1B:	$105- 175	

Location: Exit SR 1 e on Pescadero Rd 2.5 mi; s 0.7 mi on Cloverdale Rd; 2nd left Ranch Rd w is gated; paved & graded 2.5 mi; call ahead for gate access code. 700 Ranch Rd W 94060 (PO Box 96). Fax: 650/879-0656. **Terms:** Check-in 4 pm; reserv deposit, 7 day notice; handling fee imposed. **Facility:** 5 rooms. Beautifully furnished hilltop home on 60 wooded acres; some oceanviews. Hearty country breakfast. Local & home grown fruits. 2 stories; interior corridors; indoor pool. **All Rooms:** combo or shower baths. **Cards:** MC, VI.

PETALUMA—43,200

LODGINGS

BEST WESTERN PETALUMA INN
(AAA) [SAVE]
◆◆
Motel

							Phone: (707)763-0994
All Year	1P:	$72- 82	2P/1B:	$78- 88	2P/2B:	$92- 102	XP: $6 F12

Location: 1 blk e off US 101, Washington St exit. 200 S McDowell Blvd 94954. Fax: 707/778-3111. **Terms:** Reserv deposit, 7 day notice. **Facility:** 75 rooms. Few small rooms. 1 suite $4/1-10/31 $123 & 11/1-3/31 $117 for up to 2 persons; 2 stories; exterior corridors. **Dining:** Coffee shop nearby. **All Rooms:** combo or shower baths. **Cards:** AE, CB, DI, DS, JC, MC, VI. **Special Amenities:** Free local telephone calls and free newspaper. *(See color ad p 792)*

CAVANAGH INN   Phone: (707)765-4657
Rates Subject to Change
AAA
All Year [BP]   1P: $75- 135   2P/1B: $75- 135 2P/2B: $115- 125 XP: $28
Location: Exit US-101 at Washington St, 1 mi w to Keller St. 10 Keller St 94952. Fax: 707/769-0466.
◆◆◆
Bed &   **Terms:** Reserv deposit, 10 day notice. **Facility:** 7 rooms. 1912 Craftsman located near historic downtown. In-
Breakfast   terior corridors. **Dining:** Restaurant nearby. **All Rooms:** combo or shower baths. **Cards:** AE, MC, VI.

QUALITY INN-PETALUMA   Phone: (707)664-1155
AAA SAVE   7/4-9/1 [CP]   1P: $99- 150   2P/1B: $109- 165 2P/2B: $109- 139 XP: $5   F18
5/1-7/3 & 9/2-10/31 [CP]   1P: $84- 135   2P/1B: $94- 145 2P/2B: $94- 119 XP: $5   F18
◆◆◆   2/1-4/30 & 11/1-1/31 [CP]   1P: $69- 125   2P/1B: $74- 130 2P/2B: $74- 99 XP: $5   F18
Motel   **Location:** US 101 northbound exit Old Redwood Hwy-Penngrove, southbound exit Petaluma Blvd
N-Penngrove, e side adjacent to US 101. 5100 Montero Way 94954. Fax: 707/664-8566. **Facility:** 110 rooms.
2 stories; interior/exterior corridors; sauna, whirlpool. **Dining:** Restaurant nearby. **All Rooms:** combo or shower baths.
Some Rooms: whirlpools. **Cards:** AE, DI, DS, JC, MC, VI. **Special Amenities:** Free breakfast and free local telephone
calls. *(See ad p 1041 & p 738)*

RESTAURANT

FINO CUCINA ITALIANA   **Lunch:** $7-$11   **Dinner:** $7-$14   **Phone:** 707/762-5966
◆◆   **Location:** US 101, exit E Washington/Central Petaluma; corner E Washington & Petaluma Blvd N. 208
Italian   Petaluma Blvd N 94952. **Hours:** 11:30 am-2 & 5-10 pm, Sat 5 pm-10 pm. Closed major holidays & Sun.
Reservations: suggested. **Features:** beer & wine only; minimum charge-$7; a la carte. Art deco decor.
Smoke free premises. **Cards:** AE, MC, VI.

PICO RIVERA—*See Los Angeles p. 626.*

PINECREST—500

LODGING

PINECREST LAKE RESORT   Rates Subject to Change   Phone: 209/965-3411
◆◆   All Year   2P/2B: $65- 85
Motel   **Location:** Center. 421 Pinecrest Lake Rd 95364. Fax: 209/965-4032. **Terms:** Reserv deposit, 30 day notice;
handling fee imposed. **Facility:** 27 rooms. 13 two-bedroom units, 8 three-bedroom units. 14 two- & three-
bedroom townhomes, $115-$175 for up to 6 persons. & housekeeping cabins, $95-$140 for up to 6 persons; 1 story; exterior
corridors; 1 tennis court; boat dock, boat ramp. **Recreation:** swimming, boating, canoeing, charter fishing, paddleboats,
sailboating, windsurfing; downhill & cross country skiing; bicycles, hiking trails. **All Rooms:** combo or shower baths.
Some Rooms: 21 kitchens. **Cards:** MC, VI.

PINOLE—17,500

LODGING

DAYS INN-PINOLE
◆
Motel

Rates Subject to Change
All Year [CP]   1P: $59- 65 2P/1B: $59- 65 2P/2B: $59- 65 XP: $5 **Phone: 510/222-9400**
Location: I-80, exit Appian Way, 0.3 mi s. 2600 Appian Way 94564. Fax: 510/669-1614. **Facility:** 50 rooms. 2 stories; exterior corridors. **Cards:** AE, CB, DI, DS, MC, VI.

PISMO BEACH—7,700

LODGINGS

BEACHCOMBER INN
AAA
◆◆◆
Motel
VI.

Rates Subject to Change
All Year   1P: $65- 125 2P/1B: $65- 125 2P/2B: $75- 150 **Phone: (805)773-5505**
Location: Located in center of downtown Pismo Beach from US 101 & SR 1, northbound exit Price St, southbound exit SR 1. 541 Cypress St 93449. Fax: 805/773-0880. **Terms:** Reserv deposit, 3 day notice.
Facility: 7 rooms. Located 1 blk s of the pier. Tastefully decorated rooms with wet bar, microwave & refrigerator. Many rooms with ocean view. 2 stories; exterior corridors; smoke free premises. **Cards:** AE, DS, MC,

BEST WESTERN SHELTER COVE LODGE
AAA SAVE
◆◆◆
Motel

5/1-10/31 [CP]   1P: $118- 198 2P/1B: $118- 198 2P/2B: $118- 198 XP: $10 F12
2/1-4/30, 11/1-12/31 &
1/1-1/31 [CP]   1P: $88- 148 2P/1B: $88- 148 2P/2B: $88- 148 XP: $10 F12
Phone: (805)773-3511
Location: US 101 & SR 1, northbound exit Mattie Rd , southbound exit Price St. 2651 Price St 93449.
Fax: 805/773-3511. **Terms:** Reserv deposit, 3 day notice. **Facility:** 52 rooms. On a high bluff overlooking the ocean. Spacious rooms with balcony & ocean view, 4 with fireplace. 2 stories; exterior corridors; heated pool, whirlpool.
Cards: AE, DI, DS, MC, VI. **Special Amenities:** Free breakfast and free local telephone calls. *(See ad below)*

BEST WESTERN SHORE CLIFF LODGE
AAA
◆◆◆
Motor Inn

Rates Subject to Change **Phone: (805)773-4671**
4/1-10/31   1P: $139 2P/1B: $139 2P/2B: $139 XP: $10
2/1-3/31   1P: $119- 129 2P/1B: $119- 129 2P/2B: $119- 129 XP: $10
Fri & Sat 11/1-1/31 1P: $99- 129 2P/1B: $99- 129 2P/2B: $99- 129 XP: $10
Sun-Thurs 11/1-1/31 1P: $79- 99 2P/1B: $79- 99 2P/2B: $79- 99 XP: $10
Location: From US 101 & SR 1, Northbound exit Mattie Rd, southbound exit Price St. 2555 Price St 93449.
Fax: 805/773-2341. **Terms:** Reserv deposit. **Facility:** 99 rooms. Located on a high bluff with a stairway leading to a sandy cove. Spacious ocean view rooms with balcony or patio. 6 efficiencies, $10 extra charge. 6 two-bedroom suites with efficiency, $195-220 for up to 4 persons; 2-3 stories; interior/exterior corridors; heated pool, sauna, whirlpool. Fee: 2 lighted tennis courts. **Dining:** Shore Cliff Restaurant, see separate listing. **Some Rooms:** 15 efficiencies. **Cards:** AE, CB, DI, DS, JC, MC, VI. *(See color ad p 794)*

THE CLIFFS AT SHELL BEACH
◆◆
Motor Inn
Rates Subject to Change   **Phone:** (805)773-5000
All Year   1P: $110- 190   2P/1B: $110- 190   2P/2B: $110- 190   XP: $5-20
Location: Adjacent to US 101 & SR 1, northbound exit Spyglass Dr; southbound Shell Beach Rd. 2757 Shell Beach Rd 93449. Fax: 805/773-0764. **Terms:** Reserv deposit, 3 day notice; handling fee imposed. **Facility:** 165 rooms. Located on bluff 90 feet above ocean. Spacious, nicely furnished rooms, many with ocean view. 27 whirlpool rms, $275-$375; 5 stories; interior corridors; heated pool. **Services:** giftshop. Fee: massage. **All Rooms:** combo or shower baths. **Cards:** AE, CB, DI, DS, MC, VI. *(See color ad p 795)*

COTTAGE INN BY THE SEA

[FYI]

Motel

Rates Subject to Change

6/11-10/31 [CP]	1P:	$99- 179	2P/1B:	$99- 179	2P/2B:	$99- 179	XP: $10	F12
2/1-6/10 & 11/1-1/31 [CP]	1P:	$79- 159	2P/1B:	$79- 159	2P/2B:	$79- 159	XP: $10	F12

Phone: (805)773-4617

Too new to rate. **Location:** 1 mi n, adjacent to US 101 & SR 1. 2351 Price St 93449. **Facility:** 79 rooms. 1-2 stories; exterior corridors; heated pool. **Cards:** AE, DI, DS, MC, VI. *(See color ad p 797)*

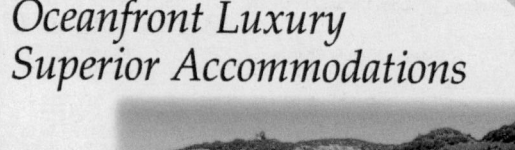

The TourBook & the AAA state map: Together they make beautiful travel music.

EDGEWATER INN & SUITES　　　　　　　　　　　　　　　Phone: (805)773-4811
(AAA) (SAVE)　All Year [CP]　　　　1P: $60- 125　2P/1B: $60- 125　2P/2B: $60- 125
◆◆　　　Location: SR 1, 2 blks w of US 101. 280 Wadsworth Ave 93449. Fax: 805/773-5121. Terms: Reserv
Motel　　deposit; weekly/monthly rates. Facility: 93 rooms. At the beach, 3 blocks n of pier. Many ocean view rooms.
1 two-bedroom unit. 20 one-bedroom apartments, $85-$135 for up to 4 persons; 2-3 stories; exterior corridors;
heated pool, whirlpool. Some Rooms: whirlpools. Cards: AE, CB, DI, DS, MC, VI. Special Amenities: Free
breakfast and free local telephone calls. (See color ad p 795)　　[icons]

KON TIKI INN　　　　　　　Rates Subject to Change　　　　　　　Phone: (805)773-4833
(AAA)　　3/19-10/3 [CP]　　　　1P: $86- 100　2P/1B: $86- 100　2P/2B: $86- 100　XP: $7-14
　　　　2/1-3/18 & 10/4-1/31 [CP]　1P: $76- 90　2P/1B: $76- 90　2P/2B: $76- 90　XP: $7-14
◆◆　　Location: From US 101, southbound exit SR 1; northbound exit Price St, 0.8 mi n. 1621 Price St 93449.
Motor Inn　Fax: 805/773-6541. Terms: Reserv deposit. Facility: 86 rooms. Nicely landscaped grounds with a private
stairway to beach. Ocean view rooms, 4 with gas fireplace. 3-4 stories; exterior corridors; heated pool, sauna,
steamroom, whirlpools; racquetball courts, 2 lighted tennis courts. Dining: Restaurant; 11:30 am-2 & 4-9 pm; $14-$25;
cocktails. Services: Fee: massage. All Rooms: extended cable TV. Cards: AE, DS, JC, MC, VI.　　[icons]

OCEAN PALMS MOTEL　　　　　　　　　　　　　　　　　　Phone: (805)773-4669
(AAA) (SAVE)　Fri & Sat [CP]　　　1P: $55- 105　2P/1B: $55- 125　2P/2B: $55- 135　XP: $5　　F18
　　　　Sun-Thurs [CP]　　1P: $42- 55　2P/1B: $45- 69　2P/2B: $45- 75　XP: $5　　F18
◆◆　　Location: US 101 northbound exit Price St, southbound Hinds St, just s. 390 Ocean View 93449.
Motel　　Fax: 805/773-4917. Terms: Reserv deposit, 3 day notice. Facility: 22 rooms. 3 blocks to beach. 2 stories; ex-
terior corridors; heated pool. Dining: Restaurant nearby. All Rooms: combo or shower baths. Cards: AE,
DS, JC, MC, VI. Special Amenities: Free breakfast and free room upgrade (subject to availability with advanced
reservations).　　[icons]

OXFORD SUITES RESORT　　　　　　　　　　　　　　　　Phone: (805)773-3773
(AAA) (SAVE)　7/1-9/5 [BP]　　　1P: $89- 99　2P/1B: $89- 109　2P/2B: $99- 129　XP: $6-10　F10
　　　　5/1-6/30 & 9/6-10/31 [BP]　1P: $79- 89　2P/1B: $79- 99　2P/2B: $89- 119　XP: $6-10　F10
◆◆◆　2/1-4/30 & 11/1-1/31 [BP]　1P: $69- 79　2P/1B: $79- 89　2P/2B: $89- 109　XP: $6-10　F10
Suite Motel　Location: Adjacent to US 101, exit 4th St. 651 Five Cities Dr 93449. Fax: 805/773-5177. Terms: Pets, $10
extra charge. Facility: 133 rooms. Nicely landscaped, tree-shaded courtyard areas. 1-bedroom suites. 2 stories; exterior corridors; heated pool, wading pool, whirlpool. Services: giftshop; complimentary evening beverages.
Cards: AE, CB, DI, DS, MC, VI. Special Amenities: Free breakfast and free newspaper. (See ad below)　　[icons]

SANDCASTLE INN　　　　　　　　　　　　　　　　　　　Phone: (805)773-2422
(AAA) (SAVE)　6/2-10/31 [CP]　　1P: $119- 179　2P/1B: $119- 179　2P/2B: $119- 179　XP: $10　F18
　　　　2/1-6/1 & 11/1-1/31 [CP]　1P: $69- 159　2P/1B: $69- 159　2P/2B: $69- 159
◆◆◆　Location: 0.3 mi w of SR 1. 100 Stimson Ave 93449. Fax: 805/773-0771. Terms: Reserv deposit; package
Motel　　plans. Facility: 60 rooms. On beach, just s of pier. Many rooms with ocean view, patio or balcony. Suites,
$159-$299; 3 stories; interior corridors; whirlpool. Cards: AE, DI, DS, MC, VI. (See color ad p 797)　　[icons]

SEA CREST RESORT MOTEL　　　Rates Subject to Change　　　　Phone: 805/773-4608
(AAA)　　5/28-9/6　　　　　　　　　　　　　　　　　　　　　　F12
　　　　2/1-5/27, 9/7-10/31 &　　　2P/1B: $79- 175　2P/2B: $79- 175　XP: $10　F12
◆◆　　1/3-1/31
Motel　　11/1-1/2　　　　　　　　　2P/1B: $70- 175　2P/2B: $70- 175　XP: $10　F12
　　　　　　　　　　　　　　　　　2P/1B: $65- 175　2P/2B: $65- 175　XP: $10　F12
Location: US 101 & SR 1, southbound exit SR 1, northbound exit Price St, 1 mi n. 2241 Price St 93449.
Fax: 805/773-4525. Terms: Check-in 4 pm; reserv deposit. Facility: 160 rooms. Many ocean view rooms. Private stairway to
beach. 5 two-bedroom units. 2-4 stories; interior/exterior corridors; heated pool, whirlpool. Dining: Restaurant nearby.
All Rooms: combo or shower baths. Some Rooms: whirlpools. Cards: AE, CB, DI, DS, JC, MC, VI. (See color ad p 798)　[icons]

SEA GYPSY MOTEL　　　　　　Rates Subject to Change　　　　　Phone: (805)773-1801
(AAA)　　7/1-9/5　　　　　　1P: $50　　　　　　　　2P/2B: $85- 110　XP: $10
　　　　3/26-6/30 & 9/6-10/31　1P: $35- 50　2P/1B: $40- 60　2P/2B: $65- 90　XP: $10
◆◆　　2/1-3/25 & 11/1-1/31　1P: $35- 45　2P/1B: $40- 55　2P/2B: $55- 80　XP: $10
Condo Motel　Location: 0.3 mi w of US 101. 1020 Cypress 93449. Fax: 805/773-9286. Terms: Check-in 3:30 pm; reserv
deposit; weekly/monthly rates. Facility: 77 rooms. At beach, 3 blks n of pier. 47 parlor units with kitchen, queen
size murphy bed & sofabed. 30 smaller rooms connect to parlor unit to make a 1-bedroom suite. 3 stories; interior/exterior corridors; small heated pool, whirlpool. All Rooms: combo or shower baths. Cards: AE, DS, MC, VI. (See ad p 798)　[icons]

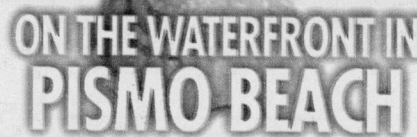

SEAVENTURE RESORT Rates Subject to Change **Phone:** (805)773-4994
◆◆◆ 6/1-8/30 [CP] 1P: $139- 349 2P/1B: $139- 349 2P/2B: $139- 349 XP: $15
Motor Inn 2/1-5/31 & 8/31-1/31 [CP] 1P: $119- 299 2P/1B: $119- 299 2P/2B: $119- 299 XP: $15
93449. Fax: 805/773-0924. **Location:** Just w of US 101, northbound exit Price St, southbound exit Hinds St. 100 Ocean View Ave **Terms:** Check-in 4 pm; reserv deposit; handling fee imposed. **Facility:** 50 rooms. On the beach. 2 blks s of pier. Attractive rooms with gas fireplace, most with balcony & whirlpool. Some ocean view rooms. 2-3 stories; interior corridors; designated smoking area; oceanview; heated pool. **Services:** Fee: massage. **Recreation:** bicycles. **All Rooms:** combo or shower baths. **Cards:** AE, CB, DI, DS, JC, MC, VI. *(See color ad p 799)*

SHELL BEACH MOTEL

Phone: 805/773-4373

AAA SAVE	Fri & Sat 6/1-10/1	1P:	$85- 130	2P/1B:	$85- 130	2P/2B:	$85- 130	XP:	$5
	Sun-Thurs 6/1-10/1	1P:	$75- 120	2P/1B:	$75- 120	2P/2B:	$75- 120	XP:	$5
◆◆	Fri & Sat 2/1-5/31 & 10/2-1/31	1P:	$65- 110	2P/1B:	$65- 110	2P/2B:	$65- 110	XP:	$5
Motel	Sun-Thurs 2/1-5/31 & 10/2-1/31	1P:	$55- 100	2P/1B:	$55- 100	2P/2B:	$55- 100	XP:	$5

Location: 2 mi n in Shell Beach; adj to US 101 & SR 1. 653 Shell Beach Rd 93449. Fax: 805/773-8625. **Terms:** Reserv deposit; pets, credit card guarantee. **Facility:** 10 rooms. 2 blocks from beach. Attractive, charming country decor. 1 small room. 1 story; exterior corridors; heated pool. **All Rooms:** combo or shower baths. **Cards:** AE, DI, DS, MC, VI.

SPYGLASS INN

Phone: (805)773-4855

AAA SAVE	6/11-9/5	1P:	$109- 189	2P/1B:	$109- 189	2P/2B:	$109- 189	XP:	$10	F12
◆◆◆	2/1-6/10 & 9/6-1/31	1P:	$69- 159	2P/1B:	$69- 169	2P/2B:	$69- 169	XP:	$10	F12

Location: Adjacent to US 101 & SR 1, Spyglass Dr exit. 2705 Spyglass Dr 93449. Fax: 805/773-5298.
Motor Inn **Facility:** 82 rooms. Many ocean view rooms. 2-3 stories; exterior corridors; heated pool, whirlpool. **Dining:** Restaurant; 7 am-9 pm, Fri & Sat -10 pm; $13-$24; cocktails. **All Rooms:** combo or shower baths. **Cards:** AE, CB, DI, DS, MC, VI. **Special Amenities:** Free local telephone calls and free newspaper. *(See color ad p 797)*

RESTAURANTS

F MCLINTOCK'S SALOON & DINING HOUSE **Dinner:** $13-$22 **Phone:** 805/773-1892
Location: Adjacent to US 101 & SR 1 between Spyglass Dr & Price St exits. 750 Mattie Rd 93449. **Hours:** 4 pm-10 pm, Sat 3 pm-10:30 pm, Sun 9 am-9:30 pm. Closed: 1/1, 11/25, 12/24 & 12/25. **Reservations:** suggested; Sun-Thurs. **Features:** casual dress; children's menu; early bird specials; carryout; cocktails & lounge; entertainment. Very popular restaurant with ocean view. Informal western atmosphere. Nice selection of steak, ribs, prime rib & seafood. Sunday Ranch Breakfast 9-11:30 am. Also gift shop & butcher shop. Smoke free premises. **Cards:** AE, DS, MC, VI.

GIUSEPPE'S CUCINA ITALIANA Lunch: $6-$9 Dinner: $10-$22 Phone: 805/773-2870
◆◆
Italian **Location:** 891 Price St 93449. **Hours:** 11:30 am-2:30 & 4:30-9:30 pm, Fri-10 pm, Sat & Sun 4:30 pm-10 pm. Closed major holidays & 1st week in Jan. **Features:** casual dress; carryout; cocktails. Southern Italian specialties including wood fired pizzas & homemade bread. Smoke free premises. **Cards:** AE, DS, MC, VI.

OLD VIENNA RESTAURANT Lunch: $5-$8 Dinner: $11-$23 Phone: 805/773-4521
AAA
◆◆
German **Location:** W side of US 101, 0.8 mi s of Spyglass Dr; in Shell Beach area. 1527 Shell Beach Rd 93449. **Hours:** 5 pm-9 pm, Sun-8 pm; also 11 am-4 pm 5/15-10/31. Closed: 1/1, 12/25 & Mon. **Reservations:** suggested. **Features:** casual dress; children's menu; carryout; beer & wine only. A delightful family owned & operated restaurant serving traditional German cuisine. **Cards:** AE, DS, MC, VI.

ROSA'S RISTORANTE ITALIANO Lunch: $6-$8 Dinner: $9-$14 Phone: 805/773-0551
AAA
◆◆◆
Italian **Location:** From US 101, northbound exit Price St, southbound exit Hinds St. 491 Price St 93449. **Hours:** 11:30 am-2 & 4-9:30 pm, Fri-10 pm, Sat 4 pm-10 pm, Sun 4 pm-9:30 pm. Closed: 11/25 & 12/25. **Features:** casual dress; children's menu; carryout; cocktails; a la carte. A charming restaurant featuring a nice selection of pasta, pizza, seafood, chicken & veal. Outdoor patio dining avail. **Cards:** AE, DI, DS, MC, VI.

SEA CLIFFS RESTAURANT Lunch: $8-$13 Dinner: $12-$23 Phone: 805/773-5000
◆◆
American **Location:** Adjacent to US 101 & SR 1, northbound exit Spyglass Dr, southbound exit Shell Beach Rd, at The Cliffs at Shell Beach. 2757 Shell Beach Rd 93449. **Hours:** 7 am-9:30 pm, Fri & Sat-10 pm. **Reservations:** suggested. **Features:** casual dress; Sunday brunch; children's menu; early bird specials; health conscious menu; cocktails & lounge; valet parking. Attractive dining room with ocean view. Selection of seafood,steaks, prime rib & pasta. **Cards:** AE, DI, DS, MC, VI.

SHORE CLIFF RESTAURANT Lunch: $6-$12 Dinner: $11-$22 Phone: 805/773-4671
◆◆
American **Location:** At Best Western Shore Cliff Lodge. 2555 Price St 93449. **Hours:** 7 am-10 pm, Sun Brunch 10 am-2 pm. **Reservations:** suggested. **Features:** casual dress; Sunday brunch; children's menu; early bird specials; cocktails & lounge; entertainment. Located on the edge of a cliff overlooking the ocean. Seafood, beef & chicken. Smoke free premises. **Cards:** AE, DI, DS, MC, VI. (See color ad p 794)

PLACENTIA—41,300 (See map p. 294; index p. 291)

LODGINGS

FAIRFIELD INN BY MARRIOTT Rates Subject to Change Phone: 714/996-4410 ⑬⓪
◆◆
Motel 5/1-9/30 [CP] 1P: $58- 61 2P/1B: $58- 61 2P/2B: $58- 61
 2/1-4/30 & 1/1-1/31 [CP] 1P: $55- 58 2P/1B: $55- 58 2P/2B: $55- 58
 10/1-12/31 [CP] 1P: $52- 55 2P/1B: $52- 55 2P/2B: $52- 55
Location: 0.3 mi w of SR 57, exit Orangethorpe Ave. 710 W Kimberly Ave 92870. Fax: 714/996-4410. **Facility:** 134 rooms. 3 stories; interior/exterior corridors; heated pool. **Cards:** AE, DI, DS, MC, VI. (See color ad p 338)

HOLIDAY INN PLACENTIA Guaranteed Rates Phone: (714)528-7778 ⑬①
◆◆◆
Motor Inn All Year [CP] 1P: $65- 75 2P/1B: $65- 75 2P/2B: $70- 80 XP: $10-20 F18
Location: Just e of SR 57; exit Orangethorpe Ave. 118 E Orangethorpe Ave 92870. Fax: 714/528-4837. **Facility:** 100 rooms. Large, well-appointed rooms. 20 two room suites with refrigerator & wet bar. 10 rooms with whirlpool tub, refrigerator & wet bar. 3 stories; interior corridors; heated pool. **Cards:** AE, CB, DI, DS, JC, MC, VI. (See color ad p 342)

PLACERVILLE—8,400

LODGINGS

BEST WESTERN PLACERVILLE INN Phone: (530)622-9100
AAA SAVE
 4/1-10/31 1P: $69- 79 2P/1B: $69- 79 2P/2B: $84- 94 XP: $10 F17
◆◆◆
Motel 2/1-3/31 & 11/1-1/31 1P: $64- 74 2P/1B: $64- 74 2P/2B: $79- 89 XP: $10 F17
Location: 2 mi w; exit US 50 at Missouri Flat Rd s. 6850 Green Leaf Dr 95667. Fax: 530/622-9376. **Facility:** 105 rooms. Some rooms with view of Sierras. Suites with fireplace, $129-$159 for up to 2 persons; 3 stories; interior corridors; heated pool, whirlpool. **Dining:** Restaurant nearby. **Cards:** AE, CB, DI, DS, MC, VI. **Special Amenities:** Free local telephone calls and free newspaper. (See color ad below)

GOLD COUNTRY INN

Phone: (530)622-3124

5/1-9/30 [CP]	1P:	$60-	74	2P/1B:	$66-	74	2P/2B:	$74-	88	XP: $5-10	F12
2/1-4/30 & 10/1-1/31 [CP]	1P:	$48-	60	2P/1B:	$48-	60	2P/2B:	$58-	64	XP: $5-10	F12

Location: US 50 exit s Schnell School Rd. 1332 Broadway 95667. Fax: 530/622-2080. **Terms:** Reserv deposit, 3 day notice. **Facility:** 45 rooms. Comfortable rooms in center of downtown. 1 two-bedroom unit. 2 stories; exterior corridors. **Dining:** Coffee shop nearby. **All Rooms:** combo or shower baths. **Cards:** AE, DS, MC, VI. **Special Amenities:** Free breakfast and free local telephone calls.

MOTHER LODE MOTEL

Phone: (530)622-0895

5/1-10/31	1P:	$36-	42	2P/1B:	$46-	52	2P/2B:	$45-	60	XP: $5
2/1-4/30 & 11/1-1/31	1P:	$28-	34	2P/1B:	$34-	42	2P/2B:	$38-	48	XP: $5

Location: 2 mi e; adjacent to US 50; exit Point View Dr. 1940 Broadway 95667. **Terms:** Reserv deposit, 3 day notice; small pets only, $5 extra charge. **Facility:** 21 rooms. Some small, modest rooms. 1 story; exterior corridors. **All Rooms:** combo or shower baths. **Cards:** DS, MC, VI. **Special Amenities:** Early check-in/late check-out and free local telephone calls.

NATIONAL 9 INN

Phone: (530)622-3884

Fri & Sat 5/16-9/30 [CP]	Rates Subject to Change									
Fri & Sat 2/1-5/15 &	1P:	$55-	75	2P/1B:	$65-	75	2P/2B:	$75-	90	XP: $5	D
10/1-1/31 [CP]	1P:	$50-	60	2P/1B:	$65-	85	2P/2B:	$75-	90	XP: $5	D
Sun-Thurs 5/16-9/30 [CP]	1P:	$45-	59	2P/1B:	$50-	65	2P/2B:	$65-	80	XP: $5	D
Sun-Thurs 2/1-5/15 &										
10/1-1/31 [CP]	1P:	$35-	49	2P/1B:	$39-	55	2P/2B:	$45-	65	XP: $5	D

Location: Exit US 50 at Schnell School Rd. 1500 Broadway 95667. **Facility:** 24 rooms. 2 stories; exterior corridors. **Dining:** Coffee shop nearby. **All Rooms:** combo or shower baths. **Cards:** AE, JC, MC, VI.

PLAYA DEL REY—*See Los Angeles p. 626.*

PLEASANT HILL—30,700

LODGINGS

COURTYARD BY MARRIOTT-PLEASANT HILL

Phone: 925/691-1444

Sun-Thurs	1P:	$99	Rates Subject to Change		
			2P/1B:	$99	2P/2B:	$99
Fri & Sat	1P:	$64	2P/1B:	$74	2P/2B:	$74

Location: W of I680; southbound exit Gregory Ln; northbound exit Monument Blvd. 2250 Contra Costa Blvd 94523. Fax: 925/691-0616. **Facility:** 135 rooms. 4 whirlpool rms, extra charge; 4 stories; interior corridors; heated indoor pool. **All Rooms:** combo or shower baths. **Cards:** AE, CB, DI, DS, MC, VI.

RESIDENCE INN BY MARRIOTT-PLEASANT HILL

Phone: 925/689-1010

All Year	1P:	$129	Rates Subject to Change		
			2P/1B:	$129	2P/2B:	$159

Location: Exit I-680 Willow Pass Rd, to Taylor W; s Contra Costa Blvd, e on Ellinwood Dr, n on Ellinwood Way. 700 Ellinwood Way 94523. Fax: 925/689-1098. **Facility:** 126 rooms. Comfortable, attractive, fully-equipped units. 28 two-bedroom units. 2 stories; interior/exterior corridors. **Services:** area transportation. **Recreation:** sports court. **All Rooms:** kitchens. **Cards:** AE, DI, DS, MC, VI.

PLEASANTON—50,600

LODGINGS

CANDLEWOOD SUITES

Phone: 925/463-1212

All Year	1P:	$109	Rates Subject to Change	
			2P/1B:	$109

Location: I-580, Hopyard S exit, w on Owen. 5535 Johnson Dr 94588. Fax: 925/463-6080. **Facility:** 126 rooms. 4 stories; interior corridors. **All Rooms:** kitchens. **Cards:** AE, CB, DI, DS, MC, VI.

COURTYARD BY MARRIOTT

Phone: (925)463-1414

All Year	1P:	$129	Rates Subject to Change	2P/2B:	$139	XP: $10	F
			2P/1B:	$129		

Location: I-580 off Hopyard Rd exit, 0.5 mi s. 5059 Hopyard Rd 94588. Fax: 925/463-0113. **Facility:** 145 rooms. Attractive, landscaped courtyard. In room coffee. 2-3 stories; interior corridors. **Cards:** AE, CB, DI, DS, JC, MC, VI.

CROWNE PLAZA-PLEASANTON
Phone: (925)847-6000
Hotel

Mon-Thurs   1P: $129- 139   2P/1B: $139- 149   2P/2B: $139- 149   XP: $10   F18
Fri-Sun   1P: $59- 69   2P/1B: $69- 79   2P/2B: $69- 79   XP: $10   F18
Location: Exit I-580 at Foothill Rd, 0.3 mi s. 11950 Dublin Canyon Rd 94588. Fax: 925/463-2585.
Terms: Monthly rates; small pets only, $50 non refundable dep. **Facility:** 244 rooms. Attractive lobby & public areas. 6 stories; interior corridors; whirlpool. **Dining:** Restaurant; 6 am-2 pm & 5:30-10 pm, Sat 6 am-11 & 5:30-10 pm; $8-$18; cocktails. **Services:** giftshop; area transportation, within 5 mi. **All Rooms:** combo or shower baths.
Cards: AE, CB, DI, DS, JC, MC, VI. **Special Amenities:** Early check-in/late check-out and free room upgrade (subject to availability with advanced reservations). *(See ad p 801)*

EVERGREEN BED & BREAKFAST
Phone: 925/426-0901
Bed & Breakfast

All Year [BP]   1P: $135- 225   2P/1B: $135- 225   Rates Subject to Change   XP: $15   F12
Location: 1680 exit Bernal Ave w; 0.3 mi s on Foothill Rd to Longview Dr. 9104 Longview Dr 94588. Fax: 925/426-9568. **Facility:** 4 rooms. Adjacent to Augustin Bernal Park & the Pleasanton Ridgeland; many hiking & biking trails. 3 stories, no elevator; interior corridors. **All Rooms:** combo or shower baths.
Cards: AE, MC, VI.

FOUR POINTS HOTEL BY ITT SHERATON
Phone: (925)460-8800
Motor Inn

All Year   1P: $199   2P/1B: $199- 209   2P/2B: $199- 209   XP: $10   F19
Location: 0.5 mi e of jct I-680 & I-580, exit I-580 at Hopyard Rd, then 0.5 mi s. 5115 Hopyard Rd 94588. Fax: 925/847-9455. **Terms:** Monthly rates. **Facility:** 214 rooms. Attractive, landscaped garden area. 2 stories; interior corridors; heated pool, whirlpool. **Dining:** Restaurant; 6:30 am-10 pm. **Services:** area transportation, within 7 mi. **Cards:** AE, CB, DI, DS, MC, VI. **Special Amenities:** Early check-in/late check-out and preferred room (subject to availability with advanced reservations). *(See color ad below)*

HILTON PLEASANTON AT THE CLUB
Phone: 925/463-8000
Hotel

Sun-Thurs   1P: $109- 149   2P/1B: $119- 159   2P/2B: $119- 159   XP: $10   Rates Subject to Change
Fri & Sat   1P: $72- 89   2P/1B: $72- 89   2P/2B: $72- 89   XP: $10
Location: In se quadrant at jct I-580 & I-680. 7050 Johnson Dr 94588. Fax: 925/463-3801. **Facility:** 294 rooms. 5 stories; interior corridors; heated pool. Fee: racquetball courts, 18 tennis courts (14 indoor, 4 lighted). **Services:** giftshop; area transportation. **Cards:** AE, CB, DI, DS, JC, MC, VI. *(See ad p 119 & below)*

SUPER 8 LODGE
Phone: 925/463-1300
Motel

All Year   1P: $75- 100   2P/1B: $78- 115   2P/2B: $82- 115   XP: $5   Rates Subject to Change
Location: Exit I-580 at Hopyard Rd, 2 blks s. 5375 Owens Ct 94588. Fax: 925/734-8843. **Terms:** Check-in 4 pm. **Facility:** 102 rooms. 3 stories; exterior corridors. **Cards:** AE, DI, MC, VI.

WYNDHAM GARDEN HOTEL-PLEASANTON
◆◆◆ Sun-Thurs [CP]   1P: $124   2P/1B: $134   2P/2B: $134   XP: $10   F18
Hotel   Fri & Sat [EP]   1P: $69   2P/1B: $69   2P/2B: $69   XP: $10   F18
Rates Subject to Change   Phone: 925/463-3330
Location: 0.5 mi sw of jct I-580 & I-680; exit I-580 at Foothill Rd, 0.3 mi s, then 0.3 mi e on Canyon Way.
5990 Stoneridge Mall Rd 94588. Fax: 925/463-3315. **Facility:** 171 rooms. Opposite Stoneridge Mall. 6 stories; interior corridors. **Cards:** AE, CB, DI, DS, MC, VI. *(See color ad below)*

RESTAURANTS

MAESTRO'S CAFFE ITALIANO   **Lunch:** $7-$20   **Dinner:** $8-$20   **Phone:** 925/463-8773
AAA   **Location:** Exit I-580 Hopyard Rd, 0.3 mi s. 5100 Hopyard Rd 94566. **Hours:** 11:30 am-2:30 & 4:30-9:30 pm,
◆◆   Sat & Sun from 4 pm. Closed major holidays. **Reservations:** suggested. **Features:** casual dress; children's
Italian menu; cocktails & lounge; a la carte. Comfortable attractive surroundings, casual atmosphere; seafood
         specialties. Smoke free premises. **Cards:** AE, DI, DS, MC, VI.

PLEASANTON HOTEL RESTAURANT   Historical   **Lunch:** $7-$15   **Dinner:** $18-$32   **Phone:** 925/846-8106
AAA   **Location:** Downtown, 2 mi e of I-680, Bernal Ave ext. 855 Main St 94566. **Hours:** 11:30 am-2 & 5-9 pm, Fri
◆◆   & Sat-10 pm, Sun 10 am-2 & 4:30-9 pm. Closed major holidays. **Reservations:** suggested.
American **Features:** casual dress; Sunday brunch; children's menu; cocktails & lounge; entertainment. Varied menu. In
         historic 1851 building. Smoke free premises. **Cards:** AE, CB, DI, DS, MC, VI.

PLYMOUTH—800

LODGING

SHENANDOAH INN   Rates Subject to Change   **Phone:** (209)245-4491
AAA   Fri & Sat [CP]   1P: $54- 63   2P/1B: $67- 75   2P/2B: $67- 75   XP: $10   F12
◆◆◆   Sun-Thurs [CP]   1P: $50- 59   2P/1B: $63- 72   2P/2B: $63- 72   XP: $10   F12
Motel   **Location:** 1 mi s on SR 49. 17674 Village Dr 95669. Fax: 209/245-4498. **Terms:** Reserv deposit. **Facility:** 47
         rooms. Comfortable rooms. View of rolling hills dotted with grazing cattle. 1 mini suite Fri & Sat, $95; Sun-
         Thurs, $85 for up to 4 persons; 2 stories; exterior corridors; whirlpool. **Cards:** AE, DI, DS, JC, MC, VI.

It's "Easy Come, Easy Go" when you have AAA's
Emergency Road Service and travel planning benefits behind you.

POINT ARENA—400—See also GUALALA.

LODGING

WHARFMASTER'S INN
◆◆◆
Motel

Guaranteed Rates
Fri & Sat   1P: $95- 175   2P/1B: $95- 175
Sun-Thurs   1P: $95- 150   2P/1B: $95- 150

Phone: 707/882-3171
XP: $20
XP: $20

Location: 1 mi w of SR 1 via Iversen or Port Rd. 785 Port Rd 95468 (PO Box 674). Fax: 707/882-4114.
Terms: Reserv deposit, 5 day notice. **Facility:** 25 rooms. On secluded, quiet hillside overlooking wharf; most units with view, fireplace. 1 two-bedroom unit. 3-bedroom Victorian, $400 for up to 6 persons. 2-room honeymoon suite with wet bar & stereo, $250; 2 stories; exterior corridors. **Recreation:** fishing; hiking trails. **All Rooms:** combo or shower baths. **Cards:** AE, DS, MC, VI.

POLLOCK PINES—1,900

LODGING

STAGECOACH MOTOR INN
(AAA) [SAVE]
◆◆◆
Motel

All Year [CP]   1P: $58- 63   2P/1B: $68- 73   2P/2B: $73- 78 XP: $5   F12

Phone: (530)644-2029

Location: 12 mi e of Placerville; eastbound exit US 50 at Pollock Pines, 1 mi e on Pony Express Tr, westbound exit Sly Park, 1 mi on Pony Express Tr. 5940 Pony Express Tr 95726 (PO Box 657). Fax: 530/644-6937. **Terms:** Reserv deposit; handling fee imposed; small pets only, $5 extra charge. **Facility:** 26 rooms. Forest setting. Nicely landscaped. Suites $105-$125; 2 stories. **Some Rooms:** 6 efficiencies, 2 kitchens. **Cards:** AE, CB, DI, DS, MC, VI. **Special Amenities:** Free breakfast and free local telephone calls.

RESTAURANT

HAVEN RESTAURANT
◆
American

Lunch: $5-$12   Dinner: $9-$19   Phone: 530/644-3448

Location: Off US 50 at Sly Park, 0.5 mi w. 6396 Pony Express Tr 95726. **Hours:** 11 am-4:30 & 5-9 pm. Closed major holidays & 12/10-12/25. **Features:** casual dress; beer & wine only; minimum charge-$4. Variety of sandwiches, omelettes & a few hot entrees. Smoke free premises. **Cards:** MC, VI.

POMONA—See Los Angeles p. 627.

PORTERVILLE—34,800

LODGING

BEST WESTERN PORTERVILLE INN
(AAA) [SAVE]
◆◆◆
Motor Inn

All Year [BP]   1P: $59   2P/1B: $64   2P/2B: $69   XP: $8   F12

Phone: (559)781-7411

Location: Adjacent to SR 190, 0.8 mi e of jct SR 65, s on Jaye St, then e. 350 W Montgomery Ave 93257. Fax: 559/781-8910. **Facility:** 116 rooms. Nicely landscaped pool & courtyard area. 2 stories; interior corridors; heated pool, whirlpool. **Dining:** Restaurant; 6 am-11 pm; $4-$12; cocktails. **Cards:** AE, CB, DI, DS, JC, MC, VI. **Special Amenities:** Free breakfast and free local telephone calls.

RESTAURANT

OAK PIT STEAK HOUSE
◆
Steakhouse

Lunch: $7-$9   Dinner: $10-$21   Phone: 559/781-7427

Location: Just n of the downtown area. 615 N Main St 93258. **Hours:** 11 am-4 & 5-9 pm, Sat 5 pm-9 pm. Closed major holidays & Sun. **Features:** casual dress; children's menu; cocktails & lounge. Western decor. Features a nice selection of steaks & barbecue specialties. Some chicken & seafood entrees also avail. Smoke free premises. **Cards:** AE, DS, MC, VI.

PORT HUENEME—20,300

LODGINGS

CASA VIA MAR INN & TENNIS CLUB
(AAA)
◆◆◆
Motel

Rates Subject to Change
Fri & Sat [BP]   1P: $59   2P/1B: $67   2P/2B: $69   XP: $10   F5
Sun-Thurs [BP]   1P: $55   2P/1B: $63   2P/2B: $65   XP: $10   F5

Phone: (805)984-6222

Location: Just w of Ventura Rd. 377 W Channel Islands Blvd 93041. Fax: 805/984-9490. **Terms:** Reserv deposit; monthly rates. **Facility:** 74 rooms. Some rooms with patio or balcony. Attractive Spanish exterior. 2 stories; exterior corridors; heated pool, whirlpool; 6 tennis courts. **All Rooms:** combo or shower baths. **Some Rooms:** 31 kitchens. **Cards:** AE, CB, DI, DS, MC, VI.

COUNTRY INN AT PORT HUENEME
◆◆◆
Motel

All Year [BP]   1P: $104   Guaranteed Rates
                              2P/1B: $104   2P/2B: $104   XP: $10   F12

Phone: (805)986-5353

Location: Port Hueneme & Ventura rds. 350 E Hueneme Rd 93041. Fax: 805/986-4399. **Facility:** 135 rooms. Nicely furnished rooms. Attractive exterior. 3 stories; interior corridors; small heated pool. **Some Rooms:** 8 kitchens. **Cards:** AE, CB, DI, DS, MC, VI. (See color ad p 765)

PORTOLA—2,200—See also GRAEAGLE.

LODGING

PULLMAN HOUSE
◆◆
Bed &
Breakfast

Rates Subject to Change
5/15-10/15 [BP]   1P: $57- 85   2P/1B: $58- 80 2P/2B: $70- 90 XP: $5-15   F3
2/1-5/14 & 10/16-1/31 [BP] 1P: $52- 63   2P/1B: $58- 70 2P/2B: $73- 80 XP: $5-15   F3

Phone: (530)832-0107

Location: Just s of SR 70 via Gulling St. 256 Commercial St 96122. Fax: 530/832-6323. **Facility:** 6 rooms. Restored 1910 boardinghouse. Deck overlooking RR yard. Small units. 2 stories; interior corridors; smoke free premises. **All Rooms:** combo or shower baths. **Cards:** AE, DI, MC, VI.

POWAY—See San Diego p. 908.

QUINCY—2,600—See also GRAEAGLE.

LODGINGS

THE FEATHERBED
◆◆
Bed &
Breakfast
Guaranteed Rates
All Year [BP]   1P: $75- 120   2P/1B: $80- 90 2P/2B: $95- 130
Phone: (530)283-0102
Location: Downtown; just s of SR 70 at Court St. 542 Jackson St 95971 (PO Box 3200).
Fax: 530/283-0167. **Terms:** Reserv deposit, 6 day notice. **Facility:** 7 rooms. 5 rooms & 2 cottages. 2 stories;
exterior corridors. **Some Rooms:** color TV. **Cards:** AE, DI, DS, MC, VI.
[VCR] [🖨] [ℹ] [✕]

LARIAT LODGE
(AAA) (SAVE)
◆
Motel
All Year [CP]   1P: $47- 50   2P/1B: $54- 57 2P/2B: $57
Phone: 530/283-1000
XP: $6   F16
Location: ON SR 70 & SR 89, south side. 2370 E Main St 95971. Fax: 530/283-2154. **Facility:** 20 rooms.
Forest setting. 1 two-bedroom unit. 2 family units, $68-$75 for 4-6 persons; 1 story; exterior corridors; seasonal
pool. **All Rooms:** combo or shower baths. **Cards:** AE, DS, MC, VI.
[🏊] [🖥] [🗔] [🖨] [🔒] [✕]

RAMONA—13,000

LODGING

RAMONA VALLEY INN
(AAA) (SAVE)
◆◆
Motel
All Year   1P: $49- 75   2P/1B: $53- 75 2P/2B: $58- 85 XP: $5-15   F12
Phone: (760)789-6433
Location: on SR 78, 0.5 mi NE of jct SR 67. 416 Main St 92065. Fax: 760/789-2889. **Terms:** Reserv
deposit; weekly rates; small pets only, $50 fee, in smoking rooms. **Facility:** 39 rooms. 1 two-bedroom unit. 4
efficiencies, $5 extra charge; 2 stories; exterior corridors. **Cards:** AE, DS, MC, VI.
[S▢] [🐾] [🏊] [🗕] [🔒] [✕]

RANCHO BERNARDO—See San Diego p. 908.

RANCHO CORDOVA—42,900   (See map p. 821; index p. 820)

LODGINGS

BEST WESTERN HERITAGE INN
◆◆◆
Motor Inn
Rates Subject to Change
All Year [BP]   1P: $59- 79   2P/1B: $64- 79 2P/2B: $59- 69 XP: $5
Phone: 916/635-4040   [68]
F
Location: 12 mi e of Sacramento; exit US 50 Sunrise Blvd S. 11269 Point East Dr 95742.
Fax: 916/635-7198. **Terms:** Reserv deposit. **Facility:** 122 rooms. Close to Sierra Foothills. 3 stories; interior
corridors; designated smoking area. **Cards:** AE, DI, DS, MC, VI.
[🐾] [🍴] [🏊] [🍴] [🍷] [🔌] [🗕] [🍴] [🖥] [🗔] [🖨] [🔒] [✕]

COMFORT INN
◆◆
Motel
Rates Subject to Change
All Year [CP]   1P: $49- 74   2P/1B: $49- 74 2P/2B: $54   XP: $10
Phone: 916/363-3344   [75]
Location: 9 mi e of Sacramento, exit US 50 at Mather Field Rd. 3240 Mather Field Rd 95670.
Fax: 916/362-0903. **Facility:** 110 rooms. 4 stories; exterior corridors; heated pool. **Some Rooms:** 8
efficiencies. **Cards:** AE, CB, DI, DS, MC, VI.
[SAVE] [🐾] [🍴] [🏊] [🍴] [🔌] [🗕] [🗔] [🖥] [🗔] [✕]

COURTYARD BY MARRIOTT
◆◆◆
Motor Inn
Rates Subject to Change
Sun-Thurs   1P: $119   2P/1B: $129   2P/2B: $129
Fri & Sat   1P: $69   2P/1B: $69   2P/2B: $79
Phone: (916)638-3800   [74]
Location: 11 mi e of Sacramento; s of & adjacent to US 50, Zinfandel Dr exit. 10683 White Rock Rd 95670.
Fax: 916/638-6776. **Facility:** 145 rooms. Attractive Landscaped Grounds. 14 suites, $76-$100 for up to 4 persons; 2-3 stories;
interior corridors; heated pool. **Cards:** AE, CB, DI, DS, MC, VI.
[ASK] [🍴] [🏊] [🍴] [🗕] [🔌] [🍴] [🖥] [🗔] [🗔] [🔒] [✕]

DAYS INN
◆
Motel
Rates Subject to Change
All Year   1P: $45   2P/1B: $50   2P/2B: $55   XP: $5
Phone: 916/638-2500   [66]
Location: US 50, exit Zinfandel Dr, just n. 10800 Olson Dr 95670. **Terms:** Reserv deposit. **Facility:** 136
rooms. 3 stories; exterior corridors. **Cards:** AE, CB, DI, DS, MC, VI.
[SAVE] [🏊] [🍴] [✕]

FAIRFIELD INN BY MARRIOTT
◆◆
Motor Inn
Rates Subject to Change
All Year [CP]   1P: $56- 79   2P/1B: $56- 79 2P/2B: $56- 79
Phone: 916/631-7500   [73]
Location: 11 mi e of Sacramento, s of & adjacent to US 50, Zinfandel Dr exit. 10713 White Rock Rd 95670.
Fax: 916/631-7500. **Facility:** 117 rooms. 3 stories; interior/exterior corridors; heated pool. **Cards:** AE, CB, DI,
DS, MC, VI.
[🏊] [🍴] [CTV] [🍴] [🗕] [🔒] [✕] [♿]

HALLMARK SUITES
◆◆◆
Hotel
Guaranteed Rates
All Year [BP]   1P: $87- 205   2P/1B: $87- 205 2P/2B: $87- 205 XP: $10
Phone: 916/638-4141   [69]
F18
Location: 12 mi e of Sacramento; exit US 50 S Sunrise Blvd. 11260 Point East Dr 95742.
Fax: 916/638-4287. **Facility:** 159 rooms. Few rooms poolside with patio. Close to Sierra Foothills. 3 stories;
interior corridors; designated smoking area; heated pool. **Cards:** AE, CB, DI, DS, MC, VI.
[ASK] [S▢] [🍴] [🍴] [🏊] [🍴] [🔌] [🗕] [🍴] [VCR] [🖥] [🗔] [🖨] [🔒] [✕]

HOLIDAY INN
◆◆◆
Motor Inn
Rates Subject to Change
All Year [CP]   1P: $110- 125   2P/1B: $110- 125 2P/2B: $110- 125 XP: $10
Phone: (916)638-1111   [72]
F19
Location: 12 mi e of Sacramento; exit US 50 via Sunrise Blvd S. 11131 Folsom Blvd 95670.
Fax: 916/635-3297. **Facility:** 130 rooms. Close to Sierra Foothills. 5 stories; interior corridors; heated pool.
Cards: AE, CB, DI, DS, JC, MC, VI.
[ASK] [🍴] [🍴] [🏊] [🍴] [🍴] [🗕] [🍴] [🖥] [🗔] [🖨] [🔒] [✕]

(See map p. 821)

INNS OF AMERICA
AAA SAVE   Phone: (916)351-1213   67
All Year [CP]   1P: $45- 50   2P/1B: $45- 50   2P/2B: $54- 60   XP: $8   F16
◆◆   Location: Exit Hwy 50 at Hazel Ave, then just s. 12249 Folsom Blvd 95670. Fax: 916/351-1817.
Motel   Terms: Pets. Facility: 123 rooms. 3 stories; exterior corridors; heated pool. Dining: Coffee shop nearby.
Cards: AE, MC, VI. Special Amenities: Free breakfast and free local telephone calls.
🛍️🐾📶🖨️🛥️🏄‍♂️🛠️🖥️❌

SHERATON SACRAMENTO RANCHO
CORDOVA HOTEL-SACRAMENTO   Rates Subject to Change   Phone: (916)638-1100   71
◆◆◆◆   All Year   1P: $176- 205   2P/1B: $187- 205   XP: $10   F17
Hotel   Location: 9 mi e of Sacramento, s of & adjacent to US 50; Sunrise Blvd exit. 11211 Point East Dr 95742.
Fax: 916/635-8356. Facility: 265 rooms. Attractive public areas, comfortable rooms. 11 stories; interior corri-
dors; small heated pool. Services: giftshop. Cards: AE, CB, DI, DS, MC, VI.
ASK 🛍️📶🖨️🛥️🏄‍♂️🛠️🖥️🖨️❌

RANCHO CUCAMONGA—101,400

LODGINGS

BEST WESTERN HERITAGE INN   Rates Subject to Change   Phone: 909/466-1111
◆◆◆   4/15-9/30 [CP]   1P: $109- 129   2P/1B: $119- 139   2P/2B: $119- 139   XP: $8   F17
Motel   2/1-4/14 & 10/1-1/31 [CP]   1P: $99- 129   2P/1B: $109- 129   2P/2B: $109- 129   XP: $8   F17
Location: 1.9 mi w of I-15, exit Foothill Blvd/SR 66. 8179 Spruce Ave 91730. Fax: 909/466-3876.
Terms: Reserv deposit, 14 day notice. Facility: 117 rooms. Across from shopping center. 12 one-bedroom suites, 5 with whirl-
pool tub; 6 stories; interior corridors; heated pool. Cards: AE, CB, DI, DS, MC, VI.
📶🖨️🛥️🏄‍♂️🛠️🖥️🖨️🖥️❌

CHRISTMAS HOUSE BED & BREAKFAST INN   Rates Subject to Change   Phone: (909)980-6450
◆◆   All Year [BP]   1P: $80- 180   2P/1B: $80- 180
Historic Bed   Location: 1.5 mi n of I-10, exit Archibald Ave. 9240 Archibald Ave 91730. Terms: Check-in 4 pm; reserv
& Breakfast   deposit, 7 day notice. Facility: 6 rooms. 1904 Queen Anne Victorian house with stained glass, wood carvings,
antique furnishings & landscaped gardens. 2 rooms with private outdoor whirlpool; 1 room with private garden
shower; 2 stories; interior/exterior corridors; designated smoking area. Some Rooms: color TV. Cards: AE, DS, MC, VI.
📺 VCR 🖨️ ❌

RESTAURANTS

CASK'N CLEAVER   Lunch: $6-$10   Dinner: $12-$24   Phone: 909-982-7108
◆   Location: 0.5 mi w of Vineyard Ave. 8689 Ninth St 91730. Hours: 11:30 am-2 & 5-9:30 pm, Fri & Sat-10
American   pm, Sun 4:30 pm-9 pm. Closed major holidays. Features: casual dress; children's menu; salad bar; cocktails
& lounge. Informal Western atmosphere. Nice selection of steak, seafood & chicken. Smoke free premises.
Cards: AE, DS, MC, VI.   ❌

CLAIM JUMPER RESTAURANT   Lunch: $8-$22   Dinner: $10-$23   Phone: 909/899-8022
◆◆   Location: just e of I-15, in Foothill Marketplace, across from Wal-Mart. 12499 Foothill Blvd 91730. Hours: 11
American   am-10 pm, Tue-Thur to 11 pm, Fri & Sat to midnight. Closed: 7/4, 11/25 & 12/25. Features: casual dress;
carryout; salad bar; cocktails & lounge. Generous portions of steak, chicken, ribs & pasta. Old West theme.
Smoke free premises. Cards: AE, DI, DS, MC, VI.   ♿❌

MAGIC LAMP INN   Lunch: $5-$12   Dinner: $10-$25   Phone: 909/981-8659
◆◆◆   Location: On SR 66, 1.3 mi e of Euclid Ave. 8189 Foothill Blvd 91730. Hours: 11:30 am-2:30 & 5-10 pm,
American   Fri-10:30 pm, Sat 5 pm-10:30 pm, Sun 5 pm-9 pm. Closed: 12/25 & Mon. Reservations: suggested.
Features: casual dress; cocktails & lounge; entertainment. Attractive early American decor. Nice selection of
prime rib, steaks, seafood & house specialties. Smoke free premises. Cards: AE, CB, DI, MC, VI.   ❌

SYCAMORE INN   Historical   Dinner: $14-$24   Phone: 909/982-1104
◆◆◆   Location: On SR 66, 1.5 mi e of Euclid Ave. 8318 Foothill Blvd 91730. Hours: 5-10 pm, Fri-11 pm, Sat 5
American   pm-11 pm, Sun 4:30 pm-8 pm. Closed major holidays. Reservations: suggested. Features: dressy casual;
children's menu; cocktails & lounge. Fine dining in historic, popular, long-established restaurant. Extensive
wine list. Smoke free premises. Cards: AE, DI, DS, MC, VI.   ❌

RANCHO MIRAGE—9,800   (See map p. 774; index p. 772)

LODGINGS

MARRIOTT'S RANCHO LAS PALMAS RESORT   Rates Subject to Change   Phone: 760/568-2727   30
◆◆◆◆   2/1-5/31 & 12/31-1/31   1P: $339   2P/1B: $339   2P/2B: $339   XP: $10   F16
9/7-12/30   1P: $259   2P/1B: $259   2P/2B: $259   XP: $10   F16
Resort Hotel   6/1-7/6   1P: $229   2P/1B: $229   2P/2B: $229   XP: $10   F16
7/7-9/6   1P: $159   2P/1B: $159   2P/2B: $159   XP: $10   F16
Location: Just n of SR 111. 41-000 Bob Hope Dr 92270. Fax: 760/568-5845. Terms: Check-in 4 pm. Facility: 450 rooms.
Early California Spanish ambiance. Most guest rooms have view of golf course fairways, lakes & pools. Beautifully landscaped.
2 stories; exterior corridors; putting green; heated pool; playground. Fee: 27 holes golf; 25 tennis courts (8 lighted).
Services: giftshop. Fee: massage. Rental: bicycles. Cards: AE, CB, DI, DS, JC, MC, VI.
🐾📶🖨️🛥️🏄‍♂️❌🛠️🖥️🖨️🖥️❌

THE RITZ-CARLTON, RANCHO MIRAGE   Rates Subject to Change   Phone: (760)321-8282   28
AAA   2/1-4/24 & 12/24-1/31   1P: $375- 525   2P/1B: $375- 525   2P/2B: $375- 525   XP: $25
4/25-6/9 & 9/10-12/23   1P: $240- 405   2P/1B: $240- 405   2P/2B: $240- 405   XP: $25
◆◆◆◆   Thurs-Sat 6/10-9/9   1P: $139- 249   2P/1B: $139- 249   2P/2B: $139- 249   XP: $25
Resort Hotel   Sun-Wed 6/10-9/9   1P: $119- 165   2P/1B: $119- 165   2P/2B: $119- 165   XP: $25
Location: 1 mi s of SR 111. 68-900 Frank Sinatra Dr 92270. Fax: 760/321-6928. Terms: Reserv deposit, 7
day notice; $6 service charge. Facility: 240 rooms. Hilltop location. Elegantly decorated public facilities & guest rooms. 3 sto-
ries; interior corridors; putting green; heated pool, saunas, steamrooms, whirlpool; playground. Fee: 10 tennis courts (6
lighted). Dining: 2 restaurants; 6:30 am-10 pm; $12-$30; cocktails; afternoon tea; also, The Dining Room, see separate
listing. Services: giftshop. Fee: massage. Recreation: basketball, volleyball, croquet court & salon on premises. Cards: AE,
CB, DI, DS, MC, VI.
📶🖨️🛥️🏄‍♂️🏊‍♂️🛠️❌🖥️🛠️🖥️🖨️🖥️❌

(See map p. 774)

THE WESTIN MISSION HILLS RESORT   Phone: (760)328-5955   ㉖

	2/1-4/30 & 1/4-1/31	1P: $359- 450	2P/1B: $359- 450	2P/2B: $359- 450	XP: $25	F18
	5/1-5/25	1P: $259- 370	2P/1B: $259- 370	2P/2B: $259- 370	XP: $25	F18
	9/13-1/3	1P: $225- 340	2P/1B: $225- 340	2P/2B: $225- 340	XP: $25	F18
Resort Hotel	5/26-9/12	1P: $149- 189	2P/1B: $149- 189	2P/2B: $149- 189	XP: $25	F18

Location: 2 mi sw of I-10, exit Bob Hope Dr. 71-333 Dinah Shore Dr 92270. Fax: 760/321-2955. **Terms:** Check-in 4 pm; reserv deposit, 7 day notice; $4 service charge; package plans; small pets only, $100 dep req. **Facility:** 512 rooms. Attractively landscaped grounds, interesting use of water, greenery & contemporary sculptures. Attractive Moroccan architecture, spacious rooms with patio or balcony. Resort service fee, $9; 2 stories; exterior corridors; heated pool, steamrooms, waterslide, whirlpools. Fee: 36 holes golf; 7 lighted tennis courts. **Dining:** Dining room, restaurant; 6 am-11 pm; $11-$24; cocktails. **Services:** giftshop. Fee: massage. **Recreation:** jogging, croquet, soccer & softball field, volleyball. Fee: bicycles. **All Rooms:** extended cable TV. **Cards:** AE, CB, DI, DS, JC, MC, VI.

RESTAURANTS

CONTINENTAL CAFE   **Lunch:** $7-$9   **Dinner:** $10-$19   **Phone:** 760/346-7113   ⑱
◆◆   **Location:** Just n of SR 111; in Rancho Las Palmas Shopping Center. 42-490 Bob Hope Dr 92270.
Continental   **Hours:** 11:30 am-2:30 & 5:30-9:30 pm, Sun 5:30 pm-9:30 pm. **Reservations:** suggested; in season. **Features:** casual dress; cocktails; a la carte. Small charming restaurant serving a selection of seafood, chicken & beef entrees. **Cards:** AE, DI, DS, MC, VI.

THE DINING ROOM   **Dinner:** $22-$36   **Phone:** 760/321-8282   ⑪
◆◆◆◆   **Location:** 1 mi s of SR 111; in The Ritz-Carlton, Rancho Mirage. 68-900 Frank Sinatra Dr 92270. **Hours:** 6
French   pm-10 pm, Fri & Sat-10:30 pm; open Fri & Sat in summer. Closed: Mon & Tues. **Reservations:** suggested. **Features:** semi-formal attire; cocktails; valet parking; a la carte. Dining in formal elegance. French Mediterranean cuisine. Smoke free premises. **Cards:** AE, CB, DI, DS, JC, MC, VI.

KOBE JAPANESE STEAK HOUSE   **Dinner:** $14-$30   **Phone:** 760/324-1717   ⑧
◆◆   **Location:** On SR 111, just e of Frank Sinatra Dr. 69-838 Hwy 111 92270. **Hours:** 5:30 pm-10 pm, Fri &
Ethnic   Sat-11 pm, Sun 5 pm-10 pm. Closed: 11/25. **Reservations:** suggested. **Features:** casual dress; children's menu; early bird specials; cocktails & lounge; valet parking; a la carte. Tepanyaki food preparation & sushi bar. Lively atmosphere. **Cards:** AE, CB, DI, DS, MC, VI.

LAS CASUELAS NUEVAS   **Lunch:** $4-$9   **Dinner:** $10-$15   **Phone:** 760/328-8844   ⑩
     Location: On SR 111, 1 mi e of Frank Sinatra Dr. 70-050 Hwy 111 92270. **Hours:** 11 am-9:30 pm; Fri &
◆◆   Sat-10 pm, Sun 10 am-9:30 pm. Closed: 11/25 & 12/25. **Reservations:** suggested; weekends.
Mexican   **Features:** casual dress; Sunday brunch; children's menu; carryout; cocktails & lounge; entertainment; a la carte. Colorfully decorated dining room & mist cooled outdoor patio. Mariachi music Fri-Sun evenings & Sunday brunch. **Cards:** AE, DI, DS, MC, VI.

LORD FLETCHER INN   **Dinner:** $18-$23   **Phone:** 760/328-1161   ⑭
◆◆   **Location:** 1 mi w on SR 111. 70-385 Hwy 111 92270. **Hours:** Open 2/1-7/2 & 9/1-1/31; 5:30 pm-10 pm, Fri
American   & Sat-11 pm. Closed: 11/25, 12/25, Sun & Mon. **Reservations:** suggested. **Features:** casual dress; children's menu; cocktails; valet parking. Fine English fare served. Old English atmosphere. Smoke free premises. **Cards:** AE, DI, MC, VI.

WALLY'S DESERT TURTLE   **Dinner:** $20-$35   **Phone:** 760/568-9321   ⑮
◆◆◆◆   **Location:** SR 111, just w of Bob Hope Dr. 71-775 Hwy 111 92270. **Hours:** Open 2/1-6/5 & 9/28-1/31; 6:30
Continental   pm-10 pm, Fri & Sat-10:30 pm; 11/1-5/1 luncheon fashion show Fri 11:30 am-2:30 pm. **Reservations:** suggested. **Features:** dressy casual; cocktails & lounge; valet parking; a la carte. Elegant decor & gracious service. Smoke free premises. **Cards:** AE, MC, VI.

RANCHO PALOS VERDES—See Los Angeles p. 628.

RANCHO SANTA FE—See San Diego p. 910.

RANDSBURG—200

LODGING

THE COTTAGE HOTEL BED & BREAKFAST   Guaranteed Rates   Phone: 760/374-2285
◆◆   All Year [CP]   1P: $75- 80   2P/1B: $80- 90   2P/2B: $85- 110   XP: $10-15
Historic Bed   **Location:** In a historical mining district. 130 Butte Ave 93554 (PO Box D). Fax: 760/374-2132.
& Breakfast   **Terms:** Check-in 4 pm; reserv deposit. **Facility:** 5 rooms. Four B&B rooms & one housekeeping cottage with kitchen. Rooms individually decorated in period themes. Antique & gift shop. 1 story; interior/exterior corridors; designated smoking area. **All Rooms:** combo or shower baths. **Cards:** AE, DS, MC, VI.

RED BLUFF—12,400—See also LASSEN VOLCANIC NATIONAL PARK.

LODGINGS

BEST WESTERN GRAND MANOR INN   Rates Subject to Change   Phone: (530)529-7060
◆◆◆   All Year [CP]   1P: $63- 91   2P/1B: $68- 96   2P/2B: $68- 96   XP: $6   F12
Motel   **Location:** Exit I-5 at SR 36E - Susanville/Lassen Park exit, 0.3 mi e to Sale Ln. 90 Sale Ln 96080. Fax: 530/529-7077. **Facility:** 67 rooms. 3 stories; interior corridors. **Cards:** AE, CB, DI, DS, MC, VI.

CINDERELLA RIVERVIEW MOTEL
Guaranteed Rates
Phone: 530/527-5490
All Year [CP] 1P: $28 2P/1B: $32- 44 2P/2B: $34- 44 XP: $4
Location: Exit I-5 at SR 36W, central district; 0.4 mi w on Antelope Blvd. 600 Rio St 96080.
Fax: 530/527-7051. **Terms:** Pets. **Facility:** 39 rooms. Some units face river. Some with balcony. 1 two-bedroom unit. 2 stories; exterior corridors. **Recreation:** fishing. **All Rooms:** combo or shower baths.
Cards: AE, DS, MC, VI.
Motel

THE FAULKNER HOUSE
Guaranteed Rates
Phone: (530)529-0520
All Year [BP] 1P: $60- 85 2P/1B: $65- 90 2P/2B: $65- 90 XP: $15
Bed & **Location:** Exit I-5 at SR 36 W (Central District), 0.5 mi w on Antelope Blvd, just n on Main St, just w to
Breakfast Jefferson St. 1029 Jefferson St 96080. Fax: 530/527-4970. **Terms:** Check-in 4 pm; reserv deposit, 3 day
notice. **Facility:** 4 rooms. 1890 Queen Anne Victorian. 2 stories; interior corridors. **All Rooms:** combo or
shower baths. **Cards:** AE, MC, VI.

I.M.A. RED BLUFF INN
Phone: (530)529-2028
All Year [CP] 1P: $37- 46 2P/1B: $41- 52 2P/2B: $45- 59 XP: $6 F12
Location: Exit I-5, SR 36W-Central District; just s on Gilmore Rd. 30 Gilmore Rd 96080. Fax: 530/527-1702.
Terms: Pets, $20 dep req. **Facility:** 60 rooms. 2 stories; exterior corridors. **Dining:** Coffee shop nearby.
Motel **Cards:** AE, CB, DI, DS, JC, MC, VI. **Special Amenities:** Early check-in/late check-out and free room
upgrade (subject to availability with advanced reservations). IMA. (See color ad p 286)

LAMPLIGHTER LODGE
Rates Subject to Change
Phone: (530)527-1150
All Year [CP] 1P: $35- 38 2P/1B: $44- 48 2P/2B: $44- 50 XP: $4 F12
Location: I-5 exit via business loop. 210 S Main St 96080. Fax: 530/527-5878. **Facility:** 50 rooms. Few large
rooms. 2 stories; exterior corridors; heated pool. **Dining:** Restaurant nearby. **All Rooms:** combo or shower
Motel baths. **Cards:** AE, CB, DI, DS, JC, MC, VI.

RELAX INN
Phone: (530)527-3545
All Year 1P: $25- 40 2P/1B: $30- 45 2P/2B: $32- 46 XP: $4 F12
Location: Exit I-5 at SR 36W (Central District), 0.5 mi w on Antelope Blvd, 0.7 mi s. 250 S Main St 96080.
Fax: 530/527-3035. **Terms:** Reserv deposit. **Facility:** 34 rooms. 1 story; exterior corridors.
Motel **Dining:** Restaurant nearby. **All Rooms:** combo or shower baths. **Cards:** AE, DS, MC, VI.
Special Amenities: Early check-in/late check-out and free room upgrade (subject to availability with
advanced reservations).

SUPER 8 MOTEL
Rates Subject to Change
Phone: (530)527-8882
All Year 1P: $39- 49 2P/1B: $45- 55 2P/2B: $45- 55 XP: $6 F12
Location: Exit I-5 at SR 36 E, Susanville/Lassen Park exit. 203 Antelope Blvd 96080. Fax: 530/527-5078.
Motel **Facility:** 72 rooms. 2 stories; interior corridors. **Cards:** AE, CB, DI, DS, MC, VI.

TRAVELODGE RED BLUFF
Phone: (530)527-6020
All Year [CP] 1P: $39- 49 2P/1B: $45- 55 2P/2B: $49- 59 XP: $6 F12
Location: Exit I-5 at SR 36W (Central District), 0.2 mi w on Antelope Blvd. 38 Antelope Blvd 96080.
Fax: 530/527-4653. **Terms:** Reserv deposit, 10 day notice; pets, $15 dep req. **Facility:** 41 rooms. Spacious
Motel grassy area located adjacent to the Sacramento River. 2 stories; exterior corridors. **Dining:** Coffee shop
nearby. **All Rooms:** combo or shower baths. **Cards:** AE, CB, DI, DS, MC, VI. **Special Amenities:** Free
local telephone calls and free room upgrade (subject to availability with advanced reservations).
(See color ad below)

RESTAURANT

J & C GREEN BARN RESTAURANT
Lunch: $5-$7 **Dinner:** $6-$15 **Phone:** 530/527-3161
Location: SR 36E, Susanville/Lassen Park exit; 1 mi e. 5 Chestnut Ave 96080. **Hours:** 11 am-9 pm, Sat-10
pm, Sun 4 pm-9 pm. Closed major holidays. **Features:** casual dress; cocktails & lounge. Long established,
family atmosphere, varied menu. **Cards:** AE, DI, MC, VI.
Steakhouse

REDCREST

LODGING

REDCREST RESORT
AAA
◆ ◆
Cottage

Rates Subject to Change   **Phone:** 707/722-4208
4/1-10/26   1P: $45- 49 2P/1B: $45- 49 2P/2B: $58- 79
2/1-3/31 & 10/27-1/31 1P: $35- 39 2P/1B: $35- 39 2P/2B: $45- 65
Location: Exit US 101 at Redcrest, just n. 26459 Avenue of the Giants 95569 (PO Box 235).
Fax: 707/722-4403. **Terms:** Pets, $5 extra charge. **Facility:** 10 rooms. 1 story; exterior corridors; designated
smoking area; whirlpool; playground. **Dining:** Restaurant nearby. **All Rooms:** shower baths.
Some Rooms: 7 kitchens. **Cards:** MC, VI.

REDDING—66,500—See also *LASSEN VOLCANIC NATIONAL PARK.*

LODGINGS

BEST WESTERN HILLTOP INN   **Phone:** (530)221-6100
AAA SAVE
◆ ◆ ◆
Motor Inn

All Year [BP]   1P: $79- 99 2P/1B: $89- 109 2P/2B: $89- 109 XP: $10   F16
Location: Exit I-5 Cypress Ave E; 0.3 mi n. 2300 Hilltop Dr 96002. Fax: 530/221-2867. **Terms:** Reserv
deposit. **Facility:** 114 rooms. Attractive comfortable rooms. 2 stories; exterior corridors; heated pool, whirlpool.
Dining: Coffee shop; 6 am-11:30 pm; $9-$16; cocktails; also, C.R. Gibbs Restaurant, see separate listing.
Cards: AE, CB, DI, DS, MC, VI. **Special Amenities:** Free breakfast and free local telephone calls.
(See ad below)

BEST WESTERN HOSPITALITY HOUSE   **Phone:** (530)241-6464
AAA SAVE
◆ ◆
Motel

All Year [BP]   1P: $69- 79 2P/1B: $69- 79 2P/2B: $69- 79
Location: W of I-5; northbound exit Lake Blvd 0.5 mi to Market, 0.5 mi s; southbound exit Market St, 2 mi s.
532 N Market St 96003. Fax: 530/244-1998. **Terms:** Pets, $25 dep req, $6 extra charge. **Facility:** 63 rooms.
2 stories; exterior corridors. **Dining:** Restaurant nearby. **All Rooms:** combo or shower baths. **Cards:** AE,
CB, DI, DS, JC, MC, VI. **Special Amenities:** Free breakfast and free local telephone calls.

BEST WESTERN PONDEROSA INN   **Phone:** (530)241-6300
◆ ◆
Motor Inn

Rates Subject to Change
All Year   1P: $44- 53 2P/1B: $50- 59 2P/2B: $52- 64 XP: $6   F12
Location: 1.5 mi w of I-5, Cypress Ave exit. 2220 Pine St 96001. Fax: 530/241-4959. **Facility:** 69 rooms. 1
two-bedroom unit. 2 stories; exterior corridors. **Cards:** AE, CB, DI, DS, MC, VI.

COMFORT INN   **Phone:** (530)221-6530
◆ ◆
Motel

Rates Subject to Change
All Year [CP]   1P: $49- 56 2P/1B: $54- 61 2P/2B: $56- 64 XP: $6   F12
Location: Exit I-5 Cypress Ave E; 0.3 mi n. 2059 Hilltop Dr 96002. Fax: 530/221-3687. **Facility:** 90 rooms. In-
room coffee. 2 stories; exterior corridors; small pool. **Cards:** AE, CB, DI, DS, MC, VI.

DOUBLETREE HOTEL   **Phone:** (530)221-8700
◆ ◆ ◆
Motor Inn

Rates Subject to Change
7/1-9/30   1P: $87- 115 2P/1B: $87- 115 2P/2B: $87- 115
2/1-6/30 & 10/1-1/31   1P: $85- 100 2P/1B: $85- 100 2P/2B: $85- 100
Location: Exit I-5 via SR 44 & 299 Hilltop Dr. 1830 Hilltop Dr 96002. Fax: 530/221-0324. **Facility:** 193 rooms.
Many large units with balcony or patio. 2 stories; interior corridors. **Services:** giftshop. **All Rooms:** combo or shower baths.
Cards: AE, CB, DI, DS, JC, MC, VI.

GRAND MANOR INN   **Phone:** (530)221-4472
◆ ◆ ◆
Motel

Rates Subject to Change
All Year [CP]   1P: $63- 83 2P/1B: $68- 93 2P/2B: $68- 93 XP: $6   F12
Location: Exit I-5 Cypress Ave E; 0.8 mi n on Hilltop Dr. 850 Mistletoe Ln 96002. Fax: 530/222-8106.
Facility: 71 rooms. 3 stories; interior corridors. **All Rooms:** combo or shower baths. **Cards:** AE, CB, DI, DS,
MC, VI.

HOLIDAY INN   **Phone:** (530)221-7500
◆ ◆ ◆
Motel

Rates Subject to Change
All Year   1P: $89- 119 2P/1B: $99- 129 2P/2B: $99- 129 XP: $10   F12
Location: I-5 exit 44/299 Hilltop just s. 1900 Hilltop Dr 96002. Fax: 530/223-9644. **Facility:** 126 rooms. 2 sto-
ries; interior corridors. **All Rooms:** combo or shower baths. **Cards:** AE, CB, DI, DS, MC, VI.

HOLIDAY INN EXPRESS

Phone: (530)241-5500

	1P:		2P/1B:		2P/2B:		XP:		
9/8-12/31 [BP]	1P:	$69- 79	2P/1B:	$69- 79	2P/2B:	$69- 79	XP: $10		F19
5/1-9/7 [BP]	1P:	$74	2P/1B:	$74	2P/2B:	$74- 79	XP: $10		F19
2/1-4/30 & 1/1-1/31 [CP]	1P:	$59- 69	2P/1B:	$59- 69	2P/2B:	$59- 69			

(AAA) (SAVE) ◆◆ Motel

Location: W of I-5, exit Twin View Blvd. 1080 Twin View Blvd 96003. Fax: 530/241-5674. **Terms:** Pets, $20 extra charge. **Facility:** 50 rooms. 4 whirlpool rms, extra charge; 2 stories; interior corridors. **Cards:** AE, CB, DI, DS, JC, MC, VI. **Special Amenities: Early check-in/late check-out and free breakfast.** *(See color ad below)*

HOWARD JOHNSON EXPRESS

Phone: (530)223-1935

	1P:		2P/1B:		2P/2B:		XP:	
All Year [CP]	1P:	$44- 49	2P/1B:	$49- 54	2P/2B:	$54- 59	XP: $5-10	F

(AAA) (SAVE) ◆◆ Motel

Location: Exit I-5 at Cypress Ave W; 0.5 mi s on Bechelli. 2731 Bechelli Ln 96002. Fax: 530/223-1176. **Facility:** 75 rooms. 2 stories; exterior corridors. **Cards:** AE, CB, DI, DS, MC, VI. **Special Amenities: Free breakfast and free local telephone calls.** *(See color ad below & opposite inside back cover)*

LA QUINTA INN

Phone: (530)221-8200

◆◆◆ Motor Inn

Rates Subject to Change

	1P:		2P/1B:		2P/2B:	
All Year [CP]	1P:	$59- 72	2P/1B:	$59- 72	2P/2B:	$59- 72

Location: Exit I-5 Cypress East, 0.5 mi n. 2180 Hilltop Dr 96002. Fax: 530/223-4727. **Facility:** 140 rooms. 3 stories; interior corridors; heated pool. **All Rooms:** combo or shower baths. **Cards:** AE, CB, DI, DS, JC, MC, VI.

OXFORD SUITES

Phone: (530)221-0100

◆◆◆ Motel

Guaranteed Rates

	1P:		2P/1B:		2P/2B:		XP:		
All Year [BP]	1P:	$76- 76	2P/1B:	$80- 84	2P/2B:	$84- 90	XP: $7		F10

Location: Exit I-5 Cypress E, 0.5 mi n. 1967 Hilltop Dr 96002. Fax: 530/221-8265. **Facility:** 139 rooms. 2 two-bedroom units. 1 whirlpool rm, extra charge; 3-4 stories; interior/exterior corridors. **Cards:** AE, CB, DI, DS, MC, VI.

RIVER INN

Phone: 530/241-9500

◆◆ Motel

All Year

	1P:		2P/1B:		2P/2B:		XP:		
	1P:	$40- 60	2P/1B:	$46- 70	2P/2B:	$50- 70	XP: $5		F16

Location: Exit I-5 at SR 299 W, 1 mi w, exit at Park Marina Dr. 1835 Park Marina Dr 96001. Fax: 530/241-5345. **Facility:** 79 rooms. Few rooms with river view. 3 king units with whirlpool, $90; 2 stories; exterior corridors. **Cards:** AE, CB, DI, DS, MC, VI.

SUPER 8 MOTEL

Phone: (530)221-8881

◆◆ Motel

Guaranteed Rates

	1P:		2P/1B:		2P/2B:		XP:		
Fri & Sat 5/1-9/6 [CP]	1P:	$53- 55	2P/1B:	$58- 60	2P/2B:	$62- 64	XP: $5		F12
Sun-Thurs 5/1-9/6 & 9/7-1/31 [CP]	1P:	$50- 52	2P/1B:	$55- 57	2P/2B:	$59- 61	XP: $5		F12
2/1-4/30 [CP]	1P:	$48- 50	2P/1B:	$53- 55	2P/2B:	$57- 59	XP: $5		F12

Location: I-5, Churn Creek Rd E exit. 5175 Churn Creek Rd 96002. Fax: 530/221-8881. **Facility:** 80 rooms. Some small rooms. 2 stories; interior corridors. **Cards:** AE, CB, DI, DS, MC, VI.

VAGABOND INN
AAA SAVE

7/1-10/15 [CP]	1P:	$66	2P/1B:	$71	2P/2B:	$76	XP: $5 F18
2/1-6/30 & 10/16-1/31 [CP]	1P:	$55	2P/1B:	$60	2P/2B:	$65	XP: $5 F18

◆◆
Motel
Phone: (530)223-1600
Location: W off I-5 via Cypress Ave. 536 E Cypress Ave 96002. Fax: 530/221-4247. **Terms:** Pets, $5 extra charge. **Facility:** 71 rooms. 2 stories; exterior corridors; seasonal pool. **Dining:** Coffee shop nearby. **Cards:** AE, CB, DI, DS, MC, VI. **Special Amenities:** Free breakfast and free local telephone calls.

RESTAURANTS

C.R. GIBBS RESTAURANT   **Lunch:** $4-$10   **Dinner:** $13-$22   Phone: 530/221-2335
◆◆
American
Location: Exit I-5 Cypress Ave E; 0.3 mi n; in Best Western Hilltop Inn. 2300 Hilltop Dr 96002. **Hours:** 6 am-10 & 11-10 pm, Sun-9 pm. Closed: 12/25. **Reservations:** suggested. **Features:** casual dress; children's menu; cocktails & lounge. Varied menu; featuring peeled shrimp appetizers. Smoke free premises. **Cards:** AE, CB, DI, MC, VI.

DE MECURIO'S RESTAURANT   **Dinner:** $10-$20   Phone: 530/222-1307
◆◆
Continental
Location: 1 mi e of I-5, exit Cypress Ave, just e to Churn Creek, 0.4 mi s to Hartnell, 05. mi e. 1647 Hartnell Ave 96002. **Hours:** 5 pm-10 pm. Closed: 12/25. **Reservations:** suggested. **Features:** casual dress; cocktails. Specializing in French, Italian & American dishes. Quiet comfortable atmosphere. Smoke free premises. **Cards:** AE, DI, DS, MC, VI.

HATCH COVER   **Lunch:** $4-$8   **Dinner:** $6-$20   Phone: 530/223-5606
◆◆
Steak and
Seafood
Location: Exit I-5 Cypress Ave W; 0.5 mi n on Hemsted Dr. 202 Hemsted Dr 96002. **Hours:** 11:30 am-2 & 5:30-9:30 pm, Fri-10 pm, Sat 5:30 pm-10 pm, Sun 5 pm-9 pm. Closed: 1/1, 11/25 & 12/25. **Features:** casual dress; cocktails & lounge; minimum charge-$6. Menu variety of fresh fish & clams, seafood, prime rib, chicken, pasta & beef. Smoke free premises. **Cards:** AE, DI, MC, VI.

REDLANDS—60,400

LODGINGS

BEST WESTERN SANDMAN MOTEL   Phone: (909)793-2001
AAA SAVE

All Year	1P:	$40- 85	2P/1B:	$45- 95	2P/2B:	$56- 66	XP: $10 F12

◆◆
Motel
Location: Adjacent to I-10, exit Tennessee St, just s, then e. 1120 W Colton Ave 92374. Fax: 909/792-7612. **Terms:** Weekly rates; small pets only, $50 dep req. **Facility:** 65 rooms. 2 stories; exterior corridors; heated pool, whirlpool. **Dining:** Restaurant nearby. **Some Rooms:** 5 efficiencies. **Cards:** AE, CB, DI, DS, JC, MC, VI. **Special Amenities:** Free breakfast and free local telephone calls. *(See ad below)*

DYNASTY SUITES-REDLANDS   Guaranteed Rates   Phone: (909)793-6648
AAA FYI

All Year [BP]	1P:	$47- 53	2P/1B:	$47- 53	2P/2B:	$55- 60	XP: $5-10 D12

Motel
Under major renovation. **Location:** Just sw of I-10, exit Tennessee St. 1235 W Colton Ave 92374. Fax: 909/798-0880. **Terms:** Weekly/monthly rates; small pets only, $10 extra charge. **Facility:** 55 rooms. 1-2 stories; exterior corridors; heated pool. **Dining:** Restaurant nearby. **Cards:** AE, CB, DI, DS, JC, MC, VI.

GOOD NITE INN   Phone: (909)793-3723
AAA SAVE

All Year	1P:	$36	2P/1B:	$42	2P/2B:	$48	XP: $6 F18

◆
Motel
Location: South side of I-10, just w of Alabama St exit. 1675 Industrial Park Ave 92374. Fax: 909/793-0172. **Terms:** Weekly rates; small pets only. **Facility:** 100 rooms. 2 large units, $57; 2 stories; exterior corridors; whirlpool. **All Rooms:** extended cable TV. **Cards:** AE, CB, DI, DS, JC, MC, VI. **Special Amenities:** Free local telephone calls.

REDLANDS MOTOR LODGE   Rates Subject to Change   Phone: 909/798-2432
AAA

All Year	1P:	$35	2P/1B:	$39	2P/2B:	$45	XP: $4 F12

◆
Motel
Location: Just n of I-10, exit Alabama St. 1151 Arizona St 92374. Fax: 909/798-4691. **Facility:** 30 rooms. 5 whirlpool rms, extra charge; 2 stories; exterior corridors. **Dining:** Restaurant nearby. **All Rooms:** combo or shower baths. **Cards:** AE, CB, DI, DS, MC, VI.

SUPER 8 MOTEL
Phone: (909)335-1612
Ⓐ ⓈⒶⓋⒺ
All Year [BP]　　1P: $35- 40　2P/1B: $38- 43　2P/2B: $43- 50　XP:$5-10　F12
Location: N side of I-10, exit Alabama Ave. 1160 Arizona St 92374. Fax: 909/792-8779. **Facility:** 80 rooms. 2
stories; exterior corridors; heated pool. **Dining:** Restaurant nearby. **All Rooms:** shower baths, extended
cable TV. **Cards:** AE, CB, DI, DS, JC, MC, VI. **Special Amenities: Free breakfast and free newspaper.**
◆
Motel

RESTAURANTS

DILLON'S　　　　**Lunch:** $7-$11　　　**Dinner:** $11-$21　　Phone: 909/793-2221
◆◆
Location: 2 mi e, adjacent to I-10, exit Ford St. 1045 Parkford Dr 92373. **Hours:** 11:30 am-9 pm, Fri &
American
Sat-10 pm, Sun 10 am-2 & 4-9 pm. **Features:** casual dress; Sunday brunch; children's menu; early bird
specials; cocktails & lounge; entertainment. Nice selection of steak, prime rib, seafood & pasta. **Cards:** AE,
DS, MC, VI.

ISABELL'S RISTORANTE ITALIANO　　**Lunch:** $7-$13　　**Dinner:** $8-$16　　Phone: 909/792-2767
◆◆
Location: Just s of I-10, westbound exit 6th St, eastbound exit Orange; in Mission Plaza. 330 N 6th St
Italian
92373. **Hours:** 11 am-2 & 4:30-9 pm, Sat & Sun 4:30 pm-9 pm. Closed major holidays. **Features:** casual
dress; carryout; beer & wine only. Nice selection of pasta, veal, seafood & chicken. Smoke free premises.
Cards: AE, CB, DI, DS, MC, VI.

JOE GREENSLEEVES　　　　　**Dinner:** $17-$25　　　　Phone: 909/792-6969
◆◆◆
Location: 3 blks s of I-10. 222 N Orange St 92373. **Hours:** 5 pm-9:30 pm, Fri & Sat II:30 am-2 & 5-9:30 pm.
American
Closed: 1/1, 12/25 & Mon. **Reservations:** suggested. **Features:** casual dress; beer & wine only. A
charming restaurant in a restored downtown building. Interesting selection of seafood, beef, pasta &
specialty items. Large selection of California wines. Smoke free premises. **Cards:** AE, DI, DS, MC, VI.

UMBERTO'S RESTAURANT　　**Lunch:** $7-$13　　**Dinner:** $10-$20　　Phone: 909/335-1466
◆◆◆
Location: Downtown, just s of I-10. 101 E Redlands Blvd 92373. **Hours:** 11:30 am-3 & 5-9 pm, Sat 5 pm-10
Italian
pm, Sun 11:30 am-2:30 & 5-9 pm. Closed major holidays. **Reservations:** suggested. **Features:** casual
dress; Sunday brunch; cocktails & lounge; a la carte. Attractive restaurant featuring a nice variety of Italian &
Continental cuisine. Smoke free premises. **Cards:** AE, CB, DI, MC, VI.

THE WILD RABBIT　　**Lunch:** $7-$14　　　**Dinner:** $15-$22　　Phone: 909/793-2038
◆◆◆
Location: Barton Rd at Alabama, in Brookside Plaza. 1502 Barton Rd 92373. **Hours:** 8 am-9 pm, Fri &
American
Sat-9:30 pm. Closed: 12/25. **Reservations:** suggested. **Features:** beer & wine only. A charming, cozy
restaurant serving a nice variety of entrees. Smoke free premises. **Cards:** AE, MC, VI.

REDONDO BEACH—See Los Angeles p. 628.

REDWAY—1,200

LODGING

DEAN CREEK RESORT
Phone: (707)923-2555
Ⓐ ⓈⒶⓋⒺ
5/1-10/31　　　1P: $62- 103　2P/1B:　$62- 103　2P/2B:　$62- 103　XP:　$5　F
2/1-4/30 & 11/1-1/31　1P: $48- 80　2P/1B:　$48- 80　2P/2B:　$48- 80　XP:　$5　F
◆◆
Location: 3 mi n, n exit US 101 Redwood Dr W; s exit US 101 Redway/Shelter Cove. 4112 Redwood Dr
Motel
95560. Fax: 707/923-2547. **Terms:** Reserv deposit. **Facility:** 11 rooms. 5 efficiencies, $72-$105 for up to 2
persons; 1 story; exterior corridors; sauna, whirlpool. **All Rooms:** combo or shower baths. **Cards:** MC, VI.
**Special Amenities: Free local telephone calls and preferred room (subject to availability with advanced
reservations).**

REDWOOD CITY—66,100　(See map p. 922; index p. 917)

LODGINGS

BEST WESTERN EXECUTIVE SUITES
Phone: (650)366-5794　🔲199
Ⓐ ⓈⒶⓋⒺ
All Year　　　1P: $89- 135　2P/1B: $99- 135　2P/2B: $99- 150
Location: Exit US 101 at SR 84 w 1 mi, 1.5 mi s on SR 82, then just e. 25 5th Ave 94063.
◆◆◆
Fax: 650/365-1429. **Facility:** 28 rooms. Attractive comfortable rooms. 2 stories; exterior corridors; sauna,
Motel
steamroom, whirlpool. **Some Rooms:** efficiency, whirlpools. **Cards:** AE, CB, DI, DS, MC, VI.
Special Amenities: Free breakfast and free newspaper.

(See map p. 922)

BEST WESTERN INN
Phone: (650)366-3808   [201]

AAA SAVE   All Year [CP]   1P: $89- 135   2P/1B: $89- 135   2P/2B: $95- 150   XP: $10   F18
◆◆◆   **Location:** US 101, exit Whipple 0.5 mi w to SR 82, n 0.3 mi. 316 El Camino Real 94062.
Motel   Fax: 650/364-9380. **Terms:** Handling fee imposed. **Facility:** 31 rooms. 2 stories; exterior corridors; small pool. **Dining:** Coffee shop nearby. **Cards:** AE, CB, DI, DS, JC, MC, VI. **Special Amenities: Free breakfast and free local telephone calls.** *(See color ad p 812)*

COMFORT INN
Rates Subject to Change   **Phone: (650)599-9636**   [204]

AAA   All Year [CP]   1P: $99- 150   2P/1B: $99- 150   2P/2B: $109- 150   XP: $15   F18
◆◆   **Location:** US 101, exit Whipple Ave, 0.5 mi w, 1 mi s. 1818 El Camino Real 94063. Fax: 650/369-6481.
Motel   **Terms:** Reserv deposit; handling fee imposed. **Facility:** 52 rooms. 10 whirlpool rms, extra charge; 2 stories; interior/exterior corridors; sauna. **Some Rooms:** 10 kitchens. **Cards:** AE, CB, DI, DS, JC, MC, VI.

DAYS INN
Phone: 650/369-9200   [203]

AAA SAVE   All Year [CP]   1P: $70- 80   2P/1B: $70- 80   2P/2B: $80- 90   XP: $12   F12
◆◆   **Location:** 1 mi s on SR 82; 0.3 mi s of jct SR 84. 2650 El Camino Real 94061. Fax: 650/363-8167.
Motel   **Terms:** Weekly rates. **Facility:** 68 rooms. Well back from highway on attractively landscaped grounds. Some units with balcony. 5 kitchen apartments, $90-$150 for 2 persons; 2 stories; exterior corridors; sauna, whirlpool. **All Rooms:** combo or shower baths. **Cards:** AE, CB, DI, DS, MC, VI.

HOLIDAY INN EXPRESS
Phone: (650)366-2000   [205]

AAA SAVE   All Year   1P: $105   2P/1B: $105   2P/2B: $105   XP: $10   F18
◆◆◆   **Location:** 0.5 mi s of jct 84 & US 101, exit US 101 at Woodside Rd (SR 84), 0.5 mi w, then just 1.3 mi s.
Motel   2834 El Camino Real 94061. Fax: 650/365-4434. **Terms:** Reserv deposit; handling fee imposed. **Facility:** 38 rooms. 2 stories; sauna, steamroom, whirlpool. **Cards:** AE, CB, DI, DS, JC, MC, VI.

HOTEL SOFITEL SAN FRANCISCO BAY
Rates Subject to Change   **Phone: (650)598-9000**   [202]

◆◆◆◆   Sun-Thurs   1P: $149- 199   2P/1B: $169- 209   2P/2B: $149- 199   XP: $20   F12
Hotel   Fri & Sat   1P: $115   2P/1B: $115   2P/2B: $115   XP: $10   F12
Location: Exit US 101 at Marine World Pkwy E, 0.5 mi s on Twin Dolphin Dr. 223 Twin Dolphin Dr 94065. Fax: 650/598-0459. **Facility:** 319 rooms. Some rooms overlooking lagoon & San Francisco Bay. 8 stories; interior corridors. **Services:** giftshop. **Cards:** AE, CB, DI, JC, MC, VI.

RESTAURANTS

BACCARAT
Lunch: $10-$20   **Dinner:** $20-$30   **Phone:** 650/598-9000   [66]
◆◆◆◆   **Location:** In Hotel Sofitel. 223 Twin Dolphin Dr 94065. **Hours:** noon-10:30 pm. Closed major holidays &
French   Sun. **Reservations:** suggested. **Features:** casual dress; cocktails & lounge; valet parking; a la carte. Elegant, sofisticated atmosphere, view of lagoon, excellent dishes, creative preparation. Smoke free premises. **Cards:** AE, CB, DI, MC, VI.

FABBRO'S
Lunch: $7-$17   **Dinner:** $11-$18   **Phone:** 650/368-1491   [65]
◆◆   **Location:** 2915 El Camino Real 94061. **Hours:** 11:30 am-3 & 5:30-10 pm. Closed major holidays & Sun.
Italian   **Reservations:** suggested. **Features:** casual dress; cocktails & lounge. Family-owned 35 years, European dishes. Smoke free premises. **Cards:** AE, DS, MC, VI.

REEDLEY—15,800

LODGING

EDGEWATER INN
Phone: (559)637-7777   F6

AAA SAVE   All Year [CP]   1P: $49- 64   2P/1B: $56- 64   2P/2B: $56- 64   XP: $7   F6
◆◆◆   **Location:** 12 mi e of SR 99 via Manning Hwy. 1977 W Manning Ave 93654. Fax: 559/637-2228.
Motel   **Terms:** Reserv deposit; handling fee imposed; weekly rates only, $7 extra charge. **Facility:** 48 rooms. 1/4 block to Kings River. 2-bedroom apt with private patio, $125 for up to 7 persons; 2 stories; exterior corridors; whirlpool. **Cards:** AE, CB, DI, DS, MC, VI. **Special Amenities: Free local telephone calls.**

RESEDA—See Los Angeles p. 630.

RIALTO—72,400

LODGING

BEST WESTERN EMPIRE INN
Phone: (909)877-0690   F16

AAA SAVE   All Year   1P: $60- 100   2P/1B: $60- 100   2P/2B: $60- 100   XP: $8   F16
◆◆◆   **Location:** I-10, exit Riverside Ave, n to Valley Blvd, 0.5 mi w. 475 W Valley Blvd 92376. Fax: 909/877-0841.
Motor Inn   **Terms:** Pets, $5 extra charge. **Facility:** 100 rooms. 10 whirlpool rms, extra charge; 3 stories; exterior corridors; sauna, whirlpool. **Dining:** Restaurant; 6 am-10 pm; $7-$15; cocktails. **Cards:** AE, CB, DI, DS, JC, MC, VI. **Special Amenities: Early check-in/late check-out.**

RICHMOND—87,400

LODGING

COURTYARD BY MARRIOTT
◆◆◆
Hotel
Guaranteed Rates
All Year   1P: $99   2P/1B: $99   2P/2B: $99   **Phone:** 510/262-0700
Location: I-80, Hilltop Dr N exit. 3150 Garrity Way 94806. Fax: 510/262-0927. **Facility:** 149 rooms. 5 stories; interior corridors. **Cards:** AE, CB, DI, DS, MC, VI.

RESTAURANTS

HOTEL MAC RESTAURANT   **Lunch:** $7-$25   **Dinner:** $14-$35   **Phone:** 510/233-0576
◆◆◆
Continental
Location: 1 blk s of Cutting Blvd; 1 mi w of Richmond-San Rafael Bridge toll booth, in Pt. Richmond. 50 Washington Ave 94801. **Hours:** 11:30 am-2:30 & 5:30-10 pm, Sat from 5:30 pm, Sun-4:30 pm-9 pm. Closed major holidays. **Reservations:** suggested. **Features:** casual dress; early bird specials; cocktails & lounge. Nicely restored building. Varied menu. Smoke free premises. **Cards:** AE, MC, VI.

SALUTE RISTORANTE AT MARINA BAY   **Lunch:** $8-$15   **Dinner:** $10-$20   **Phone:** 510/215-0803
◆◆◆
Italian
Location: Exit I-580 Marina Bay Pkwy, 0.3 mi s to Regatta; w to Melville to Esplanade. 1900 Esplanade Dr 94804. **Hours:** 11 am-10 pm, Fri-11 pm, Sat 11 am-11 pm, Sun 11 am-10 pm. Closed: 1/1 & 12/25. **Reservations:** suggested. **Features:** casual dress; cocktails & lounge; a la carte. Charming house overlooking marina. Attractive, comfortable dining rooms, wide selection of both traditional & modern dishes, emphasis on fresh ingredients & creative preparation. Smoke free premises. **Cards:** AE, DI, MC, VI.

RIDGECREST—27,700

LODGINGS

BEST WESTERN CHINA LAKE INN   **Phone:** (760)371-2300
AAA SAVE
All Year [CP]   1P: $55- 65   2P/1B: $60- 70 2P/2B: $65- 75   XP: $5   F12
Under major renovation. **Location:** 0.4 mi s of Ridgecrest Blvd, on US 395 business route. 400 S China Lake Blvd 93555. Fax: 760/375-8785. **Terms:** Check-in 4 pm; reserv deposit. **Facility:** 46 rooms. Scheduled to open October 1, 1998; 2 stories; exterior corridors; sauna, whirlpool. **Dining:** Restaurant nearby. **Cards:** AE, CB, DI, DS, JC, MC, VI. **Special Amenities: Free breakfast and free local telephone calls.**
FYI
Motel

CARRIAGE INN   **Phone:** (760)446-7910
AAA SAVE
All Year   1P: $95- 105   2P/1B: $105- 115 2P/2B: $105- 115   XP: $10   F12
Location: On SR 178 & US 395 business route. 901 N China Lake Blvd 93555. Fax: 760/446-6408. **Terms:** Reserv deposit. **Facility:** 162 rooms. 2 stories; exterior corridors; heated pool, sauna, whirlpool. **Dining:** 2 restaurants; 6 am-10 pm; $8-$17; cocktails. **All Rooms:** extended cable TV. **Cards:** AE, DI, DS, MC, VI. *(See color ad below)*
◆◆◆
Motor Inn

ECONO LODGE   **Phone:** (760)446-2551
AAA SAVE
All Year [CP]   1P: $44   2P/1B: $46   2P/2B: $50   XP: $3   F18
Location: On SR 178 & US 395 business route, just w of China Lake Blvd. 201 Inyokern Rd 93555. Fax: 760/446-5740. **Terms:** Weekly rates; small pets only. **Facility:** 54 rooms. 2 stories; exterior corridors; small pool. **Cards:** AE, CB, DI, DS, JC, MC, VI. **Special Amenities: Free breakfast and free local telephone calls.**
◆◆
Motel

HERITAGE INN & SUITES   **Phone:** (760)446-7951
AAA SAVE
Sun-Thurs [BP]   1P: $69   2P/1B: $69   2P/2B: $69   XP: $6
Fri & Sat [BP]   1P: $65   2P/1B: $65   2P/2B: $65   XP: $6
Location: On Norma St, just n of Drummond Ave. 1050 N Norma 93555. Fax: 760/446-2884. **Terms:** Pets. **Facility:** 170 rooms. 44 one-bedroom suites with kitchen; 2 stories; interior corridors; heated pool, whirlpools. **Dining:** Restaurant; 5:30 am-11 & 5-10 pm, Sat from 7 am, Sun 7 am-noon; $10-$16; cocktails. **Some Rooms:** 89 efficiencies. **Cards:** AE, CB, DI, DS, MC, VI. **Special Amenities: Free breakfast and free local telephone calls.**
◆◆◆
Motor Inn

QUALITY INN
🅰🅰🅰 SAVE
◆ ◆
Motel
All Year [CP]   1P: $40- 50 2P/1B: $42- 50 2P/2B: $49- 59 XP: $5   F18
Location: 0.5 mi s of Ridgecrest Blvd, on US 395 business route. 507 S China Lake Blvd 93555.
Fax: 760/375-4684. **Terms:** Weekly rates; pets, in designated rooms only. **Facility:** 85 rooms. 2 stories; exterior corridors. **Dining:** Restaurant nearby. **All Rooms:** extended cable TV. **Cards:** AE, CB, DI, DS, MC, VI.
Special Amenities: Free breakfast and free local telephone calls.
Phone: (760)375-9731

RESTAURANTS

LA PASTA GRILL
◆
Italian
Lunch: $6-$11   **Dinner:** $8-$17   **Phone:** 760/446-1003
Location: Just n of Drummond & e of Norma Rd, in Village Plaza. 901 N Heritage Dr 93555. **Hours:** 11 am-9 pm, Sun 11 am-8 pm. Closed: 11/25 & 12/25. **Features:** casual dress; Sunday brunch; children's menu; carryout; cocktails & lounge. Menu features a selection of pasta, seafood, steaks, chicken & veal. Smoke free premises. **Cards:** AE, DS, MC, VI.

SANTA FE GRILL
◆
Mexican
Lunch: $7-$13   **Dinner:** $7-$13   **Phone:** 760/446-5404
Location: On Drummond, just e of Norma St, in Village Plaza. 901 N Heritage Dr 93555. **Hours:** 11 am-9 pm, Fri & Sat-10 pm, Sun 10 am-8 pm. Closed: 11/25 & 12/25. **Features:** casual dress; children's menu; carryout; cocktails & lounge. Large selection of Mexican & Southwestern cuisine. Smoke free premises.
Cards: AE, DS, MC, VI.

RIO DELL—3,000

LODGING

HUMBOLDT GABLES MOTEL
🅰🅰🅰
◆
Motel
Guaranteed Rates
6/1-9/30   1P: $40- 60 2P/1B: $45- 65 2P/2B: $49- 75 XP: $6   F12
2/1-5/31 & 10/1-1/31   1P: $34- 49 2P/1B: $38- 53 2P/2B: $40- 60 XP: $4   F12
Location: Exit US 101 Rio Dell/Davis St W. 40 W Davis St 95562. **Terms:** Reserv deposit; pets, managers approval req. **Facility:** 18 rooms. 2 two-bedroom units, $54-$60 for 2 persons. 1 three-bedroom unit, $65-$80 for 3 persons; 1 story; exterior corridors. **All Rooms:** combo or shower baths. **Cards:** AE, DS, MC, VI.
Phone: 707/764-5609

RIVERSIDE—226,500

LODGINGS

BEST WESTERN OF RIVERSIDE
🅰🅰🅰 SAVE
◆ ◆
Motel
All Year [CP]   1P: $50- 55 2P/1B: $55- 60 2P/2B: $60- 70 XP: $5   F12
Location: 7 mi sw on SR 91, exit Tyler Rd, 2 blks n, then 0.3 mi w on Magnolia Ave. 10518 Magnolia Ave 92505. Fax: 909/359-6749. **Terms:** Reserv deposit, 10 day notice; weekly rates. **Facility:** 58 rooms. Just w of Tyler Mall. 1 two-bedroom unit. 2 stories; exterior corridors; heated pool, whirlpool. **Some Rooms:** 4 efficiencies, no utensils. **Cards:** AE, CB, DI, DS, MC, VI. **Special Amenities:** Early check-in/late check-out and free breakfast. (See color ad below)
Phone: (909)359-0770

COURTYARD BY MARRIOTT
◆ ◆ ◆
Motor Inn
Rates Subject to Change
All Year   1P: $79   2P/1B: $79   2P/2B: $79
Location: 0.5 mi w of I-215 & SR 60, exit University Ave. 1510 University Ave 92507. Fax: 909/787-6783. **Facility:** 163 rooms. 6 stories; interior corridors. **Cards:** AE, CB, DI, DS, MC, VI. (See color ad p 816)
Phone: (909)276-1200

DAYS INN-RIVERSIDE WEST TYLER MALL
🅰🅰🅰 SAVE
◆ ◆
Motel
All Year [CP]   1P: $44   2P/1B: $44- 69 2P/2B: $44- 79 XP: $5   F12
Location: 7 mi sw on SR 91, exit Tyler Rd, n to Magnolia, then 0.3 mi w. 10545 Magnolia Ave 92505. Fax: 909/358-0670. **Terms:** Reserv deposit. **Facility:** 66 rooms. 6 whirlpool rms, extra charge; 3 stories; exterior corridors; heated pool. **Cards:** AE, CB, DI, DS, JC, MC, VI. **Special Amenities:** Early check-in/late check-out and free local telephone calls. (See ad p 816)
Phone: (909)358-2808

DYNASTY SUITES-RIVERSIDE
Guaranteed Rates
Phone: (909)369-8200
All Year [BP] 1P: $47- 53 2P/1B: $47- 53 2P/2B: $55- 60 XP:$5-10 D12
Location: Just sw of SR 60, exit University Ave; n on Iowa Ave. 3735 Iowa Ave 92507. Fax: 909/341-6486.
Terms: Small pets only, $10. **Facility:** 34 rooms. Across from Shopping Center & Movie Theatre. 2 very spacious whirlpool rms, $90; 2 stories; exterior corridors; small heated pool. **Dining:** Restaurant nearby.
Cards: AE, CB, DI, DS, JC, MC, VI. *(See color ad below)*

Motel

HAMPTON INN
Phone: (909)683-6000
All Year [CP] 1P: $55- 65 2P/1B: $55- 65 2P/2B: $69
Location: 0.5 mi w of I-215 & SR 60, exit University Ave. 1590 University Ave 92507. Fax: 909/782-8052.
Facility: 116 rooms. 2 stories; exterior corridors; heated pool. **All Rooms:** extended cable TV. **Cards:** AE, CB, DI, DS, MC, VI. **Special Amenities:** Free breakfast.

Motel

HOLIDAY INN-EXPRESS
Rates Subject to Change
Phone: (909)688-5000
All Year [CP] 1P: $69 2P/1B: $69 2P/2B: $69
Location: 8 mi sw on SR 91, exit La Sierra; 0.5 mi n. 11043 Magnolia Ave 92505. Fax: 909/785-5655.
Facility: 42 rooms. 6 one-bedroom suites, $149; 3 stories; exterior corridors; small heated pool. **Cards:** AE, CB, DI, DS, JC, MC, VI.

Motel

HOLIDAY INN SELECT
(AAA) (SAVE) All Year   1P: $71- 129   2P/1B: $71- 129 2P/2B: $71- 129   XP: $10   F12
♦♦♦   **Phone: (909)784-8000**
Hotel   **Location:** 0.5 mi w of SR 91, exit Mission Inn/University Ave; 1 mi s of SR 60 exit Market St. 3400 Market
             St 92501. Fax: 909/369-7127. **Facility:** 291 rooms. Downtown at Riverside Convention Center. 12 stories; in-
             terior corridors; heated pool, whirlpool. **Dining:** Restaurant; 6:30 am-2 & 5-10 pm; $7-$20; cocktails.
             Services: giftshop. **Cards:** AE, DI, DS, MC, VI. **Special Amenities:** Early check-in/late check-out and
free room upgrade **(subject to availability with advanced reservations).**

(icons)

MISSION INN
(AAA)   Rates Subject to Change   **Phone: (909)784-0300**
             All Year   1P: $115- 200   2P/1B: $115- 200 2P/2B: $115- 200   XP: $15   F18
♦♦♦   **Location:** Downtown, just w of SR 91, exit Mission Inn Ave. 3649 Mission Inn Ave 92501.
Historic Hotel Fax: 909/683-1342. **Terms:** Check-in 4 pm; handling fee imposed; package plans. **Facility:** 235 rooms. A Na-
             tional Historic landmark built in stages between 1902 & 1931. Unique architecture. Elegant public areas. A wide
             variety of nicely decorated rooms & suites. 4-5 stories; interior/exterior corridors; heated pool, whirlpool.
Fee: parking. **Dining:** 2 dining rooms; cocktails; also, Duane's Prime Steaks & Seafood, Mission Inn Restaurant, see
separate listing. **Services:** giftshop. Fee: massage. **Cards:** AE, CB, DI, DS, JC, MC, VI.

(icons)

RIVERSIDE INN
(AAA)   Rates Subject to Change   **Phone: (909)686-6666**
             All Year   1P: $30- 35   2P/1B: $35- 40   2P/2B: $40- 45   XP: $5   F12
♦   **Location:** Downtown area, 0.8 mi w of SR 91, Mission Inn Ave exit. 4045 University Ave 92501.
Motel   **Terms:** Reserv deposit. **Facility:** 50 rooms. 2 stories; exterior corridors. **Dining:** Restaurant nearby.
             All Rooms: shower baths. **Cards:** AE, DI, MC, VI.

(icons)

RESTAURANTS

DUANE'S PRIME STEAKS & SEAFOOD   **Lunch:** $11-$27   **Dinner:** $17-$29   **Phone:** 909/341-6780
♦♦♦♦   **Location:** Downtown, just w of SR 91, in Mission Inn. 3649 Mission Inn Ave 92501. **Hours:** 5:30 pm-10 pm,
American   also Tues-Fri 11:30 am-1:30 pm. Closed: Sun. **Reservations:** suggested. **Features:** semi-formal attire;
             cocktails & lounge; valet parking; a la carte. A formal, beautifully decorated dining room featuring US Prime
steak & seafood. Smoke free premises. **Cards:** AE, CB, DI, DS, MC, VI.
(icon)

MARIO'S PLACE   **Lunch:** $7-$15   **Dinner:** $12-$24   **Phone:** 909/684-7755
♦♦♦   **Location:** 1725 Spruce St at Chicago Ave 92507. **Hours:** 11:30 am-2:30 & 5:30-9:30 pm, Fri-10:30 pm, Sat
Continental 5:30 pm-10:30 pm, Mon 5:30 pm-9:30 pm. Closed: Sun, 1/1 & 12/25. **Reservations:** suggested.
             Features: casual dress; cocktails & lounge; entertainment; a la carte. A comfortable, cozy restaurant. Nice
selection of French & Italian cuisine. Smoke free premises. **Cards:** AE, CB, DI, DS, MC, VI.
(icon)

MARKET BROILER   **Lunch:** $6-$10   **Dinner:** $8-$20   **Phone:** 909/276-9007
♦♦   **Location:** From SR 91, exit Central Ave, just w, then 2 blks n on Riverside Ave. 3525 Merrill St 92506.
Seafood   **Hours:** 11 am-10 pm, Fri & Sat-11 pm. Closed: 11/25 & 12/25. **Features:** casual dress; carryout; cocktails. A
             popular restaurant featuring a large variety of mesquite broiled seafood. A selection of chicken, steak &
pasta are also avail. Smoke free premises. **Cards:** AE, DS, MC, VI.
(icon)

MISSION INN RESTAURANT   **Lunch:** $9-$20   **Dinner:** $10-$22   **Phone:** 909/784-0300
♦♦♦   **Location:** Downtown, just w of SR 91, exit Mission Inn Ave; in Mission Inn. 3649 Mission Inn Ave 92501.
American   **Hours:** 6 am-10 pm. **Reservations:** suggested. **Features:** casual dress; Sunday brunch; children's menu;
             cocktails & lounge; fee for parking; valet parking; a la carte. Dining in a colorful, tiled room with vaulted
ceilings. Outdoor dining on the Spanish Patio. Smoke free premises. **Cards:** AE, CB, DI, MC, VI.
(icon)

ROCKLIN—19,000   (See map p. 821; index p. 820)

LODGINGS

DAYS INN   **Phone:** (916)632-0101   86
(AAA) (SAVE) All Year   1P: $57- 79   2P/1B: $59- 79   2P/2B: $67- 89   XP: $10   F17
♦♦   **Location:** Exit I-80 Rocklin Rd, 0.3 mi to Granite Dr then 0.5 mi e. 4515 Granite Rd 95677.
Motel   Fax: 916/632-0335. **Facility:** 65 rooms. Adjacent to freeway. Comfortable rooms. 6 whirlpool rms, extra charge;
             2 stories; exterior corridors; sauna, whirlpool. **Some Rooms:** kitchen. **Cards:** AE, CB, DI, DS, MC, VI.
             Special Amenities: Free breakfast and free local telephone calls.

(icons)

FIRST CHOICE INN   **Phone:** (916)624-4500   87
(AAA) (SAVE) 2/1-4/30 & 10/1-1/31 [BP]   1P: $80   2P/1B: $87   2P/2B: $92   XP: $7   F12
♦♦♦   5/1-9/30 [BP]   1P: $75   2P/1B: $82   2P/2B: $87   XP: $7   F12
Suite Motel **Location:** US 80 e exit Rocklin Rd; westbound exit Rocklin. 4420 Rocklin Rd 95677. Fax: 916/624-5982.
             Terms: Pets, $20 extra charge. **Facility:** 124 rooms. Close to Sierra Foothills. 3 stories; interior corridors; whirl-
             pool. **Dining:** Coffee shop nearby. **Services:** complimentary evening beverages, Mon-Fri.
All Rooms: combo or shower baths. **Some Rooms:** whirlpools. **Cards:** AE, CB, DI, DS, JC, MC, VI. **Special Amenities:**
Early check-in/late check-out and free breakfast.

(icons)

ROCKLIN PARK HOTEL   Rates Subject to Change   **Phone:** (916)630-9400   88
♦♦♦   All Year   1P: $155   2P/1B: $155   2P/2B: $155   XP: $10   F
Motor Inn   **Location:** I-80, Rocklin Rd exit, just e, s on Aguilar Rd; e on China Garden Rd. 5450 China Garden Rd
             95677. Fax: 916/630-9448. **Terms:** Reserv deposit. **Facility:** 34 rooms. Loft & beamed public areas. Terraced
rose garden. 2 stories; interior corridors. **Recreation:** bicycles, hiking trails. **Cards:** AE, CB, DI, DS, JC, MC, VI.

(icons)

ROHNERT PARK—36,300

LODGINGS

BEST WESTERN INN Phone: (707)584-7435
AAA **SAVE** 5/1-9/30 [CP] 1P: $54- 68 2P/1B: $60- 70 2P/2B: $64- 76 XP: $6 F12
2/1-4/30 & 10/1-1/31 [CP] 1P: $50- 64 2P/1B: $56- 66 2P/2B: $60- 70 XP: $6 F12
♦♦♦ **Location:** W side of US 101; exit w via Rohnert Park Expwy. 6500 Redwood Dr 94928. Fax: 707/584-3848.
Motel **Terms:** Reserv deposit, 3 day notice. **Facility:** 145 rooms. 2 stories; exterior corridors; whirlpool.
Dining: Restaurants nearby. **Cards:** AE, CB, DI, DS, MC, VI. **Special Amenities:** Free breakfast and free
room upgrade (subject to availability with advanced reservations). (See ad below)

DOUBLETREE HOTEL-SONOMA COUNTY Rates Subject to Change Phone: (707)584-5466
♦♦♦♦ All Year 1P: $132- 152 2P/1B: $157- 167 2P/2B: $157 XP: $15 F18
Hotel **Location:** 3 mi s of Santa Rosa; exit US 101, Golf Course Dr. One Doubletree Dr 94928.
Fax: 707/586-4605. **Facility:** 245 rooms. California Spanish architecture. 6 whirlpool rms, extra charge; 3 stories; interior corridors; heated pool; 2 tennis courts. **Services:** giftshop. **Cards:** AE, CB, DI, DS, JC, MC, VI.

RAMADA LIMITED Rates Subject to Change Phone: 707/584-1600
♦ All Year [CP] 1P: $39 2P/1B: $49 2P/2B: $49 XP: $5 F18
Motel **Location:** Exit US 101 via W Rohnert Park Expwy. 6288 Redwood Dr 94928. Fax: 707/584-1305.
Terms: Reserv deposit. **Facility:** 138 rooms. 2 stories; exterior corridors. **Cards:** AE, MC, VI.

ROSAMOND—7,400

LODGING

DEVONSHIRE INN MOTEL Rates Subject to Change Phone: 805/256-3454
♦♦ All Year [CP] 1P: $54 2P/1B: $54 2P/2B: $69
Motel **Location:** Just e of SR 14, exit Edwards/Rosamond. 2076 Rosamond Blvd 93560 (PO Box 2080).
Fax: 805/256-9205. **Facility:** 30 rooms. 2 suites avail, $75; 2 stories; exterior corridors; small heated pool.
Cards: AE, CB, DI, DS, MC, VI.

ROSEMEAD—See Los Angeles p. 631.

ROSEVILLE—44,700 (See map p. 821; index p. 820)

LODGINGS

BEST WESTERN ROSEVILLE INN Rates Subject to Change Phone: 916/782-4434 **80**
♦♦ All Year [CP] 1P: $59- 89 2P/1B: $59- 89 2P/2B: $59- 89 XP: $5 F17
Motel **Location:** Exit w off I-80 via Douglas, just n. 220 Harding Blvd 95678. Fax: 916/782-8335. **Terms:** Reserv
deposit. **Facility:** 126 rooms. 2 stories; exterior corridors. **All Rooms:** combo or shower baths.
Some Rooms: 4 kitchens. **Cards:** AE, DI, DS, MC, VI.

HILTON GARDEN INN Phone: 916/773-7171
[FYI] Under construction. **Location:** Jct I-80 & SR 65. 1951 Taylor Rd 95678. **Facility:** 131 rooms. (See ad p 119)

LARKSPUR LANDING Phone: 916/773-1717
[FYI] Under construction. **Location:** Jct I-80 & SR-65. 1931 Taylor Rd 95678. **Facility:** 90 rooms. Scheduled to open
January 1, 1999.

OXFORD SUITES Rates Subject to Change Phone: (916)784-2222 **81**
♦♦ All Year [BP] 1P: $73- 83 2P/1B: $80- 90 2P/2B: $83- 90 XP: $70 F10
Motor Inn **Location:** Exit e off I-80 via Douglas Blvd, 0.3 mi n. 130 N Sunrise Ave 95661. Fax: 916/782-9034.
Terms: Reserv deposit. **Facility:** 184 rooms. 6 whirlpool rms, extra charge; 3 stories; exterior corridors.
Services: giftshop. **Cards:** AE, DI, DS, MC, VI.

ROWLAND HEIGHTS—See Los Angeles p. 631.

RUTHERFORD—700

LODGING

RANCHO CAYMUS   Rates Subject to Change   **Phone:** (707)963-1777

Fri & Sat 4/1-11/30 [CP] 1P: $165- 195 2P/1B: $165- 285 2P/2B: $325   XP: $15   F5
Fri & Sat 2/1-3/31, Sun-Thurs
4/1-11/30 & Fri & Sat

Motel 12/1-1/31 [CP] 1P: $155- 185 2P/1B: $155- 275 2P/2B: $300   XP: $15   F5
Sun-Thurs 2/1-3/31 &
12/1-1/31 [CP] 1P: $145- 175 2P/1B: $145- 250 2P/2B: $275   XP: $15   F5

Location: 4 mi s of St Helena, just e of SR 29 & SR 128. 1140 Rutherford Rd 94573 (PO Box 78). Fax: 707/963-5387. **Terms:** Reserv deposit, 3 day notice; handling fee imposed; 2 night min stay, weekends 4/1-11/30. **Facility:** 26 rooms. Early California, Spanish hacienda architecture. Many rooms with woodburning fireplace. 1 two-bedroom unit. 5 whirlpool suites, $200-$295 for up to 2 persons; 2 stories; exterior corridors. **Dining:** Restaurant nearby. **Some Rooms:** 5 kitchens, whirlpools. **Cards:** AE, DI, MC, VI. *(See color ad p 738)*

SACRAMENTO

pop. 369,400

This index helps you "spot" where approved accommodations are located on the detailed maps that follow. Rate ranges are for comparison only and show the property's high season. Turn to the listing page for more detailed rate information and consult display ads for special promotions. Restaurant rate range is for dinner unless only lunch (L) is served.

✈ Airport Accommodations

Spotter/Map Pg. Number	OA	SACREMENTO METROPOLITAN AIRPORT	Rating	Rate	Listing Page
⑭ / p. 821	⊕	Host Airport Hotel, at airport entrance	◆◆	$75-117 ⬛	826

SACRAMENTO

Spotter/Map Pg.Number	OA	SACRAMENTO - Lodgings	Rating	Rate	Listing Page
❶ / p. 821	⊕	Best Western Harbor Inn & Suites - see color ad p 822	◆◆◆	$69-89 ⬛	822
❷ / p. 821	⊕	Best Western Sandman Motel - see ad p 823	◆◆◆	$72-82 ⬛	823
❸ / p. 821		Best Western Sutter House - see ad p 823	◆◆◆	$77-102 ⬛	823
❹ / p. 821		Holiday Inn Capitol Plaza	◆◆◆	$148	826
❺ / p. 821		Heritage Hotel	◆◆	$79-89	826
❻ / p. 821	⊕	Clarion Hotel - see ad p 824	◆◆	$124-139 ⬛	824
❼ / p. 821	⊕	Canterbury Inn	◆◆	$44-57 ⬛	824
❽ / p. 821		Sacramento Hilton Inn - see ad p 119 & color ad p 829	◆◆◆	$159	829
❾ / p. 821	⊕	Econo Lodge	◆	$49-89 ⬛	825
❿ / p. 821	⊕	Capitol Inn	◆◆	$48	824
⓫ / p. 821		Marriott Residence Inn	◆◆◆	$149-169	827
⓬ / p. 821		La Quinta Inn	◆◆◆	$65-82	827
⓭ / p. 821	⊕	Hyatt Regency - see color ad p 923	◆◆◆◆	$215-290 ⬛	827
⓮ / p. 821	⊕	Host Airport Hotel	◆◆	$75-117 ⬛	826
⓯ / p. 821	⊕	Crossroads Inn	◆	$50-70 ⬛	824
⓱ / p. 821	⊕	Governors Inn - see color ad p 826	◆◆◆	$84 ⬛	825
⓲ / p. 821		Days Inn-Discovery Park - see color ad p 824	◆◆◆	$69-99	825
⓳ / p. 821		Delta King River Boat Hotel - see color ad p 825	◆◆	$119-185	825
⓴ / p. 821		Howard Johnson Hotel	◆◆	$90	826
㉒ / p. 821		Fountain Suites Hotel	◆◆◆	$109-129	825
㉓ / p. 821	⊕	Ramada Inn - see color ad p 828	◆◆	$68-199	828
㉔ / p. 821		Super 8 Lodge	◆◆	$51-58	830
㉕ / p. 821	⊕	Super 8 Executive Suites	◆◆	$74-89 ⬛	830
㉗ / p. 821	⊕	Inns of America	◆◆	$45 ⬛	827

Spotter/Map Pg.Number	OA	**SACRAMENTO - Lodgings (contd.)**	Rating	Rate	Listing Page
28 / p. 821		Doubletree Hotel	◆◆◆	$134-194	825
29 / p. 821		Red Lion's Sacramento Inn - see ad p 828	◆◆◆	$89-104	829
30 / p. 821		Radisson Hotel - see color ad p 827	◆◆◆	$69-139	828
31 / p. 821		The Sterling Hotel	◆◆◆	$159-229	830
32 / p. 821	⚜	**Amber House Bed & Breakfast Inn**	◆◆◆◆	$139-269 SAVE	822
33 / p. 821	⚜	**Quality Inn - see ad p 827**	◆◆	$69-78 SAVE	827
34 / p. 821	⚜	**Best Western John Jay Inn**	◆◆	$55-110 SAVE	822
35 / p. 821		Coral Reef Lodge	◆	$46	824
36 / p. 821	⚜	**Days Inn**	◆	$68 SAVE	824
37 / p. 821	⚜	**Executive Inn**	◆◆◆	$80-130 SAVE	825
38 / p. 821	⚜	**Best Western Expo Inn - see ad p 822**	◆◆	$68-120 SAVE	822
39 / p. 821		Hartley House Bed & Breakfast	◆◆◆	$115-165	826
40 / p. 821		Vizcaya	◆◆◆	$129-229	830
41 / p. 821		Holiday Inn North East	◆◆◆	$90	826
42 / p. 821		La Quinta Inn-Sacramento Downtown	◆◆◆	$62-79	827
43 / p. 821	⚜	**Vagabond Inn**	◆◆	$98 SAVE	830
44 / p. 821		Abigail's Bed & Breakfast	◆◆◆	$105-175	822
45 / p. 821	⚜	**Gold Star National 9 Inn**	◆	$50-60 SAVE	825
46 / p. 821		Candlewood Suites	◆◆◆	$85-105	823
47 / p. 821	⚜	**Travelodge Capitol Center**	◆◆	$89-109 SAVE	830
48 / p. 821		Super 8 Motel	◆	$50	830
		SACRAMENTO - Restaurants			
1 / p. 821		Fat City Bar & Grill	◆◆	$8-16	830
3 / p. 821		Chanterelle	◆◆◆	$16-24	830
4 / p. 821		California Fats	◆◆	$12-19	830
5 / p. 821		Aldo's	◆◆◆	$12-25	830
6 / p. 821		Delta King Pilothouse Restaurant	◆◆	$11-19	830
8 / p. 821		The Firehouse	◆◆◆	$17-30	831
9 / p. 821		California Cafe Bar & Grill	◆◆	$12-18	830
10 / p. 821		Bradshaws Restaurant	◆◆	$7-14	830

Nearby Accommodations

Spotter/Map Pg.Number	OA	**CITRUS HEIGHTS - Lodgings**	Rating	Rate	Listing Page
57 / p. 821	⚜	**Olive Grove Suites**	◆◆	$75-95 SAVE	417
		RANCHO CORDOVA - Lodgings			
66 / p. 821		Days Inn	◆	$55	805
67 / p. 821	⚜	**Inns of America**	◆◆	$54-60 SAVE	806
68 / p. 821		Best Western Heritage Inn	◆◆◆	$64-79	805
69 / p. 821		Hallmark Suites	◆◆◆	$87-205	805
71 / p. 821		Sheraton Sacramento Rancho Cordova Hotel-Sacramento	◆◆◆◆	$187-205	806
72 / p. 821		Holiday Inn	◆◆◆	$110-125	805
73 / p. 821		Fairfield Inn by Marriott	◆◆	$56-79	805
74 / p. 821		Courtyard by Marriott	◆◆◆	$129	805
75 / p. 821		Comfort Inn	◆◆	$49-74	805
		ROSEVILLE - Lodgings			
80 / p. 821		Best Western Roseville Inn	◆◆	$59-89	818
81 / p. 821		Oxford Suites	◆◆	$83-90	818
		ROCKLIN - Lodgings			
86 / p. 821	⚜	**Days Inn**	◆◆	$67-89 SAVE	817
87 / p. 821	⚜	**First Choice Inn**	◆◆◆	$92 SAVE	817
88 / p. 821		Rocklin Park Hotel	◆◆◆	$155	817

AAA TourBooks and TravelBooks list and
rate more than 34,000 lodgings and restaurants.

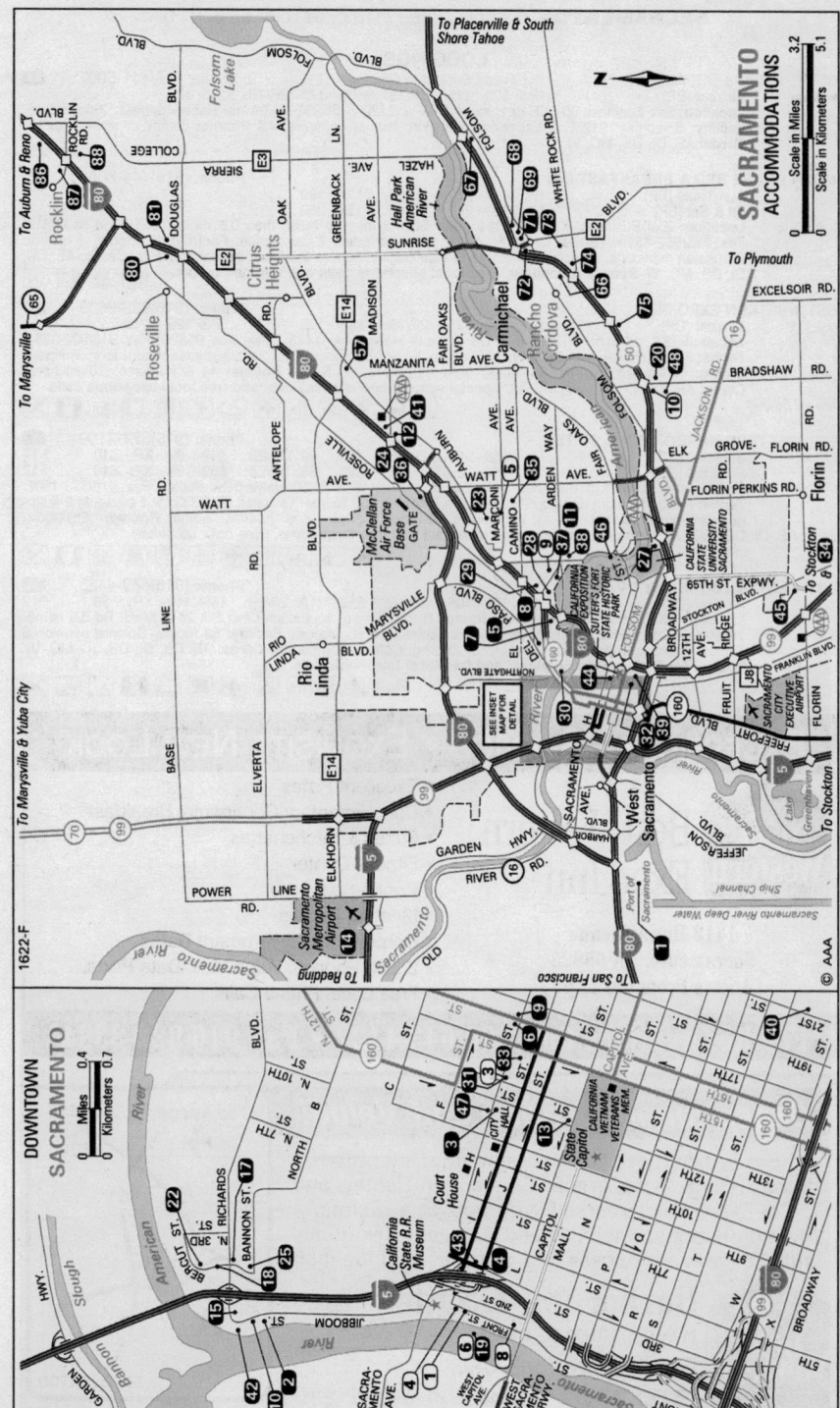

SACRAMENTO—369,400   (See map p. 821; index p. 819)

LODGINGS

ABIGAIL'S BED & BREAKFAST   Phone: 916/441-5007   [44]
◆◆◆   All Year [BP]   Rates Subject to Change
                                 1P: $99- 115   2P/1B: $105- 175 2P/2B: $105- 175
Bed &   **Location:** Exit Business 80 at E or H sts, 0.8 mi w. 2120 G St 95816. **Terms:** Reserv deposit, 7 day notice.
Breakfast **Facility:** 5 rooms. 1912 Colonial revival mansion. Interior corridors. **All Rooms:** combo or shower baths.
           Cards: AE, DI, DS, MC, VI.   [img] [X]

AMBER HOUSE BED & BREAKFAST INN   Phone: (916)444-8085   [32]
(AAA) [SAVE]   Sun-Thurs [BP]   1P: $119- 139   2P/1B: $139- 199
              Fri & Sat [BP]   1P: $139- 249   2P/1B: $139- 269
◆◆◆◆   **Location:** Exit Business 80 at SR 160 (16th St) 0.8 mi n to N St, then 0.5 mi e. 1315 22nd St 95816.
Historic Bed **Fax:** 916/552-6529. **Terms:** Check-in 4 pm; reserv deposit, 7 day notice. **Facility:** 14 rooms. 3 historic
& Breakfast   Craftsman mansions, attractively restored to their original beauty. 2 stories; interior corridors. **Cards:** AE, CB,
              DI, DS, MC, VI. **Special Amenities:** Free local telephone calls and free newspaper. [VCR] [img] [i] [X]

BEST WESTERN EXPO INN   Phone: (916)922-9833   [38]
(AAA) [SAVE]   All Year [CP]   1P: $58- 120   2P/1B: $58- 120 2P/2B: $68- 120
◆◆   **Location:** 2.5 mi n of jct SR 16 & US 50, exit Howe Ave. 1413 Howe Ave 95825. Fax: 916/922-3384.
Motel   **Terms:** Pets, $50 dep req. **Facility:** 125 rooms. 50 two-bedroom units. 2 stories; interior corridors; whirlpool.
        Dining: Restaurant nearby. **Services:** area transportation. **Some Rooms:** 44 efficiencies, 10 kitchens.
        Cards: AE, CB, DI, DS, JC, MC, VI. **Special Amenities:** Free breakfast and free local telephone calls.
(See ad below)   [S/D] [icons...] [X]

BEST WESTERN HARBOR INN & SUITES   Phone: (916)371-2100   [1]
(AAA) [SAVE]   Sun-Thurs [CP]   1P: $69- 89   2P/1B: $69- 89 2P/2B: $69- 89 XP: $10   F17
              Fri & Sat [CP]   1P: $59- 89   2P/1B: $59- 89 2P/2B: $59- 89 XP: $10   F17
◆◆◆   **Location:** 4 mi w; exit Business Loop 80 via Harbor Blvd. 1250 Halyard Dr 95691. Fax: 916/373-1507.
Motel   **Terms:** Pets, $10 extra charge, $100 dep req. **Facility:** 138 rooms. 15 suites, $75-$89 for 2 persons; 2-4 sto-
        ries; interior/exterior corridors; whirlpools. **Dining:** Coffee shop nearby. **Some Rooms:** whirlpools.
        Cards: AE, DI, DS, MC, VI. **Special Amenities:** Free breakfast and free newspaper. *(See color ad below)*
                                                        [icons...] [X]

BEST WESTERN JOHN JAY INN   Phone: (916)689-4425   [34]
(AAA) [SAVE]   All Year [CP]   1P: $50- 105   2P/1B: $55- 110 2P/2B: $55- 110 XP: $6   F12
◆◆   **Location:** Northbound exit Stockton Blvd 0.8 mi n; southbound exit SR 99 at Mack Rd 0.8 mi ne.
Motel   15 Massie Court 95823. Fax: 916/689-8045. **Terms:** Reserv deposit. **Facility:** 58 rooms. Colonial exterior. 3
        stories; interior corridors; sauna, whirlpool. **Dining:** Coffee shop nearby. **Cards:** AE, CB, DI, DS, JC, MC, VI.
        Special Amenities: Free breakfast and free local telephone calls.
                                            [S/D] [icons...] [X]

(See map p. 821)

BEST WESTERN SANDMAN MOTEL
Phone: (916)443-6515 **2**

(AAA) (SAVE) 5/1-9/30 [CP] 1P: $62- 76 2P/1B: $66- 80 2P/2B: $72- 82 XP: $6 F12
2/1-4/30 & 10/1-1/31 [CP] 1P: $59- 71 2P/1B: $62- 76 2P/2B: $66- 76 XP: $6 F12
♦♦♦ **Location:** 2.3 mi nw of Business Loop 80, off I-5 exit Richards Blvd. 236 Jibboom St 95814.
Motel Fax: 916/443-8346. **Terms:** Reserv deposit, 3 day notice. **Facility:** 116 rooms. Comfortable rooms. On the
Sacramento River next to bike trails. 2 stories; exterior corridors; whirlpool. **Dining:** Coffee shop nearby.
Cards: AE, CB, DI, DS, MC, VI. **Special Amenities:** Free breakfast and free room upgrade (subject to availability with
advanced reservations). (See ad below)

BEST WESTERN SUTTER HOUSE Phone: (916)441-1314 **3**
(AAA) (SAVE) All Year 1P: $64- 102 2P/1B: $69- 102 2P/2B: $77- 102 XP: $8 F12
♦♦♦ **Location:** Downtown, 3 blks from capitol, between 11th & 12th sts. 1100 H St 95814. Fax: 916/441-5961.
Motel **Terms:** Reserv deposit, 3 day notice. **Facility:** 98 rooms. Covered parking. 3 blocks from state capitol. 3 sto-
ries; interior/exterior corridors. **Dining:** Restaurant nearby. **Cards:** AE, CB, DI, DS, JC, MC, VI.
Special Amenities: Free breakfast and free room upgrade (subject to availability with advanced
reservations). (See ad below)

CANDLEWOOD SUITES Rates Subject to Change Phone: 916/646-1212 **46**
♦♦♦ Sun-Thurs 1P: $85- 105 2P/1B: $85- 105
Suite Motor Inn Fri & Sat 1P: $74- 94 2P/1B: $74- 94
Location: US 50, exit Howe Ave, 1.5 mi n. 555 Howe Ave 95825. Fax: 916/646-1216. **Terms:** Reserv
deposit. **Facility:** 126 rooms. 4 stories; interior corridors. **All Rooms:** kitchens. **Cards:** AE, DI, DS, MC, VI.

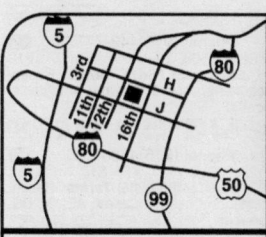

Distances indicated are from the center of town unless otherwise designated.

(See map p. 821)

CANTERBURY INN Phone: (916)927-0927 **7**
(AAA) (SAVE) All Year [CP] 1P: $39- 53 2P/1B: $44- 57 2P/2B: $44- 57 XP: $5 F15
◆ ◆ **Location:** 3 mi e of Capitol via SR 160, 16th St extension. 1900 Canterbury Rd 95815. Fax: 916/641-8594.
Motor Inn **Terms:** Check-in 4 pm; reserv deposit; pets, $100 dep req. **Facility:** 151 rooms. 5 minutes from capitol & Cal
Expo. 2 stories; exterior corridors; whirlpool. **Dining:** Restaurant; 6 am-9 pm; $8-$19; cocktails. **Cards:** AE,
CB, DI, DS, JC, MC, VI. **Special Amenities: Free breakfast and free room upgrade (subject to
availability with advanced reservations).**

CAPITOL INN Phone: 916/443-4811 **10**
(AAA) (SAVE) All Year 1P: $38 2P/1B: $43 2P/2B: $48 XP: $5 F12
◆ ◆ **Location:** 2.3 mi nw of Business Loop 80 off I-5; exit I-5 via Richards Blvd. 228 Jibboom St 95814.
Motel Fax: 916/443-4907. **Terms:** Reserv deposit. **Facility:** 69 rooms. 2 stories; interior corridors. **Dining:** Coffee
shop nearby. **All Rooms:** combo or shower baths. **Cards:** AE, DI, DS, MC, VI.

CLARION HOTEL Phone: (916)444-8000 **6**
(AAA) (SAVE) All Year 1P: $114- 129 2P/1B: $124- 139 2P/2B: $124- 139 XP: $15 F18
◆ ◆ **Location:** On SR 160; 1.3 mi n of Business Loop 80, 16th St exit. 700 16th St 95814. Fax: 916/442-8129.
Hotel **Terms:** Package plans; small pets only, $75 dep req. **Facility:** 239 rooms. Intimate atmosphere. Opposite 19th-
century governors. Mansion State Historic Park. 2-3 stories; interior corridors; designated smoking area.
Dining: Restaurant; 6:30 am-2:30 & 6-10 pm; $11-$19; cocktails. **All Rooms:** combo or shower baths.
Cards: AE, CB, DI, DS, JC, MC, VI. (See ad below)

CORAL REEF LODGE Rates Subject to Change Phone: 916/483-6461 **35**
◆ All Year [CP] 1P: $40 2P/1B: $46 2P/2B: $46 XP: $5 F12
Motel **Location:** 6 blks off Business Loop 80; exit Fulton Ave. 2700 Fulton Ave 95821. Fax: 916/488-2372.
Terms: Reserv deposit. **Facility:** 58 rooms. Beautifully landscaped courtyard with many fruit & shade trees. 2
stories; exterior corridors. **All Rooms:** shower baths. **Cards:** AE, CB, DI, DS, MC, VI.

CROSSROADS INN Phone: (916)442-7777 **15**
(AAA) (SAVE) All Year [CP] 1P: $45- 65 2P/1B: $45- 65 2P/2B: $50- 70 XP: $5 F12
◆ **Location:** 2.3 mi nw of Business Loop 80; I-5 exit Richards Blvd. 221 Jibboom St 95814. **Terms:** Reserv
Motel deposit. **Facility:** 28 rooms. Comfortable rooms. 2 stories; exterior corridors. **Some Rooms:** whirlpools.
Cards: AE, DI, DS, MC, VI. **Special Amenities: Free local telephone calls.**

DAYS INN Phone: (916)488-4100 **36**
(AAA) (SAVE) All Year [CP] 1P: $65 2P/1B: $68 2P/2B: $68 XP: $10 F12
◆ **Location:** Exit I-80 at Watt Ave, just n. 3425 Orange Grove Ave 95660. Fax: 916/489-0286. **Terms:** Reserv
Motel deposit, 3 day notice. **Facility:** 141 rooms. Exterior corridors. **Dining:** Restaurant nearby. **Cards:** AE, DI, DS,
MC, VI. **Special Amenities: Free local telephone calls and free newspaper.**

(See map p. 821)

DAYS INN-DISCOVERY PARK ◆◆◆ Motel — Rates Subject to Change — Phone: (916)442-6971 🔟8 F17
All Year [CP] 1P: $69- 99 2P/1B: $69- 99 2P/2B: $69- 99 XP: $10
Location: 2.3 mi nw of Business Loop 80; off I-5 exit, E Richards Blvd. 350 Bercut Dr 95814. Fax: 916/444-2809. Facility: 100 rooms. Comfortable atmosphere mature trees. 2 stories; exterior corridors.
Cards: AE, DI, DS, MC, VI. *(See color ad p 824)*

DELTA KING RIVER BOAT HOTEL ◆◆ Historic Hotel — Rates Subject to Change — Phone: (916)444-5464 🔟9 F6
All Year [CP] 1P: $119- 185 2P/1B: $119- 185 XP: $15-25
Location: I-5 exit J St (Old Sacramento). 1000 Front St 95814. Fax: 916/444-5314. Terms: Check-in 4 pm; reserv deposit. Facility: 44 rooms. A 1927 restored sternwheeler riverboat permanently docked on Sacramento River waterfront. On National Register of Historic Places. 5 stories; interior/exterior corridors. Services: giftshop. All Rooms: combo or shower baths. Cards: AE, CB, DI, DS, JC, MC, VI. *(See color ad below)*

DOUBLETREE HOTEL ◆◆◆ Hotel — Rates Subject to Change — Phone: 916/929-8855 2️⃣8
Sun-Thurs 1P: $119- 179 2P/1B: $134- 194 2P/2B: $134- 194 XP: $15 F16
Fri & Sat 1P: $99 2P/1B: $99 2P/2B: $99 XP: $15 F16
Location: 3.n mi e; 1 blk off Business Loop 80; exit via Arden Way. 2001 Point West Way 95815. Fax: 916/924-4913. Terms: Reserv deposit. Facility: 448 rooms. Spacious grounds. 6 two-bedroom units. 3-4 stories; interior corridors; designated smoking area. Services: giftshop. Cards: AE, CB, DI, DS, JC, MC, VI.

ECONO LODGE AAA SAVE ◆ Motel — Phone: (916)443-6631 🟨9 F18
All Year [CP] 1P: $40- 69 2P/1B: $44- 79 2P/2B: $49- 89 XP: $4
Location: SR 160, 1 mi n of Business Loop 80, I-80 business loop eastbound exit 15th St, westbound 16th St, I-5 exit J St. 711 16th St 95814. Terms: Pets, $6 extra charge. Facility: 41 rooms. 2 two-bedroom units. 3 stories; exterior corridors. Dining: Restaurant nearby. All Rooms: combo or shower baths. Cards: AE, CB, DI, DS, JC, MC, VI. Special Amenities: Free breakfast.

EXECUTIVE INN AAA SAVE ◆◆◆ Motel — Phone: (916)929-5600 3️⃣7 F12
All Year [CP] 1P: $80- 130 2P/1B: $80- 130 2P/2B: $80- 90 XP: $5-10
Location: Exit Business 80 at Arden Way; 1 mi e. 2030 Arden Way 95825. Fax: 916/929-2419. Facility: 190 rooms. Located near Cal Expo. 2 stories; exterior corridors; whirlpool. Dining: Coffee shop nearby. Some Rooms: 34 efficiencies, kitchen. Cards: AE, CB, DI, DS, JC, MC, VI. Special Amenities: Free breakfast and free local telephone calls.

FOUNTAIN SUITES HOTEL ◆◆◆ Motor Inn — Rates Subject to Change — Phone: 916/441-1444 2️⃣2 F17
All Year [CP] 1P: $94- 114 2P/1B: $109- 129 2P/2B: $114 XP: $15
Location: 2.3 mi nw of Business Loop 80; off I-5, exit Richards Blvd. 321 Bercut Dr 95814. Fax: 916/441-6530. Terms: Reserv deposit. Facility: 300 rooms. Attractive landscaped grounds. 3 stories; interior corridors; designated smoking area. Services: area transportation. Cards: AE, DI, DS, MC, VI.

GOLD STAR NATIONAL 9 INN AAA SAVE ◆ Motel — Phone: (916)399-8077 4️⃣5 F5
All Year 1P: $40- 50 2P/1B: $45- 55 2P/2B: $50- 60 XP: $8
Location: Exit SR 99 at 47th Ave, 1 mi e to Stockton Blvd, 0.5 mi s. 6610 Stockton Blvd 95823. Terms: Reserv deposit; handling fee imposed. Facility: 31 rooms. Exterior corridors. Dining: Coffee shop nearby. All Rooms: combo or shower baths. Some Rooms: 5 kitchens. Cards: AE, CB, DI, JC, MC, VI.

GOVERNORS INN AAA SAVE ◆◆◆ Motel — Phone: (916)448-7224 🔟7 D12
All Year [CP] 1P: $74 2P/1B: $84 2P/2B: $84 XP: $10
Location: 2.3 mi nw of Business Loop 80; I-5 exit E Richards Blvd. 210 Richards Blvd 95814. Fax: 916/448-7382. Terms: Reserv deposit, 3 day notice. Facility: 134 rooms. 3 stories; interior corridors; whirlpool. Dining: Coffee shop nearby. Services: complimentary evening beverages, Mon-Thurs. All Rooms: combo or shower baths. Cards: AE, CB, DI, DS, MC, VI. Special Amenities: Free breakfast.
(See color ad p 826)

(See map p. 821)

HARTLEY HOUSE BED & BREAKFAST Rates Subject to Change **Phone:** (916)447-7829 **39**
♦♦♦ Sun-Thurs [BP] 1P: $100- 120 2P/1B: $115- 165
Historic Bed Fri & Sat [BP] 1P: $115- 165 2P/1B: $115- 165
& Breakfast **Location:** Exit Business 80 at SR 160 (16th St), 0.8 mi n to N St, then 0.5 mi e. 700 22nd St 95816. Fax: 916/447-1820. **Terms:** Reserv deposit. **Facility:** 5 rooms. 1906 Colonial revival. 2 stories; interior corridors. **All Rooms:** combo or shower baths. **Cards:** AE, CB, DI, DS, JC, MC, VI.

HERITAGE HOTEL Guaranteed Rates **Phone:** 916/929-7900 **5**
♦♦ All Year 1P: $69- 74 2P/1B: $74- 79 2P/2B: $79- 89 XP: $10 F12
Motor Inn **Location:** W off Business Loop 80 via Exposition Blvd. 1780 Tribute Rd 95815. Fax: 916/921-9147. **Facility:** 206 rooms. Attractive landscaped grounds. Near Cal Expo. 3 stories; interior corridors; designated smoking area. **Cards:** AE, CB, DI, DS, MC, VI.

HOLIDAY INN CAPITOL PLAZA Rates Subject to Change **Phone:** (916)446-0100 **4**
♦♦♦ All Year 1P: $138 2P/1B: $148 2P/2B: $148 XP: $10 F16
Hotel **Location:** I-5 exit J st. 300 J St 95814. Fax: 916/446-0117. **Facility:** 364 rooms. Walking distance to Old Sacramento. Adjacent to downtown plaza shopping mall. 16 stories; interior corridors. **Services:** giftshop. **Cards:** AE, CB, DI, DS, JC, MC, VI.

HOLIDAY INN NORTH EAST Guaranteed Rates **Phone:** (916)338-5800 **41**
♦♦♦ Sun-Thurs 1P: $90 2P/1B: $90 2P/2B: $90
Hotel Fri & Sat 1P: $70 2P/1B: $70 2P/2B: $70
Location: 9 mi e; exit I-80 at Madison Ave, 0.3 mi e. 5321 Date Ave 95841. Fax: 916/334-2868. **Facility:** 225 rooms. 6 stories; interior corridors; heated indoor/outdoor pool. **Services:** giftshop. **Cards:** AE, CB, DI, DS, JC, MC, VI.

HOST AIRPORT HOTEL **Phone:** (916)922-8071 **14**
(AAA) [SAVE] All Year [CP] 1P: $75- 105 2P/1B: $75- 117 2P/2B: $75- 117 XP:$5-15 F12
♦♦ **Location:** 11 mi nw from capitol; 6 mi nw of I-80, off I-5 at the Sacramento Metropolitan Airport. 6945 Airport
Motel Blvd 95837. Fax: 916/929-8636. **Terms:** Reserv deposit; pets, $50. **Facility:** 89 rooms. Underground concourse connection direct with airport terminal. 2 stories; exterior corridors; whirlpool. **Dining:** Restaurant nearby. **Cards:** AE, DI, DS, MC, VI.

HOWARD JOHNSON HOTEL Rates Subject to Change **Phone:** 916/366-1266 **20**
♦♦ All Year 1P: $85 2P/1B: $90 2P/2B: $90 XP: $5 F17
Motor Inn **Location:** Exit US-50 at Bradshaw Rd, just s. 3343 Bradshaw Rd 95827. Fax: 916/366-1266. **Facility:** 124 rooms. Interior corridors; indoor/outdoor pool. **Cards:** AE, DI, DS, MC, VI.

(See map p. 821)

HYATT REGENCY
Phone: (916)443-1234 **13**
AAA SAVE All Year 1P: $190- 265 2P/1B: $215- 290 2P/2B: $215- 290 XP: $25 F18
Location: 1/2 blk from Capitol at 12th & L sts. 1209 L St 95814. Fax: 916/321-6699. **Terms:** Reserv deposit.
Facility: 500 rooms. Mediterranean style architecture. Restaurant & dining room smoke free. 24 suites, $350-$795 for up to 2 persons; 15 stories; interior corridors; designated smoking area; heated pool, whirlpool.
Hotel **Dining:** Dining room, restaurant; 6 am-11 pm; $15-$28; cocktails. **Services:** giftshop. **Cards:** AE, CB, DI, DS, JC, MC, VI. *(See color ad p 923)*

INNS OF AMERICA
Phone: (916)386-8408 **27**
AAA SAVE All Year 1P: $42 2P/1B: $45 2P/2B: $45 XP: $7
Location: Sw corner of jct SR 50 & Howe Ave. 25 Howe Ave 95826. Fax: 916/386-1608. **Terms:** Reserv deposit; pets. **Facility:** 102 rooms. 3 stories; exterior corridors. **Cards:** AE, MC, VI. **Special Amenities:** Free
Motel breakfast and free local telephone calls.

LA QUINTA INN Rates Subject to Change Phone: (916)348-0900 **12**
All Year [CP] 1P: $65- 82 2P/1B: $65- 82 2P/2B: $65- 82 **Facility:** 127 rooms.
Motel **Location:** 9 mi e; exit I-80 at Madison Ave. 4604 Madison Ave 95841. Fax: 916/331-7160. **Facility:** 127 rooms.
Attractive landscaped grounds. 1 suite, $85 for up to 2 persons; 3 stories; exterior corridors. **Cards:** AE, CB, DI, DS, JC, MC, VI.

LA QUINTA INN-SACRAMENTO DOWNTOWN Rates Subject to Change Phone: (916)448-8100 **42**
All Year [CP] 1P: $62- 79 2P/1B: $62- 79 2P/2B: $62- 79
Motel **Location:** 2.3 mi nw of Business Loop 80; off I-5 exit Richards Blvd W. 200 Jibboom St 95814.
Fax: 916/447-3621. **Facility:** 168 rooms. 3 stories; exterior corridors. **Cards:** AE, CB, DI, DS, JC, MC, VI.

MARRIOTT RESIDENCE INN Guaranteed Rates Phone: 916/920-9111 **11**
All Year [CP] 1P: $129- 149 2P/1B: $129- 149 2P/2B: $149- 169 XP: $10 F19
Motel **Location:** 2.5 mi n of jct SR 16 & US 50, Howe Ave eixt. 1530 Howe Ave 95825. Fax: 916/921-5664.
Terms: Reserv deposit. **Facility:** 176 rooms. 1 & 2-bedroom suites with living room & kitchen. Many with fireplace. 44 two-bedroom units. 2 stories; exterior corridors. **Cards:** AE, CB, DI, DS, MC, VI.

QUALITY INN
Phone: (916)444-3980 **33**
AAA SAVE All Year 1P: $62- 78 2P/1B: $62- 78 2P/2B: $69- 78 XP: $5 F12
Location: I-5 exit J St, 0.8 mi e to 14th, n on 14th, e on H, s on 15th; from Bus 80/SR 99 exit SR 160(16th St); 1 mi n then just w on I. 818 15th St 95814. Fax: 916/444-2991. **Terms:** Reserv deposit, 5 day notice.
Motel **Facility:** 41 rooms. 4 two-bedroom units. 3 stories; exterior corridors. **All Rooms:** combo or shower baths.
Cards: AE, CB, DI, DS, JC, MC, VI. **Special Amenities:** Free local telephone calls. *(See ad below)*

(See map p. 821)

RADISSON HOTEL
♦ ♦ ♦
Resort Hotel
Guaranteed Rates
All Year   1P: $69- 139   2P/1B: $69- 139 2P/2B: $69- 139 XP: $10
Phone: 916/922-2020 **30** F15
Location: Exit Business Route 80 at Exposition Blvd; 0.4 mi w. 500 Leisure Ln 95815. Fax: 916/649-9463.
Terms: Check-in 4 pm; reserv deposit. **Facility:** 309 rooms. Early California architecture. Some rooms with patios or decks; some rooms overlook small lake. Suites $139-$395 for up to 2 persons; 1-2 stories; exterior corridors; designated smoking area. **Services:** giftshop. Rental: paddleboats; bicycles. **Cards:** AE, CB, DI, DS, JC, MC, VI.
(See color ad p 827)

RAMADA INN
AAA
♦ ♦
Motor Inn
Rates Subject to Change
All Year [CP]   1P: $68- 119   2P/1B: $68- 199 2P/2B: $68- 119 XP: $8
Phone: (916)487-7600 **23** F17
Location: Exit Business route 80 at Fulton Ave. 2600 Auburn Blvd 95821. Fax: 916/481-7112. **Terms:** Pets, $100 dep req. **Facility:** 180 rooms. 4 stories; interior corridors. **Dining:** Restaurant; 6 am-9 pm; $7-$15.
Cards: AE, CB, DI, DS, JC, MC, VI. *(See color ad below)*

(See map p. 821)

RED LION'S SACRAMENTO INN
◆◆◆   Sun-Thurs   Rates Subject to Change   **Phone:** 916/922-8041   🔲29
Motor Inn   Fri & Sat
           1P: $89- 104   2P/1B: $89- 104   2P/2B: $89- 104   XP: $15   F16
           1P: $69- 89   2P/1B: $69- 89   2P/2B: $69- 89   XP: $15   F16
       Location: Exit Business Loop 80 via Arden Way in Arden Fair Shopping Plaza lot. 1401 Arden Way 95815.
Fax: 916/922-0386. **Facility:** 376 rooms. Spacious grounds. Some patios. Many balconies. 5 two-bedroom units. 2 stories; interior/exterior corridors; smoke free premises; putting green. **Services:** giftshop. **All Rooms:** combo or shower baths.
Cards: AE, CB, DI, DS, JC, MC, VI. *(See ad p 828)*

SACRAMENTO HILTON INN
◆◆◆   Sun-Thurs   Rates Subject to Change   **Phone:** (916)922-4700   🔲8
Hotel   Fri & Sat
           1P: $149   2P/1B: $159   2P/2B: $159   XP: $10   F18
           1P: $89   2P/1B: $99   2P/2B: $99   XP: $10   F18
       Location: At jct Business Loop 80 & Arden Way; exit W Arden Way. 2200 Harvard St 95815.
Fax: 916/922-8418. **Terms:** Reserv deposit. **Facility:** 330 rooms. 15 whirlpool rms, extra charge. 5 suites, $125-$450 for up to 4 persons; 12 stories; interior corridors; smoke free premises; heated pool. **Services:** giftshop. **Cards:** AE, CB, DI, DS, JC, MC, VI. *(See ad p 119 & color ad below)*

(See map p. 821)

THE STERLING HOTEL
◆◆◆
Historic Hotel
Guaranteed Rates
All Year [CP]   1P: $159- 229   2P/1B: $159- 229   2P/2B: $159- 229   XP: $15
Phone: (916)448-1300   **31**   F12
Location: Downtown, 3 blks n of State Capitol. 1300 H St 95814. Fax: 916/448-8066. **Facility:** 16 rooms. Attractively renovated 1894 Victorian Mansion. 3 stories; interior corridors; designated smoking area.
Cards: AE, CB, DI, MC, VI.
[ASK] [S6] [bed] [TI] [VCR] [画] [X]

SUPER 8 EXECUTIVE SUITES
(AAA) [SAVE]
◆◆
Motel
All Year [CP]   1P: $64- 79   2P/1B: $66- 79   2P/2B: $74- 89   XP: $5
Phone: (916)447-5400   **25**   F12
Location: 2.3 mi nw of Business Loop 80; I-5 exit E Richards Blvd. 216 Bannon St 95814. Fax: 916/447-5153. **Facility:** 40 rooms. 3 stories; exterior corridors; sauna, whirlpool. **Dining:** Coffee shop nearby. **Some Rooms:** whirlpools. **Cards:** AE, DI, DS, MC, VI. **Special Amenities:** Free breakfast and free local telephone calls.
[S6] [bed] [TI+] [凸] [用] [口] [画] [B] [X]

SUPER 8 LODGE
◆◆
Motel
Rates Subject to Change
All Year   1P: $45- 50   2P/1B: $49- 55   2P/2B: $51- 58   XP: $4
Phone: 916/334-7430   **24**   F12
Location: N of & adjacent to I-80; exit Madison Ave. 4317 Madison Ave 95842. Fax: 916/331-8916. **Facility:** 128 rooms. 2-3 stories; interior corridors. **Cards:** AE, DS, MC, VI.
[泳] [TI+] [用] [X]

SUPER 8 MOTEL
◆
Motel
Rates Subject to Change
All Year   1P: $39   2P/1B: $44   2P/2B: $50   XP: $5
Phone: 916/361-3131   **48**   F12
Location: Exit US 50 at Bradshaw Rd, just s. 9646 Micron Way 95827. Fax: 916/361-9674. **Terms:** Reserv deposit. **Facility:** 93 rooms. 3 stories; exterior corridors. **Cards:** AE, CB, DI, DS, MC, VI.
[泳] [TI+] [X]

TRAVELODGE CAPITOL CENTER
(AAA) [SAVE]
◆◆
Motel
All Year [CP]   1P: $69- 109   2P/1B: $79- 129   2P/2B: $89- 109   XP: $6-10
Phone: (916)444-8880   **47**   F17
Location: Downtown; between 11th & 12th sts. 1111 H St 95814. Fax: 916/447-7540. **Terms:** Reserv deposit. **Facility:** 71 rooms. 4 stories; interior corridors. **Dining:** Restaurant nearby. **All Rooms:** combo or shower baths. **Cards:** AE, CB, DI, DS, MC, VI. **Special Amenities:** Free breakfast and free newspaper.
[S6] [bed] [10'] [TI+] [口] [画] [X]

VAGABOND INN
(AAA) [SAVE]
◆◆
Motel
All Year [CP]   1P: $86   2P/1B: $93   2P/2B: $98   XP: $7
Phone: (916)446-1481   **43**   F18
Location: 8 blks w of Capitol; adjacent to Chinese Cultural Center & Old Sacramento Historic Quarter; exit J St. 909 3rd St 95814. Fax: 916/448-0364. **Terms:** Reserv deposit; pets, $5 fee. **Facility:** 107 rooms. Walking distance to old Sacramento. 3 stories; exterior corridors; heated pool. **Dining:** Coffee shop nearby. **Cards:** AE, CB, DI, DS, MC, VI. **Special Amenities:** Free breakfast and free local telephone calls.
[S6] [狗] [bed] [泳] [TI+] [凸] [口] [画] [B] [X] [2]

VIZCAYA
◆◆◆
Bed &
Breakfast
Guaranteed Rates
All Year [BP]   1P: $129- 229   2P/1B: $129- 229   2P/2B: $129- 229   XP: $15
Phone: (916)455-5243   **40**   F12
Location: Downtown, between T & U sts. 2019 21st St 95818. Fax: 916/455-6102. **Facility:** 9 rooms. Attractively renovated turn-of-the century Victorian Mansion. 2 stories; interior/exterior corridors. **Cards:** AE, DI, MC, VI.
[ASK] [S6] [bed] [画] [X]

RESTAURANTS

ALDO'S
◆◆◆
Northern
Italian
Lunch: $8-$14   **Dinner:** $12-$25   **Phone:** 916/483-5031   **5**
Location: In Town & Country Village at Fulton Ave & Marconi St. 2914 Pasatiempo Ln 95821. **Hours:** 11:30 am-10:30 pm, Sun-2:30 pm. Closed major holidays. **Reservations:** suggested. **Features:** casual dress; Sunday brunch; cocktails & lounge; a la carte. Varied selection of classic French & California specialties. Smoke free premises. **Cards:** AE, CB, DI, MC, VI.
[X]

BRADSHAWS RESTAURANT
◆◆
American
Lunch: $5-$8   **Dinner:** $7-$14   **Phone:** 916/362-3274   **10**
Location: On s side of US 50 at Bradshaw Rd. 9647 Micron Ave 95827. **Hours:** 6:30 am-10 pm, Fri & Sat-11 pm. Closed: 12/25. **Reservations:** required. **Features:** children's menu; beer & wine only. Country charm. A popular restaurant featuring a salad bar. Homemade soups, desserts & entrees. Smoke free premises. **Cards:** AE, DS, MC, VI.
[X]

CALIFORNIA CAFE BAR & GRILL
◆◆
American
Lunch: $7-$13   **Dinner:** $12-$18   **Phone:** 916/925-2233   **9**
Location: Business Loop 80 exit E Arden Way; in Arden Fair Shopping Plaza. 1689 Arden Way 95815. **Hours:** 11 am-9:30 pm, Fri & Sat-10 pm, Sun-8:30 pm. Closed: 11/25 & 12/25. **Reservations:** suggested. **Features:** casual dress; children's menu; a la carte. Contemporary California cuisine. Casual atmosphere. Smoke free premises. **Cards:** AE, CB, DI, DS, MC, VI.
[X]

CALIFORNIA FATS
◆◆
Chinese
Lunch: $8-$13   **Dinner:** $12-$19   **Phone:** 916/441-7966   **4**
Location: In Old Sacramento historic area. 1015 Front St 95814. **Hours:** 11:30 am-2 & 5-10 pm, Sun 5 pm-9 pm. Closed: 11/25 & 12/25. **Reservations:** suggested. **Features:** casual dress; Sunday brunch; children's menu; cocktails & lounge; minimum charge-$6; fee for parking; a la carte. California-Pacific cuisine, eastern seasonings; bold rustic-modern design on 3 levels. Wok & grill cooking. Smoke free premises. **Cards:** AE, MC, VI.
[X]

CHANTERELLE
◆◆◆
Continental
Lunch: $7-$12   **Dinner:** $16-$24   **Phone:** 916/442-0451   **3**
Location: In Sterling Hotel. 1300 H St 95814. **Hours:** 11:30-2 & 5:30-9 pm, Sat 5:30 pm-9 pm, Sun 8:30 am-2 & 5:30-9 pm. Closed major holidays. **Reservations:** suggested. **Features:** casual dress; children's menu; cocktails; a la carte. California French. Varied menu. Smoke free premises. **Cards:** AE, DI, MC, VI.
[X]

DELTA KING PILOTHOUSE RESTAURANT
◆◆
Continental
Lunch: $4-$12   **Dinner:** $11-$19   **Phone:** 916/441-4440   **6**
Location: On Delta King, Old Scramento Waterfront. 1000 Front St 95814. **Hours:** 11:30 am-2 & 5-10 pm, Sun 10 am-2 & 5-10 pm. **Reservations:** suggested. **Features:** casual dress; cocktails; fee for parking; valet parking; a la carte. Turn-of-the-century decor. Smoke free premises. **Cards:** AE, CB, DI, DS, MC, VI.
[X]

FAT CITY BAR & GRILL
◆◆
American
Lunch: $6-$14   **Dinner:** $8-$16   **Phone:** 916/446-6768   **12**
Location: In Old Sacramento historic area. 1001 Front St 95814. **Hours:** 11:30 am-2:30 & 4-10 pm, Fri-11 pm, Sat 10:30-2:30 & 5-11pm, Sun 10:30 am-2:30 & 5-10 pm. Closed: 11/26 & 12/25. **Features:** casual dress; Sunday brunch; children's menu; early bird specials; cocktails & lounge; minimum charge-$6; fee for parking; a la carte. Turn-of-the-century cafe. Smoke free premises. **Cards:** AE, MC, VI.
[X]

(See map p. 821)

THE FIREHOUSE   **Lunch:** $4-$12   **Dinner:** $17-$30   **Phone:** 916/442-4772 Ⓢ
♦♦♦   **Location:** In Old Sacramento historic area. 1112 2nd St 95814. **Hours:** 11:30 am-2:15 & 5:30-10 pm, Sat
Continental   from 5:30 pm. Closed major holidays & Sun. **Reservations:** suggested. **Features:** semi-formal attire;
cocktails & lounge; fee for parking; a la carte. Former quarters of Sacramento Fire Company. Period decor.
Smoke free premises. **Cards:** AE, MC, VI.   ⊗

ST. HELENA—5,000

LODGINGS

EL BONITA MOTEL   Rates Subject to Change   **Phone:** (707)963-3216
♦♦   Fri & Sat   1P: $95- 149   2P/1B: $95- 159 2P/2B: $99- 169 XP: $8-10
Motel   Sun-Thurs 4/1-10/31   1P: $89- 129   2P/1B: $99- 129 2P/2B: $99- 135 XP: $8-10
Sun-Thurs 2/1-3/31 &
11/1-1/31   1P: $75- 99   2P/1B: $75- 105 2P/2B: $75- 109 XP: $8-10
Location: 0.8 mi s on SR 29. 195 Main St 94574. Fax: 707/963-8838. **Terms:** Reserv deposit, 14 day notice. **Facility:** 42
rooms. Few small rooms with art deco motif. 6 two-bedroom units. 2 stories; exterior corridors. **All Rooms:** combo or
shower baths. **Some Rooms:** 6 efficiencies. **Cards:** AE, CB, DI, DS, MC, VI.

HARVEST INN   Rates Subject to Change   **Phone:** 707/963-9463
♦♦♦♦   Fri & Sat [CP]   2P/1B: $175- 366   XP: $20
Motor Inn   Sun-Thurs 4/15-10/31 [CP]   2P/1B: $129- 325   XP: $20
Sun-Thurs 2/1-4/14 &
11/1-1/31 [CP]   2P/1B: $99- 290   XP: $20
Location: 1.5 mi s on SR 29. One Main St 94574. Fax: 707/963-4402. **Terms:** Check-in 4 pm; reserv deposit; 2 night min
stay, weekends. **Facility:** 54 rooms. English Tudor design. Many fireplaces. Antique furnishings. 2 stories; exterior corridors.
Rental: bicycles. **Cards:** AE, DS, MC, VI.

HOTEL ST. HELENA   Guaranteed Rates   **Phone:** 707/963-4388
♦♦   All Year [CP]   1P: $145- 275 2P/1B: $145- 275 2P/2B: $145- 275 XP: $20
Historic Hotel **Location:** On SR 29, center of town. 1309 Main St 94574. Fax: 707/963-5402. **Terms:** Reserv deposit, 3
day notice. **Facility:** 18 rooms. 1888 Victorian Hotel. 2 stories; interior corridors. **Some Rooms:** color TV.
Cards: AE, DI, MC, VI.

MEADOWOOD NAPA VALLEY   Rates Subject to Change   **Phone:** (707)963-3646
♦♦♦♦   All Year   1P: $420- 702 2P/1B: $420- 702 2P/2B: $420- 702 XP: $25   F12
Resort Motor **Location:** Exit SR 29 & 128 at Pope St; 0.8 mi e to Silverado Tr, 100 ft n then 1 blk e on Howell Mountain
Inn   Rd to Meadowood Ln. 900 Meadowood Ln 94574. Fax: 707/963-3532. **Terms:** Check-in 4 pm; handling fee
imposed; 2 night min stay, weekends. **Facility:** 99 rooms. Many rooms with woodburning fireplace. Charming
country lodges on 250 acres wooded private reserve, nicely landscaped. 27 two-bedroom units, 12 three-bedroom units.
1-bedroom suites $325-$550 up to 2 persons; 2 stories; exterior corridors; heated pool. Fee: 9 holes golf; 7 tennis courts.
Services: giftshop. **All Rooms:** combo or shower baths. **Cards:** AE, DI, DS, MC, VI. A Preferred Hotel.

VINEYARD COUNTRY INN   Guaranteed Rates   **Phone:** 707/963-1000
Ⓐ   Fri & Sat 2/1-5/14, 5/15-11/15
& Fri & Sat 11/16-1/31 [CP] 1P: $220   2P/1B: $220   2P/2B: $220   XP: $15   F5
♦♦♦   Sun-Thurs 2/1-5/14 &
Suite Motel   11/16-1/31 [CP]   1P: $150   2P/1B: $150   2P/2B: $150   XP: $10   F5
Location: 0.8 mi s on SR 29. 201 Main St 94574. Fax: 707/963-1794. **Terms:** Check-in 4 pm; reserv
deposit, 3 day notice. **Facility:** 21 rooms. All rooms with wood burning fireplace, many with patio or deck, few with view of
vineyard. 2 stories; exterior corridors; heated pool, whirlpool. **Cards:** AE, CB, DI, MC, VI. *(See color ad p 739)*

RESTAURANTS

BRAVA TERRACE   **Dinner:** $12-$19   **Phone:** 707/963-9300
♦♦♦   **Location:** 2 mi n on Hwy 29. 3010 St Helena Hwy N 94574. **Hours:** noon-9 pm. Closed major holidays &
American   Wed 11/1-4/30. **Reservations:** suggested. **Features:** casual dress; cocktails; a la carte. Attractive setting
amongst the Napa Valley vineyards. Smoke free premises. **Cards:** AE, MC, VI.   ⊗

THE RESTAURANT AT MEADOWOOD   **Lunch:** $20-$35   **Dinner:** $30-$45   **Phone:** 707/963-3646
Ⓐ   **Location:** At Meadowood Resort. 900 Meadowood Ln 94574. **Hours:** 11:30 am-2:30 & 6-10 pm.
Reservations: suggested. **Features:** No A/C; semi-formal attire; Sunday brunch; cocktails & lounge; a la
♦♦♦   carte. View of wooded hillsides. Dining on deck, weather permitting. Smoke free premises. **Cards:** AE, CB,
South French DI, MC, VI.   ⊗

TRA VIGNE   **Lunch:** $7-$15   **Dinner:** $12-$24   **Phone:** 707/963-4444
♦♦♦   **Location:** 0.5 mi s on Hwy 29. 1050 Charter Oak Ave 94574. **Hours:** 11:30 am-10 pm. Closed major
Italian   holidays. **Reservations:** suggested. **Features:** casual dress; cocktails & lounge; a la carte. Attractive
location in the heart of the Napa Valley. Smoke free premises. **Cards:** DI, MC, VI.   ⊗

SALINAS—108,800

LODGINGS

BARLOCKER'S RUSTLING OAKS RANCH   Guaranteed Rates   **Phone:** 831/675-9121
♦♦♦   Fri & Sat [BP]   1P: $100- 150 2P/1B: $100- 150 2P/2B: $100- 150 XP: $50   F12
Ranch   Sun-Thurs [BP]   1P: $75- 100   2P/1B: $75- 100   2P/2B: $75- 100   XP: $50   F12
Location: 6 mi w of US 101, Chualar exit; w on River Rd, s (left) after bridge, to Limeklin, right at sign.
25252 Limeklin Rd 93908. Fax: 831/675-2060. **Terms:** Check-in 4 pm; reserv deposit. **Facility:** 4 rooms. 1932 Ranch house
& cottage, fireplace & TV in common room, with pool table. 1 two-bedroom unit. Closed 12/23-12/27; 1 story; interior/exterior
corridors; smoke free premises. **Recreation:** hiking trails. Fee: horseback riding. **Some Rooms:** shared bathrooms.
Cards: MC, VI.

BEST WESTERN JOHN JAY INN
Phone: (831)784-0176
(AAA) (SAVE)
All Year [CP] 1P: $55- 115 2P/1B: $60- 120 2P/2B: $60- 120 XP: $5 F12
◆◆
Location: N of US 101, Market St exit. 175 Kern St 93905. Fax: 831/772-0292. **Facility:** 58 rooms. Colonial
Motel facade & decor. 8 units with parlor, wet bar, microwave & refrigerator; 3 stories; interior/exterior corridors;
sauna, whirlpool. **Dining:** Coffee shop nearby. **All Rooms:** combo or shower baths. **Cards:** AE, CB, DI, DS,
JC, MC, VI. **Special Amenities: Free breakfast and free local telephone calls.**

COMFORT INN
Phone: (831)758-8850
(AAA) (SAVE)
All Year [CP] 1P: $59- 149 2P/1B: $69- 149 2P/2B: $69- 149 XP: $5 F16
◆◆
Location: Just e of US 101; Market St exit. 144 Kern St 93905. Fax: 831/758-3611. **Terms:** Reserv deposit,
Motel 3 day notice. **Facility:** 32 rooms. 1 large unit with sitting area & wet bar, $89-$159 for up to 2 persons; 3 sto-
ries; exterior corridors. **Dining:** Coffee shop nearby. **Cards:** AE, CB, DI, DS, JC, MC, VI. **Special Amenities:
Free breakfast and free local telephone calls.** *(See color ad p 702)*

DAYS INN
Phone: (831)759-9900
(AAA) (SAVE)
All Year [CP] 1P: $60- 160 2P/1B: $60- 160 2P/2B: $60- 160 XP: $12 F12
◆
Location: Just e of US 101, Airport Blvd exit. 1226 de la Torre St 93905. Fax: 831/759-2133. **Terms:** Reserv
Motel deposit, 4 day notice. **Facility:** 32 rooms. Few small rooms. 2 stories; exterior corridors. **Dining:** Coffee shop
nearby. **Cards:** AE, CB, DI, DS, JC, MC, VI. **Special Amenities: Free breakfast and free local telephone
calls.**

ECONO LODGE
Phone: (831)422-5111
(AAA) (SAVE)
All Year [CP] 1P: $46- 90 2P/1B: $50- 90 2P/2B: $55- 100 XP: $5 F18
◆
Location: Just e of US 101; Sanborn Rd or Fairview Ave exits. 180 S Sanborn Rd 93905.
Motel Fax: 831/783-0307. **Terms:** Reserv deposit, 3 day notice. **Facility:** 59 rooms. Adjacent to gas station. 3 sto-
ries, no elevator; exterior corridors. **All Rooms:** combo or shower baths. **Cards:** AE, DS, MC, VI.
Special Amenities: Free breakfast and free local telephone calls.

EL DORADO MOTEL
Phone: (831)449-2442
(AAA) (SAVE)
All Year 1P: $34- 60 2P/1B: $42- 70 2P/2B: $52- 80 XP: $8 F12
◆
Location: 1 mi ne of US 101, N Main St exit. 1351 N Main St 93906. Fax: 831/443-1722. **Terms:** Reserv
Motel deposit, 3 day notice; weekly rates; pets, $6 extra charge, $20 dep req. **Facility:** 44 rooms. Few small units.
1-2 stories; exterior corridors. **All Rooms:** combo or shower baths. **Cards:** AE, DS, MC, VI.
**Special Amenities: Free local telephone calls and preferred room (subject to availability with
advanced reservations).**

HOLIDAY INN EXPRESS
Rates Subject to Change Phone: 831/757-1020
◆◆
All Year [CP] 1P: $55- 160 2P/1B: $55- 160 2P/2B: $55- 160 XP: $10 F18
Motel **Location:** 0.5 mi w of US 101, John St exit. 131 John St 93901. Fax: 831/422-9541. **Facility:** 39 rooms. Close
to downtown. 3 stories; exterior corridors. **Cards:** AE, CB, DI, DS, JC, MC, VI.

LAUREL INN
Rates Subject to Change Phone: (831)449-2474
(AAA)
All Year 1P: $56- 110 2P/1B: $58- 120 2P/2B: $68- 150 XP: $6-8
◆◆◆
Location: Just e of US 101, Laurel Dr exit. 801 W Laurel Dr 93906. Fax: 831/449-2476. **Terms:** Reserv
Motel deposit, 10 day notice. **Facility:** 145 rooms. Some units with gas fireplace. 3 two-bedroom units. 2 stories; ex-
terior corridors; sauna, whirlpool. **Dining:** Coffee shop nearby. **All Rooms:** combo or shower baths.
Cards: AE, CB, DI, DS, MC, VI. *See ad p. 47.*

SUPER 8 MOTEL
Phone: (831)422-6486
(AAA) (SAVE)
All Year [CP] 1P: $46- 90 2P/1B: $50- 90 2P/2B: $55- 100 XP: $5
◆
Location: Just e of US 101; Sanborn Rd or Fairview Ave exit. 1030 Fairview Ave 93905. Fax: 831/422-8712.
Motel **Terms:** Reserv deposit, 3 day notice. **Facility:** 44 rooms. Adjacent to gas station. 2 stories; exterior corridors.
Cards: AE, CB, DI, DS, MC, VI. **Special Amenities: Free breakfast and free local telephone calls.**

VAGABOND INN
Phone: (831)758-4693
(AAA) (SAVE)
All Year [CP] 1P: $64 2P/1B: $69 2P/2B: $75 XP: $5 F18
◆◆
Location: Just e of US 101, Market St exit. 131 Kern St 93905. Fax: 831/758-9835. **Terms:** Pets, $5 extra
Motel charge. **Facility:** 70 rooms. Lower rates in winter; 2 stories; exterior corridors. **Dining:** Coffee shop nearby.
Cards: AE, CB, DI, DS, MC, VI. **Special Amenities: Free breakfast and free local telephone calls.**

SAN ANDREAS—2,100

LODGING

THE ROBINS NEST
Rates Subject to Change Phone: 209/754-1076
◆◆
Fri & Sat [BP] 1P: $55- 90 2P/1B: $60- 100 2P/2B: $60- 110 XP: $10
Historic Bed Sun-Thurs [BP] 1P: $55- 90 2P/1B: $60- 90 2P/2B: $60- 90 XP: $10
& Breakfast **Location:** SR 49, n end of town. 247 W St. Charles St 95249 (PO Box 1408). Fax: 209/754-3975.
Terms: Reserv deposit, 7 day notice. **Facility:** 9 rooms. 1895 Queen Ann Victorian. 2 stories; interior corridors.
Some Rooms: combo or shower baths, shared bathrooms, color TV. **Cards:** AE, DS, MC, VI.

SAN BERNARDINO—164,700

LODGINGS

COMFORT INN
Phone: (909)889-0090
(AAA) (SAVE)
All Year [CP] 1P: $59- 71 2P/1B: $65- 71 2P/2B: $65- 71 XP: $5 F18
◆◆◆
Location: Just nw of I-10, exit Waterman Ave; on Business Center Dr n of Hospitality Ln. 1909 S Business
Motel Center Dr 92408. Fax: 909/889-9894. **Terms:** Reserv deposit. **Facility:** 50 rooms. 2 two-bedroom units. 2 sto-
ries; exterior corridors. **Dining:** Restaurant nearby. **Cards:** AE, CB, DI, DS, JC, MC, VI. **Special Amenities:
Free breakfast and free local telephone calls.**

E-Z 8 MOTEL
◆
Motel
Rates Subject to Change
All Year   1P: $32   2P/1B: $37   2P/2B: $40- 45   XP: $5   F10
Location: Just n of I-10, exit Waterman Ave. 1750 S Waterman Ave 92408. **Facility:** 119 rooms. 3 stories; exterior corridors. **Cards:** AE, DI, MC, VI.
Phone: (909)888-4827

LA QUINTA INN
◆◆◆
Motel
Rates Subject to Change
All Year [CP]   1P: $62- 75   2P/1B: $62- 75   2P/2B: $62- 75
Location: Just nw of I-10, Waterman Ave exit. 205 E Hospitality Ln 92408. Fax: 909/884-3864. **Facility:** 153 rooms. 3 one-bedroom suites; 3 stories; exterior corridors; heated pool. **Cards:** AE, CB, DI, DS, JC, MC, VI.
Phone: (909)888-7571

SAN BERNARDINO HILTON
◆◆◆
Hotel
(See ad p 119)
Guaranteed Rates
All Year   1P: $135   2P/1B: $135   2P/2B: $135   XP: $10   F18
Location: Adjacent to I-10, exit Waterman Ave. 285 E Hospitality Ln 92408. Fax: 909/381-4299. **Facility:** 250 rooms. 6-7 stories; interior corridors; heated pool. **Services:** giftshop. **Cards:** AE, CB, DI, DS, JC, MC, VI.
Phone: 909/889-0133

SUPER 8 LODGE
◆◆
Motel
Rates Subject to Change
4/1-9/30   1P: $48   2P/1B: $49   2P/2B: $54   XP: $5
2/1-3/31 & 10/1-1/31   1P: $38   2P/1B: $41   2P/2B: $45   XP: $5
Location: Just n of I-10, Waterman Ave exit. 294 E Hospitality Ln 92408. Fax: 909/888-5120. **Facility:** 81 rooms. 2 stories; exterior corridors. **Cards:** AE, CB, DI, DS, MC, VI.
Phone: 909/381-1681

RESTAURANTS

BOBBY MCGEE'S
◆◆
American
Dinner: $12-$20
Location: Just nw of I-10, Waterman Ave exit. 1905 S Commerce Ctr E 92408. **Hours:** 5 pm-10 pm; Fri & Sat-10:30 pm, Sun 4-10 pm. Closed: 12/25. **Reservations:** suggested. **Features:** casual dress; children's menu; early bird specials; salad bar; cocktails & lounge. Informal service by costumed waiters & waitresses. Selection of steaks, prime rib & seafood. Smoke free premises. **Cards:** AE, CB, DI, MC, VI.
Phone: 909/884-7233

BON APPETITO
◆◆
Italian
Lunch: $5-$8   Dinner: $8-$12
Location: Just w of Waterman Ave. 246 E Baseline 92410. **Hours:** 11:30 am-2 & 4:30-9 pm, Fri-10 pm, Sat 4:30 pm-10 pm. Closed major holidays, Sun & Mon. **Reservations:** suggested. **Features:** casual dress; cocktails & lounge. A small, charming Italian restaurant. Large selection of pasta, veal, seafood, steak & vegetarian specialties. Smoke free premises. **Cards:** MC, VI.
Phone: 909/884-5054

ISABELLA'S RISTORANTE ITALIANO
◆◆
Italian
Lunch: $6-$14   Dinner: $9-$17
Location: Downtown; 0.5 mi e of I-215, Exit 2nd St. 201 N "E" St 92401. **Hours:** 11 am-2 & 4-9 pm, Sat 4-9 pm. Closed major holidays & Sun. **Features:** casual dress; cocktails; street parking. Nice selection of pasta, veal, seafood & chicken. Smoke free premises. **Cards:** AE, CB, DI, DS, MC, VI.
Phone: 909/884-2534

LE RENDEZ-VOUS RESTAURANT
◆◆
French
Dinner: $13-$23
Location: n side of town, just w of SR 18 (Waterman Ave). 4775 N Sierra Way 92404. **Hours:** 5 pm-9:30 pm. Closed: Mon. **Reservations:** suggested. **Features:** casual dress; cocktails. A charming restaurant with a European ambiance. Smoke free premises. **Cards:** AE, MC, VI.
Phone: 909/883-1231

LOTUS GARDEN RESTUARANT
◆
Chinese
Lunch: $6-$9   Dinner: $10-$14
Location: 0.5 mi nw of I-10, Waterman Ave exit. 111 E Hospitality Ln 92408. **Hours:** 11:30 am-9:30 pm, Fri & Sat-10:30 pm. Closed: 11/25. **Features:** casual dress; children's menu; cocktails & lounge. Large, nicely decorated restaurant. Extensive selection of a la carte entrees. Also, complete meals. Smoke free premises. **Cards:** AE, CB, DI, DS, MC, VI.
Phone: 909/381-6171

THE POTINIERE
◆◆
American
Lunch: $7-$13   Dinner: $7-$20
Location: Adjacent to I-10, exit Waterman Ave; in San Bernardino Hilton. 285 E Hospitality Ln 92408. **Hours:** 6:30 am-3 & 5-10 pm. **Features:** casual dress; Sunday brunch; cocktails & lounge; a la carte. A comfortable, attractive dining room. Nice selection of California cuisine. Smoke free premises. **Cards:** AE, CB, DI, DS, MC, VI.
Phone: 909/889-0133

SAN BRUNO—*See San Francisco p. 971.*

SAN CARLOS—*See San Francisco p. 972.*

SAN CLEMENTE—41,100   (See map p. 296; index p. 290)

LODGINGS

BEST WESTERN CASABLANCA INN   Phone: (949)361-1644   **74**
(AAA) (SAVE)   2/1-6/15 & 9/16-1/31 [BP]   1P: $69- 99   2P/1B: $69- 99   2P/2B: $69- 99   XP: $5   F13
♦♦♦   6/16-9/15 [BP]   1P: $74- 109 2P/1B: $74- 109 2P/2B: $74- 89   XP: $5   F13
Motel   **Location:** 0.8 mi sw of I-5, exit Avenida Pico. 1601 N El Camino Real 92672. Fax: 949/361-3825.
            Terms: Reserv deposit. **Facility:** 42 rooms. Well equipped exercise room. Some rooms with balcony. 3 sto-
            ries; exterior corridors; whirlpool. **Some Rooms:** whirlpools. **Cards:** AE, DI, DS, JC, MC, VI.
Special Amenities: Early check-in/late check-out and free breakfast.

CASA TROPICANA BED & BREAKFAST INN   Guaranteed Rates   Phone: (949)492-1234   **78**
(AAA)   Fri-Sun 2/1-10/31 [BP]   1P: $120- 350   2P/1B: $120- 350   XP: $15
        Mon-Thurs 2/1-10/31 [BP]   1P: $85- 265   2P/1B: $85- 265   XP: $15
♦♦♦   Mon-Thurs 11/1-1/31 [BP]   1P: $85- 240   2P/1B: $85- 240   XP: $15
Bed &   Fri-Sun 11/1-1/31 [BP]   1P: $110- 325   2P/1B: $110- 325   XP: $15
Breakfast   **Location:** 1 mi w of I-5 at San Clemente Pier, Avenida Palizada exit; then s on El Camino Real to Del Mar.
        610 Arendia Victoria 92672. Fax: 949/492-2423. **Terms:** Handling fee imposed. **Facility:** 9 rooms. Overlooking
the ocean, rooms decorated individually in tropical island themes, most with gas fireplace & whirlpool tub. 5 stories; exterior
corridors; designated smoking area. Fee: parking. **Dining:** Restaurant nearby. **Some Rooms:** 2 efficiencies, whirlpools.
Cards: AE, DS, MC, VI.

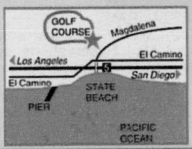

COMFORT SUITES   Phone: (949)361-6600   **82**
(AAA) (SAVE)   Fri & Sat 2/1-5/20 [CP]   1P: $59- 89   2P/1B: $64- 89   2P/2B: $79- 109 XP: $5   F14
               5/21-1/31 [CP]   1P: $69- 99   2P/1B: $69- 99   2P/2B: $89- 109 XP: $5   F14
♦♦♦   Sun-Thurs 2/1-5/20 [CP]   1P: $54- 84   2P/1B: $59- 89   2P/2B: $69- 99   XP: $5   F14
Motel   **Location:** I-5, Christianitos Rd exit; e to S El Camino Real, then n. 3701 S El Camino Real 92672.
Fax: 949/366-9745. **Terms:** Weekly rates. **Facility:** 60 rooms. 4 whirlpool rms, extra charge; 3 stories; interior
corridors; heated pool, whirlpool. **All Rooms:** combo or shower baths. **Cards:** AE, CB, DI, DS, JC, MC, VI.

(See map p. 296)

COUNTRY SIDE INN
◆◆◆   All Year [CP]   Rates Subject to Change   **Phone:** (949)498-8800   **73**
Motel   1P: $74- 84 2P/1B: $79- 84 2P/2B: $79- 84 XP: $5   F16
Location: Just w of I-5 exit Avenida Pico, just s; located behind Pico Plaza. 35 Calle de Industrias 92672.
Fax: 949/498-4840. **Facility:** 100 rooms. Some two-rm suites with microwave, refrigerator & wetbar, $99-$125;
3 stories; interior corridors; heated pool. **Cards:** AE, DI, DS, MC, VI. *(See ad p 834)*

HOLIDAY INN-SAN CLEMENTE RESORT   Rates Subject to Change   **Phone:** 949/361-3000   **76**
◆◆◆   Fri & Sat   1P: $119- 149 2P/1B: $119- 149 2P/2B: $119- 149 XP: $10   F19
Motor Inn   2/1-4/30 & Sun-Thurs   1P: $99- 139 2P/1B: $99- 139 2P/2B: $99- 139 XP: $10   F19
Location: I-5; southbound exit Ave Palizada, northbound exit Ave Presidio; 0.5 mi se. 111 S Avenida de
Estrella 92672. Fax: 949/361-2472. **Terms:** Handling fee imposed. **Facility:** 72 rooms. Many rooms with
whirlpool spa, $135-$145; 3 stories; interior corridors. **All Rooms:** combo or shower baths. **Cards:** AE, CB, DI, DS, JC, MC,
VI.

MOTEL SAN CLEMENTE   **Phone:** (949)492-1960   **77**
(AAA) [SAVE]   6/1-9/15   1P: $40- 65 2P/1B: $40- 75 2P/2B: $40- 85 XP: $5-10   D5
          2/1-5/31 & 9/16-1/31   1P: $36- 55 2P/1B: $40- 65 2P/2B: $40- 70 XP: $5-10   D5
◆◆   **Location:** Adjacent to I-5, exit El Camino Real. 1819 S El Camino Real 92672. Fax: 949/492-2618.
Motel   **Terms:** Reserv deposit; handling fee imposed. **Facility:** 18 rooms. 4 stories; exterior corridors.
All Rooms: combo or shower baths. **Cards:** AE, DS, JC, MC, VI. **Special Amenities:** Early check-in/late
check-out.

QUALITY SUITES HOTEL   **Phone:** (949)366-1000   **81**
(AAA) [SAVE]   6/1-9/28 [BP]   1P: $79- 135   2P/2B: $89- 135 XP: $10   F18
          2/1-5/31 & 9/29-1/31 [BP] 1P: $59- 129   2P/2B: $69- 129 XP: $10   F18
◆◆◆   **Location:** Adjacent to I-5, exit El Camino Real e. 2481 S El Camino Real 92672. Fax: 949/366-1030.
Motel   **Terms:** Reserv deposit; weekly/monthly rates. **Facility:** 66 rooms. 3 two-bedroom units. 4 stories; interior cor-
ridors; heated pool, whirlpool. **Cards:** AE, DI, DS, MC, VI. **Special Amenities:** Free breakfast and free
room upgrade (subject to availability with advanced reservations). *(See color ad below)*

SAN CLEMENTE BEACH TRAVELODGE   **Phone:** (949)498-5954   **80**
(AAA) [SAVE]   5/1-10/15 [CP]   1P: $45- 99 2P/1B: $49- 109 2P/2B: $49- 109 XP: $5   F17
          2/1-4/30 & 10/16-1/31 [CP] 1P: $39- 89 2P/1B: $45- 89 2P/2B: $45- 99 XP: $5   F17
◆◆   **Location:** Adjacent to I-5; southbound exit Calafia; northbound exit Magdalena. 2441 S El Camino Real
Motel   92672. Fax: 949/498-6657. **Terms:** Reserv deposit; weekly rates. **Facility:** 19 rooms. Located less than 1 mi
from the beach. 1 two-bedroom unit. 4 stories; interior/exterior corridors. **All Rooms:** combo or shower
baths. **Some Rooms:** whirlpools. **Cards:** AE, DI, DS, MC, VI. **Special Amenities:** Free breakfast. *(See color ad p 834)*

RESTAURANTS

SWISS CHALET   **Dinner:** $11-$18   **Phone:** 949-492-7931   **56**
◆◆   **Location:** Downtown, just n of Del Mar. 216 N El Camino Real 92672. **Hours:** 5 pm-9 pm, Sun from 4 pm.
Specialty   Closed major holidays Mon & Tues. **Reservations:** suggested. **Features:** casual dress; children's menu;
beer & wine only; minimum charge-$5; a la carte. Charming alpine decor. Swiss, Austrian & a few German
entrees. Smoke free premises. **Cards:** AE, MC, VI.

THE VINTAGE RESTAURANT   **Lunch:** $5-$11   **Dinner:** $9-$18   **Phone:** 949/492-3236   **57**
◆◆   **Location:** Downtown, just n of Del Mar. 110 N El Camino Real 92672. **Hours:** 7 am-10 pm; Sun-1:30 pm.
Specialty   **Features:** casual dress; cocktails & lounge; minimum charge-$5. Greek-Italian & Continental cuisine. Also
prime rib, fresh fish & pasta. **Cards:** MC, VI.

What A Long, Strange Trip It's Been . . . .

Don't make that mistake again. Let AAA's Travel Agency
Services plan your next trip.

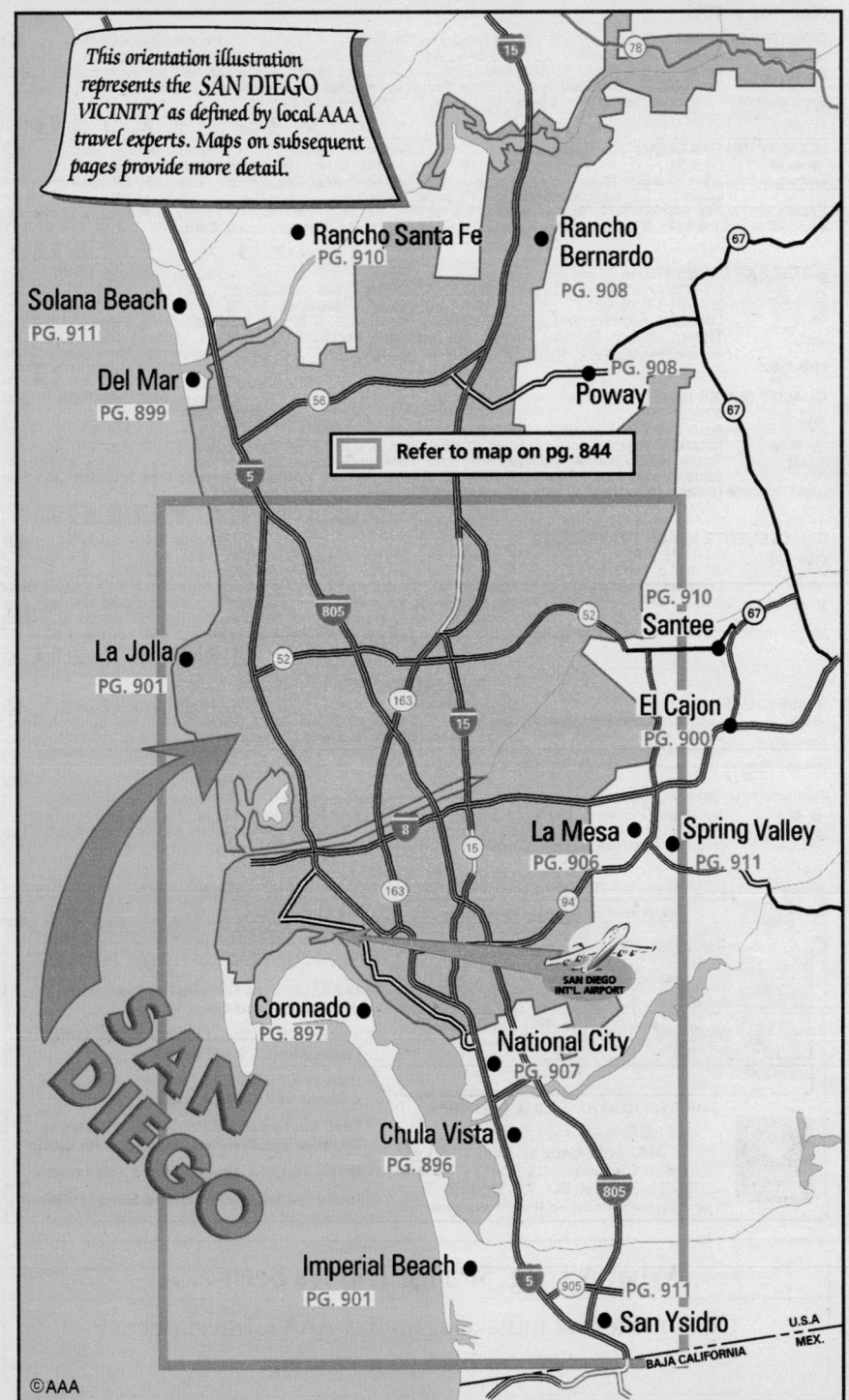

This orientation illustration represents the *SAN DIEGO VICINITY* as defined by local AAA travel experts. Maps on subsequent pages provide more detail.

Rancho Santa Fe
PG. 910

Rancho Bernardo
PG. 908

Solana Beach
PG. 911

Del Mar
PG. 899

PG. 908
Poway

Refer to map on pg. 844

PG. 910

La Jolla
PG. 901

Santee

El Cajon
PG. 900

La Mesa
PG. 906

Spring Valley
PG. 911

SAN DIEGO INT'L. AIRPORT

Coronado
PG. 897

National City
PG. 907

SAN DIEGO

Chula Vista
PG. 896

Imperial Beach
PG. 901

PG. 911

San Ysidro

U.S.A
MEX.

BAJA CALIFORNIA

©AAA

San Diego
pop. 1,110,500

This index helps you "spot" where approved accommodations are located on the detailed maps that follow. Rate ranges are for comparison only and show the property's high season. Turn to the listing page for more detailed rate information and consult display ads for special promotions. Restaurant rate range is for dinner unless only lunch (L) is served.

✈ Airport Accommodations

Spotter/Map Pg. Number	OA	SAN DIEGO	Rating	Rate	Listing Page
80 / p. 844	⟨⟩	Best Western Posada at the Yacht Harbor, 1.8 mi sw of airport	◆◆	$109-139 SAVE	850
79 / p. 844	⟨⟩	Holiday Inn-San Diego Bayside, 1.8 mi sw of airport	◆◆◆	$119-149 SAVE	875
40 / p. 844	⟨⟩	Quality Inn Airport-Seaworld Area, 1.5 mi nw of airport	◆◆	$79-119 SAVE	884
99 / p. 844	⟨⟩	Ramada Limited-Harborside, 1.8 mi sw of airport	◆◆	$69-79 SAVE	887
76 / p. 844		Sheraton San Diego Hotel & Marina, 0.3 mi s of airport	◆◆◆◆	$199	890
78 / p. 844	⟨⟩	Travelodge Hotel-Harbor Island, 0.5 mi s of airport	◆◆◆	$119-144 SAVE	891

SAN DIEGO

Spotter/Map Pg.Number	OA	SAN DIEGO - Lodgings	Rating	Rate	Listing Page
28 / p. 844		Horton Grand Hotel	◆◆	$129-219	875
29 / p. 844	⟨⟩	Best Western Inn-Miramar/San Diego	◆◆◆	$79-89 SAVE	847
30 / p. 844		Courtyard by Marriott - see color ad p 861	◆◆◆	$139	861
31 / p. 844	⟨⟩	Inn Suites Hotels San Diego Balboa Park Resort - see color ad p 877	◆◆	$99-129 SAVE	880
32 / p. 844	⟨⟩	Catamaran Resort Hotel	◆◆◆	$140-600 SAVE	853
34 / p. 844	⟨⟩	Quality Suites	◆◆◆	$95-105 SAVE	884
35 / p. 844	⟨⟩	Ramada Limited Seaworld	◆◆	$85-195 SAVE	887
36 / p. 844	⟨⟩	Heritage Park Bed & Breakfast Inn	◆◆◆	$135-225 SAVE	870
37 / p. 844	⟨⟩	San Diego Hilton Beach & Tennis Resort - see ad p 119	◆◆◆◆	$200-295 SAVE	888
38 / p. 844	⟨⟩	San Diego Paradise Point Resort - see ad p 889	◆◆◆	$185-405 SAVE	890
39 / p. 844	⟨⟩	Dana Inn & Marina - see color ad p 863, p 870	◆◆	$105-148 SAVE	861
40 / p. 844	⟨⟩	Quality Inn Airport-Seaworld Area	◆◆	$79-119 SAVE	884
41 / p. 844	⟨⟩	Goodnite Inn Sea World Area	◆◆	$57 SAVE	867
42 / p. 844	⟨⟩	Hyatt Islandia - see color ad p 565	◆◆◆	$155-250 SAVE	877
43 / p. 844	⟨⟩	Holiday Inn-Mission Bay/Sea World Area - see color ad starting on p 858, p 846	◆◆◆	$89-159 SAVE	872
44 / p. 844		Holiday Inn Select-Miramar/Mira Mesa - see color ad p 876	◆◆◆	$89-129	875
45 / p. 844	⟨⟩	Premier Inns	◆◆	$79 SAVE	882
46 / p. 844	⟨⟩	Days Inn Suites-Seaworld/Airport	◆◆	$79-109 SAVE	865
47 / p. 844		Holiday Inn Hotel & Suites-Old Town, Circa 1850 - see color ad p 873	◆◆◆	$109	872
48 / p. 844	⟨⟩	Doubletree Hotel-San Diego Mission Valley - see ad p 867	◆◆◆	$119 SAVE	867
49 / p. 844	⟨⟩	Comfort Inn & Suites-Zoo/Sea World Area - see color ad p 855, p 846	◆◆◆	$89-159 SAVE	860
50 / p. 844	⟨⟩	Hanalei Hotel - see color ad p 869	◆◆◆	$104 SAVE	868
51 / p. 844		Handlery Hotel Resort - see ad p 869	◆◆◆	$89	869
52 / p. 844	⟨⟩	Good Nite Inn	◆	$57 SAVE	867
53 / p. 844	⟨⟩	Hyatt Regency San Diego - see color ad p 565	◆◆◆◆	$264-376 SAVE	877
54 / p. 844	⟨⟩	Super 8 Motel-Mission Valley/Stadium	◆◆	$55-85 SAVE	890

Spotter/Map Pg.Number	OA	SAN DIEGO - Lodgings (contd.)	Rating	Rate	Listing Page
56 / p. 844		Wyndham Garden Hotel - see color ad p 893	◆◆◆	$121	893
57 / p. 844		Super 8 Mission Bay	◆◆	$54-69	890
59 / p. 844	⊕	Ocean Park Inn - see color ad p 881	◆◆	$129-249 SAVE	880
60 / p. 844		San Diego Marriott Mission Valley	◆◆◆	$164	888
61 / p. 844	⊕	Pacific Terrace Inn - see color ad p 883, p 870	◆◆◆◆	$215-615 SAVE	882
62 / p. 844	⊕	Radisson Hotel-San Diego - see ad p 888	◆◆◆	$105 SAVE	885
63 / p. 844	⊕	San Diego Mission Valley Hilton - see color ad p 889 & ad p 119	◆◆◆	$134-209	889
64 / p. 844	⊕	Comfort Suites Mission Valley - see color ad p 846, p 851	◆◆	$89-149 SAVE	861
65 / p. 844	⊕	Holiday Inn Select- San Diego - see color ad p 875	◆◆◆	$75-105 SAVE	875
66 / p. 844	⊕	Days Inn-Hotel Circle - see color ad p 864, p 870	◆◆	$85-149 SAVE	865
67 / p. 844	⊕	Vagabond Inn-Mission Valley	◆◆	$89-94 SAVE	892
68 / p. 844		Four Points Hotel By Sheraton	◆◆◆	$170	867
69 / p. 844	⊕	Kings Inn	◆◆	$79-109 SAVE	880
70 / p. 844	⊕	Regency Plaza Hotel - see color ad starting on p 866 , p 846	◆◆◆	$99-169 SAVE	887
71 / p. 844	⊕	Western Inn-Old town - see color ad p 892	◆◆	$79-109 SAVE	893
72 / p. 844	⊕	Ramada Plaza Hotel Circle/Sea World Area - see color ad p 852, p 846	◆◆◆	$89-119 SAVE	887
73 / p. 844	⊕	Hotel Circle Inn & Suites - see color ad starting on p 848, p 846	◆◆	$69-159 SAVE	875
74 / p. 844	⊕	Beach Haven Inn - see ad p 847	◆◆	$110-155	846
75 / p. 844	⊕	Best Western Hacienda Hotel-Old Town - see color ad p 854	◆◆◆	$145-155 SAVE	847
76 / p. 844		Sheraton San Diego Hotel & Marina	◆◆◆◆	$199	890
78 / p. 844	⊕	Travelodge Hotel-Harbor Island	◆◆◆	$119-144 SAVE	891
79 / p. 844	⊕	Holiday Inn-San Diego Bayside - see color ad p 874, p 870	◆◆◆	$119-149 SAVE	875
80 / p. 844	⊕	Best Western Posada at the Yacht Harbor - see color ad p 854	◆◆	$109-139 SAVE	850
81 / p. 844		Holiday Inn Mission Valley/Stadium - see color ad p 873	◆◆◆	$89-139	872
82 / p. 844	⊕	Shelter Pointe Hotel & Marina - see color ad p 890	◆◆◆	$119-189 SAVE	890
83 / p. 844	⊕	Humphrey's Half Moon Inn & Suites - see color ad p 878, p 870	◆◆◆	$159-299 SAVE	877
84 / p. 844	⊕	The Bay Club Hotel & Marina - see color ad p 846	◆◆◆	$119-199 SAVE	846
85 / p. 844	⊕	Best Western Island Palms Hotel & Marina - see color ad p 870, p 856	◆◆◆	$129-269 SAVE	850
86 / p. 844	⊕	Old Town Plaza Hotel	◆◆◆	$69-89 SAVE	881
87 / p. 844	⊕	Days Inn Harbor View - see color ad p 862	◆◆	$89-129 SAVE	862
88 / p. 844		Holiday Inn-Harbor View - see color ad p 873	◆◆◆	$139-169	872
89 / p. 844		Crowne Plaza-San Diego on the Bay	◆◆◆	$159-169	861
90 / p. 844	⊕	Best Western Bayside Inn - see color ad p 850	◆◆◆	$119-149 SAVE	847
91 / p. 844		Quality Inn & Suites - see color ad p 860	◆◆	$99-159	884
92 / p. 844	⊕	Rodeway Inn-Zoo/Downtown	◆◆	$79-109 SAVE	888
93 / p. 844		Comfort Inn-Downtown - see color ad p 860	◆◆	$89-149	861
94 / p. 844	⊕	The Westgate Hotel	◆◆◆◆	$205-255 SAVE	893
95 / p. 844	⊕	Vagabond Inn-Downtown	◆	$76 SAVE	892
96 / p. 844	⊕	Travelodge Sea World - see color ad p 892		$49-89	891
97 / p. 844	⊕	Vagabond Inn-Point Loma	◆	$69-74 SAVE	893
98 / p. 844		The Westin Horton Plaza	◆◆◆	$174-264	893
99 / p. 844	⊕	Ramada Limited-Harborside	◆◆	$69-79 SAVE	887
100 / p. 844	⊕	San Diego Marriott Hotel & Marina	◆◆◆◆	$215-235	888
102 / p. 844	⊕	Ramada Inn & Conference Center - see color ad p 854	◆◆	$79-109 SAVE	885
104 / p. 844		Hampton Inn-San Diego	◆◆◆	$94-99	867

Spotter/Map Pg.Number	OA	**SAN DIEGO** - Lodgings (contd.)	Rating	Rate	Listing Page
106 / p. 844	AAA	**Lamplighter Inn & Suites - see color ad p 880**	◆	$51-79	880
107 / p. 844	AAA	**Ramada Limited-Old Town - see color ad p 873**	◆ ◆ ◆	$93-102	887
108 / p. 844	AAA	**Embassy Suites-San Diego Bay**	◆ ◆ ◆	$163-269 SAVE	867
109 / p. 844	AAA	**Radisson Hotel Harbor View**	◆ ◆ ◆	$109 SAVE	884
110 / p. 844		Holiday Inn Express-Sea World Area - see color ad p 876	◆ ◆ ◆	$59-75	870
111 / p. 844	AAA	**Comfort Inn-Airport at Old Town - see color ad p 860**	◆ ◆ ◆	$79-140 SAVE	853
112 / p. 844		Clarion Hotel Bay View	◆ ◆ ◆	$119-159	853
113 / p. 844		San Diego Marriott Suites-Downtown	◆ ◆ ◆	$129	888
114 / p. 844	AAA	**Wyndham Emerald Plaza**	◆ ◆ ◆ ◆	$174 SAVE	893
116 / p. 844	AAA	**Pacific Shores Inn**	◆ ◆	$99-139 SAVE	881
117 / p. 844		Hampton Inn-Airport/SeaWorld Area - see color ad p 868	◆ ◆ ◆	$99-159 SAVE	867
119 / p. 844	AAA	**Best Western Blue Sea Lodge - see color ad p 847**	◆ ◆ ◆	$159-179 SAVE	847
120 / p. 844	AAA	**Crown Point View Suite-Hotel - see color ad p 862**	◆ ◆ ◆	$109-185 SAVE	861
121 / p. 844		Super 8 Bayview	◆	$60	890
122 / p. 844	AAA	**Town and Country Hotel - see color ad p 891**	◆ ◆ ◆	$125-210 SAVE	890
123 / p. 844	AAA	**Days Inn Downtown/Zoo**	◆ ◆	$75-105 SAVE	861
127 / p. 844	AAA	**Quality Resort-Mission Valley - see color ad p 885**	◆ ◆	$109-169 SAVE	884
129 / p. 844	AAA	**Point Loma Inn**	◆	$54-74	882
130 / p. 844	AAA	**Padre Trail Inn**	◆ ◆	$99-109 SAVE	882
131 / p. 844	AAA	**Diamond Head Inn**	◆ ◆	$99-149 SAVE	867
133 / p. 844	AAA	**Old Town Inn - see ad p 882**	◆	$55-84	880
138 / p. 844		Residence Inn by Marriott-San Diego	◆ ◆ ◆	$155	888
139 / p. 844	AAA	**Comfort Inn-Sea World Area - see color ad p 843**		$69-109	861
141 / p. 844	AAA	**Best Western Seven Seas - see color ad p 850**	◆ ◆	$89 SAVE	853
142 / p. 844	AAA	**Days Inn La Jolla & Sea World Area - see color ad p 865**	◆ ◆	$74-84 SAVE	865
144 / p. 844	AAA	**Balboa Park Inn**	◆ ◆ ◆	$99-189	846
145 / p. 844	AAA	**Ramada Limited-South Bay**	◆ ◆	$80-85 SAVE	887
		SAN DIEGO - Restaurants			
12 / p. 844		City Delicatessen	◆ ◆	$4-16	894
13 / p. 844		Old Venice Restaurant	◆ ◆	$6-16	895
15 / p. 844	AAA	**Shanghai**	◆	$8-16	896
17 / p. 844	AAA	**Casa de Bandini**	◆	$7-15	894
18 / p. 844		Cafe Pacifica	◆ ◆ ◆	$15-24	894
19 / p. 844		Islands Restaurant - see color ad p 869	◆ ◆	$6-25	895
20 / p. 844		Baci's	◆ ◆ ◆ ◆	$16-27	894
23 / p. 844	AAA	**Casa De Pico**	◆ ◆	$7-14	894
25 / p. 844		California Cafe Bar & Grill	◆ ◆ ◆	$9-19	894
27 / p. 844		Monterey Whaling Company	◆ ◆	$9-22	895
28 / p. 844		Prego	◆ ◆ ◆	$16-19	895
29 / p. 844		Dockside Restaurant	◆ ◆ ◆	$13-27	894
30 / p. 844		The Amigo Spot	◆	$6-16	894
31 / p. 844		The Tickled Trout - see color ad p 852	◆ ◆	$12-19	896
32 / p. 844		Acapulco - see color ad p 854	◆ ◆	$6-14	893
33 / p. 844		Tio Leo's	◆ ◆	$7-14	896
34 / p. 844		Hob Nob Hill	◆	$8-14	895
35 / p. 844	AAA	**Casa Guadalajara**	◆	$6-14	894
36 / p. 844		Senor Spencer's	◆ ◆ ◆	$12-22	896
37 / p. 844		Tom Ham's Lighthouse	◆	$10-30	896
38 / p. 844		Sam Choy's Hawaii at the Bali Hai	◆ ◆ ◆	$12-21	896

Spotter/Map Pg.Number	OA	SAN DIEGO - Restaurants (contd.)	Rating	Rate	Listing Page
㊴ / p. 844		Humphrey's - see color ad p 878	◆◆◆	$18-25	895
㊶ / p. 844		Anthony's Star of the Sea Room	◆◆◆	$20-40	894
㊷ / p. 844		Anthony's Fish Grotto	◆	$8-23	894
㊸ / p. 844		The Godfather Restaurant	◆◆◆	$10-23	895
㊹ / p. 844		Fio's	◆◆◆	$9-23	894
㊻ / p. 844		Harbor House Restaurant	◆◆◆	$13-23	895
㊾ / p. 844		The Fish Market & Top of The Market	◆◆	$13-30	894
㊿ / p. 844		Sally's	◆◆◆	$18-32	896
51 / p. 844		Mister A's	◆◆◆◆	$20-40	895
52 / p. 844		Kaiserhof	◆◆	$9-20	895
53 / p. 844		Molly's	◆◆◆	$18-27	895
54 / p. 844	ⓐ	**Tep's Villa Roma**	◆◆	$9-16	896
55 / p. 844	ⓐ	**Lino's Italian Restaurant**	◆◆	$7-15	895
56 / p. 844	ⓐ	**Rancho El Nopal**	◆◆	$5-9	896
59 / p. 844		China Camp	◆◆	$10-24	894
60 / p. 844		Lotsa Pasta	◆◆	$15-18	895
61 / p. 844		Dobson's Bar & Restaurant	◆◆◆	$13-25	894
62 / p. 844		Lamont St Grill	◆◆	$12-17	895
63 / p. 844		Rainwater's	◆◆◆	$18-35	895

San Diego Vicinity

Spotter/Map Pg.Number	OA	LA JOLLA - Lodgings	Rating	Rate	Listing Page
❶ / p. 844		La Jolla Marriott	◆◆◆	$189	903
❷ / p. 844	ⓐ	**Radisson Hotel La Jolla - see color ad p 886 , p 870**	◆◆◆	$149-199 🏧	904
❸ / p. 844	ⓐ	**Embassy Suites**	◆◆◆	$245 🏧	902
❹ / p. 844	ⓐ	**Sea Lodge at La Jolla Shores - see color ad p 905**	◆◆◆	$205-479 🏧	904
❺ / p. 844	ⓐ	**Andrea Villa Inn**	◆◆	$130-145 🏧	901
❻ / p. 844		Hotel La Jolla At The Shores - see color ad p 902	◆◆◆	$159-179	902
❼ / p. 844	ⓐ	**Scripps Inn**	◆◆	$145-220 🏧	904
❽ / p. 844	ⓐ	**La Valencia Hotel**	◆◆◆◆	$230-550 🏧	903
❾ / p. 844		Colonial Inn	◆◆◆	$134-225	901
❿ / p. 844	ⓐ	**Best Western Inn By The Sea - see color ad p 846**	◆◆◆	$139-219 🏧	901
⓫ / p. 844	ⓐ	**The Empress Hotel of La Jolla - see color ad p 902**	◆◆◆	$129-199 🏧	902
⓬ / p. 844	ⓐ	**La Jolla Beach Travelodge**	◆◆	$89-159	903
⓭ / p. 844	ⓐ	**Holiday Inn Express La Jolla**	◆◆◆	$89-149 🏧	902
⓮ / p. 844	ⓐ	**The Bed & Breakfast Inn at La Jolla**	◆◆◆	$135-180	901
⓯ / p. 844	ⓐ	**The Lodge at Torrey Pines**	◆◆	$110-200 🏧	903
⓰ / p. 844		Residence Inn by Marriott	◆◆◆	$155-275	904
⓱ / p. 844	ⓐ	**Sheraton Grande Torrey Pines**	◆◆◆◆	$205-280 🏧	904
⓲ / p. 844	ⓐ	**La Jolla Cove Suites - see color ad p 881**	◆	$115-325 🏧	903
⓳ / p. 844	ⓐ	**Hyatt Regency La Jolla - see color ad p 565**	◆◆◆◆	$214-325 🏧	903
⓴ / p. 844	ⓐ	**Prospect Park Inn - see color ad p 903**	◆◆	$120-185 🏧	904
21 / p. 844	ⓐ	**La Jolla Travelodge**	◆	$89-129	903
		LA JOLLA - Restaurants			
② / p. 844		Cafe Japengo	◆◆	$14-23	904
③ / p. 844		Marine Room Restaurant - see color ad p 905	◆◆◆	$18-32	904
④ / p. 844		Top O' The Cove Restaurant	◆◆◆	$33-45	906
⑤ / p. 844		Crescent Shores Grill - see color ad p 902	◆◆◆	$12-24	904
⑦ / p. 844		Sky Room	◆◆◆◆	$25-39	906
⑧ / p. 844		Coast Cafe	◆◆	$12-21	904
⑨ / p. 844		Cindy Black's	◆◆◆	$14-22	904
⑩ / p. 844		Marrakesh	◆◆	$15-23	906

Spotter/Map Pg.Number	OA	CORONADO - Lodgings	Rating	Rate	Listing Page
146 / p. 844		Hotel del Coronado	◆◆◆◆	$185-495	898
147 / p. 844	⊕	Loews Coronado Bay Resort	◆◆◆◆	$235-350	898
148 / p. 844	⊕	Glorietta Bay Inn-Coronado - see ad p 865	◆◆◆	$130-195 ▨	897
150 / p. 844	⊕	Best Western Suites-Coronado Island - see color ad p 850	◆◆◆	$120-155 ▨	897
151 / p. 844		Crown City Inn - see color ad p 884	◆◆	$89-165	897
152 / p. 844		La Avenida Inn	◆◆	$125-350	898
153 / p. 844	⊕	Coronado Island Marriott Resort	◆◆◆◆	$275-325	897
		CORONADO - Restaurants			
68 / p. 844		Crown-Coronet Room	◆◆◆	$17-25	898
69 / p. 844		Marius	◆◆◆◆	$41-54	898
70 / p. 844		Peohe's	◆◆	$19-31	898
71 / p. 844		Azzura Point	◆◆◆	$21-35	898
72 / p. 844		The Brigantine	◆◆	$13-25	898
73 / p. 844		Chez Loma Restaurant	◆◆◆	$19-26	898
74 / p. 844		Prince of Wales	◆◆◆	$23-38	898
75 / p. 844		Chameleon Cafe	◆◆◆	$9-23	898
76 / p. 844		L'Escale	◆◆◆	$14-25	898
		LA MESA - Lodgings			
156 / p. 844	⊕	La Mesa Travelodge/Centrum	◆	$69-89 ▨	907
157 / p. 844	⊕	Holiday Inn Express-La Mesa	◆◆	$69-79 ▨	907
159 / p. 844	⊕	Days Inn La Mesa Suites/S.D.S.U. - see color ad p 906	◆◆	$69-89 ▨	906
160 / p. 844	⊕	Rodeway Inn	◆◆	$60-75 ▨	907
161 / p. 844	⊕	Comfort Inn-La Mesa	◆◆	$69 ▨	906
162 / p. 844	⊕	Ramada Limited - see color ad p 906	◆◆	$59 ▨	907
		LA MESA - Restaurants			
76 / p. 844		The Brigantine	◆◆	$12-24	907
77 / p. 844		Claim Jumper	◆◆	$11-22	907
78 / p. 844		Anthony's Fish Grotto	◆	$8-15	907

Meal Plan Indicators

CP = Continental Plan of pastry, juice and another beverage or may offer expanded breakfast items
BP = Breakfast Plan of full hot breakfast
AP = American Plan of three meals daily
MAP = Modified American Plan of two meals daily
EP = European Plan, where rate includes only room

Family Plan Indicators

The establishment may limit the number of children to whom the family plan applies.

F17 = children 17 and under stay free (age displayed will reflect property's policy)
D17 = discount for children 17 and under
F = children stay free
D = discounts for children

Spotter/Map Pg.Number	OA	NATIONAL CITY - Lodgings	Rating	Rate	Listing Page
164 / p. 844	AAA	Comfort Inn San Diego/South Bay	◆◆◆	$89 [SAVE]	907
165 / p. 844	AAA	Radisson Suites-National City - see color ad p 907	◆◆◆	$79 [SAVE]	908
166 / p. 844	AAA	Holiday Inn-South Bay - see color ad p 877	◆◆	$69 [SAVE]	908
		CHULA VISTA - Lodgings			
169 / p. 844	AAA	Traveler Inn and Suites	◆◆	$89-109 [SAVE]	897
170 / p. 844	AAA	Best Western South Bay Inn - see color ad p 853	◆◆◆	$89-99 [SAVE]	896
171 / p. 844	AAA	Good Nite Inn-South Bay	◆◆	$54 [SAVE]	897
172 / p. 844	AAA	Days Inn	◆	$69-79 [SAVE]	896
173 / p. 844	AAA	La Quinta Inn	◆◆◆	$75-95 [SAVE]	897
174 / p. 844	AAA	Palomar Inn	◆	$69-99	897
176 / p. 844	AAA	Holiday Inn Express - see color ad p 871	◆◆◆	$49-89 [SAVE]	897
177 / p. 844	AAA	Chula Vista Travelodge	◆	$59-89 [SAVE]	896
		CHULA VISTA - Restaurants			
81 / p. 844		Anthony's Fish Grotto	◆	$7-17	897
82 / p. 844		Jakes-South Bay	◆◆	$12-20	897
		IMPERIAL BEACH - Lodgings			
181 / p. 844	AAA	Hawaiian Gardens Suite-Hotel - see color ad p 862	◆◆	$90-140 [SAVE]	901
		SAN YSIDRO - Lodgings			
185 / p. 844	AAA	Americana Inn & Suites	◆	$42-48 [SAVE]	911
186 / p. 844	AAA	International Motor Inn	◆	$54-59 [SAVE]	911
		SPRING VALLEY - Lodgings			
190 / p. 844	AAA	Crown Inn Suites	◆	$49-64 [SAVE]	911

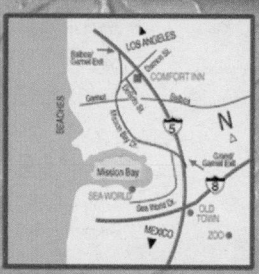

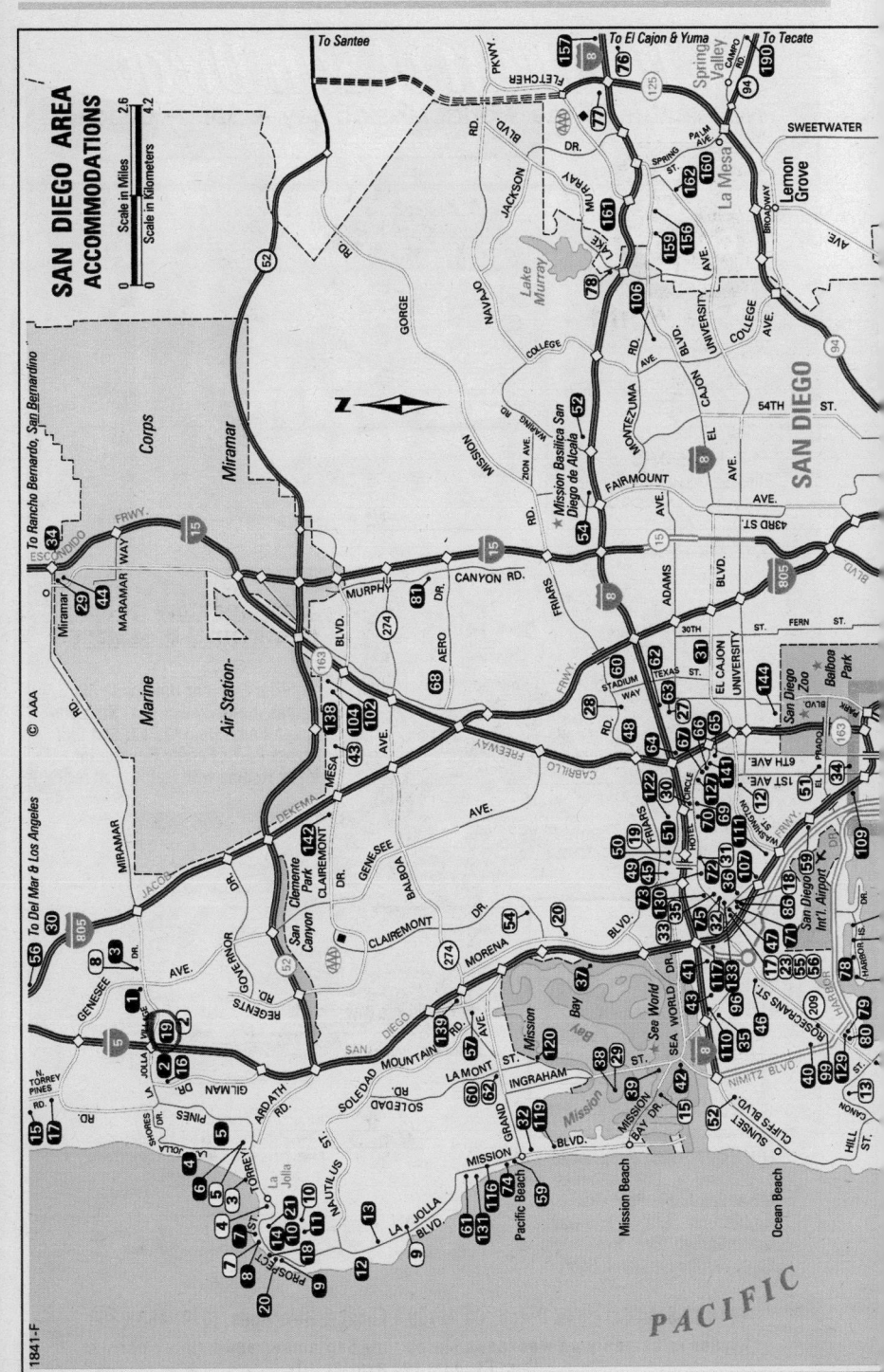

SAN DIEGO AREA
ACCOMMODATIONS

Scale in Miles

Scale in Kilometers

1841-F

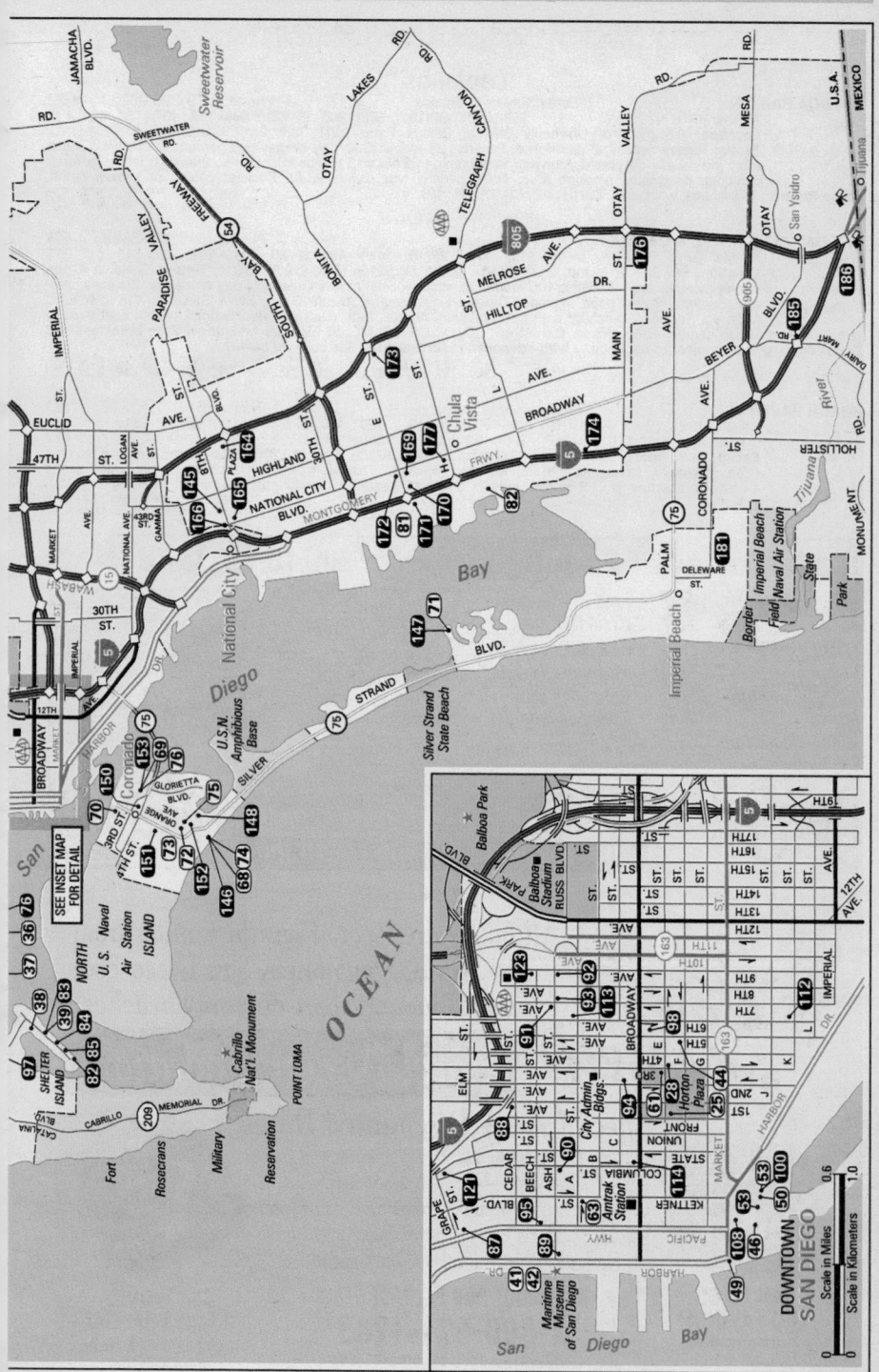

SAN DIEGO—1,110,500   (See map p. 844; index p. 837)

LODGINGS

BALBOA PARK INN
Rates Subject to Change   **Phone:** (619)298-0823   144
AAA   All Year [CP]   1P: $80- 200   2P/1B: $80- 200   2P/2B: $99- 189   XP: $8   F11
◆◆◆   **Location:** 0.5 mi s of University Blvd at Balboa Park. 3402 Park Blvd 92103. Fax: 619/294-8070.
Motel   **Terms:** Reserv deposit, 7 day notice. **Facility:** 26 rooms. Colorfully landscaped gardens & courtyard. Each room individually decorated, four with woodburning fireplace. 3 two-bedroom units. 2 stories; interior/exterior corridors; designated smoking area; street parking only; sundeck. **All Rooms:** combo or shower baths.
Some Rooms: 15 kitchens, whirlpools. **Cards:** AE, CB, DI, DS, MC, VI.   🛥️🟦💻🖥️🖨️📠🔌✕

THE BAY CLUB HOTEL & MARINA
Phone: (619)224-8888   84
AAA SAVE   All Year [BP]   1P: $109- 179   2P/1B: $119- 189   2P/2B: $119- 199   XP: $10   F12
◆◆◆   **Location:** On Shelter Island. 2131 Shelter Island Dr 92106. Fax: 619/225-1604. **Terms:** Check-in 4 pm;
Motor Inn   weekly/monthly rates. **Facility:** 105 rooms. Spacious rooms, most with view of bay or marina. 2 stories; interior corridors; heated pool, whirlpool. **Dining:** Restaurant; 6:30 am-10 pm, Sat & Sun from 7 am; $6-$18; cocktails. **Services:** giftshop; area transportation, Amtrak. Fee: massage. **Recreation:** electric boat avail to guests; in-room video games, video arcade. **Cards:** AE, CB, DI, DS, JC, MC, VI. **Special Amenities:** Free breakfast and free room upgrade (subject to availability with advanced reservations).** (See color ad below)*
🅢/🅓🔌🟦🛥️🍽️🟦🔌🛏️💻🖥️🖨️📠🔌✕

BEACH HAVEN INN
Rates Subject to Change   **Phone:** (619)272-3812   74
AAA   6/1-9/15 [CP]   1P: $85- 100   2P/1B: $90- 110   2P/2B: $110- 155   XP: $10   F12
◆◆   2/1-5/31 & 9/16-1/31 [CP]   1P: $60- 90   2P/1B: $60- 90   2P/2B: $80- 130   XP: $5   F12
Motel   **Location:** In Pacific Beach area. 4740 Mission Blvd 92109. Fax: 619/272-3532. **Terms:** Weekly/monthly rates, off-season; small pets only, $50 dep req. **Facility:** 23 rooms. 1 block to beach. Nicely decorated rooms 1-bedroom apartments. 1-2 stories; exterior corridors; heated pool, whirlpool. **Cards:** AE, CB, DI, DS, MC, VI. *(See ad p 847)*   🐾🛥️🔌🎬📺✕

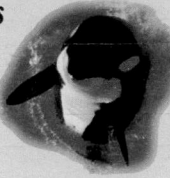

(See map p. 844)

BEST WESTERN BAYSIDE INN　　　　　　　　　　　　　　　Phone: (619)233-7500　**90**
(AAA) (SAVE)　5/1-9/30 [CP]　　1P:　$99- 129　2P/1B: $109- 129　2P/2B: $119- 149　XP: $10　F16
　　　　　2/1-4/30 & 10/1-1/31 [CP]　1P:　$99- 119　2P/1B: $109- 119　2P/2B: $109- 139　XP: $10　F16
◆◆◆　**Location:** 555 W Ash St at Columbia 92101. Fax: 619/239-8060. **Terms:** Reserv deposit; weekly/monthly
Hotel　rates. **Facility:** 122 rooms. Many rooms with harbor view, $8 additional charge; 14 stories; interior corridors;
heated pool, whirlpool. **Dining:** Restaurant; 6:30 am-2 & 5-9 pm; cocktails. **Services:** area transportation,
Amtrack & Greyhound. **Cards:** AE, CB, DI, DS, JC, MC, VI. **Special Amenities:** Free breakfast and free room upgrade
(subject to availability with advanced reservations). *(See color ad p 850)*

BEST WESTERN BLUE SEA LODGE　　　　　　　　　　　　Phone: (619)488-4700　**119**
(AAA) (SAVE)　6/1-9/30　　　　1P: $149- 169　2P/1B: $149- 169　2P/2B: $159- 179　XP: $10　F16
　　　　　2/1-5/31 & 10/1-1/31　1P:　$89- 119　2P/1B:　$89- 119　2P/2B:　$99- 129　XP: $10　F16
◆◆◆　**Location:** Pacific Beach area, just w of Mission Blvd. 707 Pacific Beach Dr 92109. Fax: 619/488-7276.
Motel　**Terms:** Reserv deposit; weekly/monthly rates. **Facility:** 100 rooms. At the beach. Many balconies & ocean
views. 3 stories; interior corridors; heated pool, whirlpool. Fee: parking. **Dining:** Restaurant nearby.
All Rooms: combo or shower baths. **Some Rooms:** 48 efficiencies. **Cards:** AE, CB, DI, DS, JC, MC, VI.
(See color ad below)

BEST WESTERN HACIENDA HOTEL-OLD TOWN　　　　　　　Phone: (619)298-4707　**75**
(AAA) (SAVE)　6/18-8/28　　　1P: $135- 145　2P/1B: $145- 155　2P/2B: $145- 155　XP: $10　F16
　　　　　2/1-6/17 & 8/29-1/31　1P: $125- 135　2P/1B: $135- 145　2P/2B: $135- 145　XP: $10　F16
◆◆◆　**Location:** Juan & Harney sts. 4041 Harney St 92110. Fax: 619/298-4771. **Terms:** Reserv deposit.
Motor Inn　**Facility:** 168 rooms. Beautifully landscaped, terraced hillside location. Rooms have a Spanish decor. 3 stories;
exterior corridors; heated pool, whirlpool. **Dining:** Restaurant; 6:30 am-10 pm; $6-$13; cocktails; also,
Acapulco, see separate listing. **Cards:** AE, CB, DI, DS, MC, VI. **Special Amenities:** Free room upgrade and preferred
room (each subject to availability with advanced reservations). *(See color ad p 854)*

BEST WESTERN INN-MIRAMAR/SAN DIEGO　　　　　　　　Phone: (619)578-6600　**29**
(AAA) (SAVE)　5/2-9/16 [CP]　　1P:　$69- 79　2P/1B:　$79- 89　2P/2B:　$79- 89　XP: $6-8　F12
　　　　　2/1-5/1 & 9/17-1/31 [CP]　1P:　$62- 72　2P/1B:　$72- 82　2P/2B:　$72- 82　XP: $6-8　F12
◆◆◆　**Location:** Just w of I-15, exit Miramar Rd. 9310 Kearny Mesa Rd 92126. Fax: 619/536-1368. **Terms:** Reserv
Motel　deposit. **Facility:** 100 rooms. 3 stories; exterior corridors; heated pool, whirlpool. **Dining:** Restaurant nearby.
Cards: AE, CB, DI, DS, JC, MC, VI. **Special Amenities:** Early check-in/late check-out and free
breakfast.

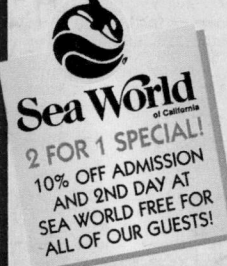

DELUXE ROOM

SPECIAL AAA FAMILY RATE

$49⁹⁵*

UP TO 4 PERSONS, PER ROOM

March, April, May & Sept. from $59⁹⁵*
June thru August from $69⁹⁵*

Higher rates during holidays & some weekends.

MINI-SUITE

$64⁹⁵*

(1 OR 2 PERSONS)

One Bed • One Bath •Full Kitchen
with Stove, Refrigerator,
Coffeemaker, Microwave and
Toaster • Utensils included

**June thru August
and Holidays from $74⁹⁵***

Higher rates on some weekends.

TWO ROOM KITCHEN SUITE

$99⁹⁵*

(UP TO 6 PERSONS)

March, April, May & Sept. from $109⁹⁵*
June, July & August from $139⁹⁵*

Higher rates during holidays & some weekends.

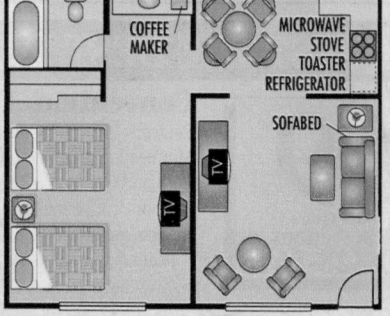

Bedroom with 2 Beds & Bath
• Spacious Living Room with
Sofasleeper • 2 TV's
• Dining Area • Full Kitchen
with Stove, Refrigerator, Toaster,
Coffeemaker and Microwave
• Utensils included

(See map p. 844)

BEST WESTERN ISLAND PALMS HOTEL & MARINA   **Phone: (619)222-0561**   85

 All Year   1P: $129- 269   2P/1B: $129- 269   2P/2B: $129- 269   XP: $10   F17
Location: On Shelter Island. 2051 Shelter Island Dr 92106. Fax: 619/222-9760. **Terms:** Check-in 4 pm; weekly rates. **Facility:** 97 rooms. Most rooms with view of marina or harbor. 29 suites with kitchen, $125-$175; 2 stories; exterior corridors; heated pool, whirlpool. Fee: marina. **Dining:** Restaurant; 6:30 am-10 pm; $9-$16; cocktails. **Recreation:** bicycles, jogging. **All Rooms:** combo or shower baths. **Cards:** AE, CB, DI, DS, JC, MC, VI. *(See color ad p 870 & p 856)*

Motor Inn

BEST WESTERN POSADA AT THE YACHT HARBOR   **Phone: (619)224-3254**   80

 6/1-9/6 [CP]   1P: $99- 129   2P/1B: $99- 129   2P/2B: $109- 139   XP: $10   F18
2/1-5/31 & 9/7-1/31 [CP]   1P: $89- 119   2P/1B: $89- 119   2P/2B: $99- 129   XP: $10   F18
Location: Point Loma area, just s of Rosecrans St. 5005 N Harbor Dr 92106. Fax: 619/224-2186. **Terms:** Weekly rates; package plans. **Facility:** 111 rooms. Many rooms with harbor view, $6 additional charge; 6 stories; interior corridors; small heated pool, whirlpool. **Dining:** Restaurant nearby. **Cards:** AE, CB, DI, DS, JC, MC, VI. **Special Amenities:** Free breakfast and free local telephone calls. *(See color ad p 854)*

Motel

(See map p. 844)

BEST WESTERN SEVEN SEAS Phone: (619)291-1300 **141**

	Fri & Sat 6/1-9/5	1P:	$89	2P/1B:	$89	2P/2B:	$89	XP: $10	F17
	Sun-Thurs 6/1-9/5	1P:	$79	2P/1B:	$79	2P/2B:	$79	XP: $10	F17
	Fri & Sat 2/1-5/31 & 9/6-1/31	1P:	$69	2P/1B:	$69	2P/2B:	$69	XP: $10	F17
Motor Inn	Sun-Thurs 2/1-5/31 & 9/6-1/31	1P:	$69	2P/1B:	$69	2P/2B:	$69	XP: $10	F17

Location: 411 S Hotel Cir 92108. Fax: 619/291-6933. **Terms:** Reserv deposit. **Facility:** 307 rooms. 2 stories; exterior corridors; heated pool, whirlpools. **Dining:** Coffee shop; 6 am-10 pm, Fri & Sat-11 pm; $6-$13. **Services:** area transportation, attractions & malls. **Recreation:** basketball court, in-room video games, playground. **Some Rooms:** 9 efficiencies. **Cards:** AE, CB, DI, DS, JC, MC, VI. **Special Amenities:** Free local telephone calls. *(See color ad p 850)*

CATAMARAN RESORT HOTEL Phone: (619)488-1081 **32**

All Year 1P: $140- 600 2P/1B: $140- 600 2P/2B: $140- 600 XP: $20 F16

Location: Just s of Grand Ave; on Mission Bay. 3999 Mission Blvd 92109. Fax: 619/488-1619.

Resort Hotel **Terms:** Check-in 4 pm. **Facility:** 313 rooms. Tropical atmosphere with many rooms overlooking the bay. 2-13 stories; interior/exterior corridors; beach, heated pool, whirlpool. Fee: parking; sailing instruction, roller skates. **Dining:** Restaurant; 6:30 am-10 pm; $7-$22; cocktails. **Services:** giftshop. **Recreation:** paddleboats. Fee: windsurfing. Rental: boats; bicycles. **Some Rooms:** 68 efficiencies, color TV. **Cards:** AE, CB, DI, DS, MC, VI.

CLARION HOTEL BAY VIEW Rates Subject to Change Phone: (619)696-0234 **112**

All Year 1P: $119- 159 2P/1B: $119- 159 2P/2B: $119- 159 XP: $20 F18

Location: 660 K St at 6th Ave 92101. Fax: 619/231-8199. **Facility:** 312 rooms. 2-room suites, extra charge; 21 stories; interior corridors. Fee: parking. **Services:** giftshop. **Cards:** AE, CB, DI, DS, JC, MC, VI.

COMFORT INN-AIRPORT AT OLD TOWN Phone: (619)543-1130 **111**

All Year [CP] 1P: $59- 110 2P/1B: $69- 130 2P/2B: $79- 140 XP: $10 F18

Location: E side of I-5, exit Old Town Ave, 0.5 mi s on San Diego Ave. 1955 San Diego Ave 92110. Fax: 619/543-0180. **Facility:** 123 rooms. Located in Old Town area. 2-3 stories; interior/exterior corridors; heated pool, whirlpool. **Some Rooms:** whirlpools. **Cards:** AE, CB, DI, DS, JC, MC, VI. **Special Amenities:** Free breakfast and free local telephone calls. *(See color ad p 860)*

BEST WESTERN
Island Palms Hotel & Marina

On Shelter Island, along the shores of San Diego Bay

800 feet of frontage along San Diego Bay

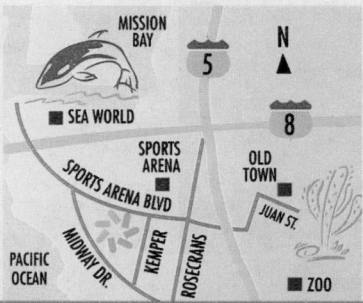

Try Our New Suites!

Mini Suite

One room suite includes a king bed & a living area with full sofa sleeper, coffeemaker, microwave, refrigerator, hairdryer, 25" TV,

$ **79** *⁹⁵

two phones, shower massager, iron/board and private in-suite safe

March, April, May, Sept. and Oct. from $89⁹⁵*
June, July, August and Holidays from $99⁹⁵*

Suite

Includes a bedroom and separate living room with sofasleeper, private in-suite safe, refrigerator, coffeemaker, microwave, iron,

$ **89** *⁹⁵

shower massager, two 25" TV's and three phones (1 in the bath)

March, April, May, Sept. & Oct. from $99⁹⁵*
June, July, August & Holidays from $119⁹⁵*

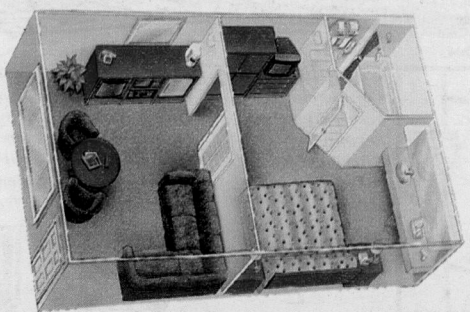

(See map p. 844)

COMFORT INN & SUITES-ZOO/SEA WORLD AREA   Phone: (619)291-7700   **49**
   All Year   1P: $89- 159 2P/1B: $89- 159 2P/2B: $89- 159 XP: $10   F12
Motel   Location: Adjacent to I-8, exit Taylor St. 2485 Hotel Circle Pl 92108. Fax: 619/297-6179. **Facility:** 200 rooms.
50 suites, extra charge; 4 stories; interior corridors; heated pool, whirlpool. **Dining:** Restaurant nearby.
◆◆◆   **Recreation:** video game room. **Some Rooms:** whirlpools. **Cards:** AE, CB, DI, DS, JC, MC, VI.
**Special Amenities: Free breakfast and preferred room (subject to availability with advanced
reservations).** (See color ad p 855 & p 846)

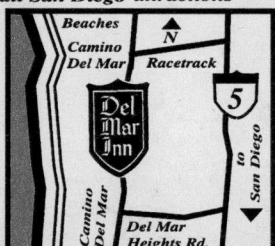

(See map p. 844)

COMFORT INN-DOWNTOWN   Rates Subject to Change   **Phone:** (619)232-2525   93
◆◆   All Year [CP]   1P: $79- 99   2P/1B: $89- 139   2P/2B: $89- 149   XP: $15-30   F18
Motel   **Location:** 719 Ash St at 7th Ave 92101. Fax: 619/238-8897. **Terms:** Reserv deposit. **Facility:** 67 rooms. 3 stories; exterior corridors. **Services:** area transportation. **All Rooms:** shower baths. **Cards:** AE, DI, DS, MC, VI.
(See color ad p 860)

COMFORT INN-SEA WORLD AREA   Rates Subject to Change   **Phone:** (619)483-9800   139
(AAA) [FYI]   4/1-4/15, 6/1-9/4 & 12/20-1/3
    [CP]   1P: $69- 109   2P/1B: $69- 109   2P/2B: $69- 109   XP: $10
Motel   2/1-3/31, 4/16-5/31,
    9/5-12/19 & 1/4-1/31 [CP]   1P: $49- 89   2P/1B: $49- 89   2P/2B: $59- 99   XP: $10
Under major renovation. **Location:** I-5; northbound exit Grand/Garnet, southbound exit Balboa/Garnet; just e of Mission Bay Dr. 4610 DeSoto St 92109. Fax: 619/483-4010. **Terms:** Reserv deposit, 3 day notice; weekly rates. **Facility:** 88 rooms. 4 stories; interior/exterior corridors; small heated pool, whirlpool. **Dining:** Restaurant nearby. **Cards:** AE, DI, DS, MC, VI.
(See color ad p 843)

COMFORT SUITES MISSION VALLEY   **Phone:** (619)294-3444   64
(AAA) [SAVE]   All Year [CP]   1P: $89- 149   2P/1B: $89- 149   2P/2B: $89- 149   XP: $10   F12
    Location: S side of I-8, Mission Center Rd exit. 631 Camino Del Rio S 92108. Fax: 619/260-0746.
◆◆   **Facility:** 122 rooms. 3 stories; interior/exterior corridors; heated pool, whirlpool. **Dining:** Restaurant nearby.
Motel   **Services:** area transportation, w/ zoo or Sea World Pkg. **Some Rooms:** whirlpools. **Cards:** AE, CB, DI, DS, JC, MC, VI. **Special Amenities:** Free breakfast and free newspaper. *(See color ad p 846 & p 851)*

COURTYARD BY MARRIOTT   Rates Subject to Change   **Phone:** 619/558-9600   30
◆◆◆   All Year   1P: $139   2P/1B: $139   2P/2B: $139
Motor Inn   **Location:** 0.5 mi e I-805; exit Mira Mesa. 9650 Scranton Rd 92121. Fax: 619/558-4539. **Terms:** Check-in 4 pm. **Facility:** 149 rooms. 3 stories; interior corridors; heated pool. **Cards:** AE, CB, DI, DS, JC, MC, VI.
(See color ad below)

CROWNE PLAZA-SAN DIEGO ON THE BAY   Rates Subject to Change   **Phone:** (619)232-3861   89
◆◆◆   9/15-1/31   1P: $149- 159   2P/1B: $159- 169   2P/2B: $159- 169   XP: $10   F18
Hotel   2/1-9/14   1P: $115- 125   2P/1B: $125- 135   2P/2B: $125- 135   XP: $10   F18
    Location: 1355 N Harbor Dr at Ash St 92101. Fax: 619/338-9737. **Facility:** 600 rooms. Many rooms with view of harbor or city skyline. 5-14 stories; interior corridors; heated pool. Fee: parking. **Services:** giftshop. **Cards:** AE, CB, DI, DS, JC, MC, VI.

CROWN POINT VIEW SUITE-HOTEL   **Phone:** (619)272-0676   120
(AAA) [SAVE]   2/1-9/14 & 12/15-1/31   1P: $85- 120   2P/1B: $90- 150   2P/2B: $109- 185   XP: $5-10
    9/15-12/14   1P: $85- 95   2P/1B: $85- 105   2P/2B: $99- 125   XP: $5-10
◆◆◆   **Location:** 0.3 blk s of Pacific Beach Dr. 4088 Crown Point Dr 92109. Fax: 619/272-0760. **Terms:** Reserv
Apartment   deposit, 14 day notice; weekly/monthly rates; 7 night min stay; $50 extra charge. **Facility:** 19
Motel   rooms. Well-equipped studios, 1- & 2-bedroom apartments. Phones issued at check-in if requested; $1 daily service charge; 3 stories; exterior corridors. **Dining:** Restaurant nearby. **Cards:** AE, CB, DI, MC, VI.
Special Amenities: Free breakfast and free local telephone calls. *(See color ad p 862)*

DANA INN & MARINA   **Phone:** (619)222-6440   39
(AAA) [SAVE]   5/28-9/25   1P: $105- 148   2P/1B: $105- 148   2P/2B: $105- 148   XP: $10   F17
    2/1-5/27 & 9/26-1/31   1P: $95- 148   2P/1B: $95- 148   2P/2B: $95- 148   XP: $10   F17
◆◆   **Location:** On Mission Bay. 1710 W Mission Bay Dr 92109. Fax: 619/222-5916. **Terms:** Check-in 4 pm;
Resort Motor   reserv deposit; 2 night min stay, wkends 31/-9/30. **Facility:** 196 rooms. Across the street from Sea World. 2
Inn   stories; exterior corridors; heated pool, whirlpool; 2 tennis courts. Fee: marina. **Dining:** Restaurant; 7 am-10 pm; $6-$15; cocktails. **Services:** area transportation, to Amtrak & bus station. **Recreation:** jet skis, wave runners; in-room video games. Fee: sailboating. Rental: boats, canoes, paddleboats; bicycles. **All Rooms:** combo or shower baths. **Cards:** AE, CB, DI, DS, MC, VI. **Special Amenities: Free room upgrade (subject to availability with advanced reservations).** *(See color ad p 863 & p 870)*

DAYS INN DOWNTOWN/ZOO   **Phone:** (619)239-9113   123
(AAA) [SAVE]   All Year [CP]   1P: $65- 95   2P/1B: $70- 100   2P/2B: $75- 105   XP: $7-10
    Location: 1449 9th Ave 92101. Fax: 619/232-9019. **Terms:** Reserv deposit. **Facility:** 45 rooms. 2 stories; ex-
◆◆   terior corridors; small pool. **Cards:** AE, CB, DI, DS, JC, MC, VI. **Special Amenities: Free room upgrade**
Motel   **and preferred room (each subject to availability with advanced reservations).**

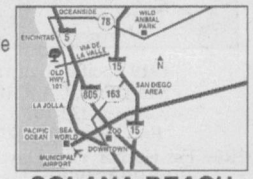

(See map p. 844)

DAYS INN HARBOR VIEW   Phone: (619)232-1077   **87**
6/11-9/30 [CP]   1P: $79- 109   2P/1B: $79- 109   2P/2B: $89- 129 XP:$5-10   F12
2/1-6/10 & 10/1-1/31 [CP]   1P: $69- 109   2P/1B: $69- 109   2P/2B: $79- 109 XP:$5-10   F12
Motel
Location: Just s of Grape St; from I-5 southbound exit Front St, northbound exit Hawthorn St. 1919 Pacific Hwy 92101. Fax: 619/233-6977. **Terms:** Reserv deposit, 3 day notice. **Facility:** 66 rooms. Close to Seaport Village, Amtrack & downtown. Dataport phones avail upon request. 2 two-bedroom units. 3 stories; exterior corridors; heated pool. **Dining:** Coffee makers and microwave available upon request. **Services:** area transportation, Amtrack & Greyhound. **Cards:** AE, DI, DS, JC, MC, VI. *(See color ad below)*

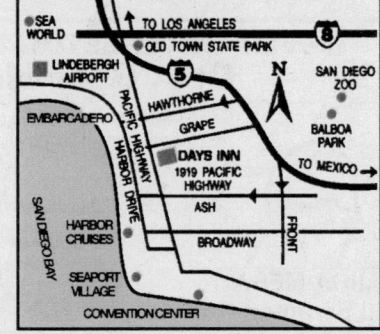

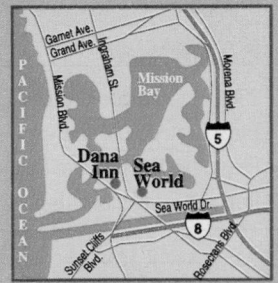

(See map p. 844)

DAYS INN-HOTEL CIRCLE Phone: (619)297-8800 66
(AAA) (SAVE) 5/28-9/24 1P: $85- 149 2P/1B: $85- 149 2P/2B: $85- 149
◆ ◆ 2/1-5/27 & 9/25-1/31 1P: $75- 149 2P/1B: $75- 149 2P/2B: $75- 149
Motor Inn **Location:** S side of I-8. 543 Hotel Circle S 92108. Fax: 619/298-6029. **Terms:** Check-in 4 pm; reserv deposit; weekly rates. **Facility:** 280 rooms. 3 stories; interior/exterior corridors; heated pool, whirlpool. **Dining:** Coffee shop; 6:30 am-9 pm, Sun 7 am-9 pm; $6-$11. **Services:** area transportation, Sea World/Zoo area. **Some Rooms:** 49 efficiencies. **Cards:** AE, CB, DI, DS, JC, MC, VI. *(See color ad p 864 & p 870)*

[icons]

DAYS INN LA JOLLA & SEA WORLD AREA Phone: (619)560-4551 142
(AAA) (SAVE) 5/17-9/7 [CP] 1P: $64- 74 2P/1B: $64- 79 2P/2B: $74- 84 XP: $6 F12
◆ ◆ 2/1-5/16 & 9/8-1/31 [CP] 1P: $49- 59 2P/1B: $49- 64 2P/2B: $59- 69 XP: $6 F12
Motel **Location:** Just w of I-805. 5550 Clairemont Mesa Blvd 92117. Fax: 619/268-4353. **Terms:** Weekly rates. **Facility:** 88 rooms. 3 stories; exterior corridors. **Dining:** Restaurant nearby. **Cards:** AE, CB, DI, DS, JC, MC, VI. **Special Amenities:** Free breakfast and free newspaper. *(See color ad below)*

[icons]

DAYS INN SUITES-SEAWORLD/AIRPORT Phone: (619)224-9800 46
(AAA) (SAVE) 6/2-9/15 [BP] 1P: $69- 99 2P/1B: $69- 99 2P/2B: $79- 109 XP: $10 F17
◆ ◆ 2/1-6/1 & 9/16-1/31 [BP] 1P: $49- 89 2P/1B: $49- 89 2P/2B: $59- 99 XP: $10 F17
Motel **Location:** 0.8 mi w of jct I-5 & I-8. 3350 Rosecrans St 92110. Fax: 619/224-0928. **Terms:** Weekly/monthly rates. **Facility:** 158 rooms. 74 one-bedroom suites with living room. 3 stories; exterior corridors; heated pool, whirlpool. **Services:** area transportation, Sea World, zoo & train. **Cards:** AE, DI, DS, MC, VI. **Special Amenities:** Free breakfast.

[icons]

(See map p. 844)

DIAMOND HEAD INN
Phone: (619)273-1900   **131**
(AAA) [SAVE]

6/2-9/15 [CP]	1P:	$99- 139	2P/1B:	$99- 139	2P/2B:	$99- 149	XP: $10		F17
2/1-6/1 & 9/16-1/31 [CP]	1P:	$79- 129	2P/1B:	$79- 129	2P/2B:	$89- 139	XP: $10		F17

♦ ♦
Motel

Location: Just w of Mission Blvd, Pacific Beach area. 605 Diamond St 92109. Fax: 619/274-3341. **Terms:** 2 night min stay, weekends; pets, $25 extra charge. **Facility:** 21 rooms. 2 stories; exterior corridors; beachfront. Fee: parking. **Some Rooms:** 20 kitchens. **Cards:** AE, DI, DS, JC, MC, VI. [icons]

DOUBLETREE HOTEL-SAN DIEGO MISSION VALLEY
Phone: 619/297-5466   **48**
(AAA) [SAVE]

All Year	1P: $119		2P/1B: $119		2P/2B: $119		XP: $10	F18

♦ ♦ ♦
Hotel

Location: Adjacent to SR 163, exit Friars Rd. 7450 Hazard Center Dr 92108. Fax: 619/297-5499. **Terms:** Reserv deposit, 3 day notice; handling fee imposed; small pets only. **Facility:** 300 rooms. 11 stories; interior corridors; heated indoor pool, sauna, whirlpool; 2 lighted tennis courts. **Dining:** Dining room; 6 am-10 pm; $8-$16; cocktails. **Services:** giftshop. **Cards:** AE, CB, DI, DS, MC, VI. *(See ad below)* [icons]

EMBASSY SUITES-SAN DIEGO BAY
Phone: (619)239-2400   **108**
(AAA) [SAVE]

6/21-9/4 [BP]	1P: $163- 269	2P/1B: $163- 269	2P/2B: $163- 269	XP: $15				F18
2/1-6/20 & 9/5-1/31 [BP]	1P: $153- 269	2P/1B: $153- 269	2P/2B: $153- 269	XP: $15				F18

♦ ♦ ♦
Suite Hotel

Location: Corner Pacific Hwy & Market St. 601 Pacific Hwy 92101. Fax: 619/239-1520. **Terms:** Check-in 4 pm; reserv deposit. **Facility:** 337 rooms. Suites with living room & efficiency. Attractive central atrium. 12 stories; interior corridors; heated indoor pool, sauna, whirlpool. Fee: parking. **Dining:** Restaurant; 11 am-midnight; $9-$15; cocktails. **Services:** giftshop; complimentary evening beverages. **Cards:** AE, CB, DI, DS, JC, MC, VI. **Special Amenities:** Free breakfast and free newspaper. [icons]

FOUR POINTS HOTEL BY SHERATON
Rates Subject to Change   Phone: (619)277-8888   **68**
♦ ♦ ♦
Motor Inn

6/16-10/31	1P: $170	2P/1B: $170	2P/2B: $170	XP: $10	F17
2/1-6/15	1P: $160	2P/1B: $160	2P/2B: $160	XP: $10	F17
11/1-1/31	1P: $150	2P/1B: $150	2P/2B: $150	XP: $10	F17

Location: From SR 163, southbound exit Balboa Ave, 1 mi se via Kearny Villa Rd, northbound exit Kearny Villa Rd, 0.8 mi ne. 8110 Aero Dr 92123. Fax: 619/279-3555. **Facility:** 225 rooms. 3 stories; interior corridors; heated pool; playground. Fee: 9 tennis courts. **Services:** giftshop; area transportation. **Cards:** AE, CB, DI, DS, JC, MC, VI. [icons]

GOOD NITE INN
Phone: (619)286-7000   **52**
(AAA) [SAVE]

5/15-9/15	1P: $45	2P/1B: $51	2P/2B: $57	XP: $6	F18
2/1-5/14 & 9/16-1/31	1P: $39	2P/1B: $45	2P/2B: $51	XP: $6	F18

♦
Motel

Location: Adjacent to I-8, Waring Rd exit. 4545 Waring Rd 92120. Fax: 619/286-8403. **Terms:** Weekly rates; pets. **Facility:** 94 rooms. 2 stories; interior corridors. **Dining:** Restaurant nearby. **Cards:** AE, CB, DI, DS, JC, MC, VI. **Special Amenities:** Free local telephone calls. [icons]

GOODNITE INN SEA WORLD AREA
Phone: (619)543-9944   **41**
(AAA) [SAVE]

5/15-9/15	1P: $45	2P/1B: $51	2P/2B: $57	XP: $6	F18
2/1-5/14 & 9/16-1/31	1P: $39	2P/1B: $45	2P/2B: $51	XP: $6	F18

♦ ♦
Motel

Location: Adjacent to I-5 & I-8; Sports Arena area. 3880 Greenwood St 92110. Fax: 619/574-1347. **Terms:** Weekly rates; package plans; small pets only, 2 days only, 30 lb limit. **Facility:** 149 rooms. 3 stories; interior/exterior corridors. **Cards:** AE, CB, DI, DS, JC, MC, VI. **Special Amenities:** Free local telephone calls. [icons]

HAMPTON INN-AIRPORT/SEAWORLD AREA
Phone: (619)299-6633   **117**
(AAA) [SAVE]

5/2-9/11 [CP]	1P: $44- 159	2P/1B: $94- 159	2P/2B: $99- 159	XP: $10				F18
2/1-5/1 & 9/12-1/31 [CP]	1P: $68- 99	2P/1B: $68- 99	2P/2B: $68- 99	XP: $10				F18

♦ ♦ ♦
Motel

Location: Adjacent to I-5 & I-8; Sports Arena area. 3888 Greenwood St 92110. Fax: 619/291-8333. **Terms:** Check-in 4 pm; reserv deposit. **Facility:** 198 rooms. 3 stories; interior corridors; heated pool, whirlpool. **Services:** giftshop. **Recreation:** in-room video games. **All Rooms:** combo or shower baths. **Cards:** AE, CB, DI, DS, MC, VI. **Special Amenities:** Free breakfast and free local telephone calls. *(See color ad p 868)* [icons]

HAMPTON INN-SAN DIEGO
Rates Subject to Change   Phone: (619)292-1482   **104**
♦ ♦ ♦
Motel

All Year [CP]	1P: $94	2P/1B: $99	2P/2B: $94- 99

Location: Adjacent to SR 163; exit Clairmont Mesa. 5434 Kearny Mesa Rd 92111. Fax: 619/292-4410. **Facility:** 151 rooms. 5 stories; interior corridors; heated pool. **Cards:** AE, CB, DI, DS, JC, MC, VI. [icons]

(See map p. 844)

HANALEI HOTEL   **Phone:** (619)297-1101   50

(AAA) (SAVE)   Fri & Sat 6/12-9/6   1P: $104   2P/1B: $104   2P/2B: $104   XP: $10   F18
         Fri & Sat 2/1-6/11, Sun-Thurs
◆◆◆   6/12-9/6 & Fri & Sat 9/7-1/31   1P: $94   2P/1B: $94   2P/2B: $94   XP: $10   F18
Hotel   Sun-Thurs 2/1-6/11 &
         9/7-1/31   1P: $84   2P/1B: $84   2P/2B: $84   XP: $10   F18

Location: N side of I-8. 2270 Hotel Cir 92108. Fax: 619/297-6049. **Terms:** Check-in 4 pm; reserv deposit; pets, $25 non-refundable dep req. **Facility:** 416 rooms. Polynesian atmosphere. 8 stories; exterior corridors; heated pool, whirlpool, children's pool. **Dining:** Coffee shop; 6:30 am-10:00 pm; $6-$25; cocktails; also, Islands Restaurant, see separate listing. **Services:** giftshop; area transportation, Old Town & Fashion Val. **Cards:** AE, CB, DI, DS, MC, VI. **Special Amenities:** Free newspaper and free room upgrade (subject to availability with advanced reservations). *(See color ad p 869)*

🛏 🐕 🚫 🎱 🏊 ⓘ 🍴 ⛳ 📺 🧺 🚪 ⊠

"San Diego's AAAdvantage"

- *Free Deluxe Continental Breakfast*
- *Free Fitness Club Access*
- *Free Parking*
- *Free Local Phone Calls*
- *Free Airport Shuttle*
- *4,000 Sq. Ft. of Meeting Space to Accommodate Groups up to 120*

Spacious accommodations with cable TV/HBO, pay-per-view movies/Super Nintendo, voice mail telephones, data ports, in-room coffeemakers, hair dryers, irons & ironing boards, deluxe rooms with microwaves, wet bar, refrigerators. Heated pool/spa, gift shop; minutes to Sea World, San Diego Zoo, beaches, Old Town, golf.

*AAA MEMBER VALUE RATES

2-1 THRU 5-1 9-19 THRU 1-31-00 **$79.00-$99.00**	5-2 THRU 9-18 **$84.00-$109.00**

Ask about our
SEA WORLD
PACKAGE

Single/double, space-available basis, tax not included, rate subject to surcharge during Holidays, Special Events and Peak Periods.

For Reservations Call:
1-800-HAMPTON
426-7866

(AAA)

♦♦♦

SEA WORLD/AIRPORT/OLD TOWN
Take I-5 So. or I-8 West to the Rosecrans Exit, right on Hancock St., right again on Greenwood St.
3888 Greenwood Street, San Diego, California 92110   (619) 299-6633

FIND THE HIDDEN MONEY!
Read TourBook advertisements carefully;
some offer special discounts for AAA members.

(See map p. 844)

HANDLERY HOTEL RESORT   Rates Subject to Change   Phone: (619)298-0511

◆◆◆   5/28-9/5   1P: $89   2P/1B: $89   2P/2B: $89   XP: $10   F1

Resort   2/1-5/27 & 9/6-1/31   1P: $79   2P/1B: $79   2P/2B: $79   XP: $10   F1

Complex   **Location:** N side of I-8. 950 Hotel Cir N 92108. Fax: 619/298-9793. **Terms:** Reserv deposit. **Facility:** 21 rooms. 2 stories; interior/exterior corridors; heated pool. Fee: 27 holes golf; 8 lighted tennis courts

Services: giftshop. Fee: massage, area transportation. **Cards:** AE, CB, DI, DS, JC, MC, VI. *(See ad below)*

(See map p. 844)

HERITAGE PARK BED & BREAKFAST INN   Phone: (619)299-6832   36
AAA SAVE   All Year [BP]   1P: $90- 225   2P/1B: $90- 225   2P/2B: $135- 225   XP: $20   F12
◆◆◆   **Location:** Off Juan St, in Old Town area. 2470 Heritage Park Row 92110. Fax: 619/299-9465.
Historic Bed   **Terms:** Reserv deposit; 7 day notice; weekly/monthly rates; 2 night min stay, weekends. **Facility:** 12 rooms.
& Breakfast   Beautifully decorated in a 1889 historic Queen Anne style mansion & Italian annex, some with whirlpool tub & fireplace. 2 stories; interior corridors; designated smoking area. **Dining:** Afternoon tea. **Services:** area transportation, to Amtrak station. **Recreation:** classic vintage films in parlor, 7 pm. **All Rooms:** combo or shower baths. **Cards:** AE, DI, DS, MC, VI. **Special Amenities:** Free local telephone calls and preferred room (subject to availability with advanced reservations).   ✈ 📺 🐾 🖨 ✕

HOLIDAY INN EXPRESS-SEA WORLD AREA   Rates Subject to Change   Phone: 619/226-8000   110
◆◆◆   All Year [CP]   1P: $59- 75   2P/1B: $59- 75   2P/2B: $59- 75   XP: $10
Motel   **Location:** 1.8 mi sw of I-5, via I-8 w, exit Sports Arena Blvd. 3950 Jupiter St 92110. Fax: 619/226-1409.
Terms: Reserv deposit. **Facility:** 70 rooms. 3 stories; interior corridors; heated pool. **Some Rooms:** 6 efficiencies. **Cards:** AE, CB, DI, DS, JC, MC, VI. *(See color ad p 876)*   🛎 🏊 🍴 🖥 🎦 🖨 ✕

You're always close to a great stay in San Diego.

As you travel through San Diego, there's always a Holiday Inn® hotel nearby. Now better than ever with brand new renovations, a great stay is always on the way.

Holiday Inn
www.holiday-inn.com

Call 1-800-HOLIDAY or these hotels directly for <u>AAA Rates</u> in the San Diego Area.

Weekend rates range from $59 – $150*

San Diego Area

Holiday Inn

1 Bayside
4875 N. Harbor Dr.
(619) 224-3621

2 Harbor View
1617 1st Ave.
(619) 239-9600

3 Mission Bay/
Sea World Area
3737 Sports
Arena Blvd.
(619) 226-3711

4 Mission Valley/
Stadium
3805 Murphy
Canyon Rd.
(619) 277-1199

5 National City
(South Bay Area)
700 National
City Blvd.
(619) 474-2800

6 Old Town
2435 Jefferson St.
(619) 260-8500

7 On the Bay
1355 N. Harbor Dr.
(619) 232-3861

8 Rancho Bernardo
(North County)
17065 W. Bernardo Dr.
(619) 485-6530

Holiday Inn EXPRESS

9 Chula Vista
(Otay Valley)
4450 Otay Valley Rd.
(619) 422-2600

10 Dana Point
34744 Coast Hwy.
(714) 240-0150

11 Encinitas
(Del Mar/Solana
Beach Area)
607 Leucadia Blvd.
(760) 944-3800

12 Escondido
1250 West
Valley Parkway
(760) 741-7117

13 La Jolla
6705 La Jolla Blvd.
(619) 454-7101

14 La Mesa
(SDSU Area)
9550 Murray Dr.
(619) 466-0200

15 Sea World Area
3950 Jupiter St.
(619) 226-8000

Holiday Inn SELECT

16 Hotel Circle
(Zoo/Old Town Area)
595 Hotel Circle S.
(619) 291-5720

17 North (Miramar)
9335 Kearny
Mesa Rd.
(619) 695-2300

(See map p. 844)

HOLIDAY INN-HARBOR VIEW ◆◆◆ Motor Inn

	Rates Subject to Change				 not — see below

HOLIDAY INN-HARBOR VIEW
◆◆◆
Motor Inn

3/29-10/1   Rates Subject to Change   Phone: (619)239-6171   88
3/29-10/1   1P: $139- 169   2P/1B: $139- 169   2P/2B: $139- 169   XP: $10   F19
2/1-3/28   1P: $129- 159   2P/1B: $129- 159   2P/2B: $129- 159   XP: $10   F19
10/2-1/31   1P: $129- 159   2P/1B: $129- 159   2P/2B: $129- 159   XP: $10   F19

Location: Adjacent to I-5; southbound exit Front St, northbound exit 6th Ave. 1617 1st Ave 92101. Fax: 619/233-6228. **Facility:** 218 rooms. Refrigerators available on request. 16 stories; interior corridors; heated pool. **Services:** giftshop. **Cards:** AE, CB, DI, DS, JC, MC, VI. *(See color ad p 873)*

HOLIDAY INN HOTEL & SUITES-
OLD TOWN, CIRCA 1850
◆◆◆
Motor Inn

   Rates Subject to Change   Phone: (619)260-8500   47
Fri & Sat   1P: $109   2P/1B: $109   2P/2B: $109
Sun-Thurs   1P: $99   2P/1B: $99   2P/2B: $99
Location: Adjacent to I-5, exit Old Town Ave. 2435 Jefferson St 92110. Fax: 619/297-2078. **Facility:** 171 rooms. 8 suites avail; 4 stories; interior corridors; heated pool. **Cards:** AE, CB, DI, DS, JC, MC, VI. *(See color ad p 873)*

HOLIDAY INN-MISSION BAY/SEA WORLD AREA   Phone: (619)226-3711   43
(AAA) SAVE
◆◆◆
Motor Inn

All Year   1P: $89- 159   2P/1B: $89- 159   2P/2B: $89- 159   XP: $10   F12
Location: 0.8 mi sw of jct I-5 & I-8; from I-5, southbound exit Rosecrans St, northbound exit I-8W, exit Sports Arena Blvd. 3737 Sports Arena Blvd 92110. Fax: 619/224-9248. **Facility:** 316 rooms. Suites, $99-$149; 3 stories; exterior corridors; heated pool, whirlpool. **Dining:** Coffee shop; 6 am-11 pm; $8-$12; cocktails. **Services:** giftshop. **Recreation:** Free access to San Diego Fitness Center, located adjacent property. **Cards:** AE, CB, DI, DS, JC, MC, VI. **Special Amenities:** Early check-in/late check-out and preferred room (subject to availability with advanced reservations). *(See color ad starting on p 858 & p 846)*

HOLIDAY INN MISSION VALLEY/STADIUM   Rates Subject to Change   Phone: (619)277-1199   81
◆◆◆
Hotel

5/27-9/6   1P: $89- 99   2P/1B: $89- 99   2P/2B: $89- 139   XP: $10   F19
2/1-5/26 & 9/7-1/31   1P: $69- 89   2P/1B: $69- 89   2P/2B: $79- 139   XP: $10   F19
Location: Adjacent to I-15, 2 mi n of I-8, exit Aero Drive. 3805 Murphy Canyon Rd 92123. Fax: 619/277-3442. **Facility:** 173 rooms. 4 stories; interior corridors; heated pool. **Cards:** AE, DI, DS, MC, VI. *(See color ad p 873)*

SET SAIL TO SAN DIEGO FOR LESS.

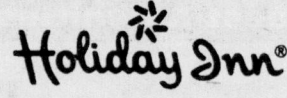

(See map p. 844)

HOLIDAY INN-SAN DIEGO BAYSIDE   Phone: (619)224-3621   79
(AAA) SAVE   All Year   1P: $119- 149   2P/1B: $119- 149   2P/2B: $119- 149   XP: $10   F19
♦♦♦   **Location:** Point Loma Area; just s of Rosecrans St. 4875 N Harbor Dr 92106. Fax: 619/224-3629.
Motor Inn   **Terms:** Check-in 4 pm; BP avail. **Facility:** 237 rooms. 2-5 stories; interior/exterior corridors; 9-hole putting
             course; heated pool, whirlpool. **Dining:** Coffee shop; 6 am-10 pm, Thurs-Sat to 11 pm; $5-$14; cocktails.
             Services: giftshop; area transportation, to Amtrack & bus station. **Recreation:** bicycles, in-room video
games. **All Rooms:** combo or shower baths. **Cards:** AE, CB, DI, DS, JC, MC, VI. **Special Amenities: Free newspaper
and free room upgrade (subject to availability with advanced reservations).** (See color ad p 874 & p 870)

HOLIDAY INN SELECT-MIRAMAR/MIRA MESA   Rates Subject to Change   Phone: (619)695-2300   44
♦♦♦   All Year [CP]   1P: $89- 129   2P/1B: $89- 129   2P/2B: $89- 129   XP: $10   F19
Motor Inn   **Location:** Adjacent to I-15; exit Miramar Rd. 9335 Kearny Mesa Rd 92126. Fax: 619/578-7925. **Facility:** 155
             rooms. 15-1 bedroom suites; 6 stories; interior corridors; heated pool. **Services:** area transportation.
Cards: AE, CB, DI, DS, JC, MC, VI. (See color ad p 876)

HOLIDAY INN SELECT- SAN DIEGO   Phone: (619)291-5720   65
(AAA) SAVE   Fri & Sat 7/1-9/5   1P: $105   2P/1B: $105   2P/2B: $105   XP: $10   F19
             Fri & Sat 5/1-6/30, Sun-Thurs
♦♦♦   7/1-9/5 & Fri & Sat 9/6-10/30 1P: $95   2P/1B: $95   2P/2B: $95   XP: $10   F19
Hotel   Sun-Thurs 5/1-6/30 &
             9/6-10/30   1P: $85   2P/1B: $85   2P/2B: $85   XP: $10   F19
             2/1-4/30 & 10/31-1/31 1P: $75- 85   2P/1B: $75- 85   2P/2B: $75- 85   XP: $10   F19
Location: S side of I-8. 595 Hotel Circle S 92108. Fax: 619/297-7362. **Terms:** Reserv deposit; package plans. **Facility:** 317
rooms. Pinball/video game room. 10 stories; interior corridors; heated pool, whirlpool. **Dining:** Restaurant; 6 am-11 pm;
$8-$18; cocktails. **Services:** giftshop. **Recreation:** video games in all rooms. **Cards:** AE, CB, DI, DS, JC, MC, VI.
**Special Amenities: Early check-in/late check-out and preferred room (subject to availability with advanced
reservations).** (See color ad below)

HORTON GRAND HOTEL   Rates Subject to Change   Phone: (619)544-1886   28
♦♦   All Year   1P: $109- 199   2P/1B: $109- 199   2P/2B: $129- 219   XP: $20   F16
Historic Hotel **Location:** In the Gaslamp Quarter. 311 Island Ave at 4th Ave 92101. Fax: 619/544-0058. **Terms:** Reserv
             deposit. **Facility:** 132 rooms. Beautifully restored historic hotel dating back to late 1800's. all rooms with gas
fireplace & ceiling fan. 4 stories; interior corridors. **Cards:** AE, DI, DS, MC, VI.

HOTEL CIRCLE INN & SUITES   Phone: (619)291-2711   73
(AAA) SAVE   All Year   1P: $69- 159   2P/1B: $69- 159   2P/2B: $69- 159   XP: $10   F12
             Location: S side of I-8. 2201 Hotel Circle S 92108. Fax: 619/542-1227. **Facility:** 196 rooms. 24 two-room
♦♦   suites with kitchen, $89-$149; 2 stories; exterior corridors; heated pool, whirlpool. **Dining:** Coffee shop; 6:30
Motor Inn   am-11:30 pm; $6-$9; cocktails. **All Rooms:** combo or shower baths. **Some Rooms:** 18 efficiencies.
             Cards: AE, CB, DI, DS, JC, MC, VI. **Special Amenities: Early check-in/late check-out and preferred
room (subject to availability with advanced reservations).** (See color ad starting on p 848 & p 846)

(See map p. 844)

HUMPHREY'S HALF MOON INN & SUITES Phone: (619)224-3411 83
(AAA) [SAVE] All Year 1P: $149- 299 2P/1B: $149- 299 2P/2B: $159- 299 XP: $10 F17
◆◆◆ **Location:** On Shelter Island. 2303 Shelter Island Dr 92106. Fax: 619/224-3478. **Terms:** Check-in 4 pm;
Motor Inn reserv deposit, 3 day notice; 2 night min stay, weekends 5/26-9/4. **Facility:** 182 rooms. Tropically landscaped
grounds. Most rooms with bay or yacht harbor view. 30 suites with kitchen, $125-$250; 2 stories;
interior/exterior corridors; heated pool, whirlpool. **Dining:** Humphrey's, see separate listing.
Services: giftshop. **Recreation:** bicycles, in-room video games, lawn games. **All Rooms:** combo or shower baths.
Cards: AE, CB, DI, DS, MC, VI. **Special Amenities: Free room upgrade (subject to availability with advanced
reservations).** (See color ad p 878 & p 870)

HYATT ISLANDIA Phone: (619)224-1234 42
(AAA) [SAVE] Fri & Sat 1P: $155- 250 2P/1B: $155- 250 2P/2B: $155- 250
Sun-Thurs 1P: $139- 215 2P/1B: $139- 215 2P/2B: $139- 215 XP: $25 F17
◆◆◆ **Location:** In Mission Bay Park; off W Mission Bay Dr. 1441 Quivira Rd 92109. Fax: 619/224-0348.
Resort **Terms:** Check-in 4 pm; package plans. **Facility:** 422 rooms. Variety of accommodations. Low rise units in
Complex garden setting, tower units with bay view & marina suites on yacht harbor. 1-16 stories; interior/exterior corri-
dors; heated pool, whirlpool. Fee: marina. **Dining:** Dining room, restaurant; 6 am-11 pm; $7-$35; cocktails.
Services: giftshop. **Recreation:** charter fishing; jogging. Fee: fishing, sailboating, scuba diving & equipment, waterskiing,
windsurfing; bicycles. Rental: boats, canoes, paddleboats. **All Rooms:** combo or shower baths. **Cards:** AE, CB, DI, DS, JC,
MC, VI. (See color ad p 565)

HYATT REGENCY SAN DIEGO Phone: (619)232-1234 53
(AAA) [SAVE] All Year 1P: $239- 351 2P/1B: $264- 376 2P/2B: $264- 376 XP: $25 F18
◆◆◆◆ **Location:** Harbor Dr & Market Pl, adjacent to Seaport Village & San Diego Convention Center. One Market
Hotel Pl 92101. Fax: 619/233-6464. **Terms:** BP avail. **Facility:** 875 rooms. Impressive skyscraper at the water front
with extensive public areas. All rooms with bay view. 40 stories; interior corridors; heated pool, saunas, whirl-
pool; 4 tennis courts. Fee: parking; marina. **Dining:** Restaurant; 6:30 am-10 pm; $10-$25; also, Sally's, see
separate listing. **Services:** giftshop. Fee: massage. **Recreation:** Fee: sailboating. Rental: boats. **Cards:** AE, CB, DI, DS, JC,
MC, VI. (See color ad p 565)

The **Resorts Index** specializes in lodgings with
extensive on-premises recreational facilities.

(See map p. 844)

INN SUITES HOTELS SAN DIEGO BALBOA PARK RESORT
Phone: (619)296-2101   **31**

AAA SAVE ◆◆ Motor Inn

Fri & Sat 6/1-9/6	1P:	$89- 129	2P/1B:	$89- 129	2P/2B:	$99- 129	XP:	$5	F18
Sun-Thurs 6/1-9/6 & Fri & Sat 9/7-1/31	1P:	$79- 119	2P/1B:	$79- 119	2P/2B:	$89- 119	XP:	$5	F18
Fri & Sat 2/1-5/31 &									
Sun-Thurs 9/7-1/31	1P:	$69- 99	2P/1B:	$79- 109	2P/2B:	$79- 109	XP:	$5	F18
Sun-Thurs 2/1-5/31	1P:	$59- 99	2P/1B:	$69- 99	2P/2B:	$69- 99	XP:	$5	F18

Location: 0.5 mi w of I-805 on El Cajon Blvd. 2223 El Cajon Blvd 92104. Fax: 619/296-0512. **Terms:** Weekly/monthly rates. **Facility:** 147 rooms. 2 three-bedroom units. 6 one & two-bedroom suites with wet bar, fireplace, living room & balcony, $129-$169; 4 stories; heated pool, whirlpool. **Dining:** Restaurant; 11 am-1 am; $8-$16. **Services:** giftshop; complimentary evening beverages; area transportation, Amtrack & San Diego Zoo. **Some Rooms:** 8 kitchens. **Cards:** AE, CB, DI, DS, JC, MC, VI. **Special Amenities: Free breakfast and free local telephone calls.** (See color ad p 877)

KINGS INN
Phone: (619)297-2231   **69**

AAA SAVE ◆◆ Motor Inn

6/1-8/31	1P:	$69- 99	2P/1B:	$69- 99	2P/2B:	$79- 109	XP:	$10
2/1-5/31 & 9/1-1/31	1P:	$59- 79	2P/1B:	$59- 79	2P/2B:	$69- 89	XP:	$10

Location: S side of I-8. 1333 Hotel Circle S 92108. Fax: 619/296-5255. **Terms:** Reserv deposit. **Facility:** 140 rooms. 2 stories; exterior corridors; heated pool, whirlpool. **Dining:** Coffee shop; 6:30 am-noon; $4-$9; cocktails; also, The Amigo Spot, see separate listing. **Cards:** AE, DS, JC, MC, VI. **Special Amenities:** Early check-in/late check-out and free room upgrade (subject to availability with advanced reservations).

LAMPLIGHTER INN & SUITES
Rates Subject to Change   **Phone:** (619)582-3088   **106**

AAA ◆ Motel

5/30-9/15 [CP]	1P:	$46- 71	2P/1B:	$51- 79	2P/2B:	$51- 79	XP:	$5	F12
2/1-5/29 & 9/16-1/31 [CP]	1P:	$43- 61	2P/1B:	$48- 66	2P/2B:	$48- 66	XP:	$5	F12

Location: 1 mi sw of I-8; exit 70th St. 6474 El Cajon Blvd 92115. Fax: 619/582-6873. **Terms:** Weekly/monthly rates; pets, by reservation only in designated rms $5 extra charge. **Facility:** 63 rooms. 2 two-room family units with kitchen $72-$85; 2 stories; exterior corridors; heated pool. **Dining:** Restaurant nearby. **All Rooms:** combo or shower baths. **Some Rooms:** 27 kitchens. **Cards:** AE, CB, DI, DS, JC, MC, VI. (See color ad below)

LA QUINTA INN & SUITES SAN DIEGO MISSION VALLEY
FYI

Under construction. **Location:** I-5 at Hotel Circle South. **Facility:** 165 rooms. Scheduled to open August 12, 1999.

OCEAN PARK INN
Phone: (619)483-5858   **59**

AAA SAVE ◆◆ Motel

3/17-9/6 [CP]	1P:	$124- 199	2P/1B:	$124- 199	2P/2B:	$129- 249	XP:	$10	F12
2/1-3/16 & 9/7-1/31 [CP]	1P:	$104- 164	2P/1B:	$104- 164	2P/2B:	$114- 204	XP:	$10	F12

Location: In Pacific Beach area, just w of Mission Blvd. 710 Grand Ave 92109. Fax: 619/274-0823. **Terms:** Reserv deposit. **Facility:** 73 rooms. Contemporary decor. All rooms with patio, most with oceanview. 7 suites $119-$189; 3 stories; interior corridors; beachfront; heated pool, whirlpool. **Dining:** Restaurant nearby. **Some Rooms:** 4 efficiencies. **Cards:** AE, DS, MC, VI. **Special Amenities: Free newspaper and preferred room (subject to availability with advanced reservations).** (See color ad p 881)

OLD TOWN INN
Rates Subject to Change   **Phone:** (619)260-8024   **133**

AAA ◆ Motel

5/30-9/15 [CP]	1P:	$47- 67	2P/1B:	$52- 76	2P/2B:	$55- 84	XP:	$5-8	F12
2/1-5/29 & 9/16-1/31 [CP]	1P:	$42- 55	2P/1B:	$47- 60	2P/2B:	$47- 60	XP:	$5-8	F12

Location: From jct I-5 & I-8, exit Morena Blvd; 0.6 mi s. 4444 Pacific Hwy 92110. Fax: 619/296-0524. **Terms:** Pets, in designated rooms. **Facility:** 83 rooms. 1-3 stories; exterior corridors. **All Rooms:** combo or shower baths. **Some Rooms:** 12 efficiencies. **Cards:** AE, CB, DI, DS, JC, MC, VI. (See ad p 882)

(See map p. 844)

OLD TOWN PLAZA HOTEL

AAA SAVE

◆◆◆
Motel

Phone: (619)291-9100

6/15-9/15 [CP]	1P:	$59- 79	2P/1B:	$59- 79	2P/2B:	$69- 89	XP: $10	F17
2/1-6/14 & 9/16-1/31 [CP]	1P:	$49- 69	2P/1B:	$49- 69	2P/2B:	$59- 79	XP: $10	F17

Location: Adjacent to I-5, exit Old Town Ave, just n via Frontage Rd. 2380 Moore St 92110. Fax: 619/291-4717. **Facility:** 78 rooms. 8 whirlpool rms, extra charge; 3 stories; interior/exterior corridors; heated pool, whirlpool. **Cards:** AE, DI, DS, MC, VI.

PACIFIC SHORES INN

AAA SAVE

◆◆
Motel

VI.

Phone: (619)483-6300

6/1-9/15 [CP]	1P:	$89- 139	2P/1B:	$89- 139	2P/2B:	$99- 139	XP: $10	F17
2/1-5/31 & 9/16-1/31 [CP]	1P:	$69- 109	2P/1B:	$69- 109	2P/2B:	$69- 109	XP: $10	F17

Location: In Pacific Beach area, 1 blk to beach. 4802 Mission Blvd 92109. Fax: 619/483-9276. **Terms:** Pets, $25 extra charge. **Facility:** 56 rooms. 1 two-bedroom unit. 6 kitchen units & 22 efficiency units, extra charge; 2 stories; exterior corridors; heated pool. **All Rooms:** combo or shower baths. **Cards:** AE, CB, DS, JC, MC,

(See map p. 844)

PACIFIC TERRACE INN   Phone: (619)581-3500 61

AAA SAVE All Year [CP]   1P: $215- 615 2P/1B: $215- 615 2P/2B: $215- 615 XP: $10 F12

◆◆◆◆ **Location:** Pacific Beach Area; just w of Mission Blvd. 610 Diamond St 92109. Fax: 619/274-3341.

Motel **Terms:** Check-in 4 pm. **Facility:** 73 rooms. Beachfront. Large rooms with balcony or patio, most with ocean view. 3 stories; interior corridors; heated pool, whirlpool. **Some Rooms:** 40 efficiencies, whirlpools.

Cards: AE, CB, DI, DS, JC, MC, VI. **Special Amenities:** Free breakfast and free newspaper.

(See color ad p 883 & p 870)

PADRE TRAIL INN   Phone: (619)297-3291 130

AAA SAVE 6/16-9/15   1P: $89- 99 2P/1B: $89- 99 2P/2B: $99- 109 XP: $5 F12

◆◆ 4/16-6/15   1P: $55- 89 2P/1B: $59- 89 2P/2B: $59- 89 XP: $5 F12

Motor Inn 9/16-10/31   1P: $55- 79 2P/1B: $59- 79 2P/2B: $59- 79 XP: $5 F12

2/1-4/15 & 11/1-1/31 1P: $55- 59 2P/1B: $59- 69 2P/2B: $59- 69 XP: $5 F12

Location: At jct I-8 & I-5, in Old Town area. 4200 Taylor St at Moreno Blvd 92110. Fax: 619/692-2080.

Terms: Weekly rates. **Facility:** 100 rooms. 2 stories; exterior corridors; whirlpool. **Dining:** Restaurant; 6:30-10:30 am, Sat & Sun 7-11 am. **All Rooms:** extended cable TV. **Cards:** AE, CB, DI, DS, JC, MC, VI.

POINT LOMA INN Rates Subject to Change   Phone: (619)222-4704 129

AAA 5/30-9/15   1P: $49- 69 2P/1B: $54- 74 2P/2B: $54- 74 XP: $5 F12

2/1-5/29 & 9/16-1/31 1P: $43- 64 2P/1B: $48- 70 2P/2B: $48- 70 XP: $5 F12

◆ **Location:** In Point Loma area, just s of Harbor Dr at Rosecrans. 2933 Fenelon St 92106.

Motel Fax: 619/222-4738. **Terms:** Weekly/monthly rates. **Facility:** 14 rooms. Near sportfishing harbor. 1-2 bedroom unit, $68-$92; 2 stories; exterior corridors. **Dining:** Restaurant nearby. **Some Rooms:** 7 efficiencies.

Cards: AE, CB, DI, DS, JC, MC, VI.

PREMIER INNS   Phone: 619/291-8252 45

AAA SAVE Thurs-Sat 6/15-9/6 [CP] 1P: $69 2P/1B: $79 2P/2B: $79 XP: $10 F12

5/27-5/31 & Sun-Wed

◆◆ 6/15-9/6 [CP] 1P: $65 2P/1B: $75 2P/2B: $75 XP: $10 F12

Motel 4/1-5/26, 6/1-6/14 &

9/7-10/31 [CP] 1P: $49 2P/1B: $59 2P/2B: $59 XP: $10 F12

2/1-3/31 & 11/1-1/31 [CP] 1P: $39 2P/1B: $49 2P/2B: $49 XP: $10 F12

Location: Adjacent to I-8, exit Taylor St. 2484 Hotel Circle Pl 92108. Fax: 619/291-8976. **Terms:** Pets. **Facility:** 111 rooms. 4 stories; exterior corridors; heated pool, whirlpool. **Dining:** Restaurant nearby. **Cards:** AE, DS, MC, VI.

(See map p. 844)

QUALITY INN AIRPORT-SEAWORLD AREA　　　Phone: (619)224-3655　🔢40
🔺🔺 (AAA) (SAVE)

	1P:		2P/1B:		2P/2B:		XP:		
6/1-9/5	$79-	99	$79-	119	$79-	119	$6	F17
2/1-5/31 & 9/6-10/31	$69-	99	$69-	99	$69-	109	$6	F17
11/1-1/31	$59-	89	$69-	99	$69-	99	$6	F17

Motor Inn　**Location:** Just e of Rosecrans St. 2901 Nimitz Blvd 92106. Fax: 619/224-4025. **Terms:** Weekly rates; AP, BP avail. **Facility:** 105 rooms. 6 stories; interior corridors; heated pool, whirlpool. **Dining:** Coffee shop; 6:30 am-2 & 6-midnight; $6-$15; cocktails. **Cards:** AE, CB, DI, DS, JC, MC, VI. **Special Amenities: Free local telephone calls and free newspaper.**

QUALITY INN & SUITES　　　Rates Subject to Change　　　Phone: (619)696-0911　🔢91
🔺🔺
All Year [CP]　　1P: $89- 109　2P/1B: $99- 149　2P/2B: $99- 159　XP:$15-30　F18
Motor Inn　**Location:** 1430 7th Ave at Ash St 92101. Fax: 619/234-9416. **Terms:** Reserv deposit; handling fee imposed. **Facility:** 136 rooms. Commercial area, many rooms with balcony, garage parking. 3 stories; interior corridors; small heated pool. Fee: parking. **Services:** area transportation. **Cards:** AE, DI, DS, MC, VI. *(See color ad p 860)*

QUALITY RESORT-MISSION VALLEY　　　Phone: (619)298-8282　🔢127
(AAA) (SAVE)

	1P:		2P/1B:		2P/2B:		XP:		
5/21-9/6	$109-	169	$109-	169	$109-	169	$10	F18
3/5-5/20 & 9/7-11/4	$99-	159	$99-	159	$99-	159	$10	F18
2/1-3/4 & 11/5-1/31	$89-	149	$89-	149	$89-	149	$10	F18

🔺🔺
Resort
Complex　**Location:** S side of I-8. 875 Hotel Circle S 92108. Fax: 619/295-5610. **Facility:** 202 rooms. 8 suites with coffeemaker, microwave, refrigerator & whirlpool, $129-$169; 2 stories; exterior corridors; heated pool, saunas, whirlpool; 5 lighted tennis courts. **Dining:** Coffee shop; 24 hrs; $6-$10. **Services:** giftshop. **Recreation:** in-room video games. **Cards:** AE, CB, DI, DS, MC, VI. **Special Amenities: Free local telephone calls and free newspaper.** *(See color ad p 885)*

QUALITY SUITES　　　Phone: (619)530-2000　🔢34
(AAA) (SAVE)
All Year [CP]　　1P: $85- 95　2P/1B: $85- 95　2P/2B: $95- 105　XP: $10　F12
🔺🔺🔺
Suite Motel　**Location:** Just e of I-15; exit Mira Mesa Blvd. 9880 Mira Mesa Blvd 92131. Fax: 619/530-2000. **Terms:** Weekly rates. **Facility:** 130 rooms. 4 stories; exterior corridors; heated pool, whirlpool. **Dining:** Restaurant nearby. **Services:** complimentary evening beverages. **Cards:** AE, DI, DS, MC, VI.

RADISSON HOTEL HARBOR VIEW　　　Phone: 619/239-6800　🔢109
(AAA) (SAVE)
All Year　　1P: $99　2P/1B: $109　2P/2B: $109　XP: $10
🔺🔺🔺
Hotel　**Location:** 1646 Front St 92101. Fax: 619/238-9461. **Terms:** Reserv deposit. **Facility:** 333 rooms. Suites avail, some rms with whirlpool; 16 stories; interior corridors; heated pool, sauna, whirlpool. Fee: parking. **Dining:** Restaurant; 6 am-10 pm; $6-$19; cocktails. **Services:** giftshop. **Cards:** AE, CB, DI, DS, JC, MC, VI.

(See map p. 844)

RADISSON HOTEL-SAN DIEGO   Phone: (619)260-0111   [62]
    (AAA) SAVE   All Year   1P: $105   2P/1B: $105   2P/2B: $105   XP: $15   F18
♦♦♦   **Location:** S side of I-8, exit Mission Center Rd. 1433 Camino Del Rio S 92108. Fax: 619/497-0813.
Hotel   **Terms:** Check-in 4 pm; reserv deposit; weekly rates; AP avail. **Facility:** 260 rooms. Many rooms with balcony.
14 stories; interior corridors; heated pool, whirlpool. **Dining:** Restaurant; 6:30 am-11 pm; $5-$12; cocktails.
Services: giftshop; area transportation, upon availability. **Some Rooms:** whirlpools. **Cards:** AE, CB, DI, DS,
JC, MC, VI. **Special Amenities:** Early check-in/late check-out and free newspaper. *(See ad p 888)*

🆂 🍽 📶 🏊 🍴 🍷 🚭 🛋 🚼 📺 📟 🖨 📠 ⓘ ✕

RAMADA INN & CONFERENCE CENTER   Phone: (619)278-0800   [102]
    (AAA) SAVE   All Year [CP]   1P: $79- 109   2P/1B: $79- 109 2P/2B: $79- 109 XP: $10   F17
♦♦   **Location:** Adjacent to SR 163; exit Clairmont Mesa. 5550 Kearny Mesa Rd 92111. Fax: 619/277-6585.
Motor Inn   **Terms:** Reserv deposit; weekly rates; AP, BP avail; pets, $150 dep req. **Facility:** 150 rooms. 2 stories; exterior
corridors; heated pool, whirlpool. **Dining:** Restaurant; 7 am-10 pm; $8-$12; wine/beer only. **Services:** area
transportation. **All Rooms:** combo or shower baths. **Some Rooms:** 13 efficiencies. **Cards:** AE, CB, DI, DS,
MC, VI. *(See color ad p 854)*

🆂 🛏 🍽 📶 🏊 🍴 🚭 🛋 🚼 🎿 📺 📟 🖥 📠 ⓘ 🅿 ✕

(See map p. 844)

RAMADA LIMITED-HARBORSIDE
Phone: (619)225-9461 [99]

(AAA) [SAVE]

All Year [CP]   1P: $59- 69   2P/1B: $69- 79   2P/2B: $69- 79   XP: $5   F12
Location: Corner of Fenelon. 1403 Rosecrans St 92106. Fax: 619/225-1163. **Terms:** Reserv deposit; pets, in assigned rooms only. **Facility:** 86 rooms. 5 two-bedroom units. 3 stories; interior corridors; heated pool.

◆◆
Motel

Dining: Cocktails. **Services:** area transportation, zoo & Sea World. **Cards:** AE, DI, DS, MC, VI.

RAMADA LIMITED-OLD TOWN
Rates Subject to Change   Phone: (619)299-7400 [107]

(AAA)

All Year [CP]   1P: $93   2P/1B: $93- 102   2P/2B: $102   XP: $3-10   F18
Location: Just e of I-5; Old Town area; exit Old Town Ave. 3900 Old Town Ave 92110. Fax: 619/299-1619.

◆◆◆
Motel

Terms: Reserv deposit. **Facility:** 125 rooms. Tastefully furnished rooms, some with terraces that overlook colorful courtyard. 3 stories; interior/exterior corridors; heated pool, whirlpool. **Dining:** Restaurant nearby. **Services:** area transportation. **Cards:** AE, DI, DS, JC, MC, VI. *(See color ad p 873)*

RAMADA LIMITED SEAWORLD
Phone: (619)225-1295 [35]

(AAA) [SAVE]

5/22-9/4 [CP]   1P: $85- 195   2P/1B: $85- 195   2P/2B: $85- 195   XP: $7-10   F17
2/1-5/21 [CP]   1P: $69- 149   2P/1B: $69- 149   2P/2B: $69- 149   XP: $7-10   F17
9/5-1/31 [CP]   1P: $59- 149   2P/1B: $59- 149   2P/2B: $59- 149   XP: $7-10   F17

◆◆
Motel

Location: 2 mi sw of I-5 via I-8 w; Sports Arena Blvd exit. 3747 Midway Dr 92110. Fax: 619/222-2123. **Terms:** Reserv deposit; weekly rates. **Facility:** 63 rooms. 2 stories; exterior corridors. **Dining:** Restaurant nearby. **All Rooms:** combo or shower baths. **Some Rooms:** whirlpools. **Cards:** AE, CB, DI, DS, JC, MC, VI.

RAMADA LIMITED-SOUTH BAY
Phone: (619)238-2788 [145]

(AAA) [SAVE]

6/1-9/30 [CP]   1P: $70- 75   2P/1B: $78- 83   2P/2B: $80- 85   XP: $8
2/1-5/31 & 10/1-1/31 [CP]   1P: $65- 70   2P/1B: $73- 78   2P/2B: $75- 80   XP: $8

◆◆
Motel

Location: Just e of I-5, Main St exit. 3878 Dalbergia Ct 92113. Fax: 619/238-1773. **Terms:** Reserv deposit; handling fee imposed. **Facility:** 64 rooms. 3 stories; exterior corridors. **Cards:** AE, CB, DI, DS, JC, MC, VI. **Special Amenities:** Early check-in/late check-out and free newspaper.

RAMADA PLAZA HOTEL CIRCLE/SEA WORLD AREA
Phone: (619)291-6500 [72]

(AAA) [SAVE]

All Year   1P: $89- 119   2P/1B: $89- 119   2P/2B: $89- 119   XP: $10   F12
Location: S side of I-8. 2151 Hotel Circle S 92108. Fax: 619/294-7531. **Facility:** 182 rooms. 4 stories; interior corridors; heated pool, whirlpool. **Dining:** The Tickled Trout, see separate listing. **Recreation:** game room.

◆◆◆
Motor Inn

Cards: AE, CB, DI, DS, JC, MC, VI. **Special Amenities:** Early check-in/late check-out and preferred room (subject to availability with advanced reservations). *(See color ad p 852 & p 846)*

REGENCY PLAZA HOTEL
Phone: (619)291-8790 [70]

(AAA) [SAVE]

All Year   1P: $99- 169   2P/1B: $99- 169   2P/2B: $99- 169   XP: $10   F12
Location: S side of I-8. 1515 Hotel Circle S 92108. Fax: 619/260-0147. **Facility:** 217 rooms. Comfortable, tastefully furnished rooms. Video game in all rooms. 29 two-room suites with wet bar

◆◆◆
Motor Inn

& refrigerator, extra charge; 8 stories; interior corridors; heated pool, whirlpool. **Dining:** Dining room; 7 am-10 pm; $7-$19; cocktails. **Services:** giftshop. **Some Rooms:** whirlpools. **Cards:** AE, CB, DI, DS, JC, MC, VI. **Special Amenities:** Early check-in/late check-out and preferred room (subject to availability with advanced reservations). *(See color ad starting on p 866 & p 846)*

(See map p. 844)

RESIDENCE INN BY MARRIOTT-SAN DIEGO Rates Subject to Change **Phone:** 619/278-2100 138
◆◆◆ 6/20-9/11 [BP] 1P: $115 2P/1B: $115 2P/2B: $155
Apartment 2/1-6/19 & 9/12-1/31 [BP] 1P: $100 2P/1B: $100 2P/2B: $140
Motel **Location:** Adjacent to SR 163, exit Clairemont Mesa. 5400 Kearny Mesa Rd 92111. Fax: 619/268-3926.
Terms: Check-in 4 pm; reserv deposit. **Facility:** 143 rooms. 1-bedroom studios & 2-bedroom suites with living
room & kitchen. 2 stories; exterior corridors; small heated pool. **Recreation:** sports court. **Cards:** AE, DI, DS, JC, MC, VI.

RODEWAY INN-ZOO/DOWNTOWN **Phone:** (619)239-2285 92
AAA SAVE 5/15-9/19 [CP] 1P: $69- 109 2P/1B: $69- 109 2P/2B: $79- 109 XP: $5-15 F18
12/26-1/31 [CP] 1P: $69- 99 2P/1B: $69- 99 2P/2B: $79- 99 XP: $5-10 F18
◆◆ 2/1-5/14 & 9/20-12/25 [CP] 1P: $49- 99 2P/1B: $49- 99 2P/2B: $59- 99 XP: $5-10 F18
Motel **Location:** Ash St at 9th Ave. 833 Ash St 92101. Fax: 619/235-6951. **Terms:** Reserv deposit; weekly/monthly
rates. **Facility:** 45 rooms. 4 stories; exterior corridors; saunas, whirlpool. **Dining:** Coffee shop nearby.
Cards: AE, CB, DI, DS, JC, MC, VI. **Special Amenities:** Free breakfast and free room upgrade (subject to availability
with advanced reservations).

SAN DIEGO HILTON BEACH & TENNIS RESORT **Phone:** (619)276-4010 37
AAA SAVE 7/1-8/31 1P: $180- 275 2P/1B: $200- 295 2P/2B: $200- 295 XP: $20
2/1-6/30 & 9/1-1/31 1P: $155- 220 2P/1B: $175- 240 2P/2B: $175- 240 XP: $20
◆◆◆◆ **Location:** Adjacent to I-5; 0.5 mi n of Sea World Dr exit. 1775 E Mission Bay Dr 92109. Fax: 619/275-7991.
Resort **Terms:** Pets, $50 dep req. **Facility:** 357 rooms. In Mission Bay Park. Attractive tropical setting. Spacious
Complex rooms with patio or balcony. 1-8 stories; interior/exterior corridors; putting green; beach, heated pool, wading
pool, sauna, whirlpools; playground. Fee: 5 lighted tennis courts; marina. **Dining:** 2 restaurants; 6 am-10 pm;
$8-$21; cocktails. **Services:** giftshop. Fee: massage. **Recreation:** jogging, Full service spa. Fee: sailboating, scuba diving &
equipment, waterskiing, windsurfing. Rental: boats, canoes, paddleboats; bicycles. **Cards:** AE, CB, DI, DS, JC, MC, VI.
(See ad p 119)

SAN DIEGO MARRIOTT HOTEL & MARINA Rates Subject to Change **Phone:** (619)234-1500 100
AAA All Year 1P: $215- 235 2P/1B: $215- 235 2P/2B: $215- 235
◆◆◆◆ **Location:** Adjacent to Seaport Village & San Diego Convention Center. 333 W Harbor Dr 92101.
Hotel Fax: 619/234-8678. **Terms:** Check-in 4 pm; BP avail; pets. **Facility:** 1354 rooms. Twin towers at the marina.
Most rooms with harbor view. 25 stories; interior corridors; heated pool, saunas, whirlpools. Fee: parking; 6
lighted tennis courts; marina. **Dining:** Dining room, restaurant, coffee shop, deli; 6:30 am-11:00 pm; $6-$27;
cocktails; also, Molly's, see separate listing. **Services:** giftshop. Fee: massage. **Recreation:** rental wave runners.
Fee: boating, sailboating; bicycles. **Cards:** AE, CB, DI, DS, JC, MC, VI.

SAN DIEGO MARRIOTT MISSION VALLEY Rates Subject to Change **Phone:** 619/692-3800 60
◆◆◆ All Year 1P: $164 2P/1B: $164 2P/2B: $164 XP: $10
Hotel **Location:** Just n of I-8: exit Stadium Way. 8757 Rio San Diego Dr 92108. Fax: 619/692-0769.
Terms: Check-in 4 pm. **Facility:** 350 rooms. 15 stories; interior corridors; heated pool; 1 lighted tennis court.
Services: giftshop; area transportation. **Cards:** AE, CB, DI, DS, JC, MC, VI.

SAN DIEGO MARRIOTT SUITES-DOWNTOWN Rates Subject to Change **Phone:** 619/696-9800 113
◆◆◆ All Year 1P: $119 2P/1B: $129 2P/2B: $129 XP: $10
Suite Hotel **Location:** Adjacent to Symphony Hall. 701 A St corner 7th Ave 92101. Fax: 619/696-1555. **Terms:** Check-in
4 pm. **Facility:** 264 rooms. 15 stories; interior corridors; heated indoor pool. **Services:** giftshop. **Cards:** AE,
CB, DI, DS, JC, MC, VI.

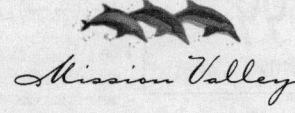

(See map p. 844)

SAN DIEGO MISSION VALLEY HILTON Rates Subject to Change **Phone:** (619)543-9000 63
All Year 1P: $124- 199 2P/1B: $134- 209 2P/2B: $134- 209
Location: Adjacent to I-8, exit Mission Center Rd. 901 Camino del Rio S 92108. Fax: 619/296-9561.
Terms: Reserv deposit; weekly rates; pets, $50 extra charge, $250 dep req. **Facility:** 350 rooms. 8 stories; interior corridors; heated pool, sauna, whirlpool. **Dining:** Restaurant; 11 am-11 pm; $9-$22; cocktails; also, Monterey Whaling Company, see separate listing. **Services:** giftshop; area transportation, within 2 mi.
Cards: AE, CB, DI, DS, MC, VI. *(See color ad below & ad p 119)*

B.Y.O. UTENSILS?
No need; they're supplied in units with cooking facilities,
unless the listing denotes otherwise.

(See map p. 844)

SAN DIEGO PARADISE POINT RESORT
Phone: (619)274-4630　③⑧

AAA SAVE

	9/2-1/31	1P: $180- 405	2P/1B: $180- 405	2P/2B: $180- 405	XP: $25	F12
	5/27-9/1	1P: $185- 395	2P/1B: $185- 395	2P/2B: $185- 395	XP: $20	F12
◆◆◆	2/1-5/26	1P: $170- 375	2P/1B: $180- 375	2P/2B: $180- 375	XP: $20	F12

Resort Complex

Location: In Mission Bay Park at W Vacation Rd & Ingraham St. 1404 W Vacation Rd 92109. **Fax:** 619/581-5929. **Terms:** Check-in 4 pm; reserv deposit, 3 day notice; handling fee imposed; monthly rates; package plans; pets, $35 dep req. **Facility:** 462 rooms. Bungalows & motel units on several acres of beautifully landscaped grounds. Studio & 2-room efficiencies, $225-$370; 1 story; exterior corridors; beach, heated pool, whirlpool. Fee: 6 lighted tennis courts; marina. **Dining:** Restaurant, coffee shop; 7 am-11 pm; $6-$24; also, Dockside Restaurant, see separate listing. **Services:** giftshop. Fee: massage. **Recreation:** jogging, 18 hole putting course. Fee: sailboating, waterskiing. Rental: canoes, paddleboats; bicycles. **Some Rooms:** 145 efficiencies. **Cards:** AE, DS, MC, VI.
(See ad p 889)

SHELTER POINTE HOTEL & MARINA
Phone: (619)221-8000　⑧②

AAA SAVE

	6/1-9/15	1P: $119- 189	2P/1B: $119- 189	2P/2B: $119- 189	XP: $10	F12
	2/1-5/31	1P: $109- 169	2P/1B: $109- 169	2P/2B: $109- 169	XP: $10	F12
◆◆◆	9/16-1/31	1P: $99- 169	2P/1B: $99- 169	2P/2B: $99- 169	XP: $10	F12

Resort Hotel

Location: On Shelter Island. 1551 Shelter Island Dr 92106. **Fax:** 619/221-5953. **Terms:** Check-in 4 pm; reserv deposit. **Facility:** 206 rooms. Waterfront rooms with view of bay or marina; all with patio or balcony. 5 two-bedroom units. 2-3 stories; interior/exterior corridors; heated pool, whirlpools. Fee: parking; 2 lighted tennis courts. **Dining:** Restaurant; 6:30 am-11 pm; $8-$25; cocktails. **Services:** area transportation, Amtrak train station. **Recreation:** sand beach with volleyball; jogging, in room video games. Fee: boating; bicycles. **Cards:** AE, CB, DI, DS, MC, VI.
(See color ad below)

SHERATON SAN DIEGO HOTEL & MARINA
Rates Subject to Change　Phone: (619)291-2900　⑦⑥

◆◆◆◆

	All Year	1P: $199	2P/1B: $199	2P/2B: $199	XP: $20	F18

Resort Hotel

Location: 1380 Harbor Island Dr 92101. **Fax:** 619/692-2337. **Facility:** 1050 rooms. Two towers and low rise buildings with shuttle service between. Most rooms overlook the bay or yacht harbor. 2-12 stories; interior/exterior corridors; heated pool; playground. Fee: parking; 4 lighted tennis courts; boat dock. **Services:** giftshop; area transportation. Fee: massage. Rental: boats; bicycles. **Cards:** AE, CB, DI, DS, JC, MC, VI.

SUPER 8 BAYVIEW
Rates Subject to Change　Phone: 619/544-0164　①②①

◆

	7/1-9/4 [CP]	1P: $50	2P/1B: $53	2P/2B: $60	XP: $4
Motel	2/1-6/30 & 9/5-1/31 [CP]	1P: $45	2P/1B: $48	2P/2B: $51	XP: $4

Location: 1835 Columbia St at Fir St 92101. **Fax:** 619/237-9940. **Terms:** Reserv deposit. **Facility:** 98 rooms. Limited parking. 4 stories; exterior corridors. **Services:** area transportation. **Cards:** AE, DI, DS, MC, VI.

SUPER 8 MISSION BAY
Rates Subject to Change　Phone: (619)274-7888　⑤⑦

◆◆

	6/6-9/12	1P: $59	2P/1B: $64	2P/2B: $69	XP: $5	F17
Motel	9/13-9/30	1P: $54	2P/1B: $59	2P/2B: $64	XP: $5	F17
	10/1-10/31	1P: $51	2P/1B: $56	2P/2B: $61	XP: $5	F17
	2/1-6/5 & 11/1-1/31	1P: $46- 49	2P/1B: $52- 54	2P/2B: $54- 56	XP: $5	F17

Location: Northbound, 0.5 mi nw of I-5, exit Grand Ave/Garnet Ave; southbound, 0.3 mi sw, exit Balboa Ave. 4540 Mission Bay Dr 92109. **Fax:** 619/274-7880. **Facility:** 117 rooms. 3 stories, no elevator; interior corridors; small pool. **Cards:** AE, CB, DI, JC, MC, VI.

SUPER 8 MOTEL-MISSION VALLEY/STADIUM
Phone: (619)281-2222　⑤④

AAA SAVE

	6/2-9/10 [CP]	1P: $45- 75	2P/1B: $45- 75	2P/2B: $55- 85	XP: $10	F17
◆◆	2/1-6/1 & 9/11-1/31 [CP]	1P: $39- 69	2P/1B: $39- 69	2P/2B: $39- 69	XP: $10	F17

Motel

Location: Adjacent to I-8, exit Mission George Rd. 4380 Alvarado Canyon Rd 92120. **Fax:** 619/280-3462. **Facility:** 103 rooms. 3 stories; exterior corridors. **Cards:** AE, DI, DS, JC, MC, VI.

TOWN AND COUNTRY HOTEL
Phone: (619)291-7131　①②②

AAA SAVE

	All Year	1P: $110- 195	2P/1B: $125- 210	2P/2B: $125- 210	XP: $15	F18

◆◆◆ Complex

Location: N side of I-8. 500 Hotel Circle N 92108. **Fax:** 619/291-3584. **Terms:** Reserv deposit. **Facility:** 964 rooms. On several acres of beautifully landscaped grounds. 2-10 stories; interior/exterior corridors; heated pool, whirlpool. **Dining:** 2 restaurants, cafeteria, coffee shop, deli; 6:30 am-1:30 am; $5-$15; cocktails. **Services:** giftshop; area transportation. **Cards:** AE, DI, DS, MC, VI. *(See color ad p 891)*

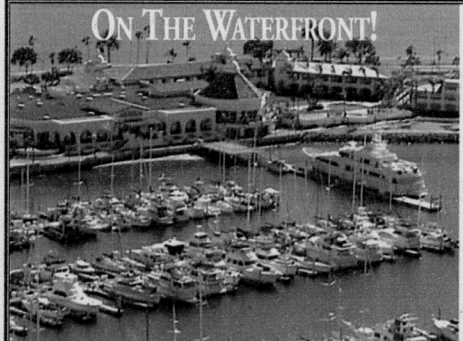

(See map p. 844)

TRAVELODGE HOTEL-HARBOR ISLAND   Phone: (619)291-6700   78
(AAA) (SAVE)   7/2-9/6 & 1/1-1/31   1P: $119- 144   2P/1B: $119- 144 2P/2B: $119- 144 XP: $10   F17
               2/1-7/1 & 9/7-12/31   1P: $109- 134   2P/1B: $109- 134 2P/2B: $109- 134 XP: $10   F17
◆◆◆   **Location:** On Harbor Island. 1960 Harbor Island Dr 92101. Fax: 619/293-0689. **Terms:** Reserv deposit.
Motor Inn   **Facility:** 207 rooms. Overlooking bay or yacht harbor. 9 stories; interior corridors; small heated pool, sauna,
               whirlpool. **Dining:** Dining room; 6:30 am-2 & 5:30-10 pm, Fri & Sat-10:30 pm; $13-$20; cocktails.
Services: giftshop. **Cards:** AE, CB, DI, DS, JC, MC, VI.

TRAVELODGE SEA WORLD   Rates Subject to Change   Phone: (619)224-3166   96
(AAA) (FRI)   6/1-9/4 & 12/20-1/4   1P: $49- 89   2P/1B: $49- 89 2P/2B: $49- 89 XP: $10
               2/1-5/31, 9/5-12/19 &
Motel   1/5-1/31   1P: $39- 69   2P/1B: $39- 69 2P/2B: $39- 69 XP: $10
               Under major renovation. **Location:** 2 mi sw of I-5 via I-8 w, Sports Arena Blvd exit. 3325 Midway Dr 92110.
Fax: 619/523-6003. **Terms:** Reserv deposit. **Facility:** 51 rooms. 3 stories; exterior corridors; heated pool, whirlpool.
Dining: Restaurant nearby. **Cards:** AE, DI, DS, MC, VI. *(See color ad p 892)*

(See map p. 844)

VAGABOND INN-DOWNTOWN　　　　　　　　　　　　　　Phone: (619)232-6391　95

								F18
Fri & Sat	1P:	$65	2P/1B:	$65	2P/2B:	$76	XP:	$5
Sun-Thurs	1P:	$54	2P/1B:	$54	2P/2B:	$70		

◆ **Location:** 1655 Pacific Hwy 92101. Fax: 619/235-4622. **Terms:** Small pets only, $5 extra charge. **Facility:** 32
Motel　rooms. 2 stories; exterior corridors. **Cards:** AE, CB, DI, DS, MC, VI. **Special Amenities:** Free breakfast and
free local telephone calls.

VAGABOND INN-MISSION VALLEY　　　　　　　　　　　Phone: (619)297-1691　67

								F18
5/15-9/14 [CP]	1P:	$71- 77	2P/1B:	$71- 77	2P/2B:	$89- 94	XP:	$5
2/1-5/14 & 9/15-1/31 [CP]	1P:	$62- 68	2P/1B:	$62- 68	2P/2B:	$79- 85	XP:	$5

◆◆ **Location:** S side of I-8. 625 Hotel Circle South 92108. Fax: 619/692-9009. **Terms:** Pets, $10 extra charge.
Motel　**Facility:** 88 rooms. 2 two-bedroom units. 2 stories; exterior corridors; heated pool, whirlpool.
　　　Dining: Restaurant nearby. **Cards:** AE, CB, DI, DS, MC, VI. **Special Amenities:** Free breakfast and free
local telephone calls.

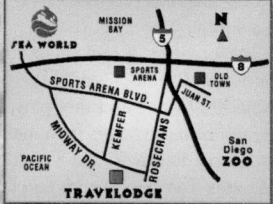

(See map p. 844)

VAGABOND INN-POINT LOMA   Phone: (619)224-3371   97

(AAA) [SAVE]   5/1-9/15 [CP]   1P: $59- 64   2P/1B: $69- 74   2P/2B: $69- 74
◆   2/1-4/30 & 9/16-1/31 [EP]   1P: $56- 61   2P/1B: $61- 66   2P/2B: $61- 66   XP: $5   F18
Motel   **Location:** Just sw of Harbor Dr. 1325 Scott St 92106. Fax: 619/223-0646. **Terms:** Pets, $10 extra charge.
      Facility: 40 rooms. Kitchens, $85-$90; 2 stories; exterior corridors; heated pool. **Cards:** AE, CB, DI, DS, MC,
      VI. **Special Amenities:** Free breakfast and free local telephone calls.

WESTERN INN-OLD TOWN   Phone: (619)298-6888   71

(AAA) [SAVE]   6/16-9/7   1P: $79- 109   2P/1B: $79- 109   2P/2B: $79- 109
◆ ◆   2/1-6/15 & 9/8-1/31   1P: $49- 79   2P/1B: $49- 79   2P/2B: $49- 79
Motel   **Location:** 3889 Arista St 92110. Fax: 619/692-4497. **Terms:** Reserv deposit. **Facility:** 35 rooms. 3 stories; ex-
      terior corridors. **Cards:** AE, DI, DS, MC, VI. **Special Amenities:** Free breakfast and free local telephone
      calls. *(See color ad p 892)*

THE WESTGATE HOTEL   Phone: (619)238-1818   94

(AAA) [SAVE]   All Year   1P: $195- 245   2P/1B: $205- 255   2P/2B: $205- 255
◆ ◆ ◆ ◆   **Location:** 1055 2nd Ave at C St 92101. Fax: 619/557-3737. **Facility:** 223 rooms. An elegant hotel; exquisite
Hotel   furnishings & decor. 19 stories; interior corridors. **Dining:** Dining room, restaurant; 6 am-10 pm; $19-$27;
      cocktails; afternoon tea. **Services:** giftshop. Fee: massage. **Recreation:** in-room video games. **Cards:** AE,
      CB, DI, DS, MC, VI.

THE WESTIN HORTON PLAZA   Rates Subject to Change   Phone: 619/239-2200   98

◆ ◆ ◆   All Year   1P: $159- 249   2P/1B: $174- 264   2P/2B: $174- 264   XP: $15
Hotel   **Location:** Just s of Broadway, adjacent to Horton Plaza. 910 Broadway Cir 92101. Fax: 619/239-0509.
      Terms: Reserv deposit. **Facility:** 450 rooms. Rooms are tastefully furnished. Contemporary decor. 16 stories;
interior corridors; heated pool. Fee: parking; 2 lighted tennis courts. **Services:** giftshop. Fee: massage. **Cards:** AE, CB, DI,
DS, MC, VI.

WYNDHAM EMERALD PLAZA   Phone: (619)239-4500   114

(AAA) [SAVE]   Sun-Thurs   1P: $174   2P/1B: $174   2P/2B: $174   XP: $10-20   F18
◆ ◆ ◆ ◆   Fri & Sat   1P: $129   2P/1B: $129   2P/2B: $129   XP: $10-20   F18
Hotel   **Location:** At Emerald-Shapery Center between Columbia & State. 400 W Broadway 92101.
      Fax: 619/239-3274. **Facility:** 436 rooms. Impressive high rise hotel, downtown. 3 two-bedroom units. 26 sto-
ries; interior corridors; heated pool, whirlpool. Fee: parking. **Dining:** Dining room, restaurant; 6 am-10 pm;
$7-$22; cocktails. **Services:** giftshop; area transportation. Fee: massage. **Cards:** AE, CB, DI, DS, JC, MC, VI.

WYNDHAM GARDEN HOTEL   Rates Subject to Change   Phone: (619)558-1818   56

◆ ◆ ◆   Sun-Thurs [EP]   1P: $121   2P/1B: $121   2P/2B: $121   XP: $10-20   F18
Motor Inn   Fri & Sat [BP]   1P: $99   2P/1B: $99   2P/2B: $99   XP: $10-20   F18
      Location: 1 mi e of I-805; exit Mira Mesa Blvd. 5975 Lusk Blvd 92121. Fax: 619/558-0421. **Facility:** 180
rooms. 7 stories; interior corridors; heated pool. **Cards:** AE, CB, DI, DS, JC, MC, VI. *(See color ad below)*

RESTAURANTS

ACAPULCO   **Lunch:** $5-$14   **Dinner:** $6-$14   Phone: 619/260-8124   32

◆ ◆   **Location:** At Best Western Hacienda Hotel-Old Town. 2467 Juan St 92110. **Hours:** 6:30 am-9 pm, Fri &
Mexican   Sat-10 pm. **Reservations:** suggested. **Features:** casual dress; Sunday brunch; carryout; cocktails & lounge.
      Patio dining overlooking Old Town. **Cards:** AE, CB, DI, JC, MC, VI. *(See color ad p 854)*

SHOW YOUR MEMBERSHIP CARD
WHEN YOU REGISTER
AT AAA APPROVED ESTABLISHMENTS.

(See map p. 844)

THE AMIGO SPOT   Lunch: $6-$16   Dinner: $6-$16   Phone: 619/297-2231   ㉚
◆   **Location:** S side of I-8; in Kings Inn. 1333 Hotel Circle 92108. **Hours:** 11:30 am-9 pm.
Mexican   **Reservations:** suggested. **Features:** casual dress; carryout; cocktails & lounge. Smoke free premises.
Cards: AE, CB, DI, DS, MC, VI.
☒

ANTHONY'S FISH GROTTO   Lunch: $6-$11   Dinner: $8-$23   Phone: 619/232-5103   ㊷
◆   **Location:** On the Embarcadero. 1360 Harbor Dr 92101. **Hours:** 11:30 am-8:30 pm. Closed major
Seafood   holidays4/12. **Features:** casual dress; children's menu; early bird specials; health conscious menu; cocktails
& lounge. Large selection of seafood served in very popular restaurant overlooking bay. **Cards:** AE, CB, DI,
DS, MC, VI.
☒

ANTHONY'S STAR OF THE SEA ROOM   Dinner: $20-$40   Phone: 619/232-7408   ㊶
◆◆◆   **Location:** On the Embarcadero. 1360 Harbor Dr 92101. **Hours:** 5:30 pm-10:30 pm. Closed major holidays &
Seafood   Easter. **Reservations:** suggested. **Features:** cocktails & lounge; fee for valet parking; a la carte. Harbor view
restaurant with Old World decor & continental service. Smoke free premises. **Cards:** AE, CB, DI, DS, MC,
VI.
☒

BACI'S   Lunch: $10-$14   Dinner: $16-$27   Phone: 619/275-2094   ㉒
◆◆◆◆   **Location:** I-5; northbound Tecolote Rd exit, southbound Clairemont Dr exit; 0.5 mi s of Clairemont Dr. 1955
Italian   Morena Blvd 92110. **Hours:** 11:30 am-2 & 5:30-10 pm, Sat from 5:30 pm. Closed major holidays & Sun.
Reservations: suggested. **Features:** casual dress; cocktails & lounge; a la carte. Small intimate Italian
restaurant featuring homemade pasta, seafood & veal specialties. **Cards:** AE, CB, DI, DS, MC, VI.
☒

CAFE PACIFICA   Lunch: $7-$12   Dinner: $15-$24   Phone: 619/291-6666   ⑱
◆◆◆   **Location:** In Old Town area. 2414 San Diego Ave 92110. **Hours:** Tue-Fri 11:30 am-2 & 5:30-10 pm, Sun 5
Seafood   pm-9:30 pm. **Reservations:** suggested. **Features:** casual dress; cocktails; valet parking. Small, charming
restaurant. Smoke free premises. **Cards:** AE, CB, DI, DS, MC, VI.
☒

CALIFORNIA CAFE BAR & GRILL   Lunch: $7-$11   Dinner: $9-$19   Phone: 619/238-5440   ㉕
◆◆◆   **Location:** In Horton Plaza-upper level. 502 Horton Plaza 92101. **Hours:** 11:30 am-9:30 pm, Fri & Sat-10
American   pm, Sun-9 pm. Closed: 11/25 & 12/25. **Reservations:** suggested. **Features:** casual dress; cocktails &
lounge; a la carte. Patio seating avail. Varied menu; some pasta & pizza selections. **Cards:** AE, DI, DS, MC,
VI.
☒

CASA DE BANDINI   Historical   Lunch: $7-$15   Dinner: $7-$15   Phone: 619/297-8211   ⑰
ⒶⒶⒶ   **Location:** In Old Town San Diego State Park, 1 blk s of Bazaar del Mundo. 2754 Calhoun St 92110.
Hours: 11 am-9 pm, Fri & Sat-9:30 pm, Sun 10 am-9 pm. Closed: 11/25 & 12/25. **Features:** casual dress;
◆   children's menu; health conscious menu; cocktails & lounge; entertainment; a la carte. Delightful dining in
Mexican   historical landmark & colorful outdoor patio area. Seafood entrees. **Cards:** AE, DI, DS, MC, VI.
☒

CASA DE PICO   Dinner: $7-$14   Phone: 619/296-3267   ㉓
ⒶⒶⒶ   **Location:** In Old Town Bazaar Del Mundo. 2754 Calhoun St 92110. **Hours:** 10 am-9 pm, Fri & Sat-9:30 pm,
10-10 in summer. Closed: 11/25 & 12/25. **Features:** casual dress; cocktails. Extensive patio seating.
◆◆   Excellent variety of Mexican dishes. **Cards:** AE, CB, DI, DS, MC, VI.
Mexican
☒

CASA GUADALAJARA   Lunch: $6-$14   Dinner: $6-$14   Phone: 619/295-5111   ㉟
ⒶⒶⒶ   **Location:** At jct I-8 & I-5, in Old Town area. 4105 Taylor St 92110. **Hours:** 11 am-10 pm, Fri & Sat-11 pm.
Closed: 12/25. **Features:** casual dress; carryout; cocktails. Good selection of Mexican dishes. Patio dining
◆   avail. **Cards:** AE, CB, DI, DS, MC, VI.
Mexican
☒

CHINA CAMP   Lunch: $5-$9   Dinner: $10-$24   Phone: 619/232-0686   ㊾
◆◆   **Location:** I 5, Laurel/Kettner Blvd exit. 2137 Pacific Hwy 92101. **Hours:** 11 am-2:30 & 5-10 pm, Sat 5-10:30
Chinese   pm, Sun 5-10 pm. Closed major holidays. **Features:** casual dress; cocktails & lounge. Nice selection of
Szechuan and Hunan beef, chicken & seafood dishes. Old west mining theme & decor. **Cards:** AE, DI, DS,
MC, VI.
☒

CITY DELICATESSEN   Lunch: $4-$8   Dinner: $4-$16   Phone: 619/295-2747   ⑫
◆◆   **Location:** At 6th Ave in Hillcrest. 535 E University Ave 92103. **Hours:** 7 am-midnight, Fri & Sat-2 am.
American   **Features:** casual dress; health conscious menu; carryout; beer & wine only; street parking & valet parking; a
la carte. Classic American deli, friendly atmosphere featuring hot & cold sandwiches. Breakfast served all
day & large selection of dessert made on premises. Smoke free premises. **Cards:** AE, CB, DI, DS, MC, VI.
☒

DOBSON'S BAR & RESTAURANT   Lunch: $6-$15   Dinner: $13-$25   Phone: 619/231-6771   ㉛
◆◆◆   **Location:** Downtown near Horton Plaza, just w of Broadway. 956 Broadway Cir 92101. **Hours:** 11:30 am-3
Continental   & 5:30-10 pm, Fri 11 am-3 & 5:30-11 pm, Sat 5:30 pm-11 pm. Closed major holidays & Sun.
Reservations: suggested. **Features:** casual dress; cocktails & lounge; fee for parking; also prix fixe. Nice
variety of meat, poultry, seafood & game dishes served in an Old World atmosphere. Smoke free premises. **Cards:** AE, DI,
MC, VI.
☒

DOCKSIDE RESTAURANT   Dinner: $13-$27   Phone: 619/274-4630   ㉙
◆◆◆   **Location:** In Mission Bay Park at W Vacation Rd & Ingraham St; in San Diego Paradise Point Resort. 1404
Seafood   W Vacation Rd at Ingraham St 92109. **Hours:** 5 pm-10 pm. **Reservations:** suggested.
Features: semi-formal attire; cocktails & lounge. Beautifully appointed restaurant overlooking Mission Bay.
Nice selection of steaks & continental entrees. **Cards:** AE, DS, MC, VI.
☒

FIO'S   Lunch: $6-$13   Dinner: $9-$23   Phone: 619/234-3467   ㊹
◆◆◆   **Location:** 801 Fifth st at F st 92101. **Hours:** 11:30 am-3 & 5-10:30 pm, Fri & Sat 5 pm-midnight, Sun 5
Northern   pm-10 pm. Closed: 11/25 & 12/25. **Reservations:** suggested. **Features:** casual dress; cocktails & lounge;
Italian   street parking & fee for valet parking; a la carte. **Cards:** AE, DI, DS, MC, VI.
☒

THE FISH MARKET & TOP OF THE MARKET   Lunch: $7-$18   Dinner: $13-$30   Phone: 619/232-3474   ㊾
◆◆   **Location:** At the Embarcadero. 750 N Harbor Dr 92101. **Hours:** 11 am-10 pm, Sun from 10 am. Closed:
Seafood   11/25 & 12/25. **Reservations:** suggested. **Features:** casual dress; Sunday brunch; cocktails; fee for parking
& valet parking. Casual dining downstairs in fish market with takeout of fresh fish avail. Menu printed daily
based on market avail of fish. Smoke free premises. **Cards:** AE, DI, DS, MC, VI.
☒

(See map p. 844)

THE GODFATHER RESTAURANT   Lunch: $6-$12   Dinner: $10-$23   Phone: 619/560-1747   ㊸
◆◆◆   **Location:** From SR 163 exit Clairemont Mesa Blvd, 0.5 mi w. 7878 Clairemont Mesa Blvd 92111. **Hours:** 11
Italian   am-2:30 & 5-10 pm, Fri & Sat-10:30 pm, Sun 4 pm-10 pm. Closed major holidays.
Reservations: suggested. **Features:** casual dress; cocktails & lounge. Old World style, Italian cuisine.
Cards: AE, CB, DI, DS, MC, VI.   ☒

HARBOR HOUSE RESTAURANT   Lunch: $7-$14   Dinner: $13-$23   Phone: 619/232-1141   ㊻
◆◆◆   **Location:** In Seaport Village. 831 W Harbor Dr 92101. **Hours:** 11 am-11 pm. **Reservations:** suggested.
Seafood   **Features:** casual dress; children's menu; cocktails & lounge; a la carte. Fine harbor view dining. **Cards:** AE,
DS, MC, VI.   ☒

HOB NOB HILL   Lunch: $6-$8   Dinner: $8-$14   Phone: 619/239-8176   ㉞
◆   **Location:** At Ivy St. 2271 First Ave 92101. **Hours:** 7 am-9 pm. Closed: 12/25. **Reservations:** suggested.
American   **Features:** casual dress; children's menu; carryout; beer & wine only; a la carte. Popular family type
restaurant featuring a large selection of entrees & daily specials. Pies & pastries baked on premises. Smoke
free premises. **Cards:** AE, DS, MC, VI.   ☒

HUMPHREY'S   Lunch: $8-$13   Dinner: $18-$25   Phone: 619/224-3577   ㊴
◆◆◆   **Location:** At Humphrey's Half Moon Inn. 2241 Shelter Island Dr 92106. **Hours:** 6:30 am-2 & 5:30-10 pm, Fri
Specialty   & Sat-11 pm. **Reservations:** suggested; Fri & Sat eveni. **Features:** casual dress; Sunday brunch; cocktails
& lounge; entertainment; a la carte. California coastal cuisine featuring nice selection of seafood, pasta &
beef. **Cards:** AE, CB, DI, DS, MC, VI. *(See color ad p 878)*   ⓕ ☒

ISLANDS RESTAURANT   Dinner: $6-$25   Phone: 619/297-1101   ⑲
◆◆   **Location:** In Hanalei Hotel. 2270 Hotel Circle 92108. **Hours:** 5 pm-10 pm, Fri & Sat 5 pm-11 pm, Sun 10
Specialty   am-2 & 5-10 pm. **Features:** children's menu; early bird specials; cocktails & lounge; entertainment.
Polynesian, also American dishes, served in an attractive South Seas atmosphere. Sat & Sun brunch.
Cards: AE, DI, DS, MC, VI. *(See color ad p 869)*   ☒

KAISERHOF   Lunch: $8-$11   Dinner: $9-$20   Phone: 619/224-0606   ㊾
◆◆   **Location:** 2253 Sunset Cliffs Blvd 92107. **Hours:** 11:30 am-3 & 5-10 pm, Sun 11 am-3 & 4:30-9 pm. Closed:
German   12/25 & Mon. **Reservations:** suggested. **Features:** semi-formal attire; Sunday brunch; children's menu; early
bird specials; cocktails & lounge. Bavarian specialties & continental dishes. **Cards:** AE, DI, DS, MC, VI.   ☒

LAMONT ST GRILL   Dinner: $12-$17   Phone: 619/270-3060   �62
◆◆   **Location:** In Pacific Beach area between Garnet & Grand Ave. 4445 Lamont St 92109. **Hours:** 5:30-10 pm,
Continental   Fri & Sat-11 pm. Closed: 7/4 & 12/25. **Reservations:** suggested. **Features:** casual dress; cocktails; street
parking. Nice selection of steak, seafood, chicken & lamb dishes. Heated patio dining avail. Smoke free
premises. **Cards:** AE, DS, MC, VI.   ☒

LINO'S ITALIAN RESTAURANT   Lunch: $4-$8   Dinner: $7-$15   Phone: 619/299-7124   �
ⒶⒶⒶ   **Location:** In Old Town's Bazaar Del Mundo. 2754 Calhoun St 92110. **Hours:** 11 am-9 pm, Fri & Sat-10 pm.
Closed: 11/25 & 12/25. **Features:** cocktails; a la carte. Traditional-style Italian cuisine featuring pastas, meat
◆◆   & seafood. Also comfortable outdoor seating in 2 patios. Smoke free premises. **Cards:** AE, DI, DS, MC, VI.
Italian   ☒

LOTSA PASTA   Lunch: $6-$13   Dinner: $15-$18   Phone: 619/581-6777   ㊿
◆◆   **Location:** Pacific Beach area, 1.05 mi e of Mission Blvd. 1762 Garnet Ave 92109. **Hours:** 11 am-9:30 pm,
Italian   Fri & Sat-10 pm. **Features:** casual dress; carryout; beer & wine only. In Pacific Plaza Shopping Center. Patio
dining avail. Smoke free premises. **Cards:** AE, CB, DI, DS, MC, VI.   ☒

MISTER A'S   Lunch: $9-$17   Dinner: $20-$40   Phone: 619/239-1377   �51
◆◆◆◆   **Location:** Top floor of Fifth Avenue Financial Center. 2550 Fifth Ave 92103. **Hours:** 11 am-2:30 & 5:30-10:30
Traditional   pm, Sat & Sun from 5:30 pm. Closed major holidays. **Reservations:** suggested. **Features:** semi-formal
Continental   attire; health conscious menu; cocktails & lounge; valet parking; a la carte. Excellent selection of meat,
poultry, seafood & pasta dishes. Commanding views of the city, airport & bay. **Cards:** AE, CB, DI, DS, MC,
VI.   ☒

MOLLY'S   Dinner: $18-$27   Phone: 619/234-1500   �53
◆◆◆   **Location:** Adjacent to Seaport Village and San Diego Convention Center; in San Diego Mariott Hotel &
Continental   Marina. 333 W Harbor Dr 92101. **Hours:** 6 pm-10 pm. **Reservations:** suggested. **Features:** casual dress;
cocktails & lounge. **Cards:** AE, CB, DI, DS, JC, MC, VI.   ☒

MONTEREY WHALING COMPANY   Lunch: $8-$12   Dinner: $9-$22   Phone: 619/543-9000   ㉗
◆◆   **Location:** In San Diego Mission Valley Hilton. 901 Camino del Rio S 92108. **Hours:** 6:30 am-2 & 5-10 pm,
Seafood   Sat & Sun 6:30-10 am & 5-10 pm. **Features:** children's menu; senior's menu; health conscious menu;
cocktails & lounge. Sun Brunch on Major Holidays. Smoke free premises. **Cards:** AE, DI, DS, MC, VI.   ☒

OLD VENICE RESTAURANT   Lunch: $5-$11   Dinner: $6-$16   Phone: 619/222-5888   ⑬
◆◆   **Location:** 2910 Canon St 92106. **Hours:** 11 am-9 pm, Fri & Sat-10:30 pm. Closed: 12/25. **Features:** casual
Italian   dress; children's menu; health conscious menu; carryout; cocktails & lounge; entertainment. Very popular
Italian Restaurant with excellent desserts. Romantic Patio seating & friendly attentive service. Smoke free
premises. **Cards:** AE, CB, DI, MC, VI.   ☒

PREGO   Lunch: $12-$19   Dinner: $16-$19   Phone: 619/294-4700   ㉘
◆◆◆   **Location:** 0.5 mi n of I-8, exit Mission Center Rd; in Hazard Center. 1370 Frazee Rd 92106. **Hours:** 11:30
Italian   am-10 pm; Fri & Sat-midnight; Sun 5 pm-10 pm. Closed: 11/25 & 12/25. **Reservations:** suggested.
Features: casual dress; cocktails & lounge; valet parking; a la carte. Northern Italian cuisine featuring
homemade pastas, mesquite-grilled fresh fish, rotisserie-grilled meats & fowl. **Cards:** AE, CB, DI, MC, VI.   ☒

RAINWATER'S   Lunch: $7-$15   Dinner: $18-$35   Phone: 619/233-5757   �63
◆◆◆   **Location:** Just s of I-5, Laurel/Kettner off Camp. 1202 Kettner Blvd 92101. **Hours:** 11:30 am-midnight, Sat
American   from 5 pm, Sun 5 pm-11 pm. Closed major holidays. **Reservations:** suggested. **Features:** semi-formal attire;
cocktails & lounge; fee for valet parking; a la carte. Excellent selection of meat, poultry & seafood.
Cards: AE, CB, DI, MC, VI.   ☒

(See map p. 844)

RANCHO EL NOPAL Lunch: $5-$9 Dinner: $5-$9 Phone: 619/295-0584 [56]
Location: In Old Town Bazaar Del Mundo. 4016 Wallace St 92110. Hours: 11 am-9:30 pm. Closed: 11/25 & 12/25. Features: casual dress; children's menu; cocktails. Nice variety of traditional Mexican dishes. Patio dining avail. Cards: AE, DI, DS, MC, VI.
◆◆
Mexican

SALLY'S Lunch: $13-$25 Dinner: $18-$32 Phone: 619/687-6080 [50]
◆◆◆ Location: Harbor Dr & Market Pl, adjacent to Seaport Village & San Diego Convention Center; in Hyatt
Seafood Regency San Diego. One Market Pl 92101. Hours: 11:30 am-2:30 & 5:30-10 pm, Fri & Sat-11 pm. Reservations: required; weekends. Features: casual dress; cocktails; fee for parking & valet parking; a la carte. Dine in contemporary setting overlooking the boardwalk & marina. Featuring nice selection of seafood with French flair; also poultry & beef. Patio dining also avail. Cards: AE, DI, DS, MC, VI.

SAM CHOY'S HAWAII AT THE BALI HAI Lunch: $8-$12 Dinner: $12-$21 Phone: 619/222-1181 [38]
◆◆◆ Location: 2230 Shelter Island Dr 92106. Hours: 11:30 am-3:30 & 5-10 pm, Fri-11 pm, Sat 5 pm-11 pm, Sun
Specialty 10 am-2 & 4-10 pm. Closed: 12/25. Reservations: suggested. Features: casual dress; Sunday brunch; cocktails & lounge. Hawaiian ambiance. Beautiful location overlooking bay & downtown skyline. Patio dining in summer, Polynesian cuisine, also beef, poultry & seafood. Cards: AE, DI, DS, JC, MC, VI.

SENOR SPENCER'S Lunch: $8-$11 Dinner: $12-$22 Phone: 619/692-2777 [36]
◆◆◆ Location: In Sheraton San Diego Hotel & Marina, West Tower. 1590 Harbor Island Dr 92101. Hours: 6:30
American am-3 & 5-10:30 pm, Fri & Sat-11 pm. Reservations: suggested. Features: casual dress; Sunday brunch; children's menu; cocktails & lounge; fee for valet parking. Nice selection of southwestern dishes. Cards: AE, CB, DI, DS, MC, VI.

SHANGHAI Lunch: $5-$7 Dinner: $8-$16 Phone: 619/226-6200 [15]
Location: In Mission Bay Park, at Marina Village. 1930 Quivira Way 92109. Hours: 11:30 am-9:30 pm, Fri-10:30 pm, Sat noon-10:30 pm, Sun 11 am-9:30 pm. Closed: 11/25. Features: casual dress; Sunday brunch; carryout; cocktails. Features Mandarin cuisine & Mongolian barbequed beef, lamb & pork. Overlooking Quivira Basin. Smoke free premises. Cards: AE, MC, VI.
◆
Chinese

TEP'S VILLA ROMA Dinner: $9-$16 Phone: 619/276-3462 [54]
Location: 3010 Clairmont Dr 92117. Hours: 5 pm-10 pm, Fri & Sat-10:30 pm, Sun 4 pm-10 pm. Closed: 11/25, Mon & Tues. Features: casual dress; children's menu; salad bar; cocktails & lounge. Nice variety of traditional Italian pasta dishes. Cards: AE, MC, VI.
◆◆
Italian

THE TICKLED TROUT Dinner: $12-$19 Phone: 619/291-6505 [31]
◆◆ Location: S side of I-8; in Ramada Plaza Hotel Circle/Sea World Area. 2151 Hotel Circle S 92108.
Seafood Hours: 6:30 am-11 pm. Reservations: suggested; weekends. Features: casual dress; cocktails & lounge. English pub decor. Smoke free premises. Cards: AE, CB, DI, DS, MC, VI. *(See color ad p 852)*

TIO LEO'S Lunch: $7-$9 Dinner: $7-$14 Phone: 619/542-1462 [33]
◆◆ Location: 0.5 mi n of Taylor via Morena Blvd. 5302 Napa St 92110. Hours: 6:30 am-10 pm, Fri & Sat-11
Mexican pm. Closed: 1/1, 11/25 & 12/25. Reservations: suggested. Features: casual dress; children's menu; carryout; cocktails & lounge. Family owned. Good food; prepared using traditional Mexican recipes. Cards: AE, DI, DS, MC, VI.

TOM HAM'S LIGHTHOUSE Lunch: $6-$11 Dinner: $10-$30 Phone: 619/291-9110 [37]
◆ Location: On Harbor Island. 2150 Harbor Island Dr 92101. Hours: 11:15 am-3 & 5-10 pm, Fri-11 pm, Sat
American 4:30-11 pm, Sun 10 am-2 & 4-10 pm. Closed: 12/25. Reservations: suggested. Features: casual dress; Sunday brunch; children's menu; early bird specials; cocktails & lounge. Early California decor; overlooks bay & city skyline. Cards: AE, DI, DS, MC, VI.

The San Diego Vicinity

CHULA VISTA—135,200 (See map p. 844; index p. 842)

LODGINGS

BEST WESTERN SOUTH BAY INN Phone: (619)420-5183 [170]

		1P:		2P/1B:		2P/2B:		XP:		
7/1-9/6 [BP]		$69-	79	$79-	89	$89-	99	$9		D
9/7-1/31 [BP]		$59-	69	$69-	79	$79-	89	$9		D
2/1-6/30 [BP]		$49-	59	$59-	69	$69-	79	$9		D

Location: Just e of I-5, E St exit. 710 E St 91910. Fax: 619/420-6254. Terms: Reserv deposit; weekly/monthly rates. Facility: 76 rooms. Next to San Diego Trolley Station. 3 two-bedroom units. 2 stories; exterior corridors; heated pool. Dining: Coffee shop nearby. Cards: AE, DI, DS, MC, VI. Special Amenities: Free breakfast and free local telephone calls. *(See color ad p 853)*

CHULA VISTA TRAVELODGE Phone: (619)420-6600 [177]
All Year 1P: $49- 79 2P/1B: $55- 85 2P/2B: $59- 89 XP: $6-10 F17
Location: 0.8 mi e of I-5; exit E St. 394 Broadway at G St 91910. Fax: 619/420-5556. Terms: Reserv deposit, weekends & summer; handling fee imposed; weekly rates; small pets only, $50 dep req. Facility: 77 rooms. 4 stories; exterior corridors; whirlpool. Cards: AE, CB, DI, DS, MC, VI. Special Amenities: Free breakfast and free newspaper.

DAYS INN Phone: (619)585-1999 [172]
All Year 1P: $59- 79 2P/1B: $69- 79 2P/2B: $69- 79 XP: $10 F11
Location: Just e of I-5, exit E St. 699 E St 91910. Fax: 619/427-3748. Terms: Reserv deposit; handling fee imposed. Facility: 102 rooms. 2 stories; exterior corridors; heated pool, whirlpool. Dining: Restaurant nearby. Cards: AE, DI, DS, MC, VI.

(See map p. 844)

GOOD NITE INN-SOUTH BAY   Phone: (619)425-8200　🔲171

(AAA) (SAVE) 5/15-9/15   1P: $42   2P/1B: $48   2P/2B: $54   XP: $6   F18
　　　　　　2/1-5/14 & 9/16-1/31   1P: $36   2P/1B: $42   2P/2B: $48   XP: $6   F18
◆◆　　　**Location:** West side of I-5, exit E St, just s. 225 Bay Blvd 91910. Fax: 619/426-7411.
Motel　　**Terms:** Weekly/monthly rates; small pets only. **Facility:** 118 rooms. 2 stories; exterior corridors.
　　　　　Dining: Restaurant nearby. **Cards:** AE, CB, DI, DS, JC, MC, VI. **Special Amenities:** Free local telephone
calls.
　　　　　　　　　　　　　　　　　　　　　　　　　　　　　　🅂⓿ 🐾 🈁 🈁 🍴 🛗 🎦 ▢ 🖥 🗑 ✕

HOLIDAY INN EXPRESS   Phone: (619)422-2600　🔲176

(AAA) (SAVE) 5/23-9/15 [CP]   1P: $49- 89   2P/1B: $49- 89   2P/2B: $49- 89   XP: $5   F17
　　　　　　2/1-5/22 & 9/16-1/31 [CP] 1P: $49- 79   2P/1B: $49- 79   2P/2B: $49- 79   XP: $10 F17
◆◆◆　　**Location:** Adjacent to I-805; exit Otay Valley Rd. 4450 Otay Valley Rd 91911. Fax: 619/425-4605.
Motel　　**Terms:** Handling fee imposed; weekly/monthly rates. **Facility:** 118 rooms. 3 stories; exterior corridors; heated
　　　　　pool, whirlpool. **Some Rooms:** 4 efficiencies. **Cards:** AE, CB, DI, DS, JC, MC, VI. *(See color ad p 871)*
　　　　　　　　　　　　　　　　　　　　　　　　　　　　　　🅂⓿ 🈁 🛗 🎦 ▢ 🖥 🗑 ✕

LA QUINTA INN   Phone: (619)691-1211　🔲173

(AAA) (SAVE) All Year [CP]   1P: $75- 95   2P/1B: $75- 95   2P/2B: $75- 95
◆◆◆　　**Location:** Just w of I-805, E St & Bonita Rd exit. 150 Bonita Rd 91910. Fax: 619/427-0135. **Terms:** Pets.
Motel　　**Facility:** 142 rooms. 3 stories; exterior corridors; heated pool. **Dining:** Restaurant nearby. **Cards:** AE, CB,
　　　　　DI, DS, JC, MC, VI. **Special Amenities:** Free breakfast and free local telephone calls.
　　　　　　　　　　　　　　　　　　　　　　　　　　　　　　🈁 🛗 🈁 🍴 🎦 🖥 ✕

PALOMAR INN   Rates Subject to Change   Phone: (619)423-8889　🔲174

(AAA)　　All Year   1P: $49- 79   2P/1B: $49- 79   2P/2B: $69- 99   XP: $5-15
◆　　　　**Location:** Adjacent to I-5, exit Palomar St. 801 Palomar St 91911. Fax: 619/575-7595. **Terms:** Small pets
Motel　　only, $25 refundable dep. **Facility:** 37 rooms. 2 two-bedroom units. 19 rms with refrigerator & microwave, $69;
　　　　　up to 2 persons; 3 stories; exterior corridors. **Cards:** AE, MC, VI.
　　　　　　　　　　　　　　　　　　　　　　　　　　　　　　🛗 🈁 ✕

TRAVELER INN AND SUITES   Phone: (619)427-9170　🔲169

(AAA) (SAVE) All Year [CP]   1P: $35- 65   2P/1B: $59- 79   2P/2B: $89- 109 XP: $10   F17
◆◆　　　**Location:** Just e of I-5, exit E St. 235 Woodlawn Ave 91910. Fax: 619/427-5247. **Terms:** Reserv deposit;
Motel　　monthly rates. **Facility:** 85 rooms. 1-bedroom suites with living rm avail; 2-3 stories; exterior corridors; heated
　　　　　pool, whirlpool. **Some Rooms:** 27 efficiencies, 57 kitchens. **Cards:** AE, DS, MC, VI.
　　　　　　　　　　　　　　　　　　　　　　　　　　　　　　🈁 🛗 🎦 (VCR) 🖥 ▢ 🗑 ✕

RESTAURANTS

ANTHONY'S FISH GROTTO   **Lunch:** $4-$17   **Dinner:** $7-$17   Phone: 619/425-4200　🔲81
◆　　　　**Location:** 0.5 blk w of I-5, E St exit. 215 W Bay Blvd 91910. **Hours:** 11:30 am-8:30 pm. Closed major
Seafood　holidays. **Features:** casual dress; children's menu; health conscious menu; cocktails & lounge. Popular
　　　　　restaurant featuring a large selection of fresh seafood. Smoke free premises. **Cards:** AE, DI, DS, MC, VI.
　　　　　　　　　　　　　　　　　　　　　　　　　　　　　　✕

JAKES-SOUTH BAY   **Lunch:** $7-$10   **Dinner:** $12-$20   Phone: 619/476-0400　🔲82
◆◆　　　**Location:** 0.5 mi w of I-5, exit J St. 570 Marina Pkwy 91910. **Hours:** 11:15 am-2:30 & 5-9 pm, Fri & Sat
Seafood　5-10 pm, Sun 9:30 am-2 & 4:30-9 pm. Closed: 11/25 & 12/25. **Features:** casual dress; Sunday brunch;
　　　　　children's menu; cocktails & lounge. Attractive yacht club decor, overlooking Chula Vista Marina. Smoke free
premises. **Cards:** AE, DI, DS, MC, VI.
　　　　　　　　　　　　　　　　　　　　　　　　　　　　　　✕

CORONADO—26,500　　(See map p. 844; index p. 841)

LODGINGS

BEST WESTERN SUITES-CORONADO ISLAND   Phone: (619)437-1666　🔲150

(AAA) (SAVE) 5/15-1/31 [CP]   1P: $115- 155 2P/1B: $115- 155 2P/2B: $120- 155 XP: $8   F12
　　　　　　2/1-5/14 [CP]   1P: $110- 145 2P/1B: $110- 145 2P/2B: $115- 145 XP: $8   F12
◆◆◆　　**Location:** Corner of SR 75 & Orange Ave. 275 Orange Ave 92118. Fax: 619/437-0188. **Terms:** Reserv
Motel　　deposit. **Facility:** 63 rooms. 3 stories; exterior corridors; small heated pool, whirlpool. **Cards:** AE, DI, DS,
　　　　　MC, VI. **Special Amenities:** Free breakfast. *(See color ad p 850)*   🈁 🖥 🎦 (VCR) 🖥 ▢ 🗑 🗑 ✕

CORONADO ISLAND MARRIOTT RESORT   Rates Subject to Change   Phone: (619)435-3000　🔲153

(AAA)　　All Year   1P: $275- 325 2P/1B: $275- 325 2P/2B: $275- 325 XP: $20   F18
◆◆◆◆　**Location:** 1.5 blks e of 4th St at Glorietta Blvd & 2nd St. 2000 2nd St 92118. Fax: 619/435-3032.
Hotel　　**Terms:** Reserv deposit, 3 day notice; BP avail. **Facility:** 300 rooms. Tastefully decorated rooms with
　　　　　balcony/patios with view of bay or lagoon. 1- & 2-bedroom villas, $235-$600; 3 stories; exterior corridors;
　　　　　heated pool, sauna, whirlpools; boat dock. Fee: parking; 6 lighted tennis courts. **Dining:** Restaurant; 6:30
am-10 pm; $14-$54; cocktails; also, Marius, L'Escale, see separate listing. **Services:** giftshop. Fee: massage.
Recreation: jogging trail. Rental: bicycles. **Cards:** AE, CB, DI, DS, JC, MC, VI.
　　　　　🅂⓿ 🈁 🈁 🈁 🍴 🈁 🈁 🈁 🈁 🈁 ✕ 🈁 🎦 🖥 ▢ 🈁 🗑 Ⓗ ✕

CROWN CITY INN   Rates Subject to Change   Phone: (619)435-3116　🔲151

◆◆　　　All Year   1P: $79- 145 2P/1B: $79- 145 2P/2B: $89- 165
Motor Inn　**Location:** 520 Orange Ave 92118. Fax: 619/435-6750. **Terms:** Reserv deposit. **Facility:** 33 rooms. 1 suite
　　　　　avail, $99.50-169.50; 2 stories; exterior corridors; small heated pool. **Recreation:** bicycles.
All Rooms: combo or shower baths. **Cards:** AE, CB, DI, DS, MC, VI. *(See color ad p 884)*
　　　　　　　　　　　　　　　　　　　　　　　　　　　　　　🐑 🈁 🍴 🈁 ✕ 🎦 (VCR) 🖥 ▢ 🗑 🗑 ✕

GLORIETTA BAY INN-CORONADO   Phone: (619)435-3101　🔲148

(AAA) (SAVE) Fri & Sat 2/1-6/30 & All Year
　　　　　[CP]   1P: $130- 195 2P/1B: $130- 195 2P/2B: $130- 195 XP: $10   F18
◆◆◆　　**Location:** On SR 75. 1630 Glorietta Blvd at Orange Ave 92118. Fax: 619/435-6182. **Terms:** Reserv deposit,
Historic Motel　3 day notice, 2 night min stay, weekends. **Facility:** 100 rooms. Around the historic Spreckel's Mansion; some
　　　　　rooms with bay view. 2 stories; exterior corridors; small heated pool, whirlpool. **All Rooms:** combo or shower
baths. **Some Rooms:** 8 efficiencies, 16 kitchens. **Cards:** AE, MC, VI. **Special Amenities:** Free breakfast. *(See ad p 865)*
　　　　　　　　　　　　　　　　　　　　　　　　　　　　　　🅂⓿ 🈁 🈁 🈁 🈁 🎦 🖥 ▢ 🗑 🗑 ✕

(See map p. 844)

HOTEL DEL CORONADO — Rates Subject to Change — **Phone:** 619/435-6611 [146]
◆◆◆◆ All Year — 1P: $185- 495 — 2P/1B: $185- 495 — 2P/2B: $185- 495 — XP: $25
Historic Hotel — **Location:** On SR 75. 1500 Orange Ave 92118. Fax: 619/522-8262. **Terms:** Check-in 4 pm. **Facility:** 692 rooms. Beautifully appointed Victorian hotel & newer towers, some poolside rooms. Some smaller rooms & baths. Shops in lower arcade. 7 two-bedroom units. 2-5 stories; interior/exterior corridors; beachfront; heated pool; marina. Fee: parking; 6 lighted tennis courts. **Services:** giftshop. Fee: massage. **Recreation:** swimming. Fee: sailboating; bicycles. Rental: boats. **Cards:** AE, CB, DI, DS, JC, MC, VI.

LA AVENIDA INN — Rates Subject to Change — **Phone:** (619)435-3191 [152]
◆◆ — 6/1-9/30 — 1P: $105- 140 — 2P/1B: $110- 145 — 2P/2B: $125- 350 — XP: $10
Motel — 2/1-5/31 & 10/1-1/31 — 1P: $95- 130 — 2P/1B: $100- 135 — 2P/2B: $115- 250 — XP: $10
Location: On SR 75 (Orange Ave). 1315 Orange Ave 92118. Fax: 619/435-5024. **Terms:** Reserv deposit. **Facility:** 29 rooms. Very tasteful, contemporary furnished rooms. 2 stories; exterior corridors. **Cards:** AE, CB, DI, JC, MC, VI.

LOEWS CORONADO BAY RESORT — Rates Subject to Change — **Phone:** (619)424-4000 [147]
ⓐ — All Year — 1P: $235- 285 — 2P/1B: $235- 285 — 2P/2B: $235- 350
◆◆◆◆ — **Location:** 5.8 mi s of Coronado Bridge, via Silver Strand Blvd. 4000 Coronado Bay Rd 92118.
Hotel — Fax: 619/424-4400. **Terms:** Reserv deposit; small pets only. **Facility:** 438 rooms. Very tasteful contemporary furnished rooms; many with view of water front. Bayside suites, $280-$475; 4 stories; interior corridors; beach, heated pool, saunas, whirlpools; marina. Fee: 5 lighted tennis courts. **Dining:** Restaurant; 6 am-11 pm; $9-$16; cocktails; also, Azzura Point, see separate listing. **Services:** giftshop; area transportation, Horton & Fashion Plaza. Fee: massage. **Recreation:** waterskiing. Rental: boats; bicycles. **Cards:** AE, CB, DI, DS, JC, MC, VI.

RESTAURANTS

AZZURA POINT — **Dinner:** $21-$35 — **Phone:** 619/424-4000 [71]
◆◆◆ — **Location:** In Loews Coronado Bay Resort. 4000 Coronado Bay Rd 92118. **Hours:** 6 pm-10 pm.
Continental — **Reservations:** suggested. **Features:** casual dress; cocktails & lounge; fee for valet parking; a la carte. Casual dining with a view of San Diego across the bay. Featuring seafood. Smoke free premises.
Cards: AE, CB, DI, DS, JC, MC, VI.

THE BRIGANTINE — **Lunch:** $5-$11 — **Dinner:** $13-$25 — **Phone:** 619/435-4166 [72]
◆◆ — **Location:** On SR 75. 1333 Orange Ave 92118. **Hours:** 11:30 am-2:30 & 5-10:30 pm, Fri-11:30 pm, Sat 5
Seafood — pm-11:30 pm, Sun 5 pm-10:30 pm. Closed: 11/25 & 12/25. **Reservations:** suggested. **Features:** casual dress; children's menu; carryout; cocktails & lounge; a la carte. Smoke free premises. **Cards:** AE, MC, VI.

CHAMELEON CAFE — **Lunch:** $9-$15 — **Dinner:** $9-$23 — **Phone:** 619/437-6677 [75]
◆◆◆ — **Location:** On SR 75. 1301 Orange Ave 92118. **Hours:** 11 am-2 & 5-10 pm. Closed major holidays.
Specialty — **Reservations:** required. **Features:** casual dress; cocktails & lounge; street parking; a la carte. A nice selection of Pacific Rim/Southwestern cuisine. Smoke free premises. **Cards:** AE, DI, MC, VI.

CHEZ LOMA RESTAURANT — **Dinner:** $19-$26 — **Phone:** 619/435-0661 [73]
◆◆◆ — **Location:** Corner of Orange Ave & Loma Ave. 1132 Loma Ave 92118. **Hours:** Sun brunch 10
French — am-2 pm. Closed major holidays. **Reservations:** suggested. **Features:** No A/C; casual dress; wine only; street parking. 1889 historical landmark home. Fresh fish, fowl, meat & pastas. Smoke free premises. **Cards:** AE, DI, MC, VI.

CROWN-CORONET ROOM — **Lunch:** $10-$15 — **Dinner:** $17-$25 — **Phone:** 619/435-6611 [68]
◆◆◆ — **Location:** In Hotel Del Coronado. 1500 Orange Ave 92118. **Hours:** 7 am-11 11:30-3 & 5-9 pm, Sat &
Continental — Sun-10 pm. **Reservations:** suggested. **Features:** casual dress; cocktails & lounge; fee for parking & valet parking. Spacious, popular dining room. Innovative cuisine includes fish, fowl, meat & pasta. **Cards:** AE, CB, DI, DS, JC, MC, VI.

L'ESCALE — **Lunch:** $10-$18 — **Dinner:** $14-$25 — **Phone:** 619/522-3039 [76]
◆◆◆ — **Location:** 1.5 blks e of 4th St at Glorietta Blvd & 2nd St; in Coronado Island Marriott Resort. 2000 Second
American — St 92118. **Hours:** 6:30 am-2 & 5-10 pm, Sun brunch 10:30 am-2 pm. **Reservations:** suggested. **Features:** casual dress; cocktails; fee for parking & valet parking; a la carte. California contemporary cuisine featuring chicken, seafood, pasta & beef. Patio dining avail with views of the bay & bridge. **Cards:** AE, CB, DI, DS, JC, MC, VI.

MARIUS — **Dinner:** $41-$54 — **Phone:** 619/522-3037 [69]
◆◆◆◆ — **Location:** 1.5 blks e of 4th St at Glorietta Blvd & 2nd St; in Coronado Island Marriott Resort. 2000 Second
French — St 92118. **Hours:** 6 pm-10 pm. Closed: Sun & Mon. **Reservations:** required. **Features:** semi-formal attire; cocktails; fee for parking & valet parking; prix fixe. Formal dining in an elegant atmosphere. Featuring contemporary French cuisine. Smoke free premises. **Cards:** AE, CB, DI, DS, JC, MC, VI.

PEOHE'S — **Lunch:** $11-$17 — **Dinner:** $19-$31 — **Phone:** 619/437-4474 [70]
◆◆ — **Location:** 2 blks e of Orange Ave; The Old Ferry Landing Plaza. 1201 First St 92118. **Hours:** 11:30 am-2:30
Seafood — & 5:30-9:30 pm, Fri & Sat 5 pm-10:30 pm, Sun 10:30 am-9:30 pm. **Reservations:** suggested. **Features:** casual dress; Sunday brunch; children's menu; cocktails & lounge; a la carte. Bay view & patio dining. Smoke free premises. **Cards:** AE, MC, VI.

PRINCE OF WALES — **Dinner:** $23-$38 — **Phone:** 619/522-8818 [74]
◆◆◆ — **Location:** In Hotel del Coronado. 1500 Orange Ave 92118. **Hours:** 5:30 pm-10 pm.
American — **Reservations:** suggested. **Features:** casual dress; cocktails; fee for parking & valet parking; a la carte. Oceanfront restaurant. Contemporary American cuisine, featuring seafood, fowl & steaks. Smoke free premises. **Cards:** AE, CB, DI, DS, JC, MC, VI.

DEL MAR—4,900

LODGINGS

BEST WESTERN STRATFORD INN Rates Subject to Change **Phone:** 619/755-1501
◆◆◆   5/25-9/14 [CP] 1P: $89- 169 2P/1B: $89- 169 2P/2B: $89- 169 XP: $10 F17
Motel   2/1-5/24 & 9/15-1/31 [CP] 1P: $79- 149 2P/1B: $79- 149 2P/2B: $79- 149 XP: $10 F17
Location: From I-5, Del Mar Heights Rd exit 1 mi w, then 0.3 mi n. 710 Camino Del Mar 92014.
Fax: 619/755-4704. **Facility:** 94 rooms. Some rooms with ocean view, balcony or patio. 2 two-bedroom units. 2 stories; interior corridors; heated pool. **All Rooms:** combo or shower baths. **Some Rooms:** 27 efficiencies. **Cards:** AE, DI, DS, MC, VI.

DEL MAR INN, A CLARION CARRIAGE HOUSE **Phone:** (619)755-9765
(AAA) [SAVE]   6/1-9/15 [CP] 1P: $105- 125 2P/1B: $105- 135 2P/2B: $115- 155 XP: $10 F16
   2/1-5/31 & 9/16-1/31 [CP] 1P: $89- 119 2P/1B: $89- 119 2P/2B: $89- 129 XP: $10 F16
◆◆◆   **Location:** From I-5, Del Mar Heights Rd exit 1 mi w, 0.3 mi n. 720 Camino Del Mar 92014.
Motel   Fax: 619/792-8196. **Terms:** Reserv deposit; weekly/monthly rates; small pets only, $20 dep req. **Facility:** 81
rooms. English Tudor design. Beautifully landscaped pool area. Many rooms with full or partial ocean view &
balcony. 3 stories; interior corridors; heated pool, whirlpool. **Dining:** Afternoon tea. **All Rooms:** combo or shower baths.
Some Rooms: 10 efficiencies. **Cards:** AE, CB, DI, DS, JC, MC, VI. **Special Amenities:** Free breakfast and free local
telephone calls. (See ad p 860)

DOUBLETREE HOTEL DEL MAR Guaranteed Rates **Phone:** (619)481-5900
(AAA)   6/13-1/31 1P: $119- 250 2P/1B: $119- 250 2P/2B: $119- 250 XP: $10 F18
   2/1-6/12 1P: $109- 250 2P/1B: $109- 250 2P/2B: $109- 250 XP: $10 F18
◆◆◆   **Location:** 0.3 mi e of I-5, exit Carmel Valley Rd. 11915 El Camino Real 92130. Fax: 619/481-0990.
Hotel   **Terms:** Reserv deposit; AP avail. **Facility:** 220 rooms. 6 suites, $150-$200; 5 stories; interior corridors; heated
pool, wading pool, whirlpool. **Dining:** Restaurant; 6-11 am, 11:30-3 & 5-10 pm; $8-$17. **Services:** giftshop;
area transportation, within 6 mi. **Recreation:** Childrens playroom. **All Rooms:** extended cable TV. **Cards:** AE, CB, DI, DS,
JC, MC, VI.

HILTON SAN DIEGO/DEL MAR **Phone:** (619)792-5200
(AAA) [SAVE]   6/11-9/4 1P: $189 2P/1B: $189 2P/2B: $189 XP: $20 F
   2/1-6/10 & 9/5-1/31 1P: $169 2P/1B: $169 2P/2B: $169 XP: $20 F
◆◆◆   **Location:** Adjacent to I-5, exit Via de la Valle, at Del Mar Race Track. 15575 Jimmy Durante Blvd 92014.
Motor Inn   Fax: 619/792-0353. **Terms:** Reserv deposit, 3 day notice. **Facility:** 245 rooms. Some rooms
with balcony or patio. 3 stories; interior corridors; heated pool, whirlpools. **Dining:** Restaurant; 6 am-2 & 5-10
pm; $10-$16; cocktails. **Services:** giftshop; area transportation, within 5 mi. **Cards:** AE, CB, DI, DS, JC, MC, VI.
Special Amenities: Free newspaper and preferred room (subject to availability with advanced reservations).
(See ad p 119 & color ad below)

L'AUBERGE DEL MAR RESORT & SPA　　　　　　　　　　　　　　　　　　Phone: (619)259-1515

　　　　7/15-9/15　　　　　　1P: $299- 379　2P/1B: $299- 379　2P/2B: $299- 379　XP: $25-50　　F12
　　　　Fri & Sat 2/1-7/14 &
◆◆◆　9/16-1/31　　　　　　1P: $255- 295　2P/1B: $255- 295　2P/2B: $255- 295　XP: $25-50　　F12
Motor Inn　Sun-Thurs 2/1-7/14 &
　　　　9/16-1/31　　　　　　1P: $165- 255　2P/1B: $165- 255　2P/2B: $165- 255　XP: $25-50　　F12
Location: I-5, Del Mar Heights Rd exit 1 mi w, 1 mi n. 1540 Camino Del Mar 92014. **Fax:** 619/755-4940. **Terms:** Check-in 4 pm; reserv deposit, 3 day notice. **Facility:** 120 rooms. City, garden or coastal view rooms, some with balcony & fireplace. 3 stories; interior corridors; heated pool, sauna, whirlpool. **Fee:** parking; 2 lighted tennis courts. **Dining:** Cocktails; also, The Dining Room, see separate listing. **Services:** giftshop; area transportation, Amtrack & racetrack. **Fee:** massage. **All Rooms:** extended cable TV. **Cards:** AE, CB, DI, DS, JC, MC, VI. **Special Amenities:** Free newspaper and free room upgrade (subject to availability with advanced reservations).

RESTAURANTS

THE DINING ROOM　　　　　**Lunch:** $10-$15　　　　　**Dinner:** $10-$25　　　　　Phone: 619/259-1515
◆◆◆　　　**Location:** I-5, Del Mar Heights Rd exit 1 mi w, 1 mi n; in L'Auberge Del Mar Resort & Spa. 1540 Camino del
Continental　Mar 92014. **Hours:** 6:30-11 am, 11:30-2:30 & 5-10 pm. **Reservations:** suggested. **Features:** semi-formal attire; children's menu; early bird specials; cocktails & lounge; fee for valet parking; a la carte. Features steak, pasta & fresh seafood. California regional cuisine. **Cards:** AE, CB, DI, DS, MC, VI.

IL FORNAIO　　　　　　　**Lunch:** $8-$25　　　　　　**Dinner:** $15-$25　　　　　Phone: 619/755-8876
◆◆　　　　**Location:** I-5, Del Mar Heights Rd exit 1 mi w, then 1 mi n. 1555 Camino Del Mar 92014. **Hours:** 11:30
Italian　　am-10:30 pm, Fri & Sat 11:30, Sun 10 am-10 pm. **Closed:** 11/25 & 12/25. **Reservations:** suggested.
　　　　　Features: No A/C; casual dress; Sunday brunch; children's menu; cocktails & lounge; a la carte. Sun brunch 10 am-3 pm. Patio dining, weather permitting. Bread & pastries baked on premises. Bakery counter. Smoke free premises. **Cards:** AE, DI, MC, VI.

EL CAJON—88,700

LODGINGS

BEST WESTERN CONTINENTAL INN　　　　　　　　　　　　　　　　　Phone: (619)442-0601
　　　　6/7-9/10 [CP]　　　1P:　$79- 139　2P/1B:　$89- 139　2P/2B:　$99- 139　XP:　$5　　F17
　　　　2/1-6/6 & 9/11-1/31 [CP]　1P:　$49- 99　2P/1B:　$59- 99　2P/2B:　$69- 99　XP:　$5　　F17
◆◆　　　**Location:** Adjacent to I-8, exit Mollison Ave. 650 N Mollison Ave 92021. **Fax:** 619/442-0152.
Motel　　**Terms:** Weekly/monthly rates. **Facility:** 97 rooms. 12 one-bedroom suites with whirlpool tub. 20 efficiencies,
$55-$85 for 2 persons; 2-3 stories; exterior corridors; whirlpool. **Dining:** Coffee shop nearby.
Some Rooms: whirlpools. **Cards:** AE, CB, DI, DS, MC, VI. **Special Amenities:** Early check-in/late check-out and free breakfast. *(See ad below)*

BEST WESTERN COURTESY INN　　　　　　　　　　　　　　　　　　Phone: (619)440-7378
　　　　All Year [CP]　　　　1P: $42　　　2P/1B: $48- 54　2P/2B: $54- 60　XP: $6　　F13
◆　　　**Location:** Business Loop I-8, 0.5 mi s of I-8; westbound exit E Main St, eastbound exit 2nd Ave, s to Main
Motel　　St, then e. 1355 E Main St 92021. **Fax:** 619/588-0582. **Terms:** Weekly rates; small pets only, $6 extra charge. **Facility:** 47 rooms. 10 two-bedroom units. 2 whirlpool rms, extra charge; 3 stories; exterior corridors; whirlpool. **Cards:** AE, CB, DI, DS, MC, VI. **Special Amenities:** Free breakfast.

PARKSIDE OF EL CAJON　　　　　　　　　　　　　　　　　　　　Phone: (619)442-4330
　　　　All Year　　　　　　1P: $42　　　2P/1B: $47　　　2P/2B: $52　　　XP: $7
◆　　　**Location:** Adjacent to I-8, exit 2nd St. 1274 Oakdale Ave 92021. **Fax:** 619/442-4330. **Terms:** Reserv
Motel　　deposit; handling fee imposed. **Facility:** 32 rooms. 2 stories; exterior corridors; heated pool.
Dining: Restaurant nearby. **Cards:** AE, MC, VI. **Special Amenities:** Free breakfast and free room upgrade (subject to availability with advanced reservations).

PLAZA INTERNATIONAL INN　　　　　　　Rates Subject to Change　　　　　Phone: (619)442-0973
　　　　All Year　　　　　　1P: $35- 40　2P/1B:　$41- 46　2P/2B:　$45- 50
◆◆　　　**Location:** Just n of I-8, exit Mollison Ave. 683 N Mollison Ave 92021. **Fax:** 619/593-0772. **Terms:** Weekly
Motel　　rates. **Facility:** 60 rooms. 4 efficiencies, weekly rental only; 2 stories; exterior corridors; saunas, indoor whirl-
pool. **Dining:** Coffee shop nearby. **Cards:** AE, CB, DI, DS, JC, MC, VI.

SINGING HILLS RESORT　　　　　　　　Rates Subject to Change　　　　　　　**Phone:** (619)442-3425
◆◆◆　All Year　　　　　　　　1P: $84- 221　2P/1B: $89- 133　2P/2B: $89- 221　XP: $14
Resort Motor　**Location:** I-8 exit SR 54 (2nd Ave), 1 mi s, 3 mi e on Washington St & Dehesa Rd. 3007 Dehesa Rd 92019.
Inn　Fax: 619/442-9574. **Terms:** Check-in 4 pm; reserv deposit, 30 day notice; handling fee imposed.
Facility: 102 rooms. Golf resort on attractive, tree-shaded grounds. Spacious, nicely decorated rooms & suites
with balcony or patio. 2 two-bedroom units. 1-2 stories; exterior corridors; heated pool. Fee: 54 holes golf; 11 lighted tennis
courts. **All Rooms:** shower baths. **Cards:** AE, DS, MC, VI.

SUPER 8 MOTEL　　　　　　　　　　Guaranteed Rates　　　　　　　　**Phone:** (619)579-1144
(AAA)　5/15-9/7　　　　　　　1P: $44　　2P/1B: $44- 45　2P/2B: $54- 59　XP: $5　F16
　　2/1-5/14 & 9/8-1/31　　1P: $41　　2P/1B: $44　　2P/2B: $49　　XP: $5　F16
◆◆　**Location:** Adjacent to I-8, exit Mollison Ave. 588 N Mollison Ave 92021. Fax: 615/579-1787. **Terms:** Pets, $5
Motel　extra charge, in designated rooms. **Facility:** 64 rooms. 2 stories; exterior corridors; heated pool, whirlpool.
Some Rooms: 6 efficiencies. **Cards:** AE, DS, MC, VI.

TRAVELODGE EL CAJON　　　　　　　　　　　　　　　　　　　　　**Phone:** (619)447-3999
(AAA) [SAVE]　5/15-9/15 [CP]　　　1P: $50- 70　2P/1B: $55- 75　2P/2B: $60- 80　XP: $5-10　F17
　　2/1-5/14 & 9/16-1/31 [CP]　1P: $40- 55　2P/1B: $45- 60　2P/2B: $50- 65　XP: $5-10　F14
◆◆　**Location:** Just s of I-8, exit Magnolia Ave. 471 N Magnolia Ave 92020. Fax: 619/447-8403. **Facility:** 47 rooms.
Motel　3 stories; exterior corridors; small pool. **Dining:** Restaurant nearby. **All Rooms:** extended cable TV.
Cards: AE, CB, DI, DS, MC, VI. **Special Amenities:** Free breakfast and free newspaper.

RESTAURANT

ECHO'S RESTAURANT　　　　　　　　Dinner: $11-$16　　　　　　　　**Phone:** 619/442-3425
◆◆　**Location:** I-8, 1 mi s on SR 54 (2nd St), then 3 mi e on Washington St & Dehesa Rd, at Singing Hills
American　Country Club. 3007 Dehesa Rd 92019. **Hours:** 5:30 pm-9 pm, Fri & Sat-10 pm. **Reservations:** suggested.
Features: casual dress; Sunday brunch; cocktails & lounge. Attractive southwestern decor. Smoke free
premises. **Cards:** AE, DS, MC, VI.

IMPERIAL BEACH—26,500　(See map p. 844; index p. 842)

LODGING

HAWAIIAN GARDENS SUITE-HOTEL　　　　　　　　　**Phone:** (619)429-5303　181
(AAA) [SAVE]　2/1-4/14, 6/15-9/14 &
　　12/15-1/31　　　　　1P: $69- 95　2P/1B: $75- 100　2P/2B: $90- 140　XP: $5-10　F
◆◆　4/15-6/14 & 9/15-12/14　1P: $65- 85　2P/1B: $70- 90　2P/2B: $85- 115　XP: $5-10　F
Apartment　**Location:** 2 mi w of I-5, Coronado Ave exit. 1031 Imperial Beach Blvd 91932. Fax: 619/429-5304.
Motel　**Terms:** Reserv deposit, 14 day notice; daily/weekly/monthly rates; small pets only, $50 extra charge.
Facility: 47 rooms. Tropically landscaped grounds. Studio 1- & 2-bedroom apartments. 3 stories; exterior corridors; heated pool, sauna. **Dining:** 5 pm-7 pm, complimentary soup & salad bar provided. **Recreation:** club house available
for reading or small meetings. **All Rooms:** kitchens. **Cards:** AE, CB, DI, DS, MC, VI. **Special Amenities: Free breakfast
and free local telephone calls.** (See color ad p 862)

LA JOLLA—28,800　(See map p. 844; index p. 840)

LODGINGS

ANDREA VILLA INN　　　　　　　　　　　　　　　　　　　**Phone:** (619)459-3311　5
(AAA) [SAVE]　6/1-9/30 [CP]　　　1P: $109- 140　2P/1B: $109- 140　2P/2B: $130- 145　XP: $10　F10
　　2/1-5/31 & 10/1-1/31 [CP]　1P: $95- 140　2P/1B: $95- 140　2P/2B: $109- 125　XP: $10　F10
◆◆　**Location:** 1.5 mi n of town. 2402 Torrey Pines Rd 92037. Fax: 619/459-1320. **Terms:** Reserv deposit, 3 day
Motel　notice; weekly/monthly rates; small pets only, $25 extra charge. **Facility:** 49 rooms. 2 stories; interior/exterior
corridors; heated pool, whirlpool. **Cards:** AE, DI, DS, MC, VI. **Special Amenities: Free breakfast.**

THE BED & BREAKFAST INN AT LA JOLLA　Rates Subject to Change　**Phone:** (619)456-2066　14
(AAA)　All Year [BP]　　　　1P: $110- 250　2P/1B: $110- 250　2P/2B: $135- 180
　　Location: 7753 Draper Ave 92037. Fax: 619/456-1510. **Terms:** Reserv deposit, 10 day notice; 2 night min
◆◆◆　stay, weekends. **Facility:** 15 rooms. 1913 "cubist" style inn, former home of the John Philip Sousa family. 2
Historic Bed　stories; interior/exterior corridors; designated smoking area. **Services:** complimentary evening beverages.
& Breakfast　**All Rooms:** combo or shower baths. **Some Rooms:** color TV. **Cards:** AE, MC, VI.

BEST WESTERN INN BY THE SEA　　　　　　　　　　　**Phone:** (619)459-4461　10
(AAA) [SAVE]　2/1-6/1 & 1/1-1/31 [CP]　1P: $139- 219　2P/1B: $139- 219　2P/2B: $139- 219　XP: $10　F12
　　6/2-9/15 [CP]　　　1P: $109- 199　2P/1B: $109- 199　2P/2B: $109- 199　XP: $10　F12
◆◆◆　9/16-12/31 [CP]　　1P: $119- 199　2P/1B: $119- 199　2P/2B: $119- 199　XP: $10　F12
Motor Inn　**Location:** In town. 7830 Fay Ave & Prospect St 92037. Fax: 619/456-2578. **Facility:** 132 rooms. Spacious
rooms. Some with ocean view & balcony. 5 stories; interior corridors; heated pool, semi-enclosed whirlpool.
Dining: Coffee shop nearby. **Recreation:** fee for health club nearby. **Cards:** AE, DI, DS, MC, VI. **Special Amenities: Free
breakfast and free local telephone calls.** (See color ad p 846)

COLONIAL INN　　　　　　　　　Rates Subject to Change　　　　　　　**Phone:** (619)454-2181　9
(AAA)　5/1-8/31　　　　　1P: $134- 225　2P/1B: $134- 225　2P/2B: $134- 225　XP: $10　F12
◆◆◆　2/1-3/31 & 1/1-1/31　1P: $114- 179　2P/1B: $114- 179　2P/2B: $114- 179　XP: $10　F12
Historic Hotel　4/1-4/30 & 9/1-12/31　1P: $109- 159　2P/1B: $109- 159　2P/2B: $109- 159　XP: $10　F12
Location: 910 Prospect St 92037. Fax: 619/454-5679. **Terms:** Reserv deposit, 3 day notice; handling fee imposed.
Facility: 75 rooms. Some ocean view rooms. 4 stories; interior corridors; heated pool. **Cards:** AE, DI, MC, VI.

(See map p. 844)

EMBASSY SUITES
Phone: (619)453-0400 **3**

6/11-9/10 [BP]	1P: $215	2P/1B: $225	2P/2B: $245	XP: $10	F18
2/1-6/10 & 9/11-1/31 [BP]	1P: $195		2P/2B: $225	XP: $10	F18

◆◆◆ **Location:** 0.8 mi e of I-5. 4550 La Jolla Village Dr 92122. Fax: 619/453-4226. **Terms:** Check-in 4 pm.
Suite Hotel **Facility:** 335 rooms. 1- & 2-bedroom suites with living room. Large central atrium with tropically landscaped koi ponds. 12 stories; interior corridors; heated indoor pool, sauna, whirlpool. Fee: parking. **Dining:** Restaurant; 11 am-11 pm; $9-$20; cocktails; deli; also, Coast Cafe, see separate listing. **Services:** giftshop; complimentary evening beverages. **Recreation:** video arcade, video game system in all rooms. **Cards:** AE, CB, DI, DS, JC, MC, VI. **Special Amenities: Free breakfast and free newspaper.**

THE EMPRESS HOTEL OF LA JOLLA
Phone: (619)454-3001 **11**

5/22-1/31 [CP]	1P: $129- 199	2P/1B: $129- 199	2P/2B: $129- 199	XP: $10	F12
2/1-5/21 [CP]	1P: $119- 189	2P/1B: $119- 189	2P/2B: $119- 189	XP: $10	F12

◆◆◆ **Location:** 7766 Fay Ave at Silverado St 92037. Fax: 619/454-6387. **Facility:** 73 rooms. 4 efficiency suites,
Hotel $350-$400; 5 stories; interior corridors; wading pool, sauna. Fee: parking. **Dining:** Dining room; 11:30 am-2 & 5:30-10:30 pm, Fri & Sat-11 pm; $17-$30; cocktails. **All Rooms:** extended cable TV. **Some Rooms:** whirlpools. **Cards:** AE, DS, MC, VI. *(See color ad below)*

HOLIDAY INN EXPRESS LA JOLLA
Phone: (619)454-7101 **13**

6/1-9/15 [CP]	1P: $89- 149	2P/1B: $89- 149	2P/2B: $89- 149	XP: $10	F17
2/1-5/31 & 9/16-1/31 [CP]	1P: $79- 109	2P/1B: $79- 109	2P/2B: $79- 109	XP: $10	F17

◆◆◆ **Location:** 1.5 mi s. 6705 La Jolla Blvd 92037. Fax: 619/454-6957. **Terms:** Weekly/monthly rates. **Facility:** 61
Motel rooms. 2-3 stories; exterior corridors; heated pool, whirlpool. **Dining:** Restaurant nearby. **Some Rooms:** combo or shower baths, extended cable TV. **Some Rooms:** 4 efficiencies, 12 kitchens, whirlpools. **Cards:** AE, DI, DS, JC, MC, VI. **Special Amenities: Free breakfast.**

HOTEL LA JOLLA AT THE SHORES
Rates Subject to Change
Phone: (619)459-0261 **6**

◆◆◆ 5/15-9/15	1P: $139- 159	2P/1B: $159- 179	2P/2B: $159- 179	XP: $20	F16
Hotel 2/1-5/14 & 9/16-1/31	1P: $129- 149	2P/1B: $149- 169	2P/2B: $149- 169	XP: $20	F16

Location: 1.5 mi n of town. 7955 La Jolla Shores Dr 92037. Fax: 619/459-7649. **Facility:** 108 rooms. Many ocean view rooms. Balconies. 11 stories; exterior corridors; heated pool. **Services:** Fee: massage. **Cards:** AE, DI, DS, MC, VI. *(See color ad below)*

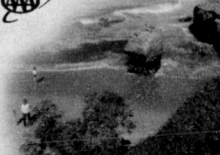

(See map p. 844)

HYATT REGENCY LA JOLLA
Phone: (619)552-1234 **19**

All Year   1P: $189- 300   2P/1B: $214- 325   2P/2B: $214- 325   XP: $25   F18

Location: Just e of I-5; exit La Jolla Village Dr. 3777 La Jolla Village Dr 92122. Fax: 619/552-6066. **Terms:** BP, CP avail; small pets only, $25 extra charge, $100 dep req. **Facility:** 419 rooms. 16 stories; interior corridors; heated pool, sauna, whirlpool; 2 lighted tennis courts. Fee: parking. **Dining:** Restaurant; 6 am-10 pm; $9-$16; cocktails; also, Cafe Japengo, see separate listing. **Services:** giftshop. Fee: massage. **Cards:** AE, CB, DI, DS, JC, MC, VI. *(See color ad p 565)*

Hotel

LA JOLLA BEACH TRAVELODGE
Rates Subject to Change   Phone: (619)454-0716 **12**

6/23-8/31   1P: $74- 129   2P/1B: $74- 129   2P/2B: $89- 159   XP: $5-6
9/1-1/31   1P: $49- 84   2P/1B: $49- 84   2P/2B: $69- 99   XP: $5
2/1-6/22   1P: $53- 84   2P/1B: $53- 84   2P/2B: $74- 99   XP: $5

Motel

Location: 1.5 mi s. 6750 La Jolla Blvd 92037. Fax: 619/454-1075. **Terms:** Weekly/monthly rates. **Facility:** 44 rooms. 2 stories; exterior corridors; heated pool, whirlpool. **Dining:** Restaurant nearby. **All Rooms:** combo or shower baths. **Cards:** AE, CB, DI, DS, JC, MC, VI.

LA JOLLA COVE SUITES
Phone: (619)459-2621 **18**

2/1-5/20 [CP]   1P: $115- 325   2P/1B: $115- 325   2P/2B: $115- 325   XP: $15   F18
5/21-9/6 & 9/7-1/31 [CP]   1P: $88- 310   2P/1B: $88- 310   2P/2B: $88- 310   XP: $15   F18

Suite Motel

Location: At La Jolla Cove, just w of Prospect St via Girard. 1155 Coast Blvd 92037. Fax: 619/454-3522. **Terms:** Reserv deposit; handling fee imposed. **Facility:** 90 rooms. Studios & suites with kitchen & balcony; most with ocean view. Roof top sundeck & solarium. 32 two-bedroom units. 1-6 stories; exterior corridors; putting green; beach, heated pool, whirlpool. **Dining:** Restaurant nearby. **Recreation:** swimming, scuba diving, snorkeling, jogging. Fee: scuba & snorkeling equipment; bicycles. **All Rooms:** kitchens. **Cards:** AE, CB, DI, DS, MC, VI. **Special Amenities:** Early check-in/late check-out and free local telephone calls. *(See color ad p 881)*

LA JOLLA MARRIOTT
Rates Subject to Change   Phone: 619/587-1414 **1**

All Year   1P: $189   2P/1B: $189   2P/2B: $189   XP: $10   F18

Hotel

Location: 0.5 mi e of I-5. 4240 La Jolla Village Dr 92037. Fax: 619/546-8518. **Facility:** 360 rooms. Comfortable, contemporary decor. Rooms furnished with equipment to meet business traveler's needs. 15 stories; interior corridors; heated indoor pool. Fee: parking. **Services:** giftshop. **Cards:** AE, CB, DI, DS, JC, MC, VI.

LA JOLLA TRAVELODGE
Rates Subject to Change   Phone: (619)454-0791 **21**

7/1-9/6   1P: $74- 84   2P/1B: $74- 94   2P/2B: $89- 129   XP: $5   F18
2/1-6/30 & 9/7-1/31   1P: $49- 79   2P/1B: $49- 89   2P/2B: $59- 99   XP: $5   F18

Motel

Location: Just s of Prospect St, via Herschel Ave. 1141 Silverado St 92037. Fax: 619/459-8534. **Terms:** Reserv deposit, 3 day notice. **Facility:** 30 rooms. 3 stories, no elevator; exterior corridors. **Dining:** Restaurant nearby. **All Rooms:** combo or shower baths. **Some Rooms:** efficiency. **Cards:** AE, CB, DI, DS, JC, MC, VI.

LA VALENCIA HOTEL
Phone: (619)454-0771 **8**

All Year   1P: $230- 550   2P/1B: $230- 550   2P/2B: $230- 550   XP: $15   F16

Historic Hotel

Location: At Herschel Ave. 1132 Prospect St 92037. Fax: 619/456-3921. **Terms:** Reserv deposit. **Facility:** 100 rooms. Charming, Spanish/Mediterranean style hotel. Rooms of varying size individually decorated in Old World style, many with ocean view. 12 suites, $500-$800; 7 stories; interior corridors; heated pool, sauna, whirlpool. **Dining:** 2 dining rooms; 6:30 am-10 pm; $14-$43; cocktails; also, Sky Room, see separate listing. **Services:** Fee: massage. **All Rooms:** combo or shower baths, extended cable TV. **Some Rooms:** 12 efficiencies, whirlpools. **Cards:** AE, CB, DI, DS, JC, MC, VI. A Preferred Hotel.

THE LODGE AT TORREY PINES
Phone: (619)453-4420 **15**

All Year   1P: $110- 200   2P/1B: $110- 200   2P/2B: $110- 200

Motor Inn

Location: 1.5 mi nw of I-5, exit Genesee Ave. 11480 N Torrey Pines Rd 92037. Fax: 619/453-0691. **Terms:** Weekly/monthly rates; package plans. **Facility:** 73 rooms. At Torrey Pines Municipal Golf Course. 2 stories; interior/exterior corridors; putting green; heated pool. Fee: 36 holes golf. **Dining:** Dining room, coffee shop; 4:30 am-10 pm; $10-$17; cocktails. **Services:** area transportation, within 5 mi. **Cards:** AE, CB, DI, MC, VI.

(See map p. 844)

PROSPECT PARK INN   Phone: (619)454-0133 ㉒
AAA SAVE   All Year [CP]   1P: $120- 185   2P/1B: $120- 185   2P/2B: $175   XP: $10
◆◆   **Location:** At Coast Blvd. 1110 Prospect St 92037. Fax: 619/454-2056. **Terms:** Reserv deposit; monthly
Motel   rates. **Facility:** 23 rooms. Ocean view from rooftop patio. Some rooms with balcony & ocean View. 2 one-
           bedroom suites with kitchen, $275-$350; 3 stories; interior/exterior corridors; smoke free premises; off site
           parking only. **Dining:** Restaurant nearby. **Some Rooms:** 3 efficiencies, 2 kitchens. **Cards:** AE, CB, DI, DS,
JC, MC, VI. **Special Amenities:** Free breakfast and free local telephone calls. *(See color ad p 903)*

RADISSON HOTEL LA JOLLA   Phone: (619)453-5500 ②
AAA SAVE   All Year   1P: $149- 199   2P/1B: $149- 199   2P/2B: $149- 199   XP: $10   F17
◆◆◆   **Location:** On hill above I-5, La Jolla Village Dr exit w to Villa La Jolla Dr, just s to Holiday Ct. 3299 Holiday
Hotel   Ct 92037. Fax: 619/453-5550. **Terms:** Reserv deposit; handling fee imposed. **Facility:** 200 rooms. Guest
           rooms surround attractively landscaped pool area. 2 stories; interior corridors; heated pool, whirlpool; 2 tennis
cocktails. courts. **Dining:** Restaurant; 6:30 am-2 & 5:30-10 pm, Sat & Sun 7 am-noon & 5:30-10 pm; $16-$26;
           Services: area transportation, within 2 mi. **Recreation:** video game system in all rooms. **Cards:** AE, DI, DS, MC,
VI. **Special Amenities:** Free newspaper. *(See color ad p 886 & p 870)*

RESIDENCE INN BY MARRIOTT   Rates Subject to Change   Phone: (619)587-1770 ⑯
◆◆◆   All Year [CP]   1P: $155- 275   2P/1B: $155- 275   2P/2B: $155- 275   XP: $10   F12
Suite Motel **Location:** 1.5 mi nw of I-5, exit Gilman Dr. 8901 Gilman Dr 92037. Fax: 619/552-0387. **Terms:** Check-in 4
           pm; reserv deposit. **Facility:** 287 rooms. 1- & 2-bedroom suites with living room. Some with fireplace. 71 two-
bedroom units. 2 stories; exterior corridors; heated pool. **All Rooms:** kitchens. **Cards:** AE, CB, DI, DS, JC, MC, VI.

SCRIPPS INN   Phone: 619/454-3391 ⑦
AAA SAVE   6/1-9/7 & 1/1-1/31 [CP] 1P: $145- 220   2P/1B: $145- 220   2P/2B: $145- 220   XP: $10
◆◆   2/1-5/31 & 9/8-12/31 [CP] 1P: $135- 195   2P/1B: $135- 195   2P/2B: $135- 195   XP: $10
Motel   **Location:** Just w of Prospect St via Cuvier St. 555 Coast Blvd S 92037. Fax: 619/456-0389. **Terms:** Reserv
           deposit, 7 day notice; weekly/monthly rates. **Facility:** 13 rooms. Across from bluff overlooking ocean. 5 one-
           bedroom efficiency suites; 2 stories; exterior corridors; designated smoking area. **All Rooms:** combo or
shower baths. **Cards:** AE, DS, MC, VI.

SEA LODGE AT LA JOLLA SHORES   Phone: (619)459-8271 ④
AAA SAVE   6/11-9/7   1P: $205- 479   2P/1B: $205- 479   2P/2B: $205- 479   XP: $20   F12
◆◆◆   3/1-6/10 & 9/8-10/16 1P: $155- 349   2P/1B: $155- 349   2P/2B: $155- 349   XP: $20   F12
Motor Inn 2/1-2/28 & 10/17-1/31 1P: $149- 339   2P/1B: $149- 339   2P/2B: $149- 339   XP: $20   F12
           Location: 1.5 mi n, on the beach; via La Jolla Shores Dr & Avenida de la Playa. 8110 Camino Del Oro
           92037. Fax: 619/456-9346. **Terms:** Check-in 4 pm; weekly/monthly rates. **Facility:** 128 rooms. Attractive, early
California decor. Balconies or patios, many with ocean view. Colorful grounds. Beachfront city park located adjacent to hotel.
3 stories; exterior corridors; beach, heated pool, sauna, whirlpool; 2 tennis courts. **Dining:** Dining room; 7 am-10 pm;
$10-$21; cocktails. **Recreation:** City boat launch adjacent to hotel. **Some Rooms:** 18 efficiencies. **Cards:** AE, DI, DS, MC,
VI. *(See color ad p 905)*

SHERATON GRANDE TORREY PINES   Phone: (619)558-1500 ⑰
AAA SAVE   All Year   1P: $205- 280   2P/1B: $205- 280   2P/2B: $205- 280   XP: $20   F17
◆◆◆◆   **Location:** 1.5 mi nw of I-5, exit Genesee Ave. Adjacent to Torrey Pines Municipal Golf Course. 10950 N
Hotel   Torrey Pines Rd 92037. Fax: 619/450-4584. **Terms:** Reserv deposit; handling fee imposed. **Facility:** 394
           rooms. Balconies or patios. Many rooms with ocean & golf course view. Complimentary butler service for all
           rooms. 4 stories; interior corridors; putting green; heated pool, saunas, whirlpool. Fee: parking; 3 lighted
tennis courts. **Dining:** Restaurant; 6:30 am-11 pm; $14-$25; cocktails. **Services:** giftshop; area transportation, within 5 mi.
Recreation: video game system in all rooms. **Rental:** bicycles. **Cards:** AE, CB, DI, DS, JC, MC, VI.

RESTAURANTS

CAFE JAPENGO   **Lunch:** $10-$13   **Dinner:** $14-$23   Phone: 619/450-3355 ②
◆◆   **Location:** Just e of I-5; exit La Jolla Village Dr; in Hyatt Regency La Jolla. 8960 University Center Ln 92122.
Ethnic   **Hours:** 11:30 am-10:30 pm, Sat-11 pm, Sun-10 pm. **Reservations:** suggested. **Features:** casual dress;
           children's menu; cocktails & lounge; fee for parking & valet parking; a la carte. Casual atmosphere. Features
contemporary Japanese dishes. Sushi bar. **Cards:** AE, CB, DI, DS, JC, MC, VI.

CINDY BLACK'S   **Dinner:** $14-$22   Phone: 619/456-6299 ⑨
◆◆◆   **Location:** 2 mi s of town. 5721 La Jolla Blvd 92037. **Hours:** 5:30 pm-9:30 pm, Sun 5 pm-8 pm. Closed
French   major holidays. **Reservations:** suggested. **Features:** semi-formal attire; cocktails & lounge; a la carte.
           Creative country French cuisine served in an intimate dining room. Prix fixe menu Sun eve. Smoke free
premises. **Cards:** AE, DI, DS, MC, VI.

COAST CAFE   **Lunch:** $7-$11   **Dinner:** $12-$21   Phone: 619/453-1418 ⑧
◆◆   **Location:** At Embassy Suites. 4550 La Jolla Village Dr 92122. **Hours:** 11 am-11 pm. **Features:** children's
American   menu; early bird specials; cocktails & lounge. Casual decor & atmosphere. Specializing in fish, steaks &
           pasta; good selection of salads. Smoke free premises. **Cards:** AE, DI, DS, JC, MC, VI.

CRESCENT SHORES GRILL   **Lunch:** $9-$13   **Dinner:** $12-$24   Phone: 619/459-0541 ⑤
◆◆◆   **Location:** 1.5 mi n of town; in Hotel La Jolla At The Shores. 7955 La Jolla Shores Dr 92037. **Hours:** 6:30
American   am-10 pm. **Reservations:** suggested. **Features:** semi-formal attire; Sunday brunch; cocktails & lounge; a la
           carte. Creative decor & menu with exhibition cooking. Panoramic ocean view. Smoke free premises.
Cards: AE, CB, DI, DS, MC, VI. *(See color ad p 902)*

MARINE ROOM RESTAURANT   **Lunch:** $8-$16   **Dinner:** $18-$32   Phone: 619/459-7222 ③
◆◆◆   **Location:** 1 mi n; adjacent to La Jolla Beach & Tennis Club. 2000 Spindrift Dr 92037. **Hours:** 11:30 am-2:30
American   & 6-10 pm, Sun from 10 am. **Reservations:** suggested. **Features:** semi-formal attire; Sunday brunch;
           children's menu; cocktails & lounge; entertainment. Located on the beach with a beautiful view of surf &
coastline. Fresh seafood, beef & veal specialties. Sun Brunch. Smoke free premises. **Cards:** AE, CB, DI, DS, MC, VI.
(See color ad p 905)

Help him build a castle and he'll help you build a bond.

- 128 guest rooms
- Secluded golden beach
- Renowned dining in The Shores and Marine Room restaurants
- Championship tennis
- Spectacular sunset view

For more information or reservations, please call 1-800-237-5211.

Sea Lodge
on La Jolla Shores Beach

See The Beach From A Fresh Perspective.

8110 Camino Del Oro · La Jolla, California 92037 · www.sealodge.com
Owned and operated by La Jolla Beach & Tennis Club Inc.

(See map p. 844)

MARRAKESH
Ethnic
◆◆
Dinner: $15-$23 **Phone:** 619/454-2500 ⑩
Location: 634 Pearl St 92037. **Hours:** 5 pm-10 pm, Fri & Sat-11 pm. **Reservations:** suggested.
Features: casual dress; children's menu; health conscious menu; carryout; cocktails; entertainment. Very colorful decor with a selection of chicken, lamb & fish served Moroccan style. Smoke free premises.
Cards: AE, DI, DS, MC, VI.
⊠

SKY ROOM
French
◆◆◆◆
Dinner: $25-$39 **Phone:** 619/454-0771 ⑦
Location: 10th floor of La Valencia Hotel. 1132 Prospect St 92037. **Hours:** 6 pm-9 pm.
Reservations: suggested. **Features:** semi-formal attire; cocktails; fee for valet parking; a la carte. Featuring fresh seafood, chicken, lamb & steak. Intimate dining with an ocean view. Prix fixe menu avail. Smoke free premises. **Cards:** AE, CB, DI, DS.
⊠

TOP O' THE COVE RESTAURANT
Continental
◆◆◆
Lunch: $8-$18 **Dinner:** $33-$45 **Phone:** 619/454-7779 ④
Location: 1216 Prospect St 92037. **Hours:** 11:30 am-3 & 5:30-10:30 pm. **Reservations:** suggested.
Features: semi-formal attire; Sunday brunch; cocktails & lounge; fee for valet parking; a la carte. Charming restaurant, ocean view from some tables. Smoke free premises. **Cards:** AE, DI, MC, VI.
⊠

LA MESA—52,900 (See map p. 844; index p. 841)

LODGINGS

COMFORT INN-LA MESA **Phone:** (619)698-7747 🄰🄰🄰 SAVE ◆◆ Motel

	1P:	2P/1B:	2P/2B:	XP:	
5/28-9/3 [CP]	$59	$59	$69	$10	F18
2/1-5/27 & 9/4-1/31 [CP]	$49	$49	$49	$10	F18

Location: Fletcher Pkwy, just e of Baltimore Dr. 8000 Parkway Dr 91942. Fax: 619/698-6347. **Terms:** Weekly rates. **Facility:** 127 rooms. 2 two-bedroom units. 3 stories; interior corridors; small pool, whirlpool. **Cards:** AE, CB, DI, DS, MC, VI. **Special Amenities:** Free breakfast and preferred room (subject to availability with advanced reservations).

DAYS INN LA MESA SUITES/S.D.S.U. **Phone:** (619)697-9005 🄰🄰🄰 SAVE ◆◆ Suite Motel

	1P:	2P/1B:	2P/2B:	XP:	
5/20-9/5	$59- 79	$59- 79	$69- 89	$5	F18
2/1-5/19 & 9/6-1/31	$49- 69	$49- 69	$59- 79	$5	F18

Location: I-8 eastbound exit 70th St, s to El Cajon Blvd, 0.8 mi e; westbound exit El Cajon Blvd, 1 mi w. 7475 El Cajon Blvd 91941. Fax: 619/461-2121. **Terms:** Reserv deposit. **Facility:** 41 rooms. All units are one-bedroom suite with kitchen. 2 stories; exterior corridors; heated pool, whirlpool. **Dining:** Restaurant nearby. **Cards:** AE, DS, MC, VI. **Special Amenities:** Early check-in/late check-out and free breakfast. *(See color ad below)*

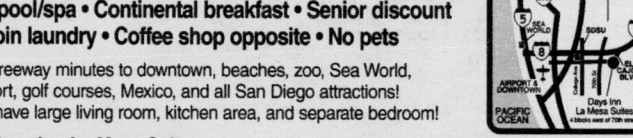

(See map p. 844)

HOLIDAY INN EXPRESS-LA MESA Phone: (619)466-0200 157
(AAA) (SAVE) All Year [CP]   1P: $69- 79 2P/1B: $69- 79 2P/2B: $69- 79 XP: $10 F
◆◆ **Location:** N side of I-8, exit Severin Dr. 9550 Murray Dr 91942. Fax: 619/460-6674. **Terms:** Weekly/monthly
Motel rates. **Facility:** 78 rooms. 4 stories; interior corridors; whirlpool. **Dining:** Restaurant nearby. **Some Rooms:** 3
efficiencies. **Cards:** AE, CB, DI, DS, JC, MC, VI. **Special Amenities:** Free breakfast.

LA MESA TRAVELODGE/CENTRUM Phone: (619)697-3444 156
(AAA) (SAVE) Fri & Sat [CP]   1P: $59- 69 2P/1B: $69- 79 2P/2B: $69- 89 XP: $5 F12
◆ Sun-Thurs [CP]   1P: $49- 59 2P/1B: $59- 69 2P/2B: $59- 79 XP: $5 F12
Motel **Location:** From I-8, westbound exit El Cajon Blvd; eastbound exit Fletcher Pkwy s to El Cajon Blvd; just w
of Baltimore Dr. 7961 El Cajon Blvd 91941. Fax: 619/668-0354. **Facility:** 39 rooms. Located in commercial
area. 3 stories; interior/exterior corridors. **Dining:** Restaurant nearby. **All Rooms:** efficiencies. **Cards:** DS,
MC, VI. **Special Amenities:** Free breakfast and free newspaper.

RAMADA LIMITED Phone: (619)466-5988 162
(AAA) (SAVE) 6/1-9/15 [CP]   1P: $49   2P/1B: $49   2P/2B: $59   XP: $5 F12
◆◆ 2/1-5/31 & 9/16-1/31 [CP] 1P: $39   2P/1B: $49   2P/2B: $59   XP: $5 F12
Motel **Location:** 0.6 mi s of I-8; eastbound exit Spring St to La Mesa Blvd; westbound e Canon Blvd, then s on
Baltimore. 7911 University Ave 91941. Fax: 619/698-0404. **Terms:** Reserv deposit. **Facility:** 57 rooms. 3 stories; interior corridors; heated pool. **Cards:** AE, CB, DI, DS, JC, MC, VI. **Special Amenities:** Early
check-in/late check-out and free breakfast. (See color ad p 906)

RODEWAY INN Phone: (619)589-7288 160
(AAA) (SAVE) All Year [CP]   1P: $50- 65 2P/1B: $50- 65 2P/2B: $60- 75 XP: $5-7 F16
◆◆ **Location:** Just n of SR 94 Frwy, exit Spring St. 4210 Spring St 91941. Fax: 619/469-0654.
Motel **Terms:** Check-out 1 am; reserv deposit; handling fee imposed. **Facility:** 44 rooms. 2 stories; interior corridors.
Dining: Restaurant nearby. **Cards:** AE, CB, DI, DS, JC, MC, VI. **Special Amenities:** Free breakfast and
free local telephone calls.

RESTAURANTS

ANTHONY'S FISH GROTTO Lunch: $6-$9   Dinner: $8-$15   Phone: 619/463-0368 78
◆ **Location:** Just n of I-8 exit Severin Dr. 9530 Murray Dr 91942. **Hours:** 11:30 am-8:30 pm. Closed major
Seafood holidays. **Features:** casual dress; children's menu; early bird specials; health conscious menu; cocktails &
lounge. Popular long established restaurant offering wide variety of fresh seafood. Smoke free premises.
Cards: AE, DI, DS, MC, VI.

THE BRIGANTINE Lunch: $8-$12   Dinner: $12-$24   Phone: 619/465-1935 76
◆◆ **Location:** South side of I-8, exit Severin/Fuerte Dr. 9350 Fuerte Dr 91941. **Hours:** 11:30 am-2:30 & 5-10
Seafood pm, Fri & Sat-11 pm, Sun 10:30 am-2:30 & 5-10 pm. Closed: 11/25 & 12/25. **Reservations:** suggested.
Features: casual dress; Sunday brunch; children's menu; early bird specials; carryout; cocktails & lounge;
valet parking. Attractive nautical decor. Nice variety of seafood. Beef, chicken, & lamb entrees also available. Oyster bar.
Cards: AE, CB, DI, MC, VI.

CLAIM JUMPER Lunch: $7-$10   Dinner: $11-$22   Phone: 619/469-3927 77
◆◆ **Location:** Just n of I-8, in Grossmont Center. 5500 Grossmont Center Dr 91942. **Hours:** 11 am-11 pm, Sun
American & Mon-10 pm, Fri & Sat to midnight. Closed: 7/4, 11/26 & 12/25. **Features:** casual dress; health conscious
menu items; salad bar; cocktails & lounge. Old mining camp atmosphere. Large selection of salads,
sandwiches & entrees. Generous portions. Smoke free premises. **Cards:** AE, DI, DS, MC, VI.

NATIONAL CITY—54,200   (See map p. 844; index p. 842)

LODGINGS

COMFORT INN SAN DIEGO/SOUTH BAY Phone: (619)474-2400 164
(AAA) (SAVE) 6/1-9/15 [CP]   1P: $84   2P/1B: $84   2P/2B: $89
◆◆◆ 2/1-5/31 & 9/16-1/31 [CP] 1P: $79   2P/1B: $79   2P/2B: $84
Motel **Location:** Just w of I-805, exit Plaza Blvd. 1645 Plaza Blvd 91950. Fax: 619/474-7403. **Terms:** Reserv
deposit. **Facility:** 91 rooms. 4 stories; interior corridors; heated pool, whirlpool. **Cards:** AE, CB, DI, DS, JC,
MC, VI. **Special Amenities:** Free breakfast and free newspaper.

(See map p. 844)

HOLIDAY INN-SOUTH BAY   Phone: (619)474-2800   166
	5/24-9/5	1P: $69	2P/1B: $69	2P/2B: $69		
	2/1-5/23 & 9/6-1/31	1P: $59	2P/1B: $59	2P/2B: $59		

Motor Inn   **Location:** Just e of I-5, southbound exit 8th St, northbound exit Plaza Blvd. 700 National City Blvd 91950. Fax: 619/474-1689. **Terms:** Monthly rates; small pets only, $25 dep req. **Facility:** 180 rooms. Some Bay view rooms. 10 stories; exterior corridors; heated pool, whirlpool. **Dining:** Restaurant; 6 am-2 & 5-10 pm; $7-$14; cocktails. **Services:** giftshop; area transportation, Amtrak, Naval Station. **All Rooms:** extended cable TV. **Cards:** AE, CB, DI, DS, JC, MC, VI. *(See color ad p 877)*

RADISSON SUITES-NATIONAL CITY   Phone: (619)336-1100   165
	5/28-9/5 [CP]	1P: $79	2P/1B: $79	2P/2B: $79	XP: $10 F17
	2/1-5/27 & 9/6-1/31 [CP]	1P: $69	2P/1B: $69	2P/2B: $69	XP: $10 F17

Suite Motor Inn   **Location:** Just e of I-5, southbound exit 8th St, northbound exit Plaza Blvd. 801 National City Blvd 91950. Fax: 619/336-1628. **Terms:** Monthly rates; pets, $25 dep req. **Facility:** 170 rooms. 1- & 2-bedroom suites, many with bay view. Restaurant & lounge across street at Holiday Inn. 19 two-bedroom units. 12 stories; exterior corridors; whirlpool. **Dining:** Restaurant nearby. **Services:** giftshop; area transportation, Amtrack, Naval Station. **All Rooms:** extended cable TV. **Cards:** AE, CB, DI, DS, JC, MC, VI. *(See color ad p 907)*

POWAY—43,500

LODGINGS

HOLIDAY INN EXPRESS   Phone: (619)748-7311
	All Year [CP]	1P: $65- 95	2P/1B: $65- 95	2P/2B: $65- 95 XP: $6

Motor   **Location:** Just e of Pomerado Rd. 12448 Poway Rd 92064. Fax: 619/679-2717. **Facility:** 47 rooms. 2 stories; exterior corridors; heated pool, whirlpool. **Some Rooms:** whirlpools. **Cards:** AE, CB, DI, DS, JC, MC, VI. **Special Amenities: Free breakfast and free local telephone calls.**

POWAY COUNTRY INN   Phone: (619)748-6320
	All Year [CP]	1P: $52- 65	2P/1B: $52- 65	2P/2B: $62- 69 XP: $4 F12

Motel   **Location:** 1 mi e of Pomerado Rd. 13845 Poway Rd 92064. Fax: 619/748-0135. **Terms:** Reserv deposit; weekly rates; small pets only. **Facility:** 43 rooms. Charming country decor. 2 stories; exterior corridors; whirlpool. **Some Rooms:** 4 efficiencies. **Cards:** AE, CB, DI, DS, MC, VI. **Special Amenities: Free breakfast.**

RESTAURANTS

THE BRIGANTINE   **Lunch:** $8-$12   **Dinner:** $11-$23   Phone: 619/486-3066
Seafood   **Location:** In Creekside Plaza Center. 13445 Poway Rd 92064. **Hours:** 11:30 am-2:30 & 4:30-9:30 pm, Fri-10:30 pm, Sat 5 pm-10:30 pm, Sun 10 am-2:30 & 4-9:30 pm. Closed: 11/25 & 12/25. **Reservations:** suggested. **Features:** casual dress; Sunday brunch; early bird specials; carryout; cocktails & lounge. Nautical decor with patio dining avail. Large variety of seafood. Also a selection of steak, pasta & chicken. Smoke free premises. **Cards:** AE, DI, MC, VI.

TRATTORIA PARADISO   **Lunch:** $6-$11   **Dinner:** $8-$16   Phone: 619/748-2900
Italian   **Location:** Just e of Pomerado Rd. 12440 Poway Rd 92064. **Hours:** 11 am-2 & 5-10 pm, Sat & Sun 5-10 pm. Closed: 7/4, 11/25, 12/25 & Mon. **Reservations:** suggested. **Features:** casual dress; carryout; cocktails. Several dining areas & outdoor patio in a former ranch style home. Smoke free premises. **Cards:** AE, DI, MC, VI.

RANCHO BERNARDO

LODGINGS

DOUBLETREE CARMEL HIGHLAND RESORT   Phone: (619)672-9100
	All Year	1P: $109	2P/1B: $109- 139	2P/2B: $109- 139 XP: $10 F18

Resort Complex   **Location:** Just w of I-15, exit Carmel Mountain Rd. 14455 Penasquitos Dr 92129 (14455 Penasquitos Dr, SAN DIEGO). Fax: 619/672-9187. **Terms:** Reserv deposit; package plans; small pets only, $150 dep req. **Facility:** 172 rooms. On several acres of nicely landscaped grounds. Rooms have balcony or patio. 2-3 stories; putting green; heated pool, sauna, whirlpools. Fee: 18 holes golf; 5 lighted tennis courts. **Dining:** Restaurant; 6:30 am-2 & 5:30-10 pm; $9-$14; cocktails. **Services:** Fee: massage. **Recreation:** short game golf practice facility. **Cards:** AE, CB, DI, DS, JC, MC, VI. **Special Amenities: Free newspaper and free room upgrade (subject to availability with advanced reservations).** *(See ad p 870)*

DOUBLETREE CLUB HOTEL   Rates Subject to Change   Phone: 619/485-9250
	Sun-Thurs	1P: $105	2P/1B: $105	2P/2B: $105 XP: $10 F12
	Fri & Sat	1P: $99	2P/1B: $99	2P/2B: $99 XP: $10 F12

Motor Inn   **Location:** From I-15, exit Rancho Bernardo Rd, just e to Bernardo Center Dr, then s to Bernardo Plaza Ct. 11611 Bernardo Plaza Ct 92128. Fax: 619/451-7948. **Facility:** 209 rooms. Attractive location with many rooms looking toward a park-like setting. 4 stories; interior corridors; heated pool, whirlpool. **Dining:** 6-9 am & 5 pm-10 pm; $9-$18; cocktails. **Services:** complimentary evening beverages. **Cards:** AE, DI, DS, JC, MC, VI.

HOLIDAY INN RANCHO BERNARDO   Rates Subject to Change   Phone: 619/485-6530
	5/23-9/2 [BP]	1P: $84	2P/1B: $84	2P/2B: $84 XP: $10
	2/1-5/22 & 9/3-1/31 [BP]	1P: $74	2P/1B: $74	2P/2B: $74 XP: $10

Motel   **Location:** Just w of I-15, Rancho Bernardo Rd exit. 17065 W Bernardo Dr 92127. Fax: 619/485-7819. **Terms:** Reserv deposit. **Facility:** 178 rooms. Some rooms with balcony or patio. 13 efficiencies, $10 extra; 2-3 stories; interior corridors; heated pool. **Cards:** AE, CB, DI, DS, JC, MC, VI. *(See color ad p 876)*

LA QUINTA INN Phone: (619)484-8800
AAA SAVE All Year [CP] 1P: $65- 85 2P/1B: $65- 85 2P/2B: $65- 85
◆◆◆ **Location:** Adjacent to I-15; exit Rancho Penasquitos Blvd/Poway Rd. 10185 Paseo Montril 92129 (10185
Motel Paseo Montril, SAN DIEGO). Fax: 619/538-0476. **Terms:** Reserv deposit; pets. **Facility:** 120 rooms. 4 stories;
exterior corridors; heated pool. **Dining:** Coffee shop nearby. **Cards:** AE, CB, DI, DS, JC, MC, VI.
Special Amenities: Free breakfast and free local telephone calls.

RADISSON SUITE HOTEL Phone: (619)451-6600
AAA SAVE 6/15-9/6 [BP] 1P: $109 2P/1B: $109 2P/2B: $109 XP: $10 F12
2/1-6/14 & 9/7-1/31 [BP] 1P: $99 2P/1B: $99 2P/2B: $99 XP: $10 F12
◆◆◆ **Location:** 0.5 mi sw of I-15 exit Rancho Bernardo Rd. 11520 W Bernardo Ct 92127 (11520 W Bernardo Ct,
Motor Inn SAN DIEGO). Fax: 619/592-0253. **Terms:** Small pets only. **Facility:** 176 rooms. Hillside location in a corporate
park area. Large rooms. 3 stories; exterior corridors; heated pool, whirlpool. **Dining:** Dining room; 6 am-9:30
& 5-10 pm, Sat & Sun 7 am-11 & 5-10 pm; $8-$12; cocktails. **Services:** complimentary evening beverages. **Cards:** AE, CB,
DI, DS, JC, MC, VI. **Special Amenities: Free breakfast and free local telephone calls.** *(See color ad p 887)*

RANCHO BERNARDO INN Phone: (619)487-1611
AAA SAVE 12/25-1/31 1P: $229- 249 2P/1B: $229- 249 2P/2B: $229- 249 XP: $15 F
2/1-12/24 1P: $189- 229 2P/1B: $189- 229 2P/2B: $189- 229 XP: $15 F
◆◆◆◆ **Location:** 2 mi ne of I-15, exit Rancho Bernardo Rd. 17550 Bernardo Oaks Dr 92128 (17550 Bernardo Oaks
Resort Dr, SAN DIEGO). Fax: 619/487-1423. **Terms:** Check-in 4 pm; reserv deposit, 3 day notice; MAP avail;
Complex package plans. **Facility:** 288 rooms. On several acres of beautifully landscaped grounds. Many rooms with
patio or balcony. 2-3 stories; interior/exterior corridors; putting green; heated pool, whirlpools. Fee: parking;
81 holes golf; 12 tennis courts (4 lighted), children's camp, major holiday weekends & 8/1-8/31. **Dining:** 2 dining rooms;
6:30 am-10 pm; afternoon tea 4 pm-5 pm; $10-$35; cocktails; also, El Bizcocho Restaurant, see separate listing.
Services: giftshop. Fee: massage. Rental: bicycles. **Some Rooms:** whirlpools. **Cards:** AE, CB, DI, DS, MC, VI.
(See ad p 179)

RANCHO BERNARDO TRAVELODGE Rates Subject to Change Phone: (619)487-0445
◆◆ All Year [CP] 1P: $49- 59 2P/1B: $54- 64 2P/2B: $63- 75 XP: $7 F16
Motel **Location:** From I-15, exit Rancho Bernardo Rd, 1 blk w, just s. 16929 W Bernardo Dr 92127.
Fax: 619/673-2062. **Facility:** 49 rooms. Located in a business park area. 2 two-bedroom units. 2 stories; ex-
terior corridors; heated pool. **Cards:** AE, DI, DS, JC, MC, VI. *(See ad below)*

RESIDENCE INN BY MARRIOTT Rates Subject to Change Phone: 619/673-1900
◆◆◆ 6/25-9/4 [CP] 1P: $144 2P/1B: $144 2P/2B: $239 XP: $10
Apartment 2/1-6/24 & 9/5-1/31 [CP] 1P: $134 2P/1B: $134 2P/2B: $134 XP: $10
Motel **Location:** Just e of I-15, exit Carmel Mountain Rd. 11002 Rancho Carmel Dr 92128. Fax: 619/673-1913.
Facility: 123 rooms. 1- & 2-bedroom suites with kitchen. 22 two-bedroom units. 2-3 stories; interior/exterior
corridors; heated pool. **Recreation:** sports court. **Cards:** AE, CB, DI, DS, JC, MC, VI.

RESTAURANTS

ANTHONY'S FISH GROTTO Lunch: $6-$10 Dinner: $8-$20 Phone: 619/451-2070
◆ **Location:** Just w of Bernardo Center Dr. 11666 Avena Pl 92128. **Hours:** 11:30 am-8:30 pm. Closed major
Seafood holidays. **Reservations:** accepted. **Features:** casual dress; children's menu; early bird specials; carryout;
cocktails & lounge. Popular family dining. Large selection of fresh seafood. **Cards:** AE, CB, DI, DS, MC, VI.

EL BIZCOCHO RESTAURANT Dinner: $22-$29 Phone: 619/487-1611
◆◆◆◆ **Location:** 2 mi ne of I-15; in Rancho Bernardo Inn. 17550 Bernardo Oaks Dr 92128. **Hours:** 6 pm-10 pm,
French Fri & Sat-10:30 pm, Sun 10 am-2:30 & 6-10 pm. **Reservations:** suggested. **Features:** semi-formal attire;
Sunday brunch; children's menu; cocktails & lounge; a la carte. A large elegant dining room serving
traditional entrees & seasonal specialties. Some tableside preparation. Smoke free premises. **Cards:** AE, CB, DI, DS, MC,
VI.

VALENTINO'S Lunch: $6-$8 Dinner: $13-$20 Phone: 619/451-3200
◆◆ **Location:** Just e of I-15; In the Mercado Center. 11828 Rancho Bernardo Rd 92128. **Hours:** 11:30 am-2:30
Italian & 5-10 pm, Sat & Sun 5 pm-10 pm. Closed major holidays. **Reservations:** accepted. **Features:** casual
dress; cocktails; a la carte. Charming restaurant serving a nice selection of Northern Italian cuisine. Patio
dining. Smoke free premises. **Cards:** AE, CB, DI, MC, VI.

RANCHO SANTA FE—7,000

LODGINGS

THE INN AT RANCHO SANTA FE
◆◆◆ All Year   1P: $95- 560   2P/1B: $95- 560   2P/2B: $95- 560   XP: $20   F18
Phone: (619)756-1131
Historic   **Location:** In village area; from I-5, exit Lomas Sante Fe Dr, 4 mi e on CR S-8(Lomas Santa Fe Dr & Linea
Complex   del Cielo). Linea del Cielo at Paseo 92067 (PO Box 869). Fax: 619/759-1604. **Terms:** Reserv deposit, 3 day
notice. **Facility:** 89 rooms. Charming long established inn. Rooms in cottages & main building on several acres
of beautifully landscaped, tree-shaded grounds. Many cottages with patio; some with fireplace. 1 three-bedroom unit, 6 two-
bedroom units. 1-2 stories; interior/exterior corridors; heated pool; 3 tennis courts. **Services:** Fee: massage.
All Rooms: combo or shower baths. **Some Rooms:** 5 efficiencies, 25 kitchens. **Cards:** AE, CB, DI, MC, VI.
(See color ad p 872)

MORGAN RUN RESORT & CLUB
◆◆◆ 5/1-10/31   1P: $149- 169   2P/1B: $149- 169   2P/2B: $149- 169   XP: $15   F18
Phone: (619)756-2471
Resort Hotel   2/1-4/30   1P: $129- 149   2P/1B: $129- 149   2P/2B: $129- 149   XP: $15   F18
11/1-1/31   1P: $119- 139   2P/1B: $119- 139   2P/2B: $119- 139   XP: $15   F18
Location: I-5, exit via De La Valle, 3 mi e to Cancha de Golf. 5690 Cancha de Golf 92091. Fax: 619/759-2150.
Terms: Check-in 4 pm; reserv deposit. **Facility:** 90 rooms. Beautiful grounds & public facilities. Traditional riding club ambi-
ance. All rooms have balcony or patio. 2 room suites with wet bar & fireplace, $285; 2 stories; interior/exterior corridors; put-
ting green; heated pool; 11 tennis courts (4 lighted). Fee: 27 holes golf. **Services:** giftshop; area transportation.
Fee: massage. **Cards:** AE, MC, VI.

RANCHO VALENCIA RESORT
◆◆◆◆ 7/1-12/31   1P: $425- 650   2P/1B: $425- 650   2P/2B: $425- 650
Phone: (619)756-1123
Resort   2/1-6/30 & 1/1-1/31   1P: $410- 600   2P/1B: $410- 600   2P/2B: $410- 600
Complex   **Location:** From I-5, take Via De La Valle 1.3 mi e, 0.5 mi s on El Camino Real, 2.5 mi e on San Dieguito
Rd, 1 mi nw on Rancho Diegueno Rd & Rancho Valencia. 5921 Valencia Cir 92067 (PO Box 9126).
Fax: 619/756-0165. **Terms:** Check-in 4 pm; reserv deposit, 7 day notice. **Facility:** 43 rooms. Nestled among rolling hills. Remi-
niscent of early California haciendas. Spacious casitas, all with fireplace & patio. 3-bedroom hacienda with pool & kitchen; 1
story; exterior corridors; putting green; heated pool; 18 tennis courts. **Services:** giftshop. Fee: massage.
Recreation: bicycles. **Cards:** AE, DI, MC, VI. A Preferred Hotel.

RESTAURANTS

DELICIAS   **Lunch:** $8-$15   **Dinner:** $18-$26   **Phone:** 619/756-8000
◆◆◆   **Location:** In village area. 6106 Paseo Delicias 92067. **Hours:** 11 am-9:30 pm, Fri-10:30 pm. Closed major
American   holidays. **Reservations:** suggested. **Features:** casual dress; Sunday brunch; carryout; cocktails & lounge; a
la carte. An attractive dining room & outdoor patio serving a nice selection of California/French cuisine.
Cards: AE, CB, DI, DS, MC, VI.

MILLE FLEURS   **Lunch:** $14-$20   **Dinner:** $38-$58   **Phone:** 619/756-3085
◆◆◆◆   **Location:** Downtown. 6009 Paseo Delicias 92067. **Hours:** 11:30 am-2:00 & 6-10 pm, Sat-5:30 pm, Sun-6
French   pm. Closed: 1/1 & 12/25. **Reservations:** suggested. **Features:** semi-formal attire; cocktails & lounge; a la
carte. Elegant country French decor. Menu changes daily. **Cards:** AE, DI, MC, VI.

SANTEE—52,900

LODGING

BEST WESTERN SANTEE LODGE
Phone: (619)449-2626
All Year [CP]   1P: $64- 105   2P/1B: $69- 105   2P/2B: $74- 105   XP: $10   F12
◆◆◆   **Location:** Just e of jct Magnolia Ave & Mission Gorge Rd. 10726 Woodside Ave 92071. Fax: 619/449-0819.
Motel   **Terms:** Reserv deposit. **Facility:** 46 rooms. 2 stories; exterior corridors; whirlpool. **Dining:** Restaurant
nearby. **All Rooms:** combo or shower baths. **Cards:** AE, DI, DS, MC, VI. **Special Amenities: Free
breakfast and preferred room (subject to availability with advanced reservations).** *(See ad below)*

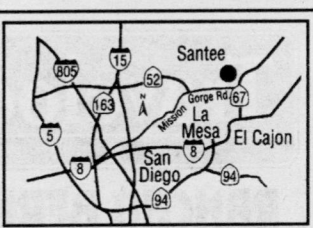

SAN YSIDRO (See map p. 844; index p. 842)

LODGINGS

AMERICANA INN & SUITES　　　　　　　　　　　　　　　**Phone:** (619)428-5521　　18Ⅸ
(AAA) [SAVE]　All Year　　　　　　1P: $40- 43　2P/1B:　$42- 48 2P/2B:　$42- 48 XP:　$5　　F1.
◆　　　**Location:** Adjacent to I-5, exit Dairy Mart Rd. 815 San Ysidro Blvd 92173. Fax: 619/428-0693
Motel　　**Terms:** Monthly rates. **Facility:** 120 rooms. 1.8 mi n of Mexican Border. 1 bedroom suites, $59-$79; 2 stories
　　　　　exterior corridors; heated pool, whirlpool. **Dining:** Restaurant nearby. **Cards:** AE, CB, DI, DS, MC, VI
　　　　　Special Amenities: Early check-in/late check-out.　　　　　　⑤卤 ➔ 🌠 🛆 🗶 ▯ 🔒 ✕

INTERNATIONAL MOTOR INN　　　　　　　　　　　　　**Phone:** (619)428-4486　　18Ⅸ
(AAA) [SAVE]　All Year　　　　　　1P: $54- 59　2P/1B:　$54- 59 2P/2B:　$54- 59 XP:　$2　　F1
◆　　　**Location:** Adjacent to I-5, exit Via de San Ysidro, then just se. 190 E Calle Primera 92173
Motel　　Fax: 619/428-3618. **Terms:** Reserv deposit, 3 day notice; pets. **Facility:** 93 rooms. 0.8 mi to Mexican borde
　　　　　2 stories; exterior corridors; heated pool, whirlpool. **Dining:** Coffee shop nearby. **Some Rooms:** 3
　　　　　efficiencies. **Cards:** AE, CB, DI, DS, MC, VI.　　　⑤卤 🐾 ➔ 🌠 🛆 🗶 ▮ 🔁 🔒 ✕

SOLANA BEACH—13,000

LODGING

COURTYARD BY MARRIOTT　　　　　Rates Subject to Change　　　　**Phone:** (619)792-820(
◆◆◆　　5/14-9/19　　　　　　1P: $119- 195　2P/1B:　$119- 195 2P/2B: $119- 195
Motel　　2/1-5/13 & 9/20-1/31　　1P: $109- 165　2P/1B:　$109- 165 2P/2B: $109- 165
　　　　　Location: 1 mi w of I-5; exit Via del La Valle. 717 S Coast Hwy 101 92075. Fax: 619/792-2370. **Facility:** 11
rooms. 1 blk from beach. Rooms with patio or balcony. 2 stories; interior corridors; heated pool. **Some Rooms:** 3
efficiencies. **Cards:** AE, CB, DI, DS, JC, MC, VI. *(See color ad p 861)*
　　　　　　　　　　　　　　⑤卤 ⑷ 🌠 ➔ 🍴 🛆 🌤 🗶 ▮ 🔁 🔒 ✕

SPRING VALLEY—55,300　(See map p. 844; index p. 842)

LODGING

CROWN INN SUITES　　　　　　　　　　　　　　　　　**Phone:** (619)589-1111　　19(
(AAA) [SAVE]　All Year　　　　　　1P: $43- 48　2P/1B:　$43- 48 2P/2B:　$49- 64
◆　　　**Location:** Just n of SR 94, exit Kenwood Dr. 9603 Campo Rd 91977. Fax: 619/460-7561. **Terms:** Reserv
Motel　　deposit; weekly/monthly rates; pets, $5. **Facility:** 44 rooms. 28 one-bedroom suites; 2 stories; exterior corri
　　　　　dors. **Dining:** Restaurant nearby. **Cards:** AE, DI, DS, MC, VI. **Special Amenities: Early check-in/late**
　　　　　check-out and free breakfast.　　　　　　🐾 ➔ 🌠 🛆 🎬 ▯ 🔒 ✕

This ends listings for the San Diego Vicinity.
The following page resumes the alphabetical listings of
cities in California.

This orientation illustration represents the SAN FRANCISCO VICINITY as defined by local AAA travel experts. Maps on subsequent pages provide more detail.

SAN FRANCISCO

San Rafael PG. 974

Larkspur PG. 970

Corte Madera PG. 967

Mill Valley PG. 971

Tiburon PG. 979

Sausalito PG. 976

Daly City PG. 967

Pacifica PG. 971

South San Francisco PG. 977

San Bruno PG. 971

SAN FRANCISCO INT'L AIRPORT

Millbrae PG. 970

Burlingame PG. 965

San Mateo PG. 973

Foster City PG. 968

Half Moon Bay PG. 968

Belmont PG. 965

San Carlos PG. 972

San Gregorio PG. 973

Refer to map on pg. 919

Refer to map on pg. 920

Refer to map on pg. 922

San Francisco

pop. 724,000

This index helps you "spot" where approved accommodations are located on the detailed maps that follow. Rate ranges are for comparison only and show the property's high season. Turn to the listing page for more detailed rate information and consult display ads for special promotions. Restaurant rate range is for dinner unless only lunch (L) is served.

✈ Airport Accommodations

Spotter/Map Pg. Number	OA	SAN FRANCISCO	Rating	Rate	Listing Page
137 / p. 922		Crowne Plaza, 1.5 mi s of airport	◆◆◆◆	$175-205	965
133 / p. 922		Doubletree Hotel-San Francisco Airport, 1.3 mi s of airport	◆◆◆	$159-229	965
132 / p. 922		Embassy Suites-SFO, 1.5 mi s of airport	◆◆◆◆	$154-234	965
129 / p. 922	◑	Hyatt Regency-San Francisco Airport, 2.5 mi s of airport	◆◆◆◆	$260-295 ☜	965
134 / p. 922		Park Plaza, 2.5 mi s of airport	◆◆◆	$180-210	965
130 / p. 922	◑	Ramada San Francisco Airport, 2.5 mi s of airport	◆◆◆	$165 ☜	966
135 / p. 922	◑	Red Roof Inn, 1.5 mi s of airport	◆◆	$121-141 ☜	966
139 / p. 922		San Francisco Airport Marriott, 2 mi s of airport	◆◆◆◆	$219	966
140 / p. 922	◑	Vagabond Inn-Airport, 1 mi s of airport	◆◆	$85-115 ☜	966
118 / p. 922	◑	Best Western El Rancho Inn, 2.5 mi sw of airport	◆◆◆	$120-140 ☜	970
122 / p. 922	◑	Comfort Inn-Airport West, 2.5 mi sw of airport	◆◆	$99-180 ☜	970
123 / p. 922	◑	Millwood Inn, 2.5 mi sw of airport	◆◆◆	$94-150 ☜	970
121 / p. 922		The Westin Hotel-San Francisco Airport, 0.5 mi s of airport	◆◆◆	$127-157	971
175 / p. 922		Courtyard by Marriott, 2 mi nw of airport	◆◆◆	$179	971
176 / p. 922	◑	Ritz Inn, 2.5 mi nw of airport	◆◆	$75-85	972
177 / p. 922	◑	San Bruno Inn, 2.5 mi nw of airport	◆◆	$80-90 ☜	972
165 / p. 922		Holiday Inn Express, 5 mi s	◆◆◆	$83-106	974
167 / p. 922		Holiday Inn-San Mateo, 5 mi s	◆◆◆	$106-167	974
156 / p. 922	◑	Best Western Grosvenor Hotel, 1.5 mi n of airport	◆◆◆	$99-169 ☜	977
152 / p. 922		Comfort Suites, 2.5 mi n of airport	◆◆◆	$99-159	977
154 / p. 922		Embassy Suites-South San Francisco, 2.5 mi n of airport	◆◆◆	$145-159	978
155 / p. 922		Holiday Inn S F O-North, 1.5 mi n of airport	◆◆◆	$119-169	978
161 / p. 922		Inn at Oyster Point, 2 mi n of airport	◆◆◆	$179-209	979
157 / p. 922		La Quinta Inn, 2.5 mi n of airport	◆◆◆	$105-129	979
150 / p. 922		Ramada Inn SFO North, 1.5 mi n of Airport	◆◆◆	$99-149	979
159 / p. 922		Super 8 Lodge, 2 mi n of airport	◆	$90	979

SAN FRANCISCO

Spotter/Map Pg.Number	OA	SAN FRANCISCO - Lodgings	Rating	Rate	Listing Page
1 / p. 919	◑	Royal Pacific Motor Inn - see color ad p 955	◆◆◆	$83-105	955
2 / p. 919	◑	Holiday Inn Select-Financial District - see ad p 943	◆◆◆	$149-189 ☜	943
3 / p. 919	◑	Hyatt Regency-San Francisco - see color ad p 923	◆◆◆◆	$295-395 ☜	946
4 / p. 919		Fairmont Hotel & Tower	◆◆◆◆	$259-369	940
5 / p. 919		The Huntington Hotel	◆◆◆	$255-375	946
6 / p. 919	◑	Mark Hopkins Inter-Continental	◆◆◆◆	$220-400 ☜	947
7 / p. 919		Renaissance Stanford Court Hotel	◆◆◆◆	$226-250	954
8 / p. 919		Petite Auberge	◆◆◆	$120-245	950
9 / p. 919		White Swan Inn	◆◆◆	$165-250	960
10 / p. 919		Palace Hotel	◆◆◆◆	$370-430	950
11 / p. 919	◑	Harbor Court Hotel	◆◆◆	$220-250	942

Spotter/Map Pg.Number	OA	**SAN FRANCISCO** - Lodgings (contd.)	Rating	Rate	Listing Page
12 / p. 919	🏨	Galleria Park Hotel	◆◆◆	$180 💲	942
13 / p. 919	🏨	Park Hyatt Hotel - see color ad p 923	◆◆◆◆	$320-510 💲	950
14 / p. 919	🏨	ANA Hotel San Francisco	◆◆◆◆	$265 💲	924
15 / p. 919		Campton Place Hotel	◆◆◆◆	$275-400	934
16 / p. 919	🏨	Grand Hyatt San Francisco - see color ad p 923	◆◆◆◆	$285-390 💲	942
17 / p. 919	🏨	Crowne Plaza-Union Square - see ad p 943		$209-249 💲	939
18 / p. 919	🏨	Sir Francis Drake Hotel	◆◆	$165 💲	957
19 / p. 919	🏨	Chancellor Hotel - see color ad p 936	◆◆◆	$143-153 💲	936
20 / p. 919	🏨	The Pan Pacific Hotel	◆◆◆◆	$315-420	950
21 / p. 919		The Donatello	◆◆◆	$159-225	940
22 / p. 919	🏨	Best Western Canterbury Hotel - see color ad p 926	◆◆	$250-450 💲	926
23 / p. 919		The Ritz-Carlton	◆◆◆◆◆	$400	954
24 / p. 919		York Hotel	◆◆	$109	960
25 / p. 919	🏨	Clarion Bedford Hotel	◆◆	$139 💲	936
26 / p. 919	🏨	Hotel Beresford - see color ad p 944	◆◆	$119-129 💲	944
27 / p. 919		Maxwell Hotel	◆◆	$155-225	947
28 / p. 919		The Westin St. Francis	◆◆◆◆	$250-280	960
29 / p. 919	🏨	Villa Florence	◆◆◆	$140-190	960
30 / p. 919	🏨	The Handlery Union Square Hotel - see ad p 942	◆◆◆	$166-195	942
31 / p. 919	🏨	Hotel Nikko	◆◆◆◆	$195	945
32 / p. 919		San Francisco Hilton & Towers - see ad p 119, p 956	◆◆◆◆	$189-269	956
38 / p. 919	🏨	Monticello Inn	◆◆◆	$110-160	947
39 / p. 919	🏨	Shannon Court Hotel - see color ad p 944	◆◆◆	$119 💲	956
40 / p. 919		San Francisco Marriott	◆◆◆◆	$275	956
41 / p. 919		The Powell Hotel - see color ad p 952	◆◆	$125	950
42 / p. 919	🏨	The Prescott Hotel	◆◆◆	$165-180 💲	952
43 / p. 919	🏨	Warwick Regis Hotel	◆◆◆	$149-169 💲	960
44 / p. 919	🏨	King George Hotel - see color ad p 946	◆◆	$160-175 💲	947
45 / p. 919	🏨	Hotel Juliana	◆◆◆	$149	944
47 / p. 919	🏨	Hotel Milano - see color ad p 944	◆◆◆	$169-189 💲	945
48 / p. 919	🏨	Hotel Monaco	◆◆◆◆	$219	945
49 / p. 919		Nob Hill Lambourne - see color ad p 924	◆◆	$200-300	948
50 / p. 919	🏨	Beresford Arms - see color ad p 925	◆◆◆	$140-150 💲	925
51 / p. 919		Savoy Hotel	◆◆	$110-149	956
52 / p. 919		Commodore International Hotel - see color ad p 924	◆◆	$99-139	939
53 / p. 919		Hotel Rex - see color ad p 924	◆◆◆	$185	945
54 / p. 919	🏨	Hotel Vintage Court	◆◆◆	$159-179	945
56 / p. 920	🏨	Redwood Inn - see color ad p 955	◆◆	$95-110	954
57 / p. 920		Inn 1890	◆◆◆	$89-109	946
58 / p. 920	🏨	Cow Hollow Motor Inn & Suites - see color ad p 938, p 939	◆◆◆	$96	939
59 / p. 920	🏨	Pacific Motor Inn	◆◆	$74-156	950
60 / p. 920	🏨	Chelsea Motor Inn - see color ad p 938	◆◆◆	$96	936
61 / p. 920	🏨	Coventry Motor Inn - see color ad p 938	◆◆◆	$96	939
62 / p. 920	🏨	Capri Motel	◆	$78-100	934
63 / p. 920	🏨	Star Motel - see color ad p 935	◆◆	$85-110	957
64 / p. 920	🏨	Francisco Bay Motel - see color ad p 949	◆◆	$95-105	941
65 / p. 920	🏨	Lombard Motor Inn - see color ad p 938	◆◆◆	$96	947
66 / p. 920		San Francisco Holiday Inn Golden Gateway	◆◆◆	$164-234	956
67 / p. 920	🏨	Vagabond Inn-Midtown	◆◆	$170-185 💲	959
68 / p. 920	🏨	Castle Inn Motel - see color ad p 949	◆◆	$95-105	936
69 / p. 920	🏨	Broadway Manor Inn - see color ad p 934	◆	$85 💲	934
70 / p. 920	🏨	Nob Hill Motel - see color ad p 949	◆◆	$95-105	948
71 / p. 920	🏨	Comfort Inn by the Bay - see color ad p 919	◆◆	$145-189 💲	939

Spotter/Map Pg.Number	OA	SAN FRANCISCO - Lodgings (contd.)	Rating	Rate	Listing Page
72 / p. 920		Queen Anne Hotel	◆◆◆	$120-275	952
73 / p. 920	⊕	Miyako Inn Best Western - see ad p 933	◆◆	$109-129	947
74 / p. 920	⊕	Laurel Motor Inn - see ad p 947	◆◆	$88-104 ⬛	947
75 / p. 920	⊕	Seal Rock Inn	◆◆	$90-118	956
76 / p. 920	⊕	Radisson Miyako Hotel	◆◆◆	$189-209 ⬛	952
77 / p. 920		Cathedral Hill Hotel - see color ad p 936	◆◆	$129-169	936
78 / p. 920	⊕	Buena Vista Motor Inn - see color ad p 935	◆◆◆	$97-140	934
79 / p. 920	⊕	Oasis Inn - see color ad p 948	◆◆	$109-119 ⬛	948
80 / p. 920	⊕	Days Inn-Geary - see color ad p 940	◆◆	$109 ⬛	940
81 / p. 920	⊕	Holiday Lodge - see color ad p 924	◆◆	$109-119	943
82 / p. 920	⊕	Holiday Inn-Civic Center - see ad p 943	◆◆◆	$145-169 ⬛	943
83 / p. 920	⊕	Best Western Civic Center Motor Inn - see color ad p 930	◆◆	$99-125 ⬛	926
84 / p. 920	⊕	Beck's Motor Lodge - see color ad p 925	◆◆	$90-125 ⬛	925
85 / p. 920	⊕	Stanyan Park Hotel	◆◆◆	$99-199	957
86 / p. 920	⊕	Atherton Hotel	◆◆	$99-129 ⬛	925
87 / p. 920	⊕	Mission Inn - see color ad p 937	◆◆	$65-80 ⬛	947
88 / p. 920		The Archbishop's Mansion - see color ad p 924	◆◆◆	$139-399	924
89 / p. 920	⊕	Super 8 Boutique Hotel - see color ad p 958	◆◆	$109	958
90 / p. 920	⊕	The Phoenix Inn - see color ad p 924	◆◆	$109	950
91 / p. 920		Days Inn at The Beach	◆	$80-85	940
92 / p. 920	⊕	Best Western Tuscan Inn at Fisherman's Wharf - see ad p 933	◆◆◆	$155-175 ⬛	931
93 / p. 920	⊕	Super 8 Motel - see color ad p 958	◆◆	$85-130 ⬛	958
94 / p. 920	⊕	Ramada Plaza Hotel International - see color ad p 954	◆◆	$139-179 ⬛	954
95 / p. 920	⊕	Pacific Heights Inn - see ad p 948	◆◆	$98-130	950
96 / p. 920	⊕	Hyatt Fisherman's Wharf - see color ad p 923	◆◆◆	$265-355 ⬛	946
97 / p. 920	⊕	Columbus Motor Inn - see color ad p 937	◆◆◆	$110	939
98 / p. 920		San Francisco Marriott Fisherman's Wharf	◆◆◆	$240	956
99 / p. 920		Ramada Plaza-Fisherman's Wharf - see color ad opposite title page	◆◆◆	$200-250	953
100 / p. 920	⊕	Holiday Inn-Fisherman's Wharf - see ad p 943	◆◆	$189-219 ⬛	943
101 / p. 920		The Sherman House	◆◆◆	$350-850	957
102 / p. 920	⊕	Best Western Americania - see color ad p 926	◆◆◆	$129-169 ⬛	925
103 / p. 920	⊕	Best Western Carriage Inn - see color ad p 930	◆◆◆	$149-179 ⬛	926
104 / p. 920	⊕	Roberts-At-The-Beach Motel	◆	$79-99	954
105 / p. 920	⊕	Days Inn-Civic Center - see color ad p 940	◆◆	$95-150 ⬛	940
106 / p. 920		Sheraton at Fisherman's Wharf - see color ad p 957	◆◆◆◆	$185	957
107 / p. 920	⊕	The Wharf Inn - see ad p 960	◆◆	$159-179	960
108 / p. 920	⊕	Best Western Flamingo Inn - see color ad p 930	◆◆	$89-109 ⬛	930
109 / p. 920	⊕	Travelodge Hotel at Fisherman's Wharf - see color ad p 959	◆◆	$145-185 ⬛	959
110 / p. 920	⊕	Howard Johnson at Fisherman's Wharf - see color ad p 945	◆◆◆	$159 ⬛	946
111 / p. 920	⊕	San Francisco Thriftlodge - see color ad p 941	◆◆	$88 ⬛	956
112 / p. 920	⊕	Travelodge By The Bay - see color ad p 959	◆◆	$115-140 ⬛	958
113 / p. 920	⊕	Ramada Limited-Golden Gate	◆◆	$99-175	952
114 / p. 920	⊕	Ramada Limited Downtown - see color ad opposite title page, p 953	◆◆	$104-189 ⬛	952
115 / p. 920	⊕	Britton Hotel - see color ad p 933	◆◆	$109-129 ⬛	933
		SAN FRANCISCO - Restaurants			
① / p. 919		The Waterfront	◆◆◆	$18-35	963
③ / p. 919	⊕	John's Grill	◆◆	$14-24	962

Spotter/Map Pg.Number	OA	SAN FRANCISCO - Restaurants (contd.)	Rating	Rate	Listing Page
4 / p. 919		Campton Place Restaurant	◆◆◆◆◆	$40-62	961
5 / p. 919		Empress of China	◆◆	$17-34	961
6 / p. 919		Kan's	◆◆	$10	962
7 / p. 919		Mason's	◆◆◆◆	$26-35	963
9 / p. 919		Carnelian Room	◆◆◆	$30-39	961
11 / p. 919		Scott's Seafood Grill	◆◆	$16-25	963
12 / p. 919		Lehr Bros Bistro & Grill	◆◆	$9-27	962
13 / p. 919		Fleur de Lys	◆◆◆◆	$25-35	961
14 / p. 919	⊛	**Cafe Majestic**	◆◆◆	$17-24	960
15 / p. 919		Cityscape	◆◆◆	$18-40	961
16 / p. 919	⊛	**New Joe's**	◆◆	$10-25	963
17 / p. 919		The Iron Horse	◆◆	$13-25	962
19 / p. 919		Palio D'Asti	◆◆◆	$16-30	963
20 / p. 919		The Dining Room	◆◆◆◆◆	$58-72	961
21 / p. 919		The Garden Court	◆◆◆◆	$36-102	961
22 / p. 919		Kuleto's	◆◆◆	$9-18	962
23 / p. 919	⊛	**L'Olivier**	◆◆◆	$15-25	962
25 / p. 919		Pacific	◆◆◆◆	$30-40	963
26 / p. 919		Farallon	◆◆◆	$18-28	961
27 / p. 919		Postrio	◆◆◆	$55-60	963
28 / p. 919		Masa's	◆◆◆◆	$72-80	962
29 / p. 920		Stars Restaurant	◆◆	$20-30	963
30 / p. 920		Chic's Seafood	◆◆	$10-24	961
31 / p. 920	⊛	**Alioto's - see ad p 205**	◆◆	$12-47	960
32 / p. 920		The Mandarin	◆◆◆	$15-25	962
33 / p. 920		Dante's	◆◆	$17-24	961
34 / p. 920	⊛	**North India Restaurant**	◆◆◆	$14-22	963
35 / p. 920		Golden Turtle	◆◆	$8-25	962
36 / p. 920		Harris'	◆◆◆	$25-33	962
37 / p. 920		House of Prime Rib	◆◆◆	$20-25	962
38 / p. 920		Maharani	◆◆	$8-25	962
39 / p. 920	⊛	**The Cliff House**	◆◆	$15-25	961
40 / p. 920	⊛	**Julius' Castle**	◆◆◆	$23-40	962
41 / p. 920	⊛	**dalla Torre**	◆◆◆	$11-20	961
42 / p. 920		Castagnola's Restaurant	◆◆	$10-34	961
43 / p. 920		Hayes Street Grill	◆◆◆	$14-22	962
44 / p. 920	⊛	**Scoma's Restaurant**	◆◆◆	$8-55	963
45 / p. 920		McCormick & Kuleto's Seafood Restaurant	◆◆◆	$14-28	963
46 / p. 920	⊛	**Pompei's Grotto**	◆◆	$16-21	963
47 / p. 920	⊛	**Fior D' Italia**	◆◆	$13-30	961
48 / p. 920	⊛	**Rick's Restaurant & Bar**	◆◆	$11-20	963

San Francisco Vicinity

Spotter/Map Pg.Number	OA	MILLBRAE - Lodgings	Rating	Rate	Listing Page
117 / p. 922	⊛	**Travelodge San Francisco Airport South**	◆◆	$85-105 🆂🅰🆅🅴	971
118 / p. 922	⊛	**Best Western El Rancho Inn - see color ad back cover, p 964**	◆◆◆	$120-140 🆂🅰🆅🅴	970
121 / p. 922		The Westin Hotel-San Francisco Airport	◆◆◆	$127-157	971
122 / p. 922	⊛	**Comfort Inn-Airport West**	◆◆	$99-180 🆂🅰🆅🅴	970
123 / p. 922	⊛	**Millwood Inn - see color ad p 970**	◆◆◆	$94-150 🆂🅰🆅🅴	970
		MILLBRAE - Restaurant			
50 / p. 922		Terrace Cafe	◆◆◆	$10-20	971
		BURLINGAME - Lodgings			
129 / p. 922	⊛	**Hyatt Regency-San Francisco Airport - see color ad p 923**	◆◆◆◆	$260-295 🆂🅰🆅🅴	965
130 / p. 922	⊛	**Ramada San Francisco Airport - see ad p 965 & color ad opposite title page**	◆◆◆	$165 🆂🅰🆅🅴	966

Spotter/Map Pg.Number	OA	BURLINGAME - Lodgings (contd.)	Rating	Rate	Listing Page
132 / p. 922		Embassy Suites-SFO - see color ad p 931	◆◆◆◆	$154-234	965
133 / p. 922		Doubletree Hotel-San Francisco Airport	◆◆◆	$159-229	965
134 / p. 922		Park Plaza	◆◆◆	$180-210	965
135 / p. 922	⊕	**Red Roof Inn - see color ad p 966**	◆◆	$121-141 SAVE	966
137 / p. 922		Crowne Plaza	◆◆◆◆	$175-205	965
139 / p. 922		San Francisco Airport Marriott	◆◆◆◆	$219	966
140 / p. 922	⊕	**Vagabond Inn-Airport**	◆◆	$85-115 SAVE	966
		BURLINGAME - Restaurants			
52 / p. 922		Gulliver's	◆◆	$22-32	966
53 / p. 922		Kuleto's Trattoria	◆◆◆	$8-17	966
		PACIFICA - Lodgings			
145 / p. 922	⊕	**Best Western Lighthouse Hotel**	◆◆◆	$120-195 SAVE	971
		PACIFICA - Restaurant			
55 / p. 922		Moonraker Restaurant	◆◆◆	$9-38	971
		SOUTH SAN FRANCISCO - Lodgings			
150 / p. 922		Ramada Inn SFO North - see color ad opposite title page & ad p 978	◆◆◆	$99-149	979
151 / p. 922	⊕	**Days Inn-SFO North**	◆◆	$99-119 SAVE	977
152 / p. 922		Comfort Suites	◆◆◆	$99-159	977
153 / p. 922	⊕	**Americana Inn Motel**	◆◆	$70-80	977
154 / p. 922		Embassy Suites-South San Francisco - see color ad p 931	◆◆◆	$145-159	978
155 / p. 922		Holiday Inn S F O-North - see ad p 977	◆◆◆	$119-169	978
156 / p. 922	⊕	**Best Western Grosvenor Hotel**	◆◆◆	$99-169 SAVE	977
157 / p. 922		La Quinta Inn	◆◆◆	$105-129	979
159 / p. 922		Super 8 Lodge	◆	$90	979
160 / p. 922	⊕	**Economy Inn - see color ad p 978**	◆	$60-70 SAVE	977
161 / p. 922		Inn at Oyster Point	◆◆◆	$179-209	979
		SOUTH SAN FRANCISCO - Restaurant			
56 / p. 922		South City Steakhouse	◆◆	$10-25	979
		SAN MATEO - Lodgings			
165 / p. 922		Holiday Inn Express	◆◆◆	$83-106	974
166 / p. 922		Villa Hotel Airport South - see ad p 974	◆◆◆	$99-119	974
167 / p. 922		Holiday Inn-San Mateo	◆◆◆	$106-167	974
169 / p. 922	⊕	**Best Western San Mateo Los Prados Inn - see ad p 977**	◆◆	$129-159 SAVE	973
170 / p. 922		Residence Inn by Marriott	◆◆◆	$179	974
171 / p. 922		Coxhead House Bed & Breakfast	◆◆◆	$119-159	973
		SAN BRUNO - Lodgings			
175 / p. 922		Courtyard by Marriott	◆◆◆	$179	971
176 / p. 922	⊕	**Ritz Inn - see color ad p 972**	◆◆	$75-85	972
177 / p. 922	⊕	**San Bruno Inn - see color ad p 978**	◆◆	$80-90 SAVE	972
		FOSTER CITY - Lodgings			
182 / p. 922		Crown Plaza Foster City	◆◆◆	$189-219	968
183 / p. 922		Courtyard by Marriott	◆◆◆	$139	968
		SAN CARLOS - Lodgings			
188 / p. 922	⊕	**Inns of America**	◆◆◆	$139 SAVE	972
189 / p. 922		San Carlos Travelodge	◆◆	$75-85	973
190 / p. 922	⊕	**Days Inn-San Carlos - see color ad p 972**	◆◆	$79-109 SAVE	972
191 / p. 922		Comfort Inn & Suites	◆◆◆	$104-139	972
		REDWOOD CITY - Lodgings			
199 / p. 922	⊕	**Best Western Executive Suites**	◆◆◆	$99-150 SAVE	812
201 / p. 922	⊕	**Best Western Inn - see color ad p 812**	◆◆◆	$95-150 SAVE	813
202 / p. 922		Hotel Sofitel San Francisco Bay	◆◆◆◆	$169-209	813
203 / p. 922	⊕	**Days Inn**	◆◆	$80-90 SAVE	813
204 / p. 922	⊕	**Comfort Inn**	◆◆	$109-150	813

Spotter/Map Pg.Number	OA	REDWOOD CITY - Lodgings (contd.)	Rating	Rate	Listing Page
205 / p. 922	⊛	Holiday Inn Express	◆◆◆	$105 ⊠	813
		REDWOOD CITY - Restaurants			
65 / p. 922		Fabbro's	◆◆	$11-18	813
66 / p. 922		Baccarat	◆◆◆◆	$20-30	813
		HALF MOON BAY - Lodgings			
208 / p. 922		Old Thyme Inn	◆◆	$99-250	969
209 / p. 922	⊛	Cypress Inn on Miramar Beach	◆◆◆	$170-275 ⊠	968
210 / p. 922	⊛	Half Moon Bay Lodge - see color ad inside back cover, p 969	◆◆◆◆	$160-220 ⊠	968
211 / p. 922	⊛	Mill Rose Inn, Spa & Garden Suites	◆◆◆◆	$165-285	969
212 / p. 922		Beach House Inn & Conference Center - see color ad p 968	◆◆◆	$165-265	968
213 / p. 922		Seal Cove Inn	◆◆◆◆	$180-260	969
214 / p. 922		Harbor View Inn	◆◆	$100	968
215 / p. 922	⊛	Ramada Limited	◆◆	$120-170 ⊠	969
217 / p. 922		Goose & Turrets Bed & Breakfast Inn	◆◆	$100-140	968
		HALF MOON BAY - Restaurants			
69 / p. 922		Miramar Beach Restaurant	◆◆	$14-24	969
70 / p. 922	⊛	The Distillery	◆◆	$14-23	969
71 / p. 922	⊛	The Shore Bird	◆◆	$16-21	969
		MENLO PARK - Lodgings			
219 / p. 922	⊛	Menlo Park Inn - see color ad p 667	◆◆◆	$95-150 ⊠	667
220 / p. 922	⊛	Stanford Park Hotel - see color ad inside back cover	◆◆◆◆	$265-375 ⊠	667
221 / p. 922	⊛	Best Western Riviera	◆◆◆	$145-175 ⊠	666
		MENLO PARK - Restaurants			
74 / p. 922		Gaylord India Restaurant	◆◆◆	$12-22	667
75 / p. 922		Fontana's Italian Restaurant	◆◆◆	$10-20	667
		DALY CITY - Lodgings			
225 / p. 922	⊛	Days Inn - see color ad p 967	◆◆	$60-200 ⊠	967
226 / p. 922	⊛	Royal Palace Inn	◆	$80-90 ⊠	967
		SAN GREGORIO - Lodgings			
230 / p. 922	⊛	Rancho San Gregorio	◆◆◆	$90-150	973
		BELMONT - Restaurant			
79 / p. 922		Pine Brook Inn	◆◆	$9-20	965
		WOODSIDE - Restaurants			
84 / p. 922		Bella Vista Restaurant	◆◆	$17-26	1085
85 / p. 922		The Village Pub	◆◆◆	$25-35	1085

Meal Plan Indicators

CP = Continental Plan of pastry, juice and another beverage or may offer expanded breakfast items

BP = Breakfast Plan of full hot breakfast

AP = American Plan of three meals daily

MAP = Modified American Plan of two meals daily

EP = European Plan, where rate includes only room

Family Plan Indicators

The establishment may limit the number of children to whom the family plan applies.

F17 = children 17 and under stay free (age displayed will reflect property's policy)

D17 = discount for children 17 and under

F = children stay free

D = discounts for children

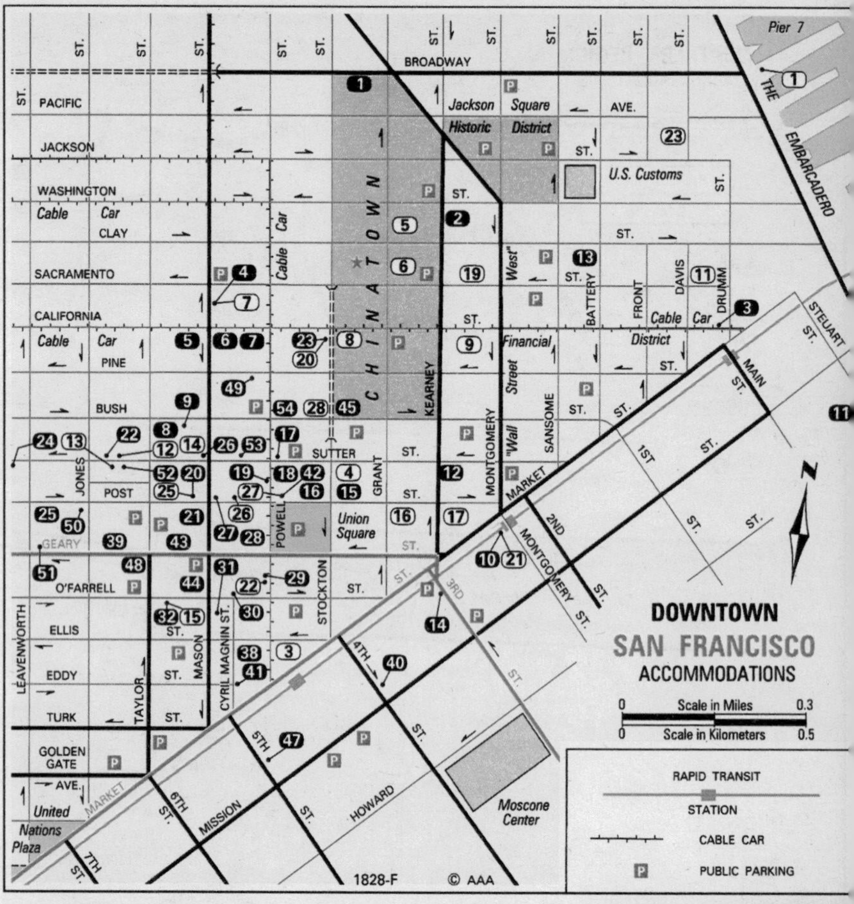

Pier 7

BROADWAY

PACIFIC

Jackson Square

AVE.

JACKSON

Historic District

WASHINGTON

U.S. Customs

Cable Car

CLAY

CHINATOWN

ST.

West

SACRAMENTO

Cable Car

CALIFORNIA

District

Cable Car

Financial District

PINE

Street

BUSH

"Wall"

SUTTER

JONES

POST

GRANT

POWELL

Union Square

GEARY

Financial Street

MONTGOMERY

SANSOME

BATTERY

FRONT

DAVIS

DRUMM

STEUART

MAIN

1ST.

2ND.

O'FARRELL

LEAVENWORTH

ELLIS

STOCKTON

3RD.

EDDY

TAYLOR

MASON

CYRIL MAGNIN ST.

4TH.

TURK

GOLDEN GATE

AVE.

United Nations Plaza

MARKET

5TH.

MISSION

6TH.

HOWARD

7TH.

Moscone Center

DOWNTOWN
SAN FRANCISCO
ACCOMMODATIONS

0   Scale in Miles   0.3
0   Scale in Kilometers   0.5

RAPID TRANSIT

STATION

CABLE CAR

P   PUBLIC PARKING

1828-F   © AAA

THE EMBARCADERO

AAA
restaurant expertise saves
you time and costly explorations.

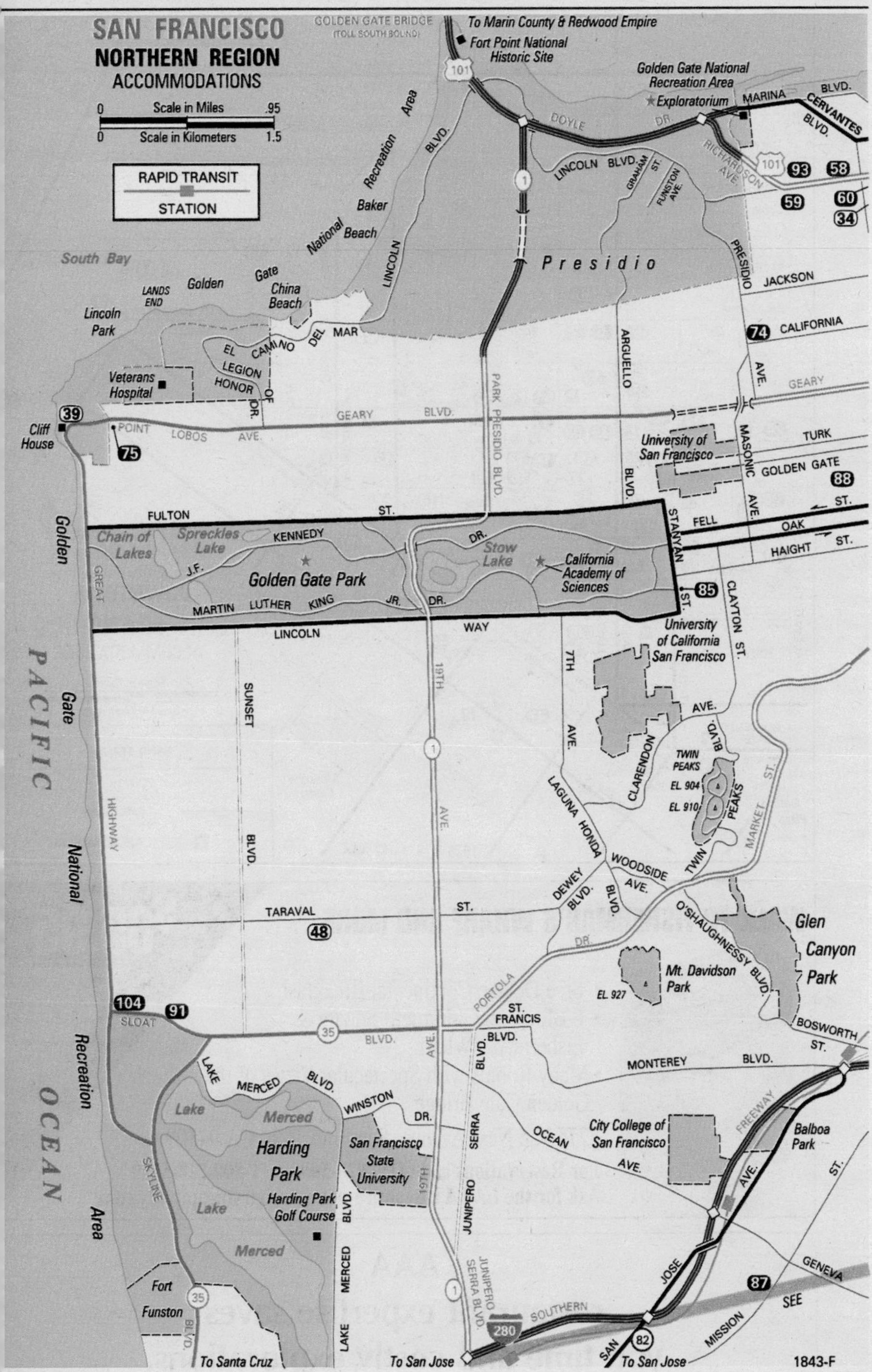

SAN FRANCISCO
NORTHERN REGION
ACCOMMODATIONS

Scale in Miles   0 — .95
Scale in Kilometers   0 — 1.5

RAPID TRANSIT
STATION

GOLDEN GATE BRIDGE
(TOLL SOUTH BOUND)

To Marin County & Redwood Empire
Fort Point National Historic Site

101

Golden Gate National Recreation Area
★ Exploratorium

DOYLE DR.

MARINA
BLVD.

CERVANTES BLVD.

Lincoln BLVD.

GRAHAM ST.
FUNSTON AVE.

RICHARDSON AVE.

101

93   58
59   60
      34

Recreation Area
National   Baker   Beach

LINCOLN   BLVD.

Presidio

South Bay

LANDS END
Golden   Gate
China Beach

DEL MAR

PRESIDIO   AVE.

JACKSON

Lincoln Park

EL CAMINO
LEGION   OF
HONOR   DR.

CAMINO DEL MAR

ARGUELLO   BLVD.

CALIFORNIA   AVE.

74   CALIFORNIA

Veterans Hospital

PARK PRESIDIO BLVD.

MASONIC   AVE.

GEARY

Cliff House
39

POINT   LOBOS   AVE.

GEARY   BLVD.

University of San Francisco

TURK
GOLDEN GATE

75

FULTON   ST.

STANYAN   ST.

FELL   ST.
OAK   ST.
HAIGHT   ST.

88

Chain of Lakes
Spreckles Lake
KENNEDY   DR.
Stow Lake
California Academy of Sciences

J.F.

Golden Gate Park

MARTIN   LUTHER   KING   JR.   DR.

CLAYTON   ST.

85

Golden   Gate   National   Recreation Area

GREAT   HIGHWAY

LINCOLN   WAY

University of California San Francisco

7TH   AVE.

PACIFIC

SUNSET   BLVD.

19TH   AVE.

CLARENDON   AVE.

TWIN PEAKS
EL 904
EL 910

TWIN PEAKS BLVD.

MARKET   ST.

OCEAN

TARAVAL   ST.

LAGUNA HONDA BLVD.

DEWEY   BLVD.

WOODSIDE   AVE.

O'SHAUGHNESSY BLVD.

Glen Canyon Park

48

PORTOLA   DR.

Mt. Davidson Park
EL 927

ST. FRANCIS BLVD.

104   91
SLOAT   BLVD.

35

MONTEREY   BLVD.

BOSWORTH ST.

LAKE MERCED BLVD.

WINSTON   DR.

SERRA   BLVD.

OCEAN   AVE.

City College of San Francisco

FREEWAY

Balboa Park

Lake Merced

Harding Park

San Francisco State University

JUNIPERO SERRA BLVD.

SKYLINE BLVD.

Lake Merced

Harding Park Golf Course

MERCED   BLVD.

19TH   AVE.

Fort Funston
35

LAKE MERCED BLVD.

SOUTHERN   FREEWAY

280

JOSE   AVE.

SAN

MISSION   ST.

GENEVA   AVE.

87

SEE

To Santa Cruz   To San Jose   To San Jose   82

1843-F

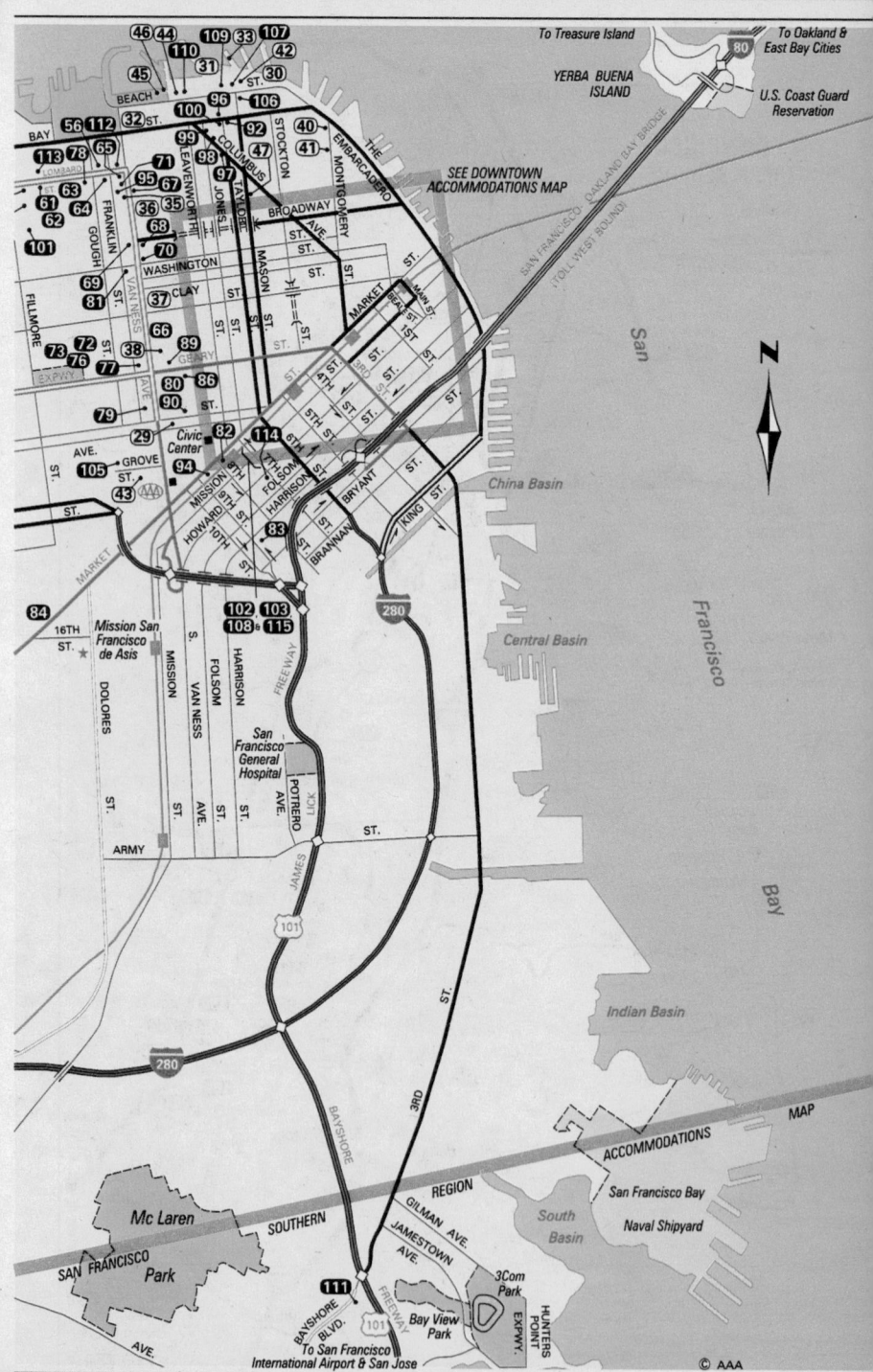

© AAA

SAN FRANCISCO
SOUTHERN REGION
ACCOMMODATIONS

Scale in Miles 0 — 3.2
Scale in Kilometers 0 — 5.1

SAN FRANCISCO

SEE SAN FRANCISCO
NORTHERN REGION
ACCOMMODATIONS MAP

Candlestick
Point State
Recreation
Area

JOHN DALY BLVD.

SOUTHERN FRWY

Daly City

San Bruno Mtn. Co. Park

225 226

GLADALUPE

HILLSIDE

CANYON PKWY.

BAYSHORE BLVD.

San Francisco Bay

OCEAN

Sharp Park Beach
145 55

Pacifica

HICKEY BLVD.

CRESTNUT AVE.

GRAND

160 159
153
South San Francisco
56 157
175
151
152 154
150 156
155
161

Oyster Point Park

Gray Whale Cove St. Beach

Montara St. Beach
217
Montara

70
213

Moss Beach

James V. Fitzgerald Marine Reserve

San Pedro Valley Co. Park

San Andreas Lake

San Francisco

State

Fish

Pilarcitos Lake

San Mateo Creek

COAST

SKYLINE BLVD.

W. BOROUGH BLVD.

SHARP PARK RD.

SAN BRUNO

San Bruno

177
176 123
122
50
Millbrae
117 118
MILLBRAE AVE.
TROUTDALE RD.
53
BROADWAY

JUNIPERO

SERRA

San Francisco International Airport

BAYSHORE

121 129 130
132 THRU 135 137
139 140 52

Coyote Point Park

82 101

Burlingame

PENINSULA AVE.

171
EL CERRITO AVE.
HAYNE RD.

167
165

San Mateo

3RD AVE.
E.

San Mateo Bridge

To Hayward

182
170
183
Foster City

71

214
Princeton
212 209
El Granada
69
Miramar
215

Half Moon Bay State Beach

Lower Crystal Springs Reservoir

CRYSTAL SPRINGS RD.
POLHEMUS RD.

HILLSDALE BLVD.
166 169
92

HALF MOON 92 BAY RD.
35

Pilarcitos

211
208
210
HIGGINS
Half Moon Bay

PURISIMA

Upper Crystal Springs Reservoir

RALSTON

79
190
191
202
188

Belmont

SAN CARLOS AVE.

66

CAMINO

HOLLY ST.

Game

CANADA

FREEWAY

San Carlos

189
201

Red wood City

ALAMEDA DE LAS PULGAS

EDGEWOOD RD.

WHIPPLE AVE.

Purisima

COAST

PURISIMA CREEK RD.

Refuge

35
84

Huddart Park

KINGS MTN. RD.

204

84

To San Jose

199
203
205 82
65 220

Menlo Park

85
Woodside

LOBITOS CR. CUTOFF

TUNITAS

To San Gregorio & Santa Cruz

To 230

1829-F

SKYLINE BLVD.

84

© AAA

To San Jose

219 221
74 & 75

PACIFIC

The Hyatt touch is applied 365 days a year.
So are these special AAA Member Services offers:

Preferred nightly rates. . .half price dinner entree!

Now through December 29, 1999, a superb dining

offer is yours to enjoy at your choice of nine

spectacular Hyatt destinations on California's north

coast. Purchase one dinner entree and receive a

second entree of equal or lesser value at

half price. Simply show your AAA card

at check-in and ask for your "Dining

 *Discount" coupon. You'll*

also sleep better at Hyatt, knowing

you will receive the lowest

Hyatt Regency Sacramento
Grand Hyatt San Francisco
Hyatt Regency San Francisco
Park Hyatt San Francisco
Hyatt at Fisherman's Wharf
Hyatt Regency San Francisco Airport
Hyatt Regency Monterey
Hyatt San Jose
Hyatt Sainte Claire

room rate available. For reservations call your

travel planner or Hyatt at 1-800 532-1496.

HYATT
HOTELS
CALIFORNIA ®

Feel the Hyatt Touch®

SAN FRANCISCO—724,000   (See map p. 919; index p. 913)

LODGINGS

ANA HOTEL SAN FRANCISCO   **Phone:** (415)974-6400   🄔
▲▲▲ [SAVE]   All Year   1P: $245   2P/1B: $265   2P/2B: $265   XP: $25
◆◆◆◆   **Location:** 1 1/2 blks n of Moscone Convention Center. 50 3rd St 94103. Fax: 415/543-8268.
Hotel   **Terms:** Handling fee imposed; package plans, Weekends. **Facility:** 667 rooms. Some units with bay view.
    Suites, $350-$1500 for up to 2 persons. 6 whirlpool rms, extra charge; 36 stories; interior corridors.
    Dining: Restaurant; 6:30 am-10:30 pm, patio dining weather permitting; $12-$19; cocktails.
Services: giftshop. Fee: massage. **Cards:** AE, CB, DI, DS, JC, MC, VI.
    🛱 🐾 🍴 ✈ 🅿 🛗 ⛴ 🕊 🐕 💻 🛗 🖨 🛄 ✕

THE ARCHBISHOP'S MANSION   Rates Subject to Change   **Phone:** (415)563-7872   🄗
◆◆◆   All Year [CP]   1P: $139- 399   2P/1B: $139- 399   2P/2B: $229   XP: $20   F12
Historic Bed   **Location:** 1.1 mi w of US 101, Van Ness Ave, at Alamo Square. 1000 Fulton St 94117. Fax: 415/885-3193.
& Breakfast   **Terms:** Reserv deposit, 7 day notice; 2 night min stay, weekends. **Facility:** 15 rooms. European antiques.
    Many rooms with fireplace. Limited parking. 1 large suite $295, Fri & Sat $385 for up to 2 persons; 3 stories;
interior corridors. **All Rooms:** combo or shower baths. **Cards:** AE, CB, DI, DS, MC, VI. *(See color ad below)*
    🛱 ✈ ⛴ [VCR] 🕊 🖨 ✕

(See map p. 919)

ATHERTON HOTEL   Phone: (415)474-5720   86

(AAA) SAVE   4/1-10/31   1P: $7- 119   2P/1B: $89- 119 2P/2B: $99- 129   XP: $10   F12
              2/1-3/31 & 11/1-1/31   1P: $69- 109   2P/1B: $79- 109 2P/2B: $79- 109   XP: $10   F12
◆◆   **Location:** 3 blks e of US 101 (Van Ness Ave). 685 Ellis St 94109. Fax: 414/474-8256. **Terms:** Reserv
Hotel   deposit. **Facility:** 75 rooms. 7 stories; interior corridors. **Dining:** Restaurant; 7 am-11 & 5-9:30 pm, Sun 8
am-2 pm. **All Rooms:** combo or shower baths. **Cards:** AE, CB, DI, DS, MC, VI. **Special Amenities:** Early
check-in/late check-out and free room upgrade (subject to availability with advanced reservations).

[SD] [3P] [Y1] [▲] [Ⓡ] [K] [▣] [✕]

BECK'S MOTOR LODGE   Phone: (415)621-8212   84

(AAA) SAVE   5/1-10/31   1P: $80- 110   2P/1B: $90- 125 2P/2B: $90- 125   XP: $10   F18
              2/1-4/30 & 11/1-1/31   1P: $76- 100   2P/1B: $80- 115 2P/2B: $80- 115   XP: $10   F18
◆◆   **Location:** 0.6 mi w of US 101(Van Ness Ave); near Castro St. 2222 Market St 94114. Fax: 415/241-0435.
Motel   **Facility:** 57 rooms. 2 gas fireplaces. Few studios. 3 stories; interior/exterior corridors. **Dining:** Restaurant
nearby. **All Rooms:** combo or shower baths. **Cards:** AE, CB, DI, DS, JC, MC, VI. *(See color ad below)*

[SD] [3P] [Y1]+ [▲] [▣] [▣] [🔒] [✕]

BERESFORD ARMS   Phone: (415)673-2600   50

(AAA) SAVE   All Year [CP]   1P: $109- 119   2P/1B: $119- 129 2P/2B: $140- 150   XP: $10   F12
◆◆◆   **Location:** 3 blks w of Union Sq. 701 Post St 94109. Fax: 415/929-1535. **Terms:** Pets, in smoking rooms,
Hotel   second floor. **Facility:** 96 rooms. Few small rooms. 57 whirlpool suites for up to 5 persons, $125-$175; 7 stories; interior corridors. Fee: parking. **Services:** complimentary evening beverages. **All Rooms:** combo or
shower baths. **Some Rooms:** 26 kitchens. **Cards:** AE, CB, DI, DS, JC, MC, VI. *(See color ad below)*

[SD] [🛏] [🔄] [3P] [✈] [▲] [Ⓡ] [VCR] [🔒] [K] [▣] [🔒] [✕]

BEST WESTERN AMERICANIA   Phone: (415)626-0200   102

(AAA) SAVE   4/1-10/31   1P: $129- 169   2P/1B: $129- 169 2P/2B: $129- 169   XP: $10   F17
              2/1-3/31 & 11/1-1/31   1P: $109- 139   2P/1B: $109- 139 2P/2B: $109- 139   XP: $10   F17
◆◆◆   **Location:** Just s of Market St. 121 7th St 94103. Fax: 415/863-2529. **Facility:** 143 rooms. Few covered & lot
Motor Inn   parking. 14 two-bedroom units. 18 family units, $90-$150 for 4-6 persons; 4 stories; exterior corridors; heated
pool, saunas. **Dining:** Dining room, coffee shop; 6:30 am-10 pm; $7-$14; cocktails. **Services:** area
transportation, to business & tourist ctr. **All Rooms:** combo or shower baths. **Cards:** AE, CB, DI, DS, JC, MC, VI.
(See color ad p 926)

[SD] [🔄] [3P] [➡] [Y1] [✈] [▲] [♿] [Ⓡ] [▣] [□] [K] [▣] [🔒] [✕]

(See map p. 919)

BEST WESTERN CANTERBURY HOTEL

Phone: (415)474-6464 [22]

(AAA) [SAVE]	12/30-1/1	1P: $225- 350	2P/1B:	$250- 450	2P/2B:	$250- 450	XP:	$25	F18
	11/1-12/29 & 1/2-1/31	1P: $125- 195	2P/1B:	$140- 225	2P/2B:	$140- 225	XP:	$15	F18
◆ ◆	5/1-10/31	1P: $125- 199	2P/1B:	$140- 215	2P/2B:	$140- 215	XP:	$15	F18
Hotel	2/1-4/30	1P: $110- 195	2P/1B:	$125- 199	2P/2B:	$125- 199	XP:	$15	F18

Location: Between Taylor & Jones sts. 750 Sutter St 94109. Fax: 415/474-5856. **Terms:** Reserv deposit. **Facility:** 253 rooms. 10 stories; interior corridors. Fee: parking. **Dining:** Restaurant; cocktails. **Services:** giftshop. **All Rooms:** combo or shower baths. **Cards:** AE, CB, DI, DS, JC, MC, VI. **Special Amenities: Preferred room (subject to availability with advanced reservations).** (See color ad below)

BEST WESTERN CARRIAGE INN

Phone: (415)552-8600 [103]

(AAA) [SAVE]	4/1-10/31 [CP]	1P: $149- 179	2P/1B:	$149- 179	2P/2B:	$149- 179	XP:	$15	F17
◆ ◆ ◆	2/1-3/31 & 11/1-1/31 [CP]	1P: $129- 149	2P/1B:	$129- 149	2P/2B:	$129- 149	XP:	$15	F17

Location: 1.5 blks s of Market St. 140 7th St 94103. Fax: 415/863-2529. **Facility:** 48 rooms. Large rooms. Victorian atmosphere. Covered parking. 5 rooms with fireplace, $25 extra; 4 stories; interior corridors; whirlpool. **Dining:** Restaurant nearby. **Services:** complimentary evening beverages; area transportation, Union Sq & Convention Ctr. **Cards:** AE, CB, DI, DS, JC, MC, VI. **Special Amenities: Free breakfast and free newspaper.** (See color ad p 930)

BEST WESTERN CIVIC CENTER MOTOR INN

Phone: (415)621-2826 [83]

(AAA) [SAVE]	5/22-9/27	1P: $85- 115	2P/1B:	$85- 115	2P/2B:	$99- 125	XP:	$10	F18
◆ ◆	4/1-5/21 & 9/28-10/31	1P: $79- 109	2P/1B:	$79- 109	2P/2B:	$89- 119	XP:	$10	F18
Motel	2/1-3/31 & 11/1-1/31	1P: $69- 95	2P/1B:	$69- 95	2P/2B:	$79- 99	XP:	$10	F18

Location: Just n off frwy; Civic Center exit, at Harrison St. 364 9th St 94103. Fax: 415/621-0833. **Terms:** Reserv deposit; small pets only. **Facility:** 57 rooms. Some studio units. 2 stories; exterior corridors; small pool. **Dining:** Coffee shop; 7 am-2 pm, Sat & Sun-11 am. **All Rooms:** combo or shower baths. **Cards:** AE, CB, DI, DS, JC, MC, VI. **Special Amenities: Early check-in/late check-out.** (See color ad p 930)

SAN FRANCISCO BAY AREA'S
FUN ATTRACTIONS

Vallejo

The New Marine World Theme Park
"Fun runs wild" at Marine World Theme Park with 35 animal shows and attractions, plus 24 family thrill rides. Inverted roller coasters, drenching water rides, dolphins, tigers and more - all at one great theme park!

Red & White Fleet
Red & White offers Land, Water and Air tours. The Bay Cruise, City Tour and Monterey trips are available in six languages. Our Yosemite trip by air is a must while touring Northern California. Cruise departure and ticket purchase at Pier 43½ in Historic Fisherman's Wharf, at the foot of Taylor St. Advance ticket purchase at (415) 447-0597.

San Francisco

San Francisco's Fisherman's Wharf

The Wax Museum at Fisherman's Wharf
The Wax Museum will be closed September 1998 thru Fall 1999 while undergoing a complete renovation. When reopened in Fall 1999, the building will house the NEW Wax Museum along with major retail and restaurants.
www.waxmuseum.com

Paramount's Great America
Northern California's largest family attraction, offering 100 acres of theme park thrills and excitement, including seven world class rollercoasters, Nickelodeon® Splat City™, and Paramount produced entertainment. New in 1999...KidZville. Park open seasonally.

Santa Clara

San Jose

Winchester Mystery House
Beautiful. Beyond Belief! Tour the beautiful but bizarre Winchester Mystery House, the 160 room Victorian mansion built by rifle heiress Sarah Winchester. the mansion is filled with beautiful craftsmanship and strange oddities such as stairs leading to the ceiling!

Roaring Camp Railroad
Two Historic Railroads! Antique steam locomotives taking passengers through the Redwoods and vintage passenger coach travel down the San Lorenzo River Canyon to the beach and boardwalk at Santa Cruz. Chuckwagon BBQ and 1880's General Store.

Felton

Santa Cruz

Santa Cruz Beach Boardwalk
It's the beach — California-style — at the West Coast's only major seaside amusement park! Sun, surf, games and over 30 great rides and attractions plus arcades, laser tag, mini golf, fun foods and shops on a beautiful mile-long beach on Monterey Bay.

SAN FRANCISCO BAY AREA'S
FUN ATTRACTIONS

A Great Vacation!

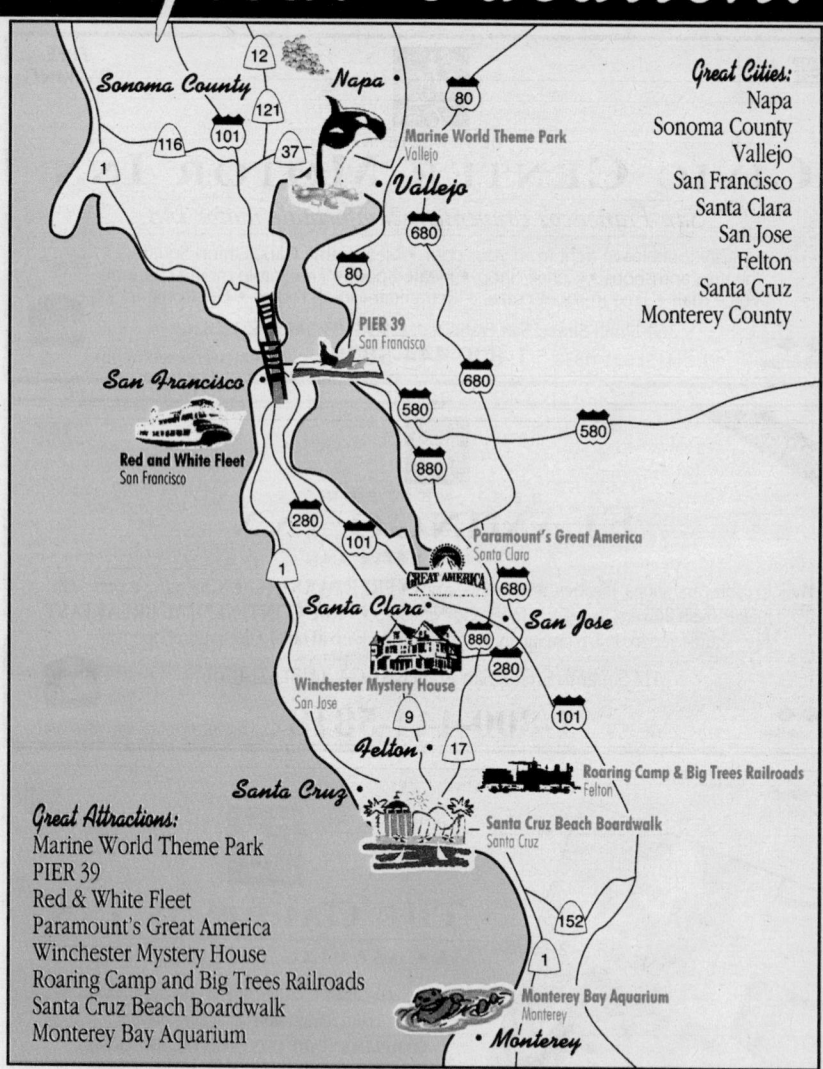

Great Cities:
Napa
Sonoma County
Vallejo
San Francisco
Santa Clara
San Jose
Felton
Santa Cruz
Monterey County

Great Attractions:
Marine World Theme Park
PIER 39
Red & White Fleet
Paramount's Great America
Winchester Mystery House
Roaring Camp and Big Trees Railroads
Santa Cruz Beach Boardwalk
Monterey Bay Aquarium

The San Francisco Bay Area

Discover Sightseeing, Shopping, Sailing and More...
For a brochure with discounts, contact our website at: sfvacations.com
or write: GSF - AAA, P.O. Box 387, Santa Clara, CA 95052

(See map p. 919)

BEST WESTERN FLAMINGO INN   **Phone:** (415)621-0701   [108]
4/1-10/31 [CP]   1P: $89- 109 2P/1B: $89- 109 2P/2B: $89- 109 XP: $10   F17
2/1-3/31 & 11/1-1/31 [CP]   1P: $79- 99 2P/1B: $79- 99 2P/2B: $79- 99 XP: $10   F17
Location: Just s of Market St; 3 blks from Civic Center. 114 7th St 94103. Fax: 415/863-2529. **Facility:** 38
Motel   rooms. Some small rooms. Lot & covered parking. 2 stories; exterior corridors. **Dining:** Restaurant nearby.
Services: area transportation, Union Square & conv. ctr. **All Rooms:** shower baths. **Cards:** AE, CB, DI, DS,
JC, MC, VI. *(See color ad below)*

(See map p. 919)

BEST WESTERN TUSCAN INN AT FISHERMAN'S WHARF   Phone: (415)561-1100   [92]

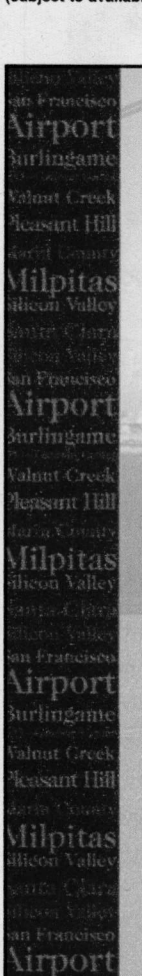

AAA SAVE   4/1-10/31 & 12/30-1/2   1P: $155- 175   2P/1B: $155- 175   2P/2B: $155- 175   XP: $10   F17
                2/1-3/31, 11/1-12/29 &
◆◆◆   1/3-1/31   1P: $135- 155   2P/1B: $135- 155   2P/2B: $135- 155   XP: $10   F17
Hotel   **Location:** Just s of the wharf at Mason St. 425 Northpoint St 94133. Fax: 415/561-1199. **Terms:** Package
            plans. **Facility:** 220 rooms. Limited pay valet parking. 12 units with VCR, CD player & parlor $238 for up to 2
persons; 4 stories; interior corridors. **Dining:** Restaurant; 7 am-10 pm & Fri-Sat till 11 pm; $12-$22; cocktails.
Services: complimentary evening beverages. **Cards:** AE, DI, DS, JC, MC, VI. **Special Amenities: Free room upgrade
(subject to availability with advanced reservations).** *(See ad p 933)*

For rave reviews check out the
Lodgings & Restaurants section of this **TourBook.**

285 Jefferson St. Want to see what all the hoopla is about at the new Marriott.

Introductory Rates From

Room	Suite
$99*	$139*
weekends	weekends

Sit back and relax. We have got the best location going and a free airport shuttle to get you there in a hurry. Just 10 minutes from San Francisco Int'l Airport. Within 30 minutes of downtown San Francisco, East Bay and Silicon Valley. Plus spacious new rooms & suites, new pool, new banquet facilities, new everything. Pull over for awhile and see how comfortable you can be.

SAN MATEO **Marriott**
SAN FRANCISCO AIRPORT

When you're comfortable you can do anything.℠

1770 South Amphlett Blvd., San Mateo, CA 94402 • (650) 573-7661 • **(800) 556-2395**

*Rate only valid on weekends. Subject to limited availability. Advanced reservations required. Rate reflects 10% AAA discount. Not valid for groups, conventions & special events.

(See map p. 919)

BRITTON HOTEL

Hotel

					Phone: (415)621-7001	115
4/1-10/31	1P: $109- 129	2P/1B: $109- 129	2P/2B: $109- 129	XP: $10		F17
2/1-3/31 & 11/1-1/31	1P: $89- 109	2P/1B: $89- 109	2P/2B: $89- 109	XP: $10		F17

Location: Just s of Market St; 3 blks s of Civic Center. 112 7th St 94103. Fax: 415/863-2529. **Facility:** 79 rooms. Convenient to cable cars, shopping & civic center. 8 two-bedroom units. 5 stories; interior corridors. Fee: parking. **Dining:** Coffee shop; 7 am-10 pm; $6-$9. **Services:** area transportation, to business & tourist ctr. **All Rooms:** combo or shower baths. **Cards:** AE, CB, DI, DS, JC, MC, VI. *(See color ad below)*

(See map p. 919)

BROADWAY MANOR INN — Phone: (415)776-7900 **69**
(AAA) SAVE — All Year — 1P: $85 — 2P/1B: $85 — 2P/2B: $85 — XP: $8 — F17
Location: On US 101, at Broadway. 2201 Van Ness Ave 94109. Fax: 415/928-0460. **Facility:** 56 rooms. Limited free parking. Lower rates in winter; 4 stories; exterior corridors. **Dining:** 7 am-2 pm; coffee shop nearby.
Motor Inn — **Cards:** AE, CB, DI, DS, JC, MC, VI. *(See color ad below)*

BUENA VISTA MOTOR INN — Rates Subject to Change — Phone: (415)923-9600 **78**
(AAA) — Fri & Sat 2/1-5/14, 5/15-11/30
& Fri & Sat 12/1-1/31 — 1P: $85- 140 — 2P/1B: $85- 140 — 2P/2B: $97- 140 — XP: $10 — F12
◆ ◆ ◆ — Sun-Thurs 2/1-5/14 &
Motel — 12/1-1/31 — 1P: $78- 120 — 2P/1B: $78- 120 — 2P/2B: $85- 120 — XP: $8 — F12
Location: On US 101, at Gough St. 1599 Lombard St 94123. Fax: 415/441-4775. **Facility:** 50 rooms. Limited free covered parking. 1 suite, $165 up to 4 persons; 3 stories; interior corridors. **All Rooms:** combo or shower baths.
Cards: AE, DI, DS, MC, VI. *(See color ad p 935)*

CAMPTON PLACE HOTEL — Rates Subject to Change — Phone: (415)781-5555 **15**
◆ ◆ ◆ ◆ — 4/1-1/31 — 1P: $275- 400 — 2P/1B: $275- 400 — 2P/2B: $365 — XP: $25 — F17
Hotel — 2/1-3/31 — 1P: $240- 360 — 2P/1B: $240- 360 — 2P/2B: $295 — XP: $25 — F17
Location: Just n of Union Square. 340 Stockton St 94108. Fax: 415/955-5536. **Terms:** Reserv deposit; handling fee imposed. **Facility:** 117 rooms. Refined atmosphere. Residential character. Suites, $450-$985 for 2 persons; 17 stories; interior corridors. **Cards:** AE, DI, JC, MC, VI.

CAPRI MOTEL — Rates Subject to Change — Phone: 415/346-4667 **62**
(AAA) — All Year — 1P: $66- 116 — 2P/1B: $66- 70 — 2P/2B: $78- 100 — XP: $8
◆ — **Location:** Just s of US 101, at Buchanan St. 2015 Greenwich St 94123. Fax: 415/346-3256. **Facility:** 46
Motel — rooms. 1 one-bedroom unit with kitchen, $90, 1 efficiency $116. 2-bedroom units with efficiency, $146 for up to 6 persons; 3 stories; exterior corridors. **All Rooms:** combo or shower baths. **Cards:** AE, DI, DS, JC, MC, VI.

(See map p. 919)

CASTLE INN MOTEL   Rates Subject to Change   **Phone:** (415)441-1155   68
    5/15-10/31 [CP]   1P: $75- 85   2P/1B: $85- 95   2P/2B: $95- 105   XP: $10-15
    2/1-5/14 & 11/1-1/31 [EP]   1P: $60- 70   2P/1B: $65- 85   2P/2B: $75- 95   XP: $8-10
Motel   **Location:** just e of US 101 (Van Ness Ave). 1565 Broadway 94109. **Fax:** 415/775-2237. **Terms:** Reserv deposit, 3 day notice. **Facility:** 26 rooms. Covered parking. 1 suite, $95-$140 up to 4 persons; 5 stories; exterior corridors. **Cards:** AE, CB, DI, DS, JC, MC, VI. *(See color ad p 949)*

CATHEDRAL HILL HOTEL   Rates Subject to Change   **Phone:** (415)776-8200   77
    4/1-10/31   1P: $129- 169   2P/1B: $129- 169   2P/2B: $129- 169   XP: $10   F18
Hotel   2/1-3/31 & 11/1-1/31   1P: $99- 129   2P/1B: $99- 129   2P/2B: $99- 129   XP: $10   F18
    Location: On US 101 between Geary & Post sts. 1101 Van Ness Ave 94109. **Fax:** 415/441-2841.
Facility: 400 rooms. Small & large units. 8 stories; interior corridors. **Services:** giftshop. **Cards:** AE, CB, DI, DS, JC, MC, VI. *(See color ad below)*

CHANCELLOR HOTEL   **Phone:** (415)362-2004   19
    All Year   1P: $128- 138   2P/1B: $143- 153   2P/2B: $143- 153   XP: $15
    Location: 0.5 blk n off Union Square. 433 Powell St 94102. **Terms:** Reserv deposit; handling fee imposed; package plans. **Facility:** 137 rooms. Few small rooms. 15 stories; interior corridors.
Hotel   Fee: parking. **Dining:** Dining room; 7 am-3 & 5-9:30 pm, Sun-3 pm; $10-$18; cocktails. **Services:** giftshop. **Cards:** AE, CB, DI, DS, JC, MC, VI. **Special Amenities: Free local telephone calls and free newspaper.**
(See color ad below)

CHELSEA MOTOR INN   Guaranteed Rates   **Phone:** 415/563-5600   60
    5/15-10/15   1P: $92   2P/1B: $96   2P/2B: $96   XP: $10   F5
    2/1-5/14 & 10/16-1/31   1P: $80   2P/1B: $84   2P/2B: $84   XP: $7   F5
Motel   **Location:** US 101 at Fillmore St. 2095 Lombard St 94123. **Fax:** 415/567-6475. **Terms:** Reserv deposit.
Facility: 60 rooms. Complimentary covered parking. 4 stories; interior corridors. **Cards:** AE, CB, DI, MC, VI. *(See color ad p 938)*

CLARION BEDFORD HOTEL   **Phone:** (415)673-6040   25
    5/1-10/31   1P: $129   2P/1B: $129   2P/2B: $139   XP: $10   F12
    2/1-4/30 & 11/1-1/31   1P: $109   2P/1B: $109   2P/2B: $119   XP: $10   F12
Hotel   **Location:** 3 1/2 blks w of Union Square. 761 Post St 94109. **Fax:** 415/563-6739. **Terms:** Reserv deposit.
Facility: 144 rooms. 16 stories; interior corridors. Fee: parking. **Dining:** Restaurant; 6:30 am-midnight; $8-$15; cocktails. **Services:** complimentary evening beverages. **Cards:** AE, CB, DI, DS, MC, VI.

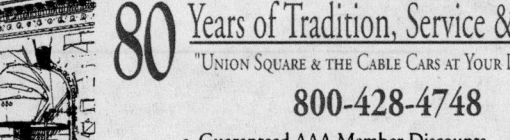

SAN FRANCISCO'S MARINA DISTRICT

(See map p. 919)

COLUMBUS MOTOR INN
AAA ◆◆◆ Motel

Guaranteed Rates   Phone: 415/885-1492   97

	1P		2P/1B		2P/2B		XP		
5/15-10/15	1P: $110		2P/1B: $110		2P/2B: $110		XP: $10		F5
2/1-5/14 & 10/16-1/31	1P: $80		2P/1B: $84		2P/2B: $84		XP: $7		F5

Location: 0.2 mi s of Fisherman's Wharf; between Francisco & Chestnut Sts. 1075 Columbus Ave 94133. Fax: 415/928-2174. **Terms:** Reserv deposit. **Facility:** 45 rooms. Complimentary covered parking. Six 2-bedroom units, $155 5/15-10/15; $120 2/1-5/14 & 10/16-1/31 for up to 4 persons; 5 stories; interior corridors. **Cards:** AE, CB, DI, MC, VI. *(See color ad p 937)*

COMFORT INN BY THE BAY
AAA [SAVE] ◆◆ Motor Inn

Phone: (415)928-5000   71

	1P	2P/1B	2P/2B	XP	
6/1-10/31 [CP]	1P: $139- 175	2P/1B: $145- 189	2P/2B: $139- 189	XP: $10	F18
3/1-5/31 [CP]	1P: $89- 155	2P/1B: $105- 165	2P/2B: $99- 169	XP: $10	F18
2/1-2/28 & 11/1-1/31 [CP]	1P: $89- 139	2P/1B: $105- 149	2P/2B: $99- 159	XP: $10	F18

Location: On US 101 at 2775 Van Ness Ave 94109. Fax: 415/441-3990. **Terms:** Handling fee imposed. **Facility:** 138 rooms. Many units with view of Bay. 11 stories; interior corridors. Fee: parking. **All Rooms:** combo or shower baths. **Cards:** AE, CB, DI, DS, JC, MC, VI. *(See color ad p 919)*

COMMODORE INTERNATIONAL HOTEL
◆◆ Hotel

Rates Subject to Change   Phone: 415/923-6800   52

	1P	2P/1B	2P/2B	XP
4/1-10/31	1P: $99- 139	2P/1B: $99- 139	2P/2B: $99- 139	XP: $10
2/1-3/31 & 11/1-1/31	1P: $89- 129	2P/1B: $89- 129	2P/2B: $89- 129	XP: $10

Location: 2 1/2 blks nw of Union Sq. 825 Sutter St 94109. Fax: 415/923-6804. **Facility:** 113 rooms. 6 stories; interior corridors. Fee: parking. **Cards:** AE, DI, DS, JC, MC, VI. *(See color ad p 924)*

COVENTRY MOTOR INN
AAA ◆◆◆ Motel

Guaranteed Rates   Phone: 415/567-1200   61

	1P	2P/1B	2P/2B	XP	
5/15-10/15	1P: $92	2P/1B: $96	2P/2B: $96	XP: $10	F5
2/1-5/14 & 10/16-1/31	1P: $80	2P/1B: $84	2P/2B: $84	XP: $7	F5

Location: US 101 at Buchanan St. 1901 Lombard St 94123. Fax: 415/921-8745. **Terms:** Reserv deposit. **Facility:** 69 rooms. Complimentary covered parking. 4 stories; interior corridors. **Dining:** Restaurant nearby. **Cards:** AE, CB, MC, VI. *(See color ad p 938)*

COW HOLLOW MOTOR INN & SUITES
AAA ◆◆◆ Complex

Guaranteed Rates   Phone: 415/921-5800   58

	1P	2P/1B	2P/2B	XP	
5/15-10/15	1P: $92	2P/1B: $96	2P/2B: $96	XP: $10	F5
2/1-5/14 & 10/16-1/31	1P: $80	2P/1B: $84	2P/2B: $84	XP: $7	F5

Location: US 101 at Steiner St. 2190 Lombard St 94123. Fax: 415/922-8515. **Terms:** Reserv deposit. **Facility:** 129 rooms. Apartments & motel rooms. Complimentary covered parking. 12 1- & 2-bedroom suites with wood burning fireplace & kitchen, $195-$245, for up to 4 persons; 4 stories; interior corridors. **Dining:** Coffee shop nearby. **Cards:** AE, CB, DI, MC, VI. *(See color ad p 938 & below)*

CROWNE PLAZA-UNION SQUARE
AAA [SAVE] [FYI] Hotel

Phone: (415)398-8900   17

	1P	2P/1B	2P/2B	XP	
7/5-11/11	1P: $189- 229	2P/1B: $209- 249	2P/2B: $209- 249	XP: $20	F18
5/1-7/4	1P: $155- 189	2P/1B: $175- 209	2P/2B: $175- 209	XP: $20	F18
11/12-1/31	1P: $145- 179	2P/1B: $165- 199	2P/2B: $165- 199	XP: $20	F18
2/1-4/30	1P: $135- 169	2P/1B: $155- 189	2P/2B: $155- 189	XP: $20	F18

Under major renovation. **Location:** Just n off Union Square, corner Powell St. 480 Sutter St 94108. Fax: 415/989-8823. **Facility:** 403 rooms. Many rooms with city views. Scheduled to open Fall, 1998. Suites, $175-$265 for up to 2 persons; 30 stories; interior corridors. Fee: parking. **Dining:** Restaurant, coffee shop; 6 am-11 pm; cocktails. **Services:** giftshop. **Cards:** AE, CB, DI, DS, JC, MC, VI. **Special Amenities:** Early check-in/late check-out and free room upgrade (subject to availability with advanced reservations). *(See ad p 943)*

(See map p. 919)

DAYS INN AT THE BEACH   Rates Subject to Change   **Phone:** 415/665-9000   91
◆   5/1-9/30 [CP]   1P: $80- 85   2P/1B: $80- 85   2P/2B: $90
Motel   2/1-4/30 & 10/1-1/31 [CP]   1P: $65- 75   2P/1B: $65- 75   2P/2B: $75- 80
    Location: 0.3 mi e of Great Hwy. 2600 Sloat Blvd 94116. Fax: 415/665-5440. **Facility:** 33 rooms. Convenient to Zoo. 3 family units, $105-$130 for up to 4 persons; 2 stories; interior corridors. **All Rooms:** combo or shower baths. **Some Rooms:** 3 efficiencies. **Cards:** AE, DI, DS, MC, VI.

DAYS INN-CIVIC CENTER   **Phone:** (415)864-4040   105
(AAA) (SAVE)   All Year   1P: $75- 95   2P/1B: $85- 100   2P/2B: $95- 150   XP: $10   D12
    Location: 2 1/2 blks w of US 101 (Van Ness Ave). 465 Grove St 94102. Fax: 415/552-4914. **Facility:** 40
◆◆   rooms. Some large rooms. Few with wet bars. 6 units with whirlpool bath, $70-$100 for up to 2 persons; 4 sto-
Motel   ries; exterior corridors. **Cards:** AE, CB, DI, DS, MC, VI. **Special Amenities: Free breakfast.**
    (See color ad below)

DAYS INN-GEARY   **Phone:** (415)441-8220   80
(AAA) (SAVE)   5/1-10/31 [CP]   1P: $89   2P/1B: $99   2P/2B: $109   XP: $10   F12
    2/1-4/30 & 11/1-1/31 [CP]   1P: $79   2P/1B: $89   2P/2B: $99   XP: $10   F12
◆◆   **Location:** Just e of US 101 (Van Ness Ave) at Larkin St. 895 Geary St 94109. Fax: 415/771-5667.
Motel   **Terms:** Reserv deposit. **Facility:** 73 rooms. Complimentary underground parking. 4 stories; interior corridors.
    Cards: AE, DI, DS, MC, VI. **Special Amenities: Free breakfast and free newspaper.**
(See color ad below)

THE DONATELLO   Rates Subject to Change   **Phone:** 415/441-7100   21
◆◆◆   All Year   1P: $159- 225   2P/1B: $159- 225   2P/2B: $159- 225   XP: $25
Hotel   **Location:** Just w of Union Square, at Mason St. 501 Post St 94102. Fax: 415/885-8842. **Facility:** 94 rooms.
    European style hotel, few studios. Suites, $315-$495 up to 6 persons; 15 stories; interior corridors.
Fee: parking. **Services:** Fee: massage. **Cards:** AE, DI, DS, MC, VI.

FAIRMONT HOTEL & TOWER   Rates Subject to Change   **Phone:** 415/772-5000   4
◆◆◆◆   All Year   1P: $229- 339   2P/1B: $259- 369   2P/2B: $259- 369   XP: $30   F12
Hotel   **Location:** Atop Nob Hill, at California St. 950 Mason St 94108. Fax: 415/837-0587. **Facility:** 596 rooms. 60
    suites, $500-$830 for up to 2 persons; 22 stories; interior corridors. Fee: parking. **Services:** giftshop.
Fee: massage. **Cards:** AE, CB, DI, DS, JC, MC, VI.

(See map p. 919)

FRANCISCO BAY MOTEL

Motel

	Rates Subject to Change						**Phone:** (415)474-3030	64
5/15-10/31 [CP]	1P: $75- 85	2P/1B:	$85- 95	2P/2B:	$95- 105	XP: $10-15		D18
2/1-5/14 & 11/1-1/31 [CP]	1P: $60- 70	2P/1B:	$65- 85	2P/2B:	$75- 95	XP: $8-10		D18

Location: On US 101 at Franklin. 1501 Lombard St 94123. Fax: 415/567-7082. **Terms:** Reserv deposit, 3 day notice. **Facility:** 39 rooms. Few small rooms. 4 stories; exterior corridors. **Cards:** AE, CB, DI, DS, JC, MC, VI. *(See color ad p 949)*

Hit the road with **AAA TourBooks,**
CampBooks and **TripTik maps.**

(See map p. 919)

GALLERIA PARK HOTEL

 SAVE

◆◆◆

Hotel

Mon-Thurs 2/1-11/14, 12/1-12/14 & 12/31-1/31	1P: $180	2P/1B: $180	2P/2B: $180	XP: $20	F17
Fri-Sun 2/1-11/14, 12/1-12/14 & 12/31-1/31	1P: $135	2P/1B: $135	2P/2B: $135	XP: $20	F17
11/15-11/30 & 12/15-12/30	1P: $119	2P/1B: $119	2P/2B: $119	XP: $20	F17

Phone: (415)781-3060 **12**

Location: 2 blks ne of Union Square. 191 Sutter St 94104. Fax: 415/433-4409. **Terms:** Reserv deposit; handling fee imposed. **Facility:** 177 rooms. Rooftop garden & jogging track; few small rooms. Suites, $195-$375 for up to 2 persons; 9 stories; interior corridors. Fee: parking. **Dining:** 2 restaurants; 7 am-10 pm; $9-$18. **Services:** complimentary evening beverages. **All Rooms:** combo or shower baths. **Cards:** AE, DI, DS, JC, MC, VI. **Special Amenities:** Early check-in/late check-out and preferred room (subject to availability with advanced reservations).

GRAND HYATT SAN FRANCISCO

SAVE

◆◆◆◆

Hotel

All Year 1P: $260- 365 2P/1B: $285- 390 2P/2B: $285- 390 XP: $25

Phone: (415)398-1234 **16** F18

Location: On Union Square at Post St. 345 Stockton St 94108. Fax: 415/391-1780. **Terms:** Package plans. **Facility:** 685 rooms. Walking distance to Financial District, Moscone Convention Center. 36 stories; interior corridors. **Dining:** Dining room, coffee shop, deli; 6:30 am-11 pm; $13-$35; cocktails. **Services:** giftshop; area transportation, within 5 mi. **Some Rooms:** whirlpools. **Cards:** AE, CB, DI, DS, JC, MC, VI.

(See color ad p 923)

THE HANDLERY UNION SQUARE HOTEL

◆◆◆

Hotel

Rates Subject to Change

All Year 1P: $150- 185 2P/1B: $160- 195 2P/2B: $166- 195 XP: $10

Phone: (415)781-7800 **30**

Location: Just sw of Union Square. 351 Geary St 94102. Fax: 415/781-0269. **Terms:** Reserv deposit; handling fee imposed; package plans. **Facility:** 377 rooms. Family owned & operated. Some large rooms. 8 two-bedroom units. 8 stories; interior corridors; heated pool, sauna. **Dining:** Restaurant nearby. **Services:** giftshop. **All Rooms:** combo or shower baths. **Cards:** AE, CB, DI, DS, JC, MC, VI.

(See ad below)

HARBOR COURT HOTEL

◆◆◆

Hotel

Rates Subject to Change

All Year 1P: $195- 215 2P/1B: $205- 220 2P/2B: $220- 250

Phone: 415/882-1300 **11**

Location: On Embarcadero, between Howard & Mission sts. 165 Stuart St 94108. Fax: 415/882-1313. **Facility:** 131 rooms. Small rooms. 8 stories; interior corridors. **Dining:** Restaurant; 11 am-3 & 5-11 pm; $14-$22. **Services:** complimentary evening beverages. **All Rooms:** combo or shower baths. **Cards:** AE, CB, DI, DS, MC, VI.

(See map p. 919)

HOLIDAY INN-CIVIC CENTER   Phone: (415)626-6103   82
AAA SAVE

	7/5-10/30	1P: $125- 149	2P/1B: $145- 169	2P/2B: $145- 169	XP: $20	F18
	5/1-7/4	1P: $109- 139	2P/1B: $129- 159	2P/2B: $129- 159	XP: $20	F18
	10/31-1/31	1P: $105- 135	2P/1B: $125- 155	2P/2B: $125- 155	XP: $20	F18
Motor Inn	2/1-4/30	1P: $99- 135	2P/1B: $119- 155	2P/2B: $119- 155	XP: $20	F18

Location: 2 blks from Civic Auditorium; just s Market St & BART Station. 50 8th St 94103.
Fax: 415/552-0184. **Terms:** Small pets only, $150 dep req, $10 extra charge. **Facility:** 394 rooms. 14 stories; interior corridors; heated pool. **Dining:** Restaurant; 6-11 am, Sat & Sun 6 am-noon & 5-10 pm; $15-$19; cocktails; breakfast buffet. **Services:** giftshop. **All Rooms:** combo or shower baths. **Cards:** AE, CB, DI, DS, JC, MC, VI. **Special Amenities:** Early check-in/late check-out and free room upgrade (subject to availability with advanced reservations). *(See ad below)*

HOLIDAY INN-FISHERMAN'S WHARF   Phone: (415)771-9000   100
AAA SAVE

	7/5-10/30	1P: $169- 199	2P/1B: $189- 219	2P/2B: $189- 219	XP: $20	F18
	5/1-7/4	1P: $129- 169	2P/1B: $149- 189	2P/2B: $149- 189	XP: $20	F18
Motor Inn	2/1-4/30 & 10/31-1/31	1P: $119- 179	2P/1B: $139- 179	2P/2B: $139- 179	XP: $20	F18

Location: 0.1 mi from the bay. 1300 Columbus Ave 94133. Fax: 415/563-4378. **Terms:** Package plans. **Facility:** 580 rooms. Limited pay garage & parking lot; 5 stories; interior corridors; small pool. **Dining:** Restaurant, coffee shop; 24 hrs; $10-$25; cocktails. **Services:** giftshop. **All Rooms:** combo or shower baths. **Cards:** AE, CB, DI, DS, JC, MC, VI. **Special Amenities:** Early check-in/late check-out and free room upgrade (subject to availability with advanced reservations). *(See ad below)*

HOLIDAY INN SELECT-FINANCIAL DISTRICT   Phone: (415)433-6600   2
AAA SAVE

| | All Year | 1P: $129- 169 | 2P/1B: $149- 189 | 2P/2B: $149- 189 | XP: $20 | F18 |

Location: 1 blk from Chinatown. 750 Kearny St 94108. Fax: 415/765-7891. **Facility:** 566 rooms. Rooms with city & bay view. 27 stories; interior corridors. Fee: parking. **Dining:** Restaurant, coffee shop; 6:30 am-10 pm; $10-$25; cocktails. **Services:** giftshop. **Cards:** AE, CB, DI, DS, JC, MC, VI. **Special Amenities:** Early check-in/late check-out and free room upgrade (subject to availability with advanced reservations).
(See ad below)

HOLIDAY LODGE   Rates Subject to Change   Phone: 415/776-4469   81
AAA

| | All Year [CP] | 1P: $99- 119 | 2P/1B: $99- 119 | 2P/2B: $109- 119 | XP: $10 | F16 |

Location: On US 101 at Jackson. 1901 Van Ness Ave 94109. Fax: 415/474-7046. **Terms:** Weekly/monthly rates, 11/1-4/30. **Facility:** 65 rooms. Some units overlook pool, garden courtyard. Complimentary covered parking. 3 stories; exterior corridors; small pool. **Dining:** Restaurant nearby. **All Rooms:** combo or shower baths. **Cards:** AE, DI, DS, JC, MC, VI. *(See color ad p 924)*

(See map p. 919)

HOTEL BERESFORD   **Phone:** 415/673-9900   26

All Year [CP]   1P: $109   2P/1B: $119   2P/2B: $119- 129   XP: $10   F12
Location: 1 blk nw of Union Square (at Mason St). 635 Sutter St 94102. Fax: 415/474-0449. **Terms:** Small
pets only. **Facility:** 114 rooms. 7 stories; interior corridors. **Dining:** Restaurant; 7 am-2 & 5-10 pm, Fri &
Sat-11 pm, closed Sun & Mon for dinner. **All Rooms:** combo or shower baths. **Some Rooms:** whirlpools.
Cards: AE, CB, DI, DS, MC, VI. *(See color ad below)*

Hotel

HOTEL JULIANA   Rates Subject to Change   **Phone:** (415)392-2540   45

2/1-11/2   1P: $139   2P/1B: $139   2P/2B: $149   XP: $20   D12
11/3-1/31   1P: $129   2P/1B: $129   2P/2B: $139   XP: $20   D12
Location: Downtown. 590 Bush St 94108. Fax: 415/391-8447. **Terms:** Reserv deposit. **Facility:** 107 rooms.
Cozy homelike atmosphere. Attractive rooms. 8 two-bedroom units. 22 suites, $140-$170 for 2 persons; 8 sto-
ries; interior corridors. **Dining:** Restaurant nearby. **Services:** complimentary evening beverages. **Cards:** AE,
CB, DI, DS, JC, MC, VI.

Hotel

(See map p. 919)

HOTEL MILANO
⬥⬥⬥ Hotel

All Year   1P: $149- 169   2P/1B: $149- 169   2P/2B: $169- 189   XP: $20   F12
Phone: (415)543-8555   **47**
Location: Just s of Market between Mission & Markets sts. 55-5th St 94103. Fax: 415/543-5843.
Terms: Reserv deposit. **Facility:** 108 rooms. 7 stories; interior corridors. Fee: parking. **Dining:** Restaurant; 6:30 am-10 pm; $15-$26; cocktails. **Some Rooms:** whirlpools. **Cards:** AE, CB, DI, DS, MC, VI.
Special Amenities: Free room upgrade and preferred room (each subject to availability with advanced reservations). *(See color ad p 944)*

HOTEL MONACO
⬥⬥⬥⬥ Hotel

Rates Subject to Change			**Phone:** (415)292-0100 **48**	
5/1-10/31	1P: $219	2P/1B: $219	2P/2B: $219	XP: $15	F17
2/1-4/30	1P: $189	2P/1B: $189	2P/2B: $189	XP: $15	F17
11/1-1/31	1P: $179	2P/1B: $179	2P/2B: $179	XP: $15	F17

Location: Just w of Union Square at Taylor St. 501 Geary St 94102. Fax: 415/292-0111. **Terms:** Pets, $150 extra charge. **Facility:** 201 rooms. Restored 1910 American Beaux Arts Hotel. Attractive public areas; few small rooms. Suites, $235-$290 for up to 2 persons; 7 stories; interior corridors; sauna, whirlpool. **Dining:** Dining room; 7 am-10 pm, Fri & Sat-11 pm; cocktails. **Services:** complimentary evening beverages. **Some Rooms:** whirlpools. **Cards:** AE, CB, DI, DS, JC, MC, VI.

HOTEL REX
⬥⬥⬥ Hotel

Rates Subject to Change   **Phone:** 415/433-4434   **53**
All Year   1P: $155   2P/1B: $155   2P/2B: $185
Location: Just nw of Union Sq. 562 Sutter St 94102. Fax: 415/433-3695. **Facility:** 94 rooms. A hotel dedicated to the arts & literary world. A few small rooms. 7 stories; interior corridors. Fee: parking. **Cards:** AE, DI, DS, MC, VI. *(See color ad p 924)*

HOTEL VINTAGE COURT
⬥⬥⬥ Hotel

Guaranteed Rates			**Phone:** (415)392-4666 **54**	
4/1-10/31	1P: $149- 169	2P/1B: $149- 169	2P/2B: $159- 179	XP: $10	F12
2/1-3/31 & 11/1-1/31	1P: $139- 159	2P/1B: $139- 159	2P/2B: $149- 169	XP: $10	F12

Location: 2 blks n of Union Sq. 650 Bush St 94108. Fax: 415/433-4065. **Facility:** 107 rooms. 8 stories; interior corridors. Fee: parking. **Services:** complimentary evening beverages. **All Rooms:** combo or shower baths. **Some Rooms:** whirlpools. **Cards:** AE, CB, DI, DS, MC, VI.

HOTEL NIKKO
⬥⬥⬥⬥ Hotel

Guaranteed Rates   **Phone:** 415/394-1111   **31**
All Year   1P: $195   2P/1B: $195   2P/2B: $195   XP: $30   F18
Location: 3 blks w of Union Square. 222 Mason St 94102. Fax: 415/394-1106. **Terms:** Package plans; pets, small dogs only. **Facility:** 523 rooms. Contemporary Japanese styling. Suites, $375-$1300 for up to 2 persons; 25 stories; interior corridors; heated indoor pool, whirlpool. Fee: parking. **Dining:** Restaurant; 6:30 am-2:30 & 6-10 pm; $15-$30; cocktails. **Services:** giftshop. Fee: massage. **Cards:** AE, CB, DI, DS, JC, MC, VI.

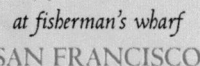

(See map p. 919)

HOWARD JOHNSON AT FISHERMAN'S WHARF

AAA SAVE

Phone: (415)775-3800   110

7/1-9/5	1P: $159	2P/1B: $159	2P/2B: $159	XP: $10	F18
4/1-6/30 & 9/6-11/13	1P: $139	2P/1B: $139	2P/2B: $139	XP: $10	F18
2/1-3/31 & 11/14-1/31	1P: $109	2P/1B: $109	2P/2B: $109	XP: $10	F18

◆ ◆ ◆
Motel

Location: Adjacent to the Cannery, between Jones & Leavenworth Sts. 580 Beach St 94133. Fax: 415/441-7307. **Terms:** Reserv deposit. **Facility:** 128 rooms. 4 stories; interior corridors. Fee: parking. **Dining:** Restaurant nearby. **All Rooms:** combo or shower baths. **Cards:** AE, CB, DI, DS, JC, MC, VI.
(See color ad p 945)

THE HUNTINGTON HOTEL   Rates Subject to Change   Phone: 415/474-5400   5

◆ ◆ ◆
Hotel

All Year   1P: $230- 350   2P/1B: $255- 375   2P/2B: $255- 375   XP: $30

Location: Atop Nob Hill at Taylor St. 1075 California St 94108. Fax: 415/474-6227. **Terms:** Reserv deposit. **Facility:** 138 rooms. Some large, richly appointed rooms. 40 units with separate parlor; 12 stories; interior corridors. **Cards:** AE, DI, DS, JC, MC, VI. A Preferred Hotel.

HYATT FISHERMAN'S WHARF   Phone: (415)563-1234   96

AAA SAVE

◆ ◆ ◆
Hotel

All Year   1P: $240- 330   2P/1B: $265- 355   2P/2B: $265- 355   XP: $25   F18

Location: Just s of the wharf; at Taylor St. 555 North Point St 94133. Fax: 415/749-6122. **Terms:** Handling fee imposed; package plans. **Facility:** 313 rooms. 5 stories; interior corridors; heated pool, sauna, whirlpool. **Dining:** Restaurant; 6:30 am-11 & noon-10:30 pm, Fri & Sat 11 pm; $10-$16. **Services:** giftshop; area transportation, Mon-Fri; limited. **Cards:** AE, CB, DI, DS, JC, MC, VI. *(See color ad p 923)*

HYATT REGENCY-SAN FRANCISCO   Phone: (415)788-1234   3

AAA SAVE

◆ ◆ ◆ ◆
Hotel

All Year   1P: $270- 370   2P/1B: $295- 395   2P/2B: $295- 395   XP: $25   F18

Location: Foot of California & Market sts. 5 Embarcadero Center 94111. Fax: 415/398-2567. **Terms:** Package plans. **Facility:** 805 rooms. 17 stories; interior corridors. Fee: parking. **Dining:** Restaurant, coffee shop, deli; rooftop dining rm 6 pm-10 pm; other 6 am-midnight; $12-$35; cocktails. **Services:** giftshop. Fee: massage. **Cards:** AE, CB, DI, DS, JC, MC, VI. *(See color ad p 923)*

INN 1890   Rates Subject to Change   Phone: (415)386-0486   57

◆ ◆ ◆
Historic Bed
& Breakfast

All Year [BP]   1P: $79- 99   2P/1B: $79- 99   2P/2B: $89- 109   XP: $10-15   F3

Location: 1 blk e of Golden Gate Park. 1890 Page St 94117. Fax: 415/386-3626. **Terms:** 2 night min stay. **Facility:** 10 rooms. 3 stories, no elevator; interior corridors; smoke free premises. **All Rooms:** shower baths. **Some Rooms:** 2 kitchens. **Cards:** MC, VI.

(See map p. 919)

KING GEORGE HOTEL
Phone: (415)781-5050   **44**
All Year   1P: $150- 165   2P/1B: $160- 175   2P/2B: $160- 175   XP: $10
Location: Just w of Union Square. 334 Mason St 94102. Fax: 415/391-6976. **Facility:** 143 rooms. Continental breakfast buffet 7-10 am. Some small rooms. Service-oriented staff. 9 stories; interior corridors. Fee: parking.
Hotel   **Dining:** 6:30 am-2:30 pm; afternoon tea. **Cards:** AE, CB, DI, DS, JC, MC, VI. *(See color ad p 946)*

LAUREL MOTOR INN
Phone: (415)567-8467   **72**
All Year [CP]   1P: $80- 96   2P/1B: $88- 104   2P/2B: $88- 104   XP: $8   F12
Location: 1 mi w of US 101 (Van Ness Ave); 1 mi e of Park Presido Blvd (SR 1) at California St. 444 Presidio Ave 94115. Fax: 415/928-1866. **Terms:** Reserv deposit; pets. **Facility:** 49 rooms. Some rooms with
Motel   view of San Francisco skyline. Complimentary covered parking. 4 stories; interior corridors. **Dining:** Restaurant nearby. **Recreation:** discount at health club across the street. **All Rooms:** combo or shower baths. **Some Rooms:** 18 kitchens. **Cards:** AE, CB, DI, DS, JC, MC, VI. **Special Amenities:** Free breakfast.
(See ad below)

LOMBARD MOTOR INN
Phone: 415/441-6000   **65**
AAA   5/15-10/15   1P: $92   2P/1B: $96   2P/2B: $96   XP: $10   F5
2/1-5/14 & 10/16-1/31   1P: $70   2P/1B: $74   2P/2B: $74   XP: $7   F5
Location: On US 101 at Franklin. 1475 Lombard St 94123. Fax: 415/441-4291. **Terms:** Reserv deposit.
Motel   **Facility:** 48 rooms. Complimentary covered parking. 4 stories; interior corridors. **All Rooms:** combo or shower baths. **Cards:** AE, CB, DI, MC, VI. *(See color ad p 938)*

MARK HOPKINS INTER-CONTINENTAL
Phone: (415)392-3434   **6**
All Year   1P: $220- 400   2P/1B: $220- 400   2P/2B: $220- 400   XP: $30   F17
Location: Corner California & Mason sts. 1 Nob Hill 94108. Fax: 415/421-3302. **Terms:** Reserv deposit.
Historic Hotel   **Facility:** 391 rooms. Panoramic view from many rooms. Refined atmosphere. 17 stories; interior corridors. **Dining:** Restaurant; 6:30 am-10:30 pm; $25-$50; cocktails; afternoon tea. **Services:** giftshop; area transportation, limited. Fee: massage. **Cards:** AE, CB, DI, DS, JC, MC, VI. **Special Amenities:** Free newspaper and preferred room (subject to availability with advanced reservations).

MAXWELL HOTEL
Rates Subject to Change   Phone: (415)986-2000   **27**
All Year   1P: $145- 215   2P/1B: $155- 225   2P/2B: $155- 225   XP: $10-20   F12
Hotel   **Location:** Just w of Union Square. 386 Geary St 94102. Fax: 415/397-2447. **Terms:** Reserv deposit.
Facility: 153 rooms. 12 stories; interior corridors. Fee: parking. **All Rooms:** combo or shower baths. **Some Rooms:** kitchen. **Cards:** AE, CB, DI, DS, MC, VI.

MISSION INN
Phone: (415)584-5020   **87**
All Year   1P: $65- 75   2P/1B: $65- 75   2P/2B: $65- 80   XP: $5   F12
Location: 5 mi s; 1 mi e of I-280; Geneva Ave exit & s on Mission St. 5630 Mission St 94112.
Fax: 415/584-1752. **Terms:** Weekly rates. **Facility:** 52 rooms. 8 two-bedroom units. 7 efficiencies & 9 kitchens,
Motel $10 extra charge; 2-4 stories; exterior corridors. **All Rooms:** combo or shower baths. **Cards:** AE, CB, DI, DS, MC, VI. *(See color ad p 937)*

MIYAKO INN BEST WESTERN
Rates Subject to Change   Phone: (415)921-4000   **73**
AAA   4/1-10/31   1P: $95- 115   2P/1B: $109- 129   2P/2B: $105- 125   XP: $10   F18
11/1-1/31   1P: $79- 109   2P/1B: $85- 115   2P/2B: $89- 109   XP: $10   F18
2/1-3/31   1P: $79- 109   2P/1B: $85- 115   2P/2B: $89- 109   XP: $10   F18
Motor Inn   **Location:** 1 mi w of Union Square; 5 blks w of US 101 at Sutter & Buchanan sts; 1 blk from the Japan Center. 1800 Sutter St 94115. Fax: 415/923-1064. **Terms:** Reserv deposit. **Facility:** 125 rooms. Limited pay garage & parking lot; 8 stories; interior corridors. **Dining:** Restaurant; 7 am-10:30 pm; $8-$17; wine/beer only. **Cards:** AE, CB, DI, DS, JC, MC, VI. *(See ad p 933)*

MONTICELLO INN
Rates Subject to Change   Phone: (415)392-8800   **38**
AAA   All Year   1P: $110- 160   2P/1B: $110- 160   2P/2B: $110- 160   XP: $15   F12
Location: Just w of Union Square. 127 Ellis St 94102. Fax: 415/398-2650. **Terms:** Reserv deposit; package
Hotel   plans. **Facility:** 91 rooms. Colonial theme. Few small rooms. 5 stories; interior corridors. **Dining:** Restaurant; 11:30 am-11:30 pm; $13-$16; cocktails. **Services:** complimentary evening beverages. **All Rooms:** combo or shower baths. **Cards:** AE, CB, DI, DS, JC, MC, VI.

(See map p. 919)

NOB HILL LAMBOURNE
◆◆
Hotel

Rates Subject to Change

Phone: (415)433-2287 **49**

2/1-6/30 [CP]	1P: $190- 290 2P/1B: $190- 290	XP: $20 F12
7/1-1/31 [CP]	1P: $200- 300 2P/1B: $200- 300	XP: $20 F12

Location: Just n of Union Square. 725 Pine St 94108. Fax: 415/433-0975. **Facility:** 20 rooms. 3 stories; interior corridors. **Cards:** AE, CB, DI, DS, MC, VI. *(See color ad p 924)*

NOB HILL MOTEL
△△△
◆◆
Motel

Rates Subject to Change

Phone: (415)775-8160 **70**

5/15-10/31 [CP]	1P: $75- 85 2P/1B: $85- 95 2P/2B: $95- 105 XP: $10-15 F18
2/1-5/14 & 11/1-1/31 [EP]	1P: $60- 70 2P/1B: $65- 85 2P/2B: $75- 95 XP: $8-10 F18

Location: Just e of US 101, Van Ness Ave. 1630 Pacific Ave 94109. Fax: 415/673-8842. **Terms:** Reserv deposit, 3 day notice. **Facility:** 29 rooms. Large rooms. 2 two-bedroom units. Covered parking; 3 stories; exterior corridors. **Dining:** Restaurant nearby. **All Rooms:** combo or shower baths. **Cards:** AE, CB, DI, DS, JC, MC, VI. *(See color ad p 949)*

OASIS INN
△△△ SAVE
◆◆
Motel

Phone: (415)885-6865 **79**

5/1-10/31	1P: $89- 99 2P/1B: $89- 99 2P/2B: $109- 119 XP: $5 F12
2/1-4/30 & 11/1-1/31	1P: $79- 89 2P/1B: $79- 89 2P/2B: $99- 109 XP: $5 F12

Location: Just w of US 101, at Eddy St. 900 Franklin St 94109. Fax: 415/474-1652. **Terms:** Reserv deposit, 3 day notice. **Facility:** 59 rooms. Free covered parking. Center garden sundeck. 1 two-bedroom unit. 4 stories; exterior corridors; whirlpool. **Cards:** AE, MC, VI. **Special Amenities:** Early check-in/late check-out and free room upgrade (subject to availability with advanced reservations). *(See color ad below)*

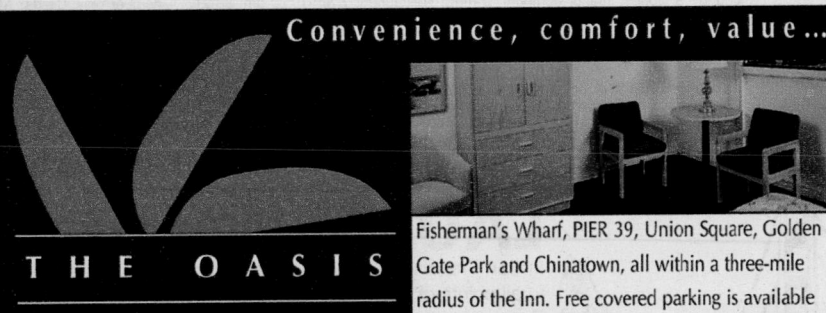

(See map p. 919)

PACIFIC HEIGHTS INN   Rates Subject to Change   Phone: (415)776-3310   95
(AAA)   All Year [CP]   1P: $85- 89   2P/1B: $89- 110   2P/2B: $98- 130
◆ ◆   **Location:** Just w of US 101 (Van Ness Ave). 1555 Union St 94123. Fax: 415/776-8176. **Terms:** Weekly
Motel   rates; small pets only, with prior approval. **Facility:** 40 rooms. Few small rooms. Free parking. 5 two-bedroom
units. 1 apartment, $95-$150 for up to 4 persons. Lower rates in winter; 2 stories; exterior corridors.
All Rooms: combo or shower baths. **Some Rooms:** 17 kitchens, whirlpools. **Cards:** AE, CB, DI, DS, MC,
VI. *(See ad p 948)*

PACIFIC MOTOR INN   Rates Subject to Change   Phone: (415)346-4664   59
(AAA)   5/14-10/15 [CP]   1P: $68- 150   2P/1B: $68- 150   2P/2B: $74- 156   XP: $6
◆ ◆   2/1-5/13 & 10/16-1/31 [CP]   1P: $54- 98   2P/1B: $54- 98   2P/2B: $60- 104   XP: $6
Motel   **Location:** On US 101; at Broderick. 2599 Lombard St 94123. Fax: 415/346-4665. **Facility:** 42 rooms. 3 stories; exterior corridors. **All Rooms:** combo or shower baths. **Cards:** AE, CB, DI, DS, JC, MC, VI.

PALACE HOTEL   Rates Subject to Change   Phone: 415/512-1111   10
◆◆◆◆   5/1-5/31 & 9/1-10/31   1P: $350- 410   2P/1B: $370- 430   2P/2B: $370- 430   XP: $20
Historic Hotel   2/1-4/30, 6/1-8/31 &
11/1-1/31   1P: $330- 390   2P/1B: $350- 410   2P/2B: $350- 410   XP: $20
Location: 0.2 mi e of Union Square; at Market St. 2 New Montgomery St 94105. Fax: 415/543-0671. **Facility:** 550 rooms. A
1909 San Francisco landmark restored to its original elegance. 32 suites, $365-$3000 for up to 2 persons; 9 stories; interior
corridors; heated indoor pool. Fee: parking. **Services:** giftshop. **All Rooms:** combo or shower baths. **Cards:** AE, CB, DI,
DS, JC, MC, VI.

THE PAN PACIFIC HOTEL   Rates Subject to Change   Phone: (415)771-8600   20
(AAA)   9/7-12/31   1P: $315- 420   2P/1B: $315- 420   2P/2B: $315- 420
◆◆◆◆   2/1-9/6 & 1/1-1/31   1P: $300- 400   2P/1B: $300- 400   2P/2B: $300- 400
Hotel   **Location:** Just w of Union Square at Mason St. 500 Post St 94102. Fax: 415/398-0267. **Terms:** Monthly
rates; package plans; small pets only, $50 dep req. **Facility:** 329 rooms. Relaxed elegance. 4 two-bedroom
units. 18 suites, $610-$1700 for up to 2 persons. 2 whirlpool rms, extra charge; 21 stories; interior corridors.
Dining: Restaurant; $27-$34; cocktails. **Services:** giftshop. **Cards:** AE, CB, DI, DS, JC, MC, VI.

PARK HYATT HOTEL   Phone: (415)392-1234   13
(AAA) [SAVE]   All Year   1P: $295- 485   2P/1B: $320- 510   2P/2B: $320- 510   XP: $25   F18
◆◆◆◆   **Location:** In Financial District; At Clay St. 333 Battery St 94111. Fax: 415/421-2433. **Terms:** AP, CP avail;
package plans. **Facility:** 360 rooms. Few rooms with view of bay, some with balcony. 24 stories; interior corri-
Hotel   dors. Fee: parking. **Dining:** Restaurant; 6 am-9:30 pm; $18-$25; cocktails. **Recreation:** discount pass &
charge privilege at nearby health club. **Cards:** AE, CB, DI, DS, JC, MC, VI. *(See color ad p 923)*

PETITE AUBERGE   Rates Subject to Change   Phone: (415)928-6000   8
◆◆◆   All Year [BP]   1P: $120- 245   2P/1B: $120- 245   XP: $15
Hotel   **Location:** Exit US 101 (Van Ness Ave) at Bush St, 6.5 blks e. 863 Bush St 94108. Fax: 415/775-5717.
Terms: Reserv deposit. **Facility:** 26 rooms. French country inn atmosphere. Some units with fireplace. 1 whirl-
pool mini-suite, $220 for 2 persons; 5 stories; interior corridors. Fee: parking. **All Rooms:** combo or shower baths.
Cards: AE, DI, MC, VI.

THE PHOENIX INN   Rates Subject to Change   Phone: (415)776-1380   90
(AAA)   All Year [CP]   1P: $109   2P/1B: $109   2P/2B: $109   XP: $10   F12
◆ ◆   **Location:** Just e of US 101 (Van Ness Ave) at Larkin. 601 Eddy St 94109. Fax: 415/885-3109. **Facility:** 44
Motel   rooms. Original artwork in all units. Landscaped courtyard with original sculpture. Limited free parking.
$139-$149 for up to 2 persons; 2 stories; exterior corridors. **Dining:** Cocktails; restaurant nearby. **Cards:** AE,
CB, DI, DS, JC, MC, VI. *(See color ad p 924)*

THE POWELL HOTEL   Guaranteed Rates   Phone: (415)398-3200   41
◆ ◆   5/15-11/14 [CP]   1P: $110   2P/1B: $125   2P/2B: $125   XP: $15   F12
Hotel   2/1-5/14 & 11/15-1/31 [CP]   1P: $95   2P/1B: $110   2P/2B: $110   XP: $15   F12
Location: Downtown at Powell St cable car turn around. 28 Cyrill Magnin St 94102. Fax: 415/398-3654.
Facility: 108 rooms. 6 stories; interior corridors. **Cards:** AE, CB, DI, DS, JC, MC, VI. *(See color ad p 952)*

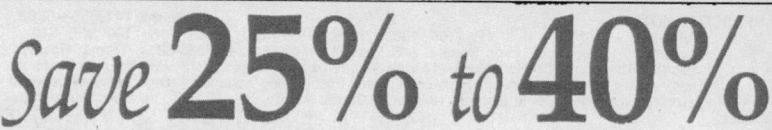

(See map p. 919)

THE PRESCOTT HOTEL
Phone: (415)563-0303 **42**

⬥⬥⬥ Hotel

All Year 1P: $165- 180 2P/1B: $165- 180 2P/2B: $165- 180 XP: $10
Location: 1.5 blk w of Union Square. 545 Post St 94102. Fax: 415/563-6831. **Terms:** Reserv deposit. **Facility:** 164 rooms. Comfortable quiet luxury. 48 one-bedroom suites, $215-$235 for up to 2 persons; 7 stories; interior corridors. **Dining:** Restaurant; also, Postrio, see separate listing. **Services:** complimentary evening beverages. **Some Rooms:** whirlpools. **Cards:** AE, DI, DS, JC, MC, VI. **Special Amenities: Free newspaper.**

QUEEN ANNE HOTEL
Rates Subject to Change **Phone:** 415/441-2828 **72**

⬥⬥⬥ Hotel

All Year [CP] 1P: $110- 275 2P/1B: $120- 275 2P/2B: $120- 275 XP: $10 F12
Location: Just w of US 101 (Van Ness Ave) at Octavia St. 1590 Sutter St 94109. Fax: 415/775-5212. **Terms:** Handling fee imposed. **Facility:** 49 rooms. Individually appointed rooms in a restored Victorian building. Few fireplaces. Limited parking opposite. 4 units with parlor, $175-$275 for 2 persons; 4 stories; interior corridors. Fee: parking. **All Rooms:** combo or shower baths. **Cards:** AE, CB, DI, DS, JC, MC, VI.

RADISSON MIYAKO HOTEL
Phone: (415)922-3200 **76**

⬥⬥⬥ Hotel

All Year 1P: $169- 189 2P/1B: $189- 209 2P/2B: $189- 209 XP: $20 F18
Location: 1 mi w of Union Square, at Laguna St in Japan Center. 1625 Post St 94115. Fax: 415/921-0417. **Facility:** 218 rooms. Japanese garden courtyard. Authentic Japanese suites, $299 & a few western-style suites with sauna, $180-$250. 4 Japanese rooms $189; 16 stories; interior corridors. **Dining:** Restaurant; 6:30 am-10:30 pm; $18-$27; cocktails. **Services:** giftshop. **Some Rooms:** whirlpools. **Cards:** AE, CB, DI, DS, JC, MC, VI. **Special Amenities: Early check-in/late check-out and free newspaper.**

RAMADA LIMITED DOWNTOWN
Phone: (415)861-6469 **114**

⬥⬥ Motel

All Year [CP] 1P: $99 2P/1B: $99- 104 2P/2B: $104- 189 XP: $10 F18
Location: Just s of Market St, between Folsom & Howard sts. 240 7th St 94103. Fax: 415/626-4041. **Terms:** Reserv deposit. **Facility:** 68 rooms. Free limited covered and lot parking. 4 two-bedroom units. 3 stories; interior/exterior corridors. **All Rooms:** combo or shower baths. **Cards:** AE, CB, DI, DS, JC, MC, VI. **Special Amenities: Free breakfast and free room upgrade (subject to availability with advanced reservations).** (See color ad opposite title page & p 953)

RAMADA LIMITED-GOLDEN GATE
Rates Subject to Change **Phone:** (415)775-8116 **113**

⬥⬥ Motel

All Year [CP] 1P: $99- 175 2P/1B: $99- 175 2P/2B: $99- 175 XP: $7 F16
Location: 0.3 mi w of US 101 (Van Ness Ave). 1940 Lombard St 94123. Fax: 415/775-9937. **Terms:** Reserv deposit; handling fee imposed. **Facility:** 37 rooms. Limited free covered parking, ground level. Lower rates in winter; 3 stories, no elevator; interior/exterior corridors. **Some Rooms:** whirlpools. **Cards:** AE, CB, DI, DS, JC, MC.

(See map p. 919)

RAMADA PLAZA-FISHERMAN'S WHARF — Rates Subject to Change — **Phone:** (415)885-4700 99
◆◆◆ — All Year — 1P: $200- 240 — 2P/1B: $200- 250 — 2P/2B: $200- 250 — XP: $10 — F17
Hotel — **Location:** Just sw of the wharf, at Columbus Ave & Jones. 590 Bay St 94133. Fax: 415/771-8945.
Terms: Reserv deposit. **Facility:** 234 rooms. 4 stories; interior corridors. Fee: parking. **Services:** giftshop.
All Rooms: combo or shower baths. **Cards:** AE, CB, DI, DS, JC, MC, VI. *(See color ad opposite title page)*

(See map p. 919)

RAMADA PLAZA HOTEL INTERNATIONAL
Phone: (415)626-8000   **94**

| | 5/1-11/15 | 1P: $119- 159 | 2P/1B: $129- 169 | 2P/2B: $139- 179 | XP: $15 | F18 |
| | 2/1-4/30 & 11/16-1/31 | 1P: $99- 129 | 2P/1B: $109- 139 | 2P/2B: $119- 149 | XP: $15 | F18 |

Location: 1 blk from Civic Auditorium. 1231 Market St 94103. **Fax:** 415/861-1460. **Facility:** 460 rooms. San Francisco landmark. 13 suites, $200-$350 for up to 2 persons; 8 stories; interior corridors. Fee: parking. **Dining:** Restaurant; 6:30 am-10 pm; $12-$25; cocktails. **Services:** giftshop; area transportation, 7 am-9 am. **All Rooms:** combo or shower baths. **Cards:** AE, DI, DS, MC, VI. **Special Amenities:** Early check-in/late check-out. *(See color ad below)*

REDWOOD INN
Rates Subject to Change   **Phone:** (415)776-3800   **56**

| | 5/1-10/31 | 1P: $80- 95 | 2P/1B: $85- 100 | 2P/2B: $95- 110 | XP: $5-10 | F5 |
| | 2/1-4/30 & 11/1-1/31 | 1P: $65- 80 | 2P/1B: $70- 85 | 2P/2B: $80- 95 | XP: $5-10 | F5 |

Location: On US 101. 1530 Lombard St 94123. **Fax:** 415/928-1934. **Terms:** Reserv deposit. **Facility:** 33 rooms. Limited parking. 4 kitchens, $8 extra charge; 2-4 stories; exterior corridors. **Cards:** AE, DI, DS, MC, VI. *(See color ad p 955)*

RENAISSANCE STANFORD COURT HOTEL
Rates Subject to Change   **Phone:** 415/989-3500   **7**

All Year   1P: $226- 250   2P/1B: $226- 250   2P/2B: $226- 250   XP: $39   F18

Location: Atop Nob Hill, at Powell St. 905 California St 94108. **Fax:** 415/391-0513. **Facility:** 400 rooms. 36 suites, $450-$925 for up to 2 persons; 8 stories; interior corridors. **Services:** giftshop. **All Rooms:** combo or shower baths. **Cards:** AE, CB, DI, DS, JC, MC, VI.

THE RITZ-CARLTON, SAN FRANCISCO
Rates Subject to Change   **Phone:** 415/296-7465   **23**

| | 9/1-12/31 | 1P: $400 | 2P/1B: $400 | 2P/2B: $400 | XP: $40 | F18 |
| | 2/1-8/31 & 1/1-1/31 | 1P: $365 | 2P/1B: $365 | 2P/2B: $365 | XP: $40 | F18 |

Location: Just n of Union Square at California St. 600 Stockton St 94108. **Fax:** 415/296-8559. **Terms:** Reserv deposit. **Facility:** 336 rooms. An exceptionally well maintained, service oriented hotel. A Neo-Classical structure. 44 suites, $525-575; 9 stories; interior corridors; heated indoor pool. Fee: parking. **Services:** giftshop; area transportation. Fee: massage. **Cards:** AE, CB, DI, DS, JC, MC, VI.

ROBERTS-AT-THE-BEACH MOTEL
Rates Subject to Change   **Phone:** 415/564-2610   **104**

	6/1-8/31	1P: $69- 85	2P/1B: $69- 89	2P/2B: $79- 99	XP: $10-15	F7
	4/1-5/31 & 9/1-10/31	1P: $59- 69	2P/1B: $59- 69	2P/2B: $69- 79	XP: $8	F7
	2/1-3/31 & 11/1-1/31	1P: $49- 63	2P/1B: $49- 63	2P/2B: $63- 73	XP: $8	F7

Location: Just e of the beach. 2828 Sloat Blvd 94116. **Fax:** 415/681-1376. **Terms:** Reserv deposit, 3 day notice. **Facility:** 30 rooms. 2 stories; exterior corridors. **All Rooms:** shower baths. **Cards:** AE, MC, VI.

(See map p. 919)

ROYAL PACIFIC MOTOR INN
Rates Subject to Change
Phone: (415)781-6661 ❶
All Year
1P: $75- 105   2P/1B: $79- 105 2P/2B: $83- 105 XP: $5
Location: Between Grant Ave & Stockton St, in Chinatown area. 661 Broadway 94133. Fax: 415/781-6688.
Facility: 74 rooms. Limited parking lot & adjacent garage, RV's not permitted; 5 stories; exterior corridors;
sauna. **Dining:** Restaurant nearby. **All Rooms:** combo or shower baths. **Some Rooms:** efficiency.
Cards: AE, CB, DI, MC, VI. *(See color ad below)*

(See map p. 919)

SAN FRANCISCO HILTON & TOWERS Rates Subject to Change **Phone: 415/771-1400** [32]
◆◆◆◆ All Year 1P: $189- 269 2P/1B: $189- 269 2P/2B: $189- 269 XP: $20 F18
Hotel **Location:** Just w of Union Square at Mason St. 333 O'Farrell St 94102. Fax: 415/771-6807. **Terms:** Reserv deposit, 3 day notice; handling fee imposed. **Facility:** 1896 rooms. Few small rooms. Some rooms with city views. Early departure fee; 19-46 stories; interior corridors; heated pool. Fee: parking. **Services:** giftshop. Fee: massage. **Cards:** AE, CB, DI, DS, JC, MC, VI. *(See ad p 119 & below)*

SAN FRANCISCO HOLIDAY INN GOLDEN GATEWAY Rates Subject to Change **Phone: 415/441-4000** [66]
◆◆◆ All Year 1P: $149- 219 2P/1B: $164- 234 2P/2B: $164- 234 XP: $15
Hotel **Location:** US 101 at Pine St. 1500 Van Ness Ave 94109. Fax: 415/776-7155. **Terms:** Check-in 4 pm. **Facility:** 498 rooms. 26 stories; interior corridors. Fee: parking. **Services:** giftshop. **Cards:** AE, DI, DS, JC, MC, VI.

SAN FRANCISCO MARRIOTT Rates Subject to Change **Phone: 415/896-1600** [40]
◆◆◆◆ All Year 1P: $275 2P/1B: $275 2P/2B: $275
Hotel **Location:** 2 blks s of Union Square; 1 blk n of Moscone Center. 55 Fourth St 94103. Fax: 415/777-2799. **Terms:** Check-in 4 pm. **Facility:** 1498 rooms. Suites, $375-$2500 for up to 2 persons; 39 stories; interior corridors; heated indoor pool. Fee: parking. **Services:** giftshop. Fee: massage. **Cards:** AE, DI, DS, JC, MC, VI.

SAN FRANCISCO MARRIOTT FISHERMAN'S WHARF Rates Subject to Change **Phone: 415/775-7555** [98]
◆◆◆ 7/1-11/15 1P: $240 2P/1B: $240 2P/2B: $240 XP: $20 F18
Hotel 2/1-6/30 1P: $175 2P/1B: $175 2P/2B: $175 XP: $20 F18
11/16-1/31 1P: $150 2P/1B: $150 2P/2B: $150 XP: $20 F18
Location: Just s of the wharf at Bay St. 1250 Columbus Ave 94133. Fax: 415/474-2099. **Terms:** Check-in 4 pm. **Facility:** 285 rooms. Limited pay valet parking. 5 stories; interior corridors. **Services:** giftshop. **All Rooms:** combo or shower baths. **Cards:** AE, CB, DI, DS, JC, MC, VI.

SAN FRANCISCO THRIFTLODGE **Phone: (415)467-8811** [111]
(AAA) (SAVE) 5/1-10/31 1P: $62 2P/1B: $62 2P/2B: $88
11/1-1/31 1P: $59 2P/1B: $59 2P/2B: $80
◆◆ 2/1-4/30 1P: $55 2P/1B: $55 2P/2B: $79
Motel **Location:** Just w of US 101, Cow Palace exit & left at first traffic light. 2011 Bayshore Blvd 94134. Fax: 415/468-3097. **Facility:** 103 rooms. Few units with small decks overlooking bay across freeway. A few small units. 4 two-bedroom units. Rate up to 4 persons; 2 stories; exterior corridors; heated indoor pool, sauna. **Dining:** Coffee shop nearby. **All Rooms:** combo or shower baths. **Cards:** AE, CB, DI, DS, JC, MC, VI.
(See color ad p 941)

SAVOY HOTEL Rates Subject to Change **Phone: 415/441-2700** [51]
◆◆ 4/1-10/31 1P: $110- 149 2P/1B: $110- 149 2P/2B: $110- 149 XP: $15
Hotel 2/1-3/31 & 11/1-1/31 1P: $95- 135 2P/1B: $95- 135 2P/2B: $95- 135 XP: $15
Location: 3 blks w of Union Square. 580 Geary St 94102. Fax: 415/441-7172. **Facility:** 83 rooms. Small rooms. Suites, $162-$248; 7 stories; interior corridors. **Cards:** AE, CB, DI, DS, MC, VI.

SEAL ROCK INN Rates Subject to Change **Phone: (415)752-8000** [75]
(AAA) 5/16-9/14 1P: $83- 110 2P/1B: $90- 118 2P/2B: $90- 118 XP: $4-8
2/1-5/15 & 9/15-1/31 1P: $73- 100 2P/1B: $80- 108 2P/2B: $80- 108 XP: $4-8
◆◆ **Location:** 5 mi w of Civic Center; 0.1 mi from beach. 545 Point Lobos Ave 94121. Fax: 415/752-6034.
Motel **Terms:** Reserv deposit; 2 night min stay, weekends. **Facility:** 27 rooms. Some fireplace. Across from Sutro Heights Park. 11 efficiencies, $6 extra charge; 4 stories; exterior corridors; small pool. **Dining:** Coffee shop; 7 am-4 pm, Sat & Sun-6 pm. **All Rooms:** combo or shower baths. **Cards:** AE, CB, DI, MC, VI.

SHANNON COURT HOTEL **Phone: (415)775-5000** [39]
(AAA) (SAVE) All Year 1P: $119 2P/1B: $119 2P/2B: $119 XP: $15 F12
Location: 3 blks w of Union Square, between Jones & Taylor sts. 550 Geary St 94102. Fax: 415/775-9388.
◆◆◆ **Terms:** Handling fee imposed. **Facility:** 171 rooms. Unique architecture. Large comfortable rooms. 15 stories; interior corridors. Fee: parking. **Dining:** Restaurant; 7 am-midnight; $9-$16. **Cards:** AE, DI, DS, JC, MC, VI.
Hotel **Special Amenities:** Preferred room (subject to availability with advanced reservations).
(See color ad p 944)

(See map p. 919)

SHERATON AT FISHERMAN'S WHARF
◆◆◆◆
Hotel
	Rates Subject to Change			Phone: 415/362-5500	106
7/1-10/31	1P: $185	2P/1B: $185	2P/2B: $185	XP: $20	F17
4/1-6/30	1P: $165	2P/1B: $165	2P/2B: $165	XP: $20	F17
2/1-3/31 & 11/1-1/31	1P: $135	2P/1B: $135	2P/2B: $135	XP: $20	F17

Location: Just se of the wharf at Beach St. 2500 Mason St 94133. Fax: 415/956-5275. **Facility:** 524 rooms. 4 stories; interior corridors. Fee: parking. **Services:** giftshop. **All Rooms:** combo or shower baths. **Cards:** AE, CB, DI, DS, JC, MC, VI. *(See color ad below)*

THE SHERMAN HOUSE
◆◆◆
Historic Hotel
| | Guaranteed Rates | | Phone: (415)563-3600 | 101 |
| | 1P: $350- 850 | 2P/1B: $350- 850 | | |

Location: US 101 (Lombard St) exit Fillmore St; 4 blks s. 2160 Green St 94123. Fax: 415/563-1882 **Terms:** Check-in 4 pm; reserv deposit, 7 day notice. **Facility:** 14 rooms. French-Italianate Victorian built in 1876. Wood burning fireplaces. 3 stories, no elevator; interior corridors. **Cards:** AE, CB, DI, MC, VI.

SIR FRANCIS DRAKE HOTEL
AAA SAVE
◆◆
Hotel
			Phone: (415)392-7755	18
4/1-10/31	1P: $155	2P/1B: $155	2P/2B: $165	XP: $15	F16
2/1-3/31 & 11/1-1/31	1P: $130	2P/1B: $135	2P/2B: $135	XP: $15	F16

Location: Just off Union Square at Sutter St. 450 Powell St 94102. Fax: 415/391-8719. **Terms:** Reserv deposit. **Facility:** 417 rooms. Few small rooms. Charm of a bygone era. 24 stories; interior corridors. Fee: parking. **Dining:** 2 restaurants; 6:30 am-11 pm; $15-$35; cocktails. **Services:** giftshop. **All Rooms:** combo or shower baths. **Cards:** AE, CB, DI, DS, JC, MC, VI. **Special Amenities:** Free newspaper and free room upgrade (subject to availability with advanced reservations).

STANYAN PARK HOTEL
AAA
◆◆◆
Historic Bed
& Breakfast
| | Rates Subject to Change | | | Phone: (415)751-1000 | 85 |
| All Year [CP] | 1P: $99- 199 | 2P/1B: $99- 199 | 2P/2B: $99- 199 | | |

Location: 2.5 mi w. 750 Stanyan St 94117. Fax: 415/668-5454. **Terms:** Reserv deposit. **Facility:** 36 rooms. Victorian; some rooms with view of Golden Gate Park; period decor with modern conveniences. 4 two-bedroom units. 4 two-bedroom suites with kitchen, $130-$180 for up to 4 persons; 3 stories; interior corridors. Fee: parking. **Some Rooms:** 6 kitchens. **Cards:** AE, CB, DI, DS, MC, VI.

STAR MOTEL
AAA
◆◆
Motel
	Rates Subject to Change			Phone: (415)346-8250	63
Fri & Sat 2/1-5/14, 5/15-11/15 & Fri & Sat 11/16-1/31	1P: $76- 99	2P/1B: $76- 99	2P/2B: $85- 110	XP: $8	F11
Sun-Thurs 2/1-5/14 & 11/16-1/31	1P: $59- 89	2P/1B: $59- 89	2P/2B: $66- 96	XP: $6	F11

Location: On US 101. 1727 Lombard St 94123. Fax: 415/441-4469. **Facility:** 52 rooms. Few small rooms. 2 stories; exterior corridors. **All Rooms:** combo or shower baths. **Cards:** AE, CB, DI, DS, MC, VI. *(See color ad p 935)*

(See map p. 919)

SUPER 8 BOUTIQUE HOTEL   Rates Subject to Change   **Phone:** (415)673-5232   89

					F15
5/1-10/31	1P: $99	2P/1B: $99	2P/2B: $109	XP: $10	F15
2/1-4/30 & 11/1-1/31	1P: $89	2P/1B: $89	2P/2B: $99	XP: $10	F15

Location: just e of US 101 (Van Ness Ave). 1015 Geary St 94109. Fax: 415/885-2802. **Facility:** 102 rooms. 6 stories; interior corridors. **Dining:** Coffee shop; 7-11 am. **Cards:** AE, CB, DI, DS, JC, MC, VI.
(See color ad below)

SUPER 8 MOTEL   **Phone:** (415)922-0244   93

All Year   1P: $55- 120   2P/1B: $69- 125   2P/2B: $85- 130   XP: $10   D8
Location: On US 101, between Scott & Divisadero sts. 2440 Lombard St 94123. Fax: 415/922-8887. **Terms:** Reserv deposit. **Facility:** 32 rooms. Limited complimentary parking on ground floor. 7 whirlpool rms, extra charge; 3 stories, no elevator; exterior corridors; sauna. **Dining:** Restaurant nearby. **Recreation:** sundeck. **Cards:** AE, CB, DI, DS, JC, MC, VI. **Special Amenities:** Free breakfast.
(See color ad below)

TRAVELODGE BY THE BAY   **Phone:** (415)673-0691   112

5/21-10/31	1P: $95- 110	2P/1B: $110- 135	2P/2B: $115- 140	XP: $10	F18
4/1-5/20	1P: $75- 85	2P/1B: $89- 105	2P/2B: $89- 105	XP: $10	F18
2/1-3/31 & 11/1-1/31	1P: $65- 85	2P/1B: $85- 95	2P/2B: $89- 99	XP: $10	F18

Location: On US 101. 1450 Lombard St 94123. Fax: 415/673-3232. **Terms:** Small pets only, $10 extra charge. **Facility:** 73 rooms. 2 two-bedroom units. 2-3 stories; exterior corridors. Fee: parking. **Dining:** Restaurant nearby. **All Rooms:** combo or shower baths. **Some Rooms:** 5 efficiencies, 2 kitchens, no utensils. **Cards:** AE, CB, DI, DS, JC, MC, VI. **Special Amenities:** Free room upgrade and preferred room (each subject to availability with advanced reservations). *(See color ad p 959)*

(See map p. 919)

TRAVELODGE HOTEL AT FISHERMAN'S WHARF   Phone: (415)392-6700   109
(AAA) (SAVE)   All Year   1P: $145- 185   2P/1B: $135- 185   2P/2B: $135- 185   XP: $10   F18
◆◆   **Location:** At Powell St. 250 Beach St 94133. Fax: 415/986-7853. **Facility:** 250 rooms. Some rooms with view
Motor Inn   of bay. Lower rates in winter; 4 stories; interior corridors. Fee: parking. **Dining:** Coffee shop nearby.
               All Rooms: combo or shower baths. **Cards:** AE, CB, DI, DS, JC, MC, VI. **Special Amenities:** Free
               newspaper. *(See color ad below)*   [icons]

VAGABOND INN—MIDTOWN   Phone: (415)776-7500   67
(AAA) (SAVE)   5/1-11/15   1P: $160- 179   2P/1B: $65- 184   2P/2B: $170- 185   XP: $5   F18
◆◆   2/1-4/30 & 11/16-1/31   1P: $114- 130   2P/1B: $119- 142   2P/2B: $125- 147   XP: $5   F18
Motel   **Location:** On US 101, at Filbert St. 2550 Van Ness Ave 94109. Fax: 415/776-5689. **Terms:** Monthly rates.
               Facility: 132 rooms. Some small rooms. Limited covered parking. 5 stories; interior/exterior corridors; small
               pool. **Dining:** Coffee shop nearby. **All Rooms:** combo or shower baths. **Some Rooms:** 6 kitchens.
Cards: AE, CB, DI, DS, MC, VI. **Special Amenities:** Free breakfast and free local telephone calls.   [icons]

(See map p. 919)

VILLA FLORENCE △△△ ◆◆◆ Hotel

Guaranteed Rates				**Phone:** (415)397-7700		29
12/31-1/31	1P: $140- 190	2P/1B: $140- 190	2P/2B: $160	XP: $15		F17
4/1-10/31	1P: $135- 185	2P/1B: $135- 185	2P/2B: $155	XP: $15		F17
11/1-12/30	1P: $115- 165	2P/1B: $115- 165	2P/2B: $135	XP: $15		F17
2/1-3/31	1P: $115- 165	2P/1B: $115- 165	2P/2B: $135	XP: $15		F17

Location: Just s of Union Square. 225 Powell St 94102. Fax: 415/397-0661. **Terms:** Handling fee imposed; package plans. **Facility:** 180 rooms. European style Hotel with Northern Italian Renaissance Decor. 7 stories; interior corridors. Fee: parking. **Dining:** Restaurant; 7 am-10:30 pm; $10-$17; cocktails. **Services:** complimentary evening beverages. **All Rooms:** combo or shower baths. **Cards:** AE, CB, DI, DS, JC, MC, VI.

WARWICK REGIS HOTEL △△△ SAVE ◆◆◆ Hotel

All Year [CP]   1P: $149- 169   2P/1B: $149- 169   2P/2B: $149- 169   XP: $10 **Phone:** (415)928-7900   43   D12

Location: 2 blks w of Union Sq. 490 Geary St 94102. Fax: 415/441-8788. **Terms:** Reserv deposit. **Facility:** 80 rooms. English & French antiques. 8 stories; interior corridors. Fee: parking. **Dining:** 7 am-9:30 & 5-11 pm, Fri & Sat-midnight; $11-$18; restaurant nearby. **Cards:** AE, CB, DI, DS, JC, MC, VI. **Special Amenities: Free breakfast and free newspaper.**

THE WESTIN ST. FRANCIS △△△ ◆◆◆◆ Hotel

Rates Subject to Change				**Phone:** (415)397-7000	28
9/1-1/31	1P: $250- 280	2P/1B: $250- 280	2P/2B: $250- 280	XP: $30	F18
2/1-8/31	1P: $240- 270	2P/1B: $240- 270	2P/2B: $240- 270	XP: $30	F18

Location: On Union Square. 335 Powell St 94102. Fax: 415/774-0124. **Facility:** 1189 rooms. Nationally famous hotel. Outstanding facilities. 12-32 stories. **Services:** giftshop. Fee: massage. **All Rooms:** combo or shower baths. **Cards:** AE, CB, DI, DS, JC, MC, VI.

THE WHARF INN △△△ ◆◆ Motel

Fri & Sat, Sun-Thurs				**Phone:** (415)673-7411	107
7/1-10/31 & 12/26-1/31	1P: $139- 149	2P/1B: $139- 159	2P/2B: $159- 179		
Sun-Thurs 4/1-6/30	1P: $115- 135	2P/1B: $125- 155	2P/2B: $135- 175		
Sun-Thurs 2/1-3/31 & 11/1-12/25	1P: $99- 109	2P/1B: $99- 129	2P/2B: $119- 139		

Location: 0.1 mi from bay, at Beach St. 2601 Mason St 94133. Fax: 415/776-2181. **Terms:** Reserv deposit. **Facility:** 51 rooms. 1 two-bedroom apartment, $250-$375 for up to 6 persons; 3 stories; exterior corridors. **Dining:** Restaurant nearby. **All Rooms:** combo or shower baths. **Cards:** AE, CB, DI, DS, MC, VI. *(See ad below)*

WHITE SWAN INN ◆◆◆ Hotel

All Year [BP]   1P: $165- 250   2P/1B: $165- 250   2P/2B: $165- 250   XP: $15 **Phone:** (415)775-1755   9

Rates Subject to Change

Location: Exit US 101 (Van Ness Ave) at Bush St. 845 Bush St 94108. Fax: 415/775-5717. **Terms:** Reserv deposit. **Facility:** 26 rooms. English country-inn atmosphere. Fireplaces. Suites, $195-$250 for up to 2 persons; 4 stories; interior corridors. **All Rooms:** combo or shower baths. **Cards:** AE, DI, MC, VI.

YORK HOTEL ◆◆ Hotel

Rates Subject to Change   **Phone:** (415)885-6800   24
All Year [CP]   1P: $99   2P/1B: $99   2P/2B: $109   XP: $10   F12

Location: Just w of Union Square. 940 Sutter St 94109. Fax: 415/885-2115. **Terms:** Reserv deposit. **Facility:** 96 rooms. European boutique style. Few small rooms. 8 stories; interior corridors. Fee: parking. **Cards:** AE, CB, DI, DS, JC, MC, VI.

RESTAURANTS

ALIOTO'S △△△ ◆◆ Seafood

Lunch: $12-$47   **Dinner:** $12-$47   **Phone:** 415/673-0183   31
Location: 8 Fisherman's Wharf 94133. **Hours:** 11 am-11 pm. Closed: 12/25. **Reservations:** suggested. **Features:** casual dress; cocktails & lounge; a la carte. On 3rd floor overlooking fishing fleet. Established 1928. Seafood specialties. Validated parking across. Smoke free premises. **Cards:** AE, CB, DI, MC, VI. *(See ad p 205)*

CAFE MAJESTIC △△△ ◆◆◆ Ethnic

Dinner: $17-$24   **Phone:** 415/441-1100   14
Location: Downtown. 1500 Sutter St 94109. **Hours:** 5 pm-9:30 pm, Sat-10 pm. **Reservations:** suggested. **Features:** semi-formal attire; cocktails & lounge; entertainment; fee for parking & valet parking; a la carte. French-inspired food with Asian undertones served in an elegant Edwardian dining room in an historical 1902 hotel. Smoke free premises. **Cards:** AE, CB, DI, MC, VI.

(See map p. 919)

CAMPTON PLACE RESTAURANT   **Lunch:** $15-$34   **Dinner:** $40-$62   **Phone:** 415/955-5555   ④
◆◆◆◆◆ **Location:** Just n of Union Square; in Campton Place Hotel. 340 Stockton St 94108. **Hours:** 7 am-10:30,
American   11:30 am, 2 & 6-10 pm, Sat 8 am-11, noon-2 & 5:30-10:30 pm, Sun 8 am-11, noon-2 & 6-9:30 pm.
Reservations: suggested. **Features:** semi-formal attire; Sunday brunch; cocktails & lounge; fee for valet
parking; a la carte. American fine dining. Inventive, eclectic dishes with an Asian influence. Artfully prepared. An intimate,
elegant atmosphere. Smoke free premises. **Cards:** AE, CB, DI, JC, MC, VI.   ✕

CARNELIAN ROOM   **Dinner:** $30-$39   **Phone:** 415/433-7500   ⑨
◆◆◆ **Location:** Atop Bank of America Center on 52 floor. 555 California St 94104. **Hours:** 6 pm-10 pm; Sun 10
Continental   am-3 & 6-10 pm. Closed major holidays. **Reservations:** suggested. **Features:** semi-formal attire; Sunday
brunch; cocktails & lounge; fee for parking; a la carte. Spectacular panoramic view. Seasonal California
cuisine. Smoke free premises. **Cards:** AE, CB, DI, MC, VI.   ✕

CASTAGNOLA'S RESTAURANT   **Lunch:** $6-$20   **Dinner:** $10-$34   **Phone:** 415/776-5015   ㊷
◆◆ **Location:** 1 blk w Fishermans Wharf; at Jones St. 286 Jefferson St 94133. **Hours:** 8 am-10 pm, Sat-10:30
Seafood   pm. Closed: 12/25. **Reservations:** suggested. **Features:** casual dress; children's menu; cocktails & lounge;
valet parking; a la carte. Since 1952. Italian specialties also. Smoking in lounge only. Smoke free premises.
Cards: AE, CB, DI, MC.   ✕

CHIC'S SEAFOOD   **Lunch:** $10-$24   **Dinner:** $10-$24   **Phone:** 415/421-2442   ㉚
◆◆ **Location:** 202-A Pier 39 94133. **Hours:** 9 am-11 pm. **Reservations:** accepted. **Features:** No A/C; casual
Seafood   dress; children's menu; cocktails & lounge; fee for parking. Early San Francisco decor. View of marina & bay.
Dinners, lite-fare all day. Smoke free premises. **Cards:** AE, CB, DI, MC, VI.   ✕

CITYSCAPE   **Dinner:** $18-$40   **Phone:** 415/923-5002   ⑮
◆◆◆ **Location:** On 46th floor; in San Francisco Hilton Tower. 333 O'Farrell St 94102. **Hours:** 5:30-10 pm, Sun 10
American   am-2 & 5:30-10 pm. **Reservations:** suggested. **Features:** semi-formal attire; Sunday brunch; cocktails;
entertainment; fee for parking; a la carte. Panoramic view. Dance music 9 pm-midnight. Smoke free
premises. **Cards:** AE, CB, DI, DS, JC, MC, VI.   ✕

THE CLIFF HOUSE   **Lunch:** $10-$20   **Dinner:** $15-$25   **Phone:** 415/386-3330   ㊴
ⒶⒶⒶ **Location:** At Ocean Beach, 6 mi w of downtown. 1090 Point Lobos 94121. **Hours:** 9 am-10:30 pm; Sat 8:30
◆◆   am-11 pm, Sun 8:30 am-10:30 pm. **Reservations:** accepted. **Features:** casual dress; cocktails & lounge;
Seafood   minimum charge-$7; street parking; a la carte. Popular landmark overlooking Seal Rocks & ocean. Seafood
& Beverage Co. downstairs. Specialty omelettes & Sunday brunch & buffet upstairs. Private rooms. Smoke
free premises. **Cards:** AE, CB, DI, MC, VI.   ✕

DALLA TORRE   **Dinner:** $11-$20   **Phone:** 415/296-1111   ㊶
ⒶⒶⒶ **Location:** Just se of Coit Tower, off Union St. 1349 Montgomery St 94133. **Hours:** 5 pm-10 pm.
◆◆◆   **Reservations:** suggested. **Features:** No A/C; casual dress; health conscious menu; cocktails & lounge; fee
Italian   for valet parking; a la carte. Northern Italian specialties. Smoke free premises. **Cards:** AE, CB, DI, DS, MC,
VI.   ✕

DANTE'S   **Lunch:** $9-$17   **Dinner:** $17-$24   **Phone:** 415/421-5778   ㉝
◆◆ **Location:** On Pier 39. 94119. **Hours:** 11 am-10 pm. Closed: 12/25. **Reservations:** suggested. **Features:** No
Seafood   A/C; casual dress; children's menu; cocktails & lounge; a la carte. Attractive decor overlooking harbor.
California cuisine with a Mediterranean twist. Smoke free premises. **Cards:** AE, CB, DI, DS, JC, MC, VI. ✕

THE DINING ROOM   **Dinner:** $58-$72   **Phone:** 415/296-7465   ⑳
◆◆◆◆◆ **Location:** Just n of Union Square at California St; in The Ritz-Carlton. 600 Stockton St 94108. **Hours:** 6
Nouvelle   pm-9 pm. Closed:Sun. **Reservations:** required. **Features:** semi-formal attire; cocktails & lounge; fee for
French   parking; valet parking; prix fixe, a la carte. Original, imaginative cuisine. Exceptional, quality ingredients;
Impeccable service in an elegant atmosphere. 3 to 5 course dinners. Smoke free premises. **Cards:** AE, CB,
DI, DS, MC, VI.   ♿ ✕

EMPRESS OF CHINA   **Lunch:** $10-$17   **Dinner:** $17-$34   **Phone:** 415/434-1345   ⑤
◆◆ **Location:** In Chinatown, on top floor of China Trade Center Building. 838 Grant Ave 94108. **Hours:** 11:30
Chinese   am-3 & 5 pm-10:30 pm, Sun 11:30 am-10:30 pm. **Reservations:** suggested. **Features:** casual dress;
cocktails & lounge; a la carte. Oriental decor; Regional specialties. Smoke free premises. **Cards:** AE, CB, DI,
MC, VI.   ✕

FARALLON   **Lunch:** $10-$18   **Dinner:** $18-$28   **Phone:** 415/956-6969   ㉖
◆◆◆ **Location:** Just w of Union Sq. 450 Post St 94102. **Hours:** 11:30 am-2 & 5:30-10 pm, Fri & Sat-10:30 pm,
Seafood   Sun 5:30 pm-10 pm. Closed major holidays. **Reservations:** suggested. **Features:** casual dress; cocktails &
lounge; fee for valet parking; a la carte. Smoke free premises. **Cards:** AE, MC, VI.   ✕

FIOR D' ITALIA   **Lunch:** $13-$30   **Dinner:** $13-$30   **Phone:** 415/986-1886   ㊼
ⒶⒶⒶ **Location:** 601 Union St 94133. **Hours:** 11:30 am-10:30 pm. **Reservations:** suggested. **Features:** No A/C;
◆◆   casual dress; cocktails; fee for parking & valet parking; a la carte, a la carte. North Beach institution since
Italian   1886. Smoke free premises. **Cards:** AE, CB, DI, MC, VI.   ✕

FLEUR DE LYS   **Dinner:** $25-$35   **Phone:** 415/673-7779   ⑬
◆◆◆◆ **Location:** between Taylor & Jones Sts. 777 Sutter St 94109. **Hours:** 6-10 pm, Fri & Sat 5:30-10:30 pm.
French   Closed: Sun, 1/1, 12/25 & a varying 2 weeks in summer. **Reservations:** required. **Features:** formal attire;
cocktails; fee for valet parking; a la carte. Elegant surroundings, contemporary French cuisine with a
Mediterranean touch. Also, two prix-fixe, one vegetarian. Smoke free premises. **Cards:** AE, CB, DI, DS, MC, VI.   ✕

THE GARDEN COURT   **Lunch:** $29-$40   **Dinner:** $36-$102   **Phone:** 415/546-5089   ㉑
◆◆◆◆ **Location:** Just e of Union Square, at Market St; in Palace Hotel. 2 New Montgomery St 94105. **Hours:** 6:30
American   am-10:30, 11:30-2 & 6-10 pm; high tea 2-4:30 pm. Closed: Sun & Mon for dinner. **Reservations:** suggested.
Features: semi-formal attire; Sunday brunch; cocktails & lounge; entertainment; fee for parking & valet
parking; a la carte. Elegantly restored 1909 landmark. Old world atmosphere in a glass-domed atrium, lavish crystal
chandeliers, marble & gold leaf decor. Classically inspired cuisine in an exceptional setting. Smoke free premises.
Cards: AE, MC, VI.   ♿ ✕

(See map p. 919)

GOLDEN TURTLE   **Dinner:** $8-$25   **Phone:** 415/441-4419   ㉟
◆◆   **Location:** On US 101. 2211 Van Ness Ave 94109. **Hours:** 5-11 pm. Closed: Mon & 12/25.
Ethnic   **Reservations:** accepted. **Features:** casual dress; beer & wine only; minimum charge-$8 per person; fee for parking; a la carte. Vietnamese cuisine & custom decor. Fee for valet parking Fri-Sun. Smoke free premises.
Cards: AE, CB, MC, VI.   ☒

HARRIS'   **Dinner:** $25-$33   **Phone:** 415/673-1888   ㊱
◆◆◆   **Location:** On US 101, at Pacific Ave. 2100 Van Ness Ave 94109. **Hours:** 6:30-11 pm, Sat & Sun from 5
Steakhouse   pm. Closed major holidays. **Reservations:** accepted. **Features:** semi-formal attire; children's menu; cocktails & lounge; minimum charge-$10; fee for valet parking; a la carte. Old San Francisco atmosphere, featuring dry-aged, Mid-Western beef & fresh seafood. Smoking in lounge only. Smoke free premises. **Cards:** AE, DI, DS, JC, MC, VI.   ☒

HAYES STREET GRILL   **Lunch:** $12-$18   **Dinner:** $14-$22   **Phone:** 415/863-5545   ㊸
◆◆◆   **Location:** 320 Hayes St 94102. **Hours:** 11:30 am-2 & 5-9:30 pm, Fri-10:30 pm, Sat 5:30 pm-10:30 pm, Sun
Seafood   5:30 pm-8:30 pm. Closed major holidays. **Reservations:** suggested. **Features:** No A/C; casual dress; cocktails; a la carte. Mesquite grilled seafood, emphasis on fresh ingredients, California style preparation. Smoke free premises. **Cards:** AE, CB, DI, MC, VI.   ☒

HOUSE OF PRIME RIB   **Dinner:** $20-$25   **Phone:** 415/885-4605   ㊲
◆◆◆   **Location:** US 101. 1906 Van Ness Ave 94109. **Hours:** 5:30 pm-10 pm, Sat 4:30 pm-10pm, Sun 4 pm-10
American   pm. **Reservations:** accepted. **Features:** casual dress; children's menu; cocktails & lounge; fee for valet parking; a la carte. Cart brought to guest's table for individual cuts. Also fresh fish, & specialty items. Smoking in lounge only. Smoke free premises. **Cards:** AE, CB, DI, MC, VI.   ☒

THE IRON HORSE   **Lunch:** $9-$15   **Dinner:** $13-$25   **Phone:** 415/362-8133   ⑰
◆◆   **Location:** Just e of Union Square. 19 Maiden Ln 94108. **Hours:** 11:30 am-10 pm, Sun from 5 pm. Closed
Northern   major holidays. **Reservations:** accepted. **Features:** casual dress; children's menu; carryout; cocktails &
Italian   lounge; minimum charge-$10; street parking; a la carte. Smoke free premises. **Cards:** AE, DI, MC, VI.   ☒

JOHN'S GRILL   **Lunch:** $7-$20   **Dinner:** $14-$24   **Phone:** 415/986-0069   ③
🆔   **Location:** 2.5 blks s of Union Square. 63 Ellis St 94102. **Hours:** 11 am-10 pm, Sun 5 pm-10 pm. Closed:
11/26 & 12/25. **Reservations:** suggested. **Features:** casual dress; cocktails; entertainment; a la carte. Since
◆◆   1908 turn-of-the-century decor. Home of the Maltese Falcon. Smoke free premises. **Cards:** AE, DI, MC, VI.
Continental   ☒

JULIUS' CASTLE   Historical   **Dinner:** $23-$40   **Phone:** 415/392-2222   ㊵
🆔   **Location:** Just e of Coit Tower. 1541 Montgomery St 94133. **Hours:** 5 pm-10 pm. **Reservations:** suggested.
Features: casual dress; health conscious menu; cocktails & lounge; fee for valet parking; a la carte.
◆◆◆   Excellent views, romantic setting. Upscale, Regional Italian specialties. Smoke free premises. **Cards:** AE, DI,
Italian   DS, MC, VI.   ☒

KAN'S   **Lunch:** $8   **Dinner:** $10   **Phone:** 415/982-2388   ⑥
◆◆   **Location:** In Chinatown. Upstairs at 708 Grant Ave 94108. **Hours:** 11:30 am-10 pm, Sun from 4 pm.
Chinese   **Reservations:** suggested. **Features:** casual dress; cocktails & lounge; street parking; a la carte.
Long-established Chinese restaurant featuring Cantonese dishes. **Cards:** AE, CB, DI, DS, VI.   ☒

KULETO'S   **Lunch:** $7-$18   **Dinner:** $9-$18   **Phone:** 415/397-7720   ㉒
◆◆◆   **Location:** SW of Union Square at the Villa Florence Hotel. 221 Powell St 94102. **Hours:** 7 am-10:30 &
Italian   11:30-11 pm, Sat & Sun from 8 am. Closed: 11/28, 12/25. **Reservations:** accepted. **Features:** casual dress; cocktails & lounge; fee for parking. In-house cured prosciutto & many other specialties; upscale, lively atmosphere. Smoke free premises. **Cards:** AE, CB, DI, MC, VI.   ☒

LEHR BROS BISTRO & GRILL   **Lunch:** $3-$17   **Dinner:** $9-$27   **Phone:** 415/474-6478   ⑫
◆◆   **Location:** Between Taylor & Jones sts, in Best Western Canterbury Whitehall Hotel. 740 Sutter St 94109.
Seafood   **Hours:** 6:30 am-10:30 pm. **Reservations:** suggested. **Features:** cocktails & lounge; fee for parking; a la carte, a la carte. Indoor garden dining. California cuisine. **Cards:** AE, CB, DI, DS, JC,
MC, VI.

L'OLIVIER   **Lunch:** $11-$15   **Dinner:** $15-$25   **Phone:** 415/981-7824   ㉓
🆔   **Location:** In Golden Gateway Center, off Jackson St. 465 Davis Ct 94111. **Hours:** 11:30 am-2:30 & 5:30-10
pm, Sat from 5:30 pm. Closed major holidays & Sun. **Reservations:** accepted. **Features:** No A/C; casual
◆◆◆   dress; early bird specials; cocktails; fee for parking & valet parking. Award-winning Bouillabaisse & other
Regional   French delights in relaxing quiet atmosphere. Smoke free premises. **Cards:** AE, CB, DI, MC, VI.   ♿ ☒
French

MAHARANI   **Lunch:** $8-$19   **Dinner:** $8-$25   **Phone:** 415/775-1988   ㊳
◆◆   **Location:** Just e of US 101, Van Ness Ave. 1122 Post St 94109. **Hours:** 11:30 am-2:30 & 5-10 pm,
Ethnic   Sat-10:30 pm. **Reservations:** required; for dinner. **Features:** No A/C; casual dress; cocktails; fee for parking; a la carte. Cuisine of India. Lunch in main dining room. Dinner also in traditional cushioned/curtained fantasy room. Smoke free premises. **Cards:** AE, CB, DI, MC, VI.   ☒

THE MANDARIN   **Lunch:** $9-$15   **Dinner:** $15-$25   **Phone:** 415/673-8812   ㉜
◆◆◆   **Location:** Nw corner of Ghirardelli Square; on top floor of Woolen Mill Bldg. 900 N Point St 94109.
Northern   **Hours:** 11:30 am-11 pm. **Reservations:** suggested. **Features:** casual dress; cocktails & lounge;
Chinese   entertainment; fee for parking; a la carte. Excellently prepared Mandarin & Szechuan cuisine. Smoke free premises. **Cards:** AE, CB, DI, DS, MC, VI.   ☒

MASA'S   **Dinner:** $72-$80   **Phone:** 415/989-7154   ㉘
◆◆◆◆   **Location:** Just s of Stockton St. 648 Bush St 94108. **Hours:** 6 pm-9:30 pm. Closed: Sun, Mon, 11/25, 12/24,
12/25 & 2 weeks in Jan; 1st wk in July. **Reservations:** required; $ guarantee req. **Features:** formal attire;
French   cocktails; fee for valet parking; prix fixe. Choice of two fixed menus; elegant, quiet atmosphere. Smoke free premises. **Cards:** AE, CB, DI, DS, MC, VI.   ♿ ☒

(See map p. 919)

MASON'S
◆◆◆◆
American
DI, MC, VI.

Dinner: $26-$35 **Phone:** 415/772-5233 ⑦
Location: Atop Nob Hill, at California St; in Fairmont Hotel & Tower. 950 Mason St 94108. **Hours:** 5:30 pm-10 pm. **Reservations:** suggested. **Features:** semi-formal attire; children's menu; early bird specials; cocktails & lounge; entertainment; fee for parking; a la carte. Softly lit, romantic atmosphere. **Cards:** AE, CB, ⊠

MCCORMICK & KULETO'S
SEAFOOD RESTAURANT
◆◆◆
Seafood

Lunch: $7-$13 **Dinner:** $14-$28 **Phone:** 415/929-1730 ㊺
Location: Ghiradelli Square. 900 North Point St 94109. **Hours:** 11:30 am-11 pm, Sun from 10:30 am. **Reservations:** suggested. **Features:** casual dress; Sunday brunch; cocktails; fee for parking; a la carte. Many tables with view of the bay. Smoke free premises. **Cards:** AE, CB, DI, DS, MC, VI. ⊠

NEW JOE'S
ⒶⒶⒶ
◆◆
Italian

Lunch: $6-$20 **Dinner:** $10-$25 **Phone:** 415/397-9999 ⑯
Location: 1/2 blk sw of Union Square. 347 Geary St 94102. **Hours:** 7 am-11 pm. Closed: 12/25. **Reservations:** suggested. **Features:** casual dress; children's menu; cocktails & lounge; street parking; a la carte, a la carte. Family restaurant; also American cuisine. **Cards:** AE, CB, DI, MC, VI. ⊠

NORTH INDIA RESTAURANT
ⒶⒶⒶ
◆◆◆
Ethnic

Lunch: $9-$16 **Dinner:** $14-$22 **Phone:** 415/931-1556 ㉞
Location: just s of US 101, Lombard St. 3131 Webster St 94123. **Hours:** 11:30 am-2:30 & 5-10:30 pm, Sat from 5 pm, Sun from 4:80 pm. Closed: 11/25 & 12/25. **Reservations:** suggested. **Features:** No A/C; casual dress; beer & wine only; fee for parking; a la carte. North Indian & Pakistani Tandoori & Moghlai cooking. Smoke free premises. **Cards:** AE, CB, DI, DS, MC, VI. ⊠

PACIFIC
◆◆◆◆
Regional
American

Lunch: $10-$20 **Dinner:** $30-$40 **Phone:** 415/929-2087 ㉕
Location: in the Pan Pacific Hotel. 500 Post St 94102. **Hours:** 6:30 am-11 am, 11:30 am-2:30 & 5:30-9:30 pm, Sat & Sun from 7 am, Sun brunch 10 am-2 pm. **Reservations:** suggested. **Features:** casual dress; Sunday brunch; children's menu; cocktails; valet parking; a la carte. California cuisine with French influence, elegant dining room, open & airy. Smoke free premises. **Cards:** AE, CB, DI, MC, VI. ⊠

PALIO D'ASTI
◆◆◆
Italian

Lunch: $10-$25 **Dinner:** $16-$30 **Phone:** 415/395-9800 ⑲
Location: In financial district. 640 Sacramento St 94111. **Hours:** 11:30 am-2:30 & 5:30-9 pm. Closed major holidaysSat & Sun. **Reservations:** suggested. **Features:** casual dress; cocktails; a la carte. Few Regional specialties. Relaxed high-tech atmosphere. Smoke free premises. **Cards:** AE, CB, DI, DS, MC, VI. ⊠

POMPEI'S GROTTO
ⒶⒶⒶ
◆◆
Seafood

Lunch: $9-$16 **Dinner:** $16-$21 **Phone:** 415/776-9265 ㊻
Location: At Fisherman's Wharf. 340 Jefferson St 94133. **Hours:** 8 am-11 pm. Closed: 12/25. **Reservations:** accepted. **Features:** No A/C; casual dress; children's menu; cocktails & lounge; minimum charge-4.00; fee for parking; a la carte, a la carte. Homemade pasta & Northern Italian dishes. Smoke free premises. **Cards:** AE, CB, DI, MC, VI. ⊠

POSTRIO
◆◆◆
American
California
MC, VI.

Lunch: $25-$30 **Dinner:** $55-$60 **Phone:** 415/776-7825 ㉗
Location: just w of Union Square; at The Prescott Hotel. 545 Post St 94102. **Hours:** 7 am-10, 11:30-2 & 5:30-10 pm, Sat & Sun 9 am-2 & 5:30-10 pm, Sat-10:30 pm. Closed: 7/4, 11/26 & 12/25. **Reservations:** required. **Features:** casual dress; Sunday brunch; cocktails & lounge; fee for valet parking. cuisine with Asian & Mediterranean influences in a lively atmosphere. Smoke free premises. **Cards:** AE, CB, DI, ⊠

RICK'S RESTAURANT & BAR
ⒶⒶⒶ
◆◆
American

Dinner: $11-$20 **Phone:** 415/731-8900 ㊽
Location: Between 29th & 30th aves. 1940 Taraval St 94116. **Hours:** 4:30 pm-10 pm, Sat 5 pm-10:30 pm. Closed: 1/1, 9/8 & 12/25. **Reservations:** accepted. **Features:** No A/C; casual dress; Sunday brunch; children's menu; early bird specials; cocktails & lounge; entertainment; minimum charge-$5; fee for parking; a la carte. Emphasis on San Francisco food. Upscale, lively atmosphere. Smoke free premises. **Cards:** AE, MC, VI. ⊠

SCOMA'S RESTAURANT
ⒶⒶⒶ
◆◆◆
Seafood

Lunch: $8-$55 **Dinner:** $8-$55 **Phone:** 415/771-4383 ㊹
Location: Fisherman's Wharf Pier 47 94133. **Hours:** 11:30 am-10:30 pm, Sat-11 pm. Closed: 11/26, 12/24 & 12/25. **Features:** casual dress; children's menu; cocktails & lounge; minimum charge-$8; valet parking; a la carte. Casual atmosphere. Popular landmark restaurant. Smoke free premises. **Cards:** AE, CB, DI, DS, MC, VI. ⊠

SCOTT'S SEAFOOD GRILL
◆◆
Seafood

Lunch: $10-$18 **Dinner:** $16-$25 **Phone:** 415/981-0622 ⑪
Location: On Promenade level. 3 Embarcadero Center 94111. **Hours:** 11 am-10 pm, Sun 4:30 pm-9:30 pm. Closed major holidays. **Reservations:** suggested. **Features:** casual dress; children's menu; health conscious menu; cocktails & lounge; a la carte. In the heart of the Financial District. Also prime steak. Smoke free premises. **Cards:** AE, CB, DI, MC, VI.

STARS RESTAURANT
◆◆
American
MC, VI.

Lunch: $10-$15 **Dinner:** $20-$30 **Phone:** 415/861-7827 ㉙
Location: 1 blk e of US 101 (Van Ness Avenue) between Redwood & Golden Gate. 555 Golden Gate 94103. **Hours:** 11:30 am-2 & 6-11 pm, Sat & Sun from 6 pm. Closed major holidays. **Reservations:** suggested. **Features:** No A/C; semi-formal attire; cocktails; entertainment; fee for valet parking; a la carte. Open kitchen & bar; local favorite serving the theatre district. Smoke free premises. **Cards:** AE, DI, DS, ⊠

THE WATERFRONT
◆◆◆
Seafood

Lunch: $14-$23 **Dinner:** $18-$35 **Phone:** 415/391-2696 ①
Location: Just n of the Ferry Bldg, on The Embarcadero. Pier 7 94111. **Hours:** 11:30 am-10:30 pm. Closed: 12/25. **Reservations:** required. **Features:** semi-formal attire; cocktails; valet parking; a la carte. Innovative cuisine at ground floor "cafe" terrace on the bay, Asian specialties at their second-story "restaurant" overlooking Bay Bridge. Smoke free premises. **Cards:** AE, DI, MC, VI. ♿ ⊠

♿ = The lodging establishment or restaurant can accommodate wheelchair travelers.

The San Francisco Vicinity

BELMONT—24,100   (See map p. 922; index p. 918)

LODGING

HOLIDAY INN EXPRESS HOTEL & SUITES   Rates Subject to Change   **Phone:** 650/654-4000
[FYI]   All Year [CP]   1P: $129- 169   2P/1B: $129- 169   2P/2B: $129- 169   XP: $10
Too new to rate. **Location:** US 101, exit Ralston Ave, w to SR 82, just s. 1650 El Camino Real 94002.
Motel   Fax: 650/654-4001. **Facility:** 82 rooms. 5 whirlpool rms, extra charge; 3 stories; interior corridors. **Cards:** AE, CB, DI, DS, MC, VI.

RESTAURANT

PINE BROOK INN   **Lunch:** $6-$13   **Dinner:** $9-$20   **Phone:** 650/591-1735   [79]
◆◆   **Location:** At Ralston Ave; in Carlmont Village Shopping Center. 1015 Alameda de las Pulgas 94002.
Continental   **Hours:** 11:30 am-2:30 & 5:30-9:30 pm, Fri-10 pm, Sat 11:30 am-10 pm, Sun 10:30 am-2 & 5-9 pm. Closed: Mon, July 4-8th, Jan 1-5th. **Reservations:** suggested. **Features:** casual dress; children's menu; early bird specials; cocktails & lounge; a la carte. Popular, long established, family owned; fresh seafood & German specialties, some tables have brookside view. Smoke free premises. **Cards:** AE, MC, VI.

BURLINGAME—26,800   (See map p. 922; index p. 916)

LODGINGS

CROWNE PLAZA   Rates Subject to Change   **Phone:** 650/340-8500   [137]
◆◆◆◆   All Year   1P: $175- 205   2P/1B: $175- 205   2P/2B: $175- 205   XP: $10   F18
Hotel   **Location:** 0.3 mi E of US 101; Broadway-Burlingame or Anza Blvd exits. 600 Airport Blvd 94010.
Fax: 650/343-1546. **Facility:** 404 rooms. Many units overlooking bay. 15 stories; interior corridors; heated indoor pool. **Services:** giftshop. **Cards:** AE, CB, DI, DS, JC, MC, VI.

DOUBLETREE HOTEL-SAN FRANCISCO AIRPORT   Rates Subject to Change   **Phone:** (650)344-5500   [133]
◆◆◆   All Year   1P: $159- 229   2P/1B: $159- 229   2P/2B: $159- 229   XP: $10   F
Hotel   **Location:** Just E of US 101; Broadway-Burlingame or Anza Blvd exits. 835 Airport Blvd 94010.
Fax: 650/340-8851. **Facility:** 391 rooms. Many rooms with bay view. Bay view rooms $10 extra charge; lower rates in winter; 8 stories; interior corridors. **Services:** giftshop. **All Rooms:** combo or shower baths. **Cards:** AE, CB, DI, DS, MC, VI.

EMBASSY SUITES-SFO   Rates Subject to Change   **Phone:** (650)342-4600   [132]
◆◆◆◆   All Year [BP]   1P: $139- 219   2P/1B: $154- 234   XP: $15   F12
Suite Hotel   **Location:** Just e of US 101; Broadway-Burlingame or Anza Blvd exits. 150 Anza Blvd 94010.
Fax: 650/343-8137. **Facility:** 340 rooms. On the bay. Many rooms with a view. Bayview units $20 extra charge; 9 stories; interior corridors; heated indoor pool. **Services:** giftshop. Fee: massage. **Cards:** AE, CB, DI, DS, JC, MC, VI.
(See color ad p 931)

HYATT REGENCY-SAN FRANCISCO AIRPORT   **Phone:** (650)347-1234   [129]
(AAA) [SAVE]   All Year   1P: $235- 270   2P/1B: $260- 295   2P/2B: $260- 295   XP: $25   F18
Fax: 650/347-5948. **Terms:** CP avail. **Facility:** 793 rooms. Some rooms with view of bay or hills. 8-story atrium with translucent-fabric roof. 11 stories; interior corridors; small pool, saunas, whirlpool. Fee: parking.
◆◆◆◆   **Dining:** Dining room, restaurant; 6:30 am-11 pm, deli 24 hrs; $15-$35; cocktails. **Services:** giftshop.
Hotel   Fee: massage. **All Rooms:** combo or shower baths. **Cards:** AE, CB, DI, DS, JC, MC, VI. *(See color ad p 923)*

PARK PLAZA   Rates Subject to Change   **Phone:** (650)342-9200   [134]
◆◆◆   All Year   1P: $180- 210   2P/1B: $180- 210   2P/2B: $180- 210   XP: $15   F18
Hotel   **Location:** Just E of US 101; Broadway-Burlingame or Old Bayshore exits. 1177 Airport Blvd 94010.
Fax: 650/342-1655. **Facility:** 303 rooms. Some rooms with bay view. 10 stories; interior corridors; heated indoor/outdoor pool. **Services:** giftshop. **Cards:** AE, CB, DI, DS, MC, VI.

(See map p. 922)

RAMADA SAN FRANCISCO AIRPORT
Phone: (650)347-2381 **130**
(AAA) (SAVE)   All Year   1P: $165   2P/1B: $165   2P/2B: $165   XP: $10   F18
◆◆◆   **Location:** Just e of US 101; Broadway-Burlingame or Old Bayshore exits. 1250 Old Bayshore Hwy 94010.
Hotel   Fax: 650/348-8838. **Terms:** Package plans. **Facility:** 146 rooms. Many rooms facing the bay. 3 stories; interior
corridors. **Dining:** Restaurant nearby. **Cards:** AE, DI, DS, MC, VI. **Special Amenities:** Free local telephone
calls and free newspaper. *(See ad p 965 & color ad opposite title page)*

RED ROOF INN
Phone: (650)342-7772 **135**
(AAA) (SAVE)   7/2-11/24   1P: $101- 121   2P/1B: $111- 131   2P/2B: $121- 141   XP: $10   F18
◆◆   4/30-7/1   1P: $81- 101   2P/1B: $91- 111   2P/2B: $101- 121   XP: $10   F18
Motor Inn   11/25-1/31   1P: $86- 96   2P/1B: $96- 106   2P/2B: $106- 116   XP: $10   F18
        2/1-4/29   1P: $71- 91   2P/1B: $81- 101   2P/2B: $91- 111   XP: $10   F18
Location: Just s of airport; US 101, Broadway-Burlingame or E Anza Blvd exits. 777 Airport Blvd 94010.
Fax: 650/342-2635. **Terms:** Pets, $10 extra charge. **Facility:** 200 rooms. Some units with bay or canal view. 5 stories; exterior
corridors. **Dining:** Coffee shop nearby. **Cards:** AE, CB, DI, DS, MC, VI. **Special Amenities:** Free local telephone calls.
(See color ad below)

SAN FRANCISCO AIRPORT MARRIOTT
Rates Subject to Change   Phone: 650/692-9100 **139**
◆◆◆◆   Sun-Thurs   1P: $219   2P/1B: $219   2P/2B: $219
Hotel   Fri & Sat   1P: $139   2P/1B: $139   2P/2B: $139
Location: Just e of US 101; Millbrae Ave exit. 1800 Old Bayshore Hwy 94010. Fax: 650/692-8016.
Facility: 684 rooms. On the Bay, many rooms with view. Max rates for up to 4 persons; 11 stories; interior corridors; heated
indoor pool. Fee: parking. **Services:** giftshop. **Recreation:** Fee: bicycles. **Cards:** AE, CB, DI, DS, JC, MC.

VAGABOND INN-AIRPORT
Phone: (650)692-4040 **140**
(AAA) (SAVE)   All Year [CP]   1P: $75- 100   2P/1B: $75- 100   2P/2B: $85- 115   XP: $5   F18
◆◆   **Location:** Just e of US 101; Millbrae Ave exit. 1640 Bayshore Hwy 94010. Fax: 650/692-5314.
Motel   **Terms:** Package plans; pets, $5 extra charge. **Facility:** 91 rooms. Some rooms overlook the bay. 3 stories; ex-
terior corridors. **Dining:** Restaurant nearby. **Cards:** AE, DI, DS, MC, VI. **Special Amenities:** Free
breakfast and free local telephone calls.

RESTAURANTS

GULLIVER'S   Lunch: $10-$19   Dinner: $22-$32   Phone: 650/692-6060 **52**
◆◆   **Location:** Just e of US 101, Millbrae Ave exit. 1699 Old Bayshore Hwy 94010. **Hours:** 11:30 am-2:30 &
American   5:30-9:30 pm, Fri & Sat 5 pm-10 pm. **Reservations:** suggested. **Features:** casual dress; children's menu;
health conscious menu; cocktails & lounge. English pub atmosphere. Prime rib & seafood. Smoke free
premises. **Cards:** AE, DI, MC, VI.

KULETO'S TRATTORIA   Lunch: $8-$17   Dinner: $8-$17   Phone: 650/342-4922 **53**
◆◆◆   **Location:** Just w of US 101, Burlingame exit. 1095 Rollins Rd 94010. **Hours:** 11:30 am-10 pm, Sat 5 pm-11
Italian   pm, Sun 4 pm-10 pm. Closed major holidays. **Reservations:** accepted. **Features:** casual dress; children's
menu; carryout; cocktails & lounge; valet parking; a la carte. Upscale atmosphere; exhibition kitchen with
oakwood grill. Smoke free premises. **Cards:** AE, CB, DI, DS, MC, VI.

Senior Discount: Some establishments offer the senior discount
with either the **Guaranteed Rates** option or the **Rates Subject to
Change** option. Where the words "senior discount" are included in
a listing, a minimum discount of
10 percent off the prevailing or guaranteed rate is available.

CORTE MADERA—8,300

LODGINGS

BEST WESTERN CORTE MADERA INN　　　　　　　　　　　　　　　**Phone: (415)924-1502**
(AAA) [SAVE]　　All Year [CP]　　　　1P: $89- 125　2P/1B:　$99- 135　2P/2B:　$99- 135　XP: $10　　　F17
◆◆◆　　**Location:** W off & adjacent to US 101; southbound exit Madera Blvd; northbound 1 blk w via Tamalpias
Motor Inn　Rd-Paradise Dr exit, then 3 blks n via Madera Blvd. 1815 Redwood Hwy 94925. Fax: 415/924-5419.
　　Facility: 110 rooms. Attractively landscaped garden area. Many rooms with patio. 6 two-bedroom units. 2 stories; exterior corridors; wading pool, whirlpools; playground. **Dining:** Coffee shop; 6:30 am-midnight; Fri &
Sat-2 am; $9-$16; cocktails. **All Rooms:** combo or shower baths. **Some Rooms:** kitchen, whirlpools. **Cards:** AE, CB, DI,
DS, JC, MC, VI. **Special Amenities: Early check-in/late check-out and free breakfast.** *(See color ad p 934)*

MARIN SUITES HOTEL　　　　　　　　　　　　　　　　　　　**Phone: (415)924-3608**
(AAA) [SAVE]　　All Year [CP]　　　　　1P: $99- 149　2P/1B: $119- 169　2P/2B: $149- 199　XP: $10　　　F17
◆◆　　**Location:** Exit US 101 via Tamalpais Rd/Paradise Dr exit. 45 Tamal Vista Blvd 94925. Fax: 415/924-0761.
Motel　　**Facility:** 100 rooms. One & two bedroom suites with fully equipped kitchens & separate living rooms. 28 two-bedroom units. 3 stories; exterior corridors. **Dining:** Restaurant nearby. **Some Rooms:** 84 kitchens.
(See ad below)　　**Cards:** AE, CB, DI, DS, MC, VI. **Special Amenities: Free breakfast and free local telephone calls.**

DALY CITY—92,300　(See map p. 922; index p. 918)

LODGINGS

DAYS INN　　　　　　　　　　　　　　　　　　　　　　**Phone: (415)467-5600**　225
(AAA) [SAVE]　　All Year [CP]　　　　　1P: $60- 100　2P/1B: . $60- 150　2P/2B: $60- 200　XP: $10　　　F12
◆◆　　**Location:** 0.5 mi w of US 101, Cow Palace/Brisbane exit. 3255 Geneva Ave 94014. Fax: 415/467-0491.
Motel　　**Terms:** Reserv deposit. **Facility:** 35 rooms. Across P G & E sub-station; near cow palace. 2 stories; exterior
corridors. **Some Rooms:** whirlpools. **Cards:** AE, CB, DI, DS, JC, MC, VI. **Special Amenities: Free
breakfast and free local telephone calls.** *(See color ad below)*

ROYAL PALACE INN　　　　　　　　　　　　　　　　　　　**Phone: (415)468-4550**　226
(AAA) [SAVE]　　All Year　　　　　1P: $67- 77　2P/1B: $67- 77　2P/2B: . $80- 90　XP: $10　　　F13
◆　　**Location:** 0.6 mi w of US 101; Cow Palace/Brisbane exit. 2929 Geneva Ave 94014. **Terms:** Reserv deposit,
Motel　4 day notice. **Facility:** 20 rooms. Across PG & E substation; near Cow Palace. Max rates for up to 4 persons;
2 stories; exterior corridors. **Some Rooms:** whirlpools. **Cards:** AE, CB, DI, DS, MC, VI.

FOSTER CITY—28,200   (See map p. 922; index p. 917)

LODGINGS

COURTYARD BY MARRIOTT
◆◆◆   All Year
Motor Inn
Rates Subject to Change   Phone: 650/377-0600   **183**
1P: $139   2P/1B: $139   2P/2B: $139   XP: $10
Location: SE of jct US 101 & SR 92, exit SR 92 at Foster City Blvd S. 550 Shell Blvd 94404.
Fax: 650/377-1983. **Facility:** 147 rooms. 3 stories; interior corridors; indoor pool. **Cards:** AE, CB, DI, DS,
MC, VI.

CROWN PLAZA FOSTER CITY
◆◆◆   Sun-Thurs
Hotel   Fri & Sat
Rates Subject to Change   Phone: 650/570-5700   **182**
1P: $189- 219   2P/1B: $189- 219   2P/2B: $189- 219   XP: $10-15   F18
1P: $89- 149   2P/1B: $89- 149   2P/2B: $89- 149   XP: $10-15   F18
Location: 1 mi e of jct US 101 & SR 92; exit SR 92 at Foster City Blvd, 0.3 mi n. 1221 Chess Dr 94404.
Fax: 650/570-0540. **Facility:** 360 rooms. Executive tower rooms have complimentary internet access unique hi-tech decor. 5
stories; interior corridors; heated indoor pool. **Services:** giftshop; area transportation. **Cards:** AE, CB, DI, DS, JC, MC, VI.

HALF MOON BAY—8,900   (See map p. 922; index p. 918)

LODGINGS

BEACH HOUSE INN & CONFERENCE CENTER   Rates Subject to Change   Phone: (650)712-3300   **212**
◆◆◆   All Year [CP]   1P: $165- 265   2P/1B: $165- 265   F16
Motor Inn   **Location:** SR 1; 3 mi n of SR 92. 4100 Hwy 1 N 94019 (PO Box 129). Fax: 650/712-0693. **Terms:** Check-in
4 pm; reserv deposit. **Facility:** 54 rooms. Wood burning fireplaces. 3 stories; interior corridors; smoke free
premises; oceanview. **Services:** Fee: massage. **All Rooms:** efficiencies. **Cards:** AE, CB, DI, DS, MC, VI.
(See color ad below)

CYPRESS INN ON MIRAMAR BEACH   Phone: (650)726-6002   **209**
(AAA) (SAVE)   All Year [BP]   1P: $170- 275   2P/1B: $170- 275   2P/2B: $170- 275   XP: $20
        Location: 3 mi n of SR 92, off SR 1; exit Medio Ave w. 407 Mirada Rd 94019. Fax: 650/712-0380.
◆◆◆   **Terms:** Reserv deposit, 10 day notice; weekly rates. **Facility:** 12 rooms. Beach opposite. Modern decor. Most
Bed &   rooms have rooms overlooking ocean; all have fireplace. Penthouse suite with fireplace, whirlpool, refrig-
Breakfast   erator, $275 for 2 persons; 3 stories, no elevator; interior corridors; smoke free premises.
        Services: complimentary evening beverages. Fee: massage. **All Rooms:** combo or shower baths.
Some Rooms: color TV, whirlpools. **Cards:** AE, DS, MC, VI. **Special Amenities: Free breakfast and free local telephone
calls.**

GOOSE & TURRETS BED & BREAKFAST INN   Guaranteed Rates   Phone: (650)728-5451   **217**
◆◆   All Year [BP]   1P: $100- 140   2P/1B: $100- 140   2P/2B: $120
Bed &   **Location:** 7.5 mi n in Montara; exit SR 1E via 2nd St, s on Main, e on 3rd, 0.5 mi becomes George St(10 mi
Breakfast   s of San Francisco). 835 George St 94037-0937 (PO Box 937, MONTARA, 94037). Fax: 650/728-0141.
        Terms: Check-in 4 pm; reserv deposit, 3 day notice. **Facility:** 5 rooms. In a quiet residential area; homey at-
mosphere; afternoon tea. 1 story; interior corridors; smoke free premises. **All Rooms:** combo or shower baths. **Cards:** AE,
DI, DS, MC, VI.

HALF MOON BAY LODGE   Phone: (650)726-9000   **210**
(AAA) (SAVE)   7/2-11/13 [CP]   1P: $160- 220   2P/1B: $160- 220   2P/2B: $160- 220   XP: $10   F17
        3/13-7/1 & 11/14-1/31 [CP]   1P: $150- 200   2P/1B: $150- 200   2P/2B: $150- 200   XP: $10   F17
◆◆◆◆   2/1-3/12 [CP]   1P: $145- 195   2P/1B: $145- 195   2P/2B: $145- 195   XP: $10   F17
Motel   **Location:** 2.5 mi s of jct SR 92 on w side of SR 1. 2400 S Cabrillo Hwy 94019. Fax: 650/726-7951.
        Terms: Check-in 3:30 pm; package plans. **Facility:** 81 rooms. Rooms with view of golf course; some with fire-
place. All rooms have patio or balcony. 4 two-bedroom units. 2 stories; exterior corridors; sauna; whirlpool.
Dining: Restaurant nearby. **Some Rooms:** whirlpools. **Cards:** AE, CB, DI, DS, JC, MC, VI. **Special Amenities: Free
newspaper and preferred room (subject to availability with advanced reservations).**
(See color ad inside back cover & p 969)

HARBOR VIEW INN   Rates Subject to Change   Phone: 650/726-2329   **214**
◆◆   2/1-10/31   1P: $70   2P/1B: $85   2P/2B: $100
Motel   11/1-1/31   1P: $65   2P/1B: $75   2P/2B: $85
        Location: 4 mi n in El Granada; just e of SR 1. 51 Ave Alhambra 94018 (PO Box 127, EL GRANADA).
Facility: 17 rooms. Across the hwy from Pillar Point Harbor. 2 stories; exterior corridors; oceanview. **All Rooms:** shower
baths. **Cards:** AE, MC, VI.

(See map p. 922)

MILL ROSE INN, SPA & GARDEN SUITES   Rates Subject to Change   **Phone:** (650)726-8750   ⓦ
All Year [BP]   1P: $165- 285   2P/1B: $165- 285   2P/2B: $165- 285   XP: $25
Location: 615 Mill St 94019. Fax: 650/726-3031. **Terms:** Reserv deposit, 7 day notice, room credit in lieu of
refund; handling fee imposed. **Facility:** 6 rooms. Elegant & charming decor; most with fireplace. Lavish flower
Bed & gardens. 2 two-room suites with fireplace & 1 with large whirlpool tub, $255-$285 for 2 persons; 2 stories; ex-
Breakfast terior corridors; enclosed whirlpool. **Services:** complimentary evening beverages. **Recreation:** stereo tape
decks. **All Rooms:** combo or shower baths. **Some Rooms:** whirlpools. **Cards:** AE, DI, DS, MC, VI.

OLD THYME INN   Rates Subject to Change   **Phone:** 650/726-1616   ⓦ
All Year [BP]   1P: $99- 250   2P/1B: $99- 250   XP: $25
Bed & **Location:** 779 Main St 94019. Fax: 650/726-6394. **Terms:** Reserv deposit, 14 day notice; handling fee
Breakfast imposed. **Facility:** 7 rooms. 1899 Queen Anne Victoria; fresh herb gardens. 2 stories; interior corridors; des-
ignated smoking area. **Some Rooms:** color TV. **Cards:** AE, DS, MC, VI.

RAMADA LIMITED   **Phone:** (650)726-9700   ⓦ
Fri & Sat 4/1-10/31 [CP]   1P: $120- 160   2P/1B: $120- 170   2P/2B: $120- 170   XP: $10   F12
Sun-Thurs 4/1-10/31 [CP]   1P: $100- 150   2P/1B: $100- 150   2P/2B: $100- 150   XP: $10   F12
Fri & Sat 2/1-3/31 &
Motel 11/1-1/31 [CP]   1P: $80- 120   2P/1B: $80- 120   2P/2B: $80- 120   XP: $10   F12
Sun-Thurs 2/1-3/31 &
11/1-1/31 [CP]   1P: $60- 100   2P/1B: $60- 100   2P/2B: $60- 100   XP: $10   F12
Location: 2 mi n of SR 92 on SR 1. 3020 N. Cabrillo Hwy 94019. Fax: 650/726-5269. **Terms:** Weekly rates. **Facility:** 20
rooms. Very attractive comfortable rooms. 3 whirlpool rms, extra charge; 2 stories; exterior corridors. **Dining:** Restaurant
nearby. **Cards:** AE, CB, DI, DS, JC, MC, VI. **Special Amenities:** Early check-in/late check-out and free breakfast.

SEAL COVE INN   Rates Subject to Change   **Phone:** (650)728-4114   ⓦ
All Year [BP]   1P: $180- 260   2P/1B: $180- 260   2P/2B: $180- 260   XP: $25
Bed & **Location:** 6.5 mi n in Moss Beach, exit SR1; at Cypress St w. (221 Cypress Ave, MOSS BEACH, 94038).
Breakfast Fax: 650/728-4116. **Terms:** Reserv deposit, 7 day notice; handling fee imposed. **Facility:** 10 rooms. Adjacent
to Fitzgerald Marine Reserve, tide pool & beach area. Closed Christmas. 2 whirlpool rms, extra charge; 2 sto-
ries; interior corridors; smoke free premises. **Cards:** AE, DS, MC, VI.

RESTAURANTS

THE DISTILLERY   Lunch: $7-$15   Dinner: $14-$23   **Phone:** 650/728-5595   ⑳
Location: 6.5 mi n of SR 92 & 1 (Pacific Coast Hwy), exit SR 1 at Cypress St & follow signs. Beach &
Ocean 94038. **Hours:** noon-3 & 5:30-8:30 pm; Sat noon-3 & 4:30 pm-10 pm; Sun 10 am-2:30 & 4:30-10 pm.
Seafood **Reservations:** required. **Features:** casual dress; Sunday brunch; children's menu; cocktails & lounge.
Established 1927. Cliff side location, spectacular ocean views. California point of historical interest. Smoke
free premises. **Cards:** CB, DI, MC, VI.

MIRAMAR BEACH RESTAURANT   Lunch: $7-$14   Dinner: $14-$24   **Phone:** 650/726-9053   ⑲
Location: W of SR 1, 2.7 mi n of SR 92. 131 Mirada Rd 94019. **Hours:** 11:30 am-3:30 & 4:30-10 pm, Sat 11
Steak and am-3:30 & 4:30-10 pm, Sun 10 am-3:30 & 4:30-10 pm. Closed: 11/25 & 12/25. **Reservations:** suggested.
Seafood **Features:** No A/C; casual dress; Sunday brunch; children's menu; cocktails & lounge; a la carte. Pasta
specialties, ocean view, busy & popular. Smoke free premises. **Cards:** DS, MC, VI.

THE SHORE BIRD   Lunch: $7-$16   Dinner: $16-$21   **Phone:** 650/728-5542   ㉑
Location: 4 mi n of jct SR 92 & SR 1 in Princeton-by-the-Sea. 390 Capistrano Rd 94019. **Hours:** 11:30
am-3:30 & 5 pm-9 pm, Sat 11 am-3:30 & 4:30-9 pm, Sun 10 am-3 & 4:30-9 pm. **Reservations:** required.
Seafood **Features:** casual dress; children's menu; cocktails & lounge; a la carte. Cape Cod cottage overlooking Pillar
Point Harbor. Steaks, chicken& pasta. Outdoor water front dining. Smoke free premises. **Cards:** AE, CB, DI,
DS, MC, VI.

LARKSPUR—11,100

LODGING

COURTYARD BY MARRIOTT   Rates Subject to Change   **Phone:** (415)925-1800
◆◆◆   4/1-10/31   1P: $159   2P/1B: $159   2P/2B: $159
Motor Inn   2/1-3/31 & 11/1-1/31   1P: $144   2P/1B: $144   2P/2B: $144
   Location: 0.3 mi e of US 101; exit E Sir Francis Drake Blvd. 2500 Larkspur Landing Cir 94939.
Fax: 415/925-1107. **Terms:** Check-in 4 pm; reserv deposit. **Facility:** 146 rooms. Attractive public areas & landscaped grounds.
3 stories; interior corridors. **Cards:** AE, DI, MC, VI.   (ASK) (SÅ) (⑭) (➜) (¶¶) (△) (➡) (♛) (🛏) (🔒) (Ġ) (✕) (✏)

RESTAURANT

LARK CREEK INN   Historical   **Lunch:** $15-$20   **Dinner:** $25-$35   **Phone:** 415/924-7766
◆◆◆   **Location:** 1.3 mi w of US 101, exit Tamalpais Dr. 234 Magnolia Ave 94939. **Hours:** 11:30 am-2:30 & 5:30-10
Regional   pm, Fri-10:30 pm, Sat 5 pm-10:30 pm, Sun 10 am-1:30 & 5-10 pm. Closed major holidays.
American   **Reservations:** suggested. **Features:** No A/C; casual dress; cocktails & lounge; a la carte. A restored
   Victorian home built in 1888. Pleasant garden setting. Smoking not permitted. Smoke free premises.
Cards: AE, MC, VI.   (✕)

MILLBRAE—20,400   (See map p. 922; index p. 916)

LODGINGS

BEST WESTERN EL RANCHO INN   **Phone:** (650)588-8500   **118**
(AAA) (SAVE)   All Year [CP]   1P: $115- 135   2P/1B: $120- 140 2P/2B: $120- 140   XP: $10   F18
   Location: 0.3 mi sw of US 101, Millbrae Ave exit; 0.8 mi n on SR 82. 1100 El Camino Real 94030.
◆◆◆   Fax: 650/871-7150. **Terms:** Weekly/monthly rates; BP avail; package plans. **Facility:** 307 rooms. Spacious
Complex   grounds. 77 two-bedroom apartments, $155-$200 for up to 8 persons. Room, park & fly
   $120-$140 up to 21 day package; 2 stories; exterior corridors; whirlpools. **Dining:** Restaurant; 6 am-2 & 5-10
pm terrace dining weather permitting; cocktails; restaurant, see separate listing. **Services:** giftshop. **All Rooms:** combo or
shower baths. **Cards:** AE, CB, DI, DS, JC, MC, VI. **Special Amenities:** Free breakfast and free room upgrade (subject
to availability with advanced reservations). (See color ad back cover & p 964)
(SÅ) (⑭) (🕓) (➜) (¶¶) (✛) (△) (➡) (♛) (VCR) (💻) (🖥) (📠) (🔒) (Ġ) (✏) (✕)

COMFORT INN-AIRPORT WEST   **Phone:** (650)952-3200   **122**
(AAA) (SAVE)   All Year [CP]   1P: $99- 150   2P/1B: $99- 180 2P/2B: $99- 180   XP: $5-7   F18
   Location: 0.3 mi sw of US 101, Millbrae Ave exit; 1 mi n on SR 82. 1390 El Camino Real 94030.
◆◆   Fax: 650/952-0474. **Terms:** Reserv deposit. **Facility:** 100 rooms. Access to rooms through central courtyard.
Motel   Subterranean parking. 3 stories; exterior corridors; sauna, whirlpool. **Dining:** Restaurant nearby.
   Some Rooms: 39 kitchens, utensils extra charge, whirlpools. **Cards:** AE, CB, DI, DS, JC, MC, VI.
Special Amenities: Free breakfast and free room upgrade (subject to availability with advanced reservations).
(SÅ) (⑭) (🕓) (➜) (¶¶) (✛) (✛) (△) (➡) (♛) (🛏) (🔒) (Ġ) (✕) (✏)

MILLWOOD INN   **Phone:** (650)583-3935   **123**
(AAA) (SAVE)   All Year [CP]   1P: $79- 150   2P/1B: $79- 150 2P/2B: $94- 150   XP: $4
◆◆◆   **Location:** 0.3 mi sw of US 101; Millbrae Ave exit; 1 mi n on SR 82. 1375 El Camino Real 94030.
Motel   Fax: 650/875-4354. **Terms:** Reserv deposit. **Facility:** 34 rooms. Exceptional amenities in all units. 5 two-
   bedroom units. 1-2 stories; exterior corridors. **Dining:** Restaurant nearby. **All Rooms:** combo or shower
   baths. **Cards:** AE, CB, DI, DS, JC, MC, VI. (See color ad below)
(🕓) (¶¶) (△) (➡) (♛) (VCR) (💻) (🖥) (📠) (🔒) (✏) (✕) (✏)

(See map p. 922)

TRAVELODGE SAN FRANCISCO AIRPORT SOUTH Phone: (650)697-7373 117
[AAA] [SAVE] All Year 1P: $75- 95 2P/1B: $85- 105 2P/2B: $85- 105 XP: $6 F18
◆ ◆ Location: 1.5 mi sw of US 101; Millbrae Ave exit; just s on SR 82. 110 S El Camino Real 94030.
Motel Fax: 650/697-7387. Facility: 58 rooms. 3 stories; interior/exterior corridors. Dining: Restaurant nearby.
All Rooms: combo or shower baths. Cards: AE, CB, DI, DS, JC, MC, VI. Special Amenities: Free local
telephone calls and free newspaper. [icons]

THE WESTIN HOTEL-SAN FRANCISCO AIRPORT Rates Subject to Change Phone: (650)692-3500 121
◆ ◆ ◆ All Year 1P: $117- 147 2P/1B: $127- 157 2P/2B: $127- 157 XP: $10-20 F18
Hotel Location: Just e of US 101, Millbrae Ave exit. 1 Old Bayshore Hwy 94030. Fax: 650/872-8111. Facility: 393
rooms. Landscaped grounds. Many rooms with bay view. 7 stories; interior corridors; heated indoor pool.
Fee: parking. Services: giftshop. Fee: massage. Recreation: hiking trails. Cards: AE, CB, DI, DS, JC, MC, VI.
[icons]

RESTAURANT

TERRACE CAFE Lunch: $6-$12 Dinner: $10-$20 Phone: 650/742-5588 50
◆ ◆ ◆ Location: 0.3 mi sw of US 101; in the Best Western El Rancho Inn. 1100 El Camino Real 94030.
American Hours: 6:30 am-2 & 5-10 pm. Closed: 11/25 & 12/25. Reservations: suggested. Features: casual dress;
Sunday brunch; cocktails; a la carte. Comtemporary ingredients & preparation, fresh seafood specials.
Smoke free premises. Cards: AE, CB, DI, DS, MC, VI. [icon]

MILL VALLEY—13,000

LODGINGS

ACQUA HOTEL Phone: 415/380-0400
[FYI] Under construction. Location: US 101, exit Seminary Dr. 555 Redwood Hwy 94941. Facility: 50 rooms.
Scheduled to open Spring, 1999;

HOLIDAY INN EXPRESS Rates Subject to Change Phone: 415/332-5700
◆ ◆ ◆ 5/1-10/31 [CP] 1P: $95- 138 2P/1B: $95- 138 2P/2B: $95- 148 XP: $8 F18
Motor Inn 2/1-4/30 & 11/1-1/31 [CP] 1P: $85- 125 2P/1B: $85- 125 2P/2B: $85- 135 XP: $8 F18
Location: 4 mi n of Golden Gate Bridge; w off US 101 at the Richardson Bay Bridge on the Stinson Beach
turn-off. 160 Shoreline Hwy 94941. Fax: 415/331-1859. Facility: 100 rooms. 2 stories; interior corridors. Cards: AE, DI, DS,
MC, VI. (See ad p 957) [icons]

MILL VALLEY/SAUSALITO TRAVELODGE Rates Subject to Change Phone: (415)383-0340
[AAA] 6/18-9/30 1P: $74- 84 2P/1B: $79- 84 2P/2B: $84 XP: $5 F17
5/1-6/17 & 10/1-10/31 1P: $69- 79 2P/1B: $74- 79 2P/2B: $79 XP: $5 F17
◆ 2/1-4/30 & 11/1-1/31 1P: $64- 74 2P/1B: $69- 74 2P/2B: $74 XP: $5 F17
Motel Location: US 101 exit Seminary Dr. 707 Redwood Hwy 94941. Fax: 415/383-0312. Facility: 45 rooms. Comfortable rooms. 2 stories; exterior corridors. Dining: Restaurant nearby. All Rooms: combo or shower baths.
Some Rooms: whirlpools. Cards: AE, CB, DI, DS, JC, MC, VI. [icons]

MILL VALLEY INN Rates Subject to Change Phone: 415/389-6608
◆ ◆ ◆ Fri & Sat [CP] 1P: $135- 259 2P/1B: $135- 259 2P/2B: $135- 259 XP: $20
Motor Inn Sun-Thurs [CP] 1P: $125- 249 2P/1B: $125- 249 2P/2B: $125- 249 XP: $20
Location: Center of town. 165 Throckmorton Ave 94941. Fax: 415/389-5051. Terms: Check-in 4 pm; 2 night
min stay, weekends. Facility: 25 rooms. Located in the heart of Mill Valley. Some rooms with fireplaces & balcony with views
of the Redwoods & Mt. Tamalpais. 3 stories; interior corridors. Cards: AE, DI, DS, JC, MC, VI. [icons]

PACIFICA—37,700 (See map p. 922; index p. 917)

LODGING

BEST WESTERN LIGHTHOUSE HOTEL Phone: (650)355-6300 145
[AAA] [SAVE] 6/1-10/31 [CP] 1P: $120- 195 2P/1B: $120- 195 2P/2B: $120- 195 XP: $10 F12
2/1-5/31 [CP] 1P: $105- 185 2P/1B: $105- 185 2P/2B: $105- 185 XP: $10 F12
◆ ◆ ◆ 11/1-1/31 [CP] 1P: $95- 175 2P/1B: $95- 175 2P/2B: $95- 175 XP: $10 F12
Motor Inn Location: Just w off SR 1. 105 Rockaway Beach Ave 94044. Fax: 650/359-4036. Facility: 92 rooms. 1 whirlpool rm, extra charge; 4 stories; interior corridors; oceanview; beach access, whirlpool. Dining: Dining room;
cocktails; also, Moonraker Restaurant, see separate listing. Services: giftshop. Cards: AE, DI, DS, MC, VI.
Special Amenities: Free newspaper and free room upgrade (subject to availability with advanced reservations).
[icons]

RESTAURANT

MOONRAKER RESTAURANT Lunch: $8-$16 Dinner: $9-$38 Phone: 650/359-0303 55
◆ ◆ ◆ Location: Just w off SR 1; in Best Western Lighthouse Hotel. 105 Rockaway Beach Ave 94044. Hours: 7
Seafood am-10, 11-2:30 & 5-10 pm; Sun 10 am-2 & 5-10 pm. Reservations: suggested. Features: No A/C; casual
dress; Sunday brunch; children's menu; early bird specials; cocktails & lounge; minimum charge-$7.50.
Excellent ocean views from most tables, seafood specialties, fresh ingredients. Smoke free premises. Cards: AE, CB, DI,
MC, VI. [icon]

SAN BRUNO—39,000 (See map p. 922; index p. 917)

LODGINGS

COURTYARD BY MARRIOTT Rates Subject to Change Phone: 650/952-3333 175
◆ ◆ ◆ All Year 1P: $179 2P/1B: $179 2P/2B: $179
Motor Inn Location: 2 mi nw of airport; US 101 to I-380 to El Camino Real S exit. 1050 Bayhill Dr 94066.
Fax: 650/952-4707. Facility: 147 rooms. Nicely landscaped.Instant potable hot water in all units. Max rates for
up to 4 persons; 3 stories; interior corridors; small heated indoor pool. Cards: AE, DI, DS, MC, VI.
[icons]

(See map p. 922)

RITZ INN
All Year   Rates Subject to Change   Phone: 650/589-3553   176
2P/1B: $75- 85 2P/2B: $85   XP: $5   F
AAA ◆◆ Motel
Location: 2.5 mi nw of airport, US 101 to I-380 to El Camino Real S exit. 151 El Camino Real 94066. Fax: 650/873-2476. **Facility:** 23 rooms. Near commercial area. 2 stories; exterior corridors. **Dining:** Restaurant nearby. **All Rooms:** combo or shower baths. **Cards:** AE, DS, MC, VI. *(See color ad below)*

SAN BRUNO INN
All Year [CP]   1P: $70- 80 2P/1B: $70- 80 2P/2B: $80- 90 XP: $5-10   Phone: 650/871-4000   177
AAA [SAVE] ◆◆ Motel
Location: 2.8 mi nw of airport; US 101 to I-380 to El Camino Real S exit. 500 El Camino Real 94066. Fax: 650/871-5754. **Terms:** Reserv deposit; handling fee imposed. **Facility:** 44 rooms. Skylighted court-yard on 2nd level. Covered parking on 1st level. 3 stories; interior corridors; sauna, whirlpool. **Dining:** Coffee shop nearby. **Some Rooms:** whirlpools. **Cards:** AE, CB, DI, DS, MC, VI. *(See color ad p 978)*

SAN CARLOS—26,200   (See map p. 922; index p. 917)

LODGINGS

COMFORT INN & SUITES
All Year [CP]   Rates Subject to Change   Phone: 650/508-1800   191
◆◆◆ Motel   1P: $89- 129 2P/1B: $99- 139 2P/2B: $104- 139 XP: $10   D
Location: SR 82, just n of Holly St. 251 El Camino Real 94070. Fax: 650/593-6100. **Terms:** Handling fee imposed. **Facility:** 50 rooms. 6 whirlpool rms, extra charge; 3 stories; interior corridors. **Cards:** AE, CB, DI, DS, JC, MC, VI.

DAYS INN-SAN CARLOS
All Year [CP]   1P: $69- 99 2P/1B: $69- 99 2P/2B: $79- 109 XP: $10   Phone: (650)591-5771   190
AAA [SAVE] ◆◆ Motel   F
Location: US 101 northbound exit Holly St w to El Camino n 0.3 mi southbound US 101 exit Ralston w to El Camino, s 0.5 mi. 26 El Camino Real 94070. Fax: 650/508-1476. **Terms:** Handling fee imposed. **Facility:** 29 rooms. 2 stories; exterior corridors. **Cards:** AE, CB, DI, DS, JC, MC, VI. **Special Amenities:** Free breakfast and free local telephone calls. *(See color ad below)*

INNS OF AMERICA
All Year [CP]   1P: $129   2P/1B: $139   2P/2B: $139   Phone: (650)631-0777   188
AAA [SAVE] ◆◆◆ Motel
Location: US 101, exit Holly St/Redwood Shores, e to Airport Blvd, then just s. 555 Skyway Rd 94070. Fax: 650/631-9610. **Terms:** Pets, $10 extra charge. **Facility:** 122 rooms. 3 stories; interior corridors. **Services:** area transportation, within 5 mi. **All Rooms:** combo or shower baths. **Cards:** AE, MC, VI. **Special Amenities:** Free breakfast and free local telephone calls.

(See map p. 922)

SAN CARLOS TRAVELODGE
◆◆   All Year [CP]
Motel
Guaranteed Rates
1P: $65- 75   2P/1B: $65- 75   2P/2B: $75- 85   XP: $5
Phone: 650/591-6655   189
F12
Location: Exit US 101, Holly St, 0.5 mi w, 1 mi s on El Camino Real (SR 82). 1562 El Camino Real 94070.
Fax: 650/802-9139. **Terms:** Reserv deposit; handling fee imposed. **Facility:** 32 rooms. 2 stories; exterior corridors. **Cards:** AE, CB, DI, DS, MC, VI.

SAN GREGORIO—400   (See map p. 922; index p. 918)

LODGING

RANCHO SAN GREGORIO
AAA   All Year [BP]
◆◆◆
Bed &
Breakfast
Rates Subject to Change
1P: $90- 150   2P/1B: $90- 150   2P/2B: $90- 150   XP: $10-15
Phone: (650)747-0810   230
D18
Location: SR 84, 5 mi e of SR 1. 5086 La Honda Rd 94074 (RT 1 Box 54). Fax: 650/747-0184.
Terms: Reserv deposit, 7 day notice. **Facility:** 4 rooms. Early California style hacienda, patios, decks & fountains. 15 acre farm, picnic barbecue area. Fruit orchards & herb gardens. 5 mi from ocean, rooms have cozy farmhouse appeal. Smoking outside. 2 stories; interior corridors. **Dining:** Harvest breakfast feast made with Rancho grown fruits. Artichoke frittata a specialty. Award winning coffee cakes. **Recreation:** hiking trails.
All Rooms: combo or shower baths. **Cards:** AE, CB, DI, DS, MC, VI.

SAN MATEO—85,500   (See map p. 922; index p. 917)

LODGINGS

BEST WESTERN SAN MATEO LOS PRADOS INN
AAA SAVE   All Year
◆◆
Motel
1P: $119- 149   2P/1B: $129- 149   2P/2B: $129- 159   XP: $10
Phone: (650)341-3300   169
F17
Location: E of & adjacent to US 101. 2940 S Norfolk St 94403. Fax: 650/341-9999. **Terms:** Reserv deposit; handling fee imposed; weekly rates; small pets only, $50 dep req. **Facility:** 113 rooms. 3 two-bedroom units. 2-3 stories, no elevator; interior/exterior corridors; indoor whirlpool. **Dining:** Coffee shop nearby.
All Rooms: combo or shower baths. **Cards:** AE, CB, DI, DS, JC, MC, VI. **Special Amenities:** Early check-in/late check-out and free newspaper. *(See ad p 977)*

COXHEAD HOUSE BED & BREAKFAST
◆◆◆   All Year [BP]
Bed &
Breakfast
Rates Subject to Change
1P: $119- 159   2P/1B: $119- 159   XP: $25
Phone: (650)685-1600   171
Location: US 101, exit 3rd Ave, w to SR 82 (El Camino Real), 0.6 mi n, then just e. 37 E Santa Inez Ave 94401. Fax: 650/685-1684. **Terms:** Check-in 4 pm; reserv deposit, 7 day notice. **Facility:** 4 rooms. 1891 Tudor Revival style. 2 stories; interior corridors; designated smoking area. **All Rooms:** combo or shower baths.
Some Rooms: color TV. **Cards:** AE, MC, VI.

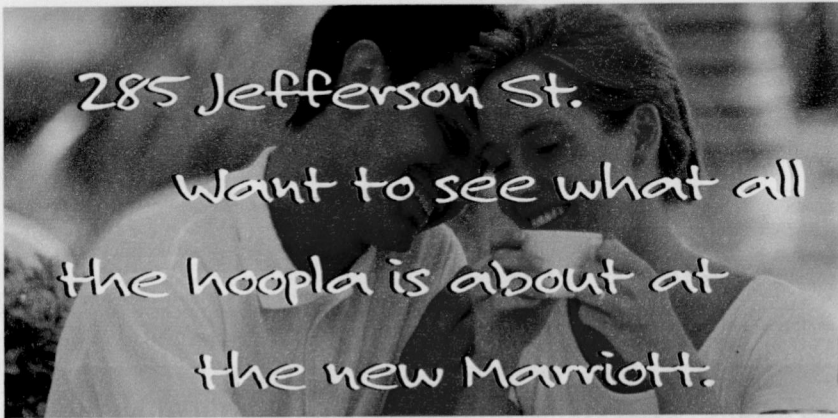

(See map p. 922)

HOLIDAY INN EXPRESS
♦♦♦ All Year [CP]
Motel   Rates Subject to Change   Phone: (650)344-6376   **165**
1P: $73- 96   2P/1B: $83- 106   2P/2B: $83- 106   XP: $10   F12
Location: Northbound exit US 101 Dore Ave; southbound exit US 101 3rd Ave E, re-enter US 101 N exit Dore Ave. 350 N Bayshore Blvd 94401. Fax: 650/343-7108. **Facility:** 111 rooms. 3 two-bedroom units. 4 stories; interior corridors. **All Rooms:** combo or shower baths. **Cards:** AE, CB, DI, DS, JC, MC, VI.

HOLIDAY INN-SAN MATEO
♦♦♦ All Year
Motor Inn   Rates Subject to Change   Phone: (650)344-3219   **167**
1P: $96- 157   2P/1B: $106- 167   2P/2B: $106- 167   XP: $10   F12
Location: Northbound exit US 101 at Dore Ave E, southbound exit 3rd Ave E, re-enter US 101 exit Dore Ave. 330 N Bayshore Blvd 94401. Fax: 650/344-9012. **Facility:** 109 rooms. Few rooms with fireplace. Very comfortable & attractive rooms. 3 two-bedroom units. 4 stories; interior corridors. **All Rooms:** combo or shower baths. **Cards:** AE, CB, DI, DS, JC, MC, VI.

MARRIOTT-SAN MATEO
(AAA) [SAVE]   Phone: (650)573-7661
[FYI]   All Year   1P: $105- 145   2P/1B: $105- 145   2P/2B: $105- 145   XP: $10   F12
Too new to rate. **Location:** Nw of jct US 101 & SR 92; exit SR 92 Delaware St, e on Concar Dr. 1770 S
Hotel   Amphlett Blvd 94402. Fax: 650/573-0533. **Facility:** 316 rooms. 3 stories; interior corridors; whirlpool. **Dining:** Dining room, coffee shop; 6 am-10:30 pm; $14-$20; cocktails. **Services:** giftshop. **Cards:** AE, MC, VI. **Special Amenities: Early check-in/late check-out and preferred room (subject to availability with advanced reservations).** *(See color ad p 973 & p 932)*

RESIDENCE INN BY MARRIOTT
♦♦♦ All Year
Suite Motel   Rates Subject to Change   Phone: (650)574-4700   **170**
1P: $161   2P/1B: $161   2P/2B: $179
Location: 0.8 mi se from jct US 101 & SR 92; exit SR 92 via Edgewater Blvd. 2000 Winward Way 94404. Fax: 650/572-9084. **Terms:** Reserv deposit. **Facility:** 159 rooms. 1-bedroom & 2-story 2-bedroom suites with living room & kitchen; patio or balcony; many fireplaces. 2 stories; exterior corridors. **Recreation:** sports court. **Cards:** AE, DI, DS, MC, VI.

VILLA HOTEL AIRPORT SOUTH
♦♦♦ All Year
Motor Inn   Rates Subject to Change   Phone: (650)341-0966   **166**
1P: $89- 109   2P/1B: $99- 119   2P/2B: $99- 119   XP: $10   F
Location: 8 mi s of San Francisco International Airport, exit US 101 W Hillsdale Blvd, 0.5 mi s on SR 82. 4000 S El Camino Real 94403. Fax: 650/573-0164. **Terms:** Reserv deposit. **Facility:** 285 rooms. 2-4 stories; interior/exterior corridors. **Services:** giftshop; area transportation. **All Rooms:** combo or shower baths. **Cards:** AE, CB, DI, DS, JC, MC, VI. *(See ad below)*

SAN RAFAEL—48,400

LODGINGS

EMBASSY SUITES HOTEL
♦♦♦♦ All Year [BP]
Suite Hotel   Guaranteed Rates   Phone: 415/499-9222
1P: $119- 174   2P/1B: $129- 199   2P/2B: $119- 209   XP: $15   F12
Location: US 101 northbound exit e San Pedro Dr, southbound exit Freitas Pkwy; adjacent to Marin County Civic Center. 101 McInnis Pkwy 94903. Fax: 415/499-9268. **Terms:** Reserv deposit. **Facility:** 235 rooms. Garden atrium. 2 two-bedroom suites, $175-$225 for up to 4 persons; 5 stories; interior corridors; heated indoor pool. **Services:** giftshop. **Cards:** AE, DI, DS, JC, MC, VI. *(See color ad p 931)*

SAN RAFAEL INN
(AAA) 6/15-9/30
♦ 2/1-6/14 & 10/1-1/31
Motel   Rates Subject to Change   Phone: 415/454-9470
1P: $54- 64   2P/1B: $58- 74   2P/2B: $65- 80   XP: $8
1P: $52- 58   2P/1B: $54- 64   2P/2B: $58- 68   XP: $8
Location: Off US 101; exit E Francisco Blvd, 1 blk n. 865 Francisco Blvd E 94901. Fax: 415/457-2512. **Terms:** Reserv deposit, 3 day notice. **Facility:** 32 rooms. Comfortable rooms. 2 two-bedroom units. 2 whirlpool rms, extra charge; 2 stories; exterior corridors; whirlpool. **All Rooms:** combo or shower baths. **Some Rooms:** 4 efficiencies, no utensils. **Cards:** AE, CB, DI, MC, VI. *(See color ad p 975)*

VILLA INN
◆ ◆
Motel
All Year [CP] Rates Subject to Change **Phone:** (415)456-4975
1P: $65- 76 2P/1B: $71- 89 2P/2B: $75- 89 XP: $8 F16
Location: Off US 101; southbound Lincoln Ave off-ramp, northbound Central San Rafael exit, 0.3 mi w on Fourth St, 0.5 mi n on Lincoln Ave. 1600 Lincoln Ave 94901. Fax: 415/456-1520. **Terms:** Reserv deposit.
Facility: 60 rooms. Attractive residential setting. Comfortable rooms centrally located. 3 two-bedroom units. 9 kitchens, 3 night min stay; $10 extra charge; 2 stories; exterior corridors; heated pool. **All Rooms:** combo or shower baths. **Cards:** AE, DI, DS, MC, VI. *(See color ad below)*

WYNDHAM GARDEN HOTEL
◆ ◆ ◆
Hotel
 Rates Subject to Change **Phone:** (415)479-8800
Sun-Thurs [EP] 1P: $104 2P/1B: $104 2P/2B: $104 XP: $10-20 F12
Fri & Sat [BP] 1P: $99 2P/1B: $99 2P/2B: $99 XP: $10-20 F16
Location: 3 mi n in Terra Linda, off US 101; exit Terra Linda off-ramp. 1010 Northgate Dr 94903.
Fax: 415/479-2342. **Facility:** 235 rooms. On knoll overlooking valley & hills. 7 suites, $200-$250 for up to 4 persons; 4-5 stories; interior corridors. **Services:** giftshop. **Cards:** AE, CB, DI, DS, JC, MC, VI. *(See color ad below)*

RESTAURANTS

LE CHALET BASQUE **Lunch:** $7-$11 **Dinner:** $13-$17 **Phone:** 415/479-1070
◆
Location: 1 mi e of Marin Civic Center. 405 N San Pedro Rd 94903. **Hours:** 11:30 am-2 & 5-10 pm, Sat
Continental from 5 pm, Sun 10:30 am-2 & 4-9 pm. Closed: Mon, 11/28, 12/25, last 2 weeks of Aug.
Reservations: suggested. **Features:** casual dress; children's menu; cocktails & lounge; a la carte. Family
dinners. Patio dining, weather permitting. **Cards:** AE, MC, VI. ⊠

SALUTE RISTORANTE **Lunch:** $8-$15 **Dinner:** $12-$23 **Phone:** 415/453-7596
◆◆
Location: US 101 exit W Central San Rafael on 3rd St to Tamalpias. 706 Third St 94901. **Hours:** 11 am-11
Italian pm. Closed: 1/1, 11/28 & 12/25. **Reservations:** suggested. **Features:** No A/C; casual dress; cocktails &
lounge; a la carte. Turn-of-the-century decor. Traditional & modern dishes. Smoke free premises. **Cards:** AE,
DI, MC, VI. ♿ ⊠

SAUSALITO—7,200

LODGINGS

CASA MADRONA HOTEL Guaranteed Rates **Phone:** (415)332-0502
◆◆◆ All Year [BP] 1P: $188- 260 2P/1B: $188- 260 2P/2B: $188- 260
Country Inn **Location:** US 101, exit Alexander Ave, 1.5 mi to Bridgeway. 801 Bridgeway 94965. Fax: 415/332-2537.
Terms: Reserv deposit. **Facility:** 34 rooms. Attractively located on a hillside overlooking the bay in Sausalito.
3 stories; interior/exterior corridors. Fee: parking. **All Rooms:** combo or shower baths. **Some Rooms:** 4 kitchens.
Cards: AE, CB, DI, DS, MC, VI. ⑪ ⌕ VCR ▣ ⚙ 🖨 🗑 ⊠

THE INN ABOVE TIDE Rates Subject to Change **Phone:** (415)332-9535
◆◆◆ All Year [CP] 1P: $195- 445 2P/1B: $195- 445 2P/2B: $195 XP: $15 F6
Motel **Location:** US 101, exit Alexander Ave, 1.5 mi to Bridgeway. 30 El Portal 94965. Fax: 415/332-6714.
Terms: Reserv deposit; handling fee imposed. **Facility:** 30 rooms. Most rooms with balconies overlooking the
bay. 3 stories; interior/exterior corridors. Fee: parking. **Cards:** AE, DI, MC, VI. 🛁 ⑪ 🖨 ⊠

RESTAURANTS

HOTEL ALTA MIRA DINING ROOM **Lunch:** $9-$18 **Dinner:** $13-$19 **Phone:** 415/332-1350
◆
Location: Center; w on Princess St from Bridgeway; n on Bulkley Ave. 125 Bulkley Ave 94966.
American **Hours:** Open 2/1-1/1; 7:30 am-11 pm. **Reservations:** suggested. **Features:** No A/C; cocktail lounge; beer &
wine only; fee for valet parking; a la carte. Hillside location with excellent view of San Francisco Bay area.
Varied menu; popular for lunch & Sun brunch. Terrace dining. **Cards:** AE, CB, MC, VI.

THE SPINNAKER **Lunch:** $7-$16 **Dinner:** $11-$19 **Phone:** 415/332-1500
◆◆
Location: 100 Spinnaker Dr 94965. **Hours:** 11 am-11 pm. Closed: 11/28 & 12/25. **Reservations:** suggested.
Seafood **Features:** casual dress; children's menu; cocktails & lounge; valet parking; a la carte. Dining room over
water. Varied menu. Smoke free premises. **Cards:** AE, MC, VI. ⊠

SOUTH SAN FRANCISCO—54,300   (See map p. 922; index p. 917)

LODGINGS

AMERICANA INN MOTEL   Rates Subject to Change   **Phone:** (650)589-0404   [153]
Ⓐ   All Year   1P: $60- 70   2P/1B: $65- 75   2P/2B: $70- 80   XP: $5   F10
◆◆   **Location:** 3 mi nw of airport, on SR 82; US 101 to I-380 to El Camino Real exit. 760 El Camino Real 94080.
Motel   **Fax:** 650/589-0404. **Facility:** 17 rooms. 2 stories; exterior corridors; sauna. **Dining:** Restaurant nearby.
Some Rooms: whirlpools. **Cards:** AE, DS, MC, VI.   ⊞ 🆅 🅱 ⊠

BEST WESTERN GROSVENOR HOTEL   **Phone:** (650)873-3200   [156]
Ⓐ Ⓢ   All Year   1P: $99- 169   2P/1B: $99- 169   2P/2B: $99- 169   XP: $15   F12
◆◆◆   **Location:** E of US 101, S Airport Blvd exit. 380 S Airport Blvd 94080. Fax: 650/589-3495. **Terms:** Package
Hotel   plans. **Facility:** 206 rooms. Few units with bay view. 8 stories; interior corridors; small pool 5/1-10/31.
Dining: Restaurant; 6 am-2 & 5-10 pm; closed for lunch Sat-Sun; $12-$20; cocktails. **Cards:** AE, CB, DI,
DS, JC, MC, VI. **Special Amenities:** Free breakfast and free newspaper.
🕏 📶 ⇆ ⊞ ⊞ 🖨 🖳 ⊡ ⊟ 🖥 ⊟ ♨ ⊠

COMFORT SUITES   Rates Subject to Change   **Phone:** 650/589-7766   [152]
◆◆◆   5/1-10/31 [CP]   1P: $99- 159   2P/1B: $99- 159   XP: $10   F16
Motel   2/1-4/30 & 11/1-1/31 [CP]   1P: $89- 139   2P/1B: $89- 139   XP: $10   F16
Location: Just E of US 101, Grand Ave exit. 121 E Grand Ave 94003. Fax: 650/589-7796. **Facility:** 169 rooms.
All units have a partitioned seating area with sofa-bed & chair. Few adjacent to RR Tracks. 3 stories; exterior corridors.
All Rooms: combo or shower baths. **Cards:** AE, CB, DI, DS, JC, MC, VI.
Ⓢ ⊞ ⇆ 🖨 🆅 🖳 ⊟ 🖥 ⊟ ♨ ⊠ ▱

DAYS INN-SFO NORTH   **Phone:** (650)873-9300   [151]
Ⓐ Ⓢ   5/1-10/31 [CP]   1P: $79- 109   2P/1B: $89- 109   2P/2B: $99- 119   XP: $10   F12
◆◆   2/1-4/30 & 11/1-1/31 [CP]   1P: $69- 79   2P/1B: $79- 89   2P/2B: $89- 99   XP: $10   F12
Motel   **Location:** Just W of US 101, Oyster Point exit. 1113 Airport Blvd 94080. Fax: 650/873-6200. **Terms:** Reserv
deposit. **Facility:** 24 rooms. 3 stories; exterior corridors. **Dining:** Coffee shop nearby. **Cards:** AE, CB, DI,
DS, JC, MC, VI. **Special Amenities:** Early check-in/late check-out and free breakfast.
💲⊘ 📶 ⊞ ⊞ 🖥 ⊟ ⊠

ECONOMY INN   **Phone:** (650)952-2505   [160]
Ⓐ Ⓢ   All Year   1P: $55- 65   2P/1B: $55- 65   2P/2B: $60- 70   XP: $5
◆   **Location:** Just w of US 101, Grand Ave or South San Francisco exits. 701 Airport Blvd 94080.
Motel   **Fax:** 650/952-8311. **Facility:** 21 rooms. 2 stories; exterior corridors. **Some Rooms:** whirlpools. **Cards:** AE,
DI, DS, MC, VI. **Special Amenities:** Free breakfast and free local telephone calls. *(See color ad p 978)*
⊠

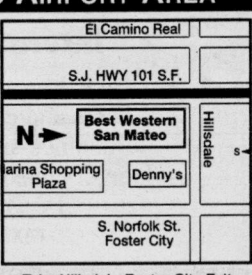

(See map p. 922)

EMBASSY SUITES-SOUTH SAN FRANCISCO   Rates Subject to Change   **Phone:** (650)589-3400   154
◆◆◆   6/1-10/31 [BP]   1P: $145- 159   2P/1B: $145- 159   2P/2B: $145- 159   XP: $10   F
Suite Hotel   2/1-5/31 & 11/1-1/31 [BP]   1P: $139- 145   2P/1B: $139- 145   2P/2B: $139- 145   XP: $10   F
Location: 2 blks e of US 101, Grand Ave exit. 250 Gateway Blvd 94080. Fax: 650/876-0305. **Facility:** 312 rooms. Some rooms with bay view. 10 stories; interior corridors; heated indoor pool. **Services:** giftshop. **Cards:** AE, DI, DS, JC, MC, VI. *(See color ad p 931)*

HOLIDAY INN S F O-NORTH   Guaranteed Rates   **Phone:** (650)873-3550   155
◆◆◆   All Year   1P: $119- 169   2P/1B: $119- 169   2P/2B: $119- 169   XP: $15   F18
Hotel   **Location:** Just E of US 101; S Airport Blvd exit. 275 S Airport Blvd 94080. Fax: 650/873-4524. **Facility:** 224 rooms. Few units with bay view; adjacent to convention center. 5 stories; interior corridors.
Services: giftshop. **Cards:** AE, DI, DS, JC, MC, VI. *(See ad p 977)*

(See map p. 922)

INN AT OYSTER POINT
◆◆◆ All Year [CP]
Motor Inn **Location:** 0.3 mi E of US 101; Oyster Point Blvd or South San Francisco exits. 425 Marina Blvd 94080.
Fax: 650/737-0795. **Terms:** Reserv deposit. **Facility:** 30 rooms. All units with bay view & gas fireplace. 3 stories; interior corridors. **Recreation:** jogging. **Cards:** AE, CB, DI, DS, MC, VI.
Rates Subject to Change
1P: $159- 199   2P/1B: $169- 209   2P/2B: $179- 209   XP: $10
Phone: (650)737-7633 `161` F12

LA QUINTA INN
◆◆◆ All Year [CP]
Motel **Location:** Just W of US 101 at S Airport Blvd exit. 20 Airport Blvd 94080. **Facility:** 174 rooms. Adjacent to industrial property & railroad tracks. 3 executive suites with refrigerator & microwave $185 for up to 2 persons; 4 stories; interior corridors; small pool. **Cards:** AE, CB, DI, DS, JC, MC, VI.
Rates Subject to Change
1P: $105- 129   2P/1B: $105- 129   2P/2B: $105- 129   XP: $10
Phone: (650)583-2223 `157`

LARKSPUR LANDING
`FYI` Under construction. **Location:** E of US 101; Grand Ave exit. 690 Gateway Blvd 94080. **Facility:** 111 rooms. Scheduled to open Spring, 1999.
Phone: 650/827-1515

QUALITY INN & SUITES
`FYI` Under construction. **Location:** E of US 101, s Airport Blvd exit. 410 S Airport Blvd 94080. **Facility:** 45 rooms. Scheduled to open spring, 1999;
Phone: 650/875-7878

RAMADA INN SFO NORTH
◆◆◆ All Year
Motor Inn **Location:** Just e of US 101, S Airport Blvd exit. 245 S Airport Blvd 94080. Fax: 650/588-5007. **Facility:** 175 rooms. Attractive courtyard landscaping. Adjacent to convention center. 2 stories; exterior corridors.
Cards: AE, DI, DS, JC, MC, VI. *(See color ad opposite title page & ad p 978)*
Rates Subject to Change
1P: $99- 149   2P/1B: $99- 149   2P/2B: $99- 149   XP: $15
Phone: (650)589-7200 `150` F18

SUPER 8 LODGE
◆ All Year
Motel **Location:** E of US 101, S Airport Blvd exit. 111 Mitchell Ave 94080. Fax: 650/871-8377. **Facility:** 117 rooms. Nice lawn area. 3 stories; interior corridors. **Cards:** AE, CB, DI, DS, JC, MC, VI.
Rates Subject to Change
1P: $79   2P/1B: $85   2P/2B: $90   XP: $5
Phone: 650/877-0770 `159` F12

RESTAURANT

SOUTH CITY STEAKHOUSE
◆◆ Location: Just w of El Camino Real. 101 Brentwood Dr 94080. **Hours:** 4:30 pm-9 pm, Fri & Sat-10 pm.
American Closed: 12/25. **Reservations:** accepted. **Features:** No A/C; casual dress; early bird specials; cocktails & lounge. Family restaurant. Smoke free premises. **Cards:** MC, VI.
Dinner: $10-$25
Phone: 650/737-7900 `56`

TIBURON—7,500

LODGING

TIBURON LODGE
`AAA` `SAVE` 5/1-10/31
2/1-4/30 & 11/1-1/31
◆◆◆ **Location:** In village; 1 blk from bay; 4 mi e of US 101; exit Tiburon-Belvedere. 1651 Tiburon Blvd 94920.
Motel Fax: 415/435-2451. **Terms:** Reserv deposit, 3 day notice; weekly/monthly rates. **Facility:** 97 rooms. Few studios. Comfortable rooms, few with vaulted ceilings. 3 apartments $125-$175 for 2-4 persons. Whirlpool rms, extra charge; 2-3 stories; exterior corridors. **Dining:** Restaurant; 7-10 am, Sat & Sun-11:30 am. **All Rooms:** combo or shower baths. **Some Rooms:** 2 efficiencies, kitchen. **Cards:** AE, CB, DI, DS, JC, MC, VI.
(See color ad p 951 & ad p 976)
Phone: (415)435-3133
1P: $139- 319   2P/1B: $154- 319   2P/2B: $154- 319   XP: $15   F12
1P: $119- 319   2P/1B: $134- 319   2P/2B: $134- 319   XP: $15   F12

This ends listings for the San Francisco Vicinity.
The following page resumes the alphabetical listings of
cities in California.

SAN GABRIEL—See Los Angeles p. 631.

SANGER—16,800

LODGING

TOWN HOUSE MOTEL
(AAA) [SAVE]   All Year   1P: $36   2P/1B: $42   2P/2B: $47   XP: $5   F12
◆   **Location:** 0.7 mi n, 1.3 mi s of SR 180 at Academy Ave. 1308 Church Ave 93657. Fax: 559/875-5201.
Motel   **Terms:** Small pets only. **Facility:** 19 rooms. 2 stories; exterior corridors. **All Rooms:** combo or shower
baths. **Cards:** AE, DS, MC, VI. **Special Amenities:** Early check-in/late check-out and free local
telephone calls.   Phone: (559)875-5531

SAN GREGORIO—See San Francisco p. 973.

SAN JACINTO—16,200

LODGING

CROWN MOTEL   Phone: (909)654-7133
(AAA) [SAVE]   All Year   1P: $32- 38   2P/1B: $38- 42   2P/2B: $42- 48   XP: $5
◆   **Location:** Just n on SR 79. 138 S Ramona Blvd 92583. Fax: 909/654-6184. **Terms:** Reserv deposit;
Motel   weekly/monthly rates; small pets only. **Facility:** 21 rooms. 2 stories; exterior corridors; whirlpool.
All Rooms: combo or shower baths. **Some Rooms:** whirlpools. **Cards:** AE, CB, DI, DS, MC, VI.

SAN JOSE—782,200

LODGINGS

ADLON HOTEL
[FYI]   Under construction. **Location:** US 101, N 1st St exit, 0.5 mi s to Rosemary St. 1275 N Fourth St 95112.
Facility: 51 rooms. Scheduled to open May 1, 1999;

ADLON HOTEL
[FYI]
Under construction. **Location:** On US 101N, 1st St exit, s 0.5 mi to Rosemary St. 1275 N Fourth St 95112. **Facility:** 51 rooms. Scheduled to open May, 1999;

AIRPORT INN-INTERNATIONAL   Rates Subject to Change   **Phone:** (408)453-5340
◆◆
Motel

Mon-Thurs [CP]	1P:	$79- 119	2P/1B:	$89- 129	2P/2B:	$89- 129	XP: $10	F12
Fri-Sun [CP]	1P:	$69- 99	2P/1B:	$79- 109	2P/2B:	$79- 109	XP: $10	F12

Location: 0.5 mi e of San Jose Airport; US 101 exit N 1st St, s 0.5 mi to Rosemary St E. 1355 N 4th St 95112. Fax: 408/453-5208. **Facility:** 194 rooms. Quiet location. 2 stories; exterior corridors; heated pool. **Cards:** AE, CB, DI, DS, JC, MC, VI. *(See color ad p 980)*

ARENA HOTEL   **Phone:** (408)294-6500
[AAA] [SAVE]

Sun-Thurs [BP]	1P: $129	2P/1B: $129	2P/2B: $149	XP: $5	F12
Fri & Sat [BP]	1P: $109	2P/1B: $109	2P/2B: $129	XP: $5	F12

◆◆◆
Motel
Location: 817 The Alameda 95126. Fax: 408/294-6585. **Terms:** Reserv deposit. **Facility:** 89 rooms. Many spacious rooms, walking distance to Arena. 3 stories; interior corridors. **All Rooms:** efficiencies. **Some Rooms:** whirlpools. **Cards:** AE, CB, DI, DS, MC, VI. **Special Amenities:** Free breakfast and free newspaper.

BEST WESTERN GATEWAY INN   **Phone:** (408)435-8800
[AAA] [SAVE]

Mon-Thurs 2/1-12/31 [CP]	1P: $109- 119	2P/1B: $109- 119	2P/2B: $109- 129	XP: $5
Mon-Thurs 1/1-1/31 [CP]	1P: $114- 124	2P/1B: $114- 124	2P/2B: $114- 124	XP: $5
Fri-Sun [CP]	1P: $89- 109	2P/1B: $89- 109	2P/2B: $99- 119	XP: $5

◆◆◆
Motor Inn
Location: Exit US 101 San Jose International Airport. 2585 Seaboard Ave 95131. Fax: 408/435-8879. **Terms:** Reserv deposit, 3 day notice. **Facility:** 146 rooms. Attractive rooms. 2 stories; interior corridors; smoke free premises; heated pool, sauna, whirlpool. **Dining:** Restaurant nearby. **Cards:** AE, DI, DS, MC, VI. **Special Amenities: Free breakfast and free local telephone calls.**

BEST WESTERN INN DOWNTOWN   **Phone:** (408)298-3500
[AAA] [SAVE]

All Year [CP]	1P: $59- 69	2P/1B: $64- 74	2P/2B: $69- 79	XP: $5	F12

◆◆
Motel
Location: Just e off SR 82. 455 S 2nd St 95113. Fax: 408/298-2477. **Facility:** 72 rooms. Convenient to convention center. 3 stories; exterior corridors. **Dining:** Restaurant nearby. **All Rooms:** combo or shower baths. **Cards:** AE, DI, DS, MC, VI. **Special Amenities: Free breakfast and free newspaper.**

BEST WESTERN SAN JOSE LODGE   **Phone:** (408)453-7750
[AAA] [SAVE]

All Year	1P: $65- 75	2P/1B: $65- 75	2P/2B: $75- 85	XP: $5	F18

◆◆
Motel
Location: 1 mi e of San Jose International Airport; s off US 101; exit via N 1st St. 1440 N 1st St 95112. Fax: 408/437-9519. **Facility:** 75 rooms. 2 stories; exterior corridors; heated pool. **Dining:** Coffee shop nearby. **All Rooms:** combo or shower baths. **Cards:** AE, CB, DI, DS, MC, VI. **Special Amenities: Free breakfast and free local telephone calls.**

THE CLARION PRESIDENT INN   **Phone:** (408)972-2200
[AAA] [SAVE]

2/1-7/30 [CP]	1P: $119	2P/1B: $119	2P/2B: $129	XP: $10	F18
7/31-11/1 [CP]	1P: $109	2P/1B: $109	2P/2B: $119	XP: $10	F18
11/2-12/1 [CP]	1P: $99	2P/1B: $99	2P/2B: $109	XP: $10	F18
12/2-1/31 [CP]	1P: $89	2P/1B: $89	2P/2B: $99	XP: $10	F18

◆◆◆
Motel
Location: Exit US 101 Tully, s on Monterey Rd. 3200 Monterey Rd 95111. Fax: 408/972-2632. **Terms:** Reserv deposit. **Facility:** 47 rooms. Attractive modern decor. 2-3 stories; interior corridors; heated pool, whirlpool. **Dining:** Restaurant nearby. **Some Rooms:** whirlpools. **Cards:** AE, CB, DI, DS, JC, MC, VI. **Special Amenities: Free breakfast and free newspaper.**

COMFORT INN AIRPORT SOUTH   Rates Subject to Change   **Phone:** 408-243-2400
◆◆◆
Motel

All Year	1P: $110- 150	2P/1B: $110- 150	2P/2B: $120- 150	XP: $10

Location: US 101 exit I-880; 1.3 mi sw of San Jose International Airport. 2118 The Alameda 95126. Fax: 408/243-5478. **Facility:** 40 rooms. 3 stories; interior corridors; heated pool. **Some Rooms:** 2 efficiencies. **Cards:** AE, CB, DI, DS, MC, VI.

COURTYARD BY MARRIOTT   Rates Subject to Change   **Phone:** 408/441-6111
◆◆◆
Motor Inn

Sun-Thurs	1P: $149	2P/1B: $149	2P/2B: $149
Fri & Sat	1P: $79	2P/1B: $79	2P/2B: $79

Location: 0.5 mi e of San Jose International Airport, via Airport Parkway, 0.3 mi w US 101 exit n 1st St, 0.3 mi w to Skyport Dr. 1727 Technology Dr 95110. Fax: 408/441-8039. **Facility:** 151 rooms. In-room coffee. 4 stories; interior corridors; heated pool. **Cards:** AE, DI, DS, MC, VI.

CROWNE PLAZA SAN JOSE
AAA SAVE
◆◆◆
Hotel
All Year 1P: $89   2P/1B: $129   2P/2B: $99- 139 XP: $10
Phone: (408)998-0400
Location: Opposite Convention Center; 6 blks n off I-280, exit via Almaden-Vine. 282 Almaden Blvd 95113. **Fax:** 408/289-9081. **Facility:** 239 rooms. 9 stories; interior corridors. **Dining:** Restaurant; 6 am-10 pm; $15-$30; cocktails. **Cards:** AE, DI, DS, JC, MC, VI. **Special Amenities:** Early check-in/late check-out and preferred room (subject to availability with advanced reservations). *(See color ad below)*

DAYS INN
AAA SAVE
◆
Motel
All Year 1P: $82   2P/1B: $82   2P/2B: $92   XP: $10   F12
Phone: (408)224-4122
Location: Just s of jct G21 (Capitol Expwy) & SR 82 (Monterey Rd). 4170 Monterey Rd 95111. **Fax:** 408/224-4177. **Facility:** 34 rooms. Convenient location. 2 stories; exterior corridors; heated pool, whirlpool. **Some Rooms:** 5 efficiencies, 4 kitchens, whirlpools. **Cards:** AE, CB, DI, DS, JC, MC, VI. **Special Amenities:** Early check-in/late check-out and free breakfast.

DOUBLETREE HOTEL
AAA SAVE
◆◆◆◆
Hotel
Mon-Thurs 1P: $245- 275   2P/1B: $245- 275 2P/2B: $245- 275
Fri-Sun 1P: $89- 109   2P/1B: $89- 109 2P/2B: $89- 109
Phone: (408)453-4000
Location: 0.3 mi e of San Jose International Airport; via airport blvd w of & adjacent to US 101 exit N 1st St; northbound, exit Brokaw Rd. 2050 Gateway Pl 95110. Fax: 408/437-2898. **Terms:** Pets. **Facility:** 505 rooms. Large rooms. 10 stories; interior corridors; heated pool, sauna, whirlpool. **Dining:** Dining room, coffee shop; 6 am-midnight; $8-$20. **Services:** giftshop. **Some Rooms:** Fee: whirlpools. **Cards:** AE, CB, DI, DS, JC, MC, VI. **Special Amenities:** Early check-in/late check-out and free newspaper.

EXECUTIVE INN-AIRPORT
AAA SAVE
◆◆
Motel
Sun-Thurs [EP] 1P: $90- 115   2P/1B: $90- 115 2P/2B: $99- 124 XP: $15   F14
Fri & Sat [EP] 1P: $75- 115   2P/1B: $75- 115 2P/2B: $75- 115 XP: $15   F14
Phone: (408)453-1100
Location: 1 mi e of San Jose Airport; at E Rosemary St. 1310 N 1st St 95112. Fax: 408/453-1890. **Facility:** 57 rooms. 2 stories; exterior corridors; heated pool, whirlpool. **Cards:** AE, DI, DS, MC, VI. **Special Amenities:** Free breakfast and free room upgrade (subject to availability with advanced reservations).

EXECUTIVE INN DOWNTOWN
AAA SAVE
◆◆
Motel
Sun-Thurs [CP] 1P: $95- 105   2P/1B: $95- 105 2P/2B: $105
Fri & Sat [CP] 1P: $85- 95   2P/1B: $85- 95 2P/2B: $95
Phone: (408)280-5300
Location: 0.8 mi s of jct I-280 & SR 82, S 1st St. 1215 S 1st St 95110. Fax: 408/280-0569. **Terms:** Reserv deposit; handling fee imposed. **Facility:** 59 rooms. Convenient to downtown. 2 stories; exterior corridors. **Some Rooms:** 22 efficiencies, no utensils, whirlpools. **Cards:** AE, DI, DS, MC, VI. **Special Amenities:** Free breakfast and free room upgrade (subject to availability with advanced reservations).

EXECUTIVE INN SUITES
AAA SAVE
◆◆
Motel
All Year 1P: $85- 95   2P/1B: $85- 95 2P/2B: $85- 95 XP: $10
Phone: (408)281-8700
Location: On SR 82, just n of jct 6-21. 3930 Monterey Rd 95111. Fax: 408/578-6799. **Facility:** 25 rooms. 2 stories; exterior corridors. **Dining:** Coffee shop nearby. **Cards:** AE, DI, DS, MC, VI. **Special Amenities:** Free breakfast and free room upgrade (subject to availability with advanced reservations).

FAIRMONT HOTEL
◆◆◆◆
Hotel
Rates Subject to Change
Phone: 408/998-1900
Sun-Thurs 1P: $199- 259 2P/1B: $199- 259 2P/2B: $199- 259 XP: $25
Fri & Sat 1P: $89- 149 2P/1B: $109- 149 2P/2B: $89- 149 XP: $25
Location: At Fairmont Plaza. 170 S Market St 95113. Fax: 408/287-1648. **Terms:** Check-in 4 pm; handling fee imposed. **Facility:** 541 rooms. 16 poolside units with lanais; elegant decor. Fax machines in all rooms. 1-bedroom suites, $400-$500 for 2 persons; 2-bedroom suites, $1300-$1800; 20 stories; interior corridors; heated pool. **Services:** giftshop. Fee: massage. **Cards:** AE, CB, DI, DS, JC, MC, VI.

HANFORD HOTEL SAN JOSE
AAA
◆◆◆
Motel
Rates Subject to Change
Phone: (408)453-3133
Sun-Thurs [CP] 1P: $169 2P/1B: $179 2P/2B: $189 XP: $10 F17
Fri & Sat [CP] 1P: $69 2P/1B: $79 2P/2B: $89 XP: $10 F17
Location: W of US 101 exit N First St. 1755 N First St 95112. Fax: 408/452-1849. **Facility:** 186 rooms. 3 stories; interior corridors; heated pool, whirlpool. **Dining:** Coffee shop nearby. **Services:** area transportation, within 3 mi. **All Rooms:** combo or shower baths. **Cards:** AE, CB, DI, DS, JC, MC, VI.

THE HENSLEY HOUSE
◆◆◆
Bed & Breakfast
Rates Subject to Change
Phone: 408/298-3537
All Year [BP] 1P: $125- 275 2P/1B: $125- 275 2P/2B: $125- 275 XP: $15
Location: Between Hensley & Empire sts. 456 N 3rd St 95112. Fax: 408/298-4676. **Terms:** Reserv deposit, 5 day notice. **Facility:** 8 rooms. French & English antiques, stained glass windows. Some off street parking. 1 room with fireplace; 2 stories; interior corridors; smoke free premises. **All Rooms:** combo or shower baths.
Some Rooms: kitchen. **Cards:** AE, CB, DI, MC, VI.

HOLIDAY INN EXPRESS CENTRAL CITY
◆◆◆
Motel
Rates Subject to Change
Phone: 408/279-6600
All Year [CP] 1P: $95 2P/1B: $100 2P/2B: $100
Location: US 101 Tully exit, w on Monterey Rd. 2660 Monterey Rd 95111. Fax: 408/279-1064. **Facility:** 57 rooms. 4 whirlpool rms, extra charge; 2 stories; exterior corridors. **All Rooms:** combo or shower baths.
Cards: AE, DI, DS, MC, VI.

HOLIDAY INN EXPRESS-SAN JOSE INTERNATIONAL AIRPORT
AAA [SAVE]
◆◆◆
Motel
Phone: (408)467-1789
All Year [CP] 1P: $89- 129 2P/1B: $89- 129 2P/2B: $89- 129 XP: $10 F16
Location: US 101 exit N 1st St, s 0.5 mi to Rosemary St E. 1350 N Fourth St 95112. Fax: 408/467-1788. **Terms:** Reserv deposit. **Facility:** 85 rooms. 3 stories; interior corridors; heated pool, whirlpool. **Dining:** Restaurant nearby. **Cards:** AE, CB, DI, DS, JC, MC, VI. **Special Amenities:** Free breakfast and free local telephone calls.

HOLIDAY INN SOUTH SAN JOSE
◆◆◆
Motor Inn
Rates Subject to Change
Phone: 408/972-7800
Sun-Thurs 1P: $119 2P/1B: $119 2P/2B: $119 XP: $10
Fri & Sat 1P: $79 2P/1B: $79 2P/2B: $79 XP: $10
Location: Exit US 101; Bernal Rd E. 399 Silicon Valley Blvd 95138. Fax: 408/972-0157. **Facility:** 210 rooms. Attractive modern decor. 3 stories; interior corridors; heated pool. **Cards:** AE, DI, DS, MC, VI. *(See ad below)*

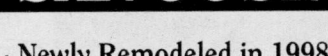

HOMEWOOD SUITES
◆◆◆
Suite Motel

Rates Subject to Change
Sun-Thurs   1P: $171- 211   2P/1B: $171- 211   2P/2B: $212- 262
Fri & Sat   1P: $89- 154   2P/1B: $89- 154   2P/2B: $134- 154

Phone: 408/428-9900

Location: Exit US 101 Trimble Rd, 1.3 mi e, 2 mi ne San Jose Int'l Airport. 10 W Trimble Rd 95131. Fax: 408/428-0222. **Terms:** Reserv deposit. **Facility:** 140 rooms. 1- & 2-bedroom suites, comfortable attractive decor. 17 two-bedroom units. 2-3 stories; interior/exterior corridors; heated pool. **Services:** giftshop; area transportation. **Recreation:** sports court. **All Rooms:** kitchens. **Cards:** AE, CB, DI, DS, JC, MC, VI.

HOTEL DE ANZA
Ⓐ
◆◆◆
Hotel

Rates Subject to Change
All Year   1P: $150- 200   2P/1B: $170- 220   2P/2B: $170- 220   XP: $15   F12

Phone: 408/286-1000

Location: 233 W Santa Clara St 95113. Fax: 408/286-0500. **Terms:** Package plans. **Facility:** 101 rooms. Elegantly restored historical 1931 hotel. Art deco & some Moorish influences with emphasis on comfort & style; complimentary video library. Penthouse suite with deck, fireplace, large whirlpool tub, $950 for 2 persons; 10 stories; interior corridors. Fee: parking. **Dining:** Restaurant; Breakfast 6:30 am, Sat & Sun 7:30 am, hotel guest; 11 am-10 pm; Complimentary deli buffet from 10 pm-5 am; cocktails. **Services:** area transportation, within 3 mi. **Cards:** AE, CB, DI, JC, MC, VI.

HYATT SAINTE CLAIRE-DOWNTOWN SAN JOSE
Ⓐ (SAVE)
◆◆◆
Historic Hotel

All Year   1P: $235- 270   2P/1B: $255- 290   2P/2B: $255- 290   XP: $20   F12

Phone: (408)885-1234

Location: Opposite convention center. 302 S Market St 95113-2889. Fax: 408/977-0403. **Facility:** 170 rooms. Historic 1926 hotel. 17 suites with wet bar, whirlpool tub, $135-$795 for 2 persons; 6 stories; interior corridors. **Dining:** Restaurant; 7 am-midnight; Sat & Sun from 8 am; $15-$35; cocktails. **Cards:** AE, CB, DI, DS, JC, MC, VI. *(See color ad p 923)*

HYATT SAN JOSE
Ⓐ (SAVE)
◆◆◆
Motor Inn

All Year   1P: $239- 259   2P/1B: $259- 279   2P/2B: $259- 279   XP: $20   F18

Phone: (408)993-1234

Location: 0.5 mi e of San Jose International Airport via Airport Pkwy; w of US 101, exit N 1st St. 1740 N 1st St 95112. Fax: 408/453-0259. **Facility:** 519 rooms. Nicely landscaped. Some compact rooms. 2-3 stories; interior corridors; heated pool, whirlpool. **Dining:** Restaurant; Patio dining open 5/1-9/30, 11 am-2; coffee shop 5:30 am-midnight; $7-$26; cocktails. **Services:** giftshop. **Recreation:** jogging. **All Rooms:** combo or shower baths. **Cards:** AE, CB, DI, DS, JC, MC, VI. *(See color ad p 923 & below)*

RADISSON PLAZA HOTEL, SAN JOSE AIRPORT
◆◆◆
Hotel

Rates Subject to Change
Sun-Thurs   1P: $159- 179   2P/1B: $159- 179   2P/2B: $159- 179   XP: $10   F17
Fri & Sat   1P: $79- 99   2P/1B: $79- 99   2P/2B: $79- 99   XP: $10   F17

Phone: 408/452-0200

Location: 0.5 mi n San Jose airport; US 101 exit n 1st St. 1471 N 4th St 95112. Fax: 408/437-8819. **Terms:** Reserv deposit. **Facility:** 185 rooms. French Provincial appointments; attractive public areas. 5 stories; interior corridors; heated pool. **Cards:** AE, CB, DI, DS, JC, MC, VI. *(See ad below)*

SAN JOSE HILTON & TOWERS
◆◆◆ All Year
Hotel
    Rates Subject to Change
1P: $130- 240   2P/1B: $145- 255 2P/2B: $145- 255 XP: $15
Phone: 408/287-2100
Location: 300 Almaden Blvd 95110. Fax: 408/947-4489. **Terms:** Check-in 4 pm; reserv deposit. **Facility:** 355 rooms. Directly connected to the San Jose McEnery Convention Center. 18 stories; interior corridors; heated pool. **Cards:** AE, CB, DI, DS, JC, MC, VI. *(See ad p 119)*

TRAVELODGE-SAN JOSE CONVENTION CENTER
◆◆ All Year
Motel
1P: $88- 100 2P/1B: $95- 105 2P/2B: $95- 105 XP: $10 F18
Phone: (408)993-1711
Location: 1 mi s of I-280 & SR 82, via S 1st St. 1415 Monterey Rd 95110. Fax: 408/993-8744. **Facility:** 26 rooms. Some small rooms. 1 two-bedroom unit. 2 stories; exterior corridors. **Dining:** Coffee shop nearby. **Some Rooms:** whirlpools. **Cards:** AE, CB, DI, DS, MC, VI. **Special Amenities:** Free room upgrade and preferred room (each subject to availability with advanced reservations).

VAGABOND
◆   7/25-7/27 [CP]
Motel 2/1-7/24 & 7/28-1/31 [CP]
    Rates Subject to Change
1P: $80   2P/1B: $85   2P/2B: $100 XP: $5 F18
1P: $75   2P/1B: $80   2P/2B: $90 XP: $5 F18
Phone: (408)453-8822
Location: I-880, exit N First St, then w. 1488 N First St 95112. Fax: 408/453-0559. **Facility:** 76 rooms. 2 stories; exterior corridors; heated pool. **Cards:** AE, DI, DS, MC, VI.

VALLEY INN
◆◆ All Year [CP]
Motel
    Rates Subject to Change
1P: $79- 89 2P/1B: $84- 94 2P/2B: $89- 99 XP: $10
Phone: (408)241-8500
Location: 0.5 mi w of I-880, 1.5 mi sw of San Jose Int'l Airport. 2155 The Alameda 95126. Fax: 408/241-8573. **Terms:** Reserv deposit; handling fee imposed. **Facility:** 26 rooms. 7 rooms with whirlpool baths $64-$109 for 2 persons; 2 stories; exterior corridors. **All Rooms:** combo or shower baths. **Cards:** AE, CB, DI, DS, MC, VI.

VALLEY PARK HOTEL
◆◆ All Year [BP]
Motel
1P: $99- 129 2P/1B: $99- 129 2P/2B: $99- 129 XP: $6 F
Phone: (408)293-5000
Location: Exit I-880, w San Carlos; 0.3 mi e. 2404 Stevens Creek Blvd 95128. Fax: 408/293-5287. **Facility:** 55 rooms. All units with extra large whirlpool tub. 3 stories; interior corridors. **All Rooms:** efficiencies. **Cards:** AE, DI, DS, JC, MC, VI. **Special Amenities:** Free breakfast and free newspaper.

WYNDHAM HOTEL-SAN JOSE
◆◆◆ Sun-Thurs
Hotel Fri & Sat
1P: $135- 165 2P/1B: $135- 165 2P/2B: $135- 165 XP: $10 F18
1P: $79   2P/1B: $79   2P/2B: $79 XP: $10 F18
Phone: (408)453-6200
Location: 0.3 mi s off US 101, exit N 1st St, 1 mi e of San Jose International Airport Pkwy, s on N 1st St. 1350 N 1st St 95112. Fax: 408/437-9693. **Terms:** Reserv deposit. **Facility:** 355 rooms. 9 stories; interior corridors; heated pool. **Dining:** Restaurant, coffee shop; 6 am-11 pm; $11-$23; cocktails. **Services:** giftshop. **All Rooms:** combo or shower baths. **Some Rooms:** whirlpools. **Cards:** AE, CB, DI, DS, JC, MC, VI. **Special Amenities:** Early check-in/late check-out and preferred room (subject to availability with advanced reservations). *(See color ad below)*

RESTAURANTS

EIGHT FORTY NORTH FIRST
◆◆◆
Continental
Lunch: $8-$26   **Dinner:** $8-$25   **Phone:** 408/282-0840
Location: 3 blks w of I-880. 840 N First St 95112. **Hours:** 11:30 am-10 pm, Sat from 5 pm. Closed major holidays & Sun. **Reservations:** suggested. **Features:** cocktails & lounge; a la carte. Extensive wine list. Smoke free premises. **Cards:** AE, DI, MC, VI.

EMILES RESTAURANT ◆◆◆ French
Lunch: $25   **Dinner:** $35   **Phone:** 408/289-1960
Location: Center. 545 S 2nd St 95112. **Hours:** 6 pm-10 pm, Fri 11:30 am-2 & 6-10 pm, Sat from 5:30 pm. Closed: Sun, Mon, 11/26 & 12/25. **Reservations:** suggested. **Features:** casual dress; cocktails; a la carte. Swiss specialties, emphasis on lite healthy preparation. Warm inviting atmosphere. Smoke free premises. **Cards:** AE, CB, DI, MC, VI.

EULIPIA RESTAURANT & BAR ◆◆ American
Lunch: $9-$12   **Dinner:** $11-$19   **Phone:** 408/280-6161
Location: 374 S 1st St 95113. **Hours:** 11:30 am-2 & 5:30-9:30 pm, Sat 5:30 pm-11 pm, Sun 4:30 pm-9 pm. Closed major holidays. **Reservations:** suggested. **Features:** cocktails & lounge; fee for parking. Creative contemporary cooking, attractive decor. **Cards:** AE, MC, VI.

LOU'S VILLAGE ⒶⒶⒶ ◆◆ Seafood
Lunch: $11-$26   **Dinner:** $17-$33   **Phone:** 408/293-4570
Location: 3.5 mi s on SR 17 from jct US 101; 1.3 mi e on W San Carlos St. 1465 W San Carlos St 95126. **Hours:** 11:30 am-10:30 pm, Sat & Sun 4:30 pm-11 pm. Closed major holidays. **Reservations:** suggested. **Features:** semi-formal attire; children's menu; cocktails & lounge; minimum charge-$7.50; a la carte. Cheerful surrounding, casual atmosphere. Varied menu including pasta, beef & poultry. Family owned since 1946. Smoke free premises. **Cards:** AE, CB, DI, MC, VI.

PASQUALE'S RISTORANTE ◆◆◆ Italian
Lunch: $8-$17   **Dinner:** $12-$20   **Phone:** 408/286-1770
Location: E of SR 82 at E Williams St. 472 S 1st St 95113. **Hours:** 11:30 am-2 & 5-10 pm, Sat from 5 pm, Sun 4 pm-9 pm. **Reservations:** suggested. **Features:** semi-formal attire; cocktails & lounge; valet parking; a la carte. Also continental cuisine, fresh seafood, chicken, veal & lamb specialties. Smoke free premises. **Cards:** AE, CB, DI, MC, VI.

SAN JUAN BAUTISTA—1,600

LODGING

SAN JUAN INN ⒶⒶⒶ ◆◆ Motel
Rates Subject to Change   **Phone:** (831)623-4380
4/1-9/30   1P: $50- 75   2P/1B: $65- 85   2P/2B: $65- 85   XP: $6   D
2/1-3/31 & 10/1-1/31   1P: $45- 60   2P/1B: $50- 75   2P/2B: $50- 75   XP: $6   D
Location: Jct SR 156. 410 Alameda 95045 (PO Box 908). Fax: 831/623-0689. **Terms:** Reserv deposit, 7 day notice; weekly/monthly rates; pets, $10 extra charge. **Facility:** 42 rooms. Quiet location, attractively landscaped grounds. 2 stories; exterior corridors; whirlpool. **Cards:** AE, DI, DS, MC, VI.

RESTAURANT

CADEMARTORI'S ◆◆ Italian
Lunch: $9-$16   **Dinner:** $13-$22   **Phone:** 831/623-4511
Location: 1st & San Jose sts, adjacent to mission grounds. 600 First St 95045. **Hours:** 11:30 am-2 & 5-9 pm, Fri & Sat-10 pm, Sun noon-9 pm. Closed: 1/1, 11/22, 12/24, 12/25 & Mon. **Reservations:** suggested. **Features:** No A/C; casual dress; children's menu; health conscious menu items; cocktails & lounge. In old adobe with beamed ceiling. Patio dining weather permitting. Homemade pastas, steaks, seafood & chicken. Smoke free premises. **Cards:** AE, MC, VI.

SAN JUAN CAPISTRANO—26,200   (See map p. 296; index p. 290)

LODGINGS

BEST WESTERN CAPISTRANO INN ⒶⒶⒶ SAVE ◆◆◆ Motel
Phone: (949)493-5661   **70**
Fri & Sat [CP]   1P: $79- 89   2P/1B: $79- 89   2P/2B: $89- 99   XP: $6   F12
Sun-Thurs [CP]   1P: $69- 79   2P/1B: $69- 79   2P/2B: $79- 89   XP: $6   F12
Location: On SR 74, just e of I-5. 27174 Ortega Hwy 92675. Fax: 949/661-8293. **Terms:** Weekly/monthly rates; small pets only. **Facility:** 108 rooms. 46 rooms with balcony. 2 stories; heated pool, whirlpool. **Dining:** Complimentary breakfast Mon-Fri; coffee shop nearby. **Services:** complimentary evening beverages, Mon-Fri. **Some Rooms:** 8 efficiencies. **Cards:** AE, CB, DI, DS, MC, VI. **Special Amenities:** Free local telephone calls and free newspaper. *(See color ad p 327)*

LAGUNA INN & SUITES ⒶⒶⒶ ◆◆◆ Motel
Guaranteed Rates   **Phone:** 949/347-8520   **71**
All Year   1P: $55- 70   2P/1B: $55- 75   2P/2B: $55- 80   XP: $5
Location: Just w of I-5, exit Avery Pkwy. 28742 Camino Capistrano 92675. Fax: 949/347-7357. **Terms:** Reserv deposit. **Facility:** 33 rooms. 3 two-bedroom units. Honeymoon suites with whirlpool, $100-$130; 3 stories; exterior corridors. **Some Rooms:** whirlpools. **Cards:** AE, DI, DS, MC, VI.

(See map p. 296)

RESTAURANTS

CAFE MOZART   **Lunch:** $4-$12   **Dinner:** $8-$20   **Phone:** 949/496-0212   53
♦♦   **Location:** In Mercado Village, 1.5 blks from Mission San Juan Capistrano. 31952 Camino Capistrano 92675.
Continental   **Hours:** 11:30 am-3 & 5:30-9 pm, Fri & Sat 5:30 pm-10 pm. Closed: 12/25, 1/1, Sun & Mon.
Reservations: suggested; weekends. **Features:** casual dress; carryout; beer & wine only. Delightful dining in casual atmosphere. Several German & fresh seafood entrees. Wild game a speciality. Dining on patio, weather permitting. Entertainment on weekends. Smoke free premises. **Cards:** AE, CB, DI, DS, MC, VI.   ✕

CEDAR CREEK INN   **Lunch:** $6-$12   **Dinner:** $13-$23   **Phone:** 949/240-2229   51
♦♦♦   **Location:** From I-5 exit Ortega Hwy, 0.5 mi w, in Mission Promenade. 26860 Ortega Hwy 92675. **Hours:** 11
American   am-9 pm, Sat-10 pm. Closed major holidays. **Features:** casual dress; Sunday brunch; cocktails. Tastefully decorated restaurant featruing a good selection of fish & meat dishes, pasta & sandwiches. Excellent desserts. Heated patio dining. **Cards:** AE, DI, MC, VI.   ✕

EL ADOBE DE CAPISTRANO   Historical   **Lunch:** $6-$11   **Dinner:** $9-$17   **Phone:** 949/493-1163   52
♦♦   **Location:** Center 1.5 blks from Misson San Juan Capistrano. 31891 Camino Capistrano 92675. **Hours:** 11
Mexican   am-9 pm, Fri & Sat-10 pm, Sun 10 am-9 pm. **Features:** Sunday brunch; children's menu; cocktails & lounge. Delightful dining in historic landmark. Also Features American cuisine. Patio dining weather permitting.
Cards: AE, DI, DS, MC, VI.   ✕

SAN LEANDRO—68,200   (See map p. 752; index p. 750)

LODGING

SAN LEANDRO MARINA INN   Rates Subject to Change   **Phone:** (510)895-1311   1
♦♦♦   All Year [CP]   1P: $89   2P/1B: $89   2P/2B: $89
Motel   **Location:** 3 mi s of Oakland Airport; w of I-880 exit Marina Blvd West, 1.3 mi w at San Leandro Marina. 68 San Leandro Marina 94577. Fax: 510/483-4078. **Facility:** 131 rooms. Attractive rooms overlooking marina. 3 stories; interior corridors. **Services:** area transportation. **Recreation:** bicycles. **All Rooms:** combo or shower baths.
Cards: AE, DI, MC, VI.

SAN LUIS OBISPO—42,000

LODGINGS

APPLE FARM INN   Rates Subject to Change   **Phone:** (805)544-2040
AAA   Fri & Sat   1P: $169- 239   2P/1B: $169- 239   2P/2B: $179- 189   XP: $20   F18
     Sun-Thurs   1P: $119- 189   2P/1B: $119- 189   2P/2B: $129- 149   XP: $20   F18
♦♦♦♦   **Location:** Just s of US 101, Monterey St exit, behind Apple Farm Restaurant. 2015 Monterey St 93401.
Motor Inn   Fax: 805/546-9495. **Terms:** Check-in 4 pm; reserv deposit. **Facility:** 69 rooms. Charming country decor & atmosphere. All rooms individually decorated in a variety of traditional or country themes with gas fireplace. Beautifully landscaped grounds. 3 stories; interior corridors; heated pool, whirlpool. **Dining:** Afternoon tea; restaurant, see separate listing. **Services:** giftshop; complimentary evening beverages; area transportation, Amtrak. **Cards:** AE, DS, MC, VI.
(See color ad p 988)

APPLE FARM TRELLIS COURT   Rates Subject to Change   **Phone:** (805)544-2040
AAA   Fri & Sat [CP]   1P: $99- 129   2P/1B: $99- 129   2P/2B: $109- 119   XP: $20   F18
     Sun-Thurs [CP]   1P: $79- 109   2P/1B: $79- 109   2P/2B: $89- 99   XP: $20   F18
♦♦♦   **Location:** Just s of US 101, Monterey St exit. 2015 Monterey St 93401. Fax: 805/546-9495.
Motel   **Terms:** Check-in 4 pm; reserv deposit. **Facility:** 34 rooms. Charming country decor. Cozy rooms with gas fireplace. Registration at Apple Farm Inn after 7 pm. 2 two-bedroom units. 2 stories; exterior corridors; heated pool, whirlpool. **Dining:** Afternoon tea; restaurant, see separate listing. **Services:** complimentary evening beverages; area transportation, to Amtrak. **All Rooms:** combo or shower baths. **Cards:** AE, DS, MC, VI. (See color ad p 988)

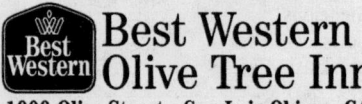

BEST WESTERN OLIVE TREE INN   Phone: (805)544-2800

AAA SAVE

◆ ◆

Motel

Fri & Sat 5/21-9/30	1P: $129- 159	2P/1B: $129- 159	2P/2B: $149- 189	XP: $10-20
Sat 2/1-5/20 & 10/1-1/31	1P: $89- 125	2P/1B: $98- 139	2P/2B: $110- 159	XP: $8-12
Sun-Thurs 5/21-9/30	1P: $69- 98	2P/1B: $69- 98	2P/2B: $79- 110	XP: $8-12
Sun-Fri 2/1-5/20 & 10/1-1/31	1P: $49- 89	2P/1B: $55- 89	2P/2B: $59- 98	XP: $5-10

Location: Just w of US 101 at jct SR 1; US 101 northbound Morro Bay exit, southbound Santa Rosa exit. 1000 Olive St 93405. Fax: 807/787-0814. **Terms:** Reserv deposit; handling fee imposed; small pets only, $25 dep req, $10 extra charge. **Facility:** 38 rooms. 6 Creekside rooms with balcony or patio. 6 efficiencies, $95; 2 stories; exterior corridors; heated pool, sauna. **Dining:** Coffee shop nearby. **Cards:** AE, CB, DI, DS, MC, VI. **Special Amenities: Free breakfast and free newspaper.** (See ad p 987)

BEST WESTERN ROYAL OAK HOTEL   Phone: (805)544-4410

AAA SAVE

◆ ◆ ◆

Motel

6/11-9/15 [CP]	1P: $69- 89	2P/1B: $69- 89	2P/2B: $69- 89	XP: $7
2/1-6/10 & 9/16-1/31 [CP]	1P: $59- 79	2P/1B: $59- 79	2P/2B: $59- 79	XP: $7

Location: Just s of US 101, Madonna Rd exit. 214 Madonna Rd 93405. Fax: 805/544-3026. **Terms:** Weekly/monthly rates; small pets only. **Facility:** 99 rooms. 2 stories; interior/exterior corridors; heated pool, indoor whirlpool. **Dining:** Restaurant nearby. **All Rooms:** extended cable TV. **Cards:** AE, CB, DI, DS, MC, VI. **Special Amenities: Free breakfast and free local telephone calls.**

BEST WESTERN SOMERSET MANOR   Phone: (805)544-0973

AAA SAVE

◆ ◆ ◆

Motor Inn

6/11-9/30 [BP]	1P: $79- 103	2P/1B: $88- 112	2P/2B: $88- 112	XP: $9	F12
2/1-6/10 & 10/1-1/31 [BP]	1P: $54- 98	2P/1B: $63- 107	2P/2B: $63- 107	XP: $9	F12

Location: On Monterey St, just s of juct US 101. 1895 Monterey St 93401. Fax: 805/541-2805. **Terms:** Reserv deposit. **Facility:** 40 rooms. 2 stories; exterior corridors; whirlpool. **Dining:** Coffee shop; 6 am-9 pm, Sun-2 pm; $5-$10; wine/beer only. **All Rooms:** combo or shower baths. **Cards:** AE, CB, DI, DS, JC, MC, VI. **Special Amenities: Free local telephone calls and free room upgrade (subject to availability with advanced reservations).** (See ad below)

CAMPUS MOTEL   Rates Subject to Change   Phone: 805/544-0881

AAA

◆

Motel

Fri & Sat 7/1-9/30 [CP]	1P: $59- 149	2P/1B: $59- 149	2P/2B: $69- 159	XP: $5-10	F12
2/1-6/30 [CP]	1P: $45- 140	2P/1B: $45- 140	2P/2B: $55- 150	XP: $5-10	F12
Sun-Thurs 7/1-9/30 [CP]	1P: $45- 130	2P/1B: $49- 130	2P/2B: $55- 140	XP: $5-10	F12
10/1-1/31 [CP]	1P: $39- 110	2P/1B: $39- 120	2P/2B: $49- 130	XP: $5-10	F12

Location: On SR 1, at jct US 101. 404 Santa Rosa St 93405. Fax: 805/544-0881. **Terms:** Reserv deposit; pets, $7-10. **Facility:** 35 rooms. 2 stories; exterior corridors; heated pool. **Some Rooms:** whirlpools. **Cards:** AE, DS, MC, VI. (See color ad below)

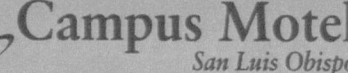

DAYS INN

Phone: (805)549-9911

AAA SAVE

◆◆◆ Motel

All Year [CP]   1P: $49- 135   2P/1B: $49- 135   2P/2B: $59- 135   XP: $5

Location: Just se of US 101, exit Monterey St. 2050 Garfield St 93401. Fax: 805/546-0734. **Terms:** Pets, $50 extra charge, $10 dep req. **Facility:** 43 rooms. 2 whirlpool rms, $65-$125; 2 rm suites, $75-$175; 3 stories; exterior corridors; whirlpool, swimming pool heated in season. **All Rooms:** combo or shower baths. **Some Rooms:** 4 kitchens. **Cards:** AE, DI, DS, MC, VI. **Special Amenities:** Free breakfast and free local telephone calls.

ECONOLODGE

Phone: (805)544-8886

AAA SAVE

◆ Motel

Fri & Sat   1P: $40- 129   2P/1B: $40- 139   2P/2B: $50- 149   XP: $8   F12
Sun-Thurs   1P: $45- 60   2P/1B: $45- 74   2P/2B: $50- 70   XP: $8   F12

Location: On Olive St, just w of US 101 at jct SR 1; US 101 northbound Morro Bay exit, southbound Santa Rosa exit. 950 Olive St 93405. Fax: 805/543-1611. **Terms:** Weekly rates. **Facility:** 32 rooms. 2 two-bedroom units. 2 stories; exterior corridors; whirlpool. **Some Rooms:** 2 efficiencies, no utensils. **Cards:** AE, CB, DI, MC, VI. **Special Amenities:** Free local telephone calls.

EMBASSY SUITES

Phone: (805)549-0800

AAA SAVE

◆◆◆ Suite Motor Inn

5/14-9/11 [BP]   1P: $109- 169   2P/1B: $114- 174   2P/2B: $114- 174   XP: $10   F18
2/1-5/13 [BP]   1P: $109- 144   2P/1B: $119- 154   2P/2B: $119- 154   XP: $10   F18
9/12-1/31 [BP]   1P: $109- 144   2P/1B: $119- 154   2P/2B: $119- 154   XP: $10   F18

Location: US 101, Madonna Rd exit; 0.5 mi s, e on Dalidio Dr. 333 Madonna Rd 93405. Fax: 805/543-5273. **Facility:** 196 rooms. At Central Coast Plaza Mall. 4 stories; interior corridors; heated indoor pool, 1 indoor whirlpool & 3 outdoor whirlpools located on second floor sun deck. **Dining:** Restaurant; 11:30-2 & 5-10 pm; $9-$16. **Services:** complimentary evening beverages; area transportation, Amtrak. **Cards:** AE, CB, DI, DS, JC, MC, VI.

GARDEN STREET INN BED & BREAKFAST

Rates Subject to Change   **Phone: (805)545-9802**

◆◆◆ Historic Bed & Breakfast

All Year [BP]   1P: $90- 180   2P/1B: $90- 180

Location: 0.5 mi e of US 101; Marsh St exit. 1212 Garden St 93401. Fax: 805/545-9403. **Terms:** Reserv deposit, 7 day notice. In downtown area. 1887 restored Italianate Queen Anne style house. Charming victorian decor. Some rooms with gas fireplace. 2 stories; interior corridors; designated smoking area. **Cards:** AE, MC, VI.

HERITAGE INN BED & BREAKFAST

Guaranteed Rates   **Phone: 805/544-7440**

AAA

◆◆ Historic Bed & Breakfast

All Year [BP]   1P: $65- 130   2P/1B: $65- 130   XP: $10

Location: Just w of US 101, at jct SR 1; Santa Rosa exit southbound,Morro Bay exit northbound. 978 Olive St 93405. Fax: 805/544-7440. **Terms:** Reserv deposit, 7 day notice; small pets only, $25 extra charge, $25 dep req. **Facility:** 7 rooms. Charming rooms in a turn-of-the-century home. 4 rooms with gas fireplace. 2 stories; interior corridors; designated smoking area. **Cards:** AE, MC, VI.

HOLIDAY INN EXPRESS

Phone: (805)544-8600

AAA SAVE

◆◆◆ Motor Inn

5/28-9/18 [CP]   1P: $99- 129   2P/1B: $99- 149   2P/2B: $99- 149   XP: $10   F18
2/1-5/27 & 9/19-1/31 [CP]   1P: $80- 129   2P/1B: $80- 129   2P/2B: $80- 129   XP: $10   F18

Location: 0.3 mi s of jct US 101; northbound Grand Ave exit, southbound Monterey St exit. 1800 Monterey St 93401. Fax: 805/541-4698. **Terms:** Reserv deposit. **Facility:** 100 rooms. 3 stories; interior corridors; heated pool, whirlpool. **Dining:** Restaurant; 11:30 am-9:30 pm; $8-$12; cocktails. **Cards:** AE, CB, DI, DS, JC, MC, VI. **Special Amenities:** Free breakfast. *(See color ad below)*

LA CUESTA MOTOR INN

Phone: (805)543-2777

AAA SAVE

◆◆◆ Motel

3/19-10/31 [CP]   1P: $85- 105   2P/1B: $95- 120   2P/2B: $95- 120   XP: $5-10   F15
2/1-3/18 & 11/1-1/31 [CP]   1P: $65- 85   2P/1B: $75- 110   2P/2B: $75- 110   XP: $5-10   F15

Location: 2 blks s of jct US 101, Monterey St exit. 2074 Monterey St 93401. Fax: 805/544-0696. **Facility:** 72 rooms. Many rooms with balcony. 4 stories; interior corridors. **Dining:** Afternoon tea; restaurant nearby. **Cards:** AE, DI, DS, MC, VI. **Special Amenities:** Free local telephone calls. *(See color ad p 991)*

LAMPLIGHTER INN   Phone: (805)547-7777

(AAA) (SAVE)   7/4-9/14 [CP]   1P: $54- 99   2P/1B: $64- 99   2P/2B: $75- 129   XP: $10   D12
            6/9-7/3 [CP]   1P: $49- 89   2P/1B: $59- 89   2P/2B: $69- 99   XP: $10   D12
◆◆   3/31-6/8 & 9/15-10/12 [CP] 1P: $45- 75   2P/1B: $49- 79   2P/2B: $59- 79   XP: $10   D12
Motel   2/1-3/30 & 10/13-1/31 [CP] 1P: $45- 59   2P/1B: $45- 69   2P/2B: $49- 75   XP: $10   D12
        Location: 0.5 mi s of US 101, Monterey St exit. 1604 Monterey St 93401. Fax: 805/547-7787.
Terms: Weekly rates. **Facility:** 40 rooms. A variety of rooms from compact to nicely decorated suites. 1 whirlpool rm, $89-$150; 11 2-room family suites with microwave & small refrigerator; $99-$225 for up to 4 persons; 2-3 stories; exterior corridors; heated pool, whirlpool. **All Rooms:** combo or shower baths, extended cable TV. **Cards:** AE, DS, MC, VI.
Special Amenities: Free breakfast and free room upgrade (subject to availability with advanced reservations).
(See color ad below)   [SB] [icons]

MADONNA INN   Rates Subject to Change   Phone: (805)543-3000
◆◆◆   All Year   1P: $87- 198   2P/1B: $97- 198   2P/2B: $97- 198   XP: $15   F18
Motor Inn   **Location:** Adjacent to US 101, Madonna Rd exit. 100 Madonna Rd 93405. Fax: 805/543-1800.
        Terms: Check-in 4 pm; reserv deposit. **Facility:** 109 rooms. On spacious grounds in a rural area. Large,
uniquely designed theme rooms. Some rock rooms with waterfall shower, some rooms with vivid colors. 2 two-bedroom units,
2 three-bedroom units. Suites, some with fireplace; 3 stories; exterior corridors; smoke free premises. **Services:** giftshop.
All Rooms: combo or shower baths. **Cards:** AE, JC, MC, VI. *(See ad p 992)*   [icons]

PEACH TREE INN   Rates Subject to Change   Phone: 805/543-3170
◆◆   All Year [CP]   1P: $69- 99   2P/1B: $79- 99   2P/2B: $79- 125   XP: $10
Motel   **Location:** Just s of jct US 101, Monterey St exit. 2001 Monterey St 93401. Fax: 805/543-7673. **Facility:** 39
rooms. 6 creekside rooms with private patio. 1 story; exterior corridors. **All Rooms:** combo or shower baths.
Cards: AE, DI, DS, MC, VI.   [icons]

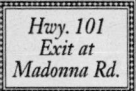

SANDS SUITES & MOTEL　　　　　　　　　　　　　　　　　　　　　　Phone: (805)544-0500

6/11-9/25 [CP]	1P:	$79-	129	2P/1B:	$79-	139	2P/2B:	$89- 139	XP: $7	F17
4/16-6/10 [CP]	1P:	$69-	109	2P/1B:	$69-	109	2P/2B:	$79- 119	XP: $7	F17
2/1-4/15 & 1/1-1/31 [CP]	1P:	$59-	89	2P/1B:	$59-	89	2P/2B:	$69- 99	XP: $7	F17
9/26-12/31 [CP]	1P:	$59-	79	2P/1B:	$59-	79	2P/2B:	$69- 89	XP: $7	F17

Motel **Location:** Just s of jct US 101, Monterey St exit. 1930 Monterey St 93401. Fax: 805/544-3529. **Terms:** Reserv deposit; pets, $5 extra charge. **Facility:** 70 rooms. 14 one-bedroom suites with microwave, refrigerator & wetbar; 2 stories; exterior corridors; heated pool, whirlpool. **Dining:** Restaurants nearby. **All Rooms:** combo or shower baths, extended cable TV. **Cards:** AE, CB, DI, DS, MC, VI. **Special Amenities: Free breakfast and free local telephone calls.** *(See ad below)*

SAN LUIS OBISPO TRAVELODGE　　　　　　　　　　　　　　　　　　Phone: (805)543-5110

5/1-9/15	1P:	$55-	79	2P/1B:	$55-	79	2P/2B:	$59-129	XP: $6
3/1-4/30	1P:	$45-	69	2P/1B:	$45-	69	2P/2B:	$52-119	XP: $6
2/1-2/28 & 9/16-1/31	1P:	$42-	69	2P/1B:	$42-	69	2P/2B:	$45- 99	XP: $6

Motel **Location:** Just s of jct US 101; exit Grand Ave. 1825 Monterey St 93401. Fax: 805/543-3406. **Terms:** Small pets only. **Facility:** 39 rooms. 2 stories; exterior corridors; heated pool. **Dining:** Restaurant nearby. **All Rooms:** combo or shower baths. **Cards:** AE, CB, DI, DS, MC, VI. **Special Amenities: Free local telephone calls and free newspaper.**

SUPER 8 MOTEL　　　　　　　　　　　　　　　　　　　　Phone: 805/544-7895

(AAA) [SAVE]

◆ ◆

Motel

6/15-9/15	1P:	$49-	89	2P/1B:	$49-	89	2P/2B:	$49-	89	XP: $3-5
2/1-6/14 & 9/16-1/31	1P:	$45-	69	2P/1B:	$45-	69	2P/2B:	$49-	69	XP: $3-5

Location: Just s of jct US 101, Monterey St exit. 1951 Monterey St 93401. **Fax:** 805/544-7895. **Facility:** 49 rooms. 2 stories; exterior corridors; small pool. **Dining:** Coffee shop nearby. **Cards:** AE, DI, JC, MC, VI.

TRAVELODGE DOWNTOWN　　　　　　　　　　　　　　Phone: (805)543-6443

(AAA) [SAVE]

◆

Motel

5/1-9/30 [CP]	1P:	$54-	72	2P/1B:	$59-	78	2P/2B:	$65-	92	XP: $5	F12
2/1-4/30 & 10/1-1/31 [CP]	1P:	$48-	50	2P/1B:	$52-	56	2P/2B:	$53-	59

Location: Just e of US 101, Marsh St exit. 345 Marsh St 93401. **Fax:** 805/545-0951. **Terms:** Reserv deposit. **Facility:** 51 rooms. 2 blks s of downtown area. 2 two-bedroom units. 2 stories; exterior corridors. **All Rooms:** combo or shower baths. **Cards:** AE, CB, DI, DS, MC, VI. **Special Amenities:** Early check-in/late check-out and free breakfast.

VAGABOND INN　　　　　　　　　　　　　　　　　　　Phone: (805)544-4710

(AAA) [SAVE]

◆ ◆

Motel

All Year [CP]	1P: $100	2P/1B:	$105	2P/2B:	$110	XP: $5	F18

Location: Just s of US 101, Madonna Rd exit. 210 Madonna Rd 93405. **Fax:** 805/541-1949. **Terms:** Small pets only, $5 extra charge. **Facility:** 60 rooms. 1 two-bedroom unit. 2 stories; exterior corridors; heated pool, whirlpool. **Dining:** Restaurant nearby. **Services:** area transportation, Amtrak station. **Cards:** AE, CB, DI, DS, MC, VI. **Special Amenities:** Free breakfast and free local telephone calls.

VILLA MOTEL　　　　　　　　　　　　　　　　　　　　Phone: (805)543-8071

(AAA) [SAVE]

◆ ◆

Motel

5/14-10/2 [CP]	1P:	$43-	110	2P/1B:	$49-	120	2P/2B:	$59-	129	XP: $5	F12
4/1-5/13 [CP]	1P:	$39-	69	2P/1B:	$42-	79	2P/2B:	$49-	89	XP: $5	F12
2/1-3/31 & 10/3-1/31 [CP]	1P:	$37-	59	2P/1B:	$40-	69	2P/2B:	$45-	79	XP: $5	F12

Location: Just s of jct US 101, Monterey St exit. 1670 Monterey St 93401. **Fax:** 805/549-9389. **Terms:** Reserv deposit, 3 day notice; handling fee imposed; weekly rates. **Facility:** 14 rooms. Weekly rates, 11/1-3/31; 1-2 stories; exterior corridors; heated pool open 4/1-10/31. **All Rooms:** combo or shower baths. **Cards:** AE, DI, DS, JC, MC, VI. **Special Amenities:** Free breakfast and free room upgrade (subject to availability with advanced reservations).

RESTAURANTS

APPLE FARM RESTAURANT　Lunch: $7-$9　　Dinner: $11-$18　　Phone: 805/544-6100

(AAA)

◆ ◆

American

Location: Just s of US 101, Monterey St, at Apple Farm Inn. 2015 Monterey St 93401. **Hours:** 7 am-9:30 pm, Fri, Sat & summer-10 pm. **Reservations:** suggested. **Features:** casual dress; children's menu; early bird specials; carryout; salad bar; beer & wine only. Country charm; a popular, busy restaurant serving homestyle cooked soups, desserts & varied entrees. Homemade ice cream. Smoke free premises. **Cards:** AE, DS, MC, VI. *(See color ad p 988 & p 991)*

BENVENUTI RISTORANTE　Lunch: $7-$11　　Dinner: $10-$19　　Phone: 805/541-5393

(AAA)

◆ ◆ ◆

Italian

Location: 0.5 mi s of downtown area; from US 101, exit Marsh St, then 0.3 mi N. 450 Marsh St 93401. **Hours:** 11:30 am-2 & 5-10 pm; Sat & Sun 5 pm-10 pm. Closed major holidays. **Reservations:** suggested. **Features:** casual dress; children's menu; cocktails; a la carte. Charming restaurant in a restored home. Nice selection of Italian cuisine. Patio seating; smoking allowed. **Cards:** AE, DI, MC, VI.

BUONA TAVOLA　　Lunch: $7-$13　　Dinner: $9-$17　　Phone: 805/545-8000

◆ ◆ ◆

Italian

Location: Downtown, next to Fremont Theater. 1037 Monterey St 93401. **Hours:** 11:30 am-2:30 & 5:30-9:30 pm, Fri-10 pm, Sat 5:30 pm-10 pm, Sun 5:30 pm-9 pm. Closed: 11/25 & 12/25. **Reservations:** suggested. **Features:** casual dress; beer & wine only; street parking; a la carte. Small restaurant with indoor or patio dining. Nice selection of well prepared pasta, fish, veal & chicken. Smoke free premises. **Cards:** AE, DS, MC, VI.

CAFE ROMA　　Lunch: $8-$12　　Dinner: $9-$19　　Phone: 805/541-6800

(AAA)

◆ ◆ ◆

Italian

Location: 0.5 mi e of downtown, adjacent to train station. 1819 Osos St 93401. **Hours:** 11:30 am-2:30 & 5:30-9:30 pm, Sat & Sun from 5:30 pm. Closed major holidays & Mon. **Reservations:** suggested. **Features:** No A/C; casual dress; cocktails & lounge; a la carte. Charming restaurant with a nice selection of pasta, veal, chicken, scampi & pizza. Outdoor patio dining avail. Smoking allowed on patio. **Cards:** AE, CB, DI, DS, MC, VI.

LINN'S RESTAURANT　Lunch: $5-$10　　Dinner: $7-$13　　Phone: 805/546-8444

◆

American

Location: Downtown. 1141 Chorro St at Marsh 93401. **Hours:** 7 am-10 pm, Fri-11 pm, Sat 8 am-11 p,, Sun 8 am-10 pm. Closed: 12/25. **Features:** No A/C; casual dress; children's menu; carryout; salad bar; beer & wine only; street parking. Popular restaurant featuring a large selection of salads, sandwiches & entrees. Chicken & beef pot pies a specialty. Gift shop & bakery. Smoke free premises. **Cards:** AE, DS, MC, VI.

MADONNA INN DINING ROOM　　Dinner: $16-$23　　Phone: 805/543-3000

◆ ◆ ◆

American

(See ad p 992)

Location: Adjacent to US 101, Madonna Rd exit, in Madonna Inn. 100 Madonna Rd 93405. **Hours:** 5:30 pm-10 pm. **Reservations:** suggested. **Features:** casual dress; children's menu; cocktails & lounge; entertainment. Ornate, uniquely decorated dining room. Smoke free premises. **Cards:** JC, MC, VI.

THIS OLD HOUSE　　Dinner: $14-$23　　Phone: 805/543-2690

◆

American

Location: 2.5 mi sw of SR 1 (Santa Rosa St). 740 W Foothill Rd 93405. **Hours:** 5 pm-9:30 pm, Fri-10 pm, Sat 4 pm-10 pm, Sun 4 pm-9:30 pm. Closed: 12/25. **Reservations:** suggested. **Features:** No A/C; casual dress; children's menu; early bird specials; cocktails & lounge. In a country location. Informal, old west atmosphere. Features oak-pit barbecue steak, ribs, chicken & seafood. Smoke free premises. **Cards:** AE, DI, DS, MC, VI.

SAN MARCOS—39,000

LODGINGS

QUAILS INN AT LAKE SAN MARCOS RESORT Rates Subject to Change **Phone:** (760)744-0120
◆◆◆ All Year 1P: $99- 149 2P/1B: $99- 149 2P/2B: $99- 149 XP: $10 F12
Motor Inn **Location:** 2 mi s of SR 78, Rancho Santa Fe Rd exit, 0.5 mi e via Lake San Marcos Dr & San Marino Dr; at Lake San Marcos. 1025 La Bonita Dr 92069. Fax: 760/744-0748. **Terms:** Reserv deposit, 3 day notice.
Facility: 140 rooms. Attractive grounds, lakefront location. Some lakeside rooms with patio or balcony. 2 1-bedroom & 2 2-bedroom lakefront apartments, $175-$299; 2 stories; interior/exterior corridors; heated pool; 4 tennis courts. Fee: 36 holes golf. Rental: boats, canoes. **All Rooms:** combo or shower baths. **Cards:** AE, CB, DI, MC, VI. *(See color ad p 884)*

🛏️🐾📞📺🅿️🏨🍴🍽️⊗➕⊛🖵🖨️🛗🔌✕

RAMADA LIMITED Rates Subject to Change **Phone:** (760)471-2800
ⒶⒶⒶ 4/1-4/15, 6/1-9/4 & 12/20-1/3
  [CP] 1P: $49- 79 2P/1B: $49- 79 2P/2B: $59- 89 XP: $6
◆◆ 2/1-3/31, 4/16-5/31,
Motor Inn 9/5-12/19 & 1/4-1/31 [CP] 1P: $44- 64 2P/1B: $44- 64 2P/2B: $49- 69 XP: $6
  Location: Just e of SR 78, exit San Marcos Blvd. 517 San Marcos Blvd 92069. Fax: 760/471-8653.
Terms: Reserv deposit; weekly/monthly rates. **Facility:** 84 rooms. Located close to freeway. 2 stories; interior/exterior corridors. **Dining:** Restaurant nearby. **Cards:** AE, DI, DS, MC, VI. *(See color ad below)*

📞📺🅿️🍴🛗🔌🖨️🛗🔌✕

RESTAURANT

FISH HOUSE VERA CRUZ **Lunch:** $6-$11 **Dinner:** $9-$16 **Phone:** 760/744-8000
◆◆ **Location:** 0.7 mi nw of SR 78, exit San Marcos Blvd. 360 Via Vera Cruz 92069. **Hours:** 11 am-9 pm, Fri & Sat-10 pm. Closed: 11/25 & 12/25. **Features:** casual dress; children's menu; cocktails & lounge. Popular restaurant featuring a large selection of fresh seafood. **Cards:** AE, MC, VI.
Seafood ✕

SAN MATEO—*See San Francisco p. 973.*

SAN MIGUEL—1,100

LODGING

WESTERN STATES INN Rates Subject to Change **Phone:** (805)467-3674
ⒶⒶⒶ Fri & Sat 5/16-9/30 1P: $55- 75 2P/1B: $65- 75 2P/2B: $75- 90 XP: $5
  Fri & Sat 2/1-5/15 &
◆ 10/1-1/31 1P: $55- 60 2P/1B: $65- 85 2P/2B: $75- 90 XP: $5
Motel Sun-Thurs 5/16-9/30 1P: $45- 59 2P/1B: $50- 65 2P/2B: $65- 80 XP: $5
  Sun-Thurs 2/1-5/15 &
  10/1-1/31 1P: $35- 40 2P/1B: $39- 45 2P/2B: $45- 65 XP: $5
Location: E side of US 101; from US 101, exit 10th St; just n on K St. 1099 K St 93451 (PO Box 58). **Terms:** Reserv deposit, 3 day notice. **Facility:** 17 rooms. Nicely furnished rooms with contemporary decor. Located just s of city park. Playground equipment & picnic tables. Public pool open June-Aug. 2 stories; exterior corridors. **Cards:** AE, MC, VI.

ASK🛏️🐾🖵🖨️🛗🔌✕

SAN PEDRO—*See Los Angeles p. 632.*

SAN RAFAEL—*See San Francisco p. 974.*

SAN RAMON—35,300   (See map p. 752; index p. 751)

LODGINGS

COURTYARD BY MARRIOTT   Rates Subject to Change   **Phone:** (925)866-2900   **55**
◆◆◆   All Year   1P: $69- 79   2P/1B: $69-   79 2P/2B: $69- 79 XP:$10-15   F18
Motor Inn   **Location:** Exit I-680 Boillinger Canyon w; s on San Ramon Valley Blvd. 18090 San Ramon Valley Blvd
94583. Fax: 925/866-8983. **Facility:** 136 rooms. 8 whirlpool rms, extra charge; 4 stories; interior corridors;
heated pool. **Cards:** AE, CB, DI, DS, MC, VI.

RESIDENCE INN BY MARRIOTT   Rates Subject to Change   **Phone:** 925/277-9292   **57**
◆◆◆   Sun-Thurs [CP]   1P: $159   2P/1B: $159   2P/2B: $199
Suite Motel   Fri & Sat [CP]   1P: $99   2P/1B: $99   2P/2B: $149
Location: E of I-680, exit Bollinger Canyon Rd. 1071 Market Pl 94583. Fax: 925/277-0687. **Facility:** 106
rooms. Some units with 2-bedrooms & 2-baths, some with fireplace. 24 two-bedroom units. 2 stories; exterior corridors.
Recreation: sports court. **All Rooms:** kitchens. **Cards:** AE, CB, DI, DS, MC, VI.

SAN RAMON MARRIOTT AT BISHOP RANCH   Rates Subject to Change   **Phone:** 925/867-9200   **56**
◆◆◆   All Year   1P: $179   2P/1B: $189   2P/2B: $199   XP: $10
Hotel   **Location:** I-680, exit Bollinger Canyon e, n on Sunset, just w. 2600 Bishop Dr 94583. Fax: 925/830-9326.
Facility: 368 rooms. Very attractive rooms & public areas. 2 whirlpool rms, extra charge; 6 stories; interior cor-
ridors; heated pool. **Services:** giftshop. **Cards:** AE, CB, DI, DS, JC, MC, VI.

SAN SIMEON—300

LODGINGS

CALIFORNIA SEACOAST LODGE   Rates Subject to Change   **Phone:** (805)927-3878
(AAA)   6/1-9/30 [CP]   1P: $65- 135   2P/1B: $65- 135 2P/2B: $65- 135 XP: $5
◆◆◆   2/1-5/31 & 10/1-1/31 [CP]   1P: $55- 125   2P/1B: $55- 125 2P/2B: $55- 125 XP: $5
Motel   **Location:** On SR 1. 9215 Hearst Dr 93452. Fax: 805/927-1781. **Terms:** Reserv deposit, 3 day notice.
Facility: 57 rooms. Some rooms with ocean view. Many with gas fireplace. Decorated in country motif. 14
rooms with whirlpool tub, $100-$185; 2 stories; interior corridors; small pool. **Cards:** AE, MC, VI.
(See color ad p 997)

EL REY GARDEN INN   Phone: (805)927-3998
7/1-9/6 [CP]   1P: $89- 109   2P/1B: $89- 109   2P/2B: $89- 109   XP: $5-10
Fri & Sat 4/1-5/31, 6/1-6/30 &
9/7-10/31 [CP]   1P: $79- 99   2P/1B: $79- 99   2P/2B: $79- 99   XP: $5-10
2/1-3/31, Sun-Thurs 4/1-5/31
& 11/1-1/31 [CP]   1P: $69- 89   2P/1B: $69- 89   2P/2B: $69- 89   XP: $5-10

Motor Inn

Location: On SR 1. 9260 Castillo Dr 93452 (PO Box 200). Fax: 805/927-8268. **Terms:** Reserv deposit. **Facility:** 56 rooms. Beautifully landscaped courtyard area. Spacious rooms with patio or balcony, many with ocean or garden view, 11 with gas fireplace. 2 two-bedroom units. 2 two-room suites with whirlpool $139-$159; 2 stories; interior/exterior corridors; small heated pool, whirlpools. **Dining:** Europa Restaurant, see separate listing. **Some Rooms:** whirlpools. **Cards:** AE, DS, MC, VI. **Special Amenities:** Free breakfast and free local telephone calls. *(See color ad below)*

MOTEL 6 PREMIERE - 1212   Rates Subject to Change   Phone: 805/927-8691
7/1-9/30   1P: $65- 75   2P/1B: $71- 81   2P/2B: $71- 81   XP: $3-6   F17
5/27-6/30   1P: $49- 59   2P/1B: $55- 65   2P/2B: $55- 65   XP: $3-6   F17
10/1-1/31   1P: $45- 55   2P/1B: $51- 61   2P/2B: $51- 61   XP: $3-6   F17
2/1-5/26   1P: $43- 53   2P/1B: $49- 59   2P/2B: $49- 59   XP: $3-6   F17

Motor Inn

Location: SR 1. 9070 Castillo Dr 93452. Fax: 805/927-5341. **Terms:** Small pets only. **Facility:** 100 rooms. 2 stories; interior corridors; heated pool. **Dining:** Restaurant; 7 am-noon & 5-10 pm; $8-$16; cocktails. **Cards:** AE, CB, DI, DS, MC, VI.

QUALITY INN

AAA SAVE

◆◆◆

Motel

Phone: (805)927-865

	1P:		2P/1B:			2P/2B:		XP:		
5/1-7/31 & 9/1-10/31	1P:	$75- 95	2P/1B:	$75- 125		2P/2B:	$83- 103	XP:	$5	F1
8/1-8/31	1P:	$85- 95	2P/1B:	$85- 125		2P/2B:	$93- 103	XP:	$5	F1
2/1-4/30 & 11/1-1/31	1P:	$60- 75	2P/1B:	$60- 115		2P/2B:	$65- 85	XP:	$5	F1

Location: On SR 1. 9280 Castillo Dr 93452. Fax: 805/927-4800. **Terms:** Reserv deposit. **Facility:** 48 rooms 4 large rms with refrigerator, microwave, VCR's & gas fireplace; 2 stories; interior corridors; indoor whirlpoo **Dining:** Restaurant nearby. **Recreation:** pool table, video games. **Cards:** AE, CB, DI, DS, JC, MC, VI. **Special Amenities** Free local telephone calls and free newspaper.

SANDS MOTEL

◆

Motel

Phone: 805/927-324

	Rates Subject to Change						
Fri & Sat 6/1-8/31 [CP]	1P:	$75- 105	2P/1B:	$75- 105	2P/2B:	$85- 110
Sun-Thurs 6/1-8/31 [CP]	1P:	$45- 95	2P/1B:	$45- 95	2P/2B:	$50- 100
Fri & Sat 2/1-5/31 & 9/1-1/31 [CP]	1P:	$45- 85	2P/1B:	$45- 85	2P/2B:	$45- 85
Sun-Thurs 2/1-5/31 & 9/1-1/31 [CP]	1P:	$39- 65	2P/1B:	$39- 65	2P/2B:	$39- 75

Location: On SR 1. 9355 Hearst Dr 93452. **Terms:** Reserv deposit. **Facility:** 33 rooms. 2 stories; exterior corridors; heate indoor pool. **All Rooms:** combo or shower baths. **Cards:** AE, DS, MC, VI.

SAN SIMEON LODGE

◆◆

Motor Inn

Phone: (805)927-460

	Rates Subject to Change							
7/1-9/6	1P:	$69- 99	2P/1B:	$69- 99	2P/2B:	$79- 99	XP: $5-10
5/1-6/30 & 9/7-9/30	1P:	$59- 89	2P/1B:	$59- 89	2P/2B:	$69- 89	XP: $5-10
4/1-4/30 & 10/1-10/31	1P:	$39- 69	2P/1B:	$39- 69	2P/2B:	$49- 69	XP: $5-10
2/1-3/31 & 11/1-1/31	1P:	$29- 49	2P/1B:	$29- 49	2P/2B:	$35- 49	XP: $5-10

Location: On SR 1. 9520 Castillo Dr 93452. Fax: 805/927-2374. **Terms:** Reserv deposit. **Facility:** 61 rooms. 2 stories; exterio corridors; heated pool. **All Rooms:** combo or shower baths. **Cards:** AE, DS, MC, VI. *(See ad below)*

SILVER SURF MOTEL

AAA SAVE

◆◆

Motel

Phone: (805)927-466

	1P:		2P/1B:		2P/2B:		XP:	
7/30-9/5	1P:	$69- 89	2P/1B:	$69- 89	2P/2B:	$74- 109	XP:	$5
3/26-7/29 & 9/6-10/31	1P:	$54- 74	2P/1B:	$54- 74	2P/2B:	$59- 94	XP:	$5
2/1-3/25 & 11/1-1/31	1P:	$39- 59	2P/1B:	$39- 59	2P/2B:	$44- 79	XP:	$5

Location: On SR 1. 9390 Castillo Dr 93452. **Terms:** Reserv deposit; pets, $5 extr charge. **Facility:** 72 rooms. Large lawn area. Some rooms with ocean view and balcony. Some small rooms 1 two-bedroom unit. 4 rooms with gas fireplace $59-89; 2 stories; exterior corridors; small heated indoor pool, whirlpoo **Dining:** Restaurant nearby. **All Rooms:** combo or shower baths. **Cards:** AE, CB, DI, DS, MC, VI. *(See color ad p 996)*

RESTAURANT

EUROPA RESTAURANT
◆◆
Continental
Dinner: $12-$18   **Phone:** 805/927-3087
Location: E side of SR 1, at El Rey Garden Inn. 9240 Castillo Dr 93452. **Hours:** 5:30 pm-9 pm. Closed:
11/29-12/26 & Sun. **Reservations:** accepted. **Features:** casual dress; children's menu; beer & wine only.
American & European food with homemade touch. Specialties include fresh seafood, pasta & desserts made
on premises. Smoke free premises. **Cards:** MC, VI.   ⊠

SANTA ANA—293,700   (See map p. 294; index p. 291)

LODGINGS

BEST WESTERN ORANGE COUNTY
AIRPORT NORTH
ⓐ
◆◆◆
Motel

	Rates Subject to Change			**Phone:** (714)432-8888	**117**
6/1-8/31 [BP]	1P: $62	2P/1B: $62	2P/2B: $62		
2/1-5/31 & 9/1-1/31 [BP]	1P: $53	2P/1B: $53	2P/2B: $53		

Location: Just w of SR 55, exit Dyer Rd W. 2700 Hotel Terrace Dr 92705. Fax: 714/434-6228. **Facility:** 148
rooms. 3 stories; exterior corridors; heated pool, whirlpool. **Cards:** AE, DI, DS, JC, MC, VI.
(See color ad p 329)   [ASK] 🅂🄳 🈵 ⊇ ⊬ 🛆 🛏 🎾 ▢ 🖨 🔒 ⊠

COMFORT SUITES - ORANGE
COUNTY AIRPORT
◆◆◆
Motel

	Rates Subject to Change			**Phone:** (714)966-5200	**112**
All Year [CP]	1P: $79	2P/1B: $79	2P/2B: $79	XP: $10	F18

Location: Just w of SR 55, exit Dyer Rd West. 2620 Hotel Terrace Dr 92705. Fax: 714/979-9650.
Facility: 130 rooms. 3 stories; exterior corridors; heated pool, whirlpool. **Dining:** Complimentary evening
beverages, Tues & Thurs; restaurant nearby. **Cards:** AE, CB, DI, DS, JC, MC, VI.
[SAVE] 🅂 🈵 ⊇ 🍴⊬ 🛆 🎾 ▢ 🖨 🔒 ⊠

COURTYARD BY MARRIOTT
◆◆◆
Motor Inn

	Rates Subject to Change			**Phone:** 714/545-1001	**113**
7/2-9/9	1P: $80	2P/1B: $80	2P/2B: $80		
2/1-7/1	1P: $62	2P/1B: $62	2P/2B: $62		
9/10-1/31	1P: $62	2P/1B: $62	2P/2B: $62		

Location: 1.5 mi n of I-405, Harbor Blvd exit. 3002 S Harbor Blvd 92704. Fax: 714/545-8439. **Facility:** 145 rooms. Nicely
landscaped courtyard & pool area. 4 stories; interior corridors; heated pool. **Cards:** AE, CB, DI, DS, MC, VI.
(See color ad p 311)   🅂 🄳 🈵 ⊇ 🍴 🛆 🛏 🎾 ▢ 🖨 🔒 ⊠

DOUBLETREE CLUB HOTEL-ORANGE
COUNTY AIRPORT
ⓐ
◆◆◆
Motor Inn
(See ad below)

	Guaranteed Rates			**Phone:** (714)751-2400	**115**
All Year	1P: $160	2P/1B: $160	2P/2B: $170	XP: $10	F18

Location: Just sw of SR 55, exit MacArthur Blvd. 7 Hutton Centre Dr 92707. Fax: 714/662-7935.
Terms: Reserv deposit. **Facility:** 167 rooms. Attractive location overlooking man-made lake & corporate office
park. 6 stories; interior corridors; heated pool, whirlpool. **Dining:** Dining room; 11 am-2 & 5-10 pm, Sat &
Sun 5-10 pm; $7-$17. **All Rooms:** combo or shower baths. **Cards:** AE, CB, DI, DS, JC, MC, VI.
[ASK] 🅂 🈵 ⊇ 🍴 🍸 ⊬ 🛆 🛏 🎾 ▢ 🖨 🔒 ⊠

EMBASSY SUITES/ORANGE COUNTY
AIRPORT NORTH
◆◆◆
Suite Motor Inn

	Rates Subject to Change			**Phone:** 714/241-3800	**114**
Mon-Thurs 6/15-9/7 [BP]	1P: $144	2P/1B: $154	2P/2B: $154	XP: $10	F18
Mon-Thurs 2/1-6/14 & 9/8-1/31 [BP]	1P: $139	2P/1B: $149	2P/2B: $149	XP: $10	F18
Fri-Sun 6/15-9/7 [BP]	1P: $124	2P/1B: $134	2P/2B: $134	XP: $10	F18
Fri-Sun 2/1-6/14 & 9/8-1/31 [BP]	1P: $119	2P/1B: $129	2P/2B: $129	XP: $10	F18

Location: Just w of SR 55; exit Dyer Rd W. 1325 E Dyer Rd 92705. Fax: 714/662-1651. **Terms:** Reserv deposit.
Facility: 301 rooms. Beautifully landscaped atrium area. Comfortable 1-bedroom suites. 10 stories; interior corridors; heated
indoor pool. **Services:** giftshop; area transportation. **Cards:** AE, CB, DI, DS, JC, MC, VI.
🅂 🄳 🈵 ⊇ 🍴 🍸 ⊬ 🛆 🛏 🎾 ▢ 🖨 🔒 ⊠

HOLIDAY INN EXPRESS
◆◆
Motor Inn

	Rates Subject to Change			**Phone:** 714/835-3051	**116**
6/1-9/6 [CP]	1P: $75- 95	2P/1B: $75- 95	2P/2B: $75- 95		
2/1-5/31 & 9/7-1/31 [CP]	1P: $72- 87	2P/1B: $72- 87	2P/2B: $72- 87		

Location: Just w of I-5, First St exit. 1600 E First St 92701. Fax: 714/543-0856. **Terms:** Reserv deposit.
Facility: 146 rooms. 10 stories; interior corridors; heated pool. **Services:** giftshop; area transportation. **Cards:** AE, CB, DI,
DS, JC, MC, VI.
🈵 ⊇ 🍴 ⊬ 🛏 🎾 ▢ 🖨 🔒 ⊠

(See map p. 294)

HOLIDAY INN-ORANGE COUNTY AIRPORT/CENTRAL BUSINESS DISTRICT   Phone: (714)966-1955 **122**
| | Mon-Thurs [BP] | 1P: $99- 129 | 2P/1B: $99- 129 | 2P/2B: $99- 129 | XP: $10 | F12 |
| | Fri-Sun [BP] | 1P: $89- 119 | 2P/1B: $89- 119 | 2P/2B: $89- 119 | XP: $10 | F12 |

◆◆◆   **Location:** Adjacent to SR 55, exit Dyer Rd W. 2726 S Grand Ave 92705. Fax: 714/966-1889. **Facility:** 180
Motor Inn   rooms. 3 stories; interior corridors; heated pool, whirlpool. **Dining:** Dining room; 6:30 am-2 & 5-10 pm;
$5-$17; cocktails. **Services:** area transportation, within 5 mi. **Cards:** AE, CB, DI, DS, JC, MC, VI.
**Special Amenities: Early check-in/late check-out and preferred room (subject to availability with advanced
reservations).** *(See color ad p 478 & p 343)*

QUALITY SUITES - ORANGE COUNTY AIRPORT   Rates Subject to Change   Phone: 314/957-9200 **120**
◆◆◆   All Year [BP]   1P: $109   2P/1B: $119   2P/2B: $119   XP: $10   F18
Suite Motel   **Location:** 1 blk w of SR 55, exit Dyer Rd West. 2701 Hotel Terrace Dr 92705. Fax: 714/641-8936.
Terms: Reserv deposit. **Facility:** 177 rooms. Attractively landscaped courtyard areas. Nicely furnished
1-bedroom suites. 3 stories; exterior corridors; heated pool. **Services:** giftshop; area transportation. **Cards:** AE, CB, DI, DS,
JC, MC, VI. *(See color ad below)*

RADISSON SUITE HOTEL-SANTA ANA   Phone: (714)556-3838 **121**
| | All Year [BP] | 1P: $105- 160 | 2P/1B: $115- 170 | 2P/2B: $115- 170 | XP: $10-20 |

◆◆◆   **Location:** Just w of SR 55, exit Dyer Rd. 2720 Hotel Terrace Dr 92705. Fax: 714/241-1008. **Terms:** Reserv
Suite Motel   deposit; weekly/monthly rates. **Facility:** 122 rooms. 4 stories; interior corridors; heated pool, whirlpool.
Services: complimentary evening beverages; area transportation, within 5 mi. **Some Rooms:** whirlpools.
Cards: AE, CB, DI, DS, JC, MC, VI. **Special Amenities: Free breakfast and free newspaper.**
(See color ad p 346 & below)

RED ROOF INN   Phone: (714)542-0311 **118**
	6/15-9/15 & 12/20-1/5	1P: $59	2P/1B: $65	2P/2B: $78	XP: $5	F18
	5/1-6/14	1P: $49	2P/1B: $54	2P/2B: $67	XP: $5	F18
	2/1-4/30, 9/16-12/19 &					
	1/6-1/31	1P: $40	2P/1B: $44	2P/2B: $58	XP: $5	F18

◆◆   **Location:** 0.3 mi n of I-5, exit Main St. 2600 N Main St 92701. Fax: 714/542-0321. **Terms:** Small pets only.
Motel   **Facility:** 126 rooms. Adjacent to Main Place shopping mall. 2 stories; interior/exterior corridors; heated pool, whirlpool.
Dining: Restaurant nearby. **Services:** area transportation, Disneyland Park. **Cards:** AE, CB, DI, DS, MC, VI.
Special Amenities: Free local telephone calls. *(See color ad p 350)*

TUSTIN SUITES   Phone: (714)558-2772 **119**
◆◆◆   All Year   1P: $49- 89   2P/1B: $49- 89   2P/2B: $54- 94   XP: $5   F12
   Location: E of I-5, exit First St. 2151 E First St 92705. Fax: 714/558-7007. **Terms:** Weekly rates; small pets
◆   only. **Facility:** 73 rooms. 2 stories; exterior corridors. **All Rooms:** combo or shower baths. **Some Rooms:** 67
Motel   kitchens. **Cards:** AE, CB, DI, DS, JC, MC, VI. **Special Amenities: Early check-in/late check-out and free
room upgrade (subject to availability with advanced reservations).**

(See map p. 294)

WOOLLEY'S PETITE SUITES HOTEL   Phone: (714)540-1111   **123**

9/16-1/31 [BP]	1P: $95	2P/1B: $95	2P/2B: $95	XP: $10	F12
6/15-9/15 [BP]	1P: $89	2P/1B: $89	2P/2B: $89	XP: $10	F12
2/1-6/14 [BP]	1P: $85	2P/1B: $85	2P/2B: $85	XP: $10	F12

Suite Motel   **Location:** Just w of SR 55, exit Dyer Rd. 2721 Hotel Terrace Rd 92705. Fax: 714/662-1643. **Facility:** 184 rooms. 3 stories; exterior corridors; heated pool, whirlpool. **Services:** giftshop; complimentary evening beverages; area transportation, to South Coast Plaza. **Cards:** AE, CB, DI, DS, MC, VI. **Special Amenities: Free breakfast and free local telephone calls.**

RESTAURANTS

ANTONELLO RISTORANTE   **Lunch:** $8-$16   **Dinner:** $16-$35   **Phone:** 714/751-7153   **35**
◆◆◆◆   **Location:** In South Coast Plaza Village just n of Sunflower w of Bristol. 1611 Sunflower 92704. **Hours:** 11:30
Northern   am-2 & 5:45-10 pm, Fri-11 pm, Sat 5:45 pm-11 pm. Closed major holidays & Sun. **Reservations:** suggested.
Italian   **Features:** semi-formal attire; cocktails & lounge; valet parking; a la carte. Fine dining in elegant, Old World ambiance. Smoke free premises. **Cards:** AE, CB, DI, MC, VI.

CRAZY HORSE STEAKHOUSE   **Lunch:** $5-$9   **Dinner:** $8-$23   **Phone:** 714/549-1512   **33**
◆◆   **Location:** Just w of SR 55 at Dyer Rd exit. 1580 Brookhollow Dr 92705. **Hours:** 11 am-3 & 5-10 pm, Sat
Steak and   5-10 pm. Closed: 1/1, 11/25, 12/24, 12/25 & Sun. **Reservations:** suggested. **Features:** casual dress;
Seafood   children's menu; cocktails & lounge; entertainment; a la carte. Beef, chicken & seafood served in a casual western atmosphere. Home of the Crazy Horse saloon. Preferential seating in saloon for restaurant guests Wed-Sat. Smoke free premises. **Cards:** AE, DI, MC, VI.

GUSTAF ANDERS   **Lunch:** $8-$20   **Dinner:** $16-$30   **Phone:** 714/668-1737   **34**
◆◆◆   **Location:** On Bear St, in South Coast Plaza Village. 1651 Sunflower Ave 92704. **Hours:** 11:30 am-2 &
Continental   5:30-10 pm, Sun 5:30 pm-10 pm. Closed: 1/1, 5/30, 7/4 & Mon. **Reservations:** suggested.
Features: semi-formal attire; cocktails; a la carte. Contemporary decor. Creative selection of California/Scandinavian cuisine. Smoke free premises. **Cards:** AE, CB, DI, MC, VI.

TOPAZ CAFE   **Lunch:** $8-$12   **Dinner:** $10-$17   **Phone:** 714/835-2002   **32**
◆◆◆   **Location:** 2002 N Main St 92706. **Hours:** 11:30 am-3, Thurs-Sat also 5-9 pm, Sun 10 am-3 pm.
Southwest   **Reservations:** accepted. **Features:** casual dress; Sunday brunch; cocktails; a la carte. At the Bowers
American   Museum of Cultural Art. Attractive sky-lighted dining room overlooking the courtyard. Southwestern cuisine. Smoke free premises. **Cards:** AE, DI, MC, VI.

SANTA BARBARA
pop. 85,600

This index helps you "spot" where approved accommodations are located on the detailed maps that follow. Rate ranges are for comparison only and show the property's high season. Turn to the listing page for more detailed rate information and consult display ads for special promotions. Restaurant rate range is for dinner unless only lunch (L) is served.

SANTA BARBARA

Spotter/Map Pg.Number	OA	SANTA BARBARA - Lodgings	Rating	Rate	Listing Page
1 / p. 1004	AAA	Summerland Inn	◆◆	$90-160	1021
2 / p. 1004		Four Seasons Biltmore	◆◆◆◆	$420-500	1011
3 / p. 1004	AAA	Montecito Inn	◆◆◆	$185-195	1016
4 / p. 1004	AAA	Coast Village Inn - see color ad p 1011	◆◆	$135-155	1010
5 / p. 1004	AAA	Old Yacht Club Inn - see ad p 1018	◆◆◆	$110-190	1018
6 / p. 1004	AAA	Radisson Hotel Santa Barbara	◆◆◆	$169-199	1019
8 / p. 1004	AAA	Fess Parker's Doubletree Resort	◆◆◆	$229-269	1010
9 / p. 1004	AAA	Harbor View Inn - see color ad p 1014	◆◆◆◆	$150-350	1012
10 / p. 1004	AAA	Pacifica Suites - see color ad p 1018	◆◆◆	$120-180	1018
11 / p. 1004	AAA	Beachcomber Inn - see color ad p 1005	◆◆◆	$115-250	1006
12 / p. 1004	AAA	West Beach Inn - see color ad p 1021	◆◆◆	$150-201	1022
13 / p. 1004	AAA	Best Western-Beachside Inn - see color ad p 1006	◆◆	$149-189	1006
14 / p. 1004	AAA	Mason Beach Inn - see color ad p 1017	◆◆	$125-155	1016
15 / p. 1004	AAA	Country Inn by the Sea - see color ad p 1008	◆◆◆	$109-229	1010
16 / p. 1004	AAA	Franciscan Inn	◆◆◆	$109-195	1011
17 / p. 1004	AAA	Tropicana Inn & Suites - see color ad p 1007	◆◆◆	$126-172	1022
18 / p. 1004	AAA	Inn by the Harbor - see color ad p 1007	◆◆	$126-172	1015
19 / p. 1004		Inn On Summer Hill - see color ad p 1015	◆◆◆◆	$190-325	1015
20 / p. 1004	AAA	Travelodge Santa Barbara Beach	◆◆◆	$65-185	1022
21 / p. 1004	AAA	The Glenborough Inn	◆◆	$225-360	1011
22 / p. 1004	AAA	Tiffany Inn	◆◆◆	$125-250	1021
23 / p. 1004	AAA	Simpson House Inn - see color ad p 1020	◆◆◆◆◆	$170-400	1021

Spotter/Map Pg.Number	OA	SANTA BARBARA - Lodgings (contd.)	Rating	Rate	Listing Page
24 / p. 1004	🏨	The Parsonage	◆◆◆	$150-305 SAVE	1019
25 / p. 1004	🏨	Olive House Inn	◆◆◆	$110-180	1018
26 / p. 1004	🏨	Marina Beach Motel - see color ad p 1016	◆◆◆	$85-250	1016
27 / p. 1004	🏨	Hotel Santa Barbara - see color ad p 1015	◆◆◆	$189-219	1012
28 / p. 1004	🏨	The Cheshire Cat	◆◆◆	$155-330	1010
29 / p. 1004	🏨	Bath Street Inn - see ad p 1005	◆◆◆	$130-150 SAVE	1005
30 / p. 1004	🏨	Eagle Inn	◆◆	$145-185 SAVE	1010
31 / p. 1004	🏨	Best Western Encina Lodge - see color ad p 1007	◆◆◆	$142-172 SAVE	1006
32 / p. 1004	🏨	Lemon Tree Inn	◆◆	$95-250 SAVE	1016
36 / p. 1004	🏨	Best Western Pepper Tree Inn - see color ad p 1007	◆◆◆	$146-168 SAVE	1006
37 / p. 1004	🏨	The Sandman Inn - see color ad p 1019	◆◆	$80-150 SAVE	1019
38 / p. 1004	🏨	San Roque Motel	◆	$85-180 SAVE	1019
39 / p. 1004	🏨	Sandpiper Lodge	◆◆	$119-139 SAVE	1019
40 / p. 1004	🏨	Mountain View Inn - see ad p 1017	◆◆	$99-169	1017
42 / p. 1004	🏨	Santa Barbara Inn - see color ad p 1020	◆◆◆	$197-302 SAVE	1020
44 / p. 1004	🏨	Villa Rosa	◆◆	$110-250	1022
45 / p. 1004	🏨	The Secret Garden & Cottages	◆◆◆	$121-214 SAVE	1021
46 / p. 1004	🏨	The Upham	◆◆◆	$140-385 SAVE	1022
47 / p. 1004		The Mary May Inn	◆◆◆	$150-200	1016
48 / p. 1004	🏨	Ramada Limited - see color ad p 1013	◆◆◆	$100-145 SAVE	1019
49 / p. 1004		Holiday Inn-Santa Barbara/Goleta	◆◆◆	$135-145	1012
50 / p. 1004	🏨	Best Western South Coast Inn - see color ad p 1009	◆◆◆	$110-114 SAVE	1006
55 / p. 1004		Circle Bar B Guest Ranch	◆◆	$186-225	1010
57 / p. 1004	🏨	El Prado Inn - see color ad p 1012	◆◆	$85-150 SAVE	1010
58 / p. 1004	🏨	Orange Tree Inn	◆	$85-220 SAVE	1018
59 / p. 1004		Blue Dolphin Inn	◆	$165-195	1006
60 / p. 1004	🏨	Blue Sands Motel - see ad p 1017	◆	$129-209	1010
61 / p. 1004	🏨	Ocean Palms Beach Resort - see color ad p 1005	◆◆	$115-250 SAVE	1017
		SANTA BARBARA - Restaurants			
1 / p. 1004		Palazzio Trattoria Italiana	◆◆	$6-12	1023
2 / p. 1004		Wine Cask Restaurant	◆◆◆	$20-30	1023
4 / p. 1004		Downey's	◆◆◆	$24-30	1023
5 / p. 1004		Andria's Harborside Restaurant - see color ad p 1006	◆◆	$11-20	1022
6 / p. 1004		Original Enterprise Fish Company	◆◆	$10-17	1023
7 / p. 1004		Montecito Cafe	◆◆◆	$7-16	1023
8 / p. 1004		Citronelle Restaurant - see color ad p 1020	◆◆◆	$19-25	1023
9 / p. 1004		The Palace Cafe	◆◆	$10-25	1023
10 / p. 1004		Chuck's of Hawaii	◆◆	$8-20	1022
11 / p. 1004		Cafe del Sol	◆◆	$9-23	1022
12 / p. 1004		Ristorante Piatti	◆◆◆	$10-18	1023
13 / p. 1004		Chad's	◆◆	$10-25	1022
14 / p. 1004		La Marina	◆◆◆◆	$20-35	1023
15 / p. 1004		Palazzio "Downtown"	◆◆	$9-16	1023
18 / p. 1004	🏨	Mousse Odile	◆◆	$13-19	1023
20 / p. 1004		Beachside Cafe	◆◆	$14-23	1022
21 / p. 1004		Alex's Cantina	◆	$5-13	1022
22 / p. 1004		Cold Springs Tavern	◆	$15-22	1023
23 / p. 1004		Tom & Jerry's American Grill - see color ad p 1019	◆	$8-20	1023

DON'T WAIT FOR THE BIG CHILL.

Check the blanket supply in your room when you arrive; you might not be able to get extras during the night.

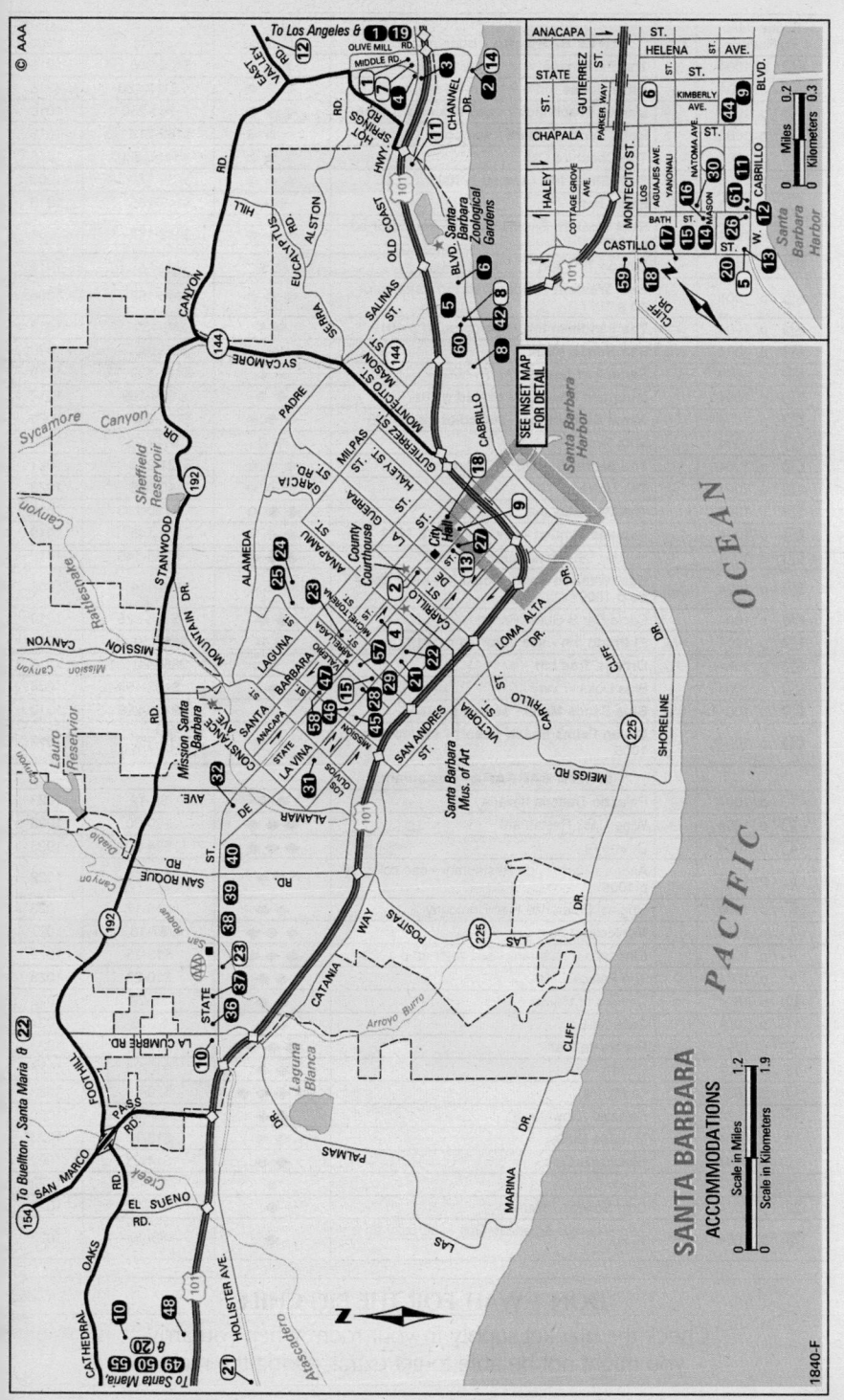

© AAA

SANTA BARBARA
ACCOMMODATIONS

Scale in Miles
0   1.2
Scale in Kilometers
0   1.9

1840-F

SEE INSET MAP FOR DETAIL

SANTA BARBARA—85,600   (See map p. 1004; index p. 1002)

LODGINGS

BATH STREET INN   **Phone:** (805)682-9680   29

AAA SAVE   Fri-Sun & Mon-Thurs
          6/15-9/15 [BP]   1P: $105- 220   2P/1B: $110- 225   2P/2B: $130- 150   XP: $20   D
◆◆◆   Mon-Thurs 2/1-6/14 &
Historic Bed 9/16-1/31 [BP]   1P: $95- 198   2P/1B: $99- 202   2P/2B: $117- 135   XP: $20   D
& Breakfast **Location:** Just s of Mission St. 1720 Bath St 93101. Fax: 805/569-1281. **Terms:** Reserv deposit, 3 day
notice; 2 night min stay, weekends. **Facility:** 12 rooms. 1890 Queen Anne Victorian house in residential area.
3 units with fireplace & whirlpool bathtub. Tea & refreshments served after 4 pm. 1 rm with private entrance, kitchen & whirlpool bathtub $175; 3 stories; interior corridors; smoke free premises. **Services:** complimentary evening beverages.
All Rooms: combo or shower baths. **Some Rooms:** whirlpools. **Cards:** AE, MC, VI. **Special Amenities: Free breakfast
and free local telephone calls.** *(See ad below)*

VCR 🖥 📠 ⓘ ✕

(See map p. 1004)

BEACHCOMBER INN
Phone: (805)965-4577   **11**

AAA SAVE

| | 6/1-10/31 | 1P: $115- 195 | 2P/1B: $115- 250 | 2P/2B: $115- 250 | XP: $10 |
| | 2/1-5/31 & 11/1-1/31 | 1P: $65- 250 | 2P/1B: $65- 250 | 2P/2B: $65- 250 | |

◆◆◆
Motel

Location: Just s of US 101, between Bath St & Chapala. 202 W Cabrillo Blvd 93101. Fax: 805/965-9937. **Terms:** Small pets only, $100 dep req, in 1st floor smoking rooms. **Facility:** 32 rooms. Across from beach. 2 sun decks with beach view. 2 stories; exterior corridors; small heated pool. **All Rooms:** combo or shower baths, extended cable TV. **Cards:** AE, CB, DI, DS, JC, MC, VI. *(See color ad p 1005)*

BEST WESTERN-BEACHSIDE INN
Phone: (805)965-6556   **13**

AAA SAVE

	5/16-9/15	1P: $109- 189	2P/1B: $129- 189	2P/2B: $149- 189
	9/16-10/31	1P: $89- 179	2P/1B: $109- 179	2P/2B: $129- 179
	3/1-5/15	1P: $89- 169	2P/1B: $99- 169	2P/2B: $119- 169
Motor Inn	2/1-2/28 & 11/1-1/31	1P: $79- 159	2P/1B: $89- 159	2P/2B: $109- 159

◆◆

Location: 4 blks s of US 101 at Castillo St. 336 W Cabrillo Blvd 93101. Fax: 805/966-6626. **Terms:** Reserv deposit. **Facility:** 60 rooms. Across from beach & yacht harbor. Some smaller rooms. 7 suites from $125-$205; 3 stories; exterior corridors; heated pool. **Dining:** Andria's Harborside Restaurant, see separate listing. **All Rooms:** combo or shower baths. **Cards:** AE, CB, DI, DS, JC, MC, VI. *(See color ad below)*

BEST WESTERN ENCINA LODGE
Phone: (805)682-7277   **31**

AAA SAVE

	5/21-9/25	1P: $142- 162	2P/1B: $142- 172	2P/2B: $142- 172	XP: $10	F12
	9/26-12/31	1P: $138- 158	2P/1B: $138- 168	2P/2B: $138- 168	XP: $10	F12
	2/1-5/20 & 1/1-1/31	1P: $132- 152	2P/1B: $132- 162	2P/2B: $132- 162	XP: $10	F12

◆◆◆
Motor Inn

Location: 0.5 mi n of US 101; exit Mission St, just s of Santa Barbara Cottage Hospital. 2220 Bath St 93105. Fax: 805/563-9319. **Terms:** Reserv deposit; weekly/monthly rates, 9/15-6/15. **Facility:** 121 rooms. Spacious grounds. Some patios & balconies. 33 one & two-bedroom kitchen apartments, 3 bi-level; 2 stories; exterior corridors; heated pool, sauna, whirlpool. **Dining:** Restaurant; 6:30 am-10 pm; $11-$19; cocktails. **Services:** giftshop. **Recreation:** complimentary access to exercise room at local hotel. **All Rooms:** combo or shower baths. **Cards:** AE, CB, DI, DS, JC, MC, VI. **Special Amenities:** Free newspaper and free room upgrade (subject to availability with advanced reservations). *(See color ad p 1007)*

BEST WESTERN PEPPER TREE INN
Phone: (805)687-5511   **36**

AAA SAVE

	5/28-9/25	1P: $146- 158	2P/1B: $146- 168	2P/2B: $146- 168	XP: $10	F12
	9/26-1/31	1P: $142- 154	2P/1B: $142- 164	2P/2B: $142- 164	XP: $10	F12
	2/1-5/27	1P: $128- 148	2P/1B: $138- 158	2P/2B: $138- 158	XP: $10	F12

◆◆◆
Motor Inn

Location: 3.5 mi nw; 0.5 mi e of jct US 101. 3850 State St 93105. Fax: 805/682-2410. **Terms:** Reserv deposit; handling fee imposed; 2 night min stay, weekends. **Facility:** 150 rooms. Attractively decorated rooms with patio or balcony. Located across from large shopping mall. 2 stories; exterior corridors; heated pool, sauna, whirlpools. **Dining:** Restaurant; 6 am-9:30 pm, Fri & Sat-11 pm; $9-$16; cocktails. **Services:** giftshop; area transportation, bus & train stations. Fee: massage. **Cards:** AE, CB, DI, DS, MC, VI. **Special Amenities:** Free newspaper and free room upgrade (subject to availability with advanced reservations). *(See color ad p 1007)*

BEST WESTERN SOUTH COAST INN
Phone: (805)967-3200   **50**

AAA SAVE

	4/30-9/25 [CP]	1P: $110- 114	2P/1B: $114	2P/2B: $118	XP: $10	F18
	9/26-1/31 [CP]	1P: $104- 108	2P/1B: $108	2P/2B: $112	XP: $10	F18
	2/1-4/29 [CP]	1P: $99- 102	2P/1B: $105	2P/2B: $106	XP: $10	F18

◆◆◆
Motel

Location: Adjacent to US 101; between Patterson & Fairview Ave exits. 5620 Calle Real 93117. Fax: 805/683-4466. **Facility:** 121 rooms. 6 two-room suites with wet bar, refrigerator & microwave, $150; 2 stories; exterior corridors; heated pool, whirlpool. **Services:** complimentary evening beverages, Mon-Thurs. **Recreation:** ping pong table. **Cards:** AE, CB, DI, DS, MC, VI. **Special Amenities:** Free breakfast and free local telephone calls. *(See color ad p 1009)*

BLUE DOLPHIN INN
Rates Subject to Change   Phone: 805/965-2333   **59**

Bed & Breakfast

| | Fri & Sat 2/1-5/14, 5/15-10/15 & Fri & Sat 10/16-1/31 [BP] | 1P: $98- 195 | 2P/1B: $98- 195 | 2P/2B: $165- 195 | XP: $15 |
| | Sun-Thurs 2/1-5/14 & 10/16-1/31 [BP] | 1P: $69- 145 | 2P/1B: $69- 145 | 2P/2B: $129- 169 | XP: $15 |

Location: Just w of Castillo St. 420 Montecito St 93101. Fax: 805/962-9470. **Terms:** Reserv deposit, 7 day notice; 2 night min stay, weekends. **Facility:** 9 rooms. Front house built in 1860. 2 blks from beach. Nicely decorated rooms. Some with private whirlpool & fireplace. 2 stories; interior/exterior corridors; smoke free premises. **All Rooms:** combo or shower baths. **Cards:** AE, DI, DS, MC, VI.

VAGABOND INNS®

"Good Value, Friendly People"™

- **FREE continental breakfast***
- **FREE incoming faxes • Local calls**
- **FREE weekday newspaper***
- **FREE Stay for children* ****

*Not available in Palm Springs. **When sharing a room with parents'

Vagabuck Savings $5 OFF

Only one VAGA-BUCK may be applied per night; may be used at any Vagabond Inn except Palm Springs; must be presented at check-in; may be applied to any rate except 50% discounts; subject to availability; may not be used in conjunction with other discount coupons; may not be available during holidays and special events. This program expires 12-31-99.

Vagabuck Savings $5 OFF

Only one VAGA-BUCK may be applied per night; may be used at any Vagabond Inn except Palm Springs; must be presented at check-in; may be applied to any rate except 50% discounts; subject to availability; may not be used in conjunction with other discount coupons; may not be available during holidays and special events. This program expires 12-31-99.

Vagabuck Savings $5 OFF

Only one VAGA-BUCK may be applied per night; may be used at any Vagabond Inn except Palm Springs; must be presented at check-in; may be applied to any rate except 50% discounts; subject to availability; may not be used in conjunction with other discount coupons; may not be available during holidays and special events. This program expires 12-31-99.

Vagabuck Savings $5 OFF

Only one VAGA-BUCK may be applied per night; may be used at any Vagabond Inn except Palm Springs; must be presented at check-in; may be applied to any rate except 50% discounts; subject to availability; may not be used in conjunction with other discount coupons; may not be available during holidays and special events. This program expires 12-31-99.

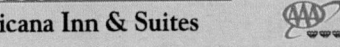

- *Heated pool and spa*
- *Air conditioning*
- *Refrigerators, coffee machines & hair dryers in room*
- *Non-smoking rooms*
- *Complimentary continental breakfast*
- *Free movie channel and local calls*

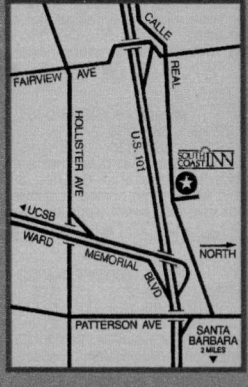

CONVENIENCE AND COMFORT

CLOSE TO SANTA BARBARA'S FINEST RECREATION

The South Coast Inn is close to all that Santa Barbara has to offer. Just minutes from beautiful beaches, championship golf, shopping and fine dining. Experience the area's famous attractions while enjoying the warm hospitality that has become our trademark.

Best Western
South Coast Inn
Santa Barbara Goleta

5620 Calle Real, Santa Barbara/Goleta, CA 93117
805-967-3200 FAX: 805-683-4466

$25 OFF *Published Rates on Sunday*

(See map p. 1004)

BLUE SANDS MOTEL — Rates Subject to Change — Phone: 805/965-1624 — 🄶

Fri & Sat 5/15-9/30 [CP]	1P: $115- 159	2P/1B: $119- 169	2P/2B: $129- 209	XP: $5
Fri & Sat 2/1-5/14 & 10/1-1/31 [CP]	1P: $75- 129	2P/1B: $79- 149	2P/2B: $85- 179	XP: $5
Sun-Thurs 5/15-9/30 [CP]	1P: $75- 85	2P/1B: $75- 90	2P/2B: $80- 159	XP: $5
Sun-Thurs 2/1-5/14 & 10/1-1/31 [CP]	1P: $54- 75	2P/1B: $54- 75	2P/2B: $57- 129	XP: $5

Motel

Location: 0.3 mi s of US 101. 421 S Milpas St 93103. Fax: 805/966-4659. **Terms:** Reserv deposit, 3 day notice; handling fee imposed; small pets only, $5. **Facility:** 11 rooms. 1 two-bedroom unit. Efficiences, $5 extra; 2-bedroom suite with kitchen, $119-$209; 2 stories; exterior corridors; designated smoking area; heated pool. **Dining:** Restaurant nearby. **All Rooms:** combo or shower baths, extended cable TV. **Some Rooms:** 4 efficiencies, kitchen. **Cards:** AE, DS, MC, VI. *(See ad p 1017)*

THE CHESHIRE CAT — Rates Subject to Change — Phone: 805/569-1610 — 🄽 F5

All Year [BP] — 1P: $155- 330 — 2P/1B: $155- 330 — 2P/2B: $155- 330 — XP: $5

Bed & Breakfast

Location: 36 W Valerio St at Chapala 93101. Fax: 805/682-1876. **Terms:** Reserv deposit, 7 day notice; handling fee imposed; 2 night min stay, weekends. **Facility:** 17 rooms. 1880 Queen Anne & Victorian homes located in residential area. 6 fireplaces. Large unit with separate living room, efficiency & large whirlpool, $190-$249; 2 stories; smoke free premises; whirlpool. **Services:** complimentary evening beverages. **All Rooms:** combo or shower baths. **Some Rooms:** 5 efficiencies, color TV, whirlpools. **Cards:** AE, DS, MC, VI.

CIRCLE BAR B GUEST RANCH — Rates Subject to Change — Phone: 805/968-1113 — 🄵

All Year [AP] — 1P: $128- 198 — 2P/1B: $186- 225 — 2P/2B: $186- 225 — XP: $60-75

Ranch

Location: 20 mi n on US 101 exit Refugio Rd, 3.5 mi n on narrow winding road. 1800 Refugio Canyon Rd 93117. **Terms:** Reserv deposit, 14 day notice; 12% service charge; 2 night min stay, weekends. **Facility:** 13 rooms. Quiet family atmosphere. Located in a scenic canyon 3.5 mi from the ocean. 1 two-bedroom unit. 1 story; exterior corridors; designated smoking area. **Recreation:** hiking trails. Fee: horseback riding. **All Rooms:** combo or shower baths. **Cards:** MC, VI.

COAST VILLAGE INN — Rates Subject to Change — Phone: (805)969-3266 — 🄸

Fri & Sat [CP]	1P: $115- 145	2P/1B: $115- 145	2P/2B: $135- 155
Sun-Thurs [CP]	1P: $67- 87	2P/1B: $67- 87	2P/2B: $87- 97

Motel

Location: In Montecito, from US 101 exit Olive Mill Rd, 0.3 mi N. 1188 Coast Village Rd 93108. Fax: 805/969-7117. **Terms:** Weekly rates. **Facility:** 27 rooms. Beautifully landscaped grounds. Few small rooms. 2 stories; exterior corridors; smoke free premises; heated pool. **Dining:** Restaurant nearby. **All Rooms:** combo or shower baths. **Some Rooms:** efficiency, kitchen. **Cards:** AE, CB, DI, DS, MC, VI. *(See color ad p 1011)*

COUNTRY INN BY THE SEA — Rates Subject to Change — Phone: (805)963-4471 — 🄵🄵

5/15-9/30 [CP]	1P: $109- 229	2P/1B: $109- 229	2P/2B: $109- 229	XP: $20
2/1-5/14 & 10/1-1/31 [CP]	1P: $89- 209	2P/1B: $89- 209	2P/2B: $89- 209	XP: $20

Motel

Location: 2 blks s of US 101. 128 Castillo St 93101. Fax: 805/962-2633. **Terms:** 2 night min stay, weekends. **Facility:** 45 rooms. Most with patio or balcony. Very attractive European country decor. 2 blocks from beach and harbor, across street from city park and tennis courts. Whirlpool suites for two persons $129-$199; 3 stories; interior/exterior corridors; small heated pool, saunas, whirlpool. **Services:** complimentary evening beverages. **Recreation:** free video library, extensive travel library. **Some Rooms:** Fee: whirlpools. **Cards:** AE, CB, DI, MC, VI. *(See color ad p 1008)*

EAGLE INN — Phone: (805)965-3586 — 🄵🄾

🄰🄰🄰 🅂🄰🅅🄴

Fri & Sat 5/28-9/18 [CP]	1P: $130- 165	2P/1B: $130- 165	2P/2B: $145- 185
Fri & Sat 2/1-5/27 & 9/19-1/31 [CP]	1P: $110- 145	2P/1B: $110- 145	2P/2B: $110- 145
Sun-Thurs 5/28-9/18 [CP]	1P: $74- 95	2P/1B: $74- 95	2P/2B: $79- 125
Sun-Thurs 2/1-5/27 & 10/1-1/31 [CP]	1P: $74- 89	2P/1B: $74- 89	2P/2B: $79- 95

Motel

Location: 3 blks s of US 101. 232 Natoma Ave at Bath St 93101. Fax: 805/966-1218. **Facility:** 27 rooms. 1 1/2 blocks to beach. Most apartments with fully equipped kitchens; 7 smaller units without kitchen have microwave, refrigerator & coffeemaker. Very clean. 2 stories; interior corridors. **All Rooms:** combo or shower baths. **Cards:** AE, DI, DS, MC, VI. **Special Amenities: Free breakfast and free room upgrade (subject to availability with advanced reservations).**

EL PRADO INN — Phone: (805)966-0807 — 🄵🄻

🄰🄰🄰 🅂🄰🅅🄴

5/15-10/31 [CP]	1P: $75- 130	2P/1B: $75- 130	2P/2B: $85- 150
2/1-5/14 & 11/1-1/31 [CP]	1P: $65- 130	2P/1B: $65- 130	2P/2B: $75- 150

Motel

Location: 1601 State St 93101. Fax: 805/966-6502. **Facility:** 68 rooms. Located in downtown area within walking distance of various restaurants, shops & theatres. Nicely landscaped pool area. 6 suites, $80-$160; 1-3 stories; exterior corridors; heated pool. **Dining:** Restaurant nearby. **All Rooms:** combo or shower baths. **Cards:** AE, CB, DI, DS, MC, VI. **Special Amenities: Early check-in/late check-out and free room upgrade (subject to availability with advanced reservations).** *(See color ad p 1012)*

FESS PARKER'S DOUBLETREE RESORT — Rates Subject to Change — Phone: (805)564-4333 — 🄴

7/1-9/5	1P: $229- 269	2P/1B: $229- 269	2P/2B: $229- 269	XP: $15	F17
3/1-6/30 & 9/6-10/31	1P: $189- 219	2P/1B: $189- 219	2P/2B: $189- 219	XP: $15	F17
2/1-2/28 & 11/1-1/31	1P: $179- 209	2P/1B: $179- 209	2P/2B: $179- 209	XP: $15	F17

Resort Hotel

Location: Just s of US 101 via Milpas St. 633 E Cabrillo Blvd 93103. Fax: 805/564-4964. **Terms:** Check-in 4 pm; reserv deposit, 3 day notice; pets, $50 dep req. **Facility:** 360 rooms. Across from beach on spacious landscaped grounds. Balcony or patio. 3 stories; interior/exterior corridors; putting green; heated pool, whirlpool; 3 lighted tennis courts. **Dining:** Restaurant, coffee shop; 6:30 am-11 pm; $7-$20; cocktails. **Services:** giftshop; area transportation, to & from State St. Fee: massage. **Recreation:** basketball & shuffleboard courts. Rental: bicycles. **Cards:** AE, CB, DI, DS, MC, VI.

(See map p. 1004)

FOUR SEASONS BILTMORE
◆◆◆◆ 5/22-12/31
Resort 2/1-5/21
Complex 1/1-1/31

Rates Subject to Change
1P: $400- 480   2P/1B: $400- 480
1P: $380- 460   2P/1B: $380- 460
1P: $420- 500   2P/1B: $420- 500

Phone: (805)969-2261   **2**
XP: $30   F18
XP: $30   F18
XP: $35   F18

Location: 0.3 mi s of US 101, in Montecito area, exit Olive Mill Rd. 1260 Channel Dr 93108. Fax: 805/969-4682. **Terms:** Reserv deposit, 3 day notice. **Facility:** 217 rooms. An impressive oceanfront resort on spacious, beautifully landscaped grounds. Spanish architecture. Large well appointed rooms in lodge & cottages. Garden or ocean views. 2 stories; interior/exterior corridors; putting green; heated pool. Fee: 3 lighted tennis courts. **Services:** giftshop. Fee: massage. **Recreation:** bicycles. **Cards:** AE, CB, DI, DS, JC, MC, VI.

🐕 🌂 🈂 🎣 🍽 🎬 🛗 🛄 🛖 🌃 🎥 VCR 💻 🛎 🎿 🖨 📠 ✕

FRANCISCAN INN
♦♦♦
Motel

Fri & Sat 5/15-9/15 [CP]
Sun-Thurs 5/15-9/15 [CP]
Fri & Sat 2/1-5/14 &
9/16-1/31 [CP]
Sun-Thurs 2/1-5/14 &
9/16-1/31 [CP]

Rates Subject to Change
1P: $81- 89   2P/1B: $89- 149   2P/2B: $109- 195   XP: $8   F5
1P: $77- 81   2P/1B: $85- 125   2P/2B: $104- 195   XP: $8   F5

1P: $72- 82   2P/1B: $80- 120   2P/2B: $95- 175   XP: $8   F5

1P: $60- 67   2P/1B: $65- 99   2P/2B: $89- 135   XP: $8   F5

Phone: (805)963-8845   **16**

Location: Just s of US 101. 109 Bath St 93101. Fax: 805/564-3295. **Terms:** Weekly/monthly rates, winter. **Facility:** 53 rooms. 1 block to beach. Guest rooms have attractive country decor; very pleasant ambiance. 2 two-bedroom units. 1-2 stories; exterior corridors; heated pool, whirlpool. **All Rooms:** combo or shower baths. **Some Rooms:** 24 efficiencies. **Cards:** AE, CB, DI, MC, VI.

🏊 🖨 🛖 VCR 💻 📠 📞 ✕

THE GLENBOROUGH INN
♦♦
Historic Bed
& Breakfast

Fri & Sat, Sun-Thurs
5/26-10/15 & 12/16-1/1 [BP]   1P: $100- 250   2P/1B: $100- 250   2P/2B: $225- 360   XP: $30
Sun-Thurs 2/1-5/25,
10/16-12/15 & 1/2-1/31 [BP]   1P: $75- 185   2P/1B: $85- 200   2P/2B: $150- 225   XP: $30

Rates Subject to Change

Phone: (805)966-0589   **21**

Location: 1327 Bath St 93101. Fax: 805/564-8610. **Terms:** Reserv deposit, 7 day notice; handling fee imposed; 2 night min stay, weekends. **Facility:** 11 rooms. 3 homes built in 1880's & early 1900's. Located in residential area. Most rooms with fireplace. 2 units with private entrance, patio & whirlpool; 2 stories; exterior corridors; smoke free premises; whirlpool. **Services:** complimentary evening beverages. **All Rooms:** combo or shower baths. **Some Rooms:** whirlpools. **Cards:** AE, CB, DI, DS, MC, VI.

🛗 💻 🖨 📞 ✕

EXTRA PERSON (XP) rates include only the standard room equipment. There may be an additional charge for cots, rollaways and baby beds.

(See map p. 1004)

HARBOR VIEW INN　　　　　　　　　　　　　　　**Phone:** (805)963-0780　[9]
All Year　　　　　　1P: $150- 350　2P/1B: $150- 350　2P/2B: $150- 350　XP: $10　F16
Location: Just s of US 101, just w of State St. 28 W Cabrillo Blvd 93101. **Fax:** 805/963-7967.
Motor Inn　**Terms:** Check-in 4 pm; reserv deposit; 2 night min stay, weekends. **Facility:** 80 rooms. Across from beach &
Steam's Wharf. Beautifully appointed rooms, many with ocean view. 2-3 stories; interior/exterior corridors;
cocktails. **Cards:** AE, CB, DI, MC, VI. **Special Amenities:** Free newspaper. *(See color ad p 1014)*

HOLIDAY INN EXPRESS-VIRGINIA HOTEL　　Rates Subject to Change　　　**Phone:** 805/963-9757
[FYI]　　All Year [CP]　　　1P: $79- 205　2P/1B: $79- 205　2P/2B: $79- 205　XP: $10
Too new to rate. **Location:** Just e of State St. 17 W Haley St 93101. **Terms:** Reserv deposit. **Facility:** 61
Motel　rooms. 3 stories; interior corridors. **Cards:** AE, CB, DI, DS, MC, VI. *(See color ad p 1014)*

HOLIDAY INN-SANTA BARBARA/GOLETA　　Rates Subject to Change　　　**Phone:** (805)964-6241　[49]
Fri & Sat 6/1-9/15　　1P: $125- 135　2P/1B: $135- 145　2P/2B: $135- 145　XP: $10　F17
Motor Inn　Fri & Sat 2/1-5/31, Sun-Thurs
6/1-9/15 & Fri & Sat
9/16-1/31　　　　　1P: $98- 108　2P/1B: $108- 118　2P/2B: $108- 118　XP: $10　F17
Sun-Thurs 2/1-5/31 &
9/16-1/31　　　　　1P: $80- 90　2P/1B: $90- 100　2P/2B: $90- 100　XP: $10　F17
Location: 7 mi nw adjacent to US 101; between Patterson & Fairview Ave exits. 5650 Calle Real 93117. **Fax:** 805/964-8467.
Facility: 160 rooms. Newly renovated, located in the foothills of the Santa Ynez Mountains. Beautiful gardens & pool areas.
2 stories; exterior corridors; heated pool. **Cards:** AE, CB, DI, DS, JC, MC, VI.

HOTEL SANTA BARBARA　　　　　　　　　　　**Phone:** (805)957-9300　[27]
5/28-9/6 [CP]　　　1P: $179- 209　2P/1B: $179- 209　2P/2B: $189- 219　XP: $15　F12
2/1-5/27 & 9/7-1/31 [CP]　1P: $109- 189　2P/1B: $109- 189　2P/2B: $119- 199　XP: $15　F12
Location: Downtown; State St at Cota St. 533 State St 93101. **Fax:** 805/962-2412. **Terms:** Reserv deposit.
Hotel　**Facility:** 75 rooms. Nicely refurbished downtown hotel built in 1926. 4 stories; interior corridors.
Dining: Restaurant; combo or shower baths, extended cable TV. **Cards:** AE, CB, DI,
DS, JC, MC, VI. **Special Amenities:** Early check-in/late check-out and free room upgrade (subject to availability with
advanced reservations). *(See color ad p 1015)*

◆　　**Diamonds are a guest's best friend.**　　◆

(See map p. 1004)

INN BY THE HARBOR   Rates Subject to Change   **Phone:** (805)963-7851   18

5/21-9/25 [CP]	1P: $96- 162	2P/1B:	$96- 172	2P/2B: $126- 172	XP: $10	F4
9/26-1/31 [CP]	1P: $190- 156	2P/1B:	$90- 166	2P/2B: $120- 166	XP: $10	F4
2/1-5/20 [CP]	1P: $84- 150	2P/1B:	$84- 160	2P/2B: $114- 160	XP: $10	F4

Motel   **Location:** Just sw of US 101, just w of Castillo St. 433 W Montecito St 93101. Fax: 805/962-9428.
Terms: Monthly rates; 2 night min stay, weekends 5/26-9/5. **Facility:** 42 rooms. 3 blks from beach, within walking distance of city park. Attractive country decor. 1 two-bedroom unit. 23 kitchens, $10 extra charge; 2 stories; exterior corridors; smoke free premises; heated pool, whirlpool. **Recreation:** Fee: bicycles. **Cards:** AE, CB, DI, DS, MC, VI.
(See color ad p 1007)

INN ON SUMMER HILL   Rates Subject to Change   **Phone:** 805/969-9998   19
♦♦♦♦   All Year [BP]   1P: $190- 325   2P/1B: $190- 325   2P/2B: $200   XP: $25
Bed & Breakfast   **Location:** N side of US 101; northbound exit Evans St, southbound exit Summerland 0.5 mi e. 2520 Lillie Ave (2520 Lillie Ave, SUMMERLAND). Fax: 805/565-9946. **Terms:** Reserv deposit, 7 day notice; 2 night min stay, weekends. **Facility:** 16 rooms. Beautifully decorated rooms in an English country motif. Ocean view. Gas fireplaces. Complimentary evening dessert & beverages. 2 stories; exterior corridors; smoke free premises. **Cards:** AE, DS, MC, VI. *(See color ad below)*

(See map p. 1004)

LEMON TREE INN   Phone: (805)687-6444   32

AAA SAVE

	Fri & Sat 5/16-10/15	1P:	$85- 230	2P/1B:	$85- 230	2P/2B:	$95- 250	XP: $10-20		F15

◆◆
Motor Inn

	Sun-Thurs 2/1-5/15 & 10/16-1/31	1P:	$70- 230	2P/1B:	$70- 230	2P/2B:	$80- 250	XP: $10		F15
	Fri & Sat 2/1-5/15 & 10/16-1/31	1P:	$80- 230	2P/1B:	$80- 230	2P/2B:	$90- 250	XP: $10		F15
	Sun-Thurs 5/16-10/15	1P:	$75- 230	2P/1B:	$75- 230	2P/2B:	$85- 230	XP: $10-20		F15

Location: 1.5 mi nw. 2819 State St 93105. **Fax:** 805/687-4432. **Terms:** Reserv deposit. **Facility:** 96 rooms. Many patios or balcony. 6 two-room suites with whirlpool tub $225-$350; 2 stories; exterior corridors; heated pool, whirlpool. **Dining:** Restaurant; 6 am-3 & 5-9 pm; $5-$16; cocktails. **All Rooms:** combo or shower baths. **Some Rooms:** whirlpools. **Cards:** AE, CB, DI, DS, JC, MC, VI. **Special Amenities:** Early check-in/late check-out and free local telephone calls.

MARINA BEACH MOTEL   Guaranteed Rates   Phone: 805/963-9311   26

AAA

	Fri & Sat 5/1-9/30 [CP]	1P:	$75- 225	2P/1B:	$75- 225	2P/2B:	$85- 250	
	Sun-Thurs 5/1-9/30 [CP]	1P:	$65- 200	2P/1B:	$65- 200	2P/2B:	$65- 225	

◆◆◆
Motel

	Fri & Sat 2/1-4/30 & 10/1-1/31 [CP]	1P:	$70- 200	2P/1B:	$70- 200	2P/2B:	$75- 225	
	Sun-Thurs 2/1-4/30 & 10/1-1/31 [CP]	1P:	$50- 100	2P/1B:	$50- 100	2P/2B:	$60- 175	

Location: 21 Bath St 93101. **Fax:** 805/564-4102. **Terms:** Weekly/monthly rates, off season; 2 night min stay, weekends 5/15-9/15. **Facility:** 32 rooms. 1/2 blk to beach. 1 story; exterior corridors. **Recreation:** bicycles. **All Rooms:** combo or shower baths, extended cable TV. **Some Rooms:** 4 efficiencies, 14 kitchens, whirlpools. **Cards:** AE, CB, DI, DS, MC, VI. *(See color ad below)*

THE MARY MAY INN   Rates Subject to Change   Phone: (805)569-3398   47

◆◆◆
Historic Bed
& Breakfast

	Fri-Sun [BP]	1P: $150- 200	2P/1B:	$150- 200		XP: $25
	Mon-Thurs [BP]	1P: $100- 125	2P/1B:	$100- 125		XP: $25

Location: At Chapala St. 111 W Valerio 93101. **Terms:** Reserv deposit, 7 day notice; handling fee imposed; 2 night min stay, weekends. **Facility:** 12 rooms. 1880's Queen Anne Victorian & 1886 Federal Style houses with gabled roof & porches. Beautifully decorated rooms, many of furnishings avail for purchase. 4 units have woodburning fireplace. Some canopy beds; cable tv in some rooms. 2 stories; interior/exterior corridors; designated smoking area. **All Rooms:** combo or shower baths. **Cards:** AE, DS, MC, VI.

MASON BEACH INN   Rates Subject to Change   Phone: 805/962-3203   14

AAA

	Fri & Sat 5/15-9/4 [CP]	1P: $125- 155	2P/1B:	$125- 155	2P/2B:	$125- 155	XP: $10	F10

◆◆
Motel

	Fri & Sat 2/1-5/14 & 9/5-1/31 [CP]	1P: $75- 135	2P/1B:	$75- 135	2P/2B:	$75- 135	XP: $10	F10
	Sun-Thurs 5/15-9/4 [CP]	1P: $75- 115	2P/1B:	$75- 115	2P/2B:	$75- 115	XP: $10	F10
	Sun-Thurs 2/1-5/14 & 9/5-1/31 [CP]	1P: $65- 95	2P/1B:	$65- 95	2P/2B:	$65- 95	XP: $10	F10

Location: Just s of US 101, southbound exit Castillo St., northbound exit Cabrillo Blvd, n to Castillo. 324 W Mason St 93101. **Fax:** 805/962-1056. **Terms:** Reserv deposit; weekly/monthly rates. **Facility:** 45 rooms. 1 block from beach. Contemporary decor. 3 suites with microwave & refrigerator, $95-$145; 2 stories; interior corridors; heated pool, whirlpool. **Cards:** AE, CB, DI, DS, MC, VI. *(See color ad p 1017)*

MONTECITO INN   Phone: (805)969-7854   3

AAA SAVE

	Fri & Sat [CP]	1P: $185- 195	2P/1B:	$185- 195	2P/2B:	$225
	Sun-Thurs 6/1-9/30 [CP]	1P: $165- 175	2P/1B:	$165- 175	2P/2B:	$205
	Sun-Thurs 2/1-5/31 [CP]	1P: $145- 155	2P/1B:	$145- 155	2P/2B:	$185
	Sun-Thurs 10/1-1/31 [CP]	1P: $105- 115	2P/1B:	$105- 115	2P/2B:	$145

◆◆◆
Historic Hotel

Location: In Montecito, adjacent to US 101, exit Olive Mill Rd. 1295 Coast Village Rd 93108. **Fax:** 805/969-0623. **Facility:** 60 rooms. Charming, historic Inn built in 1928. Located in center of town adjacent to US 101. 7 spacious suites with whirlpool, some with fireplace $325-$695; 3 stories; interior corridors; heated pool, sauna, whirlpool. **Dining:** Restaurant; also, Montecito Cafe, see separate listing. **Recreation:** bicycles. **All Rooms:** combo or shower baths. **Some Rooms:** whirlpools. **Cards:** AE, DI, DS, MC, VI. **Special Amenities:** Free breakfast and preferred room (subject to availability with advanced reservations).

MOUNTAIN VIEW INN

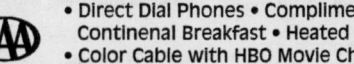

| | Rates Subject to Change | | | | Phone: 805/687-6636 | **40** |

AAA
Motel

	Fri & Sat 6/1-9/15 [CP]	1P:	$90- 159	2P/1B:	$95- 159	2P/2B:	$99- 169	XP:	$5
	Fri & Sat 2/1-5/31 & 9/16-1/31 [CP]	1P:	$75- 119	2P/1B:	$80- 139	2P/2B:	$80- 149	XP:	$5
	Sun-Thurs 6/1-9/15 [CP]	1P:	$69- 79	2P/1B:	$69- 85	2P/2B:	$72- 89	XP:	$5
	Sun-Thurs 2/1-5/31 & 9/16-1/31 [CP]	1P:	$49- 59	2P/1B:	$55- 69	2P/2B:	$60- 69	XP:	$5

Location: 1 mi e of US 101, exit Los Positas, corner of State & De La Vina sts. 3055 De La Vina St 93105. Fax: 805/682-6750. **Terms:** Reserv deposit; handling fee imposed; 2 night min stay, weekends in summer. **Facility:** 34 rooms. Adjacent to city park. Friendly atmosphere. 2 stories; exterior corridors; small pool. **Cards:** AE, DS, MC, VI.
(See ad below)

OCEAN PALMS BEACH RESORT

| | | | | | | Phone: (805)966-9133 | **61** |

AAA SAVE
Motel

| | 6/1-10/31 | 1P: | $115- 195 | 2P/1B: | $115- 250 | 2P/2B: | $115- 250 | XP: | $10 |
| | 2/1-5/31 & 11/1-1/31 | 1P: | $65- 250 | 2P/1B: | $65- 250 | 2P/2B: | $95- 250 | | |

Location: 0.3 mi e of Castillo St. 232 W Cabrillo Blvd 93101. Fax: 805/965-7882. **Terms:** Weekly rates; small pets only, $15 extra charge. **Facility:** 44 rooms. Across from beach. Some rooms with fireplace. 2 stories; interior/exterior corridors; heated pool, whirlpool. **Dining:** Coffee shop nearby. **All Rooms:** combo or shower baths, extended cable TV. **Some Rooms:** 2 efficiencies. **Cards:** AE, CB, DI, DS, JC, MC, VI.
(See color ad p 1005)

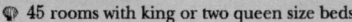

Double your pleasure with AAA Plus.

(See map p. 1004)

OLD YACHT CLUB INN   Rates Subject to Change   Phone: (805)962-1277   **5**
(AAA)
Fri-Sun & Mon-Thurs
♦♦
6/1-9/30 [BP]   1P: $105- 185   2P/1B: $110- 190   XP: $30
Historic Bed
Mon-Thurs 2/1-5/31 &
& Breakfast
10/1-1/31 [BP]   1P: $95- 165   2P/1B: $95- 175   XP: $30
Location: Just n of Cabrillo Blvd. 431 Corona Del Mar 93103. Fax: 805/962-3989. **Terms:** Reserv deposit, 7 day notice; MAP avail; 2 night min stay, weekends; weekend rates avail. **Facility:** 12 rooms. 1912 California Craftsman & 1920 Early California homes in residential area. 2 blks to beach. 8 rooms with TV hookup. 2 stories; interior/exterior corridors; smoke free premises. **Dining:** 5-course gourmet dinner served most Sat evenings; additional charge. **Services:** complimentary evening beverages. **Recreation:** bicycles. **All Rooms:** combo or shower baths. **Some Rooms:** whirlpools. **Cards:** AE, DI, DS, MC, VI. *(See ad below)*   ⊠ 𝕂 ⊠

OLIVE HOUSE INN   Guaranteed Rates   Phone: (805)962-4902   **25**
(AAA)
All Year [BP]   1P: $110- 180   2P/1B: $110- 180   XP: $25
♦♦♦
Location: 1 mi e of US 101; northbound exit Arrellaga St; southbound exit Mission St. 1604 Olive St 93101.
Historic Bed
Fax: 805/962-9983. **Terms:** Reserv deposit, 7 day notice; 2 night min stay, weekends. **Facility:** 6 rooms. 1904
& Breakfast
California Craftsman house located in a residential area. 2 rooms with private deck & whirlpool tub. 2 stories; interior corridors; smoke free premises. **Services:** complimentary evening beverages. **All Rooms:** combo or shower baths, extended cable TV. **Some Rooms:** color TV, whirlpools. **Cards:** AE, DS, MC, VI.   𝕂 ⊞ ⊠

ORANGE TREE INN   Phone: (805)569-1521   **58**
(AAA) SAVE
Fri & Sat 5/16-10/15   1P: $75- 210   2P/1B: $75- 210   2P/2B: $85- 220   XP: $10   F15
♦
Sun-Thurs 5/16-10/15   1P: $65- 200   2P/1B: $65- 200   2P/2B: $75- 210   XP: $10   F15
Motel
Fri & Sat 2/1-5/15 &
10/16-1/31   1P: $70- 200   2P/1B: $70- 200   2P/2B: $80- 200   XP: $10   F15
Sun-Thurs 2/1-5/15 &
10/16-1/31   1P: $60- 180   2P/1B: $60- 180   2P/2B: $70- 200   XP: $10   F15
Location: 0.5 mi e of US 101, exit Mission St. 1920 State St 93101. Fax: 805/682-6854. **Terms:** Reserv deposit. **Facility:** 46 rooms. 2 two-bedroom units. 3 stories; exterior corridors; pool heated 5/1-9/30. **All Rooms:** combo or shower baths. **Cards:** AE, CB, DI, DS, JC, MC, VI. **Special Amenities:** Early check-in/late check-out and free local telephone calls.   ⊠ 🛄 ⊠

PACIFICA SUITES   Phone: (805)683-6722   **10**
(AAA) SAVE
All Year [BP]   1P: $120- 180   2P/1B: $120- 180   2P/2B: $120- 180   XP: $10   F12
♦♦♦
Location: From US 101, exit Patterson Ave, 0.5 mi s, then 0.5 mi w on Hollister Ave. 5490 Hollister Ave
Suite Motel
93111. Fax: 805/683-4121. **Terms:** Small pets only, in smoking rooms only. **Facility:** 87 rooms. Nestled in a historic grove of exotic plants & trees, adjacent to the restored Sexton House built in 1880s. Attractively decorated 2-room suites. 2 stories; interior/exterior corridors; heated pool, whirlpool. **Services:** giftshop; complimentary evening beverages, Mon-Sat. **Cards:** AE, DI, DS, MC, VI. *(See color ad below)*   🆂 🛒 🍴 🍽 ⊠ ⊠ VCR 💻 ⬜ ⊞ 🔒 ⊠

(See map p. 1004)

THE PARSONAGE
Phone: (805)962-9336 ⓻

AAA SAVE

Mon-Thurs [BP]	1P: $130- 255	2P/1B: $130- 255	XP: $40
Fri-Sun [BP]	1P: $150- 305	2P/1B: $150- 305	XP: $40

◆◆◆

Historic Bed & Breakfast

Location: 1 mi e of US 101; northbound exit Arrellaga St; southbound exit Mission St. 1600 Olive St 93101. Fax: 805/962-2285. **Terms:** Reserv deposit, 7 day notice; handling fee imposed; 2 night min stay, weekends. **Facility:** 6 rooms. 1892 Victorian house in a residential area. 2 stories; interior corridors; smoke free premises. **Services:** complimentary evening beverages. **All Rooms:** combo or shower baths. **Some Rooms:** whirlpools. **Cards:** AE, DI, DS, MC, VI. **Special Amenities:** Early check-in/late check-out and free room upgrade (subject to availability with advanced reservations).

RADISSON HOTEL SANTA BARBARA
Phone: (805)963-0744 ⓺

AAA SAVE

7/1-8/31	1P: $169- 199	2P/1B: $169- 199	2P/2B: $169- 199	XP: $20	F16
4/1-6/30 & 9/1-10/31	1P: $139- 179	2P/1B: $139- 179	2P/2B: $139- 179	XP: $20	F16
2/1-3/31 & 11/1-1/31	1P: $119- 149	2P/1B: $119- 149	2P/2B: $119- 149	XP: $20	F16

◆◆◆

Motor Inn

Location: 2 blks e of Milpas St, southbound US 101 exit Milpas St; northbound exit Cabrillo Blvd. 1111 E Cabrillo Blvd 93103. Fax: 805/962-0985. **Terms:** Check-in 4 pm; reserv deposit, 3 day notice; BP avail. **Facility:** 173 rooms. Across from beach. Many ocean or mountain view rooms. Few smaller rooms. 3 stories; interior corridors; heated pool. **Dining:** Restaurant; 6:30 am-11 pm; $11-$20; cocktails. **Services:** giftshop. Fee: massage. **Recreation:** in-room video games, full service salon. **All Rooms:** combo or shower baths. **Some Rooms:** 8 efficiencies. **Cards:** AE, CB, DI, DS, JC, MC, VI.

RAMADA LIMITED
Phone: (805)964-3511 ⓽

AAA SAVE

All Year [CP]	1P: $75- 145	2P/1B: $85- 145	2P/2B: $100- 145	XP: $10	F18

◆◆◆

Motel

Location: 5 mi nw on US 101; exit Turnpike Rd, just n. 4770 Calle Real 93110. Fax: 805/964-0075. **Facility:** 126 rooms. All rooms with balcony or patio. Surrounding garden & lagoon area populated by Koi fish & ducks. 2 stories; interior corridors; heated pool, whirlpool. **Dining:** Restaurant nearby. **Cards:** AE, CB, DI, DS, MC, VI. **Special Amenities:** Free breakfast and free local telephone calls. *(See color ad p 1013)*

THE SANDMAN INN
Phone: (805)687-2468 ⓷⓻

AAA SAVE

All Year [CP]	1P: $80- 150	2P/1B: $80- 150	2P/2B: $80- 150	XP: $10	F18

◆◆

Motor Inn

Location: 3 mi nw; 0.8 mi e of US 101. 3714 State St 93105. Fax: 805/687-6581. **Facility:** 112 rooms. 6 kitchens & 11 efficiencies, $10 extra. 14 one-bedroom suites, some with kitchens, $135-149; 1-2 stories; exterior corridors; heated pool, whirlpool. **Dining:** Restaurant; $8-$20; also, Tom & Jerry's American Grill, see separate listing. **All Rooms:** combo or shower baths. **Cards:** AE, DI, DS, MC, VI. **Special Amenities:** Free breakfast and free local telephone calls. *(See color ad below)*

SANDPIPER LODGE
Phone: (805)687-5326 ⓷⓽

AAA SAVE

Fri & Sat 5/1-9/30 [CP]	1P: $109	2P/1B: $109	2P/2B: $119- 139
Fri & Sat 2/1-4/30 & 10/1-1/31 [CP]	1P: $89	2P/1B: $89	2P/2B: $99- 109
Sun-Thurs 5/1-9/30 [CP]	1P: $65	2P/1B: $65	2P/2B: $75- 89
Sun-Thurs 2/1-4/30 & 10/1-1/31 [CP]	1P: $55	2P/1B: $55	2P/2B: $65- 79

◆◆

Motel

Location: 3 mi nw, 0.8 mi e of US 101. 3525 State St 93105. Fax: 805/687-2271. **Terms:** Reserv deposit. **Facility:** 74 rooms. 16 two-bedroom units. 2 stories; exterior corridors; heated pool. **Dining:** Coffee shop nearby. **Some Rooms:** 4 kitchens. **Cards:** AE, CB, DI, DS, MC, VI. **Special Amenities:** Free breakfast and free local telephone calls.

SAN ROQUE MOTEL
Phone: (805)687-6611 ⓷⓼

AAA SAVE

Fri & Sat 5/15-9/30 [CP]	1P: $80- 150	2P/1B: $83- 160	2P/2B: $85- 180	XP: $6	F12
Fri & Sat 2/1-5/14 & 10/1-1/31 [CP]	1P: $60- 110	2P/1B: $65- 120	2P/2B: $69- 130	XP: $5	F12
Sun-Thurs 5/15-9/30 [CP]	1P: $65- 75	2P/1B: $68- 85	2P/2B: $70- 75	XP: $6	F12
Sun-Thurs 2/1-5/14 & 10/1-1/31 [CP]	1P: $45- 55	2P/1B: $48- 65	2P/2B: $52- 65	XP: $5	F12

◆

Motel

Location: 3 mi n from jct US 101. 3344 State St 93105. Fax: 805/687-7116. **Terms:** Reserv deposit. **Facility:** 32 rooms. 1-2 stories; exterior corridors. **Dining:** Restaurant nearby. **All Rooms:** combo or shower baths. **Some Rooms:** 2 efficiencies, 6 kitchens. **Cards:** AE, DS, MC, VI. **Special Amenities:** Early check-in/late check-out and free breakfast.

(See map p. 1004)

SANTA BARBARA INN   Phone: (805)966-2285   42

| | 7/1-8/31 | 1P: $187- 292 | 2P/1B: $187- 292 | 2P/2B: $197- 302 | XP: $15 | F16 |
| | 2/1-6/30 & 9/1-1/31 | 1P: $156- 259 | 2P/1B: $156- 259 | 2P/2B: $166- 269 | XP: $15 | F16 |

Motor Inn

Location: Just s of US 101, exit Milpas St. 901 Cabrillo Blvd 93103. Fax: 805/966-6584. **Terms:** Reserv deposit; 2 night min stay, weekends. **Facility:** 71 rooms. Across from beach. Spacious rooms with ocean or mountain views. 3rd floor sun deck with ocean view. 1 two-bedroom unit. 6 rooms with kitchen, $15 extra; 3 stories; interior/exterior corridors; heated pool, whirlpool. **Dining:** Citronelle Restaurant, see separate listing. **All Rooms:** extended cable TV. **Cards:** AE, CB, DI, DS, MC, VI. **Special Amenities:** Free newspaper and free room upgrade (subject to availability with advanced reservations). (See color ad below)

Simpson House Inn

Secluded on an acre of English gardens, Santa Barbara's only Historic Landmark Inn, includes restored barn and cottages. Elegantly appointed with antiques, oriental rugs, and original art. A 5-minute walk to Downtown and restaurants. Complimentary gourmet breakfast, wine and sumptuous Mediterranean hors d'oeuvres buffet, bicycles, and lawn croquet.

121 East Arrellaga St. Santa Barbara, CA 93101
Call (800) 676-1280
www.simpsonhouseinn.com

Most rooms feature: woodburning fireplaces, jacuzzi tubs, private garden patios

"Only 5 Diamond B&B in North America"

THE OCEAN IS AT OUR DOORSTEP.
THE MOUNTAINS ARE IN OUR BACKYARD.

- 71 Beautifully Appointed Guest Rooms and Suites

- Panoramic Ocean and Mountain Views

- Heated Outdoor Swimming Pool and Whirlpool Spa

- Refrigerators and Coffee Makers

- Michel Richard's Citronelle - serving fresh California French Cuisine

Santa Barbara Inn

901 East Cabrillo Boulevard
Santa Barbara, CA 93103

For reservations and information call:

1-800-231-0431
or
1-805-966-2285

www.SantaBarbaraInn.com

AAA Value Rates

$132* Value Season Sunday - Thursday

$162* July & August Sunday - Thursday

*Single or double. Per night, plus tax. Based on availability. Offer not applicable to any other discounts or special offers.

SAVE Look for this icon in the listings. These lodgings offer a minimum 10-percent discount from rates printed in the TourBook.

(See map p. 1004)

THE SECRET GARDEN & COTTAGES   Phone: (805)687-2300 ㊸
All Year [BP]   1P: $121- 214   2P/1B: $121- 214 2P/2B: $121- 214 XP: $20   F4
Location: From US 101, northbound exit Arrellaga St, southbound exit Mission. 1908 Bath St 93101.
Fax: 805/687-4576. **Terms:** Reserv deposit, 7 day notice; handling fee imposed; 2 night min stay, weekends.
Bed &   **Facility:** 11 rooms. Attractively furnished rooms in main house & cottages on tree shaded, beautifully land-
Breakfast   scaped grounds. 4 rooms with private patio & outdoor whirlpool. Complimentary dessert & hot beverages
served in evening. 1 story; interior/exterior corridors; smoke free premises. **Services:** complimentary evening
beverages. **Recreation:** bicycles. **Some Rooms:** color TV. **Cards:** AE, DS, MC, VI. **Special Amenities: Free breakfast
and free local telephone calls.**   🅢🅑 ⊠ 🆉 🅚 🖨 📲 ⊠

SIMPSON HOUSE INN   Rates Subject to Change   Phone: (805)963-7067 ㉓
All Year [BP]   1P: $170- 400   2P/1B: $170- 400 2P/2B: $170- 400 XP: $25
Location: Just e of State St. 121 E Arrellaga St 93101. Fax: 805/564-4811. **Terms:** Reserv deposit, 7 day
Historic Bed   notice; 2 night min stay, weekends. **Facility:** 14 rooms. Beautifully decorated rooms in 1874 historic Eastlake
& Breakfast   style Italianate Victorian home or in cottage or barn suites, some with whirlpool tub & fireplace. Located in a
quiet residential area on tree shaded grounds. Some small room. 2 stories; interior/exterior corridors; desig-
nated smoking area. **Services:** complimentary evening beverages. **Recreation:** bicycles, concierge, health
club & spa privileges. **All Rooms:** combo or shower baths, extended cable TV. **Some Rooms:** whirlpools. **Cards:** AE, DS,
MC, VI. *(See color ad p 1020)*   🄿 🅰 ⊠ 🆅🅲🆁 💻 🖨 📲 ⊠

SUMMERLAND INN   Phone: (805)969-5225 ❶
5/1-9/30 [BP]   1P: $90- 160   2P/1B: $90- 160 2P/2B: $135   XP: $15   F12
2/1-4/30 & 10/1-1/31 [BP] 1P: $70- 135   2P/1B: $70- 135 2P/2B: $100   XP: $15   F12
Location: Adjacent to US 101, northbound exit Evans St, southbound Summerland exit. 2161 Ortega Hill Rd
Bed &   93067 (PO Box 1209, SUMMERLAND). Fax: 805/962-0094. **Terms:** Reserv deposit, 3 day notice; 2 night
Breakfast   min stay, weekends. **Facility:** 12 rooms. Charming country inn decor. 2 units with gas fireplace. 2 stories;
interior/exterior corridors; designated smoking area; whirlpool. **All Rooms:** combo or shower baths, extended
cable TV. **Cards:** AE, MC, VI. **Special Amenities: Free breakfast and free local telephone calls.**
                                                   🅢🅑 🄿 🅰 🅚 🆅🅲🆁 🖳 🖨 📲 ⊠

TIFFANY INN   Rates Subject to Change   Phone: 805/963-2283 ㉒
All Year & Fri & Sat 2/1-5/31
[BP]   1P: $125- 250   2P/1B: $125- 250   XP: $30   D
Location: 1323 De La Vina St 93101. Fax: 805/965-0094. **Terms:** Check-in 3:30 pm; reserv deposit, 7 day
Historic Bed   notice; 2 night min stay, weekends. **Facility:** 7 rooms. 1898 Colonial Revival style house located in residential
& Breakfast   area. 5 units with woodburning fireplace. 2 rooms with private exterior entrance. 3 stories; interior/exterior cor-
ridors; smoke free premises. **Services:** complimentary evening beverages. **All Rooms:** combo or shower
baths, extended cable TV. **Some Rooms:** color TV, whirlpools. **Cards:** AE, DS, MC, VI.   🆅🅲🆁 🅚 🖨 📲 ⊠

(See map p. 1004)

TRAVELODGE SANTA BARBARA BEACH
Phone: (805)965-8527 ▨ 20
AAA SAVE | All Year | 1P: $65- 165 | 2P/1B: $65- 165 | 2P/2B: $65- 185 | XP: $10 | F17
◆◆◆
Motel
Location: Just s of US 101. 22 Castillo St 93101. Fax: 805/965-6125. **Terms:** Reserv deposit; 2 night min stay, weekends in summer. **Facility:** 19 rooms. 1/2 block from beach. 4 rooms with patios. Across from city park. 1 story; exterior corridors. **Dining:** Restaurant nearby. **All Rooms:** extended cable TV. **Cards:** AE, CB, DI, DS, JC, MC, VI. **Special Amenities:** Free local telephone calls and free newspaper.

TROPICANA INN & SUITES
Rates Subject to Change **Phone: (805)966-2219** ▨ 17
AAA
5/21-9/25 [CP]	1P: $96- 162	2P/1B: $96- 172	2P/2B: $126- 172	XP: $10
9/26-1/31 [CP]	1P: $90- 156	2P/1B: $90- 166	2P/2B: $120- 166	XP: $10
2/1-5/20 [CP]	1P: $84- 150	2P/1B: $84- 160	2P/2B: $114- 160	XP: $10
◆◆◆
Motel
Location: Northbound US 101 exit Cabrillo Blvd, 3 mi w to Castillo St, just n; southbound exit Castillo St. 223 Castillo St 93101. Fax: 805/962-9428. **Terms:** Weekly/monthly rates; 2 night min stay, Weekends 5/26-9/5. **Facility:** 31 rooms. 2 blocks to beach & harbor & near city park. Cozy country decor. 28 covered parking spaces. 1 two-bedroom unit. 1 large 2-bedroom suite with kitchen & dining room, $170 for up to 8 persons & 15-2 room suites with kitchen $106-$142; 1-3 stories; smoke free premises; heated pool, whirlpool. **Recreation:** Fee: bicycles. **All Rooms:** combo or shower baths, extended cable TV. **Cards:** AE, CB, DI, DS, MC, VI. *(See color ad p 1007)*

THE UPHAM
Phone: (805)962-0058 ▨ 46
AAA SAVE | All Year [CP] | 1P: $140- 385 | 2P/1B: $140- 385 | 2P/2B: $195 | XP: $10 | F12
◆◆◆
Historic
Country Inn
Location: US 101 exit Mission St, just n, then just e. 1404 De la Vina St at Sola 93101. Fax: 805/963-2825. **Terms:** 2 night min stay, weekends. **Facility:** 50 rooms. A historic Victorian hotel & cottages established in 1871. Beautifully landscaped garden setting. 1 suite with fireplace & whirlpool, $350; 2 stories; interior/exterior corridors. **Dining:** Restaurant; 11:30 am-2 & 6-9 pm, Sat & Sun from 6 pm; $9-$19; wine/beer only. **Cards:** AE, CB, DI, DS, JC, MC, VI. **Special Amenities:** Free breakfast and free local telephone calls.

VILLA ROSA
Rates Subject to Change **Phone: (805)966-0851** ▨ 44
AAA | All Year [CP] | 1P: $110- 250 | 2P/1B: $110- 250
◆◆
Bed &
Breakfast
Location: 1 blk from beach. 15 Chapala St 93101. Fax: 805/962-7159. **Terms:** Reserv deposit, 5 day notice; 2 night min stay, weekends. **Facility:** 18 rooms. A classic Spanish style building. Rooms decorated in an attractive southwest theme. 2 rooms with kitchenette & fireplace, $160-$190; without fireplace, $160-$165; 2 stories; interior corridors; designated smoking area; small heated pool, whirlpool. **Services:** complimentary evening beverages. **Some Rooms:** 3 efficiencies, color TV. **Cards:** AE, MC, VI.

WEST BEACH INN
Phone: (805)963-4277 ▨ 12
AAA SAVE | 2/1-6/3 & 9/5-1/31 [CP] | 1P: $106- 201 | 2P/1B: $106- 201 | 2P/2B: $119- 201 | XP: $15 | F
| 6/4-9/4 [CP] | 1P: $135- 180 | 2P/1B: $135- 180 | 2P/2B: $150- 180 | XP: $15 | F
◆◆◆
Motel
Location: Just s of US 101. 306 W Cabrillo Blvd & Bath St 93101. Fax: 805/564-4210. **Terms:** Check-in 4 pm; handling fee imposed; weekly/monthly rates; 2 night min stay, wkends 3/27-10/30. **Facility:** 44 rooms. Across from yacht harbor & beach. Some patios or balconies. Attractive pool area and large whirlpool with beach view. 2 one-bedroom apartments with kitchen, $167-$200 for 4 persons. 1 two-bedroom apartment with fireplace & refrig, $196-$250 for 6 persons; 2-3 stories; exterior corridors; heated pool, whirlpool. **Services:** complimentary evening beverages. **All Rooms:** extended cable TV. **Cards:** AE, CB, DI, MC, VI. **Special Amenities:** Free breakfast and free local telephone calls. *(See color ad p 1021)*

RESTAURANTS

ALEX'S CANTINA
Lunch: $5-$8 Dinner: $5-$13 **Phone: 805/683-2577** ▨ 21
◆
Mexican
Location: In Goleta; from SR 101 exit Fairview Ave 0.3 mi s, then w on Hollister Ave. 5918 Hollister Ave 93117. **Hours:** 11:30 am-9:30 pm, Sun 10 am-9 pm. Closed: 11/25 & 12/25. **Features:** casual dress; Sunday brunch; children's menu; senior's menu; carryout; cocktails & lounge; entertainment. Nice selection of traditional Mexican entrees. Lunch & dinner buffet also avail. Smoke free premises. **Cards:** AE, CB, DI, DS, MC, VI.

ANDRIA'S HARBORSIDE RESTAURANT
Lunch: $6-$9 Dinner: $11-$20 **Phone: 805/966-3000** ▨ 5
◆◆
Seafood
Location: At Best Western-Beachside Inn. 336 W Cabrillo Blvd 93101. **Hours:** 7 am-3 & 5-10 pm, Fri & Sat-10:30 pm. **Features:** casual dress; Sunday brunch; children's menu; carryout; cocktails & lounge; entertainment. Across from beach & yacht harbor. Nice selection of seafood & limited selection of steaks, chicken & pasta. Oyster bar. Smoke free premises. **Cards:** AE, DI, MC, VI. *(See color ad p 1006)*

BEACHSIDE CAFE
Lunch: $6-$11 Dinner: $14-$23 **Phone: 805/964-7881** ▨ 20
◆◆
Seafood
Location: In Goleta, just s of US 101 on SR 217, then 1 mi e on Sandspit Rd 93117. **Hours:** 11:30 am-4 & 5-10 pm, Fri-10:30 pm, Sat 11 am-4 & 5-10:30 pm, Sun 11 am-4 & 5-10 pm. Closed: 11/25 & 12/25. **Reservations:** suggested. **Features:** casual dress; children's menu; early bird specials; cocktails. Beachfront restaurant located adjacent to Goleta Beach County Park & Pier. Patio seating available. Oyster Bar. Smoke free premises. **Cards:** AE, MC, VI.

CAFE DEL SOL
Lunch: $6-$12 Dinner: $9-$23 **Phone: 805/969-0448** ▨ 11
◆◆
American
Location: Just s of US 101, exit Cabrillo Blvd, 1 blk s, 1 blk w. 30 Los Patos Way 93103. **Hours:** 11:30-10 pm, Sun 10 am-10 pm. Closed: 1/1, 11/25, 12/24 & 12/25. **Features:** casual dress; Sunday brunch; children's menu; carryout; cocktails; a la carte. Nice selection of seafood, chicken, steaks & Mexican specialties. Located across from Andree Clark Bird Refuge. Smoke free premises. **Cards:** AE, DS, MC, VI.

CHAD'S
Dinner: $10-$25 **Phone: 805/568-1876** ▨ 13
◆◆
American
Location: Just n of Cota. 625 Chapala St 93101. **Hours:** 5:30- 9 pm, Fri & Sat-10:30 pm. Closed: 1/1, 7/4 & 12/25. **Features:** casual dress; cocktails & lounge; entertainment; a la carte. Regional American cuisine served in a charming home built in 1876. Smoke free premises. **Cards:** AE, DI, DS, MC, VI.

CHUCK'S OF HAWAII
Dinner: $8-$20 **Phone: 805/687-4417** ▨ 10
◆◆
Steak and
Seafood
Location: 0.6 mi nw, 0.5 mi e of jct US 101. 3888 State St 93105. **Hours:** 5:30-11 pm, Fri & Sat-11:30 pm. Closed: 11/25 & 12/25. **Features:** casual dress; children's menu; salad bar; cocktails. Excellent selection of seafood, steaks & wines. Polynesian decor. Smoke free premises. **Cards:** AE, MC, VI.

(See map p. 1004)

CITRONELLE RESTAURANT   **Lunch:** $11-$16   **Dinner:** $19-$25   **Phone:** 805/963-0111   (8)
◆◆◆   **Location:** Just s of US 101, exit Milpas St; in Santa Barbara Inn. 901 Cabrillo Blvd 93103. **Hours:** 7 am-10,
French   noon-2:30 & 6-9:30 pm, Fri-10 pm, Sat 6 pm-10 pm, Sun 7-10 am, 10:30-2:30 & 6-9:30 pm.
Reservations: suggested. **Features:** casual dress; Sunday brunch; children's menu; cocktails & lounge;
valet parking; a la carte. Fine dining with a panoramic ocean view. Interesting selection of French & California cuisine.
Smoke free premises. **Cards:** AE, CB, DI, DS, MC, VI. *(See color ad p 1020)*   ⊠

COLD SPRINGS TAVERN   Historical   **Lunch:** $7-$9   **Dinner:** $15-$22   **Phone:** 805/967-0066   (22)
◆   **Location:** 15 mi n; from SR 157 (San Marcos Pass) 0.8 mi nw on Stagecoach Rd. 5995 Stagecoach Rd
American   93105. **Hours:** 11 am-3 & 5-9 pm, Fri-10 pm, Sat 8 am-3 & 5-10 pm, Sun 8 am-3 & 5-9 pm. Closed: 12/25.
Reservations: suggested. **Features:** casual dress; children's menu; carryout; cocktails & lounge. Peaceful,
tree shaded location. Rustic restaurant with ranch decor located in 100 year old stage stop. Nice selection of fish, beef,
chicken & seasonal game. Smoke free premises. **Cards:** AE, MC, VI.   ⊠

DOWNEY'S   **Dinner:** $24-$30   **Phone:** 805/966-5006   (4)
◆◆◆   **Location:** Downtown. 1305 State St 93101. **Hours:** 5:30 pm-9 pm, Fri & Sat-9:30 pm. Closed: 1/1, 12/25 &
American   Mon. **Reservations:** suggested. **Features:** casual dress; beer & wine only; a la carte. Small restaurant
serving excellently prepared & presented cuisine. Menu changes daily. Smoke free premises. **Cards:** AE,
DS, MC, VI.   ⊠

LA MARINA   **Dinner:** $20-$35   **Phone:** 805/969-2261   (14)
◆◆◆◆   **Location:** 0.3 mi s of US 101, in Montecito area, exit Olive Mill Rd; in Four Season's Biltmore. 1260
Continental   Channel Dr 93108. **Hours:** 6 pm-10 pm, Sun 10 am 2 & 6-10 pm. Closed: Mon. **Reservations:** suggested.
Features: semi-formal attire; Sunday brunch; children's menu; cocktails; valet parking; a la carte. Fine dining
in beautifully appointed dining room. Smoke free premises. **Cards:** AE, CB, DI, DS, JC, MC, VI.   ⊠

MONTECITO CAFE   **Lunch:** $7-$16   **Dinner:** $7-$16   **Phone:** 805/969-3392   (7)
◆◆◆   **Location:** In Montecito, adjacent to US 101, exit Olive Mill Rd; in Montecito Inn. 1295 Coast Village Rd
American   93108. **Hours:** 7 am-10 pm. Closed: 11/25 & 12/25. **Reservations:** suggested. **Features:** casual dress;
children's menu; health conscious menu; carryout; cocktails & lounge; entertainment. Creative upscale
selections in a California-style bistro. Smoke free premises. **Cards:** AE, MC, VI.   ⊠

MOUSSE ODILE   **Lunch:** $6-$10   **Dinner:** $13-$19   **Phone:** 805/962-5393   (18)
ⓐⓐⓐ   **Location:** Just e of State St. 18 E Cota St 93101. **Hours:** 8 am-2:30 & 5:30-9 pm, Fri & Sat-9:30 pm.
◆◆   Closed: 1/1, 11/25, 12/25 & Sun. **Reservations:** suggested; dinner. **Features:** No A/C; casual dress;
French   carryout; cocktails; street parking; a la carte. Patio Dining. Picnic baskets avail. Smoke free premises.
Cards: AE, DS, MC, VI.   ⊠

ORIGINAL ENTERPRISE FISH COMPANY   **Lunch:** $6-$9   **Dinner:** $10-$17   **Phone:** 805/962-3313   (6)
◆◆   **Location:** 1 blk s of US 101. 225 State St 93101. **Hours:** 11:30 am-9:30 pm, Fri & Sat-10 pm. Closed: 11/25
Seafood   & 12/25. **Reservations:** suggested. **Features:** casual dress; children's menu; carryout; beer & wine only.
Nautical decor. Large selection of mesquite broiled seafood. High noise level on busy nights. Smoke free
premises. **Cards:** AE, MC, VI.   ⊠

THE PALACE CAFE   **Dinner:** $10-$25   **Phone:** 805/966-3133   (9)
◆◆   **Location:** Downtown area; 3 blks nw of US 101, just e of State St. 8 E Cota St 93101. **Hours:** 5:30 pm-10
American   pm, Fri & Sat-11 pm. Closed: 11/25 & 12/25. **Features:** casual dress; children's menu; carryout; beer & wine
only; a la carte. Interesting selection of Cajun, Creole & Caribbean cuisine. Casual dining in lively
atmosphere. Smoke free premises. **Cards:** AE, MC, VI.   ⊠

PALAZZIO "DOWNTOWN"   **Lunch:** $9-$16   **Dinner:** $9-$16   **Phone:** 805/564-1985   (15)
◆◆   **Location:** Downtown. 1026 State St 93101. **Hours:** 11:30 am-3 & 5:30-11 pm, Sun 5:30 pm-10 pm. Closed
Italian   major holidays. **Features:** casual dress; carryout; cocktails & lounge; street parking. Nice selection of Italian
dishes. Large portions. Outdoor dining avail weather permitting. Smoke free premises. **Cards:** MC, VI.   ⊠

PALAZZIO TRATTORIA ITALIANA   **Lunch:** $6-$12   **Dinner:** $6-$12   **Phone:** 805/969-8565   (1)
◆◆   **Location:** In Montecito, from US 101 exit Olive Mill Rd, 0.3 mi n. 1151 Coast Village Rd 93108.
Italian   **Hours:** 11:30 am-2:30 & 5:30-11 pm, Fri & Sat-midnight, Sun from 5:30-11 pm. Closed: 11/25.
Reservations: accepted; 1st seating. **Features:** casual dress; children's menu; carryout; cocktails; street
parking; a la carte. Popular local restaurant with creative dishes in large portions, enough to share. Smoke free premises.
Cards: MC, VI.   ⊠

RISTORANTE PIATTI   **Lunch:** $8-$16   **Dinner:** $10-$18   **Phone:** 805/969-7520   (12)
◆◆◆   **Location:** 1 mi n of US 101, exit San Ysidro Rd; In Montecito Plaza Del Sol Shopping Center. 516 San
Northern   Ysidro Rd at E Valley 93108. **Hours:** 11:30 am-9 pm, Fri & Sat-10 pm, Sun 11:30 am-9 pm. Closed: 12/25.
Italian   **Reservations:** suggested. **Features:** casual dress; Sunday brunch; children's menu; carryout; cocktails &
lounge; a la carte. Selection of pasta, pizza, seafood & veal. Indoor or outdoor patio dining. Smoke free
premises. **Cards:** AE, DI, MC, VI.   ⊠

TOM & JERRY'S AMERICAN GRILL   **Lunch:** $5-$9   **Dinner:** $8-$20   **Phone:** 805/687-2828   (23)
◆   **Location:** 3 mi nw; 0.8 mi e of jct US 101; in The Sandman Inn. 3744 State St 93105. **Hours:** 11:30 am-10
American   pm. Closed: 12/24 & 12/25. **Features:** casual dress; children's menu; health conscious menu; carryout;
cocktails & lounge. Good selection of sandwiches, pasta, meat & seafood. Outdoor patio dining avail. Smoke
free premises. **Cards:** AE, DS, MC, VI. *(See color ad p 1019)*   ⊠

WINE CASK RESTAURANT   **Lunch:** $7-$13   **Dinner:** $20-$30   **Phone:** 805/966-9463   (2)
◆◆◆   **Location:** Downtown. 813 Anacapa St 93101. **Hours:** 11:30 am-3 & 5:30-9 pm, Fri-10 pm, Sat 10 am-3 &
American   5:30-10 pm, Sun 10 am-9 pm 5/31-9/15; Sun-Thurs-10 pm, Fri & Sat-11 pm. Closed: some major holidays.
Reservations: suggested. **Features:** casual dress; Sunday brunch; health conscious menu; cocktails; fee for
valet parking; a la carte, also prix fixe. California cuisine served in an attractive dining room or an outdoor courtyard.
Extensive wine list. Vegetarian entrees upon request. Located in El Paseo area. Sat & Sun brunch 10 am-2:30 pm. Smoke
free premises. **Cards:** AE, DI, MC, VI.   ⊠

SANTA CLARA—110,600

LODGINGS

BEST WESTERN INN — Guaranteed Rates — Phone: 408/244-3366
◆◆   All Year [CP]   2P/1B: $85- 120 2P/2B: $90- 130 XP: $5
Motel   **Location:** 2 blks w of Lawrence Expwy; on SR 82. 4341 El Camino Real 95051. Fax: 408/246-1387.
Terms: Reserv deposit. **Facility:** 52 rooms. Very attractive & comfortable rooms. 2 stories; exterior corridors;
heated pool. **Cards:** AE, CB, DI, DS, MC, VI.

BILTMORE HOTEL & SUITES/SILICON VALLEY — Phone: (408)988-8411
🅰 ⓢ   Sun-Thurs   1P: $129- 169   2P/1B: $139- 179   2P/2B: $149- 179   XP: $10
◆◆◆   Fri & Sat   1P: $79- 119   2P/1B: $79- 119   2P/2B: $79- 119   XP: $10
Hotel   **Location:** E of & adjacent to US 101; exit Montague Expwy; 1 mi s of Great America. 2151 Laurelwood Rd
95054. Fax: 408/988-0225. **Facility:** 262 rooms. Motel style units & tower suites. 6 two-bedroom units. 2-9 sto-
ries; interior/exterior corridors; heated pool, whirlpool. **Dining:** Restaurant; 6 am-10 pm; $10-$20; cocktails.
Services: giftshop; area transportation, within 5 mi. **Cards:** AE, CB, DI, DS, JC, MC, VI. **Special Amenities:** Free
breakfast and free local telephone calls. *(See ad below)*

DAYS INN-GREAT AMERICA — Rates Subject to Change — Phone: 408/980-1525
◆◆   All Year   1P: $139- 149   2P/1B: $149- 159   2P/2B: $149- 159   XP: $10   F17
Motor Inn   **Location:** 0.5 mi e off US 101; exit Great American Pkwy; 0.8 mi s of Great America Theme Park. 4200
Great America Pkwy 95054. Fax: 408/988-0976. **Facility:** 168 rooms. 4 stories; exterior corridors; heated pool.
Services: area transportation. **Cards:** AE, CB, DI, DS, JC, MC, VI.

EMBASSY SUITES HOTEL — Rates Subject to Change — Phone: 408/496-6400
◆◆◆   Sun-Thurs [BP]   1P: $199   2P/1B: $199   XP: $15   F17
Suite Hotel   Fri & Sat [BP]   1P: $99   2P/1B: $99   XP: $15   F17
Location: W of US 101; Great America Pkwy exit. 2885 Lakeside Dr 95054. Fax: 408/988-7529.
Facility: 257 rooms. Some small units. Suites with living room. 10 stories; interior corridors; small heated indoor pool.
Services: giftshop. **Cards:** AE, CB, DI, DS, JC, MC, VI. *(See color ad p 931)*

GRANADA INN-SILICON VALLEY — Phone: (408)241-2841
🅰 ⓢ   Mon-Thurs [BP]   1P: $90- 129   2P/1B: $90- 129   2P/2B: $90- 129   XP: $10
◆◆   Fri-Sun [BP]   1P: $69- 99   2P/1B: $69- 99   2P/2B: $69- 99   XP: $10
Motel   **Location:** Exit US 101, San Tomas Expwy; 3 mi s, then w. 2515 El Camino Real 95051. Fax: 408/241-8559.
Facility: 63 rooms. Spanish Mediterrean design. Free video library. 2 stories; interior corridors.
Dining: Restaurant nearby. **All Rooms:** efficiencies, combo or shower baths. **Cards:** AE, DI, DS, MC, VI.
(See color ad p 980)

GUEST HOUSE INN & SUITES-SILICON VALLEY USA   Phone: (408)241-3010
(AAA) (SAVE)   4/1-9/30 [CP]   1P: $99- 210   2P/1B: $99- 210   2P/2B: $109- 210   XP: $10   F17
               2/1-3/31 & 10/1-1/31 [CP] 1P: $89- 200   2P/1B: $89- 200   2P/2B: $89- 200   XP: $10   F17
◆◆   **Location:** SR 82, 0.5 mi w of San Tomas Expwy; US 101 exit s Bowers Ave. 2930 El Camino Real 95051
Motel   (PO Box 2841). Fax: 408/247-0623. **Terms:** Weekly/monthly rates; pets, $6 extra charge. **Facility:** 70 rooms.
               1 three-bedroom unit, 18 two-bedroom units. 2 stories; exterior corridors; small heated pool. **Dining:** Coffee
shop nearby. **Some Rooms:** 17 kitchens. **Cards:** AE, CB, DI, DS, JC, MC, VI. **Special Amenities:** Free breakfast and free
local telephone calls. *(See color ad p 1024)*

HAWTHORN SUITES   Rates Subject to Change   Phone: 408/241-6444
◆◆◆   Mon-Thurs [BP]   1P: $149- 189   2P/1B: $149- 189   2P/2B: $149
Motor Inn   Fri-Sun [BP]   1P: $79- 119   2P/1B: $79- 119   2P/2B: $79
               Location: Just w of San Tomas Expwy. 2455 El Camino Real 95051. Fax: 408/241-6446. **Facility:** 96 rooms.
7 whirlpool rms, extra charge; 3 stories; interior corridors; heated pool. **Cards:** AE, CB, DI, DS, JC, MC, VI.
(See color ad below)

HOWARD JOHNSON LODGE   Phone: (408)257-8600
(AAA) (SAVE)   All Year   1P: $145   2P/1B: $145   2P/2B: $145   XP: $10   F18
               Location: W of jct I-280 & Lawrence Expwy; Stevens Creek Blvd exit. 5405 Stevens Creek Blvd 95051.
◆◆◆   Fax: 408/446-2936. **Terms:** Reserv deposit; weekend rates avail. **Facility:** 96 rooms. Conveniently located. 2
Motel   stories; interior corridors; heated pool, wading pool. **Dining:** Restaurant nearby. **Cards:** AE, DI, DS, JC, MC,
               VI. **Special Amenities:** Free breakfast and free local telephone calls.
(See color ad opposite inside back cover)

MARIANI'S INN   Rates Subject to Change   Phone: (408)243-1431
(AAA)   All Year [CP]   2P/1B: $84   2P/2B: $92   2P/2B: $92   XP: $8   F12
               Location: Exit US 101, San Tomas Expwy, 3 mi s, w on ElCamino Real. 2500 El Camino Real 95051.
◆◆◆   Fax: 408/243-5745. **Facility:** 143 rooms. 4 two-bedroom units. 2 two-bedroom cottages, $150; 2 stories; ex-
Motor Inn   terior corridors; heated pool, whirlpool. **Dining:** Restaurant, see separate listing. **All Rooms:** combo or
               shower baths. **Some Rooms:** 50 kitchens. **Cards:** AE, CB, DI, DS, MC, VI.

QUALITY SUITES-SILICON VALLEY   Rates Subject to Change   Phone: (408)748-9800
◆◆◆   Mon-Thurs [BP]   1P: $179- 199   2P/1B: $189- 209   2P/2B: $189- 209   XP: $10-20   F3
Suite Motel   Fri-Sun [BP]   1P: $89- 119   2P/1B: $99- 129   2P/2B: $99- 129   XP: $10-20   F3
               Location: W of US 101, exit Lawrence Expwy, s on Oakmead, at Peterson Way. 3100 Lakeside Dr 95054.
Fax: 408/748-1476. **Terms:** Check-in 4 pm. **Facility:** 220 rooms. Nicely appointed rooms, attractive public areas. 7 stories; in-
terior corridors; heated pool. **Services:** giftshop; area transportation. **Recreation:** sports court. **Cards:** AE, CB, DI, DS, JC,
MC, VI.

SANTA CLARA DAYS INN   Rates Subject to Change   Phone: (408)244-2840
◆◆◆   All Year [CP]   1P: $102- 171   2P/1B: $102- 171   2P/2B: $113- 125
Motel   **Location:** On SR 82 at Lafayette. 859 El Camino Real 95050. Fax: 408/984-5720. **Terms:** Reserv deposit.
               Facility: 43 rooms. Very attractive decor. 25 whirlpool rms, extra charge; 2 stories; exterior corridors.
Cards: AE, CB, DI, DS, JC, MC, VI.

SANTA CLARA MARRIOTT HOTEL   Rates Subject to Change   Phone: 408/988-1500
◆◆◆   Sun-Thurs   1P: $219   2P/1B: $219   2P/2B: $219   XP: $15
Hotel   Fri & Sat   1P: $119   2P/1B: $119   2P/2B: $119   XP: $15
               Location: 0.5 mi e off US 101; exit Great America Pkwy; 0.8 mi s of Great America Theme Park. 2700
Mission College 95054. Fax: 408/727-4353. **Facility:** 758 rooms. Spanish design. Many balconies; some patios. 2-15 stories;
interior corridors; heated indoor/outdoor pool; 4 lighted tennis courts. **Services:** giftshop; area transportation.
Recreation: sports court. **Cards:** AE, DI, DS, JC, MC, VI.

THE VAGABOND INN   Phone: (408)241-0771
(AAA) (SAVE)   All Year [CP]   1P: $103   2P/1B: $108   2P/2B: $115   XP: $5   F18
◆◆   **Location:** On SR 82; se corner of Lawrence Expwy cloverleaf. 3580 El Camino Real 95051.
Motel   Fax: 408/247-3386. **Terms:** Small pets only, $5 extra charge. **Facility:** 70 rooms. Convenient location. 2 sto-
               ries; exterior corridors; heated pool. **Dining:** Coffee shop nearby. **Cards:** AE, CB, DI, DS, MC, VI.
               Special Amenities: Free breakfast and free local telephone calls.

THE WESTIN HOTEL-SANTA CLARA Rates Subject to Change Phone: 408/986-0700
◆◆◆◆

Hotel	1/1-1/31 [EP]	1P: $305- 325	2P/1B: $305- 325	2P/2B: $305- 325	XP: $20	F17
	9/1-12/31 [BP]	1P: $295- 315	2P/1B: $295- 315	2P/2B: $295- 315	XP: $20	F17
	5/1-8/31 [BP]	1P: $285- 305	2P/1B: $285- 305	2P/2B: $285- 305	XP: $20	F17
	2/1-4/30 [EP]	1P: $275- 295	2P/1B: $275- 295	2P/2B: $275- 295	XP: $20	F17

Location: 0.8 mi e off US 101, exit Great America Pkwy; at Santa Clara Convention Center. 5101 Great America Pkwy 95054. Fax: 408/980-3990. **Facility:** 501 rooms. 14 stories; interior corridors; heated pool. Fee: 18 holes golf; 4 lighted tennis courts. **Services:** giftshop. **Cards:** AE, CB, DI, DS, JC, MC, VI.

RESTAURANTS

ARTHUR'S Lunch: $7-$15 Dinner: $23-$87 Phone: 408/980-1666
◆◆◆
American **Location:** Exit US 101 Great America Pkwy W. 2875 Lakeside Dr 95054. **Hours:** 11 am-3 & 5-10 pm, Sat from 5 pm. Closed major holidays & Sun. **Reservations:** suggested. **Features:** semi-formal attire; cocktails & lounge; entertainment; minimum charge-$6; a la carte. Elegant decor, very popular; varied menu with continental flair. Smoke free premises. **Cards:** AE, CB, DI, MC, VI.

CALIFORNIA CAFE BAR & GRILL Lunch: $5-$13 Dinner: $7-$22 Phone: 408/296-2233
◆◆◆
Regional
American **Location:** Valley Fair Shopping Ctr. 2855 Stevens Creek Blvd 95050. **Hours:** 11 am-10 pm, Sun-8 pm. **Reservations:** suggested. **Features:** casual dress; Sunday brunch; children's menu; cocktails & lounge; a la carte. Smoke free premises. **Cards:** AE, CB, DI, DS, MC, VI.

MARIANI'S Lunch: $8-$16 Dinner: $10-$19 Phone: 408/243-1431
◆◆◆
Continental **Location:** On SR 82, 0.3 mi w of San Tomas, at Mariani's Inn. 2500 El Camino Real 95051. **Hours:** 6:30 am-10:30 pm; Sun-9:30 pm. Closed major holidays. **Reservations:** suggested. **Features:** casual dress; children's menu; early bird specials; cocktails & lounge; entertainment. Modern comfortable decor, varied menu featuring pasta, seafood, chops & poultry. Smoke free premises. **Cards:** AE, CB, DI, MC, VI.

PASAND INDIA CUISINE Lunch: $3-$7 Dinner: $5-$11 Phone: 408/241-5150
◆◆
Ethnic **Location:** W of Lawrence Expwy. 3701 El Camino Real 95051. **Hours:** 11:30 am-10 pm. Closed: 11/28 & 12/25. **Features:** casual dress; children's menu; beer & wine only; a la carte. Northern India specialties. Smoke free premises. **Cards:** AE, CB, DI, MC, VI.

SANTA CLARITA—*See Los Angeles p. 633.*

SANTA CRUZ—*49,000—See also APTOS, CAPITOLA, FELTON & SCOTTS VALLEY.*

LODGINGS

BABBLING BROOK BED & BREAKFAST INN Rates Subject to Change Phone: (831)427-2437
◆◆◆
Bed & Breakfast All Year [BP] 1P: $145- 195 2P/1B: $145- 195 2P/2B: $145-1952 XP: $25

Location: Just sw of SR 1. 1025 Laurel St 95060. Fax: 831/427-2457. **Terms:** Reserv deposit, 10 day notice; 2 night min stay. **Facility:** 13 rooms. 3 two-story duplexes in cozy shaded setting along brook. Many units with fireplace. 5 whirlpool rms, extra charge; 2 stories; interior corridors; smoke free premises. **All Rooms:** combo or shower baths. **Some Rooms:** color TV. **Cards:** AE, DI, DS, MC, VI.

BEACH VIEW INN Rates Subject to Change Phone: (831)426-3575
(AAA)

	5/1-9/30 [CP]	1P: $65- 160	2P/1B: $65- 160	2P/2B: $85- 175	XP: $10
◆◆	2/1-4/30 & 10/1-1/31 [CP]	1P: $45- 125	2P/1B: $45- 125	2P/2B: $60- 150	XP: $10

Motel **Location:** 1 blk from beach. 50 Front St 95060. Fax: 831/421-0143. **Terms:** Reserv deposit. **Facility:** 22 rooms. 2 whirlpool rms, extra charge; 2 stories, no elevator; exterior corridors. **Dining:** Restaurant nearby. **Cards:** AE, CB, DI, DS, MC, VI.

BEST WESTERN ALL SUITES INN Phone: (831)458-9898
(AAA) (SAVE)

	5/1-9/30 [CP]	1P: $85- 165	2P/1B: $95- 185	2P/2B: $105- 195	XP: $10	F12
◆◆◆	2/1-4/30 & 10/1-1/31 [CP]	1P: $75- 155	2P/1B: $85- 165	2P/2B: $90- 175	XP: $10	F12

Suite Motel **Location:** Exit SR 1 & 17 via Central District. 500 Ocean St 95060. Fax: 831/429-1903. **Terms:** Reserv deposit, 3 day notice. **Facility:** 40 rooms. Some units with fireplace. 3 stories; interior corridors; heated pool, sauna, lap pool. **Dining:** Restaurant nearby. **Cards:** AE, CB, DI, DS, MC, VI. **Special Amenities:** Free breakfast and free local telephone calls.

BEST WESTERN INN Phone: (831)425-4717
(AAA) (SAVE)

	6/1-9/30 [CP]	1P: $65- 150	2P/1B: $75- 160	2P/2B: $85- 175	XP: $10	F12
	4/1-5/31 [CP]	1P: $65- 140	2P/1B: $75- 140	2P/2B: $80- 150	XP: $10	F12
◆◆	2/1-3/31 & 10/1-1/31 [CP]	1P: $49- 89	2P/1B: $59- 99	2P/2B: $65- 105	XP: $10	F12

Motel **Location:** Off jct SR 1 & 17; e side of Ocean St. 126 Plymouth St 95060. Fax: 831/425-0643. **Terms:** Reserv deposit, 3 day notice. **Facility:** 26 rooms. 1 two-bedroom unit. 3 whirlpool rms, extra charge; 2 stories; exterior corridors; sauna, whirlpool. **Dining:** Coffee shop nearby. **Cards:** AE, CB, DI, DS, MC, VI. **Special Amenities:** Free breakfast and free local telephone calls.

BEST WESTERN TORCH-LITE INN Phone: (831)426-7575
(AAA) (SAVE)

	6/1-9/30 [CP]	1P: $65- 95	2P/1B: $75- 115	2P/2B: $80- 125	XP: $10
	4/1-5/31 [CP]	1P: $50- 80	2P/1B: $60- 90	2P/2B: $70- 95	XP: $10
◆	2/1-3/31 & 10/1-1/31 [CP]	1P: $50- 80	2P/1B: $55- 70	2P/2B: $65- 80	XP: $10

Motel **Location:** 3 blks from beach. 500 Riverside Ave 95060. Fax: 831/460-1470. **Terms:** Reserv deposit. **Facility:** 38 rooms. 4 kitchens, $8 extra charge; 2 stories; interior/exterior corridors; heated pool. **All Rooms:** combo or shower baths. **Cards:** AE, CB, DI, DS, MC, VI. **Special Amenities:** Free breakfast and free local telephone calls.

CAROUSEL MOTEL
AAA
◆◆
Motel

	Guaranteed Rates								Phone: (831)425-7090
5/28-9/5 [CP]	1P:	$99- 159	2P/1B:	$99- 159	2P/2B:	$119- 139	XP: $10		F12
3/1-5/27 & 9/6-10/31 [CP]	1P:	$59- 139	2P/1B:	$59- 139	2P/2B:	$69- 129	XP: $10		F12
2/1-2/28 & 11/1-1/31 [CP]	1P:	$49- 99	2P/1B:	$49- 99	2P/2B:	$59- 89	XP: $10		F12

Location: Near the boardwalk & beach. 110 Riverside Ave 95060. Fax: 831/427-3400. **Terms:** Reserv deposit; 2 night min stay. **Facility:** 34 rooms. Some rooms with view of amusement park. Balcony or patio. 2 whirlpool rms, extra charge; 3 stories; interior corridors. **All Rooms:** combo or shower baths. **Cards:** AE, DS, MC, VI. *(See ad below)*

[ASK] [S◆] [□] [K] [▦] [目] [X]

CHAMINADE AT SANTA CRUZ
AAA [SAVE]
◆◆◆
Resort
Complex

| | | | | | | | | Phone: (831)475-5600 |
| All Year | 1P: $149- 229 | 2P/1B: | $149- 229 | 2P/2B: | $149- 229 | XP: $35 | | F12 |

Location: 1.5 mi e of SR 17 & 1; exit SR 1 at Soquel Ave, just w to Paul Sweet Rd then 0.5 mi n. 1 Chaminade Ln 95063 (P.O. Box 2788). Fax: 831/476-4942. **Terms:** Check-in 4 pm. **Facility:** 152 rooms. Quiet, hillside location; overlooks Santa Cruz & the Pacific. 2 stories; interior corridors; heated pool, saunas, whirlpools, men's & women's therapy pools; 4 lighted tennis courts. **Dining:** Dining room, restaurant, coffee shop; 7 am-9:30 pm; $17-$35; cocktails. **Services:** giftshop. Fee: massage. **Recreation:** hiking trails. **Cards:** AE, CB, DI, DS, JC, MC, VI. **Special Amenities:** Free newspaper and preferred room (subject to availability with advanced reservations).

[S◆] [3P] [≈] [¶] [▦] [△] [X] [✦] [♣] [▣] [▦] [目] [X]

COMFORT INN BEACH BOARDWALK
AAA [SAVE]
◆◆
Motel

								Phone: (831)471-9999
5/23-9/6 [CP]	1P:	$69- 119	2P/1B:	$89- 119	2P/2B:	$99- 149	XP: $10-15	F18
3/1-5/22 & 9/7-10/31 [CP]	1P:	$59- 89	2P/1B:	$69- 109	2P/2B:	$79- 119	XP: $10-15	F18
2/1-2/28 & 11/1-1/31 [CP]	1P:	$55- 75	2P/1B:	$69- 99	2P/2B:	$69- 110	XP: $10-15	F18

Location: 1 blk from boardwalk. 314 Riverside Ave 95060. Fax: 831/429-5000. **Facility:** 28 rooms. Close to beach & boardwalk. 1 two-bedroom unit. 2 stories; exterior corridors; heated pool. **Dining:** Restaurant nearby. **Cards:** AE, CB, DI, DS, MC, VI. **Special Amenities:** Free breakfast and free local telephone calls.

[S◆] [≈] [¶] [X]

COMFORT INN-SANTA CRUZ
◆◆
Motel

	Rates Subject to Change						Phone: 831/426-2664
5/1-9/30	1P: $79- 109	2P/1B:	$79- 109	2P/2B:	$89- 119	XP: $10
2/1-4/30 & 10/1-1/31	1P: $69- 99	2P/1B:	$69- 99	2P/2B:	$79- 109	XP: $10

Location: Off jct SR 1 & 17; s side of Ocean St. 110 Plymouth St 95060. Fax: 831/426-0923. **Terms:** Reserv deposit. **Facility:** 63 rooms. Nicely landscaped grounds. 2 rms with gas fireplace; 2 stories; exterior corridors; heated pool. **Some Rooms:** 4 efficiencies. **Cards:** AE, DI, DS, MC, VI. *(See ad p 1028)*

[SAVE] [♣] [≈] [¶] [▣] [□] [▦] [目] [X]

DAYS INN
AAA
◆◆
Motel

	Rates Subject to Change						Phone: 831/423-8564
5/2-9/30	1P: $68- 128	2P/1B:	$68- 128	2P/2B:	$88- 165	
2/1-5/1 & 10/1-1/31	1P: $48- 98	2P/1B:	$48- 105	2P/2B:	$58- 135	

Location: 6 blks se of SR 1. 325 Pacific 95060. Fax: 831/469-0218. **Terms:** Small pets only. **Facility:** 38 rooms. Walking distance to beach, boardwalk & downtown. 4 whirlpool rms, extra charge; 1-2 stories; exterior corridors. **All Rooms:** combo or shower baths. **Cards:** AE, CB, DI, DS, JC, MC, VI.

[SAVE] [S◆] [♣] [□] [目] [X]

HOLIDAY INN EXPRESS
Phone: (831)458-9660

	1P:		2P/1B:		2P/2B:		XP:		
6/1-9/30 [CP]	1P:	$79- 199	2P/1B:	$79- 199	2P/2B:	$79- 199	XP:	$10	F19
2/1-5/31 & 10/1-10/31 [CP]	1P:	$59- 150	2P/1B:	$59- 150	2P/2B:	$59- 150	XP:	$10	F19
11/1-1/31 [CP]	1P:	$49- 150	2P/1B:	$49- 150	2P/2B:	$49- 150	XP:	$10	F19

Motel

Location: 4 blks from beach. 600 Riverside Ave 95060. Fax: 831/426-8775. **Facility:** 79 rooms. Nicely landscaped. 2 whirlpool rms, extra charge; 3 stories; exterior corridors; whirlpools. **Cards:** AE, DI, DS, JC, MC, VI. **Special Amenities:** Free breakfast and free local telephone calls. *(See color ad below)*

HOLIDAY INN-SANTA CRUZ
(AAA) (SAVE) · Motor Inn
Phone: (831)426-7100
All Year 1P: $89- 179 2P/1B: $89- 179 2P/2B: $89- 179 XP: $10 F
Location: Exit SR 1 & 17 via Central District. 611 Ocean St 95060. Fax: 831/429-1044. **Terms:** Check-in 4 pm; reserv deposit. **Facility:** 172 rooms. Some small rooms. 5 stories; exterior corridors; heated pool, whirlpool. **Dining:** Restaurant; 6:30 am-10 pm; $7-$13; cocktails. **Some Rooms:** whirlpools. **Cards:** AE, CB, DI, DS, JC, MC, VI. **Special Amenities:** Free newspaper and free room upgrade (subject to availability with advanced reservations). *(See color ad below)*

THE INN AT PASATIEMPO
(AAA) · Motor Inn
Rates Subject to Change Phone: 831/423-5000
6/1-9/30 [CP] 1P: $135- 150 2P/1B: $135- 150 2P/2B: $135- 150 XP: $10 F17
2/1-5/31 & 10/1-1/31 [CP] 1P: $89- 125 2P/1B: $89- 125 2P/2B: $89- 125 XP: $10 F17
Location: 0.8 mi n of jct SR 1 & 17; exit SR 17 via Pasatiempo Dr. 555 Hwy 17 95060. Fax: 831/426-1737. **Terms:** Pets, $10 extra charge. **Facility:** 54 rooms. Attractive landscaped garden, adjacent to Pasatiempo Golf Course. 3 two-bedroom units. 1 story; exterior corridors. **Dining:** Dining room; 11:30 am-10 pm; $12-$20; cocktails. **All Rooms:** combo or shower baths. **Some Rooms:** whirlpools. **Cards:** AE, CB, DI, MC, VI.

MISSION INN
(AAA) (SAVE) · Motel
Phone: (831)425-5455
5/1-10/1 1P: $95 2P/1B: $95 2P/2B: $110 XP: $10 F16
2/1-4/30 & 10/2-1/31 1P: $65 2P/1B: $65 2P/2B: $85 XP: $10 F16
Location: 2.5 mi sw of jct SR 1 & SR 17, on SR 1 northbound. 2250 Mission St 95060. Fax: 831/469-4870. **Terms:** Check-in 4 pm; reserv deposit; pets, manager's discretion. **Facility:** 53 rooms. Large whirlpool unit, $145 for 2 persons; 2 stories; exterior corridors; sauna, whirlpool. **Dining:** Restaurant nearby. **Some Rooms:** whirlpools. **Cards:** AE, DS, MC, VI. **Special Amenities:** Free breakfast and free local telephone calls. *(See ad below)*

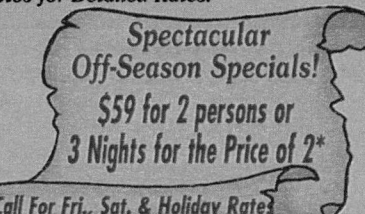

MOTEL CONTINENTAL   Rates Subject to Change   **Phone:** (831)429-1221
(AAA)   Fri & Sat 5/12-9/16 [CP]   2P/1B: $84- 104 2P/2B: $84- 124 XP: $10
               Fri & Sat 2/1-5/11 &
◆◆   9/17-1/31 [CP]   2P/1B: $64- 84 2P/2B: $64- 104 XP: $10
Motel   Sun-Thurs 5/12-9/16 [CP]   2P/1B: $74- 94 2P/2B: $84- 94 XP: $10
               Sun-Thurs 2/1-5/11 &
               9/17-1/31 [CP]   2P/1B: $48- 64 2P/2B: $48- 94 XP: $10
Location: 5 blks from beach between Broadway & Soquel aves. 414 Ocean St 95060. Fax: 408/426-8561. **Terms:** Reserv deposit. **Facility:** 47 rooms. Some small rooms. 4 whirlpool rms, extra charge; 2 stories; exterior corridors; heated pool, whirlpool. **Cards:** AE, CB, DI, DS, MC, VI.

NATIONAL 9 MOTEL   **Phone:** (831)426-4515
(AAA) (SAVE)   Fri & Sat 5/16-10/31   1P: $70- 95   2P/1B: $80- 125 2P/2B: $90- 135 XP: $10
               Fri & Sat 2/1-5/15 &
◆◆   11/1-1/31   1P: $55- 75   2P/1B: $65- 85 2P/2B: $75- 95 XP: $10
Motel   Sun-Thurs 5/16-10/31 1P: $45- 65   2P/1B: $55- 75 2P/2B: $65- 89 XP: $10
               Sun-Thurs 2/1-5/15 &
               11/1-1/31   1P: $40- 55   2P/1B: $45- 65 2P/2B: $55- 75 XP: $10
Location: Off jct SR 1 & 17; e side of Ocean St. 130 Plymouth St 95060. Fax: 831/426-4515. **Facility:** 21 rooms. 2 stories; exterior corridors. **Dining:** Coffee shop nearby. **Cards:** AE, CB, DI, MC, VI. **Special Amenities:** Free local telephone calls and preferred room (subject to availability with advanced reservations).

OCEAN PACIFIC LODGE   **Phone:** (831)457-1234
(AAA) (SAVE)   6/9-9/8 [CP]   1P: $105- 131 2P/1B: $105- 131 2P/2B: $105- 131 XP: $10   F12
               5/1-6/8 & 9/9-10/31 [CP] 1P: $75- 115 2P/1B: $75- 115 2P/2B: $75- 115 XP: $10   F12
◆◆◆   3/1-4/30 [CP]   1P: $64- 104 2P/1B: $64- 104 2P/2B: $64- 104 XP: $10   F12
Motel   2/1-2/28 & 11/1-1/31 [CP] 1P: $59- 99 2P/1B: $59- 99 2P/2B: $59- 99 XP: $10   F12
Location: 6 blks se of SR 1. 120 Washington 95060. Fax: 831/457-0861. **Terms:** Small pets only, $10 extra charge. **Facility:** 57 rooms. 3 stories; exterior corridors; heated pool, whirlpools. **Some Rooms:** whirlpools. **Cards:** AE, CB, DI, DS, MC, VI. **Special Amenities:** Free breakfast and free local telephone calls.

PACIFIC INN   Rates Subject to Change   **Phone:** (831)425-3722
(AAA)   Fri & Sat 5/12-9/16   2P/1B: $79- 138 2P/2B: $98- 168 XP: $10
               Fri & Sat 2/1-5/11 &
◆◆   9/17-1/31   2P/1B: $59- 99 2P/2B: $69- 119 XP: $10
Motel   Sun-Thurs 5/12-9/16   2P/1B: $49- 69 2P/2B: $69- 89 XP: $10
               Sun-Thurs 2/1-5/11 &
               9/17-1/31   2P/1B: $39- 59 2P/2B: $49- 69 XP: $10
Location: 1 mi from jct SR 1 & 17. 330 Ocean St 95060. Fax: 831/425-4983. **Terms:** Reserv deposit, 3 day notice; pets, $20 dep req. **Facility:** 36 rooms. 2 stories; interior corridors; heated indoor/outdoor pool, whirlpool. **Some Rooms:** whirlpools. **Cards:** AE, DS, MC, VI.

QUALITY INN   **Phone:** (831)427-1616
(AAA) (SAVE)   5/15-9/30   1P: $68- 150 2P/1B: $79- 150 2P/2B: $89- 165 XP: $10
               2/1-5/14 & 10/1-1/31   1P: $59- 129 2P/1B: $59- 129 2P/2B: $69- 139 XP: $10
◆◆   **Location:** 3 blks w off SR 1 & 17, exit Central District. 1101 Ocean St 95060. Fax: 831/427-9053.
Motel   **Terms:** Reserv deposit. **Facility:** 42 rooms. 2-3 stories; no elevator; exterior corridors. **Dining:** Restaurant nearby. **Cards:** AE, CB, DI, DS, JC, MC, VI. **Special Amenities:** Free local telephone calls and free newspaper.

RAMADA LIMITED   **Phone:** (831)423-7737
(AAA) (SAVE)   5/1-8/31 [CP]   1P: $79- 185 2P/1B: $89- 275 2P/2B: $89- 275 XP: $10   F16
               2/1-4/30 & 1/1-1/31 [CP] 1P: $59- 175 2P/1B: $69- 250 2P/2B: $69- 250 XP: $10   F16
◆◆   9/1-12/31 [CP]   1P: $49- 155 2P/1B: $59- 195 2P/2B: $59- 225 XP: $10   F16
Motel   **Location:** 2 blks from beach. 130 W Cliff Dr 95060. Fax: 831/429-6200. **Terms:** Reserv deposit, 7 day notice; handling fee imposed. **Facility:** 30 rooms. 4 whirlpool rms, extra charge; 2 stories; exterior corridors; whirlpool. **Dining:** Restaurant nearby. **Cards:** AE, CB, DI, DS, JC, MC, VI. **Special Amenities:** Free breakfast and free local telephone calls.

SANTA CRUZ INN   **Phone:** 831/475-6322
(AAA) (SAVE)   Fri & Sat 4/1-9/30   1P: $89- 120 2P/1B: $99- 130 2P/2B: $110- 169 XP: $10   D12
               Fri & Sat 2/1-3/31 &
◆◆   10/1-1/31   1P: $59- 89 2P/1B: $69- 99 2P/2B: $69- 120 XP: $10   D12
Motel   Sun-Thurs 4/1-9/30   1P: $49- 69 2P/1B: $59- 79 2P/2B: $59- 89 XP: $10   D12
               Sun-Thurs 2/1-3/31 &
               10/1-1/31   1P: $45- 65 2P/1B: $45- 65 2P/2B: $59- 79 XP: $10   D12
Location: Exit SR 1 at Soquel Ave w. 2950 Soquel Ave 95062. Fax: 831/464-6890. **Facility:** 20 rooms. 1 story; exterior corridors. **All Rooms:** combo or shower baths. **Some Rooms:** whirlpools. **Cards:** AE, CB, DI, DS, MC, VI.

SANTA CRUZ RIVIERA TRAVELODGE   **Phone:** (831)423-9515
(AAA) (SAVE)   5/15-9/15 [CP]   1P: $89- 149 2P/1B: $89- 149 2P/2B: $99- 250 XP: $10
               3/1-5/14 & 9/16-10/31 [CP] 1P: $74- 129 2P/1B: $74- 129 2P/2B: $89- 169 XP: $10
◆◆   2/1-2/28 & 11/1-1/31 [CP] 1P: $69- 119 2P/1B: $69- 119 2P/2B: $79- 149 XP: $10
Motel   **Location:** 3 blks from beach. 619 Riverside Ave 95060. Fax: 831/423-1159. **Terms:** Reserv deposit; handling fee imposed; small pets only, $5 extra charge. **Facility:** 63 rooms. 5 whirlpool rms, $99-$129 for up to 2 persons; 2 stories; exterior corridors; heated indoor pool, whirlpool. **Some Rooms:** 7 kitchens, no utensils. **Cards:** AE, CB, DI, DS, JC, MC, VI. **Special Amenities:** Free breakfast and free newspaper.

SANTA CRUZ TRAVELODGE   **Phone:** (831)426-2300
(AAA) (SAVE)   5/1-9/30   1P: $75- 150 2P/1B: $75- 150 2P/2B: $95- 165 XP: $5   F17
               2/1-4/30 & 10/1-1/31 1P: $62- 125 2P/1B: $62- 125 2P/2B: $72- 135 XP: $5   F17
◆◆   **Location:** Exit SR 1 & 17 via Ocean Street Beach. 525 Ocean St 95060. Fax: 831/426-1126. **Facility:** 55
Motor Inn   rooms. 2 stories; interior/exterior corridors; heated pool. **All Rooms:** combo or shower baths. **Cards:** AE, DI, DS, MC, VI. **Special Amenities:** Free newspaper and preferred room (subject to availability with advanced reservations).

SEA & SAND INN — Guaranteed Rates — Phone: (831)427-3400

Fri & Sat [CP]	1P: $119- 319	2P/1B: $119- 319	2P/2B: $149- 179	XP: $10	F12
Sun-Thurs 5/28-9/5 [CP]	1P: $129- 259	2P/1B: $129- 259	2P/2B: $159- 169	XP: $10	F12
Sun-Thurs 3/26-5/27 & 9/6-10/31 [CP]	1P: $109- 239	2P/1B: $109- 239	2P/2B: $129- 139	XP: $10	F12
Sun-Thurs 2/1-3/25 & 11/1-1/31 [CP]	1P: $89- 199	2P/1B: $89- 199	2P/2B: $99- 109	XP: $10	F12

ⓐ ◆◆◆ Motel

Location: Overlooking the wharf. 201 W Cliff Dr 95060. Fax: 831/427-3400. **Terms:** Reserv deposit; 2 night min stay, weekends. **Facility:** 20 rooms. On a cliff with panoramic ocean view. Country inn decor. Some small rooms. 2 housekeeping apartments, $175-$190 for up to 2 persons; 2 stories; exterior corridors; beach. **Dining:** Restaurant nearby. **All Rooms:** shower baths. **Some Rooms:** whirlpools. **Cards:** AE, DS, MC, VI. *(See ad p 1027)*

SUNSET INN — Phone: (831)423-7500

Fri & Sat 5/1-9/30 [CP]	1P: $85- 125	2P/1B: $95- 135	2P/2B: $95- 145	XP: $10	D
Sun-Thurs 5/1-9/30 [CP]	1P: $65- 95	2P/1B: $75- 105	2P/2B: $85- 125	XP: $10	D
2/1-4/30 & 10/1-1/31 [CP]	1P: $49- 89	2P/1B: $49- 89	2P/2B: $59- 99	XP: $10	D

ⓐ SAVE ◆◆◆ Motel

Location: Exit SR 1 at Mission St, 2.5 mi w. 2424 Mission St 95060. Fax: 831/423-7595. **Terms:** Reserv deposit, 3 day notice. **Facility:** 30 rooms. 1 two-bedroom unit. 4 kitchens, $10 extra charge. 4 whirlpool rms, extra charge; 2 stories; exterior corridors. **Cards:** AE, DS, MC, VI. **Special Amenities:** Free breakfast and free local telephone calls.

SUPER 8-BOARDWALK — Phone: (831)423-9449

Fri & Sat 4/1-9/30 [CP]	1P: $69- 149	2P/1B: $69- 159	2P/2B: $79- 169	XP: $8	F12
Fri & Sat 2/1-3/31 & 10/1-1/31 [CP]	1P: $49- 128	2P/1B: $49- 138	2P/2B: $59- 128	XP: $8	F12
Sun-Thurs 4/1-9/30 [CP]	1P: $49- 89	2P/1B: $59- 89	2P/2B: $59- 99	XP: $8	F12
Sun-Thurs 2/1-3/31 & 10/1-1/31 [CP]	1P: $49- 99	2P/1B: $59- 99	2P/2B: $59- 69	XP: $8	F12

ⓐ SAVE ◆◆ Motel

Location: 2 blks from beach & boardwalk. 321 Riverside Ave 95060. Fax: 831/425-5100. **Terms:** Reserv deposit. **Facility:** 23 rooms. 2 whirlpool rms, extra charge; 2 stories; exterior corridors; whirlpool. **Dining:** Restaurant nearby. **Some Rooms:** kitchen, no utensils. **Cards:** AE, DI, DS, MC, VI. **Special Amenities:** Free breakfast and free local telephone calls.

SUPER 8 MOTEL-BEACH BOARDWALK — Phone: (831)426-3707

Fri & Sat 5/1-9/30 [CP]	1P: $65- 159	2P/1B: $75- 159	2P/2B: $80- 199	XP: $8	F12
Sun-Thurs 5/1-9/30 [CP]	1P: $49- 99	2P/1B: $49- 99	2P/2B: $60- 149	XP: $8	F12
2/1-4/30 & 10/1-1/31 [CP]	1P: $39- 69	2P/1B: $43- 79	2P/2B: $49- 99	XP: $8	F12

ⓐ SAVE ◆◆ Motel

Location: 2 blks from beach & boardwalk. 338 Riverside Ave 95060. Fax: 831/426-0547. **Terms:** Reserv deposit. **Facility:** 24 rooms. 2 stories; exterior corridors; heated pool. **Dining:** Restaurant nearby. **Cards:** AE, DI, DS, MC, VI. **Special Amenities:** Free breakfast and free local telephone calls.

VILLAGER LODGE — Rates Subject to Change — Phone: 831/423-6020

Fri & Sat 3/1-9/30 [CP]	1P: $69- 130	2P/1B: $69- 130	2P/2B: $79- 150	XP: $10-20	F12
Fri & Sat 2/1-2/28 & 10/1-1/31 [CP]	1P: $49- 99	2P/1B: $49- 99	2P/2B: $59- 110	XP: $10-20	F12
Sun-Thurs 3/1-9/30 [CP]	1P: $45- 55	2P/1B: $55- 65	2P/2B: $65- 75	XP: $10-20	F12
Sun-Thurs 2/1-2/28 & 10/1-1/31 [CP]	1P: $35- 45	2P/1B: $35- 45	2P/2B: $45- 55	XP: $10	F12

ⓐ ◆◆ Motel

Location: 3 blks from beach & boardwalk. 510 Leibrandt Ave 95060. Fax: 831/426-7574. **Facility:** 26 rooms. Walking distance to the beach & boardwalk. 2 stories; exterior corridors. **All Rooms:** combo or shower baths. **Cards:** AE, DI, DS, MC, VI.

WEST COAST SANTA CRUZ HOTEL — Phone: (831)426-4330

6/12-9/6	1P: $189- 339	2P/1B: $189- 339	2P/2B: $189- 339	XP: $10
3/1-6/11 & 9/7-11/13	1P: $139- 319	2P/1B: $139- 319	2P/2B: $139- 319	XP: $10
2/1-2/28 & 11/14-1/31	1P: $109- 289	2P/1B: $109- 289	2P/2B: $109- 289	XP: $10

ⓐ SAVE ◆◆◆ Motor Inn

Location: 175 W Cliff Dr 95060. Fax: 831/427-2025. **Terms:** Check-in 4 pm. **Facility:** 163 rooms. Overlooking beach. Satellite TV. 3-10 stories; interior corridors; heated pool, whirlpool. **Dining:** Dining room, coffee shop; 6 am-10 pm; $12-$22; cocktails. **Cards:** AE, DI, DS, MC, VI. **Special Amenities:** Free local telephone calls.

RESTAURANTS

CROW'S NEST — Lunch: $6-$12 — Dinner: $8-$19 — Phone: 831/476-4560

ⓐ ◆◆ Steak and Seafood

Location: 1.3 mi e, at s shore Santa Cruz Small Crafts Harbor via Murray St bridge. 2218 E Cliff Dr 95062. **Hours:** 11:30 am-2:30 & 5:30-9:30 pm, Sat 11 am-3 & 5-10 pm, Sun 11 am-3 & 5-9:30 pm. Closed: 12/24 & 12/25. **Reservations:** suggested. **Features:** casual dress; children's menu; cocktails & lounge; entertainment; fee for parking; a la carte. Fresh seafood. View of bay. Lively atmosphere, popular with locals. **Cards:** AE, CB, DI, MC, VI.

HOLLINS HOUSE AT PASATIEMPO — Dinner: $13-$26 — Phone: 831/459-9177

◆◆ Continental

Location: 0.5 mi n of jct SR 1 & 17; w of SR 17, Pasatiempo Dr exit; at golf course. 20 Club House Rd 95060. **Hours:** 5:30 pm-9:30 pm, Sun 10 am-1:30 pm. Closed: Mon & Tues, 1/1-1/14, 12/25. **Reservations:** suggested. **Features:** No A/C; casual dress; children's menu; cocktails & lounge; a la carte, a la carte. Overlooking city & bay. Smoke free premises. **Cards:** AE, MC, VI.

SEA CLOUD — Lunch: $5-$15 — Dinner: $9-$22 — Phone: 831/458-9393

◆◆ American

Location: On 2nd floor. Municipal Wharf 49B 95060. **Hours:** 11:30 am-2:30 & 5-10 pm, Sat & Sun from 1 pm. Closed: 12/24 & 12/25. **Reservations:** suggested. **Features:** No A/C; casual dress; children's menu; cocktails & lounge; fee for parking; a la carte. California cuisine & fresh seafood. Panoramic bay & shoreline views. Smoke free premises. **Cards:** AE, CB, DI, MC, VI.

SANTA FE SPRINGS—See Los Angeles p. 634.

SANTA MARIA—61,300

LODGINGS

BEST WESTERN BIG AMERICA
Phone: (805)922-5200
All Year [CP]　　1P: $55- 95　2P/1B: $55- 95　2P/2B: $55- 90　XP: $7　F18
Location: On SR 135, 0.5 mi sw of jct US 101, exit Broadway. 1725 N Broadway 93454. Fax: 805/922-9865. **Terms:** Pets. **Facility:** 104 rooms. Attractively furnished rooms & 1-bedroom suites. 2 stories; exterior corridors; heated pool, whirlpool. **Dining:** Restaurant; 6 am-9 pm; $5-$11; cocktails. **Cards:** AE, CB, DI, DS, MC, VI. **Special Amenities:** Free breakfast and free local telephone calls. (See color ad below)

AAA SAVE ◆◆◆ Motor Inn

COMFORT INN
Phone: (805)922-5891
5/1-9/15 [CP]　　1P: $56- 66　2P/1B: $56- 66　2P/2B: $66- 76　XP: $10　F17
9/16-1/31 [CP]　　1P: $47- 57　2P/1B: $47- 57　2P/2B: $57- 67　XP: $10　F17
2/1-4/30 [CP]　　1P: $46- 56　2P/1B: $46- 56　2P/2B: $56- 66　XP: $10　F17
Location: 0.5 blk e of US 101, Main St exit. 210 S Nicholson Ave 93454. Fax: 805/928-9222. **Terms:** Small pets only, $10 per day. **Facility:** 62 rooms. 2 stories; interior corridors; heated pool, wading pool, whirlpool, playground. **Dining:** Restaurant nearby. **Cards:** AE, DI, DS, MC, VI. **Special Amenities:** Free breakfast and free newspaper. (See color ad below)

AAA SAVE ◆◆ Motel

HOLIDAY INN HOTEL & SUITES
Phone: (805)928-6000
All Year　　1P: $78- 158　2P/1B: $78- 158　2P/2B: $78- 158　XP: $10　F18
Location: Adjacent to US 101; Broadway exit. 2100 N Broadway 93454. Fax: 805/928-0356. **Terms:** Check-in 4 pm; monthly rates; BP, CP, MAP avail. **Facility:** 207 rooms. Spacious, tastefully furnished suites with efficiency. 4 two-bedroom units. 4 stories; interior corridors; heated pool, whirlpool. **Dining:** Restaurant; 6 am-10 am & 5-9 pm, 10 pm weekends; $8-$15; cocktails. **Recreation:** nintendo game in all rooms. **Cards:** AE, CB, DI, DS, MC, VI. **Special Amenities:** Early check-in/late check-out and free local telephone calls. (See ad p 1034)

AAA SAVE ◆◆◆ Hotel

SANTA MARIA HILTON
♦♦♦ All Year
Hotel
Rates Subject to Change   Phone: 805/928-8000
1P: $69   2P/1B: $69   2P/2B: $69   XP: $10
Location: From US 101, exit Betteravia Rd, 2.3 mi w, then 1.8 mi s on Skyway Dr. 3455 Skyway Dr 93455.
Fax: 805/928-5251. **Terms:** Reserv deposit. **Facility:** 190 rooms. At Santa Maria Airport. Attractive atrium
lobby. 4 stories; interior/exterior corridors; heated pool. **Cards:** AE, DI, DS, MC, VI. *(See ad p 1034 & p 119)*

SANTA MARIA INN
♦♦♦ All Year
Historic Hotel
Guaranteed Rates   Phone: (805)928-7777
1P: $99- 119   2P/1B: $99- 119   2P/2B: $99- 119   XP: $10   F12
Location: From US 101, take Main St 1 mi w, then 0.5 mi s on Broadway. 801 S Broadway 93454.
Fax: 805/928-5690. **Facility:** 166 rooms. Old English Country motif. Small, charming rooms in the original restored building to very spacious, nicely decorated rooms in the newer tower section. 2-6 stories; interior corridors; heated pool.
Services: giftshop. **Cards:** AE, CB, DI, DS, MC, VI. *(See color ad p 1034)*

RESTAURANTS

CENTRAL CITY BROILER
♦♦ American
Lunch: $6-$11   Dinner: $12-$20   Phone: 805/922-3700
Location: 0.8 mi w of US 101, exit Donovan Rd. 1520 N Broadway 93454. **Hours:** 11:30 am-2 & 5-9 pm,
Fri-10 pm, Sat 5 pm-10 pm, Sun 5 pm-9 pm. Closed major holidays. **Features:** casual dress; children's
menu; early bird specials; carryout; cocktails & lounge. Early American decor. Selection of barbecue, steaks,
chicken, seafood & prime rib. All meats cooked over open oak pit barbeque. Large portions. All you can eat crab feed,
$13.95 Tues evening. Smoke free premises. **Cards:** AE, DI, MC, VI.

FAR WESTERN TAVERN
♦ Steakhouse
Lunch: $7-$11   Dinner: $7-$30   Phone: 805/343-2211
Location: In Guadalupe, 9 mi w of US 101 via Main St. 899 Guadalupe St 93434. **Hours:** 11 am-9 pm, Fri &
Sat-10 pm, Sun 9 am-1:30 pm & 4-9 pm. Closed: 11/25 & 12/25. **Reservations:** suggested; weekends.
Features: casual dress; children's menu; carryout; cocktails & lounge. Long established family operated
steakhouse, well known for quality meats & ample portions. **Cards:** AE, DS, MC, VI.

MARIANNE'S ITALIAN VILLA
♦♦ Italian
Lunch: $6-$9   Dinner: $9-$15   Phone: 805/347-2737
Location: From US 101, take Main St w 1 mi, then 0.5 mi s. 800 S Broadway 93455. **Hours:** 11 am-9 pm,
Fri & Sat-10 pm. Closed: Sun. **Reservations:** suggested. **Features:** casual dress; children's menu; carryout;
beer & wine only. Large selection of Italian cuisine. Pasta, chicken, veal, seafood & pizza. Smoke free
premises. **Cards:** AE, DI, DS, MC, VI.

SANTA MARIA INN RESTAURANT
♦♦♦ American
Lunch: $6-$12   Dinner: $13-$21   Phone: 805/928-7777
Location: In Santa Maria Inn. 801 S Broadway 93454. **Hours:** 6:30 am-2 & 5-9 pm, Fri & Sat-10 pm.
Reservations: suggested. **Features:** Sunday brunch; early bird specials; senior's menu; cocktails & lounge.
Selection of prime rib, steaks, seafood & chicken. Patio dining avail. Wine cellar specializing in California
regional wines 4:30-10 pm Tues-Sat. Smoke free premises. **Cards:** AE, DI, DS, JC, MC, VI.

SANTA MONICA—*See Los Angeles p. 634.*

SANTA NELLA—100

LODGINGS

BEST WESTERN ANDERSEN'S INN
♦♦ Motel
6/1-1/31 [CP]   Rates Subject to Change   Phone: (209)826-5534
2/1-5/31 [CP]   1P: $61- 72   2P/1B: $61- 72   2P/2B: $72- 82   XP: $7   F12
                       1P: $61- 66   2P/1B: $61- 66   2P/2B: $72   XP: $7   F12
Location: E off & adjacent to I-5; 4 mi n of SR 152, Pacheco Pass Rd; exit I-5 via Santa Nella-Gustine SR
33. 12367 Hwy 33S 95322. Fax: 209/826-4353. **Facility:** 94 rooms. Danish architecture. 8 whirlpool rms, extra charge; 2 stories; exterior corridors; heated pool. **Cards:** AE, CB, DI, DS, MC, VI. *(See color ad below & p 1036)*

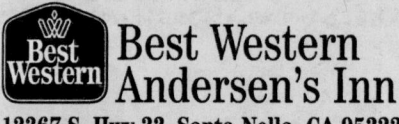

HOLIDAY INN EXPRESS Phone: (209)826-8282
(AAA) (SAVE) All Year [CP] 1P: $59- 69 2P/1B: $59- 69 2P/2B: $59- 69 XP: $8 F18
◆◆◆ **Location:** 2 blk e of I-5; SR 33 exit. 28976 W Plaza Dr 95322. Fax: 209/826-9039. **Terms:** Package plans;
Motel pets. **Facility:** 100 rooms. Surrounding nicely landscaped courtyard. 2 stories; exterior corridors; heated pool,
whirlpool. **Dining:** Coffee shop nearby. **Cards:** AE, CB, DI, DS, MC, VI. **Special Amenities:** Free breakfast
and free local telephone calls. *(See color ad below & below)*

RAMADA INN MISSION DE ORO Rates Subject to Change Phone: (209)826-4444
◆◆◆ All Year [BP] 1P: $45- 70 2P/1B: $55- 80 2P/2B: $60- 80 XP: $10 F18
Motor Inn **Location:** Adjacent to Jct I-5 & SR 33; 4 mi n of SR 152. 13070 Hwy 33S 95322. Fax: 209/826-8071.
Facility: 159 rooms. Surrounding an attractive early California-style plaza. 2 stories; interior/exterior corridors;
heated pool; playground. **Services:** giftshop. **Cards:** AE, CB, DI, DS, JC, MC, VI. *(See color ad below)*

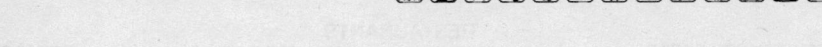

SANTA PAULA—25,100

LODGINGS

THE FERN OAKS INN
◆◆◆
Bed &
Breakfast
   All Year [BP]

Rates Subject to Change
   2P/1B: $95- 110

Phone: 805/525-7747
   XP: $20

Location: 1.5 mi n of SR 126, exit Tenth St. 1025 Ojai Rd 93060. Fax: 805/933-5001. **Terms:** Reserv deposit, 7 day notice; handling fee imposed. **Facility:** 4 rooms. An elegantly furnished 1929 Spanish Revival house on over 1/2 acre of landscaped grounds with rose gardens & oak & citrus trees. Mon-Thu, $10 per room discount; 2 stories; interior corridors; designated smoking area. **All Rooms:** combo or shower baths. **Cards:** MC, VI.

SANTA PAULA LODGE
🅰🅰🅰
◆◆
Motel
   All Year [CP]

Guaranteed Rates
1P: $45- 50 2P/1B: $52- 56 2P/2B: $62- 66

Phone: (805)525-1561
XP: $5   F15

Location: Just n of SR 126, Peck Rd exit. 350 S Peck Rd 93060. Fax: 805/525-4230. **Terms:** Weekly rates. **Facility:** 50 rooms. Mini suite, $85; 2 stories; interior corridors; small heated pool, whirlpool. **Dining:** Restaurant nearby. **All Rooms:** extended cable TV. **Some Rooms:** 3 efficiencies, no utensils, whirlpools. **Cards:** AE, DS, MC, VI.

THE WHITE GABLES INN
◆◆◆
Historic Bed
& Breakfast
   All Year [BP]

Rates Subject to Change
1P: $80- 110 2P/1B: $85- 115

Phone: 805/933-3041

Location: SR 126, exit 10th St (SR 150); 0.5 mi n, just w. 715 E Santa Paula St 93060. **Terms:** Reserv deposit, 7 day notice; handling fee imposed. **Facility:** 3 rooms. Historical 1894 Victorian Queen Anne house located in a designated historical district. 1 room with balcony. Spacious 3rd floor suite with sitting room, bedroom & bath; 3 stories, no elevator; designated smoking area. **All Rooms:** combo or shower baths. **Cards:** AE, MC, VI.

SANTA ROSA—113,300

LODGINGS

BEST WESTERN GARDEN INN
🅰🅰🅰 SAVE
◆◆◆
Motel

6/16-10/31	1P: $69- 89	2P/1B: $69- 89	2P/2B: $69- 85	XP: $6	F12
5/1-6/15	1P: $65- 85	2P/1B: $65- 85	2P/2B: $69- 75	XP: $6	F12
11/1-1/31	1P: $59- 75	2P/1B: $59- 75	2P/2B: $65- 75	XP: $6	F12
2/1-4/30	1P: $65- 79	2P/1B: $65- 79	2P/2B: $69- 75	XP: $6	F12

Phone: (707)546-4031

Location: 1 mi s on US 101 business rt; northbound exit Baker Ave; southbound exit Corby Ave. 1500 Santa Rosa Ave 95404. Fax: 707/526-4903. **Terms:** Reserv deposit; pets, $10 extra charge. **Facility:** 78 rooms. Attractive landscaped grounds. 3 two-bedroom units. 3 family units, $110-$125 5/1-10/31; $90-$96 2/1-4/30 & 11/1-1/31 for up to 2 persons; 2 stories; exterior corridors. **Dining:** Coffee shop; 6:30 am-11 am. **All Rooms:** combo or shower baths. **Cards:** AE, CB, DI, DS, MC, VI. **Special Amenities:** Free local telephone calls. (See color ad below)

COURTYARD BY MARRIOTT
🅰🅰🅰 SAVE
◆◆◆
Motor Inn

5/7-10/17	1P: $99- 139	2P/1B: $99- 139	2P/2B: $99- 139
2/1-5/6 & 10/18-1/31	1P: $89- 125	2P/1B: $89- 125	2P/2B: $89- 125

Phone: (707)573-9000

Location: US 101, exit downtown w; adjacent to Railroad Square, Old Town; 3rd & Railroad St. 175 Railroad St 95401. Fax: 707/573-0272. **Terms:** Reserv deposit; weekly/monthly rates; package plans. **Facility:** 135 rooms. 1 & 2-room suites, $119-$169; 5 stories; interior corridors; whirlpool. **Dining:** Coffee shop; 6 am-2 & 5-10 pm; $8-$14. **Cards:** AE, CB, DI, DS, JC, MC, VI. (See color ad p 1038)

FLAMINGO RESORT HOTEL
🅰🅰🅰 SAVE
◆◆◆
Motor Inn

All Year	1P: $89- 199	2P/1B: $89- 199	2P/2B: $89- 199

Phone: (707)545-8530
XP: $10   F12

Location: Off SR 12, at Farmers Ln. 2777 Fourth St 95405. Fax: 707/528-1404. **Facility:** 170 rooms. Attractively landscaped grounds. 100% non smoking public areas & meeting rooms. 14 suites, $146-$180 for up to 4 persons. 8 whirlpool rms, extra charge; 2 stories; interior corridors; heated pool, wading pool, whirlpool, 5 tennis courts. **Dining:** Dining room; 6:30 am-9 pm, Fri & Sat-10 pm; $11-$22; cocktails. **Services:** Fee: massage. **Cards:** AE, DI, MC, VI. **Special Amenities:** Early check-in/late check-out and preferred room (subject to availability with advanced reservations). (See ad p 1038)

FOUNTAINGROVE INN   Rates Subject to Change   **Phone:** (707)578-6101
QQQ   5/26-10/28 [BP]   1P: $90- 120   2P/1B: $99- 130   2P/2B: $99- 130   XP: $10   F13
◆◆◆◆   2/1-5/25 & 10/29-1/31 [BP]   1P: $82- 109   2P/1B: $92- 119   2P/2B: $92- 119   XP: $10   F13
Motor Inn   **Location:** 2 mi n off US 101; exit Mendocino Ave/Old Redwood Hwy; 0.3 mi s to Fountain Grove Pkwy. 101
Fountain Grove Pkwy 95403. Fax: 707/544-3126. **Terms:** Check-in 4 pm; package plans. **Facility:** 126 rooms.
Atrium lobby of natural wood & stone. Water cascades over stone lobby wall. 4 suites $145-$200 for up to 4
persons; 2 stories; interior corridors; whirlpool. **Dining:** Equus Restaurant, see separate listing. **Services:** giftshop.
Some Rooms: whirlpools. **Cards:** AE, DI, DS, JC, MC, VI. *(See ad below)*

ASK ⑤ ☞ ☂ ⬚ ⬚ ⑪ 🐕 ⬚ 🐕 🖨 📶 🐕 ✕ 🐾

THE GABLES INN
◆◆◆
Bed & Breakfast

Rates Subject to Change
All Year [BP]   1P: $145- 250   2P/1B: $145- 250
Location: 4 mi s of downtown Santa Rosa. 4257 Petaluma Hill Rd 95404. Fax: 707/584-5634.
Terms: Reserv deposit; handling fee imposed. **Facility:** 8 rooms. 1877 Victorian mansion. National Register of Historic Places. 2 stories; interior corridors. **Some Rooms:** kitchen. **Cards:** AE, DI, DS, MC, VI.

Phone: (707)585-7777
XP: $25

HILLSIDE INN MOTEL
ⓐⓐⓐ
◆◆◆
Motel

	Rates Subject to Change						
4/1-10/31	1P: $56	2P/1B: $61			XP: $4	F11
2/1-3/31	1P: $52	2P/1B: $56	2P/2B: $61	XP: $4	F11
11/1-1/31	1P: $52	2P/1B: $56	2P/2B: $61	XP: $4	F11

Location: 2.5 mi e off US 101 on SR 12, at Farmers Ln & 4th St. 2901 4th St 95409. **Terms:** Reserv deposit; pets, with permission only. **Facility:** 36 rooms. Some rooms with balcony & patio. 7 two-bedroom units. 17 efficiencies & 19 kitchens, $4 extra; 2 stories; exterior corridors. **Dining:** Coffee shop; 6:30 am-2:30 pm; wine/beer only. **Cards:** AE, CB, DI, DS, MC, VI. *(See ad below)*

Phone: (707)546-9353

HILTON-SONOMA COUNTY
◆◆◆◆
Motor Inn

	Guaranteed Rates					
6/1-10/31	1P: $99- 189	2P/1B: $114- 204	2P/2B: $114- 204	XP: $15	F18
2/1-5/31 & 11/1-1/31	1P: $89- 164	2P/1B: $104- 179	2P/2B: $104- 179	XP: $15	F18

Location: US 101; exit e via Mendocino-Old Redwood Hwy; 3 blks n top of the hill. 3555 Round Barn Blvd 95403. Fax: 707/569-5550. **Facility:** 247 rooms. Nestled in hills above Santa Rosa. Comfortable rooms some with patios & decks. 3 stories; interior corridors. **Cards:** AE, DI, DS, MC, VI. *(See ad below & p 119)*

Phone: 707-523-7555

HOLIDAY INN EXPRESS
ⓐⓐⓐ SAVE
◆◆◆
Motel

All Year [CP]   1P: $69- 99   2P/1B: $69- 99   2P/2B: $69- 99   XP: $10   F18
Location: Exit US 101 at Mendocino/Hopper Ave exit, just w of US 101. 870 Hopper Ave 95403. Fax: 707/571-0145. **Terms:** Pets, $50 extra charge. **Facility:** 96 rooms. 2 stories; exterior corridors. **Dining:** Restaurant nearby. **Some Rooms:** whirlpools. **Cards:** AE, CB, DI, DS, JC, MC, VI. **Special Amenities:** Early check-in/late check-out and free breakfast. *(See color ad p 1040)*

Phone: (707)545-9000

HOTEL LA ROSE
ⓐⓐⓐ SAVE
◆◆◆
Historic Hotel

All Year [BP]   1P: $139   2P/1B: $154   2P/2B: $194   XP: $10
Location: 2 blk w off US 101, exit Downtown Santa Rosa; on Railroad Square. 308 Wilson St 95401. Fax: 707/579-3247. **Terms:** Reserv deposit; package plans. **Facility:** 49 rooms. Cobblestone hotel built in 1907. Historic landmark. Member of Historic Hotels of America. 2-4 stories; interior/exterior corridors. **Dining:** Dining room; 11:30 am-2 & 5:30-9:30 pm Tues-Fri, Sat 5:30 pm-9 pm; closed Sun-Mon; $14-$21; cocktails. **All Rooms:** combo or shower baths. **Cards:** AE, CB, DI, DS, MC, VI. **Special Amenities:** Free breakfast and free local telephone calls.

Phone: (707)579-3200

LOS ROBLES LODGE   Phone: (707)545-6330

AAA SAVE   6/1-10/31   1P: $72- 87 2P/1B: $72- 87 2P/2B: $72- 87 XP: $10   F16
             2/1-5/31 & 11/1-1/31   1P: $63- 78 2P/1B: $63- 78 2P/2B: $63- 78 XP: $10   F16
◆◆◆   **Location:** 1 mi n off US 101; exit via Steele Ln. 1985 Cleveland Ave 95401. Fax: 707/575-5826.
Motor Inn   **Terms:** Check-in 4 pm; reserv deposit; package plans; pets. **Facility:** 104 rooms. Comfortable rooms, some
             with patio or deck. Adjacent to major shopping center. 2 stories; exterior corridors; wading pool, whirlpool.
Dining: Restaurant, coffee shop; 6 am-10 pm; $8-$29; cocktails. **All Rooms:** combo or shower baths.
Some Rooms: whirlpools. **Cards:** AE, CB, DI, DS, JC, MC, VI. **Special Amenities: Free local telephone calls and
preferred room (subject to availability with advanced reservations).** (See color ad below)

🐕 📶 🏊 🍴 ➕ 🛄 👷 ☕ 📼 🖥 🗄 📠 🛗 🅿 🚭 ❌

RAMADA LIMITED   Rates Subject to Change   Phone: 707/575-4600

◆◆   4/15-9/15 [CP]   1P: $50- 70 2P/1B: $55- 75 2P/2B: $60- 80 XP: $7   F12
Motel   2/1-4/14 & 9/16-1/31 [CP] 1P: $45- 60 2P/1B: $50- 65 2P/2B: $55- 70 XP: $7   F12
Location: Exit US 101 at Mendocino/Hopper Ave exit. 866 Hopper Ave 95403. Fax: 707/575-0945.
Terms: Reserv deposit. **Facility:** 34 rooms. 2 stories; exterior corridors. **Cards:** AE, CB, DI, DS, MC, VI.

🏊 🍴 🖥 🗄 📠 🛗 ❌

SANDMAN MOTEL   Phone: (707)544-8570

AAA SAVE   All Year [CP]   1P: $62- 72 2P/1B: $68- 78 2P/2B: $71- 81 XP: $6   F12
◆◆◆   **Location:** US 101; exit w Mendocino Ave. 3421 Cleveland Ave 95403. Fax: 707/544-8710. **Terms:** Check-in
Motel   4 pm; reserv deposit, 3 day notice. **Facility:** 112 rooms. Comfortable rooms. Attractive landscaping. 2 stories;
             exterior corridors; whirlpool. **Dining:** Coffee shop nearby. **Cards:** AE, CB, DI, DS, MC, VI.
**Special Amenities: Free local telephone calls and free room upgrade (subject to availability with
advanced reservations).** (See ad p 1041)

🆓 📶 🏊 🍴 🛄 ☕ 🗄 📠 ❌

SANTA ROSA DOWNTOWN TRAVELODGE   Rates Subject to Change   Phone: (707)544-4141

AAA   All Year   1P: $45- 48 2P/1B: $55- 65 2P/2B: $70- 75 XP: $5   F17
◆◆   **Location:** Exit e 3 blks off US 101 via College Ave, at Mendocino Ave. 635 Healdsburg Ave 95401.
Motel   Fax: 707/542-4403. **Facility:** 44 rooms. 2 blks from center of town & major shopping center. 3 stories; exterior
             corridors. **Dining:** Coffee shop nearby. **All Rooms:** combo or shower baths. **Cards:** AE, CB, DI, DS, JC,
             MC, VI.

🆓 🏊 🍴 ☕ 🖥 🗄 📠 ❌

SANTA ROSA TRAVELODGE   Rates Subject to Change   **Phone:** (707)542-3472
5/1-10/15   1P: $50- 55   2P/1B: $55- 60 2P/2B: $65- 70 XP: $5   F17
2/1-4/30 & 10/16-1/31   1P: $45- 50   2P/1B: $50- 60 2P/2B: $55- 60 XP: $5   F17
Location: 1.5 mi s on US 101 business route; northbound exit US 101 via Baker Ave, southbound Santa Rosa Ave-Corby. 1815 Santa Rosa Ave 95407. Fax: 707/542-5038. **Terms:** Pets, $20 dep req. **Facility:** 31 rooms. Comfortable rooms. 0.8 mi to downtown, major shopping center & fairgrounds. 4 two-bedroom units. 1 story; exterior corridors. **All Rooms:** combo or shower baths. **Cards:** AE, CB, DI, DS, JC, MC, VI.

SUPER 8 LODGE   Rates Subject to Change   **Phone:** 707/542-5544
All Year   1P: $55- 85   2P/1B: $60- 100 2P/2B: $65- 75 XP: $5   F13
Motel   **Location:** 1 mi n off US 101; exit via Steele Ln. 2632 Cleveland Ave 95403. Fax: 707/542-9738. **Facility:** 100 rooms. 3 stories; interior corridors. **Cards:** AE, DS, MC, VI.

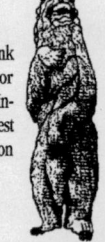

See the Sample Lodging Listing in the TourBook Navigator.

VINTNERS INN
Sun-Thurs [CP] 1P: $168- 225 2P/1B: $168- 225
Fri & Sat [CP] 1P: $178- 245 2P/1B: $178- 245
Rates Subject to Change
Phone: (707)575-7350
XP: $20 F6
XP: $20 F6
Lodge
Location: 2 mi n on US 101; exit w off US 101 via River Rd-Mark West Springs Rd. 4350 Barnes Rd 95403.
Fax: 707/575-1426. **Facility:** 44 rooms. Surrounded by vineyards & country charm; Country French decor.
Some fireplaces. 2 stories; interior corridors; whirlpool. **Cards:** AE, DI, MC, VI.

RESTAURANTS

EQUUS RESTAURANT Lunch: $6-$10 Dinner: $13-$21 Phone: 707/578-6101
Continental
Location: In FountianGrove Inn. 101 FoutainGrove Pkwy 95403. **Hours:** 11:30 am-2:30 & 5:30-9:30 pm,
Sat-5:30 pm-9:30 pm, Sun 10 am-2 & 5-9 pm. **Reservations:** suggested. **Features:** casual dress; children's
menu; cocktails & lounge; a la carte. Smoke free premises. **Cards:** AE, DI, DS, MC, VI. *(See ad p 1038)*

JOHN ASH & CO Lunch: $8-$14 Dinner: $13-$30 Phone: 707/527-7687
American
Location: At Vintners Inn. 4330 Barnes Rd 95403. **Hours:** 11:30 am-2 & 5:30-9:30 pm, Sun 10:30 am-2 &
5:30-9 pm. Closed major holidays Mon & 1st week of year. **Reservations:** suggested. **Features:** casual
dress; health conscious menu; cocktails & lounge; a la carte. Emphasis on local foods. Smoke free
premises. **Cards:** MC, VI.

LA GARE FRENCH RESTAURANT Dinner: $8-$15 Phone: 707/528-4355
French
Location: US 101, exit downtown; just w; just s of Railroad Square. 208 Wilson St 95401. **Hours:** 5:30
pm-10 pm, Sun 5 pm-9 pm. Closed: Mon, 1/1, 11/28 & 12/25. **Reservations:** suggested. **Features:** casual
dress; children's menu; beer & wine only; minimum charge-$8. Smoke free premises. **Cards:** AE, CB, DI,
MC, VI.

LISA HEMENWAY'S Lunch: $8-$17 Dinner: $12-$24 Phone: 707/526-5111
American
Location: On SR 12 in Montgomery Village; in Village Court Mall area. 714 Village Ct 95405. **Hours:** 11:30
am-2:30 & 5:30-9:30 pm, Sun 10 am-2 & 5-9 pm. Closed major holidays. **Reservations:** suggested.
Features: casual dress; Sunday brunch; beer & wine only; a la carte. California cuisine, emphasis on fresh
Sonoma County products. Smoke free premises. **Cards:** DI, MC, VI.

LOS ROBLES RESTAURANT Lunch: $5-$14 Dinner: $11-$15 Phone: 707/542-3330
American
Location: In Los Robles Lodge. 1975 Cleveland Ave 95401. **Hours:** 11 am-2 & 5-9 pm, Sun from 10 am.
Reservations: suggested. **Features:** semi-formal attire; Sunday brunch; children's menu; health conscious
menu; cocktails & lounge; a la carte, a la carte. Smoke free premises. **Cards:** AE, CB, DI, DS, MC, VI.

SANTEE—See San Diego p. 910.

SAN YSIDRO—See San Diego p. 911.

SARATOGA—28,100

LODGING

THE INN AT SARATOGA Phone: (408)867-5020
All Year [CP] 1P: $175- 250 2P/1B: $175- 250 2P/2B: $175 XP: $15 F18
Motor Inn
Location: Center; just n of SR 9. 20645 Fourth St 95070. Fax: 408/741-0981. **Facility:** 46 rooms. Tastefully
appointed. Patio or balcony overlooking adjacent park or creek. 1 two-bedroom unit. 5 stories; interior corridors.
Dining: Restaurant nearby. **Services:** complimentary evening beverages. **Some Rooms:** whirlpools.
Cards: AE, DI, MC, VI. **Special Amenities: Free breakfast and free newspaper.**

RESTAURANTS

LA MERE MICHELLE Lunch: $10-$15 Dinner: $20-$40 Phone: 408/867-5272
French
Location: On SR 9. 14467 Big Basin Way 95070. **Hours:** 11:30 am-2 & 6-10 pm. Closed major holidays &
Mon. **Reservations:** accepted. **Features:** casual dress; Sunday brunch; cocktails; a la carte. Quiet, refined
ambiance. Smoking on the terrace only. Smoke free premises. **Cards:** AE, CB, DI, MC, VI.

THE PLUMED HORSE Dinner: $25-$36 Phone: 408/867-4711
French
Location: 0.3 mi sw on SR 9. 14555 Big Basin Way 95070. **Hours:** 6 pm-10 pm. Closed major holidays &
Sun. **Reservations:** accepted. **Features:** semi-formal attire; children's menu; health conscious menu items;
cocktails & lounge; entertainment; street parking & fee for valet parking. Relaxing Old-World charm. Frequent
menu changes with a prix fixe occasionally & fresh seasonal products. Outstanding wine cellar. Smoking permitted in lounge
only. Smoke free premises. **Cards:** AE, CB, DI, MC, VI.

SAUSALITO—See San Francisco p. 976.

SCOTIA—1,300

LODGING

SCOTIA INN
◆◆◆
Historic
Country Inn
All Year [CP]   Rates Subject to Change   Phone: (707)764-5683
1P: $85- 150   2P/1B: $95- 195   2P/2B: $125- 150   XP: $20
Location: Exit US 101 W. 100 Main St 95565 (PO Box 248). Fax: 707/764-1707. **Terms:** Handling fee imposed. **Facility:** 12 rooms. Built in 1923 as boarding house for mill workers. 2 stories; interior corridors; designated smoking area. **Cards:** DS, MC, VI. *(See color ad p 445)*

SCOTTS VALLEY—8,600—See also APTOS, CAPITOLA, FELTON & SANTA CRUZ.

LODGING

BEST WESTERN INN-SCOTTS VALLEY   Rates Subject to Change   Phone: (831)438-6666
◆◆◆
Motel

	1P:	2P/1B:		2P/2B:	XP:	
6/1-9/5	$100	$100		$125	$6	F18
5/1-5/31 & 9/6-12/31	$75	$80		$85	$6	F18
2/1-4/30 & 1/1-1/31	$65	$70		$75	$6	F18

Location: Just w of SR 17, Granite Creek exit. 6020 Scotts Valley Dr 95066. Fax: 831/439-8752. **Terms:** Package plans; small pets only, in smoking rooms. **Facility:** 58 rooms. In tree-lined lot. Many units have seating area with love seat. 3 units with whirlpool $90-$125 for up to 2 persons; 2 stories; exterior corridors; small pool, whirlpool. **Dining:** Coffee shop nearby. **Cards:** AE, CB, DI, DS, MC, VI.

SEAL BEACH—25,100   (See map p. 561; index p. 551)

LODGING

RADISSON INN OF SEAL BEACH   Rates Subject to Change   Phone: (562)493-7501
◆◆◆
Motel
All Year [CP]   1P: $109   2P/1B: $118   2P/2B: $118   XP: $10   F17
Location: Just s of SR 1, Pacific Coast Hwy. 600 Marina Dr 90740. Fax: 562/596-3448. **Facility:** 71 rooms. Balconies. 3 stories; interior/exterior corridors; small pool. **Recreation:** Fee: bicycles. **Cards:** AE, CB, DI, DS, JC, MC, VI.

RESTAURANT

SPAGHETTINI   **Lunch:** $8-$15   **Dinner:** $14-$19   Phone: 562/596-2199
◆◆◆
Italian
Location: Just n of I-405, exit Seal Beach Blvd. 3005 Old Ranch Pkwy 90740. **Hours:** 11 am-3 & 5-10 pm, Sat 5 pm-10:30 pm, Sun 4:30 pm-9:30 pm. **Closed:** 11/25 & 12/25. **Reservations:** suggested. **Features:** casual dress; children's menu; early bird specials; carryout; cocktails & lounge; entertainment. Very attractive restaurant featuring a nice selection of pasta, gourmet pizza, seafood, steaks & chicken. Smoke free premises. **Cards:** AE, DI, DS, MC, VI.

SEASIDE—See Monterey Peninsula p. 722.

SEBASTOPOL—7,000

LODGING

HOLIDAY INN EXPRESS HOTEL & SUITES   Phone: (707)829-6677
Motor Inn
All Year [CP]   1P: $88- 179   2P/1B: $88- 179   2P/2B: $88- 149
Too new to rate. **Location:** Northbound US 101, exit at SR 116, 10 mi w; southbound US 101, exit at SR 12, 7 mi w to Main St. 1101 Gravenstein Hwy S 95472. **Facility:** 82 rooms. Scheduled to open August, 1998; 2 stories; interior corridors; whirlpool. **Cards:** AE, DI, DS, MC, VI. **Special Amenities:** Free breakfast and free newspaper.

SELMA—14,800

LODGINGS

BEST WESTERN JOHN JAY INN   Phone: (559)891-0300
◆◆
Motor Inn
All Year [CP]   1P: $45- 90   2P/1B: $50- 95   2P/2B: $50- 95   XP: $5   F12
Location: 10 mi s of Fresno exit Floral Ave; 2 blks e. 2799 Floral Ave 93662. Fax: 559/891-1538. **Terms:** Pets, $25 dep req. **Facility:** 57 rooms. Colonial exterior, close to freeway. 3 stories; interior corridors; sauna, whirlpool. **Dining:** Coffee shop nearby. **Cards:** AE, CB, DI, DS, MC, VI. **Special Amenities:** Free breakfast and free local telephone calls.

HOLIDAY INN-SWAN COURT   Rates Subject to Change   Phone: (559)891-8000
◆◆◆
Motor Inn
All Year   1P: $67   2P/1B: $67   2P/2B: $67   XP: $10   F12
Location: SR 99, Floral Ave exit, just w. 2950 Pea Soup Andersen Blvd 93662. Fax: 559/891-9575. **Terms:** Reserv deposit; handling fee imposed. **Facility:** 64 rooms. Attractive landscaping. Center courtyard includes a pond with swans. 3 stories; interior corridors; heated pool. **Cards:** AE, CB, DI, DS, JC, MC, VI.

SUPER 8 MOTEL   Phone: (559)896-2800
◆
Motel
All Year   1P: $45   2P/1B: $49   2P/2B: $53   XP: $5   F12
Location: SR 99, Floral Ave exit. 3142 S Highland Ave 93662. Fax: 559/896-7244. **Terms:** Pets, $20 dep req. **Facility:** 40 rooms. Interior corridors. **Dining:** Restaurant nearby. **Cards:** AE, CB, DI, DS, MC, VI.

SEQUOIA AND KINGS CANYON
NATIONAL PARKS—See also BADGER & THREE RIVERS.

LODGING

MONTECITO-SEQUOIA LODGE   Rates Subject to Change   Phone: 559/565-3388

6/21-9/6 [AP]	1P: $124	2P/1B: $188- 242	2P/2B: $188- 242	XP: $88-103	D12
2/1-4/14 & 11/24-1/31 [AP]	1P: $97- 134	2P/1B: $154- 228	2P/2B: $154- 228	XP: $59-104	D12
4/15-6/20 & 9/7-11/23 [MAP]	1P: $69- 110	2P/1B: $98- 148	2P/2B: $98- 148	XP: $39-64	D12

Lodge

Doesn't meet listing requirements. **Location:** 8 mi s of SR 180 off General's Hwy, between King's Canyon & Sequoia Nat'l Parks. 8000 General Hwy 93633 (PO Box 858, Grant Grove, KINGS CANYON NATIONAL PARK). Fax: 559/565-3223. **Terms:** Check-in 4 pm; reserv deposit, 15 day notice; package plans. **Facility:** 50 rooms. Accommodations include lodge rooms & 13 rustic cabins with central bath. Many rooms with bunk beds. Summer season reserved for groups & family retreats. No daily maid service provided. Meets AAA fire safety requirements. For reserv: (800) 227-9900; 1-2 stories; interior/exterior corridors; heated pool, whirlpool; 2 lighted tennis courts. **Dining:** Dining room; Buffet meals 7:30-9 am, noon-1 & 6-7 pm; cocktails. **Services:** giftshop. **Recreation:** canoeing, fishing, paddleboats; cross country skiing, ice skating, snowshoeing, ski school; hiking trails, jogging, volleyball, horseshoes. **Cards:** AE, DS, MC, VI. *(See ad below)*

RED ALERT!

receive from AAA members. They are telling you they're willing to go the extra mile to get your business. Some even offer special amenities designed just for you.

And don't forget to look for the establishments that display the familiar [SAVE] icon to receive discounts.

So, when you turn to the AAA TourBook to make your travel plans, be on the look out for the establishments that will give you the special treatment you deserve.

When you pick up a AAA TourBook®, be alert for the establishments that display a bright red AAA logo beside their listing. These establishments place a high value on the patronage they

SHASTA LAKE—8,800

LODGINGS

BRIDGE BAY RESORT
Phone: 530/275-3021
(AAA) [SAVE]

	1P:	$89	2P/1B:	$89	2P/2B:	$89	XP:	$6	D12
5/1-9/30									
2/1-4/30 & 10/1-1/31	1P:	$55	2P/1B:	$55	2P/2B:	$55	XP:	$6	D12

◆
Resort Motel
Location: 12 mi n of Redding, exit I-5; at Bridge Bay Rd. (10300 Bridge Bay Rd, REDDING, 96003). Fax: 530/275-8365. **Terms:** Reserv deposit, 3 day notice; pets, $5 extra charge, $25 dep req. **Facility:** 40 rooms. Overlooking Lake Shasta. Some units have lake view. 8 kitchens, $75-$150 for up to 4 persons; 2 stories; exterior corridors. Fee: boat ramp. **Dining:** Restaurant; 7 am-2 & 5-10 pm; $9-$18. **Recreation:** Fee: fishing, waterskiing, houseboats. Rental: boats. **All Rooms:** shower baths. **Cards:** DS, MC, VI. *(See ad below)*

🐴 ⛵ 🍴 🍸 ⊠ 📷 🖨

FAWNDALE LODGE & RV RESORT
Rates Subject to Change
Phone: (530)275-8000
(AAA)

		1P:	$42- 68	2P/1B:	$48- 74	2P/2B:	$53- 74	XP:	$6	D12
5/15-10/15										
2/1-5/14 & 10/16-1/31	1P:	$42- 68	2P/1B:	$42	2P/2B:	$47- 68	XP:	$6	D12

◆ ◆
Motel
Location: 1 mi s of Shasta Lake; I-5, Fawndale Rd E exit, 10 mi n of Redding. (15215 Fawndale Rd, REDDING, 96003). Fax: 530/275-1863. **Terms:** Reserv deposit; handling fee imposed; weekly rates; pets, $5 fee, $50 dep req. **Facility:** 7 rooms. Tree shaded grounds. 3 two-bedroom units. 4 kitchens, $10 extra charge; 1 story; exterior corridors. **Recreation:** badminton, BBQ pavilion, croquet, horseshoes, volleyball. **All Rooms:** shower baths. **Cards:** AE, DS, MC, VI.

(ASK) 📶 🐴 🍴 🛜 🖨 🔌 ⊠

O'BRIEN MOUNTAIN INN BED & BREAKFAST
Rates Subject to Change
Phone: (530)238-8026
◆ ◆ ◆
Bed & Breakfast

| | All Year [BP] | 1P: | $95- 125 | 2P/1B: | $95- 125 | | | XP: | $25 |

Location: 13 mi n of Redding, exit I-5 O'Brien W 0.5 mi. 18026 O'Brien Inlet Rd (PO Box 27, O'BRIEN, 96070-0027). Fax: 530/238-8026. **Terms:** Check-in 4 pm; reserv deposit, 10 day notice; handling fee imposed. **Facility:** 4 rooms. Contemporary mountain home in wooded area with tall pines. 2 stories; interior corridors; smoke free premises. **All Rooms:** combo or shower baths. **Cards:** AE, CB, DI, DS, MC, VI.

⛵ 📷 (VCR) ☎ 🖨

SHASTA DAM MOTEL
Phone: (530)275-1065
(AAA) [SAVE]

| | All Year | 1P: | $38 | 2P/1B: | $45 | 2P/2B: | $45 | XP: | $7 | F3 |

◆
Motel
Location: 7 mi n of Redding on I-5, exit Shasta Dam/Blvd, n on Union School Rd. 1529 Cascade Blvd 96079 (PO Box 71033, PROJECT CITY). Fax: 530/549-5722. **Terms:** Reserv deposit; pets, $5 extra charge, $20 dep req. **Facility:** 14 rooms. 1 two-bedroom unit. 6 efficiencies, $7 extra charge; 1 story; exterior corridors. **All Rooms:** shower baths. **Cards:** AE, CB, DI, MC, VI.

📶 🐴 ⛵ 💻 🖨 ⊠

SHERMAN OAKS—See Los Angeles p. 640.

SIERRA CITY—100

LODGING

HERRINGTON'S SIERRA PINES
Phone: 530/862-1151
(AAA) [SAVE]

| | 4/1-11/30 | 1P: | $49- 70 | 2P/1B: | $49- 70 | 2P/2B: | $55- 75 | XP: | $5 |

◆ ◆
Motor Inn
Location: 0.5 mi w on SR 49. 100 Main St 96125 (PO Box 235). **Terms:** Open 4/1-11/30; reserv deposit, 7 day notice; pets. **Facility:** 19 rooms. Spacious grounds on north fork of Yuba River. View of Sierra Buttes & river. Balconies. 1 cottage with kitchen & fireplace for up to 4 persons, $80-$100; 1 story; exterior corridors. **Dining:** Dining room; 8 am-11 & 5-9 pm; $11-$25; cocktails. **Recreation:** picnic tables by the river. Fee: trout pond fishing. **All Rooms:** shower baths. **Cards:** DS, MC, VI.

🐴 🍴 🎣 ☎ 🎿

SIERRA MADRE—See Los Angeles p. 640.

SIMI VALLEY—100,200

LODGINGS

CLARION POSADA ROYALE HOTEL
◆◆◆
Motel

| | Rates Subject to Change | | | Phone: 805/584-6300 |
Rates Subject to Change

12/21-1/5 [BP]　　1P: $85- 150　2P/1B: $85- 160　2P/2B: $85- 160　XP: $10　F18
2/1-12/20 & 1/6-1/31 [BP]　1P: $75- 150　2P/1B: $75- 160　2P/2B: $75- 160　XP: $10　F18

Location: 1 mi s of SR 118; exit Madera Rd. 1775 Madera Rd 93065. **Fax:** 805/527-9969. **Facility:** 120 rooms. Many balconies. 2 mi n of The Ronald Reagan Presidential Library. 1 two-bedroom unit. 16 one-bedroom suites with sofabed & refrigerator $120; 2 stories; interior/exterior corridors; heated pool. **Cards:** AE, CB, DI, DS, MC, VI.

HOLIDAY INN EXPRESS　　　　　　　　　　　　　　　　　**Phone:** (805)584-6006
All Year [CP]　　　1P: $59- 89　2P/1B: $59- 89　2P/2B: $59- 89　XP: $10　F17
◆◆◆
Motel

Location: Adjacent s side SR 118, exit Erringer Rd. 2550 Erringer Rd 93065. **Fax:** 805/527-5629. **Facility:** 96 rooms. 6 one-bedroom suites with & refrigerator, $79-$85; 3 stories; exterior corridors; heated pool, sauna, whirlpool. **Dining:** Restaurant nearby. **Some Rooms:** whirlpools. **Cards:** AE, DI, DS, MC, VI. **Special Amenities:** Free breakfast and free newspaper. *(See color ad below)*

RADISSON-SIMI VALLEY　　　　Rates Subject to Change　　　　　**Phone:** (805)583-2000
◆◆◆
Hotel
All Year [CP]　1P: $99　　2P/1B: $99　　2P/2B: $99　　XP: $10　F10
Location: Adjacent to SR 118; exit 1st St. 999 Enchanted Way 93065. **Fax:** 805/583-2779. **Terms:** Reserv deposit. **Facility:** 195 rooms. 6 suites with whirlpool tub, $139-$159, continental breakfast not avai on Sun; 2-4 stories; interior corridors; heated pool. **Services:** giftshop; area transportation. **Cards:** AE, CB, DI, DS, JC, MC, VI. *(See color ad below)*

RESTAURANT

DAKOTA'S MESQUITE BBQ & STEAKHOUSE　　　**Dinner:** $7-$20　　　　**Phone:** 805/582-1700
◆◆
American
Location: SR 118, exit Yosemite, just s to Cochran, then 0.5 mi e to Stow St, just n. 2525 Stow St 93063. **Hours:** 4 pm-10 pm, Fri 4 pm-11 pm, Sat 3 pm-11 pm, Sun 2 pm-10 pm. **Closed:** 11/25, 12/25. **Features:** casual dress; children's menu; early bird specials; carryout; cocktails & lounge; valet parking. Nice selection of barbecue meats, ribs, steaks & sandwiches. Smoke free premises. **Cards:** AE, DI, DS, MC, VI.

SMITH RIVER—2,000

LODGING

BEST WESTERN SHIP ASHORE MOTEL Rates Subject to Change Phone: 707/487-3141
◆◆ 6/16-10/31 1P: $58- 85 2P/1B: $64- 85 2P/2B: $71- 88 XP: $6
Motor Inn 2/1-6/15 & 11/1-1/31 1P: $49- 78 2P/1B: $55- 78 2P/2B: $62- 81 XP: $6
Location: 2.8 mi n on US 101; 3 mi s of OR-CA stateline. 12370 Hwy 101 95567 (PO Box 75).
Fax: 707/487-7070. **Facility:** 50 rooms. View of Smith River. Entrance through trailer park. 1 two-bedroom apartment with fireplace. 15 whirlpool rms, extra charge; 2 stories; exterior corridors; oceanview. Fee: boat dock, boat ramp.
Services: giftshop. **Recreation:** fishing. **Rental:** boats. **Some Rooms:** 11 efficiencies, kitchen. **Cards:** AE, CB, DI, DS, JC, MC, VI.

SOLANA BEACH—See San Diego p. 911.

SOLEDAD—7,100

LODGING

BEST WESTERN VALLEY HARVEST INN Phone: (831)678-3833
ⒶⒶⒶ ⟨SAVE⟩ All Year 1P: $70- 94 2P/1B: $79- 94 2P/2B: $79- 94 XP: $9 F12
◆◆◆ **Location:** Just e of US 101; Soledad exit. 1155 Front St 93960. Fax: 831/678-3011. **Terms:** Weekly/monthly
Motor Inn rates. **Facility:** 60 rooms. Nicely landscaped pool/whirlpool courtyard. Convenient to w entrance to Pinnacles
National Monument. Lower rates in winter; 2 stories; interior/exterior corridors; whirlpool. **Dining:** Restaurant, coffee shop; 6 am-10 pm; $9-$20; cocktails. **Some Rooms:** 4 efficiencies, no utensils. **Cards:** AE, CB, DI, DS, MC, VI. **Special Amenities:** Free local telephone calls and free newspaper.

SOLVANG—4,700

LODGINGS

BEST WESTERN KING FREDERIK INN Phone: (805)688-5515
ⒶⒶⒶ ⟨SAVE⟩ 5/1-9/30 [CP] 1P: $69- 89 2P/1B: $69- 89 2P/2B: $75- 95 XP: $10 F12
◆◆◆ 2/1-4/30 & 10/1-1/31 [CP] 1P: $54- 75 2P/1B: $54- 75 2P/2B: $60- 80 XP: $10 F12
Motel **Location:** On SR 246. 1617 Copenhagen Dr 93463. Fax: 805/688-2067. **Terms:** Reserv deposit. **Facility:** 45
rooms. Few smaller rooms. 2 stories; exterior corridors; heated pool, whirlpool. **All Rooms:** combo or
shower baths, extended cable TV. **Cards:** AE, CB, DI, DS, MC, VI. **Special Amenities:** Free breakfast.

BEST WESTERN KRONBORG INN Rates Subject to Change Phone: (805)688-2383
ⒶⒶⒶ All Year [CP] 1P: $45- 85 2P/1B: $50- 100 2P/2B: $50- 100 XP: $10 F12
◆◆◆ **Location:** Just e on SR 246. 1440 Mission Dr 93463. Fax: 805/688-1821. **Terms:** Reserv deposit, 3 day
Motel notice; small pets only, $10 extra charge, in designated rooms. **Facility:** 39 rooms. Attractive country decor. 2
whirlpool rms, extra charge; 2 stories; exterior corridors; whirlpool. **Recreation:** spa. **Cards:** AE, CB, DI, DS, JC, MC, VI.

CHIMNEY SWEEP INN Phone: (805)688-2111
AAA SAVE All Year [CP] 1P: $75- 275 2P/1B: $75- 275 2P/2B: $90- 275 XP: $10 F12
◆◆◆ **Location:** Just s of SR 246. 1564 Copenhagen Dr 93463. Fax: 805/688-8824. **Terms:** Reserv deposit;
Motel weekly/monthly rates; 2 night min stay, weekends. **Facility:** 56 rooms. Beautifully landscaped garden area.
Many rooms with fireplace. 3 two-bedroom units. 8 split-level loft rooms, $95-$185; 6 cottage units with fire-
place, some with private outdoor whirlpool $155-$275. 2-bedroom suites $115-$165; 2 stories; interior/exterior
corridors; whirlpool. **All Rooms:** combo or shower baths, extended cable TV. **Cards:** AE, DS, MC, VI.
(See color ad below)

DANISH COUNTRY INN Guaranteed Rates Phone: (805)688-2018
◆◆◆ Fri & Sat [BP] 1P: $129 2P/1B: $129 2P/2B: $129 XP: $10 F12
Motel Sun-Thurs [BP] 1P: $99 2P/1B: $99 2P/2B: $99 XP: $10 F12
Location: Just w on SR 246. 1455 Mission Dr 93463. Fax: 805/688-1156. **Facility:** 82 rooms. Spacious rooms.
6 split-level loft rooms, $180-$210 for up to 2 persons; 3 stories; interior corridors; small heated pool. **Cards:** AE, CB, DI,
DS, MC, VI. *(See color ad p 1047)*

HAMLET MOTEL Rates Subject to Change **Phone:** 805/688-4413
2P/1B: $85- 99 2P/2B: $100- 140 XP: $10
Fri & Sat [CP]
Sun-Thurs [CP] 1P: $38- 65 2P/1B: $45- 95 2P/2B: $55- 95 XP: $6
Location: Just on SR 246. 1532 Mission Dr 93463. Fax: 805/686-1301. **Terms:** Reserv deposit, 3 day
Motel notice. **Facility:** 14 rooms. Nicely furnished rooms. 2 bedroom unit, $95-$150 Fri & Sat; 2 stories; exterior cor-
ridors. **Dining:** Restaurant nearby. **All Rooms:** combo or shower baths. **Cards:** AE, DI, DS, JC, MC, VI.
(See ad p 1048)

PETERSEN VILLAGE INN **Phone:** (805)688-3121
Fri & Sat [CP] 1P: $135- 235 2P/1B: $135- 235 2P/2B: $155- 235 XP: $15
Sun-Thurs [CP] 1P: $115- 215 2P/1B: $115- 215 2P/2B: $135- 215 XP: $15
Location: In the Village Center. 1576 Mission Dr 93463. Fax: 805/688-5732. **Terms:** Package plans; 2 night
Complex min stay, most weekends. **Facility:** 40 rooms. A charming European inn complex with shops, bakery & restau-
rants. Individually decorated rooms, 2 with fireplace, many with balcony or patio. 1 smaller room. 1 two-level
suite with whirlpool, $215-$245; 3 stories; interior/exterior corridors. **Dining:** Complimentary European buffet breakfast &
evening hors d'oeuvre buffet with piano bar. **All Rooms:** combo or shower baths. **Cards:** AE, MC, VI. **Special Amenities:**
Free breakfast and free newspaper. *(See color ad below)*

THE
Petersen Village AND Inn

Four Diamond
Award

The
Petersen Village
and Inn is a family owned
complex of Shops, Sidewalk
Cafes, an authentic Danish Bakery
and a charming Old World Inn.

- A stay at the Inn includes a European Buffet Breakfast, an Evening
  Buffet in the Piano Wine Bar and Conference/Retreat Facilities
  for 6 to 40 guests.

- Enjoy Championship golf, award-winning Wineries and a
  Summer/Fall outdoor Festival Theater.

1576 Mission Drive
Solvang, CA 93463 Reservations 1-800-321-8985
1-805-688-3121

QUALITY INN OF SOLVANG

Phone: (805)688-3210

(AAA) (SAVE)
◆◆◆
Motel

		1P:		2P/1B:		2P/2B:		XP:		
5/1-10/31 [CP]		1P:	$85- 195	2P/1B:	$85- 195	2P/2B:	$90- 200	XP:	$5	F18
12/26-1/1 [CP]		1P:	$85- 195	2P/1B:	$85- 195	2P/2B:	$90- 200	XP:	$5	F18
2/1-4/30, Sun-Thurs 6/1-9/30,										
11/1-12/25 & 1/2-1/31 [CP]		1P:	$60- 155	2P/1B:	$60- 155	2P/2B:	$65- 160	XP:	$5	F18

Location: Just w on SR 246. 1450 Mission Dr 93463. Fax: 805/688-0026. **Terms:** Reserv deposit. **Facility:** 75 rooms. Rms with private spa, $105-$195; 2 stories; exterior corridors; heated indoor pool. **Recreation:** video, pinball, air hockey games & pool tables. **All Rooms:** combo or shower baths. **Some Rooms:** whirlpools. **Cards:** AE, CB, DI, DS, JC, MC, VI. **Special Amenities:** Free breakfast and free newspaper.

THE ROYAL COPENHAGEN MOTEL

Phone: (805)688-5561

(AAA) (SAVE)
◆◆◆
Motel

		1P:		2P/1B:		2P/2B:		XP:		
Fri & Sat [CP]		1P:	$79- 109	2P/1B:	$79- 109	2P/2B:	$89- 109	XP:	$5	F17
Sun-Thurs [CP]		1P:	$59- 79	2P/1B:	$59- 79	2P/2B:	$69- 79	XP:	$5	F17

Location: On SR 246. 1579 Mission Dr 93463. Fax: 805/688-7029. **Terms:** Reserv deposit, 3 day notice. **Facility:** 48 rooms. Exterior of buildings are authentic replica of Danish village. Large rooms. 4 split-level loft rooms, $110; 2 stories; interior/exterior corridors; heated pool. **All Rooms:** shower baths, extended cable TV. **Cards:** AE, DS, MC, VI. **Special Amenities:** Free breakfast and free local telephone calls. *(See color ad below)*

SOLVANG ROYAL SCANDINAVIAN INN

Phone: (805)688-8000

(AAA) (SAVE)
◆◆◆
Hotel

				2P/1B:		2P/2B:		XP:		
6/1-9/30				2P/1B:	$101- 160	2P/2B:	$101- 160	XP:	$10	F17
3/1-5/31 & 10/1-11/30				2P/1B:	$91- 131	2P/2B:	$91- 131	XP:	$10	F17
2/1-2/28 & 12/1-1/31				2P/1B:	$81- 131	2P/2B:	$81- 131			

Location: Just s of SR 246, Mission Dr. 400 Alisal Rd 93463 (PO Box 30, 93464). Fax: 805/688-0761. **Terms:** Check-in 4 pm; reserv deposit, 3 day notice; monthly rates; package plans. **Facility:** 133 rooms. Large rooms, some with balcony or patio. Attractive pool area with view of Los Padres Mountains foothills. 3 stories; interior corridors; designated smoking area; heated pool, whirlpool. **Dining:** Restaurant; 7 am-9 pm; $11-$20; cocktails. **Cards:** AE, CB, DI, DS, JC, MC, VI. **Special Amenities:** Preferred room (subject to availability with advanced reservations). *(See color ad below)*

STORYBOOK INN

◆◆◆
Bed &
Breakfast

Rates Subject to Change

Phone: (805)688-1703

		1P:		2P/1B:		
Fri & Sat [CP]		1P:	$99- 189	2P/1B:	$99- 189	XP: $25
Sun-Thurs [CP]		1P:	$89- 149	2P/1B:	$89- 149	XP: $25

Location: At Oak St. 409 1st St 93463. Fax: 805/688-0953. **Terms:** Reserv deposit, 7 day notice; 2 night min stay, weekends. **Facility:** 9 rooms. Newly constructed, tastefully decorated rooms. Most units with fireplace. 2 suites w/whirlpool tubs, $139-$189; 3 stories; interior corridors; smoke free premises. **All Rooms:** combo or shower baths. **Cards:** AE, DS, MC, VI.

SVENDSGAARD'S DANISH LODGE Rates Subject to Change Phone: (805)688-3277

◇◇◇ Fri & Sat, Sun-Thurs 6/7-9/6
& 12/20-1/4 [CP] 1P: $75- 130 2P/1B: .$81- 136 2P/2B: $85- 136 XP: $6 F10
Sun-Thurs 2/1-6/6, 9/7-12/19
Motel & 1/5-1/31 [CP] 1P: $59- 120 2P/1B: $59- 126 2P/2B: $62- 126 XP: $6 F10
Location: On SR 246, at Alisal Rd. 1711 Mission Dr 93463. Fax: 805/686-5616. **Terms:** Weekly/monthly
rates. **Facility:** 48 rooms. Many rooms with fireplace. 3 two-bedroom units. 4 kitchens, $5 extra charge; 3 stories;
interior/exterior corridors; whirlpool. **All Rooms:** combo or shower baths. **Cards:** AE, CB, DI, DS, JC, MC, VI. IMA.
(See color ad below & p 286)

THREE CROWNS INN & COTTAGES Phone: 805/688-4702

⊕ SAVE Fri & Sat [CP] 1P: $75- 165 2P/1B: $75- 165 2P/2B: $85- 165 XP: $5 F12
Sun-Thurs [CP] 1P: $45- 165 2P/1B: $45- 165 2P/2B: $60- 165 XP: $5 F12
◆◆ **Location:** Just w on SR 246. 1518 Mission Dr 93463. Fax: 805/688-6907. **Terms:** Monthly rates. **Facility:** 33
Motel rooms. Various accommodations from economy rooms to family rooms. Cottages with whirlpool tubs & efficiency
units, & fireplace. Charming waterfall & pond. Family units $90-$120, cottages $110-$180 with coffeemaker, re-
frigerator & microwave; cottages avail on monthly basis w/whirlpool tubs & Kitchenettes; 1-2 stories; exterior corridors.
Dining: Restaurant nearby. **All Rooms:** extended cable TV. **Cards:** AE, DS, MC, VI. *(See ad below)*

VIKING MOTEL Phone: (805)688-1337

⊕ SAVE Fri & Sat [CP] 1P: $52- 98 2P/1B: $52- 98 2P/2B: $58- 98 XP: $6
Sun-Thurs [CP] 1P: $30- 65 2P/1B: $35- 65 2P/2B: $38- 75 XP: $6
◆ **Location:** Just w on SR 246. 1506 Mission Dr 93463. **Terms:** Reserv deposit; small pets only, $5 extra
Motel charge. **Facility:** 12 rooms. Located in center of town. Modest rooms. 1 story; exterior corridors.
All Rooms: combo or shower baths, extended cable TV. **Special Amenities:**
Free breakfast and free local telephone calls.

RESTAURANTS

BIT 'O DENMARK RESTAURANT **Lunch:** $6-$10 **Dinner:** $9-$14 **Phone:** 805/688-5426

⊕ **Location:** Just s of SR 246. 473 Alisal Rd 93463. **Hours:** 9 am-9 pm, Fri & Sat 8 am-9:30 pm. Closed:
◆◆ 12/25. **Features:** casual dress; children's menu; carryout; cocktails. Nice selection of American & Danish
American entrees. Smorgasbord lunch & dinner. Patio dining weather permitting. Smoke free premises. **Cards:** AE,
CB, DI, DS, MC, VI.

CAFE ANGELICA **Lunch:** $5-$9 **Dinner:** $13-$20 **Phone:** 805/686-9970

◆◆ **Location:** S of Mission Rd (SR 246). 490 First St 93463. **Hours:** 11:30 am-3 & 5-8:30 pm. Closed: 4/12,
Italian 11/25, 12/25 & Wed. **Reservations:** suggested; weekends. **Features:** casual dress; children's menu; beer &
wine only; a la carte. Nice selection of freshly prepared pastas & salads. Also, Italian & California style
entrees. Patio dining also avail. Smoke free premises. **Cards:** MC, VI.

SONOMA—8,100

LODGINGS

BEST WESTERN SONOMA VALLEY INN — Rates Subject to Change — Phone: (707)938-9200

7/1-10/31 & 12/17-1/1 [CP]   1P: $129- 349   2P/1B: $129- 349   2P/2B: $129- 349   XP: $20   F16
2/1-4/10, 12/1-12/16 &

Motel
1/2-1/31 [CP]   1P: $89- 249   2P/1B: $89- 249   2P/2B: $89- 249   XP: $20   F16
4/11-6/30 & 11/1-11/30 [CP]   1P: $89- 249   2P/1B: $89- 249   2P/2B: $89- 249   XP: $20   F16
Location: 1 blk w of Town Plaza. 550 2nd St W 95476. Fax: 707/938-0935. **Terms:** Reserv deposit, 3 day notice; handling fee imposed; package plans; 2 night min stay, weekends 4/15-10/31; small pets only, $10 extra charge. **Facility:** 72 rooms. Many rooms with fireplace. 2 stories; exterior corridors; heated pool, whirlpool. **Dining:** Coffee shop nearby. **Some Rooms:** whirlpools. **Cards:** AE, CB, DI, DS, MC, VI. *(See color ad below)*

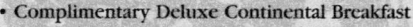

Wheelchair travelers should make reservations, since the availability of wheelchair-accessible accommodations is generally limited.

EL PUEBLO INN   Rates Subject to Change   **Phone:** 707/996-3651
AAA   5/1-10/31   1P: $73- 86 2P/1B: $73- 86 2P/2B: $73- 86 XP: $10   F16
◆◆   2/1-4/30 & 11/1-1/31   1P: $63- 73 2P/1B: $63- 73 2P/2B: $63- 73 XP: $10   F16
Motel **Location:** SR 12, 1 mi w of town plaza. 896 W Napa St 95476. Fax: 707/935-5988. **Terms:** Reserv deposit.
Facility: 38 rooms. Centrally located in the Sonoma Valley. 1 two-bedroom unit. 2 stories; exterior corridors;
heated pool. **Dining:** Restaurant nearby. **Cards:** AE, DS, MC, VI. *(See color ad below)*   [symbols]

SONOMA MISSION INN   Rates Subject to Change   **Phone:** (707)938-9000
AAA   4/14-11/10   1P: $145- 395 2P/1B: $160- 765 2P/2B: $160- 765 XP: $30   F12
◆◆◆◆   2/1-4/13 & 11/11-1/31 1P: $115- 345 2P/1B: $120- 735 2P/2B: $120- 735 XP: $30   F12
Resort Motor **Location:** 2.5 mi n on SR 12. 18140 Sonoma Hwy 95476 (PO Box 1447). Fax: 707/938-4250.
Inn   **Terms:** Check-in 4 pm; reserv deposit, 7 day notice; handling fee imposed; package plans. **Facility:** 198
rooms. A mixture of Mediterranean & Spanish-Californian architecture. Spacious, landscaped grounds. Extensive spa facilities; some with fireplace. Mineral water in pools. 10 two-bedroom units. 3 stories; interior/exterior
corridors; heated pool, sauna, whirlpools; 2 lighted tennis courts. **Dining:** 2 restaurants; 7 am-10 pm; $11-$33; cocktails.
Services: giftshop. **All Rooms:** combo or shower baths. **Cards:** AE, CB, DI, JC, MC, VI. A Preferred Hotel.   [symbols]

TROJAN HORSE INN   Rates Subject to Change   **Phone:** (707)996-2430
◆◆◆   4/14-11/30 [BP]   1P: $135- 160 2P/1B: $135- 160 2P/2B: $120- 165 XP: $20   F12
Bed & 2/1-3/31 & 12/1-1/31 [BP] 1P: $115- 140 2P/1B: $115- 140   XP: $20   F12
Breakfast **Location:** 1 mi w of Sonoma Plaza. 19455 Sonoma Hwy 95476. Fax: 707/996-9185. **Terms:** Reserv deposit,
7 day notice; handling fee imposed. **Facility:** 6 rooms. 2 stories; interior corridors. **All Rooms:** combo or
shower baths. **Cards:** AE, DI, DS, MC, VI.   [symbols]

RESTAURANTS

THE GENERAL'S DAUGHTER   **Lunch:** $7-$12   **Dinner:** $14-$24   **Phone:** 707/938-4004
AAA   **Location:** 4 blocks w of Sonoma Plaza. 400 W Spain St 95476. **Hours:** 11:30 am-2:30 & 5:30-9:30 pm, Fri
& Sat-10:30 pm. Closed major holidays. **Reservations:** suggested. **Features:** casual dress; Sunday
◆◆◆   brunch; cocktails & lounge; a la carte. Renovated Victorian built in 1864 for Natalia, third daughter of pioneer
Continental California statesman General M.G. Vallejo. Smoke free premises. **Cards:** MC, VI.   [symbol]

LA CASA   **Lunch:** $4-$11   **Dinner:** $4-$11   **Phone:** 707/996-3406
◆◆   **Location:** Opposite San Francisco Solano Mission. 121 E Spain St 95476. **Hours:** 11:30 am-9 pm, Fri &
Mexican Sat-10 pm. Closed: 11/28, 12/25 & Easter. **Reservations:** suggested. **Features:** casual dress; children's
menu; cocktails & lounge; street parking; a la carte. Traditional specialties. Smoke free premises. **Cards:** AE,
CB, DI, MC, VI.   [symbol]

SONORA—4,200

LODGINGS

ALADDIN MOTOR INN   Rates Subject to Change   **Phone:** (209)533-4971
AAA   All Year [BP]   1P: $68   2P/1B: $68- 102 2P/2B: $76- 102 XP: $8   F6
◆◆   **Location:** 3.5 mi e on SR 108. 14260 Mono Way 95370 (PO Box 356, STANDARD, 95373).
Motel Fax: 209/532-1522. **Terms:** Reserv deposit; pets, $5 extra charge. **Facility:** 61 rooms. Comfortable rooms,
some with view of surrounding hills. 1 one-bedroom suite, $99 for up to 2 persons; 2 stories; interior/exterior
corridors; heated pool, whirlpool. **Dining:** Coffee shop nearby. **Cards:** AE, DI, DS, MC, VI.   [symbols]

BEST WESTERN SONORA OAKS MOTOR HOTEL   **Phone:** (209)533-4400
AAA [SAVE] 5/1-9/30   1P: $84- 104 2P/1B: $84- 104 2P/2B: $84- 104 XP: $10   F17
1/1-1/31   1P: $79- 99 2P/1B: $84- 99 2P/2B: $79- 99 XP: $10   F17
◆◆◆   2/1-4/30 & 10/1-12/31 1P: $74- 94 2P/1B: $74- 94 2P/2B: $74- 94 XP: $10   F17
Motel **Location:** 3.5 mi e on SR 108; corner of Hess Ave. 19551 Hess Ave 95370. Fax: 209/532-1964.
Facility: 101 rooms. Country setting. 2 stories; interior/exterior corridors; heated pool, whirlpool.
Dining: Coffee shop nearby. **All Rooms:** combo or shower baths. **Cards:** AE, DI, DS, MC, VI. **Special Amenities:** Free
local telephone calls and free newspaper. *(See color ad p 1054)*   [symbols]

INNS OF CALIFORNIA   Phone: (209)532-3633

(AAA) (SAVE)   5/1-9/30   1P: $70- 155   2P/1B: $70- 155   2P/2B: $70- 155   XP: $5   F12
◆◆   2/1-4/30 & 10/1-1/31   1P: $60- 105   2P/1B: $60- 105   2P/2B: $60- 105   XP: $5   F12
Motel   **Location:** 3 blks e on SR 108 business rt. 350 S Washington St 95370. Fax: 209/532-9000. **Terms:** Reserv
                deposit; handling fee imposed. **Facility:** 112 rooms. Walking distance to downtown shops & restaurants. 3
                whirlpool suites, $90-$155 for up to 2 persons; 3 stories; exterior corridors; heated pool, whirlpool.
All Rooms: combo or shower baths. **Cards:** AE, CB, DI, DS, JC, MC, VI. **Special Amenities:** Free local telephone calls.

MINERS MOTEL   Phone: (209)532-7850

(AAA) (SAVE)   Fri & Sat 5/1-9/15   1P: $45- 55   2P/1B: $50- 55   2P/2B: $60- 75   XP: $5
◆   Sun-Thurs 5/1-9/15   1P: $40- 50   2P/1B: $45   2P/2B: $50- 60   XP: $5
Motel   Sun-Thurs 2/1-4/30 &
                9/16-1/31   1P: $37- 40   2P/1B: $37- 40   2P/2B: $45- 60   XP: $5
                Fri & Sat 2/1-4/30 &
                9/16-1/31   1P: $40- 55   2P/1B: $45   2P/2B: $55- 60   XP: $5
Location: 1 mi e of Jamestown on SR 108 & SR 49. 18740 SR 108 95327. Fax: 209/532-6401. **Terms:** Reserv deposit;
handling fee imposed; small pets only. **Facility:** 18 rooms. Comfortable rooms, few small. 1-2 stories; exterior corridors.
All Rooms: combo or shower baths. **Cards:** AE, DI, DS, MC, VI. **Special Amenities:** Free breakfast and free local
telephone calls.

SONORA DAYS INN   Phone: (209)532-2400

(AAA) (SAVE)   5/1-9/30   1P: $69- 145   2P/1B: $69- 145   2P/2B: $69- 145   XP: $5   F16
◆◆   2/1-4/30 & 10/1-1/31   1P: $55- 125   2P/1B: $55- 125   2P/2B: $55- 125   XP: $5   F16
Motor Inn   **Location:** Downtown. 160 S Washington St 95370. Fax: 209/532-4542. **Terms:** Reserv deposit, 3 day
                notice. **Facility:** 64 rooms. 3 stories; interior/exterior corridors. **Dining:** Restaurant; 7 am-9 pm; $9-$16.
                All Rooms: combo or shower baths. **Cards:** AE, CB, DI, DS, JC, MC, VI. **Special Amenities:** Early
check-in/late check-out and free local telephone calls.

SONORA GOLD LODGE   Phone: (209)532-3952

(AAA) (SAVE)   5/2-10/15   1P: $44- 64   2P/1B: $48- 74   2P/2B: $54- 79   XP: $10
◆   3/15-5/1 & 10/16-11/15 1P: $39- 49   2P/1B: $44- 64   2P/2B: $48- 64   XP: $6
Motel   2/1-3/14 & 11/16-1/31   1P: $34- 49   2P/1B: $40- 59   2P/2B: $44- 59
                Location: 0.5 mi sw on SR 108 business route & 49. 480 Stockton St 95370. Fax: 209/532-2759.
                Terms: Pets, smoking rooms extra charge. **Facility:** 42 rooms. Tree-shaded grounds. Some small rooms. Bar-
becue & picnic area. 1 story; exterior corridors; sauna, whirlpool. **All Rooms:** combo or shower baths. **Cards:** AE, DS, MC,
VI. **Special Amenities:** Free local telephone calls.

SONORA QUALITY INN
Phone: (209)984-0315
AAA SAVE   All Year [CP]   1P: $49- 89   2P/1B: $54- 99   2P/2B: $59- 99   XP: $10   F10
◆◆   **Location:** 1 mi n on SR 49/108. 18730 Highway 108 95327. Fax: 209/984-4849. **Terms:** Small pets only,
Motel $10 extra charge. **Facility:** 61 rooms. 3 stories, no elevator; exterior corridors. **Cards:** AE, CB, DI, DS, MC,
VI.   🛇🏕🛏🖨🗙

RESTAURANT

JOSEPHINE'S CALIFORNIA TRATTORIA   Historical   **Dinner:** $9-$17   Phone: 209/533-4111
◆◆◆   **Location:** SR 108 (Washington St) just s of city center behind the historic Gunn House Hotel. 286 S
Italian   Washington St 95370. **Hours:** 5:30-10 pm, Sun from 5 pm. Closed: 11/25, 12/25, 1/1-1/5 & Mon.
Reservations: suggested. **Features:** casual dress; children's menu; cocktails & lounge; a la carte. Tuscan
decor. Varied menu. Exhibition kitchen with additional view of wood fired oven. Smoke free premises. **Cards:** AE, MC, VI.
🗙

SOUTH EL MONTE—See Los Angeles p. 640.

SOUTH LAKE TAHOE—See Lake Tahoe Area p. 506.

SOUTH PASADENA—See Los Angeles p. 640.

SOUTH SAN FRANCISCO—See San Francisco p. 977.

SPRING VALLEY—See San Diego p. 911.

SPRINGVILLE—1,900

LODGING

ANNIE'S BED & BREAKFAST   Rates Subject to Change   Phone: (559)539-3827
◆◆◆   All Year [BP]   1P: $85   2P/1B: $95   XP: $25
Historic Bed   **Location:** 3.2 mi se of town on SR 190, then 0.3 mi s on Globe Dr. 33024 Globe Dr 93265.
& Breakfast   Fax: 559/539-2179. **Terms:** Reserv deposit, 15 day notice; handling fee imposed. **Facility:** 3 rooms. Country
farmhouse surrounded by pastures on 5 acres in the Sierra foothills. Television in public area. Telephones avail
on request. 1 story; interior/exterior corridors; designated smoking area. **All Rooms:** combo or shower baths. **Cards:** AE, DI,
DS, MC, VI.   🛏📺🅩🗙

STANTON—30,500   (See map p. 294; index p. 292)

LODGING

HOLIDAY INN EXPRESS-
STANTON/DISNEYLAND PARK AREA   Rates Subject to Change   Phone: 714/527-6680   [201]
◆◆   All Year [CP]   1P: $55- 85   2P/1B: $65- 85   2P/2B: $65- 85   XP: $10
Motel   **Location:** Just e of Knott Ave. 7161 W Katella Ave 90680. Fax: 714/527-7737. **Facility:** 72 rooms. 10 suites,
$71. 12 rms with whirlpool tub, $81-$91. Most rms with wetbar. All rms with refrigerator; 3 stories;
interior/exterior corridors; heated pool. **Services:** area transportation. **Cards:** AE, CB, DI, DS, JC, MC, VI.
(See color ad p 352)   🚍🅿🛏📶🖥🗙

STOCKTON—210,900

LODGINGS

BEST WESTERN INN   Phone: (209)948-0321
AAA SAVE   6/1-9/1   1P: $58   2P/1B: $62   2P/2B: $66   XP: $5   F12
2/1-5/31 & 9/2-1/31   1P: $54   2P/1B: $58   2P/2B: $62   XP: $5   F12
◆◆   **Location:** Exit I-5A at Charter Way, 0.3 mi e; 3 mi w of SR 99. 550 W Charter Way 95206.
Motel   Fax: 209/463-1638. **Terms:** Reserv deposit; small pets only. **Facility:** 80 rooms. 2 stories; exterior corridors;
whirlpool. **Dining:** Coffee shop nearby. **Cards:** AE, CB, DI, DS, JC, MC, VI. **Special Amenities: Free**
breakfast and free local telephone calls.   🛇🏕🛏📶🖥🗙

BEST WESTERN STOCKTON INN   Phone: (209)931-3131
AAA SAVE   All Year   1P: $65   2P/1B: $74   2P/2B: $76   XP: $10   F12
◆◆◆   **Location:** E off SR 99 at jct SR 88. 4219 Waterloo Rd 95215. Fax: 209/931-0423. **Facility:** 141 rooms. Spa-
Motor Inn   cious grounds. Many large rooms. 2 stories; interior corridors; wading pool, whirlpool. **Dining:** Restaurant; 6
am-2 & 5-9 pm, Sat & Sun from 7 am; $9-$18; cocktails. **Cards:** AE, CB, DI, DS, MC, VI.
Special Amenities: Free newspaper and free room upgrade (subject to availability with advanced
reservations). (See color ad p 1056)   🛇🏕🛏📶🖥🗙

CITY CENTER DAYS INN   Rates Subject to Change   Phone: 209/948-6151
◆◆   All Year [CP]   1P: $42- 55   2P/1B: $42- 55   2P/2B: $50- 65   XP: $5   F17
Motel   **Location:** 1 blk n; w off El Dorado St via Weber; southbound SR 99 traffic exit Wilson Way, northbound w
via Mariposa Rd to Charter Way; I-5 exit Downtown. 33 N Center St 95202. Fax: 209/948-1220.
Terms: Reserv deposit, 3 day notice. **Facility:** 96 rooms. 3 stories; exterior corridors. **Cards:** AE, DI, DS, MC, VI.
🛇🏕📶🛏📶📺📼🖥🗙

COMFORT INN

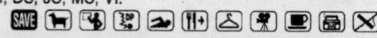

AAA [SAVE]
◆◆
Motel

Phone: (209)931-9341

All Year · 1P: $48   2P/1B: $52   2P/2B: $60   XP: $6   F12
Location: E of SR 99 at jct SR 88. 3951 E Budweiser Ct 95215. Fax: 209/931-6243. **Facility:** 67 rooms. 3 stories, no elevator; interior corridors. **Dining:** Coffee shop nearby. **All Rooms:** combo or shower baths. **Cards:** AE, CB, DI, DS, JC, MC, VI. **Special Amenities:** Early check-in/late check-out and free breakfast.

COURTYARD BY MARRIOTT
◆◆◆
Motor Inn

Guaranteed Rates   Phone: 209/472-9700

All Year [CP]   1P: $89- 104   2P/1B: 104 2P/2B: $89- 104
Location: Exit I-5; at March Ln, 0.5 mi w. 3252 W March Ln 95219. Fax: 209/472-9722. **Terms:** Reserv deposit. **Facility:** 89 rooms. 3 stories; interior corridors; heated pool. **Cards:** AE, CB, DI, DS, MC, VI.

ECONO LODGE OF STOCKTON

AAA [SAVE]
◆
Motel

Phone: (209)466-5741

5/20-5/31	1P:	$40-	45	2P/1B:	$45-	49 2P/2B:	$49- 59 XP:	$9 F12
5/1-5/19	1P:	$36-	40	2P/1B:	$38-	44 2P/2B:	$46- 52 XP:	$6-9 F12
2/1-4/30	1P:	$36-	40	2P/1B:	$38-	42 2P/2B:	$44- 49 XP:	$6-9 F12
6/1-1/31	1P:	$34-	38	2P/1B:	$38-	42 2P/2B:	$44- 48 XP:	$6-9 F12

Location: Exit I-5 w 8th St off ramp; 0.3 mi s of jct SR 4. 2210 S Manthey Rd 95206. Fax: 209/463-1255. **Terms:** Reserv deposit; handling fee imposed; small pets only, $25 dep req. **Facility:** 69 rooms. 2 two-bedroom units. 2-large units, $75-$85 for up to 6 persons; 3 stories, no elevator; interior corridors. **All Rooms:** combo or shower baths. **Cards:** AE, DI, DS, MC, VI. **Special Amenities:** Early check-in/late check-out and free local telephone calls.

GUEST INN

AAA [SAVE]
◆◆
Motel

Phone: (209)931-6675

5/1-5/31	1P:	$48-	52	2P/1B:	$48-	58 2P/2B:	$58- 64 XP:	$6-9 F12
6/1-1/31	1P:	$42-	48	2P/1B:	$44-	49 2P/2B:	$49- 56 XP:	$6-9 F12
2/1-4/30	1P:	$42-	48	2P/1B:	$44-	49 2P/2B:	$49- 56 XP:	$6-9 F12

Location: E of SR 99 at jct SR 88. 2533 N Piccoli Rd 95215. Fax: 209/931-8351. **Terms:** Reserv deposit; handling fee imposed. **Facility:** 27 rooms. Attractively decorated rooms. 2 stories; exterior corridors. **Dining:** Restaurant nearby. **Some Rooms:** whirlpools. **Cards:** AE, DI, DS, MC, VI. **Special Amenities:** Free local telephone calls and preferred room (subject to availability with advanced reservations).

LA QUINTA INN
◆◆◆
Motel

Rates Subject to Change   Phone: (209)952-7800

All Year [CP]   1P: $62- 69   2P/1B: $62- 69 2P/2B: $62- 69
Location: Just w of I-5 at March Ln exit. 2710 W March Ln 95219-6571. Fax: 209/472-0732. **Facility:** 153 rooms. 3 stories; exterior corridors. **Cards:** AE, CB, DI, DS, JC, MC, VI.

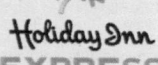

RADISSON HOTEL STOCKTON
◆◆◆   Hotel
Rates Subject to Change   **Phone: (209)957-9090**
Sun-Thurs   1P: $79   2P/1B: $79   2P/2B: $79   XP: $12   F18
Fri & Sat   1P: $69   2P/1B: $69   2P/2B: $69   XP: $12   F18
Location: Exit e off I-5 via March Ln. 2323 Grand Canal Blvd 95207. Fax: 209/473-0739. **Terms:** Reserv deposit, 3 day notice. **Facility:** 198 rooms. Some balconies. 5 stories; interior corridors; heated pool. **Cards:** AE, CB, DI, DS, JC, MC, VI.

RAMADA INN STOCKTON
◆◆   Motor Inn
Guaranteed Rates   **Phone: (209)474-3301**
All Year [CP]   1P: $49   2P/1B: $54   2P/2B: $54
Location: Exit I-5 March Ln 2 mi e, corner El Dorado St. 111 E March Ln 95207. Fax: 209/474-7612. **Facility:** 196 rooms. 3 stories; interior corridors; heated pool. **Cards:** AE, DI, DS, JC, MC, VI.

RESIDENCE INN BY MARRIOTT
◆◆◆   Apartment Motel
Guaranteed Rates   **Phone: 209/472-9800**
All Year [CP]   1P: $119- 149   2P/1B: $119- 149   2P/2B: $119- 149
Location: Exit I-5; at March Ln, 0.5 mi w. 3240 W March Lane 95219. Fax: 209/472-9888. **Terms:** Reserv deposit, 3 day notice. **Facility:** 66 rooms. 3 stories; interior corridors; heated pool. **All Rooms:** kitchens. **Cards:** AE, CB, DI, DS, MC, VI.

SUPER 8 MOTEL
◆   Motel
Rates Subject to Change   **Phone: (209)477-5576**
All Year   1P: $50- 55   2P/1B: $55- 60   2P/2B: $60- 65   XP: $10   F17
Location: Just w of I-5, exit March Ln. 2717 March Ln 95219. Fax: 209/477-5968. **Facility:** 167 rooms. 2 stories; exterior corridors. **Cards:** AE, CB, DI, DS, JC, MC, VI.

RESTAURANTS

ALBERTS
◆◆   Continental
Dinner: $12-$17   **Phone: 209-476-1763**
Location: 6 mi n; adjacent to SR 99; exit via Hammer Ln. 8103 Frontage Rd Hammer Ln N 95212. **Hours:** 5 pm-10 pm, Sun-9 pm. **Closed:** 5/27, 11/28 & 12/25. **Reservations:** suggested. **Features:** semi-formal attire; children's menu; cocktails & lounge; a la carte. Refined atmosphere. Varied menu. Featuring Portugese dishes. **Cards:** MC, VI.

LEBISTRO
◆◆◆   Continental
Lunch: $10-$14   Dinner: $19-$43   **Phone: 209/951-0885**
Location: Adjacent to I-5, exit Benjamin Holt Dr, in Village Square Center behind Lyons. 3121 W Benjamin Holt Dr 95207. **Hours:** 11:30 am-3 & 5-9 pm, Sat & Sun 5 pm-10 pm. **Closed:** 1/1 & 12/25. **Reservations:** suggested. **Features:** semi-formal attire; children's menu; cocktails & lounge; a la carte. Specializing in seafood. Smoke free premises. **Cards:** AE, DI, DS, MC, VI.

ON LOCK SAM
◆◆   Chinese
Lunch: $6-$9   Dinner: $8-$19   **Phone: 209/466-4561**
Location: 3 blks s; I-5 exit downtown. 333 S Sutter St 95203. **Hours:** 11:30 am-9:30 pm, Fri & Sat-10:30 pm. **Closed:** 11/28 & 12/25. **Reservations:** suggested. **Features:** casual dress; cocktails & lounge; a la carte. Cantonese cuisine since 1898. **Cards:** AE, MC, VI.

YE OLDE HOOSIER INN
◆   American
Lunch: $4-$8   Dinner: $6-$13   **Phone: 209/463-0271**
Location: 1 mi ne on SR 99 business rt. 1537 N Wilson Way 95205. **Hours:** 6:30 am-8:30 pm, Sat 7 am-9:30 pm, Sun 7 am-8:30 pm. **Closed:** 1/1, 7/4 & 12/25. **Features:** casual dress; early bird specials. Family restaurant. Furnished in antiques. **Cards:** MC, VI.

STUDIO CITY—See Los Angeles p. 641.

SUN CITY—14,900

LODGING

TRAVELODGE
◆   Motel
   Phone: (909)679-1133
All Year [CP]   1P: $40- 50   2P/1B: $45- 50   2P/2B: $45- 55   XP: $5   F17
Location: Just e of I-215, exit McCall Blvd. 27955 Encanto DR 92586. **Terms:** Small pets only. **Facility:** 57 rooms. 2 stories; exterior corridors; small pool, whirlpool. **Cards:** AE, DI, DS, MC, VI. **Special Amenities:** Free breakfast and free newspaper.

SUNNYVALE—117,200

LODGINGS

BEST WESTERN SUNNYVALE INN
◆◆   Motel
   Phone: (408)734-3742
5/24-11/24 [CP]   1P: $99- 113   2P/1B: $99- 113   2P/2B: $99- 113
2/1-5/23 & 1/1-1/31 [CP]   1P: $81- 99   2P/1B: $81- 99   2P/2B: $81- 99
11/25-12/31 [CP]   1P: $79   2P/1B: $79   2P/2B: $79
Location: N off & adjacent to US 101; exit via Mathilda Ave, just e on Ross Dr. 940 Weddell Dr 94089. Fax: 408/734-9519. **Facility:** 88 rooms. Few small rooms. 3 stories; interior corridors; heated pool. **All Rooms:** combo or shower baths. **Cards:** AE, CB, DI, DS, MC, VI. **Special Amenities:** Free breakfast and free newspaper.

COMFORT INN
◆◆◆   Motel
Rates Subject to Change   **Phone: 408/749-8000**
All Year [CP]   1P: $110- 125   2P/1B: $110- 125   2P/2B: $115   XP: $10   F18
Location: US 101, Mathilda Ave exit, 0.3 mi s. 595 N Mathilda Ave 94086. Fax: 408/749-0367. **Facility:** 52 rooms. Attractive decor. 2 stories; interior corridors. **Cards:** AE, CB, DI, DS, JC, MC, VI.

DAYS INN
◆◆   Motel
Rates Subject to Change   **Phone: 408/737-1177**
All Year   1P: $65- 99   2P/1B: $65- 99   2P/2B: $75- 120   XP: $10
Location: Exit US 101 at Mathilda Ave; 0.3 mi s. 590 N Mathilda Ave 94086. Fax: 408/738-6666. **Facility:** 35 rooms. Comfortable rooms. 2 rooms with large whirlpool, $75-$120 for 2 persons; 2 stories; interior corridors. **Cards:** AE, CB, DI, DS, JC, MC, VI.

FOUR POINTS HOTEL BY ITT SHERATON

Phone: (408)745-6000

		1P:	2P/1B:	2P/2B:	XP:	
Mon-Thurs		$179- 189	$184- 194	$184- 194	$5	F19
Fri-Sun		$79- 89	$79- 89	$79- 89	$5	F19

Location: US 101, Mathilda Ave exit. 1100 N Mathilda Ave 94089. **Fax:** 408/734-8276. **Facility:** 174 rooms. Attractively landscaped pool area. 2 stories; interior corridors; heated pool, whirlpool. **Dining:** Restaurant; 6:30 am-10 pm; $10-$20. **Cards:** AE, CB, DI, DS, MC, VI. **Special Amenities:** Early check-in/late check-out and preferred room (subject to availability with advanced reservations).

HOMESTEAD VILLAGE

Rates Subject to Change

Phone: 408/734-3431

	1P:	2P/1B:	XP:	
All Year Wkly	$420	$420	$5	

Location: N of Hwy 237; exit Mathilda then e on Moffett Park Dr to Orleans Dr. 1255 Orleans Dr 94089. **Fax:** 408/744-1146. **Facility:** 144 rooms. Closed major holidays. Deluxe rms, $520; for up to 2 persons; 2 stories; exterior corridors. **All Rooms:** kitchens, combo or shower baths. **Cards:** AE, CB, DI, DS, MC, VI.

LARKSPUR LANDING

Phone: 408/733-1212

Under construction. **Location:** 748 N Mathilda Ave 94086. **Facility:** 126 rooms.

MAPLE TREE INN

Rates Subject to Change

Phone: (408)720-9700

	1P:	2P/1B:	2P/2B:	XP:	
All Year [CP]	$119- 139	$129- 149	$129- 149	$10-15	F12

Location: SR 82 between Fair Oaks & Wolfe Rd, 2.5 mi W of US 101. 711 E El Camino Real 94087. **Fax:** 408/738-5665. **Facility:** 181 rooms. Some small rooms. 1 executive suite with kitchen for up to 4 persons, $149-$155; 3 stories; interior corridors; heated pool. **Recreation:** bicycles. **Some Rooms:** kitchen. **Cards:** AE, CB, DI, DS, JC, MC, VI. *(See ad below)*

QUALITY INN-SUNNYVALE

Phone: (408)744-1100

	1P:	2P/1B:	2P/2B:	XP:	
Sun-Thurs 2/1-12/18 & 1/6-1/31 [CP]	$99- 120	$99- 130	$99- 130	$10	F15
Fri & Sat 2/1-12/18 & 1/6-1/31 [CP]	$69	$79	$79	$10	F15
12/19-1/5 [CP]	$59	$69	$69	$10	F15

Location: Exit US 101 at Lawrence Expwy n, 1 mi n to Persian Dr, then 0.3 mi w. 1280 Persian Dr 94089. **Fax:** 408/744-1688. **Terms:** Reserv deposit. **Facility:** 72 rooms. Attractive rooms. 2 stories; interior corridors. **Cards:** AE, DI, DS, MC, VI. **Special Amenities:** Free breakfast and free local telephone calls.

RADISSON INN-SUNNYVALE

Rates Subject to Change

Phone: (408)247-0800

	1P:	2P/1B:	2P/2B:	XP:	
Sun-Thurs 6/1-12/31 [BP]	$170	$170	$170	$10	F13
Sun-Thurs 2/1-5/31 & 1/1-1/31 [BP]	$160	$160	$160	$10	F13
Fri & Sat [BP]	$84	$84	$84	$10	F13

Location: 0.3 mi w of Lawrence Expwy; on SR 82. 1085 E El Camino Real 94087. **Fax:** 408/984-7120. **Terms:** Reserv deposit. **Facility:** 136 rooms. Attractive rooms & public areas. 12 suites with whirlpool, $135 for 2 persons; 3 stories; interior corridors; heated pool. **Cards:** AE, CB, DI, DS, JC, MC, VI.

RAMADA INN-SILICON VALLEY

Phone: (408)245-5330

	1P:	2P/1B:	2P/2B:	XP:	
Mon-Thurs	$125	$135	$135	$15	
Fri-Sun	$79	$89	$89	$15	

Location: N off & adjacent to US 101; exit via Lawrence Expwy N. 1217 Wildwood Ave 94089. **Fax:** 408/732-2628. **Facility:** 176 rooms. Attractive landscaped grounds. 2 stories; exterior corridors; heated pool, whirlpool. **Dining:** Dining room, restaurant; 6 am-2 & 5-10 pm; $9-$19; cocktails. **Cards:** AE, DI, DS, JC, MC, VI. *(See color ad opposite title page)*

RESIDENCE INN BY MARRIOTT

Rates Subject to Change

Phone: (408)720-8893

	1P:	2P/1B:	2P/2B:	
All Year [CP]	$161- 215	$161- 215	$179- 233	

Location: US 101 exit Lawrence Expwy S, Duane Ave W, Stewart Dr S. 1080 Stewart Dr 94086. **Fax:** 408/720-8749. **Facility:** 247 rooms. 1 & 2-bedroom units with kitchen. Many with fireplace. 2 stories; exterior corridors; heated pool; 1 tennis court. **Services:** area transportation. **Recreation:** sports court. **All Rooms:** kitchens. **Cards:** AE, CB, DI, DS, JC, MC, VI.

RESIDENCE INN BY MARRIOTT
◆◆◆
Apartment
Motel

| | Rates Subject to Change | | | Phone: 408/720-1000 |
Sun-Thurs 1P: $161 2P/1B: $161 2P/2B: $179
Fri & Sat 1P: $99 2P/1B: $99 2P/2B: $119
Location: Exit US 101 Lawrence Expwy S; then e on Oakmead. 750 Lakeway Dr 94086. Fax: 408/737-9722. **Terms:** Reserv deposit. **Facility:** 231 rooms. 1 & 2 bedroom units, many with fireplace. 58 two-bedroom units. 2 stories; exterior corridors; heated pool. **Services:** area transportation. **Recreation:** sports court. **Cards:** AE, CB, DI, DS, JC, MC, VI.

SUNDOWNER INN
◆◆◆
Motel

Rates Subject to Change **Phone:** 408/734-9900
Mon-Thurs [CP] 1P: $109 2P/1B: $119 2P/2B: $129 XP: $10 F12
Fri-Sun [CP] 1P: $65 2P/1B: $65 2P/2B: $75 XP: $10 F12
Location: Sw corner of SR 237 & Mathilda Ave; e off US 101. 504 Ross Dr 94089. Fax: 408/747-0580. **Terms:** Reserv deposit. **Facility:** 105 rooms. Attractive comfortable rooms. 7 suites with wet bar, refrigerator & microwave, $150-$175 for 2 persons; 2 stories; exterior corridors; heated pool. **Cards:** AE, CB, DI, DS, JC, MC, VI.

SUNNYVALE HILTON
(AAA) [SAVE]
◆◆◆
Motor Inn

Phone: (408)738-4888
All Year 1P: $199- 269 2P/1B: $199- 269 2P/2B: $199- 269 XP: $15
Location: W off & adjacent to US 101, exit Lawrence Expwy S. 1250 Lakeside Dr 94086. Fax: 408/737-7147. **Facility:** 372 rooms. Lagoon & colorfully landscaped grounds. Spacious modern rooms. 6 two-bedroom units. 3 stories; interior corridors; heated pool, whirlpool. **Dining:** Restaurant, deli; 6:30 am-10:30 pm; $10-$20; cocktails. **Services:** giftshop; area transportation, within 5 mi. **Some Rooms:** whirlpools. **Cards:** AE, DI, DS, JC, MC, VI. **Special Amenities:** Free room upgrade and preferred room (each subject to availability with advanced reservations). *(See color ad below & ad p 119)*

SUPER 8 SUNNYVALE
(AAA) [SAVE]
◆◆
Motel

Phone: (408)244-9000
All Year [CP] 1P: $78 2P/1B: $82 2P/2B: $88 XP: $5
Location: 0.3 mi w of Lawrence Expwy; on SR 82. 1071 E El Camino Real 94087. Fax: 408/244-7354. **Facility:** 62 rooms. Well maintained, comfortable rooms. 3 stories; interior corridors; whirlpool. **Dining:** Restaurant nearby. **Cards:** AE, DS, MC, VI. **Special Amenities:** Free breakfast and free local telephone calls.

THE VAGABOND INN
(AAA) [SAVE]
◆
Motel

Phone: (408)734-4607
All Year [CP] 1P: $75 2P/1B: $80 2P/2B: $87 XP: $5 F18
Location: S off US 101; exit via Mathilda Ave S. 816 Ahwanee Ave 94086. Fax: 408/734-1675. **Terms:** Pets, $5 extra charge. **Facility:** 59 rooms. Convenient location. 1 two-bedroom unit. 2 stories; exterior corridors; heated pool. **Dining:** Coffee shop nearby. **Cards:** AE, CB, DI, DS, MC, VI. **Special Amenities:** Free breakfast and free local telephone calls.

WOODFIN SUITES
◆◆◆
Suite Motel

Rates Subject to Change

Sun-Thurs [BP]	1P: $135	2P/1B: $145	2P/2B: $150	XP: $10
Fri & Sat [BP]	1P: $94	2P/1B: $94	2P/2B: $109	XP: $10

Phone: 408/738-1700

Location: Exit US 101 at Fair Oaks; 2.5 mi w to SR 82E. 635 E El Camino Real 94087. Fax: 408/738-0840. **Terms:** Reserv deposit. **Facility:** 88 rooms. 1- & 2-bedroom suites, most with fireplace. 2 stories; exterior corridors; small heated pool. **Cards:** AE, CB, DI, DS, JC, MC, VI.

WYNDHAM GARDEN HOTEL
◆◆◆
Hotel

Rates Subject to Change

Mon-Thurs 2/1-4/2 & 11/6-1/31	1P: $149	2P/1B: $159	2P/2B: $159	XP: $10
Fri-Sun 4/3-11/5	1P: $79	2P/1B: $79	2P/2B: $79	XP: $10
Mon-Thurs 4/3-11/5	1P: $64	2P/1B: $64	2P/2B: $74	XP: $10
Fri-Sun 2/1-4/2 & 11/6-1/31	1P: $69	2P/1B: $69	2P/2B: $69	XP: $10

Phone: 408/747-0999

Location: Exit US 101 Lawrence Expwy N; at nw quadrant of SR 237 & Lawrence Expwy. 1300 Chesapeake Terr 94089. Fax: 408/745-0759. **Terms:** Reserv deposit. **Facility:** 180 rooms. Very attractive rooms & public areas. 5 stories; interior corridors; heated pool. **Services:** area transportation. **Recreation:** sports court. **Cards:** AE, CB, DI, DS, MC, VI.
(See color ad p 1059)

RESTAURANT

PEZZELLA'S VILLA NAPOLI   **Lunch:** $6-$12   **Dinner:** $7-$17   **Phone:** 408/738-2400
🆎
◆◆◆
Italian

Location: W of Mary Ave. 1025 W El Camino Real 94087. **Hours:** 11 am-2:30 & 5-10:30 pm, Sat from 5 pm. Closed major holidays, 8/10-8/31, Sun & Mon. **Reservations:** suggested. **Features:** semi-formal attire; children's menu; early bird specials; cocktails & lounge; a la carte. Comfortable attractive dining room; seafood, steak, veal & pasta specialties. Family owned for 3 generations. Smoke free premises. **Cards:** AE, CB, DI, MC, VI.

SUN VALLEY—*See Los Angeles p. 641.*

SUSANVILLE—7,300

LODGINGS

BEST WESTERN TRAILSIDE INN
🆎
◆◆◆
Motel

Rates Subject to Change

All Year [CP]	1P: $54- 59	2P/1B: $54- 59	2P/2B: $64- 79	XP: $5	F12

Phone: (530)257-4123

Location: 1.5 mi e on SR 36. 2785 Main St 96130. Fax: 530/257-2665. **Facility:** 85 rooms. 5 units with seating area & whirlpool bath, $84 for up to 2 persons; 2 stories; exterior corridors; swimming pool in summer. **Dining:** 24 hrs; complimentary telephone calls; coffee shop nearby. **Cards:** AE, CB, DI, DS, MC, VI.

HIGH COUNTRY INN
🆎 🆂🅰🆅🅴
◆◆◆
Motel

Phone: (530)257-3450

5/1-10/31 [CP]	1P: $56- 80	2P/1B: $60- 80	2P/2B: $65	XP: $5
2/1-4/30 & 11/1-1/31 [CP]	1P: $50- 75	2P/1B: $55- 75	2P/2B: $60	XP: $5

Location: 1.9 mi e, just off SR 36. 3015 E Riverside Dr 96130. Fax: 530/257-2460. **Facility:** 56 rooms. Large rooms. Few with seating area. 2 stories; interior corridors; whirlpool, pool 5/1-10/31. **Dining:** Restaurant nearby. **All Rooms:** combo or shower baths. **Cards:** AE, CB, DI, DS, MC, VI. **Special Amenities:** Free local telephone calls and free newspaper.

RIVER INN
🆎
◆◆
Motel

Rates Subject to Change

5/1-10/31	1P: $46- 52	2P/1B: $48- 54	2P/2B: $55	XP: $4
2/1-4/30 & 11/1-1/31	1P: $42- 48	2P/1B: $44- 50	2P/2B: $50	XP: $4

Phone: (530)257-6051

Location: 0.8 mi e on SR 36. 1710 Main St 96130. Fax: 530/257-4956. **Terms:** Pets, $5 extra charge. **Facility:** 49 rooms. 2 stories; exterior corridors. **Dining:** Coffee shop nearby. **Cards:** AE, CB, DI, DS, MC, VI.

SUPER 8 MOTEL
🆎 🆂🅰🆅🅴
◆◆
Motel

Phone: (530)257-2782

All Year [CP]	1P: $48- 51	2P/1B: $54- 62	2P/2B: $64	XP: $5

Location: 1.8 mi e; off SR 36. 2975 Johnstonville Rd 96130. Fax: 530/257-4956. **Terms:** Pets, $5 extra charge. **Facility:** 69 rooms. Large rooms. Lower rates in winter; 2 stories; exterior corridors; small pool open 5/1-9/30. **Cards:** AE, CB, DI, DS, MC, VI.

SUTTER CREEK—1,800

LODGINGS

THE FOXES IN SUTTER CREEK
🆎 🆂🅰🆅🅴
◆◆◆
Bed & Breakfast

Phone: (209)267-5882

All Year [BP]	1P: $125- 185	2P/1B: $125- 185

Location: Center. 77 Main St 95685 (PO Box 159). Fax: 209/267-0712. **Terms:** Handling fee imposed. **Facility:** 7 rooms. Property closed 12/25. 2 stories; interior/exterior corridors. **All Rooms:** combo or shower baths. **Some Rooms:** color TV. **Cards:** DS, MC, VI. **Special Amenities:** Free breakfast and free local telephone calls.

GREY GABLES BED & BREAKFAST INN
🆎
◆◆◆
Bed & Breakfast

Guaranteed Rates

Fri & Sat [BP]	1P: $110- 140	2P/1B: $115- 145	2P/2B: $135	XP: $20
Sun-Thurs [BP]	1P: $90- 120	2P/1B: $95- 125	2P/2B: $115	XP: $20

Phone: (209)267-1039

Location: 0.3 mi n on SR 49. 161 Hanford St 95685 (PO Box 1687). Fax: 209/267-0998. **Terms:** Reserv deposit, 7 day notice; handling fee imposed; 2 night min stay, weekends. **Facility:** 8 rooms. An English Country Manor. Some rooms have garden view. 3 stories, no elevator; interior corridors. **Services:** complimentary evening beverages. **All Rooms:** combo or shower baths. **Cards:** AE, DS, MC, VI.

RESTAURANT

RON & NANCY'S PALACE RESTAURANT & SALOON   **Lunch:** $5-$10   **Dinner:** $7-$18   **Phone:** 209/267-1355
🆎
◆◆
Continental

Location: Center on SR 49. 76 Main St 95685. **Hours:** 11:30 am-3 & 5-9 pm. Closed: 11/26. **Reservations:** suggested. **Features:** casual dress; children's menu; cocktails & lounge; minimum charge-$3. Turn-of-the-century decor. Smoke free premises. **Cards:** AE, CB, DI, DS, MC, VI.

SYLMAR—See Los Angeles p. 641.

TAFT—5,900

LODGING

HOLLAND INN & SUITES
Phone: 805/763-5211
(AAA) (SAVE)
All Year   1P: $59   2P/1B: $59   2P/2B: $59   XP: $5   F10
◆◆
Location: At 6th St & Warren, 0.3 mi n of SR 33. 531 Warren St 93268. Fax: 805/763-1536. **Facility:** 22
Motel
rooms. 2 stories; interior corridors; whirlpool. **All Rooms:** combo or shower baths, extended cable TV.
Cards: AE, DI, DS, MC, VI.

TAHOE CITY—See Lake Tahoe Area p. 527.

TAHOE VISTA—See Lake Tahoe Area p. 528.

TAHOMA—See Lake Tahoe Area p. 529.

TARANA—See Los Angeles p. 642.

TEHACHAPI—5,800

LODGINGS

BEST WESTERN MOUNTAIN INN
Phone: (805)822-5591
(AAA) (SAVE)
All Year   1P: $55   2P/1B: $60   2P/2B: $60   XP: $3
◆◆◆
Location: SR 58, exit SR 202, then 1 mi e. 416 W Tehachapi Blvd 93561. Fax: 805/822-6197.
Motel
Terms: Weekly rates; pets. **Facility:** 74 rooms. 2 stories; exterior corridors; heated pool, whirlpool.
Dining: Restaurant nearby. **All Rooms:** extended cable TV. **Cards:** AE, CB, DI, DS, MC, VI.
Special Amenities: Early check-in/late check-out. (See ad below)

TEHACHAPI SUMMIT TRAVELODGE

Phone: (805)823-8000

AAA SAVE   All Year   1P: $46- 53   2P/1B: $53- 60   2P/2B: $53- 60   XP: $7   F18

◆◆◆   **Location:** Adjacent to SR 58 eastbound exit Monolith; westbound exit Tehachapi. 500 Steuber Rd 93581
Motor Inn   (PO Box 670). **Terms:** Pets, in designated rooms. **Facility:** 76 rooms. Landscaped courtyard. 2 stories; inte-
rior corridors; heated pool, whirlpool. **Dining:** Restaurant; 6 am-9 pm, Fri & Sat-9:30 pm; $8-$20; cocktails.
Cards: AE, CB, DI, DS, JC, MC, VI. **Special Amenities: Free local telephone calls and free newspaper.**
(See ad p 1061)

TEMECULA—27,100

LODGINGS

BEST WESTERN COUNTRY INN

Rates Subject to Change   **Phone: (909)676-7378**

AAA   All Year   1P: $60- 73   2P/1B: $65   2P/2B: $73   XP: $5

◆◆◆   **Location:** W side of I-15, exit Winchester Rd, 0.5 mi s. 27706 Jefferson Ave 92590. Fax: 909/699-7995.
Motel   **Facility:** 74 rooms. 2 rms with fireplace, $95-$125; 2 stories; exterior corridors; heated pool, sauna, whirlpool.
Some Rooms: whirlpools. **Cards:** AE, CB, DI, DS, MC, VI.

BEST WESTERN GUEST HOUSE INN

Phone: (909)676-5700

AAA SAVE   Fri & Sat   1P: $79   2P/1B: $79   2P/2B: $84   XP: $5
Sun-Thurs   1P: $56   2P/1B: $60   2P/2B: $67   XP: $5

◆◆   **Location:** Just sw of I-15, Rancho California Rd exit. 41873 Moreno Rd 92590. Fax: 909/694-8520.
Motel   **Terms:** Reserv deposit. **Facility:** 24 rooms. 2 blks n of Old Town Temecula. 2 stories; exterior corridors; small
pool, whirlpool. **Dining:** Restaurant nearby. **Cards:** AE, CB, DI, DS, MC, VI.

BUTTERFIELD INN

Rates Subject to Change   **Phone: (909)676-4833**

AAA   Fri & Sat   1P: $59   2P/1B: $59- 64   2P/2B: $69- 75   XP: $5-10
Sun-Thurs   1P: $42   2P/1B: $47   2P/2B: $52   XP: $5

◆◆   **Location:** W side of I-15, exit SR 79S, then 1 mi n. 28718 Front St 92590. Fax: 909/676-2019.
Motel   **Terms:** Reserv deposit. **Facility:** 39 rooms. At south edge of Old Town Temecula. 2 stories; exterior corridors;
small pool, whirlpool. **Cards:** AE, DS, MC, VI.

COMFORT INN

Phone: (909)699-5888

AAA SAVE   All Year [CP]   1P: $48- 63   2P/1B: $59- 72   2P/2B: $69- 72   XP: $5-10

◆◆   **Location:** West side of I-15, exit Winchester Rd; just n. 27338 Jefferson Ave 92590. Fax: 909/676-3505.
Motel   **Terms:** Small pets only, $10 extra charge. **Facility:** 71 rooms. 3 stories; exterior corridors; whirlpool.
Cards: AE, CB, DI, DS, JC, MC, VI. **Special Amenities: Free breakfast and free newspaper.**

EMBASSY SUITES

◆◆◆   Rates Subject to Change   **Phone: 909/676-5656**

Suite Motor Inn   Sat [BP]   1P: $139   2P/1B: $139   2P/2B: $139   XP: $10   F18
Fri [BP]   1P: $119   2P/1B: $119   2P/2B: $119   XP: $10   F18
Sun-Thurs [BP]   1P: $99   2P/1B: $99   2P/2B: $99   XP: $10   F18

Location: Just e of I-15, exit Rancho California Rd. 29345 Rancho California Rd 92591. Fax: 909/699-3928. **Terms:** Reserv
deposit, 7 day notice. **Facility:** 176 rooms. On spacious grounds. Six 1-room studio units. 4 stories; interior corridors; heated
pool. **Cards:** AE, DI, DS, MC, VI.

LOMA VISTA BED & BREAKFAST

◆◆◆   Rates Subject to Change   **Phone: 909/676-7047**

Bed &   All Year [BP]   1P: $100- 150   2P/1B: $100- 150   XP: $25
Breakfast   **Location:** 4 mi e of I-15, exit Rancho California Rd. 33350 La Serena Way 92591. Fax: 909/676-0077.
Facility: 6 rooms. Hillside location, near area wineries. Charming, individually decorated rooms with view of
surrounding hills & vineyards. 2 stories; interior corridors; smoke free premises. **Cards:** DS, MC, VI.

RAMADA INN

Phone: (909)676-8770

AAA SAVE   All Year [CP]   1P: $55   2P/1B: $60   2P/2B: $60   XP: $5

◆◆   **Location:** W side of I-15, exit SR 79 s, then 0.3 mi. 28980 Front St 92592. Fax: 909/699-3400. **Facility:** 70
Motel   rooms. 2 stories; exterior corridors; whirlpool. **Dining:** Restaurant nearby. **Cards:** AE, CB, DI, DS, MC, VI.
**Special Amenities: Free breakfast and preferred room (subject to availability with advanced
reservations).**

TEMECULA CREEK INN

Phone: (909)694-1000

AAA SAVE   All Year   1P: $125- 165   2P/1B: $125- 165   2P/2B: $125- 165   XP: $20

◆◆◆   **Location:** I-15, use SR 79 south exit, 0.8 mi e to Pala Rd, 0.3 mi se. 44501 Rainbow Canyon Rd 92592.
Resort Motor   Fax: 909/676-3422. **Terms:** Check-in 4 pm; reserv deposit, 3 day notice; package plans. **Facility:** 80 rooms.
Inn   On attractive, tree-shaded grounds overlooking golf course. 2 stories; exterior corridors; heated pool, whirlpool;
2 tennis courts. Fee: 27 holes golf. **Dining:** Temet Grill, see separate listing. **All Rooms:** combo or shower
baths. **Cards:** AE, CB, DI, DS, MC, VI. *(See ad p 231)*

ALWAYS ASK THE HOTEL OPERATOR ABOUT **HOTEL SURCHARGES**
ON LONG DISTANCE CALLS YOU PLACE FROM YOUR ROOM.
DOING SO COULD SAVE YOU AN UNPLEASANT SURPRISE AT CHECKOUT TIME.

TEMECULA VALLEY INN
(AAA) [FYI]
Motel

	Rates Subject to Change			Phone: (909)699-2444
Fri & Sat 5/28-1/31	1P: $95- 105	2P/1B: $95- 105	2P/2B: $95- 105	XP: $10	F18

Fri & Sat 2/1-5/27 &
Sun-Thurs 5/28-1/31   1P: $85- 95   2P/1B: $85- 95   2P/2B: $85- 95   XP: $10   F18
Sun-Thurs 2/1-5/27   1P: $77- 85   2P/1B: $77- 85   2P/2B: $77- 85   XP: $10   F18

Too new to rate. **Location:** 27660 Jefferson Ave 92590. **Terms:** Check-in 4 pm; reserv deposit. **Facility:** 89 rooms. 3 stories; interior corridors; heated pool. **Dining:** Restaurant nearby. **Cards:** AE, CB, DI, DS, MC, VI.

RESTAURANTS

CAFE CHAMPAGNE   **Lunch:** $11-$18   **Dinner:** $18-$26   **Phone:** 909/699-0088
◆◆◆
American   **Location:** 4 mi e of I-15; exit Rancho California Rd; at Thornton Winery. 32575 Rancho California Rd 92591. **Hours:** 11 am-9 pm, Mon 11 am-4 pm. **Reservations:** suggested; weekends. **Features:** casual dress; Sunday brunch; wine only; a la carte. Contemporary California cuisine served in an attractive dining room or outdoor terrace. Hillside location with a nice view of surrounding area. Smoke free premises. **Cards:** AE, DI, DS, MC, VI.

CLAIM JUMPER RESTAURANT   **Lunch:** $8-$23   **Dinner:** $9-$23   **Phone:** 909/694-6887
◆◆
American   **Location:** Just e of I-15, exit Rancho California Rd. 29540 Rancho California Rd 92591. **Hours:** 11 am-10 pm, Thurs-Sat to 11 pm. **Closed:** 7/4, 11/25 & 12/25. **Features:** casual dress; children's menu; salad bar; cocktails & lounge. Western decor. Popular restaurant serving a variety of salads, sandwiches & entrees. Generous portions. Smoke free premises. **Cards:** AE, DI, DS, MC, VI.

COLOMBO'S VINEYARD COUNTRY RESTAURANT & BAKERY Lunch: $6-$9 **Dinner:** $8-$13 **Phone:** 909/695-5390
◆
American   **Location:** 0.3 mi nw of I-15, exit SR 79S. 29000 Front St 92590. **Hours:** 5 am-9 pm, Fri & Sat-10 pm. **Closed:** 11/25 & 12/25. **Features:** casual dress; children's menu; senior's menu; carryout; beer & wine only. Attractive family restaurant. Gift shop. Bakery. Smoke free premises. **Cards:** AE, CB, DI, DS, MC, VI.

MEXICO CHIQUITO   **Lunch:** $4-$11   **Dinner:** $7-$11   **Phone:** 909/676-2933
◆
Mexican   **Location:** Just sw of I-15, exit Rancho California Rd. 41841 Moreno Rd 92590. **Hours:** 11 am-9 pm, Fri-10 pm, Sat 8 am-10 pm, Sun 8 am-9 pm. **Closed:** 7/4 & 11/25. **Features:** casual dress; Sunday brunch; children's menu; carryout; cocktails & lounge. Buffet Mon-Fri 11 am-2 pm, $4.95. Sun brunch 8 am-2 pm, includes Mariachi music. **Cards:** MC, VI.

TEMET GRILL   **Lunch:** $8-$12   **Dinner:** $16-$22   **Phone:** 909/676-5631
◆◆◆
American   **Location:** From I-15, use SR 79 s exit, 0.8 mi e to Pala Rd, 0.3 mi se; at Temecula Creek Inn. 44501 Rainbow Canyon Rd 92592. **Hours:** 6:30 am-9:30 pm, Fri & Sat 6 am-10 pm. **Reservations:** suggested. **Features:** casual dress; Sunday brunch; children's menu; early bird specials; cocktails & lounge; a la carte. Overlooking golf course. Smoke free premises. **Cards:** AE, DI, DS, MC, VI.

TEMPLETON—800

RESTAURANTS

A J SPURS   **Dinner:** $15-$23   **Phone:** 805/434-2700
(AAA)
◆
American   **Location:** 1.3 mi se of 101; exit Main St. 508 Main St 93465. **Hours:** 4 pm-9:30 pm, except some major holidays. **Reservations:** suggested; except Sat. **Features:** casual dress; children's menu; early bird specials; cocktails & lounge. Casual western atmosphere. Large selection of steaks, barbecue seafood & pasta. Large portions. Smoke free premises. **Cards:** AE, DI, DS, MC, VI.

MCPHEE'S GRILL   **Lunch:** $8-$11   **Dinner:** $10-$25   **Phone:** 805/434-3204
(AAA)
◆◆◆
American   **Location:** 1.3 mi se of US 101, exit Main St. 416 Main St 93465. **Hours:** 11:30 am-2 & 5-9:30 pm, Sun champagne brunch 11:30 am-2 pm $12.95. **Closed:** 7/4 & 12/25. **Reservations:** suggested. **Features:** casual dress; Sunday brunch; children's menu; early bird specials; carryout; beer & wine only. Imaginative selection of beef, seafood, poultry, lamb, pasta & pizza. Smoke free premises. **Cards:** MC, VI.

THOUSAND OAKS—104,400

LODGINGS

BEST WESTERN OAKS LODGE   **Phone:** (805)495-7011
(AAA) [SAVE]
◆◆
Motel

All Year [CP]   1P: $53- 74   2P/1B: $57- 78   2P/2B: $57- 78   XP: $4   F17
Location: Just nw of US 101, exit Moorpark Rd, Thousand Oaks Blvd. 12 Conejo Blvd 91360. Fax: 805/495-0647. **Facility:** 76 rooms. Adjacent to shopping plazas. 7 night min stay in 6 efficiencies, $5 extra charge; 2 stories; exterior corridors; whirlpool. **Dining:** Restaurant nearby. **All Rooms:** combo or shower baths. **Cards:** AE, CB, DI, DS, JC, MC, VI. **Special Amenities:** Free breakfast and free newspaper.

DAYS INN   Rates Subject to Change   **Phone:** 805/499-5910
◆◆◆
Motor Inn

All Year   1P: $59   2P/1B: $59   2P/2B: $59   XP: $10   F17
Location: Just se of US 101, exit Ventu Park Rd. 1320 Newbury Rd 91320. Fax: 805/498-5783. **Facility:** 122 rooms. 2 units with bedroom, living room & 2 bathrooms; 3 stories; exterior corridors; heated pool.
Cards: AE, CB, DI, DS, MC, VI.

HOLIDAY INN   Rates Subject to Change   **Phone:** (805)498-6733
(AAA)
◆◆◆
Motor Inn

5/15-9/10   1P: $99- 169   2P/1B: $109- 179   2P/2B: $114- 184   XP: $10   F17
2/1-5/14 & 9/11-1/31   1P: $99- 169   2P/1B: $89- 159   2P/2B: $104- 174   XP: $10   F17
Location: Adjacent northside US 101, exit Ventu Park Rd. 495 N Ventu Park Rd 91360. Fax: 805/498-9789. **Terms:** Reserv deposit; BP avail. **Facility:** 154 rooms. Refrigerator & microwave, $10 extra charge; 2-3 stories; exterior corridors; heated pool, whirlpool. **Dining:** Dining room; 6:30 am-9:30 & 6-9 pm, Sun 6:30-9:30 am; $10-$16; cocktails. **Cards:** AE, CB, DI, DS, MC, VI.

THOUSAND OAKS INN
◆◆◆   All Year [CP]   Guaranteed Rates   Phone: (805)497-3701
Motor Inn   1P: $68- 78 2P/1B: $78- 88 2P/2B: $78- 88 XP: $10   F12
Location: Adjacent to US 101, exit Moorpark Rd, 0.3 mi w. 75 W Thousand Oaks Blvd 91360.
Fax: 805/497-1875. **Facility:** 106 rooms. Adjacent to two shopping plazas. 4 stories; exterior corridors; small heated pool. **Cards:** AE, DI, DS, MC, VI.

THOUSAND OAKS VILLAGE INN
◆◆   All Year [CP]   Rates Subject to Change   Phone: 805/496-0102
Motor   1P: $39- 55 2P/1B: $45- 59 2P/2B: $49- 65 XP: $5   F12
Location: Just ne of US 101, exit Rancho Rd; from SR 23 exit I-10 & Sand Oaks Blvd. 1425 Thousand Oaks Blvd 91362. Fax: 805/494-1295. **Facility:** 60 rooms. 2 stories; exterior corridors. **Cards:** AE, CB, DI, DS, MC, VI.

RESTAURANTS

FABRIZIO'S RISTORANTE   Lunch: $6-$13   Dinner: $12-$23   Phone: 805/496-9033
◆◆◆   **Location:** Just n of US 101, Westlake Blvd exit; in Evergreen Shopping Center. 3731 E Thousand Oaks
Continental   Blvd 91362. **Hours:** 11:30 am-2 & 6-9 pm, Fri-10 pm, Sat 6 pm-10 pm, Sun 6 pm-9 pm. Closed: 1/1 & 12/25. **Reservations:** suggested. **Features:** semi-formal attire; carryout; cocktails & lounge; a la carte. Elegant decor in an intimate setting. A variety of expertly prepared dishes. Smoke free premises. **Cards:** AE, CB, DI, DS, MC, VI.

HUNAN CHINESE RESTAURANT   Lunch: $5-$8   Dinner: $6-$15   Phone: 805/371-0075
◆   **Location:** Corner of Moorpark Rd & Janss St, s end of shopping plaza. 1352 N Moorpark Rd 91360.
Chinese   **Hours:** 11:30 am-9:30 pm, Fri & Sat-10 pm. Closed: 11/25 & 12/25. **Features:** casual dress; carryout; beer & wine only. Authentic Hunan, Cantonese, Mandarin & Szechuan style cooking. Smoke free premises. **Cards:** AE, DS, MC, VI.

RIB RANCH BBQ   Lunch: $7-$18   Dinner: $7-$18   Phone: 805/493-5522
◆◆   **Location:** SR 23, Avenida De Los Arboles exit; then just e. 1712 Avenida De Los Arboles 91362.
American   **Hours:** 11:30 am-9 pm, Fri & Sat-10 pm. Closed: 11/27-12/25. **Features:** casual dress; children's menu; carryout; salad bar; cocktails & lounge. Nice variety of sandwiches, steak, chicken & ribs. Western theme & conference atmosphere. Smoke free premises. **Cards:** MC, VI.

THOUSAND PALMS—1,700   (See map p. 774; index p. 772)

LODGING

RED ROOF INN   Phone: (760)343-1381   **14**
All Year   1P: $49   2P/1B: $56   2P/2B: $56   XP: $4   F18
◆◆   **Location:** Adjacent to I-10, exit Ramon Rd. 72-215 Varner Rd 92276. Fax: 760/343-3082. **Facility:** 114 rooms.
Motel   3 stories; exterior corridors; heated pool, whirlpool. **Dining:** Restaurant nearby. **All Rooms:** extended cable TV. **Cards:** AE, CB, DI, DS, MC, VI. **Special Amenities:** Free local telephone calls.

THREE RIVERS—1,400—See also SEQUOIA AND KINGS CANYON NATIONAL PARKS.

LODGINGS

BEST WESTERN HOLIDAY LODGE   Guaranteed Rates   Phone: (559)561-4119
4/1-10/31 [CP]   1P: $77- 91 2P/1B: $77- 91 2P/2B: $79- 93 XP: $4   F12
11/1-1/31 [CP]   1P: $59- 85 2P/1B: $59- 85 2P/2B: $63- 89 XP: $4   F12
◆◆◆   2/1-3/31 [CP]   1P: $57- 83 2P/1B: $57- 83 2P/2B: $61- 87 XP: $4   F12
Motel   **Location:** 2 mi sw on SR 198. 40105 Sierra Drive 93271 (PO Box 129). Fax: 559/561-3427. **Terms:** Pets. **Facility:** 54 rooms. Adjacent to the Kaweah River. 20 rooms with balcony or patio. 1 two-bedroom unit. 1-2 stories; exterior corridors; whirlpool; playground. **Recreation:** fishing; hiking trails. **All Rooms:** combo or shower baths, extended cable TV. **Cards:** AE, CB, DI, DS, JC, MC, VI.

BUCKEYE TREE LODGE
Phone: (559)561-5900

(AAA) (SAVE)

	4/1-10/31 [CP] Fri & Sat 2/1-3/31 &	1P: $69- 85	2P/1B: $84- 98	2P/2B: $89- 99	XP: $4	
	11/1-1/31 [CP] Sun-Thurs 2/1-3/31 &	1P: $59- 74	2P/1B: $64- 79	2P/2B: $69- 81	XP: $4	
Motel	11/1-1/31 [CP]	1P: $47- 71	2P/1B: $58- 69	2P/2B: $63- 74	XP: $4	

Location: 6 mi ne on SR 198, 0.5 mi sw of entrance to Sequoia National Park. 46000 Sierra Dr 93271. **Terms:** Reserv deposit, 3 day notice; pets, $4 extra charge. **Facility:** 12 rooms. In canyon setting. All rooms with patio or deck overlooking the Kaweah River. 1 efficiency, $8 extra. Two & a half room cottage, $140 for up to 5 persons; 1-2 stories; exterior corridors. **Dining:** Restaurant nearby. **Recreation:** fishing; video rental avail. **All Rooms:** combo or shower baths, extended cable TV. **Cards:** AE, CB, DI, DS, MC, VI. **Special Amenities: Free breakfast and free local telephone calls.**

HOLIDAY INN-EXPRESS
Phone: (559)561-9000

(AAA) (SAVE)

| | 5/1-10/31 [CP] | 1P: $89 | 2P/1B: $99 | 2P/2B: $99 | XP: $10 | F18 |
| | 2/1-4/30 & 11/1-1/31 [CP] | 1P: $69 | 2P/1B: $79 | 2P/2B: $79 | XP: $10 | F18 |

Location: SR 198. 40820 Sierra Dr 93271. Fax: 559/561-9010. **Terms:** Reserv deposit. **Facility:** 62 rooms. 6 whirlpool rms, $139-$149; 2 stories; exterior corridors; heated pool, sauna, whirlpool. **Cards:** AE, CB, DI, DS, JC, MC, VI. **Special Amenities: Free breakfast and free local telephone calls.** *(See color ad p 1064)*

LAZY J RANCH MOTEL
Phone: (559)561-4449

(AAA) (SAVE)

	4/1-10/31 Fri & Sat 2/1-3/31 &	1P: $55- 65	2P/1B: $60- 75	2P/2B: $75- 85	XP: $5	
	11/1-1/31 Sun-Thurs 2/1-3/31 &	1P: $50- 60	2P/1B: $55- 70	2P/2B: $70- 80	XP: $5	
Motel	11/1-1/31	1P: $45- 55	2P/1B: $52- 66	2P/2B: $65- 75	XP: $5	

Location: 2.5 mi sw on SR 198. 39625 Sierra Dr 93271. Fax: 559/561-4889. **Terms:** Reserv deposit, 3 day notice; pets. **Facility:** 18 rooms. Tree shaded spacious grounds in a country setting with pasture and path to river. 3 two-bedroom units. 5 cottages with kitchen, $95-$105 for 2 persons, some with fireplace. 2 two-bedroom, two-bath housekeeping suites $160-$180 for up to 8 persons; 1 story; exterior corridors; playground. **Recreation:** fishing; hiking trails. **All Rooms:** combo or shower baths, extended cable TV. **Some Rooms:** 7 kitchens. **Cards:** AE, DI, DS, MC, VI. IMA. *(See color ad p 286)*

THE RIVER INN
Rates Subject to Change   Phone: 559/561-4367

(AAA)

| | 4/1-10/31 | 1P: $51 | 2P/1B: $55 | 2P/2B: $59 | XP: $4 |
| | 2/1-3/31 & 11/1-1/31 | 1P: $38 | 2P/1B: $42 | 2P/2B: $44 | XP: $4 |

Location: 5 mi ne on SR 198, 1.5 mi sw of entrance to Sequoia National Park. 45176 Sierra Dr 93271. **Terms:** Reserv deposit, 3 day notice; handling fee imposed; pets, $4 extra charge. **Facility:** 10 rooms. Scenic mountain view. Barbecue & picnic areas. 2 stories; exterior corridors; designated smoking area. **All Rooms:** combo or shower baths. **Cards:** AE, CB, DI, DS, JC, MC, VI.

SEQUOIA VILLAGE INN
Phone: (559)561-3652

(AAA) (SAVE)

| | 6/1-10/1 | 1P: $50- 100 | 2P/1B: $61- 106 | 2P/2B: $88- 200 | XP: $5 | F6 |
| | 2/1-5/31 & 10/2-1/31 | 1P: $44- 94 | 2P/1B: $61- 100 | 2P/2B: $80- 189 | XP: $5 | F6 |

Location: 6 mi ne on SR 198; 0.5 mi sw of entrance to Sequoia National Park. 45971 Sierra Dr 93271 (Box 1014). **Terms:** Weekly rates; pets, $4 extra charge. **Facility:** 8 rooms. Cottage & duplex units in a wooded hill-side location, 2 with fireplace. Two 2-story, 3 bedroom chalets. 1 two-bedroom unit, 2 three-bedroom units. 2 stories; exterior corridors; whirlpool. **Dining:** Restaurant nearby. **All Rooms:** combo or shower baths. **Some Rooms:** 6 kitchens. **Cards:** AE, DI, JC, MC, VI. **Special Amenities: Early check-in/late check-out and free room upgrade (subject to availability with advanced reservations).**

SIERRA LODGE
Phone: (559)561-3681

(AAA) (SAVE)

| | All Year | | 2P/1B: $45- 85 | 2P/2B: $52- 85 | XP: $5 |

Location: SR 198, 3 mi sw of entrance to Sequoia National Park. 43175 Sierra Dr 93271. Fax: 559/561-3264. **Terms:** Weekly/monthly rates; pets extra charge. **Facility:** 22 rooms. Many rooms with mountain views. 1- & 2-bedroom suites with efficiency or kitchen, fireplace & private patio or balcony, $85-$195; 1-2 stories; exterior corridors. **Dining:** Restaurant nearby. **Recreation:** barbecue & picnic areas. **All Rooms:** combo or shower baths, extended cable TV. **Cards:** AE, CB, DI, DS, MC, VI. **Special Amenities: Early check-in/late check-out and free local telephone calls.**

RESTAURANTS

THE GATEWAY RESTAURANT
Lunch: $6-$10   Dinner: $11-$25   Phone: 559/561-4133

American

Location: 6 mi ne on SR 198, 0.5 mi sw of entrance to Sequoia National Park. 45978 Sierra Dr 93271. **Hours:** 11 am-9 pm, Sat 8 am-10 pm, Sun 8 am-9 pm. Closed: 12/25 & Mon. **Reservations:** suggested. **Features:** casual dress; children's menu; cocktails & lounge. Lovely mountain setting overlooking river. Variety of fish, poultry, meat & pasta dishes. Outdoor seating on deck above river, weather permitting. **Cards:** AE, DI, DS, MC, VI.

THE WHITE HORSE INN
Dinner: $12-$20   Phone: 559/561-4185

American

Location: 1 mi e on SR 198. 42975 Sierra Dr 93271. **Hours:** 6 pm-9:30 pm, Fri & Sat to 10 pm. Closed: 1/1-1/31, Mon & Tues, Mon-Thurs 10/15-3/31. **Features:** casual dress; children's menu; cocktails & lounge. Popular, long established restaurant. Menu features prime rib, steak, seafood & roast duck. Smoke free premises. **Cards:** AE, DS, MC, VI.

TIBURON—See San Francisco p. 979.

TORRANCE—See Los Angeles p. 642.

TRACY—33,600

LODGINGS

BEST WESTERN LUXURY INN
Phone: (209)832-0271
(AAA) (SAVE)
All Year [CP]   1P: $70   2P/1B: $75   2P/2B: $79 •   XP: $5   F12
◆◆◆
Location: I-205, Central Tracy exit. 811 W Clover Rd 95376. Fax: 209/832-0388. Facility: 59 rooms. 3 stories;
Motel
interior corridors; sauna, whirlpool. All Rooms: combo or shower baths. Cards: AE, CB, DI, DS, JC, MC, VI.
Special Amenities: Free breakfast and free local telephone calls.

PHOENIX LODGE
Phone: 209/835-1335
(AAA) (SAVE)
All Year   1P: $40- 60 2P/1B: $45- 65 2P/2B: $45- 65 XP: $5   F12
Under major renovation. Location: Off I-205, exit at Central Tracy. 3511 N Tracy Blvd 95376.
(FYI)
Fax: 209/835-8041. Terms: Small pets only. Facility: 59 rooms. 3 stories, no elevator; interior corridors.
Motel
Dining: Coffee shop nearby. All Rooms: combo or shower baths. Cards: AE, CB, DI, DS, JC, MC, VI.

TRINIDAD—400

LODGINGS

BISHOP PINE LODGE   Rates Subject to Change   Phone: 707/677-3314
(AAA)
4/1-10/15   1P: $70- 90 2P/1B: $70- 90 2P/2B: $75- 95 XP: $8
◆◆
2/1-3/31 & 10/16-1/31   1P: $60- 90 2P/1B: $60- 90 2P/2B: $65- 85 XP: $8
Cottage
Location: W of US 101; northbound exit Trinidad, then 2 mi n on Patricks Point Dr; southbound exit
Seawood, then 1 mi s on Patricks Point Dr. 1481 Patricks Point Dr 95570. Fax: 707/677-3444.
Terms: Reserv deposit, 7 day notice; pets, $8 extra charge. Facility: 12 rooms. Garden setting among pines
& redwoods. 2 two-bedroom units, $85-$95 for 2 persons. 1-duplex cottage with hot tub, $80 for 2 persons. 6 efficiencies & 4
kitchens; $8 extra; 1 story; interior/exterior corridors; smoke free premises. Recreation: barbecue area, individual barbecues
avail. All Rooms: combo or shower baths. Cards: AE, DS, MC, VI.

SHADOW LODGE   Rates Subject to Change   Phone: (707)677-0532
(AAA)
5/16-9/30   1P: $59- 95 2P/1B: $59- 95 2P/2B: $59- 95 XP: $5
◆
2/1-5/15 & 10/1-1/31   1P: $49- 89 2P/1B: $49- 89 2P/2B: $49- 89 XP: $5
Motel
Location: Exit US 101 at Trinidad; W to Patrick's Point Dr, 0.5 mi n. 687 Patrick's Point Dr 95570 (PO Box
540). Fax: 707/677-0532. Terms: Pets, $10 extra charge. Facility: 10 rooms. 1 story; exterior corridors.
All Rooms: combo or shower baths. Some Rooms: 5 kitchens. Cards: AE, DS, MC, VI.

TURTLE ROCKS OCEANFRONT INN   Rates Subject to Change   Phone: 707/677-3707
(AAA)
5/1-10/31 [BP]   1P: $140- 180 2P/1B: $140- 180   XP: $20
◆◆◆
3/16-4/30 & 11/1-1/31 [BP]   1P: $130- 170 2P/1B: $130- 170   XP: $20
Bed &
2/1-3/15 [BP]   1P: $110- 155 2P/1B: $110- 155   XP: $20
Breakfast
Location: Exit US 101 w at Patrick's Point Dr, 1.5 mi s. 3392 Patrick's Point Dr 95570. Terms: Reserv
deposit, 7 day notice; handling fee imposed. Facility: 6 rooms. Newly constructed traditional gabled house on
a bluff 220 ft above the pacific with views of surrounding rocks & sea stacks. 3 acres. Gourmet breakfast: sau-
sage & egg strada, yeast rolls, fresh baked coffee cake & quiche. 2 stories; interior corridors; designated smoking area; oceanfront. Services: complimentary evening beverages, & dessert. All Rooms: combo or shower baths. Cards: DS, MC, VI.

RESTAURANTS

SEASCAPE RESTAURANT   Lunch: $3-$15   Dinner: $12-$30   Phone: 707/677-3762
◆
Location: At the pier, 0.3 mi w of US 101. 95570. Hours: 7 am-10 pm. Closed: 11/25 & 12/25.
Seafood
Reservations: suggested. Features: No A/C; casual dress; children's menu; early bird specials; beer & wine
only; a la carte. On beach at Trinidad Harbor, rustic atmosphere, view of pier and bay. Fresh seafood
specials, omelets, beef, chicken & pasta. Smoke free premises. Cards: CB, DI, MC, VI.

TRINIDAD BAY EATERY & GALLERY   Lunch: $5-$7   Dinner: $5-$12   Phone: 707/677-3777
◆
Location: Exit US 101 Trinidad, w 0.5 mi. 607 Parker St 95570. Hours: 7 am-2 & 4-8 pm. Closed: 1/1,
American
11/26, 12/25, Mon & Tues. Features: No A/C; casual dress; children's menu; beer & wine only. Smoke free
premises. Cards: MC, VI.

TRINITY CENTER—500

LODGING

COFFEE CREEK RANCH   Rates Subject to Change   Phone: 530/266-3343
(AAA)
All Year Wkly [AP]   1P: $924   2P/1B: $1680   2P/2B:$1680   XP: $760   D17
◆◆◆
Location: 8 mi n of Trinity Center on SR3, 5 mi w on Coffee Creek Rd. (HC 2 Box 4940, 96091).
Cottage
Fax: 530/266-3597. Terms: Daily rates, in Spring, Fall & Winter; MAP avail, in Winter only. Facility: 15 rooms.
Smoking in designated areas. Comfortable cabins scattered above a creek on a forrested hillside, surrounded
by Trinity Alps Wilderness area. 9 two-bedroom units. 1 story; exterior corridors; seasonal pool, indoor whirl-
pool; playground. Dining: Dining room; 7:30 am-9:30, 12:30-1:30 & 5:30-7 pm; wine/beer only. Services: giftshop.
Fee: massage. Recreation: swimming, canoeing, fishing; cross country skiing; hiking trails, sports court, horseback riding in
Spring & Fall, hayrides, bonfires, trap shooting, gold panning, square dancing & line dancing. Fee: horseback riding.
All Rooms: combo or shower baths. Cards: AE, DS, JC, MC, VI.

TRUCKEE—See Lake Tahoe Area p. 530.

TULARE—33,200

LODGINGS

BEST WESTERN TOWN & COUNTRY LODGE   **Phone:** (559)688-7537
(AAA) (SAVE)   All Year [CP]   1P: $54   2P/1B: $54   XP: $6
◆ ◆ ◆   **Location:** Just w of SR 99, Prosperity Ave exit. 1051 N Blackstone 93274. Fax: 559/688-2163. **Terms:** Small
Motor Inn   pets only, $10 extra charge, for dog shows. **Facility:** 93 rooms. Across freeway from factory outlet mall. 2 sto-
              ries; interior corridors; whirlpool. **Dining:** Restaurant nearby. **All Rooms:** combo or shower baths.
(See ad below) **Cards:** AE, DI, DS, MC, VI. **Special Amenities:** Free breakfast and free local telephone calls.

GREEN GABLE INN   **Phone:** (559)686-3432
(AAA) (SAVE)   All Year [CP]   1P: $48   2P/1B: $54   2P/2B: $58   XP: F12
◆ ◆ ◆   **Location:** Just e of SR 99, Prosperity Ave exit. 1010 E Prosperity Ave 93274. Fax: 559/686-3378.
Motel   **Terms:** Reserv deposit; small pets only. **Facility:** 58 rooms. Next to factory outlet shopping mall. 6 one-
              bedroom suites, $80-$90; 3 stories; interior corridors; sauna, whirlpool. **Dining:** Coffee shop nearby.
              All Rooms: combo or shower baths. **Cards:** AE, CB, DI, DS, JC, MC, VI. **Special Amenities:** Free
breakfast and free local telephone calls.

INNS OF AMERICA   **Phone:** (559)686-0985
(AAA) (SAVE)   All Year [CP]   1P: $40   2P/1B: $46   2P/2B: $50   XP: $5
◆   **Location:** Just w of SR 99, Prosperity Ave exit. 1183 N Blackstone St 93274. Fax: 559/688-6814.
Motel   **Terms:** Pets. **Facility:** 90 rooms. Across freeway from outlet shopping. 3 stories; exterior corridors.
              Dining: Restaurant nearby. **Cards:** AE, MC, VI. **Special Amenities:** Free local telephone calls.

RESTAURANTS

APPLE ANNIE'S FAMILY RESTAURANT   **Lunch:** $5-$7   **Dinner:** $7-$10   **Phone:** 559/686-3411
(AAA)   **Location:** Just w of SR 99, Prosperity Ave exit. 1165 N Blackstone St 93274. **Hours:** 6 am-9 pm, Sun-3 pm.
◆   Closed: 1/1, 11/25 & 12/25. **Features:** casual dress; children's menu; carryout; beer & wine only. Popular
American   country style restaurant. Large selection of omelets, sandwiches, salads. Breakfast served all day. Dinner
              entrees available after 4 pm. Features a variety of apple desserts. Smoke free premises. **Cards:** AE, MC, VI.

EL DORADO MEXICAN RESTAURANT   **Lunch:** $6-$10   **Dinner:** $7-$18   **Phone:** 559/686-0061
◆ ◆   **Location:** 0.3 mi e of SR 99, exit SR 137/Central Tulare. 1776 E Tulare Ave 93274. **Hours:** 11 am-9 pm, Fri
Mexican   & Sat-10 pm, Sun-8 pm. Closed: 1/1, 11/25, 12/25 & Mon. **Reservations:** accepted. **Features:** casual dress;
              children's menu; carryout; cocktails & lounge. Long established family owned & operated restaurant with
good selection of Mexican dishes; steaks, prime rib & seafood. Smoke free premises. **Cards:** AE, DS, MC, VI.

V'S   **Lunch:** $7-$13   **Dinner:** $13-$25   **Phone:** 559/684-1264
◆ ◆ ◆   **Location:** Downtown, 1 mi w of SR 99, exit SR 137/Central Tulare. 210 E Tulare Ave 93274. **Hours:** 11
American   am-2 & 5-9 pm, Fri & Sat-10 pm. Closed major holidays & Sun. **Reservations:** suggested.
              Features: children's menu; cocktails & lounge. Elegant dining. Menu features a nice variety of steaks, veal,
pasta & seafood. **Cards:** AE, DS, MC, VI.

TURLOCK—42,200

LODGINGS

BEST WESTERN ORCHARD INN   **Phone:** (209)667-2827
(AAA) (SAVE)   Mon-Sat [EP]   1P: $54- 64   2P/1B: $59- 69   2P/2B: $60- 68 XP: $8   F17
              Sun [CP]   1P: $44   2P/1B: $49   2P/2B: $49   XP: $8   F17
◆ ◆   **Location:** 5 mi n; exit SR 99 at Taylor Rd. 5025 N Golden State Blvd 95380. Fax: 209/634-6588.
Motel   **Terms:** Small pets only, $10 extra charge, $25 dep req. **Facility:** 72 rooms. 15 efficiencies, $10 extra charge;
              4 whirlpool rms, extra charge; 2 stories; exterior corridors; whirlpool. **Dining:** Coffee shop nearby.
All Rooms: combo or shower baths. **Cards:** AE, CB, DI, DS, JC, MC, VI. **Special Amenities:** Early check-in/late
check-out and free local telephone calls. *(See color ad p 1068)*

BEST WESTERN THE GARDENS MOTOR INN
Phone: (209)634-9351
(AAA) (SAVE)   All Year [CP]   1P: $50- 60   2P/1B: $56- 66   2P/2B: $57- 67   XP: $8
◆◆◆   **Location:** Exit SR 99 at Fulkerth Rd, 1 mi e to N Golden State Blvd, just n to Pedras Rd, then right. 1119
Motor Inn   Pedras Rd 95382. Fax: 209/632-0231. **Terms:** Reserv deposit; pets. **Facility:** 94 rooms. Suburban setting.
Large rooms & attractive landscaping. Suites, $90-$100 up to 2 persons; 2 stories; exterior corridors.
Dining: Coffee shop nearby. **All Rooms:** combo or shower baths. **Cards:** AE, CB, DI, DS, JC, MC, VI.
Special Amenities: Free breakfast and free newspaper.   (icons)

COMFORT INN-TURLOCK
Phone: (209)668-3400
(AAA) (SAVE)   All Year [CP]   1P: $42- 70   2P/1B: $55- 76   2P/2B: $55- 76   XP: $7   D15
◆◆   **Location:** Exit Hwy 99, Lander exit. 200 W Glenwood Ave 95380. Fax: 209/668-0144. **Terms:** Reserv
Motel   deposit; small pets only. **Facility:** 92 rooms. Rural setting. Large comfortable rooms. 2 stories; exterior corri-
dors; whirlpool. **Dining:** Coffee shop nearby. **All Rooms:** combo or shower baths. **Cards:** AE, CB, DI, DS,
JC, MC, VI.   (icons)

TUSTIN—50,700   (See map p. 294; index p. 293)

RESTAURANTS

THE BARN RESTAURANT & SALOON
Lunch: $6-$9   Dinner: $9-$21   Phone: 714/259-0115   (110)
◆   **Location:** 0.5 mi e of SR 55, exit Edinger Ave. 14982 Red Hill Ave 92780. **Hours:** 11:30 am-2 & 5-9 pm,
American   Fri-10 pm, Sat 10 am-2:30 & 5-9 pm. Closed major holidays. **Reservations:** suggested; weekends.
Features: casual dress; Sunday brunch; children's menu; early bird specials; cocktails & lounge;
entertainment. Large restaurant with several dining areas. Casual western atmosphere. Smoke free premises. **Cards:** AE,
DI, DS, MC, VI.   (icon)

THE BLACK SHEEP BISTRO
Dinner: $14-$26   Phone: 714/544-6060   (113)
◆◆   **Location:** 303 El Camino Real at 3rd 92780. **Hours:** 5:30-9:30 pm. Closed major holidaysSun & Mon.
Ethnic   **Reservations:** suggested. **Features:** casual dress; carryout; beer & wine only. Intimate restaurant serving an
imaginative selection of French, Spanish, Italian & Mediterranean cuisine. Smoke free premises. **Cards:** AE,
DS, MC, VI.   (icon)

MIMI'S CAFE
Lunch: $7-$13   Dinner: $7-$13   Phone: 714/544-5522   (111)
◆◆   **Location:** Adjacent to SR 55. 17231 E 17th St 92780. **Hours:** 6 am-11 pm. Closed: 11/25 & 12/25.
American   **Features:** casual dress; children's menu; beer & wine only. Attractive restaurant with French cafe decor. Nice
selection of salads, sandwiches & entrees. Patio dining avail. Smoke free premises. **Cards:** AE, MC, VI.   (icon)

NIEUPORT 17 RESTAURANT
Lunch: $8-$14   Dinner: $18-$24   Phone: 714/731-5130   (112)
◆◆◆   **Location:** In Plaza Lafayette, 1 mi e of SR 55, exit 4th St/Irvine Blvd. 13051 Newport Ave at Irvine Blvd
American   92780. **Hours:** 11 am-10 pm, Fri-11 pm, Sat 5 pm-11 pm, Sun 5 pm-10 pm. Closed major holidays.
Reservations: suggested. **Features:** semi-formal attire; children's menu; cocktails & lounge; entertainment;
valet parking. Decorated with authentic aviation memorabilia. Nice selection of seafood, chicken, beef & veal. Smoke free
premises. **Cards:** AE, DI, MC, VI.   (icon)

TWAIN HARTE—1,400

LODGINGS

ELDORADO MOTEL
Phone: 209/586-4479
(AAA) (SAVE)   All Year   1P: $45   2P/1B: $54   2P/2B: $65   XP: $5
◆   **Location:** Exit SR 108 via Twain Harte; corner Twain Harte Dr & Blackhawk Dr, opposite golf course. 22678
Motel   Blackhawk Dr 95383 (PO Box 368). **Terms:** Reserv deposit, 3 day notice; pets, $10 dep req. **Facility:** 10
rooms. Rustic decor. Comfortable rooms. 2 rms with kitchens, $10 extra charge; 1 story; exterior corridors.
All Rooms: shower baths. **Cards:** DS, MC, VI.   (icons)

MCCAFFREY HOUSE B & B INN
Guaranteed Rates   Phone: (209)586-0757
◆◆◆   All Year [BP]   1P: $95- 140   2P/1B: $95- 140   2P/2B: $110- 140   XP: $10
Bed &   **Location:** 0.5 mi on SR 108; just beyond 4000' elevation marker. 23251 Highway 108 95383 (PO Box 67).
Breakfast   Fax: 209/586-3689. **Terms:** Reserv deposit, 5 day notice; handling fee imposed. **Facility:** 7 rooms. Country Inn
nesteled in a quiet forest setting. 3 stories, no elevator; interior corridors. **Cards:** AE, MC, VI.   (icons)

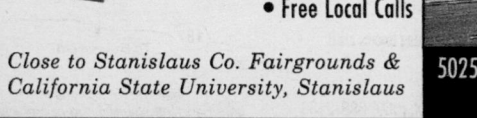

WILDWOOD INN MOTOR LODGE

Phone: (209)586-2900

AAA SAVE
◆◆
Motel

| | | 1P: | $59 | 2P/1B: | $59 | 2P/2B: | $59 | XP: | $6 | F6 |
5/25-9/15
2/1-5/24 & 9/16-1/31   1P: $50   2P/1B: $50   2P/2B: $50
Location: Center. 22960 Meadow Dr 95383 (PO Box 457). Fax: 209/586-1408. **Terms:** Reserv deposit, 3 day notice; handling fee imposed. **Facility:** 21 rooms. Comfortable rooms. 2 stories; exterior corridors. **All Rooms:** shower baths. **Cards:** MC, VI.

🚫 📺 🚗 ✕

RESTAURANT

KELLY'S KITCHEN

AAA
◆
American

Dinner: $10-$15   Phone: 209/586-3283

Location: 3 mi e on SR 108, at Sugar Pine; 14 mi e of Sonora. 24181 SR 108 95383. **Hours:** 4 pm-10 pm, Sun noon-10 pm. Closed: Tues & 12/25. **Reservations:** suggested. **Features:** children's menu; cocktails & lounge; a la carte. Family restaurant with mountain view. Varied menu; specializing in homemade pies. Patio dining, weather permitting. Smoke free premises. **Cards:** MC, VI.

✕

TWENTYNINE PALMS—11,800

LODGINGS

BEST WESTERN GARDENS INN & SUITES

Phone: (760)367-9141

AAA SAVE
◆◆◆
Motel

breakfast.

All Year [CP]   1P: $69- 109   2P/1B: $69- 109   2P/2B: $74- 109   XP: $5   F12
Location: 1.8 mi w on SR 62. 71487 Twentynine Palms Hwy 92277. Fax: 760/367-2584. **Facility:** 84 rooms. Nicely furnished rooms. 12 one-bedroom suites with efficiency, 2 suites with whirlpool $84-$140; 1-2 stories; interior/exterior corridors; heated pool, whirlpool. **All Rooms:** extended cable TV. **Some Rooms:** 12 efficiencies. **Cards:** AE, CB, DI, DS, MC, VI. **Special Amenities:** Early check-in/late check-out and free

🚫 🔄 📞 📺 🛏 🚗 🔒 ✕

CIRCLE 'C'

Phone: (760)367-7615

◆◆
Motel

Rates Subject to Change

All Year [CP]   1P: $75   2P/1B: $85   2P/2B: $85   XP: $10   D18
Location: 1.5 mi w on SR 62, just n. 6340 El Rey Ave 92277. Fax: 760/361-0247. **Terms:** Reserv deposit. **Facility:** 12 rooms. Nicely landscaped pool area. 1 story; exterior corridors; heated pool. **All Rooms:** kitchens. **Cards:** AE, CB, DI, DS, JC, MC, VI.

(ASK) 🚫 🛒 🔄 🐾 (VCR) 🚗 ✕

HOMESTEAD INN BED & BREAKFAST

Phone: 760/367-0030

AAA SAVE
◆◆
Historic Bed
& Breakfast

2/1-7/5 & 10/1-1/31 [BP]   1P: $70- 110   2P/1B: $95- 150   2P/2B: $105- 135   XP: $15
Location: 1 mi n of SR 62 on Adobe Rd, then 0.6 mi e. 74153 Two Mile Rd 92277. Fax: 760/367-1108. **Terms:** Open 2/1-7/5 & 10/1-1/31; reserv deposit, 7 day notice; weekly rates; 2 night min stay, weekends. **Facility:** 7 rooms. Historic home built in 1928. In a quiet residential desert location. Friendly, home-like atmosphere; rock fountain & cactus gardens. 2 whirlpool rms with private patio, $125-$150; interior/exterior corridors; smoke free premises. **Dining:** Wine/beer only. **Services:** Fee: massage. **Recreation:** horseshoe pits. Fee: horseback riding. **All Rooms:** combo or shower baths. **Some Rooms:** color TV, whirlpools. **Cards:** AE, JC, MC, VI.

🚫 🔄 ✕ (CTV) (VCR) 📺 🛏 🚗 🔒 ✕

UKIAH—14,600

LODGINGS

BEST WESTERN INN

Phone: (707)462-8868

AAA SAVE
◆◆◆
Motel

5/1-9/30 [CP]   1P: $55- 65   2P/1B: $58- 68   2P/2B: $65- 75   XP: $5   F12
2/1-4/30 & 10/1-1/31 [CP]   1P: $48- 58   2P/1B: $52- 62   2P/2B: $58- 68   XP: $5   F12
Location: E off US 101 bypass; exit Talmage off-ramp. 601 Talmage Rd 95482. Fax: 707/468-9043. **Terms:** Reserv deposit. **Facility:** 40 rooms. 2 stories; exterior corridors; small pool, whirlpool. **Cards:** AE, CB, DI, DS, MC, VI. **Special Amenities:** Free breakfast and free local telephone calls.

🚫 🔄 📞 🐾 📺 🔒 ✕

DAYS INN

Phone: (707)462-7584

AAA SAVE
◆◆
Motel

6/1-9/30 [CP]   1P: $59- 69   2P/1B: $65- 79   2P/2B: $75- 85   XP: $5-10   F12
2/1-5/31 & 10/1-1/31 [CP]   1P: $49- 59   2P/1B: $55- 69   2P/2B: $65- 75   XP: $5-10   F12
Location: Exit US 101 at N State St, 0.5 mi s on N State St. 950 N State St 95482. Fax: 707/463-1218. **Terms:** Small pets only, $5 extra charge. **Facility:** 55 rooms. 2 stories; exterior corridors. **Cards:** AE, DI, DS, MC, VI. **Special Amenities:** Free breakfast and free local telephone calls.

🚫 🛒 🔄 📺 ✕

DISCOVERY INN   Phone: (707)462-8873
AAA SAVE
| | 5/1-9/30 | 1P: | $58- 68 | 2P/1B: | $62- 74 | 2P/2B: | $68- 80 | XP: $6 | F12 |
| | 2/1-4/30 & 10/1-1/31 | 1P: | $48- 58 | 2P/1B: | $56- 68 | 2P/2B: | $60- 72 | XP: $6 | F12 |

◆◆◆   **Location:** 1.5 mi n on US 101 business rt; exit US 101 via N State St. 1340 N State St 95482.
Motel   **Fax:** 707/462-1249. **Facility:** 177 rooms. Some rooms with private balcony. 6 two-bedroom units. 2 stories; exterior corridors; 4 indoor whirlpools. **Dining:** Coffee shop nearby. **All Rooms:** combo or shower baths. **Some Rooms:** 7 kitchens. **Cards:** AE, CB, DI, DS, MC, VI. **Special Amenities:** Free local telephone calls and free room upgrade (subject to availability with advanced reservations). (See ad p 1069)

ECONOMY INN   Phone: (707)462-8611
AAA SAVE
| | 5/1-10/14 | 1P: | $46- 50 | 2P/1B: | $50- 58 | 2P/2B: | $52- 58 | XP: $6 | F12 |
| | 2/1-4/30 & 10/15-1/31 | 1P: | $39- 44 | 2P/1B: | $42- 48 | 2P/2B: | $44- 48 | XP: $6 | F12 |

◆◆   **Location:** 2 blks s on US 101 business rt; northbound exit US 101W via Perkins off-ramp, southbound exit
Motel   Central off-ramp. 406 S State St 95482. **Fax:** 707/468-9476. **Terms:** Reserv deposit. **Facility:** 40 rooms. 1 two-bedroom unit. 2 stories; exterior corridors. **Dining:** Restaurant nearby. **All Rooms:** shower baths. **Cards:** AE, CB, DI, DS, MC, VI. **Special Amenities:** Free local telephone calls and free room upgrade (subject to availability with advanced reservations).

HOLIDAY INN EXPRESS   Guaranteed Rates   Phone: 707/462-5745
AAA
| | 5/1-9/30 [CP] | 1P: | $65- 89 | 2P/1B: | $65- 89 | 2P/2B: | $65- 89 | XP: $5 | F18 |
| | 2/1-4/30 & 10/1-1/31 [CP] | 1P: | $55- 79 | 2P/1B: | $55- 79 | 2P/2B: | $55- 79 | XP: $5 | F18 |

◆◆◆   **Location:** US 101, exit N State St. 1720 N State St 95482. **Fax:** 707/462-8804. **Terms:** Reserv deposit.
Motor Inn **Facility:** 55 rooms. 2 stories; exterior corridors; heated pool, whirlpool. **Dining:** Restaurant nearby. **Some Rooms:** whirlpools. **Cards:** AE, DS, MC, VI.

RODEWAY INN   Phone: (707)462-2906
AAA SAVE
| | All Year [CP] | 1P: | $38- 49 | 2P/1B: | $45- 61 | 2P/2B: | $51- 65 | XP: $6 | F10 |

◆   **Location:** Exit US 101 at Talmage Rd off-ramp, 0.5 mi w. 1050 S State St 95482. **Fax:** 707/462-3040.
Motel   **Terms:** Pets, $5-$10 extra charge. **Facility:** 44 rooms. 2 stories; exterior corridors. **Dining:** Restaurant nearby. **All Rooms:** combo or shower baths. **Cards:** AE, DS, MC, VI. **Special Amenities:** Early check-in/late check-out and free breakfast.

SUNRISE INN   Rates Subject to Change   Phone: 707/462-6601
AAA
| | 6/1-9/30 | 1P: | $40 | 2P/1B: | $44 | 2P/2B: | $50 | XP: $5 |
| | 2/1-5/31 & 10/1-1/31 | 1P: | $35 | 2P/1B: | $38 | 2P/2B: | $45 | XP: $5 |

◆   **Location:** Exit US 101 at Gobbi St, 0.5 mi w to S State, just n. 650 S State St 95482. **Fax:** 707/462-6009.
Motel   **Facility:** 24 rooms. 1 story; exterior corridors. **Dining:** Restaurant nearby. **All Rooms:** combo or shower baths. **Cards:** AE, DS, MC, VI.

SUPER 8 MOTEL   Phone: (707)462-6657
AAA SAVE
	7/1-9/30 [CP]	1P:	$52	2P/1B:	$56	2P/2B:	$66	XP: $6	F12
	5/1-6/30 [CP]	1P:	$48	2P/1B:	$54	2P/2B:	$58	XP: $6	F12
	2/1-4/30 & 10/1-1/31 [CP]	1P:	$40	2P/1B:	$46	2P/2B:	$52	XP: $6	F12

◆   **Location:** Exit US 101 at Talmage exit, 1 mi w. 1070 S State St 95482. **Fax:** 707/468-8665. **Terms:** Reserv
Motel   deposit; pets, $5 extra charge, $10 dep req. **Facility:** 31 rooms. Exterior corridors. **Dining:** Restaurant nearby. **Cards:** AE, DI, DS, MC, VI.

VICHY SPRINGS RESORT   Rates Subject to Change   Phone: (707)462-9515
◆◆◆
| | All Year [BP] | 1P: | $105- 170 | 2P/1B: | $140- 205 | 2P/2B: | $140- 205 | XP: $35 |

Historic Bed **Location:** 3 mi e; exit US 101 via e Perkins St/Vichy Springs Rd. 2605 Vichy Springs Rd 95482.
& Breakfast **Fax:** 707/462-9516. **Terms:** Reserv deposit, 7 day notice; handling fee imposed. **Facility:** 19 rooms. Restored buildings circa 1854. Few smaller units in original bldg. 2 two-bedroom units. 1 story; exterior corridors; heated pool. **Recreation:** hiking trails. **All Rooms:** combo or shower baths. **Some Rooms:** 2 kitchens. **Cards:** AE, CB, DI, DS, JC, MC, VI.

WESTERN TRAVELER MOTEL   Phone: (707)468-9167
AAA SAVE
| | All Year | 1P: | $36- 52 | 2P/1B: | $42- 55 | 2P/2B: | $49- 59 | XP: $5 | F12 |

◆◆   **Location:** Exit US 101 via Gobbi St W. 693 S Orchard Ave 95482. **Fax:** 707/468-8268. **Terms:** Reserv
Motel   deposit; small pets only, $5 extra charge. **Facility:** 56 rooms. 2 two-bedroom units. 2 family units $75; 9/16-6/14 $60 for up to 5 persons. 2 stories; exterior corridors; whirlpool. **Dining:** Coffee shop nearby. **Cards:** AE, CB, DI, DS, MC, VI. **Special Amenities:** Free local telephone calls and preferred room (subject to availability with advanced reservations).

UNION CITY—53,800

LODGINGS

BEST WESTERN WELLEX INN   Phone: (510)475-0600
AAA SAVE
| | All Year [CP] | 1P: | $74- 84 | 2P/1B: | $74- 84 | 2P/2B: | $84 | XP: $6 | F12 |

◆◆   **Location:** Exit I-880 Alvarado-Niles Rd W. 31140 Alvarado-Niles Rd 94587. **Fax:** 510/475-0910. **Facility:** 77
Motel   rooms. Central pool & spa area. 4 stories; interior corridors; whirlpool. **Cards:** AE, CB, DI, DS, JC, MC, VI. **Special Amenities:** Free breakfast and free local telephone calls.

RADISSON HOTEL- UNION CITY/FREMONT   Rates Subject to Change   Phone: 510/489-2200
◆◆◆
| | All Year | 1P: | $169 | 2P/1B: | $169 | 2P/2B: | $169 | XP: $15 |

Motor Inn **Location:** Exit I-880 at Alvarado-Niles Rd, just e. 32083 Alvarado-Niles Rd 94587. **Fax:** 510/489-7642. **Facility:** 271 rooms. 6 stories; interior corridors; racquetball court. **Services:** giftshop. **All Rooms:** combo or shower baths. **Cards:** AE, CB, DI, DS, JC, MC, VI.

UNIVERSAL CITY—See Los Angeles p. 644.

UPLAND—63,400

RESTAURANTS

CAFE PROVENCAL **Lunch:** $7-$12 **Dinner:** $10-$18 **Phone:** 909/608-7100
◆◆ **Location:** Just w of San Antonio Ave. 967 W Foothill Blvd 91784. **Hours:** 11 am-2 & 5-9:30 pm, Fri & Sat-10
Continental pm. Closed major holidays & Sun. **Reservations:** suggested. **Features:** casual dress; cocktails; a la carte. A
charming restaurant serving a nice variety of Southern French cuisine. Also, a selection of wood oven pizza.
Outdoor patio dining avail. Smoke free premises. **Cards:** AE, DI, DS, MC, VI. ⊠

CHARLEY'S GRILL **Dinner:** $9-$18 **Phone:** 909/982-4513
◆◆ **Location:** Just w of Central Ave. 2035 W Foothill Blvd 91786. **Hours:** 5 pm-9 pm, Fri & Sat-10 pm, Sun
American from 4:30 pm-9 pm. Closed major holidays. **Reservations:** suggested. **Features:** casual dress; children's
menu; cocktails & lounge. Old English decor. Features prime rib, steak & seafood. Smoke free premises.
Cards: AE, DS, MC, VI. ⊠

MIMI'S CAFE **Lunch:** $6-$13 **Dinner:** $8-$13 **Phone:** 909/982-3038
◆◆ **Location:** 1 mi n of I-10, exit Mountain Ave. 370 N Mountain Ave 91786. **Hours:** 7 am-11 pm. Closed: 12/25.
American **Features:** casual dress; children's menu; health conscious menu; beer & wine only. Colorful French cafe
VI. atmosphere. Nice selection of sandwiches, salad, entrees & dessert. Smoke free premises. **Cards:** AE, MC,
⊠

UPPER LAKE—1,000

LODGING

SUPER 8 MOTEL **Phone:** (707)275-0888
(AAA) [SAVE] Fri & Sat [CP] 1P: $55- 80 2P/1B: $65- 85 2P/2B: $65- 85 XP: $10
◆ Sun-Thurs [CP] 1P: $50- 70 2P/1B: $55- 70 2P/2B: $58- 70 XP: $10
Motel **Location:** 0.5 mi e of jct SR 29. 450 E Hwy 20 95485 (PO Box 67). Fax: 707/275-2566. **Terms:** Reserv
deposit, 3 day notice. **Facility:** 34 rooms. Approximately 4 mi from the lake. 4 large units with seating area,
wet bar, refrigerator, microwave & whirlpool, $90 for up to 2 persons; 2 stories; exterior corridors; small pool,
whirlpool. **Cards:** AE, CB, DI, DS, JC, MC, VI. **Special Amenities: Free local telephone calls.** ⊠ ⊠ ⊟ ⊠ ⊿

VACAVILLE—71,500

LODGINGS

BEST WESTERN HERITAGE INN **Phone:** (707)448-8453
(AAA) [SAVE] All Year [CP] 1P: $66- 70 2P/1B: $66- 70 2P/2B: $75- 80 XP: $5 F12
◆◆ **Location:** Exit I-80 Monte Vista N. 1420 E Monte Vista Ave 95688. Fax: 707/447-8649. **Terms:** Reserv
Motel deposit; pets, $35 dep req. **Facility:** 41 rooms. 2 stories; exterior corridors. **Dining:** Coffee shop nearby.
Cards: AE, CB, DI, DS, MC, VI. **Special Amenities: Free breakfast and free local telephone calls.**
⊠ ⊠ ⊠ ⊪ ⊠ ⊟ ⊠

COURTYARD BY MARRIOTT Rates Subject to Change **Phone:** 707/451-9000
◆◆◆ Mon-Thurs 1P: $89- 109 2P/1B: $89- 109 2P/2B: $89- 109 XP: $10 F17
Motel Fri-Sun 1P: $79- 99 2P/1B: $79- 99 2P/2B: $79- 99 XP: $10 F17
Location: Eastbound exit Nut Tree Pkwy, s of & adjacent to I-80; westbound exit Monte Vista. 120 Nut Tree
Pkwy 95687. Fax: 707/449-3952. **Facility:** 127 rooms. 6 whirlpool rms. 4 two-room suites, $109; 2 stories;
interior corridors. **All Rooms:** combo or shower baths. **Cards:** AE, CB, DI, DS, MC, VI.
⊠ ⊠ ⊠ ⊪ ⊠ ⊠ ⊠ ⊟ ⊠

QUALITY INN-VACAVILLE **Phone:** (707)446-8888
(AAA) [SAVE] All Year 1P: $54 2P/1B: $99 XP: $5 F
◆◆ **Location:** S side of I-80; exit Leisure Town Rd, just e of I-505 interchange. 950 Leisure Town Rd 95687.
Motel Fax: 707/449-0109. **Facility:** 120 rooms. Large rooms. 2 stories; exterior corridors; whirlpool.
Dining: Restaurant nearby. **All Rooms:** combo or shower baths. **Cards:** AE, CB, DI, DS, MC, VI.
Special Amenities: Free breakfast and free local telephone calls.
⊠ ⊠ ⊠ ⊠ ⊪ ⊠ ⊠ ⊠ ⊿

VACAVILLE SUPER 8 Rates Subject to Change **Phone:** 707/449-8884
◆◆ 2/1-3/31 & 11/1-1/31 1P: $41 2P/1B: $46 2P/2B: $55 XP: $5 F12
Motel 4/1-10/31 1P: $46 2P/1B: $49 2P/2B: $54 XP: $5 F12
Location: N of & adjacent to I-80, exit Monte Vista Ave. 101 Allison Ct 95688. Fax: 707/449-9132.
Facility: 53 rooms. Quiet location. 3 stories; interior corridors; small pool. **Cards:** AE, CB, DI, DS, MC, VI.
⊠ ⊠ ⊠ ⊠ ⊠

RESTAURANTS

BLACK OAK RESTAURANT **Lunch:** $5-$8 **Dinner:** $6-$13 **Phone:** 707/448-1311
(AAA) **Location:** S side of I-80, at jct I-505. 320 Orange Dr 95687. **Hours:** 6 am-11 pm. **Features:** casual dress;
children's menu; beer & wine only. Booth seating, casual atmosphere, basic but varied menu. Popular
◆◆ roadside restaurant. **Cards:** AE, MC, VI. ⊠
American

VACA JOE'S RESTAURANT **Lunch:** $6-$10 **Dinner:** $8-$15 **Phone:** 707/447-4633
◆◆ **Location:** At Quality Inn-Vacaville. 980 Leisure Town Rd 95687. **Hours:** 7 am-9:30 pm, Fri & Sat-10 pm,
Italian Sun til 9 pm. Closed major holidaysMon. **Reservations:** suggested. **Features:** casual dress; children's
menu; cocktails & lounge; a la carte. Varied menu, seafood specialties. **Cards:** AE, DI, DS, MC, VI. ⊠

VALENCIA—See Los Angeles p. 645.

VALLEJO—109,200

LODGINGS

COMFORT INN
Phone: (707)648-1400

AAA SAVE | 4/1-9/3 [CP] | 1P: $59- 89 | 2P/1B: $65- 99 | 2P/2B: $75- 99 | XP: $10 | F18

◆◆ Motor Inn
| 2/1-3/31 [CP] | 1P: $49- 74 | 2P/1B: $54- 79 | 2P/2B: $64- 75 | XP: $10 | F18
| 9/4-1/31 [CP] | 1P: $49- 74 | 2P/1B: $54- 79 | 2P/2B: $64- 75 | XP: $10 | F18

Location: Exit I-80 Columbus Pkwy 0.5 mi e; 0.3 mi s on Admiral Callaghan Ln. 1185 Admiral Callaghan Ln 94591. Fax: 707/552-8623. **Terms:** Reserv deposit; handling fee imposed. **Facility:** 80 rooms. 8 whirlpool rms, extra charge; 2 stories; interior corridors; sauna, whirlpool. **Dining:** Restaurant nearby. **Cards:** AE, CB, DI, DS, JC, MC, VI. **Special Amenities:** Free breakfast and free local telephone calls.

DAYS INN
Rates Subject to Change   Phone: (707)554-8000

AAA ◆ Motel
Fri & Sat 7/1-9/7 [CP]	1P: $89	2P/1B: $89	2P/2B: $99
Fri & Sat 5/1-6/30, Sun-Thurs 7/1-9/7 & Fri & Sat 9/8-10/31 [CP]	1P: $79	2P/1B: $79	2P/2B: $89
Fri & Sat 2/1-4/30, Sun-Thurs 5/1-6/30 & 9/8-10/31 [CP]	1P: $69	2P/1B: $69	2P/2B: $79
Sun-Thurs 2/1-4/30 & 11/1-1/31 [CP]	1P: $59	2P/1B: $59	2P/2B: $69

Location: I-80 exit Redwood St, 0.5 mi s of Marine World on w side of freeway. 300 Fairgrounds Dr 94590. Fax: 707/559-8288. **Facility:** 49 rooms. 3 stories; exterior corridors. **Dining:** Coffee shop nearby. **Some Rooms:** kitchen. **Cards:** AE, DI, DS, MC, VI.

HOLIDAY INN-MARINE WORLD AFRICA USA
Rates Subject to Change   Phone: 707/644-1200

◆◆◆ Motor Inn
| 5/24-9/30 | 1P: $90- 125 | 2P/1B: $90- 125 | 2P/2B: $90- 125 | XP: $10 |
| 2/1-5/23 & 10/1-1/31 | 1P: $64- 79 | 2P/1B: $64- 79 | 2P/2B: $64- 79 | XP: $10 |

Location: N of I-80, exit Marine World Pkwy, SR 37 0.3 mi. 1000 Fairgrounds Dr 94589. Fax: 707/643-7011. **Facility:** 164 rooms. Opposite entrance to theme park. 5 stories; interior corridors. **Cards:** AE, DI, DS, JC, MC, VI.

QUALITY INN
Phone: (707)643-1061

AAA SAVE ◆◆ Motel
| 5/1-10/31 [CP] | 1P: $48- 66 | 2P/1B: $52- 70 | 2P/2B: $68- 72 | XP: $6 |
| 2/1-4/30 & 11/1-1/31 [CP] | 1P: $44- 52 | 2P/1B: $48- 66 | 2P/2B: $58- 68 | XP: $6 |

Location: E off & adjacent to I-80; exit via Tennessee St-Mare Island. 44 Admiral Callaghan Ln 94591. Fax: 707/643-4719. **Terms:** Pets, $10 extra charge. **Facility:** 78 rooms. Some smaller rooms. 2 stories; exterior corridors. **Dining:** Coffee shop nearby. **Cards:** AE, DS, MC, VI. **Special Amenities:** Free breakfast and free local telephone calls. Quality Inns.

RAMADA INN
Rates Subject to Change   Phone: (707)643-2700

◆◆ Motel
| All Year [CP] | 1P: $76- 109 | 2P/1B: $86- 119 | 2P/2B: $81- 119 | XP: $10 | F18

Location: Exit I-80 s at Columbus Pkwy; 0.5 mi w on Admiral Callaghan Ln. 1000 Admiral Callaghan Ln 94591. Fax: 707/642-1148. **Terms:** Reserv deposit. **Facility:** 130 rooms. 1 whirlpool rm, extra charge; 3 stories; exterior corridors; heated pool. **Services:** area transportation. **Cards:** AE, CB, DI, DS, JC, MC, VI. *(See color ad opposite title page)*

WINDMILL INN AT MARINE WORLD AFRICA USA
Guaranteed Rates   Phone: 707/554-9655

◆◆◆ Motel
| 5/21-9/14 [CP] | | 2P/1B: $75- 95 | 2P/2B: $75- 95 | XP: $10 | F17
| 2/1-5/20 & 9/15-1/31 [CP] | | 2P/1B: $59- 70 | 2P/2B: $59- 70 | XP: $10 | F17

Location: Exit I-80 at SR 37 N, 0.3 mi w. 1596 Fairgrounds Dr 94589. Fax: 707/554-3951. **Facility:** 116 rooms. 3 stories; interior corridors. **Services:** area transportation. **Cards:** AE, DI, DS, MC, VI. *(See color ad below)*

VAN NUYS—See Los Angeles p. 647.

VENICE—See Los Angeles p. 648.

VENTURA—92,600

LODGINGS

BELLA MAGGIORE INN Phone: (805)652-0277
All Year [BP] 1P: $75- 150 2P/1B: $75- 150 2P/2B: $75- 150 XP: $10
Location: 0.3 mi n of US 101, northbound exit California St (Downtown); southbound exit Main St. 67 S
California St 93001. Fax: 805/648-5670. **Terms:** Reserv deposit; handling fee imposed. **Facility:** 24 rooms.
Renovated historical landmark built in 1926. Attractive southern European ambiance. 2 two-room suites with
microwave & refrigerator; 3 stories, no elevator; interior corridors. **Dining:** Restaurant; 7-10 am & 11:30-2:30,
Wed & Sun 5:30 pm-9 pm; $9-$16. **Services:** complimentary evening beverages. **All Rooms:** combo or
shower baths. **Some Rooms:** whirlpools. **Cards:** AE, CB, DI, DS, MC, VI. **Special Amenities:** Free breakfast and free
local telephone calls.

Historic Bed
& Breakfast

BEST WESTERN INN OF VENTURA Phone: (805)648-3101
2/1-2/28 & 12/1-1/31 [CP] 1P: $59- 99 2P/1B: $59- 99 2P/2B: $69- 99 XP: $12 F16
3/1-10/31 [CP] 1P: $79 2P/1B: $79 2P/2B: $89 XP: $15 F16
11/1-11/30 [CP] 1P: $69 2P/1B: $69 2P/2B: $79 XP: $10 F16
Motel
Location: Just e of California St; from US 101, northbound exit California St, southbound exit Ventura Ave.
708 E Thompson Blvd 93001. Fax: 805/648-4019. **Terms:** Reserv deposit; pets, $25 dep req. **Facility:** 75
rooms. 2 stories; exterior corridors; whirlpool. **Dining:** Coffee shop nearby. **All Rooms:** combo or shower baths, extended
cable TV. **Cards:** AE, CB, DI, DS, MC, VI. **Special Amenities:** Free breakfast and free local telephone calls.

COUNTRY INN AT VENTURA Guaranteed Rates Phone: (805)653-1434
Fri & Sat [BP] 1P: $104 2P/1B: $104 2P/2B: $104 XP: $10 F12
Sun-Thurs [BP] 1P: $84 2P/1B: $84 2P/2B: $84 XP: $10 F12
Motel
Location: Just e of California St, just s of Thompson Blvd; from US 101, northbound exit California St,
southbound exit Ventura Ave. 298 Chestnut St 93001. Fax: 805/648-7126. **Facility:** 120 rooms. Some balconies, partial ocean
& mountain views. 3 stories; interior corridors; heated pool. **Cards:** AE, CB, DI, DS, MC, VI. *(See color ad below)*

DOUBLETREE HOTEL AT VENTURA Rates Subject to Change Phone: (805)643-6000

⚠️ Motor Inn ◆◆

		1P:		2P/1B:		2P/2B:		XP:		F12
Fri & Sat 7/4-9/5		1P: $99		2P/1B: $99		2P/2B: $99		XP: $10		F12
2/1-7/3, Sun-Thurs 7/4-9/5 & 9/6-11/22		1P: $79		2P/1B: $79		2P/2B: $79		XP: $10		F12
11/23-1/31		1P: $69		2P/1B: $69		2P/2B: $69		XP: $10		F12

Location: Adjacent to w side of US 101, exit Seaward Ave. 2055 Harbor Blvd 93001. Fax: 805/643-7137. **Terms:** Monthly rates. **Facility:** 284 rooms. 1 blk to San Buenaventura State Beach. Attractively landscaped courtyard & pool area. Secretarial services, extra charge; 4 stories; interior corridors; heated pool, saunas, whirlpool. **Dining:** Restaurant; 6:30 am-10 pm, Sat & Sun 7 am-10:30 pm, sports bar 4:30 pm-midnight, Fri & Sat 1 am limited menu; $9-$16; cocktails. **Services:** giftshop. **Recreation:** video game in all rooms. **All Rooms:** extended cable TV. **Cards:** AE, CB, DI, DS, MC, VI. *(See ad p 1073)*

FOUR POINTS VENTURA HARBORTOWN BY SHERATON Phone: (805)658-1212

⚠️ [SAVE] ◆◆◆ Motor Inn

		1P:		2P/1B:		2P/2B:		XP:		F18
Sat 6/1-10/31		1P: $109- 129		2P/1B: $109- 129		2P/2B: $109- 129		XP: $10		F18
Sun-Fri, Sat 2/1-5/31 & 11/1-1/31		1P: $89- 99		2P/1B: $89- 99		2P/2B: $89- 99		XP: $10		F18

Location: From US 101, exit Seaward Ave, then 1.5 mi s on Harbor Blvd, at Ventura Harbor. 1050 Schooner Dr 93001. Fax: 805/658-6431. **Facility:** 151 rooms. Many rooms with marina view & balcony or patio. 3 stories; exterior corridors; heated pool, whirlpool; 3 lighted tennis courts. **Dining:** Restaurant; 6:30 am-10 pm; $12-$30; cocktails. **Recreation:** in room video games. **Cards:** AE, CB, DI, DS, MC, VI. **Special Amenities:** Early check-in/late check-out and free newspaper. *(See ad below)*

HOLIDAY INN VENTURA BEACH RESORT Rates Subject to Change Phone: 805/648-7731

◆◆◆ Hotel

All Year 1P: $110- 125 2P/1B: $110- 125 2P/2B: $110- 125 XP: $10

Location: Adjacent to US 101; northbound exit California St, southbound exit Main St. 450 E Harbor Blvd 93001. Fax: 805/653-6202. **Terms:** Check-in 4 pm; reserv deposit. **Facility:** 260 rooms. A multi-story, beachfront hotel with balconies. 12 stories; interior corridors; heated pool; playground. **Services:** giftshop. **Cards:** AE, CB, DI, DS, JC, MC, VI.

INN ON THE BEACH Phone: 805/652-2000

⚠️ [SAVE] ◆ Motel

		1P:		2P/1B:		2P/2B:		XP:
5/22-11/1 [CP]		1P: $135- 165		2P/1B: $135- 165		2P/2B: $80- 120		XP: $5
2/1-5/21 & 11/2-1/31 [CP]		1P: $70- 110		2P/1B: $70- 110		2P/2B: $70- 110		XP: $5

Location: 0.5 mi w of US 101; exit Seaward Ave. 1175 S Seaward Ave 93001. Fax: 805/652-1912. **Terms:** Reserv deposit. **Facility:** 24 rooms. At the beach. Patio or balcony. Ocean view. 3 stories; interior corridors. **Cards:** AE, CB, DI, DS, MC, VI.

LA MER EUROPEAN BED & BREAKFAST Rates Subject to Change Phone: (805)643-3600

◆◆ Historic Bed & Breakfast

All Year [BP] 1P: $80- 180 2P/1B: $85- 185 D16

Location: 0.5 mi n of US 101; northbound exit California St, southbound exit Ventura Ave, just w of California st. 411 Poli St 93001. Fax: 805/653-7329. **Terms:** Check-in 4 pm; reserv deposit, 7 day notice; 2 night min stay, weekends. **Facility:** 5 rooms. All rooms individually furnished in a different European motif. House built in 1890. 20% discount Sun-Thurs with 2 night min stay; 2 stories; interior/exterior corridors; smoke free premises. **All Rooms:** shower or tub baths. **Cards:** AE, MC, VI.

LA QUINTA INN Phone: (805)658-6200

⚠️ [SAVE] ◆◆◆ Motel

		1P:		2P/1B:		2P/2B:
5/16-9/14 [CP]		1P: $79- 99		2P/1B: $79- 99		2P/2B: $79- 99
2/1-5/15 & 9/15-1/31 [CP]		1P: $59- 69		2P/1B: $59- 69		2P/2B: $59- 69

Location: Just s of US 101; exit Victoria Ave. 5818 Valentine Rd 93003. Fax: 805/642-2840. **Terms:** Small pets only. **Facility:** 142 rooms. 2 suites with microwave & refrigator, $99-$149; 3 stories; exterior corridors; heated pool, whirlpool. **Dining:** Restaurant nearby. **Recreation:** in room video games. **All Rooms:** extended cable TV. **Cards:** AE, CB, DI, DS, JC, MC, VI. **Special Amenities:** Free breakfast and free local telephone calls.

PIERPONT INN Rates Subject to Change Phone: (805)643-6144

◆◆ Motor Inn

All Year 1P: $99- 109 2P/1B: $99- 109 2P/2B: $99- 109 XP: $10-20 F16

Location: Adjacent to US 101; northbound Sanjon Rd exit, southbound Seaward Ave exit. 550 Sanjon Rd 93001. Fax: 805/641-1501. **Terms:** Reserv deposit. **Facility:** 72 rooms. Across freeway from beach. Attractive grounds. Many rooms with ocean view. Many rooms with balcony, 14 with fireplace. 8 ocean view suites with balcony, $129. 2 cottages, $139-$159; 2 stories; interior/exterior corridors; heated pool. Fee: racquetball courts, 12 lighted tennis courts. **Services:** Fee: massage. **All Rooms:** combo or shower baths. **Cards:** AE, CB, DI, DS, MC, VI.

RAMADA CLOCKTOWER INN Phone: (805)652-0141

AAA SAVE 5/16-9/15 [CP] 1P: $77- 85 2P/1B: $83- 90 2P/2B: $90- 108 XP: $10 D15
2/1-5/15 & 9/16-1/31 [CP] 1P: $77 2P/1B: $83 2P/2B: $90 XP: $10 D15

◆◆◆ Motor Inn **Location:** 0.5 mi nw of US 101; northbound exit California St, southbound exit Ventura Ave. 181 E Santa Clara 93001. Fax: 805/643-1432. **Terms:** Reserv deposit. **Facility:** 49 rooms. Attractive southwest decor. Adjacent to Mission San Buenaventura & Mission Park. 5 rooms with fireplace & 8 with balcony. 1 1/2 blks to beach. 2 stories; interior corridors. **Dining:** 11 am-2:30 & 5-9 pm; Sun-9 pm; also, Pastabilities, see separate listing. **Cards:** AE, DI, DS, MC, VI. **Special Amenities:** Free breakfast and free local telephone calls.
(See color ad opposite title page & below)

TRAVELERS BEACH INN Phone: (805)648-2557

AAA SAVE 5/15-9/30 1P: $49- 54 2P/1B: $49- 58 2P/2B: $55- 60 XP: $5 F18
2/1-5/14 & 10/1-1/31 1P: $39- 45 2P/1B: $43- 48 2P/2B: $45- 49 XP: $5 F18

◆ Motel **Location:** Just n of US 101, northbound exit California St; southbound exit Ventura Ave. 929 E Thompson Blvd 93001. Fax: 805/648-3408. **Terms:** Reserv deposit. **Facility:** 37 rooms. 2 stories; exterior corridors. **Dining:** Restaurant nearby. **All Rooms:** combo or shower baths. **Cards:** AE, DI, DS, MC, VI.

VAGABOND INN Phone: (805)648-5371

AAA SAVE 5/16-10/15 [CP] 1P: $70- 85 2P/1B: $75- 90 2P/2B: $83- 88 XP: $5 F18
2/1-5/15 & 10/16-1/31 [CP] 1P: $56- 61 2P/1B: $61- 66 2P/2B: $67- 73 XP: $5 F18

◆◆ Motor Inn **Location:** 0.3 mi e on US 101 business rt; from US 101 northbound exit California St, southbound exit Ventura Ave. 756 E Thompson Blvd 93001. Fax: 805/648-5613. **Terms:** Small pets only, $5 extra charge. **Facility:** 82 rooms. 2 two-bedroom units. 2 stories; exterior corridors; heated pool, whirlpool. **Dining:** Coffee shop; 5 am-10 pm; $5-$10. **Cards:** AE, CB, DI, DS, MC, VI. **Special Amenities:** Free breakfast and free local telephone calls.

RESTAURANTS

GREEK AT THE HARBOR Lunch: $7-$10 Dinner: $10-$24 Phone: 805/650-5350
◆◆ Greek **Location:** From US 101, exit Seaward Ave, 1.8 mi sw on Harbor Blvd, 0.8 mi w on Spinnaker Dr. In Ventura Harbor Village. 1583 Spinnaker Dr 93001. **Hours:** 11 am-10 pm, Fri & Sat-11 pm. **Reservations:** suggested; Fri & Sat. **Features:** casual dress; children's menu; carryout; cocktails; a la carte. Steaks, seafood, lamb, chicken, vegetarian plate, pasta & casseroles. Patio dining, dancing & harbor views. Belly Dance & Greek Dance shows. Smoke free premises. **Cards:** AE, CB, DI, DS, MC, VI.

MATTIE'S OCEAN VIEW DINING ROOM Lunch: $8-$12 Dinner: $14-$22 Phone: 805/653-6144
◆◆◆ American **Location:** In Pierpont Inn. 550 Sanjon Rd 93001. **Hours:** 6:30 am-9:30 & 11-8:30 pm, Sat 8:30 am-9:30 pm, Sun 8:30 am-8:30 pm, Sat & Sun brunch. **Reservations:** suggested. **Features:** casual dress; children's menu; cocktails & lounge; entertainment. Fine ocean view dining at family owned inn since 1928. Entrees include beef, chicken & seafood. Dessert made on premises. Smoke free premises. **Cards:** AE, CB, DI, DS, MC, VI.

OLD VIENNA RESTAURANT　　　Lunch: $6-$8　　　Dinner: $12-$22　　　Phone: 805/654-1214
⊕⊕
◆◆
German
> **Location:** 1 mi e of Main St. 3845 Telegraph Rd 92003. **Hours:** 11:30 am-2 & 5-9:30 pm, Mon from 5 pm, Sat 5 pm-10 pm, Sun 11 am-2 & 4:30-9 pm. Closed: 12/25. **Reservations:** suggested; weekends. **Features:** Sunday brunch; children's menu; early bird specials; carryout; cocktails. Large selection, including venison, roast goose in season. Smoke free premises. **Cards:** AE, CB, DI, DS, MC, VI. ⊠

PASTABILITIES　　　Lunch: $6-$12　　　Dinner: $8-$16　　　Phone: 805/648-1462
◆◆◆
Italian
> **Location:** 0.5 mi nw of US 101; northbound exit California St, southbound exit Ventura Ave; in Ramada Clocktower Inn. 185 E Santa Clara 93001. **Hours:** 11:30 am-2:30 & 5-9:30 pm, Fri-10 pm, Sat from 5 pm, Sun-9 pm. Closed major holidays. **Features:** casual dress; children's menu; cocktails; a la carte. Nice selection of Italian entrees. Menu allows individual selection of pastas & sauces. Good wine selection. Patio dining available. Smoke free premises. **Cards:** AE, CB, DI, DS, MC, VI. ⊠

SPINNAKER SEAFOOD BROILER　　　Lunch: $6-$10　　　Dinner: $8-$25　　　Phone: 805/658-6220
◆◆
Seafood
> **Location:** From US 101, exit Seaward Ave, 1.8 mi southwest on Harbor Blvd, 0.8 mi w on Spinnaker Dr; in Ventura Harbor Village. 1583 Spinnaker Dr, Suite 109 93001. **Hours:** 11 am-9:30 pm, Fri & Sat 11 am-10:30 pm. **Features:** casual dress; carryout; cocktails & lounge; a la carte. Mesquite grilled seafood, steaks, chicken & ribs. Dancing Fri & Sat 8 pm-midnight. Smoke free premises. **Cards:** AE, CB, DI, DS, MC, VI. ⊠

YOLANDA'S MEXICAN CAFE　　　Lunch: $6-$10　　　Dinner: $8-$12　　　Phone: 805/643-2700
◆◆
Mexican
> **Location:** 0.5 mi e of Seaward Ave. 2753 E Main 93003. **Hours:** 11 am-9:30 pm, Fri & Sat-10 pm, Sun 10 am-9 pm. **Closed:** 11/25 & 12/25. **Reservations:** suggested. **Features:** casual dress; children's menu; carryout; cocktails & lounge. Colorfully decorated restaurant. Southwestern cuisine. Smoke free premises. **Cards:** AE, DS, MC, VI. ⊠

VICTORVILLE—40,700

LODGINGS

BEST WESTERN-GREEN TREE INN　　　　　　　　　　　　　　　　　Phone: (760)245-3461
⊕⊕⊕ SAVE
◆◆◆
Motor Inn

	1P:		2P/1B:		2P/2B:		XP:	
1/1-1/31	$67-	82	$64-	82	$64-	82	$4-8	F12
2/1-12/31	$62-	80	$62-	80	$62-	80	$4-8	F12

> **Location:** East side of I-15, SR 18W, Palmdale Rd exit. 14173 Green Tree Blvd 92392. Fax: 760/245-7745. **Facility:** 168 rooms. Many rooms overlook a shaded lawn area & golf course. Some smaller rooms facing the parking lot. 72 one-bedroom suites with refrigerator, microwave or cooking surface & coffee makers; 2-3 stories; exterior corridors; wading pool. **Dining:** Dining room, coffee shop; 24 hrs; $7-$16; cocktails. **Services:** giftshop. **Recreation:** indoor whirlpool. **All Rooms:** extended cable TV. **Some Rooms:** whirlpools. **Cards:** AE, CB, DI, DS, MC, VI. **Special Amenities:** Early check-in/late check-out and free newspaper. 🆂🔸🛇🍽🏋🐾🏊🏌⊠

BUDGET INN　　　　　　　　　　　　　　　　　　　　　　　Phone: (760)241-8010
⊕⊕⊕ SAVE
◆
Motel

	1P:		2P/2B:		XP:	
All Year	$32		$36-	42	$5	

> **Location:** Just w of I-15, exit SR 18W; Palmdale Rd. 14153 Kentwood Blvd 92392. Fax: 760/245-8970. **Terms:** Reserv deposit; small pets only, $10 dep req. **Facility:** 40 rooms. 2 stories; exterior corridors. **Dining:** Restaurant nearby. **Cards:** AE, VI. 🆂🐾🍽🐾🔸⊠

HOLIDAY INN　　　　　　　　　　　　　　　　　　　　　　　Phone: (760)245-6565
⊕⊕⊕ SAVE
◆◆◆
Hotel

	1P:		2P/1B:		2P/2B:		XP:	
All Year	$80-	97	$80-	97	$80-	97	$6	F18

> **Location:** Just w of I-15, exit SR 18W, Palmdale Rd. 15494 Palmdale Rd 92392. Fax: 760/245-6649. **Terms:** Pets, $25 dep req. **Facility:** 162 rooms. Some rooms with patio. 3 suites, $95; 6 stories; interior corridors. **Dining:** Dining room, coffee shop; 6 am-10 pm; $6-$15; cocktails. **All Rooms:** extended cable TV. **Cards:** AE, DI, DS, MC, VI. **Special Amenities:** Free newspaper. 🆂🐾🛇🍽🏋🍸🏊🐾🏌⊠

RED ROOF INN　　　　　　　　　　　　　　　　　　　　　　Phone: (760)241-1577
⊕⊕⊕ SAVE
◆◆
Motel

	1P:		2P/1B:		2P/2B:		XP:	
5/10-6/30	$39-	50	$46-	58	$46-	60	$6	F18
7/1-9/30	$37-	48	$44-	56	$44-	58	$6	F18
2/1-5/9 & 10/1-1/31	$35-	46	$42-	54	$42-	56	$6	F18

> **Location:** E Side of I-15, between Bear Valley Rd & Palmdale Rd exits. 13409 Mariposa Rd 92392. Fax: 760/241-3627. **Terms:** Small pets only. **Facility:** 94 rooms. 14 one-bedroom suites with living room; 3 stories; exterior corridors; whirlpools. **Cards:** AE, CB, DI, DS, JC, MC, VI. **Special Amenities:** Free local telephone calls.
> *(See ad below)* 🆂🐾🔸🐾📺🐾🏊🔲🔸⊠

RESTAURANT

CASK 'N' CLEAVER
◆
American

Dinner: $12-$20
Phone: 760/241-7318
Location: West side of I-15, exit SR 18, Palmdale Rd, just w, then s on Park Ave. 13885 Park Ave 92392.
Hours: 5 pm -9 pm, Fri & Sat-10 pm, Sun 4:30 pm-9 pm. Closed: 1/1, 7/4, 11/25 & 12/25.
Features: children's menu; salad bar; cocktails & lounge. Casual dining. Features a selection of steaks, prime rib, seafood & chicken. Smoke free premises. **Cards:** AE, DS, MC, VI.

VISALIA—75,600—See also SEQUOIA AND KINGS CANYON NATIONAL PARKS.

LODGINGS

BEN MADDOX HOUSE
◆◆◆
Historic Bed
& Breakfast

Rates Subject to Change
Phone: (559)739-0721
All Year [BP]   1P: $75- 85 2P/1B: $85- 95   XP: $20
Location: Just n of downtown at corner of Encina & Race; from SR 198, exit Central Visalia. 601 N Encina St 93291. Fax: 559/625-0420. **Terms:** Reserv deposit, 3 day notice. **Facility:** 4 rooms. 1876 restored house in a neighborhood of historic homes. Furnished with period antiques. Smoking permitted on porch. 1 story; interior/exterior corridors. **Cards:** AE, DS, MC, VI.

BEST WESTERN VISALIA INN
ⒶⒶⒶ [SAVE]
◆◆
Motel

Phone: (559)732-4561
All Year [CP]   1P: $65- 72 2P/1B: $70- 76 2P/2B: $74- 80 XP: $5   F12
Location: Just w of downtown & n of SR 198. 623 W Main St 93291. Fax: 559/738-0562. **Terms:** Small pets only, $4. **Facility:** 41 rooms. Cozy, comfortable rooms. 2 stories; exterior corridors; small pool. **Dining:** Restaurant nearby. **Cards:** AE, CB, DI, DS, JC, MC, VI. **Special Amenities:** Free breakfast and free local telephone calls.

DAYS INN
ⒶⒶⒶ [SAVE]
◆
Motel

Phone: (559)627-2885
5/1-10/31 [CP]   1P: $52- 65 2P/1B: $55- 65 2P/2B: $60- 75 XP: $5   F12
2/1-4/30 & 11/1-1/31 [CP] 1P: $45- 65 2P/1B: $48- 65 2P/2B: $54- 75 XP: $5   F12
Location: On SR 198; 1.8 mi w of jct SR 63. 4801 W Mineral King Ave 93277. Fax: 559/732-7114. **Terms:** Reserv deposit. **Facility:** 39 rooms. 2 stories; exterior corridors. **Cards:** AE, CB, DI, DS, MC, VI. **Special Amenities:** Free breakfast and free local telephone calls. *(See color ad below)*

ECONO LODGE
ⒶⒶⒶ [SAVE]
◆
Motel

Phone: (559)732-6641
4/1-10/31 [CP]   1P: $59   2P/1B: $63   2P/2B: $63   XP: $5   F18
2/1-3/31 & 11/1-1/31 [CP] 1P: $55   2P/1B: $59   2P/2B: $59   XP: $5   F18
Location: On SR 63, 0.5 mi s of jct SR 198, exit SR 63 S Mooney Blvd. 1400 S Mooney Blvd 93277. Fax: 559/739-7520. **Terms:** Reserv deposit. **Facility:** 49 rooms. **Dining:** Restaurant; 5 pm-10 pm; $10-$15; wine/beer only. **All Rooms:** combo or shower baths, extended cable TV. **Cards:** AE, CB, DI, DS, JC, MC, VI. **Special Amenities:** Free breakfast and free local telephone calls.

HOLIDAY INN PLAZA PARK
◆◆◆
Motor Inn

Rates Subject to Change
Phone: (559)651-5000
All Year   1P: $79   2P/1B: $79   2P/2B: $79   XP: $10   F17
Location: Adjacent to SR 198; 0.5 mi e of jct SR 99, next to Visalia Airport. 9000 W Airport Dr 93277. Fax: 559/651-5014. **Facility:** 257 rooms. Adjacent to park and golf course. 3-5 stories; interior corridors; putting green; heated indoor pool. **Cards:** AE, CB, DI, DS, MC, VI. *(See color ad p 1078)*

LAMP LITER INN
ⒶⒶⒶ [SAVE]
◆◆◆
Motor Inn

Phone: (559)732-4511
All Year [CP]   1P: $65   2P/1B: $65   2P/2B: $65
Location: Adjacent to SR 198; 0.5 mi w of jct SR 63. 3300 W Mineral King Ave 93291. Fax: 559/732-1840. **Facility:** 100 rooms. Spacious landscaped grounds. 2 stories; exterior corridors. **Dining:** Restaurant; 6 am-10 pm; $8-$18; cocktails. **All Rooms:** combo or shower baths, extended cable TV. **Cards:** AE, CB, DI, DS, JC, MC, VI. **Special Amenities:** Free breakfast and free local telephone calls.

RADISSON HOTEL-VISALIA
ⒶⒶⒶ
◆◆◆
Hotel

Rates Subject to Change
Phone: (559)636-1111
All Year   1P: $87   2P/1B: $87   2P/2B: $87   XP: $10   F18
Location: Just N of SR 198, exit Central Visalia/SR 63 N. 300 S Court St 93291. Fax: 559/636-8224. **Facility:** 201 rooms. Adjacent to convention center. 8 stories; interior corridors; whirlpool. **Dining:** Restaurant; 6 am-11 pm; $11-$20; cocktails. **Services:** area transportation. **Cards:** AE, CB, DI, DS, JC, MC, VI.

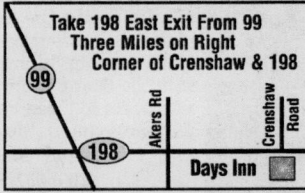

THE SPALDING HOUSE BED & BREAKFAST   Guaranteed Rates   **Phone:** (559)739-7877
◆◆◆ All Year [BP]   1P: $75   2P/1B: $85   XP: $10
Historic Bed   **Location:** Just n of downtown; from SR 198, exit Court St, n to Murray St, then w to Encina St. 631 N
& Breakfast   Encina St 93291. Fax: 559/625-0902. **Terms:** Reserv deposit. **Facility:** 3 rooms. 1901 colonial revival-style
house with library & music room with Steinway Grand Player piano. 2 stories; interior corridors; designated
smoking area; street parking only. **All Rooms:** shower baths. **Cards:** AE, MC, VI.    ⒶⓈⓀ 🆂🅳 ⒸⓉⓋ 🆉 ☒

RESTAURANTS

CAFE 225   **Lunch:** $6-$10   **Dinner:** $10-$18   **Phone:** 559/733-2967
◆◆ **Location:** Downtown. 225 W Main St 92391. **Hours:** 7 am-10 pm. Closed: 1/1, 11/25, 12/25 & Sun.
American   **Features:** casual dress; children's menu; carryout; beer & wine only; street parking. Contemporary dining.
Menu features a selection of pasta, pizza, rotisserie chicken & house specialties. Smoke free premises.
Cards: AE, CB, DI, DS, MC, VI.   ☒

THE DEPOT RESTAURANT   **Lunch:** $6-$9   **Dinner:** $13-$22   **Phone:** 559/732-8611
◆◆◆ **Location:** just ne of downtown. 207 E Oak St at Church St 93291. **Hours:** 11 am-2:30 & 5-10 pm, Fri &
American   Sat-11 pm. Closed major holidays & Sun. **Reservations:** suggested; weekends. **Features:** casual dress;
children's menu; cocktails & lounge. Elegant Spanish decor in 1897 historical railroad depot. Smoke free
premises. **Cards:** AE, DS, MC, VI.   ☒

MICHAEL'S ON MAIN   **Lunch:** $5-$9   **Dinner:** $15-$25   **Phone:** 559/635-2686
◆◆◆ **Location:** Downtown. 123 W Main St 93291. **Hours:** 11 am-3 & 5:30-10 pm, Fri & Sat-midnight. Closed:
Continental   11/25, 12/25 & Sun. **Reservations:** suggested. **Features:** casual dress; cocktails & lounge. An Italian bistro
style bar & grill serving continental dishes with an Italian influence. Smoke free premises. **Cards:** AE, CB, DI,
DS, MC, VI.   ☒

SOMETHING FRESH AMERICAN BAR & GRILL   **Lunch:** $6-$9   **Dinner:** $6-$13   **Phone:** 559/732-6572
◆◆ **Location:** 1 mi w on SR 198, just s on Chinowth Rd. 505 S Chinowth Rd 93291. **Hours:** 10:30 am-10 pm.
American   Closed major holidays. **Features:** children's menu; health conscious menu; carryout; cocktails & lounge.
Casual family type restaurant in a restored farmhouse. A variety of salads, sandwiches & entrees.
Homemade desserts. Smoke free premises. **Cards:** AE, CB, DI, DS, MC, VI.   ☒

THE VINTAGE PRESS   **Lunch:** $6-$11   **Dinner:** $13-$30   **Phone:** 559/733-3033
◆◆◆ **Location:** Downtown; just n of Main St. 216 N Willis St 93291. **Hours:** 11:30 am-2 & 6-10:30 pm, Fri &
American   Sat-11 pm, Sun 10 am-2 & 5-9 pm. Closed: 12/25. **Reservations:** suggested. **Features:** casual dress;
Sunday brunch; children's menu; cocktails & lounge. A large, popular restaurant with several attractive dining
areas & garden patio. California cuisine. Extensive wine list. Smoke free premises. **Cards:** AE, CB, DI, MC, VI.   ☒

WAGON WHEEL STEAK HOUSE   **Lunch:** $7-$11   **Dinner:** $11-$20   **Phone:** 559/734-7427
◆ **Location:** just n of downtown. 400 N Willis Ave 93291. **Hours:** 11 am-4 & 5-10 pm, Sat 5 pm-10 pm, Sun 11
American   am-9 pm. Closed: 11/25 & 12/25. **Features:** casual dress; children's menu; carryout; cocktails & lounge. Nice
selection of steak, seafood & Mexican dishes. Smoke free premises. **Cards:** AE, DS, MC, VI.   ☒

VISTA—71,900

LODGING

LA QUINTA INN   **Phone:** (760)727-8180
ⒶⒶⒶ 🆂🅰🆅🅴 All Year [CP]   1P: $59- 79   2P/1B: $59- 79   2P/2B: $59- 79
Location: Adjacent to SR 78, exit Sycamore Ave. 630 Sycamore Ave at Thibodo Rd 92083.
◆◆◆ Fax: 760/598-1732. **Terms:** Small pets only. **Facility:** 106 rooms. 3 stories; interior/exterior corridors; heated
Motel   pool. **Dining:** Restaurant nearby. **Cards:** AE, CB, DI, DS, JC, MC, VI. **Special Amenities:** Free breakfast
and free local telephone calls.   🛏 🕒 🏊 🛎 ♿ 🍴 💻 🖨 🛗 ☒

WALNUT—See Los Angeles p. 649.

WALNUT CREEK—60,600 (See map p. 752; index p. 751)

LODGINGS

EMBASSY SUITES HOTEL — Rates Subject to Change — Phone: 925/934-2500 **44**
◆◆◆◆
Suite Hotel
	Sun-Thurs [BP]	1P: $149- 169	2P/1B: $149- 169	2P/2B: $149- 169	XP: $15
	Fri & Sat 6/1-1/31 [BP]	1P: $125- 145	2P/1B: $125- 145	2P/2B: $135- 165	XP: $15
	Fri & Sat 2/1-5/31 [BP]	1P: $125- 139	2P/1B: $129- 139	2P/2B: $119- 139	XP: $15

Location: E of & adjacent to I-680, northbound exit Treat Blvd, southbound exit Oak Park Blvd at Pleasant Hill Bart Station. 1345 Treat Blvd 94596. Fax: 925/256-7233. **Facility:** 249 rooms. Attractive atrium landscaping. 8 stories; interior corridors; heated indoor pool. **Services:** giftshop. **All Rooms:** efficiencies. **Cards:** AE, DI, DS, JC, MC, VI. *(See color ad p 931)*

HOLIDAY INN OF WALNUT CREEK — Rates Subject to Change — Phone: (925)932-3332 **43**
◆◆◆
Motor Inn
| | Mon-Thurs | 1P: $94 | 2P/1B: $94 | 2P/2B: $94 |
| | Fri-Sun | 1P: $89 | 2P/1B: $89 | 2P/2B: $89 |

Location: I-680 exit N Main St, n. 2730 N Main St 94596. Fax: 925/256-7672. **Facility:** 155 rooms. Attractive courtyard setting. 2 stories; interior corridors; heated pool. **Cards:** AE, CB, DI, DS, JC, MC, VI.

MARRIOTT HOTEL — Rates Subject to Change — Phone: 925/934-2000 **41**
◆◆◆◆
Hotel
| | Sun-Thurs | 1P: $139 | 2P/1B: $149 | 2P/2B: $149 | XP: $10 |
| | Fri & Sat | 1P: $84 | 2P/1B: $84 | 2P/2B: $84 | XP: $10 |

Location: E of I-680; exit N Main St; 0.3 mi s at Parkside Dr. 2355 N Main 94596. Fax: 925/934-6374. **Terms:** Reserv deposit. **Facility:** 338 rooms. Attractive public areas. 6 stories; interior corridors; heated pool. **Services:** giftshop; area transportation. **Cards:** AE, CB, DI, DS, JC, MC, VI.

WALNUT CREEK MOTOR LODGE — Guaranteed Rates — Phone: (925)932-2811 **42**
Ⓐ
◆◆
Motel
| | All Year | 1P: $57- 60 | 2P/1B: $62- 70 | 2P/2B: $70- 75 | XP: $5 | F12 |

Location: Just e off I-680 & SR 24; northbound exit e via Ygnacio Valley Rd, southbound exit e via N Main St. 1960 N Main St 94596. Fax: 925/932-5989. **Terms:** Reserv deposit; small pets only. **Facility:** 71 rooms. 8 efficiencies, $10 extra charge; 2 stories; exterior corridors; whirlpool. **Dining:** Restaurant nearby. **Cards:** AE, DI, MC, VI.

RESTAURANTS

CALIFORNIA CAFE BAR & GRILL — **Lunch:** $8-$13 — **Dinner:** $10-$20 — Phone: 925/938-9977 **33**
◆◆◆
Regional
American
Location: exit I-680 Ygnacio Valley Rd, 0.25 mi e; s 0.75 mi on California Blvd. 1540 N California Blvd 94596. **Hours:** 11:30 am-10 pm, Sat 5-10:30 pm, Sun 10:30 am-2:30 & 5-9:30 pm. Closed: 7/4/, 11/27 & 12/25. **Reservations:** suggested. **Features:** casual dress; Sunday brunch; early bird specials; health conscious menu; cocktails; valet parking; a la carte. Casual atmosphere; innovative menus. Smoke free premises. **Cards:** AE, CB, DI, DS, MC, VI.

MASSIMO RISTORANTE — **Lunch:** $8-$16 — **Dinner:** $9-$17 — Phone: 925/932-1474 **34**
◆◆◆
Northern
Italian
Location: I-680 & SR 24, exit at Ygnacio Valley Rd; s on California Blvd, e on La Cassie. 1604 Locust St 94596. **Hours:** 11:30 am-3 & 5:30-11 pm, Sat-5:30 pm, Sun 5 pm-10 pm. Closed: 11/26 & 12/25. **Reservations:** suggested. **Features:** cocktails & lounge; a la carte. Attractive contemporary decor. Smoke free premises. **Cards:** AE, CB, MC, VI.

WATSONVILLE—31,100

LODGINGS

BEST WESTERN INN — Phone: (831)724-3367
Ⓐ SAVE
◆◆
Motel
	Fri & Sat 5/28-9/11 [CP]	1P: $119- 129	2P/1B: $119- 129	2P/2B: $129	XP: $7	F14
	Sun-Thurs 5/28-9/11 [CP]	1P: $77- 85	2P/1B: $83- 95	2P/2B: $95	XP: $10	F14
	Fri & Sat 2/1-5/27 & 9/12-1/31 [CP]	1P: $79- 85	2P/1B: $79- 85	2P/2B: $85	XP: $6	F14
	Sun-Thurs 2/1-5/27 & 9/12-1/31 [CP]	1P: $64- 73	2P/1B: $69- 75	2P/2B: $77- 85	XP: $6	F14

Location: On SR 152. 740 Freedom Blvd 95076. Fax: 831/761-1785. **Terms:** Small pets only, $5 extra charge, $50 dep req. **Facility:** 43 rooms. Few small rooms. 2 stories; exterior corridors; small pool, whirlpool. **Dining:** Coffee shop nearby. **All Rooms:** combo or shower baths. **Cards:** AE, CB, DI, DS, JC, MC, VI. **Special Amenities:** Free breakfast and free local telephone calls. *(See color ad p 711)*

ECONOMY INN — Phone: (831)724-4755
Ⓐ SAVE
◆
Motel
	Fri-Sun 5/1-9/30 [CP]	1P: $65- 99	2P/1B: $85- 109	2P/2B: $109- 129	XP: $15-25	F12
	Mon-Thurs 5/1-9/30 [CP]	1P: $49- 55	2P/1B: $55- 75	2P/2B: $65- 85	XP: $15	F12
	2/1-4/30 & 10/1-1/31 [CP]	1P: $41- 55	2P/1B: $41- 55	2P/2B: $55- 75	XP: $10	F12

Location: 1.5 mi e of SR 1, SR 152 exit. 584 Auto Center Dr 95076. Fax: 831/761-1120. **Terms:** Reserv deposit, 7 day notice. **Facility:** 30 rooms. 1 story; exterior corridors. **All Rooms:** combo or shower baths. **Cards:** AE, CB, DS, MC, VI. **Special Amenities:** Free breakfast and free local telephone calls.

INN AT MANRESA BEACH — Rates Subject to Change — Phone: (831)728-1000
◆◆
Historic Bed
& Breakfast
| | All Year [BP] | 1P: $150- 195 | 2P/1B: $150- 195 | 2P/2B: $165- 370 | XP: $25 | F10 |

Location: 2.5 mi w of SR 1, San Andreas Rd exit; near the beach. 1258 San Andreas Rd 95076. Fax: 831/728-8294. **Terms:** Reserv deposit, 10 day notice; 2 night min stay, weekends. **Facility:** 5 rooms. An 1867 replica of Abraham Lincoln's Springfield home. 2 two-bedroom units. 2 stories; interior corridors; 2 tennis courts. **All Rooms:** combo or shower baths. **Cards:** AE, DS, MC, VI.

RESTAURANT

MT MADONNA RESTAURANT   **Lunch:** $6-$12   **Dinner:** $12-$24   **Phone:** 831/724-2275
◆◆   **Location:** 7 mi e on SR 152 at summit. 1285 Hecker Pass Rd 95076. **Hours:** Thurs 4 pm, 10 pm, Fri & Sat
Continental   noon-10 pm, Sun 10 am-9 pm. Closed: 12/25 & Mon-Wed. **Reservations:** accepted. **Features:** casual
dress; children's menu; early bird specials; cocktails & lounge; entertainment; minimum charge-$10; a la
carte. Panoramic View of valley & cities below; also fresh seafood. Smoke free premises. **Cards:** AE, CB, DI, MC, VI. ✕

WEAVERVILLE—2,800

LODGINGS

49ER MOTEL   **Phone:** (530)623-4937
AAA SAVE   All Year [CP]   1P: $34- 79 2P/1B: $42- 79 2P/2B: $45- 79 XP: $5
◆◆   **Location:** On SR 299. 718 Main St 96093 (PO Box 1608). Fax: 530/623-4937. **Terms:** Pets. **Facility:** 28
Motel   rooms. Historical area, some view of Trinity Alps. 1 story; exterior corridors; seasonal pool.
Dining: Restaurant nearby. **All Rooms:** shower baths. **Some Rooms:** kitchen, whirlpools. **Cards:** AE, CB,
DI, DS, JC, MC, VI. **Special Amenities:** Free breakfast and free local telephone calls.

MOTEL TRINITY   **Phone:** (530)623-2129
AAA SAVE   6/1-10/31   1P: $39- 79 2P/1B: $49- 82 2P/2B: $50- 80 XP: $8   F12
◆   2/1-5/31 & 11/1-1/31   1P: $35- 69 2P/1B: $39- 72 2P/2B: $40- 70 XP: $7   F12
Motel   **Location:** 1112 Main St 96093 (PO Box 1179). Fax: 530/623-6007. **Terms:** Small pets only. **Facility:** 25 rooms.
Attractive mountain setting. 4 two-bedroom units. 1 story; exterior corridors; seasonal pool.
All Rooms: combo or shower baths. **Some Rooms:** 3 kitchens. **Cards:** AE, CB, DI, DS, MC, VI.
Special Amenities: Free local telephone calls and preferred room (subject to availability with advanced
reservations).

RED HILL MOTEL   Rates Subject to Change   **Phone:** 530/623-4331
◆   All Year   1P: $30- 50 2P/1B: $35- 50 2P/2B: $45- 75 XP: $5   F11
Cottage   **Location:** On SR 299, 0.5 mi w of SR 3. (PO Box 234, 96093). Fax: 530/623-4341. **Terms:** Reserv deposit.
Facility: 14 rooms. 1 two-bedroom unit. 1 story; exterior corridors. **All Rooms:** combo or shower baths.
Some Rooms: 3 kitchens. **Cards:** AE, CB, DI, DS, MC, VI.

WEAVERVILLE VICTORIAN INN   **Phone:** (530)623-4432
AAA SAVE   All Year [CP]   1P: $50   2P/2B: $59   XP: $5   F12
◆◆◆   **Location:** On SR 299. 1709 Main St 96093 (PO Box 2400). Fax: 530/623-4264. **Terms:** Small pets only, $10
Motel   dep req. **Facility:** 65 rooms. Modern comfortable rooms. 2 large rooms with wetbar & whirlpool tub, $105 for
2 persons; 2 stories; exterior corridors. **Some Rooms:** whirlpools. **Cards:** AE, CB, DS, MC, VI.
Special Amenities: Early check-in/late check-out and free breakfast.

WEED—3,100

LODGINGS

COMFORT INN   Rates Subject to Change   **Phone:** 530/938-1982
◆◆◆   All Year [CP]   1P: $69- 91 2P/1B: $74- 96 2P/2B: $74- 96 XP: $6   F12
Motel   **Location:** E of I-5 at S Weed exit. 1844 Shastina Dr 96094. Fax: 530/938-1983. **Facility:** 56 rooms. 6 suites;
2 whirlpool rms, extra charge; 3 stories; interior corridors. **All Rooms:** combo or shower baths. **Cards:** AE,
CB, DI, DS, MC, VI.

HOLIDAY INN EXPRESS   **Phone:** (530)938-1308
AAA SAVE   5/15-9/27 [CP]   1P: $65- 75 2P/1B: $65- 75 2P/2B: $75- 85 XP: $6   F18
◆◆   2/1-5/14 & 9/28-1/31 [CP]   1P: $65   2P/1B: $65   2P/2B: $65   XP: $6   F18
Motel   **Location:** I-5 exit s Weed. 1830 Black Butte Dr 96094. Fax: 530/938-1348. **Terms:** Reserv deposit; pets,
$20 fee, $20 dep req. **Facility:** 50 rooms. Very attractive rooms. 3 whirlpool rms, extra charge; 2 stories; interior corridors; indoor whirlpool. **Dining:** Restaurant nearby. **Cards:** AE, DI, DS, JC, MC, VI.
Special Amenities: Free breakfast and free local telephone calls.

SIS-Q-INN MOTEL   **Phone:** (530)938-4194
AAA SAVE   All Year [BP]   1P: $46- 54 2P/1B: $54- 62 2P/2B: $57- 65 XP: $6   D12
◆◆   **Location:** Exit I-5, s Weed. 1825 Shastina Dr 96094. Fax: 530/938-2569. **Terms:** Reserv deposit; small pets
Motel   only, $5 extra charge. **Facility:** 22 rooms. Shaded landscaped grounds with picnic tables & view of Mt Shasta.
5 two-bedroom units. 2 stories; interior corridors; indoor whirlpool. **Dining:** Restaurant nearby. **Cards:** AE,
CB, DI, DS, MC, VI. **Special Amenities:** Free breakfast and free local telephone calls.

WEST COVINA—See Los Angeles p. 650.

WEST HOLLYWOOD—See Los Angeles p. 650.

WESTLAKE VILLAGE—7,500

LODGINGS

HYATT WESTLAKE PLAZA HOTEL　　　　　　　　　　　　　　　　　　　　Phone: (805)497-9991
🔺🔺🔺 [SAVE]　All Year　　　1P: $169- 205　2P/1B: $194- 230　2P/2B: $194- 230　XP: $25　　F18
　　　Location: Adjacent to US 101; Westlake Blvd exit. 880 S Westlake Blvd 91361. Fax: 805/379-9392.
◆◆◆　**Terms:** Monthly rates. **Facility:** 262 rooms. Spacious lobby with a water fountain. 5 stories; interior corridors;
Hotel　heated pool, saunas, whirlpools. **Dining:** Restaurant; 5:30 am-11 pm; $15-$25; cocktails. **Services:** giftshop.
　　　Recreation: Fee: bicycles. **Cards:** AE, CB, DI, DS, JC, MC, VI. *(See color ad p 565)*

WESTLAKE VILLAGE INN　　　　　　Rates Subject to Change　　　　　Phone: 818/889-0230
◆◆◆　All Year　　　1P: $108- 305　2P/1B: $108- 305　2P/2B: $118- 170　XP: $10　　F17
Resort Motor　**Location:** 1.3 mi se of US 101, Westlake Blvd exit. 31943 Agoura Rd 91361. Fax: 818/879-0812.
Inn　　**Facility:** 140 rooms. Nicely landscaped grounds. Patio or balcony. Fax machine in room. 18 suites with living
　　　room, bedroom, fireplace, whirlpool bath & refrigerator. 1 villa, $750; 2 stories; exterior corridors; heated pool;
10 tennis courts (6 lighted). Fee: 18 holes golf, putting green. **Recreation:** jogging. Fee: bicycles. **Cards:** AE, DI, DS, MC,
VI.

RESTAURANT

PROVENCE AT THE WESTLAKE VILLAGE INN　　　　**Dinner:** $12-$32　　　Phone: 818/889-1662
◆◆◆　**Location:** 1.3 mi se of US 101, Westlake Blvd exit; in Westlake Village Inn. 32001 Agoura Rd 91361.
Continental　**Hours:** 5 pm-9 pm, Fri & Sat-10 pm, Sun 10 am-2 & 5-9 pm. Closed: Mon. **Reservations:** suggested.
　　　Features: casual dress; Sunday brunch; children's menu; cocktails & lounge; entertainment; a la carte.
Scenic lakeside dining. Fresh seafood, pasta, salad, chicken, steak, lamb & lobster tail. Smoke free premises. **Cards:** AE,
CB, DI, DS, JC, MC, VI.

WESTLEY—900

LODGINGS

DAYS INN　　　　　　　　　　　　　　　　　　　　　　　　　　Phone: (209)894-5500
🔺🔺🔺 [SAVE]　All Year　　　1P: $45- 60　2P/1B: $50- 65　2P/2B: $55- 75　XP: $5
　　　Location: Off & adjacent to I-5, exit Westley. 7144 McKraken Rd 95387 (PO Box 311). Fax: 209/894-3291.
◆　　**Terms:** Weekly rates; pets, $10 extra charge. **Facility:** 33 rooms. 2 whirlpool rms, extra charge; 2 stories; ex-
Motel　terior corridors; small pool, whirlpool. **Dining:** Coffee shop nearby. **Cards:** AE, DI, MC, VI.
　　　Special Amenities: Early check-in/late check-out and free breakfast.

HOLIDAY INN EXPRESS　　　　　Rates Subject to Change　　　　　Phone: 209/894-3055
[FYI]　All Year　　　1P: $49- 69　2P/1B: $49- 69　2P/2B: $54- 74
　　　Too new to rate. **Location:** I-5, exit Westley. 4525 Howard Rd 95387. **Facility:** 65 rooms. Scheduled to open
Motel　Fall, 1998. *(See color ad below)*

WESTMINSTER—78,100　(See map p. 294; index p. 292)

LODGINGS

BEST WESTERN WESTMINSTER INN　　　　　　　　　Phone: (714)898-4043　　[192]
🔺🔺🔺 [SAVE]　4/30-9/30 & 12/18-1/9　1P: $52- 92　2P/1B: $58- 98　2P/2B: $62- 108　XP: $6-10　F17
　　　2/1-4/29, 10/1-12/17 &
◆◆◆　1/10-1/31　　　1P: $46- 86　2P/1B: $52- 92　2P/2B: $58- 98　XP: $6-10　F17
Motel　**Location:** 0.3 mi w of I-405, exit Westminster Ave. 5755 Westminster Ave 92683. Fax: 714/895-6151.
　　　Terms: Reserv deposit, 5 day notice. **Facility:** 45 rooms. 2 stories; exterior corridors; whirlpool. **Cards:** AE,
CB, DI, DS, MC, VI.

TRAVELODGE WESTMINSTER/HUNTINGTON BEACH　　Rates Subject to Change　Phone: (714)373-3200　[194]
◆◆　6/1-9/30 [CP]　　1P: $45- 49　2P/1B: $49- 54　2P/2B: $55- 65　XP: $5　F12
Motel　2/1-5/31 & 10/1-1/31 [CP]　1P: $39- 42　2P/1B: $42- 47　2P/2B: $49- 55　XP: $5　F12
　　　Location: On SR 39, 0.5 mi s of jct SR 22. 13659 Beach Blvd 92683. Fax: 714/895-5801. **Facility:** 46 rooms.
2 stories; exterior corridors; heated pool. **Cards:** AE, DI, DS, MC, VI. *(See color ad p 1082)*

(See map p. 294)

WESTMINSTER GATEWAY TRAVELODGE   Phone: (714)898-5598   195
| | | | | | | | | |
6/1-9/30 · 1P: $42 · 2P/1B: $45 · 2P/2B: $55 · XP: $5 · F12
2/1-5/31 & 10/1-1/31 · 1P: $39 · 2P/1B: $42 · 2P/2B: $50 · XP: $5 · F12
Location: 0.5 mi e of I-405; exit Westminster Ave. 6601 Westminster Ave 92683. Fax: 714/895-2140. **Terms:** Reserv deposit, 3 day notice; weekly rates. **Facility:** 60 rooms. Small pool. **Some Rooms:** whirlpools. **Cards:** AE, CB, DI, MC, VI. **Special Amenities:** Early check-in/late check-out and preferred room (subject to availability with advanced reservations).

WESTMINSTER SUPER 8   Phone: (714)895-5584   196
4/1-8/31 · 1P: $45- 50 · 2P/1B: $48- 54 · 2P/2B: $55- 60 · XP: $3
2/1-3/31 & 9/1-1/31 · 1P: $40- 45 · 2P/1B: $43- 48 · 2P/2B: $50- 55 · XP: $3
Location: On SR 39, just n of I-405. 15559 Beach Blvd 92683. Fax: 714/894-0530. **Facility:** 32 rooms. 4 stories; exterior corridors. **Cards:** AE, CB, DI, DS, MC, VI. **Special Amenities:** Early check-in/late check-out and preferred room (subject to availability with advanced reservations).

WESTPORT

LODGING

DE HAVEN VALLEY FARM   Guaranteed Rates   Phone: (707)961-1660
All Year [BP] · 1P: $85- 135 · 2P/1B: $85- 135 · 2P/2B: $90- 140 · XP: $25 · F6
Location: SR 1, 18 mi n of Jct SR 20. 39244 N Highway One 95488. **Terms:** Reserv deposit, 3 day notice. **Facility:** 8 rooms. 2 stories; interior/exterior corridors; whirlpool. **Cards:** MC, VI.
Bed & Breakfast

WHITTIER—*See Los Angeles p. 652.*

WILLIAMS—2,300

LODGINGS

GRANZELLA'S INN   Phone: (530)473-3310
All Year [CP] · 1P: $60- 65 · 2P/1B: $60 · 2P/2B: $65- 75 · XP: $5 · F18
Location: Exit I-5 at main Williams exit, 0.5 mi w. 391 6th St 95987. Fax: 530/473-3486. **Terms:** Small pets only, $10 extra charge. **Facility:** 43 rooms. 2 stories; interior corridors; whirlpool. **Dining:** Restaurant; $8-$16. **Cards:** AE, CB, DI, DS, MC, VI. **Special Amenities:** Free breakfast and free local telephone calls.
Motor Inn

STAGE STOP MOTEL   Phone: (530)473-2281
All Year · 1P: $33- 35 · 2P/1B: $35- 40 · 2P/2B: $40- 45 · XP: $5 · F15
Location: Exit I-5 via SR 20 business rt, 3 blks w. 330 N 7th St 95987. Fax: 530/473-2166. **Terms:** Reserv deposit; pets, $5 extra charge. **Facility:** 25 rooms. 2 two-bedroom units. 1 story; exterior corridors; small pool. **All Rooms:** combo or shower baths. **Cards:** AE, CB, DI, DS, JC, MC, VI.
Motel

WOODCREST INN   Rates Subject to Change   Phone: 530/473-2381
All Year [CP] · 1P: $49 · 2P/1B: $54 · 2P/2B: $54 · XP: $5 · F18
Location: Adjacent to I-5, exit W SR 20 business rt; just n. 400 C St 95987 (PO Box 729). Fax: 530/473-2418. **Terms:** Small pets only, $5 extra charge. **Facility:** 60 rooms. 2 stories; exterior corridors; small pool, whirlpool. **Cards:** AE, CB, DI, DS, MC, VI.
Motel

WILLITS—5,000

LODGINGS

BAECHTEL CREEK INN   Phone: (707)459-9063
(AAA) (SAVE)   All Year [CP]   1P: $49- 98 2P/1B: $49- 98 2P/2B: $59- 108 XP: $5   F5
◆◆◆   **Location:** US 101; west on Gregory Ln. 101 Gregory Ln 95490. Fax: 707/459-0226. **Terms:** Reserv deposit,
Motel   24 day notice; small pets only, $10 extra charge, limited rooms. **Facility:** 46 rooms. 2 stories; exterior corri-
dors; heated pool, whirlpool. **Dining:** Restaurant nearby. **Cards:** AE, DS, MC, VI. **Special Amenities:** Free
breakfast and free room upgrade (subject to availability with advanced reservations).
(See color ad below)   🆂 🛏 🔧 🌊 🛎 📺 🖼 🔌 ❌

BEST WESTERN INN WILLITS   Rates Subject to Change   Phone: 707/459-5800
(FYI)   5/1-10/31 [CP]   1P: $59- 69 2P/1B: $68- 78 2P/2B: $68- 88 XP: $5   F12
2/1-4/30 & 11/1-1/31 [CP]   1P: $49- 59 2P/1B: $58- 68 2P/2B: $62- 72 XP: $5   F12
Motel   Too new to rate. **Location:** US-101, 1.3 mi s of jct SR-20. 1777 S Main St 95490. Fax: 707/459-9367.
Terms: Reserv deposit. **Facility:** 44 rooms. Scheduled to open September 1998. 2 stories; exterior corridors.
Cards: AE, CB, DI, DS, MC, VI.   🌊 🛎 🖼 🔧 📺 🔌 🔌 ❌

HOLIDAY LODGE MOTEL   Phone: (707)459-5361
(AAA) (SAVE)   5/15-10/15 [CP]   1P: $45- 55 2P/1B: $50- 60 2P/2B: $55- 65 XP: $5   F6
2/1-5/14 & 10/16-1/31 [CP] 1P: $42- 52 2P/1B: $58- 68 2P/2B: $45- 55 XP: $5   F6
◆◆   **Location:** On US-101, 1 mi s of Jct. SR-20. 1540 S Main St 95490. Fax: 707/459-2334. **Terms:** Reserv
Motel   deposit. **Facility:** 16 rooms. 1 story; exterior corridors; small pool, 5/1-9/30. **All Rooms:** combo or shower
baths. **Some Rooms:** efficiency. **Cards:** AE, DS, MC, VI. **Special Amenities:** Free breakfast and free local
telephone calls.   🌊 🔧 📺 🔌 ❌

OLD WEST INN   Phone: (707)459-4201
(AAA) (SAVE)   All Year [CP]   1P: $49- 69 2P/1B: $59- 89 2P/2B: $69- 89 XP: $10
◆◆   **Location:** On US-101, 0.5 mi s of jct SR-20. 1221 S Main St 95490. Fax: 707/459-3009. **Terms:** Reserv
Motel   deposit; handling fee imposed. **Facility:** 19 rooms. Early western theme rooms & facades. 2 stories; exterior
corridors; small pool open 5/15-9/30. **Dining:** Restaurant nearby. **Cards:** AE, CB, DI, DS, MC, VI.
Special Amenities: Free local telephone calls and preferred room (subject to availability with
advanced reservations).   🆂 🌊 🔧 📺 🔌 🔌 ❌

WILLOWS—6,000

LODGINGS

BEST WESTERN GOLDEN PHEASANT INN   Phone: (530)934-4603
(AAA) (SAVE)   All Year [BP]   1P: $59- 99 2P/1B: $69- 89 2P/2B: $79- 99 XP: $10-15   F12
◆◆◆   **Location:** E side of I-5; exit frwy via Willow-Elk Creek-Glenn Rd. 249 N Humboldt Ave 95988.
Motor Inn   Fax: 530/934-4275. **Terms:** Pets, $10 fee extra charge. **Facility:** 104 rooms. Nicely landscaped lawn area.
Spanish design. 1 story; exterior corridors; heated pool. **Dining:** Santa Fe Grill, see separate listing.
Cards: AE, CB, DI, DS, JC, MC, VI. **Special Amenities:** Free local telephone calls.
                                                      🆂 🛏 🌊 🍴 🔧 (VCR) 🔌 ❌

CROSS ROADS WEST INN   Rates Subject to Change   Phone: (530)934-7026
(AAA)   All Year   1P: $36   2P/1B: $41   2P/2B: $46
◆   **Location:** E side of I-5; exit via Willow-Elk Creek-Glenn Rd. 452 N Humboldt Ave 95988. Fax: 530/934-7026.
Motel   **Terms:** Reserv deposit; pets. **Facility:** 41 rooms. 2 stories; exterior corridors. **Dining:** Coffee shop nearby.
Cards: AE, DS, MC, VI.   🛏 🌊 🛎 ❌

SUPER 8 MOTEL   Rates Subject to Change   Phone: (530)934-2871
◆   All Year   1P: $44- 49 2P/1B: $49- 54 2P/2B: $49- 54 XP: $6   F12
Motel   **Location:** Exit I-5 via Willow- Elk Creek- Glenn Rd. 457 Humboldt Ave 95988. Fax: 530/934-5512.
Facility: 41 rooms. Interior corridors. **Cards:** AE, CB, DI, DS, MC, VI.   (ASK) 🆂 🛏 🌊 🛎 🔌 ❌

RESTAURANTS

FRANCO'S   **Lunch:** $5-$9   **Dinner:** $11-$15   Phone: 530/934-4273
◆   **Location:** 0.5 mi s on Old Hwy 99. 610 S Tehama St 95988. **Hours:** 11 am-2 & 4:30-10:30 pm, Sat 5
Italian   pm-10:30 pm, Sun 4 pm-9 pm. Closed: 1/1, 7/4 & 12/25. **Reservations:** suggested. **Features:** casual dress;
children's menu; cocktails & lounge; minimum charge-$5; a la carte. Family style, Italian American cuisine.
Cards: MC, VI.   ❌

SANTA FE GRILL   **Lunch:** $6-$11   **Dinner:** $9-$18   **Phone:** 530/934-2878
◆◆
Southwest   **Location:** At Best Western Golden Pheasant Inn. 247 N Humboldt 95988. **Hours:** 6 am-9 am, 11 am-2:30
American   pm & 5-9 pm. Sun. brunch 10 am-2:30 pm. **Reservations:** accepted. **Features:** casual dress; Sunday
brunch; cocktails & lounge; a la carte. California cuisine. **Cards:** AE, CB, DI, DS, MC, VI.

WILMINGTON—See Los Angeles p. 652.

WOODLAND—39,800

LODGINGS

BEST WESTERN SHADOW INN   **Phone:** (530)666-1251
(AAA) (SAVE)   All Year [CP]   1P: $58- 68   2P/1B: $62- 72   2P/2B: $66- 76   XP: $4   F12
◆◆◆   **Location:** I-5 exit Yuba City/Davis SR 113N, 0.3 mi w. 584 N East St 95776. Fax: 530/662-2804.
Motel   **Facility:** 123 rooms. Attractively landscaped pool area. 2 stories; exterior corridors; heated pool, whirlpools.
Dining: Coffee shop nearby. **Cards:** AE, DI, DS, MC, VI. **Special Amenities: Free breakfast.**

CINDERELLA MOTEL   **Phone:** (530)662-1091
(AAA) (SAVE)   All Year   1P: $40- 50   2P/1B: $44- 54   2P/2B: $48- 58   XP: $5
◆   **Location:** 0.8 mi w on I-5 business loop; northbound I-5 exit Main St 2 mi w, southbound exit West St, 1.5
Motel   mi s to Main St, 1 blk w. 99 W Main St 95695. Fax: 530/668-0332. **Terms:** Reserv deposit, 3 day notice;
handling fee imposed; small pets only, $25 dep req. **Facility:** 30 rooms. Centrally located. 2 stories; exterior
corridors; whirlpool. **All Rooms:** combo or shower baths. **Cards:** AE, CB, DI, DS, JC, MC, VI.
Special Amenities: Free room upgrade and preferred room (each subject to availability with advanced reservations).

COMFORT INN   **Phone:** (530)666-3050
(AAA) (SAVE)   All Year [CP]   1P: $45- 65   2P/1B: $54- 74   2P/2B: $59- 79   XP: $6-10   F12
◆◆   **Location:** I-5 northbound exit SR 113 Woodland; southbound exit Main St. 1562 E Main St 95776.
Motel   Fax: 530/666-1119. **Terms:** Reserv deposit. **Facility:** 51 rooms. Attractive comfortable rooms. 2 stories; ex-
terior corridors; whirlpool. **Dining:** Coffee shop nearby. **Some Rooms:** whirlpools. **Cards:** AE, CB, DI, DS,
JC, MC. **Special Amenities: Free breakfast and free local telephone calls.**

DAYS INN   **Phone:** (530)666-3800
(AAA) (SAVE)   All Year [CP]   1P: $45- 65   2P/1B: $56- 69   2P/2B: $59- 75   XP: $6-10   F12
◆◆   **Location:** I-5 northbound exit Woodland; southbound exit Main St; SR 113 exit Main St. 1524 E Main St
Motel   95776. Fax: 530/666-2281. **Terms:** Reserv deposit. **Facility:** 53 rooms. 3 stories, no elevator; interior corridors.
Dining: Coffee shop nearby. **All Rooms:** combo or shower baths. **Cards:** AE, CB, DI, DS, JC, MC, VI.
Special Amenities: Free breakfast and free local telephone calls.

VALLEY OAKS INN   Rates Subject to Change   **Phone:** (530)666-5511
(AAA)   All Year   1P: $42   2P/1B: $44   2P/2B: $46   XP: $2   F6
◆◆   **Location:** Exit I-5 at Yuba City exit. 600 N East St 95776. Fax: 530/666-5511. **Facility:** 62 rooms. 2 stories;
Motel   exterior corridors; whirlpool. **Dining:** Coffee shop nearby. **Cards:** AE, MC, VI.

WOODLAND HILLS—See Los Angeles p. 653.

WOODSIDE—5,000   (See map p. 922; index p. 918)

RESTAURANTS

BELLA VISTA RESTAURANT **Dinner:** $17-$26 **Phone:** 650/851-1229 ⟨84⟩
♦♦ **Location:** On SR 35, between SR 92 & 84; n of SR 84. 13451 Skyline Blvd 94062. **Hours:** 5 pm-10 pm,
Continental Sat-10:30 pm. Closed major holidays & Sun. **Reservations:** suggested. **Features:** semi-formal attire;
cocktails & lounge; minimum charge-$10; a la carte. In the redwoods. Some tables with a view. Smoke free
premises. **Cards:** AE, DI, DS, MC, VI.   ⊠

THE VILLAGE PUB **Lunch:** $8-$13 **Dinner:** $25-$35 **Phone:** 650/851-1294 ⟨85⟩
♦♦♦ **Location:** w of I-280, exit Woodside Rd, 0.7 mi. 2967 Woodside Rd 94062. **Hours:** 11:30 am-2:30 & 5:30-10
American pm, Sat 5:30-10 pm, Sun 5:30-9:30 pm. Closed major holidays. **Reservations:** suggested. **Features:** casual
dress; cocktails. Contemporary cuisine, all fresh ingredients, unique preparation. A warm, friendly
atmosphere popular with locals. **Cards:** AE, DI, DS, MC, VI.   ⊠

YORBA LINDA—52,400

LODGING

COUNTRY SIDE SUITES Rates Subject to Change **Phone:** (714)921-8688
♦♦♦ All Year [BP] 1P: $74 2P/1B: $84 2P/2B: $84 XP: $10 F12
Motel **Location:** Adjacent to SR 91, exit Weir Canyon Rd. 22677 Oak Crest Cir 92887. Fax: 714/283-3927.
Facility: 112 rooms. Attractive French country decor. Several shopping centers nearby. All rooms with whirl-
pool. 4 stories; interior corridors; heated pool. **All Rooms:** combo or shower baths. **Cards:** AE, DI, DS, MC, VI.
(See ad below)

ⒶⓈⓀ 🆂 🕸 🎄 🚪 🚶 🛏 🐟 🍴 ⛏ 🖥 🖨 🔒 ⊠

RESTAURANT

MIMI'S CAFE **Lunch:** $8-$13 **Dinner:** $8-$13 **Phone:** 714/996-3650
♦♦ **Location:** Corner of Yorba Linda Blvd, in Yorba Linda Station Shopping Center. 18342 Imperial Hwy 92886.
American **Hours:** 7 am-11 pm. Closed: 12/25. **Features:** casual dress; children's menu; beer & wine only; a la carte.
Charming French country decor. Good selection of soups, salads, pasta dishes, meat & fish entrees. Patio
dining avail. Smoke free premises. **Cards:** AE, MC, VI.   ⊠

YOSEMITE NATIONAL PARK—1,100—*See also AHWAHNEE, BASS LAKE, COULTERVILLE, EL PORTAL, FISH CAMP, GROVELAND, MARIPOSA & OAKHURST.*

Reservations should be made well in advance for all types of accommodations: write
Yosemite Concession Services, Inc., Yosemite National Park, CA 95389, or phone
(559)252-4848; also The Redwoods, PO Box 2085, Wawona, CA 95389 or phone (209)375-
6666. Rates may be revised or adjusted in fall & spring with NPS approval.

LODGINGS

THE AHWAHNEE Rates Subject to Change **Phone:** (559)252-4848
♦♦♦♦ All Year 1P: $247- 512 2P/1B: $247- 512 2P/2B: $247- 715 XP: $20 F
Historic Hotel **Location:** 0.8 mi e beyond Park Headquarters. In Yosemite Valley 95389. Fax: 559/456-0542.
Terms: Check-in 5 pm; reserv deposit, 3 day notice. **Facility:** 123 rooms. Spacious shaded setting; spectacular
views. Imposing common areas. Few small rooms. 24 duplex cottages; 7 stories; interior/exterior corridors; 2 tennis courts.
Services: giftshop; area transportation. **Recreation:** fishing; hiking trails. Fee: downhill & cross country skiing; ice skating;
bicycles, horseback riding. **All Rooms:** combo or shower baths. **Cards:** DI, DS, JC, MC, VI.

🎄 🛏 🚶 🍴 🍷 🐟 ⊠ 📼 🖥 🖨 🔒 🎿 ♿ ⊠ 🐾

THE REDWOODS IN YOSEMITE
◆◆   5/1-9/30
Resort   2/1-4/30 & 10/1-1/31
Cottage

Rates Subject to Change   Phone: 209/375-6666
1P: $105- 414   2P/1B: $105- 414   2P/2B: $105- 414   XP:$13-21   F4
1P: $82- 325   2P/1B: $82- 325   2P/2B: $82- 325   XP:$11-19   F4

Location: In Wawona, 6 mi inside the southern entrance via SR 41 & Chilnualna Falls Rd. 8038 Chilnualna Falls Rd 95389. Fax: 209/375-6400. **Terms:** Reserv deposit, 10 day notice; handling fee imposed; 2 night min stay. **Facility:** 129 rooms. Forest setting. Most units with woodburning fireplace. From rustic studio cabins to 6-bedroom deluxe homes, fully equipped. 63 two-bedroom units, 46 three-bedroom units. 3 night min stay, 6/1-8/30; 2 stories; exterior corridors. **Recreation:** swimming, fishing; hiking trails. **All Rooms:** kitchens, combo or shower baths. **Some Rooms:** color TV. **Cards:** MC, VI. *(See color ad below)*

SHOW YOUR CARD AND SAVE 10%

SeaWorld San Diego is a 150-acre adventure park on beautiful Mission Bay. Visit *Manatee Rescue* and come face to whiskers with an endangered manatee. At *Wild Arctic* where you'll encounter polar bears, beluga whales and walruses. See the ocean's top predators in the new *Shamu Adventure* killer whale show. You'll take the ride of your life on new *Shipwreck Rapids*, open May 1999.

SeaWorld
ADVENTURE PARK
San Diego

Show Your Card & Save

Hyatt Islandia

A Waterfront Resort on San Diego's Mission Bay
The closest full-service resort to SeaWorld. The Hyatt Islandia is convenient to all area attractions and beaches. Complimentary self parking. Enjoy boating, sportfishing, parasailing, swimming and bicycling. Children 18 and under stay free. A great vacation value with discount SeaWorld, Zoo and Wild Animal Park tickets.

$129
Per room, per night
Sunday - Thursday
Ask about our special AAA Tower, Marina Suite and weekend rates.

HYATT
ISLANDIA
NEXT TO SEAWORLD IN SAN DIEGO

Hyatt Regency La Jolla

Situated by scenic La Jolla, the Hyatt Regency La Jolla is close to all of the area's finest attractions. Take in a beach sunset, golf at Torrey Pines or visit the Del Mar racetrack. Enjoy the variety of facilities available to you at the Hyatt, including four award winning restaurants and the renowned 32,000 square foot Aventine Sporting Club and Spa. Just ask for the "La Jolla Getaway" special.

$169
Per room, per night Fri. - Mon.
$179 per room, per night Mon.- Fri.

HYATT
REGENCY
LA JOLLA
AT AVENTINE

Hyatt Regency San Diego

As one of the West Coast's tallest waterfront buildings, the Hyatt Regency San Diego is the centerpiece of the city's vibrant downtown area. Adjacent to Seaport Village for fantastic shopping and dining, and just a stroll to the exciting night-life of the Gaslamp district. Enjoy swimming, tennis, a healthclub, spa, boat rentals and magnificent bay views from every room. Children 18 and under stay free. Just ask for the "San Diego Getaway" special.

$189
Per room, per night

HYATT
REGENCY
SAN DIEGO
ON SAN DIEGO BAY

Catamaran Resort Hotel

Five minutes to SeaWorld. Secluded along the shores of Mission Bay, just 100 yards to the Pacific Ocean, this beachfront tropical resort offers 313 guestrooms and suites with fun activities for the entire family. Watersports, pool, spa, video arcade and fitness center. Award-winning bayside restaurant, nightclub, piano bar and sternwheeler cruises. Discounted SeaWorld, Zoo & Wild Animal Park tickets for hotel guests.

$149
Per room, per night
Sunday - Thursday

CATAMARAN
RESORT HOTEL

SAN DIEGO GETAWAY - AAA DISCOUNTS

The San Diego WILD ANIMAL PARK
There's no place like it on earth.

Save $2 On Nairobi Ticket Package

Coupon good for maximum 6 tickets. Not valid with any other offer, special ticketed events, or membership. Parking fee not included. Valid Feb.1, 1999 – April 30, 2000. PT-539

The San Diego Zoo

Save $2 On Deluxe Ticket Package

Coupon good for maximum 6 tickets. Not valid with any other offer, special ticketed events, or membership. Valid Feb.1, 1999–April 30, 2000. AT-539

YOSEMITE VIEW LODGE

Located at Yosemite's doorstep, rooms overlooking the beautiful Merced River. Fireplaces • Spa tubs for 2 • Kitchenettes • 2 pools • 3 spas • Restaurant and lounge

11156 Hwy 140 • P.O. Box "D" • El Portal, CA 95318
(209) 379-2681 • Fax (209) 379-2704

CEDAR LODGE

8 miles from Yosemite National Park across from the Merced River. Wonderful river walk area. Family units and rooms with spa tubs available • Indoor and outdoor pools • Conference facility • 2 restaurants and a lounge

9966 Hwy 140 • P.O. Box "C" • El Portal, CA 95318
(209) 379-2612 • Fax (209) 379-2712

BEST WESTERN YOSEMITE WAY STATION

In Historic Mariposa. Complimentary continental breakfast • Pool and Spa (in season) • Conference facility • Walk to restaurants

4999 Hwy 140 • P.O. Box 1989 • Mariposa, CA 95338
(209) 966-7545 • Fax (209) 966-6353

MINERS INN

In Historic Mariposa, walk to nearby History Center. Pool and Spa (in season) • In-room coffee • Some rooms with spa tubs and fireplaces • Restaurant and lounge nearby

5181 Hwy 49N • P.O. Box 1989 • Mariposa, CA 95338
(209) 742-7777 • Fax (209) 966-2343

COMFORT INN - MARIPOSA

In Historic Mariposa, just 40 minutes from Yosemite National Park. Complimentary continental breakfast • Pool and Spa (in season) • Family units available

4994 Bullion St. • P.O. Box 1989 • Mariposa, CA 95338
(209) 966-4344 • Fax (209) 966-4655

COMFORT INN - OAKHURST

15 miles from Yosemite National Park, in the center of town. Complimentary continental breakfast • In-room coffee and refrigerators • Pool and Spa (in season)

40489 Hwy 41 • Oakhurst, CA 93644
(559) 683-8282 • Fax (559) 658-7030

YOSEMITE MOTELS

Reservations
Toll Free - Nationwide
800-321-5261

reservations @yosemite-motels.com • http://www.yosemite-motels.com

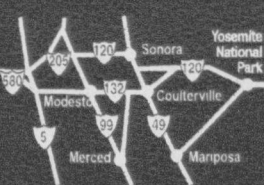

WAWONA HOTEL
Rates Subject to Change
Phone: 209/375-6556

[FYI] All Year
1P: $71- 98 2P/1B: $71- 98 2P/2B: $71- 98 XP: $13   F12
Has not been inspected. **Location:** On SR 41; 27 mi s from Yosemite Valley; 8 mi from the Mariposa Grove
Historic Hotel of Big Trees. SR 41 95389. **Fax:** 209/375-6601. **Terms:** Check-in 4 pm; reserv deposit, 3 day notice.
Facility: 104 rooms. Charming setting on spacious grounds. Modest older units. Also open weekends in winter.
Meets AAA fire safety requirements. Rates reviewed in Spring & Fall; 2 stories; interior/exterior corridors; 1 tennis court.
Fee: 9 holes golf. **Recreation:** hiking trails. **Cards:** DS, MC, VI.

YOSEMITE LODGE
Rates Subject to Change
Phone: 559/252-4848

◆◆   Fri & Sat 2/1-3/23,
Resort Motel 3/24-10/29 & Fri & Sat
10/30-1/31   1P: $87- 107 2P/1B: $87- 107 2P/2B: $87- 107 XP: $11   F12
Sun-Thurs 2/1-3/23 &
10/30-1/31   1P: $81- 86 2P/1B: $81- 86 2P/2B: $81- 86 XP: $11   F12
Location: In Yosemite Valley; 0.8 mi w of park headquarters; near Yosemite Falls. PO Box D 95318 (PO Box 1989,
MARIPOSA, 95338). **Fax:** 559/456-0542. **Terms:** Check-in 4 pm. **Facility:** 245 rooms. Rates reviewed in Spring & Fall; may
change with NPS approval; 2 stories; interior/exterior corridors. **Services:** giftshop; area transportation. **Recreation:** fishing;
hiking trails. Fee: downhill & cross country skiing, ice skating; horseback riding. Rental: bicycles. **All Rooms:** combo or
shower baths. **Cards:** CB, DI, DS, JC, MC, VI.

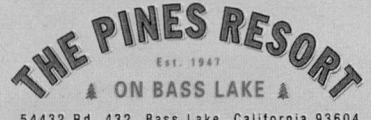

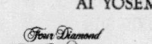
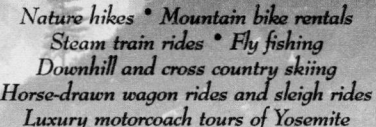

YOUNTVILLE—3,300

LODGINGS

MAISON FLEURIE   Rates Subject to Change   **Phone: 707/944-2056**
◆◆   4/1-11/30 [BP]   1P: $110- 235   2P/1B: $110- 235   XP: $15   F2
Bed &   2/1-3/31 & 12/1-1/31 [BP] 1P: $110- 205   2P/1B: $110- 205   XP: $15   F2
Breakfast   **Location:** Center; Yountville exit. 6529 Yount St 94599. Fax: 707/944-9342. **Facility:** 13 rooms. Attractively
landscaped grounds; 6 rooms with fireplace. 2 stories; interior/exterior corridors; heated pool.
All Rooms: combo or shower baths. **Some Rooms:** color TV. **Cards:** AE, MC, VI.

NAPA VALLEY LODGE   **Phone: (707)944-2468**
(AAA) (SAVE)   All Year [CP]   1P: $172- 325   2P/1B: $172- 325   2P/2B: $172- 325 XP: $25
                  Location: 0.5 mi n, off SR 29; exit Madison St. 2230 Madison St 94599. Fax: 707/944-9362. **Facility:** 55
◆◆◆◆   rooms. Many rooms with fireplaces. Some rooms overlooking vineyards & hills. Balcony or patio. 3 two-
Motor Inn   bedroom units. 2 stories; exterior corridors; heated pool, sauna, whirlpool. **Dining:** Restaurant nearby.
                  Services: complimentary evening beverages. **Cards:** AE, CB, DI, DS, MC, VI. **Special Amenities:** Free
breakfast and free newspaper. *(See color ad inside back cover & p 739)*

VILLAGIO INN & SPA   Rates Subject to Change   **Phone: 707/944-8877**
[FYI]   All Year [CP]   1P: $250- 550   2P/1B: $250- 550   2P/2B: $250- 550 XP: $25
                  Too new to rate. **Location:** SR 29, Yountville exit. 6481 Washington St 94599. **Terms:** Check-in 4 pm; reserv
Motor Inn   deposit; 2 night min stay, weekends. **Facility:** 112 rooms. Private balconies or patios & fireplaces. Scheduled
to open fall, 1998; 2 stories; exterior corridors; heated pool; 2 tennis courts. **Cards:** AE, DI, DS, MC, VI.

VINTAGE INN   **Phone: (707)944-1112**
(AAA) (SAVE)   8/1-11/15 [CP]   1P: $250- 350   2P/1B: $250- 350   2P/2B: $250- 350 XP: $25   F12
                  2/1-7/31 [CP]   1P: $225- 325   2P/1B: $225- 325   2P/2B: $225- 325 XP: $25   F12
◆◆◆◆   11/16-1/31 [CP]   1P: $200- 295   2P/1B: $200- 295   2P/2B: $200- 295 XP: $25   F12
Motor Inn   **Location:** Center; SR 29 exit Yountville. 6541 Washington St 94599. Fax: 707/944-1617. **Terms:** Check-in 4
pm; reserv deposit; 2 night min stay, weekends 4/1-11/30; pets, $25 dep req. **Facility:** 80 rooms. Vineyard,
mountain & town views. Balconies or patios, all with fireplace & whirlpool tub. 1-2 stories; exterior corridors; heated pool, whirlpool; 2 tennis courts. **Dining:** Cocktails; restaurant nearby. **Rental:** bicycles. **Cards:** AE, CB, DI, DS, MC, VI.
Special Amenities: Free breakfast and free newspaper.

RESTAURANTS

DOMAINE CHANDON   **Lunch:** $40-$55   **Dinner:** $65-$80   **Phone:** 707/944-2892
(AAA)   **Location:** W off SR 29; adjacent to Veteran's Home. 1 California Dr 94599. **Hours:** 11:30 am-2:30 & 6-9:30
                  pm. Closed: 1/1, 12/25, 12/31 & first 3 weeks in Jan, Mon & Tues for dinner. **Reservations:** required; 14-day
◆◆◆◆   advance. **Features:** semi-formal attire; wine only; a la carte, a la carte. California cuisine for lunch & French
French   for dinner. Smoke free premises. **Cards:** AE, DI, MC, VI.

NAPA VALLEY GRILLE   **Lunch:** $8-$13   **Dinner:** $11-$20   **Phone:** 707/944-8686
◆◆   **Location:** SR 29 exit Madison St; in Washington Square. 6795 Washington St 94599. **Hours:** 11:30 am-9:30
American   pm, Sat-10 pm, Sun 10 am-9:30 pm. Closed: 12/25. **Reservations:** suggested. **Features:** casual dress;
Sunday brunch; cocktails; a la carte. Contemporary California cuisine, featuring fresh grilled meats & fish.
Smoke free premises. **Cards:** AE, DI, DS, MC, VI.

PIATTI RISTORANTE   **Lunch:** $8-$15   **Dinner:** $11-$19   **Phone:** 707/944-2070
◆◆   **Location:** SR 29 exit E Yountville-Veterans Home, 1 blk n. 6480 Washington St 94599. **Hours:** 11:30 am-10
Italian   pm, Fri & Sat-11 pm. Closed: 11/27 & 12/25. **Reservations:** suggested. **Features:** children's menu;
cocktails; a la carte. Few tables with view of vineyard. Smoke free premises. **Cards:** AE, MC, VI.

YREKA—6,900

LODGINGS

AMERIHOST INN-YREKA   **Phone: (530)841-1300**
(AAA) (SAVE)   All Year [CP]   1P: $52- 57   2P/1B: $57- 67   2P/2B: $57- 67   XP: $5   F16
                  Location: Exit I-5 at SR 3/Fort Jones. 148 Moonlit Oaks Ave 96097. Fax: 530/841-0399. **Terms:** Small pets
◆◆◆   only. **Facility:** 61 rooms. Whirlpool rms, extra charge; 2 stories; interior corridors; heated indoor pool, sauna,
Motel   whirlpool. **All Rooms:** combo or shower baths. **Cards:** AE, CB, DI, DS, JC, MC, VI. **Special Amenities:**
Free breakfast and free newspaper. *(See color ad p 284)*

BEST WESTERN MINER'S INN   Rates Subject to Change   **Phone: (530)842-4355**
(AAA)   5/1-9/30   1P: $54   2P/1B: $59   2P/2B: $64   XP: $5   F12
                  2/1-4/30 & 10/1-1/31   1P: $49   2P/1B: $54   2P/2B: $60   XP: $5   F12
◆◆◆   **Location:** Just w off I-5 via Central Yreka. 122 E Miner St 96097. Fax: 530/842-4480. **Terms:** Small pets
Motel   only. **Facility:** 134 rooms. Large rooms. 15 two-bedroom units with kitchen, $85 for 2 persons; 2 stories; ex-
terior corridors; picnic area, seasonal pools; playground. **Dining:** Coffee shop nearby. **All Rooms:** combo or
shower baths. **Cards:** AE, CB, DI, DS, MC, VI.

KLAMATH MOTOR LODGE   **Phone: (530)842-2751**
(AAA) (SAVE)   5/15-9/15   1P: $45   2P/1B: $50   2P/2B: $55   XP: $5   F12
                  2/1-5/14 & 9/16-1/31   1P: $40   2P/1B: $42   2P/2B: $47   XP: $5   F12
◆◆   **Location:** Northbound exit I-5 Ft Jones N 1.3 mi; southbound exit Central Yreka s 0.8 mi. 1111 S Main St
Motel   96097. **Terms:** Reserv deposit. **Facility:** 28 rooms. Attractively landscaped grounds. 2 two-bedroom units. 2
stories; exterior corridors. **Recreation:** Picnic area. **All Rooms:** combo or shower baths. **Cards:** AE, CB, DI,
DS, MC, VI. **Special Amenities: Free local telephone calls and preferred room (subject to availability with advanced
reservations).**

MOTEL ORLEANS
◆
Motel
MC, VI.

Rates Subject to Change
All Year   1P: $29- 33   2P/1B: $35- 39   2P/2B: $36- 46   XP: $6   F12
Location: Exit I-5 at jct SR 3. 1806B Fort Jones Rd 96097 (PO Box 778). Fax: 530/842-0822. **Facility:** 53 rooms. 3 stories, no elevator; interior corridors. **All Rooms:** combo or shower baths. **Cards:** AE, CB, DI, DS,

Phone: (530)842-1612

RODEWAY INN
(AAA) [SAVE]
◆
Motel

5/15-10/15   1P: $36   2P/1B: $40   2P/2B: $44   XP: $4   F12
2/1-5/14 & 10/16-1/31 1P: $34   2P/1B: $38   2P/2B: $42   XP: $4   F12
Location: 0.3 mi s; I-5 via Central Yreka exit. 526 S Main St 96097. Fax: 530/841-0439. **Terms:** Weekly rates; pets, $4 extra charge, in designated rooms. **Facility:** 44 rooms. In-room coffee avail. 2 stories; exterior corridors. **All Rooms:** shower baths. **Cards:** AE, DS, MC, VI. **Special Amenities:** Early check-in/late check-out and free local telephone calls.

Phone: (530)842-4404

WAYSIDE INN
(AAA) [SAVE]
◆ ◆
Motel

8/1-9/8   1P: $45- 68   2P/1B: $45- 68   2P/2B: $50- 78   XP: $4   F12
5/15-7/31 & 9/9-9/30 1P: $39- 56   2P/1B: $45- 60   2P/2B: $50- 68   XP: $4   F12
2/1-5/14 & 10/1-1/31   1P: $34- 40   2P/1B: $37- 48   2P/2B: $45- 56   XP: $4   F12
Location: Northbound exit I-5 Ft Jones, 1 mi n; southbound exit Central Yreka, 1 mi s. 1235 S Main St 96097. Fax: 530/842-4412. **Terms:** Weekly rates; pets, $3 extra charge. **Facility:** 44 rooms. Attractively decorated rooms; some covered parking. 3 kitchens, $32-$48 for 2 rooms. 1 unit with whirlpool tub, fireplace, microwave, refrigerator & VCP, $135-$150; 1 story; exterior corridors; whirlpool. **Dining:** Restaurant nearby. **Recreation:** Picnic area. **All Rooms:** combo or shower baths. **Cards:** AE, CB, DI, DS, MC, VI. **Special Amenities:** Free local telephone calls.

Phone: (530)842-4412

RESTAURANT

OLD BOSTON SHAFT RESTAURANT
(AAA)
◆ ◆
Continental

Lunch: $4-$9   Dinner: $9-$16   Phone: 530/842-5768
Location: Exit I-5 at jct SR 3. 1801 Fort Jones Rd 96097. **Hours:** 11 am-2:30 & 5-9:30 pm, Sat 5 pm-9:30 pm, Mother's Day & 11/25 2 pm-9 pm. Closed: 1/1, 12/24, 12/25 & Sun. **Reservations:** suggested. **Features:** casual dress; children's menu; cocktails & lounge; a la carte. Varied menu, American/European featuring beef, seafood, veal & European desserts. Smoke free premises. **Cards:** AE, CB, DI, DS, MC, VI.

YUBA CITY—27,400

LODGINGS

BEST WESTERN BONANZA INN
(AAA) [SAVE]
◆ ◆ ◆
Motor Inn

All Year   1P: $59   2P/1B: $63   2P/2B: $68   XP: $4   F12
Location: 2 mi w of Marysville, 1 blk n off SR 20. 1001 Clark Ave 95991. Fax: 530/674-0563. **Facility:** 125 rooms. Large, comfortable rooms. 2 stories; exterior corridors; whirlpool. **Dining:** Dining room, coffee shop; 6 am-2 & 5-10 pm; $10-$25; cocktails. **Some Rooms:** whirlpools. **Cards:** AE, CB, DI, DS, MC, VI. **Special Amenities:** Free local telephone calls and free newspaper.

Phone: (530)674-8824

DAYS INN
◆
Motel
VI.

Guaranteed Rates
All Year   1P: $39- 43   2P/1B: $39- 43   2P/2B: $44- 48   XP: $5
Location: Exit SR 99 at Bridge St, 0.5 mi s of SR 20. 700 N Palora Ave 95991. Fax: 530/671-1937. **Facility:** 50 rooms. 2 stories; exterior corridors. **All Rooms:** combo or shower baths. **Cards:** AE, DS, MC,

Phone: 530/674-1711

HOLIDAY INN EXPRESS-YUBA CITY
(AAA) [SAVE]
◆ ◆ ◆
Motel

All Year [CP]   1P: $84   2P/1B: $84   2P/2B: $84   XP: $6   F18
Location: SR 99, 0.3 mi s of jct SR 20. 894 W Onstott Rd 95991. Fax: 530/674-1266. **Facility:** 88 rooms. Large comfortable rooms. 2 stories; exterior corridors; sauna, whirlpool. **Dining:** Restaurant nearby. **Cards:** AE, CB, DI, DS, MC, VI. **Special Amenities:** Free breakfast and free local telephone calls.

Phone: (530)674-1650

MOTEL ORLEANS
◆ ◆
Motel
All Rooms: combo or shower baths. **Cards:** AE, CB, DI, DS, MC, VI.

Rates Subject to Change
All Year   1P: $34- 39   2P/1B: $39- 42   2P/2B: $42- 52   XP: $6   F12
Location: E of & adjacent to SR 99, 0.5 mi s of jct SR 20, exit SR 99 at Bridge St. 730 Palora Ave 95991. Fax: 530/674-3032. **Facility:** 53 rooms. 3 stories, no elevator; interior corridors; small pool.

Phone: (530)674-1592

VADA'S MOTEL
(AAA) [SAVE]
◆ ◆
Motel

All Year [CP]   1P: $33- 48   2P/1B: $36- 50   2P/2B: $42- 55   XP: $6-8   F12
Location: SR 20, 0.5 mi e of SR 99. 545 Colusa Ave 95991. Fax: 530/673-8189. **Terms:** Reserv deposit. **Facility:** 40 rooms. 6 two-bedroom units. 2 stories; exterior corridors. **Dining:** Restaurant nearby. **All Rooms:** combo or shower baths. **Some Rooms:** 6 kitchens. **Cards:** AE, DS, MC, VI. **Special Amenities:** Early check-in/late check-out and free breakfast.

Phone: (530)671-1151

RESTAURANT

THE REFUGE RESTAURANT & LOUNGE   **Lunch:** $6-$11   **Dinner:** $13-$21   **Phone:** 530/673-7620
◆◆   **Location:** SR 99 exit; w SR 20 1 blk, 3 blks n, then 1 blk w. 1501 Butte House Rd 95991. **Hours:** 11:30
American   am-2 & 5-9 pm, Sat 5 pm-10 pm, Sun 5 pm-9 pm. Closed: 1/1 & 12/25. **Reservations:** suggested.
     Features: casual dress; children's menu; cocktails; minimum charge-$5. Prime rib, steak & fresh seafood.
Cards: AE, MC, VI.   ⊠

YUCCA VALLEY—16,500

LODGINGS

DESERT VIEW MOTEL   Rates Subject to Change   **Phone:** (760)365-9706
Ⓐ   All Year [CP]   1P: $38- 45   2P/1B: $42- 49 2P/2B: $45- 52 XP: $5   F12
     Location: Just e of jct SR 62 & 247, s on Airway Ave. 57471 Primrose Dr 92284. Fax: 760/365-6021.
◆◆   **Facility:** 14 rooms. Exterior corridors; heated pool. **All Rooms:** combo or shower baths, extended cable TV.
Motel   **Cards:** AE, CB, DI, DS, MC, VI.   (A⎯S⎯K) Ⓢ ➲ 🍴 ▣ 🖥 🔌 🔒 ⊠

OASIS OF EDEN INN & SUITES   Rates Subject to Change   **Phone:** 760/365-6321
Ⓐ   All Year [CP]   1P: $45- 199 2P/1B: $65- 199 2P/2B: $65- 199 XP: $5
◆◆◆   **Location:** 1 mi w of Jct SR 62 & SR 247. 56377 Twentynine Palms Hwy 92284. Fax: 760/365-9592.
Motel   **Terms:** Reserv deposit; weekly/monthly rates; small pets only, $10 extra charge, $25 dep req. **Facility:** 39
     rooms. 13 themed rms, 12 with whirlpool, all with VCR; 2 stories; exterior corridors; heated pool, whirlpool.
     Dining: Restaurant nearby. **All Rooms:** extended cable TV. **Some Rooms:** 6 efficiencies, whirlpools.
Cards: AE, CB, DS, MC, VI.   Ⓢ 🐾 ➲ 🍴 ▣ (VCR) ▢ 🔒 ⊠

SUPER 8 MOTEL   **Phone:** 760/228-1773
Ⓐ (SAVE)   All Year [CP]   1P: $42- 52   2P/1B: $44- 56 2P/2B: $46- 56 XP: $5   F12
     Location: SR 62, 0.3 mi w of jct SR 247. 57096 29 Palms Hwy 92284. Fax: 760/365-7799. **Terms:** Small
◆◆   pets only. **Facility:** 48 rooms. 2 stories; interior corridors; small pool. **Dining:** Restaurant nearby.
Motel   **All Rooms:** extended cable TV. **Cards:** AE, CB, DI, DS, JC, MC, VI.   Ⓢ 🐾 ➲ 🍴 ▣ ⊠

RESTAURANT

STEPHANO'S GIARDINO ITALIAN RESTAURANT   **Lunch:** $5-$16   **Dinner:** $6-$18   **Phone:** 760/228-3118
◆◆   **Location:** On SR 62, 2 mi w of jct SR 247. 55509 Twenty nine Palms Hwy 92284. **Hours:** 11 am-3 &
Italian   5-10:30 pm, Fri & Sat-11:30 pm, Sun 4 pm-10:30 pm. Closed: 11/25 & 12/25. **Reservations:** suggested.
     Features: casual dress; children's menu; carryout; cocktails. Charming, small restaurant serving traditionally
prepared Italian dishes. Smoke free premises. **Cards:** AE, DI, DS, MC, VI.   ⊠

Nevada

AMARGOSA VALLEY

LODGING

LONGSTREET INN, CASINO RV PARK & GOLF CLUB　　Rates Subject to Change　　**Phone:** (775)372-1777
◆◆◆　　All Year　　　　1P: $59- 89　2P/1B: $59- 89　2P/2B: $59- 89　XP: $6-24　F16
Motor Inn　　**Location:** 7 mi n of jct SR 127 & SR 190 (Death Valley Jct) on SR 373. HCR 70, Box 559 89020 (PO Box 559). Fax: 775/372-1280. **Facility:** 60 rooms. Attractively landscaped pool area with gazebo & pond. 2 stories; interior corridors; heated pool. **All Rooms:** shower baths. **Cards:** AE, CB, DI, DS, JC, MC, VI.　🐾 🛏 🍴 ⬜ 🐕 ✕

BATTLE MOUNTAIN—3,500

LODGINGS

BEST WESTERN BIG CHIEF MOTEL　　　　　　　　　　　　　**Phone:** (775)635-2416
(AAA) (SAVE)　　All Year [CP]　　1P: $55- 65　2P/1B: $65- 75　2P/2B: $65- 75　XP: $6　F18
◆◆　　**Location:** Just n of I-80; exit 229 or 233. 434 W Front St 89820. Fax: 775/635-2418. **Terms:** Small pets
Motel　　only, $10 dep req. **Facility:** 58 rooms. Some small units. 2 stories; exterior corridors; whirlpool, heated pool 6/1-9/7. **All Rooms:** combo or shower baths. **Some Rooms:** 8 efficiencies, no utensils. **Cards:** AE, CB, DI, DS, MC, VI. **Special Amenities:** Free breakfast and free local telephone calls.

🛏 🐾 ⬜ 🖥 🖨 ✕ 🐕

COMFORT INN　　　　　Rates Subject to Change　　　　　**Phone:** (775)635-5880
◆◆　　All Year [CP]　　1P: $49- 54　2P/1B: $54- 59　2P/2B: $54- 59　XP: $6　F12
Motel　　**Location:** Just N of I-80, exit 229 or 233. 521 E Front St 89820. Fax: 775/635-5788. **Facility:** 72 rooms. 3 stories; interior corridors. **Cards:** AE, CB, DI, DS, MC, VI.

(SAVE) 🛏 🐾 🐕 🍴 ⬜ 🖥 🖨 🖨 ✕ 🐕

BEATTY—1,600

LODGING

BURRO INN　　　　　　Rates Subject to Change　　　　　**Phone:** 775/553-2225
◆　　All Year　　　　　1P: $37　　2P/1B: $42　　2P/2B: $42　　XP: $5
Motor Inn　　**Location:** 4 blks s on SR 95. Third St & Hwy 95 89003 (PO Box 7). Fax: 775/553-2892. **Facility:** 62 rooms. Rustic Western-Style Exterior. 2 stories; exterior corridors. **Cards:** AE, MC, VI.

🛏 🍴 🍸 ⬜ 🖨 ✕

BOULDER CITY—See Las Vegas p. 1115.

CARLIN—2,200

LODGING

BEST WESTERN CARLIN INN　　　Rates Subject to Change　　　**Phone:** (775)754-6110
◆◆　　All Year [CP]　　1P: $49- 79　2P/1B: $55- 84　2P/2B: $55- 84　XP: $6　F12
Motel　　**Location:** Just s of I-80, exit 280. 1018 Fir St 89822 (PO Box 847). Fax: 775/754-6973. **Facility:** 61 rooms. Convenient to truck parking. Personal checks not accepted; 3 stories; interior corridors. **All Rooms:** combo or shower baths. **Cards:** AE, CB, DI, DS, MC, VI.

(ASK) 🛏 🐾 🖥 ⬜ 🔧 🖥 🖨 🖨 🐕 ✕ 🐕

CARSON CITY—40,400

LODGINGS

BEST WESTERN CARSON STATION HOTEL/CASINO　　Guaranteed Rates　　**Phone:** (775)883-0900
◆◆　　Fri & Sat 4/1-10/31　1P: $63- 105　2P/1B: $63- 105　2P/2B: $63- 105　XP: $5　F13
Motor Inn　　Sun-Thurs 4/1-10/31　1P: $53- 90　2P/1B: $53- 90　2P/2B: $53- 90　XP: $5　F13
　　2/1-3/31 & 11/1-1/31　1P: $45- 85　2P/1B: $45- 85　2P/2B: $45- 85　XP: $5　F13
Location: South end of town. 900 S Carson 89701. Fax: 775/882-7569. **Facility:** 92 rooms. 5 stories; interior corridors. **Cards:** AE, CB, DI, DS, MC, VI.

(ASK) 🛏 🖥 🍴 ⬜ 🖥 🖨 🖨 ✕

BEST WESTERN PINON PLAZA CASINO RESORT　　Rates Subject to Change　　**Phone:** 775/885-9000
◆◆◆　　4/1-10/31　　1P: $70　　2P/1B: $70　　2P/2B: $70　　XP: $5　F12
Motor Inn　　2/1-3/31 & 11/1-1/31　1P: $50　2P/1B: $50　2P/2B: $50　XP: $5　F12
　　Location: E end of town on Hwy 50. 2171 Hwy 50 E 89701. Fax: 775/888-8003. **Facility:** 64 rooms. 2 stories; interior corridors; heated pool. **Services:** giftshop. **All Rooms:** combo or shower baths. **Cards:** AE, CB, DI, DS, MC, VI.

🔧 🖥 🐾 🍴 ⬜ 🔧 🖨 🖨 🐕 ✕ 🐕

BEST WESTERN TRAILSIDE INN　　　Rates Subject to Change　　　**Phone:** (775)883-7300
◆◆　　All Year　　　　1P: $39- 59　2P/1B: $45- 65　2P/2B: $49- 69　XP: $6　F12
Motel　　**Location:** 0.5 mi n on US 395. 1300 N Carson St 89701. Fax: 775/883-7506. **Facility:** 67 rooms. 2 stories; exterior corridors; heated pool, small pool. **Cards:** AE, CB, DI, DS, MC, VI.

(ASK) 🛏 🖥 🐾 🍴 🖥 ⬜ 🖨 🖨 ✕

BLISS MANSION　　　　Rates Subject to Change　　　　**Phone:** 775/887-8988
◆◆◆　　All Year [BP]　　1P: $155- 165　2P/1B: $165- 175
Historic Bed　　**Location:** W of US 395 & SR 50; across from Governor's Mansion. 710 W Robinson 89703.
& Breakfast　　Fax: 703/887-0540. **Facility:** 4 rooms. 2 stories; interior corridors. **All Rooms:** combo or shower baths. **Some Rooms:** color TV. **Cards:** AE, CB, DI, DS, MC, VI.

🍴 🖥 🖨 ✕

CARSON CITY SUPER 8　　　Rates Subject to Change　　　**Phone:** (775)883-7800
◆　　All Year　　　　1P: $49- 54　2P/1B: $54　　2P/2B: $59- 70　XP: $5　F12
Motel　　**Location:** South end of town. 2829 S Carson 89701. Fax: 775/883-0376. **Facility:** 63 rooms. 2 stories; interior corridors. **Cards:** AE, DI, DS, MC, VI.

(ASK) 🛏 🖥 🖥 ⬜ 🖨 ✕

DAYS INN
AAA SAVE
◆◆
Motel

Phone: (775)883-3343

		1P:	$45-	85	2P/1B:	$45-	85	2P/2B:	$85
Fri & Sat [CP]									
Sun-Thurs [CP]	1P:	$41-	75	2P/1B:	$41-	75	2P/2B:	$75	

Location: US 395N, n end of city. 3103 N Carson St 89706. **Fax:** 775/887-0446. **Terms:** Reserv deposit; small pets only, $5 extra charge. **Facility:** 61 rooms. 2 family type units, $80-$100 for up to 4 persons; 2 stories; exterior corridors. **Dining:** Coffee shop nearby. **Cards:** AE, CB, DI, DS, JC, MC, VI. **Special Amenities:** Free local telephone calls and free newspaper.

HARDMAN HOUSE MOTOR INN
AAA SAVE
◆◆◆
Motel

Phone: (775)882-7744

All Year [CP]   1P: $82- 110 2P/1B: $82- 110 2P/2B: $82- 110 XP: $10   F12
Location: US 395, just s of US 50. 917 N Carson St 89701. **Fax:** 775/887-0321. **Facility:** 62 rooms. Centrally located in downtown area. 3 stories; interior corridors. **Dining:** Coffee shop nearby. **Cards:** AE, DI, DS, MC, VI. **Special Amenities:** Free breakfast.

MOTEL ORLEANS
◆◆
Motel

Phone: (775)882-2007

All Year   Rates Subject to Change
1P: $32- 48 2P/1B: $37- 54 2P/2B: $37- 54
Location: 1.3 mi s on US 50 & 395. 2731 S Carson St 89701. **Fax:** 775/883-4182. **Facility:** 58 rooms. 2 stories; exterior corridors; small pool. **Cards:** AE, CB, DI, DS, MC, VI.

RESTAURANT

HEIDI'S FAMILY RESTAURANT   **Lunch:** $4-$8   Phone: 775/882-0486
AAA
◆
American

Location: At jct US 395 & 50E. 1020 North Carson St 89701. **Hours:** 6:30 am-2 pm. **Features:** children's menu. Family restaurant, noted for breakfast. **Cards:** MC, VI.

COTTONWOOD COVE—*See Las Vegas p. 1115.*

ECHO BAY—*See Las Vegas p. 1115.*

ELKO—14,700

LODGINGS

BEST WESTERN AMERITEL INN   Rates Subject to Change   Phone: (775)738-8787
◆◆◆
Motel

MC, VI.

All Year [CP]   1P: $78- 120 2P/1B: $78- 120 2P/2B: $80- 150 XP: $5   F12
Location: 0.3 mi sw of I-80 exit 303. 1930 Idaho St 89801. **Fax:** 775/753-7910. **Facility:** 109 rooms. Large rooms. 3 two-bedroom units. 2 stories; interior corridors; heated indoor pool. **Cards:** AE, CB, DI, DS, JC,

BEST WESTERN ELKO INN EXPRESS   Phone: (775)738-7261
AAA SAVE
◆◆◆
Motel

All Year [CP]   1P: $49- 59 2P/1B: $54- 64 2P/2B: $59- 69 XP: $5   F12
Location: 1 mi s of I-80, exit 301 or 303. 837 Idaho St 89801. **Fax:** 775/738-0118. **Terms:** Pets, $10 extra charge. **Facility:** 49 rooms. Large rooms. 3 two-bedroom units. 2 stories; exterior corridors; heated pool 6/1-9/15 weather permitting. **Cards:** AE, DI, DS, JC, MC, VI. **Special Amenities:** Free breakfast and free local telephone calls.

BEST WESTERN GOLD COUNTRY MOTOR INN   Phone: (775)738-8421
AAA SAVE
◆◆◆
Motor Inn

All Year   1P: $59- 99 2P/1B: $59- 99 2P/2B: $69- 109 XP: $10   F12
Location: Just s of I-80 exit 303. 2050 Idaho St 89801. **Terms:** Weekly/monthly rates; pets. **Facility:** 151 rooms. Large rooms. 18 two-bedroom units. RV spaces avail with full hook-ups, extra charge; 2 stories; exterior corridors; heated pool 6/1-9/15 weather permitting. **Dining:** Coffee shop; 24 hrs & casino; $7-$15; cocktails. **All Rooms:** combo or shower baths. **Cards:** AE, DI, DS, MC, VI. **Special Amenities:** Free local telephone calls and free room upgrade (subject to availability with advanced reservations). Best Western Motels.

BUDGET INN   Phone: (775)738-7000
AAA SAVE
◆◆
Motel

		1P:	$40-	50	2P/1B:	$40-	50	2P/2B:	$55-	60	XP:	$5	F18
6/1-8/31													
2/1-5/31 & 9/1-1/31	1P:	$32-	45	2P/1B:	$32-	45	2P/2B:	$42-	50	XP:	$5	F18	

Location: 1 mi s of I-80, exit 301 or 303. 1349 Idaho St 89801. **Fax:** 775/738-1216. **Facility:** 63 rooms. 1 three-bedroom unit, 3 two-bedroom units. Personal checks not accepted; 2 stories; exterior corridors; heated pool open 6/1-9/7. **Dining:** Coffee shop nearby. **Cards:** AE, DS, MC, VI. **Special Amenities:** Free breakfast and free local telephone calls.

DAYS INN   Phone: (775)738-7245
AAA SAVE
◆◆
Motel

		1P:	$40-	49	2P/1B:	$40-	49	2P/2B:	$45-	69	XP:	$4	F12
6/1-9/15 [CP]													
2/1-5/31 & 9/16-1/31 [CP]	1P:	$34-	39	2P/1B:	$34-	39	2P/2B:	$39-	49	XP:	$4	F12	

Location: 1 mi s of I-80; exit 303. 1500 Idaho St 89801. **Fax:** 775/738-7491. **Terms:** Weekly rates. **Facility:** 33 rooms. 2 stories; exterior corridors. **Dining:** Coffee shop nearby. **Cards:** AE, DI, DS, MC, VI.

HIGH DESERT INN   Phone: (775)738-8425
AAA SAVE
◆◆◆
Motor Inn

All Year   1P: $59- 99 2P/1B: $59- 99 2P/2B: $69- 109 XP: $10   F12
Location: Just s of I-80 exit 303. 3015 Idaho St 89801. **Fax:** 775/753-7906. **Terms:** Check-in 4 pm; small pets only. **Facility:** 171 rooms. 4 stories; interior/exterior corridors; heated indoor pool, whirlpool. **Dining:** Coffee shop; 6 am-10 pm; $7-$18; cocktails. **Some Rooms:** color TV. **Cards:** AE, DI, DS, MC, VI. **Special Amenities:** Free local telephone calls and free room upgrade (subject to availability with advanced reservations). *(See color ad p 1098)*

HOLIDAY INN EXPRESS HOTEL & SUITES — Rates Subject to Change — **Phone:** 775/777-0990
[FYI]
Motel
All Year [CP]   1P: $79- 219   2P/1B: $79- 219   2P/2B: $89- 229   XP: $10   F12
Too new to rate. **Location:** Just s of I-80, exit 303. 3019 Idaho St 89801. Fax: 775/753-7906.
Terms: Check-in 4 pm. **Facility:** 77 rooms. Scheduled to open Fall, 1998; 3 stories; interior corridors.
All Rooms: combo or shower baths. **Some Rooms:** 22 efficiencies, 2 kitchens. **Cards:** AE, DI, DS, MC, VI.

NATIONAL 9 EL NEVA MOTEL — Rates Subject to Change — **Phone:** 775/738-7152
(AAA)
◆ ◆
Motel
5/16-9/10   1P: $36- 42   2P/1B: $38- 49   2P/2B: $45- 49   XP: $4   D10
2/1-5/15 & 9/11-1/31   1P: $35- 39   2P/1B: $35- 42   2P/2B: $38- 49   XP: $4   D10
Location: 1 mi s of I-80, exit 301 or 303. 736 Idaho St 89801. Fax: 775/738-3447. **Terms:** Weekly rates.
Facility: 27 rooms. 2 stories; exterior corridors. **Dining:** Restaurant nearby. **Cards:** AE, CB, DI, DS, MC, VI.

PARK VIEW INN — Rates Subject to Change — **Phone:** (775)753-7747
(AAA)
◆ ◆
Motel
All Year   1P: $44- 54   2P/1B: $44- 54   2P/2B: $54- 74
Location: 1 mi s of I-80, exit 303. 1785 Idaho St 89801. Fax: 775/753-7347. **Terms:** Weekly rates.
Facility: 61 rooms. 3 stories, no elevator; interior corridors; indoor whirlpool. **Cards:** AE, CB, DI, DS, JC, MC, VI.

RED LION INN & CASINO — **Phone:** (775)738-2111
(AAA) [SAVE]
◆ ◆ ◆
Motor Inn
4/15-1/31   1P: $69- 259   2P/1B: $69- 259   2P/2B: $79- 269   XP: $10   F12
2/1-4/14   1P: $79- 99   2P/1B: $79- 99   2P/2B: $79- 99   XP: $10   F12
Location: Just s of I-80 exit 303. 2065 Idaho St 89801. Fax: 775/753-9859. **Terms:** Check-in 4 pm; pets.
Facility: 223 rooms. Large rooms. 5 two-bedroom units. 2 suites with whirlpool, wet bar & refrigerator, $259
for 2 persons; 3 stories; interior corridors; pool heated 6/1-9/30, weather permitting. **Dining:** Restaurant,
coffee shop; 24 hrs a casino; $11-$21; cocktails. **Services:** giftshop. **Recreation:** video arcade. **Cards:** AE, DI, DS, MC, VI.
(See color ad p 1098)

SHILO INN — Rates Subject to Change — **Phone:** (775)738-5522
◆ ◆ ◆
Motel
All Year [CP]   1P: $65- 99   2P/1B: $65- 99   2P/2B: $65- 99   XP: $10   F12
Location: Just N of I-80, exit 301. 2401 Mountain City Hwy 89801. Fax: 775/738-6247. **Facility:** 70 rooms.
Across shopping center. 2 stories; interior corridors; heated indoor pool. **Cards:** AE, CB, DI, DS, JC, MC, VI.
(See ad below)

THUNDERBIRD MOTEL — **Phone:** (775)738-7115
(AAA) [SAVE]
◆ ◆
Motel
All Year   1P: $49- 79   2P/1B: $47- 79   2P/2B: $59- 89   XP: $10   F16
Location: 1 mi s of I-80, exit 301 or 303. 345 Idaho St 89801. Fax: 775/738-2694. **Terms:** Small pets only,
$25 dep req. **Facility:** 70 rooms. 2 stories; exterior corridors; heated pool 6/1-9/30, weather permitting.
Dining: Restaurant nearby. **Services:** area transportation. **Cards:** AE, DI, DS, MC, VI. **Special Amenities:**
Free breakfast and free local telephone calls.

RESTAURANT

NEVADA DINNER HOUSE — **Dinner:** $15-$22 — **Phone:** 775/738-8485
(AAA)
◆ ◆
Basque
Location: 1.5 mi s of I-80; at 4th St. 351 Silver St 89801. **Hours:** 5 pm-9:30 pm. Closed: Mon & week of
12/25. **Reservations:** accepted. **Features:** casual dress; children's menu; cocktails & lounge. Family-style
Basque cuisine. Several choices of entrees; also American fare. **Cards:** AE, MC, VI.

GIFT COUPON?

That's what it amounts to. Some establishments give
special discounts through coupons distributed by AAA clubs.
Ask your AAA club when you make your trip arrangements.

ELY—4,800

LODGINGS

BRISTLECONE MOTEL
AAA
◆◆
Motel

Rates Subject to Change
All Year   1P: $36- 38   2P/1B: $40   2P/2B: $42- 44 XP: $2
Location: Just s of jct 6, 50 & 93. 700 Ave I 89301. Fax: 775/289-6128. **Facility:** 31 rooms. 2 stories; exterior corridors. **Dining:** Restaurant nearby. **Cards:** AE, CB, DI, DS, MC, VI.
Phone: 775/289-8838

FIRESIDE INN
AAA [SAVE]
◆
Motel

4/1-10/31   1P: $39   2P/1B: $43   2P/2B: $45   XP: $5   F12
Location: 3 mi n on US 93. McGill Hwy 89301-9402 (HC 33 Box 33400, 89301). **Terms:** Open 4/1-10/31; reserv deposit; weekly rates; small pets only, $5 extra charge. **Facility:** 14 rooms. In open countryside. 1 two-bedroom unit. 1 story; exterior corridors. **Cards:** AE, DS, MC, VI. **Special Amenities:** Early check-in/late check-out and free local telephone calls.
Phone: (775)289-3765

HOLIDAY INN
◆◆◆
Motor Inn

Rates Subject to Change
6/1-10/31   1P: $75   2P/1B: $75   2P/2B: $75   XP: $4   F18
2/1-5/31 & 11/1-1/31   1P: $62   2P/1B: $62   2P/2B: $62   XP: $4   F18
Location: 1.5 mi n on US 93. 1501 Ave F 89301. Fax: 775/289-4607. **Facility:** 61 rooms. RV parking & hook-ups avail; 2 stories; interior corridors. **All Rooms:** combo or shower baths. **Cards:** AE, CB, DI, DS, JC, MC, VI.
Phone: 775/289-8900

RAMADA INN-COPPER QUEEN CASINO
AAA [SAVE]
◆◆◆
Complex

6/1-9/30   1P: $55- 69   2P/1B: $60- 74 2P/2B: $60- 74 XP: $5   F18
4/1-5/31   1P: $50- 60   2P/1B: $55- 65 2P/2B: $55- 65 XP: $5   F18
2/1-3/31 & 10/1-1/31   1P: $48- 55   2P/1B: $53- 60 2P/2B: $53- 60 XP: $5   F18
Location: 0.3 mi s of jct 6, 50 & 93. 815 7th St 89301 (701 Ave I). Fax: 775/289-1492. **Terms:** Small pets only. **Facility:** 65 rooms. Hotel rooms & slot casino in main building; motel rooms across the street. 1 unit with whirlpool & private deck, $115; 1 unit with kitchen $95; for 2 persons; 2 stories; interior/exterior corridors; heated indoor pool, whirlpool. **Dining:** Coffee shop; 6 am-9 pm; limited menu; pastas & pizzas; $8-$15; cocktails. **Recreation:** 24 hr casino. **Cards:** AE, CB, DI, DS, MC, VI. **Special Amenities:** Free local telephone calls.
Phone: (775)289-4884

STEPTOE VALLEY INN
◆◆
Bed &
Breakfast

Rates Subject to Change
6/1-10/1 [BP]   1P: $73- 82   2P/1B: $84   2P/2B: $84- 90 XP: $9
Location: Just n of US 93. 220 E 11th St 89315-1110 (PO Box 151110, 89315). **Terms:** Open 6/1-10/1; reserv deposit, 7 day 7/2 & 7/3. **Facility:** 5 rooms. Reconstructed 1907 grocery store. Private balconies, land-scaped yard with gazebo & lawn. 2 stories; interior corridors; smoke free premises. **All Rooms:** combo or shower baths. **Cards:** AE, MC, VI.
Phone: (775)289-8687

FALLON—6,400

LODGINGS

BUDGET INN OF FALLON
AAA [SAVE]
◆
Motel

All Year   1P: $35- 40   2P/1B: $40- 45 2P/2B: $45- 55 XP: $4   F12
Location: 0.5 mi s of US 50. 1705 S Taylor St 89406. Fax: 775/423-2271. **Terms:** Reserv deposit; handling fee imposed; small pets only. **Facility:** 21 rooms. 1 two-bedroom unit. 1 story; exterior corridors. **Dining:** Restaurant nearby. **All Rooms:** comb, shower or tub baths. **Some Rooms:** 4 kitchens. **Cards:** AE, CB, DI, DS, MC, VI.
Phone: (775)423-2277

COMFORT INN
◆◆
Motel

Rates Subject to Change
All Year [CP]   1P: $56- 85   2P/1B: $61- 100 2P/2B: $61- 100 XP: $5   F18
Location: US 50; 1 mi w of jct US 95. 1830 W Williams Ave 89406. Fax: 775/423-0663. **Facility:** 82 rooms. 2 stories; interior corridors; small heated indoor pool. **Cards:** AE, CB, DI, DS, MC, VI.
Phone: 775/423-5554

ECONO LODGE
AAA [SAVE]
◆
Motel

All Year [CP]   1P: $45- 53   2P/1B: $55- 60 2P/2B: $55- 60 XP: $5   F18
Location: US 50, e of US 95. 70 E Williams Ave 89406. Fax: 775/423-7187. **Facility:** 30 rooms. Lower rates in winter; 2 stories; exterior corridors; Small heated pool 5/25-10/15. **Dining:** Restaurants nearby. **All Rooms:** combo or shower baths. **Cards:** AE, CB, DI, DS, JC, MC, VI. **Special Amenities:** Free breakfast and free local telephone calls.
Phone: (775)423-2194

LARIAT MOTEL
AAA
◆◆
Motel

Rates Subject to Change
All Year   1P: $34- 36   2P/1B: $40- 44 2P/2B: $46- 48 XP: $5
Location: US 50, 0.5 mi w of US 95. 850 W Williams Ave 89406 (PO Box 649). **Terms:** Reserv deposit. **Facility:** 18 rooms. Some large rooms. 1 story; exterior corridors. **Dining:** Restaurant nearby. **All Rooms:** shower baths. **Cards:** AE, MC, VI.
Phone: (775)423-3181

WESTERN MOTEL
AAA [SAVE]
◆
Motel

All Year [CP]   1P: $37   2P/1B: $41   2P/2B: $43   XP: $8   F10
Location: Just e of US 95. 125 S Carson St 89406. **Terms:** Reserv deposit; weekly rates; small pets only, $3 extra charge, no cats. **Facility:** 22 rooms. 2 stories; exterior corridors; small heated pool 5/25-10/15. **Dining:** Restaurant nearby. **All Rooms:** combo or shower baths. **Cards:** AE, CB, DI, MC, VI. **Special Amenities:** Free local telephone calls and preferred room (subject to availability with advanced reservations).
Phone: (775)423-5118

FERNLEY—5,200

LODGINGS

BEST WESTERN FERNLEY INN
Phone: (775)575-6776

AAA SAVE

5/1-9/30 [CP]	1P:	$60-	75	2P/1B:	$65-	80	2P/2B:	$65	XP: $5 F18
3/1-4/30 & 10/1-11/30 [CP]	1P:	$59-	70	2P/1B:	$60-	75	2P/2B:	$60	XP: $5 F18
2/1-2/28 & 12/1-1/31 [CP]	1P:	$53-	63	2P/1B:	$58-	68	2P/2B:	$58	XP: $5 F18

♦ ♦
Motel
Location: Just s of I-80, exit 48. 1405 E Newlands Dr 89408. **Fax:** 775/575-6748. **Terms:** Pets, $5 extra charge. **Facility:** 42 rooms. 2 stories; exterior corridors; heated indoor pool, whirlpool. **Dining:** Coffee shop nearby. **Recreation:** RV park in back. **Cards:** AE, CB, DI, DS, MC, VI. **Special Amenities:** Early check-in/late check-out and free breakfast.

SUPER 8 MOTEL
Phone: 775/575-5555

♦
Motel

All Year [CP]	Rates Subject to Change	2P/1B:	$51	2P/2B:	$54	XP: $3

Location: Just s of I-80, exit 48. 1350 Newlands Dr W 89408. **Fax:** 775/575-6546. **Facility:** 37 stories; exterior corridors. **Cards:** AE, CB, DI, DS, MC, VI.

GARDNERVILLE—2,200

LODGINGS

TOPAZ LODGE
Phone: 775/266-3338

AAA

All Year	1P:	$39-	53	2P/1B:	$43-	53	2P/2B:	$39- 48 XP: $2 F5

♦ ♦
Motel
Location: US 395S at Topaz Lake, 22 mi s of Garderville, NV. 1979 US 395S 89410 (PO Box 187). **Fax:** 775/266-3338. **Terms:** Pets, $5 dep req, limited rooms avail. **Facility:** 102 rooms. All rooms with view of Topaz Lake. 2-3 stories; exterior corridors; small pool; playground. **Dining:** Coffee shop; 24 hrs; $7-$10; cocktails. **All Rooms:** combo or shower baths. **Cards:** AE, DS, MC, VI.

WESTERNER MOTEL
Phone: 775/782-3602

AAA

4/1-10/31	1P:	$35	2P/1B:	$40	2P/2B:	$43	XP: $3-5
2/1-3/31 & 11/1-1/31	1P:	$30	2P/1B:	$32	2P/2B:	$35	XP: $3-5

♦ ♦
Motel
Location: US 395S, south end of town. 1353 US 395S 89410 (PO Box 335). **Terms:** Reserv deposit; small pets only. **Facility:** 25 rooms. Large comfortable rooms. 1 story; exterior corridors. **Cards:** AE, DS, MC, VI.

HAWTHORNE—4,200

LODGING

EL CAPITAN RESORT CASINO
Phone: (775)945-3321

AAA

All Year	1P:	$30-	40	2P/1B:	$35-	45	2P/2B:	$35- 45 XP: $7 F12

♦ ♦
Motor Inn
Location: Just n of US 95. 540 F St 89415 (PO Box 1000). **Fax:** 775/945-2193. **Terms:** Check-in 3:30 pm; pets, $10 dep req. **Facility:** 103 rooms. Off the main roads. 4 two-bedroom units. 1-2 stories; exterior corridors; 9 holes golf. **Dining:** Coffee shop; $8-$16; cocktails. **Services:** giftshop. **Cards:** AE, CB, DI, DS, MC, VI.

HENDERSON—See Las Vegas p. 1116.

INCLINE VILLAGE—See Lake Tahoe Area p. 531.

INDIAN SPRINGS—See Las Vegas p. 1116.

JACKPOT—1,200

LODGINGS

CACTUS PETE'S RESORT CASINO
Phone: (775)755-2321

AAA SAVE

2/12-10/29	1P:	$55- 175	2P/1B:	$55- 175	2P/2B:	$55- 175
2/1-2/11 & 10/30-11/25	1P:	$45- 150	2P/1B:	$45- 150	2P/2B:	$45- 150
11/26-1/31	1P:	$40- 150	2P/1B:	$40- 150	2P/2B:	$40- 150

♦ ♦ ♦ ♦
Hotel
Location: On SR 93. 1385 Hwy 93 89825 (PO Box 508). **Terms:** Check-in 4 pm; reserv deposit, weekends. **Facility:** 293 rooms. 16 units with whirlpool bath & wet bar, $100-$175 for 2 persons; 10 stories; interior corridors; whirlpool; 2 lighted tennis courts. Fee: 18 holes golf. **Dining:** Dining room, 2 restaurants, coffee shop; 24 hour casino; $11-$40; cocktails; buffet 5 pm-10 pm, $7-$9. **Services:** giftshop; area transportation, shuttle. **Recreation:** Heated pool 5/1-9/15. **All Rooms:** combo or shower baths. **Cards:** AE, CB, DI, DS, MC, VI. **Special Amenities:** Free local telephone calls.

FOUR JACKS HOTEL & CASINO
Phone: 775/755-2491

♦ ♦

5/1-9/30	1P:	$35	2P/1B:	$35	2P/2B:	$45	XP: $5
2/1-4/30 & 10/1-1/31	1P:	$30	2P/1B:	$30	2P/2B:	$40	XP: $5

Motel
Location: On SR 73. 1702 Hwy 93 89825. **Fax:** 775/755-2934. **Facility:** 60 rooms. 4 large family units; 2 stories; interior corridors. **Cards:** AE, CB, DI, DS, MC, VI.

HORSESHU HOTEL & CASINO
Phone: (775)755-7777

AAA SAVE

2/12-10/30	1P:	$40- 85	2P/1B:	$40- 85	2P/2B:	$40- 85
2/1-2/11 & 10/31-11/25	1P:	$35- 75	2P/1B:	$35- 75	2P/2B:	$35- 75
11/26-1/31	1P:	$25- 65	2P/1B:	$25- 65	2P/2B:	$25- 65

♦ ♦ ♦
Motel
Location: On SR 93. 1385 Hwy 93 89825 (PO Box 508). **Fax:** 752/755-2740. **Terms:** Check-in 4 pm; small pets only. **Facility:** 120 rooms. 3 stories; interior corridors; whirlpool, Heated pool 5/1-9/15. Fee: 18 holes golf. **Dining:** 24 hr casino across road; cocktails; restaurant nearby. **Services:** area transportation, shuttle. **Cards:** AE, CB, DI, DS, MC, VI. **Special Amenities:** Free local telephone calls.

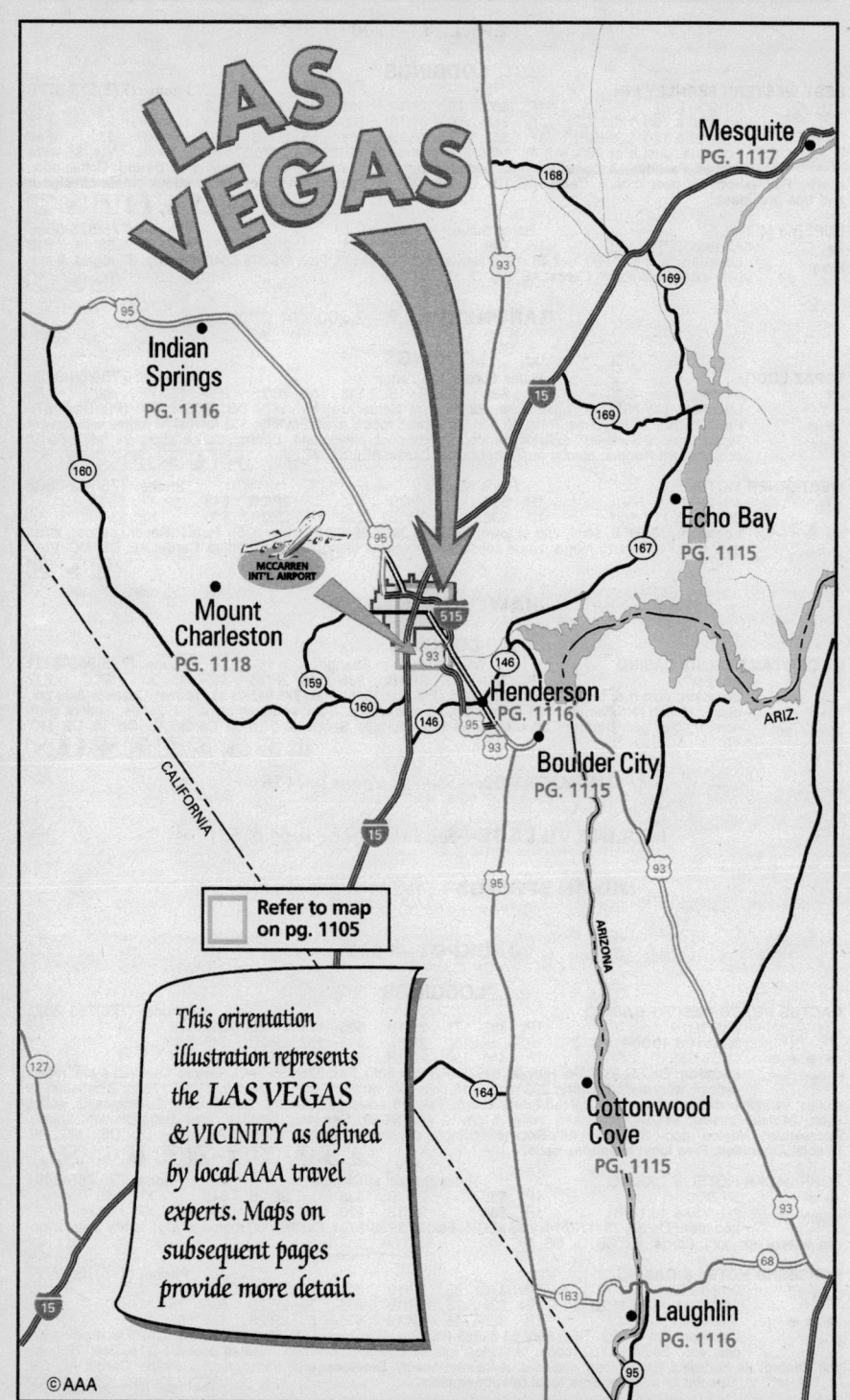

LAS VEGAS

Mesquite
PG. 1117

Indian
Springs
PG. 1116

Echo Bay
PG. 1115

MCCARREN INT'L AIRPORT

Mount
Charleston
PG. 1118

Henderson
PG. 1116

Boulder City
PG. 1115

ARIZ.

CALIFORNIA

ARIZONA

Refer to map
on pg. 1105

Cottonwood
Cove
PG. 1115

This orirentation
illustration represents
the LAS VEGAS
& VICINITY as defined
by local AAA travel
experts. Maps on
subsequent pages
provide more detail.

Laughlin
PG. 1116

©AAA

Las Vegas
pop. 258,300

> Most establishments in Las Vegas do not confirm advance reservations at a definite rate. Advance reservations for Saturday only are extremely difficult.

This index helps you "spot" where approved accommodations are located on the detailed maps that follow. Rate ranges are for comparison only and show the property's high season. Turn to the listing page for more detailed rate information and consult display ads for special promotions. Restaurant rate range is for dinner unless only lunch (L) is served.

Spotter/Map Pg.Number	OA	LAS VEGAS - Lodgings	Rating	Rate	Listing Page
1 / p. 1105	AAA	Best Western Main Street Inn	◆◆	$49-135	1106
2 / p. 1105	AAA	Best Western Heritage Inn	◆◆◆	$69-140	1106
3 / p. 1105	AAA	Comfort Inn Central	◆◆	$85	1108
4 / p. 1105		Howard Johnson Inn-Airport - see color ad opposite inside back cover	◆	$65-145	1111
5 / p. 1105		La Quinta Inn - see color ad p 1112	◆◆◆	$69-89	1111
6 / p. 1105	AAA	Best Western McCarran Inn - see color ad p 1107	◆◆	$69-139	1107
8 / p. 1105	AAA	Bally's Las Vegas - see ad p 119	◆◆◆	$103-299	1106
9 / p. 1105		Alexis Park Resort Hotel	◆◆◆	$160-375	1106
10 / p. 1105		Sam's Town Hotel	◆◆◆	$75-155	1113
11 / p. 1105	AAA	Emerald Springs-Holiday Inn	◆◆◆	$79-99	1110
12 / p. 1105	AAA	Barbary Coast Hotel	◆◆◆	$59-159	1106
13 / p. 1105		Days Inn-Airport	◆◆	$65-145	1109
14 / p. 1105	AAA	Flamingo Hilton-Las Vegas - see ad p 119	◆◆◆	$69-279	1110
15 / p. 1105		Caesars Palace	◆◆◆◆	$115-190	1107
16 / p. 1105		Harrah's-Las Vegas	◆◆◆	$50-259	1110
17 / p. 1105		Rio Suite Hotel & Casino	◆◆◆	$95-149	1113
18 / p. 1105		The Orleans	◆◆◆	$89-109	1112
19 / p. 1105	AAA	Best Western Mardi Gras Inn	◆◆	$50-120	1106
20 / p. 1105	AAA	Crowne Plaza	◆◆◆	$125-145	1109
21 / p. 1105		Treasure Island at the Mirage	◆◆◆	$59-399	1114
22 / p. 1105	AAA	Luxor Las Vegas	◆◆◆	$59-259	1112
23 / p. 1105	AAA	Somerset House Motel - see color ad p 1113	◆◆	$50	1113
24 / p. 1105	AAA	Las Vegas Hilton - see ad p 119	◆◆◆◆	$95-275	1112
25 / p. 1105		Circus Circus Hotel	◆◆	$49-119	1108
26 / p. 1105		Quality Inn & Key Largo Casino	◆◆	$39-200	1113
27 / p. 1105		Gold Coast Hotel	◆◆◆	$29-175	1110
28 / p. 1105		Arizona Charlie's Hotel	◆◆	$48-69	1106
29 / p. 1105		Silverton Hotel-Casino	◆◆	$70	1113
30 / p. 1105		Holiday Inn Casino Boardwalk	◆◆◆	$79-239	1111
31 / p. 1105	AAA	Golden Nugget Hotel	◆◆◆◆	$59-299	1110
32 / p. 1105	AAA	Boulder Station Hotel Casino	◆◆◆	$79	1107
34 / p. 1105		MGM Grand Hotel Casino & Theme Park	◆◆◆	$69-259	1112
35 / p. 1105	AAA	Days Inn Downtown	◆◆	$120-175	1109
36 / p. 1105		Hawthorn Suites - Las Vegas	◆◆◆	$99-169	1110
37 / p. 1105		The Desert Inn	◆◆◆◆	$220-300	1109
38 / p. 1105		Monte Carlo Resort & Casino	◆◆◆	$109-249	1112
39 / p. 1105		California Hotel	◆◆	$50-80	1108
40 / p. 1105	AAA	Best Western Parkview Inn	◆◆	$49-135	1107
41 / p. 1105	AAA	Best Western Nellis Motor Inn - see ad p 1107	◆◆	$56-89	1107
42 / p. 1105	AAA	Barcelona Motel	◆◆	$75-80	1106
43 / p. 1105	AAA	Carriage House - see color ad p 1108	◆◆◆	$89-165	1108
44 / p. 1105	AAA	La Quinta Inn Convention Center	◆◆◆	$69-89	1111
45 / p. 1105	AAA	Holiday Inn Express	◆◆◆	$99-250	1111
46 / p. 1105	AAA	St Tropez All Suite Hotel	◆◆◆	$115-125	1113
47 / p. 1105	AAA	Comfort Inn	◆◆◆	$69-79	1108

Spotter/Map Pg.Number	OA	**LAS VEGAS** - Lodgings (contd.)	Rating	Rate	Listing Page
48 / p. 1105	AAA	**Comfort Inn South**	◆◆	$65-85 🔲	1108
49 / p. 1105		Courtyard By Marriott-Convention Center - see color ad p 1109	◆◆◆	$89-135	1108
50 / p. 1105		Residence Inn by Marriott	◆◆◆	$95-329	1113
51 / p. 1105		The Mirage	◆◆◆◆	$109-399	1112
52 / p. 1105		Fairfield Inn by Marriott	◆◆	$62-175	1110
53 / p. 1105		Hilton Grand Vacations Club - see ad p 119	◆◆◆	$239-399	1111
54 / p. 1105	AAA	**Econo Lodge-Downtown - see color ad p 1109**	◆	$60 🔲	1110
55 / p. 1105		Excalibur Hotel & Casino	◆◆◆	$55-375	1110
56 / p. 1105		Fiesta Casino Hotel	◆◆	$45	1110
57 / p. 1105	AAA	**Howard Johnson Hotel & Casino - see color ad opposite inside back cover**	◆◆	$89 🔲	1111
58 / p. 1105		Travelodge-West Sahara	◆◆	$59-129	1114
59 / p. 1105		Riviera Hotel	◆◆	$59-145	1113
60 / p. 1105	AAA	**Texas Station Gambling Hall & Hotel**	◆◆◆	$99-129	1114
61 / p. 1105		Main Street Station	◆◆◆	$50-125	1112
62 / p. 1105	AAA	**Palace Station Hotel & Casino**	◆◆◆	$79-149	1112
63 / p. 1105		Holiday Inn Fitzgeralds Casino - see ad p 1111	◆◆◆	$50-120	1111
		LAS VEGAS - Restaurants			
① / p. 1105		Andiamo	◆◆◆	$20-30	1114
② / p. 1105		Anthony's Fine Dining	◆◆◆	$13-24	1114
③ / p. 1105		Kiefer's Atop the Carriage House	◆◆◆	$15-30	1114
④ / p. 1105		Philips Supper House	◆◆◆	$15-32	1114
⑤ / p. 1105		Battista's Hole In The Wall	◆◆	$16-30	1114
⑥ / p. 1105		Country Inn	◆◆	$4-15	1114
⑦ / p. 1105		Country Inn	◆◆	$6-15	1114
⑨ / p. 1105		Golden Steer	◆◆	$25-40	1114
⑩ / p. 1105		Yolie's Brazilian Steak House	◆◆	$15-44	1114
⑪ / p. 1105		Andre's French Restaurant	◆◆◆	$20-44	1114
⑫ / p. 1105		Cafe Michelle	◆◆◆	$15-25	1114
⑬ / p. 1105	AAA	**Monte Carlo Restaurant**	◆◆◆◆	$65-105	1114

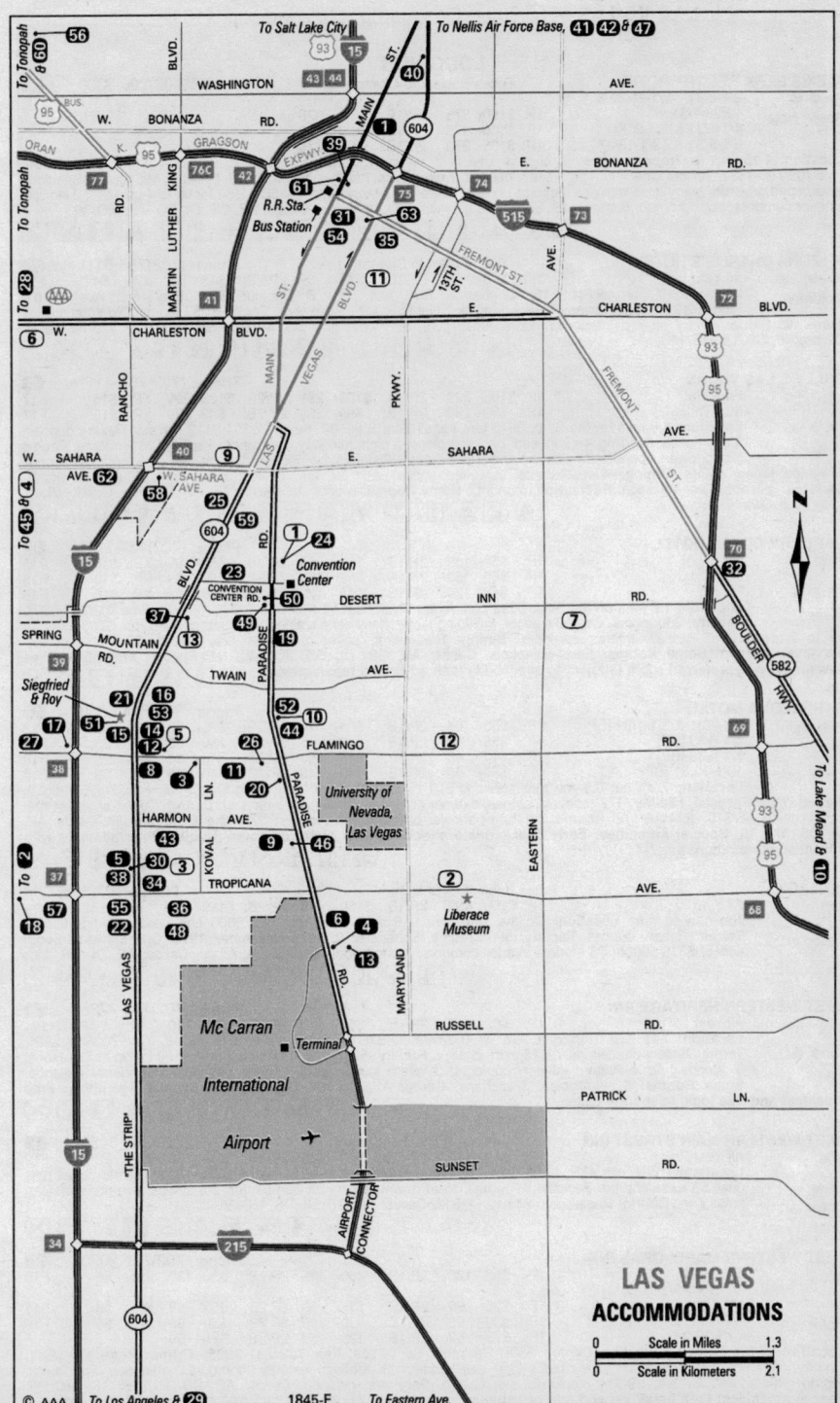

LAS VEGAS
ACCOMMODATIONS

© AAA   To Los Angeles & 29   1845-F   To Eastern Ave.

LAS VEGAS—258,300   (See map p. 1105; index p. 1103)

LODGINGS

ALEXIS PARK RESORT HOTEL
◆◆◆
Resort Hotel

Rates Subject to Change
Phone: (702)796-3300   **9**

2/1-3/31, 10/1-11/30 & 12/28-1/31	1P: $160- 375	2P/1B: $160- 375		
4/1-5/31 & 9/1-9/30	1P: $135- 375	2P/1B: $135- 375		
6/1-8/31 & 12/1-12/27	1P: $105- 270	2P/1B: $105- 270		

Location: I-15 exit e Tropicana Ave; 2 blks w UNLV, 2 mi s of Convention Center. 375 E Harmon Ave 89109. Fax: 702/796-4334. **Terms:** Check-in 4 pm; reserv deposit, 7 day notice; handling fee imposed. **Facility:** 496 rooms. Spacious landscaped grounds. Many units with gas fireplace. 12 two-bedroom, 2-story suites; $350-$1150 for up to 4 persons; 2 stories; exterior corridors; putting green; heated pool. **Services:** giftshop. Fee: massage. **Cards:** AE, CB, DI, DS, JC, MC, VI.

ARIZONA CHARLIE'S HOTEL
◆◆
Motor Inn

Rates Subject to Change
Phone: (702)258-5111   **28**

All Year   1P: $48- 69   2P/1B: $48- 69 2P/2B: $48- 69 XP: $4   F12
Location: 1 mi nw of I-15; Charleston Blvd exit. 740 S Decatur Blvd, Evergreen Ave 89107. Fax: 702/258-5192. **Terms:** Reserv deposit; 2 night min stay, weekends. **Facility:** 257 rooms. Old West atmosphere. No Sat arrivals; 7 stories; interior corridors; small pool. **Services:** giftshop. **All Rooms:** combo or shower baths. **Cards:** AE, CB, DI, DS, MC, VI.

BALLY'S LAS VEGAS
(AAA) [SAVE]
◆◆◆
Hotel

Phone: (702)739-4111   **8**

Fri & Sat	1P: $103- 299	2P/1B: $103- 299	2P/2B: $103- 299 XP: $15	F17
Sun-Thurs	1P: $99- 299	2P/1B: $99- 299	2P/2B: $99- 299 XP: $15	F17

Location: 4.5 mi s on the Strip. 3645 Las Vegas Blvd S 89109. Fax: 702/794-2413. **Terms:** Reserv deposit, 3 day notice; handling fee imposed; package plans; 2 night min stay, weekends. **Facility:** 2814 rooms. Rooms in two towers connected by casino and public areas. 26 stories; interior corridors; sauna, steamroom, whirlpool; 8 lighted tennis courts. **Dining:** 4 restaurants, 2 coffee shops, deli; 24 hrs, casino, buffet $15; $8-$34; cocktails. **Recreation:** monorail. **Some Rooms:** whirlpools. **Cards:** AE, CB, DI, DS, JC, MC, VI.
(See ad p 119)

BARBARY COAST HOTEL
(AAA) [SAVE]
◆◆◆
Hotel

Phone: (702)737-7111   **12**

2/1-6/1	1P: $59- 159	2P/1B: $59- 159	2P/2B: $59- 159 XP: $10	F15
9/2-1/31	1P: $59- 159	2P/1B: $59- 159	2P/2B: $59- 159 XP: $10	F15
6/2-9/1	1P: $49- 129	2P/1B: $49- 129	2P/2B: $49- 129 XP: $10	F15

Location: 1.8 mi s on the Strip. 3595 Las Vegas Blvd S 89109 (PO Box 19030, 89132). Fax: 702/737-6304. **Facility:** 200 rooms. Gay 90's decor, including large tiffany style stained glass mural. 12 suites $200-$350 for up to 2 persons; 5 stories; interior corridors. **Dining:** Restaurant, coffee shop; 24 hrs, casino; $7-$20; cocktails. **Services:** giftshop. **Some Rooms:** Fee: whirlpools. **Cards:** AE, CB, DI, DS, JC, MC, VI. **Special Amenities:** Free newspaper and preferred room (subject to availability with advanced reservations).

BARCELONA MOTEL
(AAA) [SAVE]
◆◆
Motor Inn

Phone: (702)644-6300   **42**

2/1-3/31 & 1/1-1/31 [BP]	1P: $60- 65	2P/1B: $65- 70	2P/2B: $75- 80	XP: $5	F18
4/1-6/30 [BP]	1P: $55- 60	2P/1B: $60- 65	2P/2B: $60- 65	XP: $5	F18
7/1-9/30 [BP]	1P: $40- 45	2P/1B: $45- 50	2P/2B: $45- 50	XP: $5	F18
10/1-12/31 [BP]	1P: $35- 40	2P/1B: $40- 45	2P/2B: $40- 45	XP: $5	F18

Location: 7 mi ne; 0.5 mi from Nellis AFB; I-15 exit 48 e. 5011 E Craig Rd 89115. Fax: 702/644-6510. **Terms:** Reserv deposit. **Facility:** 177 rooms. 2 stories; exterior corridors; small pool, whirlpool. **Dining:** Coffee shop; 24 hrs, small casino; $6-$10; cocktails. **All Rooms:** combo or shower baths. **Some Rooms:** 79 kitchens, no utensils. **Cards:** AE, DI, DS, MC, VI. **Special Amenities:** Early check-in/late check-out and preferred room (subject to availability with advanced reservations).

BELLAGIO
[FYI]
Resort Hotel

Rates Subject to Change
Phone: 702/693-7111

All Year   1P: $159- 499   2P/1B: $159- 499 2P/2B: $159- 499
Too new to rate. **Location:** On the strip, exit I-15 at E Flamingo Ave. 3600 Las Vegas Blvd S 89109. **Terms:** Reserv deposit. **Facility:** 3005 rooms. Scheduled to open November, 1998. One & two-bedroom suites; $375-$6000; 36 stories; interior corridors; heated pool. **Services:** giftshop. **Cards:** AE, DI, DS, MC, VI.

BEST WESTERN HERITAGE INN
(AAA) [SAVE]
◆◆◆
Motel

Phone: (702)798-7736   **2**

All Year   1P: $62- 110   2P/1B: $62- 110 2P/2B: $69- 140
Location: I-15 exit Tropicana Ave w; 0.025 mi. 4975 S Valley View Blvd 89118. Fax: 702/798-5951. **Terms:** Reserv deposit; pets, $15 extra charge. **Facility:** 59 rooms. 4 whirlpool rms, $150 for up to 2 persons; 3 stories, no elevator; interior corridors; heated indoor pool, indoor whirlpool. **Services:** giftshop. **Some Rooms:** 6 efficiencies, 3 kitchens. **Cards:** AE, CB, DI, DS, JC, MC. **Special Amenities:** Free breakfast and free local telephone calls.

BEST WESTERN MAIN STREET INN
(AAA)
◆◆
Motor Inn

Rates Subject to Change
Phone: (702)382-3455   **1**

All Year   1P: $49- 135   2P/1B: $49- 135 2P/2B: $49- 135 XP: $8   F12
Location: I-15N, exit 43E; I-15S, exit 44E. 1000 N Main St 89101. Fax: 702/382-1428. **Terms:** Small pets only, $8 extra charge. **Facility:** 91 rooms. Near downtown convention center. 2-3 stories; exterior corridors; small pool. **Dining:** Restaurant; 24 hrs; $8-$12. **Cards:** AE, CB, DI, DS, MC, VI.

BEST WESTERN MARDI GRAS INN
(AAA) [SAVE]
◆◆
Motor Inn

Phone: (702)731-2020   **19**

12/29-1/2	1P: $50- 120	2P/1B: $50- 120	2P/2B: $50- 120 XP: $6	F18
2/1-3/31, 9/1-11/30 & 1/3-1/31	1P: $35- 99	2P/1B: $35- 99	2P/2B: $35- 99 XP: $6	F18
6/1-8/31	1P: $30- 99	2P/1B: $30- 99	2P/2B: $30- 99 XP: $6	F18
12/1-12/28	1P: $25- 59	2P/1B: $25- 59	2P/2B: $25- 59	

Location: 0.5 mi s of Convention Center. 3500 Paradise Rd 89109. Fax: 702/731-4005. **Terms:** Reserv deposit. **Facility:** 314 rooms. Phone charge $1.50 per day added; 3 stories; exterior corridors; whirlpool, sun deck. **Dining:** Restaurant; 24 hrs; $9-$14; cocktails; slot casino. **Services:** giftshop. **Cards:** AE, CB, DI, DS, JC, MC, VI. **Special Amenities:** Free breakfast and free newspaper.

(See map p. 1105)

BEST WESTERN MCCARRAN INN   Phone: (702)798-5530   **6**

Fri & Sat [CP]   1P: $69- 139   2P/1B: $69- 139   2P/2B: $69- 139   XP: $7   F17
Sun-Thurs [CP]   1P: $49- 129   2P/1B: $49- 129   2P/2B: $49- 129   XP: $7   F17

Motel   **Location:** I-15 exit Tropicana E toward McCarran International Airport. 4970 Paradise Rd 89119. **Fax:** 702/798-7627. **Terms:** Reserv deposit. **Facility:** 99 rooms. Located directly across from airport. 3 stories; interior corridors; heated pool, seasonal pool. **Services:** area transportation, within 2 mi. **Cards:** AE, CB, DI, DS, JC, MC, VI. **Special Amenities: Free breakfast and free newspaper.** *(See color ad below)*

BEST WESTERN NELLIS MOTOR INN   Phone: (702)643-6111   **41**

All Year   1P: $48- 78   2P/1B: $56- 89   2P/2B: $56- 89   XP: $6   F12

Location: 7 mi ne; 0.3 mi from Nellis AFB; I-15, exit 48 e. 5330 E Craig Rd 89115. **Fax:** 702/643-8553.
Motel   **Terms:** Pets, $5 extra charge, $50 dep req. **Facility:** 52 rooms. 2 stories; exterior corridors; pool. **Dining:** Coffee shop nearby. **Cards:** AE, CB, DI, DS, VI. **Special Amenities: Free room upgrade and preferred room (each subject to availability with advanced reservations).** *(See ad below)*

BEST WESTERN PARKVIEW INN   Rates Subject to Change   Phone: (702)385-1213   **40**

All Year   1P: $42- 100   2P/1B: $42- 100   2P/2B: $49- 135   XP: $7-25   F12

Location: 8 blks n on US 91 & 93. 905 Las Vegas Blvd N 89101. **Fax:** 702/382-2386. **Terms:** Reserv
Motel   deposit, 3 day notice; small pets only, $8 extra charge. **Facility:** 46 rooms. 2 stories; exterior corridors; small pool. **Cards:** AE, DI, DS, JC, MC, VI.

BOULDER STATION HOTEL CASINO   Rates Subject to Change   Phone: (702)432-7777   **32**

Fri & Sat   1P: $79   2P/1B: $79   2P/2B: $79   XP: $10
Sun-Thurs   1P: $59   2P/1B: $59   2P/2B: $59   XP: $10

Hotel   **Location:** 4111 Boulder Hwy 89121 (PO Box 12027, 89112-0027). **Fax:** 702/221-6510. **Facility:** 300 rooms. 6 whirlpool rms, extra charge; 13 stories; interior corridors. **Dining:** 2 dining rooms, 2 restaurants; buffet $8-$12, casino; $10-$20; cocktails. **Services:** giftshop; area transportation, strip & related hotels. **Recreation:** Fee: movie theater. **All Rooms:** combo or shower baths. **Cards:** AE, CB, DI, DS, MC, VI.

CAESARS PALACE   Rates Subject to Change   **Phone:** 702/731-7110   **15**
◆◆◆◆   All Year   1P: $100- 175   2P/1B: $115- 190   2P/2B: $115- 190   XP: $20
Hotel   **Location:** 4.5 mi s on the Strip, I-15 exit E Flamingo Rd. 3570 Las Vegas Blvd S 89109. **Fax:** 702/731-6636. **Terms:** Reserv deposit. **Facility:** 2700 rooms. Attractively landscaped grounds & marble statuary. Large rooms. The Forum Mall resemble Roman streetscape, elegant shops, art galleries, & eateries. 29 stories; interior corridors; heated pool; 3 lighted tennis courts. **Services:** giftshop. Fee: massage. **Cards:** AE, CB, DI, DS, JC, MC, VI.

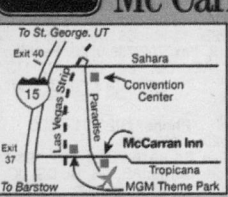

(See map p. 1105)

CALIFORNIA HOTEL — Rates Subject to Change — Phone: 702/385-1222 — **39**
◆◆
Hotel

	1P:	2P/1B:	2P/2B:	XP:
Fri & Sat	$50- 80	$50- 80	$50- 80	$5
Sun-Thurs	$40- 65	$40- 65	$40- 65	$5

Location: In downtown Casino Center Area. 1st & Ogden 89125 (PO Box 630). Fax: 702/388-2660.
Terms: Reserv deposit. **Facility:** 781 rooms. "Aloha"-style decor. 23 stories; interior corridors. **Services:** giftshop.
All Rooms: combo or shower baths. **Cards:** AE, CB, DI, DS, MC, VI.

CARRIAGE HOUSE — Phone: (702)798-1020 — **43**
AAA SAVE
◆◆◆
Condo Hotel

	1P:	2P/1B:	2P/2B:
All Year	$89- 145	$89- 145	$89- 165

Location: 1 blk e off the strip. 105 E Harmon Ave 89109. Fax: 702/798-1020. **Terms:** Reserv deposit.
Facility: 155 rooms. 15 two-bedroom units, $275-$525 for 2-6 persons; 9 stories; interior corridors; whirlpool;
1 lighted tennis court. **Dining:** Restaurant; also, Kiefer's Atop the Carriage House, see separate listing.
All Rooms: combo or shower baths. **Some Rooms:** 41 efficiencies, 114 kitchens. **Cards:** AE, CB, DI, DS,
MC, VI. **Special Amenities:** Free local telephone calls and free room upgrade (subject to availability with advanced
reservations). *(See color ad below)*

CIRCUS CIRCUS HOTEL — Rates Subject to Change — Phone: 702/734-0410 — **25**
◆◆
Hotel

	1P:	2P/1B:	2P/2B:	XP:	
Fri & Sat	$49- 119	$49- 119	$49- 119	$10-30	F17
Sun-Thurs	$29- 89	$29- 89	$29- 89	$10-30	F17

Location: 2.8 mi s on the Strip. 2880 Las Vegas Blvd S 89109 (PO Box 14967, 89114). Fax: 702/734-5897.
Terms: Reserv deposit. **Facility:** 3744 rooms. Hotel towers & motel rooms in 3-story building. 2-29 stories; interior corridors.
Services: giftshop. **All Rooms:** combo or shower baths. **Cards:** AE, CB, DI, DS, JC, MC, VI.

CLUB HOTEL BY DOUBLETREE LAS VEGAS AIRPORT — Rates Subject to Change — Phone: 702/948-4000
FYI
Hotel

	1P:	2P/1B:	2P/2B:	XP:	
Sun-Thurs	$119	$119	$1149	$15	F18
Fri & Sat	$89	$89	$89	$15	F18

Too new to rate. **Location:** I-215, exit 7, Warm Springs Rd. 7250 Pollock Dr 89119. Fax: 702/948-4100.
Facility: 190 rooms. 6 stories; interior corridors; heated pool. **Services:** area transportation.
All Rooms: combo or shower baths. **Cards:** AE, CB, DI, DS, MC, VI.

COMFORT INN — Phone: (702)399-1500 — **47**
AAA SAVE
◆◆◆
Motel

	1P:	2P/1B:	2P/2B:	XP:	
Fri & Sat [CP]	$69- 79	$69- 79	$69- 79	$10	F18
Sun-Thurs [CP]	$59- 69	$59- 69	$59- 69	$10	F18

Location: I-15 exit Cheyenne West. 910 E Cheyenne Ave 89030. Fax: 702/399-0960. **Terms:** Small pets
only, $10 extra charge. **Facility:** 59 rooms. 3 whirlpool rms, extra charge; 3 stories, no elevator; interior corri-
dors; sauna, whirlpool. **Dining:** Coffee shop nearby. **Services:** giftshop. **All Rooms:** combo or shower baths.
Some Rooms: 3 kitchens. **Cards:** AE, CB, DI, DS, MC, VI. **Special Amenities:** Free breakfast and free local telephone
calls.

COMFORT INN CENTRAL — Phone: (702)733-7800 — **3**
AAA SAVE
◆◆
Motel

	1P:	2P/1B:	2P/2B:	XP:	
Fri & Sat [CP]	$65	$75	$85	$5	F16
Sun-Thurs [CP]	$55	$65	$75	$5	F16

Location: Exit I-15 Flamingo Rd e, at Koval Rd. 211 E Flamingo Rd 89109. Fax: 702/733-7353. **Facility:** 121
rooms. 4 two-bedroom units. 2 stories; exterior corridors. **Dining:** Restaurant nearby. **Cards:** AE, CB, DI,
DS, JC, MC, VI. **Special Amenities:** Free breakfast and free newspaper.

COMFORT INN SOUTH — Phone: (702)736-3600 — **48**
AAA SAVE
◆◆
Motel

	1P:	2P/1B:	2P/2B:	XP:	
Fri & Sat [CP]	$65- 85	$65- 85	$65- 85	$5	F18
Sun-Thurs [CP]	$42- 65	$48- 65	$48- 65	$5	F18

Location: 0.5 mi e of I-15; Tropicana Ave exit. 5075 S Koval Ln 89119. Fax: 702/736-0726. **Facility:** 106
rooms. Comfortable rooms. 2 stories; exterior corridors. **Cards:** AE, CB, DI, DS, JC, MC, VI.
Special Amenities: Free breakfast and free local telephone calls.

COURTYARD BY MARRIOTT-CONVENTION CENTER — Rates Subject to Change — Phone: 702/791-3600 — **49**
◆◆◆
Motor Inn

	1P:	2P/1B:	2P/2B:
All Year	$89- 135	$89- 135	$89- 135

Location: Just e of strip; 1 blk to convention center. 3275 Paradise Rd 89109. Fax: 702/796-7981.
Facility: 149 rooms. Rates for up to 5 persons; 3 stories; interior corridors. **Cards:** AE, CB, DI, DS, JC, MC,
VI. *(See color ad p 1109)*

(See map p. 1105)

CROWNE PLAZA   **Phone:** (702)369-4400   **20**
AAA SAVE   2/1-6/30 & 9/1-1/31   1P: $125- 145   2P/1B: $125- 145 2P/2B: $125- 145 XP: $15   F18
            7/1-8/31   1P: $95   2P/1B: $95   2P/2B: $95   XP: $15   F18
♦♦♦   **Location:** Exit I-15 Flamingo, e 0.5 mi to Paradise, s 0.3 mi. 4255 S Paradise Rd 89109.
Motor Inn   Fax: 702/369-3770. **Terms:** Pets, $200 dep req, first floor only. **Facility:** 201 rooms. Atrium lobby, vibrant colors, cascading fountains. 6 stories; interior corridors; sauna, whirlpool. **Dining:** Restaurant; 6 am-10 pm; $8-$16; cocktails. **Services:** giftshop; area transportation, to strip. **Cards:** AE, CB, DI, DS, JC, MC, VI. **Special Amenities:** Free breakfast and free local telephone calls.

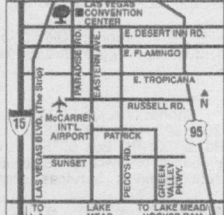

DAYS INN-AIRPORT   Rates Subject to Change   **Phone:** 702/740-4040   **13**
♦♦   Fri & Sat   1P: $65- 145   2P/1B: $65- 145 2P/2B: $65- 145
Motel   Sun-Thurs   1P: $45- 125   2P/1B: $45- 125 2P/2B: $45- 125
          Location: Exit I-15, at E Tropicana Ave, 1.8 mi e to Paradise Rd, 0.5 mi s. 5125 Swenson St 89119. Fax: 702/736-8295. **Terms:** Reserv deposit. **Facility:** 183 rooms. 2 stories; exterior corridors. **Services:** area transportation. **Cards:** AE, CB, DI, DS, MC, VI.

DAYS INN DOWNTOWN   **Phone:** (702)388-1400   **35**
AAA SAVE   11/15-11/21 & 12/27-1/1   1P: $110- 150   2P/1B: $110- 150 2P/2B: $120- 175 XP: $10
          Fri & Sat 2/1-11/14,
♦♦   11/22-12/26 & 1/2-1/31   1P: $50- 120   2P/1B: $60- 120 2P/2B: $60- 120 XP: $10
Motel   Sun-Thurs 2/1-11/14,
          11/22-12/26 & 1/2-1/31   1P: $36- 100   2P/1B: $46- 100 2P/2B: $46- 100 XP: $10
Location: On US 93 & 95 business rt. 707 E Fremont St 89101. Fax: 702/388-9622. **Facility:** 147 rooms. Few small rooms, some large. 7 one-bedroom suites, $60-$120; 3 stories; exterior corridors. **Dining:** Restaurant; 7 am-7 pm, Sat & Sun-noon; culinary training facility, motel guests only. **Cards:** AE, CB, DI, DS, JC, MC, VI. **Special Amenities:** Early check-in/late check-out.

THE DESERT INN   Rates Subject to Change   **Phone:** 702/733-4444   **37**
♦♦♦♦   All Year   1P: $220- 300 2P/1B: $220- 300 2P/2B: $220- 300 XP: $35   F17
Resort   **Location:** On the strip; I-15 northbound exit e Flamingo Ave, southbound exit e Sahara Ave. 3145 Las
Complex   Vegas Blvd S 89109. Fax: 702/733-4774. **Terms:** Reserv deposit, 3 day notice. **Facility:** 715 rooms. Lavishly landscaped grounds. 284 whirlpool suites, $1500-$5000 for 2 persons; 14 stories; interior corridors; heated pool; 4 lighted tennis courts. Fee: 18 holes golf. **Services:** giftshop. Fee: massage. **All Rooms:** combo or shower baths. **Cards:** AE, CB, DI, DS, JC, MC, VI.

(See map p. 1105)

ECONO LODGE-DOWNTOWN
(AAA) SAVE

Fri & Sat	1P:	$50	2P/1B:	$50	2P/2B: $60	XP: $10
Sun-Thurs	1P:	$40	2P/1B:	$40	2P/2B: $50	XP: $10

Phone: (702)384-8211 54 F18 F18

Motel

Location: Exit I-15 downtown Casino Center. 520 S Casino Center Blvd 89101. Fax: 702/384-8580. **Terms:** Reserv deposit. **Facility:** 48 rooms. 4 one-bedroom apartments, $69-$95 for up to 4 persons; 3 stories; interior corridors. **Some Rooms:** 4 kitchens, no utensils. **Cards:** AE, CB, DI, DS, JC, MC, VI. **Special Amenities:** Free room upgrade and preferred room (each subject to availability with advanced reservations). *(See color ad p 1109)*

EMERALD SPRINGS-HOLIDAY INN
(AAA) SAVE

All Year	1P:	$79- 99	2P/1B:	$79- 99	2P/2B: $79- 99	XP: $15

Phone: (702)732-9100 11 F19

◆◆◆ Motor Inn

Location: I-15 exit E Flamingo Rd. 325 E Flamingo Rd 89109. Fax: 702/731-9784. **Terms:** Reserv deposit; monthly rates; BP avail. **Facility:** 150 rooms. 16 suites with wet bar & whirlpool tub, $99-$250 for up to 2 persons; 3 stories; interior corridors; whirlpool. **Dining:** Restaurant; 6:30 am-10 pm, Fri & Sat-11 pm; $10-$20; cocktails. **Services:** area transportation, strip 7 am-11 pm. **Recreation:** Fee: in-room video games. **Cards:** AE, CB, DI, DS, JC, MC, VI. **Special Amenities:** Free newspaper and preferred room (subject to availability with advanced reservations).

EXCALIBUR HOTEL & CASINO
◆◆◆ Hotel

Rates Subject to Change

All Year	1P:	$55- 315	2P/1B:	$55- 375	2P/2B: $55- 375	XP: $12

Phone: 702/597-7777 55 F18

Location: I-15 exit E Tropicana Ave. 3850 Las Vegas Blvd S 89109 (PO Box 96778, 89193). Fax: 702/597-7009. **Terms:** Reserv deposit. **Facility:** 4008 rooms. Medieval castle theme. 48 whirlpool rms, extra charge; 28 stories; interior corridors. **Services:** giftshop. **All Rooms:** shower baths. **Cards:** AE, DI, DS, JC, MC, VI.

FAIRFIELD INN BY MARRIOTT
◆◆ Motel

Rates Subject to Change

11/2-1/31 [CP]	1P:	$62- 175	2P/1B:	$62- 175	2P/2B: $62- 175	
3/14-4/22 [CP]	1P:	$62- 125	2P/1B:	$62- 125	2P/2B: $62- 125	
2/1-3/13 & 4/23-11/1 [CP]	1P:	$62- 95	2P/1B:	$62- 95	2P/2B: $62- 95	

Phone: 702/791-0899 52

Location: I-15 exit E Flamingo Rd; 3 blks n of convention center. 3850 Paradise Rd 89109. Fax: 702/791-2705. **Facility:** 129 rooms. Large lobby with many tables & chairs. Comfortable rooms. Rates for up to 4 persons; 4 stories; interior corridors. **Cards:** AE, DI, DS, MC, VI.

FIESTA CASINO HOTEL
◆◆ Motor Inn

Rates Subject to Change

All Year	1P:	$39	2P/1B:	$42	2P/2B: $45 XP: $5

Phone: 702/631-7000 56

Location: 3 mi n of downtown. 2400 N Rancho Dr 89130. Fax: 702/631-7070. **Facility:** 100 rooms. 5 stories; interior corridors. **Cards:** AE, DI, DS, MC, VI.

FLAMINGO HILTON-LAS VEGAS
(AAA) SAVE

All Year	1P:	$69- 279	2P/1B:	$69- 279	2P/2B: $69- 279	XP: $20

Phone: (702)733-3111 14

◆◆◆ Hotel

Location: I-15 exit Flamingo E, n on strip. 3555 Las Vegas Blvd S 89109. Fax: 702/733-3528. **Facility:** 3642 rooms. Suites $250-$5800 up to 2 persons; 2-28 stories; interior corridors; waterslide, whirlpools. Fee: 4 lighted tennis courts. **Dining:** 5 restaurants, cafeteria, coffee shop; 24 hrs, buffet $6-$9, casino; $7-$20; cocktails. **Services:** giftshop. Fee: massage. **Cards:** AE, CB, DI, DS, MC, VI. *(See ad p 119)*

FOUR SEASONS HOTEL LAS VEGAS
[FYI]

Phone: 702/632-5000

Under construction. **Location:** I-15, E Tropicana exit, s on the strip. 3950 Las Vegas Blvd S 89119. Fax: 702/632-5222. **Facility:** 424 rooms. Scheduled to open March, 1999;

GOLD COAST HOTEL
◆◆◆ Hotel

Rates Subject to Change

All Year	1P:	$29- 175	2P/1B:	$29- 175	2P/2B: $29- 175	XP: $5

Phone: (702)367-7111 27 F16

Location: 1 blk w of I-15, exit Flamingo Rd W. 4000 W Flamingo Rd 89103 (PO Box 80750, 89180). Fax: 702/367-8575. **Terms:** Reserv deposit. **Facility:** 711 rooms. Colonial-Spanish architecture. 18 beautifully decorated suites with wet bar & refrigerator, $150-$300 for 2 persons; 10 stories; interior corridors. **Services:** giftshop. **All Rooms:** combo or shower baths. **Cards:** AE, CB, DI, DS, JC, MC, VI.

GOLDEN NUGGET HOTEL
(AAA) SAVE

All Year	1P:	$59- 299	2P/1B:	$59- 299	2P/2B: $59- 299	XP: $20

Phone: 702/385-7111 31

◆◆◆◆ Hotel

Location: In downtown Casino Center area. 129 E Fremont St 89101 (PO Box 610, 89125). Fax: 702/386-8362. **Terms:** Reserv deposit. **Facility:** 1907 rooms. Large rooms, attractive contemporary decor. 1 & 2-bedroom suites, $275-$375 for 2 persons; 10-22 stories; interior corridors; whirlpool. **Dining:** 2 dining rooms, restaurant, coffee shop; 24 hours, buffet $10, 24 hour room service, casino; $10-$35; cocktails. **Services:** giftshop. Fee: massage. **Recreation:** video arcade. **Cards:** AE, DI, DS, MC, VI.

HARRAH'S-LAS VEGAS
◆◆◆ Hotel

Guaranteed Rates

All Year	1P:	$50- 259	2P/1B:	$50- 259	2P/2B: $50- 259	XP: $10

Phone: 702/369-5000 16 F12

Location: 4 mi s on the Strip. 3475 Las Vegas Blvd S 89109. Fax: 702/369-5008. **Terms:** Reserv deposit, 3 day notice. **Facility:** 2683 rooms. 64 suites $195-$350 for up to 2 persons; 15-35 stories; interior corridors. **Services:** giftshop. Fee: massage. **Cards:** AE, CB, DI, DS, JC, MC, VI.

HAWTHORN SUITES - LAS VEGAS
◆◆◆ Suite Motor Inn

Guaranteed Rates

All Year [BP]	1P:	$99- 169	2P/1B:	$99- 169	2P/2B: $99- 169

Phone: (702)739-7000 36

Location: Exit I-15, at E Tropicana Ave, 0.8 mi e to Duke Ellington Way, just s. 5051 Duke Ellington Way 89119. Fax: 702/739-9350. **Facility:** 284 rooms. All suites include separate bedroom, living room, & full kitchen. 3 stories; exterior corridors. **Services:** giftshop. **All Rooms:** kitchens. **Cards:** AE, CB, DI, DS, JC, MC, VI.

(See map p. 1105)

HILTON GRAND VACATIONS CLUB   Rates Subject to Change   **Phone:** 702/697-2900   53
◆◆◆   All Year   1P: $109- 199   2P/1B: $109- 199   2P/2B: $239- 399
Hotel   **Location:** I-15 exit Flamingo E, n on strip; directly behind Flamingo Hilton. 3575 Las Vegas Blvd S 89109.
Fax: 702/697-2910. **Terms:** Check-in 4 pm; reserv deposit, 3 day notice; handling fee imposed. **Facility:** 291
rooms. Attractively landscaped grounds & public areas. 214 two-bedroom units. 17 stories; interior corridors.
Some Rooms: 146 efficiencies, 145 kitchens. **Cards:** AE, DI, DS, MC, VI. *(See ad p 119)*

HOLIDAY INN CASINO BOARDWALK   Rates Subject to Change   **Phone:** (702)735-2400   30
◆◆◆   Fri & Sat   1P: $79- 239   2P/1B: $79- 239   2P/2B: $79- 239   XP: $15   F19
Hotel   Sun-Thurs   1P: $49- 239   2P/1B: $49- 239   2P/2B: $49- 239   XP: $15   F19
    Location: I-15, exit Flamingo Blvd; s on Strip. 3750 Las Vegas Blvd S 89109. Fax: 702/739-8152.
Facility: 653 rooms. Whirlpool rm, extra charge; 4-16 stories; interior/exterior corridors. **Services:** giftshop.
All Rooms: combo or shower baths. **Cards:** AE, CB, DI, DS, JC, MC, VI.

HOLIDAY INN EXPRESS   **Phone:** (702)256-3766   45
AAA SAVE   Fri & Sat [CP]   1P: $99- 250   2P/1B: $99- 250   2P/2B: $99- 250   XP: $10-20   F18
   Sun-Thurs [CP]   1P: $89- 250   2P/1B: $89- 250   2P/2B: $89- 250   XP: $10-20   F18
◆◆◆   **Location:** Exit I-15 at Sahara; 6.5 mi w. 8669 W Sahara Ave 89117. Fax: 702/256-3763. **Terms:** Reserv
Motel   deposit; pets. **Facility:** 59 rooms. 3 whirlpool rms, extra charge; 3 stories; interior corridors; heated indoor pool,
whirlpool. **Dining:** Restaurants nearby. **All Rooms:** combo or shower baths. **Some Rooms:** 14 efficiencies,
3 kitchens. **Cards:** AE, DI, DS, MC, VI. **Special Amenities:** Free breakfast and free local telephone calls.

HOLIDAY INN FITZGERALDS CASINO   Rates Subject to Change   **Phone:** (702)388-2400   63
◆◆◆   Fri & Sat   1P: $50- 120   2P/1B: $50- 120   2P/2B: $50- 120   XP: $10   F18
Hotel   Sun-Thurs   1P: $34- 80   2P/1B: $34- 80   2P/2B: $34- 80   XP: $10   F18
    Location: In downtown casino center. 301 Fremont St 89101. Fax: 702/388-2181. **Terms:** Reserv deposit.
Facility: 638 rooms. 34 whirlpool rms, extra charge; 34 stories; interior corridors. **Services:** giftshop. **Cards:** AE, CB, DI,
DS, MC, VI. *(See ad below)*

HOWARD JOHNSON HOTEL & CASINO   **Phone:** (702)798-1111   57
AAA SAVE   Fri & Sat   1P: $89   2P/1B: $89   2P/2B: $89   XP: $10   F12
   Sun-Thurs   1P: $59   2P/1B: $59   2P/2B: $59   XP: $10   F12
◆◆   **Location:** Adjacent to I-15; Tropicana W exit. 3111 W Tropicana Ave 89103. Fax: 702/798-7138.
Hotel   **Terms:** Reserv deposit. **Facility:** 150 rooms. Convenient to airport & strip. 6 stories; interior corridors; whirl-
pool. **Dining:** Coffee shop; 24 hour; $6-$12; cocktails. **Cards:** AE, DI, DS, MC, VI. **Special Amenities:** Free
local telephone calls and free newspaper. *(See color ad opposite inside back cover)*

HOWARD JOHNSON INN-AIRPORT   Rates Subject to Change   **Phone:** 702/798-2777   4
◆   Fri & Sat   1P: $65- 145   2P/1B: $65- 145   2P/2B: $65- 145
Motel   Sun-Thurs   1P: $45- 125   2P/1B: $45- 125   2P/2B: $45- 125
    Location: Exit I-15 at E Tropicana Ave, 1.8 mi to Paradise Rd, 0.3 mi s. 5100 Paradise Rd 89119.
Fax: 702/736-8295. **Terms:** Reserv deposit. **Facility:** 144 rooms. 2 stories; exterior corridors. **Services:** area transportation.
Cards: AE, CB, DI, DS, MC, VI. *(See color ad opposite inside back cover)*

LA QUINTA INN   Rates Subject to Change   **Phone:** (702)739-7457   5
◆◆◆   2/1-4/30 & 12/31-1/31 [CP]   1P: $69- 89   2P/1B: $69- 89   2P/2B: $69- 89
Motel   5/1-12/30 [CP]   1P: $55- 72   2P/1B: $55- 72   2P/2B: $55- 72
    Location: 5.5 mi s on the Strip. 3782 Las Vegas Blvd S 89109-4312. Fax: 702/736-1129. **Facility:** 114 rooms.
Spanish exterior design. 3 stories; exterior corridors. **Cards:** AE, CB, DI, DS, JC, MC, VI. *(See color ad p 1112)*

LA QUINTA INN CONVENTION CENTER   **Phone:** (702)796-9000   44
AAA SAVE   2/1-4/30 [CP]   1P: $69- 89   2P/1B: $69- 89   2P/2B: $69- 89
   5/1-1/31 [CP]   1P: $52- 72   2P/1B: $52- 72   2P/2B: $52- 72
◆◆◆   **Location:** 0.8 mi s of Convention Center, exit I-15 Flamingo Ave E; 0.5 mi e of strip. 3970 Paradise Rd
Motel   89109. Fax: 702/796-3537. **Facility:** 228 rooms. Some units with balcony, few with patio. 9 two-bedroom units.
3 stories; interior corridors; whirlpool. **Dining:** Restaurant nearby. **Cards:** AE, CB, DI, DS, JC, MC, VI.
Special Amenities: Free breakfast and free local telephone calls.

(See map p. 1105)

LAS VEGAS HILTON Rates Subject to Change Phone: 702/732-5111 **24**
All Year 1P: $95- 275 2P/1B: $95- 275 2P/2B: $95- 275 XP: $20
Location: Exit 1-15 e at Sahara 2 mi; adjacent to Convention Center. 3000 Paradise Rd 89109 (PO Box 93147, 89193). Fax: 702/732-5805. **Terms:** Reserv deposit, 3 day notice. **Facility:** 3174 rooms. 300 suites, $310-$1250 for up to 2 persons; 30 stories; interior corridors; putting green; whirlpools; 6 lighted tennis courts. **Dining:** 8 dining rooms, coffee shop; 24 hours, buffet $9-$13; $8-$35; cocktails; also, Andiamo, see separate listing. **Services:** giftshop. Fee: massage. **Recreation:** video arcade. Fee: Star Trek experience. **Cards:** AE, CB, DI, DS, JC, MC, VI. *(See ad p 119)*

LUXOR LAS VEGAS Rates Subject to Change Phone: (702)262-4444 **22**
All Year 1P: $59- 259 2P/1B: $59- 259 2P/2B: $59- 259 XP: $15 F12
Location: I-15 exit E Tropicana, just s on strip. 3900 Las Vegas Blvd S 89119. Fax: 702/262-4454. **Terms:** Reserv deposit. **Facility:** 4526 rooms. A 350-foot, glass-faced pyramid crowned by a 40-billion candlepower vertical light beam. Egyptian decor theme. 30 stories; interior corridors; heated pool, wading pool, saunas, whirlpools. **Dining:** 2 dining rooms, 4 restaurants, coffee shop, deli; food court; $10-$50; cocktails. **Services:** giftshop. Fee: massage. **Recreation:** Fee: virtualand arcade, special effects attractions & "King Tut's Tomb & Museum" within the atrium, 3D Imax theater. **All Rooms:** combo or shower baths. **Some Rooms:** whirlpools. **Cards:** AE, CB, DI, DS, JC, MC, VI.

MAIN STREET STATION Rates Subject to Change Phone: 702/387-1896 **61**
All Year 1P: $50- 125 2P/1B: $50- 125 2P/2B: $50- 125
Location: In downtown casino center. 200 N Main St 89125 (PO Box 7625). Fax: 702/386-4466. **Terms:** Check-in 4 pm. **Facility:** 406 rooms. 17 stories; interior corridors. **Services:** giftshop. **All Rooms:** combo or shower baths. **Cards:** AE, CB, DI, DS, MC, VI.

MGM GRAND HOTEL CASINO & THEME PARK Rates Subject to Change Phone: 702/891-1111 **34**
All Year 1P: $69- 259 2P/1B: $69- 259 2P/2B: $69- 259 XP: $25 F12
Location: I-15 exit E Tropicana Ave. 3799 Las Vegas Blvd S 89109. Fax: 702/891-1030. **Terms:** Reserv deposit. **Facility:** 5005 rooms. Worlds largest hotel, 33 acre magical theme park. 400 suites $169-$500; rates for up to 2 persons; 30 stories; interior corridors; heated pool. Fee: 5 lighted tennis courts. **Services:** giftshop. Fee: massage. **Cards:** AE, CB, DI, DS, JC, MC, VI.

THE MIRAGE Rates Subject to Change Phone: 702/791-7111 **51**
Fri & Sat 1P: $109- 399 2P/1B: $109- 399 2P/2B: $109- 399 XP: $30
Sun-Thurs 1P: $79- 399 2P/1B: $79- 399 2P/2B: $79- 399 XP: $30
Location: 3.5 mi s on strip. 3400 Las Vegas Blvd S 89109. Fax: 702/791-7446. **Terms:** Reserv deposit. **Facility:** 3044 rooms. Lavish grounds & unique public areas, home to Siegfried & Roy & their magnificent white tigers & dolphin habitat. 1 & 2-bedroom suites, $300-$950 for 2 persons; 30 stories; interior corridors; heated pool. **Services:** giftshop; area transportation. Fee: massage. **Cards:** AE, DI, DS, JC, MC, VI.

MONTE CARLO RESORT & CASINO Rates Subject to Change Phone: 702/730-7777 **38**
Fri & Sat 1P: $109- 249 2P/1B: $109- 249 2P/2B: $109- 249 XP: $15 F13
Sun-Thurs 1P: $69- 199 2P/1B: $69- 199 2P/2B: $69- 199 XP: $15 F13
Location: On the strip between Flamingo Rd & Tropicana Ave. 3770 Las Vegas Blvd S 89109. Fax: 702/730-7250. **Terms:** Reserv deposit, 3 day notice. **Facility:** 3014 rooms. 203 whirlpool rms, extra charge; 32 stories; interior corridors; heated pool; 3 lighted tennis courts. **Services:** giftshop. Fee: massage. **Cards:** AE, DI, DS, MC, VI.

THE ORLEANS Rates Subject to Change Phone: 702/365-7111 **18**
Fri & Sat 1P: $89- 109 2P/1B: $89- 109 2P/2B: $89- 109 XP: $10
Sun-Thurs 1P: $49- 69 2P/1B: $49- 69 2P/2B: $49- 69 XP: $10
Location: Exit I-15 at Tropicana, 1 mi w. 4500 W Tropicana 89103. Fax: 702/365-7505. **Terms:** Reserv deposit. **Facility:** 840 rooms. 22 stories. **Services:** giftshop. **All Rooms:** combo or shower baths. **Cards:** AE, CB, DI, DS, JC, MC, VI.

PALACE STATION HOTEL & CASINO Rates Subject to Change Phone: (702)367-2411 **62**
Fri & Sat 1P: $79- 149 2P/1B: $79- 149 2P/2B: $79- 149 XP: $10 F17
Sun-Thurs 1P: $39- 99 2P/1B: $39- 99 2P/2B: $39- 99 XP: $10 F17
Location: Sw corner of Sahara & Rancho. Sahara exit from I-15. 2411 W Sahara Ave 89102. Fax: 702/367-2478. **Terms:** Package plans. **Facility:** 573 rooms. 20 stories; interior corridors; heated pool, whirlpools. **Dining:** 9 restaurants; 24 hrs; $12-$18. **Services:** giftshop; area transportation. **Some Rooms:** whirlpools. **Cards:** AE, CB, DI, DS, MC, VI.

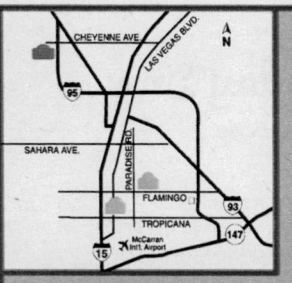

(See map p. 1105)

QUALITY INN & KEY LARGO CASINO
◆◆
Hotel
Rates Subject to Change
All Year 1P: $39- 200 2P/1B: $39- 200 2P/2B: $39- 200 XP: $10-15
Phone: (702)733-7777 **26** F18
Location: 377 E Flamingo Rd 89109. Fax: 702/369-6911. **Facility:** 315 rooms. Attractively landscaped grounds. 3 stories; interior/exterior corridors; heated pool. **Services:** giftshop; area transportation.
Cards: AE, CB, DI, DS, MC, VI.

RESIDENCE INN BY MARRIOTT
◆◆◆
Apartment
Hotel

JC, MC, VI.
Rates Subject to Change
All Year [CP] 1P: $95- 319 2P/1B: $95- 319 2P/2B: $95- 329
Phone: 702/796-9300 **50**
Location: Opposite Convention Center. 3225 Paradise Rd 89109. Fax: 702/796-9562. **Terms:** Check-in 4 pm; reserv deposit. **Facility:** 192 rooms. Complimentary snacks & beverages 5:30 pm-7 pm weekdays. 48 two-bedroom units. 2 stories; exterior corridors; heated pool. **All Rooms:** kitchens. **Cards:** AE, CB, DI, DS,

RIO SUITE HOTEL & CASINO
◆◆◆
Hotel
Rates Subject to Change
All Year 1P: $95- 149 2P/1B: $95- 149 2P/2B: $95- 149 XP: $15
Phone: 702/252-7777 **17**
Location: Exit I-15 at Flamingo Rd, 0.3 mi w. 3700 W Flamingo Rd 89103 (PO Box 14160, 89114). Fax: 702/252-8909. **Facility:** 2550 rooms. Tropical swim lagoon with white sand beach. Masquerade village, live carnival parade & show. Specialty suites, $300-$850; 41 stories; interior corridors; heated pool. **Services:** giftshop. Fee: massage. **All Rooms:** combo or shower baths. **Cards:** AE, CB, DI, DS, JC, MC, VI.

RIVIERA HOTEL
◆◆
Hotel
Rates Subject to Change
All Year 1P: $59- 145 2P/1B: $59- 145 2P/2B: $59- 145 XP: $20
Phone: 702/734-5110 **59**
Location: I-15 exit E Sahara. 2901 Las Vegas Blvd S 89109. Fax: 702/794-9451. **Terms:** Reserv deposit. **Facility:** 2073 rooms. Many large rooms. Wedding chapel. 24 stories; interior corridors; 2 lighted tennis courts. **Services:** giftshop. Fee: massage. **Cards:** AE, CB, DI, DS, JC, MC, VI.

ST TROPEZ ALL SUITE HOTEL
(AAA) (SAVE)
◆◆◆
Complex

DI, DS, MC, VI. **Special Amenities: Free breakfast and free local telephone calls.**
1P: $95- 115 2P/1B: $115- 125 2P/2B: $115- 125 XP: $10
Phone: (702)369-5400 **46** F18
All Year [CP]
Location: 2 mi s of convention center at Paradise Rd. 455 E Harmon Ave 89109. Fax: 702/369-1150. **Facility:** 149 rooms. Surrounding attractive landscaped grounds. Courtyard units with patio or deck. 34 whirlpool units, $135-$180 for up to 2 persons; 2 stories; interior/exterior corridors; whirlpool. **Dining:** Restaurant nearby. **Services:** giftshop; area transportation, to the strip. **All Rooms:** combo or shower baths. **Cards:** AE,

SAM'S TOWN HOTEL
◆◆◆
Hotel
Rates Subject to Change
Fri & Sat 1P: $75- 100 2P/1B: $75- 155 2P/2B: $75- 155 XP: $5
Sun-Thurs 1P: $50- 65 2P/1B: $50- 80 2P/2B: $50- 80 XP: $5
Phone: 702/456-7777 **10** F12
F12
Location: 1 mi e of I-515/SR 93 & 95; Flamingo exit. 5111 Boulder Hwy 89122. Fax: 702/454-8014. **Terms:** Reserv deposit. **Facility:** 650 rooms. Central indoor park with waterfall; nightly laser & water show. Southwestern decor. 9 stories; interior corridors. **Services:** giftshop; area transportation. **Cards:** AE, CB, DI, DS, MC, VI.

SILVERTON HOTEL-CASINO
◆◆
Hotel
Rates Subject to Change
Fri & Sat 1P: $70 2P/1B: $70 2P/2B: $70 XP: $5
Sun-Thurs 1P: $49 2P/1B: $49 2P/2B: $49 XP: $5
Phone: 702/263-7777 **29**
Location: I-15 exit w Blue Diamond Rd, exit 33. 3333 Blue Diamond Rd 89139. Fax: 702/896-5635. **Facility:** 300 rooms. Replica of 1800's Old West frontier mining town. 12 suites with whirlpool, $150-$195 for up to 2 persons; 4 stories; interior corridors; heated pool. **Services:** giftshop; area transportation. **Cards:** AE, CB, DI, DS, MC, VI.

SOMERSET HOUSE MOTEL
(AAA)
◆◆
Motor Inn
Rates Subject to Change
Fri & Sat 1P: $40 2P/1B: $50 2P/2B: $50 XP: $5
Sun-Thurs 1P: $32 2P/1B: $40 2P/2B: $40 XP: $5
Phone: (702)735-4411 **23** F12
F12
Location: 3 mi s, just e off the Strip. 1 blk from Convention Center. 294 Convention Center Dr 89109. Fax: 702/369-2388. **Terms:** Reserv deposit, 3 day notice; weekly rates. **Facility:** 104 rooms. Some rooms with balcony. 3 stories; interior/exterior corridors. **All Rooms:** combo or shower baths. **Some Rooms:** 17 efficiencies, 63 kitchens. **Cards:** AE, CB, DI, MC, VI. *(See color ad below)*

(See map p. 1105)

TEXAS STATION GAMBLING HALL & HOTEL Rates Subject to Change **Phone:** (702)631-1000 60
⚑ Fri & Sat 1P: $99- 129 2P/1B: $99- 129 2P/2B: $99- 129 XP:$10-15 F13
Sun-Thurs 1P: $59- 79 2P/1B: $59- 79 2P/2B: $59- 79 XP:$10-15 F13
♦♦♦ **Location:** Bus US 95, 3 mi n of downtown. 2101 Texas Star Ln 89030. Fax: 702/631-8120. **Terms:** Reserv
Motor Inn deposit; handling fee imposed. **Facility:** 200 rooms. 6 stories; interior corridors. **Dining:** Restaurant, coffee
shop; $9-$18. **Recreation:** casino, 12 screen movie theater. **Cards:** AE, CB, DI, DS, MC, VI.

TRAVELODGE-WEST SAHARA Rates Subject to Change **Phone:** (702)733-0001 58
♦♦ Sun-Thurs [CP] 1P: $39- 129 2P/1B: $39- 129 2P/2B: $39- 129 XP: $10 F17
Motor Inn Fri & Sat [CP] 1P: $59- 89 2P/1B: $59- 89 2P/2B: $59- 89 XP: $10 F17
Location: E off I-15, just w of the Strip; westbound Sahara traffic exit right via Western Ave. 1501 W Sahara
Ave 89102. Fax: 702/733-1571. **Terms:** Reserv deposit; handling fee imposed. **Facility:** 223 rooms. 3-4 stories; interior corri-
dors. **Services:** giftshop. **Cards:** AE, DI, DS, JC, MC, VI.

TREASURE ISLAND AT THE MIRAGE Rates Subject to Change **Phone:** 702/894-7444 21
♦♦♦ All Year 1P: $59- 399 2P/1B: $59- 399 2P/2B: $59- 399 XP:$25-50
Resort Hotel **Location:** 3.5 mi s on the strip. 3300 Las Vegas Blvd S 89109 (PO Box 7711, 89193). Fax: 702/894-7446.
Terms: Reserv deposit. **Facility:** 2891 rooms. A pirate theme resort & home to Cirque du Soleil. 212 suites,
$100-$500 for up to 2 persons; 36 stories; interior corridors. **Services:** giftshop; area transportation. Fee: massage.
Cards: AE, CB, DI, DS, JC, MC, VI.

RESTAURANTS

ANDIAMO **Dinner:** $20-$30 **Phone:** 702/732-5111 ①
♦♦♦ **Location:** In The Las Vegas Hilton. 3000 Paradise Rd 89109. **Hours:** 6 pm-11 pm.
Regional **Reservations:** suggested. **Features:** casual dress; cocktails & lounge; valet parking; a la carte. Comfortable
Italian & elegant surroundings, nice variety of dishes. **Cards:** AE, CB, DI, MC, VI.

ANDRE'S FRENCH RESTAURANT **Dinner:** $20-$44 **Phone:** 702/385-5016 ⑪
♦♦♦ **Location:** At Lewis St. 401 S 6th St 89101. **Hours:** 6 pm-11 pm. Closed major holidays.
French **Reservations:** suggested. **Features:** semi-formal attire; health conscious menu items; cocktails & lounge;
valet parking; a la carte. Country-French decor; several dining rooms. **Cards:** AE, CB, DI, JC, MC, VI.

ANTHONY'S FINE DINING **Lunch:** $6-$25 **Dinner:** $13-$24 **Phone:** 702/795-6000 ②
♦♦♦ **Location:** Exit I-15 Tropicana; e 3 mi. 1550 E Tropicana Ave 89119. **Hours:** 11 am-11 pm, Sat from-11 pm.
Continental Closed major holidays. **Reservations:** suggested. **Features:** semi-formal attire; early bird specials; cocktails;
a la carte. Casual elegance with an Italian flair. **Cards:** AE, DS, MC, VI.

BATTISTA'S HOLE IN THE WALL **Dinner:** $16-$30 **Phone:** 702/732-1424 ⑤
♦♦ **Location:** I-15 exit Flamingo Rd e 0.3 mi, 1 blk e of strip. 4041 Audrie 89109. **Hours:** 5 pm-10:30 pm,
Italian Sat-11 pm. Closed: 11/25 & 12/25. **Reservations:** suggested. **Features:** casual dress; cocktails & lounge.
Rustic decor. Dinners include house wine & cappuccino. **Cards:** AE, CB, DI, DS, MC, VI.

CAFE MICHELLE **Lunch:** $7-$15 **Dinner:** $15-$25 **Phone:** 702/735-8686 ⑫
♦♦♦ **Location:** In the Mission Shopping Center, at Maryland Pkwy. 1350 E Flamingo 89119. **Hours:** 11 am-11
Continental pm. Closed: 7/4, 11/26 & 12/25. **Reservations:** accepted. **Features:** casual dress; carryout; cocktails &
lounge; entertainment; minimum charge-$12; a la carte. Greek & Italian specialties, extensive menu.
Cards: AE, DS, MC, VI.

COUNTRY INN **Lunch:** $6-$15 **Dinner:** $6-$15 **Phone:** 702/731-5035 ⑦
♦♦ **Location:** 2 mi e of the strip. 2425 E Desert Inn Rd 89121. **Hours:** 7 am-10 pm, Fri & Sat-11 pm. Closed:
American 12/25. **Features:** casual dress; children's menu; beer & wine only; a la carte. Attractive country decor; casual
atmosphere. **Cards:** AE, CB, DI, DS, MC, VI.

COUNTRY INN **Lunch:** $4-$6 **Dinner:** $4-$15 **Phone:** 702/254-0520 ⑥
♦♦ **Location:** Exit I-15 Charleston, 4 mi w; s Rainbow, 0.3 mi. 1401 S Rainbow 89102. **Hours:** 7 am-10 pm, Fri
American & Sat-11 pm. Closed: 12/25. **Reservations:** suggested. **Features:** casual dress; children's menu; beer &
DS, MC, VI. wine only; a la carte. Attractive country decor, traditional dishes. Friendly atmosphere. **Cards:** AE, CB, DI,

GOLDEN STEER **Dinner:** $25-$40 **Phone:** 702/384-4470 ⑨
♦♦ **Location:** Exit I-15 Sahara, 0.3 mi e; 1 blk w of strip. 308 W Sahara Ave 89102. **Hours:** 5 pm-11:30 pm.
.Steakhouse Closed: 11/28 & 12/25. **Reservations:** suggested. **Features:** semi-formal attire; cocktails & lounge; valet
parking; a la carte. Varied menu; chicken, veal & seafood. Italian specialities. **Cards:** AE, CB, DI, MC, VI.

KIEFER'S ATOP THE CARRIAGE HOUSE **Dinner:** $15-$30 **Phone:** 702/739-8000 ③
♦♦♦ **Location:** In Carriage House. 105 E Harmon Ave 89109. **Hours:** 7 am-10 & 5-11 pm, Fri, Sat &
Continental Sun-midnight. **Reservations:** suggested. **Features:** casual dress; cocktails & lounge; minimum charge-$5; a
la carte. Views of city, very romantic atmosphere. **Cards:** AE, CB, DI, DS, MC, VI.

MONTE CARLO RESTAURANT **Dinner:** $65-$105 **Phone:** 702/733-4444 ⑬
⚑ **Location:** In The Desert Inn. 3145 Las Vegas Blvd S 89109. **Hours:** 6 pm-11 pm. Closed: Tues & Wed.
Reservations: suggested. **Features:** semi-formal attire; cocktails; valet parking; a la carte. Long established,
♦♦♦♦ service oriented dining room, very intimate atmosphere. World class food & service. **Cards:** AE, DI, DS, MC,
French VI.

PHILIPS SUPPER HOUSE **Dinner:** $15-$32 **Phone:** 702/873-5222 ④
♦♦♦ **Location:** 2.8 mi w of the Strip, between Arville St & Decatur Blvd. 4545 W Sahara Ave 89102. **Hours:** 4:30
American pm-11 pm. **Reservations:** suggested. **Features:** casual dress; early bird specials; cocktails & lounge. Prime
eastern beef, seafood & Italian specialties. **Cards:** AE, CB, DI, DS, MC, VI.

YOLIE'S BRAZILIAN STEAK HOUSE **Lunch:** $7-$13 **Dinner:** $15-$44 **Phone:** 702/794-0700 ⑩
♦♦ **Location:** On upper level, Citybank Park Plaza. 3900 Paradise Rd 89109. **Hours:** 11 am-3 & 5-11 pm; Sat &
Ethnic Sun from 5 pm. Closed: 12/25. **Features:** casual dress; children's menu; cocktails & lounge; entertainment; a
la carte. Informal atmosphere, variety of meats served from a skewer. Also lamb, chicken & fish specialties.
Cards: AE, CB, DI, DS, MC, VI.

The Las Vegas Vicinity

BOULDER CITY—12,600

LODGINGS

BEST WESTERN LIGHTHOUSE INN
Phone: (702)293-6444
AAA SAVE Fri & Sat [CP]   1P: $68- 85   2P/1B: $68- 85   2P/2B: $68- 85   XP: $10
Sun-Thurs [CP]   1P: $58- 75   2P/1B: $58- 75   2P/2B: $58- 75   XP: $10
◆◆   **Location:** 1 mi e via SR 93. 110 Ville Dr 89005. Fax: 702/293-6547. **Terms:** Reserv deposit. **Facility:** 70
Motel   rooms. Some rooms with view of Lake Mead. 3 stories, no elevator; exterior corridors; whirlpool. **Cards:** AE,
CB, DI, DS, MC, VI. **Special Amenities:** Free breakfast and free local telephone calls.

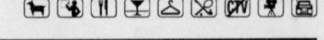

EL RANCHO BOULDER MOTEL
Rates Subject to Change   Phone: (702)293-1085
AAA   All Year   1P: $55- 70   2P/1B: $60- 70   2P/2B: $60- 100   XP: $10-20
Location: On US 93. 725 Nevada Hwy 89005. Fax: 702/293-3021. **Terms:** Reserv deposit, 17 day notice.
◆◆   **Facility:** 39 rooms. Spanish style. Attractive landscaped grounds. 7 two-bedroom units. 2 stories; exterior cor-
Motel   ridors. **Dining:** Coffee shop nearby. **Cards:** AE, CB, DI, DS, MC, VI.

SANDS MOTEL
Rates Subject to Change   Phone: (702)293-2589
AAA   All Year   1P: $37- 42   2P/1B: $42- 47   2P/2B: $47- 52   XP: $6   F12
Location: On US 93. 809 Nevada Hwy 89005. Fax: 702/294-0160. **Terms:** Reserv deposit, 3 day notice.
◆   **Facility:** 25 rooms. Some small units. 2 two-bedroom units. 1 story; exterior corridors. **All Rooms:** combo or
Motel   shower baths. **Cards:** AE, CB, DI, DS, MC, VI.

SUPER 8 MOTEL
Rates Subject to Change   Phone: 702/294-8888
◆   Fri & Sat [CP]   1P: $56- 80   2P/1B: $56- 80   2P/2B: $56- 80   XP: $5
Motel   Sun-Thurs [CP]   1P: $44- 50   2P/1B: $44- 50   2P/2B: $44- 50   XP: $5
Location: On US 93. 704 Nevada Hwy 89005. Fax: 702/293-4344. **Terms:** Reserv deposit. **Facility:** 114
rooms. 3 stories; exterior corridors; heated pool. **Cards:** AE, CB, DI, DS, MC, VI.

COTTONWOOD COVE

LODGING

COTTONWOOD COVE MOTEL
Phone: (702)297-1464
AAA SAVE 5/28-10/31   1P: $90- 95   2P/1B: $95   2P/2B: $90   XP: $8   F5
4/1-5/27   1P: $55- 60   2P/1B: $60   2P/2B: $55   XP: $8   F5
◆◆   2/1-3/31 & 11/1-1/31   1P: $35   2P/1B: $35   2P/2B: $35   XP: $8   F5
Motel   **Location:** Between Las Vegas & Needles; 14 mi e of Searchlight, off US 95. 1000 Cottonwood Cove Rd
89046 (PO Box 1000). Fax: 702/297-1464. **Terms:** Reserv deposit, 14 day notice. **Facility:** 24 rooms. Overlooking Lake Mojave. 1 story; exterior corridors; beach; boat ramp. Fee: marina. **Dining:** Coffee shop; 7 am-8 pm; 8 am-6
pm 11/1-4/1; $5-$14. **Services:** giftshop. **Recreation:** swimming, fishing, waterskiing. Fee: houseboats, powerboats &
equipment, gas station, general store. **All Rooms:** combo or shower baths. **Cards:** AE, DS, MC, VI.

ECHO BAY

LODGING

ECHO BAY RESORT
Phone: (702)394-4000
AAA SAVE 4/1-10/31   1P: $69- 74   2P/1B: $74   2P/2B: $69   XP: $6   F5
2/1-3/31 & 11/1-1/31   1P: $45   2P/1B: $45   2P/2B: $45   XP: $6   F5
◆◆   **Location:** On Lake Mead; 4 mi e of SR 167. (Lake Mead, OVERTON, 89040). Fax: 702/394-4180.
Motor Inn   **Terms:** Reserv deposit, 3 day notice; pets, $5 extra charge, $25 dep req dep req. **Facility:** 52 rooms. Some
rooms with lakeview. Many with balcony or patio. 4 family rooms, $84 for up to 4 persons; 2 stories; interior
corridors; marina. **Dining:** Restaurant; 7 am-8:30 pm; 6 am-9:30 pm, 5/1-9/30; $8-$17; cocktails. **Services:** giftshop.
Recreation: swimming, fishing, waterskiing. Fee: houseboats. Rental: boats. **Cards:** DS, MC, VI. *(See ad below)*

HENDERSON—64,900

LODGINGS

BEST WESTERN LAKE MEAD MOTEL　　　　　　　　　　　　　　　　　　　Phone: (702)564-1712

AAA SAVE	5/15-10/15 [CP]	1P: $56- 61	2P/1B: $61		2P/2B: $61		XP: $5	F12
	2/1-5/14 & 10/16-1/31 [CP]	1P: $51- 56	2P/1B: $56		2P/2B: $56		XP: $5	F12

◆◆ Motel **Location:** Exit US 93/95 Lake Mead Dr 0.5 mi e on SR 146. 85 W Lake Mead Dr 89015. Fax: 702/564-7642. **Terms:** Reserv deposit. **Facility:** 59 rooms. 2 stories; exterior corridors. **Cards:** AE, CB, DI, DS, MC, VI. **Special Amenities: Free breakfast and free local telephone calls.**

THE RESERVE HOTEL CASINO　　　　　Rates Subject to Change　　　　　Phone: 702/558-7000

◆◆◆	Fri & Sat	1P: $69	2P/1B: $69	2P/2B: $69	
Hotel	Sun-Thurs	1P: $49	2P/1B: $49	2P/2B: $49	

Location: Exit US 93/95 & Lake Mead Dr. 777 Lake Mead Dr 89015. Fax: 702/567-7373. **Terms:** Reserv deposit. **Facility:** 224 rooms. 9 stories; interior corridors; heated pool. **Services:** giftshop. **All Rooms:** combo or shower baths. **Cards:** AE, CB, DI, DS, MC, VI.

SUNSET STATION HOTEL & CASINO　　　Rates Subject to Change　　　Phone: (702)547-7777

AAA	Fri & Sat	1P: $69- 159	2P/1B: $69- 159	2P/2B: $69- 159	XP: $10	F12
	Sun-Thurs	1P: $49- 139	2P/1B: $49- 139	2P/2B: $49- 139	XP: $10	F12

◆◆◆ Hotel **Location:** From I-15 at I-215 exit to Warm Springs 7 mi e to Stephanie & Sunset Rd. 1301 W Sunset Rd 89014. Fax: 702/547-7744. **Terms:** Reserv deposit. **Facility:** 448 rooms. 21 stories; interior corridors; heated pool. **Dining:** 6 restaurants, 6 coffee shops; 24 hr buffet; $8-$18; cocktails; wine/beer only. **Services:** giftshop; area transportation. **All Rooms:** combo or shower baths. **Some Rooms:** whirlpools. **Cards:** AE, DI, DS, MC, VI.

INDIAN SPRINGS—1,200

LODGING

INDIAN SPRINGS MOTOR HOTEL　　　　　　　　　　　　　　　　　　Phone: (702)879-3700

AAA SAVE	Fri & Sat	1P: $36	2P/1B: $36	2P/2B: $40	
	Sun-Thurs	1P: $31	2P/1B: $31	2P/2B: $36	

◆ Motel **Location:** On US 95, 45 mi n of Las Vegas. 89018 (PO Box 630). Fax: 702/879-3221. **Terms:** Pets, $5 extra charge. **Facility:** 45 rooms. Adjacent to air base. Casino open 24 hours. 2 stories; interior corridors. **Dining:** Coffee shop; open 24 hours; $5-$10. **Cards:** AE, CB, DI, DS, JC, MC, VI. **Special Amenities:** Early check-in/late check-out and free local telephone calls.

LAUGHLIN—4,800

LODGINGS

AVI HOTEL & CASINO　　　　　　　　　　　　　　　　　　　　　　Phone: (702)535-5555

AAA SAVE	Fri & Sat	1P: $65- 70	2P/1B: $65- 70	2P/2B: $65- 70	XP: $5-9	D
	Sun-Thurs	1P: $30- 35	2P/1B: $30- 35	2P/2B: $30- 35	XP: $5-7	D

◆◆◆ Hotel **Location:** 9 mi s on Needles Hwy via Casino Dr from I-40 exit W Broadway, 12 mi n. 10000 AHA Macav Pkwy (PO Box 77011, 89028-7011). Fax: 702/535-5400. **Terms:** Reserv deposit; package plans; 2 night min stay, weekends. **Facility:** 300 rooms. On the Colorado River; spacious rooms. 4 stories; interior corridors; beach, whirlpool; boat ramp, marina. Fee: 18 holes golf. **Dining:** Dining room, coffee shop, deli; 24 hrs; casino, buffet, $6-$8; $10-$20; cocktails. **Services:** giftshop. **Recreation:** swimming; video arcade. Fee: sea doos. Rental: boats. **All Rooms:** combo or shower baths. **Cards:** AE, DI, DS, MC, VI.

BAYSHORE INN　　　　　　　　　Rates Subject to Change　　　　　　Phone: 702/299-9010

◆	Fri & Sat		2P/1B: $55	2P/2B: $55	
Motel	Sun-Thurs	1P: $25	2P/1B: $25	2P/2B: $25	

Location: 7 mi s of Davis Dam. 1955 W Casino Dr 89029 (PO Box 31377). Fax: 702/299-9194. **Facility:** 98 rooms. Max rate for up to 4 persons; 3 stories; interior corridors; small pool. **Cards:** DS, MC, VI.

COLORADO BELLE HOTEL & CASINO　　　Rates Subject to Change　　　Phone: 702/298-4000

◆◆	Fri & Sat	1P: $45- 60	2P/1B: $45- 60	2P/2B: $45- 60	
Hotel	Sun-Thurs	1P: $21- 39	2P/1B: $39	2P/2B: $39	

Location: 3 mi s of Davis Dam. 2100 S Casino Dr 89028 (PO Box 77000). Fax: 702/299-0669. **Facility:** 1230 rooms. On the Colorado River, riverboat design. Max rate for up to 4 persons; 6 stories; interior/exterior corridors. **Services:** giftshop. **All Rooms:** shower baths. **Cards:** AE, CB, DI, DS, MC, VI.

DON LAUGHLIN'S RIVERSIDE RESORT HOTEL & CASINO　Rates Subject to Change　Phone: (702)298-2535

◆◆◆	Fri & Sat	1P: $49- 109	2P/1B: $49- 109	2P/2B: $49- 109	
Hotel	Sun-Thurs	1P: $25- 71	2P/1B: $25- 71	2P/2B: $25- 71	

Location: 2 mi s of Davis Dam. 1650 S Casino Dr (PO Box 500, 89029). Fax: 702/298-2614. **Terms:** Reserv deposit. **Facility:** 1403 rooms. On the Colorado River. 9 whirlpool rms, extra charge. Max rates for up to 4 persons; 26 stories; interior corridors. **Services:** giftshop. **All Rooms:** combo or shower baths. **Cards:** AE, CB, DI, DS, MC, VI.

EDGEWATER HOTEL/CASINO　　　　　Guaranteed Rates　　　　　　Phone: (702)298-2453

AAA	Fri & Sat	1P: $40- 65	2P/1B: $40- 65	2P/2B: $40- 65	
	Sun-Thurs	1P: $21- 38	2P/1B: $21- 38	2P/2B: $21- 38	

◆◆◆ Hotel **Location:** 2.3 mi s of Davis Dam. 2020 S Casino Dr 89028 (PO Box 77000). Fax: 702/298-8165. **Terms:** Reserv deposit; handling fee imposed. **Facility:** 1450 rooms. Southwestern decor. Native-American art. Max rate for up to 4 persons; 3-26 stories; interior corridors; whirlpool. **Dining:** Dining room, 2 restaurants, coffee shop, deli; 24 hrs; $7-$25; cocktails; also buffet $5. **Services:** giftshop. **Recreation:** arcade. **All Rooms:** combo or shower baths. **Cards:** AE, CB, DI, DS, MC, VI.

FLAMINGO HILTON LAUGHLIN
◆◆◆
Hotel

		Rates Subject to Change					
Fri & Sat	1P:	$55	2P/1B:	$55	2P/2B:	$55	XP: $9 F12
Sun-Thurs	1P:	$25	2P/1B:	$25	2P/2B:	$25	XP: $9 F12

Phone: (702)298-5111

Location: 2 mi s of Davis Dam. 1900 S Casino Dr 89029. Fax: 702/298-5129. **Facility:** 1912 rooms. On Colorado River. Suites $75-$325 for up to 5 persons; 18 stories; interior corridors; 3 lighted tennis courts. **Services:** giftshop. Fee: massage. **Cards:** AE, CB, DI, DS, JC, MC, VI. *(See ad p 119 & color ad above.)*

GOLDEN NUGGET LAUGHLIN
◆◆◆
Hotel

		Rates Subject to Change					
Fri & Sat	1P:	$35- 95	2P/1B:	$35- 95	2P/2B:	$35- 95	XP: $7
Sun-Thurs	1P:	$21- 65	2P/1B:	$21- 65	2P/2B:	$21- 65	XP: $7

Phone: 702/298-7111

Location: 3.5 mi s of Davis Dam. 2300 S Casino Dr 89028 (PO Box 77111). Fax: 702/298-7122. **Facility:** 300 rooms. 30 foot glass topped rain forest atrium with over 500 tropical flora from around the world. Tropical motif throughout. 4 stories; interior corridors. **Services:** giftshop. **All Rooms:** combo or shower baths. **Cards:** AE, DS, MC, VI.

HARRAH'S CASINO HOTEL
◆◆◆
Hotel

		Rates Subject to Change					
Fri & Sat	1P:	$25- 180	2P/1B:	$25- 180	2P/2B:	$25- 180	XP: $5
Sun-Thurs	1P:	$25- 140	2P/1B:	$25- 140	2P/2B:	$25- 140	XP: $5

Phone: 702/298-4600

Location: 5 mi s of Davis Dam; on the river. 2900 S Casino Dr 89029. Fax: 702/298-6855. **Terms:** Reserv deposit, 3 day notice. **Facility:** 1600 rooms. Southwest architecture. On the Colorado River. 20 stories; exterior corridors. **Services:** giftshop. Fee: massage. **All Rooms:** combo or shower baths. **Cards:** AE, CB, DI, DS, MC, VI.

RAMADA EXPRESS HOTEL & CASINO
◆◆◆
Hotel

		Rates Subject to Change					
Fri & Sat	1P:	$54- 89	2P/1B:	$54- 89	2P/2B:	$54- 89	XP: $5 F18
Sun-Thurs	1P:	$23- 34	2P/1B:	$23- 34	2P/2B:	$23- 34	XP: $5 F18

Phone: 702/298-4200

Location: 3 mi s of Davis Dam. 2121 S Casino Dr 89028 (PO Box 77771). Fax: 702/298-4619. **Facility:** 1500 rooms. Turn-of-the-century railroad motif. Adults only tower. 24 stories; interior corridors. **Services:** giftshop. **All Rooms:** combo or shower baths. **Cards:** AE, CB, DI, DS, MC, VI.

RESTAURANT

WILLIAM FISK'S STEAKHOUSE
◆◆
American

Dinner: $15-$25   Phone: 702/298-6832

Location: In Harrah's. 2900 S Casino Dr 89029. **Hours:** 5 pm-10 pm, Fri & Sat-11 pm. Closed: Mon. **Reservations:** suggested. **Features:** semi-formal attire; cocktails; valet parking; a la carte. Intimate dining atmosphere overlooking Colorado River. **Cards:** AE, DI, DS, MC, VI.

MESQUITE—1,900

LODGINGS

BEST WESTERN MESQUITE STAR HOTEL & CA
FYI
Hotel

		Rates Subject to Change				
Fri & Sat	1P:	$59	2P/1B:	$59	2P/2B:	$59
Sun-Thurs	1P:	$39	2P/1B:	$39	2P/2B:	$39

Phone: 702/346-1177

Too new to rate. **Location:** At I-15 exit 122. 333 Sand Hill Blvd 89024. Fax: 702/3416-1188. **Terms:** 2 night min stay. **Facility:** 210 rooms. 1 whirlpool rm, extra charge; 4 stories; interior corridors; heated pool. **Services:** giftshop. **All Rooms:** shower baths. **Cards:** AE, CB, DI, DS, MC, VI.

BUDGET INN & SUITES
◆◆
Motel

		1P:	$45- 60	2P/1B:	$50	2P/2B:	$55	XP:	$5	F16
Fri & Sat										
Sun-Thurs		1P:	$35	2P/1B:	$40	2P/2B:	$45	XP:	$5	F16

Rates Subject to Change   Phone: 702/346-7444

Location: At exit 122. 390 N Sandhill 89024 (Box 1107). Fax: 702/346-7438. **Facility:** 67 rooms. Whirlpool rm, extra charge; 2 stories; exterior corridors. **All Rooms:** combo or shower baths. **Some Rooms:** 23 efficiencies. **Cards:** AE, DS, MC, VI.

CASA BLANCA VILLA
◆◆
Extended Stay
Motel

Rates Subject to Change   Phone: 702/346-7529

Fri & Sat	1P:	$34- 44	2P/1B:	$34- 44	2P/2B:	$34- 44
Sun-Thurs	1P:	$24- 34	2P/1B:	$24- 34	2P/2B:	$24- 34

Location: I-15, exit 120, 0.5 mi ne. 950 W Mesquite Blvd 89027 (PO Box 1620, 89024). Fax: 702/346-6888. **Facility:** 188 rooms. 18 whirlpool rms, extra charge; 9 stories; interior corridors; 1 holes golf; heated pool; 1 lighted tennis court. **Services:** area transportation. Fee: massage. **All Rooms:** combo or shower baths. **Some Rooms:** 28 efficiencies, 160 kitchens. **Cards:** AE, DI, DS, MC, VI.

HOLIDAY INN RANCHO MESQUITE
◆◆◆
Motel

Rates Subject to Change   Phone: 702/346-4600

2/1-5/31 & 1/1-1/31	1P:	$69- 89	2P/1B:	$69- 89	2P/2B:	$69- 89
6/1-12/31	1P:	$46- 59	2P/1B:	$46- 59	2P/2B:	$46- 59

Location: Exit 22W, 0.5 mi nw. 301 Mesa Blvd 89024 (PO Box 1808). Fax: 702/346-8526. **Facility:** 215 rooms. 8 two-bedroom units. 8 whirlpool rms, extra charge; 4 stories; interior corridors; heated pool. **Services:** giftshop. **All Rooms:** combo or shower baths. **Cards:** AE, DI, DS, JC, MC, VI.

MESQUITE SPRINGS MOTEL/SUITES
◆◆
Extended Stay
Motel

Rates Subject to Change   Phone: 702/346-4700

Fri & Sat	1P:	$45- 49	2P/1B:	$45- 49	2P/2B:	$45- 49
Sun-Thurs	1P:	$19- 29	2P/1B:	$19- 29	2P/2B:	$19- 29

Location: I-15, exit 122, 1 mi nw. 580 Mesa Blvd 89024 (PO Box 2785). Fax: 702/346-3500. **Facility:** 109 rooms. **All Rooms:** combo or shower baths. **Cards:** AE, CB, DI, DS, MC, VI.

VIRGIN RIVER HOTEL CASINO BINGO
◆◆
Motor Inn

Rates Subject to Change   Phone: 702/346-7777

Fri & Sat	1P:	$45		2P/2B:	$45
Sun-Thurs	1P:	$20- 35		2P/2B:	$20- 35

Location: W of & adjacent to I-15, exit 122. 100 Pioneer Blvd 89024 (PO Box 1620). Fax: 702/346-7780. **Facility:** 714 rooms. Near Utah border. 2 suites with whirlpool bath, refrigerator & wet bar $250, for up to 2 persons; 2-3 stories; exterior corridors. **Services:** giftshop. **All Rooms:** combo or shower baths. **Cards:** AE, DS, MC, VI.

MOUNT CHARLESTON

LODGING

ALMOST HEAVEN BED & BREAKFAST
◆◆◆
Bed &
Breakfast

Rates Subject to Change   Phone: 702/739-7277

Fri & Sat [BP]	1P:	$199- 349	2P/1B:	$199- 349
Sun-Thurs [BP]	1P:	$179- 299	2P/1B:	$179- 299

Location: 36 mi n of Las Vegas via US 95, w on SR 157. 123 Rainbow Canyon Blvd 89124 (PO Box 34720, 89133). Fax: 702/739-7255. **Facility:** 4 rooms. 2 stories; interior corridors; smoke free premises. **Cards:** AE, DS, MC, VI.

This ends listings for the Las Vegas Vicinity.
The following page resumes the alphabetical listings of
cities in Nevada.

LAUGHLIN—See Las Vegas p. 1116.

LOVELOCK—2,100

LODGING

RAMADA INN-STURGEON'S CASINO ◆◆◆ Motel
Rates Subject to Change
Phone: (775)273-2971

		1P:		2P/1B:		2P/2B:		XP:		
4/1-9/30		1P:	$49	2P/1B:	$59	2P/2B:	$59	XP:	$8	F18
10/1-1/31		1P:	$45	2P/1B:	$55	2P/2B:	$55	XP:	$8	F18
2/1-3/31		1P:	$39	2P/1B:	$45	2P/2B:	$45	XP:	$8	F18

Location: Just N of I-80; exits #105 or 107. 1420 Cornell Ave 89419 (PO Box 56). Fax: 775/273-2278. **Facility:** 74 rooms. Some large rooms. 2 stories; exterior corridors; heated indoor pool. **Services:** giftshop. **Cards:** AE, CB, DI, DS, MC, VI.

(ASK) 🛇 🐾 🛝 🏊 ⑪ 🗗 🛆 💻 🖨 🖥 ✕ 🕪

MESQUITE—See Las Vegas p. 1117.

MILL CITY

LODGING

SUPER 8 MOTEL
(AAA) (SAVE)
◆ Motel
Phone: 775/538-7311

All Year	1P:	$34	2P/1B:	$38	2P/2B:	$38	XP:	$4	F12

Location: Just n of I-80; exits 149. 6000 E Frontage Rd 89418. Fax: 775/538-7448. **Terms:** Pets, $5, $20 dep req extra charge. **Facility:** 50 rooms. Adjacent to Burns Brothers truck stop. 2 stories; interior corridors. **Dining:** Coffee shop nearby. **Recreation:** Small casino. **All Rooms:** combo or shower baths. **Cards:** AE, DS, MC, VI.

🐾 ⑪ 🛆 ✕

MINDEN—1,499

LODGINGS

BEST WESTERN MINDEN
(AAA) (SAVE)
◆◆◆ Motel
Phone: (775)782-7766

5/21-10/4		1P:	$75- 95	2P/1B:	$55- 75	2P/2B:	$75- 95		
2/1-5/20 & 10/5-1/31		1P:	$55- 60	2P/1B:	$40- 50	2P/2B:	$50- 55		

Location: US 395 exit Ironwood Drive w; 0.5 mi n of jct US 395 & SR 88. 1795 Ironwood DR 89423. Fax: 775/782-7756. **Terms:** Reserv deposit, 7 day notice; pets, $5 extra charge, by reservation only. **Facility:** 81 rooms. Few rooms with view of mountains. King suites Fri & Sat $75, Sun-Thur $65 for up to 2 persons; 2 stories; exterior corridors. **Dining:** Coffee shop nearby. **Cards:** AE, CB, DI, DS, MC, VI. **Special Amenities:** Free local telephone calls and free newspaper.

🛇 🐾 🔁 ⑪ 🛆 💻 🖨 🖥 ✕

CARSON VALLEY INN
(AAA) (SAVE)
◆◆◆ Motor Inn
Phone: (775)782-9711

Fri & Sat 6/27-9/25		1P:	$89	2P/1B:	$89	2P/2B:	$89	XP:	$6	F12
Fri & Sat 3/28-6/26,										
9/26-10/30 & 12/24-1/1		1P:	$79	2P/1B:	$79	2P/2B:	$79	XP:	$6	F12
Fri & Sat 2/1-3/27, Sun-Thurs										
5/21-10/28, Fri & Sat										
10/31-12/23 & 1/2-1/31		1P:	$59	2P/1B:	$59	2P/2B:	$59	XP:	$6	F12
Sun-Thurs 1/1-5/20,										
10/29-12/23 & 1/2-1/31		1P:	$49	2P/1B:	$49	2P/2B:	$49	XP:	$6	F12

Location: Center; on US 395N. 1627 US 395N 89423. Fax: 775/782-7472. **Terms:** Reserv deposit; package plans. **Facility:** 154 rooms. View of mountains or ranch land. 7 suites, $89-$149 for up to 2 persons; 4 stories; interior corridors; whirlpools. **Dining:** 3 restaurants; 24 hours; $6-$20; cocktails. **Services:** giftshop. **All Rooms:** combo or shower baths. **Cards:** AE, CB, DI, DS, MC, VI.

🛝 ⑪ 🗗 🛆 💻 🖨 🖥 🏌 ♿ ✕ 🕪

CARSON VALLEY MOTOR LODGE
(AAA) (SAVE)
◆◆◆ Motel
Phone: (775)782-9711

Fri & Sat 6/27-9/25		1P:	$69	2P/1B:	$69	2P/2B:	$69	XP:	$6	F12
Fri & Sat 3/28-6/26,										
9/26-10/30 & 12/24-1/1		1P:	$59	2P/1B:	$59	2P/2B:	$59	XP:	$6	F12
Fri & Sat 2/1-3/27, Sun-Thurs										
5/21-10/28, Fri & Sat										
10/31-12/23 & 1/2-1/31		1P:	$49	2P/1B:	$49	2P/2B:	$49	XP:	$6	F12
Sun-Thurs 2/1-5/20,										
10/29-12/23 & 1/2-1/31		1P:	$39	2P/1B:	$39	2P/2B:	$39	XP:	$6	F12

Location: Center, on US 395N. 1645 US 395N 89423. Fax: 775/782-7472. **Terms:** Reserv deposit. **Facility:** 76 rooms. 2 suites; 2 stories; exterior corridors. **All Rooms:** combo or shower baths. **Cards:** AE, CB, DI, DS, MC, VI.

🛆 🏌 💻 🖨 🖥 ♿ ✕

HOLIDAY LODGE
(AAA)
◆◆ Motel
Guaranteed Rates
Phone: 775/782-2288

Fri & Sat 5/1-10/31		1P:	$45	2P/1B:	$45	2P/2B:	$48	XP:	$5	
Fri & Sat 2/1-4/30 &										
11/1-1/31		1P:	$40	2P/1B:	$40	2P/2B:	$43	XP:	$5	
Sun-Thurs 5/1-10/31		1P:	$37	2P/1B:	$37	2P/2B:	$40	XP:	$5	
Sun-Thurs 2/1-4/30 &										
11/1-1/31		1P:	$32	2P/1B:	$32	2P/2B:	$35	XP:	$5	

Location: Center, on US 395N. 1591 US 395N 89423 (PO Box 848). Fax: 775/782-3765. **Terms:** Reserv deposit; handling fee imposed; weekly rates, 12/1-4/30; pets, $3 extra charge, $20 dep req, dogs only. **Facility:** 20 rooms. Comfortable rooms. 1 story; exterior corridors; heated pool. **Dining:** Coffee shop nearby. **Some Rooms:** 2 efficiencies, no utensils. **Cards:** AE, DS, MC, VI.

🐾 🔁 ⑪ 🏌 🖥 ✕

RESTAURANT

HEIDI'S FAMILY RESTAURANT   **Lunch:** $5-$8   **Phone:** 775/782-2930
<AAA>   **Location:** E side of US 395, 0.3 mi n of Minden-Gardnerville city limit. 1595 Hwy 395 89423. **Hours:** 6:30
◆   am-2 pm. **Features:** casual dress; children's menu. Family restaurant noted for breakfast. **Cards:** MC, VI.
American

MOUNT CHARLESTON—See Las Vegas p. 1118.

PRIMM

LODGINGS

PRIMADONNA RESORT & CASINO   **Phone:** 702/382-1212

		1P:		2P/1B:		2P/2B:		XP:		
(AAA) SAVE	Sat	1P:	$55	2P/1B:	$55	2P/2B:	$55	XP:	$5	F17
	Fri	1P:	$45	2P/1B:	$45	2P/2B:	$45	XP:	$5	F17
◆◆	Sun-Thurs	1P:	$25	2P/1B:	$25	2P/2B:	$25	XP:	$5	F17

Motor Inn   **Location:** E of & adjacent to I-15, State Line exit, 45 mi s of Las Vegas. 89019 (PO Box 19119).
Fax: 702/679-5195. **Terms:** Reserv deposit, 3 day notice; handling fee imposed; 2 night min stay, Fri & Sat.
Facility: 660 rooms. Suites, $195 for up to 2 persons; 4 stories; interior corridors; putting green; whirlpool, pool seasonal;
playground. Fee: 18 holes golf. **Dining:** Restaurant, coffee shop; 24 hours, buffet $4-$7; $5-$14; cocktails.
Services: giftshop. **Recreation:** Fee: bowling alley, ferris wheel, monorail, video game room. **All Rooms:** combo or shower
baths. **Some Rooms:** Fee: whirlpools. **Cards:** AE, DI, DS, MC, VI.

WHISKEY PETE'S HOTEL & CASINO   Rates Subject to Change   **Phone:** 702/382-4388

		1P:		2P/1B:		2P/2B:		XP:		
◆◆	Sat	1P:	$43	2P/1B:	$43	2P/2B:	$43	XP:	$5	F17
Hotel	Fri	1P:	$33	2P/1B:	$33	2P/2B:	$33	XP:	$5	F17
	Sun-Thurs	1P:	$18	2P/1B:	$18	2P/2B:	$18	XP:	$5	F17

Location: W of & adjacent to I-15, State line exit, 45 mi s of Las Vegas. (PO Box 19119, 89019-3718). Fax: 702/679-6606.
Terms: Reserv deposit, 3 day notice; handling fee imposed; 2 night min stay, Fri & Sat. **Facility:** 777 rooms. Suites $75-$195
for up to 2 persons. 12 whirlpool rms, extra charge; 2-19 stories; interior corridors. Fee: 18 holes golf. **Services:** giftshop.
All Rooms: combo or shower baths. **Cards:** AE, DI, DS, MC, VI.

RENO—133,900

LODGINGS

ATLANTIS CASINO RESORT - RENO   **Phone:** (702)825-4700

		1P:		2P/1B:		2P/2B:		XP:		
(AAA) SAVE	All Year	1P:	$89- 169	2P/1B:	$89- 169	2P/2B:	$89- 169	XP:	$10	F18

◆◆◆   **Location:** 3 mi s on US 395. 3800 S Virginia St 89502. Fax: 702/826-7860. **Terms:** 3 night min stay.
Motor Inn   **Facility:** 592 rooms. Some motel rooms. 43 suites, $125-$395 for up to 2 persons; 42 whirlpool rms, extra
charge; 18 stories; interior/exterior corridors; heated pool, sauna, whirlpool. **Dining:** Dining room, cafeteria,
coffee shop; 24 hrs, buffet dinner Sun-Thurs $9.99, Fri & Sat seafood $17.99; $7-$25; cocktails.
Services: giftshop; area transportation, Downtown 7 am-11 pm. Fee: massage. **Recreation:** Fee: game room. **Cards:** AE,
CB, DI, DS, JC, MC, VI. (See color ad p 1121)

BEST WESTERN AIRPORT PLAZA HOTEL   **Phone:** (775)348-6370

		1P:		2P/1B:		2P/2B:		XP:		
(AAA) SAVE	All Year	1P:	$69- 230	2P/1B:	$69- 230	2P/2B:	$69- 230	XP:	$10	F12

◆◆◆   **Location:** US 395, exit E Plumb Villanova. 1981 Terminal Way 89502. Fax: 775/348-9722. **Facility:** 269
Hotel   rooms. 15 two-bedroom units. 16 units with fireplace, $125-$300 for up to 2 persons; 3 stories; interior corri-
dors; 9 hole putting green; heated pool, sauna, whirlpool. **Dining:** Restaurant; 5:30 am-11 pm; $9-$20.
All Rooms: combo or shower baths. **Some Rooms:** kitchen. **Cards:** AE, CB, DI, DS, MC, VI.
Special Amenities: Early check-in/late check-out and free room upgrade (subject to availability with advanced
reservations).

BEST WESTERN CONTINENTAL LODGE   Rates Subject to Change   **Phone:** (775)329-1001

		1P:		2P/1B:		2P/2B:		XP:		
◆◆◆	All Year [CP]	1P:	$48- 110	2P/1B:	$52- 115	2P/2B:	$57- 125	XP:	$6	F12

Motor Inn   **Location:** 1 mi w of US 395, exit Plumb Villanova. 1885 S Virginia St 89502. Fax: 775/324-5402.
Facility: 103 rooms. Rooms with balcony or patio. Landscaped gardens. 2 stories; interior/exterior corridors.
All Rooms: combo or shower baths. **Cards:** AE, CB, DI, DS, MC, VI.

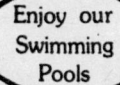

CIRCUS CIRCUS
◆◆◆
Hotel

	Rates Subject to Change				Phone: 775/329-0711	
Fri & Sat	1P: $59- 149	2P/1B: $59- 149	2P/2B: $59- 149	XP: $10	F12
Sun-Thurs	1P: $29- 120	2P/1B: $29- 120	2P/2B: $29- 120	XP: $10	F12

Location: Corner Sierra & 6th sts; just n off I-80 business rt. 500 N Sierra St 89503 (PO Box 5880, 89513). Fax: 775/329-0599. **Terms:** Reserv deposit. **Facility:** 1572 rooms. 8 whirlpool suites, extra charge; 28 stories; interior corridors. **Services:** giftshop. **Cards:** AE, CB, DI, DS, MC, VI.

COLONIAL INN HOTEL & CASINO
🛆🛆🛆 SAVE
◆◆
Motor Inn

				Phone: 775/322-3838	
Sat	1P: $73	2P/1B: $73	2P/2B: $78	XP: $10	F12
Sun-Fri 2/28-11/21	1P: $53	2P/1B: $53	2P/2B: $58	XP: $10	F12
Sun-Fri 2/1-2/27 & 11/22-1/31	1P: $51	2P/1B: $51	2P/2B: $56	XP: $10	F12

Location: Off 2nd St. 250 N Arlington 89501. Fax: 775/323-4588. **Terms:** Reserv deposit. **Facility:** 168 rooms. Comfortable rooms. Covered parking. 9 stories; interior corridors; sauna. **Dining:** Restaurant; 6 am-midnight; $6-$14. **Services:** giftshop. **Cards:** AE, CB, DI, DS, MC, VI. *(See ad p 1120)*

COLONIAL MOTOR INN-WEST
🛆🛆🛆 SAVE
◆◆
Motel

				Phone: 775/786-5038	
Sat	1P: $73	2P/1B: $73	2P/2B: $78	XP: $10	F12
Sun-Fri 2/28-11/21	1P: $53	2P/1B: $53	2P/2B: $58	XP: $10	F12
Sun-Fri 2/1-2/27 & 11/22-1/31	1P: $51	2P/1B: $51	2P/2B: $56	XP: $10	F12

Location: 1 blk off I-80 business rt; 1 blk from casinos. 232 West St 89501. Fax: 775/323-4588. **Terms:** Reserv deposit. **Facility:** 100 rooms. Comfortable rooms. Covered parking. 5 stories; exterior corridors; sauna. **Services:** giftshop. **Cards:** AE, CB, DI, DS, MC, VI. *(See ad p 1120)*

DANIEL'S MOTOR LODGE
🛆🛆🛆 SAVE
◆◆
Motel

				Phone: (775)329-1351	
Fri & Sat	1P: $35- 60	2P/1B: $54- 80	2P/2B: $60- 90	XP: $7	
Sun-Thurs	1P: $35- 60	2P/1B: $45- 70	2P/2B: $55- 80	XP: $7	

Location: In casino area, on US 395; jct I-80 business route. 375 N Sierra St 89501. Fax: 775/329-2508. **Terms:** Reserv deposit. **Facility:** 82 rooms. Many large rooms. 2-3 stories; exterior corridors. **Cards:** AE, DI, DS, MC, VI.

EASY 8 MOTEL
🛆🛆🛆
◆
Motel

	Rates Subject to Change			Phone: 775/322-4588
Fri & Sat 4/1-11/15	1P: $75	2P/1B: $75	2P/2B: $75	
Fri & Sat 2/1-3/31 & 11/16-1/31	1P: $65	2P/1B: $65	2P/2B: $65	
Sun-Thurs 4/1-11/15	1P: $35	2P/1B: $35	2P/2B: $35	
Sun-Thurs 2/1-3/31 & 11/16-1/31	1P: $30	2P/1B: $30	2P/2B: $30	

Location: From I-80 at Keystone exit, e 4 blks. 255 W 5th St 89503. **Terms:** Small pets only, $20 dep req. **Facility:** 21 rooms. 2 stories; exterior corridors.

ELDORADO HOTEL
Phone: (775)786-5700

AAA SAVE | Fri & Sat 3/19-11/20 | 1P: $89- 109 | 2P/1B: $89- 109 | 2P/2B: $99- 109 | XP: $10 | F12

Fri & Sat 2/1-3/18, Sun-Thurs
3/19-11/20 & Fri & Sat

Hotel | 11/21-1/31 | 1P: $79- 89 | 2P/1B: $79- 89 | 2P/2B: $79- 89 | XP: $10 | F12

Sun-Thurs 2/1-3/18 &
11/21-1/31 | 1P: $69- 79 | 2P/1B: $69- 79 | 2P/2B: $69- 79 | XP: $10 | F12

Location: In the casino area, 4th & Virginia sts. 345 N Virginia St 89505 (PO Box 3399). Fax: 775/322-7124. **Terms:** Reserv deposit; package plans. **Facility:** 816 rooms. Suites, $110-$750 for 2 persons; 11-26 stories; interior corridors; heated pool, whirlpool. **Dining:** 2 dining rooms, 4 restaurants, cafeteria, coffee shop; $6-$28; cocktails. **Services:** giftshop. **Cards:** AE, CB, DI, DS, MC, VI. **Special Amenities:** Early check-in/late check-out and preferred room (subject to availability with advanced reservations).

FITZGERALDS CASINO/HOTEL | Rates Subject to Change | Phone: (775)786-3663

◆◆◆ | Fri & Sat | 1P: $58- 110 | 2P/1B: $58- 110 | 2P/2B: $58- 110 | XP: $10 | F12
Hotel | Sun-Thurs | 1P: $40- 98 | 2P/1B: $40- 98 | 2P/2B: $40- 98 | XP: $10 | F12

Location: In casino area. 255 N Virginia St 89501. Fax: 775/785-3686. **Terms:** Reserv deposit, 3 day notice. **Facility:** 351 rooms. 16 stories; interior corridors. **Services:** giftshop. **Cards:** AE, CB, DI, DS, MC, VI. *(See ad below)*

FLAMINGO HILTON-RENO Rates Subject to Change Phone: 775/322-1111
◆◆◆   3/1-10/31   1P: $90   2P/1B: $90   2P/2B: $90   XP: $10   F
Hotel   2/1-2/28 & 11/1-1/31   1P: $80   2P/1B: $80   2P/2B: $80   XP: $10   F
Location: 1 blk s off I-80 business rt; 1 blk w off S Virginia St; between W 2nd & Commercial sts. 255 N Sierra St 89501 (PO Box 1291). Fax: 775/785-7086. Terms: Reserv deposit. Facility: 604 rooms. 41 suites $150-$395 for up to 2 persons; 21 stories; interior corridors. Services: giftshop. Cards: AE, CB, DI, DS, JC, MC, VI. (See ad p 119)

GATEKEEPER INN Phone: (775)786-3500
AAA SAVE   All Year   1P: $35- 80   2P/1B: $50- 80   2P/2B: $45- 75   XP: $7-8   F16
◆   Location: Adjacent to casinos, corner West & 5th sts. 221 W 5th St 89503. Terms: Check-in 4 pm; reserv
Motel   deposit. Facility: 28 rooms. Next to casinos. 3 stories; exterior corridors. Cards: AE, DS, MC, VI.
Special Amenities: Early check-in/late check-out and free local telephone calls.

HARRAH'S Phone: (775)786-3232
AAA SAVE   6/1-11/1   1P: $104- 159   2P/1B: $104- 159   2P/2B: $104- 159   XP: $10
◆◆◆   2/1-5/31 & 11/2-1/31   1P: $75- 139   2P/1B: $75- 139   2P/2B: $75- 139   XP: $10
Hotel   Location: Downtown at Center & 2nd sts. 119 N Center St 89501 (PO Box 10). Fax: 775/788-2815.
Terms: Reserv deposit; package plans; kennel avail. Facility: 973 rooms. 7 two-bedroom units. 24-26 stories; interior corridors; heated pool, saunas, whirlpools. Dining: Buffet; 24 hrs; $9-$25; cocktails; restaurants nearby. Services: giftshop. Cards: AE, CB, DI, JC, MC, VI. Special Amenities: Preferred room (subject to availability with advanced reservations). (See color ad p 1122)

HOLIDAY INN-DOWNTOWN Rates Subject to Change Phone: (775)786-5151
◆◆◆   6/2-9/1   1P: $69- 99   2P/1B: $69- 99   2P/2B: $69- 99
Hotel   2/1-6/1 & 9/2-1/31   1P: $59- 89   2P/1B: $59- 89   2P/2B: $59- 89
Location: 12 blks e; I-80 via Wells. 1000 E 6th St 89512. Fax: 775/786-2447. Facility: 286 rooms. Few small rooms. 6 suites, $125-$195 for up to 2 persons; 13 stories; interior corridors; heated pool. Services: giftshop; area transportation. Cards: AE, CB, DI, DS, JC, MC, VI.

LA QUINTA INN Rates Subject to Change Phone: (775)348-6100
◆◆◆   Fri & Sat [CP]   1P: $64- 69   2P/1B: $71- 76   2P/2B: $71   XP: $8
Motel   Sun-Thurs [CP]   1P: $61- 66   2P/1B: $62- 67   2P/2B: $62   XP: $8
Location: US 395 northbound exit airport, southbound exit Villanova Dr. 4001 Market St 89502-3110. Fax: 775/348-8794. Facility: 130 rooms. Attractively appointed rooms. 2 stories; exterior corridors. Cards: AE, CB, DI, DS, JC, MC, VI.

RENO DOWNTOWN TRAVELODGE
♦♦ Motel

Rates Subject to Change   Phone: 775/329-3451

Fri & Sat 5/1-10/31	1P: $69	2P/1B: $69	2P/2B: $69	XP: $8	F17
Fri & Sat 2/1-4/30 & 11/1-1/31	1P: $59	2P/1B: $59	2P/2B: $59	XP: $8	F17
Sun-Thurs 5/1-10/31	1P: $49	2P/1B: $49	2P/2B: $49	XP: $8	F17
Sun-Thurs 2/1-4/30 & 11/1-1/31	1P: $39	2P/1B: $39	2P/2B: $39	XP: $8	F17

Location: From I-80 at Keystone exit, 2 blks e. 655 W 4th St 89503. Fax: 775/329-3454. **Facility:** 98 rooms. 2 stories; exterior corridors. **All Rooms:** combo or shower baths. **Cards:** AE, DI, DS, MC, VI.

RENO HILTON
♦♦♦ Hotel

Rates Subject to Change   Phone: (775)789-2000

All Year   1P: $69- 149   2P/1B: $69- 149   2P/2B: $69- 149   XP: $10   F18
Location: 0.5 mi s of jct I-80 & US 395; US 395 exit Mill St. 2500 E 2nd St 89595. Fax: 775/789-1678. **Terms:** Reserv deposit. **Facility:** 2001 rooms. Spacious. Suites, $225-$795 up to 2 persons; 27 stories; interior corridors; heated pool. Fee: 8 tennis courts (5 indoor, 3 lighted). **Services:** giftshop. **Cards:** AE, CB, DI, DS, JC, MC, VI.
(See ad p 119 & p 1123)

RESIDENCE INN BY MARRIOTT
♦♦♦ Motel

Rates Subject to Change   Phone: 775/853-8800

All Year [CP]   1P: $80   2P/1B: $85   2P/2B: $103
Location: 5 mi s; exit US 395 at S Meadows Pkwy; e to Gateway Dr. 9845 Gateway Dr 89511. Fax: 775/853-8805. **Terms:** Check-in 4 pm. **Facility:** 120 rooms. 21 two-bedroom units. 3 stories; interior corridors; heated pool. **All Rooms:** kitchens. **Cards:** AE, CB, DI, DS, JC, MC, VI.

SEASONS INN
ⒶⒶⒶ
♦♦
Motel

Rates Subject to Change   Phone: (775)322-6000

Fri & Sat	1P: $69	2P/1B: $79	2P/2B: $89	XP: $6
Sun-Thurs 4/1-10/31	1P: $45	2P/1B: $49	2P/2B: $52	XP: $6
Sun-Thurs 2/1-3/31 & 11/1-1/31	1P: $38	2P/1B: $40	2P/2B: $45	XP: $6

Location: 2 blks w of casinos; corner West & 5th sts. 495 West St 89503. Fax: 775/324-6434. **Terms:** Reserv deposit. **Facility:** 56 rooms. Comfortable rooms. 4 stories; exterior corridors. **Cards:** AE, DS, JC, MC, VI.

SILVER LEGACY
ⒶⒶⒶ
♦♦♦
Hotel

Rates Subject to Change   Phone: (775)329-4777

Fri & Sat	1P: $79- 99	2P/1B: $79- 99	2P/2B: $79- 119	XP: $10
Sun-Thurs	1P: $59- 79	2P/1B: $59- 79	2P/2B: $59- 79	XP: $10

Location: I-80 exit S Virginia St; casino center. 407 N Virginia St 89501 (P.O. Box 3920, 89505). Fax: 775/325-7470. **Terms:** Reserv deposit; package plans. **Facility:** 1720 rooms. 150 whirlpool rooms, extra charge; 38 stories; interior corridors; heated pool, sauna, whirlpool. **Dining:** 5 restaurants, coffee shop; 24 hr coffee shop; buffet; casino; $6-$24; cocktails. **Services:** giftshop. **Cards:** AE, CB, DI, DS, JC, MC, VI.

SUPER 8 MOTEL
◆
Motel

Rates Subject to Change   **Phone:** (775)329-3464
All Year   1P: $28- 48   2P/1B: $31- 51 2P/2B: $33- 53
Location: Opposite University of Nevada. 1651 N Virginia St 89503. Fax: 775/329-9013. **Facility:** 71 rooms.
2 stories; exterior corridors. **Cards:** AE, CB, DI, DS, MC, VI.   ⟨ASK⟩ 〔S6〕 🐾 🛏 ⌷ 🖥 ✕

SUPER 8 MOTEL & CONVENTION CENTER-RENO
(AAA) 〔SAVE〕
◆ ◆
Motor Inn
(See color ad p 1124)

                                           Phone: (702)825-2940
All Year   1P: $45- 65   2P/1B: $45- 65 2P/2B: $45- 65 XP: $10   F17
Location: US 395 at S McCarran Blvd. 5851 S Virginia St 89502. Fax: 702/826-3835. **Terms:** Package
plans; pets, $10 extra charge. **Facility:** 153 rooms. 2 stories; exterior corridors; heated pool, whirlpool, sea-
sonal pool. **Dining:** Restaurant; 11 am-10 pm; complimentary breakfast buffet; $8-$13; cocktails. **Cards:** AE,
DS, MC, VI. **Special Amenities:** Early check-in/late check-out and free local telephone calls.
🐾 🛏 🖾 🖥 🍴 ⌷ ✕ 〔VCR〕 🖥 ⌷ 🖨 🖥 ✕ 🔧

THUNDERBIRD MOTEL
(AAA)
◆
Motel

Rates Subject to Change   **Phone:** 775/329-3578
All Year   2P/1B: $75- 100 2P/2B: $85- 150 XP: $10
Location: US 395, adjacent to casinos. 420 N Virginia St 89501. **Terms:** Reserv deposit. **Facility:** 27 rooms.
1 two-bedroom unit. 2 stories; exterior corridors. **Cards:** AE, DI, DS, MC, VI.   🖥

TRAVELODGE RENO CENTRAL
(AAA) 〔SAVE〕
◆ ◆
Motel

                                           Phone: (775)786-2500
4/1-10/31 [CP]   1P: $39- 72   2P/1B: $45- 82 2P/2B: $45- 82 XP: $9   F18
2/1-3/31 & 11/1-1/31 [CP]   1P: $34- 60   2P/1B: $43- 70 2P/2B: $43- 70 XP: $6   F18
Location: US 395 exit W Mill St. 2050 Market St 89502. Fax: 775/786-3884. **Terms:** Pets, $5 extra charge
per pet. **Facility:** 210 rooms. Comfortable rooms. 70 efficiencies, $61-$94 for up to 4 persons, no utensils; 4
stories; interior corridors; sauna, whirlpool. **Cards:** AE, CB, DI, DS, JC, MC, VI. **Special Amenities:** Free
breakfast and free local telephone calls. *(See color ad p 1124)*   〔S6〕 🛏 🖾 🖂 🖥 ✕ 🖨 ✕

VAGABOND INN
(AAA) 〔SAVE〕
◆
Motel

                                           Phone: (702)825-7134
All Year [CP]   1P: $64   2P/1B: $69   2P/2B: $75   XP: $5   F18
Location: 2.5 mi s on US 395. 3131 S Virginia St 89502. Fax: 702/825-3096. **Terms:** Small pets only, $5.
Facility: 129 rooms. Few bunk beds. 2 stories; exterior corridors; seasonal pool. **Dining:** Restaurant nearby.
Services: area transportation, downtown & Convention ctr. **Cards:** AE, CB, DI, DS, MC, VI.
Special Amenities: Free breakfast and free local telephone calls.
〔S6〕 🛏 🖾 🍴 🖂 🖥 🖨 ✕

WONDER LODGE
(AAA) 〔SAVE〕
◆
Motel

                                           Phone: (775)786-6840
Fri & Sat 7/1-10/31   1P: $46   2P/1B: $46   2P/2B: $60
Fri & Sat 2/1-6/30 &
11/1-1/31   1P: $44   2P/1B: $44   2P/2B: $57
Sun-Thurs 7/1-10/31   1P: $39   2P/1B: $39   2P/2B: $55
Sun-Thurs 2/1-6/30 &
11/1-1/31   1P: $35   2P/1B: $35   2P/2B: $49
Location: 1 blk off I-80 business rt; 2 blks from casinos. 430 Lake St 89501. Fax: 775/329-4257. **Terms:** Reserv deposit.
Facility: 63 rooms. Large rooms. 4 stories; exterior corridors; seasonal pool. **Cards:** AE, DI, DS, MC, VI.
Special Amenities: Free local telephone calls and preferred room (subject to availability with advanced
reservations).   🖾 ✕

RESTAURANTS

HEIDI'S FAMILY RESTAURANT
(AAA)
◆
American

                 Lunch: $6-$10   **Phone:** 702/826-3336
Location: On US 395 2 mi s, adjacent to Park Lane Mall. 2450 S Virginia St 89502. **Hours:** 6:30 am-2 pm.
Closed: 12/25. **Features:** casual dress; children's menu. Noted for breakfast. **Cards:** MC, VI.   ✕

PIMPAREL'S LA TABLE FRANCAISE
◆ ◆ ◆
French

                                  Dinner: $18-$35   **Phone:** 775/323-3200
Location: 1 mi w of Keystone. 3065 W 4th St 89503. **Hours:** 6 pm-9 pm, Sat-10 pm. Closed: Sun, 1/1, 7/4
& 12/25. **Reservations:** suggested. **Features:** casual dress; children's menu; cocktails & lounge; minimum
charge-$6.50; a la carte. Excellently prepared cuisine. **Cards:** AE, MC, VI.   ✕

RAPSCALLION
◆ ◆
Seafood

          Lunch: $5-$10   Dinner: $10-$20   **Phone:** 775/323-1211
Location: 1555 S Wells 89502. **Hours:** 11:30 am-10 pm, Sat 5 pm-10:30 pm, Sun 10 am-2 & 5-10 pm.
Closed: 11/25 & 12/25. **Reservations:** suggested. **Features:** casual dress; Sunday brunch; cocktails &
lounge. Fresh seafood flown in daily. **Cards:** AE, MC, VI.   ✕

STEAK HOUSE
(AAA)
◆ ◆ ◆ ◆
Continental

          Lunch: $7-$11   Dinner: $17-$25   **Phone:** 775/788-2929
Location: In Harrah's Hotel & Casino. 210 N Center St 89501. **Hours:** 11 am-2:30 & 5-10 pm, Sat-11 pm.
Reservations: required. **Features:** casual dress; cocktails; a la carte. Service oriented staff; some tableside
preparations. **Cards:** AE, CB, DI, DS, JC, MC, VI.

SPARKS—53,400

LODGINGS

BEST WESTERN MCCARRAN HOUSE
(AAA) 〔SAVE〕
◆ ◆ ◆
Motor Inn

                                           Phone: (775)358-6900
Fri & Sat 2/1-10/31   1P: $79   2P/1B: $79   2P/2B: $79   XP: $10
Fri & Sat 11/1-1/31   1P: $69   2P/1B: $69   2P/2B: $69   XP: $10
Sun-Thurs 2/1-10/31   1P: $59   2P/1B: $59   2P/2B: $59   XP: $10
Sun-Thurs 11/1-1/31   1P: $49   2P/1B: $49   2P/2B: $49   XP: $10
Location: 1.3 mi e; s off & adjacent to I-80; exit McCarran Blvd. 55 E Nugget Ave 89431.
Fax: 775/359-6065. **Terms:** Reserv deposit. **Facility:** 220 rooms. 3 suites, $110 for up to 2 persons; 9 stories; interior corri-
dors; heated pool, whirlpool. **Dining:** Restaurant; 6:30 am-9 pm; $5-$13; cocktails. **Services:** area transportation.
Cards: AE, CB, DI, DS, MC, VI. **Special Amenities:** Early check-in/late check-out and free room upgrade (subject to
availability with advanced reservations).   🖥 ⌷ 🖾 🍴 🖥 🖂 ✕ 🖨 🖥 ✕

JOHN ASCUAGA'S NUGGET COURTYARD

Phone: (775)356-3300

(AAA) (SAVE)
◆◆◆
Motel

All Year   1P: $79- 89   2P/1B: $79- 89   2P/2B: $79- 89   XP: $10
Location: On I-80 business loop; exit I-80 via Rock Blvd. 1225 Victorian Ave 89431 (PO Box 797).
Fax: 775/356-4298. **Terms:** Package plans. **Facility:** 157 rooms. Some rooms with balcony. Country french furnishings. 5 stories; interior corridors; heated pool. **Dining:** Restaurant nearby. **All Rooms:** combo or shower baths. **Cards:** AE, CB, DI, DS, MC, VI. **Special Amenities:** Free local telephone calls.

JOHN ASCUAGA'S NUGGET HOTEL

Phone: (775)356-3300

(AAA) (SAVE)
◆◆◆
Hotel

All Year   1P: $99- 125   2P/1B: $99- 125   2P/2B: $99- 125   XP: $10   F18
Location: I-80 eastbound exit Nugget Ave westbound exit Rock Blvd. 1100 Nugget Ave 89431.
Fax: 775/356-4198. **Terms:** Package plans. **Facility:** 1408 rooms. Attractively appointed and spacious new tower rooms. 96 whirlpool rooms, extra charge; 16 stories; interior corridors; heated indoor pool, whirlpool.
Dining: 2 dining rooms, 2 restaurants, 3 coffee shops; 24 hours; $5-$29; cocktails; buffet about $9-$16; Sun brunch $12. **Services:** giftshop. Fee: massage. **Cards:** AE, CB, DI, DS, MC, VI. **Special Amenities:** Free local telephone calls and free room upgrade (subject to availability with advanced reservations).

SILVER CLUB HOTEL & CASINO

Rates Subject to Change

Phone: 775/358-4771

(AAA)
◆◆
Motor Inn

Fri & Sat 7/1-10/15	1P: $69	2P/1B: $69	2P/2B: $69	XP: $10
Fri & Sat 2/1-6/30 & 10/16-1/31	1P: $59	2P/1B: $59	2P/2B: $59	XP: $10
Sun-Thurs 7/1-10/15	1P: $47	2P/1B: $47	2P/2B: $47	XP: $10
Sun-Thurs 2/1-6/30 & 10/16-1/31	1P: $40	2P/1B: $40	2P/2B: $40	XP: $10

Location: I-80 eastbound exit Nugget Ave, westbound exit Rock Blvd. 1040 Victorian Ave 89431 (P.O. Box 3567, 89432). Fax: 775/358-1639. **Terms:** Reserv deposit; 2 night min stay, Sat 5/1-9/30. **Facility:** 206 rooms. Large comfortable rooms in building behind casino. Interior corridors. **Dining:** Restaurant, coffee shop, deli; $6-$15; cocktails; buffet $7, casino. **Services:** giftshop. **Cards:** AE, CB, DI, DS, MC, VI. (See ad below)

SUNRISE MOTEL

Phone: (775)358-7010

(AAA) (SAVE)
◆
Motel

Fri & Sat	1P: $59	2P/1B: $59	2P/2B: $69	XP: $10 D
Sun-Thurs	1P: $42	2P/1B: $42	2P/2B: $48	XP: $10 D

Location: Exit I-80 at McCarren Blvd, 1 blk n to E Victorian Ave 0.1 mi w. 210 E Victorian Ave 89431.
Fax: 775/358-7566. **Terms:** Reserv deposit, 10 day notice. **Facility:** 20 rooms. 2 stories; exterior corridors.
Cards: AE, DS, MC, VI. **Special Amenities:** Free local telephone calls and preferred room (subject to availability with advanced reservations).

WINDSOR INN

Rates Subject to Change

Phone: (775)356-7770

(AAA)
◆
Motel

All Year [CP]   1P: $60   2P/1B: $60   2P/2B: $60   XP: $5
Location: Exit I-80 at McCarran Blvd, 1 blk n to E Victorian Ave. 60 E Victorian Ave 89431.
Fax: 775/355-1754. **Terms:** Reserv deposit; 2 night min stay. **Facility:** 90 rooms. 3 stories; interior corridors.
Dining: Coffee shop nearby. **Cards:** AE, DS, MC, VI.

STATELINE—See Lake Tahoe Area p. 532.

WE GO TOGETHER!
See the sights near your overnight lodging.
The front of this TourBook shows the way.

TONOPAH—3,600

LODGINGS

BEST WESTERN HI DESERT INN
AAA
♦♦♦
Motel
Rates Subject to Change
All Year   1P: $45- 49 2P/1B: $49- 59 2P/2B: $59- 69 XP: $6   F12
Phone: (775)482-3511
Location: On US 6 & 95. 320 Main St 89049 (PO Box 351). Fax: 775/482-3300. **Terms:** Small pets only, no puppies or cats. **Facility:** 62 rooms. Casino nearby. 1 two-bedroom unit. 2 stories; interior corridors; whirlpool. **Dining:** Coffee shop nearby. **Cards:** AE, CB, DI, DS, MC, VI.

JIM BUTLER MOTEL
AAA
♦
Motel
Guaranteed Rates
All Year   1P: $33- 37 2P/1B: $40- 50 2P/2B: $45- 55 XP: $5
Phone: 775/482-3577
Location: On US 6 & 95. 100 S Main St 89049 (PO Box 1352). Fax: 775/482-5240. **Terms:** Handling fee imposed; small pets only, no cats or puppies. **Facility:** 25 rooms. In downtown corner, across from casino. 2 stories; exterior corridors. **Dining:** Restaurant nearby. **Cards:** AE, CB, DI, DS, MC, VI. *(See ad below)*

VIRGINIA CITY

LODGING

GOLD HILL HOTEL
♦♦
Historic Bed
& Breakfast
Rates Subject to Change
Fri & Sat [CP]   1P: $40- 130 2P/1B: $40- 130 2P/2B: $40- 130
Sun-Thurs [CP]   1P: $40- 100 2P/1B: $40- 100 2P/2B: $40- 100
Phone: 775/847-0111
Location: 1 mi s of Virginia City on Hwy 342. 1540 Main St 89440. Fax: 775/847-0273. **Facility:** 14 rooms. Minutes away but a century back in time at Nevada's oldest hotel. 2 stories; interior corridors. **Services:** giftshop. **Some Rooms:** 2 kitchens, combo or shower baths, shared bathrooms, color TV. **Cards:** MC, VI.

WELLS—1,300

LODGINGS

BEST WESTERN SAGE INN
AAA [SAVE]
♦♦
Motel
5/1-9/30   1P: $47- 50 2P/1B: $53- 56 2P/2B: $52- 56 XP: $5   F12
2/1-4/30 & 10/1-1/31 1P: $38- 40 2P/1B: $40- 43 2P/2B: $43- 45 XP: $5   F12
Phone: (775)752-3353
Location: 0.5 mi n of I-80 exit 352. 576 6th St 89835 (PO Box 343). Fax: 775/752-3353. **Terms:** Weekly/monthly rates; small pets only, $5 extra charge. **Facility:** 24 rooms. 1 two-bedroom unit. 2 units with 3 beds $78-$88; 2 stories; exterior corridors; heated pool 6/15-9/15. **All Rooms:** combo or shower baths. **Cards:** AE, DS, MC, VI. **Special Amenities:** Free breakfast and free local telephone calls.

SUPER 8 MOTEL
AAA [SAVE]
♦♦
Motel
5/15-9/15 [CP]   1P: $40- 55 2P/1B: $42- 55 2P/2B: $44- 57 XP: $5   F12
2/1-5/14 & 9/16-1/31 [CP] 1P: $38- 55 2P/1B: $40- 43 2P/2B: $42- 47 XP: $5   F12
Phone: (775)752-3384
Location: 0.5 mi w of jct US 93, I 80 exit 352. 930 6th St 89835 (PO Box 302). Fax: 775/752-3384. **Terms:** Weekly/monthly rates; small pets only, $5 extra charge. **Facility:** 57 rooms. Some large rooms. 2 stories; exterior corridors; heated pool 6/1-9/15. **All Rooms:** combo or shower baths. **Cards:** AE, DI, DS, MC, VI. **Special Amenities:** Free breakfast and free local telephone calls.

WENDOVER—1,100

LODGINGS

BEST WESTERN SALT FLAT INN
AAA [SAVE]
♦♦♦
Motel
Sat [CP]   1P: $75   2P/1B: $75   2P/2B: $75   XP: $5   F12
Fri [CP]   1P: $65   2P/1B: $65   2P/2B: $65   XP: $5   F12
Sun-Thurs 5/16-9/15 [CP] 1P: $50- 65 2P/1B: $50- 65 2P/2B: $50- 65 XP: $5   F12
Sun-Thurs 4/1-5/15 &
9/16-3/31 [CP]   1P: $35- 45 2P/1B: $35- 45 2P/2B: $35- 45 XP: $5   F12
Phone: (435)665-7811
Location: In town; exit I-80 via Utah 2. 935 E Wendover Blvd 84083 (PO Box 400). Fax: 435/665-2383. **Facility:** 24 rooms. 2 stories; exterior corridors; heated pool, sauna, whirlpool. **Cards:** AE, CB, DI, DS, MC, VI. **Special Amenities:** Early check-in/late check-out and free breakfast.

DAYS INN OF WENDOVER   Phone: (435)665-2215

(AAA) (SAVE)   4/1-9/3 [CP]   1P: $39- 79   2P/1B: $49- 79 2P/2B: $49- 79
              2/1-3/31 & 9/4-1/31 [CP] 1P: $38- 70   2P/1B: $48- 70 2P/2B: $48- 70
♦♦♦   **Location:** In town; exit I-80 via Utah Z. 685 E Wendover Blvd 84083 (PO Box 787). Fax: 435/665-7838.
Motel   **Terms:** Package plans. **Facility:** 80 rooms. 3 stories; interior corridors; heated indoor pool, whirlpool.
             All Rooms: combo or shower baths. **Some Rooms:** whirlpools. **Cards:** AE, DS, MC, VI.
Special Amenities: Early check-in/late check-out and free breakfast.   🛏️ 🖨️ 🕹️ 🛎️ 📶 🖨️ 🔒 🔺 ✕ 🔑

STATE LINE INN   Rates Subject to Change   Phone: 435/665-2226
♦♦♦   Fri & Sat   1P: $63- 84   2P/1B: $63- 84 2P/2B: $63- 84 XP: $5   F16
Motel   Sun-Thurs   1P: $39- 63   2P/1B: $39- 63 2P/2B: $39- 63 XP: $5   F16
             Location: In town, exit 2; I-80. 295 E Wendover Blvd 84083 (PO Box 1500, WEST WENDOVER).
Fax: 435/531-4080. **Facility:** 101 rooms. 2 stories; interior/exterior corridors; heated pool. **Cards:** AE, DI, DS, MC, VI.
                                                                                         🔺 ✕

WESTERN RIDGE MOTEL   Rates Subject to Change   Phone: 435/665-2211
♦   Sat   1P: $60- 68   2P/1B: $60- 68 2P/2B: $60- 75 XP: $5   F12
Motel   Fri   1P: $45- 50   2P/1B: $45- 50 2P/2B: $45- 50 XP: $5   F12
             Sun-Thurs   1P: $26- 34   2P/1B: $30- 36 2P/2B: $30- 36 XP: $5   F12
Location: In town, exit I-80, Utah 2. 895 E Wendover Blvd 84083 (PO Box 400). Fax: 435/665-2383. **Facility:** 55 rooms. 10
two-bedroom units. 2 stories; exterior corridors; heated pool. **Cards:** AE, DI, DS, MC, VI.   🔺 📶 🔒 ✕

WEST WENDOVER—2,000

LODGING

NEVADA CROSSING HOTEL   Rates Subject to Change   Phone: 775/664-2900
(AAA)   Fri & Sat   1P: $60   2P/1B: $60   2P/2B: $60   XP: $5   F12
             Sun-Thurs   1P: $41   2P/1B: $41   2P/2B: $41   XP: $5   F12
♦♦   **Location:** I-80, exit W Wendover; 0.3 mi e. 1035 Wendover Blvd 89883 (PO Box 2457). Fax: 775/664-4024.
Hotel   **Terms:** Reserv deposit, 3 day notice. **Facility:** 137 rooms. 4 whirlpool rms, extra charge; 5 stories; interior cor-
             ridors; heated indoor pool, indoor whirlpool. **Dining:** Cocktails; restaurant nearby. **Cards:** AE, CB, DI, DS,
MC, VI.   🔺 🍴 🖨️ 🔒 ✕

WINNEMUCCA—6,100

LODGINGS

BEST WESTERN GOLD COUNTRY INN   Rates Subject to Change   Phone: (775)623-6999
♦♦♦   All Year   1P: $89- 149 2P/1B: $89- 149 2P/2B: $99- 159 XP: $10   F17
Motor Inn   **Location:** Just S of I-80; exit 176 or 178. 921 W Winnemucca Blvd 89445. Fax: 775/623-9190.
             Terms: Check-in 4 pm. **Facility:** 71 rooms. Large rooms. 1 two-bedroom unit. Personal checks not accepted;
lower rates in winter; 2 stories; interior corridors. **Some Rooms:** 15 kitchens. **Cards:** AE, DI, DS, MC, VI.
(See color ad p 1129)   (ASK) 🛏️ 🐾 🔺 🍴 📶 (VCR) 🖨️ 🗄️ 🖨️ 🔒 ✕

BEST WESTERN HOLIDAY MOTEL   Rates Subject to Change   Phone: (775)623-3684
♦♦♦   All Year   1P: $59- 64   2P/1B: $59- 64 2P/2B: $69- 74 XP: $10   F12
Motel   **Location:** Just S of I-80; exit 176 or 178. 670 W Winnemucca Blvd 89445. Fax: 775/623-4221. **Facility:** 40
             rooms. 2 stories; exterior corridors. **Cards:** AE, DI, DS, MC, VI.
                                          (ASK) 🛏️ 🐾 🔺 📶 🖨️ 🗄️ 🖨️ 🔒 ✕

"Rates Subject To Change"

The printed rates are the establishment's estimated
charges for the periods noted. The actual rates charged
may be reasonably higher or lower than those printed
in the TourBook. Any increase should not exceed 15%.

DAYS INN

🔲 🔲
◆ ◆ ◆
Motel

Phone: (775)623-3661

All Year   1P: $64- 74   2P/1B: $74- 84   2P/2B: $74- 84   XP: $10   F16
Location: Just S of I-80; exit 176 or 178. 511 W Winnemucca Blvd 89445. Fax: 775/623-4234.
Terms: Weekly/monthly rates; small pets only. **Facility:** 50 rooms. Some large rooms, few small. Lower rates
in winter; 2 stories; exterior corridors; heated pool, 5/15-9/30. **Some Rooms:** 4 efficiencies. **Cards:** AE, DI,
DS, MC, VI. **Special Amenities:** Free breakfast and free local telephone calls.

🔲 🔲 🔲 🔲 🔲 🔲 🔲 🔲

ECONOMY INN

🔲
◆
Motel

Rates Subject to Change   **Phone:** 775/623-5281
All Year   1P: $38   2P/1B: $42   2P/2B: $45   XP: $5   F12
Location: 0.5 mi w on I-80 (Business Rt), exit 176 or 178. 635 W Winnemucca Blvd 89445.
Fax: 775/625-3342. **Terms:** Small pets only. **Facility:** 29 rooms. Many large rooms. 2 two-bedroom units. 2
stories; exterior corridors. **All Rooms:** combo or shower baths. **Cards:** AE, CB, DS, MC, VI.

🔲 🔲 🔲 🔲 🔲 🔲

HOLIDAY INN EXPRESS

◆ ◆
Motel

Rates Subject to Change   **Phone:** 775/625-3100
5/1-9/30 [CP]   1P: $75- 135   2P/1B: $75- 135   2P/2B: $75- 135   XP: $5   F18
2/1-4/30 & 10/1-1/31 [CP]   1P: $55- 125   2P/1B: $55- 125   2P/2B: $55- 125   XP: $5   F18
Location: Just s of I-80, exit 176. 1987 W Winnemucca Blvd 89445. Fax: 775/625-3100. **Facility:** 72 rooms.
3 stories; interior corridors; heated indoor pool. **All Rooms:** combo or shower baths. **Cards:** AE, CB, DI, DS, MC, VI.

🔲 🔲 🔲 🔲 🔲 🔲 🔲 🔲 🔲 🔲 🔲 🔲 🔲 🔲 🔲

RAMADA LIMITED

◆ ◆
Motel

Rates Subject to Change   **Phone:** 775/623-1119
All Year [CP]   1P: $49   2P/1B: $56   2P/2B: $56   XP: $6
Location: Just s of I-80, exit 176; 0.3 mi e. 1620 W Winnemucca Blvd 89445. Fax: 775/623-1119.
Facility: 74 rooms. Large rooms, few have seating area. 2 stories; exterior corridors. **Cards:** AE, CB, DI,
DS, MC, VI.

🔲 🔲 🔲 🔲 🔲 🔲

RED LION INN & CASINO

🔲 🔲
◆ ◆ ◆
Motor Inn

Phone: (775)623-2565

All Year   1P: $69- 109   2P/1B: $69- 109   2P/2B: $79- 119   XP: $10   F17
Location: Just S of I-80; exit 176 or 178. 741 W Winnemucca Blvd 89445. Fax: 775/623-2527. **Terms:** Pets,
$50 dep req. **Facility:** 106 rooms. Some large rooms. 6 two-bedroom units. Lower rates in winter; 2 stories;
interior corridors; heated pool 5/15-9/30. **Dining:** Coffee shop; 24 hrs; $9-$20; cocktails. **Cards:** AE, DI, DS,
MC, VI. **Special Amenities:** Free local telephone calls and free room upgrade (subject to availability
with advanced reservations). Red Lion Hotels & Inns. *(See color ad below)*

🔲 🔲 🔲 🔲 🔲 🔲 🔲 🔲 🔲 🔲 🔲 🔲 🔲

TOWN HOUSE MOTEL
Guaranteed Rates
Phone: 775/623-3620

	6/1-9/30			2P/1B:	$44-	46	2P/2B:	$49	XP: $5
	4/1-5/31 & 10/1-10/31			2P/1B:	$37-	39	2P/2B:	$42	XP: $5
	2/1-3/31 & 11/1-1/31			2P/1B:	$30-	32	2P/2B:	$35	XP: $5

Motel   **Location:** Just S of I-80; exit 176 or 178; at 4 St. 375 Monroe St 89445. **Facility:** 19 rooms. 1 story; exterior corridors. **Dining:** Coffee shop nearby. **All Rooms:** combo or shower baths. **Cards:** AE, DS, MC, VI.
(See ad p 1128)

VAL-U INN
Phone: (775)623-5248

6/1-9/30	1P: $57	2P/1B: $57	2P/2B: $63	XP: $5	F12
2/1-5/31	1P: $52	2P/1B: $52	2P/2B: $58	XP: $5	F12
10/1-11/30	1P: $47	2P/1B: $47	2P/2B: $53	XP: $5	F12
12/1-1/31	1P: $40	2P/1B: $40	2P/2B: $46	XP: $5	F12

Motel   **Location:** Just S of I-80; exit 176 or 178. 125 E Winnemucca Blvd 89445. **Fax:** 775/623-4722.
Terms: Weekly rates; small pets only, $5 extra charge. **Facility:** 80 rooms. Few small rooms. 3 stories; interior corridors; sauna. **Dining:** Coffee shop nearby. **Cards:** AE, CB, DI, DS, MC, VI. **Special Amenities: Free breakfast and free local telephone calls.**

RESTAURANTS

ORMACHEA'S DINNER HOUSE
Dinner: $11-$20
Phone: 775/623-3455

Ethnic   **Location:** On US 95N at 2nd. 180 Melarkey St 89445. **Hours:** 4:30 pm-10 pm. Closed: 1/1 & 12/25. **Features:** casual dress; children's menu; cocktails & lounge. Family-style dinners. Choice of entree. Complimentary glass of wine, ice cream included. Smoking permitted in Lounge only. Basque & American cuisine. Smoke free premises. **Cards:** DS, MC, VI.

RESTAURANTE SAN FERMIN
Dinner: $10-$20
Phone: 775/625-2555

Basque   **Location:** Just s of I-80; exit 176. 485 Winnemucca Blvd 89445. **Hours:** 5 pm-10 pm. Closed: 1/1, 11/25, 12/25 & Sun. **Reservations:** accepted. **Features:** casual dress; children's menu; cocktails & lounge; minimum charge-$10. Authentic Basque cuisine & traditional tapas. Pleasant decor & background music of Spain. Conventional table seating & service. Smoke free premises. **Cards:** AE, MC, VI.

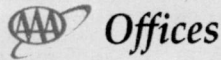 *Offices*

Cities with main offices are listed in **BOLD TYPE** and toll-free member service numbers in *ITALIC TYPE*.
All are closed Saturdays, Sundays and holidays unless otherwise indicated.
The type of service provided is designated below the name of the city where the office is located:
Auto travel services, including books/maps, marked maps and on-demand Triptik maps ✛
Auto travel services, including books/maps, marked maps, but no on-demand Triptik maps ●
Provides books/maps only. No marked maps or on-demand Triptik maps available ■
Travel agency services ▲

CALIFORNIA

ANAHEIM—AUTOMOBILE CLUB OF SO CALIFORNIA, 150 W VERMONT AVE, 92805-4699. MON-FRI 9-5. (714) 774-2392. ✛▲

ANAHEIM—AUTOMOBILE CLUB OF SO CALIFORNIA, 5500 E SANTA ANA CANYON RD, 92807-3124. MON-FRI 9-5, SAT 9-1. (714) 921-2850. ✛▲

ANGELS CAMP—CALIFORNIA STATE AUTOMOBILE ASSN, 465 S MAIN HWY 49, 95222-0594. MON-FRI 8:30-5:30. (209) 736-4517. ✛

ANTIOCH—CALIFORNIA STATE AUTOMOBILE ASSN, 1700 SOMERSVILLE RD, 94509-0951. MON-FRI 8:30-5:30. (510) 754-2210. ✛▲

ARCADIA—AUTOMOBILE CLUB OF SO CALIFORNIA, 420 E HUNTINGTON DR, 91006-3748. MON-FRI 9-5, SAT 9-1. (626) 445-5441. ✛

ARTESIA—AUTOMOBILE CLUB OF SO CALIFORNIA, 18642 S GRIDLEY RD, 90701-5408. MON-FRI 9-5, SAT 9-1. (562) 924-6636. ✛▲

AUBURN—CALIFORNIA STATE AUTOMOBILE ASSN, 2495 BELL RD, 95603-4198. MON-FRI 8:30-5:30. (530) 885-6561. ✛▲

BAKERSFIELD—AUTOMOBILE CLUB OF SO CALIFORNIA, 1500 COMMERCIAL WAY, 93309. MON-FRI 9-5. (805) 327-4661. ✛▲

BERKELEY—CALIFORNIA STATE AUTOMOBILE ASSN, 1775 UNIVERSITY AVE, 94703-1582. MON-FRI 8:30-5:30. (510) 845-8890. ✛

BISHOP—AUTOMOBILE CLUB OF SO CALIFORNIA, 187 W PINE ST, 93514-2641. MON-FRI 9-5. (760) 872-8241. ✛

BLYTHE—AUTOMOBILE CLUB OF SO CALIFORNIA, 221 E HOBSON WAY, 92225-1730. MON-FRI 9-5. (760) 922-3194. ✛

BURBANK—AUTOMOBILE CLUB OF SO CALIFORNIA, 1111 W ALAMEDA AVE, 91506-2805. MON-FRI 9-5, SAT 9-1. (818) 843-2833. ✛▲

CAPITOLA—CALIFORNIA STATE AUTOMOBILE ASSN, 4400 CAPITOLA RD, 95010-0250. MON-FRI 8:30-5:30. (831) 479-9830. ✛▲

CHICO—CALIFORNIA STATE AUTOMOBILE ASSN, 2221 FOREST AVE, 95928-2404. MON-FRI 8:30-5:30. (530) 891-8601. ✛▲

CHINO—AUTOMOBILE CLUB OF SO CALIFORNIA, 5402 PHILADELPHIA ST #A, 91710-1906. MON-FRI 9-5, SAT 9-1. (909) 591-9451. ✛

CHULA VISTA—AUTOMOBILE CLUB OF SO CALIFORNIA, 569 TELEGRAPH CANYON RD, 91910-6495. MON-FRI 9-5, SAT 9-1. (619) 421-0410. ✛

CLOVIS—CALIFORNIA STATE AUTOMOBILE ASSN, 1595 SHAW AVE, 93611-4040. MON-FRI 8:30-5:30. (209) 298-9121. ✛▲

CONCORD—CALIFORNIA STATE AUTOMOBILE ASSN, 2055 MERIDIAN PARK BLVD, 94520-5767. MON-FRI 8:30-5:30. (925) 671-2708. ✛▲

COSTA MESA—AUTOMOBILE CLUB OF SO CALIFORNIA, 3350 HARBOR BLVD, 92626-1502. MON-FRI 9-5. (714) 427-5950. ✛▲

CRESCENT CITY—CALIFORNIA STATE AUTOMOBILE ASSN, 785 E WASHINGTON BLVD #1, 95531. MON-FRI 8:30-5:30. (707) 464-7428. ✛

CULVER CITY—AUTOMOBILE CLUB OF SO CALIFORNIA, 4512 SEPULVEDA BLVD, 90230-4833. MON-FRI 9-5. (310) 390-9866. ✛

CUPERTINO—CALIFORNIA STATE AUTOMOBILE ASSN, 1601 S DE ANZA BLVD #148, 95014. MON-FRI 8:30-5:30. (408) 996-3553. ✛▲

DALY CITY—CALIFORNIA STATE AUTOMOBILE ASSN, 455 HICKEY BLVD, 94015-2699. MON-FRI 8:30-5:30. (650) 994-8400. ✛▲

DEL MAR—AUTOMOBILE CLUB OF SO CALIFORNIA, 12835 POINTE DEL MAR WAY, 92014. MON-FRI 9-5. (619) 481-7181. ✛▲

DIAMOND BAR—AUTOMOBILE CLUB OF SO CALIFORNIA, 2843 DIAMOND BAR BLVD, 91765-7469. MON-FRI 9-5. (909) 444-0299. ✛▲

DOWNEY—AUTOMOBILE CLUB OF SO CALIFORNIA, 8223 FIRESTONE BLVD, 90241. MON-FRI 9-5. (562) 861-2231. ✛

DUBLIN—CALIFORNIA STATE AUTOMOBILE ASSN, 7035 DUBLIN BLVD, 94568-3099. MON-FRI 8:30-5:30. (925) 829-2021. ✛▲

EL CENTRO—AUTOMOBILE CLUB OF SO CALIFORNIA, 300 S IMPERIAL AVE #12, 92243-3149. MON-FRI 9-5. (760) 352-6731. ✛

ESCONDIDO—AUTOMOBILE CLUB OF SO CALIFORNIA, 800 LA TERRAZA BLVD, 92025-3898. MON-FRI 9-5, SAT 9-1. (760) 745-2124. ✛▲

EUREKA—CALIFORNIA STATE AUTOMOBILE ASSN, 707 L ST, 95501-1135. MON-FRI 8:30-5:30. (707) 443-5087. ✛

FAIRFIELD—CALIFORNIA STATE AUTOMOBILE ASSN, 222 ACACIA ST, 94533-3800. MON-FRI 8:30-5:30. (707) 422-1820. ✛

FORT BRAGG—CALIFORNIA STATE AUTOMOBILE ASSN, 179 BOATYARD DR SUITE A, 95437. MON-FRI 8:30-5:30. (707) 964-0659. ✛

FRESNO—CALIFORNIA STATE AUTOMOBILE ASSN, 5040 N FORKNER AVE, 93711-2899. MON-FRI 8:30-5:30. (209) 435-8450. ✛▲

FULLERTON—AUTOMOBILE CLUB OF SO CALIFORNIA, 2101 N HARBOR BLVD, 92635-3895. MON-FRI 9-5. (714) 871-2333. ✛

GILROY—CALIFORNIA STATE AUTOMOBILE ASSN, 1395 FIRST ST, 95020-4790. MON-FRI 8:30-5:30. (408) 847-2300. ✛

GLENDALE—AUTOMOBILE CLUB OF SO CALIFORNIA, 1233 E BROADWAY, 91205-1496. MON-FRI 9-5. (818) 240-2200. ✛▲

GLENDORA—AUTOMOBILE CLUB OF SO CALIFORNIA, 1301 S GRAND AVE, 91740. MON-FRI 9-5. (626) 963-8531. ✛▲

GRASS VALLEY—CALIFORNIA STATE AUTOMOBILE ASSN, 113 DORSEY DR, 95945-5201. MON-FRI 8:30-5:30. (530) 272-9011. ✛

GREENBRAE—CALIFORNIA STATE AUTOMOBILE ASSN, 100 DRAKES LANDING RD, 94904-2496. MON-FRI 8:30-5:30. (415) 925-1200. ✛▲

HANFORD—CALIFORNIA STATE AUTOMOBILE ASSN, 780 N IRWIN ST, 93230. MON-FRI 8:30-5:30. (209) 582-9071. ✛

HAYWARD—CALIFORNIA STATE AUTOMOBILE ASSN, 1580 CHABOT CT, 94545-2498. MON-FRI 8:30-5:30. (510) 784-0900. ✛▲

HEMET—AUTOMOBILE CLUB OF SO CALIFORNIA, 450 W STETSON AVE, 92543-7045. MON-FRI 9-5. (909) 652-6202. ✛▲

HOLLISTER—CALIFORNIA STATE AUTOMOBILE ASSN, 351 TRES PINOS RD SUITE D, 95023. MON-FRI 8:30-5:30. (831) 637-7457. ✛

HUNTINGTON BEACH—AUTOMOBILE CLUB OF SO CALIFORNIA, 16160 BEACH BLVD, 92647. MON-FRI 9-5, SAT 9-1. (714) 848-2227. ✛▲

INGLEWOOD—AUTOMOBILE CLUB OF SO CALIFORNIA, 1234 CENTINELA AVE, 90302-1138. MON-FRI 9-5. (310) 673-5170. ✛

JACKSON—CALIFORNIA STATE AUTOMOBILE ASSN, 11974 STATE HWY 88 #2092, 95642-9472. MON-FRI 8:30-5:30. (209) 223-2761. ✛

KINGS BEACH—CALIFORNIA STATE AUTOMOBILE ASSN, 7717 N LAKE BLVD, 96143. MON-FRI 8:30-5:30. (530) 546-4245. ✛

LAFAYETTE—CALIFORNIA STATE AUTOMOBILE ASSN, 3390 MT DIABLO BLVD, 94549. MON-FRI 8:30-5:30. (925) 283-9450. ✛▲

LAGUNA HILLS—AUTOMOBILE CLUB OF SO CALIFORNIA, 25181 PASEO DE ALICIA, 92653-4670. MON-FRI 9-5, SAT 9-1. (714) 951-1400. ✛▲

LA HABRA—AUTOMOBILE CLUB OF SO CALIFORNIA, 1700 W LA HABRA BLVD, 90631-5130. MON-FRI 9-5. (562) 694-3711.✦▲

LAKEPORT—CALIFORNIA STATE AUTOMOBILE ASSN, 1464 PARALLEL DR, 95453-9712. MON-FRI 8:30-5:30. (707) 263-4807.✦

LA MESA—AUTOMOBILE CLUB OF SO CALIFORNIA, 8765 FLETCHER PKY, 91942. MON-FRI 9-5. (619) 464-7001.✦▲

LANCASTER—AUTOMOBILE CLUB OF SO CALIFORNIA, 1055 W AVE J, 93534-3395. MON-FRI 9-5. (805) 948-7661.✦

LA QUINTA—AUTOMOBILE CLUB OF SO CALIFORNIA, 46-050 WASHINGTON ST, 92253. MON-FRI 9-5. (760) 771-1162.✦▲

LODI—CALIFORNIA STATE AUTOMOBILE ASSN, 1335 S FAIRMONT AVE, 95240-5599. MON-FRI 8:30-5:30. (209) 334-9671.✦▲

LOMPOC—AUTOMOBILE CLUB OF SO CALIFORNIA, 816 E OCEAN AVE, 93436-7017. MON-FRI 9-5. (805) 735-2731.✦

LONG BEACH—AUTOMOBILE CLUB OF SO CALIFORNIA, 4800 AIRPORT PLZ DR, 90815-1274. MON-FRI 9-5. (562) 496-4130.✦▲

LOS ANGELES—AUTOMOBILE CLUB OF SO CALIFORNIA, 2601 S FIGUEROA ST, 90007-3299. MON-FRI 9-5. (213) 741-3686.✦▲

LOS ANGELES—AUTOMOBILE CLUB OF SO CALIFORNIA, 5550 WILSHIRE BLVD #101, 90036-3886. MON-FRI 9-5. (213) 525-0018.✦

LOS ANGELES—AUTOMOBILE CLUB OF SO CALIFORNIA, 4835 VENICE BLVD, 90019. MON-FRI 9-4, FRI 10-6, SAT 10-2. (213) 634-8680.▲

LOS ANGELES—AUTOMOBILE CLUB OF SO CALIFORNIA, 4143 CRENSHAW BLVD, 90008. MON-FRI 9-4:30, FRI 9-6, SAT 9-1. (213) 290-8980.▲

LOS BANOS—CALIFORNIA STATE AUTOMOBILE ASSN, 919 W PACHECO, 93635-3931. MON-FRI 8:30-5:30. (209) 826-1773.✦

LOS GATOS—CALIFORNIA STATE AUTOMOBILE ASSN, 101 BLOSSOM HILL RD, 95032. MON-FRI 8:30-5:30. (408) 395-6411.✦▲

MADERA—CALIFORNIA STATE AUTOMOBILE ASSN, 221 N G ST, 93637-3188. MON-FRI 8:30-5:30. (209) 673-3586.✦

MANHATTAN BEACH—AUTOMOBILE CLUB OF SO CALIFORNIA, 700 S AVIATION BLVD, 90266-7106. MON-FRI 9-5. (310) 376-0521.✦▲

MANTECA—CALIFORNIA STATE AUTOMOBILE ASSN, 145 TREVINO AVE, 95337. MON-FRI 8:30-5:30. (209) 239-1252.✦

MARYSVILLE—CALIFORNIA STATE AUTOMOBILE ASSN, 1205 D ST, 95901-0430. MON-FRI 8:30-5:30. (530) 742-5531.✦

MERCED—CALIFORNIA STATE AUTOMOBILE ASSN, 3065 M ST, 95348-3213. MON-FRI 8:30-5:30. (209) 723-9143.✦▲

MODESTO—CALIFORNIA STATE AUTOMOBILE ASSN, 3525 COFFEE RD, 95355-1341. MON-FRI 8:30-5:30. (209) 523-9171.✦▲

MONTEBELLO—AUTOMOBILE CLUB OF SO CALIFORNIA, 2444 W BEVERLY BLVD, 90640-2306. MON-FRI 9-5. (213) 725-6545.✦

MONTEREY—CALIFORNIA STATE AUTOMOBILE ASSN, 53 SOLEDAD DR, 93940-6094. MON-FRI 8:30-5:30. (831) 373-3021.✦▲

MONTROSE—AUTOMOBILE CLUB OF SO CALIFORNIA, 2112 MONTROSE AVE, 91020-1508. MON-FRI 9-5. (818) 249-3971.✦

MOUNTAIN VIEW—CALIFORNIA STATE AUTOMOBILE ASSN, 900 MIRAMONTE AVE, 94040-2457. MON-FRI 8:30-5:30. (650) 965-7000.✦

NAPA—CALIFORNIA STATE AUTOMOBILE ASSN, 800 TRANCAS ST, 94558. MON-FRI 8:30-5:30. (707) 226-9961.✦▲

NEWARK—CALIFORNIA STATE AUTOMOBILE ASSN, 39600 BALENTINE DR, 94560-0324. MON-FRI 8:30-5:30. (510) 770-9280.✦

NEWPORT BEACH—AUTOMOBILE CLUB OF SO CALIFORNIA, 3880 BIRCH ST, 92660-2669. MON-FRI 9-5. (714) 476-8880.✦▲

NORTHRIDGE—AUTOMOBILE CLUB OF SO CALIFORNIA, 9440 RESEDA BLVD, 91324-2987. MON-FRI 9-5. (818) 993-1616.✦▲

OAKLAND—CALIFORNIA STATE AUTOMOBILE ASSN, 380 W MACARTHUR BLVD, 94609-2899. MON-FRI 8:30-5:30. (510) 652-1812.✦▲

OCEANSIDE—AUTOMOBILE CLUB OF SO CALIFORNIA, 3330 VISTA WAY, 92056-3799. MON-FRI 9-5. (760) 433-6261.✦▲

OROVILLE—CALIFORNIA STATE AUTOMOBILE ASSN, 1430 FEATHER RIVER BLVD, 95965. MON-FRI 8:30-5:30. (530) 533-3931.✦

PALM SPRINGS—AUTOMOBILE CLUB OF SO CALIFORNIA, 300 S FARRELL DR, 92262-7993. MON-FRI 9-5. (760) 320-1121.✦▲

PALO ALTO—CALIFORNIA STATE AUTOMOBILE ASSN, 430 FOREST AVE, 94301. MON-FRI 8:30-5:30. (650) 321-0470.✦▲

PARADISE—CALIFORNIA STATE AUTOMOBILE ASSN, 6332 CLARK RD, 95969-4152. MON-FRI 8:30-5:30. (530) 872-2236.✦

PASADENA—AUTOMOBILE CLUB OF SO CALIFORNIA, 801 E UNION ST, 91101-1732. MON-FRI 9-5. (626) 795-0601.✦▲

PETALUMA—CALIFORNIA STATE AUTOMOBILE ASSN, 111 LYNCH CREEK WAY, 94954-2338. MON-FRI 8:30-5:30. (707) 763-0973.✦

PLACERVILLE—CALIFORNIA STATE AUTOMOBILE ASSN, 1323 BROADWAY, 95667. MON-FRI 8:30-5:30. (530) 622-4084.✦

PORTERVILLE—AUTOMOBILE CLUB OF SO CALIFORNIA, 24 W MORTON AVE, 93257-2331. MON-FRI 9-5. (209) 784-6500.✦

QUINCY—CALIFORNIA STATE AUTOMOBILE ASSN, 20 CRESCENT ST, 95971. MON-FRI 8:30-5:30. (530) 283-1014.✦

RED BLUFF—CALIFORNIA STATE AUTOMOBILE ASSN, 151 SALE LN, 96080-2909. MON-FRI 8:30-5:30. (530) 527-4304.✦

REDDING—CALIFORNIA STATE AUTOMOBILE ASSN, 943 MISSION DE ORO DR, 96003-3883. MON-FRI 8:30-5:30. (530) 222-2722.✦▲

REDLANDS—AUTOMOBILE CLUB OF SO CALIFORNIA, 413 E PALM AVE, 92373-6135. MON-FRI 9-5. (909) 793-3357.✦▲

REDWOOD CITY—CALIFORNIA STATE AUTOMOBILE ASSN, 20 EL CAMINO REAL, 94062-1796. MON-FRI 8:30-5:30. (650) 364-0620.✦

RICHMOND—CALIFORNIA STATE AUTOMOBILE ASSN, 3060 HILLTOP MALL RD, 94806-2494. MON-FRI 8:30-5:30. (510) 223-8080.✦

RIDGECREST—AUTOMOBILE CLUB OF SO CALIFORNIA, 114 S GEMSTONE #A, 93555-4198. MON-FRI 9-5. (760) 375-8426.✦

RIVERSIDE—AUTOMOBILE CLUB OF SO CALIFORNIA, 3700 CENTRAL AVE, 92506. MON-FRI 9-5, SAT 9-1. (909) 684-4250.✦

ROSEVILLE—CALIFORNIA STATE AUTOMOBILE ASSN, 2100 PROFESSIONAL DR, 95661-3700. MON-FRI 8:30-5:30. (916) 784-3232.✦

SACRAMENTO—CALIFORNIA STATE AUTOMOBILE ASSN, 15 BICENTENNIAL CIR, 95826-2899. MON-FRI 8:30-5:30. (916) 381-3355.✦

SACRAMENTO—CALIFORNIA STATE AUTOMOBILE ASSN, 4333 FLORIN RD, 95823-2569. MON-FRI 8:30-5:30. (916) 422-6511.✦▲

SACRAMENTO—CALIFORNIA STATE AUTOMOBILE ASSN, 4745 CHIPPENDALE DR, 95841-2596. MON-FRI 8:30-5:30. (916) 331-7610.✦▲

SALINAS—CALIFORNIA STATE AUTOMOBILE ASSN, 1019 POST DR, 93907. MON-FRI 8:30-5:30. (831) 424-2521.✦

SAN BERNARDINO—AUTOMOBILE CLUB OF SO CALIFORNIA, 590 NORTH D ST, 92401-1329. MON-FRI 9-5. (909) 381-2211.✦

SAN CLEMENTE—AUTOMOBILE CLUB OF SO CALIFORNIA, 638 CAMINO DE LOS MARES, 92673-2856. MON-FRI 9-5. (949) 489-5572.✦▲

SAN DIEGO—AUTOMOBILE CLUB OF SO CALIFORNIA, 4973 CLAIREMONT DR #C, 92117-2793. MON-FRI 9-5, SAT 9-1. (619) 483-4960.✦▲

SAN DIEGO—AUTOMOBILE CLUB OF SO CALIFORNIA, 815 DATE ST, 92101-2899. MON-FRI 9-5. (619) 233-1000.✦▲

SAN DIEGO—AUTOMOBILE CLUB OF SO CALIFORNIA, 12630 SABRE SPGS PKY 301, 92128-9896. MON-FRI 9-6. (619) 486-0786.✦

SAN FRANCISCO—CALIFORNIA STATE AUTOMOBILE ASSN, 150 VAN NESS AVE, 94102-5279. MON-FRI 8:30-5:30. (415) 565-2012.✦

SAN GABRIEL—AUTOMOBILE CLUB OF SO CALIFORNIA, 215 S MISSION DR, 91776-1125. MON-FRI 9-5. (626) 289-4491.✦

SAN JOSE—CALIFORNIA STATE AUTOMOBILE ASSN, 5340 THORNWOOD DR, 95123-1274. MON-FRI 8:30-5:30. (408) 629-1911.✦▲

SAN LUIS OBISPO—AUTOMOBILE CLUB OF SO CALIFORNIA, 1445 CALLE JOAQUIN, 93405-7203. MON-FRI 9-5. (805) 543-6454.✦

SAN MATEO—CALIFORNIA STATE AUTOMOBILE ASSN, 1650 S DELAWARE ST, 94402. MON-FRI 8:30-5:30. (650) 572-1160.✦▲

SAN RAFAEL—CALIFORNIA STATE AUTOMOBILE ASSN, 99 SMITH RANCH RD, 94903. MON-FRI 8:30-5:30. (415) 472-6700.✦▲

SAN RAMON—CALIFORNIA STATE AUTOMOBILE ASSN, 1081 MARKET PL, 94583. MON-FRI 8:30-5:30. (510) 830-9797. +▲

SANTA BARBARA—AUTOMOBILE CLUB OF SO CALIFORNIA, 3712 STATE ST, 93105-3135. MON-FRI 9-5. (805) 682-5811. +▲

SANTA CLARA—CALIFORNIA STATE AUTOMOBILE ASSN, 80 SARATOGA AVE, 95051-7398. MON-FRI 8:30-5:30. (408) 985-9300. +▲

SANTA CLARITA—AUTOMOBILE CLUB OF SO CALIFORNIA, 23770 VALENCIA BLVD, 91355. MON-FRI 9-5, SAT 9-1. (805) 259-6222. +▲

SANTA MARIA—AUTOMOBILE CLUB OF SO CALIFORNIA, 2033 B SO BROADWAY, 93454-7809. MON-FRI 9-5, SAT 9-1. (805) 922-5731. +

SANTA ROSA—CALIFORNIA STATE AUTOMOBILE ASSN, 1500 FARMERS LN, 95405-7596. MON-FRI 8:30-5:30. (707) 544-1010. +

SIMI VALLEY—AUTOMOBILE CLUB OF SO CALIFORNIA, 2837 COCHRAN ST, 93065-2766. MON-FRI 9-5, SAT 9-1. (805) 522-7330. +

SONOMA—CALIFORNIA STATE AUTOMOBILE ASSN, 650 2ND ST W, 95476. MON-FRI 8:30-5:30. (707) 996-1083. +

SONORA—CALIFORNIA STATE AUTOMOBILE ASSN, 1071 SANGUINETTI RD, 95370. MON-FRI 8:30-5:30. (209) 532-3134. +

SOUTH LAKE TAHOE—CALIFORNIA STATE AUTOMOBILE ASSN, 961 EMERALD BAY RD, 96150. MON-FRI 8:30-5:30. (530) 541-4434. +

SOUTH LOS ANGELES—AUTOMOBILE CLUB OF SO CALIFORNIA, 9621 S VERMONT AVE, 90044-3296. MON-FRI 9-5. (213) 754-2831. +

STOCKTON—CALIFORNIA STATE AUTOMOBILE ASSN, 3116 W MARCH LN SUITE 100, 95219-2335. MON-FRI 8:30-5:30. (209) 952-4100. +▲

SUNNYVALE—CALIFORNIA STATE AUTOMOBILE ASSN, 755 S BERNARDO AVE, 94087-1022. MON-FRI 8:30-5:30. (408) 739-4422. +

SUSANVILLE—CALIFORNIA STATE AUTOMOBILE ASSN, 550 ASH ST, 96130. MON-FRI 8:30-5:30. (530) 257-6144. +

TEMECULA—AUTOMOBILE CLUB OF SO CALIFORNIA, 26403 YNEZ RD, 92591-4654. MON-FRI 9-5. (909) 694-9403. +▲

THOUSAND OAKS—AUTOMOBILE CLUB OF SO CALIFORNIA, 100 E WILBUR RD, 91360-5589. MON-FRI 9-5. (805) 497-0911. +▲

TORRANCE—AUTOMOBILE CLUB OF SO CALIFORNIA, 23001 HAWTHORNE BLVD, 90505-2997. MON-FRI 9-5, SAT 9-1. (310) 325-3111. +▲

TURLOCK—CALIFORNIA STATE AUTOMOBILE ASSN, 2160 GEER RD, 95382. MON-FRI 8:30-5:30. (209) 668-2722. +

TUSTIN—AUTOMOBILE CLUB OF SO CALIFORNIA, 13331 JAMBOREE RD, 92782. MON-FRI 9-5. (714) 973-1211. +▲

UKIAH—CALIFORNIA STATE AUTOMOBILE ASSN, 601 KINGS CT, 95482. MON-FRI 8:30-5:30. (707) 462-3861. +

UPLAND—AUTOMOBILE CLUB OF SO CALIFORNIA, 1021 E FOOTHILL BLVD, 91786-4048. MON-FRI 9-5. (909) 981-2961. +▲

VACAVILLE—CALIFORNIA STATE AUTOMOBILE ASSN, 555 MASON ST SUITE 150, 95688. MON-FRI 8:30-5:30. (707) 453-0260. +

VALLEJO—CALIFORNIA STATE AUTOMOBILE ASSN, 1183 ADMIRAL CALLAGHAN LN, 94591-3701. MON-FRI 8:30-5:30. (707) 552-0592. +▲

VAN NUYS—AUTOMOBILE CLUB OF SO CALIFORNIA, 6725 KESTER AVE, 91405-4595. MON-FRI 9-5. (818) 997-6230. +▲

VENTURA—AUTOMOBILE CLUB OF SO CALIFORNIA, 1501 S VICTORIA AVE, 93003-6583. MON-FRI 9-5. (805) 644-7171. +▲

VICTORVILLE—AUTOMOBILE CLUB OF SO CALIFORNIA, 12490 AMARGOSA RD, 92392-5469. MON-FRI 9-5. (760) 245-6666. +

VISALIA—AUTOMOBILE CLUB OF SO CALIFORNIA, 300 S MOONEY BLVD, 93291-4510. MON-FRI 9-5. (209) 732-8045. +

WATSONVILLE—CALIFORNIA STATE AUTOMOBILE ASSN, 1195 S GREEN VALLEY RD, 95076-0615. MON-FRI 8:30-5:30. (831) 722-8151. +

WEST LOS ANGELES—AUTOMOBILE CLUB OF SO CALIFORNIA, 1900 S SEPULVEDA BLVD, 90025. MON-FRI 9-5. (310) 914-8500. +▲

WHITTIER—AUTOMOBILE CLUB OF SO CALIFORNIA, 8522 S PAINTER AVE, 90602-3335. MON-FRI 9-5. (562) 698-3721. +

WILLOWS—CALIFORNIA STATE AUTOMOBILE ASSN, 855 W WOOD ST, 95988. MON-FRI 8:30-5:30. (530) 934-4648. +

WOODLAND—CALIFORNIA STATE AUTOMOBILE ASSN, 95 W LINCOLN AVE, 95695-3719. MON-FRI 8:30-5:30. (530) 662-9344. +

WOODLAND HILLS—AUTOMOBILE CLUB OF SO CALIFORNIA, 22708 VICTORY BLVD, 91367-1697. MON-FRI 9-5, SAT 9-1. (818) 883-2660. +▲

YREKA—CALIFORNIA STATE AUTOMOBILE ASSN, 500 N MAIN ST, 96097-0410. MON-FRI 8:30-5:30. (530) 842-4416. +

NEVADA

CARSON CITY—CALIFORNIA STATE AUTOMOBILE ASSN, 2901 S CARSON ST, 89701-5527. MON-FRI 8:30-5:30. (702) 883-2470. +

ELKO—CALIFORNIA STATE AUTOMOBILE ASSN, 705 RAILROAD ST, 89801. MON-FRI 8:30-5:30. (702) 777-3800. +

HENDERSON—CALIFORNIA STATE AUTOMOBILE ASSN, 601 WHITNEY RANCH DR #A, 89014. MON-FRI 8:30-5:30. (702) 458-2323. +▲

LAS VEGAS—CALIFORNIA STATE AUTOMOBILE ASSN, 3312 W CHARLESTON BLVD, 89102-1892. MON-FRI 8:30-5:30. (702) 870-9171. +▲

LAS VEGAS—CALIFORNIA STATE AUTOMOBILE ASSN, 8440 W LAKE MEAD STE 203, 89128. MON-FRI 8:30-5:30. (702) 360-3151. +▲

RENO—CALIFORNIA STATE AUTOMOBILE ASSN, 199 E MOANA LN, 89510-7020. MON-FRI 8:30-5:30. (702) 826-8800. +▲

Dead battery? Call AAA.
We'll boost your battery, change a flat, deliver fuel or give you a tow. When you're a member, the answer to your car problems is as simple as that.
Contact your local AAA Club for more information.

Temperature Averages - Maximum/Minimum
From the records of the National Weather Service

Values shown as maximum/minimum.

	JAN	FEB	MAR	APR	MAY	JUN	JUL	AUG	SEP	OCT	NOV	DEC
CALIFORNIA												
Bakersfield	57/37	63/41	69/45	76/50	85/56	92/62	100/68	98/66	92/61	81/53	69/43	59/39
Barstow	59/31	63/34	70/40	77/45	84/51	96/60	101/67	100/65	92/57	80/47	70/37	60/30
Bishop	53/21	56/25	64/30	73/38	81/44	90/50	97/55	95/52	89/47	77/37	64/28	55/23
Bridgeport	38/9	41/12	48/19	59/27	66/33	74/38	84/45	83/44	77/37	65/29	53/21	44/15
Chico	54/36	60/39	67/41	73/44	82/49	91/55	98/59	96/58	88/53	79/47	66/40	55/36
Eureka	54/41	54/42	55/43	56/45	58/48	60/51	61/52	61/53	62/51	60/49	58/45	55/43
Fresno	55/36	61/39	67/42	75/47	83/52	90/57	99/63	97/60	91/56	80/48	67/39	56/37
Indio	70/39	75/45	80/50	86/57	93/63	102/72	107/78	106/76	101/69	91/58	80/46	71/39
Los Angeles	65/47	66/48	69/50	71/53	74/56	77/59	83/63	83/63	82/61	77/57	73/52	68/49
Merced	55/36	62/39	66/41	73/45	81/50	91/56	97/61	95/59	88/54	79/47	67/39	56/35
Mount Shasta	41/25	47/28	52/30	60/35	68/40	75/46	85/51	85/49	78/45	66/38	53/31	45/27
Needles	64/39	70/45	77/49	86/55	94/63	104/71	108/80	105/78	98/67	85/55	72/46	63/40
Redding	54/37	59/40	64/43	71/48	80/54	88/61	97/67	95/65	87/59	77/52	64/44	56/38
Sacramento	53/39	59/42	65/44	72/47	80/52	89/56	95/59	94/58	90/57	79/51	65/44	55/40
San Diego	65/46	65/48	67/50	68/54	70/57	72/60	76/63	77/65	77/62	73/58	71/51	67/48
San Francisco	55/42	58/43	62/45	64/47	67/50	70/52	72/54	72/54	74/54	71/51	64/46	57/43
Santa Barbara	64/43	65/44	66/46	68/48	69/50	72/53	76/56	77/57	76/55	74/51	72/46	67/43
Truckee	38/16	38/16	46/21	53/29	60/36	73/41	81/43	81/41	73/37	63/30	52/24	40/15
Willits	49/31	53/34	56/35	64/39	70/43	77/47	86/52	86/50	83/49	71/44	57/38	50/34
NEVADA												
Beatty	55/25	59/30	66/33	73/39	81/46	92/55	99/61	97/59	89/52	76/43	65/33	55/26
Elko	35/10	40/16	49/22	60/29	69/35	79/41	91/48	89/45	80/36	66/28	49/19	39/14
Ely	37/9	40/13	47/20	58/28	67/34	77/40	87/48	85/47	77/38	63/29	49/18	41/13
Hawthorne	45/23	49/26	57/31	64/36	72/44	82/52	90/59	89/59	79/51	67/40	57/31	46/24
Las Vegas	55/32	60/36	69/42	79/51	88/60	98/69	105/76	102/73	95/66	81/53	66/40	57/33
Reno	47/17	51/21	57/25	65/30	73/34	81/39	91/45	90/43	83/37	71/29	58/21	49/17

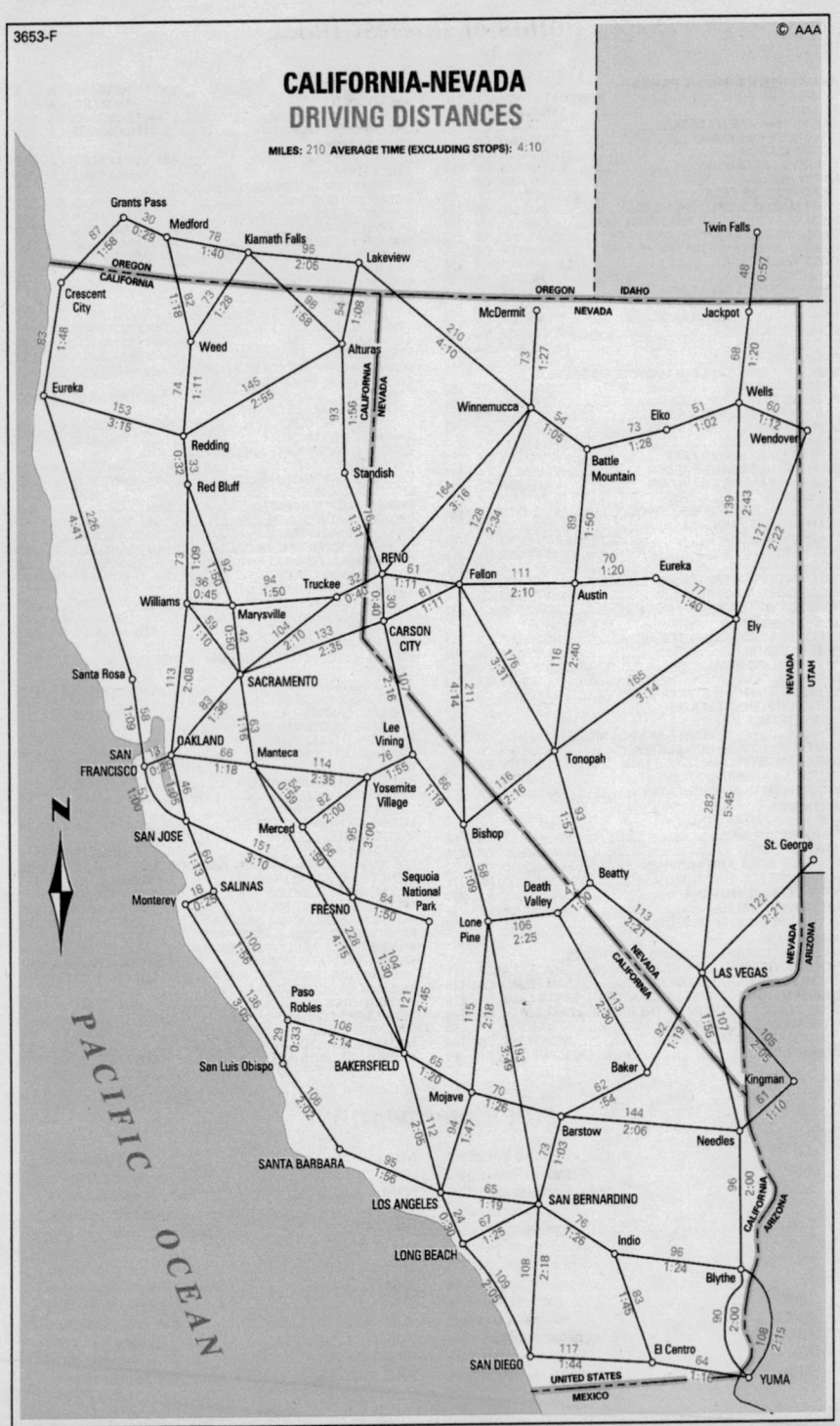

CALIFORNIA-NEVADA
DRIVING DISTANCES

MILES: 210 AVERAGE TIME (EXCLUDING STOPS): 4:10

3653-F

© AAA

Points of Interest Index

INDEX ABBREVIATIONS

NB.. national battlefield	NR...national river
NBP............................ national battlefield park	NS.. national seashore
NC..................................... national cemetery	NWR............................ national wildlife refuge
NF...national forest	PHP.................... provincial historic(al) park
NHM................... national historic(al) monument	PHS....................provincial historic(al) site
NHP............................ national historic(al) park	PP..................................... provincial park
NHS.............................. national historic(al) site	SF... state forest
NL..................................... national lakeshore	SHM................ state historic(al) monument
NME.................................national memorial	SHP..................... state historic(al) park
NMO................................. national monument	SHS..................... state historic(al) site
NMP............................ national military park	SME............................... state memorial
NP...national park	SP... state park
NRA......................national recreation area	SRA............... state recreation area

SIGHTSEEING-AIRCRAFT RIDES & TOURS

SIGHTSEEING TOURS

SIGHTSEEING TOURS-BOATS

SOUND & LIGHT PRESENTATIONS

WALKING TOURS

WATERFALLS

WATER PARKS

SAVE Attraction Admission Discount Index

Bed & Breakfast Lodgings Index

Some bed and breakfasts listed below might have historical significance. Those properties are also referenced in the Historical index. The indication that continental [CP] or full breakfast [BP] is included in the room rate reflects whether a property is a Bed-and-Breakfast facility.

BED & BREAKFAST LODGINGS (CONT'D)

NEVADA
ACCOMMODATIONS

Country Inns Index

Some of the following country inns can also be considered as bed-and-breakfast operations. The indication that continental [CP] or full breakfast [BP] is included in the room rate reflects whether a property is a Bed-and-Breakfast facility.

Historical Lodgings & Restaurants Index

Some of the following historical lodgings can also be considered as bed-and-breakfast operations. The indication that continental [CP] or full breakfast [BP] is included in the room rate reflects whether a property is a Bed-and-Breakfast facility.

Resorts Index

Many establishments are located in resort areas; however, the following places have extensive on-premises recreational facilities:

Comprehensive City Index

Here is an alphabetical list of all cities appearing in this TourBook. Cities are presented by state/province. Page numbers under the POI column indicate where points of interest text begins. Page numbers under the L&R column indicate where lodging and restaurant listings begin.

COMPREHENSIVE CITY INDEX (CONT'D)

COMPREHENSIVE CITY INDEX (CONT'D)

COMPREHENSIVE CITY INDEX (CONT'D)

Photo Credit Index

When traveling in the United States and Canada...

Member Services Call Center

SUPERNUMBER®

1-800-AAA-HELP

1-800-955-4TDD (Hearing Impaired)

a 24-hour, toll-free, Emergency Road Service information system.

It's easy to use:

Look in the white pages of the telephone book for a listing under "AAA" in the United States or "CAA" in Canada, since road service is dispatched by the local club in many communities.

If there is no listing, have your membership card handy and call *SUPERNUMBER®*, **1-800-AAA-HELP,** for the nearest road service facility. *Hearing Impaired call* **1-800-955-4TDD.**

SUPERNUMBER®, is available in the United States and Canada 24 hours a day, but **only** for Emergency Road Service and **only** when traveling outside the area served by your home club. Contact the nearest club office regarding other services you may require.

NOTE: NOT AVAILABLE WHEN TRAVELING IN MEXICO.

CALIFORNIA

Anaheim
Howard Johnson Plaza-Hotel
SE corner of I-5 & Harbor Blvd.
From LAX: Century Blvd E to I-405 S
to 22 Fwy E, exit Harbor Blvd N to
Anaheim, 4 mi. From John Wayne
Airport: 55 Fwy N to I-5 N, exit
Harbor Blvd, turn left.

Los Angeles
Howard Johnson Hotel
405 North: exit Manchester, West
1 mi, left Airport Blvd. 405 South: exit
Manchester, west 1 mi, left Airport Blvd.

Los Angeles
Howard Johnson Plaza –
Hotel & Suites
From LAX Airport: 405 N to 10 E,
Hoover Exit N, left 2 mi to Wilshire
Blvd., right to hotel. From I-5 to 170 S
to 101 S, Vermont Exit, right on
Vermont to Wilshire, left 2 mi to hotel.

Modesto
Howard Johnson Express Inn
From 99S: Hatch Rd. exit, right on
Herndon. From 99N: Hatch Rd. exit,
left on Hatch, right on Herdon.

Montebello
Howard Johnson Hotel
Fwy 5 at Slauson Ave Exit.

North Hills
Howard Johnson Inn
405 Fwy, exit Devonshire, East to
Sepulveda Blvd, turn right, approx
1/2 mi south, on right.

Redding
Howard Johnson Express Inn
From I-5, exit Cypress. Follow west to
Bechelli Lane, south on Bechelli for
two blocks·

Reseda
Howard Johnson Express Inn
I-101, north on Reseda Blvd; I-118,
south on Reseda Blvd; I-405 take
Sherman Way west to Reseda, 2
blocks north·

San Mateo
Howard Johnson Express Inn
Hwy 101 N or S to Hwy 92 W, exit El
Camino Real S, 2 blks on right.

Santa Clara
Howard Johnson Inn
North 280: exit on Lawrence Expwy.,
West on Stevens Creek Blvd. South
280: exit on Stevens Creek at
Lawrence Expwy.

NEVADA

Las Vegas
Howard Johnson Plaza-Hotel
At I-15 & Tropicana Exit.

Las Vegas
Howard Johnson Inn
I-15 to Tropicana East, right on
Paradise South.

AAA members save 10-20% off regular rates!

From California To Nevada, All Roads Lead To Howard Johnson.

Enjoy all that today's Howard Johnson® offers when you stay at any of our convenient locations in the West. From a clean, comfortable room at a great price, to the warm, friendly service, Howard Johnson makes you feel at home. Plus, seniors get discounts and kids stay free.* For reservations call your travel agent or **1-800-I-GO-HOJO**® and ask for **"SA3"** to receive your AAA Discount. Or visit us at **www.hojo.com**.

Howard Johnson®
MAKES YOU FEEL AT HOME℠

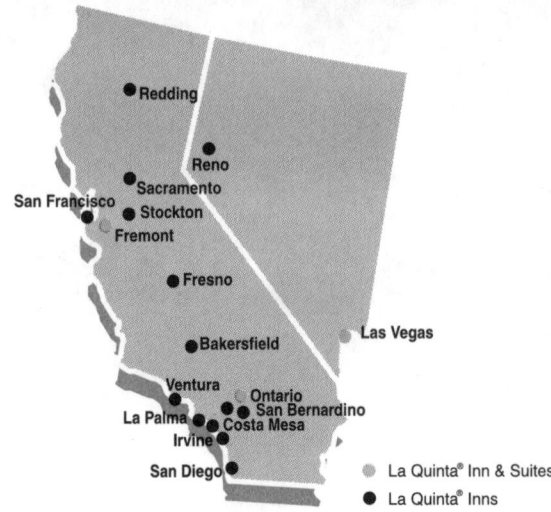

(See map p. 680)

CARMEL RIVER INN   Rates Subject to Change   **Phone:** (831)624-1575   82
All Year   1P: $89- 110   2P/1B: $90- 150   2P/2B: $100- 170   XP: $20   F
Location: 1 mi s on SR 1; n of Carmel River Bridge at Oliver Rd. 93922 (PO Box 221609).
Fax: 831/624-0290. **Terms:** Reserv deposit, 3 day notice; 2 night min stay, on weekends. **Facility:** 43 rooms.
Motel   Many balconies & patios overlooking river-bed. 24 Cottages (some small) 9 with woodburning fireplaces. 6
two-bedroom units. Cottages $65-$130 for up to 4 persons; 2 stories; exterior corridors; heated pool.
All Rooms: combo or shower baths. **Some Rooms:** 10 efficiencies, 3 kitchens. **Cards:** MC, VI. *(See color ad p 683)*

CARMEL SANDS LODGE   Rates Subject to Change   **Phone:** 831/624-1255   100
5/1-10/31   1P: $75- 145   2P/1B: $75- 145   2P/2B: $75- 145   XP: $10
2/1-4/30 & 11/1-1/31   1P: $69- 125   2P/1B: $69- 125   2P/2B: $69- 125   XP: $10
Location: 2 blks n off Ocean Ave; on San Carlos St & 5th ave. (PO Box 951, 93921). Fax: 831/624-2576.
Terms: 2 night min stay, weekends & in summer. **Facility:** 38 rooms. Few small rooms, few fireplace & bal-
Motel   cony. 2 stories; interior/exterior corridors. **Dining:** Simpson's Restaurant, see separate listing.
All Rooms: combo or shower baths. **Cards:** AE, CB, DI, DS, MC, VI. *(See color ad p 688)*

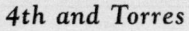

(See map p. 680)

CARMEL TRADEWINDS INN ◆◆
Motel

	Rates Subject to Change			
6/1-9/30 [CP]	1P: $159- 225	2P/1B: $159- 225	2P/2B: $159- 250	XP: $15-30
2/1-5/20, 4/1-5/31 &				
10/1-11/1 [CP]	1P: $139- 200	2P/1B: $139- 200	2P/2B: $139- 225	XP: $15-30
2/1-3/31 & 11/2-1/31 [CP]	1P: $79- 189	2P/1B: $79- 189	2P/2B: $99- 200	XP: $15-30

Phone: (831)624-2776 **87**

Location: 4 blks n off Ocean Ave at Mission St & 3rd Ave. (PO Box 3403, 93921). Fax: 831/624-0634. **Terms:** Reserv deposit, 3 day notice; handling fee imposed; 2 night min stay, weekends. **Facility:** 27 rooms. Large units, many gas fireplaces. View of ocean or mountains; balconies. 1 whirlpool rm, extra charge; 1-3 stories, no elevator; exterior corridors; smoke free premises; heated pool. **All Rooms:** combo or shower baths. **Cards:** AE, MC, VI.

CARMEL VALLEY RANCH (AAA) (SAVE)
◆◆◆◆
Resort
Complex

7/1-10/31	1P: $255- 615	2P/1B: $255- 615	2P/2B: $255- 615	XP: $20	F18
4/1-6/30	1P: $235- 565	2P/1B: $235- 565	2P/2B: $235- 565	XP: $20	F18
2/1-3/31 & 11/1-1/31	1P: $215- 505	2P/1B: $215- 505	2P/2B: $215- 505	XP: $20	F18

Phone: (831)625-9500 **116**

Location: 6.3 mi e of SR 1 via Carmel Valley Rd, exit at Robinson Canyon Rd & follow signs. One Old Ranch Rd 93923. Fax: 831/624-2858. **Terms:** Check-in 4 pm; reserv deposit, 21 day notice; $15 service charge; package plans, golf/tennis; pets. **Facility:** 144 rooms. Hillside location overlooking valley & golf course. Woodburning fireplaces. 2 two-bedroom units. 20 suites with outdoor whirlpool, $340-$700 for 2. 24 suites with whirlpool, $225-$520 for up to 2 persons; 1 story; exterior corridors; saunas, whirlpools; 2 clay tennis courts; 1 grass tennis court. Fee: 18 holes golf; 13 tennis courts. **Dining:** 3 restaurants; 7 am-2 & 6-10 pm; $25-$45; cocktails. **Services:** giftshop. Fee: massage. **Recreation:** Fee: horseback riding. **Cards:** AE, CB, DI, DS, MC, VI. **Special Amenities:** Free newspaper.

CARMEL VILLAGE INN & ANNEX (AAA)
◆◆◆
Motel

	Rates Subject to Change			
Fri & Sat & Sun-Thurs				
3/1-10/31 [CP]	1P: $79- 150	2P/1B: $79- 150	2P/2B: $129- 200	XP: $15
Sun-Thurs 2/1-2/28 &				
11/1-1/31 [CP]	1P: $79- 150	2P/1B: $79- 150	2P/2B: $98- 149	XP: $15

Phone: 831/624-3864 **108**

Location: At Ocean Ave & Junipero St. (PO Box 5275, 93921). Fax: 831/626-6763. **Terms:** Handling fee imposed. **Facility:** 53 rooms. Attractive, comfortable rooms. 2 studio apartments with kitchen or efficiency & gas burning fireplace, $89-$189 for up to 5 persons; 2 stories; exterior corridors. **Dining:** Restaurant nearby. **Cards:** AE, MC, VI.
(See color ad p 689)

Our **bold type** listings have a special interest in serving you!

(See map p. 680)

CARMEL WAYFARER INN   Phone: (831)624-2711   92

	7/1-10/31 [CP]	1P: $92- 162	2P/1B: $102- 172	2P/2B: $142- 192	XP: $16
	3/1-6/30 [CP]	1P: $82- 142	2P/1B: $92- 162	2P/2B: $132- 182	XP: $14
	2/1-2/28 & 11/1-1/31 [CP]	1P: $72- 132	2P/1B: $82- 152	2P/2B: $122- 172	XP: $12

Bed & Breakfast

Location: 3 blks n off Ocean at 4th Ave & Mission St. (PO Box 1896, 93921). Fax: 831/625-1210. **Facility:** 15 rooms. Most units with gas burning fireplace; few with ocean view. 2 units with living room & sleeper sofa $132.50-$145.50 for up to 2 persons. 2 rm suites, $155-$195 for up to 4 persons; 2 stories; exterior corridors; smoke free premises. **All Rooms:** combo or shower baths. **Some Rooms:** 3 kitchens. **Cards:** AE, CB, DI, DS, MC, VI. **Special Amenities:** Free breakfast and free local telephone calls. *(See color ad below)*

All information in this TourBook is accurate at press time.
Changes may occur between publications.
Be sure to use the latest edition for the most recent information.

(See map p. 680)

CARRIAGE HOUSE INN Phone: 831/625-2585 [113]
AAA SAVE Fri & Sat & Sun-Thurs
7/2-10/30 [CP] 1P: $234- 304 2P/1B: $234- 304 XP: $15 F14
◆◆◆◆ Sun-Thurs 2/1-7/1 &
Bed & 10/31-1/31 [CP] 1P: $185- 234 2P/1B: $185- 234 XP: $15 F14
Breakfast **Location:** 2 blks s off Ocean Ave, on Junipero St between 7th & 8th aves. (PO Box 1900, 93921).
Fax: 831/624-0974. **Terms:** Reserv deposit, 3 day notice; 2 night min stay, weekends. **Facility:** 13 rooms. All
units with fireplace. 1 suite, $209-$289 for up to 2 persons. 1 large unit, $209-$289 for up to 2 persons; 2 stories; exterior cor-
ridors; smoke free premises. **Dining:** Restaurant nearby. **Services:** complimentary evening beverages.
Some Rooms: whirlpools. **Cards:** AE, DS, MC, VI. *(See color ad p 685)*

CHATEAU CARMEL Phone: 831/624-1900 [98]
AAA SAVE 5/15-10/31 [CP] 1P: $155- 245 2P/1B: $155- 245 2P/2B: $155- 245 XP: $10-20
2/1-5/14, Sun-Thurs
◆◆◆ 11/1-1/31 & 11/1-1/31 [CP] 1P: $95- 225 2P/1B: $95- 225 2P/2B: $95- 225 XP: $10-20
Motel **Location:** 2 blks n of Ocean Ave at Junipero St & 5th aves. (PO Box 1295, 93921). Fax: 831/624-1571.
Terms: Handling fee imposed; 2 night min stay, weekends 5/15-10/21. **Facility:** 20 rooms. 2 stories; exterior
corridors; smoke free premises; small pool. **Dining:** Restaurant nearby. **All Rooms:** combo or shower baths.
Some Rooms: 9 efficiencies. **Cards:** AE, CB, DI, DS, MC, VI. *(See color ad p 691)*

COACHMAN'S INN Phone: (831)624-6421 [107]
AAA SAVE All Year [CP] 1P: $85- 145 2P/1B: $85- 160 2P/2B: $95- 160 XP: $10 F12
◆◆◆ **Location:** Just s of Ocean Ave, San Carlos St between 7th & 8th aves. 93921 (PO Box C-1).
Fax: 831/624-3311. **Terms:** Small pets only, $15 extra charge; dogs only. **Facility:** 30 rooms. Attractive, large
Motel comfortable rooms. 3 stories, no elevator; exterior corridors; smoke free premises. **Some Rooms:** 2
efficiencies. **Cards:** AE, MC, VI. **Special Amenities: Free breakfast and preferred room (subject to
availability with advanced reservations).** *(See ad below)*

COBBLESTONE INN Rates Subject to Change Phone: 831/625-5222 [114]
◆◆◆ All Year [BP] 1P: $95- 175 2P/2B: $95- 175 XP: $15
Bed & **Location:** On Junipero St between 7th & 8th aves. 93921 (PO Box 3185). Fax: 831/625-0478. **Facility:** 24
Breakfast rooms. Quaint appointments. All rooms with gas fireplace. 1 king suite with 4-poster bed, fireplace & window
seat, $180; 2 stories; interior/exterior corridors; smoke free premises; street parking only. **All Rooms:** combo
or shower baths. **Cards:** AE, DI, MC, VI.

COLONIAL TERRACE INN Rates Subject to Change Phone: (831)624-2741 [79]
AAA All Year [CP] 1P: $90- 250 2P/1B: $90- 250 2P/2B: $120- 300 XP: $20 F
Location: On San Antonio between 12th & 13th aves. (PO Box 1375, 93921). Fax: 831/626-2715.
◆◆ **Terms:** Reserv deposit, 3 day notice; 2 night min stay, weekends. **Facility:** 25 rooms. All
Motel rooms with gas burning fireplace. Some rooms with ocean view. 1 two bedroom family unit w/fireplace $235,
for up to 6 persons; 2 stories; exterior corridors. **All Rooms:** combo or shower baths. **Some Rooms:** 6
efficiencies, 2 kitchens, whirlpools. **Cards:** MC, VI. *(See color ad p 683)*

CRYSTAL TERRACE INN BED & BREAKFAST Phone: 831/624-6400 [78]
AAA SAVE 5/15-10/31 [CP] 1P: $140- 275 2P/1B: $140- 275
2/1-5/14 & 11/1-1/31 [CP] 1P: $95- 250 2P/1B: $95- 250
◆◆◆ **Location:** W of SR 1, exit Carpenter St; 0.5 mi. 24815 Carpenter St 93921 (PO Box 2623).
Bed & Fax: 831/624-5111. **Terms:** Reserv deposit, 7 day notice; handling fee imposed. **Facility:** 16 rooms. Some
Breakfast small rooms. 1 story; exterior corridors; smoke free premises. **Services:** complimentary evening beverages.
Cards: AE, CB, DI, DS, JC, MC, VI. *(See color ad p 691)*

CYPRESS INN Phone: (831)624-3871 [106]
AAA SAVE All Year [CP] 1P: $110- 285 2P/1B: $110- 285 2P/2B: $145- 285 XP: $15
Location: 1 blk s off Ocean Ave; at Lincoln St & 7th Ave. (PO Box Y, 93921). Fax: 831/624-8216.
◆◆◆ **Terms:** Reserv deposit, 3 day notice; 2 night min stay, weekends; pets, $17 extra charge. **Facility:** 34 rooms.
Historic Hotel Mediterranean setting with garden courtyard. Afternoon tea Mon-Fri. 2 stories; interior/exterior corridors; street
parking only. **All Rooms:** combo or shower baths. **Cards:** AE, DS, JC, MC, VI.

(See map p. 680)

DOLPHIN INN
Phone: 831/624-5356   91

AAA SAVE

◆◆◆

Motel

| | Fri & Sat & Sun-Thurs 7/2-10/30 [CP] | 1P: $114- 234 | 2P/1B: $114- 234 | 2P/2B: $154- 234 | XP: $15 | F14 |

Sun-Thurs 2/1-7/1 & 10/31-1/31 [CP]   1P: $94- 194   2P/1B: $94- 194   2P/2B: $124- 194   XP: $15   F14

Location: 3 blks n off Ocean Ave at San Carlos St & 4th Ave. (PO Box 1900, 93921). Fax: 831/624-2967. **Terms:** Reserv deposit, 3 day notice; 2 night min stay, weekends. **Facility:** 26 rooms. Many gas fireplaces, some rooms balcony or patio. 2 suites, $165-$219 for up to 2 persons. 1 family unit, $169-$229 for up to 6 persons. 1 whirlpool unit, extra charge; 2 stories; exterior corridors. **Dining:** Restaurant nearby. **Some Rooms:** efficiency. **Cards:** AE, DS, MC, VI. *(See color ad p 685)*

HIGHLANDS INN
Phone: 831/624-3801   80

AAA SAVE

◆◆◆◆

Motor Inn

| | All Year | 1P: $290- 450 | 2P/1B: $325- 450 | 2P/2B: $600- 800 | XP: $25 |

Location: 4 mi s on SR 1, in Carmel Highlands. 93921 (PO Box 1700). Fax: 831/626-1574. **Terms:** Check-in 4 pm; package plans, mid week & weekend; small pets only, $75. **Facility:** 142 rooms. Outstanding ocean view. Units with woodburning fireplace & CD player. Some small rooms. All suites with whirlpool bath. 2-3 stories, no elevator; exterior corridors; whirlpools. **Dining:** Dining room, restaurant; also, Pacific's Edge, see separate listing. **Services:** giftshop; area transportation, within 10 mi. **Recreation:** bicycles. **All Rooms:** combo or shower baths. **Some Rooms:** 103 kitchens, whirlpools. **Cards:** AE, CB, DI, DS, MC, VI.

HOFSAS HOUSE
Rates Subject to Change   Phone: (831)624-2745   85

AAA

◆◆

Motel

| | 6/15-11/1 [CP] | 1P: $80- 150 | 2P/1B: $80- 150 | 2P/2B: $80- 150 |
| | 2/1-6/14 & 11/2-1/31 [CP] | 1P: $65- 120 | 2P/1B: $65- 120 | 2P/2B: $65- 120 |

Location: 3 blks n off Ocean Ave, between 3rd & 4th aves, on San Carlos St. (PO Box 1195, 93921). Fax: 831/624-0159. **Terms:** Reserv deposit, 3 day notice. **Facility:** 38 rooms. Partial ocean view, some woodburning fireplaces. 5 two-bedroom units. 12 units with fireplace. 2-bedroom units, $150-$180 for 2 or more persons; 4 stories, no elevator; exterior corridors; sauna. **All Rooms:** combo or shower baths. **Some Rooms:** 15 efficiencies, 5 kitchens. **Cards:** AE, MC, VI.

HORIZON INN & OCEAN VIEW LODGE
Phone: 831/624-5327   88

AAA SAVE

◆◆◆

Motel

| | 6/2-11/1 | 1P: $99- 250 | 2P/1B: $99- 250 | 2P/2B: $99- 250 | XP: $15 | F12 |
| | 2/1-6/1 & 11/2-1/31 | 1P: $69- 180 | 2P/1B: $69- 190 | 2P/2B: $69- 180 | XP: $15 | F12 |

Location: 4 blks n off Ocean at Junipero St & 3rd Ave. 93921 (PO Box 1693). Fax: 831/626-8253. **Terms:** Reserv deposit, 3 day notice; 2 night min stay, weekends. **Facility:** 26 rooms. Some rooms with fireplace. 4 units with large whirlpool tub & fireplace $159-$209 for 2 persons; 2 stories; exterior corridors; small pool. **Dining:** Restaurant nearby. **All Rooms:** combo or shower baths. **Some Rooms:** 6 kitchens. **Cards:** AE, DS, MC, VI. *(See color ad p 687 & below)*

LA PLAYA HOTEL
Rates Subject to Change   Phone: (831)624-6476   110

AAA

◆◆◆

Historic Hotel

| | All Year | 1P: $140- 240 | 2P/1B: $140- 240 | 2P/2B: $155- 185 | XP: $15 | F12 |

Location: Just s of Ocean Ave. Camino Real at 8th Ave 93921 (PO Box 900). Fax: 831/624-7966. **Terms:** 2 night min stay, weekends. **Facility:** 80 rooms. Mediterranean-style architecture. Beautifully landscaped grounds, few small rooms. Some with view of ocean. 5 cottages, 1- to 3-bedrooms with fireplace & kitchen, $230-$495 for up to 8 persons; 4 stories, no elevator; interior/exterior corridors. **Dining:** Dining room; 7 am-10 pm. Outside dining on protected terrace; $16-$24; cocktails. **All Rooms:** combo or shower baths. **Some Rooms:** whirlpools. **Cards:** AE, DI, MC, VI.

LOBOS LODGE
Rates Subject to Change   Phone: (831)624-3874   101

AAA

◆◆◆

Motel

| | All Year | 1P: $99- 185 | 2P/1B: $99- 185 | 2P/2B: $99- 185 | XP: $25 |

Location: Ocean Ave & Monte Verde. 93921 (PO Box L-1). Fax: 831/624-0135. **Terms:** Reserv deposit, 3 day notice; 2 night min stay, weekends. **Facility:** 30 rooms. Some rooms with ocean view, all with gas fireplace. 2 stories; exterior corridors. **Some Rooms:** kitchen. **Cards:** AE, MC, VI.

(See map p. 680)

NORMANDY INN Rates Subject to Change **Phone: 831/624-3825** [105]
All Year [CP] 1P: $98- 200 2P/1B: $98- 200 2P/2B: $98- 200 XP: $10 F6
Location: Ocean Ave between Monte Verde & Casanova. (PO Box 1706, 93921). Fax: 831/624-4614.
Motel **Terms:** 2 night min stay, weekends. **Facility:** 48 rooms. 3 three-bedroom units. 3 family cottage units with
woodburning fireplace, & kitchen, $250-$400 for up to 8 persons. Suites, $165-$300; 2 stories; exterior corri-
dors; small pool. **Dining:** Restaurant nearby. **All Rooms:** combo or shower baths. **Cards:** AE, MC, VI.
(See color ad below)

(See map p. 680)

PINE INN

 ◆◆◆ Historic Hotel

Rates Subject to Change **Phone:** (831)624-3851 **102**

All Year 1P: $95 2P/1B: $95- 230 2P/2B: $125- 230 XP: $10 F18

Location: Ocean Ave; between Lincoln & Monte Verde. (PO Box 250, 93921). Fax: 831/624-3030. **Terms:** Check-in 4 pm; 2 night min stay, weekends. **Facility:** 49 rooms. 1889 Hotel; elegant furnishings & fabrics. 3 stories, no elevator; interior/exterior corridors. **Dining:** Dining room, coffee shop; 8 am-10 pm, outdoor patio dining; $10-$20; cocktails. **Cards:** AE, CB, DI, DS, JC, MC, VI. *(See color ad p 693)*

QUAIL LODGE RESORT & GOLF CLUB

◆◆◆◆ Resort Complex

Phone: (831)624-1581 **84**

4/1-11/28 1P: $295-1350 2P/1B: $295-1350 2P/2B: $295-1350 XP: $25 F12

2/1-3/31 & 11/29-1/31 1P: $225-1350 2P/1B: $225-1350 2P/2B: $225-1350 XP: $25 F12

Location: 3.5 mi e of SR 1, via Carmel Valley Rd. 8205 Valley Greens Dr 93923. Fax: 831/624-3726. **Terms:** Check-in 4 pm; reserv deposit, 3 day notice; handling fee imposed; pets, one pet per room. **Facility:** 100 rooms. On manicured country club grounds. Some rooms with fireplace, patio or balcony. 2 stories; exterior corridors; putting green; whirlpool. Fee: 18 holes golf; 4 tennis courts. **Dining:** Dining room, restaurant; at clubhouse, 0.3 mi; 7 am-3 pm; 17% service charge. **Services:** giftshop. **Recreation:** jogging. **Some Rooms:** whirlpools. **Cards:** AE, CB, DI, JC, MC, VI. **Special Amenities:** Free newspaper. A Preferred Hotel. *(See color ad below)*

SUNSET HOUSE

◆◆◆ Bed & Breakfast

Phone: (831)624-4884 **104**

All Year [CP] 1P: $150- 170 2P/1B: $170- 190 2P/2B: $170- 190 XP: $20-30 F4

Location: S off Ocean on Camino Real. (PO Box 1925, 93921). Fax: 831/624-4884. **Terms:** Reserv deposit, 10 day notice; handling fee imposed; 2 night min stay, weekends; pets, dogs only. **Facility:** 4 rooms. Wood-burning fireplace, cathedral ceilings in most rooms. Some rooms have partial ocean view some antiques. 2 stories; interior/exterior corridors; smoke free premises. **All Rooms:** combo or shower baths. **Some Rooms:** whirlpools. **Cards:** AE, CB, DI, DS, JC, MC, VI. **Special Amenities:** Early check-in/late check-out and free breakfast.

SVENDSGAARD'S

◆◆◆ Motel

Phone: 831/624-1511 **115**

Fri & Sat & Sun-Thurs
7/2-10/30 [CP] 1P: $124- 214 2P/1B: $124- 214 2P/2B: $124- 214 XP: $15 F14

Sun-Thurs 2/1-7/1 &
10/31-1/31 [CP] 1P: $94- 174 2P/1B: $94- 174 2P/2B: $94- 174 XP: $15 F14

Location: 3 blks n off ocean at San Carlos St & 4th Ave. (PO Box 1900, 93921). Fax: 831/624-5661. **Terms:** Reserv deposit, 3 day notice; 2 night min stay, weekends. **Facility:** 34 rooms. Landscaped grounds. Some large rooms, some gas burning fireplace. 1 two-bedroom unit. 2 suites, $149-$199 for up to 2 persons. 1 family unit, $149-$199 for up to 4 persons; 1 whirlpool unit, $159-$209 for up to 2 persons; 2 stories; exterior corridors. **Dining:** Restaurant nearby. **All Rooms:** combo or shower baths. **Some Rooms:** 14 efficiencies. **Cards:** AE, DS, MC, VI. *(See color ad p 685)*